# Music
# Since
# 1900

# MUSIC
# SINCE
# 1900

*Nicolas Slonimsky*

*Fourth Edition*

CHARLES SCRIBNER'S SONS

*New York*

Fourth Edition
Copyright © 1971 Nicolas Slonimsky

Copyright 1937, 1938, 1949 Coleman-Ross Company, Inc.;
renewal copyright © 1965, 1966 Nicolas Slonimsky

This book published simultaneously in the
United States of America and in Canada—
Copyright under the Berne Convention

A-9.71(C)

Printed in the United States of America
Library of Congress Catalog Card Number 70-114929
SBN 684 10550-0

# Table of Contents

# PREFACE

# TO

# MUSIC SINCE 1900

"This is a book in the first place of materials, in the second of evaluation. The main body of the book, a DESCRIPTIVE CHRONOLOGY, is intended to be a sort of newsreel reflecting the 'inner headlines' of musical events that may not be at the moment of their occurrence of any significance, and yet contain elements of evolutionary power that subtly but surely influence the entire future of music. Thus, the date of completion of *Le Sacre du Printemps* or of *Pierrot Lunaire,* while quite unnoticed by the music world at large, is an inner headline of extreme importance; such dates, when ascertainable, are given particular attention. . . . Spectacular performers, great singers, big impresarios have been left out of the picture almost entirely, although their power in the musical world and their hold on the outer headlines are incomparably superior to that of a composer-inventor.

"DESCRIPTIVE CHRONOLOGY is here unrolled without national subdivisions. An event of musical interest may happen today in America, tomorrow in Russia; it is their contiguity in time alone that places them one after another. This method has the disadvantage of lumping together unrelated phenomena, but so has every chronology.

"A history of the modern musical idiom is yet to be written. Here we may cautiously draw a general outline of musical evolution since 1900, and post its milestones. We must remember that all musical innovation, no matter how extreme, is useful in that it indicates potentialities heretofore overlooked. Thus, composers thoroughly averse to the spirit of the twelve-tone technique may find its methods of great value within the tonal framework. The exploration of quarter-tone music may be an isolated phenomenon, and yet it subtilizes our perception of chromatic harmony.

"Selection of landmarks in modern music is perforce arbitrary, but no more so than the designation of historical eras. It was not announced in Rome in A.D. 476 that the Middle Ages had then and there begun; yet historians accept this date as a convenient chronological landmark. Similarly, we are justified in selecting an important event in 20th-century music as a chronological symbol of esthetic evolution. The first performance of Debussy's *Pelléas et Mélisande,* on 30 April 1902, may be considered such a symbol, signalizing the advent of impressionist opera. The outbreak of World War I brought about a musico-psychological realignment, with the romance of the machine replacing the romance of sentiment. The era of machine music came abruptly to an end with the economic collapse of 1929, when musicians abandoned the cult of the discredited machine and turned to composing pure music in a neo-classical manner. As if by general consent, pictorial and descriptive titles disappeared from the pages of musical scores. Honegger's first 'mouvement symphonique,' composed in December 1923, was subtitled *Pacific 231,* and was intended to glorify the American locomotive of that designation; his second 'mouvement' was *Rugby,* written in 1928 as a musical picture of a fashionable game; but his third work in the same genre, composed between October 1932 and January 1933, is entitled simply *Mouvement Symphonique.*

"The process of forming a new technique is illuminated in a remarkable letter from Arnold Schoenberg (in the section LETTERS AND DOCUMENTS) regarding the origin of his method of composition with twelve tones related only to one another. This letter shows how an idea latent in a musician's mind crystallizes, by the logic of true intuition, into a definite formula, at a definite point in time."

The foregoing paragraphs are extracted, with minor alterations, from the introduction to the first edition of *Music Since 1900,* published in 1937. There was a second printing in 1938 and an enlarged edition in 1949. An eventful third of a century has passed since this introduction was written. *Music Since 1900* was designed as a history of the future, a future which has now come to pass. Schlegel has said: "Der Historiker ist ein rückwärts gekehrter Prophet." What events are memorable enough to be included in such a prophetic history? I have established a simple criterion: when in doubt, do not delete. Better to have a hundred bits of musical flotsam and jetsam in circulation than to omit a single potentially important event. The fear of leaving out an interesting work has even invaded my dreams. One particularly vivid nightmare was that I had overlooked a really sensational item—the "Red Army Symphony" by Brahms, written in 1938 and dedicated by him to Marshal Voroshilov. Commenting on the perishable quality of new works commissioned by the New York Philharmonic on the occasion of its quasisesquicentennial, a British music critic wrily observed that these pieces "may well disappear into that impeccably kept graveyard of our century—*Music Since 1900.*" The burial may be premature. The composers interred herein may yet arise in glory at the sound of the last trump. *Et exspecto resurrectionem mortuorum,* etc.

Many ghosts of these pale *morituri,* opaque luminaries of music, are gathered on these pages from all over the world, including the *partes infidelium* not often visited by music historians—Rumania, Bulgaria, even Albania. Nearer the center of musical culture, virtually all operas of Siegfried Wagner, "the little son of a great father," are recorded here with a brief summary of content for each. The dates of completion and first performances of all 27 symphonies of Miaskovsky are faithfully tabulated. He fell into the habit in his later years of notifying me in regular succession of the progress made in adding yet another symphony to his enormous catalogue of works. Miaskovsky's Soviet biographers report that when he was hard pressed for information, he would tell them, only half-facetiously, to write Slonimsky in America for details. It would be unchivalrous not to make full use of these data.

A perspicacious, and on the whole sympathetic critic, reviewing the third edition of *Music Since 1900,* detected a streak of sensationalism in its choice of material. Why, he wondered, had I eliminated the entry on the natural death of an American music critic from the earlier editions, but retained that of his colleague who died by a self-inflicted gunshot wound in the mouth? Why did I quote a personal letter from Percy A. Scholes in which he frankly admits his role in the suicide of Arthur Eaglefield Hull? "Hull's suicide was the result of my exposure of his thefts in his book," Scholes wrote. "He threw himself under a train." But why shouldn't I have? This book is a historical study of factual romanticism, and violence and tragedy are part of the romance of our times.

Admittedly, some entries are frivolous—endurance records for piano-fortitude, underwater harp playing, a competition of singing canary birds, the timetable of the Chopin Express between Vienna and Warsaw, a horoscope of Scriabin, the arrest of a Rumanian diva for spying during World War I, etc., etc., etc. But these are passing sights and sounds of the general musicorama of the period, and as such are of illustrative value.

The scenes unreeled in Descriptive Chronology are so expansive that concision of technical analysis of each individual item becomes an economic necessity. A program annotator of the Boston Symphony Orchestra nodded approval of my summary description of the last movement of Béla Bartók's *Music for Strings, Percussion and Celesta* as a "paradoxical rondo with a non-recurrent subject." But he also cautioned the reader to beware of my loquacity when upon occasion I am prolix rather than terse, discursive rather than curt, rhetorical rather than pert. To illustrate the point he quoted a non-stop sentence purporting to describe another movement of the same Bartók piece—a sentence which I, most reluctantly, had to leave out in the present edition for the simple reason that, upon examination, I could not justify it on technical grounds.

"Brevitate moderni gaudent," is a frequent incipit in medieval treatises on music. Brevity still remains a desideratum, but no one has ever approached the utmost succinctness of expression of two fabled Renaissance scholiasts tied in a contest for the briefest possible non-nonsensical statement—in Latin, of course. "Eo rus," wrote one, tersely announcing his decision to depart for the country. "I," replied the other in a magnificently vertical imperative of the Latin verb "ire," to go, winning the match.

A measure of prolixity is inherent in the format of Descriptive Chronology, inasmuch as each entry is arranged in the form of a continuous paragraph without intermediate full stops, ramifying autogenetically, with subsidiary excrescences and efflorescences, into a network of ancillary clauses (a stylistic idiosyncrasy which I developed in the first edition of the book in order to achieve a would-be Aristotelean unity of place, time and action within each item, and which necessitates frequent recourse to long parenthetical enclaves so as to secure clear articulation of separate rubrics without dislocating the grammatical succession of substantives and predicates with their adverbial modifiers), all this further ornamented by hyphenated appositions, creating at times a veritable ziggurat of interdependent verbal structures with topical gradients traversing historical, biographical, analytical and proleptic matters, consciously invoking alliteration's artful aid in a plasma of seemingly untenable paronomasia (if not incontinent logorrhea), while striving to preserve a technically correct syntactical arrangement so as to make it possible for the constituent parts of speech to be retrieved and placed in proper perspective in the pervasive quagmire of quaquaversal qualifiers.

Errors and misprints can make a fortune for a lucky philatelist who chances upon an airmail stamp with an inverted airplane. But to a lexicographer, they are so many poltergeists—furtive, diabolically inventive, grimacing with self-contented malice while going about their mischievous business. Still one can't deny a certain appositeness to such typographical accidents as Charminade for Cécile Chaminade (caught in time and purged of the intrusive *r*), orbits for obits (inspired perhaps by a master mortician's plan to dispose of a surplus of cadavers by shooting them into outer space), or loverlooking for overlooking (positively inspirational). The first prize must go to the poltergeist who caused the author of a book dealing with the preparation of a manuscript for publication to express his gratitude to his secretary for her careful reading of the . . . *poofs!*

Far more menacing than these playful sprites are doublegangers, the chronological revenants that, thanks to an inadvertent substitution of a digit, stage a reappearance a year or several years later on the same day of the month. Most of these chimeras have been exorcised. Let us hope that none will slip through the crack of time to haunt the distraught chronicler.

Alfred Einstein, who had a plentiful share of his own Sisyphean struggle for accuracy, wrote me once, wondering whether we—"und natürlich vor allem Sie"—would receive our just reward in Heaven for having cleansed the world of some lexicographical *Ungenauigkeiten*. Would fain that the present edition of *Music Since 1900* would merit such a heavenly accolade. I should like to be able to emulate with some confidence the wording of the festooned banner on my favorite 17th-century map, which proudly proclaims itself "Orbis Terrarum Nova et Accuratissima Tabula." But even in this "most accurate chart," California is detached from the North American continent and sent drifting off into the Pacific, and Hollandia Nova—not yet Australia—is allowed to fade away into the terra incognita of the Antarctic. My fond hope is that no such peninsular islands or insular isthmuses will be encountered in my own "Orbis Musicae Modernae Nova et Accuratissima Tabula."

Most entries in DESCRIPTIVE CHRONOLOGY are world premières of significant works, even if they take place inconspicuously in some small town prior to a gala vernissage in a metropolitan center. American musical comedies are usually tried out in Boston, Philadelphia or some other perfectly respectable but not very glamorous spot. Soviet operas and symphonies are often performed first in Leningrad before coming to Moscow for a grand opening. In each case, it is the *prima assoluta* that is recorded here.

The dating of opera premières poses a problem. In European opera houses, particularly in Paris, two *premières auditions* are usually presented—one a *répétition générale* for the élite and the press, and one for the paying public. It is the press première that is given chronological priority in this book.

Any attempt at rational chronology crumbles in reporting the manifestations of the avant-garde of the last third of the 20th-century. Some composers blithely advise the performer that the duration of this or that composition is a matter of personal discretion; it may last a day or a minute, a year or a chiliad, a hebdomad of lustra, a quadrillion of milliseconds, a sextillion of nanoseconds, or a quindecillion of non-zero moments—all these temporal segments to be fragmented, quadrated or quaquadrated at will. And how are we to date a work of duration zero? Unheard for the first time? Here we reach the Ultima Thule of uncertainty and passivity. The experience of the Greek philosopher Cratylus comes to mind: he passed days and nights moving his forefinger to and fro in front of his nose to demonstrate the only verity of the world. Another precursor of

20th-century modernism was St. Simeon the Stylite who spent sixty-eight years in the sixth century perched on a number of successively taller pillars, the last one being 66 feet in elevation. His career could provide a fitting subject for a symphonic poem with leitmotifs based on a series of gradually increasing intervals.

Verbalization without musical notation as it is practiced by the avant-garde is almost Hesychastic in its contemplative solipsism. The title itself becomes a composition. Karlheinz Stockhausen draws a parabolic curve with this inscription: "Sound a note. Continue sounding it as long as you please. It is your prerogative." John Cage has made verbalization a cardinal discipline in his aleatory scores. In the coalition of music with theater, motion pictures, art, literature and drama that constitutes the program of the contemporary avant-garde, every action, every "happening," becomes a musical event. Nam June Paik gives explicit instructions for the performance of his piece entitled *Playing Music*: "Cut your left arm very slowly with a razor (more than 10 centimeters)." This has been executed. Philip Corner issues a simple command: "One anti-personnel type CBU (Cluster Bomb Unit) will be thrown into the audience." This composition has not been performed.

Then there are musical non-events that may be described by the term *Unwasity*, something that never was. A historical instance of such an un-wasity was the announced first performance of Prokofiev's *Scythian Suite* at a Koussevitzky concert in Moscow in December 1916, which was can-celled because of wartime conditions. This did not deter the Russian critic Leonid Sabaneiev from publishing a scathing review of the piece, going so far in his reporting of an unwasity as to mention that Prokofiev him-self conducted the work with "barbaric abandon."

The period of time covered in DESCRIPTIVE CHRONOLOGY traverses the biblical span of three score and ten. Actuarial statistics make it almost inevitable that total lifetimes of several 20th-century composers should be encompassed within these years. Dates of birth and death are here given in local time. When Schoenberg died in Los Angeles late at night on the 13th of July of 1951, it was past midnight in New York and early morning of the next day in Europe. As a result, Schoenberg's death was reported in European newspapers as having taken place on the 14th. Yet in Schoenberg's case, local time is of dramatic import, for he was seriously afflicted with triskaidecaphobia, and feared number 13 with grave appre-hension. He thought it was an evil omen that he was born on the 13th of the month of September in 1874. When he reached his 76th birthday, his last, he fell to brooding on the numerological fact that the sum of the digits of 76 is 13. During the last conscious hours of his life he re-marked that all would be well if he would survive the fatefully num-bered day. But he died 13 minutes before midnight on that 13th day of July of 1951.

The famous prima donna Melba died in Australia on 23 February 1931, but her death was reported in New York newspapers dated the previous day! This preposthumous calendarization was the consequence of Australia's position on the other side of the International Dateline. Melba died while the Western Hemisphere was still rotating under the sun of the preceding day—hence the anachronological paradox.

All Russian musical events between March 1900 and 1918, when the Soviet government adopted the Western calendar, have been adjusted by adding 13 days to equalize the Julian and the Gregorian styles. The difference between the two calendars increased from 12 to 13 days in 1900 because of the intercalation of 29 February in 1900, a bissextile year in Russia, but not in the West.

Spelling of names poses a knotty problem. Not infrequently, changes are made in the first or last names of persons during their lifetimes. Before Schoenberg came to America he spelled his last name with an umlaut, Schönberg, which is still the form used in German reference books. For uniformity's sake, the later spelling Schoenberg has been adopted throughout. Sibelius signed his first name Jean, and this form has been adopted in the present edition, not Jan as in the earlier editions and in some biographical sources. The baptismal name of Varèse was Edgard. He dropped the final *d* early in his career, and all original editions of his scores are signed Edgar Varèse, but about 1950 he restored the missing letter. However, I decided to retain the more familiar *d*-less form. Even in America, Varèse kept the grave accent in the middle of his last name, but his close contemporary and friend Carlos Salzedo, whose last name originally had an *accent aigu* on *e*, removed it in the process of Americanization.

Eugen Zádor jettisoned his tonic Hungarian accent and anglicized his first name to Eugene in his American avatar. In this case I made a compromise, listing his works first performed in Europe under the Hungarian cognomen, and those produced in America in the naturalized spelling. For some reason Leoncavallo's forename is commonly spelled Ruggiero, whereas the official Italian form is Ruggero. The latter form is adopted here.

The transliteration of Russian names is as insoluble a proposition as the squaring of the circle, because of the non-correspondence of the sounds represented by the letters of the Cyrillic alphabet and those of the Latin vocables. Since Russian music was first published in Germany, Russian composers became embedded in Germanic matrices. Tchaikovsky was Tschaikowsky in American concert halls, even though the initial Russian consonant of his name has the exact phonetic equivalent in the English diphthong "ch." Even more intractable is the Cyrillic symbol for the sound "shch." To locate Shcherbachev in a German music lexicon one must start with the acervulus of seven consonants, Schtsch. It was thanks to the former premier of the Soviet Union Nikita Khrushchev that the phonetically accurate transliteration of the Russian "shch" sound became finally crystallized in American and British usage.

The introductory "T" persists in the common American spelling of Tchaikovsky, even though most library catalogues list him under "Ch." But familiarity breeds respect, and Chaikovsky looks queer. A similar ambivalence exists in the spelling of Tcherepnin. On the other hand, the adequate "ch" is gradually superseding the nimiety of "tch" in the middle and at the end of Russian names. Shostakovich is no longer Shostakovitch, as he was in the early editions of *Music Since 1900*. The former Khatchaturian has been slenderized into Khachaturian. But considerations of preeminent usage dictate the retention of the supererogatory "t" in Gretchaninoff. Igor Markevitch, though born in Russia, made his professional career as composer and conductor in Paris. He signs his name in the form containing "tch," and there is no reason for tampering with it.

It is most unfortunate that the English alphabet has no symbol for the German guttural sound "ch" or the Spanish "j" (as in José). No difficulty exists in spelling the name of the Soviet composer Tikhon Khrennikov in German (Tichon Chrennikow) or in Spanish (Tijon Jrennikov). The Spanish spelling Jachaturian for Khachaturian is an exact phonetic equivalent of the Russian sound. Conceivably, the spelling Hrennikov and Hachaturian could be proposed in English, but the visual aspect of such a rendering would be forbidding.

There are musical Russian names whose spelling is sanctified by usage and cannot be altered without giving offense. Rachmaninoff is Rachmaninoff is Rachmaninoff. This is the way he invariably signed his name, and this is the spelling retained in this book. To adopt the phonetically consistent but repulsively unmusical spelling Rakhmaninov would be as unnatural as calling Rachmaninoff's C-sharp minor Prelude D-flat minor.

Objections have been raised, principally by British music editors, to the spelling of Koussevitzky, on the ground that it is a mixture of French and German. But this is the way Koussevitzky used to sign his name, and this is the way it is preserved in this book. Besides, I acquired the habit of spelling it this way during the years of my service as Koussevitzky's personal secretary.

As a matter of common sense, names of Russian composers of French or German origin retain their ancestral spelling. It is César Cui, not the ridiculous Tsezar Kyui. It is Maximilian Steinberg, not the abnormal Shteinberg. In their determination to square the Cyrillic circle the cataloguers of the Library of Congress went so far as to retransliterate the names of classical composers in the titles of Russian publications, resulting in such monstrosities as Shooman, Shoobert, Dzhyakomo Poochchini, and even Betkhoven. No person of healthy constitution can stomach any of these.

As a natural corollary of the commanding lead that America is beginning to assume in the world of music, increasing representation of works by American composers has been given in the present edition of *Music Since 1900*. A contributing factor to this enhancement is the massive migration of European composers to the United States during the period between wars and revolutions. The list of names is imposing: Rachmaninoff, Stravinsky, Schoenberg, Hindemith, Toch, Krenek, Kurt Weill, all of whom became naturalized if not totally Americanized. Béla Bartók wrote some of his most significant scores during his few years in America before his death in 1945. At the same time, native American composers began to impress themselves on the surprised world. As late as 1948, *Le Guide du Concert* of Paris could declare with an air of pompous condescension: "L'Amérique n'est plus une nation a-musicale: elle compte une cinquantaine de compositeurs de talent." Soon Europe discovered the greatness of Charles Ives. It is with understandable pride that I am including in DESCRIPTIVE CHRONOLOGY the programs of my European concerts at which I conducted works by Ives and other American composers for the first time on the continent.

Even a history of the future must have a temporal finis. I have resolved to mark it by the romantically realistic landing of men on the moon. But what, one may ask, is the connection between the soundless moon and music? The Harmony of the Spheres, of course. This Pythagorean link provides a perfect ending.

In the first edition of *Music Since 1900* I introduced the term of my own invention, Pandiatonicism, intended to describe the free use in melody and harmony of all seven degrees of the diatonic scale. The term has since been widely adopted, and its success encouraged me to follow up with additional neologisms that may prove useful. As a result, the modest glossary of terms of earlier editions has grown into a propaedeutical compendium of rather formidable dimensions. For good measure, I threw in some parerga—or perhaps offal (awful offal?)—of my purely linguistic elucubrations. The modus operandi in making up new terms is simple. I first determine in my mind the area to be covered. Then, in the best tradition of scientific logodaedaly, I put together a Graeco-Latin compound corresponding to the nascent concept. I have felt, for instance, the necessity of a term to describe modern idioms peculiar to the 20th century, and I hit upon the word Vigesimosecular, which would supplement such crescively vaguescent descriptions as Modern, New, Contemporary, Advanced, Avant-Garde, Ultra-modern, etc., and which by the ponderous sound of its sesquipedalian Latinity would suggest progressive modernism. Among other functional terms in the present glossary are Asomatous

Variations (variations without a theme), Aud Music (an auditory analogy of Op Art), Demotic Music (a generic rubric covering vernacular, urban and country music) and Icositetraphonic Harmony (relating to quarter-tones).

Much new material has been added to the last section of the book, LETTERS AND DOCUMENTS. The text of the dramatic interrogation of Hanns Eisler by the House of Representatives Committee on Un-American Activities has been extracted from the official transcript of the hearings. A comical pendant to this grim inquisition is the Resolution of the Fire and Police Research Association of Los Angeles, urging Congress to ban folk music festivals as hotbeds of Communist activity, and the hilarious debate that followed in the Senate, proving that legislators can display upon occasion an exquisite sense of the ridiculous. On the more serious side, there is a message addressed to the Subcommittee on the Environment by that tireless ecological gadfly Ralph Nader, sounding alarm at the noise pollution generated by Rock 'n' Roll bands. One of the most important documents in this section is the Charter of the Union of Soviet Composers, setting forth the guiding principles for the desirable type of Soviet composition. Also included is an ideological article in *Peking Review*, dealing with the correct application of Chairman Mao's thoughts to the domain of fine arts and music.

Not without some hesitation, I have decided to publish the letters I received through the years from Charles Ives. My scruples arise from his extreme praise of me as a person and as a conductor. There is something inexpressibly poignant in what he writes about my courage in "ferreting out a nonentity." In his last letter he congratulates me on the publication of the first edition of *Music Since 1900*. He wrote all his letters to me in his seismic handwriting—his muscular coordination was badly affected by chronic diabetes. But Charles Ives is a great spirit of the age and a towering genius of American music. This correspondence, so personal in its expression, offers a revealing glance into his heart and mind. As such it must be made known.

Quite different in tone are the letters from Varèse, also included in the last section of the book. They demonstrate a sense of unflinching purpose, a firm confidence in the validity of his musical ideals in the face of disheartening hostility towards his music on the part of the press and the public. A single letter from Anton von Webern betrays his crying need for sympathy.

My list of acknowledgments will be brief but global. I am deeply grateful to a legion of anonymous (for their signatures are usually illegible) archivists, librarians, embassy officials and municipal clerks in many parts of the world for their willingness to search musty files on dusty shelves in damp basements for some chronological minutiae essential in the preparation of this book. Along more personal lines, the overwhelming share of my overflowing gratitude goes to Wayne Shirley of the Music Division in the Library of Congress, whose instant and multilingual erudition has saved me from many an embarrassing imbroglio. He is also an *acharné* collector of musical and literary curiosa, and last but not least, a born grammarian—inestimable qualities of a true editorial mind. Viva Wayne Shirley!

Help came also from the 6'3", 130 lbs. astronomer and meteorologist David Cloud, a cumulus of non-nebulous data, teeming with a lot o' news, not only about the square of the hypotenuse, but about a fantastic amount of things musical.

On an entirely different level, untutored in the niceties and technicalities of the subject, Joyce Knapp, a California blonde, born in Hollywood in 1946, lent decisive support by typing, retyping and overtyping, albeit defiantly and often petulantly, the harrowing immensity of the continually fluctuating text of the manuscript, spotting a duplication here and a pleonasm there, pointing out unwarranted unintelligibilities and suggesting workable substitutions for inordinately involved auxiliary clauses. For this I owe her a sempiternal debt of gratitude.

Then came Teri, or to spell her out in full, Mary Thérèse Friedrichs, who entered the scene on her 21st birthday during the semifinals in the assembly of "insticks" (a Swedish word I adopted for last-minute inserts) in the manuscript. She applied herself to this task with a devotion to the cause that would have given credit to the "little flower" from whom she received her middle name. Thanks, Teri. (You're welcome, Nicolas.)

NICOLAS SLONIMSKY
December 1970

# Descriptive
# Chronology
# 1.1.1900-7.20.1969

# ❧ *1900* ❧

1 JANUARY 1900

The first volume of the collected works of Hector BERLIOZ, true precursor of 20th-century music, whose grandeur of design and subjective programmaticism engendered new and fertile non-classical forms marked by an associative thematic development and an expansive inflation of symphonic sonorities, is issued by Breitkopf & Härtel, on the symbolic day when the 1900's begin. (The 20th century proper did not open until January 1901)

13 JANUARY 1900

*Hiawatha*, overture by Rubin GOLDMARK, American-born nephew of the grand master of Central European romanticism Carl Goldmark, inspired by Longfellow's famous poem of Indian lore, and couched in a Germanically effusive style with occasional pentatonic themes to depict the redskins, is performed for the first time by the Boston Symphony Orchestra, Wilhelm Gericke conducting.

14 JANUARY 1900

At the Costanzi Theater in Rome the world première is given of *Tosca*, opera in three acts by Giacomo PUCCINI, after Victorien Sardou's poignant melodrama *La Tosca* (the definite article is used in the title of the French play but not in the title of the opera); wherein a voluptuously desirable Italian songstress Floria Tosca, mistress of an artist member of a Napoleonic conspiracy of June 1800 at the time of Napoleon's surprising victory at Marengo, slays the lecherous, treacherous chief of Roman police at a private dinner as she feigns a willingness to submit to his desires as a price to save her lover, but is posthumously outwitted by him when the secret order of execution is carried out, and in despair throws herself to her death from a high parapet, the score couched in the most effective manner of Italian Verismo, containing such harmonic innovations as systematic progressions of parallel triads, parallel progressions of inverted seventh-chords, and ominously sounding whole-tone scales.

Last evening at the Costanzi Theater the first performance of Puccini's new opera was given before an immense audience, the largest that ever filled that theater. Early in the evening the crowd began to assemble. Every seat and every ticket had been sold for days previous, so that when the curtain rose, the house was packed from top to bottom to its fullest capacity, even standing room being at a premium. The boxes were filled with a dazzling array of richly dressed women, while celebrities of all kinds—the court, diplomats, artists, literary men, critics, clerics, army and navy men, musicians— were seen on every side. Never has such interest been shown any first representation as upon this occasion. . . . After the close of the first act the composer was called out eight times in response to the demands of the audience. (*The Musical Courier,* New York, 31 January 1900)

The great musical event of the New Year in Rome is over, and Giacomo Puccini, the young composer, has launched a new opera. . . . The general opinion seems to be that the story is somewhat too dramatic for an opera, that the music is lost in the general interest of the development of the plot. However, difficult as the situations are from a musical standpoint, the "maestro" has handled them in a masterly manner. (*Pall Mall Gazette*, London, February 1900)

Signor Puccini's opera *Tosca* is a typical example of the proclivity of Italian composers to seek inspiration in the crudest forms of elemental passion, and of their apparent inability to perceive that ignoble sentiment is a fatal bar to the creation of noble music. In *Tosca* another degradation has certainly been put on music by seeking to make it express physical torture. Although the music consists of little more than growls and screams from the orchestra and declamatory passages of little meaning from the soloists, the gruesomeness of this portion of the play is invested with peculiar objectionableness by force of contrast. (An unidentified London newspaper, February 1900)

Those who were present at the performance of Puccini's opera *Tosca* were little prepared for the revolting effects produced by musically illustrating the torture and murder scenes of Sardou's play. The alliance of a pure art with scenes so essentially brutal and demoralizing . . . produced a feeling of nausea. . . . What has music to do with a lustful man chasing a defenseless woman or the dying kicks of a murdered scoundrel? (A London newspaper, 13 July 1900)

*Tosca* is a melodrama in the truest sense. The music is almost entirely subordinated to the drama. . . . The *parlando* is employed continually. It is as if a broken mirror was made to reflect and distort bits of sunlight; both eye and ear are often offended by the consecutive fifths, raw harmonic progressions and alterations of the tawdry with the solemn. . . . Indeed, the short bursts of sustained melody are generally formless. Here is the Wagner theory skeletonized, almost reduced to an absurdity. (New York *Sun*, 5 February 1901)

At the first hearing, much, perhaps most, of Puccini's *Tosca* sounds exceedingly, even ingeniously ugly. Every now and then one comes across the most ear-flaying succession of chords. . . . To my ear, the most complex dissonant harmonies of Wagner or Richard Strauss—"chords" (so-called) of six or seven notes perhaps—have not half the rasp that some perfectly consonant triad progressions have. (W. F. Apthorp, Boston *Evening Transcript*, 12 April 1901)

### 18 JANUARY 1900

*Thyl Uylenspiegel,* opera in three acts by the Flemish composer Jan BLOCKX, dealing with the Dutch rebellion against the Spanish rule in the Netherlands in 1568–1573 and the patriotic role of the legendary jester Till Eulenspiegel, set to music in an opulently Wagneromantic vein, with refreshing interludes of Flemish folk dances, is produced in Brussels.

### 20 JANUARY 1900

*Raquel,* opera in four acts by the Spanish composer Tomás BRETÓN, after Grillparzer's play *Die Jüdin von Toledo,* dealing with the loves and tragedies of a Toledan Jewess and set in a fastidiously dramatic musical idiom, is produced in Madrid.

### 22 JANUARY 1900

*Es war einmal,* three-act opera by the 28-year-old Vienna-born composer of Polish origin, Alexander ZEMLINSKY, based on a triptych of Danish folk tales of pastoral imprint with grim overtones, set to music in a freshly Wagnerized fluent idiom, is produced at the Vienna Opera, Gustav Mahler conducting.

### 27 JANUARY 1900

The final volume of the monumental edition of the collected works of Johann Sebastian BACH is published by Breitkopf & Härtel under the auspices of the Bach-Gesellschaft, which was founded on 28 July 1850, the centennial of Bach's death.

### 2 FEBRUARY 1900

*Adonais*, elegiac overture by the Boston composer George Whitefield CHADWICK, inspired by Shelley's threnody to the memory of Keats, "The Pard-like spirit, beautiful and swift," and composed in a fine Germanic manner acquired by Chadwick during his apprentice years in Leipzig, is performed for the first time by the Boston Symphony Orchestra.

### 2 FEBRUARY 1900

*Louise*, "roman musical" in four acts by Gustave CHARPENTIER, his first opera, to his own libretto (his mistress at the time was also named Louise and, like the heroine, was employed in a dressmaking shop), portraying with sensuous melodiousness and sentimental harmoniousness the pleasures of Paris, "cité de lumière, cité d'amour," amid lovable nyctophiliacs, amorous artists, grisettes, soubrettes and midinettes, alive with city noises and precisely notated cries of vegetable vendors, is produced at the Opéra-Comique in Paris, destined to become the most popular French opera of the 1900's and the first successful example of French operatic naturalism.

### 7 FEBRUARY 1900

*Lancelot du lac*, lyric drama in four acts by the French composer Victorin de JONCIÈRES, to a libretto dealing with Sir Lancelot of the Lake and his love for Queen Guinevere, with a conventional musical score in the style of Gounod, is performed for the first time at the Paris Opéra.

### 9 FEBRUARY 1900

*Der Bärenhäuter*, opera in three acts by Arnold MENDELSSOHN, son of a cousin of Felix Mendelssohn, to a libretto derived from a grim Grimm brothers' tale wherein a handsome German soldier is turned by the devil into a repellent monster covered by a bearskin (hence the title *The Bearskinned*), and is saved from his ursine deformation by the love of a maiden to whom he cleaves despite the repeated attempts of a succession of seductive she-devils to abduct him, is produced in Berlin.

### 10 FEBRUARY 1900

Riccardo DRIGO, Italian conductor of the Russian Imperial Ballet, conducts at the Hermitage Theater in St. Petersburg the first performance of his most successful ballet *Les Millions d'Arlequin,* which includes the perennially popular *Sérénade d'Arlequin* fashioned in the finest Italian vein for a soulful solo by the cello.

### 16 FEBRUARY 1900

Vása SUK, Czech composer of the romantic school, conducts in Kharkov, Russia, during his sojourn there as an operatic director and teacher, the first performance of his opera *The Forest King,* dealing with the bold adventures of an endearing bandit chief and containing effective dances in the Slavic vein. (The first performance to the original libretto in the Czech language took place in Prague on 5 April 1903, the composer conducting)

### 17 FEBRUARY 1900

*Kain,* one-act opera by Eugen D'ALBERT, to the biblical story of the first human murder, in which Abel is slain to the ominous sounds of chromatically heaving diminished seventh-chords, with the voice of avenging Jehovah represented by a mighty chorus in unison, is produced in Berlin.

### 17 FEBRUARY 1900

*Anton,* opera in three acts by the 27-year-old Italian composer Cesare GALEOTTI, wherein a young Libyan, whose pagan mistress slays his early Christian concubine known as the "Flower of the Catacombs," flees to the Egyptian desert, suppresses his sensuous memories, resists a series of diabolically contrived temptations and becomes sanctified as Saint Anthony, to a musical score gushing out crimson floods of curvilinear melos, is produced at La Scala, Milan.

### 18 FEBRUARY 1900

Charles Russell DAY, English soldier who was gazetted to Light Infantry in India in 1882 and became an authority on Hindu music, is killed in the battle of Paardeberg in South Africa during the Boer War.

### 22 FEBRUARY 1900

*Cenerentola,* opera in three acts by the 24-year-old half-German half-Italian composer Ermanno WOLF-FERRARI, recounting in harmonious tones the ever-inspiring tale of a lowly maid who rises from domestic cinders to princely incense, is produced in Venice with some cuts necessitated by the enormous length (1007 manuscript pages) of the original score.

### 2 MARCH 1900

Kurt WEILL, composer of highly functional theater music throbbing with modern rhythms in energizing march time alternating with ruefully nostalgic waltzes against a dissonant but tonally stable harmonic background, is born in Dessau, Germany.

## 6 MARCH 1900

Carl BECHSTEIN, founder of the piano manufacturing company bearing his name, whose handsomely wing-shaped Flügel are distinguished by a velvet-like tone and resilient key action, dies in Berlin in his 74th year.

## 10 MARCH 1900

*Atahualpa,* grand opera in four acts by the Italian composer Ferruccio CATTELANI (1867–1932) who settled in South America in 1886, to a libretto about the last king of the Incas betrayed by the conquistadores and garroted on 29 August 1533, is produced in Buenos Aires.

## 10 MARCH 1900

Johann Peter Emilius HARTMANN, patriarch of Danish opera composers and the last representative of the Hartmann musical dynasty in Denmark, the son of August Wilhelm Hartmann and grandson of Johann Ernest Hartmann, dies in his native Copenhagen at the age of 94 years, 9 months and 25 days.

## 12 MARCH 1900

Lady Jane Douglas SCOTT, who in 1834 wrote the air *Annie Laurie,* the most famous song of nostalgic loyalty among British and American swains, dies at her estate at Spottiswode, Berwickshire, at the age of ninety.

## 17 MARCH 1900

*Norwegische Hochzeit,* opera in two acts by the Norwegian composer Gerhard SCHJELDERUP, to his own libretto in German dealing with a Norwegian wedding, is performed for the first time in Prague.

## 19 MARCH 1900

Charles-Louis HANON, French composer and pedagogue whose books of piano exercises are second in ubiquitous immortality only to Czerny's, and who, like Czerny, remained a childless célibataire, dies at Boulogne-sur-Mer at the age of eighty-one.

(Hanon was born at Rénescure, district of Dunkerque, Département du Nord, on 2 July 1819, according to a certificate of birth obtained by the author from the Mairie of Rénescure. All dictionaries and reference works give wrong date and wrong place of Hanon's birth)

## 11 APRIL 1900

*Le Juif polonais,* opera in three acts by Camille ERLANGER, after a ghostly no-vella from Erckmann-Chatrian's tales, detailing the murder in an Alsatian inn of a transient Jew who comes back to torment his murderer in a realistic post-humous appearance, is produced at the Opéra-Comique in Paris.

## 15 APRIL 1900

The 1900 Exposition Universelle opens in Paris, offering among its attractions the spectacles, dances and music of Cambodia, Annam, Java, Japan and

China, bringing to Europe a cornucopia of exotic scales and asymmetrical rhythms deeply impressive to the impressionable impressionists.

### 29 APRIL 1900

*Vikingeblod* (*Viking Blood*), last opera in four acts by the Danish composer Peter Erasmus LANGE-MÜLLER (1850–1926), is produced in Copenhagen.

### 1 MAY 1900

*Mazeppa*, grand opera in four acts by the Polish composer Adam MINHEJMER (1831–1904), based on the dramatic story of the Ukrainian chieftain who fought a losing battle against Peter the Great, receives its belated production in Warsaw a quarter of a century after its composition.

### 7 MAY 1900

A century has passed since the death in Paris of Niccolò PICCINNI who went down into oblivion as a hapless rival of Gluck in their contest for Parisian favors, but who was a knowledgeable opera composer in his own right.

### 15 MAY 1900

The Paderewski Fund of $10,000 is established in New York by Ignace PADEREWSKI, universally idolized Polish genius of the piano, to award annual prizes to American composers for the best orchestral works.

### 22 MAY 1900

Edwin S. VOTEY patents a "pneumatic piano attachment" constituting the basic principle of the Pianola. (Patent filed in Washington on 25 January 1897; renewed application on 5 February 1900; patent granted on 22 May 1900. Dates in the official Gazette of the U.S. Patent office of 22 May 1900, No. 650,285, p. 1572)

### 28 MAY 1900

Sir George GROVE, grand seigneur of British musical scholarship, the begetter, with the aid of continental contributors, of the monumentally famous *Dictionary of Music and Musicians*, dies in his native London eleven weeks before his 80th birthday.

### 30 JUNE 1900

The Schweizerischer Tonkünstlerverein is formally organized in Zürich by Joseph LAUBER, Carl VOGLER and other Swiss composers, with the object of promoting the cause of national music in Switzerland.

### 1 JULY 1900

The music publishing firm of Breitkopf & Härtel issues the first volume of the collection *Denkmäler der Tonkunst in Bayern*, devoted to the publication of works by composers of Bavaria. (Date of the preface)

6

## 2 JULY 1900

*Finlandia,* patriotic symphonic poem by Jean SIBELIUS, proclaiming in force-fully somber melodies and granitically noble harmonies the right of Finland to national independence, profoundly expressive of the spiritual essence of the Finnish people, is performed for the first time in Helsingfors, under its origi-nal title *Suomi* (Finnish for Finland), with Robert Kajanus conducting.

## 2 JULY 1900

*Second Symphony,* op. 115, by the Swiss composer Hans HUBER, composed in 1897 under the impression of an exhibition of Böcklin's paintings and for that reason known as Böcklinsinfonie, in four movements, of which the last is a theme with eight variations each named after a Böcklin picture, written in an expansive Wagneromantic manner within a formal Brahmsogenic framework, is performed for the first time at the first Swiss Music Festival in Zürich. (The Symphony was tentatively scheduled for performance in Basel on 20 March 1898, but was withdrawn by the composer after one rehearsal for further revi-sions)

## 4 JULY 1900

Louis ARMSTRONG, the Great Satchmo (i.e. Satchel Mouth), trumpeter ex-traordinary who was to cut a powerful swath through decades of hot jazz and swing and whose unlearned art combined spontaneity of expressive perform-ance and fantastic technical prowess (he set a record by hitting High C 280 times in succession) with an immediacy of popular appeal characteristic of Dixieland Negro music, is born in New Orleans on Independence Day.

## 8 JULY 1900

George ANTHEIL, self-styled "Bad Boy of Music," whose *Ballet mécanique* glorified the spirit of the machine age with magnificently contrived acousma, is born in Trenton, New Jersey.

## 14 JULY 1900

On Bastille Day the Opéra-Comique presents in Paris a patriotic opera by Lu-cien LAMBERT entitled *La Marseillaise,* melodramatically depicting the scene purported to have taken place in Strasbourg on the night of 24 April 1792 when Rouget de l'Isle is supposed to have improvised the famous tune of the French National Anthem. (It is almost certain that Rouget de l'Isle was the author of only the text, not the music)

## 22 JULY 1900

*I due fratelli,* opera by the Greek composer Denis LAVRANGAS, to an Italian li-bretto, is produced for the first time by an Italian opera company in Athens.

## 23 AUGUST 1900

Ernst KRENEK, whose versatile musical talent epitomizes the mutations of the 20th-century style in composition, ranging from satire in jazz to the mathe-

7

matically involved complexities of the dodecaphonic technique and integral serialism, is born in Vienna.

### 25 AUGUST 1900

Friedrich NIETZSCHE, whose scant musical production lacks the proud virility that his philosophy glorifies, dies in Weimar at the age of 55 in a pathetic state of dementia praecox consequent upon syphilitic infection contracted by him during his student days.

### 26 AUGUST 1900

*Prométhée*, "tragédie lyrique" in three acts by Gabriel FAURÉ, his first opera, wherein Prometheus (who has only a spoken part) deters Pandora from opening her baleful box, thus assuring a temporary tranquillity in a strife-torn world, set to an austerely economic score in neo-Grecian modalities, is performed for the first time in the ancient Roman Arena at Béziers.

### 15 SEPTEMBER 1900

*Princessen paa Aerten*, one-act opera by the Danish composer August ENNA (1860–1939), after Hans Christian Andersen's fairy-tale about a royal princess who proves her highborn supersensitivity by sensing the presence of a pea under a score of fluffy mattresses on her ample bed and thus qualifies for marriage to the heir-apparent of a neighboring kingdom, is performed for the first time at the opening of the new municipal theater in Aarhus.

### 28 SEPTEMBER 1900

*Asya*, opera in three acts by Mikhail IPPOLITOV-IVANOV, after Turgenev's story of a short-lived but profoundly felt summer romance in a pastoral German town blossoming forth between a vacationing Russian student and an expatriate Russian girl named Asya, set to an emotionally heaving score in a Tchaikovskian manner, is performed for the first time in Moscow.

### 3 OCTOBER 1900

*The Dream of Gerontius*, sacred oratorio in two parts by Edward ELGAR (completed on 7 June 1900), to Cardinal Newman's devoutly Catholic poem, wherein the dying Gerontius (i.e. oldster) prays in English and Latin for divine intercession against the "sour and uncouth dissonance" of chromatically vocal demons, and after an agonizingly protracted suspension of a minor thirteenth-chord ("for one moment must every instrument exert its full force") arrives at a D-major apotheosis, with harps arpeggiating, the organ pealing and the celestially confident chorus saying Amen, is performed for the first time at the Birmingham Festival, Hans Richter conducting.

What every connoisseur of orchestration must have said at the first hearing of Elgar's *Gerontius* (among other things) was, "What a devil of a fortissimo." Here was no literary paper instrumentation, no muddle, no noise, but an absolutely new energy given to the band by a consummate knowledge of what it could do and how it could do it. (George Bernard Shaw, *Music and Literature*, 1920)

#### 4 OCTOBER 1900

*Janek,* opera in two acts by the 63-year-old Polish composer Wladislaw ZELEŃSKI, is produced in Lwów.


#### 6 OCTOBER 1900

Three centuries have passed since the production of the earliest opera of which the music is extant, *Euridice* by Jacopo PERI, presented at the Pitti Palace in Florence at the wedding feast of Maria de' Medici and King Henri IV of France, with Peri himself singing the part of Orpheus. (Peri was also the composer of the musical drama *Dafne,* produced at the Palazzo Corsi in Florence during the carnival of 1597; its music is lost)


#### 15 OCTOBER 1900

Symphony Hall, acoustically one of the finest concert auditoriums in the world, along with Carnegie Hall, Musik-Verein-Saal in Vienna and Concertgebouw in Amsterdam, is formally inaugurated in Boston as the permanent home of the Boston Symphony Orchestra.

Musical Boston has lost its real music hall forever, and Symphony Hall is its la-di-da substitute. But why not Nocturne Hall, or Kapellmeister Hall, or Sostenuto Hall, or, in fact, why not Oratorio Hall? These titles are no sillier than Symphony Hall. (From a column signed *Chatterer* in the Boston *Herald,* 16 September 1900, before the official inauguration)

You have proved here that the Science of Acoustics certainly exists in a definite form. (From a letter to the architect Wallace Sabine from Major Lee Higginson, founder of the Boston Symphony Orchestra)


#### 15 OCTOBER 1900

Zdeněk FIBICH, Czech composer of 376 works, among them a trilogy of music dramas and a number of highly playable concert pieces for the violin, of which the *Romance* (composed in 1879) became a perennial favorite, dies in Prague at the age of forty-nine.


#### 1 NOVEMBER 1900

*Petru Rareş,* opera in three acts by the Rumanian composer Eduard CAUDELLA, wherein a heroic bastard son of a 16th-century Moldavian voyevoda regains his ancestral throne and frees his beloved from the villainous clutches of a wily gospodar, set to music in an Italianate Wagneromantic manner retouched with colorful Balkanized orientalisms, is produced in Bucharest.


#### 2 NOVEMBER 1900

Vincent D'INDY reads his Inauguration Speech as new President of the Schola Cantorum in Paris.

Where shall we find the quickening life that will give us fresh forms and formulas? The source is not difficult to discover. Do not seek it anywhere but in the decorative art of the plainsong singers, in the architectural art of the age of Palestrina, and in the expressive art of the great Italians of the seventeenth century. It is there, and there alone, that we shall find melodic craft, rhythmic cadences, and a harmonic magnificence that is really new—if our modern spirit can only learn how to absorb their nutritious essence. And so I prescribe for all pupils in the School the careful study of classic forms, because they alone are able to give the elements of a new life to our music, which will be founded on principles that are sane, serious and trustworthy. (Quoted from *Tribune de Saint-Gervais*, November 1900, by Romain Rolland in his *Musiciens d'aujourd'hui*)

### 3 NOVEMBER 1900

*Sémiramis, "scène lyrique"* by Florent SCHMITT, which won him the Premier Prix de Rome, dedicated *"à mes chers Maîtres Massenet et Fauré,"* is performed for the first time in Paris.

I had to compete five times for the Prix de Rome to win it once. And if in the end I was not left out in the cold, it was thanks to Gabriel Fauré, my much lamented teacher, who managed to gather for me enough votes among sculptors and painters to counterbalance the animosity of musicians, who, with the exception of Massenet, Reyer and Saint-Saëns, turned thumbs down on me. So it was not really a music prize. But I have no shame for all that, for the other musicians among committee members were Paladilhe, Dubois and Lenepveu. The important thing was the thirty thousand gold francs. (Florent Schmitt, in *Cinquante ans de musique française*, Paris, 1925, vol. II p. 51)

### 3 NOVEMBER 1900

*The Tale of Tsar Saltan,* opera in four acts with a prologue by RIMSKY-KORSAKOV (completed on 31 January 1900), after Pushkin's poem, wherein the heir to the throne of a mythical kingdom exiled by a camarilla led by his mother's sisters, learns magic, turns into a bumblebee, revisits his native land and in buzzingly painful chromatics repeatedly stings his perfidious aunts, and eventually regains his rightful throne accompanied by a beautiful swan-bride whose life he had saved from a predatory falcon, is performed for the first time in Moscow, Ippolitov-Ivanov conducting.

### 9 NOVEMBER 1900

*Pád Arkuna (Fall of Arcona),* opera by Zdeněk FIBICH in the Czech language, relating the royally dramatic love of Dargun and Helga in 1168 A.D., is posthumously produced in Prague, 25 days after Fibich's death.

### 9 NOVEMBER 1900

*Atzimba,* opera in three acts by the 36-year-old Mexican composer Ricardo CASTRO, dealing with the depredations of the Spanish conquistadores in Mexico, is produced in Mexico City.

## 10 NOVEMBER 1900

*Zazà,* lyric comedy in four acts by Ruggero LEONCAVALLO, dealing with a Parisian chanteuse whose yearning for matrimonial respectability is shattered by the revelation that her lover is a married man and a father, with a score in an effective veristic manner redolent of melorhythmic patterns of his famous opera *Pagliacci,* is produced in Milan, Arturo Toscanini conducting.

## 14 NOVEMBER 1900

Aaron COPLAND, American composer who has set a new norm for an integrated national style of 20th-century composition, widely varied in technical resources, ranging from jazzy asymmetries to symphonic serenity, from ethnic melorhythms to dodecaphonic serialism and from triadic pandiatonicism to polyharmonic quadritonality, is born in Brooklyn.

## 16 NOVEMBER 1900

The Philadelphia Orchestra presents its inaugural concert under the direction of Fritz SCHEEL in a program of symphonic favorites including Beethoven's *Fifth Symphony,* with the participation of the 22-year-old Russian pianist Ossip GABRILOWITSCH playing Tchaikovsky's *First Piano Concerto.*

## 17 NOVEMBER 1900

*Medio Evo Latino,* operatic triptych by the 25-year-old Argentine composer Ettore PANIZZA, in which the action takes place in three Latin countries in medieval times, is performed in a world première at Genoa.

## 20 NOVEMBER 1900

*The House of Ice,* opera in four acts by the Russian composer Arseny KORESHCHENKO, to a libretto based on a horrendous tale about an 18th-century Russian landlord who punishes a recalcitrant serf by pouring water on his naked body in midwinter until he becomes a human icicle, with a musical score imitative of Tchaikovsky, is produced for the first time in Moscow.

## 22 NOVEMBER 1900

Edward ELGAR is awarded the honorary degree of Doctor in Music by the University of Cambridge, England.

## 22 NOVEMBER 1900

Sir Arthur SULLIVAN, English composer of superb mock-Italian operettas to the exhilarating quasi-Shakespearean texts of Sir William Gilbert, as well as of two imperishable vocal favorites, *The Lost Chord* and *Onward, Christian Soldiers,* dies in London at the age of fifty-eight.

The death of Sir Arthur Sullivan may be said without hyperbole to have plunged the whole of the Empire in gloom; for many years he has ranked with the most distinguished personages rather than with ordinary musicians. Never in the history of the art has a position such as his been held by a composer. For all the English-speaking races, with the exception of a very small and, possibly, unimportant class, Sullivan's name stood as a synonym for music in England. (*The Times*, London, 23 November 1900)

### 24 NOVEMBER 1900

*First Symphony* in E minor by Alexander SCRIABIN, couched in a Russianized Wagnerian idiom presaging the proclamatory style of his later music, is performed, without its sixth choral movement, at the Russian Symphony Concerts in St. Petersburg, under the direction of Anatoli Liadov. (A complete performance, including the last choral movement, entitled *Hymn to Art*, was given in Moscow on 29 March 1901)

### 9 DECEMBER 1900

The first two sections of the symphonic suite *Nocturnes* by Claude DEBUSSY, *Nuages*, an impressionistic evocation containing only 102 bars, diaphanously set for divided strings and paired woodwinds, and *Fêtes*, an animated movement in ternary form, evanescently concluding until nothing remains of the festal sound but a faintly percussive rhythm, are performed for the first time at the Concerts Lamoureux in Paris, Camille Chevillard conducting.

### 21 DECEMBER 1900

*Festival of Pan*, the first of the three symphonic romances by the efficaciously competent American composer Frederick S. CONVERSE, suggested by *Endymion* of Keats, a romantically fluent musical score infused with Wagneromorphic ninth-chords and augmented triads, is performed for the first time by the Boston Symphony Orchestra, Wilhelm Gericke conducting.

### 26 DECEMBER 1900

*Ollanta*, by José María VALLE-RIESTRA, the first truly national Peruvian opera by a native composer, dealing with the rebellion of an Inca general against the emperor whose daughter he loves, and employing authentic pentatonic chants of pre-Columbian times, is produced in Lima.

# ❦ *1901* ❦

### 11 JANUARY 1901

Vassili KALINNIKOV, Russian composer of melodious symphonic and other works, imitative of Borodin and Tchaikovsky but breathing a lyrical sentiment of individual grace, dies at Yalta in the Crimea, succumbing to tuberculosis two days before his 35th birthday.

## 17 JANUARY 1901

*Le Maschere,* opera in three acts by Pietro MASCAGNI (originally dedicated "to myself, with my distinguished consideration and unaltering esteem"), wherein the familiar characters of the commedia dell'arte are embroiled in conflicting emotions, culminating in a wedding feast when Arlecchino weds his Colombina, with a musical setting in a traditional Italian manner, is produced in a sextuple première on the same day in Milan, Venice, Turin, Genoa, Verona and Rome (where Mascagni himself conducted the performance)

## 18 JANUARY 1901

Victor HERBERT conducts the Pittsburgh Symphony Orchestra in the first performance of his symphonic poem *Hero and Leander,* inspired by the classical legend about a Greek youth swimming the Hellespont every night to visit Hero, a vestal of Venus (Lord Byron duplicated Leander's feat in 1810 in one hour and ten minutes)

## 27 JANUARY 1901

Giuseppe VERDI, great Italian operatic composer whose 26 operas range from Bellinian simplicity to symphonic drama, dies in Milan at the age of 87 years, 3 months and 17 days.

Signor Verdi died at Milan today, 27 January, at 2:50 A.M. . . . The Senate was specially convoked this afternoon in order to commemorate the great musician to whom it was decided to grant the same honors as those paid in 1873 to Alessandro Manzoni—namely, a State funeral, and the execution of a bust of Verdi for the Senate . . .

In person Verdi was the ideal of a well-bred Italian: the finely-cut features, the piercing black eyes, and the expressive face which are familiar to all, were associated with a figure of a height unusual among his countrymen and a bearing of the utmost dignity. (*The Times,* London, 28 January 1901)

The maestro is dead. He carried away with him a great quantity of light and vital warmth. We had all basked in the sun of his Olympian old age. He died magnificently like a fighter redoubtable and mute. This silence of death fell on him a week before he died. With his head bent, his eyebrows set, he seemed to measure with half-shut eyes an unknown and formidable adversary, calculating in his mind the force that he could summon up in opposition. Thus he put up a heroic resistance. The breathing of his great chest sustained him for four days and three nights; on the fourth night the sound of his breathing still filled the room; but what a struggle, poor Maestro! How magnificently he fought up to the last moment! (Giuseppe Giacosa, quoted by Francis Toye, in *Giuseppe Verdi and His Works,* New York, 1931)

## 29 JANUARY 1901

*Divertissement espagnol* by the Alsatian-born Americanized composer Charles Martin LOEFFLER for orchestra with alto saxophone obbligato, written in the form of a rhapsody based on a hispanoid rhythmic theme, is performed for the first time in Boston by the Orchestral Club of 75 amateur musicians "from select social circles, at least half of them being attractive young women," with Georges Longy, prime oboist of the Boston Symphony Orchestra, conducting.

*El Náufrago,* opera by the Cuban composer Eduardo SÁNCHEZ DE FUENTES, to a libretto from Tennyson's *Enoch Arden,* wherein a shipwrecked sailor given up for dead returns home only to find his supposed widow married to another, and nobly goes back to sea, is produced in Havana.

### 2 FEBRUARY 1901

Jascha HEIFETZ (properly Jacob, Jascha being a diminutive form used in application to children), one of the few child prodigies who, having taken up the violin in early infancy, achieved merited fame as a virtuoso of the modern school of "cold tonal beauty," is born in Vilna, the Polish-Lithuanian town which by some arcane magic spawned a disproportionate number of Jewish violinists.

### 3 FEBRUARY 1901

*Pelléas et Mélisande,* orchestral suite by Gabriel FAURÉ drawn from his incidental music to Maeterlinck's drama, in three movements: (1) *Prélude,* depicting in a serenely modal idiom the finding of Mélisande by Golaud (2) *Fileuse,* where Mélisande weaves a gentle fabric of unwarped woof in sextuple semiquavers (3) *Molto Adagio,* a somber threnody as her life ebbs slowly away from grievous wounds inflicted in a jealous rage by Golaud after he has slain his half-brother Pelléas, is performed for the first time at the Concerts Lamoureux in Paris.

### 7 FEBRUARY 1901

*Chansons de Bilitis* by Claude DEBUSSY (a different work from his songs on the same poems of Pierre Louÿs), scored for two flutes, two harps and celesta, is performed for the first time in the Salon of *Le Journal* in Paris, in the form of a mimo-melodrama, with the poems read to music while a mime interprets in eloquently symbolic gestures the sensual content of the verses. (The musical material of this score was incorporated later in Debussy's *Six Épigraphes antiques* for piano duo)

### 15 FEBRUARY 1901

*Astarté,* opera in four acts by Xavier LEROUX, depicting in Gallically Wagnerian colors the story of the Lydian queen Omphale, the worshipper of the moon-goddess Astarte, who subjects Hercules to humiliatingly effeminate work at her spinning wheel while she struts girt in a lion-skin as lady paramount, is produced at the Paris Opéra.

The score is one of the noisiest ever heard. From the first note to the last it rattles along a ceaseless interminable flow of ear-splitting clangor and hullabaloo, thundering, clanking, jangling, without a single moment of respite or instant's pause in the deafening clatter. Then the subject is repugnant, indecent. (*Era*, London, 23 February 1901)

### 17 FEBRUARY 1901

Gustav MAHLER conducts the Vienna Philharmonic in the first performance of his youthful cantata *Das klagende Lied*, completed in 1880, to his own text after a harrowing fairy-tale by Ludwig Bechstein, in which the male heir to the throne murders his brother to remove a rival in royal succession, a crime that comes to haunt him horrifyingly when a shepherd fashions a flute out of one of the victim's extant bones which miraculously sings out the tale, set to music in a Wagneromantic spirit but illuminated by proleptic Mahlerian flashes.

### 17 FEBRUARY 1901

Ethelbert NEVIN, American composer of melodious songs of great sentimental appeal, of which *The Rosary* attained extraordinary popularity, and of harmonious piano pieces, of which the melliferous *Narcissus* is a perfect specimen, dies of apoplexy in New Haven, Connecticut, at the age of thirty-eight.

### 20 FEBRUARY 1901

*La Fille de Tabarin*, lyric comedy in three acts by Gabriel PIERNÉ, dealing with the amours and heartbreaks of the daughter of a celebrated 17th-century mountebank, is performed for the first time at the Opéra-Comique in Paris.

### 23 FEBRUARY 1901

*Picarol*, zarzuela by Enrique GRANADOS, is produced in Barcelona.

### 3 MARCH 1901

*Der polnische Jude*, opera in two acts by the Bohemian composer Karel WEIS, his most successful work, to a libretto from Erckmann-Chatrian's tale of the robbery and murder of a rich Polish Jew by an Alsatian innkeeper, avenged fifteen years later on a wintry Candlemas day in 1833 when another rich Polish Jew arrives at the inn, inducing in the murderer a fatal nightmare, the curtain falling as the reincarnated Polish Jew gazes meaningfully at the dead body, is performed for the first time at the German Opera in Prague.

### 4 MARCH 1901

*Gugeline*, opera in five acts by the German composer Ludwig THUILLE, set in an expansive Wagneromorphic idiom depicting the happy romance of a rustic damsel with a democratic prince who rejects three potential royal-blooded mates in her favor, is produced in Bremen.

### 6 MARCH 1901

*Charlotte Corday*, music drama in three acts by Alexandre GEORGES, portraying the stabbing in the bathtub of the *"ami du peuple"* Marat by aristocratic

15

Charlotte Corday, after she declines the honorable attentions of Count de Lux, and culminating in her death on the guillotine, is produced at the Opéra-Populaire in Paris. (The title page of the printed score gives a premature date, 16 February 1901. The correct date is given in *Le Ménestrel* of 10 March 1901)

### 8 MARCH 1901

Peter BENOIT, ardent cultivator of Flemish music in Belgium, whose durable and endurable operas and cantatas to original Flemish texts are written in a chromaticized musical idiom of Gounod and César Franck, but are enlivened by the use of authentic melorhythms of his native Flanders, dies in Antwerp at the age of sixty-six.

### 14 MARCH 1901

*Herzog Wildfang,* second opera in three acts by Siegfried WAGNER, to his own libretto wherein an 18th-century German girl accidentally wounded by a young duke during a deer hunt recovers in his castle and promises her heart to the fastest runner in a local foot race, which is won by her former sweetheart, whereupon the disappointed duke returns to his profitable trade of supplying Hessian mercenaries for use against American colonists in the Revolutionary War, set to a filially faithful Wagneromantic score, is produced in Munich.

### 20 MARCH 1901

*Nausikaa,* opera in three acts with a prologue by the German composer August BUNGERT to his own libretto, constituting the second part of his ambitious Homeric tetralogy covering the Mediterranean travels of Ulysses, is produced in Dresden.

### 31 MARCH 1901

*Rusalka,* lyric folk tale in three acts by Antonín DVOŘÁK, wherein a mermaid, miraculously turned into a complete girl and subsequently debauched by a young profligate, gives him the lethal kiss of a nix and then returns to her undine home in a central European lake, with a score permeated by bittersweet melodiousness of Slavic folksongs, is produced in Prague.

### 1 APRIL 1901

Claude DEBUSSY publishes in the Paris journal, *La Revue Blanche* his first article on music under the nom de plume Monsieur Croche (i.e. Mr. Quaver, or Mr. Eighth-Note)

### 13 APRIL 1901

*Lorenzo,* opera in three acts by the Italian opera conductor Edoardo MASCHERONI, is produced in Rome.

## 26 APRIL 1901

*Le Roi de Paris*, grand opera in three acts by Georges HÜE, dealing with the abortive rebellion of the Duc de Guise against Henri III of France (at the end of the opera, the king delivers his historic *mot* as he looks down upon the prostrate body of the assassinated duke: *"Il ne m'a jamais paru si grand"*), is performed for the first time at the Paris Opéra. (Date on the title page of the printed score, confirmed by the cable dispatch to the New York *Herald*)

## 29 APRIL 1901

*L'Ouragan*, lyric drama in four acts by Alfred BRUNEAU, to a libretto from Émile Zola's stormy tale of raging passions on a French island in the tempestuous English Channel, wherein a 40-year-old seaman, loved by his 25-year-old sister-in-law and her 35-year-old sister, sails away from them for the French West Indies with his tropical 15-year-old shipmate Lulu, the music heaving in tidal waves of Gallic recitative supported by the pillars of major ninth-chords and anchored deep in sustaining pedal points, is produced at the Opéra-Comique in Paris.

## 3 MAY 1901

On his fifteenth birthday the precocious French organist Marcel DUPRÉ plays the organ part in the domestic first performance in his parental home in Rouen of his oratorio *La Vision de Jacob* (with a fugal treatment of the celestial stairway), his father leading a local choral society named *L'Accord Parfait*, and his mother filling in the requisite harmonies at the piano.

## 17 MAY 1901

Pope Leo XIII publicly commends the erudite Benedictine monks of Solesmes for their reconstitution of Gregorian modes by diligent collation and intelligent summation of authentic manuscripts.

## 17 MAY 1901

Werner EGK, German composer whose compact operas and ballets contributed to the formulation of the modern style of utilitarian musical theater, is born in Auchsesheim, in Bavaria. (The story circulated in the 1950's that Egk's name was an arrogantly self-aggrandizing pseudonym formed by the acronym *Echt grosser Künstler* is a scurrilous canard, confuted by Egk's birth certificate obtained by the author, which proves that Egk's family name was Egk)

## 29 MAY 1901

*Manru*, tragic opera in three acts by Ignace PADEREWSKI, wherein an adventurous gypsy named Manru shares his leisure with a wife in the Tatra Mountains and a belle in a village, culminating in his wife's suicide and his own death at the hands of the belle's suitor, set to a competently synthetic score with undertones by Chopin and overtones by Wagner, and containing several boisterous Gypsy dances for orchestra, is produced in a German version at the Dresden Opera.

### 30 MAY 1901

*Much Ado About Nothing,* opera in four acts after Shakespeare by Charles Villiers STANFORD, written in a melodious and harmonious manner with some humorous touches, but otherwise steeped in a plasma of traditional music, is produced at Covent Garden in London.

*Much Ado About Nothing* was strangled at birth. It was given twice in all at Covent Garden and then withdrawn. Judged on its merits, this was a rank injustice. Full of the loveliest tunes, sparkling with humour, beautifully scored, and sung and acted by a splendid cast, it made a great hit. I was there and can testify to this. (Harry Plunket Greene, *Charles Villiers Stanford,* London, 1935)

### 1 JUNE 1901

Universal Edition, music publishing firm dedicated in a truly universal spirit to the support and encouragement of modern music, in Austria and anywhere, is formally established at the constitutional assembly of its founders in Vienna.

From C major to the *Mutterakkord,* containing all the 12 different notes and all the different intervals, runs the range of works published by Universal Edition. (Alban Berg in *Die Musik,* Berlin, November 1929)

### 19 JUNE 1901

The German Ministry of Justice promulgates a law of literary and musical property, in which Article 13 expressly forbids "the utilization in musical works of a recognizable melody from another work, taken as a base of a new musical composition."

### 20 JUNE 1901

Edward ELGAR conducts the London Philharmonic in the world première of his concert-overture *Cockaigne (In London Town),* set in a descriptive sonata form, the first subject reflecting London gaiety, the second a London romance; the development projecting loud fanfares in artful antiphony with a church service, the recapitulation and coda resounding with Cockney hubbub (Cockaigne being the name of a mythical country, connected with the Cockneys only through whimsical alliteration).

### 23 JUNE 1901

*Vivre Aimer,* symphonic diptych by the 20-year-old Swiss composer Ernest BLOCH, dedicated to his teacher Jaques-Dalcroze, consisting of two large sections, *La Vie* and *L'Amour,* developed thematically in a Lisztian manner, is performed for the first time during the Second Festival of Swiss music in his native Geneva.

## 30 JUNE 1901

The Académie des Beaux-Arts, composed of Saint-Saëns, J. P. Lourens, Reyer, Massenet, Paladilhe, Théodore Dubois, with Duvernoy, Hillemacher, Lefevre, Fauré and Widor as supplementary judges, awards, after one hour of deliberation at their annual session in Paris, the "deuxième second" Prix de Rome to Maurice RAVEL for the composition of the cantata *Myrrha* (the assigned subject), while the first Grand Prix goes to André Caplet, and the "premier second" to Gabriel Dupont.

(*Le Temps* of 1 July 1901 states that the deliberation proceeded in the "ultra-Senegalian heat, of which the hot-air furnace can give only a slight approximation." Yet, from the meteorological bulletin in the same issue, it appears that the Paris temperature on 30 June 1901 stood at 24° centigrade, only 6° above normal, so that the passing-up of Ravel in favor of Caplet cannot be excused on the grounds of thermal debilitation of the jury)

## 4 JULY 1901

*Dona Mecia,* "lyrical novelette" in two acts by the 31-year-old Portuguese pianist-composer Oscar DA SILVA, is performed for the first and last time in Lisbon.

## 28 JULY 1901

Rudy VALLÉE (*recte* Hubert Prior Vallée), American prototypal protagonist of the fine art of crooning, i.e. singing in head-tones in approximate pitch while maintaining a blandly suggestive expression without a perceptible movement of facial muscles, is born in Vermont.

## 17 AUGUST 1901

Edmond AUDRAN, French composer of gay and popular Parisian operettas, of which *La Mascotte* was performed about 2000 times in twenty years since its production in 1880, whose funeral march on the death of Meyerbeer provoked, according to plausible reports, a winged bon mot of Rossini ("it would have been better if he had died and Meyerbeer had written a funeral march"), dies in Tierceville at the age of sixty-one.

## 20 SEPTEMBER 1901

*Die Musik,* an illustrated bi-monthly, begins publication in Berlin, the first issue containing 104 pages.

Our publication was born out of a clear consciousness of the fact that there is lacking, in the art of Music to which hundreds of thousands pledge their devotion, an organ that might favorably compare with the foremost magazines of literature, pictorial and applied arts. (From the "Praeludium" in the first issue)

## 20 SEPTEMBER 1901

*Os Saldunes,* opera in three acts by the Brazilian composer Leopoldo MIGUEZ (1850–1902), to a libretto romantically elaborated from Caesar's *De Bello Gal-*

*lico* and relating the noble sufferings of a group of Roman soldiers in Gallia (*saldunes,* i.e. comrades) banded together in a pact of mutual fidelity in life, in war, and in death, with a servilely Wagneromorphic musical setting, is performed for the first time in Rio de Janeiro.

### 26 SEPTEMBER 1901

*Judith,* lyric drama in three acts by George Whitefield CHADWICK, after the biblical story of a heroic Hebraic widow who enters the tent of the Assyrian chieftain Holofernes laying siege on her home town of Bethulia in 656 B.C., and, after making him drunk with lust and wine, decapitates him with his own sword, returning in triumph to her people with the bearded head of the foe concealed under her mantle, to a musical score competently imitative of the best varieties of European biblical operas, is performed for the first time in concert form at the Worcester, Massachusetts, Music Festival.

### 19 OCTOBER 1901

The first two of the five imposingly imperialistic symphonic marches by the uncrowned musical laureate of Great Britain, Edward ELGAR, united under the Shakespearean title *Pomp and Circumstance* (in Othello's farewell speech), are performed for the first time in Liverpool.

### 23 OCTOBER 1901

*Les Barbares,* lyric drama in three acts with a prologue by Camille SAINT-SAËNS, dealing with the assault upon the last refuge of the vestal virgins during the siege of Orange in southern Gaul by the Cimbri and Teutones in 105 B.C., wherein the conquering chieftain takes the priestess as his wife, but is in the last act stabbed to death by the widow of the fallen Roman commander, with the musical score harmoniously arranged in a series of dramatic scenes and lyrical arias, is produced at the Paris Opéra.

### 26 OCTOBER 1901

*Toussaint L'Ouverture,* concert-overture by the mulatto composer Samuel COLERIDGE-TAYLOR, inspired by the career of the mulatto Haitian leader who assumed the name L'Ouverture to celebrate his military coup in forcing an opening (ouverture) in the French camp during the island war of liberation in 1796, is performed for the first time in London.

### 27 OCTOBER 1901

The first integral performance of DEBUSSY's symphonic triptych, *Nocturnes* (composition completed at 3:00 A.M. on 15 December 1899), with a third movement, *Sirènes,* presenting a mistily mystical tonal painting in impressionistically modulative aquamarine colors including a wordless chorus of alluring female voices intercalated with instrumental cascades of whole-tone scales, is given by the Lamoureux Orchestra in Paris under the direction of Camille Chevillard who was also the conductor of the first performance of the initial two movements of *Nocturnes* on 9 December 1900.

## 3 NOVEMBER 1901

One hundred years have elapsed since the birth in Catania of Vincenzo BELLINI, composer of dramatically songful operas, of which *Norma* and *La Sonnambula* have become perennial favorites.

(Exact date of birth is deduced from his baptismal certificate a copy of which was obtained by the author from the registry of birth in Catania. The baptism certificate is dated 4 November 1801, and contains the notation by the priest: "Infantem *hieri natum* baptisavi," "born yesterday," i.e. on 3 November 1801)

## 4 NOVEMBER 1901

*Maid Marian,* comic opera in three acts by the American composer Reginald de KOVEN, being a sequel to his 19th-century opera *Robin Hood,* wherein the champion of the poor embarks on a Crusade to the Holy Land, but eventually returns to England and his bride Marian, is produced in Philadelphia.

## 9 NOVEMBER 1901

Seven months and eight days after his 28th birthday, Serge RACHMANINOFF plays at a Moscow Philharmonic concert, with his cousin Alexander Siloti conducting, the solo part in the first complete performance of his *Second Piano Concerto* in C minor, dedicated to Dr. Nicholas Dahl in gratitude for the cure by neuropsychotherapy of a nervous tremor in his fingers, a work destined to become the new century's most celebrated piano concerto, set in three equilibrated movements:

(1) *Allegro,* in C minor, opening with spacious chordal formations rooted in the deepest subdominant, and plagally passing to a series of broadly rolling arpeggios in the tonic and the dominant, while the orchestra intones a ruminating theme, growing in expansive harmonic waves and leading to a soaring second theme in the relative major key, then hastening on to a rhythmically pulsating coda (2) *Andante,* in E major, with the piano monodically chanting a nostalgic lament, presently gathering momentum and spreading through the entire range of the keyboard in precipitous diatonic cascades (3) *Finale,* in restive festive C major, undimmed in its luminous élan by the constant flatting of the submediant, in a peculiarly Russian, inexorably wistful harmonic major mode, and culminating in a sky-high display of C major jubilation.

(A partial performance of the *Second Piano Concerto,* without the first movement, which was written after the second and third movements, was given by Rachmaninoff in Moscow on 15 December 1900 at a special concert organized by the Moscow Prison Philanthropic Committee)

## 9 NOVEMBER 1901

Hans PFITZNER conducts in Elberfeld the world première of his romantic opera *Die Rose vom Liebesgarten,* a modern German fairy-tale in two acts with a prologue and an epilogue, in which the rose from the garden of love grows amid starmaidens, sunchildren, little woodwomen, giants, elves, mossmen, marshmen, minnesingers, as well as some incorporeal mystical abstractions, with a musical setting suggesting woodsy murmurings, watery drip-

*21*

pings, aerial meanderings and cosmic maunderings in a polythematically allusive idiom of deep Wagneromantic colors. (A shortened version was produced in Frankfurt on 5 May 1939)

### 14 NOVEMBER 1901

*Ib and Little Christina,* opera in three acts by Franco LEONI, to a libretto from Hans Christian Andersen, is produced in London.

### 17 NOVEMBER 1901

*Fantaisie* for piano and orchestra by Louis AUBERT, set in an impressionistically florid style in which tangential modalities and tonalities serve as asymptotes for a series of thematic fragments, is performed for the first time by the Colonne Orchestra in Paris, with Aubert's teacher Louis Diémer conducting.

### 20 NOVEMBER 1901

*Grisélidis,* opera in three acts by Jules MASSENET, derived from Boccaccio's whimsical tale about a submissively acquiescent woman whose sadistically pietistic husband subjects her to a series of calculated humiliations to test her uxorial devotion, with a musical score abounding in melodiously florid and harmoniously dramatic scenes, is performed for the first time at the Opéra-Comique in Paris.

### 21 NOVEMBER 1901

Richard STRAUSS conducts at the Dresden Opera the first performance of his third opera *Feuersnot* (completed on 22 May 1901), with a libretto derived from a poem by Ernst von Wolzogen dealing with a preternatural deprivation of phlogiston in medieval Munich, relieved when a virginal town belle accedes to a Tristanesque tryst with the local magus whose philosophy is that only a warm young woman's body can give light, with the promise fulfilled in a tremendous climax in an instrumental interlude building up into a single silent post-coital measure at which moment all the fires—the pyres before the doors, the lanterns of the townsfolk, the torches of the men of armor, the lamps in the house—flare up simultaneously, set to music marked by Wagneromantic fervor, with a sly intent to berate the Munich society, which disdained Richard I (Wagner) and failed to appreciate Richard II (Strauss).

### 24 NOVEMBER 1901

*A Feast in Time of Plague,* one-act opera in an effective lyrico-dramatic style by César CUI, the least mighty of the "Mighty Five" of Russia, to the text of Pushkin's play derived from John Wilson's tragedy *The City of the Plague* which describes the London pestilence of 1665, is performed for the first time in Moscow.

### 25 NOVEMBER 1901

Gustav MAHLER conducts in Munich the world première of his *Fourth Symphony* in G major, scored for a large orchestra with the significant omission of trombones, in four movements, each bearing descriptive indications of tempo and mood, with the inclusion of a soprano solo in the finale to the text from the old German collection of folk poems *Des Knaben Wunderhorn*:

(1) *Bedächtig, Nicht eilen*, in G major, in 4/4 time, opening in presumptive B minor with an exaltation of a quartet of resonant flutes, heterophonically joined by the clarinet, and gently accompanied by a rhythmic tinkling of sleighbells (a vignette that is to recur in the final movement) followed by the appearance of a bright vernal melody, "as inconspicuous as a dewdrop on the petals of a flower before sunrise," in Mahler's own words, "but breaking out in a thousand luminous colors in every pearl of the dew as the first rays of the sun fall on the field so that a sea of sunbeams greets us in reflection" (2) *In gemächlicher Bewegung, ohne Hast* in C minor, in 3/8 time, comprising three scherzo-like expositions and two trio-like interludes separating them, set in the measure of a melancholy *Ländler*, introduced by a surrealistic violin *scordatura* with all four strings raised a whole tone up "so that it would sound strong and raw, as if Death herself struck the tune," the entire movement conjuring up "a kaleidoscopic tourbillion of a myriad sparkling gems, like so many dancing, changing drops of the rainbow," occasionally disrupted by staccato points of wandering *ignis fatuus* "that will make your hair stand on end with horror" (3) *Ruhevoll*, in 4/4, in G major, designed as a set of variations that "vary thoroughly as true variations ought to do, with the entire movement pervaded by a divinely merry and profoundly mournful melody, so that one can only laugh and weep listening to it," comprising so many radical changes of tempo that "the movement could be marked *Andante, Adagio, Allegro,* or *Presto,* in the most diversified mixture of instrumental colors ever devised, resulting in the type of sound that is *spherical,* in an almost ecclesiastically Catholic spirit" (4) *Sehr behaglich,* a vocal ballad, originally entitled *Das himmlische Leben,* envisioned by Mahler as "an undifferentiated expanse of cerulean sky color," with a soprano solo limning the life in Heaven in terms of a prosperous Bavarian home, with St. Peter as the celestial majordomo looking down bemusedly upon a fiddle-riddled firmament, St. Martha serving as cook and St. Cecilia taking charge of the heavenly music in Gregorian organum-like polyphony arranged in bare consecutive fifths, and containing such innovations as glissandi in the cellos, finally subsiding in a solemn hymnal incantation in E major, significantly remote from the principal key of the symphony, G major, thus making a definite departure from the cyclical Aristotelian unity of symphonic tonalities. (The earliest case of symphonic heterotonality was probably that of the *First Symphony* by Carl Nielsen, composed in 1892)

(Originally, Mahler entitled the Fourth Symphony *Humoresque*, and planned it in six movements: (1) *Die Welt als ewiges Jetztsein* (*The World as Eternal Now*), in G major (2) *Das irdische Leben* (*Earth Life*), in E-flat minor (3) *Caritas* (*Love*), in B major (4) *Morgenglocken* (*Morning Bells*), in F major (5) *Die Welt ohne Schwere* (*The World Without Trouble*), in D major (6) *Das himmlische Leben* (*Heavenly Life*), in G major)

Those who hoped that with his Fourth Symphony Mahler would return to a healthier musical idiom, to the prime sources of all art and natural expression, must have been disappointed. There is no spontaneity, no original ideas, no individual feeling, not even genuine colors for artificial tonal images. Everything is technique, calculation and inner falseness, a morbid tasteless supermusic. The budding weeds of Mahler's Third Symphony, which has some of his better qualities, are grown in this new work to thorny tares. Everywhere the exploitation of all possible orchestral devices to dress up a formless stylistic monster made up of superficial details indiscriminately thrown together. (Theodor Kroyer, *Die Musik*, Berlin, December 1901)

*Richard Strauss hat die Gegenwart, Mahler die Zukunft.* (Ernst Otto Nodnagel in his account of Mahler's *Fourth Symphony* in *Jenseits von Wagner und Liszt,* Königsberg, 1902, pp. 185–192)

It is not fair to the readers of *The Musical Courier* to take up their time with a detailed description of that musical monstrosity which masquerades under the title of Gustav Mahler's *Fourth Symphony.* There is nothing in the design, content or execution of the work to impress the musician, except its grotesquerie. . . . The writer of the present review frankly admits that to him it was one hour or more of the most painful musical torture to which he has been compelled to submit. (*The Musical Courier,* New York, 9 November 1904)

### 25 NOVEMBER 1901

*Chopin,* opera arranged from Chopin's piano works by Giacomo OREFICE, depicting in four acts the four great loves of Chopin (who sings in tenor voice), from his adolescence to his death in the arms of the first and the fourth, is produced in Milan.

### 25 NOVEMBER 1901

Josef RHEINBERGER, German musician of superhuman industry, accomplished composer and famous piano teacher whose career was never marred by a worldly setback from the time when he as a mere child was church organist in his native Vaduz, capital of the Duchy of Liechtenstein, dies in Munich at the age of sixty-two after a protracted decline of his health and an even more precipitous caducity of his symphonies, chamber music and innumerable piano pieces.

### 30 NOVEMBER 1901

*De Bruid der Zee (The Bride of the Sea),* Flemish national opera in three acts by Jan BLOCKX, foremost representative of operatic modernism of the Belgian Flanders, depicting the tempestuous passions among shrimp fishermen, crayfish fisherwomen and adolescent catchers of marine macruran decapod crustaceans, wherein a brawny prawn monger vanishes on a fishing expedition to Iceland, and his betrothed, hearing his disembodied voice from a fog bank, leaps into the sea, while her rejected suitor plunges a knife into the heart of an importunate lobster girl who proffers herself as a substitute for the "bride of the sea," the arpeggiated Wagnerian ocean waves engulfing the scene in a score in which dramatic events are ingratiatingly alternated with authentic Flemish melorhythms, is produced at the Flemish Opera in Antwerp.

### 5 DECEMBER 1901

Walt DISNEY, originator of the animated cinematic cartoons *Silly Symphonies,* of which the polyscopic *Fantasia* of 1940 is the silliest, is born in Chicago.

### 11 DECEMBER 1901

The first transatlantic radio signal is transmitted by Guglielmo MARCONI from Poldhu, Cornwall, to St. John's, Newfoundland.

On Monday 9 December 1901, Marconi cabled the Poldhu station to begin sending signals at 3 P.M. daily, and to continue them until 6 P.M., these hours being, respectively, 11:30 A.M. to 2:30 P.M. St. John's time. During these hours Wednesday, 11 December, Signor Marconi elevated a kite with an aerial wire, by means of which signals are sent or received. He remained at the recorder attached to the receiving apparatus, and to his profound satisfaction, signals were received by him at intervals, according to the programme arranged previously with the operator at Poldhu. These signals consisted of repeating at intervals the letter S, which, in Marconi's code, is made by three dots or quick strokes." (New York *Tribune* in the story headlined: "Signor Marconi's Triumph. Wireless Messages Flashed Over the Ocean From Cornwall to Newfoundland. Most Wonderful Achievement of the Electric Age," published in the issue of 15 December 1901, and reprinted in the centennial issue of the New York *Herald Tribune* of 13 April 1941.)

### 20 DECEMBER 1901

On the thirtieth birthday of Henry HADLEY, his *Second Symphony,* subtitled *The Four Seasons: (1) Winter,* "deflowering Nature's grassy robe" in coldly self-confident, intervalically masculine tonal strides (2) *Spring,* marking the reappearance of diatonically ambulating ants and chromatically busy bees (3) *Summer,* projecting pentatonic Indian madrigals in a pastoral scene with birdcalls of the flutes and gurgling brooks in the strings (4) *Autumn,* heralded by invigorated hunting horns against the seasonally deciduous violins, is performed for the first time as the winner of the 1901 Paderewski Prize, by the New York Philharmonic, Emil Paur conducting.

### 26 DECEMBER 1901

Georgy RIMSKY-KORSAKOV, grandson of the great Rimsky from whose legacy he deviated far afield to become a foremost Russian exponent of quarter-tone music, is born in St. Petersburg.

# ❧ *1902* ❧

### 4 JANUARY 1902

*I Pirenei,* first part of an operatic trilogy by the "Spanish Wagner" Felipe PEDRELL (the second part, *La Celestina* and the third, *Raimundo,* remaining unperformed), dealing with the feudal feuds between France and Aragon (separated by the Pyrenees, hence the title) in the 13th century, in three historic scenes, *Il Conde de Foix* (1218), *Rayo de Luna* (1245) and *La Jornada de Panissares* (1285), eloquently projected in a Wagneromorphically Iberomantic manner of a music drama, with thematic motives descriptive of people and places identifiable also by vivid folkloristic allusions in hispanistic dances and eclectically ecclesiastical chants, is produced in Barcelona in an Italian version of the original Catalan libretto.

### 12 JANUARY 1902

*Till Eulenspiegel,* opera in two parts with an epilogue by Emil von REZNIČEK, to his own libretto about the roguish but lovable transgressor of medieval mores, is performed for the first time in Karlsruhe.

### 17 JANUARY 1902

*Les Guelfes,* grand opera by Benjamin GODARD, to the story of political strife between the Guelfs and the Ghibellines in medieval Italy, is produced posthumously in Rouen.

### 18 JANUARY 1902

Filippo MARCHETTI, Italian composer of grandiose operas in which the gentle afflatus of Gounod is Italianized in the spirit of Mercadante, whose transitory art of lyric invocation and dramatic concitation had its luster of popular success, and who as Director of the Liceo Musicale in Rome was the appreciated teacher of a generation of aspiring Italian musicians, dies in Rome at the age of seventy.

### 25 JANUARY 1902

*First Symphony* by the 27-year-old Austrian composer Franz SCHMIDT, completed in 1899, in the romantic key of E major, in four Brahmsogenic movements with Wagnerophiliac excrescences, is performed for the first time in Vienna.

### 25 JANUARY 1902

*Second Symphony* in C minor by Alexander SCRIABIN, in five movements, the idiom of which is characterized by irresolutions of amplified ninth-chords and ecstatic upward leaps of sensuous melody premonitory of the "jeux divins" and the orgiastic yearnings of his ultimate symphonic style, is performed for the first time at the Russian Symphony Concerts in St. Petersburg, Anatoli Liadov conducting.

Some Symphony! The Devil knows what it is! Scriabin may well join hands with Richard Strauss. God, what happened to music?! Decadents crawl in from every hole. Holy Saints, help!! Police!!! I am all beaten up, like Don Quixote by the shepherds. Next to Scriabin, Wagner is just a suckling babe in the arms mumbling sweet nothings. I am going crazy! Where can I flee from such music? Help! (Liadov in an apparently jocular letter to Belaieff after receiving the score of Scriabin's Second Symphony which he was assigned to conduct)

The Russian Symphony Society put on the program of its last concert the Second Symphony by Scriabin. I believe that it was a gross typographical error; instead of Symphony the program should have read Cacophony, because in this so-called Symphony there seem to be no consonances whatsoever. The peace is disturbed for 30 or 40 minutes by dissonances piled up one upon another with no sense at all. I cannot understand why Liadov consented to perform such an absurdity. I went to hear it only to amuse myself. Glazunov never showed up. Rimsky-Korsakov, whom I asked what he thought of it, said that he could not understand why any composer should want to depreciate consonances to such an extent as Scriabin. (From a letter by Anton Arensky to Sergei Taneyev, written shortly after the concert)

Scriabin deliberately flaunts dissonances at the public and they saturate his Second Symphony to the point that the music offends the ear. (From a review in the *Russian Musical Gazette*, St. Petersburg, 1 February 1902)

### 1 FEBRUARY 1902

Salomon JADASSOHN, learned German music pedagogue, nicknamed "musical Krupp" (he wrote canons, Krupp made cannons), dies in Leipzig at the age of seventy.

### 9 FEBRUARY 1902

Hans HUBER conducts in Basel the first performance of his *Third Symphony*, surnamed *Heroische*, but set in the key of C major, thus differing in tonality from a similarly surnamed and identically numbered Beethoven symphony, with the funeral movement *Totentanz* being third of the four, whereas Beethoven put a corresponding movement second.

### 15 FEBRUARY 1902

*Orestes*, opera by the German conductor Felix WEINGARTNER in three acts, to a text from the trilogy of Aeschylus, is produced in Leipzig.

### 18 FEBRUARY 1902

*Le Jongleur de Notre-Dame*, a miracle play in three acts by Jules MASSENET, from a medieval fable about a monk who, having nothing of material value to offer on the altar of the Virgin, sings and dances before her statue which comes to life and blesses him whereupon he dies of ecstasy, is performed for the first time at Monte Carlo.

### 22 FEBRUARY 1902

*La Pompadour*, first opera in two acts by the Hungarian composer Emanuel MOÓR, after Alfred de Musset's poem about the politically powerful mistress of Louis XV, written in an effective pseudo-classical settecento style, is performed in a German version for the first time in Cologne.

### 25 FEBRUARY 1902

*Der Improvisator*, opera by Eugen D'ALBERT, to a libretto from 16th-century Italy wherein a minstrel, accidentally sentenced to death for treason, turns out to be a nobleman who saved Padua from Venetian domination, is liberated and marries the Paduan podestà's daughter, is performed for the first time in Berlin.

### 1 MARCH 1902

*The Legend of the Great City of Kitezh and the Calm Lake Svetoyar,* dramatic cantata by Sergei VASSILENKO, after an ancient Russian tale of a city which saves itself from the invading Tatar hordes by submerging in a lake, tolling the church bells underwater, is performed for the first time in Moscow.

(An operatic version of the cantata was produced in Moscow on 3 March 1903; a famous opera on the same subject by Rimsky-Korsakov was brought out in St. Petersburg on 20 February 1907)

### 8 MARCH 1902

Jean SIBELIUS conducts in Helsingfors the first performances of his early *Overture* in A minor and of his lofty masterpiece, the tumultuously serene and rhapsodically lyric *Second Symphony* in D major, in four movements:

(1) *Allegretto,* progressing in mounting waves of string sonorities antiphonally contrasted with independent parts for wind instruments and reaching a harmonious coalition in a final dynamic recession (2) *Tempo andante, ma rubato,* with a pair of lugubrious bassoons initiating a rhythmically excited motion of melodic phrases built at singularly angular thematic intervals (3) *Vivacissimo,* a fugal gigue with lyrical interludes (4) *Finale, Allegro moderato,* wherein a simple progression in D major is exalted by dint of relentless repetition in varying registers to a dramatic proclamation of extraordinary power, concluding on a vibrant plagal cadence.

### 10 MARCH 1902

*Bucolic Suite* for orchestra by Ralph VAUGHAN WILLIAMS, in four movements imbued with English folksong inflections, is performed for the first time in Bournemouth.

### 10 MARCH 1902

Gustav MAHLER, 41 years old, marries Alma Maria Schindler, 23, ten weeks after the pre-marital consummation of their union. (Alma Schindler wrote on 4 January 1902: "Wonne über Wonne!")

### 11 MARCH 1902

*Germania,* lyric drama in two acts by the 41-year-old German-educated Italian composer Baron Alberto FRANCHETTI, wherein a German girl, seduced by a university student, marries his comrade in an atmosphere of continued seething rivalry, and in the epilogue conciliates them as they lie dying of patriotic wounds on the battleground of Leipzig on 19 October 1813, to a Wagneromantic setting strongly impregnated with a Tristanesque fluid, is produced at La Scala in Milan.

18 MARCH 1902

*Verklärte Nacht*, string sextet for two violins, two violas and two cellos by Arnold SCHOENBERG, completed by him on 1 December 1899 at the age of 25, and inspired by a poem of Richard Dehmel—a rare example of a chamber music work with a definite literary link—wherein a woman confesses to her beloved in a walk through a darkened forest that she is with child which is not by him (the words "Ich trag ein Kind, und nicht von dir" fit precisely into the melorhythmic figure of a corresponding motive in the music, and further identification is suggested by the notation "mit schmerzlichem Ausdruck" and "wild, leidenschaftlich"), to which he serenely replies (and the score contains the expression marks "weich, zart, warm" to depict his soft tenderness towards her, marked by a passionate flow into the illumined key of F-sharp major, in perfect prosodical concordance with the words of the poem, "Das Kind das Du empfangen hast sei deiner Seele keine Last") that the warmth within him will transfigure the alien child within her to become his own, with the music rooted in the profoundest intimacy of twilit romanticism, from the opening measures in sad D minor almost literally suggestive of two people walking, to the spiritual conciliation in the "transfigured night" of the title, concluding in pendulously swaying harmonious arpeggios in the lucent key of D major, is performed for the first time in Vienna by the Rosé String Quartet and two players from the Vienna Philharmonic. (All books on Schoenberg and all music dictionaries give the erroneous year 1903 for the first performance)

Lieber Herr Schönberg! Last night I heard *Verklärte Nacht*, and I would be guilty of the sin of omission were I not to send you a word of thanks for your wonderful sextet. I expected to peruse the motives of my poem in your composition, but I soon forgot about it, so bewitched was I by your music . . . Ein Wörtlein Dank—o schönster Schall: des Schöpferwortes Widerhall . . . (From Richard Dehmel's letter from Hamburg dated 12 December 1912)

25 MARCH 1902

*Urvasi*, opera in two acts by the 45-year-old Polish-born composer Erasmus DLUSSKI, wherein a Hindu princess loves a disembodied but exceedingly handsome spirit and is turned into a morning star with her astral soul enjoying an orbital Nirvana, to a score saturated with tangible recollections from Tchaikovsky and Rimsky-Korsakov, is performed for the first and last time at a charity performance at the Imperial Opera in St. Petersburg.

29 MARCH 1902

William Turner WALTON, English composer of grandiloquent symphonies and romantic overtures, with an incisive satirical strain in lighter works, is born in Oldham, Lancashire.

31 MARCH 1902

Paul LINCKE conducts in Berlin the first performance of his two-act operetta *Lysistrata*, after Aristophanes, suggesting an effective anti-war deterrent by a female strike against marital relations during wartime, the score containing the famous *Glühwürmchen* (*Glow-Worm*) song.

29

## 2 APRIL 1902

*Merrie England,* operetta in two acts by Edward GERMAN, lightly picturing the affairs of Sir Walter Raleigh, Queen Elizabeth et al., is produced in London.

## 5 APRIL 1902

*Jeux d'eau* by Maurice RAVEL, a historically significant piano piece forcefully written in a new technique of massed sonorities, harmonically based on the principle of counter-position of two mutually exclusive scales, heptatonic (white keys) and pentatonic (black keys), equitably distributed over the entire range of the keyboard (the nonexistent G-sharp in the lowest bass register in the black-key avalanche of the cadenza is replaced by its acoustical approximation A), is performed for the first time by the Spanish pianist Ricardo Viñes at a concert of the Société Nationale de Musique in Paris.

## 9 APRIL 1902

*Der Wald,* one-act music drama by the English composeress Ethel SMYTH, to her own libretto in German, dealing with an unholy passion of a feudal lady for a young forester whom she orders to be shot as a trespasser when he scorns her ardor in favor of the love of a peasant girl (who dies with him in the attempt to protect him with her interposed body), with mystical hamadryads drenched in Wagnerian fluid in the role of a Grecian chorus, is performed for the first time at the Royal Opera in Berlin, Karl Muck conducting.

At the final rehearsal, Dr. Muck laid down his baton and uttered the ominous words: "So geht's nicht!" His Majesty Emperor William II, however, insisted upon a production of the work at the Royal Opera House, where his wish, of course, is command. Who, however, is Miss Smyth that she could prevail upon the Emperor so as to have her opera produced? She is a prim, neat and cold-looking spinster, high in the thirty-nine, as they say. Her sister is first lady-in-waiting upon the present Queen of England. Be that as it may, Miss Smyth's influence must be a very potent one, and she used it for her own discomfort, for she brought upon her virginal head a fiasco the like of which I have never witnessed. (*The Musical Courier,* New York, 14 April 1902)

## 11 APRIL 1902

*Chonchette,* opéra-bouffe in one act by the 35-year-old French composer Claude TERRASSE, dealing with a ravishing Parisian laundress and her multiple swains, including a whistled arioso, the first of its kind in any opera, is produced in Paris.

## 14 APRIL 1902

Two weeks before the dress rehearsal of Claude DEBUSSY's opera *Pelléas et Mélisande,* the Paris daily *Le Figaro* publishes an open letter from Maurice Maeterlinck, author of the drama, sharply denouncing both Carré's libretto and Debussy's setting and expressing a wish that the production should result in a "prompt and resounding failure," his wrath aroused because Debussy preferred Mary Garden in the title role to Georgette Leblanc, Maeterlinck's common-law wife.

Paris 13 April 1902

DEAR SIR: The direction of the Opéra-Comique announces the impending performance of *Pelléas et Mélisande.* This performance will take place against my will, for Messrs. Carré and Debussy have ignored my legitimate rights.

I should have solved this difference in the courts, which would probably rule once more that a poem belongs to the poet, if a particular circumstance had not altered the *espèce* as they say in the courts.

Indeed, Monsieur Debussy, having first agreed with me on the choice of the interpreter whom I judged the sole person capable of creating the role of Mélisande in conformity with my intentions and desires, decided, when confronted with unjustifiable opposition to this choice on the part of Monsieur Carré, to deny me the right of intervention in the casting, by taking advantage of an all-too-confident letter I wrote him more than six years ago.

Bizarre practices followed this inelegant gesture, as proved by the receipt record of the work, manifestly antedated in an attempt to establish that my protests had been tardy.

Thus, they managed to oust me from my own work, and thenceforth it has been treated as conquered territory. Arbitrary and absurd cuts have been made in the play, rendering it incomprehensible; on the other hand, they have left intact the parts that I intended to delete or improve as I did in a booklet just published, and from which one can see how much the text adopted by the Opéra-Comique differs from the authentic text.

In a word, the *Pelléas* under discussion is a piece which has become an almost enemy alien to me. Barred from all control of my work, I am compelled to wish that its failure should be resounding and prompt.

I beg you, dear Sir, to accept the expression of my highest regard.

MAURICE MAETERLINCK

## 28 APRIL 1902

A public rehearsal is held at the Opéra-Comique in Paris of DEBUSSY's sublime masterpiece, *Pelléas et Mélisande,* lyric drama in five acts and twelve tableaux, portraying with translucent penetration the peripeteia of Maeterlinck's poignantly symbolic play, from the mysterious finding of Mélisande forlorn in a medieval forest to the insensate murder by the jealously deluded Golaud of his young half-brother Pelléas, and to the serene death of Mélisande in childbirth, with a musical setting of startling originality and concentrated power of latent expressiveness, the voices singing the poetic lines according to the inflections of natural speech following every nuance of sentiment in a continuously diversified declamation, the melodic curves tending towards their harmonic asymptotes in tangential proximity and forming chords of quasi-bitonal consistency, the modal intervalic progressions with their concomitant cadential plagalities imparting a nostalgically archaic sound to the music, the frequent parallel motion of triadic units, seventh-chords and ninth-chords providing instant modulatory shifts, extensive vertical edifices in fourths and fifths reposing on deeply anchored pedal-points giving stability in fluidity, while the attenuated orchestra becomes a multicellular organism in which the instrumental solos are projected with pellucid distinction echoing the text in allusive symbolism (when light is mentioned, the strings are luminously tremulous; for water, harps respond), and the psychologically adumbrative motives reflect the appearances of dramatic characters in graphically imprecise identifications. (Composition begun in August 1893; the score completed in August 1895, but revised; the second version finished in 1898, reorchestrated in December 1901; some symphonic interludes written shortly before the first performance, in 1902)

The theater programs that the noisy boys are in the habit of peddling at the entrance usually expatiate on the merits of the production. Yesterday, at the rehearsal at the Opéra-Comique, those privileged to attend the first audition of Claude Debussy's work were not a little astonished at reading the program sold at the door which contained an ironic description of Maeterlinck's work. This little drama is a chef-d'oeuvre, and Maeterlinck is a genius. At least, they say so. Is it a mystification? Is there anything behind this? There was a great deal of talk about this and very singular stories have been heard with great curiosity in the lobby. Some propose to call the play Pelléas et Médisances. (*Le Figaro*, Paris, 29 April 1902)

The copyist was conscientious but very inexperienced; he wrote sharps for flats so that Debussy himself could not make out which was which; frequently the change of clef or time-signature after a rest was left out. Result: exasperating rehearsals; impossible to proceed; every time a stop. "Is this a sharp?" . . . A first-desk player declares that the music makes no sense, but after the twenty-first rehearsal admits that the enthusiasts were right. The trombone player, speaking for the brass section, opines: "We have little to play here, but what we do play is great!" . . . To gain time, the scenery is entrusted to two great specialists, Jusseaume and Ronsin. Catastrophe! *Pelléas* demands thirteen changes of scenery, but it is impossible to accomplish in the hall. The stage technicians swear a thousand oaths, and, to save the situation, Debussy sits down to compose, between two rehearsals, the necessary interludes; it is a miracle that the stitches do not show. . . . After the end, the assistant secretary of the Ministry of Education demands the deletion of fifteen bars on account of the portion of the dialogue inadmissible on the stage of a subsidized theater:
   "Golaud: Et . . . et le lit? Sont-ils près du lit?
   Yniold: Le lit, petit père? Je ne vois pas le lit."
(Robert Jardillier, *Pelléas*, Paris, 1927)

Here is a work of art outside the beaten path, a new impression, a subtle expression, in which the critics, to their joy, found no imitation of Wagner, Gounod or Massenet. In our times such works are not daily occurrences. The music of *Pelléas et Mélisande* possesses originality so specialized that it would be strange if it would not encounter its detractors. Since the right to deny merit to a musical work is an absolute right, and since in this particular case impression is everything, one should not be particularly surprised that the remarkable score of Debussy should suffer the destiny that pursued long ago the masterpieces of Wagner or *Carmen* of Bizet. We are not trying to establish any comparison between Wagner and Bizet with Debussy. We simply wish to remind ourselves that works debated at their first appearance are apt to become most pleasing to the connoisseurs and to the general public later on. While we find it quite natural that not everybody relishes the exquisite savor of Debussy's music, while we can explain very well that the noble allure and the unusual terms of the lyric drama presented yesterday might exasperate and annoy some listeners, while we concede that we must above all respect the opinion of everyone, we humbly demand for ourselves the liberty to be charmed by this curious, delicious, poetic music of Debussy. It does not resemble anything we have ever heard. You would look in vain in the 283 pages of the score for a piece that can be extracted for separate performance. There are no arias so greatly favored. The personages on the stage avoid singing. They declaim in a sort of melodic speech, summarily notated, what they have to say, and the task of expressing and of communicating their sentiments is left entirely to the orchestra.

The changes of scenes do not interrupt the musical current. Instrumental playing ceases only at the end of an act. The orchestra, in which the images rise and vanish, where clear visions and troubling apparitions pass with a light touch, murmurs of the breeze, fluttering of wings, sound of waves, the pallor of the moon, the crimson of the twilight, the tenderness, the impatience, the timidity, the spasms of passion, the malaise, the fragrance of the roses, the lure, the contained impulses, the freshness of dew, the agonies of light, the bluish reflections and the indecisive movement, this atmosphere is created in the orchestra which bathes the action in a sonorous vapor exquisitely tinted with the most elusive nuances. The souls of the actors seem to float like fine dreams on a sea of harmony.

One should not conclude, however, that the score of *Pelléas et Mélisande*, in which melody, at least what one generally understands as melody, is absent, and in which the rhythm disappears in intentionally imprecise harmonic aggregations, is devoid of character or shape. From the initial prelude, the delicately poetic music is invested with an adorably remote color and leaves in the ear an evanescent echo of faraway things . . . for Debussy's music constantly floats above the realities of life. Its emotion is poetic, and its suffering is without a human outcry. This dream music never escapes the world of reverie. (André Corneau, in *Le Matin*, Paris, 1 May 1902)

Debussy has imparted to Maeterlinck's tragic legend his own musical atmosphere. He was not preoccupied with the musical expression which formulates with precision, rhythm and movement the psychological states which are devoid of action. One would seek in vain in *Pelléas et Mélisande* either the arias with their time-honored strophes and refrains or the Wagnerian leitmotif and its transformations. In his orchestral commentary, which is rich and sonorous, the composer creates, we repeat, an atmosphere of the drama and its characters. This word, atmosphere, is the only one which fits the fluidity of this music. It does not resemble in any of its parts a configuration, an ordonnance, a development. The composer understands the alliance of music with the words as a color that is applied to a point in order to make it come out with greater emphasis, or, better still, as a light placed behind an object or drawing to illuminate a detail with greater clarity. It remains to be seen whether in this system of "spoken music" the art does not lose all it has to offer by absorbing itself in another art. We believe, on our part, that it is a dangerous system. Others may find it excellent, but they will refuse to imitate it. (Montcornet, *Le Petit Parisien*, 1 May 1902)

Pelléas c'est encore de la musique à écouter la figure dans les mains. Toute musique à écouter dans les mains est suspecte. Wagner c'est le type de la musique qui s'écoute dans les mains. (Jean Cocteau, *Coq et l'Arlequin*, Paris, 1918)

Claude Debussy is a representative of the most advanced school of music. His *Nocturnes* and particularly a prelude entitled *L'Après-midi d'un faune* indicate a very extensive knowledge of the orchestra, but also an absolute disdain for all the rules transmitted to us by musical masters. M. Debussy has a horror of the perfect triad, and if by chance he uses one, it is almost always in an antitonal progression, as if to say "This is a perfect triad, to be sure, but you must admit that it does not look it!" Besides, M. Debussy covers with gauze his coarsest passages. The use of a mute and of pianissimo allow him to take greater risks for the good reason that one hears less. . . . The production of *Pelléas et Mélisande* proves once more that the world of music is divided into two camps, on the one hand a group of *arrivistes* who have noisy friends determined to defend them in spite of everything, and on the other, a company of fervent devotees of art who believe that music is a Holy Trinity whose three parts, melody, harmony and rhythm, are regulated by laws which cannot be continually infringed to the detriment of reason and of the ear. . . . *Pelléas et Mélisande* marks the limit that, I believe, can not be transgressed, and it certainly merits a place, as a curiosity, in all music libraries. (Eugène d'Harcourt, in *Le Figaro*, Paris, 1 May 1902)

M. Debussy's score defies description, being such a refined concatenation of sounds that not the faintest impression is made on the ear. The composer's system is to ignore melody altogether, and his personages do not sing, but talk in a sort of lilting voice to a vague musical accompaniment of the text. No solo, no detached phrase ever breaks the interminable flow of commonplace sound. The effect is quite bewildering, almost amusing in its absurdity. (Paris dispatch in *Era*, London, 1 May 1902)

The public is tired of hearing music which is not music; it is weary of this heavy, continuous declamation, without air and light; it is sated with this unsupportable abuse of chromatics, thanks to which all sense of tonality disappears along with the melodic sense. . . . Rhythm, melody, tonality—these are three things that are unknown to M. Debussy. His music is vague, without color or nuance, without motion, without life. It is not even declamation, but a continual dolorous melopoeia, without vitality or vigor, deliberately shunning all semblance of precision. . . . And what a delightful series of false relations! What adorable progressions of consecutive triads, with the inevitably resulting fifths and octaves! What a collection of dissonances, sevenths and ninths, ascending even by disjunct intervals! I recommend to music lovers a ninth-chord on page ten of the full score, where the voice sings the fifth of that ninth, so that only one note is missing to complete the scale in this chord. Very pretty! No, I will never have anything to do with these musical anarchists! (Arthur Pougin, in *Le Ménestrel*, Paris, 4 May 1902)

The music is such as one could expect from the composer of *L'Après-midi d'un faune*, *Damoiselle élue*, *Trois Nocturnes*, etc., i.e. indefinite, strange, escaping, full of harmonic hardness, particularly in the preludes and postludes of the orchestra. . . . We know too well that one shouldn't be scandalized by notes not in the harmony, for examples of such attempts one might find in the works of the greatest masters. But, with them, it is an exception, and the ear relishes their bold innovations as long as they are tempered by tonalities pure of all accidents. With Debussy, it is exactly the reverse: harmonic simplicity is a rare thing in his score. (H. Imbert, in *Le Guide musical*, Paris, 4 May 1902)

Music is the final religion of these last centuries without faith. The disciples of Wagner were at least sincere. They were recruited from all classes of society, and the poverty of their dress, the ugliness, sometimes sublime, of their drawn faces, bore witness to the fervor and fury of their faith. The religion of Mr. Claude Debussy has more elegance. The neophytes affect especially the orchestra fauteuils, the first boxes, the orchestra stalls; they are found by the side of the young blonde girls, too delicate, too white, too blonde, in evident imitation of the type to which Mary Garden belongs.
*"Je regardais Lucie, elle était pâle et blonde."* And turning over with a lazy hand the score placed on the rail of the box there is a whole class of beautiful young men (nearly all the Debussyites are young, O, so young), ephebes with long hair cunningly brought in stringy locks over the forehead, with dull, smug faces, with deep-sunken eyes. Their

dress coats have a velvet collar and puffed sleeves; their frock coats are a little too pinched in the waist; their satin cravats are mussy over the neck or they float loosely, tied carelessly to the turnover collar when the Debussyite is "en veston." They all wear on their little fingers (for they all have pretty hands) precious rings of Egypt or Byzantium, rings of turquoise or of twisted greenish gold. Thus adorned, they go in couples. Orestes and Pylades commune together, or the model son accompanies his mother. They are archangels with visionary eyes, and under the spell of an impression they whisper in each other's ears, and their whispers go to the lowest depths of the soul. "The Pelléastres!" (Jean Lorrain, in *Le Journal*, Paris, May 1902)

Not the least originality of M. Debussy is his ability to write a whole musical composition without a single melodic phrase, without a single measure of melody. . . . In *Pelléas et Mélisande* there are no leitmotifs for the good reason that it has no motifs of any kind. . . . Rhythm is no less detestable to him. In his doubly formless art, the abolition of rhythm corresponds to the suppression of melody. . . . M. Debussy's orchestration appears sickly and gaunt. When it intends to caress, it scratches and bruises. *Il fait peu de bruit, je l'accorde, mais un vilain petit bruit.* No one is more qualified than the author of *Pelléas et Mélisande* to preside over the decomposition of our art. . . . M. Debussy's music contains the seed not of life and progress but of decadence and death. (Camille Bellaigue, in *Revue des Deux Mondes*, Paris, 15 May 1902)

A work of singular novelty and beauty has been presented at the Opéra-Comique, and it was received, naturally, with surprise, scandal, mockery and hostility. . . . The play that M. Claude Debussy set to music was not an adaptation for the stage, but the actual text of Maurice Maeterlinck. Only a few scenes were cut from it. . . . One might have feared that the opera would appear disjointed, divided into small episodes, agreeable and brilliant, but disparate. To the contrary, it possesses a style, a consistency, a continuity, a unity quite out of the ordinary, a line of admirable simplicity and purity . . . a sobriety, a limpidity of a classical art. . . . M. Claude Debussy is a poet; all is poetry and all is music in his work; and all of his music is poetry. (Pierre Lalo, in *Le Temps*, Paris, 20 May 1902)

The vocal parts are written without any attention being paid to the characteristics of the singing voices. In fact, the singers recite their roles to notes without the composer's having cared as to whether the sequence of these notes shall prove agreeable to the ear. Of melody there is not the slightest pretension. In fact, the same results would be obtained exactly if the singers were to declaim their parts instead of singing them, provided they kept the pitch of the voice quite distinct from the tonality of the orchestra. (*The Musical Courier*, New York, 28 May 1902)

Through the intellectual refinement of a crazy pursuit for novelty, Debussy has arrived at the greatest negation of every doctrine. He disowns melody and its development, and despises the symphony with all its resources. The opinion of the best musical critics is unanimous in declaring *Pelléas et Mélisande* a work of musical decline. . . . France may be still congratulated upon possessing Reyer, Massenet, Saint-Saëns and Charpentier. They cannot certainly prevent the decline of the musical art; but they will delay it for a while. (S. Marchesi, *Monthly Musical Record*, London, 1 June 1902)

In Debussy's opera consecutive fifths, octaves, ninths and sevenths abound in flocks, and not only by pairs but in whole passages of such inharmonious chords. . . . Such progressions sound awful, and as they come out in the strings one gives an involuntary start, as when the dentist touches the nerve of a sensitive tooth. (Arthur Bles, *The Musical Courier*, New York, 16 July 1902)

I met Debussy at the Café Riche the other night and was struck by the unique ugliness of the man. His face is flat, the top of his head is flat, his eyes are prominent, the expression veiled and somber, and, altogether, with his long hair, unkempt beard, uncouth clothing and soft hat, he looked more like a Bohemian, a Croat, a Hun, than a Gaul. His high, prominent cheek bones lend a Mongolian aspect to his face. The head is brachycephalic, the hair black. . . . Debussy is not a stylist, but an impressionist. Like Claude Monet he seems to delight in giving us the complementary hue of every tone. There are no purples on his palette—no blacks. His colors occasionally screech, so "high" are they, and their vibrations never cease. If the Western World ever adopted Eastern tonalities, Claude Debussy would be the one composer who would manage its system, with its quarter-tones and split quarters. . . . The music to Maeterlinck's *Pelléas et Mélisande* is so absolutely incidental that as music *qua* music it is unthinkable. At first hearing you set the composer as lacking ear. But Richard Strauss *via* the music of Wagner, Liszt and Berlioz has set the pace for the cacophonists. Since his *Don Quixote* there has been nothing new devised—outside of China—to split the ears of diatonic lovers. . . . *Pelléas* is a perfect specimen of decomposition. The musical phrase is dislocated; the rhythms are decomposed; the harmonic structure is pulled to pieces, melts before our eyes, or ears; is resolved into its constituent parts. And his themes are often developed in opposition to all laws of musical syntax. . . . His future should be viewed with suspicion from all the critical watchtowers. (James Gibbons Huneker, in the New York *Sun,* 19 July 1903)

In *Pelléas et Mélisande* Debussy has come closer than most artists to the goal of all conscious art, be it in words or tones, in line or in color—the nearly perfect fusion of the manner of utterance with the thing to be uttered. (H. T. Parker, in the Boston *Evening Transcript,* 8 April 1909)

### 30 APRIL 1902

DEBUSSY's opera *Pelléas et Mélisande* is presented at the Opéra-Comique in Paris, in an official première, with the Scottish soprano Mary Garden singing the part of Mélisande betraying a strong English accent, supported by a cast of French singers conducted by André Messager to whom the work is dedicated.

### 7 MAY 1902

*Circe,* opera in three acts by the Spanish composer Ruperto CHAPÍ, dealing with the enchantress of the island of Aeaea who holds Ulysses in sensual thrall after turning his shipmates into swine, is produced at the inaugural spectacle of the Teatro Lírico in Madrid.

### 21 MAY 1902

*Orsola,* lyric drama in three acts by P. L. (initials of two Prix-de-Rome-winning brothers Paul and Lucien) HILLEMACHER, dealing with a Venetian courtesan Orsola who induces her lover to kill the reigning Doge and is in the end stabbed to death herself by the assassin who is led to the execution block in the choral finale, set to a turbulently chromatic score densely inseminated with concatenations of dramatic diminished seventh-chords, is produced at the Paris Opéra.

*36*

## 30 MAY 1902

*La Troupe Jolicœur,* "comédie musicale" in three acts, the last stage work by Arthur COQUARD, completed by him on Christmas Day 1899, to his own libretto involving a quadrangular love triangle, wherein the strongman and the clown in an itinerant circus headed by a kind-hearted Mme Jolicœur courting a pretty street singer lose out to a composer who teaches her elementary solfeggio, is produced at the Opéra-Comique in Paris.

## 9 JUNE 1902

Twenty-eight days before his forty-second birthday, Gustav MAHLER conducts in Krefeld the first complete performance of his *Third Symphony,* composed in 1893–1896, subtitled in the original manuscript *Ein Sommermorgentraum,* and designated "F-dur" (rather than D minor, as stated in most analytical notes), in six principal sections with an introduction, bearing programmatic descriptions in the original manuscript but not in the printed score:

Introduction: *Pan erwacht,* announcing the awakening of Pan, with eight horns in unison; I. *Der Sommer marschiert ein,* a dramatic pastorale full of Dionysiac outbursts in emphatic major seventh-chords, alternating with episodes of intense serenity; II. *Was mir die Blumen auf der Wiese erzählen,* a minuet in the most ingratiating Viennese manner, elaborated by four variations; III. *Was mir die Thiere im Walde erzählen,* presenting in rondo form a fairly naturalistic para-Wagnerian forest idyll with bird-like flutes and wolf-like barks and howls, until a posthorn signalizes the end of the outing; IV. *Was mir der Mensch erzählt,* with a dark, deep and sonorous contralto voice intoning the *Nachtwanderers Lied* from Nietzsche's *Also sprach Zarathustra,* warning transients to beware of ineffable woe; V. *Was mir die Engel erzählen,* for contralto, women's chorus and boys' chorus, to a text from the German anthology of children's verses *Des Knaben Wunderhorn,* with chimes characterizing the angelic advice to those who innocently break the Ten Commandments; VI. *Was mir die Liebe erzählt,* peacefully advancing to full-throated sound, scaling the heights and plumbing the depths of pantheistic joy.

## 10 JUNE 1902

Horatio PARKER is awarded the honorary degree of Doctor in Music by the University of Cambridge, England. (Date and information received from the Registrar of the University of Cambridge)

## 20 JUNE 1902

*Kryse,* lyric drama in four acts by the 40-year-old Argentinian composer Arturo BERUTI, to a libretto dealing with a virtuous courtesan who flourished in Alexandria in 60 B.C., set in Wagneromorphic harmonies with Verdian melodies, is produced in the Italian language in Buenos Aires.

## 1 AUGUST 1902

Oscar SONNECK, American music scholar, is appointed to organize a Music Division at the Library of Congress in Washington.

### 17 AUGUST 1902

*Parysatis,* incidental music of operatic proportions by Camille SAINT-SAËNS, to a play taking place in Persia in 401 B.C. dealing with the Persian Queen Parysatis and the struggle between her son Artaxerxes and her grandson Darius for love of the Greek concubine of her slain son Cyrus, is performed for the first time at the Grand Roman Arena in Béziers, France, by a grandiose ensemble of 450 orchestra players plus 20 harps, 15 trumpets, 12 cornets, 250 choristers and 60 dancers.

### 6 OCTOBER 1902

*Das war ich,* a "village idyll" in one act by Leo BLECH, after Boccaccio's tale of an amorous farmer making love to a milkmaid in the barnyard and to a neighbor's wife in the house, using both affairs as alibis against each other, is performed for the first time at the Dresden Opera House.

### 6 OCTOBER 1902

*When Johnny Comes Marching Home,* "spectacular military opera in 3 acts" by Julian EDWARDS, from the time of the Civil War, wherein a Southerner steals important documents from a Northern general during a vocal quintet, Negro slaves sing spirituals, while twelve Southern belles try to undermine the vigilance of twelve federal officers, and though the latter succumb en masse, the North wins the war to the strains of a final chorus *My Own United States,* is produced in Detroit.

### 14 OCTOBER 1902

*Rymond,* opera by the 18-year-old Polish piano prodigy Raul KOCZALSKI, dealing with a Lithuanian chieftain converted to Christianity during the crusade of 1217 through the love of a well-born lady, is performed for the first time at Elberfeld.

### 14 OCTOBER 1902

*Servilia,* opera in five acts by RIMSKY-KORSAKOV, completed on 12 June 1901, one of the four of his stage works not on Russian subjects (the others being *Mozart and Salieri, Mlada* and *Pan Voyevoda*) wherein a beauteous maiden's love for a noble tribune in Nero's Rome is thwarted by a wily centurion, causing her to die of a broken heart, is performed for the first time at the Imperial Opera in St. Petersburg.

### 21 OCTOBER 1902

Tor AULIN conducts the inaugural concert of the Stockholm Symphony Orchestra, *Konsertfoerening,* incorporated on 27 May 1902. (Dates from *Stockholms Konsertfoerening, 1902-1927,* a 25-year anniversary booklet, Stockholm, 1927)

## 22 OCTOBER 1902

A century has elapsed since the death in London of Samuel ARNOLD, English composer of stately oratorios and sedate operas, and learned editor of the collected works of Handel.

O shade rever'd! Our nation's loss and pride! For mute was harmony when Arnold died! (From a poem engraved on a plaque near the tombstone of Arnold in Westminster Abbey)

## 1 NOVEMBER 1902

The Philadelphia Orchestra Association is incorporated "to exist perpetually" with the aim of encouraging performances of first-class orchestral music in Philadelphia. (Date from Appendix A, in F. Wister's *Twenty-Five Years of the Philadelphia Orchestra, 1900-1925*)

## 6 NOVEMBER 1902

*Adriana Lecouvreur,* lyric drama in four acts by Francesco CILÈA, his most celebrated work, to a libretto dealing in a highly dramatized manner with the life and the loves of the French actress Adrienne Lecouvreur (1692–1730), who undergoes a series of misadventures including mistaken identities, misdirected letters, mislaid jewels, and misfired amourettes, and dies from the fumes of poisoned violets sent to her by a jealous rival (the real Adrienne died of an internal hemorrhage), with a musical setting luxuriating in sonorous cantilena and throbbing with melodramatic diminished seventh-chords, is produced at the Teatro Lirico in Milan.

## 9 NOVEMBER 1902

*Andreas Hofer,* opera in two acts by the Hungarian composer Emanuel Moór, to his own German libretto dealing with the Tyrolese patriot Andreas Hofer who valiantly opposed Napoleon in the interests of the Austrian cause and then was betrayed into the hands of the French and executed in Mantua in 1810, is produced in Cologne.

## 12 NOVEMBER 1902

*Dornröschen (Sleeping Beauty),* short opera by Engelbert HUMPERDINCK, written in the ingratiating manner of his fairy-tale classic *Hänsel und Gretel* and similarly Wagneromantic in its style, is produced in Frankfurt.

## 21 NOVEMBER 1902

*Wiener Frauen (Der Klavierstimmer),* operetta in three acts by Franz LEHÁR, dealing with a versatile piano tuner, who instructs his exclusively female pupils in both music and love, is produced in Vienna, with an overture artfully reproducing the tuning in fifths of a grand piano.

## 27 NOVEMBER 1902

*Theodore Körner,* opera in four acts by the 23-year-old Sicilian composer Stefano DONAUDY, to a libretto by his brother dealing with the short, dramatic and lyric life of the German poet Karl Theodore Körner who fell on the field of battle in Schwerin in 1813 at the age of twenty-one is performed for the first time in Hamburg in the German version of its originally Italian libretto.

## 28 NOVEMBER 1902

*Saul og David,* first opera in four acts by the 37-year-old Danish composer Carl NIELSEN, conceived in a grandly oratorical manner and articulated into a series of symphonically designed dramatic tableaux, in which the biblical characters of Saul and David assume a veristic psychological coloration, is produced in Copenhagen.

## 1 DECEMBER 1902

Carl NIELSEN conducts in Copenhagen the first performance of his *Second Symphony,* subtitled *The Four Temperaments,* and reflecting in its four movements the four putative humors (yellow bile, phlegm, black bile, blood): (1) *Allegro collerico,* wherein the eruptive choleric mood is mitigated by gently lyric interludes (2) *Allegro comodo e flemmatico,* based on a phlegmatic two-note motive (3) *Andante malincolico,* in which the pervading melancholy is expressed by unstable intervalic maundering (4) *Allegro sanguineo,* marching in sanguine major keys through ostentatious syncopation to an optimistic conclusion.

## 4 DECEMBER 1902

Feodor Ignatievich STRAVINSKY, father of Igor Stravinsky, Russian operatic bass of velvety vocal magnificence and dramatic grandiloquence, dies in St. Petersburg, the scene of his many operatic triumphs, at the age of fifty-nine. (Previous additions of *Music Since 1900* mistakenly give the place of Feodor Stravinsky's death as Wildungen, Germany, where he lived during the summer of 1902 and whence he was brought *in extremis* to St. Petersburg on 28 October 1902)

My father died on 21 November (old style, 4 December new style) 1902. After death, the body was frozen like a piece of meat, dressed in evening clothes, and photographed. The funeral procession started from our house on an unseasonably humid day. The artists and directors of the Maryinsky Theater were present, and Rimsky-Korsakov stood by my mother. (Igor Stravinsky & Robert Craft, *Expositions and Developments,* New York 1962, p. 56)

## 9 DECEMBER 1902

*Francesca da Rimini,* after Dante, the last opera, in four acts, by the famous Russian conductor, Eduard NAPRAVNIK, is produced in St. Petersburg.

## 16 DECEMBER 1902

*Götz von Berlichingen,* opera in five acts by Karl GOLDMARK, based on Goethe's famous story, is produced in a Hungarian version in Budapest.

16 DECEMBER 1902

*Potemkin Holiday,* opera in four acts by Mikhail IVANOV, Russian music critic of ultra-conservative tendencies, to a libretto by the reactionary editor of a right-wing St. Petersburg newspaper, descriptive of the celebration in 1791 of Fieldmarshal Potemkin's victories, and set to music in abecedarian harmonies, is produced in St. Petersburg.

16 DECEMBER 1902

*La Carmélite,* opera in four acts by the Venezuelan-born French composer Reynaldo HAHN, to a libretto by Catulle Mendès patterned after the life of Madame de la Vallière, the country girl who became the favorite mistress of Louis XIV, but was eventually replaced by the more worldly Madame de Montespan, and in her chagrin joined the decalced order of Carmelites, the musical score written in the manner of Massenet with some pleasing neo-Lullyan dance music in the ballet interludes, and employing rhythmed speech in the religious scene in the last act, is performed for the first time at the Opéra-Comique in Paris.

The taking of the veil was reproduced with such fidelity on the stage of the Opéra-Comique that it wounded the religious scruples of many spectators, and one or two critics expressed in vigorous language their objections to such a masquerade. The immediate result has been that the director has cut out the first part of the last act, which in the future will commence after Madame de la Vallière has taken the veil, the objectionable mimicry being thus suppressed. (*Era,* London, December 1902)

25 DECEMBER 1902

*Kashchey the Immortal,* "little autumn tale" in one act and three tableaux by RIMSKY-KORSAKOV (composition begun in St. Petersburg on 9 July 1901 and completed there on 1 April 1902), wherein a beauteous Russian princess kept in oppressive durance by a malevolent white-bearded wizard is rescued by the fair-headed princely youth Ivan, written in a harmonic idiom rich in surprising innovations such as "cross-relations formed by consecutive major thirds, deceptive cadences on unresolved dissonances and a multitude of passing chords" (as Rimsky-Korsakov himself characterized the modernism of the score), is performed for the first time in Moscow, Ippolitov-Ivanov conducting.

# ～ *1903* ～

1 JANUARY 1903

Claude DEBUSSY receives the Cross of Chevalier de la Légion d'Honneur, through the efforts of the musicographer Jules Combarieu, an official of the French government.

## 2 JANUARY 1903

Victor HERBERT conducts the Pittsburgh Symphony Orchestra in the first performance of his symphonic sketch *Columbus.*

## 3 JANUARY 1903

Jane FOSTER, Stephen Foster's wife who inspired the song *Jeanie with the Light Brown Hair,* composed during their period of separation, but published in June of 1854 after their reconciliation, dies in Pittsburgh as Mrs. Matthew D. Wiley (she remarried in 1879).

## 3 JANUARY 1903

Alexander GLAZUNOV conducts at the second of the annual series of Russian Symphony Concerts in St. Petersburg the world premières of two of his works: *Seventh Symphony* in F major (completed on 16 July 1902) in four movements, *Allegro moderato, Andante, Scherzo, Finale,* couched in a combined sonata-variation form, and distinguished by soaringly songful lyricism, deep-grounded and opulent harmonies, ingenious contrapuntal interplay of thematic elements, and majestic modality in the epic Russian manner, with an ending on a festive fanfare with clanging bells; and an orchestral suite *From the Middle Ages* (completed 3 October 1902), in four parts: *Prelude, Scherzo, Serenade of a Troubadour,* and *The Crusaders,* written in a proclamatory style of nearly operatic eloquence.

## 6 JANUARY 1903

Boris BLACHER, composer of abstract chamber operas and concrete instrumental music, who was to identify himself with the cause of German modernism, is born in Newchwang, China, of Russian-bred ethnically Estonian-German parents.

## 7 JANUARY 1903

*L'Étranger,* "action musicale" in two acts by Vincent D'INDY, to his own libretto from an ancient French legend about a shipwrecked mariner who exercises mystical attractive power on an affianced local maiden and sails away with her on his miraculously navigable shipwreck as the awed villagers sing *De Profundis,* with a setting in which Wagnerian harmonies are veiled in an impressionistic mist and thematic materials are enriched by Gallic virelais, is performed for the first time at the Théâtre de la Monnaie in Brussels.

*L'Étranger* is what dogmatic people call an example of pure and lofty art, but in my humble opinion it is more than that. It is the working out of formulas which are admittedly pure and lofty, but which have the coldness, blueness, delicacy, and hardness of steel. Beautiful music is there, but it is, as it were, cloaked; and the mastery is so amazing that one hardly ventures to feel anything so incongruous as emotion. Say what you will, Wagner's influence on Vincent d'Indy was never really profound. If *Fervaal* owes something to the influence of the Wagnerian tradition, it is protected from it by its conscientious scorn of the grandiloquent hysteria which ravages the Wagnerian heroes. (Debussy, *Monsieur Croche, Anti-Dilettante*)

## 16 JANUARY 1903

*First Symphony* in E-flat major by Reinhold GLIÈRE, Russian composer of remote Belgian extraction, in four movements, *Andante, Allegro molto vivace, Andante* and *Finale,* conceived in a grand epic manner with the application of a totality of favorite Russian melodic, rhythmic, harmonic and instrumental devices, short folk-like refrains within the compass of a pentachord, a major hexachord with a lowered submediant, drones on the dominant, deep pedal-points, and symmetrically compounded meters, is performed for the first time in Moscow.

## 19 JANUARY 1903

*Het Eerekruis (The Cross of Honor),* one act opera by the Dutch composer Cornelis DOPPER, is produced in Amsterdam.

## 22 JANUARY 1903

*Oceana,* short opera by Antonio SMAREGLIA, 48-year-old Italian composer who lost his eyesight in 1900 but continued to compose Wagneromantic Italianate music by dictating it note by note while improvising at the piano, is performed for the first time at La Scala in Milan.

## 27 JANUARY 1903

*La Botte secrète,* opéra-bouffe in one act by Claude TERRASSE, in which a pair of shoes serves as evidence to trap the blackguard who kicked an aristocratic customer's derrière, set to music with Gallic elegance, is produced in Paris, on the composer's 36th birthday.

## 28 JANUARY 1903

Four French musicians die on the same day: Augusta Mary HOLMÈS, Parisian-Irish composer and pupil of César Franck, pianistic wonder-child of the Second Empire, in Paris in her fifty-sixth year; Robert PLANQUETTE, composer of celebrated operettas, among them *Les Cloches de Corneville,* in his native Paris in his fifty-fifth year; Edmond NEUKOMM, writer on music, in Paris in his sixty-third year; and one AUGEUZ, a singer in his fifty-sixth year.

"Funereal, indeed, is this week, which had brought the news on the same day, Wednesday, of the death of four artists meriting recognition! Our poor friend Augusta Holmès is gone. . . . She was older than it was believed. The year 1854 was given for her birth. But, it was in 1847 that she was born. I am absolutely certain of this. . . . It is quite a distance to the author of *Cloches de Corneville.* They rejuvenated him, too, making him appear in this world in 1850. The truth is, he was born on 31 July 1848. . . . I must also give the final farewell to my old comrade, Edmond Neukomm, who was nephew of the two Haydns. . . . His most curious and original work is the one he will not see accomplished: *Le Tour de France en musique.* . . . He was a gentleman and an artist of rare talent, this excellent Auguez. . . . Ah! If only his voice had equalled his talent!" (Arthur Pougin in *Le Ménestrel,* Paris, 1 February 1903)

## 7 FEBRUARY 1903

Two symphonic poems, *Minnehaha* and *Hiawatha*, by the German composer Hugo KAUN (1863–1932), a tribute to America where he dwelt from 1887 to 1902, was cherished by German friends and made happy by Theodore Thomas and Frederick Stock who loyally conducted his competently fashioned sub-Wagnerian post-Mendelssohnian symphonies with the Chicago Symphony Orchestra, are performed for the first time in Chicago.

## 11 FEBRUARY 1903

Six years and four months after the death of the great Austrian symphonist Anton BRUCKNER, his unfinished *Ninth Symphony* in D minor, dedicated "An meinem lieben Gott," is performed for the first time in Vienna under the direction of Bruckner's devoted friend and disciple Ferdinand Loewe, considerably edited, altered and reorchestrated by him, with the substitution for the unfinished finale of Bruckner's *Te Deum*, in three movements:

(1) *Feierlich*, hurling anguished defiance at the dedicatee, the "lieber Gott," with 8 horns blasting heavenwards in challenging octave leaps, while the violins voice their lament in languorous chromatics, the commotion ultimately subsiding in ascetic hollow fifths and meek minor thirds (2) *Bewegt, lebhaft*, a sensuous septuagenarian fantasy in the spirit of a lambent Scherzo, with fluvial flutes, clarion clarinets and bacchanalian bassoons indulging in insouciant dalliance (3) *Sehr langsam, feierlich*, a solemn *Adagio*, in which the rebellious spirit of theomachy is revealed in mounting minor ninths and tortured minor seconds, ending in a harmonious conciliation with the Deity in a poignant motive marked "Abschied vom Leben." (On 2 April 1932 the original version of the three extant movements was performed for the first time in Munich before an invited audience under the direction of Siegmund von Hausegger; a public performance of these movements was first given in Vienna under the direction of Clemens Kraus on 23 October 1932. Hans Redlich and Robert Simpson assembled and organized Bruckner's sketches for the finale, and had the synthetic result performed in London on 17 September 1948)

## 14 FEBRUARY 1903

*Le Tasse*, opera in three acts by the French composer-nobleman Count Eugène D'HARCOURT, dealing with the fateful passion of the famous poet Torquato Tasso for the duchess Leonora d'Este, which drove him to self-imposed celibacy in a monastery and her to a loveless marriage and an early death, with an appropriately emotional but harmonically static and dramatically constricted score, is produced in Monte Carlo.

## 20 FEBRUARY 1903

*Bruder Straubinger*, operetta in three acts by Edmund EYSLER, wherein a virginal child of nature in a sinful Teutonic town is unwittingly procured by a dissimulating panderer to satisfy the perverted lust of a licentious landgrave but is rescued from debauched perdition by a young peasant impersonating his own 114-year-old grandfather who volunteers to marry her, ostensibly to provide matrimonial cover, is produced in Vienna.

## 21 FEBRUARY 1903

*Moharózsa (Moss-Rose)*, after Ouida's fairly tale *Two Little Wooden Shoes*, opera in four acts by the famous Hungarian violinist Jenö HUBAY, is produced in Budapest.

## 22 FEBRUARY 1903

Hugo WOLF, the Wagner of the Lied, who was to the last quarter of the 19th century what Schubert was to the first quarter, and who developed the art of accompanied song into a polyphonic form wherein the voice becomes a contrapuntal strand in the highly chromaticized tonal fabric and the piano part is a harmonic determinant, dies 19 days before his 43rd birthday in an insane asylum in Vienna where he was kept with some intermissive remissions from 20 September 1897.

## 4 MARCH 1903

*Jean-Michel*, opera in four acts by the Belgian composer Albert DUPUIS, is produced in Brussels.

## 8 MARCH 1903

Gheorge ENESCU (who to acclimatize himself in Europe adopted the French form of his name Georges ENESCO), prodigiously gifted 21-year-old Rumanian violinist and composer, conducts in Bucharest the first performances anywhere of his *First Suite* for orchestra in C major and his two *Rumanian Rhapsodies*, the first (which was to become his most famous work) based on the popular tunes *Am un leu si vreau să-l beau* (I have a leu and I want to buy a drink), *La moara* (At a Mill), a "hora," *Ciocilia* (A Lark) and *Banu Mărăcine* (a quick dance in alternating tones and semitones) and the second being an essay in Balkan orientalism pregnant with sesquitonal melismas. (Date from actual program in the Georges Enesco Museum in Bucharest, 23 February 1903 according to old style calendar then valid in Rumania)

## 18 MARCH 1903

*Muguette*, opera in four acts by the French composer Edmond MISSA, after Ouida's tale *Two Little Wooden Shoes*, wherein a flower girl, poetically nicknamed after the lily of the valley and seasonally blossoming in Flanders in May 1820, succumbs to the savoir-faire of a French painter for whom she poses, and when he acquires another model in Paris, trudges in her two little wooden shoes to join him there, and surprisingly achieves an emotional reunion with wedding overtones (in Ouida's original story she dies), with an unassuming musical setting in the manner of Missa's teacher Massenet, gaining much by the ingratiating infusion of authentic Flemish folksongs, is performed for the first time at the Opéra-Comique in Paris.

## 21 MARCH 1903

*La Vita Nuova*, oratorio after Dante by Ermanno WOLF-FERRARI, is performed for the first time in Munich.

President Theodore ROOSEVELT inaugurates East Room Musicales in the White House, with a special concert given by Paderewski.

9 APRIL 1903

*Endymion's Narrative,* the second of the two symphonic romances by Frederick S. CONVERSE, suggested by the allegorical poem of Keats, wherein the solo violin narrates to a mildly Wagnerian orchestral accompaniment the sad tale of the legendary Greek youth loved for one terrestrial night by the goddess of the moon and thenceforth doomed to dream of her as a thing of beauty without attainment in a magically induced sleep, is performed for the first time by the Boston Symphony Orchestra, Wilhelm Gericke conducting.

16 APRIL 1903

*Le Sire de Vergy,* opera in three acts by the French composer Claude TERRASSE, to a story of a trusting Provençal crusader who hands the key to his wife's corselet of chastity to his best friend before going to the wars, and having found out that his friend betrayed him and misused the key, serves his wife a slice of calf's liver, pretending it was the cooked heart of her lover, and yet himself picks up a comely medieval midinette from Paris, is performed for the first time at the Théâtre des Variétés in Paris.

17 APRIL 1903

Nicolas NABOKOV, Russian composer of operas, ballets and instrumental works of euphonious facture, embellished with prudential dissonant counterpoint, is born in an ancient castle, near Lubcha, in the Minsk region, ancestral seat of his family, tracing his genealogy back to a Russian concubine of Genghis Khan.

19 APRIL 1903

Edvard GRIEG conducts the Colonne Orchestra in Paris in a program of his works at his first appearance in France since his angry rejection of Colonne's invitation in 1899 accompanied by a denunciation of French justice in the Dreyfus Affair (Dreyfus had in the meantime been released from his detention at Devil's Island).

Did you read about my concert with the Colonne Orchestra in Paris? Never in my life did I experience anything like that. When I appeared on the stage, there were hisses and boos. But I had my full revenge, for my artistic victory was as great as I could have desired. (From Grieg's letter to Alexander Siloti, dated Paris, 30 April 1903, and published in *A. Siloti, Letters and Documents,* Leningrad, 1963)

1 MAY 1903

Luigi ARDITI, Italian composer of celebrated arias of which the vocal waltz *Il Bacio* is an imperishable favorite, and who eventually settled in England, dies in Hove, Sussex, at the age of eighty.

## 5 MAY 1903

Gino MARINUZZI, 21-year-old Italian composer, conducts in his native Palermo the first performance of his first opera *Barberina*, in three acts.

## 6 JUNE 1903

Aram KHACHATURIAN, Armenian composer of orientally inflected and rhythmically bubbling music in all genres, is born in Tiflis.

## 7 JUNE 1903

*Ilsebill*, "dramatic symphony" in five operatic scenes by the German composer Friedrich KLOSE, to a tale by the brothers Grimm about an overweeningly ambitious fisherwoman whose outrecuidance leads her to proclaim herself divine and demand absolute obedience to her wishes until the whole presumption collapses as in a dream, written in a faithfully Wagneromorphic idiom in resonant harmonies, with the oceanographic key of E major as the guiding tonality, is performed for the first time in Klose's native town of Karlsruhe. (The date, 29 October 1905, given in some reference works as absolute premiere is the first Munich production.)

## 17 JUNE 1903

*Babes in Toyland*, musical extravaganza in three acts by Victor HERBERT, populated with familiar characters from Mother Goose, who aid and abet the rebellion of toys in the nursery against the toymaker, is performed for the first time in Chicago.

## 27 JUNE 1903

Académie des Beaux-Arts in Paris awards the first Grand Prix de Rome to Raoul LAPARRA, from six contestants admitted to the finals, passing up Ravel, who applied for the second time, having received the Deuxième Second Prix de Rome in 1901.

## 30 JUNE 1903

Harry Lawrence FREEMAN, American Negro composer, conducts in Chicago the first performance of his opera *African Kraal*, with an all-Negro cast.

## 14 JULY 1903

*Viy*, short opera by the Czech composer Karel MOOR, after Gogol's horrifying tale of a nightmarish monster preying on human blood to sustain his posthumous existence, is performed for the first time in Prague.

## 20 JULY 1903

*Maguelone*, lyric drama in one act by the facile French composer Edmond MISSA, wherein a superbly desirable orphan girl in a fishing village of southern France, irrationally infatuated with a nefarious but masculine ship-wrecker, enters on a shameful bargain with a sleuthing customs official ("ton corps pour le sauver," he sings), but is saved by her lover who stabs him in the back at the critical moment and lets her accept the blame as acting in self-defense, with a songful but unoriginal score pleasingly interspersed with endearing Provençal airs, is performed for the first time on any stage at Covent Garden in London.

### 24 JULY 1903

At the centennial celebration of the birth of Charles-Adolphe ADAM, his melodious opera *Le Postillon de Lonjumeau*, dealing with the adventures of the post coachman whose vocal prowess in announcing arrivals and departures led to his engagement by Louis XV at the court opera, is performed for the first time in Longjumeau itself. (The spelling of the town's name as it appears on the title page of the opera is Lonjumeau, but it is Longjumeau in French geography books)

### 3 AUGUST 1903

*Sarrona; or the Indian Slave,* one-act opera by the American composer William Legrand HOWLAND to his own libretto, wherein the queen of a kingdom on the Ganges River, preparing to plunge a dagger into the dissipated flesh of her treacherous royal husband embroiled with a Greek dancer, is prevented in her design by a slave who demands carnal gratification as a price for his silence but, deterred by her reminder of his untouchability to a person of her caste, stabs himself to death, is performed for the first time on any stage in Bruges, Belgium, in an Italian version.

### 25 AUGUST 1903

*Second Symphony* by the 23-year-old English composer Cyril SCOTT is performed for the first time in London, at a Promenade Concert conducted by Henry Wood. (It was subsequently converted into *Three Symphonic Dances* —Gavotte, Eastern Dance, English Dance—and ceased to exist as a separate work)

### 1 SEPTEMBER 1903

Erik SATIE writes a piece for piano four hands entitled *3 Morceaux en Forme de Poire avec une Manière de Commencement, une Prolongation du même et un en plus suivi d'une Redite,* caricaturing the pedantry of musical terminology and of impressionistic preciosity.

Impressionist composers cut a pear in twelve pieces and gave each of them the title of a poem. Then Satie composed twelve poems and entitled the whole: *Morceaux en forme de poire.* (Jean Cocteau, *Le Rappel à l'ordre,* Paris, 1926)

This title, Satie explained, had been given to them because Debussy had declared them shapeless: "So I called them 'pear-shaped'—and *that* ought to show him and everybody that they are *not* shapeless." (M. D. Calvocoressi, *Musicians' Gallery,* London, 1935)

## 1 OCTOBER 1903

*Alpenkönig und Menschenfeind,* opera in three acts by Leo BLECH, is produced in Dresden. (It was revived in a new version under the title *Rappelkopf* in Berlin on 2 October 1917.)

## 8 OCTOBER 1903

Carl NIELSEN conducts in Copenhagen the first performance of his concert-overture *Helios,* inspired by the sunset over the Aegean Sea, and completed during his visit in Athens on 23 April 1903, when, as he wrote in a letter to a friend, "Helios burned all day long."

## 10 OCTOBER 1903

*Prinses Zonneschijn,* Flemish opera in four acts by the Belgian composer Paul GILSON, to the libretto from an old German legend of a lovely princess radiating sunshine in the darkest feudal forests, loved by a young Teutonic commoner, with the path to their union strewn with necessary royal cadavers, to a mildly Wagnerian setting full of foreboding horn calls, mystical reverberations among the flutes, and muted tremolos in the strings, is performed for the first time at the Flemish Opera in Antwerp.

## 14 OCTOBER 1903

*The Apostles,* oratorio by Edward ELGAR, to the text depicting the apostolic missions at the birth of Christianity, and the establishment of the church among the Gentiles, making use of an authentic Hebrew melody set to traditional Western harmonies, is performed for the first time at the Birmingham Festival.

## 17 OCTOBER 1903

*The Vagabond and the Princess,* the first opera, in one act, by the Hungarian composer Ede POLDINI, after Hans Christian Andersen's fairy tale, is produced in a Hungarian version translated from the original German libretto, at the Royal Opera in Budapest.

## 17 OCTOBER 1903

*The Duchess of Dantzic,* operetta in three acts by Ivan CARYLL (1861–1921), prolific Belgian-born British-bred American composer, to a libretto based on Sardou's play *Madame Sans-Gêne* dealing with an ambitious laundress who marries into nobility and becomes an influential intrigante at Napoleon's court, is performed for the first time in London.

## 27 OCTOBER 1903

*Dobrinya Nikititch,* opera in three acts by Alexandre GRETCHANINOFF, depicting in a grandiloquently Russian manner the daring exploits and ardent loves of a fabled figure of Russian folklore, is produced in Moscow.

### 30 OCTOBER 1903

*Odysseus' Tod,* the last part of the operatic tetralogy *Homerische Welt* by the Wagneromantic German composer August BUNGERT, to his own libretto from *The Odyssey,* in three acts with a prologue, is produced in Dresden.

### 1 NOVEMBER 1903

*The Christmas Tree,* one-act opera by the 37-year-old Russian composer Vladimir REBIKOV, to a libretto from various sources depicting the heart-rending misery of an orphan girl deprived of Christmas joys, with a musical setting boldly applying novel devices, such as whole-tone scales, pentatonic scales, nefarious parallel fifths and progressions of unresolved dissonances, ending defiantly on an augmented triad, but containing several pleasing arias and a Chopinesquely Tchaikovskyan waltz (which later became popular), is performed for the first time in Moscow, on the same bill with his earlier opera entitled *In the Storm.*

### 5 NOVEMBER 1903

The Minneapolis Symphony Orchestra makes its first appearance as a permanent organization under the direction of Emil OBERHOFFER, the conductor of the parent Philharmonic Club, or, as it was formerly called, Philharmonic Choral Society.

### 7 NOVEMBER 1903

*Liebeswogen,* "spoken opera" in one act by Theodor GERLACH, after Heinrich Heine's poem, with some singing passages and short choruses, all in an asthmatically post-Wagnerian vein, is produced in Bremen.

### 15 NOVEMBER 1903

*Tiefland,* lyric drama in three acts by the Scottish-born but self-Germanized composer Eugen D'ALBERT, to a libretto drawn from the play *Terra Baixa* (*Lowlands*) by the Catalan writer Angel Guimerá, wherein a young shepherd descends from his mountain pastures into the valley to marry a village maiden only to find that she is his master's mistress, a revelation that drives him to such homicidal fury that he strangles her seducer as he once strangled a prowling wolf, and carries his bride to the highlands where they can breathe the unpolluted air and enjoy unviolated love, set to music in an effective Wagneromantic style in which the contrapuntal woof is thematically enlaced with chromatic warp in the dramatically tense scenes that take place in the iniquitous lowlands while the episodes in the highlands are exalted in the spacious intervals of the natural scale, a contrast that made the opera a durable product despite the derivativeness of its eclectic idiom of composition, is produced at the German Opera House in Prague.

### 17 NOVEMBER 1903

*Mam'zelle Fifi,* one-act opera by César CUI, after a celebrated novelette by Maupassant in which a Prussian lieutenant, nicknamed Mam'zelle Fifi for his ephebic beardlessness, stationed with an occupational squad near Rouen in 1871, is stabbed to death by a patriotic fille de joie when he dares to speak slightingly of France, is performed for the first time in Moscow.

### 17 NOVEMBER 1903

*Storia d'amore*, opera in three acts by the Greek composer Spiro SAMARA, is performed for the first time in Milan. (It was produced under a changed title *La Biondinetta*, in Gotha, on 1 April 1906.)

### 22 NOVEMBER 1903

Pope PIUS X issues the epoch-making encyclic *Motu proprio*, in which he sets down the basic precepts for the interpretation and performance of Gregorian Chant in the light of the findings by the Benedictine monks of Solesmes. (Full text in LETTERS AND DOCUMENTS)

As regards the reforms of the Pontiff, in brief, all this seems very wonderful to me in substance, but not realizable in practice. This return to primordial purity of Gregorian Chant seems very difficult to me. Who can define essentially the difference between sacred and secular styles? Why proscribe the cymbals and the drums when angels play them in the old paintings? In all this I see words, phrases of excellent effect, but not much else. The world will go on as before. (Camille Saint-Saëns in *Le Figaro*, Paris, 1905, quoted by Arthur Dandelot, in *La Vie et l'œuvre de Saint-Saëns*, Paris, 1930)

### 27 NOVEMBER 1903

*Le donne curiose*, musical comedy in three acts by Ermanno WOLF-FERRARI, whose name hyphenates that of his German father and his Italian mother, with a libretto drawn from a play by Carlo Goldoni, wherein a bevy of inquisitive Venetian wives intent upon discovering the agenda of an exclusive men's club where their husbands habitually congregate, enter it by ruse only to find that, contrary to their suspicions, the club is indeed womanless, written in a merry settecento vein with Wagneromimic simulation, is performed for the first time in Munich, in a German version under the title *Die neugierigen Frauen*.

### 3 DECEMBER 1903

*Acté*, opera in four acts by the Catalan violinist Joan MANÉN, to his own libretto in the Catalan language, wherein a Christian maiden, coveted by Nero, defies and scorns him, whereupon he burns Rome to the accompaniment of a lyre and accuses her of complicity, with an Italianate setting utilizing stylized Greek modalities to depict early Christian rites, is performed for the first time in Barcelona. (A new version to a libretto in German was produced on 3 February 1928 in Karlsruhe, under the title *Nero und Akté*)

### 7 DECEMBER 1903

*Muirgheis*, Irish opera in three acts by O'Brien BUTLER (1870–1915), the first to be written to a libretto in the Gaelic language, is produced in Dublin.

## 8 DECEMBER 1903

In a pontifical letter to Cardinal Respighi, Pope Pius X expresses his apostolic disapproval of "endless musical compositions to the words of the Psalms . . . in a traditional theatrical manner, which are of so little artistic value that they would not be acceptable even at mediocre secular concerts," and urges the return to a proper musical treatment of sacred texts.

## 11 DECEMBER 1903

A century has passed since the birth of Hector BERLIOZ.

## 14 DECEMBER 1903

The Presbyterian Churches of Chicago adopt a resolution condemning the announced production of Wagner's *Parsifal* in New York as contributing to the promotion of a blasphemous work.

## 16 DECEMBER 1903

The Richard Wagner Society of America issues a protest against the intended production of *Parsifal* by the Metropolitan Opera of New York for audiences to whom "the essential character of Wagnerian art has never been and probably never will be revealed."

## 19 DECEMBER 1903

At the Teatro alla Scala in Milan, a gala première is given of *Siberia*, opera in three acts by the 36-year-old Italian composer Umberto GIORDANO, dealing with the deepest passions in darkest Tsarist Russia, wherein the lover of the mistress of a St. Petersburg nobleman nearly kills him in a duel and is dispatched to Siberia, whither she follows him and stabs herself to death after a failure to engineer his escape, the musical setting constituting a veritable anthology of Russian songs and dances wherein the doleful Volga Boatmen's song ungeographically serves as a Siberian motto and a complete rendition of the Tsarist national anthem is given by a police band during the hero's arrest, while the composer's own contribution is limited to Italianate mimicry of Russian sentimental ballads and to instrumental interludes such as a chromatic blizzard in the Siberian "Hungry Steppes."

## 20 DECEMBER 1903

*Taras Bulba*, opera in five acts by Nicolai LISSENKO, the "Ukrainian Glinka," to a libretto in the Ukrainian language based on Gogol's epical novel, wherein an unflinchingly stern Cossack leader embroiled in a 17th-century fight against Poland shoots down his own son treasonably infatuated with a Polish beauty, receives its belated first production in Kiev, a dozen years after its composition.

## 24 DECEMBER 1903

The first performance of WAGNER's *Parsifal* outside Bayreuth is given by the Metropolitan Opera in New York despite the formal objections of Cosima and

Siegfried Wagner made through their New York attorneys, asserting that no production of the opera can be given under the German copyright law until fifty years after Wagner's death, i.e. before 13 February 1913.

No one can deny that the production of *Parsifal* under the circumstances will justify the condemnation that will be uttered against us, and the efforts of all those to restore to us an opinion favorable to our character will now go for naught. This full-blooded American stock will point to the fact that those who have been engaged in the name of the people of the United States in committing this offense against ethics are chiefly foreigners. . . . Taking the opera house personnel we would find that the men who conducted the stage work were foreigners; that the orchestra consists of foreigners or their children; that the conductor was a foreigner; that the manager was foreign born; that his assistants were, to a great extent, foreign born, or the children of foreigners in the first generation. The whole scheme is essentially anti-American . . . and the newspapers of Germany which have denounced this production so vehemently should not forget to mention the names of those people who were identified with it, and those names will disclose the origin and the character of the people who are called American "Parsifalites." (*The Musical Courier*, New York, 30 December 1903)

### 27 DECEMBER 1903

*Sweet Adeline*, "echo song" by Henry ARMSTRONG, beloved by Manhattan inebriates as they travel from bar to bar banded in small groups, leaning mutually to maintain an unstable equilibrium, the title derived from the great Adelina Patti, is launched on its glorious career at the Sure Pops Sunday Nights in New York.

### 28 DECEMBER 1903

*La Reine Fiammette*, opera in four acts by Xavier LEROUX, French composer of Italian extraction on the maternal side, to a semidemihistorical novel of Catulle Mendès, wherein a young monk is induced by a wily secular cardinal in medieval Bologna to assassinate the local reigning queen for dynastic reasons, but upon penetrating into her chambers recognizes in her his hebdomadal inamorata of a suburban convent and falls into her passionate embrace, whereupon a more reliable hired killer slays them both at the crucial moment, with a musical setting in the lyrico-dramatic manner of Leroux's master, Jules Massenet, is produced at the Opéra-Comique in Paris.

# ~ 1904 ~

### 2 JANUARY 1904

Stanislav BINICKI, 31-year-old Serbian composer, conducts in Belgrade the first performance of his one-act opera, *Na uranku* (*At Dawn*), the first national opera to a libretto in the Serbian language, dealing with a Balkan love rivalry between a Turk and a Serbian under Ottoman rule, ending tragically when the girl of their choice throws herself in the path of the slow but lethal Turkish bullet to protect her lover, with the score vitalized by Balkanized orientalisms and native rhythmic asymmetries within a German harmonic framework.

## 2 JANUARY 1904

Peter JURGENSON, German-born founder of the Russian music publishing firm bearing his name, enlightened publisher and true friend of Tchaikovsky and a pleiad of other Russian composers, dies in Moscow at the age of sixty-seven.

## 8 JANUARY 1904

In a decree of the Congregation of Rites, Pope PIUS X sanctions the *cantus traditionalis* according to the restored texts transcribed by the Benedictine monks of Solesmes, in preference to the reformed Gregorian chant.

## 9 JANUARY 1904

The Spanish pianist Ricardo VIÑES gives the first performance at the Société Nationale de Musique in Paris of *Estampes* by DEBUSSY, a suite in three movements: *Pagodes,* an impressionistic distillation of Cambodian pentatonicism ornamented with Orientalistic tintinnabulations; *Soirée dans Grenade,* in a refined hispanistic idiom; and *Jardins sous la pluie,* an alliteratively pluvious tableau with raindrops in the treble watering the flower roots of the pedal-points.

## 10 JANUARY 1904

Mitrofan Petrovich BELAIEFF, Maecenas of national Russian music, founder and munificent supporter of the Belaieff publishing firm, which printed in its Leipzig shop a series of magnificently engraved operas, symphonies, chamber music, piano pieces and songs by a galaxy of Russian luminaries of varying magnitudes, among them Balakirev, Borodin, Glière, Liadov, Gretchaninoff, Scriabin, Taneyev, Liapunov, Maximilian Steinberg, Wihtol, Nicolas Tcherepnin and his son Alexander, as well as a number of resplendent obscurities—Akimenko, Alferaki, Amani, Artzibushev, Kalafati and Zolotarev—dies in his native St. Petersburg, where his father made a fortune in lumber export, at the age of sixty-seven.

## 13 JANUARY 1904

*Kossuth,* first truly symphonic work by the 22-year-old Béla BARTÓK, in ten tableaux glorifying the leader of the Hungarian uprising against Austria in 1848 with a mockingly atonalized version of Haydn's Austrian anthem *Gott, erhalte Franz den Kaiser,* is performed for the first time in Budapest.

## 15 JANUARY 1904

Eduard LASSEN, Danish-born, Belgian-trained, German-domesticated conductor, and himself composer of competent operas and symphonies, dies at the age of 73 in Weimar, where he settled as Court Music Director in 1858, and where he led important operatic premières including the first performance of *Samson et Dalila* of Saint-Saëns.

### 21 JANUARY 1904

*Její Pastorkyňa* (*Her Foster Daughter;* also known as *Jenufa*), opera in three acts by Leoš JANÁČEK, in which young Jenufa, loved by two brothers, is made pregnant by one whom she loves but who refuses to marry her, and knifed by the other whose true love she rejects but who remains loyal to her even when her infant is found drowned in a nearby lake and she is accused of infanticide until her adoptive mother confesses guilt, to a musical setting richly imbued with modally Slavic melorhythms plastically adapted to depict transient joy, black melancholy and stark tragedy, is performed for the first time in Brno.

### 28 JANUARY 1904

Modest ALTSCHULER conducts the first concert, at Cooper Union Hall in New York City, of the Russian Symphony Orchestra founded by him in America to promote the cause of Russian symphonic music.

### 29 JANUARY 1904

*Der Kobold,* opera in three acts by Siegfried WAGNER, to his own libretto dealing with sprites and fays, nymphs and sylphs, dryads and hamadryads, oreads and limoniads, kobolds, gnomes and other elfenfolk puckishly intervening in the otherwise realistic events taking place in a small German town early in the 19th century, with the paternal ghost of the composer's great father determining the shaping of musical themes and the formation of harmonies, is performed for the first time in Hamburg.

I am well aware that of the applause bestowed upon my *Kobold* only 20% is due me, and 80% due my father. If my name were not Siegfried Wagner, but Müller or Schulz, this distinguished assembly would not be gathered here. (Siegfried Wagner's remark at a banquet given in his honor after the production of *Der Kobold* in Graz on 3 December 1904)

The tragedy of sons of great fathers is not that they lack talent but precisely because they possess a talent. (Julius Korngold, *Neue Freie Presse,* 20 January 1905, after the Vienna production of *Der Kobold*)

### 1 FEBRUARY 1904

Enrico CARUSO makes his first phonograph recording in America for the Victor Company, singing the aria *Vesti la giubba* from *Pagliacci,* which he made famous by the application of the "Caruso sob," known technically as *coup de glotte.*

### 3 FEBRUARY 1904

Luigi DALLAPICCOLA, whose inventive skill and stylistic flexibility has enabled him to integrate the dodecaphonic technique into a neoclassical Italian framework in his instrumental and vocal compositions, is born in Pisino, Italy.

#### 4 FEBRUARY 1904

*La Cigale,* ballet by Jules MASSENET, wherein the improvident grasshopper of La Fontaine's fable is transformed into a Parisian coquette and the industrious ant into a bourgeois matron, with the moral propounded by a bank clerk, is produced at the Opéra-Comique in Paris.

#### 8 FEBRUARY 1904

Jean SIBELIUS conducts in Helsingfors, with Victor NOVÁČEK as soloist, the first performance of his *Violin Concerto* in three movements, *Allegro moderato, Adagio di molto,* and *Allegro ma non tanto,* rooted in the German romantic tradition, treating the violin with a philosophical disregard for self-propelled virtuoso play, yet constantly maintaining interest by relentlessly propulsive rhythms and somberly colorful instrumentation. (A revised final version of the Violin Concerto was performed for the first time in Berlin, Carl Halir soloist, on 19 October 1905)

All the heights of the violin are furiously scaled in this new concerto of Sibelius, and all its most lugubrious depths explored. There are few opportunities for the violin to speak in tones of beauty while the accompaniment is for the greater part either a mutter or a growl. Solo instrument and orchestra do not love each other in this new work. (New York *Tribune,* 1 December 1906)

#### 13 FEBRUARY 1904

Edward MACDOWELL addresses the following letter to Felix Mottl on the status of American composers:

I see by the morning papers a so-called American Composers' Concert advertised for tomorrow evening at the Opera House. I have for years taken a strong stand against such affairs, and though I have not seen the program, fearing there might be something of mine in it, I write to protest earnestly and strongly against the lumping together of American composers. Unless we are worthy of being put on programs with other composers, to stand or fall, leave us alone. By giving such a concert, you tacitly admit that we are too inferior to stand comparison with composers of Europe. If my name is on the program and it is too late to have new ones made, I beg of you to have a line put through the number, crossing it off the programs. If necessary, I will pay the expense of having this done. (Quoted by Alfred Frankenstein in the *Juilliard Review,* New York, Winter, 1955–56)

#### 16 FEBRUARY 1904

*Marya,* opera in three acts by the Polish composer Henryk MELCER, is produced in Warsaw.

#### 17 FEBRUARY 1904

At the Teatro alla Scala in Milan, the world première (unsuccessful to the point of a resounding fiasco) is given of *Madama Butterfly,* "Japanese tragedy" by Giacomo PUCCINI, in two acts (the second subdivided into two parts), to a libretto by Giacosa and Illica, after an American play by David Belasco, based on a short story by John Luther Long purported to be derived from an actual event but seemingly influenced by the French novelette *Madame Chrysanthème*, telling the piteous tale of a 15-year-old Nagasaki geisha married in a ceremony of dubious legality (for a consideration of 100 yen) to a U.S. Navy lieutenant Francis Blummy Pinkerton (thus in the original libretto; later changed to Benjamin Franklin Pinkerton; yet even in the revised editions, Butterfly herself refers to him as F. B., rather than B. F., Pinkerton; in German productions, the name invariably appears as Linkerton in order to avoid the urinary associations of the verb *pinkeln*), with the tragically predictable harakiri ensuing when Pinkerton revisits Japan with his American wife, the curtain falling upon the self-eviscerated body of his ephemeral Butterfly as their Nipponese-American infant stands uncomprehendingly by, holding a tiny American flag, the musical score abounding in authentic Japanese songs (including the Imperial Anthem) in pentatonic and para-Phrygian modes, while the American side is represented by snatches from *The Star-Spangled Banner*, to which Pinkerton sings in English, "America Forever!"—all this enveloped in soaringly passionate Puccinian melos accoutred in harmonies often moving in parallel formations and consolidated in powerful unisons at dramatically climactic points.

Growls, roars, laughter, animal noises, giggling, such was the reception that the audience of La Scala gave to the new work of Maestro Puccini. This performance in the hall seemed as well organized as the one on the stage, for it started precisely as the opera began. It had an air of actuality, as if the Russians, in serried battalions, attacked to rout Puccini's Japanese from the stage. Afterwards, Puccini, Giacosa, Illica, in agreement with the publisher Ricordi, withdrew *Madama Butterfly* and reimbursed the management of the theater for the amount of the rights of performance. (Giulio Ricordi, in *Musica e Musicisti*, March 1940)

Fiasco . . . but good Lord, how can anyone expect to set to music episodes which have no lyric substance? The personality of Puccini sins on the side of uniformity. The heroes and heroines of his musical dramas do not present variety of type or sentiment. Almost all of them resemble each other. *Butterfly* is a replica of *La Bohème*, but with less freshness. . . . Instead, there is exaggerated emphasis and musical fragmentation. (Gian Battista Nappi, *Perseveranza*, February 1904)

A long, too long, first act was received coldly. After the first stage call for the singers, Maestro Puccini, leaning on a cane (he broke his leg during an automobile accident on 25 February 1903) appeared twice in front of the curtain. The public, gathered in the theater in the expectation of a new victory by a favorite composer, changed its mood from excessive approbation to harsh condemnation. . . . Even Butterfly's aria *Un bel dì vedremo*, which possesses a fine romantic quality, ended amid protests. . . . Yet it is a page of most delicate texture and of immediate effectiveness. . . . I persist in believing that the opera, condensed and lightened up, will come back to life. (Giovanni Pozza, in *Corriere della Sera*, 19 February 1904)

*Butterfly* is coated with Japanese lacquer amalgamated with American rubber. . . . It is Japanese more in appearance than in substance. . . . Puccini resorts to the Parisianism of *La Bohème*, to Romanism of *Tosca*, to Franco-Americanism of *Manon*, making use of his favorite musical phrases. He obtains local color by allusions and patterns of the singing line, and by quotations of Japanese songs. But these elements are merely photographic, and do not convey the true essence. (*La Lombardia*, 19 February 1904)

A terrible evening. The failure of *Madama Butterfly* struck me deeply, for it was totally unexpected. But I met this rebuke with a sense of rebellion. . . . On that night of sorrow, I had the pride of protest, but the next morning I felt annihilated, and this feeling was deepened by endless humiliation. It was not the labor of three years that I mourned, but the destruction of my hopes. It was the sorrow of seeing this poetic dream, which I cherished with so much love, crushed. For a while it seemed to me that I would never again be able to write a single note. On that morning, the newsboys passing under my windows in the vicinity of La Scala shouted: "Il fiasco del Maestro Puccini!" For two weeks I did not want to go out of the house. I was ashamed. (Puccini's words of recollection quoted by Arnaldo Fraccaroli in his *La vita di Giacomo Puccini*, Milan, 1925)

The press and the public can say whatever they want, they can hurl at me all their darts as at St. Stephen, but they will not bury me and destroy my Butterfly. She will rise again, alive and well. . . . You shall see if I am telling the truth. (Puccini's letter to Alfredo Vandini, 21 February 1904)

(Puccini's faith was justified. On 28 May 1904, a slightly revised version of the opera was given in Brescia, with triumphant success; seven numbers were encored)

All the telegrams which I have received, accord faithfully and exactly with the colossal, clamorous and genuine success. It is only right that today it is our turn to laugh a little! And it is just that the enemy horde should be compelled to swallow the rust of their casseroles and of their fury. In the meantime: Viva Butterfly forever! (Puccini's letter to Giulio Ricordi, 2 June 1904)

18  FEBRUARY 1904

*Hélène,* lyric poem in one act and four tableaux by Camille SAINT-SAËNS, to his own libretto in rhymed verse detachedly detailing the fateful flight of Helen and Paris in a boat propelled by the "double caresse des zéphires et des baisers" undeterred by the monitory and minatory vision of burning Troy conjured up by Pallas Athena, who sides with the forces of conjugal fidelity against Aphrodite's aphrodisiac proddings, the music bathed in impeccably fluid harmonies, is performed for the first time at Monte Carlo, as a commissioned work dedicated "to His Serenest Highness Prince Albert I of Monaco."

18  FEBRUARY 1904

*Second Symphony* in B-flat major by the master of Gallic neo-classicism, Vincent D'INDY, in four movements: (1) *Extrêment lent—Très vif* (2) *Modérément lent* (3) *Modéré—Très animé* (4) *Lent—Fugue et Final,* in a cyclic construction with passages in whole-tone scales, consecutive major ninth-chords, instantaneous modulations by means of parallel motion, and other modernistic paraphernalia contrasted with folkloric references to regional songs of France, is performed for the first time in Paris.

29  FEBRUARY 1904

An orchestral *Scherzo* by Béla BARTÓK, composed in 1902 at the age of 20, is performed for the first time in Budapest.

## 5 MARCH 1904

*String Quartet* in F by Maurice RAVEL, in four movements: (1) *Allegro moderato—Très doux* (2) *Assez vif—Très rythmé* (3) *Très lent* (4) *Vif et agité,* monothematic in substance but polyharmonic and allorhythmic in variations, with widely ranging technical resources, from modal pandiatonicism to chordal parallelism and opulent Andalusian cadences wherein a descending Phrygian tetrachord is harmonized in major triads, concluding in an ascending series of major six-four chords along a sesquitonal root progression, is performed for the first time at a concert of the Société Nationale de Musique in Paris.

## 12 MARCH 1904

Thirteen centuries have elapsed since the death of Pope GREGORY THE GREAT, organizer of sacred music of the church into a great code known as Gregorian Chant.

## 16 MARCH 1904

*La Fille de Roland,* "tragédie musicale" in four acts by Henri RABAUD, wherein a young warrior in Charlemagne's ranks loves the daughter of the great paladin Roland, unaware that it was his own father who betrayed his beloved's father to the infidels at the battle of Roncesvalles in 778 A.D., with a musical score set in two-dimensional heterophony to impart the feeling of the period but exploding in ample arpeggios in the scenes of passion, is performed for the first time at the Opéra-Comique in Paris. (The title page of the printed score gives the date of the first performance as 15 March 1904, but the account of the production in *Le Ménestrel* gives 16 March 1904)

## 18 MARCH 1904

*Baba-Yaga,* symphonic poem by Anatoly LIADOV, picturing in uninterrupted presto motion the flight through the air of a fabulous Russian witch Baba-Yaga in a mortar propelled by a pestle and navigated with a broom, taking off in a whirlwind of whole-tone scales and disappearing beyond the horizon in a chromatic pianissimo, is performed for the first time in St. Petersburg.

## 21 MARCH 1904

On his first visit to the United States, Richard STRAUSS conducts in New York a concert of his music with the Wetzler Symphony Orchestra, in a program including *Don Juan, Also Sprach Zarathustra,* and the world première of his enormously protracted *Symphonia Domestica* (completed by him in Charlottenburg on the last day of 1903), scored for a huge orchestra and dedicated "to my beloved wife and our young one," presenting a systematic chronological account of 24 hours of domestic felicity, the psychomusical material containing 67 distinct but tonally interrelated motives in constant mutation and mutual adaptation through inversion, augmentation, diminution, canon and fugue, the whole work articulated into four sections:

*Introduction,* presenting the four principal aspects of the composer himself (genial, dreamy, sullen, fiery), three sides of his wife's nature (graceful, angry, gay), and, intoned by the oboe d'amore accompanied by the softest violins, the entirely lovable child, whose countenance is commented upon by the aunts (muted trumpets and assorted clarinets in unison), "Ganz der Papa!" and by the uncles (oboes, oboe d'amore, English horn, muted horn and muted bass trombone), "Ganz die Mama!" (the words are written out in the score); *Scherzo,* in which the child's theme is accelerated fourfold and intertwined with the father's bugle-like motive in inversion, until the infantile lallation subsides, as the old-fashioned clock's peal in glockenspiel announces the time for the evening bath with 7 strokes; *Adagio,* with an emotional upsurge of marital love through the night in artfully connubial braces of complementary leitmotivs and harmonious contrapuntal osculation, culminating in a soaring fortissimo after which the flutes, out of breath, the whispering harps, and the moan of stifled violins *sul ponticello* veil the domestic scene; the clock's peal in glockenspiel is heard again at 7 o'clock in the morning, ushering in the *Finale* with a new day's vigor, with all the 67 motives in all their mutations, and the parental themes merging into a mighty double fugue, with the child's motive trumpeted for the full-blown coda.

I see no reason why I should not write a symphony about myself. I find the subject as interesting as Napoleon or Alexander the Great. (Richard Strauss quoted in Romain Rolland's *Musique française et Musique allemande* in *Richard Strauss et Romain Rolland,* Paris, 1951)

The Symphonia Domestica—Home Sweet Home as Written by Richard Strauss— Papa and Mama and Baby Celebrated in a Huge Conglomeration of Orchestral Music. (Headlines in the New York *Sun,* 22 March 1904)

In the whole of the *Domestic Symphony* there is only one particularly individual melody, the one which represents the baby; and even that is rather commonplace. It is developed and orchestrated with much skill, and towards the end it is built up into a climax which suggests a megalosaurian monster rather than a Bavarian baby. . . . So far as there is any relation between music and subject, the *Domestic Symphony* might be called quite as appropriately A Trip to Constantinople or A Day at Vladivostok. . . . The whole thing is either a deplorable aberration of taste or else a clever method of courting publicity. (Henry T. Finck, in the New York *Evening Post,* 22 March 1904)

It is not every family which has double fugues for breakfast, but this Strauss family is a peculiar one. If *Symphonia Domestica* were a true biographical sketch, we fancy that the wife would be portrayed on trombones and tubas while the husband would be pictured on the second violin. (Louis C. Elson, in the Boston *Daily Advertiser,* 12 January 1917)


## 25 MARCH 1904

*Armida,* the last opera by Antonín DVOŘÁK (begun on 11 April 1902 and completed on 29 June 1903), in four acts, derived from Tasso's *La Gerusalemme liberata,* wherein the crusader Rinaldo, held in voluptuous thrall by the magically seductive daughter of the infidel commander, mortally wounds her as she meets him in combat incognito accoutred in a black cuirass, to a dramatically effective score replete with chromatically moving diminished seventh-chords, and closing with a chorale as Armida is baptized by Rinaldo before expiring in his arms, is produced in the original Czech version in Prague.

## 30 MARCH 1904

*Koanga,* opera in three acts by Frederick DELIUS, recounting the story of a royal African prince Koanga abducted from his proud equatorial domain and sold into slavery in 18th-century Louisiana under the Spanish rule, of his ardently reciprocated love for the mulatto half-sister of the planter's wife, his death in a futile uprising and the consequent suicide of his beloved, to a score brightened by authentic creole rhythms and pentatonically stylized Negro tunes, with an ensemble of banjos integrated into the orchestra, while the harmonic setting adheres to the conventional German-Italian formula in its chromaticized idiom, is performed for the first time anywhere, in Elberfeld, to a German translation of the originally English libretto.

## 20 APRIL 1904

*Le Fils de l'Étoile,* music drama in five acts by Camille ERLANGER, to a libretto of Catulle Mendès, wherein the legendary "son of the star" leading the Hebrews in their last rebellion against the Roman rule becomes entangled with the malignantly passionate imprecatrix Lilith and loses the battle, set to a Wagneromantically luxuriant score, is produced at the Paris Opéra.

## 25 APRIL 1904

Jean SIBELIUS conducts in Helsingfors the first performance of the chamber-orchestra version of his perennial favorite *Valse Triste.* (In the original score of incidental music to Järnefelt's play *The Death, Valse Triste* was orchestrated for strings only)

## 1 MAY 1904

Antonín DVOŘÁK, great Czech composer, the Verdi of Bohemia, who by his consummate art of harmonic universalization of natural melodic resources of his native land contributed to the creation of a national school of Czech music, and who was the first European to write an American symphony, *From the New World,* in which he made use of melorhythms adumbrative of the Negro spirituals, dies suddenly at the dinner table in his home in Prague, at the age of 62 years, 7 months and 3 weeks.

## 15 MAY 1904

*Manuel Menendez,* one-act opera by Lorenzo FILIASI, is produced in Milan.

## 15 MAY 1904

*Rübezahl und der Sackpfeifer von Neisse,* opera in four acts by the 66-year-old German composer Hans SOMMER, is produced in Brunswick.

## 16 MAY 1904

Exactly one month before "Bloomsday" proclaimed by James JOYCE in his novel *Ulysses,* replete with musical anamneses, he enters a contest at the

Dublin *Feis Ceoil,* judged by Luigi Denza, the composer of *Funiculi-Funi-cula,* and sings adequately in a tenorized baritone voice the two test pieces (*Come Ye Children* by Arthur Sullivan and the Irish air *A Long Farewell*), but refuses to try his unconsummate skill at sight reading, and so loses the potential gold medal, although he obtains a second prize when its original winner is in turn disqualified.

### 17 MAY 1904

At a concert of the Société Nationale de Musique in Paris the first performance is given of *Shéhérazade,* song cycle for voice and orchestra, by the 29-year-old Maurice RAVEL, to the texts of three exotic poems of Tristan Klingsor: (1) *Asie,* breathlessly exhaling puffs of Gallically perfumed Orientalistic vapors, apostrophizing in hypnotic glossolalia the distant "Asie, Asie, vieux pays merveilleux," enticing by its very longuinquity, tonally illustrated by rapid melismatic arabesques and delicately dissonant instrumental couplings against a deeply resonant foundation of open fifths (2) *La Flûte enchantée,* depicting a timeless girl standing immobile listening as the sounds of a flute fall on her cheek with the intangible caress of a wafted kiss (3) *L'indifférent,* a fleeting image of an effeminate youth whose lips shape the vocables of an alien language ("comme une musique fausse") intimated by a linear discord in false modality, and terminating on a pandiatonically extended triad with a major ninth. (At the same concert, Albert ROUSSEL's symphonic prelude *Résurrection,* his first orchestral work, inspired by Tolstoy's moralistic novel of that name and written in a congenially religious mood concluding with a liturgical chorale from the Catholic Easter service, is performed for the first time anywhere)

### 17 MAY 1904

*La Cabrera,* opera in two acts by the 26-year-old French composer Gabriel DUPONT, to a libretto wherein a Spanish cabrera (i.e. goatherdess), seduced and left pregnant by a dissolute villager and rejected by her betrothed upon his return from the Cuban front in the Spanish-American war of 1898, leaves her village and goes into the mountains with her child which dies of inanition, and she dies, too, as the two men in her life tardily try to console her, to a somewhat Italianate setting enlivened by the inclusion of authentic Basque dances in asymmetrical meters, is performed for the first time at the Teatro Lirico in Milan as the prize-winning opera (50,000 Italian lire in gold) in the International Competition of the Italian music publisher Sonzogno, selected among 237 entries in 1902, the last of the series of these competitions, the first of which, held in 1889, propelled into world fame Mascagni's opera *Cavalleria rusticana.*

### 17 MAY 1904

*Choral varié* for saxophone and orchestra by Vincent D'INDY, one of the earliest examples of the use of the saxophone as a solo instrument, is performed for the first time in Paris.

## 9 JUNE 1904

The London Symphony Orchestra, organized by dissident members of the Queen's Hall Orchestra on a democratic basis as a "commonwealth" with players sharing financial risks but controlling the artistic policy, presents its inaugural concert under the direction of the bearded Hungarian master Hans RICHTER.

## 14 JUNE 1904

*Sergeant Brue*, a musical farce by Liza LEHMANN, English-born soprano of German extraction, dealing with a London policeman's desperate stratagems to get promoted to inspector in order to satisfy the terms of a whimsically conditioned bequest of a fortune, is produced in London.

## 15 JUNE 1904

Otto NUSSBAUMER makes the first transmission by wireless telegraphy of music and speech from Salzburg. (Date and claim on the plaque on the municipal building in Mozartplatz, Salzburg)

## 16 JUNE 1904

Leopold BLOOM, Irish-Jewish Ulysses of James Joyce's novel of that name, fulfills in a single Bloomsday the exagminations round his factification for incamination as a Dublin newspaper advertisement canvasser, in the course of which he experiences a number of musical impressions, viz. (1) hears a barmaid intone a tune from the vaudeville show *Florodora* (2) befriends a blind piano tuner (3) overhears a Jesuit priest sing Lionel's aria *M'appari* from Flotow's opera *Martha* (4) hears a bass "barreltone" render a ballad in native Doric (5) punningly recollects his wife's chamber music ("empty vessels make most noise, and the resonance . . . is equal to the law of falling water, like those rhapsodies of Liszt's Hungarian, gypsy-eyed diddle-iddle-addle"), follows "chordsdark lumpmusic" harping slower, paronomastically muses that "tenors get women by the *score*" (6) attends a gathering to bid farewell to Hungarian printers as a band of Irish pipers strikes up *Come Back to Erin* and the *Rákóczy March* (7) chants medieval Latin hymns in church (8) listens attentively to a recurrent playing of Ponchielli's *Dance of the Hours* on a pianola in a local brothel in the drunken belief that the clanking timepieces are his parcae.

## 22 JUNE 1904

At the close of a performance in the courtyard of the Schola Cantorum at Rue Saint-Jacques, Paris, of Rameau's pastorale *Guirlande*, Claude DEBUSSY suddenly rises from his seat and cries, "Vive Rameau! A bas Gluck!"

## 28 JUNE 1904

Daniel Decatur EMMETT, the Northerner whose song *Dixie* became the fighting hymn of the Confederacy during the Civil War, dies in his native Mount Vernon, Ohio, at the age of eighty-eight.

## 4 JULY 1904

Charles E. IVES sketches a *March 1776* (later incorporated in the second movement of his symphonic suite *Three Places in New England*), an amazingly proleptic leap into the musical future, illustrating the coming together of two marching bands in a New England village playing march tunes at two different speeds, polymetrically constructed in the ratio of velocities of 4:3, resulting in a fantastic imbroglio of fractional rhythms and heterotonal harmonies. (Date in the manuscript lent by Ives to the author)

## 5 JULY 1904

Edward ELGAR is knighted at the King's investiture.

When he was a small boy at school he was asked a question and to his reply the master said: "What is your name?" "Edward Elgar," said the boy. "Say *Sir*," said the master. "Sir Edward Elgar," said the boy. (W. H. Reed, *Elgar*, London, 1939)

## 14 JULY 1904

Rosalie ("Lily") TEXIER, the first wife of Debussy whom he deserted for the more socially desirable and financially prosperous matron Madame Bardac, shoots herself in Paris, inflicting a grave but not fatal wound in the heart.

Debussy loved few women. Each brought him what he needed spiritually at the moment of their meeting. In Lily Texier, Debussy loved her ravishing beauty, boyish vivacity, ardor of devotion. This midinette was, according to the opinion of those who had known her, a model of patience, tact, discretion. When Debussy seemed perturbed and preoccupied, she always managed to divert him with a pleasantry and never spared an effort to bring him cheer. Nonetheless Lily Texier's spirit of a petite Parisienne could not make up for the almost complete absence of culture. Very soon Debussy began to suffer from her lack of refinement and intellectual poverty. . . . Against his will, he ceased to love her. Her voice became repulsive to him to the point that his blood congealed in his veins when he heard it. It was in this state of mind that he met the woman who was to become the second Madame Debussy. She was an accomplished femme du monde, brilliant conversationalist, a singer of compelling talent. She presented a complete contrast to Lily. . . . As Debussy would leave the salon of Madame Bardac to join Lily, silent and brooding, suspicious, ready to burst into the violent passions of a woman of the people that she always remained, he could measure the chasm that separated them. He hesitated a long time. Several times he left her and then came back, until he finally decided to abandon his ruined household forever. For those who have followed this psychological crisis there cannot be any question of cold calculation on Debussy's part. It is beyond doubt that he suffered cruelly even as he made suffer. (Henry Prunières, in an article *Autour de Debussy* in *La Revue Musicale*, Paris, May 1934)

## 6 AUGUST 1904

Eduard HANSLICK, Austrian music critic who earned an unenviable fame through his venomous assaults on the moderns of his day, and above all on Wagner (the name of Beckmesser, the giftless caviller of *Die Meistersinger,* was originally Hans Lick) but whose esthetic treatise *Vom Musikalisch-Schönen*, published in 1854, had tremendous reverberations in musical philosophy despite its dogmatic formalism, dies in Vienna at the age of seventy-eight.

### 7 SEPTEMBER 1904

*The Love that Casteth Out Fear,* "sinfonia sacra" for contralto, bass, semichorus and orchestra by the professorial English composer Sir Hubert PARRY, to his own hermeneutically evangelical text descriptive of the Passion of Christ, set to music in a grand and lofty Handelian style, is performed for the first time at the Gloucester Musical Festival.

### 14 SEPTEMBER 1904

*Filenis,* two-act opera by the Polish composer Roman STATKOWSKI (1859–1925), is produced in Warsaw.

### 21 SEPTEMBER 1904

Edward GERMAN (whose real name was Edward German JONES) conducts at the Cardiff Music Festival the first performance of his *Welsh Rhapsody*, an amalgam of gay Welsh tunes calculated to find eager response in Celtic hearts.

When the last bar of the *Welsh Rhapsody* had been played, there was an outburst of applause. Women waved their handkerchiefs and the men shouted lustily . . . Three times was the composer recalled to acknowledge the enthusiastic cheers of the crowded assembly. (From a Cardiff paper, 22 September 1904)

### 29 SEPTEMBER 1904

Sigurd LIE, Norwegian composer of precocious and versatile gifts who wrote Grieg-like music, occasionally elaborated by contrapuntal artifice, a facility he acquired during his apprentice days in Leipzig, dies in Drammen at an early age of thirty-three.

### 10 OCTOBER 1904

*The Sho-Gun,* comic opera in two acts by the 38-year-old German-born American composer Gustav LUDERS, wherein a mythical Korean island is invaded by an American chewing-gum salesman who is accidentally appointed the Sho-Gun of Korea, but is rescued from his high office by the U.S. Marines, is produced in New York.

### 14 OCTOBER 1904

*Pan Voyevoda,* opera in four acts by the Russian titan of Russian operatic art, RIMSKY-KORSAKOV, to a libretto dealing with a feudal Polish lord who captures a comely peasant maiden while hunting wild animals in a forest, and decides to marry her, but is poisoned in the last act by the rejected lover of his former favorite, with a score written in a conventionally effective manner including several symphonic Polish dances, is produced in St. Petersburg.

## 15 OCTOBER 1904

*Zeevolk*, Flemish opera in two acts by the Belgian composer Paul GILSON, to a libretto drawn from Victor Hugo's tale of poverty and passion among mariners, *Les pauvres Gens*, is performed for the first time in Antwerp.

## 18 OCTOBER 1904

Gustav MAHLER conducts in Cologne the first performance of his *Fifth Symphony*, known as *The Giant*, for indeed it is a sprawlingly extensive body of music comprising three principal parts but alternatively divisible into five distinct movements, each one in turn constituting a multicellular organism of many interlocking functions, opening in a mournful C-sharp minor and ending heterotonally in a resounding D major, with every major and minor key explicitly employed between the outer termini, and every key signature from zero to six flats or sharps explicitly staved, while evading the quintal consecution of adjacent modulatory sections and similarly avoiding the use of enharmonism, a calculated distributive pantonality of symphonic design of a decisive philosophical and musico-theoretical significance:

(1) *In gemessenem Schritt. Streng. Wie ein Kondukt—Plötzlich schneller. Leidenschaftlich. Wild,* opening with a solemnly somber trumpet solo and proceeding "in measured steps, rigorously, like a funeral procession," quickly accumulating sonorous energy and suddenly accelerating in an impassioned display of controlled wildness eventually subsiding in percussive pianissimo (2) *Stürmisch bewegt—Mit grösster Vehemenz,* stormily entering with utmost vehemence in triple forte on a clonic motivic convulsion, rending the tonal firmament with protracted anguished implorations in tormented suspensions of falling semitones in a series of modulatorily unrelated keys with A minor paramount (3) *Scherzo—Kräftig, nicht zu schnell,* an enormously expanded (fully 800 bars) movement occasionally relaxing in ironic waltzing but otherwise powerfully self-assertive, formally constructed in concentric annular triptychs, circumscribing one another, with some tangential excrescences, and terminating abruptly in a volcanically explosive cadence (4) *Adagietto,* a poetic invocation in a pastoral key of F major, scored only for harp and strings, with thematic material related to Mahler's tragic *Kindertotenlieder* of 1902 (5) *Rondo-Finale,* a series of resonant rounds, rotundly rotated, with forceful fugues separating chorale-like proclamations and concluding, after a torrential rush of whole-tone scales, on a triumphantly unisonal D.

Mahler is in the noblest sense of the word a tone poet. . . . Yet to believe that he intends to set down specific and narrowly circumscribed ideas in his works is to misinterpret him completely. . . . For Mahler is an enemy of programmatic descriptions and painstaking analytical studies. The following episode is singularly indicative of his train of thought. In October 1900, after a concert which he conducted in Munich, an illustrious company of artists, men of learning, and writers gathered together in a joyful circle to spend the rest of the evening with him. The conversation touched on the subject of program annotations. Suddenly, like a bolt of lightning on a hot and sunny day, Mahler's eyes lightened up, his countenance rose, he sprang excitedly from the table, and cried out: "Away with program notes that generate false ideas! The concertgoers must be allowed to form their own opinions about the music! They should not be urged to read during the concert and to be prejudiced by what they read. If a composer succeeds in impressing upon the listeners the sensations that went through his own mind when he wrote his music then he will have attained his goal. The language of tones will then have come close to words, but it will have infinitely more to communicate than words." . . . Then Mahler raised his glass and emptied it exclaiming, *"Pereant the program books!"* And all of us exchanged meaningful glances. (Ludwig Schiedermair, *Gustav Mahler, biographisch-kritische Würdigung,* Leipzig, 1900)

It is a matter of extreme difficulty to detect tangible themes in the second movement of Mahler's Fifth Symphony, and it is an almost impossible task to follow them through the tortuous mazes of their formal and contrapuntal development. One has to cling by one's teeth, so to speak, to a shred of theme here and there, which appears for an occasional instant above the heavy masses of tone, only to be jumped upon immediately by the whole angry horde of instruments and stamped down into the very thick of the orchestral fray. The fighting grows so furious toward the finish that one is compelled to unclose one's teeth on a morsel of themes and lo and behold! it is seized upon, hurled through the screaming and frenzied ranks of the combatants, and that is the last seen or heard of the poor little rag of a theme. (*The Musical Courier* New York, 21 February 1906)

Mahler had not much to say in his Fifth Symphony and occupied a wondrous time in saying it. His manner is ponderous, his matter imponderable. (New York *Sun,* 5 December 1913)

### 2 NOVEMBER 1904

*Monsieur de la Palisse,* operetta in three acts by Claude TERRASSE, dealing with a French aristocrat so deeply engrossed in advancing his career in diplomacy that he totally neglects his desirable wife and tardily begins to appreciate her attractions only after she irretrievably plunges into an illicit liaison, is performed for the first time at the Théâtre des Variétés in Paris.

### 10 NOVEMBER 1904

Ferruccio BUSONI plays in Berlin with an orchestra conducted by Karl Muck, the solo part in the first performance of his *Piano Concerto* (completed on 3 August 1904, with the title page of his own design, showing three buildings, Greek, Egyptian and Assyrian, a miraculous mythical flower, a bird, Mt. Vesuvius and a group of cypress trees), in five movements conceived as an architectonic pentacle, with the odd-numbered movements symbolizing the apexes of spirituality, while the second movement, a scherzo, and the fourth, a tarantella, represent terrestrial transience, with a hidden chorus intoning a *Hymn to Allah* for an ending, the music gravid with Lisztian fustian but often illumined by felicitous transparencies in the finest Busonian manner.

During the five movements of Busoni's *Piano Concerto* we were submerged in a flood of cacophony; a *pezzo giocoso* painted the joys of barbarians lusting in war, and a tarantella, the orgies of absinthe drinkers and of harlots. (*Die Tägliche Rundschau,* Berlin, 12 November 1904)

### 12 NOVEMBER 1904

*Die lustigen Nibelungen,* a gaily irreverent operetta by Oskar STRAUS, wherein the Teutonic divinities of Valhalla frolic in a most unseemly manner hurling portentous Wagnerian quotations in the brass, is produced in Vienna.

**13 NOVEMBER 1904**

*Caprice andalou* for violin and orchestra, a musical souvenir of a visit in Andalusia by Camille SAINT-SAËNS, is performed for the first time in Paris.

**16 NOVEMBER 1904**

At the invitation of the Coleridge-Taylor Society of Washington, Samuel COLERIDGE-TAYLOR, 28-year-old London-born composer whose father was a native of Sierra Leone and whose mother was an Englishwoman, conducts in Washington, D.C., the first integral performance of his choral trilogy *Hiawatha,* after Longfellow's classic Amerindian poem, with a cast of Negro singers.

**21 NOVEMBER 1904**

*It Happened in Nordland,* comic opera in two acts by Victor HERBERT, wherein an American ambassadress to an operettically mythical court is compelled to impersonate the queen whom she physically resembles to save Nordland from scandal when the real queen stages a disappearance, is performed for the first time in Harrisburg, Pennsylvania, preliminary to the New York opening two weeks hence.

**29 NOVEMBER 1904**

Ernst von DOHNÁNYI plays in Vienna the first performances of his four Rhapsodies for piano solo.

**30 NOVEMBER 1904**

*Risurrezione,* opera in three acts by Franco ALFANO, after Tolstoy's moralistic tale wherein an inoffensive Russian orphan girl, seduced on a wintry Easter day by a young city wastrel and abandoned by him in a railroad station, is driven by despair to further degradation through drink and petty crime, and is marched off to Siberia after rejecting the offer of honorable marriage by her now penitent seducer so as to expiate her fall by condign suffering, the score adhering to the esthetics of the Italian verismo in a traditional idiom sprinkled with a few whole-tone scales at dramatically tense moments, a slightly altered Russian church hymn serving as an identifying national motto, is performed for the first time in Turin.

**7 DECEMBER 1904**

*Byron,* symphonic poem by the 26-year-old English composer Josef HOLBROOKE, with a choral ending to the words of Keats, "Byron, how sweetly sad thy melody . . . ," is performed for the first time at the Leeds Festival.

**10 DECEMBER 1904**

The first distribution of the Glinka Prizes from the income of the basic capital of 75,000 rubles willed by the publisher Belaieff for annual prizes to best compositions by Russian composers, is held on the exact anniversary of the productions of Glinka's operas, *Life for the Tsar* (produced on 10 December 1836) and *Russlan and Ludmila* (10 December 1842) with prizes awarded by Rimsky-Korsakov, Liadov, and Glazunov, as executors of the Belaieff fund, to Anton ARENSKY for his Piano Trio, op. 32 (500 rubles), to Sergei LIAPUNOV for his Piano Concerto (500 rubles), to Serge RACHMANINOFF for his Second Piano Concerto (500 rubles), to Alexander SCRIABIN for his Third and Fourth Piano Sonatas (500 rubles) and to Sergei TANEYEV for his Symphony, op. 12 (1000 rubles)

### 13 DECEMBER 1904

*Der Roland von Berlin,* opera in four acts by Ruggero LEONCAVALLO, the subject of which, relating to the strife among burghers and knights in medieval Berlin, was suggested to him by Emperor Wilhelm II himself, the musical substance and treatment remaining incongruously Italianate, is produced at a gala performance in Berlin.

### 14 DECEMBER 1904

*Vlasty Skon (The Death of Vlasta),* the first opera, in three acts, by Otakar OSTRČIL, dealing with a women's rebellion in medieval Bohemia whose leader Vlasta is treacherously slain by a male assassin, is performed for the first time in Prague.

### 19 DECEMBER 1904

*Il re si annoia,* opera by Ausonio de LORENZI-FABRIS, is produced in Trieste.

### 19 DECEMBER 1904

*Cristo Alla Festa di Purim,* one-act opera by the Neapolitan composer Giovanni GIANNETTI, who settled in Brazil, is produced in Rio de Janeiro.

### 31 DECEMBER 1904

*Die Dorfmusikanten,* a gay fable with singing and dancing by the Czechoslovak composer Karel WEIS, dealing with a village fifer traveling around to finance his wedding to a girl at home and in the process curing a congenitally unsmiling royal princess from perennial melancholy, entertaining ghosts, phantoms and other disembodied creatures by playing rhythmic Slavic dance tunes, is performed for the first time at the German Theater in Prague.

# ᴽ *1905* ᴾ

### 2 JANUARY 1905

Michael TIPPETT, English composer of nobly designed choral and instrumental music, whose pacifistic passions led him to prison during World War II but did not prevent him from being knighted in 1966, is born in London.

## 4 JANUARY 1905

Theodore THOMAS, American conductor, founder in 1891 of the Chicago Symphony Orchestra, who was taken to the United States from his native Hannover at the age of ten, toured the Southern states as a precocious violinist advertising himself in handwritten posters as "The Prodigy," went on to play chamber music in New York, and eventually achieved fame as a competent, conscientious and circumspect conductor, dies in Chicago at the age of sixty-nine.

## 8 JANUARY 1905

*Le Palais hanté*, symphonic poem by Florent SCHMITT, effectively conjuring up the "vast forms that move fantastically to a discordant melody" in the haunted palace of Edgar Allan Poe's eerie tale of horror by means of tritone-compassed motives coursing and recoursing through somberly sonorous corridors echoing with impressionistic harmonies, is performed for the first time at the Concerts Lamoureux in Paris.

## 8 JANUARY 1905

*Irrlicht*, the only opera by the Austrian composer of successful operettas, Leo FALL, relating in three acts the melancholy tale of a lad's love for a lass who turns out to be his illegitimate half-sister thus making their amorous intimacy but a will-o'-the-wisp (hence the title), set to an emotionally Wagneromorphic score, is produced in Mannheim.

## 18 JANUARY 1905

*La Croisade des Enfants*, "légende musicale" by Gabriel PIERNÉ for soli, children's chorus and orchestra, depicting in an effective oratorio style the semi-legendary crusade of 1212 when thousands of children fled their homes in Flanders, embarked in unseaworthy ships for the Holy Land and perished in a storm, is performed for the first time in Paris, with a chorus of 200 school children, under the direction of Édouard Colonne.

## 26 JANUARY 1905

Arnold SCHOENBERG conducts in Vienna the first performance of his symphonic poem *Pelleas und Melisande* (completed in Berlin on 28 February 1903; sketches begun on 4 July 1902), inwardly and expressionistically rather than explicitly and impressionistically paralleling the peripeteia of Maeterlinck's poignant drama, conceived in a quadripartite form approximating that of a sonata, couched in a highly chromaticized idiom without abandoning the tonal system (the principal key is D minor, and appropriate key signatures are used in modulatory sections), forming a complex contrapuntal web of para-Wagnerian leitmotivs, and using novel instrumental sound colors (including the first instance of trombone glissandos to express the horror and the pity of the fate befalling the innocent lovers).

70

Schoenberg's *Pelleas und Melisande* is not just filled with discords, in the sense that *Don Quixote* by Strauss is, but constitutes in itself a protracted discord lasting fifty minutes. This is to be taken literally. What else might be concealed behind this cacophony is impossible to guess. (Ludwig Karpath, *Signale für die musikalische Welt*, Berlin, 1 March 1905)

## 28 JANUARY 1905

*Giovanni Gallurese*, historic melodrama in three acts by Italo MONTEMEZZI, portraying in glowing colors with a quasi-Wagnerian emphasis the noble career of a Sardinian patriot from the province of Gallura who in 1662 repeatedly rescues his beloved from the evil clutches of a Catalan bravo during the seething warfare against the alien Spanish rule, only to die in an ambush in the end, is produced in Turin.

## 2 FEBRUARY 1905

Robert EITNER, scholarly and persistent German archivist who spent a life time in the dusty recesses of German and other European libraries compiling a gigantic list of music manuscripts and published the results in a monumental ten-volume edition, *Biographisch-Bibliographisches Quellenlexikon der Musiker und Musikgelehrten,* which in spite of laughable errors (phantom composers are spontaneously generated, e.g. Berger, Ungay, whose name was formed from a *Chanson d'un gai berger* and L'Auberge, Isolée, similarly conjured up from a *Chanson de l'auberge isolée*) is of unique documentary value, dies in Templin at the age of seventy-two.

## 5 FEBRUARY 1905

*Second Concerto* for cello and orchestra by Camille SAINT-SAËNS in four distinct sections combined into two parts, is performed for the first time in Paris.

## 13 FEBRUARY 1905

*Les Dragons de l'Impératrice*, comic opera in three acts by André MESSAGER, detailing in exhilarating Offenbachian tunes the multiplex imbroglio wherein a resplendently uniformed captain of the guards of the Third Empire steals the affections of the mistress of a captain of the dragoons, and the latter avenges himself twelvefold by seducing a dozen of his rival's former mistresses, with a conciliatory ending when a chorus of seducers, adulteresses and cuckolds chant a hymn to love in perfect harmony, is performed for the first time at the Théâtre des Variétés in Paris.

## 14 FEBRUARY 1905

*Chérubin,* "comédie chantée" in three acts by Jules MASSENET, depicting in euphonious harmonies the light-hearted adventures of a youthful amorist who makes love in quick succession to an ingénue, a countess, a baroness and a famous Spanish ballerina, with an allusive quotation from Mozart's *Don Giovanni* in the finale, is performed for the first time at Monte Carlo.

## 15 FEBRUARY 1905

RIMSKY-KORSAKOV, RACHMANINOFF, TANEYEV, GRETCHANINOFF, GLIÈRE, CHALIAPIN, SILOTI and 25 other Russian musicians sign a declaration protesting against the political oppression of the Tsar's government.

When life itself is in chains, art cannot be free. When there is no freedom of thought, of religion, of expression, of the press, artistic ideals of the nation are also repressed and creative art withers. The title of "free artist" (conferred on Conservatory graduates) becomes a bitter mockery. We are not free artists but victims of the present abnormal situation. Along with the rest of the Russian population we are deprived of our civil rights. There is but one way out of this impasse for Russia, namely, a program of radical political reforms. (Quoted from the *Russian Musical Gazette*, St. Petersburg, No. 7, 1905)

## 23 FEBRUARY 1905

Amid vast revolutionary tremors in Russia, the general assembly of St. Petersburg Conservatory students votes 451 to 146 to discontinue attendance of classes for the remainder of the academic year, and adopts the following resolution: "We reject the false doctrine of the separation of art from political life. Believing that the continuation of classes is incompatible with our civic and human dignity under present conditions, we resolve not to return to the Conservatory until the demands of the Russian people for political liberty are satisfied by the government."

I implore you not to reveal the names of Conservatory students who attended their meeting to the Board of Education. Police measures have no place in a temple of art. What can be accomplished by handing lists of names to those bemedaled and beribboned generals who preside over the board? This would ruin the careers of many talented students. The Jews would particularly suffer, for they would probably be subjected to much harsher reprisals than the Christians. Eventually the Conservatory would have to be placed under administrative authority in which case many of its best teachers would probably resign. (From a letter addressed by Glazunov on 25 February 1905 to the administrative director of the St. Petersburg Conservatory, A. R. Bernhardt)

## 25 FEBRUARY 1905

Serge KOUSSEVITZKY plays the double-bass solo in the first performance in Moscow of his *Concerto for Double-Bass and Orchestra* in F-sharp minor, dedicated to his recent wife Natalie Ouchkoff, in three movements, *Allegro, Andante, Allegro*, with thematic materials (betraying obvious derivation from Dvořák and Tchaikovsky) organized, developed, harmonized and orchestrated by Reinhold Glière.

## 27 FEBRUARY 1905

*The Knights of the Road*, operetta by Sir Alexander Campbell MACKENZIE, is produced in London.

3 MARCH 1905

*Martylle,* opera by Albert DUPUIS, is performed for the first time in Brussels.

3 MARCH 1905

*The Mystic Trumpeter,* symphonic fantasy by Frederick S. CONVERSE, inspired by Walt Whitman's poetic vision of a strange musician hovering unseen in the air, vibrating capricious tunes, incarnating haply some dead composer in whom musical oceans chaotically surge, the musical score articulated, like Whitman's poem itself, into five distinct sections—serene, amorous, warlike, sullen, joyful—with the solo trumpet carrying the mystic message, is performed for the first time by the Philadelphia Orchestra, Fritz Scheel conducting.

3 MARCH 1905

*L'Enfant-Roi,* lyric comedy in five acts by Alfred BRUNEAU, after a posthumous novelette of Émile Zola, wherein a Paris baker, wondering where his wife goes every Tuesday, follows her to a clandestine rendezvous with a young man who turns out to be her pre-maritally conceived natural son and magnanimously agrees to adopt him, to a musical setting in a veristic Gallic vein containing an interestingly syncopated bread-baking episode ("C'est Paris qui toujours mange"), is performed for the first time at the Opéra-Comique in Paris.

4 MARCH 1905

Alexander GLAZUNOV conducts in St. Petersburg the first performance of his *Violin Concerto* in A, with Leopold Auer, to whom it is dedicated, as soloist, the violin entering in the very first bar on a germinal theme out of which a songful subject is artfully evolved through the mechanism of intervalically precise inversions, the two themes presently interlocked in a contrapuntal mesh until a rhythmically propulsive violin cadenza breaks into the open, leading to a clarion fanfare in the orchestra, and, after momentary divagations into major keys situated at the right angles in the circle of scales in relation to the principal tonality of A major, concluding with a triumphant finale. (Mischa Elman's performance of the Concerto in London on 17 October 1905 is erroneously cited in most reference works as its world première)

8 MARCH 1905

Edward ELGAR conducts the London Symphony Orchestra in a program of his works, including the first performances of his Welsh-inspired *Introduction and Allegro* for string quartet and string orchestra, with a fugato ending, and of his imperial march *Pomp and Circumstance* No. 3.

12 MARCH 1905

*Re Enzo,* first opera by Ottorino RESPIGHI, in three acts, presenting in a droll manner of the commedia dell' arte the otherwise tragic episode from the turbulent times of 13th-century Italy, is performed for the first time in Bologna, where the real Enzo, poet and nominal Emperor of Sardinia, was imprisoned after losing a battle.

### 16 MARCH 1905

*Amica*, opera by Pietro MASCAGNI, in two acts separated by an orchestral intermezzo, to a French libretto recounting a torridly Mediterranean tale wherein a young married woman pursues her brutish lover through a precipitous mountain pass, stumbles and, oblivious to her loyal husband's anguished pleas, perishes in a torrent, to a musical setting in a dramatic manner of the Italian verismo foreshadowed in his famous *Cavalleria rusticana*, is performed for the first time in Monte Carlo.

### 18 MARCH 1905

Two operas by the prodigiously precocious 17-year-old Italian composer Renzo BIANCHI, *In Umbria*, in two acts, and *Il Canto di Francesca*, in one act, written in flamboyantly inflatable Italianate harmonies, are produced in Pavia.

### 25 MARCH 1905

*Les Girondins*, lyric tragedy in four acts by Fernand LE BORNE, dealing with sanguinary events in Paris in 1793, with several interpolated pieces of the period (e.g. Gossec's *Hymn to Nature* and *Hymn to Liberty*), concluding with the singing of the *Marseillaise* by the chorus of doomed moderates from the province of La Gironde with the bloodthirsty women of the people supplying a cunningly elaborate motet *Ça ira, ça ira, aristocrates à la lanterne*, is produced in Lyon.

### 30 MARCH 1905

Emil Nikolaus REZNIČEK, 44-year-old Vienna-born composer, conducts the Berlin Philharmonic in the first performance of his *Symphonietta* in B flat major, in four movements, later subtitled by him *Ironische Symphonie*, with reference to some innocuous whimsicalities contained in the Scherzo.

### 30 MARCH 1905

*Nemo*, the second part of an ambitious operatic trilogy by Géza ZICHY on the life of the famous Magyar patriot Rákóczy, is produced in Budapest (the first and the third parts were staged, also in Budapest, respectively on 30 January 1909 and 20 March 1912)

### 1 APRIL 1905

RIMSKY-KORSAKOV is discharged from his professorship at the St. Petersburg Conservatory as a disciplinary measure for his public protest made in a letter to the newspaper *Russia* on 19 March 1905 against the reprisals of the Tsarist-appointed Directorate of the Conservatory in the affair of the student strike.

14 APRIL 1905

*Die Heirat wider Willen,* comic opera in three acts by Engelbert HUMPERDINCK, to a libretto by Frau Humperdinck freely adapted from *Les Demoiselles de Saint-Cyr* by Alexandre Dumas, wherein two young men are forced to marry two inmates in a nunnery whom they were visiting and after the initial consternation find marriage a desirable condition, with a musical score containing elements of ribald burlesque, is performed for the first time at the Royal Opera in Berlin.

15 APRIL 1905

The first public demonstration of Eurhythmics, a method developed by Émile JAQUES-DALCROZE "to create with the help of rhythm a rapid and regular current of communication between brain and body" is given at the Conservatory of Geneva. (See LETTERS AND DOCUMENTS for the history of the Dalcroze method)

15 APRIL 1905

*Fischer und Kalif,* opera by Felix DRAESEKE, is produced in Prague.

16 APRIL 1905

*Jessica,* opera in three acts by the prime Czech opera composer Josef Bohuslav FOERSTER (after Shakespeare's *The Merchant of Venice*) is produced in Prague.

27 APRIL 1905

On his eleventh birthday Sol MYSNIK stages, in the recreation hall of High School No. 11 in St. Petersburg, in which he is a student, the world première of his politico-revolutionary opera in eleven scenes, *The X-Ray Vindicator,* scored for three countertenors, basso profundo, piano, balalaika, toy pistol and a static electricity generator, the action dealing with a young scientist confined in the dreaded Peter-and-Paul Fortress for advocating the extermination of the Tsar and the termination of the Russo-Japanese war, who escapes by directing a stream of Röntgen rays at himself from a hidden cathode tube as a Secret Police officer enters his cell to question him, putting him to flight in superstitious horror by appearing as a skeleton, and then calmly walking through the open gate to resume his terroristic propaganda, with pettybourgeoisie characterized by insipid arpeggios on the balalaika and the playing of the waltz *On the Dunes of Manchuria* on the phonograph, revolutionary fervor by the songs "The Sun Goes Up, the Sun Goes Down, I Wish the Tsar Would Lose his Crown" and "We Fell as Martyrs to Our Cause Because We Scorned the Tsarist Laws," the X-rays by chromatically advancing sequences of diminished seventh-chords, and Freedom through Terror by blazingly incandescent C major.

## 2 MAY 1905

On his third and last attempt to qualify for the Grand Prix de Rome before the age limit of thirty, Maurice RAVEL fails to pass even the preliminary test of admission at the Académie des Beaux-Arts, all six winning entries being by students of Lenepveu, an influential professor at the Paris Conservatory.

## 14 MAY 1905

*Danze piemontesi,* suite of two symphonic dances by Leone SINIGAGLIA, artfully fashioned from folksongs of his native Piedmont in a bouquet of florid melodies harmoniously scented with finely distilled perfumery and wafted from colorfully assembled instrumental solos, is performed for the first time in Turin, under the direction of Arturo Toscanini.

## 20, 21 & 22 MAY 1905

A three-day Music Festival of Alsace-Lorraine, the first of its kind under German government, is held in Strasbourg, presenting programs of German and French music as a token of reconciliation between the two national elements of the region wrested from France in 1871, with Richard STRAUSS conducting his autobiographical *Symphonia Domestica* and Gustav MAHLER his cyclopean *Fifth Symphony* in C-sharp minor (the orchestra paid tribute to Mahler by playing a congratulatory *Tusch* in D major, the concluding tonality of the Symphony), Camille CHEVILLARD conducting César FRANCK's *Les Béatitudes* and Gustave CHARPENTIER his *Impressions d'Italie,* the Festival closing with Beethoven's Ninth Symphony under Mahler's direction, with a pointed political stress on the line "Alle Menschen werden Brüder" in the choral finale.

Music accomplishes its highest mission when it serves as a link between nations, races and governments . . . In such festivals as this there can be no pursuit of victory of one esthetic tendency over another. The purpose is to assemble all that is great, noble and ageless in the art of different epochs and different nations. (From a program note of the Festival)

It was a noble design to inaugurate these Olympic Games of Europe in Alsace, that perpetual battlefield of nations. In actual fact, this congress became a contest on the musical ground between two civilizations and two arts: French and German. And it is right, for these two arts represent at this time all that is truly vital in the music of Europe. (Romain Rolland, in *Musique française et musique allemande,* reprinted in his *Musiciens d'aujourd'hui*)

## 25 MAY 1905

*Onkel Dazumal,* one-act opera by Émile JAQUES-DALCROZE, to a German libretto after a French play *Le Bonhomme Jadis,* is produced in Cologne.

## 29 MAY 1905

*Third Symphony* by Alexander SCRIABIN, *Poème Divin,* his first orchestral work of mystical connotations, in three linked movements bearing pregnantly meaningful subtitles in French: *Luttes,* opening with a brass proclamation of tremendous majesty and then proceeding to develop within the framework of sonata form, the second subject soaring heavenwards in the trumpets; *Voluptés*, replete with caressing trills and thrills; and *Jeu Divin*, marked "avec une joie éclatante," inexorably moving towards immarcessible, immaculately virginal, divinely white tonality of C major, with a harmonically figurated plagal cadence ending on a sustained and concentrated unison, is performed for the first time in Paris, Arthur Nikisch conducting.

### 31 MAY 1905

Franz STRAUSS, one of the greatest players upon the French horn, whose heroic *Eroica* tones, nocturnal poesy of *Tristan* solos, and the glowing lyrical quality of romantic horn passages in German symphonic music aroused universal admiration, father of Richard Strauss (he was too old to essay the acrobatic horn part in *Till Eulenspiegel*), himself a composer of ten trios for Bavarian postillion horns and other estimable pieces, dies in Munich at the age of eighty-three.

### 26 JUNE 1905

Gabriel FAURÉ is appointed Director of the Paris Conservatory to succeed Théodore DUBOIS, its Director since 6 May 1896.

### 28 JUNE 1905

*L'Oracolo*, opera in one long act by Franco LEONI, Italian composer resident in London, to a libretto based on the short story *The Cat and the Cherub* by C. B. Fernald, dealing with multiplex villainy in San Francisco's Chinatown, wherein a wily opium-den keeper kidnaps the child of the uncle of a girl he covets, kills her young lover, and is in the end strangled by the latter's father (a passing policeman mistakes his death rattle for Chinese talk), with a local astrologer delivering remarkably accurate oracles, an Italianate musical score tinkling with tiny bells, booming with deep gongs, and bubbling with orientalistic pentatonicisms, is performed for the first time at Covent Garden, London.

### 2 JULY 1905

Having eliminated Maurice RAVEL in the preparatory test, the French Académie des Beaux-Arts selects winners of the Prix de Rome from the number of six young composers, awarding two Premier Grand Prix (to make up for the 1904 defection of composer Pech who broke the celibacy clause by getting married), and two Second Grand Prix to the following men, all pupils of Professor Lenepveu, influential member of the Academy: Premier Grand Prix, Victor-Léon GALLOIS; Premier Grand Prix (vacated by Pech) to Marcel-Auguste SAMUEL-ROUSSEAU; Premier-Second Prix to Philippe GAUBERT; Deuxième-Second Grand Prix to Charles-Louis DUMAS.

It is not against the law to be an imbecile, for this is a congenital affliction, but when people suffer from it, they are treated by psychotherapy which has made considerable progress thanks to the new techniques of trepan and thyroid serum. (Jean Marnold, commenting on the members of the jury in his article *Le Scandale du Prix de Rome*, in *Le Mercure Musical*, Paris, June 1905)

The competition for the Prix de Rome is preceded by a preparatory test which serves to eliminate students insufficiently prepared. The jury for this test is formed by the music section of the Académie des Beaux-Arts, which coopts several composers who are not members of the Academy. Teachers of competing students cannot be members of the jury unless they are members of the Institut de France as well, in which case they are jury members by virtue of their status. There are three professors of composition. One is Fauré who has in the meantime become Director of the Conservatory, and who is one of the most original and fine artists of our time. The second is Widor, admirable organist and learned composer. Neither of the two is a member of the Institute. The third is a poor musician, author of a few worthless compositions; without ideas, or art: but he is a member of the Institute; it is unnecessary to mention him by name. Each of these three professors presented for the preliminary test their best pupils. But the first two, not being members of the jury, could not defend the interests of their students, while the third protected his pupils well, which was amply repaid by the outcome. As if by coincidence, his pupils were the only ones to be admitted at the final competition, from which it naturally follows that they divided all the prizes, and that their class would get all the honors of the competition and their professor would derive a great luster from it. Inasmuch as the poor musician in question schemed at the time to obtain the directorship of the Conservatory, he counted on this glory so acquired to be designated as the choice of the administration, a profound calculation which was upset by the events. This story is in itself rather extraordinary; but certain details make it scandalous. Among students who were not passed in the preliminaries there was Ravel, pupil of Fauré, and Mademoiselle Fleury, pupil of Widor, who not only were admitted to the finals in previous years, but who were each awarded a second Grand Prix. But this is not all. Mlle Fleury's adventure is painful; but Ravel's is even more so. Mlle Fleury can compete again in the future; but Ravel will not be able to do so for he has reached the age limit this year. Then, whatever are the qualities of Mlle Fleury, she has not heretofore disclosed exceptional talents, while Ravel, through a singular and deplorable coincidence for the Institute, is one of two or three young men on whom French music can rightfully put her highest hopes. (Pierre Lalo, *Le Temps*, Paris, 11 July 1905)

In 1901 Ravel obtained the second Prix de Rome; but since then the Institute has refused him not only the prize but even the entry to the finals. Hence, the scandal, resignation of Théodore Dubois, utter ruin of the hopes of another official hack, and the arrival at the director's post at the Conservatory of Gabriel Fauré. (M. D. Calvocoressi, in *Le Courier Musical*, Paris, 1 March 1907)


11 AUGUST 1905

The Sacred Congregation of the Rites of the Vatican issues a decree approving the Vatican edition of Gregorian Chant.


15 AUGUST 1905

Gustave-Adolphe KOËLLA, the youngest of the four precocious Swiss brothers who, under the aegis of their covetous and tyrannous father, toured Europe from 1829 (when their respective ages were 12, 11, 10 and 7) until 1834 as the

Koëlla String Quartet, gathered ducats from ducal courts and were graciously commended by Paganini, dies at the Nestorian age of eighty-three in Lausanne, where he founded in 1861 the prestigious Institut de Musique.

## 27 AUGUST 1905

*Les Hérétiques,* opera in three acts by Charles LEVADÉ, dealing with the struggle of Albigensian antisacerdotalists and Catharist anticonsubstantialists against the sanguinary crusader Monfort, set to a melodramatically exploding score, generously sprinkled with multiple drops of whole-tone scales, is produced in the open-air Arena of Béziers in southern France, the town where the action of the opera itself evolved seven centuries before.

## 31 AUGUST 1905

*Miss Dolly Dollars,* Victor HERBERT's operetta light-heartedly detailing the losing contest of a dollar-laden American canned-soup heiress with an Aristotle-quoting stenographer for the love of a semi-intellectual male, is produced in Rochester, New York.

## 13 SEPTEMBER 1905

*Lilia,* first opera by the future futurist Francesco Balilla PRATELLA, still safely embedded in the traditional Italianate songfulness, is produced at Lugo, the composer's birthplace.

## 29 SEPTEMBER 1905

*Cleopatra,* symphonic poem by the Boston composer George Whitefield CHADWICK, focused on the story of Cleopatra's dalliance with Anthony, and written in a luscious Wagneromantic idiom, is performed for the first time at the Worcester, Massachusetts, Music Festival.

## 7 OCTOBER 1905

*Mlle Modiste,* comic opera by Victor HERBERT, wherein a Paris hat shop model is launched on a singing career by an American millionaire, and surprisingly becomes a prima donna, thus qualifying for the marriage with a French nobleman, the score containing the perennially popular waltz *Kiss Me Again,* is performed for the first time in Trenton, New Jersey, preliminary to the New York opening on Christmas Day of 1905.

## 8 OCTOBER 1905

*Sinfonietta* in A major, op. 90, by Max REGER, set in a post-classical idiom heavily romanticized by harmonic suspensions and contrapuntal elaborations, is performed for the first time in Essen, Felix Mottl conducting.

I shall make music, and only music. . . . My *Sinfonietta* ought to prove most resoundingly that the classical form is not obsolete. And since my technical demands are quite modest compared to Richard Strauss, no one can say that the music suffers the malady of unplayability. (Max Reger in a letter to Karl Straube of 2 May 1905)

In this discordantly hatched tonal pap of Reger's *Sinfonietta* there is not a single distinct theme, not a single melodically compact idea, but only thematic fragments of astounding aridity and poverty of invention. (Carl Krebs, *Der Tag*, Berlin, 12 November 1905)

Reger has manifestly wished to be simple. But it remained only a wish; he has been unable to carry out this intention. . . . The *Sinfonietta* is not inherently a significant work; its tonal language depends mainly on conjuring up the illusion of significance by a thousand contrapuntal tricks. (Rudolph Louis, in *Münchener Neueste Nachrichten*, 7 February 1906)

I am sitting in the smallest room of my house. I have your review before me. In a moment it will be behind me. (From Max Reger's letter to Rudolph Louis)

### 13 OCTOBER 1905

*Bruder Lustig*, opera in three acts by Siegfried WAGNER, to his own libretto from a 10th-century German legend with a historical background, wherein a Frankish knight nicknamed Brother Lusty for his virile joy of life desecrates the person of King Otto by pulling his red beard, communes with witches and nixes and takes one of them for a bride, then makes peace with the King, helps him to capture an important Rhenish town, and in the last act of lustful generosity gives his soldiers the freedom of all unattached local women and maidens; with a musical setting in a ripe style of *Die Meistersinger*, from its C-major overture to its C-major ending, and 88 leading motives serving to identify the characters and concepts, is produced in Hamburg.

### 15 OCTOBER 1905

Camille Chevillard conducts the Lamoureux Orchestra in Paris in the first performance from manuscript of DEBUSSY's impressionistic masterpiece *La Mer*, "trois esquisses symphoniques" (completed at six o'clock in the evening of 5 March 1905), a triptych of symphonic aquatints etched with the finest precision of tonal craftsmanship suggesting the minutissimic equilibration of Japanese prints (Hokusai's blue wave delicately suspended on the rim of white foam like an unresolved major ninth-chord serves as the cover of the publishe d score of *La Mer*), each of the three symphonic sketches illustrating a marine scene:

(1) *De l'aube à midi sur la mer,* compressing the six hours from dawn to noon into a relatively few minutes, with a somberly susurrant seascape, pierced by an insistent rhythmic wavelet, then suddenly erupting into a multicolored aquatic musicorama of concerted instrumental splendors, while pentatonic melodies soar high above anchored basses (2) *Jeux de vagues,* with submarine tritones serving as prickly mainstays of the harmonic structure through which whole-tone chords softly glide in swift cascades, while aquamarine melodies undulate on the surface and luminescent animalcules of the cymbals and the fatuous lights of the flutes flicker in the interplay of randomly colliding wavering waves (3) *Dialogue du vent et de la mer,* with windy gusts stirring up chromatic wails while the oceanic motto is sounded in whole-tone steps, ending in a sonorous apotheosis in the parent D-flat major tonality.

One would seek in vain in these "three symphonic sketches" not only an appearance of an inner structure but an idea, a clearly outlined design. The composer, by a pre-conceived notion, avoids all that might resemble a melody, a leading theme, however short; rather, he superposes and intermingles an infinity of designs so as to form a sort of sonorous complex which the ear is incapable of disentangling. (J. Jemain, *Le Ménestrel*, Paris, 29 October 1905)

## 21 OCTOBER 1905

Ferruccio BUSONI conducts in Berlin the first performance of an orchestral suite in eight movements arranged from his incidental music to the play *Turandot* by Gozzi, making use of stylized Asian melorhythms, both of the pentatonic and ultra-chromatic variety, to tell the story of a beautiful but inscrutable Chinese princess whose eager suitors are given a chance to possess her orientally desirable self, with death as an alternative should they fail to supply correct answers to three preposterous riddles.

## 22 OCTOBER 1905

*Hjoerdis*, opera in four acts by the Czech composer Karel MOOR, is produced in Prague.

## 7 NOVEMBER 1905

*Miarka*, opera in four acts by Alexandre GEORGES, after Jean Richepin's novel about a nomadic girl, strangely born in a Gypsy camp in medieval Picardy without a mother but with a grandmother, who upon reaching the flower of eager nubility dreams prophetically of becoming the Queen of Rumanian Gypsies, and after repulsing the inopportune advances of a locally amorous peasant, marches eastward as her grandmother dies on the dusty roadway within sight of royal glory heralded by slightly orientalized fanfares, the score incorporating primitivistic hymns to the sun, to the clouds, to the running water, to love and to other natural things, set in unisonal or quintal harmonies (these hymns were originally published by the composer in a successful song album), is staged at the Opéra-Comique in Paris.

## 9 NOVEMBER 1905

*Mademoiselle de Belle-Isle*, opera in three acts by the Greek composer Spiro SAMARA, after Alexandre Dumas, is produced in Genoa, with an Italian libretto.

## 12 NOVEMBER 1905

*Flauto solo*, one-act musical "lustspiel" by the Scottish-born self-Germanized composer Eugen D'ALBERT whose father was a Frenchman and mother a Scotchwoman, to a whimsical play by the Wagnerian theorist Hans von Wolzogen, wherein a flute-playing Francophile Prussian Prince (obviously the future Frederick the Great) holds a contest of skill in composition with participants from France, Italy and Germany in order to prove the superiority of French art, but is compelled to give the palm of greatness to Germany as represented by Dr. Pepusch, with a score containing imitations of various national styles to illustrate the story, is performed for the first time at the German Opera in Prague.

14 NOVEMBER 1905

A *Tigris* (*The Tiger*), one-act opera by the Hungarian composer Peter Lazar STOJANOVITS, is produced in Budapest.

22 NOVEMBER 1905

*Fourth Symphony,* subtitled *Easter Eve,* by the Czech romanticist Josef Bohuslav FOERSTER, in four movements, purporting to express the philosophical and religious implications of the eschatological doctrine of bodily resurrection, and containing appropriately devout hymnal sections, is performed for the first time in Prague.

1 DECEMBER 1905

*Zenobia,* grand opera in three acts by Louis Adolphe COERNE, American composer of German extraction, wherein Queen Zenobia of the Syrian city of Palmyra is defeated by the Roman Emperor Aurelian in 272 A.D., and dies in the arms of her Greek lover, scorning Aurelian's offer of freedom and imperial status as his consort, to a score steeped in Wagneromantic harmonies, is produced in a world première in Bremen, Germany, the first opera by a native American to be staged in Europe.

3 DECEMBER 1905

*L'Albatro,* "northern legend" in two acts by the 28-year-old Italian composer Ubaldo PACCHIEROTTI, is produced in Milan.

3 DECEMBER 1905

An appeal to unionize Russian musicians is launched in St. Petersburg, with unauthorized signatures of many prominent musicians, among them RIMSKY-KORSAKOV, GLAZUNOV and SILOTI:

COMRADES! Now that workers in many fields are organized to protect their rights, only we, musicians, remain without protection. We are not free servants of our art but slaves of our daily bread. We are serfs of managers and contractors. Not so long ago musicians were treated like chattel. A bourgeois landlord, in his desire to achieve importance, used to keep horses, hounds and musicians. And now, when all Russia is engaged in a struggle for a happier future, many of us are thrown out of work and are starving. Organization is imperative. Let this day, the third of December 1905, be a historic day, the day of decision for St. Petersburg musicians to unite and organize the nucleus of the first all-Russian Musicians' Union. We appeal to you, our comrades, to join us in this undertaking. (Text in the *Russian Musical Gazette,* St. Petersburg, No. 7–8, 1906)

5 DECEMBER 1905

*Cassandra,* opera in two parts with a prologue by the 29-year-old Italian composer Vittorio GNECCHI, telling the classical tale of the prophetically minded

Trojan princess in Greek captivity, culminating in the murder of Agamemnon predicted by her, the score luxuriating in exclamatory incandescence of spasmodic dissonance in a concentrated post-Wagnerian un-Italian style, is performed for the first time in Bologna, Arturo Toscanini conducting.

The opera obtained a dubious success and would have been quickly forgotten had it not become at a later date the subject of a widespread controversy. A few months after the first performance of *Elektra* by Richard Strauss, the well-known critic Tebaldini published an essay with a comparative table of musical examples, demonstrating a very close analogy between the themes and motives of *Elektra* and those of *Cassandra*. The curious coincidence, or whatever else it might have been, was elusively described by Tebaldini as a case of musical telepathy (cf. his two articles in No. 2 and No. 3, 1909, of the *Rivista Musicale Italiana: Telepatia musicale; a proposito dell'Elettra di R. Strauss,* and *Telepatia musicale? Sempre a proposito,* etc.) which aroused great interest in European musical circles and provoked peremptory defense of Strauss by numerous critics. Despite the unquestionable chronological precedence of Gnecchi's opera over *Elektra,* and the fact that Gnecchi presented to Strauss a copy of his score already in 1905 during their meeting in Turin, American newspapers openly accused Gnecchi of plagiarism. But apart from these misadventures, Gnecchi did not succeed in his ambitious project to evoke the tragic Aeschylean atmosphere, even though he resorted to Greek modes to attain an austere style, agitated here and there by "modern violence." (*Enciclopedia dello Spettacolo,* vol. V, 1958)

### 5 DECEMBER 1905

The Flonzaley Quartet, organized in 1903 by Edward J. de Coppet of New York City, the name derived from the Villa Flonzaley, his summer home in Switzerland, where the quartet was first assembled (the word "Flonzaley" means little river in the local Swiss dialect), with the original personnel comprising Adolfo Betti, Alfred Pochon, Ugo Ara and Ivan d'Archambeau, presents its first American concert in Carnegie Chamber Music Hall, New York City.

### 9 DECEMBER 1905

At the Dresden Opera, the world première is given of *Salome,* one-act opera by Richard STRAUSS (completed by him in Berlin on 20 June 1905), to a German libretto drawn from Oscar Wilde's French play, exhibiting with horrendous naturalism Salome's immund passion for the imprisoned John the Baptist who curses her variously and powerfully when she implores him to let her kiss his mouth, with murderous vengeance swiftly forthcoming as she prevails upon her stepfather Herod, the tetrarch of Judea, who covets her himself to deliver to her, as a pledged reward for dancing before him a voluptuous dance of the seven veils during which she casts off one cover after another from her body (a ballerina actually performing the dance by adroit substitution on the stage), the severed head of the prophet, which she proceeds to kiss avidly after it is brought in on a silver platter, sinking her teeth into the dead mouth "as into a ripe fruit" in an ecstasy so hideous that Herod, appalled and frustrated in his own lust, orders his soldiers to slay her, with the score embodying all the resources of the modern orchestra (a newly constructed baritóne oboe, the Heckelphone, is here used for the first time), scaling the heights and plumbing the depths of vocal expression in a Wagnerogenic psycho-musical identification of characters (the prophet vociferating in piously wrathful monody, Herod raising his voice in whole-tone steps, Salome writhing in anguishedly languishing, lasciviously languorous orientalistic chromatics), with acervative polyharmony reaching its maximal embroilment in a well-nigh unresolvable tonal tangle of five unsympathetic Jews, and eventually leading, through a plethora of labyrinthine peripeteia, to a long-deferred catharsis in a magniloquently protracted cadence.

For a long time no work has been awaited here with such expectancy as Strauss's *Salome*. It has been an open secret that the censor's prohibition in Vienna has only served as a cloak wherewith to hide the real reason for abandoning the performance— i.e. the refusal of the singers to devote themselves to its insane difficulties. It was expected that a similar condition might arise here even at the eleventh hour, but no obstacle intervened and everything went off in perfect order. The singers and orchestral musicians who accomplished almost supernatural deeds received full reward. First, the public accorded them an ovation that lasted ten minutes by actual count, and culminated in twenty recalls, and secondly, the triumph was witnessed by all the managers of Germany's largest opera houses and by the most representative audience, intellectually, that could be gathered together in this country. There is no doubt that all the leading opera houses in Germany will give *Salome*. The public will be fascinated and awed. Men of the world and tender virgins, in unanimous accord, will applaud until the palms of their hands ache. In spite of the unwillingness with which I say it, I feel impelled to point out that it is a sign of the most dangerous decadence that such a work is able to achieve a success so complete. Strauss and his school have reached the limit of this kind of music, and further progress in the same direction must end in the destruction of all musical law and order, where tonal anarchy reigns supreme, where cacophony, ugliness and dissonance become a sport, and where everything that has been regarded as beautiful, true, poetical, artistically satisfying and uplifting must be left behind. The musicians in the orchestra say that in *Salome* they themselves often are not sure whether they are playing correctly or not. Some of the orchestral sections play unconcernedly in keys that are a semitone removed from the tonality used at the same time by other groups. At one place the orchestra plays B-flat major while Salome sings insistently in B natural. (Paul Pfitzner, *Musikalisches Wochenblatt*, Berlin, 15 December 1905)

Seldom has the première of a new opera been expected more eagerly than the first performance of Richard Strauss's *Salome* at the Dresden Royal Opera. It was considered almost certain that the intelligent and educated Dresden public, accustomed as it is to the best in art, would protest angrily and loudly at an opera whose story exceeds in gruesomeness and perverted degeneracy anything that has been offered in a musical work for the stage. These fears were not realized, for the opera had a thunderous, stormy and unanimous success. The public would not rest until the composer and the officiating conductor had come before the curtain and bowed their thanks at least a dozen times. This proves that the most perverted, the most degrading and revolting vice that was ever conceived by human mind and put into an art form, can be presented on the stage today. Merely to bring the severed head on the stage was not suggestive and grim enough for Oscar Wilde; he felt the need of presenting the public with a new and extraordinarily stimulating nerve sensation. Salome, who has been instructed in all the ways of sexual vice by her mother, saw in the white body of the innocent young prophet a new gratification of her lustful instincts. As he repulses her, there ripens in her a devilish plan, and she nurses her lewd imagination with the thought at once bestial and voluptuous that if she may not kiss the living man, then at least she shall satisfy her desires with the quivering head of her decapitated victim. To this story Strauss has composed music which fascinates one not so much with the importance of its themes as through the masterful manner in which he uses his thematic material and the glittering brilliancy of its orchestral dress. One of the phenomenal gifts possessed by Strauss is his faculty for imitating the sounds of nature and picturing external occurrences. For instance, when Salome, attracted by the voice of the prophet, looks into the pit where he is imprisoned, the double basses play the notes C, E-flat, F-sharp, and G, mysteriously and pianissimo, while the rest of the strings play an insistent tremolo on E-flat *sul ponticello*. This remarkable combination of tones conveys the feeling of the gruesome atmosphere of the underground prison. Even more impressive is the ghastly quiet when Salome, shortly before the end of the opera, looks into the pit once more to assure herself that the executioner has done his bloody deed. There are short staccato sounds which suggest, for all the world, the falling of drops of blood. (Arno Kleffel, *Allgemeine Musik-Zeitung*, Berlin, 15 December 1905)

The chromatics in *Salome* begin with the second note of the score. At times we find the bass in a flat key and the other harmonies in sharps. All rhythms are interwoven with a strong predilection for 5/4 and 7/4. As regards tonality, it is utterly unnecessary for Strauss to give any key signature to his music. It is impossible to know whether one is playing true or false, and misprints could not be detected by any known musical rule. The libretto is a compound of lust, stifling perfumes and blood, and cannot be read by any woman or fully understood by anyone but a physician. (Louis C. Elson, Boston *Advertiser*, 27 February 1906)

*Salome* is a real work of genius which belongs to the most important productions of our time! There labors and lives under a lot of rubbish a volcano, a subterranean fire— not mere fireworks! And it is so with the whole personality of Strauss! That is why it is so difficult to separate wheat from chaff in him. But I have gained enormous respect for this entire phenomenon. (From a letter from Gustav Mahler to Alma Mahler, after he heard a performance of *Salome* in January 1907)


### 17 DECEMBER 1905

At the first meeting of the Autonomous Artistic Council of the St. Petersburg Conservatory, organized as a result of concessions on the part of the Tsarist-appointed directorate, RIMSKY-KORSAKOV is asked to rejoin the faculty from which he was expelled on 1 April 1905, and Alexander GLAZUNOV is unanimously elected Director of the Conservatory.


### 26 DECEMBER 1905

*Les Pêcheurs de Saint-Jean,* opera in four acts by Charles-Marie WIDOR, portraying the turbulent scenes among mariners at Saint-Jean-de-Luz, in the course of which the young suitor of a local belle spurned by her imperious father unselfishly rushes into a stormy Bay of Biscay to save him and thus wins the girl, with a musical score swimming in the majestic waves of resonant arpeggios and basking in well-proportioned melodic curves, is produced at the Opéra-Comique in Paris.

## 28 DECEMBER 1905

*La Mort de Tintagiles,* lyric drama in three acts by Jean Nouguès, after the poem of Maeterlinck, written in neo-medieval modalities and depicting the horror of a little boy's death at the hands of unknown malefactors, is produced in Paris.

## 28 DECEMBER 1905

*Die lustige Witwe,* famous operetta by Franz Lehár, that embodies, in a series of rollicking, nostalgic, sentimental and eminently waltzable or polkable tunes, the Weltanschauung of the irrepressibly cozy world of glory and pleasure, dealing with a free-loving prince of a mythical kingdom gallivanting in Paris and eventually finding stable happiness with a rich and merry widow, is performed for the first time in Vienna.

# ☙ *1906* ❧

## 6 JANUARY 1906

*Černé Jezéro (The Black Lake),* opera in three acts by the Czech composer Josef Richard Rozkošný, is produced in Prague.

## 20 JANUARY 1906

*Emporium,* opera in three acts by the Catalan composer Enrique Morera, in which a fugitive male slave is purchased by a benevolent Roman philosopher as a gift to his favorite concubine, with a romance growing between them interrupted by the slave's legitimate wife arriving unexpectedly from the country of his origin, all this drenched in Wagnerian harmonies, is produced in Barcelona.

## 21 JANUARY 1906

*First Symphony* in E-flat major by the Rumanian composer Georges Enesco, in three movements, *Assez vif et rythmé* (in marching waltz time opening with proclamatory brass), *Lent* (permeated with chromaticized melismas of Balkanized orientalism, with muted strings and fluent harps), and *Vif et vigoureux* (in propulsive rhythms rising excelsiorly to a fiery plagal conclusion) is performed for the first time in Paris, at a Colonne concert, with Colonne himself conducting. (The first Rumanian performance of the Symphony took place under Enesco's own direction in Bucharest on 19 January 1908)

People are puzzled and annoyed because they cannot classify me, for my musical education was not confined to one locality. I was born in Rumania; studied in Vienna, then went to Paris, and absorbed French influence which, combined with German ingredients, imparted a novel quality to my Rumanian music. (Enesco quoted in a contemporary interview)

### 24 JANUARY 1906

Serge RACHMANINOFF conducts in Moscow the world première of his two short operas, *The Miserly Knight,* after Pushkin, dealing with a morbidly avaricious baron who refuses to help even his own son, and dies in his dingy cellar stingily guarding his purposeless gold; and *Francesca da Rimini,* after Dante, telling the piteous tale of Paolo and Francesca slain by her jealous husband, the music of both operas throbbing with Tchaikovskian anxiety in somberly suspenseful harmonies.

### 26 JANUARY 1906

*William Ratcliff,* opera by the French composer Xavier LEROUX, disciple of Massenet, to a libretto drawn from a sanguinary ballad of the same title by Heinrich Heine, wherein a medieval Scottish knight slays a succession of suitors of his beloved, and after a licentious explosion of illicit passion, stabs her to death (so that she would belong to no one else), murders her father and then kills himself, is produced for the first time in Nice.

### 27 JANUARY 1906

Ernest BLOCH conducts in Geneva the world première of his symphonic diptych *Hiver-Printemps,* composed in 1905 as a study in contrasts between hibernal somberness and vernal exultation, and concluding on a resolutely unresolved E major tonic seventh-chord, symbolic of heliotropic elliptical turn in the Northern hemisphere after solstice. (The date 16 October 1916, cited in reference works as the world première was the first performance in America, conducted by Bloch in New York.)

### 31 JANUARY 1906

*The Pipe of Desire,* "romantic grand opera" in one act by Frederick S. CONVERSE, to a diffusely symbolic libretto dealing with an old man with a magical pipe ruling over a forestful of sylphs, a riverful of undines and a swampful of salamanders, who wreaks dire punishment upon a defiant shepherd who seizes the pipe (corno di bassetto) and by playing tunes disastrously harmonized by inverted major seventh-chords and augmented triads, inadvertently causes his young bride to wither and die of malaria, set to an ambitiously Wagnerian score, is performed for the first time in Boston. (This was also the first opera by an American composer to be produced by the Metropolitan Opera Company, in New York, on 18 March 1910)

### 4 FEBRUARY 1906

*Slovácká Suite* for orchestra by the 35-year-old Czech composer Vítězslav NOVÁK, based on Slovak songs, is performed for the first time in Prague.

## 5 FEBRUARY 1906

In a letter addressed to Pierre Lalo, music critic of *Le Temps*, Maurice RAVEL affirms his priority in evolving new functional techniques of writing for the modern piano:

You have commented at great length upon a rather special method of writing for piano, the invention of which you attribute to Debussy. I wish to point out that my *Jeux d'eau* appeared early in 1902, when there were no piano works by Debussy except his three pieces *Pour le Piano*, which I admire very much but which contain nothing new from the pianistic point of view. (Quoted from *Le Temps*, Paris, 9 April 1907)

## 6 FEBRUARY 1906

*Concert Overture*, by the 23-year-old Polish composer Karol SZYMANOWSKI, based on two contrasting themes with much chromatic involution, is performed for the first time in Warsaw, Gregor Fitelberg conducting.

## 11 FEBRUARY 1906

*Fifth Symphony* by Hans HUBER, subtitled *Romantische*, with an important violin solo, making it practically a concerto (another subtitle describes it as *Der Geiger von Gmünd*), is performed for the first time in Basel.

## 14 FEBRUARY 1906

President Theodore ROOSEVELT receives at the White House a delegation of Negro students from the Industrial Institute of Manassas, Virginia, and declares, after hearing them perform some songs for him, that "gradually out of the capacity for melody that the Negro race has, America shall develop some school of national music." (President Says Negro Makes American Music— May Furnish the Foundation of the True National Music—captions in the New York *Times*, 15 February 1906)

## 18 FEBRUARY 1906

*Jour d'Été à la Montagne*, symphonic triptych by Vincent D'INDY, an impressionistic evocation of a day in the Cevennes Mountains, wherein chromatic violins and joyful trumpets mark the progress of *Aurore* from mistily mystical C minor to sun-drenched B major; the advent of *Jour* under the pine trees is portrayed in cool E major with tarantellic rhythms punctuated by drumbeats and the *Soir* reverses the auroral modulating scheme falling from the cinquefoil of invigorating B major into a crepuscular C minor, introducing partly inverted themes of *Aurore*, is performed for the first time at a Colonne concert in Paris.

## 21 FEBRUARY 1906

*Benvenuto Cellini*, opera in three acts by the 33-year-old Apulian composer Angelo TUBI, based on the autobiographical adventures of the famous Florentine artist and multifutuent lover, is produced in Parma.

## 21 FEBRUARY 1906

*Sanga,* lyric drama in three acts by Isidor de LARA wherein a vindictive village girl in Savoy prays for the Alpine glaciers to melt and flood her inconstant lover's farm, but illogically rushes to his rescue, when her prayer is answered, resulting in the death of both in the darkly churning waters to the accompaniment of Valkyrian augmented triads, is produced in Nice.

## 24 FEBRUARY 1906

*L'Ancêtre,* lyric drama in three acts by Camille SAINT-SAËNS, dealing with a family vendetta in Corsica circa 1810, wherein the implacable grandmother of a feuding clan takes aim to kill the youthful slayer of her grandson, but misses and fatally wounds her own granddaughter, set to a luxuriantly prolix score ingratiatingly adorned with Corsican melodies, is produced in Monte Carlo.

## 25 FEBRUARY 1906

Anton ARENSKY, Russian composer of wistful songs and brilliant piano pieces, limner of twilight moods in minor keys, poet of nostalgic indetermination, dies at the melancholy age of 44, in Terijoki, a Finnish resort near St. Petersburg.

Arensky was a student of mine. After graduating from the St. Petersburg Conservatory, he became a professor of the Conservatory of Moscow. . . . His life was spent in dissipation, drunkenness and gambling. . . . At one time he became mentally ill. . . . He languished for a time in Nice, and died of tuberculosis in Finland. . . . In his youth he was somewhat influenced by my music, and later by Tchaikovsky. He will be forgotten soon . . . (Rimsky-Korsakov, *The Chronicle of My Musical Life,* St. Petersburg, 1909)

## 1 MARCH 1906

*Greysteel,* or *The Bearsarks Come to Surnadale,* first opera in one act by the English composer Nicholas Comyn GATTY, to his brother's libretto, wherein an Icelandic carl defeats, with the aid of his trusted runic sword Greysteel, the fierce Bearsarks and restores the rule of the gentle Princess of Soursop, is produced in London.

## 7 MARCH 1906

*Concerto* for cello and orchestra by Ernst von DOHNÁNYI is performed for the first time by Hugo Becker and the Budapest Philharmonic, under the direction of the composer.

## 10 MARCH 1906

*Hugdietrichs Brautfahrt,* operetta in three acts by Oscar STRAUS, dealing with a Byzantine potentate in search of an adequate wife who is helped in his pursuit by various preternatural personages, is produced in Vienna.

## 10 MARCH 1906

*Don Procopio*, an early opera in two acts by Georges BIZET, written by him in 1858 to an Italian libretto, receives its first performance, in a French version, at Monte Carlo.

## 11 MARCH 1906

*Russian Fantasy*, by Alexander GLAZUNOV, scored for an ensemble of balalaikas, and composed especially for the Great-Russian Orchestra founded and conducted by the virtuoso balalaikist Vasily Andreyev, is performed for the first time at his concert in St. Petersburg.

## 19 MARCH 1906

*I Quattro Rusteghi*, opera buffa in three acts by Ermanno WOLF-FERRARI, after Goldoni's comedy dealing with four brutish Venetians who try putting obstacles into the course of love between the son of one of them and a daughter of another, but are outwitted by their more humane wives, with a hedonistic score in the manner of the Italian baroque, is performed for the first time anywhere in Munich, in a German version under the title *Die vier Grobiane*.

## 22 MARCH 1906

Martin WEGELIUS, German-trained grandmaster of Finnish music, composer of competent symphonic works and esteemed pedagogue who counted Sibelius among his students, dies in his native Helsingfors at the age of fifty-nine.

## 26 MARCH 1906

*The Free Lance*, comic opera by the American "March King" John Philip SOUSA, to a story wherein the Prince of Graftiana and the Princess of Braggadocia, slated for a diplomatically convenient marriage sight unseen, run away from their palaces in peasant dress to escape the forced wedding, meet accidentally and fall in love incognito, thus arranging things to universal satisfaction, is performed for the first time in Springfield, Massachusetts.

## 27 MARCH 1906

*Aphrodite*, music drama in six tableaux by Camille ERLANGER, after a novella by Pierre Louÿs, set in humid Alexandria in 57 B.C., wherein a Greek sculptor forsakes Cleopatra's older sister in favor of a Hebrew enchantress who is put to death for abstracting sacred objects from the temple of Aphrodite, with a musical setting full of oppulent Wagnerian sonorities, is produced at the Opéra-Comique in Paris.

## 29 MARCH 1906

*La Figlia di Jorio*, opera in three acts by Alberto FRANCHETTI, to a libretto drawn from the pastoral tragedy by Gabriele d'Annunzio, wherein a mystical virgin, seeking protection from a group of sensually inflamed harvesters at the home of a young affianced villager, is taken by him to an Apennine cave, where he kills his own father when the latter in an unexpected intrusion tries to possess her by force, and is condemned to death but is replaced at the burning stake by the heroine who dies exclaiming appreciatively, "La fiamma è bella!", all this set to a facile Italianate score in which ecclesiastical chants and folk tunes of the Abruzzi mountains are freely intermingled, is produced at La Scala in Milan.

### 3 APRIL 1906

*Déidamia*, the first opera, in four acts, by the Belgian composer François RASSE, to a libretto drawn from Alfred de Musset's poem *La Coupe et les lèvres*, wherein the multifutuent vagabond lover of a chaste Alpine girl claims her for a bride, and is stabbed to death by a former mistress on his wedding night, is performed for the first time at the Théâtre de la Monnaie in Brussels.

### 6 APRIL 1906

*Chopiniana*, ballet in one act, music by CHOPIN, orchestrated by various hands, is performed for the first time at the Imperial Opera House in St. Petersburg. (*Chopiniana* was produced under the title *Les Sylphides* by Diaghilev's Ballet Russe in Paris on 2 June 1909)

### 8 APRIL 1906

*Medea*, opera in three acts by Vincenzo TOMMASINI, to his own libretto, is produced in Trieste.

### 10 APRIL 1906

*Tess*, opera in four acts by Frédéric D'ERLANGER after Thomas Hardy's *Tess of the d'Urbervilles*, is produced in an Italian version in Naples.

### 14 APRIL 1906

*Hans, le Joueur de flûte*, comic opera in three acts by Louis GANNE, wherein a medieval Flemish piper arranges the marriage of a loving couple against the opposition of their parents by threatening to lure away all cats in town and let the local mice proliferate unimpeded, is produced in Monte Carlo.

### 17 APRIL 1906

On the eve of the San Francisco earthquake and fire that destroyed its opera house, the Metropolitan Opera Company gives its second and, by fatal inevitability, last production of its San Francisco season, playing *Carmen*, with Enrico Caruso as Don José, to a packed house.

The fact that Caruso was announced packed the building on the second night, and it is terrible to contemplate the awful results had the earthquake surprised the community during the operatic performance. The loss of the Metropolitan Company was not as great as may be expected. The two houses brought in about $15,000, if not more. . . .

In sixteen performances the company should have taken in $160,000. . . . There has been considerable talk about contributing the advance sale to the relief fund, but this is all nonsense. The money must be returned to the purchasers of tickets, who need the funds more than the city at large. The purchasers of opera tickets are in far more distress than the poorer classes of people, who are no strangers to adversity. So it is certain that the money will be returned to the purchasers of tickets. Notwithstanding his $1,200 performance, Caruso had to sleep in Golden Gate Park on Wednesday and Thursday nights, April 18 and 19. (*The Musical Courier,* New York, 9 May 1906.)

### 25 APRIL 1906

John Knowles PAINE, American composer, chairman of the first American faculty of music at Harvard University, whose own music was exquisitely Mendelssohnian in its flowing harmonies (he studied in Berlin), dies in Cambridge, Massachusetts at the age of sixty-seven.

### 1 MAY 1906

At the graduation exercises of the Bucharest Conservatory, 17-year-old Rumanian violinist Grigoras DINICU plays as an encore for a regular academic program his newly-composed, contagiously rhythmical *Hora Staccato,* a stylized rustic dance in a gypsified Mixolydian mode, destined to become a perennial prestidigital violinistic favorite.

### 8 MAY 1906

*Le Roi aveugle,* opera in two acts by Henry FÉVRIER, wherein a Nordic princess, abducted in front of her blind father, falls in love with her ravisher and sails away with him in his kayak, set to a musical score which justifies the dedication of the opera to Février's teacher Gabriel Fauré (there are freely flowing modalities, consecutive melodic fourths and other Fauréisms as well as some incongruous whole-tone progressions), is produced at the Opéra-Comique in Paris.

### 24 MAY 1906

*Sea Drift,* coloristic rhapsody by Frederick DELIUS, set for baritone solo, chorus and orchestra to Walt Whitman's impressionistically autobiographical poem of the sea, sea birds and sea bird tragedy, is performed for the first time at the Music Festival in Essen, Germany.

### 27 MAY 1906

Six weeks before his 46th birthday, Gustav MAHLER conducts in Essen the first performance of his autobiographically tragic *Sixth Symphony,* with a symbolic motto heralded by an A major triad, which is depressed into A minor by a pessimistic lowering of the mediant, in four clearly delineated movements:

(1) *Allegro energico,* treading in heavy marching steps, slowly mounting the diatonic ladder to the sounds of a metronomical drum, until the sonorous climax is reached in

the triadic metamorphosis from major to minor, followed by a fleeting relaxation before returning to the original somber mood (2) *Scherzo,* a rapid succession of powerfully stressed rhythmic figures, apocopated by the alternation of the metrical compasses of 3/8 and 4/8, relieved by smiling interludes of gracefully acknowledged irony, but ineluctably striving for a restatement of the major-minor chiaroscuro motto, falling by consecutive triadic steps into the profundity of the tonic A minor (3) *Andante moderato,* in an outspoken optimistic mood established by the alternation of the resonant major keys of E and E-flat, with horn calls and cowbells painting a pastoral scene (4) *Finale,* constituting the antithesis of the first three movements, equalling their combined length and over-shadowing them in elemental power generated by a Berliozian orchestra, and culminating in a fateful stroke of a heavy hammer.

The classical form is not abandoned; the traditional number of movements is retained. And an allegro is really an allegro, the andante is an andante, the scherzo is a scherzo, and the finale a finale. Only in the orchestra is there an innovation; percussion is employed with a completeness hitherto unheard of, and constitutes an organized invasion of rhythmic noises into the symphonic field. A hammer clashes in the last movement which has a duration of 30 minutes. A colossal structure built up in a thoroughly thematic style, and at the same time in a strict unity of sentiment. This sentiment Mahler designates as a tragic one. The new symphony surpasses its predecessors in the solidity of structure but also in its realism and nerve-wracking intensity. It operates like an alarm. Friend and foe rush to arms. (Julius Korngold, *Neue Freie Presse,* Vienna, 30 May 1906)

Mahler's *Sixth Symphony* contains not one original thought of moment. Its themes, when they are Mahler's own, are commonplace and banal, and nearly always in march time. And as to reminiscences, the Symphony is full of them. One hears a few notes of Goldmark's *Sakuntala Overture,* of the Liszt E flat and Tchaikovsky B flat minor concertos, of *Carmen,* of Spohr, of the *Faust Overture* by Wagner. Mahler's weakness is his lack of continuity in style; and he patches together these stray scraps from ancient and modern music with a conventional thread or two of his own, making a heterogeneous crazyquilt of music. (Arthur M. Abell, *The Musical Courier,* New York, 20 June 1906)

### 28 MAY 1906

*Snow Man,* musical fairy tale in one act by César CUI written for school children, receives its first performance in Yalta.

### 29 MAY 1906

Edvard GRIEG receives the degree of Doctor of Music *honoris causa* from Oxford University.

### 14 JUNE 1906

Samuel COLERIDGE-TAYLOR, British mulatto composer, conducts in London the first performance of his symphonic *Variations on an African Air,* in which he makes use of ancestral tetraphonic themes.

### 1 JULY 1906

Manuel GARCÍA, member of a singing Spanish family, brother of the fabulous María Malibran and of Pauline Viardot-García, teacher of Jenny Lind, and the inventor of the laryngoscope enabling him to look into the human larynx and, if need be, pharynx, to see what might be wrong with the vocal cords of an imperfect prima donna, dies in London, where he settled in 1848, at the incredible age of 101 years, 3 months and 14 days.

## 1 JULY 1906

*New Music for an Old World,* article by Ray Stannard Baker, describing a Dynamophone, "an extraordinary electrical invention for producing scientifically perfect music," constructed by Dr. Thaddeus CAHILL at the cost of 200 dollars, is published by McClure's Magazine in New York.

Dr. Cahill's new invention suggests a complete change in the system by which a comparatively few rich people enjoy the best music to the exclusion of all others. Instead of bringing the people to music, the new method sends music to the people. The instrument itself produces no music; it merely gives out electrical waves of various sorts which are carried over wires like a telegraph message. Highly skilled musicians, located in a quiet room distant from the whir of the machinery, regulate the production of these waves by playing upon keyboards similar to those of the pipe-organ. Connected with the central plant, cables are laid in the streets, from which wires may be run into your house or mine, or into restaurants, theaters, churches, schools, or wherever music is desired. Upon our table, or attached to the wall, we have an ordinary telephone receiver with a funnel attached. By opening a switch we may 'turn on' the music. . . . You and I may sit in our homes on Easter morning and hear the same music that is being produced in the churches, or in the evening, dining at the restaurant, we may enjoy identical selections given in the opera house or the theater. It is the dream of the inventor that in the future we may be awakened by appropriate music in the morning, and go to bed at night with lullabies. (Extract from the article)

(The machine was patented as No. 580.035 on 6 April 1897, under the name of "Art of an apparatus for generating and distributing music electrically." The briefer description is given in the *Official Gazette,* vol. 79, pp. 32–42; the full description in the volume of *Specifications,* April, 1906, Part I, pp. 155–200, and the drawings are appended at the end of Part II, volume of the *Specifications* for the same month on pp. 34–36)

## 29 JULY 1906

Alexandre LUIGINI, French composer of the popular pseudo-oriental *Ballet égyptien* and of numerous other attractive symphonic confections, dies in Paris at the age of fifty-six.

## 2 AUGUST 1906

*Zino-Zina,* ballet-pantomime in two acts by the 43-year-old French composer Paul VIDAL, written in an elegant Gallic idiom, dealing with an 18th-century Calabrian poet Zino who kills himself for the love of a socially impregnable and physically insurmountable Signora, and is avenged by his sister Zina who seduces and marries the lady's royal lover, is produced in Paris.

## 23 AUGUST 1906

*Norfolk Rhapsody No. 1* in E minor by Ralph VAUGHAN WILLIAMS, thematically based on five Norfolk tunes, contrapuntally elaborated, fugued and intervalically dislocated, with a pentatonically piping clarinet for a bucolic motto, is performed for the first time at a Promenade Concert in London.

(*Norfolk Rhapsody* No. 2 and ditto No. 3 were first performed at the Cardiff Festival, on 27 September 1907, but later were discarded by the composer)

## 24 AUGUST 1906

Josef HOLBROOKE conducts the Kursaal Orchestra at Ostend in the first performance of his symphonic poem *Dreamland.* (The performance at the Three Choirs Festival of 12 September 1906 is erroneously listed as the absolute première in the official Festival history)

## 3 SEPTEMBER 1906

*The Red Mill,* comic opera in two acts by Victor HERBERT, telling a tale of two American youths staying at a Dutch inn named The Sign of the Red Mill who help the burgomaster's daughter escape via a revolving wing of a windmill from her room where she was locked by her irascible father intent on keeping her away from her chosen mate, with a desired consummation vouchsafed by the discovery that the bridegroom is heir to a vast fortune, is performed for the first time in Buffalo. (The New York production followed on 24 September 1906)

## 4 SEPTEMBER 1906

RIMSKY-KORSAKOV completes the manuscript of his *Chronicle of My Musical Life,* with the following confession: "The chronicle of my musical life is now at its end. It is disorganized, uneven in details, badly written, and frequently too dry; but it tells the truth, and this alone justifies the reader's interest."

## 25 SEPTEMBER 1906

Dmitri SHOSTAKOVICH, prime composer of the Soviet period of Russian music, whose many symphonies, profoundly spiritual in their philosophical overtones but grandly Russian in the broad vistas of their thematic landscape, have contributed powerfully to the formation of a characteristically national and yet distinctly individual type of Soviet music, is born in St. Petersburg.

## 10 OCTOBER 1906

On his first American tour Ruggero LEONCAVALLO conducts in New York a concert of his own music, concluding with a march *Viva l'America,* dedicated to President Theodore Roosevelt, and consisting of varied repetitions of *Yankee Doodle* and *Dixie.*

## 10 OCTOBER 1906

Joseph GUTTOVEGGIO, American composer of Italian parentage, who adopted the name Paul CRESTON after a high-school nickname as an Anglo-Saxon assonance of Crespino, a role he acted in a play, and whose many instrumental works are distinguished by rational dissonances in the framework of basic tonality, is born in New York City.

### 23 OCTOBER 1906

Vladimir STASOV, white-bearded Russian music critic, grandiloquent champion of enlightened nationalism in art, whose winged phrase in a newspaper article in 1867 affixed the honoring appellation "The Mighty Five of Russian Music" to Balakirev, Borodin, Cui, Mussorgsky and Rimsky-Korsakov, dies at St. Petersburg at the patriarchal age of eighty-two.

### 27 OCTOBER 1906

*Gaziel,* zarzuela by Enrique GRANADOS, is produced in Barcelona.

### 31 OCTOBER 1906

*Ariane,* opera in five acts by Jules MASSENET, to a libretto by Catulle Mendès, wherein the familiar story of a helpful Cretan girl abandoned by an ungrateful Greek hero is expanded to include his island romance with her sister and Ariadne's death in the sea, with the music flowing unimpeded through waves of melodious passion, is produced at the Paris Opéra.

### 6 NOVEMBER 1906

*Birute,* melodrama in two acts by the Lithuanian composer Mikas PETRAUSKAS, constituting the first attempt in Lithuanian to create a national opera, is produced in Vilna. (An expanded version was produced in Kaunas on 16 February 1921.)

### 8 NOVEMBER 1906

*La Légende de Rudel,* opera in three episodes and 12 scenes by the Mexican composer Ricardo CASTRO, dealing with the medieval Provençal troubadour who deserts a devoted French maiden for a futile crusade and dies at the feet of a haughty Countess of Tripoli after a shipwreck, written in a conventional melodramatic idiom embellished by orientalistic arabesques, is produced for the first time in Mexico City, in an Italian version of the original French libretto, in the presence of the permanent president dictator Porfirio Diaz.

### 8 NOVEMBER 1906

*Les Armaillis,* dramatic legend in two acts by the Swiss composer Gustave DORET, recounting the tragic story of an Alpine "armailli" (shepherd) who pushes a friend to his death down a precipice to secure for himself a shepherdess they both love, but is driven to suicide by remorse and jumps into the same chasm that swallowed his rival, is produced for the first time anywhere at the Opéra-Comique in Paris.

### 10 NOVEMBER 1906

The world première is given at the Leipzig Opera of a German version of the three-act opera *The Wreckers,* composed by the mannish English suffragette

Ethel SMYTH, after the original French drama *Les Naufrageurs* by Henry Brewster, wherein a youth and a maid who light fires to warn off mariners on stormy nights in a Cornish seacoast village are left to die in a cave at high tide by looters of wrecked ships, with a score full of Wagnerian sound and fury. (An English version was first performed in London in concert form, on 30 May 1908, and on the stage on 22 June 1909; a revised version was produced at Sadler's Wells, London, on 19 April 1939)

### 11 NOVEMBER 1906

Carl NIELSEN conducts at the Danish Royal Opera House in Copenhagen the première of his opera in three acts, *Maskarade,* wherein a young man betrothed by parental decision to a young lady he has never met falls in love with a girl behind a mask at a masked ball, and proceeds to arrange a series of illicit meetings with her, only to find that, happily, she is his chosen fiancée.

### 11 NOVEMBER 1906

*Third Symphony* by the bearded Breton composer Guy ROPARTZ, for soli, choruses and orchestra, in three Wagneromantically pantheistic movements, depicting the sunlit serenity of nature, the gloom of men and the philosophic synthesis of life and humanity through love, is performed for the first time at the Paris Conservatory.

### 12 NOVEMBER 1906

*The Vicar of Wakefield,* a romantic light opera by Liza LEHMANN, London-born soprano of German extraction, to Goldsmith's classical novel dealing with a commendably equanimous Dr. Primrose who unostentatiously rescues his venturesome daughter from the primrose path of dalliance with an unscrupulous squire by proving to him that he cannot escape legal marriage, and judiciously arranges his other daughter's marriage to the squire's uncle, is produced in London.

### 13 NOVEMBER 1906

*Christmas Overture* by Cyril SCOTT, with a choral ending a cappella, is performed for the first time by the London Symphony Orchestra.

### 13 NOVEMBER 1906

*Il Battista,* "azione sacra" in three acts by Giocondo FINO, depicting the holy life and decapitation of John the Baptist, is produced in Turin.

### 23 NOVEMBER 1906

Enrico CARUSO is found guilty of molesting a woman in the monkey house in the Central Park Zoo in New York City by touching her left forearm with his right elbow, and is fined ten dollars in a New York City Municipal Court. (Caruso cabled his father in Italy after the verdict: "I swear upon thy white hair that I am innocent")

## 1 DECEMBER 1906

*Vendetta*, opera in three acts by Emilio PIZZI, is produced in Cologne, with a German libretto. (It was performed in Italian as *Ivania* at Bergamo on 14 September 1926.)

## 3 DECEMBER 1906

Oscar HAMMERSTEIN, 60-year-old German born operatic impresario, opens in New York the first season of his ambitious Manhattan Opera House, with a roster of celebrated *prime donne* in his company, and with an avowed intention to offer bold commercial competition to the Metropolitan Opera. (He sold the Manhattan Opera House to the Metropolitan Opera Company in April 1910 for $1,200,000)

## 8 DECEMBER 1906

*Moloch*, musical tragedy in three acts by Max von SCHILLINGS, to a libretto dealing with a priest of the Moloch cult in Carthage who leaves the ruins of his city destroyed by the Romans and goes to Ultima Thule where he instructs the sub-arctic natives in agriculture, viniculture and apiculture, but, frustrated in his attempt to organize a local army against Roman rule, leaps from a cliff into the cold North Sea, with a score of viscously Wagneromantic music, is produced in Dresden.

## 14 DECEMBER 1906

The French Chamber of Deputies votes against the taxation of private motor cars, but instead imposes special taxes on privately owned pianos as being more numerous than automobiles and therefore more productive of revenue.

## 22 DECEMBER 1906

Alexander GLAZUNOV conducts in St. Petersburg the first performance of his *Eighth* (and last) *Symphony* in E-flat major, set as usual in four movements (*Allegro moderato, Mesto, Scherzo, Finale*) with stately oscillations between two contrasting musicosophical ideals (it has been described as his Ormuzd-Ahriman symphony), harmonically rich without inordinate turgidity, diatonic in its melos and somberly chromatic in its labyrinthine polyphony. (The Symphony was begun on 12 August 1905 and completed on 13 November 1906)

## 26 DECEMBER 1906

The Bohemian Club, dedicated to the promotion of good music, is organized in New York City, the founding members being benefactors of great wealth and important social figures.

## 27 DECEMBER 1906

*Psalm XLVII* by Florent SCHMITT for orchestra, chorus and organ, remarkably proleptic in its innovating techniques, with asymmetrical meters and unresolved dissonant structures and starkly primitivistic vocal lines, is performed for the first time at a concert of Prix de Rome winners in Paris.

*98*

The *Psalm XLVII* holds a singular place in the history of modern music. . . . We are in the presence of a grandiose work. Certainly, this score of 120 orchestral pages, notated on 32 staves generously blackened with notes, has not been filled with music by means of a dropper. The performers have no time to read their newspapers between two passages in *forte*, and the Women of Israel must not spare their high B's. But all this edifice is so neat and so well balanced that it should not frighten anybody. (Emile Vuillermoz, *Musiques d'aujourd'hui*, pp. 111–112, Paris, 1923)

### 29 DECEMBER 1906

Three weeks after his 41st birthday Jean SIBELIUS conducts in St. Petersburg, at one of the Siloti concerts, the first performance anywhere of his symphonic fantasy *Pohjola's Daughter*, based, as so many of his works are, on the Finnish epic *Kalevala*, painting in majestically modal melodies and granitically stable harmonies the rune of mighty Väinämöinen on his ride through northernmost Lapland (in smoothly gliding rhythmic passages in the strings), who is struck by the arctic beauty of the Virgin of the Air, Daughter of the North, as she spins reclining on the rainbow (in spirally involuted melismas), and asks her to come down and share his sled with him (jingling the sleighbells by instantaneous grace notes in the wind), to which she agrees on condition that he split a horsehair for her (by chromatically halving the diatonic steps), tie an egg in knots (by involuting arpeggiated augmented triads), peel a stone (by enharmonic compression of brass chords) and build a boat out of her spindle, which latter he fails to accomplish, only bruising his fingers against prickly whole-tone scales, and sadly slides away under the midnight sun foreglimpsing perhaps her hideous end when the Finnish Zeus Kullervo lets loose a pack of wolves on her, and she is devoured.

(Date, 16 December 1906 old style, corresponding to 29 December 1906 new style, is taken from the original program of the Siloti concert at which Sibelius appeared as guest conductor. That this performance was indeed the world première is corroborated by Karl Ekman in his biography of Sibelius, published in Helsinki in 1935, stating that *Pohjola's Daughter* was completed in the autumn of 1906, and that Sibelius conducted its first performance in St. Petersburg "shortly before Christmas," referring of course to old-style calendar)

# 1907

### 3 JANUARY 1907

The first Bulgarian symphonic work of European stature, the overture *Ivailo* by the Bulgarian composer Dobry KHRISTOV, who studied in Prague with Dvořák, inspired by the heroic tale of a medieval Balkan peasant who wrested the power from Byzantine usurpers and ascended his rightful throne as Tsar of Bulgaria, is performed for the first time in Sofia.

## 5 JANUARY 1907

*Mytislaw der Moderne,* operetta by Franz LEHÁR with the background of amorous intrigue among modernized Slavs, is produced in Vienna.

## 12 JANUARY 1907

*Histoires naturelles,* song cycle by Maurice RAVEL to a set of animal fables of Jules Renard, depicting in anthropomorphic imagery the idiosyncrasies of the peacock (panpentatonically preening himself for a wedding ceremony that never takes place), the cricket (grinding its extremities in high frequency over chords of the thirteenth), the swan (diving under the surface of the lake, with resonant ninth-chords reposing on deep submarine pedal points), the kingfisher (insouciantly alighting on a fishing rod with piscivorous expectations on sustained upper notes and volatile arpeggios underneath), the guinea hen (neurotically clucking in semitones and nearly suffocating in rapid pianissimos), is performed for the first time at a concert of the Société Nationale de Musique in Paris, eliciting indignant animal noises from the conservative sections of the audience.

The Société Nationale de Musique played a useful part in French music, but after 1900 it fell under the influence of Vincent D'Indy so completely that compositions by mediocre students of the Schola Cantorum, which he headed, were constantly performed while works of real value were often rejected. Even Ravel's music was regarded with suspicion, and the whole clan of the Schola expressed its hostility to the point of discourtesy at its performances. (From a 1936 letter to the author from Charles Koechlin, one of the secessionists who left the Société Nationale de Musique and organized the more open-minded Société Indépendante de Musique)

There are few subjects more alien to music than these *Histoires naturelles.* . . . M. Ravel furnished them with appropriate settings, laborious, affected and dry, almost devoid of real essence, a collection of diligently worked-out curiosities. . . . When M. Ravel encounters in the texts a particularly important point or a word, the piano ceases to play, the complex harmonies disappear and the solo voice presents the narrative. After a while the piano resumes with a succession of altered chords. It makes one think of the café-concert, a café-concert with a ninth-chord. But I should be inclined in favor of the café-concert pure and simple. (Pierre Lalo, *Le Temps,* Paris, 19 March 1907)

## 22 JANUARY 1907

*Salome,* notoriously famous opera by Richard STRAUSS, after Oscar Wilde's French play, is performed for the first time in America by the Metropolitan Opera Company in New York, precipitating a moralistic explosion among the wealthy, the proper and the self-righteous members of New York society.

4000 Survive The Most Appalling Tragedy Ever Shown on the Mimic Stage—Composer Who Out-Herods Richard Wagner Conquers Every Hearer of His Incomparable Score—The Last Touch of Genius that Germany's Tone-Poet Achieves by the Dramatic Dynamite of Britain's Unforgiven Oscar Wilde Such a Rehabilitation as No Music Ever Gave a Poet Before—And in a Half-Hour Horror of Death's-Head Embrace the Young American Star, Olive Fremstad, Wins Her Place Among the Greatest Dramatic Singers in the World (Subheadlines in the New York *Sun,* 23 January 1907)

A reviewer . . . should be an embodied conscience stung into righteous fury by the moral stench with which *Salome* fills the nostrils of humanity, but, though it makes him retch, he should be sufficiently judicial in his temperament calmly to look at the drama in all its aspects and determine whether or not as a whole it is an instructive note on the life and culture of the times and whether or not this exudation from the diseased and polluted will and imagination of the authors marks a real advance in artistic expression. . . . There is a vast deal of ugly music in *Salome*—music that offends the ear and rasps the nerves like fiddlestrings played on by a coarse file. . . . There is not a whiff of fresh and healthy air blowing through *Salome* except that which exhales from the cistern. . . . The orchestra shrieked its final horror and left the listeners staring at each other with smarting eyeballs and wrecked nerves. (H. E. Krehbiel, New York *Tribune*, 23 January 1907)

Strauss has a mania for writing ugly music; a modern harpy, he cannot touch anything without besmearing it with dissonance. What more natural then that he should cast about for a subject which imperatively demands hideous din to correspond with and justify his concatenated discords? And what more natural than that the noisome Salome should seem an ideal companion for his noisy music? The presentation of such a story is ethically a crime; Richard Strauss's music is esthetically criminal or at least extremely coarse and ill-mannered. His music often suggests a man who comes to a social reception unkempt, with hands unwashed, cigar in mouth, hat on, and who sits down and puts his feet on the table. No boor ever violated all the laws of etiquette as Strauss violates all the laws of musical composition. There is one consolation. Thanks to the prevailing dissonance, nobody knows—or cares—whether the singers sing the right notes—that is, the notes assigned to them—or not. Who can fail to see the stupendous originality of Richard Strauss? What composer before him has been so clever as to be able to write music in which it makes no difference whether or not you sing or play correctly? (W. J. Henderson, New York *Sun*, 23 January 1907)

I am a man of middle life who has devoted upwards of twenty years to the practice of a profession that necessitates a daily intimacy with degenerates. I say after deliberation that *Salome* is a detailed and explicit exposition of the most horrible, disgusting, revolting and unmentionable features of degeneracy that I have ever heard, read of or imagined. (From a physician's letter, New York *Times*, 24 January 1907)

Mr. Clemens has never been able to sit through any production of grand opera. He is very fond of good acting and of good music, but he wants the one divorced from the other. The spectacle of a beautiful singer trying to earn a large salary as an actor while he or she is getting good pay as a musician, he says, has always made him nervous. . . . (Statement by Mark Twain's secretary in the New York *Herald*, 24 January 1907)

I know an old lady in Germany who has heard *Salome* twenty-seven times, and she likes it very much. It never did her any harm. (An unidentified statement in the New York *Times*, 25 January 1907)

## 25 JANUARY 1907

*Hesperia*, one-act opera by Juan Lamote de GRIGNON, is produced in Barcelona.

## 27 JANUARY 1907

Yielding to the protests of the Board of Directors of the Metropolitan Opera and Real Estate Company of New York City (among them such notables as J.

P. Morgan, William K. Vanderbilt and A. D. Juilliard), the Executive Committee of the Metropolitan Opera Company takes *Salome* off the repertory and makes arrangements to refund the tickets already bought for the three scheduled performances.

Salome Not Immoral Says Its Composer—Strauss Amazed at the Opposition to his Play in New York (Headlines in the Boston *Advertiser*, 28 January 1907)
Shaw, Praising Salome, Says People Don't Understand Him or Wilde (Headline in the Boston *Post*, 28 January 1907)

### 28 JANUARY 1907

The New England Watch and Ward Society launches an investigation with a view of ascertaining the degree of obscenity in the text and the music of *Salome* so as to forestall attempts to present the opera in Boston.

Boston Anxious to Hear Salome—Salome Named an Indecent Opera—The Rev. McElveen Condemns Music Which Appeals to Beast in Man—Clergy Opposed to Salome—Strauss's Opera Disgrace to Civilization Is View—Dragging Sacred Things Down to Mire—Mayor Intimates That Show May Not Come—Doubts If Theater Will Do Anything Offensive to Public Opinion—No Salome for Boston—Too Many Stumbling Blocks Stop Presentation (Assorted headlines in Boston newspapers of 29 January 1907)

### 29 JANUARY 1907

Mayor John F. FITZGERALD of Boston (grandfather of President John F. Kennedy), in reply to the petition of the New England Watch and Ward Society seeking to prevent possible performances of *Salome* in Boston, issues the following statement:

The Mayor's office does not interfere as a rule with the productions in the Boston theaters. Licenses are issued under such conditions as the office makes, and we insist at all times that the productions be up to the proper standard. If any theater violates public decency by the presentation of anything offensive, we can revoke the license. If the people of Boston do not want the opera *Salome* presented and give expression to that view, I do not think that the opera will be given. No theater manager will fly in the face of public opinion.

### 2 FEBRUARY 1907

*Naïs Micoulin*, opera in two acts by Alfred BRUNEAU, after Zola's novelette *La Douleur de Toine*, wherein a Marseille fisherman's daughter, infatuated with a Parisian wastrel, is unrequitedly admired by an honest toiler of the sea and embraces virtue in the end by pushing the former off a precipitous cliff and marrying the latter, set in effectively gallicized Wagneromantic harmonies, is performed for the first time at Monte Carlo.

### 3 FEBRUARY 1907

*Asrael*, second symphony, in C minor, by Dvořák's son-in-law Josef SUK, dedicated to the memory of his wife and of Dvořák himself, set in five movements of funereally fatalistic music, with themes consisting of mournfully falling fifths and sobbingly suspended semitones in minor keys, intermittently utilizing passages in whole tones suggestive of facelessly untonal horrors, and progressing mostly in slow motion except for the central scherzo despairingly waltzing around the skeletons of tritones, is performed for the first time in Prague.

Dvořák criticized his son-in-law severely for attempting to erect this pentagonal monument of a symphony. "God gave us five fingers," he said, "not four or six. Beethoven gave four movements to a symphony. Three is too few; five is too many." (William Ritter, in *Mercure Musical et S.I.M.*, Paris, 15 January 1907)

### 3 FEBRUARY 1907

*Une Barque sur l'Océan*, Maurice RAVEL's orchestral version of a movement from his piano suite *Miroirs*, is performed for the first time at a Concert Colonne in Paris, Gabriel Pierné conducting.

*Une Barque sur l'Océan* presents, one might say, a number of lessons in orchestration, demonstrating various methods of altering the original instrumental color. In Ravel's orchestra no instrument keeps its natural sound; to him there are no trumpets but muted trumpets. Despite all this, Ravel fails to evoke an impression of nature. There is no boat, no ocean; there are only notes and instruments; there is nothing suggesting the sea. (Pierre Lalo in *Le Temps*, Paris, 19 March 1907)

Ravel has fallen upon this defenseless city ere now with piano music of the decayed school, but never before did he launch at us such extraordinary roulades of false notes as in his *Barque sur l'Océan*. For a time it sounded as if the upper half of the piano had suddenly gone out of tune with the lower half, but it was only a progressive composer being "intensely modern" and writing in two keys at the same time. The little boat—such a tiny bark—was groaning at every seam, bravely battling the discordant gale, but eventually fell apart, and all on board were lost. The composer unfortunately did not sail on the ship. (W. J. Henderson, the New York *Sun*, 9 November 1907)

### 5 FEBRUARY 1907

*Cavalleria Rusticana*, one-act opera by Domenico MONLEONE, to a libretto by his brother Giovanni Monleone derived from the same play by Verga as the celebrated opera of Mascagni, is performed for the first time in Amsterdam.

(Mascagni and his publishers sued Monleone for infringement of copyright and succeeded in preventing further performances, but not before a production in London took place under the disputed title; eventually a new libretto was provided by Giovanni Monleone, and the opera was produced in Florence on 18 February 1914 as *La Giostra dei Falchi*)

Although the outlines of the two libretti and most of the details are identical, the text is not quite the same, and one or two small points are slightly modified. Still, in spite of these differences and the absence of any obvious telepathic communications on the matter of themes between the two composers, it all comes very much to the same thing in the end. In both operas the melodies are either laden with sugar or torn to the usual shreds with the usual passion, and in both operas the orchestration is the conventional mixture of harp and muted strings and very unmuted brass. (London *Times*, 11 May 1910)

## 5 FEBRUARY 1907

Ludwig THUILLE, Tyrolean-born German-bred composer of Wagneromantic operas and of some durable chamber music, master pedagogue whose composition classes at the Munich School of Music have attracted aspiring apprentices from many lands, dies in Munich at the age of forty-five.

## 7 FEBRUARY 1907

*Thérèse*, music drama in two acts by Jules MASSENET, expertly put together in his most effective style, to a libretto drawn from the events of the French Revolution, wherein the heroine's loyalty is torn between her husband, a Girondin, and her pre-nuptial lover, a royalist, both of whom are seized as the tide of terror rises in 1793, and greet her as their open cart passes under her window on the way to the guillotine whereupon she shouts "Vive le Roi!" to provoke arrest, and joins them in death, is produced at Monte Carlo.

## 8 FEBRUARY 1907

*Kammersymphonie*, for 15 solo instruments, op. 9, by Arnold SCHOENBERG, completed on 25 July 1906, and constituting the turning point in his methodical evolution from explicit tonality to implicit atonality, with a key signature still firmly impaled on the staff, its four sharps designating the principal key of E major, but with melodic and harmonic elements built horizontally and vertically in fourths and fifths connoting a departure from the traditional tertian system and the abundant whole-tone scales utilized structurally rather than coloristically, while each instrument is treated as a soloist in the contrapuntal matrix of thematic tissues, is performed for the first time in Vienna.

## 15 FEBRUARY 1907

*String Quartet No. 1*, in D minor, op. 7, by Arnold SCHOENBERG (completed on 26 September 1905), set entirely within a tonal framework as the explicit designation of the key indicates, comprising a single continuous movement, sonatically divisible into at least four well demarcated sections, including a simulacrum of a scherzo and a slow lyric episode, and ending, after a series of intensely emotional chromatically involved stresses and interstitial precipitations of whole-tone scales, in unequivocal D major, is performed for the first time in Vienna.

## 20 FEBRUARY 1907

*Legend of the Invisible City of Kitezh and of the Maiden Fevronia*, opera in four acts by RIMSKY-KORSAKOV, to a libretto from ancient Russian chronicles telling the tale of a Russian city that disappears under the surface of a lake in the year 6751 after the Creation to save itself from Tatar invasion while the saintly maiden Fevronia is taken prisoner, with an apotheosis in which she joins her slain bridegroom in a transfigured eternal Kitezh, with church bells pealing majestically, the score rich in Wagnerian undertones (which caused it to be described as the Russian *Parsifal*), employing the scale of alternating tones and semitones to depict the Mongolian horde in a symphonic interlude, asymmetrically divided meters in modal chants, and a highly colorful orchestration, is produced at the Imperial Theater in St. Petersburg.

### 21 FEBRUARY 1907

*A Village Romeo and Juliet,* fourth and the most important opera by Frederick DELIUS, in three acts with a prologue, after a story (based on an actual event that occurred in Germany in 1847) dealing with two neighboring children of opposite sexes forbidden by their feuding parents to intermingle, who hold secret trysts and, upon maturity, become lovers and elope on a stolen river barge but, perturbed by the wickedness of their unsanctified bliss, scuttle it and in the last ecstatic embrace float to their chilly deaths, the score presenting a musicorama of romantic nature painting contrasted with the brooding quality of human peripeteia elaborated with the aid of para-Wagnerian thematic identifications and tesselated with artful canonic developments, is performed for the first time in a German version by Mrs. Jelka Delius (translated from a discarded English version made by a friend of Delius) under the title *Romeo und Julia auf dem Dorfe,* at the Kroll Opera House in Berlin.

### 22 FEBRUARY 1907

*Introduction et Allegro* by Maurice RAVEL, for harp solo, string quartet, flute and clarinet, wherein contrasting sonorities float atmospherically suspended in an exquisitely incorporeal equilibrium, with the principal tonality of six flats assuming pentatonic or modal guises by facile tonal elision, while thematic phrases waft over the columnar shafts of ninth-chords, is performed for the first time at the Cercle Musical in Paris.

### 1 MARCH 1907

DEBUSSY's *La Mer* receives its first American performance as the impeccably Germanic Dr. Karl Muck courageously conducts it with the Boston Symphony Orchestra for an audience of easily discomfited dowagers, quiet academically-minded New England music lovers and irascible music critics. (The first New York performance of *La Mer* took place on 21 March 1907, given also by Dr. Muck with the Boston Symphony)

When we read the title of the first of the sea sketches Debussy—*From Dawn till Noon* —we feared that we were to have a movement seven hours long. It was not so long, but it was terrible while it lasted. . . . Frenchmen are notoriously bad sailors, and a Gallic picture of the sea is apt to run more to stewards and basins and lemons than to wild majesty of Poseidon. We clung like a drowning man to a few fragments of the tonal wreck, a bit of a theme here, and a comprehensible figure there, but finally this muted-horn sea overwhelmed us. If this be Music, we would much prefer to leave the Heavenly Maid until she has got over her hysterics. (Louis C. Elson, Boston *Daily Advertiser,* 4 March 1907)

*The Sea* is persistently ugly. . . . It is prosaic in its reiteration of inert formulas. . . . Debussy fails to give any impression of the sea. . . . There is more of barnyard cackle in it than anything else. (New York *Times*, 22 March 1907)

*The Sea* of Debussy does not call for many words of comment. The three parts of which it is composed are entitled *From Dawn till Noon, Play of the Waves* and *Dialogue of the Wind and the Sea*, but as far as any pictorial suggestiveness is concerned, they might as well have been entitled *On the Flatiron Building, Slumming in the Bowery* and *A Glimpse of Chinatown During a Raid*. Debussy's music is the dreariest kind of rubbish. Does anybody for a moment doubt that Debussy would not write such chaotic, meaningless, cacophonous, ungrammatical stuff, if he could invent a melody? . . . Even his orchestration is not particularly remarkable. M. Loeffler of Boston is far more original from this point of view. (New York *Post*, 22 March 1907)

New York heard a new composition called *The Sea*, and New York is probably still wondering why. The work is by the most modern of modern Frenchmen, Debussy. . . . Compared with this, the most abstruse compositions of Richard Strauss are as primer stories to hear and to comprehend. (New York *World*, 22 March 1907)

We believe that Shakespeare means Debussy's ocean when he speaks of taking up arms against a sea of troubles. It may be possible, however, that in the transit to America the title of this work has been changed. It is possible that Debussy did not intend to call it *La Mer*, but *Le Mal de Mer*, which would at once make the tone-picture as clear as day. It is a series of symphonic pictures of seasickness. The first movement is *Headache*. The second is *Doubt*, picturing moments of dread suspense, whether or no! The third movement, with its explosions and rumblings, has now a self-evident purpose. The hero is endeavoring to throw up his boot-heels! (Louis C. Elson, Boston *Daily Advertiser*, 22 April 1907)

### 1 MARCH 1907

*La Faute de l'Abbé Mouret,* "pièce avec musique" in four acts by Alfred BRUNEAU, set for spoken dialogue accompanied by orchestra, to his own libretto from Zola's novelette of the same name, wherein a young unbeneficed secular ecclesiastic in Provence, seduced by flesh in the person of a 16-year old parishioner, suffers agonies of spirit before rebounding to his prelapsarian prelature, with a score illustratively contrasting the two sundering forces in tumescently sonorous harmonies and ascetically repressive monodies, is performed for the first time in Paris.

### 2 MARCH 1907

*Ein Walzertraum,* operetta in three acts by Oskar STRAUS, dealing with the foundering marriage of the princess of Snobia happily salvaged after she takes a course of exotic *ars amandi* from her husband's Gypsy mistress, is produced in Vienna.

### 2 MARCH 1907

*Monna Vanna,* opera in three acts by Emil ABRÁNYI, after the play by Maeterlinck, is produced in Budapest.

## 2 MARCH 1907

*O Amor e Perdicão* (*Love and Perdition*), opera in three acts by João Marcelino ARROYO, Minister of Education and Fine Arts in the cabinet of the last King of Portugal Manuel, composed in a Wagneromantically Tristanomorphic parachromatic idiom, is produced in Lisbon.

## 5 MARCH 1907

Lee DE FOREST, the American wizard of the cathode rays, succeeds in transmitting by wireless a performance of Rossini's *William Tell* overture from Telharmonic Hall in New York to the Brooklyn Navy Yard, marking the first broadcast of a musical composition.

There's music in the air about the roof of the Hotel Normandie these days. A good deal of it is being collected by wireless telephone ready for distribution to possible purchasers. (New York *Tribune*, 7 March 1907)

## 9 MARCH 1907

Arnold SCHOENBERG finishes the composition of *Friede auf Erden*, a Christmas ballad for chorus a cappella set in dissonantly harsh harmonies obliquely tending towards ultimate tonality and depicting the peace on earth of the title by explicit key signatures.

## 14 MARCH 1907

*Stara Baśń* (*An Old Tale*), opera by the 69-year-old Polish composer Wladislaw ZELEŃSKI, is produced in Lwów.

## 17 MARCH 1907

*Théodora*, music drama in three acts by Xavier LEROUX, to a libretto dealing with the adventurous life of the 6th-century Empress Regnant of Byzantium, with a musical setting rich in allusive orientalisms, is produced in Monte Carlo.

## 19 MARCH 1907

Edward ELGAR, the Edwardian English composer of marvelously outspoken and hearty symphonic and choral music, makes his first American appearance conducting the Oratorio Society of New York City in a performance of his reverentially reverberant oratorio *The Apostles*.

## 19 MARCH 1907

*Das ewige Feuer*, one-act opera by Richard WETZ, is produced in Düsseldorf.

## 22 MARCH 1907

*Second Symphony* by the Norwegian composer Christian SINDING is performed for the first time in Berlin.

## 12 APRIL 1907

*Salome*, tone poem by Henry HADLEY, inspired by Oscar Wilde's play and composed in 1905 before the production of Strauss's famous opera, wherein Salome moans concupiscently in quasi-oriental but neatly arranged arabesques, the prophet curses her in trombones, Herod enters with heraldic fanfares, and the decapitation is accomplished with shocked pauses, is performed for the first time by the Boston Symphony Orchestra, Karl Muck conducting.

## 13 APRIL 1907

*Les Enfants à Bethléem*, Christmas oratorio by Gabriel PIERNÉ, to a poetic story of children guided by a soprano-voiced star to the manger where the Christ Child, pale and underweight, is tenderly tended by a devout ox (tenor) and a perspicacious ass (baritone) exhaling animal warmth in the December chill, the musical idiom eclectically combining quasi-Gallic folksong melos with solemn organum-like harmony, is performed for the first time in Amsterdam.

## 15 APRIL 1907

*Gloria*, lyric drama in three acts by Francesco CILÈA, dealing with the internecine strife in 14th-century Siena, ending in a double tragedy when Gloria's young husband is slain and she kills herself, is produced at La Scala in Milan.

## 17 APRIL 1907

*Circé*, lyric drama in three acts by P. L. HILLEMACHER (actually two brothers, Paul and Lucien, both former Prix de Rome winners), a conventional operatic portrait of the Homeric enchantress from whose dehumanizing magic Ulysses was protected by a fabulous herb, receives its belated first production, ten years after its composition, at the Opéra-Comique in Paris on the same bill with *La Légende du point d'Argentan*, one-act opera by the 27-year-old French composer Félix FOURDRAIN, to a story about a poor lacewoman trying to win a prize for needle point such as was practiced in Argentan (hence the title) supernaturally helped by a chorus of angels who weave a divinely inspired mantle under the instructions of a Gothic Madonna descended from a Fra Angelico fresco.

## 17 APRIL 1907

*Tom Jones*, comic opera by Edward GERMAN after the celebrated novel by Fielding, *The History of Tom Jones, a Foundling*, in which the multifutuent hero turns out to be the natural son of the sister of a highly puritanical moralist, the libretto and the musical setting couched in the style made familiar in the operettas of Gilbert and Sullivan, is produced at the Apollo Theater in London.

## 20 APRIL 1907

*Souvenirs*, symphonic threnody by Vincent D'INDY in memory of his wife, the *bien aimée* of the dedication, with the principal theme (taken from his youthful *Poème des Montagnes*) intoned by a griefstricken English horn, followed by an agitated section characterizing Madame d'Indy's vitality in life, and concluded with a solo on a muted small trumpet, is performed for the first time at a concert of the Société Nationale in Paris.

### 27 APRIL 1907

*First Symphony* by Igor STRAVINSKY, dedicated "to my dear teacher Nicolai Andreyevich Rimsky-Korsakov," in E-flat major, set in four traditional movements: (1) *Allegro moderato,* in 4/4 time in strict sonata form (2) *Scherzo,* in 2/4 time, with a trio section very Russian in melody, somewhat akin to the folksong *Down the Street,* utilized in *Petrushka* (3) *Largo,* in 2/4 time in G-sharp minor and (4) *Finale, Allegro molto,* with a triumphant ending in glorious E-flat major, in the style of Glazunov, is performed for the first time in St. Petersburg, at a private concert of the orchestra of the Imperial Chapel. (The first public performance was given by the same orchestra on 22 January 1908)

### 27 APRIL 1907

*Sperduti nel buio (Lost in the Dark),* opera in three acts by the 28-year-old Sicilian composer Stefano DONAUDY (who had his first opera performed at the age of 13) is produced in Palermo.

### 9 MAY 1907

Two centuries have passed since the death in Lübeck of Dietrich BUXTEHUDE, the great organist of Danish extraction, whom to hear Handel and Bach made arduous journeys.

### 10 MAY 1907

*Stára pravá (Ancient Rights),* opera by the Czech composer František SPILKA, is produced in Prague.

### 10 MAY 1907

The first performance is given at the Opéra-Comique in Paris of *Ariane et Barbe-bleue,* fairy tale in three acts by Paul DUKAS, depicting in liquescent sonorities the elusively symbolic drama of Maurice Maeterlinck, wherein Ariane, the sixth wife of Bluebeard, opens not only the five doors behind which she finds sparkling jewels, but also the forbidden sixth door which leads to a darksome casement where Bluebeard's five former wives are kept, and sets them free, emaciated but alive (among them one named Mélisande whose appearance is signalized by a quotation from Debussy's *Pelléas et Mélisande,* Act I. Scene III), while the crowd outside assaults Bluebeard who is brought bleeding into the castle, arousing unexpected pity among his abused wives who elect to stay with him and let Ariane depart alone from the scene of the "délivrance inutile" (the original subtitle of the play), to a symphonically conceived setting, with voices singing in prosodically measured recitative, their delicate melorhythms gliding radiantly across the columnar supports of ninth-chords and of finely equilibrated pandiatonic structures while opulent whole-tone scales flow alongside in recurrent streams.

The Maeterlinck drama might perhaps dispense with a musical commentary, but these personages in *Ariane et Barbe-bleue* move about in a somewhat imprecise atmosphere and express themselves in a rather remote manner. The music of Paul Dukas, so strong, so precise, so eloquent, does it not shed a little light that enables us to gain better grasp of their nature, does it not bring us closer to their actions and make their utterances more vibrant and more articulate? In a dreamy world, conjured up by the poet, what marvelous aid is this pictorial music! What magical sonorities, what variety, what invention in this phantasmagoria of precious stones falling in a cataract of emeralds, sapphires, pearls, rubies! . . . How I rejoice in seeing our music enriched by such a gem! (Gabriel Fauré in *Le Figaro*, Paris, 11 May 1907)

The score of Paul Dukas is very significant from the standpoint of the present state of mind. Written with rare technical ability, it floats between two opposite tendencies: here and there, classical in the noble sense of the word, it is subject to influences of the current fashion that one could call *modern style*. In what does it consist? First of all, and particularly, in one characteristic fact: *an absolute exclusion of melody*. Note that the question does not concern those sugary vocalizations that one justly despises. No, we speak of the expressive and inspired melody, such as was understood by Rameau and Gluck, Beethoven and Schumann, as well as César Franck and Wagner. And by what is it replaced? It is a grave question, because the entire future of music is at stake. I am not praising, I am not condemning. I merely expound the situation. (Arthur Coquard, *Écho de Paris*, 11 May 1907)

### 16 MAY 1907

Miller R. HUTCHISON files at the U.S. Patent Office the original application for his invention, a motor-driven Diaphragm Actuated Horn and Resonator, for use as a signal in automobiles, which under the trade name Klaxon became a musical instrument used in various orchestral scores of the automobile age, including Gershwin's symphonic tableau *An American in Paris*. (The patent was granted on 3 May 1910; it was subsequently acquired by F. Hallett Lovell, manufacturer and distributor, who died on 19 May 1962 at the age of ninety-four)

### 16 MAY 1907

Under the auspices of the Société des Grandes Auditions Musicales de France, Serge DIAGHILEV presents in Paris the first of the five "historic concerts" of Russian music, with RIMSKY-KORSAKOV and GLAZUNOV conducting their own works, RACHMANINOFF playing his *Second Piano Concerto*, Arthur Nikisch and Camille Chevillard conducting orchestral and operatic excerpts by Glinka, Borodin, Balakirev, Mussorgsky, Cui, Tchaikovsky, Scriabin, Liapunov, Liadov and Alexander Taneyev (uncle of Sergei Taneyev and holder of an influential position at the Tsarist Court who obtained a subsidy of 70,000 rubles in gold for the concerts), and featuring the first appearance in Paris of Feodor Chaliapin. (The other four concerts took place on 19, 23, 26 and 30 May 1907)

Chaliapin made such an impression at the opening concert that the audience, containing many Russians, insisted upon endless recalls. Nikisch finally emerged and, mounting the podium, awaited an opportunity to begin the closing number. But he was not permitted to make a start. Finally, with a gesture of despair, he descended from the podium and beckoned the orchestra to leave (*The Musical Courier*, New York, 5 June 1907)

In May 1907 Richard Strauss conducted in Paris several performances of his opera *Salome*; Rimsky-Korsakov attended one of them. He met Strauss at a reception, but their personal acquaintance did not go beyond an exchange of a few chance remarks. For Rimsky-Korsakov knew Strauss's comments on Russian music: "We are no longer children." (Annotations to the Russian Edition of Rimsky-Korsakov's *Chronicle of My Life*, Moscow, 1935, by Andrei Rimsky-Korsakov)

Our American composers, if they had as good an opportunity at home as have Russians who are supported financially and morally by the government, by society, by the Court, and by the people, would produce as good and palatable music. . . . The Russians have said au revoir, but the Russian music has said good-bye; it is gone never to return to Paris. (*The Musical Courier*, New York, 19 June 1907)

## 24 MAY 1907

*La Catalane*, lyric drama in four acts by the Belgian-born Paris-educated 45-year-old composer Fernand LE BORNE, after the celebrated Catalan play *Terra Baixa* by Angel Guimerá (which also supplied the libretto for Eugen d'Albert's opera *Tiefland*) wherein a simple-minded mountain shepherd who innocently marries the discarded mistress of a rich farmer in the valley avenges her dishonor by strangling him to death, set to music in an effective lyrico-dramatic manner of the composer's master Massenet, is produced at the Paris Opéra.

## 26 MAY 1907

The Bach Museum is formally dedicated in the house where he was born in Eisenach on 21 March 1685, the permanent collection containing the old clavichord on which Bach played, contemporary portraits, manuscripts, letters and other pertinent documents.

## 4 JUNE 1907

*Otho Visconti*, opera in three acts by the German-bred American composer Frederick Grant GLEASON, to his own libretto dealing with the monstrous "viper of Milan" who founded in the 13th century the politically powerful Visconti family, with a score dramatically luxuriating in the uncoagulated plasma of Germanic romanticism, is performed for the first and last time, two and a half years after his death, in Chicago where he dwelt as a respected pedagogue from 1876. (According to the terms of his will, other operas left among his manuscripts were not to be studied or performed until fifty years after his death, which occurred in Chicago on 6 December 1903)

## 5 JUNE 1907

*Fortunio*, "comédie musicale" in five acts by André MESSAGER, after Alfred de Musset's play *Le Chandelier*, dealing with gallant intrigues among 18th-century immoralists, wherein a clerk in the office of a middle-aged notary serves as a candle carrier to light the way for clandestine meetings between his employer's young wife and a dashing army captain, with Fortunio's fortune brightened when he becomes the lover and the captain the chandelier, to an appropriately gay setting abounding in grandiloquently humorous arias and vocal ensembles, is produced at the Opéra-Comique in Paris.

### 12 JUNE 1907

Alexander GLAZUNOV is awarded the honorary degree of Doctor in Music by the University of Cambridge, England.

Gaudium nostrum cumulavit hodie vir in arte musica insignis, qui Russorum in imperio maximo iam per annos quinque et viginti in luce publica versatus, primum abhinc annos decem Britanniae innotuit. Argumenta magna vir magnus aggressus, popularium suorum artis musicae hodiernae in "Raymonda" praesertim documentum splendidum protulisse dicitur. Inter peritos vero constat, "nympham pulchram dormientem" illiam a Tschaikovskio, doctore olim nostro, musicis modis accommodatam, quasi statuarum elegantissimarum ordinem effingere; viri huius autem "Raymondam" figuris potius ex aere fusis immensis comparari. Iuvat nunc iterum ex imperio Russorum ad nos advectum salutare magistrorum in arte musica magnorum aemulum, qui artis suae genus pulchrum, genus severum et sobrium repraesentat, patriaeque cantus populares non minus fideliter quam feliciter exprimit. (Text of the speech delivered by the Public Orator in presenting to the Chancellor the recipient of the honorary degree of Doctor in Music)

### 18 JUNE 1907

Alexander GLAZUNOV is awarded the honorary degree of Doctor in Music by Oxford University.

### 26 JUNE 1907

Camille SAINT-SAËNS is awarded the honorary degree of Doctor in Music by Oxford University.

### 1 JULY 1907

*Kaleidoskop: Original Theme and Variations* for orchestra by the Austrian-born composer Heinrich NOREN, with the last variation, dedicated "to a celebrated contemporary," making use of the themes of the hero and the antagonists from *Ein Heldenleben* by Richard Strauss, is performed for the first time in Dresden. (Although Strauss graciously accepted the homage, his publishers sued Noren for infringement of copyright, but lost when the Royal Court of Dresden ruled that the Strauss motives represent "a conscious negation of melody" and therefore cannot be construed as recognizable musical materials subject to protection by copyright)

### 27 JULY 1907

*Der fidele Bauer*, operetta in two acts by Leo FALL, in which an inhibited German professor tries to conceal his peasant origin but is freed from his acquired snobbishness when his semi-aristocratic wife welcomes his demi-rustic relatives as equals, is produced in Mannheim.

### 15 AUGUST 1907

Joseph JOACHIM, Hungarian violin virtuoso, one of the greatest interpreters of classical music, whose playing, according to the acoustical measurements made by Helmholtz, was more precise in just intonation than any other's, the founder in Berlin in 1869 of the superlative Joachim Quartet, devoted friend of Brahms who dedicated his violin concerto to him, and teacher of two generations of ascending violinists, dies in Berlin at the age of 76 years, one month and 18 days.

### 22 AUGUST 1907

*La Princesse Maleine,* symphonic poem by Cyril SCOTT, inspired by the poignant drama of Maurice Maeterlinck, set in impressionistic harmonies interspersed with neo-archaic modalities (the organ enters in open fifths when the Beguines begin their sermon), evolving into a polychromatic tempest and concluding with a matutinal cockcrow solo, is performed for the first time in London.

### 24 AUGUST 1907

*Pomp and Circumstance* No. 4, the most famous of the grandly imperial orchestral marches by the sublimely British composer Edward ELGAR, containing the stirring middle section, later adapted to the rousing text, *Song of Freedom* by A. P. Herbert, is performed for the first time in London.

### 4 SEPTEMBER 1907

Edvard GRIEG, "Chopin of the North," whose strikingly colorful and romantically saturated piano pieces, songs and symphonic suites reflect and enhance the lyric poetry and rhythmic vivacity of Norwegian folk songs and dances, and who made the characteristic cadential fall from the leading tone to the fifth in a minor key the true hallmark of Scandinavian modality, dies in his native Bergen at the age of sixty-four.

Mr. Grieg stayed at the Hotel Norge in Bergen during the last few days, and intended to leave for Christiania yesterday; his luggage had already been taken on board. At noon, however, he complained of feeling ill, and, as the symptoms appeared to be serious, was removed to the hospital. His wife was with him all night, and at half-past three in the morning he passed away peacefully. (London *Times,* 5 September 1907)

### 25 SEPTEMBER 1907

Jean SIBELIUS conducts in Helsingfors the first performance of his *Third Symphony* (composed in 1904–1907), concisely set in three compact movements, with the principal key of C major:

(1) *Allegro moderato,* with a foreboding motto in low register, gathering strength in proclamatory brass while the strings are engaged in rhythmed propulsion, ending with

113

a plagally cadenced chorale (2) *Andantino con moto quasi Allegretto,* in G-sharp minor, a somberly questioning, modally inflected musical essay (3) *Allegro,* with dramatically crisscrossing chains of parallel thirds and sixths in oblique modalities teleologically tending towards the ultimate catharsis of immaculate C major.

### 27 SEPTEMBER 1907

Ralph VAUGHAN WILLIAMS conducts at the Cardiff Festival the world premières of his *Norfolk Rhapsody No. 2,* in D minor, and *Norfolk Rhapsody No. 3* in G minor. (Both works were subsequently discarded by Vaughan Williams, and remained unpublished.)

### 8 OCTOBER 1907

*For Valor,* concert overture by the 31-year-old English composer Havergal BRIAN, composed in 1902 and inspired by a passage from Walt Whitman's *Drum Taps,* is performed for the first time in London, Henry Wood conducting.

### 15 OCTOBER 1907

*Variationen und Fuge über ein lustiges Thema von Johann Adam Hiller* (the inviting adjective "lustiges" was added by the publisher to original title), op. 100, by Max REGER, a series of eleven variations elaborating an unassuming folk-like tune from a singspiel written by Hiller in 1771 to a maximum of polyphonic density through canonic imitation, thematic augmentation, contrapuntal permutation and harmonic inspissation, concluding with a magisterial double fugue, is performed for the first time in Cologne.

### 15 OCTOBER 1907

Gustav MAHLER conducts his last performance at the Vienna Opera as its Music Director, before departure for America as conductor of the New York Philharmonic Orchestra.

The hour has come marking the end of our work together. I am now taking leave of a place that has become dear to me. . . . Not always have my efforts been crowned with success. No one bears greater responsibility for the overcoming the resistance of the material and attaining a treacherously elusive objective than a practicing artist. . . . I have done my best to subordinate my person to the task at hand and my inclinations to my duty. I have not spared myself, and I felt that I could demand also from others that they exert their strength to the utmost. Under the pressure of the battle, in the heat of the moment, neither you nor I have escaped injuries and errors. But the work has been done and the task has been fulfilled. (From Mahler's letter addressed to the orchestra of the Vienna Opera, published in *Signale für die musikalische Welt,* Berlin, 18 December 1907)

### 26 OCTOBER 1907

*Die Rote Gret,* first opera in three acts by the Vienna composer Julius BITTNER, to his own libretto derived from an Austrian folk tale, is produced in Frankfurt.

*114*

## 1 NOVEMBER 1907

RIMSKY-KORSAKOV completes the composition of his orchestral piece *Neapolitan Song*, a fantasy on the celebrated ballad *Funiculi, funicula* by Luigi Denza, mistaken for a genuine anonymous folksong, as it was also mistaken by Richard Strauss in an early symphonic poem *Aus Italien*. (*Neapolitan Song* was put in rehearsal at a concert conducted by Siloti in St. Petersburg on 10 December 1907, but Rimsky-Korsakov found the piece unsatisfactory and cancelled its performance)

## 2 NOVEMBER 1907

*Die Dollarprinzessin*, operetta by Leo FALL, exhilaratingly propounding the legend of the Plenipotential Dollar, personified by a Chicago heiress who regards European nobility as a purchasable commodity but in the end marries an untitled German for love, while her widowed father enters matrimony with a moderately voluptuous Russian songstress, is produced in Vienna.

## 6 NOVEMBER 1907

*Le Chemineau*, lyric drama in four acts by Xavier LEROUX, after a poem by Jean Richepin, wherein a rootless wayfarer seduces a farm girl in a Burgundian village, leaves her pregnant, but exhibits sudden paternal interest in his son while passing through the same village twenty years later and succeeds in mending the latter's broken romance with a girl whose family discovers the young man's bastardy, to a dramatically effective score with some lyrically pleasing arias, is produced at the Opéra-Comique in Paris.

## 9 NOVEMBER 1907

*Marcella*, opera by Umberto GIORDANO, in three episodes bearing descriptive subtitles: (1) *Trovata*, wherein a disillusioned artist's model is found in a Paris café-chantant by a young expatriate painter (2) *Amata*, wherein she is loved by him (3) *Abandonnata*, wherein she is abandoned by her lover who confesses that he is no painter but the legitimate heir to a distant Slavic throne to which he is summoned by his oppressed people to wrest the reins of the reign from the imbecilic hands of his senile father fallen under the sway of greedy and cruel ministers, with a musical setting expertly synthesizing the Parisian music of other Italian operas, from *La Traviata* to *La Bohème*, is produced at La Scala in Milan.

## 9 NOVEMBER 1907

*Tragédie de Salomé*, "mute drama" by Florent SCHMITT, in five symphonic episodes (*Prélude, Danses de perles, Les enchantements sur la mer, Danse des éclairs, Danse de l'effroi*) with serpentine melismas and asymmetrical rhythms illustrating the fibrillar spasms of Salomé's body as she strives to please Herod with her voluptuous whirlings, and culminating in the horror of the decapitation of John the Baptist portrayed in a "dance of fear" in an asymmetric time signature notated $\dfrac{3 + \frac{1}{2}}{4}$, and savagely dissonant harmonies, is performed for the first time in Paris in a version for chamber orchestra. (A performance for large orchestra took place in Paris at a Colonne concert on 8 January 1911)

### 11 NOVEMBER 1907

*Paolo e Francesca,* one-act opera by Luigi MANCINELLI, AFTER Dante's tale of the two unfortunate lovers, is produced in Bologna.

### 21 NOVEMBER 1907

Gaetano BRAGA, Italian composer of eight operas and of the perennially nostalgic song *Angel's Serenade,* dies in Milan at the age of seventy-eight.

### 22 NOVEMBER 1907

*A Pagan Poem* for orchestra and piano obbligato by the Alsatian-born American composer Charles Martin LOEFFLER, inspired by the 8th Eclogue of Virgil written in 39 B.C., wherein a country girl sings magic songs to bring her truant lover back from the city (three trumpets off stage represent the imploration, "Ducite ab urbe domum, mea carmina, ducite Daphnim"), the pagan timelessness being conjured up by the inclusion of a pair of antique cymbals and tam-tam in the orchestra, while the spirit of the young 20th century is sustained by impressionistically fluid streams of arpeggios in the piano part and intermittent precipitation of whole-tone scales elsewhere, with columnar ninth-chords resonantly placed to attain temporary harmonic stability and interstitial chromatics supplying the needs of greater cohesion within a basically tonal framework bearing a permanent key signature of two flats, is performed for the first time by the Boston Symphony Orchestra, Karl Muck conducting. (Originally written for a chamber group in 1901, and first performed at the home of Isabella Stewart Gardner in Boston on 13 April 1903)

We consider *A Pagan Poem* to be Mr. Loeffler's greatest work. Its mastery of orchestration is wonderful, and its ingenuity of figure development equally phenomenal. Surely, if the modern school becomes permanent, Mr. Loeffler will be reckoned among its greatest exponents. He is not so purely cerebral as the bitter Vincent d'Indy and he is fully as romantic as the fawning Debussy. He is as great as either of them—or greater. (Louis C. Elson, Boston *Advertiser,* 27 November 1907)

Mr. Loeffler's music will not stale with many repetitions for in substance and in expression *A Pagan Poem* is a masterpiece of musical eloquence. Mr. Loeffler before this has composed music of indisputable originality. With it, he has risen to a still greater height, and at the same time he has sounded a still more emotional depth—a composer of true genius. (Philip Hale, the Boston *Herald,* 15 March 1908)

The text of Mr. Loeffler's *Pagan Poem* ran: "Fetch water forth and twine the altars here with the soft fillet and burn resinous twigs and male frankincense that I may try by magic rites to turn my lover's sense from sanity" from Virgil's 8th Eclogue; that is to say, something uncanny was happening, and this was emphasized by the ominous sound of trumpets in three-part harmonies. It was an effort to listen for nearly half an hour. (London *Times,* October 1917)

*116*

## 24 NOVEMBER 1907

*Lady Godiva*, overture by the Czech composer Vítězslav Novák, celebrating in luscious romantic tones the legendary English noblewoman who ignored the trombone threats of her 11th-century feudal husband and took a noontime ride through the streets of Coventry totally denuded, caressed by four solo violins and bathed in the coda in warm E major, pianissimo, to win the human rights and freedom from excessive taxation for her vassals, is performed for the first time in Prague.

## 25 NOVEMBER 1907

*Le Pavillion d'Armide*, ballet by Nicolas Tcherepnin, after Théophile Gautier's poem *Omphale*, in which a French viscount dreams of a Gobelin tapestry in his bedroom coming to life and imagines himself to be the crusader Rinaldo held in a delectably oriental subjection at the pavilion of the seductive Armida, as Hercules was held by Omphale, to a musical score full of agreeable Franco-Russian sounds, is performed for the first time in St. Petersburg.

## 1 DECEMBER 1907

Two centuries have elapsed since the death by his own hand of Jeremiah Clarke, English composer, and real author of the celebrated *Trumpet Voluntary* whose authorship was long ascribed to Purcell.

## 3 DECEMBER 1907

*Tragaldabas (Der geborgte Ehemann)*, one-act opera by the Germanized Scottish-born composer Eugen d'Albert, wherein a professional pauper hired to pose socially as a wealthy lady's husband, is dismissed when he becomes unduly familiar with her, and is given the job to impersonate a recently deceased ape in a circus, is produced in Hamburg.

## 7 DECEMBER 1907

*V Tatrach (In the Tatras)*, symphonic poem by the Czech composer Vítězslav Novák, painting in romantically dramatic Smetanesque tones the beauty and the eerie mystery of the Tatra mountains of the Carpathian range (Novák was an ardent Alpinist), is performed for the first time in Prague.

## 14 DECEMBER 1907

*The Wand of Youth*, subtitled *Music to a Child's Play*, symphonic suite in seven movements by Edward Elgar, originally composed by him for piano at the age of twelve and orchestrated 37 years later, is performed for the first time in London.

## 19 DECEMBER 1907

*Soléa*, lyric drama in four acts by Isidore de Lara, London-born composer whose original name was Cohen, to a libretto by Jean Richepin, set in the island of Rhodes in 1522, wherein a proudly virginal Gypsy girl single-handedly foils a local traitor in dramatic recitative, slays a spy to the accompaniment of muted trumpets, fires a fairly effective cannon shot at the besieging Turkish flotilla to the roll of a bass drum, inspires a transitory naval victory in a symphonic interlude bristling with syncopated Ottoman melodies, and in the last act blows up an enemy magazine in a loud explosion of descending chromatic scales while locked in a harmonious embrace with a noble Greek-born Knight Hospitaller of St. John of Jerusalem, is produced with a German libretto in Cologne.

## 27 DECEMBER 1907

Henry HADLEY conducts the Berlin Philharmonic Orchestra in the first performance anywhere of his *Third Symphony* in B minor (completed in Munich on 1 August 1906), conceived in an exuberantly Germanic vein, in four movements: *Moderato e maestoso; Andante* (in the spirit of an Angelus, with three large church bells in the orchestra), *Scherzo* and *Allegro*.

## 27 DECEMBER 1907

*Matteo Falcone,* dramatic scene by César CUI, after a novella of Prosper Mérimée, dealing with the passions and perils among Corsican contrabandists during Napoleonic wars, is produced in Moscow.

# ∂ *1908* ∂

## 1 JANUARY 1908

Gustav MAHLER makes his first appearance in the United States, conducting *Tristan und Isolde* at the Metropolitan Opera in New York.

## 2 JANUARY 1908

At the aristocratic Paris salon of Armande de Polignac, patroness of arts and herself a composer of songs, the avant-garde pianist Blanche SELVA plays for the first time the three pieces of the third book from the piano suite *Iberia* by Isaac ALBÉNIZ, *El Albaicín, El Polo* and *Lavapiés.*

In *El Albaicín* one finds the atmosphere of those Spanish nights that radiate the fragrance of carnation and aguardiente. . . . It is like the muffled sounds of a guitar complaining in the night. (Claude Debussy, in the *Bulletin français de la Société Indépendante de Musique,* Paris, 1 December 1913)

## 18 JANUARY 1908

*Brigg Fair,* "English Rhapsody" for orchestra by Frederick DELIUS, in variation form, with some interstitial unrelated materials, based on a Lincolnshire country tune in lilting pastoral time, in a Dorian mode with a characteristic cadential plagal subtonic, dedicated to Percy Grainger who originally notated the song (the title of the piece being derived from the line in the refrain, "Unto Brigg Fair I did repair"), is performed for the first time in Liverpool, Granville Bantock conducting.

(Sir Thomas Beecham in his biography of Delius, New York, 1960, states, on p. 149, that *Brigg Fair* was first performed at Basel, Switzerland, in January 1908, by Hermann Suter, preceding its initial English performances. This is in error, for Hermann Suter, who was conductor of the Basel concert series from 1902, did not produce *Brigg Fair* until 13 November 1910; the original program of that concert states that it was the first local performance in Basel of the piece. Perhaps Beecham confused *Brigg Fair* with another work by Delius, *Dance Rhapsody*, written in 1908, which was dedicated to Hermann Suter)

### 20 JANUARY 1908

DEBUSSY marries the affluent and socially influential divorcée Mme Bardac after divorcing the poor and socially inadequate Rosalie Texier, who was his mistress and subsequently wife during the years of composition of *Pelléas et Mélisande*.

### 21 JANUARY 1908

*Der Mann mit den drei Frauen*, operetta by Franz LEHÁR, positing in gayly waltzing and polkaing rhythms the horns of the modern trilemma of de facto trigamy among philogynous men, is produced in Vienna.

### 21 JANUARY 1908

*Sternengebot (The Stars' Command)*, opera in three acts by Siegfried WAGNER, son of Richard Wagner and grandson of Liszt, to his own libretto dealing with the power struggle among the Ripuarian Franks of the 10th century, wherein a German ruler, informed by an astrologer that the house of his chief tribal rival is to inherit his throne, orders the whole enemy clan slain but lets a youngling inadvertently escape only to discover that he is his own bastard son, the score presenting a weird simulacrum of the composer's father's music dramas and his grandfather's mystical rhapsodism, is performed for the first time in Hamburg.

### 23 JANUARY 1908

At his debut as conductor outside Russia, Serge KOUSSEVITZKY presents in Berlin an orchestral concert of Russian music including the world première of the *Second Symphony* of Reinhold GLIÈRE, conceived in an epical style, with occasional orientalisms imparting an exotic touch to the broadly diatonic Russian melodies, in four movements:

(1) *Allegro pesante*, in 4/4 time, in majestically flowing C minor (2) *Allegro giocoso*, a scherzo in 2/4 time in G minor (3) *Andante con variazioni*, in F minor, in 3/4 time, with a fugally propulsive last variation (4) *Allegro vivace*, returning to the initial C minor, in 12/8 time, presenting a sonorous panorama of Russian laetification.

## 23 JANUARY 1908

Edward MacDowell, the first truly national composer of America, whose talent, fostered in German institutions of musical learning, retained none the less the spirit of free American rhythmic song, but whose mind collapsed, reducing him to a pathetic state of second infancy, dies in New York at the age of 46 years, one month and 5 days.

E. A. MacDowell Dead—Noted Composer and Pianist Passes Away at Home Here.— Dr. Edward A. MacDowell, the composer and pianist, died about 8 o'clock last night in his apartment at the Westminster Hotel, Irving Place and 16th Street, following a long illness. . . . In the spring of 1905 overwork and insomnia brought on what eminent medical specialists pronounced to be a hopeless case of cerebral collapse. This it proved to be. Under the devoted care of his wife, he lived on, spending the summer months at Peterboro, New Hampshire, the winter at his apartment in the Westminster Hotel, in New York, oblivious to all the things which had once occupied a peculiarly active and sensitive mind. (New York *Tribune*, 24 January 1908)

## 25 JANUARY 1908

*Baldie*, lyric drama in three acts in Flemish by the Belgian composer Jean Blockx, wherein an unscrupulous but prosperous 18th-century Flemish farmer named Baldie insidiously abuses the innocence of a village belle during the temporary absence of her artistic fiancé (he sculpts), plunging her into melancholy, inappetence and terminal inanition, with condign punishment meted out to him by her sister who stabs him to death with a kitchen knife during a colorful kermess, set to tumultuous music enlivened by Netherlandish dance tunes, is performed for the first time in Antwerp.

(A completely revised version of the story which replaces the violation of chastity by an honest rivalry between two suitors of unimpeachable integrity culminating in a bloodless duel with bows and arrows and a subsequent triumph of selective love, with the musical score essentially unaltered, was staged for the first time under the title *Liefdelied*, i.e. *Song of Love*, in Antwerp, on 14 January 1912)

## 25 JANUARY 1908

*Leili and Medzhnun*, first opera by the 23-year-old Shusha-born Azerbaijan composer Uzeir Gadzhibekov, to his own libretto, after an ancient Caucasian legend dealing with the tragic love of a fearless warrior for a beauteous mountain maiden, written in a homophonic style making use of native instruments in the orchestra, is produced in Baku, the heroine's part being sung by a man in deference to the Moslem customs forbidding the appearance of women on the stage, and conducted by an amateur musician ignorant of written notes.

## 1 FEBRUARY 1908

Claude Debussy conducts, in Queen's Hall, London, his *Prélude à l'Après-midi d'un Faune* and *La Mer*.

With all the wealth of picturesque orchestration and piquant harmony and rhythm, we are inclined to doubt whether a second hearing of *La Mer* pieces would make us feel that they are the equal to the Prelude in imaginative impression. . . . The breath of freshness that came with Schubert's "Unfinished" Symphony, which Mr. Wood conducted immediately after Mr. Debussy's work, was a tribute to older methods of expression, and showed up one defect at any rate in the French composer's music, its monotonous orchestral coloring. (An unidentified London paper—not *The Times*—3 February 1908)

### 7 FEBRUARY 1908

The first complete performance is given by the Boston Symphony Orchestra, Karl Muck conducting, of *Symphonic Sketches* by George Whitefield CHADWICK, in four movements: *Jubilee* (with a "Juba" horn call imitating a Southern plantation Negro "breakdown"), *Noël* (a simple Christmas offering), *Hobgoblin* (a quasi-Mendelssohnian scherzo) and *A Vagrom Ballad* ("a tale of tramps and railway ties, of old clay pipes and rum") which includes an irreverent quotation from Bach's great G-minor organ fugue. (The first performances of two separate movements, *Jubilee* and *A Vagrom Ballad*, were conducted by Chadwick himself at a Chickering Production concert in Boston on 23 March 1904)

### 8 FEBRUARY 1908

RACHMANINOFF conducts the orchestra of the Moscow Philharmonic Society in the first performance of his *Second Symphony* in E minor, completed by him in Dresden in January 1908, in four movements all in 4/4 or 2/2 time:

(1) *Largo*, a mournful lamentation enhanced in its pessimism by recurrent lapses into the homonymous Phrygian mode, reluctantly rising from its fatalistic depths to an *Allegro moderato* marked by a strongly symmetric rhythmic pulse, entering the bright landscape of E major, and concluding abruptly in a chordal cadence (2) *Allegro molto*, in A minor, suggesting in its animated motion *alla breve* a modified scherzo, with the middle section fugally developed (3) *Adagio*, in A major, with ascending suspensions against plagally somber harmonies (4) *Allegro vivace*, in optimistic E major qualified by characteristically Russian declination of the submediant while the glockenspiel dispiritedly tolls its intermittent chimes, but recovering its primal strength in richly sonorous harmonies supported by resonant pedal points.

### 13 FEBRUARY 1908

*Espada*, Spanish ballet by Jules MASSENET, forming a concentration of sword dances (espadas), card dances, marches of toreros, a bolero, a corrida, a fandango, etc., is performed for the first time at Monte Carlo.

### 15 FEBRUARY 1908

Giuseppe MARTUCCI conducts the dedicatory program at the inauguration of a new concert series at the Augusteo in Rome.

### 16 FEBRUARY 1908

*Eliána*, opera in three acts by the Hungarian composer Ödön MIHALOVICH, his last stage work, after Tennyson's *Idylls of the King*, is produced in Budapest.

## 19 FEBRUARY 1908

DEBUSSY's *Pelléas et Mélisande* is performed for the first time in America at the Manhattan Opera House in New York.

Lyric Drama Dazes New York—Debussy's Opera Exquisite But Creepy—Characters Do Not Sing, They Intone to Wonderful and Mystic Harmonies. (Headlines in the New York *American*)

Preraphaelite Opera—Pelléas et Mélisande a Study in Glooms—A Mass of Shifting and Inessential Details—The Fundamentals of Music Left Out of Account. (Headlines in the New York *Sun*)

## 26 FEBRUARY 1908

*La Habanera*, lyric drama in three acts by Raoul LAPARRA, 31-year-old composer of Hispanic antecedents (he was destined to be killed in an Allied air raid on a Paris suburb on 4 April 1943), to his own libretto wherein an insanely jealous young Castillian stabs to death his own brother for the love of a woman as a habanera is danced by the populace, is haunted by its tune and by the hallucinatorily realistic form of his victim on each anniversary of the murder, and, when in the last act he finds their beloved lying dead on his brother's grave, goes mad, to a musical setting abounding in Spanish and Basque refrains, with moderately modern *fin-de-siècle* harmonies and appropriately colorful orchestration, is performed for the first time at the Opéra-Comique in Paris.

In my opera, singing must not be aimed to produce conventional effects, but must depend intimately on the prosody and expression. Therefore, the roles must be declaimed, and the vocalization must be made part of this declamation. . . . All soft sonorities must be excluded from the orchestra. The power and the accents must be conveyed with the energy of the dance itself that seems to circumscribe the entire Spanish character. (From *Quelques opinions de l'auteur sur la manière d'interpréter son œuvre*, printed in the score)

M. Raoul Laparra's opera *La Habanera* has much in common with the half-hour shockers at the Grand Guignol in Paris. From the first strenuous phase of the prelude to the final drum tap the chief aim of the composer seems to be hair-raising. . . . The melodramatic plot of *La Habanera* might have excused the employment of the most villainous discords, but the author-composer in moments of the greatest hurly-burly contents himself with discords that pass into good resolutions and in some of the most exciting situations he uses the orchestra with reticence and a powerful effect little short of genius. (From a review of the production of *La Habanera* at Covent Garden, London, published in *Referee*, 24 July 1910)

How the management could present such a horrible piece of dilettante workmanship at the Royal Opera in Berlin must ever remain a conundrum. Where the audience were intended to be impressed with horror, they roared with laughter. (From a review of the Berlin production of *La Habanera*, in *Era*, London, 10 December 1908)

## 27 FEBRUARY 1908

*Eidelberga Mia!*, an operatic tribute in three acts by a romantic Italian composer Ubaldo PACCHIEROTTI (1877–1916) to the glories of the old German university town of Heidelberg, is produced in Genoa.

29 FEBRUARY 1908

*Le Faune et la Bergère*, suite of three songs for mezzo soprano and orchestra by 25-year-old Igor STRAVINSKY, to poems by Pushkin: (1) *The Shepherdess*, depicting in pneumatically triadic harmonies and curvilinear melodies the post-adolescent flowering of an ancient Greek maiden (2) *The Faun*, wherein the lusty hircine creature disports himself in his sylvan retreat in characteristically Russian tritonal capers with occasional excursions into whole-tone configurations (3) *The River*, an operatically dramatic scene wherein the incensed faun pursues the shepherdess in precipitate syncopated rhythms and chromatically rising diminished seventh-chords enharmonically resolving into beatific aqueous harmonies in the finest manner of Stravinsky's teacher Rimsky-Korsakov to illustrate the protective waters of the river whither the maiden hastens to plunge, is performed for the first time in public at a concert of the Russian Symphony Society in St. Petersburg. (A semi-private performance was given in 1907 in St. Petersburg by the Imperial Court Orchestra)

I received your letter containing the most delightful and joyful news that *Le Faune et la Bergère* is to be performed by the Russian Symphony Society. I rejoice, and mentally I bow low before my benefactors, and especially before you, my dear Nicolay Andreyevitch. You say in your letter in regard to the progress of *Le Coq d'or* that in old age work goes rather slowly. Would that I, in my young age, could work as fast as you do! How wonderful it would be! (From Stravinsky's letter to Rimsky-Korsakov written in July 1907)

13 MARCH 1908

Nikita BALIEV inaugurates, in a house next to the Church of Christ the Savior in Moscow, his intimate cabaret, later to be known in Western Europe as *Le Chauve-Souris*, devoted to verbal and musical persiflage of self-important social and literary figures.

15 MARCH 1908

*Rapsodie espagnole*, symphonic suite by Maurice RAVEL in four contrasting movements: (1) *Prélude à la Nuit*, in 3/4 time, based on a hauntingly recurrent descending motive of four notes, F, E, D, C-sharp, in a nocturnal setting in which muted instruments predominate (2) *Malagueña*, an infectiously rhythmic Spanish dance in very rapid 3/4 time, artfully presented in a continuous crescendo from an accentuated susurrus in the low register to a multicolored orchestral fireworks display (3) *Habanera* (originally written for two pianos in 1895), a hesitatingly sensuous Hispano-Cuban air acidulated by softly discordant minor seconds in the pendulously swinging accompaniment (4) *Feria*, spectacular tableau of a Spanish fiesta in a typical dual meter of 6/8 and 3/4, with a cornucopia of Iberian drums and shakers, and the use of novel coloristic instrumental devices, such as tangent glissandos *sul ponticello* and the unprecedented glissandos on natural harmonics in the viola and cello, is performed for the first time at a Colonne concert in Paris, the near-septuagenarian Edouard Colonne himself ineffectually leading the orchestra.

The work received a courteous welcome from the audience, which turned to enthusiasm at the end of the *Malagueña*, encored at a request from the upper gallery. This encore was followed by certain ironical murmurs from the orchestra stalls. It was then that the thunderous voice of Florent Schmitt asked from the top of the gallery for a second encore "just once more, for the gentlemen below who haven't been able to understand." (Roland-Manuel, *Maurice Ravel*, London, 1947)

Not mere impressionism, but "pointillisme" in music is Mr. Maurice Ravel's *Spanish Rhapsody*. Even Mr. Claude Debussy's musical poem *La Mer* is painted in broader strokes. Mr. Ravel throws tiny little dabs of color in showers upon his canvas. There is not an outline nor an expanse in the sketch; everything is in spots. In the third part, a fête, the first violins, literally mewing like a rather deep-voiced tom-cat, brought laughs from the audience. (From the Paris dispatch in *Era*, London, 21 December 1909)

## 22 MARCH 1908

*First Symphony* by Albert ROUSSEL, subtitled *Le Poème de la Forêt*, in four descriptive movements corresponding to the four seasons (*Forêt d'Hiver, Renouveau, Soir d'été, Faunes et Dryades*, evoking a winter forest, the rebirth of nature in the spring, a pastoral summer evening and an autumnal frolic of sylvan divinities) is performed for the first time in Brussels.

## 23 MARCH 1908

Ferruccio BUSONI plays in Berlin the solo part in the world première of the *Ukrainian Rhapsody* for piano and orchestra by the Russian composer Sergei LIAPUNOV, written in an expansive Lisztian manner without loss of the lyric and rhythmic flavor of the Ukrainian songs used as basic material.

## 30 MARCH 1908

*Les Jumeaux de Bergame*, two-act opera by the prophet of eurhythmics, Émile JAQUES-DALCROZE, his last stage work, is produced in Brussels.

## 5 APRIL 1908

*Toman a lesní panna* (*Toman and the Forest Nymph*), symphonic poem by the romantic Czech composer Vítězslav NOVÁK, inspired by an absorbingly horrifying folk tale of murder by massive osculation, wherein a faithless lover is kissed to death by a congregation of forest nymphs to avenge his kissing betrayal of one of their trusting sisters, set to an ingratiatingly titillating score punctuated by bradyseismic rhythms, is performed for the first time in Prague.

## 11 APRIL 1908

*Rhea*, opera in three acts by the Greek composer Spiro SAMARA, to an Italian libretto recounting the tale of multilateral passion, bilateral jealousy, intentional adultery, murder, suicide and general human turbulence, projected against the paradisiac scenery of the fabled Greek island Chio, wrested in 1346 from the infidel Saracens by an Apollo-like Greek warrior in the service of the podestà of Genoa, who is loved by the podestà's young Greek wife

Rhea and is affianced to her stepdaughter, with the tragic denouement as an envious love rival stabs him to death, and Rhea, falling on his lifeless body, takes a potently poisonous potion contained in her votive ring, to a singingly Italianate score saturated with dramatic chromatics occasionally relieved by ethnically Grecian, orientally florid arabesques, is produced in Florence.

## 17 APRIL 1908

*Piano Concerto* in D-flat major by Emanuel MoÓR is performed in a world première by Harold Bauer and the Boston Symphony Orchestra.

Emanuel Moór, a Hungarian by birth, married a Miss Burke, the daughter of the famous bottler of ale, and has thus been enabled to write music at his leisure. Whether it would not have been as profitable for him to tipple his ale in the shade is a question for posterity to decide. (Philip Hale, Boston *Herald,* 19 April 1908).

I played Moór's piano concerto with the Boston Symphony Orchestra while Karl Muck was the conductor. "Es klingt," he said to me, screwing up his face in that Mephistophelian manner for which he was famous. (Harold Bauer, *His Book,* New York, 1948) (Muck did not conduct the Concerto, however, but delegated the task to his assistant Carl Wendling)

## 1 MAY 1908

*Frühlingsnacht,* one-act opera by the Germanically educated Norwegian composer Gerhard SCHJELDERUP, to his own German libretto romantically descriptive of gentle love on a spring night, set in warmly Mendelssohnian harmonies, is performed for the first time in Dresden. (Expanded to three acts, it was produced in Lübeck on 18 October 1934 under the more explicit title *Liebesnächte*)

## 4 MAY 1908

*The Garden of Death,* symphonic poem by Sergei VASSILENKO, tonalizing Oscar Wilde's story of a disenchanted phantom with orientalistically twisted scales conjuring up an air of ultramundane mysteries and promises of millennial tranquility, is performed for the first time in Moscow.

## 10 MAY 1908

Arthur LEMBA, 22-year old Estonian graduate of the St. Petersburg Conservatory under Rimsky-Korsakov, conducts in Tartu the first performance of his Estonian opera *Lembitu Tütar* (*Lembitu's Daughter*), in which the valorous daughter of the commander of pagan but noble Estonians resists to the death the wiles of the victorious leader of the well-caparisoned crusaders of the Teutonic Order of the Knights of the Sword intent on converting her after Lembitu himself falls on the field of honor in 1217.

## 1 JUNE 1908

*Overture* to Heine's drama of Scottish passion, *William Ratcliffe* by the Swiss composer Othmar SCHOECK, a work of abecedarian Mendelssohnian harmonies and Meyerbeerish foudroyance, is performed for the first time in Dresden.

### 4 JUNE 1908

*Flagellantenzug*, symphonic poem by the German composer Karl BLEYLE, depicting in marching rhythms the scenes of massive self-flagellation of medieval penitents, men, women and children, perambulating the German city streets in long processions in double file and scourging themselves with leathern thongs to exorcise the pestilence on earth and perdition in afterlife, is performed for the first time in Munich.

### 13 JUNE 1908

BLIND TOM, American Negro slave who amazed the world as a musical child prodigy playing whole concerts of piano pieces of moderate difficulty (a brochure, *Le merveilleux prodigue musical Tom l'Aveugle*, published in Paris in 1867, adequately glorified his achievements), dies at the age of 59, in Hoboken, New Jersey, in the family home of Colonel Bethune to whom he was originally sold as a suckling.

Tom was born in Georgia, owned by a man named Jones. He was an idiot from birth. His father and mother were offered for sale. Price: $1,500 without Tom, $1,200 with him." (Dwight's *Journal of Music*, ca. 1880)

### 15 JUNE 1908

Erik SATIE, the eccentric genius of Parisian musical sophistication, belatedly determined to acquire an academic education, obtains at the age of 42 a certificate of the satisfactory completion of a course in counterpoint at the Schola Cantorum in Paris, with a notation by his professor Albert Roussel, "très bien."

### 17 JUNE 1908

On Igor STRAVINSKY's twenty-sixth birthday, his symphonic *Fireworks*, realistically descriptive of Roman candles, pinwheels and other pyrotechnical devices, for a large orchestra luxuriating in the contrasted sonorities of flutes, harps, bells and individualized strings playing high harmonics, and dedicated to Maximilian Steinberg and Rimsky-Korsakov's daughter Nadezhda, is performed in St. Petersburg, a few hours after their marriage in a village church near Kritzi.

The modern tonal coruscations and explosions entitled *Fireworks* seemed unartistic enough. One could hear the flashes and (very decidedly) the final bombs. What some of the brass dissonances meant we could not imagine unless the man who lit the pieces had burned his fingers and made a few resultant remarks. (Louis C. Elson, the Boston *Advertiser*, 1914)

Arthur Brock, the head of a firm of pyrotechnics, was invited to hear Igor Stravinsky's *Fireworks* performed in London on 28 February 1914. He made the following comments: "It was a wonderful impressionistic rendering of pyrotechnic effects, in beautiful colors, sparkling scintillations, graceful forms and movements, leading up to the Grande Mêlée and an impressive Final Bouquet. As a pyrotechnist, I am grateful to Stravinsky as the first musical composer to recognize the absorbing beauties of the pyrotechnic art." (London *Observer*, 1 March 1914)

20 JUNE 1908

Federico CHUECA, prolific and popular Spanish composer, described as "the barrel-organ of his generation," among whose penetratingly infectious zarzuelas *La Gran Vía* attained enormous success, and whose patriotic march from the operetta *Cádiz* became in the 1880's an unofficial national anthem of Spain, dies in his native Madrid at the age of sixty-two.

21 JUNE 1908

RIMSKY-KORSAKOV, the professorial tone poet of Russian music, whose epically designed operatic spectacles reflect with civilized definition the grandeur of Russian history and legend, who enriched the technical vocabulary of musical resources by some extraordinary innovations such as the scale of alternating whole-tones and semitones (in Russia it came to be known as the Rimsky scale), venerated teacher of two generations of Russian composers, dies of angina pectoris at his summer home in Lubensk in the vicinity of St. Petersburg, the capital where he spent his life in domestic tranquillity and social respectability, at the age of 64 years, 3 months and 3 days.

1 JULY 1908

Max REGER receives an honorary degree of Doctor of Music from the University of Vienna, presented to him as "modorum musicorum inventori novorum cultissimo . . . qui Joannis Sebastiani Bach divinis vestigiis ingressus Artis organariae fines inopino successu propagavit," giving an academic imprimatur to Hugo Riemann's declaration that Reger could become the Bach of the twentieth century.

7 JULY 1908

*Horrida Nox*, one-act opera by the 46-year-old Argentinian composer Arturo BERUTI, the first opera by a native composer to a libretto in Spanish to be publicly performed in Argentina, in which a rebel patriot dies in the arms of his beloved after his escape from the dungeon where he was held by henchmen of the tyrannical South American dictator Rosas, is performed for the first time in Buenos Aires.

2 AUGUST 1908

*Hochzeitsglocken*, one-act opera by the Hungarian pianist and composer Emanuel MOÓR, in which the felicitous wedding bells chime incessantly, is produced in Kassel.

## 5 SEPTEMBER 1908

Ettore PANIZZA, Argentine-born composer of Italian extraction, conducts at the inauguration of the renovated Teatro Colón in Buenos Aires the first performance of his patriotic opera *Aurora*, in three acts, expressly commissioned for the occasion by the Argentine government and competently written in an effective Italian idiom, to a libretto wherein Aurora, daughter of the Spanish Governor of Argentina, enamored of a young rebel imprisoned by her father during the war of liberation in 1810, is fatally shot in a pre-auroral encounter and dies in her temporarily unchained lover's arms, pointing at the rubescent horizon symbolically incarnadined by her blood as the harbinger of national independence (the initial strains of the Argentine National Anthem are here sounded in the orchestra).

## 12 SEPTEMBER 1908

*Uku and Vanemujne*, opera by the Estonian composer Karl August HERMAN (1851–1908), based on Estonian mythology, is produced in Tartu.

## 19 SEPTEMBER 1908

Gustav MAHLER conducts in Prague the first performance of his *Seventh Symphony*, written during the summers of 1904 and 1905, but revised and refurbished in detail many times, variously designated by unauthorized exegeticists as "Song of the Night," "Romantic Symphony," etc., in five movements, of which the two outer ones, connoting the diurnal states of pessimistic introspection and pantheistic convection, spherically encycle the nocturnally romantic inner three, the heterotonal embrasures of the entire work being the initial indeterminate E minor and the ultimate triumphant C major:

(1) *Langsam—Allegro con fuoco*, the slow exordium optically suggesting a funeral march, interrupted by an impulsive attack of four fiery horns joined by trumpets apostrophizing in fanfares of calculated tonal obliquity in quartal and tritonal ascents (2) *Nachtmusik—Allegro moderato*, a bucolic tone poem with flutey birdcalls and resonant cowbells, converging tonally on a philosophically homonymous C, in minor and in major (3) *Schattenhaft—Fliessend aber nicht schnell*, a crepuscular scherzo, with emotional implosions so intense that at one point the cellos and the doublebasses are explicitly exhorted to snap the strings in quintuple forte to cause them to rebound forcibly against the fingerboard (4) *Nachtmusik—Andante amoroso*, an idyllic serenade, with a guitar and a mandolin suggesting the amorous dalliance of the *amoroso* section, the principal key being the traditionally pastoral F major (5) *Rondo-Finale—Allegro ordinario*, with kettledrums introducing a series of exultant fanfares ascending along the entire scale of harmonic tones and driving in impatient exaltation towards a self-assertive apotheosis in the pantheistically foudroyant key of C major.

## 20 SEPTEMBER 1908

Pablo SARASATE, grandly artistic Spanish violinist who for nearly half a century fascinated all of Europe by the brilliance of his technique and the beauty of his singing tone, composer of numerous prestidigital concert pieces for the violin, of which the Gypsy dance known under the German title *Zigeuner-*

*weisen* has become a perennial favorite, dies in his villa at Biarritz at the age of sixty-four.

### 4 OCTOBER 1908

*Durchs Fenster,* opera by Iwan KNORR, is produced in Karlsruhe.

### 8 OCTOBER 1908

*Olav Trygvason,* unfinished early opera by Edvard GRIEG, his only attempted work for the musical theater, dealing with the first Christian king of Norway who after many heroic exploits perished in a naval battle in 1000, is produced in Christiania.

### 13 OCTOBER 1908

Max REGER's hour-long *Violin Concerto* in A major, op. 101, thickeningly vortical in its labyrinthine polyphony, in three movements, the outer two fast and the inner slow, with a formidable cadenza at the end of the first movement, is performed for the first time by Henri Marteau with the Gewandhaus Orchestra of Leipzig conducted by Arthur Nikisch.

Your concerto is of the highest significance to our violin literature; it is simply *kolossal.* (Henri Marteau in a letter to Reger)

In his powerful presentation of polyphonic forms and in the expressive mobility of his melismatic writing, Reger appears as the blessed inheritor of Bach's treasure. Through the confluence of the richest sources of the musical past and present his music streams towards a sea of sounds which will perhaps be the musical ocean of the future. (*Leipziger Zeitung,* 16 October 1908)

### 24 OCTOBER 1908

*Lamia,* symphonic poem by Edward MACDOWELL (after Keats), depicting in chromatic harmony, laden with successive diminished seventh-chords, the enchantress who lures a youth to her magical palace and then reverts to her original form of a serpent, shocking him to death, is performed posthumously for the first time by the Boston Symphony Orchestra.

*Lamia* was written in 1888. When we came to America, we ran up against the fact that it would be impossible to get an orchestra to try over a composition in a rehearsal. In Germany it would have been a simple and easy thing to accomplish. I can see, as if it were yesterday, the kindly faces of the members of different orchestras in Wiesbaden, Darmstadt, Frankfurt, so willing to help out the young American. The only grumble I ever heard was over the parts. I copied most of them, and the early ones must have been awful. I can hear an old musician say under his breath: "Schrecklich copiert." (From a letter of Mrs. Edward MacDowell to Philip Hale, editor of the Boston Symphony Program Notes)

### 30 OCTOBER 1908

Antoine MARIOTTE conducts in Lyon the first production of his lyric tragedy in one act, *Salomé,* to the original text of Oscar Wilde's French play (its composition was begun before Mariotte knew that Richard Strauss was writing an opera on the same libretto), a dramatically inflated score strewn with whole-tone scales and their concomitant augmented triads to convey a sense of horror, with pseudo-oriental jangle accompanying Salomé's septuple dance, suggesting orectic aprosexia rather than erotic parorexia.

### 4 NOVEMBER 1908

*Versiegelt*, one-act comic opera by Leo BLECH, to a Falstaffian story of a jolly widow who conceals a philandering burgomaster in a cupboard containing her friend's wardrobe subject to confiscation for debts, and when the bailiffs have it sealed (hence the title) uses his discomfiture to force his consent to the marriage of his daughter to a disapproved swain, is produced in Hamburg.

### 14 NOVEMBER 1908

*Der tapfere Soldat*, operetta in three acts by Oskar STRAUS, fashioned from George Bernard Shaw's Voltairean play *Arms and the Man*, cynically glorifying a reluctant soldier who prefers chocolates to bayonets (in England and America the operetta became famous as *The Chocolate Soldier*) is produced in Vienna.

### 16 NOVEMBER 1908

Arturo Toscanini makes his first American appearance, conducting *Aida* at the Metropolitan Opera House in New York City.

### 25 NOVEMBER 1908

*Kunálovy ocj* (*Kunala's Eyes*), opera in three acts by the Czech composer Otakar OSTRČIL, to a libretto from an old Indian legend dealing with the incestuous passion of a queen for her stepson whom she blinds by magic when he rejects her overtures but who regains his eyesight through countermagic, is produced in Prague.

### 28 NOVEMBER 1908

*Il Grillo del focolare*, first opera in three acts by Riccardo ZANDONAI, to a libretto freely adapted from the Dickens tale *The Cricket on the Hearth*, is produced in Turin.

### 3 DECEMBER 1908

*Hero and Leander*, tone poem by the 32-year-old English composer Havergal BRIAN, inspired by Leander's fabled trans-Hellespontine non-stop swimming trek to see his beloved across the strait (Byron duplicated this mythological feat to prove it could be done), is performed for the first time in London conducted by Thomas Beecham. (The score and parts disappeared after this performance without a trace)

## 3 DECEMBER 1908

Hans RICHTER conducts in Manchester, England, the première of the *First Symphony* in A-flat major by Edward ELGAR, dedicated to him as "a true artist and true friend" and set in four movements:

*Andante nobilmente e semplice* leading to the main *Allegro* moving along in energetic para-Brahmsian melorhythms towards a climactic *Grandioso*, then receding, idiosyncratically for Elgar, to a soft ending; *Allegro molto* in a remote key of F-sharp minor, in effect a scherzo, bearing a curious time signature 1/2, debouching into an *Adagio* in D major, the very slow initial theme of which is identical with the initial 24 notes of the rapidly evolving motto of the preceding movement, but aurally is beyond recognition owing to rhythmic deformation and harmonic dislocation; *Lento*, in D minor, opening with an ominously distant roll of the bass drum as a prelude to an agitated *Allegro*, leading, after many an artful modulatory exploration, to the main key of the work and, aided and abetted by beatific sonorities of the arpeggiating harps, reaching the final *Grandioso* and a powerful chordal ending.

## 10 DECEMBER 1908

Olivier MESSIAEN, "compositeur de musique et rythmicien," is born in Avignon to Cécile Sauvage, the poetess, who immediately wrote the poem *L'Âme en bourgeon,* dedicated to the infant's "burgeoning soul."

## 10 DECEMBER 1908

The Russian Symphony Orchestra of New York City, under the direction of its founder Modest ALTSCHULER gives the first performance anywhere of SCRIABIN's Fourth Symphony, *Le Poème de l'Extase,* completed in Lausanne in the summer of 1907, reflecting in a solipsistically erotic and pantheistically expansive continuous movement the mystic intent to "possess the Cosmos as a man possesses a woman," the music traversing eight initially passive but progressively active states of ecstasy—languor, yearning, volitation, emergent creativeness, anxiety, volition, postulation of self, challenge—symbolized by thematic figures mutually combining in augmentation, diminution, truncation, apocopation, intervalic torsion and rhythmic contortion in an ambience of tonal obliquity yet adhering to fundamental tonality with a purposive predominance of major triads and cohering in the formal symmetry of cyclic unity, bearing the following designations of tempo and sentiment:

*Andante, Languido,* wherein the temporary passivity of the dormant spirit is suggested by a symmetrically rotated theme, and the nascent activity by melodic nutation and rhythmic libration; *Lento, Soavemente,* in which the clarinet yearns for the ineffable in quartal ascension over a tonally dominant pedal point, forming an altered chord of the major 13th; *Allegro volando,* flying at asymptotic tangents from the tonal coordinates in volitient volitation; *Lento, Allegro non troppo,* wherein the imperious trumpet postulates "avec une noble et douce majesté" the primacy of self; *Moderato,* "avec délice," intensifying and torrefying the senses in egocentric rhythmic implosions and spastic melodic exhalations, oriented "avec une ivresse toujours croissante, presque en délire" towards a delectable goal of consciously savored self-intoxication; *Allegro drammatico, Tragico, Tempestoso,* with the trumpet, ever the protagonist, resuming its spasmodically mounting calls "avec une noble et joyeuse émotion" as a prelude to a grand recapitulation of languorously passive, sensuously sinuous, volantly exultant declarations, and after an episode marked *Charmé* and a transitory *Scherzando* leading to the majestic consummation of the final *Maestoso,* with the French horns chanting orgiastically holding their infundibula aloft, the powerful organ entering in majesty followed by the sonorous large campana, with a tremendous tension sustained over an undeviatingly powerful deep C for 53 long measures, erecting a compound plagal cadential structure before dissolving in ultimate ectasy in the purest of triadic harmonies in cosmically apocalyptic C major.

The nerves of the audience were worn and racked as nerves are seldom assailed even in these days. Scriabin's *Poème de l'Extase* was the cause. This composition was heralded as a foster child of theosophy. Certainly it conveyed a sense of eeriness and uncanny connotation. Most of the time, the violins were whimpering and wailing like lost souls, while strange, undulating and formless melodies roved about in the woodwinds. A solo violin spoke occasionally, growing more and more plaintive, and finally being swallowed in a chaos of acid harmonies with violins screaming in agony overhead. There were three such climaxes in the composition, all built upon a basis of cymbals, drums and inchoate blarings of the brass. It all seemed far more like several other things than ecstasy. (W. J. Henderson, New York *Sun,* 11 December 1908)

(The première of *Le Poème de l'Extase* was scheduled by the Russian Symphony Concert Society for its concert of 29 February 1908, but was cancelled for ambiguously stated reasons that the parts had not arrived in time. The first performance of the work in Russia took place on 1 February 1909 by the Court Orchestra in St. Petersburg)

The ultra-moderns all resemble each other. When one of these extreme gentlemen comes at you with a *Poem of Ecstasy,* you may be sure of one thing, he is going to use every known instrument. Some of this ecstasy was extremely bitter, while some of it reminded of the ecstasy of the too convivial gentleman who thought that the air was filled with green monkeys with crimson eyes and sparkling tails, a kind of ecstasy that is sold in Russia at two rubles a bottle. (Louis C. Elson, Boston *Daily Advertiser,* 22 October 1910)

In Paris, in May 1907, when concerts of Russian music were presented, Scriabin played on the piano some excerpts from his *Poème de l'Extase,* in the presence of Rimsky-Korsakov and others. This music impressed Rimsky-Korsakov as morbid eroticism. "Is he losing his mind?" he remarked half-facetiously. (From annotations by Andrei Rimsky-Korsakov in his edition of his father's *Chronicles of My Life,* Moscow, 1935)

*Le Poème de l'Extase* is the Joy of Liberated Action. The Cosmos, i.e. Spirit, is Eternal Creation without External Motivation, a Divine Play with Worlds. The Creative Spirit, i.e. the Universe at Play, is not conscious of the Absoluteness of its creativeness, having subordinated itself to a Finality and made creativity a means towards an end. The stronger the pulse beat of life and the more rapid the precipitation of rhythms, the more clearly the awareness comes to the Spirit that it is consubstantial with creativity, immanent within itself, and that its life is a play. When the Spirit has attained the supreme culmination of its activity and has been torn away from the embraces of teleology and relativity, when it has exhausted completely its substance and its liberated active energy, the Time of Ecstasy shall then arrive. (From a program note of a concert of Scriabin's music given in Moscow by the Imperial Russian Music Society on 6 March 1909)

## 11 DECEMBER 1908

Elliott CARTER, American composer who has developed a masterly modern style of composition by imaginative hyperclassical and serial methods, is born in New York City.

## 11 DECEMBER 1908

Frederick DELIUS conducts the London Philharmonic in the first performance of his symphonic poemette *In a Summer Garden,* dedicated to his wife Jelka Rosen, and justifying by its unpretentious musical setting, with simple symmetric tunes of folksong lilt and flowery melismas in the frequent instrumental solos, the insertion of a motto from Rossetti in the printed score: "All are my blooms; and all sweet blooms of love/To thee I gave while spring and summer sang."

Very much may happen in a summer garden, and, truth to tell, the presence of 3 bassoons, 3 tenor trombones, chromatic timpani and 3 tubular bells led me to expect a summer thunderstorm; but the prevailing tone color was somber and suggested an autumn rather than a summer atmosphere. (*Referee,* London, 12 December 1908)

As there is no organic idea in the piece, no thematic germ of any consequence, *In a Summer Garden* is a little like a play in which there is nothing but scenery and limelight, or like the efforts of an unimaginative country organist who is obliged to extemporize until the clergyman is ready to begin the service. . . . The list of extra instruments in the program leads ordinary hearers to wonder what is the object of employing so many players to say so very little. (*The Times,* London, 12 December 1908)

## 18 DECEMBER 1908

Harold BAUER gives the first performance, at the Cercle Musical in Paris, of DEBUSSY's *Children's Corner,* "petite suite pour piano seul" composed in July 1908, and touchingly dedicated to his small daughter—"à ma chère petite Chouchou avec des tendres excuses de son père pour ce qui va suivre" (Chouchou was not destined to live beyond adolescence), in six movements furnished with English titles (Chouchou had an English governess):

(1) *Doctor Gradus ad Parnassum,* an ironically affectionate stylization of Clementi's famous didactic studies set in sterling C major acidulated by pandiatonic mixtures, with a meditative middle section in melodic augmentation (2) *Jimbo's Lullaby* (Chouchou's elephant toy Jumbo, mispronounced Jimbo with nasal French semi-vowel) marked "doux et un peu gauche," stepping awkwardly but cautiously in secundal harmonies on pachydermatous pentatonic basses, with a mock-exotic interlude in whole-tone scales (3) *Serenade of the Doll,* musical aquatint of a porcelaneously delicate, orientally slant-eyed idol inaudibly nodding in quartal harmonies on pentatonically black keys reposing on the tonic-dominant pedal point in E major (4) *The Snow Is Dancing,* an animated pantomime of rhythmically cadent snowflakes with fleeting whole-tone images passing softly and sadly by over the thematic phrase of a Phrygian tetrachord (5) *The Little Shepherd,* a modally inflected Grecian air in tenuously bucolic harmonies (6) *Golliwogg's Cake Walk,* a gently syncopated piece of ragtime inspired by the American dance popular in Paris vaudeville theaters, with a sly interpolation of the

opening motive of *Tristan und Isolde,* irreverently disharmonized in a modern lilting rhythm sarcastically marked "avec une grande émotion" and followed by a sardonic un-Wagnerian cachinnation.

(Golliwoggs are children's dolls, extremely popular early in the twentieth century, inspired by the series of "golliwogg" books by the American-born British writer Florence Upton, who published her first Golliwogg story in collaboration with her mother, Mrs. Bertha Upton, in London in 1895, at the age of 22; the word itself is Welsh in its phonetical make-up, but it was invented by Florence Upton. Golliwogg dolls manufactured in England were usually dark-skinned to provide "exotic" color. Debussy's daughter apparently had such a colored Golliwogg, which led Debussy to use the rhythms of a Negro dance in his *Golliwogg's Cake Walk*)

After I played the last piece, *Golliwogg's Cake Walk,* Debussy remarked: "You don't seem to object today to the manner in which I treat Wagner." I had not the slightest idea what he meant, and asked him to explain. He then pointed out the pitiless caricature of the first measures of *Tristan und Isolde* that he had introduced in the middle of the *Cake Walk.* It had completely escaped me. I laughed heartily. (Harold Bauer: *His Book,* New York, 1948) (Léon Vallas asserts in his biography of Debussy that Harold Bauer learned about the *Tristan* quotation in 1932, after reading the biography, an implausible assertion in the light of Harold Bauer's story)

21 DECEMBER 1908

*String Quartet No. 2,* op. 10, in F-sharp minor, by Arnold SCHOENBERG (begun 9 March 1907 and completed on 11 July 1908), the last of his works designated with an express key signature in the title, apart from some didactic compositions, in four movements: (1) *Moderato,* embalmed in a dissolvent chromatic fluid with condoling convergences into cadential triads and set in a discernible sonata form (2) *Sehr rasch,* a rash tourbillon of perturbing sonorities off center of the 16 strings of the quartet suddenly interrupted by a macabre strain of disharmonized Viennese tune "Ach du lieber Augustin, alles ist hin!" (3) *Litanei,* with a soprano part singing the introspective verses of the Viennese poet Stefan George, rising to the highest range of plaintive agony, with Hebraistic semitone sighs in the instrumental interludes (4) *Entrückung,* with a soprano solo intoning an extraterrestrial poem by Stefan George ("I feel the air of other planets") set to a nostalgically Tristanesque accompaniment, leading to a serene conclusion on a submissive major tonic triad, is performed for the first time in Vienna.

It was a veritable *Katzenmusik.* Nevertheless the audience kept quiet. After the end of the first movement, there were heard some signs of approval. This gave a signal for a regular *scandale,* which increased like an avalanche, subsided, again grew in force, and finally reached fortissimo . . . Someone said: "Now they will play Beethoven, so let us first ventilate the hall!" (*Wiener Tageszeitung,* Vienna, 23 December 1908)

During the performance of a new string quartet by the ultraviolet musical secessionist Arnold Schoenberg, there was some booing and laughter. Suddenly the music critic Karpath rose and cried out, "Stop it! Enough!" His colleague Specht countered by shouting, "Quiet! Continue to play!" The majority of the public was against the music. Some discords made elegantly dressed ladies cringe under the painful impact on their delicate ears, and elderly gentlemen were at the point of tears from fury. In the middle of all this tumult stood the figure of the composer who gestured towards the performers in an expression of gratitude and encouragement. (Richard Batka, *Prager Zeitung*, 28 December 1908)

25 DECEMBER 1908

Eva WAGNER, Wagner's natural daughter born to Cosima Liszt, the then undivorced wife of Hans von Bülow, marries the Germanized British Wagnerite and proponent of the doctrine of Teutonic racial supremacy, Houston Stewart CHAMBERLAIN.

31 DECEMBER 1908

Sergei PROKOFIEV makes his first public appearance at the age of 17, as a pianist and composer at a concert of the Society for Contemporary Music in St. Petersburg, playing seven short piano pieces of his own, including the provocatively dissonant and rhythmically impulsive *Suggestions diaboliques*, earning for himself the sobriquet of the *enfant terrible* of modern Russian music.

Young Prokofiev belongs to the extreme radical wing of modernism, and in his boldness and originality goes even farther than contemporary French modernists. (*Slovo*, St. Petersburg, 2 January 1909)

*Suggestions diaboliques* ought to have a more concrete title. I suggest *Wild Pandemonium of Dirty Devils in Hell*, or *Savage Fight of Two Infuriated Gorillas*. (*Novy Den*, St. Petersburg, 2 January 1909)

# ‿ *1909* ‿

13 JANUARY 1909

*Monna Vanna*, lyric drama in four acts by Henry FÉVRIER, to a play by Maurice Maeterlinck set in 15th-century Italy, wherein the virtuous wife of the defender of Pisa offers herself to the commander of the besieging forces as the price of the city's relief, but is spared defilement as the latter recognizes in her his childhood sweetheart and she decides to remain with him, set to a resonantly throbbing score in which the elements of French romanticism and Italian verismo are touched with impressionistic colorism, is produced at the Paris Opéra.

14 JANUARY 1909

*Bon-Bon Suite*, cantata for baritone, chorus and orchestra in six movements by the British mulatto composer Samuel COLERIDGE-TAYLOR, confected in an infantiloquent idiom, is performed for the first time in its complete orchestral version at the Brighton Music Festival. (An arrangement for voices with two pianos was played previously on 9 December 1908 at the Hampstead Conservatoire)

## 15 JANUARY 1909

Ernest REYER, French composer who added "er" to his real name Rey out of Wagnerolatrous devotion and whose Nordic opera *Sigurd* remains a Nibelungian homunculus of singular incongruity, dies at Le Lavandou, Hyères, at the age of eighty-five.

## 21 JANUARY 1909

*Ein Herbstmanöver*, first operetta in three acts by the 26-year-old Hungarian composer Emmerich KÁLMÁN, portraying in coyly waltzing Vindobonic melodies the smiling dalliance of the Austrian Hussars with the obliging countryside damsels during the time of autumn maneuvers (hence the title), is performed for the first time in Vienna. (Originally, it was performed in Budapest in the Hungarian language, under the title *Tatárjárás*, on 22 February 1908)

## 25 JANUARY 1909

The world première is given at the Dresden Royal Opera House of *Elektra*, opera in one act by Richard STRAUSS, scored for a huge orchestra including the Heckelphone, a bass oboe specially constructed by Heckel, to a libretto by Hugo von Hofmannsthal, marking their first collaboration, in which the terrifying story of the daughter's vengeance for the assassination of her father through the murder, with the aid of her brother, Orestes, of their guilty mother and her lover, is told in terms not of inexorable fate but of personal will, pervaded by unremitting and unresolved dissonances, set in a network of identifying motives, characterizing Elektra's hatred by a venomously disfigured fanfare of royal pride, the bloody footsteps by inspissatedly clotted chromatic progressions of hissingly discordant bitonalities, her resolve of matricide by a stately ascent along the major scale stumbling midway into chromatic blocks, her dance of joy by maniacally triumphant battology, and her sudden collapse by an abrupt chordal spasm; Klytemnestra's remembered misdeed by an atonally rising syncopated figure, her imperiousness by dark successions of unrelated triadic harmonies, her tinkling jewelry by futile flights of flutes against incongruously broken chords, her spiritual decay by cadential dejections into exhausted minor heteroharmonies in low register, and her fear of death by tense, prolonged and discordant suspensions; the revelation that Orestes lives by rapid knocks along the notes of major triads, and the virginal virtue of Elektra's sister Chrysothemis by concordantly harmonized implorations.

*Elektra* was produced for the first time on any stage before a brilliant international audience at the Saxon Royal Opera tonight. . . . With one act lasting an hour and forty minutes and 122 players in the orchestra, for thrilling histrionic vocal and orchestral effects *Elektra* outrivals *Salome*. It is a prodigious orchestral orgy, with nothing that can be called music in the score, and makes superhuman demands upon the physical and mental powers of the singers and players. . . . The marvelous imitative effects of the orchestra are bloodcurdling, drastic and gruesome to the last degree. It is fortunate for hearers the piece is no longer for it would else be too nerve racking. (From the cable dispatch from Dresden by H. E. Krehbiel, in the New York *Times* of 26 January 1909)

Violent, Lurid *Elektra*—First Impressions of Richard Strauss's New Opera—A Remarkable Work Whatever May Be Thought of the Theme—Gruesome Expressions in Music of Mysterious Moments of Horror. (Headlines in the New York *Sun*, 26 January 1909)

Elektra has known for some time that her papa was killed by mamma's gentleman friend. . . . She screams and then gets down and digs up out of the dirt the axe her papa was killed with. . . . Her mother is afraid of her. Elektra keeps on howling. . . . The orchestra breaks into strange and unearthly noises. . . . Muted trumpets, woodwinds in the lowest register and strings leaping in intervals of ninths and sevenths mingle in a medley of sounds which gives the idea of a snarling frightened animal. In the great scene in which Elektra accuses her mother of murdering her father, the music ends with a long shrill whistle like that of a locomotive entering a tunnel. Elsewhere the music reproduces sounds of smashing glass and china, the bursting of bottles, the clashing of shovels and tongs, the groaning and creaking of rusty hinges and stubborn doors, avalanches in the mountains, the crying of babies, the squealing of rats, the grunting of pigs, the bellowing of cattle, the howling of cats and the roaring of wild beasts. . . . I didn't pick out a tune that I should imagine would be later on included in "Gems from the Opera for the Parlor Organ." (Dispatch from New York City in the Boston *Herald*, 31 January 1910)

In *Elektra* Strauss lets loose an orchestral riot that suggests a murder scene in a Chinese theater. He has a constitutional aversion to what sounds beautiful. . . . If the reader who has not heard *Elektra* desires to witness something that looks as its orchestral score sounds, let him poke a stick into an ant hill and watch the black insects darting, angry and bewildered, biting and clawing in a thousand directions at once. (H. T. Finck in the New York *Post*, 2 February 1910)

Is it progress to use the human voice as Strauss does? Madame Schumann-Heink, who is noted for her big robust voice, found the strain of singing Klytemnestra in Dresden so great that she resigned after the first performance. She has related how, at the rehearsals, when Conductor Schuch, out of regard for the singers, moderated the orchestral din, Strauss declared: "But, my dear Schuch, louder, louder the orchestra; I can still hear the voice of Frau Heink!" (H. T. Finck, *Richard Strauss*, Boston, 1917)

In *Elektra* of Strauss, jarring discords, the desperate battle of dissonances in one key against dissonances in another, settle themselves down into total delineation of shrieks and groans, of tortures physical in the clear definition and audible in their gross realism. Can you conceive of the inward scream of a conscience in the flames of the inferno being translated into the polyphonic utterances of instruments writhing in a counterpoint no longer required to be the composition of two or more melodies which shall harmonize with one another but of melodies which shall spit and scratch and claw at each other, like enraged panthers? Snarling of stopped trumpets, barking of trombones, moaning of bassoons and squealing of violins are but elementary factors in the musical system of Richard Strauss. (W. J. Henderson, New York *Sun*, 2 February 1910)

## 3 FEBRUARY 1909

A century has passed since the birth in Hamburg of Felix MENDELSSOHN, the felicitously facile genius of Romantic music, endowed with a superb melodic gift, a natural sense of mellifluous harmony, a penetrating musical intelligence and an unfailing mastery of the art of composition in all its aspects.

## 3 FEBRUARY 1909

*Il Principe Zilah,* opera by Franco ALFANO in two acts, with a prologue and an epilogue, is produced in Genoa.

## 3 FEBRUARY 1909

*Hircus Nocturnus,* symphonic poem by Sergei VASSILENKO, inspired by an episode in Dmitri Merezhkovsky's novel *The Resurrected Gods,* wherein the nocturnal goat suddenly throws off his animal vesture and, brandishing a thyrsus and a cluster of grapes, reveals himself as Dionysius, the orgiastic god of vinous revelry, and flies away surrounded by a nymphomaniacal swarm of witches whirling under the full moon, to a score written in the fine tradition of Russian musical demonism with ominously syncopated thematic pronouncements intervalically based on the "diabolus in musica" of medieval lore, the tritone, is performed for the first time in Moscow.

## 6 FEBRUARY 1909

*Scherzo fantastique* by Igor STRAVINSKY, scored for a luxuriant orchestra including three harps and a celesta, suggesting by its entomologically buzzing chromatics the intense activity of a beehive, the nuptial flight of the queen bee in the soaring piccolos, the death of her discarded mate in sonorously Wagnerian augmented triads, and the return of the cycle of life and death in tremulous diminished seventh-chord harmonies, is performed for the first time in St. Petersburg, Alexander Siloti conducting.

## 8 FEBRUARY 1909

Mieczyslaw KARLOWICZ, Polish composer of romantically inspired choral and symphonic pieces written in a consciously national manner closely associated with authentic folk melodies, perishes in a snowy avalanche while mountain climbing in Zakopane, Galicia, at the age of thirty-two.

## 9 FEBRUARY 1909

*Quo Vadis?,* opera in five acts by Jean NOUGUÈS, after the celebrated historical novel from Nero's time by Henryk Sienkiewicz, panoramically depicting with a fine sense of dramatic theatricality and an easily accessible inventory of effective melodies, resonant harmonies and nicely calculated vocal effusions and instrumental colorations, the immoral Roman ways, the burning of Rome while Nero sings to the accompaniment of an anachronistic lute, the martyrdom of the Christians and the salvation of a young maiden loved by a

Roman patrician whom she has converted to Christianity, as her giant of a slave slays the bull to whose back she was tied as a bait for carnivorous beasts in the Coliseum, with the central episode recounted by Apostle Peter—his vision of Jesus returning to Rome to be crucified again to whom he poses the famous question of the title—all these varied scenes fittingly characterized by hymnal harmonies, ominous progressions of chromatically ascending diminished seventh-chords and reservedly orgiastic wide-ranging arpeggios, is performed for the first time anywhere in Nice.

### 11 FEBRUARY 1909

*Boleslaw Smialy,* the first opera, in three acts, by Ludomir Różycki, relating in majestically romantic Wagneromorphic tones the turbulent events in the life of the 11th-century King of Poland, Boleslaw the Bold, grandson of Boleslaw the Brave, who tried to impose his will on the Russians in Kiev and on the clergy in Cracow, and who was excommunicated by Pope Gregory VII for the murder of a bishop during a solemn mass, is produced in Lwów.

### 12 FEBRUARY 1909

At a concert of the Boston Symphony Orchestra conducted by Max Fiedler, Ignace Paderewski plays the *Fourth Concerto* for piano and orchestra by Saint-Saëns and hears the first performances anywhere of his *Symphony* in B minor expressing his grief for the extinction of Poland's sovereignty but voicing his faith that, in the words of the patriotic air sung at the time of the third partition of Poland in 1795 "jeszcze Polska nie zginela" (this hope that Poland had not yet perished was to be vindicated eight years after the performance of the symphony when Paderewski himself became Prime Minister of the resurrected Polish Republic), set in three movements:

(1) *Adagio maestoso,* serving as a somber introduction to the main section *Allegro vivace e molto appassionato* invoking in a well-calibrated sonata form the past glories of Poland, and ending with a solemn chorale played by the organ solo (2) *Andante con moto,* a lyric dedication to the Polish people in B flat minor (3) *Vivace,* in B minor, an impassioned commemoration of the heroically ineffectual Polish uprising of 1863, with courageous fanfares and optimistic tambourines crushed by assembled sarrusophones marching in heavy Russian steps, while distant thunder of resistance is heard in the foudroyant tonitruones, specially constructed at Paderewski's instructions, ending in a grand finale wherein the patriotic Polish hymn, disfigured and debilitated by intervalic alterations, emerges in all its autonomous power.

Great is Paderewski's New Symphony—It will Insure Piano Virtuoso Fame as a Composer (Headlines in the Boston *Globe* of 13 February 1909)

Paderewski's Symphony—The Disappointment That It Brought and a Lukewarm Reception For It—The Monotony of Mood and Color and the Lack of Vital Emotional Appeal (Headlines in the Boston *Evening Transcript* of 13 February 1909)

### 12 FEBRUARY 1909

F. T. Marinetti, Italian protagonist of *Futurismo,* publishes in the Paris newspaper *Le Figaro* his First Futurist Manifesto promulgating the militant ideals of futurist drama, literature, art and music—irrealistic, irrational, illogical, intuitive, improvisatory, autocephalous, synthetic, abstract, fantasmic, cerebral, unpredictably fulminating and stupefying. (See LETTERS AND DOCUMENTS for full text)

### 13 FEBRUARY 1909

*Le vieil Aigle,* lyric drama in one act by the Rumanian-born French impresario Raoul GUNSBOURG, to his own libretto from the tumultuous history of the Tatar khanate in 14th-century Crimea, wherein the Khan throws his favorite concubine into the Black Sea when he discovers his son's infatuation for her, and as he belatedly realizes that by this impetuous act he has alienated his son's affections, he plunges into the dark waters himself, is produced at the Monte Carlo Opera under Gunsbourg's own management, in an arrangement from disparate musical materials supplied by the nominal composer, made by Léon Jehin, and with Chaliapin in the title role of the "old eagle."

(Loewenberg in his *Annals of Opera,* Grove's *Dictionary of Music and Musicians,* Baker's *Biographical Dictionary of Musicians* edited by Nicolas Slonimsky, and *Die Musik in Geschichte und Gegenwart,* all incorrectly state that the libretto is taken from a story by Maxim Gorky)

### 16 FEBRUARY 1909

*Le Cobzar,* one-act lyric drama by Gabrielle FERRARI, a pupil of Gounod and one of the very few female composers of opera in France, depicting a Rumanian itinerant musician whose strumming on his four-stringed backbent-necked *cobza* fascinates a local matron so irresistibly that she kills her husband and follows the Cobzar to hard labor in the salt mines whither he has been sent for the previous murder of his Gypsy mistress, with both going blind from the reflected white light of the saline rocks while their hypersalinated bodies disintegrate into painful compounds of flesh, to a musical setting in a competently imitative style with some coloristic Rumanian dances appearing in a symphonic intermezzo, is produced in Monte Carlo.

### 19 FEBRUARY 1909

Arnold SCHOENBERG composes the first piece of *Drei Klavierstücke,* op. 11, which marks the historic departure from tonality and the inception of conscious atonality, leading eventually to the new method of composition with twelve tones related only to one another.

I am striving towards a goal that seems to be a certainty, and I already feel the opposition that I shall have to overcome. . . . It is not any lack of invention, of technical skill, or the knowledge of postulates of other contemporary systems of esthetics that has impelled me in this direction. . . . I am following an inner compulsion that is stronger than my education, stronger than my artistic training. (Arnold Schoenberg in a program note)

(Date, from Josef Rufer's *Das Werk Arnold Schoenbergs,* Kassel, 1959, refers to the first manuscript, in pencil; the date of 19 March 1909 given in previous editions of *Music Since 1900* is that of a final copy)

### 21 FEBRUARY 1909

*Enchanted Lake,* "fable-tableau" by Anatoli LIADOV, a concentrically symmetric symphonic cinquefoil, in which the serene surface of the water is gently agitated by a summer wind on a starlit Russian night, calling forth a lyrical round of romantic Russian mermaids, with fleeting thematic motives following a tertian modulatory scheme shifting either by minor or major thirds in the characteristic manner of Rimsky-Korsakov's marine music, and rich harmonies of ninth-chords supported by deeply anchored pedal points, scored for an orchestra vibrant with airy harps, celesta raindrops and fluid flute figurations, is performed for the first time in St. Petersburg, Nicolas Tcherepnin conducting.

Ah, how I love my *Enchanted Lake!* How picturesque it is, how clear, with its stars and mystery in its depths! (From Liadov's letter to a friend written during the composition of the work in 1908)

### 22 FEBRUARY 1909

Arnold SCHOENBERG composes the second piece of *Drei Klavierstücke,* op. 11, with a vestigial basso ostinato remaining as the unsevered umbilical link with the tonal past.

(Date from the manuscript in pencil, without expression marks and tempo indications, as given in Josef Rufer's *Das Werk Schoenbergs,* Kassel, 1959; the date 20 February 1909, given in previous editions of *Music Since 1900,* is apparently less substantiated)

### 22 FEBRUARY 1909

*In the Fen Country,* symphonic impression by Ralph VAUGHAN WILLIAMS, composed in 1904, written in a folk-like English fashion, is performed for the first time in London at a concert conducted by Sir Thomas Beecham.

### 24 FEBRUARY 1909

*Margarita la Tornera,* last opera, in three acts, by Ruperto CHAPÍ is produced in Madrid.

### 27 FEBRUARY 1909

*Katharina,* dramatic legend in three acts by the Belgian composer Edgar TINEL, dealing with the life and death of Saint Catherine, the Egyptian virgin of Alexandria converted to Christianity in 307 A.D., who became so steadfast in her new faith that she confuted the court philosophers charged with her repaganization (she is the tutelary saint of philosophers) and rejected the passionate proposal of the Emperor Maximinus to be his concubine, whereupon he ordered her to be drawn and quartered on a specially constructed wheel (she is the patron saint of wheelwrights), and when the wheel was providentially split by a bolt of lightning, had to resort to decollation, and in despair took poison himself, the score being constructed in the style of a religious oratorio, with the martyred saint's ecstasy illustrated by harp arpeggios and the Emperor's anger by trumpet fanfares, the Christian spirit being reflected in noble triadic harmonies imitative of *Tannhäuser* and *Parsifal,* and paganism represented by a fugal counterpoint derivative of *Die Meistersinger,* is produced in Brussels.

### 28 FEBRUARY 1909

*Suite Française* for orchestra by ROGER-DUCASSE, in four movements, *Ouverture, Bourrée, Récitatif et Air, Menuet vif,* an elegant stylization of 18th-century French dances, is performed for the first time at the Concerts Colonne in Paris.

### 1 MARCH 1909

Giovanni TEBALDINI publishes in the *Rivista Musicale Italiana* an article sarcastically entitled *Telepatia Musicale* purporting to prove, by tabulating some fifty musical examples, that Richard Strauss made use in his opera *Elektra* of a number of thematic patterns and harmonic progressions from the opera *Cassandra* by Vittorio GNECCHI produced three years and one and a half months before *Elektra.*

What should I do? Is there a better way to combat hatred and envy than noble silence? You know the story of Hercules and the hydra. I had already decided not to make any reply even before I had read the article of Tebaldini in which he makes publicity in behalf of Gnecchi. Now that I have read it, I am even more determined to remain silent. This whole affair is too silly to discuss, not to mention the chauvinistic undertones distinctly noticeable in these attacks. . . . (From a letter dated 5 May 1909 from Richard Strauss to Romain Rolland, published in a French translation in *Richard Strauss et Romain Rolland,* Paris, 1951)

### 6 MARCH 1909

*Et Bryllup i Katakomberne (The Wedding in the Catacombs),* opera in three acts by the Danish composer Georg HOEBERG, is produced in Copenhagen.

### 9 MARCH 1909

*Sinfonischer Prolog zu einer Tragödie* by Max REGER, his op. 108, a rhapsodically sprawling overture to an unnamed and unimplied tragedy, is performed for the first time in Cologne.

The whole vapid *Prologue to a Tragedy,* overladen with the ballast of laborious counterpoint and overheated by straining after tragic pathos, is utterly artificial. It lacks, as does all of Reger's music, the warm rays of a more genuine, greater and simpler art. (Walter Niemann, *Leipziger neueste Nachrichten,* April 1909)

### 16 MARCH 1909

Serge KOUSSEVITZKY and his wife Natalie establish in Moscow, with branches in Germany and France, the Russian Music Publishing House (*Editions*

*Russes de Musique, Russischer Musikverlag*), with a capital of 1,250,000 French francs in gold currency, founded for the purpose of publishing works by important Russian composers. (Scriabin's *Prometheus*, Stravinsky's *Pétrouchka, Le Sacre du Printemps,* and *Symphonie de Psaumes,* Prokofiev's *Classical Symphony* were among its publications).

17 MARCH 1909

*Hellera,* opera in three acts by Italo MONTEMEZZI, is produced in Turin.

25 MARCH 1909

*Prinzessin Brambilla,* first opera in two acts by the German composer Walter BRAUNFELS, after a whimsical tale of E. T. A. Hoffmann in which European royalty and characters from the commedia dell'arte commingle, set to a thoroughly conventional musical score, with some metrical asymmetries as a token of modernity, is produced in Stuttgart.

25 MARCH 1909

Ruperto CHAPÍ, Spanish composer of 168 zarzuelas and some operas in a grander manner, dies in Madrid two days before his 58th birthday.

26 MARCH 1909

*First Symphony* in F minor by Karol SZYMANOWSKI is performed for the first time by the Warsaw Philharmonic Orchestra, Gregor Fitelberg conducting.

2 APRIL 1909

Mayor Hibbard of Boston bans the announced local production by the Manhattan Opera Company of *Salome* by Richard STRAUSS, giving for a reason a telephone call from a woman acquaintance who had heard the opera in New York, was shocked by it, and declared that its presentation would endanger Boston morality.

4 APRIL 1909

Henry HADLEY conducts in Mainz (where he held the post of Kapellmeister) the first, and last, performance of his one-act opera *Safié,* to a German libretto dealing with a Persian princess poisoned by the court magician after she refuses to submit to the amorous blandishments of his son, with a musical score comprising sinuous oriental melismas and exotic colorisms set in Wagnerian harmonies.

9 APRIL 1909

In a historic first wireless transmission of the human voice Enrico CARUSO's singing is broadcast from the Metropolitan Opera House in New York through two microphones placed in the footlights of the stage to the home of Lee DE FOREST, inventor of the Audion, three-element vacuum tube which made radio possible.

## 9 APRIL 1909

DEBUSSY conducts at the Concerts Colonne in Paris the first performance of his *Trois chansons de Charles d'Orléans*, for a chorus a cappella, conceived in a medievally restrained idiom with a revealing infusion of bleakly heterophonic elements.

## 10 APRIL 1909

*The Beauty Spot*, a musical play by Reginald DeKoven, revolving around a revealing birthmark on the knee of a Paris model married to a Tsarist envoy General Samovar who spends a fortune tracking down her portraits showing the compromising feature, is produced in New York City.

## 19 APRIL 1909

*Dido*, opera by the Greek composer Denis Lavranges, derived from Virgil's *Aeneid* and depicting in effective Italianate cantilena the self-immolation of the Carthaginian Queen abandoned by Aeneas, is produced in Athens.

## 23 APRIL 1909

*Second Symphony*, in D minor, by the sage dean of the Russian Mighty Five, Mily Balakirev, written at the age of 70, and set in four movements: (1) *Allegro ma non troppo*, lively and direct in its classical symmetry (2) *Scherzo alla Cosacca*, containing quotations from Ukrainian dance tunes (3) *Romanza*, frankly romantic in its Schumannesque inspiration (4) and *Finale*, marked *Tempo di Polacca*, a vigorous orchestral polonaise, is performed for the first time in St. Petersburg, Sergei Liapunov conducting.

## 24 APRIL 1909

*La Perugina*, last opera by Edoardo Mascheroni, in four acts, is produced in Naples.

## 26 APRIL 1909

*Samson et Dalila*, celebrated opera of Camille Saint-Saëns, is at long last presented on an English stage, at Covent Garden, London, after the Lord Chamberlain at a special request of Queen Alexandra rescinds the ban imposed on theatrical plays and operas portraying biblical characters.

## 1 MAY 1909

Serge Rachmaninoff conducts in Moscow the first performance of his symphonic poem *The Island of the Dead* (completed on 17 April 1909), inspired by Böcklin's tenebrous painting in which shrouded human figures cross in a somber boat the Stygian waters to a cypress-lined island resembling one of the Ponza Islands north of the Gulf of Naples ("It must produce a stillness such that one would be awed by a knock at the door," Böcklin once said), set in a pantheistic A minor with asymmetrical rhythms within the meter of 5/8, softly eddying in the strings until the minatory tones of Dies Irae are heard, and after a tide of inexorable mortuary waves of diminished-seventh chords, lapsing into the cadential caducity of the sempiternal tonic A.

## 5 MAY 1909

*Bacchus,* opera in four acts by Jules MASSENET, to a libretto after Catulle Mendès in which Bacchus takes Ariadne to India where a local queen tries to seduce him with the aid of holy monkeys but is fulminated down by Zeus, and Bacchus with Ariadne are apotheosized on Olympus, with both the Greek and Indian mythological figures characterized uniformly by ecclesiastic plain-chant melos, is produced at the Paris Opéra.

## 5 MAY 1909

*Robin's Ende,* first opera, in two acts, by the German composer Eduard KÜNNECKE, is produced in Mannheim.

## 15 MAY 1909

*Zoraide,* opera by the Argentinian composer Juan Bautista MASSA, is produced in Buenos Aires.

## 15 MAY 1909

Giuseppe BLANC, 23-year-old Italian student, composes the song *Giovinezza,* destined to become the official anthem of the Fascists.

On the 15th of May 1909, we students were to have a farewell dinner before gradua-tion, and on that morning several students came to me and said: "You must write a song for the dinner tonight." I said I would if somebody would write the words. Nino Oxilia volunteered, and in five minutes completed the verse. It took me no longer than that to write the music. (From an interview with Giuseppe Blanc in the New York *Times* of 10 October 1934; the story is corroborated in the article on Blanc in *Di-zionario dei musicisti* by Alberto de Angelis, 3rd edition, Rome, 1930)

## 18 MAY 1909

Isaac ALBÉNIZ, Spanish composer, the first among his countrymen to develop a national style of composition in which the festive spirit of the dance and the nocturnal poetry of the land are transmuted in all their variety into the virtu-oso idiom of modern piano music, dies in Cambo-les-Bains, in the French Py-renees, eleven days before reaching his 49th birthday.

## 21 MAY 1909

Wassili LEPS, 39-year-old Russian pianist, conducts the Philadelphia Operatic Society in the first performance of his grand Japanese opera *Hoshi-San,* in three acts, with the action evolving in 1688 and dealing with a dancing girl of the Buddhist temple who is imprisoned without food or water because of her love for a desecrator of shrines, but whose prayer-dance redeems her soul and permits her to rejoin him in a hill of skulls, to a musical score presenting an amalgam of pentatonic orientalisms with Russian-style harmonies.

### 22 MAY 1909

Richard H. STEIN completes, in a brochure meaningfully dated "am Geburtstage Richard Wagners 1909" (i.e. 22 May 1909), a detailed exposition of his system of composition in quarter-tones, elaborating the introduction to his *Zwei Konzertstücke* of 1906, for cello and piano, the first composition containing quarter-tones ever to be published.

### 23 MAY 1909

*Fourth Symphony* by the Swiss composer Hans HUBER, subtitled *Akademische,* in four movements couched in the form of a concerto grosso for string orchestra, is performed for the first time in Basel. (A revised version, for two string orchestras, organ and piano, was first performed in Zürich on 3 February 1919)

### 30 MAY 1909

Benny David GOODMAN, "The King of Swing," magnetic killer-diller on the "licorice stick" (clarinet), by his art capable of moving cats and jitterbugs of the 1930's to ritualistic frenzy, is born in Chicago.

### 1 JUNE 1909

Giuseppe MARTUCCI, Italian pianist, conductor and educator, one of the most ardent adherents to the cause of German music in Italy, the composer of Wagneromantic symphonies and chamber music, dies in Naples, at the age of fifty-three.

### 2 JUNE 1909

Lucien HILLEMACHER, French composer who amalgamated his musical personality with that of his brother Paul, both being Prix de Rome winners, and wrote passable operas in fraternal collaboration under the name P. L. Hillemacher, dies in his native Paris eight days before reaching 49 years of age, destined to be survived by his older brother by 24 years.

### 7 JUNE 1909

*A Mass of Life,* grandiose oratorio for soloists, chorus and large orchestra by Frederick DELIUS, pagan rather than Christian in its pantheism, written to selected passages from Nietzsche's *Also sprach Zarathustra,* and couched in a solemn romantic style with occasional modernistic discordancies, is performed for the first time in its entirety in London, under the direction of Thomas Beecham. (The second part only of *A Mass of Life* was performed in Munich on 4 June 1908)

Mr. Delius was not happy in naming his work *A Mass of Life,* for the composition refers neither to the ritual of the Church of Rome nor to any particular seething mass of vitality. Its essence is the personality of Nietzsche, who, it may be added, died in a lunatic asylum. (*Referee*, London, 13 June 1909)

The ear in listening to the choral climaxes in *A Mass of Life* is bewildered that any man should consider this ugly featureless noise as music. (Glasgow *Herald*, 9 June 1909)

(In his book *Frederick Delius*, New York, 1960, Sir Thomas Beecham writes (p. 155): "The climax in the crescendo of interest was attained in the performance at Queen's Hall on June 10th of *A Mass of Life*; this being the first time the complete work had been given anywhere." The date is in error, for an extensive account of the concert of 7 June 1909 at which *A Mass of Life* was performed for the first time is found in *The Times* London, 8 June 1909, concluding as follows: "There was a fairly large and appreciative audience and Mr. Delius was called to the platform and heartily applauded.")

### 9 JUNE 1909

*Ode to Discord*, "a chimerical bombination in four bursts" by Charles Villiers STANFORD, dedicated to the Amalgamated Society of Boiler Makers, for voices and a large orchestra which includes a hydrophone and a dreadnaught drum, with all kinds of modernities such as the whole-tone scale and ninth-chords strewn over the score, and featuring the aria, "Hence, loathed Melody!—Divine Cacophony, assume—The rightful overlordship in her room—And with Percussion's stimulating aid—Expel the Heavenly but no longer youthful Maid!" is performed for the first time in London.

### 1 JULY 1909

United States Copyright Law, securing exclusive rights to composers and/or publishers to print, publish, copy, vend, arrange, record by means of a gramophone or any other mechanical device, and perform publicly for profit original musical compositions, and affording protection against infringement for a period of 28 years and a renewal period of the same length, enacted by Congress on 4 March 1909, comes into force. (Information and wording from *The Copyright Law of the United States of America*)

### 4 JULY 1909

Erik SATIE is presented an honorary academic degree at Arcueil-Cachan, a suburb of Paris, for his services to the cause of local musical education, and, presaging the formation of a mythically realistic École d'Arcueil, to which Milhaud, Poulenc, Auric and many other young musical rebels subsequently flocked, adopts the long-winded title of *Président d'Honneur du Comité de Pupilles Artistes et Directeur du Service Intérieur du Patronage Laïque.*

### 13 JULY 1909

*Elegy* for orchestra by Edward ELGAR, written in memory of a junior warden of the English Worshipful Company of Musicians, is performed for the first time in London.

## 15 JULY 1909

The name of Igor STRAVINSKY appears for the first time in a European press review, in a dispatch from St. Petersburg, published in the *Bulletin français de la Société Indépendante Musicale:*

The young Stravinsky was a private pupil of Rimsky-Korsakov. He is the composer of a symphony in E-flat major and of a suite *La Bergère et le Faune.* This suite contains interesting pages of music, and it will draw attention to its young composer whose talent will develop still further.

## 3 AUGUST 1909

*Eithne,* "romantic opera" in two acts by Robert O'DWYER, founded on the Irish folk story *Ean an Ceoil Binn,* the first opera to words in the Erse language, dealing with the king of Eirinn whose heir is unjustly accused of killing the royal hound, but is exonerated, meets a mysterious princess named Eithne, fights a tournament with his step-brothers for her possession, defeats them, marries her and is crowned when the old ruler dies, written in an unpretentious style of folk-like balladry, with occasional thematic uses of the Celtic pentatonic scale, is produced by the Irish Company of the Oireachtas in Dublin. (Date communicated by the composer. The date given in Loewenberg's *Annals of Opera,* refers to a later production at the Gaiety Theatre in Dublin on 16 May 1910, which is also cited in the printed score of the opera)

## 7 AUGUST 1909

Arnold SCHOENBERG composes the third of *Drei Klavierstücke,* op. 11, completing the suite of three piano pieces marked by a conspicuous absence of a key signature and a decisive recession from tonality.

## 12 AUGUST 1909

*Maïda,* first opera by the 36-year-old French composer André BLOCH, is performed for the first time at Aix-les-Bains.

## 7 SEPTEMBER 1909

Frederick DELIUS conducts at the Hereford Music Festival the first performance of his *Dance Rhapsody No. 1,* derived in its thematic material from English countryside tunes, and scored for a colorful orchestral ensemble, including the novel baritone oboe, the Heckelphone.

The Dance Rhapsody is an extremely brilliant piece. . . . Although it is the work of a thoroughly modern composer, it was warmly applauded, and Mr. Delius, who conducted, had repeatedly to bow his acknowledgements to the audience. (*Manchester Guardian,* 8 September 1909)

The performance of the *Dance Rhapsody* by Frederick Delius under the composer's direction only served to impress the mind with the second-rate and second-hand character of the tunes. The duet between the English horn and the Heckelphone (a kind of bass oboe) at the beginning was robbed of its misty atmospheric effect by the fact that the player had to struggle with the Heckelphone to produce the notes in any way possible. Then the prosaic dance tune and the still more commonplace pendant to it were emphasized without a gleam of humor or rhythmic lightness. It is really unkind to allow a composer to dissect his score in public. (*The Times*, London, 8 September 1909)

Mr. Percy Grainger believes that Delius is the greatest living composer. . . . He was not heated by wine when he made this statement, for he is a total abstainer. . . . Delius is a strange apparition in the musical world, not easily classified. Take this *Dance Rhapsody*, for instance. The chief theme is of a jig-like nature; this is repeated in a scrappy fashion, and then suddenly we are in the East, and there is the thought of Russians waiting for languorous dancing girls. What, pray, has the little introduction to do with what follows? We have yet to be persuaded that Delius warrants Mr. Grainger's perfervid admiration. (Philip Hale, Boston *Herald*, 25 February 1916)


## 11 SEPTEMBER 1909

*Bacchus triomphant,* opera by Camille ERLANGER, is produced in Bordeaux.


## 14 SEPTEMBER 1909

Sergei PROKOFIEV graduates from the St. Petersburg Conservatory in the classes of pianoforte (with Anna Essipova) and composition (with Rimsky-Korsakov, Wihtol and Liadov), and receives a diploma as a "free artist." (Date communicated to the author in 1936 by Maximilian Steinberg, professor of the St. Petersburg Conservatory, and later its director)


## 6 OCTOBER 1909

Dudley BUCK, American organist, pianist and composer of competent organ music and impressively sounding cantatas, who, like so many serious American musicians of his generation, went to Leipzig for his training, and upon return taught younger Americans the Germanic science of music, dies in Orange, New Jersey, at the age of seventy.


## 7 OCTOBER 1909

A posthumous production is given in Moscow of RIMSKY-KORSAKOV's last opera *Le Coq d'or* (*The Golden Cockerel*), subtitled "impersonated fable," after Pushkin's versified tale, in three acts:

(1) wherein a gluttonous and somnolent tsar withdraws his armies from the borders to the immediate vicinity of the capital and for security obtains from the court astrologer a magically alert weathervane in the shape of a cock who would crow an alarm in a gaily fanfarous trumpet call of a major triad soaring into a lamentably unrelated key the moment the enemy attacks (2) wherein the tsar arrives too late on the battlefield strewn with the corpses of his soldiers, the stillness and the corruption of death signalized by the creeping motion of diminished seventh-chords colliding in strident dissonance with a procession of augmented triads moving in the opposite direction, while inverted whole-tone scales stride in the basses in gigantic steps of minor sevenths and mournful progressions of alternating semitones and sesquitones enhance the tonal ambiguity of the music, when suddenly an oriental queen makes an appearance and sings

a radiant hymn to the sun embroidered with serpentine melismas of such seductive power that the tsar forgets his disasters and takes her home for a bride (3) wherein the wedding march combining the intervalic obliquity of orientalistic melos with sonorous Russian harmonies heterophonically embedded in well-lined pedal points is rudely interrupted by the astrologer who demands as his payment for the golden cockerel the cession of the bride herself, so infuriating the tsar that he slays him with a baton, whereupon the cock flies off his perch and administers a fatal peck at the tsar's occipital fissure.

### 17 OCTOBER 1909

Nicola SPINELLI, Italian composer of melodramatic operas, a minor master of the Verismo who explored the rustic chivalries and the caustic rivalries among passionate Sicilians in search of inspiration, dies in Rome at the age of 44, a victim of dementia praecox induced by youthful incontinence and intemperance.

### 19 OCTOBER 1909

*William Ratcliff,* last opera in two acts by the Dutch composer Cornelis DOPPER, after Heine's melodramatic ballad detailing the gory murders in a Scottish family, is produced in Weimar.

### 4 NOVEMBER 1909

Serge RACHMANINOFF makes his first appearance in the United States as a pianist, in a recital at Smith College, Northampton, Massachusetts.

### 6 NOVEMBER 1909

*Izeÿl,* music drama in three acts by the Germanized Scottish-born composer Eugen D'ALBERT, dealing with a venomously mouthed Hindu princess of 600 B.C., who implants a kiss of death on the lips of her suitors but perishes of her own labiodental poison when she attempts to seduce an osculatorily immune stranger, set to an artificially flavored orientalistic musical score inspissated with Wagneromantic harmonies, is produced in Hamburg.

### 8 NOVEMBER 1909

The Boston Opera House, erected in the fashionable Fenway Park section of the town, opens under the management of Henry Russell, with a gala performance of Ponchielli's *La Gioconda.*

### 10 NOVEMBER 1909

Ludvig SCHYTTE, German-trained Danish pianist, whose ingratiatingly pianistic pieces with programmatic titles are eminently suitable for teaching purposes, dies in Berlin at the age of sixty-one.

### 11 NOVEMBER 1909

*Pierrot and Pierrette,* allegorical fantasy in two scenes by the English composer Josef HOLBROOKE, wherein Pierrot, incited by the devil, temporarily plunges into the vice-ridden tourbillon of urban life, but remorsefully returns to his irreproachable and unreproaching Pierrette, is produced in London, under the direction of the composer.

## 12 NOVEMBER 1909

*Der Graf von Luxemburg,* operetta in two acts by Franz LEHÁR, wherein a Russian Grand Duke, infatuated with a complaisant girl in a European spa, engages an accommodating local count to marry her incognito so that after a quick divorce she would, as a titled lady, be eligible to marry his royal self, but is frustrated as the count and the lady unpremeditatedly fall in love at a masked ball, with a musical score rich in singingly swinging waltz tunes, is performed for the first time in Vienna.

## 15 NOVEMBER 1909

*On Wenlock Edge,* suite in six sections for tenor, piano and string quartet by Ralph VAUGHAN WILLIAMS, after A. E. Housman's poem *A Shropshire Lad,* reflecting thoughts on life, love and death, set to music in spacious modalities of English country folksongs, is performed for the first time in London.

## 22 NOVEMBER 1909

*Second Suite* for small orchestra by Béla BARTÓK, based on Hungarian rural dance tunes, is performed for the first time in Budapest. (A two-piano arrangement made 30 years later was performed by Bartók and his wife in Chicago on 6 January 1942)

## 26 NOVEMBER 1909

*The Wasps,* incidental music to a play by Aristophanes, by Ralph VAUGHAN WILLIAMS, scored for tenor, baritone, male quartet and orchestra, is performed for the first time at the University of Cambridge, England. (A symphonic suite was drawn from this score in 1912, and first performed in London on 23 July 1912, under the composer's direction)

## 28 NOVEMBER 1909

During his first tour of the United States, Serge RACHMANINOFF gives in New York the first performance anywhere, with the New York Symphony Orchestra conducted by Walter Damrosch, of his *Third Piano Concerto,* in D minor, in three movements, composed in Moscow between June and October 1909:

(1) *Allegro ma non tanto,* in 4/4 time, opening with a contemplative alternation of the tonic and the supertonic, in homophonically lyric tones, efflorescing into garlands of arpeggios leading to an exuberant cadenza covering the entire range of the keyboard, then returning to the initial mood in a philosophical recapitulation (2) *Intermezzo,* 3/4, ostensibly in A major with a characteristically Russian chromatic declination of the submediant tending towards the basic D minor, then evolving into a magniloquent D-flat harmonic major and finally, through enharmonic change, returning to A major and D minor, concluding on a plagal cadence (3) *Finale,* attacked without pause, set in *alla*

*breve* time, in the initial key of D minor, palpitating in rhythms similar to the opening, then digressing into C major, and ending with a typical rhythmic figure of one long, two short and one long note in fortissimo, identical with the melorhythmic ending of the *Second Piano Concerto.*

The title Fantasy would seem to suit Rachmaninoff's *Third Piano Concerto* better. It is rambling in texture and unstereotyped in its makeup. . . . The first movement is neither long nor brilliant. . . . A wailing Russian note pervades not only this movement but the other two. Mr. Rachmaninoff has labeled the second movement an Intermezzo. It is in several tonalities and several tempos, and leads into the finale, which is the longest and the most brilliant movement of the work. When the composer had finished, he received a well-deserved ovation from the audience, and it is likely that the concerto will be heard soon again. (New York *Times,* 29 November 1909)

### 30 NOVEMBER 1909

*Sheikh Senan,* opera in four acts by the 24-year-old Tatar composer Uzeir GADZHIBEKOV, to his own libretto dealing with a muezzin's love for a beautiful Georgian maiden inconveniently betrothed to a local prince, is performed for the first time in Baku, the composer conducting.

### 1 DECEMBER 1909

*Zeppelins grosse Fahrt,* dramatic symphony by the 64-year-old German composer August BUNGERT, subtitled *Genius triumphans,* and depicting in grandiosely Wagneromantic tones the proud flight of an early dirigible airship, with engines working in fugal counterpoint, the propeller whirring in the kettledrums, and the lyrical Zeppelin leitmotiv soaring over Germany until the landing at Echterdingen where it is torn asunder at its mooring mast by a sudden gust of ascending chromatic thirds, is performed for the first time in Coblenz.

### 4 DECEMBER 1909

*La Sina d'Vargöun,* opera in three acts by the vocal spokesman of Italian Futurism, Francesco Balilla PRATELLA, to his own libretto depicting the amorous turbulences in the life of Rosselina dei Vergoni (whose name in the Romagnese dialect is represented by the title of opera), written in a realistic manner of the Italian Verismo (the heroine stabs her unfaithful lover to death in church during his wedding to her successor), the score abounding in folk melodies, in a harmonic idiom, utterly non-Futurist and non-antimelodic, closely emulating that of Mascagni, is produced in Bologna, as the winner of the Baruzzi prize.

A year ago, a jury composed of Pietro Mascagni, Giacomo Orefice, Guglielmo Mattioli, Rodolfo Ferrari, and the critic Gian Battista Nappi, selected my futurist opera *La Sina d'Vargöun,* to my own libretto in free verse, as the winner in a competition for the prize of 10,000 lire, willed by the Bologna Citizen Cincinnato Baruzzi to cover the expenses of production of a superior and worthy operatic work. The performance that took place in December 1909 at the Teatro Comunale in Bologna brought me a success, marked by stupid and despicable criticisms, generous defense by friends and unknowns, honors and a host of enemies. Having thus made my entrance in triumph upon the Italian musical scene, and placed in contact with the public, music publishers and critics, I could judge with utmost composure the intellectual mediocrity, the mercantile baseness and misoneism which reduce Italian music to a single immutable form of vulgar melodrama, placing Italy in the position of absolute inferiority in the futurist evolution of music among nations. (Francesco Balilla Pratella in his *Manifesto dei Musicisti Futuristi,* issued in Milan on 11 October 1910)

4 DECEMBER 1909

*Il Segreto di Susanna,* one-act musical comedietta, or Intermezzo, by Ermanno WOLF-FERRARI (the horrifying secret being that Suzanne indulged in smoking—a dreadful offense to the morality of the 1900's), with music written in a pleasantly neo-classical Italian style, is produced for the first time in Munich, under the German title *Susannens Geheimnis.*

5 DECEMBER 1909

Ebenezer PROUT, English music theorist, author of detailed and magnificently ponderous tomes dealing with harmony, counterpoint, form and orchestration, himself the composer of symphonic and chamber music in which no academic rule is ever broken, dies in London at the age of seventy-four.

8 DECEMBER 1909

*Le Cœur du Moulin,* "pièce lyrique" in two acts by the aristocratic French composer Déodat DE SÉVERAC (he descended from the kings of Aragon), to a libretto dealing with an 18th-century villager in Languedoc who leaves home and a fiancée in quest of better fortunes and upon return tries to win her back from his friend who in the meantime has honorably married her, but is dissuaded from his treacherous design by the miraculously audible voices emanating from the heart of the local mill (hence the title), to a musical setting in which the intrinsic operatic monotony is relieved by the intercalation of melodic refrains from old French songs, is produced at the Opéra-Comique in Paris.

10 DECEMBER 1909

*Aino,* opera by the Finnish composer Erkki MELARTIN, his only stage work, inspired by an episode in the *Kalevala,* is produced in Helsingfors.

12 DECEMBER 1909

*Kikimora,* fantastic scherzo for orchestra by Anatoly LIADOV, depicting the posthumous pranks of an unbaptized infant girl, in two sections, a poetic *Adagio* wherein the kikimora is incubated in a crystal carriage tended by a cat, in gently swinging feline cradle rhythms, and a demoniacal tritone-laden *Presto,* representing her emergence into a life of mischief, is performed for the first time in St. Petersburg, Alexander Siloti conducting.

153

### 15 DECEMBER 1909

Francisco TÁRREGA, the Spanish guitarist who elevated the guitar to the stature of a classical instrument by writing for it works of formal elegance, dies in Barcelona at the age of fifty-seven.

### 16 DECEMBER 1909

*Duke or Devil*, a farcical opera in one act by the English composer Nicholas Comyn GATTY, dealing with a ruling duke of 15th-century Bologna mistaken for the devil because of his black cloak and nearly put to death, is produced in Manchester.

### 23 DECEMBER 1909

*Das Tal der Liebe*, a musical comedy in three acts by Oskar STRAUS, set in 1770, wherein a stern Prussian Markgraf announces a contest for the best wet nurse for his newly-born son, thus giving a chance for a young bride to join her soldier husband in a valley of love (hence the title), is produced in Vienna.

### 26 DECEMBER 1909

*Den Lille Havfrue*, ballet by the Danish composer Fini Valdemar HENRIQUES, after Hans Christian Andersen's melancholy tale about a little mermaid who had her fishtail bifurcated for the love of a riparian prince but returns to her native aquatic element when she realizes that she can never be more than an unsexual companion, is produced in Copenhagen.

(The ballet provided the inspiration for the famous bronze statue *The Little Mermaid* in Copenhagen harbor, made by the sculptor Edvard Eriksen, for which Ellen Price, the original prima ballerina of the ballet, was the model until she became pregnant, and Eriksen's wife finished the modeling. The statue was installed on a rock in Copenhagen harbor in August 1913. On the night of 25 April 1964, the statue was mysteriously decapitated by vandals, but a new head was cast from the plaster original, with the neck reinforced with an extra layer of bronze to prevent a recurrence of vandalism, and the completed statue reinstalled on 1 June 1964)

### 26 DECEMBER 1909

Kôsçak YAMADA, 23-year-old Japanese composer, conducts in Tokyo the first performance of his oratorio *The Star of Promise*.

*The Star of Promise* is the first attempt to render a dramatic theme musically by a Japanese composer by means of a Japanese orchestra, chorus and soloists. (*Japan Advertiser*, Tokyo, 28 December 1909)

# ❧ 1910 ❧

### 8 JANUARY 1910

*Zigeunerliebe*, operetta in three acts by Franz LEHÁR, wherein a Gypsy girl tempted by a vagrant guitar strummer in a Hungarian camp is saved from perdition through a prophetic dream exposing her lover's future perfidy, richly spangled with Csárdás melorhythms and cymbalom clangs, is performed for the first time in Vienna.

## 10 JANUARY 1910

*Rumanian Symphony* for piano and orchestra by the Paris-educated Rumanian composer Stan GOLESTAN is performed for the first time in Bucharest, with Georges Enesco playing the piano part.

## 13 JANUARY 1910

The first radio broadcast of operatic selections is made from the stage of the Metropolitan Opera House in New York, with Caruso singing arias from *Cavalleria Rusticana* and *Pagliacci*, "trapped and magnified by the dictograph directly from the stage and borne by wireless Hertzian waves."

## 15 JANUARY 1910

*Maia*, lyric drama in three acts by Ruggero LEONCAVALLO, to a melodramatic libretto by his French publisher Paul Choudens, culminating in a fatal encounter between two competitors for Maia's favors on the island of Camargue and her suicide by drowning in the delta of the Rhône River, with an undistinguished musical score palely reminiscent of his striking *Pagliacci*, is produced in Rome, with Pietro Mascagni conducting.

## 17 JANUARY 1910

Fritz Stein conducts in Jena the first performance of the so-called *Jena Symphony* in C major, attributed to BEETHOVEN in an old inscription in the orchestral parts copied by an unknown hand and found in the archives of the College of Music in Jena, in four movements, *Adagio-Allegro vivace, Adagio cantabile, Menuetto* and *Finale*, in a style about 75% Haydn, 20% Mozart and 5% early Beethoven. (The symphony proved to be the work of Beethoven's close contemporary Friedrich Witt when C. Robbins Landon discovered in 1956 the original manuscript signed by Witt)

## 19 JANUARY 1910

*Malbruk*, comic fantasy in three acts by Ruggero LEONCAVALLO after a story from Boccaccio, dealing with a semi-legendary king of Lower Navarra who woos the Damsel of the White Goose but is diverted into a crusade and ends up as the master of a Turkish harem with 49 odalisques, is produced in Rome.

## 22 JANUARY 1910

*Der Schleier der Pierrette*, pantomime in three scenes by the Hungarian composer Ernst von DOHNÁNYI, to the bittersweet story of modern Vienna in terms of a fairy tale by Arthur Schnitzler, is performed for the first time at the Dresden Opera, conducted by Ernst von Schuch.

### 23 JANUARY 1910

*Banadietrich,* opera in three acts by Siegfried WAGNER, to his own libretto wherein a Germanic youth (Banadietrich means Dietrich of Bern in the Wendish language) trades away to a realistically East Prussian devil his true devotion to a swan-white undine Schwanweiss but is redeemed in the end and joins her in the waters of her native river, the score genetically derived from the musical substance of his father Richard Wagner and his grandfather Franz Liszt, exhaling dramatic valor and exuding lyric emotion from the deepest recesses of major ninth-chords, is performed for the first time in Karlsruhe.

When one bears the name of Wagner, a certain degree of diffidence attends one's efforts, and one has greater difficulties to overcome than other musical composers. I hope, however, that in the course of time this distrust of my own efforts will disappear. (Siegfried Wagner's statement at the Vienna production of *Banadietrich* on 15 May 1912)

### 24 JANUARY 1910

*La Glu,* musical drama in four acts by the 31-year-old French composer Gabriel DUPONT, to a highly melodramatic libretto wherein a Parisian cocotte, the Glu, glues herself nefariously to the only son of a pious widowed lady in a heretofore sinless seacoast village in Brittany and in the last act is slain by her with an axe while a local doctor rushing in to lend tardy medical aid is revealed as the Glu's separated husband, set to a suitably emotive musical score in the manner of Dupont's teacher Massenet, with symphonic interludes painting the desolate landscape in bleakly vacuous fifths, is performed for the first time in Nice.

### 3 FEBRUARY 1910

*Endymion's Dream,* cantata by the British mulatto composer Samuel COLERIDGE-TAYLOR, for women's voices, chorus and orchestra, to the words of Keats dealing with the selenophilic infatuation of a Greek youth kissed by the moon goddess, is performed for the first time in Brighton, England.

(Date from *The Times,* London, 4 February 1910. W. C. Berwick Sayers, in his monograph on Coleridge-Taylor, published in 1915, gives the correct date on p. 229, 4 February 1910 on p. 318, and 5 February 1910 on p. 231. The list of works appended to the memoir on Coleridge-Taylor by his widow gives the erroneous 4 February)

### 16 FEBRUARY 1910

*Piemonte,* symphonic suite by Leone SINIGAGLIA, based on authentic tunes of his native Piedmont, in four colorful movements: a countryside idyll with violins and harp sustaining the pastoral mood; a rustic ballet throbbing with delicate vulgarity; a religious intermezzo in which an old chant sacred to the Madonna is heard; and a fast festive fair with piercing trumpets and punctuating drums, is performed for the first time anywhere in Utrecht, Holland.

## 16 FEBRUARY 1910

*La Fête chez Thérèse,* ballet-pantomime by Reynaldo HAHN, Venezuelan-born Parisian composer, to a story from the world of haut monde and haute couture in Paris in the 1840's, where duchesses, seamstresses, grisettes and ballerinas jealously pullulate, with Carlotta Grisi dancing the *Valse de Giselle* by Friedrich BURGMÜLLER (which Adam actually incorporated in his famous ballet created by her in 1841), to a musical score of high hedonistic piquancy, is performed for the first time at the Grand Opéra in Paris.

## 19 FEBRUARY 1910

*Don Quichotte,* "heroic comedy" in five acts by Jules MASSENET, written in a floridly melodious style, wherein Dulcinea disports herself in melismatic coloratura, while guitars, tambourines and castanets strum, jangle and clap, and the harmonies luxuriate in pseudo-Iberian Phrygian cadences, is produced in Monte Carlo, with Chaliapin in the title role providing the tragic idealism absent in the music.

(Date on the printed score is 24 February 1910, but *Le Ménestrel* of 26 February 1910 gives the date 19 February, which is also the date accepted by Loewenberg in his *Annals of Opera*)

## 20 FEBRUARY 1910

At a Colonne concert in Paris, under the direction of Gabriel Pierné, the world première is given of DEBUSSY's *Ibéria,* second of his three orchestral works under the general title *Images* (the first being *Gigues,* the third *Rondes de Printemps*), completed on 25 December 1908, and consisting of three sections evoking the sights, the odors, and the sounds of Spain:

(1) *Par les rues et par les chemins,* animated walk through the Spanish countryside in whole tones peculiar of Debussy's general musical vocabulary (2) *Les Parfums de la nuit,* a stilled *tableau odorant,* with the ethereal oil of divided and muted strings dissolving in the rhythms of nocturnal tambourines and flowery melismas adorned in fragrantly soft harmonies (3) *Le Matin d'un jour de fête,* a joyful festival of Iberian sound, in gentle march time sonorous with chimes and castanets and overflowing with incipient whole-tone scales, reaching an internal climax when the violinists are instructed to hold their instruments under the arms and strum four-part chords like guitar players.

The Iberia of M. Debussy is no longer the Spain of Bizet or Chabrier! What fog! Can there be a typographical error in the program? But surely! The first letter of the title must have fallen out. It should be Siberia! Then everything becomes clear. (René Brancour, *Le Ménestrel,* Paris, 28 June 1913)

## 21 FEBRUARY 1910

*L'Auberge Rouge,* lyric novella in two acts by Jean NOUGÈS, after a story by Balzac dealing with a French soldier stationed at Andernach on the Rhine in 1806 who is accused and summarily executed for a murder he did not commit (the killer was his German companion), to a melodramatically effective score (the murder is illustrated by a series of augmented triads), is performed for the first time in Nice.

21 FEBRUARY 1910

Ernst von DOHNÁNYI, 32-year-old Hungarian romanticist, conducts in Budapest the first performance of his *Suite for Orchestra* in F sharp minor, in four movements:

(1) *Andante con variazioni,* on a modally inflected theme with six amiably confectioned Brahmsophiliac variations (2) *Scherzo,* wafting pulverized Mendelssohnophonic molecules of euphonious dust, with paired harps providing the gossamer environment (3) *Romanza,* a Schumannonymous interlude (4) *Rondo,* a vigorous Brahmsonorous finale.

23 FEBRUARY 1910

Max REGER conducts at Chemnitz the first complete performance of his *Psalm 100* for chorus and orchestra, dedicated to the University of Jena on the occasion of three and a half centuries of its existence.

1 MARCH 1910

The Superior Court of Boston orders the management of the Lenox Hotel to desist from using the name of the Russian prima donna Lydia Lipkovska in the chef Niccolo Sabattini's special "soufflé de fraises à la Lipkovska," charging $2 for it à la carte.

1 MARCH 1910

A century has passed since the birth in Zelazowa Wola, a village near Warsaw, of Fredryk CHOPIN, supreme poet of piano music, originator of a mode of technical expression that in its melismatic complexity borders on polytonality of polar keys in the tritone relationship (as in the B-minor Sonata), atonality (as in the E-minor Prelude) and polyrhythmy (as in *Fantaisie Impromptu*).

(Chopin's baptism certificate of 23 April 1810 gives his date of birth as 22 February 1810, but it is in all probability an error, perhaps through confusion with the day and month of birth of his godfather Fryderyk Skarbek. Chopin's mother always celebrated his birthday on 1 March, and Chopin himself gives this date in his letter of acceptance of membership in the Polish Literary Society in Paris, dated 16 January 1833)

2 MARCH 1910

DEBUSSY conducts in Paris, at the third of the four Concerts de Musique Française, organized by the French publisher Durand, the first performance of *Rondes de Printemps,* third movement of his orchestral suite *Images.*

These are real pictures in which the composer has endeavored to convey aurally the impressions received by the eye. He attempts to blend the two forms of sensory perception in order to intensify them. The melody, with its infinitely varied rhythms, corresponds to the multiplicity of lines in drawing; the orchestra represents a large palette where each instrument supplies its own color. Just as a painter delights in contrasts of colors, in the interplay of light and shade, so the musician takes pleasure in the shock of unexpected dissonances and the fusion of unusual timbres; he wants us to visualize what he intends us to hear, and the pen he holds in his fingers becomes a brush. This is musical impressionism of a very special kind and of a very rare quality. (From a program note by Charles Malherbe written for this concert)

M. Claude Debussy conducted a new *Image* of his suite in three parts. *Rondes de Printemps* is a relatively short composition, luminous and colorful, always free in form and imprecise in its design, according to the familiar procedure of the composer. However, an ingenious use of the popular round "Nous n'irons plus au bois" lends to this piece some cohesion and unity. (J. Jemain, *Le Ménestrel*, Paris, 12 March 1910)

### 6 MARCH 1910

*Symphonie française,* an academically Gallic work by the professorial Théodore DUBOIS, in four movements with allusions to the *Marseillaise* in the Finale, is performed for the first time at the Concerts Colonne in Paris.

### 7 MARCH 1910

*Éros Vainqueur,* lyric fairy tale in three acts by Pierre DE BRÉVILLE, wherein Eros, vagabonding in search of unprobed hearts, kidnaps two out of three well-guarded princesses but releases them after instructing them in the art of love while the third princess dies of emotional inanition, to a semi-Wagnerian demi-Debussyan hemi-Straussian musical score containing a ballet wherein nymphs and aegypans descend from a medieval tapestry in a dream and participate in the action, is produced in Brussels.

### 7 MARCH 1910

*Léone,* lyric drama in four acts by Samuel ROUSSEAU, wherein a Corsican bandit so fascinates the daughter of a local voltigeur that when he is arrested by her father she falls into deep melancholy and dies of vulvar atrophy, set to music in a harmoniously dramatic vein with a patina of Tristanesque chromaticization, is performed posthumously at the Opéra-Comique in Paris, five and a half years after the composer's death. (Rousseau died on 1 October 1904)

### 9 MARCH 1910

Samuel BARBER, American composer whose symphonic, vocal and chamber music is fired by a powerful romantic imagination sustained by a consummate mastery of modern technical means, is born in West Chester, Pennsylvania.

### 11 MARCH 1910

*Malířský Nápad (A Painter's Whim),* one-act opera buffa by the Czech composer Otakar ZICH, dealing with life in Bohemia, is produced in Prague.

### 17 MARCH 1910

*Mese mariano (Mary's month,* i.e. May), one-act opera by Umberto

GIORDANO, to a libretto describing the pathetic life of inmates in an orphan asylum, is performed for the first time in Palermo, Sicily.

### 26 MARCH 1910

*Finnish Fantasy* for orchestra by Alexander GLAZUNOV, derived thematically from authentic Finnish sources and accoutred in sonorous Russian harmonies, is performed for the first time in St. Petersburg.

### 27 MARCH 1910

Franz MIKOREY, Munich composer and conductor of the Opera of Dessau, conducts there the first performance of his musical fable in two acts, *Der König von Samarkand,* wherein a young bridegroom dreams of taking possession of the Samarkand throne through fraud, murder and royal marriage, but awakens happily in his native Caucasus and, having exorcised the sinister side of his nature symbolized by the blackness of the skin of his blameless Negro helper, marries his appointed bride and forgets the illusive Orient.

### 28 MARCH 1910

Édouard COLONNE, French conductor, founder of the renowned series of concerts hospitable to French composers in search of performances, dies in Paris at the age of seventy-one.

### 6 APRIL 1910

A *Somerset Rhapsody* by Gustav HOLST, founded on three folksongs, a pastoral tune played by an oboe, a march with trumpets and drums, and a love song introduced by the cello, ending softly, is performed for the first time in London.

### 10 APRIL 1910

*Madame Sherry,* musical comedy in three acts by the Bohemian-born naturalized American composer Karl HOSCHNA, dealing with a profligate nephew of an eccentric American millionaire who feigns an Irish marriage to induce his ethnically Gaelic uncle to will him his fortune, featuring a vivacious *Dublin Rag,* is produced in Chicago.

### 12 APRIL 1910

*Der Musikant,* a Wagneromantic opera in two acts by Julius BITTNER to his own libretto in which a musician in 1780 loses his favorite coloratura soprano to a petty duke, but quickly finds a less temperamental replacement, is produced in Vienna.

### 13 APRIL 1910

*Arnljot,* opera in three acts by the 43-year-old Swedish composer Wilhelm PETERSON-BERGER, to his own libretto, is produced in Stockholm.

## 13 APRIL 1910

Julius Ferdinand BLÜTHNER, founder of the German piano manufacturing company bearing his name and patent holder of the Aliquot system of stringing in which sympathetic strings are added above the strings in the upper register to increase resonance, dies in Leipzig at the age of eighty-six.

## 14 APRIL 1910

*Boure (The Tempest)*, cantata by the Czech composer Vítězslav NOVÁK, depicting in turbulent Wagnerian tones the sinking of a slave ship in mid-Atlantic with one of the abducted Africans himself abducting the slave trader's woman, is performed for the first time in Brno.

## 15 APRIL 1910

*Daniel Hjört*, opera in five acts by the Finnish composer Selim PALMGREN, to his own libretto in Swedish dealing with the Finnish attack on a Swedish castle in the 16th century complicated by a Swedish officer's love for a rebel daughter of the Finnish chief, is produced in Abo. (First production in the Finnish language took place in Helsinki on 20 February 1929)

## 17 APRIL 1910

Gustav MAHLER makes his first appearance in Paris, conducting the orchestra of Concerts Colonne in a performance of his *Second Symphony*.

## 18 APRIL 1910

*La Dorise,* lyric drama in three acts by Cesare GALEOTTI, 37-year-old Italian composer permanently resident in Paris, with a libretto wherein a chanteuse at a Paris café-concert uses her immoral earnings to bring up her daughter as an honorable bourgeoise and who poisons herself when her double status is disclosed by her former customer, the uncle of her respectable son-in-law, to a musical score turbulent with chromatic harmonies obstructing the flow of Italianate arias, is produced in Brussels.

## 18 APRIL 1910

*Margherita*, opera in four acts by the 37-year-old German composer Alfred BRÜGGEMANN, to a libretto adapted from Goethe's *Faust* and constituting the second part of an unperformed Faustian trilogy, is produced at La Scala in Milan.

## 20 APRIL 1910

At the first concert of the secessionist Société Musicale Indépendante in Paris, founded by a group of dissident members of the academically disposed Société Nationale de Musique, two female infants, Christine Verger, age six, and Germaine Durant, age ten, give the first performance of the original version for piano four hands of Maurice RAVEL's suite *Ma mère l'Oye,* "cinq pièces enfantines":

(1) *Pavane de la Belle au bois dormant,* a gently drawn pastel evoking in the Aeolian mode the dormant belle awaiting in the woods the arrival of her Prince Charming (2) *Petit Poucet,* a lightfooted promenade of Tom Thumb melodiously scattering thematic bread crumbs across the keyboard to guide him on his way back unsuspecting that the birds discanting in melismatic twirls in the treble would pick them up, and completing his promenade on a self-contented third of Picardy in the candidly white key of C major (3) *Laideronnette, Impératrice des pagodes,* wherein the unbeautiful (*laide*) Empress of China pentatonically arrays her china, shaped like male and female pagodas, on the black keys in euphonious tertian, quartal and quintal counterpoint (4) *Les Entretiens de la Belle et de la Bête,* a dialogue in gentle waltz time between the Belle in dulcet treble and the beast in the saturnine bass (5) *Le Jardin féérique,* wherein the dormant belle of the first piece is awakened by her Prince Charming in gladsomely pandiatonic C major, and other characters of Mother Goose join them in quiet jubilation.

### 23 APRIL 1910

Alfredo CASELLA, 26-year-old Italian composer, conducts in Paris a concert of his orchestral works, all performed for the first time: *Second Symphony* in C minor, *Suite* in C major in three movements (*Prelude, Sarabande, Bourrée*) and a symphonic rhapsody entitled simply *Italia,* employing various Sicilian and Neapolitan airs, a lover's exhortation, a lament of a pulmonary sulphur miner, Mario Costa's *Lariula,* Paolo Tosti's *A Marechiare,* and Luigi Denza's perennially popular *Funiculi-Funicula,* glorifying the funicular train of Mt. Vesuvius.

### 23 APRIL 1910

At the Royal Opera of Berlin the world première is given of the three-act Indian opera *Poia* (in a German version) by the 39-year-old American composer Arthur NEVIN, the first opera by an American to be staged in Berlin, and dealing with an American Blackfoot Indian who journeys to the court of the Sun God to cure himself of an evil scar which renders him ineligible for the hand of a beautiful squaw, is made clean in his sleep by the magical intercession of The Four Seasons, but loses his bride who is slain by a rival's arrow aimed at Poia himself, the score strewn with authenticated pentatonic tunes in sterilized Wagnerian harmonies.

(*Poia* had four performances in Berlin; none in the United States, except in excerpts presented by the Pittsburg Symphony Orchestra on 15 January 1906, and at a White House reception on 23 April 1907 in the presence of President Theodore Roosevelt, with the composer at the piano in lieu of an orchestra)

### 23 APRIL 1910

*La Dolorosa,* opera in two acts by the Cuban composer Eduardo SÁNCHEZ DE FUENTES, to a melodramatically religious libretto depicting the symbolic transsubstantiation of an ailing peasant girl into Virgin Mary, is performed for the first time in Havana.

## 1 MAY 1910

*Das Gelöbnis* (*The Pledge*), two-act opera by the Berlin-rooted Java-born Dutch composeress Cornelie van OOSTERZEE (1863–1943), to a libretto dealing with an Italian girl briefly flourishing circa 1800, whose bandit lover kills her rich bridegroom on their wedding night well before the consummation of their marriage, who unwittingly betrays him to the police, and after he is executed joins him in death in his open grave, written in a thoroughly Germanic idiom relieved by sporadic tarantellas, is produced in Weimar.

## 4 MAY 1910

*Le Mariage de Télémaque*, lyrical comedy in five acts by Claude TERRASSE, wherein Ulysses forces his son smitten with adulterous love for Helen of Troy to marry Nausicaa, the princess who had saved Ulysses when he was shipwrecked on her father's island, to a musical score in a candidly Offenbachian vein, is produced at the Opéra-Comique in Paris.

## 9 MAY 1910

Serge KOUSSEVITZKY opens in Tver a month-long tour of the Volga River travelling in a specially chartered steamer, conducting 19 concerts of old and new music in eleven towns, with an orchestra of 65 musicians mostly from the personnel of the Bolshoi Theater of Moscow (where he himself played the double-bass earlier in his career), and Scriabin as composer-soloist in his own *Piano Concerto*.

## 18 MAY 1910

Pauline VIARDOT-GARCÍA, French mezzo-soprano, daughter of the famous Spanish operatic singer and impresario Manuel del Popolo Vicente García, sister of the fabulous Maria Malibran and of the centenarian laryngoscopist Manuel García, wife of the French impresario Louis Viardot whom she married in 1841, and intimate friend of the Russian novelist Turgenev, dies in her native Paris at the age of 88 years and 10 months.

## 21 MAY 1910

*Mendi Mendiyan*, lyric pastorale by the 23-year-old Basque composer José María USANDIZAGA, to a libretto in Spanish dealing veristically with life among the Basques, with a tragic denouement as rural passions collide, is produced in Bilbao.

## 25 MAY 1910

Claude DEBUSSY plays at a concert of the Société Musical Indépendante in Paris a group of pieces from his newly completed first book of piano *Préludes*:

*Danseuses de Delphes,* a sybillic evocation of the Grecian sacred dance through a series of archaically homophonic triadic parallelisms with a strong pedal support for the slow motion of the vestal virgins; *Voiles,* an impressionistic tableau of a congregation of slender sailboats gently balanced in a light breeze on the crest of whole-tone waves in parallel major thirds, with a brief pentatonic interlude providing for black-key glissandos; and *La Cathédrale engloutie,* inspired by an old legend of an Armorican city submerged after a princess, out of suicidal jealousy for her sister's successful romance, lets the enemy open the dykes, the music reverberating with marble echoes over the gothically sustained ostinatos creating a stained-glass texture of pandiatonic mosaics; and *Puck,* a mischievously light Shakespearean scherzo.

### 29 MAY 1910

Mily BALAKIREV, dean of the Russian National School, the most venerable of the Mighty Five, teacher of Rimsky-Korsakov, mentor of Moussorgsky, initiator of the peculiar type of Russian symphonic poem, protagonist of Russian orientalism with its melismatic fiorituras accoutred in opulent harmonies, dies in St. Petersburg at the age of seventy-three.

### 30 MAY 1910

Gabriel PIERNÉ conducts at the Opéra-Comique in Paris the première of his lyric comedy in three acts, *On ne badine pas avec l'amour,* after Alfred de Musset's story of true love that by excess of sensual passion literally kills its object, with a musical score in a fine Gallic manner of harmonious hedonism.

### 4 JUNE 1910

Percy GRAINGER completes the piano version (begun on 19 May 1908) of his dance *Mock Morris,* one of the series of "Room-Music Tit-Bits," to be played at "fast jog-trotting speed." (Dates on Grainger's manuscripts in the British Museum).

No folk-music tune-stuffs at all are used herein. The rhythmic cast of the piece is Morris-like, but neither the build of the tunes nor the general lay-out of the form keep to the Morris dance shape. (Grainger's remarks on the manuscript)

### 8 JUNE 1910

A century has passed since the birth in the Saxon town of Zwickau of Robert SCHUMANN, generator of romantic music in its most subjective form, who was driven into the world of total insanity in his last years of life.

### 25 JUNE 1910

A week after STRAVINSKY's 28th birthday, his first ballet *The Firebird,* "conte dansé en 2 tableaux" completed on 18 May 1910 and dedicated to Rimsky-Korsakov's son Andrei, to a libretto fashioned from a familiar Russian folk tale by Michel Fokine, the balletmaster, wherein Ivan Tsarevitch armed with a magic feather from the flaming plumage of the Firebird liberates his beloved Princess Never-To-Be-Looked-Enough-At Beauty from the enchanted domain of Kashchei the Immortal by breaking the mysterious egg holding the secret of his perennial vitality in its yolk, is produced in a world première by Serge DIAGHILEV's splendorous company, Ballet Russe, at the Grand Opéra in Paris, the coruscating score subdivided into the following tableaux:

(1) *Introduction,* opening with an eerie ostinato within the compass of a tritone, the *diabolus in musica* of medieval musical theology (2) the *Magic Garden of Kashchei,* an orientalistic tonal painting with a striking novel effect of glissandos on natural harmonics in the strings over the range of 12 overtones (3) *Appearance of the Firebird pursued by Ivan Tsarevitch,* a cornucopia of dazzling luminous colors in rhythmic scintillation with a broadly Russian theme for Ivan (4) *Dance of the Firebird,* marked *Allegro rapace* (for the Firebird is of a rapacious nature), with a dramatic precipitation of tritone-pivoted scales over a colonnade of firmly anchored ninth-chords (5) *Capture of the Firebird by Ivan Tsarevitch,* a brief interlude of contrasting character (6) *Supplication of the Firebird,* a poignantly chromaticized plaint embellished with melismatic bird songs, her release and her gift of the magic feather to Ivan in a descending progression of two semitones, a major third, two semitones, and a major third again in tritonal harmonic formation (7) *Appearance of Thirteen Enchanted Princesses,* in a quiet narrative exposition (8) *The Princesses' Game With Golden Apples,* a resilient melo-rhythmic saltation in aurific instrumental sonorities (9) *Sudden Appearance of Ivan Tsarevitch,* an expressively Russian interlude in the Aeolian mode (10) *Round Dance of the Princesses,* a poetic Russian melodic figure canonically treated (11) *Dawn of the New Day* (12) *Magic Carillon,* with paganized chimes in spiralling centripetal and centrifugal intervals (13) *Apparition of the Monster Guardians of Kashchei,* with such abominations as unbaptized female infants—the Kikimoras, midget Russian homunculi—the Boliboshki, bicephalous abortions, etc., accompanied by grossly tritonal brass figures in bleakly homophonic harmonies (14) *Capture of Ivan Tsarevitch* (15) *Entrance of Kashchei the Immortal,* marked by ominous progressions in the lowest bass leading to an explosion of demoniac power in triple forte (16) *Dialogue with Ivan.* (17) *Intercession of the Princesses in Ivan's Behalf,* with futile but melodious entreaties (18) *Appearance of the Firebird* with her appanage of vermillion colors (19) *Dance of Kashchei's Henchmen Bewitched by the Firebird,* pounding discordant tonal groups (20) *Infernal Dance of Kashchei's Kingdom,* a savagely syncopated orgy in triple time with an intervalic thrust of the thematic tritone (21) *Berceuse of the Firebird,* a plumed cadent melodic strain in a minor key (22) *Death of Kashchei,* a monstrously malformed threnody as the egg yolk of his soul oozes out in slowly diverging melodic particles with outer darkness ensuing as the polar tonalities of C and F sharp major approximate a conjunction (23) *Coming Back to Life of Petrified Knights,* a powerful revival of vital forces from their dormant state (24) *Universal Joy* in a hymnal Russian song reaching a stretto and concluding on a coda in asymmetrical septuple time.

### 29 JUNE 1910

Aloys OBRIST, 53-year-old custodian of the Liszt Museum in Weimar, kills the singer Anna Sutter in a fit of jealous passion, and then lays a violent hand upon himself.

### 4 JULY 1910

Louis BOURGAULT-DUCOUDRAY, French composer and enlightened aesthetician, one of the earliest Western theorists to make a first-hand study of non-European music and demand recognition for "all possible modes, old or new, European or exotic," dies in Paris in his 71st year.

## 23 JULY 1910

*A Summer Night,* one-act opera by the English composer George H. CLUTSAM, is produced in London.

## 4 AUGUST 1910

William SCHUMAN, American composer of tense but basically hedonistic music in various genres is born in New York City.

## 17 AUGUST 1910

*Comedy Overture on Negro Themes* by Henry F. GILBERT, an enthusiastic pioneer of autochthonous American music, containing a fugue based on the tune *Old Ship of Zion,* is performed for the first time by the Municipal Symphony Orchestra of New York in an open-air concert in Central Park.

## 21 AUGUST 1910

*Héliogabale,* lyric tragedy in three acts by Déodat DE SÉVERAC, the action taking place during the brief rule (218–222 A.D.) of the profligate Roman Emperor who assumed the name of the Syrian sun-god Elagabalus whom he worshipped and who was slain by his praetorian guard as the Christians whom he persecuted passed by singing Alleluia, with a musical score containing amid operatic banalities some interesting ballet numbers, in the oriental style, and incorporating the twelve instruments (reeds, drums, trumpets) of the Catalan cobla of deep antiquity in the orchestra, is performed for the first time at the Théâtre des Arènes, itself going back to the Roman times, in Béziers.

## 27 AUGUST 1910

*Aura,* first opera by the 37-year-old Italian composer Amilcare ZANELLA, in three acts, after an ancient fable of incarnated atmospheric phenomena, is produced in Pesaro, where Zanella succeeded Mascagni as director of the Liceo Rossini.

## 29 AUGUST 1910

Pietro FLORIDIA, 50-year-old Italian composer who migrated to America in 1904, conducts in Cincinnati the first performance of his grand opera in four acts, *Paoletta,* completed 19 days before its production, commissioned by the City of Cincinnati on the occasion of the Ohio Valley Exposition to a non-Ohioan story of a necromancer infatuated with the daughter of the King of Castile, who drinks from a fountain of youth to woo her but is reduced to his primordial debility when a concave sacred mirror focuses sunrays on his body and shrinks it, whereupon princess Paoletta marries a genuinely youthful don, to an Italianate score of such mellowness as to evoke 48 curtain calls for the singers.

## 31 AUGUST 1910

Pierre AUBRY, French musicologist and paleographer, collector of folksongs and codifier of oriental modes, dies in Dieppe as a result of a fencing accident, at the age of thirty-six.

## 6 SEPTEMBER 1910

Ralph VAUGHAN WILLIAMS conducts in the Gloucester Cathedral in the course of the Gloucester, England, Music Festival, the first performance of his *Fantasia on a Theme by Thomas Tallis*, "father of English Cathedral Music," who flourished in the reign of Elizabeth I, set for double stringed orchestra in homophonically sonorous intermodal progressions antiphonally opposed to a melismatically contrapuntal section, the theme being the third of the eight written in 1567, and characterized as "raging and braying" in a contemporary verse: "The first is meeke, devout to see; the second sad in majesty; the third doth rage and roughly brayeth . . ."

## 12 SEPTEMBER 1910

Two months and five days after his 50th birthday, Gustav MAHLER conducts at the Exposition Concert Hall in Munich the world première of his Eighth Symphony, announced as the Symphony of a Thousand, and indeed employing 1003 performers (146 orchestral players, two mixed choruses of 250 voices each, a children's choir of 350, and seven vocal soloists, with 5 harps, organ, piano, harmonium, mandolin, bells, tam-tam and four kettledrums in the score) set in two parts:

(1) *Veni, creator spiritus*, on a Latin ninth-century hymn for two combined choruses and orchestra, in clear E-flat major, and (2) Concluding Scene from Goethe's *Faust*, conceived as a symphonic poem with chorus, opening in E-flat minor and ending in E-flat major, very diatonic throughout, on a consciously reduced modulatory plan, with a magniloquently sonorous chorale to the philosophical and enigmatic words of Goethe, "All that passes is a parable, all that is unattainable is a true event; the eternal feminine draws us near."

This is the greatest work that I have produced so far, and so unique in content and form that it is impossible to describe it. You must imagine that the Universe itself is set to sound and to song. These are no longer voices of man, but of orbiting planets and suns. (Mahler in a letter to Willem Mengelberg, 1910)

This symphony is a gift to the nation. All my previous works are but preludes to this. In other works there is still present a subjective tragic quality, but this one is a grand dispenser of joy. (Mahler in a conversation with Richard Specht, 1910)

Flames seemed to dart from Mahler as he conducted; a thousand wills obeyed his will. (*Neue Freie Presse*, Vienna, 13 September 1910)

The Damascus blade matched with 1000 fencing spears. (*Frankfurter Zeitung*, 13 September 1910)

Eight trumpeters and 4 trombone players stood up in a row at the top of the platform and blew for all they were worth into the faces of the audience. . . . A faithful

Achates, busy with tinkling triangles, ringing bells and banging big drums, would drop his own work, sprint 20 feet across the platform, never once upsetting a music desk, snatch up a pair of sticks and let loose on the kettledrums. There was also a gentleman who played on a large concert grand piano. He was very industrious. I know it because I saw him. Unfortunately, in the general clamor, none of his notes even got as far as my ear. Max Reger was there and Richard Strauss, who sat in the front of a box and read the piano score—through a lorgnette! (*The Musical Courier*, New York, 28 September 1910)

### 12 SEPTEMBER 1910

Antonio MARTELLO pleads guilty in a New York court to playing a guitar and singing Neapolitan ballads to women in the Bronx, and is sentenced to serve 20 days in the workhouse as a common nuisance.

### 18 SEPTEMBER 1910

Richard STRAUSS issues a declaration asserting that the stipulation in his contracts with opera houses wishing to produce his highly desirable new opera *Der Rosenkavalier* must guarantee the production of his less desirable operas *Salome* and *Elektra* four times annually for ten years is not motivated by financial considerations but by a morally compelling reason to give a composer a fair chance to promote all his works. (The Dresden Opera Company notified Richard Strauss on 7 September 1910 of its refusal to produce *Der Rosenkavalier* on such terms)

### 18 SEPTEMBER 1910

*Liebelei*, opera in three acts by the Czech-born composer Franz NEUMANN, to a play by the Viennese writer Arthur Schnitzler dealing with a pleasant love-let indulged in by a reasonably congenial couple, is produced in Frankfurt in the presence of Schnitzler himself.

### 20 SEPTEMBER 1910

*The Veil*, oratorio by Sir Frederic Hymen COWEN, is performed for the first time at the Cardiff Festival.

### 24 SEPTEMBER 1910

*La Maja de Rumbo*, grand opera by the Spanish composer Emilio SERRANO (1850–1939), dealing with an 18th-century Madrid damsel, liberal in love, charity and hope-giving conduct, is produced at the Teatro Colón in Buenos Aires.

### 25 SEPTEMBER 1910

*Askepot* (*Cinderella*), ballet by the Danish composer Otto MALLING, is performed for the first time in Copenhagen.

## 3 OCTOBER 1910

JAQUES-DALCROZE, creator of eurhythmics, as a revival in a modern form of Grecian gymnopaedia, contributing to musical education through graceful bodily motion in coordinated rhythms, leaves Geneva with fifteen of his best disciples for Hellerau, Germany, to establish an Institute of Eurhythmics there. (Date obtained from the Secretariat of the Dalcroze School in Geneva. See history of the Dalcroze movement in the section LETTERS AND DOCUMENTS)

## 4 OCTOBER 1910

*Der Schneemann,* pantomime by the prodigiously precocious musically mature adolescent Erich Wolfgang KORNGOLD, written by him in piano score at the age of eleven and orchestrated by his teacher Alexander Zemlinsky, to a story wherein Pierrot paints himself white, stands as a snowman in front of the house of Pantalon who keeps his beloved Colombine in durance vile, horrifies him into submission as he suddenly begins to move, and captures the enraptured Colombine, is produced at the Vienna Opera, with Zemlinsky himself conducting.

The music to the pantomime *The Snow Man,* young Korngold wrote as a piano solo when he was eleven years old. . . . When it had received a most favorable reception at some aristocratic houses here, the authorities of the Imperial Opera resolved to have it performed. Till then Dr. Korngold (father of Erich, musical critic at the Vienna *Neue Freie Presse,* successor of Hanslick) had purposely kept a knowledge of his prodigy from the public. Finally he came to the conclusion that he had no right any longer to conceal his son's marvelous achievements. . . . So extraordinary are they that they have been made the subject of theoretical study at the Berlin University, and Professor Arthur Seidl has lectured on them at the Leipzig Conservatoire (Vienna dispatch in the *Musical Standard,* London, 5 November 1910)

## 8 OCTOBER 1910

An exhibition of paintings by Arnold SCHOENBERG, marked by expressionist intensity of geometric forms and opulence of color, opens at the Heller Bookstore in Vienna. (Date from an announcement in the *Neue Freie Presse,* Vienna, 2 October 1910)

What Schoenberg represents in his paintings are not impressions of so-called reality, but its reflections on a higher psychic plane. These paintings are the realizations of completely transcendental phenomena made perceptible through outer senses. (Anton von Webern, *Rheinische Musik- und Theater-Zeitung,* 24 February 1912, reprinted by Willi Reich in *Melos,* January 1969)

When Schoenberg paints he does not intend to produce a "pretty" or an "attractive" picture. Scorning the objective result he seeks only to fix his own subjective "apperception" and therefore needs only such means as appear to him indispensable at the moment. Not every professional painter can boast of such a creative method! In his painting, as in his music, Schoenberg avoids the superfluous, that is, detrimental, and takes the direct path to the essential, that is, necessary. (Wassily Kandinsky, 1912)

### 11 OCTOBER 1910

Francesco Balilla PRATELLA issues in Milan a *Manifesto dei Musicisti Futuristi*, in which he makes an appeal to young composers to desert music schools, conservatories and academies, to combat with assiduous contempt the venal and ignorant critics, to abstain from the participation in any competition that requires payment of fees for admission, to denounce publicly the incompetence of contest juries usually composed of idiots and senile mental defectives, to stay aloof from academic circles, preferring a modest life to rich profits from art for sale, to condemn loathsome Neapolitan ballads and sacred music which has no reason for existence now that faith has declined, and which has become the monopoly of impotent conservatory directors and unordained priests, to exalt all that is original and revolutionary in music, and to regard the insults and the sarcasms of the moribund reactionaries and opportunists as a signal honor. (See complete text in LETTERS AND DOCUMENTS)

### 12 OCTOBER 1910

Max REGER receives the honorary degree Dr. med. from the Faculty of Medicine at the University of Berlin in appreciation of the fact that "the harmoniousness of his music raises the spirits of those stricken with melancholy and heals sick minds."

### 12 OCTOBER 1910

Ralph VAUGHAN WILLIAMS conducts at the Leeds Festival the first performance of his *Sea Symphony (First Symphony)*, scored for soprano, baritone, mixed chorus and orchestra, to texts from poems of Walt Whitman, set to music in an elevated narrative style mirroring the varying aspects of the sea and the human characteristics of the intrepid sea-farers, in four movements: (1) *A Song for All Seas, all Ships, Moderato maestoso* (2) *On the Beach at Night Alone, Largo sostenuto* (3) *The Waves,* a scherzo, *Allegro brillante* (4) *The Explorers, Grave e molto adagio.* (A revised version of the score was first performed in London on 4 February 1913)

### 15 OCTOBER 1910

*Lord Giorgio Byron,* opera in three acts by the 42-year-old Italian composer Luigi Stefano GIARDA, is performed for the first time in Santiago, Chile.

### 20 OCTOBER 1910

*Ivan le Terrible,* opera in three acts by the Bucharest-born French impresario Raoul GUNSBOURG, to his own gory story wherein the depraved Russian ruler orders the daughter of an impenitent boyar dissenter to be deflowered in the presence of her father who then blurts out the terrible secret that she is the tsar's own daughter produced as a result of a violation of the boyar's wife's hospitality sixteen years before, the horrifying revelation followed by the strangling of the girl's fiancé by the tsar's henchmen, her death of a broken heart and the tsar's collapse in the mortal throes of tardy repentance, is produced in Brussels.

## 23 OCTOBER 1910

The Orquesta Sinfónica of Barcelona, Spain, gives its inaugural concert.

## 24 OCTOBER 1910

*Naughty Marietta,* light opera in two acts by Victor HERBERT in which a boyishly exuberant French "Casket Girl" named Marietta, sent to New Orleans in mid-18th century, nearly weds a pirate but ultimately finds her true love in the person of an upright young American captain, offering such musically communicative airs as *Ah, Sweet Mystery of Life!, Tramp, Tramp, Tramp, Naughty Marietta* and the *Italian Street Song,* is performed for the first time in Syracuse, New York.

## 10 NOVEMBER 1910

*Concerto for Violin and Orchestra* by Edward ELGAR, with an enigmatic epigraph from Le Sage's *Gil Blas,* "aquí está encerrada el alma de . . ." in three movements, *Allegro, Andante,* and *Allegro molto,* all in 4/4 time, but in varied moods, from stately contemplation to dignified hedonism, and some novel effects, such as pizzicato tremolando, is performed for the first time in London by Fritz KREISLER to whom the *Concerto* is dedicated, with Elgar himself conducting the London Philharmonic.

## 12 NOVEMBER 1910

Gabriel FAURÉ appears as guest conductor in a concert of his orchestral works in St. Petersburg, on his first visit to Russia.

## 17 NOVEMBER 1910

*Piano Trio* in D major, op. 1, by the 13-year-old Vienna prodigy Erich Wolfgang KORNGOLD, composed between December 1909 and April 1910, marked by a modern quasi-Straussian idiom, is performed for the first time anywhere by the Margulies Trio in New York.

Maybe his papa is trying to bring him up to be a real modern composer, but if he is not, then something ought to be done. If we had a little boy of 12 who preferred writing this sort of music to hearing a good folk tune or going out and playing in the park, we should consult a specialist. (W. J. Henderson, New York *Sun,* 18 November 1910)

## 17 NOVEMBER 1910

*Elinan Surma (Elina's Death),* opera by the Finnish composer Oskar MERIKANTO, is produced in Helsingfors.

## 19 NOVEMBER 1910

*Der Talisman,* opera in four acts by the 44-year-old English composeress Adela MADDISON, is produced in Leipzig.

## 20 NOVEMBER 1910

*Semirama,* lyric tragedy in three acts by Ottorino RESPIGHI, is performed for the first time in Bologna.

### 25 NOVEMBER 1910

*Stella Maris*, opera in three acts by the Belgian composer Alfred KAISER (who changed his name to De Keyser during World War I to dispel the odium attached to the Kaiser) is produced in Düsseldorf in a German version.

### 25 NOVEMBER 1910

*Liturgy of St. John Chrysostom*, for chorus a cappella, by Serge RACHMANINOFF, is performed for the first time in Moscow.

### 30 NOVEMBER 1910

*Macbeth*, the only opera by Ernest BLOCH, composed in 1902, preserving the most essential parts of Shakespeare's tragedy, in an expressively illustrative modernistic idiom, using harsh secundal dissonances to describe the murder, augmented triads and combinative whole-tone chords to express the horror of premonition, naturalistic applosive rhythms to characterize Lady Macbeth's attempts to take the damned spot off her hands, and sinister tritone-laden progressions for the appearance of Banquo's ghost, is produced at the Opéra-Comique in Paris.

New Opera is Called Barbaric—Composer of Macbeth is Accused of Sacrificing Art to Brutal Sincerity (Wireless dispatch published in the New York *Sunday Herald* of 3 December 1910)

This music is an indecipherable rebus, rhythmically as well as tonally, and I wonder how the singers and the orchestra found their way through it. As for the rhythm, it is not only capricious but downright incoherent as a result of incessant changes of meter. Judge for yourself. In one place in the score I find this succession of time signatures: 3/4, 4/4, 3/4, 4/4, 6/4, 4/4; in another I find a measure of 4/4, followed by 5/4, 6/4 and 4/4. What becomes of rhythmic unity, and how can accuracy of performance be secured under such circumstances? As for harmonic progressions, they are no less extraordinary, and one can only qualify them as savage. . . . It is noise for the sake of noise, and the abuse of trumpets would break the sturdiest ear drums. (Arthur Pougin, in *Le Ménestrel*, Paris, 3 December 1910)

### 2 DECEMBER 1910

*Kleider machen Leute*, opera in three acts by Alexander ZEMLINSKY, with a satirical point that all men are created equal, but that different clothes make them unequal in society, is produced in Vienna.

### 4 DECEMBER 1910

Claude DEBUSSY conducts a concert of his works in Budapest.

### 5 DECEMBER 1910

At a student concert of the St. Petersburg Conservatory, 19-year-old Sergei PROKOFIEV conducts the first performance of his symphonic poem *Dreams* and plays his first *Piano Sonata* in F minor.

172

10 DECEMBER 1910

The world première of Puccini's opera in three acts, *La Fanciulla del West,* after a play by David Belasco, *The Girl of the Golden West,* wherein a golden-hearted and brave Western girl, working in a California mining town in 1849, wins the life of her reformed robber-lover from a duty-conscious but love-smitten sheriff in a game of poker during which she produces an extra pair of aces from her stocking, and who subsequently persuades the uncouth but noble-minded miners not to hang him on a tree, finally departing with him sadly singing "addio, mia California," with a musical score full of dramatic progressions of augmented triads and their concomitant whole-tone scales, harmonious pandiatonic sequences and emotionally suspended ninth-chords, including also some velvet-toned Italianate arias and love duets, with the American motives represented by pentatonic tunes and ragtime rhythms, is given at the Metropolitan Opera House in New York, with Arturo Toscanini conducting, and Caruso singing the lover's part.

Great Welcome for New Opera—Brilliant Audience Wildly Applauds Puccini's Girl of the Golden West—Composer, Originator and Conductor Have a Triumph After Each Act—The Opera House Thronged—Ticket Speculators Got Some Seats But Had to Sell Out at Less Than Cost (New York *Times,* 11 December 1910)

An International Premiere—America Proud of The Girl of the Golden West—Under Two Flags, a $22,000 House Riots Over Puccini, the Opera Directors Send a Silver Wreath to the Stage—Caruso Looks and Acts His Best—Emmy Destinn Sings Heroically the Most Powerful Woman's Role in Recent Melodrama—Sheriff Pasquale Amato Shares the Big Scene Where the Composer Gives Native Playwright a Free Hand—Fifty Curtain Calls and a Forest of Flowers Too. (New York *Sun,* 12 December 1910)

The Girl of the Golden West is an apotheosis of the barroom and of gambling. The play caters to a depraved taste, and the music is without any appeal beyond that of emphasizing the meretricious elements in the libretto. Puccini's harmonic scheme is extremely limited and consists of intervals studiously made unconventional and tonal succession arbitrarily distorted to titillate the senses. . . . Of course, there is nothing American about the music. Puccini had no models to go to when he undertook to make music to this American play, for not even the composers who were born in this country have ever written any music different from the music of Europe. (*The Musical Courier,* New York, 14 December 1910)

15 DECEMBER 1910

*Bourgogne,* a symphonic poem by the 26-year-old French composer Edgar Varèse, temporarily residing in Berlin, written in a flamboyantly romantic vein, with some ethnic allusions to folk songs of Bourgogne, is performed for the first time in Berlin, under the direction of Josef Stransky.

Varèse wants to say everything at once, and gets so confused in the process that it is impossible to discover even a single clear idea in this work. (*Signale für die musikalische Welt,* Berlin, 21 December 1910)

15 DECEMBER 1910

*Concerto for Piano and Orchestra* in F minor, op. 114, by Max Reger, in three movements, *Allegro moderato, Largo* and *Allegretto con spirito,* completed on

16 July 1910, and written in a luxuriant romantic manner of high viscosity, is performed for the first time by the Gewandhaus Orchestra in Leipzig, Arthur Nikisch conducting, Frieda Kwast-Hodapp soloist.

The Piano Concerto is another abortion of Reger's Muse degenerated through constant inbreeding. (*Leipzig Tageblatt,* 16 December 1910)

In his latest work, the Piano Concerto, op. 114, Professor, Dr. phil. h. c. and Dr. med. h. c. Max Reger demonstrates that the painful complication of asthmatic invention and dropsical swelling of facture of which he is known to have suffered for a long time, has now become chronic. In the first movement, amid the familiar commotion there stare at us some thematic fragments reminiscent of Brahms, Liszt and Grieg. . . . In the Finale, an insane army of churlish tonality-free chords blunder into a somewhat more amiable kobold of a fugato and trample underfoot a frightened little elf of a melody which becomes somehow entangled in all this. (Arthur Smolian, *Signale für die musikalische Welt,* Berlin, 21 December 1910)

### 28 DECEMBER 1910

*Königskinder,* an operatic version in three acts of incidental music by Engelbert HUMPERDINCK to a play by Ernst Rosmer (pseudonym of the wife of a Munich lawyer, Dr. Max Bernstein, originally produced on 23 January 1897), to a grim Grimm-like fairy tale wherein a goose girl, who is really a royal princess, held in durance vile by a witch, is rescued by a swineherd, who is really a royal prince, but both die in the cold night most piteously when they fail to persuade the authorities that they are indeed of royal blood, to a Wagnerian score of great chromatic intensity, is produced for the first time on any stage at the Metropolitan Opera House in New York.

### 30 DECEMBER 1910

*Le Miracle,* lyric drama by Georges HÜE, to the story of a medieval courtesan who saves a besieged city by bewitching the besieger, poses for a statue of St. Agnes, becomes enamored of the young sculptor, kills an unwelcome suitor, petulantly strikes the statue and falls dead at its feet, whereupon the statue changes miraculously into a real likeness of St. Agnes, is produced at the Grand Opéra in Paris.

# ⚘ *1911* ⚘

### 16 JANUARY 1911

Maurice RAVEL performs at the Société Musicale Indépendante de Paris three piano pieces by Erik SATIE, written in 1888, as an act of homage to (in Ravel's words) "a precursor of genius whose music astounds by its prescience of the modern vocabulary and by the almost prophetic character of its harmonic innovations."

As the Tsar Nicholas II of All the Russias enters the imperial box during a performance of Mussorgsky's opera *Boris Godunov* at the Imperial Opera House in St. Petersburg, the great Russian bass singer Feodor CHALIAPIN, as Boris, in a sudden frenzy of patriotic fervor, falls to his knees and begins to sing *God Save the Tsar.*

You rose from the depths of democracy, and you were to us a symbol of the growing creative forces of that democracy. You have now sullied the name of Chaliapin by the dust on your knees, when you prostrated yourself before the Tsar. (From a letter addressed to Chaliapin by a group of Russian workers)

Let me tell you that my soul and my heart did not take part in what happened on that occasion. I am guilty only on two counts: (1) that I became distracted (2) that I was employed in an organization in which, unfortunately, such surprises as crawling on one's knees are always possible. (From Chaliapin's letter to Maxim Gorky dated July 1911)

### 19 JANUARY 1911

*Knez Ivo od Semberije (Count Ivo of Semberija),* one-act opera by the Serbian composer Isidor BAJIĆ, dealing with a Bosnian patriot who purchases Slav slaves from Turks during the Ottoman domination of Serbia and sets them free, selling even the family icon to raise funds, which shocks his pious mother so much that she dies of a cardiac arrest, is performed for the first time in Belgrade under the direction of the composer.

### 25 JANUARY 1911

*La Vendetta,* lyric drama in three acts by the 35-year-old French romantic opera composer Jean NOUGUÈS, dealing with a bitter family vendetta in Italy and culminating in the murder of a woman who challenged the warring factions, is produced in Marseilles.

### 25 JANUARY 1911

*Poupě (The Bud),* one-act opera by the Czech composer Otakar OSTRČIL, dealing with a neurotically reluctant bride, is produced in Prague.

### 26 JANUARY 1911

*Der Rosenkavalier,* "Komödie für Musik" in three acts by Richard STRAUSS (completed on 26 September 1910; begun on 1 May 1909), full of sophisticated waltzes and ironically sentimental arias, to Hugo von Hofmannsthal's tale placed in 18th-century Vienna, in which a conniving dowager designates her young lover as the bearer of a symbolic silver rose sent from her aging cousin to a young coquette in proposing marriage, with a characteristic reversal of roles as the cavalier of the rose woos and wins her after many a transvestiture (in the third act the Rosenkavalier, a mezzo-soprano, is disguised as a maid thus reverting to her natural sex), the score containing 118 identifiable leitmotivs, according to officious exegetes, is produced at the Dresden Opera, Ernst Schuch conducting.

On the eve of the 28th anniversary of WAGNER's death, his youthful *Symphony in C Major*, written at the age of 19 in a prevalent idiom of early 19th-century music, is published for the first time in Leipzig.

Gustav MAHLER conducts the New York Philharmonic Orchestra for the last time, twelve weeks before his death.

*From Shakespeare*, symphonic suite by the Germanic Czech composer Josef Bohuslav FOERSTER, illustrating five Shakespearean characters in a proleptic prelude and four movements (*Perdita, Viola, Lady Macbeth, Katharine and Petruchio*), is performed for the first time in Prague.

*Natoma*, opera by Victor HERBERT in three acts, dealing with amorous entanglements in the wilds of Spanish California in 1820 wherein an Indian princess, nurturing self-sacrificial love for an American lieutenant, kills the Spanish suitor of the girl he loves and then enters a convent, is performed for the first time in Philadelphia.

*Natoma* Performed—A dull Text Set to Mediocre Music—The Comparative Failure of the First Performance in Philadelphia in Spite of the Able Cast and Thorough Preparation—An Antiquated "Book" Written in Stilted Speech and Silly Verse That Contains Neither Operatic Drama nor Operatic Characters—The Mediocrity and the Dull Commonplace of Mr. Herbert's Music Except Where It Approximates Operetta—Its Undramatic and Untheatrical Quality (Headlines in the Boston *Evening Transcript*, 27 February 1911)

*Aux Étoiles*, the second and last orchestral piece by Henri DUPARC, written in the atmospheric manner of his evocative songs, is performed for the first time at a Lamoureux concert in Paris.

*The Captain's Daughter*, opera in four acts by César CUI, after Pushkin's tale dealing with the peasant rebellion against Catherine the Great (who sings mezzo-soprano), is produced in St. Petersburg.

*The Sacrifice*, opera in three acts by Frederick S. CONVERSE, to his own melo-dramatic libretto, wherein the commander of an invading U.S. detachment becomes deeply enamored of a beauteous señorita in a desecrated Mexican Mission in Southern California in 1846, but lets himself be stabbed to death by an intruding bravo when he realizes that the interloper is his inamorata's prior lover, is produced in Boston.

### 3 MARCH 1911

On the fiftieth anniversary of the liberation of Russian serfs, a cantata by Alexandre GRETCHANINOFF entitled *19 February 1861* (the date of the issuance of the Tsar's manifesto of emancipation, according to old-style calendar) is performed for the first time in St. Petersburg.

### 4 MARCH 1911

*Borislav*, opera in three acts by the Italian-trained 28-year-old Bulgarian composer Georgy ATANASOV, written in a verdantly Verdian manner, and dealing with a medieval Bulgarian commander's patriotic love for the Bulgarian Tsar's daughter, is produced in Sofia.

### 11 MARCH 1911

Francesco Balilla PRATELLA issues in Milan a "Manifesto Tecnico della Musica Futurista" in which he advocates the creation of new music that would synthesize melody and harmony in a chromaticized continuum, confidently predicting the eventual victory for an ideal enharmonic mode to be discovered by true harbingers of the future and a universal emergence of a "futurist melody" similar to an ideal line formed by the "incessant flowering of thousands of ocean waves." (Full text in LETTERS AND DOCUMENTS)

### 11 MARCH 1911

Enrique GRANADOS plays in Barcelona the first performance of his piano suite *Goyescas*, magically congenial translations of Goya's paintings into rhythms and melodies of Spain, and comprising two books of colorfully descriptive pieces: *Los Requiebros, Coloquio en la reja, El Fandango del Candil, Quejas, o la Maja y el Ruisenor, El Amor y la Muerte* and *La Serenada del espectro.*

In *Goyescas*, I tried to convey a personal note, a mixture of bitterness and grace, of rhythm, color and life that are typically Spanish, of a sentiment at once amorous, passionate, dramatic and tragic, such as can be perceived in Goya's works. (Granados quoted by Henri Collet in *Albéniz et Granados*, Paris, 1926)

### 13 MARCH 1911

*The Pink Lady*, operetta by the Belgian-born American composer Ivan CARYLL, dealing with a dandy who takes his sweetheart to a restaurant and there runs into his current fiancée, containing the famous waltz *My Beautiful Lady*, is produced in New York.

## 14 MARCH 1911

*Déjanire,* opera in four acts by Camille SAINT-SAËNS, expanded from incidental music to a tragedy by Louis Gallet (first performed at Béziers on 25 August 1898), dealing with the hapless wife of Hercules induced by the centaur Nessus to give his bloody shirt to Hercules to wear as an aphrodisiac, thus poisoning him, is performed for the first time in its full-fledged operatic form in Monte Carlo.

## 15 MARCH 1911

Alexandre SCRIABIN plays the piano part, with Serge Koussevitzky conducting, in the world première in Moscow of his tremendous symphonic work *Promethée, Poème du Feu,* his fifth symphony, scored for a large orchestra, piano, organ, voices, and a special instrument of light, *Luce,* or *clavier à lumières,* designed to immerse the concert hall in a kaleidoscopic scintillation of multicolored lights, reflecting the inner progress of the music, with the harmonic and melodic content derived from a basic "mystic chord" (C, F-sharp, B-flat, E, A, D), corresponding to the high ethereal primary tones of the harmonic series (1, 45, 7, 5, 27, 9), in a single continuous movement symbolizing five quintessences (Will, Movement, Anxiety, Contemplation, Mystery) in a series of constantly contrasting moods, all furnished with ecstatic expression marks in French:

*Lent, brumeux,* with an oriflamme of French horns announcing a Promethean motto drawn from the "mystic chord," epitomizing the idea of a "creative principle" emerging from a "cosmic mist," clearing the way to the entrance of piano solo marked *impérieux,* exemplifying will-power, followed by a variety of spiritual states and sensual materializations: *voluptueux, presque avec douleur, avec délice, avec un intense désir, avec émotion et ravissement, voilé, mystérieux, avec enthousiasme, limpide, sourd, menaçant, étrange, charmé,* giving rise to a Promethean uplift in the piano part, in a crescendo of esthetic concepts and their emotional incarnation, *soudain très doux et joyeux, avec un effroi contenu, avec défi belliqueux, orageux, avec un splendide éclat, déchirant, comme un cri,* vesuviating in a spasmodic outburst of instrumental colors in thrice triple time, driving to the coda by a cumulative assault, frustrated by sudden relapses into a debilitating softness, indicated by the expression marks, *extatique, étincelant, de plus en plus large, avec un éclat éblouissant, ailé, dansant, flot lumineux, dans un vertige,* accomplishing the mystical synthesis of Self and All and the incorporation of human ideals and cosmic laws into the perfect musical form of a sphere yielding a maximum of volume with a minimum of surface in bright-blue F-sharp major, a color associated with this tonality in Scriabin's chromotonal scheme. (Because of technical difficulties, the part of *Luce* was not included in the performance)

## 20 MARCH 1911

Russia promulgates its first copyright law, extending the protection of composers and authors in all countries previously bound by an international copyright treaty.

## 22 MARCH 1911

*Symphonie antique* by the prime French organist Charles-Marie WIDOR, inspired by the poem of Sophocles written on the night of the Greek victory over the Persians at Salamis in 480 B.C., in four grandiloquent movements, concluding with a choral *Te Deum*, with thematic materials set in Grecian modes, is performed for the first time in Paris.

### 23 MARCH 1911

At a meeting of militant English Suffragettes in Albert Hall in London, a *March of the Women*, written by Ethel SMYTH for the cause, with its main tune derived from an Italian folksong she heard in Abruzzi, is intoned by the Suffragette Choir, aided and abetted by a cornet and organ, to keep them in tune.

### 25 MARCH 1911

Claude DEBUSSY conducts in Paris the orchestral version of his piano suite *Children's Corner* arranged by André CAPLET, and first performed by Caplet in New York a year earlier.

### 29 MARCH 1911

Alexandre GUILMANT, French organist, co-founder with Charles Bordes and Vincent d'Indy of the Schola Cantorum of Paris on 6 June 1894, dies at Meudon at the age of seventy-four.

### 1 APRIL 1911

The word "dodecafonia" is used for the first time to describe synthetic chords of 12 chromatic degrees, in an article by the Italian theorist and composer Domenico ALALEONA, entitled *L'armonia modernissima*, published in *Rivista musicale italiana*, in which he advances the idea of a "neutral" tonality, effected by an "art of stupefaction" by means of consecutive diminished seventh-chords.

### 2 APRIL 1911

In anticipation of a complete ballet performance of *Daphnis et Chloé* by Maurice RAVEL, Gabriel Pierné conducts a Colonne Concert in Paris in the first performance of the first suite drawn from the score, in three sections:

*Nocturne*, set in nebulously quartal harmonies reposing on resonant pedal points while a wordless chorus intones Grecian chants with lips closed, in the first tremor of love as Daphnis meets Chloé; *Interlude*, with ominously piercing fanfares introducing a savage *Danse guerrière* bristling with prickly tritones and asymmetrical rhythms as alien invaders abduct Chloé, who is rescued as a company of fawning fauns fights feral foes to the accompaniment of Pan's panpentatonic panpipes delectably simulated by reedy roulades in the woodwinds.

The score of the first suite from Ravel's *Daphnis et Chloé* has strength, rhythm, brilliance. Voices mingle with the instruments, mysterious and fervid voices. . . . The freedom of form and of texture surpasses imagination. Harmonic and polytonic anarchy here reign supreme, and I must confess that I cannot accept this music without hesitation. (Alfred Bruneau, *Le Matin*, Paris, 3 April 1911)

The *Nocturne*, with its multiple *divisi* of various instrumental groups produces a curious effect of transparence and dreamlike atmosphere; the *Interlude* with its chorus placed backstage sounding with great tenderness, its trumpet calls and an adroitly wrought gradation leading to a barbarically rhythmed *Danse guerrière*, are pages of unusual music which must astonish, attract and please the public. (*Le Ménestrel*, Paris, 2 April 1911)

Ravel's suite from *Daphnis and Cloë* is a series of what the Futurists might call rhythmic pictures. There is no characterization and no drama, but the score pulsates with a life that is now sensitive and subtle, now vigorous and wild. (London *Times*, 3 August 1912)

3 APRIL 1911

Jean SIBELIUS conducts a concert of his music in Helsingfors, including the first performance of his *Fourth Symphony*, his most modernistic work, in four movements:

(1) *Tempo molto moderato, quasi adagio*, opening with brooding somberness in low strings and bassoons in a characteristic Lydian mode accentuating its thematic tritone, leading to a main subject in A minor, and after six dynamic implosions and an interlude for soft strings, vanishing towards a unisonal A (2) *Allegro molto vivace*, maintaining the tritone emphasis, soaring dancingly in ascending strophes towards a claritonal cadence (3) *Il Tempo Largo*, a poetic nocturne with characteristically Sibelian solos of the woodwinds, containing a considerable incidence of whole-tone scales with their concomitant tritones, ending in a pianissimo unison on C (4) *Allegro*, reviewing and reassessing the thematic materials of the previous movements in a tersely brusque manner, with slowly rising dynamics in the strings leading towards a sonorous climax, then subsiding into nothingness and concluding on eight funereal A minor chords in the strings.

6 APRIL 1911

*Mot Nordpolen (To the North Pole)*, opera in three acts by the Norwegian composer Johan HALVORSEN, is produced in Christiania.

7 APRIL 1911

The first performance is given in Warsaw of *Second Symphony* in B-flat major by Karol SZYMANOWSKI, in three long, connected movements:

(1) *Allegro moderato*, in contrapuntal harmonies progressing along disparate paths, with a multiplicity of appoggiatured stresses and constant tonal deviations, reaching telestically for a plagal cadence (2) *Lento*, a chromatically involuted theme with six variations leading to a magistrally projected quintuple fugue (3) *Allegro moderato molto energico*, cyclically reverting to the principal theme of the first movement and, after an eloquent development, concluding on a triumphal tonic chord.

19 APRIL 1911

*Le Spectre de la Rose*, choreographic tableau from a poem by Théophile Gautier, to the music of Carl Maria Weber's *Invitation to the Waltz*, wherein the spectre of the rose, in a sensuously roseate contact with a sleeping maiden vanishes with her dream, is mimed by Nijinsky who performs a leap through the window with a preternatural power of levitation, is produced for the first time by Diaghilev's Ballet Russe in Monte Carlo.

He upsets the law of gravitation. He seems to be painted on the ceiling. He reclines softly in space, he makes a thousand little assaults on the sky, and his dancing has the appearance of beautiful poems written in capital letters. (Jean Cocteau on Nijinski, *Comœdia Illustré*, Paris, 1911)

26 APRIL 1911

The cornerstone of the JAQUES-DALCROZE INSTITUTE is laid at Hellerau-Dresden, the "garden city" of eurhythmic education.

26 APRIL 1911

*La Jota*, lyric opera in two acts by the 34-year-old French composer Raoul LAPARRA, a sequel to his opera *La Habanera*, to his own libretto wherein a young soldier and his fiancée, torn apart by conflicting allegiances during the Aragon-Navarre clash of 1835, are reunited in a ruined church and dance a sanguinary jota in a mortal embrace as a renegade priest monstrously lusting after the bride is nailed by the invading soldiery to a life-size crucifix from which the figure of Christ has been wrested by an explosion, is produced for the first time at the Opéra-Comique in Paris, on the same program with the first performance of *Le Voile du Bonheur*, a lyric scene in two acts by the 40-year-old Charles Pons, to a libretto from a play by the French statesman Georges Clemenceau.

26 APRIL 1911

*Narcisse*, choreographic tone poem to music by Nicolas TCHEREPNIN, portraying in melodious Russian modalities the melancholy tale of Narcissus, infatuated with his own image in the waters and oblivious to the anguished appeals of the forlorn nymph Echo, with the poetic justice of Greek mythology transforming him into a bulbous amaryllidaceous flower with a fluffy corona, while the hapless nymph is reduced to a disembodied sound, is produced by Diaghilev's Ballet Russe in Monte Carlo, with the composer conducting the orchestra.

5 MAY 1911

James BLAND, Negro minstrel composer of the famous song *Carry Me Back to Old Virginny*, dies in Philadelphia at the age of fifty-six.

8 MAY 1911

Two weeks before the scheduled production of Claude DEBUSSY's musical setting of Gabriele d'Annunzio's mystery play *Le Martyre de Saint-Sébastien*, the Archbishop of Paris enjoins Catholics to refrain from attending a spectacle in which Ida Rubinstein, an Israelite, is to take the part of the perforated Saint, an injunction causing many pious customers to ask for refunds of purchased tickets, and the refusal of the critic Camille Bellaigue to review the performance.

In his recent edict, the Archbishop of Paris ill-advisedly attacked our work, with which he is unfamiliar. We wish to express our regret over this strange attitude undeserved by us, and we affirm upon our honor and upon the honor of all who are acquainted with the score and the scenario of *Le Martyre de Saint-Sébastien* that this work is deeply religious in spirit and is the lyric glorification not only of the admirable "athlete of Christ," but of all Christian heroism. (From a joint declaration signed by Gabriele d'Annunzio and Debussy)

## 9 MAY 1911

*Concert des auteurs anonymes,* with the audience playing the game of guessing the names of the composers, is given by the Société Indépendante de Musique in Paris, with the intention of probing the stylistic understanding of cultivated audiences.

| TITLES AND TRUE NAMES OF COMPOSERS | MAJORITY OPINION | OTHER GUESSES |
|---|---|---|
| *1st Vocal Quartet* (Leo Sachs) | Dubois, Sachs | Labey, Charpentier |
| *2nd Vocal Quartet* (Leo Sachs) | Sachs, Schmitt, Debussy | Labey, Chausson, Samazeuilh |
| *3 Poèmes* (Ingelbrecht) | Ingelbrecht, Debussy | Dupin, Philippe, Delage |
| *Valses nobles et sentimentales* (Ravel) | Ravel, Satie Kodály | Blanche Selva, Szántó, Salomon |
| *Poème de pitié* (Mariotte) | Huré, Wurmser, Sachs | Leroux, Chabrier, Roussel, Max d'Ollone |
| *J'aime l'âne* (Fraggi) | Ravel, Koechlin | Botrel, Saint-Saëns, Terrasse, Messager, Bruneau, Vincent d'Indy |
| *Vocal Quartet* (Büsser) | Auber, Saint-Saëns, Hahn | Caussade, Lalo, Pillois, Caplet |
| *Vocal Quartet* (Mignan) | Locard, Duparc, Debussy | Widor, Delage, Gaubert |
| *Deux Rondels* (Wurmser) | Wurmser, Ravel | Madame de Polignac Dalcroze, Dubois |
| *Concert* (Couperin) | Rameau, Casella | Schmitt, Enesco, Dubois |

(Date and table from *Le Courier Musical,* Paris, 15 May 1911, p. 365)

The outcome of this referendum was appalling. Professional critics cautiously abstained from voting, and failed to publish a single line about this concert, which must have been so disconcerting to them. As for the rest of the audience, they naively ascribed works, in which personality of our extreme modernists was clearly reflected, to Mozart, Schumann, Chopin, Gounod, Wagner or Mendelssohn. And not one of those present discerned the hand of Ravel in a succession of waltzes, which bear so clearly Ravel's distinctive imprint. (Émile Vuillermoz, in *Maurice Ravel par quelques-uns de ses familiers*, Paris, 1939. Vuillermoz's memory was inexact, as is apparent from the above chart of guesses, which were not so wide of the mark)

Ravel was in a loge in the midst of a group of society dilettantes who habitually swooned when they heard even a few bars of Ravel's music. Heroically faithful to his oath of a conspirator, the composer of *Valses nobles et sentimentales* had not forewarned them that his unpublished work was included in the program. When they heard this composition played with an imperturbably serious mien by Louis Aubert, the composer's sycophantic companions began to jeer, hoping to give Ravel pleasure by assailing ferociously these "ridiculous pages." Stoically, but no doubt somewhat bitterly, Ravel accepted these remarks in silence. (*ibidem*)

The title *Valses nobles et sentimentales* is a sufficient indication that my intention was to compose a chain of waltzes following the example of Schubert. *Valses nobles et sentimentales* were performed for the first time, amidst protests and booing, at the concert without the names of composers given by the Société Indépendante de Musique. The listeners voted for the authorship of each piece. The paternity of the *Valses* was correctly attributed to me, but by a weak majority. (From Ravel's autobiographical sketch, written in 1928 and published in the memorial Ravel issue of *La Revue Musicale*, Paris, December 1938)

## 17 MAY 1911

Joseph STRANSKY is appointed conductor of the New York Philharmonic Orchestra, succeeding Gustav Mahler.

## 18 MAY 1911

Gustav MAHLER, the last of the great romantic composers of Vienna, who strove to translate his inner spiritual struggles into symphonic works of cosmic grandeur, dies in Vienna at 11:05 in the evening, of heart disease complicated by septic poisoning resulting from inflammation of the throat and pneumonia, 50 days before his 51st birthday.

WORRIED BY NEW YORK WOMEN.—Mahler was taken gravely ill in Paris and went to a sanitarium in Neuilly. When an American correspondent called there on the 4th of May he met Madame Mahler, who said that she attributed her husband's illness to nervous prostration and its consequences caused by his unfortunate relations with the Philharmonic Society of New York. "You cannot imagine," she said, "what he has suffered. In Vienna my husband was all-powerful. Even the Emperor did not dictate to him. But in New York, to his amazement, he had ten women ordering him about like a puppet. He hoped, however, by hard work and success to rid himself of his tormentors. Meanwhile he lost health and strength. Then, after an excursion to Springfield, he contracted angina pectoris. At his last concert in New York, rather than disappoint the public, he conducted while he was in a high fever. (New York *American*, 20 May 1911)

It was generally understood that Mr. Mahler had frequent struggles with the women managers of the New York Philharmonic Orchestra who assembled the large guarantee fund which was needed to cover the deficits of the orchestra. His physical breakdown was said to be the result of these disagreements although this has been denied even by the conductor himself. His wife, however, repeated the charges when it was thought that Mr. Mahler was about to die in a Paris sanitarium. (New York *Sun*, 20 May 1911)

"It is easy to kill a man through witchcraft, provided it be helped out with a little arsenic." So said Voltaire. "Nobody dies of a broken heart," say we, unconvinced when we are not able to find the germ or "bug." There were some expressions of derision when it was reported that Gustav Mahler, late of this city, was dying in Europe of "worry." His wife was the authority for the statement. Mahler, Tchaikovsky, Dvořák and Richard Strauss were the most distinguished men to conduct in our Carnegie Hall. Perhaps if the first had had some amiable peculiarities, if he had used no baton in conducting, or had had a huge family, or had gone to afternoon teas, he would have been more popular, and would be alive today. (Editorial in the New York *Evening Sun*, 20 May 1911)

He was looked upon as a great artist, and possibly he was one, but he failed to convince the people of New York of the fact, and therefore his American career was not a success. . . . In his treatment of the simple melodies of his symphonies (some of them borrowed without acknowledgment) he was utterly inconsiderate of their essence. . . . We cannot see how any of his music can long survive him. (New York *Tribune*, 21 May 1911)

The extremity which plunged us into the deepest mourning, no longer to possess the revered Gustav Mahler, has still left for our lives the imperishable ideal of his art and his living work. (Arnold Schoenberg's inscription on the wreath he brought to Mahler's funeral in Vienna on 21 May 1911)

19 MAY 1911

*L'Heure Espagnole*, one-act opera by Maurice RAVEL, after a play of Franc-Nohain of that name, wherein a vivacious Spanish señora in 18th-century Toledo conceals two of her lovers in the clock cabinets in the shop of her horologist husband, and when they are discovered by him, explains that they are customers interested in the workings of the mechanism and, while he is preoccupied with making a sale, takes a muscular muleteer to her upstairs chamber for an interlude of amours, set to music with horological precision, wherein the tiniest rhythmic wheels transmit melodic motion to the metrical cogs in nicely calculated kinetic impulses, with spacious tertian harmonies integrating in the chord of the 13th, and human voices declaiming in finely inflected prosody imparting the sense of continuous action, is produced at the Opéra-Comique in Paris.

*L'Heure Espagnole* is a curious and peculiar work. Its humor, precious, dry and stiff, does not relax for a single moment. Its characters lack vitality. Their declamation, strangely stressed, compressed and savored, possesses inflections and intervals peculiar to *Pelléas et Mélisande* but it has none of the fluidity, vivacity and suppleness of M. Debussy's musical language. It sounds like *Pelléas* played on a phonograph at a greatly reduced speed. This increases the resemblance of M. Ravel's characters to speaking and singing automatons. Everything is congealed and glacial; all elements are small, minuscule, narrow, foreshortened—the stature, the manner, the gestures, the words themselves and their intonation. They are cabinet puppets, figurines of a music clock. As for musical materials, chord progressions and harmonic subtleties, it is obvious that M. Ravel owes much to M. Debussy. But the soul of his music and of his art is absolutely different. M. Debussy is all sensibility, M. Ravel, all insensibility. (Pierre Lalo, *Le Temps,* Paris, 28 May 1911)

We find ourselves in the presence of pure music in the "chorus of little voices" of the horlogerie, this delectable prelude where the singing soul of familiar objects is harmoniously exhaled, where the whole childish mystery, the secret and distant poetry of minute organisms of steel is enriched by the power of the musical talisman possessed by the suave sorcerer Ravel. (Émile Vuillermoz, *La Revue Musicale,* Paris, 15 June 1911)

### 20 MAY 1911

Two short symphonic pieces by the 38-year-old French composer Déodat DE SÉVERAC, *Fête des Vendanges* and *Danse des Treilles et du Chevalet,* the latter being a ballet number from his opera *Cœur du Moulin,* are performed for the first time at the Société Nationale de Musique in Paris.

### 22 MAY 1911

The world première is given in Paris of *Le Martyre de Saint-Sébastien,* mystery play by Gabriele d'Annunzio, set to music by Claude DEBUSSY, with Ida Rubinstein miming the part of the punctured saint, in five parts:

(1) *The Court of the Lilies,* in which Saint Sebastian sends an arrow into infinity and performs an ecstatic dance on burning coals, accompanied by lambent strings pizzicato and incandescent woodwinds around a median C-sharp (2) *Magic Chamber,* wherein Christian maidens are exquisitely tortured in the Roman Coliseum by parallel augmented triads, with the thematic C-sharp providing a focal rack (3) *The Council of False Gods,* with triadic fanfares announcing a sinister pagan theme, yielding to the Christian tonal center on C-sharp (4) *The Wounded Laurel Tree,* in which the master archer Sebastian becomes a passive target for whole-tone missiles (5) *Paradise,* wherein Sebastian's perforated body is carried away by lamenting women, with the lethal arrows remaining miraculously affixed to the trunk of the laurel tree sacred to Apollo, while the portals of Paradise are thrown wide open as choruses of virgins, Apostles and angels intone reverential chants in Gregorian modalities.

No matter what the opinion of the critics and the public may be of my play, I am convinced that all will recognize in the score of Debussy the most divine source of emotion. (Gabriele d'Annunzio in a summation of the production)

Ida Rubinstein is beneath the level of being merely repellent. She even failed to present a plastic composition of her role. She offered a series of unconnected poses, lacking in continuity. (Henri Bidou, *Journal des Débats,* Paris, 29 May 1911)

Ida Rubinstein makes one think of a miraculously animated stained-glass window whose image is full of immobile memory, mute, translucid and sacred. (Jean Cocteau, *Comœdia,* Paris. 1 June 1911)

Debussy's score is characteristic in its expression of religious respect, discretion, mystic contemplation. It seems that it disappointed certain "Debussyites." They expected infinite subtleties of nuance, curious sonorous refinements, morbid search for rare effects. But Debussy is not a slave to formula. His style is always the same, but here it is amplified, matured, ennobled. It expands gloriously in the orchestra, flows in powerful waves in the voices. (Special issue of *Le Théâtre,* Paris, June 1911)

*Le Martyre de Saint-Sébastien* represents barbarism, all the more dangerous because it wears the Mediterranean mask of beauty. (Henri Ghéon, *Nouvelle Revue française,* Paris, July, 1911)

## 24 MAY 1911

Edward ELGAR conducts at the London Music Festival the first performance of his *Second Symphony* in E-flat major, dedicated "to the memory of His Late Majesty King Edward VII" and consisting of four movements:

(1) *Allegro vivace e nobilmente,* eloquently Brahmsogenic in its contrapuntal rigor, vigor and fervent nobility, with a brace of vivacious harps providing a confection of dulcet arpeggios (2) *Larghetto,* a solemn march punctuated by mortuary strokes of the bass drum, gradually rising to the altitude of predictable grandeur "nobilmente e semplice" (3) *Rondo—Presto,* in an invigorating triple measure (4) *Moderato e maestoso,* arriving through a series of well-equilibrated climaxes to a soft finish.

## 24 MAY 1911

Granville BANTOCK conducts in Glasgow the first performance of his symphonic poem *Dante and Beatrice,* opening with three bars solo on three kettledrums, then embarking on a romantically flowing course in Lisztogenic harmonies towards a pianissimo conclusion.

## 24 MAY 1911

*Americanesque,* a symphonic movement by Henry F. GILBERT, based on three Negro minstrel tunes, is performed for the first time at a concert of the Boston Pops.

Numerous scraps of melody and of rhythm are at present drifting about in the musical atmosphere of America. Without inquiring too closely into their origin, I have tried to bind a few such scraps together into an art form. It may easily be said: that is not necessarily American music which merely uses American tunes as themes on which to build. But America itself was not discovered unpremeditatively. Its ultimate discovery was the result of many attempts. So it will undoubtedly be with American music. And when real American music does arrive, it will be the result of many attempts to write it, each of which considered by itself may be far afield, but all of which, taken together, will form the soil from which it must spring. (From Gilbert's statement, quoted in *Musical America,* New York, 3 June 1911)

## 29 MAY 1911

Sir William S. GILBERT, the satirical disestablishmentarian whose marvelously versified lines in the comic operas of the unheavenly twins Gilbert & Sullivan poked irreverent fun at the most formidably dignified and impregnable Victorian institutions, including the House of the Lords and even Windsor Castle itself, dies at the age of 74 of a cardiac syncope induced by an excessive exertion in assisting an inexpert girl swimmer in the artificial lake on his estate in Harrow Weald, Middlesex.

### 2 JUNE 1911

*Isabeau,* opera in three acts by Pietro MASCAGNI, to a libretto based on a modified version of the famous horseback ride of the medieval Lady Godiva, wherein the daughter of a tyrannical feudal lord parades through town mounted on a white horse completely naked to protest against being forced into a physically and morally abhorrent marriage, and when a fervent swain who throws roses on her unclad figure from a balcony is condemned to death at the stake, leaps into the flames herself on a sudden impulse, set to music full of incandescent Italianate emotionalism, is produced at the Teatro Colón in Buenos Aires.

We intended to have Isabeau appear naked, but not every soprano would consent to this. Besides, she might catch a cold. (Mascagni in an interview with an American correspondent in November 1911)

On his arrival in Buenos Aires, Mascagni was met at the pier by a crowd of 50,000 people. Women threw flowers at him, and he threw kisses in return—another portable commodity no Italian composer or prima donna can afford to travel without. Seventy-five banquets were arranged in his honor. "If my Isabeau is a success, I am a dead man—dead of indigestion" was Mascagni's despairing cry. (*Musical America,* New York, July 1911)

### 6 JUNE 1911

Henry HADLEY conducts at the Norfolk, Connecticut, Music Festival the world première of his *Fourth Symphony,* subtitled *North, East, South, West,* wherein the North blows arctic blasts in brass while frigid strings moan, the Orient is lavish with exotic flutes, the American South fiddles away in ragtime rhythms, and the West exhibits a parade of pentatonic Indians attired in Wagneromorphic augmented triads.

### 13 JUNE 1911

*Silence,* a romantic symphonic poem by the 30-year-old Russian composer Nicolai MIASKOVSKY, inspired by the poetry of Edgar Allan Poe, is performed for the first time in Moscow. (Composition completed on 20 February 1910; date communicated by the composer)

### 13 JUNE 1911

Four days before Igor STRAVINSKY's 29th birthday, his ballet *Pétrouchka* (completed by him in Rome on 26 May 1911) glorifying the pathetic Russian puppet (Pétrouchka is the French spelling of the rustic Russian diminutive of Peter, Petrushka), subtitled "Scènes burlesques en 4 tableaux," to the scenario of Alexandre Benois in collaboration with Stravinsky himself, is produced by Serge Diaghilev's Ballet Russe at the Théâtre du Châtelet in Paris, with Pétrouchka mimed by Nijinsky, and the orchestra conducted by Pierre Monteux.

BRIGHT WINTER DAY IN ADMIRALTY SQUARE IN ST. PETERSBURG IN THE 1830's. At the height of Shrovetide, a puppeteer of an oriental cast of countenance presents an exhibition of his animated puppets, Pétrouchka, a Ballerina and a Moor, who perform a frenetic dance before an astounded public. The puppeteer's art imbues the puppets with the sentiments and passions of real people. Pétrouchka is so strongly endowed with these qualities that he feels more deeply than the Ballerina and the Moor. He bitterly resents the cruelty of the puppeteer, and his own subjection to him, his separation from the outside world, his ungainly and ludicrous appearance. He seeks solace in his love for the Ballerina, and he imagines that in her heart she reciprocates his sentiments, while in reality she is frightened by his strange behavior and avoids him. The life of the stupid and malevolent Moor presents a complete contrast to Pétrouchka's existence. The Ballerina likes the Moor and seeks to allure him in various ways. She finally succeeds, but Pétrouchka is furiously jealous and interrupts their rendezvous. The Moor, enraged by the intrusion, throws him out. The gaiety of the fair reaches its height. A merchant makes merry with Gypsy girls and throws coins to the crowd; the coachmen of the court dance with fashionably attired nurses; an animal trainer enters with a dancing bear; a band of maskers appears and the crowd follows them in a wild dance. At the climactic moment, screams are heard from the theater booth. The contest between the Moor and Pétrouchka reaches its critical point. The animated puppets run out into the street. The Moor cuts Pétrouchka with his saber, and he dies pitifully in the snow amid the crowd of celebrants. The puppeteer is summoned by a guard to calm the crowd. At his hands Pétrouchka becomes once more a puppet. The crowd sees that his broken skull is made of wood and his torso is filled with sawdust, and disperses. But the affair is not over for the wily puppeteer. To his horror, the ghost of Pétrouchka appears over his booth making threatening gestures at his tormentor and mocks the people who believed in his magic tricks. (Translation by Nicolas Slonimsky from the Russian text of the scenario printed in the score)

FIRST SCENE: *Popular Festivities at Shrovetide Fair,* with the thematic four notes D-E-G-A dominating the scene and establishing the elements of the tonic (D-A) and the dominant (E-G) in a cardiac diastolic-systolic accordion-like dominant-tonic pulsation within the triadic spectrum of D major. *Intoxicated Revelers Pass Dancingly,* in consecutive triads, in inebriated duple time. *The Old Man of the Fair* entertains the crowd from his theater booth in asymmetrically propulsive 5/8 time within a heavily accented Dorian mode. *Organ Grinder and a Street Dancer,* marking time with a triangle, presently competing with another street dancer singing a sentimental romance. *Gay Revelers Return,* recapitulating the accordion music in consecutive triads, in constantly changing meters of 2/8, 3/8, 4/8 and 5/8 time. *The Puppeteer Plays the Flute,* wherein Pétrouchka, the Moor and the Ballerina come to life as the puppeteer touches them with his flute during the *fermate* of a luxuriant cadenza, while *flautando* violins, inwardly spiralling within a narrow compass produce a highly concentrated series of 12 different notes out of a group of 14, canonically distributed in sequential cellular figures. *Russian Dance,* with Pétrouchka, the Moor and the Ballerina gloriously bursting out into an overwhelmingly vitalistic symmetric step in accordion-like dominant-tonic pulsations rooted in a deep dominant pedal G, the piano prancing, leaping and thumping pandiatonically on white keys, the dance presently modulating up a whole tone, producing some acidulated accidentals and dashing off a fistful of Russian refrains before returning to pandiatonically embroidered C major festivities and ending on a tonic chord enriched by a major sixth.

Second Scene: *At Pétrouchka's,* a torturous succession of spasmodic outcries, during which a bitonal chord combining C major and F-sharp major is outlined in closely overlapping arpeggios in the paired clarinets and in the piano cadenza, constituting the earliest use in music history of overt bitonality of two major triads whose tonics are related by a tritone. *Adagietto,* wailing in spiral convolutions as Pétrouchka's unrequited love for the Ballerina drives him to distraction, presently erupting in furibund malediction of bitonally copulated muted trumpets and muted cornets, vociferating imprecations in the top register of a maddened clarinet, and finally collapsing on a fatalistic plagal cadence.

Third Scene: *At the Moor's,* wherein the Moor, attired in a sumptuous oriental gown, juggles coconuts to exotically ornate susurrations, presently joined by the Ballerina introduced by a flourish on a cornet, whereupon they indulge in a hypersentimental display of ostentatious pseudo-vulgarity to a stylized salon waltz. *Appearance of Pétrouchka and His Quarrel with the Moor,* with Pétrouchka restraining his desperation in depressing minor arpeggios in the muted trumpets, growing into open conflict at the ominous entrance of bitonally arpeggiated trombones, causing the Ballerina to faint.

Fourth Scene: *Popular Festivities at Shrovetide,* returning to the initial merry-making, with the four principal thematic tones D-E-G-A again forming the dominant-tonic complex suggesting the diastolic-systolic accordion rhythms. *Dance of the Nurses,* with their sentimental singing of the Russian urban tunes "Down the Street" and "Oh, my gates, my brand-new gates" in stimulatingly discordant harmonies. *Muzhik with a Dancing Bear,* lumbering to the accompaniment of a ponderous tuba in whole-tone progressions within the compass of a tritone. *A Merchant Carousing,* squeezing a gay accordion with two Gypsy girls. *Dance of the Coachmen and Stable Boys,* accentuated by heavy brass in a Mixolydian mode and crude syncopation. *Dance of Nurses and Coachmen,* with sentimental ballad tunes tenderly nursed against the rudely masculine encroachments of the male menials. *The Maskers,* in an animated asymmetrical march movement, leading to uninhibited revelry in 5/8 time. *General Dance,* once more returning to the spirit of the initial scene, with its thematic 4-note motto, while foreboding chromatics rise from the depths presaging disaster, as Pétrouchka runs out of the theater booth screaming bitonally in his attempt to evade the pursuing Moor, who overtakes him and smites him down with his Ottoman scimitar, cracking Pétrouchka's skull to the accompaniment of a dull thud of a tambourine dropped on the floor in the orchestra pit, and followed by a stifled bitonal spasm of the piccolos. *Pétrouchka's Death,* as sawdust oozes out of his wooden head to a pathetic dirge of a dulcet clarinet and a dolorous bassoon, expiring in residual bitonalities; the puppeteer appears and shakes Pétrouchka to the shivering sound of *spiccato* violins, and, as the crowd disperses, drags the cadaver away, but flees in horror when Pétrouchka's ghost materializes over the theater booth and thumbs his nose in a caducous tritone.

In my unbounded admiration for the unquestionable genius of Stravinsky's music, I was quite willing to minimize my own part in the creation of *Pétrouchka.* The subject of the ballet was entirely Stravinsky's idea, and I only helped him to organize it in a concrete dramatic form. But the libretto, the cast of characters, the plot and the dénouement of the action, as well as a number of other details, were almost wholly mine. My share in the production, however, seems trivial in comparison with Stravinsky's music. I do not know a single work which flows in such an uninterrupted current (or rather in continuous cascades, jets and rivulets) as this. The collision of Pétrouchka's lonely soul with the mass of humanity is linked and intertwined with a sense of profound inevitability, and therein lies its tragic quality. All this does not follow from the words of the scenario but from the essence of the music itself. In fact, it is quite impossible to translate this drama into words; its meaning can be expressed only in music. When at a rehearsal Stravinsky asked me who should be listed as the author of *Pétrouchka*, I replied without a moment's hesitation, "You, of course." Stravinsky objected to this verdict and insisted that I should be named as the actual author of the libretto. Our *combat de générosité* was resolved by putting both our names on the program as co-authors, but I succeeded in having Stravinsky's name placed first, despite my alphabetical precedence. Still, my name appears twice in the score, because Stravinsky decided to dedicate *Pétrouchka* to me, which touched me infinitely . . . From my earliest childhood I carried the vivid memories of the riotous turmoil and merrymaking of the "plain people" of St. Petersburg at the Shrovetide, the peepshows and the excitement of the street fair, where my friends used to come "to learn what Russia really is like." These unforgettable scenes of a vanishing world remain dear and near to me in many ways. Some will say that these memories are colored by the remoteness of my childhood, and that in reality it was just dirt, brawling and lust. Naturally, these street fairs were not idyllic events conforming with the bittersweet ideals of virtue so dear to our temperance societies. But no matter how much drunkenness, how much crudity there was in these scenes, the street life had its own rights, and set its own rules of conduct and its own code of decency. (Alexandre Benois, *Rech*, St. Petersburg, 17 August 1911)

*Pétrouchka* is a marvel. The scenario of these "scènes burlesques" is of no consequence. The important thing is what the composer, co-author with Benois of this scenario, has retained of it. It does not seem possible to achieve a stronger, richer, and more intense evocation of the story. It is simply astonishing. Apart from an abundance of musical themes, original and "classical" and a profusion of fantastic rhythms, Igor Stravinsky's orchestral scoring is extraordinary. Instrumental timbres flow in a stream in a most novel fashion. These sonorities engender among the audience a sense of inexpressible exhilaration. Not a single measure remains indifferent. And what boldness in the handling of the instruments! What eloquence! What life! What youthfulness! (*Comœdia*, Paris, 14 June 1911)

### 14 JUNE 1911

Johan SVENDSEN, Norwegian composer of romantic music with ingratiating Scandinavian inflections, including the ubiquitous *Romance* for violin, dies in Copenhagen, where he was court conductor, at the age of seventy.

### 22 JUNE 1911

At the conclusion of the coronation of King George V and Queen Mary, Edward ELGAR's *Coronation March,* expressly written for the occasion, is performed for the first time.

### 1 JULY 1911

Arnold SCHOENBERG completes in Vienna his significant pedagogical work, *Harmonielehre,* dedicated to the memory of Gustav Mahler.

No art has been so hindered in its development by its teachers as music. For no one watches more jealously over his property than that man who knows that, strictly speaking, it does not belong to him. (From the opening chapter of *Harmonielehre.*)

## 2 JULY 1911

Felix Mottl, Austrian conductor whose knowledgeable devotion to Wagner (he took part in the preparatory work of the first Wagner Festival in Bayreuth) elevated him to the highest rank among conductors of Wagner's music dramas and whose congenial orchestral transcriptions of ballet music by Lully, Rameau, Grétry and Gluck have contributed greatly to the popularity of these works, dies in Munich at the age of fifty-four.

## 7 JULY 1911

Gian Carlo Menotti, composer of expertly made operatic melodramas to his own librettos in the English language, is born in Cadegliano, Italy. (He has retained faithfully his Italian citizenship during his long and successful career in America.)

## 19 JULY 1911

Anton von Webern composes in Vienna the shortest piece of orchestral literature, the fourth of his *Five Pieces for Orchestra*, op. 10, scored for clarinet, trumpet, trombone, mandolin, celesta, harp, small drum, violin and viola, containing 6 1/3 measures in 3/4 time lasting 19 seconds according to the metronome mark. (The date of composition of No. 1 of the *Five Pieces* is 28 June 1911; of No. 2, 13 September 1913; of No. 3, 8 September 1913; of No. 5, 6 October 1913. All these dates communicated by Anton von Webern himself in a personal letter to the author)

## 1 AUGUST 1911

*Autumn,* symphonic tableau by 20-year-old Sergei Prokofiev, is performed for the first time in Moscow.

## 5 AUGUST 1911

A century has passed since the birth in Metz of Ambroise Thomas, French composer of the Gallic operatic classic *Mignon* and of other mellifluous music for the stage.

## 27 AUGUST 1911

Three centuries have elapsed since the death in Madrid of Tomás Luis de Victoria, great Spanish composer of the Renaissance, whose masses, motets, hymns, psalms, antiphons, canticles, and other sacred vocal works are, in grandeur, spiritual elevation, and polyphonic virtuosity, all but equal to the sublime creations of his contemporary Palestrina.

## 25 SEPTEMBER 1911

*The Little Millionaire,* musical comedy with book, lyrics and music by George M. Cohan, dealing with the predicament of an heir to a fortune who has to make sure that his fiancée loves him for his physical and mental distinctions and not for his gold, is produced and staged by George M. Cohan at the Cohan Theater in New York, with George M. Cohan starring in the title role.

### 14 OCTOBER 1911

*Conchita*, opera in four acts by Riccardo ZANDONAI, written to a story adapted from the erotic novella, *La Femme et le Pantin* by Pierre Louÿs, in which a Carmen-like girl, employed in a Seville cigar factory, taunts her wealthy admirer into a rage of unconsummated passion, is produced in Milan.

### 22 OCTOBER 1911

A century has passed since the birth of Franz LISZT, titanic pianist and fantastically productive composer whose expansive romanticism bore a seed of futurity in the bold projections of his musical speculations revealed in the polytonal and atonal usages in his posthumous keyboard pieces.

### 1 NOVEMBER 1911

At a benefit performance of Massenet's opera *Cendrillon* by the Chicago Opera Company, Mary GARDEN, the Prince Charming of the cast, sells kisses to young men for charity.

Mary Garden's kiss lasts a long time and makes the world look sort of different. Mary looks squarely in your eyes, and, believe me, she is some kisser! (From a testimonial report by "Tough" Darnum, one of the seven men who bought Mary Garden's kisses)

### 4 NOVEMBER 1911

E. H. CRUMP is reelected Mayor of Memphis, Tennessee, after an arduous campaign, helped along by a song *Mr. Crump* especially composed for him by the Negro balladeer W. C. Handy, and later renamed *Memphis Blues*, which created a new style of American popular music technically distinguished by a flatted "blue" seventh and a flatted "blue" third in a major key.

(The following statement from Mr. Crump's secretary obtained by Mrs. Frances Fink at the author's request seems to contradict the story of *Memphis Blues*: "Mr. Crump did not use Handy's song in either of his elections. The song was written a couple of years after Mr. Crump was elected Mayor the first time. . . . He was elected the second time in November 1911, and again in November 1915. I do not think Handy wrote the song as a campaign song, but simply used Mr. Crump's name in the composition of same." But from Mr. W. C. Handy comes a rejoinder: "I did not write the *Memphis Blues* as a campaign song for Mr. Crump but wrote *Mr. Crump* as a campaign song for Mr. Crump and then changed the title for publication to the *Memphis Blues* and published it in 1912 myself . . . I then followed that with the *St. Louis Blues*, copyrighted on 14 September 1914")

### 4 NOVEMBER 1911

*Symphony in G* by Walford DAVIES, renowned English musical educationist, is performed for the first time in London. (The originally scheduled performance on 15 May 1911, with Arthur Nikisch conducting the London Symphony Orchestra, was cancelled)

## 9 NOVEMBER 1911

*Der Bergsee,* Wagneromantic opera in two acts with a prelude by the Austrian composer Julius BITTNER, to his own libretto in the Austrian dialect, from the time of peasant uprisings in the Austrial Tyrol, wherein a frustrated maiden crushes the wall of a dam with an axe to drown her uncertain lover and herself in a flood of augmented triads, is performed for the first time at the Vienna Opera.

## 11 NOVEMBER 1911

The AEROPHOR, a tone-sustaining instrument, consisting of a rubber bulb with a tube appliance, enabling the player on a wind instrument to hold a note indefinitely, is given its first demonstration by the inventor, Bernard Samuels, in Berlin.

## 19 NOVEMBER 1911

*Sixth Symphony* by the Swiss composer Hans HUBER is performed for the first time in Basel.

## 20 NOVEMBER 1911

*Thor kører til Jotunheim (Thor Drives to Jotunheim Mountains),* orchestral fantasy by the Danish composer Hakon BÖRRESEN, his first and most successful work, written at the age of 19 in 1895, reaches its belated first performance in Copenhagen.

## 20 NOVEMBER 1911

Six months and two days after the death of Gustav MAHLER, Bruno Walter conducts in Munich the first performance of his pantheistic song-symphony *Das Lied von der Erde,* in six sections, scored for tenor, contralto and orchestra, to texts of a German translation of 8th-century Chinese poems, with the basic tetraphonic motto, A,G,E,C, undergoing motivic metamorphosis through augmentation, diminution, inversion, rhythmic alteration, permutation and, in the final chord integration into a vertical complex rooted in deep C:

(1) *Das Trinklied vom Jammer der Erde (Drinking Song of Earthly Anguish),* for tenor and orchestra with a pentatonic horn call of the ageless Song of the Earth intoned in fatalistic A minor, achieving antinomial catharsis by enharmonic equivocation of modal structure (2) *Der Einsame im Herbst (Solitary Soul in Autumn),* for contralto and orchestra, a resigned plaint in philosophical D minor with caducous cadences in the Phrygian mode (3) *Von der Jugend (Of Youth),* for tenor and orchestra, an exhilarating interlude set in optimistic B-flat major mitigated by the pentatonicism of its melodic structure to avoid the inexorable finality of the leading tone (4) *Von der Schönheit (Of Beauty)* for contralto and orchestra, set in mundane G major with pentatonic melos outlined in the thematic pattern E, G, A, B, D, in the orchestra (5) *Der Trunkene im Frühling (The Drunkard in Springtime),* for tenor and orchestra, a bitter-sweet soliloquy in ostentatiously cheerful A major, descriptive of the dual intoxication by

wine and singing birds (6) *Der Abschied* (*The Farewell*), for contralto and orchestra, a symphonic concept abounding in instrumental flourishes, melismatically centered on the pessimistic C minor, and slowly progressing in the direction of the redemptive tonality of C major, with the ultimate 90° turn from the horizontal melody to the vertical harmony in the chord of the unresolved tonic sixth.

"Is it safe to have this music performed? Will not the people, after hearing my work, go out in the streets and kill themselves?" (Mahler's question reportedly addressed to a friend.)

### 23 NOVEMBER 1911

*Kuhreigen*, seventh opera by the Austrian composer Wilhelm KIENZL, dealing with a Swiss soldier in the service of Louis XVI, condemned to death for singing the associatively subversive nationalistic Alpine air *Kuhreigen*, but pardoned thanks to the intercession of a humanistic marquise (to whom he subsequently offers consolation after the French Revolution, when she herself goes to the guillotine), is produced in Vienna.

### 24 NOVEMBER 1911

*Eva*, operetta in three acts by Franz LEHÁR, to a story of a Paris factory girl who acquires sophistication from an experienced soubrette, fascinates a grand duke and eventually marries her young industrialist employer, is produced in Vienna.

### 27 NOVEMBER 1911

*Esvelia*, the first opera in one act, by the 27-year-old Italian composer Iginio ROBBIANI, after a poem by Heinrich Heine, is performed for the first time in Rome.

### 6 DECEMBER 1911

*A Tale of Old Japan*, an orientalistic cantata by Samuel COLERIDGE-TAYLOR, employing a simulacrum of pentatonic modalities of Japanese court dances, is performed for the first time in London.

### 8 DECEMBER 1911

The San Francisco Symphony Orchestra, established as a "permanent orchestral body along the lines of those maintained by the larger cities of Europe and the East," opens its first season of six concerts, in a program of works by Wagner, Tchaikovsky, Haydn and Liszt, under the direction of Henry Hadley, the first American to head a major symphony orchestra.

### 14 DECEMBER 1911

*Schauspiel Ouvertüre*, op. 4, by the remarkably precocious 14-year-old Austrian composer Erich Wolfgang KORNGOLD, whose Mozartomorphic middle name was given to him by his father, eminent Vienna music critic, is performed for the first time at the prestigious Gewandhaus (so named because it was originally a warehouse), in Leipzig, under the direction of Arthur Nikisch.

Mozart and Korngold are two geniuses who began to write music in their earliest childhood. Why does Mozart spontaneously lisp music in the simple idiom of his own day, while Korngold lisps in the complex idiom of his? Korngold can hardly have derived his harmonic system from the study of other composers, for in what composer's work could he have found it? It is the spontaneous product of a most subtly organized brain that at the first span embraces practically all we know and feel today in the way of harmonic relation. (Ernest Newman, in *The Nation*, London, quoted in *Musical America*, 5 October 1912)

Korngold's *Overture* deserves an honorable place in the Museum of Infant Prodigies. If Master Korngold could make such a noise at fourteen, what will he not do when he is twenty-eight? The thought is appalling. (Philip Hale, Boston *Herald*, 16 February 1914)

## 15 DECEMBER 1911

*Bérénice*, "tragedy in music" in three acts by Albéric MAGNARD, to his own libretto fashioned from Racine's play about the Jewish concubine of the Roman Emperor Titus, who, like the legendary Egyptian queen of the same name, surrenders her luxuriant tresses to Aphrodite in exchange for an aphrodisiac potion she desperately needs to lure back an errant lover, set to music, according to Magnard's own admission, "dans le style wagnérien," but containing some enticing illustrative inventions such as canons in the octave to illustrate a consummated amour, is produced at the Opéra-Comique in Paris.

## 19 DECEMBER 1911

At a gala spectacle staged at the Paris Opéra under the auspices of the Aero-Club de France, Camille ERLANGER conducts the première of a mimed "épopée lyrique" *Icare*, glorifying the pioneer of man-powered winged flight, competently arranged by Erlanger from raw materials contributed by a wealthy amateur musician named Henri Deutsch de la Meurthe.

## 23 DECEMBER 1911

*The Miracle*, a Catholic mystery play to a scenario by Max Reinhardt in two acts and an intermezzo, with music by Engelbert HUMPERDINCK to a libretto derived from medieval Marian cult poems, dealing with an excitable nun who runs away with a knight errant, whereupon the Virgin descends from her altar to fill the vacancy created by her sinful trespass, is performed for the first time in London, calling forth street demonstrations of Protestant groups brandishing placards proclaiming No POPERY.

## 23 DECEMBER 1911

*I Gioielli della Madonna*, tragic opera in three acts by the paternally Bavarian and maternally Venetian composer Ermanno WOLF-FERRARI, to a highly charged melodramatic story of his own invention wherein a maddened lover lays the jewels stolen from the Madonna's altar at the feet of his beloved, who thereupon surrenders herself to him, but jumps into the Bay of Naples when she realizes the enormity of the sacrilege, and her suitor stabs himself to death, is performed for the first time anywhere at the Berlin Opera, in a German version under the title *Der Schmuck der Madonna.*

### 29 DECEMBER 1911

*L'Aube rouge,* lyric drama in four acts by Camille ERLANGER, dealing with a group of romantic Russians on the French Riviera idealistically plotting to liquidate an Imperial Grand Duke to advance the "red dawn" in Russia over the objections of a girl conspirator enamored of the appointed assassin (he dutifully throws his bomb in Moscow, and is shot down by the Tsarist police), set to an appropriately dynamitic score, with some incidental Russianisms such as Greek Orthodox church hymns and asymmetrical meters of 7/4, is performed for the first time anywhere in Rouen.

# ✑ *1912* ✎

### 8 JANUARY 1912

A century has passed since the birth in Geneva of Sigismond THALBERG, piano virtuoso and composer of brilliant waltzes and études, whose steely octaves, meteoric chromatics and gurgling trills captivated the salons of Europe.

(Date of birth, 8 January 1812, obtained from the registry of births in Geneva, certifying that Thalberg was a legitimate son of Joseph Thalberg, and not an illegitimate offspring of a titled nobleman as stated in most reference works, and as Thalberg himself chose to proclaim.)

### 10 JANUARY 1912

*First Symphony* by the prime Swedish symphonist Kurt ATTERBERG is performed for the first time in Stockholm.

### 18 JANUARY 1912

*Oberst Chabert,* opera in three acts by the 29-year-old German composer Hermann von WALTERSHAUSEN, to a libretto from a novella by Balzac wherein a Napoleonic colonel given up for dead after the wars returns to Paris only to shoot himself after he finds that his wife is married to another is produced in Frankfurt.

### 21 JANUARY 1912

*Ma Mère l'Oye,* orchestral version of RAVEL's suite of children's pieces (first performed in the original setting for piano 4 hands in Paris on 20 April 1910), distinguished by a delicate equilibrium of instrumental forces, and featuring a uniquely expressive solo by the double-bassoon as the shy Beast who becomes a princely youth when the flute, as Beauty, accepts his love, is presented for the first time in Paris.

26 JANUARY 1912

*Ormazd,* symphonic poem by Frederick S. CONVERSE, depicting in Wagneromantic colors Ormazd's victory over the forces of evil, is performed for the first time by the St. Louis Symphony Orchestra, Max Zach conducting.

1 FEBRUARY 1912

*Le Pays,* opera in three acts by the French composer Guy ROPARTZ, wherein a French fisherman married to an Icelandic girl pines for his native Brittany and in the end plunges to his death into the arctic waters to the accompaniment of Wagneromantic brass, is produced in Nancy, conducted by the composer, the director of the local conservatory of music.

2 FEBRUARY 1912

*L'Aigle,* "lyric epic" in three acts by Jean NOUGUÈS, an illustrated musical chronicle of revolutionary events in France, from the thunderous fall of Robespierre in 1794 to the death of Napoleon in 1821, with quotations from suitable popular tunes, is produced in Rouen.

3 FEBRUARY 1912

*Der liebe Augustin,* operetta in three acts by the Austrian composer Leo FALL, involving an accidental exchange of two female babies, one of them of princely birth, who when grown fall in love with their music teacher Augustin, who marries the presumptive princess who turns out to be of lowly birth, is produced in Berlin.

6 FEBRUARY 1912

*Die verschenkte Frau,* comic opera in three acts by Eugen D'ALBERT, in which a susceptible 18th-century Italian innkeeper finds his wife acting a loving columbine with a harlequin in a company of visiting comedians, explodes in fury and offers her to him in perpetuity, but relents as he realizes that it was all a play, set to music in an automatized abecedarian idiom of the opera buffa, is produced in Vienna.

6 FEBRUARY 1912

*Die Geburt des Herrn,* first part of the triple oratorio *Christus* by the 76-year-old German composer Felix DRAESEKE, traversing the life of Jesus in three subdivisions, composed between 1896 and 1899 in a grandiosely Germanic and lutulently pietistic manner, is performed for the first time in Berlin. (The second part of the trilogy, *Christus der Prophet,* was first performed in Berlin on 13 February 1912; the third, *Tod und Sieg des Herrn*, on 20 February 1912.)

### 7 FEBRUARY 1912

*La Lépreuse*, opera in three acts by the Tyrol-born French composer of Italian extraction Sylvio LAZZARI, wherein a beauteous yet piteously leprous girl contaminates her vacillating lover to secure his fidelity and settles with him on an isolated mountain retreat conducted thither by a Wagneromantic chorus of monks, nuns and peasants in a triadically harmonized procession, is produced at the Opéra-Comique in Paris.

### 11 FEBRUARY 1912

*Second Symphony* by the foremost Swedish symphonist Kurt ATTERBERG is performed for the first time in Stockholm.

### 15 FEBRUARY 1912

*Rhéna*, opera in four acts by the Belgian composer Jean Baptiste van der EEDEN, is produced in Brussels.

### 17 FEBRUARY 1912

*Roma*, opera in five acts by Jules MASSENET, set in Rome in 216 B.C. and focused on the tragic fate of a vestal virgin who becomes the concubine of a legionnaire and is doomed to die just as the Roman soldiers return after their victory over Carthage, is produced in Monte Carlo.

### 22 FEBRUARY 1912

*Der Simplicius*, opera in three acts by the Swiss composer Hans HUBER, written in 1899, to a libretto dealing with a noble simpleton who pacifies the rebellious Westphalian peasantry in 1640 and marries his feudal lord's daughter, set to music in a turbulent Wagnerogenic idiom, receives its belated first performance in Basel.

### 24 FEBRUARY 1912

*Les trois masques*, opera in four acts by Isidore de LARA, is produced in Marseilles.

### 28 FEBRUARY 1912

Carl NIELSEN conducts in Copenhagen the first performance of his *Third Symphony*, subtitled *Sinfonia Espansiva* (completed on 30 April 1911), comprising four movements, *Allegro espansivo, Andante pastorale, Allegretto non troppo* and *Allegro pomposo*, written in an expansively romantic idiom replete with impatient modulations, sudden inturgescences of orchestral sonorities, and sequential detumescences of harmonic substance; and on the same program, the first performance of his *Violin Concerto* (completed on 13 December 1911) in two connected movements, *Praeludium* and *Poco Adagio* and an appended *Rondo*, with Nielsen's son-in-law Emil Telmányi as soloist.

### 29 FEBRUARY 1912

*Lelia*, first opera in four acts by the 33-year-old Swedish composer Natanael BERG, after Byron's exotic poem *The Giaour*, is produced in Stockholm.

### 1 MARCH 1912

*Sangre y sol*, opera by the French composer Alexandre GEORGES, is produced in Nice.

### 6 MARCH 1912

*I Dispettosi Amanti*, one-act opera by the 37-year-old Italian composer Attilio PARELLI (whose real name at birth was Paparella), is produced in Philadelphia.

### 7 MARCH 1912

*Édénie*, opera in three acts by the Belgian composer Léon DU BOIS, his last, is produced at Antwerp with a Flemish version of the original French libretto.

### 11 MARCH 1912

*The Crown of India*, an "imperial masque" with music by Edward ELGAR, written to celebrate the visit to India by King George V, is performed for the first time at the London Coliseum.

### 12 MARCH 1912

On the day after his fifteenth birthday Henry COWELL presents at the San Francisco Music Club the first demonstration of his "tone-clusters," pandiatonic and panpentatonic, played on the white or on the black keys of the piano keyboard with fists or forearms. (In a remarkable synchronization of invention the Russian composer Vladimir REBIKOV published in 1912 a *Hymn to the Sun* for piano, in special columnar notation, indicating that the conglomeration of keys are to be encompassed with the edge of the palm of the hand)

### 14 MARCH 1912

*Mona*, opera in three acts by Horatio PARKER, the winning work in a competition for the Metropolitan Opera Prize of $10,000, to a gory libretto wherein an early British noblemaiden stabs her Roman lover to death in 99 A.D. when he meddles in her druidic rites, set to a Wagneromantic score chockful of suspended ninth-chords and anguished chromatics, is produced at the Metropolitan Opera House in New York, destined to vanish from the repertory after only four performances.

One device which I have used in *Mona* is that of associating the different personalities of the drama with definite tonalities. For instance, Gwynn, the hero, is associated with the key of B major. With Mona herself I carried the idea still further, assigning separate keys to the two distinct aspects of her personality. In her character of a Druid priestess she is associated with the key of E minor, while in her character as a woman she is assigned to the key of E-flat major. (Horatio Parker in a statement to the press)

### 17 MARCH 1912

Gabriel Pierné conducts in Paris the first performance of the symphonic picture *Thèbes* by Ernest FANELLI, a music copyist and drummer, written in 1883, which anticipates in a tentative manner some impressionistic devices of tone painting, such as progressions of ninth-chords and whole-tone scales.

### 21 MARCH 1912

*La Farce du Cuvier,* opera in two acts by the French composer Gabriel DUPONT based on a 15th-century mystery-play, is produced in Brussels.

### 23 MARCH 1912

*Ilya Murometz,* third symphony by the Russian composer Reinhold GLIÈRE, illustrating in epically grandiloquent four movements the four phases in the legendary career of the 11th-century giant of Russian folklore, (1) *Ilya Murometz's Confrontation with a Rival* (2) *The Highwayman named Nightingale* (3) *At the Court of the Sun Prince Vladimir* (4) *Heroic Exploits of Ilya and his Petrification* (introduced by ominous tritone progressions), is performed for the first time in Moscow.

### 29 MARCH 1912

*Útok na Mlýn,* opera in three acts by the 50-year-old Czech composer Karel WEIS, after Émile Zola's novel *L'Attaque du Moulin,* is produced in the Czech version in Prague.

### 6 APRIL 1912

*Pompeii,* opera in four acts by Marziano PEROSI, after Bulwer Lytton's historic novel, is produced in Vienna.

### 6 APRIL 1912

A thousand years have elapsed since the death of NOTKER (BALBULUS), the St. Gall monk who was one of the earliest church musicians to develop the ecclesiastical sequence.

### 11 APRIL 1912

*Oudelette,* opera in three acts by the Belgian composer Charles RADOUX, is produced in Brussels.

### 12 APRIL 1912

*Cyrano de Bergerac,* symphonic poem for horn and orchestra by the 25-year-old Belgian composer Robert HERBERIGS, in three movements picturing Cyrano as frondeur, lover and warrior, is performed for the first time in Brussels.

13 APRIL 1912

*Die Brautwahl*, opera in three acts with an epilogue by Ferruccio Busoni (completed by him in Berlin on 8 October 1911) after a fantastic tale by E.T.A. Hoffmann, scored in an opulent polyphonic idiom in which the choice of the bride becomes entangled in invertible counterpoint, is performed for the first time in Hamburg.

*Die Brautwahl* is suffering from constipation, like the composer himself. (Busoni, in a letter quoted in Edward J. Dent's *Ferruccio Busoni, A Biography*, London, 1933)

15 APRIL 1912

Eight British musicians, W. Hartley, J. Hume, P.C. Taylor, J.W. Woodward, R. Bricoux, F. Clarke, G. Krius and W.T. Brailey, members of the ship's band on the White Star liner, S.S. *Titanic*, go down with the iceberg-ripped ship playing *Nearer My God to Thee*.

15 APRIL 1912

*Hoffmann*, opera in three acts by the Italian composer Guido Laccetti, dealing with the life and literary productions of E.T.A Hoffmann, is produced in Naples.

16 APRIL 1912

*La Baronessa di Carini*, one-act opera by Giuseppe Mulè, his first, is produced in Palermo.

22 APRIL 1912

Mary Carr Moore conducts in Seattle the first performance of her four-act opera *Narcissa*, to the libretto by her mother, detailing the missionary exploits of Marcus Whitman in the American Northwest culminating in his and his wife Narcissa's murder on 29 November 1847 at the hands of Oregon Indians armed with authentic-sounding pentatonic war cries when they suspect that an outbreak of measles is the result of the white man's pale-faced sorcery.

22 APRIL 1912

Four French composers conduct their own works in Paris at a dance recital of the Russian ballerina Natacha Trouhanova: (1) Paul Dukas, the first performance of his symphonic poem *La Péri*, a score of rarefied exoticism with a fluid enharmonic modulatory chord employed as a sonorous "block" (2) Vincent d'Indy, his orientalistic symphonic variations *Istar* (3) Florent Schmitt, his barbaric ballet *La Tragédie de Salomé* (4) Maurice Ravel, the first performance of *Adélaïde, ou le Langage des fleurs*, a delicate orchestral version of his *Valses nobles et sentimentales*.

22 APRIL 1912

*Nail*, lyric drama in three acts by the English-Parisian composer Isidor de Lara, dealing with an Algerian nautch-girl enamored of an anti-French guer-

rilla fighter, resisting to the death the lewd advances of a multifutuent Moroc-
can emir, written in a rhapsodically expansive manner with a melismatic patina of orientalistic arabesques and containing a hymn to Allah in the whole-
tone scale, is produced in Paris.

## 1 MAY 1912

*Beni Mora,* oriental suite in three movements for orchestra by Gustav HOLST,
inspired by a 4-note motive he heard played on a bamboo flute in Algeria for
two and a half hours without stopping, and which he incorporated verbatim
for 163 bars, taking only 5 minutes and 26 seconds to play, in the third movements of the suite, is performed for the first time in London.

## 3 MAY 1912

*Vasksenje (Resurrection),* by the Serbian composer Stevan HRISTIĆ, to a romantically interpreted biblical story, is performed for the first time in Belgrade.

## 14 MAY 1912

*Le Dieu bleu,* Hindu ballet in one act with music by the Venezuelan-born Parisian composer Reynaldo HAHN, is produced by Diaghilev's Ballet Russe in
Paris.

## 18 MAY 1912

*Évocations,* symphonic suite in three movements by Albert ROUSSEL, evoking
in impressionistic colors the sights and sounds of India which he visited in
1909, is performed for the first time in Paris:

(1) *Les Dieux dans l'ombre des cavernes,* painting in tones the feral aspects of the murderous gods carved in the rock, their animal joy and their passions (2) *La Ville rose,*
portraying the festive noises of a sundrenched Hindu village (3) *Aux Bords du fleuve
sacré,* reflecting the scenes of ritual ablutions in the Ganges River, with a chorus glorifying the aromatic spirits of human love.

## 26 MAY 1912

Jean BLOCKX, Flemish composer of romantic operas, choruses and songs perfused with the melorhythms of Flemish folkways, dies in his native Antwerp
in his 62nd year.

## 29 MAY 1912

The choreographic tableau *L'Après-midi d'un Faune,* to the music of
DEBUSSY, is presented for the first time by Diaghilev's Ballet Russe in Paris.

## 4 JUNE 1912

*Aphrodite,* symphonic fantasy by the Boston romanticist George Whitefield
CHADWICK, inspired by the contemplation of the head of Aphrodite in the

Boston Museum of Fine Arts, in nine well-defined sections, with foamy harps, humid strings, and zephyr-wafted woodwinds assaulted by Wagnerophallic trombones and mating trumpets before coming to a plagally pastoral F-major cadence, is performed for the first time at the Norfolk, Connecticut, Music Festival.

### 8 JUNE 1912

Three centuries have passed since the death of Hans Leo HASSLER, German composer who was the first to apply the polyphonic style of Italian madrigals to works derived from German folk music.

### 8 JUNE 1912

*Daphnis et Chloë*, ballet in one act and three tableaux by Maurice RAVEL, with a scenario fashioned after a Greek erotic tale of pastoral love, wherein Daphnis plays the alto flute to lure Chloë, as Pan once lured Syrinx, and leopard-skinned Bacchantes burst out in a corybantic dance in rapid quintuple meters while delicate drums and poetic harps suffuse the scene in a translucid neo-archaic gauze, suspended in an aerostatically euphonious equilibrium above deep-rooted pedal points, is produced by Diaghilev's Ballet Russe in Paris.

### 14 JUNE 1912

The first solo performance on a PIANOLA is given in London playing Grieg's *Piano Concerto*, manipulated by Easthope MARTIN, and accompanied by Arthur Nikisch with the London Symphony Orchestra.

### 15 JUNE 1912

*The Children of Don*, opera in three acts with a prologue by the 33-year-old English composer Josef HOLBROOKE, constituting the first part of his Wagneromorphic Welsh trilogy *The Cauldron of Annwyn*, wherein the children of the earth goddess wrest a magical cauldron from the Druids to bring about a millennium, is performed for the first time in London. (The second part, *Dylan, Son of the Wave*, was produced in London on 4 July 1914; the third part, *Bronwen*, on 1 February 1929)

### 20 JUNE 1912

Twenty-five days after his 19th birthday, Eugene GOOSSENS, London-born composer, son of Eugene Goossens, French-born operatic conductor, grandson of Eugene Goossens, Belgian-born operatic conductor, conducts at a students' concert at the Royal College of Music in London the first performance of his first orchestral composition *Variations on a Chinese Theme*, with a pentatonic melodic figure accoutred in an exotically impressionistic harmonic garb.

### 24 JUNE 1912

*La Reginetta delle Rose (The Little Rose Queen)*, operetta in three acts by Ruggero LEONCAVALLO, to a libretto opaquely allusive to the events of the

Portuguese Revolution of 1910, wherein the heir to the throne of a transparently named Kingdom of Portowa plots to depose himself and marry an English flower girl, is produced simultaneously in Rome and in Naples, but fails to arouse interest even remotely comparable to the spontaneous success of Leoncavallo's youthful opera *Pagliacci*.

### 26 JUNE 1912

A year, a month and eight days after the death of Gustav MAHLER, Bruno Walter conducts in Vienna the first performance of Mahler's posthumous *Ninth Symphony*, in four movements, the outermost two pantheistically contemplative, the inner two choreographic, with a significantly heterogeneous tonal relationship between the first movement in D major and the last movement in D-flat major:

(1) *Andante comodo*, opening with a foreboding pianissimo on the unison A in the low register, then introducing the seminal theme of three notes, building up towards multiple climaxes with recurrent outcries of dynamic pulsation at shorter and shorter intervals of time forming a "dynamic stretto," and concluding on a unison D, thus encasing the whole movement in a dominant-tonic clause (2) *Im Tempo eines gemächlichen Ländlers*, a scherzo in the form of a chain of angularly anamorphosed and ostentatiously vulgarized waltzes wandering through many keys but converging on the central C major (3) *Rondo. Burlesque*, a restless concatenation of polkas and marches around an axial tritone (4) *Adagio*, an impassioned invocation holding on faithfully to the principal key of D-flat major, soaring to resonant heights, then subsiding into the softest triadic ending.

### 5 JULY 1912

In the presence of qualified witnesses in a photographer's studio at 42nd Street and Sixth Avenue, New York City, Professor Charles MUNTER hypnotizes an admittedly inept vocal student Marian Graham into performing a series of thrillingly Trilbyesque trills.

### 18 JULY 1912

In Milan, Francesco Balilla PRATELLA issues a manifesto entitled *Destruction of Quadrature*, inveighing against the hegemony of binary meters and postulating the liberating principle of a "new musical order of disorder."

### 23 JULY 1912

Ethel SMYTH, English composeress and militant suffragette, is arrested in London on a charge of complicity in an attempt, made on 13 July 1912 during a suffragist demonstration, to burn the historic country house of Lewis V. Harcourt, Secretary of State for the Colonies.

### 24 JULY 1912

*Second Symphony* by Nicolai MIASKOVSKY, set in the melancholy Russian key of C-sharp minor, in three movements (completed on 22 December 1911), is performed for the first time in Moscow.

All my works of this period bear the imprint of deep pessimism. It is difficult for me to analyze the reason for it. (Miaskovsky in his *Autobiographical Notes*, published in *Sovietskaya Musica*, No. 6, 1936)

## 7 AUGUST 1912

Sergei PROKOFIEV appears in Moscow as soloist in the first performance of his *First Piano Concerto* in D-flat major, in a single movement marked by rhapsodically explosive energy with an intimately lyric middle section. (He played this Concerto also at the commencement at the St. Petersburg Conservatory on 24 May 1914, and won the Rubinstein Prize, a grand piano, for his performance)

This energetically rhythmed concerto, coarse and crude, primitive and cacophonic, scarcely merits its honorable title. The composer, in his quest of novelty, but lacking it in the depth of his nature, has apparently contorted himself to the ultimate limit. This sort of thing does not happen with real talents. (Leonid Sabaneyev, *Voice of Moscow*, No. 173, 1912)

## 10 AUGUST 1912

Under the auspices of the Bohemian Club of San Francisco, Henry HADLEY conducts, amidst the millennial trees of the Redwood Grove in northern California, the first performance of his music drama in three scenes, *The Atonement of Pan*, in which Pan expiates the wickedness of his past deeds by fostering the romance of Zephyr and Flora and overcoming the sinister quintal harmonies of the harpies by the Arcadian pastorality of panpipe music.

## 13 AUGUST 1912

Jules MASSENET, French composer of melodious and harmonious operas usually centering on an attractive though sinful feminine figure lyrically outpouring her amorous distresses while dramatic events bearing on her ultimate fate are ominously suggested in perilously concatenated diminished seventh-chords and violent orchestral strokes (his father was the inventor of a steel hammer), dies in Paris, the scene of his many triumphs, three months and a day after his 70th birthday.

". . . Mais aussi, Massenet, tu tiens le violon
Dans l'orchestre divin où Mozart tient la flûte . . ."
(From a sonnet by Edmond Rostand read at a celebration in Massenet's honor at the Paris Opéra on 11 November 1911)

## 17 AUGUST 1912

*Anush*, opera in four acts by the Armenian composer Armen TIGRANIAN (1879–1950), dealing with a bloody feud in an Armenian village, leading to a lover's murder and his betrothed's suicide in a precipitous mountain river, is produced in Alexandropol.

## 18 AUGUST 1912

*Der ferne Klang*, first opera, in three acts, by the Monaco-born Austrian composer Franz SCHREKER (his real name was Schrecker but he excised the letter

C before K to exorcise the frightening spectre of *Schreck*) to his own libretto, dealing with a beautiful girl, who, after a temporary stay in a Venetian bordello, joins her musician lover at the production of his unsuccessful opera *Die Harfe*, during which he expires in her arms to the thematic "far clang" of whole-tone clusters suspended in a sonorous cloud formed by high violins, tambourine and celesta, is produced in Frankfurt.

### 23 AUGUST 1912

Erik SATIE completes the composition of his cycle of three piano pieces entitled *Véritables Préludes flasques*, with a subtitle *"pour un chien,"* in barless notation. (The first piece was written on 12 August 1912; the second on 17 August 1912)

### 1 SEPTEMBER 1912

Samuel COLERIDGE-TAYLOR, son of a West African Negro and his white English wife, and named after the English poet Samuel Taylor Coleridge, dies at Croydon, 16 days after his 37th birthday.

### 2 SEPTEMBER 1912

*Caio Petronio*, "Roman scenes" in three acts by the 34-year-old Argentine composer Constantino GAITO, glorifying Gaius Petronius, *arbiter elegantiarum* of Nero's time and the author of *Satyricon*, is produced at the Teatro Colón in Buenos Aires.

### 3 SEPTEMBER 1912

Arnold SCHOENBERG's epoch-making score *Fünf Orchesterstücke*, op. 16 (completed on 11 August 1909), receives its world première in London, conducted by Sir Henry Wood:

(1) *Vorgefühle*, forefeelings of unnamed but fearful events in a tonifugal hyperchromatic idiom laden with horizontally arrayed heterotonal tritones within quartal and quintal harmonies (2) *Vergangenes*, looking back in time with serene recollection of faces seen and emotions experienced (3) *Der wechselnde Akkord*, centering on a thematically static chord in quartal structure surrounded by kaleidoscopically changing spectral tone colors in subtle dynamic shades never rising above *mezzo piano*, with a notice in the score warning that "the change of harmonies should occur gently, without emphasis on instrumental entries, so that only the difference in color is perceived" (4) *Peripetie*, marked *Sehr rasch*, rashly exposing a series of vertiginous peripeteia charged with secundal progressions and periodically detonating in bright explosions (5) *Das obligate Recitativ*, wherein paired mirror-imaged symbols are introduced for the first time in musical notation to designate principal and secondary themes thus outlining intellectually the emotionally inventive melodies.

(In an entry in his diary of 27 January 1912 Schoenberg states that the titles were added at the request of the publisher C. F. Peters for business reasons: "I will probably give in, for I have found titles that at least are plausible. But otherwise, the idea does not appeal to me. For music is wonderful in that one can express in it everything that one wishes to express, so that the knowing will understand all. Yet it has its mysteries which ought not to be revealed. Titles are too garrulous. Music has already said what was to be said. Why add words? Were words needed, they would have been used. Art says more than words. Titles, which I may use in my pieces, communicate without betraying, for they are partly obscure, partly technical: (1) *Vorgefühle* (everyone has premonitions) (2) *Vergangenes* (everyone has a past, too) (3) *Akkordfärbungen* (chord colors; technical) (4) *Peripetie* (common enough) (5) *Das obligate* (perhaps better said 'ausgeführte' or 'unending') *Recitativ*. But in any case, all this with an annotation that this is a publishing technicality, and not a suggestion of 'poetic' content")

(In a new version of the score, 1950, for a reduced orchestra, the third piece was retitled *Sommermorgen an einem See* (*Summer Morning by the Lake*); other movements retained their original titles)

The greatest difficulty in performing these pieces is that this time it is really impossible to read the score. It would be almost imperative to perform them through blind faith. I can promise you something really colossal, especially in sound and mood. For that is what they are all about—completely unsymphonic, devoid of architecture or construction, just an uninterrupted change of colors, rhythms and moods. (Schoenberg's letter to Richard Strauss, dated 14 July 1909, relating to the *Fünf Orchesterstücke*, translated from the original in the Strauss-Archive in Garmisch)

This music seeks to express all that swells in us subconsciously like a dream; which is a great fluctuant power, and is built upon none of the lines that are familiar to us; which has a rhythm, as blood has its pulsating rhythm, as all life in us has its rhythm; which has a tonality, but only as the sea or the storm has its tonality; which has harmonies, though we cannot grasp or analyze them nor can we trace its themes. All its technical craft is submerged, made one and indivisible with the content of the work. (From a program note for the first performance)

It was like a poem in Tibetan; not one single soul could possibly have understood it at a first hearing. We can, after all, only progress from the known to the unknown; and as the program writer, who had every reason to know, said, there was not a single consonance from beginning to end. Under such circumstances the listener was like a dweller in Flatland straining his mind to understand the ways of that mysterious occupant of three dimensions, man. . . . At the conclusion half the audience hissed. That seems a too decisive judgment, for after all they may turn out to be wrong; the other half applauded more vehemently than the case warranted, for it could hardly have been from understanding. (London *Times*, 4 September 1912)

The program of last Tuesday's Promenade Concert included *Five Orchestral Pieces*, op. 16, by Arnold Schoenberg, who evidently revels in the bizarre. According to Dr. Anton von Webern, his music "contains the experience of his emotional life," and that experience must have been of a strange, not to say unpleasant character. . . . Is it really honest music or merely a pose? We are inclined to think the latter. If music at all, it is music of the future, and we hope, of a distant one. There is plenty of interesting and noble music to enjoy. Why, then, should the ears of the Promenade audience be tortured with scrappy sounds and perpetual discord? (London *Daily Mail*, 7 September 1912)

Imagine the scene of the bleating of sheep in *Don Quixote*, the sacrificial procession in *Elektra*, and the scene of the opponents in *Heldenleben*, all played together, and you will have a faint idea of Schoenberg's idea of orchestral color and harmony. As to theme or subject, it must be supposed that he would consider it an insult to be told that he has any traffic with such things. . . . The pieces have no program or poetic basis. We must be content with the composer's own assertion that he has depicted his own experiences, for which he has our heartfelt sympathy. (London *Daily News*, 4 September 1912)

Schoenberg's music is a return to an elemental condition. It is a collection of sounds without relation to one another. It is the reproduction of the sounds of nature in their crudest form. Modern intellect has advanced beyond mere elementary noise: Schoenberg has not. If the mind of man is superior to that of beast, then it should be able to improve and not rest content with imitation. The course adopted by Schoenberg is retrograde. (*Morning Post*, London, 4 September 1912)

It is impossible to give an idea of the music. The endless discords, the constant succession of unnatural sounds from the extreme notes of every instrument, and the complete absence of any kind of idea, which, at one hearing at least, one can get hold of, baffle description. Herr Schoenberg, in short, is to Strauss at his wildest what Strauss is to Mozart, and he is never for a bare space normal. He does not even end his pieces with recognizable chords. He is a Futurist painter, and he scores as he paints. (*Manchester Guardian*, 5 September 1912)

It is not often that an English audience hisses the music it does not like; but a good third of the people the other day permitted themselves that luxury after the performance of the five orchestral pieces of Schoenberg. Another third of the audience was not hissing because it was laughing, and the remaining third seemed too puzzled either to laugh or to hiss. . . . Nevertheless, I take leave to suggest that Schoenberg is not the mere fool or madman that he is generally supposed to be. . . . May it not be that the new composer sees a logic in certain tonal relations that to the rest of us seem chaos at present, but the coherence of which may be clear enough to us all some day? (Ernest Newman, *Nation*, London, September 1912)

### 5 SEPTEMBER 1912

John CAGE, revolutionary American composer and experimenter, pioneer of the concept of "total music" embracing not only tonal parameters but also environmental acoustical phenomena, incidental noises, and other aleatory elements, inventor of the "prepared piano" in which the tone color is altered by placing screws, bolts, coins and other unpianistic objects on the strings, is born in Los Angeles.

### 5 SEPTEMBER 1912

*Music Pictures*, symphonic suite by the 31-year-old English theorist and composer John FOULDS, in four movements, inspired by the paintings of William Blake and others, significant because the second movement makes use, perhaps before any other orchestral work, of quarter-tones, is performed for the first time at the Promenade Concerts in London.

In the year 1898 I had tentatively experimented in a string quartet with smaller divisions than usual of the intervals known to musicians. In 1912, having set myself to paraphrase in music the sensations received from certain pictures, I again found it necessary to call upon this item in my musical vocabulary. I was forced over the old border-lines and produced a piece described as *Study in Whole-Tones, Half-Tones, and Quarter-Tones*, No. 2 of *Music Pictures*. (*Music Today* by John Foulds, London, 1934)

## 8 SEPTEMBER 1912

Bernhard ZIEHN, German-American music theorist who developed some original ideas about harmonic relations in modern music, and who taught two generations of American musicians, dies at the age of 67 in Chicago, his home since 1868.

## 16 SEPTEMBER 1912

*Zingari,* opera in two acts by Ruggero LEONCAVALLO, after Pushkin's poem depicting the ardors and internecine passions of a Bessarabian Gypsy camp, is produced for the first time in London.

## 24 SEPTEMBER 1912

*The Sea,* suite for orchestra by Frank BRIDGE, enlightened and progressive-minded English professor of music, in four impressionistic movements, *Seascape, Seafoam, Moonlight* and *Storm,* containing a distillation of Debussyan aquamarine harmonies, is performed for the first time in London, Sir Henry Wood conducting.

## 4 OCTOBER 1912

*Konzert im alten Stil* for orchestra, op. 123, by Max REGER, in three sections marked by considerable contrapuntal commotion, in the manner of a concerto grosso, with a lyrical middle movement, is performed for the first time in Frankfurt, Willem Mengelberg conducting.

## 11 OCTOBER 1912

*Romantische Suite* for orchestra by Max REGER, op. 125, in three evocative movements, *Notturno, Scherzo* and *Finale,* set in intricate polyphonic patterns, blossoming forth unexpectedly into impressionistic floridity, and including sonorous progressions in whole-tone scales, is performed for the first time in Dresden.

## 11 OCTOBER 1912

Leopold STOKOWSKI, 30-year-old London-born organist, son of an émigré Polish cabinetmaker and a Scottishwoman, leads the opening concert of the season of the Philadelphia Orchestra as its new music director.

Every seat was taken and the extra chairs had been placed within the orchestra rail. There was much enthusiasm, manifesting itself at the beginning in prolonged applause as Stokowski came forward with bowed head, evidently pondering the content of his musical message. Those who went forth to see a hirsute eccentric were disappointed. They beheld a surprisingly boyish and thoroughly business-like figure, who was sure of himself, yet free from conceit, who dispensed with the score by virtue of infallible memory, and held his men and his audience from first note to last firmly in his grasp. (*Public Ledger,* Philadelphia, 12 October 1912)

### 14 OCTOBER 1912

*The Firefly,* operetta by Rudolf FRIML, dealing with an Italian street singer who gets a job as a cabin boy on a yachting trip to Bermuda to be near a young man with whom she is secretly in love, and two years later suddenly emerges as a prima donna, finally capturing her beloved, is performed for the first time in Syracuse, New York. (Date on the title page of the score; first New York performance was given on 2 December 1912)

### 15 OCTOBER 1912

*The Dove of Peace,* "a satire on the dream of universal peace," with music by Walter DAMROSCH, with scenes taking place in Portsmouth, New Hampshire, where the Russo-Japanese peace treaty was signed, in the United States Senate Chamber, and on Guam Island during the Spanish-American war, is produced, unsuccessfully, at Philadelphia.

### 16 OCTOBER 1912

After forty rehearsals, Arnold SCHOENBERG's *Pierrot Lunaire,* "cycle of thrice seven melodramas," opus (significantly!) 21, to texts by the Belgian poet Albert Giraud, rendered into German by Otto Erich Hartleben, "set to tones" (*vertont*) for a spoken voice (*Sprechstimme*), piano, flute (interchangeable with piccolo), clarinet (or bass clarinet), violin (or viola) and cello, containing in its three septuple parts $(39 + 41 + 31 + 18 + 44 + 24 + 27 = 224) + (26 + 20 + 20 + 29 + 13 + 36 + 22 = 166) + (31 + 27 + 32 + 19 + 53 + 30 + 30 = 222) = 612$ measures, in quarternote meters 2/4, 3/4, 4/4, 6/4 (with the exception of No. 20 which is in 6/8) written in a supremely expressionistic, articulately crystalline, dissonantly atonal idiom, replete with mutually precipitating canonic devices crowned by a magistrally symbolistic retrograde canon in No. 18, *Der Mondfleck,* mirroringly halved in the paired groups of clarinet with piccolo, and violin with cello, to paint the inerasable reflection of the bright moon on the back of the lunar Pierrot's black jacket, is performed for the first time in Berlin, with Albertine Zehme, to whom the score is dedicated "in heartfelt friendship," as the speakingly singing recitalist, the individual 21 "melodramas" bearing the following titles and completed on the following dates in 1912, according to the original manuscript in the Library of Congress (the dates in the printed edition are erroneously listed according to the sequence of the titles rather than the non-consecutive chronology of actual times of composition):

(1) *Mondestrunken* (29 March) (2) *Colombine* (20 April) (3) *Der Dandy* (2 April) (4) *Eine blasse Wäscherin* (5) *Valse de Chopin* (7 May) (6) *Madonna* (9 May) (7) *Der kranke Mond* (18 April) (8) *Nacht* (21 May) (9) *Gebet an Pierrot* (12 March) (10) *Rauh* (9 May) (11) *Rote Messe* (24 April) (12) *Galgenlied* (12 May) (13) *Enthauptung* (23 May) (14) *Die Kreuze* (9 July) (15) *Heimweh* (22 May) (16) *Gemeinheit* (6 June) (17) *Parodie* (4 May) (18) *Der Mondfleck* (28 May) (19) *Serenade* (25 April) (20) *Heimfahrt* (9 May) (21) *O alter Duft* (30 May).

Hermann Helmholtz speaks somewhere about so-called "metamathematical spaces," that is, spaces wherein the known axioms of Euclid's geometry are not valid. I think of these remarkable spaces when I tread on the tone-space of the latest Schoenberg: I feel translated into "metamusical" spaces. To breathe in this new atmosphere one must leave behind all that is considered axiomatic in things musical. One must first learn the new alphabet to approach this new frightful Schoenberg, to get the bearings of this "Prose of Music," as Herr von Webern calls it. (*Signale für die musikalische Welt*, Berlin, 2 November 1912)

To arouse any kind of a sensation in these days is of itself an extraordinary feat. Arnold Schoenberg may be either crazy as a loon, or he may be a very clever trickster who is apparently determined to cause a sensation by writing music that in its hideousness and illogical ear-splitting ugliness defies description . . . His music to Albert Giraud's poems entitled *Pierrot Lunaire* is the last word in cacophony and musical anarchy. Some day it may be pointed out as of historical interest, because it represents the turning point, for the outraged muse surely can endure no more of this; such noise must drive even the moonstruck Pierrot back to the realm of real music. Albertine Zehme, a well-known Berlin actress, dressed in a Pierrot costume, recited the "Three Times Seven" poems, as the program announced, while a musical, or rather unmusical, ensemble, consisting of a piano, violin, viola, cello, piccolo and clarinet, stationed behind a black screen and invisible to the audience, discoursed the most ear-splitting combinations of tones that ever desecrated the walls of a Berlin music hall. Schoenberg has thrown overboard all of the sheet anchors of the art of music. Melody he eschews in every form; tonality he knows not and such a word as harmony is not in his vocabulary. The remarkable part of the whole farce is that Schoenberg is taken seriously . . . The critics have written columns about Schoenberg. To be sure, they condemn him almost to a man, but they give him space—from four to five times the space that other more deserving composers get, and they do this for the same reason that I am now doing it, because there is an element of interest for the readers . . . Schoenberg even has adherents who rally round his standard and swear by his muse, declaring that this is music of the future. Otto Taubmann, the critic of the *Börsen Courier*, expressed the feelings of all sane musicians when he wrote, "If this is music of the future, then I pray my Creator not to let me live to hear it again." (Arthur M. Abell, *The Musical Courier*, New York, 6 November 1912)

What is Arnold Schoenberg? An Altruist Laboring for the Second and Third Generations or a Colossal Joker? A Berlin Hearing of His *Pierrot Lunaire* Fails to Shed Light on the Problem (Headlines in *Musical America*, New York, 16 November 1912)

### 25 OCTOBER 1912

Richard STRAUSS conducts in Stuttgart the world première of his incidental music to Molière's *Le Bourgeois Gentilhomme*, with a one-act opera *Ariadne auf Naxos* as a play within a play (composition completed on 24 April 1912), to the text by Hugo von Hofmannstahl, wherein Ariadne, abandoned on an Aegean island, is revitalized by Bacchus, set in a neo-archaic homophonic idiom for a small ensemble of 39 highly individualized instruments, while the Molière comedy, representing the nouveau-riche society in quest of theatrical entertainment, is characterized by burlesqued polyphony.

### 25 OCTOBER 1912

On the 48th birthday of Alexandre GRETCHANINOFF, his three-act opera *Sœur Béatrice*, after Maeterlinck's play, is produced in Moscow, followed by an outcry in the monarchist press about the blasphemy of the theme, and resulting in the opera's suppression after three performances.

The Moscow newspapers report a new affront against our religious feelings. On the same stage where naked women disport themselves night after night, there will appear—it is horrible to utter!—the image of the Purest Virgin, More Glorious than the Seraphim. . . . As if this were not enough, the Purest Virgin will be represented on the stage by a godless and depraved actress. . . . What is Moscow coming to? Is it being transformed into a dissolute Babylon, invoking the wrath of God upon Holy Russia? (From an article in the monarchist daily *Kolokol,* quoted in Gretchaninoff's *My Life,* New York, 1952)

### 25 OCTOBER 1912

*Radda,* opera in one act by Giacomo OREFICE, after a story by Maxim Gorky, is produced in Milan.

### 26 OCTOBER 1912

*Meduza,* opera in three acts by the 28-year-old Polish composer Ludomir RÓŻYCKI, dealing with episodes in the life of Leonardo da Vinci, is produced in Warsaw.

### 29 OCTOBER 1912

*La Danseuse de Pompei,* opera-ballet in five acts by the French composer Jean NOUGÈS, depicting the destruction of Pompeii, is produced at the Opéra-Comique in Paris.

### 1 NOVEMBER 1912

Holland announces its adherence to the international copyright law guaranteeing performance and publication rights to composers.

### 6 NOVEMBER 1912

Nikolai LISSENKO, Ukrainian composer of several operas to Gogol's tales (*Taras Bulba, Night Before Christmas, The May Night*), and an ardent collector of Ukrainian folksongs, which he harmonized in congenial arrangements, dies in Kiev at the age of seventy.

### 7 NOVEMBER 1912

*La Dubarry,* opera by Ezio CAMUSSE, dealing with the famous courtesan and influential mistress of Louis XV, in three acts and an epilogue of her death on the guillotine on 7 December 1793, is produced in Milan.

### 10 NOVEMBER 1912

*Nattergallen (The Nightingale),* opera in three acts by the Danish composer August ENNA, after Hans Christian Andersen's tale, is produced in Copenhagen.

## 12 NOVEMBER 1912

*Liebesketten,* ninth opera by the self-Germanized English-born composer Eugen D'ALBERT, wherein the tangled chains of adulterous love among fisherfolk of Brittany are tragically resolved by the brown-skinned castaway maiden who dies of stab wounds protecting her lover from the cuckolded husband of his former mistress, is produced in Vienna.

## 13 NOVEMBER 1912

*Melenis,* third opera in three acts by Riccardo ZANDONAI, to a gory story dealing with a Greek courtesan who kills herself when her gladiator lover marries another, is produced in Milan.

## 15 NOVEMBER 1912

*Lebenstanz,* tone-poem by Frederick DELIUS, known in England as *Life's Dance* and constituting a revision of his French-titled work *La Ronde se déroule,* composed in 1900, and revealing traits of vague impressionism superimposed on a Germanically conceived program piece, receives its belated first performance in Berlin.

## 17 NOVEMBER 1912

Suffering from an excruciating toothache, exactly five months after his 30th birthday, Igor STRAVINSKY completes in Clarens, Switzerland, the composition of *Le Sacre du Printemps,* in piano score, with indications as to instrumentation.

(Date and description from Stravinsky's own contemporary notation in the manuscript title page reproduced in facsimile in *Melos,* June 1962, and reading, in Russian "Today, 4/17 XI 1912, Sunday, while having an excruciating toothache, finished the music of *Le Sacre.* Igor Stravinsky, Clarens." The scoring was completed on 8 March 1913)

## 30 NOVEMBER 1912

*Chrysis,* ballet by the romantic nationalist of Russian music Reinhold GLIÈRE, inspired by an exotically erotic tale by Pierre Louÿs, set to music replete with luscious orientalistic modalities, is produced in Moscow.

## 5 DECEMBER 1912

Sir Charles Hubert Hastings PARRY, eminent British academician of music, conducts in London the first performance of his *Symphony-Fantasy* in B minor, couched in a Germanically tumescent romantic idiom, in four linked movements, with psychological subtitles: (1) *Stress* (2) *Love* (3) *Play* (4) *Now!*

## 8 DECEMBER 1912

*From the Apocalypse,* last symphonic poem by the Russian composer of evocative symphonic poems, Anatoli LIADOV, written in an exalted neo-ecclesiastical manner, opening with a descending double major tetrachord with tritonally related roots, followed by modally harmonized Russian hymns, and ending with seven thunderclaps of grandisonant apocalyptic sounds in the brass and drums, raising aloft the oriflamme of Russianized Revelation, is performed for the first time in St. Petersburg, conducted by Alexander Siloti.

### 11 DECEMBER 1912

*Isabelle et Pantalon,* opera buffa by the 21-year-old French composer Alexis ROLAND-MANUEL (whose real name was Roland Alexis Manuel Lévy), to a modernized commedia dell'arte libretto in which the old Doctor Pantalon keeps his young ward Isabelle isolated in a hydrotherapeutic institution, whence she in spite of all precautions is abducted by Arlequin, is performed for the first time in Paris.

### 12 DECEMBER 1912

Harald SAEVERUD, precocious 15-year-old Norwegian composer, conducts in Bergen a concert consisting entirely of his symphonic works.

### 18 DECEMBER 1912

*La Sorcière,* opera in four acts by Camille ERLANGER, is performed for the first time at the Opéra-Comique in Paris.

### 21 DECEMBER 1912

During his first and only Russian tour, Arnold SCHOENBERG conducts in St. Petersburg the first local performance of his romantic symphonic poem *Pelleas und Melisande,* composed in 1903.

### 22 DECEMBER 1912

*Le Chant de la Cloche,* dramatic legend by Vincent D'INDY, to Schiller's text, in seven scenes with a prologue, is performed for the first time as a stage work in Brussels. (A concert version was first played at a Lamoureux concert in Paris on 25 February 1886)

### 28 DECEMBER 1912

*Megae,* first opera in three scenes to a libretto from an old Japanese legend, by Adam Tadeusz WIENIAWSKI, Polish composer of romantic music, nephew of the famous violinist Wieniawski, is produced in Warsaw.

# ᘒ *1913* ᘒ

### 3 JANUARY 1913

*Doctor Merryheart,* comedy overture by the 36-year-old English composer Havergal BRIAN, an extended piece of program music constructed as a set of symphonic variations, is performed for the first time in Birmingham as part of the Annual Conference of the Incorporated Society of Musicians.

## 7 JANUARY 1913

*La Forêt bleue,* opera in three acts by the 35-year-old French composer Louis AUBERT, to a libretto in which several characters from fairy tales of Perrault meet in social intercourse, set to music in an ingratiatingly harmonious vein, is performed for the first time in Geneva, Switzerland.

## 11 JANUARY 1913

Camille SAINT-SAËNS receives the Grande Croix of the Légion d'Honneur, the highest decoration of the Order.

## 15 JANUARY 1913

*Gala plácida,* lyric drama by the Catalan composer Jaime PAHISSA, dealing with a heterogenetic passion of a patrician Roman matron for a chieftain of the barbarian Goths, symbolizing the conflict between Mediterranean and Teutonic cultures, with a musical setting in a sumptuous modernistic idiom, is produced in Barcelona.

## 20 JANUARY 1913

*Tante Simona,* comic opera in one act by the 35-year-old Hungarian composer Ernst von DOHNÁNYI, wherein a misandronous Italian spinster keeps her inno-cent niece from treacherous heterosexual contacts, but undergoes a psycho-logical rejuvenation when an ancient beau appears after a lapse of decades and offers her his superannuated heart, set to music in a conventional Ger-manic manner, is performed for the first time in Dresden.

## 29 JANUARY 1913

*La Festa dei Fiori,* "idyllic operetta" by the 26-year-old Italian composer Giuseppe BLANC (the future author of the Fascist hymn *Giovinezza*), is pro-duced in Rome.

## 10 FEBRUARY 1913

Hamilton HARTY conducts in London the first performance of his *Variations on an Irish Folk Tune,* for violin and orchestra, with Paul Kochanski as soloist.

## 12 FEBRUARY 1913

*Madame Roland,* opera by Félix FOURDRAIN, is produced in Rouen.

## 20 FEBRUARY 1913

*Uguale Fortuna,* an opera buffa by the 34-year-old Italian composer Vincenzo TOMMASINI, centered on a pair of aspiring balladeers serenading a widow under her balcony, only to lose out to a stranger already embedded in her room, is produced as a prize-winning work in the Verdi Contest, in Rome.

### 21 FEBRUARY 1913

*Sinfonia della Vita* by the Italian Futurist composer Francesco Balilla PRATELLA, is performed for the first time at a Futurist exposition in Rome, with the futuristic element represented by whole-tone scales.

### 22 FEBRUARY 1913

*Kaatje,* opera in three acts by the 45-year-old Belgian composer Victor BUFFIN, to a libretto dealing with the patriotic struggle in Flanders against Spanish rulers in the 16th century, is produced in Brussels.

### 23 FEBRUARY 1913

Fifteen and a half months after the completion of Arnold SCHOENBERG's vocal cycle *Gurre-Lieder,* which occupied his creative energies from March 1900 until May 1901, to the text of the German translations of poems by the Danish poet Jens Peter Jacobsen written by him in 1868 at the age of 21, traversing the tragic events in the life of King Waldemar IV of Denmark, his eternal love for a commoner Tove who waits for him at the Gurre Castle on the Esrom Sea in North Zealand, his anguish when he learns of her death and his mystical expectation of her resurrection, set in richly resonant harmonies and progressing along chromatically unwinding Wagneromorphic paths leading to an apotheosis in diatonic splendor, scored for 5 solo voices, a speaking voice, 3 male choirs, a mixed chorus of 8 parts and a tremendously expanded orchestra (Schoenberg had to order special manuscript paper of 48 staves to accommodate the instrumental parts), including a large iron chain to be shaken with concussive effect, and introducing for the first time a trombone glissando, is performed for the first time in Vienna, Franz Schreker conducting, the work subdivided into three parts:

PART I, opening with an E-flat major chord enriched by an upper sixth, from which the thematic elements unfold in fanfare-like tones, comprising nine arias sung in dialogue by Waldemar and Tove, and concluding with the song of a woodland dove announcing in mournfully chromaticized melismas the death of Tove.—PART II, wherein Waldemar hurls defiant imprecations at the cruel god of death.—PART III, *Die wilde Jagd,* an episode of a satanically wild chase, the choruses lamenting lost peace, but ultimately finding diatonic solace in a joyous hymn to the ever-returning sun, leading to a 28-bar coda in which the thematic sixth on the C-major triad resolves after an eon of suspensions into a revitalized, immaculately white C major.

### 24 FEBRUARY 1913

*Carmosine,* "conte romanesque" in four acts by Henry FÉVRIER, after Alfred de Musset's poem dealing with a 13th-century girl who suffers pernicious ane-

mia as a result of her love for King Pedro of Aragon, but is saved from ultimate inanition by her appointment as a lady-in-waiting at the palace where
she is enabled to observe her royal idol in daily proximity, and by a subsequent marriage to her old admirer willing to act as a vicarious substitute, set
to music in harmonious sonorities, is produced at the Théâtre-Lyrique in
Paris.

### 26 FEBRUARY 1913

*Deux images,* symphonic diptych by Béla BARTÓK, the first titled *En pleine
fleur* representing the rebirth of nature in late spring with flowery muted
strings and trilling avian flutes, the second, *Danse campagnarde,* robustly
rhythmical in a propulsive Hungarian manner, is performed for the first time
in Budapest.

### 26 FEBRUARY 1913

Felix DRAESEKE, German composer of grandly academic instrumental music,
dies in Dresden at the age of seventy-seven.

### 27 FEBRUARY 1913

*Cyrano de Bergerac,* opera in four acts by the German-American conductor
Walter DAMROSCH, to a libretto fashioned from the famous play of Edmond
Rostand dealing with the nasute 17th-century poet and soldier whose long
nose makes him repugnant to the lady of his adoration but who wins her love
for an inarticulate friend by writing eloquent letters to her in his behalf, set to
an amiably melodious score fatally handicapped by a lack of verve, is performed for the first and preantepenultimate time by the Metropolitan Opera
Company in New York.

### 28 FEBRUARY 1913

*Coco-Chéri,* operetta in one act with music by Erik SATIE, is performed for
the first time in Monte Carlo.

### 2 MARCH 1913

*La Leggenda delle sette torri,* one-act opera by the Italian music critic and occasional composer Alberto GASCO (1879–1938), inspired by two pre-Raphael-
ite paintings of Dante Gabriel Rossetti, *The Tune of Seven Towers* and *Boni-
facio's Mistress,* is performed for the first time in Rome.

### 3 MARCH 1913

*Elektra* by Richard STRAUSS is produced for the first time in St. Petersburg,
evoking a vehement denunciation in the monarchist newspaper *Novoye
Vremya:* "It is inadmissible that in this year when Russia celebrated the 300th
anniversary of the ruling Romanov dynasty, the Imperial Opera House should
produce an opera in which royal personages are brutally slain."

### 4 MARCH 1913

*Pénélope*, opera in three acts by Gabriel FAURÉ, presenting in quasi-Grecian modalities the Homeric episode of the virtuous wife of Ulysses, his homecoming in the disguise of an ancient mendicant and his victory over her intrusive suitors, with a serenely dolorous theme for Pénélope and a heroically valorous theme for Ulysses forming the principal materials, and ending in marble-white C major, is performed for the first time at the Opera of Monte Carlo, in the principality of Monaco.

### 6 MARCH 1913

The word JAZZ appears in print for the first time as a synonym for pep, in the San Francisco *Bulletin*, in a sports column written by "Scoop" Gleeson. (See complete text in LETTERS AND DOCUMENTS)

### 11 MARCH 1913

Luigi RUSSOLO, Italian futurist musician and painter, issues in Milan a defiant manifesto legislating the fundamental tenets of Art of Noises. (See full text in LETTERS AND DOCUMENTS)

### 15 MARCH 1913

*Das Spielwerk und die Prinzessin*, opera by the Monegasque-born German composer Franz SCHREKER, in two acts with a prologue, wherein an ailing princess perishes in a conflagration when a maddened suitor destroys a specially constructed therapeutic music box designed to warn her of dangerous body symptoms, set to a Wagneromantic score, diversified by archaizing modalities and impressionistic nebulosities, is produced simultaneously in Frankfurt and Vienna. (A revised version in one act was produced in Munich on 30 October 1920, in the form of a mystery play, under the shortened title *Das Spielwerk*)

### 20 MARCH 1913

*Le Carillonneur*, lyric opera in four acts by Xavier LEROUX, depicting the turbulent life of an ambitious bell ringer who wins a prize in a professional contest but suffers emotional failures in his personal life, is produced at the Opéra-Comique in Paris.

### 24 MARCH 1913

*Sweethearts*, romantic opera in two acts by Victor HERBERT, dealing with a Neapolitan damsel adopted by a 15th-century laundress with six daughters of her own who discovers that royal blood courses in her veins and opportunely marries the heir-presumptive to the throne of Zilania, containing the melodious duet *The Angelus* and the irresistibly harmonious waltz tune *Sweethearts*, is produced in Baltimore. (Its first New York performance took place on 8 September 1913)

## 28 MARCH 1913

*Le Château de la Bretèche,* lyric drama in four acts by the Belgian composer Albert DUPUIS, after the lugubrious novella by Balzac, wherein a cuckolded husband immures his wife's paramour in his castle, set to music in an egalitarian harmonic idiom using conventional resources of Gallic operatic art, is produced in Nice.

## 30 MARCH 1913

*La Procesión del Rocío,* symphonic poem by Joaquín TURINA in two sections, descriptive of Triana, the colorful suburb of Seville, and the Procession of the Dew carrying the image of the Virgin in an ox-driven cart, set to music in typically Iberian melorhythms, with alternating isotopic meters 3/4 and 6/8, is performed for the first time in Madrid.

## 31 MARCH 1913

The Academic Society for Literature and Music in Vienna presents a concert of advanced music, Arnold SCHOENBERG conducting, comprising the following:

(1) *6 Stücke für Orchester* by Anton von Webern, the "dynamic psychographer" of new music, dedicated "in greatest love" to Arnold Schoenberg, "teacher and friend," written in 1910 and anticipating the serialistic code of non-repetition of thematic tones (the opening melody is composed of nine different notes in atonally oriented intervals) and of non-recurrence of instrumental colors (2) *Four Songs* for voice and orchestra to poems of Maeterlinck by Schoenberg's teacher and brother-in-law Alexander Zemlinsky (3) *Kammersymphonie* by Schoenberg himself, in one continuous movement, written in 1906 and still well within the tonal framework despite the quartal harmonic structure (4) Two songs out of *5 Orchesterlieder* by Alban Berg, to text by the Vienna café poet Peter Altenberg jotted by him on the back of picture postcards, and therefore referred to sometimes as "postcard songs."

A certain section of the audience attended the concert for the sake of sensation seeking and with the obvious intention of provoking a scandal. There were present, for instance, some operetta composers who usually stay away from performances of new music. Already during the playing of Webern's orchestral pieces and Schoenberg's *Kammersinfonie* there were clashes between the enthusiastically applauding young students and individuals who tried to interfere with the music by hissing and shouting "Pfui!" During the performance of Alban Berg's songs the noise became so deafening that it was impossible to hear anything . . . The whole thing ended in a wild melée which found its sequel in court. There, a well-known operetta composer summoned as a witness, declared to the judge: "I, too, laughed, and why shouldn't I laugh when something really comic is going on?" Another, a physician by profession, asserted that the effect of this type of music is "unnerving for a major part of the public and therefore harmful to the nervous system, so that many among those who attend such concerts show outward symptoms of profound mental depression." (Egon Wellesz, *Arnold Schoenberg,* Vienna, 1921)

The Grosser Musikverein-Saal audience has an air of expectancy. Vienna prides itself on being "advanced," and this is no joke either. There are more things possible with the modern orchestra, so we find out, than Strauss ever dreamed of. These strange whimpers and sighs, the growls of the basses underneath the peculiar wheezes which the clarinet can produce by pressing the lower lip in a certain way—can they be the birth pangs of a new art, these zoological expressions that would make a real menagerie seek cover with drooping tails and ears in their general disgust at nature's provision to them of such inadequate vocal talents? As for the key, gracious! people wrote in "keys" far back in 1910. We thought we knew all the discords which human ingenuity could devise, but here even the wisest can learn something. It is without doubt "original" music. It is, to be specific, the music of some of Schoenberg's pupils being performed under the auspices of the Akademischer Verband für Literatur and Musik, with the master himself conducting. They may be called "Ultraists," though by any other name they could by no means lose any of their fragrance. If this concert was intended to be a "memorable occasion" it surely succeeded, for it occasioned the greatest uproar which has occurred in a Vienna concert hall in the memory of the oldest critics. Laughter, hisses and applause continued throughout a great part of the actual performance of the disputed pieces. After the Berg songs the dispute became almost a riot. The police were called and the only officer who could be found actually threw out of the gallery one noisemaker who persisted in blowing on a key for a whistle. But this policeman could not prevent one of the composers from appearing in a box and yelling to the crowd, "Heraus mit der Baggage!" ("Out with the trash!"), whereat the uproar increased. Members of the orchestra descended from the stage and entered into spirited controversy with the audience. And finally the president of the Akademischer Verband came and boxed the ears of a man who had insulted him while he was making an announcement. (Vienna dispatch in *The Musical Courier*, New York, 23 April 1913)

### 1 APRIL 1913

*La Vida breve,* lyric drama in two acts by Manuel DE FALLA, dealing with the pathetically brief life of a Gypsy girl in Granada who dies of a broken heart after denouncing the perfidy of her seducer on the day of his marriage to a street vendor, to a score vibrant with Andalusian modalities, fandango rhythms and orientalistically chromaticized arabesques, against the background of strumming guitars, clapping castanets and outcries of "Olé," is performed for the first time in Nice.

### 2 APRIL 1913

Maurice RAVEL completes the orchestration of the piano part of the first of his *Trois Poemés* to Mallarmé's texts, *Soupir,* for two flutes, two clarinets, piano and strings, in ethereally delicate sonorities. (The second song was orchestrated in May 1913; the third in August 1913. Dates at the end of each song in the printed score)

J'ai pris à peu près pour cette œuvre l'appareil instrumental du *Pierrot Lunaire* de Schoenberg. (Ravel in his autobiographical sketch, in *Le Ménestrel*, Paris, 26 May 1939)

It was with special interest that I marked the dates given in *Music Since 1900* for Schoenberg's *Pierrot Lunaire* . . . It has been said that Ravel's *Trois Poèmes de Mallarmé* (1913) were composed under the influence of this work, an allegation against which I have already protested. *Pierrot Lunaire* was not given outside Germany and Austria until after the war, and Ravel visited neither country in 1912–1913 . . . I had questioned Ravel before this piece of information came to me, and his reply was that he had not heard or read Schoenberg's work at the time, but only heard of it (probably through Stravinsky, who attended the Berlin performance). On the other hand, he knew the *Kammersymphonie* and this knowledge coupled with the information about *Pierrot Lunaire* gave rise to the idea of composing the *Trois Poémes* for voice and nine instruments. (M. D. Calvocoressi in his review of the first edition of *Music Since 1900*, in *Musical Opinion*, London, June 1938)

### 3 APRIL 1913

*Le Festin de l'Araignée*, ballet-pantomime by Albert ROUSSEL, an arachnoid drama wherein an inhumanly voracious spider lures a multicolored butterfly into his net by deceptively ingratiating melodies wrapped in a gauze of impressionistic harmonies but, as he prepares his cannibalistic feast, is killed in turn by a vigilant praying mantis attacking in dramatically detonating dissonant chords, is performed for the first time in Paris, two days before Roussel's 44th birthday.

### 10 APRIL 1913

*L'Amore dei tre re*, opera in three acts by Italo MONTEMEZZI, set in 10th-century Italy, wherein a blind barbarian king strangles his daughter-in-law whom he rightly suspects of infidelity to his son, and puts poison on her dead lips so that when her princely lover kisses her in her crypt, he dies, as does her husband who kisses her too, leaving the old man alone with three cadavers, set to music in the style of Italian Verismo in opulent Wagneromorphic harmonies, is produced at La Scala, in Milan.

### 14 APRIL 1913

*Mimi Pinson*, lyric comedy in four acts by Ruggero LEONCAVALLO, a new version of his 1897 opera *La Bohème*, is produced in Palermo, under a new title in order to disassociate it from Puccini's famous homonymous opera.

### 18 APRIL 1913

*Au Jardin de Marguerite*, symphonic poem with chorus by the French romantic composer ROGER-DUCASSE, written in 1901–1905, describing Faust's visit, in his second old age, to Marguerite's garden, where the scent of fragrant flowers excites his debile flesh with aphrodisiac memories, while gentle marguerites envelop him in their chaste petals, set to florid impressionistic music, is performed for the first time in Paris.

### 18 APRIL 1913

*Merlin*, music drama in three acts by the German composer Felix DRAESEKE (completed on 13 May 1905), wherein Satan begets Merlin by a celestial virgin but is foiled in his design to use his hybrid offspring in the service of his anti-Christian crusade, despite the contributory seduction of Merlin by King Arthur's sister-in-law, set in a turbulent Wagnerolatrous idiom, is produced posthumously in Gotha. (Date from *Signale für die Musikalische Welt*, Berlin, of 30 April 1913; in his worshipful Nazigenic biography of Draeseke published in Berlin in 1937, Erich Roeder gives the erroneous date 10 May 1913)

### 25 APRIL 1913

*Panurge*, "high musical farce" in four acts by Jules MASSENET, retailing the licentious adventures, tempered by philosophical divinations, of the gay rogue Panurge, devious and cunning companion of the hirsute and multifutuent giant Pantagruel in the celebrated satirical chronicle by Rabelais, is performed posthumously in Paris.

### 26 APRIL 1913

Three weeks before his forty-seventh birthday Erik SATIE composes *Sur un Casque*, the third and last piece of his piano suite *Descriptions automatiques*, in barless notation, interspersed with self-congratulatory marginal remarks such as *C'est magnifique!* and nonsensically mocking exhortations such as *Léger comme un œuf.*

(The first piece, *Sur un vaisseau*, written on 21 April 1913, contains this annotation: *Le Captiaine dit: Très beau voyage;* the second, composed on 22 April 1913, entitled *Sur une lanterne*, warns the player: *N'allumez pas encore: vous avez le temps!*)

The public is shocked by the charming mockery of the titles and expression marks used by Erik Satie, but it has respect for the formidable nonsense of the *Parsifal* libretto. The same public accepts the craziest titles of François Couperin: *Le tic-tic choc ou Les Maillotins, Les Culbutes JXCXBXNXS, Les Coucous bénévoles, Calotins et Calotines ou la Pièce à tretous, Les Vieux galants, Les Trésorières surannées.* (Jean Cocteau, *Le Rappel à l'ordre*, Paris, 1926)

### 27 APRIL 1913

*Arianna*, musical intermezzo by Benedetto MARCELLO, written by him in 1727 and rediscovered in 1885, is performed for the first time in concert form at the Liceo Benedetto Marcello in Venice.

### 15 MAY 1913

The first set of *Impressioni dal Vero*, a symphonic triptych by Gian Francesco MALIPIERO, in three sections, illustrating the sound of a warbler, a woodpecker (repeatedly pecking at a high F-sharp), and an owl (represented by an intermittent hoot in the low register of the flute), in impressionistically succulent harmonies, is performed for the first time in Milan.

### 15 MAY 1913

*Jeux*, ballet by Claude DEBUSSY, representing a tennis match during which a ball bouncing off the grass court gives the pretext for a country lad to chase girls running after the ball, written in a rhythmically hedonistic manner with brief explosive motives suggesting the action, is performed for the first time by Diaghilev's Ballet Russe in Paris, with Nijinsky as the principal dancer and choreographer.

## 22 MAY 1913

A century has passed since the birth in Leipzig of Richard WAGNER, originator of music drama in which the orchestra is elevated to symphonic significance and a network of leitmotivs is established to characterize personages, objects and even abstract concepts.

## 29 MAY 1913

Diaghilev's Ballet Russe presents in Paris the world première of Igor STRAVINSKY's epoch-making ballet *Le Sacre du Printemps* (in the original Russian, *Vesna Sviashchennaya*, i.e. Spring the Sacred), "scenes of pagan Russia" (completed in piano score on 17 November 1912; orchestration finished on 8 March 1913), with choreography by Nijinsky, in two parts:

Part I: THE KISS OF THE EARTH, opening with a bassoon solo in the uppermost reaches of its range; *Fortune-Telling in the Spring*, in stamping duple time; *Dance of Smartly-Dressed Young Women*, with the melodies confined within the compass of a perfect fifth, characteristic of very old Russian folksongs; *The Game of Abduction*, primitivistic and brusque with truncated meters, pullulating rhythmic patterns and asymmetric chordal ejaculations; *Spring Rounds*, a syncopated march, opening and closing with six bars of serene folk refrains; *Game of Two Camps*, a polytonal and polyrhythmic display of primitive strength in a millennial bowling game; *Procession of the Oldest and Wisest Chieftain*, stupefyingly persistent in crutch-pounding in the low brass; *Dance of the Earth*, with a stolid terrestrial solo in triple time, accompanied by seismic activities throwing out enormous boulders of blunt sonorities into the instrumental stratosphere, with a subterranean motto on the primeval pedal point C. Part II: THE GREAT SACRIFICE, opening with a polyharmonic reedy murmuration in volatile timbres; *Secret Rites and Rounds of Young Maidens*, in a major-minor bitonal complex, ending with a series of eleven identical bitonal chords; *The Glorification of the Chosen Maiden*, in constantly changing meters, with the eighth-note as the lowest common metrical denominator, dynamically and rhythmically vitalized into a frenzied dance; *Appeal to the Ancestors*, a turgidly treading, ominously austere vision of stony men-idols; *Rites of Old Men, Human Forebears*, with D as the keynote, projecting a sinuously chromatic solo of the English horn against a rhythmic duple-time figure, culminating in a cadential petrification; *The Great Sacred Dance* in ternary form, with a 16th-note as the lowest common denominator in the first and third sections, and the eighth-note in the middle section; *Sostenuto e Maestoso*, with a quarter-note as the main unit, in triplets or duplets, reverting to the *Great Sacred Dance* in constantly changing meters of 1, 2, 3, 4 and 5 16th notes in a measure, until, after a scratch on a Cuban guiro (used here for the first time in European orchestral music) and a fertilizing seminal ejaculation from the piccolos and flutes, the music comes to a stop on the keynote D, topped by the tritone G-sharp in the highest register, acoustically constituting the 45th overtone.

Does Stravinsky really believe that a melody would become more intense and eloquent if it is doubled for 50 bars by a second above it, a second below it, or both? The innovations embodied in the score of *Le Sacre du Printemps* are mostly of this type. (H. Quttard, *Le Figaro*, Paris, 31 May 1913)

The most important distinction achieved by *Le Sacre du Printemps* is its claim to be the most discordant composition ever written. Never has the cult of the wrong note been applied with such industry, zeal and ferocity. From the first measure to the last, whatever note one expects is never the one that comes, but the nearest one to it; whatever harmony is suggested by a preceding chord, it is always another chord that is heard; and this chord and this note are used deliberately to produce the sensation of acute and almost cruel dissonance. When two melodies are superimposed, far be it from the composer's mind to use those that fit together; quite to the contrary, he selects them so that their superposition should produce the most irritating friction and squeaking that can be imagined. (Pierre Lalo, *Le Temps*, Paris, 3 June 1913)

Igor Stravinsky is displeased. The audience of the Ballets Russes reacted to his new work *Le Sacre du Printemps* with discordant outcries and laughter, interrupted by the applause of a few initiates. But in all fairness I must say that the composer was not very much upset and did not fulminate too violently against his detractors when we interviewed him yesterday.

Stravinsky is small in stature, but looks tall because he holds his forehead high, so that he dominates his interlocutor; he speaks from an elevation, and his eyes rove over objects and people with a mobility that engulfs them like a sudden shower.

"That my music could not be immediately accepted, I quite understand," he declared backstage at the Théâtre des Champs-Elysées. "What is unjustifiable, however, is the lack of good will on the part of the audience. It seems to me that they should have waited for the end of the performance to express their disapproval. This would have been courteous and honest. I gave them something new, and I fully expected that those who had applauded *Pétrouchka* and *The Firebird* would be somewhat dismayed, but I also expected an understanding attitude. I have acted in good faith; my previous works which have been well received were a guarantee of my sincerity, and should have proved that I had no intention whatsoever of making fun of the public. During the première, when the commotion made it impossible for the dancers to hear the music, we all were quite unhappy, not only because of our own pride, but because we feared that we would not be able to go on with the show. And this was the reward for 130 rehearsals and of a year of work!"

"Nijinsky was criticised for his choreography; some said it was alien to the music."

"They were wrong. Nijinsky is an admirable artist. He is capable of revolutionizing the art of ballet. He is not only a marvelous dancer, but he is able to create something new. His contribution to *Le Sacre du Printemps* was very important. However, I am confident that some day, perhaps soon, my music will be fully understood. An unexpected novelty disconcerts Paris, but Paris knows how to regain its composure and forget its bad humor."

Paris, which admires Nijinsky as a dancer, does not admire him at all as a choreographer. It is regrettable, but it is a fact. Recall his staging of *L'Après-midi d'un Faune* and *Jeux*, when Debussy went through some pretty bad moments, watching the spectacle in silence, philosophically and prudently. Let Nijinsky dance, for he dances like a young god. But for the sake of all of us, poor French art lovers, he must stop trying to direct the dancing of others, interpreting poetic texts and transforming *Le Sacre* into a *Massacre du Printemps*. (Henri Postel du Mas, *Gil Blas*, Paris, 4 June, 1913)

The music of *Le Sacre du Printemps* baffles verbal description. To say that much of it is hideous as sound is a mild description. There is certainly an impelling rhythm traceable. Practically, it has no relation to music at all as most of us understand the word. (*The Musical Times*, London, 1 August 1913)

The Paleozoic Crawl turned into tone with all the resources of the modern orchestra

. . . the primitive run riot, almost formless and without definite tonality, save for insistently beating rhythms that made the tom-tom melodies of the gentle Congo tribes seem super-sophisticated in comparison . . . Without description or program, *Le Sacre du Printemps* might have suggested a New Year's Eve rally of moonshine addicts and the simple pastimes of early youths and maidens, circumspectly attired in a fig leaf apiece. (Philadelphia *North American*, 4 March 1922)

The public played the role that it had to play. It laughed, spat, hissed, imitated animal cries. They might have eventually tired themselves of that if it had not been for the crowd of esthetes and a few musicians who, carried by excess of zeal, insulted and even pushed the occupants of the loges. The riot degenerated into a fight. Standing in her box, her diadem askew, the old Comtesse de Pourtalès brandished her fan and shouted: "It is the first time in sixty years that anyone has dared to make a fool of me!" The good lady was sincere. She really thought it was a mystification. (Jean Cocteau, *Le Rappel à l'ordre*, Paris, 1926)


## 2 JUNE 1913

Luigi RUSSOLO, 28-year-old Italian Futurist musician and painter, presents in Modena for the first time in public his ensemble of noise-makers, *Intonarumore,* invented by him and constructed in collaboration with Ugo Piatti.


## 2 JUNE 1913

*Julien,* or *La Vie du Poète,* opera in four acts with a prologue by Gustave CHARPENTIER, a sequel to his masterwork *Louise,* to his own libretto depicting in naturalistic colors the decline, despair and ultimate dissolution of a philosophically disposed artist, marked by ethereal mysticism and eclectic pantheism (a bearded priest discourses in a Temple of Beauty, Julien challenges Nature on a Hungarian plain, an artistic festival is held in Montmartre), is presented at the Opéra-Comique in Paris in a special public rehearsal. (The official world première took place on 4 June 1913)

Paris Sees Charpentier's *Julien*—Enthusiasm Evoked by Sheer Beauty and Lyric Passion of the Music and Superb Stage Setting—Long Expected Continuation of Louise Is a Success—Critics Disappointed, However, by the Failure of the Composer to Produce Any Really New Note (Headlines in the New York *Sun,* 3 June 1913)


## 3 JUNE 1913

Edgar Stillman KELLEY conducts at the Norfolk, Connecticut, Music Festival the first performance of his *Second Symphony,* subtitled *New England,* 24 years before the first performance of his *First Symphony.*


## 5 JUNE 1913

Henry F. GILBERT, American composer, ardent champion of musical Americanism, conducts the New York Philharmonic at the 25th Meeting of the Litchfield County Choral Union in Norfolk, Connecticut, in the first performance of his *Negro Rhapsody,* subtitled *Shout,* inspired by the exalted outcries at Negro religious gatherings and making use of themes from Negro spirituals.

## 7 JUNE 1913

*First Symphony* by Josef Matthias HAUER, subtitled *Nomos,* in seven movements for 2 pianos 4 hands, derived from the putative law (nomos) of Terpandros, Greek philosopher who flourished circa 700 B.C., is performed for the first time in Sankt Pölten, Austria.

## 10 JUNE 1913

Tikhon KHRENNIKOV, Russian composer whose healthy diatonic style represents the optimistic philosophy underlying the Soviet doctrine of Socialist Realism unobscured by pre-revolutionary ambiguities and ambivalences, is born in Eletz.

## 19 JUNE 1913

A concert of music by Claude DEBUSSY, prefaced by a lecture "Claude Debussy et la Pensée contemporaine" by Émile Vuillermoz, takes place in Paris, with Debussy at the piano playing the first performances in public of three pieces from his newly completed second book of *Préludes: Canope,* inspired by the Grecian urn in his workroom ("canope" is the cover of a funerary receptacle), in which mortuary outcries interrupt stately progressions of parallel triads; *La Terrasse des audiences du clair de lune,* an impressionistic evocation of the terraced approaches to a moonlit Buddhist temple in Indo-China; and *Hommage à Pickwick, Esq.,* opening with the strains of *God Save the King* in the bass and progressing through a series of portentously portly harmonies, with incidental discords suggesting the risible gaucheries of Pickwick's figure.

## 30 JUNE 1913

*Abul,* opera on a biblical subject by the Brazilian composer Alberto NEPOMUCENO, is produced for the first time at the Teatro Colón in Buenos Aires.

## 30 JUNE 1913

Erik SATIE composes *Holothurie,* the first of his three piano pieces under the general title *Desiccated Embryos,* in barless notation, urging the player to perform "comme un rossignol qui aurait mal aux dents" in order to adequately paint in tones the ossicles and the spicules of the echinodermic sea cucumber.

## 1 JULY 1913

Erik SATIE composes *Edriophthalmia,* the second piano piece of his suite *Desiccated Embryos,* portraying a group of crustaceans with sessile eyes, with a quotation from Chopin's Funeral March waggishly labeled "citation de la célèbre mazurka de Schubert."

## 4 JULY 1913

Erik SATIE writes the third and last number of his piano suite *Desiccated Embryos,* entitled *Podophthalmia,* in barless notation, purported to represent the order of malacostracan crustaceans with eyes supported on movable stalks, in humorously trite F-major arpeggios.

## 6 JULY 1913

At the annual audition of works submitted for the Prix de Rome, the Académie des Beaux-Arts in Paris awards the Premier Grand Prix de Rome to Lili BOULANGER, nineteen years and ten and a half months old, the first woman to receive this high award.

The Academy of Fine Arts assembled yesterday for the final audition of cantatas submitted for the Prix de Rome in music. The contestants, five in number, were to set to music the text *Faust and Helen* after Goethe. Upon the requisite drawing of lots, the cantata by Claude Delvincourt was heard first; the cantata by Marc Delmas followed. Mademoiselle Lili Boulanger, a pupil of Paul Vidal came next. Her cantata was accompanied by her sister Nadia Boulanger. Then cantatas of Marcel Dupré and Edouard Mignan were performed. After a long deliberation, the Academy adjudged the Grand Prix de Rome, by 31 votes to 5, to Mlle Lili Boulanger and the Second Grand Prix to Claude Delvincourt by 29 votes to 7. Marc Delmas received the first Second Grand Prix. The result was greeted by a long ovation. Mlle Boulanger, who is not quite twenty, is the first woman to be awarded the Grand Prix in music. Her elder sister, Nadia Boulanger, had also entered the competition for the Grand Prix. She obtained the Second Grand Prix in 1908, but was less fortunate than her younger sister and did not succeed in carrying the Grand Prix in 1909. (*Le Temps*, Paris, 7 July 1913)

## 18 JULY 1913

Nine centuries have passed since the birth of Hermannus CONTRACTUS (nicknamed "contracted" because he was a hunchback), enlightened musical scientist and inventor of a system of intervalic notation that anticipated equal temperament.

## 7 AUGUST 1913

David POPPER, Prague-born virtuoso cellist and composer of numerous celebrated pieces for his instrument, dies in Baden at the age of seventy.

## 25 AUGUST 1913

Erik SATIE composes *Españaña*, the third and last of the series of piano pieces in barless notation under the general title *Croquis et Agaceries d'un gros Bonhomme en Bois*, a sarcastic bisyllabilization of *España*, containing anamorphosed quotations from Chabrier's famous *España*.

(The first number of the series, heteroethnically entitled *Tyrolienne turque*, was written on 28 July 1913; the second, *Danse maigre*, a quasi-homonymous phonetic variant of *Danse nègre*, was written on 2 June 1913)

## 5 SEPTEMBER 1913

At a summer concert in Pavlovsk, a suburb of St. Petersburg, 22-year-old Sergei PROKOFIEV plays the solo part in the first performance of his *Second Con-*

*certo* in G minor for piano and orchestra, in four movements, alternatively lyric and energetic, marked by widely leaping melodic intervals in resonant harmonies and instantaneous modulations into keys a semitone off the principal tonic, resulting in a playful barbarization of the classical modalities, and culminating in the finale in overt polyharmony. (A revised version of the *Second Concerto* was first performed by Prokofiev on 8 May 1924 in Paris, at a concert conducted by Serge Koussevitzky)

The debut of the pianistic cubist and futurist Prokofiev has brought excitement in the public. In the train going to Pavlovsk, one hears on all sides: "Prokofiev, Prokofiev, Prokofiev . . . a new star of the piano!" A youngster appears on the podium. It is Sergei Prokofiev. He sits at the piano and proceeds to make motions as though he were dusting the keys or tuning the instrument. All this he does with a sharp dry touch. The audience is puzzled. Some are outraged. A couple leaves and runs for the exit: "This kind of music will drive you crazy!" "What is this? A deliberate persiflage?!" After the first exits, other listeners begin to leave their seats. Prokofiev is now playing the second movement of his Concerto. Once more, a rhythmic jumble of sounds. The more audacious members of the audience begin to hiss. The hall is gradually emptying. Finally, with a mercilessly dissonant combination of brass instruments, the young artist concludes his Concerto. Most listeners react by booing. Prokofiev bows defiantly, then plays an encore. The public flees. On all sides one hears, "To the devil with this futurist music! My cat can play like that!" Prokofiev's Concerto is cacophony which has nothing to do with cultural music. His cadenzas are insufferable. The *Concerto* is filled to overflow with musical mud, produced, one may imagine, by accidental spilling of ink on music paper. (*St. Petersburg Gazetta*, 7 September 1913)

Young Prokofiev outdid the "man of wisdom and light" Scriabin. His Concerto is a torrent of muddy water. (*Novoye Vremya*, St. Petersburg, 7 September 1913)

The audience hissed. This is in the order of things. Some ten years from now it will expiate these hisses by unanimous applause for Sergei Prokofiev, famous composer with a European reputation. (*Rech*, St. Petersburg, 7 September 1913)

2 OCTOBER 1913

Edward ELGAR conducts at the Leeds Festival the first performance of his "symphonic study in C minor with two interludes in A minor" titled *Falstaff*, an affectionate tonal portrait of Shakespeare's amiable fat hero whose pomposity is epitomized in a bassoon cadenza marked "full tone, coarse" bestriding in large awkward intervals the entire range of the instrument, and his tragedy in repudiation and death signalized by a puny solo on the small sidedrum.

2 OCTOBER 1913

*A Shropshire Lad*, orchestral rhapsody by the 28-year-old English composer George BUTTERWORTH, expanded from his song *The Cherry Tree*, to the words of A. E. Housman, poetically reflecting the brooding meditations of a rustic lad away from his native place, in a tranquil modal manner with occasional outbursts of quasi-impressionistic harmonies, is performed for the first time at the Leeds Festival, Arthur Nikisch conducting.

## 2 OCTOBER 1913

Two pastoral symphonic pieces by Frederick DELIUS, *On Hearing the First Cuckoo in Spring* and *Summer Night on the River,* permeated with the folkloric spirit of English song and set in euphonious Germanic harmonies, are performed for the first time anywhere in Leipzig.

(The first English performance of both pieces took place on 20 January 1914, played by the London Philharmonic Orchestra, under the direction of Willem Mengelberg)

## 8 OCTOBER 1913

*The Fair at Sorotchintzy,* unfinished opera by MUSSORGSKY, after Gogol's tale depicting the lusty merriment of a Ukrainian market day, supplemented by music from other works of Mussorgsky, and arranged by various hands, is performed for the first time in Moscow in a three-act version. (Another version, by César Cui, was produced in Petrograd on 26 October 1917; still another, edited by Vissarion Shebalin, using only Mussorgsky's own materials, was first performed in Leningrad on 21 December 1931; a version with supplementary materials by Shebalin, was brought out in Moscow on 13 March 1952)

## 12 OCTOBER 1913

The Gesellschaft der Musikfreunde of Donaueschingen (organized on 18 September 1913) presents its first concert of an annual series intended to foster general interest in modern music, and destined to continue, with some interruptions by wars and political upheavals, for more than half a century.

## 12 OCTOBER 1913

Max REGER conducts in Essen the world première of his *4 Tondichtungen nach Arnold Böcklin:*

(1) *Der geigende Eremit,* picturing in folk-like tones a violin-playing hermit before the statue of the Madonna (2) *Im Spiel der Wellen,* a waltztime seascape representing Böcklin's picture of mermaids and merlads porpoising purposefully amid gentle waves (3) *Die Toteninsel,* a thanatological evocation of Böcklin's volcanic island lined with funereal cypress trees, with the horns sounding a sepulchral fanfare (4) *Bacchanal,* a riotous dance of vinous Romans.

## 19 OCTOBER 1913

*Festliches Præludium* by Richard STRAUSS (completed on 11 May 1913) for orchestra and chorus, making use of the novel device Aerophor, helping to sustain breath playing long notes in the brass instruments, is performed for the first time at the inauguration of the Konzert-Haus in Vienna, for which occasion the work was commissioned.

## 19 OCTOBER 1913

*Moscou,* third symphony by Charles TOURNEMIRE, is performed for the first time anywhere in Amsterdam.

## 25 OCTOBER 1913

*Polenblut,* operetta by the 39-year-old Czech composer Oskar NEDBAL, outlining a love quadrangle wherein an impoverished Polish count disdains an eager heiress who thereupon therapeutically dons peasant skirts and approaches him incognito stirring his Polish blood (hence the title) sufficiently to lure him into marriage, is produced in Vienna.

## 26 OCTOBER 1913

Erik SATIE composes three piano pieces in one day, under the general title *Peccadilles importunes,* with a self-deprecating marginal note in the manuscript "Si le bon Dieu voit cela il sera furieux."

## 30 OCTOBER 1913

*Der Abenteurer,* musical play in four acts by the 39-year-old Austrian composer Julius BITTNER, to his own libretto dealing with a semi-legendary adventurer named Jerome de Montfleury in which he makes use of a psychological "tendency motive" serving as a monothematic melorhythmic motto of the entire score, is performed for the first time in Cologne.

## 1 NOVEMBER 1913

*Are you there?,* musical farce in three acts by Ruggero LEONCAVALLO, to an English text, is produced in London.

## 5 NOVEMBER 1913

*Men on the Line,* cantata by the 30-year-old English operetta composer Hubert BATH, containing in the score some onomatopeic sounds descriptive of the bustle and commotion of a large railway in operation, is performed for the fist time by the Great Eastern Railway Musical Society in London.

## 22 NOVEMBER 1913

Benjamin BRITTEN, magus of modern English music, whose operas, symphonies, oratorios and chamber music are imbued with the imperishable spirit of musical Englishry and marked by technical expertise, astutely incorporating the most viable elements of cosmopolitan modernism, is born in Lowestoft.

## 22 NOVEMBER 1913

*Shylock,* opera in three acts by the Belgian composer Flor ALPAERTS, to a libretto after Shakespeare in the Flemish language, is produced in Antwerp.

## 28 NOVEMBER 1913

*Sinfonietta* by the 16-year-old Viennese wonder boy Erich KORNGOLD, a score of Straussian complexity with a "motive of the cheerful heart" built on ascending fourths as a thematic nucleus, is performed for the first time in Vienna, Felix Weingartner conducting.

Occasion: the third Philharmonic concert. Scene: the great concert hall of the Mus-ikverein in Vienna. Prophets to the right, prophets to the left, and the wonder child, young Korngold, in the middle. . . . His *Sinfonietta* performed for the first time before what is perhaps the most critical audience in the world went the way of most productions destined to outlive the praise or blame of the day: it evoked storms of applause and protests. (*The Musical Courier,* New York, 7 January 1914)

### 3 DECEMBER 1913

*Second Symphony* by the 38-year-old Austrian romantic composer Franz SCHMIDT, in the heroic key of E flat major, in three movements, the middle one being a theme with ten variations, and the Finale containing a magisterial fugue, is performed for the first time in Vienna.

### 4 DECEMBER 1913

*L'Amore Medico,* opera in two acts by the German-Italian composer Ermanno WOLF-FERRARI, after Molière's comedy *L'Amour médecin,* is performed for the first time in Dresden, in the German version under the title *Der Liebhaber als Arzt.*

### 9 DECEMBER 1913

*Der Rosenkavalier* by Richard STRAUSS is presented for the first time in America by the Metropolitan Opera in New York.

Richard Strauss Turns His Hand to a Comedy Opera—Von Hofmannsthal's Sprightly Libretto Filled with Music Which is Mozartian in Terms of the Modern Orchestra—The Altogether New and Different Strauss of This Score—Its Waltz Tunes Not Distinguished—Its Humor Often Exaggerated, but Remarkable in His Union of Intricacy and Simplicity. (Headlines in the Boston *Evening Transcript,* 10 December 1913)

*Rosenkavalier* at Metropolitan—A Vapid and Salacious Comedy Given with Great Earnestness—From Necrophilism to Lubricity—The Policy of Such a Production at the Opera Questioned (Headlines in the New York *Tribune,* 10 December 1913)

### 9 DECEMBER 1913

Franz KULLAK, German piano pedagogue and highly conscientious and competent editor of piano classics, son of Theodor KULLAK, nephew of Adolf KULLAK, first cousin of Ernst KULLAK, respectively respectable pianists and teachers, dies in Berlin in his 70th year.

### 10 DECEMBER 1913

Morton GOULD, American composer of modernistic symphonies, concertos and chamber music, as well as inventive pieces in a popular vein, is born in New York City.

### 10 DECEMBER 1913

In his first appearance in Russia as a symphonic conductor, Claude DEBUSSY leads Serge Koussevitzky's orchestra in Moscow in a program of his works, including *Nocturnes, Clarinet Rhapsody, La Mer, L'Après-midi d'un Faune, Images* and *Marche écossaise.*

### 13 DECEMBER 1913

Serge RACHMANINOFF conducts in St. Petersburg the first performance of his choral symphonic poem *Kolokola (The Bells)*, completed by him on 9 August 1913, to the text of Edgar Allan Poe's onomatopoeic ode to tintinnabulating bells translated into Russian, in four movements: a merrily jangling *Allegro*, an epithalamian *Lento* adorned by caressing orientalistic melismas, a *Presto*, ringing the chimes of alarums, and a sepulchrally funereal *Lento lugubre.*

### 15 DECEMBER 1913

*Parisina,* opera in four acts by Pietro MASCAGNI, to a libretto by Gabriele d'Annunzio, wherein the Duke of Ferrara orders his natural son to be beheaded when he learns that his favorite concubine Parisina was his son's clandestine inamorata, set to an emotionally Italianate score in the Verismo manner, scaling the operatic heights and plumbing dramatic depths, is performed for the first time at La Scala, Milan.

### 19 DECEMBER 1913

*Flup!,* the first and the most popular operetta in three acts by Jósef Zygmunt SZULC, 38-year-old Warsaw-born Parisianised composer of light music, with action taking place in Ceylon in May 1913, wherein a British Duke exchanges identities with a waterfront porter known under the quasi-canine appellation Flup (the exclamation point in the title indicates the vocative case suitable to Flup's profession) in order to win by proxy the hand of the British Colonial Resident's daughter, a royalty-hating militant suffragette, is produced in Brussels.

# ～ 1914 ～

### 17 JANUARY 1914

Erik SATIE composes a *Choral hypocrite* for violin and piano, ten bars in length, set in acerbic harmonies, with a verbal declaration, "My chorales are equal to those of Bach, with this difference that they are fewer and less pretentious," this being the first of his three violin pieces, under the general title *Choses vues à Droite et à Gauche (Sans Lunettes)* calculated to present a monocular view of bars dexter and bars sinister.

(The second piece, *Fugue à tâtons,* a tentative fugue on a French nursery tune, bears the date of 21 January 1914; the third, *Fantaisie musculaire,* consisting of a series of flexed arpeggios and debile trills, with a pompously inane violin cadenza ending "very contritely" on a succession of 13 low G's, is dated 30 January 1914)

## 17 JANUARY 1914

At his first appearance in London as composer-conductor, Arnold SCHOENBERG conducts his *5 Orchesterstücke.*

London Baffled by Schoenberg's *Orchestral Pieces*—Composer Himself Conducts and He at Least Is Pleased—Reminiscent of a Nightmare (Headlines in *Musical America,* New York, 14 February 1914)
To one critic, the music of Schoenberg's *Five Orchestral Pieces* suggested feeding time at the zoo; also a farmyard in great activity while pigs are being ringed and geese strangled. On another the identical section of the work produced the impression of a village fair with possibly a blind clarinetist playing at random. The same listener heard sounds as of sawing steel and the distant noise of an approaching train alternately with the musical sobs of a dynamo. (*Daily Telegraph,* London, 24 January 1914)

Sir: Any one acquainted with music history would find little cause for surprise at the incoherent criticism following on the performance of Schoenberg's *Five Orchestral Pieces.* The vulgarity of the writer who stated that "long hair used to be indispensable but now has been superseded by the bald head" (an obvious and disgraceful attack on the personality of Herr Schoenberg) and the even more stupid remark of the other person who wrote that "they (the Schoenberg pieces) were so ridiculous in their cha-otic formlessness that the orchestra sometimes laughed down their instruments instead of blowing down them," may be dismissed as examples of ignorance and lack of de-cency. It is, however, surprising to find this bewilderment on the part of our most sin-cere critics. May I venture to suggest that it is a lack of constructive vision in regard to musical psychology? (Letter to the Editor of the *Daily Telegraph,* London, by Leigh Henry, 17 February 1914)

In January 1914 we repeated Schoenberg's *Five Orchestral Pieces* with Schoenberg conducting. The performance drew a large and appreciative audience who may or may not have been surprised by the following notice in the programme: "Herr Arnold Schoenberg has promised his cooperation at today's concert on condition that during the performance of his *Orchestral Pieces* perfect silence is maintained." (Henry J. Wood, *My Life in Music,* London, 1938)

## 24 JANUARY 1914

*Canossa,* musical scene by Gian Francesco MALIPIERO, based on the episode of the Emperor Henry IV's genuflected submission to the Pope in Canossa in 1077, is given its first and last performance in Rome, after which Malipiero destroyed the manuscript.

## 24 JANUARY 1914

*Madeleine,* lyric opera in one act by Victor HERBERT, dealing with a tempera-mental prima donna whose friends insist on spending New Year's day with their mothers, is produced at the Metropolitan Opera in New York, with con-siderable acclaim and 16 curtain calls.

### 31 JANUARY 1914

*Orphée*, lyric mimodrama in three acts by the 50-year-old French composer Jean-Jules Aimable ROGER-DUCASSE, for orchestra, solo voices and choruses, depicting Orpheus as a virtuous virtuoso on the lyre, who is dismembered by furibond mænads when he scorns their nymphomaniacal advances, set in an evocatively neo-archaic manner, with explosive rhythmic asymmetries, is performed for the first time, without choreography, in St. Petersburg, Alexander Siloti conducting. (First stage performance of *Orphée* as a ballet was given at the Paris Opéra on 11 June 1926)

### 4 FEBRUARY 1914

*Las Golondrinas* (*The Swallows*), opera in three acts by the 26-year-old Basque composer José María USANDIZAGA, dealing with passionate turbulence among members of a traveling circus, and culminating in the murder of a fickle equestrienne by the director of the troupe, set to music in a pleasingly Italianate idiom, seasoned with stimulating Pyrenean melorhythms, is produced in Madrid, less than two years before Usandizaga's untimely death.

### 6 FEBRUARY 1914

A year after the death of the Germanic romantic composer Felix DRAESEKE, his last symphony, completed on 22 August 1912, and entitled *Symphonia comica*, in four movements, the humor of which reaches its high point in an episode called *Fliegenkrieg*, with flies battling chromatically against a background of buzzing tremolos, is performed for the first and last time from manuscript, in Dresden.

A musician's lot in Germany is a canto missing in Dante's *Inferno*. But I did not allow my sense of humor to be ruined, as I proved in my latest opus. (From Draeseke's letter written in June, 1912, to a friendly symphonic conductor.)

### 10 FEBRUARY 1914

*Abisso*, last opera in three acts by the 59-year-old blind Italian composer Antonio SMAREGLIA, couched in a Wagnerophylic idiom refreshed by sprays of florid Mediterranean melos, is produced at La Scala, Milan.

### 12 FEBRUARY 1914

*Estrellita*, nostalgic song by the 31-year-old Mexican composer Manuel PONCE, so authentically Latin in its expansive melorhythmic expression that it became mistakenly identified as a folk song, is published in Mexico City.

### 13 FEBRUARY 1914

The American Society of Composers, Authors and Publishers (ASCAP), established to protect performing rights and to distribute annual fees to members according to the frequency of performance of their music, is formally organized at a dinner meeting in the Hotel Claridge in New York under the directorship of Victor HERBERT.

234

## 14 FEBRUARY 1914

*La Chanson d'Halewyn,* musical legend by the Belgian composer Albert DUPUIS, depicting in Wagneromantic tones a series of mystical events in a medieval castle, is produced in the Flemish language, under the title *Det Lied van Heer Halewyn.* (It was first produced as a cantata for which Dupuis won the Prix de Rome, in Brussels, on 25 November 1903; the printed score gives the apparently premature date of 6 December 1913 for the performance of the operatic version.)

## 17 FEBRUARY 1914

Ernst von DOHNÁNYI, 36-year-old Hungarian composer and pianist, plays in Berlin the solo piano part in the first performance of his *Variationen über ein Kinderlied* (*Variations on a Nursery Song*), dedicated "to the enjoyment of lovers of humor and to the annoyance of others," containing eleven variations on the 18th-century French air *Ah, Vous dirai-je, maman,* introduced by the theme played bidigitally on the piano solo, and replete with polychromatic pianistic pyrotechnics in a Brahmsogenetic vein.

Dohnányi's *Variations* must rank high among the modern classics in one of the severest of art forms. (Sir Donald Tovey, *Essays in Musical Analysis,* vol. 3, London, 1939)

Dohnányi's wit can be very ponderous, as in the *Variations on a Nursery Song,* where the comic effect of the deliberately portentous introduction, followed by the thin, schoolgirlish delivery of the theme by the soloist, has no more subtlety than the mountain delivering the ridiculous mouse. (Eric Blom, in the article on Dohnányi in the Fifth Edition of Grove's *Dictionary of Music and Musicians,* London, 1954)

## 19 FEBRUARY 1914

*Francesca da Rimini,* fourth and most successful opera in four acts by Riccardo ZANDONAI, to a libretto after a tragedy by Gabriele d'Annunzio, inspired by the famous episode in Dante's *Inferno,* is produced in Turin.

## 23 FEBRUARY 1914

*Cléopâtre,* "drame passionel," last opera by Jules MASSENET, in four acts, to a libretto introducing a historically undocumented emancipated Greek slave as Cleopatra's last lover, is produced posthumously in Monte Carlo.

## 23 FEBRUARY 1914

*The Midnight Girl,* first American operetta by the 26-year-old Hungarian-born composer Sigmund ROMBERG, is produced in New York.

## 10 MARCH 1914

*La Fille de Figaro,* operetta in three acts by Xavier LEROUX, is performed for the first time in Paris.

## 11 MARCH 1914

*Hashish,* symphonic poem by the Russian composer Sergei LIAPUNOV, illustrating the vividly sensual visions of lissome oriental beauties seductively disporting themselves in serpentine chromatics induced by the smoking of hashish, is performed for the first time in St. Petersburg.

### 11 MARCH 1914

At Carnegie Hall, New York, Jim EUROPE conducts a Negro symphony orchestra in an instrumental ensemble anticipatory of jazz bands, sans oboes, bassoons or second violins, but with a cornucopia of clarinets, trumpets, trombones, banjos, a set of drums and a phalanx of ten pianos.

### 17 MARCH 1914

*I Mori di Valenza,* opera by Amilcare PONCHIELLI, written by him in 1879, and rediscovered in 1902, is performed for the first time at Monte Carlo.

### 20 MARCH 1914

*The Banks of Green Willows,* orchestral idyll by the English composer George BUTTERWORTH with melodic materials inspired by English countryside tunes, is performed for the first time in London.

### 27 MARCH 1914

The world première is given in London of *A London Symphony* by Ralph VAUGHAN WILLIAMS, his *Second Symphony,* descriptive of the sights and sounds of London, scored for a very large orchestra with an extensive set of percussion including tam-tam and a pod of jingles, in four movements:

(1) *Lento; Allegro risoluto,* opening at dawn on the Thames River with the solemn sound of the Big Ben leading to the busy London day, newspaper boys shouting the headlines, costermongers singing their refrains, clerks whistling confidently, while the residential section of the town remains dreamily lyrical and tonally relaxed (2) *Lento,* a Bloomsbury vigil in November fog, an old fiddler playing in front of a pub, the distant voice of a lavender vendor forming an antiphonal contrast, concluding in a modally inflected diatonic mist (3) *Scherzo (Nocturne): Allegro vivace,* a Saturday night near the Houses of Parliament, with the sounds of muted merriment wafted by a slow wind from the other side of the Thames, coster girls dancing a double-shuffle jig accompanied by a mouth harmonica, a hurdy-gurdy grinding its ballads, until the sempiternal London fog lowers its veil upon the scene (4) *Andante con moto; Maestoso alla Marcia. Epilogue: Andante sostenuto,* revealing the London of the lower classes, still struggling against economic oppression, with the strains of a "Hunger March" colliding with the crowds in the wealthy districts of the city, gradually resolving into silence, in which the philosophical sound of the Westminster Chimes is heard again.

The title might run *A Symphony by a Londoner.* Various sights and sounds of London may have influenced the composer, but . . . if the hearers recognize a few suggestions of such things as the Westminster chimes, or the lavender cry, these must be treated as accidents and not essentials of the music. (Vaughan Williams in a statement)

The composer of the *London Symphony* understood that music begins where realistic noise leaves off. If his thoughts are not all pleasant or all hopeful individually, in their relations to one another he builds up something which is beautiful in its entirety. (London *Times,* 28 March 1914)

29 MARCH 1914

Alfredo CASELLA conducts the orchestra of the Concerts Colonne in Paris in the first performance of his *Notte di Maggio* for voice and orchestra, in which his "second style" of composition, polytonal and polymodal, is definitely established. (In his review of *Notte di Maggio* in *Comœdia*, Paris, on 30 March 1914, Émile Vuillermoz suggested that the term "polyharmony" might be advantageously used in place of polytonality to describe the superposition of two or more chords or melodic figures in different keys)

29 MARCH 1914

*Variations for Orchestra*, the first important work by the 32-year-old Dutch composer Sem DRESDEN, is performed for the first time by the Concertgebouw Orchestra in Amsterdam, Willem Mengelberg conducting.

1 APRIL 1914

*Madame Roland*, lyric drama in three acts by Felix FOURDRAIN, to the dramatic story of the French lady of progressive views who perished on the guillotine on 8 November 1793, ending with her famous cry "Oh Liberty, how many crimes are committed in your name," is produced in Paris.

1 APRIL 1914

*Notre Dame*, opera in two acts by Franz SCHMIDT, to a libretto from Victor Hugo's famous novel, is performed for the first time in Vienna. (An orchestral suite from the opera, characteristically titled *Zwischenspiel aus einer unvollständigen romantischen Oper*, was first performed in Vienna on 6 December 1903)

2 APRIL 1914

Five months before his tragic death, Albéric MAGNARD conducts, at a concert of the Union des Femmes Professeurs et Compositeurs in Paris, the first performance of his magnum opus, the resplendently expansive *Fourth Symphony*, in C-sharp minor, in four movements: (1) *Modéré*, with an oriflamme of fanfaric calls against the rumble of multidivisional harmonic figurations (2) *Vif*, a scherzo in 1/2 time in F minor (3) *Sans lenteur et nuancé* in E major (4) *Animé*, homonymically passing from the basic key of C-sharp minor to the eloquent tonality of D-flat major.

2 APRIL 1914

*L'Ombra di Don Giovanni*, opera in three acts by Franco ALFANO, is produced in Milan.

5 APRIL 1914

STRAVINSKY's *Le Sacre du Printemps* receives its first performance as a symphonic composition without stage action, at the Casino de Paris, conducted by Pierre Monteux.

12 APRIL 1914

A century has elapsed since the death of the great English music historian Charles BURNEY.

Full of years and full of virtues, the pride of his family, the delight of society, the unrivalled chief and scientific HISTORIAN of his tuneful Art! Beloved, revered, regretted, breathed in Chelsea College his last sigh! Leaving to posterity a fame unblemished, raised on the noble basis of intellectual attainments. High principles and pure benevolence, goodness with gaiety, talents with taste, were of his gifted mind the blended attributes; while the genial hilarity of his airy spirits animated or softened his every earthly toil; and a conscience without reproach prepared in the whole tenour of his mortal life, through the meditation of our Lord Jesus Christ his soul for heaven. Amen. Born April 7th Old Style 1726. Died April 12th 1814. (From the inscription on Burney's tombstone in Westminster Abbey)

19 APRIL 1914

*Der Heilige Berg,* the only opera by the Norwegian composer Christian SINDING, in two acts with a prologue, is produced, in a German version, in Dessau.

21 APRIL 1914

Luigi RUSSOLO, Futurist composer, inventor of *Intonarumori* (intonators of noises), presents in Milan the first performance of his bruitistic *Networks of Noises.* (The first public demonstration of *Intonarumori* as an instrumental medium was given by Russolo in Modena on 2 June 1913)

The program of the first concert of 4 *Networks of Noises* comprised the following works: (1) *The Awakening of the Capital* (2) *A Meeting of Automobiles and Airplanes* (3) *A Dinner on the Terrace of the Casino* (4) *A Skirmish in an Oasis.* Russolo conducted the orchestra composed of 19 bruiteurs:

| | | |
|---|---|---|
| 3 bumblers | 2 exploders | 2 gurglers |
| 3 thunderers | 3 whistlers | 2 rufflers |
| 1 fracasseur | 2 stridors | 1 snorer |

There was an enormous crowd. Boxes, the orchestra and balcony seats were filled to capacity. A deafening uproar of "passéistes" greeted us. They arrived with the express purpose of interrupting the concert at all costs. For an hour, the Futurists offered passive resistance. But an extraordinary thing happened just at the start of *Network of Noise No. 4*: five Futurists—Boccioni, Carra, Amando Mazza, Piatti and myself—descended from the stage, crossed the orchestra pit, and, right in the center of the hall, using their fists and canes, attacked the "passéistes," who appeared to be stultified and intoxicated with reactionary rage. The battle lasted fully half an hour. During all this time Luigi Russolo continued to conduct imperturbably the nineteen bruiteurs on the stage. It was a display of an amazing harmonic arrangement of bloody faces and dissonances, an infernal mêlée. Our previous battles took place in the streets or backstage after the performance. For the first time on this occasion the performing artists were suddenly divided into two groups: one group continued to play, while the other went down into the hall to combat the hostile and rioting audience. It is thus that an escort in the desert protects the caravan against the Touaregs. It is thus that the infantry sharpshooters provide cover for the construction of a military pontoon. Our skill in boxing and our fighting spirit enabled us to emerge from the skirmish with but a few bruises. But the "passéistes" suffered eleven wounded, who had to be taken to a first-aid station for treatment. (F. T. Marinetti, *L'Intransigeant*, Paris, 29 April 1914)

Real battles took place during my concerts. The incomprehension of the very serious principles underlying my music on the part of the public and the critics was exasperating. Only a few musicians of stature—among them Ravel and Stravinsky—understood the value of my innovations, as yet realized only in part. The financial impossibility to do my research compelled me to discontinue my work several years ago. I regret that I did not have an occasion to give a demonstration of my instruments when I had the pleasure of meeting you in Paris, at the time you conducted concerts of modern American music there. (Letter to Nicolas Slonimsky from Luigi Russolo, dated 24 August 1934)

### 23 APRIL 1914

*Madelon*, song by Camille ROBERT glorifying an amiable, accommodating and cooperative French barmaid, destined to become the most popular ballad of the battle-scarred poilus of World War I, is performed for the first time at the café-concert Eldorado in Paris.

### 6 MAY 1914

*Scemo*, lyric drama in five acts by Alfred BACHELET, his first opera, written in a mild Wagneromorphic idiom, dealing with a Corsican village idiot (*scemo* is a mental defective in a local dialect) who inspires a perverted passion in the bosom of a young matron in spite of his reputation as a *jettatore* (evil-eye), is produced at the Paris Opéra.

Composers of M. Bachelet's ilk are in my view the most savage enemies of music, who would inevitably lead it to total perdition if they were allowed to go on without a protest against their criminal activities . . . The most complex difficulties of Wagner's music are nothing in comparison with obstacles posed at every step in M. Bachelet's score. (Arthur Pougin, *Le Ménestrel*, Paris, 9 May 1914)

### 9 MAY 1914

A "Moderner Musikabend" is given in Wiener-Neustadt, with a program including the first performance of the *Third Symphony* by Josef Matthias HAUER.

### 10 MAY 1914

Lillian NORTON, American soprano, who was given a euphonious operatic name Giglia Nordica (Lily of the North) by her Italian teacher, possessor of a resonant Wagnerian voice and solid femininity (her first husband Frederick A. Gower vanished in a balloon flight over the English Channel), *diva assoluta* of prideful temperament (she once told the Boston Symphony Orchestra men that they played like a Kalamazoo band, thus alienating the affections of both Boston and Kalamazoo) and an authority on international cuisine (she baptized a delicacy, Chicken à la Nordica), dies at the age of fifty-six in Batavia, Java, on a concert tour around the world.

### 10 MAY 1914

*Die Marketenderin,* opera by Engelbert HUMPERDINCK, is produced in Cologne.

### 11 MAY 1914

*Don Juans Letztes Abenteuer,* opera in three acts by Paul GRAENER, depicting Don Juan's final affair with a Venetian patrician's young daughter, and postulating the supremacy of carnal love in chromatically Wagnerophallic harmonies is produced in Leipzig.

### 14 MAY 1914

Richard STRAUSS conducts, at Diaghilev's Ballet Russe in Paris, the first performance of his ballet in one act *Josephs Legende,* to the biblical story of Joseph's virtuous rejection of Potiphar's wife, set to music in the characteristic idiom of his tone poems, with stolid virtue painted in cerulean major tonalities and strident polyharmonies depicting the abomination of carnality.

### 15 MAY 1914

*Marouf, Savetier du Caire,* opera in four acts by the French romanticist Henri RABAUD, generally regarded as his chef d'œuvre, after the Arabian tale wherein a poor Cairo cobbler marries the Sultan's daughter under false pretenses, but makes his prevarication come true when, at the behest of a sympathetic genie, a caravan he boasted of owning materializes in time to save him from the execution block, is performed for the first time at the Opéra-Comique in Paris.

### 15 MAY 1914

Erik SATIE composes (in the morning, before breakfast) his dyspeptic *Choral inappétisant,* set in regurgitating modalities with ecclesiastical borborygmuses, concluding on a cathartic C major cadence, serving as a postlude to a series of short piano pieces under the general title *Sports et Divertissements.*

(The other pieces of the suite are, in the chronological order of composition: *La Pêche,* 14 March 1914; *La Pieuvre,* 17 March 1914; *Le Yachting,* 22 March 1914; *Les Courses,* 26 March 1914; *Le Flirt,* 29 March 1914; *La Balcançoire,* 31 March 1914; *Le Carneval,* 3 April 1914; *Le Feu d'artifice,* 6 April 1914; *La Chasse,* 7 April 1914; *La Bain de mer,* 11 April 1914; *Le Water-Chute,* 14 April 1914; *Le Pique-Nique,* 19 April 1914; *Les Quatre Coins,* 24 April 1914; *La Comédie italienne,* 29 April 1914; *Le Tennis,* 21 April 1914; *Colin-Maillard,* 27 April 1914; *Le Traineau,* 2 May 1914; *Le Tango,* 5 May 1914; *Le Réveil de la Mariée,* 16 May 1914; *Le Golf,* 20 May 1914)

### 17 MAY 1914

*Kain und Abel,* one-act opera by the prestigious German conductor Felix WEINGARTNER, to his own libretto presenting a romantically dramatic version of the biblical story dealing with the first murder committed on earth, is produced in Darmstadt.

### 26 MAY 1914

*Le Rossignol*, opera-ballet in three tableaux by Igor STRAVINSKY, after the tale of Hans Christian Andersen, in which a manically depressed Emperor of China, mortified by the metallic tintinnabulations of a mechanical nightingale made in Japan, with its Nipponese pentatonicism polluted by chromatic impurities, is restored to life by the thrilling trills and therapeutically euphonious atonal melismata of a sinologically authentic philomel brought back from the woods whither he fled from his insular rival, written in a dissonantly bitonal idiom rooted in quartal harmonies superimposed on structures of major sevenths and tritones, is produced in Paris by Diaghilev's Ballet Russe, with the orchestra under the direction of Pierre Monteux. (A symphonic poem extracted from *Le Rossignol*, was first performed, under the title *Le Chant du Rossignol*, by the Orchestre de la Suisse Romande in Geneva, conducted by Ernest Ansermet on 6 December 1919. It was given as a ballet in Paris on 2 February 1920)

One recalls the scandalous spectacle of *Le Sacre du Printemps*—or rather *Massacre du Printemps*—a year ago. Never were human ears assailed more defiantly. One cannot say that *Le Rossignol* is quite as outrageous as that. Apart from some croaking of frogs and the mooing of a young cow, the music holds together, more or less. One finds in it quite as many offensive dissonances as in *Le Sacre*, but they are presented in a more dissimulated manner, more shamefacedly, without conviction, as if the composer in his embarrassment wished to apologize but had no strength to repudiate them. But all is changed in the second act, where we enter the new manner of Mr. Stravinsky. There reigns insufferable cacophony, an accumulation of bizarre chords which succeed one another without rhythm or justification; it seems like a wager that one can make the gullible public and the snobs swallow anything at all in our concert halls. We will say nothing about the delirium of some enthusiasts lodged on top of the gallery who cried out loudly for the author, but the latter had the good sense not to appear. (H. Moréno, *Le Ménestrel*, Paris, 6 June 1914)

### 28 MAY 1914

*Maruxa*, lyric eclogue in two acts by the prolific Spanish composer of light opera Amadeo M. VIVES, to a story of tumescent rustic passions, wherein a farmer's daughter covets a simple-minded shepherd while her male cousin cozens the shepherd's favorite shepherdess, all this vitalized by a cornucopia of Iberian melorhythms, is produced in Madrid.

### 1 JUNE 1914

The fifth, and last, Congress of the International Music Society is held in Paris, two months before the outbreak of World War I puts an end to it as to many other international cultural enterprises, so auspiciously flourishing during a century of major peace since the Congress of Vienna.

## 2 JUNE 1914

*First Symphony* by the foremost Russian symphonist Nicolai MIASKOVSKY in G minor (completed on 21 September 1908), in three contrasting movements representing the formation of his early romantic style of composition, is performed for the first time at a summer concert in Pavlovsk, near St. Petersburg.

The summer of 1908 brought the First Symphony and earned me a scholarship at the St. Petersburg Conservatory. Were it not for this scholarship, I would have been forced to leave the Conservatory for I could not afford the annual tuition of 250 rubles. The composition of the First Symphony determined my future, for prior to that time I was afraid to tackle orchestral writing. And I was never interested in composing operas or ballets. (From Miaskovsky's *Biographical Notes*, published in *Sovietskaya Musica*, June 1936)

## 4 JUNE 1914

On his first visit to America, Jan SIBELIUS conducts at the 28th meeting of the Litchfield County Choral Union, held at Norfolk, Connecticut, a concert of his orchestral works, including *Pohjola's Daughter, Christian II, The Swan of Tuonela* and *Oceanides*, the last being a world première.

## 14 JUNE 1914

Seven weeks before the outbreak of Franco-German hostilities, the French government confers the order of Chevalier of the Légion d'Honneur on Richard STRAUSS.

## 17 JUNE 1914

The degree of Doctor of Music is conferred upon Jean SIBELIUS by Yale University, with the following summary of his position:

By his music, intensely national in inspiration, and yet in sympathy with the mood of the West, Doctor Jan Sibelius long since captured Finland, Germany and England, and on coming to America to conduct a symphony concert found that his fame had already preceded him also. Still in the prime of life, he has become, by the power and originality of his work, one of the most distinguished of living composers. What Wagner did with Teutonic legend, Dr. Sibelius has done in his own impressible way with the legends of Finland as embodied in her national epic. He has translated the Kalevala into the universal language of music, remarkable for its breadth, large simplicity, and the infusion of a deeply poetic personality.

## 19 JUNE 1914

The Bavarian Civil Court rejects the suit brought by Isolde Beidler against her mother Cosima Wagner seeking legal recognition of her status as a natural daughter of Richard WAGNER, and an equal share with her brother Siegfried and her sister Eva in the proceeds from Wagner's estate.

(Isolde was born on 10 April 1865, and was registered as a legitimate daughter of Hans von Bülow, then legal husband of Cosima Wagner. The court found no proof that Cosima had not carnally cohabited with Von Bülow between the dates of 12 June and 12

October 1864, the limits for conception of a child born on 10 April 1865, according to Bavarian law, and that consequently Isolde might have been a legitimate issue. This period corresponds to the time when Wagner was a guest of Hans and Cosima von Bülow at Villa Pellet in Starnberg. Isolde's husband, Franz Beidler, acting as her lawyer, published on 26 May 1914 a report citing contemporary accounts tending to establish Wagner's intimacy with Cosima at the time, including a neighbor's report that von Bülow, returning one evening to his villa from Munich, found Wagner's bedroom locked with Cosima inside, became despondent, began to shriek, banged on the furniture and rolled on the floor. Beidler also proposed phrenological and hemological tests of Isolde and Siegfried to establish their total consanguinity)

### 24 JUNE 1914

Three hundred years have passed since the completion of the first music encyclopedia, *Syntagma Musicum* by Michael PRAETORIUS, planned in four volumes, of which only three were published.

(Date of the preface of the first volume, in Latin, dealing with sacred music, is 24 June 1614. The second volume, in German, was published in 1619, and has the subtitle, *De Organographia*, dealing with organ playing and construction. The preface is curiously dated: "in the year after Christ, *stylo Vulgari*, 1616, but, according to exact calculation, 1621; since the creation of the world, 5568; since the exodus from Egypt, 3116; since the foundation of Rome, 2371; in the 599 Olympiad." The third volume, also in German, has the date 14 May 1619 in the preface and contains an explanation of French and Italian terms, description of dances, and numerous musical examples)

### 25 JUNE 1914

Erik SATIE composes *Obstacles vénimeux*, the first number in his suite of three barless piano pieces bearing the oxymoronic title *Heures Séculaires et instantanées*, with the following text accompanying the music:

This vast part of the world is inhabited by a single man, a Negro. He is bored to the point of dying of laughter. The shadow of millennial trees marks 9:17 o'clock. [The time of the day is indicated in the music by 9 chords in the bass for the hours, and 17 notes in the treble for the minutes]. The toads call each other by name. For better cogitation the Negro holds his cerebellum in his outstretched right hand. From a distance he looks like a distinguished physiologist. Four anonymous serpents hold him captive, suspended on the tails of his uniform, deformed by suffering and loneliness. An old mangrove tree slowly bathes its repulsively filthy roots at the riverside. It is not the hour of the shepherd. (A footnote reads: To Whom it May Concern: I forbid to recite the text aloud during the musical performance. Failure to comply will cause justified indignation on my part against the transgressor.)

### 2 JULY 1914

Two centuries have passed since the birth at Erasbach of Christoph Willibald GLUCK, audacious reformer of operatic traditions, who put dramatic ideals above vocal virtuosity and vindicated the poetic essence in theatrical music.

### 3 JULY 1914

Erik SATIE composes *Crépuscule matinal (de midi)*, the second piece of his oxymoronic piano suite, entitled *Heures séculaires et instantanées*, to ridicule the impressionistic fashion of musical landscape painting, with the following text in the music:

The sun rose early, in good humor. The temperature is expected to be above normal, for this is an antediluvian sunrise. The sun is now high in the sky and it looks like a nice fellow. But do not trust the sun. It may burn the harvest or administer a stroke: a sun-stroke. Behind the hangar a bull gorges himself on fodder to the point of nausea.

(The third piece, entitled *Affolements granitiques*, wherein some noxious miasmata disport themselves in heteronymous pseudo-bitonalities of E-sharp and F major while the clock strikes metachronistic 13, bears no date of composition in the printed edition)

### 4 JULY 1914

*Dylan, Son of the Wave*, opera by the British composer Josef HOLBROOKE, being the second part of his Wagneromorphic trilogy, wherein the hero is slain by a blackguard uncle, who perishes in turn, as the ocean waves invade his moated castle to avenge the death of his kith and kin, is produced in London.

### 10 JULY 1914

*Piano Concerto* in C minor by the 21-year-old English composer Herbert HOWELLS is performed for the first time in London, with Arthur Benjamin as soloist.

### 2 AUGUST 1914

Gabriel DUPONT, French composer of youthful promise and great expectations, dies at the age of 36 in war-oppressed Paris.

### 15 AUGUST 1914

The annual series of Promenade Concerts opens its first war season in London with the playing of national hymns of the Allied powers, in a changed program substituting ELGAR's *Sospiri* for strings, harp and organ and TCHAIKOVSKY's *Italian Capriccio* for the previously scheduled performance of the symphonic poem *Don Juan* by Richard STRAUSS, removed from the program in agreement with the general wartime concert policy in England to ban music by living German composers. .

### 17 AUGUST 1914

A program of French and Russian music is substituted for the announced all-Wagner evening at the Promenade Concerts in London.

The taboo of Wagner is much to be regretted. Apparently, the directors of the Queen's Hall and of the Orchestra feared a demonstration by non-musical super-patriots. (*Musical Times*, London, September 1914)

In London during August 1914 the usual cheap evening orchestral concerts, so-called Promenade Concerts, were announced in a patriotic manner, with the comment that

244

no German musician would be represented on the program. Everybody applauded this announcement, but nobody attended the concert. A week later a program of Beethoven, Wagner and Richard Strauss was announced. Everybody was indignant and everybody went to hear it. It was a complete and decisive German victory without a single man being killed. (From George Bernard Shaw's letter to a friend in Vienna, published in the *Frankfurter Zeitung* of 21 April 1915 and reprinted in the New York *Times* of May 1915)

### 17 AUGUST 1914

Edward ELGAR volunteers to serve in the Hampstead Special Constabulary, and is sworn in, receiving an armlet and a heavy baton as the symbol of authority.

### 26 AUGUST 1914

*The Immortal Hour*, opera in two acts by the 36-year-old English composer Rutland BOUGHTON, to a libretto from Irish legendary tradition, wherein the King of Shadows arranges for the young King of Ireland to meet his immortal bride from the Land of Youth and Heart's Desire only to lose her and be left with the Dream of Death at an Immortal Hour, set to music of Celtic provenance, thematically derived from ancient pentatonic modalities, yet bleak and stark in facture, is performed for the first time at Glastonbury.

### 28 AUGUST 1914

Anatoly LIADOV, Russian composer of miniature symphonic poems inspired by Russian folklore, distinguished by an imaginative melodic and harmonic presentation, dies at his family estate, near the ancient Russian capital of Novgorod, at the age of fifty-nine.

### 3 SEPTEMBER 1914

Albéric MAGNARD, French composer of four symphonies, three operas and other works conceived in a rhapsodically grandiloquent style representing the French counterpart of Wagnerianism, perishes in his house on the Marne, in the act of armed resistance to the advancing Germans.

At 9:45 in the morning, the Germans appeared at my place and told me that there was a sniper in the village. It was Albéric Magnard, who killed a hussard and wounded another. The Germans threatened to burn the village in reprisal and to shoot down any inhabitants who would try to flee. At 11:40 A.M., they took me to Magnard's villa and set it on fire. As the smoke began to rise, we heard a shot inside the house. A German officer remarked: "He chose the best way out." (From the testimony of F. J. Robert, notary at Baron, given on 28 January 1915, and quoted in Gaston Garraud, *La Vie et la Mort d'Albéric Magnard*, Paris, 1921, pp. 284–285)

I swear to tell the truth. On 3 September I was returning to our house at Baron, when I noticed a detachment of German soldiers on the terrace. Approaching the house, they shouted: "Komm heraus! Einmal, zweimal, dreimal!" At that moment my father-in-law fired two shots through the blinds of the window in the first floor. Two Germans fell in the garden, some five meters from where I stood. Thereupon the soldiers fired at the house. A superior officer was called, and he ordered the house burned. It was set afire by grenades. While the house was burning I heard a shot, and my impression was that my father-in-law had killed himself. He had said before that he had four bullets for the enemy and one for himself. (Testimony of R. Creston, son-in-law of Magnard, given in Paris on 6 February 1915, and quoted in Garraud's book, pp. 285–286)

On 4 October 1914 I went to Baron to try to find the remains of my poor husband in the ruins of our house, of which only a pile of rubble within the four walls was left. The position in which I found his remains makes it possible for me to state that he was standing behind the window when he died. I am convinced, therefore, that he was killed by the Germans. I also found, near his body, the blackened and burned pages of the manuscript of his opera *Bérénice*. (Testimony of Mme Magnard, given in Paris on 3 November 1914, and quoted in Garraud's book, pp. 287–288)

### 10 SEPTEMBER 1914

Two centuries have passed since the birth in Aversa, near Naples, of Niccolò JOMMELLI, "the Italian Gluck."

### 19 SEPTEMBER 1914

Camille SAINT-SAËNS publishes in *L'Écho de Paris* the first of a series of articles denouncing German art and music under the title *Germanophilie,* vehemently denouncing Wagner (whom he knew in Paris and who admired Saint-Saëns) and urging a total ban on Wagner's operas in France.

What Hohenzollernian fly has stung Saint-Saëns? Was it perhaps during his recent trip to Berlin, after which an inscribed photograph of the Kaiser was seen adorning his piano? We can explain his present Wagnerophobia only by senile debility. (Jean Marnold, *Le Cas Wagner,* Paris, 1920)

### 27 SEPTEMBER 1914

Frédéric Masson of the French Academy publishes in *L'Écho de Paris* an article, *L'art sans patrie,* ferociously attacking WAGNER, "the composer of that miserable rhapsody, *Die Meistersinger,*" and urges Frenchmen to banish Wagner from French musical life "by law, by persuasion, by force, or even by violence if need be."

### 29 SEPTEMBER 1914

Stevan MOKRANJAĆ, Serbian composer of fine church music, including a devotional *Serbian Liturgy,* dies in Skoplje at the age of fifty-eight.

### 30 SEPTEMBER 1914

The German publishing house of BREITKOPF & HÄRTEL announces the dissolution of the International Music Society because of the wartime breakdown of international cooperation.

### 10 OCTOBER 1914

*Margot,* lyric comedy by Joaquín TURINA, is produced in Madrid.

## 12 OCTOBER 1914

The Berlin Philharmonic Orchestra opens its first wartime season in a program of Beethoven and Brahms conducted by Arthur Nikisch.

## 13 OCTOBER 1914

*Perseus,* second symphonic work by the 21-year-old English composer Eugene GOOSSENS, is performed for the first time at the Promenade Concerts in London.

## 14 OCTOBER 1914

Walford DAVIES, 45-year-old English composer and educationist, plays at the Promenade Concerts in London the piano part in the first performance of his *Conversations* for piano and orchestra, in four movements, fancifully labelled *Genial Company, A Passing Moment, Intimate Friends* and *Playmates.*

## 22 OCTOBER 1914

*Britain's War March,* patriotic orchestral piece by Cyril SCOTT, is performed for the first time at the Promenade Concerts in London.

## 28 OCTOBER 1914

Richard HEUBERGER, Austrian composer of numerous respectable musical works in the manner of Brahms (whose worshipful friend he was), who achieved his more or less durable fame mainly with an operetta *Das Opernball,* dies in Vienna at the age of sixty-four.

## 3 NOVEMBER 1914

Thomas Beecham conducts in London the Royal Philharmonic Orchestra in the first performance of *Two Passacaglias* by Cyril SCOTT, the first based on the pentatonic *Irish Famine Song,* the second on the medievally lugubrious tetratonic tune *Poor Irish Boy,* liberally bestrewn by whole-tone scales, and lavishly orchestrated, reaching an exalted climax with massed sonorities of gliding harps, crashing piano chords, drums, violins glissando along the natural series of overtones, and the organ in a grandly resonant C-major peal.

## 6 DECEMBER 1914

Middle-aged French musicians, members of the Lamoureux and Colonne orchestras in Paris, who are not subject to military service, combine forces to present their initial concert in wartime Paris under the auspices of both orchestras.

## 7 DECEMBER 1914

*Carillon* for voice and orchestra by Edward ELGAR, to patriotic words by a Belgian poet, is performed for the first time at the Promenade Concerts in London.

247

## 8 DECEMBER 1914

*Watch Your Step,* "a syncopated musical show" by Irving BERLIN, in which Giuseppe Verdi appears on the stage to protest against the syncopation of his arias, but is eventually won over to the novel zip of ragtime, is produced in New York.

## 12 DECEMBER 1914

*Three Poems from the Japanese* by Igor STRAVINSKY, scored for soprano, 2 flutes, 2 clarinets, piano and string quartet are performed for the first time in Petrograd.

## 14 DECEMBER 1914

Giovanni SGAMBATI, Italian composer, pianist and renowned pedagogue, dies in his native Rome at the age of seventy-three.

## 16 DECEMBER 1914

Giovanni von ZAYTZ, whose real name was Ivan Zajc, Croatian composer of about 1200 works of all kinds and author of the first Croatian national opera *Nikola Šubrič Zrinski* (1876), dies in Zagreb at the age of eighty-three.

## 27 DECEMBER 1914

The Academy of Santa Cecilia in Rome confers honorary membership on Vincent D'INDY.

# ᕲ 1915 ᕲ

## 1 JANUARY 1915

The first issue of *The Musical Quarterly,* devoted to both the human and theoretical aspects of music, is published in New York by G. Schirmer, Inc., under the editorship of Oscar George SONNECK, Chief of the Music Division of the Library of Congress.

Publisher and editor are agreed not to throttle *The Musical Quarterly* at birth with a "program" . . . The policy of the magazine? That may best be defined by this subtle alteration of a good, old doctrine: *Audietur et altera pars.* The foundations of this magazine were laid months before the European War broke out. Since then many foreign collaborators have been called to the colors, and the editor suddenly found himself under the necessity of changing the distribution of his forces and of adjusting his plans to unwelcome circumstances. While the war lasts, of necessity, articles by continental contributors will be fewer than were solicited and promised. Indeed, the editor fears that the pen of more than one valued contributor rests forever. (From the preface to the first issue)

## 1 JANUARY 1915

Florent SCHMITT conducts his *Chant de Guerre* for tenor, chorus and orchestra at a patriotic matinée in Toul, given for the wounded French soldiers, early victims of the first few months of the great senseless war between civilized nations.

## 2 JANUARY 1915

Karl GOLDMARK, Austrian composer of effective orchestral and operatic music, in a romantic idiom midway between Mendelssohn and Wagner, dies in Vienna in his 85th year.

## 4 JANUARY 1915

*I Didn't Raise My Boy to be a Soldier*, sentimentally pacifistic tune by Al PIANTADOSI, to the words by A. Bryan, challenging, in quick-step time, anyone to place a musket on his shoulder and to make him shoot some other mother's darling boy, with a garish cover representing a gray-haired American mother babying a boy about twenty years old and protecting him with an upraised hand from bombs exploding in an alien war on a transatlantic continent, is copyrighted by Leo Feist, publishers, bearing a dedication "respectfully to every mother everywhere." (650,000 copies were sold in the first three months of 1915)

After America's entry into World War I in 1917, numerous sequels were published reflecting the changing sentiment toward war; dates in parentheses are copyright dates: *I Didn't Raise My Dog to Be a Sausage* (21 April 1915); *I Did Not Rear My Boy to Be a Coward* (18 October 1915); *I Did Not Raise My Girl to Be a Soldier's Bride* (24 June 1916); *I Didn't Raise My Boy to Be a Soldier, I'll Send My Girl to Be a Nurse* (17 January 1917); *America, Here's My Boy* (16 February 1917); *I'm Glad I Raised My Boy To Be a Soldier* (14 April 1917); *I'm Raising My Boy to Be a Soldier to Fight for the U.S.A.* (28 April 1917); *I Didn't Raise My Boy To Be a Molly-Coddle* (4 May 1917); *I Want to Be a Soldier Boy* (11 May 1917); *I'm Raising My Boy for a Soldier* (15 May 1917); *I'll Give My Boy to My Country* (7 June 1917); *I Raised My Boy to Be a Soldier* (12 June 1917); *I Didn't Raise My Boy to Be a Soldier, But He'll Fight for the U.S.A.* (13 June 1917); *I Didn't Raise My Boy to Be a Slacker* (13 July 1917); *I Did Give My Boy to Uncle Sammy* (31 December 1917); *I Raised You For a Soldier Lad* (13 June 1918); *I Didn't Raise My Boy to Be a Soldier, But!* (10 August 1918); *I Wish I Had a Thousand Sons to Fight for U.S.A.* (6 September 1918); *I Raised My Darling Boy to Be a Soldier* (21 October 1918)

## 14 JANUARY 1915

*Notte di Leggenda*, one-act opera by Alberto FRANCHETTI, is produced at La Scala, in Milan.

## 24 JANUARY 1915

*Sinfonia drammatica* by Ottorino RESPIGHI, in three movements of intensive tone painting, ranging in mood from muted premonitions to sonorous implosions, is performed for the first time in Rome.

## 25 JANUARY 1915

*Madame Sans-Gêne,* opera by Umberto GIORDANO in three acts, taking place respectively, on 10 August 1792 in the laundering establishment of Madame Sans-Gêne in turbulent revolutionary Paris, at Compiègne in September 1811, and finally in the private quarters of Napoleon whose temporary mistress she had become, the musical score containing a number of inserted dances in the French *style galant,* while the harmonic and orchestral idiom follows the precepts of Italian Verismo in the manner of Giordano's preceding opera from the period of the French Revolution, *Andrea Chénier,* is produced at the Metropolitan Opera in New York for the first time anywhere, Arturo Toscanini conducting.

## 5 FEBRUARY 1915

Max REGER conducts in Berlin the first performances of his *Variationen und Fuge über ein Thema von Mozart,* op. 132, for orchestra, wherein the ingenuous theme of Mozart's piano sonata in A major, itself in the form of variations, is subjected to torturous melodic anamorphoses, contrapuntal contortion, canonic dislocation, rhythmic incrustation and harmonic inspissation, and of *Eine vaterländische Ouvertüre,* dedicated to the German Army, then in the flush of its initial successes in World War I, with the German national anthem *Deutschland, Deutschland über alles* and the patriotic song *Die Wacht am Rhein* trumpeted mightily against polyphonic countercurrents.

## 6 FEBRUARY 1915

*La Candidata,* operetta by Ruggero LEONCAVALLO, is produced in Rome.

## 8 FEBRUARY 1915

*The Birth of a Nation,* ultra-patriotic film produced by the egomaniacal cinemagus D. W. GRIFFITH (called during its first engagement *The Clansman* after the Negrophobic novel by Thomas Dixon on which it was based), with a special score for orchestra and chorus nominally supplied by the American composer Joseph Carl Breil, but actually constituting a medley of popular classical and semi-classical selections in the established tradition of the silent cinema accompaniment, with the heroic Klan Call taken bodily from *The Ride of the Valkyries* by Richard Wagner, opens a successful run across the United States.

## 8 FEBRUARY 1915

Sociedad Nacional de Música, formed in Madrid for the purpose of promoting native music, presents its first concert with works by Manuel de FALLA, Enrique GRANADOS and Joaquin TURINA.

## 11 FEBRUARY 1915

The New York District Court grants but suspends an injunction of sales to Charles T. Boosey, publisher of the song *I Hear You Calling Me,* against the

Empire Music Company, Inc., publishers of the song *Tennessee, I Hear You Calling Me,* for infringement of copyright, in the following ruling:

The composition which plaintiffs own is of a dignified character, has been sung by a distinguished singer, and has at its basic theme a living person standing on the grave of his dead loved one and hearing her voice. The composition owned by defendant is in syncopated time (familiarly known as ragtime), has been sung by a master of that art, and expresses the desire of a Negro to go back to his old home in Tennessee. The two compositions are considerably different, both in theme and execution, except as to this phrase *I hear you calling me,* and, as to that, there is a marked similarity. . . . The words *I hear you calling me* and the music accompanying those words are practically identical in both compositions, and the real controversy in the case is whether the use of this similar phraseology and the similar bars of music is sufficient to warrant the charge of piracy and infringement of copyright. I have had someone, indifferent to the controversy, play both songs for me, and the sentiment of one song is about the same as the other.

### 16 FEBRUARY 1915

Emil WALDTEUFEL, Alsatian-born waltz composer, who became a successful dance director at the court of Napoleon III, dies in Paris, his adoptive home, at the age of seventy-seven.

### 19 FEBRUARY 1915

Jules ÉCORCHEVILLE, 42-year-old French musicologist, editor of the music catalogue of the Bibliothèque Nationale de Paris, falls in combat at Perthes-les-Hurlus in Champagne while leading his company against the advancing Germans.

### 27 FEBRUARY 1915

*Third Symphony* in A minor by Nicolai MIASKOVSKY, in two movements, composed in 1914, and couched in a brooding Russian style characteristic of his romantic inspiration, is performed for the first time in Moscow.

### 10 MARCH 1915

*Vesper Mass* for chorus a cappella by Serge RACHMANINOFF is performed for the first time in Moscow.

### 15 MARCH 1915

Alexander GLAZUNOV conducts at the Petrograd Conservatory the second "Patriotic Concert" of a series inaugurated during the first season of wartime, giving the first performance of his orchestral *Paraphrases of the National Anthems of the Allied Nations,* including those of Russia, Serbia, Montenegro, France, England, Belgium and Japan.

### 19 MARCH 1915

*Adventures in a Perambulator,* orchestral suite by the American composer and railroad industrialist John Alden CARPENTER, describing in modernistic modalities with a vocabulary of the impressionist palette six typical scenes as seen and heard from the vantage point of a baby carriage, *En voiture!*, *The Policeman*, *The Hurdy-Gurdy*, *The Lake*, *Dogs* and *Dreams*, is performed for the first time by the Chicago Symphony Orchestra.

### 20 MARCH 1915

The Russian Symphony Orchestra of New York, directed by its founder and conductor Modest ALTSCHULER, gives the first American performance of Scriabin's symphonic poem *Prometheus*, including the part of *Luce* (light) ineffectively executed on a rudimentary "color organ" projecting blurred color images on the screen.

### 20 MARCH 1915

*Fedra*, the first opera in three acts by the 34-year-old Italian composer Ildebrando PIZZETTI, to a libretto by Gabriele d'Annunzio, depicting the heroine's unnatural passion for her stepson that leads to the tragic death for both, set to music with a novel technique of non-Wagnerian melosomatic psychomotives, Fedra herself being characterized by an involuted chromatic theme, recitatives austerely drawn in a luminescent musical prosody, opulent pedal points supporting the aerostatically buoyant upper harmonies, the whole marking a significantly new type of modern Italian music drama, is produced at La Scala in Milan.

In the score of *Fedra* not a single note is at variance with the spontaneous rhythm that marks every line. Indeed, each note makes the rhythmic group of words with which it is associated more expressive, without dislocating or distorting it. (Gabriele d'Annunzio on *Fedra*, quoted in Guido M. Gatti, *Ildebrando Pizzetti*, London, 1951)

### 28 MARCH 1915

Georges ENESCO, 33-year-old Rumanian composer, conducts in Bucharest the first performance of his *Second Symphony* in A major, couched in a Gallic romantic manner along neo-baroque lines, with rural melorhythms of his native Rumania providing a welcome local color.

### 3 APRIL 1915

*Fedra*, "tragic rhapsody" in one act by the Italian composer Romano ROMANI on the classical subject of quasi-incestuous love, is produced in Rome.

### 8 APRIL 1915

*Evangelio*, symphonic poem by the Spanish romantic composer Joaquín TURINA, is performed for the first time in Madrid.

### 9 APRIL 1915

*La Chasse aux Boches*, patriotic French operetta by F. PERPIGNAN showing the brave French poilus chasing the panicked boches, is staged at the Folies-Bergère in Paris.

## 14 APRIL 1915

*Upon Reading the Psalms*, cantata by Sergei TANEYEV, his last work (completed on 12 January 1915), inspired by the modes of the Russian liturgy and accoutred in fine 19th-century harmonies, is performed for the first time in Moscow, Serge Koussevitzky conducting in the presence of the composer.

## 15 APRIL 1915

*El Amor Brujo* (*Love the Sorcerer*), ballet-pantomime with voices by Manuel de FALLA, based on an old Andalusian tale wherein the courtship of a young widow by an ardent swain is systematically interrupted by the ghostly apparition of her husband claiming posthumous marital rights, which his harassed widow finally provides by proxy in the warming flesh of a Gypsy girl, set to music with a profusion of Spanish melorhythms, and reaching its greatest impact in the *Ritual Fire Dance*, destined to become one of the most popular numbers in orchestral literature, is produced in Madrid.

## 15 APRIL 1915

Twelve days before his death, Alexander SCRIABIN plays at the Petrograd Conservatory his last piano recital in a program of his works, including his last composition, the hauntingly atonal and polytonal 5 *Préludes*, op. 74.

## 27 APRIL 1915

Alexander SCRIABIN, Russian composer who sought to create new music of pantheistic universality and who believed himself to be an instrument of divine will whose works are steeped in deep solipsistic theosophy and bear titles expressive of these associations—*Divine Poem, Poem of Ecstasy, Satanic Poem*—who constructed a six-note "Mystic Chord" as a medium of preternatural harmonies and who evolved a unique piano technique of resonant power and subtly equilibrated dynamics, dies in Moscow from a fulminatingly rapid blood infection (which could be, thirty years later, unfailingly remedied by the administration of sulfa drugs), at the lamentable age of 43 years, 3 months, 20 days, 17 hours and 55 minutes.

I treasure the devotion you feel for the One who dwells within me. You have faith in Him, because He is great, even though I myself am often meek, small, weak and exhausted. I am not yet He, but I will soon become that which is He! . . . I am carried aloft to extraordinary heights by the immense wave of my inspiration! I suffocate! I am in a state of blessedness! I write music that is divine! (From Scriabin's letter to his common-law wife Tatiana Schloezer)

On 20 April Scriabin was forced to stay in bed as he developed a small furunculus on the upper lip. This caused no alarm at first, particularly since he had suffered a similar infection a year before and it disappeared without ill effects. On 26 April the swelling diminished somewhat and Scriabin felt better. But towards noon he began to complain of pain in the chest and his doctor diagnosed symptoms of pleurisy. At one o'clock the following night Scriabin began to lose consciousness. At three o'clock he was given the last Sacrament, and on 27 April, at 8:05 in the morning he died. (Y. Engel, *Musical*

*Contemporary,* Moscow, December 1915) (Scriabin's exact age at the time of his death can be established because it is known that he was born at 2:10 P.M. on Christmas Day 1871, according to old style calendar; he attached considerable significance to the fact that he was born on the day of Nativity)

Scriabin's life and death can be analyzed astrologically with great accuracy. He is known to have been born at 2:10 P.M. local Moscow time, when the mystic star Betelgeuze was in ascendance in the zodiacal sign of Gemini, and Mars almost exactly at the zenith. His was a difficult birth chart to live up to: great tensions, great power, very poor health, home tragedies, a most difficult marriage with the sign of inevitable separation. A weaker soul would have broken down at once. His mother's sickness before his birth is found as sowing seeds of ill health, probably through glandular disturbances. Strong series of blood poisoning are shown, anemia and digestive difficulties. His life was sustained entirely by faith and inner inspiration. His death closes a cycle begun as he entered the Moscow Conservatory in 1888. As he died, Uranus was exactly at the zenith point of his birth chart, Saturn exactly at the Eastern horizon point. His was indeed a mystic's death, a token of personal immortality. (Horoscope of Scriabin drawn at the author's request in 1937 by Dane Rudhyar, French-born American composer, mystic and astrologer)

### 5 MAY 1915

The German music weekly *Signale für die musikalische Welt* publishes an editorial appeal to extreme German patriots to heed Bismarck's dictum, *quieta non movere,* not to disturb quiescent objects, and stop advocating the forcible Germanization of Italian musical terminology as long as Italy remains neutral. (Italy declared war on Germany and Austria 18 days after the publication of this article)

### 7 MAY 1915

O'Brien BUTLER, composer of the first Irish opera with Gaelic words, *Muirgheis,* perishes on the S.S. *Lusitania,* torpedoed by a German submarine not far from the coast of Kerry, where the first act of *Muirgheis* is laid.

### 7 MAY 1915

A group of commuters waiting at the Hanover Square Station of New York's Third Avenue Elevated Railroad, moved by the news of the sinking of the S.S. *Lusitania* by a German submarine, and prompted by the sound of a hurdygurdy playing *In the Sweet Bye and Bye,* begins spontaneously singing the song in memory of the dead, causing Charles IVES, one of the commuters, to commemorate the incident in the last movement of his Second Orchestral Set, entitled *From Hanover Square North at the End of a Tragic Day the Voice of the People Again Arose.*

### 10 MAY 1915

Two one-act operas by the 30-year-old Italian composer Adriano LUALDI, *La Rosa di Saaron (Rose of Sharon)* and *Le furie di Arlecchino,* an "intermezzo giocoso," are performed for the first time at the Teatro Carcano in Milan.

(Loewenberg in his *Annals of Opera* gives a much later date for the production of *Le Furie d'Arlecchino,* 19 June 1924, in Buenos Aires, and adds: "Stated sometimes to have been produced at the T. Carcano, Milan, as early as 1915, a statement which I could not verify." *Enciclopedia dello Spettacolo* lists the exact dates of first performances of both operas)

## 14 MAY 1915

The Boston Symphony Orchestra, under the direction of Karl MUCK, presents the first of thirteen daily concerts at the Panama-Pacific International Exposition in San Francisco in programs of music of all nations.

## 15 MAY 1915

Cyril SCOTT plays with the Royal Philharmonic Orchestra in London, Thomas Beecham conducting, the piano part in the world première of his *Piano Concerto* in C major, in three contrasting movements, *Allegro maestoso, Adagio* and *Allegro poco moderato*, couched in an eclectic para-modernistic style, containing elements of neo-classical formalism, impressionistic rhapsodism and exotic pentatonicism, described by one listener as "impressions of Bach taken while on a supposed journey to China."

Cyril Scott's music has passed through many phases and exhibited almost every kind of inchoate experiment, but in his piano concerto he seems to have entirely emerged from the experimental stage. The untiring vitality of his own playing, of course, helped it immensely. (London *Times*, 17 May 1915)

## 29 MAY 1915

The Lewisohn Stadium, gift to the College of the City of New York by Adolph LEWISOHN, is dedicated and officially opened. (The regular summer symphony concerts were inaugurated in 1917 with an eight-week season)

## 2 JUNE 1915

Botho SIGWARD, Count of Eulenburg, German composer of orchestral and vocal music in a romantic vein, is killed in Galicia during the retreat of the Austrian and German armies before a temporary Russian offensive.

## 9 JUNE 1915

The Italian composer Riccardo ZANDONAI, born in Tyrol as an Austrian subject, is accused of high treason by the Austrian Governor of the province of Trieste for composing and circulating a student hymn calling for the return of the lost provinces of *Italia irredenta*.

## 19 JUNE 1915

Sergei TANEYEV, Russian composer, theorist and pedagogue, teacher of 135 students at the Moscow Conservatory and at his home (he never accepted payment from private pupils), whose vocal and instrumental works possess an architectural solidity of design in a fine classical tradition barely touched by Russian folk element, compiler of an imposingly scientific tome *Mobile Coun-*

*terpoint in Strict Style,* dies on his estate in the village of Dyudkovo in the Zvenigorod District, near Moscow, at the age of fifty-eight.

### 19 JUNE 1915

Camille SAINT-SAËNS conducts in San Francisco, as an invited guest at the Panama-Pacific International Exposition, the first performance of his orchestral ode composed for the occasion, *Hail, California!*

### 1 JULY 1915

*Fairyland,* allegorical opera by Horatio PARKER, winner of the $10,000 prize of the National Federation of Women's Clubs (his second large prize, the first being for *Mona,* produced by the Metropolitan Opera on 14 March 1912), to a story of a medieval novitiate nun who contrary to ecclesiastical regulations took unto herself a lover (albeit a supernatural fairy), is condemned to be burned at the stake, but is saved when the faggots are miraculously extinguished and all witnesses become fairies, set to music in magniloquently Wagneromorphic tones, is performed for the first, and practically last, time in Los Angeles.

It may be that many men—perhaps some of genius (if you won't admit that all are geniuses)—have been started on the downward path of subsidy by trying to write a thousand-dollar prize poem or a ten-thousand-dollar prize opera. . . . If a bishop should offer a "prize living" to the curate who will love God the hardest for fifteen days, whoever gets the prize would love God the least. (Charles Ives, from *Essays Before a Sonata,* New York, 1920)

### 6 JULY 1915

*Polonia,* symphonic poem by Edward ELGAR written especially for the benefit of the Polish Relief Fund, is performed for the first time in London.

### 15 JULY 1915

The West Virginia Folkore Society is organized with the purpose of ascertaining the possible derivation of Negro spirituals from the songs of mountain white folks.

### 5 AUGUST 1915

*The Blue Paradise,* operetta by the 28-year-old Hungarian composer Sigmund ROMBERG, who settled in the United States in 1909, with additional music by the Viennese composer Edmund EYSLER, to a libretto wherein an Americanized native revisits Vienna in quest of nostalgic memories centered on a flower girl whom he first met at the café called The Blue Paradise, and featuring one of Romberg's most popular songs, *Auf Wiederseh'n,* is produced for the first time in New York.

### 15 AUGUST 1915

*Concerto* for cello and orchestra by the Chilean composer Humberto ALLENDE, containing some impressionistic touches in the general framework of classical form, is performed for the first time in Santiago, Chile.

## 18 AUGUST 1915

*Anfion y Zeto*, opera by the Italian-born Argentine composer Pascual de ROGATIS, to a libretto dealing with the twin brothers Amphion (the lyre-player) and Zethus (the shepherd) who capture the town of Thebes and fortify it telekinetically by charming the stones into place by music, is produced in Buenos Aires.

## 23 AUGUST 1915

Erik SATIE writes *Idylle, à Debussy*, first of three piano pieces in barless notation in the suite under the general title *Avant-dernières pensées*, with an affectionately derisive text mockingly imitative of impressionistic verbal imagery:

What do I see? The rivulet is all wet and the woods are inflammable like matches. But my heart is very small. The trees resemble crooked combs and the sun has attractively gilded rays. But my heart has a cold in its back. The moon has quarreled with her neighbors and the rivulet is wet to the bone.

(On 3 October 1915 Satie wrote an *Aubade, à Paul Dukas*, with some marginal notes such as *Do not sleep, Sleeping Beauty*; on 6 October 1915 he wrote *Méditation, à Albert Roussel*)

## 25 SEPTEMBER 1915

Fritz JÜRGENS, 27-year-old German composer of songs in a lyrico-dramatic Wagneromantic manner, is killed in action on the Champagne front.

## 26 SEPTEMBER 1915

Max von SCHILLINGS conducts in Stuttgart the first performance of his two-act opera *Mona Lisa*, composed in the Wagnerian system of contrapuntal leit-motifs, the most important of which is that of the mysterious smile of Madonna Lisa del Giocondo, which appears on her lips only as the aftermath or the foretaste of a gratifying love experience, a phenomenon which enables her husband, del Giocondo, to trap one of her lovers in a casemate of his Florentine plazzao, where he himself becomes immured after La Gioconda tricks him into entering it, with an epilogue taking place four centuries later, in which a woman tourist stops at Leonardo da Vinci's famous portrait in the Louvre in Paris and pays a guide to say a prayer for the salvation of Mona Lisa's soul and then departs wearing a mysterious smile on her lips.

## 29 SEPTEMBER 1915

Rudi STEPHAN, 28-year-old German composer of neo-classical music, is killed on the Russian front, near Tarnopol.

## 5 OCTOBER 1915

José María USANDIZAGA, Basque composer of sensitive vocal music redolent of Iberian melorhythms, dies in Yanti of tuberculosis at the age of twenty-eight.

## 10 OCTOBER 1915

*Zvíkovský Rarášek* (*Der Burgkobold,* or *The Imp of Zvíkov*), the first opera by Vítězslav Novák, in one act, to a story about a poet who in 1585 attempted a disloyal seduction of the wife of his best friend in the town of Zvíkov, but was foiled in his hazardous undertaking by her precociously perspicacious son, is produced in Prague.

## 12 OCTOBER 1915

After the closure, due to the exigencies of war, of the Jaques-Dalcroze Institute for Eurhythmics in its original site of Hellerau, Germany, it transfers its activity to neutral Geneva.

## 24 OCTOBER 1915

*Berceuse Héroïque* for small orchestra, a musical tribute to King Albert of Belgium by Claude DEBUSSY, is performed for the first time in Paris.

## 26 OCTOBER 1915

August BUNGERT, German composer of a turgidly Wagnerolatrous teratological tetralogy based on the *Odyssey* and a similarly monstrous trilogy on the *Iliad,* dies disillusioned and unappreciated in Leutesdorf, at the age of seventy, the biblical span of life vouchsafed also to his idol Wagner.

## 28 OCTOBER 1915

Richard STRAUSS conducts the Berlin Philharmonic Orchestra in the first performance of his *Alpensinfonie,* "a hundred days' symphony," for it had taken Strauss exactly that time to complete this Baedeker in tones (the date at the end of the score is 9 February 1915), the most literal piece of program music in orchestral literature, embanked within one continuous movement and subdivided into the following illustrative episodes:

(1) *Night,* a peaceful descent along the B-flat minor scale over the entire bassoon range, while the strings slide slowly in pandiatonic tone-clusters (2) *Sunrise,* in crimson-faced brass sonorities rooted in a deep pedal point on A (3) *Ascent,* a glorified fanfare in the foothills sounded in the natural harmonics of E-flat major (4) *Entrance in the Forest,* in romantically sylvan C minor (5) *Wandering by the Brook,* in a shimmering display of colors in A-flat major (6) *At the Waterfall,* with a flourish of trumpets in oxygenated D major (7) *Apparition,* a sudden lapse into a dramatic series of diminished seventh-chords, with the violins in a state of commotion resorting to *glissando* (8) *On Blossoming Meadows,* with snow-white edelweiss springing up staccato in the woodwind section (9) *On Mountain Pastures,* wherein the postillion horns announce a halt in E-flat major (10) *Through Thicket and Underbrush, on the Wrong Way,* with angular melodic intervals in heterotonally baleful harmonies (11) *On the Glacier,* in cycloramically sunlit D minor (12) *Perilous Moments,* with chromatic avalanches leaving behind them a conglomerate of fused semitones (13) *On the Summit,* set in pastoral F major leading in plagal triumph to the apotheosis in the heretofore unapproached, sublimely Alpine and virginally immaculate, sharpless and flatless C major (14) *Vision,* with illusionistic trills and harmoniously arpeggiated harps (15) *Rising Mists,* an incho-

ate agitation of darksomely low tones in the primordial key of B-flat minor (16) *Gradual Darkening of the Sun*, in premonitory tritones against a rumblingly muted instrumental ground (17) *Elegy*, in the romantic key of F-sharp minor (18) *Stillness Before the Storm*, recalling the thematically descending B-flat minor scale with foreboding large drops of pizzicato strings and cohesive pandiatonic clusters forming in the increasingly sharp wind section (19) *Thunderstorm and Descent*, wherein a novel wind machine and a roaring thunder machine are introduced for naturalistic effect, with flutes flutter-tonguing in cascades rushing towards the home key of B-flat minor but resolving deceptively into the opaque submediant G-flat major (20) *Sunset*, with scattered thematic fragments clashing in a clatter of dissonant counterpoint (21) *Ausklang*, sounding out in unadulterated E-flat major (22) *Night*, descending along the path of the parent B-flat minor scale forming opulent pandiatonic clusters consolidated in the final seven-note chord.

A work like the Alpine Symphony could be created only in a German land. Its place in history will be for posterity to evaluate. For us it is at present the first and the only towering musical monument from the great era in which we live. (Leopold Schmidt, *Berliner Tageblatt*, 29 October 1915)

### 5 NOVEMBER 1915

The Sociedad Nacional de Música is inaugurated in Buenos Aires with a concert of chamber music by composers of Argentina.

### 10 NOVEMBER 1915

Marguerite LONG gives at the Société Nationale de Musique in Paris the first performance of DEBUSSY's piano études, among them *Les Arpèges composées, Pour les Sonorités opposées* and *Pour les cinq doigts*, ranging in technical application from five-finger exercises, "according to Monsieur Czerny" (in which the left hand mischievously crosses over into the treble to place a discordant A-flat amid the snow-white landscape of C major), to prestidigital double-thirds, double-fourths, double-sixths, chromatics, rapidly repeated notes, altered arpeggios, and antiphonally distributed massive harmonic aggregations.

### 13 NOVEMBER 1915

*Die Czardasfürstin*, operetta by Emmerich KÁLMÁN dealing with a dancing chanteuse who marries a prince and is nicknamed the *Czardas Princess*, is produced in Vienna.

### 13 NOVEMBER 1915

Heitor VILLA-LOBOS, 28-year-old Brazilian composer, presents in Rio de Janeiro the first concert of his instrumental and vocal pieces, including a piano trio, a cello sonata and several songs.

### 13 NOVEMBER 1915

Leo FEIST, commercial American music publisher, still making money from the sales of the anti-war song *I Didn't Raise my Boy to Be a Soldier*, copyrights the patriotic song *Don't Bite the Hand That's Feeding You*, with words by Thomas Hoier, and music by Jimmie Morgan, counseling foreign-born residents of the United States that "if you don't like your Uncle Sammy, then go back to your home o'er the sea" and, by implication, advising them to cease their pacifist agitation.

### 14 NOVEMBER 1915

Theodor LESCHETIZKY, Polish-born great man of piano pedagogy, originator of the *Kugelhand* (arched hand) method of piano playing, pupil of Czerny, and through him a grand-pupil of Beethoven (with whom Czerny studied), teacher of Paderewski and of a multitude of other celebrities of the piano, composer of virtuosistic piano studies, and successive husband of four of his female pupils, dies in Dresden at the age of eighty-five.

### 20 NOVEMBER 1915

In conformity with the decree of the Imperial Government of Russia banning performances of works by German and Austrian composers during the war, Alexander SILOTI is compelled to replace works of Bach, technically an enemy alien, he was to conduct in Petrograd by a program of orchestral music by Russian composers. (On a later date Siloti was forced to cancel a performance of Beethoven's *Seventh Symphony*)

### 21 NOVEMBER 1915

*Piano Concerto* by Vítězslav NOVÁK, in one movement subdivided into three sections (fast, slow, fast), richly arpeggiated and solemnly cadenced in a characteristic virtuoso manner of central European music, is performed for the first time in Prague.

### 26 NOVEMBER 1915

*Kudeyar,* ballad opera in five acts by the Russian composer Alexander OLENIN, to his own libretto dealing with an imaginative and attractive bandit who flourished in 17th-century Russia, conquered feminine hearts and befriended ambitious youths, to a musical score flowingly rolling with Russian folksong material, is produced in Moscow.

### 30 NOVEMBER 1915

*Die Geschwister,* opera by Ludwig ROTTENBERG, father-in-law of Paul Hindemith, is produced in Frankfurt.

### 1 DECEMBER 1915

The American inventor Lee DE FOREST publishes an article entitled *Audion Bulbs as Producers of Pure Musical Tones* in *The Electrical Experimenter,* in which he refers for the first time to music produced by vacuum tubes:

In my laboratory there are a number of small spherical incandescent bulbs, from which I am able to obtain a succession of musical notes, clear and sweet, of surprising volume, the pitch and timbre of which can be varied almost at will to imitate any musical tone of an orchestra. Here, then, in the laboratory we have for the first time the Music of the Lamps.

(The term Electronic Music was used for the first time in print in an article by Hugo Gernsback in *Radio-Craft*, March 1933)

## 2 DECEMBER 1915

*Katinka* (Russian diminutive of Catherine), musical comedy by Rudolf FRIML, to a story dealing with a pompous Tsarist ambassador who loses his flighty fiancée to a younger Russian, is produced in Morristown, New Jersey. (The New York performance followed on 23 December 1915)

## 8 DECEMBER 1915

On his fiftieth birthday, the great Finnish composer Jean SIBELIUS conducts in Helsingfors a concert of his orchestral music, including two *Serenades*, the symphonic poem *Oceanides*, and the first performance of his Fifth Symphony in E-flat major, marked by the cumulative thematic grandeur of its form and granitic poetry of his national sentiment, in three movements:

(1) *Tempo molto moderato; Allegro moderato*, beginning with a four-note phrase as a formative nucleus amid a variety of scattered themes, cast in somber hues and favoring the low registers of the instrumental range (2) *Andante mosso, quasi Allegretto*, a scherzo evolving from the first movement by thematic links, with the profusion of fluvial flutes and clarion clarinets in aquamarine harmonies (3) *Allegro molto; un pochettino largamente*, building up tension through persuasive iteration of a sharply contoured melody appearing in multiple instrumental guises, until the cumulative thematic drive attains a critical saturation, leading to a series of spasmodic chords in the simplest terms of the dominant and the tonic, and concluding in a blaze of tonal brass. (The Symphony was revised considerably, and the new version was conducted by Sibelius for the first time in Helsingfors on 14 December 1916)

## 11 DECEMBER 1915

Willem PIJPER, 21-year-old Dutch composer of impressionistic proclivities, plays the solo part in the first performance, in Utrecht, of his *Piano Concerto* in one movement.

## 25 DECEMBER 1915

*Les Cadeaux de Noël*, opera in one act by the 52-year-old French composer Xavier LEROUX, described as a "heroic tale" and dedicated to his son, a French army soldier, is performed, fittingly so, on Christmas Day at the Opéra-Comique in Paris.

## 28 DECEMBER 1915

*Bethlehem*, choral drama by Rutland BOUGHTON based on the Coventry Nativity Play, is produced at an annual Christmas Festival he inaugurated in the town of Glastonbury in Southwest England in the forlorn hope of establishing there a Bayreuth-like Wagnerian site for his grandiose music dramas.

28 DECEMBER 1915

*Everyman,* one-act opera by Liza LEHMANN, is produced in London.

31 DECEMBER 1915

*Impressions from an Artist's Life in Form of Variations on an Original Theme* for piano and orchestra by Ernest SCHELLING, with 21 variations marked by initials of his famous friends, Karl Muck, Hans Pfitzner, Paderewski, Mahler, Kreisler, Anna Pavlova, Mengelberg and others, is performed for the first time by the Boston Symphony Orchestra, Karl Muck conducting, with Schelling playing the piano part.

# ◈ *1916* ◈

11 JANUARY 1916

On his 60th birthday, Christian SINDING is awarded by the Norwegian government a purse of 30,000 crowns in appreciation of his services to Norwegian music as "the greatest national composer since Grieg."

14 JANUARY 1916

*Der Sterngucker (The Star Gazer),* operetta by Franz LEHÁR, is produced in Vienna.

14 JANUARY 1916

*Le Poilu,* a military operetta in two acts by Maurice JACQUET, glorifying the courage of the French *poilu* (the "hairy one," in the affectionate argot of World War I for French soldiers), is produced in Paris.

14 JANUARY 1916

*The Critic, or an Opera Rehearsed,* a comic opera in two acts by Charles Villiers STANFORD, after Sheridan's play (but Sheridan's subtitle was "a tragedy rehearsed"), wherein the author Puff and critic Sneer engage in a deep philosophical discourse on the meaning of art, with a Spanish soldier Don Whiskerandos providing exotic color, is produced in London, conducted by Eugene Goossens (who is himself included in the cast of characters, pretending that something has gone wrong with the music.)

15 JANUARY 1916

*Das Dreimäderlhaus (The House of Three Maidens),* operetta by the Hungarian composer Heinrich BERTÉ, a pasticcio of Schubert's melodies to a romanticized tale of his emotional frustrations in a Vienna cottage inhabited by three coquettish girls named Hederl, Haiderl and Hannerl, none of whom would yield to Schubert's amorous importunities (he sings tenor), is performed for the first time in Vienna, becoming Berté's most popular stage work, destined to achieve fame in England and America under the title *Lilac Time* (first produced in that particular version in London on 22 December 1922)

### 15 JANUARY 1916

Modest TCHAIKOVSKY, loyal biographer of his famous brother, the librettist of *The Queen of Spades* and a competent dramatist in his own right, dies in Moscow at the age of sixty-five.

### 17 JANUARY 1916

Ferruccio BUSONI appears as soloist in Zürich in the first performance of his *Indianische Fantasie* for piano and orchestra, written in an expansively rhapsodic vein with extensive cadenzas covering the entire range of the piano keyboard, and making use of authentically pentatonic American Indian melodies in opulently harmonic dressing.

### 17 JANUARY 1916

*Hebridean Symphony* by Granville BANTOCK (completed on 23 November 1915) in four linked movements, depicting in stark pentatonic melodies embanked within chromaticized Wagneromimic harmonies the romantically bleak landscape of the islands off the coast of western Scotland, with a rare sunny day portrayed by 40 bars of cloudless C major, is performed for the first time in Glasgow.

### 19 JANUARY 1916

At a meeting of the Russian cult of Abstainers in Vyritza, near Petrograd, twenty phonographs and several recordings of Bach and Beethoven are solemnly burned in a bonfire as products of "German abomination." (Date and circumstances found in the weekly *Russian Musical Gazette*, St. Petersburg, No. 3, 1916, p. 78)

### 20 JANUARY 1916

*Le Tambour*, a brief lyric poem by Alfred BRUNEAU, nostalgically depicting in ballad-like tones the outbreak of war and the conscription of sons and husbands into the French army, with the military drum beating ominously repetitious rhythms, is produced at the Opéra-Comique in Paris.

### 22 JANUARY 1916

Iwan KNORR, Prussian-born composer who spent many years in Russia and absorbed some Slavic inflections in his melodic writing, champion of invertible counterpoint, assiduous scholar and teacher of a generation of composers, dies in Frankfurt, at the age of sixty-three.

## 28 JANUARY 1916

*Goyescas,* one-act opera by Enrique GRANADOS, to a libretto inspired by scenes from Goya's paintings wherein a young captain of the Royal Guards of the Spanish Court is killed by a bull fighter over the affections of an aristocratically desirable young lady, the music derived from Granados's suite of piano pieces *Goyescas* and containing the popular aria *La Maja y el Ruiseñor* (*The Lady and the Nightingale*), is produced for the first time anywhere by the Metropolitan Opera in New York.

*Goyescas* Seen for First Time—Standing Room at Premium—If Applause Counts for Aught, Latest Production Will Be Palpable Hit (Headlines in the New York *Times*)

Opera in Spanish First Sung Fails to Impress—*Goyescas* a Series of Tapestry Pictures Lacking in True Character and Without Real Consistency (Headlines in the New York *World*)

## 28 JANUARY 1916

*The Boatswain's Mate,* two-act opera by England's most prominent woman composer Ethel SMYTH, to her own libretto dealing with an ex-boatswain who asks a friend to fake a burglary of a pub owned by a comely widow, intending to pose as her rescuer and thus impress her into marrying him, the plot miscarrying when she surprises the pretended burglar and decides to marry him instead, is performed for the first time in London.

## 29 JANUARY 1916

Sergei PROKOFIEV conducts in Petrograd the first performance of his *Scythian Suite,* subtitled *Ala and Lolli,* originally intended for a ballet wherein an ancient Slav warrior saves the sun-god Ala from the spirit of darkness, in four movements depicting Scythian sun-worshipping rites (in primitivistic rhythmic iteration), the dance of evil spirits (in bleak quartal harmonies), a nocturnal scene (in sonorous pandiatonic complexes) and the sunrise (in magnificently swelling brass sonorities in solar B-flat major), and his Conservatory teacher Nicolas TCHEREPNIN leads the orchestra in the première of his own choreographic poem *The Masque of the Red Death,* after the horror story of Edgar Allan Poe (the ominous pendulum swings at the regular human pulse rate, while the chimes are illustrated by an eerie ensemble of gusli, mandolines and zithers).

It is probable that our remote ancestors would have accepted Prokofiev's *Scythian Suite* as their very own for the music is really wild . . . It produces some kind of aggressive, crude sound which expresses nothing but infinite braggadoccio. (*Petrograd Listok,* 30 January 1916)

## 1 FEBRUARY 1916

Carl NIELSEN conducts in Copenhagen the first performance of his *Fourth Symphony,* completed on 14 January 1916, subtitled *The Inextinguishable,* in four linked movements (*Allegro, Poco allegretto, Poco adagio* and *Allegro*), the title being a subjective expression of the inextinguishability of life in its evolutionary process, the struggle for survival reflected in fluctuating tonalities, with portentous beats of the kettledrums significantly tuned at the interval of the tritone, the medieval "diabolus in musica."

## 4 FEBRUARY 1916

The Paris periodical *La Renaissance* publishes a symposium of opinions by musicians and artists on the question whether the music by Richard WAGNER should be performed in France after the war, with five in favor and 16 against Wagner, including the sculptor Rodin, who wrote, "Wagner a été trop mêlé à nos affaires".

## 8 FEBRUARY 1916

Tristan TZARA invents the word DADA expressive of utter mental nihilism in the domains of art, literature and music.

Dada is something newer, different, a bewilderment that affected the art world of Europe for a few shell-shocked years during and immediately after the War. The object of Dadaism was a conscious attack on reason, a complete negation of everything, the loudest and silliest expression of post-War cynicism. "I affirm," wrote early Dadaist Hans Arp, "that Tristan Tzara discovered the word Dada on the 8th of February, 1916, at 6 o'clock in the evening in the Terrace Café in Zürich. I was there with my twelve children when Tzara pronounced for the first time this word, which aroused a legitimate enthusiasm in all of us." Later, Dadaist Richard Hülsenbeck claimed: "It was I who pronounced the word Dada (hobby-horse) for the first time." In moments of Harmony and Logic which they affected to despise, Dadaists admitted that their object was "to spit in the eye of the world." (TIME, 14 December 1936)

## 10 FEBRUARY 1916

*First Symphony* by the Finnish composer Leevi MADETOJA, written in an intelligent Sibelian manner, is performed for the first time in Helsingfors.

## 11 FEBRUARY 1916

The Baltimore Symphony Orchestra gives its inaugural concert in Baltimore, under the direction of its permanent conductor, the German musician Gustav STRUBE.

## 18 FEBRUARY 1916

*First Symphony* in C minor by the American composer Daniel Gregory MASON, in three cyclic movements "conceived dramatically in the interplay of musical ideas and emotions," stating its three principal themes in the slow introduction, and distinguished by a stolid solidity of Brahmsogenic polyphony with frequent outbursts of Wagneromorphic fanfares, is performed for the first time by the Philadelphia Orchestra. (The Symphony was subsequently revised, and first performed in its new version in New York on 1 December 1922)

## 23 FEBRUARY 1916

*Dame Kobold,* opera in three acts by Felix WEINGARTNER, to his own libretto after Calderón, is produced in Darmstadt.

## 24 FEBRUARY 1916

*L'Ultimo dei Mohicani,* grand opera in five acts by the Bostonian composer Paul ALLEN, written in an eloquent Italianate style with an admixture of Indian pentatonic elements to characterize the action of the libretto after James Fenimore Cooper's famous novel, is produced in Florence.

## 26 FEBRUARY 1916

The word DADA, eloquently meaningless slogan of the anti-esthetical nihilistic movement arising from cumulative frustrations of the immobile trench war and stagnation in belles-lettres, beaux-arts and music, appears for the first time in print in a poster exhibited at the Cabaret Voltaire in Zürich, the cradle of Dadaism.

Grande soirée—Poème simultané 3 langues protestations bruit musique nègre Hoosenlatz Hoosenlatz piano Tipperary Lanterna magica démonstration proclamation dernière!! Invention dialogue!! DADA!! Dernière nouveauté!!! Syncope bourgeoise, musique BRUITISTE, dernier cri, chanson Tzara, danse, protestations—la grosse caisse —lumière rouge, policemen—chansons tableaux cubistes, cartes postales, chanson Cabaret Voltaire—poème simultané breveté Tzara Hoosenlatz et van Hoddis Hülsenbeck Hoosenlatz tourbillon Arp-two-step réclame alcool fument vers les cloches—on chuchote! arrogance—silence Mme Hennings, Janco déclaration, l'art transatlantique —peuple se réjouit, étoile projetée sur la danse cubiste en grelots.—Collaborateurs: Apollinaire, Picasso, Modigliani, Arp, Tzara, van Hoddis, Hülsenbeck, Kandinsky, Marinetti, Cangiulio, Van Rees, Slodky, Ball, Hennings, Janco, Cendrars, etc. Dialogue DaDaDa dada dadadadadada—la vie nouvelle—contient un poème simultané—la critique carnivore nous plaça platoniquement dans la maison des vertiges de génies trop mûrs. Évite l'appendicite éponge l'intestin. J'ai constaté que les attaques venaient de moins en moins et qui veut rester jeune évite les rhumatismes (From *Dada Almanach,* Berlin, 1920)

## 5 MARCH 1916

*Die toten Augen (Sightless Eyes),* opera in one act with a prologue by the self-Germanized Scottish-born composer Eugen D'ALBERT, his most successful production (composition completed on 20 August 1913), wherein a blind woman of Corinth is cured by Jesus on Palm Sunday A.D. 29, through a persistent application of curative C major, and when her sightless eyes are opened, impulsively embraces a handsome Roman centurion mistaking him for her malformed husband, whereupon the latter kills the former in blind rage and the woman commits oculocide by deliberately staring at the incandescent sun to make the outside world black again, set to music in an eloquent Wagneromantic style, seasoned by modernistic whole-tone progressions, impressionistic triadic parallelisms and occasionally unresolved prudential discords, is performed for the first time in Dresden.

## 10 MARCH 1916

*Concertino* for piano and orchestra by John Alden CARPENTER, designed as a "light-hearted conversation between piano and orchestra as between two friends," is performed for the first time by Percy Grainger with the Chicago Symphony Orchestra.

## 13 MARCH 1916

Frank BRIDGE conducts in London the first performance of his tone-poem *Summer.*

## 24 MARCH 1916

Enrique GRANADOS perishes with his wife at sea as the S.S. Sussex is sunk by a German submarine between Folkestone and Dieppe, at three o'clock in the afternoon.

Abandon Hope for Goyescas Composer—Sr. and Sra. Granados Lost in Sussex Disaster, Friends fear—No Trace of Either—When Last Seen Sr. and Sra. Granados Were Clinging to a Small Raft Which, It Is Thought, Was Unable to Weather the Heavy Sea or the Couple Was Washed Overboard to Drown (Headlines in the London *Morning Telegraph,* 28 March 1916)

## 24 MARCH 1916

*Protomastoras (Master-Builder),* musical drama in two acts by Manolis KALOMIRIS, first opera by a Greek composer on a Hellenic subject, dealing with an architect who relinquishes the love of a young bride to devote his life to the building of a Bridge of Arts, is produced in Athens.

## 28 MARCH 1916

Two one-act operas by the 18-year-old Vienna *wunderkind* Erich Wolfgang KORNGOLD are produced in a single evening in Munich:

(1) *Violanta,* wherein a young Venetian matron intent on avenging the violation of her sister's chastity, arranges a clandestine assignation with its perpetrator and asks her husband to come, too, and slay him with impunity vouchsafed by the Venetian adultery law, but is overcome at the critical moment by an overwhelming sexual desire for the seducer and throws herself between him and her husband, receiving a mortal dagger blow, set to music replete with vibrant dissonances and suspended melodic resolutions (2) *Der Ring des Polykrates,* inspired by Schiller's ballad about the tyrant of Samos whose ill-starred ring which he throws into the ocean returns to him inside a fish he caught, with the action transferred to Saxony in 1797 and centered on a married kapellmeister, his drummer and an attractive maidservant embroiled in an imbroglio of triangular emotions, with a musical setting of the type of neo-Mozartean rococo.

## 2 APRIL 1916

*Die schöne Bellinda,* romantic opera in three acts by the Swiss composer Hans HUBER, is performed for the first time in Bern.

## 9 APRIL 1916

*Noches en los jardines de España,* symphonic suite for piano and orchestra by Manuel DE FALLA, in three sections (1) *En el Generalife,* unveiling in atmospheric harmonies the panorama of the hillside gardens in Generalife near the Alhambra in Granada, with Andalusian melorhythms palpitating in brief motivic themes and pyrotechnically exploding in piano cadenzas (2) *Danza lejana,* with a serpentine Moorish dance tune sounded at a distance (3) *En los jardines de la Sierra de Córdoba,* an enfilade of Andalusian cantillation abutting in Phrygian cadences on the major dominant, is performed for the first time by the Orquesta Filarmónica of Madrid, Enrique Fernández Arbós conducting, José Cubiles pianist.

## 11 APRIL 1916

Alberto GINASTERA, Argentinian composer of operas, ballets, symphonic and vocal music in a hypermodern style, employing serial techniques and nostalgic melorhythms nurtured on native ethnic resources, is born in Buenos Aires.

## 27 APRIL 1916

*Goffredo Mameli,* one-act opera by Ruggero LEONCAVALLO, is produced in Genoa.

## 27 APRIL 1916

*Suite Brève* for orchestra by the 39-year-old French composer Louis AUBERT, in three movements, *Menuet, Berceuse* and *Air de Ballet,* is performed for the first time in Paris.

## 11 MAY 1916

Max REGER, formidably industrious and prolific German composer and master organist whose extraordinary polyphonic prowess caused his teacher Hugo Riemann to earnestly opine that Reger was the Bach of the 20th century and whose palindromic name suggested an invertible versatility, but whose aridity of imagination and infertility of invention made his massive music lifeless, is found dead at the age of 43, in a hotel room in Leipzig, with his spectacles still in position and an evening newspaper of the day before in his rigid hands.

(Reger went to his hotel in Leipzig, where he was on a visit, at 10:30 P.M. on the night of 10 May 1916, after complaining to friends of an indisposition, and must have died of a sudden heart failure, during the night, i.e. on 11 May 1916)

## 23 MAY 1916

Learned HAND, United States District Judge in New York City, rules in favor of the plaintiff Harry Haas who claimed that the tune of the popular song *I Didn't Raise My Boy to Be a Soldier* was plagiarized by its supposed composer Al Piantadosi from a previously published song by Haas, *You Will Never Know How Much I Really Cared.*

The defendant Feist has a large publishing house in the city of New York, and employed the defendant Piantadosi as a casual composer of melodies, though he has small knowledge of musical notation and small skill in playing. His custom was, when he composed a song, to play it over to some other employee of Feist, who took down the simple theme upon a "lead sheet" as it is called, and afterwards worked it up into so much musical form as was necessary. Piantadosi's piracy of the chorus seems to me sufficiently established. . . . I am aware that in such simple and trivial themes as these it is dangerous to go too far upon suggestions of similarity. For example, nearly the whole of the leading theme of Piantadosi's song is repeated literally from a chorus of *Pinafore*, though there is not the slightest reason to suppose that the plaintiff ever heard of the opera. . . . It is said that such similarities are of constant occurrence in music and that little inference is permissible. . . . Nevertheless, between (the) two choruses in question (by Piantadosi and by Haas), there is a parallelism which seems to my ear to pass the bounds of mere accident.

(However, Judge Learned Hand, upon a re-hearing on 8 June 1916, ruled for the defendant on a technicality, since the plaintiff's publishing firm was not properly incorporated and hence not legally entitled to seek damages)

## 28 MAY 1916

Albert LAVIGNAC, French musical encyclopedist and popularizer, editor of the voluminous *Encyclopédie de la musique et Dictionnaire du Conservatoire*, which started publication on 30 May 1913, dies in his native Paris at the age of seventy.

## 7 JUNE 1916

In a letter to the Ligue Nationale pour la Défense de la Musique Française, Maurice RAVEL, employed by the French Army as a military camion driver, voices his repugnance towards the current campaign in France against performances of contemporary German and Austrian music.

I do not believe that it is necessary to ban public performances in France of works by contemporary German and Austrian composers in order to protect the French artistic commonwealth. It would be dangerous for French composers to ignore systematically the production of their foreign colleagues and to create a national coterie of the arts. Our music, so rich now, would then degenerate into stereotyped formulas. It matters little to me that Schoenberg is an Austrian. He is a musician of high merit whose interesting experiments exercise a healthy influence on composers of the allied nations, and on us. I am glad that Bartók, Kodály and their followers are Hungarian nationalists, and that they show this adherence with such excellent taste in their music. (From Ravel's letter quoted in *La Revue Musicale*, Paris, December 1938)

## 8 JUNE 1916

At the Litchfield County Choral Union Festival in Norfolk, Connecticut, Percy GRAINGER plays the piano part in the world première of his suite *In a Nutshell*, scored for orchestra, wood and steel marimbas and a synthetic Nabimba (a marimba with an admixture of clarinet timbre), in four movements: (1) *Arrival Platform Humlet* (inspired by Grainger's travel between the Liverpool Street and Victoria stations of the London railway system on 2 February

1908 and his humming a "humlet)" (2) *Gay but Wistful,* inspired by contradictory moods induced by riding a train in America (3) *Pastoral* (4) *The Gum Suckers' March* (gum suckers being Australian slang for natives of Victoria, Grainger's home state)

### 7 JULY 1916

Jules COMBARIEU, eminent French music historian, dies in Paris at the age of fifty-seven.

### 14 JULY 1916

The Dadaists present in Zürich their first public show.

Pour la première fois dans tout le monde DADA-SOIRÉE (Musique, Danses, Théories, Manifeste, Poèmes, Tableaux, Costumes, Masques)

Devant une foule compacte Tzara manifeste, nous voulons nous voulons nous voulons pisser en couleurs diverses, Hülsenbeck manifeste, Ball manifeste, Arp Erklärung, Janco meine Bilder, Heusser eigene Kompositionen—Les chiens hurlent et la dissection du Panama sur piano et embarcadère—Poème crié—on crie dans la salle, on se bat, premier rang approuve, deuxième rang se déclare incompétant, le reste crie, qui est plus fort, on apporte la grosse caisse, Hülsenbeck contre 200, Hoosenlatz accentué par la très grosse caisse et les grelots au pied gauche—on proteste, on crie, on casse les vitres, on se tue, on démolit, on se bat, la police interruption.

Reprise du boxe: Danse cubiste, costumes de Janco, chacun sa grosse caisse sur la tête, bruits, musique nègre—trabatgea bonoooooo ooooooo—5 expériences littéraires: Tzara en frac explique devant le rideau, sec sobre pour les animaux, la nouvelle esthétique: poème gymnastique, concert de voyelles, poème bruitiste, poème statique, arrangement chimique des notions, Biribum Biribum saust der Ochs im Kreis herum (Hülsenbeck), poème de voyelles a a o, i e o, a i i, nouvelle interprétation, la folie subjective des artères, la danse du cœur sur les incendies et l'acrobatie des spectateurs. De nouveau cris, la grosse caisse, piano et canons impuissants, on se déchire les costumes de carton, le public se jette dans la fièvre puerpérale interomprrrre. Les journaux, mécontents, poème simultané à 300 idiotisés définitivs (From multilingual and heterotypographical *Dada Almanach,* Berlin, 1920)

### 15 JULY 1916

*Gott strafe England,* German hymn of hate for England, is published in Leipzig.

### 22 JULY 1916

*Huémac,* one-act opera to the story of the Toltecs of ancient Mexico by the Italian-born naturalized Argentinian composer Pascual DE ROGATIS, is produced at the Teatro Colón in Buenos Aires.

### 27 JULY 1916

Karl KLINDWORTH, German pianist, conductor, pedagogue, erudite musical scholar, renowned editor of piano literature, arranger of Wagner's *Ring des Niebelungen* in piano score, dies at Stolpe at the age of eighty-five.

## 5 AUGUST 1916

George BUTTERWORTH, 31-year-old English composer of evocative instrumental pieces imbued with the melorhythms of the English countryside, is killed in action near Pozières on the Somme, after successfully capturing a German trench.

## 21 AUGUST 1916

*The Happy Ending,* a play with music by Eugene HAILE, wherein a girl summons at a spiritual séance the ghost of her aviator lover fallen in aerial combat and is told that he did not suffer when he was shot down because "life was instantaneous," a "spoken opera" in which words are accompanied by the orchestra, with the melodic line calculated to follow the rhythmic verbal inflections, is produced in New York City.

## 31 AUGUST 1916

Arturo TOSCANINI conducts a military band on the hilltop of Monte Santo after its capture by Italian soldiers, and is subsequently awarded a medal of valor for courage under fire.

## 2 SEPTEMBER 1916

*Prestami tua moglie,* operetta by Ruggero LEONCAVALLO, is produced in Montecatini.

## 9 OCTOBER 1916

Incensed by his anti-German feelings, Pierre MONTEUX refuses to conduct *Till Eulenspiegel* by Richard Strauss at the Ballet Russe presentation at the Manhattan Opera House in New York, and the German conductor Anselm Goetz takes his place at the podium. (Monteux conducted the rest of the program consisting of works by Russian composers.)

## 10 OCTOBER 1916

K-K-K-Ka—ty, Beautiful Katy, stuttering and stammering ballad by Geoffrey O'Hara, inspired by a lady named Katy Richardson, is copyrighted in Washington. (A pedicular parody on this song, dedicated to the typhoid carrier, C-C-C-Coo—tie, *Horrible Cootie, you're the only B-B-B—Bug that I Abhor,* dedicated to the typhoid carrying *parasita vestimenti,* became popular in the American Expeditionary Force in 1918)

## 15 OCTOBER 1916

*Das Höllisch Gold,* a "German Singspiel" in one act by the Austrian composer Julius BITTNER, his most successful opera, to his own libretto after a medieval fairy tale of Hans Sachs, centered on a simple-minded devilkin sent from the nether regions to the surface of the earth with a mission to corrupt a virtuous couple by gold, but becoming converted himself by their purity of soul, written in the manner of a folk play with simple illustrative motives forming its thematic substance, is performed for the first time in Darmstadt.

### 17 OCTOBER 1916

*Violin Concerto* by Ernest SCHELLING, in one movement subdivided into several autonomous sections, interludes and variations (some of them borrowed and rearranged from his own *Impressions from an Artist's Life* for piano and orchestra), traversing through classical, romantic, Scottish and Spanish moods, with an occasional application of asymmetric meters, and fertilized by non-toxic dissonances, is performed for the first time at a concert by the Boston Symphony Orchestra in Providence, Rhode Island, with Fritz Kreisler (to whom the Concerto is dedicated) as soloist.

### 27 OCTOBER 1916

The earliest mention in print of jazz bands (spelled jass band) is made in *Variety.*

Chicago has added another innovation to its list of discoveries in the so-called *Jass Bands.* The *Jass Band* is composed of three or more instruments and seldom plays regulated music. The College Inn and practically all the other high-class places of entertainment have a *Jass Band* featured, while the low cost makes it possible for all the smaller places to carry their *Jass* orchestra (*Variety,* 27 October 1916, p. 18)

Re the Original Dixieland Jazz Band. This band was organized in New Orleans about the year 1912 and played under the name Dixieland Band and the word Jazz was not added until after we played in Chicago in 1914 for Harry James at the Booster Club. He billed us as The Original Dixieland Jazz Band coming to Reisenweber's in New York City in 1916 to 1918 . . . Re any information you wish I am the man that can give you same, being the leader and manager for this band till we disbanded in 1927 in New York City (From a letter from D. Jas. La Rocca dated 6 April 1936)

The Original Dixieland Jazz Band was the first band in the world to be called a Jazz Band. Our first billing was in the year of 1914, month of March, place Booster Club, Chicago, Illinois, Manager Henry James. It occurred one night while we played for dancers, one frenzied couple kept yelling for more jazz. Mr. James, hearing them call out "play some more jazz" or "jazz it up!" gave him the idea to bill us as such a band . . . The word Jazz is of northern origin. We never before had heard this word Jazz down south. It was used in the theatrical profession, meaning various things, one meaning to pep or excite one . . . The word was not known widely until the release of our Victor Records around the latter part of 1916 or first part of 1917. Our records sold in the millions. (From a subsequent letter from La Rocca dated 19 April 1936)

(Inquiries from the Victor Company established that the first jazz record was issued in March 1917. The Columbia Phonograph Company issued their first jazz record at a later date. The following letter from Mr. A. W. Toos, of the Columbia Phonograph company, written in reply to the author's inquiries, and dated 11 March 1937, stated in part: "In the Columbia record catalog issued October 1st, 1918, the following record is listed, and it was not included in the previously issued catalog dated January 1st, 1918, and accordingly, was released during that interval. Columbia 10-inch Record A-2297 *Darktown Strutters Ball* (Brooks)—Fox Trot, coupled with *Indiana* (Hanley)—

One-Step, played by the Original Dixieland Jass Band . . . In the October 1st, 1919, Columbia catalog, that is the next following complete catalog, the spelling of the artist for Record A-2297 is changed to Original Dixieland Jazz Band. In that 1918 catalog and in many other places we have many uses of the word Jazz but never any other of Jass . . . I have carefully examined our record catalogs for 1914, 1915, 1916 and 1917, but find no use of the word Jass or Jazz before the entry of Record A-2297, evidently released by us about the middle of 1918.")

### 29 OCTOBER 1916

*Two Indian Dances* for orchestra by Charles Sanford SKILTON, based on American Indian melodies, and comprising Part I of his *Suite Primeval* (Part II was first performed in Minneapolis on 13 November 1921), is performed for the first time in Minneapolis.

### 30 OCTOBER 1916

Silas Gamaliel PRATT, eccentric American composer who in his heyday produced a series of patriotic musical spectacles, but who is chiefly remembered by his probably apocryphal remark to Richard Wagner, "Herr Wagner, you are the Silas G. Pratt of Germany," dies in Pittsburgh at the age of seventy.

### 11 NOVEMBER 1916

LILIUOKALANI, Queen of the Sandwich Islands, author of the Hawaiian national anthem *Aloha Oe*, who claimed English blood "because my grandfather ate Captain Cook," dies in Honolulu, her quondam capital, at the age of seventy-eight (she was born on 2 September 1838)

### 13 NOVEMBER 1916

Frederick Septimus KELLY, Australian composer of versatile gifts, a popular athlete and a prize-winning oarsman, is killed in action at Beaucourt, on the Ancre, France, at the age of thirty-five.

### 18 NOVEMBER 1916

*Karlštejn,* comic opera in three acts by the Czech composer Vítězslav NOVÁK, to a libretto about Emperor Carl IV who forbade women to enter his castle only to be outwitted by his Queen who gains entrance in a man's attire to make sure that she is the only one whom he really loves, is performed for the first time in Prague.

### 18 NOVEMBER 1916

Arcady DUBENSKY, 26-year-old Russian composer, conducts in Moscow the first performance of his one-act opera *A Romance with a Contrabass,* after Chekhov's story wherein a Russian girl takes a swim in the nude, cannot find her clothes when she emerges from the water, and takes shelter in a string-bass case which is picked up by her fiancé, a clarinet player, with ensuing imbroglios reflected in a duet of clarinet and string bass in the orchestra.

## 19 NOVEMBER 1916

During the playing of *Siegfried's Funeral Music* from *Götterdämmerung* in Rome under Toscanini's direction, an Italian soldier shouts from the balcony: "In memory of our battalions!" an incident that leads to the prohibition of performance of German music in Italy for the duration of the war. (Information and date obtained from Alfredo Casella)

## 21 NOVEMBER 1916

*Ole from Nordland,* opera in four acts by the Russian composer Mikhail IPPOLITOV-IVANOV, to a story about a young Norwegian fisherman whose unsuccessful love rival kills him on the eve of his wedding, is produced in Moscow.

## 23 NOVEMBER 1916

Eduard NAPRAVNIK, Russianized Czech composer of operas in a lyrically Tchaikovskian vein, and from 1869 chief conductor of the Imperial Opera Theater in St. Petersburg, where he acquired fame as a fanatical disciplinarian intolerant of the slightest deviation from fidelity of pitch and rhythm (in *The Brothers Karamazov* Dostoevsky uses his name, which in Slavic languages suggests directive authority, as a synonym for instructor), dies in St. Petersburg at the age of seventy-seven.

## 24 NOVEMBER 1916

Josef HOFMANN plays with the Cincinnati Symphony Orchestra the piano part in the world premiere of his pseudonymous *Chromaticon* programmed as a work by Michel Dvorsky (Dvor is Russian for Hof which is German for courtyard) described in the program notes as a "semi-Polish composer born in France in 1890."

## 28 NOVEMBER 1916

*Third Symphony* by the Swedish composer Kurt ATTERBERG is performed for the first time in Stockholm.

## 2 DECEMBER 1916

*Die Rose von Stambul,* operetta in three acts by Leo FALL, dealing with a pasha's daughter who discovers to her delight that her family-imposed Turkish fiancé is the novelist with a French nom de plume with whom she has conducted an amorous correspondence, is produced in Vienna.

## 5 DECEMBER 1916

*Sāvitri,* one-act opera by Gustav HOLST, based on an episode from the Hindu epic poem *Mahabharata,* with Death singing an introductory solo and a hidden female chorus vocalizing on the symbolic vowel "U", is performed for the first time in London.

## 5 DECEMBER 1916

Hans RICHTER, monumentally corpulent and luxuriantly bearded Hungarian-born conductor, a benevolent autocrat of the baton, dies at the age of 73 in Bayreuth where he led the rehearsals and the productions of Wagner's music dramas during the first Wagner Festival of 1876.

## 6 DECEMBER 1916

*Elga,* opera in seven scenes by Erwin LENDVAI, to a libretto from Gerhart Hauptmann's play of the same name, is produced in Mannheim.

## 6 DECEMBER 1916

*Das Testament,* opera by Wilhelm KIENZL, is produced in Vienna.

## 10 DECEMBER 1916

A concert of music by Sergei PROKOFIEV is given in St. Petersburg, featuring the first performance of his narrative ballad for voice and piano *The Ugly Duckling,* telling the story, after Hans Christian Andersen, of a swan hatched by a duck and regarded as ugly by anatine standards (Maxim Gorky, hearing the piece, said: "Prokofiev meant himself in this music!") and *Humorous Scherzo* for a quartet for bassoons.

## 15 DECEMBER 1916

*American Negro Suite* by the Danish composer Thorvald OTTERSTRÖM, dwelling in Chicago from 1892, consisting of a group of instrumental pieces based on Negro spirituals, is performed for the first time by the Chicago Symphony Orchestra.

## 25 DECEMBER 1916

*Les Quatre Journées,* opera in four acts by Alfred BRUNEAU, to his own libretto inspired by a story by Émile Zola, is produced at the Opéra-Comique in Paris, in which each act is represented by a season of the year, projecting the calendar far into the future:

(1) *Spring 1914,* picturing pastoral life in Provence rumbling with undertones of the imminent war (2) *Summer 1920,* with war unprophetically scheduled as still continuing, and describing the encounter after a battle between a French farmer-soldier and an Alsatian in a German uniform who become friends (3) *Autumn 1938,* portraying peace and growing families (4) *Winter 1956,* painting in tones a disastrous flood overtaking an aging family, with only two friends and a small child surviving.

## 25 DECEMBER 1916

Leonid Sabaneyev, Russian music critic, publishes in the Moscow newspaper *News of the Season* a devastating review of the *Scythian Suite,* by Sergei PROKOFIEV, originally scheduled for performance at a Koussevitzky concert on 12 December 1916 in Moscow, but cancelled owing to the dispersion of orchestral musicians conscripted into the army.

275

At a current Koussevitzky concert one of the main attractions was the first performance of the *Scythian Suite* by a young composer Prokofiev, under his own direction . . . . If one says that this music is bad, that it is cacophonous, that a listener with a well differentiated auditory organ cannot tolerate it, people will say "but this is supposed to be barbaric music." And the critic is forced to retreat in shame. So I will not condemn this music. Quite to the contrary, I shall say that it is magnificently barbaric, the world's best barbaric music. But if I am asked whether this music gives me pleasure or artistic satisfaction, if it produces a profound impression, I must categorically say no. The composer himself conducted with barbaric abandon. (Excerpts from Sabaneyev's review)

In the preliminary announcement of Koussevitzky's concerts my *Scythian Suite* was programmed for the 12th of December 1916, under my direction. In view of the impossibility to assemble a large orchestra in wartime, the performance was cancelled. Nevertheless, the Moscow periodical *News of the Season*, whose music department is headed by Leonid Sabaneyev, published a review signed L.S. I hereby state (1) that I have never appeared as conductor in Moscow (2) that my *Scythian Suite* has never been performed in Moscow (3) that the critic could not possibly acquaint himself with the music because the only manuscript score of the work is in my possession. (From Prokofiev's statement published in *Musikalny Sovremennik*, Petrograd, 30 January 1917)

# ~ *1917* ~

## 1 JANUARY 1917

*Eileen*, romantic comic opera in three acts by Victor HERBERT, dealing with the Irish agitation for home rule in 1798, and including a miscegenating romance between an English lady and an Irish rebel, generating in the process a lot of fine Irish tunes (*My Little Irish Rose, Too-re-loo-re, In Erin's Isle*), concluding with the prophetic proclamation, *When Ireland Stands Among the Nations of the World,* is performed for the first time in Cleveland under the original title *Hearts of Erin*.

## 5 JANUARY 1917

*Variety* marks the progress of JAZZ (spelled JAZ) in Chicago's night clubs.

The most popular attractions in Chicago cabarets are now the Jaz Bands or Orchestras, and every cabaret, regardless of its size has a Jaz aggregation. Bert Kelly is credited with the introduction of the Jaz Orchestra in and around Chicago, Kelly featuring his own organization at the College Inn. The College Inn Jaz combination is probably the best of the local outfits, with Kelly at the banjo and Gus Mueller playing the saxophone. At Harry James' Casino on the North Side, the Jaz Band is also a big drawing card, but James has strengthened his amusement end there with a so-called Jug-Band. The Jug-Band is a Jaz Band with a "Juggist" blowing bass notes into an ordinary whiskey jug. The tone resulting resembles the music of a bass viol.

## 17 JANUARY 1917

Leo SOWERBY, 21-year-old composer from Grand Rapids, Michigan, presents in Chicago a program of his works, billed "Leo Sowerby: His Music" including the world premieres of the concert overture *Comes Autumn Time,* an orchestral scherzo entitled *The Irish Washerwoman,* a cello concerto, and a piano concerto with a soprano obbligato, with the composer at the piano, Eric De Lamarter conducting.

I took the advice of a not-too-friendly critic, stole out one dark night and deposited the cello concerto in an ashcan. (From a letter by Leo Sowerby to the author dated 22 June 1961)

(The piano concerto, condensed and exuviated of its ectoplasmic soprano part was performed by Sowerby for the first time in the new version with the Chicago Symphony Orchestra on 5 March 1920)

## 17 JANUARY 1917

The ORIGINAL DIXIELAND JAZZ BAND, the first ensemble to make use of the word Jazz, consisting of cornet played by the leader James (Nick) LaROCCA, trombone, clarinet, piano and drums, billed as "Creators of Jazz," opens at Reisenweber's Restaurant at 8th Avenue and 58th Street in New York.

## 20 JANUARY 1917

*Der Eiserne Heiland,* opera in three acts by Max von OBERLEITHNER, is produced in Vienna.

## 20 JANUARY 1917

*Third Symphony* by Karol SZYMANOWSKI, subtitled *Song of the Night,* in three connected movements for orchestra, chorus and tenor solo, to the words of the mystical *divan* by the Persian poet Jalal al-Din Rumi (1207–1273), with an orientalistic ambience suggested by serpentine melodic arabesques, alternating with whole-tone progressions and pedal-pointed bitonalities, ultimately reaching the firmament of celestially cerulean C major, with glissandi along the overtone series in the cellos and violas leading to a sempiternal moment of vibrant silence, is performed for the first time in Petrograd, conducted by Alexander Siloti.

## 21 JANUARY 1917

*Elegia Eroica* by Alfredo CASELLA, a symphonic tribute to the soldiers of the Allied Armies, is performed for the first time in Rome.

## 22 JANUARY 1917

In a historic decision, Victor Herbert vs. the Shanley Co., Justice Oliver Wendell HOLMES of the United States Supreme Court rules that "the performance in a restaurant or hotel of a copyrighted musical composition, for the entertainment of patrons without charge for admission to hear it, infringes the exclusive right of the owner of a copyright under the act of 4 March 1909, to perform the work publicly for profit."

The plaintiff owns the copyright on a lyric comedy in which is a march called *From Maine to Georgia*. The defendant hotel company caused this march to be performed in the dining room of the Vanderbilt Hotel for the entertainment of guests during meal times, in the way now common, by an orchestra employed and paid by the company. It was held by the circuit court of appeals, reversing the decision of the district court, that this was not a performance for profit within the meaning of the act. If the rights under the copyright are infringed only by a performance where money is taken at the door, they are imperfectly protected. Performances not different in kind from those of the defendants could be given that might compete with and even destroy the success of the monopoly that the law intends the plaintiffs to have. It is enough to say that there is no need to construe the statute so narrowly. The defendant's performances are not eleemosynary. They are part of a total for which the public pays, and the fact that the price of the whole is attributed to a particular item which those present are expected to order is not important. It is true that the music is not the sole object, but neither is the food, which probably could be got cheaper elsewhere. The object is a repast in surroundings that to people having limited powers of conversation or disliking the rival noise give a luxurious pleasure not to be had from eating a silent meal.

### 26 JANUARY 1917

The DIXIE JASS BAND (so spelled) of New Orleans opens at Reisenweber's Cabaret in Chicago.

(Date and facts from *Variety* of 2 February 1917, p. 8: "The Dixie Jass Band, five pieces, is at Reisenweber's, brought on by Max Hart. The band opened last Friday. It is said to have come from New Orleans")

### 30 JANUARY 1917

*Eine florentinische Tragödie*, one-act opera by Alexander ZEMLINSKY, to a libretto after Oscar Wilde, is performed for the first time in Stuttgart.

### 2 FEBRUARY 1917

*I Love the Neutral U.S.A.*, a pacifistic song reflecting the lingering isolationist spirit on the eve of America's entry into World War I, is copyrighted in Washington. (Another pacifistic song *It is the Mothers Who Pay the Price of War* was copyrighted on 13 June 1917, when America was already in the war)

### 2 FEBRUARY 1917

The first full-fledged JAZZ BAND makes its first appearance in New York City.

The Jazz Band has hit New York at last, but just how popular it will become here is a matter that is going to be entirely in the hands of certain authorities that look after the

278

public welfare. There is one thing that is certain, and that is that the melodies as played by the Jazz organization at Reisenweber's are quite conducive to making the dancers on the floor loosen up and go the limit in their stepping. Last Saturday night the Jazz musicians furnished the bigger part of the music for dancing at the 400 Club, and the rather "mixed" crowd that was present seemed to like it, judging from the encores that were demanded, and from the manner in which the dancers roughened up their stepping. The band carries its strongest punches in the trombone and the piccolo, the latter hitting all the blues. (*Variety*, 2 February 1917)

### 9 FEBRUARY 1917

Walter DAMROSCH, German-born conductor of the New York Symphony Orchestra, whose acquired Americanism was the product of his sincere devotion to the cause of democracy, lectures his mostly Germanic players at a rehearsal on the necessity of being loyal to their adoptive country.

I gave the men a lecture . . . on their patriotic duties toward the country in which they made their living. The last was necessary because a few German members objected to being made to play *America* so often, "as if they were an American orchestra." I told them plainly that that was just what we were. (From Damrosch's letter to his wife, in the archives of the Library of Congress)

### 10 FEBRUARY 1917

Emile-Louis-Fortuné PESSARD, amiable French harmony teacher and Prix de Rome winner, composer of pleasingly pre-Impressionistic songs, one of which (*Chanson d'un fou*) was copied by Debussy when he was a student at the Paris Conservatory, the manuscript in Debussy's handwriting being published erroneously as Debussy's own work, dies in Paris at the age of seventy-three.

### 10 FEBRUARY 1917

*The Kairn of Koridwen*, dance-drama by Charles T. GRIFFES, dealing with a druidess who defies the moon goddess Koridwen in her kairn by refusing to slay an intruding non-druidical Gaul and is forced to take poison from the sacred caldron brewing deadly belladonna, with an impressionistic score colorfully arranged for five wind instruments, celesta, harp and piano, is performed for the first time in New York.

### 25 FEBRUARY 1917

Lazare SAMINSKY, 34-year-old Russian composer, conducts in Petrograd the first performance of his *First Symphony*, surnamed *Symphony of the Great Rivers*, and designated as being in the key of *E-frimoll* (free E minor).

### 28 FEBRUARY 1917

*Kullervo*, opera in three acts by the Finnish composer Armas LAUNIS, after the *Kalevala*, is produced in Helsinki.

### 7 MARCH 1917

The world's first jazz recording is issued by the Victor Company, with *Livery Stable Blues* on one side and *Dixieland Jazz Band One-Step* on the other.

### 7 MARCH 1917

Antonina Ivanovna TCHAIKOVSKAYA, née Milyukova, widow of Tchaikovsky, from whom she was never divorced (their nominal cohabitation lasted only six weeks in the summer of 1877 before Tchaikovsky fled from unconsummated heterosexual horrors) and who had two surviving sons, fruits of a liaison with her solicitor, dies in a psychiatric clinic in Petrograd where she was confined in 1896.

### 8 MARCH 1917

*The Canterbury Pilgrims,* opera in four acts by the American composer Reginald DE KOVEN, after Chaucer, the action taking place in the late afternoon of 16 April 1387, with the musical score commenting lightly on the characters including Chaucer himself, is produced by the Metropolitan Opera in New York.

(Five performances only were given; during the fifth performance an announcement was made from the stage of America's entry into the war, whereupon the German soprano cast as the Wife of Bath fainted and could not go on; other German members became similarly distracted, and as a result further performances of the opera had to be cancelled)

### 10 MARCH 1917

*Eros und Psyche,* opera in five acts by the Polish composer Ludomir RÓŻYCKI, his most successful stage work, is performed for the first time in Breslau, in the German version translated from the Polish original.

### 11 MARCH 1917

*Fontane di Roma,* symphonic poem by Ottorino RESPIGHI, descriptive of four contrastingly inspiring Roman fountains, at dawn, in the morning, at midday and at sunset, is performed for the first time at the Augusteo in Rome:

(1) *La Fontana di Valle Giulia all'alba,* a pastoral scene at dawn, opening with an oboe solo in the Phrygian mode and developing into a cycloramic tableau with atmospheric changes at dawn reflected in tremulously rising warm air in the strings and gentle drops of rain in the celesta (2) *La Fontana del Tritone al mattino,* in which the marine demigod blows his conch shell in a mighty unison of four French horns and summons a school of naiads riding on sea-horses (3) *La Fontana di Trevi al meriggio,* with declaratory trumpet calls and proclamatory trombone announcements, followed by poetic effusions in the harps and strings (4) *La Fontana di Villa Medici al Tramonto,* pensive and archaic, as befits a fountain in the vicinity of a museum, marking the sunset in attenuated sonorities.

(Date of first performance obtained from the Augusteo in Rome. The performance conducted in Rome by Arturo Toscanini on 10 February 1918 is often erroneously given as the première)

### 11 MARCH 1917

Second part of *Impressioni dal Vero* by Gian Francesco MALIPIERO, a triptych of musical cameos: (1) *Colloquio di Campane,* an intimate confabulation of tintinnabulating carillons (2) *I Cipressi e il Vento,* a study of stately cypresses wafted gently by the zephyr (3) *Baldoria campestre,* a festive scene of rustic laetification, is performed for the first time in Rome.

### 17 MARCH 1917

La Société Française de Musicologie is founded in Paris, with Lionel de La Laurencie as its first President. (Exact date obtained from the Secretary of the Society)

### 17 MARCH 1917

The world's first jazz phonograph record is advertised in the catalogue of Victor Records: "Spell it Jass, Jas, Jaz or Jazz—nothing can spoil a Jass band."

### 22 MARCH 1917

Four centuries have passed since the birth in Chioggia of Gioseffo ZARLINO, grandmaster of the Venetian school of composition and influential teacher of a multitude of disciples who flocked to him from many lands.

### 23 MARCH 1917

Ernest BLOCH conducts the Boston Symphony Orchestra in the first performance of his *Trois Poèmes juifs,* dedicated to the memory of his father:

(1) *Danse,* a somberly distant rhythmic evocation of the Jewish spirit of dance, devoid of literal melismatic Hebraicisms and set in modal harmonies (2) *Rite,* a solemn ceremonial service in emotionally insistent melodic sequences interrupted by sudden anguished outcries (3) *Cortège funèbre,* in mournfully vacant organum-like quartal and quintal harmonies with trumpeted theomachian imprecations.

Strange and Signal Music of Ernest Bloch—Three Jewish Poems That Evoke a Composer of Remarkable Idiom and Procedure, Invention, Imagination and Power— Pieces of a Singing Vehemence (H. T. Parker's headlines in the Boston *Evening Transcript,* 24 March 1917)

### 27 MARCH 1917

*La Rondine,* "lyric comedy" in three acts by Giacomo PUCCINI, dealing with a Parisian grisette flourishing circa 1860 who fascinates and captivates a decent provincial youth but, overcome by scruples, rejects his offer of marriage and flies away, like a swallow—*la rondine*—back to her natural demi-monde, the musical score approaching light opera in its popular dance style, but retaining the characteristically Puccinian modalities and chordal parallelisms, is produced in Monte Carlo.

The production of Puccini's opera *La Rondine* was accompanied by fierce political polemics, as a result of an article by Léon Daudet in *L'Action française,* in which he asserted that the idea of the opera was suggested to Puccini by a Vienna editor and that the libretto was written by another Viennese, and demanded that the producer of the opera Raoul Gunsbourg be indicted for unlawful commerce with the enemy. The controversy ended in the courts, where Daudet's accusation was found unjustified. From an artistic point of view the work was criticized as an uncertain compromise between grand opera and operetta and for its numerous lapses into the waltz-type of light opera of Lehár and his followers. (Alberto de Angelis, *Dizionario dei musicisti*, Rome, 1918)

## 30 MARCH 1917

*Il Macigno*, opera in two acts by Victor DE SABATA, is performed for the first time at La Scala, in Milan. (A new version was produced under the title *Driada*, in Turin, on 12 November 1935)

## 3 APRIL 1917

Arthur HONEGGER, 25-year-old French modernist, and a student in Vincent d'Indy's orchestration class, conducts at the Paris Conservatoire his first symphonic work, *Aglavaine et Sélisette*, an overture to Maeterlinck's drama of that name.

## 4 APRIL 1917

At a "metachoreographic" dance recital of abstract miming in New York, the modernistic French choreographer Valentine de Saint-Point presents the first orchestral works of Daniel CHENNEVIÈRE, 22-year-old French-born American composer, theosophist and astrologer, later known under his adopted astral name Dane RUDHYAR, *Poèmes ironiques* and *Vision végétale*, influenced by the impressionistically nihilistic manner of Parisian sophisticates and touched by the rhythmic dynamism of primitivistic Russian ballets, with Pierre Monteux conducting the orchestra.

## 6 APRIL 1917

On the day of the declaration of war on Germany by the United States, George M. COHAN composes the famous song *Over There*, based on the three notes of the bugle call. (The song was copyrighted by Leo Feist, publishers, on 1 June 1917; Cohan received a check for $25,000 from the publishers on 31 October 1917 in full payment for the song; this money he gave to soldiers' funds and civic charities)

## 7 APRIL 1917

*El Corregidor y la Molinera* (*The Governor and the Miller's Wife*), "mimic farce" with music by Manuel de FALLA, the scenario derived from *El Sombrero de tres picos* by Alarcón, dealing with a philandering local governor whose emblem of authority is the three-cornered hat, and whose amorous entanglement with a miller's wife leads to adulterous imbroglios, with the fate motive from Beethoven's Fifth Symphony quoted ominously as the miller knocks at the door during their assignation, is performed for the first time in Madrid. (In the final version of the score, the ballet was produced under the English title *The Three-Cornered Hat* by Diaghilev's Ballet Russe in London on 22 July 1919)

9 APRIL 1917

At a gala performance of Diaghilev's Ballet Russe in Rome, given for the benefit of the Italian Red Cross, Igor STRAVINSKY's orchestral arrangement of the *Volga Boatmen's Song*, especially made as a substitute for the Russian Imperial National Anthem rendered obsolete by the Revolution, is played for the first time, conducted by Ernest Ansermet. (Date from *Il Giornale d'Italia*, Rome, 10 April 1917)

9 APRIL 1917

*Tabu*, comic opera in three acts by the Polish composer Lucjan KAMIEŃSKI, is produced in Königsberg.

12 APRIL 1917

*Les Femmes de Bonne Humeur*, choreographic comedy after Carlo Goldoni, to the music of Domenico Scarlatti, arranged and orchestrated by Vincenzo TOMMASINI, is produced by Diaghilev's Ballet Russe in Rome.

15 APRIL 1917

*Gloria Arsena*, opera in four acts by the Danish composer August ENNA (after Alexandre Dumas), is produced in Copenhagen.

25 APRIL 1917

*Ženidba Miloša Obilića* or *Vilin Veo* (*The Wedding of Miloš Obilić*, or *The Fairy's Cloak*), opera in three acts by the foremost Serbian composer Petar KONJOVIĆ, to a story inspired by a popular ballad wherein Miloš invades a fairy dance and pulls the magic cloak off one of the doll-like creatures who is then instantly transformed into an earthly maiden and eagerly accepts his offer in marriage, the music following the early models of German romantic operas, against the pastoral background of Slavic folkwise inflections, in a normal harmonic setting, is produced in Agram (Zagreb).

(The original title of the opera centering on the name of a folk hero of Serbian folklore was changed to the neutral description *The Fairy's Cloak* at the demands of the wartime Austrian authorities to suppress any ethnic sentiments among the people in Croatia, then a part of the Austro-Hungarian Empire)

28 APRIL 1917

*Where Do We Go From Here*, a patriotic American song by Howard JOHNSON and Percy WENRICH, with the boast to "slip a pill to Kaiser Bill and make him shed a tear," is published in New York.

30 APRIL 1917

*Lodoletta* (*Little Skylark*), lyric drama by Pietro MASCAGNI, his third opera, in three acts, after Ouida's sentimental tale of an innocent Dutch girl who is seduced by a Parisian painter and when, seized by scruples, he goes to Holland to find her, she is dead and her native wooden shoes are all that is left for him, written in an effectively Italian manner but falling short of his unsurpassed *Cavalleria rusticana* despite attempts at modernization by means of whole-tone scales and augmented triads, is produced in Rome.

### 3 MAY 1917

The New York Society of the Friends of Music presents a concert of orchestral works by Ernest BLOCH, with Bloch himself conducting two movements of his *Israel* symphony, the rest of the program (led by Artur Bodanzky) including *Three Jewish Poems, Three Psalms* for solo voices and orchestra, and the world première of *Schelomo* (Solomon), "Hebrew rhapsody" for cello and orchestra composed in Geneva in February 1916 and inspired by the wax sculpture by Catherine Barjansky (to whom the score is dedicated), the cello representing King Solomon as a songful monarch and the orchestra as his collective concubines submissively attentive to the constantly fluctuating moods of the music, nostalgic in its orientalized scale passages, despairing and defiant in its wide intervalic leaps, fearfully palpitating in the *saltando* violins and tapping drums, fatalistically bleak in open fifths and fourths, poetically meditative in arpeggiating harps, and sorrowfully gay in dance-like interludes.

It is not my purpose, not my desire, to attempt a reconstitution of Jewish music. . . . It is the Jewish soul that interests me, the complex, glowing, agitated soul that I feel vibrating throughout the Bible. It is this that I endeavor to hear in myself and to transcribe in my music: the venerable emotion of the race. (From Ernest Bloch's letter to Philip Hale published in Philip Hale's Boston Symphony Program Notes, New York, 1935)

Mr. Bloch's ideal of the Jewish music of the future is apparently the grotesque, hideous, cackling dispute of the Seven Jews in Richard Strauss's *Salome* . . . Nearly all of Bloch's music is hot in the mouth with curry, ginger and cayenne, even where one has a right to expect vanilla and whipped cream . . . Even the mellifluous Mozart can be made to sound like Bloch or Schoenberg by simply changing all flats to sharps and all sharps to flats. Mr. Bloch seems to be really in need of such a method . . . An interminably long "Hebrew rhapsody" called Solomon (Schelomo) does not reveal that monarch in all his glory. (New York *Evening Post*, 4 May 1917)

### 5 MAY 1917

In his last public appearance in Paris, Claude DEBUSSY, already ravaged by cancer, plays the piano part with Gaston Poulet as violinist in the first performance of his *Violin Sonata*, completed by him on 14 April 1917.

### 8 MAY 1917

The Provisional Government of Russia, headed by Alexander Kerensky, offers to Serge KOUSSEVITZKY the position of musical director and conductor of the former Imperial Court Orchestra in Petrograd, which he accepts.

### 11 MAY 1917

Two short operas by Ferruccio BUSONI to his own libretti are produced in Zürich:

(1) *Turandot,* in two acts derived from his incidental music for Max Reinhardt's production of Carlo Gozzi's play of that name in Berlin on 27 October 1911, and dealing with the cruelly nubile Chinese lady whose condition for marrying is that the suitor should give correct answers to three ambiguously worded riddles on areane subjects, but who relents at the sight of a nameless young pretender who successfully passes his examination, with a passionately rhapsodic score including orientalistic pentatonic progressions (2) *Arlecchino,* "a theatrical capriccio" set in Bergamo in the 19th century, in four connected scenes wherein Harlequin appears in four different guises, as adventurer, soldier, family man and army general.

## 11 MAY 1917

*Gloemenkind,* fairy-tale opera by the Dutch composer Frits Adriaan KOEBERG, is performed for the first time in Amsterdam.

## 12 MAY 1917

*A fából faragott királyfi (Tale of the Wooden Prince),* ballet in one act by Béla BARTÓK, dealing with a xylophilic young lady, who fetishistically caresses an invultuated wooden simulacrum of her beloved prince and a malevolent melanoptic forest sprite who shakes the trees to prevent the prince from reaching her chamber, set to music palpitating with strong asymmetrical rhythms and weighed down with knotted secundal chord formations but resolving into a seamlessly planed two-dimensional C major as the heroine surrenders herself to carnal delights, is performed for the first time in Budapest.

## 18 MAY 1917

Serge Diaghilev's Ballet Russe presents in Paris the first performance of "ballet réaliste" *Parade* by Erik SATIE, to a surrealist scenario by Jean Cocteau, wherein three frantic American managers advertise their rival shows, featuring a Chinese prestidigitator, a girl dancing ragtime, two acrobats passing "in parade" before the public, and a battery of American-made typewriters in the orchestra pit, with a cubistic curtain by Pablo Picasso, set to music in an ostentatiously "dépouillé" style, as a reaction against both the luxuriant impressionism of Debussy and the primitivistic *fauvisme* of Stravinsky.

Paris is an enfant terrible. Parisians always break the toys given to them. But *Parade* is an unbreakable toy. In 1917, the haste, the turmoil, the defective lighting prevented us from giving to the audience a spectacle planned by us. As a result, the public judged us through a misunderstanding: it mistook its own *scandale* for the show and its own noisy demonstration for the music. That is why even fair-minded critics spoke of the orchestral sound as a charivari, because it had the audacity of being simple, of dispensing with stuffing, with musical surplus, with harmonic tinsel and the pulverized gold of impressionism. Satie's orchestra is a false straw-man. Don't break *Parade* to find out what is inside. There is nothing. It does not conceal anything. *Parade* has no meaning. *Parade* is a parade. *Parade* contains no symbols. *Parade* is as simple as bonjour, as frank as gold, as fresh as a rose, as free as air. After a performance of *Parade,* with a fight going on in the audience, I heard a man say to a friend: "If I knew it was so silly, I would have taken the children along!" This was the best tribute. (Jean Cocteau, *Paris-Midi,* 21 December 1920)

It was a *scandale*. All Paris was there and rioted. Satie was delighted: they fought on account of him! . . . The press was charming: Satie, Cocteau and Picasso were called "boches." One review provoked Satie to such an extent that he sent an insulting postcard to the critic. Dragged to court, the author of *Parade* was sentenced to eight days in jail for "public insults and defamation of character." (P. D. Templier, *Erik Satie*, Paris, 1932. The critic was Jean Poueigh. The text of Satie's letter contained but a single sentence: "Vous n'êtes qu'un cul, mais un cul sans musique." Satie never served the imposed sentence)

## 31 MAY 1917

*We're Going to Take the Germ from Germany*, the first of the punning jingo songs of the war is copyrighted in Washington. (Others using the same pun are *When we Take the Germ out of Germany* (26 September 1917), *We're Going to Take the Germ out of Germany* (7 November 1917), *When the Yanks Yank the Germ out of Germany* (23 July 1918), *Our Yankee Boys Have Yanked the Germ out of Germany* (7 October 1918) and finally, *There'll be no Germ in Germany*, copyrighted on 23 November 1918.

## 7 JUNE 1917

*Ardid de Amor*, lyric comedy in one act by the Uruguayan composer Carlos PEDRELL, nephew of the "Spanish Wagner" Felipe Pedrell, to a story of conquering love in 19th-century Spain, is produced in Buenos Aires.

## 7 JUNE 1917

*We Are Out for the Scalp of Mister Kaiser Man*, the first of a series of 88 American Kaiser-hanging war songs, is copyrighted in Washington, to be followed by such titles as *We Will Make the Kaiser Wiser* (copyrighted 25 August 1917; several other songs used the same rhyme); *We're Going to Hang the Kaiser Under the Linden Tree* (1 October 1917); *We're Going to Whip the Kaiser* (12 November 1917); *We're Truly on Our Way to Can the Kaiser* (19 December 1917); *We're Going to Show the Kaiser the Way to Cut Up Sauerkraut* (14 March 1918); *We'll Lick the Kaiser If It Takes Us Twenty Years* (2 April 1918); *Ropin' the Kaiser* (11 April 1918); *We All Want a Separate Piece of Kaiser Bill* (16 April 1918); *I'd Like to See the Kaiser with a Lily in His Hand* (8 May 1918); *We'll Give the Stars and Stripes to the Kaiser* (15 May 1918); *We're Going to Kick the Hell Out of Will-Hell-em* (15 May 1918); *I'd Kill the Kaiser for You* (15 July 1918); *If I Only Had My Razor Under the Kaiser's Chin* (20 July 1918); *We'll Take the I Out of Kaiser* (24 July 1918); *Shoot the Kaiser* (3 August 1918); *We'll Yank the Kaiser's Moustache Down* (19 August 1918); *When We've Taken the Kaiser's Scalp* (22 August 1918); *The Kaiser's Pants Afire* (14 September 1918); *We'll Swat the Kaiser for Uncle Sam* (30 September 1918); *If I Catch That Kaiser in de Chicken Coop* (16 October 1918); and—after the Armistice—*Hang the Kaiser to a Sour Apple Tree* (23 November 1918); and *Kaiser Now Is Wiser* (16 December 1918)

(The Kaiser died, unscalped and unhung, of a heart attack in his exile home in Doorn, Holland, at 11:30 A.M. on 4 June 1941, in territory occupied by Hitler's armies)

## 9 JUNE 1917

*Seventh Symphony,* surnamed *Schweizerische,* by Switzerland's foremost symphonist Hans HUBER, based on melodic materials from Swiss folksongs, with particular distinction given to *Ranz des vaches,* a national air dating back to 1710 and used by Liszt in his nostalgic piano piece *Le mal du pays* from *Années de pèlerinage,* first series, devoted to reminiscences of his travels in Switzerland, is performed for the first time in Basel.

## 11 JUNE 1917

*Der liebe Augustin,* "scenes from the life of a Vienna talent" in four acts by the Austrian composer Julius BITTNER, to his own libretto centered on the amorous adventures of Augustin, the mythical hero of the famous popular song of unknown origin, is performed for the first time in Vienna.

## 12 JUNE 1917

*Palestrina,* "musical legend" in three acts by Hans PFITZNER, to his own libretto related to the dramatic twenty-two days in Palestrina's life in 1563 when the Council of Trent ruled that his florid type of polyphonic composition was unsuitable for liturgy (Palestrina's vindication came with his *Missa Papae Marcelli,* the theme of which was sung to him by an angel in a dream), with intrinsic allusions identifying Palestrina's strife with Pfitzner's own artistic discomfitures, the musical score written with an application of modernized ecclesiastical modes, is performed for the first time in Munich, Bruno Walter conducting.

## 12 JUNE 1917

Teresa CARREÑO, Venezuelan-born "Valkyrie of the Pianoforte," so nicknamed because of her massive personal appearance and powerful chordal technique, dies in New York at the age of sixty-three.

## 16 JUNE 1917

*We'll Soon Be in Old Berlin,* the first of a series of Berlin-capturing songs, is copyrighted in Washington, to be followed by numerous similar titles: *We'll Take Old Berlin or Bust* (copyrighted 26 October 1917); *We'll Go A-Whirling to Berlin in an Airship Built for Two* (18 March 1918); *We're Going to Get to Berlin Through the Air* (2 April 1918); *Berlin or Bust* (21 October 1918); *A Hot Time Down in Old Berlin* (18 November 1918) and finally, as an accomplished fact but without reference to forcible physical capture, *Berlin Has Fallen* (29 November 1918).

## 19 JUNE 1917

Two centuries have passed since the birth in Deutsch-Brod, Bohemia, of Johann STAMITZ, grandmaster of the Mannheim School, whose 74 symphonies stabilized the form of sonata in orchestral music, thus anticipating and strengthening the direction taken by Haydn and Mozart.

## 2 JULY 1917

*Rapsodia Satanica* for orchestra by Pietro MASCAGNI, arranged from music written to accompany a motion picture, is performed for the first time in Rome.

## 5 JULY 1917

*Ghismonda,* lyric tragedy in two acts with a sexual intermezzo entitled *Incubus,* by the 30-year-old Italian composer Renzo BIANCHI, in which a beauteous medieval damsel falls into the dark powers of demoniac debauchery, is produced in Rome.

## 15 JULY 1917

Erik SATIE composes in Paris a *Sonatine bureaucratique* for piano, depicting an office bureaucrat who hums "an old Peruvian air which he picked up from a deaf-mute in Lower Brittany" while a pianist next door practices a Clementi sonata.

## 16 JULY 1917

Philipp SCHARWENKA, Polish-born but thoroughly Germanized composer and pedagogue, whose romantic piano pieces provided eupeptic pabulum for sentimental piano teachers, co-founder with his younger brother Franz Xaver Scharwenka, of the once-renowned Scharwenka Conservatory in Berlin, dies at Bad Nauheim at the age of seventy.

## 16 AUGUST 1917

*Maytime,* operetta in four acts by Sigmund ROMBERG, dealing with two youthful lovers who married unloved mates in 1840, after burying a valuable property deed near Washington Square in New York, and its accidental discovery two generations later by her granddaughter and his grandson, who fall in love and get married thus gaining happiness denied to their respective grandparents, the score containing the famous love duet *Will You Remember?* sung transchronically by both couples separated by two generations, is performed for the first time in New York City.

## 25 AUGUST 1917

*Schwarzwaldmädel,* operetta by Leon JESSEL, set in early 20th century wherein an ardent maiden from Schwarzwald pursues a vacillating musician whose tastes are for chambermaids, is produced in Berlin.

## 28 AUGUST 1917

*Leave It to Jane,* musical comedy by Jerome KERN, in which a co-ed induces a college football quarterback to remain in the college of her choice and then seduces him into marriage, featuring the songs *Cleopatterer, Just You Watch My Step,* and *Leave It to Jane,* is produced in New York.

## 18 SEPTEMBER 1917

The UKULELE is patented by the Honolulu Ad Club as "a musical instrument made in Hawaii." (Date from the U.S. Patent Bureau, Washington, D.C.)

## 25 SEPTEMBER 1917

*Three Pieces for Cello and Piano,* op. 8, by the 21-year-old German composer Paul HINDEMITH, his first printed work, is published by Breitkopf & Härtel in Leipzig. (Information and date obtained from the publishers)

## 13 OCTOBER 1917

The Board of Education of New York City rules that operas by German composers, being products of enemy provenance, are not to be used as subjects for school and college lectures under its jurisdiction.

## 25 OCTOBER 1917

In a speech before the opening concert of the New York Symphony Society, the German-born but sincerely Americanized conductor and composer Walter DAMROSCH voices an earnest plea that Bach, Beethoven and Brahms should not be treated like enemy aliens and that their music should be allowed to be heard in America.

## 26 OCTOBER 1917

*The Fair of Sorochintzy,* the unfinished opera by MUSSORGSKY, inspired by an episode from Gogol's Ukrainian tale *Evenings on a Farm Near Dykanka,* abounding in fine melodies and infectious dancing rhythms (the Hopak has become famous as an independent dance number), with musical interstices filled in by César Cui, Mussorgsky's comrade-in-arms in the group of Mighty Five, is performed for the first time in Petrograd.

## 27 OCTOBER 1917

Jascha HEIFETZ, 16-year-old Russian-Jewish prodigy of the violin, makes his first appearance in America in his concert at Carnegie Hall, New York, producing a sensation by the virtuosity and maturity of his playing.

(During the intermission, Mischa Elman, a whilom *Wunderkind* himself, remarked to Leopold Godowsky, the sharp-witted pianist, that it was hot in the hall, to which Godowsky replied "Not for pianists." The accuracy of this story was confirmed to the author by Godowsky himself.)

## 1 NOVEMBER 1917

Elena TEODORINI, Rumanian prima donna, is arrested on a steamer en route from Buenos Aires to France, as it neared Cadiz, by a boarding party of British officers on suspicion of pro-German espionage, is transferred to a British destroyer, stripped by a female attendant and immersed in a chemical bath to verify an informer's report that a message in invisible ink was tattooed on her bare shoulders.

You know already about the adventure, both painful and grotesque, that I went through on the boat last year. Fortunately, after being held for 24 hours, I was finally permitted to continue my voyage and enter France. But the rival professional clique in Buenos Aires hastened to take advantage of this incident to fill the local newspapers with all sorts of lies, even saying that I was in a Paris jail and was going to be . . . executed! (From Elena Teodorini's private letter dated 30 November 1918 and preserved in the archives of the Rumanian Academy in Bucharest)

I certify that the accusation that Madame Elena Teodorini was involved in espionage is absolutely false, an infamous calumny made out of whole cloth by her enemies in Buenos Aires. (Statement signed on 12 December 1921 by the Rumanian consul in Rio de Janeiro, preserved in the archives of the Rumanian Academy in Bucharest, manuscript No. 5,366, p. 56)

### 3 NOVEMBER 1917

*Lanzelot und Elaine*, opera in four acts by the German conductor Walter COURVOISIER (after Tennyson), is produced in Munich.

### 9 NOVEMBER 1917

The management of the Philadelphia Orchestra announces that it is "heartily in accord with any movement directed by patriotic motives" and will "conform with pleasure" to the request of the Pittsburgh Orchestra Association to eliminate German music from the program of its Pittsburgh concert of 19 November 1917, and will devote it entirely to works by American composers.

### 11 NOVEMBER 1917

Alexander GLAZUNOV conducts in revolutionary Petrograd a matinée concert at the Conservatory, in a program including the first performance of his *Second Piano Concerto* in B major (the nucleus of which originated in 1894), in a single movement, built on a cyclical model and couched in a network of erudite polyphony.

### 14 NOVEMBER 1917

*Šumařovo dítě (Fiddler's Child)*, symphonic poem by Leoš JANÁČEK, foremost composer of Czechoslovakia, is performed for the first time in Prague.

### 17 NOVEMBER 1917

At a war benefit performance of the Chicago Opera Company, a German named Reinhold Faust rolls a bomb down the aisle from his seat in Row K in the hall as a demonstration against America's entry into the war. (The bomb failed to go off; four more bombs were found in Faust's safe in the National Safe Deposit Company during another German war, 22 years later, in 1939)

## 24 NOVEMBER 1917

*The Spirit of England,* a choral triptych by Sir Edward ELGAR to the text from three patriotic ballads connected with the war—*The Fourth of August, To Women* and *For the Fallen*—is given for the first time in its entirety in London.

## 6 DECEMBER 1917

*An allem ist Hütchen Schuld,* opera in three acts by Siegfried WAGNER, the "little son of a great father," to his own libretto, containing a spoken scene in which Jakob Grimm, the fabulist, complains to the composer (or his Thespian simulacrum) that the abstruse events going on in the opera constitute an inexcusable falsification of his simple fairy tale, is produced in Stuttgart.

## 8 DECEMBER 1917

Ernst KUNWALD, German conductor of the Cincinnati Symphony Orchestra, is arrested as an enemy alien and immediately freed on bail and even allowed to conduct concerts before internment. (Kunwald conducted two more weekly concerts and rehearsals and then was asked to resign)

(An announcement appeared in the Cincinnati Symphony program book of 16–17 November 1917, with a waving American flag in color on the cover, that the American National Anthem would be played at the beginning of each concert, and Kunwald complied with this requirement)

## 10 DECEMBER 1917

The Vatican issues a decree, signed by the Secretary of the Consistorial Congregation, enjoining Catholics against dancing the tango and the maxixe, at home, in public, in the daytime or at night.

## 11 DECEMBER 1917

*Rapsodie nègre* by the 18-year-old French composer Francis POULENC, scored for piano, string quartet, flute, clarinet and baritone voice, in five movements: (1) *Prélude* (2) *Ronde* (3) *Honoloulou* (*"le chant sans nuances"*) syllabilizing pseudo-Hawaiian words *Patata, Bananalou,* etc. (4) *Pastorale* and (5) *Final,* based on pentatonic progressions in saccadic rhythms, is performed for the first time in Paris, with Poulenc himself being forced to sing the vocal solo in *Honoloulou,* after the scheduled singer refused to appear.

## 11 DECEMBER 1917

*Das Christ-Elflein,* Christmas opera in two acts by Hans PFITZNER (derived from his incidental music to a play produced exactly 11 years before, on 11 December 1906, in Munich), to a story combining elements of pagan Germanic magic and the Christian concept of divinity, wherein the Christ Child befriends an elfin scion of an old fir tree, and together they fetch a Christmas tree to bring cheer to an ailing girl, set to music in a pleasingly harmonious style, is performed for the first time in Dresden.

13 DECEMBER 1917

*Sortilegi,* symphonic poem for piano and orchestra by the 35-year-old Bohemian-born Italian composer Riccardo PICK-MANGIAGALLI, with the spirit of sortilege illustrated by the lambent saltation of igneous instrumental colors, is performed for the first time in Milan.

26 DECEMBER 1917

Henry HADLEY conducts in Chicago the first performance of his opera *Azora, Daughter of Montezuma,* in three acts wherein an Aztec princess, condemned to death with her lover, is saved when Cortez rides on a white charger into the Aztec temple where she awaits her fate, and the conquistadores intone *Gloria in Excelsis Deo,* set to music in an effective melodramatic style with a modicum of pentatonic progressions to illustrate the Indian modalities.

# ~ *1918* ~

5 JANUARY 1918

A *Daughter of the Forest,* one-act opera by the American composer Arthur Finley NEVIN, brother of the song composer Ethelbert Nevin, dealing with the life of animal trappers in Pennsylvania at the time of the Civil War, with tragedy ensuing when the daughter of one of them becomes illegitimately pregnant and kills herself, whereupon her lover joins the Federal troops to seek death in combat, is produced in Chicago.

5 JANUARY 1918

Serge RACHMANINOFF leaves Russia, never to return.

15 JANUARY 1918

An auspicious public presentation of music by the "nouveaux jeunes" of France is made at an intimate concert in Paris under the benevolent tutelage of Erik Satie, in a program of music by 26-year-old ROLAND-MANUEL, 25-year-old Arthur HONEGGER, 25-year-old Germaine TAILLEFERRE, 19-year-old Francis POULENC and 18-year-old Georges AURIC.

19 JANUARY 1918

Sylvio LAZZARI, 60-year-old French composer born in Tyrol of Italian parents, conducts the Chicago Opera in the world première of his three-act opera *Le Sauteriot,* an epic of life among lowly Lithuanians, in which an illegitimately conceived girl surnamed *sauteriot* (grasshopper) for her saltatory amours, commits suicide by poison when her desirable beau, after spending a night with her, joins his regular mistress in the morning, set to music in a Wagnero-genically Gallic vein, with some exotic supplements such as a Lithuanian Bear Dance.

21 JANUARY 1918

The directors of the Philharmonic Society of New York issue a public statement banning all works by living German composers from its programs.

22 JANUARY 1918

Mrs. William Jay, superpatriotic Boston dowager, dispatches the following letter to Major Henry Lee Higginson, founder and director of the board of trustees of the Boston Symphony Orchestra, protesting against the continuance of Karl Muck's tenure as conductor of the orchestra:

As a result of the intense feeling regarding a man who bears the German Emperor's decoration and whose sympathies are most palpably opposed to the United States, the Boston Symphony concerts in New York have become a gathering place for everyone who hopes for a defeat of Allied arms. In our opinion even art must stand aside so that every possible influence can be brought to bear to terminate the war with an Allied victory. To this end, there seems no swifter means of emphasizing the whole-heartedness of the United States than by terminating the German influence in musical affairs. (Higginson replied on 30 January 1918 as follows: "Dr. Muck is probably German in feeling, but he has done nothing wrong. He has been eminently satisfactory to me as a conductor and as a man. His industry, knowledge and power are great, and his place cannot be supplied in this country." Mrs. Jay retorted in a letter dated 25 February 1918, demanding the removal of "the last tentacle of the German octopus" from American musical life)

23 JANUARY 1918

François CASADESUS conducts at the Opéra-Comique in Paris the first performance of his "évocation dramatique et lyrique" entitled *Au beau jardin de France.*

24 JANUARY 1918

Gottfried von EINEM, Austrian composer of operas in a modern romantic vein, is born in Bern, Switzerland, the son of an attaché at the Austrian Embassy.

25 JANUARY 1918

*Peintures,* a set of three impressionistic sketches for orchestra (*Portrait d'une jeune fille, Le Jardin de Nuit, La Fête*), by the English-born violinist Felix BOROWSKI is performed for the first time by the Chicago Symphony Orchestra, Frederick Stock conducting.

27 JANUARY 1918

The first part of *Pause del Silenzio,* "seven symphonic expressions" by Gian Francesco MALIPIERO, portraying in eloquent sonorities the spirit of softness, crudity, melancholy, gayety, mystery, war and savagery, concluding on a thematic pause of silence, is performed for the first time in Rome.

George Moore knew in his sojourn in Paris a strange musician, poor, but wearing silk shirts . . . He should be remembered by a remark he made: "To express silence in music I should need at least three brass bands." There were moments when one might be pardoned for thinking that Malipiero had pondered that theory. (Philip Hale, Boston *Herald,* 5 April 1919)

### 1 FEBRUARY 1918

*Wo die Lerche singt,* operetta in three acts by Franz LEHÁR, dealing with a morally unstable painter whose picture of an Austrian *milchmädel* wins him a prestigious prize but who loses her as a model and as a prospective inamorata after his promiscuous dalliance with a sexually experienced actress, is produced in Budapest.

### 7 FEBRUARY 1918

*Doreya,* opera by the Cuban composer Eduardo SÁNCHEZ DE FUENTES, to a libretto from the life and legend of pre-Columbian Indians in Spanish America, containing authentic pentatonic material from ancient tribal chants, is produced in Havana.

### 11 FEBRUARY 1918

*Pan and Syrinx,* symphonic poem by the Danish composer Carl NIELSEN, depicting in romantic tonalities the poetic Greek myth of an Arcadian nymph who changed into a reed to escape the pursuit of Pan and whose hollow stem Pan fashioned into a panpipe, is performed for the first time in Copenhagen.

### 14 FEBRUARY 1918

*Swanee,* the first successful song by the 19-year-old American composer George GERSHWIN, is performed for the first time as a number in the revue *Sinbad* produced in New York.

### 17 FEBRUARY 1918

*A Child's Garden of Verses,* symphonic suite by the American composer Edward Burlingame HILL, inspired by Robert Louis Stevenson's cycle of poems, in four sections: (1) *March,* a merry procession with some chromatic acerbities (2) *The Land of Nod,* a sophisticated lullaby ornamented by resolvable discords (3) *Where Go the Boats,* a stylized tarantella (4) *The Unseen Playmate,* a romantic reverie, is performed for the first time by the New York Symphony under the direction of its permanent conductor Walter Damrosh.

### 20 FEBRUARY 1918

*Schaaban,* opera in three acts by Vittorio RADEGLIA, who was the composer of the Turkish national anthem, is produced in Vienna, to a German libretto translated from an original text in Turkish.

## 10 MARCH 1918

*Der Stier von Olivera,* opera in three acts by the deracinated Germanized English-born composer Eugen D'ALBERT, is produced in Leipzig.

## 10 MARCH 1918

*Ritorna Vincitor,* opera in Italian by the Philippine composer Antonio J. MOLINA, is performed for the first time in Manila, the composer conducting.

## 14 MARCH 1918

Karl MUCK conducts the Boston Symphony Orchestra in Carnegie Hall, New York, despite the frenetic efforts of ultra-patriots to prevent his appearance.

City Is Confident Ban Will Be Put on Doktor Muck—Loyal Foes of Prussian Direktor Expect Action Today—Trinity Rector Writes Concert Should Be Prohibited—Condemns Tolerance—Mrs. William Jay Moves to Stop Muck's Concerts—Patronage of Boston Symphony Is Largely Pro-German, She Says, Moving to Silence Orchestra—Muck and His Enemy Aliens Here Tonight—Patriotic Societies and Loyal Citizens by Thousands Protest in Vain—Kaiser's Direktor and Band Reach City—Carnegie Hall Swings Wide Its Doors to German Doktor—Nine Austrians in Orchestra—Muck Plays Here Guarded by Police—Only Subscribers Admitted to Concert Which Was Not Interrupted—Opens With Our Anthem—New York Bows Head in Shame as Muck Leads—Germans Applaud Their Hero Loudly (Assorted consecutive headlines in the New York newspapers of March 1918).

## 15 MARCH 1918

Lili BOULANGER, first woman composer ever to receive the Premier Grand Prix de Rome annually awarded by the lofty Institut de France, whose delicate vocal and instrumental works were cast in a fine impressionistic manner of the *fin de siècle,* dies in her native Paris at the lamentably unfulfilled age of 24 years, 6 months and 3 weeks, only 4 years, 8 months and 9 days after receipt of the prize.

## 23 MARCH 1918

A century has passed since the death in Paris of Nicolò ISOUARD, Malta-born composer of many melodious and harmonious operas to fanciful French libretti, often set in exotic lands.

## 23 MARCH 1918

John POWELL, 35-year-old American composer, plays with the Russian Symphony Orchestra in New York the solo part in the world première of his *Rapsodie nègre* for piano and orchestra, inspired by Joseph Conrad's novel *Heart of Darkness.*

## 23 MARCH 1918

The Paris Opéra cancels the evening performance of *Rigoletto* and *Coppélia* owing to the bombardment of Paris by the German long-range gun, manufactured by the Krupp Company and known as "the Big Bertha" with an affectionate allusion to Frau Bertha Krupp, the matriarch of the Krupp family.

### 23 MARCH 1918

Two new American works are performed for the first time at the Metropolitan Opera in New York:

*Shanewis, or The Robin Woman,* opera by Charles Wakefield CADMAN, in two acts, dealing with a beautiful Indian girl brought up in an aristocratic Californian home, whose American lover follows her to an Indian Reservation in Oklahoma where he is killed by a poisoned arrow shot by her brother after it becomes clear that he could not marry Shanewis because of laws and customs against miscegenation, set to music in an effectively melodious and harmonious vein, abounding in pentatonically stylized arias and duets; and *The Dance in Place Congo,* ballet-pantomime by Henry F. GILBERT, evoking in stark ethnic colors the tribal Negro festivals in Place Congo in ante-bellum New Orleans and making thematic use of French Creole songs of the period.

### 24 MARCH 1918

Despite daily bombardment, the Paris Opéra opens its doors with the performance of Gounod's *Faust,* taking in 8,262 francs 10 centimes at the box office. (Information from *Cinquante ans de musique française,* Paris, 1926)

### 25 MARCH 1918

Claude DEBUSSY, sublime poet of new French music, originator of a distinctive style of composition that came to be called Impressionism, even though he himself deprecated the term, dies of cancer in war-saddened Paris, as cannons thunder, at ten o'clock at night, having lived 55 years, 7 months and 3 days.

Il est mort, Claude de France, l'Orphée des songes interrompus. *Le miel mélodieux ne coule plus des alvéoles* . . . (Gabriele d'Annunzio's lines upon learning of Debussy's death)

### 25 MARCH 1918

Karl MUCK, German conductor of the Boston Symphony Orchestra, is arrested in Boston as an enemy alien.

Dr. Karl Muck Arrested as Alien Enemy—Symphony Conductor Taken As He Leaves Motor Car at His Home—Locked Up in Back Bay Police Station—Federal Authorities Silent Regarding Possible Recent Evidence.

Dr. Karl Muck, director of the Boston Symphony Orchestra, was arrested at his home, 50 Fenway, at 11:30 o'clock last night, by policemen and agents of the Department of Justice . . . The arrest was decided upon late last evening. Policemen and Department of Justice agents kept vigil on the Fenway residence from about 8:30 until 11:30. Dr. Muck, they learned, was either at a play or at some social affair. Immediately upon the arrival of his limousine at his home a policeman stepped to his side, identified him, and told him he was under arrest. (Boston *Herald,* 26 March 1918)

It is evident that the federal authorities view Dr. Muck as an important prisoner. They consider it established that his Boston residence was part of the Kaiser's policy of some years ago of "planting" musicians, college professors and other men of great accomplishments and culture in various countries as part of his gorgeous scheme of eventual world-wide conquest. Dr. Muck, claiming Swiss citizenship, was "loaned" by the Kaiser to the Boston Symphony Orchestra and constantly expressed his pride in the fact that his orchestra was composed almost wholly of Germans and Austrians (Boston *Herald*, 28 March 1918)

## 26 MARCH 1918

César Cui, the last surviving and least mighty of the Mighty Five of Russia, composer of poetic miniatures of which *Orientale* is a paradigm, whose father, a French officer in Napoleon's army taken prisoner in 1812 married a Russian woman, and who was himself a general in the Tsarist Army and instructor in the science of military fortification to the last Russian Tsar Nicholas II, dies in Petrograd at the age of 83, surviving Balakirev by nearly 8 years, Rimsky-Korsakov by nearly 10, Borodin by 31 and Mussorgsky by 37 years.

(24 March 1918 was cited erroneously as the date of Cui's death in the previous editions of *Music Since 1900*, in Baker's *Biographical Dictionary of Music and Musicians, Fifth Edition*, edited by Nicolas Slonimsky, in *Die Musik in Geschichte und Gegenwart*, in Grove's *Dictionary of Music and Musicians* and *Enciclopedia dello Spettacolo*. The correct date, 26 March 1918, is verified by obituaries in the Petrograd newspapers and published announcements by the family)

## 27 MARCH 1918

*If He Can Fight Like He Can Love, Good Night, Germany*, a jingoistic popular song, with a suggestive erotic angle, is copyrighted in Washington, D.C.

## 4 APRIL 1918

*Kjartan und Gudrun*, opera in three acts by the German composer Paul von KLENAU, is produced in Mannheim.

## 6 APRIL 1918

*1814*, opera by Xavier LEROUX, to a libretto depicting the decline and fall of Napoleon, is produced in Monte Carlo.

## 7 APRIL 1918

Karl MUCK is interned as an enemy alien at Fort Oglethorpe, Georgia, for the duration of the war.

Dr. Muck's Boast in Berlin His Undoing—Letters Show His Propaganda Connection and Contempt for America and Boston—Written to a Young Boston Woman He Deceived by Promise of Marriage—Complete Wireless Outfit in Muck's House—Muck Active German Spy Many Years—Boston People Gave Cash to Dr. Muck to Help Germany in War—Dr. Muck Was Audacious in Use of Cipher—Complained Code was Muddled by Telegraph Co.—Listed Women with Phone Calls—Kept Record of Names and Activities in German Cause (Assorted headlines in the Boston *Post*)

## 21 APRIL 1918

Two days before his 27th birthday Sergei PROKOFIEV conducts in Petrograd the first performance of his *Classical Symphony* in D major (completed on 23 September 1917), ostentatiously classical in form but unorthodox in its wide melodic leaps, curt plagal cadences, asymmetrical rhythms and modulatory detours, in four movements:

(1) *Allegro*, in energetic sonata form, with the recapitulation in the lateral tonality of C major (2) *Larghetto*, in A major, with a songful theme in the violin projected upon the murmurations and susurrations of the rest of the ensemble (3) *Gavotte*, a courtly dance in D major, with a Musette in G major, a delicate rococo creation, suggesting a Parisian music box in its fragile sonorities, but providing a sharply scented snuff in deceptive cadences thumbing the nose at the classics (4) *Finale*, in D major, a spirited mobile rondo.

When you appeared on the podium to conduct your sunlit symphony, a ray of sun illumined your dear features. Was it a smile of sympathy towards your kindred element? I cannot tell, but I believe it might be. (From a note in Prokofiev's album by Nicolas Tcherepnin, his teacher of conducting, inscribed on 20 April 1918 after the final rehearsal of the *Classical Symphony*)

## 23 APRIL 1918

*First Symphony* by the 23-year-old Dutch modernist Willem PIJPER (completed on 14 October 1917), in four movements: (1) *Allegro burlesca*, set in a rustically rhythmic idiom (2) *Lento*, a neo-romantic nocturnal intermezzo (3) *Giocoso*, in the manner of a modern minuet and (4) *Andante maestoso*, an animistic representation of Pan's funeral procession, is performed for the first time by the Concertgebouw Orchestra in Amsterdam, Willem Mengelberg conducting.

## 25 APRIL 1918

*Die Gezeichneten* (*The Stigmatized*), opera in three acts by Franz SCHREKER, to his own libretto dealing with an unconsummated passion of a cripple with a beautiful soul for a girl with a beautiful body in 16th-century Genoa, set to music in a tensely dramatic expressionistic idiom presaging the emancipated chromatic syle of the immediate future, is produced in Frankfurt.

## 27 APRIL 1918

*Russian Rag*, ragged version of RACHMANINOFF's famous C-sharp minor *Prelude*, one of the earliest examples of jazzification of respectable music, perpetrated by George L. Cobb, is copyrighted in Washington, D.C.

## 7 MAY 1918

*What General Pershing Will Do to Germany Is Just What Dewey Did at Manila Bay*, a patriotic song, is copyrighted in Washington.

## 18 MAY 1918

Toivo KUULA, Finnish composer of music based on East-Bothnian melodic resources organized within Western contrapuntal and harmonic confines, is murdered in a tavern brawl in Vyborg, seven weeks before his 35th birthday, and three weeks after the brief occupation of the city by the White Finnish Army fighting the Bolsheviks.

## 22 MAY 1918

*Grab a Gun, Put the Hun on the Run,* one of the many anti-Hun songs of World War I, is copyrighted in Washington.

## 24 MAY 1918

*A Kékszakállú Herceg Vára (Duke Bluebeard's Castle)*, one-act opera by the foremost modern composer of Hungary Béla BARTÓK, written in 1911, and depicting the fabled polygamist and his inquisitive fourth wife who opens the forbidden seventh door where she finds Bluebeard's previous three wives kept in an anabiotic state, set to a tortuously dramatic score with strident discords stressing the cumulatively melodramatic peripeteia, is performed for the first time at the Budapest Opera.

*Bluebeard's Castle* is for Hungarians what *Pélléas* is for the French . . . The seven doors, opened one after another, give occasion for as many musical images, not through external characterization but by means of intimate sentiment . . . Bartók's opera may be called a "symphonie à tableaux," or a drama with symphonic accompaniment, but what is certain is that the combination is a masterpiece, a musical geyser of sixty minutes of compressed tragedy. (Zoltán Kodály in *La Revue Musicale*, Paris, March 1921)

## 1 JUNE 1918

Jaroslav NOVOTNÝ, Czech composer of impressionistic songs in the French manner, is killed at the age of 32 in the Ural mountains during a skirmish between the Red Army and former Austrian prisoners of war of Bohemian extraction forming a unit in the anti-Soviet White Army.

## 5 JUNE 1918

*Theophano,* opera in three acts by the German composer Paul GRAENER, dealing with the illicit passion of Theophano, twin sister of the Roman Emperor in Byzantium, for his trusted aide, with the lovers saved from execution for immorality by the intercession of the people of the country, written in a lutulent Wagneromimic idiom, fertilized by non-toxic dissonances, is performed for the first time in Munich. (A new version, under the title *Byzanz*, was produced in Leipzig on 22 April 1922)

## 10 JUNE 1918

Arrigo BOITO, Italian opera composer and librettist, himself a poet of superior literary gifts, dies in Milan at the age of seventy-six.

## 17 JUNE 1918

A century has passed since the birth of Charles GOUNOD, the lyric genius of the French musical theater.

### 23 JUNE 1918

The New York Philharmonic Orchestra inaugurates an annual series of summer concerts in open air financed by Adolph Lewisohn, and presented in a stadium that was to bear his name.

### 29 JUNE 1918

*Tucumán,* opera by the Argentine composer Felipe BOERO, based on an episode of the South American war of independence in the town of Tucumán, set to music in a conventional Italian manner, brightened by the injection of authentic folk dance rhythms, is produced at the Teatro Colón in Buenos Aires.

### 6 JULY 1918

On his way from Russia via Siberia to the United States, Sergei PROKOFIEV presents in Tokyo a recital of his piano music, introduced in the English-language program as "The Gigantic Russian Composer & Pianist Virtuoso, The Another Prizz Winner."

### 12 JULY 1918

By decree of the Soviet of People's Commisars, the conservatories of Petrograd and Moscow are nationalized and put under the authority of the Department of Education.

### 27 JULY 1918

Gustav KOBBÉ, 61-year-old New York music critic and compiler of books on opera, is killed in his sailboat by a Navy seaplane maneuvering in the bay near Babylon, Long Island, New York.

### 11 AUGUST 1918

Gino MARINUZZI conducts in Buenos Aires the first performance of his opera in three acts, *Jacquerie,* on the subject of the bloody peasant rebellion in 14th-century France.

### 18 AUGUST 1918

*Fernando,* opera written by Franz SCHUBERT in 1815, has its first stage performance 103 years later, in Magdeburg.

### 19 AUGUST 1918

*Yip, Yip, Yaphank,* revue with book, music and lyrics by the 30-year-old Russian-born musician Irving BERLIN, is performed for the first time in Camp Upton, New York, with Berlin himself taking the part of a reluctant recruit singing *Oh, How I Hate to Get Up in the Morning* and voicing homicidal intentions towards the army bugler who sounds the reveille, and including also the inspirational hymn *God Bless America,* destined to achieve immense patriotic popularity.

## 25 AUGUST 1918

Leonard BERNSTEIN, uniquely versatile pianist-composer-conductor, destined to be as successful in the domain of exalted music-making at the helm of a great orchestra as in the composition of melodiously rhythmic and harmoniously stimulating Broadway shows, is born in Lawrence, Massachusetts, to a family of second-generation Jewish immigrants from Russia.

## 28 AUGUST 1918

*Shanghai,* operetta in two acts by Isidore WITMARK, picturing in a conventional stylized form the life in imperial China, with a couple of American characters, Flash Pansy (female) and Pete Dark (male), indulging in some crooked deals, is performed for the first time in London.

## 9 SEPTEMBER 1918

*Caramurú,* symphonic poem by the 21-year-old Brazilian composer Francisco MIGNONE, descriptive of the anthropophagic rites of the Brazilian Indians, is performed for the first time in São Paulo, conducted by Mignone's father.

## 15 SEPTEMBER 1918

*Meister Guido,* comic opera in three acts by the German composer Hermann NOETZEL, dealing with a poor music teacher who wins the hand of a Florentine lady by assuming the air of a nobleman dabbling in arts, is produced in Karlsruhe.

## 16 SEPTEMBER 1918

One thousand, nine hundred and twenty-five years after the death of Gaius Maecenas, Mrs. Elizabeth Sprague COOLIDGE, American encourager of the arts, opens on her estate in the Berkshires, near Pittsfield, Massachusetts, a Temple of Music dedicated to concerts of classical and modern music by American and European composers.

## 18 SEPTEMBER 1918

Sergei PROKOFIEV arrives in New York from Petrograd via Japan and declares that Russian musicians keep working despite intolerable conditions of famine and civil dislocation.

## 18 SEPTEMBER 1918

Ernest Bristow FARRAR, 33-year-old English composer of fine-textured music in a neo-Elizabethan manner, is killed during the Battle of the Somme.

## 18 SEPTEMBER 1918

*Carillon magico,* mimo-symphonic comedy by the 36-year-old Bohemian-born Italian composer Riccardo PICK-MANGIAGALLI, to his own libretto, is produced at La Scala, Milan.

19 SEPTEMBER 1918

Liza LEHMANN, English singer and accomplished composer whose melodious song cycle *In a Persian Garden*, a setting for 4 voices and piano of assorted verses from the *Rubaiyát* of Omar Khayyam, has become a favorite of easily satisfied lovers of semi-classical music, its antepenultimate movement, *Ah Moon of My Delight*, possessing the deepest emotional appeal to tenors of all descriptions, dies in her native London at the age of fifty-six.

28 SEPTEMBER 1918

The first performance is given in Lausanne under the direction of Ernest Ansermet of Igor STRAVINSKY's ballet with narration, *L'Histoire du Soldat*, a morality play to the text of C. F. Ramuz, "to be read, played and danced," centering on a demoralized soldier who gives away his violin to the benevolent-looking devil in exchange for wisdom, loses his soul in a card game, and after many an adventure returns home to surrender himself to the devil, with a speaker accompanied by an ensemble of seven instruments selected so as to achieve a maximum efficiency with a minimum of means and yet to cover the entire useful range in a given timbre, namely, two string instruments (violin and contrabass), two woodwinds (clarinet and bassoon), two brasses (cornet and trombone), and a monticule of percussion manned by a single player, the work having the following distinctive parts:

(1) *Soldier's March*, a polymetric grotesque with the contrabass maintaining an unchanging four-note *ostinato* while the melody parts are variously apocopated, generating cross-rhythms and shift of stress (2) *Soldier's Violin*, a musette-like intermezzo with a steady drone on the dominant, simulating an untutored fiddler's dance tune, while the narrator queries querulously: "Where is he going?" (3) *Pastorale*, a serene interlude of philosophical contemplation in statically sonorous harmonies (4) *Royal March*, a discordant asymmetrical military march in which the trumpet and the trombone perform melodic acrobatics against a persistent march-time rhythm (5) *Little Concert*, using the entire available ensemble, and marked by distinctly Russian melodic and rhythmic inflections (6) *Tango*, for violin, clarinet and percussion, a nostalgically discordant modern dance (7) *Waltz*, a caricature of an old-fashioned dance in mock-serious blanched, bland and blank C major (8) *Ragtime*, an Americanized syncopated number played by a ragged violin accompanied by agitated drums (9) *Devil's Dance*, recalling the *Soldier's March* and his violin, and foreshadowing the Devil's triumph (10) *Little Chorale*, an osculatory intermezzo, accompanying the soldier's silent embrace with a princess (11) *The Devil's Song*, a melodrama in denuded thumping rhythms as background for the spoken text (12) *Grand Chorale*, replete with multicadential *fermate*, a majestically Gothic and statically chordal presentation (13) *Triumphal March of the Devil*, in which artful disharmonies serve to express the satanic lure of profitable evil, ending with a protracted solo for percussion, in constantly changing meters, in rapid tempo, varying from 2 to 6 eighth-notes to a bar.

*L'Histoire du Soldat* was born of opportunistic preoccupations. The war was still continuing; no one could foretell when it would end. The Ballet Russe had suspended its productions; the theaters were virtually inactive. I myself was in difficult circumstances because of my inability to find what is known commercially as an outlet. I recall that one day, rather naively, Stravinsky and I wondered: Why not write something simple, something that would not require a large theater or a large audience to produce? It may be a piece for a few instruments with two or three actors on the stage. Since the theaters were no longer available, we could create a theater of our own, with scenery which could be set up anywhere, even in the open air. We would then resume the tradition of itinerant players. . . . *L'Histoire du Soldat* was the outcome of these practical ideas. As for the scenario, all we had to do was to peruse a few volumes of an enormous collection of fairy tales by a famous Russian folklorist. Among a multitude of stories, in which the devil seemed to play the dominating part, we selected one about a soldier and his violin, perhaps for the very reason that it was so completely incoherent (C. F. Ramuz, *Souvenirs sur Igor Stravinsky*, Paris, 1929)

### 7 OCTOBER 1918

Sir Hubert PARRY, English composer of an enormous quantity of music written in a culturally romantic and academically competent style, author of books and erudite scholar, dies at Rustington at the age of seventy.

### 18 OCTOBER 1918

Henry HADLEY conducts in New York the first performance of his one-act opera *Bianca*, to a libretto based on Carlo Goldoni's comedy *La Locandiera*, taking place in Florence in 1760 and dealing with the desirable proprietess of an inn where two cavaliers, fighting a duel over her favors, are stopped by a brave interloper who strikes their swords out of their hands with Bianca's ironing board and wins her love for his resourceful action.

### 20 OCTOBER 1918

Joseph BOULNOIS, 34-year-old French composer of melodious and harmonious songs and instrumental pieces, is killed in battle at Chalaines.

### 22 OCTOBER 1918

All music publishing firms of the Russian Soviet republic are nationalized and declared State property.

### 24 OCTOBER 1918

Charles LECOCQ, French composer of the celebrated operettas *Giroflé-Girofla* and *La Fille de Madame Angot*, dies in Paris at the age of eighty-six.

### 30 OCTOBER 1918

The word GEBRAUCHSOPER (practical opera) is used for the first time in an article by the composer Heinrich Noren in the Berlin music periodical *Signale für die musikalische Welt*.

### 30 OCTOBER 1918

*Zrání*, symphonic poem by the Czech composer Josef SUK, is performed for the first time in Prague.

## 1 NOVEMBER 1918

The VEREIN FÜR MUSIKALISCHE PRIVATAUFFÜHRUNGEN, a society for private performances from which newspaper critics were excluded and where applause was forbidden, is formed in Vienna, with Arnold SCHOENBERG as president. (See Declaration of the Society in LETTERS AND DOCUMENTS section)

## 1 NOVEMBER 1918

*La Nave,* opera by Italo MONTEMEZZI, consisting of a prologue and three episodes, to Gabriele d'Annunzio's poem, the action taking place in Venice in A.D. 552, centering on a fearless girl who takes vengeance on the murderous Venetian tyrant for having gouged the eyes of her parents and brothers by arousing in him the sensation of unappeasable lust for her but in the end suffers horrible death when he affixes her alive to the prow of his proud ship (hence the title) as its figurehead, the music illustrating the hideous plot by hyper-dramatic vocalization and explosively rising waves of orchestral sonorities, is produced at La Scala in Milan.

## 4 NOVEMBER 1918

One of a series of army love songs, *She's Teaching Me to Parlez-Vous Français, and I'm Learning More and More Each Day,* is copyrighted in Washington, on the same day with the song *Let Us Make the World Safe for Democracy.*

## 5 NOVEMBER 1918

*Schwarzschwanenreich,* Wagnerofilial opera in three acts by Siegfried WAGNER, describing a legendary land of black swans, is performed for the first time in Karlsruhe.

## 11 NOVEMBER 1918

On the morning of the Armistice, Igor STRAVINSKY completes in neutral Morges, Switzerland, the composition of his *Ragtime,* scored for eleven instruments, including the cimbalom (a Hungarian dulcimer used in Gypsy bands), a symbolic recognition of the growing spread of American syncopated music and the post-war necessity for economy in orchestration. (The first performance of *Ragtime* was given in London on 27 April 1920, Arthur Bliss conducting)

## 14 NOVEMBER 1918

A Provisional Central Musical Council is formed in Berlin after the German revolution and assumes the jurisdictional authority over musical affairs of the German Republic.

## 15 NOVEMBER 1918

*Russians,* a cycle of five songs with orchestra by Daniel Gregory MASON, to verses by Witter Bynner, characterizing in imitatively Mussorgskian models a group of supposedly typical Russians—a drunkard (on diluted vodka), an accordion player (apparently on a foreign-made instrument), a revolutionist (mystically self-doubting), a boy (prematurely debile) and a prophet (balefully proclamatory)—is performed for the first time by Reinald Werrenrath (to whom the cycle is dedicated) with the Chicago Symphony Orchestra.

## 16 NOVEMBER 1918

Hugo ALFVÉN's *Fourth Symphony* in C minor is performed for the first time in Stockholm.

## 17 NOVEMBER 1918

An American jazz band under the direction of Harry PILCER appears for the first time in Europe, playing in Paris at the Casino de Paris. (Date communicated by the management of the Casino de Paris)

In 1918 the first jazz band arrived from New York . . . I recall the shock, the sudden awakening that its staggering rhythm and its new sonorities brought to France . . . This influence from North America has given us the *Ragtime du Paquebot* in Satie's *Parade*, and *Adieu New York* by Georges Auric. In these compositions we have a portrait of a ragtime and of a foxtrot seen through a symphonic glass. (Darius Milhaud, *Études*, Paris, 1927)

## 20 NOVEMBER 1918

Sergei PROKOFIEV makes his American debut as pianist-composer in New York in a program of his own works.

New ears for new music! The new ears were necessary to appreciate the new music made by Sergei Prokofiev in his first pianoforte recital at Aeolian Hall yesterday afternoon. He is younger looking than his years, which are patriarchal, twenty-seven. He is blond, slender, modest as a musician, and his impassibility contrasted with the volcanic eruptions he produced on the keyboard. We have already one musical anarch here, Leo Ornstein, but that youth's *Wild Man's Dance* is a mere exercise in euphony, a piece positively Mozartian, in comparison with the astounding disharmonies gentle Sergei extorted from his suffering pianoforte. The young man's style is orchestral, and the instruments of percussion rule in his Scythian brains. His fingers are steel, his wrists steel, his biceps and triceps steel, his scapula steel . . . As a composer he is cerebral. His music is volitional and essentially cold, as are all cerebral composers . . . The finale of his second sonata evoked visions of a charge of mammoths on some vast immemorial Asiatic plateau. Rebikov seems a miniaturist after this. Prokofiev uses, like Arnold Schoenberg, the entire modern harmonies. He is a psychologist of the uglier emotions—hatred, contempt, rage—above all rage—disgust, despair, mockery, and defiance . . . His scale scheme is omnitonic—or is it omphalic? But now and then we get a glimpse of a recondite region, a No Man's Land wherein wander enigmatic and fascinating figures, an unearthly landscape, an atmosphere, murky and ominous, but painted in bold feverish strokes. (Richard Aldrich, New York *Times*, 21 November 1918)

## 21 NOVEMBER 1918

*Mr. Wilson, You're a Wonderful Man*, a tuneful tribute to the wartime President, is copyrighted ten days after the Armistice.

## 24 NOVEMBER 1918

*Frutta di Mare*, opera in three acts by the Swiss composer Hans HUBER is produced in Basel.

## 27 NOVEMBER 1918

Four centuries have elapsed since the publication of the musical treatise *De Harmonia musicorum instrumentorum* by the Italian music theorist Franchinus GAFURIUS.

## 29 NOVEMBER 1918

*Booze, Booze, Booze*, the first song of the Prohibition era, is copyrighted in Washington.

## 30 NOVEMBER 1918

The Société de l'Orchestre de la Suisse Romande gives its inaugural concert in Geneva under the direction of Ernest ANSERMET.

## 2 DECEMBER 1918

*Le Dit des Jeux du Monde*, incidental music by Arthur HONEGGER to Paul Meral's play, in the form of a suite of ten dances, two interludes and a coda, is performed for the first time in Paris.

## 11 DECEMBER 1918

*Das heisse Eisen*, one-act opera by the 26-year-old Swiss composer Werner WEHRLI, to a text from a play by Hans Sachs, is produced in Bern.

## 14 DECEMBER 1918

The Metropolitan Opera of New York presents the absolute world premiere of three one-act operas by Giacomo PUCCINI, *Il Tabarro, Suor Angelica* and *Gianni Schicchi*, often described as *Il Trittico* despite Puccini's specific and emphatic disavowal of such collective title inasmuch as there is no common theme uniting the three:

*Il Tabarro (The Cloak)*, inspired by a play from the Paris Grand Guignol, taking place on a barge on the Seine, where its owner strangles the trespassing lover of his wife and then invites her to lie down under the cloak hiding the body, set to music in a characteristically melodramatic style, marked by resonant modal harmonies and ingratiating melorhythmic sequences.

*Suor Angelica*, dealing with a formerly noble young lady of Florence flourishing circa 1600 whose loss of chastity induces her family to send her to a convent, and who takes poison when she learns that her illegitimate child is dead, prays to the Virgin to save her soul while discordant carillon tolls, is rewarded by the vision of the Mother of God leading a blond boy—her child—and dies in peace while the angels sing a hymn of salvation in virginally immaculate C major.

*Gianni Schicchi*, whose name appears in the tenth chasm of Dante's *Inferno* as a cunning deceiver, a Florentine peasant active in 1299 who helps his daughter and her young suitor to unite by posing as the latter's rich relative and dictating a will leaving most of his estate to himself but later handing the illicit patrimony to the happy lovers, stylistically treated as a traditional Italian opera buffa, with modernistic polytriadic harmonies revealing its vigesimosecular provenance.

## 15 DECEMBER 1918

*Hieroglyphs* by the Dutch modernist Daniel RUYNEMAN, scored for a sonorously uncommon group of three flutes, celesta, harp, piano, two mandolines, two guitars and a series of chromatically tuned, hemispherical cup-bells with a compass of $2\frac{1}{2}$ octaves specially made in England according to the composer's specifications, set in an exotically hieroglyphic style calculated to evoke the pictorial writing of ancient Egypt, making liberal use of tinklingly disparate whole-tone progressions and atonal melismas, is performed for the first time in Amsterdam on the same program with Ruyneman's choral work *De Roep (The Call)* for a "color scale of mixed voices" a cappella, in a polyphony of contrasting vowels with occasional consonants to intensify the plastic accent.

## 17 DECEMBER 1918

*Second Symphony* by the Finnish composer Leevi MADETOJA, written in somber colors and couched in Sibelian harmonies, is performed for the first time in Helsinki.

## 19 DECEMBER 1918

*Nepřemožení (The Invincibles)*, opera in four acts by the Czech composer Josef Bohuslav FOERSTER, to his own libretto in which an ailing musician nurses an insurmountable passion for an unattainable countess, is produced in Prague.

## 24 DECEMBER 1918

*Le Cochon qui sommeile*, operetta by Claude TERRASSE, is produced in Paris.


# ❧ *1919* ❧


## 11 JANUARY 1919

*Eventyr (Once Upon a Time)*, a symphonic poem by Frederick DELIUS, inspired by Norwegian fairy tales and couched in a Grieg-like manner, with Impressionistic harmonies coloring the unassuming thematic substance, is performed for the first time at the London Promenade Concerts, Sir Henry Wood conducting.

### 14 JANUARY 1919

*Gismonda,* lyric drama in three acts by Henry FÉVRIER, to a play by Victorien Sardou, wherein the Florentine duchess, ruler of Athens in 1451, impelled by anti-pagan zeal, orders the destruction (to a whole-tone scale) of a newly-found ancient statue of Aphrodite and is condemned by the outraged goddess to submit to a falconer (whom she however learns to love after a preliminary night), to a score of Wagneromorphic resplendence, rich in grandiosely arpeggiated sonorities and cascading chromatic scales (one of them going fully five octaves down to illustrate the falling into a lion's den), is produced for the first time anywhere by the Chicago Opera Company as a commissioned work, with Mary Garden, the current directress of the enterprise, in the title role.

### 17 JANUARY 1919

Ignace PADEREWSKI becomes Premier of Poland, the first musician to head a modern state.

### 26 JANUARY 1919

After two years of a ludicrously chauvinistic ban on German music in Italy, Beethoven's *Egmont* Overture is performed in Rome without incident.

### 26 JANUARY 1919

*Poème de la Maison,* oratorio by the French composer Georges Martin WITKOWSKI, written in a neo-Renaissance polyphonic idiom, is performed for the first time in Lyons, France.

### 30 JANUARY 1919

*Requiem,* suggested by Lincoln's Gettysburg Address, by the New York-born German-trained 46-year-old romantic composer Rubin GOLDMARK, in five connected sections, appropriately opening with a trumpet solo, and concluding with an assertive peroration in the militant key of E flat major subliminally alluding to Beethoven's *Eroica,* is performed for the first, and antepenultimate, time by the New York Philharmonic Orchestra.

### 30 JANUARY 1919

*Ferhuda,* opera in one act by the Italian composer Francesco SANTOLIQUIDO, based on a North African tale of passionate violence, is performed for the first time in Tunis, where the composer himself has long dwelt.

### 2 FEBRUARY 1919

Xavier LEROUX, French composer of melodramatic operas in a competent traditional style, pupil of Massenet, teacher of Alfredo Casella and other modern composers, dies in Paris at the age of fifty-five.

### 5 FEBRUARY 1919

*Legend of Shota Rustaveli,* opera in four acts by the Georgian composer Dmitri ARAKISHVILI, after the medieval Georgian epic, is produced in Tiflis.

## 15 FEBRUARY 1919

Carl NIELSEN conducts in Copenhagen the first performance of his symphonic suite *Aladdin,* in five movements inspired by the *Arabian Nights*: (1) *Oriental Festival March* (2) *Aladdin's Dream and Dance of the Morning Mists* (3) *Dance of the Captives* (4) *Market Place in Ispahan* and (5) *Negro Dance.*

## 18 FEBRUARY 1919

*Through the Looking Glass,* suite for small orchestra by Deems TAYLOR, after the classic tale of Lewis Carroll, written in a pleasingly Gallic vein and vividly orchestrated (the clarinet paints the brillig afternoon in *Jabberwocky,* and the vorpal blade of a xylophone snickersnacks the Jabberwock in the bassoon) is performed for the first time by the New York Chamber Music Society. (The suite was subsequently revised for full orchestra; the first performance in this amplified version took place in New York on 10 March 1923, with Walter Damrosch conducting the New York Symphony Society Orchestra)

## 21 FEBRUARY 1919

*Abesalom e Etheri,* opera in four acts by the Georgian composer Zakhar PALIASHVILI, to an Italian libretto dealing with a dynastic struggle in ancient Georgia, wherein the heir to the throne becomes involved in a morganatic liaison with the king's adopted daughter, is produced in Tiflis.

## 3 MARCH 1919

*Passa la Ronda!,* one-act opera by Renzo BOSSI, is produced in Milan.

## 8 MARCH 1919

Three pieces for orchestra, *Chinoiserie, Valse sentimentale* and *Cossack Dance* by Lord BERNERS, the Satie of England, set in a characteristically British ironic manner seasoned with acrid harmonies, pungent rhythms and cultivated exoticisms, are performed for the first time in Manchester.

## 8 MARCH 1919

*El Avapiés,* opera in three acts, written in collaboration by the Spanish composers Angel BARRIOS and Conrado del CAMPO, with the action taking place in the densely populated district around the Calle de Lavapiés (colloquially transmogrified into El Avapiés) in Madrid, around 1800, with thematic materials assembled from old street airs, is produced in Madrid.

## 12 MARCH 1919

The Metropolitan Opera produces in New York two American one-act operas:

(1) *The Legend* by the 48-year-old composer Joseph Carl BREIL, with action evolving in a mythical Balkan country Muscovadia where a brave girl, defending her bandit fa-

ther, stabs to death her affianced police officer and is shot down herself as the curtain falls rapidly while the orchestra plays a rousing finale (2) *The Temple Dancer* by the 46-year-old Connecticut composer John Adam Hugo, to a story of a Hindu priestess who steals the jewels of a monstrously cruel idol originally purchased at the price of her carnal abasement, but is struck by lightning as she undulates with a holy snake around her waist to the accompaniment of sinuously serpentine orientalistic scales.

### 14 MARCH 1919

Gabriel FAURÉ conducts in Paris the first performance of his *Ballade* for piano and orchestra, with Alfred Cortot as soloist.

### 18 MARCH 1919

*Gaudeamus,* "scenes from German student life" by Engelbert HUMPERDINCK, with the famous hedonistic Latin student song providing a resonant climax, is performed for the first time in Darmstadt.

### 22 MARCH 1919

*Habanera,* symphonic dance in the Spanish vein by Louis AUBERT, set in Parisian harmonies of bitonal implications, is performed for the first time in Paris.

### 27 MARCH 1919

*Fourth Symphony* by Kurt ATTERBERG is performed for the first time in Stockholm.

### 7 APRIL 1919

André MESSAGER conducts in Birmingham, England, the world première of his three-act opera *Monsieur Beaucaire,* in an English version translated from the original French libretto derived from a story by the American writer Newton Booth Tarkington, dealing with a cousin of Louis XV masquerading as a barber during an incognito visit to England, contemptuously rebuked by an English noblewoman who is subsequently dismayed when he is re-introduced to her as the Duke of Orleans, to a score full of musical galanteries characterizing the variously animated peripeteia of the action.

### 8 APRIL 1919

At the 8th Soirée Dada in Zürich, Tristan TZARA, the inventor of both the word and the concept of DADA, issues his *Proclamation sans prétention,* in which he launches the destructive exhortation, "Musiciens, Cassez Vos Instruments Aveugles Sur la Scène," and asseverates his thesis that Dada is but a natural process of urinal relief: "J'écris parce que c'est naturel comme je pisse."

### 10 APRIL 1919

*Nausicaa,* opera in two acts by the Venezuelan-born Parisian composer Reynaldo HAHN, to the story of the Homeric princess who befriends Odysseus on

her father's Aegean island, set in a pleasingly perfumed idiom with a proliferation of sonorously marshalled ninth-chords, is produced in Monte Carlo, on
the same bill with the first performance of Gabriel FAURÉ's "divertissement
lyrique" in one act *Masques et Bergamasques,* the title alluding to the alliterative line from a poem of Paul Verlaine.

### 13 APRIL 1919

*Starý král (The Old King),* opera after Rémy de Gourmont's play by the
Czech composer Jaroslav JEREMIÁŠ, who died on 19 January 1919 at the age
of 29, is produced posthumously in Prague.

### 16 APRIL 1919

*Don Ranudo de Colibrados,* comic opera in four acts by the Swiss composer
Othmar SCHOECK, to a libretto from a Danish play by Ludwig Holberg, dealing with a fatuous Spanish grandee who indignantly rebukes a colored aspi-
rant for his daughter's hand, only to find that the latter is a Royal Ethiopian
prince, which makes him accept his offer with supine obsequiousness, set to
music in a Wagneromantic manner with a profusion of flamboyant sonorities,
is produced in Zürich.

### 18 APRIL 1919

A century has passed since the birth in Spalato, Dalmatia, of Franz von
SUPPÉ, an aristocrat of Germanic-Italian descent whose full name was Francesco Ezechiele Ermenegildo SUPPÉ-DEMELLI, composer of ingratiatingly melodious light operas, whose harmonious overture *Poet and Peasant* has become
permanently embedded in the popular orchestra repertory.

### 24 APRIL 1919

Camille ERLANGER, French composer of several effective operas, of which *Le
Juif polonais* has proved viable, dies in Paris at the age of fifty-five.

### 25 APRIL 1919

Augustus D. JUILLIARD, self-made millionaire and generous supporter of the
arts, dies in New York six days after reaching his 83rd birthday (he was born
at sea in a sailing vessel in which his French Huguenot parents embarked on
their way to America), leaving the bulk of his great estate for the establishment of a Juilliard Music Foundation, "to aid all worthy students of music."

### 29 APRIL 1919

*Blodwen (White Flower),* Welsh opera in three acts by Joseph PARRY (1841–
1903), first performed in concert form in Swansea, Wales, on 20 June 1878,
dealing with the abortive attempt of the Welsh to gain independence from
England in the 14th century, wherein Blodwen, the daughter of a Welsh patriot, is reunited with her imprisoned lover to the triumphant strains of a

Welsh national march, receives its first stage performance in Colwyn Bay, with the original libretto in the Welsh language.

### 6 MAY 1919

*Notturno e Rondo fantastico,* a diptych for piano and orchestra by Riccardo PICK-MANGIAGALLI, is performed for the first time in Milan.

### 8 MAY 1919

*Ihre Hoheit, die Tänzerin,* popular operetta by the German composer Walter W. GOETZE, is produced in Stettin.

### 9 MAY 1919

Jim EUROPE, Negro leader of the jazz band "Hell Fighters," is mortally stabbed at 9:15 P.M. in his dressing room at Mechanics Hall, Boston, by the drummer of his band, and dies two hours later in a Boston hospital.

### 11 MAY 1919

Thirteen and a half months after DEBUSSY's death, his *Rhapsody* for saxophone, sketched out at the behest of Mrs. Elisa Hall of Boston in 1903, receives its first performance at a concert of the Société Nationale de Musique in Paris, in a version completed and orchestrated by Roger-Ducasse.

### 12 MAY 1919

The Royal Opera of London resumes its regular season at Covent Garden, after its closure during the war.

### 14 MAY 1919

*Fantaisie,* op. 111, for piano and orchestra by Gabriel FAURÉ, in a single movement, opening with a piano solo, in the key of G major, with characteristic excursions into plagal modalities, is performed for the first time at the Société Nationale de Musique in Paris, with Alfred Cortot, to whom the score is dedicated, at the piano.

### 20 MAY 1919

*Sœur Béatrice,* opera in three acts by the 23-year-old Greek composer and conductor Dimitri MITROPOULOS, written by him at the age of 19, after Maeterlinck's religious play, and set in impressionistic colors, is produced in Athens.

### 25 MAY 1919

Georges ENESCO conducts in Bucharest the first performance of his *Third Symphony* in C major, scored for organ, piano, wordless chorus and orchestra, in three movements portraying three periods of the first two decades of the 20th century—the ephemeral nearly warless world before 1914, the advent of the war, with men of different nations marching mindlessly to their deaths, and the ultimate arrival of precarious peace. (The Paris performance on 26 February 1921 is erroneously listed in some references works as the world première)

### 29 MAY 1919

*Xenia*, opera by Alexander SAVIN, Belgrade-born naturalized American conductor, written to his own Serbian libretto, is performed for the first time anywhere in Zürich, in a German version, with his wife, the American soprano Lillian Blauvelt, in the title role.

### 5 JUNE 1919

*La Boutique fantasque*, ballet in one act on themes from Rossini's posthumous piano pieces, assembled and prismatically orchestrated by Ottorino RESPIGHI in an attractively heterogeneous "fantastic shop" is produced in London by Diaghilev's Ballet Russe.

### 15 JUNE 1919

Poland issues a 20-pfenning postage stamp (1/5 of a zloty) with the head of Premier PADEREWSKI. (Date obtained in 1936 from the Philatelic Division of the Post Office in Warsaw)

### 15 JUNE 1919

*Les Choéphores*, musical tragedy after Aeschylus and Paul Claudel by Darius MILHAUD, is performed for the first time in concert form in Paris. (The first stage performance was given in Brussels on 27 March 1935)

### 16 JUNE 1919

The 1919 edition of The Ziegfeld Follies, introducing Irving BERLIN's famous song *A Pretty Girl Is Like a Melody*, is produced in New York.

### 20 JUNE 1919

A century has elapsed since the birth in Cologne of Jacques OFFENBACH, the gayest spirit of the comic opera during the Second Empire in Paris.

### 22 JUNE 1919

*The White Peacock*, first of the four pieces in the piano suite Roman Sketches by the American composer Charles Tomlinson GRIFFES, depicting in fine Impressionistic harmonies the exotic bird of Southeast Asia displaying its multicolored tail in a luxuriant kaleidoscope of ninth-chords, is performed for the first time in an orchestral version as a ballet, in New York. (The first concert performance of *The White Peacock* was given by Leopold Stokowski conducting the Philadelphia Orchestra on 19 December 1919)

## 22 JUNE 1919

Julian SCRIABIN, 11-year-old son of Alexander Scriabin, who as a student of Glière, wrote several preludes (later published in Moscow) in a terse and tense quasi-atonal manner suggestive of the last opus numbers of his father, drowns during an outing in the Dnieper River at Kiev.

## 5 JULY 1919

*Balada de Carnaval,* one-act opera by Amadeo VIVES, is produced in Madrid.

## 7 JULY 1919

Samuel GARDNER, Russian-born violinist and composer, conducts at a concert in New York City the first performance of his symphonic poem *New Russia.*

## 10 JULY 1919

Hugo RIEMANN, German music scholar and illustrious pedagogue, author of books on harmony, counterpoint, fugue, orchestration and form, compiler of the redoubtably compendious *Musik-Lexikon,* firm believer in the uniqueness of solutions of all musical problems according to strict Hegelian modes, so that music history could be interpreted as a coalition of opposing premises, dies in Leipzig, where he taught a generation of worshipful students, 8 days before reaching the Biblical span of 70 years of age.

## 14 JULY 1919

CHOUCHOU, Debussy's 14-year-old daughter to whom he tenderly dedicated his *Children's Corner,* succumbs to diphtheria in Paris, after the failure of a desperate attempt to relieve her pulmonary congestion by tracheotomy.

## 20 JULY 1919

Guillermo URIBE-HOLGUÍN, prime composer of Colombia, who acquired a fine impressionistic flair as a student of Vincent d'Indy in Paris, conducts in Bogotá the first performance of his harmonious *First Symphony.*

## 22 JULY 1919

The first complete performance of Manuel DE FALLA's ballet *El Sombrero de Tres Picos,* is presented in London by Diaghilev's Ballet Russe, under the English title, *The Three-Cornered Hat.* (Absolute world premiere of the work in its original version was given in Madrid on 7 April 1917 under the title *El Corregidor y la Molinera*)

## 27 JULY 1919

*La Via della finestra,* fifth opera in three acts by the Italian veristic composer Riccardo ZANDONAI, is produced at Pesaro. (A revised version, compressed into two acts, was produced in Trieste on 18 January 1923)

### 9 AUGUST 1919

Ruggero LEONCAVALLO, pioneer of Italian Verismo, who cultivated dramatic verisimilitude in operatic libretti and musical characterization, and who as a young man wrote an immortal opera *Pagliacci*, but could never duplicate this success in his many subsequent theatrical works, dies at Montecatini at the age of sixty-one.

### 20 AUGUST 1919

MANA-ZUCCA (née Augusta Zuckermann), 28-year-old American pianist, soprano and composeress, plays the solo part in the first performance of her *Piano Concerto* in New York.

### 22 AUGUST 1919

The Academy of Santa Cecilia in Rome is "regificated," and is renamed Regio Conservatorio Musicale di Santa Cecilia.

### 23 AUGUST 1919

*Los Heroes,* grand opera in three acts by the 57-year-old Argentine composer Arturo BERUTI, to an Italian libretto glorifying the heroic march over the Andes of the patriotic armies of San Martín during the war of Liberation of Spanish America in 1810 (the composer's grandfather fought in their ranks), making use of native melorhythms in an Italianate setting, is produced at the Teatro Colón in Buenos Aires.

### 29 AUGUST 1919

Josef Matthias HAUER completes in Vienna the first of his series of *Nomos* for piano, in which his self-promulgated law (nomos) that each theme should consist of 12 different tones, subdivided into symmetrical tropes, is applied for the first time, without, however, attaining the integrality of Schoenberg's method of composition with 12 tones related only to one another.

### 2 SEPTEMBER 1919

*Caio Petronio,* an effectively Italianate opera in three acts by the Argentinian composer Constantino GAITO, to a libretto centering on the fate of the *arbiter elegantiarum* Petronius who was ordered to commit suicide by Nero in 66 A.D., is produced at the Teatro Colón in Buenos Aires.

### 27 SEPTEMBER 1919

Adelina PATTI, fabulous Spanish-born coloratura soprano, the *prima donna assoluta* who moved audiences to frenzied raptures by her thrilling trills and enchanting bel canto, and who continued to inspire adulation on her multiple farewell tours in both hemispheres, dies at the age of seventy-six at Brecknock, Wales, where she was married to her third husband.

## 29 SEPTEMBER 1919

*Härvard Harpolekare* (*Härvard the Potter*), first opera in two acts by the 31-year-old Swedish composer Kurt Atterberg, is produced in Stockholm. (A revised version, with a new third act, was produced in Linz, Austria, on 14 June 1952)

## 10 OCTOBER 1919

*Die Frau ohne Schatten,* opera in three acts by Richard STRAUSS, to a mystically symbolic libretto of Hugo von Hofmannsthal, wherein a supernatural queen of a group of mythical islands, reincarnated from a white gazelle, casts no shadow and is therefore unable to bear offspring, since progeny is an umbilically umbral projection, but who becomes fertile after she demonstrates her superior humanity by refusing to purchase a shadow from a poor woman at the price of her perdition, and is saluted by a chorus of their unborn children, is produced in Vienna.

## 16 OCTOBER 1919

*A chi la giarettiera?,* operetta by Ruggero LEONCAVALLO, centered on an anonymous garter of unidentified provenance and possibly audlterous implications, is produced posthumously in Rome.

## 21 OCTOBER 1919

*Kronburden,* opera in four acts by the Swedish composer Ture RANGSTRÖM, after Strindberg's play, is produced for the first time, in a German version, under the title *Die Kronbraut* (*The Crown Bride*), in Stuttgart.

## 21 OCTOBER 1919

*Fennimore und Gerda,* the last opera by Frederick DELIUS, completed in 1910, in two individually separable acts, to a libretto after a psychological novel by the Danish writer Jens Peter Jacobsen, detailing the passionate contention between a poet and a painter for a girl named Fennimore, happily resolved when the poet finds solace with his childhood sweetheart Gerda, set to music in a characteristically Deliusian manner, ingenuously combining German neo-romanticism with Gallic quasi-impressionism, is performed for the first time in Frankfurt, to a German libretto by the composer.

## 24 OCTOBER 1919

The newly-formed Los Angeles Philharmonic Orchestra gives its initial concert under the direction of Walter Rothwell.

## 26 OCTOBER 1919

*Revolutionshochzeit,* opera in three acts by the Germanized English-born composer Eugen D'ALBERT, the action taking place near Condé in France in April 1793, focused on the self-sacrifice of the one-night bride of an unjustly

*316*

condemned young Jacobin, who throws herself in front of the firing squad set to execute him, and both perish, with the score containing some innovations (a speaking chorus, realistic instrumental onomatopeia of string glissandi to illustrate the consummation of wedded love), is produced in Leipzig.

### 27 OCTOBER 1919

Edward ELGAR, the prime Edwardian romanticist of English music, conducts in London the first performance of his *Concerto for Violoncello and Orchestra*, in E minor, with Felix Salmond as soloist, in four discursive movements:

(1) *Adagio—Moderato*, where the cello plays a pensive soliloquy, leading to a slow jig in a bland Aeolian mode (2) *Lento—Allegro molto*, erupting after some artful vacillation into a coruscating perpetuum mobile (3) *Adagio*, a spirited romanza with decorative undulating convolutions in the solo part (4) *Allegro*, featuring a rhapsodic recitative in the cello, followed by a decisive *Allegro molto*, in dancing steps with propulsively symmetric rhythms, ending with gentlemanly gentility in peaceful E minor.

### 28 OCTOBER 1919

The Star Opera Company of New York City, organized with the intention of presenting German operas in the German language, voluntarily cancels its season after a series of violent ultrapatriotic demonstrations organized by the American Legion.

The Star Opera Co. has retired, egg-stained, from the lyric stage of America, and the attempt of German propagandists to storm the fortress of American post-bellum opinion is a thing of the past. The genial insolence of the Star Opera Co. and its Teutonic associates in testing American tolerance gave New York a series of thrills. Even the New York Supreme Court became interested—to the final regret of Fritz, the uncomprehending and still dazed personification of Germanism. The season opened on 20 October 1919 despite adverse public opinion. On 21 October Mayor Hyland exercised police power to keep the theater closed, but he was overruled by a temporary injunction of the New York Supreme Court and Lortzing's opera *Czar und Zimmermann* was given. Only 150 persons had dared to run the gauntlet of the street. A pitched battle between police and patriots ebbed and flowed down Lexington Avenue. Although the former were supported by Cavalry, the latter sent out a motor truck, preceded by a barrage of milk bottles. Next night rioting was renewed. On 28 October the Star Opera abandoned its plan to sing German opera. (*The Musical Leader*, Chicago, 30 October 1919.)

### 1 NOVEMBER 1919

*L'Invasion*, opera in three bloody acts with a victorious epilogue by the 31-year-old Belgian composer Fernand BRUMAGNE, whose house and musical manuscripts were burned by the invading Germans in 1914, is performed for the first time at the Théâtre de la Monnaie in Brussels.

### 8 NOVEMBER 1919

Three days before the first anniversary of the Armistice, WAGNER is played again in Paris for the first time by the Pasdeloup Orchestra, after a vote taken in the audience gives 4,983 in favor of re-Wagnerization of the French musical theater and only 213 for de-Wagnerization.

## 12 NOVEMBER 1919

*Ein Fest zu Haderslev,* opera by the 33-year-old Alsatian composer Robert HEGER, is produced in Nuremberg.

## 15 NOVEMBER 1919

*Den Kongelige Gast (The Royal Guest),* one-act opera by the Danish composer Hakon BÖRRESEN, is produced in Copenhagen.

## 15 NOVEMBER 1919

Henry Lee HIGGINSON, munificent founder of the Boston Symphony Orchestra, dies in Boston, three days before his 85th birthday.

## 16 NOVEMBER 1919

*Poem* for flute and orchestra by the American composer Charles Tomlinson GRIFFES, written in a delicately Impressionistic manner, is performed for the first time in New York, with Georges Barrère as soloist.

## 18 NOVEMBER 1919

*Irene,* musical comedy by Harry TIERNEY on a tale of a modern Cinderella who makes her nonchalant way from the slums of Ninth Avenue in New York to the plush mansions of Long Island, is produced in New York.

## 22 NOVEMBER 1919

*Taras Bulba,* opera in five acts by the French composer Marcel SAMUEL-ROUSSEAU, son of Samuel Rousseau whose first name he subjoined to his last, to a libretto from Gogol's powerful novel dealing with a fiercely patriotic Ukrainian Cossack who fought the invading Poles so intransigently that he had no hesitation to shoot his own son for having become infatuated with a Polish beauty, is produced in Paris.

## 23 NOVEMBER 1919

*Grajek (The Player),* opera in two acts by the Polish composer Tadeusz JOTEYKO, dealing with the life of a dedicated church organ player, is produced in Warsaw.

## 25 NOVEMBER 1919

*Boudour,* ballet-pantomime in one act by the 47-year-old English-born American composer Felix BOROWSKI relating the story of intermingled infidelity and mutual poisoning, with a caliph's concubine named Boudour plotting his overthrow in complot with a muscular male slave, is performed for the first time by the Chicago Opera Company. (An instrumental suite drawn from the ballet was first performed by the Chicago Symphony Orchestra on 14 February 1919)

27 NOVEMBER 1919

After ten months and ten days in office Ignace PADEREWSKI resigns as Premier of Poland.

28 NOVEMBER 1919

*The Pleasure Dome of Kubla Khan,* symphonic poem for orchestra by Charles Tomlinson GRIFFES, inspired by the celebrated verses of Coleridge, and depicting the sacred river flowing "through caverns measureless to man down to a sunless sea" in characteristically bleak tone colors, changing to prismatic fountain music with sounds of dancing merriment heard from the Pleasure Dome "decreed" by the mighty monarch, and returning to the somber evocation of "caves of ice" once more overwhelmed by Mongolian revelry, is performed for the first time by the Boston Symphony Orchestra, Pierre Monteux conducting.

30 NOVEMBER 1919

*La Mafia,* sanguinary opera in two acts by Georges de SEYNES, in which a member of the Sicilian Mafia gouges out the eyes of a suspected traitor and nails his wife's right hand to the table whereupon the blinded victim knifes the killer to death, is produced in Paris.

2 DECEMBER 1919

The former Imperial Opera House in Petrograd announces the discontinuance of further performances owing to extreme winter cold and the utter impossibility to obtain fuel in the disruption of communications during the raging civil war.

13 DECEMBER 1919

*Sí,* operetta in three acts by Pietro MASCAGNI, described as a "duetto americano" and caricaturing the modern dances of transatlantic provenance, with the purported aim of "safeguarding light Italian music from the enslavement by alien fashions," is produced in Rome.

14 DECEMBER 1919

*Sinfonia brevis de Bello Gallico (Third Symphony)* by Vincent D'INDY, written during World War I (hence the title), in four movements (thus not very "brevis") abounding in rhapsodically contrasting episodes, and ending in a victorious fanfare, is performed for the first time at the Société Nationale de Musique in Paris.

*Premier mouvement*—la mobilisation, la Marne; *Scherzo*—la gaîté au front; *Andante,* l'art latin et l'art boche; *Finale,* la victoire avec l'hymne de Saint-Michel comme peroraison. . . . *La Symphonie de Bello Gallico* n'a rien de Stravinsky—tant pis! (From Vincent d'Indy's letter to Guy Ropartz, dated 4 January 1918)

## 18 DECEMBER 1919

Horatio PARKER, American composer of a series of works distinguished by an impressive Germanic technique, whose pedagogical gift brought profound satisfaction to a generation of grateful students at Yale University where he was a long-term professor of music, dies at Cedarhurst, New York, at the unfulfilled age of fifty-six.

## 20 DECEMBER 1919

*La Boîte à joujoux,* "ballet pour enfants" by Claude DEBUSSY, written in 1913 in piano score and subsequently arranged for orchestra by his intimate collaborator André Caplet, to a scenario in which a wooden soldier parades to the burlesqued sounds of the military march from Gounod's *Faust,* woos and wins a handsome doll in mortal combat with the wily Polichinelle, set to music of diaphonous infantiloquy and harmonized in gently archaic open fifths and translucently fragile ninth-chords, with the application of whole-tone scales and chromatically moving consecutive major seconds to depict scenes of infantile terror, and incorporating an exotic episode based on an authentic Hindu elephant-training chant in 5/4 time, is performed posthumously for the first time in Paris, under the direction of André Caplet.

## 23 DECEMBER 1919

*The Birthday of the Infanta,* ballet-pantomime by the Chicago composer and railroad man John Alden CARPENTER, after the short story by Oscar Wilde, depicting the tragedy of a Spanish court dwarf who is horrified as he accidentally sees himself in the mirror and, after a grotesque dance that pleases the young princess at her birthday party, drops dead at her feet from exhaustion, is performed for the first time in Chicago.

## 27 DECEMBER 1919

Albert WOLFF conducts at the Metropolitan Opera House in New York the world première of his opera *L'Oiseau Bleu,* in four acts, after Maeterlinck's play about mystical children yearning for a bluebird of happiness and fulfillment.

## 29 DECEMBER 1919

The Council of People's Commissars of the Russian Soviet Socialist Republic issues an order to close all vaudeville and light music theaters as detrimental to the educational needs of the proletarian masses.

# ∿ 1920 ∿

*Music and Letters*, a quarterly publication devoted impartially and equally to problems of musical todays and yesterdays, begins publication in London, under the editorship of Arthur Henry Fox-Strangways.

It is just six years over the century since the first musical quarterly in the English language was born and six since the last one died. Between these there have been half a dozen, but their united ages have amounted to a bare fifty years. So that a musical quarterly may have a merry life but is evidently a thing that people get tired of in time. (From the editorial in the first issue)

2 JANUARY 1920

*Rip Van Winkle*, opera in three acts by Reginald DE KOVEN, to a libretto derived from a colonial American legend made famous by Washington Irving, wherein a narcoleptic Dutch villager in the Catskills of 1750 hunts for a magic flask in possession of the phantom of Hendrik Hudson, discoverer of the Hudson River, and falls asleep for twenty years, but returns to marry his old sweetheart, is produced by the Chicago Opera Company, two weeks before DE KOVEN's sudden death.

2 JANUARY 1920

*La Veglia*, one-act opera by Arrigo PEDROLLO based on J. M. Synge's *The Shadow of the Glen*, is produced in Milan.

3 JANUARY 1920

*Le Chant de Nigamon*, symphonic poem by Arthur HONEGGER, descriptive of the internecine war between Indian tribes, in which the victorious Huron warrior issues the order to burn the defeated Iroquois alive, but listens in awe as their chief Nigamon intones his own funeral chant, making use in the score of authentic war songs in the pentatonic mode interspersed with agonizingly wistful chromatic laments, and ending on a minor chord with added major sixth and major seventh, is performed for the first time in Paris.

10 JANUARY 1920

*La Terra del sogno*, opera by Franco LEONI, is produced in Milan.

12 JANUARY 1920

*La Rôtisserie de la Reine Pédauque*, opera in four acts by Charles LEVADÉ, after Anatole France's story of convivial encounters in a popular refectory, is produced at the Opéra-Comique in Paris.

### 13 JANUARY 1920

*Quentin Durward,* opera in three acts after Walter Scott by the unappreciated but honorable English composer Alexander Morvaren (known mostly as Alick) MACLEAN, is produced in its second (revised) version at Newcastle-on-Tyne (the first version, unproduced, was written in 1892).

### 16 JANUARY 1920

Reginald DE KOVEN, 60-year-old American composer of several lively operettas, whose immortality was secured by a single song *Oh, Promise Me,* dies suddenly of an apoplectic stroke, after a banquet given in his honor by Mrs. Joseph Fish, patroness of art, in her South Side mansion in Chicago.

### 16 JANUARY 1920

Henri COLLET writes in the Paris theatrical daily newspaper *Comœdia* a historic article *Les Cinq Russes, Les Six Français et Erik Satie,* drawing an esthetic and numerical parallel between the Russian Mighty Five and a group of six young French composers—Darius MILHAUD, Louis DUREY, Georges AURIC, Arthur HONEGGER, Francis POULENC and Germaine TAILLEFERRE.

"I want a French music for France," writes Jean Cocteau in his remarkable little volume *Le Coq et l'Arlequin.* We are happy that he did write that, for it is precisely what we preach ourselves in our tribune of *Comœdia.* "Music that is not national does not exist," writes Rimsky-Korsakov in *My Musical Life,* and continues: "Indeed, all music that is regarded as universal is in fact national." Jean Cocteau and Rimsky-Korsakov tell us what no conservatory can teach: it is necessary to belong to a nation and to unite with compatriots. Russian music, cultivated by the illustrious Five—Balakirev, Cui, Borodin, Mussorgsky, Rimsky-Korsakov—was united in its aims and became the object of universal admiration because these composers appreciated the initiative of Glinka. The Six Frenchmen, Darius Milhaud, Louis Durey, Georges Auric, Arthur Honegger, Francis Poulenc and Germaine Tailleferre, henceforth inseparable as it was demonstrated by an interesting collection of their compositions as Le Groupe de Six, have by their splendid decision to return to simplicity, brought about a renaissance of French music, because they appreciated the phenomenon of Erik Satie and because they followed the precepts, so lucid, of Jean Cocteau. The above-mentioned album of Le Groupe de Six is a suite of six pieces: *Prélude* by Georges Auric, *Romance sans paroles* by Louis Durey, *Sarabande* by Arthur Honegger, *Mazurka* by Darius Milhaud, *Valse* by Francis Poulenc and *Pastorale* by Germaine Tailleferre. The different temperaments of these six composers clash without conflict, and their works, individual and distinctive, reveal a unity of approach to art that conforms to the ideas of the spokesman of Le Groupe de Six: Jean Cocteau. (Excerpts from Collet's article)

### 17 JANUARY 1920

Maurice RAVEL refuses to accept his nomination as a Chevalier of the Légion d'Honneur.

What a ridiculous proposition! Who could have played such a joke on me? . . . Members of the Légion d'Honneur are like morphine addicts who would use trickery to force others to share their passion, perhaps to justify it in their own eyes. (From Ravel's letter to Roland-Manuel)

17 JANUARY 1920

*Fantasy Scenes from an Eastern Romance* for orchestra by Hamilton HARTY is performed for the first time at Leeds.

21 JANUARY 1920

*Der Schatzgräber (The Treasure Digger)*, opera in four acts by Franz SCHREKER to his own libretto from the realm of German fable, in which a minstrel, guided by a sensitive lute which raises its pitch and accelerates the tempo in the vicinity of gold, locates a treasure-trove and presents it to his Queen who graciously commutes his long-standing death sentence and enables him to rejoin his bride who, however, succombs to anemia, set to music with Wagneromantic fervor, with an inventory of seminal motives immersed in sebaceously pregnant sonorities, is produced in Frankfurt.

24 JANUARY 1920

*Il Monaco nero*, opera in one act by the Spanish composer Joaquín CASSADÓ, dealing with the "black monk" Schwartz who invented gunpowder in 1340 and blew up the house of his faithless inamorata, killing her and himself, is produced in Barcelona in an Italian version of the original Spanish libretto.

26 JANUARY 1920

*Overture on Hebrew Themes* by Sergei PROKOFIEV, for piano, clarinet and string quartet, based on authentic Jewish folk songs and arranged in a characteristic Russian manner with plagal cadences and agitated trochaic rhythms, is performed for the first time anywhere in New York by a Jewish-American group of former students of the St. Petersburg Conservatory, which supplied Prokofiev with the thematic material for the work.

27 JANUARY 1920

On his American visit, Maurice MAETERLINCK hears DEBUSSY's *Pelléas et Mélisande* for the first time, in a performance by the Chicago Opera Company at the Lexington Theater in New York, with Mary Garden as Mélisande, 17 years and 9 months after the original production in Paris, which Maeterlinck opposed so strongly and which he believed to be a travesty of his play, an additional annoyance to him being the refusal of the management of the Opéra-Comique to cast his mistress Georgette Blanc as Mélisande.

29 JANUARY 1920

*Ritter Blaubart*, opera in three acts by Emil REZNIČEK, to a libretto dealing with the uxoricidal bluebeard, set in an effectively synthetic idiom of German folk romance, Italian Verismo and Gallic Impressionism, is produced in Darmstadt.

30 JANUARY 1920

*Regina von Emmeritz*, the last opera, in five acts, by the Finnish composer Oskar MERIKANTO, is produced in Helsinki.

323

### 30 JANUARY 1920

*First Symphony* by the American composer Frederick S. CONVERSE, set in an academically solid cosmopolitan romantic style, is performed for the first time by the Boston Symphony Orchestra.

### 31 JANUARY 1920

*Cleopatra's Night*, opera in two acts by the American composer Henry HADLEY, adapted from Théophile Gautier's story *Une Nuit de Cléopâtre*, wherein Cleopatra grants a night of Egyptian delights to a muscular freeman on condition that it will be his last, whereupon her favorite maid who loves him stabs herself to death and is thrown to the crocodiles, and her lover dutifully drinks a flask of venom as Anthony arrives to join Cleopatra, seasoned with pseudo-exotic whole-tone progressions and serpentine orientalistic arabesques and supported by bombastic Wagneromantic harmonies, is produced at the Metropolitan Opera in New York.

### 1 FEBRUARY 1920

*Melos*, fortnightly German magazine devoted to modern music, starts publication in Berlin under the general editorship of the modern-minded conductor Hermann SCHERCHEN, shortly after his return from Russia where he was interned as an enemy alien during World War I.

### 2 FEBRUARY 1920

*Le Chant du Rossignol*, ballet in one act adapted from the opera *Le Rossignol* by Igor STRAVINSKY, is produced by Diaghilev's Ballet Russe in Paris.

### 5 FEBRUARY 1920

Leopold GODOWSKY, the scholarly pianist of prodigiously prestidigital powers, completes the composition in New York of his piano cycle of thirty pieces *Triakontameron*, so named by analogy with Boccaccio's *Decameron*, each piece having been written on a single day, containing his most popular piece, the perennial light classic *Alt Wien*.

### 7 FEBRUARY 1920

*Der türkisenblaue Garten*, "a play of love and death" in one act by the 35-year-old Hungarian composer Aladar SZENDREI, taking place amid vermillion pillows and sensuous Persian rugs in a turquoise blue garden wherein the Shah's young wife restores the life of her poisoned lover by a protracted oriental kiss to the accompaniment of chromatic Wagneromantic roulades, is produced in Leipzig.

### 14 FEBRUARY 1920

*Nocturne de Printemps*, symphonic poem by the 46-year-old French composer ROGER-DUCASSE, contrasting the exterior impressions of a spring night with the interior emotions of two conjointed human beings, set to music in impressionistic colors, is performed for the first time in Paris.

## 14 FEBRUARY 1920

*Socrate,* "symphonic drama" by Erik SATIE, scored for four sopranos and orchestra, set in an artfully archaic, gymnopedically Hellenistic idiom stripped of all melismatic ornamentation, is performed for the first time at the Société Nationale de Musique in Paris in a version for voices and piano. (A complete orchestral performance was first given in Paris on 7 June 1920)

Those who fail to understand *Socrate* are asked by me to observe a most respectful silence and to manifest an attitude of total obsequiousness and inferiority. (Satie's inscription under the beard of his drawing of Socrates reproduced on the cover of *Le Guide du Concert,* Paris, 15 February 1920)

Satie gestated *Socrate* and beat the bass drum around it. The score is strung together in a succession of melodic fragments of two or four bars each, in the manner of salon chatter. Impotence would not be too harsh a word to characterize the nullity of the whole thing. (Jean Marnold, *Le Mercure de France,* Paris, March 1920)

Dans *Socrate,* du génie. (Charles Koechlin)

## 21 FEBRUARY 1920

A program of modern ballet performances by the "nouveaux jeunes" of French music is presented at the Comédie des Champs-Elysées in Paris, comprising the first performances of the following productions:

*Le Bœuf sur le Toit (The Bull on the Roof)* by the 27-year-old Darius MILHAUD, completed by him on 21 December 1919, and subtitled, in the original English, "The Nothing Doing Bar," a "cinéma-fantaisie, imagined and arranged by Jean Cocteau," with an appropriately cinematic variety of choreographic and musical materials, including a Brazilian scene (Milhaud served as an attaché at the French Embassy in Rio de Janeiro during the last year of World War I), a policeman's dance in waltz time, a sketch ridiculing the follies of American Prohibition (a bartender hangs out a sign, "Only Milk is Served Here"), couched in an advanced technical idiom, including the first systematic use of bitonality in a section entirely written in the synchronized triadic harmonies of C major and F sharp major, and an authentically sounding excursion into early American jazz (Art influenced life when the proprietor of a Paris bistro renamed his establishment, with Milhaud's permission, "Le Bœuf sur le Toit"); *Cocarde* by the 21-year-old Francis Poulenc; *Foxtrot* by 21-year-old Georges Auric, and *Trois petites pièces montées* by the perpetual vieux-jeune Erik Satie.

## 23 FEBRUARY 1920

*Der Fremde,* opera in four scenes by the German composer Hugo KAUN, after Grimm's grim tale *Gevatter Tod,* in which death plays the role of Godfather, is produced in Dresden.

## 24 FEBRUARY 1920

*Poèmes bouddhiques* by the Siamese-born Parisian composer Eugène GRASSE, an oriental triptych of impressionistic tableaux, *Les Oiseaux inspirés, La Procession* and *Le Réveil des Bouddhas,* is performed for the first time at the Concerts Colonne in Paris. (The last movement was performed previously in Paris on 20 February 1920)

*Le Tombeau de Couperin* by Maurice RAVEL, an orchestral suite arranged from four of Ravel's six piano pieces, *Prélude, Forlane, Rigaudon* and *Menuet,* a stylized tribute to Couperin's Gallic muse set in pandiatonically enriched harmonies, is performed for the first time by the Pasdeloup Orchestra in Paris.

6 MARCH 1920

*L'Uomo che ride,* opera by Arrigo PEDROLLO (after Victor Hugo's *L'Homme qui rit*), is produced in Rome.

8 MARCH 1920

Erik SATIE presents at the Galéries Barbezanges in Paris his provocative *Musique d'Ameublement,* dedicated to the proposition that music should be regarded as a utilitarian object of immediate environment, like furniture (hence the title), a potpourri of unrelated tunes performed by musicians stationed in separate parts of the hall so as to enable the public to hear the playing of individual instruments while walking.

10 MARCH 1920

*Fifth Symphony,* subtitled *Dans les Alpes,* by the French organist Charles TOURNEMIRE, is performed for the first time anywhere at The Hague.

21 MARCH 1920

*Balada blanická (The Ballad of Blaník)*, symphonic poem by Leoš JANÁČEK, is performed for the first time in Brno.

31 MARCH 1920

*Mirra,* opera in two acts by the Italian modernist Domenico ALALEONA, wherein a young woman of Cyprus, possessed by incestuous love for her young father, neglects her ardent husband causing him to wither in utter inanition in gymnosophistical naked fifths, while her father curses her in highly chromaticized dissonances, driving her to suicide by stabbing herself with the aid of perpendicularly integrated columns of whole-tone scales, making use also of non-tempered "pentafonia" dividing the octave into five equal intervals, is produced in Rome.

8 APRIL 1920

*Komedianter,* opera in three acts by the Danish composer August ENNA, after Victor Hugo's story *L'homme qui rit,* is produced in Copenhagen.

8 APRIL 1920

Charles Tomlinson GRIFFES, American composer of Impressionistically flavored music with delicately poetic invocations of distant lands and exotic creatures, written in a style directly influenced by Debussy and Ravel, but containing elements of individual tonal perceptivity, dies in New York at the age of thirty-five.

### 11 APRIL 1920

*Ballata delle Gnomidi*, symphonic poem by Ottorino RESPIGHI, written in his characteristically picturesque style, is performed for the first time at the Augusteo in Rome, Bernadino Molinari conducting.

### 17 APRIL 1920

*Marche française*, symphonic poem by ROGER-DUCASSE, descriptive of peace, summons to arms, and victorious marching, written during World War I and dedicated to Georges Clemenceau and Marshal Foch, is performed for the first time at the Pasdeloup Concerts in Paris.

### 23 APRIL 1920

*Výlety páně Broučkovy (Flights of Mr. Brouček)*, opera in two acts by Leoš JANÁČEK, to a satirical libretto ridiculing the extraterrestrial fantasies of a central European burgher, who in a state of inebriation imagines trips both through time to the 15th century and through space to the moon, reaching it a full 49 years before the actual lunar landing of 20 July 1969, vigorously set to music pulsating with asymmetrical rhythms and stimulatingly angular melodies, is produced in Prague.

### 24 APRIL 1920

*Amy Robsart*, opera in three acts by the Argentine composer Alfredo SCHIUMA, to a libretto from Walter Scott's historical novel *Kenilworth*, focused on the unhappy fate of Lady Leicester whose husband murdered her in the hope of marrying Queen Elizabeth, is produced at the Teatro Colón in Buenos Aires.

### 24 APRIL 1920

*Isabella Orsini*, lyric tragedy in four acts by the Italian composer Renato BROGI, dealing with the internecine struggle between powerful family groups in medieval Tuscany, is produced in Florence.

### 28 APRIL 1920

*Schirin und Gertraude*, opera in four acts by Paul GRAENER, dealing with a German feudal lord who imports a Turkish odalisque from a Crusade and persuades his wife to acquiesce in a triangular concubinage, set to music in a luxuriantly Wagneromorphic vein in ponderous harmonies inspissated with gravid dissonant combinations, is produced in Dresden.

### 13 MAY 1920

Two one-act operas by the German conductor Felix WEINGARTNER, *Die Dorfschule* and *Meister Andrea*, are produced in Vienna.

15 MAY 1920

*Pulcinella*, "ballet avec chant" by Igor STRAVINSKY, based on the musical materials of various instrumental pieces attributed to Pergolesi (but in fact suspected to be works by other Italian 18th-century composers), is produced at the Paris Opéra by Diaghilev's Ballet Russe, with a scenario centering on the famous character of Neapolitan commedia dell'arte, who perseveres in his pursuit of a girl he fancies above all others, with the musical score following the form of a classical dance suite:

(1) *Overture*, set in a strict manner of the Italian Baroque, in a major mode (2) *Serenata* (a tenor solo) (3) *Scherzino*, leading to *Allegro*, followed by *Andantino*, *Allegro* and *Presto* (4) *Allegretto* with soprano solo, *Allegro assai*, followed by *Allegro* with a bass solo, *Largo*, *Allegro*, with a duet for soprano and tenor, *Presto* with a tenor solo, *Allegro*, *Andantino* with a soprano solo and *Allegro* (5) *Gavotte* with two variations (6) *Vivo*, *Minuetto* and *Finale*, concluding on a sumptuously emblazoned, triumphantly festive, pandiatonically enriched, fiercely white C major.

19 MAY 1920

*Lorenzaccio*, opera in four acts by the French composer Ernest MORET, based on the play by Alfred de Musset depicting a life of debauchery and murder in 16th-century Florence, centering on the dissolute member of the Medici family Lorenzaccio (a contemptuous Italian diminutive for Lorenzo), whose misdeeds included the slaying of the first Medici who claimed the title of Duke, is produced at the Opéra-Comique in Paris.

20 MAY 1920

A festival of music by Camille SAINT-SAËNS opens in Athens, with the participation of the 84-year-old composer as pianist and conductor. (Three more concerts were given on 22, 28 and 29 May 1920)

22 MAY 1920

*Amaya*, opera in three acts by Jesús GURIDI, the first ever written in the Basque language, dealing with the conflict of pagan and Christian doctrines and mores in the Pyrenees, with dance interludes set in characteristic dual meters, 3/4 and 6/8, is produced in Bilbao.

24 MAY 1920

Pablo PICASSO makes a three-quarter drawing of Igor STRAVINSKY showing him as a seated figure, with hands enlarged by natural perspective and left forefinger hooked around the right middle finger. (Picasso drew Stravinsky in profile on 31 December 1920)

24 MAY 1920

The British Music Society adopts the standard pitch A = 435.4 vibrations per second at 59° Fahrenheit.

328

## 28 MAY 1920

*Die blaue Mazur,* operetta by Franz LEHÁR, in which a virginal Austrian damsel is compelled to marry a dissolute Polish count after she accepts the invitation to dance the matrimonially binding blue mazurka with him at an aristocratic ball, but flees in horror from their bridal chamber when it is invaded by a procession of ci-devant concubines, returning to him only when he solemnly abjures recidival pluralistic fornication, is produced in Vienna.

## 29 MAY 1920

*Banjuta,* opera in four acts by Alfreds KALNINŠ, the first national Latvian opera to a libretto from medieval Livonian life, involving rape, murder and the bereaved woman's sudden passion for the killer of her husband, is produced at the newly opened (inaugurated on 2 December 1919) Latvian National Opera House in Riga.

## 6 JUNE 1920

The Austrian Government adopts a new national anthem to replace the old Imperial hymn written in 1797 by Haydn, with the text by Austria's Chancellor Karl Renner and music by Wilhelm KIENZL. (On 13 December 1929, the Haydn melody was reinstated with a different set of words eliminating imperial references)

## 6 JUNE 1920

*La Légende de Saint Christophe,* sacred drama by Vincent D'INDY, set in the form of a triple triptych, containing three acts of three scenes each, depicting the conversion of Christopher by the Infant Jesus whom he carried across a stream (hence the name Christopher, Christ-Bearer), his temptation in a prison cell by the Queen of Lust (who becomes herself converted as her pagan whole-tone motto is transmuted into an ecclesiastical mode), his uninflammability (the flames are diverted by celestially pure medieval harmonies at the stake), his invulnerability (diatonic arrows rebound from his skin) and his ultimate martyrdom, is performed for the first time at the Paris Opéra, with the omission of an episode in which Satan stages a procession of false savants, Jews, socialists and composers of ultra-modern music. (Date from the review in *Le Ménestrel;* the same date is given in Loewenberg's *Annals of Opera.* But the printed score of the work cites 8 June 1920 for the first performance, as does Grove's *Dictionary of Music and Musicians*)

## 6 JUNE 1920

*Lešetínský Kovář (The Blacksmith of Lešetín),* opera by the Czech composer Karel WEIS, is produced in Prague.

## 1 JULY 1920

*Die ersten Menschen,* two-act opera by Rudi STEPHAN, German composer killed on the Russian front on 29 September 1915, is produced in Frankfurt.

## 7 JULY 1920

*De Triomfeerende Min (Love's Triumph)* in one act, first opera in the Dutch language, written and published in 1680, by Carolus HACQUART, is performed in a newly rearranged version by P.A. van Westhreen, in Arnheim.

## 18 JULY 1920

*Fifth Symphony* in D major by Nicolai MIASKOVSKY, completed in the summer of 1918, in four classically outlined movements, written in a more objectively optimistic style than his somberer works of previous years, and showing a preponderance of major keys, is performed for the first time in Moscow.

## 20 JULY 1920

The first experiment in broadcasting music by wireless telephony from a ship is made during the passage from England to Canada of the S.S. *Victoria*.

## 21 JULY 1920

*Saika*, operatic fairy tale by the Argentine composer Floro UGARTE, to his own libretto, similar to the story of *Hänsel und Gretel*, in which two children are lured into an enchanted forest by the witch Saika, and are saved from immolation by angelic intercession, is produced at the Teatro Colón in Buenos Aires.

## 4 AUGUST 1920

Vladimir REBIKOV, Russian composer and experimenter, who introduced such innovations as systematic sequences of unresolved discords, chordal integration of whole-tone scales (as in his piano piece *Les Démons s'amusent*), counterpoint in open fourths and fifths, and pandiatonic matrices of sound (as in his *Hymn to the Sun*, for piano solo composed in 1912 synchronously with Henry Cowell's experiments in tone-clusters, and using identical notation as Cowell), dies in Yalta, Crimea, of a brain hemorrhage, at the age of fifty-four.

(Date according to the death certificate in the Russian Orthodox Church of Autka, Yalta; the date 1 December 1920, given in the previous editions of *Music Since 1900* and in all music dictionaries is wrong)

## 5 AUGUST 1920

Leon THEREMIN, 23-year-old Russian electrical engineer, presents at the Physico-Technical Institute in Petrograd an experimental demonstration of his historic invention, AETHEROPHONE (later renamed THEREMINOVOX, and known in America simply as THEREMIN), the first musical instrument to produce musical tones by electronic impulses, effected by the interaction of two ultra-sonic circuits passing through a set of oscillating radio tubes, one circuit operating at a constant frequency, the other being altered by the movement of the player's hand through the air in front of an antenna, with the resulting differential tones falling in the audible range.

## 5 AUGUST 1920

*Ariana y Dionisios,* opera by the Argentine composer Felipe BOERO, relating Ariadna's peripeteia after she is abandoned by Theseus and restored to life by Dionysus, is produced at the Teatro Colón in Buenos Aires.

## 20 AUGUST 1920

The first commercial radio broadcast featuring musical numbers, is made by the Detroit Station WWJ.

On the night of 20 August 1920, the first commercial radio broadcast station in all the world was opened. And every night and every day since that momentous beginning WWJ has maintained this service. . . . Not until eleven weeks after its founding did WWJ share the channels of the air with a rival broadcasting station. The honor of being second fell to KDKA of Pittsburgh . . . and, though it has erroneously claimed and been credited with priority among broadcasters, it is still entitled to a place of distinction. (From an announcement by Lee de Forest, American inventor and pioneer of broadcasting, on the occasion of the 16th anniversary of the initial broadcast, on 20 August 1936)

## 23 AUGUST 1920

*The Sunset Trail,* Indian music drama by Charles Wakefield CADMAN, is produced for the first time by the California Theater Ensemble at San Diego, California.

## 5 SEPTEMBER 1920

Peter Racine FRICKER, English composer of symphonic and chamber music in a lyrically dramatic modernistic style verging on atonal melos and polytonal harmonies, with a fine texture of non-toxic dissonance, is born in London.

## 11 SEPTEMBER 1920

*Sinfonía sevillana* by Joaquín TURINA, a symphonic integration of Andalusian melorhythms, is performed for the first time at San Sebastian, Spain, under its original title *Sevilla,* with Fernández Arbós conducting.

## 1 OCTOBER 1920

Henri RABAUD is appointed Director of the Paris Conservatory.

## 2 OCTOBER 1920

Max BRUCH, industrious and competent German composer whose *Kol Nidrei,* a romance for violin and orchestra, written in 1880 for a Jewish community of Liverpool, is so intimately impregnated with the spirit of Hebrew cantillation that he was mistakenly listed as a Jew in the early editions of Grove's *Dictionary* and other reference books, and whose *Violin Concerto* in G minor is still cherished by romantically inclined virtuosos, dies in Berlin at the age of eighty-two.

### 19 OCTOBER 1920

Anatoly LUNACHARSKY, People's Commissar of Education of the Russian Soviet Socialist Republic, declares the continued maintenance of the Petrograd Philharmonic Orchestra to be of national importance:

I herewith serve notice that the Philharmonic Orchestra of Petrograd is the only exemplary symphonic institution of the Republic. Any attempt at the disorganization of its activities is a criminal offense. The Petrograd Philharmonic must remain intact as an institution of prime national importance. All musicians who were included in the orchestra personnel before 1 January 1919 are to be regarded as original members whose principal obligation is to the Philharmonic, and employment elsewhere is to be allowed only as an inevitable concession to the prevailing conditions of our time. (Date and text from *The Leningrad Philharmonic,* Leningrad, 1935)

### 24 OCTOBER 1920

At a Colonne concert in Paris, the first performance is given of Darius MILHAUD's *Second Orchestral Suite,* from the materials of his incidental music to Paul Claudel's play *Protée,* comprising the following movements:

(1) *Overture,* in a protean bitonal idiom, with D major serving as an axis and an anchor (2) *Prelude and Fugue,* based on a grotesquely iterative figure originating in the low wind instrument register (3) *Pastorale,* set in the compound meter of 8/8 separated into asymmetrical groups of 3, 3 and 2 eighth-notes, alternating with simple 3/4 time (4) *Nocturne,* in a propulsively steady 5/8 time (5) *Finale,* in square time, with polytonal excursions, reverting in the end to a concentrated, unisonally assertive C.

### 29 OCTOBER 1920

*The Garden of Fand* by Arnold BAX, his best known and valid symphonic poem, written in 1913 and illustrating the Irish legend of an enchanted garden on a mid-Atlantic island, ruled by a beautiful Irish girl, who captures an enthralled boat crew and causes the island to submerge amid dance and sensuous revelry under the aquamarine waves of impressionistic ninth-chords, amethyst triadic inversions and pearly arpeggios on the celesta, is performed for the first time anywhere by the Chicago Symphony Orchestra.

### 1 NOVEMBER 1920

*La Revue Musicale,* "Revue mensuelle internationale d'art musical ancien et moderne," starts publication in Paris, edited by Henry PRUNIÈRES, inaugurating a fruitful period of informative and elegant musical journalism.

### 2 NOVEMBER 1920

*Des Kaisers Dichter,* opera in three acts by Clemens von FRANCKENSTEIN, to a libretto dealing with the life of the Chinese poet Li Tai Po, is produced in Hamburg.

## 4 NOVEMBER 1920

*L'Aviatore Dro,* "futurist opera" by the Italian composer Francesco Balilla PRATELLA, to his own libretto in which the aviator Dro abandons his beauteous mistress to be alone with his beloved biplane, and flies aloft to merge with the universe, with a motorcycle engine included in the score to illustrate the revving up of an airplane, is performed for the first time in the composer's native town of Lugo.

## 4 NOVEMBER 1920

*Zeelandia,* symphonic poem descriptive of the lowlands of Holland by the Dutch composer Frits Adriaan KOEBERG, is performed for the first time in Amsterdam.

## 5 NOVEMBER 1920

On his first visit to the United States, Cyril SCOTT appears as soloist with the Philadelphia Orchestra conducted by Leopold Stokowski in the first American performance of his *Piano Concerto,* and also conducts his two orchestral *Passacaglias.*

## 5 NOVEMBER 1920

*Suite* for viola and orchestra by Ernest BLOCH, an orchestral version of his suite for viola and piano, in four movements (1) *Lento-Allegro* (2) *Allegro ironico* (3) *Lento* (4) *Molto vivo,* with the music redolent of quasi-Oriental exoticism in its melismatic arabesques, is performed for the first time in New York.

## 7 NOVEMBER 1920

On the third anniversary of the Soviet Revolution, *The Conquest of the Winter Palace,* spectacle with music, is enacted with a cast of thousands in Winter Palace Square in Petrograd.

## 15 NOVEMBER 1920

The first complete public performance of the astrological symphonic suite *The Planets* by the English composer Gustav HOLST (he studied astrology assiduously in 1913) takes place in London under the direction of Albert Coates. (A private performance of *The Planets* was first given in London on 29 September 1918):

*Mars, the Bringer of War,* with hollow chords portraying the vacuous inexorability of martial endeavor against the restless agitation of the strings in asymmetrical 5/4 time; *Venus, the Bringer of Peace,* with a tender violin solo introduced by a pacific harp, and some contention between rival factions manifested by clashing seventh-chords; *Mercury, the Winged Messenger,* in dual meters of 6/8 and 3/4 alternating with choreographic agility; *Jupiter, the Bringer of Jollity,* projecting a powerful high-gravity central theme in ponderously sententious harmonies; *Saturn, the Bringer of Old Age,* a debile progression of emasculated quintal harmonies; *Uranus, the Magician,* opening with a passage of catarrhal bassoons, developing non-thematically into a sonorous bubble, and, after an organ glissando, exploding into the solar whiteness of februated C major before subsiding into inaudible timelessness; *Neptune, the Mystic,* an impressionistic study with discursive arpeggios rolling along over the angular intersections of 5/4 time while a wordless chorus of female voices intones measured syllables of expressionless communication.

### 18 NOVEMBER 1920

*El Greco,* ballet by the French conductor and composer Désiré Émile INGHELBRECHT, to a scenario on the life and art of the great Greco-Hispanic painter whose ascetically limned saints and somberly contemplative landscapes presage the expressionistic configurations of the modern era, set to music incorporating elements of Spanish and ecclesiastical modalities, is produced by the Ballets Suédois in Paris.

### 23 NOVEMBER 1920

*Pilgrim Vision* by John Alden CARPENTER, a symphonic poem written to celebrate the tercentenary of the landing of the Pilgrims at Plymouth, Massachusetts, is performed for the first time by the Philadelphia Orchestra.

### 27 NOVEMBER 1920

*Scherzo veneziano,* choreographic comedy by Ottorino RESPIGHI, is performed for the first time in Rome.

### 1 DECEMBER 1920

*Le Roi Candaule,* lyric comedy in four acts by Alfred BRUNEAU, wherein a dissolute ruler of the rich kingdom of Lydia is assassinated by his prime minister who then marries his queen giving rise to the last Lydian dynasty, set to music in a pseudo-exotic manner brightened by naturalistic dramatic touches, such as a quasi-Debussyan croaking of frogs in sharply accentuated secundal counterpoint, and impressionistic chordal parallelisms, is produced at the Opéra-Comique in Paris.

### 4 DECEMBER 1920

*Die Vögel,* opera in two acts by the German composer Walter BRAUNFELS, after Aristophanes, is produced in Munich.

### 4 DECEMBER 1920

*Die tote Stadt,* opera in three acts by the 23-year-old Austrian composer Erich Wolfgang KORNGOLD, after Rodenbach's novel *Bruges-la-Morte,* wherein a grieving widower meets a ballerina who resembles his wife in every respect but the quality of virtue, and in a reverie strangles her with his wife's golden tresses preserved in a crystal container, to the accompaniment of a baleful "hair motive" in the trombones, whereupon he wakes up and decides to leave the "city of the dead," is produced on the same night in Hamburg and Cologne.

### 6 DECEMBER 1920

Karel Kovařovic, Czech composer, conductor of the National Opera in Prague, who wrote operas on historical subjects in an effective dramatic manner slightly touched by Wagneromantic effluvia, dies in Prague, three days before reaching his 58th birthday.

### 12 DECEMBER 1920

*La Valse*, "choreographic poem for orchestra in the tempo of the Viennese waltz" by Maurice RAVEL, presenting a nostalgic panorama of old Vienna, opening with fragments of waltz tunes and developed with calculated hesitation into a flamboyant ball, richly supported by deeply anchored pedal points and gothic columns of ninth-chords, and suggesting a gauze-covered painting in muted colors, is performed for the first time in Paris, by the Lamoureux orchestra, Camille Chevillard conducting.

Whirling clouds give glimpses, through rifts, of couples waltzing. The clouds scatter little by little. One sees an immense hall peopled with a twirling crowd. The scene is gradually illuminated. The light of the chandeliers burst forth in fortissimo. An Imperial Court about 1855. (From the description in the printed score)

### 13 DECEMBER 1920

*Edipo rè*, posthumous one-act opera, after Sophocles, by Ruggero LEONCAVALLO, is produced for the first time anywhere in Chicago.

### 21 DECEMBER 1920

*Sally*, musical comedy by Jerome KERN, in which a waitress crashes a society party in Long Island pretending to be a Russian ballet dancer, and using her meretricious snob appeal lures a gullible millionaire into matrimony, containing the hit songs *Sally, Look for the Silver Lining* and *The Little Church Around the Corner*, is produced at the Ziegfeld Follies in New York.

### 28 DECEMBER 1920

Arturo TOSCANINI conducts in New York the first concert of his American tour with the orchestra of La Scala, Milan.

### 31 DECEMBER 1920

The Lithuanian National Opera is organized in Kaunas, the capital of the Lithuanian Republic.

# ☙ *1921* ❧

### 1 JANUARY 1921

Fritz KLEIN completes the score of his symphonic poem for chamber orchestra *Die Maschine, Eine extonale Selbstsatire*, signing it *Heautontimor-*

*umenos* (*Self-tormentor*), containing nine innovating musico-mathematical devices: (1) a 12-note rhythm (2) a 12-note modal theme (3) a chord containing 12 different intervals, from a minor second to an octave (4) a "neutral" scale of alternating minor and major seconds (5) a theme composed of the three preceding intervalic arrangements (6) a Pyramid Chord constructed of 12 intervals in an arithmetical progression (7) *Mutterakkord,* containing 12 different notes and 11 different intervals (8) a mirror reflection of a symmetrically arranged chord-theme (9) a contrapuntally combined development of all themes and intervalic arrangements of the piece.

### 2 JANUARY 1921

*Das Wandbild,* scene and pantomime by the foremost lyric composer of Switzerland, Othmar SCHOECK, to a story by Ferruccio Busoni, wherein a youthful swain pursues an oriental girl in a picture on the wall in a Paris shop into the land of erotogenic delights set to music in Wagneromantic harmonies, is performed for the first time in Halle.

### 2 JANUARY 1921

For the first time, a complete radio broadcast is made of a church service from Calvary Church in Pittsburgh. (The date is commemorated on the plaque at the entrance of Calvalry Church)

### 5 JANUARY 1921

For the first time since the war, the Paris Opéra presents a Wagner music drama, *Die Walküre,* collecting the unprecedented sum of 35,977 francs at the box office.

### 10 JANUARY 1921

By order of municipal authorities of Zion City, Illinois, the playing of jazz music is forbidden in all public places.

### 10 JANUARY 1921

*Third Symphony* by the Norwegian composer Christian SINDING is performed for the first time anywhere in Berlin.

### 19 JANUARY 1921

*Nemici,* opera in three acts by Guido GUERRINI, to his own libretto, is produced in Bologna.

### 28 JANUARY 1921

The Federal Court of New York City orders an injunction restraining J. H. Remick & Co., music publishers, from selling copies of *Avalon,* a popular song about a beautiful ocean island of the Arthurian romances, set to music identical with Cavaradossi's anguished lines *O dolci baci, o languide carezze,* from the aria *E lucevan le stelle* in Puccini's *Tosca* (with the line "I found my love in Avalon," hideously altered to a major key), and imposes a fine of $25,000 for damages in favor of the plaintiff, G. Ricordi & Co., owners of the copyright.

### 9 FEBRUARY 1921

James Gibbons HUNEKER, American author of brilliant essays on music, self-confessed "old fogey" (the expression which he applied to himself in the title of one of his books), believer in an absolute standard of esthetics, urbane demolitionist of ultra-modern composers, such as Debussy and Strauss, dies in Brooklyn nine days after his 61st birthday.

### 12 FEBRUARY 1921

*Pastorale d'été*, Arcadian evocation for a small ensemble of instruments by Arthur HONEGGER, is performed for the first time in Paris.

### 13 FEBRUARY 1921

*Per una Favola cavalleresca*, "symphonic illustration of legendary love scenes, tournaments and battles" by Gian Francesco MALIPIERO, written in a characteristic dual idiom of Italian musical modernism, affecting archaic forms in pandiatonic harmonies, is performed for the first time in Rome.

### 3 MARCH 1921

*Les Trois Mousquetaires*, opera in six scenes by the Anglo-French composer Isidore DE LARA, after the famous novel of flamboyant adventure of Alexandre Dumas, is produced in Cannes.

### 4 MARCH 1921

*Indian Sketches*, orchestral suite by the American composer Henry F. GILBERT, making use of authentic Indian tunes, is performed for the first time by the Boston Symphony Orchestra, Pierre Monteux conducting.

### 5 MARCH 1921

*Violin Concerto* in three movements by the 21-year-old Bulgarian composer Pantcho VLADIGEROV, written in an expansively romantic melodious manner powdered with Balkanized rhythmic asymmetries, is performed for the first time by his older nonidentical twin brother Luben with the Berlin Philharmonic, under the direction of Fritz Reiner. (Luben was born in Zürich, whither Mother Vladigerov sped before parturition mistrustful of Bulgarian obstetrical skill in multiple birth cases, late on 12 March 1899, with Pantcho following into the world 16 hours later on 13 March 1899; these dates have been obtained by the author from the registeries of birth in Zürich)

### 12 MARCH 1921

*The Rebel Maid*, light opera by the 35-year-old English organist and harmony teacher Montague PHILLIPS, dealing with a militant girl supporter of William of Orange on his landing in England on 5 November 1688, who witnesses him crowned as King of England in joint sovereignty with his wife Mary, written in a melodiously harmonious academic manner, is produced in London.

### 14 MARCH 1921

*Antar,* "heroic narrative" in four acts by the French composer Gabriel DUPONT (1878–1914), to a libretto in which a desert sheik's nomadic marriage is rescinded when he is struck down by an arrow shot by a blinded love rival whose guidance in archery was made possible by an accurate vectorial measurement of his foe's loud voice, set to music contrasting the cerulean brilliance of the aquamarine colors of the Mediterranean melorhythms with the sandy monotony of the orientalistically oriented chants of the Sahara, is posthumously produced at the Paris Opéra.

### 16 MARCH 1921

*Kaddara,* opera by the Danish composer Hakon BÖRRENSEN, to a libretto set in Greenland, wherein Kaddara, an intransigent Arctic housewife, locks out her whaling husband when he comes home without booty, whereupon he reembarks in his kayak, harpoons a giant whale and takes it to a local widow whose daughter bites his shoulder according to the ancient Greenlandian welcoming ritual, which fails to fascinate him, and he returns to his igloo, as his wife sings a lullaby for their child and the sun appears on the horizon after a long polar night, set to music with the application of authentic modes of Eskimo songs, is performed for the first time in Copenhagen.

### 17 MARCH 1921

Pantcho VLADIGEROV, 22-year-old Bulgarian composer, plays the solo part with the Berlin Philharmonic in the first performance of his *First Piano Concerto,* written in a romantic manner with injections of typical Bulgarian melorhythms.

### 17 MARCH 1921

*Ramuntcho,* lyric drama in four acts by the 42-year-old Sicilian composer Stefano DONAUDY, is performed for the first time in Milan.

### 19 MARCH 1921

Two and a half centuries have passed since the opening of the first public opera theater in Paris by the poet Pierre PERRIN and the court musician Robert CAMBERT.

### 21 MARCH 1921

*La Colombe de Bouddha,* one-act opera by the Venezuelan-born Parisian composer Reynaldo HAHN, to a libretto dealing with the sacred dove of the Buddha, is performed for the first time in Cannes.

## 24 MARCH 1921

Déodat DE SÉVERAC, French composer of delicately wrought impressionistic music in various forms, dies of chronic albuminuria, at Céret in the Pyrenees, at the age of forty-eight. (He was born on 20 July 1872, as proved by his birth certificate, not on 20 July 1873 as he liked to believe.)

## 27 MARCH 1921

*Kyra Frossini,* opera by the Greek composer George SKLAVOS, is performed for the first time in Athens.

## 29 MARCH 1921

*La Jane,* one-act opera by the Belgian composer Armand MARSICK, to a story of a piteously seduced damsel who avenges herself by killing her corrupter on the day of his marriage to another, is produced in Liège.

## 5 APRIL 1921

Alfons DIEPENBROCK, Dutch composer, ardent polyphonist and guardian of the old Flemish tradition, dies in his native Amsterdam at the age of fifty-eight.

## 9 APRIL 1921

*Die Kohlhaymerin (Kohlhaymer's Spouse),* opera in four acts by the Austrian composer Julius BITTNER, to his own libretto, focused on a well-preserved Viennese widow who flourished in 1810, with an element of fantasy intruding as her deceased husband steps out of the frame of his portrait to the accompaniment of ominous progressions in whole-tone scales to warn her against a predatory local Don Juan, is produced in Vienna.

## 15 APRIL 1921

*Anima allegra,* lyric comedy in three acts by the Italian composer Franco VITTADINI, in which a girl from Granada, the "merry soul" of the title, invades circa 1830 the dank premises of her suburban aunt's home, introduces her male cousin to a Gypsy camp, and eventually marries him, the score set in a conventional Mediterranean style with the insertion of Andalusian dance episodes, is produced in Rome.

## 22 APRIL 1921

Serge KOUSSEVITZKY inaugurates in Paris the annual series of Concerts Koussevitzky.

## 28 APRIL 1921

*Die Krähen (The Crows),* "Lustspiel" in one act by the German conductor Walter COURVOISIER, to a libretto from Benvenuto Cellini's autobiography, portraying a gathering of young artists and their "crows" (female friends) at the height of the plague in Rome in the early 16th century, at which Cellini brings a male apprentice dressed as a woman to mock the unjustified jealousy of his suspicious inamorata, is performed for the first time in Munich.

### 2 MAY 1921

Pietro MASCAGNI conducts in Rome the first performance of his three-act opera *Il piccolo Marat*, in which a young French nobleman infiltrates the ranks of terrorists in Arras about 1793 so successfully that he earns the sobriquet "Little Marat," and in the last act rescues his widowed mother from the Revolutionary sans-culottes and elopes with the niece of the dreaded chairman of the local Committee of Public Safety, ending in an aristocratic display of royally immaculate C major.

### 7 MAY 1921

*Il Mistero*, opera by Domenico MONLEONE, is performed for the first time in Venice.

### 9 MAY 1921

*Pan Twardowski*, ballet by the Polish composer Ludomir RÓZICKI, after the classical poem of Adam Mickiewicz, is performed for the first time in Warsaw.

### 11 MAY 1921

*Middelalderig (The Middle Ages)*, opera by the 36-year-old Swedish composer Ture RANGSTRÖM, is produced in Stockholm.

### 15 MAY 1921

*Die Prinzessin Girnara*, first opera, in two acts, by Egon WELLESZ of Vienna, to a mystical play by Jakob Wassermann in which the real and symbolic characters intermingle in somnial ambulation, set to music in nervously implosive dissonant harmonies, is performed for the first time in Hannover. (A revised version was produced in Mannheim on 2 September 1928)

The opera is blatant nonsense of unspeakable hideousness. We must refuse to tolerate in the future such criminal assaults in art and on the public. (Richard Ohlekopf, *Signale für die musikalische Welt*, Berlin, 25 May 1921.)

### 16 MAY 1921

*Sirocco*, opera in three acts by Eugen D'ALBERT, wherein a Parisian cocotte, nicknamed after the devastating desert wind, demoralizes the stalwart soldiers of fortune in North Africa and is ultimately throttled by a member of the French Foreign Legion, set to a synthetic score, incestuously combining elements of German romanticism and Italian Verismo, is performed for the first time anywhere in Darmstadt.

## 17 MAY 1921

Diaghilev's Ballet Russe presents in Paris the first performance of *Chout* (French spelling of the Russian word for Buffoon) by the 30-year-old Sergei Prokofiev, derived from a medieval Russian folk tale, *The Buffoon Who Outwitted Seven Other Buffoons,* set to a grotesquely agitated musical score bristling with asymmetrical rhythms against a steady marching beat and diversified by the interpolation of ironically lyric episodes, in six compact scenes interlarded with five symphonic interludes:

(1) *Buffoon's Room,* in brusque bombastic rhythms and melodies set in pandiatonic harmonies (2) *At the House of Seven Buffoons,* a boisterously discordant burlesque in which the buffoons slaughter their wives trusting their colleague's assurances that it would improve their character after they are brought back to life with the aid of his magic wand (3) *In the Backyard,* illustrating the onset of doubt and anxiety on the part of the bereaved buffoons in a nervously chromaticized idiom, changing to a furious diatonic *prestissimo* and concluding on an *Andante innocente* (4) *Reception Room,* with a polka-like dance of the seven daughters of the seven buffoons (5) *Merchant's Bedroom,* wherein the scoundrel buffoon in a woman's clothes is taken to the merchant's quarters, accompanied by a sentimental ballad, but at the crucial moment substitutes a she-goat with whom the merchant dances an animated cossack step (6) *Merchant's Garden,* in which the she-goat, succumbing to the exhaustion of the dance, is buried to the strains of a dissonant funeral march, interrupted by the invasion of the seven buffoons starting a frenzied dance, abruptly ending on a unisonal C.

## 20 MAY 1921

*La Voz de las Calles,* symphonic poem by the foremost modern composer of Chile, Humberto ALLENDE, in which he employs authentic melodies of street vendors as thematic material, thus justifying the title, *The Voice of the Streets,* is performed for the first time in Santiago.

## 21 MAY 1921

*Prince Ferelon,* or *The Princess's Suitors,* one-act musical extravaganza by the English composer Nicholas Comyn GATTY, to his own libretto in which a wandering minstrel enters a contest for the hand of the princess in the guise of a musician, dress designer and a dancer, and after being rejected in all three assumed identities, succeeds when he reveals his true self, is produced in London.

## 24 MAY 1921

*Le Piège de Méduse,* lyric comedy in one act by Erik SATIE, with dance interludes, to his own libretto, composed in 1913, and facetiously scored for a surrealist ensemble of two piston flutes, two slide clarinets, a siphon in C, three keyboard trombones, a group of "cephalophones" with a range of 30 octaves, interspersed with such expression marks as "silencieusement, je vous prie," is performed for the first time in a modest arrangement for realistic musical instruments, in Paris.

26 MAY 1921

*Uguns un Nakts* (*Fire and Night*), opera in four acts by the Latvian composer Jānis MEDIŅŠ, is produced in Riga.

31 MAY 1921

Edgar VARÈSE organizes in New York the International Composers' Guild with the purpose of promoting the cause of 20th-century music. (The date of the charter)

The composer is the only one of the creators of today who is denied direct contact with the public. When his work is done, he is thrust aside, and the interpreter enters, not to try to understand the composition but impertinently to judge it. Not finding in it any trace of the conventions to which he is accustomed, he banishes it from his programs, denouncing it as incoherent and unintelligible . . . In every other field, the creator comes into some form of direct contact with his public. The poet and novelist enjoy the medium of the printed page; the painter and sculptor the open doors of a gallery; the dramatist the free scope of the stage. The composer must depend upon an intermediary, the interpreter . . . It is true that in response to public demand, our official organizations occasionally place on their programs a new work surrounded by established names. But such a work is carefully chosen from the most timid and anemic of contemporary productions, leaving absolutely unheard the composers who represent the true spirit of our times . . . Dying is the privilege of the weary. The present day composers refuse to die. They have realized the necessity of banding together and fighting for the right of each individual to secure a fair and free presentation of his work. It is out of such a collective will that the International Composers' Guild was born . . . Its aim is to centralize the works of the day, to group them in programs intelligently and organically constructed, and, with the disinterested help of singers and instrumentalists, to present these works in such a way as to reveal their fundamental spirit . . . It refuses to admit any limitation, either of volition or action . . . disapproves of all "isms"; denies the existence of schools; recognizes only the individual. (From the Manifesto of the International Composers' Guild)

4 JUNE 1921

Two one-act operas by Paul HINDEMITH are produced for the first time in Stuttgart:

(1) *Mörder, Hoffnung der Frauen,* a duodrama involving a nameless Man and an equally nameless Woman, developing the thesis that only by murder can women achieve self-fulfillment, set to a grindingly dissonant score (2) *Das Nusch-Nuschi,* a musical play for Burmese marionettes in which a monster born of a giant rat and an alligator assumes the role of deus ex machina, while the King, the Crown Prince, the Hangman, a falsetto-singing Eunuch and assorted bayaderes disport themselves in an astutely discordant musical setting with the interpolation of some parodistic elements (King Mark's motive from *Tristan und Isolde* makes its appearance in the orchestra when the King of Burma finds out that his aide-de-camp has seduced four of his wives).

6 JUNE 1921

*La Esclava,* opera by the Cuban composer José MAURI (1856–1937), to a libretto dealing with a mulatto girl imported into Cuba as a slave in 1860, set to music replete with Afro-Cuban melorhythms within the harmonic framework of Italian operatic convention, is produced in Havana.

## 6 JUNE 1921

*L'Homme et son désir,* surrealist ballet by Darius MILHAUD, to a scenario fashioned from Paul Claudel's "plastic poem," picturing a symbolic modern man debilitated by ineffectual fantasies of half-materialized nudes, scored for a multifarious ensemble, including iron castanets and a wooden plank struck with a hammer, with the stereophonic placement of instruments in five quasi-autonomous groups, is produced in Paris.

*L'Homme et son désir* was the fruit of the collaboration of three friends in 1917 who exchanged ideas about music and art on the heights of the Serra which dominates Rio de Janeiro. This "plastic drama" drew out of the ambiance of the Brazilian jungle forest in which we were, so to say, submerged. (Paul Claudel in *La Danse,* Paris, June 1921)

## 10 JUNE 1921

*Symphonies d'instruments à vent* by Igor STRAVINSKY, dedicated to the memory of Debussy, in which the word symphony denotes a polyphonic ensemble of instrumental voices, set in static and placid harmonies with its central idea formed by a reverential chorale, is performed for the first time at Koussevitzky's third concert of Russian music given in London.

To us, the *Symphonies of Wind Instruments* spelt nothing but senseless ugliness. (*The Times,* London, 12 June 1921)

## 10 JUNE 1921

*Passacaglia* for orchestra, op. 1, by Anton von WEBERN, written in 1908 in a firmly tonal idiom in the explicitly indicated key of D minor, but already containing the foretaste of the atonal principle of non-repetition of thematic notes in the subject (D, C-sharp, B-flat, A-flat, F, E, A, D) is performed for the first time at Bochum, Germany, at a concert of modern Austrian music.

After Schoenberg's more or less tolerable *Verklärte Nacht* and Erich Korngold's music of real genius to *Much Ado About Nothing,* Anton von Webern's *Passacaglia* seemed like an evil spirit, not to say a bad joke and wretched pretentiousness. (Joseph Schwermann, *Signale für die musikalische Welt,* Berlin, 27 July 1921)

## 11 JUNE 1921

*Le Roi David,* symphonic psalm by Arthur HONEGGER (begun on 25 February 1921 and completed on 28 April 1921), in three parts, after the drama of René Morax, scored for chamber orchestra, chorus, soloists and a narrator, in the manner of a modern oratorio, making free use of stridently frictional harmonies and atonally oriented melodies while remaining within the framework of basic tonality, tracing King David's career from the smiting of Goliath, through the defeat of discordantly marching Philistines and to the point of

*343*

death on a pandiatonic major chord, is performed for the first time at Jorat, Switzerland.

## 14 JUNE 1921

The British Music Society gives its inaugural concert of symphonic music in London, presenting *The Planets* by Gustave HOLST, the overture to the opera *The Children of Don* by Josef HOLBROOKE, *The Eternal Rhythm* by Eugene GOOSSENS, *Piano Concerto* by Cyril SCOTT and *The Lark Ascending* by Ralph VAUGHAN WILLIAMS.

## 16 JUNE 1921

*Legenda z Erinu (The Legend of Erin)*, opera by the Czech composer Otakar OSTRČIL, to a story dealing with an Irish king's bride who flees from matrimony to join her former lover, with retribution vouchsafed to them when the king refuses to save his mortally wounded rival by the miraculous powers of the imposition of royal hands and lets him die, whereupon the distracted girl kills herself, is produced in Brno.

## 18 JUNE 1921

Luigi RUSSOLO, Italian musician and painter, conducts in Paris a concert of Futurist music with a noise orchestra, consisting of Thunderclappers, Exploders, Crashers, Splashers, Bellowers, Whistlers, Hissers, Snorters, Whisperers, Murmurers, Mutterers, Bustlers, Gurglers, Screamers, Screechers, Rustlers, Buzzers, Cracklers, Shouters, Shriekers, Groaners, Howlers, Laughers, Wheezers, and Sobbers.

## 19 JUNE 1921

*Les Mariés de la Tour Eiffel*, a synthetic spectacle devised by Jean COCTEAU, combining drama, comedy, vaudeville, pantomime and opera, in two scenes, *Marche Nuptiale* and *Fugue du Massacre*, with the music by five of the French Six (HONEGGER, MILHAUD, AURIC, POULENC, TAILLEFERRE), is presented by the Ballets Suédois in Paris.

## 24 JUNE 1921

The American Conservatory of Music is established at Fontainebleau, near Paris, to serve the growing needs of American music students gravitating towards France after the twilight of the German musical gods during the First World War.

## 7 JULY 1921

*El Caminante*, lyric drama in one act, on a religious theme, by the Cuban composer Eduardo SÁNCHEZ DE FUENTES, is produced in Havana.

## 20 JULY 1921

A pageant to commemorate the tercentenary of the Pilgrims' landing is given in Plymouth, Massachusetts, with music provided by George CHADWICK,

Henry F. GILBERT, Frederick S. CONVERSE, Arthur FOOTE, Edward Burlingame HILL, Edgar Stillman KELLEY, John POWELL, Leo SOWERBY and Chalmers CLIFTON.

### 31 JULY 1921

The first Festival for Promotion of Contemporary Music opens in Donaueschingen, Germany, with the following programs:

(1) Morning concert: first performance of *String Quartet No. 4* by the Czech pioneer of fractional music Alois HÁBA, making use of quarter-tones and multiples of quarter-tones ($3/4$, $1\frac{1}{4}$ tones and resulting icositetraphonic complexes), piano pieces by the Austrian modernist Wilhelm GROSZ played by himself; first performance of *Serenade* for clarinet and string quartet by the 20-year-old Viennese composer, thenceforth destined for fame, Ernst KRENEK. (2) Evening concert: *Piano Quartet* by the German neo-romanticist Franz PHILIPP; *Lieder* by the Austrian atonalist Karl HORWITZ; *Six Fugues* for piano by the German neo-classical composer Arthur WILLNER; *String Quartet* by the French-born Catalonian composer active mainly in Germany, Philipp JARNACH.

While there exists today a lively debate regarding the innovations in plastic arts, prose, poetry and drama, young composers must struggle against overwhelming odds to secure a public hearing of their works. Interpreters and publishers, on whom composers depend for self-expression, usually refuse to aid unknown talents. Considering the situation, the Gesellschaft der Musikfreunde of Donaueschingen decided to contribute its modest effort to the promotion of the creative work of the young generation of composers . . . When a series of chamber music concerts was organized in this little Schwarzwald town of Donaueschingen, it was not an artificially planted seed in an uncultivated soil, but a continuation of a long and fine tradition established through 150 years of the Dukedom . . . The programs are arranged without partisan bias. Only the inner worth of each work and its craftsmanship were the determining factors for acceptance. Emphasis is laid, however, on giving priority to unknown or little known names; mature works by established composers may be passed over in favor of music by younger men struggling for recognition, even if their efforts show for the time being more ardor than accomplishment (From the declaration of the Donaueschingen Committee for the Promotion of Contemporary Music, published in the *Neue Musik Zeitung*, 21 July 1921)

### 1 AUGUST 1921

At the third concert of the first Donaueschingen Music Festival, three chamber-music works are performed for the first time: *Sonata* for violin and piano by the 19-year-old German composer Rudolf PETERS, with him playing the piano part; *Piano Sonata* by Schoenberg's disciple Alban BERG, his opus No. 1, written in 1908, and first performed in Vienna on 24 April 1911, in a single movement, in classical form, but intervalically emancipated and tending to wide distribution of thematic notes in quartal, tritonal and quintal leaps; and *String Quartet No. 3* by the 25-year-old master of German neo-classicism Paul HINDEMITH. (Information from the original programs, obtained from the Secretariat of the Gesellschaft der Musikfreunde in Donaueschingen)

## 2 AUGUST 1921

Enrico CARUSO, the most celebrated Italian tenor of all time, whose art of bel canto moved audiences to a frenzy of adulation, and whose notorious "coup de glotte," known as the "Caruso sob," became his throatmark, who was also a gifted caricaturist, a gastronomic gourmet (a brand of macaroni was named after him), a lover of women, and despite his corpulence, an agile and convivial celebrant of good living, dies at the age of 48 years, five months and one week, at 9 o'clock in the morning at the Hotel Vesuvius in his native Naples, a victim of a combination of ailments, which first manifested themselves when he suffered a throat hemorrhage during a performance at the Brooklyn Academy of Music on 11 December 1920.

## 8 AUGUST 1921

Arthur Pougin, scholarly French music critic, inveterate denouncer of modern ways in music, who hurled jovian thunderbolts against Debussy and all those who broke the inviolable rules of traditional music, dies in Paris two days after his 87th birthday.

## 27 AUGUST 1921

Four centuries have passed since the death of Josquin DES PREZ, great precursor of modern polyphony. (The spelling Des Prez appears in a contemporary acrostic, and must therefore be regarded as authentic, although the spellings Des Prés and Desprès are encountered in various sources)

## 14 SEPTEMBER 1921

Six centuries have passed since the formation of the first musicians' union, when 29 minstrels and 8 female jugglers banded together in Paris on 14 September 1321.

## 25 SEPTEMBER 1921

A State Institute of Musical Science is organized in Moscow.

## 27 SEPTEMBER 1921

Engelbert HUMPERDINCK, German composer whose fairy-tale opera *Hänsel und Gretel* is a dramatic projection of Wagner's methods into musical infantiloquy, dies at Neustrelitz at the age of sixty-seven.

## 29 SEPTEMBER 1921

*Blossom Time*, operetta by Sigmund ROMBERG, adapted from *Das Dreimäderlhaus*, a romanticized story of Schubert's life, made up of Schubert's tunes, with the hit number *Song of Love* set to the famous cello tune in the *Unfinished Symphony*, is produced in New York.

## 4 OCTOBER 1921

The American Academy in Rome is founded and grants its first fellowship in musical composition to Leo SOWERBY.

*Taras Bulba,* symphonic rhapsody by Leoš JANÁČEK, after Gogol's tragic tale from the period of savage struggle between the Cossacks of the Dnieper and the Poles in the early 17th century, in three movements, describing the death of two sons of Taras—Andrei, slain by Taras for betraying the Cossack cause for the sake of a beautiful Polish girl, and Ostap, captured by the Poles and executed after torture in Warsaw—and finally Taras himself, crucified and burned alive, written in a tense quasi-modern idiom, irrigated by streams of Slavic melorhythms, is performed for the first time in Brno. (The first Prague performance on 9 November 1924 is erroneously listed in reference works as the world première)

13 OCTOBER 1921

*Study for Pianola* by Igor STRAVINSKY is performed for the first time in London from the pianola roll recorded expressly by him for the Aeolian Company.

16 OCTOBER 1921

Three centuries have elapsed since the death of Jan Pieterszoon (i.e. Peter's son) SWEELINCK (or Swellinck; 24 variants of his name are known, and he himself used three), superb organist of the Old Church in Amsterdam, teacher of a generation of North European organists, composer of exalted vocal and instrumental music in the superlative manner of autochtonous Flemish florid counterpoint, independent of the dominant Venetian School (contrary to a persistent error, Sweelinck never went to Venice).

*M. Joannes Petri Swellingus Amstelo-batavus*
*Musicus et Organista toto orbe celeberrimus*
*Vir singulari modestia ac pietate cum in vita*
*Tum in morte omnibus suspiciendus*
(Inscription on a copper engraving by Joh. Müller made in 1624, three years after Sweelinck's death)

28 OCTOBER 1921

Alfredo CASELLA makes his first American appearance with the Philadelphia Orchestra, in the triple capacity of composer, conductor and pianist.

29 OCTOBER 1921

*Eighth Symphony* by the 69-year-old Swiss composer Hans HUBER, being an orchestral arrangement of his only string quartet, is performed for the first time in Basel, eight weeks before his death.

29 OCTOBER 1921

*Pour une Fête de Printemps,* symphonic poem by Albert ROUSSEL, formed out of the materials originally intended for a scherzo of his *Second Symphony,* written in the vernal spirit of Gallic modernism and harmonically based on the euphonious bitonality of major triads at a tritone's distance, is performed for the first time at a Colonne concert in Paris under the direction of Gabriel Pierné.

### 30 OCTOBER 1921

*Horace Victorieux,* "mimed symphony" by Arthur HONEGGER, depicting in starkly dissonant tones the legendary encounter between the three Horatii and three Curiatii, in which the surviving Horatius slays all three of the Curiatii and then smites, in thunderous anger spouted by the maximal discord formed by two contiguous diminished seventh-chords, his own sister who loved a Curatius, is performed for the first time in Lausanne, Ernest Ansermet conducting.

### 17 NOVEMBER 1921

Henry HADLEY conducts the New York Philharmonic Orchestra in the first performance of his symphonic poem *The Ocean,* with the syncopated waves of chromatics in the strings lashing at Wagneroaring brasses while the chant of the high wind instruments is counterposed by the sustained foghorn of the nethermost tuba.

### 20 NOVEMBER 1921

*Mon Lac,* symphonic poem for piano and orchestra by Georges Martin WITKOWSKI, 54-year-old Algerian-born French composer of remote Polish origin, a romantically illustrative impression, in three sections, of a provincial lake Paladru, near Lyons, is performed for the first time in Lyons.

### 23 NOVEMBER 1921

*Katá Kabanová,* opera in three acts by Leoš JANÁČEK, after Ostrovsky's play *The Storm,* depicting the illicit love affair of a married mid-19th-century Russian woman repressed by her tyrannical mother-in-law, her voluntary confession and her suicide in the waters of the Volga River, set to a romantically saturated score, with strong melodic and rhythmic inflections of Russian folk music (the cadential falling fourth in a minor mode is thematically manifest), is produced in Brno. (Date from the actual program, confirmed by a newspaper review; 23 October 1921 is erroneously given in Loewenberg's *Annals of Opera*)

### 1 DECEMBER 1921

Vincent D'INDY conducts the New York Symphony in the world première of his symphonic suite *Poème des rivages,* dedicated to his second wife whom he married in 1918, and set in four geographic movements recalling his travels with her: (1) *Agay,* a poetic view of the coastal line (2) *Majorca,* a glorification of the cerulean waters of the Mediterranean (3) *Falconara,* with an audibly puffing Italian train (4) *Gascogne,* an expansive cyclorama of the Basque country in Gascogne.

## 7 DECEMBER 1921

*Dans l'ombre de la Cathédrale,* lyric drama in three acts by Georges Hüe, after a mystically realistic story of Blasco Ibañez wherein the guardian of the jewels of the Madonna in the cathedral of Toledo is killed by his former revolutionary associates when he, seized by sudden loyalty, resists their planned expropriation, is produced at the Opéra-Comique in Paris.

## 8 DECEMBER 1921

On his first American tour, the prime French organist Marcel Dupré improvises at the Wanamaker organ in Philadelphia a complete *Symphonie-Passion* in four movements, on six themes offered by musicians in the audience. (The improvisation was subsequently written down and performed in a definitive form at Westminster Abbey, London, on 9 October 1924)

## 10 DECEMBER 1921

*La Leggenda di Sakuntala,* opera in three acts by Franco Alfano, to a libretto from the 5th-century play by Kalidasa, the Shakespeare of India, centered on a marine girl searching for the father of her child, finding it was the King and becoming the Queen, to a conventionally orientalized score with serpentine melodies and free rhythms within the framework of modernistic harmonies, is performed for the first time in Bologna.

## 16 DECEMBER 1921

Sergei Prokofiev appears as soloist with the Chicago Symphony Orchestra in the world première of his *Third Piano Concerto* in C Major, in three movements:

(1) *Andante—Allegro* opening with a very Russian songful theme and then suddenly attacking the keyboard in a vehement exercise of the whitest C major scales and arpeggios with a maximum of cumulative effect (2) *Theme and Variations,* based on a lyric melody notated in 1913, lending itself to flowing and translucid transformations (3) *Allegro ma non troppo,* a precipitous rondo charged with animal vitality alternating with romantically colored thematic episodes and ending in an irresistibly rhythmical display of optimistically impeccable C major, Prokofiev's favorite pianistic tonality.

## 16 DECEMBER 1921

Camille Saint-Saëns, French composer, the Victor Hugo of music, apostle of clarity and immediacy of communication, prolific creator of operas, symphonies, concertos and other works that endure in posterity despite their essentially neutral esthetic quality, universal musician, virtuoso pianist and organist, cultured writer and occasional poet, dies at his winter home at Hôtel de l'Oasis in Algiers, at the age of eighty-six.

Il est possible d'être aussi musicien que Saint-Saëns, mais il est impossible de l'être davantage (Liszt)

## 23 DECEMBER 1921

*Krazy Kat,* an orchestral suite from the "jazz pantomime" by John Alden CARPENTER, inspired by the famous newspaper comic strip, in which the misspelled cat, "Don Quixote and Parsifal rolled into one," is driven to madness by a bouquet of catnip presented with malice aforethought by an impudently aggressive mouse, set to music replete with jazzy inflections, constituting the first such jazzification of a piece of concert music, is performed for the first time by the Chicago Symphony Orchestra, Frederick Stock conducting.

## 25 DECEMBER 1921

Hans HUBER, foremost Swiss symphonist of Switzerland, music educator and teacher of a generation of Swiss musicians, dies in Locarno at the age of sixty-nine.

## 26 DECEMBER 1921

La Scala of Milan, closed since 1917, reopens with a performance of Verdi's *Falstaff* conducted by Arturo TOSCANINI.

## 30 DECEMBER 1921

Sergei PROKOFIEV conducts in Chicago the world première of his opera in four acts *The Love for Three Oranges,* fashioned after the 18th-century comedy of Carlo Gozzi wherein a hypochondriac prince is doomed to fall in love with three gigantic oranges which he pursues to the end of the earth and in one of them finds a beautiful princess, the dream of his life since infancy, whom, after many a tragicomic peripeteia, in which the spectators placed in a loge participate, he happily marries, set to a musical score compactly filled with energetic grotesqueries alternating with moments of lyric exuberance, and containing a march destined to become Prokofiev's most popular creation, ending on an assertively positivistic C major triad.

The music of Love for Three Oranges is, I fear, too much for this generation. After intensive study and close observation at rehearsals and performances, I detected the beginnings of two tunes. . . . For the rest of it, Mr. Prokofiev might well have loaded up a shotgun with several thousand notes of varying lengths and discharged them against the side of a blank wall. (Edward Moore, *The Chicago Tribune,* 31 December 1921.)

# ꙮ *1922* ꙮ

## 9 JANUARY 1922

*Four Orchestral Pieces,* a suite by Béla BARTÓK, in four movements, *Preludio, Scherzo, Intermezzo* and *Marcia funebre,* composed in 1912 and orchestrated in 1921, is performed for the first time by the Philharmonic Society in Budapest, under the direction of Ernst von Dohnányi.

### 10 JANUARY 1922

Thomas WILFRED presents in New York the first demonstration of his CLAVILUX, an instrument which throws colors on a screen according to the key struck on the keyboard, thus correlating the visual and auditory sensations.

### 17 JANUARY 1922

Ferruccio BUSONI addresses an open letter to the editor of the modern-minded German magazine *Melos*, expressing his strong views against excesses in modern music:

When a physician recommends wine to a patient, he does not intend to make him drunk. Anarchy is not liberty. Liberality must not become libertinism, and free love must not be turned into prostitution. An attractive idea does not constitute a work of art; a talented person does not become a master at once; a seed, however vigorous and fertile, is not the harvest. I do not wish to deprecate the use of novel effects in art, but I believe that such effects should be applied esthetically, with proper regard for balance and rhythm, with sonorities achieved through skill, so that a musical work in whatever idiom it is written is raised to the level of classical art in the original sense of the word as ultimate perfection.

### 20 JANUARY 1922

*Skating Rink*, "danced poem" by Arthur HONEGGER, of strongly bitonal consistency reflecting the sensual anxiety of mutual attraction and revulsion, and proceeding through a series of angularly pirouetted melorhythms to a climax when the patineur captures his patineuse "like a holocaust consuming all the beauty and intoxication of life," is performed for the first time by the Ballets Suédois in Paris.

### 23 JANUARY 1922

Arthur NIKISCH, whose passionate interpretation of German symphonic masterpieces in finely controlled performance earned for him an exalted position among conductors, dies in Leipzig at the age of sixty-six.

### 24 JANUARY 1922

Nine days after the completion of the score, Carl NIELSEN, prime modernist of Denmark, conducts in Copenhagen the first performance of his *Fifth Symphony*, in two movements:

(1) *Tempo giusto*, opening with a viola tremulating on two successive notes, A and C, upon which the conjugated wind instruments engender heterophonic patterns, leading to a pacification of emotions in *Adagio*, with a snare-drum part "to be played in its own rhythm as though intended at all costs to disrupt the music," followed by a cadenza drummed independently of the steady flow of the music elsewhere "in complete

freedom and in all possible rhythmic figures with occasional fermatas," the movement finally disintegrating into a *sotto voce* dialogue between the clarinet and the sempiternal drum (2) *Allegro,* marked by angular intervalic patterns, subsiding into an *Andante poco tranquillo,* and then returning to the initial tempo and ending in an eloquently rhetorical E-flat major epilogue.

### 26 JANUARY 1922

Luigi DENZA, Italian composer of some 500 songs and ballads, among which *Funiculi-Funicula* written to celebrate the opening of the funicular railway on Mt. Vesuvius, attained universal popularity, dies in London, where he made his home in 1879, at the age of seventy-five.

### 26 JANUARY 1922

The first performance is given in London, under the direction of Adrian Boult, of *Pastoral Symphony (Third Symphony)* by Ralph VAUGHAN WILLIAMS (completed on 25 November 1921) in four movements:

(1) *Molto moderato,* with dulcet woodwinds and a bucolic harp setting the mood while the divided strings move in parallel triadic harmonies (2) *Lento moderato,* an idyllic scene of quiet contemplation, containing solo passages by a natural trumpet in E flat and a natural French horn using non-tempered 7th and 9th partials of the harmonic series (3) *Moderato pesante,* an optimistic jig (4) *Lento,* with a wordlessly distant voice in a hexatonically transparent melodic line opening and closing the movement.

### 30 JANUARY 1922

*La Megère apprivoisée,* opera in four acts by the French composer Charles SILVER, to a libretto from Shakespeare's play *The Taming of the Shrew,* is produced at the Paris Opéra.

### 4 FEBRUARY 1922

*L'Amour en quatrième vitesse,* operetta by H. MORISSON, glorifying the automotive sport combined with love in fourth gear (overdrive), is produced at the Variétés Parisiennes, in Paris.

### 5 FEBRUARY 1922

*Concerto gregoriano* for violin and orchestra by Ottorino RESPIGHI in three movements (1) *Andante tranquillo—Allegro molto moderato* (2) *Andante expressivo e sostenuto* (3) *Allegro energico,* with the solo violin symbolizing the cantor and the orchestra the congregation, concluding on a universal Alleluia in the spirit of medieval jubilation, is performed for the first time in Rome.

### 5 FEBRUARY 1922

*Romantisches Klavierkonzert* in E major by the Viennese composer Joseph MARX, in three movements exuding the aroma of tardigrade romanticism, is performed for the first time in Vienna, Felix Weingartner conducting.

*Ciottolino,* musical fable in two acts by Luigi FERRARI-TRECATE, is produced by the Teatro dei Piccoli in Rome.

## 13 FEBRUARY 1922

PERSYMFANS (PERVYI SYMPHONICHESKY ENSEMBLE), first conductorless ensemble, opens its initial season in Moscow in a program of Beethoven's music, intent on demonstrating that in a proletarian state orchestra men do not need a musical dictator.

(The Persymfans received the nomination of an Honored Collective of the Russian Socialist Soviet Republic awarded by the Soviet Government in 1927 and continued its leaderless activities for another lustrum sans lustre, until it fell into a state of innocuous desuetude, languished and finally was discontinued in 1932, the year when militant opposition to all guidance ceased to be regarded as ideologically correct, and when once more conductors, wearing full dress and white ties, assumed their imperious attitudes and privileges on the podium.)

## 14 FEBRUARY 1922

*Giulietta e Romeo,* opera in three acts by Riccardo ZANDONAI, to Shakespeare's tragedy, supplemented by interpolations from Italian versions of the story, set in a harmoniously euphonious manner, replete with chromatic progressions of diminished seventh-chords, the "accorde di stupefazione" of the Italian operatic stage, is produced in Rome.

## 14 FEBRUARY 1922

*The Two Sisters,* opera in three acts by the English composer Cyril ROOTHAM, based on the Scottish ballad *The Twa Sisters o'Binnorie,* telling the bleak tale of a maid of the moors who drowns her sister to take possession of her fiancé, but goes mad at her wedding when a minstrel plays a threnody on a harp strung with the dead girl's hair, is produced in Cambridge.

## 25 FEBRUARY 1922

*Carnaval des Animaux,* "grande fantaisie zoologique" by Camille SAINT-SAËNS, scored for two pianos, strings, flute, clarinet, harmonium, xylophone and celesta, in 14 colorful tableaux illustrating the lions, hens and a rooster, hémiones, turtles (portrayed by Offenbach's cancan in multiple augmentation), elephants (pachydermic borborygmuses in the basses derived from *La Valse des Sylphes* of Berlioz), kangaroos, an aquarium, a "personage with long ears," a cuckoo, an aviary, pianists (treated as an animal species in a run of mindless scales), fossils, and the cellifluous swan, followed by a rollicking finale, originally composed in 1886, receives the first public hearing in its entirety at the Concerts Colonne in Paris, under the direction of Gabriel Pierné, two months and nine days after the composer's death. (Saint-Saëns forbade public performances of the *Carnaval des Animaux* during his lifetime, with the sole exception of *The Swan.*)

### 4 MARCH 1922

*Symphonie en Si bémol,* second symphony by Albert ROUSSEL, in three movements: *Introduction et Allegro, Scherzo, Adagio et final,* suggesting the three stages of man—youthful aspirations, emotional gaiety and disillusioned age—and set in a neo-classical idiom, with tritonally oriented melodies within quartal and quintal harmonies propelled by asymmetric syncopation, is performed for the first time in Paris.

### 7 MARCH 1922

*The Rose of Stamboul,* operetta in three acts by the Austrian composer Leo FALL, with additional songs by Sigmund Romberg, depicting in rousing melodies the adventures of a companionate international girl on the banks of the Bosporus, is performed for the first time in New York City.

### 9 MARCH 1922

*Olivier le Simple,* lyric drama in three acts by the Belgian composer Victor VREULS, his first opera, to a libretto in which the simple-minded knight Olivier is bewitched by the oriental charms of a captive girl brought back by the crusaders in the 13th century, and, against the insistent advice of his family and his fiancée, flees with her to her distant home in the mysterious East, set to music in a dramatically Gallic manner with a patina of conventional exoticisms, is produced in Brussels.

### 14 MARCH 1922

*Vina (Guilt),* opera in three acts by the Czech composer Otakar ZICH, is produced in Prague.

### 16 MARCH 1922

*English Suite No. 3* by the 46-year-old English composer Havergal BRIAN, in five folkloric movements (*Ye Ancient Village, Morris Dance, Postillions, The Stone-Breaker, The Merry Peasant*), written in a modernistically Straussian vein flaunting its incongruity with English dance rhythms, is performed for the first time in Bournemouth, England.

### 18 MARCH 1922

*La Figlia del Rè,* opera in three acts by Adriano LUALDI, to his own libretto depicting the mystical and amorous career of a Hindu princess and abounding in episodes of exotic color set in effective Italianate forms, is produced in Turin.

### 19 MARCH 1922

*A Vajda Tornya (The Tower of the Voivod),* opera in three acts by the Hungarian composer Ernst von DOHNÁNYI, to the subject of a clash between a powerful Valachian chieftain and the oppressed masses of the countryside, is produced in Budapest.

## 23 MARCH 1922

*Requiem* for chorus and orchestra by Frederick DELIUS, composed in 1914–1916 "to the memory of all young artists fallen in the war" to a text in German, with Latin interpolations from Ecclesiastes, set to music in an effective romantic idiom, with spacious harmonies in minor modes projected against austerely receding chromatic bases forming terse dissonances, comes to a belated first performance in London.

## 26 MARCH 1922

Selim PALMGREN, Finnish composer in the tradition of Grieg and Sibelius, plays the piano part in the world première of his *Metamorphoses* (*Third Piano Concerto*) with the Minneapolis Symphony Orchestra.

## 26 MARCH 1922

*Sancta Susanna,* one-act opera by Paul HINDEMITH, for two large singing roles (and a minuscule third), two speaking parts, a female chorus and orchestra, to a mystical libretto wherein a youthful nun, known as Saint Susan for her constant piety, strips the loincloth from the figure on a Crucifix as a spider crawls down her neck and reveals herself as the spiritual sister of another nun who was immured in a corner of the cathedral for a similar offense long before, set to music in a neo-ecclesiastical vein making use of authentic Gregorian chants in dissonant counterpoint, with flutes offstage and celesta limning the intoxicating sensuality of the secular world outside while a sustained C-sharp in the organ part suggests the singleness of the nun's idolatrous obsession, is produced for the first time in Frankfurt.

## 27 MARCH 1922

*The Flaming Arrow,* one-act opera by the abecedarian American composeress Mary Carr MOORE, is produced in San Francisco.

## 29 MARCH 1922

*San Francesco d'Assisi,* mystery play by Gian Francesco MALIPIERO, for solo voices, chorus, and orchestra, completed on 25 May 1921, in four linked sections illustrative of the life of St. Francis, set in a translucidly diatonic idiom, symbolic of his vows of animistic asceticism, with deep pedal points expressive of the profundity of his religious conscience, is performed for the first time anywhere in New York.

## 1 APRIL 1922

*Amadis,* opera in four acts by Jules MASSENET, dealing with a cenobite knight who dreams about a distant Saxon princess, flees his monastic cell to contend in a tournament for her hand, and after mortally wounding his opponent recognizes in him his long-lost twin brother, but marries the princess and participates in the repulsion of Danish invaders from the British coast, is produced posthumously in Monte Carlo.

1 APRIL 1922

The Benedictine monks of Solesmes, restorers of authentic Gregorian usage in French ecclesiastical practice, return to their Solesmes home after twenty-one years of virtual exile on the Isle of Wight.

1 APRIL 1922

*Ta Bouche,* operetta by Maurice YVAIN, centering on a rich American tourist who could submit dispassionately to any feminine enchantments, but could not remain indifferent to French kisses on the mouth, is produced in Paris.

7 APRIL 1922

*First Symphony* by the 26-year-old American composer Leo SOWERBY, in three movements marked *With Restless Energy, With Quiet Languor* and *With Triumphal Sweep,* is performed for the first time by the Chicago Symphony Orchestra, Frederick Stock conducting.

11 APRIL 1922

The New York Philharmonic Orchestra makes its first recording for the Victor Co., with Willem Mengelberg conducting Beethoven's *Coriolan* Overture on two 12-inch single-faced discs.

13 APRIL 1922

*La bella addormentata nel bosco,* operatic fairy tale for marionettes, by Ottorino RESPIGHI, to the perennially alluring subject of a beauty sleeping in the woods, is produced in Rome by the imaginative puppeteer Vittorio Podrecca and his Teatro dei Piccoli, with the singers off stage.

21 APRIL 1922

*Second Symphony* by the American composer Frederick S. CONVERSE, written in a consolidated Brahmsogenic idiom, in three competent movements expressive of "suffering, resolute defiance and solace in hope," is performed for the first time by the Boston Symphony Orchestra.

21 APRIL 1922

Alessandro MORESCHI, the last of the *castrati,* whose voice was of such celestial purity that he became known as *l'Angelo di Roma,* dies in Rome at the age of sixty-three.

24 APRIL 1922

The Austrian Post Office issues a series of stamps with portraits of BEETHOVEN (7½ kronen), BRUCKNER (25 kronen), HAYDN (2½ kronen), MOZART (5 kronen), SCHUBERT (10 kronen), Johann STRAUSS (50 kronen) and Hugo WOLF (100 kronen.)

## 25 APRIL 1922

*La Fiamminga,* last opera, in one act, by the 43-year-old Italian composer Stefano DONAUDY, is performed for the first time in Naples.

## 29 APRIL 1922

*First Symphony* by Georges MIGOT, subtitled *Agrestides* and extolling the pleasures of rural life, is performed for the first time in Paris.

## 4 MAY 1922

At its convention in Rochester, New York, the Society of St. Gregory of America issues a "Black List" of music regarded as unsuitable for performances at sacred services of the Catholic Church. (See complete Index Expurgatorius in LETTERS AND DOCUMENTS section)

## 9 MAY 1922

*Hagoromo,* choreographic symphony by Georges MIGOT is performed for the first time in Monte Carlo.

## 10 MAY 1922

Othmar SCHOECK, foremost lyric composer of Switzerland, conducts in Zürich the first performance of his three-act opera *Venus,* after a tale of Prosper Merimée set in Paris in 1820, wherein a newly unearthed ancient statue of Venus materializes as an ectoplasmic apparition between the bridegroom and his bride on their wedding night effectively preventing the consummation of their marriage, and crushes him to death in her marmoreal embrace, set to music in a lyrico-dramatic vein of romantic opera.

## 12 MAY 1922

*Scaramouche,* "tragic pantomime" by Jan SIBELIUS, composed in 1913, to a scenario in which Scaramouche is stabbed by Blondelaine, the dancing wife of a cardiac sufferer who dies of emotional upset, as does Blondelaine herself, is performed for the first time in Copenhagen.

## 13 MAY 1922

*Hagith,* one-act opera by the prime modernist of Poland Karol SZYMANOWSKI, to a dramatic libretto paralleling the Biblical story of David and his last untouched concubine Abishag, wherein a young country damsel, summoned to the royal palace to give the dying King the comfort of her bodily warmth, becomes enamored of the heir to the throne and lets the old King die, in consequence of which impiety she is stoned to death at the orders of the priests, set to music in turbulent modernistic harmonies and coloristic orchestration, is performed for the first time in Warsaw.

## 18 MAY 1922

*Renard,* "a fable about a fox, a rooster, a cat and a ram, a merry spectacle with singing and music after popular Russian fairy tales" by Igor STRAVINSKY (completed by him in Morges, Switzerland, on 1 August 1916, "at noon, under cloudless skies"), in which the proverbially wily fox is outfoxed and garroted with his own tail by animals it has tried to trap, with dancers and jugglers miming the action, while the parts for the four animals are sung in the orchestra pit by two tenors and two basses, set to music in astringent dissonant harmonies, apocopated meters and angular rhythms, profoundly Russian in intervalic construction within a hexachordal diatonic range, is performed for the first time by Diaghilev's Ballet Russe in Paris. (In the earlier editions of *Music Since 1900*, the date of the first performance of *Renard* is given as 3 June 1922; and the same erroneous date is cited in Stravinsky's *Autobiography*, in Loewenberg's *Annals of Opera*, and in a number of other reference works)

### 20 MAY 1922

*Staerstikkeren*, opera by the Danish composer Fini Valdemar HENRIQUES, is produced in Copenhagen.

### 21 MAY 1922

*Doktor Eisenbart* (*Doctor Iron Beard*), opera in three acts by the German composer Hermann ZILCHER, dealing with a medical charlatan who guarantees the birth of a male heir to a childless ducal couple in Germany circa 1680, and is sentenced to hang when no pregnancy results from his ministrations, but is saved from the gallows when the duchess reveals that her gestation period is elephantine in duration, set to music in an infra-modern idiom containing a modicum of prophylactic dissonances, is performed in a double premiere on the same day in Leipzig and Mannheim.

### 23 MAY 1922

*Deevi un Cilveki* (*Gods and Men*), opera in four acts on a subject from Egyptian mythology by the foremost Latvian composer Jānis MEDIŅŠ, is produced in Riga in the Latvian language.

### 27 May 1922

A century has passed since the birth of Joseph Joachim RAFF, once revered German composer of expertly manufactured symphonies exuding the romantic spirit from every contrapuntal pore.

### 28 MAY 1922

*Der Zwerg*, one-act opera by Alexander ZEMLINSKY, after Oscar Wilde's story *The Birthday of the Infanta*, in which the court dwarf dances himself to death to please the Infanta on her 16th birthday, is produced in Cologne.

### 3 JUNE 1922

*Mavra*, comic opera in one act by Igor STRAVINSKY after Pushkin's poem *A House in Colomna*, dealing with an amorous hussar who disguises himself as a *cuisinière* and is hired by his sweetheart's mother, with a catastrophic denouement when he is surprised while shaving and thus exposed as an intruding transvestite, set to music in a typical Stravinskian neo-Russian manner, marked by lyrical ariosos in compact pandiatonic harmonies with off-base basses, is produced by the Diaghilev Ballet Russe in Paris, on the same bill with *Renard*, *Pétrouchka* and *Le Sacre du Printemps*. (A private performance of *Mavra* was first presented at the Hotel Continental in Paris on 29 May 1922)

### 6 JUNE 1922

*Smrt majke Jugovića* (*Death of the Mother of the Brothers Jugović*), symphonic poem by the Yugoslav composer Miloje MILOJEVIĆ (1884–1946), inspired by a legend of the savage battle of Kosovo Pole in 1389 in which the Turks slew countless Slavs, and its aftermath when the mother of nine Serbian soldiers finds their bodies, with a grisly addendum as two black ravens bring her the hands of her youngest son, causing her death from supernumerary horror, all this immersed in a plasma of chronic chromatics mitigated by scoriaceous and vesicular diatonic cavities and interspersed with thematic leading motives, is performed for the first time in Belgrade.

### 13 JUNE 1922

A two-day festival of *Cante Hondo*, or *Canto Jondo*, or Flamenco (literally, "Flemish"), or gypsified music, of southern Spain, with its characteristically deciduous Phrygian cadences, accompanied by the onomatopeic ejaculation "Olé" (corrupted from Allah, indicative of Moorish influence), organized by the Spanish poet Federico GARCÍA LORCA and Manuel DE FALLA, opens in the Alhambra, in Granada.

### 11 JULY 1922

The Hollywood Bowl, open-air auditorium built in a natural canyon in the Los Angeles area, is inaugurated with a symphonic concert conducted by the bearded German conductor Alfred HERTZ.

### 11 JULY 1922

*The Shepherds of the Delectable Mountains*, "pastoral episode" by Ralph VAUGHAN WILLIAMS, his first operatic work, after John Bunyan's classic *The Pilgrim's Progress*, is performed for the first time in London. (The music was later incorporated in his full-scale opera *The Pilgrim's Progress*, produced in London on 26 April 1951)

### 30 JULY 1922

The Second Chamber Music Festival for the Promotion of Contemporary Music, organized by the Gesellschaft der Musikfreunde in Donaueschingen, presents two Sunday concerts consisting of first performances of works by young composers:

Morning concert: *Symphonic Music for 9 Solo Instruments* in an abstract formalistic idiom with masterly technique by 21-year-old Ernst KRENEK; *Michelangelo Lieder* by the German composer Edmund SCHRÖDER; *Fuga Grotesca* for string quartet by the German composer Rudolf DINKEL; *Quintet* in a Reger-like linear idiom by the German composer Richard ZÖLLNER; and *Trio-Sonata* for violin, viola and piano in a competent contrapuntal style by the Austrian-born Reger disciple Hermann GRABNER.

Evening concert: *String Quartet* by Bernard VAN DIEREN, philosophical Dutchman living in London, set in a neo-Flemish polyphonic style; *Clarinet Sonata* by the 28-year-old Swiss-Italian composer Reinhold LAGUAI; *Lieder* by the Prussian composer Hans VON DER WENSE, and *Sextet* for clarinet, string quartet and piano, in one condensed movement, rhythmically and atonally advanced in the direction of Schoenberg's ideals by the Viennese composer Felix PETYREK.

### 31 JULY 1922

On the second day of concerts of the Chamber Music Festival at Donaue-schingen, the following program of new chamber music works is given:

*Quintet* for oboe, clarinet, violin, viola and cello by the German composer Max BUTTING, set in a polyphonically elaborate neo-classical style; *String Quartet* by the Bohemian-born German-influenced polyphonist Fidelio FINKE; and the first performance of the thematically concise, contrapuntally heterotonal *Kammermusik No. 1* for chamber orchestra by the 26-year-old master of modern German music, Paul HINDEMITH. (Programs and dates from the Donaueschingen issue of the *Neue Musik-Zeitung* of 20 July 1922)

### 3 AUGUST 1922

The first artificially contrived sound effect on radio is introduced at Station WGY in Schenectady with the aid of two strips of wood slapped together to imitate a door slammed in anger. (Date from an article by Lucille Fletcher in *The New Yorker*, 13 April 1940)

### 3 AUGUST 1922

*Flor de Nieve*, opera by the Argentine composer Constantino GAITO, to the story of a 16-year-old Italian Gypsy girl, nicknamed a snow flower, who is accused by the villagers of ruining the harvest by black magic, and is stoned to death, expiring in the arms of her faithful suitor, is produced at the Teatro Colón in Buenos Aires.

### 7 AUGUST 1922

The First International Festival of Contemporary Music opens in Salzburg with the following program:

*Five Songs* by Richard STRAUSS; a militantly hedonistic polytonal *Sonata* for flute, oboe, clarinet and piano by the 29-year-old Darius MILHAUD; a *Lied*, with flute and piano, by the Austrian composer Joseph MARX, set in a traditional neo-romantic idiom; a neo-classical pandiatonic *Passacaglia* for piano by the Austrian composer Felix PETYREK; *Rout*, a linguistically modernistic futuristic piece by Arthur BLISS for soprano and ten instruments to a text consisting of meaningless but phonetically sonorous syllables; and *Sonata No. 1* for violin and piano by Béla BARTÓK, in three movements, a rhapsodically oriented *Allegro appassionato,* a speculative *Adagio* with a long atonal recitative by the solo violin, and the stormy *Allegro molto,* in stamping Hungarian rural rhythms, percussively accentuated and heterotonally harmonized.

## 8 AUGUST 1922

Two concerts of modern chamber music take place in the course of the First Festival of Contemporary Music in Salzburg:

In the morning concert: *Quintet* for woodwind and piano by Albéric MAGNARD, performed in commemoration of his tragic death eight years before at the outset of World War I; songs by Gian Francesco MALIPIERO, Ildebrando PIZZETTI and Mario CASTELNUOVO-TEDESCO; *Six Impromptus* for piano by 23-year-old French modernist Francis POULENC, played by the composer himself; *Piano Rag Music* by Igor STRAVINSKY (composed on 28 June 1919), a stylized piece of American pre-jazz syncopation; *Syrinx,* DEBUSSY's heretofore unpublished composition for unaccompanied flute rhapsodically reciting in Grecian modalities, billed on the program under the title *La Flûte de Pan* (it was Pan who invented the musical pipe of seven reeds which he named Syrinx in memory of the nymph of that name whom he loved and who was changed into a reed to help her escape him); *Sonata* for two flutes by the master composer of France Charles KOECHLIN, set in a Baroque manner; three songs from RAVEL's cycle *Mélodies populaires grecques;* five songs by Manuel DE FALLA and *Rapsodie* for two flutes, clarinet and piano by Arthur HONEGGER, written in a lyrically expansive idiom marked by broad cantilena, acrid harmonies and propulsive rhythm.

In the evening concert: *Sonata* for violin and piano by the Danish neo-romanticist Carl NIELSEN; four songs by the Swedish composer Ture RANGSTRÖM; *Gaspard de la Nuit,* piano suite by Maurice RAVEL, in three movements of extraordinary illustrative brilliance and impressionistic evocation, entitled *Ondine, Le Gibet* and *Scarbo; Sonatina* for piano by Ferruccio BUSONI; *Tantris le bouffon* for piano by the Polish modernist Karol SZYMANOWSKI; *String Quartet* by Schoenberg's disciple Egon WELLESZ; a pleasing burlesque for piano, entitled *Marionettes,* by Fidelio FINKE; 5 *Sätze für Streichquartett,* op. 5, by Anton von WEBERN, composed in 1909, a set of aphoristic and laconic essays for string quartet (the middle piece, a *Scherzo,* takes only 35 seconds to play), in a sharply atonalized idiom in which the generating chromaticism is inverted so as to form intervalic progressions in major sevenths, and dynamic range extended from the faintest pianissimo to the most thundering triple forte, while the technical applications include swiftly changing effects of virtuoso performance; and a poetically impressionistic *Sonata* for violin and piano by the Dutch composer Willem PIJPER.

Anton von Webern appears. I never saw an angrier man; he is about 35, dry and thin, as though pickled in perennial fury, and erect as a ramrod. It was amusing to see him face up to each of the four executants of his five pieces for string quartet, as if he were going to kill them, then relent, wring his hands bitterly, glare defiance at the audience, and rush off stiffly into the artists' room. Thereupon, one suddenly became aware of the sixth furious man (who I subsequently learned was an architect and stone-deaf), passionately reproaching the audience, and more especially a certain Kapellmeister there present, for laughing and spoiling everything. Most ungrateful, since but for those ever-recurring scenes, the school, whom no one takes seriously except Schoenberg, would have fizzled out long ago. Webern's five pieces follow his very subjective formula. One long-drawn note on the bridge of the first violin (pause); a tiny scramble for viola solo (pause); a pizzicato note on the cello. Then another pause, after which the four players get up very quietly, steal away and the thing is over. And now, snorts and laughter are heard in the audience, while four furious admirers clap and yell amid not ill-natured giggles. (*Daily Telegraph,* London, 9 September 1922)

### 9 AUGUST 1922

A "Viennese Matinée" is given in the course of the Salzburg Festival of Contemporary Music in a program of songs and chamber music by the modernists of Vienna: Walter KLEIN, Ernst KANITZ, Hugo KAUDER, Egon LUSTGARTEN, Carl HORWITZ, Karl ALWIN, Wilhelm GROSZ and Karl WEIGL, all writing in an idiom marked by neo-romantic subjectivism, retaining the native predilection for ternary form and waltzing rhythms.

### 9 AUGUST 1922

At the evening concert of the Salzburg Festival for Contemporary Music, the following program of chamber music is presented:

Piano music by Joseph MARX, Adolfo SALAZAR, Manuel DE FALLA and Egon KORNAUTH; *Odelette* by Dame Ethel SMYTH; Ernest BLOCH's *Schelomo* for cello, played with piano accompaniment, since an orchestra could not be had; *Second String Quartet* in three movements—*Allegro, Lento, Vivace*—by 26-year-old Paul HINDEMITH, written in an acutely chromaticized melodic idiom but maintaining a translucidly diatonic triadic substratum; and *Violin Sonata* in three movements by Ernest BLOCH, written in 1920, and set in a highly personal, strongly rhythmic and tangentially bitonal idiom combining the tonics of two polar major triads at a tritone's distance.

### 10 AUGUST 1922

The Salzburg Festival of Contemporary Music concludes with two concerts of modern chamber music, in the morning and in the evening:

Morning concert: *Serenade* for two violins and viola by the foremost master of national Hungarian music Zoltán KODÁLY; four songs with violin obbligato by Gustav HOLST; a song by the English composer Gerrard WILLIAMS; three songs by Arnold BAX; *Sonata* for violin and piano by the American composer Leo SOWERBY; two songs by the Danish neo-romantic composer Poul SCHIERBECK; *Summer,* a song by the Danish neo-classicist Ebbe HAMERIK; *Nod,* for voice with string quartet by the English composer Armstrong GIBBS, performed coincidentally on his 33rd birthday; and two songs with string quartet by Eugene GOOSSENS.

Evening concert: *Variations and Fugue on a Theme by Schumann* for piano by the German contrapuntist Guido BAGIER; *Molly on the Shore,* a stylized dance tune by the Australian composer Percy GRAINGER, arranged for string quartet; six songs by the Austrian composer of vanguard ideas, Rudolf RETI; three songs for voice and string quartet by the scholarly Viennese modernist Paul A. PISK; songs by the Czech composers Jaroslav KŘIČKA and Ladislav VYCPÁLEK; and *Second String Quartet* by Arnold SCHOENBERG.

It seems almost incredible that one can have heard so much music in four days, but the programs are there to vouch for it: Fifty-four composers of fifteen different nationalities! If we include Strauss who arrived later to conduct the Mozart operas, there were more than twenty composers present. Beginning at 7 o'clock, not any of the evening concerts were over before ten, and the matinees, at the unearthly hour of half past ten, made it difficult to keep luncheon appointments at one. Twenty hours of music! (Edwin Evans, *Musical Times*, London, September 1922)

### 11 AUGUST 1922

At a meeting held after the conclusion of the Salzburg Festival of Contemporary music, a resolution was unanimously brought out to organize a permanent body for the promotion of modern music, to be named International Society for New Music, with the central office in London and branches in all musical capitals of the world, with Edward J. Dent as President.

The plan is that in each country either an existing body, or one to be created for the purpose, shall draw all those interested in new music, that is to say contemporary music, regardless of tendency. These national organizations pledge themselves to mutual aid by the transmission of information, of books and music, of programs, and of anything further that appears likely to spread the knowledge of contemporary music . . . Each of them will elect a delegate to the committee of the International Society for New Music as the new concern is to be called. There will be an annual Festival, provisionally at Salzburg. Wherever it takes place, it will be under the control of the International, which will, however, delegate to the local section the duty of technical organization (Edwin Evans, *Musical Times*, London, September 1922)

### 12 AUGUST 1922

*Escenas Argentinas*, symphonic suite by the Argentinian composer Carlos LOPEZ-BUCHARDO, consisting of three authentically ethnic native soundscapes *Día de Fiesta*, *El Arroyo*, and *La Campera*, is conducted in a world premiere by Felix Weingartner in Buenos Aires.

### 15 AUGUST 1922

Lukas Fuchs, later destined to gain modernistic fame in America and the world under the anglicized name Foss, is born in Berlin.

### 19 AUGUST 1922

Felipe PEDRELL, the "Spanish Wagner" who entertained Wagnerian ideas of music drama and who attempted to compose an operatic cycle of Nibelungan dimensions, enlightened music scholar and pioneer of theoretical Spanish nationalism in his conviction that all true art ought to derive its essential inspiration from folk music, teacher of Manuel de Falla and Isaac Albéniz, who brilliantly carried out his lofty ideals, dies in Barcelona at the age of eighty-one.

### 26 AUGUST 1922

*Alkestis*, opera after Euripides, by Rutland BOUGHTON, is produced in Glastonbury, England, at a theater founded by himself in the forlorn hope of establishing a British Bayreuth.

**7 SEPTEMBER 1922**

Arthur BLISS conducts at the Three Choirs' Festival in Gloucester, England, the first performance of his *Colour Symphony*, in four sections representing four heraldic colors:

(1) *Purple,* the color of amethysts, pageantry, royalty, and death, proudly imperial in its neo-Handelian mantle, parading sonorously in triadic harmonies (2) *Red,* the color of rubies, wine, revelry, furnaces, courage, and magic, compulsively discordant, then subsiding into pastoral contemplation (3) *Blue,* the color of sapphires, deep water, skies, loyalty, and melancholy, aquatically impressionistic, containing a Falstaffian marching waltz (4) *Green,* the color of emeralds, hope, joy, youth, spring, and victory, melorhythmically involute in the spiral patterns of the music, with rich basses descending chromatically towards the ultimate synthesis of the complementary colors of the preceding movements, the color of White, symbolized by the unpigmented key of C major, and ending triumphantly on the parapandiatonically lucid chord of the tonic sixth.

**15 SEPTEMBER 1922**

*Pierozzo,* lyric poem in two parts by Luigi FERRARI-TRECATE, is produced in Alexandria.

**11 OCTOBER 1922**

*Il Barbiere di Siviglia,* lyric comedy in three acts by the Italian composer Leopoldo CASSONE, an attempt to create a new version of the famous Beaumarchais comedy according to the principles of the school of Verismo, is performed for the first and last time in Turin.

**13 OCTOBER 1922**

*Sedlak Jakub,* opera by the Czech composer and conductor Oskar NEDBAL, is performed for the first time in Brno.

**19 OCTOBER 1922**

Serge KOUSSEVITZKY conducts in Paris the first performance of MUSSORGSKY's graphic *Pictures at an Exhibition* in the orchestration of Ravel, specially commissioned by Koussevitzky for the sum of 10,000 francs, magically scored with coruscating aptness, as exemplified by the use of a lumbering tuba solo to represent a slow-moving Polish horse-wagon, and rising to a climax of sonorous magnificence in the bell-filled finale The Great Gate of Kiev. (3 May 1923 given in the earlier editions of *Music Since 1900* was not the date of the first performance)

**22 OCTOBER 1922**

*Ballade de la geôle de Reading,* first significant orchestral work by the 32-year-old French composer Jacques IBERT, in three interconnected sections, inspired by Oscar Wilde's anguished poem written during his imprisonment, and set in a correspondingly dark impressionistic idiom, in

*364*

astringent harmonies chained to immovable pedal points, and leading to the desperate conclusion that "each man kills the thing he loves" in the dim central key of F-sharp minor, is performed for the first time at the Concerts-Colonne in Paris, Gabriel Pierné conducting.

### 23 OCTOBER 1922

Mayor Curley of Boston bars Isadora DUNCAN from further appearances on the Boston stage on the grounds of immorality (she wore a transparent Grecian dress) and political outrage (she addressed the audience at Symphony Hall the night before, praising the Soviet regime and her Soviet husband, the poet Sergei Essenin).

### 2 NOVEMBER 1922

*Second Symphony* by the prime Dutch modernist Willem PIJPER (completed on 18 August 1921), in two movements separated by sixty seconds of silence: a polyharmonically tense *Allegro maestoso,* punctuated by persistent ictus of a varied monothematic motto, and *Lento molto rubato,* with chromatic convolutions in secundal harmonies, ending in an abrupt rhythmic figure, is performed for the first time by the Concertgebouw Orchestra in Amsterdam, Willem Mengelberg conducting.

### 3 NOVEMBER 1922

Jacques BIZET, son of Georges Bizet, shoots himself dead in Paris in consequence of hopeless frustrations in art, literature, music and multiple loves, succeeding only in automobilism (he was instrumental in building the first small French car, named Zèbra.)

### 3 NOVEMBER 1922

The Société des Compositeurs in France issues a protest against the attempts of visiting American jazz bands to jazz up Chopin's *Funeral March.*

### 6 NOVEMBER 1922

*Quand la cloche sonnera,* one-act opera by the French composer Alfred BACHELET, centering on the tragic dilemma of a Russian bellringer's daughter whose soldier friend waits for her on a bridge over the Niemen River which is to be blown up to stop Napoleon's invading army in 1812 at a signal given by the bell rung by her father, whose tone, a low E, becomes the crucial motto of the opera, is performed for the first time at the Opéra-Comique in Paris.

### 7 NOVEMBER 1922

On the fifth anniversary of the Soviet Revolution, "Symphony for Factory Whistles" is performed for the first time in Baku with the participation of the foghorns of the entire Caspian Fleet, all local factory sirens, two batteries of artillery, several infantry regiments, a machine-gun section, real hydroplanes, and finally choirs, with participation of spectators.

## 11 NOVEMBER 1922

The British Broadcasting Corporation commences the transmission of musical programs by wireless telephony.

## 16 NOVEMBER 1922

*Second Symphony* by Lazare SAMINSKY, subtitled *Symphony of the Summits,* and designated as being in the key of H-fridur (free major tonality on B), is performed for the first and last time by the Concertgebouw Orchestra in Amsterdam, under the direction of Willem Mengelberg.

## 23 NOVEMBER 1922

After eighteen years of intermittent litigation between the two brothers Pierre and Adolphe DEGEYTER over the authorship of the music to the *Internationale,* the song of the rising proletarian masses written in 1888, the Appellate Court in Paris decides in favor of Pierre. (Date and information from Alexandre Zévaés, *Chants révolutionnaires, l'Internationale, ses auteurs, son histoire,* in *Le Monde,* Paris, 27 April 1929)

## 23 NOVEMBER 1922

*La Tempesta,* opera by Felice LATTUADA in three acts with a prologue to a libretto from Shakespeare's play *The Tempest,* is performed for the first time in Milan.

## 4 DECEMBER 1922

*First Symphony* in E-flat major by the English composer Arnold BAX, scored for a very large orchestra, which includes the heckelphone and a sarrusophone, in three movements cast in a neo-Celtic mood and opaque harmonies, subjectively related to the horrors of war and laden with naked tritones in the thematic structure, in three movements, *Allegro moderato e feroce, Lento solenne* and *Allegro maestoso,* all set in 4/4 time with momentary excursions into other meters, is performed for the first time in London.

## 7 DECEMBER 1922

Two Chorale Preludes by BACH, *Schmücke dich, O liebe Seele* and *Komm, Gott, Schöpfer, Geist,* arranged by Arnold SCHOENBERG for large orchestra, including a triangle, celesta and glockenspiel, faithfully preserving Bach's original melody and harmony, are performed for the first time, from the manuscript, by the New York Philharmonic, Josef Stransky conducting.

## 10 DECEMBER 1922

A century has passed since the birth in Liège of César FRANCK, grandmaster of French romanticism, whose works, few in number but impeccable in the purity of style and cleanliness of harmonies maintaining a fluid course amid constant enharmonic modulations, whose influence on the French musicians maturing at the *fin de siècle* felicitously counterbalanced the Wagnerian wave, virtuoso organist and teacher of several generations of composers gathered in his classes from many lands.

## 11 DECEMBER 1922

*Isabelle et Pantalon,* two-act opera by the French composer ROLAND-MANUEL (Roland Alexis Manuel Lévy), inspired by the familiar characters and situations of the commedia dell'arte, is produced in Paris.

## 15 DECEMBER 1922

*Fantasia dos Movimentos Mixtos* for violin and orchestra by the prime composer of Brazil, Heitor VILLA-LOBOS, in three movements subtitled *Serenity, Butterfly in Sunlight* and *Contentment,* set in an impressionistic but highly individual idiom, is performed for the first time in Rio de Janeiro. (In a later version the first movement was renamed *Convulsed Soul; Serenity* was shifted to second place, a permutation which partly accounts for the general title *Fantasy of Mixed Movements*)

## 16 DECEMBER 1922

*Dèbora e Jaele,* three-act opera by Ildebrando PIZZETTI, constituting the first part of an operatic triptych (the second and the third are *Fra Gherardo* and *Lo Straniero*), written to the biblical story dealing with a patriotic maiden who seduces the hostile chieftain to ruin him but learns to love him unto death, is produced at La Scala in Milan.

## 19 DECEMBER 1922

*Fredigundis,* opera in three acts by the Austrian romantic composer Franz SCHMIDT, dealing with the mistress of a sixth-century king of the Merovingian dynasty whom she inadvertently poisons with a potion prepared by her for the queen and perishes as her golden tresses become enmeshed in the lid of his coffin, dying in the arms of her previous lover, a bishop, is produced in Berlin.

## 29 DECEMBER 1922

*Polyphème,* lyric drama in four acts by the French composer and a captain in the French Navy, Jean CRAS, in which cyclopean amourettes are developed against the oceanic sonorities of the orchestra and each situation is assigned a protoplasmic musical motto, is produced at the Opéra-Comique in Paris.

# ⊗ *1923* ⊗

## 4 JANUARY 1923

The first radio network program is given when the Boston station WNAC transmits the radio program of the New York station WEAF.

**6 JANUARY 1923**

*Fifth Symphony* by Kurt ATTERBERG is performed for the first time in Stockholm.

**8 JANUARY 1923**

MOZART's opera *The Magic Flute* is broadcast direct from a London concert hall by the British Broadcasting Corporation, marking the first wireless transmission of a complete opera.

**15 JANUARY 1923**

*Odalise et le Chèvre-pied,* ballet by Gabriel PIERNÉ, after a tale of Rémy de Goncourt, in which a young demigod demi-goat strays away from the herd and falls in love with an 18th-century damsel, is performed for the first time at the Paris Opéra.

**18 JANUARY 1923**

*Negro Rhapsody* by the 50-year-old New York-born Germanic composer Rubin GOLDMARK, based on seven Negro Spiritual themes, developed in the manner of a romantic prelude, is performed for the first time by the New York Philharmonic, Josef Stransky conducting.

**24 JANUARY 1923**

*Il Principe e Nuredho,* one-act opera by Guido BIANCHINI, is produced in Venice.

**7 FEBRUARY 1923**

*Wildflower,* musical comedy by Vincent YOUMANS, wherein a richly promiscuous heiress is restrained by the terms of the inheritance from all sexual activity for six months before the probate, is produced in New York.

**9 FEBRUARY 1923**

*Die gelbe Jacke,* romantic operetta in three acts by Franz LEHÁR, dealing with a Viennese girl of 1912 who goes to China to marry a technically polygamous mandarin, but soon becomes disenchanted with exotic living, obtains an instant oriental divorce and weds her original Viennese suitor, lieutenant of the Imperial Hussars, set to music with pseudo-Sinological pentatonic melodic patterns lending local color to a typically Viennese score, is performed for the first time in Vienna. (The operetta was revised and produced under the title *Das Land des Lächelns* in Berlin on 10 October 1929)

**15 FEBRUARY 1923**

*L'Amour masqué,* operetta by André MESSAGER, in which a Parisian amourette is unmasked at a masquerade, is produced in Paris.

## 16 FEBRUARY 1923

Bessie SMITH, archetypal blues singer, makes her first recording, *Downhearted Blues*, for Columbia Records.

## 17 FEBRUARY 1923

*La Monacella della Fontana*, one-act opera by Giuseppe MULÈ, is produced in Trieste.

## 19 FEBRUARY 1923

Jean SIBELIUS conducts in Helsinki the first performance of his *Sixth Symphony*, op. 104, in four movements:

(1) *Allegro molto moderato*, set in steady motion of thematic molecules, placidly diatonic in its Dorian mode (there is only one accidental in 62 bars), developing by simple doubling of voices paired in characteristically Sibelian thirds (2) *Allegretto moderato*, a syncopated scherzo in an increasing rhythmic frequency of 3, 6, 9 and 12 notes to a 3/4 measure (3) *Poco vivace* in the rhythm of a jig (4) *Allegro molto*, a modal rondo, in vigorous duple time, ending softly on the tonic D minor.

My *Sixth Symphony* is wild and impassioned in character, somber in its pastoral contrasts . . . The orchestra rises in a menacing roar, in which the main theme is completely drowned. (From a letter dated 20 May 1918, long before its composition was actually begun, sent by Sibelius to a friend and quoted in Karl Ekman's biography of Sibelius published in 1935)

## 22 FEBRUARY 1923

The Juilliard Musical Foundation of New York City receives a $10,000,000 fund bequeathed by Frederick A. JUILLIARD for furtherance of music education in the United States.

## 23 FEBRUARY 1923

*A Victory Ball*, fantasy for orchestra, after the poem of Alfred Noyes, by the American composer Ernest SCHELLING, "a vision of troops marching on irresistibly, inexorably . . . to victory or disaster," dedicated "to the memory of an American soldier," a macabre musicorama traversing a tragic military march, a languid tango and a mortuary waltz, with the organ "playing as many notes as possible with flat hands and arms" at the climactic point, and concluding on a distant trumpet call, is performed for the first time by the Philadelphia Orchestra, under the direction of Leopold Stokowski.

## 2 MARCH 1923

*Madame Pompadour*, operetta by Leo FALL, presenting the gay Paris of Louis XV and his legendary mistress in a rollicking Viennese manner, is produced in Vienna.

## 4 MARCH 1923

*La Primavera*, cantata for soloists, chorus and orchestra by Ottorino RESPIGHI, is performed for the first time in Rome.

## 4 MARCH 1923

*Hyperprism* by Edgar VARÈSE, 39-year-old French-born genius of new music, illustrating in abstractly expressionistic musical terms the geometric projection of a prism into the fourth dimension, athematically composed as a matrix of "organized sound" in a totality of dissonant counterpoint, scored for 9 wind instruments and 18 percussion devices and exploring extreme registers of the instrumental range, ending in fortissississimo, is performed for the first time at a concert of the International Composers' Guild in New York.

## 6 MARCH 1923

*Jardín de Oriente,* opera by Joaquín TURINA, written in a brilliant Hispanic style, is produced in Madrid.

## 9 MARCH 1923

*Le Hulla,* lyric oriental tale in four acts by the 40-year-old French composer Marcel SAMUEL-ROUSSEAU, in which a Persian polygamist dismisses his favorite wife and gives her to a *hulla,* a nominally anonymous transitional husband, who unexpectedly develops a sensual attachment for her and is sentenced to death for his failure to live up to his pledge of continence, but is saved from the gallows by the shah in plain clothes and awarded the disputed wife in permanent possession, while the original husband becomes himself a *hulla,* with flutes purring serpentine oriental melismas and drums providing an exotic ambiance, is produced at the Opéra-Comique in Paris.

## 18 MARCH 1923

*Das Rosengärtlein,* opera to his own libretto by the 48-year-old Austrian composer Julius BITTNER, with the action taking place on the banks of the Danube in the 13th century, wherein a Turkish odalisque occupying a castle on the Danube under the Ottoman Imperial rule loses her love match for the heart of the feudal castellan to a fishmaiden, is produced in Mannheim.

## 18 MARCH 1923

Sixty years after its composition, Anton BRUCKNER's *Symphony in F minor* is performed for the first time in Klosterneuburg, Germany.

## 20 MARCH 1923

*Mahit,* symphonic ballet with voices by the 40-year-old Bohemian-born Italian composer Riccardo PICK-MANGIAGALLI, is produced at La Scala in Milan.

## 31 MARCH 1923

*Marianela,* opera in three acts by the Catalan composer Jaime PAHISSA, to the story of a blind man who miraculously recovers his sight, is produced in Barcelona.

## 7 APRIL 1923

*Ciboulette*, light opera by the Venezuelan-born Parisian composer Reynaldo HAHN, dealing with a milkmaid nicknamed *ciboulette* ("little garlic girl") working in the Halles, "the belly of Paris" in 1867, who becomes an actress and wins the love of a young aristocrat of the Second Empire, set to music in an Offenbachian vein, replete with hedonistic melorhythms, is produced in Paris.

## 10 APRIL 1923

*I Compagnazzi (Companions)*, opera in one act by the 47-year-old Italian composer Primo RICCITELLI, with the action set in 15th-century Florence, wherein a company of determined young men preaching the doctrine of free sensuous love confute the obscurantic monastic penitents led by the fanatical ascetic Savonarola, written in a harmonious Italian vein contrasted with ecclesiastical chants in parsimonious counterpoint, is produced in Rome.

## 11 APRIL 1923

A group of American composers secedes from the International Composers' Guild of New York to form a League of Composers in order to gain equal representation to moderate as well as radical tendencies of modern music.

The presentation in America of contemporary music is an undertaking that has rapidly outgrown the capacities of existing musical organizations. The media recently formed to promote modern music have been adequate only to offer a special phase of the whole movement. No organization exists today which proposes to bring the entire range of modern tendencies before the public . . . It is for this purpose that the League of Composers has been organized. It believes not only that the creative artist needs contact with the public, but that the public is willing to give him a hearing . . . The League intends to encourage and give support to the production of new and significant works. It will promote the publication of new music. It will effect cooperation between composers of all nations, and it will give well planned performances of new music selected from every school. (From the *Foreword to the Season of 1923–1924* issued by the League of Composers)

## 22 APRIL 1923

*Poéme symphonique sur le nom de Gabriel Fauré* by ROGER-DUCASSE, dedicated "à mon Maître Gabriel Fauré" and based on the three musical notes in Fauré's name, F-A-E, with an insertion of G for U and D for R, is performed for the first time in Paris.

## 26 APRIL 1923

*Belfagor*, lyric comedy in two acts with a prologue and epilogue by Ottorino RESPIGHI, wherein the archdemon Belfagor, fittingly characterized in the score by the leading motive of the tritone, the medieval "diabolus in musica," is sent to earth to test the theory that wives make marriage a living hell, and flees to real hell to escape impending matrimony, with a setting of functional modernity, periodically relaxing into Italianate neo-classicism, is performed for the first time at La Scala in Milan.

### 27 APRIL 1923

*Maria,* opera in three acts written in 1904 by the Polish composer Henryk OPIEŃSKI, is produced in Poznan.

### 29 APRIL 1923

*Die Heilige Ente,* opera in three acts by the 32-year-old Austrian composer Hans GÁL, is produced in Düsseldorf.

### 29 APRIL 1923

*Il primo bacio,* one-act opera by Ruggero LEONCAVALLO, treating lightly the solemn subject of the first kiss, is produced posthumously in Montecatini.

### 3 MAY 1923

*Chant de joie,* symphonic movement for orchestra by Arthur HONEGGER, in three sections, the first and the third vigorous and joyful, the middle one meditative and lyrical, is performed for the first time in Paris, under the direction of Serge Koussevitzky.

### 3 MAY 1923

*Casanova,* opera in three acts by the 39-year-old Polish composer Ludomir RÓŻYCKI, dealing with Casanova's abduction of the Algerian Bey's favorite concubine and his subsequent affair with the mistress of the chief of police in Venice, set in a melodiously Italianate manner, is produced in Warsaw.

### 5 MAY 1923

Society of Quarter-Tone Music is organized in Petrograd under the direction of Georg RIMSKY-KORSAKOV, grandson of the composer, to promote icositetraphony in Russia.

### 13 MAY 1923

*Lucerna (The Lantern),* musical legend in four acts by the Czech composer of the modern romantic school Vitězslav NOVÁK, in which a lantern lit by a linden tree, a symbol of the feudal vassalage of a local miller, is destroyed by a pair of sympathetic male water sprites, who subsequently force the landlord to surrender his fief, set to music in a vivacious Bohemian vein, is produced in Prague.

### 14 MAY 1923

*The Perfect Fool,* one-act opera by Gustav HOLST, wherein a maleficently thaumaturgic wizard standing on top of a Stonehenge trilithon brews a potion to make himself irresistible to women, but is outwitted by a mentally retarded narcoleptic youth who drinks it first and marries a nubile princess, with two secondary characters, a Troubadour singing a Verdian aria and a Traveler intoning baleful Wagnerogenic incantations, is produced at Covent Garden in London. (A symphonic suite from *The Perfect Fool* was performed at a London concert on 11 December 1921)

The Characters of this opera (excepting the Troubadour and Traveler whose origins are obvious) belong to no particular country or period. The author asks that the spirit of high comedy shall be maintained throughout. (Gustav Holst's prefatory note in the printed score)

### 17 MAY 1923

Peter MENNIN, American composer of symphonies and oratorios written in a civilized neo-classical idiom with the application of prudential dissonances, is born in Erie, Pennsylvania, of Italian parents. (His real name was Mennini.)

### 21 MAY 1923

*Ninna nanna della bambola,* children's opera by the futuristically-minded Italian composer Francesco Balilla PRATELLA, is produced in Milan.

### 30 MAY 1923

Howard HANSON, 26-year-old American composer, conducts in Rome, during his residence there as holder of the American Rome Prize, the first performance anywhere of his *First Symphony* in E minor, surnamed *Nordic Symphony,* expressive of his intimate sentiment for the Scandinavian North of his ancestors, "its solemnity, austerity and grandeur, its restlessness and surging and strife, its somberness and melancholy," with a predilection, Sibelius-like, for the lowest reaches of the instrumental compass, in three movements: a philosophical *Andante solenne* leading to a dramatic *Allegro con fuoco,* a tenderly simple *Andante* (dedicated to his mother), and an energetic *Finale* (dedicated to his father). (The first American performance, conducted by Hanson with the Rochester Philharmonic on 19 March 1924 was erroneously listed in the previous editions of *Music Since 1900* as an absolute first performance)

### 30 MAY 1923

Camille CHEVILLARD, French conductor, son-in-law of Charles Lamoureux and his successor as permanent conductor of the famed Lamoureux concerts in Paris, dies in his native Paris at the age of sixty-three.

### 1 JUNE 1923

*Padmâvatî,* opera-ballet in two acts by Albert ROUSSEL, to a libretto based on the story of the legendary 13th-century Hindu queen who refuses to submit to the desires of a conquering Mongol khan (the instructions in the text specify that the role of Padmâvatî demands "une grande beauté physique"), stabs the wounded King to death and dies with him, ascending his funeral pyre as the frustrated invader enters the temple, set to music in acrid modern harmonies without ostentatious orientalization, is produced at the Paris Opéra.

### 4 JUNE 1923

*Fête galante,* operatic "dance dream" in one act by the foremost musical suffragette of England Dame Ethel SMYTH, is produced in Birmingham.

### 5 JUNE 1923

*Old King Cole,* ballet for orchestra and chorus by Ralph VAUGHAN WILLIAMS, to a scenario dealing with the Saxon King of Colchester whose daughter became a Roman empress and organized a music contest, is performed for the first time in Cambridge, England.

### 12 JUNE 1923

*Façade,* "an entertainment for reciting voice and instruments" by the 21-year-old English composer William WALTON, to the texts of syntactically nonsensical but syllabically meaningful blank verses by Edith Sitwell, is performed for the first time in London, with Edith Sitwell herself speaking her lines through the "sengerphone," a decorated megaphone protruding through the mouth of a monstrous head painted on the curtain. (A private performance of *Façade* was given first in the London home of Sir Osbert Sitwell, brother of Edith Sitwell, on 24 January 1922; the title *Façade* was an intrafamilial joke, Edith Sitwell being described as clever, but "only a façade")

### 13 JUNE 1923

Serge Diaghilev's Ballet Russe presents in Paris the first performance of *Les Noces,* "choreographic scenes with singing and music" by Igor STRAVINSKY (completed in Monaco on 6 April 1923), scored for chorus, vocal soloists, four pianos and 17 percussion instruments, a stylized portrayal of a Russian village wedding, to a text garnered from authentic peasant locutions, marked by asymmetrical rhythms within changing meters united by a constant mutual beat, and set in pandiatonically extended modalities in desiccated sonorities, containing two principal parts and four tableaux:

(1) *In the Bride's Room,* a ritual lamentation for the maiden about to become a bride, interrupted by other maidens proffering gratuitous encouragement in angular melodic intervals and syncopated rhythms, with the eighth-note as a metrical constant (2) *In the Bridegroom's Room,* an ode in starkly bland counterpoint suggesting a modernized organum in quartal and quintal harmonies, followed by the parental lament, in a triadic compass, with an ambivalent mediant of a fluctuating major-minor third, succeeded by a rudely intoned choral chant (3) *The Bride's Farewell,* an intense static epithalamium set against an *ostinato* within the range of a minor ninth (4) *The Wedding Repast,* a hocket in stridently dissonant counterpoint, with the metrical invariant of an eighth-note, brutalized into rhythmic speech and followed by an instrumental postlude in slow, bell-like sounds of widely spaced chords on the pianoforte.

## 14 JUNE 1923

The "École d'Arcueil" is formally organized and in all seriousness announced by Erik SATIE, a resident of Arcueil, a placid sub-Parisian village, at a Paris concert of his young admirers, Henri CLIQUET-PLEYEL, Roger DÉSORMIÈRE, Maxim JACOB and Henri SAUGUET, founding members of the new sodality dedicated to Satie's esthetic ideals.

*J'ai toujours fait crédit à la jeunesse.* (Satie's declaration at the occasion)

They chose the name "School of Arcueil" because of their affection for an old inhabitant of that suburban locality. I shall not discuss their merits, being happily neither a sycophant nor a professional critic. The public must be their critic, for it is the public that has real powers to pass judgment upon them. Personally, I am happy at the arrival of the School of Arcueil in the musical arena. They will replace the Group of Six, some of whom have already won a reputation despite the absurd attacks on them by parlor artists, envious second-raters and criticasters. (From Erik Satie's letter to Rolf de Mare, director of the Ballets Suédois in Paris)

## 17 JUNE 1923

In the course of the Third Festival of Modern Chamber Music at Donaueschingen, the first performance is given of *Das Marienleben*, cycle of 15 songs for voice and piano by 27-year-old Paul HINDEMITH, to the poems of Rainer Maria Rilke, depicting the life of Virgin Mary in diatonically lucid melodic lines against dissonant contrapuntal progressions in the piano part, conjuring up an attractive neo-medieval ambience but revealing emotional intensity beneath the austere surface of the music.

## 24 JUNE 1923

*Die Chinesische Flöte*, a chamber symphony in six sections for 14 solo instruments and soprano by Ernst TOCH, to a German version of ancient Chinese poetry, wherein Buddhist monks intone a polytonal chorale and Confucius introduces a series of aphorisms in an ascending progression of wholetone scales, is performed for the first time in Frankfurt.

## 25 JUNE 1923

In the Paris salon of the Princesse de Polignac, the first stage production is given of the marionette opera *El Retablo de Maese Pedro* by Manuel DE FALLA, after an episode in *Don Quixote* where the errant knight wrecks a little theater trying to save a noble damsel from a pack of maleficent puppet Moors, realistically including spoken parts for the director of the theater and a singing role for Don Quixote seated in the orchestra, the music palpitating with Andalusian melorhythms in a gibbous tonality astutely maintained by recurrent Phrygian cadences on a major dominant. (The first concert performance was given in Seville on 23 March 1923)

## 4 JULY 1923

*English Folk Song Suite* by Ralph VAUGHAN WILLIAMS, scored for military band, in three movements of fanciful variations on popular English ditties,

*Seventeen Come Sunday, Pretty Caroline, Dives and Lazarus, My Bonny Boy, Green Bushes, Blow Away the Morning Dew, High Germany, The Tree so High* and *John Barleycorn,* is performed for the first time in London as a commissioned work by the Royal Military School of Music.

### 4 JULY 1923

Three hundred years have passed since the death of the great Elizabethan madrigalist William BYRD.

### 13 JULY 1923

Asger HAMERIK, Danish composer of seven symphonies, four operas, two choral trilogies and other music in a respectable romantic idiom, who for 26 years (1872–1898) was director of the Peabody Conservatory of Baltimore, brother of the music historian Angul Hammerich (which is the original Germanic family surname), dies at Frederiksberg at the age of eighty.

### 13 JULY 1923

*Ilse,* opera by the Argentine composer Gilardo GILARDI, to a story of a Bavarian maiden fatefully involved in a melodramatic romance with an improvident painter, is produced at the Teatro Colón in Buenos Aires.

### 25 JULY 1923

*Sruth na Maoile (The Sea of Moyle),* one-act opera by the 40-year-old English-born Irishman Geoffrey PALMER, to a libretto founded on the Irish saga *The Children of Lir,* is produced in Dublin with the original libretto in the Gaelic language.

### 2 AUGUST 1923

The First Festival of the International Society for Contemporary Music (first, because the parent 1922 Salzburg Festival took place before the formation of the Society) opens in Salzburg with the following program of chamber music:

*String Quartet* by Alban BERG, written in 1910 in an anamnestically Wagnerian and consciously Mahlerophiliac manner and revised in 1920 under the impact of the Schoenbergian concepts, emancipated in its use of unresolved chords and independent from central tonality; Arnold SCHOENBERG's cycle of 15 songs *Das Buch der hängenden Gärten* for voice and piano, to poems by the Viennese expressionistic poet Stefan George, written in 1909 and representing the inception of the atonal period, free from key-signatures, consistently dissonant in harmonic complexes, ending on unresolved chords, and favoring the acoustically inharmonious intervals of major sevenths and tritones while avoiding all triadic implications; and *Second Violin Sonata* by Béla BARTÓK, composed in 1922, in two movements in which the melodic structure is based on the technique of octave displacement so that the semitones of the chromatic scale become intervalic leaps of major sevenths, but concluding paradoxically on a candid and purified C-major triad.

## 3 AUGUST 1923

At the second concert of the First Festival of the International Society for Contemporary Music in Salzburg, the following program of chamber music is given:

*Sonate libre en deux parties enchaînées* (*ad modum clementis aquae*) for violin and piano by Florent SCHMITT (so titled with reference to Clemenceau's newspaper originally appearing as *l'Homme Libre* and later, when censorship began to intervene, *L'Homme Enchaîné*), in two movements separated in their principal tonalities by the "diabolus in musica," the first being in G-sharp minor, the second in D minor, symbolically reflecting the diabolical horrors of the war of 1914–1918 during which it was partly written, the harmonic idiom marked by a considerable incidence of polytonality, sharpened by polyrhythmic asymmetry and melodic angularity; *Hafislieder*, a cycle of five songs by the foremost Swiss lyric composer Othmar SCHOECK, inspired by Persian poetry but devoid of ostentatious musical orientalism, performed with the composer at the piano; *Sonata for Violin Solo* by the Latvian-born German-educated romantic composer Eduard ERDMANN; songs by Yrjö KILPINEN, the "Hugo Wolf of Finland"; and *Third String Quartet* by the 22-year-old Viennese modernist Ernst KRENEK.

## 4 AUGUST 1923

At the third concert of the First Festival of the International Society for Contemporary Music in Salzburg, the following program of chamber music is presented:

*Overture on Hebrew Themes* for clarinet, string quartet and piano by Sergei PROKOFIEV, based on authentic modern Jewish songs and first performed in New York on 26 January 1920; *Délie*, a cycle of three songs by ROLAND-MANUEL; *Eine Reiterburlesque* for piano by the Czech-born German composer of lyric music, Fidelio FINKE; 2 *Hafis Songs* by Karol SZYMANOWSKI, inspired by Persian legends; 2 Songs by Manuel DE FALLA; *Duo* for violin and cello by RAVEL; *Sonatina* for flute and piano by the French-born half-German half-Catalan composer Philipp JARNACH; 2 *Sacred Songs* for voice and organ by the Viennese composer Paul A. PISK; and *First String Quartet*, written in an ingratiatingly hedonistic neo-classical idiom by the 21-year-old English composer William WALTON.

## 5 AUGUST 1923

At the fourth concert of the First Festival of the International Society for Contemporary Music in Salzburg, the following program of chamber music is presented:

Austere and somber *Sonata* for violin and piano by the foremost Czech romanticist Leoš JANÁČEK; colorful *Rhapsody* by Arthur BLISS, a nonet for soprano, tenor, flute, English horn, two violins, viola, cello and double-bass, set in an Arcadian mood with two voices vocalizing on an open syllable "Ah"; *Divertissement* for flute, oboe, clarinet, bassoon, French horn and piano by Albert ROUSSEL, written in 1906, ingeniously intertwining rhythmic strains in a kaleidoscopic variety of melodic turns in semi-impressionistic harmonies; *Sonata* for flute and harp by the Dutch composer Sem DRESDEN, in three movements inspired by folk-like melorhythms and accoutred in Debussyan harmonies, performed with the composer at the piano replacing the harp;

*Valses bourgeoises* for two pianos by the British musical wit Lord BERNERS; *New York Days and Nights* for piano solo by the American composer Emerson WHITHORNE, descriptive of the turmoil of the great city of skyscrapers with the Woolworth Building, the tallest in the world, towering over the populace riding in the new model T Ford automobiles; *Il Raggio verde* for piano by the Italian lyric composer Mario CASTELNUOVO-TEDESCO; *Three Pieces for String Quartet* by Igor STRAVINSKY, composed in 1914, and based on brief Russian-like refrains in apocopated meters, with triadic melodic conformations; and Stravinsky's *Concertino for String Quartet*, written in 1920, in one monolithic but not monothematic compressed movement, with open quartal and quintal melodic progressions set in neolithically crude harmonies.

### 6 AUGUST 1923

At the fifth concert of the First Festival of the International Society for Contemporary Music in Salzburg, the following program of chamber music is presented:

*Sonata* for viola and piano by Arthur HONEGGER; *2 Sonetti del Berni* for soprano and piano by Gian Francesco MALIPIERO; *Second String Quartet* in quarter-tones by Alois HÁBA, the Czech icositetraphonic pioneer, making use not only of quarter-tones, but also of 3/4-tones, 5/4-tones, etc., and notated with the aid of specially designed symbols; *Sonata* for violin and cello by Maurice RAVEL, in four movements, cyclically conceived and monothematically centered on an intervalic sequence of major or minor sevenths constituting the melodic inversion of consecutive notes in the chromatic and diatonic scales; and the first performance of the two-piano version of Ferruccio BUSONI's monumental *Fantasia contrappuntistica*, originally written for piano solo during his American tour of 1910 in emulation of Bach's *Kunst der Fuge*, set in 12 interdependent sections, and architectonically designed as a grandiose triptych of fugues, variations and intermezzi, extending the resources of the keyboard technique to the utmost neo-classical limits, while remaining within the larger confines of conceptual tonality.

### 7 AUGUST 1923

At the sixth concert of the First Festival of the International Society for Contemporary Music in Salzburg, the following program is presented:

*Fourth String Quartet* by Darius MILHAUD, written in an Arcadian pastoral mood, with the bucolic melodies translucidly attired in polytonal harmonies; *Promenades* for piano by Francis POULENC; *Piano Sonata* by Charles KOECHLIN; *Five Songs* by the neo-romantic German musician Manfred GURLITT for voice with chamber orchestra, the composer conducting; *Sonata* for cello solo by Zoltán KODÁLY, a tour de force of modern instrumental writing, with an ingenious and esthetically justified application of *scordatura*, with the C and G strings lowered a semitone to provide a B-minor tonic chord for basic harmony; and *Quintet* for clarinet and string quartet by Paul HINDEMITH, in five movements, of which the last is a free retrograde canon of the first.

### 10 SEPTEMBER 1923

*The Ajanta Frescoes*, ballet by Alexander TCHEREPNIN portraying the Buddha's renunciation of the world as depicted in the mural paintings in the caves of Ajanta, India, is performed for the first time in London, with Anna Pavlova in the role of the princess.

## 29 SEPTEMBER 1923

*Schwanenweiss*, opera in three acts by the German composer Julius WEISMANN, to a libretto from a play by August Strindberg, is produced in Duisburg.

## 17 OCTOBER 1923

*Doña Francisquita*, opera in three acts by the Spanish composer Amadeo VIVES, based on Lopez de Vega's comedy *La discreta enamorada*, is produced in Madrid.

## 18 OCTOBER 1923

Two world premières are given at a Koussevitzky concert in Paris:

*Octet* by Igor STRAVINSKY (conducted by him), scored for flute, clarinet, 2 bassoons, 2 trumpets and 2 trombones, marking a new turn in his creative evolution in the neo-classical direction of parsimonious economy of means, with a dynamic scheme of chiaroscuro precision, limited to stark contrasts of annunciatory forte and antiphonal piano, set in three movements of great frugality of expression and flaming frigidity of consequential exposition: (1) *Sinfonia*, opening with a reserved *Lento*, leading to a decisively styled *Allegro moderato* (2) *Tema con variazioni*, a carefully equilibrated study in controlled variants of a robust melorhythmic statement (3) *Finale*, a sturdy piece of polyphonic sonification with a terminal C major chord in second inversion; *First Violin Concerto* in D major by Sergei PROKOFIEV (performed by Marcel Darrieux, with Koussevitzky conducting), written in Russia in 1917, in three movements: (1) *Andantino*, commencing with a lyrically inflected theme for solo violin and developed with structural and emotional logic along rhapsodically drawn lines (2) *Scherzo*, constituting a characteristic display of Prokofiev's rhythmic verve and restrained irony in the intervalic saltation of the melody (3) *Moderato*, a nostalgic meditation, reverting to the elegiac mood of the initial movement and concluding with a poetic peroration.

## 25 OCTOBER 1923

*La Création du Monde*, ballet by Darius MILHAUD, to a scenario depicting the creation of the world by three Central African gods and the fashioning of primitive men out of hairy primates, the first symphonic work based on jazz rhythms and melodic inflections of the Blues, anticipating Gershwin's symphonic jazz, is produced by the Ballets Suédois in Paris.

## 25 OCTOBER 1923

Third part of *Impressioni dal Vero* by Gian Francesco MALIPIERO in three divisions: (1) *Festa in Val d'Inferno*, a bolero-like multicolored bacchanale (2) *I Galli*, a barnyard scene, with gallivanting roosters strutting in descending consecutive minor triads and nervous hens emitting explosive hockets, and (3) *La Tarantella a Capri*, symphonic exteriorization of a Dionysiac dance once believed to possess curative powers against the venomous bite of the tarantula, is performed for the first time in Amsterdam, Alfredo Casella conducting.

### 27 OCTOBER 1923

*Holofernes*, biblical opera in two acts by Emil Nikolaus von REZNIČEK, depicting the bloody deed of Judith in the decapitation of the enemy commander, is produced in Berlin.

### 31 OCTOBER 1923

*Le Jardin du Paradis*, lyric tale in four acts by Alfred BRUNEAU, fashioned after a tale by Hans Christian Andersen, dealing with a young prince whose beloved tests his faith in her by confessing untruthfully that she has once been inadvertently kissed and shocks him to such an extent that he goes to the garden of Eden to avenge his disgrace on Eve as the source of the original sin, but finds that Eve is identical with his beloved who finally consoles him by admitting her absolute immaculacy, is produced at the Paris Opéra.

### 31 OCTOBER 1923

*Mareike von Nymwegen*, opera by Eugen D'ALBERT, to a subject from a medieval Dutch folk tale, is produced in Hamburg.

### 1 NOVEMBER 1923

Hugo GERNSBACK, Luxembourg-born inventor and science fiction writer, gives a demonstration over Radio Station WJZ in New York unveiling his STACCATOPHONE, an electronic piano with vacuum tubes instead of strings, capable of producing the pitch of all 88 notes of the keyboard.

### 10 NOVEMBER 1923

*Anna Karenina*, opera in three acts by the Hungarian violinist Jenö HUBAY, based on Tolstoy's novel of sin and retribution and ending in the heroine's suicidal death under the wheels of a locomotive, set to a dramatically Wagnerogenic score with an injection of Russianized melodies as *couleur locale*, is produced in Budapest.

### 11 NOVEMBER 1923

At the inaugural concert in New York of the League of Composers, the first performance is given of Ernest BLOCH's *Quintet* for piano and string quartet, in three movements, *Agitato, Andante mistico* and *Allegro energico*, introducing quarter-tones used as "affective" devices to enhance the emotional elements of individual melodic tones, without consecutive icositetraphonic progressions, but in the manner of instantaneously close appoggiaturas, while the main thematic material is grounded in expressive cantillation and deep pedal-points.

### 11 NOVEMBER 1923

The 43-year-old English composer and conductor John FOULDS leads, on Armistice Day in London, the first performance of his oratorio *A World Requiem*, written in an aridly reverential spirit to commemorate those fallen in World War I.

*380*

## 12 NOVEMBER 1923

*Vendetta,* grand opera by the American Negro composer Harry Lawrence FREEMAN, is produced in New York.

## 15 NOVEMBER 1923

*Srdce (The Heart),* opera in two acts by the Czech composer of German extraction Josef Bohuslav FOERSTER, to his own libretto dealing with an actor who decides to devote his life to helping the poor after an unrequited love affair with a frigid-hearted young lady, is produced in Prague.

## 19 NOVEMBER 1923

On the occasion of the 50th anniversary of the union of the twin cities of Buda and Pest, three specially commissioned works by three eminent Hungarian composers are performed for the first time in Budapest:

(1) *Festival Overture* by the Hungarian academic romanticist Ernst von DOHNÁNYI (2) *Psalmus Hungaricus* for tenor, mixed chorus, children's chorus and orchestra by Zoltán KODÁLY, to an old Hungarian text adapted from the Penitential Psalms, with a pentatonic unison chant in the ancient Magyar manner as a choral ritornello, developing by cumulative accretion of contrapuntal and harmonic elements and reaching a grandiloquent expansion of astutely applied modern harmonies (3) *Five Dances* by Béla BARTÓK, composed in a folksong idiom on original themes melorhythmically derived from various national elements of southeastern Europe: oriental motives in the first and fourth dances, Magyar inflections in the second and third dances, and Gypsy refrains in the fifth dance, building a multi-colored sonic quincunx.

## 26 NOVEMBER 1923

*Bubbles,* one-act opera by the Irish composer Hubert BATH, a farce in which the bubbles of gossip are burst when a farm hand presumed to have been slain as a victim of adulterous fornication appears in the court room where his rustic inamorata is being tried for his murder, in a jigful Irish setting, is performed for the first time in Belfast, Ireland, conducted by the composer.

## 26 NOVEMBER 1923

The American barefoot dancer Isadora DUNCAN presents in Moscow a ceremonious choreographic monodrama to the music of Schubert's *Ave Maria* to celebrate the civil christening of a Communist baby girl, with the matriarch of German Communism Klara Zetkin acting as an atheistic godmother and the Soviet theorist Bukharin, who was to be shot by Stalin in 1938, as a dialectical godfather.

## 10 DECEMBER 1923

*La Brebis égarée,* "roman musical" in three acts by Darius MILHAUD, wherein the wayward wife of a lenient husband contritely returns home, like the lost sheep of the biblical parable, after a disillusioning affair with an insubstantial bravo in Spain, during which she has to undergo a prosaic operation of appendectomy, is performed for the first time at the Opéra-Comique in Paris.

### 18 DECEMBER 1923

*Scarecrow Sketches,* symphonic suite by the American composer Frederick S. CONVERSE, assembled from materials of his "photo-music-drama" *Puritan Passions,* is performed for the first time in Boston.

### 19 DECEMBER 1923

*Daisi (Twilight),* opera in three acts by the Georgian composer Zachar PALIASHVILI, dealing with the struggle for national independence in the Caucasian dukedom of Georgia in the 18th century, and making use of old native folk rhythms harmonized in the framework of Russian orientalism, is produced in Tiflis.

### 22 DECEMBER 1923

*La Dame en décolleté,* operetta in three acts by Maurice YVAIN is produced in Paris.

### 22 DECEMBER 1923

*Diana,* one-act opera by the 29-year-old Hungarian composer Eugen ZÁDOR, wherein a gruesome medieval knight slays his wife's lover and then serves her a glass of his coagulated blood as a mockery of the wine of the Eucharist, is produced in Budapest.

### 28 DECEMBER 1923

The first Hebrew opera house is opened in Tel Aviv with the intention of launching a series of classical and romantic operas in the Hebrew language.

### 31 DECEMBER 1923

*Kid Boots,* American musical comedy by Harry TIERNEY, dealing with a gifted crook and featuring (by interpolation) the famous song *Dinah* sung by Eddie Cantor, is produced in New York.

# ᕫ *1924* ᕬ

### 5 JANUARY 1924

*Faust en ménage,* operetta by Claude TERRASSE, a sequel to Gounod's opera, in which Faust marries and becomes a becalmed bourgeois, is produced in Paris.

## 6 JANUARY 1924

*Les Biches*, "ballet avec chant" by Francis POULENC, in which a bevy of human does and roes presents a succession of stylized dances, classical and new, pure and hybrid (such as Rag-Mazurka), in a musical idiom eclectically combining elements of Scarlatti, Delibes and Stravinsky, is produced in Monte Carlo by the Ballet Russe on the eve of Poulenc's 25th birthday.

## 6 JANUARY 1924

*Escales*, symphonic suite by Jacques IBERT, in three movements descriptive of his Mediterranean cruise as a winner of the Prix de Rome, with stops at three ports of call, not specifically mentioned in the printed score, but presumed to be (1) Palermo, marked *Calme-Assez animé*, suggesting a poetically humid and warmly fragrant atmosphere of Sicily followed by a sudden outburst of dancing energy (2) Tunis, *Modéré, très rythmé*, with a solitary oboe on a high minaret broadcasting his prayerful message to the faithful while drums beat distantly (3) Valencia, *Animé*, an exulting fandango full of Mauretanian vigor and Andalusian vivacity, vibrating with impressionistic colors, is performed for the first time at the Concerts Lamoureux in Paris.

## 11 JANUARY 1924

*La plus forte*, opera in four acts by Xavier LEROUX, wherein a passionate woman of the people, married to a harried tiller of the soil, engages in an affair with a sensuously supercharged youth, who turns out to be her own stepson, whereupon she hurls herself into the sea, while father and son return to their fertile earth, the "stronger one" of the title, is produced posthumously at the Opéra-Comique in Paris, in a version completed and orchestrated by Henri Busser.

## 14 JANUARY 1924

Count Géza ZICHY, Hungarian pianist who at the age of fourteen lost his right arm in a hunting accident, and subsequently became a virtuoso left-hand pianist, composed sinistro-manual piano pieces and performed a three-hand arrangement of Liszt's *Rakóczy March* with Liszt himself playing the other two hands, dies in Budapest at the age of seventy-four.

## 19 JANUARY 1924

*Les Fâcheux*, ballet after Molière's comedy, with the music by the youngest of the French Six, 24-year-old Georges AURIC, in the form of a dance suite, classical in movement and rhythm, modernistically bitonal or pandiatonic in harmony, is produced by Diaghilev's Ballet Russe in Monte Carlo. (Exact date obtained from the management of the Monte Carlo Opera)

## 26 JANUARY 1924

Alexander TCHEREPNIN plays at the Société Nationale de Musique in Paris the solo part in the first performance of his *Second Piano Concerto*, with Nadia Boulanger conducting.

## 2 FEBRUARY 1924

The sinistro-manual *Concertante Variationen über ein Thema von Beethoven* for left-hand piano and orchestra by the Austrian composer Franz SCHMIDT, based on the theme of the Scherzo from Beethoven's F-major Violin Sonata, with its pointed syncopation, is performed for the first time in Vienna, with the amputated Viennese pianist Paul Wittgenstein, for whom the work was written, as soloist. (The work was subsequently arranged in a bimanual version, and first performed in Wuppertal on 12 April 1940.)

## 9 FEBRUARY 1924

*Le Petit Elfe Ferme-l'Œil,* "une semaine dansée" by Florent SCHMITT, after Hans Christian Andersen's fairy tale, traversing seven days in a child's life and dealing with the poetic image of a little elf who closes the eyes of good children going to sleep and puts an imaginative assortment of pleasant dreams under their eyelids—mice getting married, armored knights fighting wooden soldiers, the alphabet staging a dance—but lets bad children go dreamless, to a score saturated with impressionistically opulent sonorities, is produced at the Opéra-Comique in Paris. (A concert performance was given earlier, on 1 December 1923, at the Concerts Colonne in Paris)

## 10 FEBRUARY 1924

*Věčný Návrat (Eternal Return),* "poem in music" for orchestra by the Czech romantic composer Villém PETRŽELKA, is performed for the first time in Brno.

## 12 FEBRUARY 1924

George GERSHWIN, 25-year-old Brooklyn-born composer of inspired popular songs in an authentically modern American style, appears as piano soloist in the first performance, at a concert conducted by Paul Whiteman in Aeolian Hall in New York, of his epoch-making *Rhapsody in Blue,* completed by him in piano score on 7 January 1924, and arranged for piano and a jazz-type ensemble by Ferde Grofé, the title indicating its derivation from the soulful "blues" of urban American melos, and permeated with the spirit of nostalgic Negritude, comprising the following subdivisions:

*Molto Moderato,* opening with an acrobatic clarinet climb from low F to the stratospheric B-flat, stating the principal "blue" subject in a Mixolydian mode with a lowered sixth; *Moderato assai,* with the piano presenting the principal theme in a hedonistically optimistic and virtuosistically Lisztian manner in three keys whose tonics are distanced by minor thirds—G-flat major, A major and C major—succeeded by the exposition of two new themes; *Meno Mosso e poco scherzando,* with a jazzily dancing chromatic arabesque; a recapitulation in which the principal subject appears successively in G, C and E-flat major, with a new rhapsodic theme in a hypo-Ionian hexachord, soon jazzed up along the successive degrees of the whole-tone scale; *Agitato e misterioso,* in which the 2/4 meter is subdivided into asymmetrical groups of 3/16, 3/16 and 2/16 producing an effect of natural syncopation; *Molto slendando,* insistently stressing the songful C-major theme; *Grandioso,* in an expansively Lisztian manner in which the *scherzando* motive appears in diminution, concluding with the final triumphant enunciation of the primary subject in the original key of B-flat major, with a "blue" seventh converting the major scale into a Mixolydian mode.

The audience was stirred, and many a hardened concertgoer excited with the sensation of a new talent finding its voice, and likely to say something personally and racially important to the world. A talent and an idiom, also rich in possibilities for that generally exhausted and outworn form of the classic piano concerto (Olin Downes, New York *Times,* 13 February 1924)

This music is only half alive. Its gorgeous vitality of rhythm and of instrumental color is impaired by melodic and harmonic anemia of the most pernicious kind. . . . How trite and feeble and conventional the tunes are, how sentimental and vapid the harmonic treatment, under the disguise of fussy and futile counterpoint! (Lawrence Gilman, New York *Tribune,* 17 February 1924)

He is a link between the jazz camp and the intellectuals. His *Rhapsody* had all the faults one might expect from an experimental work . . . It was crude, but it hinted at something new, something that has not hitherto been said in music. Mr. Gershwin will bear watching; he may yet bring jazz out of the kitchen. (Deems Taylor, New York *World,* 17 February 1924)

There had been so much chatter about the limitations of jazz. . . . Jazz, they said, had to be in strict time. It had to cling to dance rhythms. I resolved, if possible, to kill that misconception with one sturdy blow. Inspired by this aim, I set to work composing with unwonted rapidity. No set plan was in my mind, no structure to which my music would conform. The *Rhapsody,* as you see, began as a purpose, not a plan. At this stage of the piece, I was summoned to Boston for the première of *Sweet Little Devil.* I had already done some work on the *Rhapsody.* It was on the train with its steely rhythms, its rattlety-bang that is so stimulating to a composer. . . . I frequently hear music in the very heart of noise. And then I suddenly heard—and even saw on paper—the complete construction of the *Rhapsody,* from beginning to end . . . as a sort of musical kaleidoscope of America. (Gershwin quoted in Isaac Goldberg's book, *George Gershwin, a Study in American Music,* New York, 1931)


14 FEBRUARY 1924

*Thomas l'Agnelet, Gentilhomme de Fortune,* opera in four acts by the Belgian composer Léon JONGEN, to a story of adventure wherein a corsair in the employ of Louis XIV during the Franco-Spanish war, frustrated by the refusal of a captive Spanish beauty to reciprocate his ardor, kills all male members of her family whereupon she decides to seduce him to gain an opportunity to slay him, when his conscience unexpectedly compels him to confess his misdeeds to the authorities with the result that he is sentenced to hang on the mast of his own depredatory frigate, all these peripeteia set to sonorously Wagneromantic music, is produced in Brussels.


16 FEBRUARY 1924

*Farsangi Lakodalom (Carnival Wedding),* comic opera in three acts by the Hungarian composer Ede POLDINI, is produced in Budapest.

## 21 FEBRUARY 1924

*Sandha,* one-act opera by the Italian composer Felice LATTUADA, depicting the tragedy of an Indian woman compelled to abide by the humiliating customs of her caste, as an untouchable Pariah, an object of animal male concupiscence, is produced in Genoa.

## 25 FEBRUARY 1924

The first number of the quarterly *The League of Composers' Review,* later renamed *Modern Music,* is issued in New York as the official organ of the League of Composers.

## 28 FEBRUARY 1924

*Gräfin Mariza,* operetta in three acts by Emmerich KÁLMÁN, Hungarian composer of light music, with the action taking place in Hungary in 1922, wherein a nubile countess is shocked by the amorous advances of her own majordomo, but acquiesces when he turns out to be an impoverished but titled nobleman, is produced in Vienna.

## 1 MARCH 1924

*Tycho Brahes Dröm,* ballet by the Danish composer Hakon BÖRRESEN, wherein the Danish astronomer Tycho Brahe (1546–1601) achieves his cherished dream in building the famous Uranienborg observatory, is produced in Copenhagen.

## 2 MARCH 1924

A century has passed since the birth in Leitomischl of Bedřich SMETANA, great nationalist composer of Bohemia and musical innovator in his use of modal melodies and asymmetrical rhythms redolent of authentic music of his people.

## 6 MARCH 1924

*The White Bird,* one-act opera by the American composer Ernest CARTER, wherein a forester passionately involved with his employer's wife shoots her by accident mistaking the white scarf around her bosom for a low-flying white bird, and in desperate fury strangles the husband, making use of American songs peculiar to the scene in upper New York State, arranged in abecedarian harmonies, is performed for the first time in Chicago.

## 8 MARCH 1924

*Clo-clo,* musical farce in three acts by Franz LEHÁR, dealing with a temperamental star of the Folies-Bergère in Paris sexually pursued by her piano teacher, a provincial sexagenarian politician, and other libidinously inclined gentlemen, who eventually finds a congenial soul and adequate physique in the person of a cultured French nobleman, is produced in Vienna.

## 17 MARCH 1924

*Yugoslav Symphony* by the Serbian composer Milenko PAUNOVIĆ, in three movements thematically based on native melorhythms and unified by a "motive of fate", esthetically derived from Bruckner and Dvořák, is performed for the first time in Ljubljana, shortly before the composer's death at the age of thirty-five.

## 18 MARCH 1924

August FOERSTER, German piano manufacturer, receives the patent for his quarter-tone piano, the first ever issued for such an instrument. (Exact date communicated to the author by Foerster)

## 19 MARCH 1924

*Les Dieux sont morts,* opera in two acts by the French organist Charles TOURNEMIRE, composed in 1912, based on a mystic concept that Pan and other poetically attractive pagan gods died when Christ was born, is produced at the Paris Opéra, on the same program with *Siang-Sin,* ballet-pantomime by Georges HÜE, wherein an old king of magical powers punishes a recalcitrant concubine by inducing a case of accelerated senescence in her body, but reverses the process when she promises to satisfy his exotic proclivities in amorous congress.

## 20 MARCH 1924

*Alkestis,* one-act opera after Euripides by Egon WELLESZ, is produced in Mannheim.

## 24 MARCH 1924

Jean SIBELIUS conducts in Stockholm the world première of his *Seventh Symphony,* op. 105, his last, completed on 2 March 1924, in a single compressed movement containing four contrasting sections, crystalizing in it the stylistic and musico-philosophical ideals of his entire creative life, set within the tonal confines of serene C major, opening with a kettledrum on the dominant, picking up an ascending scale in the strings in a measured procession of quarter-notes, maintaining this configuration with remarkable consistency, the scales ascending, reaching upper range, dropping a few octaves and ascending again, while ever new melodies spring up in solo instruments, the enharmonic modulations leading to remote keys, the rhythmic pulse being tripled in further developments, and dynamic levels abruptly shifted, Beethoven-like, with the rhythmic agitation reaching its maximum frequency in strings tremolando in 1/128-notes, and finally coming to rest on a long appoggiatura on the sensible leading tone and its consequent catharsis on the tonically pure, self-sufficient C.

On the 2nd of March 1924, at night, as I entered it in my diary, I completed the composition of my *Fantasia sinfonica*—the title that I had thought of giving my one-movement *Seventh Symphony*. (Sibelius, quoted by Ekman in his biography of Sibelius, Helsinki, 1936)

### 27 MARCH 1924

*Irrelohe*, opera in three acts by Franz SCHREKER, to his own libretto centering on the curse of the house of Irrelohe (etymologically divisible into Irre Lohe, errant flame) continuing through the centuries and involving lycanthropy, with a deadly rivalry developing between two half-brothers for the possession of a maidenly guest until a general conflagration engulfs their ancestral castle leaving only her and the better of the two brothers alive, set to music with Wagnerogenic fervor, is produced in Cologne.

### 29 MARCH 1924

Sir Charles Villiers STANFORD, English composer of seven operas, seven symphonies, six Irish rhapsodies, and many other works in a spirited academic manner, full of workable but easily forgettable musical ideas, dies in London at the age of seventy-one, after a stroke suffered twelve days before.

### 29 MARCH 1924

*Noc letnia* (*Summer Night*), comic opera by the Polish conductor and composer Emil MLYNARSKI, is produced in Warsaw.

### 10 APRIL 1924

*L'Appel de la Mer,* one-act opera by Henri RABAUD, fashioned from J. M. Synge's drama *Riders to the Sea*, depicting the tragic loss of young men to the cruel ocean on a desolate island west of Ireland, set in naked vocalization and bleak harmonies, relieved by occasional injection of Irish jig rhythms, and ending on a tormented unresolved chord of the thirteenth, is produced at the Opéra-Comique in Paris.

### 16 APRIL 1924

*Saint John's Eve,* one-act opera by the 76-year-old Scotch composer and educator Sir Alexander Campbell MACKENZIE, a dream story in which a tinker and a poacher both dream concomitant dreams of a seductive wood nymph making her home in a tree and a nixie dwelling in the River Severn, is produced in Liverpool.

### 24 APRIL 1924

*Le Carrosse du Saint-Sacrement,* one-act opera by Lord BERNERS, to a story from Mérimée, is produced in Paris.

### 26 APRIL 1924

At a concert of RAVEL's music in London, Jelly d'Arányi, Hungarian violinist, presents the first performance of *Tzigane* for violin and piano with Ravel himself playing the accompaniment on the "lutheal," a hybrid keyboard instrument with an organ attachment, composed for her and completed only two days before the performance, and written in an unabashed bravura style with just a half-smile behind the violinistic pyrotechnics, ending abruptly after many a rhapsodic episode, in a vertiginous dash of 488 sixteenth-notes.

To hear a whole program of Ravel's works is like watching some midget pygmy doing clever but very small things within a limited scope. Moreover, the almost reptilian cold-bloodedness, which one suspects of having been consciously cultivated, of most of M. Ravel's music is almost repulsive when heard in bulk; even its beauties are like the markings on snakes and lizards . . . In *Tzigane* one is puzzled to understand what M. Ravel is at. Either the work is a parody of all the Liszt-Brahms-Joachim school of Hungarian violin music, or it is an attempt to infuse into his work a little of that warm blood it needs. But in neither case does it greatly matter. (London *Times*, April 28, 1924)

## 1 MAY 1924

Arturo Toscanini conducts at La Scala, Milan, the posthumous world première of *Nerone*, opera in four acts by Arrigo BOITO, to his own libretto depicting the persecution of the Christians under the Emperor Nero, with the emotional interest centered on a Roman girl of dual allegiance as a pagan Vestal and a devout Christian, who is absolved of sin in the end as she is carried into the solarium, mangled by pagan lions in the Coliseum, while Rome burns. (Boito began the composition of *Nerone* in 1879, but left the music unfinished at his death in 1918; the score was completed and partly orchestrated by Vincenzo Tommasini and Arturo Toscanini.)

## 1 MAY 1924

*Miroir de Jésus*, chamber oratorio by André CAPLET, in fifteen religious tableaux, is performed for the first time in Paris.

## 2 MAY 1924

*Symphonic Mystery* by the Soviet composer Andrei PASHCHENKO, scored for the Thereminovox and orchestra, the first symphonic work ever written for an electronic instrument as soloist, is performed for the first time in Leningrad.

## 3 MAY 1924

*Panie Kochanku*, comic opera in three acts by the Polish composer Mieczyslaw SOLTYS, is produced in Lwów.

## 4 MAY 1924

The first performance is given in Moscow of the *Sixth Symphony* by the polysymphonic Soviet composer Nicolai MIASKOVSKY, completed on 3 July 1923, one of his most significant works from the esthetic and technical standpoint, set in the symphonically rare key of E-flat minor, reflecting his individual conception of the Russian Revolution as a martyrdom, and set in four movements:

(1) *Poco largamente, Allegro feroce*, in 4/4 time, replete with chromatic lamentations (2) *Presto tenebroso*, a tenebrous scherzo employing explicit bitonality of C major combined with G-flat major (3) *Andante appassionato*, a lyrical confession of inner turmoil (4) *Allegro vivace*, making use of the French revolutionary songs *Carmagnole* and *Ça ira*, and the medieval hymn of Doomsday *Dies irae*, concluding with an ancient Russian religious chant, "The parting of the soul from the body," with chorus ad libitum.

In spite of my instinctively correct ideological orientation, the absence of a theoretically firm and rational philosophy of life has generated in my mind a neurotic and submissive attitude towards the Revolution, not uncommon among the Russian intelligentsia. This attitude affected the embryo of my *Sixth Symphony* . . . The first stimulus for its composition was provided by an accidental hearing of the French revolutionary songs *Ça ira* and the *Carmagnole* sung by a French artist. When I began work on my *Sixth Symphony* in 1922, these melodies came back to me. My somewhat confused state of mind at that time made me think of a program, which now seems strange to me, involving a "sacrificial offering," the "parting of the soul from the body" and some sort of apotheosis of eternal salvation at the end. Still, it seems to be capable of stirring the listener, as I can judge from its frequent performances abroad, particularly in America. (From Miaskovsky's *Autobiographical Notes* published in *Sovietskaya Musica*, Moscow, June, 1936)

## 6 MAY 1924

*Anna Karenina*, melodrama in four acts by the 40-year-old Italian composer Iginio ROBBIANI, his most successful opera, to a libretto after Tolstoy's famous novel dealing with an obsolescently dramatic carnal passion, adulterous imbroglio, anguished compunction, moral retribution and pathetic suicide as the guilty woman throws herself under the wheels of a slowly puffing Russian train, set to music with an Italianate flamboyance and incorporating some ethnic elements from Russian folksongs, is produced in Rome.

## 8 MAY 1924

Angel MENCHACA, Paraguayan-born music theorist who invented a keyboard with the black keys sloping towards the white keys so as to make the playing of chromatic scales more comfortable, and who also devised a system of musical notation to make sight reading more uncomfortable, dies in Buenos Aires, where he served as an emigration officer, at the age of sixty-nine.

## 8 MAY 1924

*Pacific 231*, "symphonic movement" by Arthur HONEGGER, rhapsodically glorifying the robust energy of the great American locomotive (the digits 2-3-1 stand for 2 front trucks, 3 pairs of driving wheels and 1 rear truck), "an intelligent monster, a joyous giant," is performed for the first time in Paris by Serge Koussevitzky and his specially assembled orchestra, the music traversing the following stages from start to full speed and to the final stop:

The friction of the wheels against the rails is demonstrated by playing *sul ponticello* on the upper strings against the trilled dominant G-sharp in the bass, with the flutes

*390*

assisting by artful flutter-tonguing, the engine slowly starting in rhythmic pulsations, first in whole-notes, then, in measured acceleration, in dotted half-notes, undotted half-notes, half-notes in triplets, quarter-notes, eighth-notes, eighth-notes in triplets, finally reaching full speed in 16th-notes while the trumpets and the horns intone the chant of the rails and the switches in angular melodies, bursting into a fugato of telegraph poles, while the solemn trombones roar warnings to the unwary at the top of their muscular range, the piccolos emit continuous steam whistles and the violins haw and yaw sideways in wide jerking intervals, until the whole orchestra begins to throb with the steady beat of the piston engine, the restraining brakes are applied and the rhythmic pulsations retard from 16th-notes to eighth-notes in triplets to eighth-notes in duplets to quarter-notes in triplets to quarter notes in duplets to half-notes to dotted half-notes, pulling into the terminal station in whole-notes and coming to a full stop on the tonic unison of C-sharp, forming a cyclic design from the initial presumed dominant to the tonic of the implied key of C-sharp minor in the absence of a key signature.

I have always loved locomotives passionately. For me they are living beings whom I love as others love women or horses. What I sought to achieve in *Pacific 231* was not the imitation of the noises of the locomotive but the translation of a visual impression and of physical enjoyment through a musical construction. It opens with an objective observation, the calm respiration of the machine at rest, the effort of the start, a gradual increase in speed, ultimately attaining the lyric stage, the pathos of a train 300 tons in weight launched in the dark of night at 120 kilometers an hour. For my subject I selected a locomotive of the Pacific type, bearing the number 231. (From Honegger's interview published in the Geneva magazine *Dissonances* and reproduced in the printed score)

## 9 MAY 1924

Richard STRAUSS conducts in Vienna the first performance of his *Schlagobers*, "gay Viennese ballet in two acts," completed by him on 16 October 1922, a series of adventures in a Vienna pastry shop under the guidance of Schlagobers (whipped cream liberally laid on Viennese desserts) presented as gauze-clad girls, with chocolate creams, ginger cookies, pralinés and other delectable confections waltzing dreamily, and exotic liqueurs dancing in French, Russian and Polish rhythms, blissfully unaware that the proletarian buns, Vienna batons and matzos conspire to overturn the hegemony of the upper baking classes.

## 17 MAY 1924

*Salade*, "ballet chanté" by Darius MILHAUD (composed between 5 and 20 February 1924), a gay salad of miscellaneous ingredients seasoned with sophisticatedly vulgarized exotic condiments, is presented for the first time, in the form of a "contrepoint chorégraphique" in Paris.

## 21 MAY 1924

*Léontine Sœurs*, "comédie musicale" in three acts by the French composer Antoine MARIOTTE, dealing with a patriotic manicurist who poses as the King's daughter when a dastardly republican conspiracy to kidnap her is discovered, thus enabling the royal family to take a vacation in Norway unmolested, is produced in Paris.

22 MAY 1924

Igor STRAVINSKY appears as piano soloist at a concert with Serge Koussevitzky's orchestra in Paris, in the world première of his *Concerto* for piano, wind instruments and double-basses, written in his newly promulgated neo-Baroque style of composition, in three classically balanced movements:

(1) *Largo*, an austere exordium leading to *Allegro* in a pellucid manner of the Italian settecento (2) *Larghissimo*, a fantasia, with cadenzas in successively astringent diminutions (3) *Allegro*, couched in pandiatonic harmonies and marked by asymmetric rhythmic patterns punctuated by recurrent bradyseismic implosions.

25 MAY 1924

The first concert of Latin American music to be given a radio performance is broadcast from Washington under the auspices of the Pan American Union.

26 MAY 1924

Victor HERBERT, 65-year-old Irish-born creator of the special genre of American sentimental light opera possessing an immediacy of communication as certain as its continental counterparts, dies in New York at 4 P.M. of heart disease while climbing the stairs of his doctor's apartment at 57 East 77th Street.

Instead of sending for his doctor, he decided that he was well enough to go there himself. He left his automobile unassisted, but weighing over 250 pounds, the extra effort of walking up the stairs caused him to collapse. (New York *Times*, 27 May 1924)

27 MAY 1924

*From the Northland*, orchestral suite by Leo SOWERBY, composed in Italy in 1922–1923, but recording earlier impressions of the Lake Superior country in Canada, in four movements (*Forest Voices, Cascades, Burnt Rock Pool, The Shining Big-Sea Water*), pleasingly neo-Romantic, Sibelian, sylvan, pastoral or rhapsodically hydropathic, with some harsh dissonances mitigated by deep-seated pedal points, is performed for the first time at the Accademia Americana in Rome, Howard Hanson conducting.

29 MAY 1924

*Memories of My Childhood*, symphonic poem by Charles Martin LOEFFLER, a rhapsody of reminiscences of a small town in Russia where the composer spent his childhood, is performed for the first time at the North Shore Festival in Evanston, Illinois.

29 MAY 1924

Alexandre GRETCHANINOFF conducts in Kiev the first performance of his *Symphony in E major*, op. 100, written in a broad Russian manner, with epic, lyric and dramatic episodes neatly balanced and effectively orchestrated.

## 29 MAY 1924

*Seven Are They*, "Chaldean incantation" for tenor solo, chorus and orchestra by Sergei PROKOFIEV, composed in Russia in 1918, to words by the symbolist Russian poet Constantin Balmont, an apocalyptic vision of seven giant deities commanding the world, set in eight contrasting episodes with thundering silences and mute explosions, and abounding in special effects, such as a whispering chorus *glissando*, the whole constituting the most extremely modernistic work in Prokofiev's creative evolution, is performed for the first time in Paris, under the direction of Serge Koussevitzky.

## 31 MAY 1924

The Second Festival of the International Society for Contemporary Music opens in Prague with the following program of symphonic music:

*Introduction and Polonaise* from the unfinished opera, *The Carnival of Prague* by SMETANA, written during his last torturous years of deafness and creeping madness, performed here to mark the centennial of his birth; *Sinfonietta* by the Czech neo-romantic composer and violinist Otakar OSTRČIL, belying its diminutive title by its inordinate symphonic length; a cycle of songs by the Austrian Schoenberg disciple Carl HORWITZ who had the misfortune of losing his hearing shortly before the Festival; *Concerto* for wind quintet and orchestra, a lively neo-classical piece in the pandiatonic technique by the Italian composer Vittorio RIETI, a disciple of Casella; the passionate *22nd Psalm* by Ernest BLOCH, revealing his deep consciousness of racial and religious participation in the eternal spiritual life of the Jews through the millennia; *Bacchanale* from Florent SCHMITT's score of incidental music to Shakespeare's play *Anthony and Cleopatra*, produced in Paris in André Gide's version on 14 June 1920; and Arthur HONEGGER's kinetic locomotive piece *Pacific 231*.

## 1 JUNE 1924

At the second concert of the Second Festival of the International Society for Contemporary Music in Prague, the following program of orchestral works is presented:

*Second Symphony* by the Latvian-born German-educated composer Eduard ERDMANN, written in a ponderous polyphonic and moderately discordant idiom; *First Violin Concerto* by Sergei PROKOFIEV, composed in 1917 and first performed in Paris on 18 October 1923; *Le Chant du Rossignol*, symphonic poem by Igor STRAVINSKY, first performed in Geneva, on 6 December 1919; and the emotive, impassioned and somewhat Russianized *First Symphony* by Arnold BAX.

## 2 JUNE 1924

At the third concert of the Second Festival of the International Society for Contemporary Music in Prague, the following program of symphonic music is performed:

*Zrání (Maturity)*, a romantically autobiographic symphonic poem by Josef SUK, son-in-law of Dvořák, descriptive of the provincial life of a contented middle-aged musician; *First Violin Concerto* by Poland's foremost modern composer Karol

SZYMANOWSKI, in a single movement written in the spirit of virtuoso display, articulated into three sections—fast, slow, fast—and written in a richly ornamental melorhythmic idiom, with harmonies tending towards bitonality of major keys whose tonics are set at a tritone's distance from each other; the third suite of *Impressioni dal Vero* by Gian Francesco MALIPIERO; and Albert ROUSSEL's austere and masterly *Symphonie en Si bémol*.

## 6 JUNE 1924

*Erwartung,* monodrama in four scenes by Arnold SCHOENBERG, his first stage work, and the first opera ever written for a single character, a woman, to a poem by Marie Pappenheim, depicting the protagonist wandering in a dark forest in a state of surrealistic irrationality, expressionistically exteriorized in an *Angsttraum* (as Schoenberg himself described it) until she stumbles and falls over the body of her lover whom she had gone to meet, with a score of anguished atonality, containing an early adumbration of dodecaphony, is performed for the first time at the Prague Festival of the International Society for Contemporary Music, almost fifteen years after the completion of the work (composition begun 27 August 1909 and completed on 12 September 1909).

## 8 JUNE 1924

The Orquesta Filarmónica of Havana, Cuba, opens its first season under the direction of Pedro SANJUÁN, Spanish conductor and composer.

## 9 JUNE 1924

*Der Sprung über den Schatten,* comic opera in three acts and ten episodes by the 23-year-old Vienna-born composer Ernst KRENEK, to his own libretto, written in the sophisticated manner of a modern detective story, with a musical setting in an amalgamated neo-classical and constructivistic idiom, encompassing a variety of forms, from passacaglia to foxtrot, is produced in Frankfurt.

This is a comic opera partly with a satirical tendency directed against the aberrations of modern society (corruption, occultism, snobbism, dance craze, etc.), musically combining seriously treated atonal elements with deliberate banality. (From Krenek's statement in a letter to the author dated 5 February 1938)

## 10 JUNE 1924

*Fra Angelico,* "tableau musical" by Paul HILLEMACHER, the surviving member of the composing team of two French brothers who produced their many stage works under the composite name P. L. Hillemacher, is performed for the first time at the Opéra-Comique in Paris.

## 15 JUNE 1924

*Mercure,* "poses plastiques" in three tableaux and 12 scenes by Erik SATIE, in which various Grecian deities playfully disport themselves to the accompaniment of modern dance rhythms, Mercury steals pearls from the

Three Graces during their ablutions and is chased by the three-headed dog Cerberus in ragtime, and Pluto abducts Persephone to the strains of a jazzy march, is produced in Paris.

## 17 JUNE 1924

*Abenteuer des Casanova,* opera in four acts by the Swiss conductor Volkmar ANDREAE, depicting four of Casanova's international amourettes, taking place in Italy, France, Spain and Germany, is performed for the first time in Dresden.

## 18 JUNE 1924

*George White's Scandals of 1924,* is produced in New York, with a score by George GERSHWIN, including the celebrated song *Somebody Loves Me.*

## 19 JUNE 1924

*Nazdah,* opera by the Argentine composer Athos PALMA, to the story of a devoted Hindu nurse who defeats the treacherous scheme of a wily courtier to kidnap the heir to the throne by substituting her own child for him and stabs herself to death after the child is found murdered, is produced at the Teatro Colón in Buenos Aires.

## 20 JUNE 1924

*Le Train bleu,* "operette dansée" by Darius MILHAUD, named after the "blue train" that carried the rich and the idle from Paris to the Riviera, illustrating in a harmonious and melodious manner the confused inaction on the beach, with *poules,* gigolos, sailors and elderly lechers milling around (Picasso's curtain design showed two enormous females fleeing from invisible pursuers), is produced in Paris by Diaghilev's Ballet Russe.

## 1 JULY 1924

Nicolas OBOUHOV, 32-year-old Russian expatriate, "Nicolas l'Illuminé" as he liked to be called, completes in Paris the full score of his mystical magnum opus *Le Livre de Vie,* some 2,000 pages long, in the composer's own notation of 12 notes named after syllables found in Guido d'Arezzo's original hymn, Do-Lo-Re-Te-Mi-Fa-Ra-Sol-Tu-La-Bi-Si, with expression marks marked in red in his own blood as a symbol of the blood shed in the Russian Revolution.

Nicolas Obouhov m'a fait entendre des fragments du *Livre de Vie;* j'ai été frappé par la force pathétique géniale, à vrai dire, de cette œuvre singulière. Sans doute l'idée conductrice en est bien loin des miennes, aussi bien que la mystique russe peut l'être du sensualisme français, mais je ne dois tenir compte ici que des qualités musicales qui sont d'une profondeur et d'une élévation des plus rares. (From Maurice Ravel's letter to Nicolas Slonimsky written in 1928 at his request to help raise some money for Obouhov in his desperate financial situation; about $250 was collected and sent to him in Paris by the author)

## 4 JULY 1924

*Hugh the Drover*, ballad opera by Ralph VAUGHAN WILLIAMS, to a story of true love opposed by the girl's father who favors a rival John the Butcher, with Hugh the Drover winning out in a boxing match between them, set in England in the year 1812 (political overtones are superinduced when Hugh is unjustly accused of being in Napoleon's pay as a spy), is performed for the first time at the Royal College of Music in London. (The first public performance took place at His Majesty's Theater, London, on 14 July 1924)

## 20 JULY 1924

In the course of the Fourth Festival of Chamber Music in Donaueschingen the first public performance is given of the historic *Serenade*, op. 24, by Arnold SCHOENBERG, for baritone, violin, cello, clarinet, bass clarinet, mandolin and guitar, the first work in which the method of composition with 12 tones was definitely established, in seven sections:

(1) *March* (2) *Minuet* (3) *Variations* (4) *Sonett 217* of Petrarca, in which the row of 12 different notes appears for the first time, horizontally in the vocal line, the work having been completed on 16 April 1923 (5) *Tanzszene* (6) *Lied ohne Worte* (7) *Finale*, a modified recapitulation of the introductory March.

## 22 JULY 1924

After ten years of Wagnerian "Götterdämmerung" caused by war and revolution, the Bayreuth Festival House opens its doors with a performance of *Die Meistersinger von Nürnberg*.

## 24 JULY 1924

On the occasion of the quadricentennial of the founding of Guatemala City, *Quiché Vinák*, opera by the Guatemalan composer Jesús CASTILLO, after the legend of an Indian *brujo* who foretells the ruin of the Quiché empire at the hands of European invaders, with a liberal application in the score of authentic Indian melodies, is produced in Guatemala City. (Date and description communicated by Jesús Castillo)

## 27 JULY 1924

Ferruccio BUSONI, Italian composer, pianist and teacher, who introduced a new symphonic dimension into piano playing simulating the sonorities of orchestral instruments by an infinitely sensitive use of the 18 possible gradations of sound on the keyboard and an ingenious application of the pedals, who aggrandized Bach's works into grandiose pianistic cycloramas, and himself composed music of rare romantic consciousness, postulated on a sui generis esthetic philosophy, dies in Berlin, where he spent most of his later years, of chronic inflammation of the cardiac muscles, at the age of fifty-eight.

At the time of Busoni's death and for some years previously so many unfounded rumors were in circulation as to his alleged intemperance that it is necessary to give a medical account of his last illness on the authority of his physician, Dr. Hans Meyer of Berlin. It was commonly reported in Switzerland that Busoni was taken home every night from the station restaurant at Zürich in a state of complete intoxication. Directly after his death, Italian papers asserted that he had died of *delirium tremens* in an inebriates' home. It cannot be too emphatically stated that these stories were utterly untrue. Busoni was Italian by birth and breeding; he was naturally brought up from infancy to regard wine as his normal beverage. He was always fond of wine and appreciated wines of fine quality, but he never drank to excess at any time of his life. The disease of which Busoni died was chronic inflammation of the kidneys together with chronic inflammation of the muscles of the heart. (Edward J. Dent, *Ferruccio Busoni*, London, 1933)

### 6 AUGUST 1924

A supplementary Festival of the International Society for Contemporary Music opens in Salzburg, with the following program of chamber music:

*Viola Sonata* by Arnold BAX, in three movements, written in a surprisingly energetic manner, with one episode, *feroce*, and the concluding bars marked by eruptive power; *Cello Sonata* by Ildebrando PIZZETTI, an instrumental litany comprising two adagios interrupted by an agitated movement, with bitonalities accumulating in dramatic interludes; *Drei geistliche Lieder* for voice, clarinet and violin, by the German lyric polyphonist Heinrich KAMINSKI, set in stylized ecclesiastical modalities; *Frauentanz* for soprano, viola, flute, clarinet, horn and bassoon by Kurt WEILL, German composer of palpitatingly vital music, elemental in the directness of its impact; a group of songs by the Viennese neo-romantic composer Ernst KANITZ; songs by the Czech composer Ladislav VYCPÁLEK; and *Fourth String Quartet* by Ernst KRENEK.

### 7 AUGUST 1924

At the second concert of the supplementary Festival of the International Society for Contemporary Music in Salzburg the following program of chamber music is presented:

*Septet* for flute, oboe, clarinet, horn, double-bass and piano by Willem PIJPER, Dutch composer of impressionistically colored romantic music suspended on the brink of atonality and polytonality, favoring especially the scale of alternating whole-tones and semitones (which his disciples termed Pijper's scale, unaware that Rimsky-Korsakov used it in the 19th century); *The Curlew*, a song by Philip HESELTINE, English musician who adopted the characteristically witching nom de plume Peter Warlock; *On Wenlock Edge*, song with string quartet accompaniment by Ralph VAUGHAN WILLIAMS; *Duo for Violin and Cello* by the Hungarian master of modern music Zoltán KODÁLY, in four contrasting movements making artful use of the available sonorities, wherein broad lyrical episodes of pentatonic spaciousness alternate with dance-like moments in asymmetric rhythms; a song by the Russian composer Alexander SHENSHIN; and *String Trio* by the 28-year-old master of modern German polyphony Paul HINDEMITH, containing instances of natural polytonality and polyrhythmy and a highly complex fugue applying a variety of learned devices of canonic writing.

### 8 AUGUST 1924

At the third concert of the supplementary Festival of the International Society for Contemporary Music in Salzburg the following program of chamber music is presented:

397

*Second String Quartet,* subtitled *Stornelli e Ballate* by Gian Francesco MALIPIERO, comprising a theme and 14 stanzas derived in spirit from the popular types of Italian ritornello and danced ballads; *Socrate,* symphonic drama by Erik SATIE written in ostentatiously arid modalities, making use in the vocal part of monotonously scanned speech rhythms; *4 Pieces* for string quartet by the Czech composer Erwin SCHULHOFF, written in a pleasingly modernistic vein; *Sonata* for clarinet and bassoon by Francis POULENC, composed in a hedonistic Parisian vein of facile *contrepoint sans peine* and dispensing attractively confectioned puerilities of the Satiesque *art dépouillé;* 12 *Etudes* for piano by Karol SZYMANOWSKI, written in a trans-Lisztian virtuoso technique; *Sonata* for cello and piano, in three movements, by the English composer John IRELAND, conceived in a broadly melodic manner, but dramatically departing from strict tonal procedures; and *Gaselen,* a song cycle for baritone, flute, oboe, bass clarinet, trumpet, percussion and piano by the neo-romantic Swiss composer Othmar SCHOECK.

### 9 AUGUST 1924

At the fourth concert of the supplementary Festival of the International Society for Contemporary Music in Salzburg, the following program of chamber music is given:

*String Quartet* by the French-born German-Catalan composer Philipp JARNACH, highly contrapuntal in texture and relentlessly developed from homuncular motives; piano pieces by Boleslav VOMÁČKA and Karl Boleslav JIRÁK of Czechoslovakia, and by Francis POULENC; *Catalogue de Fleurs* for voice and piano by Darius MILHAUD, a surrealistic florilegium with melodious characterizations of seven flowers, set to music with a fine Parisian flair; *Short Suite* for seven instruments by the Viennese modernist Egon WELLESZ; songs by Mario CASTELNUOVO-TEDESCO; and Igor STRAVINSKY's neo-Baroque *Octet* for wind instruments, first performed under Stravinsky's direction in Paris on October 18, 1923.

### 21 AUGUST 1924

*The Queen of Cornwall,* opera in two acts by the English composer Rutland BOUGHTON, after Thomas Hardy's play on the subject, is performed for the first time in Glastonbury.

### 2 SEPTEMBER 1924

*Rose Marie,* musical play in two acts by the Prague-born American-rooted operetta composer Rudolf FRIML, dealing with an irresistibly attractive French-Canadian damsel who cuts the swath of adoration in male hearts from Vancouver to Quebec, containing the famous songs *Rose Marie, I Love You* and the somewhat chromaticized but still authentically pentatonic *Indian Love Call,* is produced in New York.

### 4 SEPTEMBER 1924

A century has passed since the birth in Ansfelden, Austria, of Anton BRUCKNER, the "Wagner of the Symphony," whose music, grandiose in design and supremely romantic in its essence, marked the summit of the heroic esthetics of the 19th century.

### 19 SEPTEMBER 1924

PUCCINI's opera *Tosca* is produced at the Mamont (MAstershop of MONumental Theater) in Leningrad, with a new libretto fashioned by the Moscow stage director Nikolai Vinogradov, entitled *Struggle for the Commune,* in which the action is transferred from 1800 to 1871, Tosca is metamorphosed into a Russian revolutionary émigrée, Cavaradossi into a leader of the Communards, and Scarpia into the anti-Commune General Gallifet, duly murdered by Tosca in the second act. (The real General Gallifet died peacefully in his bed on 8 July 1909 and not murdered in 1871. There were only 14 performances of *Struggle for the Commune;* on 25 May 1929 *Tosca* reappeared on the Leningrad stage in its original Puccinian form)

### 20 SEPTEMBER 1924

*Contractador dos Diamantes,* first opera by the 27-year-old Brazilian composer Francisco MIGNONE, dealing with the gay adventures of a diamond merchant in 18th-century colonial Brazil and containing the rousing Brazilian dance *Congada* often performed as a separate symphonic piece, is produced in Rio de Janeiro.

### 27 SEPTEMBER 1924

*The Seal Woman,* opera in two long acts by the English composer Granville BANTOCK, wherein a Celtic islander catches a beautiful female seal, skins her, attires her in woman's clothes and marries her in church, with their domestic tranquility unhappily interrupted by her septennial estrous calls to the sea until she dons her exuviated sealskin kept in the attic and swims away in the bay, is produced in Birmingham.

### 1 OCTOBER 1924

Paul Schwers, editor-in-chief of the *Allgemeine musikalische Zeitung,* is found guilty in a Berlin court of having defamed Eugen D'ALBERT in print by erroneously asserting that he was writing an operetta on the subject of a polygamous nobleman (Eugen d'Albert had at least eight successive wives), and is fined 500 gold marks, with an alternative of 15 days in jail.

### 10 OCTOBER 1924

Two and a half months after his 50th birthday, Serge KOUSSEVITZKY leads the initial concert of the season as permanent conductor of the Boston Symphony Orchestra.

Four-fold Comes New Conductor to Boston Stage—The Quality and the Rank of Mr. Koussevitzky—Master of Line, Color, Tone, and Characterization in Music—The new conductor somewhat belies report oral, textual, pictorial. He is in the flower of middle years; but no lingering aura of youth seems to gild them; while to one pair of eyes he was less romantic presence than twentieth-century musician in unglamored practice of his profession. . . . Koussevitzky Superbus, as the old Romans might have written; but Koussevitzky passioning for his music—not for himself. (H. T. Parker, Boston *Evening Transcript,* 11 October 1924)

## 12 OCTOBER 1924

Anton BRUCKNER's early symphony in D minor, composed in 1864 and revised in 1869, which he designated as *Symphony No. Zero,* is brought out for the first time in public performance in Klosterneuburg, Germany.

## 12 OCTOBER 1924

Gustav MAHLER's unfinished *Tenth Symphony,* faithfully and intelligently edited by Ernst Krenek, in two movements: *Adagio* (a slowly developing musical peroration culminating on the chord of the diminished 19th (C-sharp, G-sharp, B, D, F, A, C, E-flat, G) and *Purgatorio* haunted by the spectre of death (the manuscript contains this inscription in Mahler's handwriting: "Madness seizes me, annihilates me so that I cease to exist"), is performed in Vienna for the first time, Franz Schalk conducting.

## 14 OCTOBER 1924

*Die glückliche Hand,* drama with music by Arnold SCHOENBERG, in one brief act to his own words, in which a symbolic Man vainly struggles for the possession of a symbolic Woman who rejects him definitively by kicking a large rock down a ravine at the bottom of which he lies prostrate (her role is songless and wordless), set to music of extreme anguish, integrally dissonant and atonal, beginning with a discord of seven different notes and ending on a discord of ten different notes, with the application of a unique expressionistic effect of "color crescendo" accompanying the scene in which the Man emerges from a tenebrous grotto brandishing a bloodied sword as a chromatic wind begins to blow and the illumination changes from rubiginous to grayish blue, to violet, to deep red, which becomes brighter until it reaches crimson, and then subsides to yellow and serenely cerulean blue, is brought to public performance in Vienna almost eleven years after the completion of the work.

## 16 OCTOBER 1924

*Zwingburg,* scenic cantata in one act by the 24-year-old Austrian modernist Ernst KRENEK, to a story by Franz Werfel, in which a tyrannical lord, invisibly ruling the populace (only his hideous laughter betrays his presence in the castle), is overthrown by a revolutionary coup, but ironically the new masters establish the same regime of inaccessibility and absolute power, set to music in incisively dissonant harmonies, is produced in Berlin.

*Zwingburg* is an essay in "social" opera without a concrete political tendency. Its theme is the separation of the masses from the individual; there is a large choral participation—hence the title of a scenic cantata. A revival of *Zwingburg* was planned in the later 1920's in Stuttgart, but was cancelled because of its supposed "revolutionary" character. At the same time it was also rejected in Russia on account of its "reactionary" tendency. (Krenek's statement in a letter to the author dated 5 February 1938)

## 20 OCTOBER 1924

Guillermo URIBE-HOLGUÍN, prime composer of Colombia, conducts in Bogotá the first performance of his *Second Symphony.*

The newly organized Society of Rumanian Composers opens its active program by a concert honoring Béla BARTÓK who appears as pianist in his *Second Violin Sonata* with Georges Enesco as violinist.

The Society of Rumanian Composers begins its activities inspired by high ideals. The concerts organized by the Society will give an opportunity to all gifted Rumanian composers to acquaint the public with their works. Responding to a long-felt need the Society will also establish a music publishing press as soon as it becomes financially possible. The Society of Rumanian Composers intends to develop and strengthen friendly ties with foreign musicians, endeavoring to spread the knowledge of Rumanian music abroad. The Society expresses its firm assurance that its efforts in the direction of promoting national music will find support among music lovers of the land. (Declaration signed by Georges Enesco, Mihail Jora, Alfons Castaldi, George Enacovici, Ion Brediceanu, Ion Vidu, Alfred Alessandrescu, Dmitri Kiriac, Filip Lazar and Ion Nonna-Ottescu)

23 OCTOBER 1924

*Third Symphony* in one movement by the 36-year-old German composer Max TRAPP, is performed for the first time by the Gewandhaus Orchestra in Leipzig, Furtwängler conducting.

25 OCTOBER 1924

*Pohjalaisia*, folk opera by the Finnish composer Leevi MADETOJA (1887–1947) from the life of the Finnish peasantry, with action evolving, circa 1850, in the northernmost land of Pohjola (hence the title), wherein an impetuous bridegroom kills a friend for making objectionable remarks about the bride but escapes with the aid of her brother, set to music in a Sibelian style, with technical devices largely derived from Rimsky-Korsakov's operas, is produced in Helsinki.

27 OCTOBER 1924

*Nerto*, lyric drama in four acts by the dean of French organists Charles-Marie WIDOR, dealing with a medieval maiden who seeks the intercession of the dissident Pope of Avignon to save her soul sold to the devil by her father, but is unexpectedly pursued by the Pope's lecherous nephew, and flees to the convent where she perishes resisting Satan's claims on her, set to music with Gallic savoir-faire and some originality as manifested in the quaint quodlibets in the medieval celebration of the Advent of the Ass, is produced at the Paris Opéra.

29 OCTOBER 1924

*The Red Whirlwind*, ballet by the Soviet composer Vladimir DESHEVOV, subtitled "a synthetic poem in two processes," the first process being a choreographic representation of growing revolutionary consciousness, and the second depicting a proletarian unification of working men and women, is produced in Leningrad.

## 29 OCTOBER 1924

*John Reed,* opera in four acts by the 26-year-old Soviet composer Vladimir KASHNITSKY, depicting the life and experiences of the American reporter John Reed who witnessed the Soviet Revolution and wrote *Ten Days That Shook the World,* died in Russia, and was buried in the Kremlin, is produced in Leningrad.

## 4 NOVEMBER 1924

*Intermezzo,* "domestic comedy with symphonic interludes" by Richard STRAUSS, in two acts (completed in Buenos Aires on 21 August 1923 during his South American journey), to his own libretto with transparent autobiographical allusions, wherein the court conductor named Robert Storch gets into trouble when a love letter addressed to his colleague named Stroh is mistakenly delivered at his home and is intercepted by Frau Storch, is performed for the first time in Dresden.

## 4 NOVEMBER 1924

Gabriel FAURÉ, French composer of poetic music profoundly national in the source of its inspiration, creator of a new transitional style of neo-archaic modal harmony, touched with pre-impressionistic imagery, great educator and teacher of two generations of French musicians, dies in Paris at the age of seventy-nine.

## 8 NOVEMBER 1924

Sergei LIAPUNOV, Russian composer, worthy epigone of the national school of composition, whose brilliant piano pieces are almost Lisztian in virtuosity of technical writing, dies as an émigré in Paris at the age of sixty-four.

## 11 NOVEMBER 1924

*Ilseino Srdce (Else's Heart),* lyric comedy in three acts by the Czech composer Rudolf KAREL, is produced in Prague.

## 13 NOVEMBER 1924

*Irish Symphony* by Sir Hamilton HARTY is performed in Manchester for the first time in its final version, after several revisions.

## 14 NOVEMBER 1924

*Le Miracle des loups,* a French film with a musical score specially composed by Henri RABAUD to accompany the action on the screen, showing an attack on travelers by wolf packs in the snow, is presented at the Paris Opéra, the first demonstration of a motion picture with music ever to be given in an opera house.

## 14 NOVEMBER 1924

*First Symphony,* subtitled *Assyrian,* by the American composer Frederick JACOBI is performed for the first time in San Francisco.

## 15 NOVEMBER 1924

*Don Gil von den grünen Hosen,* comic opera in three acts by Walter BRAUNFELS, after a play by Tirso de Molina, is produced in Munich.

## 15 NOVEMBER 1924

*Khamma,* "légende dansée" by Claude DEBUSSY, originally written for piano in 1912 and orchestrated by Charles Koechlin, dealing with an ancient Egyptian virgin who dances to propitiate a cruel stone god and to invoke his aid against the enemy besieging the city, and is struck dead by the carnally aroused idol as it begins to melt from unexpected passion, couched in a characteristically Debussyan idiom of exotic Impressionism, is performed for the first time in Paris.

## 16 NOVEMBER 1924

*Příhody Lišky Bystroušky (Cunning Little Vixen),* comic opera in three acts by Leoš JANÁČEK to his own libretto in the form of an animal parable, in which a schoolmaster and a parson contend for the love of a Gypsy girl while a vixen entices hens to rebellion and is finally shot by the forester who fashions from its skin a fox muff for his wife, with an epilogue in which the vixen's progeny symbolizes the renewal of the life cycle, set to music in vivid melorhythms of the Bohemian countryside, is produced for the first time in Brno.

## 16 NOVEMBER 1924

Ernst von DOHNÁNYI conducts in Budapest the first performance of his symphonic suite, *Ruralia Hungarica,* in five sections, arranged from his piano pieces, and reflecting the changing melorhythms of rural Hungarian songs, making use of Gypsy scales with their characteristic ambiguity of the supertonic placed either a major or a minor second above the tonic and their abundance of augmented seconds, harmonized with the application of occasional circumspect dissonances.

## 19 NOVEMBER 1924

*La Giara,* "choreographic comedy" by Alfredo CASELLA, after Pirandello's Sicilian tale about a hunchback who crawls inside a large jar to repair it and becomes caught in it so that he has to break the jar again in order to get out, set to music with the idea of creating a "modern synthesis of the old type of Neapolitan comedy with the elements of Italian folklore," and written in the refreshing idiom of modernistically elaborated Italian Baroque, is performed for the first time at the Ballets Suédois in Paris.

## 28 NOVEMBER 1924

*A Baltic Legend,* opera by the 47-year-old Polish composer Felix NOWOWIEJSKI, is produced in Poznań.

## 29 NOVEMBER 1924

*Relâche,* "ballet instantanéiste" by Erik SATIE, in two acts (the title means "release," i.e. no performance) with an ostentatiously vulgarized musical score illustrating the irrational behaviour of the characters on the stage, including a cinematographic entr'acte by René Clair in which Satie is shown by trick photography firing a cannon from the roof of the theater, is produced in Paris by the Ballets Suédois, with the curtain bearing the inscription: "Erik Satie est le plus grand musicien du monde."

## 29 NOVEMBER 1924

Giacomo PUCCINI, Italian genius of operatic craft, creator of striking melodramas destined to become immortal masterpieces of the musical theater, who was not averse to experimentation and who used modern devices in his operas, including whole-tone scales, parallel progressions of massed chords, and instantaneous modulatory procedures, dies in Brussels of cancer of the throat at the age of sixty-five.

## 29 NOVEMBER 1924

*Typhoon,* opera in three acts by the Hungarian pianist and composer Theodor SZÁNTÓ, dealing with the tragic devastation brought upon a Japanese village by the destructive forces of the wind and the sea, and making use of authentic Japanese melorhythms, is performed for the first time in Mannheim.

## 30 NOVEMBER 1924

*Stepan,* "revolutionary" opera in three acts by the 26-year-old Danish composer Ebbe HAMERIK, in which a band of atheist Ukrainians crucifies a lapsed Bolshevik on a cross made of liquidated furniture from the comfortably appointed hut of a local kulak, to the accompaniment of a semi-dissonant pseudo-proletarian march, is produced in a German version in Mainz.

## 1 DECEMBER 1924

*Lady Be Good,* musical revue by George GERSHWIN with lyrics by Ira Gershwin, containing one of his most important, musicologically speaking, songs, *Fascinating Rhythm,* in which an apocopated 7/8 theme generates off-beat ictuses as it overlaps the barlines in 4/4 time, is produced in New York.

## 2 DECEMBER 1924

*The Student Prince,* operetta in four acts by Sigmund ROMBERG, based on Mansfield's play *Old Heidelberg,* a bittersweet story of the heir to a small throne, who, while studying and drinking beer at Heidelberg University, loses his heart to the maid of the inn, but unexpectedly becomes King, and weds a staid princess, with a score containing some of Romberg's most memorable songs (*Golden Days, Deep in my Heart, Dear, Serenade* and *Drink, Drink, Drink*), is performed for the first time in New York.

## 3 DECEMBER 1924

*For the Hammer and the Sickle,* a revised Soviet version of the opera *A Life for the Tsar,* by GLINKA, wherein a Communist peasant scarifices his life to lead astray a gang of Polish spies sent to assassinate Lenin during the undeclared Soviet-Polish war of 1921, is performed for the first and last time in Odessa.

(Glinka's classical opera was revived after the Revolution at the Bolshoi Theater in Moscow on 21 February 1939, under the title *Ivan Susanin,* after the hero's name in the original opera, which had indeed been the original title, changed by Glinka to please the Tsar Nicholas I)

## 7 DECEMBER 1924

*Men and Mountains,* symphonic suite by the nonconformist individualistic 48-year-old New Englander Carl RUGGLES, with a motto from William Blake, "Great things are done when men and mountains meet," in three movements: (1) *Men,* a succession of monumental unisons unshaken by the sky-rending discords (2) *Lilacs,* a cameo of melodic color for strings alone (2) *Marching Mountains,* growing more discordant with every bar, scaling heights, plumbing depths, proclaiming polysyllabical millennia, is performed for the first time in New York.

## 8 DECEMBER 1924

Franz Xaver SCHARWENKA, Polish-born German pianist and pedagogue, co-founder with his older brother Philipp Scharwenka of the prestigious Scharwenka Conservatory in Berlin, author of numerous finger-building and octave-mastering exercises in a hyper-Czernian style, and composer of a plethora of technically effective and melodically pleasing piano pieces, among which his early *Polish Dance* became the rage in both hemispheres in the last quarter of the 19th century, dies in Berlin at the age of seventy-four.

## 10 DECEMBER 1924

*American Symphonic Suite* by the 48-year-old St. Louis-born composer Walter STOCKHOFF, an orchestral version of his piano suite *In the Mountains: Seven Impressions,* is performed for the first time in Frankfurt, Germany, Hermann Scherchen conducting.

Stockhoff is America's most original composer. A distinct and genuine American note is sounded in his *Seven Impressions* for pianoforte. A European hearkens spellbound, forgets the traditions of his schooling and his art, and is enthralled by the virginal quality and authenticity of this language. (From the testimonial given to Stockhoff by Ferruccio Busoni in 1915 upon hearing him play the *Seven Impressions*)

## 14 DECEMBER 1924

*Pini di Roma,* symphonic poem by the foremost master of Italian Impressionism Ottorino RESPIGHI, limning the inspiring vistas of nobly erect colonnades of pine trees in the gardens and roads of Rome, with the inclusion in the score of six ancient crooked horns, *buccinae*, and, for a naturalistic touch, a phonograph record of a real nightingale, listed in the catalogue of the Concert Record Gramophone Co. under No. 6,105 as *Il canto dell' usignuolo*, is performed in Rome for the first time, conducted by Bernardino Molinari, and comprising the following four tableaux:

(1) *I Pini di Villa Borghese*, with children disporting themselves happily in the park near the famous Renaissance villa, singing popular nursery songs accompanied by harps in crisscrossing *glissandos*, strings *saltando*, wind instruments *tremolando*, self-important brass and exuberant drums (2) *Pini presso una catacomba*, in a devotional Hypodorian mode set in arid organum-like counterpoint, recalling the Christian vigils near the catacombs and gradually rising in religious fervor until a state of ecstatic exultation is reached (3) *I Pini del Gianicolo*, a crepuscular idyl, in which, for the first time in orchestral literature, a phonograph record is introduced singing the song of a nightingale against faint muted strings and a distant clarinet (4) *I Pini di Via Appia*, a march starting in the deep recesses of the somber low region of the instrumental range, and mounting in measured steps to a rousing triumph of militant national pride recalling the glories of the Roman consular army ascending the Capitoline Hill and, by historic association, the successful march on Rome of Benito Mussolini's Fascist legions.

### 20 DECEMBER 1924

*La Cena delle Beffe (The Feast of the Jests)*, opera in four acts by Umberto GIORDANO, dealing with a tubercular poet scorned by a fishmonger's daughter in favor of a muscular army captain, with the grim operatic jest delivered in the last scene when the captain kills his own brother believing him to be the poet lurking in the bride's room, is produced at La Scala, Milan, Arturo Toscanini conducting.

### 24 DECEMBER 1924

*L'Arlequin*, lyric comedy in five acts by the French composer Max D'OLLONE, dealing with an actor who arouses the passion of a young heiress from the Fortunate Isle but decides to send her back to her parents, whereupon she languishes and dies, and he accepts the offer to become the successor to the ruler of the now Unfortunate Isle, is produced at the Opéra-Comique in Paris.

# ❧ *1925* ❧

### 1 JANUARY 1925

Fritz KLEIN publishes a significant article in *Die Musik*, entitled *Frontiers of the Semitone World*, suggesting new ways of combining tones and intervals, as part of his theory of "musical statics," applied in his piece *Die Maschine* of 1921 and giving the formula for the construction of a *Mutterakkord*, which includes all 12 different notes and all 12 different intervals, forming an invertible series of 11, 8, 9, 10, 7, 6, 5, 2, 3, 4, 1 semitones. (Klein's *Mutterakkord* is not the only matrix; several other "mother chords" are given in the *Thesaurus of Scales and Melodic Patterns* by Nicolas Slonimsky)

Although I saw Mr. Klein's 12-tone composition about 1919, 1920, or 1921, I am not an imitator of him. I wrote a melody for a scherzo which was composed of 12 tones. This was in 1915, as Webern knows. It was planned as a movement of a long symphony, the finale of which was part of what became later *Jakobsleiter*. Besides, I wrote piano pieces, op. 23, which I called "composing with the tones of the basic motif." In these pieces I used a technique which is certainly a first step towards composing with 12 tones. Besides, you will find that in the first edition of my *Harmonielehre* (1911) there is a description of the new harmonies and their application, which has probably influenced all these men who now want to become my models. At least I know that Hauer used it almost literally in the first edition of his book and eliminated it later. It states the reasons that led me to this new technique in these words: "The repetition of a tone produces the danger of lending it the importance of a *Grundton*, which ought to be avoided." I have not much interest in originality, and that is why I never objected to misstatements. (Schoenberg's letter, in English, to the author dated Los Angeles, 2 January 1940)

## 8 JANUARY 1925

Igor STRAVINSKY makes his first appearance in America as conductor with the Philharmonic Orchestra of New York, in a program of his works.

## 11 JANUARY 1925

*Symphony* for organ and orchestra by the 24-year-old Brooklyn-born composer Aaron COPLAND, in three movements, *Prelude*, *Scherzo*, and *Finale*, cast in a declarative diatonic idiom, with widely ambulant melodic intervals and assertive melismas around strategic points, static tonal harmonies in chorale-like episodes, and incisive asymmetrical rhythms with ragtime-like syncopation in dance-like sections, is performed for the first time by the New York Symphony, Walter Damrosch conducting, with Nadia Boulanger, Copland's teacher during his Parisian period of apprenticeship, at the organ. (The score, dedicated "with admiration" to Nadia Boulanger, was revised in 1928, and the organ part absorbed into the new orchestration)

Mr. Copland is a child of his time. Naturally enough, his speech is the atonal, polytonal speech of today. Why anyone should expect him or his fellows to write in any other idiom than that which is characteristic of 1925, is more than we can understand. Let us get used to the fact that it is as normal for the youth of 1925 to write in two keys simultaneously as it was for the youth of 1825 to confine himself frugally to one . . . Mr. Damrosch, hearing some hisses at the end of the piece, remarked to his audience that a youth who could write such a symphony at twenty-four would be capable some day of murder. That was a bit rough on Mr. Copland. He does not strike us as one of the murderous kind. (Lawrence Gilman, New York *Herald Tribine*, 12 January 1925)

## 23 JANUARY 1925

*Bäckahästen* (*The River Horse*), opera in four acts by the foremost Swedish symphonist Kurt ATTERBERG, is produced in Stockholm.

### 23 JANUARY 1925

Igor STRAVINSKY makes his first American appearance as pianist, in the first American performance of his neo-baroque *Piano Concerto*, with the Boston Symphony Orchestra, Serge Koussevitzky conducting. (The absolute first performance took place at a Koussevitzky concert in Paris on 22 May 1924)

### 31 JANUARY 1925

A suite of three pieces of Jacques IBERT, orchestrated by him from *Les Rencontres: petite suite en forme de ballet:* (1) *Les Bouquetières,* a gracefully stylized evocation of flower girls in peppery harmonies and jogging rhythms (2) *Créoles,* in tango-like see-saw manner (3) *Les Bavardes,* in quick quintuple time, is performed for the first time in Paris.

### 31 JANUARY 1925

*Zéphyr et Flore,* the first ballet by the 21-year-old Russian composer Vladimir DUKELSKY, written in a pleasingly stylized bucolic manner of neo-Baroque dance music, is performed for the first time, for an invited audience, by Diaghilev's Ballet Russe in Monte Carlo.

### 7 FEBRUARY 1925

*Il Convento veneziano,* "choreographic comedy" by Alfredo CASELLA, composed in 1912, has its first stage performance at La Scala, Milan. (A symphonic suite extracted from this score was first performed under the title *Le couvent sur l'eau,* in Paris on 23 April 1914, Casella conducting)

### 8 FEBRUARY 1925

Two symphonies by Russia's most prolific symphonist Nicolai MIASKOVSKY, the *Fourth,* in E minor, subjective and somber albeit with an optimistic ending, in three contrasting movements (composed in 1918), and the *Seventh,* in B minor (composed in 1922), animated and extrovert, and more harmoniously adhering to the Soviet ideals of healthy music, are performed at the same concert for the first time in Moscow.

### 13 FEBRUARY 1925

Leo ORNSTEIN, 32-year-old Russian-born modernistically minded composer, experimenter in meta-pianistic sonorities, plays the first performance with the Philadelphia Orchestra, Leopold Stokowski conducting, of his *Second Piano Concerto,* arranged from his earlier sonata for two pianos of 1921, its modernity expressed by the absence of key signature and the abundance of metrical shifts, the finale pursuing its course in rapid 5/8 time.

### 13 FEBRUARY 1925

*Le Mariage de Rosine,* comic opera after Beaumarchais by the Belgian composer Robert HERBERIGS, is produced in Ghent.

## 14 FEBRUARY 1925

Giuseppe DONATI DE BUDRIO, the inventor (in 1867) of the ocarina, the bird-shaped (ocarina means, literally, a little goose) hollow-sounding whistleflute, known in U.S. parlance as "sweet potato," dies in poverty in Milan, at the age of eighty-eight (he was born on 2 December 1836), with part of his ocarina glory usurped by Luigi Silvestri, who even got himself nicknamed "papa dell'ocarina."

(Luigi Silvestri died at an even more advanced age, well over ninety, at Camisano, on 1 March 1927. Information from the article by Mario Sandri, *Storia dell' ocarina di Budrio* in *Gazetta del Popolo*, Turin, 25 April 1927)

## 15 FEBRUARY 1925

*Preludio a Cristóbal Colón*, overture to an unwritten opera on Christopher Columbus by Julián CARRILLO, Mexican pioneer of music in fractional intervals, scored for a quarter-tone soprano and orchestra playing in quarter-tones, eighth-tones and 16th-tones, is performed for the first time in Mexico City.

## 18 FEBRUARY 1925

*Pas sur la bouche*, operetta by Maurice YVAIN, dealing with a middle-aged American businessman gallivanting in Paris in quest of exotic amours, who stoutly resists the implantation of specialized French kisses on the mouth which render him helpless against nuptial inducements, the score containing a delectably explicit song detailing the mechanism of male sexual response by a young Frenchman, "Je fais ça machinalement sans savoir comment," is produced in Paris.

## 19 FEBRUARY 1925

*Gli Amanti Sposi*, opera in three acts by Ermanno WOLF-FERRARI, after Goldoni's comedy *Il Ventaglio*, is produced in Venice.

## 20 FEBRUARY 1925

Enrico BOSSI, 63-year-old Italian composer of operas and oratorios in a fine Verdian manner, dies on board the S.S. *De Grasse* on his return from an American tour. (Date from a letter to the author from the Compagnie Générale Transatlantique: "Marco Enrico Bossi, de nationalité italienne, né le 25 avril 1861, est décédé à bord du *De Grasse* le 20 février 1925, à 13 heures G.M.T.)

## 4 MARCH 1925

Moritz MOSZKOWSKI, Silesian-born virtuoso pianist, composer of the perennial piano favorites *Spanish Dances* and *Serenata*, and numberless pieces of romantically spiced salon music, dies of stomach cancer in Paris, at the age of seventy.

## 7 MARCH 1925

*I Cavalieri di Ekebù*, seventh opera by Riccardo ZANDONAI, to a libretto from Selma Lagerlöf's novel *Gösta Berling*, focused on the turbulent passion of a disorganized youth who eventually marries a divorced countess, is produced at La Scala, Milan, conducted by Arturo Toscanini.

## 10 MARCH 1925

*Thermidor*, opera in four acts by the Apulian composer Angelo TUBI, focusing on the overthrow of Robespierre on the 9th of Thermidor (27 July 1793), is produced in Cagliari, Sardinia.

## 11 MARCH 1925

*No No Nanette*, musical comedy by Vincent YOUMANS, in which a compiler of hymn anthologies with an insecure penchant for semi-pregnant young girls, finds himself enmeshed with three abandoned damsels and a jealous wife, but extricates himself thanks to a cunning lawyer, containing the famous songs *Tea for Two* and *I Want to be Happy*, is produced for the first time in London, England, before its New York opening on 16 September 1925. (A brief tryout of *No No Nanette* took place in Chicago in 1924)

## 21 MARCH 1925

The world première is given at Monte Carlo of *L'Enfant et les Sortilèges*, opera in two parts by Maurice RAVEL, to a tale based on a "fantaisie lyrique" by Colette, with animated characters of house furniture, in which a mischievous six-year-old boy smashes the Chinese mezzo-contralto cup, pulls the pendulum off the baritone horloge, breaks the tenor teapot, rips the bass armchair, and pulls the tail of the mezzo-soprano cat, set to music in an asymmetrically rhythmic idiom, reaching the climax when the crockery accompanied by a sofa, the ottoman and the wicker chair, joined by exercises from his torn arithmetic book, engage themselves in all kinds of baleful sortileges, aided and abetted by an amorous duo of the baritone tomcat under the window meowing in nasal glissandos in ascending intervals and the female domestic cat responding in feline glissandos in descending intervals, the whole score attaining the illustrative quality of a children's picture book in its imaginative and poetic infantiloquy.

## 26 MARCH 1925

Pierre BOULEZ, French composer of abstract constructivist music based on serial principles and exploring the ultimate of structural potentialities in the tempered scale, is born in Montbrison.

## 29 MARCH 1925

*Le Marchand de Venise*, opera by Reynaldo HAHN, after Shakespeare, is performed for the first time at the Paris Opéra.

30 MARCH 1925

*Trio* for violin, viola and cello, by the Russian expatriate composer Jef GOLYSCHEFF, in four movements indicating the dynamic values as serialistic entities: (1) *Mezzo-forte* (2) *Fortissimo* (3) *Piano* (4) *Pianissimo*, and written according to a *sui generis* system of twelve non-repeated thematic tones, termed by him *12 Tondauer-Musik*, is published in Berlin a year after the promulgation, on 1 March 1924, of Schoenberg's epoch-making dodecaphonic *Serenade*, op. 24, but elaborated independently.

(Herbert Eimert states in his *Atonale Musiklehre*, Leipzig, 1924, that Golyscheff experimented in dodecaphonic composition as early as 1914, but gives no proof; Golyscheff himself became a painter, and in 1968 was living in Brazil)

1 APRIL 1925

Three Soviet composers, Alexander DAVIDENKO, Boris SCHECHTER and Victor BYELY, organize in Moscow a Society for Promotion of Proletarian Music, Production Collective (PROCOLL).

3 APRIL 1925

*At the Boar's Head*, one-act opera by Gustav HOLST, to his own libretto arranged from Shakespeare's play *King Henry IV*, musically derived from old English melorhythms and accoutred in circumspect dissonances, is produced in Manchester, England.

21 APRIL 1925

*Il Diavolo nel Campanile*, one-act opera by the 40-year-old Italian composer Adriano LUALDI, to a libretto from Edgar Allan Poe's fantastic tale *The Devil in the Belfry*, is produced in La Scala, Milan.

22 APRIL 1925

André CAPLET, French composer of impressionistic pieces of chamber music, sensitive conductor of opera and symphony, an intimate friend and collaborator of Debussy, dies in Paris at the age of forty-six.

24 APRIL 1925

*For Red Petrograd*, opera in three acts by Arseny GLADKOVSKY and Eugene PRUSSAK, the first opera ever written on a Soviet subject, dealing with the defense of Petrograd in October 1919 against the massive assault of the White Army, which is characterized in the score by an eerie progression of ominous whole-tone scales, is produced in Leningrad. (A revised version, in four acts, under the title *Front and Rear*, was produced in Leningrad on 7 November 1930)

30 APRIL 1925

*The Traveling Companion*, posthumous four-act opera by Charles Villiers STANFORD, to a libretto from Hans Christian Andersen's fairy tale, is produced in Liverpool by an amateur group in a makeshift orchestration, with a piano filling in the missing instrumental parts. (The first tolerably professional performance was given in Bristol on 25 October 1926)

### 30 APRIL 1925

Howard HANSON, newly appointed as Director of the Eastman School of Music in Rochester, New York, conducts the first of an annual series of concerts devoted exclusively to American music.

### 1 MAY 1925

*Scie Musicale,* a musical saw capable of sounding melodies in tempered or non-tempered scales in the range of three octaves, is demonstrated for the first time at the Gervex Pavilion at the Paris Exposition.

### 4 MAY 1925

*Esther, Princesse d'Israël,* opera in three acts by Antoine MARIOTTE, to a libretto dealing with the resourceful biblical damsel who makes herself so desirable to the oppressive king Ahasuerus that he delivers into her hands his murderously antisemitic minister Haman, is produced at the Paris Opéra.

### 7 MAY 1925

A century has passed since the death, insane, of Antonio SALIERI, fine Italian craftsman of great musical expertise, author of many melodious and harmonious operas, whose destiny was to be unjustly accused of poisoning Mozart.

### 9 MAY 1925

Four centuries have elapsed since the birth of Giovanni Pierluigi PALESTRINA, the "Saviour of Liturgical Music;" founder of modern counterpoint, universalizer of modern polyphony.

(The date of Palestrina's birth, 9 May 1525, is derived from his inscription in a manuscript music book, "Libro de' ricordi scritto da me, Giovanni Pierluigi da Palestrina, commenzato a dì 19 di settembre 1578, per memoria da Iginio mio figluolo, di età de' 53 anni, mesi 4, giorni 10, perconto de' stampe de' Messe con messer Dorico," cited by Raffaele Casimir, in *Noto d'Archivio* of March 1924)

### 10 MAY 1925

All records for precocious musical wunderkindism are broken by the 2¼-year-old Spanish girl Giocasta CORMA (born in Barcelona on 4 February 1923), at her public concert in a program of ten classical pieces in the Salle Mozart in Barcelona. (Dates from *Diccionario de la Música Ilustrado,* Barcelona, 1930)

### 15 MAY 1925

The Third Festival of the International Society for Contemporary Music opens in Prague with the following program:

Ferruccio BUSONI's early *Serenata* for cello and piano, composed in 1892; *5 Pieces for Chamber Orchestra* by Ernst TOCH, lyrically modal in its slow episodes, boisterously chromatic in rapid passages, astringently rhythmed and diaphanously orchestrated; *Tempo di Ballo,* a Gallic pastiche by ROLAND-MANUEL; a symphonic suite from the ballet *Noah's Ark* by the Italian composer Vittorio RIETI, representing a panorama of vivacious animal scenes; *Demon,* a somberly conceived symphonic poem by the Czech composer Rudolf KAREL; and *Concerto Grosso* for double orchestra by the German master of polytechnical polyphony Heinrich KAMINSKI.

## 17 MAY 1925

At the second concert of the Third Festival of the International Society for Contemporary Music in Prague, the following program of orchestral music is presented:

A neo-classical *Partita* by Paul A. PISK of Vienna, dissonant and complex in its polyphonic texture; *6 Pieces for Orchestra* by the Hungarian composer Georg KÓSA, with expressionistically pessimistic titles, such as *Seul, Prière sceptique* and *Sans Espoir;* a formalistic *Concertino* for piano and orchestra by the Serbian-born Austrian composer and theorist Rudolf RETI; *Les Adieux,* for soloists and orchestra, by the Czech-born German-educated romantic composer Fidelio FINKE; *Half-Time,* a symphonic impression of a soccer game by the Czech composer Bohuslav MARTINU, written in his Parisian style of hedonistic constructivism; and *Pastoral Symphony* by Ralph VAUGHAN WILLIAMS (first performed in London on 26 January 1922)

## 19 MAY 1925

At the third concert of the Third Festival of the International Society for Contemporary Music in Prague, the following program of orchestral music is given:

*Concerto Grosso* by Ernst KRENEK, written in a modernistic neo-Baroque style; *Variazioni senza tema* for piano and orchestra by Gian Francesco MALIPIERO (completed by him on 29 July 1923), the title being selected "not for the sake of a paradox, but because the component parts of this work actually possess the character of variations on an absent theme"; *Toman a lesní panna (Toman and the Forest Nymph),* symphonic poem by the Czech romanticist Vítězslav NOVÁK (first performed in Prague on 5 April 1908); *Protée,* symphonic suite by Darius MILHAUD, from incidental music to Paul Claudel's play; and the infectiously rhythmogenic *Dance Suite,* by Béla BARTÓK, consisting of five movements linked by ritornels, on original themes patterned on Slavic, Hungarian and Rumanian melorhythms.

## 19 MAY 1925

*Jacob chez Laban,* biblical pastoral in one act by Charles KOECHLIN, dealing with the mutual deception practiced by Laban (who contrary to his covenant with Jacob placed an older daughter in the bridal bed of Jacob instead of the younger one) and Jacob (who schemed to secure a majority of speckled cattle by holding crossed rods in front of copulating animals, in the belief that this would alter their genes so as to produce striped offspring which were to be his by a previous agreement), all this set to music with the application of audacious dissonances, is performed for the first time in Paris, many years after its composition.

## 21 MAY 1925

Nine months and three weeks after the death of Ferruccio BUSONI, his unfinished opera *Doktor Faust*, in six scenes, to his own text, drawn from an old marionette play, in which Mephistopheles appears in six different hypostasies—a man clad in black, a chaplain, a monk, a messenger, a courier and a night watchman—all these encounters projected against the realistic background of 16th-century German student life (the actual Dr. Faustus was a university alchemist), is performed for the first time at the Dresden Opera, in a version completed by Busoni's pupil, French-born half-Catalan half-German composer Philipp Jarnach.

## 23 MAY 1925

*Concertino* for piano and orchestra by Arthur HONEGGER, a hedonistic modernistic piece in three movements, *Allegro molto moderato*, an antiphonal interplay with fugal developments, *Larghetto sostenuto*, a bucolic air with variations, and *Allegro*, containing some infectious Gallic jazz, is performed for the first time in Paris at a concert directed by Serge Koussevitzky, with Honegger's fiancée, Andrée Vaurabourg, at the piano.

## 28 MAY 1925

*Der Alchimist*, opera in three scenes by Cyril SCOTT, 45-year-old English composer educated in Germany, to his own text focused on a young alchemist in the pursuit of the *lapis philosophorum*, who is compelled to count the hairs on his head to summon a cooperative demon, set to music in romantic colors, is performed for the first time in Essen, in a German version of the original English libretto.

## 30 MAY 1925

Germaine TAILLEFERRE, French composer, the only woman in the group *Les Six*, appears as soloist with Serge Koussevitzky and his orchestra in Paris in the first performance of her *Piano Concerto*, written in a lively French style.

## 1 JUNE 1925

Ernest BLOCH conducts in Cleveland the first performance of his *Concerto Grosso* for piano obbligato and string orchestra, composed in a neo-Baroque idiom as a didactic piece for his students at the Cleveland School of Music during the last year of his directorship there, in four contrasting movements:

(1) *Prelude,* set in energetically massive chordal complexes with bitonal ramifications (2) *Dirge,* a solemn invocation in plagal modes (3) *Pastorale and Rustic Dances,* a bucolic essay followed by a controlled outburst of feral rural rhythms (4) *Fugue,* a modernistic exercise in bitonal polyphony.

## 5 JUNE 1925

Eric DeLAMARTER, 45-year-old American composer, conducts at John Wanamaker's store in Philadelphia the first performance of his *Second Sym-*

*phony*, set in conventional modalities vivified by jazzy American balladry, in three movements inspired by lines from Walt Whitman: (1) *I Sound My Barbaric Yawp* (2) *Glistening Perfumed South* (3) *Robust, Friendly, Singing With Open Mouths.*

### 6 JUNE 1925

*Second Symphony* by Sergei PROKOFIEV, in D minor, in two movements, (1) *Allegro ben articolato*, set in metallic tones of primitivistic constructivism (2) *Tema con variazioni*, marked by melodic saltation, trochaic rhythms and progressively dense harmonic concentrations in septuple counterpoint, with a thematic recapitulation after six variations, concluding on a structure of three minor triads suspended over the fundamental D in pianissimo, is performed for the first time in Paris by Serge Koussevitzky and his orchestra.

My *Second Symphony* sounded overloaded. Although one critic commended my septuple counterpoint, my friends preserved an embarrassed silence. (Prokofiev, in his *Autobiography;* he planned to rewrite the work, as op. 136, during the last year of his life in 1953, but the project remained incomplete)

### 11 JUNE 1925

Arthur HONEGGER conducts in Mezières, Switzerland, the first performance of his incidental music to *Judith*, a play by René Morax, telling the famous biblical story of a Jewish widow of "goodly countenance" who penetrated the camp of the besieging Assyrians as a refugee, captivated and inebriated their chief Holofernes, decapitated him with his own falchion, packed the severed head in her maidservant's meat bag, returned in triumph to her people and lived in total chastity until the age of 105, set to music of anguished intensity in starkly dissonant polyphony. (*Judith* was produced as an "opéra sérieux" in an amplified version, in Monte Carlo on 13 February 1926)

### 14 JUNE 1925

Alexander LÁSZLÓ, 29-year-old Hungarian composer, gives at the Music Festival in Kiel the first public demonstration of his specially constructed "color pianoforte" (*Farblichtklavier*) as an experiment in controlled subjectivism of sensory impressions of synchronized light and sound.

### 15 JUNE 1925

On the occasion of the 60th birthday of Paul GILSON, Belgian composer and esteemed pedagogue, eight of his pupils—René BERNIER, Gaston BRENTA, Francis de BOURGUIGNON, Théo de JONCKER, Robert OTLET, Marcel POOT, Maurice SCHOEMAKER and Jules STRENS proclaim their esthetical credo in conformity with their teacher's ideals, and designate themselves as SYNTHÉTISTES whose aim is to "couler dans les formes bien définies tous les apports de la musique actuelle" and to abandon "les longs développements, les froides et pédantes rhétoriques au profit d'un art clair et vivant." (Quotations from a speech by Brenta at a concert of the Synthétistes broadcast by Radio-Belgique on 1 October 1930)

### 17 JUNE 1925

*Les Matelots,* ballet by the 26-year-old French composer Georges AURIC, is produced by Diaghilev's Ballet Russe in Paris, depicting in five concise tableaux, set to hedonistically facile music, the story of a sailor and his girl:

(1) *Engagement and Departure,* a hornpipe frolic (2) *Solitude,* the girl's lament (3) *Return,* a sensuous waltz during which the sailor and his two friends try to seduce the bride as a test of her fidelity (4) *Temptation,* in which the sailors fail to induce the girl to have a drink with them (5) *Finale,* the scene of recognition and reconciliation between the lovers in jig-time.

### 17 JUNE 1925

*La Forêt païenne,* ballet by Charles KOECHLIN, is presented for the first time, in concert performance, in Paris.

### 17 JUNE 1925

*Concerto* for cello and chamber orchestra by Ernst TOCH, in four movements marked by a hyperchromatic tension and devoid of key signature, but with a clearly sensed barycenter on B, is performed for the first time in Kiel.

### 26 JUNE 1925

*La maschera nuda,* three-act operetta arranged by Salvatore ALLEGRA from posthumous fragments of an unfinished opera by Ruggero LEONCAVALLO, is performed for the first time in Naples.

### 27 JUNE 1925

*Sous-marine,* constructivistic ballet by Arthur HONEGGER, is produced at the Opéra-Comique in Paris.

### 1 JULY 1925

*La Naissance de la Lyre,* "conte lyrique" in one act and three scenes by Albert ROUSSEL (completed by him on 14 September 1923), to a subject from the writings of the French Hellenist Théodore Reinach, based on a recently discovered play by Sophocles, *The Bloodhounds,* dealing with the invention of the lyre by Hermes from the guts and horns of sheep stolen by him from Apollo and its appropriation by Apollo in exchange for his entire flock, set to music in neo-Grecian modalities, is produced at the Paris Opéra.

### 1 JULY 1925

Erik SATIE, French composer whose life, like his art, was a carefully calculated series of aphorisms and paradoxes, but who in spite of the lack of substance in his music exercised an incommensurately great influence on the 20th-century generation of French composers, dies in Paris in his sixtieth year. (Date communicated by the Saint-Joseph Hospital in Paris where he was confined)

### 1 JULY 1925

*Gergana,* opera in three acts by the pioneer Bulgarian composer Georgi ATANASOV, wherein a 19th-century Bulgarian maiden, obsessed by the fear that a Turkish overlord might force her into his harem, dies of inanition in the temporary absence of her faithful suitor, who, upon learning of her death, succumbs himself to shock and grief, written in a facile Italianate manner, is produced in Stara Zagora, Bulgaria.

### 25 JULY 1925

*Concerto* for orchestra with oboe, bassoon and violin soli, by Paul HINDEMITH, is performed for the first time in Duisburg.

### 6 AUGUST 1925

*Tabaré,* opera by the Argentine composer Alfredo SCHIUMA, in a setting from the time of the Conquistadores, dealing with the story of a mestizo named Tabaré who is loved by the sister of a Spanish captain, and expires in her arms in the last act, is produced at the Teatro Colón in Buenos Aires.

### 24 AUGUST 1925

Arnold DOLMETSCH, English musician and manufacturer of replicas of obsolete old instruments, inaugurates his first Festival of Old Music in his home town of Haslemere.

### 3 SEPTEMBER 1925

A supplementary Chamber Music Festival of the International Society for Contemporary Music opens in Venice with the following program:

*String Quartet* by the Czech composer of Schoenbergian music, Erwin SCHULHOFF; *L'Horizon chimérique,* a song cycle by Gabriel FAURÉ performed to commemorate his death ten months before; *Nocturnal Impressions of Peking* and *Korean Sketch* for chamber orchestra by the 55-year-old American traveler and collector of oriental instruments, Henry EICHHEIM; *Jassband* for violin and piano, a Central European version of American syncopated music by the Austrian composer Wilhelm GROSZ; songs by the prime Brazilian composer Heitor VILLA-LOBOS; and *Concerto,* op. 36, No. 1, for pianoforte and 12 instruments by Paul HINDEMITH, in four movements of propulsively rhythmical neo-classicism, with the eighth-notes as metrical constants.

### 4 SEPTEMBER 1925

At the second concert of the supplementary Chamber Music Festival of the International Society for Contemporary Music in Venice, the following program is presented:

*Sonata* for cello and piano by the Catalan cello virtuoso Gaspar CASSADÓ; a Scriabinesque *Piano Sonata* by the Russian composer Samuel FEINBERG; *Sonata* for unaccompanied violin by the Hungarian musician Zoltán SZÉKELY; *5 Pieces* by the German composer Max BUTTING; *Songs* by the Czech composer Ladislav VYCPÁLEK; *Duo* for violin and cello by Hanns EISLER, a disciple of Schoenberg whose proletarian political predilections has deterred him from whole-hearted adoption of total dodeca-phony; and *String Quartet* by the grandmaster of Czech music, Leoš JANÁČEK.

5 SEPTEMBER 1925

At the third concert of the supplementary Chamber Music Festival of the International Society for Contemporary Music in Venice, the following program is given:

*String Quartet* by the whilom *Wunderkind*, now 28 years old, Erich KORNGOLD; *2 Mouvements* for two flutes, clarinet and bassoon by Jacques IBERT; *Sonata* for cello and piano by Arthur HONEGGER in his most felicitous lyrico-dramatic style combined with an artfully applied modern instrumental technique; *Joueurs de Flûte* for flute and piano by Albert ROUSSEL, in four movements evoking the images of Pan, Virgil, Krishna and a literary personage, set in a stylized quasi-exotic manner; *Tzigane* for violin and piano by RAVEL, a virtuosistic vision of Gypsy vitality; and *Sonata* for piano, flute, oboe and bassoon by Vittorio RIETI.

7 SEPTEMBER 1925

At the fourth concert of the supplementary Chamber Music Festival of the International Society for Contemporary Music in Venice, the following program is given:

*String Quartet* in A minor by Mario LABROCA, pupil of Respighi and Malipiero, in three movements, conventionally but pleasingly written; *Piano Sonata* by the celebrated pianist Arthur SCHNABEL composed in a surprisingly advanced quasi-atonal idiom; *Merciless Beauty*, three rondels for tenor and strings by VAUGHAN WILLIAMS, and *Serenade* for clarinet, bass clarinet, mandolin, guitar, violin, viola, cello and bass voice by Arnold SCHOENBERG, op. 24, the historic work which establishes within the confines of a classical suite a new style and technique of organized method of composi-tion in twelve tones.

8 SEPTEMBER 1925

At the fifth and last concert of the supplementary Chamber Music Festival of the International Society for Contemporary Music in Venice, the following program is performed:

*String Quartet* by Karol SZYMANOWSKI, in three movements, written in a lyrico-dramatic style with passing allusions to Polish folksongs, concluding with an un-compromisingly polytonal movement *Scherzando alla burlesca*, with the key signatures of A major, C-sharp major, E-flat major and C major in the four string instruments; *Le Stagioni italiche*, cycle of four songs for soprano and piano by Gian Francesco MALIPIERO, traversing four contrasting moods of Italian lyric poetry; *Angels* for six trumpets by the self-taught and aggressively individual American composer Carl RUGGLES, opening in angelically soft dissonances but fissioning forthwith into raucous atonalities; *Piano Sonata* by STRAVINSKY, his second work of purposive neo-classicism, played by himself; and *Daniel Jazz* by the Russian-born American composer Louis GRUENBERG, a stylized essay in jazzification for a Negro voice, string quartet, trumpet, piano and percussion, first performed in New York on 22 February 1925.

## 14 SEPTEMBER 1925

*Tango Jalousie* by the Danish composer Jacob GADE, inspired by an actual drama of passion with a fatal outcome that took place in Denmark in 1925, a tune destined to become celebrated all over the world, is performed for the first time at the Paladsteatret in Copenhagen, in connection with the showing of the Douglas Fairbanks film *Don Q.*

## 15 SEPTEMBER 1925

Leo FALL, Austrian composer of numerous operettas, among them the celebrated *Dollar Princess*, poking fun at America's cult of the Almighty Dollar, dies in Vienna at the age of fifty-two.

## 21 SEPTEMBER 1925

*The Vagabond King*, musical play in two acts by the Czech-born American composer Rudolf FRIML, after Justin Huntly McCarthy's novel *If I Were King*, inspired by the legend of the medieval French poet François Villon who was made king for a day by Louis XI and was ordered to generate love in the frigid bosom of a stolid lady-in-waiting, under penalty of death in case of failure, set to music with abundant élan, including in the score such perennial favorites as *Love Me Tonight*, *Some Day*, *Waltz Huguette*, *Only a Rose*, and the *Song of the Vagabonds*, is produced in New York.

## 22 SEPTEMBER 1925

*Sunny*, musical comedy by Jerome KERN, in which Sunny, a comely British lass employed as a horseback rider in a circus, marries, divorces and remarries an American doughboy, featuring a popular duet *Who?* is produced in New York.

## 7 OCTOBER 1925

*Choral Symphony* by Gustav HOLST for soprano, chorus and orchestra, to poems of Keats, is performed for the first time at the Leeds Festival.

## 11 OCTOBER 1925

Two jazz pieces for orchestra by Leo SOWERBY, *Monotony* and *Syncopata*, are performed for the first time in Chicago, Paul Whiteman conducting.

## 12 OCTOBER 1925

*Monodía* for orchestra by the Catalan composer Jaime PAHISSA, written exclusively in unisons, octaves, and multiple octaves, but creating an impression of intricate polyphony through the ingenious use of contrary motion, atonal melodic lines, asymmetrical rhythms and quick transitions from one instrument to another, is performed for the first time in Barcelona by the Casals Orchestra.

### 16 OCTOBER 1925

Paul WITTGENSTEIN, amputated Austrian pianist who lost his right arm on the Russian front during World War I, plays in Dresden the world première of *Parergon zur Symphonia Domestica* by Richard STRAUSS, for left-hand piano and orchestra, dedicated to Wittgenstein and commissioned by him, the thematic materials being by-products (parergon) of the *Symphonia Domestica*. (Date from *Signale für die musikalische Welt*, Berlin, 21 October 1925, p. 1622. The performance in Leipzig on 29 October 1925, given in the article on Strauss in Nicolas Slonimsky's edition of Baker's *Biographical Dictionary of Musicians*, 1958, was not the first).

### 19 OCTOBER 1925

*Flos Campi*, suite for viola, small chorus and small orchestra by Ralph VAUGHAN WILLIAMS, suggested by lines from the Song of Solomon, which are entered into the score as captions but are not sung, the chorus being wordless, is performed for the first time in London.

### 25 OCTOBER 1925

*La Nuit de Saint-Jean*, ballet by the Swedish composer Hugo ALFVÉN, to the music of his most popular symphonic work *Midsommarvaka* written in 1904, is produced by the Ballets Suédois in Paris.

### 25 OCTOBER 1925

The centennial anniversary of the birth of Johann STRAUSS, the splendidly mustachioed Waltz King, is observed in Vienna by a gala performance of his operetta *Der Zigeunerbaron*.

### 28 OCTOBER 1925

The first Festival of Chamber Music opens at the Library of Congress in Washington under the auspices of the Elizabeth Sprague Coolidge Foundation, in a program containing the first performances of three specially commissioned works by American composers:

*Canticle of the Sun* for voice and chamber orchestra by Charles Martin LOEFFLER of Boston, and *Rhapsodic Fantasy* for chamber orchestra by Frederick A. STOCK, conductor of the Chicago Symphony Orchestra; and *Two Assyrian Prayers* for voice and chamber orchestra by Frederick JACOBI.

### 29 OCTOBER 1925

*Menandra*, opera in three acts by the German composer Hugo KAUN, is produced in Brunswick, Kiel, Osnabrück and Rostock, all on the same night.

### 30 OCTOBER 1925

*Paganini,* light opera by Franz LEHÁR in which Nicolò Paganini, singing in tenor voice, pursues an ardent love affair with Napoleon's sister Maria-Anna-Elisa, Duchess of Lucca, but abandons her in the end to devote himself to his violin, is performed for the first time in Vienna.

### 5 NOVEMBER 1925

*L'Orfeide,* opera in three parts to his own texts by Gian Francesco MALIPIERO: (1) *La Morte delle Maschere* (completed 15 January 1922) in which the old masks of the ancient drama are taken out of a trunk to revitalize the artificial modern art (2) *Sette Canzoni,* seven "dramatic expressions" (completed in February 1919) gathered from Malipiero's personal observations (3) *Orfeo,* "musical representation in one act" (completed 14 June 1920), a philosophical continuation of the *Sette Canzoni,* is performed for the first time in its entirety in Düsseldorf. (*Sette Canzoni* was performed separately in Paris on 14 July 1920)

### 6 NOVEMBER 1925

*Concerto accademico* in D minor for violin and string orchestra by Ralph VAUGHAN WILLIAMS, in three movements, *Allegro pesante, Adagio, Presto,* systematically flaunting a series of flagrantly unacademic consecutive fifths in a highly unorthodox modulatory scheme, and ending with a violin cadenza presenting an ostentatious display of tonal ambiguity of homonymous major and minor thirds, is performed for the first time in London, with the modernistically-minded Hungarian violinist Jelly d'Arányi, to whom the work is dedicated, as soloist.

### 7 NOVEMBER 1925

*Eagles in Revolt,* opera in five acts by the Soviet composer Andrei PASHCHENKO, to a libretto based on the historic Volga Cossack rebellion against Catherine the Great, is produced in Leningrad.

### 11 NOVEMBER 1925

*Šárka,* opera in three acts by Leoš JANÁČEK, written in 1887, is belatedly brought to performance in Brno, after many revisions of the original score.

### 13 NOVEMBER 1925

*Volpino il Calderaio,* one-act opera by Renzo BOSSI, son of Enrico Bossi, after Shakespeare's play *The Taming of the Shrew,* is produced in Milan.

### 21 NOVEMBER 1925

*La Fête chez la Bergère* by Georges MIGOT, orchestral version of his *3 Epigrammes* for piano, is performed for the first time at a Pasdeloup concert in Paris.

21 NOVEMBER 1925

*L'Île désenchantée,* comic opera in two acts by Henry FÉVRIER, is produced in Paris.

24 NOVEMBER 1925

*The Asra,* one-act opera by the American composer Joseph Carl BREIL, to his own libretto after Heine's orientalistic poem *Der Asra,* wherein a low-caste musician is seized with a strangling paroxysm during an illicit embrace with a high-caste damsel and gives up the ghost, is performed for the first and last time in Los Angeles, two months before the composer's death precipitated by acute neurasthenia.

26 NOVEMBER 1925

*Suton (Twilight),* music drama in one act by the Croatian composer Stevan HRISTIĆ, focused on a Dalmatian girl of 1830 who enters a convent after she is prevented by her class-conscious aristocratic mother from marrying a soldier of her heart's desire, is produced in Belgrade.

28 NOVEMBER 1925

"Grand Ole Opry", a series of Saturday night broadcasts lasting $4\frac{1}{2}$ hours each and embodying a medley of cowboy tunes, country ballads, and rustic jazz, is inaugurated in Nashville, Tennessee, on Radio Station WSM, under its initial appellation "Barn Dance".

28 NOVEMBER 1925

*Music for the Theatre,* suite for small orchestra with piano by the 25-year-old American composer Aaron COPLAND, in five imaginative movements (*Prologue, Dance, Interlude, Burlesque, Epilogue*), a fine study in contrasts, almost austere in its classical formulation and making use of jazz rhythms in the *Dance,* is performed for the first time at a concert of the League of Composers in New York, conducted by Serge Koussevitzky to whom the score is dedicated.

2 DECEMBER 1925

*Mozart,* "musical comedy" by Sacha Guitry with a Mozartian musical score by the Venezuelan-born Parisian composer Reynaldo HAHN, depicting Mozart's imaginary amourettes during his sojourn in Paris as a youth of 22, with a variety of women from the former mistress of Rousseau to a chambermaid, is performed for the first time in Paris.

3 DECEMBER 1925

George GERSHWIN appears as soloist with the New York Symphony Orchestra, under the direction of Walter Damrosch, in the world première of his *Concerto in F* for piano and orchestra, in three movements of classical formulation, but deeply American in the blue chromaticism of the music and asymmetrical rhythms within square meters:

(1) *Allegro,* opening with a jazzy motive contrasted with a rousing emotional theme (2) *Adagio,* serving as an introduction to an elegiac *Andante con moto,* building up to a sonorous climax and then subsiding to a harmonious ending (3) *Allegro con brio,* with the most conspicuous theme of the initial movement returning in Tchaikovskian splendor for a brilliant ending.

6 DECEMBER 1925

*Féerique,* symphonic poem by Jacques IBERT, an artful evocation of the Ravelesque phantasmagoria in a fine form of "petit art," is performed for the first time at the Concerts Colonne in Paris, Gabriel Pierné conducting.

11 DECEMBER 1925

*Barabau,* ballet in one act with chorus by Vittorio RIETI, is performed for the first time by Diaghilev's Ballet Russe in London.

11 DECEMBER 1925

Carl NIELSEN, prime Danish modernist, conducts in Copenhagen the first performance of his *Sixth Symphony,* entitled *Sinfonia semplice,* completed barely six days before the performance, in four classically designed movements: (1) *Tempo giusto* (2) *Humoresca* (3) *Proposta seria* (4) *Tema con variazioni,* set in nutritious triadic harmonies, with some surprisingly audacious excursions into the realm of emancipated dissonances, suggesting that the simplicity proclaimed in the subtitle may have been an irony.

11 DECEMBER 1925

*Namiko-San,* lyric drama in one act by the naturalized American Italian-born composer Aldo FRANCHETTI, to his own libretto in English from a French translation of an ancient Japanese tale, wherein an adolescent geisha in the household of a warrior prince in the valley of Fujiyama is slain by him when he surprises her in the company of a young itinerant monk, is produced by the Chicago Civic Opera, with the composer conducting.

13 DECEMBER 1925

*Rustic Symphony* by Alexander KASTALSKY, written in a Russian folk-song manner, is performed for the first time in Moscow.

14 DECEMBER 1925

After one hundred and thirty-seven rehearsals, the State Opera in Berlin presents the world première of Alban BERG's expressionistic masterpiece *Wozzeck,* opera in three acts to the libretto from a play by the early 19th-century romantic German writer Georg Büchner (his original spelling of the name of the protagonist was *Woyzeck*), focused on a private soldier whose mistress Marie has a child by him but keeps company with a swashbuckling drum major, a situation leading to a fateful dénouement when the desperate Wozzeck stabs her to death and then accidentally drowns while trying to retrieve his bloody murder weapon from a pond, with a poignant epilogue in which their uncomprehending child rocks on a hobby-horse urging it on with infantiloquent interjections, set to music in a style of emancipated melody and harmony, employing both atonal and tonal media in a free flow of the sonic liquid, unified by a conscious formal scheme of classical organization in a Baroque-like triptych, evolving in these peripeteia:

ACT I. EXPOSITION, portraying Wozzeck's relationship to his environment, in five scenes: (1) *Classical Suite*, comprising Prelude, Pavane, Gigue, Gavotte, Air, and a recapitulation of the Prelude, partly in retrograde motion (2) *Fantasy* on three thematic chords (3) *March and Berceuse* (4) *Passacaglia*, based on a 12-tone series, and containing 21 variations (5) *Rondo*. ACT II. DEVELOPMENT, a symphony descriptive of Wozzeck's torments, in five sections: (1) *Sonata*, cast in a strict classical form with a repeat of the exposition (2) *Prelude and Triple Fugue* (3) *Adagio*, scored for chamber orchestra using the same instrumentation as Schoenberg's *Kammersymphonie*, and intended as homage to Berg's revered master (4) *Scherzo*, illustrating Wozzeck's distress as he sees Marie dallying with the drum major (5) *Rondo*, wherein Wozzeck is taunted by his successful rival. ACT III. CATASTROPHE, in the form of a suite of six Inventions: (1) *Theme and Variations* (2) Invention on a single note, B natural, alphabetically alluding, in German notation, to the initial letter of the word *Hilfe*, which Marie sings out, crying for help to ward off the knife-wielding Wozzeck (3) Invention on a rhythm, a realistically constructed improvisation, with a deliberately mistuned pianino on the stage suggesting the irony, pity and horror of Wozzeck's fate (4) Invention on a 6-note chord (5) Invention on a key, in the traditionally romantic tonality of D minor, culminating in a 12-tone conglomerate formed by three contiguous diminished-seventh chords (6) *Moto perpetuo*, marked by a precipitation of rapid triplet eighth-notes in continuous motion and terminating with a serene catharsis symbolic of the eternal cycle of life.

Opera of Noisy Dissonance Gets Composer Called a genius.—The State Opera at Berlin has become a storm center of musical discussion through its production of the opera *Wozzeck* by Alban Berg, which breaks all records for dissonance and cacophony. The composer is acclaimed by critics in terms varying from "musical mountebank" to "inspired genius." Not content with having the orchestra attack the ears with noises so inharmonious that some listeners aver they suffer physical pain, the composer prescribes that the tin-pan piano used in one of the scenes must be out of tune and that the singers must sing off key (Associated Press dispatch in the New York *Times*, 15 December 1925)

Splitting the convulsively inflated larynx of the Muse, Alban Berg produces tortured and mistuned cackling, a pandemonium of dismembered orchestral sounds, mishandled men's throats, bestial outcries, bellowing, rattling, and all sorts of other hideous noises . . . Berg is the poisoner of the fountainhead of German music. (*Germania*, Berlin, 15 December 1925)

As I left the State Opera last night I had a sensation not of leaving a public institution, but an insane asylum. On the stage, in the orchestra, in the hall, everywhere, plain madmen. Among them, in defiant squadrons, the shock troops of atonalists, the dervishes of Arnold Schoenberg. *Wozzeck* by Alban Berg was the battle cry. It is a work by a Chinaman from Vienna. For with European music and music history this massive assault of instrumental sounds has nothing in common. In Berg's music there is not a trace of melody. There are only scraps, shreds, spasms, snorts. Harmonically, the work is beyond debate, for everything in it sounds wrong. The perpetrator of this opera counts with assurance on the stupidity and human kindness of his fellow-men, and relies for the rest on God Almighty and the Universal Edition of Vienna. I regard Alban Berg as a musical swindler, one who represents a musical danger to the community. I might go even further. Unprecedented occurrences demand new steps. We must in all seriousness pose the question as to what extent the profession of music may be criminal. We are confronted here, in the field of music, with a capital offense. (Paul Zschorlich, *Deutsche Zeitung*, Berlin, 15 December 1925)

One cannot imagine without having lived through the dissonant orgy of *Wozzeck* the murderous demands made on the voice, the torture to which the ears of the poor singers and members of the State Opera Orchestra were subjected during the rehearsals of the opera. (Adolf Diesterweg, *Die Zeitschrift für Music*, Berlin, January 1926)

Alban Berg is the creator of sounds which horrify the ear accustomed as it is to all manner of excesses. . . . Dissonance has been elevated to the point of principle in this music. Forms resolve into a continuous flow, colors coalesce, but the result is something that, by its constant fluctuation and nebulous substance, is the kind of music that justifies the transformation of *Wozzeck* into an opera. (Max Marschalk, *Die Vossische Zeitung*, Berlin, 15 December 1925)

Alban Berg's *Wozzeck*, born of his tragic consciousness of the reality of life, and grown out of the expressionistic transformation of the living tissue, reflecting the hopelessness of human suffering in the clutches of the monstrous and inhuman capitalist society, reveals the helplessness of the Western European petty-bourgeois intelligentsia before the imminent Fascist assault, proving that Europe is going through a crisis not alone in the individual consciousness of a Western European bourgeois composer, but in its general music culture. (Boris Asafiev, *Sovietskaya Musica*, Moscow, 1934)

23 DECEMBER 1925

Reinhold GLIÈRE conducts in Odessa the first performance of his symphonic tableau *The Cossacks of Zaporozh*, inspired by the famous painting of Repin showing the indomitable Cossacks dictating to a scribe an insulting letter to the Turkish Sultan Mahomet IV in reply to his demand to submit to his rule.

24 DECEMBER 1925

*Le Joueur de Viole*, opera in four acts by Raoul LAPARRA, to his own libretto focused on a philosophical player on a magical viol who strives to fulfill his destiny by harmonizing the vibrations of the four strings of his instrument with the four seasons of the year and the four dominant human events—love, glory, sorrow and death—is produced at the Opéra-Comique in Paris.

26 DECEMBER 1925

*The Decembrists*, opera in four acts by the Russian composer Vasily ZOLOTAREV, is produced in Moscow to mark the centennial of the abortive revolt of the "Decembrists" against the incumbent Tsar Nicholas I in

December 1825, led by a group, subsequently hanged, of liberal officers and literary men.

### 31 DECEMBER 1925

Ottorino RESPIGHI appears as soloist with the New York Philharmonic Orchestra in the world première of his *Concerto in modo misolidio* for piano and orchestra, a stylized neo-archaic work set in the consistently employed Mixolydian mode.

### 31 DECEMBER 1925

Arnold SCHOENBERG completes the composition of the second of a group of three satires, entitled *Vielseitigkeit,* for chorus a cappella, set in the form of invertible retrograde canon (symmetrical in relation to its axis so that, allowance made for the position of sharps and flats, it is identical when read upside-down, from the last bar to the first) to his own text deriding a transparently pseudonymous contemporary, "der kleine Modernsky" who wears "authentic false hair" and looks quite like "der Papa Bach."

I wrote these satires when I was very angry over the attacks against me by some of my younger contemporaries. I wanted to warn them that it does not pay to tangle with me. (From Schoenberg's letter dated 13 May 1949, quoted in Josef Rufer's *Das Werk Schoenbergs,* 1959)

Immediately after the war I received some very cordial letters from Schoenberg . . . Then, in 1925, he wrote a very nasty verse about me (though I almost forgive him for setting it to such a remarkable mirror canon). I do not know what had happened in between. (*Conversations with Igor Stravinsky* by Igor Stravinsky and Robert Craft, New York, 1959)

# ᗌ 1926 ᗍ

### 1 JANUARY 1926

An Association for Contemporary Music is founded in Leningrad, stating the following theses and beliefs:

(1) That during the transitional period of Socialist construction contemporary music can play a socially organizing role along with other arts (2) That our music should utilize all technical and formal attainments of modern music in the West in order to achieve the fullest musical expression and the greatest technical mastery (3) That the absorption of serious Western music must be effected by means of a critical selection of products of practical value. Tendencies that are purely esthetical and decadent are strongly opposed by the Association . . . With these reservations, contemporary music may become a powerful factor of Socialist culture and a fitting medium of self-expression of the class responsible for that culture. (From the Declaration of Aims of the Association for Contemporary Music published in S. Korev, *Disposition of Class Forces on the Musical Front,* Moscow, 1930)

## 8 JANUARY 1926

Émile PALADILHE, French composer and educator who began his musical career as a child prodigy amazingly endowed by the external gifts of absolute pitch, retentive memory and precocious facility for composition, won the Prix de Rome at the age of sixteen, and then lapsed into didactic mediocrity and became an unimaginative professor at the Paris Conservatory, dies in Paris at the unenviable age of eighty-one.

## 15 JANUARY 1926

Enrico TOSELLI, Italian composer of the celebrated *Serenade,* by which he is solely remembered, dies in Florence at the age of forty-two.

## 16 JANUARY 1926

*Děduv Odkaz (Old Man's Bequest)*, opera in three acts by the Czech composer Vítězslav NOVÁK, dealing with a village fiddler married to a wood nymph who flees from him after he offends her chastity, but endows him with a charismatic virtuosity on the violin so that he becomes famous, is produced in Brno.

## 16 JANUARY 1926

*Passionnément,* musical comedy by André MESSAGER dealing with an American lady who finds romance in Paris, divorces her uninteresting American husband, and marries a passionate Frenchman, is produced in Paris.

## 30 JANUARY 1926

The Prefect of Police in Paris decrees a ban on jazzing up the *Marseillaise* by dance hall bands.

## 30 JANUARY 1926

*Aeroplane,* symphonic movement by the American composer Emerson WHITHORNE, the first orchestral composition on an aeronautical subject, arranged from his piano piece of the same title written in 1921, is performed for the first time anywhere in Birmingham, England, Adrian Boult conducting.

## 31 JANUARY 1926

*Concerto Italiano,* for violin and orchestra, by Mario CASTELNUOVO-TEDESCO, is performed for the first time in Rome.

## 5 FEBRUARY 1926

André GEDALGE, French theorist and pedagogue, author of the prestigious *Traité de fugue,* dies in Paris at the age of sixty-nine.

## 6 FEBRUARY 1926

*Quodlibet, eine Unterhaltungsmusik* by Kurt WEILL, a modern counterpart of the medieval improvisatory quodlibet (literally, "what pleases"), and in this sense constituting true *Unterhaltung* (entertainment), is performed for the first time in Coburg, Germany, signalizing a significant advance in the generic concept of *Gebrauchsmusik* (utilitarian music).

## 10 FEBRUARY 1926

*Salinieki (The Islanders)*, patriotic opera in four acts by the Latvian composer Alfred KANINŠ, to a Latvian libretto, is performed for the first time in Riga. (A revised version of the opera, retitled *Dzimtenes Atmoda*, i.e. *The Awakening of Fatherland*, was produced in Riga on 9 September 1926. Loewenberg, in his *Annals of Opera*, gives a much later date, 9 September 1933, as that of the première)

## 11 FEBRUARY 1926

*Mr. Pepys*, ballad-opera in three acts by the English composer Martin SHAW, to a libretto based on the famous 17th-century diary of Samuel Pepys, is produced in London.

## 13 FEBRUARY 1926

Arthur HONEGGER conducts at the Monte Carlo Opéra the first performance of his three-act opera *Judith*, "opéra sérieux" expanded from the incidental music he wrote for a play by René Morax, first performed nine months and two days before.

## 16 FEBRUARY 1926

*Concertino* for piano, two violins, viola, clarinet, bassoon and horn by Leoš JANÁČEK, completed by him on 29 April 1925 at the age of seventy, in four contrasting movements, written in a modernistic manner, without key signatures, and yet tonally gravid, marked by brusque asymmetric rhythms and an artful intervalic nutation in heterotonal counterpoint, accoutred in audacious dissonances, and permeated by national Moravian melorhythms, is performed for the first time in Brno.

## 19 FEBRUARY 1926

*Skyscrapers*, "ballet of modern American life" by the 49-year-old American composer John Alden CARPENTER, polyrhythmically reflecting in agitated motion the sights and sounds of megalopolitan New York City, vibrating in nervous foxtrot time, seeking oblivion in narcoleptic Broadway ballads, submerging in the ceaseless rattle of subways and puffing flivvers, scored for a large orchestra with the inclusion of such vernacular instruments as banjo and saxophones, is performed for the first time by the Metropolitan Opera Company in New York.

## 28 FEBRUARY 1926

*Concerto* for cello and wind instruments by Jacques IBERT is performed for the first time in Paris.

## 3 MARCH 1926

*Général d'Amour*, operetta in a pseudo-Parisian manner by the Austrian composer Julius BITTNER, is produced in Vienna.

## 13 MARCH 1926

*Saturday's Child*, "an episode in color" for mezzo-soprano, tenor and chamber orchestra by the 41-year-old American composer Emerson WHITHORNE, to the texts from *Color* by the Negro poet Countee Cullen, with reference to the nursery rhyme predicting children's careers according to the day of the week of their births ("Saturday's child works hard for its living"), with melorhythmic materials freely fashioned from Negro spirituals, ragtime and the Blues, is performed for the first time at a concert given by the League of Composers in New York.

## 17 MARCH 1926

*The Girl Friend*, musical comedy by Richard RODGERS, in which a gambler's attempt to fix a bicycle race is foiled by a prime contestant whose rectitude receives its award when he wins first prize and the heart of his favorite girl, featuring besides the title song, an ingratiating ballad *The Blue Room*, is produced in New York.

## 20 MARCH 1926

*La Bella e il Mostro*, fairy tale opera by the 41-year-old Italian composer Luigi FERRARI-TRECATE, to the age-old story of the dramatic confrontation between a beauty and an ostensible monster (who is transmuted into an aristocratic youth as soon as she pledges her love for him), is produced at La Scala, Milan.

## 21 MARCH 1926

*Foules*, symphonic poem by the 26-year-old French composer Pierre Octave FERROUD, marked by a systematic application of the scale in alternating tones and semitones to represent an animated movement of city crowds, is performed for the first time in Paris.

## 24 MARCH 1926

*Tre Commedie goldoniane*, three one-act operas by Gian Francesco MALIPIERO, to plays by Goldoni: *La bottega da Caffè*, *Sior Todaro Brontolon* and *Le Baruffe Chiozzotte*, evoking the atmosphere of old Venice, with considerable additions and alterations made by Malipiero in the original texts, and making liberal use of *parlando*, are performed for the first time anywhere in Darmstadt.

26 MARCH 1926

*Die Zirkusprinzessin,* operetta by Emmerich KÁLMÁN, is produced in Vienna.

26 MARCH 1926

Franz KNEISEL, Rumanian-born violinist, who organized in 1885 the prestigious Kneisel Quartet responsible for first performances of numerous works by European and American composers, dies in New York at the age of sixty-one.

27 MARCH 1926

*Der Protagonist,* one-act opera by Kurt WEILL, in which the protagonist in a drama being performed at a duke's palace in Elizabethan England kills the leading actress out of jealousy while the spectators admire the realism of the acting, is staged for the first time in Dresden.

3 APRIL 1926

*Rapsodie grecque* for piano and orchestra by the Greek composer Manolis KALOMIRIS, orchestrated by Gabriel Pierné, is performed for the first time in Paris, Pierné conducting.

6 APRIL 1926

*Tamar Tsbieri (Perfidious Tamar),* opera in three acts by the 63-year-old Georgian composer Meliton BALANTCHIVADZE, in which an imperious 17th-century Georgian queen throws a reluctant young folk poet, who rejects her advances, into a dungeon, and then takes poison, is produced in Tiflis.

8 APRIL 1926

*Third Symphony* by the Finnish composer Leevi MADETOJA (1887–1947), conceived in a Sibelian manner, with folklike melodies enveloped in bleakly static harmonies, is performed for the first time in Helsinki.

9 APRIL 1926

*Amériques,* symphonic poem by the French-American composer Edgar VARÈSE, titled in plural to embrace all Americas, abstract and concrete, present and future, scored for a huge orchestra and set in dissonant harmonic counterpoint built of functional thematic molecules, proceeding by successive crystallizations in the sonorous mass of organized sound, is performed for the first time anywhere by the Philadelphia Orchestra, Leopold Stokowski conducting.

15 APRIL 1926

*Pageant of P. T. Barnum,* symphonic suite by Douglas MOORE, delineating Barnum's fantastically successful career as promoter of "the greatest show on earth," in five illustrative episodes: (1) *A Boyhood at Bethel* (2) *Joyce Heth,*

*161-year-old Negress* (3) *General and Mrs. Tom Thumb,* in the rhythm of a midget march (4) *Jenny Lind,* with the flute reaching high A for which Jenny Lind was famous (5) *Circus Parade,* is performed for the first time by the Cleveland Orchestra.

## 22 APRIL 1926

Four months after the production of Alban BERG's sensational opera *Wozzeck,* another *Wozzeck,* to the same play by Büchner, composed independently and synchronously by Manfred GURLITT, comprising 18 scenes with an epilogue and couched in a modernistic but not radically atonal style, is produced in Bremen.

## 24 APRIL 1926

*Das Lied der Nacht,* opera by Hans GÁL, is produced in Breslau.

## 25 APRIL 1926

PUCCINI's three-act opera *Turandot,* left unfinished at his death, completed by Franco Alfano who added the last duet and the brief final scene, dealing with a cruelly beautiful Chinese princess who, to avenge the abusive treatment of her ancestress at the hands of male invaders, rules that all suitors unable to solve the three riddles of her invention ("What is it that is born at night and dies during the day?"—*Hope;* "What is it that blazes like a fever and grows cold at death?"—*Blood;* "What is the ice that sets you on fire?"—*Turandot*) are to be executed, but who is herself challenged by the heroically astute youth to guess his name after he has successfully answered the riddles, replies *"Amore"* and succumbs to his charms, to a score filled with ultra-modernistic usages, such as frank bitonalities, concatenations of unresolved discords, angularly atonal melodic deviations and asymmetric rhythms, is performed for the first time at La Scala, Milan, conducted by Arturo Toscanini, up to the last measure written by Puccini himself, omitting Alfano's ending.

## 29 APRIL 1926

*Castle Agrazant,* opera in three acts by the American composer Ralph LYFORD (1882–1927), to his own libretto dealing with a noble crusader whose beautiful wife is forcibly abducted with vile intent by a former suitor, but who returns to his castle from his holy mission disguised as a monkish minstrel and slays the blackguard, the bride herself being mortally wounded when she tries to intervene and dies as he sings in Wagneromimic tones of the land of eternal sunshine, is produced in Cincinnati under the composer's direction and at a cost of $15,000 raised by the American Opera Foundation there.

## 4 MAY 1926

*La Mandragola,* opera in three acts by the 31-year-old Italian composer Mario CASTELNUOVO-TEDESCO, to a libretto fashioned from a story by Machiavelli wherein a licentious bravo seduces a pudent, prudent matron by immobilizing her with a potent potion of narcotic mandragora administered to her under the pretext that it would cure her barrenness, is produced in Venice.

## 4 MAY 1926

*Romeo and Juliet*, the first ballet by the 20-year-old English composer Constant LAMBERT, is produced by Diaghilev's Ballet Russe in Monte Carlo.

## 7 MAY 1926

*Sancta Civitas*, oratorio by Ralph VAUGHAN WILLIAMS, to a text from the Revelation of St. John, scored for tenor, baritone, mixed chorus, semi-chorus and distant chorus, is performed for the first time in Oxford.

## 7 MAY 1926

*Les Malheurs d'Orphée*, short opera by Darius MILHAUD, in three minuscule acts, with Orpheus pictured as "having long hair and wearing a sheepskin cloak" and Eurydice presented as a "jeune Bohémienne," is performed for the first time anywhere in Brussels.

## 12 MAY 1926

The Leningrad Philharmonic, under the direction of Nikolai Malko, gives the first performance of the *First Symphony*, in F minor, by the 19-year-old Soviet composer Dmitri SHOSTAKOVICH, written by him as his graduation work at the Leningrad Conservatory in 1925, and marked by motoric vivacity, contemplative lyricism and relentless rhythmic drive within a classical consistency of formal structures, in four movements:

(1) *Moderato*, opening with a muted trumpet solo, gradually gathering momentum and developing to a high climax before returning to the initial lyric sentiment (2) *Allegretto*, an animated succession of thematically related motives (3) *Lento*, a reflective elegy with instrumental solos against the shimmering strings (4) *Allegro molto* prefaced by a slow meditation, accumulating latent energy and pressing sonorously towards an electrically charged finale.

(On the same program, a *March of the Orient* for large orchestra by scientifically-minded Joseph SCHILLINGER, and a symphonic cantata *The Twelve* by Julia WEISSBERG, wife of Rimsky-Korsakov's son Andrei, to the poem by Alexander Blok likening a patrol of twelve Red Army soldiers to twelve apostles, were performed)

A bright outstanding creative talent. There is a great deal of imagination and invention in his music . . . His *First Symphony* is accepted as graduation work for a diploma. (From the transcript of remarks adjudging Shostakovich's qualifications for graduation made in 1926 by Alexander Glazunov, Director of the Leningrad Conservatory of Music)

## 15 MAY 1926

Four symphonic pieces by the Greek composer Petro PETRIDIS based on authentic Greek melorhythms, *Danse de Kleftes, Prélude de Zemfira,*

*Berceuse* and *Le petit vaisseau*, are performed for the first time at the Concerts Colonne in Paris, Gabriel Pierné conducting.

## 23 MAY 1926

*Eighth Symphony* in A major by Nicolai MIASKOVSKY, conceived as an objective reflection of Russian life and containing melorhythmic formations peculiar to Russian folksongs of the Volga region, in four movements, *Andante, Allegro risoluto e con spirito, Adagio* and *Allegro deciso* (completed on 29 June 1925) is performed for the first time in Moscow.

## 26 MAY 1926

*La Pastorale,* ballet by Georges AURIC, to a scenario in which a messenger boy falls asleep after a swim and is caught in the camera-grinding turmoil when a cinema company moves in, with a happy ending provided by a starlet who rides off with him on his bicycle, is produced by Diaghilev's Ballet Russe in Paris.

## 27 MAY 1926

Alexandre TANSMAN, 28-year-old Parisianized Polish composer, plays with the Koussevitzky Orchestra in Paris the first performance of his *First Piano Concerto*, in four movements, *Allegro molto, Lento, Intermezzo* and *Finale*, written in a neo-classical form, with harmonies enhanced by pandiatonic quartal excrescences and bitonal superimpositions on resonantly spaced triadic basses, and distinguished by authentically inflected Polish dance melorhythms. (The date 27 May 1925 given in previous editions of *Music Since 1900* is in error.)

## 29 MAY 1926

*Masquerade,* "American rhapsody for orchestra" by the 30-year-old American composer Carl McKINLEY, is performed for the first time at the Chicago North Shore Festival.

## 3 JUNE 1926

*Préface au Livre de Vie,* the initial fragment of the pantheistic *Livre de Vie* by the Russian expatriate Nicolas OBOUHOV, scored for orchestra, two pianos and four soloists, making use of shrieking and hissing sounds to express religious ecstasy, is performed for the first time in public, at a Koussevitzky concert in Paris, with the composer and Nicolas Slonimsky playing the piano parts.

"I suggest that, for your own safety, you'd better put up a sign, 'I am not the composer.'" (A remark made to Nicolas Slonimsky at the concert)

## 5 JUNE 1926

A century has passed since the death in London of the protagonist of German operatic romanticism, Carl Maria von WEBER.

## 11 JUNE 1926

*Orphée*, lyric mimodrama in three acts by ROGER-DUCASSE, written in 1913, depicting the classical story of the divine singer, culminating in the horrifying spectacle of the Bacchantes tearing his body limb from limb when he refuses to satisfy their carnal desires (in the final scene his head floats in the water on a luminous lyre), the score adhering to the principle of identifying leading motives in a synthetic Wagnerian manner, is performed for the first time at the Paris Opéra. (The first concert performance of *Orphée* took place on 31 January 1914, in St. Petersburg, at one of Siloti's concerts)

## 18 JUNE 1926

The Fourth Festival of the International Society for Contemporary Music opens in Zürich with the performances of two modern oratorios: Zoltán KODÁLY's *Psalmus Hungaricus* and Arthur HONEGGER's *King David*.

## 19 JUNE 1926

*Ballet Mécanique* by the 25-year-old Parisian-American avant-garde composer George ANTHEIL, originally written for an abstract motion picture by Léger, scored for eight pianos, a player piano and assorted percussion, is presented for the first time anywhere in Paris, Vladimir Golschmann conducting, on the same program with the first performance of his unassumingly tonal, triadically nurtured, academically titled *Symphony in F*.

If America has given or is to give anything to general esthetics, it is presumably an esthetic of machinery . . . Antheil has made a beginning; that is in writing music that couldn't have been written before. His musical world is a world of steel bars, not of old stone and ivy. With the performance of the *Ballet Mécanique* one can conceive the possibility of organizing the sounds of a factory, let us say, of boiler plate or any other clangorous noisiness, the actual sounds of the labor, the various tones of the grindings, according to the needs of the work. (Ezra Pound, *George Antheil and Harmony*, 1927)

## 19 JUNE 1926

At the second concert of the Fourth Festival of the International Society for Contemporary Music in Zürich the following program of chamber music is presented:

*String Trio* by the Swiss composer Walther GEISER, cast in a neo-Baroque idiom; Arnold SCHOENBERG's *Quintet*, op. 26, for flute, oboe, clarinet, bassoon and horn (begun on 21 April 1923 and completed on 26 July 1924), hard on untutored ears because here the relentless logic of the method of composition with 12 tones attains its intellectual perfection; and *String Quartet* making use of authentic Indian themes by the American composer Frederick JACOBI.

## 19 JUNE 1926

*Król Roger*, opera in three acts by Karol SZYMANOWSKI, dealing with the 12th-century Norman king of Italy, and involving the participation of supernatural forces in the historic events, set to an expansively sonorous lyrico-dramatic score rich in dissonant content, is produced in Warsaw.

## 21 JUNE 1926

At the Fourth Festival of the International Society for Contemporary Music in Zürich, two choral works are given:

*Le Miroir de Jésus*, a fervently religious work in an austere neo-medieval setting by the French composer André CAPLET commemorating his death 14 months before; *Litanies* by the Czech composer Felix PETYREK, scored for a boys' chorus, singing in their low register, accompanied by two trumpets, two harps and percussion.

## 22 JUNE 1926

At the Fourth Festival of the International Society for Contemporary Music in Zürich the following program of orchestral music is given:

(1) World première of *Portsmouth Point*, pictorial overture by William WALTON, inspired by an 18th-century print of Thomas Rowlandson representing the quayside of Portsmouth in a state of great animation in varied modalities, with a finale in an unpigmented key of C; *Concerto for Orchestra* by Paul HINDEMITH, in a neo-classical idiom revitalized by propulsive rhythm; *Partita* for piano and orchestra, in a neo-baroque manner, by Alfredo CASELLA; the long, and grandiose *Fifth Symphony* for violin, trumpet and orchestra by the Swiss composer Ernst LÉVY, written in an obsolescent but erudite idiom; *Foules*, symphonic movement by the French composer Pierre Octave FERROUD, couched in a utilitarian impressionistic style; and *Danse de la Sorcière*, a ballet suite in attractive quartal harmonies by the Parisian-Polish composer Alexandre TANSMAN.

## 23 JUNE 1926

At the Fourth Festival of the International Society for Contemporary Music in Zürich the following program is presented:

*Fourth Piano Sonata*, in C minor, in three movements, by the Russian romanticist Nicolai MIASKOVSKY; *Septet* for soprano, flute, piano and strings written in a Ravelesque manner by the Parisian Belgian music critic and composer Arthur HOERÉE; the charismatic *Fünf Stücke für Orchester*, op. 10, by the Viennese master Anton von WEBERN, composed in 1911–1913, consisting of five miniatures containing only $12 + 14 + 11\frac{1}{2} + 6\frac{1}{3} + 32 = 75\frac{5}{6}$ measures, scored for most uncommon instrumental combinations, including a harmonium, a mandolin, a guitar, sheep bells besides the ordinary orchestral instruments, written in a pointillistic manner, each instrument playing mostly alone, all essence of counterpoint, sequence or harmony being practically eliminated, while the changing timbres acquire a new melodic significance (Schoenberg writes about this "timbre-melody": "subtle, indeed, are the senses that can differentiate between these elements; fine is the mind that is capable of finding pleasure in things so recondite"); *Concerto* by the 26-year-old German composer Kurt WEILL, for violin, woodwinds, double-bass and percussion in three neo-classical movements: (1) *Andante con moto*, with the violin solo of an atonal design, sparked by asymmetrical rhythms and agitated dissonant counterpoint (2) *Notturno-Cadenza-Serenata*, an unromantic interlude replete with syncopated pulsations (3) *Allegro*, a spirited tarantella, coming to an end with dominant-tonic postscripts in the timpani; and *Pastorale and March*, set in dispirited dissonant counterpoint, by the Czech composer Hans KRÁSA.

## 29 JUNE 1926

*Sinfonietta* by Leoš JANÁČEK, Czech national composer, written by him at the age of 72, in five movements, originally subtitled *Fanfares, The City, The Cloister of the Empress, The Street* and *City Hall* (the subtitles were removed in the published edition), a colorful cinquefoil of illustrative musical vignettes perfused by whole-tone scales and asymmetrical rhythms, is performed for the first time in Prague under the title *Sokol-Sinfonietta*, at a festive concert in honor of the Czechoslovak Sokol (Eagle) Youth Society.

## 1 JULY 1926

Hans Werner HENZE, German composer of symbolistically realistic stage works and instrumental pieces couched in a modern idiom within a free network of rational dissonances, is born in Gütersloh.

## 4 JULY 1926

A century has passed since the birth in Lawrenceville, Pennsylvania, on the 50th anniversary of the Declaration of Independence, of Stephen Collins FOSTER, creator of songs glorifying in words and music the spirit of antebellum America, its masculine men, its lovely women and its contented Negro slaves.

## 17 JULY 1926

*First Symphony* by the 29-year-old Danish composer Knudaage RIISAGER, in three movements, is performed for the first time in Copenhagen.

## 23 JULY 1926

*Ollantay,* grand opera by the Argentine composer Constantino GAITO, dealing with the heroic rebel Ollantay who leads a patriotic struggle against the tyrannical king of the Incas whose daughter he adores, is produced at the Teatro Colón in Buenos Aires.

## 25 JULY 1926

The SPHÄROPHON, electronic musical instrument constructed by Jörg MAGER and named with reference to the mystical "music of the spheres," is demonstrated for the first time at the Donaueschingen Festival of New Music.

## 30 JULY 1926

At the Sesquicentennial International Exposition in Philadelphia, the first complete performance is given of the orchestral suite *New York Days and Nights* by Emerson WHITHORNE (originally written for piano and performed at the First Festival of the International Society for Contemporary Music in Salzburg on 5 August 1923), in five movements:

*436*

(1) *On the Ferry*, an early morning scene picturing a daily voyage to Manhattan from across the East River in clangily dissonant harmonies (2) *The Chimes of Saint Patrick*, with the bell sonorities represented by a progression of parallel minor ninth-chords, the organ intoning the melody of *Dies Irae* (3) *Pell Street* (*Chinatown*), set in the pentatonic scale making use of an authentic old Chinese tune *The Fifteen Bunches of Blossoms* (4) *A Greenwich Village Tragedy*, depicting an idyllic love affair beginning *fervente* and *con esaltazione* in rhapsodically expansive tones and ending on a hateful discord in grindingly incompatible frictional disharmonies (5) *Times Square*, megalopolitan apotheosis of the Great White Way with its electric signs and the mass of moving flivvers and flappers, the tumult illustrated by chromatic rows of dominant seventh-chords on a pedal tone. (A partial performance, of the 2nd, 3rd and 5th movements, was given in Paris on 24 June 1923)

### 6 AUGUST 1926

The first "100% sound motion picture," *Don Juan*, made by the Vitaphone Company and featuring Henry HADLEY, American composer and conductor, leading the New York Philharmonic Orchestra, is shown for the first time in New York City (An invitation performance was given at the Warner Theater, New York, on 5 August 1926)

### 15 SEPTEMBER 1926

Jelly Roll MORTON and his RED HOT PEPPERS (George Mitchell, cornet; Kid Ory, trombone; Omer Simeon, clarinet; Johnny St. Cyr, banjo; John Lindsay, bass; Andrew Hilaire, drums) hold their first recording session in Chicago for R.C.A. Victor, cutting among other pieces their famous *Black Bottom Stomp*, whose rollicking swing beat artfully conceals the total absence of the tonic chord in the entire opening section.

### 18 SEPTEMBER 1926

*Deep River*, "native opera with jazz" by the American composer W. Franke HARLING, in three acts focusing on a New Orleans ball in 1830, at which a lovely quadroon girl tries to bewitch a wealthy plantation owner with the aid of a voodoo amulet, set to a Puccinian score filled with pseudo-exotic effusions, is produced for the first time anywhere at Lancaster, Pennsylvania.

### 19 SEPTEMBER 1926

*Sturmvogel*, opera by the Germanized Norwegian composer Gerhard SCHJELDERUP, is produced in Schwerin.

### 20 SEPTEMBER 1926

*Corimayo*, grand opera by the Argentine composer Enrique CASELLA to a libretto from the time of the Incas is produced at the Teatro Colón in Buenos Aires.

### 1 OCTOBER 1926

The German Post Office issues stamps with portraits of Bach at 50 pfennigs and of Beethoven at 20 pfennigs.

## 8 OCTOBER 1926

*First Piano Concerto* by Ernst TOCH, in three movements, *Allegro, Adagio, Rondo disturbato,* set in a modernistic and richly rhythmical style in fluid tonality, is performed for the first time in Düsseldorf.

## 15 OCTOBER 1926

*The Leper's Flute,* one-act opera by the English composer Ernest BRYSON, to a grim South African tale in which a flutist avenges himself on his perfidious fiancée through whose machinations he has been placed in a leprosaurium by passing a leprosy-riddled flute to her new flutist lover, resulting in her contamination through labial contact in defiance of medical opinion that leprosy is not a contagious disease, set to music in a coloristic manner of abecedarian impressionism containing a plethora of fluvial flute airs, is performed for the first time in Glasgow. (A concert performance of the work was given in the spring of 1926 at Golder's Green Hippodrome in London.)

## 16 OCTOBER 1926

*Háry János,* opera by Zoltán KODÁLY, relating in a brilliant musicorama the imaginary exploits of a fabulous Hungarian folk liar whose wild tales of royal love and martial glory are introduced by a dynamic sneeze, a traditional Hungarian indication that the tale to follow is absolutely true, illustrated by a chromatic ascension in the woodwinds and a sternutatory glissando in the horns, is performed for the first time in Budapest.

## 20 OCTOBER 1926

*Entente Cordiale,* a "post-war comedy" by England's suffragette composer Ethel SMYTH, dealing with a group of British soldiers taking leave of France, one of whom gets married to a French girl through a linguistic misunderstanding when he asks for a *poule* instead of a *poulet,* the *entente cordiale* being restored when a horde of British wives descend on the port of disembarcation to claim their lawful husbands, is produced in Bristol.

## 21 OCTOBER 1926

*Concerto* for flute and orchestra by the prime Danish composer Carl NIELSEN, in two movements: *Allegro Moderato* and quadripartite *Allegretto* (with an intervening *Adagio* and the final *Tempo di marcia*), is performed for the first time in Paris, 20 days after the completion of the score. (Nielsen arranged another ending after this first performance, and the revised score was first heard in Oslo on 9 November 1926)

## 24 OCTOBER 1926

*Suite Intertonal* in four movements by the 46-year-old Catalan composer, Jaime PAHISSA, written (with the exception of the third movement), according to the "intertonal" system of pure "di-sonancy" (di-sonant, twice-sounded), is performed for the first time by the Casals Orchestra in Barcelona.

## 28 OCTOBER 1926

*Third Symphony* by the 32-year-old Dutch composer Willem PIJPER in four movements—a persistently rhythmic *Allegro,* an atonally attenuated *Molto Adagio,* a rustically saltatory *Scherzo* and a vigorously polyrhythmic *Molto Allegro*—written in a somberly heroic mood, the philosophical intent summarized in the appended motto from the Aeneid, "Flectere si neque superos, Acheronta movebo," conceding the inability to deflect the gods, but trying instead to move the Acheron, thematically symbolized by aggressive descending fourths harmonically amalgamated into quartal harmonies and further enriched by sonorous bitonalities, is performed for the first time by the Concergebouw Orchestra in Amsterdam, Pierre Monteux, to whom the score is dedicated, conducting.

## 29 OCTOBER 1926

*Tzigane,* symphonic poem by the Parisian-Rumanian composer Filip LAZAR, based on Gypsy melorhythms of Southeast Europe, is performed for the first time by the Boston Symphony Orchestra, Serge Koussevitzky conducting.

## 1 NOVEMBER 1926

*Der Krämerspiegel,* a self-satirizing musical pastiche written for the amusement of friends by Richard STRAUSS, in which themes and phrases from his symphonic and operatic works collide and recoil in witty counterpoint, to a set of texts attacking various music publishers for their mercenary attitude towards composers (hence the title, *A Mirror for Merchants*), is performed for the first time at a semi-private gathering in Berlin.

## 5 NOVEMBER 1926

Eighteen days before his fiftieth birthday Manuel DE FALLA conducts in Barcelona the first performance of his neo-classical *Concerto* for harpsichord, flute, oboe, clarinet, violin and cello, with Wanda Landowska at whose suggestion the work was written and to whom the score is dedicated taking part at the harpsichord, in three movements:

(1) *Allegro,* in a vigorous Baroque manner with asymmetrically propulsive rhythms in a laconic sonata form (2) *Lento (giubiloso ed energico),* containing a long old-style cadenza for the harpsichord (3) *Vivace (flessibile, scherzando),* in the dual Spanish meters of 3/4 and 6/8, proceeding relentlessly toward a sonorous conclusion in D major.

## 8 NOVEMBER 1926

*Oh Kay,* musical revue by George GERSHWIN, which includes the celebrated tunes *Clap Yo' Hands* and *Do, Do, Do, What You Done, Done, Done, Before, Baby,* is produced in New York.

## 9 NOVEMBER 1926

*Cardillac,* opera in three acts by Paul HINDEMITH, after the horrendous tale of E. T. A. Hoffman, dealing with an insanely possessive Paris goldsmith named

Cardillac who murders his customers in order to get back the jewels he sold them, until his daughter's fiancé buys a necklace for her and valiantly resists Cardillac's attempt to murder him too, so that a mob gathers and slays the chronic slayer, set to music in a neo-classical form of 18 discrete numbers (indicating a rejection of the Wagnerian esthetic of "thorough composition"), written in a satirically dissonant polyphonic idiom, is produced at the Dresden Opera, a week before Hindemith's 31st birthday.

### 13 NOVEMBER 1926

Two new works by Soviet composers are performed for the first time in Leningrad: *Symphony in F minor* by the 24-year-old Vissarion SHEBALIN and *Revolutionary Episode,* symphonic poem by the 27-year-old Lev KNIPPER.

### 14 NOVEMBER 1926

*Der Golem,* music drama in three acts by the self-Germanized English-born composer Eugen D'ALBERT, to a fantastic tale of a 17th-century rabbi of Prague, who builds with the aid of black magic an android figure (called a Golem in Hebrew folklore), and in his exultation and pride of God-like powers, tells his daughter to teach him to express himself in an artificial language sung syllabically in consecutive tritones and whole-tone scales, with a tragic dénouement when she dies of a ghostly infection and the Golem is turned into stone, is performed for the first time in Frankfurt.

### 15 NOVEMBER 1926

The first chain broadcast over the newly-organized National Broadcasting Company network is inaugurated in New York, with a concert by the New York Symphony Orchestra conducted by Walter DAMROSCH, the New York Oratorio Society led by Albert STOESSEL, and the Goldman Band directed by its founder Edwin Franko GOLDMAN.

### 16 NOVEMBER 1926

*Delitto e castigo,* opera in three acts by the 47-year-old Italian composer Arrigo PEDROLLO, after Dostoyevsky's novel *Crime and Punishment,* written in the melodramatic style of the Italian Verismo, is produced in Milan.

### 27 NOVEMBER 1926

*The Miraculous Mandarin,* pantomime by Béla BARTÓK, composed in 1918, dealing with a prostitute who lures an inexhaustible Chinese *homo libidinus* into a den of iniquity where he is set upon by her accomplices, robbed, suffocated by cushions, thrice stabbed by a rusty knife and hanged from a collapsible lamp hook, but rebounds each time with renewed chromatic inturgescence and tremulous tremolos in artfully copulated intussusceptions in dissonant double counterpoint, with the emphasis on the angst-ridden intervals of the tritone and major sevenths, in a relentlessly monistic élan, culminating in a series of monstrous orgasms *fortississimo,* followed by a labile sonic detumescence in trombones and strings glissando, is performed for the first time in Cologne. (An orchestral suite extracted from the score was first performed on 1 April 1927 by the Cincinnati Symphony Orchestra under the direction of Fritz Reiner).

### 27 NOVEMBER 1926

*The Creation,* a "Negro Sermon" for voice, clarinet, flute, bassoon, horn, trumpet, percussion, viola and piano, by the Russian-born American composer Louis GRUENBERG, to the text by James Weldon Johnson, presenting an ingenuous picture of the Creator ("I'm lonely, I'll make me a world"), set to music in an intellectualized jazz idiom, arranged in euphonious dissonant harmonies, is performed for the first time at a concert of the League of Composers in New York.

### 27 NOVEMBER 1926

*Don Pistacchio,* a newly-exhumed comic opera by Luigi CHERUBINI, is produced for the first time in Dresden.

### 28 NOVEMBER 1926

*Darker America,* by the American Negro composer William Grant STILL, a litany of racial sorrow expressed in the melodious modalities of Negro spirituals, is performed for the first time in New York.

### 29 NOVEMBER 1926

*La Tisseuse d'Orties,* lyric drama in four acts by the Swiss composer Gustave DORET, wherein the concubine of a royal prince usurps the throne during his absence and denounces him upon his return, with a mystical dénouement when a beauteous webster of polygamous apetalous urticaceous flower tissues rescues him after he assents to submit to the purgatory of carnal love, is produced at the Opéra-Comique in Paris during Doret's brief tenure of its directorate.

### 29 NOVEMBER 1926

The municipal authorities of Prague ban further performances of Alban BERG's opera *Wozzeck* to forestall the repetition of disturbances that attended the first Prague performance of the Czech version of the opera on 11 November 1926.

### 30 NOVEMBER 1926

*The Desert Song,* operetta in two acts by Sigmund ROMBERG, set in the locale of the Riff War in North Africa in 1925, wherein a mustachioed Riff chieftain clandestinely romances with a highborn French beauty, whom he eventually weds as war actions subside, containing a number of rousing tunes, among them the swashbuckling *Riff Song,* the masculine *Sabre Song* and the rhapsodic title song *My Desert is Waiting,* is produced in New York City.

3 DECEMBER 1926

*The Triumph of Neptune,* "English pantomime in ten tableaux" by Lord BERNERS, to a scenario by Sacheverell Sitwell, with Britannia dancing the hornpipe, shipwrecks occurring to the accompaniment of a wind machine and a battery of drums, and a suddenly materialized inebriated singer drunkenly intoning *The Last Rose of Summer,* culminating in a pandiatonically white C-major apotheosis of Neptune, is produced in London.

5 DECEMBER 1926

*Diptyque méditerranéen* by Vincent D'INDY, a symphonic impression of sunrise and sunset on the Mediterranean, is performed for the first time in Paris.

8 DECEMBER 1926

A *Witch of Salem,* one-act opera by Charles Wakefield CADMAN, to a story of the Puritan struggle against the prevalence of witches in Salem of 1682, in which a local maiden accuses her love rival of witchcraft on the evidence of a blood-red cross on her breast, but confesses her perjury as the other is brought to the gallows, and is stoned to death by the infuriated populace cheated of the hanging spectacle, written in a melodious and harmonious style with a considerable display of dramatic chromatic progressions of diminished seventh-chords, is produced by the Chicago Civic Opera Company.

9 DECEMBER 1926

Darius MILHAUD plays the piano part in the world première of his hedonistic piece of sophisticated urban music *Le Carnaval d'Aix* on themes from his ballet *Salade* (he was born in Aix-en-Provence), with the New York Philharmonic, Willem Mengelberg conducting.

15 DECEMBER 1926

*Chôros No. 10* by Heitor VILLA-LOBOS, for mixed chorus and orchestra, subtitled *Rasga o Coracão,* is performed for the first time in Rio de Janeiro.

18 DECEMBER 1926

*Věc Makropulos,* opera in three acts by the 72-year-old grandmaster of modern Czech music, Leoš JANÁČEK (begun 11 November 1923 and completed 12 November 1925) after a play by Čapek, *The Makropulos Affair,* centering on a litigation involving Elina Makropulos, 342 years of age, whose father, the court alchemist to the Emperor Rudolf II, gave her an elixir of indefinite longevity, and who became a famous singer in the 20th century, set to a musical score of pointed modernity in its thematic brevity, rhythmic asymmetry and dramatic precipitation, is performed for the first time in Brno.

26 DECEMBER 1926

*Tapiola,* symphonic poem by Jean SIBELIUS (composed between March and May 1926), the title relating to the forest god of Finnish demonology, Tapio, set in the somber and austere tones of Nordland, somnolent but dreaming savage dreams within a monothematic structure in which variety is achieved by a constant fluctuation of instrumental colors and occasional insertions of whole-tone passages, culminating in a chromatic rise in a 56-bar crescendo of cumulative string sonorities, is performed for the first time anywhere as a commissioned work by Walter Damrosch and the New York Symphony Society Orchestra.

# ❧ *1927* ❧

8 JANUARY 1927

*Penthesilea,* one-act melodrama by Othmar SCHOECK, after Kleist's play wherein the Amazon queen captured by Achilles is engaged in a game of hostile passion with him and after Achilles is slain to the sound of an excurciatingly dissonant polychord, falls dead on his body while secundal disharmonies clash, is performed for the first time in Dresden.

8 JANUARY 1927

The first performance is given in Vienna by the Kolisch String Quartet of *Lyrische Suite* by Alban BERG, written in a distinctive individual style, wherein the Schoenbergian method of 12-tone composition is applied in alternation with non-dodecaphonic, tonal and even triadic procedures, melodically and harmonically anchored on additive intervalic complexes of fourths and tritones summing up to major sevenths, and fifths and tritones summing up to minor ninths, in six movements:

(1) *Allegretto giovale,* a hedonistic dodecaphonic essay, concluding with a canon of two mutually exclusive major hexachords at distances of minor thirds and tritones, resulting in a surprising melodramatic precipitation of consecutive diminished-seventh chords (2) *Andante amoroso,* in a free lyrico-dramatic vein (3) *Allegro misterioso,* containing a *Trio estatico* with a dodecaphonic episode of mutually exclusive whole-tone scales (4) *Adagio appassionato,* with a melodic quotation from the *Lyrische Symphonie* by Alexander von Zemlinsky, Schoenberg's teacher and brother-in-law, to whom the score is dedicated (5) *Presto delirando,* a scherzo employing diamond-shaped notes to indicate sustained tones (6) *Largo desolato,* with the insertion of the initial motive from *Tristan und Isolde,* terminating in a series of despondent tertian oscillations in one instrument after another, trailing off into inaudibility. (Berg subsequently arranged three movements of the *Lyrische Suite* for chamber orchestra; the first performance of this version took place in Berlin on 21 January 1929)

9 JANUARY 1927

Houston Stewart CHAMBERLAIN, English-born Wagnerite who married Wagner's daughter Eva and who expanded Wagner's pan-Teutonic philosophy into a political doctrine, dies in his spiritual home, Bayreuth, at the age of seventy-one, only six years before the advent of the Wagnerogenic Nazi millennium.

### 15 JANUARY 1927

*Iñes de Castro,* opera in three acts by the prime Portuguese opera composer Ruy COELHO, to a libretto presenting a melodramatized story of the mistress of the Emperor Pedro I of Portugal, put to death in 1355 by a coterie of perfidious courtiers but posthumously rehabilitated in her martyrdom in a grisly scene of the coronation of her exhumed cadaver, set to music in an expansive Italianate vein, is produced in Lisbon in the original Portuguese version. (An Italian version was produced in Lisbon on 27 April 1951.)

### 16 JANUARY 1927

*Fonctionnaire MCMXII: Inaction en Musique,* symphonic skit by Florent SCHMITT, deriding old-fashioned bureaucracy of the 1912 vintage whose slogan was "never do today what you can make someone else do tomorrow," is performed for the first time in Paris.

### 21 JANUARY 1927

*Suite en fa* for orchestra by Albert ROUSSEL, his first work written in a neo-classical manner, in three movements, *Prélude, Sarabande* and *Gigue,* completed on 21 August 1926, is performed for the first time anywhere by the Boston Symphony Orchestra, under the direction of Serge Koussevitzky to whom it is dedicated.

### 22 JANUARY 1927

*Scarlattiana,* a divertimento based on 88 themes from 545 sonatas of Domenico Scarlatti by Alfredo CASELLA, for piano and chamber orchestra, is performed for the first time anywhere by the New York Philharmonic Orchestra, conducted by Otto Klemperer, with the composer at the piano.

### 28 JANUARY 1927

Aaron COPLAND, 26-year-old Brooklyn-born composer, appears as soloist with the Boston Symphony Orchestra, Serge Koussevitzky conducting, in the first performance of his *Piano Concerto,* in two connected movements, evolving, after an elegiac exordium, into a boldly polyrhythmic essay in jazz, with the nervously syncopating melody set against a steady ostinato in the manner of the Blues, then erupting in a series of angular intervalic leaps, while maintaining a clearly identifiable classical sonata form.

Copland's Piano Concerto shows a shocking lack of taste, of proportion. After thunderous, blaring measures in which one brass instrument vies with another in arrogant announcement, there are gentle purposeless measures for the piano, which is struck by fingers apparently directed at random, as a child amuses itself by making noises when it is restless in the room. (Philip Hale, Boston *Herald,* 29 January 1927)

If there exists anywhere in the world a stranger concatenation of meaninglessly ugly sounds and distorted rhythms than Mr. Copland's *Piano Concerto,* Boston has been spared it. (Warren Storey Smith, Boston *Post,* 29 January 1927)

From all Copland Concertos and others of the same sort, Good Lord deliver us. . . . Last Saturday night the generous audience politely laughed. It ought to have been a case of tears rather than laughter. I fear that the listeners didn't appreciate how insulting the piece was. We hear so much about prohibition nowadays; let us have a little prohibition against the awful sounds made sometimes in the name of music. (Letter to the Editor of the Boston *Herald,* 2 February 1927, signed by Clayton Johns, a Boston musician and composer of songs)

Mr. Copland, for aught anyone can affirm, may be the merest freak or a composer of eminence in embryo. A serene and distant future, not a clamoring present, will give judgment. Meanwhile, he speaks for a "chapel" of young American composers, for a new and experimental sort of American music. . . . Not prejudice, but perception, will reduce Mr. Copland to his level. (H. T. Parker, Boston *Evening Transcript,* 4 February 1927)

All sorts of things are said about the Boston Symphony Orchestra's performance of an extraordinary piano concerto by Aaron Copland—among them that Mr. Koussevitzky, as a cynical foreigner, is seeking only to satirize American music, to bring it into contempt, by the production of such a musical monstrosity. . . . The Listener acquits Mr. Koussevitzky of cynicism, but he finds no music at all in the Copland composition. To him, it is a harrowing horror from beginning to end. . . . There is no rhythm in the so-called concerto. The piano part is not played, but merely happened upon at random, as it might be if the performer struck the keyboard with his elbows instead of his fingers. At least that is the way the piece impressed persons in the audience who have welcomed and enjoyed the newer developments that have come since Strauss, Debussy and Stravinsky dawned on the world. The Listener believes that the Boston Symphony audiences are tolerant to the point of docility; but this performance was too much for them. (The Listener, in a column in the Boston *Evening Transcript,* 5 February 1927)

Dear Kolya—You're a darling to have sent all those delightful write-ups. After reading them I went to the mirror to see if I could recognize myself. How flattering it was to read that the 'Listener' can understand Strauss, Debussy, Stravinsky—but not poor me. How instructive to learn that there is 'no rhythm' in this 'so-called concerto!' Only one thing got my nanny: how dare H. T. Parker talk of *reducing* me to my level, while I am waiting to be *raised* to my level. And all that really worries me is whether or not the Maestro will ever again have sufficient courage to perform me anywhere. When the Concerto is played again (O horrid thought!) we must see if we can't get the police to raid the concert hall to give a little added interest to this 'horrible' experiment.—Till Soon, Aaron. (Letter to Nicolas Slonimsky from Aaron Copland, dated New York, 10 February 1927)

## 28 JANUARY 1927

*Angélique,* musical farce in one act by Jacques IBERT, dealing with a shrew whom not even the devil himself could tame, set to a modernistic score with the inclusion of a jazzy interlude to portray the ethnological consciousness of a voodooistic tribal chief in the African interior, is performed for the first time in Paris.

## 29 JANUARY 1927

*Herrn Dürers Bild*, opera in three acts by the Czech-born German-educated composer Joseph Gustav MRACZECK, in which a Nuremberg girl infatuated with Albrecht Dürer who painted her portrait in 1520 is mortally wounded by her blind father as he seeks to kill the painter, set to a romantically expansive musical score, is produced in Hanover.

## 29 JANUARY 1927

Second movement of the *Fourth Symphony*, a work of prophetic modernity by the New England composer of genius Charles E. IVES, set in a polymetrical notation comprising improvisational instrumental parts, forming a monumental counterpoint of two symphonic units, independent in concept and design but coalescing into a dual entity, while the harmonic complications arising therefrom exemplify a complete emancipation of dissonance, is performed for the first time in New York, Eugene Goossens conducting.

## 30 JANUARY 1927

*Beatrix Cenci*, tragic opera in five acts by the Polish composer Ludomir RÓZYCKI, dealing with the beautiful Roman gentlewoman executed in 1599 as an accomplice in the murder of her father, is performed for the first time in Warsaw.

## 2 FEBRUARY 1927

*Rio Rita*, vivacious musical comedy by Harry TIERNEY, dealing with a Texas Ranger in hot pursuit of a Mexican bandit, gaining a girl in the process, is produced in New York.

## 6 FEBRUARY 1927

*Kolo*, symphonic dance by the Croatian composer Jakov GOTOVAC, set in propulsively asymmetric rhythms peculiar to the Slavic Balkan regions, is performed for the first time in Zagreb.

## 9 FEBRUARY 1927

*Variations on a Hungarian Folksong*, orchestral suite by the 32-year-old Hungarian composer Eugen ZÁDOR, based on a Hungarian army song popular during World War I, is performed for the first time in Vienna.

## 10 FEBRUARY 1927

*Jonny Spielt Auf*, opera in two acts and eleven scenes by the 26-year-old Viennese composer Ernst KRENEK (completed 19 June 1926), to his own libretto portraying in an astutely dissonant idiom, liberally spiced with jazzified polyrhythms, the adventures of the Negro jazzband leader Jonny, indulging in miscegenating amourettes with an accessible prima donna and a Paris chambermaid, appropriating a Stradivarius from an anachronistically long-haired violin virtuoso, entering into a lucrative business relationship with a euphoric American concert manager, set against the background of mystically humanized nature, singing glaciers and other supernatural phenomena, employing the scientific marvels of radio loudspeakers, and culminating in Jonny's apotheosis as he triumphantly straddles a revolving terrestrial globe, dancing jazz on top of the world, is performed for the first time at the Leipzig Opera House.

The main idea of *Jonny Spielt Auf* is the split between the historically overburdened and brooding European, and especially central European, spirit and the fresh life-asserting mentality of the West symbolized by America. At the time, this conflict appeared to me in such a simple formulation. I used jazz elements only by way of quotation to characterize a certain sphere of action, and jazz affects the entire opera only in passing. Naturally, it never occurred to me to call it a "jazz opera." While in Europe it was often held as an offensive glorification of Americanism, many Americans took it as a contemptuous criticism of their own country. (Ernst Krenek's statement in a letter to the author dated 5 February 1938)

## 12 FEBRUARY 1927

*La Rosiera,* "tragic idyll" in three acts by Vittorio GNECCHI, after Alfred de Musset's play *On ne badine pas avec l'amour,* telling the piteous tale of a country girl who kills herself with a scythe after her defilement and betrayal by a philandering feudal baron, the music seasoned with opulent modernities, with occasional quarter-tones to express erotic anxiety, is performed for the first time, sixteen years after its composition, in a German version, in Gera. (The first performance in Italian was given in Trieste, on 24 January 1931)

## 17 FEBRUARY 1927

*The King's Henchman,* first opera, in three acts, by the American composer Deems TAYLOR, to the text of Edna St. Vincent Millay, from a Tristanesque legend of Eadgar, King of England who incautiously entrusts his foster brother with the task of bringing the ineffably beautiful Aelfrida of Devon to be his consort, with a mellifluously Wagneromantic score, is produced by the Metropolitan Opera House in New York, bringing in $15,504 at the box office, the only opera by an American composer to retain its place in its repertory for three consecutive seasons before vanishing into limbo.

## 17 FEBRUARY 1927

*Hanneles Himmelfahrt,* opera in two acts by the 55-year-old German composer Paul GRAENER, to a libretto drawn from a play by Gerhart Hauptmann, relating the mystical story of an ailing girl who succumbs in a plasma of Wagnerogenic chromatic harmonies, undergoes a diatonic transfiguration and is carried to heaven in celestial D major, is produced simultaneously in Dresden and Breslau.

## 21 FEBRUARY 1927

*Le Poirier de Misère,* a musical fable in three acts by the French composer Marcel DELANNOY, in which the pear tree shelters personified Misery, which

447

captures everyone that climbs on it, trapping Death itself in its fruit-laden branches and releasing it only at the demand of the human *morituri* desperate at the prospect of ineluctable immortality, is produced at the Opéra-Comique in Paris.

21 FEBRUARY 1927

*Der Zarewitsch,* light opera in three acts by Franz LEHÁR, in which the Russian Tsarevich's dalliance with a complaisant damsel in Naples is unhappily broken when the Tsar dies, and the Tsarevich obeys the call of duty and returns to St. Petersburg to ascend the Russian throne, set to music in a vivacious Viennese manner, with interludes of balalaika music supplying local color, is produced in Berlin.

21 FEBRUARY 1927

*Sophie Arnould,* lyric comedy in one act by Gabriel PIERNÉ based on apocryphal anecdotes about the stormy life of the Paris soprano Sophie Arnould (1740–1802), is performed for the first time at the Opéra-Comique in Paris.

25 FEBRUARY 1927

*Vetrate di Chiesa,* four impressions for orchestra by Ottorino RESPIGHI, inspired by stained-glass windows in Italian churches: (1) *La Fuga in Egitto,* depicting in reverently illustrative tones the flight of the Holy Family into Egypt (2) *San Michele Arcangelo,* a trumpetingly wrathful invocation of the Archangel Michael smiting the legions of the rebellious ex-angel Lucifer (3) *Il Mattutino di Santa Chiara,* a poetic elegy suggested by the contemplation of a morning in the life of Saint Clara (1191–1212) (4) *San Gregorio Magno,* the apotheosis of Gregory the Great blessing the crowds, is performed for the first time anywhere by the Boston Symphony Orchestra, Serge Koussevitzky conducting.

27 FEBRUARY 1927

*Adils och Elisiv,* opera in three acts by the Swedish composer Wilhelm PETERSON-BERGER, is produced in Stockholm on his sixtieth birthday.

1 MARCH 1927

Poland issues a CHOPIN commemorative stamp with his portrait of the denomination of 40 groschen.

2 MARCH 1927

*Royal Palace,* one-act opera by Kurt WEILL, dealing with an international charmer named Deianira (symbolically identified with the wife of Hercules whom she inadvertently poisoned with the blood of the centaur slain by him) who holds in sensuous thrall three men of her past, present and future on vacation at the Royal Palace Hotel on a South Pacific island, to a score in a satiric idiom vibrating with derisive syncopation and stylized balladry, is produced in Berlin.

### 3 MARCH 1927

*Basi e Bote,* comic opera in three acts by the Bohemian-born Italian composer Riccardo PICK-MANGIAGALLI, to a libretto, in the Venetian dialect, by Arrigo Boito, with characters of old commedia dell'arte depicted in a mellifluous Donizettian score orchestrated with Wagneromantic lusciousness, is produced in Rome.

### 4 MARCH 1927

*Concertino* by the 52-year-old Mexican composer Julián CARRILLO, written for special instruments capable of producing fractional tones (quarter-tones, eighth-tones, sixteenth-tones), is performed for the first time anywhere by the Philadelphia Orchestra, Leopold Stokowski conducting.

### 5 MARCH 1927

*Concerto* for violin, horn and orchestra by the foremost English composeress Ethel SMYTH, is performed for the first time in London, Henry Wood conducting, Jelly d'Arányi and Aubrey Brain soloists.

### 5 MARCH 1927

*Second Symphony* in one movement by the Danish composer Knudaage RIISAGER is performed for the first time in Copenhagen, on the eve of his 30th birthday.

### 9 MARCH 1927

*Madama di Challant,* opera in three acts by the 33-year-old Italian composer Carmine GUARINO, is produced at La Scala in Milan.

### 11 MARCH 1927

On his fourth American tour, Alfredo CASELLA conducts at the Wanamaker department store in New York the first performance anywhere of his *Concerto Romano* for organ, brass, percussion and strings, commissioned by the manager of the store and set in a neo-Baroque style intended to recreate in music the plastic monumentality of classical Roman architecture.

### 13 MARCH 1927

Nikolai MEDTNER appears as soloist in the first performance in Moscow of his *Second Piano Concerto* in C minor.

### 17 MARCH 1927

*Shah-Senem,* opera in four acts by Reinhold GLIÈRE, commissioned by the Soviet Socialist Republic of Azerbaijan, to a legend dealing with the love of a beautiful Caucasian maiden for a young folksinger who arrives on a white charger to claim her at the last moment before the expiration of a seven-years' test period granted to Shah-Senem by her father intent on giving her in marriage to a feudal lord, set to an astutely orientalistic score glowing with serpentine fioriuras and based on original native folksongs, is performed for the first time to a Russian libretto in Baku.

(Date from *The Worker of Baku* of 18 March 1927; a new version, to a libretto in the Tatar language, was produced in Baku on 4 May 1934. Previous editions of *Music Since 1900*, Loewenberg's *Annals of Opera* and Baker's *Biographical Dictionary of Musicians*, 5th Edition, 1958, edited by Nicolas Slonimsky, all give the date of the revised version)

### 18 MARCH 1927

Serge RACHMANINOFF appears as soloist with the Philadelphia Orchestra, Leopold Stokowski conducting, in the first performance of his *Fourth Piano Concerto*, in G minor (begun in Russia in 1914, and completed on 25 August 1926 in New York), dedicated to his spiritually and esthetically close friend Nikolai Medtner, in three movements:

(1) *Allegro vivace (alla breve)*, with a spacious opening gradually increasing in rhythmic frequencies per metric unit and expanding in pianistic virtuosity (2) *Largo*, in C major, with a mournfully flatted submediant, set in a pessimistically elegiac mood, and leading directly to the finale (3) *Allegro vivace*, a rondo in 3/4 time, moving energetically along its foreseeable course, and ending in the assertive G major.

(The Finale was totally revised in 1941, with the first two movements reorchestrated, and the new version performed by Rachmaninoff with the Philadelphia Orchestra, Eugene Ormandy conducting, on 12 October 1941)

### 18 MARCH 1927

*Third Symphony* by the Chicago composer Arne OLDBERG, written in a competent Germanic manner, in three movements, is performed for the first and last time by the Chicago Symphony Orchestra, Frederick Stock conducting.

### 18 MARCH 1927

*First Symphony* in A minor by Alexandre TANSMAN, in four contrasting movements, set in a romantically classical style, with acrid bitonalities in its harmonic structure and a suggestion of incisive Polish rhythms, is performed for the first time anywhere by the Boston Symphony Orchestra, under the direction of Serge Koussevitzky to whom the score is dedicated.

### 20 MARCH 1927

*Kammerkonzert* for piano, violin and 13 wind instruments by Alban BERG, completed on 23 July 1925, thematically based on the modified musical letters, in German notation, present in the names of his friend and teacher Arnold Schoenberg (ArnolD SCHönBErG, where S = Es = E-flat), to whom the score is dedicated, Anton Webern (Anton wEBErn) and his own (AlBAn BErG), wherein the coincidence of the initial letters in their first names creates a simulacrum of a tonal center in an otherwise atonal matrix, cast in three movements, each naturally divisible into three sections (the figure 3 acquires here a magical significance), *Thema scherzoso con variazioni,* scored for piano and wind instruments, *Adagio* for violin and wind instruments, and *Rondo ritmico con Introduzione,* for all fifteen instruments as a Hegelian synthesis of thesis and antithesis, is performed for the first time in Berlin, Hermann Scherchen conducting.

20 MARCH 1927

*From the Black Belt,* a suite of character pieces for small orchestra by the American Negro composer William Grant STILL, in seven sections, (1) *Lil' Scamp,* lasting only eight measures (2) *Honeysuckle,* in dulcet melodies and facile rhythms (3) *Dance* (4) *Mah Bones Is Creakin'* wherein an old man bemoans his rheumatic pain in rattling syncopation (5) *Blue,* in the style of Negro spirituals (6) *Brown Girl,* a musical tribute to a handsome mulatto (7) *Clap Yo' Han's,* with musicians clapping their hands rhythmically as in a children's game, is performed for the first time by the Barrère Little Symphony in New York.

22 MARCH 1927

*Canto a Sevilla,* poem for voice and orchestra by Joaquín TURINA, is performed for the first time in Madrid.

26 MARCH 1927

A century has passed since the death of BEETHOVEN.

31 MARCH 1927

*Lilacs,* poem for orchestra (after Amy Lowell) by Edward Burlingame HILL, written in a cerulean impressionistic manner marked by intertonal freedom but free of chromatic complexities, is performed for the first time by the Boston Symphony Orchestra, Serge Koussevitzky conducting.

1 APRIL 1927

The world première of the second part of *Pause del Silenzio,* "five symphonic expressions" by Gian Francesco MALIPIERO, is given by the Philadelphia Orchestra, Leopold Stokowski conducting.

(The score was published under the title *L'esilio dell'eroe,* suggested by Gabriele d'Annunzio, and later renamed by the composer *Sul fiume del tempo,* and again renamed *Il grillo cantarino,* eventually reverting to its original title *Pause del Silenzio,* none of which renaming helped the fortunes of the piece, which, as Malipiero remarked in 1952, should have perhaps been titled *Silenzio senza pause*)

2 APRIL 1927

*Concerto* for flute, cello and string orchestra by Vincent D'INDY, is performed for the first time in Paris.

*Naila,* opera in three acts by Philippe GAUBERT, is produced at the Paris Opéra, under the direction of the composer, chief conductor there from 1920.

8 APRIL 1927

*Arcana,* symphonic poem by Edgar VARÈSE, French-American builder of "organized sound," inspired by the hermetic philosophy of Paracelsus in probing the arcane essence of the arts, designed as a macrocosmic passacaglia developing through an athematic concatenation of melorhythmic molecules, wherein melody (in spacious atonally oriented intervalic progressions), rhythm (precise in its complexity within variable meters), harmony and counterpoint (dissonant with the exception of two measures of pure C-G fifths inserted to achieve the paradoxical effect of maximal discordance) and instrumental color (exploiting extreme ranges) are integral parts of the formal matrix, scored for a tremendously large orchestra including 40 percussion instruments, is performed for the first time by the Philadelphia Orchestra, under the direction of Leopold Stokowski.

Varèse's *Arcana* plunged the listener into morasses of sound which seemingly had little relation to music. . . . There was no mercy in its disharmony, no pity in its successions of screaming, clashing, clangorous discords. . . . A series of gunpowder explosions might similarly overawe the ear . . . but their musical quality would be open to question. (Oscar Thompson, *Musical America,* New York, 23 April 1927)

10 APRIL 1927

Shortly after his return from Europe, George ANTHEIL presents at Carnegie Hall, New York, a program of his works which includes a *Jazz Symphony,* a *String Quartet,* a *Sonata* for violin, piano and drums, and his monumental *Ballet Mécanique.*

Antheil Art Bursts on Startled Ears—First Performance of Ballet Mécanique in This Country Draws Varied Response—Hisses, Cheers Greet Him—Concatenation of Anvils, Bells, Horns, Buzzsaws Deafens Some Pleases Others. (Headlines in the New York *Times,* 11 April 1927)

I personally consider that the *Ballet Mécanique* was important in one particular and that it was conceived in a new form, that form specifically being the filling out of a certain time canvas with musical abstractions and sound material composed and contrasted against one another with the thought of time values rather than tonal values. . . . In the *Ballet Mécanique* I used time as Picasso might have used the blank spaces of his canvas. I did not hesitate, for instance, to repeat one measure one hundred times; I did not hesitate to have absolutely nothing on my pianola rolls for sixty-two bars; I did not hesitate to ring a bell against a certain given section of time or indeed to do whatever I pleased to do with this time canvas as long as each part of it stood up against the other. My ideas were the most abstract of the abstract. Still I was totally misunderstood by the morons who listened to the *Ballet Mécanique* in 1926. Although I had *very clearly* published exactly what I had intended way back in 1923 and 1924 in many *avant-garde* magazines, practically all of the *dumbbells* in New York went to listen to the *Ballet Mécanique* expecting to see me grind out pictures of the machine age! Some imbeciles expected to see a kind of Buck Rogers fantasy of the future. I was totally misunderstood, so deeply misunderstood that I have never made any attempt whatever of explanation what I was after in America. I realized that it was hopeless. Today, almost ten years afterwards I am making my first explanation to you. (From Antheil's letter to Nicolas Slonimsky, dated 21 July 1936)

## 15 APRIL 1927

*Flivver 10,000,000, a Joyous Epic: Fantasy for Orchestra* Inspired by the Familiar Legend *The Ten Millionth Ford Is Now Serving Its Owner* by Frederick S. CONVERSE, the main stops in the course of the music being Dawn in Detroit, The Call to Labor, Birth of the Hero (in a whole-tone trumpet fanfare), Trying His Metal, May Night by the Roadside (America's romance), The Joy Riders (America's Frolic) and The Collision (America's Tragedy), with frictional secundal harmonies illustrating the close call, concluding on an apotheosis, Phoenix Americanus, with the Hero recovering from the shock of the accident proceeding on his way "with redoubled energy, typical of the indomitable American spirit," the music set in a modestly modernistic vein, and the score including the wind machine and the Ford auto horn, is performed for the first time by the Boston Symphony Orchestra, Serge Koussevitzky conducting.

## 16 APRIL 1927

*Agamemnon,* musical play after Aeschylus and Paul Claudel by Darius MILHAUD, is performed for the first time in Paris.

## 17 APRIL 1927

Carlos SALZEDO plays the harp in the first performance in New York of his *Concerto* for harp and seven wind instruments, introducing novel effects, such as percussive taps on the frame, glissandi obtained by means of the pedals and xylophonic sounds.

## 21 APRIL 1927

*Veste di cielo,* opera by Ermanno WOLF-FERRARI, is performed for the first time in Munich, in a German version entitled *Das Himmelskleid.*

## 22 APRIL 1927

*Symphony in E minor* by the 30-year-old American composer Roger SESSIONS (completed in Florence on 31 January 1927) in three neo-classical movements: (1) *Giusto* with eighth-notes as invariables through a succession of changing meters, in the manner of a symphonic toccata (2) *Largo,* in pandiatonically expanded modalities (3) *Allegro vivace* in synocopated polyphony, in the homonymous initial key of E major, is performed for the first time by the Boston Symphony Orchestra, Serge Koussevitzky conducting.

## 23 APRIL 1927

Three centuries have passed since the production of the first opera by a German composer, *Dafne* by Heinrich SCHÜTZ (its music is lost), presented at the wedding of Princess Sophie of Saxony at Hartenfels Castle in Torgau, to a text from the same play by Rinuccini which served as the libretto for the first opera ever written, *La Dafne* by Jacopo PERI, composed in 1597, the music of which is also lost.

### 25 APRIL 1927

*Hit the Deck*, musical comedy by Vincent YOUMANS, dealing with the circumnavigatory passion of a wealthy society lady from Newport, Rhode Island, for a sailor, containing the famous sailor's chorus *Hallelujah* and the love duet *Sometimes I'm Happy*, is produced in New York.

### 27 APRIL 1927

*Švanda Dudák* (*Schwanda the Bagpiper*), comic opera in two acts by the 31-year-old Czech composer Jaromír WEINBERGER, to a libretto from a folk tale dealing with a minstrel who falsely assures his wife that he has never kissed the queen at a court entertainment, is dispatched to Hell for perfidy and throws the local devils into a choreographic pandemonium by the infectious virtuosity of his bagpipe playing, redeeming his soul and returning to the earth for a life of domestic tranquility, is produced in Prague in the Czech language obtaining the greatest acclaim accorded to any native opera of the 20th century, and marking a start of world-wide successes.

### 28 APRIL 1927

The first Russian Jazz Band ever to perform in public is introduced in a program of miscellaneous jazz numbers in Leningrad.

### 30 APRIL 1927

*La Chatte*, ballet by Henri SAUGUET, wherein a felinophilic youth, whose favorite kitten, happily metamorphosed into a young girl, reverts to her atavistic instincts when she sees a mouse, is produced in Monte Carlo.

### 5 MAY 1927

*Madonna Imperia*, comic opera in one act by Franco ALFANO, to a libretto derived from Balzac's tale, dealing with a young man enamored of a noblewoman at the Council of Constance in 414 A.D. who encounters two rivals, a bishop and a cardinal, in her boudoir (although clerical continence was decreed in 386 A.D., concubinage among ordained priests of the Church was not formally prohibited until the twelfth century), but wins her love through intellectual cunning, set to music in a passionately Italianate and lux-uriantly sonorous manner, is produced in Turin, with a chancellor and an am-bassador substituted for the parts of bishop and cardinal.

### 15 MAY 1927

*La Fata Malerba*, opera by Vittorio GUI, is produced in Turin.

454

## 20 MAY 1927

The Nicaraguan composer Luis A. DELGADILLO conducts in Caracas the first performance of his *Sinfonia Incaica*, based on ancient Peruvian themes.

## 21 MAY 1927

*Der Sprung über den Schatten* by Ernst KRENEK, the first modern European opera to be given on the Soviet stage, is presented in Leningrad.

With Mozart-like power of observation, nonchalance, and directness, Krenek portrays an astutely chosen group of people who have lost the healthy attitude towards life, and are seeking sensuous excitement at any price . . . Krenek is a master of the stage and a musician who has succeeded in returning the opera to healthy Mozartean traditions. (Igor Glebov in *Krasnaya Gazeta*, Leningrad, 20 May 1927, reproduced in Bogdanov-Berezovsky's *Soviet Opera*, Leningrad, 1940, p. 82).

Krenek's opera is rather confused in its plot, and it is in this respect a perfect counterpart of contemporary European culture, which is incapable of creating anything of the least value. (Lunatcharsky, Soviet Commissar of Education, in *Krasnaya Gazeta*, Leningrad, 7 March 1928, quoted in Bogdanov-Berezovsky's *Soviet Opera*, Leningrad, 1940, p. 83)

## 30 MAY 1927

Maurice RAVEL plays the piano part, with Georges Enesco as violinist, in the first performance, in Paris, of his *Sonata* for violin and piano, in three movements:

(1) *Allegretto*, in which a quasi-pentatonic theme is tensed by acrid major sevenths (2) *Blues*, a nervously syncopated melody with a "blue" flatted mediant in a major key (3) *Allegro*, a waltzed summary of melorhythmic materials of the first two movements, with a precipitate *perpetuum mobile* of scale passages against a harmonic background of secundal and septimal dissonance.

## 30 MAY 1927

Igor STRAVINSKY conducts in Paris for Diaghilev's Ballet Russe the world première of the concert version of his opera-oratorio *Œdipus Rex* (completed in vocal score on 14 March 1927; orchestration finished on 10 May 1927, at 4 o'clock in the morning), in two acts, to the text (in French) by Jean Cocteau, after Sophocles, translated into impersonal Latin (in order to make the drama stand out as timeless and non-geographic) by J. Danielou, the action explained to the audience by a Speaker in the vernacular (French in the original score) without musical accompaniment, providing a connective tissue between the successive episodes, from the supplication of the people to save them from the plague to the final revelation of the enormity of the King's guilt in killing his father and marrying his mother, with the music suggesting the atmosphere of a medieval mystery play along the precepts of *Ars Antiqua*, replete with recurrent thematic statements in stark, bleak harmonies stripped of all accoutrements of modernity, aridly dissonant in their open intervalic spaces and proleptic canonic progressions, cast in Gothic sonorities creating the impression of passionate immobility.

## 7 JUNE 1927

*Le Pas d'Acier*, ballet by Sergei PROKOFIEV, a choreographic interpretation of the "Leap of Steel" in industrialized new Russia, with hydraulic hammers illustrated by moving pillars of dissonant harmonies, sailors gallivanting on the stage to the strains of revolutionary songs, a former countess selling her garments at a flea market to the tune of a sentimental ballad, boys peddling cigarettes in polka time, and commissars orating in marching rhetorics, conjuring up a panorama of Bolshevistic exhilaration in an urbanistically constructivist vein, is produced by Diaghilev's Ballet Russe in Paris.

The tense, dramatic struggle, rich in great deeds of heroism and examples of supreme sacrifice, has apparently failed to impress Prokofiev's consciousness. . . . The musical characterizations in his ballet *Leap of Steel* are so monotonously similar, so completely submerged in buffoonery and persiflage that it is difficult to distinguish among them. . . . In the eyes of the bourgeoisie, Soviet Russia appears as a backward, half-civilized country populated by idiots, and its Bolshevik inhabitants as crude barbarians living according to pre-historic morals and customs. Consciously or unconsciously, Prokofiev adopts this hostile attitude in his musical descriptions of Soviet types. (Yuri Keldysh, *The Proletarian Musician*, Moscow, June 1929)

Q. Why is the last scene of *Leap of Steel* so saturated with mechanical, machine-like rhythms? A. Because machines are more attractive than people. Q. Is the factory represented in your ballet a capitalistic factory where workers are slaves, or a Soviet factory where the worker is master? If it was your intention to represent a Soviet factory, where and when did you study its operations, seeing that you lived abroad since 1918 and visited Soviet Russia for the first time in 1927, and then only for two weeks? A. This is a political and not a musical question, and I will not answer it. (Questions and answers during an interview with Prokofiev in the spring of 1929 in Moscow arranged by the Association of Proletarian Musicians and reported in *The Proletarian Musician*, Moscow, June 1929)

## 10 JUNE 1927

*Le Rêve de Cyniras*, lyric comedy in three acts by Vincent D'INDY, is produced in Paris.

## 12 JUNE 1927

*Piccola Suite* for orchestra by Riccardo PICK-MANGIAGALLI, in three minuscule movements, *I piccoli soldati*, *Berceuse* and *La Danza d'Olaf*, is performed for the first time in Milan.

## 14 JUNE 1927

*The Red Poppy*, ballet in three acts by Reinhold GLIÈRE, focused on a gallant Soviet crew at a Chinese port of call, featuring an infectious sailors' dance in the polka rhythms of the popular Soviet song *Little Apple*, which inspires the downtrodden coolies to break the chains of oppressive minor seconds and rise in rebellion in the ascending fourths of the *Internationale*, containing a lyric episode of a beautiful proletarian cabaret singer who sacrifices her life to foil a counter-revolutionary plot against a valiant Soviet army captain, with the apotheosis proclaiming the victory of the Chinese people over the feudal lords and their imperialist allies and an unbreakable fraternal friendship with Soviet Russia, is produced with an appropriate socialist enthusiasm at the Bolshoi Theater in Moscow.

## 23 JUNE 1927

Igor STRAVINSKY presents in Paris a performance on the specially constructed "piano pneumatique" of the four-hand piano arrangement of his ballet score *Le Sacre du Printemps*, amplified by the PANOTROPE, "le plus fort phonographe du monde."

## 30 JUNE 1927

The Fifth Festival of the International Society for Contemporary Music opens in Frankfurt with the following program of chamber music:

*String Quartet* in an optimistically polyphonic manner by the Soviet composer Alexander MOSSOLOV; a subtly impressionistic *Flute Sonata* by the Dutch modernist Willem PIJPER; *Concertino* for piano and six instruments by the 72-year-old grandmaster of Czech music Leoš JANÁČEK, first performed in Brno on 16 February 1926, cast in a hedonistically modernistic form; *Le Danze del Re David*, a Hebraic suite for piano in a stylized neo-paleographic idiom by the Italian neo-romanticist Mario CASTELNUOVO-TEDESCO.

## 1 JULY 1927

The second concert of the Fifth Festival of the International Society of Contemporary Music in Frankfurt presents the following program of symphonic music:

*Dance in Place Congo*, a symphonic panorama of a Negro and Creole street festival in New Orleans by the New England composer Henry F. GILBERT, the "Ur-Amerikaner," as a German critic has described him; *Seventh Suite* by the Viennese theorist and dodecaphonic pioneer Josef Matthias HAUER, based on a series of two mutually exclusive six-note tropes; the world première of the *First Piano Concerto* by Béla BARTÓK, completed by him on 12 November 1926, played by Bartók himself with Wilhelm Furtwängler conducting the orchestra, distinguished by barbaric rhythmic power and couched in dissonant counterpoint, with the major seventh becoming a substitute for the octave, within a modal framework in which E and C-sharp assume the function of strong barycenters, and making use of tone-clusters (borrowed by personal permission from Henry Cowell's pianistic innovation), in three movements: (1) *Allegro moderato*, marked by cumulative kinetic energy, with the eighth-note as the least common denominator within the matrix of changing meters, in a dissonant idiom intensified by the process of gradual accretion of non-harmonic notes (2) *Andante*, a colloquy between the piano and a consortium of drumlets in the manner of an antiphonal concertino, with the strings conspicuously absent and wind instruments arriving at the very end (3) *Allegro molto*, an essay in spontaneous motility, with distinctive thematic molecules passing back and forth between the piano and the orchestra, concluding with a terse, crisp and sharp coda, accentuated by hard desiccated strokes of sonic matter; *Fifth Symphony* by the Danish neo-romantic composer Carl NIELSEN (first performed in Copenhagen on 24 January 1922.)

457

## 2 JULY 1927

The third concert of the Fifth Festival of the International Society for Contemporary Music in Frankfurt presents the following program of chamber music:

*Third String Quartet* by the Swiss neo-classicist Conrad BECK; *String Quartet* by the Russian-born German-educated romantic modernist Wladimir VOGEL; the logical, austere, and yet emotionally intense *Kammerkonzert* by Alban BERG, first performed in Berlin on 20 March 1927; and the neo-ecclesiastical *Magnificat* by the German master of choral polyphony Heinrich KAMINSKI.

## 3 JULY 1927

Two concerts are presented during the course of the Fifth Festival of the International Society for Contemporary Music held in Frankfurt, in the morning and in the evening:

Morning concert: a Slavic oratorio by the Croatian composer Božidar ŠIROLA, *The Lives and Remembrance of the Holy Brethren and Apostles to the Slavs, Cyril and Methodius.*

Evening concert: *Offrande à Siva,* choreographic poem with pleasingly orientalistic music expressing in artful arabesques the spirit of Hindu rituals, by the French composer Claude DELVINCOURT; *Il Cantico del Sole,* to the poem of St. Francis, by the Parisian composer Raymond PETIT; the dynamic and transcendentally modernistic *Piano Concerto* by Ernst TOCH; and the academically competent *Second Symphony* by the Czech composer Emil AXMAN.

## 3 JULY 1927

Wanda LANDOWSKA, superbly endowed modern mistress of the harpsichord, inaugurates at her summer home in St.-Leu-la-Forêt, near Paris, a series of concerts of old music performed on the replicas of ancient instruments manufactured under her supervision, with splicitous regard for authenticity of tone production.

## 4 JULY 1927

The Fifth Festival of the International Society for Contemporary Music in Frankfurt concludes with the following program of chamber works:

*Fourth String Quartet,* in a neo-Flemish contrapuntal manner by the Dutch-born London resident Bernard van DIEREN; *Sonatina* for flute, clarinet and bassoon by the romantically disposed Danish composer Jörgen BENTZON, a pupil of Carl Nielsen; an attractive *Trio* for piano, violin and cello by the Spanish composer Joaquín TURINA; *Psalm 139,* for chorus a cappella by the English composer William WHITTAKER; the consistently atonal *Sonata* for violin and piano by the Hungarian composer Alexander JEMNITZ; and *Music for the Theater,* an energetic and poetic suite for chamber orchestra by the 26-year-old American composer Aaron COPLAND, first performed in Boston on 20 November 1925.

## 17 JULY 1927

Four short modern chamber operas are produced in the course of a Festival of New Music in Baden-Baden:

World première of *Hin und Zurück* by Paul HINDEMITH, a 'film sketch' in which the action proceeds in a crab canon after reaching the middle (hence the title, 'forth and back'): an adulteress is killed by her husband, returns to life, the attending physician backs out of the door, the husband pockets the revolver and the scene reverts to the *status quo ante; Mahagonny,* a satirical skit by Kurt WEILL, picturing the degradation in an imaginary capitalist city named Mahagonny with specifications suggesting Florida; first performance of *Die Prinzessin auf der Erbse,* fable after Hans Christian Andersen by Ernst TOCH, picturing a highly sensitive princess who could feel a pea through twenty layers of mattresses; and the world première of *L'Enlèvement d'Europe,* 'opéra-minute' by Darius MILHAUD, to Paul Claudel's imaginative libretto wherein Europa prefers the company of cattle to that of men, taking particular fancy to a bull, who is Jupiter in disguise, with a happy ending secured as she elopes with him while the chorus sings encouragingly in thematic ascending sevenths and ninths.

## 12 AUGUST 1927

Half a century has passed since the day that Thomas Alva EDISON patented the phonograph.

## 14 AUGUST 1927

Two centuries have passed since the English organist William Croft, composer of pious hymn music, "at cælum demigravit chorum praesentior angelorum concentibus suum additurus Hallelujah" as his entry into Heaven is phrased on his tombstone in Westminster Abbey in London.

## 24 AUGUST 1927

The Soviet Government deprives the famous Russian bass singer Fedor CHALIAPIN of his honorary title as a People's Artist for his anti-Soviet declarations in the émigré circles.

## 27 AUGUST 1927

*We,* symphonic poem by the American composer James DUNN, celebrating Lindbergh's transatlantic flight (the first person plural of the title refers to Lindbergh's collective identification with his plane, the Spirit of St. Louis), is performed for the first time by the New York Philharmonic.

## 3 SEPTEMBER 1927

*T-DOXC,* "poème mécanique" for orchestra by the 30-year-old Danish composer Knudaage RIISAGER, is performed for the first time in Copenhagen.

## 9 SEPTEMBER 1927

*Pomona,* ballet by Constant LAMBERT, a bucolic idyll depicting the courtship of Pomona, the goddess of fruit, by the god Vertumnus, is produced in Buenos Aires.

## 12 SEPTEMBER 1927

*My Maryland,* operetta in three acts by Sigmund ROMBERG, in which Barbara Frietchie, rejuvenated from Whittier's poetic image of her as "bowed with her fourscore years and ten" to a luxuriant and sensuous Southern Rebelle who captivates the Yankee captain of the Union troops that captured her town, is produced in New York.

### 19 SEPTEMBER 1927

*Third String Quartet* by Arnold SCHOENBERG, op. 30, completed on 8 March 1927, cast in a consciously elaborated method of composition with 12 tones, in four classically correlated movements, (1) *Moderato* (2) *Adagio* (3) *Intermezzo, Allegro moderato* (4) *Rondo, Molto moderato,* is performed for the first time by the Kolisch String Quartet in Vienna.

### 30 SEPTEMBER 1927

A new International Musicological Society is formed in Basel under the honorary chairmanship of Guido Adler to supplant the International Music Society dissolved at the outbreak of the war in 1914. (The first issue of the trilingual Bulletin of the International Musicological Society was published on 1 October 1928)

### 6 OCTOBER 1927

*The Jazz Singer,* first film with a synchronized optical sound track, starring Al JOLSON, opens at the Warner Brothers' Theater in New York. (This was only partly a sound film; the first motion picture with sound throughout, also starring Al Jolson and titled *The Singing Fool,* opened in New York on 19 September 1928)

### 7 OCTOBER 1927

*Das Wunder der Heliane,* opera-mystery in three acts by the once wonder boy of modern music Erich Wolfgang KORNGOLD of Vienna, now 30 years old, wherein the angelic Heliane enrolls the aid of an archangelic stranger to combat the sinister designs of a Lucifer-like demon, set to music of mystically Wagneromantic effusiveness replete with Straussian harmonic protuberances, is produced in Hamburg.

### 15 OCTOBER 1927

*New Music,* a quarterly for publication of ultra-modern American music, edited by Henry COWELL, publishes its first issue, the full score of *Men and Mountains,* 'symphonic ensemble' in a poignantly atonal idiom by Carl RUGGLES, rugged individualist from Vermont.

*New Music* affords a means of publication of ultra-modern works, and also insures their distribution among its subscribers. It publishes works for orchestra, piano, voice, violin, chamber music, etc., specializing in the music of Americans, but not excluding occasional foreign works. It is not a profit-making plan, and any profits which may accrue will be equitably divided among the contributing composers. (From the publisher's statement in the first issue)

## 24 OCTOBER 1927

*Chôros No. 8* for large orchestra and two pianos by Brazil's foremost composer Heitor VILLA-LOBOS, is performed for the first time anywhere in Paris.

## 29 OCTOBER 1927

*First Symphony* by the 28-year-old Russian composer Alexander TCHEREPNIN, marked "en Mi," but lacking a key signature, in four well-balanced movements, of which the second, *Vivace,* scored for pitchless percussion instruments, reinforced by gentle taps with the bow on the body of violins, violas, cellos, and double-basses, constitutes the earliest known example of an integral percussive movement in a symphony, and the third, *Andante,* exemplifies Tcherepnin's personal technique of *Interpunctus,* leading to a finale, *Allegretto con anima,* concluding on a coagulated major-minor triad on E, and making consistent use of the "Tcherepnin Scale" of nine notes in a variety of permutations, is performed for the first time in Paris.

## 3 NOVEMBER 1927

*A Connecticut Yankee,* musical comedy, fashioned after Mark Twain's story by Richard RODGERS, wherein a skeptical American anachronistically blunders into King Arthur's court in Camelot, and decides to modernize the place by introducing the telephone and radio, featuring the popular songs *My Heart Stood Still* and *Thou Swell,* is produced in New York.

## 5 NOVEMBER 1927

Salle PLEYEL, the largest concert hall in Paris, is officially opened to the public.

## 6 NOVEMBER 1927

*To October,* Second Symphony in one movement by 21-year-old Dmitri SHOSTAKOVICH, "a symphonic dedication," concluding with a choral ode to the Soviet Revolution "the herald of the awaited Sun, the will of the centuries in revolt, the happiness of fields and work benches and the banner of living generations" containing numerous instrumental and technical innovations, (1) a factory whistle (2) polyrhythmic counterpoint combining 2, 3, 4, 5, and 6 notes to a beat (3) chromatic canon in the major seventh in nine parts, resulting in the progression of chords comprising nine different chromatic tones, is performed for the first time in Leningrad, at the Festival on the occasion of the tenth anniversary of the Soviet Revolution, on the same program with the cantata *October* by Nicolas ROSLAVETZ and an orchestral suite from the ballet *Zavod (The Iron Foundry)* by Alexander MOSSOLOV, which includes in its orchestration a sheet of steel to simulate the sound produced by industrial machines at work.

## 13 NOVEMBER 1927

*Komödie für Orchester* by Ernst TOCH is performed for the first time by the Berlin Philharmonic Orchestra, Furtwängler conducting.

### 18 NOVEMBER 1927

*La Campana sommersa,* opera in four acts by Ottorino RESPIGHI, after the drama of Gerhart Hauptmann, dealing with a bell maker whose masterpiece, a large church bell, falls accidentally into a lake, and who is lured to follow it beneath the waters by a mysterious mountain maiden, is produced, in a German version, in Hamburg.

### 18 NOVEMBER 1927

*La Bagarre,* symphonic rondo by Bohuslav MARTINU, illustrating in realistically impressionistic tones the emotional commotion that greeted Lindbergh at his landing at Le Bourget airport after his transatlantic flight, is performed for the first time anywhere by the Boston Symphony Orchestra, Serge Koussevitzky conducting.

### 22 NOVEMBER 1927

*Funny Face,* musical revue with a score by George GERSHWIN, featuring among others the celebrated song *'S Wonderful,* is produced in New York.

### 23 NOVEMBER 1927

*Zulumćar (The Tyrant),* opera in three acts by the Serbian composer Petar KRSTIĆ, based on rustic life in Ottoman-dominated Bosnia, is performed for the first time in Belgrade.

### 27 NOVEMBER 1927

*Les Euménides,* opera in three acts by Darius MILHAUD, the third of the three parts of his operatic trilogy after Aeschylus' *Oresteia* (the first two being Agamemnon and *Les Choéphores*) dealing with Orestes pursued by the furies, Erinys, to punish him for the murder of his mother committed by him to avenge the murder at her hands of his father Agamemnon, but protected by Athena and Apollo, and declared innocent by the people of Athens by reason of justifiable matricide, whereupon the Erinys change their name to Eumenides (meaning benevolent ones), is performed for the first time in Antwerp.

### 4 DECEMBER 1927

*Satuala,* opera in three acts by Emil von REZNIČEK, involving a fair-skinned Hawaiian girl-spy who lures a captain of the landing American forces in Sandwich Islands in 1893 in order to delay the operation but becomes enamored of him in earnest and stabs herself to death as he, realizing his delinquency, shoots himself to the strains of the *Star-Spangled Banner,* in an effective theatrical setting including a hula-hula ballet accompanied by secundal harmonies and syncopated rhythms, is produced in Leipzig.

### 5 DECEMBER 1927

Somdet Phra Chao Yu Hua Bhumibol Adulyadej, King ANANDA of Siam, composer of American jazz tunes, among them *Blue Night* to the lyrics by the Royal Chamberlain, is born in the Grand Palace in Bangkok.

## 5 DECEMBER 1927

*Le Bon Roi Dagobert*, opera in four acts by Marcel SAMUEL-ROUSSEAU, after the old French fable about the good old King Dagobert, who loves his queen in the daytime but fails to notice that another woman plays the succuba at night, and when he finds out, cannot decide which one he prefers, is produced at the Opéra-Comique in Paris.

## 5 DECEMBER 1927

*Glagolithic Mass* (*Slavonic Mass*), the last work of the Czech grandmaster Leoš JANÁČEK, completed by him on 15 October 1926 at the age of 72, to the orthodox text in old Slavonic, scored for soloists, chorus, organ and orchestra (thus violating the tradition of the Eastern Church admitting only a cappella singing), making use of undiatonic melodies in whole-tone scales and occasional polytonalities, with the rhythmic line often in asymmetric patterns, comprising eight sections, five of which are choral, with a final apotheosis consisting of an organ solo and an instrumental envoi, is performed for the first time in Brno.

## 10 DECEMBER 1927

*Fantaisie basque* for violin and orchestra by Gabriel PIERNÉ is performed for the first time in Paris, with Jacques Thibaud as soloist and the composer conducting.

## 11 DECEMBER 1927

*La Principessa di Perepepè*, musical comedy by the Italian composer Mario LABROCA, is produced in Rome.

## 13 DECEMBER 1927

The Bromberg Jazz Orchestra in Warsaw, Poland, establishes the world's endurance record by playing thirty-three hours and ten minutes, with only forty-five seconds' intermission between the numbers, bettering the previous record by two hours.

## 15 DECEMBER 1927

Arthur SHEPHERD conducts the Cleveland Orchestra in the first performance of his first symphony, *Horizons*, in four movements representing four geographically psychological scenes of the American West: (1) *Westward* (2) *The Lone Prairie*, with the song *The Dying Cowboy* played by a saxophone (3) *The Old Chisholm Trail*, making use of the old tune of that name (4) *Canyons*, painting a spacious musicorama of a famous Western landmark.

## 16 DECEMBER 1927

*Le Pauvre Matelot*, "a complaint in three acts" in the form of an opera, by Darius MILHAUD (completed on 7 September 1926), to a libretto by Jean

Cocteau, wherein a sailor returning home after many years at sea represents himself to his wife as a stranger to test her fidelity and is murdered by her for his money which she hopes to save for his return, is produced at the Opéra-Comique in Paris.

### 21 DECEMBER 1927

*Jakub lutnista (Jacob the Lutenist)*, opera by the 57-year-old Polish composer Henryk OPIEŃSKI, is produced in Poznan.

### 22 DECEMBER 1927

Willem PIJPER, 33-year-old Dutch modernist, plays the piano solo with the Concertgebouw Orchestra in Amsterdam, Pierre Monteux conducting, in the first performance of his *Second Piano Concerto* (completed on 26 August 1927), consisting of four symphonic pieces with piano obbligato separated by three unaccompanied piano solo sections.

### 27 DECEMBER 1927

*Show Boat*, musical comedy by Jerome KERN, his masterpiece of the American musical theater, with book and lyrics by Oscar Hammerstein II, based on the novel by Edna Ferber of the same name, presenting a romantic story of events on a Mississippi showboat in the 1880's, wherein the captain's daughter elopes with a gambler, featuring one of the most authentically inspired songs in American popular music, the hymnal *Ol' Man River*, conceived in the tones of a Negro spiritual, is performed for the first time in New York, produced by Florenz Ziegfeld.

### 28 DECEMBER 1927

*Dinara*, comic opera in three acts by the 54-year-old Georgian composer Dmitri ARAKISHVILI, to a libretto in the Georgian language, after the Arabian tale *Caliph for an Hour*, is produced in Tbilisi.

### 28 DECEMBER 1927

*Antigone*, "musical tragedy" by Arthur HONEGGER, to a libretto by Jean Cocteau after Sophocles, couched in a stylized neo-Grecian idiom, vitalized by astringent secundal discords, is produced in Brussels.

### 29 DECEMBER 1927

*Sly*, opera in three acts by Ermanno WOLF-FERRARI, founded on the prologue to Shakespeare's *The Taming of the Shrew*, descriptive of the drunken sot named Sly, is produced at La Scala in Milan.

### 29 DECEMBER 1927

Alexandre TANSMAN, 30-year-old Polish-Parisian composer, appears as soloist with the Boston Symphony Orchestra, Serge Koussevitzky conducting, in the world première of his *Second Piano Concerto*, in three movements, of which the last opens with a *Berceuse* set in nostalgic Polish inflections and then erupts into a rhythmic finale.

# ∽ *1928* ∾

### 1 JANUARY 1928

*Legend*, symphonic poem by the totally blind Bulgarian composer Petko STAINOV, dealing with a medieval maiden who is passionately importuned by an incontinent monk but is appropriated by a brutal Tatar, set to music in purple colors redolent of Russian orientalisms, is produced in Sofia.

### 9 JANUARY 1928

Jean Eugène Gaston LEMAIRE, Paris composer of light theater music, commits suicide at the age of seventy-three by jumping into the Seine.

### 16 JANUARY 1928

*Angelo, Tyran de Padoue*, opera in five acts by Alfred BRUNEAU, after Victor Hugo's drama wherein a tyrannical podestà of Padua orders his wife to be poisoned on suspicion of adultery, but is circumvented when she drinks a sleeping potion instead, and upon awakening flees with the knight of her desire, set to a melodramatic score in the best tradition of French theatrical realism, is produced at the Opéra-Comique, in Paris.

### 16 JANUARY 1928

*La Tour de Feu*, opera in three acts by the Tyrol-born composer of Italian extraction Sylvio LAZZARI, to his own libretto wherein the passion-ridden wife of the lighthouse keeper in a small island off the coast of Brittany, whose Portuguese seaman lover is shipwrecked when her husband extinguishes the guiding beacon in a stormy night, jumps to her death in the raging waters and he sets the lighthouse afire and perishes in the "tower of fire," set to a musical score of effective melodramatic power, is produced for the first time at the Paris Opéra.

### 27 JANUARY 1928

*Violin Concerto* by Cyril SCOTT, in one movement, marked by a considerable interjection of unresolved dissonances with polytonal implications employed in chromatic blocks in the orchestral accompaniment, while the violin part moves along exotic scales, is performed for the first time in Birmingham, May Harrison soloist, Sir Adrian Boult conducting.

### 29 JANUARY 1928

*Traumwandel,* opera in two acts by the Swiss composer Karl Heinrich DAVID (based on a story by Turgenev), is produced in Zürich.

### 31 JANUARY 1928

*Ol-Ol,* opera in three acts by Alexander TCHEREPNIN, after a drama by Leonid Andreyev depicting the mores of pre-revolutionary Russian students, with the heroine Olga (nicknamed Ol-Ol) representing the element of intellectual love, is produced in Weimar.

### 12 FEBRUARY 1928

*Egdon Heath,* symphonic poem by Gustav HOLST, inspired by Thomas Hardy's description of it as "a place perfectly accordant with man's nature . . . singularly colossal and mysterious in its swarthy monotony," is performed for the first time by the New York Symphony Orchestra under the direction of Walter Damrosch who commissioned the work.

### 16 FEBRUARY 1928

More than fifty-eight years after MUSSORGSKY completed the full score of *Boris Godunov* on 15 December 1869 according to old-style calendar, the opera is performed in Leningrad for the first time in its original form, without Rimsky-Korsakov's mellificent alterations.

### 18 FEBRUARY 1928

*Der Zar lässt sich photographieren,* one-act opera buffa by Kurt WEILL, in which a tsar vacationing in Paris visits a photographer's studio and is charmed by its female operator who, on orders from a revolutionary group, shoots him dead with a gun concealed in her camera, is produced in Leipzig.

### 26 FEBRUARY 1928

*Violin Concerto* by the Venezuelan-born Parisian composer Reynaldo HAHN is performed for the first time in Paris with the composer conducting.

### 28 FEBRUARY 1928

The THEREMINOVOX, electronic apparatus generating musical sounds by rheostatic regulation of the electric current through the motion of a hand in front of an antenna, is patented in Washington by its inventor, the Russian engineer Leo THEREMIN.

### 2 MARCH 1928

*Capriccio* by Leoš JANÁČEK, for piano-left hand, flute, two trumpets, three trombones and tuba, written for the Czech pianist Otakar Hollmann whose right hand was badly mutilated in World War I, is performed for the first time by him and an instrumental ensemble in Prague.

### 3 MARCH 1928

The Government of Cuba rescinds its prohibition of the jungle drum BONGO used by Afro-Cuban villagers for communication and potential clarion calls for a rebellion.

### 8 MARCH 1928

*Il Finto Arlecchino,* opera buffa in two acts by Gian Francesco MALIPIERO, constituting the second part of the trilogy *Il mistero di Venezia,* is produced separately in Mainz, to a German libretto.

### 11 MARCH 1928

*Lied der Sturmkolonnen,* Hitlerite storm troop song, to the tune of the *Internationale,* is sung for the first time at a Nazi rally in Bernau, with a new set of words extolling Hitler's love of freedom, his solicitude for workers and determination to end unemployment. (Date and information from *Die Musik,* Berlin, December 1936, p. 174)

### 11 MARCH 1928

*Preludio e Fuga* for orchestra by Riccardo PICK-MANGIAGALLI (the fugue theme being a monorhythmic ascending C major scale) is performed for the first time in Milan.

### 14 MARCH 1928

*Dafni,* opera in three acts by Giuseppe MULÈ, a "pastoral poem" recounting the flight of Daphné from Apollo, is produced in Rome.

### 16 MARCH 1928

*Latavra,* opera in three acts by the 57-year-old Georgian composer Zakhar PALIASHVILI, is performed for the first time in Tiflis, in the Georgian language.

### 20 MARCH 1928

*Chirurgie,* one-act opera by Pierre Octave FERROUD, to Chekhov's play about painful Russian dentistry, with a musical score illustrating abortive tooth extraction in a naturalistic Mussorgskyan manner, is performed for the first time at Monte Carlo.

### 21 MARCH 1928

A group of conscientious objectors to modern music and jazz hurl a stink bomb in the Budapest Opera Theater during the Hungarian première of the opera *Jonny spielt auf* by Ernst KRENEK.

### 23 MARCH 1928

*Symphonic Piece* by the Boston classicist Walter PISTON, written in an 'absolute idiom' of modern polyphony with a justifiable admixture of tolerable dissonance, is performed for the first time by the Boston Symphony Orchestra, on the same program with the first performance of a similarly conceived but quite differently executed piece, *Music for an Orchestra* by the Rumanian composer Filip LAZAR.

24 MARCH 1928

*Beatrix*, Flemish opera in three acts by the 30-year-old Flemish composer Ignaz LILIEN, is produced in Antwerp.

25 MARCH 1928

At a festival of Bulgarian music in Prague, the first performance is given of *Vardar*, symphonic rhapsody by the 29-year-old Bulgarian composer Pantcho VLADIGEROV, with thematic materials derived from authentic popular songs of the Vardar River valley.

27 MARCH 1928

Armand GIVELET, Vice-President of the French Radio Club gives the first public demonstration in Paris of a heterodyne instrument capable of producing musical tones of definite pitch by the movement of the hand, similar to the principle of the Thereminovox, but securing greater accuracy of intonation within the tempered scale.

27 MARCH 1928

Leslie STUART (real name T. A. Barrett), English composer of light operas, of which *Florodora* (a fancied name of a tropical island), featuring a famous sexy sextet of Victorian girls, has attained enormous success, dies in London at the age of sixty-four. (The statement in previous editions of *Music Since 1900* that Leslie Stuart was the author of the song *It's a Long, Long Way to Tipperary* is erroneous; its composer and lyricist were respectively Jack Judge and Harry Williams)

29 MARCH 1928

A new harp model perfected by the French-American master harpist Carlos SALZEDO (in comparison with which the old harp was said to be "as an ox to an airplane") is demonstrated for the first time in public at the eighth annual National Harp Festival in Philadelphia.

29 MARCH 1928

*A Holtak Szigete* (*The Isle of Death*), two-act opera by the 33-year-old Hungarian composer Eugen ZÁDOR, inspired by the famous painting of Arnold Böcklin, wherein Böcklin himself is taken to the funereal cypress-lined isle of death by the jealous lover of his beloved, whither she follows him in a rowboat on a stormy afternoon and is dashed to her death against the rocky shore, is produced in Budapest.

## 30 MARCH 1928

The Philharmonic Society of New York is merged with the New York Symphony Society, forming the New York Philharmonic-Symphony Society, with Arturo Toscanini as the principal conductor and Walter Damrosch, former music director of the New York Symphony, as guest conductor.

## 30 MARCH 1928

*Symphony* by the American composer Edward Burlingame HILL, in three movements, *Allegro moderato, Moderato maestoso* and *Allegro brioso,* written "with no descriptive basis, no dramatic conflict or spiritual crisis" in the cerulean key of B-flat major, with excursions into the impressionistic regions of enhanced tonality, is performed for the first time by the Boston Symphony Orchestra under the direction of Serge Koussevitzky, to whom the score is dedicated.

## 31 MARCH 1928

*Filomela e l'Infatuato,* music drama in three parts by Gian Francesco MALIPIERO (completed on 22 June 1925), to a libretto dealing with a man infatuated with a human philomel whose thrilling trilling fascinates him, is produced in Prague.

## 4 APRIL 1928

MUSSORGSKY's piano suite *Pictures at an Exhibition* is presented in Dessau as an abstract ballet, with a highly stylized, surrealistic décor by the Russian painter Wassily Kandinsky, wherein *Gnomus* is symbolized by a cellular circle surrounded by triangular hemoglobins, the *Old Castle* is built on superimposed spherical segments, and the *Great Gate of Kiev* is represented by a heavenward-reaching tower flanked by a lunar crescent and an eclipsed sun.

Mussorgsky's work is not program music merely because it was inspired by pictures. If this music mirrors anything at all, it is not the painted image but some inner experiences of Mussorgsky himself, which rise much higher than the subject of the actual paintings and are expressed in pure musical forms. With the exception of the sketch portraying Samuel Goldenberg and Schmuyle and that of the Market of Limoge, my entire décor is abstract. (Wassily Kandinsky in *Kunstblatt,* August 1930)

## 5 APRIL 1928

*Danças Africanas,* orchestral suite by Brazil's prime composer Heitor VILLA-LOBOS, subtitled *Danças dos Indios mestisos do Brasil* and based on the melorhythmic figurations of the Brazilian jungle songs, in three sections: (1) *Farrapos,* a dance of youths (2) *Kankikis,* a dance of old men, and (3) *Kankukus,* a children's dance, all set in 2/4 time in asymmetric rhythms, with a liberal infusion of whole-tone scales, but differing in tempo and kinetic energy, is performed for the first time in Paris.

## 5 APRIL 1928

*Die Herzogin von Chicago,* operetta by Emmerich KÁLMÁN, dealing with the wilful daughter of a Chicago sausage magnate who gives a $5,000 tip to a Budapest Gypsy band to play Charleston for her dance with a jazz-hating crown prince of Sylvaria and wins a million-dollar bet from the Young Ladies' Eccentric Club of New York for this achievement, is made a Duchess of Chicago by the aged King of Sylvaria so as to enable the crown prince to marry her without demeaning his royal status, and is contracted by Fox Films of New York to act out her princely romance on the screen, is produced in Vienna.

## 6 APRIL 1928

*California,* "festival scenes" by Frederick S. CONVERSE, is performed for the first time by the Boston Symphony Orchestra.

## 7 APRIL 1928

*Tenth Symphony* by Russia's most prolific symphonist Nicolai MIASKOVSKY, in F minor, completed by him on 29 December 1927, in one movement consisting of two sections, *Un poco sostenuto* and *Allegro tumultuoso,* inspired by Pushkin's poem *The Bronze Knight,* descriptive of the mad challenge to the bronze statue of Peter the Great hurled by a humble clerk whose betrothed perished in the 1824 inundation in St. Petersburg, the town which Peter built, is performed for the first time in Moscow.

## 9 APRIL 1928

*Thien-Hoa (Fior di cielo),* opera in three acts, to a pseudo-Sinological libretto, by the 42-year-old Italian composer Guido BIANCHINI, is produced at La Scala, in Milan.

## 12 APRIL 1928

*Six Symphonic Epigrams,* orchestral suite by the foremost Dutch modernist Willem PIJPER, written for the 40th anniversary of the Concertgebouw Orchestra in Amsterdam and inspired by Shakespeare's line, "Brevity is the soul of wit" (the entire suite lasts less than five minutes when played at the proper tempo), is performed for the first time in Amsterdam.

## 14 APRIL 1928

*Frühlings Erwachen,* opera in three acts by Max ETTINGER, to a libretto based on Frank Wedekind's vivid story of torments of adolescent sexuality, is produced in Leipzig.

## 20 APRIL 1928

Two 'minute operas' by Darius MILHAUD, *La Délivrance de Thésée,* depicting the deliverance of Theseus with the help of Ariadne, from the labyrinth of Minotaur in Crete, and *L'Abandon d'Ariane,* illustrating the abandonment of Ariadne by Theseus on the island of Naxos, are produced in Wiesbaden.

## 20 APRIL 1928

ONDES MUSICALES, electronic musical instrument, invented by the French musician and engineer Maurice MARTENOT, known also as ONDES MARTENOT, is demonstrated for the first time in Paris. (The instrument was patented in Paris on 30 March 1929)

## 25 APRIL 1928

René BERTRAND gives in Paris a demonstration of an orchestra of six dynaphones, producing sounds by heterodynamic frequencies, the first instance of multiple employment of electronic instruments.

## 26 APRIL 1928

*Present Arms*, musical comedy by Richard RODGERS, in which an American Marine in Hawaii, dishonorably discharged for impersonating an officer, salvages a British yacht and wins the hand of a peer's daughter, featuring the song *You Took Advantage of Me*, is produced in New York.

## 27 APRIL 1928

*Apollon Musagète*, ballet in two scenes by Igor STRAVINSKY for string orchestra, written in a gymnosophistical, Delphically austere, stately neo-Baroque style, with meaningful pauses at the points of harmonic congeries when dissonant chords are ominously suspended, with a motto-chord C, F, B, D, F-sharp symbolizing Apollo, set in a highly choreographable rhythmic design, depicting Apollo as the leader of the muses of poetry, mimic action, and dance, is performed for the first time at the Library of Congress in Washington, D.C., as a work commissioned by the Elizabeth Sprague Coolidge Foundation.

## 29 APRIL 1928

*Ninth Symphony*, in E minor, by Nicolai MIASKOVSKY (completed 21 July 1927), in four movements, *Andante sostenuto, Presto, Lento molto*, and *Allegro con grazia*, conceived as a lyric and contemplative work, is performed for the first time in Moscow, three weeks and a day after the performance of his *Tenth Symphony*.

## 6 MAY 1928

At a festival of modern music in Wiesbaden, three satirical one-act operas by Ernst KRENEK, to his own texts, are given for the first time:

(1) *Der Diktator*, wherein a woman, trying to murder a Mussolini-type modern dictator, suddenly asks him to kiss her and is accidentally killed by a bullet fired at him by his wife (2) *Das geheime Königreich*, wherein a coloratura singer becomes the queen of a Utopian kingdom and falls in love with a political dissenter planning the king's assassination, with a happy ending ensuing when the rebel returns to his revolutionary comrades and the queen reconciles herself to monarchy (3) *Schwergewicht, oder die Ehre der Nation* (completed on 14 June 1927), a burlesque inspired by the contempla-

tion of the adulation extended to sport figures and a German statesman's declaration that "a prize fighter or a channel swimmer does more for the glory of the nation than all the artists and scientists put together," the story evolving around a muscular heavyweight champion loved by a habitual adulteress and an erratic medical student who disguises herself as a boxing trainee and to her great delight is knocked out by him in a gym.

For some time I pursued the stylistic direction of *Jonny Spielt Auf.* The three one-act operas that I wrote immediately afterwards may be regarded as a kind of marginal observation to it. *Der Diktator* treated a bloody episode from the private life of a Duce type character. *Das geheime Königreich* was a fairy tale which was to demonstrate that all worldly might was a *vanitas vanitatum* and recommended a return to innocent nature. *Schwergewicht, oder die Ehre der Nation,* was a satirical operetta, which attacked hero worship in the field of sports, exposing a heavyweight world champion as a helpless idiot despite an honorary doctor's degree bestowed upon him by the department of philosophy in a university. (Ernst Krenek, in *Selbstdarstellung,* Zürich, 1948)

6 MAY 1928

*Die Freunde von Salamanca,* opera written by Franz SCHUBERT in 1815, is produced posthumously in Halle.

9 MAY 1928

*Sarati le Terrible,* opera in four acts by the 37-year-old French composer Francis BOUSQUET, dealing with an Algerian coal merchant named Sarati, incestuously infatuated with his young niece, who kills himself after she marries a mysterious young stranger, is produced at the Opéra-Comique in Paris.

9 MAY 1928

*Blackbirds of 1928,* an all-Negro revue by Jimmy McHUGH, with a locale placed in Harlem, and containing the celebrated song *I Can't Give You Anything But Love, Baby,* is produced in New York.

10 MAY 1928

*Anathema,* opera in three acts by Alfred TOFFT (founded on a story by Mérimée), his second and last opera, is produced in Copenhagen.

15 MAY 1928

*Napasta (Disaster),* opera in three acts by the 33-year-old Rumanian composer Sabin DRAGOI, written in a passionately romantic manner and depicting the horrors of a hidden murder when the second husband of a rural widow is revealed as the killer of her first husband, a crime for which an innocuous village idiot was unjustly convicted, is produced in Bucharest.

16 MAY 1928

*Fra Gherardo,* opera in three acts by Ildebrando PIZZETTI, to his own text dealing with an actual flagellant friar burned at the stake for heresy about

1260 in Parma, with fictional additions involving a local girl seduced and abandoned by him, and in the end stoned as a witch, to a musical score artfully applying elements of authentic medieval modalities, with empty fifths illustrating monastic asceticism, recurrent rhythmic strokes in dissonant harmonies suggesting penitential self-flagellation, and luxuriant Italianate outbursts of flowing melodies depicting the incontinence of earthly passions, is produced at La Scala, Milan, Arturo Toscanini conducting.

### 19 MAY 1928

Henry F. GILBERT, American composer of native-conscious philosophy, a primordial American who refused to regard American music as a colonial by-product of the art of Europe, and whose own instrumental and vocal works draw amply upon Indian, Negro and Creole resources for thematic material, dies in Cambridge, Massachusetts, at 3:42 A.M. of cerebral hemorrhage (he was born as a 'blue baby' with imperfect cardiac walls) at the age of fifty-nine.

### 25 MAY 1928

The new building of the Teatro Colón is opened in Buenos Aires.

### 6 JUNE 1928

Die Ägyptische Helena, opera in two acts by Richard STRAUSS, to a libretto by Hugo von Hofmannsthal, wherein the cuckolded King Menelaus intends to kill Helen after the destruction of Troy, but is given to drink a potion of oblivion which makes him believe that she was not with Paris in Troy but in Egypt waiting for a marital reunion, making it possible for them to return to Sparta together after some additional complications when he drinks a potion of remembrance, with a musical score much less complex than the highly charged Salome and Elektra, but still revealing the familiar Straussian flights into empyrean harmonies, is produced in Dresden.

### 6 JUNE 1928

Ode, or Meditation at Night on the Majesty of God as Revealed by the Aurora Borealis, ballet-cantata by the 25-year-old Russian émigré composer Nicolas NABOKOV, to the text of a poem by the Russian scientist-poet Mikhail Lomonosov written by him on the occasion of the coronation of Empress Elizabeth, daughter of Peter the Great, is produced in Paris by the Ballet Russe directed by Serge Diaghilev, great-great-grandson of one of Elizabeth's several illegitimate children.

### 7 JUNE 1928

Concerto for piano and orchestra by Albert ROUSSEL, in three movements, a propulsive Allegro molto, a contemplatively somber Adagio and a precipitate Allegro con spirito in the form of a rondo with variations, is performed for the first time at a Koussevitzky concert in Paris, with Alexander Borovsky as piano soloist.

473

## 9 JUNE 1928

*Belkis,* biblical opera by the Portuguese composer Ruy COELHO, is produced in Lisbon.

## 13 JUNE 1928

Wolfgang GRAESER, youthful Swiss composer and able music scholar, editor of *Die Kunst der Fuge* in the *Neue Bach-Gesellschaft* edition, kills himself in Berlin at the age of twenty-one.

## 15 JUNE 1928

Alexander GLAZUNOV leaves Leningrad for Vienna as a delegate to the Schubert Centennial, never to return. (Exact date of Glazunov's departure obtained from Maximilian Steinberg, Glazunov's successor as Director of the Leningrad Conservatory)

## 16 JUNE 1928

During his Brazilian tour Ottorino RESPIGHI conducts in São Paulo the first performance of his newly composed symphonic suite *Impressioni Brasiliane,* in three sections:

(1) *Notte tropicale,* an impressionistic tableau of a tropical night with humidly sliding chord blocks and violins glissando as an atmospheric background for a soft echo of a Brazilian carnival song (2) *Butantan,* a tonal painting of a snake garden in Butantan near São Paulo, with a bassoon introducing a serpentine tune, the clarinet responding in colubrine arabesques and sibilant violins in sforzando puffs, ending on a hissing solo in the bass clarinet (3) *Canzone e Danza,* a stylization of popular Brazilian rhythms subtly accompanied by syncopated drumbeats, without specifically Brazilian percussion instruments, and concluding on a pizzicato chord in A major in the strings. (The performance was first announced for 9 June 1928, but was postponed until a week later. Information received from the Music Section of the Biblioteca Nacional in Rio de Janeiro.)

## 19 JUNE 1928

*Frenos,* four-act opera by the Argentine composer Raul ESPOILÉ, dealing with a reincarnated Greek philosopher Frenos (from *phrenos,* mind) working in a biological laboratory in Argentina, and becoming involved intellectually with a reincarnated Sappho and carnally with a reincarnated Helen of Troy, with a score set in lush Pucciniesque harmonies, is performed for the first time at the Teatro Colón in Buenos Aires.

## 28 JUNE 1928

Louis ARMSTRONG and his Hot Five record *West End Blues,* a milestone in the history of Jazz.

## 14 JULY 1928

*Actualités,* suite for a small orchestra by Darius MILHAUD, subtitled 'Musique de film,' a series of stylized musical pictures of a newsreel—an official reception for aviators, a boxer, industrial application of water, a murder attempt in a train, the Derby horse race—is performed for the first time at a music festival in Baden-Baden.

## 15 JULY 1928

*The Hero,* satirical opera in one act by the Soviet composer Alexander MOSSOLOV, to his own text ridiculing bourgeois hero worship in capitalist Germany, is produced for the first time anywhere in Baden-Baden, unique occasion of the world première of a Soviet work outside of the Soviet Union.

## 1 AUGUST 1928

*Detvan,* opera by the Slovak composer Viliam FIGUŠ-BYSTRÝ, the first stage work to a text in the Slovak language on a subject from Slovak folklore, is produced in Bratislava.

## 9 AUGUST 1928

Percy GRAINGER marries the Swedish poet and painter Ella Viola Ström in a public ceremony performed by a Swedish Lutheran minister, at the Hollywood Bowl, with a lighted cross atop a nearby mountain illuminating the amphitheater, and conducts for an audience of 22,000 his orchestral dedication *To a Nordic Princess.*

## 10 AUGUST 1928

In a public address Mustafa KEMAL PASHA, the founder of modern Turkey, urges the adoption of Western dances and jazz to relieve the traditional homophony and rhythmic indeterminacy of Turkish folk music.

## 12 AUGUST 1928

Leoš JANÁČEK, modern grandmaster of Czech music, great animator of native musical culture whose works are built on the realistic concept of melody as spoken music, and harmony as a product of moving voices, dies at Ostrava at the age of seventy-four.

## 31 AUGUST 1928

*Die Dreigroschenoper,* ballad-opera in eight scenes with an epilogue by the 28-year-old German composer Kurt WEILL, modeled after *The Beggar's Opera* of John Gay (produced 200 years, 7 months, and 2 days before, in London—Dr. Johnson remarked to Boswell after attending a performance: "Sir, there is in it such a labefaction of all principles that it may be injurious to morality"), to a libretto by Bertolt Brecht, with the action transferred to the year of Queen Victoria's coronation, 1837, telling a story of Mackie Messer (Mack the Knife) and his girl friend from a low London bordello, and his rise to social eminence and prosperity with the connivance of corrupt officials, set to music vibrating with the honky-tonk melorhythms of Americanized popular tunes (the song *Mack the Knife* was to become a world hit), ending with a mock-solemn chorale propounding the cynical moral "Combat the wrong, but not too strong," is produced for the first time in Berlin.

### 5 SEPTEMBER 1928

*L'Innocente,* second opera by the Brazilian composer Francisco MIGNONE, written to an Italian libretto, is produced in Rio de Janeiro.

### 7 SEPTEMBER 1928

*Królowa Jadwiga (Queen Jadwiga),* opera by the Polish composer Tadeusz JOTEYKO, is produced in Warsaw.

### 10 SEPTEMBER 1928

Harry Lawrence FREEMAN, American Negro composer, conducts in New York the first performance, with an all-Negro cast, of his opera *Voodoo,* to the story of a Louisiana snake-cult queen who kidnaps her rival for the affections of a Creole lover, and is about to put her to death in a voodoo orgy when the lover arrives, rescues the victim and slays the prospective murderess, set to music compounded of Negro spirituals, barn dance tunes and jazz, with recitatives in southern dialect.

### 10 SEPTEMBER 1928

The Sixth Festival of the International Society for Contemporary Music opens at Siena, Italy, under the auspices of its Italian branch, CORPORAZIONE DELLE NUOVE MUSICHE, in a program of old Italian music under the direction of Bernardino Molinari.

### 11 SEPTEMBER 1928

At the Sixth Festival of the International Society for Contemporary Music in Siena, the following program of chamber music is given:

*String Quartet* by the Italian neo-classicist Vincenzo TOMMASINI; a neo-romantic *Flute Sonata* by Karel HÁBA, brother of the pioneer of quarter-tone music Alois Hába; *Suite* for piano by Paul HINDEMITH; *Violin Sonata* by RAVEL, with a slow movement, *Blues,* emulating American ballad modalities; and a *String Quartet* by the rightfully venerated Austrian composer Alexander ZEMLINSKY.

### 12 SEPTEMBER 1928

In the course of the Sixth Festival of the International Society for Contemporary Music in Siena, Emil František BURIAN of Prague presents his "Voice Band" in wordless vocalization, accompanied by piano and drums, and creating harmonic effects by adroit combinations of vowels (treated as consonances) and consonants (treated as dissonances).

### 13 SEPTEMBER 1928

The Sixth Festival of the International Society for Contemporary Music in Siena presents the following program of chamber music:

*476*

*Third String Quartet* by the English romantic composer Frank BRIDGE, originally commissioned by the Elizabeth Sprague Coolidge Foundation and first performed in Washington on 17 September 1927, in three movements, with an elegiac quasi-atonal *Andante* flanked by two kinetic *Allegros; Duo* for violin and piano by the German composer of Wagnerogenic music Heinz TIESSEN; *String Trio,* op. 20 by Anton von WEBERN, in two movements, his first instrumental work integrally planned according to the Schoenbergian method of composition with 12 tones related only to one another, with the basic tone-row thematically stressing the interval of minor second, the music evolving in the classical forms of sonata and rondo, wherein the principle of variation form is extended to the ultimate in the aspects of metrical asymmetry, rhythmical diminution and augmentation, melodic inversion, octave translocation, retrograde movement and thematically construed pauses of silence; *Concerto* for harpsichord, flute, oboe, violin and cello by Manuel DE FALLA, with the composer at the harpsichord, its performance greatly delayed in view of the turbulence in the audience, aroused by the hearing of Webern's *Trio,* so that Manuel de Falla openly voiced his apprehension at the possibility of a physical attack on composers, whether guilty or innocent of dodecaphony or cacophony, and hesitated to appear on the podium until assured that the passions had subsided; and *Music for Eight Instruments* by the Swiss composer Robert BLUM.

After the performance of Anton von Webern's *String Trio* there was a disturbance, hisses and boos. The correspondent of the Milan newspaper *Popolo d'Italia* roared: "This is the music of the savages!" (*Breslauer Neueste Nachrichten,* Breslau, 15 September 1928)

### 14 SEPTEMBER 1928

In the course of the Sixth Festival of the International Society for Contemporary Music in Siena, Alfredo CASELLA conducts, in the morning, two consecutive performances of *Façade* by William WALTON, and, in the afternoon, his own *Serenata* for five instruments and Stravinsky's scenic cantata depicting the Russian wedding ritual, *Les Noces.*

### 15 SEPTEMBER 1928

At the last concert of the Sixth Festival of the International Society for Contemporary Music in Siena, the following program of chamber music was given:

*Second String Quartet* by the master polyphonist of Czech music Bohuslav MARTINU; a florid *Cello Sonata* by the Italian composer Franco ALFANO; and *Piano Quintet* (with affective quarter-tones) by Ernest BLOCH. (Prokofiev's *Quintet* for oboe, clarinet, bassoon, viola and double-bass was announced in the program, but could not be performed because the instrumental parts failed to arrive in time)

### 19 SEPTEMBER 1928

The first "100% all-talking, all-singing" motion picture, *The Singing Fool,* with the title role performed by Al Jolson in blackface, and an animated cartoon *Steamboat Willie* by Walt Disney, introducing Mickey Mouse, both with a newly perfected synchronized musical sound track, are shown for the first time in New York City.

477

*The New Moon,* musical romance in two acts by Sigmund ROMBERG, wherein a young revolutionary arrested by the French Royal authorities of New Orleans in 1788 and taken aboard the French ship *New Moon,* escapes detention and establishes a settlement on a small West Indies island with his sweetheart and a group of comrades-in-arms until the French Revolution liberates them, with a musical score containing the popular osculatory ballads *One Kiss* and *Lover, Come Back to Me,* the masculine chorus *Stout-Hearted Men* and the mutually optative duet *Wanting You,* is produced in New York.

28 SEPTEMBER 1928

*Coups de roulis,* operetta in three acts by the 74-year-old French composer André MESSAGER, is produced in Paris.

1 OCTOBER 1928

*Mariette,* gay operetta in an Offenbachian manner by Oscar STRAUS, to a libretto by Sacha Guitry, dealing with a fictional story of a young enchantress (acted by Yvonne Printemps, Sacha Guitry's wife) who captivates Prince Louis Napoleon (acted by Sacha Guitry), only to lose his love when he becomes Emperor Napoleon III, is produced in Paris.

2 OCTOBER 1928

*Concerto* for clarinet and orchestra by the Danish grandmaster Carl NIELSEN (completed on 15 August 1928), in one compact movement, set in a quasi-modernistic idiom, stressing the dichotomy of the polar tonalities at a tritone's distance, while thematic melorhythms remain well within the traditional forms, is performed for the first time in Copenhagen.

4 OCTOBER 1928

*Friederike,* operetta in three acts by Franz LEHÁR based on an episode in Goethe's life, when as a law student in Strassburg in 1771 he formed a deep attachment for a village pastor's daughter actually named Friederike, and revisited her eight years after going through three more romances, with some of his tenor arias in waltz time set to his poems actually inspired by Friederike, is performed for the first time in Berlin.

8 OCTOBER 1928

*Concerto* in A minor for violin and orchestra by Alfredo CASELLA, a work representing a concession to the romantic trends in modern music, is performed for the first time anywhere by the conductorless orchestra in Moscow, Josef Szigeti soloist.

8 OCTOBER 1928

*Bratři Karamazovi,* opera in three acts by the Czech composer Otakar JEREMIÁŠ, in which the drama of the Karamazov brothers depicted in

Dostoyevsky's psychological novel receives a romantic interpretation, is produced in Prague.

10 OCTOBER 1928

*L'Eau du Nil*, the first French 'film sonore' with a synchronized sound track, is demonstrated in Paris.

10 OCTOBER 1928

*Hold Everything*, a musical comedy by Ray HENDERSON, wherein a welterweight champion dejected by a psychological misunderstanding with his girl friend is sufficiently aroused by jealousy against the challenger to knock him out in the prize ring, featuring the perennially alluring song *You're the Cream in My Coffee*, is produced in New York.

15 OCTOBER 1928

*Symphony in C Major* by the Swedish composer Kurt ATTERBERG, winner of the $10,000 Schubert Memorial Prize offered by the Columbia Phonograph Company of New York awarded to him on 17 August 1928 by an International Grand Jury of eminent composers and scholars—Franz Schalk, Donald Francis Tovey, Alfred Bruneau, Max von Schillings, Franco Alfano, Emil Mlynarski, Alexander Glazunov, Carl Nielsen, Adolfo Salazar and Walter Damrosch—as the best work conceived in the spirit of the lyrical genius of Schubert, written to commemorate the centennial of his death, is performed for the first time in Cologne.

Every one was busy spotting reminiscences in the Symphony; and it can not be denied that they are plentiful and obvious. Atterberg may have looked down the list of judges, and slyly made up his mind that he would put in a bit of something that would appeal to each of them in turn—a bit of *Scheherazade* for the Russian Glazunov, a bit of *Cockaigne* for Mr. Tovey, a bit of the *New World Symphony* for Mr. Damrosch, a bit of *Pétrouchka* for the modernist Alfano, a bit of Granados for Salazar. . . . But I wonder if there may not be another explanation. . . . Atterberg is not merely a composer. He is a musical critic. . . . Suppose he looked round with the cynical smile that, as all the world knows, all critics wear, and decided to pull the world's leg? (Ernest Newman, Sunday *Times*, London, 18 November 1928)

(Kurt Atterberg published an article in the *Musical Digest*, Chicago, February 1929, entitled *How I Fooled the Music World*, admitting that his symphony was a satirical challenge to Schubert worshippers)

19 OCTOBER 1928

The Orchestre Symphonique de Paris gives its inaugural concert in Paris, in a program comprising the world première of the "symphonic movement" *Rugby*, by Arthur HONEGGER descriptive of the restless animation of the game. (*Rugby* was subsequently performed during the intermission of the International Rugby Match between France and England on 31 December 1928)

## 20 OCTOBER 1928

The French Academy rules that celibacy is to be no longer a *conditio sine qua non* for applicants for the Prix de Rome.

## 20 OCTOBER 1928

*Suite Canadienne* for orchestra and chorus by the 37-year-old Canadian composer Claude CHAMPAGNE is performed for the first time in Paris.

## 25 OCTOBER 1928

Joaquín TURINA conducts in Barcelona the first performance of his orchestral choreographic fantasy *Rítmos*.

## 25 OCTOBER 1928

*Tuhotulva (Deluge)* opera in three acts by the Finnish musicologist Ilmari KROHN, is produced in Helsinki.

## 27 OCTOBER 1928

*El Giravolt de Maig (Round Dance of May)*, one-act opera in the Catalan language by Eduardo TOLDRÁ, is produced in Barcelona.

## 1 NOVEMBER 1928

The National Opera House is inaugurated in Tashkent, capital of the Uzbek Soviet Republic in Central Asia.

## 4 NOVEMBER 1928

Dr. Arthur Eaglefield HULL, English musicologist, champion of Scriabin and modern music in general, dies in London at the age of fifty-two, in consequence of the injuries sustained in his suicide attempt (fractured ribs and amnesia) on 18 September 1928 when he jumped under the train at the Huddersfield Railway Station, driven to this desperate act by the public exposure of extensive plagiarism perpetrated in his book *Music, Classical, Romantic and Modern,* published by J. M. Dent & Sons, Ltd., on 8 April 1927 and withdrawn from its catalogue on 28 August 1928 after the evidence of Hull's literary expropriations became irrefutable.

Hull's suicide was the result of my exposure of his thefts in his book *Music, Classical, Romantic and Modern.* He threw himself under a train. (Percy A. Scholes in a letter to the author dated 21 March 1948)

## 4 NOVEMBER 1928

Carlos CHÁVEZ conducts in Mexico City the first performance of his ballet *El fuego nuevo,* in the form of a suite of four dances, the action of which unfolds around an Aztec pyramid, making use of primitive Mexican instruments of percussion in the score.

## 10 NOVEMBER 1928

*Los Hijos del Sol,* opera by the Argentine composer Athos PALMA, based on a story of the Inca priests, 'Sons of the Sun', in an appropriately pentatonic melodic setting, is produced at the Teatro Colón in Buenos Aires.

## 13 NOVEMBER 1928

*Mondnacht,* opera in three acts by Julius BITTNER, to his own libretto, dealing with a lieutenant of the German Army, in love with a somnambulist, who steals and sells a portfolio containing information pertaining to the military plans of 1865, is apprehended and ordered to commit suicide, with the sound of the shot on a moonlit night upsetting the equilibrium of his beloved walking precariously on a ledge who falls to her death, is produced in Berlin.

## 16 NOVEMBER 1928

Igor STRAVINSKY conducts the Orchestre Symphonique in Paris in the first performance of the orchestral version of his *Étude* for pianola composed in 1917.

## 19 NOVEMBER 1928

A century has passed since Franz SCHUBERT, genius of the German lied and youthful creator of immortal symphonies, dies at his brother's house in Vienna, at the age of thirty-one.

## 22 NOVEMBER 1928

Ida Rubinstein presents at her dance recital at the Paris Opéra the world première of *Boléro* by Maurice RAVEL, specially written for her, a fantastically varied rondo comprising eighteen recurrences of a binary subject of a Hispanic melorhythmic nature, the first section in pure C major, the second in the Mixolydian mode on C, culminating in a fulminant digression into E major in the coda, with triadic harmonies in parallel motion (in one variation the high harmonics create an overtone complex that forcibly changes the color of the solo instrument), scored for a large and diversified orchestra including an oboe d'amore, three saxophones and an important percussion ensemble.

*Boléro* is an experiment in a very special and limited direction . . . a piece lasting seventeen minutes and consisting entirely of orchestral fabric without music, of one long, very gradual crescendo. There are no contrasts, and practically no inventive ideas except in the design and manner of execution. The themes are impersonal folk-like melodies of the common Spanish-Arabian sort. (From Ravel's statement to M. D. Calvocoressi, published in the *Daily Telegraph,* London, 16 July 1931, and reprinted in the article *Ravel's Letters to Calvocoressi* in *The Musical Quarterly* of January 1941)

## 23 NOVEMBER 1928

*Chanticleer,* festival overture by Daniel Gregory MASON, with a motto from Thoreau's *Walden:* "I do not propose to write an ode to dejection but to brag as lustily as Chanticleer in the morning," faithfully portraying a rooster crowing on the notes of an arpeggio, then yielding to the chromatic cackling of a hen, is performed for the first time by the Cincinnati Symphony Orchestra.

### 23 NOVEMBER 1928

*Pilgrim's Progress*, oratorio by Sir Granville BANTOCK, written in commemoration of Bunyan's tercentenary, illustrating the scenes of Bunyan's moralistic dream in luxuriantly Wagneromantic tones, is performed for the first time in London.

### 27 NOVEMBER 1928

Ida Rubinstein stages at the Paris Opéra the world première of the allegorical ballet in four tableaux *Le Baiser de la Fée*, by Igor STRAVINSKY, dedicated "to the memory of Tchaikovsky, identifying his Muse with the Fairy whose genius has marked his music with a magic kiss," the subject being inspired by Hans Christian Andersen's fairy tale *The Snow Maiden*, with the thematic material built on songs and piano pieces by Tchaikovsky, masculated and invigorated by converting his feminine phrase endings into monosyllabic rhythmic thrusts.

### 27 NOVEMBER 1928

*Jazz Poem* for piano and orchestra by Randall THOMPSON, is performed for the first time by the Rochester Philharmonic, Howard Hanson conducting, and Thompson himself playing the solo part.

### 30 NOVEMBER 1928

A Union of Young Composers is organized at the Central House of Art Workers in Moscow "to collectively guide the young unorganized creative talents, to eradicate by means of comradely advice any undesirable aberrations and to create artistically valid musical works that would reflect the Soviet scene and are suitable for mass audiences."

### 1 DECEMBER 1928

*Die schwarze Orchidee*, opera-grotesque in three acts by Eugen D'ALBERT, focused on a gentleman-thief who customarily leaves a rare black orchid in apartments he robs in New York, then suddenly inherits an English estate and a title of nobility, and marries an eccentric American lady whose house, situated on Fiftieth Avenue, No. 5, he has once burglarized, the cast of characters including "Tanzgirls" dancing the "Eros Foxtrot" at the Mount Everest Bar, a reporter named Schmuckele and an ensemble of "Jazz-Neger" playing syncopated banjo music, all this immersed in a heterogeneous compost of pre-fabricated discords and whole-tone scales, is produced in Leipzig.

### 2 DECEMBER 1928

*Variationen für Orchester*, op. 31, by Arnold SCHOENBERG (completed on 20 September 1928), his first orchestral work written according to his method of composing in twelve tones related only to one another, with the thematic series (B-flat, F-flat, G-flat, E-flat, F, A, D, C-sharp, G, G-sharp, B, C) treated in 48 different configurations (melodic inversion, retrograde, inversion of the retrograde, besides the original basic form), and integrated vertically and diagonally in canon, polyphonic imitations, harmonic combinations, with the barycenter on the initial note of the series, B-flat, producing a simulacrum of tonality, even though no triads or triadic melodic progressions ever occur and the emancipation of dissonance is complete, the orchestral score including exotic instruments (mandolin, flexaton, etc.), is performed for the first time by the Berlin Philarmonic, Wilhelm Furtwängler conducting.

The majority of the audience remained silent, but two excitable minorities engaged in combat. The exchange of remarks for and against the Schoenberg Variations soon assumed a more violent form than we ever experienced even at a Schoenberg première, and we are accustomed to almost anything. (Max Marschalk, *Die Vossische Zeitung*, Berlin, 4 December 1928).

Arnold Schoenberg's work, *Variations* for orchestra, is calculated and excogitated musical mathematics, dictated by the intellect of someone who is obsessed with a fixed idea. I have a complete understanding of the stubborn and almost tragic determination with which Schoenberg undeviatingly pursues his path. And yet I cannot take him and his music seriously, for its logic must lead to nonsense because its premises are false. (Fritz Ohrmann, *Signale für die musikalische Welt*, Berlin, 12 December 1928)

Straying from the main road, Schoenberg goes along his lost pathways a lonesome figure, a fanatic, a martyr of his intellectual eccentricity; one who is lost in himself, a madman, if you will, but still a character. I therefore do not laugh when I hear these unnatural sounds; rather I am impressed by the tragedy of a man who deliberately chooses the road to oblivion, which will probably overtake him still during his lifetime . . . His music, insofar as these tonal combinations excogitated by their own laws can be described as such, creates a world of sounds which are inaccessible to our ears and our brains . . . At the public rehearsal and at the concert itself the playing of Schoenberg's *Variations* led to a mighty uproar. The public begins to protect itself against assaults on its better nature. Such incidents are to be deplored, but they are understandable in the light of the torture inflicted on the nervous system. For Schoenberg and the few faithful beneficiaries of his speculations the performance of his *Variations* was a catastrophe. . . . I am sorry for him, and yet I must pose a serious question: How long can the untenable situation be tolerated whereby a person like Arnold Schoenberg, lost to the world of music, continues to lead a master class in composition in a State-supported academic institution where he may cause incalculable harm to innocently trustful youth? When will an energetic interpellation be finally submitted to the Prussian Ministry of Education demanding steps to prevent such cultural damage in the future? Let Schoenberg be given a decent financial settlement, or a state pension, but let us, for God's sake, remove him, and very soon, from his teaching post. (Paul Schwers, *Allgemeine Musikzeitung*, Berlin, 7 December 1928)

2 DECEMBER 1928

*Anacaona*, symphonic poem by the Cuban composer Sánchez DE FUENTES, inspired by the melodramatic self-sacrifice of a patriotic 16th-century Indian queen, is performed for the first time in Havana.

## 2 DECEMBER 1928

*Third Symphony* by the 53-year-old Austrian composer Franz SCHMIDT in the youthful key of A major, in four movements written in a Schubertogenic romantic manner, is performed for the first time in Vienna as winner of the Schubert Centennial Prize for the Austrian Section awarded by the Columbia Phonograph Company of New York, on the same program with the *Sixth Symphony* by the Swedish composer Kurt ATTERBERG, the absolute winner of the contest.

## 9 DECEMBER 1928

*First Piano Concerto* by Mario CASTELNUOVO-TEDESCO is performed for the first time in Rome.

## 10 DECEMBER 1928

*Der singende Teufel,* opera in four acts by Franz SCHREKER, to his own libretto dealing with a magister organum in darkly medieval Germany passionately attached to an inconvertibly pagan Frankish maiden who destroys his organ as a singing devil, written in the *al fresco* manner of an archaically stylized static counterpoint of Hucbaldian aridity, is produced in Berlin.

## 11 DECEMBER 1928

The Society of Friends of Music is founded at the Library of Congress, Washington, D.C., "to provide a link among serious lovers of music in our country by associating them, through the National Library, in musical activities devoted to artistic and educational ends."

(Date from the stenographic report of the first meeting of the Society; but the Society's brochure of 1930 gives the date of the foundation as 16 December 1928)

## 13 DECEMBER 1928

*An American in Paris,* an 'orchestral tone poem' by George GERSHWIN (completed on 18 November 1928), a touristic musicorama, with identifiable 'walking themes' of nostalgic, wistful, joyful, nonchalant and amorous (when a solo violin approaches the tourist in a suggestively inviting manner) implications and illustrative quotations such as the Paris vaudeville tune *La Sorella,* with four Paris taxi horns for realistic effect, is performed for the first time by the Philharmonic-Symphony Society of New York, Walter Damrosch conducting.

The honks have it. Four automobile horns, vociferously assisted by three saxophones, two tom-toms, rattle, xylophone, wire brush, wood blocks, and an ensemble not otherwise innocent of brass and percussion blew or thumped the lid off in Carnegie Hall when *An American in Paris* by George Gershwin had its first performance. . . . For those not too deeply concerned with any apparently outmoded niceties of art, it was an amusing occasion . . . To conceive of a symphonic audience listening to it with any degree of pleasure or patience twenty years from now, when whoopee is no longer even a word, is another matter. Then . . . there will still be Franck with his outmoded spirituality. (Oscar Thompson, New York *Evening Post,* 14 December 1928)

*An American in Paris* is nauseous claptrap, so dull, patchy, thin, vulgar, long-winded and inane, that the average movie audience would be bored by it . . . This cheap and silly affair seemed pitifully futile and inept. (Herbert F. Peyser, New York *Telegram*, 14 December 1928)

### 14 DECEMBER 1928

*La Symphonie* by Bohuslav MARTINU, written in memory of the occasion when the first national Czechoslovak flag was presented to the first Czech regiment at Darney, France, in June 1918, and conceived as a jubilant, but lyrical procession of musical colors, is performed for the first time anywhere by the Boston Symphony Orchestra, Koussevitzky conducting, on the same program with *Two Pieces for String Orchestra* by Aaron COPLAND (originally written for string quartet), in two movements, *Lento molto* and *Rondino*, which latter is based on a theme derived (as far as alphabetically possible) from the name of Gabriel Fauré.

### 20 DECEMBER 1928

On the occasion of the ninth centenary of the coming of Guido d'Arezzo to Rome and his reception by Pope John XIX, Pope PIUS XI issues the Apostolic Constitution, *Divini Cultus Sanctitatem*, establishing the laws of performance of the Liturgy and other sacred music, and confirming the principles laid down in the papal decree of 22 November 1903, *Motu Proprio*.

### 20 DECEMBER 1928

*America,* 'an epic rhapsody in three parts' for orchestra, a national American musicorama by the Swiss-American composer Ernest BLOCH, winner of the prize offered by the magazine *Musical America* for the best symphonic work glorifying the ideals of the United States, tracing the history of the land beginning with serene pentatonic chants of the Indian aborigines through the landing of the Pilgrims to the auspicious advent of the Machine Age in the 1920's and culminating with an anthem, "America! America! Thy Name is in my Heart!" is performed by the New York Philharmonic for the first time anywhere. (Performances by the Boston, Philadelphia, Chicago and San Francisco Symphony orchestras were given simultaneously on 21 December 1928)

### 21 DECEMBER 1928

*Riquet à la Houppe,* musical comedy in three acts by Georges HüE, after the fable of Perrault dealing with an ugly prince who becomes beautiful when a beauteous princess, ignoring his temporarily repulsive exterior, accepts his love, is produced at the Opéra-Comique in Paris.

### 23 DECEMBER 1928

Maurice MARTENOT appears as a soloist on his electronic keyboard instrument ONDES MARTENOT at a Pasdeloup concert in Paris, in the first performance of a work specially written for this instrument by the Parisian-Greek composer

Dimitri Levidis, entitled *Poème symphonique pour solo d'Ondes Musicales et Orchestre*.

### 28 DECEMBER 1928

Domenico Alaleona, Italian composer and music theorist whose ideas of potential new techniques in composition were vindicated by the rapidly advancing future, dies in his native town of Montegiorgio, at the age of forty-seven.

### 29 DECEMBER 1928

*Kejserens nye Klaeder* (*The Emperor's New Clothes*), first opera, in three scenes, by the 29-year-old Danish composer Finn Höffding, after the famous skeptical tale of Hans Christian Andersen in which a court tailor makes a suit of clothes for his Emperor of the finest possible material, as thin as air, thus exposing the essential nakedness of his body and soul to the populace, deceiving everyone except an innocent child who cries out that the Emperor has no clothes on, is produced in Copenhagen.

# ℒ *1929* ℒ

### 1 JANUARY 1929

*The Proletarian Musician,* a monthly journal of the Russian Association of Proletarian Musicians (RAPM), dedicated to the militant propaganda of a constrictive ideology of utilitarian musical optimism in major keys, coercing Soviet composers to relinquish their freedom of creative self-expression in favor of a peremptory dogma, begins publication in Moscow.

The Marxist ideology of the Association of Proletarian Musicians and the necessity of pursuing ideological propaganda on the musical front make it imperative to create a special publication for these purposes . . . *The Proletarian Musician* will (1) oppose the influence of decadent bourgeois music among young Soviet musicians (2) impress on them the necessity of absorbing the best, the healthiest and the most acceptable ideological elements of the musical legacy of the past (3) prepare the ground for the creation of a new specifically proletarian type of music. (From the declaration of policy in the first issue of *The Proletarian Musician*)

### 6 JANUARY 1929

Ernesto Lecuona, the Cuban composer of dance melodies, writes four songs destined to become popular hits, all in one day: *Blue Night, Siboney, Say Si Si* and *Two Hearts That Pass in the Night*.

### 8 JANUARY 1929

*First Symphony* by the Russian-born composer of neo-classically melodious and modernistically stimulating music, Nicolai Lopatnikoff, is performed for the first time in Karlsruhe.

## 11 JANUARY 1929

*The Golden Goose,* choral ballet by Gustav HOLST, based on a German folk tale by the Grimm Brothers, is performed for the first time in Liverpool.

## 12 JANUARY 1929

*Il Rè,* one-act opera by Umberto GIORDANO, the Italian composer of the Veristic school, is produced at La Scala, Milan.

## 14 JANUARY 1929

*Strike Up the Band,* satirical musical comedy by George GERSHWIN, focused on American ultra-patriots striking up the band in their campaign for war on Switzerland over the issue of chocolate imports, featuring the ballad *Soon,* is produced in New York.

## 17 JANUARY 1929

The Red Army Ensemble is founded in Moscow to stimulate spontaneous musical activities among soldiers, with a nucleus of twelve army men, among them performers on the balalaika, accordion and mandolin, under the direction of Alexander Alexandrov.

## 18 JANUARY 1929

*The Path of October,* the first collective symphonic work by nine Soviet composers: Victor BIELY, Henrik BRUCK, Alexander DAVIDENKO, Marian KOVAL, Zara LEVINA, Sergei RIAUSOV, Vladimir TARNOPOLSKY, Nicolai TCHEMBERDZHI and Boris SCHEKHTER, all members of the Production Collective (Procoll), is performed for the first time in Moscow.

## 19 JANUARY 1929

Ernst KRENEK's "jazz opera" *Jonny Spielt Auf* is produced in English for the first time at the Metropolitan Opera in New York, with the role of the miscegenating Negro bandleader performed by a black-faced white singer in deference to the segregationist susceptibilities of patrons from the southern states.

## 19 JANUARY 1929

*Casanova a Venezia,* 'choreographic action' by the 46-year-old half-Bohemian half-Italian composer Riccardo PICK-MANGIAGALLI, portraying in eight scenes the multifutuent lover's carnival of Venetian amours and amourettes in an appropriately hedonistic style fertilized by aphrodisiacally syncopated rhythms, is produced at La Scala, Milan. (An orchestral suite drawn from it was first performed under the title *Scene carnevalesche* in Milan on 6 February 1931)

## 25 JANUARY 1929

*Balkanofonia,* orchestral suite by the 32-year-old Serbian composer Josip SLAVENSKI, in seven parts, an artful Balkanophonic stylization of Serbian,

Albanian, Turkish, Greek, Rumanian, Istrian and Bulgarian melorhythms, is performed for the first time in Berlin. (The date 18 November 1929, cited in K. Kovačević's authoritative volume *Hrvatski Kompozitori i njikova djela*, published in Zagreb in 1960, is that of the first Zagreb performance)

### 25 JANUARY 1929

*Cello Concerto* by Frederick STOCK, in three movements, written in an eclectically romantic idiom, with Spanish melorhythms accoutred in Germanic harmonies, is performed for the first time by the Chicago Symphony Orchestra, with Alfred Wallenstein, first cellist of the orchestra, as soloist under the direction of the composer, as permanent conductor of the Orchestra.

### 1 FEBRUARY 1929

*Bronwen, Daughter of Llyr,* opera in three acts by the English composer Josef HOLBROOKE, third part of his Wagneromorphic Celtic trilogy *The Cauldron of Annwyn,* wherein a Siegfried-like blond hero named Dylan, reincarnated as a son of Bronwen, perishes in the final battle between the British and Irish human divinities, is performed for the first time at Huddersfield. (Part I was produced on 15 June 1912; part II, on 4 July 1914)

### 9 FEBRUARY 1929

*Der Tenor,* opera in three acts by Ernst DOHNÁNYI, to a libretto dealing with a provincial German tenor who captivates multiple feminine hearts but fails to achieve artistic success, is produced in German in Budapest.

### 9 FEBRUARY 1929

*Le Preziose Ridicole,* one-act opera by the 47-year-old Italian composer Felice LATTUADA, after Molière, is produced at La Scala in Milan.

### 21 FEBRUARY 1929

*Feste Romane,* symphonic poem in four movements by Ottorino RESPIGHI, illustrating four festive actions in Rome: (1) *Circenses,* the great spectacles in the Circus Maximus (2) *Il Giubileo,* a jubilee celebration (3) *L'ottobrata,* an excursion to Roman suburbs (4) *La befana,* the Feast of Epiphany, the manifestation of a benevolent sorceress, the musical score drawing upon a variety of resources, from ancient Greco-Roman modalities to highly chromaticized dissonances, is performed for the first time by the New York Philharmonic Orchestra, conducted by Arturo Toscanini.

### 22 FEBRUARY 1929

*Bunte Suite* for orchestra by the 41-year-old Viennese composer Ernst TOCH, in six unamalgamated movements (hence the title), *Marschtempo, Intermezzo, Adagio espressivo, Marionetten-Tanz, Galante Passacaglia, Karussel,* set to music in a characteristic hedonistic manner of lyrical grotesquerie, is performed for the first time in Frankfurt.

24 FEBRUARY 1929

André MESSAGER, French composer of comic operas in the best Gallic tradition, brilliant symphonic and operatic conductor and a tolerant interpreter of modernistic works, dies in Paris at the age of seventy-five.

24 FEBRUARY 1929

*Živí Mrtvým (The Living to the Dead)*, oratorio by the Czech composer Boleslav VOMÁČKA, is performed for the first time in Prague.

28 FEBRUARY 1929

*Concerto dell'Estate (Summer Concerto)* by Ildebrando PIZZETTI, a symphonic triptych: (1) *Mattutino,* a joyful matutinal overture (2) *Notturno,* a pensive nocturnal eclogue in 5/4 time (3) *Gagliarda,* a rustic round in vivacious triple time, is performed for the first time by the New York Philharmonic Orchestra under the direction of Arturo Toscanini. (The first Italian performance of the work took place in Rome on 10 November 1929)

1 MARCH 1929

Frederick DELIUS, paralyzed and blind, is made a Companion of Honour by Royal decree "for conspicuous national service," the only musician among the forty members of this British order instituted in 1917, whose motto is 'in action faithful and in honour clear.'

4 MARCH 1929

*L'Éventail de Jeanne (Jeanne's Fan)*, a tenfold symphonic offering to the Parisian hostess Mme Jeanne Dubost by ten French composers—Florent SCHMITT, Albert ROUSSEL, Maurice RAVEL, Jacques IBERT, ROLAND-MANUEL, Darius MILHAUD, Marcel DELANNOY, Francis POULENC, Georges AURIC, and Pierre Octave FERROUD—each contributing an elegant Gallic dance as a souvenir of musical congregations in her salon, is performed for the first time as a ballet at the Paris Opéra. (The first performance of the suite in its original form for piano took place in Mme Dubost's Paris salon on 16 June 1927; it was then that the idea came to name the collection *Jeanne's Fan,* each dance by each composer being an individual 'plait' of her *éventail*)

11 MARCH 1929

*Concerto* for piano and wind octet by the 27-year-old Canadian composer Colin McPHEE, is performed for the first time in Boston.

20 MARCH 1929

*Der verlorene Sohn,* one-act opera by the 28-year-old German composer Hermann REUTTER, to Rainer Maria Rilke's story adapted from André Gide's novelette *Le Retour,* is produced in Reutter's native town, Stuttgart. (A later version in the form of a chamber oratorio, *Die Rückkehr des verlorenen Sohnes,* was performed for the first time in Munich on 15 February 1952)

21 MARCH 1929

*Sir John in Love,* opera in four acts by Ralph VAUGHAN WILLIAMS, after Shakespeare's play *The Merry Wives of Windsor,* focused on the incongruity of Falstaff's image as a lover and making liberal use of English folk-tunes in the process, with *Greensleeves* (specifically mentioned by Shakespeare) as a recurrent motive, is produced at the Royal College of Music in London. (A *Fantasia on Greensleeves,* adapted by Vaughan Williams from *Sir John in Love,* became a highly popular symphonic piece)

22 MARCH 1929

*Jazz Suite* for orchestra by the American composer Louis GRUENBERG, in four movements, (1) *Fox-Trot Tempo,* (2) *Boston Waltz-Tempo,* (3) *Blues Tempo, Slow Drag* and (4) *One-step Tempo,* is performed for the first time by the Cincinnati Symphony Orchestra.

23 MARCH 1929

*La Femme nue,* lyric drama in four acts by the 53-year-old French composer Henry FÉVRIER, to a play written in 1908 by Henri Bataille, wherein a Paris midinette, modeling for her lover's painting "La Femme nue," shoots herself in the breast after he decides to marry a rich femme du monde (precisely as Debussy's mistress Lily did on 14 July 1904 when he deserted her for Madame Bardac), but recovers from her carnal and spiritual wounds and marries her old sweetheart, also a painter, set to a melodious score laden with dramatically suspenseful ninth-chord harmonies, is produced in Monte Carlo.

24 MARCH 1929

*Tupeyny Khudozhnik (Toupée Artist,* i.e. master barber), opera in four acts by the Soviet composer Ivan SHISHOV, depicting a fanciful episode from the era of Russian serfdom about 1820, wherein a serf wig maker elopes with a serf actress, is produced in Moscow.

29 MARCH 1929

*Second Symphony,* in B minor, in three movements, by the 33-year-old American composer Leo SOWERBY, is performed for the first time in Chicago.

3 APRIL 1929

*Le Mas,* opera in three acts by the 49-year-old French composer Joseph CANTELOUBE (who added the name of his ancestral family estate Malaret to his patronymic, making it Canteloube de Malaret), written in 1910–1913, dealing with the grandson of a wealthy farmer who abandons his Parisian fiancée in favor of a more rustic and uncomplicated provincial cousin, set to music redolent of the melorhythms of the composer's native Auvergne and arranged in tasteful quasi-impressionistic harmonies, is performed for the first time in Paris.

## 6 APRIL 1929

The Seventh Festival of the International Society for Contemporary Music opens in Geneva with the following program of orchestral music:

*Symphony in E minor* by Roger SESSIONS, written in a neo-classical vein, the first symphony by an American to be performed by the International Society for Contemporary Music; *Concertino* for piano and orchestra by the Dutch composeress Henriette BOSMANS, set in a refined idiom of Dutch impressionism; *Le Fou de la Dame,* ballet-cantata by Marcel DELANNOY, an animated tableau of a chess game conceived in the manner of a medieval "chanson de geste," with the white Queen's Bishop (*fou* in French chess terminology) falling lifeless at her feet after fighting a valiant combat in her name along the musical diagonal; and *Rythmes,* an ingenious study in asymmetric linear counterpoint and vertical polyharmonies by the Swiss composer Frank MARTIN.

## 7 APRIL 1929

At the Seventh Festival of the International Society for Contemporary Music in Geneva, the following program of chamber music is presented:

*String Quartet* in one slow movement by the Viennese composer Julius SCHLOSS; *Piano Sonatina* by the English composer John IRELAND, played by himself; *Songs to the Virgin Mary* by the Parisian Russian composer Nicolas NABOKOV; *Five Variations and a Double Fugue on a Theme by Schoenberg* for chamber orchestra by Schoenberg's disciple Viktor ULLMAN; and a neo-romantic *Violin Sonata* by the Czech composer Erwin SCHULHOFF.

(In the afternoon of the same day, choral works by Karl MARX of Germany, and Krsto ODÁK and Leoš JANÁČEK of Czechoslovakia were performed.)

## 8 APRIL 1929

At the Seventh Festival of the International Society for Contemporary Music in Geneva, the following program is given:

*Serenade* for violin, viola, and cello by the Hungarian composer Alexander JEMNITZ, written in a highly economical (maximum sonority with minimum of means) atonal idiom; *Sonatina* for two violins and piano by the Parisian composer Manuel ROSENTHAL, conceived in a neo-classical manner with an injection of euphoniously pleasurable dissonances; *Piano Sonata* by Berthold GOLDSCHMIDT of Germany; 7 *Haï-Kaïs,* a song cycle by Maurice DELAGE, to the texts of laconic Japanese tristichs, written in a reticent orientalistic manner; and *Second String Quartet* by the Polish composer Jerzy FITELBERG, set in a pellucid neo-classical style. (In the evening of the same day, vocal works of MONTEVERDI, CIMAROSA and Adriano LUALDI were given)

## 9 APRIL 1929

The Seventh Festival of the International Society for Contemporary Music in Geneva concludes with the following concert of orchestral music:

*Flos Campi,* suite for viola solo, wordless chorus and orchestra by Ralph Vaughan Williams, inspired by the Song of Songs, and written in a neo-medieval polyphonic style with impressionistic touches; *Concerto* for piano and chamber orchestra by the German operetta composer Johannes Müller; *Dance* for clarinet and orchestra by the Dutch lady composer Emmy Heil-Frensel-Wegener; and a ponderous *Third Symphony* by Max Butting of Germany.

### 12 APRIL 1929

*Bérengère,* opera written in 1912 by the French composer Marcel Labey, is performed for the first time in Le Havre.

### 13 APRIL 1929

*Maschinist Hopkins,* opera in three acts with a prologue by the Austrian composer Max Brand, to his own libretto, with the action taking place in factories and nightclubs in New York, wherein a cuckolding libertine pushes the husband of his mistress to his death in the cogs of a monstrous machine and strangles her when he finds out that she has become a promiscuous prostitute, whereupon the foreman Machinist Hopkins, dismisses him from his job ostensibly for inefficiency, set to a polytonally jazzy score, is produced in Duisburg, Germany.

### 24 APRIL 1929

*La Peau de chagrin,* "comédie lyrique" in four acts by Charles Levadé, after Balzac's fantastic tale dealing with a young Paris poet bent on suicide who acquires in a curiosity shop a magic piece of leather which carries out his wishes but shrinks with every fulfillment and concomitantly diminishes his days of life until he dies of consumption at the feet of his beloved whom he has thoughtlessly neglected in favor of a mundane noblewoman, with a score written in a functionally romantic style, is produced at the Opéra-Comique in Paris.

### 27 APRIL 1929

*Jürg Jenatsch,* drama with music in six scenes by the German composer Heinrich Kaminski, to a story from the period of the Thirty Years' War, focused on the tragic dilemma of a soldier-politician named Jürg Jenatsch who is given the order to kill the father of a woman he loves, set to music in a sharply dissonant idiom containing spoken recitative and a Greek-like chorus commenting on the action, is performed for the first time in Dresden.

### 29 APRIL 1929

*The Gambler,* opera in four acts by Sergei Prokofiev, composed in 1916 and revised in 1927, after Dostoyevsky's novel of that name, dealing with an imperious Russian grandmother who, to the horror of her descendants, gambles away the family fortune in European spas, written in a lyrico-dramatic vein, and containing a realistic tonal illustration of the roulette wheel in a dissonant counterpoint of minor seconds, is performed for the first time at the Théâtre Royal de la Monnaie in Brussels.

3 MAY 1929

*Concert champêtre* for harpsichord and orchestra by Francis POULENC, in three movements, *Allegro, Andante* and *Finale*, set in a hedonistically pastoral manner of the French "style galant," with asymmetric rhythmic figurations pleasingly stimulating the senses, is performed for the first time by the Orchestre Symphonique de Paris, under the direction of Pierre Monteux, with Wanda Landowska, to whom the score is dedicated, as soloist on a clavecin manufactured according to her instructions.

4 MAY 1929

*Il Gobbo del califfo*, one-act opera by the formerly futuristic Italian composer Franco CASAVOLA, portraying the misadventures of a hunchbacked Caliph in the manner of an opera buffa, the sole manifestation of futuristic modernity being an occasional use of whole-tone scales, is produced in Rome as the winner of a municipal prize.

7 MAY 1929

German students, members of Hitler's brownshirted Nazi gang, hurl stink bombs during the performance of *Dreigroschenoper* by Kurt WEILL at the Berlin State Opera to express their olfactory reaction to modern music by Jewish composers.

15 MAY 1929

*Persée et Andromède ou le plus heureux des trois,* opera in two acts by Jacques IBERT with Andromeda modernized as a Parisian cocotte who subdues her monster captor and frustrates her destined rescuer Perseus, is produced at the Paris Opéra on the same program with the ballet *L'Écran des jeunes filles* by ROLAND-MANUEL, in which an itinerant movie actor induces a schoolmistress to let him give a demonstration of his films at her school and then, with other actors, materializes from the screen and joins the delighted schoolgirls in a frenzied dance.

17 MAY 1929

*Third Symphony* by Sergei PROKOFIEV, in four movements, *Moderato, Andante, Allegro agitato (Scherzo), Andante mosso,* with most of the thematic material taken from his opera *The Flaming Angel,* so that the heroine's chromatic anguish and her diatonic love for the Flaming Angel form the contrasting subjects of the first movement, the scene in the convent contributes its archaically stylized harmonies to the second movement, the demonological orgy of the opera is incorporated in the Scherzo and the apocalyptic medieval visions of pandemonium provide the inspiration for the finale, is performed for the first time by the Orchestre Symphonique de Paris, Pierre Monteux conducting.

Sergi PROKOFIEV conducts at Diaghilev's Ballet Russe in Paris the first performance of his ballet *The Prodigal Son,* after the biblical parable, traversing the scenes of the prodigal son's departure from his home, his polyrhythmic meeting with dubious wayfarers, a polytonally organized robbery, a quasi-atonal drinking orgy, a diatonic romance, and an ascetically harmonized penitent home-coming.

21 MAY 1929

*Les Enchantements d'Alcine,* ballet by Georges AURIC, picturing Alcina as the personification of carnal delights in Ariosto's epic poem *Orlando Furioso,* with the terrifying prospect that Orlando, like other beneficiaries of her enchantments, might be turned to stone, set to music in neo-medieval quartal and quintal harmonies, is produced at the Paris Opéra by Ida Rubinstein and her dance group.

23 MAY 1929

Sergei VASSILENKO conducts the world première in Moscow of his grand opera *Son of the Sun,* in four acts, with the action taking place during the Boxer Rebellion of 1900 in Pekin, wherein a Chinese scientist nicknamed "Son of the Sun" successfully counters the diplomatic representations of the British ambassador, American Navy, German Army officers and a bevy of sanctimonious missionaries, with the score employing authentically pentatonic Chinese-style themes.

25 MAY 1929

*Knez od Zete (Duke of Montenegro)* music drama in four acts by the prime romantic composer of Yugoslavia Petar KONJOVIĆ, to a fictional historic episode concerning the marriage arranged for political reasons between the daughter of the Doge of Venice and a Montenegrin duke, ending in a tragedy as the bridegroom deformed by smallpox asks his friend to act as his proxy and the double suicide of the bride and groom, incorporating in the score the ethnic elements of the Adriatic Montenegrin mountain songs, is produced in Belgrade.

30 MAY 1929

*Amazonas* by the prime Brazilian composer Heitor VILLA-LOBOS, a symphonic poem to a story by his father, depicting primeval life in the Amazon River basin in Brazil, wherein an Indian virgin is pursued by the monsters of the jungle, written in luxuriantly tropical harmonies, with the application of novel orchestral effects such as playing on string instruments below the bridge, is performed for the first time in Paris.

8 JUNE 1929

*Neues vom Tage,* journalistic 'Gebrauchsoper' in three acts by Paul HINDEMITH, wherein a married couple performs a Hate Duet, the chorus sings a Divorce March, and, in the second act, the wife takes a naked bath in her hotel room in the presence of witnesses and a detective impersonating a lover to establish a case of adultery, with a number of other news items, including stenographers taking atonal dictation in dissonant counterpoint, typewriters clicking in asymmetric rhythms, etc., is performed for the first time in Berlin.

19 JUNE 1929

*Aubade*, a "choreographic concerto for piano and 18 instruments" by Francis POULENC, is performed for the first time at the Paris home of the Vicomtesse de Noailles, to whom the work is dedicated.

25 JUNE 1929

Eugene GOOSSENS conducts at Covent Garden in London the first performance of his one-act opera *Judith*, to a libretto based on the biblical novel by Arnold Bennett, composed in a bold modernistic idiom (the opening motto contains ten different notes) and set in dissonant counterpoint, without resorting to pseudo-exotic melodic effects.

12 JULY 1929

*El Matrero*, dramatic legend in three acts by the Argentinian composer Felipe BOERO, to a story dealing with a nomad gaucho enamored of the daughter of a village elder, is produced at the Teatro Colón in Buenos Aires.

28 JULY 1929

At the concluding concert of the *Musiktage* in Baden-Baden, a *Hörspiel* ("hearing play," i.e. a radio cantata), entitled *Lindberghflug*, with music by Kurt WEILL and Paul HINDEMITH, to the text by Bertolt Brecht, is performed for the first time, illustrating the realistic and surrealistic aspects of Lindbergh's transatlantic solo flight of 21 May 1927:

The voice of the ocean (monodically); Lindbergh's thoughts (in the syncopated manner of the Blues); New York radio stations urging ships to report sighting of Lindbergh's plane (canonically); the formation of fog (in nebulously opaque, somberly static harmonies); inventory of equipment (flashlight, food rations, etc.); a dialogue with the clouds (in Baroque counterpoint); the waltz of falling snow (a soft scherzo); Erlkönig-like cajolery of the elements lulling Lindbergh to sleep, chanting in bass voice, 'Schlaf, Charlie . . . ,'; sensation-mongering American reporters (in jazz accents); the French newspapermen (an anxious chorus a cappella); Lindbergh's apostrophe to the sputtering motor (*tremolando*, in asymmetric rhythms); sighting of the plane by Scottish fishermen (in jig-time); waiting crowd at Le Bourget airport at night (in agitated foxtrot time); the landing (a triumphant hymn-like march); epilogue (Lindbergh's philosophical musings on the 'unattainable' that has been attained).

(In 1930 Brecht revised the text of his play as *Der Flug der Lindberghs*, i.e., Flight of the Lindberghs, treating the flyer as a representative of the general species of *Homo volans*. In 1950 he changed the title to the impersonal description *Der Ozeanflug*, eliminating Lindbergh's name as politically repugnant. The radio performance included musical numbers contributed by Paul Hindemith; his name appeared in the program as co-composer, but he withdrew his music shortly afterwards, and at the first concert performance of the score, which took place in Berlin on 5 December 1929, under the direction of Otto Klemperer, Kurt Weill only was named as the composer of the work)

### 11 AUGUST 1929

Leo SOWERBY conducts at Interlochen, Michigan, the first performance of his symphonic poem *Prairie*, inspired by Carl Sandburg's vision of the great open American spaces.

### 19 AUGUST 1929

Serge DIAGHILEV, magister elegantiarum of the world of modern dance, sophisticated, cultured and imaginative animator of choreographers, dancers, mimes, composers, artists and stage directors, creator of the great Ballet Russe that received its artistic baptism in Paris and influenced profoundly the evolution of the modern Terpsichorean art, under whose tutelage, marked by an impeccable taste, Stravinsky, Prokofiev and a host of others contributed some of their most significant works for the stage, great-great-great-great-grandson, through an illegitimate line, of Peter the Great whom he resembled physically, dies in Venice at the age of fifty-seven.

### 21 AUGUST 1929

*Bitter Sweet*, operetta in three acts, with words and music by the English playwright Noel COWARD, in which a sophisticated lady helps her inexperienced niece to engage in free love with a sexually competent and potent band leader, is produced in London.

### 25 AUGUST 1929

*Chapultepec*, symphonic triptych by Manuel PONCE, first Mexican composer of the advanced modern school, in three contrasting movements, *Primavera*, *Nocturno Romántico* and *Canto y Danza*, written in an impressionistic style, but profoundly Mexican in thematic substance (the title refers to the historic suburb of Mexico City), is performed for the first time in Mexico City, conducted by Carlos Chávez, who was one of Ponce's many Mexican pupils. (A new, radically revised version, was first performed by Chávez in Mexico on 24 August 1934)

### 2 SEPTEMBER 1929

*Sweet Adeline*, a musical romance by Jerome KERN, dealing with a chorus girl in a beer garden during the Spanish-American War who sincerely lends her charms to a succession of male admirers, is produced in New York.

### 21 SEPTEMBER 1929

*Engelbrekt*, opera in four acts by the Swedish composer Natanael BERG, to his own libretto, is produced in Stockholm.

## 3 OCTOBER 1929

*Viola Concerto* by William WALTON, in three movements, *Andante comodo, Vivo* and *Allegro moderato,* neo-classically diversified by asymmetrical rhythmicalities and accoutred in polyharmonic dress, is performed for the first time in London, with Paul Hindemith playing the viola solo part. (The work was revised for a smaller orchestra, with an added harp part, and was first performed in the new version in London on 18 January 1962)

## 10 OCTOBER 1929

*Il Carnevale di Venezia,* symphonic poem by Vincenzo TOMMASINI, is performed for the first time anywhere by the New York Philharmonic under the direction of Arturo Toscanini.

## 12 OCTOBER 1929

A festival of music by Frederick DELIUS opens in London, with Sir Thomas Beecham conducting the London Symphony Orchestra in the following program: *Brigg Fair, A Late Lark* for tenor and orchestra (first performance), *Dance Rhapsody No. 2, Sea Drift, In a Summer Garden,* and an excerpt from the opera *A Village Romeo and Juliet.*

Delius, blind and helpless though he was, was determined to be present. The distance to be traveled from France, where he lived, was 400 miles, and included a long car journey and a sea crossing . . . He was carried in his invalid chair, propped up with cushions, down the gangway to a waiting ambulance. (Clare Delius, *Frederick Delius, Memories of My Brother,* London, 1935)

Delius had suffered a heavy blow in the defection of his favorite goddess Aphrodite Pandemos who had returned his devotions with an affliction which, although temporarily alleviated, was to break out again incurably some twenty-five years later. (Sir Thomas Beecham, *Frederick Delius,* New York, 1959, p. 119)

(The second concert of Delius' music, on 16 October 1929, comprised the first performance of his *Air and Dance* for string orchestra; the third concert, on 18 October 1929, included the first performance of *Cynara* for baritone and orchestra; a revised version of his *Piano Concerto;* Norwegian-inspired symphonic ballad *Eventyr; Arabesque* for baritone, chorus and orchestra; and *Appalachia,* variations on an old Negro song for chorus and orchestra, named after the extinct Indian tribe of northwestern Florida where Delius briefly sojourned in 1884; the fourth concert, on 23 October 1929, included a performance of his *String Quartet,* songs and choruses; the fifth concert, on 24 October 1929, programmed the orchestral *Dance Rhapsody No. 1;* two scenes from the opera *Fennimore and Gerda; Songs of Sunset* for orchestra; *Violin Concerto;* and the symphonic suite *North Country Sketches*)

## 25 OCTOBER 1929

*Jungle,* symphonic movement by the Alsatian-born American composer Werner JOSTEN, inspired by Henri Rousseau's primitivistic painting *Forêt exotique,* using a rich fauna of African drums and a lion's roar (a drum with a rosined cord drawn through the drumhead), is performed for the first time by the Boston Symphony Orchestra, Serge Koussevitzky conducting.

## 1 NOVEMBER 1929

The London Festival of music by Frederick DELIUS concludes with a performance of *A Mass of Life*, Sir Thomas Beecham conducting, followed by the composer's brief word of leave-taking from his invalid chair.

The strength and weakness of Delius is his solitariness. He belongs to no school, follows no tradition, and is like no other composer in the form, content, or style of his music . . . This spiritual isolation is reflected in his technique. Variation form offers endless scope for reflecting on a subject without getting any farther. Delius is not happy in his use of sonata form, which demands progressive development of the thought; his use of variations is masterly. Other symptoms of his lack of vigour are a rhythmic languor and the absence of counterpoint. His harmony, moreover, is curiously static: it belongs to a world from which time and movement have been banished. (*A Retrospect*, editorial in *The Times*, London, 2 November 1929)

## 4 NOVEMBER 1929

A new building for the Chicago Opera is inaugurated by Samuel INSULL, utility magnate.

## 12 NOVEMBER 1929

*Violin Concerto* in one movement by Josef Matthias HAUER, subtitled *Zwölf-tonmusik for Orchestra with a Solo Instrument*, with 112 derivative tone-rows formed by permutations of the original dodecaphonic series, and ending on a typical Hauerian seventh-chord B-D-sharp-F-sharp-B-flat, is performed for the first time in Berlin.

## 20 NOVEMBER 1929

*Fifth Symphony* in D minor, op. 141, by the 69-year-old Czech composer of German extraction Josef Bohuslav FOERSTER, in four movements, the first of which, *Moderato solenne*, is derived from the musical acrostic on the four letters (AFED) in the name of his only son Alfred who died at the age of fifteen in 1921, is performed for the first time in Prague.

## 21 NOVEMBER 1929

Alexander GLAZUNOV makes his first American appearance as conductor leading his *Sixth Symphony* with the Detroit Symphony Orchestra.

## 27 NOVEMBER 1929

*Fifty Million Frenchmen*, musical comedy by Cole PORTER, in which an American playboy woos and wins a footloose American girl in Paris against the formidable competition of an expatriated Russian Grand Duke, is produced in New York.

## 27 NOVEMBER 1929

*Bilý Pán* (*Gentleman in White*), opera in two acts by the Czech composer Jaroslav KŘIČKA, to a libretto derived from Oscar Wilde's story *The*

*Canterville Ghost,* wherein Mr. and Mrs. Hollywood of U.S.A. rent a haunted castle in Bohemia and, intent on capturing a local ghost for the museum of their midwestern home town, instruct their daughter to kiss the apparition, which turns out to be the prankish owner of the castle dressed in ghostly white, with a happy dénouement vouchsafed to both when the ci-devant phantom marries the girl, is produced in Brno. (A revised version in German, entitled *Spuk im Schloss, oder Böse Zeiten für Gespenster,* was produced in Breslau on 14 November 1931.)

28 NOVEMBER 1929

*The First Airphonic Suite* by Joseph SCHILLINGER, written for the electronic instrument Thereminovox and orchestra, is performed for the first time anywhere in Cleveland, with its Russian inventor Leon Theremin, as the soloist, manipulating the instrument by the wave of the hand, to and fro, thus changing the heterodyne frequency and producing the desired tone.

28 NOVEMBER 1929

A century has elapsed since the birth in a small village, Vikhvotinetz, in Southwestern Russia, of Anton RUBINSTEIN, great pianist of the romantic school, composer of grandiloquent operas and virtuoso piano pieces.

(Rubinstein was born a Jew but was baptized, along with thirty other members of the Rubinstein family, on 6 August 1831; the act of Baptism was published in the *Russian Musical Gazette,* No. 45, 1909. Altmann's *Künstlermusiklexicon,* 1936, erroneously states that Rubinstein was a Siberian of Aryan extraction)

29 NOVEMBER 1929

The Stephen Foster Society is organized in New York City with the aim of collecting and publishing American folksongs.

3 DECEMBER 1929

*The Depraved Heavenly Maid,* opera written in 1908 by the Japanese composer Kôsçak YAMADA, is produced in Tokyo.

6 DECEMBER 1929

Igor STRAVINSKY plays the solo part with the Orchestre Symphonique de Paris, under the direction of Ernest Ansermet, in the first performance of his *Capriccio* for piano and orchestra, set in the "style galant" of the French Baroque, in three well-demarcated movements, *Presto, Andante rapsodico* and *Allegro capriccioso,* wherein episodes in varied genres are arrayed in free succession with capricious logic.

11 DECEMBER 1929

*Atsumori,* one-act Japanese opera by Charles W. LAWRENCE is performed for the first time, in concert form, in Seattle. (First stage performance, in the Japanese language, took place in Tokyo, on 9 December 1950.)

## 12 DECEMBER 1929

Constant LAMBERT, 24-year-old English composer, conducts in Manchester, England, the first performance of his symphonic cantata *The Rio Grande*, scored for piano, mixed chorus, strings, brass and five percussion sections, to the poem by Sacheverell Sitwell, glorifying the tropical luxuriance of the great Rio Grande of Brazil ("By the Rio Grande they dance no sarabande"), in artful jazzy rhythms.

## 13 DECEMBER 1929

*Second Symphony* by Arnold BAX, designated as being in E minor and C, in three movements; (1) *Molto moderato*, set in arid Celtic fifths and abounding in consecutive triadic progressions, exploding "riotously" into great rhapsodic turbulence (2) *Andante*, in B major, with alternating meters of 3/4 and 4/4, lyric, mystical, mounting rebelliously in sonorous waves of symphonic color (3) *Poco largamente*, leading to *Allegro feroce*, with the ferocity of angular melodies and apoplectic rhythms mitigated by the deep pedal points of the organ, the entire work being unified by a thematically pregnant three-note figure, is performed for the first time by the Boston Symphony Orchestra under the direction of Serge Koussevitzky, to whom the score is dedicated.

## 14 DECEMBER 1929

*Ijola*, opera by the 45-year-old Polish composer Piotr RYTEL, to his own libretto, is produced in Warsaw.

## 15 DECEMBER 1929

*La Légende de Bebek*, symphonic poem by the Turkish composer Djemal RECHID, after a gruesome Turkish fairy tale about a young mother whose infant child falls from a camel and is devoured by vultures, is performed for the first time in Paris.

## 15 DECEMBER 1929

*Viola Concerto* in four movements by Darius MILHAUD is performed for the first time by the Concertgebouw Orchestra in Amsterdam, with Paul Hindemith playing the solo part and Pierre Monteux conducting.

## 18 DECEMBER 1929

*Symphonie*, op. 21, by Anton von WEBERN, written in the sylleptically polyphonic, canonic, palindromic, dodecaphonic techniques, thematically derived from the guiding series A, F-sharp, G, A-flat, E, F, B, B-flat, D, C-sharp, C, E-flat consisting of two mutually reflexive groups of six notes each, in which the second is formed by the transposed inversion of the first, the central interval being the tritone and the equidistant intervals from it (first and last, second and penultimate, third and antepenultimate, fourth and preantepenultimate, fifth and quasipreantepenultimate) standing also in the relationship of a tritone, in two movements, (1) *Ruhig schreitend,* opening with great liberality of dodecaphonic legalities, so that the 12-tone series is not assembled until 23 notes are distributed among the instruments of the orchestra (2) *Variationen,* comprising a theme with seven variations, each constructed quasipalindromically, with the central fourth variation being a self-reflecting longitudinally broken mirror, all these elements arrayed in pointilistically propulsive rhythms, the entire work presenting a paradigm of dodecaphonic chirality, is performed for the first time as a commissioned work by the League of Composers in New York.

In Goethe's primordial plant the root is no different from the stalk, the stalk from the leaf, the leaf from the flower—these are all variations of the same idea. . . . The same law is valid for all living things. Variations on a theme represent a primordial form which underlies everything, something that is apparently something else, and yet always the same. . . . In my *Symphonie* the second movement is the crab form of the first. . . . There are therefore only 24 forms, because each pair represents one unit. The accompaniment of the theme is also a crab form. The first variation is a double canon. No greater intimacy of relationship can be imagined. Even the Flemish polyphonists never achieved such union. The fourth Variation is a mirror reflection. It is the middle point of the entire movement, after which the music turns backwards again, so that it becomes itself a double canon in crab motion! (Anton von Webern, *Der Weg zur neuen Musik,* Vienna, 1960)

*Symphonie for Chamber Orchestra* of Schoenberg's pupil Anton von Webern is one of those whispering, clucking, picking little pieces which Webern composes when he whittles away at small and futile ideas, until he has achieved the perfect fruition of futility . . . Webern's little orchestra suggested nothing so much as a cat that, arching its back, glared and bristled its fur, and moaned or growled or spat . . . Yells of laughter came from all over the hall and nearly drowned the sounds of Webern's whimpering orchestra. (Olin Downes, New York *Times,* 19 December 1929)

Mr. Webern's Symphony was composed of fractional sounds uttered at night by the sleeping inhabitants of a zoo. (Samuel Chotzinoff, New York *World,* 19 December 1929)

### 21 DECEMBER 1929

*Samuel Pepys,* one-act opera by Albert COATES, depicting in an astutely stylized manner the times and the mores of the famous London diarist, with topical citations from 17th-century English songs, is performed for the first time with a German libretto, in Munich.

### 22 DECEMBER 1929

Sergei PROKOFIEV conducts in Paris the first performance of his symphonic *Divertissement,* in four movements, *Moderato, Nocturne, Dance, Epilogue,* of which the first and the third were salvaged from the discarded music of the ballet *Trapeze* written in 1925.

My *Divertissement* was called 'a little abstract.' Why? I think now that it was my new conception of melody which caused the impression of abstraction. (Prokofiev quoted by Olin Downes in the New York *Times,* 2 February 1930)

# ꧁ *1930* ꧂

*Cuauhtémoc,* symphonic poem by the Mexican composer José ROLÓN, inspired by the historic legend of the last Indian Emperor of Mexico, is performed for the first time by the Orquesta Sinfónica de Mexico, Carlos Chávez conducting, in Mexico City.

12 JANUARY 1930

*The Nose,* the first opera by 23-year-old Dmitri SHOSTAKOVICH, in three acts, scored for large orchestra, chorus and 78 singing and speaking personages, after Gogol's fantastic tale about a humble government clerk whose nose vanishes from his face to be reincarnated as an important official, set to music of great comic impact, including an octet of janitors in dissonant canonic counterpoint, a sentimental romance with a deliberately incompatible accompaniment, and a thunderous orchestral sneeze, in the realistically grotesque tradition of Mussorgsky, solicitously safeguarding the natural inflections of common Russian speech, is produced in Leningrad.

I took Gogol's story for my opera because I believe that classical literature possesses a sense of actuality. As a satire on the era of Tsar Nicolas I, *The Nose* is one of Gogol's strongest works. But my music does not exaggerate the parody. Gogol reports his comic episodes in a very serious tone. Similarly, my music does not indulge in deliberate witticisms. (Shostakovich in his declaration, *Why The Nose?* published in the original program book for the première)

15 JANUARY 1930

*Le Roi d'Yvetot,* comic opera in four acts by Jacques IBERT, dealing with an insouciant king who loses a war but preserves the affection of his people and marries his favorite concubine, is performed for the first time at the Opéra-Comique in Paris.

19 JANUARY 1930

*Leben des Orest,* opera in five acts by the 29-year-old Austrian modernist Ernst KRENEK, to his own version of the famous story of the infamous Atridae, in which the lover of Klytemnestra, mother of Elektra and Orestes, gives a cup of venomous potion to Elektra who unwittingly tenders it to her father Agamemnon, is caged for her involuntary deed, retaliates by inciting Orestes to kill Klytemnestra and is subsequently slain herself by an outraged mob, is produced in Leipzig.

*Third Symphony,* subtitled *May First,* by the 23-year-old Soviet composer Dmitri SHOSTAKOVICH, in a single exuberant movement, set in an optimistic idiom rooted in major modalities and maintaining a proletarian marching rhythm, with a choral ending to an anonymous text celebrating in confident revolutionary terms the annual Day of International Labor, accompanied by an oriflamme of French horns, an ovation of trumpets and proclamatory trombones, with an industrious sibilation of the piccolos, is performed for the first time in the Leningrad House of Culture by the Leningrad Philharmonic, conducted by Alexander Gauk.

(A second performance of the *Third Symphony* was given on the following day in Leningrad for a special audience of Communist Youth groups; the earlier editions of *Music Since 1900* cite a much later production that took place in Leningrad on 6 November 1931, on the 14th anniversary of the Soviet Revolution, as the first; the same date is given in most Soviet reference works. The *Third Symphony* was judged ideologically inadequate to its theme and was allowed to lie fallow for 34 years until its revival in Leningrad on 12 May 1964)

May First! Burning in the whistle of bullets, in the bayonets and rifles leading assault on the Tsar's Winter Palace! Our turn has come! Listen, proletarian masses, to the voice of our factories! Burn the old! Ignite the flames of new reality! With the sun emblazoned on our uplifted banners, let our march thunder in the ears of the world! Revolution, stamp the march of the millions! (From the text of the chorus in the finale of the *Third Symphony*)

## 26 JANUARY 1930

A series of concerts for the proletariat, with admission free, is inaugurated by the Orquesta Sinfónica in Mexico City.

## 26 JANUARY 1930

*Galatea,* one-act opera by Walter BRAUNFELS, to the old Greek tale of a sculptor becoming enamored of the marmoreal beauty of his own creation, is produced in Cologne.

## 1 FEBRUARY 1930

*Von Heute auf Morgen,* one-act opera by Arnold SCHOENBERG (completed at 3:15 P.M. on 1 January 1929), scored for voices and orchestra including two saxophones, mandolin, guitar and flexaton, limning a modern mismarriage, wherein the husband indulges in a mental flirtation with a seductive soprano and his wife dissimulates as a potential mistress of a tenor, with both abandoning their fantasies in favor of life 'from day to day', set in an anguished dissonant idiom, with the thematic materials based on a dodecaphonic series, is performed for the first time in Frankfurt. (Schoenberg remarked to the orchestra after the performance: "Gentlemen, the difference between what you played tonight and what I actually wrote in my score would make a new opera.")

## 6 FEBRUARY 1930

*Petite Suite* for orchestra by Albert Roussel, in three movements, *Aubade, Pastorale* and *Mascarade,* in the "style galant" of the rococo period, is performed for the first time in Paris.

## 15 FEBRUARY 1930

*Çançunik* (phonetic transcription of the French traffic sign *Sens unique,* one-way street), a humorous symphonic sketch by Florent Schmitt, is performed for the first time in Paris.

## 16 FEBRUARY 1930

*Symphonie lyrique* by the 26-year-old expatriate Russian composer Nicolas Nabokov, in three classically designed movements, *Allegro, Largo, Allegro,* is performed for the first time in Paris by the Orchestre Symphonique de Paris, Pierre Monteux conducting.

## 20 FEBRUARY 1930

*First Symphony* by the 30-year-old American composer Randall Thompson (completed by him on 29 December 1929) is performed for the first time by the Rochester Philharmonic, under the direction of Howard Hanson.

## 23 FEBRUARY 1930

Horst Wessel, "martyred poet" of the Nazi cause, author of the text of the Storm Troopers' marching song, set to music plagiarized from a Hamburg waterfront ballad, which as the *Horst-Wessel-Lied* became a Nazi anthem, extolling in lofty syllables the glories of the sanguinary SA (one version had a stanza "When Jewish blood drips off your trusted pen-knife/ We march ahead with twice as steady step"), dies at the age of 22 in a Berlin hospital, of blood poisoning resulting from a revolver wound suffered by him on the night of 14 January 1930, in a Berlin street brawl over the favors of a "Lucie of Alexanderplatz".

(Sol Epstein, a painter, Peter Stoll, a tailor, and Hans Ziegler, a barber, sentenced to prison terms by the Republican German court, as accomplices in the murder, were later retried by the Nazi court, which, on 15 June 1934, sentenced Epstein and Ziegler to death, and Peter Stoll to $7\frac{1}{2}$ years of hard labor. Epstein and Ziegler were decapitated on 10 April 1935)

## 25 FEBRUARY 1930

John Hays Hammond, Jr., American musical inventor, presents in New York the first demonstration of his Crea-Tone, a pianoforte capable of sustaining and increasing the strength of a tone.

## 27 FEBRUARY 1930

*Rondo veneziano* for orchestra by the foremost proponent of Italian tradition in modern music Ildebrando Pizzetti, is performed for the first time anywhere by the New York Philharmonic, Arturo Toscanini conducting. (It was staged in the form of a ballet at La Scala, Milan, on 8 January 1931)

9 MARCH 1930

*Aufstieg und Fall der Stadt Mahagonny (Rise and Fall of the City of Mahagonny),* opera in three acts by Kurt WEILL, to a libretto by the fiery denunciator of inequities and iniquities of modern life, Bertolt Brecht, expanded from the one-act *Singspiel* originally produced at the Baden-Baden Music Festival on 17 July 1927 under the title *Mahagonny,* and portraying scenes of rapacious capitalist society in a Miami-like American town, ruled by three loan sharks to whom financial irregularities are graver crimes than murder, but whose order to execute a citizen for non-payment of a bill precipitates popular revolt, with an apotheosis in which Mahagonny goes up in flames like a modern Sodom, set to a musical score flaunting its ostentatiously sophisticated vulgarity and polytonally harmonized jazz ballads to texts in pseudo-American English ("Oh Moon of Alabama, We now must say goodbye, We've lost our good old Mamma, And must have whiskey, oh you know why!"), is performed for the first time in Leipzig, accompanied by shouts from the audience: 'Es stinkt!' and 'Schweinerei!'

13 MARCH 1930

*Fantasia on Sussex* for violoncello and orchestra by Ralph VAUGHAN WILLIAMS, based on the hymn-tune *Sussex,* is performed for the first time in London, with Pablo Casals as soloist with the Royal Philharmonic Orchestra, conducted by Sir John Barbirolli.

14 MARCH 1930

*Third Symphony* by Arnold BAX, couched in somber Northern colors of static turbulence, in three movements with an epilogue, (1) *Lento moderato,* with a motto proffered by a sad bassoon, erupting suddenly in the energetically controlled *Allegro moderato* (2) *Lento dolcissimo,* in which a brooding horn solo is accompanied by plucked muted strings (3) *Moderato,* leading to a slow *Epilogue* and ending on a pietistically white C-major triad, "the basic idea of the music being adumbrated as through a dark haze," is performed for the first time in London, Sir Henry Wood conducting.

15 MARCH 1930

*Boruta,* opera by the 56-year-old Polish composer Witold MALISZEWSKI, is produced in Warsaw.

19 MARCH 1930

*Georges Dandin,* one-act opera by Max D'OLLONE, after Molière's comedy of manners in which a merchant marries above his social status and has to supply money to his aristocratic in-laws, is produced at the Opéra-Comique in Paris, on the same program with another short opera after Molière, *Le Sicilien ou l'amour peintre,* by Omer LETOREY.

### 26 MARCH 1930

*The Golden Hoop,* music drama in four acts by the Ukrainian composer Boris LIATOSHINSKY, dealing with the struggle for liberation of mountain tribes in the Caucasus during the Mongol invasion of 1241, is produced in Odessa.

### 28 MARCH 1930

Walter PISTON conducts the Boston Symphony Orchestra in the first performance of his *Suite for Orchestra,* in three movements, derived from old forms of absolute music, but containing an American section with a syncopated blues-type tune over an *ostinato* suggesting the popular type of ragtime accompaniment.

### 29 MARCH 1930

The Music Supervisors National Conference, held in Chicago, unanimously adopts the following resolution opposing the bill pending in Congress for the nomination of *The Star-Spangled Banner* as the National Anthem of the United States:

WHEREAS, this Conference is informed that a bill is to be considered by Congress which would make *The Star-Spangled Banner* our national anthem, and

WHEREAS, the approval of this bill would signify to our people and to the people of the world at large a unique endorsement of this song as embodying the ideals of our nation, and

WHEREAS, the text of this song is largely the reflection of a single war-time event which cannot fully represent the spirit of a nation committed to peace and good will, and

WHEREAS, the music of this song, while thrilling and effective when well sung on occasions of high patriotic fervor, is not suitable for frequent singing in school rooms and assemblages of many kinds where a national anthem is needed;

THEREFORE, the Music Supervisors National Conference, with a membership of 7,500 and with the support of the great body of music educators who direct the musical activities of millions of children in our schools and deeply affect spiritual values in our communities, does hereby

RESOLVE, that while recognizing the legitimate place of *The Star-Spangled Banner* as one of our historic patriotic songs, the Conference still vigorously opposes its adoption as our national anthem.

### 29 MARCH 1930

*Meine Schwester und ich,* operetta by Ralph BENATZKY, wherein a music librarian inadvertently marries a French heiress who poses as her own non-existent sister, becomes inhibited by their social disparity but eventually overcomes his inferiority complex and consummates the marriage, is produced in Berlin.

### 30 MARCH 1930

*The Football Players,* ballet by the 30-year-old Soviet composer Victor ORANSKY (whose real name was Gershov), a choreographic social tract contrasting the healthy Soviet love of a football player for a proletarian scrubwoman with the degenerate romance between an unliquidated bourgeois individual and an obsolete noblewoman, is produced in Moscow.

### 31 MARCH 1930

*North Wind,* tragic opera in three acts by the Soviet composer Lev KNIPPER, dealing with the historic episode of the execution in 1918 of a group of Soviet commissars by the British occupation army in the "windy city" of Baku on the Caspian Sea, is performed for the first time in Moscow.

### 1 APRIL 1930

Cosima WAGNER, imperious matriarch of Wagner's musical domain, daughter of Franz Liszt and former wife of Hans von Bülow whom she left for Wagner, dies in her Bayreuth domain at the age of ninety-two, surviving Wagner by forty-seven years and one and a half months.

### 3 APRIL 1930

*Summer Evening,* symphonic poem by the Hungarian master Zoltán KODÁLY, reorchestrated and remodeled from his early graduation piece of 1906, scored for a soft orchestra, sans trumpets or trombones, thematically derived from spaciously pentatonic melorhythms redolent of the folk patterns of immemorial Pannonia, and including a vivacious fugato in the Dorian mode touched by Magyar syncopation in felicitously diaphonous contrapuntal harmonies, is performed for the first time by the New York Philharmonic, Arturo Toscanini conducting.

### 3 APRIL 1930

The violinistic Hungarian sisters Adila Fachiri and Jelly d'Aranyi give in London the first performance of *Double Concerto* for two violins and orchestra, by Gustav HOLST, written especially for them.

### 9 APRIL 1930

*Variazioni sinfoniche,* a set of orchestral variations by Mario CASTELNUOVO-TEDESCO, in forms and idioms ranging from the Renaissance to vigesimosecular America, comprising four sections (1) *Chaconne e Corrente* (1) *Minuetto e Pastorale* (3) *Notturno* (4) *Fox-trot ed Epilogo,* is performed for the first time by the New York Philharmonic Orchestra, Arturo Toscanini conducting.

### 12 APRIL 1930

*Z mrtvého domu,* last opera, in three acts, by Leoš JANÁČEK, to his own libretto after Dostoyevsky's semi-autobiographical novel *From the House of the Dead,* describing the horrors of life in a Tsarist Siberian prison camp, set to music in an expressionistic idiom with tangential allusions to Russian folksong modalities, and concluding with an ode to freedom, is produced posthumously in Brno, a year and eight months after Janáček's death.

## 14 APRIL 1930

The first complete performance of the final version of *Drei Orchesterstücke*, op. 6, by Alban BERG, bearing the dedication "To my teacher and friend Arnold Schoenberg in immeasurable gratitude and love," conceived as a symphony, in which the first section, *Präludium*, which opens with a consortium of pitchless drumlets, tam-tams and cymbals, presenting a rich assortment of varied atonal themes in opulent polyphonic treatment, corresponds to the first movement; the second, *Reigen*, has the combined function of Scherzo and a slow movement, and the finale, *Marsch*, is a grotesque stylization of a Prussian military tune, concluding on a pyramidal tritone consisting of low E's and high B-flats fortissississimo with a chasm of three and a half octaves in between, is performed for the first time in Oldenburg. (The score was completed on 23 August 1914, and revised in 1929; the first two sections, *Präludium* and *Reigen*, were performed previously in Berlin on 5 June 1923)

## 17 APRIL 1930

*The Sun Bride*, one-act opera to a libretto derived from American Indian folklore, by Charles Sanford SKILTON, the most industrious cultivator among American composers of Indian-inspired theatrical and orchestral music, receives its world première in a radio performance in New York.

## 19 APRIL 1930

*L'Ultimo Lord*, opera in three acts by Franco ALFANO, is produced in Naples.

## 26 APRIL 1930

*La Sagredo*, opera in three acts by the 46-year-old Italian composer Franco VITTADINI, is produced at La Scala, Milan.

## 29 APRIL 1930

*Lo Straniero*, opera in two acts by Ildebrando PIZZETTI, the third part of his operatic triptych, of which *Dèbora e Jaele* and *Fra Gherardo* are the first two, wherein an Oedipus-like parricide, the Stranger of the title, is doomed to travel through the deadly desert pursued by the Furies, but finds spiritual support in the company of a shepherd's young daughter who follows him through his fateful journey to the end, set in the manner of a Greek tragedy, with the chorus commenting on the events and their meaning, and with a candidly melodious and harmonious musical score in the emotive Italian tradition, is performed for the first time in Rome.

## 5 MAY 1930

*Christophe Colomb*, opera by Darius MILHAUD, to a text by Paul Claudel, in two parts, containing 27 scenes, with elements of Greek drama (in the moralistic use of a suasive chorus), mystery play (in allegorical parables), music

508

drama (in the use of identifying though non-Wagnerian musical phrases), sur-realist projection (Columbus conversing with his second self), modern realism (through insertion of cinematic sequences) and symbolistic allusions (doves are released on the stage, the name of Columbus in French being almost iden-tical with *colombe*, a dove), set to music in an eloquently rhetorical style, with passing quotations of Spanish refrains, is produced for the first time at the Berlin Opera, in a German version.

### 15 MAY 1930

*Ice and Steel*, opera in four acts by the 41-year-old Soviet composer Vladimir DESHEVOV, dealing with the 1921 rebellion of a politically immature contingent of the Red Fleet against the Soviet government, with much incidental action descriptive of the life in Petrograd at the time—commotion on the black market illustrated by a rapid tarantella on a 12-tone theme, an obsolete lady-in-waiting begging alms in French in the intonations of a sentimental romance, a disfranchised officer of the liquidated Tsarist Army playing a bourgeois guitar number, a former courtier selling the anachronistic trousers of his abolished uniform—with a grand climax picturing the victorious assault on the dissident citadel of Kronstadt across the frozen surface of the Gulf of Finland led by the class-conscious proletariat to the accompaniment of stridently dissonant music reinforced by acervative tone-clusters played on the piano with the forearms (a technical device demonstrated by Henry Cowell during his tour of Russia in 1928) is produced in Leningrad.

### 24 MAY 1930

*X-mal Rembrandt*, opera-burlesque by the Hungarian composer Eugen ZÁDOR, dealing with a painter copying a self-portrait of Rembrandt in a German museum, and then substituting his copy for the original, only to discover that the supposed original was also a fake placed on exhibition by the museum director after selling the original to an American lady, and that even that was a fake supplied years back by an old man, who chants philosophically: 'One time Rembrandt, two times Rembrandt, X times Rembrandt' (hence the title of the opera), is performed for the first time in Gera.

### 25 MAY 1930

*Transatlantic*, opera in three acts by George ANTHEIL, subtitled *The People's Choice*, depicting the turbulent events during an American presidential campaign, with the president-elect attempting to strangle a promiscuous lady friend, set to music against the background of jazz and booze, flappers and flivvers, is produced in Frankfurt, Germany.

In general, the story of *Transatlantic* is one of political corruption in the U.S.A.; a character something like J. P. Morgan (basso) who backs a presidential candidate only to have this candidate turn traitor to the powers of blackness. There is, of course, a love story, too: J. P. Morgan (let us say) uses a woman, a very beautiful one, to try and induce our hero to come along to his way of thinking. But she loves our president-to-be and turns coat to J. P. Morgan, too. The whole thing shows the horrible whirlwind of 1927 in the U.S.A.; a Happy End is practically posted on the opera to make it even more ironic; I wanted to have rose petals falling all over the stage at the end. A satire, and the first modern political opera. (From George Antheil's letter to the author, dated 21 July 1936)

### 29 MAY 1930

*Zagmuk,* oriental opera in four acts by Alexander KREIN, dealing with the struggle of Babylonian slaves against their Assyrian oppressors in 703 B.C., is presented for the first time in Moscow.

### 2 JUNE 1930

*Rayon de soieries,* comic opera in one act by Manuel ROSENTHAL, wherein a young silk hosiery salesman is temporarily deflected from his constant girl friend by the munificent matronage of the Queen of the Island of Aloha who appoints him her exclusive purveyor of silk garments in the "rayon de soieries," of a Paris department store, is produced at the Opéra-Comique in Paris, on the same bill with the first stage performance of *Le Fou de la Dame,* ballet-cantata by Marcel DELANNOY, a neo-medieval allegory in the framework of a chess game in which the queen's bishop (*fou de la dame*) makes a supreme sacrifice for his sovereign, originally performed in concert form at the Geneva Festival of the International Society for Contemporary Music on 6 April 1929.

### 4 JUNE 1930

*Der Wein,* concert aria for voice and orchestra by Alban BERG, to the words of three poems by Baudelaire (*L'Âme du vin, Le vin des amants,* and *Le vin du solitaire*) in German translations by Stefan George, written in a dodeca-phonic idiom, is performed for the first time in Königsberg.

### 8 JUNE 1930

*Der Fächer* (*The Fan*), opera-capriccio in three acts by Ernst TOCH, to a whimsical story dealing with a Chinese widow who swears a binding oath to remain chaste as long as the earth covering her old husband's grave retains moisture, and then speeds up the drying process by ventilating it with a magically efficient fan so as to be able to yield herself to a cinemactor during a radio performance of Toch's own opera *Die Prinzessin auf der Erbse,* while China is in the throes of revolutionary disorders, with a finale in which the rebels and the dispossessed classes dance a universal foxtrot in the spirit of syncopated solidarity, to an ingeniously contrived musical setting containing quasipentatonic chinoiseries, is performed for the first time at the festival of the Allgemeiner Deutscher Musikverein in Königsberg.

### 17 JUNE 1930

A modern music festival, *Fest der neuen Musik,* opens in Berlin, with the professed aim of exploring various forms of utilitarian music, mechanically produced (by phonograph recording, radio transmission, electronically generated by heterodynamic frequency modulation) and socially applied (*Hausmusik*, community music, amateur music, school music, *Sprechstimme*), featuring the first performances of *Sabinchen*, a "Hörspiel" by Paul HINDEMITH and *Fuge aus der Geographie* for chorus a cappella, and a piece of "Gesprochene Musik" by Ernst TOCH, articulating in syllabic counterpoint a number of names of exotic geographical places.

### 18 JUNE 1930

*Das Wasser*, a "Lehrstück" by Ernst TOCH for a speaker and chorus reciting a disquisition on the chemical and physiological virtues of $H_2O$, is performed for the first time during the course of the *Fest der neuen Musik* in Berlin.

### 19 JUNE 1930

*Ombre Russe*, grand opera by the Neopolitan-born American composer Cesare SODERO, written in 1909 when he was 23 years old, and dealing with the dramatic dilemma of a Russian nihilist student assigned to assassinate the Tsarist chief of police with whose daughter he is in love (he accidentally kills her taking aim at her father and goes mad in the final act), set to music in a passionately inflated Italianate manner, is produced in Venice.

Cesare Sodero Acclaimed as Composer of Genius.—Success was great and affirms the genius of the composer. There were 30 recalls. The applause was delirious. (Dispatch from Sodero's manager to *The Musical Courier*, New York, 28 June 1930)

### 20 JUNE 1930

A millennium has elapsed since the death of the Benedictine monk HUCBALD who codified and amplified the Gregorian modes and warned church composers against the explicit or implied use of the tritone, the "diabolus in musica," credited also with the invention of a system of notation with 18 lines.

### 21 JUNE 1930

*Wir bauen eine Stadt*, children's opera by Paul HINDEMITH, a modernistic piece of utilitarian music with a simple story about building a city, recited in an infantiloquent vein to a neo-Baroque accompaniment in clearly separated tonal pictures containing just a modicum of acescent dissonance and asymmetric rhythms, is performed for the first time in Berlin.

### 23 JUNE 1930

*Almast*, opera in four acts by the foremost Armenian composer Alexander SPENDIAROV, to the legend of the 18th-century Armenian princess Almast who betrays her people to the besieging Persians in the hope of becoming the Persian queen, but is captured, placed in the royal harem, and is killed when she tries to stab the libidinous shah, set to music in an orientalistic manner, replete with serpentine augmented seconds and helical melismas, is posthumously produced in Moscow.

### 30 JUNE 1930

*Der Jasager,* school opera in two acts by Kurt WEILL, to a libretto by Bertolt Brecht derived from an ancient Japanese tale of fatalistic feudalism, wherein a young boy crossing the mountains into a valley in quest of a miraculously curative herb to combat an epidemic, falls ill himself and, according to a pre-arranged ritual does not resist when his companions push him into the precipice (hence the title, *The Yea-Sayer*), so as to enable them to accomplish their laudable purpose, set to music in a relentless rhythmic style, with grimacing discords stressing the irony of the action, is performed for the first time in the course of the *Fest der neuen Musik* in Berlin, by schoolchildren seemingly undeterred by the grimness of the subject.

(When the pupils of the Karl Marx Schule in Berlin pointed out to Brecht that the death of the boy in obedience to a feudal custom is against socialist humanity, he rewrote the play as *Der Neinsager,* in which the boy refuses to die, proclaims the necessity of a new way of thinking, and is taken safely home. The new version of the play was subsequently performed by the same schoolchildren in the same Berlin school.)

### 6 JULY 1930

*First Symphony* by the Dutch composer Henk BADINGS is performed for the first time in Amsterdam.

### 15 JULY 1930

Leopold AUER, celebrated Hungarian-born violin teacher, trainer of a flock of *Wunderkinder* including Mischa Elman and Jascha Heifetz, for many years the mainstay of the violin master class at the St. Petersburg Conservatory, a virtuoso in his own right, to whom Tchaikovsky dedicated his violin concerto (Auer criticized it and Tchaikovsky dejectedly took back the dedication), dies in Loschwitz, near Dresden, at the age of eighty-five.

*When we began, our notes were sour,*
*Until a man, Professor Auer,*
*Set out to show us, one and all*
*How to pack 'em in the Carnegie Hall.*
(Initial quatrain from George Gershwin's song, *Mischa, Jascha, Toscha, Sascha*)

### 22 JULY 1930

Carlos CHÁVEZ conducts in Mexico City the world première of his ballet *Los Cuatros Soles,* derived from the Mexican cosmogony, in four ages of the sun (of fire, of air, of water, of earth), with the music presenting a symphonic reflection of the austere and yet expressive nature of the people of Mexico.

### 4 AUGUST 1930

Siegfried WAGNER, "Little son of a Great Father," whose birth Wagner celebrated by writing his passionate *Siegfried Idyll,* dies in the shrine of the Wagner cult, Bayreuth, at the age of 61, surviving his mother by four months and three days.

## 1 SEPTEMBER 1930

The Eighth Festival of the International Society for Contemporary Music opens in Liège with a concert of band music played by the First Regiment of Les Guides, in the following program:

*Fanfare pour une Corrida* by the Belgian composer Raymond MOULAERT; *Spiel* by Ernst TOCH; *Konzertmusik*, in military march rhythms, by Paul HINDEMITH; *Pièce symphonique* for piano and band by the Belgian composer and pedagogue Joseph JONGEN; *Dionysiaques*, a symphonic bacchanale by Florent SCHMITT; *Symphonies d'instruments à vent à la mémoire de Claude-Achille Debussy* by STRAVINSKY; *Danse funambulesque* by the Belgian composer Jules STRENS; and *Feu d'artifice* by the Flemish-Belgian composer Maurice SCHOEMAKER.

## 2 SEPTEMBER 1930

At the second concert of the Eighth Festival of the International Society for Contemporary Music in Liège, the following program of chamber music is presented:

*Musique pour Piano* by the German-Czech composer Erhard MICHEL; *Septet* for violin, clarinet, viola, horn, cello, bassoon and piano by Karel HÁBA, semi-atonal brother of the quarter-tonalist Czech modernist Alois Hába; *Chansons Françaises*, in an ingratiating neo-Lullyan vein, by the sole lady composer of the Group of Six, Germaine TAILLEFERRE; a neo-romantic *Sonata* for two pianos by Arnold BAX; and *Second String Quartet* by the Belgian neo-classical polyphonist Albert HUYBRECHTS.

## 3 SEPTEMBER 1930

At the third concert of the Eighth Festival of the International Society for Contemporary Music in Liège the following program of chamber music is presented:

*Quintet* for wind instruments by the Czech polyphonist Karel Boleslav JIRÁK; *Moralités non légendaires* for voice and divers instruments, set in a satirically dadaistic vein, by the Belgian composer Fernand QUINET; *Trio* for flute, viola and cello by Albert ROUSSEL, in three movements, marked by his customary expertise and elegance; *Quintet* for saxophone and string quartet by Karl STIMMER of Germany; and the precisely fashioned *Serenata* for clarinet, bassoon, trumpet, violin and cello by Alfredo CASELLA, written in a fine style of Italian neo-Baroque.

## 4 SEPTEMBER 1930

At the fourth concert of the Eighth Festival of the International Society for Contemporary Music in Liège the following program of orchestral music is given:

*Music for Orchestra* by the Swiss conductor-composer Volkmar ANDREAE, set in a neo-Straussian vein, the non-programmatic title of the work concealing a variety of illustrative allusions; *Sinfonietta* by the Dutch-born American composer Bernard

WAGENAAR, in a neo-Beethovenian idiom, vigorous and dramatic; *Concerto for Viola and Orchestra* by the brilliant representative of the English neo-Baroque school, William WALTON; *Sinfonia Italiana* in a rhapsodically conceived Mediterranean style by Antonio VERETTI; *Rondo Burlesque* by Florent SCHMITT; and *Poème de l'Espace*, a modernistically dissonant and rhythmically propulsive ode to transatlantic fliers by the Belgian composer Marcel POOT.

6 SEPTEMBER 1930

At the fifth and last concert of the Eighth Festival of the International Society for Contemporary Music in Liège the following program of symphonic music is given:

*Praeludium,* a neo-Bachian piece of *Augenmusik* by the German constructivist composer Ernst PEPPING; *Start,* a 'symphonic Allegro' descriptive of a sports event by the Czech urbanistic composer Pavel BOŘKOVEC; *Chant funèbre* by the French composer of new music in old forms Jean RIVIER; *Temptation,* a Gaelic marching piece by Henry GIBSON; *Violin Concerto* by the Viennese atonalist Josef Matthias HAUER, built on a dodecaphonic series of two mutually exclusive six-tone tropes, a method of composition initiated by him in parallel development with Schoenberg's ideas; a hedonistically utilitarian symphonic *Suite* by the Polish-born German-educated composer Karol RATHAUS; *Fantaisie* by the Parisian-Rumanian composer Marcel MIHALOVICI; and the stupendous *Steel Foundry* by the Soviet enfant terrible Alexander MOSSOLOV, including in the score a metal sheet shaken longitudinally for realistic onomatopoeia.

20 SEPTEMBER 1930

The fifth and last march of the orchestral series *Pomp and Circumstance* by Edward ELGAR, is performed for the first time in London.

24 SEPTEMBER 1930

Henry HADLEY conducts in Tokyo the world première of his symphonic suite *Streets of Pekin,* in seven touristic movements, illustrating Great Stone Men's Street, Sweet Rain Street, Ricksha Boy No. 309, Jade Street, Shoemaker Street, Sleeping Lotuses, and The Forbidden City, replete with simulated orientalisms, pentatonic tintinnabulations, sinuous Sinologicalities and various other auricular bombilations accoutred in Germanic harmonies.

2 OCTOBER 1930

*Concerto* for piano and orchestra by the 51-year-old English composer John IRELAND, written in the rejuvenating tonality of E-flat major, in two movements, *In tempo moderato* and *Lento espressivo,* of highly romantic music barely tinged with amiable modernities, maintaining an almost unvarying, dreamily waltzing, 3/4 time throughout, leading to an optimistic finale, *Allegretto giocoso,* and concluding in an embracing unison, is performed for the first time in London by Ireland's pupil, 20-year-old pianist Helen Perkin, for whom the work was written. (The dedication to Helen Perkin was removed by the composer in 1950, long after she married another.)

## 3 OCTOBER 1930

*Vom Fischer un seiner Fru,* operatic fantasy by the Swiss composer Othmar SCHOECK, to his own libretto in the *plattdeutsch* dialect, after a fairy tale by the Grimm brothers, dealing with the overweening wife of a fisherman, who in seven consecutive scenes asks the demiurgical flounder her husband has befriended to fulfill her increasingly presumptuous wishes—a new hut, a castle, a kingdom, an empire, the papacy, and finally divinity—until her sacrilegious outrecuidance impels the outraged fish to take away from her all her acquisitions and to send her back to her dilapidated waterfront shack to the sounds of a magisterial double fugue with a symbolically inverted second subject in the *stretto,* is performed for the first time in Dresden.

## 10 OCTOBER 1930

Sir George HENSCHEL, first conductor of the Boston Symphony Orchestra, leads the Boston Symphony Orchestra at the opening concert of its 50th season in a program almost identical with the one he gave on its inaugural concert on 22 October 1881, with the exception of Weber's *Jubel Overture,* replaced by the Prelude to Wagner's opera *Die Meistersinger von Nürnberg.*

## 14 OCTOBER 1930

*Girl Crazy,* musical comedy by George GERSHWIN, dealing with a Park Avenue playboy sent by his rich father to a desert town in Arizona, which he promptly transforms into a den of iniquity, although he later renounces vice and marries the local postmistress, containing a number of syncopatingly stimulating songs, one of which, *I Got Rhythm,* presents a fascinating study in infra-metrical asymmetry (measures in 4/4 time are subdivided into the rhythmic molecules of 2/16, 3/16, 3/16, 3/16, 3/16, 2/16), is produced in New York.

## 15 OCTOBER 1930

*Three's a Crowd,* "intimate revue," by Arthur SCHWARTZ, with additional songs by Vernon Duke and others, featuring some mildly scabrous sketches (a young lady inadvertently stumbles into the bathroom while a gentleman performs ablutions in the tub and by instant observation of his intimate anatomy recognizes him as an old sexual acquaintance), is produced in New York.

## 16 OCTOBER 1930

Nikolai LOPATNIKOFF plays in Düsseldorf the piano part in the first performance of his *Second Piano Concerto,* in three movements, a propulsive *Allegro energico,* an angularly lyrical *Andantino,* and a neo-Baroque *Allegro molto.*

## 20 OCTOBER 1930

In a Berlin court, Kurt WEILL wins a lawsuit brought against the Nero Film Company to prevent it from altering the musical score for a screen version of his *Dreigroschenoper*, at the same session at which Bertolt Brecht, the author of the play, is denied the right to restore the anti-capitalist ending of his original in which the villain-hero Mack the Knife becomes a bank president.

### 20 OCTOBER 1930

Hitlerite students throw stink bombs during the performance of the opera *Mahagonny* by Kurt WEILL at the Frankfurt Opera House, as a gesture of protest against the alleged immorality of its plot and the racial impurity of its Jewish composer, with a post-theatrical fracas resulting in the killing of a Communist student by a Nazi-operated beer stein.

### 22 OCTOBER 1930

*Morning Heroes*, symphony for orator, chorus and orchestra by Arthur BLISS, dedicated to the memory of the composer's brother "and all other comrades killed in battle," in six sections: (1) *Hector's Farewell to Andromache* from Homer's *Iliad* (2) *The City Arming*, after Walt Whitman (3) *The Bivouac's Flame*, after Walt Whitman (4) *Achilles Goes Forth to Battle* (5) *Spring Offensive*, after Wilfred Owen, English poet killed in battle (6) *Dawn on the Somme*, after Robert Nichols, English poet killed in battle, is performed for the first time at the Norwich Festival in England.

### 24 OCTOBER 1930

*Symphony in G minor* by Albert ROUSSEL, his *Third*, completed on 29 March 1930, in four movements, *Allegro vivo*, *Adagio*, *Vivace* and *Allegro con spirito*, a "symphony of energy" suffused with an *élan vital* and evolving along lucidly Gallic lines, with a central motive of five notes as a guiding musical idea, is performed for the first time by the Boston Symphony Orchestra, as a commissioned work for its 50th anniversary, under the direction of Serge Koussevitzky, to whom the score is dedicated.

### 25 OCTOBER 1930

*Missa in Dedicatione Ecclesiae* by Ernst von DOHNÁNYI, for soloists, chorus and orchestra, is performed for the first time at the consecration of the Cathedral of Szeged.

### 26 OCTOBER 1930

*The Age of Gold*, ballet by the 24-year-old Soviet composer Dmitri SHOSTAKOVICH, is produced in Leningrad, to a satirical scenario picturing the capitalist way of life in the West, with the cast of characters including a racist referee discriminating against a Negro challenger in a prize fight, an immoral operatic diva, an imperialist *agent-provocateur*, and—on the virtuous side of the ledger—a young girl Communist, a downtrodden shoeshine boy, and a host of oppressed proletarians, with a discordant polka portraying the international disarmament conference in Geneva, and an optimistic finale projecting a *Solidarity Dance* of Soviet and Western workers.

## 31 OCTOBER 1930

Serge Koussevitzky conducts the Boston Symphony Orchestra in the first performance of his *Overture*, modestly listed in the program book as a work by an unknown composer, written in an apologetically unprofessional manner and concluding with a slightly modified finale of Glinka's opera *A Life for the Tsar.*

## 6 NOVEMBER 1930

*Begleitungsmusik zu einer Lichtspielszene*, op. 34, by Arnold Schoenberg (completed in Berlin on 14 February 1930), designed as the musical score for a typical cinematic scene, in three expressive sections—*Drohende Gefahr, Angst, Katastrophe*—with mounting dynamic tension indicating the transition from an objective imminent danger through subjective anxiety to the ultimate catastrophe, written according to Schoenberg's method of composition with twelve tones related only to one another, the basic tone-row being E-flat, G-flat, D, E, C-sharp, C, A, B, B-flat, A-flat, G, F, which is developed both melodically and harmonically with classical clarity of structure, is performed for the first time in Berlin, Otto Klemperer conducting the orchestra of the Berlin State Opera.

Whether Schoenberg's score is to be regarded as an accompaniment to an imaginary motion picture or as absolute music is entirely immaterial. This is absolute Unmusic. (Walter Herschberg, in an article published in *Signale für die musikalische Welt*, Berlin, 12 November 1930)

## 7 NOVEMBER 1930

*Metamorphoseon, Modi XII*, orchestral theme and variations by Ottorino Respighi, set in neo-medieval modalities, is performed for the first time by the Boston Symphony Orchestra as a commissioned work for the 50th anniversary of its founding, under the direction of Serge Koussevitzky.

## 7 NOVEMBER 1930

*4 Etudes* by Igor Stravinsky, orchestral arrangements made by him in 1928 of his *Three Pieces for String Quartet* (composed in 1914 and first performed in New York on 30 November 1915 by the Flonzaley Quartet) and a *Study for Pianola* (composed in 1917 and first performed on a piano roll in London on 13 October 1921), to which he appended descriptive titles, *Dance, Excentrique* (inspired by the spastic miming of the English dancer Little Tich), *Cantique* and *Madrid* (a souvenir of Stravinsky's visit to Spain in 1916), are performed for the first time in Berlin.

## 7 NOVEMBER 1930

*Second Symphony* in A major by the dean of the American academic school of composition Daniel Gregory Mason, written in a competent Brahmsogenic manner, is performed for the first time by the Cincinnati Symphony Orchestra, Fritz Reiner conducting.

517

## 8 NOVEMBER 1930

*Im weissen Rössl,* operetta in three acts by the Bohemian-born composer Ralph BENATZKY, focused on the durable landlady of a hostelry called "The White Stallion", at an Austrian summer resort circa 1900, whose middle-aged passion for a lawyer who courts a lingerie manufacturer's daughter whose eligible fiancé prefers the company of an impoverished professor's daughter, creates a multilateral interamorous imbroglio resolved by a deus ex machina in the person of Emperor Franz Joseph who visits the inn and advises its proprietress to marry her faithful headwaiter, and helps to pair off the other two couples according to their emotional choices, set to a hedonistic score abounding in romantic waltzes, erotic tangos and virile foxtrots, is produced in Berlin.

## 9 NOVEMBER 1930

*Soldaten,* opera in three acts by the German composer Manfred GURLITT, to his own libretto, is produced in Düsseldorf.

## 11 NOVEMBER 1930

*Spiel oder Ernst?* by Emil von REZNIČEK, one-act comic opera with the action taking place during a rehearsal of Rossini's opera *Otello,* dealing with a dishonorable pianist-répétiteur, who, lusting after the soprano who sings the part of Desdemona and who is in private life the wife of the tenor who sings Otello, insinuates that she is cuckolding him with the bass who sings Iago, but is exposed and dismissed from his job, is produced in Dresden.

## 14 NOVEMBER 1930

Serge Koussevitzky conducts the Boston Symphony Orchestra in the first performance of the *Fourth Symphony* in C major by Sergei PROKOFIEV, in four movements, with considerable portions of its materials taken from Prokofiev's unsuccessful ballet *L'Enfant prodigue* of 1929, in four movements:

(1) *Andante,* drawn in epically spacious modalities in a heroic mold, with a ballad-like contrasting theme, and ending with an impetuous march-toccata (2) *Andante tranquillo,* a pastoral episode in which a bucolic chant alternates with ominous proclamations in the somber bass register (3) *Moderato quasi allegretto,* a lyrical scherzo with characteristic passages of intervalic saltation (4) *Allegro risoluto,* a rondo finale, animated by propulsive motion culminating in a sonorous apotheosis in the whitest sound of C major.

## 28 NOVEMBER 1930

*Second Symphony* by the 34-year-old American composer Howard HANSON, subtitled *Romantic* as a candid declaration of faith, but employing masculine melodic configurations in angular rhythms and bold bitonal superpositions of major triads related by a tritone and written in an enlightened modernistic manner, in three movements (1) *Adagio—Allegro Moderato,* opening with a gentle recitation, leading to the epical annunciation of the main theme (2)

*Andante con tenerezza*, a bucolic eclogue in tones of tender gentility (3) *Allegro con brio*, an energetic exposition of romantic ideals with triumphant sonorous fanfares, is performed for the first time by the Boston Symphony Orchestra, Serge Koussevitzky conducting, as a commissioned work for its 50th anniversary.

### 28 NOVEMBER 1930

*Dances of Marosszék*, symphonic rondo with variations by Zoltán KODÁLY, based on folksong materials collected by him in the Marosszék region of Transylvania, some of them couched in the millennial modes of immemorial Pannonia, characterized by the ambiguous major-minor modes with raised subdominants and lowered submediants, is performed for the first time in Dresden.

### 29 NOVEMBER 1930

*Morana*, national romantic opera by the 35-year-old Croatian composer Jakov GOTOVAC, to a libretto centered on rural lovers who flee into the hills and settle in healthy concubinage to elude the perfidious machinations of their avaricious relatives scheming to marry them off into advantageously affluent families, set to music pregnant with asymmetric Slavic melorhythms and gravid with ponderous harmonic layers, is produced in Brno. (The first performance in Yugoslavia took place on 3 October 1931 in Zagreb)

### 30 NOVEMBER 1930

*Divertissement*, symphonic suite by Jacques IBERT, extracted from his score of incidental music for a farce, *Le Chapeau de paille d'Italie*, produced in Paris in 1929, in six sections (1) *Introduction* (2) *Cortège*, a discordantly vulgarized march with a sudden irruption of Mendelssohn's *Wedding March* (3) *Nocturne* (4) *Valse*, containing an episodic allusion to *The Blue Danube Waltz* (5) *Parade* (6) *Finale*, a stimulatingly noisy cancan, is performed for the first time in Paris.

### 1 DECEMBER 1930

Kaikhosru SORABJI, 38-year-old English-born composer of Parsi and Spanish extraction, whose real baptismal names are Leon Dudley, plays in Glasgow, under the auspices of the Active Society for the Propagation of Contemporary Music, the first performance of his monumental *Opus Clavicembalisticum* (completed by him on 25 June 1930), written in a fantastically complex polyphonic idiom, in three parts and twelve subdivisions, two of which have 44 and 81 variations respectively, the printed score containing 252 pages, making it the longest individual piano composition ever written, and bearing a dedication "to the everlasting glory of those few men blessed and sanctified in the curses and execrations of those many whose praise is eternal damnation."

I am of Parsi, i.e. Persian, and Spanish-Sicilian descent. . . . Do not dare to call me an *Indian* composer. We Parsis repudiate that description indignantly. We are *not* Indians, we are Persians. . . . My *Opus Clavicembalisticum* has been described as the greatest and most important work for piano since the *Art of Fugue,* the *Forty-Eight,* or the *Diabelli Variations,* as indeed it is. I have no false modesty nor mock humility in my make-up, so do not be surprised at the calm way in which I recognize the importance of my own work!! (From Sorabji's letter to Nicolas Slonimsky, dated 23 March 1933)

### 5 DECEMBER 1930

*Concerto* for percussion and chamber orchestra by Darius MILHAUD, in two contrasting movements, is performed for the first time in Paris.

### 5 DECEMBER 1930

*The Black Maskers,* symphonic suite by Roger SESSIONS from his incidental music to Leonid Andreyev's symbolistic play of that name (written for the production of the play at Smith College, Northampton, Mass., in June 1923), in four movements, *Dance, Scene, Dirge, Finale,* with the black maskers invading a man's castle symbolic of his soul, culminating in a general conflagration in which he finds his death and redemption, set to music with great romantic fervor, in a contrapuntally dissonant but firmly tonal idiom, is performed for the first time by the Cincinnati Symphony Orchestra, Fritz Reiner conducting.

### 9 DECEMBER 1930

*Námořník Mikuláš (Mariner Nicholas),* symphonic drama by the 41-year-old Czech composer Vilém PETRŽELKA, dealing with a romantic sailor, his faithful dog and his unfaithful wife, scored for narrator, chorus, organ, orchestra and jazz band, with occasional passages in quarter-tones to express anxiety, is performed for the first time in Brno.

### 10 DECEMBER 1930

*Camille,* opera in three acts by the 29-year-old American composer Hamilton FORREST, to his own libretto, based on *La Dame aux Camélias,* the play used by Verdi in *La Traviata,* but brought up to date by placing the action in a dual plane of 1850 and 1930, containing passages in half-sung half-spoken recitative, with interludes in the rhythms of foxtrot, Charleston and other modern dances, is performed for the first time by the Chicago Civic Opera Company, with Mary Garden, who commissioned the score, in the title role, to a French version of the original English libretto.

### 10 DECEMBER 1930

*Fremde Erde,* first opera in four acts by the 35-year-old Polish-born composer Karol RATHAUS, portraying a group of Russian immigrants on board a ship bound for America inspired by false hopes of making a fortune, written in a modernistically dissonant Central European idiom, and seasoned with the rhythms of ragtime and blues, is produced in Berlin.

## 12 DECEMBER 1930

*Les Aventures du Roi Pausole,* the first operetta by Arthur HONEGGER, after a novel by Pierre Louÿs, dealing with extra-marital adventures of the leader of a nudist kingdom who has 365 queens of high fidelity and a supernumerary bissextile queen whom he can use only once in a quadrennium on 29 February, and whose daughter reared in utter innocence elopes with a trousered danseuse unaware of her technical gender, is performed for the first time in Paris.

## 13 DECEMBER 1930

*Symphonie de Psaumes* by Igor STRAVINSKY (completed on 15 August 1930), "composed for the glory of God and dedicated to the Boston Symphony Orchestra on the occasion of the 50th anniversary of its existence," scored for chorus and orchestra without violins and violas, using the Latin text of the Psalms, is performed for the first time in Brussels, six days before its production by the Boston Symphony Orchestra (a chronological displacement owing to the illness of the conductor Serge Koussevitzky, forcing the postponement of the scheduled performance from 12 December to 19 December 1930, in three sections originally designated *Prélude, Double Fugue* and *Allegro symphonique* but changed in the published edition to impersonal metronomic markings:

(1) *quarter-note = 92,* an accompanied chorale paragraphed by powerful columns of E-minor chords and couched in a devotional neo-ecclesiastical style in Baroque techniques, with groups of repeated eighth-notes followed by a precipitation of 16th-notes (2) *eighth-note = 60,* a magisterial four-part double fugue, in C minor, with the first subject in oscillating major sixths and the second subject based on a motive of two disjunct minor thirds confined within the compass of a perfect fifth (3) *quarter-note = 48,* opening with a devotional Alleluia in humbly dissonant counterpoint, the tempo accelerating to 80 half-notes per minute and the contrapuntal design traversing the heterophony of the second species, the Baroque mobility of the third species, the syncopated agility of the fourth species and culminating in the florid quaquaversality of the fifth species, at 48 half-notes per minute, crowned with a medievally canonized solemn coda in seraphic C major.

## 13 DECEMBER 1930

*Die Massnahme (The Measures Taken),* didactic play for tenor, three speakers, chorus and orchestra by the 32-year-old German composer of music of social significance, Hanns EISLER, to words by Bertolt Brecht, a series of songs for the agitation and propaganda section of the German Communist Party, set in strong proletarian marching rhythms invigorated by belligerent discords, is performed for the first time in Berlin.

The singers must strive to perform *Die Massnahme* without expression or sympathetic insight as in a love song; rather the music must be treated only for its reference values, in the manner of a militant progress report at a mass meeting, cool, sharp, and incisive. Each singer must fully understand the political import of the text. (From an instruction supplied by Hanns Eisler for performances of *Die Massnahme.*)

Here is at least an ideologically mature and artistically perfect choral work for workers. There is no musical grasshopping here, no mechanical game of leitmotivs, but a vigorous appeal to revolutionary action. (*Die rote Fahne*, Berlin, 20 January 1931.)

### 14 DECEMBER 1930

*Leggenda sinfonica*, tone poem by the 30-year-old Boston-born composer Alexander STEINERT, written in an impressionistic style replete with luscious minor ninth-chords and neo-archaic modalities, is performed for the first time anywhere in Rome, Howard Hanson conducting.

### 17 DECEMBER 1930

Philip HESELTINE, 36-year-old English composer and writer on music, brilliant exponent of hedonistic modernity in the arts, who had selected the nom de plume Peter Warlock to indicate the subliminal witchery of his motivations, is found dead in his London apartment, suffocated by escaping gas. (Although suicide was widely suspected, it was not conclusively proved.)

### 22 DECEMBER 1930

Franco ALFANO conducts in Caracas, Venezuela, the world première of his Hymn to Bolivar, as part of the centennial commemoration of the death of the liberator of South America Simon Bolívar.

### 23 DECEMBER 1930

*Victoria und ihr Hussar*, operetta in three acts by Paul ABRAHAM, in which Victoria's hussar husband, given up for dead in World War I, suddenly turns up in Tokyo after escaping from a Siberian prisoner camp and confronts his wife who in the meantime has mistakenly married an American diplomat stationed there, with the marital *status quo* eventually restored to all concerned, is produced in Vienna.

### 24 DECEMBER 1930

Oscar NEDBAL, Czech composer and conductor, commits suicide by defenestration, jumping to his death from the third floor of the National Theater in Zagreb.

### 26 DECEMBER 1930

*Benzin*, industrial ballet by the 33-year-old Danish composer Knudaage RIISAGER, is performed for the first time in Copenhagen.

### 28 DECEMBER 1930

Henry COWELL plays with the Havana Philharmonic the first complete performance of his *Piano Concerto* in three movements, *Polyharmony, Tone Cluster* and *Counter Rhythm*, in which tone clusters, invented and named by him, are produced by pounding the keys with the fists, plastering them with the palms of the hands, and loudly depressing them with extended forearms, pandiatonically covering two octaves on the white keys or, panpentatonically, two octaves on the black keys. (A squad of Cuban policemen guarded the hall to forestall threatened disturbances by local anti-modernists.)

(A performance of the first two movements with a repetition of the first serving as a finale was given by the Conductorless Orchestra in New York on 26 April 1930, with the composer at the piano)

# ꙮ *1931* ꙮ

2 JANUARY 1931

*Sonido 13*, a fantasy by the Mexican pioneer of fractional music Julián CARRILLO (*Sonido 13* denotes the domain beyond the twelve notes of the chromatic scale), scored for violin, horn, guitar, piccolo, cello and harp, tuned to play quarter-tones, eighth-tones and (for the harp) sixteenth-tones, is performed for the first time in Mexico City, Leopold Stokowski conducting.

4 JANUARY 1931

The Bruckner Society of America is founded in New York with the expressed purpose "to develop in the public an appreciation of the music of Bruckner, Mahler, and other moderns."

7 JANUARY 1931

*Virginie,* lyric comedy in three acts by Alfred BRUNEAU, 73-year-old French composer of the realistic operatic school, depicting an episode from the life of the French actress and singer Virginie Déjazet who left, in 1825, a gallant lover to form a more profitable liaison with his courtier father, set to music with eclectic savoir-faire, is produced at the Paris Opéra.

10 JANUARY 1931

The absolute world première is given in New York by Nicolas Slonimsky, conducting his Chamber Orchestra of Boston, of *Three Places in New England* by the prophetic genius of American music Charles E. IVES, limning three tonal images of historic American sites, landscapes and monuments, written between 1906 and 1914 but never performed heretofore, anticipating by many years such novel usages as emancipated harmony, atonal extensions of essentially triadic structures, asymmetrical rhythms and polymetrical superpositions, and palimpsests of folksongs, creating a sense of pantechnical freedom in an individual style of national expression:

(1) *Colonel Shaw and his Colored Regiment,* evoked by the famous basrelief on Boston Common, opening with a lyric recollection of the Civil War victory song, *Marching Through Georgia* with its refrain, "Hurrah! Hurrah! We Bring the Jubilee!" in a polyharmonic setting, gradually growing into a rousing march, then subsiding into a memory and an echo (2) *Putnam's Camp,* suggested by martial relics of the American Revolution, making ingenious use of old songs and march tunes refracted into angular atonal configurations in a polymetric arrangement making it imperative for the conductor to beat four bars in *alla breve* time with his left hand against three bars in 4/4 time in the right hand to illustrate the episode in which two marching bands meet in a village square while playing tunes at two different tempi (3) *The Housatonic at Stockbridge,* painting the majestic flow of the great New England river in polymetric designs of great complexity, mathematically precise as to rhythmic values and yet spacious and free in its poetic progress, with the main motto formed by Zenner's *Missionary Chant* and the "Fate motive" of Beethoven's Fifth Symphony, annexing in its course a number of old American tunes, expanding into a fantastic panoply of simultaneous melodies and polytriadic harmonies, and after a thunderous climax ending suddenly in a residual hymnal chorale, a unique effect of colorful sonority.

### 16 JANUARY 1931

*Perkin,* 'legende basque' in three acts by the French composer Jean POUEIGH, is performed for the first time in Bordeaux.

### 20 JANUARY 1931

*Brummel,* operetta in three acts by the Parisianized Venezuela-born composer Reynaldo HAHN, dealing with the life of the London dandy George Bryan Brummel (1778–1840) whose Byronic adventures and effeminate beauty earned him the sobriquet Beau Brummel, is produced in Paris.

### 31 JANUARY 1931

*La Notte di Zoraima,* tragic opera in one act by Italo MONTEMEZZI, dealing with a 16th-century Inca princess who offers her body to the commander of the besieging Spanish forces in Peru in exchange for the safe conduct of her wounded lover, and when the bargain is carried out by the enamored conquistador, she stabs herself to death, set to music with Italianate eloquence, is produced at La Scala, in Milan.

### 4 FEBRUARY 1931

*Piano Concerto* by the Venezuela-born Parisian composer Reynaldo HAHN is performed for the first time in Paris, with Magda Tagliaferro soloist under the direction of the composer.

### 5 FEBRUARY 1931

*Evocation* by the Alsatian-American composer Charles Martin LOEFFLER, scored for speaker, women's chorus and orchestra, descriptive of the erection of a temple of the Muses, and illustrating in neo-archaic tones Pan's playing on the syrinx for his beloved naiad Syrinx, echoed by his favorite nymph

Echo, is performed for the first time as a dedication piece at the inauguration of Severance Hall, the permanent home for the Cleveland Orchestra, named after a local philanthropist who financed the building project.

### 7 FEBRUARY 1931

*Peter Ibbetson*, lyric drama in three acts by the American composer Deems TAYLOR, to a libretto after George du Maurier's novel of the same name, dealing with a young London architect "dreaming true" of a childhood sweetheart whom he meets years later when she, as an influential Duchess, saves his life by securing the commutation of his death sentence to life imprisonment for killing his adoptive uncle with a stroke of his cane, with a final dream scene in Elysian Fields suggestive of the garden in Paris where he grew up, to a musical setting of turbulent sentimentality and harmoniously consistent spissitude, is performed for the first time at the Metropolitan Opera in New York, culminating in 36 curtain calls.

### 9 FEBRUARY 1931

*Cantegril*, comic opera in four acts by ROGER-DUCASSE dealing with a shrewd villager Cantegril around 1880 in the French Pyrenees who lures the temporary fiancée of a rich local boy into a compromising situation in his bed and wins her over as his wife, with a musical score sprinkled with Pyrenean rhythms and colored with quasi-impressionist harmonies, is performed for the first time at the Opéra-Comique in Paris.

### 9 FEBRUARY 1931

*Kleine Theater-Suite* for orchestra by Ernst TOCH, in five movements suggesting five theatrical situations—*Overture, Timid Approach, Dance, Night, Finale*—is performed for the first time by the Berlin Philharmonic, Wilhelm Furtwängler conducting.

### 12 FEBRUARY 1931

*La Bisbetica Domata*, opera in four acts by Mario PERSICO, after Shakespeare's play *The Taming of the Shrew*, is produced in Rome.

### 13 FEBRUARY 1931

Marcel DUPRÉ improvises in Brussels an organ symphony, *Le Chemin de la Croix* (he performed it in a definitive version in Paris, March 18, 1932).

### 13 FEBRUARY 1931

*Symphonie* by Arthur HONEGGER (his *First Symphony*), without a key signature, but with the tonal barycenter audibly sensed as C for the first movement, *Allegro marcato;* F-sharp for the second, *Adagio;* and C again for the last, *Presto,* with the thematic structure largely derived from the inversion of the chromatic scale into an intervalic series of major sevenths, is performed for the first time by the Boston Symphony Orchestra, Serge Koussevitzky conducting, as a commissioned work for the 50th anniversary of its existence.

### 16 FEBRUARY 1931

*L'illustre Fregona,* opera in three acts by Raoul LAPARRA, to his own libretto derived from a story by Cervantes, is produced in Paris.

### 19 FEBRUARY 1931

*Les Offrandes oubliées* by the 22-year-old French composer Olivier MESSIAEN, a "symphonic meditation" on the "forgotten offerings," to Jesus on the cross, is performed for the first time in Paris.

### 21 FEBRUARY 1931

*Mlyn diabelski (The Diabolical Mill),* opera in six scenes by the Polish composer Ludomir RÓZYCKI, is produced in Poznan.

### 23 FEBRUARY 1931

Nellie MELBA, grand prima donna whose sonorous voice and queenly presence enthralled opera audiences all over the world, holder of the imposing title of a Dame Commander of the British Empire, whose fame reached even the realm of gastronomy in the shape of *Peach Melba* and *Melba Toast,* and whose consecutive farewell tours in England and America continued until 1926, dies in Sydney in her native Australia, at the age of sixty-nine.

### 26 FEBRUARY 1931

*Az Alarc (The Mask),* last opera, in three acts, by the Hungarian violinist Jenö HUBAY, is produced in Budapest.

### 27 FEBRUARY 1931

*Second Symphony* in C major by Edward Burlingame HILL in four movements (composition completed 11 February 1930) is performed for the first time by the Boston Symphony Orchestra, Serge Koussevitzky conducting.

### 28 FEBRUARY 1931

*Sonatine transatlantique* by Alexandre TANSMAN, in three sections (*Fox-Trot, Spiritual et Blues, Charleston*), inspired by his American journeys, and reflecting the genre of sophisticated Parisian jazz, set in succulent bitonal harmonies, is performed for the first time in its orchestral version at the Concerts Pasdeloup in Paris, Rhené-Baton conducting. (The first performance of the original version for piano solo was given by José Iturbi in Boston on 10 November 1930. The music was used by Kurt Jooss in his ballet *Impressions of a Big City,* first performed in Cologne on 21 November 1932)

### 28 FEBRUARY 1931

*Die geliebte Stimme,* opera in three acts by Jaromír WEINBERGER, dealing with a Balkan belle fascinated by a lovable singing voice she hears from afar, who devotes three acts to trace its possessor only to discover that the singer is her family-appointed fiancé whom she has repeatedly spurned, set to music in a felicitous vein, rich in folklike asymmetrical meters, is produced in Munich, with a German libretto translated from the Czech original by the composer, derived from a contemporary German novel.

### 1 MARCH 1931

Igor MARKEVITCH, 18-year-old Russian-born pianist, composer and conductor, plays the solo part with the Orchestre Symphonique de Paris, Pierre Monteux conducting, in the first performance of his *Piano Concerto* in three vivaciously lyric movements, written in a Gallic neo-Baroque manner.

### 3 MARCH 1931

A bill designating *The Star-Spangled Banner* as the national anthem of the United States of America is passed by the Senate, and sent to President Hoover for his signature, thus sanctioning the *de facto* status of the hymn written by lawyer Francis Scott Key on 12 September 1814, and sung to an old English drinking tune.

### 4 MARCH 1931

*Piér li Houïeu (Peter the Collier)*, one-act opera in the Walloon dialect by the famous Belgian violinist Eugène YSAŸE, is produced in Liège, in the presence of the composer *in extremis*, brought in to attend the performance in an invalid chair, suffering from diabetes which necessitated the amputation of his left foot and led to his death eleven weeks after the presentation of this opera.

### 5 MARCH 1931

*La Vedova scaltra*, comic opera in three acts by Ermanno WOLF-FERRARI, after Goldoni's comedy dealing with a shrewd widow who maneuvers skillfully to her advantage, among four suitors, a phlegmatic Englishman, an incontinently passionate Spaniard, an ebullient Frenchman and a scheming Italian of low birth but high virility, is performed for the first time in Rome.

### 8 MARCH 1931

*Symphonie en La* by Pierre-Octave FERROUD, in three well-constructed movements, astutely varying moments of lyricism with explosions of drama in a placidly romantic manner, is performed for the first time by the Orchestre Symphonique de Paris, Pierre Monteux conducting.

### 19 MARCH 1931

*The Canterbury Pilgrims*, oratorio for chorus, soloists and orchestra by George DYSON, depicting in harmoniously melodious tones the pilgrimage of the travelers from the Prologue to Chaucer's *Canterbury Tales* to the grave of the sainted Archbishop of Canterbury Thomas à Becket, is performed for the first time in Winchester, England, a few miles from the scene of Becket's assassination.

### 26 MARCH 1931

*Moineau,* best-known operetta by the French composer Louis BEYDTS, wherein an unscrupulously immoral Paris painter attracts his consecutive mistresses by displaying suggestive exhibits of his art in an open window of his Montmartre apartment, baiting passing girls into conversation and subsequent intimacy, like so many sparrows (hence the title) with crumbs of bread, but who eventually is trapped by one of them into a solidified marriage, thus becoming himself a moineau, is produced in Paris.

### 3 APRIL 1931

*Konzertmusik* for string orchestra (with the two violin sections coalesced into one) and brass instruments by Paul HINDEMITH (completed on 27 December 1930) in two compound parts, the antiphony of the participating choirs being the philosophical idea animating the music, set in a grandly rhetorical Baroque style, with a tonal barycenter firmly established on C-sharp (D-flat), while the ambiguity of major and minor thirds creates a fluid modulatory atmosphere, is performed for the first time by the Boston Symphony Orchestra under the direction of Serge Koussevitzky.

### 4 APRIL 1931

George Whitefield CHADWICK, American composer of symphonic music of a grand romantic design containing occasional Americanisms in thematic sources, director of the New England Conservatory of Music, educator of a generation of American musicians, dies in Boston at the age of seventy-six.

### 4 APRIL 1931

*Corradino lo Svevo,* lyric drama in two acts by the 23-year-old Italian composer Pino DONATI, dealing with the youthful prince Conradin, Duke of Swabia, the last of the Hohenstaufens, who following an abortive attempt to wrest the crown of the Kingdom of the Two Sicilies from the usurper Charles d'Anjou, was captured and beheaded in 1268 at the age of sixteen, set to music in the elevated modalities suitable to the solemnity of the story, is produced in Verona.

### 5 APRIL 1931

*Comedians,* ballet by Reinhold GLIÈRE, freely after the play *La Fuente ovejuna* of Lopez de Vega, wherein a feudal lord who takes advantage of the medieval *jus primae noctis* forcing young brides of his fief to spend their virginal night with him at the castle, is foiled by a troupe of comedians who mimic the revoltingly immoral practice so realistically that the populace rises, slays the violator and liberates the captive maidens, with local color furnished by a number of Spanish-accented dances, is produced in Moscow.

8 APRIL 1931

*In the Captivity of Apple Trees*, opera in five acts by the Ukrainian composer Oles TCHISHKO, with the action taking place during the multilateral civil war in 1918–19, involving the Red Army, the White Army, and the Green Army of anarchistic Ukrainian nationalists, is produced in Odessa.

8 APRIL 1931

*Three Chinese Pieces* (originally written for piano) by Abram CHASINS (*A Shanghai Tragedy, Flirtation in a Chinese Garden* and *Rush Hour in Hong Kong*), set in a pentatonically tintinnabulating vein, is performed in an orchestral version by the New York Philharmonic under the direction of Arturo Toscanini.

8 APRIL 1931

*Bolt,* "choreographic spectacle" in three acts and seven scenes by the 24-year-old Soviet composer Dmitri SHOSTAKOVICH, to a scenario dealing with attempted sabotage by an anti-Soviet worker who sticks a bolt into a vital piece of machinery but is foiled by the vigilant Communist Youth Brigade, with an *Enthusiasm Dance* concluding the ballet, is produced in Leningrad.

16 APRIL 1931

*Koštana,* folk opera in three acts by the Serbian composer Petar KONJOVIĆ, wherein a Gypsy girl in Ottoman-ruled Serbia in 1870 inflames the passions of a youthful Turk, his aging father and sundry local dignitaries, creating an emotional commotion of such sexual dimensions that the mayor orders her to marry a deaf mute from her own tribe to pacify the local male population, set to music in a vivaciously ethnic vein and containing a number of orientalized Balkan dances in asymmetrical rhythmic sequences, is produced in Zagreb.

17 APRIL 1931

*Sinfonia Dialectica,* first symphony by the Russian esthetician Arthur LOURIÉ, cast in an ascetic neo-scholastic style of vacuous musical rhetoric, is performed for the first time by the Philadelphia Orchestra.

18 APRIL 1931

*Dornröschens Erwachen,* fairy opera in two acts by the Hungarian composer Eugen ZÁDOR, a variant of the story of *Sleeping Beauty,* is performed for the first time in Saarbrucken.

24 APRIL 1931

*Guercœur,* posthumous opera in three acts by Alberic MAGNARD, to his own libretto, dealing with a valiant fighter for liberty who dies in combat, goes to

Heaven where he communes with divine personages, returns to earth to visit his mistress who has in the meantime joined a popular dictator, leads a crusade for freedom for the second time and is slain once more, achieving the highest order of celestial beatitude, with a romantic score restored and re-scored by Guy Ropartz from the partially preserved drafts of the manuscript charred by fire when the Germans burned down Magnard's house and killed him on 3 September 1914, is produced at the Paris Opéra.

### 5 MAY 1931

*Bacco in Toscana,* dithyramb in one act, for voices, chorus and ballet by Mario CASTELNUOVO-TEDESCO, dealing with the myth of Ariadne who, after being abandoned by Theseus, is restored to life and temporary ecstasy by Bacchus, is performed for the first time at La Scala in Milan.

### 12 MAY 1931

Eugène YSAŸE, Belgian violinist who elevated the art of violin playing to an intellectually contained display of emotional powers, to whom César Franck dedicated his famous violin sonata, dies in Brussels at the age of 72, after a long struggle with diabetes, which necessitated the amputation of his left foot.

### 14 MAY 1931

A young Fascist strikes TOSCANINI in Bologna for his refusal to conduct the Fascist song *Giovinezza* before his symphonic concert. (On 18 May 1931 the Musicians' Syndicate of Bologna condemned Toscanini's refusal to conduct *Giovinezza* as "absurd and unpatriotic")

### 15 MAY 1931

*Torneo Notturno,* music drama by Gian Francesco MALIPIERO (completed by him on 10 December 1929), set in the form of a septuple nocturnal tournament, depicting seven psychologically connected scenes, landscapes and moods, with symphonic portions alternating with singing episodes, *Le Serenate, La Tormenta, La Foresta, La Taverna del Buon Tempo, Il Focolare spento, Il Castello della Noia,* and *La Prigione,* is performed for the first time in Munich, in a German version, under the title *Komödie des Todes.*

### 17 MAY 1931

*Die Mutter,* opera in ten scenes by Alois HÁBA, the first stage work making systematic use of quarter-tones and their multiples, dealing with a self-denying second wife of a Czech peasant whose children of the first marriage are hostile to the new children and to her, is produced for the first time in Munich. (The original Czech version was produced in Prague on 23 May 1947)

My first quarter-tone opera *Die Mutter* proves that it is humanly possible to build large musical forms on an athematical principle. Harmonically, I have used combinations ranging from two to 24 different sounds. Melodically, I have applied multiples of quarter-tones (3/4-tones and 5/4-tones), as well as neutral thirds, sixths, fourths and sevenths. This may be described as diatonic music in the quarter-tone system. For the first performance of my opera in Munich, the piano manufacturer August Förster has built a special quarter-tone piano, Kohlert has constructed two new clarinets in quarter-tones, and Heckel has furnished two quarter-tone trumpets. (Alois Hába, *Anbruch*, Vienna, May 1931)

### 18 MAY 1931

Count Alexander Dmitrievitch SHEREMETIEV, founder and conductor of a series of symphonic concerts of Russian music in St. Petersburg in the heyday of the Russian autocracy, when money and noble blood could buy fame, dies at the age of 72 in exile in a Russian charity home at Ste-Geneviève-des Bois, near Paris.

### 19 MAY 1931

*Wagadus Untergang durch die Eitelkeit,* oratorio for three solo voices, singing and speaking chorus, and five saxophones by the Moscow-born half-German half-Russian composer Vladimir VOGEL, inspired by a North African legend of the decline and fall of a proud Berber kingdom, is performed for the first time in Munich.

### 22 MAY 1931

*Sahdji,* ballet by the American Negro composer William Grant STILL, with chorus singing comments on the action and a bass voice reciting African proverbs, to a scenario dealing with an adulterous favorite wife of an ancient central African chieftain punished for her sins by the jungle deities beating the ritual drums, is performed for the first time in Rochester, New York.

### 22 MAY 1931

*Bacchus et Ariane,* ballet in two acts by Albert ROUSSEL, dealing with Theseus's abandonment of Ariadne (who had saved him from the Minotaur) on the island of Naxos, where she finds solace in the arms of Bacchus, and takes part in a Bacchanale, is performed for the first time at the Paris Opéra.

### 2 JUNE 1931

*Cris du monde,* stage oratorio by Arthur HONEGGER, portraying a peaceful recluse trying to elude the modern world chanting in propulsively dissonant harmonies of its urban accessories, the twinkling electric signs, the automobiles, the Métro, "Join us! Join us!" is performed for the first time in Paris.

### 3 JUNE 1931

*Deep Forest,* prelude for chamber orchestra by the 52-year-old American composeress Mabel DANIELS, who enjoyed the benefit of German musical training under the tutelage of Thuille, thus becoming the most erudite among American women composers of her generation, written in a romantic vein with some impressionistic daubs of color, is performed for the first time in New York.

### 3 JUNE 1931

*The Band Wagon*, a musical revue by Arthur SCHWARTZ, featuring the celebrated song *Dancing in the Dark*, is produced in New York.

### 6 JUNE 1931

Under the auspices of the Pan American Association of Composers, Nicolas SLONIMSKY conducts in Paris the first of his two concerts of modern American music:

*American Life*, an overture by the Baltimore-born American composer Adolph WEISS, written in a lively but erudite manner, combining jazzy inflections of the American life in the first quarter of the century with atonal and paradodecaphonic devices of his master Arnold Schoenberg; *Three Places in New England* by the greatest musical genius of modern America Charles E. IVES, composed between 1906 and 1914, but not performed until Nicolas Slonimsky conducted it in New York on 10 January 1931; *Men and Mountains*, symphonic poem by the individualistically intractable Vermont composer Carl RUGGLES, set in an uncompromisingly severe tonal, polytonal and atonal style (one of the viola players in the Paris orchestra added the words *Il* before *viola* in his part and *la musique* after the word *viola*, to record his opinion that Ruggles has violated music); the world première of *Synchrony*, a study in functional simultaneity of tones, timbres and rhythms by the indomitable innovator Henry COWELL, with the application of symphonic tone-clusters in chromatic compacts of homogeneous instrumental elements; and *La Rebambaramba*, a multicolored musicorama by the fiery Cuban mulatto composer Amadeo ROLDÁN, depicting an Afro-Cuban fiesta in a gorgeous display of Caribbean melorhythms, with the participation of a multifarious fauna of native percussion effects, including a polydental glissando on the jawbone of an ass.

It seems that polyrhythmic and polyharmonic experiments are conducted in America in a spirit more sane, more candid, and more youthful than here. One needs to possess a certain amount of savagery to march with easy steps in this new kind of music administered by hammer blows. With us, in Europe, a burdensome artistic heritage takes away the element of joyous insouciance from this spontaneous display. (Emile Vuillermoz, *Excelsior*, Paris, 8 June 1931)

Nicolas Slonimsky of Boston, indefatigable in furthering the cause of the extreme radical composers, has brought out in Paris orchestral compositions by Americans who are looked on by our conservatives as wild-eyed anarchists. He thus purposed to acquaint Parisians with contemporaneous American music. But the composers represented were not those who are regarded by their fellow-countrymen as leaders in the art, nor have they all been so considered by the conductors of our great orchestras. If Mr. Slonimsky had chosen a composition by Loeffler, Hill; one of Deems Taylor's suites, Foote's suite, or music by some who, working along traditional lines, have nevertheless shown taste, technical skill and a suggestion at least of individuality, his audience in Paris would now have a fairer idea of what Americans are doing in the art. Are these Parisians to be blamed if they say that the American composers thus made known to them are restless experimenters, or followers of Europeans whose position in the musical world is not yet determined, men who show ingenuity chiefly by their rhythmic inventions and orchestral tricks; men who apparently have no melodic gift, or, having it, disdain it for the tiresome repetition and transformation of an insignificant pattern; who neglect the sensuous charm of stringed instruments and put their trust for startling effects in combinations of wind and percussion choirs? (Philip Hale, in an editorial entitled *Mr. Slonimsky in Paris,* in the Boston *Herald,* 7 July 1931)

The Paris concerts given by Slonimsky were better received than I expected they would be; the only unfavorable comment which I saw was by a Prof. Pruniéries—it wasn't so unfavorable as unfair or weak-eared. He says that I "know my Schoenberg" —interesting information to me as I have never heard nor seen a note of Schoenberg's music. Then he says that I haven't applied the lessons as well as I might. This statement shows almost human intelligence. It's funny how many men, when they see another man put the breechin' under a horse's tail, wrong or right, think that he must be influenced by someone in Siberia or Neurasthenia. No one man invented the barber's itch. But one thing about the concerts that everyone felt was that Slonimsky was a great conductor. (Letter from Charles Ives to Robert E. Schmitz, dated 10 August 1931)

### 11 JUNE 1931

Nicolas SLONIMSKY conducts in Paris his second concert of American music in the following program of works for chamber orchestra:

*Sones de Castilla,* suite by the Spanish-Cuban composer Pedro SANJUÁN, in expansive melodic forms of Castillian songs and dances modernized by Stravinskian rhythms; the first performance anywhere of *Energía* by the Mexican composer Carlos CHÁVEZ, primitivistically virile in its rejection of common esthetics; *Préambule et Jeux* for harp and nine instruments by the Franco-American innovator Carlos SALZEDO; *Bembé,* Afro-Cuban movement in powerfully asymmetrical rhythms and discordant harmonies by the 25-year-old Cuban composer Alejandro CATURLA; *Three Canons* in dissonant counterpoint by the American modern polyphonist Wallingford RIEGGER; and *Intégrales* for wind instruments, double-bass and percussion by Edgar VARÈSE, an essay in organized sound expressing in the abstract terms of condensed and static emotion the concept of integral calculus.

### 14 JUNE 1931

*The Black Cliff,* opera in four acts by Andrei PASHCHENKO, to a story dealing with the civil war raging in 1919 in Central Asia, couched in a homophonic idiom with abundant melorhythmic allusions to Kirghiz folksongs, is produced in Leningrad.

### 20 JUNE 1931

*Die Bakchantinnen,* opera in two acts by Egon WELLESZ, after the last play of Euripides, *The Bacchae,* dealing with the hideous vengeance of Bacchus upon the townspeople of Thebes for their rejection of the bacchanals and persecution of the maenads, is performed for the first time in Vienna.

### 23 JUNE 1931

*Amphion,* scenic melodrama in one act by Arthur HONEGGER to a text by Paul Valéry wherein Apollo orders Amphion to invent music, which he does by creating a scale of two major tetrachords disjunct by a semitone, thus dividing the octave bitonally into tritones, and playing a fugue on the lyre so powerfully that stones are moved telekinetically to erect a temple to Apollo in Thebes, is produced at the Paris Opéra, with Ida Rubinstein miming Amphion.

### 5 JULY 1931

*Job*, "masque for dancing" by Ralph VAUGHAN WILLIAMS, inspired by William Blake's illustrations to the Book of Job and delineating the increasingly dramatic tests of faith administered by the implacable God of the Old Testament, set to music in old modalities, with Satan's irruptions of cachinnating rhythms, is performed for the first time in London.

### 21 JULY 1931

Hans BARTH registers the patent for his quarter-tone piano.

This instrument has two keyboards of 88 notes each and appears to be much larger than the present-day piano. The upper keyboard is tuned to the regular international pitch and has the usual five black keys and seven white keys. The other keyboard is a quarter-tone lower and has five blue keys and seven red keys. The A, a quarter-tone lower than the regular 440 pitch, is 427½ pitch. The music written for this instrument sounds weird at first to the average listener, but after a while it gives one a new feeling of tone color never experienced before. (From a letter to the author by Hans Barth, 1936)

### 23 JULY 1931

The Ninth annual Festival of the International Society for Contemporary Music opens at Oxford, England, with the following program of symphonic music:

*Lyric Suite* for small orchestra in the classical four movements by the Soviet composer Lev KNIPPER, written in a Scriabinesque manner and subtilized instrumentation; *Piano Sonata* in a continuous four-segmented movement, marked by a cumulatively rising dissonant tension, by the American neo-classicist Roger SESSIONS; *String Trio* in an atonally constructivistic idiom by the Polish composer Jozef KOFFLER; *Ame en peine* for unaccompanied chorus by the French composer Jean HURÉ, who died a year and a half before this performance; *3 Choruses a cappella* by Schoenberg's disciple and Byzantine scholar Egon WELLESZ, couched in an austerely dissonant polyphonic idiom; *4 Japanese Songs* for voice and orchestra, set in the "Tokyo scale" (with quarter-tones) by the Polish composer Jan MAKLAKIEWICZ; and *Sinfonietta* in three movements in a hedonistic neo-Rococo manner by the 26-year-old Spanish composer Ernesto HALFFTER.

### 24 JULY 1931

At the second concert of the Ninth Festival of the International Society for Contemporary Music in Oxford, the following program of choreographic music is given:

534

Orchestral suite from *Pomona* by Constant LAMBERT, conducted by the composer; *La Somnambule,* a grotesque dance by the Prague-born atonal neo-classicist Erwin SCHULHOFF, designed as an absolute piece of music with an abstract expressionist scenario, conducted by the composer; and *Job,* "being Blake's vision of the Book of Job," by Ralph VAUGHAN WILLIAMS, arranged for theater orchestra by Constant Lambert and conducted by him.

24 JULY 1931

*Die Blume von Hawaii,* operetta by Paul ABRAHAM dealing with the exotic shenanigans of a jazz singer named Jim Boy, and taking place in Honolulu and Monte Carlo, is performed for the first time in Leipzig.

25 JULY 1931

During the Ninth Festival of the International Society for Contemporary Music in Oxford, a musical play for children by Paul HINDEMITH, *Wir bauen eine Stadt,* his most characteristic piece of *Gebrauchsmusik,* with simple stage action and a neo-Baroque score seasoned with temperate discords, is presented in the afternoon, and the following program of chamber music is given at the evening concert:

*String Quartet* in four descriptive movements (*Calme, Rythmique, Douloureux, Rigaudon*) by Marcel DELANNOY, French impressionist composer turning towards neo-classicism; *Sonatina* for piano in three movements by Otto JOKL of Vienna, in a light neo-classically polytonal vein; *Sonatina* for flute and clarinet by the young French composer Jean CARTAN, in a concise utilitarian manner of Gallic neo-classicism; the ultra-chromatic, harmonically tense and dynamically explosive *Second Sonata* for violin and piano by Eugene GOOSSENS; and a discursive *Piano Quintet* by the Italian composer Mario PILATI.

27 JULY 1931

As part of the Ninth Festival of the International Society for Contemporary Music, with its principal site at Oxford, a concert of symphonic music is given at Queen's Hall in London with the following program:

*Symphonic Music* in an ostentatiously non-programmatic absolute style by the Polish composer Roman PALESTER; *Symphony* for chamber orchestra, op. 21, by Anton von WEBERN (first performed in New York on 18 December 1929), built on a series of twelve different notes in two mutually exclusive and symmetrically disposed tropes related by a tritone; a neo-romantic *Rapsodia* by the Italian composer Virgilio MORTARI; *Second Symphony* by the cosmopolitan Russian composer Vladimir DUKELSKY (first performed in Boston on 25 April 1930), in three classically outlined movements with the subject matter approximating a stylization of Glinka's melodic concepts; *Music for Orchestra,* non-programmatic in its neo-classical orthodoxy, by Constant LAMBERT, conducted by the composer; and *An American in Paris,* a nostalgic piece of symphonic tourism by George GERSHWIN.

28 JULY 1931

At the Ninth Festival of the International Society for Contemporary Music in London, the following program of symphonic and choral works is given:

*3 Symphonic Pieces* by the Argentinian composer Juan José CASTRO; *3 Symphonic Movements* by the Belgian composer Fernand QUINET; *Polish Songs* for chorus a cappella by Karol SZYMANOWSKI; *Songs of the Wolves* for chorus a cappella by the Hungarian composer Ferencz SZABÓ; *Benedicite* for soprano solo, chorus and orchestra by VAUGHAN WILLIAMS; 2 *Studies for Orchestra* (*Ritmica funebre, Ritmica scherzosa*) by the Russian-born German-bred neo-romanticist Vladimir VOGEL, written in an expansively sonorous musical language; and *Psalm 80* for chorus and orchestra by Albert ROUSSEL.

### 15 AUGUST 1931

The first annual Festival of Mountain White Folk Music ("White Top Folk") is held at Marion, Virginia.

### 30 AUGUST 1931

*Cinderella,* ballet by Marcel DELANNOY, is performed for the first time anywhere in Chicago. (A revised version was first performed in Paris on 14 May 1935, under the title *Pantoufle de vair,* i.e. *Fur Slipper,* the probably correct title of Perrot's classical tale, the word *vair* having been misspelled through the centuries as *verre* leading to the popular misinterpretation of Cinderella's being shod in glass rather than in a much more likely material, fur)

### 17 SEPTEMBER 1931

*A Song of Summer,* orchestral piece by blind and bedridden Frederick DELIUS, dictated by him to his musical amanuensis, Eric Fenby, who wrote it down note by note, is performed for the first time at a concert of Delius's music in London, the composer listening in by radio from his retreat in Grez, in France.

### 3 OCTOBER 1931

*Armastus ja surm* (*Love and Death*), opera in three acts by the Russian-educated Estonian composer Arthur LEMBA, with the action taking place on a Baltic island where a wrecked seaman finds local love interrupted by sea death, is produced in Reval (Tallin), capital of Estonia.

### 3 OCTOBER 1931

Carl NIELSEN, prime modernist of Denmark, whose romantically impassioned symphonies with mystically inspired programmatic designs written in a singularly peninsular manner, half-detached from the musical continent, half-surrounded by an impressionistic sea, yet distinctly of the twentieth century in the austerities and asperities of the idiom, dies in Copenhagen at the age of sixty-six.

### 10 OCTOBER 1931

*Belshazzar's Feast,* neo-Handelian oratorio for baritone, chorus and orchestra by William WALTON, to a text arranged from Biblical sources by Osbert Sitwell, beginning with the shattering prophecy by Isaiah and ending with the Babylonian king's death and jubilation by the captives, is performed for the first time at the Leeds Festival in England.

### 15 OCTOBER 1931

*The Cat and the Fiddle,* musical comedy by Jerome KERN, to the story of a chorus girl who marries a Rumanian opera composer to the tune *The Night Was Made for Love,* is produced in New York.

### 20 OCTOBER 1931

Emanuel Moór, Hungarian pianist, composer, inventor of the Duplex Pianoforte with two keyboards, the upper sounding an octave above the lower, with a coupler uniting both keyboards so as to enable a pianist to play octave passages with unisonal dexterity, dies at Mont-Pélerin, near Vevey, Switzerland, at the age of sixty-eight.

(All music dictionaries give the erroneous date of Moór's death as 21 October 1931; Max Pirani, in his monograph on Moór, published in London in 1959, states that he died shortly after 5:00 P.M. on 20 October 1931, and this date has been confirmed by Moór's niece from documentary evidence)

### 23 OCTOBER 1931

The American composer Harold MORRIS plays the solo part in the first performance with the Boston Symphony Orchestra, Serge Koussevitzky conducting, of his ultra-romantic infra-modern *Piano Concerto,* in three movements, *Allegro-Andante, Variations on the Negro Pilgrim Song* and *Rondo,* distinguished by a somberly evocative quasi-impressionistic style, with an enchorial sentiment in the melorhythmic configurations of thematic content.

### 23 OCTOBER 1931

Igor STRAVINSKY conducts in Berlin the first performance, with Samuel Dushkin as soloist, of his *Concerto en Ré* for violin and orchestra, in four movements, *Toccata, Aria I, Aria II,* and *Capriccio,* set in an austere neo-Baroque idiom, with pandiatonic harmonies adding resonance to the ascetically shaped spacious melodies.

### 24 OCTOBER 1931

*Au Béguinage,* symphonic tableau by the 58-year-old French composer André BLOCH, suffused with the tropical scents of the island of Martinique, with its native dance, the béguine, providing the vitalizing spark to his conventionally designed score, is performed for the first time in Paris.

### 25 OCTOBER 1931

*L'ospite inatteso,* lyrical opera buffa in one act by the Bohemian-born 49-year-old Italian composer Riccardo PICK-MANGIAGALLI to a libretto describing the emotional and social imbroglios created by an unexpected visitor, is performed for the first time on the Milan-Turin-Genoa radio network, the first opera to be premièred on the radio.

## 29 OCTOBER 1931

*Afro-American Symphony* by William Grant STILL, in four movements depicting in melodious and harmonious tones the authentically racial musical world of the black people of America, is performed for the first time by the Rochester Philharmonic Orchestra, Howard Hanson conducting.

## 29 OCTOBER 1931

*Der Gondoliere des Dogen,* opera in one act by Emil Nikolaus von REZNIČEK, is produced in Stuttgart.

## 1 NOVEMBER 1931

The first piece in *Klavarskribo* notation, based on the tablature principle with the position of each note indicated on the diagram of the piano keyboard, is published in Slikkerveer, near Rotterdam, Holland.

(Klavarskribo is the Esperanto word for piano writing. The idea was worked out by C. Pot between 1905 and 1931, and copyrighted on 6 September 1933. A similar method was proposed earlier by Gustave Neuhaus in his book *Zur Einführung in die Neuhaussche Notenschrift Natürliches Notensystem,* published in Nuremberg in 1906. Richard Zeiler published several works in this notation in 1906)

## 10 NOVEMBER 1931

*Der Freikorporal,* opera in three acts by Georg VOLLERTHUN, is produced in Hannover.

## 12 NOVEMBER 1931

*Das Herz,* music drama in three acts by Hans PFITZNER to a supernatural story of cadaverous and astral heart transplants, suggested by Pfitzner himself and elaborated by his pupil Hans Mahner-Mons, dealing with a 17th-century German doctor, who successfully transplants a healthy heart from a corpse he saw in a dream into the body of a prince with a hopelessly damaged heart, only to discover that the heart he so recklessly used was his wife's (she dies, and her heart in the prince's body dies too, precipitating his death and the doctor's political downfall), with a happy ending provided by her astral body with the heart restored, carrying him into the realm of heavenly dreamland, is produced for the first time simultaneously in Berlin and Munich.

## 13 NOVEMBER 1931

*Five Picture Studies,* a symphonic arrangement by Ottorino RESPIGHI of five *Etudes-Tableaux* by RACHMANINOFF, with gratuitous fortuitous descriptive titles attached to each (*The Sea and the Gulls, The Fair, Funeral March, Red*

*Riding-Hood and the Wolf, March*), is performed for the first time by the Boston Symphony Orchestra, Serge Koussevitzky conducting.

### 13 NOVEMBER 1931

*Friedemann Bach,* opera in three acts by Paul GRAENER, depicting in ostentatiously Bachian polyphony the hedonistic Dresden years of Bach's profligate eldest son Wilhelm Friedemann, after his appointment as court organist in Saxony in 1733, is produced in Schwerin.

### 19 NOVEMBER 1931

*Jack and the Beanstalk,* "a fairy opera for the childlike" by the 47-year-old Russian-born American-bred composer Louis GRUENBERG, to the book by John Erskine, with a modernistic musical setting imparting a surrealist touch to the old nursery tale, in which the cow sings tenor, and the giant countertenor in falsetto, while golden eggs are laid in impressionistic harmonies, is performed for the first time at the Juilliard School of Music in New York.

### 21 NOVEMBER 1931

*Das Unaufhörliche,* oratorio by Paul HINDEMITH to the text of a mystically idealistic poem by Gottfried Benn, written in a neo-medieval manner, modal in its melodic teleology, compact in its intricate polyphony, and starkly pandiatonic in harmony, is performed for the first time in Berlin.

### 22 NOVEMBER 1931

*Grand Canyon Suite,* a rotating musicorama by Ferde GROFÉ, presenting in vivid orchestral colors the changing tableaux: *Sunrise, Painted Desert, On the Trail, Sunset* and *Cloudburst,* is performed for the first time by Paul Whiteman and his orchestra in Chicago.

### 25 NOVEMBER 1931

*Sonata* for chamber choir by the Dutch composer and innovator Daniel RUYNEMAN, with vocal instrumentation built on the differentiation of tonecolor of vowels, is performed for the first time in Vienna.

### 25 NOVEMBER 1931

*Die Heilige aus U.S.A.,* a play by Ilse LANGNER dealing with the life of the founder of Christian Science, Mary Baker Eddy, presenting her career as the commercial undertaking by a made-in-America "saint" with incidental music by Ernst TOCH, applying discordant hymnal harmonies to characterize the building of The Mother Church in Boston, jazz rhythms for the prying reporters, and a grand fugue for the symbolic confrontation with Mark Twain and other early critics of Christian Science, is produced in Berlin.

### 27 NOVEMBER 1931

Paul WITTGENSTEIN, one-armed Austrian pianist (his right arm was amputated in a Russian hospital where he was a prisoner of war during World War

I), plays in Vienna the first performance anywhere of RAVEL's *Piano Concerto for the Left Hand* and orchestra, specially written for him, in a triune movement:

*Lento,* majestic and sonorous, covering the entire range of the keyboard creating aurally an impression of bimanual technique reaching a climax in a deceptively dexterous quinquedigital cadenza; *Allegro,* a curiously hybrid blues episode with a Hispanic motto akin to that of Ravel's *Boléro* in which the third and the seventh of the major scale are lowered while the major harmony is maintained elsewhere, shifting to a merrier jazzy idiom; *Lento,* in an improvisatory mood, first lyrical then rushing towards a precipitate ending in full orchestral and pianistic sonority.

In a work of this kind, it is essential to give the impression of a texture no thinner than that of a part written for both hands. For the same reason, I resorted to a style that is much nearer to that of the more solemn kind of traditional concerto. A special feature is that after the first section in this traditional style a sudden change occurs and the jazz music begins. Only later does it become manifest that the jazz music is built on the same theme as the opening part. (Ravel's statement to M. D. Calvocoressi, published in the *Daily Telegraph,* London, on 16 July 1931, and reprinted in the article *Ravel's Letters* to *Calvocoressi* in *The Musical Quarterly,* New York, January 1941)

### 1 DECEMBER 1931

*The Devil Take Her,* a farcical musical comedy in one act with a prologue by the 38-year-old Australian-born English composer Arthur BENJAMIN, is performed for the first time in London.

### 2 DECEMBER 1931

Vincent D'INDY, grand master of French music, whose academically pure musical language is a model of clarity while conveying evocative images of landscapes and moods through astute use of folksong inflections, dies in his native Paris at the age of eighty.

### 8 DECEMBER 1931

*The Blonde Donna, or The Fiesta of Santa Barbara,* opera in three acts by the 65-year-old American composer Ernest CARTER, first performed in concert form in New York in February 1912, to his own libretto involving an uprising of Mission Indians in Santa Barbara, California, in 1824, against the obtusely beneficent Padres, with the Blonde Donna of the title persuading the rebels to desist and take part in a general dance, receives its first complete stage production in Brooklyn.

### 11 DECEMBER 1931

Dmitri KABALEVSKY, 26-year-old Soviet composer, plays the solo part in the world première in Moscow of his *First Piano Concerto* in A minor in three movements, written in a lyrico-heroic manner, with recurrent eruptions of kinetic energy in an optimistic tonal ambience, vitalized by prudential and temperate dissonances.

540

## 15 DECEMBER 1931

Igor MARKEVITCH, 19-year-old Russian-born Parisian composer, conducts the Orchestre Symphonique de Paris in the first performance of his ballet suite *Rebus*, dedicated to the memory of Serge Diaghilev, in six neo-Rococo movements: *Prélude, Danse, Gigue, Variations, Fugue* and *Parade de vices* (The solution of the rebus is the Russian proverb "Poverty is not a Vice.")

## 20 DECEMBER 1931

*Rotative*, symphonic poem by the 26-year-old Italian composer Giacinto SCELZI, inspired by the phrase from a poem by Rupert Brooke: "the keen impassioned beauty of a great machine" and written in a mechanistically romantic manner to portray the transformation of the reciprocating motion of the piston into a continuous rotary motion of a steam engine, with the rhythmic pulsation humanly faulted by occasional asymmetrical meters, is performed for the first time by the Orchestre Symphonique de Paris, Pierre Monteux conducting.

## 21 DECEMBER 1931

*Schön ist die Welt* (*The World is Beautiful*), optimistic operetta by Franz LEHÁR, is produced in Vienna.

## 26 DECEMBER 1931

*Of Thee I Sing*, a musical comedy with book by Morris Ryskind and George Kaufman, lyrics by Ira Gershwin and music by George GERSHWIN, describing in tones of supreme persiflage the presidential campaign of Wintergreen and Throttlebottom running on the platform of Love, with embarrassing problems ensuing when the President-elect jilts his fiancée of Imperial lineage being the illegitimate granddaughter of an illegitimate nephew of Napoleon and marries a country girl who can cook, so that it devolves upon the Vice-President to marry his chief's former fiancée, is produced in New York.

*Of Thee I Sing* is funnier than the government, and not nearly so dangerous (Brooks Atkinson, New York *Times*, 27 December 1931)

# ❧ *1932* ❧

## 4 JANUARY 1932

*Maximilien*, opera in three acts by Darius MILHAUD, after Franz Werfel's play *Juarez und Maximilian*, portraying the sad fate of the unfortunate Archduke of Austria set up as Emperor of Mexico by Napoleon III and executed by the forces of the Mexican popular leader Juárez in 1867, with a turbulently dramatic score rich in topical rhythmic materials arranged in intensely dissonant harmonies, is produced by the Paris Opéra.

### 9 JANUARY 1932

*La Jungle*, a "polyphonie" for organ and orchestra by Georges MIGOT, is performed for the first time in Paris.

### 10 JANUARY 1932

A year and three weeks before Hitler's advent to power, the National Socialist Symphony Orchestra, organized by Nazi party members, gives its inaugural concert at a Munich circus, not far from the beer cellar where Hitler embarked on his road to infamy.

### 14 JANUARY 1932

Maurice RAVEL conducts in Paris a concert of his music, including the world première, with Marguerite Long as soloist, of his *Concerto* in G major for piano and orchestra, for both hands (composed before its left-handed companion which was performed on 27 November 1931), in three movements:

(1) *Allegramente*, in which the basically pentatonic melodic line is embanked in polytonal arpeggios, with the second tonality, F-sharp major, gaining ascendancy and, ultimately, supremacy (2) *Adagio assai*, in a poetically Chopinesque vein, and (3) *Presto*, set in pandiatonic harmonies and containing elements of jazzy syncopation in energetic motion.

### 14 JANUARY 1932

*Innominata*, symphonic movement by the 30-year-old Swiss composer Conrad BECK, so named to emphasize the namelessness of its musical form and content, written in an austerely dissonant idiom without a key signature, but with tangibly set tonal barycenters, is performed for the first time in Geneva by the Orchestre de la Suisse Romande, Ernest Ansermet conducting.

### 23 JANUARY 1932

*Belkis, regina di Saba*, "choreographic spectacle with musical illustrations" by Ottorino RESPIGHI, written in a resplendently eclectic style, with orientalistically undulant arabesques characterizing the Queen of Sheba and pentatonic scales depicting the populace, is produced at La Scala, in Milan.

### 27 JANUARY 1932

*Plameny (Flames)*, opera in two acts by the Czech composer Erwin SCHULHOFF, is produced in Brno.

### 28 JANUARY 1932

Lady Dean PAUL, Brussels-born posthumous daughter of the Polish pianist Henryk Wieniawski, composeress, under the pen-name Poldowski, of im-

542

pressionistic songs to French texts and of innocuous piano miniatures, dies in London at the age of fifty-two.

### 29 JANUARY 1932

George GERSHWIN plays the solo part with the Boston Symphony Orchestra, Serge Koussevitzky conducting, in the world première of his *Second Rhapsody* for piano and orchestra, commissioned for the 50th anniversary of the Boston Symphony and picturing in polyrhythmic constructivist sonorities diversified by lyric interludes in rutilant hues, the "eternal tattoo" of the skyscraper riveters of Manhattan erecting the tallest buildings in the world, the nucleus of thematic inspiration being derived from his score for the motion picture *Delishious*.

I wanted to write a serious composition and found the opportunity in California to do it. Nearly everybody comes back from California with a Western tan and a pocketful of moving-picture money. I decided to come back with both those things, and a serious composition—if the climate would let me. (From Gershwin's letter of 30 June 1931 to Philip Hale, program annotator of the Boston Symphony Orchestra.)

### 14 FEBRUARY 1932

Cemal Reshid REY, 27-year-old Turkish composer, conducts in Paris the first performance of his *Karagueuz*, a symphonic suite in 12 movements illustrating 12 tableaux of Turkish shadow silhouette marionettes (*karagueuz* means black eyes).

### 14 FEBRUARY 1932

*Der Gewaltige Hahnrei*, opera in three acts by the 29-year-old German composer Berthold GOLDSCHMIDT, extolling the virtues and generosities of a "powerful cuckold," is produced in Mannheim.

### 18 FEBRUARY 1932

*Helvetia, the Land of Mountains and its People*, a symphonic fresco by Ernest BLOCH, composed intermittently between 1900 and 1929, with the multinational diversity of his native Switzerland exemplified by some thirty motives derived from Helvetian folksongs, is performed for the first time anywhere by the Chicago Symphony Orchestra, Frederick Stock conducting, as the winning work of one-fifth of a prize of $25,000 offered by the Victor Talking Machine Company, shared with four other works submitted for this contest.

### 18 FEBRUARY 1932

*Tragödie in Arezzo*, a melodramatic opera in three acts with a prologue and epilogue by the Dutch-born American composer Richard HAGEMAN, after Robert Browning's poem *The Ring and the Book*, dealing with the trial for murder, conviction and execution of a uxoricidal nobleman of Arezzo who in 1698 slew his wife whom he suspected of carnal intercourse with the young priest named Caponsacchi, is performed for the first time at Freiburg-im-

Breisgau, in a German translation, with 25 curtain calls for the composer. (The opera was produced in the original version in English, under the title *Caponsacchi*, by the Metropolitan Opera in New York on 4 February 1937, conducted by the composer)

### 19 FEBRUARY 1932

*Symphonic Ode* by Aaron COPLAND, with thematic materials drawn from an earlier *Nocturne* for violin and piano, is performed for the first time by the Boston Symphony Orchestra as a commissioned work for its 50th anniversary, Serge Koussevitzky conducting.

### 21 FEBRUARY 1932

*Jazz Music* by the Belgian composer Marcel POOT, a symphonic movement with a saxophone and a trombone syncopating in American rhythms, is performed for the first time in Brussels.

### 25 FEBRUARY 1932

*Sun-Treader,* symphonic poem by Carl RUGGLES, 55-year-old rugged American individualist, inspired by Robert Browning's line, "Sun-treader, life and light be thine forever," written in a tense atonal idiom, in unrelentingly driven march time from the initial drum beats to the final solar illumination in revelatory C major (Browning spoke of "the C major of life"), with powerful tonal protuberances forming a pandiatonic corona, is performed for the first time anywhere, by the Orchestre Symphonique de Paris conducted by Nicolas Slonimsky.

### 3 MARCH 1932

Eugen D'ALBERT, Scottish-born pianist and composer, who renounced his insular birthright to return to the land of his German ancestors, dies in Riga, Latvia, during one of his many tours, at the age of sixty-seven.

### 6 MARCH 1932

John Philip SOUSA, American March King, Washington-born son of a Portuguese father and a Bavarian mother, whose marching tune *Stars and Stripes Forever* provided a vitalizing bio-musical stimulus to generations of American soldiers, dies in Reading, Pennsylvania, at the age of seventy-seven, forty years after the first concert of the Sousa Band which he led in Plainfield, New Jersey, on 26 September 1892. (The story, generated by an unknown mythologist, that SOUSA is an acrostic for SUPER OMNES USA, is a fantasy)

### 10 MARCH 1932

*Die Bürgschaft (The Pledge)*, musical play in three acts with a prologue by Kurt WEILL, wherein an abandoned cache of gold bullion is appropriated by the state to finance an aggressive war, scored for voices, two electrically amplified pianos and a jazz band, is produced in Berlin.

12 MARCH 1932

The Vatican Congregation of the Council issues a warning against the singing and playing in Catholic churches of sacred music written in the modern idiom, and forbidding such performances altogether in case royalties are to be paid to the composer.

14 MARCH 1932

A Congress of Arab musicians opens in Cairo to discuss the adoption of a uniform method of musical notation capable of indicating with precision the non-tempered intervals in oriental scales.

14 MARCH 1932

George EASTMAN, inventor of Kodak (he coined the word himself), munificent patron of music, although tone-deaf himself, founder of the Eastman School of Music in Rochester, New York, commits suicide by shooting himself, because of incurable cancer.

16 MARCH 1932

*Fourth Symphony* by Arnold BAX, in E-flat, in three movements: (1) *Allegro moderato,* marked by an energetically fanfarous sound with epically narrative undertones (2) *Lento moderato,* in a pentatonically Celtic melodic structure, suggesting by its muted colors a mystically distant realm of thought (3) *Allegro,* a cyclic return to the initial mood of affirmation through doubt, is performed for the first time anywhere by the San Francisco Symphony Orchestra under the direction of the English conductor Basil Cameron.

16 MARCH 1932

Ottorino RESPIGHI conducts in New York the world première of his mystery play *Maria Egiziaca,* a neo-medieval triptych relating an old legend of Mary of Egypt, first a dissolute woman in sinful Alexandria, then a penitent, and finally a devout Christian, cleansed of her sins by baptismal ablutions in the river Jordan, set to music in an appropriately Gothic manner, in archaic modalities of naked fifths and palpitant rhythms.

17 MARCH 1932

Alfredo CASELLA conducts in Rome the world première of his first opera *La Donna Serpente,* in three acts (begun on 16 October 1928 and completed on 22 October 1931), to a fantastic play by Carlo Gozzi wherein a fairy donna is turned into a serpent for a period of 200 years as punishment for carnal intercourse with a mortal, but is transformed into a human female when a lover divines her true self, set to music in a pandiatonically translucent and energetically rhythmic style.

The audience was full of beautiful half-naked women, but there was perfidy and menace in the air. A stage box was occupied by a "madmen's gang" intent on sabotaging the opera. I was aware of their presence and had a group of muscular young friends placed in their vicinity. My appearance on the podium was greeted by applause, interrupted by catcalls. For a composer making his debut as an opera conductor at the age of forty-nine the performance presented a real endurance test, but it was concluded in an atmosphere of cordiality. (Alfredo Casella, *I Segreti della Giara*, Florence 1941)

(In his monograph on Casella, published in Genoa in 1936, Luigi Cortese gives on p. 120, the erroneous year, 1931, for the first performance of the opera)

### 17 MARCH 1932

*On the Market Place*, ballet by the 40-year-old Rumanian composer Mihail JORA, who despite his training with Max Reger in Leipzig succeeded in preserving his Balkan rhythmic vivacity, wherein vendors of oriental sweets are depicted by melismatic arabesques, knife sharpeners by strident trumpets, junk dealers by heavy brass and inebriates by slippery bassoons, with flower girls tempting casual military men by the promissory floridity of their orientalistic modalities, with harsh heterophony characterizing the crowds, is produced in Bucharest.

### 17 MARCH 1932

*Il Favorito del Rè*, first opera, in three acts, by the 32-year-old Italian composer Antonio VERETTI, wherein the king's favorite courtier and his wife feign their own death in order to collect funeral expenses, set to music in a modern opera buffa manner, incorporating a jazz episode, is produced at La Scala, in Milan. (A compressed version, in one act, was produced in Rome on 29 January 1955 under the title *Burlesca*)

### 23 MARCH 1932

Pietro MASCAGNI conducts in San Remo the first performance of his youthful two-act opera *Pinotta*, written in 1880, the manuscript of which was lost for fifty years and recovered by chance, on the same bill with the 13,000th performance of his perennial favorite, *Cavalleria Rusticana*.

### 24 MARCH 1932

*Second Symphony* by the 32-year-old American composer Randall THOMPSON (completed by him in Switzerland on 6 September 1931), in four contrasting movements: (1) *Allegro*, in a forceful motoric drive (2) *Largo*, set in spaciously pentatonic modalities (3) *Vivace*, containing fugal episodes in asymmetric rhythms (4) *Andante moderato*, leading to *Allegro con spirito*, marked by frenzied jazzy ejaculations, is performed for the first time by the Rochester Philharmonic Orchestra under the direction of Howard Hanson.

### 24 MARCH 1932

*Hop! Signor*, lyric drama in three acts by the French composer Manuel ROSENTHAL, to a libretto dealing with a medieval woman who sends her crippled husband to his death to save him from lifelong torment, is performed for the first time in Toulouse.

*546*

## 31 MARCH 1932

*Caballos de Vapor,* or *H.P.* (*Horsepower*), constructivistic ballet of the modern age by the prime composer of Mexico Carlos CHÁVEZ, drawing a sharp contrast between the industrialized, capitalistic society of the United States and the pauperized but primitivistically vigorous Americas to the south, constructed in the form of a symphony, in four movements, with the northern foxtrot expressing the technological drive of advanced civilizations, and the southern huapango and tango depicting the languorous but purposeful ontology of homogenized tropical populations, set to music in an emancipated dissonant idiom, with harmonies anchored in focal tonalities, is performed for the first time anywhere, in Philadelphia, under the direction of Leopold Stokowski.

## 31 MARCH 1932

Two centuries have passed since the birth at Rohrau of Joseph HAYDN, whose intuitive genius for musical organization made the 18th century the era of the instrumental Sonata, the String Quartet and their orchestral counterpart, the Symphony, the forms brought by him to the summit of perfection.

## 2 APRIL 1932

Three completed movements of the posthumous *Ninth Symphony,* by Anton BRUCKNER, in their original version cleansed of the gratuitous emendations made by Ferdinand Loewe (who conducted his adulterated edition of the work in Vienna on 11 February 1903), are performed for the first time before an invited audience in Munich under the direction of Siegmund von Hausegger.

(The first public performance of these three authentic movements took place in Vienna on 23 October 1932, conducted by Clemens Kraus. The finale of the *Ninth Symphony,* assembled and synthesized by Hans Redlich and Robert Simpson from materials contained in the 184 manuscript pages on which Bruckner worked until the very day of his death on 11 October 1896, was performed for the first time in London on 17 September 1948.)

## 2 APRIL 1932

Hugo KAUN, German composer of highly respectable operas and other romantically colored music, dies in his native Berlin at the age of sixty-nine.

## 4 APRIL 1932

Jascha HEIFETZ performs for the first time in Vienna his brilliant violin arrangement of *Hora Staccato,* a dance tune written in 1906 by the 17-year-old Rumanian violinist Grigoraş DINICU.

## 5 APRIL 1932

Gino MARINUZZI, 50-year-old Italian composer, conducts at La Scala in Milan, the first performance of his opera in three acts, *Palla de' Mozzi,* dealing

547

with the leader of the Black Band in 16th-century Siena whose son falls in love with the daughter of a castellan imprisoned by him, and who, horrified by this act of filial disloyalty, kills himself, set to music in a quasi-impressionistic idiom with a considerable admixture of hard chromaticized disharmonies.

8 APRIL 1932

*Der Bettler Namenlos,* opera in three acts by the Austrian composer Robert HEGER, to a Homeromorphic story of the return of Odysseus to his native island of Ithaca as a nameless beggar, set in grandisonous Wagneromantic harmonies, is performed for the first time in Munich, under the composer's direction.

15 APRIL 1932

*Philharmonisches Konzert (Variationen für Orchester)* by Paul HINDEMITH, written in a euphonious manner of neo-classical stylization, is performed for the first time by the Berlin Philharmonic Orchestra, under the direction of Wilhelm Furtwängler, as a commissioned work on the occasion of its 50th anniversary.

23 APRIL 1932

The Central Committee of the Council of People's Commissars of the Russian Soviet Socialist Republic announces the dissolution of the RUSSIAN ASSOCIATION OF PROLETARIAN MUSICIANS (RAPM), along with related organizations in literature and art, as factional, divisive and detrimental to progressive ideology in Soviet culture.

April twenty-third 1932. Seven o'clock in the evening. An air of expectancy reigns in the hall of the Collegium of the People's Commissariat for Education . . . Different generations and different trends of creative musical craft are represented, from Ippolitov-Ivanov to the leaders of the RAPM . . . On the serious faces, there is a question: what is going to happen? It is apparent that something very unusual is in the air, perhaps a decisive battle . . . The Commissar for Education, Comrade Bubnov, opens the discussion dealing with problems of Soviet culture . . . He asks for a frank debate. The floodgates are open. Those present take the floor one after another, attacking the RAPM with extraordinary vehemence. Its theoretical, creative, tactical attitudes are under fire. In some speeches there is bitterness; theoretical contentions give way to echoes of recent squabbles. Personal feelings run high. It becomes clear that the RAPM by its policies, limiting the sphere of creative musical activity, has caused unhealthy conditions for the development of Soviet music. It is clear also that these conditions cannot be allowed to continue. On the 24th of April, the Moscow newspapers publish the decree of the Central Committee announcing the dissolution of all Proletarian Art Associations. The announcement is laconic and unexpected. It is read and discussed everywhere. A new responsibility is given to all. A new path has been opened for creative work. (*Sovietskaya Musica,* Moscow, No. 3, 1933, p. 132. See also the Declaration of Aims of the RAPM in the section, LETTERS AND DOCUMENTS)

24 APRIL 1932

*Székely Fonó (The Spinning Room of the Szeklers),* operatic ballad by Zoltán KODÁLY, composed of a series of 27 connected authentic songs of Transylvanian Szeklers (known, in Magyar, as Székely, descendants of Atilla's Huns or of Black Ugrians), to the texts of madrigal-like salutes to love as a socially liberating force, scored for chorus and orchestra applying Kodály's favorite device of "Hungarian counterpoint" wherein two different songs are combined canonically, is performed for the first time in Budapest.

## 25 APRIL 1932

*The Bride of Dionysus*, mythological opera in three acts by the erudite British musicologist Sir Donald TOVEY, is produced in Edinburgh.

## 30 APRIL 1932

The First Festival of Contemporary American Music opens at Yaddo (the name being derived in memory of a child's palatalized pronunciation of "shadow"), private estate near Saratoga Springs, New York, presenting 18 chamber works on two consecutive evenings and one afternoon:

*Piano Variations* by Aaron COPLAND, played by himself, written in a maximally economical and sparse idiom of reflexive dissonant counterpoint, with variations formed by the interpolations of non-thematic elements thus generating new melodic configurations; *Sonata* for flute and piano in a compact neo-Baroque idiom by Walter PISTON; a song with string quartet accompaniment by Virgil THOMSON; seven songs by Charles IVES, ranging from the obliquely romantic *Serenity* to the highly dissonant swashbuckling Western ballad *Charlie Rutlage;* songs by Paul BOWLES written in a subtilized quasi-impressionistic vein; songs with string quartet accompaniment by Robert Russell BENNETT; a polyphonically designed and economically worked out *Piano Sonata* by Roger SESSIONS; the tersely individualistic *Piano Sonata* by Roy HARRIS; *Unidad* and *36* for piano by the prime Mexican composer Carlos CHÁVEZ, written in a constructivistic percussive idiom; *Suite* for unaccompanied flute by Wallingford RIEGGER, in four movements, the last of which contains a group of 36 different notes as a triple dodecaphonic series; *Four Diversions* for string quartet by Louis GRUENBERG; *String Quartet* by Nicolai BEREZOWSKY; *String Quartet* by Marc BLITZSTEIN; *String Quartet* by Israel CITKOWITZ; a dissonantly racial *String Quartet* by the Mexican composer Silvestre REVUELTAS; and piano pieces by Vivian FINE, Oscar LEVANT and Henry BRANT.

## 1 MAY 1932

Five winning orchestral works by five American composers, Philip JAMES, Max WALD, Carl EPPERT, Florence GALAJIKIAN and Nicolai BEREZOWSKY, selected from 573 manuscripts in a contest for the best American compositions organized by the National Broadcasting Company, are broadcast under the direction of Eugene Goossens, and the prize of $5,000 is awarded to Philip JAMES for his topical score *Station WGZBX*, in four movements, *In the Lobby, Interference, A Slumber Hour, Mikestruck*. (*Traffic*, a movement from *Symphony of a City* by Carl EPPERT, composed in 1929 while he was working in a Cleveland cigar store observing the vehicular traffic in the street, received the third prize)

## 2 MAY 1932

The Pulitzer Committee of Columbia University announces the award of its annual prize to George KAUFMAN and George GERSHWIN for their political musical extravaganza *Of Thee I Sing*, the first such distinction bestowed on a musical comedy.

This award may seem unusual, but the play is unusual. Its effect on the stage promises to be very considerable, because musical plays are always popular, and by injecting genuine satire and point into them, a very large public is reached. (From the statement issued by the Pulitzer Committee)

### 4 MAY 1932

*Striženo-Košeno (Cut-Mown)*, opera in three acts by the 37-year-old Croatian composer Krešimir BARANOVIĆ, dealing with a quarrelsome couple who argue interminably whether it is more proper to say that grass is cut or mown, finally bringing the philological discussion to the attention of the court, set to an appropriately humorous musical score with numerous allusions to popular songs of Serbo-Croatia, is produced in Zagreb.

### 22 MAY 1932

*The Marriage of Aude*, one-act opera by the American composer Bernard ROGERS, is produced in Rochester, New York.

### 26 MAY 1932

*David Rizzio*, opera in two acts by the abecedarian American composeress Mary Carr MOORE, active in women's clubs, is produced in Los Angeles.

### 26 MAY 1932

*Sinfonia Technica*, industrial symphony by the 37-year-old Hungarian composer Eugen ZÁDOR, in four illustrative sections, (1) *The Bridge*, thematically constructed on spacious fourths and fifths unruffled by disequilibrating rhythmic syncopation but reasserting its stability on the final D-minor chord with an added ninth *fortississimo* (2) *The Telegraph Pole*, with fluted birds reposing nonchalantly on wires chromatically buzzing with important messages in divided string instrument parts, finishing off pianississimo (3) *Water Works*, wherein the cluttered trombones, glissando strings and trilling woodwinds create hydraulic power (4) *The Factory*, getting to production in dissonantly clashing brass and culminating in a sonorous A minor, is performed for the first time in Paris, conducted by Ivan Boutnikoff.

### 1 JUNE 1932

*Twelfth Symphony* in G minor by the most prolific Russian symphonist of all time, Nicolai MIASKOVSKY, completed on 31 January 1932, known popularly as "Collective Farm Symphony," reflecting in its three movements, *Andante*, *Presto agitato* and *Allegro festivo*, the three stages of the process of agricultural collectivization—its beginnings, the high point of rural struggle and the successful abolition of individual ownership, making use of folksong materials for realistic representation, is performed for the first time in Moscow.

The 10th Festival of the International Society for Contemporary Music opens in Vienna with the following program of orchestral music:

*Innominata*, neo-classical work in dissonant counterpoint by the Swiss composer Conrad BECK, performed by coincidence on his 31st birthday; *Piano Concerto* in a vigorously diatonic and rhythmically propulsive manner by the Russian-educated composer Nicolai LOPATNIKOFF; *Overture to an Ancient Tragedy* by Miroslav PONC of Czechoslovakia, based on the Greek enharmonic mode, which includes quarter-tones in the upper degrees of tetrachords; *Violin Concerto* by Karel HÁBA, brother of the quarter-tone pioneer Alois Hába, set in a discursive instrumental idiom without recourse to fractional intervals; *Melodies of Catalonia* by Roberto GERHARD of Barcelona; and an impressionistically romantic score, *Bal Vénitien*, by the French composer Claude DELVINCOURT.

17 JUNE 1932

At the second concert of the 10th Festival of the International Society for Contemporary Music in Vienna, the following program of chamber music is presented:

*Cantàri alla Madrigalesca*, third string quartet by Gian Francesco MALIPIERO, so named to indicate that the participating string instruments sing in the melodic madrigal manner without development; *Flute Sonata* by the Czech-born German composer Fidelio FINKE; *Viola Sonata* by Walter LEIGH of England; *Piano Sonata* by the Austrian composer Julius SCHLOSS, set in an eclectic style embodying elements of Liszt's rhapsodism in Americanistic jazz rhythms; *Children's Cantata*, in modernized ecclesiastical modes by the Polish composer and pianist Boleslaw WOYTOWICZ; and *Quintet* for wind instruments, a piece of abstraction in counterpoint, by the Croatian composer Josef MANDIĆ.

20 JUNE 1932

At the third concert of the 10th Festival of the International Society for Contemporary Music in Vienna, the following program of orchestral music is presented:

*Serenade* for small orchestra by the Latvian-born German-bred composer Eduard ERDMANN, in a melodious neo-classical vein touched with dissonance; *Piano Concerto* in a percussive modernistic manner by the German composer Norbert von HANNENHEIM; a vigorously accented neo-Baroque *Violin Concerto* by the Polish composer Jerzy FITELBERG, son of the conductor Gregor Fitelberg; *Durch die Nacht*, a song cycle in a post-romantic Mahlerian mood by Ernst KRENEK; and a *Symphony for Brass* in a slightly jazzified manner by the Vienna atonalist Hans JELINEK.

21 JUNE 1932

At the fourth, and last, concert of the 10th Festival of the International Society for Contemporary Music in Vienna, the following program of chamber music is given:

*Quintet* for oboe and strings in a lyric neo-Elizabethan manner by the English modernistic romanticist Arthur BLISS; a percussively discordant *Kleine Sonate* for piano by the not quite 22-year-old Czech composer Karel REINER; *Serenata* by the Italian composer of neo-classical music Vittorio RIETI; *String Trio* in academically worked out five movements by the Austrian composer Leopold SPINNER; *8 Bagatelles* for string quartet and piano by the 20-year-old Parisian hedonist Jean FRANÇAIX; and *Nonet* for flute, oboe, clarinet, bassoon, horn and string quartet by the Hungarian-Parisian composer Tibor HARSÁNYI. (On the same day, Anton von Webern conducted the Workers' Orchestra of Vienna, the Arbeiter-Sinfonie, in a program containing works by Mahler, Schoenberg and Berg)

### 3 JULY 1932

*The Green Table*, "dance of death in eight scenes" by the German choreographer Kurt Jooss, with music by Fritz COHEN, depicting scenes at the diplomats' green table, recruits' departure from sweethearts and wives, military brothels, and survivors' recessional, is produced at the Théâtre des Champs-Elysées in Paris, as a prize-winning ballet (25,000 francs) in a competition of the *Archives Internationales de la Danse* in Paris.

### 16 AUGUST 1932

*Cuban Overture* by George GERSHWIN, in three distinct sections, the first in propulsive rhumba rhythms, the second in an elegiac manner, and the third in an explosive outburst of Caribbean colors brought to the point of sonic saturation by the use of Cuban percussion instruments, is performed for the first time at an all-Gershwin concert at the Lewisohn Station in New York, Albert Coates conducting, under its original title *Rhumba*.

(Gershwin renamed the piece *Cuban Overture* for a performance at a benefit concert of the Metropolitan Opera in New York on 1 November 1932, in order to avoid the association with the popular type of Cuban music manufactured on Broadway. The first performance of the *Cuban Overture* in Cuba was conducted by Nicolas Slonimsky in Havana on 10 April 1933)

### 17 AUGUST 1932

*La Sangre de las Guitarras*, opera by the Argentine composer Constantino GAITO, to a libretto based on the internal struggles in Argentina in 1840, with the "blood of the guitars" luxuriantly blended with the dulcet wine of the Italianate score, is produced in Buenos Aires.

### 28 AUGUST 1932

The management of the Philadelphia Orchestra issues a statement to the effect that "debatable" new works will be severely rationed in future concert programs so as not to antagonize those among its patrons who prefer approved music of a melodious nature.

### 6 SEPTEMBER 1932

Two short operatic works are performed for the first time at the Fifth Music Festival in Venice: *La Favola di Orfeo*, in one act, by Alfredo CASELLA, a classically proportioned score in a homophonic monochrome, to the mythological play by Poliziano, first produced with incidental music at the ducal court of Mantua on 18 July 1472; and *Pantea*, symphonic drama by Gian Francesco MALIPIERO, for a ballerina solo, baritone, chorus and orchestra.

## 8 SEPTEMBER 1932

*Golem*, orchestral suite by Joseph ACHRON, in which the last movement is the exact reversal of the first movement, note by note, and in the same orchestration, symbolizing the making and the destruction of the Golem, the mechanical monster of the medieval Jewish legend, is performed for the first time anywhere in Venice, Fritz Reiner conducting.

## 12 SEPTEMBER 1932

*Bachianas Brasileiras No. 1*, scored for an orchestra of violoncellos by Heitor VILLA-LOBOS, the first of his nine works in which Brazilian thematics are subjected to Bachian treatment, in three movements with classical titles (*Prelude, Aria* and *Fugue*) and Brazilian subtitles (*Embolada, Modinha* and *Conversa*), is performed for the first time by the Philharmonic Orchestra of Rio de Janeiro, conducted by Burle Marx, to whom the work is dedicated. (Villa-Lobos conducted the work in Rio de Janeiro ten days later on 22 September 1932)

## 15 SEPTEMBER 1932

*Paris*, a suite for chamber orchestra by Jacques IBERT arranged from his incidental music to *Donogoo*, a play by Jules Romains, is performed for the first time in Venice.

## 25 SEPTEMBER 1932

*Romanticismo*, opera in three acts by the 48-year-old Italian composer Iginio ROBBIANI, the first part of his "Trittico lirico italiano," is performed for the first time in concert form, on the Italian Radio. (The first stage performance took place in Venice on 10 January 1933)

## 29 SEPTEMBER 1932

Leo Blech conducts in Dresden the posthumous first performance of an unfinished opera by Eugen D'ALBERT, *Mister Wu* (in Blech's own completed version), dealing with a vengeful mandarin who beheads his own daughter when she admits having been innocently dishonored by an Englishman, and then kidnaps the seducer's mother to wreak a corresponding abuse on her in retaliation, his plot failing when she puts poison into his tea, set to vapidly romantic music scented with pentatonic themes and sprinkled with a Chinese shower of gong sonorities.

## 10 OCTOBER 1932

*Quartet for Strings and Orchestra* by Bohuslav MARTINU, scored for the string quartet as a quadruple soloist with orchestra, in three movements, in a luminously lyrical mood, is performed for the first time anywhere as a commissioned work in London by the Pro Arte String Quartet with the London Philharmonic, Malcolm Sargent conducting.

### 10 OCTOBER 1932

*Symphonie Concertante (Fourth Symphony)* by Karol SZYMANOWSKI, for piano and orchestra, in three movements, *Moderato, Andante molto sostenuto* and *Allegro non troppo*, with thematic materials derived from Polish songs and dances of the Tatra Mountains region, treated in asymmetric rhythms and accoutred in bitonal harmonies, is performed for the first time in Poznan, Gregor Fitelberg conducting, with Szymanowski as soloist.

### 21 OCTOBER 1932

John Alden CARPENTER plays the piano part in the first performance by the Boston Symphony Orchestra, Serge Koussevitzky conducting, of his *Patterns* for piano and orchestra, in one movement of eclectic hedonism, comprising waltzes, jazzy discursions and bits of Spanish dances.

### 23 OCTOBER 1932

Wilhelm Hintze, the banker husband of the 38-year-old Wagnerian soprano Gertrud BINDERNAGEL, exasperated by true and false reports of her systematic infidelities, shoots her fatally in the kidney at the Charlottenburg Opera House in Berlin after a performance of *Siegfried*, in which she sang the part of Brünnhilde. (She died of her wounds on 3 November 1932)

### 28 OCTOBER 1932

At a radio concert in Berlin, Igor STRAVINSKY plays the piano part, with Samuel Dushkin as violinist, in the first performance of his *Duo Concertant* (completed on 15 July 1932), in five movements in the decorative style of the French Rococo, inspired by the classical serenity of ancient bucolic poetry.

### 29 OCTOBER 1932

*Der Schmied von Gent*, fairy opera in three acts by Franz SCHREKER, to his own libretto dealing with a Ghent blacksmith who sells his soul to the devil to save himself from political persecution by the Spanish authorities of the Netherlands in the late Middle Ages, but refuses to carry out his bargain and instead opens a restaurant at the heavenly gates, ingratiating himself by his culinary art with St. Peter and the Holy Family, until he is finally granted admission to Heaven, is produced in Berlin.

### 31 OCTOBER 1932

Sergei PROKOFIEV appears as soloist with the Berlin Philharmonic under the direction of Wilhelm Furtwängler, in the world première of his *Fifth Piano Concerto* in G major, in five movements: *Allegro con brio, Moderato ben ac-*

*centuato, Allegro con fuoco (Toccata), Larghetto* and *Vivo,* written in a classically modernistic manner saturated with euphonious discords in a grand manner of percussive virtuosity alternating with passages permeated by lyric
irony.

1 NOVEMBER 1932

Charles MUNCH (original spelling, Münch), Alsatian-born violinist, makes his
first appearance as conductor in Paris at the unusually advanced age of forty-
one.

3 NOVEMBER 1932

*Un Jardin sur l'Oronte,* lyric drama in four acts by the French composer Alfred BACHELET, after a melodramatic novel by Maurice Barrès, in which a devout Christian crusader is ensorceled by a sultry sultana and dies entrammeled in her arms in a garden on the Syrian river Oronto, under siege by his
former comrades-in-arms, is produced at the Paris Opéra.

6 NOVEMBER 1932

*Symphonie* by the 20-year-old French composer Jean FRANÇAIX, in four
movements, written in a neo-Rococo "style galant" seasoned with melodic
angularities, harmonic asperities and rhythmic asymmetries, is performed for
the first time by the Orchestre Symphonique de Paris, Pierre Monteux conducting, with two interruptions by booing and hissing conscientious objectors
to dissonant counterpoint, using housekeys as resonators, and causing Monteux to plead with them for the freedom of modernistic musical expression.

7 NOVEMBER 1932

*The Flames of Paris,* ballet in four acts by the Russian musicologist and composer Boris ASAFIEV, to a scenario from the French Revolution, focused on a
dramatic episode wherein an obsolete Marquis is slain by the brother of a
peasant girl whose virtue he tried to corrupt, with topical quotations from the
*Marseillaise, La Carmagnole* and other popular songs of the time, is produced
in Leningrad, on the 15th anniversary of the Soviet Revolution.

8 NOVEMBER 1932

*Music in the Air,* musical comedy by Jerome KERN, featuring a turbulent romance between a Bavarian music master and an aspiring comic opera songstress, is produced in New York.

9 NOVEMBER 1932

*First Symphony,* in C-sharp minor, by Dmitri KABALEVSKY, originally conceived as a historical cantata representing the contrast between Tsarist and
Soviet Russia, but ultimately crystallized as an instrumental work in two
parts, the somberly oppressed tone picture of "the crown and the knout"

(*Andante molto sostenuto*) and the optimistic *Allegro molto agitato,* symbolizing the struggle for freedom and better life, with a ballad about Lenin forming a finale, is performed for the first time in Moscow.

### 9 NOVEMBER 1932

*Concerto* for string quartet and wind instruments by the 38-year-old Czech composer Erwin SCHULHOFF, in three movements, *Allegro moderato, Largo,* and *Allegro con brio,* composed in the manner of a Baroque concerto grosso, with a vitalizing intrusion of fugal jazzification, is performed for the first time in Prague.

### 19 NOVEMBER 1932

*Lidé z Pokerflatu* (*The Outcasts of Poker Flat*), opera in five acts by Jaromir WEINBERGER, after the Californian tale of adventure and love by Bret Harte, with local color introduced in the form of old-fashioned American dance rhythms, is produced in Brno.

### 24 NOVEMBER 1932

*Resan till Amerika* (*The Journey to America*), comic opera by the Swedish composer Hilding ROSENBERG, is produced in Stockholm.

### 25 NOVEMBER 1932

On his first and only American tour, Florent SCHMITT appears as pianist, playing the solo part in the first performance of his *Symphonie Concertante* for piano and orchestra, with the Boston Symphony Orchestra, Serge Koussevitzky conducting, as a commissioned work on its 50th anniversary, written in a highly congested polyphonic idiom in three contrasted movements:

(1) *Assez animé,* a polyharmonic essay in modernity, with the major seventh as the thematic interval (2) *Lent,* in a pensively elegiac mood, gaining momentum in a series of pianistically varied scale passages (3) *Animé,* with an energetic fugato containing quasi-improvisatory trilled cadenzas in asymmetrical meters, gravitating towards the tonal barycenter of G.

### 28 NOVEMBER 1932

Three centuries have elapsed since the birth of Jean-Baptise LULLY, the Florentine master of French ballet and opera.

(*Notice historique* in the authorized edition of Lully's complete works states erroneously that Lully was born on Monday, 29 November 1632, at 9 o'clock in the morning, which was the day and hour of Lully's baptism. He was born on the day before, 28 November 1632, at 4 o'clock in the afternoon, as testified by the following document obtained by the author from the registries of the births and baptisms in Florence: "L'anno 1632 a dì 29 del mese di Novembre è stato battezzato Gio. Battista di Lorenzo di Nalolo Lulli e di Caterina di Gabriello del Sera. Nato il dì 28 Novembre 1632 a ore 16:30 nel popolo di St. Lucia sul Prato." All new editions of music dictionaries have amended the date accordingly after the publication of Lully's birth certificate by Nicolas Slonimsky in *Le Guide Musical,* Paris, 1 February 1952)

556

## 29 NOVEMBER 1932

Two days after the 65th birthday of the venerably bearded, orally admired but seldom performed French master of modern composition, Charles KOECHLIN, a concert of his music is given by the Orchestre Symphonique de Paris, under the direction of Roger Desormière, in a program containing first performances of his *Trois Poèmes du Livre de la Jungle,* for voices and orchestra, composed in 1899–1910, inspired by Rudyard Kipling's *Jungle Book, Cinq Chorals dans les modes du moyen-âge* and *Fugue symphonique,* both written in 1932.

## 29 NOVEMBER 1932

*The Gay Divorcee,* a musical comedy by Cole PORTER, in which a divorce-bound actress enters a collusion with a professional corespondent who falls in love with her after faking a scene of adultery, containing Cole Porter's greatest song *Night and Day,* is produced in New York.

## 7 DECEMBER 1932

*Walk a Little Faster,* a revue by Vernon DUKE (né Vladimir Dukelsky), containing the nostalgic and sinuously sensuous song *April in Paris,* is produced in New York.

## 11 DECEMBER 1932

The English Folk-Dance Society and the Folk Song Society are amalgamated in London under the combined name English Folk-Dance and Song Society.

## 15 DECEMBER 1932

*Il Mistero di Venezia,* trilogy by Gian Francesco MALIPIERO, is produced for the first time in its totality in Coburg, in a German version under the title *Mysterium Venedigs,* comprising the following individual three parts:

*Le Aquile di Aquileia* (completed on 12 May 1928), a music drama in three episodes glorifying the heroic origins of Venice as the home of eagles in their aerie; *Il Finto Arlecchino,* musical comedy in two parts ( completed on 15 December 1925, and first performed separately in a German version in Mainz on 8 March 1928); and *I Corvi di San Marco,* music drama in pantomime without words (completed on 23 December 1928), depicting the decline and fall of Venice's greatness under the symbolic image of the ravens of San Marco Square.

## 16 DECEMBER 1932

TRITON, Paris society dedicated to the propagation of modern chamber music, the name referring both to the sea demigod whose attribute is a trumpet made of a conch shell with which he raises or calms the waves, and to the interval of the augmented fourth, basic to atonal melody and bitonal harmony, presents its first concert comprising the first performances of the *Third String Quartet* by the Hungarian-Parisian composer László LAJTHA, *Sonatine* for violin and cello by Arthur HONEGGER and a *String Quartet* by Albert ROUSSEL, as well as the non-premières of FAURÉ's song cycle *L'Horizon chimérique* and PROKOFIEV's *Sonata* for two violins, in his favorite key of C major, originally performed in Moscow on 27 November 1932.

(The *Triton* concerts continued for seven seasons, until World War II stopped them. Complete programs of all concerts are reproduced in Claude Rostand's *L'œuvre de Pierre-Octave Ferroud*—who was one of the founders of *Triton*—published in Paris in the form of a catalogue in 1957)

### 16 DECEMBER 1932

*Sur le Borysthène,* ballet by Sergei PROKOFIEV, to a love story on the banks of the Dnieper (Borysthène is the old Greek name of the river inserted because no Frenchman could pronounce its Slavic name Dnyepr), wherein a soldier wins back his beloved after a fight at her wedding with another, is produced unsuccessfully by the choreographer Serge Lifar at the Paris Opéra.

(Prokofiev sued Lifar to collect the remaining sum of 30,000 francs out of the total fee of 100,000 francs for the composition and exclusive rights, when the latter refused to pay it claiming that the music was inferior and that the production failed because of this, and on 5 January 1937 won his suit, the Paris court ruling that "any person acquiring a musical work puts faith in the composer's talent, since there is no dependable criterion for the evaluation of the quality of a work of art, which is received according to individual tastes, history teaching us that the public is often mistaken")

### 17 DECEMBER 1932

Ten Italian composers, two of them eminent, Ottorino RESPIGHI, Giuseppe MULÈ, Ildebrando PIZZETTI, Riccardo ZANDONAI, Alberto GASCO, Alceo TONI, Riccardo PICK-MANGIAGALLI, Guido GUERRINI, Gennaro NAPOLI and Guido ZUFFENATO issue a manifesto deploring the cerebrality of modern music.

We take the stand against this art which cannot have and does not possess any human content and tends to be only a mechanical experiment and a cerebral conundrum. In the musical world today there reigns the biblical Babel. For twenty years the most diverse and disparate trends have been consolidated in an uninterrupted revolutionary chaos. . . . A logical connection must bind the past with the future, and the romanticism of yesterday must become the romanticism of tomorrow. (From the manifesto, as quoted in the New York *Times* of 7 January 1933)

### 28 DECEMBER 1932

The United States District Court in New York City rules that George GERSHWIN's musical comedy *Of Thee I Sing* does not infringe on the copyright issued on 17 February 1930 to the authors of the musical revue *U.S.A. With Music,* and that the similarity in the political plot between them is purely coincidental and in no way constitutes an act of plagiarism.

### 29 DECEMBER 1932

Two children's operas by the Czech composer Jaroslav KŘIČKA, *Tlustý Pradědeček (Fat Great-Grandfather)* and *Lupici a Detektyvove (Robbers and Detectives),* are performed for the first time in Prague.

# ∿ *1933* ∿

6 JANUARY 1933

Vladimir de PACHMANN, eccentric Russian pianist, who charmed world audiences by his poetic renditions of Chopin and stormy interpretations of Beethoven, and unnerved them by looking for wrong notes under the piano, applauding himself, or grimacing (James Gibbons Huneker called him Chopinzee), dies in Rome at the age of eighty-four.

7 JANUARY 1933

*The Emperor Jones,* opera in two acts with a prologue and an interlude by Louis GRUENBERG, to his own libretto after Eugene O'Neill's play, centered on a former Pullman porter wanted for murder during a dice game who becomes an imperial potentate on a Caribbean island but is forced to flee into the jungle as his people rebel against his rule, and sends a magical silver bullet into his heart when the cumulative crescendo of voodooistic drums leaves him no escape, with a highly dissonant but basically homophonic setting, is produced at the Metropolitan Opera House in New York.

The Emperor Jones Triumphs as Opera—World Première of Gruenberg's Version of O'Neill's Play Hailed at Metropolitan—Drama Swift, Tense, Emotional, with Fantastical Music, and Spectacular Finale (Headlines in the New York *Times,* 8 January 1933)

16 JANUARY 1933

*Eleventh Symphony* by Nicolai MIASKOVSKY, completed on 19 March 1932, in three movements: (1) *Lento-Allegro agitato* (2) *Andante-Adagio* (3) *Precipitato-Allegro,* set in the "Russian" key of E minor, alternating with its tritonal apotone, B-flat minor, thus producing an intermittent rotatory polarization in the modulatory scheme conjuring up a sense of ineffable melancholy, but reaching a more optimistic relationship of major modes in the finale, is performed for the first time in Moscow.

19 JANUARY 1933

Rudolf GANZ conducts the Detroit Symphony Orchestra in the first performance of his symphonic suite, *Animal Pictures,* with onomatopoeic zoological effects in the orchestra.

29 JANUARY 1933

*First Symphony* by the French composer Jean RIVIER, in three movements, with an impetuously energetic finale, is performed for the first time by the Orchestre Symphonique de Paris under the direction of Pierre Monteux.

## 1 FEBRUARY 1933

*Piano Concerto* in C major by Ralph VAUGHAN WILLIAMS, in four movements: (1) *Toccata*, in 7/8 time, a kinesthetic essay in a free rhapsodic vein, containing a luxuriantly arpeggiated cadenza (2) *Romanza*, set in a serenely monodic idiom, in which a central tone effloresces into a songful instrumental arioso (3) *Fuga cromatica*, based on an involuted chromatic subject with a clear tonal epicenter (4) *Finale alla tedesca*, a rhythmic German dance in rondo form, is performed for the first time in London by the BBC Symphony Orchestra conducted by Sir Adrian Boult, with Harriet Cohen as soloist. (A quotation from the *Third Symphony* by Arnold Bax, incorporated in the *Finale* after a cadenza, as a friendly gesture to an admired colleague, was eliminated after the first performance for reasons of esthetical congruity)

## 3 FEBRUARY 1933

The first performance is given in Brno of *Smrt Kmotřička* (*Godmother Death*), opera in three acts by the Czech composer Rudolf KAREL, wherein a fecund musician invites Death to be godmother of his thirteenth child, a boy, to promote his career as a doctor by her infallible medical prognosis (she would stand at the patient's feet as a signal of recovery, and at the head if the disease is fatal), who circumvents the scheme when Death takes the stand at the head of the sick girl he loves by turning the bed around.

## 5 FEBRUARY 1933

Alexander TCHEREPNIN plays in Paris the piano part in the first performance of his *Third Piano Concerto* in three movements, with the principal motive derived from a song of Egyptian oarsmen on the Nile and other motives inspired by Eurasian chants, while the fugue in the second movement is derived from Tcherepnin's own technique of Interpunctus, in which coupled voices enter the intussusception between two other voices placed at extreme registers so as to avoid overlapping.

## 5 FEBRUARY 1933

*Vocero,* symphonic poem by the 31-year-old Corsican composer Henri TOMASI, depicting a professional mourner who intones a vociferous *vocero* at the funeral of a vendetta victim, is performed for the first time in Paris under the composer's direction.

## 11 FEBRUARY 1933

*Il Galante tiratore,* "choreographic action" by the 32-year-old Italian composer Antonio VERETTI, is performed for the first time in San Remo.

## 11 FEBRUARY 1933

*Rossknecht,* one-act opera by the 27-year-old German composer Winfried ZILLIG, dealing with a hippophilic maniac who murders a tractor dealer to deter him from undermining the rural rule of horsepower by machinery, set to a constructivistically satirical musical score, is produced for the first time in Düsseldorf.

## 12 FEBRUARY 1933

Lev KNIPPER conducts in Moscow the first performance of his *Third Symphony* for orchestra, chorus and military band, written in a socialistically optimistic mood, mostly in major keys, with thematic elements partly derived from Siberian folksongs, and patriotically dedicated to the Soviet Army of the Far East having continuous skirmishes on the Manchurian frontier with the encroaching Japanese.

## 12 FEBRUARY 1933

Henri DUPARC, French composer of pre-impressionistic songs of historic interest since they represent the earliest examples of a truly symphonic treatment of piano parts, dies in Paris at the age of 85, nearly half a century after he stopped composing any music.

## 12 FEBRUARY 1933

*Le Tombeau resplendissant,* a thanatological symphonic poem by Olivier MESSIAEN, is performed for the first time in Paris.

## 16 FEBRUARY 1933

*Grazina,* opera in four acts by the Lithuanian composer Jurgio KARNEVICIUS, with the action focused on the 15th-century Lithuanian queen who dons the armor of her effeminate husband to fight the German Knights, falls in battle and is cremated on a solemn pyre, to a musical score replete with folk refrains, is produced in Kaunas on the occasion of the 15th anniversary of the independence of Lithuania.

## 17 FEBRUARY 1933

At a concert of modern music in Vienna, a man in the fifth row who shouted after the performance of a work by Josef Matthias HAUER, "Das ist Musik! Pfui Mozart!," is promptly arrested for interfering with a public function and disturbing the peace.

## 21 FEBRUARY 1933

*La Berceuse,* ballet by Riccardo PICK-MANGIAGALLI, to a story from the time of Louis XV, in which a handsome marchioness plays an adulterous practical joke on her somnolent husband (hence the sly title), is performed for the first time in San Remo.

## 22 FEBRUARY 1933

*La Farsa amorosa,* opera in three acts, five scenes and three comic interludes by Riccardo ZANDONAI, to the Spanish tale by Alarcón dealing with a town official who wears a three-cornered hat as a symbol of authority, indulges in an unsuccessful attempt to seduce a miller's wife and misplaces his evidential hat in the process, is performed for the first time in Rome.

## 23 FEBRUARY 1933

The first issue of the monthly *Sovietskaya Musica,* serving not only professional interests but helping to build the ideological foundations of Soviet music, examining, dissecting and interpreting every quiddity and every haecceity of the dogma and the pragma of Socialist Realism to provide correct guidance to Soviet composers, theorists and historians, swerving neither to the left in the direction of the discredited and abolished Russian Association of Proletarian Musicians, nor to the right of the Western orientation with its tantalizing decadence and ultimate laissez-faire, is published in Moscow under the dateline January-February 1933. (Date of the actual release)

Our periodical starts publication at a time of extraordinary significance. Our Soviet land, under the guidance of the Party, its Central Committee, and the leader of the world proletariat Comrade Stalin, has completed the first 5-year plan in 4 years, and is now entering its second 5-year plan. . . . We will fight relentlessly against the danger of the rightist interpretation of the decree of 23 April 1932 in the sense that the Central Committee has "amnestied" all bourgeois idealistic theories. Under the pretense of studying Western European techniques, the rightist musicians are trying to smuggle in the ideological baggage of the rotting bourgeois world, "atonalities," jazz harmonies, etc. . . . But with equal determination our periodical will fight "leftist" distortions of Marxism-Leninism, vulgarization and pseudo-simplification, which was the practice and theory of the now liquidated Russian Association of Proletarian Musicians. (From an editorial statement of aims published in the first issue of *Sovietskaya Musica*)

## 2 MARCH 1933

At a concert of works by Lev KNIPPER, given at the Moscow Conservatory, his *Fourth Symphony,* subtitled *Four Etudes for Orchestra: Improvisation, March, Aria, Finale,* is performed for the first time.

(Knipper subsequently destroyed the manuscript of the *Fourth Symphony,* and wrote a new symphony, *Ballad About a Komsomol Fighter,* designating it as his Fourth; it is in that new *Fourth Symphony,* first performed on the Moscow Radio on 23 February 1934, that the famous song *Polyushko-Polye (Meadowland)* appears in the choral finale)

## 5 MARCH 1933

*Violin Concerto* by Gian Francesco MALIPIERO, completed on 10 March 1932, in three movements, in which "rhetorical virtuosity is avoided like a contagious disease," technically based on pandiatonic concepts, in which the seven notes of the heptatonic scale are superimposed freely over a functional bass (thus the opening chordal complex is C-G-E-A-D-G-B, with the semantical value of a C-major triad), is performed for the first time in Amsterdam, Viola Mitchell soloist, Pierre Monteux leading the Concertgebouw Orchestra.

## 6 MARCH 1933

*Ionisation,* epoch-making work by Edgar VARÈSE, scored for instruments of percussion, friction and sibilation, all of indeterminate pitch (kettledrums being excluded), completed by him on 13 November 1931 in Paris and portraying in a recognizably classical sonata form the process of atomic change as electrons are liberated and molecules are ionized, the main subject suggesting a cosmic-ray bombardment introduced by an extra-terrestrial rhythmic figure on the tambour militaire while two sirens slide in contrary motion over the whole spectrum of audible frequencies, much in the manner of harp glissando, the second subject, of an ominously lyrical nature, reflecting in palpitating rhythms the asymmetrical interference pattern of heterodyne frequencies, the development section being marked by the appearance of heavy nuclear particles in the metal group (anvils, gongs, tamtams), as contrasted with the penetrating but light wood-and-membrane sonorities of the exposition, and after an artfully abridged recapitulation arriving at a magistral coda, with tubular chimes ringing as new atomic polymers are created and the residual thermal energy of vigorous tone-clusters on the piano keyboard serving as a cadential ostinato, is performed for the first time anywhere at a concert of the Pan American Association of Composers in New York, with Nicolas Slonimsky (to whom the score of *Ionisation* was eventually dedicated) conducting an ensemble of fourteen professional composers and innate rhythmicians manning 41 multifarious instruments, among them Carlos Salzedo playing the Chinese blocks, Henry Cowell pounding the tone-clusters on the piano, Paul Creston striking the gongs and William Schuman pulling the cord of the lion's roar.

### 7 MARCH 1933

*Lili Spiewać*, comic opera in three acts by the Polish composer Ludomir RóZICKI, is produced in Poznan.

### 11 MARCH 1933

*Rapsodia sinfónica* for piano and string orchestra by the Spanish composer Joaquín TURINA, discursively ambling through sonorous passes and impasses of Mediterranean melorhythms, with whole-tone scales floating in a plasma of impressionistic harmonies, is performed for the first time in Madrid.

### 11 MARCH 1933

Carl EBERT, director of the Berlin Municipal Opera, and Fritz STIEDRY, its conductor, are summarily removed from their posts by the Ministry of Propaganda of the Nazi Government as non-Aryans.

### 12 MARCH 1933

Cemal Reşid REY, 28-year-old Turkish composer, plays the solo part of his Concerto chromatique for piano and orchestra, with the Orchestre Symphonique de Paris, Dmitri Mitropoulos conducting.

### 15 MARCH 1933

The Berlin Radio issues an absolute ban on broadcasting of "Negro Jazz."

## 16 MARCH 1933

The municipal authorities in Leipzig cancel a scheduled symphony concert under the direction of Bruno WALTER, on the grounds that the appearance of a Jew on the podium might create public disturbances.

## 17 MARCH 1933

*Die Hochzeit der Sobeide,* opera in three acts by the 34-year-old Russian composer Alexander TCHEREPNIN, to the play by Hugo von Hofmannstahl, wherein the beautiful Sobeide, married to an elderly merchant, elopes with a virile youth, and in the despondence of guilty feeling jumps from the garden tower, expiring in her loving husband's arms, set to music thematically derived from Tcherepnin's favorite scale of nine notes, with dramatic points marked by tolerable dissonance, is produced in Vienna.

## 25 MARCH 1933

*Guido del Popolo,* a megadramatic lyric tragedy in four acts by the 48-year-old Italian composer Iginio ROBBIANI, a second part of his "Trittico lirico italiano," to his own libretto from the times of medieval strife in Italy, is produced at La Scala, in Milan.

## 27 MARCH 1933

*Mouvement symphonique No. 3* by Arthur HONEGGER, significantly lacking a programmatic subtitle (its predecessors were the pointedly illustrative *Pacific 231* and *Rugby*), signalizing his transition from programmatic to absolute music, is performed for the first time anywhere by the Berlin Philharmonic, Wilhelm Furtwängler conducting.

## 1 APRIL 1933

Arturo TOSCANINI, Walter DAMROSCH, Frank DAMROSCH, Serge KOUSSEVITZKY, Arthur BODANZKY, Alfred HERTZ, Fritz REINER, Ossip GABRILOWITSCH, Harold BAUER, Charles Martin LOEFFLER and Rubin GOLDMARK dispatch the following cable to Adolf Hitler, newly elevated chancellor of Germany, urging him to cease racial persecution:

The undersigned artists who live and execute their art in the United States of America feel the moral obligation to appeal to your Excellency to put a stop to the persecution of their colleagues in Germany for political or religious reasons. We beg you to consider that the artist all over the world is estimated for his talent alone and not for his national or religious convictions. . . . We are convinced that such persecutions as take place in Germany at present are not based on your instructions, and that it cannot possibly be your desire to damage the high cultural esteem Germany, until now, has been enjoying in the eyes of the whole civilized world. Hoping that our appeal in behalf of our colleagues will not be allowed to pass unheard, we are, respectfully yours, etc. (signatures follow)

I am not enchanted over the idea of addressing as "your Excellency" a man for whom I have not the slightest respect, nor do I think it quite truthful to say, "We are convinced that such persecutions as take place in Germany at present are not based on your instructions," whereas in reality I am thoroughly convinced that Hitler is personally responsible for all that is going on in Germany at the present time. I also want to make it clear that I am not in the least bit afraid to add my signature. (From a letter by Ossip Gabrilowitsch, New York *Times*, 2 April 1933)

2 APRIL 1933

*Kaa*, symphonic poem by the 60-year-old French composer André BLOCH, portraying the sly serpent of Kipling's *Jungle Book* in a sinuously undulating saxophone solo and the threatened monkeys by nervous jazz rhythms, is performed for the first time in Paris.

4 APRIL 1933

The Nazi director of the Berlin Radio issues the following order in connection with the protest of American musicians against the racial German policies:

According to newspaper reports, several conductors and musicians in the United States have lodged a complaint with the Chancellor because of the rejection of certain Jewish and Marxist fellow-musicians in Germany. . . . Pending clarification of this matter I direct that the compositions and recordings of these gentlemen shall no longer find a place on the programs of German broadcasting stations and that no musical performance in which they have a part in any capacity shall be transmitted from concert halls.

6 APRIL 1933

*Inni (Hymns)*, symphonic piece by Gian Francesco MALIPIERO, completed on 14 May 1932, marking his turn from rhetorical romanticism towards a linear style of absolute music in a classical Italian manner, is performed for the first time in Rome.

9 APRIL 1933

Sigfrid KARG-ELERT, German organist and composer of versatile pieces, some touched with un-German impressionistic colors (his real name was simply Karg, but he added the hyphenated second name to dispel the unpleasant connotations of the word which suggests covetousness and avidity), dies in Leipzig at the age of fifty-five.

10 APRIL 1933

Dr. Goebbels, Nazi Minister of Propaganda, rejects the appeal by Wilhelm Furtwängler, conductor of the Berlin Philharmonic, not to exclude Jewish musicians and artists, specifically Max Reinhardt, Otto Klemperer and Bruno Walter, from German cultural life.

12 APRIL 1933

*Second Violin Concerto* by Mario CASTELNUOVO-TEDESCO, subtitled *The Prophets*, in three movements that purport to give musical characterizations of Isaiah, Jeremiah and Elijah, is performed for the first time by Jascha Heifetz and the New York Philharmonic under the direction of Arturo Toscanini.

## 24 APRIL 1933

*Momus,* symphonic scherzo by the Brazilian composer Francisco MIGNONE, depicting a Brazilian carnival character Momus named after the Greek god of satire, and abounding in typical rhythms of Brazilian dances, is performed for the first time in Rio de Janeiro, Villa-Lobos conducting.

## 27 APRIL 1933

At the initiative of the International Music Bureau, the Moscow Radio presents its first broadcast dedicated to the international revolutionary musical movement, with a program consisting of two works by the Hungarian Communist composer Ferenc SZABÓ: a symphonic poem significantly entitled *Class Struggle,* and a chorus a cappella, *November Seventh,* the day of the Soviet Revolution according to the Western calendar.

## 27 APRIL 1933

*Jeunesse,* ballet by Pierre-Octave FERROUD, wherein amorous young men meet casual young girls in bars and dancing halls in a Riviera resort, uniting after initial comedies of error in recognition, set to easily choreographable music with a touch of dissonant sophistication, is produced at the Paris Opéra.

## 2 MAY 1933

*Bootleggers,* satirical operetta by Manuel ROSENTHAL, to a story from the period of American Prohibition, in which a group of thespian bootleggers organize a theatrical company in Canada to import liquor into the dry United States, is performed for the first time in Paris.

## 5 MAY 1933

*La Guiablesse,* ballet by William Grant STILL, with the action taking place on the island of Martinique, in which the demoniac guiablesse (meaning she-devil in local patois) lures a young lover away from his beloved and frightens him to death in the mountain abyss when she reverts to her original hideous exterior, to a score based on authentic Creole refrains of the West Indies, is performed for the first time in Rochester, New York.

## 7 MAY 1933

A century has elapsed since the birth in Hamburg of Johannes BRAHMS, the epigonic genius of German classical music, the third B of the trinity Bach, Beethoven, Brahms, as nominated by his staunch admirer Hans von Bülow (the B's in Bülow's canonized witticism referred not to the second letter of the alphabet, but to the colloquial German designation for a flat; in his opin-

ion, Bülow said, the greatest work was the *Eroica* Symphony with its three
B's—*Be'en*—in the key signature, for Bach, Beethoven and Brahms)

11 MAY 1933

*Symphony* by Yuri SHAPORIN, in four movements with chorus, portraying the
confrontation of a human being with the demands of a great social upheaval:
(1) *The Past*, a non-lamenting recollection of obsolete society and the implantation of the revolutionary seed in the form of the popular song, "Little
Apple, where are you going? If you go too far, you will never come back,"
treated in tragic tones (2) *Dance*, a realistic festival of latent dynamism of the
people (3) *Lullaby*, representing the eternally feminine aspect of life (4)
*March*, symbolizing the revolution as energy transformed into action, is performed for the first time in Moscow.

18 MAY 1933

*Verlobung im Traum*, opera by the Czech composer Hans KRÁSA, after Dostoyevsky's short story *Uncle's Dream*, is performed for the first time in a German version in Prague.

25 MAY 1933

*The Three Little Pigs*, famous "Silly Symphony" of a series of cinematic animated cartoons created by Walt DISNEY, containing the greatly popular song
"Who's Afraid of the Big Bad Wolf?" is shown for the first time in New York.

26 MAY 1933

*The Fugitive*, opera in four acts by the Soviet composer Nicolai STRELNIKOV,
after Leo Tolstoy's short story *What For?* depicting the escape of a political
prisoner from Siberia in 1830, is performed for the first time in Leningrad.

30 MAY 1933

Arnold SCHOENBERG and Franz SCHREKER are dismissed from the faculty of
the Prussian Academy of Arts in Berlin, as unfit to teach music in Nazi Germany.

31 MAY 1933

Twenty-nine American composers band together in a Composers' Protective
Society and issue a militant statement protesting against the inferior social position in which composers in America find themselves vis-a-vis conductors and
instrumentalists, citing the following obstacles in the path to a better future:

(1) The attitude which has reduced the composer to a minor position in the modern
musical world (2) The usurpation of the dominant position in modern musical life by
interpreters—instrumentalists, singers, conductors (3) The consequently unhealthy atmosphere for the nurturing of new music—the apathy of the public, the limitations of
the press, the lack of organized encouragement of new music (4) The concentration of

power in the hands of an average conductor, a self-confessed autocrat at whose mercy the average composer invariably is (5) The exaggerated attention bestowed upon a new reading of a familiar masterpiece, as compared with the grudging, inadequate notice of a new work (6) The operation of petty prejudices in directorial circles and nationalistic loyalties on the part of conductors, resulting frequently in the performance of inferior works which reflect discredit on the whole of modern music (7) The familiar practice of conductors and virtuosi in making up their season's repertoire while abroad during the summer months, with the result that the American composer is deprived of the opportunity of acquainting the public with his works via the programs of these artists who provide the bulk of our musical activity during the winter (8) The lack of opportunity for the composer (unless he is also an interpreter) to earn a living through the serious pursuit of his profession (9) The paucity of informed discussion of new works in the periodical press as compared with the attention devoted to new literature and painting. (New York *Times*, 1 June 1933)

### 5 JUNE 1933

Arturo TOSCANINI cancels his engagement to conduct at the Bayreuth Festival as a protest against Nazi persecution of Jewish musicians.

### 9 JUNE 1933

The 11th Festival of the International Society for Contemporary Music opens in Amsterdam with the following program of orchestral works:

*Symphonic Suite* by the 32-year-old Alsatian composer Leo Justinus KAUFFMANN, written in a neo-Baroque manner; *15 Variations* for strings by the 35-year-old Polish composer Josef KOFFLER, derived from a governing 12-tone series; *Piano Concerto* by the 29-year-old Hungarian neo-romanticist Paul KADOSA, set in a propulsively percussive manner, consanguineous with the music of Béla Bartók, with Kadosa at the piano; *First Symphony* by the Dutch composer Guillaume LANDRÉ, composed along neo-Flemish polyphonic lines; and a *Symphonic Suite* by the Czech composer František BARTÓŠ.

### 10 JUNE 1933

In the course of the 11th Festival of the International Society for Contemporary Music in Amsterdam, the Catalan composer Roberto GERHARD conducts the following program of choral and orchestral music:

GERHARD's own *Passacaglia and Chorale*, from his cantata derived thematically from a 14-note figure which serves alternatively as a cantus firmus or an ostinato; *Pater Noster* for chorus a cappella by Jean CARTAN, French composer who died young the year before; and *Belshazzar's Feast*, powerful neo-Handelian cantata by William WALTON.

### 11 JUNE 1933

At the 11th Festival of the International Society for Contemporary Music in Amsterdam a concert of choral music a cappella by Dutch composers is given, including works by the great polyphonists of the Renaissance, Obrecht, Orlando Lasso, Jan Tollins and Sweelinck, and by modern composers Bernhard van den SIGTENHORST-MEYER, J. N. MUL and Willem PIJPER.

## 12 JUNE 1933

*Die Sieben Todsünden der Kleinbürger* (*The Seven Mortal Sins of the Petty-Bourgeois*), ballet by Kurt WEILL, with song lyrics and spoken dialogue by Bertolt Brecht, depicting an unselfish Louisiana girl who successfully plies her utilitarian profession in order to provide her backwoods family with a decent home but is reviled by petty-bourgeois townspeople for alleged immorality, is performed for the first time in Paris, where both Brecht and Weill fled after Hitler's accession to power in their native Germany.

## 13 JUNE 1933

The world première is given in Amsterdam of *Halewijn,* symphonic drama in nine scenes by the prime Dutch modernist Willem PIJPER, to a libretto in Dutch, dealing with a preternaturally macrophallic and diabolically multi-futuent demigod-like archdemon who is symbolically emasculated by an imperious princess after he refuses to sing his magic song for her except at the price of complete carnal submission, set to music in a coloristically vigesimo-secular style intensified by chromatic torques and transintervalic saltation.

My symphonic drama is not synonymous with music drama. The music is here completely self-contained, with all problems of a psychological, metaphysical or esthetic nature already solved in the music. I would call *Halewijn* a monothematic work. The germinal cell is the principal motive consisting of a perfect fourth containing in it a minor third (F, B-flat, A-flat) and its melodic inversion G, D, E. There are also present some melodies derived from Dutch folksongs. (Willem Pijper, in his article published in *De Telegraaf,* Amsterdam, 11 June 1933)

## 13 JUNE 1933

The 31-year-old French composer Henri TOMASI conducts in Paris the first performance of his orientalistic symphonic poem *Tam-tam.*

## 13 JUNE 1933

At the 11th Festival of the International Society for Contemporary Music in Amsterdam, the following program of symphonic music is given:

*Second Symphony,* a brief work in a pleonastically polyphonic manner by the Dutch composer Bertus VAN LIER; *5 Orchesterstücke,* set in a neo-Baroque manner supercharged with dissonant counterpoint by the 27-year-old German composer Edmund VON BORCK, destined to die in war a decade later; *Concertino* for piano and orchestra by the half-French half-Russian composeress Marcelle DE MANZIARLY, with herself at the piano; *Partita* by the Italian modernist Goffredo PETRASSI, in a neo-classical manner characteristic of the young school of composers in Italy; and *Theme and Variations* for orchestra by the Scottish composer Erik CHISHOLM.

## 15 JUNE 1933

At the last concert of the 11th Festival of the International Society for Contemporary Music in Amsterdam the following program of chamber music is presented:

Tense, terse and sparse *Piano Variations* by Aaron COPLAND; *Sonatina* for flute and clarinet by Juan Carlos PAZ of Buenos Aires; *Sonatina* for clarinet and piano by the Czech neo-romanticist Isa KREJČI; *Lieder* by Ernst KRENEK; *Three Songs* by the modernistically minded American composer Ruth CRAWFORD, to Carl Sandburg's three surrealistic poems: *Rat Riddles* ("*Why do you sneeze on Tuesdays?*" to the accompaniment of a bass drum), *Prayers of Steel* and *Tall Grass*; and a remarkably involute but molecularly coherent *Quintet* for wind instruments by the 24-year-old Croatian girl composer Ljubica MARIĆ.

## 25 JUNE 1933

*L'Envoi d'Icare*, ballet by the 21-year-old Russian-born Parisian composer Igor MARKEVITCH, depicting in cerulean melodies and airy harmonies the fateful flight of Icarus, is performed for the first time in Paris.

## 26 JUNE 1933

*Vercingétorix*, lyric drama in four acts by Joseph CANTELOUBE, poignantly descriptive of the heroic saga of the great Gaul defeated by Caesar and carried off in ignominy to Rome, set to music in austere harmonies, with the application for the first time in an opera of the electronic instrument *Ondes Musicales* to limn the ethereal mysteries of the Druid cult, is produced at the Paris Opéra.

## 1 JULY 1933

*Arabella*, lyric comedy in three acts by Richard STRAUSS, to a libretto by Hugo von Hofmannstahl, with the action taking place in Vienna circa 1860, in which Arabella's sister, dressed in boy's clothes, plays Cupid on Arabella's behalf to a youth and becomes enamored of him herself, the confusion being compounded by Arabella's sudden passion for an exotic Slav, with a finale in which the couples are paired according to their altered tastes, to a lissome musical setting in the waltzingly tuneful manner of *Der Rosenkavalier*, is produced in Dresden.

## 13 JULY 1933

*Columbus*, radio opera by Werner EGK, is produced in Frankfurt. (Its first stage presentation took place in Frankfurt on 13 January 1942)

## 24 JULY 1933

At a ceremony in a Paris synagogue, Arnold SCHOENBERG returns to the Hebrew faith which he abandoned in 1921 when he became converted to Catholicism.

## 24 JULY 1933

Max von SCHILLINGS, German composer whose operas absorbed the Wagneromorphic doctrines of music drama, with features of the Italian Verismo, dies in Berlin at the age of sixty-five.

## 29 JULY 1933

Gerhard SCHJELDERUP, Norwegian composer of romantic operas, symphonic pieces, songs, and instrumental music, competently manufactured in an unadventurous Germanic vein, dies at the age of eighty-three at Benediktbeuren in Bavaria, his home for many years.

## 30 JULY 1933

A Wagner museum is opened at Triebschen, Switzerland, in a villa occupied by Wagner when he wrote *Tristan und Isolde.*

## 13 AUGUST 1933

Paul HILLEMACHER, the older of the two Hillemacher brothers who wrote collective operas under the joint initials P. L. (for Paul and Lucien), dies in Versailles, at the age of eighty, having survived his younger brother by more than 24 years.

## 17 AUGUST 1933

*Godiva,* second opera in three acts by the German composer Ludwig ROSELIUS, depicting in a Wagneromantic manner with an admixture of Straussian melodramatic ecstasies, Pfitznerian austerity and Schrekerian colorism, the legendary naked ride of the medieval British housewife on a propaganda mission against high taxes, is produced in Nuremberg.

## 30 AUGUST 1933

*The School for Scandal,* overture after Sheridan's play by the 23-year-old American composer Samuel BARBER, written in a blithely Baroque manner suitable for the 18th-century subject of the music, is performed for the first time at a summer concert of the Philadelphia Orchestra in Robin Hood Dell.

## 13 SEPTEMBER 1933

In reply to Wilhelm FURTWÄNGLER's invitation to resume his concert appearances in Germany, Bronislaw HUBERMANN sends him a reasoned refusal:

My dear friend, you write that "someone must make a beginning to break down the wall that separates us!" Oh, if it were only a wall in a concert hall! The question is not just of giving violin recitals; it is not a question concerning the Jews as such. No, the issue touches on the elementary pre-conditions of our European culture, of freedom of personal expression regardless of class or race.

## 15 SEPTEMBER 1933

*Kamarinsky Muzhik,* opera by Valery ZHELOBINSKY, dealing with the rebellion of the fugitive serf Bolotnikov against the provisional Tsar Shuisky during the troubled times in Russia in 1607, with mass scenes à la Mussorgsky, and some comic episodes such as a quartet of princes to the accompaniment of four double-basses, is produced in Leningrad.

*Špaliček*, cycle of folksongs, games and enacted fables with miming and dancing for orchestra and women's chorus, by Bohuslav MARTINU, derived principally from Czech melorhythmic patterns and diversified by acrid but invariably tonal harmonies, is performed for the first time in Prague.

28 SEPTEMBER 1933

*In Terra di Leggenda*, opera in three acts by the Italian composer Lodovico ROCCA, wherein a maiden in a legendary land, given in marriage to an overbearing overlord, succumbs to acute anaphrodisia after her youthful lover is caught during their illicit meeting and cruelly put to death, is performed for the first time in concert form, in Milan. (The first stage production of the opera was given in Bergamo on 1 October 1936)

30 SEPTEMBER 1933

*Zwei Herzen im 3/4 Takt*, subtitled *Der verlorene Walzer*, operetta in three acts by the Austrian composer Robert STOLZ, wherein an operetta composer suffers waltzing amnesia when the source of his inspiration, a singer named Fee Florabella, vanishes from his horizon and the production of his operetta is held up until she suddenly reappears, sings the lost waltz, their hearts beat together again in perfect 3/4 time, while the tune is written down by an arranger (the composer being illiterate), and, after a tremendous success of the piece, they are happily united in matrimony, is produced for the first time in Zürich.

30 SEPTEMBER 1933

*As Thousands Cheer*, a topical revue with book by Moss Hart and music by Irving BERLIN, darting slings and arrows at political and social figures of the day, and containing an imperishable song *Easter Parade* (unsuccessfully used by Irving Berlin in 1917 with different words, *Smile and Show Your Dimple*), is produced in New York.

3 OCTOBER 1933

*Idyll* by Frederick DELIUS for soprano, baritone and orchestra, after Walt Whitman ("I once passed through a populous city"), is performed for the first time at the London Promenade Concerts, Sir Henry Wood conducting.

5 OCTOBER 1933

*O mon bel inconnu*, musical comedy in three acts by Reynaldo HAHN, to a libretto by the Paris actor Sacha Guitry, is performed for the first time in Paris.

5 OCTOBER 1933

*Second Symphony* by Henk BADINGS is performed for the first time in Amsterdam.

## 6 OCTOBER 1933

*Second Violin Concerto* by Karol SZYMANOWSKI in one movement embodying varied musical materials, archaically modal, orientalistically chromatic and rhythmically resilient, with fleeting motives appearing, vanishing, and reappearing in assorted instrumental solos, set in the key of A minor but departing from it to the remotest tonalities and bitonalities, and resonantly supported by pedal points, is performed for the first time by Paul Kochanski (to whom the Concerto is dedicated, and who wrote a virtuosistic cadenza for it), with Gregor Fitelberg conducting the Warsaw Philharmonic Orchestra.

## 14 OCTOBER 1933

*Der Kreidekreis,* opera in three acts by Alexander ZEMLINSKY, to his own libretto after a vertistically modernized Chinese tale of a mystical "chalk circle" circumscribing the murderous events in the Manchurian court, to a musical setting in which perfunctory pentatonicisms are presented in quasi-atonal quartal and secundal harmonies, is performed for the first time in Zürich, as a musical drama with spoken dialogue and mimo-plastic interludes.

## 14 OCTOBER 1933

Alexander GLAZUNOV conducts in Paris the first performance of his *Concerto-Ballata* for cello and orchestra, with Maurice Eisenberg as soloist.

## 15 OCTOBER 1933

Twenty days after his 27th birthday, Dmitri SHOSTAKOVICH plays the piano part with the Leningrad Philharmonic in the first performance of his *First Concerto* for piano, solo trumpet and strings, in four contrasting movements: an optimistic *Allegro Moderato,* a meditative *Lento,* a short transitional *Moderato,* and a rollicking *Allegro con brio,* ending endlessly in an unceasing display *(style pompier)* of trumpeted C major.

## 21 OCTOBER 1933

*Let 'em Eat Cake,* a musical comedy by George GERSHWIN, titled after Marie-Antoinette's famous but spurious saying, "Qu'ils mangent de la brioche," when told that her people had no bread (Rousseau quotes a similar remark in his *Confessions* published before the unfortunate Queen of France was born), brought up to date as a sequel to Gershwin's *Of Thee I Sing,* with a proletarian dictatorship established in New York and shaggy revolutionists singing "Down with music by Stravinsky! Down with shows except by Minsky!", is produced in New York.

## 21 OCTOBER 1933

*Madame Liselotte,* opera in three acts by Ottmar GERSTER, dealing, in a melodiously harmonious folklike manner, with the patriotic princess of Pfalz (1652-1721) who marries a brother of Louis XIV but remains German at heart despite her French adhesions, is produced in Essen.

### 23 OCTOBER 1933

*Hermann Göring March*, composed by Horst GERLACH, in the martial key of E-flat major, with a self-complacent *Trio* in A-flat, a grandiose Coda, and a subtitle, *Hakenkreuz stets voran* (*The Swastika ever onward!*), is published in the Third Reich.

### 31 OCTOBER 1933

Arnold SCHOENBERG arrives in the United States, leaving Germany forever.

### 4 NOVEMBER 1933

*Michael Kohlhaas*, opera in three acts by the Danish-born but completely Germanized composer Paul von KLENAU, to his own libretto after Heinrich von Kleist's novel dealing with oppression of common people in medieval Germany, to a musical score of a singularly angular structure, opening with a thematically important 12-tone motto, containing passages of *Sprechstimme*, and concluding in B minor, the favorite key of German romantic composers, is produced in Stuttgart. (A revised version was produced at the Berlin Opera on 7 March 1934)

### 5 NOVEMBER 1933

*Aurora*, opera written in 1811 by the great fabulist E. T. A. HOFFMANN, who was also a fairly competent composer, the manuscript of which was discovered in 1907, is performed for the first time in Bamberg in a slightly refurbished version.

### 12 NOVEMBER 1933

A century has passed since the birth in St. Petersburg of Alexander BORODIN, registered officially as a son of the serf butler named Boroda (The Beard), but in fact the illegitimate son of the 62-year-old Georgian prince Luke Gedeonov and his 25-year-old mistress, a physician's wife named Avdotia Antonova, the child so procreated destined to become one of the Mighty Five of the Russian National School of composition.

### 15 NOVEMBER 1933

A revised version of *Donna Diana*, the best known opera by Emile-Nicolas von REZNIČEK, originally produced in Prague on 16 December 1894, and dealing with a coquettish Spanish damsel playing a double game with a shrewd torero, who finally overcomes her wiles by the simple expedient of exciting her jealousy, is produced in Wuppertal.

### 15 NOVEMBER 1933

The Reichsmusikkammer, affiliated with the German Ministry of Propaganda, is organized in Berlin by Dr. Joseph Goebbels, to supervise the esthetic and racial problems of German music, and the following officers are named: President, Richard STRAUSS; Vice-President, Paul GRAENER; General Music Director, Wilhelm FURTWÄNGLER; members, Fritz STEIN, Gustav HAVEMANN; Secretary, Heinz IHLERT.

(The general Reichskulturkammergesetz, a decree empowering the Ministry of Propaganda to establish six Reich Culture Chambers for literature, press, radio, theater, music and fine arts, was signed by Hitler on 22 September 1933; the provisional Filmkammer for the cinema industry was established on 14 July 1933. The text of the general decree, along with other regulations relating to musical activities in the Third Reich, was contained in *Musikrecht*, compiled by Karl Friedrich Schrieber and Karl Heinz Wachenfeld, and published in Berlin in 1936)

### 15 NOVEMBER 1933

*1929, A Satire*, symphonic sketch by David Stanley SMITH, Dean of the Yale School of Music, depicting with gentle professorial humor the emotions preceding and following the disastrous stock market crash, is performed in New York for the first time.

### 17 NOVEMBER 1933

*Concerto* for piano, violin, cello and orchestra by Alfredo CASELLA is performed for the first time in Berlin.

### 18 NOVEMBER 1933

*Roberta*, musical comedy by Jerome KERN, dealing with an American football player who takes over the management of a Paris dress shop owned by his Aunt Roberta, and falls in love with a model who turns out to be a Russian Princess, featuring the famous ballad *Smoke Gets In Your Eyes*, is produced in New York.

### 20 NOVEMBER 1933

*Värmlandsrhapsodie* for orchestra by Kurt ATTERBERG, based on the folk music of Värmland, the northern region glorified in the novels of Selma Lagerlöf, is performed on the Swedish radio for the first time as a tribute on her 75th birthday.

### 30 NOVEMBER 1933

*Sea-Drift*, symphonic poem after Walt Whitman, by the American industrialist-composer John Alden CARPENTER, is performed for the first time by the Chicago Symphony Orchestra, Frederick Stock conducting.

### 30 NOVEMBER 1933

*Feier der neuen Front*, a cycle of four choral movements a cappella by Richard TRUNK, professor of the Musikhochschule in Cologne, titled *Hitler, Des Führers Wächter, O Land*, and *Horst Wessel*, to the text by the youth leader of the Third Reich, Baldur von Schirach, is performed for the first time in Berlin.

575

A folklike penetrating melos which comes unmistakably from the heart, the working out of specific sonorous materials that is wholly admirable, make this composition of Richard Trunk, written in February and March 1932, a worthy tribute to the Führer and serves as the mirror of his spirit and his deeds. (Arthur Egidi, *Musik im Zeitbewusstsein*, 16 December 1933)

In that turbulent year 1933 many German poets and composers contributed, quite spontaneously, occasional pieces which can be understood only in the light of the political reality of the time. That a weird error was thus committed was realized sooner or later by everyone. (From a letter by Richard Trunk to Fred K. Prieberg, dated 7 November 1961)

### 2 DECEMBER 1933

Maximilian STEINBERG, Russian composer and teacher, son-in-law of Rimsky-Korsakov, conducts the Leningrad Philharmonic in the first performance of his *Fourth Symphony*, surnamed *Truksib*, glorifying in a rhapsodically heroic style the construction of the Turkestan-Siberian railroad.

### 6 DECEMBER 1933

*Münchhausen*, opera in three acts by Mark LOTHAR, depicting the career of the famous liar in a sympathetic light, leaning towards the conclusion that imaginative falsehoods are the essence of great art, set to music in the style of old Italian opera buffa is produced in Dresden.

### 12 DECEMBER 1933

Theodore MOSES-TOBANI, American song writer who wrote the celebrated ballad *Hearts and Flowers* in 1893, which reflects with florid cordiality the sentiments of the era, dies in New York of apoplexy at the age of seventy-eight.

### 15 DECEMBER 1933

Carlos CHÁVEZ, prime composer of Mexico, conducts in Mexico City the first performance of his *Sinfónia de Antígona*, inspired by Greek mythology, but paradoxically redolent of Mexican melorhythms in the framework of austere quasi-Grecian modalities.

### 15 DECEMBER 1933

*Moon Trail*, suite of four symphonic sketches by Emerson WHITHORNE (completed 26 April 1933) depicting in impressionistic colors the western American landscape, is performed for the first time by the Boston Symphony Orchestra, Serge Kousevitzky conducting.

### 16 DECEMBER 1933

*Der Heidenkönig*, opera in three acts by Siegfried WAGNER, dealing with the pagan king of East Prussia during the Polish invasion in the 12th century whose queen, unfaithful with a Christian, is fatally stabbed by her brother-in-law for her un-pagan attitude, with Christianity winning over when a miraculous monk dispels a choreographic pandemonium, is posthumously produced in Cologne, with a musical score marked by harmonic chromaticism and orchestral sonorities characteristic of Wagner-père.

## 31 DECEMBER 1933

An anti-jazz parade is held at Mohall, Ireland, with banners proclaiming "Down with Jazz and Paganism."

# ℒ 1934 ℒ

## 1 JANUARY 1934

The German State Philharmonic Orchestra of the German Soviet Republic of the Volga basin is established by a Soviet decree.

## 6 JANUARY 1934

Ralph VAUGHAN WILLIAMS conducts at the National Folk Dance Festival in London the first performance of his orchestral work, *The Running Set*, based on traditional dance tunes.

## 10 JANUARY 1934

*Le Astuzie di Bertoldo*, opera in three acts by the Italian composer Luigi FERRARI-TRECATE, set in a neo-Baroque manner, modernized by polytonal rococo harmonies, is produced in Genoa.

## 10 JANUARY 1934

*Fourth Symphony* in C major by the 59-year-old Austrian composer Franz SCHMIDT, his last, opening and closing with a pessimistic trumpet solo funereally matted by flatting the supertonic, mediant and submediant, inspired by the death of his only daughter, and therefore also known as *Requiem Symphony*, in four movements—*Allegro molto moderato, Adagio, Molto vivace* and *Poco sostenuto*—unified by an integrated sonatomorphic design in which the first movement is the exposition, the two middle movements represent the development, and the last movement corresponds to the recapitulation, is performed for the first time in Vienna, conducted by Oswald Kabasta, to whom the score is dedicated.

## 12 JANUARY 1934

*First Symphony* by the American composer Emerson WHITHORNE is performed for the first time by the Cincinnati Symphony Orchestra.

## 12 JANUARY 1934

Ernest BLOCH conducts in Turin, Italy, the world première of his *Sacred Service,* in five movements, inspired by the Hebrew cantillation of the old ritual, but set in modern harmonies.

## 13 JANUARY 1934

*La Favola del Figlio Cambiato,* opera in three acts by Gian Francesco MALIPIERO, to Pirandello's play dealing with a dynastic switch wherein a mentally defective heir to the throne is replaced by a normal but non-royal young man, is performed for the first time in Brunswick, Germany, in a German version as *Die Legende vom vertauschten Sohn.*

## 14 JANUARY 1934

George GERSHWIN plays the solo piano part, with the Leo Reisman Orchestra in Boston, in the first performance of his *Variations on "I Got Rhythm"* for piano and orchestra, derived from the song of that name in his revue *Girl Crazy,* and built on a palindromic tetratonic rhythmic figure of four dotted eighth-notes flanked by two eighth-note rests in square time, with variations traversing the entire spectrum of ethnic American expression, from propulsive aggressiveness to poignant melancholy of the Blues.

## 15 JANUARY 1934

*Madrisa,* folk opera in three acts by the Swiss composer Hans HAUG, is performed for the first time in Basel.

## 15 JANUARY 1934

*Fifth Symphony* by Arnold BAX, revealing a selective consanguinity to Sibelius, to whom the score is dedicated, in its tenebrous harmonies and self-generating rhythmic motives, in three romantic movements: (1) *Poco lento,* followed by an ignescent *Allegro con fuoco* vesuviating in an eruption of tonal lava before subsiding into C-sharp minor (2) *Poco lento,* again, a rhapsodically contemplative essay, focused on B-flat minor, containing a whimsical solo of the muted bass tuba, disparting itself in a rude rustic manner (3) *Poco moderato,* in pregnant unisons in strong strings, leading to a dancing *Allegro,* potently exhibiting an array of muscular rhythms, with brass and drums supplying the generative power for polythematically cyclic development until a coda on a plagally approached unison D-flat in fortissimo, is performed for the first time by the London Philharmonic, Sir Thomas Beecham conducting.

## 17 JANUARY 1934

Albert EINSTEIN makes his American debut as a violinist in the New York home of the financier and music patron Adolph Lewisohn, at a private concert for the benefit of Jewish and other scientists in Nazified Berlin, with Einstein playing the second violin in Bach's *Concerto* for two violins and in a Mozart *Quartet.*

## 18 JANUARY 1934

Otakar Ševčík, Czech violinist and pedagogue, compiler of famous manuals of violin playing, who taught some five thousand aspiring violinists in Prague, Vienna, London and New York, dies at the age of 81 in the small Bohemian town of Písek, in retirement from his Herculean labors in cleansing the Augean stables of the four fiddle strings.

## 20 JANUARY 1934

*Giuditta,* operetta by Franz Lehár, dealing with the depredations inflicted by the irresistible titular heroine on male Mediterranean hearts, set to music in a grandiloquently emotional style, is performed for the first time in Vienna.

## 21 JANUARY 1934

To commemorate the tenth anniversary of the death of Vladimir Lenin, *Lenin,* dramatic symphony with narrator and chorus by Vissarion Shebalin, to texts of Vladimir Mayakovsky, opening with a fugal movement symbolizing the cumulative impact of the Revolution, followed by a threnody mourning Lenin's death, and ending with a choral shout "Lenin!", is performed for the first time in Leningrad. (A partial performance of the work was given in Moscow on 21 January 1933)

## 21 JANUARY 1934

*Third Symphony,* the "Lenin Symphony" by Dmitri Kabalevsky (completed on 26 December 1933 before his *Second Symphony*), in two conjunct movements *Allegro impetuoso* and *Andante marciale lugubre,* written in the somber tones befitting the subject, and concluding with a dirge for "one who fell silent, but who is more alive than ever," is performed for the first time in Moscow, on the tenth anniversary of Lenin's death.

## 22 JANUARY 1934

*Lady Macbeth of the District of Mzensk,* opera in four acts by the 27-year-old Soviet composer Dmitri Shostakovich, to the libretto from a short story of that name by the 19th-century Russian writer Leskov, dealing with an emotionally frustrated Russian woman who murders her merchant husband in a complot with her lover, goes to Siberia with him for their crime and stabs him to death when he leaves her for another murderess, set to music in a powerful dramatic style, rich in satirical grotesquerie, including a naturalistic symphonic interlude illustrating, with realistic slide trombone glissandos, sexual intercourse on the marital bed behind the curtains on an open stage, is performed for the first time in Leningrad.

I have tried to make the musical language of my opera as simple as possible. I do not agree with the once fashionable theory that the operatic vocal line should be nothing more than recitation with accented inflection. An opera is by definition a vocal work. Accordingly, the voice parts in my opera are built on broad cantilena, making use of all available resources of the human voice, which is the richest musical instrument we have. The musical development of the opera follows a symphonic plan, proceeding in a continuous flow. Musical interludes between the scenes form a part of this continuous flow; they serve the purpose of developing basic musical ideas and illustrating the action. (Shostakovich in an article published in the program book of the first performance of his opera)

Shostakovich reveals himself in his opera as a powerful satirist. He exposes the bestiality of the merchant class of all Russia, the stupidity of the priests, the crudity of the soldiery, the greed of the bourgeoisie, the corruption of the lackeys of the aristocracy. He applies the method of vulgarizing his musical material to characterize social phenomena. The scene at the police station, for instance, is illustrated by a deafening march. The coarseness of such intentionally blatant music reveals the animalistic nature of the repellent bourgeoisie of Old Russia. (A. Ostretzov, in an article in the program book of the first performance of the opera)

*Lady Macbeth of the District of Mzensk*, later renamed *Katerina Izmailova*, after the name of the heroine, held me spellbound when I first heard it at my home with Shostakovich playing it at the piano. All those present understood at once that we were witnessing the birth of a work of the highest creative caliber. The silence that followed after he stopped playing lasted several minutes and expressed the depth of our emotional response. No one wished to indulge in easy words of praise. (Boris Mordvinov, director of the first production of the opera, in an article published in the program book)

### 23 JANUARY 1934

*La Fiamma*, musical melodrama in three acts by Ottorino RESPIGHI, dealing with the flaming passion of a woman for her young stepson, set to music in the manner of "ritorno all 'antico" making use of ancient modes in modern pandiatonic dress, is performed for the first time in Rome.

### 24 JANUARY 1934

*L'Alba della Rinascità*, opera by the 47-year-old Italian composer Nino CATTOZZO (real name Cattozzo Luigi), is produced at La Scala, in Milan.

### 26 JANUARY 1934

*First Symphony*, subtitled *1933*, by the 35-year-old American composer Roy HARRIS, in three movements, portraying respectively the moods of "adventure and physical exuberance, the pathos underlying human existence and a positive will to power and action," is performed for the first time by the Boston Symphony Orchestra, Serge Koussevitzky conducting.

### 27 JANUARY 1934

*Fanal*, opera in three acts by the Swedish composer Kurt ATTERBERG, to a romantic subject from Heine's ballad *Der Schelm von Bergen*, is produced in Stockholm.

### 5 FEBRUARY 1934

Four centuries have elapsed since the birth in Florence of Giovanni de' BARDI, founder of the Florentine Camerata whose gatherings at his palatial home led to the formation of the art of opera.

## 8 FEBRUARY 1934

*Four Saints in Three Acts*, surrealist opera by the 37-year-old American composer Virgil THOMSON, to Gertrude Stein's ostentatiously simplicistic book replete with inventive incongruities (there are in the cast sixteen, not four, saints, two hypostases of Ste. Theresa, and the number of acts is four, not three), with the high point of magnificent inanity reached in the choral lament "Pigeons on the grass—Alas!" set to music in a congenially coy, triadically sophisticated style, is performed for the first time anywhere in Hartford, Connecticut, by a Negro cast wearing cellophane clothes, and presented under the auspices of the Society of Friends and Enemies of Modern Music.

Gertrude Stein loved these saints because they were Spanish, and I loved them because they were saints. (Virgil Thomson in *This Week*, New York, 28 April 1952)

## 10 FEBRUARY 1934

*First Symphony* by Louis GRUENBERG, composed in 1919 and revised in 1929, set in orthodox four movements, reaches a belated first performance at a Boston Symphony concert, Serge Koussevitzky conducting.

## 10 FEBRUARY 1934

*Merry Mount*, opera in four acts by Howard HANSON, after Hawthorne's tale *The Maypole of Merry Mount*, dealing with the Puritan leader of colonial Massachusetts, immolated in fiery death with the woman infidel who corrupted him to ungodly practices at the pagan rites of the Maypole, set to music in colorful contrasts of religious chants artfully spiked by the tritone, the "diabolus in musica" of medieval demonology, with hedonistic songs and paganistic dances marked by acute but euphonious discordancies and vitalized by rhythmic asymmetries, ending hyperplagally in a tritonally cadenced E major, is produced by the Metropolitan Opera Company in New York.

(The first performance of the opera, in concert form, took place at the University of Michigan, Ann Arbor, on 20 May 1933)

## 14 FEBRUARY 1934

*El castillo de Almodovar*, three symphonic impressions by the Spanish composer Joaquín TURINA, orchestrated by him from his three piano pieces bearing the same title, is performed for the first time in Madrid.

## 15 FEBRUARY 1934

*Cecilia*, "sacred action" in three episodes by Licinio REFICE, dealing with the life and martyrdom of Santa Cecilia, patron saint of music, ending in sonorous B-flat major in the apotheosis, is performed for the first time in Rome.

## 16 FEBRUARY 1934

*Second Symphony* by the Russian-born American composer Nicolai BEREZOWSKY, neo-romantic in essence but modernistic in substance (he forgoes the key signature), is performed for the first time by the Boston Symphony Orchestra, Richard Burgin conducting.

### 23 FEBRUARY 1934

Sir Edward ELGAR, uncrowned laureate of English music, creator of a powerful national style of composition, supremely British in its stately pomp and its dignified humor, and expressed in a technically impeccable, romantically inspired idiom, dies in Worcester at the age of seventy-six.

### 23 FEBRUARY 1934

*Ballad About a Komsomol Fighter,* by Lev KNIPPER, his Fifth Symphony, renumbered No. 4 (after he destroyed the manuscript of the original *Fourth Symphony* first performed in Moscow on 2 March 1933), containing the famous song *Polyushko-Polye (Meadowland)*, is performed for the first time on the Moscow Radio.

### 23 FEBRUARY 1934

*Jánošík,* opera in three acts by the Czech modernist Karel HÁBA, brother of the famous ultra-modernist Alois Hába, dealing with a rebellion led by the historic Jánošík against the feudal lords of medieval Bohemia, ending in a victorious defeat as he is treacherously slain after he has enriched the poor by expropriating the rich, is produced for the first time in Prague.

### 25 FEBRUARY 1934

Georges ENESCO conducts in Bucharest the first performance of his *Symphony in D minor,* written by him in 1896 when he was 14 years old.

### 25 FEBRUARY 1934

*Concerto* for flute and orchestra by Jacques IBERT, in three flautogenic movements set in impressionistic harmonies, is performed for the first time in Paris.

### 28 FEBRUARY 1934

*Helen Retires,* opera in three acts by George ANTHEIL, freely derived from John Erskine's novel *The Private Life of Helen of Troy,* wherein Helen announces her retirement from erotic activities after seducing Achilles in the Elysian Fields, but breaks her vow when she meets a virile youth, set to music in an appropriately sophisticated idiom, ranging from mock-classicism to jazz, is produced at the Juilliard School of Music in New York.

### 6 MARCH 1934

Walter PISTON conducts the Boston Symphony Orchestra at a concert in Cambridge in the first performance of his *Concerto for Orchestra,* in three movements, marked by neo-Baroque effervescence with an admixture of stimulatingly tolerable dissonances.

## 11 MARCH 1934

Sergei PROKOFIEV conducts in Paris the first performance of his symphonic suite *Sur le Borysthène*, derived from his ballet of the same name and picturing pagan Russian scenes on the banks of the Dnieper River.

## 12 MARCH 1934

*Mathis der Maler*, symphony by Paul HINDEMITH, in three movements formed from the materials of his future opera of that name inspired by the altar triptych of the 16th-century painter Mathias Grünewald in the Alsatian town of Isenheim, in three movements: (1) *Engelkonzert*, written in an austerely open diatonic idiom, with the old German folk theme *Es sungen drei Engel* as a permeating motto (2) *Grablegung*, brief threnody in agonized muted discords ending on a fatalistic major triad (3) *Versuchung des Heiligen Antonius*, opening with a rhapsodic invocation in polymodal unisons and free measure, leading through a tense section of high motility to the victorious chorales *Lauda Sion Salvatorem* and *Alleluia* in broad chordal harmonies concluding on the thematic tonic of D-flat major, is performed for the first time by the Berlin Philharmonic, Wilhelm Furtwängler conducting. (A partial performance of the symphony was conducted by Paul Hindemith with the British Broadcasting Company in London on 21 December 1933)

## 15 MARCH 1934

*Elga*, opera in five scenes, with a prologue and an epilogue, by the Russian-trained Estonian composer Arthur LEMBA, after the homonymous drama by Gerhart Hauptmann, with the action taking place in Poland in the 17th century, is performed for the first time in Tallin.

## 15 MARCH 1934

*First Symphony* by the French composer Marcel DELANNOY is performed for the first time in Paris.

## 16 MARCH 1934

Arnold SCHOENBERG makes his first American appearance as conductor with the Boston Symphony Orchestra, in a program limited to his early works.

(Schoenberg was scheduled to conduct the Boston Symphony Orchestra in a program of his works on 12 and 13 January 1934, but was unable to appear on account of a severe cold)

## 20 MARCH 1934

*Uzbekistan*, symphonic suite on native themes by the Russian nationalist composer Mikhail IPPOLITOV-IVANOV, is performed for the first time at the inauguration of the Uzbek Symphony Orchestra in Tashkent.

## 21 MARCH 1934

Franz SCHREKER, Monaco-born Vienna-bred German composer of expressionistic music dramas of meaningful literary and musical content (he wrote his own libretti) and influential teacher of a generation of modernists, dies in Berlin two days before his 56th birthday.

## 22 MARCH 1934

*Giration,* choreographic divertissement by Gabriel PIERNÉ, with the participation of talking machines in the stage action, is performed for the first time in Paris.

## 24 MARCH 1934

*Il Dibuk,* opera in three acts by the Italian composer Lodovico ROCCA, inspired by the mystically realistic Jewish tale of a girl possessed by the mental complex of her suicidal suitor to such an extent that she absorbs his mentality and dies herself, is produced at La Scala, Milan.

## 26 MARCH 1934

On the occasion of the semicentennial of the death of the national Bohemian composer Bedřich SMETANA, the government of Czechoslovakia issues a commemorative postage stamp of 50 kronen.

## 26 MARCH 1934

*La Princess lointaine,* opera in four acts by the 67-year-old French composer of remote Polish extraction Georges-Martin WITKOWSKI, to a libretto after Rostand's play in which an aging crusader undertakes an arduous voyage to Tripoli to meet his appointed young bride but expires from cardiac arrest induced by her first embrace, while his loyal henchman suppresses his own hidden passion for her and continues on his way to Jerusalem, is performed for the first time in Paris.

## 26 MARCH 1934

Two days after the Rome production of the opera *La Favola del figlio cambiato* by Gian Francesco MALIPIERO, first performed in Brunswick on 13 January 1934, the Fascist Government forbids its further representations by an express order of Mussolini for reasons of "moral incongruity" of the Pirandello play on which the libretto is based.

## 2 APRIL 1934

The 12th Festival of the International Society for Contemporary Music opens in Florence with the following program of Italian orchestral music, arranged by its Italian branch, the Corporazione delle Musiche Nuove:

*Second Symphony* by the romantic composer Franco ALFANO, written in the characteristically expansive and grandiloquent idiom of his operas; *Partita* by the 30-year-old Luigi DALLAPICCOLA, marking a tonal trend toward neo-Casellan Scarlattianism; the world première of the *First Symphony* by Gian Francesco MALIPIERO, subtitled "in quattro tempi come le quattro stagioni" (in four movements like four seasons): (1)

*Quasi andante, sereno* (Spring) (2) *Allegro* (Summer) (3) *Lento ma non troppo* (Autumn) (4) *Allegro quasi allegretto* (Winter), conceived in a refined ottocento style with pandiatonically enriched Italianisms and seasoned with spicy percussion effects; *Two Sicilian Songs* by Giuseppe MULÈ; and the neo-Baroque *Introduction, Aria, and Toccata* by Alfredo CASELLA.


### 3 APRIL 1934

At the second concert of the 12th Festival of the International Society for Contemporary Music in Florence the following program of chamber music is presented:

*String Quartet* in a somewhat impressionistic manner by the French composer Henri MARTELLI; *Suite* for trumpet (mostly muted), bass clarinet, saxophone and piano by Rudolf HOLZMANN, 24-year-old German expatriate composer, written in a sophisticated *style pompier* (this piece replaced a work by Hindemith withdrawn by him from performance to avoid the aggravation of his situation in Nazi Germany); *Four Songs* on national themes by the Yugoslav composer Slavko OSTERC; a vigorous and loud *Piano Sonata* by the young Dane, Knudaage RIISAGER; Alban BERG's *Lyric Suite* for string quartet, written in a technique largely within the system of 12-tone composition; and *Sonata* for two violins and cello in a neo-classical vein by a typical *jeune français* Jean FRANÇAIX.


### 4 APRIL 1934

At the third concert of the 12th Festival of the International Society for Contemporary Music in Florence, the following program of orchestral music is presented:

Arthur HONEGGER's *Mouvement Symphonique No. 3* (sequel to his *Pacific 231* and *Rugby,* respectively Symphonic Movements No. 1 and No. 2), devoid of a descriptive subtitle and representing Honegger's renunciation of programmatic composition in favor of neo-classical conceptions; RAVEL's *Concerto* for left hand alone with orchestra, commissioned by the one-armed Austrian pianist Paul Wittgenstein, and performed by him; *Rhapsody* for violin and orchestra by Béla BARTÓK; *Psalm* for soprano and orchestra by the 21-year-old Russian-born Paris-bred composer Igor MARKEVITCH, written in a strident neo-diatonic idiom, conducted by the composer himself, and shocking the audience into shouts of esthetic indignation; *Turkmenia,* symphonic suite on Central Asian themes by the Soviet composer Boris SCHECHTER.


### 5 APRIL 1934

At the fourth concert of the 12th Festival of the International Society for Contemporary Music in Florence, the following program of chamber music is given:

*Phantasy Quartet* for oboe, violin, viola and cello, Op. 2, by Benjamin BRITTEN, written by him at the age of 19 in 1932 in a rhapsodically cyclic form of symmetrically positioned imaginative variations, his first work to attract attention at an international gathering of musicians; *Piano Trio* by the Hungarian composer Heinrich NEUGEBOREN; *Quartettino* for strings by the Austrian composer Leopold SPINNER, written in an expressionistically introspective quasi-atonal manner; explosively percussive *Sonata* for violin and piano by the Czech composer Jaroslav JEŽEK; 5 *Lyric Pieces* by the Viennese composer Hans Erich APOSTEL, couched in a neo-romantic style with an injection of bland atonalities; *Cantata* for mezzo-soprano, flute, oboe d'amore, lute, viola d'amore, viola da gamba and cello in a neo-archaic modal idiom by the Swiss composer Richard STÜRZENEGGER; and the neo-classically burnished *Sinfonietta* by the Swedish composer Lars-Erik LARSSON.

### 6 APRIL 1934

*Union Pacific,* ballet by Nicolas NABOKOV, 30-year-old Russian composer newly resident in America, depicting in rhythmically impulsive and lyrically discursive diatonic images the completion of the transcontinental railroad and making occasional use of American western tunes for local color, is produced for the first time by the Monte Carlo Ballet in Philadelphia.

### 7 APRIL 1934

At the fifth and last concert of the 12th Festival of the International Society for Contemporary Music in Florence the following program of Italian chamber music is given:

*Second Quartet,* by Mario LABROCA, in an unpretentious tonal manner; *Concertino* for wind instruments, percussion, and piano, in a hedonistic urban style, by the 20-year-old Venetian Gino GORINI; *Songs* by the Italian romanticist Mario CASTELNUOVO-TEDESCO; *Divertimento* for string trio, clarinet, bassoon and trumpet, by Riccardo NIELSEN of Bologna; and the poetically dramatic *String Quartet in D* by the grand-master of the modern Italian school of composition, Ildebrando PIZZETTI.

### 12 APRIL 1934

Thaddeus CAHILL, American inventor of the futuristic-looking machine called Telharmonium, patented by him early in the century, and capable of generating sounds by electro-magnetic induction which he proposed to broadcast by telephone, whose eccentrically prophetic notions earned for him an admiring mention in Busoni's book on new musical esthetics, dies in New York at the age of sixty-seven.

### 12 APRIL 1934

*Macbeth,* Shakespearean opera in three acts by the English composer Lawrence Arthur COLLINGWOOD, is performed for the first time in London.

### 14 APRIL 1934

*Symphonic Song* by Sergei PROKOFIEV, written after his return to Russia from Paris, and despite the compulsory demodernization of Soviet music still betraying in its idiom the acuity and acridity of his naturally aggressive manner, is performed for the first time in Moscow.

### 15 APRIL 1934

*Ecuatorial,* symphonic poem for bass voice, brass ensemble, percussion and Thereminovox by Edgar VARÈSE, to texts from the sacred book of the Mayan priests of Mexico, describing the horrifying tribulations of a group of mountain people lost on their way to the City of Abundance, is performed for the first time in New York, under the direction of Nicolas Slonimsky.

## 22 APRIL 1934

By a decree of the Nazi government, all German singing societies are incorporated into the national Sängerbund, to which the practical policy of using music as a tool of racial propaganda is arrogated.

## 30 APRIL 1934

Igor STRAVINSKY conducts in Paris the first performance of his *Perséphone*, ballet-melodrama in three parts to the text by André Gide, dealing allegorically with the abduction of Perséphone by Pluto, scored for orchestra, tenor, chorus and a children's choir, and set in a gymnosophistical idiom marked by an austere polyphonic design, with Ida Rubinstein appearing in the title role as dancer and speaker. (On the same program, the first performance took place of *Diane de Poitiers*, ballet by Jacques IBERT, hedonistically depicting the royal pastimes of a favorite concubine of Louis XIV, with musical interludes of exotic Russian and Peruvian dances)

Inasmuch as I have been asked to present my own attitude towards my ballet *Perséphone*, I should like to call the attention of the public to a word that summarizes my entire program: Syllable. This comprises everything that I intend to communicate in *Perséphone*: beautiful strong syllables, and action. Music is not thinking. I do not exteriorize. The function of music is, in my view, something entirely different from what it is to others. The art of music is given to us with the purpose of putting things in order, arranging them in an organized state of perfect consciousness that insures vitality and durability. . . . When one becomes conscious of an emotion, it is already cold. It becomes like lava, converted to trivial substance used to manufacture souvenirs sold in the foothills of Mt. Vesuvius. . . . I abhor instrumental effects used solely for the sake of color. In *Perséphone* the listener should not expect to be dazzled by seductive sonorities, for I have long ago realized the futility of *brio*. I recoil from the idea of courting the public. It embarrasses me. Let those who make a profession of this honorable practice, in composing as well as in conducting, indulge in it to the point of complete saturation. The public expects the artist to disembowel himself and to exhibit his entrails. This action is regarded as the noblest expression of art, and is termed variously as Personality, Individuality, or Temperament. My score to *Perséphone* must remain in the musical annals of our era as I conceived it. *Perséphone* forms an indissoluble link with my ideas expressed in my previous works. It follows *Oedipus Rex, Symphonie de Psalmes, Capriccio, Violin Concerto* and *Duo Concertant* as a sequel of a series, and my abstention from spectacular effects in these works does not diminish in the least the autonomous life of the music. Things that are felt and things that are true are susceptible to projections on an enormous scale. I follow a very definite path, which cannot be the subject of a debate or criticism. One does not criticize somebody, or something, that functions. The nose is not manufactured. The nose *is*. So is my art. (Igor Stravinsky, in *Excelsior*, Paris, 29 April 1934, reprinted in *Le Monde Musical*, Paris, 31 May 1934)

M. Stravinsky warns us that his way in art is not to be debated or criticized. Such self-assurance is probably without precedent in music history. Bach, Mozart, Beethoven, Wagner, Debussy, Fauré, were all conscious of the validity of their art, but none of them presumed to guarantee the vitality and the durability of their works. Curiously, it is not as the composer of such scores as *Petrouchka, L'Oiseau de feu, Le Rossignol* or *Le Sacre du Printemps,* which have earned him world renown, that Stravinsky aspires to enter the Pantheon. No, it is his works which even his most fervent admirers hesitate to glorify, works written during the period of his "return to Bach," that he regards as "enormous projections." At its first performance, *Perséphone* received meager signs of appreciation from the audience. During the last scene, in which Persephone descends into Hell for the second time, someone was heard to whisper: "Let's hope she stays there." (A. Mangeot, *Le Monde Musical,* Paris, 31 May 1934)

### 7 MAY 1934

*Kykunkor, the Witch,* African opera by Asadata Dafora HORTON of Sierra Leone, derived from West African songs and dances, is produced for the first time at the Unity Theatre Studio in New York, with a Negro cast, accompanied by an instrumental ensemble including a large section of African percussion instruments.

### 11 MAY 1934

*Sémiramis,* ballet by Arthur HONEGGER, to Paul Valéry's dramatic poem, dealing with the fabulous queen of Babylon who orders the execution of a captive king because he has failed to satisfy her orgiastic expectations, and then exposes herself to the murderous rays of the sun after consulting a quartet of astrologers, to the mystically sounding vibrations of the Ondes Martenot in the orchestra, is performed for the first time at the Paris Opéra, with Ida Rubinstein, the Parisian Terpsichore who also mimed St. Sebastian in Debussy's mystery play, Ravel's *Boléro* and Stravinsky's Persephone, in the title role.

### 11 MAY 1934

Çemal ERKIN, 28-year-old Turkish composer, conducts in Ankara the first performance of his symphonic poem *Bairam,* depicting the whirling dervish dances of the Moslem holiday.

### 15 MAY 1934

Nicolas OBOUHOV, Russian expatriate composer and religious mystic, who has adopted the signature "Nicolas l'Illuminé," presents in Paris the first demonstration of the *Croix Sonore,* an electronic musical instrument in the form of a cross, in a program of his works designed to accomplish a theosophic synthesis of divinity by means of demiurgic aggregations of twelve chromatic notes in a non-dodecaphonic order and to achieve instant communication on a telepathic musical wavelength with the extra-terrestrial intelligences of the Spiritus Mundi.

M. Obouhov has no other pretensions except to let us hear True Music, the Music of the Inspired, which crowns the Divine Spirit and guides mankind to the eternal abyss on the mystical accents of Verity. (*Le Ménestrel,* Paris, 1 June 1934)

## 25 MAY 1934

Gustav HOLST, English composer of romantically elevated symphonic and choral pieces, whose real name was Gustavus Theodore von Holst (he was of Swedish extraction) but who removed the embarrassing Germanic nobiliary particle after the outbreak of World War I, dies in London in his sixtieth year.

## 25 MAY 1934

*Cantata Profana* for chorus and orchestra by Béla BARTÓK (completed in Budapest on 8 September 1930), to the text relating the fantasmagoria of nine enchanted stags, set to music in a neo-primitivistic percussive idiom, is performed for the first time in London.

## 26 MAY 1934

*Honzovo Královstvi (Ivan's Kingdom)*, opera in seven scenes by the 55-year-old Czech composer Otakar OSTRČIL, after Tolstoy's fairy tale in which a simple peasant succeeds in curing an incurable princess, accedes to the throne and distributes land to indigent workers of the soil, following the precepts of Tolstoy's favorite American economist Henry George, advocate of a single tax, is produced in Brno.

## 28 MAY 1934

*Rolande et le mauvais garçon*, opera in five acts by the French composer Henri RABAUD, dealing with a mythical Mediterranean queen who is embroiled in a passionate affair with a lowly "mauvais garçon," loses all interest in him when she discovers that the philosophically inclined king openly condones her affair, and returns to her queenly chores in the royal garden, set to music in a mellifluously harmonious and melodious Gallic manner, is produced at the Paris Opéra.

## 1 JUNE 1934

Belgium issues a postage stamp for 75 Belgain francs in honor of the national Flemish composer Peter BENOÎT on the centennial of his birth.

## 2 JUNE 1934

The first performance is given in Belgrade of *Oriental Symphony*, subtitled *Religiofonia*, by the 38-year-old Serbian composer Josip SLAVENSKI, scored for soloists, chorus and orchestra, in seven movements intended to represent five religions of the East and two other socio-historical categories:

(1) *The Pagans*, or *Musica Ritmica*, derived from a primitive motive of three notes, C, D and F, in widely varied rhythmic patterns, with singers intoning the exhortatory syllable "Ha" (2) *The Hebrews*, or *Musica Coloristica*, representing a stylized version of the Hebrew chant of death, *Kaddish* (3) *The Buddhists*, or *Musica Architectonica*, set in the conventionally oriental pentatonic scale subjected to canonic treatment (4) *The Christians*, or *Musica Melodica*, a solemn consecration with melodic references to me-

dieval religious hymns (5) *The Moslems,* or *Musica Articulatiae,* illustrated by muezzin's anguished laments in the orientalistic scale of anfractuous semitones and sesquitones (6) *Musica Poliphonia,* set in dissonant counterpoint, recapitulating the principal motive, C, D, F, in quadruple canonic treatment (7) *Pjesma Radu (Song of the Popular Assembly),* or *Musica Harmoniae,* an ode to socialistic joy and realistic comradeship, concluding with a sonorously optimistic jubilation.

### 3 JUNE 1934

The American Musicological Society is organized and formally incorporated in New York City, with Carleton Sprague Smith as chairman.

### 7 JUNE 1934

*Oratorio über die Sprüche des Angelus Silesius* by the 32-year-old Swiss composer Conrad BECK, to the texts gathered from the pantheistic aphorisms of Johannes Scheffler, 17th-century gnomic poet from Silesia, who assumed the name Angelus Silesius (Messenger from Silesia) when he was ordained to priesthood, is performed for the first time by the Basel Chamber Orchestra, Paul Sacher conducting.

### 9 JUNE 1934

*Maschinenmensch,* ballet by the 39-year-old Hungarian composer Eugen ZÁDOR, dealing with a superhumanly efficient robot who, at his inventor's command, kidnaps a famous violinist's mistress, written in an ostentatiously mechanistic style in polytonal harmonies bristling with asymmetric rhythms, culminating in a grandly copulative C major chord, is performed for the first time in Braunschweig, Germany.

### 10 JUNE 1934

Frederick DELIUS, English composer of German extraction, whose pictorial symphonic essays are marked by a unique combination of sentimental Germanic romanticism, Gallic impressionism and English folklorism, with a modicum of modernistic devices such as whole-tone scales and consecutive major ninth-chords, dies in his French retreat near Fontainebleau, at the age of 72, after a long period of paresis, blindness and pathetic inanition.

### 10 JUNE 1934

Igor STRAVINSKY becomes a French citizen by decree of the French Ministry of Justice. (Date from *Le Journal officiel* for 1934, p. 5769, col. 3)

### 11 JUNE 1934

On his 70th birthday, Richard STRAUSS receives from Hitler his framed picture with the inscription: "Dem grossen Komponisten Richard Strauss in aufrichtiger Verehrung, Adolf Hitler" and a framed photograph of the Nazi Minister of Propaganda Goebbels, inscribed: "Dem grossen Meister der Töne in dankbarer Verehrung zum 70. Geburtstag."

## 15 JUNE 1934

Alfred BRUNEAU, prolific French composer, initiator of a realistic operatic Gallic style, dies in Paris at the age of seventy-seven.

## 1 AUGUST 1934

*Merlino mastro d'organi*, musical drama in two parts by the Italian master of the national modern style of composition Gian Francesco MALIPIERO, dealing with a malevolent organist who kills his unfaithful inamorata by lethal vibrations of his powerful organ, and is killed in turn by a deaf mendicant impervious to sonic impact, is performed for the first time in Rome.

## 20 AUGUST 1934

Self-exiled from Germany after its Hitlerization, Ernst TOCH, in London on his way to America, plays the piano solo part in the world première of his *Symphony* for piano and orchestra.

## 31 AUGUST 1934

A century has passed since the birth of the Italian composer Amilcare PONCHIELLI, whose opera *La Gioconda*, with its sempiternally popular ballet interlude *The Dance of the Hours*, has never lost its appeal.

## 4 SEPTEMBER 1934

The Music Therapy Project, the first of its kind since the tarantella was played to cure tarantula bites in Taranto, is inaugurated at the Veterans' Administration Hospital in Lyons, New Jersey, with the establishment of a 24-piece band under the direction of W. J. Borland, himself seeking melosomatic medication to cure his own neurosis which he developed during his service as a psychological interrogator in the United States Army.

## 10 SEPTEMBER 1934

Sir George HENSCHEL, German conductor, who began his career as a singer and was the first conductor of the Boston Symphony Orchestra in 1881, became naturalized in England in 1890 and was knighted on the eve of the war against his fatherland in 1914, dies in Aviemore in Scotland at the age of eighty-four.

## 10 SEPTEMBER 1934

*The Lily Maid*, opera in two acts by the romantic English composer Rutland BOUGHTON, to his own libretto centered on Elaine, the "lily maid" of the Arthurian romance, is performed for the first time in Stroud, Gloucester. (The first London production took place on 12 January 1937)

## 11 SEPTEMBER 1934

*Concerto* for cello and orchestra by Ildebrando PIZZETTI, written in a songful Italian style emblazoned in kaleidoscopic instrumental colors, is performed for the first time in Venice.

### 27 SEPTEMBER 1934

Ralph VAUGHAN WILLIAMS conducts the BBC Symphony Orchestra in London in the first concert performance of his *Fantasia on Greensleeves* for strings and harp, adapted from his opera *Sir John in Love,* and based on an old Shakespearian tune, twice mentioned in *The Merry Wives of Windsor,* set in euphoniously flowing triadic modalities, with an interpolation of another folk melody, of newer provenance, *Lovely Joan,* and then returning to the dulcet rusticity of *Greensleeves* to form a perfect symmetry of ternary design.

### 28 SEPTEMBER 1934

The Council of People's Commissars of the Union of Soviet Socialist Republics issues a list of ratings of payment for musical composition: 10,000 to 12,000 rubles for an opera, 6,000 to 8,000 rubles for a symphony, 3,000 to 5,000 rubles for a piece of chamber music and 500 to 1,000 rubles for a chorus.

### 28 SEPTEMBER 1934

*The Fountain of Bakhchisarai,* ballet after Pushkin's poem by the Russian music scholar and composer Boris ASAFIEV, marked by an abundance of anfractuously orientalized melodies and languorous rhythms characteristic of the Tatar folk music in the Crimea, where the action of the ballet takes place, is produced in Leningrad.

### 29 SEPTEMBER 1934

The Nazi Ministry of Propaganda issues an order prohibiting the use by musicians of foreign-sounding pseudonyms, setting the date 31 October 1934 as final for restoring original German names of such users.

### 29 SEPTEMBER 1934

Carlos CHÁVEZ conducts in Mexico City the first performance of his *Llamadas (Calls),* subtitled *Sinfonía Proletaria,* scored for chorus and small orchestra and written in a virile proletarian manner marked by alternating duple and triple meters and terse harmonic formations.

### 1 OCTOBER 1934

The Mutual Broadcasting System, the third American Radio network, is inaugurated in New York City. (It was extended to a coast-to-coast network on 29 December 1936)

### 3 OCTOBER 1934

*Pacat Boieresc (The Boyar's Sin),* opera by the 41-year-old Rumanian composer Martian NEGREA, wherein a vicious Balkan overlord villainously dishonors a villager's wife and daughter and is ultimately slain by the aroused populace, in a musical setting in an ingenuously indigenous manner vitalized by asymmetrical Balkan rhythms, is produced in Cluj.

## 11 OCTOBER 1934

*Second Symphony* by Kurt WEILL, written in a euphoniously modernistic manner in three movements: (1) *Sostenuto*, 4/4, with a somber introduction emerging into a pantonal waltz (2) *Largo*, 4/4, a romanza on a funereal march rhythm (3) *Allegro vivace*, a neo-romantic rondo in 2/4 followed by a hedonistic tarantella, is performed for the first time by the Concertgebouw Orchestra in Amsterdam, Bruno Walter conducting.

## 13 OCTOBER 1934

Theodore BAKER, German-educated American musicologist, who compiled in 1900 the original edition of the prestigious *Baker's Biographical Dictionary of Musicians,* which listed a number of Americans theretofore not accorded lexicographical honors, and who was also the author of a pioneer work on American Indian music in the German language, dies in Dresden at the age of eighty-three.

## 15 OCTOBER 1934

The Pageant of Labour opens at Crystal Palace in London, presenting a Marxist ballet in six scenes: (1) *Capital Enslaves the Worker* (2) *Martyrdom of the Children* (3) *Consolation of Philanthropy and Religion* (4) *London Receives the Chartists* (5) *The Triumph of the Trade Unions* (6) *Fletcher Family, 1900,* set to music in a properly socialistic idiom by Alan Bush, member of the left wing of the Labour Party, based on a system of leading motives, each characterizing a personage or a political idea.

## 16 OCTOBER 1934

*Thirteenth Symphony* by Nicolai MIASKOVSKY, in B-flat minor (completed on 20 October 1933), in three continuous movements, *Andante moderato, Agitato molto tenebroso* and *Andante nostalgico,* abounding in somber tonal fluxions with tritone-laden melodies asymptotically approaching the acknowledged tonal focus, is performed for the first time by the Musikkollegium in Winterthur, Switzerland, Hermann Scherchen conducting. (Exact date obtained from the Musikkolegium in Winterthur. The date 15 November 1934, given in previous editions of *Music Since 1900* and other reference works as the world première, is that of the first American performance in Chicago)

## 17 OCTOBER 1934

*Fragonard,* comic opera by Gabriel PIERNÉ, depicting the ambience of 18th-century France, as reflected in the rococo art of Jean-Honoré Fragonard, is produced at the Opéra-Comique in Paris.

## 20 OCTOBER 1934

*Lucedia,* opera in three acts by the 31-year-old American composer Vittorio GIANNINI, telling in harmoniously melodramatic tones the story of a vestal virgin who violates her oath of chastity and is sent to her death in a leaking boat, is produced in Munich, with a German version of the original Italian libretto.

*La Leyenda de Urutaú*, opera by the 45-year-old Argentinian composer Gilardo GILARDI, with action taking place at the time of the Spanish conquest of South America, written in a competent ethnomusical manner, making use of authentic Inca and Spanish melorhythms, is produced in Buenos Aires.

### 1 NOVEMBER 1934

The German monthly *Die Musik* discloses that the National-Socialist Kulturgemeinde has, through its leader Dr. Walter Strang, commissioned from the impeccably Aryan German composers Rudolf WAGNER-RÉGENY and Julius WEISMANN new musical settings for Shakespeare's *A Midsummer Night's Dream* to replace the racially tainted Mendelssohn's score. (These new scores came to performance respectively on 6 and 11 June 1935, during the Reichstagung of the National-Socialist Kulturgemeinde at Düsseldorf)

The National-Socialist Kulturgemeinde has discharged an important obligation of the National-Socialist Revolution in commissioning a new score for *A Midsummer Night's Dream* of Shakespeare. Mendelssohn's music is inadmissible in the Third Reich, where the unalienable laws of racial purity must be uncompromisingly maintained. (Wilhelm Herzog in *Die Musik*, 1 November 1934)

### 6 NOVEMBER 1934

*Iernin*, Celtic saga-opera in three acts by the 21-year-old Welsh composer George LLOYD, to his father's libretto wherein a benevolent Faery of the Shining People of the Hills helps a brave youth to win a beauteous maiden away from the sinister blandishments of a hideous seventh-century Saxon overlord, is produced in Penzance.

### 7 NOVEMBER 1934

*Kyz-Zhibek*, the first national opera of Kazakhstan by the 28-year-old Soviet composer Evgeny BRUSILOVSKY, in four acts, to the story of the suicide of a beautiful medieval Central Asian lass named Kyz-Zhibek, who leaps to her death into a lake from a cliff after her lover, a proletarianized son of a khan, is slain in jealous rage by a feudal Mongolian knight, set to music in abecedarian but ethnomusicologically authentic monody vivified by a rhythmical whine, plink and plunk of assorted native instruments, is produced in Alma-Ata, capital of Kazakhstan, on the 17th anniversary of the Soviet Revolution.

### 7 NOVEMBER 1934

Serge RACHMANINOFF plays at a concert of the Philadelphia Orchestra in Baltimore, conducted by Leopold Stokowski, the piano part in the first performance anywhere of his *Rhapsody on a Theme by Paganini*, composed between 3 July and 24 August 1934, in A minor, consisting of 24 variations on Paganini's *Caprice No. 24* (the same that Brahms used for his piano variations), written in a superlative virtuoso manner, covering the entire range of the keyboard, with the 18th variation presenting an ingenious inversion of the subject, so that the ascending minor phrase becomes the descending major motive, curiously resulting in a Slavic-flavored ballad-like melody, the whole work culminating in a grandiose invocation of the thematically related medieval hymn *Dies Irae* (which had already been introduced in the piano part of the 7th variation).

## 8 NOVEMBER 1934

*Arctic Symphony* by the Russian composer Sergei VASSILENKO, his fourth symphony, glorifying in its five chronologically programmatic movements the Arctic explorations of Soviet scientists, is performed for the first time in Moscow.

## 10 NOVEMBER 1934

Czechoslovakia issues a commemorative stamp at 50 kronen for Antonín DVOŘÁK.

## 12 NOVEMBER 1934

*Suite* for viola and small orchestra by Ralph VAUGHAN WILLIAMS, comprising three groups of stylized English dances, is performed for the first time in London, with Lionel Tertis as soloist.

## 16 NOVEMBER 1934

*First Symphony* by the American composer Harl MCDONALD, subtitled *The Santa Fe Trail*, illustrating in pleasingly harmonious tones his impressions of the Western desert, the mountains, and the pioneer explorations in the American West, is performed for the first time by the Philadelphia Orchestra, Leopold Stokowski conducting.

## 21 NOVEMBER 1934

*Anything Goes*, musical comedy by Cole PORTER, with the action taking place on a transatlantic ship, marshalling a multiplicity of incompatible international characters involved in a puzzling web of incongruous events, including in its score the rollicking tunes, *Blow, Gabriel, Blow, You're the Top, I Get a Kick Out of You*, is produced in New York.

## 22 NOVEMBER 1934

Pablo Casals gives the first performance of the affably competent *Cello Concerto* by the erudite Sir Donald Francis TOVEY, with the composer conducting the Reid Symphony Orchestra in Edinburgh.

Le 22 novembre 1934 sera la plus importante date de ma vie de musicien. Joachim a dû ressentir la même joie et l'honneur le jour qu'il a remis sur pied le concerto pour violon de Beethoven et celui de la première audition du concerto de Brahms. (From a letter by Casals to Tovey written on the eve of the performance, and quoted in the original French in Mary Grierson's monograph on Tovey, London, 1952, p. 181)

### 23 NOVEMBER 1934

*First Concerto* for piano and orchestra by Darius MILHAUD, in three movements: (1) *Très vif,* marked by euphonious bitonalities (2) *Barcarolle,* a harmonious aquatic piece set in furfuraceous chromatic harmonies (3) *Finale,* a hedonistic rondo, is performed for the first time in Paris, with the modernistically minded French pianist Marguerite Long as soloist.

### 25 NOVEMBER 1934

*Concerto for Saxophone,* op. 109, by the venerable classicist of the Russian National School Alexander GLAZUNOV, his last work, written in the spring of 1934, in E flat major, in a single movement articulated into three sections, an *Allegro,* an *Andante* with a florid cadenza, and a concise *Fugato,* is performed for the first time anywhere with a local orchestra in an old church in Nyköping, Sweden, by the Danish saxophone virtuoso Sigurd Rascher, to whom the work is dedicated.

I met Glazunov in Paris early in 1934 and went to visit him at his home. . . . "Alors, jouez!" he said. I played, soft, loud, in cascades and ripples. "Merveilleux!" Glazunov exclaimed. I timidly explored the idea of his composing a saxophone concerto for me. He looked benevolent, shook the ashes off his cigar and asked me to come again. When I saw him next, the Concerto was almost ready. For a whole wonderful afternoon, and late into the evening, we worked together on the score, changing a note here and a note there, and fixing the cadenza. Thanks to his patience I had the opportunity of receiving his instructions on every point in the Concerto. It was one of the greatest lessons I had ever had. (Sigurd Rascher in a letter to the author, dated 29 December 1960)

### 30 NOVEMBER 1934

*Symphonic Suite* from the unfinished opera *Lulu* by Alban BERG to Frank Wedekind's plays, *Erdgeist* and *Die Büchse der Pandora,* dealing with an inflammable seductress whose three husbands and a Lesbian admirer all meet violent death, and who herself is disemboweled in London in 1889 by Jack the Ripper to the harrowing sound of a dodecaphonic chord symbolizing the tearing of her entrails in the duodenum measuring 12 fingerbreadths between the stomach and the jejunum, the entire score deriving from a basic 12-tone series, is performed for the first time in Berlin under the direction of Erich Kleiber.

The accounts of the performance of Alban Berg's symphonic suite from his opera *Lulu* demonstrate the ideological confusion and lack of artistic understanding of the majority of Berlin critics. It is significant that one of the most degraded foreign yellow newspapers, the *Neues Wiener Journal,* was able to quote several Berlin reviews which seemed favorably inclined toward the émigré *Musikjuden.* . . . Such reviews are inadmissible in our age of directed public opinion, for they befuddle the mind and hinder the rebuilding of our culture. The National Association of the German Press would do well to reexamine basically the fitness of these reviewers for their jobs. (*Die Musik*, Berlin, January 1935)

## 1 DECEMBER 1934

*Don Quichotte à Dulcinée,* three songs with orchestral accompaniment by Maurice RAVEL, his last work written before the onset of his final illness, characterized by apraxia and aphasia, is performed for the first time in Paris, in the vacuous presence of the semi-amnesiac composer.

## 4 DECEMBER 1934

Wilhelm FURTWÄNGLER resigns as conductor of the Berlin Philharmonic, Deputy President of the Reichsmusikkammer and as Director of the Berlin State Opera, as a result of his failure to establish a modus vivendi with the Nazi regime, and specifically because of his objections to the Nazi drive to exclude Paul Hindemith from German musical life as a *Kulturbolschevist.*

State Counsellor Dr. Wilhelm Furtwängler has asked the Minister of the Reich Dr. Goebbels to relieve him from his duties as Deputy President of the Reichsmusikkammer and conductor of the Berlin Philharmonic Orchestra. At the same time he requested the Prussian First Minister to release him from the post of Director at the Berlin State Opera. Both ministers have granted his requests. (From an official statement)

The Hindemith Case has broadened itself into a Furtwängler Case. In this problem we are faced with two conflicting ideologies. One of them regards everything in the light of pure artistic pursuit. The other, represented by National Socialism, realizes that an artist reflects a political situation. So when a man like Hindemith, after a few German beginnings, lives and works for fourteen years among Jews and feels himself at ease in such company, consorts almost exclusively with Jews, and is loved by them; when he, following the ideology of the Weimar Republic, commits the foulest perversions of German music, we have a right to reject him and his environment. The accomplishments of such a person under the Weimar Republic, and the laurels bestowed upon him by that now overthrown regime are of no value to our movement. . . . It is a great pity that so great an artist as Dr. Wilhelm Furtwängler entered this controversy, and chose to identify himself with Hindemith's cause. Herr Furtwängler clings to his 19th-century ideas and has manifestly lost all sense of the national struggle of our times. (Excerpts from the article *Esthetics or National Struggle?* by Alfred Rosenberg, foremost theorist of National Socialism, in *Die Musik,* Berlin, January 1935)

## 6 DECEMBER 1934

Dr. GOEBBELS, Minister of Propaganda of the Third Reich, delivers a thunderous denunciation of the "moral decay of atonal composers" with specific reference to the bathtub aria in Hindemith's opera *Neues vom Tage.*

Technical mastery is not an excuse but an obligation. To misuse it for meaningless musical trifles is to besmirch true genius. Opportunity creates not only thieves but also atonal musicians, who in their eagerness to make a sensation exhibit naked women in the bathtub on the stage in the most disgusting and obscene situations and further befoul such scenes by the most atrocious dissonance of musical impotence. (Excerpt from the statement by Goebbels)

## 8 DECEMBER 1934

*Das Veilchen*, two-act opera by the 60-year-old Austrian composer Julius BITTNER, is produced in Vienna.

## 15 DECEMBER 1934

While conducting a rehearsal of the musical comedy *Feodora* at the Rio de Janeiro Opera Theater, the Italian conductor Franco PAOLANTONIO is shot to death by a disgruntled orchestra musician.

## 15 DECEMBER 1934

Jean FRANÇAIX, precocious 22-year-old French composer (he published a piano piece at the age of nine) plays the piano part in the first performance in Paris of his *Concertino* for piano and orchestra, in four movements animated by the spirit of the Gallic rococo, *Presto leggiero, Lento, Allegretto, Rondo*.

## 17 DECEMBER 1934

Eleven days after losing his position as musical director of Radio Station WTIC, Christian KRIENS, Dutch-born violinist and composer, who had a precocious career in Holland, shoots himself to death in a fit of despondency, in Hartford, Connecticut.

No wealth, no friends, no influence, Christian Kriens, composer tells how he made his way despite handicaps—Advantages of America over Europe—Mr. Kriens is not only optimistic, he is enthusiastic, and his enthusiasm is upheld by an activity that bids well for his own future. (Unprophetic headlines in an interview with Christian Kriens published upon his arrival in the United States, in *Musical America*, New York, 19 November 1910)

## 18 DECEMBER 1934

*Podzimní Symfonie (Autumn Symphony)* by the 64-year-old Czech composer Vítězslav NOVÁK, for tenor, chorus and orchestra, in three movements, each ending on a pandiatonically amplified triad, and portraying the sadness, the joy and the wisdom of autumn, is performed for the first time in Prague.

## 19 DECEMBER 1934

Francis PLANTÉ, eccentric French pianist (in 1915 he gave a concert in Paris hidden from the audience by a screen, in conformance with his solemn vow "never to be seen again in public"), dies at St. Avit, near Mont-de-Marsan, at the age of ninety-five.

## 20 DECEMBER 1934

*Big Ben*, fantasy with variations on the melody of the Westminster chimes, by the 47-year-old Vienna-born romantic composer Ernst TOCH, now resident of America, written in a sophistically elaborated neo-romantic idiom, is performed for the first time anywhere at a concert of the Boston Symphony Orchestra in Cambridge, Massachusetts, Richard Burgin conducting.

## 25 DECEMBER 1934

*Second Symphony* by the 29-year-old Soviet composer Dmitri KABALEVSKY (completed on 8 November 1934, after he finished his *Third Symphony*), in the key of C minor, in three movements (1) *Allegro*, built on an artful contrast of dramatic and lyric moods (2) *Andante*, an eloquently serene elegy, and (3) *Prestissimo*, an optimistically dynamic Russian finale, is performed for the first time in Moscow, with the Russian-born Englishman Albert Coates conducting.

## 27 DECEMBER 1934

*Bayönder*, one-act opera by the 26-year-old Turkish composer Necil KÂZIM AKSES, and *Taşbebek*, one-act opera by the 27-year-old Turkish composer Ahmed Adnan SAYGUN, are produced in Ankara.

## 31 DECEMBER 1934

GOUNOD's *Faust* is given at the Paris Opéra for the 2,000th time.

# ≈ *1935* ≈

## 1 JANUARY 1935

SWING appears in print for the first time in the American monthly *Down Beat*, defined as "a musician's term for perfect rhythm," with pragmatic connotations as a free improvisation on a clarinet or a jazz trumpet, accompanied by steady square beat in the piano and drums.

## 8 JANUARY 1935

*Mount Mihara, the Suicide Volcano*, symphonic poem by the Kansas-born composer Claude LAPHAM, inspired by suicides of Japanese lovers jumping into the mouth of Mihara, is performed for the first time by the Tokyo Symphony Orchestra under the direction of Klaus Pringsheim, German musician long resident of Japan.

## 13 JANUARY 1935

*When Johnny Comes Marching Home*, overture by Roy HARRIS, in the form of variations of the famous Civil War tune, is performed for the first time in its definitive version, by the Minneapolis Symphony Orchestra, Eugene Ormandy conducting. (An earlier version, entitled *Overture from the Gayety and Sadness of the American Scene*, was first performed by Nicolas Slonimsky conducting the Los Angeles Philharmonic Orchestra on 29 December 1932)

## 14 JANUARY 1935

Heinrich SCHENKER, Polish-born Austrian music theorist, originator of the analytical concept of *Urlinie*, according to which the essence and the substance of every composition can be reduced to a melorhythmic prototype, dies in Vienna at the age of sixty-six.

### 16 JANUARY 1935

Pietro MASCAGNI conducts at La Scala in Milan the first performance of his opera *Nerone*, traversing in three acts the imperial career of Nero amid scenes of Roman debauchery and meretricious artistry, set to music throbbing with melodramatic flamboyance and exuberant bel canto.

### 23 JANUARY 1935

A concert of music from Iceland is broadcast by the Danish Radio in Copenhagen, featuring *Icelandic Dances* for orchestra and an overture *Iceland* by Jón LEIFS, German-bred prime Icelandic composer, written in an appropriately glacial pentatonic idiom harmonized by slow processions of naked fifths.

### 24 JANUARY 1935

*In the Pasha's Garden*, one-act opera by the American composer John Laurence SEYMOUR, his ninth in chronological order, the previous eight remaining unperformed, to the story of a Turkish effendi who correctly surmises that the large coffer in his beautiful French wife's chamber is used as the hiding place for her lover, and gleefully buries it, with the adulterer inside, in his garden, to the accompaniment of whole-tone scale runs, with some exotically inflected arias providing local color, is performed for the first and last time by the Metropolitan Opera House in New York.

### 26 JANUARY 1935

*Second Piano Concerto* by Ernst TOCH, in four movements—*Allegro, Lebhaft, Adagio* and *Cyclus variabilis*—is performed for the first time in Frankfurt, at a concert of the *Kulturbund deutscher Juden* (according to Nazi racial laws, Toch, as a Jew, could not be represented on any programs except those given by explicitly designated Jewish cultural organizations in Germany), by Heida Hermanns, pianist, Wilhelm (William) Steinberg conducting, in the absence of the composer, emigrated to the United States.

### 28 JANUARY 1935

Mikhail IPPOLITOV-IVANOV, Russian composer of operas and orchestral works couched in an expansively romantic Russian style saturated with folkloric melorhythms, dies in Moscow in his sleep (he was found dead in his bed by his wife at 2:30 A.M.) at the age of seventy-five.

### 31 JANUARY 1935

The first American performance of the opera *Lady Macbeth of the District of Mzensk* by Dmitri SHOSTAKOVICH is given in Cleveland, conducted by Artur Rodzinsky.

*600*

## 31 JANUARY 1935

*Concerto* for violoncello and orchestra by the 39-year-old Italian composer Mario CASTELNUOVO-TEDESCO, written in a melodious and harmonious Mediterranean idiom, is performed for the first time by Gregor Piatigorsky with the New York Philharmonic conducted by Arturo Toscanini.

## 31 JANUARY 1935

*Primavera,* concert overture by the 37-year-old Danish composer Knudaage RIISAGER, portraying the season of spring in a resounding aviary of woodwind instruments in secundal formations of atonally arrayed melodies, is performed for the first time in Copenhagen.

## 1 FEBRUARY 1935

*Ungarisches Capriccio,* symphonic sketch in the Hungarian style by the 40-year-old Hungarian composer Eugen ZÁDOR, is performed for the first time in Budapest.

## 2 FEBRUARY 1935

*Liola,* lyrico-comic opera in three acts by the Italian composer Giuseppe MULÈ, after Luigi Pirandello's play dealing with a young Sicilian peasant Liola whose pregnant mistress marries a rich old man who takes pride in rumors that the prospective child is his own, is performed for the first time in Naples. (Pirandello disowned the opera because of its licentious departures from the symbolic theme of his original play)

## 7 FEBRUARY 1935

In reply to a query from Olin Downes, the music critic of the New York *Times,* Fritz KREISLER admits in a cable from Venice that the violin pieces published as his purported arrangements of works by various 18th-century composers are in fact his own original compositions.

The entire series labelled classical manuscripts are my original compositions, with the sole exception of the first eight bars from the Chanson Louis XIII, taken from a traditional melody. Necessity forced this course on me thirty years ago when I was desirous of enlarging my programs. I found it inexpedient and tactless to repeat my name endlessly on the programs. (From Kreisler's cable to Olin Downes)

## 10 FEBRUARY 1935

*Second Piano Concerto* in E flat major for left-hand piano and orchestra by the Austrian composer Franz SCHMIDT, in three movements, with the vivacious finale containing a virtuosistic sinistromanual cadenza, is performed for the first time in Vienna by Paul Wittgenstein, the amputated Viennese pianist for whom it was written, with the composer conducting the orchestra. (The work was subsequently arranged in a bimanual version, which was performed for the first time in Vienna on 5 February 1940.)

## 13 FEBRUARY 1935

*Gargantua,* opera in four acts by the 59-year-old French composer Antoine MARIOTTE, subtitled "Rabelaisian scenes" and traversing in conventionally lyrico-dramatic terms the story of the fantastic adventures of the gigantically dissolute Gargantua, is produced in Paris.

## 17 FEBRUARY 1935

*Juha,* opera by the Finnish composer Leevi MADETOJA, to his own libretto inspired by Finnish sagas, is produced in Helsinki.

## 20 FEBRUARY 1935

*Der Günstling,* opera in three acts by the German composer Rudolf WAGNER-RÉGENY, subtitled *Die letzten Tage des grossen Herrn Fabiani,* derived from Victor Hugo's play *Marie Tudor* and dealing with the stormy career of the Italian adventurer Fabiano at the court of Bloody Mary in 16th-century England, is produced in Dresden.

## 24 FEBRUARY 1935

*Fourteenth Symphony* by the prime Russian symphonist Nicolai MIASKOVSKY (completed on 11 October 1933), in five movements of varied moods and rhythms, resolutely set in the optimistic and socialistically realistic key of C major, in contrast to his previous symphonies, twelve of which are in minor keys, is performed for the first time in Moscow.

## 26 FEBRUARY 1935

The youthful *First Symphony* by Georges BIZET, in four classically proportioned movements, set in the primordial key of C major, written by him at the age of 17 but discarded as naive, is performed for the first time anywhere, 80 years after its composition, in Basel, Switzerland, conducted by Felix Weingartner from a copy of the manuscript kept in the Paris Conservatory. (The date 26 February 1933 given in the earlier editions of *Music Since 1900* is erroneous)

## 2 MARCH 1935

*A Milói Vénusz (Venus of Milo),* romantic opera by the Hungarian violinist Jenö HUBAY, is produced in Budapest.

## 7 MARCH 1935

In a campaign against street noise, Mayor WALKER of New York City cancels licenses of all local organ grinders.

## 14 MARCH 1935

*Der Prinz von Homburg,* opera in four acts by the 63-year-old German composer Paul GRAENER, to Heinrich von Kleist's story dealing with a Prussian princeling who achieves a military victory by defying the judgment of his general staff and wins the hand of a gallant lady, written in the style of a "dialogue opera" immersed in Regeromantically lutulent Prussianized polyphony, is produced in Berlin.

### 16 MARCH 1935

*Orfeo*, opera by Claudio MONTEVERDI, arranged in a discreetly modernized style by Ottorino Respighi, is performed for the first time at La Scala in Milan.

### 23 MARCH 1935

*Music for a Scene from Shelley* for orchestra by the 25-year-old American composer Samuel BARBER, written in a poetic neo-romantic idiom, is performed for the first time by the New York Philharmonic.

### 24 MARCH 1935

*Concerto Grosso* by the 33-year-old Soviet composer Mikhail STAROKA-DOMSKY, one of the few Soviet works written in a neo-classical idiom, is performed for the first time in Moscow.

### 25 MARCH 1935

*Le Marchand de Venise*, opera in three acts by the Venezuelan-born Parisianized composer Reynaldo HAHN, set in an elegant Gallic style, to a libretto modelled very freely after Shakespeare, ending with a septet of three happy couples joined by the Merchant of Venice himself, is produced at the Paris Opéra, on the same day with the dress rehearsal at the Paris theater Gaîté-Lyrique, of Hahn's operetta *Malvina*, depicting the gay Paris life of the eve of the Revolution of 1830, which overthrew the last of the Bourbon dynasty.

### 26 MARCH 1935

*Her Name Day*, opera in three acts by the 22-year-old Soviet composer Valery ZHELOBINSKY, in which an emancipated Russian serf kills himself after he is rejected by his former owner's daughter on her name day, is performed for the first time in Leningrad.

### 2 APRIL 1935

*Second Concerto* for violoncello and orchestra by the 39-year-old American composer Leo SOWERBY, is performed for the first time in New York.

### 3 APRIL 1935

*First Piano Concerto* by Gian Francesco MALIPIERO, in a continuous movement in three distinct sections, with the piano treated in a translucent Baroque idiom enlivened by modernistically percussive effects, is performed for the first time in Rome.

## 4 APRIL 1935

*The Limpid Stream*, ballet by Dmitri SHOSTAKOVICH, depicting in optimistic tones the scenes of Soviet life on a collective farm named Limpid Stream and situated on the Kuban River in North Caucasus, is performed for the first time in Leningrad.

In the ballet by Shostakovich, the characters are tinsel puppets who pretend to be enjoying a dance, but whose activities have nothing to do with authentic folk dances on the Kuban River or any other place. (From an article *Choreographic Misrepresentation*, in *Pravda*, 6 February 1936)

## 8 APRIL 1935

*Maria Malibran*, opera in three acts by the American composer Robert Russell BENNETT, inspired by the life story of the young Spanish singer María García (1808–1836) who was forced to marry an elderly New York merchant named Malibran to save her family from ruin is produced in New York.

## 10 APRIL 1935

*Fourth Symphony* in F minor by the dean of English composers Ralph VAUGHAN WILLIAMS, in four movements: (1) *Allegro*, a rhapsodically free essay built on a tensely chromaticized theme alternating with spacious diatonic progressions (2) *Andante moderato*, marked by a moderate cornucopia of folk-like themes, with a concluding flute solo set in dolorous accents redolent of muezzin-like arabesques (3) *Scherzo*, a highly syncopated jig in rapidly modulating keys (4) *Finale, con epilogo fugato*, a coruscating mosaic of artfully varied folk-like themes, culminating in a magisterial fugal epilogue and concluding on the focal F, is performed for the first time in London by the British Broadcasting Corporation Symphony, Sir Adrian Boult conducting.

## 13 APRIL 1935

*Variazioni coreografiche*, ballet by the Italian composer Riccardo PICK-MANGIAGALLI, is performed for the first time at San Remo.

## 16 APRIL 1935

Petar STOJANOVIĆ, Hungarian-born Serbian composer, conducts in Belgrade the first performance of his symphonic poem *Sava*, an ethnic musicorama of Serbia's great river, from its source in the Triglav mountains to its confluence with the mighty Danube.

## 17 APRIL 1935

*Brothers Karamazov*, opera in five acts, after Dostoyevsky's famous novel, by the Czech composer Otakar JEREMIÁŠ, is produced in Prague.

## 25 APRIL 1935

As a result of a temporary reconciliation with the Nazi Government of Germany Wilhelm FURTWÄNGLER is allowed to resume his post as conductor and music director of the Berlin Philharmonic.

## 28 APRIL 1935

Riccardo ZANDONAI, minor master of the Italian Verismo, composer of grand operas throbbing with exuberant melodrama, regarded by some as a legitimate successor to Puccini, is awarded the Mussolini Prize from the Royal Academy of Rome.

Riccardo Zandonai has glorified the lyric Italian theater in which he has maintained its sacred traditions in a modern design. (From Respighi's valedictory speech on the occasion of the presentation of the Prize)

## 2 MAY 1935

*Third Symphony* by the modern Dutch composer Henk BADINGS is performed for the first time in Amsterdam.

## 5 MAY 1935

*Orsèolo,* opera in three acts by the Italian composer Ildebrando PIZZETTI, to a libretto depicting the emotional conflict between the Venetian doge Orsèolo and a young nobleman who courts his daughter, is performed for the first time in Florence.

## 11 MAY 1935

*Harnasie,* ballet in three tableaux by the romantic Polish composer Karol SZYMANOWSKI, dealing with the picaresque leader of "harnasies", the patriotically inspired Polish brigands active in the igneous chain of Central Carpathian Mountains, who elopes with a villager's bride on her scheduled wedding day, with authentic regional melorhythms set to sonorous bitonal harmonies and anchored in deeply rooted pedal points, is performed for the first time anywhere in Prague.

## 14 MAY 1935

*La Pantoufle de vair,* "conte dansé" by the French composer Marcel DELANNOY, after the famous fairy-tale of Charles Perrault, in which Prince Charming recognizes his Cinderella by her dainty slipper made of fur (*vair*, not *verre,* as commonly misinterpreted, a fur slipper being aristocratic whereas a glass slipper is unwearable), is produced at the Opéra-Comique, as an expanded version of Delannoy's ballet *Cinderella,* originally produced in Chicago on 30 August 1931.

## 17 MAY 1935

Paul DUKAS, "Degas of Music," French composer of impressionistically rarefied symphonic works, master of illustrative evocation revealed in full power in his celebrated orchestral scherzo *L'Apprenti Sorcier,* dies in Paris in his 70th year, having destroyed in his last lucid moments all his unpublished manuscripts, including a violin sonata, an overture, and an unfinished work commissioned by the Boston Symphony Orchestra.

## 18 MAY 1935

*Suite for String Orchestra* by Arnold SCHOENBERG (originally titled *Suite im alten Stile für Streichorchester*), completed in Hollywood on 26 December 1934, and bearing, for the first time since his *Second String Quartet* of 1908, a definite key signature, in five movements, (1) *Ouverture* in G major (2) *Adagio* in E minor (3) *Minuet* in G major (4) *Gavotte* in B-flat major and (5) *Gigue* in G major, is performed for the first time by the Los Angeles Philharmonic, Otto Klemperer conducting.

The spots in this score are Klemperer's drops of perspiration. (Schoenberg's inscription on the title page of the original manuscript)

I have become convinced that every modern composer, and particularly myself, ought to be interested in satisfying the demands of American high school orchestra in these respects: Without momentarily exposing the student to the "poison of atonality" to build the foundation of a modern technique leading to modern sensitivities, in fingering, articulation, form, counterpoint and phrase structure so as to enable him to acquire gradually a feeling for something more than the primitive symmetric construction, the unvaried and undeveloped melody, which give pleasure to mediocrities of all lands and peoples. Even in this music there should be room for higher forms which belong to a higher species of art not only from a technical but also from a spiritual standpoint. (From Schoenberg's foreword, translated from German)

## 19 MAY 1935

Charles Martin LOEFFLER, Alsatian-born American composer, whose art of sensitive decalcomania in reproducing the coloristic images of cultured French impressionism made him a minor master of American modernism, dies in Medfield, near Boston, at the age of seventy-four.

## 20 MAY 1935

*Die Zaubergeige*, opera in three acts by the 34-year-old German composer Werner EGK, to a libretto derived from a Bavarian folk tale dealing with a farmhand who receives a magic violin from the Prince of the Elements, becomes an instant virtuoso, is entrammeled in an affair with an aristocratic belle, and finally returns to the peaceful life with his plain peasant wife, set to music in Germanically stolid harmonies, is produced in Frankfurt.

## 20 MAY 1935

*The Rake's Progress*, ballet by the 33-year-old Scottish singer Gavin GORDON, inspired by Hogarth's moralistic drawings, is produced in London.

## 25 MAY 1935

*Uirapurú*, symphonic poem by the prime Brazilian composer Heitor VILLA-LOBOS, in which the Brazilian jungle bird Uirapurú (*Levolepis modulator*), incarnated in an Amazon Indian playing the nose flute, reverts to its ornithological prototype after the Indian is slain by a youth, the latter being himself a product of reincarnation induced by a non-metamorphosed jungle maiden, written in an idiom saturated with tropical melorhythms, against which Uirapurú intones a pentatonic cantus firmus, is performed for the first time in Buenos Aires.

### 29 MAY 1935

Josef SUK, Czech composer, son-in-law of Dvořák and continuator of his musical heritage, dies at Benešovo at the age of sixty-one.

### 2 JUNE 1935

Henry HADLEY conducts at the Norfolk, Connecticut, Festival, the world première of his *Fifth Symphony,* commemorating the tercentenary of the State of Connecticut and depicting in its three movements the three centennial landmarks in its history: *A.D. 1635,* with pentatonic allusions to aboriginal Indians; *A.D. 1735,* portraying in pastoral tones the agricultural period of the colonial settlement; and *A.D. 1935,* a musicorama of modern Connecticut vivified by jazzy rhythms.

### 9–10 JUNE 1935

*First Labor Olympiad* is held in Strasbourg, with concerts of orchestral and choral music given by proletarian groups from Switzerland, Holland, England, Czechoslovakia and France, and sponsored by radical-minded composers and writers of Europe and America.

### 13 JUNE 1935

*La Novia del Hereje (Heretic's Bride),* opera in three acts by the 54-year-old Italian-born Argentinian composer Pascual de ROGATIS, written in a melodramatically Italianate operatic idiom, is performed for the first time in Buenos Aires.

### 17 JUNE 1935

Holland issues a postage stamp of 5 centimes in honor of the national Flemish composer Alfons DIEPENBROCK (1862–1921).

### 19 JUNE 1935

*Training,* ballet by the 36-year-old Russian composer Alexander TCHEREPNIN, symphonically and choreographically illustrating the training of sportsmen, is performed for the first time in Vienna.

### 20 JUNE 1935

Holland issues a postage stamp of 12½ centimes in honor of the great Dutch organist and composer Jan Pieterszoon SWEELINCK (1562–1621), whose works mark a historic advance in polyphonic instrumental writing.

## 24 JUNE 1935

*Die schweigsame Frau,* eleventh opera by Richard STRAUSS (completed by him on 20 October 1934 at the age of seventy), in three acts, to a libretto by Stefan Zweig, based on Ben Jonson's comedy *Epicene,* wherein a retired mariner, oversensitive to noise, is tricked by a designing nephew into a fraudulent marriage to an ostensibly silent woman who is actually the nephew's own wife, and who stages at once a wild charivari, driving the victim to distraction, set to music full of effervescent badinage, containing sly quotations from *Rigoletto* and *Tannhäuser,* with a happy ending vouchsafed to all in idyllic E-flat major when true identities are revealed, is produced in Dresden.

## 13 JULY 1935

Richard STRAUSS resigns his post as President of the Reichsmusikkammer, ostensibly on account of lack of time and advanced age, but reportedly because of profound distaste for Nazi interference in artistic life and reluctance to part with his favorite Jewish librettist Stefan Zweig. (Peter Raabe was appointed to succeed Richard Strauss)

## 17 JULY 1935

Emile RIADIS, "the Greek Ravel," whose instrumental music preserves the modal ethos of eternal Hellas under the glitter of impressionistic coloristic devices, dies in Saloniki at the age of forty-five.

## 31 JULY 1935

*Aeneas,* ballet with chorus by Albert ROUSSEL, after Virgil's epic poem *The Aeneid,* is performed for the first time in Brussels.

## 1 AUGUST 1935

The Federal Music Project is organized in Washington as a branch of the Emergency Relief Bureau to provide work for unemployed American musicians.

## 2 AUGUST 1935

Mikola KOLIADA, 28-year-old Ukrainian Soviet composer, whose symphonic poem *Assault on Tractorstroy* provided a classical specimen of Socialist Realism in its optimistic portrayal of agricultural industrialization, perishes in a fall in the Caucasus during a mountain climbing trip.

## 30 AUGUST 1935

The Nazi Reichsmusikkammer issues a decree forbidding Jews and other non-Aryans to play in German orchestras.

## 1 SEPTEMBER 1935

The 13th Festival of the International Society for Contemporary Music opens in Prague with the following program of orchestral music:

*Miserae* by Karl Amadeus Hartmann of Germany, set in a brooding introspective mood and marked by atonal melos; *Piano Concerto* by the Yugoslav composer Slavko Osterc, in three movements, written in a modernistically percussive style, enlivened by asymmetric Balkan rhythms; *Variations* for orchestra, op. 31, by Arnold Schoenberg, a masterpiece of logical construction as instructive in its application of the method of composition with 12 tones as Bach's *Kunst der Fuge* is for Baroque counterpoint; *Cello Concerto* by the Prague composer Karel Hába, brother of the quarter-tone pioneer Alois Hába, written in an athematic modern idiom and governed solely by contrasts of adhesive mood-motifs; and *Second Symphony* by the Soviet composer Vissarion Shebalin, set in an expansive rhapsodic style, instinct with broad Russian melos.

### 2 SEPTEMBER 1935

At the second concert of the 13th Festival of the International Society for Contemporary Music in Prague the following program of chamber music is presented:

*Sonata* for violin and piano by the Dutch composer Henk Badings, in a motoristically modernistic and lyrically implosive idiom; *Berceuse* for voice, flute, clarinet, and harp by the Polish composer Boleslaw Woytowicz, written in a dramatic neo-Mussorgskyan vein; *Four Songs* for voice and string quartet by H. W. Suesskind of Czechoslovakia, conceived in a fresh lyric manner; *Concertino* for two pianos by the German composer Fidelio Finke, in three characteristically archaizing neo-classical movements, *Alla Marcia, Nocturno* and *Quodlibet; Dialectic* for string quartet by the English composer Alan Bush, written in a lucid polythematic vein; *Divertimento in Four Studies* for soprano, flute, oboe, clarinet, viola and cello by the Italian modernist Luigi Dallapiccola, set in a rationally pantonal style, depicting four basic tempers—melancholy, gaiety, joy, despair—of the medieval system of four humors; and *Fantasy* for string orchestra by the Swiss composer Willy Burkhard, in a neo-classical setting.

### 4 SEPTEMBER 1935

At the third concert of the 13th Festival of the International Society for Contemporary Music in Prague the following program of chamber music is presented:

*String Quartet* by Sándor Veress of Hungary, in a synthetic style set in the matrix of Bartók and Kodály; *Introduction and Allegro* for violin and eleven instruments by the Italian modernist Goffredo Petrassi, in a hedonistic neo-Scarlattian style, performed under the composer's direction; *String Quartet* by the Belgian composer Raymond Chevreuille, written according to the expressionistic concordance of harmony-moods; *Concerto* for 9 instruments by Anton von Webern, op. 24, dedicated to Arnold Schoenberg on his 60th birthday, and based on a dodecaphonic series of four 3-note segments, related to one another by reversion, inversion and reversed inversion, with the minor second and its inversion, the major seventh, as cybernetical intervals governing the melodic and harmonic formations, in linear and vertical dimensions, arranged in a characteristically subtilized instrumentation of maximum expressive power achieved by a minimum of sonorous means; *Sonata for Harp* by Alexander Jemnitz of Hungary, set in an atonal manner marked by the minutest discrimination of dynamic elements; *Prelude, Interlude and Fugue* for two violins by the Scottish composeress Elizabeth Maconchy, in a neo-Bachian style; *Chaconne* and *Etude-Toccata* for piano by Vladimir VOGEL, of Moscow and Berlin, written in a neo-Baroque style trammeled with neo-Busonian polyphony; and *Wind Quintet* in a hedonistically utilitarian vein by Alexander MOYZES of Czechoslovakia.

### 6 SEPTEMBER 1935

At the fourth concert of the 13th Festival of the International Society for Contemporary Music in Prague the following program of symphonic music is given:

*Poème héroique* by Jef van DURME of Belgium, set in a neo-romantic pseudo-programmatic vein allowing occasional excursions into harmonic modernities; *Symphony in A Major* by the French neo-romanticist Pierre Octave FERROUD, performed less than a year before his tragic death, written in a polyphonically imbricated, harmonically dense style influenced by his teacher Florent Schmitt; *Piano Concerto* by Pavel BORKOVEC of Czechoslovakia, in a modernistic virtuoso style of the Prokofiev type; *Symphonic Suite* from the opera *Lulu* by Alban BERG, played less than four months before his untimely death; and *Cesta života (The Road of Life)*, symphonic fantasy in seven connected sections by Alois HÁBA of Prague, atonal and athematic in structure, set in a densely polyphonic dissonant idiom, and portraying in varying intervallic formations the three dominant anthroposophic figures of the universe, Christ (the most diatonic), Lucifer (the most atonal) and Ahriman (the most compressed).

### 12 SEPTEMBER 1935

A century has elapsed since the bass tuba was patented by Wilhelm Wieprecht, Director of the Berlin Gardes du Corps-Musik.

### 30 SEPTEMBER 1935

*Porgy and Bess*, folk opera in three acts by George GERSHWIN, his last major work (completed by him on 2 September 1935), to the libretto by his brother Ira Gershwin drawn from the play *Porgy* by Du Bose and Dorothy Heyward, portraying in nostalgic blues and neurotically vibrant jazz modalities the dark peripeteia of Negro life in Catfish Row in Charleston, South Carolina, focusing on the cripple Porgy who kills the former lover of his beloved Bess but loses her in the end when she goes off to New York with a character called Sportin' Life, containing such perennial classics as *Summertime, I Got Plenty of Nuttin'* and the skeptical exposure of biblical tales, *It Ain't Necessarily So*, is performed for the first time in Boston. (The first New York production took place on 10 October 1935. The European première took place in Copenhagen, in Nazi-infested Denmark, on 27 March 1943)

### 4 OCTOBER 1935

*Second Symphony* by the 36-year-old American composer Harl McDONALD, subtitled *Reflections of an Era of Turmoil*, with a *Rumba* movement replacing the conventional scherzo, is performed for the first time by the Philadelphia Orchestra, Leopold Stokowski conducting.

### 10 OCTOBER 1935

*First Symphony* in B-flat minor by the 22-year-old Soviet composer Tikhon KHRENNIKOV, his graduation piece at the Moscow Conservatory, in three movements, *Allegro, Adagio,* and *Molto Allegro,* set in an enticingly melodious, ingratiatingly harmonious and exuberantly rhythmic vein, in commendable accord with the symphonic precepts of Socialist Realism, is performed for the first time in Moscow.

#### 12 OCTOBER 1935

Eugen HADAMOWSKI, director of the Nazi Radio Network issues the order to ban jazz music from the German air waves in order to "eliminate the last vestige of Jewish Kultur-Bolschewismus."

#### 13 OCTOBER 1935

Klaus PRINGSHEIM, German conductor long resident in Japan conducts in Tokyo the first performance of his *Piano Concerto* in C major, employing Japanese pentatonic melodies set in accommodating Western harmonies.

#### 15 OCTOBER 1935

On the approximate centennial of the death in France of the great Italian opera composer Vincenzo BELLINI, the Italian post office issues a series of postage stamps in his honor, at 20, 30, 50, 125, and 275 lire and at six denominations of airmail stamps.

#### 18 OCTOBER 1935

Carlos CHÁVEZ conducts in Mexico City the first performance of his *Obertura Republicana,* making thematic use of three revolutionary Mexican songs of the 19th-century—*Marcha Zacatecas, Club Verde* and *La Adelita.*

#### 19 OCTOBER 1935

*Radio-Panoramique,* symphonic sketch by Arthur HONEGGER, a mechanistic radiorama burlesquing the multi-channeled versatility of the radio, switching stations from symphony to jazz, from Viennese waltzes to sacred music in kaleidophonic profusion, is performed for the first time in public in Paris. (The first radio broadcast of *Radio-Panoramique* was given by Radio-Geneva as a commissioned work in March 1935)

#### 19 OCTOBER 1935

*Fourth Symphony* in A major by Albert ROUSSEL, in four classically contrasted movements: an incisive *Allegro con brio*; a wistfully pensive *Lento molto*; a tersely mobile *Allegro scherzando*; and a graceful *Finale,* marking a historical turn away from obsolescent Impressionism in the direction of enlightened Gallic neo-classicism, with sparkling polytonalities projected on the clear surfaces of tonal writing, is performed for the first time in Paris.

#### 22 OCTOBER 1935

*Quiet Flows the Don,* opera in four acts by the 27-year-old Soviet composer Ivan DZERZHINSKY, after the novel of Mikhail Sholokhov, detailing the dramatic events in the Don basin during the turbulent early months of the Revolution, written in an esthetically proper idiom with ethnic undertones, in accordance with the tenets of Socialist Realism, diversified by euphonious dissonances and stark progressions in consecutive triads, is performed for the first time in Leningrad. (The title is usually given in English as *Quiet Flows the Don*; the Russian title, *Tikhy Don*, is literally *Pacific Don*)

The success of Dzerzhinsky's opera is explained by the fact that its dramatic backbone is constructed firmly and effectively. There is no unnecessary psychologizing, no annoying digging into the hero's soul, no leftist oversimplification in the portrayal of significant social phenomena. Striving towards the realistic truth, Dzerzhinsky remains uncontaminated by the extremes of musical expressionism with its morbid exposure of psychic aberrations. He does not ignore individual heroic personages to put emphasis solely on mass action, as some Soviet composers are apt to do. *Don, the Pacific* is superior as a historical opera to the propaganda type of certain other Soviet operas. One of its great advantages is the accessibility of its musical language. The score is distinguished by simplicity, expressive vigor and fine characterization of action. The composer does not resort to musical quotations from revolutionary songs, but rather endeavors to recreate the revolutionary genre in accordance with historical truth. The folksong intonations in the opera are products of complex transformations of materials underlying the melos of popular songs and dances. Naturalistic ethnology and artificial folksiness are alien to the realistic method of Ivan Dzerzhinsky. (A. Ostretzov in the program book for the performance of the opera at The Bolshoi Theater in Moscow in 1936)

### 26 OCTOBER 1935

*O noapte furtunoasa*, comic opera by the 26-year-old Rumanian composer Paul CONSTANTINESCU, based on a modern Rumanian farce, wherein a gallant beau inadvertently enters the darkened bedroom of a policeman's wife instead of that of her sister with whom he had a nocturnal assignation, written in a vivacious Gallic manner seasoned with native gitanesque rhythms, is produced in Bucharest.

### 28 OCTOBER 1935

*Fifteenth Symphony* in D minor by the most prolific Russian symphonist Nicolai MIASKOVSKY, in four movements (completed on 29 November 1934), exhaling an optimistic air with relatively few introspective digressions, ostentatiously Russian in its rhapsodic expanse, but free from explicit folkloric references, is performed for the first time by the Moscow Radio Orchestra.

Many praise my *Fifteenth Symphony* for its optimism and lyricism. But this is not the proper language in order to express the feelings of an artist of the present day. I do not know what this language ought to be, and I possess no recipe for its formation. Neither folksong patterns nor city ballads can be the exclusive ingredients of the musical language of Socialist Realism. (Nicolas Miaskovsky, *Autobiographical Notes*, in *Sovietskaya Musica*, No. 6, 1936)

### 30 OCTOBER 1935

The Composers' Forum-Laboratory, a branch of the Federal Music Project, designed to provide a pragmatic outlet for creative activities of American composers in the depths of economic and moral depression, opens in New York with a program of compositions by Roy Harris.

Here music expressive of every shade of thought and feeling peculiar to this movement in history will have a hearing. The purpose of these Forums is to provide an opportunity for serious composers residing in America, both known and unknown, to hear their own compositions and to test audience reaction. (From the statement of aims of the Composers' Forum-Laboratory)

## 2 NOVEMBER 1935

*Ero s onoga Svijeta* (*A Rogue from the World Beyond*), comic opera in three acts by the 40-year-old Croatian composer Jacov GOTOVAC, wherein a playful revenant causes posthumous mischief in his native village, is produced in Zagreb.

## 6 NOVEMBER 1935

The first complete performance is given by the British Broadcasting Corporation Symphony Orchestra in London, with Sir Hamilton Harty conducting, of the *First Symphony* by the 33-year-old English composer William WALTON, in four classically delineated movements, marked by the conspicuous absence of a key signature, but with the music firmly rooted in tonal foundations:

(1) *Allegro assai,* opening and closing on B flat in unison, moving gently along a swift Baroque current of kinetic energy, with a dynamic design following the logarithmic curve ranging from pianissimo to fortissimo (2) *Presto, con malizia,* focused on a unison E, an ironic scherzo in rustic modalities, with the "malice" of the title implied by an episodic use of obsolete diminished-seventh chords and obsolescent whole-tone progressions and the ostentatious employment of the tritone, the "diabolus in musica" of the medieval theorists, the dynamic curve being that of a catenary (3) *Andante con malinconia,* opening and closing on C sharp in unison, a stylized eclogue permeated by unpessimistic melancholy, the dynamic design following the outline of the arching "Witch of Agnesi" oscillating between piano and forte (4) *Maestoso,* opening and closing on B flat in unison, coming to a standstill on a pause, then plunging into a precipitous *Brioso ed ardentemente,* culminating in a pyrotechnical fugue on a subject built on ascending fourths, the dynamic design being that of a catenary extending from fortissimo to fortississimo. (The first three movements, without the Finale, were first performed in London by the BBC Orchestra, Sir Hamilton Harty conducting, on 3 December 1934)

## 14 NOVEMBER 1935

Paul HINDEMITH plays the solo viola part with the Concertgebouw Orchestra in Amsterdam, Willem Mengelberg conducting, in the world première of his concerto for viola and orchestra, entitled *Der Schwanendreher.*

## 16 NOVEMBER 1935

*Jumbo,* American musical comedy by Richard RODGERS, in which the circus elephant Jumbo becomes the object of contention between two rival impresarios, featuring also the non-pachydermic songs *The Most Beautiful Girl in the World* and *My Romance,* is produced in New York.

## 21 NOVEMBER 1935

*Sixth Symphony* by the English neo-romantic composer Arnold BAX, in three movements: (1) *Moderato,* set in opulent secundal harmonies over deep pedal-points (2) *Lento molto espressivo,* marked by a cornucopia of crepuscular melismas in tenebrous polyphony with a plethora of sepulchral cadences (3) *Introduction, Scherzo and Trio, Epilogue,* successively pensive, somberly exulting, and funereally festive, is performed for the first time by the London Philharmonic Orchestra, Sir Hamilton Harty conducting.

## 21 NOVEMBER 1935

Igor STRAVINSKY plays in Paris, with his son Sviatoslav Soulima-Stravinsky, the first performance of his *Concerto for Two Pianos,* without orchestral accompaniment, couched in a terse neo-Baroque idiom, in four movements: (1) *Con moto,* focused on the tonic E in the pandiatonic matrix of a toccata (2) Notturno, a neo-Scarlattian eclogue (3) *Quattro Variazioni,* in a pellucid percussive manner (4) *Preludio e Fuga,* set in sharply clashing tonalities, with a magistral coda concluding on a tonic seventh E major chord.

## 21 NOVEMBER 1935

*Malaisie,* symphonic triptych by the 50-year-old neo-romantic Belgian composer Léon JONGEN, reporting in exotically coloristic tones the impressions of his travels in Malaya, is performed for the first time in Brussels.

## 21 NOVEMBER 1935

*Third Symphony* by the 38-year-old Danish composer Knudaage RIISAGER, in three vehement movements, *Feroce, Violente e fantastico, Tumultuoso,* is performed for the first time in Copenhagen.

## 23 NOVEMBER 1935

Ethel LEGINSKA, English-born Americanized composeress and conductoress (who added a feminine Slavic ending *ka* to her unappealingly Anglo-Saxon name Liggins, and also modulated the initial vowel, in the hope of having a better chance for a career in a music world riddled with Polish-Russian aspirants) conducts in Chicago the first performance of her opera in two scenes *Gale,* subtitled *The Haunting,* dealing with a sailor named Gale who drowns his brother in a pool to secure his part in the family fortune, but is lured by his victim's ghost to his death in the same watery grave.

## 28 NOVEMBER 1935

The Italian Ministry of Propaganda issues a decree forbidding performances in Italy of works by authors and composers of nations members of the Council of the League of Nations which have voted punitive sanctions against Italy for its aggressive war on Ethiopia.

The Ministry of Propaganda has issued precise instructions to all its branches to define the proper attitude in the field of artistic activities adopted by Italy towards nations

614

which have voted sanctions against it. On the basis of these instructions, plays by the nationals of the sanctionist powers are to be excluded from the repertory of Italian theaters, with the exception of Shakespeare and George Bernard Shaw. Special provisions have been made in regard to French drama, in consideration of the respectful attitude towards Italy taken by the majority of French intellectuals. Italian opera companies are to cancel productions of works by composers belonging to the sanctionist nations, except for French operas, with a reduced number of presentations. . . . In the concert field, music by composers of the sanctionist nations is to be eliminated entirely from the programs with the exception of a limited number of symphonic and chamber works by French and Spanish composers. In the field of light music, however, all works by representatives of sanctionist countries are to be taken off the repertory. Prohibitions and limitations will also be imposed on the activities in Italy. of artists from the sanctionist nations. Performers of vaudeville, musical revues, operettas, operas, dancers, concert artists and conductors will no longer be allowed to appear in Italy, with some exceptions of individual French artists. The production of works by all expatriate living Russian authors who carry White Russian passports, is allowed without any restrictions, and Russian artists traveling on such passports are free to engage in professional activities in Italy. In the field of radio, Italian music and the music of nations that are not signatories to the sanctions agains Italy are the only works allowed to be broadcast, although a limited quantity of French music may be included. Regulations similar to those applied to radio programs will be enforced also to cinema orchestras and public functions in general. (Excerpts from the order of the Italian Ministry for the Press and Propaganda obtained by the author in 1936)

1 DECEMBER 1935

*Second Violin Concerto* in G minor by Sergei PROKOFIEV (completed in Baku on 16 August 1935) in three movements: an impulsively exuberant *Allegro Moderato,* set in sonata form, with lyrical discursions imparting a characteristic touch of poetic irony; *Andante assai,* an eclogue, in which an artfully exfoliating melody in the violin solo is accompanied by rhythmic figurations, and a waltzing Finale, *Allegro ben marcato,* is performed in Madrid, Spain, for the first time anywhere.

5 DECEMBER 1935

*May Wine,* musical play by Sigmund ROMBERG, exploring in uninhibitedly enticing accents the psychoanalytic aspects of marital infidelity, is produced in New York.

8 DECEMBER 1935

*Pamir,* a geographically scenic symphonic suite by the French composer Claude DELVINCOURT, extracted from his film score *La Croisière jaune,* and depicting in its four movements the alpestrine Central Asian mountains of Pamir, known as "Top of the World," a caravan ascending the snow-covered trails, the nomadic Kirghiz horsemen, and the Great Wall of China, is performed for the first time in Paris. (Another symphonic suite from the same film score entitled *Films d'Asie,* was first performed in Paris on 16 January 1937)

## 12 DECEMBER 1935

*La Spirale*, a group of modern-minded French composers, organized to promote French music, presents its initial concert at the Schola Cantorum in Paris, in a program of chamber music by Claire DELBOS, André JOLIVET, Paul LE FLEM, Jules LEFEBVRE, Édouard SCIORTINO, Georges MIGOT, DANIEL-LESUR, and Olivier MESSIAEN.

*La Spirale* does not limit itself to first performances but will rather strive to give repeated hearings of significant works. The name *La Spirale* was adopted because a spiral is infinite and symbolizes the spirit of progress, being constantly attached to its point of origin and yet tracing a new path at its every turn. (From the declaration of the organizational committee of *La Spirale* printed in the program book of its inaugural concert)

## 15 DECEMBER 1935

*La Passione*, oratorio for soloists, chorus and orchestra by Gian Francesco MALIPIERO, to the text of the second part of the 16th-century mystery play by Pierrozzo Castellani, *Rappresentazione della Cena e Passione*, written in a deliberately archaic two-dimensional monodic perspective, in the manner of a religious fresco, is performed for the first time in Rome.

## 16 DECEMBER 1935

The Metropolitan Opera Company of New York issues a ruling banning the paid claque and forbidding its singers to hire claqueurs, and a fortiori, hissers and booers of rival artists.

## 21 DECEMBER 1935

*Divertissement* for chamber orchestra by the 23-year-old "jeune français" Jean FRANÇAIX, written in a hedonistic neo-rococo manner of Gallic modernism, is performed for the first time in Paris.

## 24 DECEMBER 1935

*Nerghiz*, opera in four acts by the 50-year-old Azerbaijan composer Muslim MAGOMAYEV, relating in epical tones and ethnically Caucasian accents the story of a native village girl named Nerghiz, who fights in the Bolshevik ranks against the imperialist forces operating in the Caucasus in 1919, shoots to death a lecherous landlord who tries to lure her to his capitalistic habitat and subvert her proletarian consciousness, and liberates her shepherd lover, as the Red Army batters down the last bastion of the enemy's defense, is produced in Baku. (A new version, orchestrated by Reinhold Glière, was produced at the Festival of Azerbaijan Music in Moscow on 11 April 1938)

## 24 DECEMBER 1935

Alban BERG, Austrian composer whose expressionistic music penetrates deeply into the subliminal recesses of the human consciousness and at whose hands the twelve-tone method of composition promulgated by his teacher Arnold Schoenberg has become the emotional language of modern man, dies in Vienna of blood poisoning at the age of fifty.

In the first days of September 1935, Alban Berg had to cancel his trip to Prague to participate in the Festival of the International Society for Contemporary Music on account of an abscess on his back. The abscess was removed by surgical means and soon healed, but it proved to be the beginning of a fatal illness. On 17 December 1935 he was taken to the hospital; a blood transfusion brought about a slight improvement. He expressed a wish to thank the blood donor personally. After he saw him—it was a young Viennese boy—he turned to me and observed with an ineffable expression, "I only hope that his blood will not make an operetta composer out of me!" On 22 December the illness took a catastrophic turn: the heart refused to function. On 24 December 1935, 15 minutes after one o'clock, Alban Berg died in the arms of his wife. (Willi Reich, *Alban Berg,* Vienna, 1937)

## 25 DECEMBER 1935

A triple opera, in three acts, *Das almachtige Gold, Harla,* and *Dame in Traum,* by Franz SALMHOFER, is produced in Vienna.

# ᘓ 1936 ᘔ

## 3 JANUARY 1936

*Third Symphony* by the 36-year-old American composer Harl McDONALD, subtitled *Lamentations of Fu Hsuan,* for soprano solo, chorus and orchestra, is performed for the first time by the Philadelphia Orchestra.

## 11 JANUARY 1936

On the eightieth birthday of the Norwegian composer Christian SINDING, his *Fourth Symphony,* subtitled *Winter and War,* is performed for the first time in Oslo, as a tribute to his earnest achievements in advancing the cause of Norwegian music.

## 12 JANUARY 1936

Theodore METZ, American composer of the celebrated inebriating song hit *There'll Be a Hot Time in the Old Town Tonight,* dies in New York in his 89th year.

## 19 JANUARY 1936

At the dedication ceremony of the Theodore Roosevelt Memorial at the American Museum of Natural History in New York, Vittorio GIANNINI, 32-year-old American composer of Italian parentage, conducts the first performance of his symphonic work commissioned for the occasion, entitled *In Memoriam: Theodore Roosevelt.*

### 22 JANUARY 1936

*Cyrano de Bergerac,* opera in four acts by the 59-year-old Italian composer Franco ALFANO, to a libretto fashioned after Edmond Rostand's dramatic play dealing with the nasute poet's vicarious romance as an epistolary alter ego of an untutored but sexually balanced army soldier, is produced in Rome.

### 22 JANUARY 1936

Two days after the death of King George V of England, Paul HINDEMITH plays in London the solo part in the first performance of his *Funeral Music* for viola and string orchestra, written on the day before as a tribute to the innocuous old British sovereign.

### 22 JANUARY 1936

*Quadruple Concerto* for woodwind quartet and orchestra by the "jeune français" Jean FRANÇAIX is performed for the first time in Paris.

### 23 JANUARY 1936

Carlos CHÁVEZ conducts the Columbia Broadcasting Symphony Orchestra in New York in the first performance of his *Sinfonia India,* his second symphony, employing a large array of primitive Mexican percussion instruments (Yaqui drums, water gourd, a string of desiccated butterfly cocoons, a chain of deer hooves, two teponaxtles, a huehuetl, claves, maracas, guïro, etc., interchangeable, if necessary, with more common drums and rattles), in one continuous movement, making use of three authentic pentatonic Mexican tunes, in a treatment abounding in changing meters, but with the eighth-note as the least common denominator maintaining a uniform beat, with a coda of 125 bars of relentless reiteration of a tune from the island of Tiburon in the gulf of Baja California over the firm pedal-point on tonic F, and concluding on a pandiatonic chord.

### 24 JANUARY 1936

*The Nations of the Soviet Land,* "vocal symphony" by the 36-year-old Soviet composer Klimenty KORCHMAREV, in five choral movements, each representing an ethnic section of the Soviet Union, *Sonata* (Kazakhstan), *Andante* (Russian), *Scherzo* (Jewish), *Canzona* (Ukrainian) and *Danza-Finale* (Moldavian), is performed for the first time in Moscow.

### 28 JANUARY 1936

An ominously anonymous article entitled *Confusion Instead of Music,* bearing all the signs of a centrally inspired authoritative declaration of policy, is published in *Pravda,* organ of the Communist Party of the USSR, condemning

SHOSTAKOVICH's opera *Lady Macbeth of the District of Mzensk* as the product of Western-oriented un-Soviet activities in the field of music.

As culture continues to advance in our land, there has been an increasing demand for good music. Never in history have composers enjoyed such public support as in our country. Popular masses are eager to hear new songs, instrumental works, good operas. . . . Several Soviet theaters have presented the opera *Lady Macbeth of the District of Mzensk* by Dmitri Shostakovich. Officious music critics have praised the opera to the skies, spreading its fame far and wide. But audiences were bewildered by a stream of deliberately discordant sounds in the music. Melodic fragments, bits of musical phrases popped up on the surface here and there but were immediately drowned, emerging only to disappear once more in the general uproar. To follow this sort of music is difficult, and to enjoy it is impossible. . . . Singing is replaced by screaming. If by some lucky chance the composer happens to hit upon an attractive melodious tune, he hastens, as though horrified by such a calamity, to plunge back into the jungle of musical confusion, at times degenerating into complete cacophony . . . All this is done not because of the composer's lack of talent, not because of his inability to express simple and profound emotions in musical tones. No, his music is distorted deliberately, so as to obliterate all resemblance to classical opera, all connection with natural musical speech. The fundamental concept of this music is a total negation of opera, by analogy with the ideas dominating leftist drama which rejects simplicity and realism in the theater, and scorns imagery and the normal sounds of human speech. It transfers the most pernicious methods of Meyerhold's theatrical productions into the field of music. It is a leftist bedlam instead of human music. The inspiring quality of good music is sacrificed in favor of petty-bourgeois formalist cerebration, with pretense at originality by cheap clowning. This game may end badly . . . The peril of such distortion for Soviet music is clear. Leftist monstrosities in the opera are derived from the same sources as leftist monstrosities in art, in poetry, in pedagogy and in science. The petty-bourgeois "innovations" lead to the renunciation of true art, true science, true literature . . . While our press and our music critics swear by the ideas of Socialist Realism, the musical theater serves us in Shostakovich's opera the coarsest kind of naturalism. Landlords and workers are painted in the same color, emphasizing their most bestial aspects. The predatory merchantwoman who gains a fortune and power through murder is represented as a victim of the bourgeois state . . . The orchestra squeals, grunts, growls, and chokes itself to express love scenes as realistically as possible. This "love" is smeared all over the opera in the most vulgar manner imaginable. The merchant bed occupies the center of the stage, and on it all "problems" are solved . . . The composer apparently is not interested in the wishes and expectations of the Soviet public. He scrambles his notes together in order to appeal to formalistic esthetes who have lost all taste for good art long ago . . . Some critics call this glorification of merchant lust a satire. But there are no satirical elements in the opera. The composer is trying to involve his audience in the lurid and vulgar passions and actions of the merchantwoman, making use of the entire arsenal of his musical and dramatic resources . . . *Lady Macbeth* is highly successful with the bourgeois audiences abroad. It may be that this success is owing to the fact that Shostakovich's opera is utterly devoid of all political meaning, and that it titillates the perverted tastes of the bourgeoisie with its fidgeting, screaming, neurasthenic music. (From the *Pravda* article)

## 28 JANUARY 1936

*Astuzie d'Amore*, opera in three acts by the 44-year-old Italian composer Franco CASAVOLA, is produced in Bari.

## 2 FEBRUARY 1936

*Farhad and Shirin,* music drama in four acts by the Russian composer Victor USPENSKY (1879–1949), to a romantic libretto dealing with the tribulations of a loving couple in Central Asia, written with a declared purpose of promoting ethnological music, and including numerous native instruments in the score, is produced in Tashkent. (The second enlarged version was staged for the first time in Tashkent on 22 March 1937)

## 4 FEBRUARY 1936

The plenary meeting of the Union of Soviet Composers unanimously votes to expel Alexander MOSSOLOV for staging drunken brawls in public places, beating up a waiter in a restaurant and generally behaving "in the glorious old Russian manner" utterly unbecoming to a citizen of a Socialist country.

Having heard the testimony by several comrades revealing a picture of civil and moral decay of Alexander Mossolov, and considering that his disgraceful conduct in the Press Building restaurant on the night of 31 January 1936 was not an isolated instance, but one of numerous episodes that corroborate the above estimate of his character, the plenum of the Union of Soviet Composers, regarding Mossolov's actions as incompatible with the honorable status of a Soviet composer and inadmissible for a Soviet musician, unanimously resolves to expel him from the Union. (*Sovietskaya Musica,* Moscow, March 1936)

## 8 FEBRUARY 1936

*Giulio Cesare,* opera in three acts by Gian Francesco MALIPIERO, to his own libretto after Shakespeare's play, is produced in Genoa.

## 10 FEBRUARY 1936

The Italian Ministry of Propaganda rescinds its ban against the authors and composers of nations, members of the League of Nations, which have voted for the application of sanctions against Italy for its invasion of Ethiopia, but leaves in force the prohibition of appearances by artists from such nations.

Effective on 10 February 1936, provisions regarding the foreign plays and operas promulgated on 28 November 1935 are abrogated . . . Performances of all foreign works may take place if they are approved by the censor's office and receive special authorization issued by the Italian Society of Authors and Publishers. The provision regarding performing artists remains unchanged. (From the text of the order of the Italian Ministry of Propaganda)

## 12 FEBRUARY 1936

*Il Campiello (The Intersection),* comic opera in three acts by the German-Italian composer Ermanno WOLF-FERRARI, after a comedy by Carlo Goldoni, detailing a trivially triangular contention among three girls in a three-way intersection for the favors of a handsome stranger, is produced in Milan.

## 15 FEBRUARY 1936

*Asra*, one-act opera by the 41-year-old Hungarian composer Eugen ZÁDOR, wherein the sociologically inadmissible passion of a young soldier of Yemen for the Caliph's daughter is unexpectedly requited, precipitating a dual cardiac palpitation of such amplitude that they both die, is produced in Budapest.

## 17 FEBRUARY 1936

*Sixth Symphony* by the Soviet composer Lev KNIPPER is performed for the first time in Moscow.

## 17 FEBRUARY 1936

*Hamlets* (Latvian for *Hamlet*), Shakespearean opera in three acts by the Latvian composer Janis KALNIŅŠ, to a libretto in the Latvian language, is produced in Riga.

## 18 FEBRUARY 1936

*Das Gesicht Jesajas (Isaiah's Vision)*, biblical oratorio by the 35-year-old Swiss composer Willy BURKHARD, set in a grand Handelian manner with a discreet admixture of euphonious discords, is performed for the first time by the Chamber Orchestra of Basel, under the direction of its founder Paul Sacher.

## 21 FEBRUARY 1936

A century has passed since the birth of Léo DELIBES, French master of delectably harmonious ballets and appealingly melodious operas.

## 22 FEBRUARY 1936

*Judith*, biblical opera in five acts by the 57-year-old romantic Swedish composer Natanael BERG, is produced in Stockholm.

## 27 FEBRUARY 1936

*Fourth Symphony* in B-flat major by the 33-year-old Soviet composer Vissarion SHEBALIN, in two movements scored for orchestra and military band, couched in the expansive modalities of Slavic melos and dedicated to the heroes of the Russian Civil war of 1918–1920, is performed for the first time in Moscow.

## 28 FEBRUARY 1936

*Bloud (The Simpleton)*, opera in three acts by the dean of Czech composers Josef Bohuslav FOERSTER, to his own libretto after Tolstoy's moralistic tale, contrasting the Pharisaical ostentation of two sanctimoniously eleemosynary mendicants with the sincere goodness of a simple youth who comes to the aid of a blind girl with a sick grandmother, is performed for the first time in Prague.

## 28 FEBRUARY 1936

Two new works by the 38-year-old American composer Roy HARRIS are performed for the first time on the same day, one in Boston and one in Philadelphia: *Second Symphony* in three movements, presented by the Boston Symphony Orchestra, Richard Burgin conducting; and *Prelude and Fugue* for string orchestra, played by the Philadelphia Orchestra, Werner Janssen conducting.

## 1 MARCH 1936

*Guignol,* opéra-bouffe by the 63-year-old French composer André BLOCH, is produced in Lyon.

## 1 MARCH 1936

The once respectable German music monthly, *Die Musik,* now designated as the official organ of the Nazi Cultural Community, issues a special anti-Semitic number featuring articles on such repulsive subjects as *Der Jude als Musik-Fabrikant,* illustrated by portraits and photographs of MENDELSSOHN, MEYERBEER, OFFENBACH, MAHLER, SCHOENBERG, TOCH, WEILL and KLEMPERER, retouched to make their facial expressions appear sinister, with the pupils of their eyes dilated darkly, prefaced by quotations in bold Gothic type from Adolf Hitler's utterances, e.g. "The Jew possesses no culture-building power whatsoever," and quoting also, without documentation, the statement of the long-dead German composer Felix Draeseke, "Our sole salvation lies in anti-Semitism."

## 6 MARCH 1936

Rubin GOLDMARK, New York-born nephew of the Austrian composer Karl Goldmark, and himself the composer of a considerable number of competently fashioned romantic pieces for orchestra, renowned chiefly as a useful pedagogue and compassionate teacher of a generation of American composers, dies in New York, where he settled in 1891, at the age of sixty-three.

## 8 MARCH 1936

*Pagan Symphony* by the 67-year-old romantically inclined British composer Granville BANTOCK, with a motto "Et ego in Arcadia vixi," implying his consanguinity with the world of pre-Christian innocence, completed on 20 June 1928, in a single movement in four sections, a tranquil exordium in denuded harmonies of bare fifths, a scherzoid "dance of satyrs" for frolicking wood-wind instruments, a fast episode with a lot of drum thrumming and a finale concluding in a resonantly unpagan C major, is performed for the first time by the BBC Orchestra in London, conducted by Sir Adrian Boult.

## 10 MARCH 1936

*Œdipe,* lyrical tragedy in four acts by the prime Rumanian composer Georges ENESCO, traversing the tragic peripeteia in the life of Oedipus and the consummated prophecy of parricide and incest, written in a grand romantic style, diversified by numerous modernistic effects, including a brief passage in quarter-tones in the strings to illustrate the psychotomic anguish of the king, with instrumental interludes serving as philosophical commentary on events, is produced at the Paris Opéra.

### 14 MARCH 1936

In consequence of a storm of protest in the United States against the announced engagement of Wilhelm FURTWÄNGLER as conductor of the New York Philharmonic for the season 1936–1937, aroused by his ambiguous relationship with the Nazis and his willingness, however reluctant, to continue his artistic activities in Germany, he releases the management of the New York Philharmonic from its contract in the following cablegram from Luxor, Egypt:

Political controversies disagreeable to me/am not politician but exponent of German music which belongs to all humanity regardless of politics/propose postpone my season in the interests of Philharmonic society and music until the public realizes that politics and music are apart.

### 18 MARCH 1936

The Theater of People's Art, organized for the purpose of promoting musical activities of European and Asian nations, members of the Union of Soviet Socialist Republics, is established in Moscow.

### 21 MARCH 1936

Alexander GLAZUNOV, last great symphonist of old Russia, who wrote his first symphony at the age of sixteen, heir to the glorious national traditions of Balakirev, Borodin and Rimsky-Korsakov, grandmaster of the arts of counterpoint, harmony and orchestration, noble defender of time-honored musical precepts of beauty, euphony and formal perfection, for many years beloved director of the St. Petersburg Conservatory, and teacher of a pleiad of Russian composers, dies at the age of 70 in Paris where he settled after leaving Russia on 15 June 1928.

### 26 MARCH 1936

A Decade (ten days) of Music for National Defense, organized at the initiative of the Political Council of the Union of Soviet Composers, concludes in Moscow its series of four public concerts and three radio broadcasts, in programs of works by 37 composers, each portraying an event of the Soviet Revolution, the Civil War, a phase of domestic economic policy, or a signal achievement in Soviet industry.

### 27 MARCH 1936

*Rossini in Neapel*, light opera in three acts by the 48-year-old Austrian conductor Bernhard PAUMGARTNER on the subject of Rossini's purported amorous adventures in Naples, couched in a congenially songful Neapolitan manner, is performed for the first time in Zürich.

### 3 APRIL 1936

The International Music Festival in Baden-Baden is inaugurated by the Reichsmusikkammer of Nazi Germany to compete with the racially impure International Society for Contemporary Music, in programs of works by composers of untainted Aryan blood, representing eight nations.

### 4 APRIL 1936

Thirteen centuries have elapsed since the death of the Spanish musician and theologian ISIDOR of Seville who said that musical sounds could never be reproduced on paper in precise notation (*scribi non possunt*).

### 9 APRIL 1936

American Guild of Musical Artists (AGMA) is incorporated in New York, the first of its kind in the United States, empowered to act as a bargaining agent for musical performers, on the basis of equality with all labor unions.

### 11 APRIL 1936

*On Your Toes*, musical comedy by Richard RODGERS with book and lyrics by Lorenz Hart, incorporating a jazz ballet *Slaughter on Tenth Avenue*, featuring a love duet *There's a Small Hotel* and a mock-classical number, *The Three B's*, is produced in New York.

### 18 APRIL 1936

Ottorino RESPIGHI, Italian composer of flamboyantly colorful symphonic poems, whose tonal portrayals of the Roman landscape, the pines of its ancient roadways, the fountains of Rome and the stained glass paintings of its churches, coruscate with an almost panoptical brilliance, dies in Rome at 6:10 A.M. at the age of fifty-six.

### 19 APRIL 1936

The 14th Festival of the International Society for Contemporary Music opens in Barcelona, presenting two concerts, one in the morning and one in the evening, with the following programs:

*Three Symphonic Movements (Pastorale, Dance, Nuptial)* for wind instruments by the Catalan composer Josep M. RUERA, set in a neo-archaic style, making use of ancient Greek modes; *Devise* by the Moscow-born German resident composer Wladimir VOGEL, based on a pentaphonic motto-device and a marching tune, the two subjects uniting in the Finale in sextuple counterpoint; *Joan of Os*, symphonic legend for solo singers, chorus and wind instruments by the director of the Municipal Band of Barcelona, Ricard LAMOTE DE GRIGNON, written in a frugal neo-medieval style; and *Dionysiaques*, corybantically turbulent symphonic poem by Florent SCHMITT.

*Prelude and Fugue* by the German neo-classical composer Edmund von BORCK (fated to be killed on 16 February 1944 on the German front in Italy); *Ariel*, ballet suite by the Catalan composer Roberto GERHARD, subdivided into four sections, expressing

624

the four moods of the Shakespearean sprite of *The Tempest;* three fragments from the historical opera *Karl V* by Ernst KRENEK, his first work in the 12-tone style; and the world première of the *Violin Concerto* by Alban BERG, completed by him on 11 August 1935 shortly before his death, and dedicated "to the memory of an angel" (Manon Gropius, 18-year-old daughter of Alma Mahler and her second husband, the architect Gropius), in two bipartite movements, *Andante/Allegretto* and *Allegro/Adagio,* based on a remarkably tonal 12-tone series—G, B-flat, D, F-sharp, A, C, E, G-sharp, B, C-sharp, E-flat, F—representing four conjunct alternating minor and major triads ending with a succession of three whole tones, undergoing a variety of transformations in retrograde and inverted forms, the concluding section being a set of variations on Bach's chorale *Es ist genug* from the cantata *O Ewigkeit, du Donnerwort,* which opens with three whole tones, thus corresponding to the ending of the 12-tone series in the work, played by the American violinist Louis Krasner, who commissioned the Concerto, and conducted by Hermann Scherchen replacing Anton von Webern who in his dogmatic insistence on perfection spent several hours rehearsing the introductory measures of the work, and had to resign from his task; and three fragments from Berg's opera *Wozzeck.*

## 20 APRIL 1936

In the course of the 14th Festival of the International Society for Contemporary Music in Barcelona the following program of chamber music is given:

*Piano Sonata,* Op. 1, in one tripartite movement by the Viennese dodecaphonist Ludwig ZENK; *Four Psalms* for soprano and chamber orchestra by the Swiss neo-classicist Robert BLUM; *Two Movements for String Quartet,* Op. 1, by the 34-year-old New York composer Mark BRUNSWICK, set in a neo-classical idiom; *5 Berceuses* by the Slovak composer Václav KAPRÁL, inspired by memories of cradle songs his mother sang for him and for his eleven brothers and sisters; and *Concertino da Camera* for alto saxophone and small orchestra by the master of French tone-painting Jacques IBERT, in three movements in the compact manner of modern rococo, with explosive cross-accents punctuating the asymmetrically juxtaposed thematic phrases.

## 20 APRIL 1936

*Tsar Kaloyan,* opera in four acts by the 37-year-old Bulgarian composer Pantcho VLADIGEROV, to the story of the Bulgarian 13th-century tsar who slays the non-Bulgarian seducer of the tsarina who thereupon kills herself, in a musical setting enlivened by the influx of asymmetrical Balkan polyrhythms and titivated by Italianate melodic fioriture, is produced in Sofia.

## 21 APRIL 1936

In the course of the 14th Festival of the International Society for Contemporary Music in Barcelona, the following program of chamber music is given:

*Sonata* for flute and piano by the American master contrapuntist Walter PISTON in three classically contrasted movements, written in a rationally lucid, rhythmically virile melodic style; *5 Sonnets of Elizabeth Browning* by the erudite Vienna composer Egon WELLESZ, for soprano and string quartet set in the style of an instrumental Lied; *Suite* for violin and piano by the rising 22-year-old Englishman Benjamin BRITTEN, in four movements, *March, Moto Perpetuo, Lullaby,* and *Waltz,* based on a thematic 4-

note motto; *Quelques Airs de Clarisse Juranville* for soprano, string quartet and piano by the Belgian composer André Souris, couched in a surrealistic but tonal style of "kinesthetic action"; *Les Ombres perennes* for piano by the Catalan composer Manuel Blancafort, in three neo-classical movements; and *String Quartet No. 5* by Béla Bartók in sharply contrasted five movements permeated with resiliently asymmetrical Transylvanian rhythms, composed in a month between 6 August and 6 September 1934 as a commission by Elizabeth Sprague Coolidge, and first performed on 8 April 1935 at the Coolidge Festival, at the Library of Congress in Washington.

## 22 APRIL 1936

At the 14th Festival of the International Society for Contemporary Music in Barcelona the following program of orchestral music is given:

*Sun-Treader* by the American composer Carl Ruggles, with a motto from Robert Browning, written in an intensely emotional, dissonantly atonal style (first performed in Paris on 25 February 1932); *Fourth Symphony* by Albert Roussel, in four movements written in a translucid neo-classical style; *Concerto* for piano and orchestra by the Swiss composer Frank Martin, in a contained romantic style marked by propulsive rhythms; *Don Lindo de Almería*, choreographic tone poem by the 35-year-old Spanish modernist Rodolfo Halffter; *Concerto quasi una Fantasia* for violin and orchestra by the Parisianized Rumanian, Marcel Mihalovici; and *Danse Polonaise*, based on Carpathian melorhythms, by the Polish composer Roman Palester.

## 23 APRIL 1936

In the course of the 14th Festival of the International Society for Contemporary Music in Barcelona, the following program of orchestral music is presented:

*Overture*, a piece of abstract theatrical music by the 32-year-old Englishman Lennox Berkeley, written in the pandiatonic technique of freely intermingled and superimposed tones of the major scale resulting in a cornucopia of multitriadic harmonies; *Symphony* in two movements by the Austrian composer Karl Alfred Deutsch, resident in Paris, set in a melodiously atonal idiom; *Second Concerto* for violin and orchestra by the prime composer of modern Poland, Karol Szymanowski, thematically derived from Carpathian folk songs; *Sinfonía* with piano concertante by the Manila-born Spanish composer, Federico Elizalde, in four movements bristling with Hispanic melorhythms; and a neo-classical *Overture* by the 27-year-old Swedish composer Lars-Erik Larsson.

## 25 APRIL 1936

*Notturno romantico*, lyric drama by the Italian composer Riccardo Pick-Mangiagalli, is produced in Rome.

## 25 APRIL 1936

The 14th Festival of the International Society for Contemporary Music in Barcelona concludes with a concert of modern Spanish music in the following program:

*La Nochebuena del Diablo*, cantata by the prime Spanish romanticist Oscar Esplá, to a text derived from a popular children's story dealing with the prowling devil at

Christmas time; *Sonatina,* in the form of a ballet by the 31-year-old Spanish composer Ernesto HALFFTER, brother of Rodolfo Halffter; three dances from the ballet *Sombrero de los Tres Picos* by Manuel de FALLA; *Bailada* for piano and orchestra by the 37-year-old Spanish composer Salvador BACARISSE; *Por el Rio Guadalquivir* by the Spanish colorist Joaquín TURINA; *Triana* by Isaac ALBÉNIZ, orchestrated by Fernández ARBÓS; *Iniciación* from *Liturgía Negra* by the 49-year-old Spanish composer Pedro SANJUÁN, inspired by the Afro-Cuban ritual; *Sardana* by the Catalan composer Juli GARRETA (1875–1925); fragments from *Goyescas* by Enrique GRANADOS; and *El Comte Arnau,* lyric poem for voices, chorus and orchestra by the founder of Spanish ethnomusicology Felipe PEDRELL.

### 1 MAY 1936

The Soviet *Wind Massive,* instrumental ensemble of 3,150 wind and percussion players, gives its inaugural performance in Leningrad in celebration of May Day.

### 2 MAY 1936

At a children's concert of the Moscow Philharmonic, the first performance is given of *Peter and the Wolf,* symphonic fairy tale by Sergei PROKOFIEV, with a speaker recounting the ingenuous story, set to music in an euphoniously infantiloquent style with acrid dissonances at dramatic points, wherein each character is portrayed by a musical instrument: Peter by the violins, his grouchy grandfather by the bassoon, the predatory wolf by three massed horns, the bird, which helps Peter to fling the rope around the wolf's head and capture him, by the flute, the hapless duck, temporarily swallowed by the wolf, by the oboe, the unreliable cat by the clarinet in the low register, and the hunters by the kettledrums and the bass drum. (First sketches were completed on 15 April 1936; full score was finished on 24 April 1936; these dates were communicated to the author by Prokofiev in 1938)

### 7 MAY 1936

The first flying piano recital is given by the German pianist Franz WAGNER of Dresden, who presents a program of romantic music on the aluminum grand piano installed in the German dirigible *Hindenburg* during its first transatlantic crossing from Hamburg to New York.

### 12 MAY 1936

*Second Piano Concerto* in G minor, by the Soviet composer Dmitri KABALEVSKY, in three movements, an optimistic *Allegro moderato,* a philosophical *Andante semplice* and a tempestuous *Allegro molto,* written in an idiom gravitating towards the conjugate foci of tonality, but making use also of 20th-century devices such as concatenations of consecutive triads, instant modulation and juxtapositions of unresolved dissonances, is performed for the first time in Moscow.

### 12 MAY 1936

*The Poisoned Kiss,* or *The Empress and the Necromancer,* romantic extravaganza in three acts by Ralph VAUGHAN WILLIAMS, to a libretto drawn from

Richard Garnett's story *The Poison Maid,* wherein a magician's daughter named Tormentilla, who is inured to poisons but whose veneniferous kiss is lethal to admirers, is decontaminated by the antitoxic love of the son of the Empress, is produced in Cambridge, England.

### 13 MAY 1936

The last concert is given at the Teatro Augusteo in Rome before its demolition to uncover the tomb of the Emperor Augustus presumed to lie under the site of the hall. (1,935 concerts had been given at the Teatro Augusteo, producing 940 works by Italian composers, of which 531 were first performances, and 1,492 non-Italian compositions.)

### 26 MAY 1936

*Doktor Johannes Faust,* opera by the 35-year-old German composer Hermann REUTTER, to a libretto in which the devil guarantees to Faust 24 years of uninhibited fulfillment of all his desires, is produced in Frankfurt.

### 27 MAY 1936

The Orquesta Sinfónica Nacional of Bogotá is formally established by the Colombian government, with Guillermo ESPINOSA as its conductor.

### 29 MAY 1936

Igor MARKEVITCH, 23-year-old Russian-born Parisian composer and conductor, leads in Paris the first performance of his oratorio *Paradis Perdu,* inspired by Milton's classic poem, in two parts, of which the first portrays the fall of Adam and Eve in tumultuously discordant harmonies and the second depicts their redemption in relatively euphonious tones.

### 3 JUNE 1936

*La Jeune France,* a group of young French composers, united in their determination to promote modern French music, presents in Paris a program of orchestral compositions, by its founding members, Olivier MESSIAEN, DANIEL-LESUR, Yves BAUDRIER, André JOLIVET, and, in a matripotestal capacity, Germaine TAILLEFERRE, a member of the young French group of a previous generation, Les Six.

As life becomes increasingly strenuous, mechanized and impersonal, musicians ought to endeavor to contribute spiritual excitement to music lovers. *La Jeune France,* reviving the name once used by Berlioz, sets out on the intransigent course taken by him long ago. Its membership consists of four young French composers working in friendly association: Olivier Messiaen, Daniel-Lesur, Yves Baudrier, and André Jolivet. The aim of the group is to promote performances of musical works which are youthful and free, standing aloof from revolutionary slogans or academic formulas . . . The personal tendencies of the members of the group are diverse; their common agreement lies in their desire to cultivate sincerity, gnerosity and artistic good faith . . . The society intends to encourage performances of new French works which suffer from neglect through the indifference of official institutions, or lack of funds, and to continue in this century the tradition of the great composers of the past who have made French music one of the purest gems of civilization. (From the manifesto of *La Jeune France* printed in the program of its inaugural concert)

### 15 JUNE 1936

*Le Roi nu,* ballet with music by the young Gallic musical hedonist Jean FRANÇAIX, after the celebrated ironic tale by Hans Christian Andersen about a vain king wearing invisible clothes, is performed for the first time in Paris.

### 29 JUNE 1936

The Congress of the United States presents a gold medal to George M. Cohan in recognition of his meritorious service as the composer of the rousing World War I song *Over There* and of the patriotic ballad *You're a Grand Old Flag.*

### 11 JULY 1936

On the occasion of the centennial of the birth of the Brazilian national composer Antonio Carlos GOMES, the Brazilian Post Office issues a series of stamps with musical quotations from his works, marking the first use of musical notation in philatelic history.

### 14 JULY 1936

On the French national holiday, two plays by Romain Rolland, *Danton* and *Le 14 Juillet* are presented in public performance at the Paris Arena, with incidental music especially written for the occasion by Albert ROUSSEL, Arthur HONEGGER, Jacques IBERT, Daniel LAZARUS, Darius MILHAUD, Georges AURIC, and Charles KOECHLIN.

### 17 JULY 1936

*La Ciudad roja,* patriotic opera in three acts by the Argentinian composer Raúl ESPOILE, dealing with the blockade of the littoral of Argentina by the French fleet in 1840, ending on a major triad with an added sixth as a symbol of victory, is produced at the Teatro Colón in Buenos Aires.

### 17 JULY 1936

Nie ER, 23-year-old Chinese Communist composer of the revolutionary song *Along the Yangtze River,* accidentally drowns in the Sea of Japan.

### 12 AUGUST 1936

The great Polish pianist and statesman Ignace PADEREWSKI appears for the first time in a cinematic performance, with sound, playing Beethoven's *Moonlight Sonata* in a London film studio.

## 16 AUGUST 1936

At the Olympiad in Berlin, first performances are given of the following works by certified Aryan composers belonging to the German-Italian political axis, prize winners of the Olympic competition, organized by the Nazi Ministry of Propaganda with the aid of the subservient Reichsmusikkammer.

*Olympic Hymn* by Richard STRAUSS, based on the leading motive "Olympia"; *Il Vincitore* by the 34-year-old Italian composer Lino LIVIABELLA, written in an amplified Respighian manner; *Olympic Cantata 1936* by the 32-year-old German composer Kurt THOMAS, based on chants from Protestant hymnology; *Olympic Festival Music* by the 35-year-old German composer Werner EGK written in an appropriately exuberant marching vein; and *Olympic Pledge* by Paul HOEFFER, set in officiously hymnal Handelian harmonies.

## 17 AUGUST 1936

Pierre-Octave FERROUD, 36-year-old French composer of symphonic and chamber music written in a sophisticated modernistic idiom, is killed while motoring near Debrecen, Hungary.

## 29 AUGUST 1936

The National Bureau of Standards in Washington starts broadcasting the 440-cycle standard A for tuning purposes. (The broadcast continued until 11: 40 A.M., 13 September 1936)

## 4 SEPTEMBER 1936

*Second Symphony* by the Mexican composer of Indian extraction Candelario HUÍZAR, subtitled *Ochpaniztli* (the ancient name for the month of October), in three movements, *Sacrificial Dance, Dance of Birds and Butterflies* and *Mask Dance*, set in stark primitivistic modalities, is performed for the first time in Mexico City by the Orquesta Sinfónica de Mexico under the direction of Carlos Chávez.

## 11 SEPTEMBER 1936

*Te Deum of Budavár* by Zoltán KODÁLY, thanksgiving hymn for soloists, chorus and orchestra, written for the celebration of the 250th anniversary of the successful defense of the city of Buda against the Turks, opening with an exultant fanfare of victory to the majestic Latin lines of the ancient Christian hymn *Te Deum laudamus,* combining the pentatonic modes of immemorial Pannonia with devotional ecclesiastical tropes set in freely modulating triadic harmonies, is performed for the first time in Budapest.

## 14 SEPTEMBER 1936

The first music typewriter is patented in Berlin under the trade name *Nototyp Rundstatler,* possessing 44 keys in four rows: (1) upper row: clefs, numerals for time signatures, sharps, flats and bar lines (2) second row: notes on the staff up to the third line (3) third row: notes above the middle line (4) lowest row: stems. (Rests, dots, crescendo, diminuendo, etc. are distributed among all four rows)

The work on which I am now engaged would have been finished long ago, were it not for the fact that my hand gets weary of putting notes on paper. I wish that some ingenious person would invent a machine enabling tired composers to write music faster and less laboriously. (From Haydn's letter to a friend, quoted in the article *Die Sonate auf der Schreibmaschine*, published in the *Hamburger Fremdenblatt* of 13 September 1936)

## 14 SEPTEMBER 1936

Ossip GABRILOWITSCH, 58-year-old Russian-born pianist of the golden age of virtuosistic exuberance, and since 1918 conductor of the Detroit Symphony Orchestra, dies of cancer in Detroit.

## 15 SEPTEMBER 1936

The Federal Music Project of the Works Progress Administration in Washington announces the figures of attendance for the period from 1 January to 15 September 1936: 15 WPA orchestras gave concerts throughout the United States with an estimated attendance of 32 million people; the grand total of 10,797 performances were given before audiences aggregating 11,167,173 persons in July and August 1936.

## 22 SEPTEMBER 1936

*L'Amante in Trappola,* one-act opera by the 57-year-old Italian composer Arrigo PEDROLLO, is performed for the first time in Verona.

## 25 SEPTEMBER 1936

At the 34th Norwich Triennial Festival Ralph VAUGHAN WILLIAMS conducts the first performance of his choral suite, *Five Tudor Portraits,* for soloists, chorus and orchestra, to the text by John Skelton. (The printed program listed Dr. Heathcote Statham as the conductor, but he only prepared the chorus; Vaughan Williams conducted the actual concert)

## 4 OCTOBER 1936

*The Bells of Zlonitz,* an early unnumbered symphony by Antonín DVOŘÁK, the manuscript of which was discovered in the Prague archives, is performed for the first time by the Czechoslovak State Radio Orchestra in Prague.

## 8 OCTOBER 1936

*First Symphony* in D minor by the dean of Canadian composers Healey WILLAN is performed for the first time in Toronto.

## 15 OCTOBER 1936

*Die schwarze Spinne,* radio opera in one act by the 26-year-old Swiss composer Heinrich SUTERMEISTER, to a horrendous Swiss folk tale of arachnoid deviltry, in which a woman is forced to give birth to a litter of black spiders, is performed for the first time in Bern. (First stage production of the opera took place in St. Gall, Switzerland, on 2 March 1949)

### 16 OCTOBER 1936

*Concertino* for piano, violin, cello and orchestra by the 45-year-old Czech composer Bohuslav MARTINU, written in a neo-Baroque style with the thematic elements permeated by vigorous Bohemian melorhythms, is performed for the first time in Basel.

### 18 OCTOBER 1936

*Le Jeu sentimental* for orchestra by the 24-year-old French composer Jean FRANÇAIX, a symphonic stylization of 19th-century salon music, is performed for the first time in Paris.

### 20 OCTOBER 1936

*First Symphony* by the 26-year-old American composer William SCHUMAN is performed for the first time by the Gotham Symphony Orchestra in New York.

### 22 OCTOBER 1936

*Partita* for orchestra by the 40-year-old Austrian composer Johann Nepomuk DAVID, in six movements, based on a single subject in four interrelated forms (direct, specular reflection, retrograde and reflected specular retrograde), is performed for the first time in Leipzig.

### 24 OCTOBER 1936

*Sixteenth Symphony* in F major by the prime Russian symphonist Nicolai MIASKOVSKY (completed on 5 April 1936), dedicated to the Soviet Air Force, and reflecting in its four movements (1) social optimism and faith in progress (2) gaiety of youth (3) sorrow at the loss of the giant Soviet plane *Maxim Gorky* during its inaugural flight (4) contemplation of Russia's greatness as revealed in folk music, is performed for the first time in Moscow.

### 29 OCTOBER 1936

*Russian Overture* by Sergei PROKOFIEV (completed on 25 September 1936), based on three contrasting Russian melodies, a dance, a city ballad and a lyric chant, and emulating in its orchestration the sound of Russian folk instruments (balalaika, domra, accordion), is performed for the first time in Moscow.

### 29 OCTOBER 1936

*Bogatyri (Giants)*, operatic pasticcio with music put together by BORODIN in 1867, consisting of 22 numbers partially borrowed from Meyerbeer, Rossini,

Offenbach, Verdi and Serov, and first performed in Moscow on 18 November 1867, is produced in Moscow with a new militantly atheistic text by the proletarian Soviet poet Demian Biedny, burlesquing the Christianization of Russia in 988.

### 6 NOVEMBER 1936

*Third Symphony* in A minor by Serge RACHMANINOFF (completed on 30 June 1936), in three movements: (1) *Allegro moderato,* in a characteristic Russian style with a three-note motto (2) *Adagio ma non troppo,* a set of discreet variations on a slow theme, gradually increasing in mobility, then subsiding and reiterating the three-note motto of the first movement (3) *Allegro,* a vivacious Russian dance in triumphant A major with a tritonally cadenced ending, is performed for the first time by the Philadelphia Orchestra, Leopold Stokowski conducting.

### 8 NOVEMBER 1936

*Enoch Arden,* opera in three acts by the 39-year-old German composer Ottmar GERSTER, after Tennyson's poem about a sailor shipwrecked on a desert island, who returns to his native village after many years to find his wife married to another, and decides to go away without revealing his identity, set to a Wagneromorphic score with leading motives assigned to each character and subject, is performed for the first time in Düsseldorf.

### 8 NOVEMBER 1936

Jean FRANÇAIX, 24-year-old French composer, appears as piano soloist with the Berlin Philharmonic in the world première of his elegantly hedonistic *Piano Concerto,* set in the fashionable neo-classical vein, in four movements distinguished by glittering melodic surfaces adorned with asymmetric rhythmic designs.

### 11 NOVEMBER 1936

Edward GERMAN, English composer of effective light operas, whose real name was Edward German Jones, dies in London at the age of seventy-four.

### 12 NOVEMBER 1936

*Das Opfer,* opera by the 31-year-old German composer Winfried ZILLIG, written in an advanced Wagneromantic style, but embodying some daring dodecaphonic structures, with the tone row vertically integrated in the form of four mutually exclusive triads, is produced in Hamburg.

### 14 NOVEMBER 1936

*Le Testament de la Tante Caroline,* comic opera in three acts by Albert ROUSSEL, in which an eccentric aunt wills her considerable fortune to the first of her three nieces to bear a child, starting a trilateral pregnancy race during which a barren niece unsuccessfully tries to pass an adopted child for her own, and another niece has a furious affair with her chauffeur endowed with an exceptional spermatozoic fertility who turns out to be the missing natural son of the third niece who, upon verification of her maternity, gains the entire contested estate, is produced for the first time in Olomouc, Czechoslovakia, in a Czech version. (The first French production of the opera took place at the Opéra-Comique in Paris on 11 March 1937)

### 14 NOVEMBER 1936

The Council of People's Commissars of the Union of Soviet Socialist Republics cancels all performances of the opera *Bogatyri*, based on music of Borodin, produced in Moscow on 29 October 1936, on the grounds that the abusive attitude in the libretto by the proletarian Soviet poet Demian Biedny towards the objectively progressive conversion of Russia to Christianity in 988 is ideologically incorrect.

Considering that the opera-farce *Bogatyri* by Demian BIEDNY making use of music by Borodin (1) glorifies the bandit chiefs of Kiev as positive revolutionary characters, falsifying the historical truth and propagating erroneous political views (2) tarnishes the image of Russian epic heroes, *Bogatyri*, who personify in the popular imagination the inherent traits of the people of Russia (3) gives an un-historic and offensive interpretation of the conversion of Russia to Christianity, which was in fact a positive factor of Russian history and which contributed to cultural relations of Slavic nations with other countries of superior civilizations . . . the Committee for the Arts at the Council of People's Commissars resolves that the opera shall be removed from the theatrical repertory as inimical to the ideals of Soviet art. (*Pravda*, Moscow, 14 November 1936)

### 16 NOVEMBER 1936

France issues a Berlioz postage stamp valued at 40 francs.

### 19 NOVEMBER 1936

*Johnny Johnson*, a fable with music by Kurt WEILL, his first theatrical score written in America, dealing with a helplessly pacifistic American soldier who feeds laughing gas to his superior officers to deter them from making war, and is eventually sent to an insane asylum for his bizarre behavior, is produced in New York.

### 20 NOVEMBER 1936

*Pickwick*, opera in three acts, after Dickens, by the English conductor Albert COATES, written in an engagingly vivacious style, with clever topical quotations from contemporary English balladry, is produced in London.

### 22 NOVEMBER 1936

*Concerto* for cello and orchestra by Holland's prime modernist Willem PIJPER (completed on 27 October 1936), with the Latin motto "Vulnerant omnes, ultima necat" suggesting an increasing vulnerability of man, culminating in the ultimate mortal wound, in five movements played without pause, employing polycentric tonalities in resonant superposition, and embroidering the thematic quasi-atonal melodies with coloristic arabesques, is performed for the first time in Amsterdam.

## 24 NOVEMBER 1936

*The Astrology of Personality* by Dane RUDHYAR, French-born American composer who changed his original name Daniel Chennevière to a more theosophic cognomen, is published in New York, the first book on astrology ever written by a professional musician.

*The Astrology of Personality* is said to be for the future of astrology what Ptolemy's *Tetrabiblos* has been for astrology of the past. It reveals a new philosophy of Creative Time, of an Algebra of Life. (Rudhyar's self-appraisal made shortly after the publication of the book)

## 25 NOVEMBER 1936

*Slaraffenland (Fool's Paradise)*, ballet by the 39-year-old Danish composer Knudaage RIISAGER, dealing with a fatuous boy who ventures into the land of King Sauce where he gets indigestion from immoderate consuming of condiments, is produced in Copenhagen.

## 27 NOVEMBER 1936

The German Minister of Propaganda Dr. Joseph Goebbels issues a circular letter to newspaper reviewers with an injunction to confine themselves to factual accounts of artistic events, eschewing excessive praise or sharp criticism, and establishing a minimum age of thirty to qualify as purveyors of directed opinion in the Third Reich.

Among professional critics who write their reviews objectively in a business-like manner and who regard their function as that of intermediaries between the performing artists and the public, the order of Dr. Goebbels to replace criticism by an observation of art (*Kunstbetrachtung*) ought to meet with full agreement. Germany of today enables artists and critics to be comrades again, united in the service of a common cause and workers for a common purpose. (Richard Ohlekopf in *Signale für die Musikalische Welt*, Berlin, 9 December 1936)

What are the present conditions of literary, artistic and theatrical criticism in Germany? What was the motive that impelled the German government to forbid young men less than thirty years of age to be employed as critics? Italy whose national song is *Giovinezza*, would never exclude the young. . . . In a country where art thrives on polemical discussion, it would be quite impossible to replace a critical review by an "objective account." We are told in school that every sentence, even such as "This beefsteak is good" or "The yolk of an egg is yellow," is a judgment expressed in words. This is fully corroborated when we consider that to a vegetarian, beefsteak is not good, and that to Italians the yolk of an egg is *rosso* (red) but to the French it is *jaune* (yellow). (From the article *Abolire la critica?* in *La Tribuna*, Rome, 3 December 1936)

### 30 NOVEMBER 1936

*Second Piano Concerto* by the 41-year-old American composer Leo SOWERBY is performed for the first time by the Boston Symphony Orchestra, with Serge Koussevitzky conducting.

### 1 DECEMBER 1936

To mark the centennial of the death of the Swiss composer Hans Georg NÄGELI, the Swiss post office issues a 5-franc postage stamp with his romanticized portrait.

### 8 DECEMBER 1936

The Nazi Ministry of Propaganda issues a directive limiting all outdoor performances of Gottfried Sonntag's *Nibelungen-Marsch*, based on motives from Wagner's *Ring* cycle, only to important meetings under the aegis of the Nazi party. (A supplementary order, signed by Hitler himself on 6 July 1937, made the playing of the March compulsory at all *Parteitage*)

### 10 DECEMBER 1936

*Pinocchio,* "a merry overture" by Ernst TOCH, his first orchestral work written after he settled in California, inspired by the beguiling children's fable of Carlo Collodi about a mendacious pine-ocular fibber whose nasal longitude grew proportionately to the enormity of each tale told, set to music in relaxed march time vivified by fugal imbroglios in a slightly disoriented tonality, is performed for the first time by the Los Angeles Philharmonic under the direction of Otto Klemperer.

### 13 DECEMBER 1936

*First Symphony* by the 26-year-old American composer Samuel BARBER, in a single pluralistic movement, with a tarantella forming a vivacious interlude between the dramatic first section and the lyrically rhapsodic finale, converging from quasi-atonal approaches onto a resonant E-minor coda, is performed for the first time in Rome, Bernardino Molinari conducting. (First American performance of the work was given by the Cleveland Orchestra on 21 January 1937)

### 15 DECEMBER 1936

*The Dream of Wei Lien,* Chinese ballet by the China-rooted expatriate Russian composer Aaron AVSHALOMOV, making use of pentatonic Chinese melodies in Russianized harmonies and Germanized counterpoint, is produced in Shanghai with a Chinese cast.

### 19 DECEMBER 1936

Joseph ACHRON plays the solo part in the first performance of his *Second Violin Concerto* with the Los Angeles Philharmonic, under the direction of Otto Klemperer.

## 20 DECEMBER 1936

*Bret Harte,* symphonic overture by the 46-year-old American composer Philip JAMES, inspired by Bret Harte's tales of adventure, is performed for the first time by the New York Philharmonic.

## 26 DECEMBER 1936

The newly organized Palestine Symphony Orchestra, consisting mainly of refugees from Nazi Germany, presents its inaugural concert at Tel Aviv, under the direction of Arturo Toscanini, in a program of German classics and Rossini.

Toscanini refused any remuneration, not even traveling expenses. He said that at the time when dark forces were seeking the destruction of the Jewish people he felt it his duty to prove his sympathy with the Jews within his own domain of music. (New York *Times,* 27 December 1936)

## 31 DECEMBER 1936

*First Symphony* by the Cyprus-born American composer Anis FULEIHAN is performed for the first time by the New York Philharmonic.

# ᴐ *1937* ᴐ

## 2 JANUARY 1937

A century has passed since the birth in Nizhny-Novgorod, on the Volga River, of Mily BALAKIREV, the genial Amphitryon of the Russian National School of Composers and friendly mentor of Mussorgsky and Rimsky-Korsakov.

## 21 JANUARY 1937

*A Voice in the Wilderness,* symphonic poem in six movements for orchestra and cello obbligato by Ernest BLOCH with the sections "bound together by a barely perceptible thematic relationship or reminiscence" wherein the cello has "an aggressive role without endless displays of virtuosity, like the character in a drama," written in Bloch's typical expansive harmonic vocabulary of contrasting polar tonalities distanced by a tritone, is performed for the first time by the Los Angeles Philharmonic, Otto Klemperer conducting.

(The well-known passage in Isaiah 40:3, from which the title is taken is actually a mistranslation; correct meaning is found in Powis Smith's "American Translation" of the Bible: "Hark! one calls: In the wilderness clear the way of the Lord.")

637

## 21 JANUARY 1937

The Chamber Orchestra of Basel, Switzerland, under the direction of its founder Paul Sacher, gives the world première of *Music for Strings, Percussion and Celesta* (containing also harp and piano) by Béla BARTÓK (completed on 7 September 1936), in four movements:

(1) *Andante tranquillo,* a fugue on a highly chromaticized subject centering on A, in propulsive asymmetrical rhythms firmly maintaining the common denominator of an eighth-note (2) *Allegro,* wherein the strings are subdivided in two groups operating in antiphonal variations, coalescing in vigorous, rigorous polyphony, with glissandos in the strings, harp and piano, imparting an exotic ambiguity to the strong tonality gravitating towards the focal C (3) *Adagio,* with a xylophone chiming on a single high F introducing a chromaticized subject related to that of the initial movement, and followed by a spectacular panpentatonic exhibition on the black keys of the piano accompanied by similar exhibitions in the celesta and the harp, leading to a restatement of the chromatic subjects with an epitaph on the high F of the xylophone (4) *Allegro molto,* a paradoxical rondo, with a non-recurrent theme leading to a magisterial coda in which the chromatic fugal subject of the first movement is conformally expanded into a diatonic statement, concluding with a Lydian cadence in fortissimo.

## 21 JANUARY 1937

*Third Symphony* in three movements by the 36-year-old Siberian-born American composer Nicolai BEREZOWSKY, written in a brightly tonal idiom marked by perceptible Russianisms, is performed for the first time in Rochester.

## 23 JANUARY 1937

*Rembrandt van Rijn,* opera in four acts by the Germanized Danish-born composer Paul von KLENAU, to his own libretto, relating the story of Rembrandt's marital sorrows, financial troubles and other misfortunes, set to music of multiple resources, including polyharmony and quasi-dodecaphonic atonalities, with episodes of spoken commentary to attenuated orchestral accompaniment, is performed for the first time, simultaneously in Berlin and Stuttgart.

## 24 JANUARY 1937

*Divertissement pour une fête de nuit* for piano and orchestra by Reynaldo HAHN is performed for the first time in Paris.

## 25 JANUARY 1937

Ivan WYSCHNEGRADSKY, expatriate Russian composer of experimental music, conducts in Paris a concert of his works in quarter-tones: *Symphonic Fragments,* in an arrangement for four pianos, two of which are tuned a quarter-tone higher than the others; *Thus Spake Zarathustra,* in a similar arrangement for four pianos; *Etude en forme de Scherzo* for two pianos tuned a quarter-tone apart; and *Preludes* in quarter-tones.

## 25 JANUARY 1937

*Second Symphony* by Gian Francesco MALIPIERO, subtitled *Elegiaca*, in four movements, an energetic *Allegro non troppo*, a meditative *Lento*, a brisk *Mosso* and an elegiac *Finale*, is performed for the first time as a commissioned work by the Seattle Symphony Orchestra, under the direction of Basil Cameron.

I wrote my *Elegiaca* in the anxious and tragic months of 1936, a year full of sadness. I wish to point out that the word *Elegiaca* does not signify an intention to write program music. (From Malipiero's note in the program book of the Seattle Symphony Orchestra)

## 26 JANUARY 1937

The Brazilian Parliament patriotically votes a bill stipulating that "musical programs performed in Brazil shall include compulsory works by Brazilian-born composers."

## 6 FEBRUARY 1937

*Concertino* for cello and orchestra by the French master Albert ROUSSEL, in three movements, *Allegro moderato, Adagio, Allegro molto,* following the classical models but imbued with the Gallic spirit of vigorous hedonism, is performed for the first time in Paris.

## 8 FEBRUARY 1937

*Tanzsymphonie* by Eugen ZÁDOR is performed for the first time in Budapest.

## 20 FEBRUARY 1937

*Mirjana,* opera in three acts by Josef MANDIĆ, Croatian composer active in Prague as a prosperous lawyer, to the macabre story of a young man's visit to his dead fiancée's grave on the day of his marriage to another girl, his subsequent disappearance for a hundred years and his adventure with Mirjana rediviva as a noblewoman with whom he circumnavigates the world, is performed for the first time at Olmütz.

## 20 FEBRUARY 1937

Sergei PROKOFIEV conducts in Paris the first performance of his symphonic suite *Lieutenant Kijé* from film music of that name, dealing with a mythical army officer whose last name was the product of the accidental typographical coupling of two Russian verbal particles, disgorging a cornucopia of wittily dislocated marching tunes and mock-sentimental ballads.

## 22 FEBRUARY 1937

*Fernando del Nonsensico,* operatic satire in three acts by the English-born 64-year-old Chicago composer Felix BOROWSKI, with its shafts aimed at the absurdities of Italian opera, containing distorted quotations from Bellini and

Verdi and ending with the death of all participants, is presented for the first time in Los Angeles.

*Garrick*, opera in three acts by the 42-year-old American composer Albert STOESSEL, to a libretto recounting the professional and amorous ventures of the Shakespearean actor David Garrick, is performed for the first time by the Opera Department of the Juilliard School of Music in New York, conducted by the composer.

*Lucrezia*, one-act opera by Ottorino RESPIGHI, to a libretto recounting the sad story of Lucretia who killed herself in 508 B.C. after she was ravished by an unscrupulous princeling, is performed posthumously for the first time in Rome, in a version completed and edited by Respighi's widow, Elsa Olivieri Respighi.

*Scènes Ibériennes*, symphonic suite by the Hispanically inclined French composer Raoul LAPARRA, is performed for the first time in Paris.

*Massimila Doni*, opera in four acts by the 50-year-old Swiss composer Othmar SCHOECK, after Balzac's novelette of that name, wherein a Venetian lady conducts in 1830 an intellectualized love affair with an emotional man from Genoa, set in a Wagneromorphic style of composition with identifying motivs and the inclusion of spoken song to gently orchestrated accompaniment, is produced for the first time at the Dresden Opera.

*Le Rossignol en Amour*, chamber opera by the 46-year-old French composer Georges MIGOT, is performed for the first time in Geneva.

*The Headless Horseman*, one-act operetta by Douglas MOORE, after *A Legend of Sleepy Hollow* by Washington Irving, is performed for the first time at Bronxville, New York.

*L'Aiglon*, opera in five acts after Edmond Rostand's nostalgic play about Napoleon's tubercular son, "the eaglet," with music by Arthur HONEGGER (Acts II, III, and IV) and Jacques IBERT (Acts I and V), written in a style midway between post-Wagnerian expansiveness and ante-Debussyan colorism, is produced at the Opera of Monte Carlo.

## 12 MARCH 1937

Charles-Marie WIDOR, Nestor of French music, last surviving pupil of Rossini, master organist, composer of operas, symphonies, and organ works, teacher of three generations of French composers, dies in Paris 19 days after his 93rd birthday.

## 18 MARCH 1937

*Veselohrz na mostě*, one-act opera by the prime Czech composer Bohuslav MARTINU, after an old Czech parable dealing with a group of civilians trapped on a bridge between two opposing armies, with the resulting stalemate giving an opportunity for social satire and amorous gunplay, is performed for the first time on the Prague radio. (The opera was performed with an English libretto under the title *Comedy on the Bridge*, at Hunter College in New York on 28 May 1951)

## 19 MARCH 1937

*Oedipus Rex*, tragedy by Sophocles, with music arranged from works of the great Venetian madrigalist Andrea Gabrieli by Fernando LIUZZI (1884–1940), is performed for the first time in Sabratha, Libya, at the inauguration of the Teatro Romano, reconstructed from the ruins of an ancient Roman coliseum.

## 19 MARCH 1937

*Second Symphony* by the modernistic American composer Emerson WHITHORNE, is performed for the first time by the the Cincinnati Symphony Orchestra, Eugene Goossens conducting.

## 24 MARCH 1937

*Violin Concerto* by the 21-year-old American composer David DIAMOND, written in a romantically flavored classical style, is performed for the first time in New York with Nicolai Berezowsky as soloist, the composer conducting.

## 28 MARCH 1937

Karol SZYMANOWSKI, "20th-century Chopin," whose music, written in the modern manner, employs with discrimination the valid devices of polyharmony and dissonant counterpoint while faithfully retaining the melorhythmic elements of ancestral Polish songs and dances, dies near Lausanne, Switzerland, at the age of fifty-four.

## 1 APRIL 1937

*Amelia Goes to the Ball*, one-act opera-buffa by the 25-year-old Italian-born American composer Gian Carlo MENOTTI, to his own Italian libretto *Amelia al Ballo*, dealing with social tourbillions at the cotillions of Milan at the turn of the century, with a score written in a dynamically propulsive and expansively Italianate manner, is performed for the first time, in an English version, at the Philadelphia Academy of Music, Fritz Reiner conducting.

## 8 APRIL 1937

Arthur FOOTE, American composer of instrumental and vocal music of a fine-textured romantic quality, dies in Boston at the age of eighty-four.

It is difficult to realize that Arthur Foote is no longer among us with his sunny smile and cheerful manner . . . He always made everyone happy and at ease in his presence—the hallmark of a true gentleman. This broad humility appeared in his compositions which struck a note not likely to be duplicated. (Walter R. Spalding, in a letter published in the Boston *Evening Transcript*, 13 April 1937)

## 9 APRIL 1937

Five days before the 80th birthday of the American composer Edgar Stillman KELLEY, his symphony *Gulliver*, traversing in its four movements Gulliver's first voyage, his visit to the land of Lilliput and his return, set to music in an unpretentious romantic manner, is performed for the first time by the Cincinnati Symphony Orchestra, Eugene Goossens conducting.

## 10 APRIL 1937

Algernon ASHTON, English composer of 24 elaborate string quartets in all 24 major and minor keys, known to the British public mainly as an inveterate writer of letters on every conceivable topic to the editors of London newspapers, with an especial fondness for the subject of neglected tombstones, dies in London at the age of seventy-seven.

## 10 APRIL 1937

Paul HINDEMITH makes his first appearance in America at the 8th Festival of Chamber Music given at the Library of Congress in Washington, under the auspices of the Elizabeth Sprague Coolidge Foundation playing his own *Sonata* for viola solo.

## 13 APRIL 1937

Music for strings in 1/6 tones and other fractional intervals by the Czech pioneer of microtonal composition Alois HÁBA and his pupils is presented in Prague by the modern music society *Pritomnost* (*The Present*).

## 14 APRIL 1937

*Babes in Arms*, musical comedy by Richard RODGERS, with book and lyrics by Lorenz Hart, dealing with a gang of abandoned children who make good as producers of adolescent ballets, the score including the perennially popular songs *My Funny Valentine* and *The Lady Is a Tramp*, as well as *Where or When* and *Johnny One-Note*, is produced in New York.

## 14 APRIL 1937

*The Bleeding Heart of Timpanogos*, opera in three acts by William F. HANSON, professor of music at Brigham Young University, Utah, dealing with the sacrifice of an Indian virgin made in order to induce the rain god Timpanogos to end the draught, momentarily delayed when the virgin's lover impersonates the god but is exposed and mortally wounded by the medicine woman of the tribe as the virgin leaps to her death from a high cliff and the rain begins to fall, the score teeming with Indian pentatonicisms and supernumerary whole-tone scales, is performed for the first time in Provo, Utah, conducted by the composer.

## 19 APRIL 1937

*Five Incapacitated Preludes,* a symphonic suite by the 35-year-old Canadian-born American Byron ARNOLD, is performed in Rochester, Howard Hanson conducting, with the following specifications:

(1) *For a One-Armed Man* (the conductor to lead with his left arm only) (2) *For a Blind Man* (to be conducted gropingly with arms extended full length) (3) *For a Cross-Eyed Man* (crossing the baton with the left arm) (4) *For a Deaf Man* (the players to simulate the motions of playing from the notes actually written out, without making any sounds) (5) *For a Lame Man* (the conductor being instructed to limp on the downbeat).

## 21 APRIL 1937

*The Second Hurricane,* school opera by Aaron COPLAND, designed for performance by boys and girls between the ages of 8 and 18, to a libretto dealing with a rescue team of highschool students flying in a chartered airplane to help victims of a hurricane in the Ohio Valley, who become stranded there themselves as a second hurricane strikes, so that another airplane has to be sent to bring them back, set to music with deceptive simplicity in abecedarian triadic harmonies fertilized by incisive asymmetric rhythms, is performed for the first time by a cast of 150 children at the Henry Street Music School in New York, Lehman Engel conducting.

## 24 APRIL 1937

*La Morte di Frine,* one-act opera, subtitled *Leggenda tragica,* by the 41-year-old Italian composer Lodovico ROCCA, to the legend of a famous courtesan Phryne, on trial in Athens for the profanation of Eleusinian mysteries, who presented her own defence by taking off her robe to show that her beauty was sufficient justification for her act, is performed for the first time on the stage of La Scala, Milan. (A radio performance of *La Morte di Frine* was given in Turin on 31 May 1936)

## 27 APRIL 1937

Igor STRAVINSKY conducts at the Metropolitan Opera House in New York the world première of his ballet *Jeu de Cartes,* representing three deals of straight poker (of which Stravinsky is a devotee), with the situation complicated in each deal "by the endless guiles of the perfidious Joker who believes himself invincible because of his ability to become any desired card":

(1) First Deal: *Introduction, Pas d'action, Dance of the Joker, Little Waltz* (one player is out; two remain in the game, both holding straights) (2) Second Deal: *Introduction,*

*March, Variations of the Four Queens, Variations of the Jack of Hearts and Coda, March and Ensemble* (three aces and a joker beat four queens) (3) Third Deal: *Introduction, Waltz-Minuet, Combat Between Spades and Hearts, Triumph of the Hearts* (climactic gamble with each player holding a flush, culminating in a monumental duel in which the joker heading a straight in spades is defeated by a royal flush in hearts), each of the deals opening with a neo-baroque exordium, and the entire score possessing an elastic quality of eclectic classicism, containing latent quotations from Rossini, Delibes and Johann Strauss, all this vitalized by constant rhythmic mobility, at times suggesting the syncopation of early ragtime.

### 30 APRIL 1937

Uzeir GADZHIBEKOV, prime composer of Azerbaijan, conducts in Baku the first performance of his three-act opera *Kyor-Oglu* (*A Blind Man's Son*), dealing with a 17th century uprising of the Tatar population in the region of the Caspian Sea against their Turkish overlord, the brutal perpetrator of the monstrous act of blinding Kyor-Oglu's father, set to music in a simple ethnic style, making use of the authentic pentatonic and chromatically angular folk tunes.

(The present date is verified by the original program and contemporary reviews in the Baku newspapers. The date 13 January 1937 given in the previous editions of *Music Since 1900* is erroneous)

### 30 APRIL 1937

*First Symphony* by the 35-year-old English composer Edmund RUBBRA, in three classically contrasted movements: (1) *Allegro moderato e tempestoso*, written in a sharply dissonant emotionally charged style (2) *Perigourdine*, a set of variations marked *Allegro bucolico e giocoso*, on a French tune taken from an old Paris anthology (3) *Lento*, leading to a magistral fugue, and ending on a resonant coda, is performed for the first time in London.

### 6 MAY 1937

On the eve of the first anniversary of the proclamation by the Fascist government of the Italian Empire, *Il Deserto tentato*, opera in one act by Alfredo CASELLA, presenting a mystical interpretation of Mussolini's conquest of Ethiopia, is performed for the first time at the May Festival in Florence.

*Il Deserto tentato* is a mystery play in one act, in the manner of a secular oratorio in which both poet and composer have tried to invoke the Ethiopian war into a totally unreal and mythical plane . . . It exalts, in the elevated language of poetry, the humanitarian mission of a great nation in taking possession, thanks to the exploits of her aviators, of a barren desert, carrying to it the fruits of civilization it has been waiting for since time immemorial. The music, at least in appearance, is simple, monumental and severe, with important choruses. I should like to add that in my opinion this opera is my best work. (From Alfredo Casella's letter to the author, dated Rome, 1 June 1937)

### 7 MAY 1937

*The Ordering of Moses*, biblical oratorio by the Negro composer Robert Nathaniel DETT, is performed for the first time in Cincinnati.

The Moses here depicted is not the Moses familiarized to us by the other arts, especially by the work of Michelangelo, whose statue of the patriarch has become symbolic. At the time of this "ordering" Moses was a shepherd, undoubtedly a young man, which explains the part being assigned to a tenor voice. (Composer's foreword to the printed score)

### 9 MAY 1937

*Crown Imperial,* coronation march by William WALTON, inspired by William Dunbar's poem "In beawtie beryng the crone imperiall," marked *Allegro real* and set in a royally festive honi-soit-qui-mal-y-pense key of C major, is performed for the first time by the British Broadcasting Corporation in anticipation of the actual ceremony on the day of coronation of George VI, 12 May 1937, in Westminster Abbey, when the march was repeated.

### 12 MAY 1937

Walter DAMROSCH, 75-year-old German-born American conductor and composer, conducts at the Metropolitan Opera House in New York, where he made his debut as conductor 52 years before, the world première of his grand opera in two acts, *The Man Without a Country,* to Edward Everett Hale's famous story of an American Navy lieutenant involved in Aaron Burr's imperial conspiracy, who insolently damns the United States, and is sent away on maritime exile on the high seas with an injunction to everyone in his entourage never to mention America in his presence, his redemption coming at last when he is allowed to participate in military action against the Berber pirates and is mortally wounded, while the feminine voice of a woman who took pity on him sings an unseen lullaby, in a commensurately emotional musical setting in a lushly Wagneromantic manner.

### 12 MAY 1937

At the end of the ceremonies in the Coronation of King George VI and Queen Elizabeth of Great Britain, the first performance of the *Festival Te Deum,* specially written for the occasion by Ralph VAUGHAN WILLIAMS, is given in the Abbey Church of St. Peter Westminster in London.

### 23 MAY 1937

*Lenox Avenue,* symphonic musicorama of life in the Negro district of Harlem in New York, by the Negro composer William Grant STILL, is given its first performance in a radio broadcast by the Columbia Broadcasting System in New York.

### 24 MAY 1937

The International Society for Promoting Cooperation among Composers, created in 1933 under the presidency of Richard Strauss to replace the International Society for Contemporary Music from which Nazi Germany withdrew, opens a Music Festival of its own in Dresden, with works by hematologically unadulterated Aryan composers from 18 nations, among them Henk Badings of Holland, Hugo Alfvén of Sweden, Carl Nielsen of Denmark, Paul Graener of Germany, Jón Leifs of Iceland, Leevi Madetoja of Finland, Božidar Kunz of Czechoslovakia, Joseph Haas of Austria, Adriano Lualdi of Italy, Jean Rivier of France, Béla Bartók of Hungary, and, by special dispensation, the half-Jewish half-German Pantcho Vladigerov of Bulgaria.

### 26 MAY 1937

*Requiem* by the Philadelphia-born composer Vittorio Giannini, written in memory of his mother, is given its first performance anywhere in Vienna, with the composer's sister Dusolina Giannini as soprano soloist.

### 30 MAY 1937

The Moscow State Radio broadcasts a special concert of salutatory music on a directional short wavelength for the Soviet polar party of scientists slowly floating on an ice floe in the vicinity of the North Pole.

### 2 JUNE 1937

Louis Vierne, 66-year-old French master organist and composer of melodious and harmonious music for his instrument, collapses and dies while playing his *Stèle pour un enfant défunt* at Notre Dame de Paris, where he was organist since 1900.

### 2 JUNE 1937

Two acts and two fragments of the third act of Alban Berg's unfinished opera *Lulu,* to his own libretto after Frank Wedekind's macabre plays of rapine, perversion, lust and crime, *Erdgeist* and *Die Büchse der Pandora,* in which Lulu ends up in a London garret abdominally ripped by Jack the Ripper in 1889 to the accompaniment of an eviscerating dodecaphonic chord made up of minor seconds and perfect fourths, the music derived from a 12-tone matrix and yet allowing for liberal employment of tonality (Frank Wedekind's own folk-like tune in C major is used as a theme for a set of variations) and of uniform chromatic progressions (Lulu kills her third husband by five consecutive bullets on the ascending chromatic scale, C-sharp, D, E-flat, E and F), the entire score being cast in ostentatiously classical forms (Sonata, Rondo, Variations), with the central Ostinato, marked *Filmmusik,* forming a strict cancrizans outlining Lulu's arrest and imprisonment and, in the retrograde section, her escape, are given for the first time in Zürich, Switzerland. (A symphonic suite for *Lulu* was first performed in Berlin prior to the stage production, on 30 November 1934)

### 5 JUNE 1937

The British Broadcasting Corporation gives the first successful demonstration of televising opera, transmitting the entire third act of Gounod's *Faust* to a television receiver in its London studio.

This was not a special television production but rather a presentation by television of a regular performance. The first opera to be televised in its entirety was *La Serva Padrona* by Pergolesi on 23 December 1937. In the case of *Hänsel und Gretel,* the experiment was tried for the first time with two casts. The singers were not seen, the acting casts were silent, and their movements consisted largely of miming specially devised for the music of the opera. The next special television production, again with two casts, was Act II of *Tristan* on 25 January 1938. (From a letter to the author from the Assistant Director of Television of the BBC)

### 5 JUNE 1937

W. J. HENDERSON, American "reporter with a specialty, music," as he liked to style himself, commits suicide in New York at the age of 81, by shooting himself in the mouth with his old 38-caliber army pistol which he carried as a soldier in the Spanish-American war of 1898.

### 8 JUNE 1937

*Carmina Burana* for soloists, choruses, orchestra and a battery of percussion by the 41-year-old German composer Carl ORFF, the first of a trilogy of "scenic cantatas" under the collective title *Trionfi,* with the Latin subtitle, *Cantiones profanae cantoribus et choris cantandae comitantibus instrumentis atque imaginibus magicis,* to the texts in vulgar Latin, French and Bavarian dialects in a macaronic linguistic mixture, drawn from a book of ribald medieval student songs discovered in 1803 at the Bavarian monastery of Benediktbeuren (the adjective Burana is from the Latin name of the town), in three parts relating to springtime, drinking and love, set to music in an amalgam of heterogeneous neo-medieval, ecclesiastical, ethnic and popular melodic and rhythmic elements, accoutred in bland modalities and marked by a hypnotically repetitive asymmetrical cantillation alternating with monometrical ululation and syncopated hockets, is performed for the first time in Frankfurt.

### 8 JUNE 1937

*Jeanne d'Arc,* "symphonie concertante" for soprano and orchestra by Maurice JAUBERT, 37-year-old French composer fated to be killed in combat on 19 June 1940, in three parts depicting three principal stages of Joan's life—*Domrémy, Les Batailles, Rouen*—set to music in a severely reverential idiom in which the voice assumes the role of a chronicler, is performed for the first time in Paris.

### 8 JUNE 1937

Georges ENESCO, prime composer of Rumania, conducts in Paris a concert of Rumanian symphonic music, including the first performance of *Caprice roumain* by the Parisianized Rumanian composer Marcel MIHALOVICI.

### 10 JUNE 1937

Georges ENESCO conducts in Paris a second concert of Rumanian symphonic music, including the first performance of an elegantly proportioned *Divertissement* by the precocious 20-year-old Rumanian pianist Dinu LIPATTI.

## 12 JUNE 1937

MANETO (acronym for Manifestatie Van Nederlandsche Toonkunst), organized in Holland as the "manifestation of Netherlandish tonal art," presents in Amsterdam its first concert of Dutch music featuring works by Johan WAGENAAR, Henk BADINGS, Bertus van LIER and Guillaume LANDRÉ.

## 12 JUNE 1937

The German Tonkünstler Verein, founded by Liszt, is dissolved after its 68th Annual Music Festival held in Darmstadt and Frankfurt, in silent protest against the imposition of the doctrine of *Gleichschaltung* by the Nazi Ministry of Propaganda leveling all musical activities to the arbitrary norms of racist nationalism.

## 15 JUNE 1937

*Checkmate,* dramatic ballet in one scene and prologue by the English composer Arthur BLISS, to his own scenario suggesting the Vienna opening of the chess game, in six moves, Dance of the Four Knights, Entry of the Black Queen, The Red Knight, Ceremony of the Red Bishops, Death of the Red Knight and Checkmate, and set in a lyrico-dramatic neo-Baroque idiom, is produced in Paris by the visiting opera and ballet company of Sadler's Wells of London.

## 16 JUNE 1937

*Tá Mar,* opera by the Portuguese composer Ruy COELHO, is produced in Lisbon.

## 16 JUNE 1937

*The Cradle Will Rock,* proletarian opera in two acts by Marc BLITZSTEIN, to his own libretto, picturing class warfare between a rapacious capitalist Mr. Mister and a group of workers trying to organize a union in Steeltown, U.S.A., the score consisting of a series of vernacular ballads, such as *Croon-Spoon,* or *The Nickel Under the Foot,* is given its first performance in New York in a makeshift production, without scenery or costumes, with Blitzstein himself at the piano and singers stationed in the hall, to circumvent the ban imposed by the Federal Theater, branch of the Works Progress Administration, on account of the radical nature of the play. (It was finally presented as an opera in a Broadway theater in New York on 27 December 1947, and later by the New York City Opera, on 11 February 1960)

## 17 JUNE 1937

*Emek (The Valley)* symphonic poem by the 33-year-old Latvian-born Palestinian composer Marc LAVRY, descriptive of pioneer work in cultivating the agricultural resources of the Jezreel Valley in the Gilboa Mountains, in the form of variations on an authentic Emek folksong, culminating in an agitated Hora dance, is performed for the first time in Tel-Aviv.

## 20 JUNE 1937

Walter Piston conducts the first performance, broadcast from New York over the CBS network, of his *Concertino* for piano and chamber orchestra, "an adventure of a musical idea," as he characterized it in his introductory speech.

## 21 JUNE 1937

*Dreadnaught Potemkin*, realistic opera in four acts by the Soviet composer Oles Tchishko, to a libretto from the historical naval mutiny during the abortive Russian revolution of 1905, containing such naturalistic lines as "Our borsht is full of vermin," set to music according to the Soviet doctrine of Socialist Realism, in broad Russian harmonies, is performed for the first time in Leningrad. (An amplified version, with a sharpened political point, in which the part of a wily Menshevik has been introduced into the libretto, was produced in Leningrad on 30 December 1955)

## 21 JUNE 1937

The 15th Festival of the International Society for Contemporary Music opens in conjunction with the Paris Exposition of 1937 presenting the following program of chamber music:

*Second String Quartet* by Arthur Honegger; *La voix de Yamato* for soprano, two flutes, clarinet, bassoon and cello by the Japanese woman composer Michigo Toyama; *Nonet* by the young Czech composer Karel Reiner; *Duo* for flute and clarinet by the Catalan composer Joaquín Homs; *Morceau de Concert* for cello and piano by the English leftist composer Alan Bush, calculated to secure compositional accessibility of its idioms; and *Suite en Rocaille* for flute, violin, viola, cello and harp in an elegant rococo style by the dean of French modernists, Florent Schmitt.

## 22 JUNE 1937

At the second concert of the 15th Festival of the International Society for Contemporary Music in Paris, the following program of orchestral music is presented:

*Symphonie Concertante* by Karol Szymanowski of Poland (his fourth symphony) for piano and orchestra, written in an opulent quasi-impressionistic manner (it was first performed in Poznan on 9 October 1932); *Concerto for Orchestra* in a vigorous neo-classical idiom by the Soviet composer Mikhail Starokadomsky; *Fantasy* for string orchestra by Norbert von Hannenheim, who represented Republican Germany at the Vienna Festival of 1932, but changed his allegiance to Rumania after the Nazification of German music; *Second Violin Concerto* by the young Polish neo-classicist Jerzy Fitelberg, conducted by his father Gregor Fitelberg; *Hommage à Babeuf* for wind instruments and percussion by the Belgian modernist André Souris; *Symphonie Concertante* by the Swedish neo-romantic composer Hilding Rosenberg; and *Second Symphony*, subtitled *Elegiaca*, in four movements, by Gian Francesco Malipiero.

## 23 JUNE 1937

At the third concert of the 15th Festival of the International Society for Contemporary Music in Paris, the band of the Garde Républicaine de Paris presents a concert with the following program:

*Prélude* from the *Suite in F* by Albert ROUSSEL, written in a neo-classical Gallic manner, in which clarity and logic are paramount; *Canción y Movimiento* by the Spanish composer Ernesto LOVREGLIO; *Gulliver au pays de Lilliput*, a Swiftian intermezzo by Gabriel PIERNÉ; and *Chorale and March* by the foremost master of Italian modern music Alfredo CASELLA.

### 24 JUNE 1937

*Don Juan de Mañara*, second opera by Eugene GOOSSENS, in four acts, after Arnold Bennett's story dealing with the 17th-century sensualist Miguel de Mañara to whom "the alcove was the altar," composed in an eminently cohesive modernistic idiom with some naturalistic touches (Don Juan's sexual excitement is illustrated by asymmetrical staccato beats), is produced in London.

### 24 JUNE 1937

At the fourth concert of the 15th Festival of the International Society for Contemporary Music in Paris the following program of chamber music is given:

*Second String Quartet* by the Hungarian composer Sándor VERESS; *Ninth String Quartet* by Darius MILHAUD; *Four Melodies* by the Austrian atonalist Hans Erich APOSTEL; *Trio* for piano, violin and cello by the Dutch neo-classicist Henk BADINGS. (*Two Pieces* for clarinet and piano by the German composer Peter SCHACHT were scheduled for performance on this program, but withdrawn at the last moment by the composer in deference to the official opposition by the Nazi Ministry of Propaganda to the International Society for Contemporary Music)

### 25 JUNE 1937

At the fifth concert of the 15th Festival of the International Society for Contemporary Music in Paris, the following program of orchestral music is presented:

*Overture* from the opera *Nova Zeme (New Land)* by the Czech modernist Alois HÁBA, a political music drama expressing unlimited faith in the ability of collective labor to build a happy future, with the injection of fragments of the *Internationale; Concerto* for piano and orchestra by the *jeune français* Jean FRANÇAIX, written in the newly fashionable style of neo-classical mannerism; *Passacaglia* by Juan Carlos PAZ of Argentina, written in the 12-tone technique; two movements from *German Symphony* by Hanns EISLER, a politically and musically radical disciple of Schoenberg; *Concerto* for string quartet and orchestra by the Catalan composer Josep VALLS; and *Toccata* by the Serbian neo-classical composer Demetrij ZEBRE.

### 25 JUNE 1937

*La Samaritaine*, lyric drama by Max d'OLLONE, depicting in three tableaux the meeting of Christ with the Samaritan woman at the well, composed in an orthodox style, with some orientally serpentine melodies for local color, is produced at the Paris Opéra.

## 26 JUNE 1937

The 15th Festival of the International Society for Contemporary Music closes with its sixth concert presenting the following program of chamber music:

*Second String Quartet* by Elizabeth MACONCHY of England, written in an advanced modernistic idiom tending towards integral atonality; *Grimaces rythmiques* for piano by the Serbian impressionist Miloje MILOJEVIĆ, written with considerable Parisian verve; *Musica per tre pianoforti*, hymns with the motto "Il paradiso è all'ombra delle spade," by the 33-year-old Italian modernist Luigi DALLAPICCOLA; and *Divertimento* for chamber orchestra by the Swedish neo-classicist Lars-Erik LARSSON.

## 1 JULY 1937

*Scaramouche*, suite for two pianos by Darius MILHAUD, in three movements, *Vif, Modéré* and *Brasileira*, abounding in tropical melorhythms set in bitonal harmonies, is performed for the first time in Paris.

## 5 JULY 1937

*Piano Concerto* by the 34-year-old Soviet Armenian composer Aram KHACHATURIAN, in three movements, *Allegro ma non troppo e maestoso, Andante con anima* and *Allegro brillante,* abounding in quasi-oriental melismatic adornments and sonorous cadenzas of an improvisatory nature, set in acrid harmonies of major and minor seconds, and ending with a triumphant Caucasian dance, is performed for the first time in Leningrad.

## 11 JULY 1937

George GERSHWIN, American genius of jazz, whose epoch-making *Rhapsody in Blue*, written at the age of 24, has become an American classic, whose folk opera *Porgy and Bess* has set a new mark in the American musical theater, whose songs embody with piercing vividness the sadness and gladness of the American scene and whose polyrhythmic syncopation has caught the American musical pulse beat, dies in Hollywood at 10:35 A.M., following an operation on a cystic brain tumor, at the age of thirty-eight.

Music was to George Gershwin not a mere matter of ability. It was the air he breathed, the dream he dreamed. I grieve over the deplorable loss of music, for there is no doubt that he was a great composer. (Arnold Schoenberg in a radio broadcast from Hollywood at the Gershwin memorial service at 9 P.M. on 12 July 1937)

## 17 JULY 1937

*Mekhano*, mechanical ballet by the modern Argentinian composer Juan José CASTRO, featuring a dance of the hammer, a dance of seduction, and a realistic transfusion of blood to a robot (illustrated by runs of whole-tone scales), is produced at the Teatro Colón in Buenos Aires, conducted by the composer.

## 17 JULY 1937

Gabriel PIERNÉ, French composer of elegant music in various genres, distinguished also as an opera conductor, dies in Ploujean, Brittany, at the age of seventy-three.

## 25 JULY 1937

*Music for Radio* by Aaron COPLAND is performed for the first time as a commissioned work by the Columbia Broadcasting System Orchestra. (A national contest for a descriptive title of *Music for Radio* was held after the initial performance, and *Saga of the Prairie* was selected as the most fitting title, reflecting the melodic expansiveness, metrical tranquility and triadic resonance of the music)

## 27 JULY 1937

Igor STRAVINSKY is awarded by a Paris Tribunal the token sum of one French franc in compensation for the "moral damage" sustained by him through the illicit use of his music in Warner Brothers' motion picture *The Firebird,* in which a virtuous girl is systematically ruined by a roué while under the aphrodisiac influence of the playing of a phonograph recording of the syncopated pagan dance of the immund teratological creatures from the finale of Stravinsky's ballet of the same tile.

"Mais, Monsieur Stravinsky, c'est le plus grand compliment du monde pour un compositeur!" (Purported comment by the Paris judge on the moral issue involved in the use of Stravinsky's music as an instrument of seduction)

The musician Stravinsky claimed damages of 300,000 francs from a motion picture company which has incorporated in its film *The Firebird* a few musical fragments taken from Stravinsky's ballet of that name. Among the various complaints in the suit only one was considered valid by the Tribunal de la Seine, namely that Stravinsky's music was preceded without explanation by a Viennese waltz. The judge found in this a regrettable incomprehension of the music by a great artist and adjudged to him the damages for the sum of one French franc as a mark of their disapproval. (Tribunal Civil de la Seine, 27 July 1937, Stravinsky v. Société Warner Bros., reproduced in *La Semaine juridique,* Paris, 1937, p. 392) (The date 3 February 1938, given in the previous editions of *Music Since 1900,* is erroneous, taken from a delayed report in the American press)

## 1 AUGUST 1937

*Anti-Fascist Symphony* for orchestra, chorus and military band by 28-year-old Soviet composer Boris MOKROUSOV, a sharp symphonic warning to the Nazis and Fascists not to underestimate the musical and military strength of the Soviet Union, counterposing in the score a powerful expansion of Russian folksong modalities to the mechanical themes of the Nazi machine, is performed for the first time in Moscow, less than four years before the Hitlerized hordes moved madly into Russia.

## 17 AUGUST 1937

*A London Overture* by John IRELAND, with a rhythmic motto inspired by a bus conductor's cry "Piccadilly!" and containing other topical allusions to the melodious turmoil of London streets, set to music in an unpretentiously harmonious manner, is performed for the first time at the Promenade Concerts in London, Sir Henry Wood conducting.

## 23 AUGUST 1937

The Works Progress Administration announces in Washington that the Federal Music Project under its aegis gave 4,360 musical presentations for audiences aggregating to 4,346,705 listeners during the month of July 1937, and that the highest monthly attendance was reached in August 1936 with a total of 6,178,093 listeners.

## 23 AUGUST 1937

Albert ROUSSEL, French master composer of nobly conceived and expertly realized instrumental and vocal works, whose early evocations of the Orient where he travelled as a marine officer and his symphonies set in classical forms have contributed to the formation of a peculiarly identifiable modern French style of composition, in which elements of impressionism, romanticism and neo-classicism coalesce in a fine synthesis, dies in Royan at the age of sixty-eight.

On 28 July 1937 Albert Roussel went to Royan in quest of much needed rest. On 13 August he was compelled to take to bed, interrupting the composition of his Trio for oboe, clarinet and bassoon. Of this Trio, only the middle section was completed; it is a stirring swan song. He bore valiantly the terrible suffering caused by a heart attack. On Monday, 23 August 1937, shortly before 4 o'clock in the afternoon, the great composer died. (Arthur Hoérée, *Albert Roussel*, Paris, 1938)

## 27 AUGUST 1937

*El Salón Mexico,* symphonic sketch by Aaron COPLAND named after a popular night club in Mexico City, thematically based on authentic Mexican ballads and dance tunes set in astute juxtaposition, with apocopated melorhythms emphasizing the polymetric nature of Mexican folk music, unobtrusively harmonized and orchestrated with congenial economic coloration, is performed for the first time by the Orquesta Sinfónica de Mexico, Carlos Chávez conducting.

## 6 SEPTEMBER 1937

Henry HADLEY, American composer of operas and symphonies, on programmatic subjects of geographical categories, ranging from the state of Connecticut to the deep Orient depicted in median Germanized harmonies, conductor of various orchestras, including a term with the New York Philharmonic, dies in New York at the age of sixty-five.

## 8 SEPTEMBER 1937

*Mizú,* operetta by the Brazilian composer Francisco MIGNONE, is produced in Rio de Janeiro.

## 9 SEPTEMBER 1937

*Maria d'Alessandria,* opera in three acts by the 45-year-old Italian composer Georgio Federico GHEDINI, centered on a historically authentic demi-vierge

653

of Alexandria, Egypt, whose perverse delight was to inflame dark passions in the guarded groins of minifutuent pilgrims passing through on their way to the Holy Land, but who repented in holy horror after a monk corrupted by her was struck down by a punitive bolt of lightning, is produced in Bergamo.

## 12 SEPTEMBER 1937

*Partisan Days,* ballet in three acts by the Russian music scholar and imitative composer Boris ASAFIEV, dealing with the civil war in the Caucasus in 1919–1920, centering on the heroism of a Bolshevik girl guerrilla captured by a squad of White Army officers, is produced in Leningrad.

## 12 SEPTEMBER 1937

Darius MILHAUD conducts in Venice the first performance of his *Suite Provençale,* a tasteful symphonic confection of Mediterranean melorhythms in a bouillabaisse of spicy bitonalities.

## 14 SEPTEMBER 1937

*The Marriage,* unfinished comic opera by MUSSORGSKY, completed and orchestrated by Alexander TCHEREPNIN, is performed for the first time in this version in Essen, Germany.

## 19 SEPTEMBER 1937

*Yanina's Nine Brothers,* opera in four acts by the Bulgarian composer Lubomir PIPKOV, to a libretto from Bulgarian rustic life, abounding in asymmetric dancing rhythms of Balkan folkways in a euphonious solution of nutritious triadic harmonies, is produced in Sofia.

## 19 SEPTEMBER 1937

Howard HANSON conducts the orchestra of the Columbia Broadcasting System in New York in the first performance of three movements, (1) *Andante lamentando–Agitato* (2) *Andante tranquillo* (3) *Tempo scherzando* (without the finale) of his *Third Symphony,* written in commemoration of the 300th anniversary of the first Swedish settlement on the shores of Delaware in 1638, and conceived as a tribute to the epic qualities of the Swedish pioneers in America (of which Hanson himself was a descendant), with their "rugged and turbulent character alternating with a religious mysticism." (The Finale, *Largamente e pesante,* was added to the Symphony later, and the work was performed in its entirety in a broadcast of the NBC Symphony Orchestra on 26 March 1938, the composer conducting. First concert performance was conducted by Hanson with the Boston Symphony Orchestra on 3 November 1939)

## 22 SEPTEMBER 1937

Silvestre REVUELTAS, Mexican composer of impassioned music in which his innate Mexicanism harmonizes with the modern techniques of polyharmony

*654*

and polyrhythmy, conducts in Madrid, under siege by the Franco forces, his orchestral *Homenaje a Federico García Lorca,* an homage to the great Spanish poet executed by the Falangists.

### 26 SEPTEMBER 1937

Refused admission to a white hospital after being gravely injured in an automobile accident, Bessie SMITH, the greatest of Blues singers, dies in Memphis, Tennessee, before the arrival of a properly segregated Negritudinal ambulance.

### 1 OCTOBER 1937

*Eighteenth Symphony* by the prime Soviet symphonist Nicolai MIASKOVSKY, in three movements, *Allegro, Lento* and *Allegro giocoso,* written for the celebration of the 20th anniversary of the October Revolution, and completed during the night of 7–8 September 1937, set in the optimistic and socially realistic key of C major, with thematic material derived from the intervalic and rhythmic elements of national Russian songs and dances, is performed for the first time in Moscow, nearly three months before the first performance of Miaskovsky's earlier *Seventeenth Symphony.*

### 1 OCTOBER 1937

*Orači (Harvesters),* "symphonic meditation" by the Croatian composer Jacov GOTOVAC, is performed for the first time in Zagreb.

### 6 OCTOBER 1937

*In Honour of the City of London* for chorus and orchestra by William WALTON, set in variation form, to the words of William Dunbar, is performed for the first time at the Leeds Festival.

### 7 OCTOBER 1937

The Society of Recorder Players is incorporated in London, England, with the purpose to revive the vertical flute of the Renaissance, with Arnold DOLMETSCH, inventor of the modern recorder, as president, and his son Carl as musical director.

### 17 OCTOBER 1937

*Green Mansions,* "non-visual radio opera" by the American composer Louis GRUENBERG, after a novel of the same name by W. H. Hudson, dealing with a South American explorer whose malarial hallucinations include the voice of a jungle girl calling to him in the language of the birds (her voice is represented by a solo on the musical saw, the first such use in an opera), as well as the voices of trees, insects and the hisses of snakes, is performed for the first time over the Columbia Broadcasting System in New York.

### 23 OCTOBER 1937

*Soil Upturned,* second opera, in four acts, by the 28-year-old Soviet composer Ivan DZERZHINSKY, a sequel to his first opera *Quiet Flows the Don,* after the epic novel by Mikhail Sholokhov, depicting in sonorously moving modalities the roaring rural rumbles during the collectivization of agriculture in the Don basin in 1930, is performed for the first time at the Bolshoi Theater in Moscow.

### 25 OCTOBER 1937

Italy issues two postage stamps in honor of Pergolesi, at 30 and 75 centesimi, and two stamps in honor of Spontini, at 10 centesimi and 1 lire 75 centesimi.

### 27 OCTOBER 1937

*Third Symphony* by Bernard ROGERS, the American composer, set in four contrasting movements, is performed for the first time in Rochester, Howard Hanson conducting.

### 1 NOVEMBER 1937

The Central Committee on Arts of the Council of People's Commissars of the Union of Soviet Socialist Republics issues a tabulation of fees to be paid to concert artists, ranging from 50 to 600 rubles per concert according to four categories of merit.

### 2 NOVEMBER 1937

*I'd Rather Be Right,* musical comedy by Richard RODGERS, in which a couple cannot afford to marry until the national budget is balanced and the groom receives a salary raise, is produced in New York.

### 4 NOVEMBER 1937

*First Symphony* in A minor by the 24-year-old American composer Gardner READ, set in four movements in cyclic relationship, wherein the three principal themes explicitly stated in the first movement are restated by virtually every instrument, with an ending on a chord of muted cellos and basses in the low register, is performed for the first time by the New York Philharmonic, John Barbirolli conducting, as the winner of a $1000 prize of the New York Philharmonic Society.

### 4 NOVEMBER 1937

After many a weary month of research, international correspondence and painful collation of divergent data culled from purportedly authoritative reference works, the first edition of *Music Since 1900* by Nicolas SLONIMSKY, a chronological panorama of musical events since the turn of the century, is published in New York by W. W. Norton Co.

### 6 NOVEMBER 1937

*Il Festino,* comic opera in one act by Gian Francesco MALIPIERO, is performed for the first time in concert form over the Turin Radio.

## 17 NOVEMBER 1937

A *Lincoln Symphony* by Daniel Gregory MASON, dean of American academic symphonists, set in four musico-biographic movements, in the historiosophic key of B-flat major unified by a stolid fugue: (1) *The Candidate from Springfield*, in syncopated quadrille tempo (2) *Massa Linkum*, a Negro lament voiced by the English horn (3) *Old Abe's Yarns*, in playful waltz time (4) *1865*, *Lento serioso*, in *tempo di marcia funebre*, in the key of Chopin's funeral march, B-flat minor, ending with a memorial trumpet fanfare, is performed for the first time by the New York Philharmonic, John Barbirolli conducting.

## 18 NOVEMBER 1937

*Violin Concerto* by the American composer John Alden CARPENTER, in a single movement articulated into several contrasting sections, couched in a conventional style of instrumental writing, with occasional excursions into modernistic bitonalities, and ending on a naked tritone, is performed for the first time by the Chicago Symphony Orchestra, Zlatko Baloković soloist.

This is the Concerto of a gentleman. (Oscar Thompson, New York *Sun*, 10 March 1939)

## 18 NOVEMBER 1937

*Wallenstein*, fourth opera by the Czech composer Jaromir WEINBERGER, in six episodes, after Schiller's play, focused on the dramatic career of Wallenstein, the valiant Austrian general assassinated in 1634 during the Thirty Years' War, and dedicated to the Austrian Chancellor Schuschnigg, in allegorical reference to his continued resistance to the encroaching Nazis, is produced in Vienna in a German version translated from the original Czech libretto.

## 21 NOVEMBER 1937

The Leningrad Philharmonic presents the first performance of the *Fifth Symphony* by Dmitri SHOSTAKOVICH, his first publicly performed work after the denunciation of his music by *Pravda* on 28 January 1936, approved in advance by the Union of Soviet Composers and sanctioned by Soviet spokesmen as a sincere manifestation of his redemption in the spirit of Socialist Realism, set, as most of his symphonies, in four classically disposed movements:

(1) *Moderato*, opening with majestic Beethoven-like tones, and then embarking on a vibrantly agitated *Allegro non troppo*, in steady 4/4 time, reverting to a slower tempo for a soft ending in D minor (2) *Allegretto*, a vivaciously dissonant scherzo, with constant shifts of tonal epicenters, and stentorian trumpets proclaiming an optimistic credo (3) *Largo*, a dramatic soliloquy, dynamically ranging from expressive pianissimo to grandiloquent fortississimo, concluding on a moribundly muted F-sharp major chord (4) *Allegro non troppo*, a triumphant peroration on a determined course culminating in a magistral coda, with the brass blaring blatant D major fanfares against 251 eighth-notes on the dominant A in the high strings and woodwinds.

The subject of my *Fifth Symphony* is the evolution of an individual. The music is conceived in a lyrical vein. The finale resolves on an optimistic plane the tragic tension of the first three movements. The question is sometimes asked whether tragedy should have a place in Soviet art at all; but tragedy is not to be confused with hopelessness and pessimism. It is my belief that Soviet tragedy is entirely valid as a genre. But its essence must be suffused with a positive ideal, as in the life-asserting pathos of Shakespeare's tragic plays. (From Shostakovich's statement *My Creative Reply*, published in *Vetchernaya Moskva*, Moscow 25 January 1938)

Shostakovich's *Fifth Symphony* consists of four movements, each presenting a clear formulation of psychological moods. At the same time, the work is an artistic monolith . . . There is a feeling of joy, of happiness bubbling in the orchestra, and spreading throughout the concert hall like a spring breeze. The audience feels the sense of gratitude to the composer whose music has the sound of truth. The Soviet listener rejects decadent, somber or pessimistic art, but he responds enthusiastically to joyful, optimistic, self-asserting artistic declarations. The artistic optimism of Shostakovich's *Fifth Symphony* was communicated to and unreservedly accepted by the public. (Alexei Tolstoy in *Izvestia*, Moscow, 23 November 1937)

### 24 NOVEMBER 1937

*Tobias Wunderlich*, opera in three acts by the 58-year-old German composer Joseph HAAS, dealing with a Bavarian cobbler and town councilman who refuses to agree to the sale of a wooden church figurine of Santa Barbara to an American tourist for half a million dollars, and is rewarded for his devotion when the Gothic saint descends from her wall and offers her services to him as a *Mädchen für alles*, gets back on the wall when he incautiously reveals her identity to the council, but returns to his household to alleviate his sincere distress while the American millionaire assuages his financial troubles by an annual order of 10,000 wooden shoes, set to music in Regeromantic harmonies with an infusion of pietetic modalities and dietetic dissonances, is produced in Kassel.

### 26 NOVEMBER 1937

Three days after the 75th birthday of the dean of Argentinian composers Alberto WILLIAMS, whose English patronymic was derived from his grandfather Benjamin Williams of Exeter, England, a concert of his works, including the first performances of his *Sixth Symphony*, surnamed *Death of the Comet*, and *Seventh Symphony, Eternal Repose*, written in an expansive romantic style, marked by sonorous chromaticism redolent of the mannerisms of César Franck who was his teacher, is presented in Buenos Aires.

### 26 NOVEMBER 1937

Schumann's *Violin Concerto*, written by him between 21 September and 3 October 1853, as he was struggling against the Stygian darkness of mental disease, unperformed hereto because of the stipulation in the will of the violinist Joseph Joachim, who owned the manuscript, barring its performance before the expiration of 100 years after Schumann's death, is brought to performance in Berlin 19 years in advance of that centennial term.

Before the performance of Schumann's *Violin Concerto* takes place, a remarkable book will have been published and reviewed, *Horizons of Immortality* by Baron Erik Palmstierna. The last pages of this book contain a detailed account of spirit messages that have been conveyed to Miss Jelly d'Aranyi expressing Schumann's personal wish that this Concerto should be produced . . . I assert my positive conviction that the spirit of Schumann is inspiring Jelly d'Aranyi's production of Schumann's posthumous *Violin Concerto*. (Donald Tovey in a letter to the London *Times*, 24 September 1937. But Schumann's spirit, which spoke to his communicant in a peculiarly ungrammatical German, had apparently failed to impress the Nazis, and the revival of the Concerto was entrusted not to Jelly d'Aranyi but to an obscure violinist, a member of the Nazi Party.)

### 30 NOVEMBER 1937

*Riders to the Sea*, one-act opera by Ralph VAUGHAN WILLIAMS, to a play by J. M. Synge, depicting the recurrent tragedies of seamen lost off the coast of Ireland, set in recitative following natural inflections of normal human speech, economically harmonized, but resorting, when dramatically expedient, to harsh bitonalities, with the inclusion of a wordless female chorus, is produced in London.

### 3 DECEMBER 1937

*Third Symphony* in G major by Edward Burlingame HILL, in three movements, completed on 19 February 1937, "with no descriptive background, but aiming merely to present musical ideas according to the traditional forms," is performed for the first time by the Boston Symphony Orchestra under the direction of Serge Koussevitzky.

### 6 DECEMBER 1937

*Concertante Musik* for orchestra by the China-born Russo-Estonian composer Boris BLACHER, domiciled in Berlin, written in an economic polyphonic idiom with strong asymmetrical rhythmic beats, is performed for the first time in Berlin.

### 16 DECEMBER 1937

*Lambeth Walk*, jaunty cockney dance in which the participants are instructed to slap their knees, point thumbs over their shoulders while loudly shouting "Hoy!" and strut in an uninhibited manner of the lower classes of society, makes its sensational appearance in the London musical revue *Me and My Girl*, with the score by Noel GAY. (1,065 performances were given in a continuous run until 2 September 1939 when all London theaters were closed at the outbreak of World War II)

### 17 DECEMBER 1937

*Vodník* (*Water Spirit*), opera in three acts by the Czech composer Boleslav VOMÁČKA, to the popular legend about a man from the river who lures a village girl to his watery domain, allows her to come up to the dry surface for a visit, and kills their submarine child when she refuses to rejoin him, set to music in the manner of Smetana, with realistic Czech tunes and folk rhythms, is produced in Prague.

### 17 DECEMBER 1937

*Seventeenth Symphony* by Nicolai MIASKOVSKY, in the mournful tonality of G-sharp minor (completed on 25 June 1937), set in the orthodox four movements in contrasting moods, is performed for the first time in Moscow, several weeks after the première of his *Eighteenth Symphony,* given on 1 October 1937.

### 18 DECEMBER 1937

Two centuries have passed since the death in Cremona, at the age of 92, of the mirific reifier of ideal violins, Antonio STRADIVARI.

### 18 DECEMBER 1937

An exhibition of 39 paintings by George GERSHWIN opens in New York.

George had a way of regarding his painting and music as almost interchangeable phenomena. They sprang, he felt, from the same Freudian elements in him—one emerging as sight, the other as sound. . . . There were, indeed, periods when the palette almost weaned him from the piano; when he willingly stopped composing to paint, and only grudgingly stopped painting to compose. (From the introductory article by Frank Crowningshield in the catalogue of the Gershwin Memorial Exhibition)

### 19 DECEMBER 1937

Forty-eight representative American composers assemble in New York with the purpose of establishing the new protective organization, American Composers' Alliance, protecting the performing rights of composers who are not members of the American Society of Composers, Authors and Publishers.

### 21 DECEMBER 1937

*A Boy Was Born,* choral set of six variations by the 24-year-old English composer Benjamin BRITTEN, is broadcast for the first time by the British Broadcasting Corporation in London.

### 21 DECEMBER 1937

The German *Reichsmusikkammer* forms a board of examiners to weed out phonograph recordings made wholly or partly by Jewish and Negro musicians in order to protect the racial purity and mental integrity of true Aryans in the Nazi Reich.

### 25 DECEMBER 1937

The first concert of the newly formed National Broadcasting Company Symphony Orchestra, with Arturo TOSCANINI as music director, is broadcast by the National Broadcasting Company in New York.

## 28 DECEMBER 1937

Transatlantic radio transmission of a musical score is successfully made when, in consequence of the loss in the mails of the string parts of *Origin of Fire* by SIBELIUS, scheduled for performance by the Boston Symphony Orchestra, its management arranges with Breitkopf and Härtel, publishers, to transmit the missing parts from Leipzig by radio photo.

## 28 DECEMBER 1937

Maurice RAVEL, great French composer, supreme artificer of tonal art whose masterly precision in handling exquisitely molded melodies and fine-textured impressionistic harmonies has creaഄed a magic world of translucently oscillating rhythmic images suffused with the prismatic light of instrumental coloration, described in the citation of the honorary degree of Doctor of Music conferred upon him by the Oxford University as "Musarum interpretes modorum daedalus Mauritius Ravellus," dies in Paris at the age of sixty-two, nine days after brain surgery made necessary by an acute state of apraxia and dysphasia.

The perfection of Ravel's art may be likened to that of Chopin, Mozart or Bach. Ravel recalls particularly the composer of *Le Nozze di Figaro* by his astounding combination of a child's simplicity of soul with a musical technique of such completeness that it would be no exaggeration to call it magical. (Alfredo Casella in the memorial Ravel issue of *La Revue Musicale*, Paris, December 1938)

From the political and cultural standpoint, Hungary has for centuries suffered from the immediate proximity of Germany. But young Hungarian musicians since the turn of this century have been directing themselves towards the culture of France. And that is the reason, from our Hungarian point of view, that the genius of Ravel, along with that of Debussy, has such significance for us. (Béla Bartók; *ibidem*)

Maurice Ravel was one of those rare creative artists who possessed the power of revolutionizing the very foundations of his art while remaining faithful to its immutable laws. . . . Among the many reasons for our admiration for Ravel in Greece, that makes his memory sacred, is that one of our best composers, Emil Riadis, prematurely taken from us, was a fervent disciple and admirer of Ravel. (Manolis Kalomiris, director of the Conservatory of Athens, Greece; *ibidem*)

The great respect that I have for Ravel's art increases my regret that I am not sufficiently informed about the particulars of his life to write a tribute that would do justice to the stature of this great composer. (Richard Strauss; *ibidem*)

It has been said more than once in the present publication that Albert Roussel is much closer to the spirit of the French people than Ravel, and no wonder, for we learn from a reliable source that Maurice Ravel, whose real name was Rawelowitsch, was a descendant from a family that had emigrated from the Near East, and so cannot be regarded as *urfranzösisch*. (*Signale für die musikalische Welt*, Berlin, 9 March 1938)

Ravex, Ravez and Ravet are fairly current in Savoie. The form Ravel probably originated in a misreading of the final *t*. The hypothesis that the name can be traced back to the Jewish patronymic Rabbele is unfounded. Ravel's mother, née Marie Délouart, was born in 1840 in the Bassess-Pyrénées, France, the descendant of a Basque family whose name was Deluarte or Eluarte. (M.D. Calvocoressi, in the 1940 Supplement to Grove's *Dictionary of Music and Musicians*)

# ∽ *1938* ∾

### 1 JANUARY 1938

*Margherita da Cortona*, lyric drama in three acts by the 54-year-old Italian composer Licinio REFICE, dealing with a 13th-century woman in Umbria who expiates her carnal sins by inducing the seductive murderer of her former lover to join the Holy Land Crusade, is produced in La Scala, Milan.

### 5 JANUARY 1938

*Songs of Our Day*, a set of nine choral pieces with orchestra by Sergei PROKOFIEV, written in a socialistically realistic idiom fertilized by felicitous harmonic acerbities, to texts from Soviet poems, including a solemn piece about Stalin, is performed for the first time in Moscow.

### 6 JANUARY 1938

*Filling Station*, automobilistic ballet by Virgil THOMSON, wherein a courteous filling station attendant welcomes passing motorists in an immaculately clean gasoline palace, set to a vernacular score, with thematic elements "like all the familiar tunes, though there is no direct quotation," is performed for the first time in Hartford, Connecticut.

### 7 JANUARY 1938

*Oriane et le Prince d'Amour*, choral ballet by the 67-year-old dean of French modernists Florent SCHMITT, dealing with a polyandrous Renaissance lady who successively seduces a poet, a Mongol merchant and a Prince of Love, but perishes when she dances at a masked ball with Death, in a musical setting saturated with polyharmonies and marked by incisive asymmetrical rhythms, is produced at the Paris Opéra.

(The original title of the work was *Oriane la Sans-Égale;* it was changed to *Oriane et le Prince d'Amour* at the suggestion of Serge Lifar, the choreographer of the Paris Opéra. An orchestral suite drawn from the ballet was first performed in Paris on 12 February 1937. Florent Schmitt's "tragédie dansee" entitled simply *Oriane*, and containing materials later used in the present ballet, was first performed at a dance recital of Ida Rubinstein in Paris on 11 May 1934)

### 13 JANUARY 1938

*Symphony in G Minor* by the 43-year-old English composer of Irish descent Ernest John MOERAN, in four movements closely adhering to the romantic formulae, but enlivened by melodic elements of Irish and East Anglian origin, is performed for the first time in London.

### 13 JANUARY 1938

Maurice MARTENOT takes out the patent No. 841,128 for a microtonal keyboard of his electronic instrument ONDES MUSICALES, which can produce 1/12 tones, constructed especially to approximate the intervallic scale of the Hindu *ragas*.

## 16 JANUARY 1938

Béla BARTÓK and his wife Ditta play in Basel, Switzerland, the solo parts in the first performance of his *Sonata for Two Pianos and Percussion*, in three movements: (1) *Assai lento—Allegro molto* (2) *Lento ma non troppo* (3) *Allegro non troppo*, written in a tersely economic, scintillatingly dissonant idiom, attaining the utmost degree of subtilization in the coloristic employment of percussion instruments, and containing extensive xylophone solos, with the pianos themselves treated as specialized percussion media.

(Bartók made an orchestral arrangement of his sonata in 1940, and renamed it *Concerto for Two Pianos, Percussion and Orchestra*. The first performance of this version took place in London on 14 October 1942, with the Royal Philharmonic Orchestra, Sir Adrian Boult conducting; the pianists were Louis Kentner and Llona Kabos. The first American performance of the *Concerto* was given by the New York Philharmonic, Fritz Reiner conducting, on 21 January 1943, with Béla Bartók and his wife as soloists; it is erroneously listed as the *Uraufführung* in the authoritative edition, *Béla Bartók, Weg und Werk, Schriften und Briefe* by Bence Szabolcsi, published in Budapest in 1957.)

## 18 JANUARY 1938

*Un Drame sous Philippe II*, historical opera in three acts by the 60-year-old Belgian composer Albert DUPUIS, written in the grandiloquent manner of Wagneromantic music drama, is produced for the first time in Brussels.

## 27 JANUARY 1938

*Horoscope*, ballet by the urbanely mundane 32-year-old English composer Constant LAMBERT, to a scenario dealing with an astrologically incompatible love of a boy, born under the sign of Leo, for a zodiacally divergent girl born under the sign of Virgo, with a happy ending provided by their discovery of a mutual selenological congruence since both were born with the moon in Gemini, set to music in an eclectically modernistic manner, is produced in London. (An orchestral suite from *Horoscope* was performed for the first time in London under Lambert's direction on 8 August 1938)

## 29 JANUARY 1938

*Suite sans esprit de suite*, a whimsical orchestral sketch by Florent SCHMITT, written in an anti-baroque manner, is performed for the first time in Paris.

## 30 JANUARY 1938

Darius MILHAUD conducts in Paris the world première of his choreographic poem *L'Oiseau*.

## 30 JANUARY 1938

*Ocean*, ballet by the Japanese composer Shiro FUKAI, is performed for the first time in Tokyo.

## 2 FEBRUARY 1938

*Le Cantique des cantiques,* ballet by Arthur HONEGGER, is produced at the Paris Opéra.

## 10 FEBRUARY 1938

*Die Wirtin von Pinsk,* opera in three acts by the 33-year-old German composer Richard MOHAUPT, to the story of a clever hostess of an inn in Pinsk during its occupation by Napoleon's retreating armies in 1812, modeled after Goldoni's play *Mirandolina,* to a musical setting in an effective polyharmonic idiom fertilized by strong asymmetrical rhythms, is performed for the first (and last) time at the Dresden Opera.

For some time I have been attacked on account of the fact that my wife is Jewish. The sensational success of my opera *Die Wirtin von Pinsk* in Dresden was followed by protests against its further performances. The opera was immediately banned, and a few months later an official directive was issued by the Nazi authorities forbidding performances of any of my works. (From Mohaupt's letter to the author, dated Berlin, 28 June 1938)

## 11 FEBRUARY 1938

*Evocations,* orchestral suite by Ernest BLOCH, composed between 1930 and 1937, written in an effectively exotic style, in three tableaux: a buddhistically serene *Contemplation;* a pentatonically vibrant tone poem *Houang-Ti, God of War;* and an onomatopeically tintinnabulating musicorama of San Francisco's Chinatown, *Renouveau-Spring,* is performed for the first time by the San Francisco Symphony Orchestra, Pierre Monteux conducting.

## 13 FEBRUARY 1938

While listening to the radio broadcast of Tchaikovsky's *Fourth Symphony* by the New York Philharmonic, Nicolas SLONIMSKY suddenly discovers, at 4:30 P.M., the formula for the "Grossmutterakkord," containing all twelve tones (C, B, D-flat, B-flat, D, A, E-flat, A-flat, E, G, F and G-flat, in this order) and eleven different intervals, the equidistant intervals from the central interval being inversions of one another, and the central interval, the tritone, being the inversion of itself, with even-numbered intervals forming an increasing arithmetical progression, and the odd-numbered intervals forming a decreasing arithmetical progression, with a semitone as a unit.

(The melodic version of the "Grossmutterakkord" is the principal motto of the interplanetary opera *Aniara* by Karl-Birger Blomdahl; it also appears in other dodecaphonic works of the 1950's and 1960's. It is known among American dodecaphonists as the "screw row" because of its spiral winding out and in towards its axis)

I wish great prosperity and more progeny to the "Grossmutterakkord." (Paul Hindemith in a guest album of Nicolas Slonimsky, 1938)

To the devil with Grandmother! Let us write real music! (Sergei Prokofiev, *ibid.*)

*664*

## 15 FEBRUARY 1938

The ashes of Teresa CARREÑO, Venezuelan pianist who died in New York in 1917, are repatriated in Caracas by the Government of Venezuela.

## 19 FEBRUARY 1938

Bruno Walter conducts the Vienna Philharmonic for the last time before the infamous Nazi *Anschluss* of Austria, in a program comprising the original version of *Fourth Symphony* by Anton BRUCKNER and the world première of *Prosperos Beschwörung*, symphonic poem after Shakespeare's play *The Tempest* by Egon WELLESZ, in the presence of the composer, also destined soon to leave Nazified Austria.

## 20 FEBRUARY 1938

*Les Petites Cardinal*, light opera in two acts composed jointly by Arthur HONEGGER and Jacques IBERT, is performed for the first time in Paris.

## 21 FEBRUARY 1938

*Ulysse et les Sirènes*, symphonic poem with female voices by the French impressionist composer Jean-Jules Aimable ROGER-DUCASSE, with the sirens weaving seductive chromatic arabesques around a focal D-flat symbolizing the firm course of the ship, while Ulysses struggles diatonically to free himself from self-imposed restraining pentatonic ropes, ignoring the warnings of anxious trumpets, is performed for the first time in Paris.

## 22 FEBRUARY 1938

*Colas Breugnon*, opera in three acts by the Soviet composer Dmitri KABALEVSKY, after Romain Rolland's novel *Le Maître de Clamecy*, dealing with a French wood carver, a man of the people who rebels against a feudal lord who fails to appreciate humble folk art, written in a socialistically realistic idiom marked by lucid tonalities and clear symmetric rhythms and incorporating quotations from authentic old French melodies, is performed for the first time in Leningrad.

I received the vocal score of your opera *Le Maître de Clamecy* and played it over several times with great pleasure. You have succeeded very well in your treatment of the French folk songs; you have absorbed their essence and recreated it in your music. My ear of a Frenchman has caught these songs without difficulty in your lively tableaux. Your opera is one of the best works for the stage I know in new Russian music. (From Romain Rolland's letter to Kabalevsky, dated 27 November 1937)

## 28 FEBRUARY 1938

*Ramona*, opera in three acts by the German-American composer Gustave STRUBE, is produced in Baltimore.

## 4 MARCH 1938

Alan BUSH, 37-year-old English composer, plays the solo part in the first performance in London of his *Piano Concerto*, in four movements of resolutely diatonic, rhythmically propulsive music, with a choral ending containing a triadic message of social significance in major keys.

## 9 MARCH 1938

*Ivan Sergejewitsch Tarassenko,* lyric drama in two acts by the Viennese composer Franz SALMHOFER, to a sentimental libretto from Russian life, is produced in Vienna.

## 15 MARCH 1938

*Chansons populaires juives,* a "collectivistic distillation" for orchestra of seven East-European Jewish songs by the 30-year-old Palestinian composer Uriah BOSCOVICH, is performed for the first time by the Palestine Symphony Orchestra in Haifa.

## 16 MARCH 1938

*Julietta,* fantastic opera in three acts by Bohuslav MARTINU, to a libretto wherein a young man exteriorizes his three dreams about an ethereally beauteous maiden amid oneiristically fluctuating scenes involving Arabian camel riders, pawnbrokers and blind souvenir vendors, in a musical setting full of languorous polyharmonies, is performed for the first time in Prague.

## 17 MARCH 1938

Ernst KRENEK plays the piano part in the first performance, with the Concertgebouw Orchestra in Amsterdam, under the direction of Bruno Walter, of his *Second Piano Concerto* (composed between 25 May and 22 August 1937) in four movements without pause, written according to the 12-tone system of composition, adopted by Krenek in 1931 as a method which "by the nature of its historical development has supplanted the harmonic scaffolding of tonality by a new unifying force."

"Conditions in Europe must be dreadful." (Comments of a Boston lady after Krenek's performance of his *Concerto* with the Boston Symphony Orchestra on 4 November 1938, overheard and reported by H. W. Heinsheimer in his *Menagerie in F Sharp,* New York, 1947)

## 18 MARCH 1938

Cyril ROOTHAM, English composer of sonorous symphonic music in a stately Elgarian vein, dies in Cambridge at the age of 62, leaving behind an unorchestrated manuscript of his *Second Symphony,* which he, stricken with paralysis, had dictated to his friends and pupils, note by note, instrument by instrument. (Rootham's *Second Symphony* was orchestrated by Patrick Hadley and performed for the first time in London on the eve of the first anniversary of Rootham's death, on 17 March 1939)

## 23 MARCH 1938

*Proserpina,* opera in three acts by the 52-year-old Italian composer Renzo BIANCHI, is produced at La Scala in Milan.

## 24 MARCH 1938

*De Snoek (The Pike)*, comic opera in one act by Guillaume LANDRÉ, 33-year-old Dutch composer, son and namesake of the 63-year-old dean of Dutch composers Guillaume (or Willem) Landré, dealing with the fishing trip of an inmate in a modern penological institution, and couched in an appropriately progressive harmonic idiom, with some atonal discursions in the vocal parts, is produced in Amsterdam.

## 24 MARCH 1938

*Grossdeutschland zum 10. April,* hymn-fanfare by the Nazi composer Paul WINTER, urging the Austrian populace in the grip of the Hitlerian Anschluss, to vote on 10 April 1938 for the incorporation of Hitler's native Austria in the Third Reich, is performed for the first time on the Vienna Radio.

I was the happy witness of the Führer's first journey through his liberated fatherland. I watched the indescribable and tumultuous jubilation of the enthusiastic Austrians. As I drove back to Linz from Vienna, the day after the Führer's arrival in the Austrian capital, I suddenly decided to write a fanfare as an expression of my profound joy inspired by the events and the magnificent consummation of Greater Germany. (Paul Winter, *Die Musik,* Berlin, May 1938)

## 2 APRIL 1938

Quincy PORTER, 41-year-old American composer, conducts the New York Philharmonic in the first performance of his *First Symphony* in three movements, "an attempt to find expression for feelings and emotions which the composer knew no other way of setting down," written in an aggressively rhythmic, opulently massive harmony, but lyrical in melodic outline and impressionistically colorful in instrumentation.

## 8 APRIL 1938

Walter PISTON conducts the Boston Symphony Orchestra in the first performance of his *First Symphony* (completed on 25 September 1937), in three movements constituting an essay in absolute forms, "devoid of any pictorial, narrative, political or philosophical intent," revolving around a focal theme and ending with its sonorous restatement in the euphoniously euphorious key of C major.

## 11 APRIL 1938

Society for the Preservation and Encouragement of Barbershop Quartet Singing in America is organized in Tulsa, Oklahoma, by the oil millionaire O. C. CASH.

For a year or more, I have been collecting words to all the old barbershop favorites. I decided to have a meeting of twelve men who on occasion had been caught in the throes of a barbershop chord. Much to my surprise, 35 men showed up instead of twelve . . . Attendance doubled for the next three or four meetings . . . Within two months chapters were formed all the way from Hollywood, with Bing Crosby as President, to New York, Mayor La Guardia, President. (From a letter to the author from O. C. Cash, dated 11 April 1940)

(A barbershop quartet contest was held in July 1940 at the New York World's fair, with the first prize, consisting of radio receivers and phonograph recording machines, awarded by Mayor La Guardia, President of the New York chapter of the SPEBSQSA, to the Flat Four, a police team. Other contestants were Melody Maulers, Frog Hollow Four, Chromatic Canaries, and Phillip's 6 Barflies)

### 12 APRIL 1938

Feodor CHALIAPIN, great Russian bass whose fabulous career, from peasant beginnings to world glory, embraced half a century of singing, and whose portrayal of Boris Godunov constitutes, in its dramatic power, one of the greatest achievements of operatic art, dies in Paris at the age of sixty-five.

Chaliapin suffered from chronic diabetes aggravated by acute anemia. His doctors recommended blood transfusion. The first was given by his wife, the second by his youngest daughter. The third transfusion was given by a professional blood donor whose name was Chien. Chaliapin joked: "Since his name is Dog, I am afraid I will be barking tomorrow." But the transfusions were futile. In the morning of 12 April 1938 he became delirious. He kept asking, "Where am I? In a theater in Russia? To sing, I must breathe, but I cannot . . ." At 5:15 P.M. he died. (*Les Dernières Nouvelles*, Russian émigré newspaper, Paris, 13 April 1918)

Chaliapin betrayed his people and sold his fatherland for petty cash. Having lost contact with his native soil, he failed to create a single new character on the stage during his stay abroad. His great talent faded long ago. He left nothing behind him after his death. (*Izvestia*, Moscow, 14 April 1938)

Only those are really dead who are forgotten . . . I read this inscription on a tombstone somewhere. If so, then Chaliapin will never die. He cannot die! For this amazing artist, who had a truly fabulous talent, is unforgettable. Forty-one years ago, almost at the beginning of his career, the development of which I witnessed myself, he had stood on a pedestal, from which he had never come down, never even stumbled . . . Chaliapin was a giant. To future generations he will be a legend. (Rachmaninoff, in *Les Dernières Nouvelles*, Paris, 17 April 1938)

### 14 APRIL 1938

*The Captive of the Caucasus*, ballet by the erudite 53-year-old Russian music scholar and prolific composer of theatrical music, Boris ASAFIEV, after a poem by Pushkin, dealing with a prisoner's passion for a Circassian girl, whom he encounters while serving in the Russian army during periodical skirmishes with bellicose Caucasian tribes, is produced in Leningrad.

### 22 APRIL 1938

*Concerto for Organ and Orchestra* by the 42-year-old American composer Leo SOWERBY, in three contrasting movements, ending in a triumphantly academic C-major finale, is performed for the first time by the Boston Symphony Orchestra, under the direction of Serge Koussevitzky, with E. Power Biggs as organ soloist.

## 27 APRIL 1938

The French master organist Marcel DUPRÉ plays the organ solo in the first performance of his *Concerto* for organ and orchestra in Groningen, Holland. (The first Paris performance of the *Concerto* took place on 27 October 1938)

## 1 MAY 1938

The REICHSMUSIKKAMMER, the governing organ of Nazified German music, issues a directive ruling that no Aryan music instructors are to be allowed to teach Jewish pupils.

## 4 MAY 1938

*Antonio e Cleopatra,* opera in three acts by Gian Francesco MALIPIERO (completed on 2 April 1937) to his own libretto after Shakespeare, written in a pandiatonically enriched harmonic style, is performed for the first time at the May Festival in Florence.

## 6 MAY 1938

To celebrate Hitler's state visit to Mussolini in Rome, the Italian opera composer Gino MARINUZZI conducts an open air concert with a Fascist ensemble comprising an orchestra of 900 players, 45 military bands and 111 choruses, aggregating to 10,000 performers.

## 8 MAY 1938

*Dumbarton Oaks* for chamber orchestra by Igor STRAVINSKY, named after the estate of the American music patron Robert Woods Bliss, in three neo-classical movements, characteristically reviving the Baroque custom of dedicating works to munificent patrons, is performed for the first time in Dumbarton Oaks, Washington, D.C., under the direction of Nadia Boulanger. (At the first Paris performance on 16 June 1938 the piece was programmed under the title *Concerto,* without reference to Dumbarton Oaks)

Stravinsky's *Concerto* sounds strangely dull. It abounds in scholastic clichés and banalities. Every vestige of imaginative effect is systematically eliminated. This type of music may signify its final decline, its mortal illness, unless it is the radical reincarnation and rejuvenation of the art. There is no other alternative. (Boris Schloezer in *Les Dernières Nouvelies,* Russian émigré paper, Paris, 21 June 1938)

## 11 MAY 1938

*I Married An Angel,* musical comedy by Richard RODGERS with lyrics by Lorenz Hart dealing with a mystical Count who vows never to marry except an angel, actually finds one but experiences trouble when she proves to be angelically truthful with people, thus causing him embarrassment, presenting, besides the attractive title number, a lovely duet, *Spring Is Here,* is produced in New York.

## 12 MAY 1938

*Jeanne d'Arc au Bûcher,* dramatic oratorio by Arthur HONEGGER (completed on 30 August 1935) and conceived as a modern *chanson de geste,* to the text by Paul Claudel, set to music of high tension and dissonant consistency, including spoken dialogue, with Joan of Arc tied to the stake throughout the play, is performed for the first time in concert form by the Chamber Orchestra of Basel, Switzerland, with Paul Sacher, its founder, conducting, and with Ida Rubinstein in the role of Joan.

## 16 MAY 1938

*Uprising,* opera in three acts by the Azerbaijan composer Lev KHODZHA-EINATOV, dealing with social upheavals during the civil war in Central Asia in 1920, written in the idiom of socialist realism and containing musical quotations from indigenous melodies, is produced in Leningrad.

## 22 MAY 1938

Emil GILELS, 21-year-old Odessa-born Soviet pianist, wins the first prize of 50,000 Belgian francs at the Concours Ysaÿe in Brussels, an international competition of 95 pianists from 23 countries, the *pièce de résistance* among the 12 finalists being a new piano concerto by the Belgian composer Jean ABSIL, in three contrasting movements, written in a moderately modern, rhythmically intricate and harmonically opulent idiom, handed to the contestants only seven days before the public performance with an orchestra, for study in isolated rooms of a suburban castle. (Second prize was awarded to Mary JOHNSTON of England; third prize to Jacob FLIER of Russia)

Gilels literally fought his way through the impasse of Absil's piano concerto. He and Flier were particularly at a disadvantage since they had no experience in performing modernistic music, or even listening to such music. The atonal constructions of Absil's concerto, with its constant rhythmic changes, appeared to them absolutely devoid of meaning. Gilels wrote to his teacher in Moscow: "I am completely isolated from the outside world. They handed me a tremendously difficult concerto. I am working on it six or seven hours every day. Very difficult!" (S. Hentova, *Emil Gilels,* Moscow, 1959)

## 22 MAY 1938

An exhibition of ENTARTETE MUSIK (Debased Music) opens in Düsseldorf under the auspices of the Nazi Ministry of Propaganda, with the declared aim to forestall the proliferation of "microbes of musical decomposition, Marxist, Bolshevist, Jewish and other un-German tendencies, such as atonal music and jazz," with special alcoves containing phonograph recordings of modernistic music and published scores by such "cultural Bolsheviks" as Stravinsky, Paul Hindemith, Franz Schreker, Arnold Schoenberg, Alban Berg, Josef Matthias Hauer, Ernst Toch, Ernest Bloch, Ernst Krenek, Kurt Weill and Hanns Eisler, as well as books and articles by Schoenberg, Hindemith, Alfred Einstein, Her-

670

mann Scherchen, and other Aryan and non-Aryan proponents of alleged *Kulturbolschewismus.*

### 22 MAY 1938

*Ostmark-Overture* by the German composer Otto BESCH, a nationalistic piece written to celebrate the nazification and annexation of Austria, now renamed Ostmark, by the Third German Reich, is performed for the first time at the opening of a Nazi music festival in Düsseldorf.

### 25 MAY 1938

*Second Symphony* by the 27-year-old American composer William SCHUMAN is performed for the first time by the Greenwich Orchestra in New York.

### 28 MAY 1938

The first air-conditioned opera theater opens at Dessau, Germany, enabling singers and audience to act and react in a purified atmosphere at comfortable temperatures.

### 28 MAY 1938

*Mathis der Maler,* opera in seven scenes by Paul HINDEMITH, to his own libretto inspired by the triptych painting of the altar piece in Isenheim, Alsace, by Mathis Grünewald (1470–1531), with symphonic and choral tableaux limning the three thematic scenes—*Angels' Concert, Entombment* and *Temptation of St. Anthony* (in which Mathis dreams of himself being tempted by seductive visions)—set against the realistic background of peasant rebellion in Germany, which Mathis led, with the musical score in a tense contrapuntal idiom, culminating in a theodicy in grandiloquent triadic harmonies, is produced in Basel, Switzerland, after Hindemith had been declared a persona non grata in Nazi Germany. (Symphony *Mathis der Maler,* incorporating the interludes from the opera, was first performed in Berlin on 12 March 1934)

### 30 MAY 1938

*Lusabatzin (At Dawn,)* opera in five acts by the 41-year-old Armenian composer Aro STEPANIAN, with the action taking place during the civil war in Armenia in 1920, illustrating in socialistically realistic tones the Bolshevik magnanimity, Menshevik pusillanimity, and bourgeois parvanimity, is produced in Erevan.

### 30 MAY 1938

*The Incredible Flutist,* ballet by Walter PISTON, to a story about a circus player who could charm not only snakes but also snake charmers, in an uninhibited hedonistic medium in luxuriant orchestration ranging from pseudo-sentimental to ostentatiously romantic, at one point inserting a dodecaphonic tune (recording of a barking dog has been sanctioned by the composer at some performances), is played for the first time by the Boston Pops Orchestra, Arthur Fiedler conducting.

## 2 JUNE 1938

Hans von WOLZOGEN, fervent Wagnerophile who popularized the term *Leitmotiv* to designate the identifying leading motifs in Wagner's music dramas (Wagner's own term was *Grundthema*), dies in his beloved Bayreuth in his 90th year.

## 2 JUNE 1938

*La Femme à Barbe,* pogonological musical farce by the 50-year-old French composer Claude DELVINCOURT, recounting the transsexual adventures of a bearded woman, is performed for the first time in Versailles.

## 2 JUNE 1938

*The Scarlet Letter,* opera in two acts, after Hawthorne's classic tale, by the 34-year-old Philadelphia-born composer Vittorio GIANNINI, to his own libretto in Italian, is produced for the first time at the State Opera of Hamburg, in the German version as *Das Brandmal,* with the composer's sister Dusolina Giannini in the role of the young matron of Salem, Massachusetts, whose unhallowed affair with a Puritan clergyman was stigmatized with the embroidered initial A for Adulteress on her dress, set to music in an impassionate dramatic manner, with ingratiating modernities within the matrix of the Italianate operatic idiom.

## 12 JUNE 1938

Venezuela issues a 25-centavo postage stamp to commemorate the Venezuelan pianist Teresa CARREÑO, "the Valkyrie of the piano."

## 15 JUNE 1938

*Das Buch mit Sieben Siegeln,* oratorio by the Austrian romantic composer Franz SCHMIDT, his last and most ambitious work, to the text from the Revelation of St. John, in two parts, culminating in the opening of the seventh seal and revealing the awesome panorama of the Last Judgment with horrendous explosions of dissonant tonite, is performed for the first time in Vienna.

## 15 JUNE 1938

*Karl V,* allegorical historical music drama in two parts by Ernst KRENEK, in which the dying Emperor of the Holy Roman Empire is questioned by God speaking to him from Titian's painting *La Gloria,* while his mundane enemies —Martin Luther, King Francis I of France, the Sultan and the Pope—offer philosophical comments, Krenek's first work written entirely according to the method of composition with 12 tones, completed by him on 24 May 1933, and embodying some non-dodecaphonic illustrative devices, including a naturalistic quartet of preternatural voices and pendulum clocks, is performed for the first time in Prague, in the absence of Krenek himself, who could not take the risk of flying over Hitler's Germany from London where he was staying as an exile from Nazi-infested Austria.

The story of my opera embraces the entire life of Emperor Charles V, who first took America under his rule, fought the Turks and got in trouble with the Pope. The scenes of his life appear on a second stage. Musical recitative is often interrupted by spoken dialogue. *Karl V* is my first composition in the 12-tone system. (From Ernst Krenek's letter to the author, dated 5 february 1938)

17 JUNE 1938

*Zadig*, opera in four acts by the French composer Jean DUPÉRIER, after Voltaire's novel of that name, is produced at the Paris Opéra-Comique.

17 JUNE 1938

The 16th Festival of the International Society for Contemporary Music opens in London with the following program of orchestral works:

*Military Symphonietta* by Vítězslava KAPRÁLOVÁ, 23-year-old daughter of the Czech composer Vaclav Kaprál, conducted by herself, and dedicated to the President of Czechoslovakia Beneš, with a notation that the word "military" in the title "is not an appeal for war but rather a conscious defensive posture in mobilizing physical sensations and the determination to preserve the national independence of one's own country"; *Third Symphony*, in four classically designed movements by the Polish modernist Józef KOFFLER, who was to perish tragically five years hence, killed by the Nazis with his wife and child; *Domini est Terra*, a psalm for chorus and orchestra, by the 35-year-old English neo-classicist Lennox BERKELEY, written in neo-ecclesiastical modalities; *Das Augenlicht* for mixed chorus and orchestra by Anton von WEBERN, with a seemingly conventional four-part harmonic setting ingeniously made up of three statements of the fundamental 12-tone row and its inversion, replete with characteristically Webernian major sevenths, the total creating an impression of hierophantic solemnity; *Jeanne d'Arc*, symphonic suite in five movements by the nearly 34-year-old French composer Manuel ROSENTHAL, a hedonistically anachronistic evocation of the canonized virgin-whore, concluding with a contorted version of the *Marseillaise* (the third movement was omitted at this performance); *Tres Ciudades* for voice and orchestra by the 37-year-old Spanish composer Julián BAUTISTA, to the text by Federico García Lorca, the radical poet murdered by the Falangists during the Spanish Civil War; and *Le Nouvel Âge*, "symphonie concertante" by the Russian-born Parisian composer and conductor Igor MARKEVITCH, conceived in a neo-classical idiom, in clear tonalities with pandiatonic incrustations.

18 JUNE 1938

At the second concert of the 16th Festival of the International Society for Contemporary Music in London, the following program of chamber music is presented:

*Quintet* for flute, clarinet, violin, viola and cello by the Swedish composer Franz SYBERG; *String Quartet* by the German neo-classical composer Karl Amadeus

HARTMANN, written in the neo-baroque technique of dissonant counterpoint; *Theme and Variations* for two violins by the 33-year-old English composer Alan RAWSTHORNE (the festival program book states: "The composer is convinced that the theme appears in each variation"); *String Quartet* by the 42-year-old Polish composer Karol RATHAUS, written in a Schoenbergian atonal idiom; *Violin Sonata*, by the 53-year-old German-born American composer Werner JOSTEN, in an academically effective neo-romantic style; *String Quartet* by the 40-year-old Austrian composer Viktor ULLMAN; and *Pianoforte Quintet* by the Berlin-born Spanish-Cuban composer Joaquín NÍN-CULMELL, couched in a neo-classical Hispanic idiom.

### 19 JUNE 1938

At the third concert of the 16th Festival of the International Society for Contemporary Music in London, two old English operas are presented: *Venus and Adonis* by Dr. John BLOW (1649–1708), newly arranged by Anthony Lewis, and *The Ephesian Matron* by Charles DIBDIN (1745–1814).

### 20 JUNE 1938

At the fourth concert of the 16th Festival of the International Society for Contemporary Music in London, the following program is given:

*Suite* for strings and piano by the dean of Dutch composers Willem LANDRÉ; two movements from *Suite* for female voices, oboe and strings by the 25-year-old Australian neo-classical composeress Peggy GLANVILLE-HICKS; *Variations on a Theme of Frank Bridge* for string orchestra by the 24-year-old English composer Benjamin BRITTEN, a set of ten imaginative metamorphoses on a melodious subject by Britten's revered teacher, replete with whimsical allusions to Italian operatic arias and Viennese waltzes; *Music for Radio* by František BARTOŠ of Czechoslovakia; *Concerto for Trumpet and Strings* by the Danish neo-classicist Knudaage RIISAGER; *Cantata* for soprano, chorus and piano by Ernst KRENEK; and *Sonata for Two Pianos and Percussion* by Béla BARTÓK, first performed by him and his wife in Basel on 16 January 1938.

### 22 JUNE 1938

At the fifth concert of the 16th Festival of the International Society for Contemporary Music in London the following program of chamber music is presented:

Two pieces from *La Nativité du Seigneur* for organ by the 29-year-old French composer Olivier MESSIAEN, set in a stark neo-medieval idiom, played by the composer himself; three movements from *Nonet* by the 31-year-old Lithuanian composer Jeronimas KAČINKAS, written in a neo-classical manner with some impressionistic touches; *Nachtklänge*, a set of songs for voice and wind quintet by the Czech composer Isa KREJČI; *Little Suite* for violin and piano by the Dutch composer Bertus VAN LIER; *Racconto* for flute, saxophone, bassoon and doublebass by the 41-year-old Danish neo-classicist Jörgen BENTZON; *Two Songs* for soprano, oboe, clarinet and bassoon by the 27-year-old Serbian composer Vojislav VUČKOVIĆ, fated to be murdered by the Nazis on Christmas Day four years hence; *Composition* for violin and viola by the Swedish composer Sten BROMAN, written in a deliberate two-dimensional idiom, in strict two-part counterpoint without double-stops for either instrument; and *Suite dans le goût espagnol* for oboe, bassoon, trumpet and harpsichord by the French composer ROLAND-MANUEL, with profusion of coloristic Hispanic melorhythms.

674

## 24 JUNE 1938

The 16th Festival of the International Society for Contemporary Music in London presents its last concert in the following program of orchestral music:

*Concerto for Orchestra* by the Italian modernist Riccardo NIELSEN set in a neo-classical style with atonal excrescences; *Mouvement Symphonique* by the Serbian composer Slavko OSTERC, written in a highly chromaticized idiom, thematically diversified with an express avoidance of repetitious melodic patterns and sequences; *El Salón Mexico*, a brilliant Latin American pasticcio by Aaron COPLAND, first performed in Mexico City on 27 August 1937; *Aubade, Interlude and Dance* by the 41-year-old Catalan composer Roberto GERHARD; excerpts from the opera *Mathis der Maler* by Paul HINDEMITH; *Danses* by the Swiss composer Jean BINET; fragments from the oratorio *Das Gesicht Jesajas* by the Swiss composer Willy BURKHARD, written in a linear neo-classical style of vigesimosecular dissonant counterpoint.

## 21 JULY 1938

*St. Francis*, choreographic legend for orchestra by Paul HINDEMITH, on the life and the natural philosophy of St. Francis of Assisi, set in a stark neo-medieval idiom in sinewy linear counterpoint, is performed for the first time in London by the Ballet Russe of Monte Carlo. (A suite for orchestra drawn from this ballet, in three movements, is catalogued under the title *Nobilissima Visione*)

## 24 JULY 1938

*Friedenstag*, one-act opera by Richard STRAUSS, with its action taking place on 24 October 1648, the day of the conclusion of the Westphalian Peace Treaty ending the Thirty Years' War, illustrated in the finale by a militantly concordant display of demonstratively peaceful C major, is produced in Munich before an international audience, with 16 curtain calls for the composer, but in the conspicuous absence of Nazi officials. (In his speech of 30 January 1940, Hitler described the Westphalian Peace Treaty, which dismembered Germany into a number of small royal and ducal states, as treasonable)

## 28 JULY 1938

Jack JUDGE, a music hall singer, whose popular song *Tipperary*, written jointly with Harry J. Williams in 1912, became a favorite of the British Tommies in World War I, dies at West Bromwich at the age of sixty.

## 31 JULY 1938

Morton GOULD, 24-year-old American composer, conducts the New York Philharmonic at the Lewisohn Stadium in the first performance of his *Second American Symphonette*, "entertainment music attempting to utilize the elements of American swing in the classical form of the sinfonietta," in three movements, the second of which, entitled *Pavanne*, fuses elements of jazz in swing time with the form of a classical court dance.

I know that the spelling *Pavanne* is incorrect, but at the time I wrote the piece, the *Pavanne* was not a well-known word. Those who knew Ravel's *Pavane* could spell the name right, but the people who knew mine had difficulty in pronouncing the title. Among the misspellings were "Pavayne," "Puvunie," and even "Parvenu," and I decided to use two n's to give at least some idea of what the phonetic sounds were. (Morton Gould in a letter to the author dated 26 July 1961, in reply to an orthographic inquiry)

## 31 JULY 1938

A century has elapsed since the death, on board the brig *Otis* bound from the West Indies to the United States, of Johannes Nepomuk MAELZEL, eccentric inventor of the useful metronome and of the futuristic Panharmonicon (for which Beethoven wrote his *Wellington's Victory*) and the perpetrator of the Chess Automaton Hoax, which he promoted in both hemispheres with the aid of a midget chess master hidden inside among pieces of collapsible machinery, and moving the magnetized chessmen from beneath the board.

## 18 AUGUST 1938

Benjamin BRITTEN, 24-year-old English composer, plays the piano part in the first performance of his *Piano Concerto* in four movements, *Toccata, Waltz, Recitative and Aria* (replaced in 1945 by an *Impromptu*) and *March* (consisting of a series of march tunes, played, in the words of the composer, "full of confidence by the pianoforte and then by the orchestra"), at the Promenade Concerts in London, Sir Henry Wood conducting.

The Concerto was conceived with the idea of exploiting various important characteristics of the pianoforte, such as its enormous compass, its percussive quality, and its suitability for figuration; so that it is not by any means a symphony with pianoforte, but rather a bravura concerto with orchestra. (From Britten's annotations in the program book of the concert)

## 1 SEPTEMBER 1938

*Shchors*, opera in five acts by the 43-year-old Ukrainian composer Boris LIATOSHINSKY, with the action taking place during the civil war in the Ukraine in 1918, centering on the heroic figure of Nicolai Shchors, commander of the partisan group fighting against the troops of the Hetman, the German army of occupation and the nationalist Ukrainian bands, couched in the heroic tones of socialist realism with a liberal utilization of Ukrainian folksongs, is performed for the first time in Kiev.

## 3 SEPTEMBER 1938

At the opening concert of the Nordic Music Festival in Copenhagen, Jón LEIFS, prime composer of Iceland, conducts the first performance of the orchestral suite from his music to the drama *Loftr*.

## 3 SEPTEMBER 1938

*Conquest of the Air*, symphonic suite from incidental music for the London Films Production, by the English modernist Arthur BLISS, in six illustrative movements, *The Wind, The Vision of Leonardo da Vinci, Stunting, Over the Arctic, Gliding* and *March*, is performed for the first time in London, the composer conducting.

676

## 7 SEPTEMBER 1938

*Los Amos del Barrio*, a "sainete" (burlesque) by the 48-year-old Spanish violinist Manuel QUIROGA, is performed for the first time in Madrid.

## 23 SEPTEMBER 1938

Aurelio GIORNI, Italian-born American composer, vanishes at 6:30 P.M. near the Housatonic River in Western Massachusetts (his body was recovered) in a state of profound depression, induced by exceedingly bad reviews of his symphony, at its first performance in New York on 25 April 1938.

## 23 SEPTEMBER 1938

Phonograph recordings and full orchestral scores of *Finlandia* by SIBELIUS, *Stars and Stripes Forever* by John Philip SOUSA, and a swing piece *Flat Foot Floogie*, are deposited, along with other memorabilia of 20th-century civilization, in a Time Capsule, encased in an indestructible metal tube, buried underground in the area of the New York World's Fair, with engraved instructions to posterity to open it in A.D. 6938.

## 25 SEPTEMBER 1938

Eugenie SCHUMANN, last surviving daughter of Robert Schumann, dies in Bern, Switzerland, five weeks before her 87th birthday.

## 26 SEPTEMBER 1938

*Knickerbocker Holiday*, opera in two acts by Kurt WEILL, 38-year-old German composer of bimusical talent, excelling both in modern symphonic and light theatrical genres, his first stage work written in America, with the book and lyrics by Maxwell Anderson, after Washington Irving's chronicle *Father Knickerbocker's History of New York*, wherein the Dutch Governor Peter Stuyvesant appears as a proto-Fascist, including among many melodious arias, the celebrated *September Song*, is produced for the first time at Hartford, Connecticut. (The first New York performance took place on 19 October 1938)

## 1 OCTOBER 1938

Walter KAUFMANN, 31-year-old Czech composer, conducts in Bombay, India, where he found temporary employment after flight from Czechoslovakia overhung by the dark cloud of Nazi menace, the first performance of his radio opera *Anasuya*, on the subject of an Indian maiden struggling in a world of multidirectional perils.

## 2 OCTOBER 1938

*Lancillotto del Lago*, opera in three acts by the 31-year-old Italian composer Pino DONATI, telling the eternally fascinating story of Lancelot of the Lake, knight of King Arthur's Round Table, and set to music in an unpretentiously abecedarian triadic idiom, is performed for the first time in Bergamo.

## 5 OCTOBER 1938

*Serenade to Music* by Ralph VAUGHAN WILLIAMS, scored for vocal soloists, chorus and orchestra, to the text from Shakespeare's play *The Merchant of Venice* ("Soft stillness and the night become the touches of sweet harmony"), set to music in sonorously resonant triadic harmonies, is performed for the first time at the Promenade Concerts in London, under the direction of Sir Henry Wood.

## 10 OCTOBER 1938

*Trepak,* ballet by the 39-year-old Russian modernist composer Alexander TCHEREPNIN, is performed for the first time anywhere by the Mordkin Russian Ballet in Richmond, Virginia.

## 15 OCTOBER 1938

*Daphne,* bucolic tragedy in one act by Richard STRAUSS (completed in Taormina, Italy, on 24 December 1937), derived from the Greek myth of Daphne's metamorphosis into a laurel tree (Daphne means laurel in Greek), to escape Apollo's amorous pursuit, and ending with Daphne's voice heard from the branches of the tree, set in characteristically Straussian harmonic sonorities mellowed by a high incidence of triadic consonances, is performed for the first time at the Dresden Opera House, on the same program with his opera, *Friedenstag,* first produced in Munich on 24 July 1938.

## 16 OCTOBER 1938

*Billy the Kid,* ballet in one act by Aaron COPLAND, to a scenario by Lincoln Kirstein, nostalgically depicting the short life of William H. Bonney, picaresque badman of the Old West who was trapped and killed in 1881, permeated with incisive American frontier melorhythms and incorporating several authentic cowboy songs, among them *Git Along Little Dogie, Old Chisolm Trail,* and *O Bury Me Not on the Lone Prairie,* traversing the Kid's life beginning with his killing, at the age of 12, of the murderers of his mother, through episodes of card games with his outlaw friends, his jailing and his escape from prison, and finally his death after a posse led by his former friend tracks him down as he rests in the desert with his girl, is produced by Ballet Caravan in Chicago. (A symphonic suite in 7 sections, *The Open Prairie, Street in a Frontier Town, Card Game at Night, Gun Battle, Celebration Dance, Billy's Death,* the *Open Prairie Again,* was performed for the first time on 9 November 1940 in New York by the NBC Symphony under the direction of William Steinberg)

## 20 OCTOBER 1938

*The Serf,* opera in three acts by the 25-year-old English composer George LLOYD, to his father's libretto, dealing with the tragic love of a Saxon vassal youth for a Saxon maiden in 11th century Britain, who discover to their incestuous horror that they are both natural children of the old Norman King, is produced in London.

## 22 OCTOBER 1938

*Preludio e Scherzo Sinfonico* by the 56-year-old Czech-born Italian composer Riccardo PICK-MANGIAGALLI, written in a propulsively rhythmic idiom, is performed for the first time in Milan.

## 24 OCTOBER 1938

THE BACH SOCIETY of New Jersey sends a letter of protest to the Federal Communications Commission in Washington against the practice of jazzing up the classics by swing bands on the radio.

Recently we heard a jazz orchestra giving a rendition of Bach's *Toccata in D Minor*. All the beautiful fugue effects were destroyed by the savage slurring of the saxophone and the jungled discords of the clarinet. As a group interested in bringing the best music to the people in our state, we must protest against the jazzing of Bach. (An excerpt from the letter of the Bach Society)

Why should the jazzing of Bach's music be any more profane than the mundane treatment it receives at the hands of theater orchestra arrangers? I dare say that the well-fed salty, beerdrinking, begetting Bach might have delighted in some of the glamorous virtuoso performances of our American jazz transcriptions. (Roy Harris in an open letter to the Bach Society of New Jersey)

## 25 OCTOBER 1938

A century has elapsed since the birth in Paris of Georges BIZET, whose sunny Mediterranean music enchanted the world and captivated even the tenebrous mind of ruminant Friedrich Nietzsche as an antidote to the octopus-like embrace of Wagner's Teutonic genius.

## 5 NOVEMBER 1938

Arturo Toscanini conducts the Orchestra of the National Broadcasting Company in New York in the first performances of two works by the 28-year-old American composer Samuel BARBER: *First Essay for Orchestra,* a romantically compact narrative in poetically inflected musical paragraphs, forming a compound of three contrasting sections, *Andante sostenuto, Allegro molto, Scherzando*; and *Adagio for Strings,* an orchestral version of the slow movement from Barber's early *String Quartet,* written in an austerely eloquent manner of a polyphonic chorale, destined to become one of the most frequently performed American works, particularly favored on funereal occasions (it was played on the radio after the official announcement of President Roosevelt's death on 14 April 1945).

## 9 NOVEMBER 1938

*Leave It to Me,* a musical comedy by the harmonious tunesmith Cole PORTER, dealing with a bumptious American correspondent stationed in Moscow who constantly gets in trouble with both Russians and Americans, featuring the famous song *My Heart Belongs to Daddy,* and the pseudo-political ditties *I'm*

*Taking the Steps to Russia* and *From U.S.A. to U.S.S.R.*, is produced in New York.

### 11 NOVEMBER 1938

*Violin Concerto* by Edward Burlingame HILL, a cultured New Englander, an enlightened Harvardman of music, wrought in an expert manner imbued with an impressionistic aura, is performed for the first time by the Boston Symphony Orchestra, Serge Koussevitzky conducting, with Ruth Posselt as soloist.

### 11 NOVEMBER 1938

On the 20th anniversary of the end of World War I, Kate SMITH, the voluminous songstress of the radio, broadcasts Irving BERLIN's anthem-like song *God Bless America,* originally composed in 1918 for the musical revue *Yip Yip Yaphank* at Camp Upton, New York, where he served as a draft sergeant, but never performed in public.

(On 29 November 1940, an octogenarian song writer Alfred M. Aarons filed a lawsuit in Los Angeles against Irving Berlin and Kate Smith charging plagiarism from his own song *America, My Home So Fair,* copyrighted in 1918 and allegedly similar in melody and rhythm with Berlin's song, but lost the case)

### 14 NOVEMBER 1938

*Violin Concerto* in D minor by Nicolai MIASKOVSKY, in three movements (completed on 20 July 1938), couched in a lyrico-dramatic style, with luscious melodies in the solo instrument harmoniously supported by a resonant orchestra, is performed for the first time in Leningrad.

### 21 NOVEMBER 1938

Leopold GODOWSKY, fabulously endowed Polish-born pianist virtuoso, composer of transcendentally difficult piano pieces and polypianistic arrangements, such as an ambidextrous palimpsest of Chopin's *Black-Key Etude* in the left hand and the *Butterfly Etude* in the right hand, whose aphoristic verbal wit matched his digital agility, dies in New York at the age of sixty-eight.

### 21 NOVEMBER 1938

Ruby HELDER, American woman-tenor with vocal cords masculine in size and resonant power, capable of singing an octave lower than a normal soprano, dies in Hollywood at the age of forty-eight.

### 23 NOVEMBER 1938

*The Boys from Syracuse,* musical comedy by Richard RODGERS, derived from Shakespeare's play *A Comedy of Errors,* wherein the mistaken identities of the translocated spouses result in fortuitous adultery, including in the score the popular waltz tune *Falling in Love with Love* and the ballad *This Can't Be Love,* is produced in New York.

### 24 NOVEMBER 1938

*Beauty and the Beast,* one-act opera by Vittorio GIANNINI, is produced in concert form on the CBS radio. (The first stage performance took place in Hartford, Connecticut on 14 February 1946)

680

## 24 NOVEMBER 1938

Werner EGK, 37-year-old German composer, conducts at the Berlin State Opera the first performance of his opera in three acts, *Peer Gynt*, to a libretto amplified from Ibsen's dramatic allegory, including an episodic voyage to America, set to music in a fairly modernistic manner, boldly challenging the supremacy of Grieg's celebrated score from incidental music written for the same Ibsen play.

The Nazi press made an assault upon *Peer Gynt* by Werner Egk, and declared it to be unfit for the Nationalist Socialist outlook on the world. Then something quite unexpected occurred: at one of the more recent presentations of the opera in Berlin there appeared—a *deus ex machina*, so to speak—Führer Adolf Hitler himself. The work pleased him extremely. He asked to have the composer introduced, and is said to have made the statement that he was happy to have met such talent. The direct result of this was the proposal of the opera to the executive board of the Reich Music Festival (and thereby the prospect of numerous productions throughout the Reich) and also the bestowal upon Egk of a government prize of 10,000 marks for the composition of a new opera. (From a Düsseldorf dispatch in the *Christian Science Monitor* of 15 July 1939)

## 26 NOVEMBER 1938

*Concerto* for cello and orchestra in E minor by Sergei PROKOFIEV, sketched in Paris in 1934 and completed in Moscow on 18 September 1938, in three movements, *Andante, Allegro giusto* and *Reminescenza*, the finale being a later addition, a thematic metempsychosis, containing a "reminiscence" of the first two movements, the music being of an expressively tonal and rhythmically propulsive facture, is performed for the first time in Moscow by Mstislav Rostropovich.

(Prokofiev incorporated the materials of this concerto in his Second Cello Concerto, which he entitled *Symphony-Concerto for Violoncello and Orchestra,* and which was performed for the first time by Mstislav Rostropovich in Moscow on 18 February 1952)

## 28 NOVEMBER 1938

The State Jazz Orchestra of the Union of Soviet Socialist Republics is inaugurated in Moscow, signalizing official Soviet acceptance of jazz as legitimate popular art, in a program of jazzified pieces by Tchaikovsky and Rachmaninoff, and a suite for jazz orchestra expressly written for the occasion by Dmitri SHOSTAKOVICH.

## 28 NOVEMBER 1938

Vano MURADELI, 30-year-old Georgian Soviet composer, conducts in Moscow the first performance of his *First Symphony*, dedicated to the memory of Sergei Kirov (whose real name was Kostrikov), the Soviet leader assassinated in 1934, who was in his pre-revolutionary past a theater critic and had a pleasing tenor voice.

### 29 NOVEMBER 1938

A *Poem About Stalin*, symphonic dedication by Aram KHACHATURIAN, set in a loyally devotional lyrico-dramatic manner, with thematic allusions to the native melorhythms of Georgia in the Caucasus, where both Stalin and Khachaturian were born, is performed for the first time at the Second Festival of Soviet Music, in Moscow, with a choral ending to the words of the Caucasian folk poet Ashug Mirza:

Leader of our land! Higher than the mountain rises your glory among nations! Like the sun itself you spread your light through space! The entire globe will soon open its eyes and raise your banner! Ashug Mirza knows that it is true, and that is why he sings so freely! With a song of joyous labor the open pathways will resound! Your name will be our banner forever, O Comrade Stalin!

### 2 DECEMBER 1938

*First Piano Concerto* by Darius MILHAUD, composed in 1933, in three contrasting movements, marked *Très Vif, Mouvement de Barcarolle* and *Final*, is performed for the first time by the Minneapolis Symphony Orchestra, with Dimitri Mitropoulos acting in the dual capacity as piano soloist and conductor.

### 4 DECEMBER 1938

The Bishop of the Fejervar Diocese in Hungary issues a directive forbidding the playing of the wedding marches from *Lohengrin* and *A Midsummer Night's Dream* in the Catholic churches under his jurisdiction, reminding his parishioners that Wagner's march is a prelude to adultery and that Mendelssohn's music illustrates the transformation of the bridegroom into a jackass.

### 11 DECEMBER 1938

President Franklin Delano ROOSEVELT gives an official sanction to the placing of a new Steinway grand piano in the East Room of the White House to replace the old-fashioned gold-cased instrument installed in 1903 by Theodore Roosevelt, and voicing the hope that future Presidents would make actual use of it. (His successor, Harry Truman, was the first President since Jefferson able to play the piano)

### 11 DECEMBER 1938

Orquesta Sinfónica Nacional, the first Peruvian orchestra capable of playing the entire repertory of classical works is inaugurated in Lima, with the Austrian musician Theo Buchwald as conductor and music director.

### 15 DECEMBER 1938

*Violin Concerto* by Ernest BLOCH, in three movements: (1) *Allegro deciso*, in which a broad pentatonic foundation is ornamented with melismatic arabesques (2) *Andante*, a rhapsodic cantillation in Hebraic plagal modes (3) *De-*

682

*ciso—Allegro moderato,* harmonically rooted in stark naked parallel fifths, and concluding on a pandiatonic A minor chord, is performed for the first time by Joseph Szigeti and the Cleveland Orchestra conducted by Dimitri Mitropoulos.

### 16 DECEMBER 1938

*Dédicaces* by Vladimir DUKELSKY, for piano, orchestra and soprano, in five pleasingly concatenated movements, is performed for the first time by the Boston Symphony Orchestra, Serge Koussevitzky conducting.

### 16 DECEMBER 1938

*Second Symphony* by the 37-year-old English composer Edmund RUBBRA, in four movements, *Lento, Scherzo, Adagio tranquillo* and *Rondo,* written in a classically designed and modernistically accoutred idiom, with an ending in unobstructed D major, is performed for the first time in London.

### 16 DECEMBER 1938

*An Outdoor Overture,* a functional orchestral piece by Aaron COPLAND, written in an ozonically spacious pandiatonic idiom, designed for painless musicalization by school orchestra, "optimistic in tone" and calculated to "appeal to the adolescent youth in the country", is performed for the first time at the High School of Music and Art in New York.

### 23 DECEMBER 1938

*Boogie-Woogie,* a new way of "swinging the 88" (that is, disporting oneself freely on the 88 keys of the piano keyboard), with a "walking bass" following the rigid metro-harmonic formula—Tonic, Subdominant, Tonic, Dominant—while the right hand promenades along the keys in rhythmically diversified improvisations, is given its first public demonstration at Carnegie Hall, New York, in a historical exposition "from Spiritual to Swing."

The originator of boogie-woogie was Pine Top SMITH of Chicago, who died a few years ago after a barroom brawl. We don't know where his name came from, but the music's name is based on an old phrase, 'pitch a boogie,' which simply meant 'throw a party.' It was at 'houseparties' in the prohibition days that boogie-woogie flourished; a crowd would gather around while the boogie-woogie boys, who bore such names as Crippled Clarence and Toothpick, held a little cutting session. (Maybe we ought to explain that cutting means trying to outplay your predecessor.) (*The New Yorker,* 31 December 1938)

Boogie-woogie is a kind of blues piano playing in which the left hand drones a set bass phrase over and over, while the right hand goes to town with whatever variations the player can think up. Its form is identical with that of the classical *passacaglia,* a kind of dance music (of Spanish origin) that was old stuff to Bach's grandfather. Though boogie-woogie's mournful thump and clatter has long been heard in the humbler dives of New Orleans and Chicago, it was not taken up by the connoisseurs until 1938. In Manhattan, the temple of boogie-woogie has been a subterranean leftist cabaret in Greenwich Village called *Café Society.* Its high priests: Negroes Albert Ammons, Pete Johnson, Meade Lux Lewis. (*Time,* 4 March 1940)

# ⚘ *1939* ⚘

## 5 JANUARY 1939

VODER (vo-coder, i.e. voice-coder), the first machine ever to produce the sound of the human voice electronically synthesized from primary sibilant and buzzing elements, is demonstrated publicly for the first time at the Franklin Institute in Philadelphia.

## 5 JANUARY 1939

*Horus*, opera in four acts by the 60-year-old Hungarian-American composer Baron Gabriel WAJDITSCH VERBOVAC VON DÖNHOFF, to his own libretto, in which the Egyptian god Horus incarnates himself to make love to a beautiful woman, written in a fairly dissonant quasi-impressionistic monodic manner, is performed for the first time by the Philadelphia-LaScala Opera Company at the composer's own expense ($7,500), Fritz Mahler conducting.

The music (if it may justly be called that) of *Horus* was discordant from beginning to end, with an occasional consonant chord occurring so rarely that it seemed as though the composer had made a mistake. He showed an ability bordering upon genius for selecting orchestral combinations which entirely drowned the voices, for there is no chorus in *Horus*. (Samuel L. Laciar, Philadelphia *Record*, 6 January 1939)

It was a shoemaker's performance. The orchestra was too small. But my *Horus* is *really* a modern opera, not like one by Stravinsky, who knows very little, and is an imitator of Strauss. I have little respect for him. (Baron Gabriel Wajditsch von Dönhoff in a letter to the author, dated 17 November 1963)

## 9 JANUARY 1939

Béla BARTÓK plays in New York the piano part in the first performance of his *Contrasts* for violin, clarinet and piano (completed in Budapest on 24 September 1938), assisted by Josef Szigeti, violinist, and Benny Goodman, jazz clarinetist, in three movements derived from Hungarian folk melorhythms, the first being the Hungarian recruiting dance *Verbunkos*, the second a slow lyrical piece, and the third a fast rondo, with the violinist making use in its opening bars of an extra violin in *scordatura* tuning, G-sharp, D, A and E-flat calculated to facilitate the playing of open-string tritones, fundamental to Bartók's Lydian modalities and polarized tonalities.

## 10 JANUARY 1939

*The Darvaz Pass*, opera in four acts by the 30-year-old Soviet composer Lev STEPANOV, subtitled *The Border Guards*, to his own libretto, dealing with class struggle in pre-revolutionary Central Asia, in which hirelings of feudal Tadzhik overlords unnecessarily murder a non-political girl on her wedding day, thus precipitating a popular revolt, is performed for the first time in Moscow.

*684*

## 10 JANUARY 1939

Julius BITTNER, Austrian composer of neo-romantic operas, dies in Vienna at the age of sixty-four, after the amputation of both legs due to varicose veins.

## 19 JANUARY 1939

David VAN VACTOR, 32-year-old American composer, conducts the New York Philharmonic in the first performance of his *Symphony in D*, winner of the $1,000 prize of the American Composers' Contest.

## 20 JANUARY 1939

John Kirkpatrick gives in New York the first complete performance of the *Second Pianoforte Sonata*, entitled *Concord, Mass. 1840–1860*, by the great American individualist Charles IVES, a work of transcendental music in the philosophical conception of the word, constituting a new type of impressionism in which ideas and convictions, even politics, are used as programmatic and descriptive elements, written between 1909 and 1915 and anticipating, in a flash of genius, the musical developments of the future years, published by Ives himself and distributed gratis to anyone with a companion volume, *Essays before a Sonata*, dedicating it "to those who can't stand his music," dedicating the music "to those who can't stand the essays," and "respectfully dedicating" both "to those who can't stand either," in four immensely varied and yet dialectically cohesive movements, each named after a Concord writer:

(1) *Emerson*, with the material derived from a projected "Emerson Piano Concerto," transcendentally complex in texture, with tremendous dissonances enveloped in the lyric substance of cerulean transparency (2) *Hawthorne*, "trying to suggest some of his wilder, fantastical adventures into the half-childlike, half-fairylike phantasmal realms," in which for the first time in piano literature, clusters of notes are played by pressing a strip of board, 14¾ inches long, on the keyboard to convey the idea of Hawthorne's dream of a celestial railroad (3) *The Alcotts*, a gentle pastorale incorporating the thematic four notes of the "Fate" motive from Beethoven's Fifth Symphony as though played on "the little old spinet-piano Sophia Thoreau gave to the Alcott children" (4) *Thoreau*, embodying "a transcendental tune of Concord," with an optional flute part, for Thoreau "much prefers to hear the flute over Walden."

This Sonata is exceptionally great music—it is, indeed, the greatest music composed by an American, and the most deeply and essentially American in impulse and implication. (Lawrence Gilman, the New York *Herald Tribune*, 21 January 1939)

## 23 JANUARY 1939

*Alt-Danzig*, orchestral suite by the 62-year-old German composer Georg VOLLERTHUN, written with the nationalistic purpose of extolling the spirit of German Danzig, and making use of a number of local German songs, is broadcast for the first time in Berlin as part of the Nazi propaganda campaign to annex the Free City of Danzig.

## 26 JANUARY 1939

*Re Hassan*, opera in three acts by the 46-year-old Italian composer Giorgio Federico GHEDINI, to a libretto dealing with the fall of the last Moorish bastion in Granada at the time when the Moorish King Hassan arranged his son's alliance with Spain, in a musical setting containing verisimilitudinarian Mauretanian arabesques, is performed for the first time in Venice.

### 28 JANUARY 1939

*Die Bürger von Calais,* opera in three acts by the 35-year-old German composer Rudolf WAGNER-RÉGENY, to a libretto concerning the siege of Calais by the English in 1347, wherein a group of prominent citizens volunteer to be executed as hostages in exchange for the permit to import food for 6,000 inhabitants of the town to save them from starvation, is performed for the first time in Berlin.

### 31 JANUARY 1939

*Cello Concerto* by Gian Francesco MALIPIERO is performed for the first time anywhere in Belgrade, Yugoslavia.

### 1 FEBRUARY 1939

*La Dama boba,* comic opera in three acts by Ermanno WOLF-FERRARI, subtitled *La Ragazza sciocca (The Foolish Girl),* after Lope de Vega's comedy of old Spanish mores and amores, written in the manner of the Italian Baroque, is produced at La Scala in Milan.

### 2 FEBRUARY 1939

NOVACHORD, an electronic musical instrument invented by Laurens HAMMOND, capable of reproducing the timbre of any instrument, from the Hawaiian ukulele to the clavichord, from the piccolo to the trombone, from the violin to the double-bass, is given the first public demonstration in Washington.

### 3 FEBRUARY 1939

*Cotillon,* a suite of symphonic dances by the Australian-born composer Arthur BENJAMIN, derived from melodies in the old collection, *The Dancing Master* (London, 1719), in nine dancing figures: (1) *Lord Hereford's Delight* (2) *Daphne's Delight* (3) *Marlborough's Victory* (4) *Love's Triumph* (5) *Jig It* (6) *The Charmer* (7) *Nymph Divine* (8) *The Tattler* (9) *Argyle,* is performed for the first time in London.

### 5 FEBRUARY 1939

*Der Mond,* "theatrical macrocosm" in three acts by the 43-year-old German composer Carl ORFF, to a libretto adapted from a tale of Brothers Grimm about four village boys who capture the moon for the private illumination of their lodgings and take it underground after their deaths, waking up neighboring corpses by lunar luminosity, until St. Peter retrieves the satellite by dispatching a supersonic comet to reinstate it in the firmament to the accompaniment of a zither solo, scored for a modernistically economic instrumental ensemble vivified and rhythmically enriched by a diversified flora and fauna of exotic percussion, is produced in Munich.

11 FEBRUARY 1939

Franz SCHMIDT, romantic Austrian composer of rhapsodically impassioned symphonies and oratorios, dies in Perchtoldsdorf, near Vienna, at the age of 64, largely ignored by an unappreciative musical world.

11 FEBURARY 1939

*Nuptiae Catulli,* cantata by the 31-year-old German composer Wolfgang FORTNER after poems by Catullus, is performed for the first time by the Basel Chamber Orchestra.

11 FEBRUARY 1939

*Die pfiffige Magd (A Sly Maid),* comic opera in three acts by the 59-year-old German composer Julius WEISMANN, is produced in Leipzig.

15 FEBRUARY 1939

*Nineteenth Symphony* by the prime Soviet symphonist Nicolai MIASKOVSKY, composed between 3 and 26 January 1939, and scored for military band in the optimistic key of E-flat major, in four movements suggesting, respectively, a folk dance, a symphonized waltz, a lyric meditation and constructive rejoicing, is performed for the first time at the Comintern Radio Station in Moscow.

16 FEBRUARY 1939

Wiktor LABUNSKI, 43-year-old Polish-American composer, plays the solo part with the Kansas Symphony Orchestra in the first performance of his *Piano Concerto,* in three movements, *Krakowiak, Nocturne* and *Mazurek,* inspired by Polish dance forms.

16 FEBRUARY 1939

*Cynthia Parker,* short opera by the American composeress Julia SMITH, relating the story of an American girl kidnapped by the Indians in Old Texas who marries an Indian chief and becomes completely Indianized, with local color supplied by stylized pentatonic songs and dances, is produced at North Texas State Teachers' College in Denton, Texas.

20 FEBRUARY 1939

*Two Choric Dances,* symphonic diptych in a neo-Grecian manner by the 32-year-old American composer Paul CRESTON, scored for orchestra, piano and tom-tom, with the first dance being slow and stately, and the second impulsive and precipitous, is performed for the first time by the Cleveland Federal Orchestra, Arthur Shepherd conducting. (Originally, the work was scored for chamber orchestra, and performed at the Yaddo Festival in Saratoga Springs, New York, in 1938)

24 FEBRUARY 1939

*Third Symphony* by Roy HARRIS, set in a single continuous movement articulated into five contrasting sections, with the first section incorporating materials from an aborted violin concerto written for Jascha Heifetz but rejected by him for lack of violinisticality, opening with a spacious melody in the concerted cellos autogenetically evolving through translucid mazes of contrapuntal configurations, pausing for a pastoral episode with woodwinds pollinating the receptive strings in synchronized motion, reaching a grandiloquent climax in the magisterial fugue in the clarion key of D major (although no key signature is used in any part of the work), and concluding on a somberly powerful G-minor chord, is performed for the first time by the Boston Symphony Orchestra, under the direction of Serge Koussevitzky.

The *Third Symphony* by Harris is America's most successful work in that form. . . . It is earnest, clumsy, pretentious, imaginative, and terribly sincere. (Virgil Thomson, New York *Herald Tribune,* 17 January 1949)

Let's not kid ourselves. My *Third Symphony* happened to come along when it was needed. The first season it was greeted with the same boos and bravos as have been all my works. Then *Time* magazine hailed it as the most important American symphony, and the Third Symphony was in. (Roy Harris in a statement to the author in 1951)

### 26 FEBRUARY 1939

Aaron COPLAND's *Sextet* for clarinet, piano and string quartet (arranged from his *Short Symphony*), is performed for the first time in New York.

### 26 FEBRUARY 1939

On his 20th tour of the United States, Ignace Jan PADEREWSKI gives his first radio recital at Radio City in New York, playing Beethoven's *Moonlight Sonata,* a group of works by Chopin and his own compositions. (The program was printed on silk to prevent audible rustling by the studio audience during the broadcast)

### 27 FEBRUARY 1939

Mrs. Eleanor ROOSEVELT resigns her membership in the society of Daughters of the American Revolution in protest against the refusal of the patriotic society, proprietor of Constitution Hall in Washington, to lease it to Marian ANDERSON, Negro contralto, for a public concert.

(Marian Anderson gave an Easter Sunday open-air concert in Lincoln Memorial Park in Washington on 9 April 1939, with 75,000 people in attendance. Eventually she succeeded in overcoming the resistance of the reactionary elements among the membership of the Society, and was enabled to sing in Constitution Hall on 7 January 1943)

### 27 FEBRUARY 1939

A *Life for the Tsar,* GLINKA's epoch-making national Russian opera is performed in Moscow for the first time after the Revolution, under the title *Ivan Susanin,* the name of the peasant hero of the opera, who led a group of Polish men bent upon the assassination of the newly elected Tsar Mikhail Romanov in 1606 into an impassable wintry forest and sacrificed his own life by so doing.

(The text of the final chorus, "Glory be to our Russian Tsar" was demonarchized into an acceptably patriotic "Glory be to our Russian land." A preview of *Ivan Susanin* was given on 21 February 1939 in Moscow for a select audience and another special presentation took place in Moscow on 24 February 1939 for the members of the Red Army and Navy)

### 28 FEBRUARY 1939

*Qarrtsiluni,* symphonic poem on Eskimo themes by the 41-year-old Danish composer Knudaage RIISAGER, is performed for the first time in Copenhagen. (A ballet version of *Qarrtsiluni* was first produced in Copenhagen on 21 February 1942)

### 1 MARCH 1939

Hamilton HARTY conducts in London the first performance of his symphonic poem *The Children of Lir,* inspired by the ancient Irish saga in which two pairs of twins are transformed into swans by their malevolent stepmother, but are restored to human shape by the sound of a church bell, enabling them to die a Christian death at 1,000 years of age, written in an ambitiously modernistic idiom full of augmented triads and their concomitant whole-tone scales, and including a wordlessly distant soprano voice intoning a pentatonic Celtic chant.

### 2 MARCH 1939

Amadeo ROLDÁN, Cuban mulatto composer of Afro-Cuban music, including the ballet *La Rebambaramba* productive of tremendous kinesthetic energy, dies of cancer in Havana, at the age of thirty-eight.

### 6 MARCH 1939

*Second Piano Concerto* by Gian Francesco MALIPIERO is performed for the first time in Duisburg.

### 8 MARCH 1939

*Third Symphony* by the Czech composer and conductor Karel Boleslav JIRÁK is performed for the first time in Prague.

### 11 MARCH 1939

*Pogromes,* symphonic poem by the French composeress Elsa BARRAINE, depicting in vivid colors the horrors of anti-Semitic outrages in Tsarist Russia, is performed for the first time in Paris.

### 16 MARCH 1939

*La Chartreuse de Parme,* first opera in four acts by the 37-year-old French composer Henri SAUGUET, after Stendhal's famous novel, dealing with a young adventurer roaming Italy in 1815, who escapes after imprisonment for murder, rejoins his faithful inamorata but eventually withdraws into the Carthusian monastery in Parma, set to music in a modernistically renovated Italianate idiom, is produced at the Paris Opéra.

### 21 MARCH 1939

A century has passed since the birth of Modest MUSSORGSKY, the mightiest of the Mighty Five of Russia, who introduced in his operas and songs a true realistic style of melodic expression, faithful to the prosody of Russian speech.

### 22 MARCH 1939

*Laurencia,* ballet by the Soviet composer Alexander KREIN, after Lopez de Vega's play *Fuente Ovejuna,* dealing with a 15th-century peasant girl who leads a rebellion against a local feudal lord, making use of genuine Spanish folk songs in an epically rhapsodic and romantically sonorous musical setting, is performed for the first time in Leningrad, as a tribute to the defeated republican cause in the Spanish Civl War of 1936–1939.

### 25 MARCH 1939

Heitor VILLA-LOBOS conducts in Rio de Janeiro the first performance of his *Bachianas Brasileiras* No. 5, scored for voice and eight (or any multiple of eight) cellos.

### 29 MARCH 1939

REICHS-MUSIKPRÜFSTELLE, a Nazi agency in charge of musical policy, declares the American ballad *Frankie and Johnny* and all music by Ignace Paderewski inadmissible for performance in Germany.

### 29 MARCH 1939

The EARL OF CLARENDON, Lord Chamberlain and Supervisor of the London stage, bans the song *Even Hitler Had a Mother,* scheduled for first performance in a musical revue opening in London on 20 April 1939, as discourteous to the head of a foreign nation. (The ban was lifted after the outbreak of World War II in September 1939)

### 29 MARCH 1939

*Elisabeth von England,* opera in four acts by the Danish-born German composer Paul von KLENAU, to his own libretto picturing the Queen torn between love for power and love for Essex, written in a sui generis 12-tone idiom with a high incidence of dissonance and the application of *Sprechgesang,* is performed for the first time in Kassel. (After the outbreak of World War II, the title was changed to the non-committal designation *Die Königin*)

### 31 MARCH 1939

A 50-schilling stamp, bearing the portrait of Josef RHEINBERGER, the estimable German composer and teacher who was born in Vaduz, capital of Liechtenstein, on 17 March 1839, is issued by the government of Liechtenstein to commemorate, with a fortnight's delay, the centennial of his birth. (A large souvenir sheet of 20 multicolored Rheinberger stamps was issued as an accompanying collection)

## 1 APRIL 1939

A Festival of Music for the People opens in London with the professed intention of mobilizing music in the service of peace, freedom and labor, featuring a pageant in ten episodes, with the participation of 500 singers, 100 dancers and the People's Festival Wind Band, in performances of works especially written by pacifically inclined English composers, among them Frederic AUSTIN, Alan BUSH, Erik CHISHOLM, Arnold COOKE, Christian DARNTON, Norman DEMUTH, Elizabeth LUTYENS, Elizabeth MACONCHY, Alan RAWSTHORNE, Edmund RUBBRA, Victor YATES and Ralph VAUGHAN WILLIAMS.

## 3 APRIL 1939

*L'Intransigeant Pluton,* one-act opera by the 40-year-old Parisian Rumanian composer Marcel MIHALOVICI, is performed for the first time in Paris.

## 3 APRIL 1939

The second concert of the Festival of Music for the People is given in London with the following program:

*Two English Folk Songs* by Ralph VAUGHAN WILLIAMS; *British Folk-Music Settings* by Percy GRAINGER; *Matra,* a set of Hungarian folksongs by Zoltán KODÁLY; a militantly satirical suite for voice and instruments by the expatriated leftist Austrian composer Hanns EISLER, in three movements (1) *News from Vienna, 1938* (2) *Cantata of Exile* (3) *Prison House; Friede auf Erden* by Arnold SCHOENBERG for chorus a cappella, composed in 1907; and *Popular Tunes of the Day in USSR* by several Soviet composers arranged for an ensemble of balalaikas.

## 5 APRIL 1939

The third concert of the Festival of Music for the People in London presents the following program:

BEETHOVEN's *Egmont Overture,* as a symbol of popular struggle for national freedom; the first performance of Benjamin BRITTEN's *Ballad of Heroes* for tenor, chorus and orchestra, composed as a tribute to the men of the British Battalion of the International Brigade, killed while fighting Fascism during the Spanish Civil War; *Lento and Finale* from the *Concerto* for piano and orchestra, baritone and male chorus, by the leftist member of the British Parliament Alan BUSH, ending with a chorus of social significance, with the composer at the piano; and an optimistically eschatological cantata, *These Things Shall Be* by John IRELAND.

## 5 APRIL 1939

Ferruccio BURCO, precocious boy maestro who, barely out of diapers and into velvet pants, was to conduct professional orchestras, is born in Milan, destined to die in an automobile crash on 27 April 1965.

## 6 APRIL 1939

*Symphonie* by the 26-year-old Polish composer Witold LUTOSLAWSKI, written in a neo-classical idiom, is performed for the first time by the Radio Orchestra of Katowice, Gregor Fitelberg conducting.

## 9 APRIL 1939

*Concerto a tre* for violin, cello, piano and orchestra, by Gian Francesco MALIPIERO, is performed for the first time in Florence.

## 14 APRIL 1939

Four and a half months before the Nazi attack on Poland, the 17th Festival of the International Society for Contemporary Music opens in Warsaw, with the following program of orchestral music:

*Symphony* by the 35-year-old Catalan composer Josep VALLS, written in polyrhythmically vitalized asymmetrical meters (the finale is a dance in 7/8); *5 Orchestral Pieces* by the English composer Christian DARNTON, all extremely short, lasting an average time of 96 seconds each; *Epic Legend* by the Belgian composer Marcel POOT, designed as a modern version of an old-fashioned romantic ballad; *Passacaglia-Chorale* by the Serbian neo-classicist Slavko OSTERC; Scherzo and Finale from the *Violin Concerto* by the Moscow-born half-German, half-Russian composer Wladimir VOGEL, based on a 24-tone theme derived from a 12-tone series and its melodic inversion, culminating with a double fugue, advisedly modeled with a declared intention after Mozart's overture to *Die Zauberflöte;* and *First Symphony* in D major by the French composer Jean RIVIER.

## 15 APRIL 1939

The first national Kirghiz opera *Aytchurek* composed by Abdylas MALDYBAYEV with the aid of two Russian ethnomusicologists Vladimir VLASOV and Vladimir FERE, to a libretto from an old Kirghiz folk tale concerned with a young maiden nicknamed Lunar Beauty and her beloved fighting for a better life in their benighted land, with the application of genuine melorhythms of the Mongolian tribes of Kirghizstan, is produced in Frunze.

## 15 APRIL 1939

At the second concert of the 17th Festival of the International Society for Contemporary Music in Warsaw the following program is presented:

*Chamber Cantata* by the Swiss neo-classicist Conrad BECK; *Concertino* for saxophone and chamber orchestra by the Danish composer Knudaage RIISAGER; *Mass in G Major* for chorus a cappella by the quadrigenarian member of the once youthful Groupe des Six, Francis POULENC; *Suite* for four trombones in quarter-tones by the Serbian composer Milan RISTIĆ; *Tre Laudi* for voice and chamber orchestra by the Italian modernist Luigi DALLAPICCOLA; *Rengaines* for wind quintet by the Belgian musical surrealist

André Souris; and *Five Etudes* for piano and orchestra by the Dutch composer Robert DE ROOS.


16 APRIL 1939

Two ancient Egyptian trumpets, one 22½ inches in length made of silver and gold, and one 19½ inches in length made of copper, found in the sarcophagus of King Tutankhamen, are sounded on a world-wide radio broadcast from Cairo after a silence of 3,297 years.


16 APRIL 1939

At the third concert of the 17th Festival of the International Society for Contemporary Music in Warsaw, the following program of choral music by Polish composers is given: *Cantate Romantique* by Stanislaw WIECHOWICZ; *Cantata Ecclesiastica* by Michal KONDRACKI; and *Stabat Mater* by Karol SZYMANOWSKI.


17 APRIL 1939

At the fourth concert of the 17th Festival of the International Society for Contemporary Music in Warsaw, the following program of chamber music is presented:

*String Quartet* by the English atonal composeress Elizabeth LUTYENS; *Sonatina* for violin and piano by the Czech neo-romanticist Eugen SUCHOŇ; *String Quartet*, op. 28, by Anton VON WEBERN, commissioned by the Elizabeth Sprague Coolidge Foundation, and first performed at the Berkshire Festival of Chamber Music in Pittsfield, Massachusetts, on 22 September 1938, in three movements, with the fundamental series derived from the intervallic figure BACH, its inversion and its transposition; *String Quartet* by the Japanese composer Kojiro KOBUNE; *Coplas Sefardies* for voice and piano by Alberto HEMSI of Egypt; *Two Songs* by Honorio SICCARDI of Argentina; and *String Quartet* by the Dutch composer Henk BADINGS.


19 APRIL 1939

*Zvezdoliki* (*The Star-Faced*), cantata by Igor STRAVINSKY, usually catalogued under the French title *Le Roi des Etoiles*, written in 1911–12, to words by the Russian poet Constantin Balmont from his cycle *The Vigil of the White Doves*, wherein a Nietzschean superman arises in Apocalyptic glory to lead mankind towards a mystical consummation of faith, set to music in subtilized sonorities using special effects such as glissandos on harmonics in the divided strings, and ending on a dissonant chord of an augmented eleventh, is performed for the first time anywhere in Brussels, 27 years after its composition, by the Belgian State Radio Orchestra and male chorus, on the date of the solar eclipse (partial in Belgium).

(*Zvezdoliki* was announced for performance in the printed program of the Philadelphia Orchestra, under the direction of Leopold Stokowski, for 9–10 December 1932, but the performance was canceled at the last moment owing to the difficulty in obtaining clearance of performance rights)

## 20 APRIL 1939

At the fifth concert of the 17th Festival of the International Society for Contemporary Music in Warsaw, the following program of chamber music is presented:

*String Quartet* by the Polish composer Jerzy FITELBERG; *Trois Poèmes Lyriques* for violin and piano by the Yugoslav composer Demetrij ZEBRE; *String Quartet* by the Catalan composer Joaquín HOMS; *Petite Suite* for violin and piano by the Czech composer Jozef ZAVÁDIL; *Fugue* for piano by the Dutch composer Piet KETTING; *String Quartet* by the Czech composer Vladímir POLÍVKA.

## 21 APRIL 1939

The 17th Festival of the International Society for Contemporary Music concludes in Warsaw with the following program of orchestral works:

*20 Variations in Symphonic Form* by the Polish composer Boleslaw WOYTOWICZ, based on the principle of cumulative accretion of thematic material, each variation containing added components of the gradually integrated subject; *Le Savetier et le Financier,* aria for baritone and orchestra by Gaston BRENTA of Belgium; *Ostinato* for orchestra by Lars-Erik LARSSON of Sweden; *Prélude et Invention* for string orchestra by the Parisianized Rumanian composer Marcel MIHALOVICI; *Symphonic Studies* by the English composer Alan RAWSTHORNE; and *Overture* by the Polish composer Antoni SZALOWSKI.

## 22 APRIL 1939

*The Old Maid and the Thief*, grotesque opera by Gian Carlo MENOTTI, to his own libretto in English, depicting in 14 episodes in merry Rossinian tones, the picaresque adventures of a sexy intruder in the bedroom of an American spinster who becomes fascinated by his physique ("tall and burly, black hair and curly, light complexion, Southern inflection") and joins him in his kleptophilic profession, is performed for the first time in concert form by the National Broadcasting Company in New York. (First stage performance was given by the Philadelphia Opera Company on 11 February 1941)

## 23 APRIL 1939

*Violin Concerto* by Béla BARTÓK, completed by him on 31 December 1938, is performed for the first time by Zoltán Székely in Amsterdam, with Willem Mengelberg conducting the Concertgebouw Orchestra, in three movements:

(1) *Allegro non troppo*, written in a varied sonata form, based on a spacious theme centering on B and developing by cumulative ornamentation into a colorful tapestry of chromatic designs, including a theme of 12 different notes in the solo part without an overt dodecaphonic treatment and some incidental quarter-tones in the recapitulation (2) *Andante tranquillo*, a set of six variations on a Transylvanian-shaped tune fo-

cused on G, subjected to artful translocations and intervallic contractions and expansions, with a fugal episode leading to a tonal pacification, and the violin solo restating the main theme at the end (3) *Allegro molto*, a precipitous Rondo, where in a folklike subject is topologically dislocated, followed by a fanfaric canon in proclamatory fourths accumulating vertically in quartal pillars, and after a tremendous crescendo leading to a coda with an epicenter on the tonic B colliding with an avalanche of C's, and culminating in an unobstructed terminal B major triad.

### 28 APRIL 1939

*Paul Bunyan*, ballet for puppets and solo dancers by the 18-year-old American composer William BERGSMA, is performed for the first time in Rochester, New York.

### 29 APRIL 1939

*Gudrun*, ballad opera in two acts by the 36-year-old German composer Ludwig ROSELIUS, is performed for the first time in Graz.

### 30 APRIL 1939

The New York World's Fair inaugurates its Music Hall, with Olin DOWNES, the music critic of The New York *Times*, as its director. (He resigned on 24 May 1939 after the administration of the Fair announced a new policy of presenting only popular musical programs)

### 2 MAY 1939

*Suite variée* for symphony orchestra by the American composer Ernest SCHELLING, in six descriptive movements couched in a romantically old-fashioned idiom—*Catalonian Evocation* (written in memory of Enrique Granados), *The Fountains of Garengo* (a tonal impression of Shelling's estate in Switzerland), *Cradle Song for a Sick Child, Tarantella* (for strings only), *Irlandaise* (a musical portrait of a vivacious Irishwoman) and *The Last Flight*, subtitled *Aviation Field, October 10, 1918* (commemorating the fatal flight of an aviator friend over Verdun at the end of World War I), is performed for the first time by the San Francisco Symphony Orchestra, Pierre Monteux conducting.

### 12 MAY 1939

Luis A. DELGADILLO, prime composer of Nicaragua, conducts in Managua the intermittently active Orquesta Sinfónica de Nicaragua in the first performances of his colorful symphonic suites, *Escenas Pastoriles* and *Los Tincos*, based on Nicaraguan folk melodies.

### 17 MAY 1939

Sergei PROKOFIEV conducts in Moscow the world première of his cantata *Alexander Nevsky*, completed by him on 7 February 1939, with the music expanded from the material of his film score of the same name, in seven sections:

(1) *Russia under the Mongolian Yoke*, written in an ostentatiously static Asiatic melismatic style (2) *Song About Alexander Nevsky*, commemorating the Russian victory against Sweden on the banks of the River Neva, which gave Alexander his honorary surname Nevsky (3) *Teutonic Knights in Pskov*, a medieval Latin chant in mock-Gregorian monotone (4) *Arise, Russian People*, a patriotic marching song with characteristic folksong inflections and plagal cadences (5) *Battle on Ice*, a triumphant proclamation of the Russian victory over the Teutonic knights on the frozen surface of Lake Peipus on 5 April 1242, constituting a meaningful reminder to the latter-day Nazi Teutons not to venture into Russia (6) *The Field of the Dead*, a lyrical lament in gently modulated minor tonalities (7) *Alexander's Entry in Pskov*, a grandiloquent celebration of the victory by ringing church bells and singing Russian songs.

### 18 MAY 1939

*The Devil and Daniel Webster*, American folk opera in one act by Douglas MOORE, to a libretto by Stephan Vincent Benét, wherein a young New England farmer incautiously signs a contract selling his soul to the Devil incarnated in the affable shape of a Boston lawyer named Scratch, but is saved from perdition by the forensic eloquence of the great Webster, who proves the Devil legally wrong, set to music in an artfully simplicistic melodious and harmonious manner, is produced in New York.

### 19 MAY 1939

Under the auspices of the Society of Friends and Enemies of Modern Music of Hartford, Connecticut, Ernst KRENEK conducts his first major work written in America, *Eight-Column Line*, a newspaper ballet in the 12-tone technique, with the principal tone-row emblematic of the pressure in meeting the daily deadline.

### 24 MAY 1939

*München Walzer*, orchestral suite of nostalgic waltzes by Richard STRAUSS, composed on 3 January 1939 for a film about Munich, is performed for the first time at a Munich municipal ball.

(The film itself was never shown. The second version of the music was completed by Strauss on 24 February 1945, with the inclusion of a supplementary section in G minor marked "trauernd einverlebt" as a mourning *Gedächtniswalzer* after the devastating fire air raid on Munich by the Allied Air Force. This second version was performed for the first time in Vienna on 31 March 1951)

### 24 MAY 1939

*Pocahontas*, ballet-legend in one act by the 30-year-old American composer Elliott CARTER, dealing with the Indian maiden of that name (1595–1617) who reportedly saved the valiant Virginian settler John Smith from death at the hands of her segregationist antimiscegenating father, is performed for the first time in New York.

696

## 2 JUNE 1939

Josef REITER, Austrian composer, sadly remembered as one who wrote a *Festgesang an den Führer des deutschen Volkes*, dedicated to Hitler, and published by the Nazi-dominated Universal Edition, but never performed, dies in Vienna at the age of seventy-seven.

## 5 JUNE 1939

Two stamps at 10 and 70 centimes with portraits of Claude DEBUSSY are issued by the French Post Office.

## 9 JUNE 1939

The British Week at the New York World's Fair is inaugurated with a concert by the New York Philharmonic conducted by Sir Adrian Boult, featuring the world première of the *Seventh Symphony* in A-flat by the English romantic composer Arnold BAX, dedicated to the American people, in three movements, alternatingly muscular, lymphatic and melancholic, along with the first American performance of the *Concerto for Oboe and Orchestra* by Eugene GOOSSENS, with the composer's brother Leon playing the solo part (first performed by him in London on 2 October 1930).

## 10 JUNE 1939

Sir Adrian Boult conducts the New York Philharmonic in the second concert under the auspices of the British Council for the British Week at the New York World's Fair, featuring the world première of the *Piano Concerto* by Arthur BLISS, dedicated "to the people of the United States of America," in three movements, *Allegro con brio, Adagietto* and *Andante maestoso,* written in a grandly pianistic manner, chromatically opulent but firmly anchored in tonality, with sonorous explosions mitigated by lyric interludes; and the world première of *Five Variants on Dives and Lazarus* for string orchestra by Ralph VAUGHAN WILLIAMS.

## 11 JUNE 1939

On his 27th birthday, Mukhtar ASHRAFI, Bukhara-born Soviet composer, conducts in Tashkent the first performance of the first national Uzbek opera *Buran,* in five acts, written with the help of his teacher Sergei Vassilenko, to a libretto dealing with the Uzbek rebellion against Tsarist rule in Central Asia in 1916 led by an indigent proletarian named Buran and his son whose young wife, violated by the soldiery, goes insane.

## 17 JUNE 1939

*Variations Symphoniques* by the 26-year-old Polish composer Witold LUTOSLAWSKI, with a theme in E major of Chopinesque facture evolving in its variations into complex configurations adorned by neo-Baroque frills and trills, long scales with migratory tonics and tritone-terraced canons, ending on a major seventh tonic chord, is performed for the first time in Cracow.

## 17 JUNE 1939

*Katchkyn (The Fugitive)*, opera by the 28-year-old Tatar composer Nazib ZHIGANOV, first national Tatar opera, in three acts, to a libretto in the Tatar language, dealing with Pugatchov's rebellion against Catherine the Great, is produced at the opening of the National Tatar Opera House in Kazan, once the main stronghold of the Golden Horde of the conquering Mongols to whom Russia paid tribute for centuries.

## 20 JUNE 1939

*Las Vírgenes del Sol,* opera by the Argentine composer Alfredo SCHIUMA, in three acts, glorifying in sonorous Italianate tones the desperate stand of the Sun Virgins in an Inca temple in Peru in 1532, during the final assault of the Conquistadores, is produced at the Teatro Colón in Buenos Aires.

## 23 JUNE 1939

By the order of the War Department in Washington, the marching cadence of the United States Army is reduced from 128 to 120 steps per minute, effective as of September 1939.

## 24 JUNE 1939

$H_2O$, symphonic poem by the 31-year-old Belgian composer Robert ROUSSEAU, winner of the competition for the best aquatic composition for the Exposition Internationale de l'Eau at Liège, written in a scientifically illustrative idiom, in a fine fluvial vein, with melodious hydrogen atoms and harmonious oxygen particles combining in double counterpoint in an effective chemical reaction producing a molecule of water, is performed for the first time at the inaugural of the Liège Exposition.

## 18 JULY 1939

The Spanish composer Manuel PALAU conducts the inaugural concert of the newly established Orquesta de Falange Española Tradicionalista in Valencia, organized and supported by the Falangist party.

## 24 JULY 1939

The Nazified municipality of Vienna expropriates the personal estate and royalties of the family of Johann STRAUSS in order to deprive his non-Aryan step-daughter of her rights to the inheritance, overruling her claim that she was an illegitimate daughter of Johann Strauss himself, and therefore an Aryan in good standing.

## 8 AUGUST 1939

The Fascist Department of Education issues in Rome a directive aimed at the elimination of French musical terminology, arguing that "just as omelette can be replaced by the Italian word *frittata*," so the French form *Ouverture* can and ought to be changed to *Introduzione,* and *Suite* to *Sequenza.*

## 28 AUGUST 1939

*Chasca*, lyric opera by the Argentinian composer Enrique M. CASELLA, with an orchestra of native wind and percussion instruments concealed behind the scenery, is produced at Tucumán.

## 28 AUGUST 1939

*Drygva (Woodland Thicket)*, national Byelorussian opera in four acts by the 26-year-old Vitebsk-born composer Anatoly BOGATYREV, to a libretto in the Byelorussian (White Russian) language, portraying in socialistically realistic tones the partisan resistance of Byelorussian peasants against the Polish occupation army during the civil war of 1919, with an ending paralleling that of Glinka's opera *A Life for the Tsar*, as the peasant hero dies chanting "Voroshilov leads us forward," is performed for the first time in Minsk, the capital of Byelorussia.

## 11 SEPTEMBER 1939

The song writers Jimmy KENNEDY and Michael CARR of London compose the first British World War II marching song *We're Gonna Hang Out the Washing on the Siegfried Line, If the Siegfried Line's Still There*, with a traditional 32-bar refrain. (As fate would have it, the Siegfried Line wasn't there, militarily speaking, when the Allied armies reached it during the last weeks of the war in 1945)

## 27 SEPTEMBER 1939

The initial eleven notes of CHOPIN's *Military Polonaise*, serving as signature of the Warsaw State Radio, are sounded on the xylophone for the last time before the final occupation of the burning Polish capital by the Nazi war machine.

## 6 OCTOBER 1939

*American Festival Overture* by the 29-year-old American composer William SCHUMAN, an animated musical fresco of modern American life, with the initial three notes imitating the teenage call of New York Streets, evolving into a tetrahedron of quadruple counterpoint punctured by explosive polyrhythms, is performed for the first time by the Boston Symphony Orchestra, Serge Koussevitzky conducting, at a special concert "in honor of the American composer" on the same program with George GERSHWIN's *Piano Concerto*, Randall THOMPSON's *Second Symphony* and the *Third Symphony* of Roy HARRIS.

## 7 OCTOBER 1939

*Médée*, opera in three scenes, after Euripides, by Darius MILHAUD, portraying in ominous bitonalities and tragically translocated asymmetric rhythms the terrorizing story of the mythological Greek mother avenging herself on her perfidious husband by killing her children, is produced for the first time in Antwerp.

## 7 OCTOBER 1939

*Die Kathrin,* opera in three acts by Erich Wolfgang KORNGOLD, erstwhile musical prodigy from Vienna, forced to go into exile in Hollywood, to a libretto dealing with the amorous military life in a garrison town in Southern France, is produced in Stockholm, after its planned first performance in Vienna scheduled for spring 1938 was canceled by the invading Nazis as a work by a Jewish composer.

## 8 OCTOBER 1939

*Columbus,* one-act opera by Eugen ZÁDOR, 44-year-old Hungarian composer, who arrived in the United States as war clouds began to gather in Europe in the spring of 1939, written originally to a Hungarian libretto by Archduke Joseph Franz of Hungary, grandson of the Emperor Franz Joseph, depicting in five episodes the successive stages leading to the discovery of America, receives its world première in an English version, over the National Broadcasting Company Network in New York.

## 8 OCTOBER 1939

Unwilling to continue to live in Spain conquered by the Falangist regime, Manuel DE FALLA arrives in Buenos Aires after a sea voyage of 16 days, destined to remain in Argentina until his death.

## 10 OCTOBER 1939

*During the Storm,* opera in four acts by the 26-year-old Soviet composer Tikhon KHRENNIKOV, dealing with the turbulent events during the communization of agriculture in the Tambov region in 1919–1921, incorporating a romantic love story between two militant young collectivists, with the epicenter occupied, for the first time in Soviet opera, by the vigilant but benevolent figure of Lenin in his Kremlin office, couched in a socialistically realistic, melodious and harmonious idiom, is produced in Moscow. (A second version of this opera was produced in Moscow on 12 October 1952)

## 12 OCTOBER 1939

*Variations and Fugue* by the expatriate Czech composer Jaromir WEINBERGER, on the melody *Under the Spreading Chestnut Tree* by William Sterndale Bennett (1816–1875), made newly popular by King George VI who sang it at a boys' camp in London shortly after the outbreak of World War II, is performed for the first time by the New York Philharmonic, John Barbirolli conducting.

## 14 OCTOBER 1939

The new American musical protective society, BROADCAST MUSIC, INC. is organized in New York City, "pursuant to a resolution to carry out the building of an alternate source of music suitable for broadcasting," thereby entering competition with the hitherto practically monopolistic American Society of Composers, Authors and Publishers (ASCAP), established in 1914.

## 21 OCTOBER 1939

*Die Nacht,* symphonic suite written in a lyrical Germanic idiom by the expatriate octogenarian American composer George Templeton STRONG, who took up permanent residence in Switzerland in 1892 as a gesture of protest against the neglect of American music in the United States, is performed for the first time anywhere by the NBC Symphony Orchestra in New York conducted by Arturo Toscanini.

## 24 OCTOBER 1939

*Third Symphony* for string orchestra by the French composer Jean RIVIER, in four movements of gallantly Gallic music elegantly projecting nostalgic, vivacious, ruminant and declarative moods, is performed for the first time at Hartford, Connecticut, Leon Barzin conducting. (The French première of the work took place in Paris on 25 September 1940)

## 28 OCTOBER 1939

*Concerto in D* for guitar and orchestra by the 44-year-old Italian composer Mario CASTELNUOVO-TEDESCO is performed for the first time by Andrés Segovia in Montevideo, Uruguay.

## 31 OCTOBER 1939

*Overture* by the Soviet composer Lev KNIPPER, written to celebrate "the liberation of the Western Ukraine and Byelorussia," heretofore Eastern Polish provinces, by the Red Army, is performed for the first time on the Moscow Radio.

## 2 NOVEMBER 1939

Mario CASTELNUOVO-TEDESCO, Italian composer who was compelled to leave Italy in 1939 when the Fascist officialdom under pressure from Hitler adopted discriminatory measures against Jews, plays the solo part with the New York Philharmonic conducted by John Barbirolli, in the world première of his *Second Piano Concerto,* in three contrasting movements, *Vivo, Romanza* and *Vivo e impetuoso,* written in an effective manner of the modern Italian Baroque.

## 5 NOVEMBER 1939

*Sixth Symphony* by Dmitri SHOSTAKOVITCH, in three movements: (1) *Largo,* proceeding from a unisonal opening through contrapuntal involvements and pastoral discursions to a quiet ending in D minor (2) *Allegro,* a scherzo in 3/8 time, neatly symmetrical in outline, marked by an incessant rhythmic propulsion and ending in a pianississississimo in D major (3) *Presto,* a perpetually self-generating rondo in socialistically realistic 4/4 time, with an interlude in 3/4, ending in a sonorous D major, is performed for the first time in Leningrad.

### 9 NOVEMBER 1939

The Palestine Symphony Orchestra inaugurates in Haifa a series of conductorless concerts under the motto "The Orchestra Conducts Itself," in a program of classical works.

### 17 NOVEMBER 1939

*Kleine Sinfonie* for strings, woodwinds, trumpet, harp and cymbals, by the aging conservative German composer Hans PFITZNER, written in an engagingly old-fashioned romantic manner, is performed for the first time in Hamburg.

### 18 NOVEMBER 1939

Upon his arrival in Argentina from Spain, Manuel DE FALLA conducts at the Teatro Colón in Buenos Aires the first complete performance of his *Homenajes*, a symphonic suite of four homages: *Pour le Tombeau de Debussy* (originally composed for guitar in 1920); *Fanfare pour Arbós* (written in 1933 as a friendly offering to the Spanish conductor Enrique Fernández Arbós); *Pour le Tombeau de Paul Dukas* (originally a piano piece written as an elegy on the death of Dukas in 1935); and *Pedrelliana*, a dedication to the Spanish composer and folklorist Felipe Pedrell, composed in 1938.

### 18 NOVEMBER 1939

The Third Soviet Music Festival opens in Moscow with the first performances of the symphony-cantata *On the Field of Kulikovo* by the 52-year-old Soviet composer Yury SHAPORIN, glorifying in grandly resonant harmonies the Russian victory over the entrenched Mongols in 1380, and dedicated to the ideal of "immortal national heroism and eternal all-conquering patriotic love of the Russian people for our fatherland," and of a *Harp Concerto* by Alexander MOSSOLOV, regenerated Soviet ex-modernist, chastened into a frame of mind suitable for composing music for the harp.

### 20 NOVEMBER 1939

Lev KNIPPER, 40-year-old Soviet symphonist, conducts in Moscow the first performance of his *Seventh Symphony*, subtitled *Military Symphony*, signalizing "the readiness of the Soviet people to answer, blow for blow, the agitation of the warmongers," and presenting in its three movements a series of musical episodes in the life of the Red Army, on the same program with a similarly monitory cantata *Alexander Nevsky* by Sergei PROKOFIEV.

### 20 NOVEMBER 1939

Désiré PÂQUE, Belgian composer of eight symphonies and a number of pieces of chamber music, inventive excogitator of the athematic method of composition, "adjonction constante" who wrote the first atonal pieces for children, dies in Bessencourt, France, at the age of seventy-two.

## 22 NOVEMBER 1939

*Blennerhassett*, radio opera by the 36-year-old American composer Vittorio GIANNINI, written in a flowingly melodious and ingratiatingly harmonious idiom, dealing with the seditious ruminations of the imperial-minded Vice President of the United States Aaron Burr on the island of Blennerhassett on the Ohio River, is performed for the first time by the Columbia Broadcasting Company in New York.

## 23 NOVEMBER 1939

*Peacock Variations* for orchestra by Zoltán KODÁLY, a set of sixteen very short pieces in various forms, meters and rhythms, all derived melodically from the pentatonic Hungarian folk song *Fly, Peacock, Fly*, prefaced with an Introduction and capped by a Finale, arranged in brilliant instrumental colors, is performed for the first time by the Concertgebouw Orchestra in Amsterdam as a commissioned work for its 50th anniversary, with Willem Mengelberg conducting.

## 25 NOVEMBER 1939

*Emelian Pugatchov*, historical oratorio by the Soviet composer Marian KOVAL, glorifying the Russian cossack who led a rebellion against Catherine the Great, and even taunted her by impersonating her husband Peter III, assassinated by a band of her lovers, but who was eventually cornered, drawn and quartered in Moscow on 11 January 1779, set to music in appropriately heroic tones, with dramatic plagal cadences and resonant Russian harmonies, is performed for the first time at the Moscow Festival.

## 6 DECEMBER 1939

*Du Barry Was a Lady*, musical revue by Cole PORTER, in which an American washroom attendant dreams of being Louis XIV, in hot pursuit of Madame Du Barry (who appears to him as the incarnation of a nightclub entertainer after whom he lusts) and is shot in the groin by the Dauphin, is produced in New York.

## 7 DECEMBER 1939

*Violin Concerto* by the 37-year-old English composer William WALTON, in three movements, *Andante tranquillo*, *Presto capriccioso alla napolitana* and *Vivace*, written in a resonant cosmopolitan, inframodern idiom, with firm tonal epicenters reposing above the modulatory lyric turbulence, is performed for the first time by Jascha Heifetz, by whom it was commissioned, with the Cleveland Orchestra, Artur Rodzinski conducting.

## 8 DECEMBER 1939

Ernest SCHELLING, American erstwhile child prodigy of the piano, and in his maturity a successful conductor of concerts for children, composer of urbane albeit unnecessary symphonic pieces, dies in New York at the age of sixty-three.

### 9 DECEMBER 1939

*Imaginary Landscape No. 1,* first of a series of surrealistic compositions by the 27-year-old Californian apostle of the musical avant-garde, John CAGE, scored for two phonograph turntables, muted piano and a suspended cymbal, comprising four 15-bar sections, each divided into three equal parts, alternating with three interludes, respectively one, two and three bars in length, is performed for the first time in Seattle, Washington.

### 21 DECEMBER 1939

*Zdravitza (Health Toast),* salutatory cantata by Sergei PROKOFIEV composed for Stalin's 60th birthday, to words in the Russian, Ukrainian, Byelorussian, Kurd, Mari and Mordva languages, is performed for the first time in Moscow, on the same program with a *Birthday Overture* by Nicolai MIASKOVSKY, also written for Stalin, and cast in the appropriately optimistic, socialistically realistic, flatless and sharpless key of C major.

### 22 DECEMBER 1939

*Second Symphony* by the 36-year-old Russian-American composer Nikolai LOPATNIKOFF, written in a cheerfully neo-classical manner, in the traditional four movements, is performed for the first time by the Boston Symphony Orchestra, Serge Koussevitzky conducting.

### 23 DECEMBER 1939

*Monte Ivnor,* opera in three acts by the 44-year-old Italian composer Lodovico ROCCA, to a libretto derived from Franz Werfel's novel *Die vierzig Tage des Mussa Dagh,* wherein a tribal group ensconced in the caves of an impregnable Caucasian mountain defends itself for forty days against a fearful enemy assault, set to music in a bleak homophonic idiom inspissated by drops of dissonant blobs, is performed for the first time in Rome.

# ❦ *1940* ❧

### 2 JANUARY 1940

Jacques HEUGEL, descendant of the founder of the French music publishing firm Heugel, publishes an editorial in *Le Ménestrel,* cautioning Frenchmen against emotional Wagnerophobia justified by Hitler's annexation of Wagner's racial notions, and urging the detractors of "le grand Saxon" to devote their patriotic energies to the safeguarding of the Rhine frontier (here two lines were deleted in the magazine by the French military censor) and to the fight against Bolshevism.

## 5 JANUARY 1940

The linking of radio stations by short wave is successfully demonstrated by an experimental connection between the local radio station in Worcester, Massachusetts, and New York City, using frequency modulation techniques developed by Major Edwin H. Armstrong, effectively eliminating background noises produced by static electricity.

## 7 JANUARY 1940

Effie Canning CARLTON, American lady who wrote in 1886, when she was 15, the famous berceuse *Rock-a-Bye, Baby,* whose somnific cadences lulled generations of American children to restful sleep, dies in Boston at the age of sixty-nine.

## 7 JANUARY 1940

*Violin Concerto* by the Dutch modernist Willem PIJPER (completed on 8 February 1939), in three movements, monothematically designed and polyharmonically evolved, ending on a bitonal chord with D as epicenter, is performed for the first time in Amsterdam.

## 8 JANUARY 1940

*Violin Concerto* by the 43-year-old American composer Roger SESSIONS, rationally neo-classical in form, imaginatively dissonant in contrapuntal harmony, fundamentally tonal in its centripetal mobility and asymmetrically kinesthetic in rhythmic patterns, cast in four movements, *Largo e tranquillo, Scherzo, Romanza* and *Molto vivace,* is performed for the first time in Chicago.

## 9 JANUARY 1940

*La Rosa rossa,* opera by Renzo BOSSI, after Oscar Wilde's tale of a mysteriously potent red rose, is performed for the first time in Parma.

## 11 JANUARY 1940

*Romeo and Juliet,* ballet by Sergei PROKOFIEV, in three acts and 13 tableaux, with a prologue and epilogue, wherein the multiple aspects of Shakespeare's play are reflected in a musical mirror resplendent with lyrical sentiment, dramatic tension and tragic somberness, and presented in an infinite variety of artful melodious settings, vitalized by a propulsive current of vivacious rhythms and colorful instrumentation, is produced in Leningrad. (Three orchestral suites, drawn from the ballet score, were performed respectively in Moscow on 24 November 1936, in Leningrad on 15 April 1937 and in Moscow on 8 March 1946)

### 20 JANUARY 1940

*Joan von Zarissa,* ballet by the 38-year-old German composer Werner EGK, is produced in Berlin.

### 27 JANUARY 1940

After playing a piano recital in Town Hall, New York City, in a program consisting exclusively of works in minor keys, and concluding with *Totentanz* by Liszt, Alexander KELBERINE, 36-year-old Russian-born American pianist, takes a lethal overdose of sleeping drugs to end a life made intolerable by financial troubles and marital disharmony (his wife, Jeanne Behrend, was also a pianist). (His body was found in his New York apartment on 30 January 1940)

There were distortions in rhythmic patterns, blurred pedal effects and exaggeration of inner voices . . . A psychic turmoil seemed to be reflected in Mr. Kelberine's performances. (Robert Lawrence in the New York *Herald Tribune,* 28 January 1940)

Kelberine Suicide After Recital That Revealed Psychic Turmoil—Pianist's Condition Noted in Critic's Review. (Headlines in the New York *Herald Tribune,* 31 January 1940)

### 30 JANUARY 1940

*Les Illuminations,* suite of ten pieces for high voice and string orchestra by the 26-year-old English composer Benjamin BRITTEN (completed on 25 October 1939 in Amityville, New York, where he was staying, having left England as a conscientious objector to the war), to French poems by Arthur Rimbaud, set in delicately luminous tonal transparencies, is performed for the first time in London.

### 1 FEBRUARY 1940

The first issue of the British magazine *The Music Review,* intended to provide a forum for the free expression of every shade of critical opinion, exclusive of patent prejudice or blatant vulgarity, is published in Cambridge, England, under the editorship of Geoffrey Sharp.

### 2 FEBRUARY 1940

*Dance Symphony* for orchestra and women's chorus by the 55-year-old Flemish composer Arthur MEULEMANS, is performed for the first time in Brussels.

### 4 FEBRUARY 1940

*Ghirlino,* fairy-tale opera by the 55-year-old Italian composer Luigi FERRARI-TRECATE, in two acts, dealing with an adolescent hero who slays the monster kidnapper of his sister and of other little girls, is produced in Milan.

### 4 FEBRUARY 1940

*The Ballad of Magna Carta,* cantata by Kurt WEILL, foremost proponent of European political theater music, now living in the United States, to the text by Maxwell Anderson, relating in rhythmic speech and vocal narration the events accompanying the signing of the Magna Carta by King John of England in 1215 A.D., marking the advent of modern democratic concepts, set to music in marching and waltzing motion, in triadic harmonies seeded with pandiatonic dissonance, is performed for the first time on the Pursuit of Happiness Radio Program of the Columbia Broadcasting System in New York, as an expression of concerted determination of free nations to oppose European dictators.

## 6 FEBRUARY 1940

*Barbershop Ballad* for orchestra by the American composer Ross Lee FINNEY, a sophisticated medley of enticingly vulgar tunes beloved by the mustachioed celebrants of the gay nineties, is performed for the first time on a Columbia Broadcasting System radio program in New York.

## 9 FEBRUARY 1940

*Double Concerto* for two string orchestras, piano and timpani by the prime Czech composer Bohuslav MARTINU, completed by him in Switzerland on 29 September 1938, the day on which his country was dismembered at the appeasement conference in Munich, written in a neo-Baroque style, with searching atonal melodic leaps, impatient and yet restrained rhythmic pulse, basically tonal and bitonal, triadic in harmony, though key signature is never applied, in three movements, *Poco Allegro, Largo, Allegro,* the first two ending on major triads, the last on an agonizingly polytonal chord, is performed for the first time as a commissioned work by the Chamber Orchestra of Basel, Paul Sacher conducting.

With anguish we listened every day to the news bulletins on the radio. During this time I was at work on my *Double Concerto;* but all my thoughts were constantly with my endangered country . . . It is a work written under terrible circumstances, but the emotions it voices are not those of despair, but rather of revolt, courage and unshakable faith in the future . . . The foreboding of approaching tragedy anticipated the character of the whole composition, like a warning against unleashed destructive elements, as if it were in my power to hold them back. (Martinu's words quoted in the article *Music and War* by Gerald Larner in *The Listener,* London, 17 March 1966)

## 15 FEBRUARY 1940

*La Pulce d'Oro,* opera buffa in one act and three scenes by the 47-year-old Italian composer Giorgio Federico GHEDINI, dealing with an aurific flea with a Midas touch whose bite produces a golden pimple on the thigh of an innkeeper's daughter, whereupon the flea's owner asks the girl's hand in marriage, and departs with her and the flea, is produced in Genoa.

## 20 FEBRUARY 1940

*Il Revisore,* comic opera by Amilcare ZANELLA, after Gogol's comedy descriptive of civic corruption and official subservience in a provincial Russian town early in the 19th century, is produced in Trieste.

## 24 FEBRUARY 1940

*Irek (Freedom)*, opera in four acts by the 29-year-old Soviet composer Nazib ZHIGANOV, to a libretto in the Tatar language, dealing with the revolutionary events of 1917 in the Tatar villages on the Volga, is produced in Kazan.

## 28 FEBRUARY 1940

Arnold DOLMETSCH, "Musical Confucius," restorer of old instruments and scholarly interpreter of Baroque music (in medieval German, Dolmetsch means interpreter), founder of the Haslemere Festivals presenting concerts of new music specially composed for his instruments, dies in Surrey, England, four days after his 82nd birthday.

## 1 MARCH 1940

*La Danse des Morts*, dramatic oratorio for solo voices, chorus and orchestra, by Arthur HONEGGER to the text by Paul Claudel, inspired by Holbein's drawings of macabre skeleton dances, fusing choral polyphony and spoken psalmody in exchatological pageantry, in which the majestic voice of Jehovah thunders supulchral reminders of man's mortality, and the tune of the French song *Sous le Pont d'Avignon* is interwoven with the strains of the revolutionary ballad *La Carmagnole* and the ominous sounds of *Dies Irae* in a pandemoniac *quodlibet*, is performed for the first time by the Chamber Orchestra of Basel, Paul Sacher conducting.

## 3 MARCH 1940

Karl MUCK, imperious and authoritative German conductor (Philip Hale described him as "calm, undemonstrative, graceful, elegant, aristocratic") whose interpretations of German symphonic masterpieces were marked by strict fidelity to the composer's score, dies in Stuttgart at the age of eighty.

## 7 MARCH 1940

Arthur SHEPHERD, 60-year-old Idaho-born composer, conducts the Cleveland Orchestra in the first performance of his *Second Symphony*, in four classically organized movements, interspersed with a few American tunes.

## 7 MARCH 1940

*Pennsylvania Symphony* by the American romanticist Charles Wakefield CADMAN, depicting in a vast musicorama the history of Pennsylvania, from its founding by William Penn in the sylvan wilds of the American Atlantic Coast to the dawn of the industrial age (illustrated by banging on an iron plate in the orchestra), is performed for the first time by the Los Angeles Philharmonic, Albert Coates conducting.

## 10 MARCH 1940

The first American television broadcast of an operatic work takes place in New York, presenting a condensed version of Leoncavallo's opera *Pagliacci* performed by members of the Metropolitan Opera Company.

## 10 MARCH 1940

Paul PARAY conducts in Paris a concert of the combined orchestras of Concerts Colonne and Lamoureux, composed of musicians not drafted into the French Army, in a program of works by Berlioz, Debussy and Ravel, and, despite a general clamor against performances of Wagner's music in wartime France, including also the overture to Wagner's opera *Tannhäuser*.

(The concert was originally announced as a Berlioz-Wagner Festival, but the program was changed on the advice of the French Minister of Finance, replacing three Wagner selections by works of Debussy and Ravel, and retaining only the Overture to *Tannhäuser* as a gesture of artistic impartiality, reasoning that the annexation of Wagner by Hitler should not impair the intrinsic value of Wagner's art)

## 14 MARCH 1940

*Dame Kobold*, comic opera by the Latvian-born German composer Kurt von WOLFURT, written in a fairly modernistic vigesimosecular idiom, is performed for the first time in Kassel.

## 14 MARCH 1940

*Violin Concerto* by Paul HINDEMITH, in three movements, marked *Mässig bewegte Halbe*, *Langsam* and *Lebhaft*, written in free tonality, with spacious quartal melodies contracting into tense chromatics in the development, is performed for the first time by the Concertgebouw Orchestra in Amsterdam, under the direction of Willem Mengelberg.

## 16 MARCH 1940

*Singoalla*, opera by the 31-year-old Swedish composer Gunnar de FRUMERIE, is performed for the first time in Stockholm.

## 18 MARCH 1940

*Violin Concerto* by the American master of neo-classical composition, Walter PISTON, in three movements, an acidly energetic *Allegro*, a reticently modal *Andantino* and a spirited *Allegro*, cast in ternary tonality (D major, F minor, D major) is performed for the first time in New York, with Ruth Posselt as soloist.

## 20 MARCH 1940

The German music periodical *Signale für die musikalische Welt* publishes the article *Angst vor Richard Wagner*, deploring the "fear of Wagner" in France during the period of so-called "phony war" on the Western front when neither the French nor the Germans initiated aggressive military action as though observing a tacit armistice:

In the absence of military activity at the West Wall (our adversaries call it the Siegfried Line), the French government has opened an offensive against German art and issued orders against playing Wagner's music. The strange association between the

Siegfried Line and Wagner is explained in the Paris daily *Le Jour:* "Wagner's art is a mirror of the brutal and rapacious German soul. Now that the front line, where our sons may be fighting tomorrow, bears the name of Siegfried, it seems hardly fitting for us to participate in Wagner's glorification."

### 23 MARCH 1940

ANNA, veteran white mare of the Metropolitan Opera House in New York, an honored member of the cast, distinguished particularly for her supporting role in *Aida*, and once mounted by Caruso himself, dies of old age at the Pegasus Club in Rockleigh, New Jersey.

### 24 MARCH 1940

Edouard BRANLY, French inventor of the coherer, an essential element in wireless telegraphy, who sent the first radio signals from one room to another (he reported his experiment to the Paris Académie des Sciences on 24 November 1890), dies in war-darkened Paris at the age of ninety-five.

### 3 APRIL 1940

Masao OKI, 38-year-old Japanese composer, conducts in Tokyo the first performance of his symphonic ballet suite *Hagoromo* inspired by an old Japanese legend.

### 6 APRIL 1940

Heitor VILLA-LOBOS conducts in Rio de Janeiro the first complete performance of his opera *Izaht*, to the story of an American Indian girl in Paris who unselfishly saves the life of the bride of the French viscount she loves, incidentally revealing the fact that the winning bride is the natural daughter of an Apache chieftain, set to a harmonious score enlivened by heteroousian Brazilian rhythms.

### 7 APRIL 1940

*New York Skyline*, "symphonic millimetrization" scientifically contrived by Heitor VILLA-LOBOS, with its melorhythmic shape derived from the diagram of a photograph of the New York skyline, is broadcast from Rio de Janeiro to New York on the occasion of the opening of the Brazilian Pavilion at the New York World's Fair.

### 9 APRIL 1940

Stereophonic reproduction of recorded music from sound film, producing an illusion of multidirectional life-like performance and three-dimensional listening, is demonstrated in public for the first time by the Bell Telephone Laboratories in Carnegie Hall in New York.

### 11 APRIL 1940

*Moby Dick*, dramatic cantata by the 29-year-old American composer Bernard HERRMANN, a sonorous characterization of the cetacean hero of Melville's famous novel, employing an appropriately leviathanic orchestra, including a set of radio thunder drums, is performed for the first time by the New York Philharmonic, John Barbirolli conducting.

### 12 APRIL 1940

*A Tale About the Land,* ballet by the 33-year-old American composer Paul CRESTON, is performed for the first time in Philadelphia.

### 12 APRIL 1940

Eugene GOOSSENS conducts the Cincinnati Symphony Orchestra, of which he is the music director, in the world première of his *First Symphony* in four movements, written in a characteristically cosmopolitan modern manner, brightened by a cornucopia of colors from his impressionistic palette, and dedicated to "my colleagues of the Cincinnati Symphony Orchestra."

### 13 APRIL 1940

*Romeo und Julia,* opera in two acts, after Shakespeare, by the 29-year-old Swiss composer Heinrich SUTERMEISTER, is produced in Dresden.

### 16 APRIL 1940

*Aotearoa,* overture on the themes of the aboriginal Maori tribes by the 24-year-old New Zealand composer Douglas LILBURN, is performed for the first time in London.

### 17 APRIL 1940

*Suite Georgienne* by the 41-year-old expatriate Russian composer Alexander TCHEREPNIN, in four movements, a symphonic evocation of the mountainous landscape of Georgia in the Caucasus, is performed for the first time in Paris, Charles Munch conducting.

### 17 APRIL 1940

*Christophe Colomb,* radio drama by Arthur HONEGGER, portraying in philosophical terms the search by Columbus of the way to the Indies, is performed for the first time by the Radio Lausanne, under the direction of Ernest Ansermet.

### 18 APRIL 1940

*Pravo Horo,* symphonic dance by the 28-year-old Bulgarian-born American composer Boris KREMENLIEV, employing asymmetrical meters peculiar to Balkan music, and utilizing a battery of native percussion, is performed for the first time in Rochester, New York, Howard Hanson conducting.

### 19 APRIL 1940

*Concertino* for string orchestra by the Boston composer Edward Burlingame HILL, in three balanced movements, the last being in the form of a quadruple concerto, is performed for the first time by the Boston Symphony Orchestra, Serge Koussevitzky conducting.

### 24 APRIL 1940

*The Wise Virgins,* ballet by the English composer William WALTON, to a scenario from the parable of ten virgins in the New Testament, making use of themes from Bach's cantatas, is performed for the first time in London.

### 25 APRIL 1940

*America Was Promises,* cantata by the 37-year-old Russian-born American composer Nicolas NABOKOV, to a text by Archibald MacLeish, with the application of rhythmic speech, is performed for the first time on the radio in New York.

### 28 APRIL 1940

Luisa TETRAZZINI, Italian prima donna, voluminous of torso and mighty of lungs, who could pick up a carnation from a bouquet on the floor while singing a high C without losing power, and whose turbulent life story included a provisional marriage to a professional gigolo, dies in Milan at the age of sixty-eight.

### 29 APRIL 1940

*Concertino* for marimba and orchestra by the American composer Paul CRESTON is performed for the first time in New York.

### 3 MAY 1940

As part of the American Composers' series, a one-cent Stephen FOSTER stamp and a two-cent John Philip SOUSA stamp are issued by the United States Post Office.

### 7 MAY 1940

A century has elapsed since the birth of Peter Ilytch TCHAIKOVSKY, great Russian melodist whose contagious emotionalism flowing in the harmonious streams of his symphonies, concertos and songs has endeared him to Old and New Russia alike, and made his music a perennial art. (The Soviet government commemorated the Tchaikovsky centennial by renaming a Moscow street Tchaikovsky Boulevard, and by issuing a series of postage stamps with Tchaikovsky's portraits)

### 7 MAY 1940

The New York Song Writers Protective Association overwhelmingly adopts a vote of censure against commercial exploitation of pornography in popular American music, and orders the expulsion of all members purveying lewd, lascivious, licentious and libidinous songs for juke boxes, but reserves judgment on sophisticated songs with an optional double meaning, such as *She Had to Go and Lose It at the Astor*, or *I Don't Know How He Does It But He Does It*.

## 9 MAY 1940

Two centuries have passed since the birth in Taranto of Giovanni PAISIELLO, Italian composer of melodious operas who enjoyed a fine success not only in Italy but in Russia, whither he went at the invitation of Catherine the Great, and whose setting of *Le Barbier de Séville* enjoyed considerable popularity until displaced by Rossini's masterpiece on the same subject.

## 11 MAY 1940

*Kleopatra*, opera in two acts by the Yugoslav composer Danilo SVARA, depicting the familiar tragedy of the Egyptian Queen, is produced in Ljubljana.

## 13 MAY 1940

As part of the American Composers Postage Stamps Series, 2,200,000 Victor HERBERT 3-cent stamps are placed on sale in New York, and the same number of 5-cent Edward MACDOWELL stamps are issued at the MacDowell Colony in Peterborough, New Hampshire.

## 16 MAY 1940

Carlos CHÁVEZ conducts at the Museum of Modern Art in New York an ensemble of Mexican musicians in a program of modern Mexican music, including the first performance of his piece for percussion orchestra *Xochipili-Macuilxochitl*, named after the Aztec god of music.

## 17 MAY 1940

*Marie Grubbe*, opera by the Danish composer Ebbe HAMERIK, to a libretto based on the life story of a cunning Danish intrigante who wrought havoc in the dynastic affairs of Scandinavia in the second half of the 17th century, is produced in Copenhagen.

## 18 MAY 1940

*Volo di Notte*, one-act opera by the Italian composer Luigi DALLAPICCOLA (completed on 18 April 1939), to a libretto after *Vol de nuit* by the French aviator Antoine de Saint-Exupéry, describing a dramatic night flight over the Andes, fighting the winds and the cold in a single-engine fabric monoplane, written in a tense atonal idiom, with incidental dodecaphonic passages (a wordless voice speaks to the pilot in 12-tone phrases) and spoken dialogue, is performed for the first time in Florence.

## 27 MAY 1940

*Amerindia*, ballet by the foremost Bolivian composer José María VELASCO MAIDANA, glorifying "the new Indian of tomorrow," is produced in La Paz, an event described by the President of Bolivia as "of transcendent significance in the history of Bolivia's artistic culture."

## 27 MAY 1940

Adrian LEVERKÜHN, the fictional inventor of the 12-tone method of composition in Thomas Mann's novel *Doktor Faustus*, dies in Munich at the age of forty-four, after suffering a catatonic seizure while giving a lecture on his symphonic cantata *The Lamentation of Dr. Faustus*, written in the 12-tone system of composition, with a mystical fundamental verbal tone-row containing 12 syllables, "Denn ich sterbe als ein böser und guter Christ," set to a melody consisting of 12 different notes and all different intervals between successive tones, with numberless ramifications in which "the ordering of basic materials becomes total," so that "there is no longer a free note," concluding on a high G *pianissimo*.

## 27 MAY 1940

A century has passed since the death in Nice of Niccolò PAGANINI, the Mephistophelean wizard of the violin.

## 30 MAY 1940

*Rosas de Todo o Ano*, opera by the Portuguese composer Ruy COELHO, is produced in Lisbon.

## 31 MAY 1940

Arturo TOSCANINI and the National Broadcasting Company Symphony Orchestra sail from New York on the S.S. *Brasil* on a good-will tour of South America, with the first concert stop in Rio de Janeiro, where Toscanini made his debut as opera conductor in 1886 at the age of nineteen.

## 7 JUNE 1940

*Král Lávra* (*King Laurence*), opera by the Czech composer Jaroslav KŘIČKA, is produced in Prague.

## 10 JUNE 1940

As part of the American Composers' postage stamp series, the United States Post Office issues a ten-cent stamp for Ethelbert NEVIN.

## 11 JUNE 1940

*Genug ist nicht genug*, cantata for mixed chorus, string orchestra, two trumpets and kettledrums by the Swiss composer Willy BURKHARD, written in an effective neo-ecclesiastical vein, is performed for the first time by the Chamber Orchestra of Basel, Paul Sacher conducting.

## 11 JUNE 1940

*Divertimento* for string orchestra by Béla BARTÓK, in three movements, *Allegro non troppo*, *Molto adagio*, and *Allegro assai*, written in an ebullient neo-Baroque vein, with an insistent rapid pulse in triple meters governing the outer, fast movements and the slow middle part marked by rhythmic fibrillation in dissonant secundal harmonies, is performed for the first time by the Chamber Orchestra of Basel, Paul Sacher conducting.

12 JUNE 1940

*Durad Branković,* music drama in five scenes by the Serbian composer Svetomir NASTASIJEVIĆ, to a libretto depicting the misfortunes of a medieval Balkan maiden abducted by the Turkish Sultan for his harem, is produced in Belgrade.

19 JUNE 1940

Maurice JAUBERT, French composer of theater music for cinema and dance, is killed leading a company of soldiers at Azérailles, near Baccarat, during the last days of fighting on the Western front, before the French capitulation to the overpowering Nazi might.

20 JUNE 1940

Jéhan ALAIN, 29-year-old French composer of 127 organ pieces, a young keeper of the ornate Franckian tradition, is killed a few days before the end of hostilities in France while leading a motorcycle patrol near Saumur.

21 JUNE 1940

Jean VUILLERMOZ, 33-year-old French composer, is killed during the last hours of military action before the surrender of France, while on patrol duty at Lobsonn, Alsace.

23 JUNE 1940

*Semyon Kotko,* opera in five acts by Sergei PROKOFIEV, to a libretto dealing with the dramatic events of the Civil War in the Ukraine in 1918–1920, written in a heroically realistic manner thematically imbued with native melorhythms, in a framework of typical Prokofievian harmonies, is produced in Moscow.

25 JUNE 1940

Three American works: *And They Lynched Him on a Tree,* cantata by the Negro composer William Grant STILL; *1940* by Roy HARRIS, a choral work to the text of the Preamble of the Constitution of the United States; and *Ballad for Americans,* "a statement of democracy" for voice and orchestra by Earl ROBINSON, are performed for the first time in public by the New York Philharmonic at the Lewisohn Stadium in New York, Artur Rodzinski conducting. (*Ballad for Americans* had a previous radio performance on 5 November 1939)

1 JULY 1940

A lawsuit brought by Jack DARRELL against the authors and publishers of the popular song *It Happened on the Beach at Bali Bali* charging infringment of copyright of his tune, *Does Anybody Want a Kew Pie?* is dismissed by the United States Circuit Court of Appeals on the ground that "the infantile demands of the popular ear" reduce the choice of available combinations of tones to a very low number, and that apparent plagiarism is easily explicable by a probable coincidence.

### 5 JULY 1940

*This Is Our Time,* cantata of social consciousness by the 29-year-old American composer William SCHUMAN, is performed for the first time at the Lewisohn Stadium in New York by the New York Philharmonic, assisted by the workers' chorus of the People's Philharmonic Choral Society, composed of members of many trades, among them house painters, carpenters, laundrymen, and furriers, with Artur Rodzinski conducting. (The performance was originally scheduled for Independence Day, 4th of July, but had to be postponed on account of rain)

### 8 JULY 1940

The Berkshire Music Center opens its first academic summer session at Lenox, Massachusetts, with Serge Koussevitzky as its founder and director, as the outgrowth of the annual Berkshire Music Festivals, established by him in 1934.

### 10 JULY 1940

Sir Donald TOVEY, hyper-cultured British musical essayist, master of elegant English prose, and incidentally a composer of romantic pieces of all descriptions, able conductor and a pianist, dies in Edinburgh a week before his 65th birthday.

### 12 JULY 1940

*Panambí,* ballet by the 24-year-old Argentine composer Alberto GINASTERA, written in a modernistically stylized Latin American idiom, bristling with asymmetrical rhythms projected against steady meters, is performed for the first time in Buenos Aires. ( A symphonic suite from *Panambí* was performed in Buenos Aires for the first time on 27 November 1937)

### 26 JULY 1940

Ernst TOCH becomes an American citizen.

### 4 AUGUST 1940

Twenty days after his arrival in New York from subjugated France, Darius MILHAUD conducts the first performance, broadcast over the Columbia network, of his orchestral elegy, *Le Cortège funèbre,* written by him in his native Aix-en-Provence shortly before the French surrender to the overwhelming Nazi forces.

#### 4 AUGUST 1940

Charles Naginski, 31-year-old Egyptian-born American-Jewish composer of brilliant eclectic music, drowns himself in the Housatonic River near Lenox, Massachusetts, in a fit of despondency over his inability to meet the strict contrapuntal test in Paul Hindemith's composition class at the Berkshire Music Center.

#### 9 AUGUST 1940

*Ferial*, symphonic divertimento by the Mexican composer Manuel Ponce, bearing the simple dedication "A México," and depicting the colorful commotion of a Mexican fiesta, introduced by a reverent church scene, is performed for the first time in Mexico City, under the direction of Carlos Chávez.

#### 16 AUGUST 1940

As a result of a statistical survey conducted by the Parliamentary Secretary to the Ministry of Information of Great Britain, regarding the catalytic property of suitable music in wartime factory work, it is announced in London that the playing of music by Chopin and Rachmaninoff produces an increase of the munitions output from 6 to 12 percent.

#### 27 AUGUST 1940

Meredith Willson, 38-year-old American composer of popular music, conducts the San Francisco Symphony Orchestra on Treasure Island, California, in the world première of his *Prelude to The Great Dictator*, arranged by him from the background music of Chaplin's motion picture *The Great Dictator*, the thematic material of which was "composed," by whistling and humming, by Charlie Chaplin himself, and set on paper, organized and harmonized by Hanns Eisler and others, with Hynkel (Hitler) represented by a hoarse trumpet. (The program included also Willson's own *Second Symphony*, subtitled *The Missions of California*)

#### 11 SEPTEMBER 1940

*Hold On to Your Hats*, a musical comedy by Burton Lane, centered on a radio singer who goes off to Mexico to capture a bandit as an advertising stunt, the score containing the popular song *There's a Great Day Coming Mañana*, is produced in New York.

#### 15 SEPTEMBER 1940

*Stabat Mater*, a newly discovered work by Domenico Scarlatti, scored for a ten-part chorus, a rare example of a truly polyphonic work in his catalogue, is performed for the first time at the opening of the Musical Festival in Siena.

#### 19 SEPTEMBER 1940

*De två Kungadöttrarna (Two Princesses)*, radio opera by the Swedish composer Hilding Rosenberg, is performed for the first time in Stockholm.

## 1 OCTOBER 1940

Nadezhda PLEVITSKAYA, Russian singer of folk ballads, who once sang for the Tsar and who had appeared at a concert in New York with Rachmaninoff at the piano as an accompanist, dies in a prison cell in Rennes, France, where she was confined for her involvement in a conspiracy to kidnap and murder an expatriate Russian general in Paris.

## 6 OCTOBER 1940

Silvestre REVUELTAS, jovial 40-year-old Mexican composer (he was born on the last day of the 1800's), fervent believer in the political function of music (his posthumous ballet *La Coronela* centers on a female colonel leading the Mexican revolution against the dictatorial President Diaz), dies in Mexico City of pneumonia, aggravated by chronic alcoholism, at ten minutes after midnight (and thus, technically speaking, on 6 October), on the night of the performance of his last completed ballet *El Renacuajo Paseador* (*Promenading Pollywog*).

## 7 OCTOBER 1940

*Guslar*, symphonic poem by the Croatian composer Jacov GOTOVAC, a tonal biography of a player on the Balkan instrument *gusla*, depicting the peripeteia of his life and concluding in an ethnic catharsis, is performed for the first time in Zagreb.

## 10 OCTOBER 1940

The Jubilee season of the Chicago Symphony Orchestra, celebrating its 50th anniversary, is inaugurated by its German-born music director and conductor Frederick STOCK with the first performance of his own *Festival Fanfare* scored for a vociferous ensemble including the Schellenbaum, a luxuriantly ornamented percussion and concussion instrument, known also as Turkish Crescent, Chinese Pavilion, or Jingling Johnny, used in Turkish Janizary music and introduced into European military bands to provide visual and auditory exotic effects.

## 17 OCTOBER 1940

Darius MILHAUD conducts the Chicago Symphony Orchestra in the world première of his *First Symphony* in neatly articulated four movements, completed on 19 December 1939 in his native Aix-en-Provence, and conceived in a broadly rhapsodic style, based on native melorhythms.

## 17 OCTOBER 1940

*Nele Dooryn*, lyric opera in three acts by the 64-year-old French composer Antoine MARIOTTE, is produced at the Opéra-Comique in Paris.

## 20 OCTOBER 1940

At the opening of a ten-day festival of Buriat-Mongol music in Moscow, two four-act operas in the Buriat language are given for the first time:

*Enkhe-Bulat-Bator* (*Enkhe, the Steel Giant*), first national opera of the Buriat-Mongol Republic, written on native themes by the Byelorussian-born composer Markian Frolov (1892–1944), dealing with the overthrow of a repressive Siberian Khan by his adopted son of proletarian parentage, whose perilous struggle is diversified by his lyrical love for the daughter of a downtrodden blacksmith; and *Bair* by the 40-year-old Soviet composer Pavel Berlinsky, centering on the heroic rescue of a beauteous peasant girl kept in a golden cage in the expectation of her transportation to the harem of a Mongol warlord. (*Bair* was first performed in the form of incidental music to a play in Ulan-Ude on 3 July 1938)

### 22 OCTOBER 1940

A revised version of *Guntram* by Richard Strauss, his first opera, to a medieval story of the chivalrous love of the German knight Guntram, a member of the Holy Society of Peace, for a duke's daughter, is performed for the first time in Weimar, where it was originally staged on 10 May 1894.

### 24 OCTOBER 1940

*Fourth Symphony* subtitled *Sinfonia gaia,* by the 43-year-old Danish composer Knudaage Riisager, in three hedonistic movements, is performed for the first time in Copenhagen.

### 24 OCTOBER 1940

*Symphony in C* by the American composer and successful railroad executive John Alden Carpenter, a single movement of romantic inspiration, articulated into sections, with occasional excursions into the colorful realm of impressionistic tone painting, is performed for the first time by the Chicago Symphony Orchestra as a commissioned work for its golden anniversary.

### 25 OCTOBER 1940

*Cipressi,* a symphonic suite by the 45-year-old Italian composer Mario Castelnuovo-Tedesco, an orchestrated version of his romantically colored dendrological piano suite written in 1921, is performed for the first time by the Boston Symphony Orchestra, Serge Koussevitzky conducting.

### 25 OCTOBER 1940

*Cabin in the Sky,* musical fantasy by Vernon Duke (né Vladimir Dukelsky), containing among its tunes the memorable ballad *Taking a Chance on Love,* is produced in New York.

### 26 OCTOBER 1940

*Gherman,* symphonic poem by the Bulgarian composer Filip Kutev, a ritual prayer for rain during which a stone idol nicknamed Gherman is mourned to the refrain "Gherman died of drought, send a drop of water, o God," melo-rhythmically derived from orientalized Balkan motives in asymmetrical rhythms, is performed for the first time in Sofia.

### 27 OCTOBER 1940

*Festmusik* by Richard STRAUSS, composed on the occasion of the 2,600 years of the Imperial dynasty of Japan, is performed for the first time in Tokyo. (Strauss completed the score on 22 April 1940 and handed it over to the Japanese Ambassador in Berlin on 11 June 1940 as an act of solidarity to an ally in the political Axis of Germany, Italy and Japan)

### 28 OCTOBER 1940

*Hamlet,* Shakespearean symphonic poem by the Manchurian-born German composer Boris BLACHER, is performed for the first time by the Berlin Philharmonic Orchestra.

### 29 OCTOBER 1940

*Violin Concerto* by the Soviet master of instrumental music Vissarion SHEBALIN, in three movements, *Introduction and Fugue, Aria* and *Rondo,* is performed for the first time in Leningrad.

### 30 OCTOBER 1940

*Panama Hattie,* a musical comedy by Cole PORTER, in which an American diplomat shocks society by marrying a Panama nightclub hatcheck girl but proves the wisdom of his choice when she foils an anarchist plot to blow up the Panama Canal, is produced in New York.

### 6 NOVEMBER 1940

After an arduous journey from Switzerland through Nazi-occupied France and Falangist Spain, in a flight from the "unbearable moral atmosphere of the European continent," the grand old man of Polish music Ignace PADEREWSKI lands in New York on the S.S. *Excambion* from Lisbon, Portugal.

### 7 NOVEMBER 1940

*Sixth Symphony,* by the New England composer of Wagneromantic orchestral music Frederick S. CONVERSE (1871–1940), is performed posthumously for the first time by the Indianapolis Symphony Orchestra, Fabien Sevitzky conducting.

### 7 NOVEMBER 1940

Igor STRAVINSKY conducts the Chicago Symphony Orchestra in the world première of his *Symphony in C,* completed by him in Beverly Hills, California, on 19 August 1940, commissioned by the Chicago Symphony Orchestra to mark its semicentennial, bearing a dedication identical in wording with Stravinsky's dedication of the *Symphony for Psalms* to the Boston Symphony Orchestra ten years before: "This Symphony, composed for the glory of God, is dedicated to the Chicago Symphony Orchestra on the occasion of the 50th anniversary of its existence," in four movements:

(1) *Moderato alla breve,* set in a classical bithematical form of a sonata, in pandiatonic tonality (2) *Larghetto concertante,* an aria, "simple, clear and tranquil" (3) *Allegretto,* "white music," in Stravinsky's words, comprising the neo-classical counterparts of a *Minuet,* a *Passepied* and a *Fugue* (4) *Largo, Tempo giusto,* distributed in spacious harmonies, and concluding on a medievally oblique cadence, coming to rest on a pandiatonic complex, with a G-major triad superimposed on the C-major sixth-chord.

### 9 NOVEMBER 1940

*Concierto de Aranjuéz* for guitar and orchestra by the blind Spanish composer Joaquín RODRIGO, in three movements, *Allegro con spirito, Adagio, Allegro gentile,* painting the fragrant ambience of the streets and plazas of the town of Aranjuéz in the fertile plain near Madrid in an artlessly harmonious and melodious manner, rich in an authentic feeling for Spanish folkways, and distinguished by virtuoso cadenzas for the guitar, is performed for the first time in Barcelona.

### 12 NOVEMBER 1940

Alejandro García CATURLA, Cuban composer of aggressively modernistic music of Afro-Cuban inspiration, saturated with primitivistic rhythms of the jungle in a modernistic setting of sonorously dissonant harmonies, is assassinated with two bullets fired in his chest, by a petty criminal about to be sentenced to a prison term by Caturla acting as district judge of his native town of Remedios.

### 12 NOVEMBER 1940

The French Post Office issues two DEBUSSY stamps, at 10 and 80 centimes.

### 13 NOVEMBER 1940

*Fantasia,* a cosmogonic "silly symphony" contrived for the motion picture screen in full color by Walt Disney, opens its presentations at the Broadway Theater in New York with special "fantasound" equipment creating the illusion of a realistically stereophonic sound, conducted by Leopold Stokowski (whose coattails are occasionally pulled by Mickey Mouse), with Deems Taylor supplying urbane comments, set to a musical score zeugmatically arranged from the following sources:

Abstract animation for Bach's *Toccata and Fugue;* vesuviating mushroom dance for Tchaikovsky's *Nutcracker Suite;* Mickey Mouse as *Sorcerer Apprentice* for Paul Dukas's symphonic scherzo; mesozoic monsters disporting themselves in the primordial slime for Stravinsky's *Le Sacre du Printemps* (with an anachronism of some 90,000,000 years occurring in the animation, in which a giant Tyrannosaurus Rex of the Cretaceous period is locked in combat with a Stegosaurus of the Jurassic period); flirting centaurs and centaurettes for excerpts from Beethoven's *Pastoral Symphony;* alligators and hippopotamuses choreographically cavorting to the music of Amilcare Ponchielli's *Dance of the Hours;* a nocturnal sortilege to Mussorgsky's symphonic tableau *Night on the Bald Mountain;* and an angelic apotheosis in a sonorously amplified and flamboyantly devotional rendition of Schubert's *Ave Maria.*

## 16 NOVEMBER 1940

At the Moscow Festival of Soviet Music in Moscow, three new works are performed for the first time:

*Twenty-First Symphony* in F-sharp minor by Nicolai MIASKOVSKY (composed between 28 May and 1 July 1940), a lyrico-dramatic work in one cyclic movement, with distinct subdivisions marked by contrasting moods (which was performed, as a commissioned work, by the Chicago Symphony Orchestra on a later date, 26 December 1940, under the title *Symphonie-Fantaisie*); *Violin Concerto* by Aram KHACHATURIAN, in three movements, *Allegro con fermezza, Andante sostenuto* and *Allegro vivace*, embodying orientalistic elements of Caucasian melorhythms, ultra-chromatic in nostalgic lyrical episodes, diatonic in volitional dramatic passages and orgiastic in the dancing finale; and excerpts from the unfinished opera *The Decembrists* by Yury SHAPORIN.

## 17 NOVEMBER 1940

*Gualicho,* one-act opera by the Italian-Argentinian composer Alfredo PINTO, is produced in Buenos Aires.

## 21 NOVEMBER 1940

*Die Walküre* is brilliantly staged at the Moscow Opera House, marking the first Russian performance of a WAGNER opera since 6 December 1925, staged as a conciliatory gesture towards Wagnerophilic Germany, in harmony with the non-aggression and rapprochement pact, concluded by the Union of Soviet Socialist Republics with the Third Reich on the eve of World War II in August, 1939.

## 23 NOVEMBER 1940

At the Moscow Festival of Soviet Music, Dmitri SHOSTAKOVICH plays the piano part in the world première of his *Quintet* for piano and strings (which was to win for him a Stalin prize of 100,000 rubles), in five movements:

(1) *Prelude*, with a slow introduction leading to an infectiously rhythmic gigue, and cyclically reverting to the slow statement (2) *Fugue*, a stately projection, entirely orthodox in the tonal imitation of the subject (3) *Scherzo*, in a boisterously furfuraceous spirit (4) *Intermezzo*, gaunt in its philosophic rumination (5) *Finale*, in the manner of toccata, with whimsically percussive episodes, concluding with an exuberant circus-like march tune.

## 25 NOVEMBER 1940

*Third Symphony* for string orchestra by the French romantic composer Jean RIVIER, set in four movements in classical forms and marked by impressionistic procedures, is performed for the first time in Paris.

## 28 NOVEMBER 1940

*Twentieth Symphony* by Nicolai MIASKOVSKY, in E major (completed on 20 September 1940), in three contrasting movements, is performed for the first time in Moscow, twelve days after the first performance of his *Twenty-first Symphony*.

*Don João IV*, opera by the Portuguese composer Ruy COELHO, is produced in Lisbon.


5 DECEMBER 1940

Jan KUBELÍK, Czech violin virtuoso, raven-locked darling of feminine audiences of the early years of the century, dies in Nazified Prague at the age of sixty.


6 DECEMBER 1940

The world première is given by Louis Krasner, soloist, with the Philadelphia Orchestra, Leopold Stokowski conducting, of the *Violin Concerto* by Arnold SCHOENBERG, completed by him in Hollywood on 23 September 1936, and written according to the method of composition with 12 tones related only to one another, carried out with classical lucidity and precision, with the basic tone row, A, B-flat, E-flat, B, E, F-sharp, C, D-flat, G, A-flat, D and F, containing in its configuration three significantly consecutive tritones, in three movements:

(1) *Poco Allegro*, rich in isorhythmic thematic phrases, gaining momentum as incidence of notes per time unit increases, while the basic tone row is solidified in vertical formations, culminating in a flowery violin cadenza, before subsiding into a euphonious coda (2) *Andante grazioso*, gently swaying in waltzing Viennese rhythms, with characteristically Schoenbergian choriambic sighs, while sternly maintaining the unrelentingly dissonant harmonies and steadfastly evading any tonal connotations (3) *Allegro*, marked by an extraordinary prevalence of dry drum rolls, giving rise to passionate discords and eventuating in a stentorian restatement of the original tone row.

Schoenberg: I believe that in my Violin Concerto I have created the necessity for a new kind of violinist.

José Rodriguez: A virtuoso recently told me that the concerto is unplayable until violinists can grow a new fourth finger especially adapted to play on the same string at the same stop as three other fingers.

Schoenberg (laughing like a pleased child): Yes, yes, that will be fine. The Concerto is extremely difficult, just as much for the head as for the hands. I am delighted to add another unplayable work to the repertoire. I want the Concerto to be difficult and I want the little finger to become longer. I can wait. (From a dialogue between José Rodriguez and Schoenberg in the anthology *Arnold Schoenberg*, edited by Merle Armitage, New York, 1937)

The new Violin Concerto by Arnold Schoenberg combines the best sound effects of a hen yard at feeding time, a brisk morning in Chinatown, and practice hour at a busy music conservatory. The effect on the vast majority of hearers is that of a lecture on the fourth dimension delivered in Chinese. (Edwin H. Schloss, Philadelphia *Record*, 7 December 1940)

The violinist slithers his bow around, apparently at random, pauses to pluck at a string here and poke at another three there. While this is going on, the orchestra is busy playing a game that sounds like every man for himself. (Philadelphia *Inquirer*, 7 December 1940)

For thirty years, bald, parchment-faced, Austrian-born composer Arnold Schoenberg has written music so complicated that only he and a couple other fellows understand what it is all about. This music, which sounds to the uninitiated not only queer, but accidental, has been enjoyed by very few. But it has thrown the world of music into a Kilkenny cat fight. One cat camp maintains that Schoenberg's music, like Einstein's theory, sounds queer because it is way over the average man's head; opponents swear that Schoenberg is pulling everybody's leg, including his own, and that his miscalled music is a gibberish of wrong notes. Gibberish or no, Arnold Schoenberg's music is fearfully difficult to play. The main difficulty is to get all of Schoenberg's wrong notes in the right places. (*Time*, 16 December 1940)

### 15 DECEMBER 1940

*Third Symphony* by the English composer Edmund RUBBRA, in four classically contrasted movements, with its academic substance enriched by sonorous polyharmonies and colorful instrumentation, is performed for the first time in Manchester. (Its first performance, announced for 23 September 1940 in London, was cancelled on account of German air raids)

### 15 DECEMBER 1940

*Chamber Symphony No. 2*, op. 38, by Arnold SCHOENBERG, marking a deliberate regression to his tonal past, in two movements (1) *Adagio*, in 2/4 time, with a key signature of six flats centered on E-flat minor (originally sketched out in Vienna in 1906; radically revised in 1939 and completed in Los Angeles on 16 August 1939) and (2) *Con fuoco*, in 6/8 time, with a key signature of one sharp in the clear ambience of G major, reverting in a subsequent *Molto Adagio* to the tonality and the spiritual atmosphere of the initial movement and terminating on an E-flat minor triadic configuration (composition completed in Los Angeles on 21 October 1939), is performed for the first time by the New Friends of Music in New York under the direction of Fritz Stiedry.

The difficulties that Schoenberg faced were enormous. As he had meanwhile advanced to an entirely different level, he found that his personal contact with his work had been disrupted: it was remote from him from the point of view both of time and style. He solved his task in a brilliant way: he finished the *Kammersymphonie* in his former style, but with his new technique developed by his compositions based on the chromatic scale. He used all his knowledge of musical development and orchestration he had acquired in recent years. So the work underwent a reformation more far reaching than, for instance, a classical work does when it is orchestrated by a modern composer. It was *Schoenberg interpreted by Schoenberg.* (From a program note written by Schoenberg's pupil and son-in-law Felix Greissle)

### 24 DECEMBER 1940

On the second Christmas Eve of World War II, the British Broadcasting Corporation broadcasts a program of Christmas carols from Coventry Cathedral reduced to ruins by Nazi air raids.

## 25 DECEMBER 1940

*Pal Joey,* musical comedy by Richard RODGERS, based on stories by John O'Hara, revolving around an amiably tough Chicago character, who sacrifices love for cash, the most popular number being *Bewitched, Bothered and Bewildered,* is produced in New York.

## 26 DECEMBER 1940

*Folk-Song Symphony* for chorus and orchestra by Roy HARRIS, his fourth symphony, with thematic material of its seven sections derived from American country tunes, is performed for the first time in its entirety by the Cleveland Orchestra.

(Four choral movements from the *Folk-Song Symphony* were performed for the first time at the American Spring Festival in Rochester on 25 April 1940, Howard Hanson conducting. On 9 March 1941 the New York Philharmonic performed the two orchestral *Interludes* from the *Folk-Song Symphony* plus an extra *Interlude)*

# ❧ *1941* ☙

## 1 JANUARY 1941

As a result of a disagreement between ASCAP (American Society of Composers, Authors and Publishers) and the radio networks, a trained canary named Cheerio whose repertoire included an arrangement of *Yankee Doodle,* copyrighted by ASCAP, and Sharkey, the trained seal who has learned to play the tune *Where the River Shannon Flows* on the mouth harmonica, also an ASCAP property, are barred from appearances as guest artists on the radio.

## 2 JANUARY 1941

*Sinfonia Biblica* by Nicolas NABOKOV, 37-year-old Russian composer living in the United States, in four movements: (1) *Ecclesiasticus* (Wisdom) (2) *Solomon* (Love) (3) *Absolom* (Fear) (4) *Hosannah* (Praise), intended as "a piece of music first of all, the Old Testament being the stimulus," with principal subjects thematically interrelated (e.g., the motive of Absalom's flight is a rhythmically accelerated intervallic inversion of the theme of Wisdom), is performed for the first time by the New York Philharmonic, Dimitri Mitropoulos conducting.

## 3 JANUARY 1941

*Symphonic Dances,* a suite by Serge RACHMANINOFF, originally planned as a triptych describing the passage of twelve hours of the day, *Midday, Twilight* and *Midnight,* with germinal materials taken from his unfinished ballet *The*

*Scythians* of 1915, is performed for the first time by the Philadelphia Orchestra, under the direction of Eugene Ormandy to whom the score is dedicated.

## 5 JANUARY 1941

*No for an Answer,* second opera of social significance by the American composer Marc BLITZSTEIN (Blitzstein means lightning-stone), to his own libretto dealing with the attempts of a group of unemployed Greek waiters to organize a union, whose leader is murdered by the police and whose gathering place, the Diogenes Social Club, is burned down by hired arsonists, is performed for the first time in New York City, with Blitzstein acting as a one-man orchestra at the piano and simultaneously conducting the singers on the stage.

*No for an Answer* is a labor drama leaning so far to the left that it is practically horizontal. (Brooks Atkinson in the New York *Times,* 6 January 1941)

## 10 JANUARY 1941

Frank BRIDGE, cultured English composer of romantically colored pieces in various genres, gently touched with tantalizing atonalities, dies in Eastbourne at the age of sixty-one.

## 10 JANUARY 1941

*Concerto* for two pianos and orchestra by the 40-year-old Cyprus-born American composer Anis FULEIHAN is performed for the first time in Hempstead, New York.

## 11 JANUARY 1941

*Ecuba,* tragic opera by Gian Francesco MALIPIERO, in three acts after Euripides, dealing with the dreadful misfortunes of Hecuba, the Queen of Troy, written in the neo-Renaissance manner of accompanied monody, is produced in Rome.

## 11 JANUARY 1941

*Alexandru Lapuşneanu,* sociological opera by the Rumanian composer Alexandru ZIRRA, dealing with the leader of a 16th-century Balkan rebellion against the Turks, written in a strong dramatic style influenced by Mussorgsky's national realism, is produced in Bucharest in its final revision. (The early version was performed in Bucharest in 1934)

## 12 JANUARY 1941

*The Virgin of Sparta,* short opera with spoken dialogue by the dean of Greek composers Manolis KALOMIRIS, is performed for the first time in Athens.

## 15 JANUARY 1941

*Quatuor pour la fin du temps* by the 32-year-old French composer MESSIAEN, scored for violin, cello, clarinet and piano, in eight movements, inspired by the Apocalypse, is performed for the first time at the German prisoners' camp, Stalag VIII-A in Görlitz, with Messiaen, himself a prisoner of war, playing the piano part.

### 19 JANUARY 1941

*Architectura,* a symphonic concerto in seven connected movements by the 48-year-old Italian composer Giorgio Federico GHEDINI, so named to emphasize the architectonic evolution of the basic themes of the piece, is performed for the first time in Rome.

### 19 JANUARY 1941

Mukhtar ASHRAFI, Bukhara-born Soviet composer, conducts in Tashkent the first performance of his opera *The Great Canal,* in five acts, in the Uzbek language, composed in collaboration with his teacher Sergei Vassilenko, with the action taking place in 1939 during the building of the great Fergana Canal in Uzbekistan.

### 23 JANUARY 1941

*Lady in the Dark,* musical play by Kurt WEILL, in which a lady magazine editor goes through the torments and absurdities of a psychoanalytic treatment, is produced in New York.

### 24 JANUARY 1941

Albert EINSTEIN plays a program of violin music at the Present Day Club in Princeton, New Jersey, at a benefit concert to raise funds for the American Friends Service Committee for Refugee Children in England, in a program including the E minor *Sonata* of Mozart and first performances of two pieces by Frida S. Bucky of New York, *Old Indian Song* and *Russian Dance.*

### 25 JANUARY 1941

Iver HOLTER, Nestor of Norwegian composers, dies in Oslo six weeks after his 90th birthday.

### 28 JANUARY 1941

*Quiet City,* instrumental suite by Aaron COPLAND, scored for trumpet, English horn and string orchestra, arranged from incidental music to a play of that name, conjuring up a fine tonal picture of urban serenity, is presented by the Saidenberg Little Symphony in New York.

### 1 FEBRUARY 1941

Under the megadollar threat of a lawsuit for the infringement of copyright, Western Union and Postal Telegraph discontinue the use of the song *Happy Birthday to You* in their telephoned "singing telegrams," upon the disconcerting discovery that the tune, with the original words *Good Morning Dear*

*Teacher,* is taken from *Song Stories for the Kindergarten* by the sisters Patty S. and Mildred J. HILL, copyrighted by Clayton F. Summy Publishing Company of Chicago.

### 1 FEBRUARY 1941

*Gli Orazi,* one-act opera by the 31-year-old Italian composer Ennio PORRINO, on the subject of the legendary combat between three heroic Roman Horatii and three equally valorous Albanian Curiatii, is produced at La Scala, Milan.

### 5 FEBRUARY 1941

*Fürstin Tarakanowa,* opera in three acts by the 38-year-old Manchurian-born German composer of Russian-Estonian parentage Boris BLACHER, on the subject of the hideous death of the Russian Countess Tarakanova, imprisoned for political opposition, who perished in a rat-riddled dungeon during the 1824 flood in St. Petersburg, is performed for the first time in Wuppertal, Germany.

### 6 FEBRUARY 1941

*Concerto for Orchestra* by Zoltán KODÁLY, commissioned by the Chicago Symphony Orchestra for its 50th anniversary, with thematic materials derived isochronically from pentatonic modes of immemorial Pannonia and popular Magyar dance rhythms, while preserving the Baroque form of a classical concerto in antiphonal structure, is performed for the first time by that orchestra, with Frederick Stock conducting.

### 7 FEBRUARY 1941

*Violin Concerto* by the 30-year-old American composer Samuel BARBER, in three movements: (1) *Allegro molto moderato,* introducing a broad narrative theme in the solo violin, developed in a free rhapsodic form with a cornucopia of contrasting melodies, with tension subsiding in a metempsychosis of the initial theme (2) *Andante sostenuto,* a bucolic sarabande (3) *Presto, in moto perpetuo,* an impetuous tarantella with the rhythmic stimulus provided by the unaccompanied kettledrums, is performed for the first time by the Philadelphia Orchestra, Albert Spalding soloist, Eugene Ormandy conducting.

### 7 FEBRUARY 1941

*Concerto for Violoncello and Orchestra* by Paul HINDEMITH, his first major work written in America (completed in Tanglewood, Massachusetts, on 9 September 1940), in three classically framed movements, (1) *Moderato,* opening with an assertive G major chord but oscillating widely in tonality, rhythm and mood (2) *Andante con moto,* an elegy in meditative E major (3) *Allegro marciale,* a hedonistic finale containing a set of variations on an old march tune and concluding in the focal tonality of G major, is performed for the first time by Gregor Piatigorsky and the Boston Symphony Orchestra, Serge Koussevitzky conducting.

## 9 FEBRUARY 1941

Morton GOULD conducts in New York the first performance of his *Spirituals for String Choir and Orchestra*, in five movements, *Proclamation, Sermon, A Little Bit of Sin, Protest* and *Jubilee*, reflecting the entire gamut of American Negro music, from devotional hymns to secular jazz.

## 15 FEBRUARY 1941

Guido ADLER, eminent Austrian musicologist, mercifully allowed by fate to draw his earthly days to a natural close without the lethal catalysis of a Nazi extermination camp for Jews, dies in Nazi-infested Vienna at the age of eighty-five.

## 15 FEBRUARY 1941

*Tata Vasco*, opera in five acts by the Mexican composer Bernal JIMÉNEZ, written on the occasion of the quadricentennial of the arrival in Michoacán of Vasco de Quiroga, to a libretto based on the turbulent events of the time of the conquistadores, with the music fusing the disparate elements of Indian pentatonic modes and Spanish hymnal liturgy, is performed at Patzcuaro, Mexico, on the eve of the composer's 31st birthday.

## 19 FEBRUARY 1941

Sir Hamilton HARTY, English conductor of eloquent powers, cultured keeper of British traditions in music, dies in Brighton at the age of sixty-one.

## 20 FEBRUARY 1941

Rudolph GANZ plays with the Chicago Symphony Orchestra, under the direction of Frederick Stock, the piano part in the world première of his *Piano Concerto*, set in four romantically inspired movements, with the two subjects of the *Scherzo* intervallically derived from the numbers of Ganz's automobile licenses for 1940 (280893, in A minor) and for 1941 (501127, in A major).

## 21 FEBRUARY 1941

Eugene Goossens conducts the Cincinnati Symphony Orchestra in the world première of the *First Symphony* by the Manila-born 31-year-old American composer John HAUSSERMANN, in four movements, of which the third, an elegy, is inspired by the mournful news of the death of Maurice Ravel.

## 22 FEBRUARY 1941

The National Youth Administration Symphony Orchestra presents in Brooklyn, under the direction of Fritz Mahler, nephew of Gustav Mahler, a program of first performances of American symphonic works, including the following:

*First Symphony* by the 34-year-old American composer Paul CRESTON (whose real name was Joseph Guttoveggio, and who adopted the name Creston by assonance with

Crespino, a role he acted in a high school performance, which his schoolmates simplified to Crest), in four movements, marked *With Majesty,* in free sonata-allegro form; *With Humor,* a lyrically animated scherzo; *With Serenity,* in which the muted strings sustain a tranquil mood; *With Gayety,* a hedonistic rondo in a rhapsodic manner; *Ballad of a Railroad Man* for chorus and orchestra by Roy HARRIS; *Violin Concerto* by Henry BRANT; and *Latin-American Symphonette* by Morton GOULD, in four dance movements, *Rumba, Tango, Guaracha* and *Conga. (Jazz Poem* for orchestra by Randall THOMPSON, first performed in Rochester on 27 November 1928, was also included in the program)

### 23 FEBRUARY 1941

*Rebus* by the romantic English composer Frank BRIDGE, a symphonic movement illustrating the murmuration of a rumor in which an explicitly stated subject becomes metamorphosed into a number of remote shapes, a sort of variations *ad absurdum,* is given a posthumous first performance by the London Philharmonic Orchestra under the direction of Sir Henry Wood.

### 25 FEBRUARY 1941

*Der Uhrmacher von Strassburg,* opera in three acts by the 36-year-old German composer Hans BREHME, is produced in Kassel.

### 1 MARCH 1941

Seth FLINT, the bugler who played the bugle call marking the end of the Civil War, at Appomattox on 9 April 1865, dies at Worcester, New York, at the age of ninety-three.

### 4 MARCH 1941

Wesley LAVIOLETTE conducts the San Francisco Symphony Orchestra in the first performance of his symphonic poem *Music from the High Sierras,* melo-rhythmically derived from the old Spanish chants of the mountains.

### 5 MARCH 1941

*Kristoffer Columbus,* opera by the 41-year-old Danish composer Finn HÖFFDING, is produced in Copenhagen.

### 6 MARCH 1941

*Third Symphony* by the 45-year-old American composer Leo SOWERBY, in three movements marked (1) *With Vigor and Drive* (2) *Slowly, with Warmth of Expression* (3) *Fast and with Fiery Energy,* is performed for the first time by the Chicago Symphony Orchestra under the direction of Frederick Stock.

### 7 MARCH 1941

Camargo GUARNIERI, a leading composer of modern Brazil, conducts in São Paulo the first performance of his incisive symphonic *Dansa Brasileira,* a coruscating modern realization of the tropically rhythmed Brazilian samba.

11 MARCH 1941

Sir Henry Walford DAVIES, the 20th keeper of the office of Master of the King's Musick since its creation by Charles II in 1660, whose duties comprised the arrangement of musical programs for royal weddings, coronations and funerals, composer in his own right of a variety of symphonic and vocal works written in an impeccably British academic idiom, and, in his later years, wireless lecturer on school music with "a perfect radio voice," dies at his home near Bristol at the age of seventy-one.

18 MARCH 1941

*Aladdin,* opera in three acts by Kurt ATTERBERG, is produced in Stockholm.

20 MARCH 1941

*Ferghana Holiday,* symphonic poem by Reinhold GLIÈRE, inspired by the building of the Ferghana Canal and based on authentic nomad tunes of Central Asia, is performed for the first time anywhere by the Chicago Symphony Orchestra as a commissioned work for its semicentennial.

23 MARCH 1941

*Fantaisie Portugaise* for orchestra, by the half-German, half-Spanish composer Ernesto HALFFTER, long resident of Portugal, is performed for the first time in Paris.

27 MARCH 1941

*Third Symphony* by Alfredo CASELLA (completed by him in Siena on 24 August 1940), in four neo-classically conceived movements, is performed for the first time anywhere by the Chicago Symphony Orchestra as a commissioned work, with Frederick Stock conducting.

29 MARCH 1941

*Sinfonia da Requiem* by the 27-year-old English composer Benjamin BRITTEN, originally commissioned in 1939 by the Japanese Government as a jubilee piece for the 2600th anniversary of the reigning dynasty of Japan, but rejected as being excessively Christian in nature, written by him under the impression of the death of his father during his stay in the as yet neutral United States as a pacifist and conscientious objector to all war however righteous, in three parts: (1) *Lacrymosa,* "a slow marching lament in a persistent 6/8 rhythm with a strong tonal center on D" (2) *Dies Irae,* "a form of dance of death, with occasional moments of quiet marching rhythm" (3) *Requiem Aeternam,* a devotional imploration for eternal peace after righteous death, is performed for the first time by the New York Philharmonic, under the direction of John Barbirolli.

3 APRIL 1941

*Scapino,* comedy overture by William WALTON, inspired by a 1622 etching of Jacques Callot depicting the mischievous character of the Italian commedia dell'arte, composed in a correspondingly hedonistic manner with a lot of drumfire in the orchestra, and ending in a triumphantly self-righteous unison C, is performed for the first time by the Chicago Symphony Orchestra as a commissioned work for its semicentennial, Frederick Stock conducting.

### 4 APRIL 1941

*Johanna Balk*, opera in three acts by the 37-year-old German composer Rudolf WAGNER-RÉGENY, dealing with a pacific 17th-century German matron who succeeds in bringing peace among feuding households, is produced in Vienna.

### 11 APRIL 1941

Arnold SCHOENBERG becomes an American citizen.

### 17 APRIL 1941

The first national Tadzhik ballet, *Two Roses*, by the 31-year-old Soviet composer Alexander LENSKY, dealing with the revolutionary struggle of the Tadzhik people against feudal overlords, is staged in Moscow.

### 20 APRIL 1941

Igor MARKEVITCH, 28-year-old Russian-born Parisian composer and conductor, whose precocious gifts as composer caused some of his incautious admirers to call him Igor the Second (the first being, of course, Stravinsky), conducts in Rome the first performance of his historic oratorio *Lorenzo the Magnificent*.

### 5 MAY 1941

*Paul Bunyan*, "a choral operetta" in five scenes by Benjamin BRITTEN, to the text by W. H. Auden, conceived in a whimsically modernistic vein, updating the legendary lumberjack of American folkways who blares his sylvan ballads through a radio loudspeaker, while a Western Union messenger rides by on a bicycle, is performed for the first time at Columbia University in New York City.

### 10 MAY 1941

Queen's Hall, the historic London theater, is destroyed by incendiary bombs dropped by the Nazi Luftwaffe during a night air raid.

At 10 o'clock in the morning of Sunday, May 11, 1941, the members of the London Philharmonic Orchestra arrived for the rehearsal. They found clouds of smoke pouring from the ruined building and "water, water everywhere." Many of them had left their instruments there overnight. Arrangements were then made to transfer the concert to the Duke's Hall of the Royal Academy of Music, and an emergency box-office was established at a table outside the wrecked building. At 3 o'clock that afternoon the concert was given as advertised, but unrehearsed and largely with borrowed instruments.

732

Queen's Hall was gone; music carried on. (From *Queen's Hall, 1893–1941*, by Robert Elkin, London, 1943)

### 10 MAY 1941

Robert WARD, 23-year-old American composer of versatile gifts, conducts the Juilliard Graduate School Orchestra in New York in the first performance of his *First Symphony*, in three movements, written in a concise and compact neo-Baroque idiom, vitalized by asymmetrical American rhythms and occasional pandiatonic bitonalities.

### 11 MAY 1941

*Tales of the Countryside*, suite for piano and orchestra by Henry COWELL, in four movements, each written in a different state of the Union, *Deep Tides* (in California), *Exultation* (in New York), *The Harp of Life* (in Iowa cornfields) and *Country Reel* (on a Kansas farm), conceived in a pleasingly folk-like manner, with the application of Cowell's tone-clusters (pandiatonic and panpentatonic columns of notes, played respectively on white and on black keys), arranged from original piano pieces of c. 1920, is performed for the first time by the All-American Youth Orchestra, organized and conducted by Leopold Stokowski, at its inaugural concert in Atlantic City, New Jersey, with Cowell himself at the piano.

### 12 MAY 1941

*Die Windsbraut*, opera in three scenes by the 36-year-old German composer Winfried ZILLIG, to a story of sylvan elves and the Wind Bride, daughter of Storm, written in a fundamentally Wagnerogenic but rationally dissonant idiom, containing tangential dodecaphonic passages and other atonal approximations, but concluding in an unambiguously tonal F-sharp major, is produced in Leipzig.

### 13 MAY 1941

*Tarquin*, "a new opera for the modern stage" in two acts, with a prologue and epilogue, by Ernst KRENEK (completed by him in Hollywood on 13 September 1940) to a libretto in English, is produced by the Experimental Theater at Vassar College, Poughkeepsie, New York, with the composer, as member of the faculty, playing the piano part of the reduced version, originally scored for four vocal soloists, four speakers, clarinet, trumpet, violin, percussion and two pianos. (A complete stage performance of *Tarquin* was given in Cologne on 16 July 1950)

### 16 MAY 1941

*A Symphony in D for the Dodgers* by the 46-year-old American composer Robert Russell BENNETT, in four movements, entitled (1) *Allegro con brio: Brooklyn Wins* (2) *Andante lamentoso: Brooklyn Loses* (3) *Scherzo* (4) *Finale: The Giants Come to Town*, with a choral final glorifying the composer's favorite baseball team, is played for the first time in a radio performance in New York.

733

## 17 MAY 1941

The 18th Festival of the International Society for Contemporary Music, blacked out of war-torn Europe, opens in New York with a broadcast of modern chamber music over the Columbia Braodcasting System, in a program including *Three Sonnets from Shakespeare* for voice and piano by Piet KETTING of Holland, and the miniaturistically brief *Third String Quartet* by Antoni SZALOWSKI of Poland.

## 18 MAY 1941

In the course of the 18th Festival of the International Society for Contemporary Music, the following program is presented by the Columbia Broadcasting System in New York:

*Prelude to a Tragedy* by Henk BADINGS of Holland, for string orchestra, written in a rationalized neo-classical idiom, with fugal elements animating the musical action; *Les Illuminations* by Benjamin BRITTEN for high voice and string orchestra to texts from ten poems by Arthur Rimbaud (first performed in London on 30 January 1940)

## 19 MAY 1941

In the course of the 18th Festival of the International Society for Contemporary Music, the following program of chamber music is given at Columbia University in New York:

*Second String Quartet* by Paul KADOSA of Hungary, written in a neo-classical idiom; *Psalm 54* for voice and piano by the German atonal composer Stefan WOLPE, who settled in New York after the advent of the Nazis; *Second Piano Sonata* by René LEIBOWITZ, leading French modernist of the Schoenbergian persuasion; *Divertimento* for solo flute by the British composer William ALWYN; and *Fourth String Quartet* by the Polish neo-classicist Jerzy FITELBERG, resident in New York City.

## 20 MAY 1941

In the course of the 18th Festival of the International Society for Contemporary Music, at Columbia University, Bernard WAGENAAR, Dutch-born American composer of neo-Baroque music, conducts a broadcast performance of his *Triple Concerto* for flute, cello, harp and orchestra.

## 21 MAY 1941

In the course of the 18th Festival for the International Society for Contemporary Music, the following program of chamber music is presented at the New York Public Library:

*Second String Quartet* by the 36-year-old Hungarian composer Mátyás SEIBER, now resident of London, couched in a neo-classical idiom with high incidence of atonal dissonance; *Piano Sonata* by the 43-year-old Austrian composer Viktor ULLMAN; *String Quartet* op. 28, by Anton VON WEBERN (described in the program book as "independent" but still living in Nazified Vienna despite his being blacklisted as a Kultur-Bolschewik in the Nazi brochure *Entartete Musik*), originally commissioned by the Elizabeth Sprague Coolidge Foundation and first performed at the Berkshire Chamber Music Festival in Pittsfield, Massachusetts, on 22 September 1938, in three movements, based on a 12-tone row of the intervallic pattern of BACH appearing in inversion, several transpositions and retrograde forms; *Les Voix de Paul Verlaine à Anatole France* by Paul DESSAU, a German refugee living in New York, scored for voice, two pianos and percussion, and written in a sharply dissonant quasi-dodecaphonic idiom; and atonally inflected Regeromantic *Piano Pieces in Seven Parts*, by the renowned pianist Artur SCHNABEL.

## 22 MAY 1941

During the 18th Festival of the International Society for Contemporary Music held in New York, *Tre Ricercari* for orchestra by Bohuslav MARTINU and *Saga of the Prairie* for orchestra by Aaron COPLAND are broadcast by Radio Station WOR.

## 23 MAY 1941

In the course of the 18th Festival of the International Society for Contemporary Music, a concert of chamber music by American and Latin American composers is presented at the Museum of Modern Art in New York, in the following program:

*Theme with Variations and Finale* for violin and piano, by the 24-year-old composer Edward T. CONE, from North Carolina, written in a stable neo-classical style with a modicum of atonal digressions; *Three Songs* by Russel G. HARRIS; *Piece for String Quartet* by the Mexican composer Salvador CONTRERAS; *Theme and Variations* for cello and piano by Paul NORDOFF; *String Quartet* by Emil KOEHLER; *Music for Trio* (clarinet, saxophone and trumpet), by the Argentinian modernist Juan Carlos PAZ, written in the orthodox 12-tone technique; and *Música de Feria* for string quartet, a posthumous work by the Mexican composer Silvestre REVUELTAS.

## 24 MAY 1941

As part of the 18th Festival of the International Society for Contemporary Music in New York, two works by Hungarian composers, *Concerto for String Quartet* by Edmund PARTOS and *Second String Quartet* by Zoltán KODÁLY, are broadcast by the Columbia Broadcasting System.

## 25 MAY 1941

At the 18th Festival of the International Society for Contemporary Music in New York, three orchestral works are broadcast over the Columbia Broadcasting System:

*Little Overture* by Roman PALESTER of Poland, written in an optimistically bland neo-Baroque idiom; *Obertura Concertante* by Rodolfo HALFFTER, Spanish composer settled in Mexico after the defeat of the anti-Fascist forces in Spain; and *Hymnus, Der Tag und Die Nacht* by the Swiss composer Willy BURKHARD, set in a hymnally devotional style.

## 27 MAY 1941

*Bal vénitien*, ballet by the French composer Claude DELVINCOURT, is produced at the Opéra-Comique in Paris.

## 27 MAY 1941

At the conclusion of the 18th Festival of the International Society for Contemporary Music in New York, the National Broadcasting Company Orchestra presents a posthumous performance of *Sinfonietta* by Charles NAGINSKI, who suicidally drowned himself in the Housatonic River on 4 August 1940, and *Two Preludes* for orchestra by the Mexican composer Blas GALINDO.

## 5 JUNE 1941

Paul BEN-HAIM, 43-year-old Palestinian composer (who changed his real name, Frankenburger, when he fled the Nazis), conducts in Tel-Aviv the first performance of his *First Symphony*, opening with a lament depicting the despair of Nazi victims, but concluding with an optimistic tarantella expressive of the faith in the victory against the ideological and military menace of Fascism.

## 8 JUNE 1941

*Nine-minute Overture* by the 21-year-old American composer Harold SHAPERO, written in a propulsive neo-Baroque manner, is performed for the first time by the Columbia Broadcasting Symphony Orchestra.

## 10 JUNE 1941

*Concerto* for organ, strings, and kettledrums by the most hedonistic of the French Six, Francis POULENC, in one quadripartite movement, based on a melorhythmic motto of four notes, written in an uninhibitedly synthetic idiom freely combining old-fashioned salon music with suggestive modernities and aggravated by a periodically tumescent organ part, is performed for the first time in Paris, Charles Munch conducting.

## 12 JUNE 1941

On the occasion of the official birthday of King George VI of Great Britain (his real birthday was 14 December), the pianist Myra HESS is named Dame Commander of the British Empire for her musical service in wartime.

## 13 JUNE 1941

*Sunčanica (Sunflower)*, opera in three acts by the 35-year-old German-born Croatian composer of Greek origin, Boris PAPANDOPULO, relating the pathetic peripeteia of a Serbian girl nicknamed Little Sunflower, recruited for the Sultan's harem at the time of the Turkish domination of the Balkans, written in a nostalgically dramatic idiom combining elements of Slavonic folksongs and colubrine Oriental melorhythms, is produced in Zagreb.

## 27 JUNE 1941

The British Broadcasting Company urges the subjugated populations of France, Holland, Belgium, Luxembourg, Denmark, Norway and other countries submerged under the Nazi military occupation, to adopt the Morse signal for the letter V for Victory (three short taps and one long) or whistle the opening motive of Beethoven's *Fifth Symphony*, rhythmically corresponding to the V code word, whenever Nazi soldiers are around.

(On 8 July 1941 the British Press Service reported that the radio station at Hilversum in occupied Holland pointedly substituted a recording of Beethoven's *Fifth Symphony* for a previously scheduled work. The day of 20 July 1941 was proclaimed by Winston Churchill to be a symbolic V Day in Nazified Europe. The Nazis retaliated by adopting the symbol themselves and advertising the V sign as the initial letter of the German nonce word Viktoria, and persistently featured broadcasts of the first four notes of Beethoven's *Fifth Symphony*. The same four notes were added to the hours of the Westminster chimes in London)

### 28 JUNE 1941

Francisco MIGNONE conducts in São Paolo the first performance of his orchestral suite *Sonho de um Menino Travesso* (*Dream of a Spoiled Child*), in four movements descriptive of the pranks of an inventively mischievous infant.

### 29 JUNE 1941

Ignace Jan PADEREWSKI, grand seigneur of the piano whose romantic genius and the mangificence of personal stature inflamed the hearts of millions in Europe and America, composer of celebrated piano pieces, Polish patriot and statesman, who briefly served as Prime Minister of Poland after its resurrection in 1918, dies in New York at the age of eighty during the dark days of a new subjugation of his native country. (At President Roosevelt's orders, Paderewski's body was laid to rest under the mast of the battleship *Maine* in Arlington Cemetery pending its return to Poland after its liberation from the Nazis)

### 4 JULY 1941

Jean SIBELIUS sends an impassionate appeal to the government and the people of the United States imploring for assistance in Finland's unequal fight against the Red Army seeking to prevent the military occupation of Finland by the Nazis:

In 1939 my country was attacked by the Bolsheviks. The enlightened American opinion realized then that we were fighting not only for our national freedom, but for Western civilization itself, and they gave us valued assistance. Now once more the barbaric hordes from the East are attacking us in their attempt to bolshevize Europe. I am convinced that freedom-loving and intelligent Americans will understand and judge the present situation correctly, and will oppose the bolshevization of Europe which would annihilate freedom and civilization on the entire continent.

### 5 JULY 1941

Lorin MAAZEL, 11-year-old boy wonder, "a chubby little chap with a big shock of black hair and a round, earnest face," born of American parents at

Neuilly, France, on 5 March 1930, actually conducts from memory a concert of the National Broadcasting Symphony Orchestra in an adult program, including a complete Mendelssohn symphony, and succeeds in maintaining a steady tempo throughout the performance.

### 6 JULY 1941

Two weeks after the German invasion of Russia, Reinhold GLIÈRE addresses the following message to American musicians:

In this portentous hour, when savage Fascist bands are attacking my native land, I wish to send my greetings to my colleagues beyond the ocean who are supporting the Soviet people in its struggle for human rights. We, Soviet composers, in common with the entire nation, are using the medium of our art to help the Red Army carry on its fight against the brutal enemy. Like the rest of the country, we have put ourselves on a war footing. I have already written a marching song to the words, *Hitler's End Will Come.*

### 10 JULY 1941

*Tango,* orchestral version of a piano piece of Igor STRAVINSKY by a professional arranger is performed for the first time at the Robin Hood Dell Concerts in Philadelphia, under the direction of the "King of Swing" Benny Goodman, beating time with a pencil. (Stravinsky made his own orchestration of the *Tango* in 1953, and it was first performed in Los Angeles on 19 October 1953 under the direction of Robert Craft)

### 12 JULY 1941

*Altyntchetch (The Golden-Haired),* opera in four acts by the 30-year-old Tatar composer Nazib ZHIGANOV, in the Tatar language, to a story from the time of the Mongol invasion of the Volga region in the 13th century, wherein a golden-tressed native maiden magically sprouts wings to flee the lecherous pursuit of a predatory Mongol warlord, and summons a flock of golden-winged swans to strike him down and to liberate the land from his rapacious depredations, is performed for the first time in Kazan, the capital of the Tatar Soviet Socialist Republic.

### 18 JULY 1941

*Concierto Argentino* for piano and orchestra by the 25-year-old Argentinian composer Alberto GINASTERA, written in classical form with the thematic use of indigenous melorhythms, is performed for the first time in Montevideo.

### 27 JULY 1941

Two orchestral works by the 34-year-old American composer Paul CRESTON, *Prelude and Dance* and *A Rumor,* are performed for the first time in New York.

### 28 JULY 1941

"Defense Swing," a new ballroom dance in which the male makes a covertly libidinous advance towards the female who parries him off with the crook of her elbow, is accepted as a legitimate dance form at the sixth Annual Convention of the Dance Educators of America.

## 29 JULY 1941

*El Indio*, a group of dance tunes by the untutored Peruvian composer Daniel Alomía ROBLES (1871–1942), arranged in the form of a symphonic suite by Rudolf Holzmann, German conductor resident in Peru, is performed for the first time by the Orquesta Sinfónica Nacional of Lima, under Holzmann's direction.

## 4 AUGUST 1941

Eleven years after Siegfried WAGNER's death, his *Symphony in C Major*, completed in 1927, in four movements couched in a loyally filial Wagnerogenic style, with additive Weberomantic and Brahmsomorphic turns, is performed for the first time in the baronial site of Wagnerocracy, the medievally Germanic town of Bayreuth.

## 8 AUGUST 1941

*Lin-Calel*, one-act opera by the Italian composer Arnaldo D'ESPOSITO resident in Argentina, to a libretto dealing with a legendary Indian Queen of the Andes, is produced at the Teatro Colón in Buenos Aires.

## 10 AUGUST 1941

Dean DIXON, 26-year-old Negro musician, first member of his race to lead a major American orchestra, conducts a concert of the New York Philharmonic during its summer season at the Lewisohn Stadium in a program of works by Brahms, Berlioz and Liszt.

## 25 AUGUST 1941

In anticipation of the centennial of the birth of Antonin DVOŘÁK, the government of Czechoslovakia issues two commemorative postage stamps of 60 hellers and 1 krone 20 hellers.

## 7 SEPTEMBER 1941

Eleazar de CARVALHO, 29-year-old Brazilian conductor of Dutch-Indian extraction, conducts in Rio de Janeiro the first performance of his opera *Tiradentes* (*The Tooth Puller*), dealing with a revolutionary dentist during Brazil's war for independence from Portuguese rule, written in a national Brazilian style and containing orchestral interludes onomatopoeically evoking the heterotonally jumbled sounds of the jungle.

## 13 SEPTEMBER 1941

Franz IPPISCH, Austrian composer who settled in Guatemala after the seizure of Austria by the Nazis in 1938, conducts in Guatemala City the first performance of his *Sinfonía Guatemalteca*, composed as a tribute to his adoptive country and based on the folksongs of Guatemala, organized in an expectedly academic Germanic manner.

### 15 SEPTEMBER 1941

*Festival of Insects*, ballet by the 31-year-old Japanese composer Kozaburo HIRAI, is produced in Tokyo.

### 28 SEPTEMBER 1941

Goffredo PETRASSI conducts in Venice the first performance of his dramatic madrigal *Coro di Morti*, for male voices, brass instruments, three pianos, double-basses and percussion, to the text of the pessimistic Italian poet Giacomo Leopardi, proclaiming that the dead fear life as much as those living fear death, set to music in suitably asomatous monodic harmonies, to depict the chants of the dead and an instrumental fugue to reflect the mechanical mobility of biological existence.

### 30 SEPTEMBER 1941

The Brazilian composer Oscar Lorenzo FERNANDEZ, described as the "brasileirissimo" for the authenticity of his native inspiration, conducts in Rio de Janeiro the world première of his five-act opera *Malazarte*, to the story of a legendary Master of the Evil Arts (Malazarte = Malas artes) active in colonial Brazil, written according to a sui generis system of motivic themes, identifying the principal moods—Destiny, Seduction, Love, Death—and thematically derived from authentic Brazilian melorhythms.

### 1 OCTOBER 1941

Dmitri SHOSTAKOVICH, his wife, son and daughter, fly to Moscow from besieged Leningrad over the Nazi lines encircling the city.

### 3 OCTOBER 1941

Wilhelm KIENZL, Austrian composer of Wagneromantic operas and lyric songs, author of the short-lived Austrian National Anthem, officially adopted in 1920 and relinquished in 1929, appreciated for the rectitude of his musical intentions and honored by his intimates, dies in Nazi-depressed Vienna at the age of 84, having long outlived his ephemeral fame.

### 4 OCTOBER 1941

Manuel PONCE, pioneer of modern music in Mexico, conducts in Montevideo, Uruguay, the world première of his *Concierto del Sur* (*Concerto of the South*) for guitar and orchestra, with Andrés Segovia, to whom the work is dedicated, as soloist.

## 9 OCTOBER 1941

*De profundis,* symphonic poem by the Czech composer Vítězslav NOVÁK, expressive of national hope amid misery in his subjugated fatherland under Nazi occupation, is performed for the first time in Brno.

## 11 OCTOBER 1941

*Die Hexe von Passau (The Witch of Passau),* opera in four acts by Ottmar GERSTER, to a verisimilitudinarian story wherein an inspired woman of mantic powers induces the pious mayor of Passau to join her in leading the German peasant rebellion of 1489, is performed for the first time in Düsseldorf.

## 11 OCTOBER 1941

Nicolai BEREZOWSKY, Russian-American composer of romantic music, plays the viola part with the Columbia Broadcasting Symphony Orchestra in New York in the first performance of his *Concerto* for viola and orchestra.

## 17 OCTOBER 1941

*Third Symphony* by the 31-year-old American composer William SCHUMAN (completed on 11 January 1941), conceived in an energetically neo-classical idiom, with the component structures oscillating axially in the vicinity of variable tonal asymptotes, in two parts (1) *Passacaglia,* adhering to its basic formula in stating the dominating subject as the cantus firmus of an enfilade of variations, leading to a *Fugue,* marked by ingeniously contrived canonic unisons (2) *Chorale,* a stately hymnal utterance, and *Toccata,* in a furfuraceous flux of string sonorities, is performed for the first time by the Boston Symphony Orchestra, Serge Koussevitzky conducting.

## 17 OCTOBER 1941

*The Lincoln Symphony* by Jaromir WEINBERGER, Czech composer of the famous comic opera *Schwanda,* who settled in the United States after the Nazi occupation of Czechoslovakia in 1938, in four biographically arranged movements: (1) *The Hand on the Plough* (2) *Scherzo Heroïque* (3) *O Captain! My Captain!* (4) *Deep River,* is performed for the first time by the Cincinnati Symphony Orchestra, Eugene Goossens conducting.

## 19 OCTOBER 1941

*Baal Shem* (so named after the Jewish-Polish founder of the religious sect of Hassids) by Ernest BLOCH, for violin and orchestra, is performed for the first time by Joseph Szigeti and the Works Progress Administration Orchestra in New York.

## 21 OCTOBER 1941

Aaron COPLAND plays in Buenos Aires the world première of his *Piano Sonata* in three movements, based on the principle of evolving melodic and rhythmic patterns, an architectonic study of balanced sonorities and interrelated formal divisions, in austerely contrapuntal textures with widely spaced chordal axes marking moments of tonal rarefaction.

## 28 OCTOBER 1941

*Roma dei Cesari,* opera in four acts by the 57-year-old Italian composer Iginio ROBBIANI, the third part of his "Trittico lirico italiano," is performed for the first time in Rome.

## 29 OCTOBER 1941

*Let's Face It,* a musical comedy by Cole PORTER, dealing with three Army wives who acquire gigolos for sexual congress in retaliation of the libertine ways of their philandering husbands, is produced in New York.

## 31 OCTOBER 1941

Nicolas SLONIMSKY conducts in Buenos Aires the world première of his instrumental *Suite,* written according to a system of integral consonant counterpoint in mutually exclusive pentatonic and heptatonic tonal matrices, in 8 movements: *Jazzelette, Penny for Your Thoughts, Happy Farmer, Fugato, Anatomy of Melancholy* (originally scored for a domestic cat solo whose tail is pulled to induce high-register meows, or a small lion's roar if a cat is unobtainable, or if local police regulations forbid the abuse of animals in musical performance on the stage), *Bitonal March, Valse très sentimentale* and *Typographical Errors* with a typewriter solo.

## 5 NOVEMBER 1941

*Czech Rhapsody* for orchestra by the 45-year-old Bohemian composer Jaromir WEINBERGER, now making his home in America, is performed for the first time by the National Symphony Orchestra in Washington.

## 13 NOVEMBER 1941

*A Bird's Opera,* symphonic fantasy by Jaromir WEINBERGER, depicting in illustrative tunes and rhythms the animal life in a barnyard, in four movements: *Overture, Nuptial Ceremonies, Junior Reception* and *Fugue on Many Subjects* "with undue interference by a dog," is performed for the first time in Detroit.

## 14 NOVEMBER 1941

*Rapsodie Polonaise* by Alexandre TANSMAN, dedicated to the defenders of Warsaw, set in propulsive rhythms of the Polonaise and Mazurka and containing thematic allusions to the Polish national anthem, "Poland has not perished yet," is performed for the first time by the St. Louis Symphony, Vladimir Golschmann conducting.

## 14 NOVEMBER 1941

*Concerto Grosso* for chamber orchestra, in three movements, *Allegro non troppo, Lento, Allegretto,* by Bohuslav MARTINU, originally scheduled to be played in Vienna in 1938, but canceled after the Anschluss; later announced for a performance in Prague but taken off the program after the Nazi invasion of Czechoslovakia; subsequently scheduled for a performance in Paris in May 1940, only to be called off once more as the Nazis invaded Belgium and Holland, is finally performed for the first time anywhere by the Boston Symphony Orchestra, under the direction of Serge Koussevitzky.

### 17 NOVEMBER 1941

*Second Symphony* by Virgil THOMSON in three movements: (1) *Allegro militaire* (2) *Andante* (3) *Allegro,* based on a continuous transformation of the musical materials of the opening statement, is performed for the first time in its entirety by the Seattle Symphony Orchestra under the direction of Sir Thomas Beecham.

### 21 NOVEMBER 1941

*Symphony in E-flat* by Paul HINDEMITH (completed by him in New Haven on 15 December 1940), in four classically contoured movements marked *Sehr lebhaft, Sehr langsam, Lebhaft, Mässig schnell Halbe,* devoid of key signature except for the indication of the tonic in the title, but concluding on a full-blooded E-flat major chord, written in a propulsive rhythmic idiom, with lyrical episodes providing some elegiac digressions, and combining in its melodic structure triadic elements and spacious quartal leaps, while the harmonic fabric preserves its essential diatonicism, is performed for the first time by the Minneapolis Symphony Orchestra, Dimitri Mitropoulos conducting.

### 25 NOVEMBER 1941

*Wiener Symphonie* by the 69-year-old German composer Paul GRAENER, in three movements written in an eclectic Viennese style, traversing the idioms from Haydn to Johann Strauss, and ending in the affirmative key of C major, is performed for the first time by the Berlin Philharmonic.

### 28 NOVEMBER 1941

*Scottish Ballad* for two pianos and orchestra by Benjamin BRITTEN, in three linked sections thematically derived from old Scottish tunes, *Lento, Adagio* and *Allegro,* in which the strains of *Dundee* are heard, leading to a lament for the Scottish soldiers who fell in the battle of Flodden, based on a funereal song *The Flowers of the Forest,* and concluding with a lively *Scottish Reel* (after funerals in Scotland, a merry military tune is often played), is performed for the first time by the Cincinnati Symphony Orchestra, under the direction of Eugene Goossens, with Ethel Bartlett and Rae Robertson as piano soloists.

### 28 NOVEMBER 1941

*Ballade* for flute, string orchestra and piano by the Swiss composer Frank MARTIN is performed for the first time by the Basel Chamber Orchestra, Paul Sacher conducting.

## 3 DECEMBER 1941

Christian SINDING, Norwegian romantic composer, whose piano piece *Rustles of Spring* has become a perennial favorite, dies in Oslo at the age of eighty-five.

## 6 DECEMBER 1941

Alan BUSH, 40-year-old English composer, ardent anti-Fascist, conducts the London String Orchestra in the first performance of his *Meditation on a German Song of 1848*, symbolic of the ancient revolutionary spirit of Germany as contrasted with the Nazi savagery of the day.

## 9 DECEMBER 1941

For the first time since the Russian Revolution, TCHAIKOVSKY's *1812 Overture*, expressive of the patriotic dedication to eternal Russia, brandishing the glorious oriflamme of sonorous brasses as the symbol of victory over the invader, is performed in the famine-stricken city of Leningrad under Nazi siege as a symphonic pledge that Hitler would suffer the fate of Napoleon, in an arrangement made by the Soviet composer Vissarion SHEBALIN, with the chorus from GLINKA's opera *Ivan Sussanin* (originally titled *A Life for the Tsar*) isoharmonically substituted for the unacceptable Tsarist national hymn in Tchaikovsky's score.

## 11 DECEMBER 1941

*Canti di Prigionia*, vocal cycle by the 37-year-old Italian composer Luigi DALLAPICCOLA, scored for chorus, two pianos, two harps and a phalanx of percussion, in three tableaux depicting with vigesimosecular Angst the agonies of three exalted personages put to death at three points of history, and set to Latin texts: (1) *Prayer of Mary Stuart* (2) *Invocation of Boethius* (3) *Farewell of Savonarola*, is performed for the first time in its entirety in Rome, on the day when Mussolini declared war on the United States. (*Prayer of Mary Stuart* was performed separately in Brussels for the first time anywhere on 10 April 1940)

## 15 DECEMBER 1941

The Red Army recaptures the town of Klin, near Moscow, and proceeds to repair the depredations committed by the Nazis in the Tchaikovsky Museum there.

A pack of mad swine could not have befouled the house of Tchaikovsky as much as the Germans did. They tore off the wall panels and used them for fuel, even though there was plenty of wood in the backyard. Fortunately, Tchaikovsky's manuscripts, his library, his favorite piano, his writing desk, all had been previously evacuated. I saw with my own eyes a Beethoven portrait torn down from the wall and carelessly thrown on a chair. Near this chair, the German soldiers excreted on the floor. The German army men made a latrine next to an excellent portrait of Beethoven! (Eugene Petrov in *Izvestia*, Moscow, 17 December 1941)

## 18 DECEMBER 1941

Darius MILHAUD plays with the Chicago Symphony Orchestra the piano part in the world première of his *Second Concerto* for piano and orchestra, in three contrasting movements, *Animé, Romance* and *Bien modérément animé*, with the finale suggesting the rhythms of the rumba.

## 21 DECEMBER 1941

*First Symphony* by the 26-year-old American composer David DIAMOND, in three movements, based on a motto of three notes constituting the thematic nucleus of the entire work, is performed for the first time by the New York Philharmonic, conducted by Dimitri Mitropoulos.

# ᴈ 1942 ᴈ

## 1 JANUARY 1942

*Piano Concerto* by the foremost Mexican composer Carlos CHÁVEZ, written in a kinetically energetic idiom, economically compact in its flinty parallelisms of strident bitonalities, with lyrical statements of quasi-monastic austerity and occasional glimpses of Mexican folkways, in three movements: (1) *Largo non troppo*, leading to *Allegro agitato* (2) *Molto lento* (3) *Allegro non troppo*, is performed for the first time by the New York Philharmonic under the direction of Dimitri Mitropoulos, with Eugene List as soloist.

## 4 JANUARY 1942

*Schwanhild*, lyric opera in three acts by the German composer Paul GRAENER, to a libretto after a German folk tale, in which a young maiden, moved by religious fervor, flies to the Holy See using the aerodynamic attachment of a swan's wings and fuselage, only to be shot down by a misguided bürgher on her way home, set in a Regeromantic idiom, expressionistically enhanced by atonal angularities, is performed for the first time in Cologne, a week before the composer's 70th birthday.

## 4 JANUARY 1942

*Nestenarka,* ballet on national Bulgarian themes by the 33-year-old Bulgarian composer Marin GOLEMINOV, is produced in Sofia.

## 6 JANUARY 1942

*Eight Etudes for Orchestra* by the American composer Robert Russell BENNETT, intended to provide "specific problems to overcome, in the same way that etudes for solo instruments present technical difficulties to the per-

745

former or student," is performed for the first time at a concert of the Philadelphia Orchestra in New York.

## 7 JANUARY 1942

*Statements for Orchestra*, a symphonic suite by Aaron COPLAND, in six brief sections, *Militant, Cryptic, Dogmatic, Subjective, Jingo, Prophetic*, with the descriptive titles intended "as a help to the public in understanding what the composer had in mind when writing these pieces," is performed for the first time in its entirety by the New York Philharmonic, Dimitri Mitropoulos conducting.

## 9 JANUARY 1942

*O Espantalho (Scarecrow)*, symphonic essay by the 44-year-old Brazilian composer Francisco MIGNONE, making use of a train whistle and a police siren in the score, is performed for the first time in São Paolo.

## 10 JANUARY 1942

*La Dispute des Orgues* for chorus and orchestra by the Belgian composer Raymond CHEVREUILLE is performed for the first time in Brussels.

## 12 JANUARY 1942

*Twenty-Second Symphony* (subtitled *Symphonie-Ballade*), in B minor, by the prime Soviet symphonist Nicolai MIASKOVSKY, written in Naltchik, Caucasus, where Miaskovsky betook himself, as the Nazi armies drove relentlessly toward the Caucasian mountain range, in three movements, with thematic material largely derived from Caucasian folk melodies, is performed for the first time in Tbilisi, capital of Georgia.

## 13 JANUARY 1942

*Kilderejsen*, opera by the Danish composer Finn HÖFFDING, is produced in Copenhagen.

## 14 JANUARY 1942

Fred FISHER, 66-year-old composer and lyricist, author of an early aeronautical courtship song *Come Josephine in My Flying Machine*, a man of the world who served in the German Navy and in the French Foreign Legion, hangs himself in New York.

## 16 JANUARY 1942

Paul WITTGENSTEIN, left-handed, amputated Austrian pianist who lost his right arm on the Russian front in World War I, plays the solo part with the Philadelphia Orchestra under the direction of Eugene Ormandy, in the first performance anywhere of *Diversions on a Theme* by Benjamin BRITTEN, written especially for him, and consisting of eleven variations on a simple musical theme.

*746*

## 21 JANUARY 1942

*Blood of the People,* one-act opera by the Soviet composer Ivan DZERZHINSKY, extolling the heroism of a Soviet girl guerrilla captured and hanged by the Nazis in 1941, with the concluding chorus chanting "Rise, Soviet People, defend your native land! Never will our people be captives of the Fascist foe!" is produced in the town of Tchkalov (formerly Orenburg), in the Ural region, by the Leningrad Opera Company, moved there from the besieged city of Leningrad.

## 21 JANUARY 1942

*La Doncella Ixquic,* ballet suite by the Guatemalan composer Ricardo CASTILLO, a "mythological tragedy" revolving around 'an Indian maiden pursued by beastly creatures, is performed for the first time in Guatemala City, Nicolas Slonimsky conducting.

## 21 JANUARY 1942

*Jamaican Rumba* by the 48-year-old Australian-born English composer Arthur BENJAMIN, a rollicking stylization of the infectious Caribbean dance, is performed for the first time anywhere by the WOR Radio Orchestra in New York, under the direction of Alfred Wallenstein.

## 22 JANUARY 1942

*Fourth Symphony* by the 31-year-old American composer William SCHUMAN (completed on 17 August 1941), in three movements, with a strong axial tonality diversified by chromatic episodes and vitalized by jazz rhythms, is performed for the first time by the Cleveland Orchestra, Artur Rodzinski conducting.

## 23 JANUARY 1942

*Concerto da camera,* in F minor, by Bohuslav MARTINU, for violin and string orchestra, with piano and timpani, in three movements of a classical consistency, (1) *Moderato, poco Allegro* (2) *Adagio* (3) *Poco Allegro,* with a motivic character redolent of Czech melorhythms, is performed for the first time in Basel, with Gertrude Flügel as soloist, and Paul Sacher conducting the Basel Chamber Orchestra.

## 28 JANUARY 1942

*Enriquillo,* symphonic poem by the Dominican composer José CERÓN, portraying in pentatonic melodies the story of an Indian chief in the Caribbean converted to Catholicism, is performed for the first time by the Orquesta Sinfónica Nacional in Ciudad Trujillo, Casal Chapí conducting.

## 8 FEBRUARY 1942

Igor STRAVINSKY conducts the Janssen Symphony Orchestra in Los Angeles in the first performance anywhere of his *Danses Concertantes* (completed on 13

747

January 1942 in Los Angeles), in five movements, with the introductory march identically repeated in the last movement, the second movement being a *Pas d'Action,* the third a theme with variations, and the fourth a *Pas de Deux,* written in an elegant manner of the French galanterie, with coquettish musical Gallicisms, neo-classical mannerisms and choreographic affectation of measured rhythmic steps.

### 10 FEBRUARY 1942

Felix POWELL, English composer of the optimistic war song *Pack Up Your Troubles in Your Old Kit Bag and Smile, Smile, Smile,* pessimistically shoots himself to death in Brighton.

### 10 FEBRUARY 1942

*Ramuntcho,* fourth opera by the American composer Deems TAYLOR, in three acts, to a libretto from the picaresque tale of Pierre Loti dealing with a Basque smuggler Ramuntcho whose patrician fiancée becomes a nun, set to music in an urbanely craftsmanlike style, with snatches from Basque folk songs lending an aura of authenticity to the score, is produced for the first time in Philadelphia. (A public dress rehearsal of *Ramuntcho* was given on 7 February 1942 for an invited audience)

### 17 FEBRUARY 1942

Oscar LEVANT, American pianist, composer, causeur and raconteur, author of a self-deprecating autobiography, *A Smattering of Ignorance,* plays the piano part in the world première in New York of his impressively competent *Concerto in One Movement,* with the National Broadcasting Company Symphony Orchestra, Alfred Wallenstein conducting.

### 19 FEBRUARY 1942

*Das Jahr,* oratorio by the 41-year-old Swiss composer Willy BURKHARD, is performed for the first time by Paul Sacher and his Chamber Orchestra of Basel.

### 20 FEBRUARY 1942

*The Island God,* one-act opera by the 30-year-old Italian-born American composer Gian Carlo MENOTTI, to his own libretto, dealing with a married couple marooned on a Mediterranean island during World War II and a young fisherman who seduces the wife, starting a tumult and rousing an obsolescent Greek god from his musty antiquity in a ruined temple, who hurls an Olympian thunderbolt at the offenders, but loses so much electric potential by this violent discharge that he lapses into an ontologically primordial nihility, is produced by the Metropolitan Opera Company in New York.

### 20 FEBRUARY 1942

*Philatelie,* chamber cantata by the 48-year-old Belgian composer Jean ABSIL, in five movements, passing in review the philatelic rarities of Europe, Asia,

Africa, America and Oceania, scored for a vocal quartet and small orchestra, with a variety of exotic sounding instruments of percussion, friction and sibilation, including a siren, is performed for the first time in Brussels.

## 21 FEBRUARY 1942

*Suvorov*, opera in four acts by Sergei VASILENKO, written in a grand Russian national style, patriotically glorifying the generalissimo who fought Napoleon in the Italian Alps, subtly drawing the inference that Russians cannot be defeated by Napoleon or Hitler, is performed for the first time in Sverdlovsk.

## 26 FEBRUARY 1942

David VAN VACTOR, 35-year-old American composer, conducts the Chicago Symphony Orchestra in the first performance of his *Gothic Impressions*, a set of twelve variations on an "aggressive" theme.

## 1 MARCH 1942

The first performance is given in Kuibischev on the Volga (formerly called Samara) of the *Seventh Symphony* by Dmitri SHOSTAKOVICH, glorifying the heroic city of Leningrad, where he was born, and partly composed under Nazi siege, in four movements:

(1) *Allegretto* (completed in Leningrad on 3 September 1941), depicting in lyrically majestic C major the socialist labor in Soviet Russia ominously menaced by the distant drumbeat of the invasion, with an insipid marching tune of the Nazi hordes growing into a monstrous machine, but held back by the irrepressible counterflow of Russian melos, and eventually reduced to a pathetic metric relic (2) *Moderato* (completed in Leningrad on 17 September 1941), an elegiac scherzo reflecting the peaceful life before the June solstice of 1941 when the Nazis struck (3) *Adagio* (completed in Leningrad on 29 September 1941), an agonizing chronicle of suffering and death, in a slow rhythmic step (4) *Allegro non troppo* (completed on 27 December 1941 in Kuibishev), marking the growing glorious tide of Russian might struggling through a field of minor keys towards the apotheosis of victorious C major.

My *Seventh Symphony* is inspired by the great events of our patriotic war, but it is not battle music. The first movement is dedicated to the struggle and the fourth to victory. . . . No more noble mission can be conceived than our fight against the dark powers of Hitlerism. That is why the roar of the cannon does not keep the muse of our people from lifting their powerful voice. (From Shostakovich's statement of March, 1942)

## 1 MARCH 1942

John CAGE, 29-year-old American experimenter in rhythmed sounds, conducts in Chicago the first performance of his metamusical *Imaginary Landscape No. 3*, scored for an electric oscillator, buzzers of variable frequency, Balinese gongs, generator whine, tin cans, plucked coil and a marimbula.

## 10 MARCH 1942

*Caribbean Concerto* for mouth harmonica and orchestra, the first of its kind, by the 32-year-old German-born American composer Jean BERGER, is performed for the first time by Larry Adler, harmonica virtuoso, with the St. Louis Symphony Orchestra.

## 12 MARCH 1942

*Das Märchen vom Aschenbrödel*, ballet on the subject of Cinderella by the Swiss composer Frank MARTIN, is produced in Basel.

## 15 MARCH 1942

*King John*, Shakespearean overture by the Italian composer Mario CASTELNUOVO-TEDESCO, now living in America, is performed for the first time anywhere by the New York Philharmonic, John Barbirolli conducting.

## 16 MARCH 1942

Alexander VON ZEMLINSKY, Austrian composer of fervently romantic music in a progressive Viennese tradition, first teacher of Schoenberg, who came to America in 1938 after the Nazi Anschluss, dies in musical oblivion, in Larchmont, New York, at the age of seventy.

(Zemlinsky was born in Vienna on 14 October 1871, according to the irrefutable evidence of the registries of birth in Vienna and in the Jewish Cultural Community there, not on 4 October 1872 as stated in all reference works)

The one to whom I owe most of my knowledge of the technique and the problems of composing was Alexander von Zemlinsky. I have always thought and still believe that he was a great composer. I do not know one composer after Wagner who could satisfy the demands of the theater with better musical substance than he. His ideas, his forms, his sonorities, sprang directly from the action, from the scenery, and from the singers' voices, with a naturalness and distinction of supreme quality. (Arnold Schoenberg, *My Evolution*, in *The Musical Quarterly*, October 1952)

## 16 MARCH 1942

*Sinfonietta giocosa* by Bohuslav MARTINU, Czech composer now making his home in America, is performed for the first time in New York.

## 26 MARCH 1942

*Le Vin herbé*, oratorio in three parts, with a prologue and an epilogue, by the 51-year-old Swiss composer Frank MARTIN, to the text from the perpetually moving legend of Tristan and Iseut whose nefarious passion is inflamed by a potent wine philter filtered through a compost of aphrodisiac herbs, set to music in the austere narrative manner of a mystery play, with a chorus commenting on the passing events, and sustained by the compact texture of neo-medieval polyphony, is performed for the first time in Zürich, Switzerland.

## 28 MARCH 1942

During an Allied air raid on Lübeck, a bomb falls on the Marienkirche destroying the great organ on which Buxtehude gave his concerts and Bach played in 1705.

## 29 MARCH 1942

*Solomon and Balkis,* one-act opera by the 42-year-old American composer Randall THOMPSON, to a libretto adapted from Kipling's story *The Butterfly That Stamped,* dealing with a magical butterfly that stamped its feet with great uproar to deter Solomon's 999 wives from quarreling, set to music in a mock-heroic Handelian manner, with sinuously orientalistic arabesques characterizing Balkis, the Queen of Sheba, is performed for the first time over the radio in New York. (The first stage performance of the opera was given at Harvard University, Cambridge, Massachusetts, on 14 April 1942)

## 8 APRIL 1942

Two and a half centuries have passed since the birth of Giuseppe TARTINI, great violin virtuoso and composer of numerous violin pieces, including the vertiginous *Trillo del Diavolo,* inspired by a tune played by Satan in Tartini's dream.

## 12 APRIL 1942

*Hymne Védique,* cantata by the 78-year-old French composer Alfred BACHELET, to the text by Leconte de Lisle invoking the ancient Vedic ritual of the sun, set to music in an exotically melodious idiom in fluid Wagneromorphic harmonies, is performed for the first time in Paris.

## 13 APRIL 1942

Two centuries have passed since the first performance in Dublin, Ireland, of HANDEL's *Messiah.*

## 16 APRIL 1942

*Second Essay for Orchestra* by the 32-year-old American composer Samuel BARBER, a miniature symphonic drama, opening with a spacious Celtic theme accompanied by an ominous rumble of the bass drum, erupting into an impetuous tarantella, and concluding with a solemn chorale, is performed for the first time by the New York Philharmonic, Bruno Walter conducting.

## 17 APRIL 1942

*Violin Concerto* by Nikolai LOPATNIKOFF, Russian-born, German-educated, American composer, in three movements of neo-classical proportions, is performed for the first time by Richard Burgin with the Boston Symphony Orchestra, under the direction of Serge Koussevitzky.

## 22 APRIL 1942

On his tour of the United States, the Brazilian composer Francisco MIGNONE conducts the National Broadcasting Company Symphony Orchestra in New York in the first performance of his symphonic suite *Festa das Igrejas (A Festival of Churches),* portraying in its four movements the impressions of four Brazilian cathedrals.

## 30 APRIL 1942

*Concerto* for violoncello and orchestra by the 26-year-old American composer David DIAMOND, written in an expansively rhapsodic, tensely modernistic manner, with aggressive discords stridently striding across the score, is performed for the first time in Rochester, New York, by Luigi Silva, with Howard Hanson conducting the orchestra.

## 2 MAY 1942

Ernst BACON, 43-year-old American composer, conducts in Spartanburg, South Carolina, the first performance of his opera in four scenes, *A Tree on the Plains,* to a libretto by Paul Horgan, dealing with an emotionally disturbed family in the American Southwest during a drought and abounding in authentic Americanisms, including a hitch-hiking call and a chewing-gum ballad, culminating in a hymn of praise in the final scene, as the eagerly awaited rainfall refreshes the thirsty land.

## 3 MAY 1942

*Twelve Tribes of Israel,* symphonic poem by the 50-year-old Jewish-German composer Erich Walter STERNBERG, is performed for the first time by the Palestine Symphony Orchestra in Tel Aviv.

## 5 MAY 1942

*Le Rossignol de Saint-Malo,* one-act opera by the French composer Paul LE FLEM, is produced in Paris.

## 12 MAY 1942

*Sinfonía Porteña* (that is, Symphony of the port of Buenos Aires) by the 26-year-old Argentine composer Alberto GINASTERA is performed for the first time in Buenos Aires.

## 14 MAY 1942

*Lincoln Portrait,* symphonic poem by Aaron COPLAND for speaker and orchestra (completed on 16 April 1942), to texts from Lincoln's sayings, linked by the recurring phrase "This is what Abe Lincoln said," making use of melodies from two contemporary songs, *Camptown Races* and *The Pesky Sarpent,* set in a compact tonal idiom with pandiatonic connotations, is performed for the first time as a commissioned work by the Cincinnati Symphony Orchestra, André Kostelanetz conducting, on the same program with symphonic portraits of other great Americans, *Mark Twain* by Jerome KERN, and *The Mayor La Guardia Waltzes* by Virgil THOMSON.

(The printed program of the first performance had an indefinite article prefacing the title; most symphony programs designate the work as *A Lincoln Portrait,* but the published score omits the article. In a letter to the author dated 20 August 1960, Aaron Copland confirms that the title should be *Lincoln Portrait*)

The composition is roughly divided into three sections. In the opening section I wanted to suggest something of the mysterious sense of fatality that surrounds Lincoln's personality. Also, near the end of that section, something of his gentleness and simplicity of spirit. The quick middle section briefly sketches in the background of the times he lived in. This merges into the concluding section where my sole purpose was to draw a simple but impressive frame about the words of Lincoln himself. (Copland's statement in the program book)

### 18 MAY 1942

The French government issues two postage stamps, of 2 and 3 francs, in honor of Emmanuel CHABRIER, in a belated commemoration of the centennial of his birth on 18 January 1841.

### 23 MAY 1942

*Second Symphony* by Arthur HONEGGER, scored for string orchestra, is performed for the first time by the Chamber Orchestra of Basel, Switzerland, Paul Sacher conducting, in three movements:

(1) *Molto moderato,* opening in somber tones and leading to an energetic atonal fugato (2) *Adagio mesto,* a chromatic lamentation yielding to a diatonic chant (3) *Vivace non troppo,* a discordant gigue, bitonally notated with 6 sharps in the first violins and none in the other string instruments, concluding on a devotional chorale, reinforced by an optional trumpet and coming to rest on a pandiatonically enriched D-major chord.

### 25 MAY 1942

*Salomon,* grand opera by the Italian-Argentinian composer Arturo LUZZATTI, to the biblical story of King Solomon's multiple concubines, is produced in Buenos Aires.

### 2 JUNE 1942

*By Jupiter,* musical comedy by Richard RODGERS and Lorenz HART, the last product of their fruitful collaboration, with the action taking place in prehistoric Asia Minor at the time when the roles of the sexes were reversed, with women making war, and men keeping house, is produced in New York.

### 6 JUNE 1942

Heitor VILLA-LOBOS conducts in New York the first performance of his *Bachianas Brasileiras No. 4* for orchestra, in four movements reflecting the duality of the music, Brazilian in essence and Bachian in substance: *Preludio, Aria, Coral* (in which a recurrent B-flat in high treble is intended to reproduce the jungle cry of the Brazilian bird arapunga) and *Dança.*

### 11 JUNE 1942

*L'Apocalypse,* oratorio by Jean FRANÇAIX, written in 1939, is performed for the first time in Nazi-oppressed Paris.

On the centennial of the birth of the Norwegian composer Rikard NORDRAAK, who during his very short life gave a vital impetus towards the formation of truly national Norwegian music, and who wrote the Norwegian National Anthem, the government of Norway issues a series of stamps in his honor, of 10, 15, 20, and 30 øre.

12 JUNE 1942

*Yusup and Akhmed,* heroic opera in four acts by the Soviet composer Boris SHEKHTER, to a libretto from a 12th-century Mongolian epic, in which a young romance flowers among the downtrodden Central Asian masses who rise in rebellion against their feudal overlords, is produced in Ashkhabad, the capital of Turkmenistan.

12 JUNE 1942

Walter LEIGH, English composer of tasteful instrumental and choral music written in an urbanely diatonic idiom, is killed in combat near Tobruk, Libya, during a tank encounter with the Nazi forces.

14 JUNE 1942

*A Ceremony of Carols* by Benjamin BRITTEN, scored for a chorus of adolescent boys, tenderly accompanied by a gentle harp, to texts from medieval poetry, set in a restrained, but polyphonically strong idiom, is performed for the first time in Aldeburgh.

15 JUNE 1942

*Cinq Danses rituelles,* suite for orchestra by the 36-year-old French composer André JOLIVET, a founder of the optimistically self-proclaimed group "La Jeune France," dedicated to the propaganda of French music young in spirit, is performed for the first time in Paris.

20 JUNE 1942

*Die Geschichte vom schönen Annerl,* opera in nine scenes, to a libretto from a German folk tale, by the 40-year-old Alsatian composer Leo Justinus KAUFFMANN, his last, for he was destined to be killed in an Allied air raid on Strasbourg on 25 September 1944, is performed for the first time in Strasbourg, now occupied by Germany.

22 JUNE 1942

*Kabelia,* last opera by the Cuban composer Eduardo SÁNCHEZ DE FUENTES, to a libretto from Hindu mythology, set to music in an Italianate manner with the infusion of some orientalistic melismas, is performed for the first time in Havana.

22 JUNE 1942

On the occasion of the centennial of the birth of the supremely melodious and sublimely harmonious French master of mellifluous operas Jules MASSENET, the French government issues a commemorative 4-franc postage stamp bearing his portrait.

26 JUNE 1942
*Violin Concerto* in four movements by the Spanish composer Rodolfo HALFFTER, resident in Mexico since the defeat of the Spanish anti-Fascist forces in 1939, is performed for the first time by Samuel Dushkin with the Orquesta Sinfónica de México under the direction of Carlos Chávez.

3 JULY 1942
Harl McDONALD, manager of the Philadelphia Orchestra and a symphonic composer in his own right, conducts the National Symphony Orchestra in Washington in the first performance of his symphonic poem *Bataan*, illustrating in cinematically vivid tones, the dramatic retreat of Americans on Bataan Peninusla in the Philippines before the overpowering Japanese pressure.

14 JULY 1942
*My Toy Balloon*, a set of symphonic variations of a Brazilian folk song by Nicolas SLONIMSKY, scored for a regular orchestra supplemented by one hundred multicolored toy balloons to be perforated with hatpins at the final *sforzando*, is performed for the first time by the Boston Pops Orchestra, Arthur Fiedler conducting.

14 JULY 1942
*Newsreel*, symphonic suite "in five shots" by the 31-year-old American composer William SCHUMAN, illustrating in cinematic modalities a prestipedal *Horse Race*, a sentimentally waltzing *Fashion Show*, a primitivistic *Tribal Dance*, syncopatingly grimacing *Monkeys at the Zoo*, and a plangently circensian *Parade*, is performed for the first time in New York City.

15 JULY 1942
Heitor VILLA-LOBOS conducts in Rio de Janeiro the first performances of three of his orchestral *Chôros*: No. 6, No. 9 and No. 11, exhaling the rhythms, the perfumes and the colors of the Brazilian scene, with tropical birds exotically chanting in the woodwinds against the measured beats of jungle drums.

20 JULY 1942
*Twenty-Third Symphony* by the prime Soviet symphonist Nicolai MIASKOVSKY, composed by him in Tbilisi, Georgia, in three movements based on ten folk melodies of the Caucasus, is performed for the first time in Moscow.

24 JULY 1942
Alan BUSH conducts the London Philharmonic in the first performance of his *First Symphony*, set in the firmly proletarian key of C major as a symbol of so-

cial directness and popular action, in harmony with the dialectical philosophy of his socialistic convictions.

25 JULY 1942

*Ginevra,* comic opera by Marcel DELANNOY, to a libretto after Boccaccio, is produced in Paris.

31 JULY 1942

*First Symphony* by the 42-year-old Mexican composer Eduardo HERNÁNDEZ MONCADA, in four movements containing melorhythmic allusions to the huapango and other Mexican folk dances, is performed for the first time by the Orquesta Sinfónica de México under the direction of Dimitri Mitropoulos.

1 AUGUST 1942

*Bridegroom from the Embassy,* political operetta by the Soviet composer Vissarion SHEBALIN, is produced in Sverdlovsk.

1 AUGUST 1942

The American Federation of Musicians enjoins its members to boycott radio stations and recording companies that refuse to respect the performing rights of American composers. (The Government of the United States instituted a suit against the American Federation of Musicians, its members and its president James C. Petrillo for violation of the Anti-Trust Act, but its suit was dismissed by the Chicago Federal District Court on 12 October 1942)

1 AUGUST 1942

The 19th Festival of the International Society for Contemporary Music opens in Berkeley, California, representing 34 composers from thirteen nations, including those subjugated by the Nazis, in the following program of orchestral music:

*Divertimento* for string orchestra by Béla BARTÓK; *Viola Concerto* by Nicolai BEREZOWSKY (first performed by him in New York on 11 October 1941); *Canon and Fugue* for string orchestra by the progressive American composer Wallingford RIEGGER; the world première of the *Piano Concerto* by the Polish composer Karol RATHAUS, now making his home in America; and *Symphonic Sketch on Three American Folk Tunes* by the American composer Arthur KREUTZ.

2 AUGUST 1942

At the second concert of the 19th Festival of the International Society for Contemporary Music at Berkeley, California, the following program of orchestral music is presented:

*Concerto* for small orchestra by the 27-year-old American composer Robert PALMER; Sinfonietta by the English composer Stanley BATE, temporarily residing in the United States; *Sinfonietta* by Nikolai LOPATNIKOFF; and *Suite for String Orchestra* by Felix LABUNSKI.

## 3 AUGUST 1942

At the third concert of the 19th Festival of the International Society for Contemporary Music at Berkeley, California, the following program of music for string quartet is presented:

*Introduction and Scherzo* by the 37-year-old English composer Norman SUCKLING; *Informal Music* by the 36-year-old American composer Normand LOCKWOOD; *Divertimento* by the Hungarian composer Frederic BALAZS; and *Fifth String Quartet* by the Polish-born Parisian composer, temporarily in the United States, Alexandre TANSMAN.

## 5 AUGUST 1942

At the fourth session of the 19th Festival of the International Society for Contemporary Music at Berkeley, California, Darius MILHAUD presents an informal talk dealing with the French Six, of whom he was an important representative, with musical illustrations from his ballet *Le Bœuf sur le toit,* and the *Concerto for Two Pianos* by Francis POULENC.

## 6 AUGUST 1942

At the fifth concert of the 19th Festival of the International Society for Contemporary Music at Berkeley, California, the following program of chamber music is presented:

*Sonata* for oboe and piano by the Russian-born Argentinian composer Jacobo FICHER; *Sonata de Primavera* for piano by the Argentinian composer José María CASTRO, written in an ingratiatingly vernal pianistic idiom with a stimulating infusion of euphonious dissonances; *Prelude, Allegro* and *Pastorale* for clarinet and viola by the English violist Rebecca CLARKE; *Three Songs* by the Yugoslav-born composer André SINGER; and *Sonatina* for oboe, clarinet and piano by the 23-year-old pupil of Darius Milhaud, Donald FULLER.

## 7 AUGUST 1942

At the sixth concert of the 19th Festival of the International Society for Contemporary Music at Berkeley, California, the following program of chamber music is presented:

*Sonatina* for violin and piano by Charles JONES, 30-year-old American student of Darius Milhaud; *6 kleine Klavierstücke,* op. 19, by Arnold SCHOENBERG, written in 1911, in which the organization of the tonal material and dynamic nuances presages the imminent dodecaphonic future and the coming age of serial composition; *Poems of the Sea* for piano and *Piano Sonata* by Ernest BLOCH; *Three Songs* by Carlos CHÁVEZ of Mexico; *Música para niños,* a piano suite for sophisticated infants by the Argentinian composer Luis GIANNEO; *7 Miniatures on Brazilian Folk Themes,* a set of colorful piano pieces by the Brazilian composer Fructuoso VIANNA, written in delicately scented tropical modalities in an appealingly romantic manner; and *Toccata* for piano by Jacques de MENASCE, 36-year-old Austrian disciple of Alban Berg, resident of New York from 1941.

## 8 AUGUST 1942

*Les Animaux modèles,* ballet in six scenes by Francis POULENC, inspired by six fables of La Fontaine, wherein distinctive animal characteristics serve as masks of human types, set to music in a neo-archaic manner with a modernistic patina barely covering the rococo surface of old Gallic dance music, is performed at the Paris Opéra.

## 8 AUGUST 1942

At the seventh concert of the 19th Festival of the International Society for Contemporary Music at Berkeley, California, the following program of orchestral music is performed:

*Fanfare, Chorale and Finale* for brass by the 29-year-old English composer Godfrey TURNER (fated to kill himself in New York on 7 December 1948 for the love of a woman); *Sinfonia da Requiem* by Benjamin BRITTEN (first performed by the New York Philharmonic on 29 March 1941); *Concerto du Loup* by the Italian composer Vittorio RIETI (Loup in the title being a French river, not a wolf); *Folk Tunes of Castille* by Pedro SANJUÁN, Spanish composer domiciled in Cuba, coloristically portraying the scenes of eternal Spain; and a *Concerto for Orchestra* by the 26-year-old Chicago composer Ellis KOHS.

## 9 AUGUST 1942

At the eighth and last concert of the 19th Festival of the International Society for Contemporary Music at Berkeley, California, the following program of orchestral music is given:

*Prelude to a Holiday* by Arthur BENJAMIN, Australian-born composer of hedonistic and optimistic music; *Symphony in E-Flat* by Paul HINDEMITH, now professor of music at Yale University, set in a didactically classical vein; *Concerto for Chamber Orchestra* by the 27-year-old American composer David DIAMOND, written in a tense neo-classical technique; and *Allegro Symphonique* by the Belgian composer Marcel POOT, a founder in Brussels of the modernistic group Synthesistes dedicated to enlightened eclecticism.

## 11 AUGUST 1942

Richard Heinrich STEIN, German music theorist and composer who was the first to publish a work containing quarter-tones in 1906, and who built a quarter-tone clarinet, dies at the age of 60 at Santa Brigida in the Canary Islands, whither he fled from Nazified Germany.

## 13 AUGUST 1942

*Musiques liliputiennes* for four flutes (hence the diminutive title) by the Belgian composer Raymond CHEVREUILLE, is performed for the first time in Brussels.

## 14 AUGUST 1942

*Fourth Symphony* by the 41-year-old English composer Edmund RUBBRA, in three movements: (1) *Con moto,* characterized by impulsive melorhythmic anapests in a dissonant atmosphere of clashing bitonalities mitigated by moments of candid lyricism (2) *Intermezzo,* a graceful scherzo in measured waltz time (3) *Grave e molto calmo,* leading to an impetuous *Allegro Maestoso,* and ending on a forceful E major chord, is performed for the first time in London.

### 18 AUGUST 1942

Erwin SCHULHOFF, Austrian composer of expressionistic music, author of a cantata to the text of the Communist Manifesto, dies at the age of 48 in a German concentration camp in Wülzburg. (Date communicated by his widow)

### 8 SEPTEMBER 1942

João GOMES DE ARAUJO, Nestor of Brazilian composers, whose Italianate operas were favorably received in Italy at the time when Verdi and Wagner still flourished, dies in São Paulo at the age of ninety-six.

### 20 SEPTEMBER 1942

*Violin Concerto* by the 35-year-old Brazilian composer Camargo GUARNIERI is performed for the first time in Rio de Janeiro.

### 20 SEPTEMBER 1942

*Napoleon,* opera by the 36-year-old German composer Edmund von BORCK, destined to be killed in combat in Italy in 1944, is performed for the first time in Gera.

### 4 OCTOBER 1942

*Festliche Toccata* for orchestra by the 45-year-old German composer Ottmar GERSTER is performed for the first time in Düsseldorf.

### 7 OCTOBER 1942

*Odysseus,* opera in three acts by the 42-year-old German composer Hermann REUTTER, is produced in Frankfurt.

### 15 OCTOBER 1942

*Leningrad,* suite for chorus and orchestra by Dmitri SHOSTAKOVICH, written as a tribute to the courage of the citizens of Leningrad during the still continuing siege of their city, is performed for the first time in Moscow.

### 16 OCTOBER 1942

*Rodeo,* or *The Courting at Burnt Ranch,* one-act ballet by Aaron COPLAND, a lyrico-dramatic musical stereopticon of the American west, in which a cowbelle outdoes the cowboys in bronco busting, and wins her favorite roper at a ranch house dance, utilizing in the score two western ballads and two square-dance tunes, is produced, as a commissioned work, by the Ballet Russe de

Monte Carlo in New York. (An orchestral suite drawn from *Rodeo*, in four dancing movements, was first performed on 28 May 1932, by the Boston Pops Orchestra, with Arthur Fiedler conducting)

### 18 OCTOBER 1942

*Concerto for String Orchestra* by the 39-year-old Chinese-born Estonian-German composer Boris BLACHER, is performed for the first time in Hamburg.

### 22 OCTOBER 1942

*Second Symphony* by the American composer John Alden CARPENTER, in three movements, *Allegro, Andante, Allegro*, with some allusions to Algerian tunes among its themes (Carpenter had visited Algiers upon his retirement as Vice-President of the Carpenter Railway and Ship Supplies Co.), is performed for the first time by the New York Philharmonic conducted by Bruno Walter.

### 22 OCTOBER 1942

*Ankara Castle*, symphonic suite by the Turkish composer Necil KAZIM AKSES, is performed for the first time in Ankara.

### 24 OCTOBER 1942

*I Capricci di Callot*, comic opera in three acts by Gian Francesco MALIPIERO, inspired by the carnavelsque masques in the etchings of Jacques Callot (1592–1635) as transmuted in Hoffmann's tales, is produced in Rome.

### 28 OCTOBER 1942

*Capriccio*, opera in one act by Richard STRAUSS (completed on 3 August 1941) to a libretto by Clemens Krauss and the composer, set as a conversation piece in Paris of 1775, debating the problem of relative importance of words and music in an opera, with interpolations of anachronistic musical quotations—including passages from Strauss's own operas, specifically *Ariadne auf Naxos* —is produced in war-darkened Munich.

### 28 OCTOBER 1942

*La Tentation dernière*, cantata by André JOLIVET, depicting the trial of Joan of Arc, is performed for the first time in Paris.

### 30 OCTOBER 1942

*Die Zauberinsel*, opera in two acts by the Swiss composer Heinrich SUTERMEISTER, after Shakespeare's play *The Tempest*, is performed for the first time in Dresden.

### 1 NOVEMBER 1942

Hugo DISTLER, 36-year-old German composer of an imposing array of cantatas, oratorios, motets and organ works, written in a massive polyphonic manner of neo-classical rhetoric, commits suicide in Berlin.

## 1 NOVEMBER 1942

*A Lincoln Legend,* symphonic paragraph by Morton GOULD, ambidextrous American composer of serious and popular music, is performed for the first time by the National Broadcasting Company Symphony Orchestra in New York.

## 3 NOVEMBER 1942

Walter DAMROSCH, 80-year-old German-born American composer and conductor, leads in New York the first performance of his one-act opera *The Opera Cloak,* to a fanciful libretto by his daughter, dealing with a sad seamstress languishing in New York in 1915, who finds vicarious enjoyment in reading a passionate love letter inadvertently left in the pocket of an opera cloak given to her for repairs, accidentally rings a fire alarm and is rescued from loneliness by a handsome fireman who takes her to a dance, written in a synthetically competent operatic idiom replete with subliminal recollections of fragments from Wagner, Verdi and Puccini, galvanized in some scenes by ragtime rhythms.

## 5 NOVEMBER 1942

George M. COHAN, American song and dance man, the "Yankee Doodle Dandy" of the vaudeville stage, who wrote the rousing popular song of World War I, *Over There,* dies of cancer in New York at the age of sixty-four. (A motion picture portraying his life, with James Cagney cast as Cohan, was shown to him in New York five months before his death)

## 7 NOVEMBER 1942

*At the Approaches to Moscow,* opera in four acts by the 37-year-old Soviet composer Dmitri KABALEVSKY, to a libretto dealing with the Soviet counter-offensive against the Nazis in the suburbs of Moscow in December 1941, written in a militantly patriotic manner, is produced in Moscow less than a year after the events depicted in the score, and coincidentally celebrating the 25th anniversary of the Soviet Revolution. (The second version of the opera was produced for the first time in Moscow under the title *Under Fire* on 19 September 1943)

## 7 NOVEMBER 1942

*Ildar,* opera in four acts by the 31-year-old Soviet composer Nazib ZHIGANOV, dealing with the earnest love pact between a tractor driver and a collective farm milkmaid in the midst of Nazi war, is performed for the first time, in the Tatar language, in Kazan, former stronghold of the Tatar kingdom crushed by Ivan the Terrible in 1582.

## 7 NOVEMBER 1942

*Emelian Pugatchov,* opera in five acts by the Soviet composer Marian KOVAL, depicting in heroic Russian harmonies the bold rebellion led against Catherine the Great by the ambitious Ural cossack Pugatchov, who eventually was caught, and publicly drawn and quartered in Moscow, is performed for the first time in the Ural town of Perm by an opera group moved from besieged Leningrad.

### 13 NOVEMBER 1942

*First Symphony* by Bohuslav MARTINU, in four movements, *Moderato, Allegro, Largo, Allegro vivace,* notated without key signatures but teleologically directed towards the tonal centers of B and B-flat, with the neo-classical idiom enriched by the intussusception of secundal harmonies, while deep-rooted pedal points provide basses for euphonious bitonalities, and ending in sonorous B-flat major, is performed for the first time by the Boston Symphony Orchestra, Serge Koussevitzky conducting.

### 13 NOVEMBER 1942

*Concerto* for two pianos and orchestra by Darius MILHAUD, in three movements, *Animé, Funèbre, Vif et précis,* is performed for the first time by the Pittsburgh Symphony Orchestra, Fritz Reiner conducting, with Vitya Vronsky and Victor Babin as soloists.

### 14 NOVEMBER 1942

*Marco Takes a Walk,* a set of symphonic variations by Deems TAYLOR, depicting a child's walk through a busy street, transforming the passing scene in his fantasies into a world of fabulous creatures, set to music in an affectionately coloristic idiom, is performed for the first time by the New York Philharmonic.

### 18 NOVEMBER 1942

A millennium has elapsed since the death of Odo DE CLUGNY, the Benedictine monk who expanded the hexachordal system of the ancients into a continuous diatonic scale from A to G, and formulated the distinction between B-flat (*b rotundum,* so named from its shape, and later developed into the modern flat sign) and B natural (*b quadratum* which evolved into the modern natural sign)

### 19 NOVEMBER 1942

*Minnie la Candida,* opera by Riccardo MALIPIERO, nephew of Gian Francesco Malipiero, is performed for the first time in Parma, Italy.

### 20 NOVEMBER 1942

The General Government of Poland, under Nazi occupation, issues a postage stamp of 50 Groschen honoring the memory of Chopin's teacher Joseph Xaver ELSNER.

### 23 NOVEMBER 1942

The Italian Government issues four postage stamps at 25, 30, and 50 centesimi and one lira, belatedly commemorating the sesquicentennial year of the birth of ROSSINI, who was born on 29 February 1792.

## 27 NOVEMBER 1942

*Cantata de los Rios de Chile* for chorus and orchestra by the prime Chilean modernist Domingo SANTA CRUZ, descriptive of the great mountain stream Maipo and Mt. Aconcagua, written in a grand polyphonic idiom, with occasional topical allusions to the Chilean scene, such as the imitation of a policeman's whistle by the oboe, is performed for the first time in Santiago.

## 27 NOVEMBER 1942

A *Fanfare for Paratroopers* by Paul CRESTON is performed by the Cincinnati Symphony Orchestra, under the direction of Eugene Goossens, as one of several musical salutations by American composers to the United States Armed Forces.

## 3 DECEMBER 1942

The Boston Symphony Orchestra, the last surviving non-union orchestra in the United States, joins the American Federation of Musicians under the pressure of a virtual boycott by all union-controlled institutions and recording companies.

## 4 DECEMBER 1942

*Concierto sinfónico* for violin and orchestra by the Chilean composer Humberto ALLENDE, set in three contrasting movements within a neo-classical framework, is performed for the first time in Santiago.

## 9 DECEMBER 1942

*Gayane,* ballet by Aram KHACHATURIAN, in which a class-conscious Armenian girl worker on a Soviet collective farm foils the insidious machinations of her anti-Soviet husband, and after he is liquidated, marries his valorous executioner, with a series of orientalistic Caucasian dances in the score (of which the *Saber Dance,* with its sinuous melorhythms, has become universally popular), is produced in the town of Molotov, renamed in honor of the Soviet Minister of Foreign Affairs from its ancient name of Perm, in the Ural region.

## 11 DECEMBER 1942

*Fanfare de la Liberté,* a brief symphonic tribute by Darius MILHAUD to the undaunted spirit of France under Nazi occupation, is played for the first time by the Cincinnati Symphony Orchestra, Eugene Goossens conducting.

## 25 DECEMBER 1942

Vojislav VUČKOVIĆ, Croatian composer of mass songs, among them *Chorus of 10,000 Strikers,* author of scholarly monographs on Marxism in music, is shot by the Nazi police as he emerges from his secret hiding place in occupied Belgrade, dying a few hours later, on the same day that his wife was captured and tortured to death in another Gestapo dungeon.

## 28 DECEMBER 1942

*Stronger than Death*, opera in three acts by the 37-year-old Soviet composer Victor VOLOSHINOV, depicting the heroism of Soviet men and women in a Nazi-occupied village in 1941, is produced in Orenburg.

## 31 DECEMBER 1942

Yakob ORLANSKY, Russian accordion player, who in 1905 designed the BAYAN, so named after the legendary Russian minstrel, destined to become universally popular in Russia under that name, manufactured according to his instructions by the Russian instrument builder Peter Sterligov, and completed after two years of experimentation in August 1907, consisting of 58 spade-shaped keys chromatically arranged in three manuals for the right hand and four groups of buttons regulating triads and dominant-seventh-chord harmonies in the left hand, is found dead in his apartment in besieged, famine-stricken Leningrad.

# ❧ 1943 ❧

## 7 JANUARY 1943

*Something for the Boys*, a musical comedy by Cole PORTER, in which two nightclub songstresses and a New York street vendor unexpectedly inherit a Texas ranch, with intermingled love affairs entering their financial squabbles, further diversified by the discovery that one of the trio is a human radio receiver through the carborundum fillings in her bridgework, featuring besides the title song a popular ditty *Hey, Good Looking*, is produced in New York.

## 10 JANUARY 1943

*Second Symphony* in C minor by Tikhon KHRENNIKOV, expressing "the irresistible will to defeat the Fascist foe," and depicting in its four movements the purposeful Socialist labor of the Soviet man, a lament for the victims of the Nazi aggression, the undaunted spirit of young Soviet soldiers and the victorious military impetus, culminating in a triumph, in gloriously shining C major, over the Nazi war machine, is performed for the first time in Moscow. (The *Finale* was later revised, and the new version performed in Moscow on 9 June 1944)

## 13 JANUARY 1943

*Concerto* for piano and small orchestra by William SCHUMAN (completed by him on 18 July 1942) is performed for the first time in New York.

## 15 JANUARY 1943

*Fanfare for France* by Virgil THOMSON is performed by the Cincinnati Symphony Orchestra.

## 19 JANUARY 1943

The Shoestring Opera Company, a non-profit corporation formed "to demonstrate that artistic, dramatic music can be presented without the prohibitive cost of present-day grand opera," opens its first season with a performance of *Tales of Hoffmann,* at Hunter College in New York.

*"Shoestring.* Colloq. a very small amount of money or capital used to start or carry on an enterprise or business." (*The American College Dictionary*)

## 21 JANUARY 1943

*1941,* a symphonic suite by Sergei PROKOFIEV in three movements, *Battle, At Night,* and *For the Brotherhood of Nations,* depicting the anxieties of the Nazi invasion, the determination to win the war, and the hope for the creation of a new world of universal peace, is performed for the first time at Sverdlovsk.

## 22 JANUARY 1943

*Fanfare for Freedom* by Morton GOULD is sounded by the Cincinnati Symphony Orchestra.

## 31 JANUARY 1943

*Divertimento* for chamber orchestra by Richard STRAUSS, on the themes from piano pieces by François Couperin (the score completed on 12 September 1941), is performed for the first time in Vienna.

## 1 FEBRUARY 1943

Serge RACHMANINOFF becomes an American citizen.

## 2 FEBRUARY 1943

Alexandre TANSMAN, 45-year-old Parisian Polish composer, a musical refugee in America during the Nazi occupation of France, conducts the National Symphony Orchestra of Washington at its concert in Baltimore, in the first performance of his *Fifth Symphony* in D minor, in four classically outlined movements: (1) *Lento, Allegro con moto* in simple harmonious polyphony (2) *Intermezzo,* a bucolic eclogue (3) *Vivo,* a scherzo palpitating with jazzy rhythms in asymmetrical meters (4) *Lento, Allegro con moto,* coming to an assertive ending in the tonic major.

## 13 FEBRUARY 1943

*Prayer in Time of War* for orchestra by William SCHUMAN is performed for the first time in Pittsburgh.

## 14 FEBRUARY 1943

*Seventh Symphony,* surnamed *Sinfonia Romantica,* by the prime symphonist of Sweden, Kurt ATTERBERG, is performed for the first time in Frankfurt.

## 18 FEBRUARY 1943

*Die Kluge,* "a story of the King and the wise woman," in six scenes by the 47-year-old German composer Carl ORFF, to his own text derived from Grimm's fairy tale *Die kluge Bauerntochter* and synthesized with tales from China and Afghanistan, in which a rural damsel cunningly solves three crucial riddles propounded by a simple-minded king, written in a characteristically denuded solitonic melologue employing rhythmed speech, spoken song and singing melody, replete with obstinate ostinati and ostentatious repetition of ostensibly monothematic motives symbolizing the rough-shod wisdom of German peasantry, containing whimsical quotations in orchestral ritornelli from Mozart's *Entführung aus dem Serail,* is performed for the first time in Frankfurt.

## 23 FEBRUARY 1943

*Tania,* opera in one act by the 32-year-old Soviet composer Vasily DEKHTEREV, depicting the heroism of a Soviet girl guerrilla during the Nazi invasion of Russia in 1941, is produced in Moscow.

## 23 FEBRUARY 1943

*Violin Concerto* by the Dutch modernist Daniel RUYNEMAN is performed for the first time at a concert of the Concertgebouw Orchestra in Amsterdam.

## 26 FEBRUARY 1943

*Fifth Symphony* by Roy HARRIS, in three classically formal movements, *Prelude, Chorale* and *Fugue,* dedicated "to the heroic and freedom-loving people of our great ally, the Union of Soviet Socialist Republics, as a tribute to their strength in war, their staunch idealism for world peace, their ability to cope with stark materialistic problems of world order without losing a passionate belief in the fundamental importance of the arts," is performed for the first time by the Boston Symphony Orchestra, conducted by Serge Koussevitzky.

## 28 FEBRUARY 1943

*Complaintes du Soldat,* a melancholy triptych for voice and orchestra by André JOLIVET, is performed in Nazi-oppressed Paris.

## 28 FEBRUARY 1943

*Michelangelo,* oratorio by the 42-year-old Swiss composer Hans HAUG, is performed for the first time at Solothurn, Switzerland.

## 1 MARCH 1943

Three centuries have passed since the death in Rome of the great contrapuntist and master organist Girolamo FRESCOBALDI.

## 3 MARCH 1943

*Variationen für Orchester,* op. 30 by Anton VON WEBERN, comprising a theme with six variations, based on a symmetric 12-tone series, divisible into three segments of four notes each, of which the middle tetrad is identically self-invertible and self-reversible, while the outer tetrads are mutually invertible in their intervallic structure, the entire series consisting of two six-note intervallically mirrorable tropes, all these materials being treated in augmentation, diminution, canonic imitation and chordal integration of dodecaphonic ingredients, is performed for the first time in Winterthur, Switzerland, under the direction of Hermann Scherchen. (Exact date obtained from the Municipality of Winterthur)

Imagine this: six tones are given in a basic form, which is determined in respect to successive ordering and rhythm, and what follows is nothing but this same basic form over and over again!!! Goethe says about the "Primal Phenomenon" that it is "Ideal, because it is the last we can know/ Real, because we know it/ Symbolic, since it comprises all events/ Identical with all events." This is also the essence of my *Variations.* (Anton von Webern, in a letter written in 1943)

## 5 MARCH 1943

Morton GOULD, 29-year-old American composer of symphonic and light music, conducts the Pittsburgh Symphony Orchestra in the first performance of his *First Symphony.*

## 11 MARCH 1943

*Capriccio* for orchestra by the 25-year-old Austrian composer Gottfried VON EINEM is performed for the first time by the Berlin Philharmonic Orchestra.

## 12 MARCH 1943

*Fanfare for the Common Man* by Aaron COPLAND is sonorously heralded by the Cincinnati Symphony Orchestra.

## 23 MARCH 1943

Joseph SCHILLINGER, Russian musical scientist and composer, who devised a leviathanic Schillinger System of Composition, in which music is treated as a technology of sound, and proposed to train composers like mechanical engineers, dies in New York at the age of 47, at the peak of an astonishingly successful teaching career during which a whole pleiad of Broadway composers, including George Gershwin, flocked to his gadget-filled studio-laboratory in quest of instant musical knowledge.

## 26 MARCH 1943

*A Free Song,* secular cantata by William SCHUMAN (completed on 16 October 1942), to the text from Walt Whitman, couched in a propulsive rhythmic style as a 20th-century counterpart of old Handelian forms, is performed for the first time by the Boston Symphony Orchestra, Serge Koussevitzky conducting.

## 28 MARCH 1943

Serge RACHMANINOFF, last giant of the golden age of Russian music, great virtuoso pianist, composer of emotionally stirring, supremely pianistic concertos and preludes imperishable in their romantic appeal to successive generations of music lovers all over the world, dies of cancer and terminal pneumonia, at Beverly Hills, California, at 1:30 A.M. four days before his seventieth birthday.

## 31 MARCH 1943

*Oklahoma!*, a musical play by Richard RODGERS, with book and lyrics by Oscar Hammerstein, based on the play *Green Grow the Lilacs* by Lynn Riggs, depicting with ineffable nostalgia the rustic joys of 1900 in the virgin countryside of Oklahoma, containing such perennial favorites of the American musical theater as the bucolic opening number *Oh, What a Beautiful Mornin'*, and *The Surrey with the Fringe on Top*, is produced in New York. (Its run of 5 years and 9 weeks established a record for any Broadway musical play; prior to the New York production it was given a try-out in New Haven, under the title *Away We Go*, on 11 March 1943, and in Boston, under the same title, on 15 March 1943; it was only in New York that it acquired its permanent title with an exclamation point at the end)

## 1 APRIL 1943

*Das Schloss Dürande*, opera in four acts by the lyrical Swiss composer Othmar SCHOECK, to a romantic libretto from the time of the French Revolution, wherein a young Jacobin sets a royalist castle on fire circa 1790 to avenge his sister's ruin by its aristocratic owner, but realizes that their love was reciprocal and joins them in the holocaust himself, is performed for the first time at the Staatsoper in Berlin.

## 4 APRIL 1943

Raoul LAPARRA, 66-year-old French composer of romantic operas and Spanish-flavored symphonic music, is killed in an American air raid upon the Renault works near Paris.

## 13 APRIL 1943

*The Testament of Freedom* by Randall THOMPSON, for men's voices and orchestra, written for the 200th anniversary of the University of Virginia at Charlottesville, to a text from the writings of Thomas Jefferson, the University's founder, with a musical score conceived in the spirit of simplicity, leaving not a discord untamed in its prevalent C major, is presented for the first time by the Virginia Glee Club, with the composer at the piano.

## 17 APRIL 1943

*Le Nozze di Haura*, one-act opera by Adriano LUALDI, is performed for the first time in Rome, 35 years after its composition. (A radio performance of the opera was given in Rome on 19 October 1939)

768

## 12 MAY 1943

*Concerto* for coloratura soprano and orchestra by Reinhold GLIÈRE, in two movements of singable vocalization and considerable lyrical power without words, the first full-fledged vocal concerto of this genre, is performed for the first time in Moscow.

## 12 MAY 1943

Albert STOESSEL, 48-year-old American conductor and composer, collapses and dies of heart failure while conducting the ballad-poem *Dunkirk* by Walter Damrosch at the National Institute of Arts and Letters in New York, scored for baritone solo, solo chorus, piano and chamber orchestra, and dedicated to the heroes of the evacuation of Dunkirk by the British, with Walter Damrosch himself at the piano. (The world première of *Dunkirk* was given by the NBC Symphony Orchestra under the direction of the composer on 2 May 1943)

## 18 MAY 1943

José ARDÉVOL, 32-year-old Spanish-born Cuban composer, conducts in Havana the first performance of his choral ballet *Forma,* inspired by a solipsistic concept of an ego in flux, and arranged in a formal classical instrumental suite of court dances.

## 22 MAY 1943

To commemorate the 130th anniversary of WAGNER's birth, the Nazi occupation authorities of Bohemia and Moravia issue three commemorative postage stamps, with Wagner's portraits, in the denominations of 60 hellers, one krone 20 hellers and 2 kronen 50 hellers.

## 27 MAY 1943

The 46-year-old Norwegian composer Harald SAEVERUD conducts in Bergen the first performance of his *Sixth Symphony,* subtitled *Sinfonia Dolorosa,* in a single movement conceived in a national Scandinavian vein, with drums and bells marking the fortissimo ending.

## 1 JUNE 1943

To circumvent the prohibition by the Nazi authorities in occupied Paris to play music by Darius MILHAUD as a non-Aryan Frenchman making his home in America, Milhaud's *Scaramouche* for two pianos is performed by two Aryan French pianists at the École Normale de Musique in Paris, anagrammatically programmed as Mous-Arechac by Hamid-al-Usurid.

## 2 JUNE 1943

The Brazilian composer Camargo GUARNIERI conducts in São Paulo the first performance of his *Abertura concertante,* an orchestral overture in a baroque style seasoned with Brazilian melorhythms.

## 12 JUNE 1943

The American Army Task Force presents at Kiriwina Island in the Pacific, captured from the Japanese, the first concert of military band music, terrifying the natives by the jazzy sounds of brass instruments shining in the tropical sun.

## 15 JUNE 1943

To commemorate the centennial of the birth of Edvard GRIEG, the Nazi-dominated Quisling government of Norway issues a series of special stamps in the denominations of 10, 20, 40 and 60 øre.

## 21 JUNE 1943

Michael TIPPETT, 38-year-old English composer, director of music at Morley College, London, and a militant pacifist, is sentenced to three months' imprisonment in Wormwood Scrubs, Surrey, for violation of terms of his registration as a conscientious objector, and for failing to perform farm labor tasks assigned to him by the British Army.

## 24 JUNE 1943

VAUGHAN WILLIAMS conducts at the London Promenade Concerts the first performance of his *Fifth Symphony* in D major, dedicated "in sincere flattery" to Sibelius, marked by a somber serenity of musical utterance and developed by measured accretion of thematic substance, concomitant with cumulative rise and recession in dynamic strength, in four classically conceived movements: *Preludio, Scherzo, Romanza* (bearing an epigraph from Bunyan's *Pilgrim's Progress,* and using some thematic material from the subsequent opera of that title) and *Passacaglia.*

## 30 JUNE 1943

*La Vita è Sogno,* three-act opera, after Calderón, by Gian Francesco MALIPIERO, is performed for the first time anywhere in a German version, in Breslau.

## 5 JULY 1943

*Gli Dei a Tebe,* opera in three acts by the half-German half-Italian composer Ermanno WOLF-FERRARI, based on a Greek myth wherein Hera grants to Zeus a night of love with Amphitryon's wife, until the cuckoo in the Temple sacred to Hera signalizes the coming of dawn, is performed for the first time in Hannover, Germany, in the German version, under the title *Der Kukuck von Theben.*

## 8 JULY 1943

Lennox BERKELEY, 40-year-old English composer, conducts in London the first performance of his *First Symphony,* in four classically designed movements.

## 13 JULY 1943

The German ethnomusicologist Kurt HUBER, distinguished by his profound and valuable research in the field of German folk music, is beheaded by the Nazi executioner in Munich, on the charge of participation in student demonstrations and circulating anti-Hitlerian proclamations. (Exact date obtained from the Oberbürgermeister of Munich. Riemann's *Musiklexikon* gives the erroneous date 13 May 1943)

## 11 AUGUST 1943

*Second Concerto* for French horn and orchestra by Richard STRAUSS (completed on 28 November 1942) is performed for the first time in Salzburg.

## 15 AUGUST 1943

*Tivoli-Tivoli,* orchestral suite by the modern Danish composer Knudaage RIISAGER, a musical tribute to the famous central park Tivoli Gardens in Copenhagen, is performed for the first time at the summer concert series in the Tivoli Gardens in Copenhagen.

## 16 AUGUST 1943

During an Allied air attack on the industrial installations of Milan, a direct bomb hit is made on the Teatro alla Scala, destroying the auditorium, but, thanks to the protection of the steel curtain, leaving the stage intact. (The theater was restored after the war; the first post-war season was inaugurated on 11 May 1946, with Arturo Toscanini conducting)

## 19 AUGUST 1943

Ernest John MOERAN, 48-year-old English composer, plays at the London Promenade Concerts the solo part in the first performance of his *Rhapsody* for piano and orchestra.

## 20 AUGUST 1943

*Concerto* for violin and orchestra by the Mexican composer Manuel PONCE, in three movements, which incorporates his famous song *Estrellita* in the slow second movement, is performed for the first time in Mexico City, under the direction of Carlos Chávez.

## 25 AUGUST 1943

Morton GOULD conducts the first performance in New York of his *Interplay* for piano and orchestra, with José Iturbi as soloist, in four movements designated *With drive and vigor, Gavotte, Blues,* and *With verve and gusto,* written in a jaunty jazzy idiom replete with brave atonalities and saturated with non-harmonic additives (a section in the *Blues* is marked "Slow and dirty").

## 8 SEPTEMBER 1943

*Nadezhda Svetlova,* lyric opera in three acts by the Soviet composer Ivan DZERZHINSKY, to his own libretto dealing with the heroism of a surgeon and his daughter, an art student, in besieged Leningrad in 1941, is produced in Orenburg by members of the evacuated staff of the Leningrad Opera.

## 15 SEPTEMBER 1943

Hans HUMPERT, 42-year-old German composer of romantic symphonies and choral music, is killed in combat at Salerno, Italy, fighting in the German ranks against the American landing forces.

## 26 SEPTEMBER 1943

*Brébeuf and His Brethren,* historical musical pageant by the Canadian composer Healey WILLAN, scored for speaker, chorus and orchestra, is performed for the first time in Toronto as a commissioned work by the Canadian Broadcasting Corporation.

## 26 SEPTEMBER 1943

*The Four Freedoms,* symphonic suite by the American composer Robert Russell BENNETT, inspired by the famous speech of President Roosevelt, with Freedom of Speech exemplified by a tonal portrait of a street orator; Freedom of Worship by a stately anthem; Freedom from Want illustrated by a prosperous dance tune; and Freedom from Fear by a confident cradle song gradually evolving into a happy march, is performed for the first time in New York by the National Broadcasting Company Symphony Orchestra.

## 28 SEPTEMBER 1943

*Freedom Morning,* symphonic poem by the 38-year-old American composer Marc BLITZSTEIN for orchestra, tenor and chorus, dedicated to "all Negro troops in the service of the United States" and containing Negro spirituals in its thematic material, is performed for the first time at an Anglo-American concert in London with the participation of the London Symphony Orchestra, the Negro tenor Roland Hayes, and a Negro chorus of 200 members of aviation engineering units stationed in England.

## 7 OCTOBER 1943

*One Touch of Venus,* musical comedy by Kurt WEILL, dealing with a jesting New York barber who puts an engagement ring on the finger of a statue of Venus, whose marmoreal body thereupon changes to warm flesh, and who becomes his statuesque companion for life, is produced in New York.

## 8 OCTOBER 1943

*Ode* by Igor STRAVINSKY, in three parts *Eulogy, Eclogue, Epitaph,* "an elegiac chant" dedicated to the memory of Natalie Koussevitzky, wife of Serge Koussevitzky, as "an appreciation of her spiritual contribution to the art of the eminent conductor, in which the second part is a kind of concert champêtre, suggesting out-of-door music, an idea cherished by Natalie Koussevitzky," is performed for the first time by the Boston Symphony Orchestra, Serge Koussevitzky conducting.

## 9 OCTOBER 1943

Italo MONTEMEZZI conducts in New York the first performance of his opera *L'Incantesimo (Enchantment)*, in a radio broadcast over the network of the National Broadcasting Company.

## 10 OCTOBER 1943

*Barbe-Bleue*, comic opera by Jacques IBERT in which the fabled uxoricide (he painted his beard blue) is outwitted by his six wives and is reduced in the end to the humiliating status of the head of a bourgeois household with his seventh bride, is performed for the first time on the radio in Lausanne.

## 14 OCTOBER 1943

*Frontiers*, a symphonic musicorama in three tableaux by Paul CRESTON, depicting in rhapsodic tones "the westward American migration achieved through the vision, constancy and indomitable spirit of the pioneers," is performed for the first time by the Toronto Symphony Orchestra, André Kostelanetz conducting.

## 15 OCTOBER 1943

*Serenade* for tenor voice, horn solo and string orchestra by Benjamin BRITTEN, to poems of Ben Jonson, Blake, Keats, Tennyson and others, is performed for the first time in London.

## 15 OCTOBER 1943

*The Prairie*, orchestral suite by the 21-year-old Berlin-born American composer Lukas Foss, extracted from his cantata to the poem of Carl Sandburg of the same name, suggesting "vast open landscapes, and lots of fresh air," is performed for the first time by the Boston Symphony Orchestra, Serge Koussevitzky conducting. (The entire cantata was performed for the first time in New York on 15 May 1944 by the Collegiate Chorale, Robert Shaw conducting)

## 17 OCTOBER 1943

*Invasion*, symphonic sketch by Bernard ROGERS, portraying the hope and anxiety of the expectation of the imminent landing by the Allied forces in Nazi-infested Europe, cast in ominously somber harmonies, is performed for the first time by the New York Philharmonic, Artur Rodzinski conducting.

## 18 OCTOBER 1943

The National Theater of Munich, housing the Staatsoper built in 1818, is destroyed during an incendiary bomb attack by the Allied air forces.

## 22 OCTOBER 1943

Nicolai BEREZOWSKY, 43-year-old Russian-born American composer of euphoniously modernistic instrumental music, conducts the Boston Symphony Orchestra in the first performance of his *Fourth Symphony*, in four movements of cyclic design, with well-planned thematic retrospection at strategic musical points.

## 28 OCTOBER 1943

On the 25th anniversary of the establishment of Czechoslovakia as an independent republic after World War I, two orchestral works by the prime Czech composer Bohuslav MARTINU, making his temporary home in America, are given their world premières on the same day: *Memorial to Lidice*, a symphonic tribute to the martyrs of the Czech village destroyed by the Nazis, performed by the New York Philharmonic under the direction of Artur Rodzinski; and *Second Symphony* (composed between 29 June and 24 July 1943), played by the Cleveland Orchestra, Erich Leinsdorf conducting.

## 29 OCTOBER 1943

*Cupid and Psyche,* ballet overture by Paul HINDEMITH, inspired by an old Roman fresco, is performed for the first time by the Philadelphia Orchestra, Eugene Ormandy conducting.

## 29 OCTOBER 1943

*Commando March* by Samuel BARBER, originally written for military band and used on American short-wave broadcast throughout the world, is performed for the first time in its symphonic form by the Boston Symphony Orchestra, Serge Koussevitzky conducting.

## 29 OCTOBER 1943

Percy GOETSCHIUS, grand old man of American musical education, confirmed believer in the imminent goodness of Germanic academic classicism (he used to call the C-major scale "God's own scale"), dies in Manchester, New Hampshire, at the patriarchal age of ninety.

## 4 NOVEMBER 1943

*Eighth Symphony* by Dmitri SHOSTAKOVICH, conceived as a symphonic tragedy and reflecting the growing hope of liberation from the dark power of Nazi Germany, in five movements, of which the last three are played without pause: (1) *Adagio,* a demanding challenge to humanity locked in a mortal struggle, leading to a vigorous *Allegro* charged with kinetic energy in a fugally developed motion (2) *Allegretto,* a rondo in five distinct sections, throbbing with militant energy (3) *Allegro non troppo,* based on a persistent triadic motive achieving tremendous power, with the kettledrums repeating it 29 times and eventually subsiding to an echo of a military drum (4) *Largo,* a philosophical passacaglia and (5) *Finale,* set in resolutely optimistic C major, is performed for the first time in Leningrad conducted by Evgeny Mravinsky.

## 5 NOVEMBER 1943

*Concerto for Two Pianos and Orchestra* by Bohuslav MARTINU (composed in New York between 3 January and 23 February 1943), evocative of the poignant melorhythms of Moravian folk music, in three movements in the contrasting styles of brisk toccata, lyrical contemplation and propulsive rondo form, with lengthy cadenzas for each of the two pianos, is performed for the first time by the Philadelphia Orchestra under the direction of Eugene Ormandy, with Pierre Luboshutz and Genia Nemenoff as soloists.

## 6 NOVEMBER 1943

*Catulli Carmina,* scenic cantata to Latin texts from the poems of Catullus, by Carl ORFF, scored for voices, 4 pianos and percussion, with a cast of characters that includes Catullus himself, his beloved Lesbia, his friend Caelius (who surreptitiously takes Lesbia's place in the slumbering poet's bed), and assorted courtesans, couched in a percussively modernistic manner, with protracted iteration of single notes accompanied by polytonal harmonies, is performed for the first time in Leipzig.

## 12 NOVEMBER 1943

*Symphony for Strings* by William SCHUMAN, his *Fifth Symphony,* set in three movements: (1) *Molto agitato ed energico,* evolving from a theme played in unison by violins on the G string (2) *Larghissimo,* set in bitonal harmonies, and employing a novel effect of *fortissimo* on muted strings (3) *Presto leggiero,* written in a sophisticated jazz manner, is performed for the first time by the Boston Symphony Orchestra, Serge Koussevitzky conducting.

## 13 NOVEMBER 1943

On the 75th anniversary of the death of ROSSINI (whose acute triskaidekaphobia was aggravated by a superstitious fear of Fridays, and who died on 13 November 1868 which was a Friday), the Italian government issues a series of four postage stamps in his honor, of denominations of 25, 30 and 50 centesimi and one lira.

## 14 NOVEMBER 1943

Leonard BERNSTEIN, 25-year-old native of Lawrence, Massachusetts, youthful disciple of Serge Koussevitzky, makes a spectacular debut as associate conductor of the New York Philharmonic when he is called upon short notice as a substitute for the ailing Bruno Walter, and acquits himself sensationally in a challenging program including *Don Quixote* of Richard STRAUSS and an artfully intricate set of *Variations on a Hungarian Peasant Song* by the Hollywoodized Hungarian composer Miklós RÓZSA.

There are many variations of one of the six best stories in the world: the young corporal takes over the platoon when all the officers are down; the captain, with the dead

775

admiral at his side, signals the fleet to go ahead; the young actress, fresh from Corinth or Ashtabula, steps into the star's role; the junior clerk, alone in the office, makes the instantaneous decision that saves the firm from ruin. The adventure of Leonard Bernstein, 25-year-old assistant conductor of the Philharmonic, who blithely mounted the podium at Carnegie Hall Sunday afternoon when Conductor Bruno Walter became ill, belongs in the list. The corporals and captains must be brave, the young actress beautiful and talented, the clerk quick on his feet. Likewise, Mr. Bernstein had to have something approaching genius to make full use of his opportunity. It's a good American success story. The warm, friendly triumph of it filled Carnegie Hall and spread far over the air waves. (*A Story Old and Ever New,* Editorial in the New York *Times,* 16 November 1943)

### 15 NOVEMBER 1943

With the German Army in full retreat only a few miles away, the San Carlo Opera House in Naples reopens its season after the theater is cleaned up and the bomb damage repaired.

### 17 NOVEMBER 1943

*The Anxious Bugler,* orchestral sketch by the American composer-industrialist John Alden CARPENTER, depicting in folksy tones the emotions of "any boy anywhere, who finds himself a soldier," is performed for the first time by the New York Philharmonic, Artur Rodzinski conducting.

### 25 NOVEMBER 1943

*Fredlös (The Outlaw),* opera by the 56-year-old Swedish composer Oskar LINDBERG, after a short story by Selma Lagerlöf, is produced in Stockholm.

### 26 NOVEMBER 1943

Gardner READ, 30-year-old American composer, conducts the Boston Symphony Orchestra in the first performance of his *Second Symphony* in three movements, cast in impressively somber, somewhat Nordic, sonorities in the manner of Sibelius, with concealed rhythmic energies periodically released in frenetic eruptions.

### 29 NOVEMBER 1943

Three centuries have passed since the death in Venice of Claudio MONTEVERDI, initiator of the true operatic style of stage music as a glorified elaboration of the dramatic madrigal achieving an inspired coalescence of instrumental polyphony with vocal monody.

### 2 DECEMBER 1943

*Carmen Jones,* a Negro version of Bizet's *Carmen,* to a new Americanized libretto by Oscar HAMMERSTEIN II, with the score reorchestrated by Robert Russell BENNETT, and the scene of action transferred from Seville to an American parachute factory during World War II, in which Carmen is employed,

776

Don José is a military guard who goes AWOL for her sake, and the toreador a prize fighter, is produced in New York with an all-Negro cast.

### 3 DECEMBER 1943

Howard HANSON conducts the Boston Symphony Orchestra in the first performance of his *Fourth Symphony*, subtitled *Requiem*, dedicated to the memory of his father and written in a fervid devotional style, in four movements named after the parts of the Latin service for the dead, *Kyrie, Requiescat, Dies Irae* and *Lux Aeterna*, and ending softly on a mysteriously inconclusive first inversion of the C-major triad as a pledge of faith in an eventual conversion to the eternal tonic.

### 4 DECEMBER 1943

The stockrooms and the building of the historic German publishing firm Brietkopf & Härtel are destroyed in an Allied air raid on Leipzig, cremating many engraved treasures of past musical glories, with only a few copper plates of the works by great composers recovered from the ashes. (Manuscripts and precious memorabilia had been saved from destruction through the heroic efforts of employees who had deposited them in rural air-raid shelters)

### 6 DECEMBER 1943

*Opus Americanum*, a symphonic tribute to America by Darius MILHAUD in gratitude for American hospitality to him in a temporary refuge from subjugated France, is performed for the first time by the San Francisco Symphony Orchestra, Pierre Monteux conducting.

### 8 DECEMBER 1943

*Twenty-Fourth Symphony* by the most prolific 20th-century symphonist Nicolai MIASKOVSKY (completed on 3 September 1943), in F minor, in three movements, written in a lyrical Russian style contrasted with dramatic episodes in fanfare-like sonorities, is performed for the first time in Moscow.

### 10 DECEMBER 1943

*Biblical Scenes*, triptych for orchestra by the Hungarian-American composer Eugene ZÁDOR, with three sections portraying Joseph as the symbol of innocence, David as a symbol of victory over superior forces and Paul in his dual role as Saul, persecutor of Christ, and as Paul, Christ's great disciple, is performed for the first time by the Chicago Symphony.

### 16 DECEMBER 1943

Bernard HERRMANN, 32-year-old American composer, conducts the New York Philharmonic in the first performance of his symphonic elegy *For the Fallen*, "a berceuse for those who lie asleep on the many alien battlefields," with a consolatory quotation from Handel's *Messiah* in the coda.

The first performance is given in Moscow of the *Second Symphony* by the 40-year-old Soviet Armenian composer Aram KHACHATURIAN, described as *Symphony of Bells* by some Soviet commentators on account of the introduction of large church bells in the score suggesting the impact of bombs on bronze, a war-generated work in four movements:

(1) *Andante maestoso,* in which the "bell motive" dominates the musical scene alternating with a songful theme, and ending in a resolute march (2) *Allegro risoluto,* a somber dance with macabre overtones relieved briefly by lyric interludes (3) *Andante sostenuto,* a tragic elegy reflecting the immense sufferings of the Soviet people inflicted by the brutal Nazi war machine, with the ominous tones of *Dies irae* rising from the depths as a universal motive of death and lamentation (4) *Andante mosso; Allegro sostenuto,* voicing the faith in ultimate triumph over the dark enemy forces in sonorous fanfares and culminating in a grand declaration of expected victory raising the oriflamme of the confident brass to the sound of great church bells symbolic of eternal impregnable and holy Russia.

## 31 DECEMBER 1943

*Concerto* for violin and orchestra by Bohuslav MARTINU in three movements, (1) *Andante; Allegro* (2) *Poco moderato* (3) *Poco allegro,* cast in a lyrico-dramatic vein, alternating between classically terse and rhapsodically emotional moods, tonally lucid but occasionally ramifying into euphonious bitonalities, is performed for the first time by Mischa Elman, for whom it was written, and the Boston Symphony Orchestra, under the direction of Serge Koussevitzky.

# ✑ *1944* ✑

## 5 JANUARY 1944

*In Memoriam: The Colored Soldiers Who Died for Democracy,* symphonic paragraph by William Grant STILL, the American Negro composer, one of a series of works commissioned by the League of Composers of New York in dedication to an aspect of World War II, is performed for the first time by the New York Philharmonic, Artur Rodzinski conducting.

## 13 JANUARY 1944

Igor STRAVINSKY conducts the Boston Symphony Orchestra in Cambridge, Massachusetts, the first performances of his symphonic suite *Four Norwegian Moods* (originally designed for a motion picture about Norway), written "without any assumption of ethnological authenticity," and making use of Norwegian folk tunes "only as a rhythmic and melodic basis," and the orchestral version of his *Circus Polka,* written in Hollywood on 15 February 1942 for the elephant dance commissioned by the Ringling Brothers Circus, and devised in the manner of sophisticated grotesquerie with the insertion of a quotation from Schubert's *Marche Militaire* in a polyharmonic arrangement, prefacing the concert with his own version of *The Star-Spangled Banner*, containing an unorthodox modulation into the subdominant in the cadence, thereby running afoul of a Massachusetts statute forbidding any tampering with the national anthem.

Searching about for a vehicle through which I might best express my gratitude at becoming an American citizen, I chose to harmonize and orchestrate as a national chorale the beautiful sacred anthem *The Star-Spangled Banner*. It is a desire to do my bit in these grievous times toward fostering and preserving the spirit of patriotism in this country that inspires me to tender this, my humble work, to the American people. (Stravinsky's statement in English, upon completing his arrangement on 4 July 1941)

Mr. Stravinsky's harmonies seemed a little queer to the New Englanders of today. In response to complaints, Boston Police Commissioner Thomas F. Sullivan and Police Captain Thomas F. Harvey appeared at the Saturday concert, 15 January 1944, flanked by six members of the "radical squad" prepared to sign a complaint charging Mr. Stravinsky with violation of chapter 264, Section 9, of the Massachusetts laws which forbids rearrangement of the national anthem and provides a penalty of $100. But the performance of the new version was cancelled, the police refrained from taking action, and quiet was restored to the banks of the Charles. (*Musical America*, New York, January, 1944)

### 20 JANUARY 1944

*Symphonic Metamorphoses on Themes of Carl Maria von Weber* by Paul HINDEMITH, in four movements: (1) *Allegro,* an astute variation derived from four-hand piano music of Weber (2) *Turandot-Scherzo,* with thematic material taken from Weber's score of incidental music to Schiller's play of that name, titivated by percussive chinoiserie, and containing a jazzy fugue launched by the trombones in unison (3) *Andantino,* an artful transmogrification of an innocent Weber piece for piano duet (4) *March,* a magnisonant fanfaronade of vigesimosecular polyphony, is performed for the first time by the New York Philharmonic under the direction of Artur Rodzinski.

### 21 JANUARY 1944

André JOLIVET conducts in Nazi-held Paris the first performance of his first "radiophonic legend" *La Queste de Lancelot,* inspired by Arthurian legends.

### 27 JANUARY 1944

*Concerto for Saxophone and Orchestra* by Paul CRESTON, in three movements designated (1) *Energetic* (2) *Meditative* (3) *Rhythmic,* is performed for the first time by the New York Philharmonic with Vincent Abato as soloist and William Steinberg conducting.

### 28 JANUARY 1944

*Mexican Hayride,* musical comedy by Cole PORTER, in which an American female bullfighter, sensationally successful in Mexico, abandons her New York

779

gangster lover in favor of a well-mannered American diplomat, set to music in an ingratiating Mexican-flavored style, is produced in New York.

### 28 JANUARY 1944

Leonard BERNSTEIN, 25-year-old American composer and conductor, leads the Pittsburgh Symphony Orchestra in the première of his *First Symphony* entitled *Jeremiah*, in three movements, *Prophecy, Profanation, Lamentation*, intended "to parallel in feeling the intensity of the prophet's pleas with his people," embodying in its thematic content both the ritualistically devotional and primitivistically orgiastic elements of Hebrew music, with the voice of the prophet in the finale intoning sacred verses in the original Hebrew.

### 30 JANUARY 1944

*Summer Rhapsody*, by the 46-year-old Danish composer Knudaage RIISAGER, based on Danish folksongs, is performed for the first time in Copenhagen.

### 2 FEBRUARY 1944

Yvette GUILBERT, Paris chanteuse who was erotically immortalized by Toulouse-Lautrec in his flamboyant posters depicting her with flying petticoats and multi-plumed chapeaux, dies in Aix-en-Provence at the age of seventy-seven.

### 5 FEBRUARY 1944

*Prinzessin Turandot*, ballet by the 26-year-old Austrian composer Gottfried VON EINEM, on the subject of a cruel Chinese princess who put to death a number of unlucky suitors, is performed for the first time in Dresden.

### 6 FEBRUARY 1944

*Piano Concerto* by Arnold SCHOENBERG, op. 42 (completed in Hollywood on 30 December 1942), in a single movement articulated into four classically contrasted sections, containing distinct elements of an introduction, a scherzo, a slow interlude and a rondo, thematically built on a unifying 12-tone series, E-flat, B-flat, D, F, E, C, F-sharp, G-sharp, C-sharp, A, B, G, and displaying despite its strict dodecaphonic organization a surprising liberality towards tonality and even triadic permissiveness, terminating with an incandescently white major seventh-chord anchored in deep C, is performed for the first time in New York with Eduard Steuermann as soloist and Leopold Stokowski conducting the Orchestra of the National Broadcasting Company.

### 7 FEBRUARY 1944

Lina CAVALIERI, Italian lyric soprano, renowned at the turn of the century as "la donna più bella del mondo," and whose first three husbands were a Russian prince, an American millionaire and a French tenor, perishes tragically with her fourth husband, an Italian nobleman, when a bomb falls on her villa near Florence during an American air raid.

## 8 FEBRUARY 1944

*Violin Concerto* by the Soviet composer Lev KNIPPER is performed for the first time in Moscow.

## 11 FEBRUARY 1944

*Third Symphony* by the Soviet composer Vissarion SHEBALIN, in four classically symmetric movements, culminating in a magisterial fugue in the optimistic key of C major, is performed for the first time in Moscow.

## 13 FEBRUARY 1944

*Fourth Symphony* by the 43-year-old American composer George ANTHEIL, erstwhile *enfant terrible* of music, cast in his newly adopted un-modern idiom, adhering to explicit tonality and rhythmically symmetric, concluding on a jubilant E-flat major triad, is performed for the first time in New York, with Leopold Stokowski conducting the Symphony Orchestra of the National Broadcasting Company.

## 15 FEBRUARY 1944

*Ludus Tonalis,* piano suite by Paul HINDEMITH, subtitled "Studies in Counterpoint, Tonal Organization and Piano Playing," a "tonal game" without key signatures, cast in dissonant linear counterpoint, with the Prelude and the Postlude being upside-down retrograde conjugates of each other (allowing for non-retroactive accidentals), is performed for the first time at the University of Chicago.

## 16 FEBRUARY 1944

Edmund VON BORCK, German composer of neo-classical instrumental music, is killed in the ranks of the German Army during the fighting in Italy near Nettuno, six days before his 38th birthday.

## 17 FEBRUARY 1944

*William Billings Overture* by William SCHUMAN, built on themes from three choral works by "America's first professional composer, William Billings," is performed for the first time by the New York Philharmonic, Artur Rodzinski conducting.

## 19 FEBRUARY 1944

Nicolai MEDTNER, 64-year-old romantic Russian pianist and composer, expatriated in England since the Revolution deprived him of his native habitat, plays, with the London Philharmonic under the direction of Sir Adrian Boult, the solo part in the first performance of his *Third Piano Concerto* in E minor, subtitled *Ballade,* dedicated to the Maharaja of Mysore "with deep gratitude for the appreciation and furtherance of my work" (the Maharaja, like a Rex ex machina manifested himself at a most critical moment of Medtner's financial distress and gave him munificent support), conceived in an ascetically re-strained contrapuntal idiom, in three movements:

(1) *Con moto largamente,* freely modulating from austere hexatonic modalities into keys situated in chromatic propinquity, and spreading copious pianistic cadenzas across the breadth of the keyboard (2) *Interludium,* a diptych of variations on pre-viously stated themes (3) *Finale: Allegro molto, svegliando eroico,* in rondo form, cul-minating in a heroically rhetorical declaration of musical faith in E major.

### 19 FEBRUARY 1944

Burnet TUTHILL conducts the St. Louis Symphony Orchestra in the first per-formance of his orchestral rhapsody *Come Seven,* intended not as "a musical description of the well-known gutter game," but reflecting "an attempt to compose in seven rhythm," with 11/8 ending, emblematic of the consumma-tion of the ardent wishes of all players of crap, "seven, come eleven."

### 21 FEBRUARY 1944

*Ballad of a Boy Who Remained Unknown,* cantata by Sergei PROKOFIEV, in-spired by the real story of a young Soviet partisan who blew up the Nazi staff automobile in a Nazi-occupied Russian village where his mother and sister were murdered by the invaders, is performed for the first time in Moscow.

### 23 FEBRUARY 1944

*Ode to the Red Army,* cantata by Sir Arnold BAX, to a poem by John Masefield, British Poet Laureate, written in homage to Soviet soldiers ("Though flanks were turned and center gone/ You stood for home and strug-gled on/ And now you reap reward; the line/ Comes west again; the foes de-cline"), is performed in London as a tribute to the Red Army on the 26th an-niversary of its founding.

### 25 FEBRUARY 1944

*Missa Oecumenica* for soli, chorus, organ and orchestra by Alexandre GRETCHANINOFF, 79-year-old Russian expatriate composer living in New York, "inspired by the idea of the ecumenic significance of the church," set to the Latin words of the Mass and containing the characteristics of both the Russian orthodox church and the Roman Catholic ritual, is performed for the first time by the Boston Symphony Orchestra, Serge Koussevitzky conducting.

### 1 MARCH 1944

Hans KRÁSA, 44-year-old Prague-born Jewish composer of finely wrought music sensitized by anguished atonalities, perishes in the Nazi concentration camp at Auschwitz.

### 1 MARCH 1944

*Hudson River Legend,* ballet by the 44-year-old American composer Joseph WAGNER, to a scenario after Washington Irving's story of supernatural phenomena in colonial America, with a moderately modernistic score featuring among other things a Geometry Dance, is performed by the Boston Civic Symphony Orchestra, Arthur Fiedler conducting.

## 3 MARCH 1944

*Second Symphony* by Samuel BARBER, in three movements gravitating towards the focal tonic F-sharp: (1) *Allegro ma non troppo* (2) *Andante un poco mosso* (3) *Presto,* dedicated to the U.S. Army Air Forces and incorporating in the second movement an electrical tone generator simulating the rhythmic radio signal code, with a spirally mounting melody in the finale expressing the rapid ascent in flight, is performed for the first time by the Boston Symphony Orchestra, Serge Koussevitzky conducting.

(The Symphony was revised in 1947, eliminating all navigational allusions, and first performed in this new demilitarized version at the Curtis Institute of Music in Philadelphia on 5 January 1949, and publicly by the Philadelphia Orchestra on 21 January 1949)

## 5 MARCH 1944

*Second Symphony* by Walter PISTON in three movements, a bithematically classical *Moderato,* a candidly lyrical *Adagio,* and a trithematical *Allegro,* with some Americanisms audible despite the composer's rejection of conscious musical nationalism ("Is the Dust Bowl more American than, say, a corner in the Boston Athenaeum? . . . The composer cannot afford the wild-goose chase of trying to be more American than he is"), is performed for the first time, as a commissioned work, by the National Symphony Orchestra in Washington, Hans Kindler conducting.

## 13 MARCH 1944

VILLA-LOBOS conducts in Rio de Janeiro the first performance of his *Bachianas Brasileiras No. 7* for string orchestra, designed to express his fervid Brazilianism in terms of Bach's polyphony, in four sections, with Bachian titles, *Prelude, Gigue, Toccata, Fugue,* and Brazilian subtitles, *Ponteio, Quadrilha, Desafio, Conversa.*

## 15 MARCH 1944

*Hymn of the Bolshevik Party* by Alexander ALEXANDROV, conductor of the Red Army Band, with a new set of words stressing the national rather than the political point, is adopted by the Soviet Government as the official anthem of the Union of Soviet Socialist Republics to replace the Internationale, reserved only for purely Communistic functions.

## 18 MARCH 1944

A century has passed since the birth in Tikhvin, at 4:53 P.M., local time, of Nicolas RIMSKY-KORSAKOV, supreme artificer of gorgeously painted Russian musicscapes limned in luminously bright orchestral colors.

19 MARCH 1944

*A Child of Our Time,* oratorio for chorus and orchestra by the 39-year-old English composer Michael TIPPETT, to his own libretto, inspired by the act of a young Jewish boy who shot a German diplomat in Paris in November 1938, in three parts symbolizing (1) General state of the world as it affects nations, societies and individuals (2) Conflict between personal destiny and over- whelming social forces (3) Synthesis of a man's shadow with a man's light, with a musical setting of multiple derivations, incorporating five Negro spirit- uals in the score as symbols of inhumane persecution, is performed for the first time at Morley College, London, under the direction of the expatriate German conductor Walter Goehr.

14 APRIL 1944

*Sixth Symphony* by Roy HARRIS, in four movements subtitled *Awakening, Conflict, Dedication, Affirmation,* symbolizing the four states of Abraham Lin- coln's mind during the Civil War (the score was completed on Lincoln's birthday, 12 February 1944, which also was the composer's 46th birthday), set in the appropriate tones of civic exaltation, with tense bitonal harmonies ex- pressing moods of expectation, strife, devotion and faith, is performed for the first time by the Boston Symphony Orchestra, Serge Koussevitzky conducting.

14 APRIL 1944

*Führerworte,* oratorio by the 29-year-old German composer Gottfried MÜLLER, dedicated to the "heroes of the German fight of destiny" to texts reverently selected from Hitler's speeches, with the Führer's applosive sen- tences nearly submerged in a magma of neo-gothic polyphony, with a brassy ending in the key of C major intended to symbolize the purity of Nazi ideals, is performed for the first time in Dresden.

18 APRIL 1944

Leonard BERNSTEIN, 25-year-old American-born conductor and composer, conducts at the Metropolitan Opera House in New York the première of his one-act ballet *Fancy Free,* written in a popular Broadway manner, with a sce- nario in which three sailors, with only two girls on their hands, play a roman- tic American roulette for their favors and in the end set off to chase after a third girl.

18 APRIL 1944

*Tale of the Battle for the Russian Land,* a patriotic cantata in twelve scenes by the Soviet composer Yury SHAPORIN: (1) *A Spring Day* (2) *Invasion* (3) *Women's Lament* (4) *An Old Man's Word* (5) *Red Army Singing* (6) *Letter to a Friend* (7) *Ballad of the Partisans* (8) *On the Banks of the Volga River* (9) *On the Steppes of the Don River* (10) *Eternal Glory* (11) *The Oath* (12) *The Re- turn of Spring,* picturing in heroic Russian modalities the awesome chronology of the Nazi invasion of Russia in 1941, the crucial battles of 1942 and the turn of the tide in 1943, is performed for the first time in Moscow.

## 18 APRIL 1944

Cécile CHAMINADE, French composeress of ingratiatingly harmonious piano pieces adorned with endearingly sentimental titles, possessing a perennial appeal to frustrated spinsters and emotional piano teachers, dies in war-darkened Monte Carlo at the hopeless age of eighty-six.

## 24 APRIL 1944

P. Kilian KIRCHHOFF, learned German analyst of Byzantine hymnography, translator of the complete Kanons and Stichera of the Byzantine Triodion and Pentekostarion, is beheaded by the Nazi executioner in Brandenburg for his militant opposition to the infamous deeds of the Nazi government.

## 26 APRIL 1944

*Arctic Forest,* symphonic poem by the Japanese composer Akira IFUKUBE, is performed for the first time in Chungchung, in Japanese-occupied China.

## 27 APRIL 1944

*Night Flight,* tone poem by the 31-year-old American composer Gardner READ, depicting in impressionistic harmonies and coloristic instrumentation the flight of Antoine de St.-Exupery, is performed for the first time in Rochester, New York, under the direction of Howard Hanson, on the same program with the *First Symphony* by the 35-year-old American composer Elliott CARTER, in three movements designated *Moderately and Wistfully, Andante serioso, Rondo,* and inspired by "the characteristic beauties of Cape Cod" where the work was written.

## 29 APRIL 1944

*Guignol et Pandore,* surrealist ballet in one act by André JOLIVET, in which Guignol, the director of a puppet theater, himself becomes a marionette, culminating in the seduction of Guignol's wife by one of the puppets named Pandore, is produced in Nazi-occupied Paris.

## 6 MAY 1944

Carl ENGEL, Paris-born American writer of urbane musical prose, librarian, editor, bibliographer, dies in New York at the age of sixty.

## 8 MAY 1944

Dame Ethel Mary SMYTH, British composeress who was periodically gaoled as a militant suffragette, and whose Wagneromantic operas reflected her distinctly mannish personality, dies in Woking, Surrey, at the purposeless age of eighty-six.

## 12 MAY 1944

*The Passion,* oratorio by the American composer Bernard ROGERS, aiming at expressionistic realism (non-tempered scales are employed in the prayer on the Cross), with an ending on an integral quintal tonal pillar containing all the 12 notes of the cycle of fifths from low C to high F, is performed for the first time at the May Festival in Cincinnati, under the direction of Eugene Goossens.

### 12 MAY 1944

*Obertura para el Fausto Criollo*, symphonic overture by the 28-year-old Argentinian composer Alberto GINASTERA, portraying the strange sensations of a gaucho from the pampas attending a production of Gounod's *Faust* at the Teatro Colón in Buenos Aires, is performed for the first time anywhere in Santiago, Chile.

### 12 MAY 1944

To commemorate the 60th anniversary of the death of the national Czech composer Bedřich SMETANA, the Nazi-controlled government of Bohemia and Moravia issues a series of postage stamps with his portrait at the denominations of 60 hellers, one krone 40 hellers, one krone 70 hellers and 3 kronen 80 hellers.

### 30 MAY 1944

To commemorate the centennial of the birth of RIMSKY-KORSAKOV, the Soviet government issues a series of postage stamps at the denominations of 30 kopecks, 60 kopecks, one ruble and 3 rubles.

### 4 JUNE 1944

*Symphony on Marching Tunes* by Morton GOULD, composed in celebration of the centennial of the Young Men's Christian Association, in four movements, *March Variations, Bivouac, Quickstep, Memorial*, derived mainly from Civil War campfire ballads and fast dances, is performed for the first time by the New York Philharmonic, during its summer concerts in New York.

### 5 JUNE 1944

Riccardo ZANDONAI, Italian composer of romantically flamboyant operas in the tradition of modern Verismo, dies in Pesaro at the age of sixty-one.

### 11 JUNE 1944

On his 80th birthday, Richard STRAUSS conducts the Vienna Philharmonic in a program of his works in the afternoon and attends a broadcast performance of his opera *Ariadne auf Naxos* at the Vienna Staatsoper in the evening.

### 18 JUNE 1944

Sylvio LAZZARI, French composer of Wagneromorphic operas to melodramatic librettos from contemporary life, glossed over with a fine impressionistic patina, dies in Nazi-infested Paris at the superannuated age of eighty-six.

## 18 JUNE 1944

*Sonatina No. 1* for 16 wind instruments by Richard STRAUSS (completed by him on 22 July 1943) is performed for the first time in war-darkened Dresden.

## 30 JUNE 1944

As the twilight of the Nazi gods draws near, WAGNER's *Götterdämmerung* is performed at the Vienna Opera House, marking with symbolic irony the conclusion of the last wartime season in that glorious edifice of obsolete Austrian splendor before its utter destruction during the Allied air raid of 12 March 1945.

## 2 JULY 1944

A few days before the closure of all theaters in Germany as a war measure, the comic opera *Die Hochzeit des Jobs* in four acts by the academically romantic German composer Joseph HAAS, dealing with a German university student who fails in his examination in Roman law in 1800 but wins the hand of his landlady's daughter, is produced in Dresden.

## 3 JULY 1944

*The Song of Norway*, a musical pastiche of Grieg's music, macerated by Robert Wright and George Forrest to make it accessible to public taste, with Grieg's *Piano Concerto* serving as the motto, wherein Grieg himself appears as a romantic hero saved from the immoral clutches of a scheming Italian prima donna by the constructive devotion of his future wife, is produced in San Francisco. (The first New York production took place on 21 August 1944)

## 4 JULY 1944

*La Gageure imprévue,* one-act comic opera by the 43-year-old French composer Henri SAUGUET, is produced at the Opéra-Comique in Paris.

## 22 JULY 1944

*Berlenhemd,* opera in two acts by the Alsatian composer Leo Justinus KAUFFMANN, is produced in Strasbourg, during the German occupation.

## 29 JULY 1944

*Of New Horizons,* overture by the 27-year-old Arizona-born American Negro composer Ulysses S. KAY, written in an optimistic Americanistic manner maintaining a hedonistic momentum of positivistic 4/4 time throughout the work, opening and ending in clear D major, but devoid of an explicit key signature to allow freedom of modulatory action, is performed for the first time by the New York Philharmonic at the Lewisohn Stadium in New York.

## 19 AUGUST 1944

Sir Henry WOOD, English symphonic and choral conductor, indefatigable champion of British music, who in the words of Arnold Bax "purified and en-

riched the musical taste of at least two generations," dies in Hitchin, Hert-
shire, at the age of seventy-five.

## 23 AUGUST 1944

Nicolai ROSLAVETZ, Russian composer who early in the century wrote atonal
music and was subsequently hounded by the reactionary Association of Proletarian Musicians for his progressive musical ideas, dies in obscurity in Moscow
at the age of sixty-three.

## 3 SEPTEMBER 1944

*Theme and Variations According to the Four Temperaments* by Paul
HINDEMITH, scored for string orchestra and piano, depicting in spacious neo-
Baroque modalities the four "humors" of medieval biology—melancholy (in
muted violins, followed by a manic-depressive march), sanguine (a hedonistic
waltz), phlegmatic (in turgid motion), and choleric (in vigorously impassioned
rhythms)—is performed for the first time in Boston under the direction of
Richard Burgin.

## 25 SEPTEMBER 1944

Leo Justinus KAUFFMANN, 43-year-old German composer and professor of the
Strasbourg Conservatory under the Nazi regime since the German occupation
of the city in 1940, is killed in Strasbourg at noon during an Allied air raid.

## 30 SEPTEMBER 1944

*Concerto* in A minor for oboe and string orchestra by Ralph VAUGHAN
WILLIAMS in three movements, *Rondo pastorale, Minuet* and *Finale-Scherzo*,
is performed for the first time by Leon Goossens, to whom it is dedicated,
with the Liverpool Philharmonic Orchestra conducted by Malcolm Sargent.

## 8 OCTOBER 1944

*Capricorn Concerto* for flute, oboe, trumpet and strings by Samuel BARBER, so
named after the composer's house at Mt. Kisco, New York, is performed for
the first time in New York.

## 13 OCTOBER 1944

*Second Symphony* by David DIAMOND, in four movements, *Adagio funebre,
Allegro vivo (Scherzo), Andante espressivo quasi adagio, Allegro vigoroso*,
traversing the moods of elegiac lyricism, mocking gayety, somber reflection
and optimistic expectation, making use of atonally inclined melodies in tren-
chantly multitonal harmonies vivified by aggressively tilted rhythms, is performed for the first time by the Boston Symphony Orchestra, Serge Koussevitzky conducting.

It was in no way my intention to have the musical substance represent specific emotional reactions or to conjure up programmatic fantasies. I have a horror of anything as

788

prosaic as that. My emotional life and reactions to certain events and situations have worked hand in hand with purely abstract musical conception and manipulation of material; and it was always the material that remained foremostly important to me in my working stages. (From David Diamond's declaration in the Boston Symphony program book)

## 16 OCTOBER 1944

The first version of the opera *War and Peace* by Sergei PROKOFIEV after Tolstoy's epic novel, in eleven scenes, to his own libretto written in a collaboration with his second wife Myra Mendelson, set to music in a heroic Russian style, with grandly developed panoramic musical tableaux in strongly tonal but constantly fluctuating harmonies, containing arias in an expansively melodic idiom, vitalized by vibrant rhythmic flow, is produced in Moscow.

(Composition began on 15 August 1941 in Nalchik, Caucasus, where Prokofiev stayed as the Nazis approached Moscow; vocal score completed in Tbilisi on 13 April 1942; orchestration finished in Alma-Ata, Turkmenia, in April 1943. The number of scenes was subsequently extended to 13, with a symmetrical division of subject matter, the first 6 scenes describing the period of peace and emphasizing the lyric, personal and psychological qualities in arias, duets and vocal ensembles; the middle scene representing transition to war, and the last six scenes portraying the war itself in its dramatic, social and national aspects, mainly in massive choral episodes. Part I, comprising eight scenes, was performed for the first time in Leningrad on 12 June 1946, forming a nucleus of the second version, which was completed in 1947; the third and final version, calculated to compress the entire opera into a single evening, was completed in 1952; it preserves the original 13 scenes with many cuts in secondary episodes; the cast of characters numbers 72 dramatis personae)

## 17 OCTOBER 1944

*Letter from Home* by Aaron COPLAND, an unpretentious symphonic recitative for chamber orchestra, reflecting the emotions associated with the receipt of reassuring news, is performed for the first time by Paul Whiteman and the Philco Radio Orchestra in New York. (A version for full orchestra was first performed by the Cleveland Symphony Orchestra, on 27 February 1947, under the direction of George Szell)

## 19 OCTOBER 1944

*First Symphony* by the 44-year-old American composer Joseph WAGNER, in three cyclic movements, is performed for the first time in Rochester, Howard Hanson conducting.

## 20 OCTOBER 1944

*Theme and Variations for Orchestra*, op. 43b (op. 43a is scored for band) by Arnold SCHOENBERG, bearing the explicit key signature of G major, and constituting his second reversion to tonal writing in ten years (the first was his *Suite for String Orchestra,* also in G major, composed in 1934), with a march-like subject non-atonally transfigured in seven variations, and the Finale "using motival and harmonic features of the themes, thus producing new themes of contrasting character and mood," is performed for the first time by the Boston Symphony Orchestra, Serge Koussevitzky conducting.

When I had finished my first *Kammersymphonie,* op. 9, I told my friends: "Now I have established my style. I know now how I have to compose." But my next work showed a great deviation from this style; it was a first step toward my present style. My destiny had forced me in this direction—I was not destined to continue in the manner of *Verklärte Nacht* or *Gurrelieder* or even *Pelléas und Mélisande.* The Supreme Commander had ordered me on a harder road. But a longing to return to the older style was always vigorous in me; and from time to time I had to yield to that urge. This is how and why I sometimes write tonal music. To me stylistic differences of this nature are not of special importance. I do not know which of my compositions are better; I like them all, because I liked them when I wrote them. (From Schoenberg's article *One Always Returns* in the New York *Times,* 19 December 1948)

### 21 OCTOBER 1944

*Fugue on a Victory Tune* by Walter PISTON, one of a long series of wartime pieces commissioned by the League of Composers of New York, is performed for the first time by the New York Philharmonic, Artur Rodzinski conducting.

### 22 OCTOBER 1944

*Chant de Libération* for baritone, chorus and orchestra by Arthur HONEGGER, composed in German-occupied Paris in 1942, is performed for the first time in liberated Paris.

### 24 OCTOBER 1944

*A Stopwatch and an Ordnance Map,* a realistic piece of wartime music by Samuel BARBER, scored for men's chorus and kettledrums, is performed for the first time in Columbus, Ohio.

### 26 OCTOBER 1944

*Miracle in the Gorbals,* ballet by Sir Arthur BLISS, dealing with the miraculous resuscitation of a completely dead suicide wrought by a mysterious stranger in the Gorbals slums of Glasgow, is produced in London.

### 30 OCTOBER 1944

Martha Graham and her dance group give in Washington the first performance of *Appalachian Spring,* "ballet for Martha" by Aaron COPLAND, named after the title of a poem by Hart Crane (though unrelated to its content), a vivid musicorama in seven scenes depicting in tonally pellucid harmonies equipped with unequivocal key signatures the time of spring in the Appalachian foothills in early 19th-century Pennsylvania, around a farmhouse built for a newly married couple, with the groom, the bride and a counselling old neighbor in the cast of characters, and concluding in a hymnal jubilation of the pious sect of Shakers, shaking before the Lord and chanting their ancient song, "When true simplicity is gained/ To bow and to bend we shan't be ashamed/ To turn, turn will be our delight/ Till by turning, twining we come round right," set in the immaculate white key of C major. (The ballet version was scored for 13 instruments; Copland later arranged it for full orchestra as a symphonic suite, which was first performed by the New York Philharmonic on 4 October 1945, and on the next day by the Boston Symphony Orchestra and the Cleveland Orchestra)

### 1 NOVEMBER 1944

Manuel Rosenthal, 40-year-old French composer, conducts in Paris the first performance of his oratorio *Saint Francis d'Assisi*, with the inclusion in the orchestra of the electronic musical instrument Ondes Martenot.

### 11 NOVEMBER 1944

*Ozark Set* for orchestra by the 35-year-old American composer Elie Siegmeister, in four movements, *Morning in the Hills, Camp Meeting, Lazy Afternoon* and *Saturday Night*, portraying the folkways of the Ozark mountain people of Missouri and Arkansas and employing authentic American melorhythms set in rational harmonies spiced with endurable dissonances, is performed for the first time by the Minneapolis Symphony Orchestra, Dimitri Mitropoulos conducting.

### 13 NOVEMBER 1944

Paul Graener, one of the few German composers who cultivated an impressionistic manner of harmony and orchestration and whose operas reveal a modern expressionistic character with an occasional earnest utilization of dodecaphonic methods, dies in the war-depressed Mozartean town of Salzburg at the age of seventy-two.

### 17 NOVEMBER 1944

Virgil Thomson conducts the Philadelphia Orchestra in the first performance of a symphonic suite from his *Portraits,* composed by him with the subject sitting for his likeness as he would for a painter, featuring among them *Bugles and Birds* for Picasso, *Tango Lullaby* for a young girl, and *Percussion Piece* for a California lady.

### 22 NOVEMBER 1944

The first annual Day of Music, established by a decree of General Trujuillo, self-styled permanent President and benefactor of the Dominican Republic before his final assassination, is celebrated throughout the land, on the feast day of St. Cecilia, patron saint of music.

## 23 NOVEMBER 1944

*Ode to Napoleon Buonaparte,* op. 41 by Arnold SCHOENBERG, for string orchestra, piano and speaker, to Byron's poem ruefully reflecting on the fall of Napoleon, written according to a novel version of Schoenberg's method of composition for 12 tones, enhanced by an allegorical code of intervallic semantics, wherein the motto of an ascending fourth and a descending minor second, thrice repeated, symbolizes presumptuous dictators of any historic period, ending in an unobstructed chord of E-flat major, as an emblem of eventual liberation, is performed for the first time by the New York Philharmonic, Artur Rodzinski conducting.

## 24 NOVEMBER 1944

*Rounds* for string orchestra by the 29-year-old American composer David DIAMOND, a "spherical" work in three movements played without pause, with the middle section *Adagio* "acting as a resting point between the two fast movements," is performed for the first time by the Minneapolis Symphony Orchestra, Dimitri Mitropoulos conducting.

## 24 NOVEMBER 1944

Ernst VON DOHNÁNYI flees Budapest as the Russian Army penetrates its environs.

## 30 NOVEMBER 1944

Antoine MARIOTTE, French composer of romantic operas, dies in Izieux, Loire at the age of sixty-eight.

## 1 DECEMBER 1944

The Boston Symphony Orchestra, under the direction of Serge Koussevitzky, gives the world première of *Concerto for Orchestra* by Béla BARTÓK, his last symphonic work, composed between 15 August and 8 October 1943 in New York during recuperation from his next-to-last illness, in five movements bearing Italian titles:

(1) *Introduzione,* opening with sylvan murmuration of strings and flutes and developing like a scherzo in rondo form (2) *Giuoco delle Coppie,* a game of couples, so named because the wind instruments are copulated at specific intervals, the bassoons in sixths, the oboes in thirds, the clarinets in sevenths, the flutes in fifths, the muted trumpets in major seconds, while the time signature, 2/4, represents still another couple (3) *Elegia,* a sepulchral threnody, almost oriental in its profusion of melorhythmic arabesques (4) *Intermezzo interrotto,* derived from two asymmetrical subjects, the interruption being a sly intrusion of a refrain from the Nazi theme in the *Seventh Symphony* by Shostakovich which Bartók heard on the radio in obsessive quantity (5) *Finale,* based on a persistently repetitive fugal subject, developed in single, double and triple augmentation, single, double and triple diminution and multiple stretti in quadruple counterpoint, culminating in a magisterial coda in an oriflamme of brass sonorities.

## 1 DECEMBER 1944

*Violin Concerto* by the American composer Louis GRUENBERG, in three movements: (1) *Rhapsody* (2) *With Simplicity and Warmth* (3) *Lively and With Good Humor,* derived in its thematic contents Negro spirituals and rustic American songs, is performed for the first time by Jascha Heifetz, who commissioned the work, with the Philadelphia Orchestra.

## 2 DECEMBER 1944

Josef LHÉVINNE, Russian pianist of formidable technical powers and lyrically romantic Musikanschauung, dies in New York, eleven days before his 70th birthday.

## 7 DECEMBER 1944

*The Seven Lively Arts,* revue produced by Billy Rose, containing parts of a score he commissioned to Igor STRAVINSKY for a fee of $5,000 (the material of which was later utilized by Stravinsky in his *Scènes de Ballet* conducted by him with the New York Philharmonic on 3 February 1945), opens in New York.

(The preview took place in Philadelphia a few days earlier; after the opening night there, Billy Rose telegraphed to Stravinsky: YOUR MUSIC GREAT SUCCESS STOP COULD BE SENSATIONAL SUCCESS IF YOU WOULD AUTHORIZE ROBERT RUSSELL BENNETT RETOUCH ORCHESTRATION STOP BENNETT ORCHESTRATES EVEN THE WORKS OF COLE PORTER. Stravinsky wired back: SATISFIED WITH GREAT SUCCESS)

## 7 DECEMBER 1944

*Poem for Orchestra* by the American Negro composer William Grant STILL, expressing the despair of humanity "on the rim of a desolate world," is performed for the first time by the Cleveland Orchestra.

## 10 DECEMBER 1944

*Nocturne* by George ANTHEIL, a movement from his symphonic suite *Decatur at Algiers,* reflecting an American boy's vision of an American hero, illustrated by a profusion of orientalistic inflections, is performed for the first time by the St. Louis Symphony Orchestra, under the direction of Vladimir Golschmann.

## 15 DECEMBER 1944

*Saturnalia,* opera by the 47-year-old Danish composer Jorgen BENTZON, to a libretto inspired by the erotic epic, *The Golden Ass* of Apuleius, is produced in Copenhagen.

## 16 DECEMBER 1944

*Sinfonia Tripartita* by the Italian composer Vittorio RIETI, now resident in New York, his fourth symphony, dedicated to Igor Stravinsky, and set in an austere neo-Baroque idiom, is performed for the first time by the St. Louis Symphony Orchestra, Vladimir Golschmann conducting.

### 25 DECEMBER 1944

*Burevesnik (Stormy Petrel)*, symphonic poem after Maxim Gorky by the Serbian composer Vojislav VUČKOVIĆ, is performed for the first time in liberated Belgrade exactly two years after the composer's death at the hands of the Nazis.

### 28 DECEMBER 1944

*On the Town,* musical comedy by Leonard BERNSTEIN, to a libretto suggested by the scenario of his ballet *Fancy Free,* in which three sailors, engaged in the pursuit of happiness in New York City, find gratification by pairing off with a female taxi driver, an anthropology student and a dancer, set to music with a rollicking hedonistic élan, is produced in New York.

### 30 DECEMBER 1944

Romain ROLLAND, French novelist and inspired writer on music, whose serial novel *Jean-Christophe* was the first literary work ever written in which the central character is a professional composer, dies at his home in Vézelay, France, at the age of seventy-eight.

### 31 DECEMBER 1944

*Alesia,* opera in four acts by the 51-year-old Byelorussian composer Evgeny TIKOTSKY, dealing with a heroic Byelorussian girl who inspired the fight against the invading Nazis in 1941, is produced in Minsk, capital of Byelorussia, shortly after the expulsion of Nazi troops from Byelorussia by the Red Army.

# ❧ 1945 ❧

### 1 JANUARY 1945

Vít NEJEDLÝ, 32-year-old Czech composer, son of the musicologist Zdenek Nejedlý (who was appointed Minister of Education of Czechoslovakia in 1948), dies of typhoid fever near Dukla, in the ranks of the Liberation army advancing with the Soviet Red Army into Slovakia.

### 13 JANUARY 1945

Sergei PROKOFIEV conducts in Moscow a concert of his orchestral music, including the first performance of his *Fifth Symphony,* op. 100, "a symphony about the spirit of man," composed during the summer of 1944, set in the victoriously optimistic key of B-flat major, in four movements exuding fervid Russian lyricism and rhythmic energy:

(1) *Andante,* in B-flat major, in 3/4, opening with a soaring Russian melody in thematically controlled variations with fugal excrescences scaling the heights of sonorous exuberance, and then receding to the depths of a dramatic envoi, anchored on the pedal point in the bass (2) *Allegro marcato,* in D minor, in 4/4 time, a scherzo maintaining its relentless momentum with a drumfire beat evoking the recent memories of war and tragedy, changing to a more affective 3/4 time, and then returning to the initial square beats, culminating in a tremendous explosion of vital forces (3) *Adagio,* a somber elegy in 3/4 time, in F major, with dotted rhythms emphasizing the inner tension within a steady metrical division (4) *Allegro giocoso,* in B-flat major in 2/2 time, depicting a scene of pastoral contentment, in anticipation of a victory over the brutality of Fascism, now within a few months of achievement, in an apotheosis, marked by an ovation of trumpets, an irresistible advance of trombones and the brandished oriflamme of horns reinforced by a cotillion of drums, and nailed down by a triumphant beat of the bass drum.

### 24 JANUARY 1945

Ernst KRENEK becomes a citizen of the United States.

### 26 JANUARY 1945

*Violin Concerto* by the Swiss neo-classical composer Willy BURKHARD is performed for the first time in Zürich.

### 26 JANUARY 1945

*First Symphony* by the 28-year-old Swedish modernist Karl-Birger BLOMDAHL is performed for the first time in Stockholm.

### 26 JANUARY 1945

*Concerto* for doublebass and orchestra by the expatriate Russian composer Thomas DE HARTMANN is performed for the first time in Paris.

### 27 JANUARY 1945

*Up in Central Park,* musical play in two acts by Sigmund ROMBERG, dealing with the real-life exploit of a New York *Times* reporter who in 1870 exposed the sinister machinations of Tammany Hall and married the widow of a slain crook, with the song *Close as Pages in a Book* serving as a romantic motto, is produced in New York.

### 1 FEBRUARY 1945

*Lycksalighetens (Isle of Felicity),* opera by the 52-year-old Swedish composer Hilding ROSENBERG, is performed for the first time in Stockholm.

### 1 FEBRUARY 1945

*Concerto for Orchestra* by Morton GOULD, in three American-flavored movements, with a boogie-woogie finale, is performed for the first time by the Cleveland Orchestra.

### 3 FEBRUARY 1945

Igor STRAVINSKY conducts the New York Philharmonic in the first performance of his *Scènes de Ballet* for orchestra, consisting of eleven terpsichorean poses proffered in the elegant manner of the gallant era of French choreography, "patterned after the forms of the classical dance, free of any given literary or dramatic argument."

(The work was originally written for Billy Rose's production *The Seven Lively Arts*, which opened in New York on 7 December 1944, but was not presented in its entirety; the score was subsequently revised and adjusted for concert performance)

### 4 FEBRUARY 1945

Lukas Foss, 22-year-old Berlin-born (his original surname was Fuchs) American pianist and composer, conducts the Pittsburgh Symphony Orchestra in the first performance of his romantically inspired and pleasurably eclectic *Symphony in G*, written in a variety of styles ranging from Handelian harmony to prudential jazzification.

### 5 FEBRUARY 1945

*Takhir and Zukhra*, opera in four acts by the Soviet composer Alexander LENSKY, dealing with a dramatic romance of a Tadzhik couple in medieval Central Asia, is performed for the first time at the Tadzhik Opera House in Stalinabad.

### 9 FEBRUARY 1945

*Eighth Symphony* by the prime symphonist of Sweden Kurt ATTERBERG is performed for the first time in Helsinki.

### 11 FEBRUARY 1945

*Leonora Tellez*, opera by the Portuguese statesman and amateur musician João Marcelino ARROYO, is produced posthumously in Lisbon.

### 15 FEBRUARY 1945

*Second Symphony* by the American composer Paul CRESTON, "conceived as an apotheosis of the two foundations of all music: song and dance," in two movements: (1) *Introduction and Song* (2) *Interlude and Dance*, is performed for the first time by the New York Philharmonic, under the direction of Artur Rodzinski.

### 17 FEBRUARY 1945

Marc LAVRY, Latvian-born Palestinian composer, conducts the world première in Tel Aviv of his Hebrew opera *Dan the Guard*, to Max Brod's libretto dealing with the kibbutz movement of Palestinian settlers working towards the goal of building a national Jewish state.

## 21 FEBRUARY 1945

Heitor VILLA-LOBOS conducts the Boston Symphony Orchestra in the first performance anywhere of his *Chôros No. 12*, scored for a gargantuan orchestra with a large assortment of Brazilian drums and shakers to suggest the popular impression of a *chôros*, a "sui generis form of musical composition in which are synthesized the different modalities of Brazilian, Indian and modern popular music."

## 22 FEBRUARY 1945

Virgil THOMSON conducts the New York Philharmonic in the first performance of his *Symphony on a Hymn Tune*, derived from two pentatonic hymns of the Southern Baptists, in four movements:

(1) *Introduction*, "a conversational passage for solo instruments and pairs of instruments followed by a statement of the hymn tune in half-in and half-out-of-focus harmonization," leading to *Allegro*, "a succession (and superposition) of dance-like passages derived from the main theme," ending with a heteroousian cadenza for piccolo, violin, cello and trombone (2) *Andante*, a series of variations with a simulated locomotive whistle alliterated by a total glissando of all brass instruments (3) *Allegretto*, "a passacaglia of marked rhythmic character on the hymn-tune bass" (4) *Finale*, "a canzona on a part of the main theme."

## 26 FEBRUARY 1945

*Concerto* for the Thereminovox, electronic musical instrument invented by the Russian engineer Leon Theremin, and orchestra by the Cyprus-born American composer Anis FULEIHAN, is performed for the first time by the New York City Symphony Orchestra, Leopold Stokowski conducting, with Clara Rockmore at the Thereminovox, producing the alteration of pitch by wafting her hand to and fro thus altering the heterodynamic field, resulting in a differential frequency within the audible range.

## 5 MARCH 1945

Rudolf KAREL, 64-year-old Czech composer of folkloristically inspired music, dies in a Nazi concentration camp at Teresin near Prague.

## 12 MARCH 1945

During an air raid on Vienna by American bombers, five bombs fall on the Vienna Opera House, three of them destroying the iron curtain separating the stage from the orchestra, one exploding above the right proscenium box, and one bursting in the adjacent street Operngasse, opening a gap of 120 square yards in the left side of the building and reducing it to a heap of twisted debris.

## 17 MARCH 1945

*Cello Concerto* in C minor by Nicolai MIASKOVSKY, in two movements, *Lento ma non troppo* and *Allegro vivace*, written in an elegiac lyric manner, with

797

moments of rhythmic tension creating a dramatic contrast, is performed for the first time in Moscow.

## 22 MARCH 1945

*Concerto* for string orchestra, piano and percussion by Alfredo CASELLA is performed for the first time in Basel, Switzerland.

## 25 MARCH 1945

*Figure Humaine*, cantata for double chorus a cappella by Francis POULENC, written by him in Paris in 1943 under Nazi occupation, to the text by Paul Eluard, expressing the silent wrath of a subjugated people yearning for liberty, is performed for the first time by the British Broadcasting Company in London, whose wartime broadcasts to France were, in Poulenc's words, "the unfailing source of hope during the German occupation."

## 26 MARCH 1945

*Symphony of the Brave Young Men*, a patriotic piece by the dean of Greek composers Manuel KALOMIRIS, is performed for the first time in Athens.

## 6 APRIL 1945

Gunther SCHULLER, 19-year-old first horn player of the Cincinnati Symphony Orchestra, plays the solo part in the world première of his *Concerto for Horn and Orchestra*, in two movements, *Rhapsody* and *Scherzo*.

## 8 APRIL 1945

At the approach of the final hour of Nazidämmerung, the Austrian conductor Leopold REICHSWEIN, one of the few musicians who was lured by the opportunities for individual and racial aggrandizement offered by the Nazi doctrine, kills himself in Vienna.

## 10 APRIL 1945

*Undertow*, a suite of choreographic psychological episodes for orchestra by the 34-year-old American composer William SCHUMAN, traversing the "emotional development of a transgressor" from a Freudian infancy through the anxiety-riddled period of puberty, reflected in a sonorously discordant, angularly rhythmed music, is performed for the first time in New York.

## 12 APRIL 1945

Peter RAABE, German esthetician and music theorist, who in 1935 succeeded Richard Strauss as President of the inglorious Reichsmusikkammer, dies in Weimar at the age of 72, on the day of the entry of American troops into the town.

Peter Raabe did not commit suicide, as was rumored; he was ill for weeks, perhaps for years, distressed by his long struggle against the regime which was imposed upon him and whose views were alien to him. . . . I myself was present at his sickbed a few days before his death, and I spoke at his funeral. (From a letter to the author, dated 24 July 1947, from Prof. Dr. Wahl, Director of the Goethe Museum in Weimar)

## 15 APRIL 1945

The Polish Music Publishing Society is founded in Cracow, shortly after the liberation of the city from the Nazis.

## 16 APRIL 1945

*The Canticle of the Sun* for chorus and orchestra by the 49-year-old American composer Leo SOWERBY, to the text of the hymn by St. Francis, is performed for the first time in New York.

## 19 APRIL 1945

*Carousel,* a musical play by Richard RODGERS, with book and lyrics by Oscar Hammerstein II, to an Americanized story from Ferenc Molnár's play *Liliom,* with the original Hungarian locale transferred to the New England of 1873, wherein the circus barker Liliom becomes Billy Bigelow, is involved in a robbery, kills himself, but is given a pass to Heaven to fetch a star for his small daughter on earth, containing the hit tunes *June Is Bustin' Out All Over* and *You'll Never Walk Alone,* is produced in New York.

## 21 APRIL 1945

*Trois petites liturgies de la Présence Divine* by Olivier MESSIAEN, for female chorus in unison and instruments, to his own texts on subjects from theology, botany, geology and astronomy, scored for "a Europeanized Hindu or Balinese ensemble," including celesta, vibraphone, maracas, Chinese cymbals, gong, piano, Ondes Martenot and strings, and couched in Messiaen's individual polymodal and polyrhythmic language, is performed for the first time in Paris.

## 1 MAY 1945

*Deda da Shvili (Mother and Son),* opera in two acts by the 31-year-old Georgian composer Alexei MACHAVARIANI, is performed for the first time in Tbilisi.

## 2 MAY 1945

*Monte Carlo,* ballet by the 30-year-old Spanish composer Carlos SURINACH, depicting in humorous tones the aleatory alternations of fortunes and misfortunes at the gambling tables of the Casino in Monte Carlo, is produced in Barcelona.

## 7 MAY 1945

*In terra Pax,* oratorio by Frank MARTIN, is performed for the first time in Geneva.

## 8 MAY 1945

*Thanksgiving for Victory* by Ralph VAUGHAN WILLIAMS, scored for speaker, soprano, chorus and orchestra, to texts from Shakespeare's *Henry V*, the Bible and patriotic poems of Kipling, is performed for the first time by the British Broadcasting Corporation on the day of victory over Nazi Germany.

## 8 MAY 1945

*Veten (Fatherland)*, opera in four acts by the Azerbaijan composers Dzhevdet GADZHIEV and Kara KARAEV, to a patriotic libretto in the Tatar language dealing with the desperate struggle against the Nazi invasion of Azerbaijan in 1943, is produced in Baku.

## 9 MAY 1945

*The Scarecrow*, one-act opera by the American composer Normand LOCKWOOD, in which Beelzebub transforms a scarecrow in a 17th-century New England village into a man and commands him to corrupt a Puritan maiden, but is foiled when true love blossoms forth between them, is performed for the first time in New York.

## 12 MAY 1945

The First Annual Festival of Contemporary American Music opens at Columbia University in New York in a program including *Rounds for Strings* by David DIAMOND, *Fourth Symphony* by Howard HANSON, *Saxophone Concerto* by Henry BRANT and *Second Symphony* by Walter PISTON.

## 7 JUNE 1945

*Peter Grimes*, opera in three acts by England's prime 20th-century composer Benjamin BRITTEN, to a libretto from Crabbe's poem *The Borough* (1810), wherein a young Suffolk fisherman, suspected of murder after the successive but accidental drownings of his two apprentices, sails away to a certain death in his small boat to escape the vengeance of the villagers, written in a tense expressionistic idiom, with tonal harmonies drowned in tempestuous waves of chromatic dissonances, relieved only by realistic "sea interludes" of stormy winds and crying gulls, with uninhibited use in the libretto of such hitherto unoperatic vocables as "bitch" and "hell," is performed for the first time at the opening of the first post-war season at the Sadler's Wells Theatre in London. (Five orchestral tableaux from *Peter Grimes—Passacaglia, Dawn, Sunday Morning, Moonlight, The Storm*—forming a symphonic suite, were performed for the first time under Britten's direction in Cheltenham on 13 June 1945)

## 13 JUNE 1945

*Suite Française* for band by Darius MILHAUD, a pentaptych of musical picture postcards depicting five typical French provinces—Normandy, Brittany, Ile-de-France, Alsace-Lorraine and Provence—is performed for the first time in New York.

## 21 JUNE 1945

*Tuleelegid (Flames of Vengeance)*, Estonian opera in five scenes by Eugen KAPP, dealing with the historic rebellion of Estonian patriots against Teutonic Crusaders on the night of 23 April 1343, after a young village bride is ravished by a brutal Teuton, whereupon the people storm his castle and slay him and his henchmen, and once the flames of vengeance are lit, go forth to the final battle for liberation from the feudal yoke, set to music in flamboyantly rousing modalities with an influx of lyric Estonian strains to depict the sorrows of oppression and the sempiternity of the patriotic fervor, is produced in Tallin.

## 24 JUNE 1945

*Tulyak*, opera in five scenes, in the Tatar language, by the 34-year-old Soviet composer Nazib ZHIGANOV, dealing with the bloody events of the Mongol invasion of Central Asia in the 12th century, is produced in Kazan.

## 3 JULY 1945

As a gesture of good will toward America, the State Symphony Orchestra of Moscow presents a concert of modern American symphonic music in a program including *Ode to Friendship* by Roy HARRIS, *March in Memoriam* by Wallingford RIEGGER, *First Essay for Orchestra* by Samuel BARBER, *Ozark Set* by Elie SIEGMEISTER and *Rhapsody in Blue* by George GERSHWIN.

## 9 JULY 1945

*L'appel de la montagne*, ballet in three tableaux by Arthur HONEGGER, dealing with a Scotsman who loves a Swiss lass but loses her to a Swiss shepherd and in his despair climbs an inaccessible Swiss mountain, falling into a moderately precipitous abyss where droll trolls mock him until he is rescued by the Virgin of the Fairies, is produced in Paris.

## 14 JULY 1945

The Allied Occupation Authorities in Germany issue an order forbidding playing military music or singing Nazi songs.

## 27 JULY 1945

Alan BUSH, 44-year-old English composer of socially significant music and a left-wing member of Parliament, conducts the London Symphony Orchestra in the world première of his orchestral *Fantasia on Soviet Themes*.

## 31 JULY 1945

Ralph VAUGHAN WILLIAMS conducts in London the first performance of his symphonic suite *The Story of a Flemish Farm*, drawn from incidental music to a film about a group of patriotic Belgian airplane pilots escaping to England after the German occupation of Belgium.

## 2 AUGUST 1945

Pietro MASCAGNI, Italian opera composer whose *Cavalleria Rusticana*, written in his early youth, earned him an enduring place in music history as a pioneer of Verismo and operatic realism, but whose honor was tarnished by his willful association with Mussolini's Fascists, dies in Rome at the age of eighty-one.

## 2 AUGUST 1945

Emil Nikolaus VON REZNIČEK, 85-year-old Austrian-born composer of romantic operas, succumbs in devastated Berlin to typhoid fever aggravated by starvation.

No coffins were available in Berlin when Rezniček died, and his body remained unburied for four days in the upper story of a tenement house in Charlottenburg; finally a coffin was procured; Rezniček was buried on the day the atom bomb fell on Japan. (From a memoir of Rezniček's daughter, *Gegen den Strom, Leben und Werk von E. N. Rezniček*, Vienna, 1960)

## 17 AUGUST 1945

Gino MARINUZZI, 63-year-old Italian conductor and composer of Wagneromorphic operas and of a jubilee piece on the occasion of Hitler's meeting with Mussolini, is murdered in the streets of the disoriented and turbulent city of Milan by Italian resistance fighters on the justified suspicion of being a militant Fascist.

## 23 AUGUST 1945

Leo BORCHARD, conductor of the Berlin Philharmonic Orchestra, is accidentally shot and killed by an American sentry in Berlin when the driver of the car in which he is riding ignores the order to stop.

## 1 SEPTEMBER 1945

*Grünewald*, patriotic symphonic poem by the Polish composer Jan MAKLAKIEWICZ, glorifying the battle of 1410 in which the presumptuous Teutonic Knights were routed by the Polish Army on the fields of Grünewald, is performed for the first time in Cracow, to mark the liberation of Poland from Nazi occupation.

## 3 SEPTEMBER 1945

The Union of Polish Composers is organized in Warsaw.

## 15 SEPTEMBER 1945

Anton VON WEBERN, 61-year-old Austrian composer of music so subtle and succinct that not only notes, but intervals, dynamic marks and durations assume thematic significance, philosopher-musician and pioneer of integral seri-

alism as an expansion of the dodecaphonic concept formulated by his master
Arnold Schoenberg, is accidentally shot and killed by an American soldier of
the army of occupation in Mittersill, near Salzburg, in the house of his son-in-
law suspected of black market speculation. (Webern's son-in-law was subsequently sentenced to one year's imprisonment; the unwitting killer of Anton
von Webern, though cleared of blame, died in 1950 of acute alcoholism induced by remorse.)

### 16 SEPTEMBER 1945

John McCORMACK, golden-voiced Irish tenor whose emotional ballad-singing
made the hearts of millions in Europe and America beat faster, dies near
Dublin at the age of sixty-one.

### 17 SEPTEMBER 1945

The heart of CHOPIN, hidden during the war in the Polish provincial town of
Milanowek, is returned to its sanctified place in the wall of the Holy Cross
Cathedral in Warsaw, with a plaque bearing the inscription in French: "Où
se trouve mon trésor, là se trouve mon cœur."

### 26 SEPTEMBER 1945

Béla BARTÓK, great composer of modern Hungary, explorer in his symphonic
and chamber music of the outermost frontiers of tones, rhythms and dynamic
nuances, indefatigable collector and codifier of ethnically diversified folksongs
and dances of his native Transylvania, dies of leukemia in New York, where
he settled after fleeing Fascist-infested Europe in 1940, at the age of sixty-
four.

The man whose music had elemental sweep, barbaric rhythm and penetrating force,
never weighed more than 116 pounds and sometimes as little as 90. His constant battle
with ill health started as a youth when he had lung trouble. His body remained delicate, and other difficulties—asthma, skin trouble, stomach disorders and fever made
their appearance. The fever increased and in the spring of 1944 it was diagnosed as
leukemia. In September 1945 there was an abrupt rise in his white cell count, and the
doctors knew he was near the end. He died on 26 September 1945, shortly before
noon. ASCAP paid the funeral expenses, for, following the tradition set by so many
other great composers, Bartók left no estate save the boundless wealth of his music.
(Ernö Balogh in *Musical Digest,* Chicago, September 1947)

(Bartók's body was cremated and the ashes kept in parcel No. 470 of the Ferncliff
Cemetery near Hartsdale, N.Y., sans headstone, sans marker, sans everything. Not
until the third anniversary of Bartók's death was this mortuary anonymity broken and
a memorial tablet placed on his grave)

### 4 OCTOBER 1945

*First Symphony* by the 39-year-old Norwegian composer Klaus EGGE (completed on 17 May 1942), dedicated to Norwegian sailors who served in World
War II, set in his personalized key of E minor (the score is signed in musical

letters E-G-G-E) and immersed in romantically dulcet modalities, is performed for the first time in Oslo.

### 12 OCTOBER 1945

*Third Symphony* by Bohuslav MARTINU, in three movements: (1) *Allegro poco moderato* (2) *Largo* (3) *Allegro-Andante*, with literal recapitulations in each movement, ending pianissimo, is performed for the first time by the Boston Symphony Orchestra, Serge Koussevitzky conducting.

### 14 OCTOBER 1945

*Prière pour les condamnés à mort*, a tragic evocation of the victims of the Nazi executions, for narrator and orchestra, by the Belgian composer Raymond CHEVREUILLE, is performed for the first time in Brussels.

### 19 OCTOBER 1945

*Put u pobedu (The Road to Victory)*, symphonic poem by the 45-year-old Serbian composer Mihailo VUKDRAGOVIĆ, depicting in heroic triadic harmonies the partisan struggle in occupied Yugoslavia against the Nazis during World War II, culminating in the singing of the triumphant socialist song, the Internationale, is performed for the first time in Belgrade, under the direction of the composer.

### 23 OCTOBER 1945

Vincent PERSICHETTI plays the solo part, with the Eastman Orchestra in Rochester, under the direction of Howard Hanson, of his *First Piano Concerto*, in one movement, written in a prudential neo-classical idiom, spiced with judiciously cultivated dissonant counterpoint.

### 26 OCTOBER 1945

*Suite Symphonique* by Ernest BLOCH in three movements: (1) *Overture* (2) *Passacaglia* (3) *Finale*, culminating in "a grotesque sardonic fugue," is performed for the first time by the Philadelphia Orchestra, conducted by Pierre Monteux.

### 27 OCTOBER 1945

*Harvest* for harp, vibraphone and strings by Morton GOULD, employing chordal counterpoint leading to agreeable polytonality, with American-flavored melodic materials of a cheerful nature suitable for singing at harvest time, is performed for the first time by the St. Louis Symphony Orchestra, Vladimir Golschmann conducting.

### 28 OCTOBER 1945

*Neustupujte (Do Not Yield!)*, cantata of resistance by the Czech composer Miloslav KABELÁČ, written on the eve of Hitler's invasion of Czechoslovakia in the spring of 1939, is performed for the first time in liberated Prague.

## 30 OCTOBER 1945

*Victory,* overture by Reinhold GLIÈRE, written to commemorate the final rout of Fascism in all its forms, is performed for the first time in Moscow.

## 2 NOVEMBER 1945

*Piano Concerto* by the 34-year-old Italian-born American composer Gian Carlo MENOTTI, in F major, in three movements: *Allegro, Lento, Allegro moderato,* exuding the baroque aura of the Italian classical period, is performed for the first time by the Boston Symphony Orchestra, Rudolf Firkušny soloist, Richard Burgin conducting.

## 3 NOVEMBER 1945

*Ninth Symphony* by Dmitri SHOSTAKOVICH (completed on 30 August 1945), designated as being in E-flat major, and indeed adhering more closely to the principal key than an average classical symphony, in five movements, *Allegro, Moderato* (a waltz), *Presto, Largo* (a very brief meditation) and *Allegretto* (a symmetric rondo), a varicolored musicorama ranging in mood from philosophical lyricism to quasi-choreographic rapture, conceived as a joyous postlude to a devastating but ultimately victorious war, is performed for the first time in Leningrad.

## 4 NOVEMBER 1945

*Third Symphony* by Gian Francesco MALIPIERO, completed on 14 February 1945, subtitled *Delle Campane (Of the Bells),* in four movements, *Allegro moderato, Andante molto moderato, Vivace,* and *Lento,* is performed for the first time in Florence.

War refuses to live in peace, even with itself. The composition of my *Third Symphony* relates to that ominous day, 8 September 1943, when Mussolini was rescued by the Nazis and set up a new Fascist government in Northern Italy. The bells of San Marco in Venice rang at sunset but they could not deceive those who knew their true voice. They tolled not for peace but for new torments, new horrors. (Malipiero in a statement quoted in *L'Opera di Gian Francesco Malipiero,* Treviso, 1952)

## 10 NOVEMBER 1945

*Ode to the End of the War* by Sergei PROKOFIEV, scored for a victoriously grandiose orchestra comprising woodwinds, brass, percussion, four pianos, eight harps and 16 doublebasses, but no violins, violas or cellos, is performed for the first time in Moscow.

## 10 NOVEMBER 1945

Ivan VYSHNEGRADSKY, Russian pioneer of quarter-tone music, conducts in Paris the first performance of his symphonic poem *Cosmos* for four pianos, two of which are tuned a quarter-tone higher than the other two, his mimo-drama *Linnite* and *5 Variations* on the single note C.

## 11 NOVEMBER 1945

Jerome KERN, American composer of melodious operettas and musical revues, among them the classic of the American musical theater, *Show Boat*, dies in New York at the age of sixty.

## 16 NOVEMBER 1945

*Suite for Violin and Orchestra* by Darius MILHAUD, in three sections, *Gigues, Sailor Song* and *Hornpipes*, with thematic materials taken from popular 18th-century English tunes, is performed for the first time by Zino Francescatti as violin soloist with the Philadelphia Orchestra under the direction of Eugene Ormandy.

## 18 NOVEMBER 1945

*Genesis* for narrator and orchestra, a suite of seven scenes by seven composers: (1) Arnold SCHOENBERG: *Prelude* (2) Nathaniel SHILKRET: *Creation* (3) Alexandre TANSMAN: *Adam and Eve* (4) Darius MILHAUD: *Cain and Abel* (5) Mario CASTELNUOVO-TEDESCO: *Noah's Ark* (6) Ernst TOCH: *The Covenant* (7) Igor STRAVINSKY: *The Tower of Babel*, is performed for the first time by the Janssen Symphony in Los Angeles, under the direction of its founder Werner Janssen.

The Prelude to *Genesis* was by Arnold Schoenberg, the text for which was "The Earth was without form, and void." This reviewer has never heard music that had less form or was more nearly void than Mr. Schoenberg's contribution. It was simply a succession of ugly sounds bearing no relation whatsoever to the thing generally known as music . . . Stravinsky's *Babel* vindicated this writer's belief that except when Stravinsky uses borrowed thematic material he has not composed anything of real value since *The Firebird*. Truly this was Babel to the nth degree . . . *Creation* was one of the very engaging sections of the work; it was composed by Nathaniel Shilkret, who commissioned the entire work. (*Pacific Coast Musician*, Los Angeles, 15 December 1945) (The first performance of *Genesis* was originally scheduled for 21 October 1945, but was postponed until 18 November 1945; the date 15 December 1947 given in the 3rd edition of *Music Since 1900* is that of a later performance)

## 21 NOVEMBER 1945

*Cinderella*, opera-ballet by Sergei PROKOFIEV, completed in 1943, an earthy Russian version of the classic wish-fulfilling fairy tale, in which a mysophiliac Russian girl Mascha Chernushka (literally, "Dirty Black Little Mary," the name for Cinderella used in Russian children's books), wins her prince charming, scored in the traditional manner of Russian classical ballet, featuring a *pas de deux*, a mazurka, waltzes, etc., with twenty arias interspersed between choreographic numbers, is performed for the first time in Moscow.

## 21 NOVEMBER 1945

Two hundred and fifty years have passed since the death of the great English composer Henry PURCELL.

*806*

23 NOVEMBER 1945

*Symphonie des Souvenirs* for voices, narrator and orchestra by the Belgian composer Raymond CHEVREUILLE, written in a cultured vigesimosecular manner, is performed for the first time in Brussels.

25 NOVEMBER 1945

Arturo Toscanini conducts the National Broadcasting Symphony Orchestra in the world première of *Western Suite* by the 36-year-old American composer Elie SIEGMEISTER, in five descriptive Americanistic movements, *Prairie Morning, Round-up, Night-Herding, Buckaroo,* and *Riding Home,* hippophiliac in content and ostentatiously folkloric in derivation containing quotations from a number of authentic prairie songs, stylized in fertilizingly non-toxic harmonies.

26 NOVEMBER 1945

Aaron AVSHALOMOV, Russian-American composer of Chinese-inspired works, conducts in Shanghai the first performance of his music drama in five acts *The Great Wall,* dealing with the tragedy of a young woman tortured to death at the Great Wall on orders of the Chinese Emperor whose celestial lechery she has imprudently spurned.

29 NOVEMBER 1945

*The Seven Ages,* symphonic suite by John Alden CARPENTER, inspired by the famous lines spoken by Jaques in Shakespeare's *As You Like It,* in seven musical episodes, ending with "sans eyes, sans teeth, sans everything," is performed for the first time by the New York Philharmonic, Artur Rodzinski conducting.

30 NOVEMBER 1945

*Fourth Symphony* by the expatriate Czech composer Bohuslav MARTINU, temporarily making his home in the United States, written without a key signature but strongly gravitating towards tonal centers, in four movements: (1) *Poco moderato,* calibrated in the mercurial melorhythms of a Siciliana (2) *Allegro vivo,* in the spirit of a tarantella, with a lyrical middle part (3) *Largo,* a moribund dumka erupting into a furibund furiant (4) *Poco Allegro,* a vigorous finale ending in a victorious display of unencumbered C major, is performed for the first time by the Philadelphia Orchestra, Eugene Ormandy conducting.

2 DECEMBER 1945

Hans HENKEMANS, 31-year-old Dutch composer, plays in Amsterdam the piano part in the first performance of his neo-classical *Passacaglia and Gigue* for piano and orchestra, with the Concertgebouw Orchestra under the direction of Eduard van Beinum.

## 5 DECEMBER 1945

*Majova Symphonie* by the Czech composer Vítězslav NovÁK, for chorus and orchestra, in three movements, begun under the Nazi occupation in 1943, and completed after the liberation of Czechoslovakia in May, 1945 by the Soviet armies, and for this reason named *Majova* (i.e. of the month of May), graphically portraying the historic event by the quotation of the Volga Boatmen's song which reduces the Nazi brawling Hort Wessel tune and the pan-Germanic hymn *Deutschland über alles* to pathetic shreds in a minor key alternating with an apocalyptic chant of Dies Irae, is performed for the first time in Prague.

## 6 DECEMBER 1945

Darius MILHAUD conducts the New York Philharmonic in the world première of his Caribbean diptych *La Bal Martiniquais*, in two divisions, *Chanson Créole* and *Biguine*, inspired by the creole rhythms of the French-governed island of Martinique, with the thematic material derived from Milhaud's *La Libération des Antilles*, for voice and piano, a setting of poems by the islanders expressing their joy at the liberation of the French West Indies from the repugnant regime of Vichy.

## 8 DECEMBER 1945

On the 80th birthday of Jean SIBELIUS, Finland issues a postage stamp of five marks with his portrait, a unique philatelic honor for a living composer.

## 8 DECEMBER 1945

Alexander SILOTI, Russian pianist and conductor, keeper of the best traditions of the Russian performing arts, a pupil of Liszt, teacher and first cousin of Rachmaninoff, dies in New York at the age of eighty-two.

## 9 DECEMBER 1945

*Violin Concerto* by Ildebrando PIZZETTI, in three movements: (1) *Molto mosso e appassionato*, an impassionately lambent lament with lachrymally cadent semitones forming the principal thematic figures (2) *Aria*, a frugal baroque theme with rococo variations (3) *Andante largo*, on the subject from Pizzetti's choral work *Recordare*, written in the spirit of devout imploration, is performed for the first time in Rome.

## 14 DECEMBER 1945

The Hungarian Ministry of Justice removes the name of Ernst VON DOHNÁNYI from the list of war criminals and exonerates him from the charge that he was a member of the pro-Nazi Hungarian Arrow-Cross Party. (The Communist Budapest newspaper *Az Ember* of 15 March 1947 revived the charge, but it was decisively refuted by a number of Hungarian refugees in America, some of them of Jewish extraction, who would be the first to militate against anyone tainted with Nazi affiliations)

## 19 DECEMBER 1945

*Concerto* for flute and orchestra by the Dutch composer Marius FLOTHUIS, floatingly fluvial in flute passages, is performed for the first time in Utrecht.

## 19 DECEMBER 1945

*Thunderbolt P-45,* orchestral scherzo by Bohuslav MARTINU is performed for the first time in Washington.

## 28 DECEMBER 1945

Igor STRAVINSKY becomes an American citizen, renouncing his previous allegiance to France whose citizen he had become on 10 June 1934.

## 30 DECEMBER 1945

*The Enchanted Kiss,* one-act radio opera by Robert Russell BENNETT, is performed for the first time in New York.

# ᐁ *1946* ᐂ

## 5 JANUARY 1946

*Rejsekammeraten,* opera by the 47-year-old Danish composer Ebbe HAMERIK, to a libretto after Hans Christian Andersen, is produced in Copenhagen.

## 10 JANUARY 1946

Harry von TILZER, American composer of sentimental ballads (his real name was Harry Gumm), purported originator of the expression "Tin Pan Alley" (he used to put strips of paper on the strings of a grand piano, making it sound like a tin pan), dies a lonely death in a New York hotel at the age of seventy-three.

## 23 JANUARY 1946

*Dark Meadow,* ballet choreographed by Martha Graham to the score of *Hija de Cólquide* by Carlos CHÁVEZ, is produced by her dance group in New York.

## 24 JANUARY 1946

Igor STRAVINSKY conducts the New York Philharmonic Orchestra in the first performance of his *Symphony in Three Movements* (parenthetically directed in the program book to be played without a pause, but actually containing a double-bar at the end of the first movement automatically requiring a stop), with its three sections evolving in the following forms:

(1) *Symphony-Overture* (so titled in the program book, but replaced in the printed score by a scholastic metronomic tempo indication of 160 quarter-notes per minute), set in a propulsive neo-Baroque style, in 4/4 time, punctuated by frequent rhetorical aposiopeses causing the metrical bars to collapse into irregular units, with thematic groupings rotating around the migratory tonal foci of G, A and C, the entire melo-rhythmic momentum having been suggested to Stravinsky by viewing a newsreel of the Japanese invasion of China, and after multiple instrumental monologues and di-alogues terminating on a spacious chord of a major seventh anchored on deep C (2) *Andante*, a terse concertino, thematically utilizing the flotsam and jetsam from Stra-vinsky's unrealized score for the motion picture of Franz Werfel's *Song of Bernadette* (3) *Con moto*, a rondo, reverting to Stravinsky's primitivistic avatar with its volcani-cally disequilibrated meters, convulsive silences and quaquaversal quick quivers of asymmetrical rhythms, culminating with a magisterial fugue suggested to Stravinsky by the films of the Allies' victorious march into Germany, and concluding with a glori-ously grandisonant D-flat major chord pandiatonically enriched by an added sixth and an added ninth and spread in the orchestra upon a range of six octaves and a fifth.

Each episode in the Symphony is linked in my imagination with a specific cinemato-graphic impression of the war. But the Symphony is not programmatic. Composers combine notes—that is all. How and in what form the things of this world are im-pressed upon their music is not for them to say. (Stravinsky in his annotations for a re-cording of the *Symphony in Three Movements,* issued by Columbia Phonograph Rec-ords)

### 25 JANUARY 1946

*Metamorphosen* for 23 solo string instruments by Richard STRAUSS, composed between 13 March and 12 April 1945, in the dying throes of the great Ger-man Reich, inscribed *In Memoriam* and containing thematic quotations from Beethoven's Funeral March of the *Eroica*, is performed for the first time in Zürich, Switzerland, where Strauss took refuge after the final German deba-cle.

### 29 JANUARY 1946

Sidney JONES, English composer of light music, whose operetta *The Geisha* portraying the accessible delights of Japanese femininity as judged by British visitors, produced in 1896, became a world favorite, dies in his native city of London at the age of eighty-four.

### 30 JANUARY 1946

*Concerto* for clarinet and orchestra by Darius MILHAUD, in four contrasting movements marked *Animé, Très décidé, Lent, Animé*, is performed for the first time at the Marine Barracks in Washington.

### 2 FEBRUARY 1946

*Ballad* for harp and orchestra by the 42-year-old Odessa-born Palestinian composer Joseph KAMINSKI, is performed for the first time by the Palestine Symphony Orchestra in Tel Aviv.

*810*

## 6 FEBRUARY 1946

Oswald KABASTA, 49-year-old Austrian conductor who without circumspection or prescience joined the Austrian Nazi party during its early suppuration, kills himself in Munich, as retribution and professional disgrace became imminent.

## 8 FEBRUARY 1946

*Third Concerto* for piano and orchestra by Béla BARTÓK, his last work, completed by him with the exception of the final 17 bars which had to be deciphered from sketches by his friend Tibor Serly (Bartók wrote *Vege* in the last bar of the *Concerto,* a Hungarian word meaning End, which he had never used before in his music), conceived in a surprisingly simplified idiom, replete with baroque sequences and symmetrically arrayed cadences, in three movements, *Allegretto, Adagio religioso* and *Allegro vivace,* which form a satisfying neo-Baroque triptych, is performed posthumously for the first time by György Sándor with the Philadelphia Orchestra, Eugene Ormandy conducting.

## 13 FEBRUARY 1946

*Edge of the World,* symphonic poem by the 32-year-old Canadian composer John WEINZWEIG, is performed for the first time in Toronto.

## 15 FEBRUARY 1946

*Makar Čudra,* symphonic poem for bass voice and orchestra by the Croatian composer Petar KONJOVIĆ, inspired by the novella of Maxim Gorky, dealing with the passion of a Gypsy singer for a proud Russian beauty, whom he stabs when she rebukes his professions of love, and then is himself killed by her father, written in a melodramatically romantic idiom with occasional adumbrations of Russian folk songs, is performed for the first time in Belgrade.

## 17 FEBRUARY 1946

*Danzón Cubano* by Aaron COPLAND, a symphonic movement derived from the asymmetrical rhythms of popular Afro-Cuban dances, maintaining a steady beat as a common denominator of constantly shifting meters, is performed for the first time by the Baltimore Symphony Orchestra, Reginald Stewart conducting. (In its original form for two pianos, *Danzón Cubano* was first performed by Aaron Copland and Leonard Bernstein on 17 December 1942, at a concert of the League of Composers in New York)

## 18 FEBRUARY 1946

Four centuries have passed since the death of the great religious reformer and composer of hymns Martin LUTHER, who created the German Protestant chorale, the *Kirchenlied,* in the vernacular, to justify his apocryphal dictum that the devil should not have all the best tunes.

## 25 FEBRUARY 1946

*Legend of Tariel,* opera in four acts to a libretto in the Georgian language by the 41-year-old Georgian composer Shalva MSHVELIDZE, after the classical epic of the Georgian 12th-century poet Shota Rustaveli, dealing with the return of the warrior Tariel on the wedding day of his beloved to a tribal chieftain, whom he manfully slays to regain her, is produced in Tbilisi.

## 26 FEBRUARY 1946

*Concerto* for oboe and chamber orchestra by Richard STRAUSS, completed by him on 25 October 1945 in Switzerland, in three classically equilibrated movements, *Allegro, Andante, Rondo* is performed for the first time in Zürich, in the presence of Strauss himself.

## 6 MARCH 1946

*Second Symphony* by the Dutch composer Guillaume LANDRÉ is performed for the first time in The Hague.

## 7 MARCH 1946

Halsey STEVENS, 37-year-old American composer, conducts in San Francisco the first performance of his *First Symphony.* (A revised version of the work was first performed in Los Angeles on 3 March 1950, under the composer's direction)

## 9 MARCH 1946

*Les Amours de Jupiter,* a hedonistically mythological ballet by Jacques IBERT, is performed for the first time in Paris.

## 22 MARCH 1946

Igor STRAVINSKY conducts the San Francisco Symphony Orchestra in the first performance of the version for full orchestra of his *Scherzo à la Russe,* a symphonic pasticcio on popular Russian refrains, originally written for Paul Whiteman's band and performed by him on the radio in 1944.

## 23 MARCH 1946

*Airborne,* oratorio for narrator, singers and orchestra, by the American composer Marc BLITZSTEIN, depicting in twelve vivid musical tableaux the history of human flight from Icarus to the fighting airmen of World War II, with brassy detonations punctuating the terse declarative prose of the narration, is performed for the first time by the New York City Symphony Orchestra, Leonard Bernstein conducting.

## 25 MARCH 1946

Edward LA VINE, popular vaudeville actor, whose performance in Paris in 1910 inspired DEBUSSY to write his prelude, *General Lavine-Eccentric,* dies at the desert town of Twenty-Nine Palms in California.

## 25 MARCH 1946

*Sonatina No. 2* for 16 wind instruments by Richard STRAUSS (completed by him on 22 June 1945) is performed for the first time in Winterthur, Switzerland.

## 25 MARCH 1946

*Ebony Concerto* by Igor STRAVINSKY, scored for "ebony stick" (swing term for clarinet) and band, written in a highly stylized but not condescendingly sophisticated jazz idiom, with fitful instrumental sternutations creating a stimulatingly neurotic ambience, while the harmony remains parsimoniously austere in its tonal foundations within a classical form of three movements, is performed for the first time by Woody Herman and his band as a commissioned work, in Carnegie Hall, New York.

## 1 APRIL 1946

*Arlequin Radiophile*, chamber opera by the 47-year-old French composer Marcel DELANNOY, combining the spirit of commedia dell'arte with the 20th century, is performed for the first time in Paris.

## 5 APRIL 1946

Forty-two years after its composition, the first performance is given by the Little Symphony of New York, Lou Harrison conducting, of the *Third Symphony* by Charles IVES, in three movements bearing titles of remembered American events:

(1) *Old Folks Gatherin'*, opening with an original hymnal tune of a devotional pentatonic structure, leading to the prime thematic mover, *Azmon* (commonly sung to the words "O For a Thousand Tongues to Sing"), constituting, with its characteristic falling thirds, the main motivic material of the movement, the second subject being *Erie* by Charles Crozat Converse (1832–1918), widely known by the incipit "What a Friend We Have in Jesus," used as countersubject to the original theme and to *Azmon* (2) *Children's Day*, a tender memory of childhood in the 1880's with the hymnal tune *Naomi* as a guiding cantus firmus combined with Lowell Mason's pentatonically constructed melody *Fountain* ("There is a Fountain Filled with Blood"), switching to a march-like anthem *Happy Land*, also pentatonic in structure, popular among children of several generations with parody words, "There is a Boarding-House Far, Far Away/ Where They Have Ham and Beans Three Times a Day/ Oh, How Those Boarders Yell/ When They Hear That Dinner Bell!" harmonized in audacious polytonalities, but returning in the end to the serenity of children's tranquil joys (3) *Communion*, based principally on the tune known as *Woodworth* identifiable by the incipit "Just as I Am, Without One Plea," written by an actress named Charlotte Elliott after a personally experienced epiphany, and ever since used as the standard closing anthem at revival meetings, the movement concluding with falling minor thirds in the cello solo, as though evoking the voice repeating, "I Come, I Come . . ." (On 5 May 1947, Ives was notified that the Pulitzer Prize was awarded to him for his *Third Symphony*; he accepted, but murmured a demurrer: "Prizes are for boys—I'm grown up!")

## 5 APRIL 1946

*Cello Concerto* by the 36-year-old American composer Samuel BARBER, written in a rhapsodically discursive manner with an astute injection of jazzy rhythms, in three movements, *Allegro moderato, Andante sostenuto, Molto allegro e appassionato*, evolving along a centripetal melodic spiral with a tritone as the focal interval, and ending on a unison A, is performed for the first time by Raya Garbousova with the Boston Symphony Orchestra, Serge Koussevitzky conducting.

## 5 APRIL 1946

Vincent YOUMANS, American composer of musical comedies, whose *Tea for Two* became a perennial favorite, dies of tuberculosis in Denver at the age of forty-seven.

## 8 APRIL 1946

The first *Concerto portugues* for piano and orchestra by the Portuguese composer Ivo CRUZ, is performed for the first time in Lisbon. (The second *Concerto portugues* was first performed in Lisbon on 16 December 1946.)

## 8 APRIL 1946

*Adam Zero*, choreographic spectacle in 16 scenes by the 54-year-old English composer Arthur BLISS, in which the life cycle of a symbolic Adam is traced, from birth to death, adding up to Zero, which God, personified by a stage director, marks on a blackboard, with the creation of Adam illustrated by agonizingly chromaticized harmonies and his illicit acquisition of the knowledge of good and evil by jazzy percolation of thematic fragments, is produced in London.

## 9 APRIL 1946

August LUDWIG, German composer and journalist who attained dubious fame by completing Schubert's *Unfinished Symphony*, adding two movements, entitled *Philosopher's Scherzo* and *March of Fate* (it had its first and last performance at the concert of the Berlin Philharmonic on 8 December 1892), dies in Dresden at the age of eighty-one.

## 10 APRIL 1946

The Government of Rumania issues a series of stamps at 10, 20, 55, 80 and 160 lei in homage to the Bucharest Philharmonic and two large souvenir sheets with music from George ENESCO's *Second Rumanian Rhapsody* (the initial three notes of which were erroneously reproduced on the stamps as B, D, D, instead of A, B, C)

*814*

## 20 APRIL 1946

*Deirdre of the Sorrows*, first Canadian grand opera, dealing with a Celtic love triangle in Ulster in A.D. 1, composed by Healey WILLAN, himself an Ulster Celt, is performed for the first time, in concert form, by the Canadian Broadcasting Corporation in Toronto.

## 26 APRIL 1946

*The Bells*, symphonic suite by Darius MILHAUD, in five movements, *Overture, Silver Bells, Golden Bells, Brazen Bells* and *Iron Bells*, inspired by the versicular tintinnabulations of Edgar Allan Poe's celebrated alliterative poem, is performed for the first time in Chicago.

## 5 MAY 1946

*Second Symphony in A major* by the American composer Douglas MOORE, in four movements, (1) *Andante con moto, Allegro giusto* (2) *Andante quieto e semplice* (3) *Allegretto* (4) *Allegro con spirito*, written in an "objective modified classical style, with emphasis on rhythmic and melodic momentum," is performed for the first time in Paris. (The first American performance of the work took place in Los Angeles on 16 January 1947)

## 5 MAY 1946

*L'Homme à la Peau de Léopard*, ballet in three acts based on the famous epic by the 12th-century Georgian poet Shota Rustaveli, with music collectively written by Arthur HONEGGER (first act), Alexander TCHEREPNIN (second act), and Tibor HARSÁNYI (third act), is produced in Monte Carlo.

## 8 MAY 1946

*The Medium*, opera in two acts by the 34-year-old Italian-American composer Gian Carlo MENOTTI, to his own libretto in English, dealing with a fraudulent spiritualist who falls victim of her own deception when she begins to experience tactile hallucinations and in her terror murders her deaf-mute boy assistant believing him to be a ghost, set to music in a highly dramatic manner enhanced by artful modernistic devices safeguarding a basic tonal design, is produced in New York. (The National Spiritualist Association protested against a Chicago production of *The Medium* in January 1948 as an attempt "to discredit honest and sincere mediums of the Spiritualist Religion at the time of its 100th birthday.")

## 8 MAY 1946

Boris PAPANDOPULO, German-born Croatian composer of Greek origin, conducts in Zagreb the first performance of his *Second Symphony*, in five movements depicting five states of his own mind: optimistic, resigned, hallucinatory, lyrical and libertarian, combining neo-romantic traits with earthy asymmetrical Balkan rhythms.

## 10 MAY 1946

*The Serpent Heart,* ballet by Samuel BARBER to a Freudianized story of Medea's possessive and destructive love "which feeds upon itself like a serpent heart," with the principal characters designated as One Like Medea and One Like Jason, set to music applying both archaic modal patterns and modern idioms, with agonizing dramatic tension achieved by the thematic use of atonally arrayed major sevenths and colubrine sinuosities of the melodic line, is produced at the opening presentation of the Second Annual Festival of Contemporary American Music at Columbia University, with choreography by Martha Graham.

(Barber revised the ballet, and it was produced under the title *Cave of the Heart,* with choreography again by Martha Graham, in New York on 27 February 1947. A symphonic suite in 7 movements from this version was first performed by the Philadelphia Orchestra, Eugene Ormandy conducting, on 5 December 1947. Finally, a scoring for large orchestra was made of sections from the ballet and published under the title *Medea's Meditation and Dance of Vengeance.* This final version was first performed by the New York Philharmonic Orchestra under the direction of Dimitri Mitropoulos on 2 February 1956)

## 11 MAY 1946

At the Teatro alla Scala in Milan, restored after the aerial bombardment of 16 August 1943, with its six candelabra and a huge central chandelier of Bohemian glass comprising 365 electric bulbs installed in the hall, Arturo TOSCANINI conducts the music of Rossini, Verdi, Boito and Puccini. (The official reopening took place on 26 December 1946, with Tullio Serafin conducting *Nabucco* of Verdi)

## 11 MAY 1946

*Koreanisches Märchen (A Korean Fairy-Tale),* one-act opera by the German composer Waldemar WENDLAND, is produced in Altenburg.

## 12 MAY 1946

*Phoenix,* mythological ballet by the Danish composer Knudaage RIISAGER, is performed for the first time in Copenhagen.

## 14 MAY 1946

*When Lilacs Last in the Dooryard Bloom'd,* "American Requiem" by Paul HINDEMITH for soprano, contralto, baritone, chorus and orchestra, written under the impression of the sudden death of President Roosevelt on 14 April 1945, to the words of Walt Whitman's threnody on Abraham Lincoln, in four sections, couched in a stately polyphonic idiom, is performed for the first time in New York by The Collegiate Chorale under the direction of its founder Robert Shaw.

## 16 MAY 1946

*Annie Get Your Gun,* musical comedy in three acts by Irving BERLIN, dealing with Annie Oakley, sharp-shooting star of Buffalo Bill's Wild West Show, who falls in love with an even sharper shooter of a rival show, with a score including the suggestive ballad *Doin' What Comes Naturally*, and many other infectious songs (*The Girl That I Marry, You Can't Get a Man with a Gun, Anything You Can Do I Can Do Better*) culminating in the apotheosis of the American theater, *There's No Business Like Show Business*, is produced in New York.

## 17 MAY 1946

*Petite Symphonie Concertante* for harp, harpsichord, piano and two string orchestras by the 55-year-old Swiss composer Frank MARTIN, in four movements, set in an elegant neo-classical style with momentary episodes in the 12-tone technique, embellished by coloristic daubs of the impressionistic palette is performed for the first time as a commissioned work by the Basel Chamber Orchestra in Zürich, Paul Sacher conducting.

## 25 MAY 1946

The Turkish composer Ahmet Adnan SAYGUN conducts the Presidential Philharmonic Orchestra and chorus in Ankara in the first performance of his oratorio *Yunus Emre*.

## 26 MAY 1946

*Third Piano Concerto* by Darius MILHAUD, in three contrasting movements, is performed for the first time at the Spring Festival in Prague.

## 31 MAY 1946

*Sinfonia Elegiaca* by the 30-year-old Argentinian composer Alberto GINASTERA, in one movement divided into four sections, depicting the state of serenity in coruscatingly colorful harmonies, is performed for the first time in Buenos Aires.

## 1 JUNE 1946

Leo SLEZAK, great Austrian tenor, famous also for his brilliant wit (when the mechanical swan in the last act of *Lohengrin* swam away ahead of schedule, Slezak inquired of a stage hand, "When does the next swan leave?"), dies on his estate in Egern on the Tegernsee at the age of seventy-two.

## 16 JUNE 1946

Miloje MILOJEVIĆ, Serbian composer of agreeably impressionistic piano pieces, dies in his native Belgrade at the age of sixty-one.

## 21 JUNE 1946

*Vergilii Aeneis*, heroic symphony by Gian Francesco MALIPIERO for voices and orchestra, inspired by Virgil's *Aeneid*, is performed for the first time in Turin.

## 22 JUNE 1946

A century has passed since the patenting of the saxophone, invented by the French instrument-maker Adolphe SAX, and named after him.

## 22 JUNE 1946

*Niobe,* monodrama in two acts for soprano, double chorus, orchestra and dancers by the Swiss composer Heinrich SUTERMEISTER, depicting the tragic story of Niobe who lost her 14 children when her defiant boasting of fecundity aroused the lethal wrath of the relatively infertile Leto, mother of Apollo and Artemis, is produced in Zürich.

## 7 JULY 1946

After four years of inactivity during World War II, the International Society for Contemporary Music resumes the presentation of its annual festivals, inaugurating its 20th Festival in London in the following program of symphonic music:

*Stadtpfeiffermusik* by the German composer Richard MOHAUPT, a hedonistic utilitarian score stylizing the merry music-making of old German town fifers; *Three Symphonic Preludes* by the quadrigenarian English composeress Elizabeth LUTYENS, written in a neo-classical idiom; *Piano Concerto* by the 39-year-old Dutch composer Robert de Roos; *Second Symphony* by the 36-year-old French composeress Elsa BARRAINE; and *Ode to the End of the War* by Sergei PROKOFIEV.

## 8 JULY 1946

The second concert of the 20th Festival of the International Society for Contemporary Music is given in London, presenting the following program of chamber music:

*Fifth String Quartet* by the Polish composer Jerzy FITELBERG resident in New York; Sonatina for clarinet and piano by the Swiss impressionist composer Albert MOESCHINGER; *Canti di Prigionia* for chorus, two pianos, two harps and percussion by the prime Italian modernist Luigi DALLAPICCOLA, first performed in Rome on 11 December 1941, and written in the idiom of expressionistic atonality; *Sonata for Two Pianos* by Igor STRAVINSKY, written in a compact and concise neo-classical idiom, first performed on 8 August 1944 at a "Concert with Commentaries" given by Nadia Boulanger at the University of Indiana in Bloomington; and *String Quartet* in E-flat by Paul HINDEMITH.

## 10 JULY 1946

The third concert of the 20th Festival of the International Society for Contemporary Music in London presents the following program of chamber music:

*String Quartet* No. 7 by Ernst KRENEK; *Suite* for violin and piano by Jozef ZAVADIL of

Czechoslovakia; *Quatuor pour la Fin du Temps* for violin, clarinet, cello and piano by Olivier MESSIAEN (originally performed, with the composer at the piano, on 15 January 1941 in a German prisoner-of-war camp in Silesia); and *Ode to Napoleon Buonaparte* for string quartet, piano and reciter by Arnold SCHOENBERG (first performed in a version with a string orchestra in New York on 23 November 1944).

## 12 JULY 1946

The fourth concert of the 20th Festival of the International Society for Contemporary Music is presented in London with the following program:

*Symphony for Strings* by the 35-year-old American composer William SCHUMAN, his fifth symphony (originally performed by the Boston Symphony Orchestra on 12 November 1943); *5 Folk Tunes* for childrens' voices and instruments by the 31-year-old Polish composer Andrzej PANUFNIK; *First Cantata*, op. 29, for soprano, chorus and orchestra by Anton von WEBERN, composed in 1939, in three movements, conceived as an exercise in Hegelian dialectics in music, with the melodic thesis opposed by antithesis, resolving in thematic synthesis, derived from a bisected 12-tone series, in which the second half is the retrograde inversion of the first; and *Divertimento No. 2* for string orchestra and solo trumpet by the 48-year-old Hungarian-Parisian composer Tibor HARSÁNYI.

## 12 JULY 1946

*The Rape of Lucretia*, opera in two acts by Great Britain's glorified composer, 32-year-old Benjamin BRITTEN, based on a French play derived from Shakespeare's poem dealing with the monstrous rape in 509 B.C. of the virtuous Roman matron, who kills herself after her ordeal, scored for an economical ensemble of 8 singers and 17 solo instruments, wherein atonal elements are polarized by pedal-pointed polyharmonies, and dramatic impact is attained by strong and spacious rhythmic dispositions while the text itself flaunts such erotically realistic lines as "let me rise to my first sepulchre, which is your thighs," is produced at the Glyndebourne Festival in England.

## 14 JULY 1946

The fifth concert of the 20th Festival of the International Society for Contemporary Music is presented in London in the following program of symphonic music:

*Cortèges* by the British composer Alan RAWSTHORNE; *Nocturne* by Raymond LOUCHEUR of France; *Violin Concerto* by Roman PALESTER of Poland; *Concerto for Orchestra* by Béla BARTÓK.

## 19 JULY 1946

*Puhajarv (Holy Lake)*, opera in three acts by the 37-year-old Estonian composer Gustav ERNESAKS, to a libretto in the Estonian language, dealing with the Estonian peasant rebellion against German feudal lords in 1840, is performed for the first time in Tallin, as a parabolic allusion to the Nazi invasion of Estonia in 1941.

## 12 AUGUST 1946

*The Mikado,* comic opera by GILBERT and SULLIVAN, making flippant fun of Japanese Emperor worship and heretofore banned in Japan for its disrespectful treatment of the Emperor, is produced for the first time in Tokyo by the Special Services Detachment of General Headquarters of the American Army of Occupation, with a new overture on oriental themes especially written by Klaus PRINGSHEIM, German musician long resident of Japan. (The production, originally scheduled for 22 July 1946, was postponed until 12 August 1946 on account of extremely hot weather which made the wearing of heavy ceremonial robes uncomfortable)

There was considerable discussion as to the propriety of doing *The Mikado* in Japan. Permission was finally obtained and production began in May 1946. The principals were all members of the United States Armed Forces, with the exception of the women's roles which were sung by the Civilian Actress Technicians, American women employed in the Special Services Soldier Show Program . . . The Corps de Ballet was entirely Japanese . . . At no time was any performance open to the Japanese public. However, on 11 August 1946 a dress rehearsal was held and passes were issued to 111 Japanese artists, singers, theater producers, newspaper editors and columnists. These were the only Japanese authorized at any time to see *The Mikado.* (From a letter to the author, dated 14 May 1948, from Gerald J. Cameron, Executive Officer of the Entertainment & Recreation Branch of the United States Army)

## 17 AUGUST 1946

*Symphonie Liturgique* by Arthur HONEGGER, his *Third Symphony,* in three movements: (1) *Dies Irae,* evoking the apocalyptic vision of an atonal Doomsday (2) *De Profundis clamavi,* tortuously rising from the somber depths of the bass register and scaling the heights of desperate clamor in chromatic anxiety (3) *Dona Nobis Pacem,* an imploration for peace against the distant drumfire of war, with diatonic aspirations gradually overcoming the chromatic waves of despair, is performed for the first time in Zürich under the direction of Charles Munch to whom the score is dedicated.

## 18 AUGUST 1946

*Corrobboree,* ballet suite by the 42-year-old Australian composer John ANTILL, depicting in primitivistically modernistic modalities the traditional festival of Australian aborigines: (1) *Welcome Ceremony* (2) *Dance to the Evening Star* (3) *Rain Dance* (4) *Procession of Totems and Fire Ceremony,* is performed for the first time in Sydney.

## 3 SEPTEMBER 1946

Moriz ROSENTHAL, "little giant" of the piano, one of the two remaining pupils of Liszt (the last survivor being the Portuguese pianist José Vianna Da Motta), whose wit matched his digital dexterity (asked for biographical information, he wrote: "I was born at an early age and sang a chromatic scale when I was one hour old. I am never nervous when I play in public, but pianists in the audience usually are"), dies in New York at the age of eighty-three.

## 27 SEPTEMBER 1946

First performances of two symphonic works by Polish composers are given by the Cracow Philharmonic:

*Concerto* for string orchestra by 42-year-old Tadeusz KASSERN, written in a neo-Polonian manner of classical constructivism; *Second Symphony* by 46-year-old Boleslaw WOYTOWICZ, dedicated to his stepson killed in the Warsaw uprising of 1944, in four movements: (1) *Disaster*, growing out of an embryo motive of three notes, C-D-F, rising to great exertions but soon receding into forced passivity (2) *Insurrection*, an energetic scherzo, quoting a Polish resistance tune of 1863 (3) *Contra spem spero*, a double fugue, containing rhythmic allusions to the radio signals for help sent to the Allies in the "hope against hope" as Poland was being crushed by the Nazi war machine in September 1939 (4) *Jubilation*, a polymetric rondo in Krakowiak rhythms, ending with a bitonal chord of F-sharp major superimposed on F major, symbolic of victory against impossible odds.

## 7 OCTOBER 1946

Two centuries have elapsed since the birth in Boston of William BILLINGS, the first professional American composer who created a *sui generis* type of American "fuguing tunes" (which gave rise through an imaginative misspelling, to "fudging" tunes of the hill country in Kentucky and Tennessee)

## 8 OCTOBER 1946

RCA Victor releases its billionth recording: John Philip SOUSA's perennial patriotic favorite, the march *Stars and Stripes Forever*.

## 10 OCTOBER 1946

*Musique de Table*, symphonic suite by the French composer Manuel ROSENTHAL, composed in 1942 in France as a salivating gastronomic fantasy relishing the then unobtainable products of the French cuisine, with a menu of eight dishes in eight movements: Salade russe, Eels in Red Wine, Quenelles, Beef Tenderloin, Mixed Fresh Vegetables, Loin of Venison, Salade de saison and Fromage de montagne, set to music in an appetizingly hedonistic manner of tonal gourmandise, is performed for the first time in America by the New York Philharmonic, Artur Rodzinski conducting.

## 16 OCTOBER 1946

Sir Granville BANTOCK, English composer of impeccable gentility and stately competence, whose oratorios and symphonic pieces command admiration for their irreproachable academic solidity, dies in London at the age of seventy-eight.

## 18 OCTOBER 1946

*Third Symphony* by Aaron COPLAND, in four movements (1) *Molto moderato*, containing three principal themes and presented in an unambiguous tonal setting (2) *Allegro Molto*, in the form of a classical cyclic scherzo (3) *Andantino quasi Allegretto,* a set of three variations (4) *Molto deliberato,* the longest movement of the work, containing a quotation from Copland's *Fanfare for the Common Man,* and set in sonata form, the whole work revealing proclamatory lyricism, alternating with nervously asymmetric rhythms creating the impression of jazzy turbulence under its finely equilibrated surface, is performed for the first time by the Boston Symphony Orchestra, Serge Koussevitzky conducting.

### 22 OCTOBER 1946

After 28 years of vacillation and violent political peripeteia, the government of Austria adopts a melody from Mozart's *Little Masonic Cantata* as its new national anthem, with words by Paul Preradovic, *Land der Berge, Land am Strome,* selected in a special contest.

(The original Austrian anthem was Haydn's *Gott erhalte unsern Kaiser,* adopted in 1797. From 1920 until 1929 an anthem with words by Karl Renner, prime minister of Austria, and music by Wilhelm Kienzl was in use; on 13 December 1929, the Haydn tune was reinstated with a different set of words, and was current in that form until 1946)

### 22 OCTOBER 1946

*Sinfonietta* by the 45-year-old Belgian composer Marcel POOT, a member of Synthétistes, a group promoting music as a synthesized product of classical forms and modern content, is performed for the first time by the Chicago Symphony Orchestra, under the direction of the Belgian conductor Désiré Defauw.

### 24 OCTOBER 1946

Leonard BERNSTEIN conducts in New York the first performance of his ballet *Facsimile,* set to music in a rambunctiously modernistic manner, with an existentialist scenario dealing with the intersected passions of two men contending for the favors of one woman.

### 30 OCTOBER 1946

*Cello Concerto* in E major by Aram KHACHATURIAN, in three classically proportioned movements, *Allegro moderato, Andante sostenuto* and *Allegro a battuta,* written in an attractively coloristic manner, with orientalistic arabesques set in luxuriant harmonies, is performed for the first time in Moscow.

### 3 NOVEMBER 1946

*Betrothal in a Convent,* opera in four acts by Sergei PROKOFIEV, to a libretto by Prokofiev's second wife Myra Mendelson, after Sheridan's comedy *The Duenna,* dealing with intersected amours, mistaken identities and various other embroilments of 18th-century Seville, set to music in a hedonistic lyrico-dramatic manner, with sharp rhythmic thrusts perforating the tonal surface of vocal and instrumental fabric, is produced in Leningrad.

## 12 NOVEMBER 1946

*Les Sirènes*, ballet by Lord BERNERS, depicting in modulatory fluxions and asymmetric rhythms an encounter of two mermaids with a group of masculine human swimmers on a beach in 1910 "when spirits were high and skirts were low," is produced in London.

## 14 NOVEMBER 1946

Manuel DE FALLA, great Spanish composer whose ballets and operas are vibrant with the melorhythms of rural and urban Spain set in resonant modern harmonies, dies nine days before his 70th birthday at Alta Gracia, Argentina, where he went in 1938 leaving Spain torn asunder by civil war.

## 14 NOVEMBER 1946

*Fifth Symphony* by Guy ROPARTZ, 82-year-old French composer of melodious and harmonious music in the tradition of César Franck, is performed for the first time in Paris, Charles Munch conducting.

## 15 NOVEMBER 1946

On his first visit to the United States, Zoltán KODÁLY, foremost living composer of Hungary, conducts the Pittsburgh Symphony Orchestra in a performance of his symphonic *Dances of Galánta* composed in 1933, inspired by the memories of his childhood spent in the polyethnic western Hungarian village of Galánta, set in characteristically amygdaline Magyar modalities.

## 22 NOVEMBER 1946

*Third Piano Concerto* by Ernst KRENEK, in five movements, written in a basically tonal idiom, with the application of some special effects (at one point the soloist silently presses down the keys while playing glissando on the strings inside the grand piano), is performed for the first time by Dimitri Mitropoulos with the Minneapolis Symphony Orchestra, playing and conducting simultaneously from memory.

## 28 NOVEMBER 1946

*Sevastopoltzy*, opera in four acts by the Soviet composer Marian KOVAL, extolling the courage of Sebastopol guerrilla fighters during the invasion of the Crimea by the Nazis in 1942, is produced in Molotov (Perm).

## 28 NOVEMBER 1946

*Second Concerto* for violoncello and orchestra by Darius MILHAUD, in three movements, marked *Gai, Tendre* and *Alerte*, is performed for the first time by the New York Philharmonic, Artur Rodzinski conducting.

## 29 NOVEMBER 1946

*Instruments of the Orchestra*, educational English film with music by Benjamin BRITTEN, from which he has fashioned an instrumental suite *The Young Person's Guide to the Orchestra*, is produced for the first time in London.

### 29 NOVEMBER 1946

Camargo Mozart GUARNIERI, Brazilian composer, who usually omits his given middle name out of modesty, conducts the Boston Symphony Orchestra in the world première of his *Symphony* in three movements marked *Rude, Profundo, Radioso,* set in classical form but containing colorful references to Brazilian dance rhythms.

### 11 DECEMBER 1946

*Sérénade à Angélique* by Arthur HONEGGER, a fanciful symphonic scherzo, wherein the trombone's stentorian passion is pipingly rebuked by a flute-like Angélique, is performed for the first time in Paris.

### 13 DECEMBER 1946

*First Symphony* by the internationally renowned pianist and pedagogue Artur SCHNABEL, in four traditional movements cast in an uncompromising idiom of dissonant counterpoint, with the principal decaphonic and hendecaphonic themes on the verge of dodecaphonic extension, is performed for the first time by the Minneapolis Symphony Orchestra, Dimitri Mitropoulos conducting, preceded, to assuage the tonal feelings of the audience in advance, by Schnabel's exuberantly romantic rendition of Beethoven's chaste *Fourth Piano Concerto.*

### 13 DECEMBER 1946

*Three Cyprus Serenades,* symphonic triptych by the Cyprus-born American composer Anis FULEIHAN, marked by luxuriantly expressive Mediterranean arabesques but without "too much mustard," is performed for the first time by the Philadelphia Orchestra, Eugene Ormandy conducting.

### 14 DECEMBER 1946

As part of musical festivities marking the 8ooth anniversary of the foundation of the city of Moscow, *Moscow,* patriotic cantata by Vissarion SHEBALIN, glorifying in five movements the city and its people ("7 times 7 roads, 7 times 7 blue rivers . . . all lead to the wonderful town of Moscow"), with a magnivocal climax in grandiose Russian homophony accompanied by an aggregation of pealing church bells, is performed for the first time in Moscow.

### 15 DECEMBER 1946

*Les Saisons et les Jours,* "allegoric symphony" by Henri SAUGUET, is performed for the first time in Paris.

### 17 DECEMBER 1946

At a session of the Berlin Tribunal charged with denazification proceedings in the field of art and music, Wilhelm FURTWÄNGLER, former conductor of the Berlin Philharmonic, is found not guilty of passive participation in the criminal activities of the Nazi regime.

What made me remain in Germany was my anxious desire to preserve the integrity of German music. When Thomas Mann asks, "How can Beethoven be played in Himmler's Germany," I answer, "When was the music of Beethoven more needed than in Himmler's Germany?" I could not therefore leave Germany in her hour of greatest need, and I have no regrets for having stayed at my post. (From Furtwängler's statement to the world press)

## 17 DECEMBER 1946

*Kamenik,* opera by the Yugoslav composer Jacov GOTOVAC, is performed for the first time in Zagreb.

## 19 DECEMBER 1946

Norman DELLO JOIO, 33-year-old American composer of Neapolitan extraction, plays the solo part, with the New York Philharmonic under the direction of George Szell, in the first performance of his *Ricercari* for piano and orchestra, written in a Baroque idiom vitalized by melorhythmic asymmetries.

## 20 DECEMBER 1946

*Die Flut,* one-act chamber opera by Boris BLACHER, to a libretto fashioned after a short story by Guy de Maupassant, *Mademoiselle Henriette,* in which a group of travelers becomes stranded on a sandbar at high tide, a young man murders and robs a banker and runs away with his mistress, with a chorus supplying a moralistically cynical commentary, set to music in stark lines of direct action in hard polytriadic harmonies, is performed for the first time on the Berlin Radio. (First stage performance took place in Dresden on 4 March 1947)

## 20 DECEMBER 1946

Darius MILHAUD conducts the Boston Symphony Orchestra in the first performance of his *Second Symphony,* in five movements: (1) *Paisible,* pacific, despite some bellicose outbursts of the trumpet and the piccolo (2) *Mystérieux,* with arcane atonalities in the high register of the violins (3) *Douloureux,* a dolorous manifestation in roaring fortissississimo (4) *Avec Sérénité,* wherein serenity is portrayed in jig time (5) *Allélouia,* a fugal laetification in modernistic psalmody.

## 21 DECEMBER 1946

*Minstrel Show* by the 33-year-old American composer Morton GOULD, "a musical impression of the old minstrel tunes," scored in a coloristic folksy manner, with the application of special effects such as sandpaper blocks imitating the shuffling sound of the soft-shoe dance, is performed for the first time by the Indianapolis Symphony Orchestra, Fabien Sevitzky conducting.

## 27 DECEMBER 1946

Charles MUNCH, Alsatian-born, German-educated French conductor makes his American debut with the Boston Symphony Orchestra, of which he was to become the conductor and Music Director in 1949–1962, in a program of French music, featuring a *Sonata a due* by Maurice JAUBERT, killed at the front on 19 June 1940, during the last days of French military resistance to the Nazis.

### 28 DECEMBER 1946

Carrie Jacobs BOND whose ultra-sentimental tunes such as *The End of a Perfect Day*, which she published herself on borrowed money, stirred millions of American hearts and sold millions of copies, dies in Glendale, California, at the age of eighty-four, and is buried in the Forest Lawn Memorial Court of Honor, Hollywood's Westminster Abbey.

### 30 DECEMBER 1946

Charles Wakefield CADMAN, American composer of melodious and harmonious songs, among them *At Dawning*, rejected by 14 publishers before it became a perennial best seller, dies in Los Angeles at the age of sixty-five.

# ᘛ *1947* ᘚ

### 2 JANUARY 1947

*L'Oro*, music drama in three acts by the prime Italian romantic modernist Ildebrando PIZZETTI, to his own libretto, dealing with the idealistic mayor of a medieval Italian village who refuses to reveal the location of a hidden gold treasure lest sudden prosperity should undermine the morality of its heretofore frugal inhabitants, is produced at La Scala, Milan.

### 4 JANUARY 1947

*Dolores*, opera-buffa in one act by André JOLIVET, subtitled *Miracle de la Femme laide*, in which a repellently ugly woman conquers men by irresistible subcutaneous attractions, is performed for the first time on the Paris Radio.

### 9 JANUARY 1947

*Street Scene*, dramatic folk opera by Kurt WEILL, after the play of the same name by Elmer Rice, portraying in idiomatically functional tones the drab life in a New York tenement district tragically disrupted when a jealous husband kills his wife and her milkman lover, is produced in New York.

### 9 JANUARY 1947

*Second Symphony* by the 50-year-old American composer Roger SESSIONS, in four movements: (1) *Molto agitato; Tranquillo e misterioso; Molto agitato* (2)

*Allegretto capriccioso* (3) *Adagio, tranquillo ed espressivo* (4) *Allegramente,* dedicated to the memory of President Roosevelt, written in a highly dissonant polyphonic idiom within a classical formal scheme, is performed for the first time by the San Francisco Symphony Orchestra, Pierre Monteux conducting.

### 10 JANUARY 1947

*Finian's Rainbow,* a fantastic musical play by Burton LANE, involving mysterious Irishmen, a leprechaun, Southern racists and Negro sharecroppers, and including the hit songs *How Are Things in Glocca Morra* and *Look to the Rainbow,* is produced in New York.

### 11 JANUARY 1947

*The Warrior,* opera by Bernard ROGERS, "a drama in which the characters speak musically," to the biblical story of Samson and Delilah, cast in an advanced non-operatic style midway between colorful Parisian impressionism and somber Viennese expressionism, is produced at the Metropolitan Opera in New York.

### 16 JANUARY 1947

*Violin Concerto* by the Parisian-Hungarian composer Tibor HARSÁNYI is performed for the first time in Paris.

### 18 JANUARY 1947

*Prairie Legend,* "a midwestern set" for orchestra by the American composer Elie SIEGMEISTER, "inspired by the quietness and simple beauty of endless fields and the black earth," is performed for the first time in its entirety by the New York Philharmonic, Leopold Stokowski conducting. (The second part, *Harvest Evening,* was performed separately on 29 December 1946 by Stokowski and the New York Philharmonic)

### 21 JANUARY 1947

Paul Sacher conducts the Basel Chamber Orchestra in the world premières of three works written to mark its twentieth anniversary:

*Toccata e due Canzoni* by Bohuslav MARTINU; *Concerto in D* for string orchestra by Igor STRAVINSKY, in three movements, *Vivace, Arioso, Rondo,* set in an austere chiaroscuro manner of the modern baroque; *Fourth Symphony* by Arthur HONEGGER, subtitled, to honor the Swiss city for which it was written, *Deliciae Basilienses,* in three movements: (1) *Lento e misterioso—Allegro,* a lyrically discursive instrumental confabulation expressing a relish and a delight of the artistic ambience of Switzerland (2) *Larghetto,* built on the old Basel tune "Z'Basel an mim Rhy" and (3) *Allegro-Finale,* a tripartite Rondo, Passacaglia, and Fugue, intoning a fife fanfare on the tune *Basler Morgenstreich* and concluding with a Lutheran chorale and a brief coda.

### 26 JANUARY 1947

Grace MOORE, American opera star, perishes in an airplane crash, two minutes after taking off from Copenhagen for Stockholm on a concert tour.

## 28 JANUARY 1947

Reynaldo HAHN, Venezuelan-born Parisian composer of urbane theater music, mundane entertainment pieces, and daintily cadenced, lavender-scented chansons, who was the slender model of the delicately perfumed, sensitively capricious character of Vinteul in Proust's *À la recherche du temps passé*, dies in Paris at the age of seventy-one.

## 28 JANUARY 1947

*The Birthday of Infanta*, symphonic suite in seven sections after Oscar Wilde, by the Italian neo-romantic composer Mario CASTELNUOVO-TEDESCO, who settled in Hollywood in 1939, is performed for the first time in New Orleans.

## 31 JANUARY 1947

*Third Symphony* for string orchestra by the 42-year-old Soviet composer Gavriil POPOV, based on Spanish themes, written in homage of the heroic resistance of the Loyalist forces to the overwhelming Fascist bands of the Falange in the Spanish Civil War of 1936-1939, is performed for the first time in Moscow.

## 1 FEBRUARY 1947

*Symphonia Serena* by Paul HINDEMITH, in four movements of glorified *Hausmusik*: (1) *Moderately fast*, a neo-classical essay set in energetic rhythms (2) *Geschwindmarsch by Beethoven*, a paraphrase of a Beethoven military march (3) *Colloquy*, in which two groups of strings engage in an antiphonal exchange of sentiments, containing a recitative for violin solo played backstage (4) *Gay*, a polythematic finale, is performed for the first time by the Dallas Symphony Orchestra, under the direction of Antal Dorati.

## 3 FEBRUARY 1947

Artur RODZINSKI resigns from his post as conductor of the New York Philharmonic in protest against the monopolistic policies of the manager Arthur Judson, and shortly afterwards accepts an appointment as conductor and music director of the Chicago Symphony Orchestra, without signing a legally binding contract.

## 4 FEBRUARY 1947

Luigi RUSSOLO, far-seeing Italian futurist, imaginative pioneer of the Art of Noises, signatory along with four futurist painters of the original Futurist Manifesto of 11 February 1910, and himself the painter of flamboyant surrealistic canvasses under such fantastically phrased titles as *The Solidity of Fog* and *Plastic Synthesis of the Actions of a Woman*, dies at Cerro di Laveno on Lago Maggiore at the age of sixty-one.

## 8 FEBRUARY 1947

*Le Malade Imaginaire*, comic opera after Molière by the Swiss composer Hans HAUG, is produced in Zürich.

*Concerto in D* for violin and orchestra by the reformed *enfant terrible* of American music, 46-year-old George ANTHEIL, written in a socially accepta- ble melodious idiom, perfused with the nutritious extract of triadic harmonies, is performed for the first time in Dallas.

15 FEBRUARY 1947

*Violin Concerto* in D major, in 3 movements, by the 49-year-old Vienna-born composer Erich Wolfgang KORNGOLD, once hailed as a 20th-century Mozart (his given name Wolfgang underlining the kinship), but now living in un-Mo- zartean Hollywood, is performed for the first time by Jascha Heifetz who commissioned the work, with the St. Louis Symphony Orchestra, Vladimir Golschmann conducting.

The work was contemplated for a Caruso of the violin rather than for a Paganini. It is needless to say how delighted I am to have my Concerto performed by Caruso and Pa- ganini in one person: Jascha Heifetz. (From a statement by Erich Wolfgang Korngold)

In this Concerto there was more corn than gold. (Irving Kolodin in the *Saturday Re- view of Literature*, after the New York performance of the work)

16 FEBRUARY 1947

Morton GOULD, 33-year-old American composer of popular semi-classical pieces as well as impressive symphonic works, conducts the Dallas Symphony Orchestra in the first performance of his *Third Symphony* (completed on 27 January 1947) in four movements, stylistically ranging from rhapsodic roman- ticism to fugal frugality. (The last movement was revised in the form of a pas- sacaglia, and a new version performed for the first time on 28 October 1948 by the New York Philharmonic, Dimitri Mitropoulos conducting)

18 FEBRUARY 1947

Gian Carlo MENOTTI, 35-year-old Italian-born composer, conducts in New York the first performance of his one-act opera *The Telephone*, to his own li- bretto in English, bearing the subtitle *L'Amour à trois* (the third member of the amorous equilateral triangle being the telephone whose raucous ring keeps interrupting the timorous suitor until he goes out and uses his rival, the telephone, to propose to his beloved), set to music in a humorously melodious idiom peppered with euphonious dissonances, together with a revised version of his opera *The Medium*, which was originally produced in New York on 8 May 1946.

19 FEBRUARY 1947

Heitor VILLA-LOBOS conducts the orchestra of the Columbia Broadcasting System in New York in the first performance of his *Bachianas Brasileiras No. 3* for piano and orchestra, which artfully combines Brazilian musical folkways with baroque devices of Bachian polyphony.

### 21 FEBRUARY 1947

André JOLIVET conducts the Paris Radio Orchestra in the world première of his second "radiophonic legend" *Le Livre de Christophe Colomb,* to the text from a poem of Paul Claudel.

### 27 FEBRUARY 1947

*Third Symphony* by the 23-year-old American composer Peter MENNIN, in three movements, *Allegro robusto, Andante moderato, Allegro assai,* with the energetic first and precipitous third movements contrasted with lyrical "voice-weaving" in the slow middle movement, is performed for the first time by the New York Philharmonic, with Walter Hendl conducting.

### 27 FEBRUARY 1947

*Concerto for Piano and Orchestra* by Paul HINDEMITH (completed on 29 November 1945), in three movements, *Moderately fast, Slow, Medley on the Medieval Dance Tre Fontane,* the latter consisting of a canzone for solo piano developing into a non-medieval march and a romantic waltz, written in a neo-classical idiom, tonal at its core but resonantly amplified by chromatic counterpoint, is performed for the first time by Jesús María Sanromá with the Cleveland Orchestra under the direction of George Szell.

### 5 MARCH 1947

Alfredo CASELLA, scholarly animator of new Italian music, civilized composer of astutely calibrated symphonic and chamber music, operas and ballets, perspicacious observer of the contemporary musical scene, dies of cancer in Rome, at the age of sixty-three.

### 5 MARCH 1947

*Folk Symphony* by MAHLER-KALKSTEIN, 39-year-old Jewish-Polish composer (he later changed his German-sounding name to its near-Hebrew equivalent Menahem Avidom), in six movements with thematic material derived from Palestinian dance rhythms, is performed for the first time by the Palestine Symphony Orchestra in Tel Aviv.

### 6 MARCH 1947

*Twenty-Fifth Symphony* by Nicolai MIASKOVSKY, in D-flat major, set in three symmetrically contrasting movements, *Adagio, Moderato* and *Allegro impetuoso,* is performed for the first time in Moscow.

### 7 MARCH 1947

*The Song of Songs,* biblical solo cantata by the 24-year-old Berlin-born American composer Lukas Foss (whose original name was Fuchs), in four sections, written in an appropriately Solomonesque manner of devotional sensuality, is performed for the first time by the Boston Symphony Orchestra, Serge

Koussevitzky conducting, Ellabelle Davis, Negro soprano, to whom the work is dedicated, soloist.

### 13 MARCH 1947

*Brigadoon,* whimsical musical fantasy by the Viennese-born American operetta composer Frederick LOEWE, set in a mythical village in Scotland, which magically vanishes in 1747 to escape a plague of witches, but reappears once in a century for twenty-four hours, leading to a fantastic situation when an American tourist anachronistically wanders into it during its periodical time corridor in 1947 and falls in love with a ravishing bicentennial Scottish lass, is produced in New York.

### 14 MARCH 1947

*Lestenitza,* one-act opera by the 58-year-old Greek composer George SKLAVOS, is performed for the first time in Athens.

### 14 MARCH 1947

*Habeyssée* (whimsical phonetic homonym of ABC, pronounced in French) for violin and orchestra by the venerable French modernist Florent SCHMITT, is performed for the first time in Paris.

### 19 MARCH 1947

*The Minotaur,* ballet by the 38-year-old American composer Elliott CARTER, depicting in somberly dramatic tones the classical horrors of the gluttonously carnivorous Cretan bull, with Ariadne unwinding her quaquaversally labyrinthine thread to lead the heroic but ungentlemanly tauricide Theseus out to safety, is performed for the first time by the New York Ballet Society.

### 19 MARCH 1947

Willem PIJPER, Dutch composer of atmospheric symphonies, coloristic chamber music and impressionistic chansons, whose persistent use of the scale of alternating whole tones and semitones caused it to be known in Holland as the "Pijper scale" (Rimsky-Korsakov had a long established priority on it, and in Russia it is known as "Rimsky-Korsakov scale"), dies at Leidschendam at the age of fifty-two.

### 26 MARCH 1947

*Khamma,* "légende dansée" by Claude DEBUSSY in the orchestration of Charles Koechlin, is produced for the first time as a ballet at the Opéra-Comique in Paris. (Its first concert performance took place at the Concerts-Colonne in Paris, on 15 November 1924)

### 28 MARCH 1947

*Tic-Tac,* operetta by the Swiss composer Willy BURKHARD, is performed for the first time in Zürich.

1 APRIL 1947

*Europa und der Stier,* opera by the synthetic composer Siegfried SITZPLATZ, conjured up by synchronous playing of several different phonograph records in heteroousian disharmony interspersed with unauthentic singing commercials, is broadcast on April Fool's Day over radio station WQXR in New York, for the delectation of the cognoscenti and consternation among the untutored radio masses.

11 APRIL 1947

Ernst KRENEK conducts at the University of Chicago the first performance of his choral work a cappella, *The Santa Fe Time Table,* to the text from the time table of the Santa Fe Railroad, covering all stops between Albuquerque and Los Angeles.

12 APRIL 1947

*La follia di Orlando,* ballet by the 42-year-old Italian modernist Goffredo PETRASSI, is given for the first time at La Scala, Milan.

16 APRIL 1947

*Marion, ou la Belle au Tricorne,* radio opera by the 31-year-old Swiss composer Pierre WISSMER, is performed for the first time in Geneva.

16 APRIL 1947

*Fourth Symphony* by the 56-year-old Czech composer Karel Boleslav JIRÁK is performed for the first time in Prague.

18 APRIL 1947

*The Trial of Lucullus,* opera in one act by Roger SESSIONS, to the radio play written in 1939 by Bertolt Brecht, an anti-Hitler allegory involving a predatory Roman general brought to trial before the tribunal of common people at the entrance to the Elysian Fields, and condemned for his crimes against humanity despite his proud claims of having dethroned seven kings and destroyed 53 cities, set to music in a structurally compact, texturally dissonant, melodically atonal and rhythmically asymmetric idiom, is performed for the first time at the Berkeley Campus of the University of California.

19 APRIL 1947

*Rachel,* one-act opera by Reinhold GLIÈRE, after Guy de Maupassant's short story *Mademoiselle Fifi,* dealing with the assassination by a patriotic French tart of an obnoxious Prussian lieutenant nicknamed Mademoiselle Fifi during the occupation of Rouen in 1871 by the Prussian Army (who are characterized in the score by a grotesquely dislocated Austrian tune *Ach du lieber Augustin*), receives its first stage performance in Moscow. (A radio performance of *Rachel* was given in Moscow in 1943 as a propaganda production at the height of the Soviet-Nazi war)

## 19 APRIL 1947

*Veronika,* opera by the 32-year-old Czech composer-conductor Rafael KUBELÍK, son of the once idolized violin virtuoso Jan Kubelík, is produced in Brno.

## 23 APRIL 1947

*Symphony in A* by the American composer John POWELL, in four movements, reflecting four different genres of American folkways—*Country Dance, Folksong, Ballad, Ritual Dance*—as "a synthesis of American folk music tradition" is performed for the first time by the Detroit Symphony Orchestra.

## 24 APRIL 1947

*Two Rustic Dances,* symphonic set by the 62-year-old German-Czech novelist, playwright, philosopher and occasional composer Max BROD, who immigrated into Palestine in 1939, is performed for the first time in Tel Aviv, with Charles Munch conducting the Palestine Symphony Orchestra.

## 1 MAY 1947

A three-day Symposium on Music Criticism intended "to help the new army of listeners by providing them with a greater number of competent guides," and "to initiate a fundamental reexamination of the principles of music criticism," opens at Harvard University in Cambridge, Massachusetts with introductory remarks by various musicologists, followed by first performances of specially commissioned works: *Third String Quartet* by Walter PISTON, professor of composition at Harvard University; *String Trio,* op. 45, by Arnold SCHOENBERG, in one movement divided into three sections by two intervening "episodes" providing formal and stylistic contrasts; and *Sixth String Quartet* by Bohuslav MARTINU.

## 2 MAY 1947

On the second day of the Harvard Symposium on Music Criticism, three choral works commissioned for the occasion are performed for the first time: *Apparebit repentina Dies* for mixed chorus and brasses by Paul HINDEMITH, to the text of a medieval hymn; *La Terra* for chorus and organ by Gian Francesco MALIPIERO, to words from Virgil's *Georgics*; and *In the Beginning* by Aaron COPLAND for mezzo-soprano and chorus, to words from the opening chapters of *Genesis*.

## 3 MAY 1947

The Harvard Symposium of Music Criticism concludes with the first performance by Martha Graham and her dance group of *Night Journey,* obstetrical ballet by William SCHUMAN, in which an allegorical umbilical cord is tangled up prior to parturition in a discordant coil of atonal filaments and spasmodically jactitating rhythms within an amniotic sac of constantly colliding acrid bitonalities.

## 7 MAY 1947

*The Mother of Us All,* opera in three acts by the subtle symphonizer of sophisticated simplicities Virgil THOMSON, to words by Gertrude Stein (before a single note was put on paper, she called it "the greatest American tragic opera"), dealing with the story of the American pioneer of women's suffrage Susan B. Anthony, and introducing such historic figures as Ulysses S. Grant, Daniel Webster and Lillian Russell, as well as Gertrude S. and Virgil T. "to supply comment and interpretation," set to music in an ostentatiously triadic idiom with allusive old American melodic turns ("jamais de banalité, le plus possible de lieux communs," as the composer put it in French), is produced at Columbia University in New York.

## 12 MAY 1947

At the opening concert of the Third Annual Festival of Contemporary American Music given at Columbia University in New York, the 46-year-old Russian-American composer Nicolai BEREZOWSKY conducts the first performance of his oratorio *Gilgamesh,* relating the proud chronicle of King Gilgamesh of Babylon who in 1750 B.C. refused to submit to a Sumerian tyrant, set to music in an effective blend of archaic and modern devices.

## 13 MAY 1947

*The Seasons,* ballet by the 34-year-old American musical experimentalist John CAGE, reflecting the traditional view of the seasons of the year as quiescence (winter), creation (spring), preservation (summer) and decay (autumn), with thematic components arranged serially in single tones, intervals and chords, is performed for the first time in New York.

## 27 MAY 1947

*Fifth Symphony* by Bohuslav MARTINU, in three movements: (1) *Adagio-Allegro-Adagio-Allegro-Adagio,* shimmeringly dissonant and bitonal, set in nervously asymmetrical rhythms (2) *Larghetto,* a study in serenely nostalgic modalities (3) *Lento,* a Moravian dumka, is performed for the first time in Prague under the direction of Rafael Kubelík.

## 28 MAY 1947

Larry ADLER, American virtuoso performer on the oral harmonica, gives the world première in Paris of the *Suite for Harmonica and Orchestra* by Darius MILHAUD, in three dance-like movements: *Gigues, Sailor's Song, Hornpipes.* (The *Suite* was originally performed in Philadelphia on 16 November 1945, in a version for violin and orchestra, by Zino Francescati with the Philadelphia Orchestra, Eugene Ormandy conducting)

## 29 MAY 1947

The 21st Festival of the International Society for Contemporary Music opens in Copenhagen with the following program of symphonic music:

*Fifth Symphony* by the 37-year-old Danish composer Vagn HOLMBOE; *Variations symphoniques* by the 53-year-old Belgian composer Jean ABSIL, conceived monothematically, in three parts with 12 variations; *Concerto for String Orchestra* by Sweden's most prolific composer Hilding ROSENBERG; *De Profundis* for chorus and orchestra by the Slovak composer Vítězslav NOVÁK (first performed in Brno on 20 November 1941 as a mute litany of Czechoslovakia under the Nazi domination); and *Galdreslätten*, symphonic dance by the Norwegian nationalistic modernist Harald SAEVERUD, inspired by a perdurable childhood memory of his great-grandfather who was a village fiddler and maker of fiddles.

### 31 MAY 1947

At the second concert of the 21st Festival of the International Society for Contemporary Music in Copenhagen, the following program of chamber music is given:

*Second String Quartet* in one movement by the neo-classical Swiss composer Willy BURKHARD; *Toccata* for two pianos by the 23-year-old Austrian composer Anton HEILLER; *Trio* for two violins and viola by György KÓSA of Hungary; *Piano Sonata* by Jan KAPR of Czechoslovakia, written in an atonally inflected neo-classical idiom; and *Sextet* for wind instruments and piano by Herman KOPPEL of Denmark.

### 1 JUNE 1947

At the third concert of the 21st Festival of the International Society for Contemporary Music in Copenhagen, the following program of chamber music is presented:

*Trio* for string instruments by the 30-year-old Swedish composer Karl-Birger BLOMDAHL; *Piano Sonata* by Aaron COPLAND, a meticulously calculated study in thematic patterns and percussively pianistic sonorities, in three movements of austerely passionate music (first performed in Buenos Aires on 21 October 1941); *Second Violin Sonata* by Sergei PROKOFIEV, written in a characteristic, ironically lyrical vein (in a postcard of 3 February 1948, addressed to the *Musical Digest* of Chicago, George Bernard Shaw describes this Sonata as "a humorous masterpiece of authentic violin music," unaware of the fact that Prokofiev originally composed it for flute and piano, later arranging it for violin); *Partita* for piano by the 27-year-old Dane Niels Viggo BENTZON, couched in a peculiarly Hindemithish neo-classical idiom; and *Second String Quartet* by the 41-year-old English composer Benjamin FRANKEL.

### 2 JUNE 1947

At the fourth concert of the 21st Festival of the International Society for Contemporary Music in Copenhagen, the following program of instrumental music is given:

*Serenades* for piano and chamber orchestra by David van de WOESTYNE of Belgium; *Concerto* for clarinet and strings by the modernistic 40-year-old neo-Elizabethan Elizabeth MACONCHY of England; *Duae fugae novem compositae sonis quattuor sine nomine vocibus* by Adone ZECCHI of Italy, based on a 9-note subject and scored for four anonymous instrumental or vocal parts; *Sonetto di Michelangelo* for chamber orchestra

by the Norwegian modernist Fartein VALEN; *Concerto* for bassoon and orchestra by
Michal SPISAK of Poland; and *Préludes joyeux* by Camille SCHMIT of Belgium.

### 2 JUNE 1947

Herman DAREWSKI, Russian-born pianist, inventor of Kiddie Music Notation,
in which the notes of the scale are designated by animal names, who used this
method as music instructor of Princess Elizabeth, later Queen Elizabeth II of
England, dies in London at the age of sixty-four.

### 3 JUNE 1947

At the fifth concert of the 21st Festival of the International Society for Contemporary Music in Copenhagen the following program of chamber music is
presented:

*Arcana Musae Dona* by the 35-year-old Dutch composer Rudolf ESCHER, combining
urbane impressionism with conscious neo-medieval modalities; *Trio* for oboe, clarinet
and bassoon by Klement SLAVICKÝ of Czechoslovakia; *Second String Quartet* by Ernest
BLOCH, marked by passionate expressiveness with modernistically acerbic departures
from tonality; *Piano Sonata* by André JOLIVET, 41-year-old representative of the group
"La jeune France"; and three sacred choruses, *Cade la sera, Ululate* and *Recordare
Domine* by the Italian master of neo-ecclesiastic modern music Ildebrando PIZZETTI.

### 3 JUNE 1947

*Les Mamelles de Tirésias,* opéra bouffe in two acts by the 48-year-old French
modernist Francis POULENC, after the surrealist play by Guillaume Apollinaire, wherein a lady's *mamelles* are detached and float away in the form of
inflated mammary balloons, exploding when ignited, which induces her to assume a male identity under the name of Tirésias, whereupon her outraged
husband retaliates by effecting a transsexual change of his own, leading to
such embroilment in a series of incongruous peripeteia that both decide to resume their original sexual denominations and functions to the strains of a
"metamorphosis waltz" and address a fervent plea to the audience to multiply freely for the glory of France ("Faites des enfants . . ."), announcing
proudly that in his female avatar, the husband produced from his womb fully
40,000 offspring, is performed for the first time at the Opéra-Comique in
Paris. (Date from the announcement in *Le Figaro,* Paris, of the date of the
première, 3 June 1947; the date of the répétition générale, 31 May 1947, is
given in some reference works as the première.)

### 4 JUNE 1947

At the sixth and last concert of the 21st Festival of the International Society
for Contemporary Music in Copenhagen the following program is presented:

*Sinfonia breve,* in five neo-classical movements by the 56-year-old Swedish composer
Gösta NYSTROEM; *Spoon River Anthology,* oratorio for soloists, chorus and orchestra
by Gino NEGRI of Italy, to the text from the American modern classic by Edgar Lee
MASTERS; *Petite Symphonie Concertante* for harp, harpsichord, piano and two string
orchestras by the 56-year-old Swiss composer Frank MARTIN (first performed in Zürich
on 17 May 1946); and a symphonic suite from the ballet *Don Quixote* by Roberto
GERHARD, Catalan expatriate modernist now living in London.

## 8 JUNE 1947

*Fourth Symphony* by the Austrian composer Max BUTTING is performed for the first time in Berlin.

## 12 JUNE 1947

Nina MAKAROVA, wife of Aram Khachaturian, and composeress in her own right, conducts in Moscow the first performance of her optimistically feminine *First Symphony*.

## 15 JUNE 1947

*Die Bernauerin,* folk opera in two parts and seven scenes by the German composer Carl ORFF, dedicated to the memory of Kurt Huber, German ethnomusicologist executed by the Nazis on 13 July 1943, to a libretto revolving around the Bavarian duchess of low birth, Agnes Bernauer, known as die Bernauerin, who was set upon and drowned by her tyrannical father-in-law in 1435, set to music of maundering monodies, scored for a stringless orchestra floating despondently in a pond of quintal homophony (the bass voices are programmed to sing la-la-la on a single note 75 times), is produced in Stuttgart.

## 20 JUNE 1947

Benjamin BRITTEN conducts at the Glyndebourne Festival in England the first performance of his fourth opera *Albert Herring,* in three acts, to a libretto after Guy de Maupassant's story *Le Rosier de Madame Husson,* with its locale transferred to an English town, wherein a shy and over-chaste citizen named Albert Herring is crowned as May King as the sole virginal person in the area, but is declassified when he undergoes a scandalous deterioration in his character after drinking an alcoholic potion (a *Tristan* chord is sounded in the orchestra at this point) under the impression that it was lemonade.

## 20 JUNE 1947

LEMONADE OPERA, a cooperative enterprise, so named after the beverage served during theater intermissions, opens in New York its first and last season with a tepid production of Mozart's *Don Giovanni.*

## 25 JUNE 1947

*Symphony No. 5½* by the Democritically cachinnigenous Missourian Don GILLIS, so named because it was written between his 5th and 6th symphonies, subtitled *Symphony for Fun,* in four movements, *Perpetual Emotion, Spiritual, Scherzophrenia* and *Conclusion,* is performed for the first time by the Boston Pops Orchestra, Arthur Fiedler conducting.

## 2 JULY 1947

In the Denazification Court in Bayreuth, Winifred WAGNER, widow of Wagner's son Siegfried, is declared guilty of willing participation in the criminal actions of Hitler's Third Reich. (60% of her personal property, including shares in the Bayreuth Festival Company, was ordered to be confiscated, but the ruling was rescinded in March 1949 by the Bavarian Bureau for Political Exoneration)

### 9 JULY 1947

Two hundred years have passed since the death in Vienna, in abject poverty, of Giovanni BONONCINI, the Italian rival of Handel for operatic supremacy in London, who was exalted in a contemporary jingle, "Some say, compared to Bononcini/ That Mein Herr Handel's but a ninny."

### 6 AUGUST 1947

Heitor VILLA-LOBOS conducts in Rome the first performance of his orchestral *Bachianas Brasileiras* No. 8, in four movements combining the baroque techniques of Bach with the native melorhythms of Brazil, *Preludio, Aria (Modinha), Toccata (Catira Batida)* and *Fuga*.

### 6 AUGUST 1947

*Dantons Tod,* opera in two acts by the 29-year-old Swiss-born Austrian composer Gottfried von EINEM, to a libretto by the Manchurian-born half-Estonian, half-German composer Boris Blacher, after a play by the short-lived German romanticist Georg Büchner (1813–1837), expressive of human futility and individual ineluctability during major historical upheavals, such as the French Revolution, with a score of two-dimensional monody in opaquely discordant harmonies and statically coalescent polyphony, marking Danton's death on the guillotine by impassive choral commentary, and concluding with a philosophical stroke of a tam-tam, is produced in Salzburg. (Waggish tongues commented, with reference to the eclectic nature of the music, "Nicht von Einem sondern von vielen")

### 20 AUGUST 1947

*Song of the Antipodes,* symphonic poem by the 31-year-old New Zealand composer Douglas LILBURN, is performed for the first time in Wellington, New Zealand.

### 22 AUGUST 1947

*The Free Wind,* operetta by the Soviet composer Isaak DUNAYEVSKY, dealing with an Italian anti-Fascist resistance member during World War II, who is persecuted again, after Allied victory, by the American occupation army in Italy as a Communist, with a happy ending as he joins his proletarian girl companion, is produced in Moscow.

### 27 AUGUST 1947

*Heimferd,* opera by the Norwegian composer Ludvig Irgens JENSEN, is produced in Oslo.

## 20 SEPTEMBER 1947

El Salvador issues a commemorative stamp of 12 centavos to honor Felipe SOTO, native bandleader who composed the music of the Salvadorean national anthem.

## 28 SEPTEMBER 1947

*Great Friendship,* opera in four acts by the Georgian composer Vano MURADELI, depicting in luxuriantly orientalistic tones the turmoil of the Civil War in North Caucasus in 1919, is produced in Stalino (Donetz).

(It was produced under the title *Friendship of Peoples* in Perm on 24 October 1947, and under the original title in Leningrad on 5 November 1947; and on 7 November 1947, on the 30th anniversary of the Soviet Revolution, simultaneously in Moscow, Gorky, Novosibirsk and Saratov. These productions led to the denunciation of the opera for the erroneous interpretation of the role of Caucasian ethnic groups, for the modernistically simplicistic musical characterizations and the fallaciously formalistic technical treatment. See complete text of the denunciation in the section LETTERS AND DOCUMENTS)

## 9 OCTOBER 1947

*High Button Shoes,* musical comedy by Jule STYNE, dealing with a couple of imaginative crooks in the pacific world of 1913, containing a song *Papa Won't You Dance with Me,* is produced in New York City.

## 10 OCTOBER 1947

*Allegro,* a musical play by Richard RODGERS with book and lyrics by Oscar Hammerstein II, dealing with a small town doctor who rises to social eminence in Chicago, but becomes disillusioned and returns to his point of origin and humble but honest practice, containing the popular number *The Gentleman Is a Dope,* and including extended excursions into the domain of grand opera in ensembles written for chorus, soloists and orchestra, is produced in New York.

## 10 OCTOBER 1947

*Sixth Symphony* by Sergei PROKOFIEV, set in the explicitly designated and symphonically rare key of E-flat minor, in three movements: (1) *Allegro moderato,* lyrically austere but propulsively energetic (2) *Largo,* a songfully bright and harmoniously contemplative elegy (3) *Vivace,* cyclically reminiscent of the first movement, precipitating into a cataract of major keys, is performed for the first time in Leningrad. (The first Moscow performance, on 25 December 1947, is erroneously listed as the absolute first hearing in the Third Edition of *Music Since 1900*)

## 13 OCTOBER 1947

*Fourth Symphony* by the Dutch composer Henk BADINGS is performed for the first time in Rotterdam.

## 20 OCTOBER 1947

Thomas K. SCHERMAN inaugurates in New York a series of concerts of the Little Orchestra Society, founded and conducted by him, with the aim of providing a convenient outlet for contemporary composers and opaque luminaries of the Baroque past, presenting during its first season the première of music for *Romeo and Juliet* by David DIAMOND; a brisk neo-classical *Concerto* for harp and orchestra by Norman DELLO JOIO; *Farm Journal,* a suite by the smiling philosopher of American music Douglas MOORE, which includes such pastoral symphonic tableaux as *Up Early, Sunday Clothes, Lamplight* and *Harvest Song*; and sundry pieces by Georges ENESCO, Ferruccio BUSONI and others.

## 21 OCTOBER 1947

*First Symphony* by the 32-year-old American composer Vincent PERSICHETTI, in one movement, written in 1942, and set in a humanistically deployed neo-classical idiom with discreetly discrete dissonances and emanations of chromatic vapors liberated by diatonic vesicles in nutritious polytriadic harmonies, is performed for the first time in Rochester, New York, under the direction of Howard Hanson.

## 24 OCTOBER 1947

*Short Symphony* by Henry COWELL, his fourth, in four movements: (1) *Hymn* (2) *Ballad* (3) *Dance* (4) *Fuguing Tune,* oriented towards American melodic and rhythmic materials and concluding with a stylization of fuguing tunes developed from the shaped-note style of *Southern Harmony* (1854), is performed for the first time by the Boston Symphony Orchestra, Richard Burgin conducting.

## 24 OCTOBER 1947

*Seventh Symphony* by the 50-year-old Polish-born Parisian composer Alexandre TANSMAN, in four linked movements, opening with a slow meditative introduction, followed by an energetic main portion, and, after an *Andante cantabile* connecting with a scherzo, ending cyclically with a reversion to the initial movement, is performed for the first time by the St. Louis Symphony Orchestra, Vladimir Golschmann conducting.

## 25 OCTOBER 1947

*Genoveva,* opera in three acts by the Swedish composer Natanael BERG, to the Germanic legend (previously used by Schumann for his identically named opera) of a crusader's immaculately chaste bride monstrously charged with inconceivable adultery by a scheming henchman coveting her with licentious lust, aided and abetted by a diabolical magus who conjures up lascivious visual tableaux calculated to incense his lecherous fantasies, with virtue triumphant at the end and the collusive villains foiled, set to music in constantly tumescent Straussian harmonies, is produced in Stockholm.

*Beautiful Season,* symphonic poem by the Japanese composer Hisaharu WATANABE, is performed for the first time in Tokyo.

30 OCTOBER 1947

*Third Symphony* by Darius MILHAUD, subtitled *Hymnus Ambrosianus,* in four movements, concluding with a *Te Deum,* is performed for the first time in Paris. (Although *Te Deum* is commonly ascribed to St. Ambrose, and is often called Ambrosian Hymn, it was probably the work of the Bishop of Remesiana; Milhaud followed the general assumption in subtitling his symphony *Ambrosianus*)

30 OCTOBER 1947

*First Symphony* by the 38-year-old American composer Elie SIEGMEISTER, in four movements, *Andante, Vivace brioso, Moderato cantabile, Maestoso,* expressive of "the spirit, the struggle and the hope of man," permeated by the American melos without actual quotations from folk tunes, is performed for the first time by the New York Philharmonic, Leopold Stokowski conducting.

31 OCTOBER 1947

*Toccata for Percussion Instruments* by Carlos CHÁVEZ, in three movements: *Allegro* for drums only; *Largo* for metallic instruments and a xylophone, and *Allegro un poco marziale* for small drums, maracas, claves and glockenspiel, is performed for the first time in Mexico City.

3 NOVEMBER 1947

*Fifth Symphony* by Gian Francesco MALIPIERO (completed on 25 September 1947), subtitled *Concertante, in eco* (with reference to two conspicuous piano parts echoing each other and "dominating the music like a dual spinal column of the instrumental organism"), without a key signature, but with clear tonal intent, in four sections, *Allegro agitato* (in traditional sonata form), *Lento* (projecting a series of bell-like chords in the piano parts), *Allegro vivace* (opening with a consortium of drumlets accompanied by a triangle) and *Lento ma non troppo* (ending in an evanescently pandiatonic chord), is performed for the first time by the orchestra of the British Broadcasting Corporation in London.

7 NOVEMBER 1947

*The Young Guard,* opera in four acts by the Ukrainian composer Yuli MEITUS, depicting in epic Russian modalities the heroic resistance against the brutal Nazi occupation by a group of young boys and girls in a mining locality in the Don basin in 1943, who perish with the name of Stalin on their lips as the red dawn heralds liberation, is produced in the Ukrainian language in Kiev, on the 30th anniversary of the Soviet Revolution.

## 8 NOVEMBER 1947

The first Estonian ballet, *Kalevipoeg,* by the Estonian composer Eugen KAPP, to a scenario derived from the medieval Estonian tale of a peasant girl abducted by a demon who in turn is destroyed by a benevolent Estonian god, while the girl is transformed into a stone image, is performed for the first time in Tallin.

## 9 NOVEMBER 1947

*Les Douze,* cantata by Alexander TCHEREPNIN, for narrator, strings, harp, piano and percussion, to the text of the religiously revolutionary ballad by the Russian poet Alexandre Blok, in which twelve Red Army Guards are likened to the Twelve Apostles led by Jesus Christ, is performed for the first time in Paris.

## 9 NOVEMBER 1947

During the radio festival of Slavic music in Cracow, Andrzej PANUFNIK, 33-year-old Polish composer, conducts the first performance of his *Berceuse,* scored for 29 string instruments and two harps, and making use of icositetraphonic harmonies in quarter-tones.

## 17 NOVEMBER 1947

*Cosmogonie,* symphonic prelude by André JOLIVET, is performed for the first time, nine years after it was composed, by the Paris Radio Orchestra.

## 20 NOVEMBER 1947

*Mediator Dei,* encyclical letter by Pope PIUS XII, is issued at the Vatican, promulgating a new and more liberal view (as compared with *Motu Proprio* of 1903) regarding the use of secular music in Catholic liturgy and allowing the inclusion in church services of "modern music and singing . . . if such is not profane and does not spring from a desire of achieving extraordinary and unusual effects," while reaffirming the supremacy of the Gregorian chant, "which the Roman Catholic Church considers her own as handed down from antiquity and kept under her close tutelage," and further urging "that the faithful take part in the sacred ceremonies, alternating their voices with the priest and the choir, according to the prescribed norms" (Full text is given in the section LETTERS AND DOCUMENTS)

## 21 NOVEMBER 1947

*Third Symphony* by the 32-year-old American composer Vincent PERSICHETTI, in four movements bearing subtitles expressive of mood and tempo: (1) *Somber,* built on two dotted-note figures and ending on a 12-tone chord (2) *Spirited,* in a dancing mode (3) *Singing,* centered on a sustained melody in the English horn (4) *Fast and Brilliant,* an exuberant exposition of varied themes, concluding with a chorale, is performed for the first time by the Philadelphia Orchestra, Eugene Ormandy conducting.

## 25 NOVEMBER 1947

A waterproof Irish harp, manufactured by Melville CLARK of Syracuse, New York, strung with pre-shrunk nylon strings, is given its first public demonstration in New York by a mermaid-shaped harpist enclosed in a glass tank filled with water, in a fluvially fluent demonstration of marine arpeggios, underwater glissandos and aquatic passages of enharmonic liquidity.

## 27 NOVEMBER 1947

*Fourth Symphony* by Ernst KRENEK, in three movements, the inner meaning of which is the materialization of an ideal detached from reality and the victory of that ideal over the menace of disruptive forces, written in the 12-tone technique to secure a "very high amount of logical coherence and intelligible significance," within the framework of classical divisions, the first movement following a sonata-allegro form, the second, an *Adagio*, being a dual variation and the last, a triune *Allegro* constituting an abstract rondo, is performed for the first time by the New York Philharmonic, Dimitri Mitropoulos conducting.

## 27 NOVEMBER 1947

*Variations for Orchestra on a Theme by Paganini*, a set of 16 variations by the 44-year-old Manchurian-born Russian-bred, genetically Estonian-German composer Boris BLACHER, using the same theme as the famous variations of Brahms and Rachmaninoff, each variation posing a distinct structural problem in which the melorhythmic parameters are arranged in different arithmetical proportions, with the exploitation of sophisticated crudity to dispel the illusion of euphony, is performed for the first time in Leipzig.

## 29 NOVEMBER 1947

*The Legend of Ohrid*, ballet in four acts by the 62-year-old Serbian composer Stevan HRISTIĆ, depicting the abduction of a Serbian bride by Turkish janissaries for the Sultan's harem and her liberation as she is magically transformed into a turtle dove, with a colorful score making use of asymmetrical Balkan melorhythms, is performed for the first time in Belgrade, under the composer's direction.

## 30 NOVEMBER 1947

On the day of the official proclamation at the United Nations of the independence of Israel, Avner CARMI, a Jewish piano technician, completes his repair work on the so-called Siena Piano, the sounding board of which, according to legend, contained wood from King David's harp (thus fulfilling the prophecy that Israel would be reborn when David's harp is sounded again in the land), which became part of the two pillars, known as Joachim and Boaz, of King Solomon's Temple, was carried away from Jerusalem by Roman soldiers after the destruction of the Temple in 70 A.D., subsequently used as material for a Roman Caesarian sanctuary, and after its destruction by an earthquake eventually found its way to Italy and was embedded in the Siena Piano constructed in the 18th century.

### 1 DECEMBER 1947

The Spanish Government issues a series of postage stamps at 15, 20, 25, and 80 centavos, honoring Manuel DE FALLA, great Spanish composer who died in Argentina in exile on 14 November 1946.

### 3 DECEMBER 1947

Ernst von DOHNÁNYI, Nestor of Hungarian composers, plays in Sheffield, England, the piano part in the first performance of his *Second Piano Concerto* in B minor, with Thomas Beecham conducting the orchestra.

### 4 DECEMBER 1947

*Song of the Dead Proletarians,* cantata by the 36-year-old Slovenian composer Ivan RUPNIK, glorifying in sonorous triadic modalities the heroism of Yugoslav partisans during the Nazi occupation, is performed for the first time in Belgrade, conducted by the composer.

### 11 DECEMBER 1947

*Trilogy* by the 50-year-old American composer Leroy ROBERTSON, a symphonic poem inspired by the ambience of the high plateaus of his native Utah where he tended sheep as a youth, and written in an effective abecedarian idiom, vitalized by some realistic onomatopeia, such as the sound of male tobacco expectorations into brass spittoons, winner of the $25,000 prize for the best symphonic work by an American composer donated by the chemical magnate Henry Reichhold (Robertson submitted his score under the nom de plume Nostrebor, i.e. Robertson spelled backwards), is performed for the first time by the Detroit Symphony Orchestra.

### 14 DECEMBER 1947

*Exodus,* biblical choreographic poem for baritone solo and orchestra by the 37-year-old Polish-born composer Josef GRÜNTHAL (who later abbreviated his name to Tal), is performed for the first time by the Palestine Symphony Orchestra in Tel Aviv.

### 15 DECEMBER 1947

*Les Mirages,* choreographic fairy-tale for symphony orchestra by the 46-year-old French composer Henri SAUGUET, to a scenario in which a youth invades the palace of the moon and rouses the ethereal maidens of the night only to find that his mirage of love is the image of death, is produced at the Paris Opéra.

### 18 DECEMBER 1947

*Rosa de Papel,* opera by the Portuguese composer Ruy COELHO, is produced in Lisbon.

21 DECEMBER 1947

*Saul,* opera in five scenes by the German composer Hermann REUTTER, to the biblical story of a tortured superstitious king of the Hebrews, punctuated by Handelian trumpet calls and tinctured by modern Angst, expressed by tumid dissonances and corrosive orientalistic chromatics, is produced by the Hamburg State Opera.

29 DECEMBER 1947

*Militza,* heroic ballet by the Russian composer Boris ASAFIEV, written in 1942 to glorify the name of a Serbian girl guerrilla, leader of the resistance movement against the Nazi occupation troops in Yugoslavia, with the authenticity of the music enhanced by the use of Serbian dance tunes, is performed for the first time in Leningrad.

# ◈ *1948* ◈

1 JANUARY 1948

*Buduj Vlast, Posíliš mír (Build Your Nation, and You Will Strengthen Peace)* cantata by the Czech composer Václav DOBIÁŠ, suffused with patriotically socialistic sentiments in the virile rhythms of Bohemian rustic dances, is performed for the first time in Prague.

9 JANUARY 1948

*Third Symphony* in E by Walter PISTON, in four movements: (1) *Andantino* (2) *Allegro* (3) *Adagio* (4) *Allegro,* designated respectively as being in Tonality C, Tonality F, Tonality G and Tonality C, and constructed on a network of interdependent thematic "phrases" is performed for the first time by the Boston Symphony Orchestra, Serge Koussevitzky conducting.

10 JAUNARY 1948

*El Mozo que casó con mujer brava,* one-act comic opera by the Spanish composer Carlos SURINACH, is produced in Barcelona.

13 JANUARY 1948

The board of trustees of the Chicago Symphony Orchestra peremptorily dismisses its conductor and music director Artur RODZINSKI in the middle of his first season, charging him with "last-minute program changes causing confusion in rehearsals, staging of operatic productions in place of regular concerts, exceeding the budget by $30,000 and attempting to secure a three-year contract."

## 15 JANUARY 1948

*Étude,* ballet by the Danish composer Knudaage RIISAGER, with the music based on Czerny's celebrated finger exercises, is performed for the first time in Copenhagen.

## 21 JANUARY 1948

Ermanno WOLF-FERRARI, Italian opera composer whose *Il Segreto di Susanna* (the secret is Suzanne's shocking indulgence in cigarette smoking) has created a new type of comic *verismo,* dies in Venice at the age of seventy-two.

## 21 JANUARY 1948

The Austrain Government issues a 20-groschen postage stamp in honor of Karl Michael ZIEHRER (1843–1922), Austrian band leader and composer of a myriad of Viennese waltzes.

## 23 JANUARY 1948

*Fourth Symphony* by the 32-year-old American composer David DIAMOND, his "smallest large symphony," in three movements: (1) *Allegretto,* symbolizing a state of uninterrupted sleep (2) *Andante,* illustrative of the transition from sleep to wakefulness and (3) *Allegro,* signifying eternal awakening in death, is performed for the first time by the Boston Symphony Orchestra, Leonard Bernstein conducting.

## 23 JANUARY 1948

*Mandu-Carará,* symphonic poem by Heitor VILLA-LOBOS, scored for two pianos, percussion, mixed choir and children's chorus, inspired by a Brazilian legend of two resourceful Indian children who, like their European analogues Hänsel and Gretel, kill the malevolent ogress while her ogre husband goes into the jungle in search of two fat monkeys, is performed in a world première in New York.

## 25 JANUARY 1948

*Second Symphony* by the 30-year-old American composer Robert WARD, intended to demonstrate the validity of music "in older forms treated in a new way," in three movements: (1) *Fast and energetic* (2) *Slowly* (3) *Fast,* is performed for the first time by the National Symphony Orchestra in Washington, Hans Kindler conducting.

## 30 JANUARY 1948

*Symphony for Classical Orchestra* by the 27-year-old American composer Harold SHAPERO, premeditatedly cast in the traditional four movements, set in the proclamatory key of B-flat major, the natural tonality of the bugle, and ending in a display of tonic major triads, is performed for the first time by the Boston Symphony Orchestra, Leonard Bernstein conducting.

## 30 JANUARY 1948

*First Symphony* in B-flat major by the American composer Henry BRANT, inspired by the jazzy ambience of modern America, in four movements, *Sermon, Ballad, Skit* and *Procession,* is performed for the first time by the Cincinnati Symphony Orchestra, Thor Johnson conducting.

## 2 FEBRUARY 1948

*Second Symphony* by the 50-year-old Palestinian composer Paul BEN-HAIM (Paul Frankenburger) who adopted his Hebraic name after leaving Hitlerized Germany in 1933, in four movements, is performed for the first time by the Palestine Symphony Orchestra in Tel Aviv.

## 8 FEBRUARY 1948

*Symphonie expiatoire* by the 46-year-old French composer Henri SAUGUET, written at the end of World War II as an act of expiation of the unconscious guilt in the national apathy and helplessness during the Nazi subjugation of France, in four movements, concluding with a "berceuse des morts," is performed for the first time in Paris.

## 10 FEBRUARY 1948

The Central Committee of the Communist Party of the Union of Soviet Socialist Republics issues a resolution condemning "decadent formalism" (i.e. formulism, adherence to cerebral formulas in art) in Soviet music, naming SHOSTAKOVICH, PROKOFIEV and KHACHATURIAN as the principal culprits, and MIASKOVSKY and SHEBALIN as conscious inculcators of inharmonious music at the Moscow Conservatory. (Full text in the section LETTERS AND DOCUMENTS)

## 11 FEBRUARY 1948

*Fifth Symphony* by the German composer Hermann ZILCHER, who died on 1 January 1948, is performed posthumously for the first time in Hamburg.

## 12 FEBRUARY 1948

*Fantasy* for trombone and orchestra by the 41-year-old American composer Paul CRESTON, in one continuous movement esthetically articulated in three sections (lively, lyric and fugally agitated), is performed for the first time by the Los Angeles Philharmonic.

## 20 FEBRUARY 1948

*L'Âme heureuse,* ballet by the 80-year-old patriarch of French modern music Charles KŒCHLIN, is performed for the first time in Paris.

## 21 FEBRUARY 1948

*Mosquito Serenade,* an orchestral scherzo by the American composer Arthur KREUTZ, onomatopoeically imitating the enervating buzz of the *Culex pipiens,* is performed for the first time by the New York Philharmonic.

## 22 FEBRUARY 1948

*Le Baccanti*, opera in three acts, after Euripides, by the 55-year-old Italian composer Giorgio Federico GHEDINI, is produced at La Scala, Milan.

## 22 FEBRUARY 1948

Wilhelm FURTWÄNGLER conducts with the Berlin Philharmonic the first performance of his own exuberantly romantic *Second Symphony*, modelled after the German symphonic masterpieces of the 19th century, and set in a formally cohesive and academically competent manner.

## 24 FEBRUARY 1948

*The Seine at Night*, symphonic poem by the transsequanic Missourian Virgil THOMSON, the "Lutecian Maro" who (as he himself phrased it) "wrote in Paris music that was always, in one way or another, about Kansas City," is performed for the first time by the Kansas City Philharmonic.

## 25 FEBRUARY 1948

*Les Malheurs de Sophie*, ballet by the 35-year-old "jeune français" Jean FRANÇAIX, to a scenario after the French children's classic detailing a series of misfortunes that ultimately bring a fortune to a peculiarly susceptible young girl, written in an insouciantly hedonistic manner, is produced at the Paris Opéra.

## 27 FEBRUARY 1948

*Fourth Symphony* (*In Memoriam*) by Gian Francesco MALIPIERO, in four movements, all ending in minor keys, the first, *Allegro moderato*, and the third, *Allegro*, expressive of a timid hope; the second, *Lento funebre*, lamenting the loss of friends in the war, and the fourth, *Lento*, being a set of six variations on a funereal enfilade of chimes of church bells, written in an idiom in which "the musical dissonance is linear, developed with the spontaneous logic of Italian classicism" is performed for the first time by the Boston Symphony Orchestra, under the direction of Serge Koussevitzky, as a commissioned work written for the Koussevitzky Foundation, and dedicated to the memory of Mrs. Natalie Koussevitzky.

## 29 FEBRUARY 1948

*First Violin Concerto* by the 32-year-old American composer David DIAMOND is performed for the first time in Vancouver.

## 29 FEBRUARY 1948

*Die Nachtschwalbe*, "dramatic nocturne" in one act by the 45-year-old Manchurian-born German-Estonian composer Boris BLACHER, to a libretto centered on a company of pimply pimps and putative putains in a small German town, during which the head of the vice squad finds out that one of the "night swallows" is his orphaned daughter, set to music in poignant dissonant harmonies and asymmetrically angular rhythms, is produced in Leipzig.

## 2 MARCH 1948

An orchestral suite of stage music for Ibsen's *Peer Gynt* by the 50-year-old Norwegian composer Harald SAEVERUD, boldly departing from Grieg's sanctified treatment of the same subject, is performed for the first time in Oslo.

## 13 MARCH 1948

*Third Symphony* by the American composer Harold MORRIS, subtitled *Amaranth*, after a poem of that name by Edwin A. Robinson relating to a perennially blossoming flower, in four movements, expressive of (1) joy and freedom (2) play and humor (3) exaltation, and (4) triumph, written without key signatures, but centripetally gravitating towards the terminal albification of C major, the alpha and the omega of the work, is performed for the first time in Houston, Texas.

## 15 MARCH 1948

*Czinka Panna,* one-act opera by the prime Hungarian composer Zoltán KODÁLY, to the story of a Gypsy girl who inspired Rákóczi's fighting men in the Hungarian struggle against the Austrians in 1703, featuring an originally conceived Magyar-rhythmed *Rákóczi March,* is performed for the first time at the Budapest Opera. (On the same day, Kodály was awarded the newly-instituted Kossuth Prize "for signal services in the arts.")

## 18 MARCH 1948

*Posledni Hejtman (The Last Captain)*, opera by the Czech composer Miroslav KREJČÍ, is produced in Prague.

## 20 MARCH 1948

*Piano Concerto* by Boris BLACHER is performed for the first time in Göttingen.

## 20 MARCH 1948

Five days before his 81st birthday, Arturo TOSCANINI conducts the Symphony Orchestra of the National Broadcasting Company in New York in a program of Wagner's music, televised by a network including Washington, Philadelphia, Schenectady and Buffalo.

(This was to be the first television broadcast of a major symphony orchestra, but it was anticipated by one hour by the Columbia Broadcasting System in a televised concert of the Philadelphia Orchestra, Eugene Ormandy conducting, transmitted from Philadelphia to New York by the newly-laid coaxial cable)

## 23 MARCH 1948

Hilding ROSENBERG, prolific Swedish composer of vocal music, conducts in Stockholm the first performance of the last portion of his eight-hour-long opera-oratorio *Joseph and His Brethren,* after. Thomas Mann's biblical novel.

### 26 MARCH 1948

Hanns EISLER, German composer of atonal symphonies and optimistically triadic proletarian songs, who came to the United States in 1942, leaves America as a "voluntary deportee," after the House of Representatives Committee on Un-American Activities, in its campaign directed mainly against Eleanor Roosevelt and other liberals who helped to save Eisler's life by obtaining an American visa for him, uncovers the fact of his brief membership in the German Communist Party in 1926, and thunders that "he has perjured his way in and out of the United Sates at will, going to Soviet Russia and other countries when he pleased." (See extracts from *Hearings Regarding Hanns Eisler* in LETTERS AND DOCUMENTS)

I recall reading in a French newspaper in 1933 that Hitler put a price on my head. I was not surprised. But I never dreamed that I would experience the same sort of thing in the United States, a country that I love. (Eisler's statement in Los Angeles upon posting $1,000 bail for himself and $500 for his wife pending a hearing with the Commissioner of Immigration to answer charges of perjury)

### 1 APRIL 1948

*First Symphony* by the 35-year-old Polish composer Witold LUTOSLAWSKI is performed for the first time in Katowice.

### 2 APRIL 1948

The newly erected State Opera in Ankara, Turkey, is inaugurated with a concert of Turkish music including *Symphony* by Cemal REŞID REY, *Violin Concerto* by Ulvi CEMAL ERKIN, *Ballade* by Necil KAZIM AKSES and a fragment from the opera *Kerem* by Ahmed Adnam SAYGUN. (The first complete performance of *Kerem* was given in Ankara on 1 March 1953)

### 2 APRIL 1948

*Fourth Symphony* for strings by the foremost German polyphonist Karl Amadeus HARTMANN, in three movements written in a tense dramatic idiom marked by tremendous melorhythmic peripeteia (1) *Lento assai, con passione,* (2) *Allegro di molto, risoluto* (3) *Adagio apassionato,* the latter exfoliating in an explicit dodecaphonic statement, and ending in a precipitous dynamic descent, from *fortissississimo* to *pianississimo,* is performed for the first time in Munich.

### 4 APRIL 1948

*Fifth Symphony* in one movement by the German composer Max BUTTING is performed for the first time in Berlin.

### 4 APRIL 1948

*Vision dramatique,* symphonic movement by the Polish composer Karol RATHAUS, is performed for the first time by the Palestine Symphony Orchestra in Tel Aviv.

## 4 APRIL 1948

*Duett-Concertino* for clarinet, bassoon, string orchestra and a harp, by Richard STRAUSS, written by him in Switzerland where he went after the German débacle, and built upon the contrast between the "gay clarinet" and the "sad bassoon," is performed for the first time over the network of the Radio-Swizzera Italiana.

## 9 APRIL 1948

*Knoxville: Summer of 1915* for soprano and orchestra by Samuel BARBER, to the text of the prose poem in the novel *A Death in the Family* by James Agee, bearing the legend: "We are talking now of summer evenings in Knoxville, Tennessee, at the time when I lived there so successfully disguised to myself as a child," metempsychotically conjuring up the simple life of the obsolescent American past in a musical idiom combining elements of folkloric melodiousness with poignant atonalities and realistic details, as in illustrating the electric sparks of a streetcar antenna by pizzicati glissando in the lower strings, is performed for the first time by Eleanor Steber with the Boston Symphony Orchestra, Serge Koussevitzky conducting.

## 15 APRIL 1948

Pierre SCHAEFFER, French radio engineer, conjures up the concept of *Musique Concrète*, a phono-montage of recordings of random sounds, including speech, heterogeneous noises and bits of music.

Pour la musique classique un *do* est un *do* quelle que soit sa situation dans sa tessiture. Pour la musique concrète, un *son* est un *son* (qu'il soit pur ou complexe) et il est inséparable de sa situation dans le spectre sonore.

|  MUSIQUE HABITUELLE  (dite *abstraite*) | MUSIQUE NOUVELLE  (dite *concrète*) |
|---|---|
| Phase I.    Conception (*mentale*) | Phase I.    Composition (*matérielle*) |
| Phase II.   Expression (*chiffrée*) | Phase II.   Esquisses (*experimentation*) |
| Phase III.  Exécution (*instrumentale*) | Phase III.  Matériaux (*fabrication*) |
| (de l'abstrait au concret) | (du concret à l'abstrait) |

(*Introduction a la Musique Concrète* by Pierre Schaeffer, *Polyphonie*, Paris, 1950)

## 21 APRIL 1948

*Sixth Symphony* by the 75-year-old dean of British composers Ralph VAUGHAN WILLIAMS, in four movements, interconnected so that "each of the first three has its tail attached to the head of its neighbor": (1) *Allegro* (2) *Moderato* (3) *Scherzo* (4) *Epilogue*, opulently magniloquent in its triadic sonorities, revitalized by energetic syncopation and tonally subordinated to the commanding unity of the key of E minor despite numerous excursions into the penumbra of atonality (the fugue in the scherzo is built on a series of disjunct tritones), is performed for the first time by the Royal Philharmonic in London, Sir Adrian Boult conducting.

### 22 APRIL 1948

Morton GOULD conducts in New York the first performance of his ballet *Fall River Legend*, after the celebrated Lizzie Borden parricide case ("Lizzie Borden took an axe and gave her mother forty whacks; when she saw what she had done, she gave her father forty-one"), with thematic materials ranging from New England hymnody to stylized social dances and balladry. (A symphonic suite from the ballet was performed for the first time on 6 January 1949 by the San Francisco Symphony, under the direction of Pierre Monteux)

### 23 APRIL 1948

*Concerto for Ondes Martenot and Orchestra* by the 42-year-old French composer André JOLIVET, scored for large orchestra with a substantial percussion section, in three movements, *Allegro moderato, Allegro vivace* and *Largo Cantabile*, with an extended cadenza for the Ondes Martenot, is performed for the first time anywhere in Vienna.

### 24 APRIL 1948

Manuel PONCE, pioneer of Mexican modern music, composer of ephemeral symphonic works imbued with the spirit of *Mexicanismo*, whose song *Estrellita* achieved universal popularity (he never collected royalties on it owing to a faulty copyright registration), dies in Mexico City at the age of sixty-five.

(Ponce gave his date of birth as 8 December 1886, but he was in fact born at 11:45 P.M. on 8 December 1882, and baptized on 12 December 1882, as proved by Jesús Romero in his solidly documented calendar of Ponce's life, *Efemérides de Manuel M. Ponce* in the periodical *Nuestra Música*, Mexico City, No. 2, 1950)

### 24 APRIL 1948

*Momtchil*, opera in three acts by the 43-year-old Bulgarian composer Lubomir PIPKOV, to a libretto dealing with a 14th-century rebellion of Balkan peasants against their feudal oppressors, romanticized by the gratuitous episode of a requited passion of the rebel leader for the overlord's virginal daughter, written in an emphatic national idiom making artful use of Balkan asymmetrical dance rhythms, is produced in Sofia.

### 24 APRIL 1948

Joseph WIHTOL (or, in Latvian, Vitols), foremost Latvian composer, who taught at the St. Petersburg Conservatory (among his pupils were Prokofiev and Miaskovsky), went after the Russian Revolution to Riga, where he established a Latvian Conservatory, and fled Riga for Germany at the approach of the Soviet Armies in 1944, dies in Lübeck at the age of eighty-four.

### 25 APRIL 1948

Wonsik LIM conducts the Korean Symphony Orchestra in Seoul in the first performance of his *Korean Dance Fantasy.*

### 28 APRIL 1948

*Orpheus,* choreographic poem by Igor STRAVINSKY, cast in a Hellenistic idiom of static monody ornamented by melodious mannerisms of the baroque era and irrigated by warm streams of Tchaikovskian sentiment with a somberly inharmonious G sharp protruding in the bass through an A-minor triad in the opaque peroration, culminating in an overwhelming vesuviation of the Bacchantes as they set upon Orpheus to tear him apart in their nymphomaniacal fury, is performed for the first time in New York.

### 30 APRIL 1948

*Inside U.S.A.,* a revue by Arthur SCHWARTZ, a wildly whimsical musical show in which a Broadway mermaid is melodically wooed by Chopin, Liszt and Tchaikovsky, who lavish their famous tunes on her, is produced in New York.

### 4 MAY 1948

*Fourth Symphony* in four movements by the American composer Bernard ROGERS, written in 1945 "to trace a line leading from darkness and despair to affirmation," is performed for the first time by the Rochester Philharmonic Orchestra, Howard Hanson conducting.

### 5 MAY 1948

At the opening of the Fourth Annual Festival of Contemporary Music at Columbia University, New York, Otto LUENING conducts the belated world première of his three-act opera *Evangeline,* written 16 years previously after Longfellow's celebrated poem, embodying in the score a variety of thematic elements pertaining to the life in early New England, including church anthems and Indian war cries.

### 7 MAY 1948

*Gli Incatenati,* one-act opera, with three characters, by the 61-year-old Italian composer Renzo BIANCHI, to his own libretto, is performed for the first time at La Scala, Milan.

### 9 MAY 1948

The Experimental Theater in New York presents the first performance of *Ballet Ballads,* a novel synthetic art show, with lyrics by John LATOUCHE and music by Jerome MOROSS, esemplastically fusing instruments and voices, dance and lighting effects, into a recognizably Americanoid product, in three tableaux:

(1) *Susannah and the Elders,* a folkloristic fresco exposing under a biblical guise the

lechery and treachery in the deep South (2) *Willie the Weeper,* "12-tone Willie with his sexy sax" dreaming terpsichorean marijuana dreams (3) *The Eccentricities of Davy Crockett,* a musical portrait of the popular American hero who fishes a mercurial mermaid out of the Tennessee River, catches Halley's Comet by the tail, goes to Congress, and returns to Texas to suffer martyrdom in the Alamo massacre.

## 9 MAY 1948

*Jugoslovenska partizanska rapsodija (Yugoslav Partisan Rhapsody),* cantata on Yugoslav guerrilla songs by the Yugoslav composer Jovan BANDUR (1899–1956), is performed for the first time in Belgrade, on the same program with his *Poem 1941* for bass solo, chorus and orchestra, lamenting the massacre of patriotic schoolboys by the Nazis in occupied Serbia in 1941.

## 12 MAY 1948

*Le Roi de Camargue,* opera by the 72-year-old French composer Jean POUEIGH, is performed for the first time in Marseilles.

## 13 MAY 1948

*The Hospital,* musico-medical suite for orchestra by Dr. Herman M. PARRIS of Philadelphia, portraying a young woman's appendectomy in ten prophylactic vivisections, introducing a smiling nurse (*Allegro e amabile*), anxious intensive care (*Andantino* ), the operating room (*Allegro,* realistically followed by *Molto agitato*) and anesthesia (*Presto*), set to music in an impartially bland idiom, imitative of Handel, Tchaikovsky and Gershwin, is performed for the first time by the Doctors' Orchestral Society in New York.

## 16 MAY 1948

*Third Symphony* by the progressive American composer Wallingford RIEGGER, in four movements, *Moderato, Andante affettuoso, Moderato, Passacaglia and Fugue,* employing modified dodecaphonic techniques, each movement containing a fugal development, and ending with a resonant array of thematic forces, is performed for the first time by the Columbia Broadcasting System Symphony Orchestra in New York, Dean Dixon conducting, on the same program with the first performance of *Concerto* for viola and orchestra, in four movements, by Quincy Porter.

## 20 MAY 1948

Darius MILHAUD conducts in Paris the first performance of his *Fourth Symphony,* subtitled *1848,* in four movements marked *Insurrection, To the Dead of the Republic, The Peaceful Joys of Liberty Regained* and *Commemoration 1948,* commissioned by the French government to commemorate the 1848 revolution against King Louis Philippe, making use of fragments of French revolutionary songs and marches of the time, with the notation at the end of the score reflecting Milhaud's geographical mobility: "Pacific Ocean, Atlantic Ocean, August-September, 1947; orchestrated at Genval and Aix-en-Provence, October-December, 1847."

## 20 MAY 1948

*Les Demoiselles de la nuit,* dramatic ballet in three scenes by Jean FRANÇAIX, a fantasy about a female cat which for one *nuit d'amour* becomes a human girl, but, disgusted by the physical crudity of men's love, goes back to prowl on rooftops with her pliable feline companions, is produced in Paris.

## 24 MAY 1948

Benjamin BRITTEN conducts in Cambridge, England, the first performance of his modernized version of John Gay's *Beggar's Opera,* with the 200-year-old tunes of its first harmonizer, the Prussian musician Johann Christoph Pepusch, pepped up and contrapuntally rejuvenated.

## 28 MAY 1948

*First Symphony* by the 35-year-old Polish composeress Grazyna BACEWICZ is performed for the first time in Cracow.

## 29 MAY 1948

The Second International Congress of Composers and Musicologists, assembled in Prague, issues a declaration of aims of contemporary composers of the Socialist bloc and its sympathizers, urging the adoption of a program of conciliation and coordination of creative effort in the art of music, aiming at its accessibility to the masses. (Complete text in the section LETTERS AND DOCUMENTS)

## 2 JUNE 1948

*Le Carrosse du Saint Sacrement,* one-act lyric comedy by Henri BÜSSER, is produced at the Opéra-Comique in Paris.

## 5 JUNE 1948

*Saint Nicolas,* cantata by Benjamin BRITTEN (completed on 31 May 1948), scored for tenor solo, mixed chorus, two pianos, strings, percussion and organ, in nine movements, to the text by Eric Crozier, traversing in devotional but urbane tones, not devoid of secular gaiety, the career of the Saint, his birth, his dedication, his pilgrimages, his bishopric, his imprisonment, the miraculous resuscitation of the butchered "pickled" boys, his piety, his death and his sainthood in glorious D major, making artful use of old English tunes to create an atmosphere of familiarity and intimacy, is performed for the first time in the course of the Aldeburgh Music Festival. (The cantata was written for the Centenary celebration of Lancing College, Sussex, where it was performed on 24 July 1948, but the absolute priority of the world premiere was pre-empted in Aldeburgh)

## 5 JUNE 1948

The 22nd Festival of the International Society for Contemporary Music opens in Amsterdam with the following program of symphonic music:

*Concerto for Orchestra* by Raymond CHEVREUILLE of Belgium, in four movements, written in a neo-baroque idiom with sporadic atonal discursions; *Second Violin Concerto* by the Dutch composer Sem DRESDEN; and *Fifth Symphony,* subtitled *Concertante, in eco,* by Gian Francesco MALIPIERO, in four movements set in an emotionally romanticized Vivaldian style, first performed in London on 3 November 1947. (*Second Symphony* by Miloslav KABELÁČ of Czechoslovakia was programmed but not performed)

## 6 JUNE 1948

In the course of the 22nd Festival of the International Society for Contemporary Music in Amsterdam two works by Hendrik ANDRIESSEN of Holland are presented: *Christus Rex* for double choir and organ and the first part of a *Sinfonia* for organ solo.

## 6 JUNE 1948

*Abraxas,* ballet by Werner EGK, to a scenario derived from a pre-Goethean representation of Faust as a magus in possession of the abracadabramorphic charm abraxas, receives its first stage performance in Munich. (A concert performance was first given on the Baden-Baden radio on 7 December 1947)

## 7 JUNE 1948

At the 22nd Festival of the International Society for Contemporary Music in Amsterdam the following program of orchestral music by modern Dutch composers is presented:

*Little Suite* on the notes E-F by Willem LANDRÉ (1874–1948), written in a tensely chromatic idiom and first performed in Rotterdam on 11 June 1943; *Sinfonia Sacra In Memoriam Patris* by Willem Landré's son Guillaume LANDRÉ, composed as a tribute of filial devotion shortly after the elder Landré's death on 1 January 1948; *Sinfonia piccola* by Léon ORTHEL, cast in an energetically polyrhythmic idiom, in six interconnected sections, first performed in Rotterdam on 31 October 1941; *Six Symphonic Epigrams* by Willem PIJPER (1894–1947), a set of variations on a 16th-century Dutch song; and *Symphonic Variations* by Henk BADINGS, set in a modernistic neo-classical idiom of melorhythmically angular intervallic facture. (Daniel RUYNEMAN's *Amphitryon Overture* was programmed but not performed)

## 8 JUNE 1948

In the course of the 22nd Festival of the International Society for Contemporary Music in Amsterdam the following program of chamber music is presented:

*Trio* in four movements by Klaus EGGE, Norwegian composer of tightly knit polyphonic music; *Put Away the Flutes* for tenor, flute, oboe, and string quartet by Humphrey SEARLE of England, to a poem by the Irish poet W. R. Rogers, written during World War II as an ironic sermon of psychological renunciation in wartime: "Put away the flutes into their careful clefts, and cut the violins that like ivy climb flat to their very roots"; *Sonata* for two pianos by Hans HENKEMANS of Holland; *Sonatina* for oboe and piano by Antoni SZALOWSKI of Poland; *Eight Poems by Michelangelo* by the

Swiss cellist Richard Sturzenegger, designed as "a group of musical sculptures"; and *Quintet* for wind instruments by Finn Høffding of Denmark.

## 8 JUNE 1948

At a denazification court in Munich Richard Strauss is officially absolved of the taint of his passive collaboration with the Nazi regime in Germany.

## 9 JUNE 1948

At the 22nd Festival of the International Society for Contemporary Music in Amsterdam the following program of orchestral music is given:

*Second Symphony* by Roger Sessions, in four movements of tensely wrought polyphony; *Violin Concerto* by Karl-Birger Blomdahl of Sweden; *Symphonic Etudes* for piano and orchestra by the Polish composer Artur Malawski (first performed on 30 April 1948, in Sopot, Poland), in six sections cast in a luscious quasi-Rachmaninoffian virtuoso manner; and *Musique pour l'Esprit en Deuil*, a somber threnody dramatized by xylophone and drums by the Dutch composer Rudolf Escher, written during the war years but not given its mournful title until 1945, and first performed in Amsterdam on 19 January 1947.

## 9 JUNE 1948

Six hundred and sixty-four years after the mass abduction of children by the fabled Pied Piper of Hamelin, the British Broadcasting Corporation broadcasts an audition of a flute, manufactured by John Heywood, imitating the mating call of rats, making use of rodent sex appeal to lure them into an electric death trap, but unlike the flute used by the Pied Piper in 1284, having no harmful effect on impressionable children.

## 10 JUNE 1948

In the course of the 22nd Festival of the International Society for Contemporary Music in Amsterdam, the following program of chamber music is given:

*Three Songs* for soprano and piano by Sándor Jemnitz, Hungarian composer of atonally inflected music; *Concertino da Camera* for flute, clarinet, bassoon and piano by the Australian composeress Peggy Glanville-Hicks; *4 Poemas Callegos* for voice and chamber orchestra by Julián Bautista, Spanish composer living in Argentina; and *Quintet* for wind instruments by Stepan Lucký of Czechoslovakia, a survivor of a Nazi concentration camp, and an enlightened experimentalist in icositetraphonic structures. (*Primavera* for harp, flute and strings by the French grandmaster of modern music Charles Kœchlin was included in the printed program but not played owing to lack of rehearsal time)

## 12 JUNE 1948

At the concluding concert of the 22nd Festival of the International Society for Contemporary Music in Amsterdam the following program of symphonic music is given:

*40th May,* heterochronistically titled symphonic suite in three movements by the Austrian composer Alexander SPITZMUELLER, living in Paris, written ostensibly for a "birthday of a beloved friend," and set in an imbricatingly complex polyphonic idiom with a proliferation of palindromic canons; *Lullaby* for 29 string instruments and two harps by Andrzej PANUFNIK of Poland, derived from a folk tune fragmentized by a prevalence of singultation and hockets and punctuated by icositetraphonic glissandos; *Violin Concerto* in one movement by the atonally tense Norwegian composer Fartein VALEN whose early years were spent in tropical Madagascar; *Horn Concerto* by Elizabeth LUTYENS of England; and *Sinfonietta* in three movements by Walter PISTON, first performed in Boston on 10 May 1941.

### 14 JUNE 1948

*La Femme et son Ombre,* ballet by the Russian-Parisian composer Alexander TCHEREPNIN, is performed for the first time in Paris.

### 18 JUNE 1948

Columbia Records, jointly with the Columbia Broadcasting System and Philco, presents in New York the first public demonstration for the press of LP (long playing) Microgroove, a non-breakable 12-inch vinylite disc, capable of playing recorded music for 45 minutes, perfected by Dr. Peter GOLDMARK, Director of CBS Engineering Research and Development Laboratories.

### 24 JUNE 1948

*La Farce du Maître Pathelin,* one-act comic opera by Henry BARRAUD, is produced at the Opéra-Comique in Paris.

### 27 JUNE 1948

George Templeton STRONG, cantankerous American composer who, discouraged by the general lack of interest in native music in America, settled in 1892 in Switzerland where he took up watercolor painting, dies in Geneva at the patriarchal age of ninety-two.

### 30 JUNE 1948

*First Symphony* by the Australian composer Arthur BENJAMIN, written "to reflect the feelings, the hopes and despairs of the times," and cast in an appropriately ambivalent mood, is performed for the first time at the Cheltenham Festival of Contemporary British Music, John Barbirolli conducting.

### 1 JULY 1948

*Violin Concerto,* by the 43-year-old English composer Alan RAWSTHORNE, in two movements, is performed for the first time at the Cheltenham Festival.

### 14 JULY 1948

*Down in the Valley,* folk opera, named after a Kentucky mountain song, by the Americanized German expressionist Kurt WEILL, to a libretto dealing with a condemned murderer who kills his old sweetheart's new beau, is produced at the University of Indiana at Bloomington.

### 26 JULY 1948

Patriarch ALEXEI of the Russian Orthodox Church in Moscow issues an edict condemning the "worldliness" in Russian church music and urging the appointment of a religious censor to preserve the purity of Russian church singing and to prevent performances of modern or uneuphonious choral works at the services.

### 26 JULY 1948

*Magdalena,* "a musical adventure" for the stage by Heitor VILLA-LOBOS, dealing with the amours of an equatorial dictator and a Parisian cocotte on the banks of the Colombian river Magdalena, involving the theft of a statue of the Holy Virgin by the heathen Indian fiancé of a Christian native girl, set to music in languorously tropical modalities and humid harmonies, diversified by mechanistic effects (a broken-down pianola accompanies a frenetic jungle dance; an old Ford motor car is cranked up to raucously polytonal harmonies) is given its world première in Los Angeles.

### 29 JULY 1948

Igor STRAVINSKY files in Los Angeles a lawsuit for $250,000 against the Leeds Music Corporation of New York for using his name as the composer of *Summer Moon,* a denatured version of a theme from Stravinsky's uncopyrighted score of *The Firebird,* equipped with mawkish lyrics, thereby damaging his standing as "world famous composer of serious and sincere music."

(The suit was dismissed by the Superior Court of Los Angeles on 9 March 1949, with a finding that Stravinsky had voluntarily entered into a valid contract with the defendant corporation in full knowledge that the tune would be used for commercial purposes in the form of a popular song.)

### 9 AUGUST 1948

*Shur* and *Kurdy-Ovshary,* a symphonic diptych by the 25-year-old Azerbaijan composer Fikret AMIROV, based on Caucasian ballad forms and consisting of an integrated series of coloristic dances, is performed for the first time in Baku.

### 13 AUGUST 1948

At the opening of the American Dance Festival on the campus of Connecticut College in New London, Martha Graham presents the first performance of *Wilderness Stair,* ballet by Norman DELLO JOIO, subtitled *Diversion of Angels,* cupidophilously portraying "games, flights, fancies, configurations of the lover's intention" in its choreography, and neo-classically hedonistic in its musical score.

### 19 AUGUST 1948

*Eloise,* symphonic poem by Ernest Clyde SALISBURY, former inmate of the Wayne County General Hospital in the town of Eloise, Michigan (after which the piece was named), where he was treated for chronic alcoholism and manic depression by the musical therapist Dr. Ira M. Altshuler, who also helped him in supplying maudlin Tchaikovskian themes as material for his work, is performed for the first time by the Detroit Symphony Orchestra, as a demonstration of confidence in mental therapy which, in the ineffable composer's own words, "done me good."

### 25 AUGUST 1948

*First Symphony* by the 21-year-old German composer Hans Werner HENZE is performed for the first time in its entirety at Bad Pyrmont. (A revised version was first performed in Berlin on 9 April 1964)

### 26 AUGUST 1948

Oscar Lorenzo FERNANDEZ, 50-year-old Brazilian composer of nostalgically poetic, tropically languorous music in all genres and forms, described as "Brasileirissimo" for his intimate communication of the spirit of "Brasilidad," dies during sleep in his native Rio de Janeiro.

### 8 SEPTEMBER 1948

*Concerto* for string orchestra "alla memoria di Béla BARTÓK," by the Italian composer Guido TURCHI, is performed for the first time in Venice.

### 9 SEPTEMBER 1948

*Marsia,* ballet in one act by the 44-year-old Italian modernist Luigi DALLAPICCOLA, in three parts: (1) *La presentazione di Marsia* (2) *Dramma di Marsia,* including a Magic Dance, a Dance of Apollo and Last Dance of Marsia (3) *La Morte di Marsia,* depicting the fate of a legendary satyr, who dared to challenge Apollo in a music contest and was put to death after he lost, is performed for the first time at the Venice Music Festival.

### 12 SEPTEMBER 1948

*L'Incubo,* opera by the Italian dodecaphonic composer Riccardo NIELSEN, is performed for the first time in Venice.

### 13 SEPTEMBER 1948

*Oboe Concerto* by Cyril SCOTT is performed for the first time in London.

### 30 SEPTEMBER 1948

In compliance with the will of the Italian-born violinist Louisa TERZI of Los Angeles, her Stradivarius violin, which she won at a contest in Milan in 1888, is buried with her in her coffin.

## 5 OCTOBER 1948

The first *Concert de bruit*, in five sections arranged by the inventor of *Musique concrète* Pierre Schaeffer by simultaneous playing of several phonograph records selected at random—a recitation of Sacha Guitry, incidental coughing in the studio, a harmonica solo, Balinese ritual music, acoustically denatured piano—is broadcast by the Paris radio.

## 11 OCTOBER 1948

*Where's Charley?*, a musical comedy by Frank Loesser after Brandon Thomas' farce, *Charley's Aunt*, in which a youth impersonates his mythical aunt, acts as a chaperon for couples in love in Oxford, England, and eventually remasculinizes himself to woo a British college girl, is produced in New York.

## 14 OCTOBER 1948

The Orchestre National de France, under the direction of Charles Munch, conductor-elect of the Boston Symphony Orchestra, presents the first concert on its first American tour (and first by any French orchestra since 1919), at Bridgeport, Connecticut, in a program of French music plus a specially written American work, a terse symphonic *Toccata* by Walter Piston.

## 14 OCTOBER 1948

*Raskolnikoff*, music drama in two acts by the Swiss composer Heinrich Sutermeister, after Dostoyevsky's psychological novel *Crime and Punishment*, is performed for the first time in Stockholm.

## 22 OCTOBER 1948

*Suite delphique* by the French modernist André Jolivet, scored for wind instruments, harp, Ondes Martinot and percussion, is performed for the first time anywhere in Vienna.

## 23 OCTOBER 1948

Two Mexican one-act operas, *Carlota*, by Luis Sandi and *La Mulata de Córdoba* by Pablo Moncayo, are performed for the first time in Mexico City.

## 24 OCTOBER 1948

*Sinfonietta* by Francis Poulenc, written in his newly adopted neo-classical vein, is performed for the first time anywhere by the British Broadcasting Corporation Orchestra in London.

## 24 OCTOBER 1948

Franz Lehár, 78-year-old Austrian composer, melodious fashioner of elegant Viennese operettas extolling the light amours and innocent intrigues of merry widows, Gypsy lovers and Balkan princes expensively romancing in plush

Paris, dies in Bad Ischl, at 2:45 P.M., of the combined effects of cancer, double pneumonia, gastric ulcers and heart disease.

### 27 OCTOBER 1948

*Mass* according to the Catholic ritual by Igor STRAVINSKY, comprising *Kyrie, Gloria, Credo, Sanctus* and *Agnus Dei*, for a chorus of treble and alto voices (sung by children), tenors and basses (sung by adults), and a double wind quintet (5 woodwind instruments and 5 brasses), set in archaically austere gymnosophistical harmonies with rosary-like melorhythmic iteration, is performed for the first time in Milan, Ernest Ansermet conducting.

### 28 OCTOBER 1948

*Tři Vlasy Děda Vševěda (Three Hairs of Old Wise Man)* musical fairytale by the Czech composer Rudolf KAREL (his last work, written in a concentration camp, where he died), receives its posthumous first performance in Prague.

### 29 OCTOBER 1948

*Violin Concerto* by the Soviet composer Dmitri KABALEVSKY, the first of a "trilogy of concertos" dedicated to the Soviet youth (the second being a cello concerto, the third a piano concerto), in three movements, *Allegro Molto, Andantino cantabile* and *Vivace giocoso*, alternatively lyric and boisterous, evolved in strong melodic structures with bitonally enriched triadic formations, is performed in a double première in Leningrad and Moscow.

### 4 NOVEMBER 1948

*A Survivor of Warsaw,* cantata by Arnold SCHOENBERG, scored for narrator, men's chorus and orchestra, to a text in English by Schoenberg himself, with chillingly realistic interpolations of shouted Nazi commands in brutal German slang making a count of the decimated remnants of Warsaw ghetto Jews to be sent to the gas chambers, written in an expressively inflected *Sprechstimme*, and concluding with a shatteringly dramatic chorus intoning a Hebrew prayer, with the entire work couched according to Schoenberg's method of composition with twelve tones, symbolic in its chromatic dispersal of the diaspora of the twelve tribes of Israel, is performed for the first time by the Albuquerque Civic Symphony Orchestra, Kurt Frederick conducting.

### 7 NOVEMBER 1948

*Second Violin Concerto* by Darius MILHAUD (composed at Mills College, Oakland, California, in ten days between 6 February and 16 February 1946), in three movements: *Dramatique, Lent et sombre, Emporté*, is performed for the first time in Paris.

### 12 NOVEMBER 1948

Umberto GIORDANO, Italian composer who at the age of 28 wrote his only successful opera *Andrea Chenier*, veristically dramatizing the tragic life of the guillotined French poet, dies in Milan at the age of eighty-one.

Arnold SCHOENBERG addresses an indignant letter to the editors of the *Satur-day Review of Literature* protesting against the unlicensed use of his method of composition with twelve tones related only to one another, in Thomas Mann's musicosophical novel *Doctor Faustus* featuring a mythical German composer of 12-tone music, Adrian Leverkühn (1885–1943), who wrote disso-nances to express hope and gladness and used consonant triadic harmonies to portray deep anguish.

In his novel *Doctor Faustus*, Thomas Mann has taken advantage of my literary prop-erty. He has produced a fictitious composer as the hero of his book; and in order to lend him qualities a hero needs to arouse people's interest, he made him the creator of what one erroneously calls my 'system of twelve tones,' which I call 'method of com-posing with twelve tones.'

He did this without my permission and even without my knowledge. In other words, he borrowed it in the absence of the proprietor. The supposition of one reviewer, that he obtained information about this technique from Bruno Walter and Stravinsky, is probably wrong; because Walter does not know anything of composition with twelve tones, and Stravinsky does not take any interest in it.

I have still not read the book itself, though in the meantime Mann had sent me a Ger-man copy, with a handwritten dedication, 'To A. Schoenberg, dem Eigentlichen.' As one need not tell me that I am an 'Eigentlicher,' a real one, it was clear that he wanted to tell me that his Leverkühn is an impersonation of myself.

Leverkühn is depicted, from beginning to end, as a lunatic. I am seventy-four and I am not yet insane, and I have never acquired the disease from which this insanity stems. I consider this an insult.

When Mrs. Mahler-Werfel discovered this misuse of my property, she told Mann that this was my theory, whereupon he said: 'Oh, does one notice that? Then perhaps Mr. Schoenberg will be angry!' This proves that he was conscious of his guilt, and knew it was a violation of an author's right.

Finally I sent him a letter and showed him the possible consequences of ascribing my creation to another person which, in spite of being fictitious, is represented like a liv-ing man, whose biography is told by his friend Serenus Zeitblom.

One knows the superficiality and monomania of some historians who ignore facts if they do not fit in their hypotheses. Thus I quoted from an encyclopedia of the year 2060, a little article in which my theory was attributed to Thomas Mann, because of his Leverkühn.

Much pressure by Mrs. Mahler-Werfel had still to be exerted to make Mann promise that every forthcoming copy of *Doctor Faustus* will carry a note giving me credit for the twelve-notes composition. I was satisfied by this promise, because I wanted to be noble to a man who was awarded the Nobel Prize. "But Mr. Mann was not as gener-ous as I, who had given him good chance to free himself from the ugly aspect of a pi-rate. He gave an explanation: a few lines which he hid at the end of the book on a place on a page where no one ever would see it. Besides, he added a new crime to his first, in the attempt to belittle me: He calls me 'a (a!) *contemporary* composer and the-oretician.' Of course, in two or three decades, one will know which of the two was the other's contemporary." (From Schoenberg's letter, published in the *Saturday Review of Literature*, New York, 1 January 1949)

Arnold Schoenberg's letter both astonished and grieved me. If his acquaintance with the book were not based exclusively on the gossip of meddling scandal mongers, he would know that my efforts to give the central figure of the novel 'qualities a hero needs to arouse people's interest' were neither limited to the transfer of Schoenberg's 'method of composing with twelve tones,' nor was this characteristic the most important one.

It is quite untrue that it required 'much pressure' to induce me to give him due credit. As soon as I understood his concern I gave instructions to include in all translations, as well as in the German original, the statement which now appears in the English edition of *Doctor Faustus*. The statement does not raise the question who is whose contemporary. If Schoenberg wishes, we shall, all of us, consider it our greatest and proudest claim to be his contemporaries.

Instead of accepting my book with a satisfied smile as a piece of contemporary literature that testifies to his tremendous influence upon the musical culture of the era, Schoenberg regards it as an act of rape and insult. It is a sad spectacle to see a man of great worth, whose all-too-understandable hypersensitivity grows out of a life suspended between glorification and neglect, almost wilfully yield to delusions of persecution and of being robbed, and involve himself in rancorous bickering. It is my sincere hope and wish that he may rise above bitterness and suspicion and that he may find peace in the assurance of his greatness and glory! (From Thomas Mann's reply to Schoenberg in the *Saturday Review of Literature*, 1 January 1949)

### 14 NOVEMBER 1948

*Suite palestinienne* for cello and orchestra by the 75-year-old French composer André BLOCH, based on Jewish and Arabian tunes of Palestine, is performed for the first time in Paris.

### 20 NOVEMBER 1948

*Shunko-Den,* opera by the Japanese composer Toroko TAKAGI, to a melodramatic libretto in which a virtuous 18th-century Korean geisha, enamored of a virginal nobleman, suffers a cardiac collapse as a result of his persistent respect for her chastity, set to music built on pentatonic patterns of oriental folk melodies, is produced in Tokyo.

### 23 NOVEMBER 1948

*Second Symphony* in E major by Ernst von DOHNÁNYI, distinguished by a flow of Brahmsogenic exuberance, is given its world première by the Chelsea Symphony Orchestra in London, Norman Del Mar conducting.

### 25 NOVEMBER 1948

*In Praise of Peace,* symphonic poem by the 28-year-old Japanese composer Shin-ichi TAKATA, written in turgid Straussian harmonies, is performed for the first time in Tokyo.

### 26 NOVEMBER 1948

*Suite for Orchestra* from incidental music for the film *Louisiana Story* by Virgil THOMSON in four sections: (1) *Pastoral—The Bayou and the Marsh Buggy*

(2) *Chorale—The Derrick Arrives* (3) *Passacaglia—Robbing the Alligator's Nest* (4) *Fugue—Boy Fights Alligator,* with local color provided by verisimilitudinarian regional melorhythms organized in vigesimosecular counterpoint with occasional application of tonal dodecaphony in serial groups of four mutually exclusive triads, is performed for the first time by the Philadelphia Orchestra, Eugene Ormandy conducting.

### 29 NOVEMBER 1948

The British-made film, *Scott of the Antarctic,* with a musical score by Ralph VAUGHAN WILLIAMS in 23 sections depicting "the terror and fascination of the South Pole," reflected in the diaries of Robert Falcon Scott who perished on his return from the South Pole in 1912, is demonstrated for the first time in London.

### 7 DECEMBER 1948

Godfrey TURNER, 35-year-old English-born composer of sanely euphonious, harmonious, optimistic and even hedonistic symphonic and chamber music, driven to the depths of despondency by the agony of unrequited love, shoots himself to death in New York City.

### 7 DECEMBER 1948

Virgil THOMSON conducts the Louisville Orchestra in the world première of his "landscape piece," *Wheat Field at Noon,* conceived as a series of free variations on a theme containing all twelve tones of the chromatic scale arranged in four mutually exclusive triads (C minor, F-sharp minor, B-flat major, and E major).

### 8 DECEMBER 1948

*Lucifer,* cantata-mimodrama by the 60-year-old French composer Claude DELVINCOURT, in which the mutely mimed stage action is sententiously commented upon by a chorus seated in the orchestra pit, to a scenario dealing with the mighty fall of dissident angels and incidentally with the first human murder (the original title of the opera was *Le Mystère de Caïn*), is produced in Paris.

### 8 DECEMBER 1948

*Istrian Suite* for orchestra by the 34-year-old Croatian composer Natko DEVČIČ, in four movements, arranged in the style of Istrian folksongs and dances, and marked by characteristic asymmetric meters mitigated by Italianate mellowness, is performed for the first time in Zagreb.

### 12 DECEMBER 1948

*Violin Concerto* by the 22-year-old German composer Hans Werner HENZE is performed for the first time in Baden-Baden.

## 18 DECEMBER 1948

Werner EGK, 47-year-old German composer conducts in Berlin the first performance of his opera *Circe* in three acts, after the Homeric story dealing with the seductive siren who perfidiously lured the fascinated Greek sailors to her island and perdition.

## 18 DECEMBER 1948

The Austrian government issues a postage stamp of 60 groschen in honor of Franz Xaver GRUBER, the author of the perennially popular Christmas song *Stille Nacht, Heilige Nacht.*

## 28 DECEMBER 1948

*Twenty-Sixth Symphony* on Russian themes by the prime Soviet symphonist Nicolai MIASKOVSKY (completed on 2 October 1948), set in the socialistically realistic key of C major calculated to eliminate all formalistic impurities in the totality of tonal albification, so as to satisfy the demands of the edict of the Central Committee of the Communist Party of the USSR promulgated on 10 February 1948, in three movements: (1) *Adagio sostenuto-Allegro* (2) *Andante quasi lento* (3) *Adagio maestoso,* is performed for the first time in Moscow.

## 29 DECEMBER 1948

The Union of Soviet Composers completes in Moscow a nine-day Plenum on Soviet Music, commending some composers for proper application of the principles of Socialist Realism in their music, condemning others for unregenerate formalism, and concluding with this pronouncement: "Only Bolshevik art, the mighty lever of our national enlightenment in the spirit of Communism is capable of truthfully reflecting the greatness of the Leninist-Stalinist era."

The works by composers mentioned in the Resolution of the Central Committee of the All-Union Soviet Communist Party (Bolsheviks) of 10 February 1948 as representatives of the formalistic trend, naturally attracted the attention of the Plenum of the Union of Soviet Composers. Among recent works by these composers the most successful were the score for the film *Young Guard* by SHOSTAKOVICH and some choruses by MURADELI. The effort to enter the path of realistic creativeness and its partial success are demonstrated in Khachaturian's score for the film about V. I. Lenin, MIASKOVSKY's *Symphony on Russian Themes* and SHEBALIN's *Seventh String Quartet.* The Plenum concedes that the creative reorientation of these composers is proceeding at a very slow pace, as shown by the presence of some unliquidated formalistic elements in their music. Defeated ideologically, formalism still lingers in Soviet music. This is demonstrated by the new opera of PROKOFIEV, *Tale of a Real Man.* In the modernistic, anti-melodic music of this opera, in its treatment of the Soviet characters, the composer perseveres in his old positions, condemned by the Party and by the Soviet public. The spiritual world of the Soviet man who performs miracles of valor and heroism for the love of his Fatherland, fails to attract the composer's attention. He is still interested only in the external sharpness of stage action and in naturalistic details. (Tikhon Khrennikov, Secretary General of the Union of Soviet Composers, in his article, *Soviet Music in Its New Period,* in *Pravda,* Moscow, 4 January 1949)

## 30 DECEMBER 1948

*Kiss Me Kate,* a musical comedy by Cole PORTER, dealing with an estranged couple who regain their mutual love after acting in a musical version of Shakespeare's comedy *The Taming of the Shrew,* and containing in the score an ingratiatingly tuneful waltz in a continental manner, *Wunderbar,* is produced in New York.

## 30 DECEMBER 1948

*Curtain Raiser to an American Play,* symphonic appetizer in a fugal style with a lyric interlude, by the Constantinople-born half-Austrian Americanized 45-year-old composer Frederick PIKET, is performed for the first time by the Minneapolis Symphony Orchestra, Dimitri Mitropoulos conducting.

## 31 DECEMBER 1948

Howard HANSON conducts the Boston Symphony Orchestra in the first performance of his *Piano Concerto,* in four brief movements, with Rudolf Firkušny as soloist, and Lukas Foss conducts the first performance of his symphonic threnody *Recordare,* dedicated to the memory of Mahatma Gandhi.

## 31 DECEMBER 1948

*Fifth Symphony* by the 48-year-old whilom *enfant terrible* of American music George ANTHEIL, subtitled "Joyous," and voicing in its three well-contrasted movements the spirit of euphonious euphoria in triadic laetification, is performed for the first time by the Philadelphia Orchestra, Eugene Ormandy conducting.

# ❧ *1949* ❧

## 2 JANUARY 1949

Dynam-Victor FUMET, French organist and composer, whose flamboyant career as a dynamic fumer (he was once arrested for making bombs for anarchist purposes) carried him from the piano bench of a café chantant to the console of a church organ, and who wrote a number of multifarious pieces in various genres couched in a Gallicized Wagneromantic vein, dies in Paris at the age of eighty-one.

## 3 JANUARY 1949

The first performance of a work announced as the *21st Symphony* by an early 19th-century composer Dmitri OVSIANNIKO-KULIKOVSKY, with the finale in the rhythms of a Ukrainian dance, but in reality a stunning fabrication perpetrated by the Soviet violinist and composer Michael Goldstein whose original works have been systematically rejected for performance or publication in the Soviet Union, is played for the first time in Odessa.

### 4 JANUARY 1949

*Kentuckiana*, a symphonic divertimento on twenty Kentucky airs by Darius MILHAUD, is performed in a world première by the Louisville Orchestra.

### 5 JANUARY 1949

*Fifth Symphony* by Henry COWELL is performed for the first time in Washington.

### 7 JANUARY 1949

*Fourth Symphony* by the 53-year-old American composer Leo SOWERBY, in three movements marked: *Fast and Violently; Slowly and Wistfully; Agitated*, expressive of "the excitement and gusto, noise and glamour of a big city, sprawling and youthful—perhaps Chicago," is performed for the first time by the Boston Symphony Orchestra, Serge Koussevitzky conducting.

### 14 JANUARY 1949

Joaquín TURINA, Spanish composer of colorful symphonic pieces throbbing with languorously applosive Iberian rhythms and accoutred in luxuriant inframodern harmonies, dies in Madrid at the age of sixty-six.

### 16 JANUARY 1949

*Mirandolina*, ballet by the venerable 76-year-old master of Russian romantic music, Sergei VASSILENKO, based on Carlo Goldoni's comedy *La Locandiera* (*The Mistress of the Inn*), is produced in Moscow.

### 26 JANUARY 1949

*Fifth Symphony* in B-flat minor by the 47-year-old English composer Edmund RUBBRA, in four movements: a sepulchrally lugubrious *Adagio* leading to a turbidly kinetic *Allegro energico;* a bucolic *Allegro moderato;* a stately passacaglia, *Grave;* and an *Allegro vivo*, is performed for the first time in London.

### 27 JANUARY 1949

Boris ASAFIEV, Russian composer of neo-romantic operas, and author, under the nom de plume of Igor Glebov, of voluminous tomes on musical esthetics, dies in Moscow at the age of sixty-four.

### 29 JANUARY 1949

*Puck*, fairy opera by the 50-year-old French composer Marcel DELANNOY, after Shakespeare's play *A Midsummer Night's Dream*, is performed for the first time in Strasbourg.

## 4 FEBRUARY 1949

*Second Symphony* by the 34-year-old American composer Cecil EFFINGER is performed for the first time in Cincinnati.

## 9 FEBRUARY 1949

*White Wings*, chamber opera by the 55-year-old American composer Douglas MOORE, to a libretto concerning an incompatible romance blossoming up in 1900 in the fetid fragrance of unpaved New York streets between a sanitation department worker assigned to the removal of equine merde (the title *White Wings* refers to the antiseptic uniform of the corps), and the daughter of an automobile manufacturer whose horseless carriages threaten the abolition of his job, written in a sophisticated simplicistic idiom combining elements of mock-grand opera, ragtime rhythms, and sentimental balladry, with a patina of euphoniously pandiatonic non-odoriferous dissonant counterpoint, is performed for the first time in Hartford, Connecticut.

## 10 FEBRUARY 1949

*Sixth Symphony* by the 48-year-old American whilom modernist George ANTHEIL, written in a candidly tonal idiom sprinkled with non-toxic dissonances, in three romantically sociological movements, the first *Maestoso*, inspired by the painting of Delacroix, "Liberty Leading the People," depicting in tones "the smoke of battle, courage, despair and hope, all marching into the future;" the second, *Larghetto*, being a "breath of Autumn;" and the third, *Allegro*, "a triumph of joy," set in ozonized triadic harmonies, is performed for the first time by the San Francisco Symphony Orchestra, Pierre Monteux conducting.

## 11 FEBRUARY 1949

*Sixth Symphony* (*degli archi*) by Gian Francesco MALIPIERO, scored for strings only in the manner of a Concerto Grosso, and set in the classical four movements, *Allegro, Piuttosto Lento, Allegro vivo* and *Lento ma non troppo*, ending on a wistfully vanishing dissonant chord, is performed for the first time in Basel, Paul Sacher conducting.

## 12 FEBRUARY 1949

*Concerto* for marimba, vibraphone and orchestra by Darius MILHAUD is performed for the first time by the St. Louis Symphony Orchestra.

## 19 FEBRUARY 1949

*The Emperor's New Clothes*, opera by Douglas MOORE, based on the famous fairy tale by Hans Christian Andersen about a naked king, who was attired in garments so fine as to be invisible, a tailoring finesse dispelled by a child's outcry of astonishment at royal nakedness, set to music in an appropriately grand mock-imperial manner, is performed for the first time, in concert form, by the New York Philharmonic.

## 19 FEBRUARY 1949

*Movements,* symphonic suite for orchestra by the 22-year-old Israeli composer Ben-Zion ORGAD, is performed for the first time by the Israel Philharmonic Orchestra in Tel Aviv.

## 23 FEBRUARY 1949

*Prima Donna,* one-act opera by Arthur BENJAMIN, set in 18th-century Venice, and featuring a singing contest between rival prima donnas, is produced in London.

## 25 FEBRUARY 1949

*Symphony* in B major by the Brazilian composer Oscar Lorenzo FERNANDEZ (1897–1948), in four movements, suffused with Brazilian melorhythms, is performed posthumously for the first time by the Boston Symphony Orchestra, Eleazar de Carvalho conducting.

## 27 FEBRUARY 1949

*Sixth Symphony* by the 38-year-old American composer William SCHUMAN, in one movement divided into six sections, the initial and the final sections being in slow tempo, with atonal, quasi-dodecaphonic themes developed in passacaglia-like variations, is performed for the first time by the Dallas Symphony Orchestra, Antal Dorati conducting.

## 2 MARCH 1949

*Red Ear of Corn,* ballet by the 35-year-old Canadian composer John WEINZWEIG, is performed for the first time in Toronto.

## 2 MARCH 1949

*Die Schwarze Spinne,* one-act opera by the Swiss composer Heinrich SUTERMEISTER, after a chimerical Swiss tale in which the devil, trying to obtain an unbaptized child for his diabolical ritual, transforms a local woman into a black spider, with poisonous arachnids pouring forth out of her defiled womb, is produced for the first time in St. Gall, Switzerland.

## 6 MARCH 1949

*Sosi* for violin, piano, percussion and strings, by the half-Armenian, half-Scottish American composer Alan HOVHANESS, is performed for the first time in New York, two days before his 38th birthday.

## 8 MARCH 1949

*Third Piano Concerto* by Gian Francesco MALIPIERO, in three linked sections, *Allegro, Lento,* and *Allegro agitato,* couched in a transparent contrapuntal manner of the Italian settecento, is performed for the first time, as a commissioned work, by the Louisville Orchestra.

*870*

### 14 MARCH 1949

*The Bronze Knight*, ballet in four acts by Reinhold GLIÈRE, after Pushkin's poem centering on a St. Petersburg youth driven to despair when his beloved perishes in the catastrophic inundation of the river Neva in 1824, and who hurls imprecations at the equestrian statue of Peter the Great, the founder of the city, whereupon the bronze giant chases him down the streets to his death, is produced in Leningrad.

### 15 MARCH 1949

*Concerto* for cello and orchestra in G minor by Dmitri KABALEVSKY, the second of his "trilogy of concertos," and like the other two (the *Violin Concerto* and the *Third Piano Concerto*) set in three cyclic movements (fast, slow, very fast), designed for performances by young players and rooted in the modal variations of major and minor thirds in homonymic triads, nostalgically poetic in slow interludes, impetuously alert in rapid passages, is performed for the first time, in Moscow.

### 17 MARCH 1949

*Regina Uliva*, opera in three acts by the 42-year-old Italian composer Giulio Cesare SONZOGNO, to a libretto from the history of Castille, is produced at La Scala, in Milan.

### 24 MARCH 1949

*Tragic Overture* by the 34-year-old Polish composer Andrzej PANUFNIK, written in memory of the victims of the Warsaw uprising of 1943, is performed for the first time in New York.

### 31 MARCH 1949

*The Troubled Island*, opera in three acts by the 53-year-old American Negro composer William Grant STILL, to a libretto from the time of the Haitian struggle for independence against Napoleonic France, is produced at the New York City Center of Music and Drama.

### 5 APRIL 1949

Roy HARRIS conducts the Louisville Orchestra in the first performance of his symphonic scherzo *Kentucky Spring*, reflecting the "soft air of Kentucky, filled with bird song, and earth clothed in a riot of colors," and containing thematic references to Stephen Foster's song *My Old Kentucky Home*.

### 7 APRIL 1949

*South Pacific*, musical play by Richard RODGERS, with lyrics by Oscar Hammerstein II, based on James A. Michener's *Tales of the South Pacific*, wherein a French planter dwelling in paradisiac contentment on a south Pacific island sires two Polynesian children, performs other deeds of valor during World

War II, and subsequently woos and wins an American girl in marriage, containing the ineffably mellifluous tropical songs *Bali Ha'i, Happy Talk, I'm in Love With a Wonderful Guy, Younger Than Springtime,* and *There is Nothing Like a Dame,* is produced in New York.

### 8 APRIL 1949

Leonard BERNSTEIN, 30-year-old pianist, conductor and composer, plays the piano part with the Boston Symphony Orchestra, Serge Koussevitzky conducting, in the world première of his *Second Symphony,* subtitled *The Age of Anxiety,* for piano and orchestra, inspired by W. H. Auden's poem *The Age of Anxiety: a Baroque Eclogue,* "a dream-odyssey through common experience and alcohol," couched in an omnimusical syncretic idiom, from existentialistic melologues to urbanistic jazz, containing also a dodecaphonic episode, in six sections (1) *Prologue,* a merry scene in a New York bar (2) *The Seven Ages,* in seven athematic variations (3) *The Seven Stages,* with seven variations making "an inner and highly symbolic journey," (4) *The Dirge,* a dodecaphonic lamentation of three men and a girl in a taxicab, voicing their need of a protective father figure, the "colossal Dad" (5) *The Masque,* "a fantastic piano-jazz" in the form of a scherzo (6) *Epilogue,* wherein the entire orchestra makes "a positive statement of the newly-recognized faith."

### 22 APRIL 1949

The 23rd Festival of the International Society for Contemporary Music opens in Palermo, Sicily, with a performance of the opera *King Roger* by Karol SZYMANOWSKI (first produced in Warsaw on 19 June 1926), to a libretto from the time when King Roger the Norman (1093–1154) ruled Sicily.

### 23 APRIL 1949

At the 23rd Festival of the International Society for Contemporary Music in Palermo the following program is given:

*String Quartet* in one neo-classical movement by the 28-year-old Swiss composer Armin SCHIBLER; *Piano Sonata* by the 33-year-old French composer Henri DUTILLEUX; *Fifth String Quartet* by the prime Dutch impressionist Willem PIJPER (1894–1947); *Canti di Morte* for chorus by the 42-year-old Italian composer Gino CONTILLI; and *14 Different Ways of Describing Rain* for speaker and chamber orchestra by the German disciple of Schoenberg Hanns EISLER, written in 1944 in honor of Schoenberg's 70th birthday, based on a 12-tone series, and scored for the same ensemble as Schoenberg's *Pierrot Lunaire.*

### 24 APRIL 1949

At the 23rd Festival of the International Society for Contemporary Music in Palermo the following program of stage music is presented:

*La Favola d'Orfeo,* opera in one act by Alfred CASELLA (first performed in Venice on 6 September 1932); *Le Diable boiteux,* a musical dialogue for two male voices by Jean

872

FRANÇAIX (first performed in the Paris salon of Princess Polignac in 1937); *The Pit*, a dramatic scene for tenor and bass by the English composeress Elizabeth LUTYENS, to the story of a coal mine disaster; and *Qarrtsiluni*, ballet from Eskimo life by the Danish composer Knudaage RIISAGER (*Qarrtsiluni* is an Eskimo word expressing the mysterious moment of apprehensive silence before disaster strikes), first performed in Copenhagen on 21 February 1942.

## 24 APRIL 1949

*The Inn Hostess*, comic opera in three acts by the 41-year-old Odessa-born Russian composer of Italian parentage Antonio SPADAVECCHIA, after Carlo Goldoni's play *La Locandiera*, with the music couched in an appropriate style of the Italian settecento, is produced in Moscow.

## 25 APRIL 1949

At the 23rd Festival of the International Society for Contemporary Music in Palermo, the following program of chamber music is presented:

*Fourth String Quartet* by the 54-year-old Czech composer Pavel BOŘKOVEC (first performed by the League of Composers in New York on 11 April 1948); *3 Pieces* for Ondes Martenot, voice and percussion by the Algerian-born French composeress Yvette GRIMAUD, making use of quarter-tone polyphony in icositetraphonic harmonies; *String Quartet* by the 48-year-old Austrian composer Hans Erich APOSTEL; *Sonetto a Dallapiccola* for piano by the 46-year-old Russian-born Belgian composer Wladimir WORONOW, written according to his own system of "polyvariations"; *Nocturnes* for contralto and string quartet by the 33-year-old German-Brazilian dodecaphonic composer Hans Joachim KOELLREUTTER; and *Primavera* for five instruments by the patriarch of French modern music Charles KŒCHLIN, composed in 1936, and couched in bitonal harmony.

## 26 APRIL 1949

The following program of orchestral music is presented at the 23rd Festival of the International Society for Contemporary Music in Palermo:

*Fuga giocosa* by the 33-year-old English composer Humphrey SEARLE; *Concerto* for piano and orchestra in three movements by the 45-year-old English composer Lennox BERKELEY; *Second Suite* from the oratorio *Thyl Claes* (after the medieval folk-tale about Till Eulenspiegel) by the 53-year-old Russian-born Swiss composer Wladimir VOGEL; and *Second Symphony* by the 40-year-old Czech composer Miloslav KABELÁČ (first performed in Prague on 17 April 1947), in three movements opening with a funereal dirge as a memorial of the Nazi occupation of Czechoslovakia, and concluding with an optimistic finale.

## 27 APRIL 1949

The following program of Italian music is presented at the 23rd Festival of the International Society for Contemporary Music in Palermo:

*Concerto* for string orchestra in three movements by Vincenzo TOMMASINI; suite from the ballet *Ritratto di Don Chisciotte* by Goffredo PETRASSI; *Tre tempi* from *Musica d'Archi* by 41-year-old Riccardo NIELSEN; and *Concerto dell'albatro* in five movements by Giorgio Federico GHEDINI, scored for a narrator, violin, cello, piano and small orchestra. (Alfredo CASELLA's *Paganiniana*, originally programmed for this concert, was not performed)

### 28 APRIL 1949

The following program is presented at the 23rd Festival of the International Society for Contemporary Music in Palermo:

*Variations* for brass and string instruments by the 50-year-old Rumanian-French composer Marcel MIHALOVICI; *Fourth Symphony* for string orchestra, in three movements, *Lento con passione, Allegro di molto (Scherzo)* and *Adagio appassionato,* by the 43-year-old German master of modern polyphony Karl Amadeus HARTMANN; *Miniature Symphony* in four short movements by the 33-year-old Belgian composer Victor LEGLEY; and *Symphonic Suite* from the ballet *Orphée* by the French composer Jean Louis MARTINET.

### 29 APRIL 1949

The first concert of a newly formed *Groupe du Zodiaque,* dedicated to "the defense of the freedom of the musical language from all sorts of tyrannical esthetics," is presented in Paris.

### 29 APRIL 1949

At the 23rd Festival of the International Society for Contemporary Music held at the Teatro Greco-Romano in Taormina, a performance is given of *The Cyclops* by Euripides, with stage music and choruses by Giuseppe MULÈ. (It was at Taormina that, according to Homer's *Odyssey,* Ulysses met and smote the Cyclops Polyphemus)

### 29 APRIL 1949

*Golgotha,* oratorio by Frank MARTIN, to the text of St. Augustine, with a neo-baroque musical score based on a three-note motto evolving into triadic harmonies in luminous hymn-like tones, is performed for the first time in Geneva.

### 30 APRIL 1949

The 23rd Festival of the International Society for Contemporary Music concludes with a concert in Taormina, presenting the following program:

*Fantasia concertante* for violin solo and string accompaniment by the 43-year-old expatriate Hungarian composer Mátyás SEIBER, resident in England since 1935, written in an expressionistic paradodecaphonistic idiom; *Canciones castellanas* for soprano and 8 instruments by the 30-year-old Chilean composer Juán ORREGO SALAS; *Variations* for piano and 10 instruments, in classical forms of dodecaphonic content, by the 24-year-old French composer Serge NIGG (first performed in Paris on 29 January 1947); *6 Canzoni* for tenor, strings, and piano by the 55-year-old Swiss composer Jean BINET; and *Concerto* for two pianos with chamber orchestra, in three movements, in a neo-baroque manner, by the 29-year-old Italian conductor and composer Bruno MADERNA.

#### 4 MAY 1949

Ildebrando PIZZETTI conducts in Florence his music drama, *Vanna Lupa*, in three acts, to his own libretto garnered from Florentine chronicles of the 14th century, focused on a widowed lady alienated from her sons because of political and social disparity, written in an eloquently dramatic Italian manner with a tropism towards post-Verdian cantilena.

#### 7 MAY 1949

*Das Wundertheater*, operatic melodrama by the 22-year-old German composer Hans Werner HENZE, to a libretto from Cervantes, written in an exuberantly rubicund rhythmic style, with an artfully disoriented vocal line accoutred in acerb but non-corrosive harmonies and orchestrated in the hedonistic manner of the utilitarian German musical theater, is produced in Heidelberg.

#### 8 MAY 1949

*Sinfonia* by the 35-year-old Rumanian composer Ion DUMITRESCU is performed for the first time in Bucharest.

#### 9 MAY 1949

*Don't We All*, one-act opera by Burrill PHILLIPS, is produced in Rochester, New York.

#### 9 MAY 1949

*A Drumlin Legend*, opera in three acts by Ernst BACON, is performed for the first time, in concert form, at Columbia University in New York.

#### 12 MAY 1949

*Il Cordovano*, one-act opera buffa by the 44-year-old Italian modernist Goffredo PETRASSI, to a libretto from Cervantes, in which a bravo intrudes into the chambers of a respectable matron by pretending to be a vendor of tanned goatskins (*cordovano*), is produced at La Scala in Milan.

#### 13 MAY 1949

*Till Eulenspiegel*, opera by the 56-year-old Czech composer Otakar JEREMIÁŠ, is produced in Prague.

#### 13 MAY 1949

*Paris-Magie*, ballet in one act by the only woman member of the group of the French Six Germaine TAILLEFERRE, is produced at the Opéra-Comique in Paris.

#### 13 MAY 1949

Andrzej PANUFNIK, 34-year-old Polish composer, conducts in Warsaw the world première of his *Sinfonia Rustica*, in four movements: *Con tenerezza,*

*Con grazia, Con espressione, Con vigore,* scored for a small orchestra with the strings divided into two groups, couched in an optimistic diatonic idiom, with a recurring chromatic motive serving as a nostalgic counterfoil.

15 MAY 1949

*Third Symphony* in A minor by the 50-year-old American composer Randall THOMPSON, in four movements (1) *Largo elegiaco,* suffused with nostalgic modalities (2) *Allegro appassionato,* in rondo form inspired by a sense of tonal defiance, but collapsing in desolate wistfulness in an episode entitled *Calmato ma triste assai* (3) *Lento tranquillo,* a bucolic eclogue (4) *Allegro vivace* in which the somber introspection of the preceding movements is dispelled by exuberant extroversion of triadic jubilation, is performed for the first time as part of the American Music Festival in New York.

17 MAY 1949

The First Congress of Dodecaphonic Music opens a four-day session in Milan, presenting (with the telegraphic blessing from Arnold Schoenberg who sent this message: "Proudly I greet my companions who aim to present musical ideas with new tools of musical logic—good luck!") works by Arnold SCHOENBERG (*Piano Suite,* op. 25); Ernst KRENEK (*Kafka Lieder*); Hans Erich APOSTEL (*Quartet* for flute, clarinet, horn and bassoon); Wallingford RIEGGER (*Third Symphony*); Luigi DALLAPICCOLA (5 *Fragments from Sappho* for voice and orchestra), and *Zwölftonmusik* for orchestra by Josef Matthias HAUER.

18 MAY 1949

Darius MILHAUD conducts at Temple Emanuel in San Francisco the world première of his *Sabbath Morning Service,* written according to a free Hebrew ritual, without precise quotations of liturgical chants.

22 MAY 1949

Hans PFITZNER, romantic German composer of operas and instrumental music wrought with masterly art but lacking vitality, dies in Salzburg, at 6:30 in the morning, 17 days after his 80th birthday.

27 MAY 1949

*Ulysses,* cantata for tenor solo, mixed chorus and orchestra, by the 44-year-old expatriate Hungarian composer, now residing in London, Mátyás SEIBER, to the text from the famous surrealist novel by James Joyce, reaching climactic heights in the fugue: "our system plunging towards the constellation of Hercules," with an atonally oriented setting (the first two chords from Schoenberg's *Klavierstück,* op. 19, No. 6, are quoted in the score), is performed for the first time in London.

28 MAY 1949

*Die schwarze Spinne,* opera in two acts by the Swiss composer Willy BURKHARD, after a nightmarish little tale by the Swiss cleric Albert Bitzius

*876*

(1797–1854), wherein a village woman, preternaturally impregnated by the devil, procreating a pack of poisonous black spiders is redeemed from perdition by a normally gravid maiden who exorcises the monstrous arachneous progeny at the time of her own parturition, is performed for the first time in Zürich. (The same story was used in Heinrich Sutermeister's identically named opera, produced in St. Gall on 2 March 1949, and by Josef Matthias Hauer in his opera produced in Vienna on 23 May 1966)

### 10 JUNE 1949
*Ouanga,* three-act opera by the American Negro composer Clarence Cameron WHITE, to a libretto dealing with a Haitian voodoo priestess who refuses to surrender her fetish *ouanga* (hence the title) to a presidential usurper, is performed by an all-Negro cast in South Bend, Indiana.

### 14 JUNE 1949
*Let's Make an Opera,* an "entertainment for young people" by Benjamin BRITTEN, incorporating a miniature opera *The Little Sweep,* dealing with a child chimney sweep, a pathetic victim of the inhuman exploitation of little boys in England early in the 19th century used as living brushes to go through the chimney and clean the soot with their small bodies, is performed for the first time at the Aldeburgh Music Festival, with the audience invited to participate in singing a few simple songs "rehearsed" in the first part of the play.

### 15 JUNE 1949
*Die Bremer Stadtmusikanten,* opera by the 44-year-old German composer Richard MOHAUPT, is produced in Bremen.

### 18 JUNE 1949
*Fourth Symphony,* subtitled *Metamorphoses,* by the 29-year-old Danish composer Niels Viggo BENTZON, is performed for the first time in Copenhagen.

### 20 JUNE 1949
*Stradivario,* "a choreographic fantasy of instruments that dance" for orchestra, by Gian Francesco MALIPIERO, picturing the telekinetic conduct of antique instruments at the Palazzo Pisani in Venice, which attack an old beggar who attempts to steal a Stradivarius violin, is performed for the first time at the Maggio Musicale in Florence.

### 21 JUNE 1949
*Le Oui des Jeunes Filles,* lyric comedy in three acts by Reynaldo HAHN, is produced posthumously at the Opéra-Comique in Paris, with the last act orchestrated by Henri Büsser.

### 25 JUNE 1949
*Das verzauberte Ich,* comic opera by the 51-year-old German composer Ottmar GERSTER, is performed for the first time in Wuppertal.

## 27 JUNE 1949

*Second Symphony* by the 48-year-old English composer Alan Bush, *The Nottingham*, in four movements, subtitled *Sherwood Forest, Clifton Grove, Castle Rock* and *Goose Fair*, glorifying the liberating movement of Robin Hood, is performed at Nottingham, England, to mark the city's semimillennium.

## 28 JUNE 1949

*Illusion*, radio opera by the Parisianized Hungarian composer Tibor Harsányi, is performed for the first time in Paris.

## 30 JUNE 1949

The Bärenreiter Verlag in Kassel launches the publication of the most voluminous encyclopedia of music ever undertaken, *Die Musik in Geschichte und Gegenwart*, edited by Friedrich Blume. (The article on Bach was not to be reached until column No. 962)

## 8 JULY 1949

Riccardo Pick-Mangiagalli, Bohemian-born Italian composer of effective ballets and lyrical instrumental pieces, dies in Milan two days before his 67th birthday.

## 14 JULY 1949

*Spring Symphony* by Benjamin Britten, for soprano, alto, tenor, mixed chorus and orchestra, consisting of twelve vocal numbers, to vernal texts by English poets from the 13th to the 20th century, is performed in a world première at the Holland Festival in Amsterdam.

## 15 JULY 1949

Francisco Mignone, 51-year-old Brazilian composer, conducts in Rio de Janeiro the first performances of his ballet suite *Quadros Amazonicos* and his oratorio *Alegrias de Nossa Senhora*.

## 18 JULY 1949

Vítězslav Novák, Bohemian composer pupil of Dvořák and teacher of a generation of Czechoslovak musicians, whose own operatic and symphonic music is suffused with national thematic materials on a flow of romantic harmonies, dies in Skuteč, Slovakia, at the age of seventy-eight.

## 22 JULY 1949

*Rapsodie provençale* by the 53-year-old French composer Jean Rivier, an unpretentious piece of pastoral symphonic music, is performed for the first time at the International Festival in Aix-en-Provence.

## 2 AUGUST 1949

*Paw i dziewczyna* (*The Peacock and the Maiden*), ballet by the 52-year-old Polish composer Tadeusz Szeligowski, is produced in Wroclaw (Breslau).

878

## 9 AUGUST 1949

*Antigonae,* musical play by the 54-year-old German composer Carl ORFF, with the text adapted from Sophocles, relating the tragic story of a loyal sister who violated her father's order and gave a decent burial to her brother who fought and fell in the enemy camp during the siege of Thebes, in the German version by the poet Friedrich Hölderlin, scored for a modernistically primitivistic ensemble of six pianos (to be played also on their insides, hitting the strings by mallets of various sizes), four harps, African drums, ten Javanese gongs, several large xylophones, an anvil and vocalists, assigned cephalotriptic single-note parts (in one scene the watchman has 174 consecutive D's before interrupting his solipsistic iteration, is performed for the first time in Salzburg.

## 10 AUGUST 1949

*String Octet* in three movements: *Animé, Modéré, Vif,* by Darius MILHAUD, an ingenious musical palimpsest of his 14th and 15th string quartets (which can also be played separately), is performed for the first time at Mills College, California, Milhaud's principal American teaching place, by the combined Budapest and Paganini Quartets.

## 15 AUGUST 1949

*Prayer for Peace,* choral symphonic poem by the Japanese composer Shiro FUKAI, is performed for the first time in Tokyo.

## 27 AUGUST 1949

The Government of the Federal German Republic commemorates the centennial of the death of the German opera composer Konradin KREUTZER by issuing a postage stamp of 10 marks with his picture.

## 3 SEPTEMBER 1949

Charles KELLOGG, "California Nature Singer," reputed to be able to reproduce the song of any bird, thanks to his congenitally ornithomorphic syrinx in addition to the normal larynx (his tessitura encompassed $12\frac{1}{2}$ octaves, reaching into the ultrasonic range beyond 14,000 cycles), dies at the age of 80 at Morgan Hill, California. (On 6 September 1926 he broadcast a shrill note over radio station KGO, which extinguished a candle in Hawaii and a chemical flame on the Berkeley campus of the University of California, where the test was made)

## 3 SEPTEMBER 1949

At the Edinburgh Music Festival, Ernest BLOCH conducts the BBC Scottish Orchestra in the world première of his *Concerto Symphonique* for piano and orchestra in three movements: *Pesante* (chime-like unison progressions); *Allegro Vivace* (a scherzo with a contrasting songful section); and *Allegro deciso* (rhapsodic and energetic).

### 3 SEPTEMBER 1949

On the eve of the 125th anniversary of the birth of Anton BRUCKNER, the Austrian Government issues a commemorative stamp of 40 groschen in his honor.

### 7 SEPTEMBER 1949

*Billy Budd,* one-act opera by the Italian veristic composer Giorgio Federico GHEDINI, after Melville's tragic tale of an unjustly hanged seaman, is produced in Venice. (Benjamin Britten's opera on the same subject was produced in London on 1 December 1951)

### 8 SEPTEMBER 1949

Richard STRAUSS, "Richard the Second" (so nicknamed by Hans von Bülow to dub him the inheritor of Wagner's mantle), the last of the titans of German musical romanticism, creator of the sui generis philosophical tone poem, daring explorer of the extreme regions of tonality, dies in his home at Garmisch-Partenkirchen, at the age of eighty-five.

### 11 SEPTEMBER 1949

Henri RABAUD, French composer of effective operas and symphonic poems (of which *La Procession Nocturne* for orchestra was a transitory favorite), dies in Paris in his 76th year.

### 15 SEPTEMBER 1949

*King's Rhapsody,* operetta by the 56-year-old English composer Ivor NOVELLO, in which a modern-minded prince marries a conventional Scandinavian princess but carries an illicit affair with a Riviera temptress with such flagrant nonchalance that he is forced to abdicate, is produced in London.

### 18 SEPTEMBER 1949

*Naši furianti (Our Wild Ones),* opera in three acts by the Czech composer Rudolf KUBÍN, is produced at Ostrava.

### 19 SEPTEMBER 1949

Nikos SKALKOTTAS, Greek composer, disciple of Schoenberg who elaborated the 12-tone method in an imaginatively personal manner in his numerous instrumental works, dies in Athens at the age of forty-five.

### 19 SEPTEMBER 1949

*Stormen,* opera by the dean of Swedish composers Kurt ATTERBERG, after Shakespeare's play *The Tempest,* is performed for the first time in Stockholm.

### 24 SEPTEMBER 1949

On the eve of the centennial of the death of Johann STRAUSS, SR., "Father of the Waltz," the government of Austria issues a commemorative 30-groschen stamp in his honor.

## 29 SEPTEMBER 1949

*Tormida Rand* (*Stormy Coast*), opera in five acts by the 40-year-old Estonian composer Gustav ERNESAKS, to a libretto dealing with the oppression of 19th-century Estonian fishermen by a feudal landlord who deliberately sets false signals to ships on stormy nights to lure them to destruction and then rob the wreckage, but is eventually hurled over a cliff into the sea by a shipwrecked Russian sailor, is produced in Talinn.

## 29 SEPTEMBER 1949

*The Olympians*, fanciful opera in three acts by the urbane English modernist Arthur BLISS, to a story about a couple of lovers whose happiness is arranged by the intercession of Jupiter, Venus, Mars, Mercury, Bacchus and other Greek deities convivially gamboling in an English seaport in 1810, in the guise of travelling players, returning to Mt. Olympus one night every year, is produced in London.

## 30 SEPTEMBER 1949

*Fourth Symphony* by the 61-year-old Dutch romantic composer Matthijs VERMEULEN is performed for the first time in Rotterdam.

## 4 OCTOBER 1949

Edmund EYSLER, Austrian composer of vivacious operettas, dies in his native city of Vienna at the age of seventy-five.

## 11 OCTOBER 1949

*Regina*, musical drama in three acts by the American composer Marc BLITZSTEIN, to his own libretto based on Lillian Hellman's play *The Little Foxes*, focused on a vulpine covey of contentious siblings of an ante-bellum Southern family torn by avarice and pride, with Regina outfoxing the other little foxes in obtaining the largest share in a lucrative contract for building a cotton mill, set to music in a diversified but distinctly vigesimosecular idiom with a lively influx of antique ragtime, is produced in Boston. (The first New York performance of *Regina* took place on 30 October 1949)

## 13 OCTOBER 1949

*Fourth Symphony* by the 53-year-old Austrian composer Johann Nepomuk DAVID, in four movements, *Adagio, Allegro moderato, Scherzo* and *Finale*, monothematically conceived but pluralistically carried out, so that the basic intervallic ascent increases from the second to a third, a fourth, a fifth and a sixth, reaching the ultimate expansion in the tumescent finale, is performed for the first time in Leipzig.

## 16 OCTOBER 1949

Carl Emil SEASHORE, Swedish-born American psychologist who devised the "Seashore Test," a method for rating musical ability by measuring instruments of his own invention, such as audiometer, tonoscope, and chronograph, dies in Lewiston, Idaho, at the age of eighty-three.

### 17 OCTOBER 1949

On the centenary of CHOPIN's death, Paulina CZERNICKA, a middle-aged Polish lady pathologically obsessed with the image of Chopin, who manufactured and circulated a number of letters purportedly written by Chopin to Delfina Potocka, which represented him as a pornographic sensualist using anachronistic verbal vulgarity (some obscene Polish slang found in the letters were of World War I vintage), shoots herself to death in Warsaw. (In October 1961 the Chopin Institute in Warsaw officially declared the correspondence to be a forgery)

### 20 OCTOBER 1949

*Des Simplicius Simplicissimus Jugend,* "scenes from German destiny," by Karl Amadeus HARTMANN, in three parts, to an allegorical scenario from the time of the Thirty Years War (1618–1648), in which a young wanderer Simplicius voices his incomprehension of internecine carnage, stumbles into the governor's palace during an orgy, and survives because "he is not worth a bullet," scored for speaking and singing voices, ten instruments and percussion, and marked by a stark rhythmic pattern of atonal melodies, with episodic Germanic folksongs in triadic harmonies pandiatonically amplified, and distinguished in the text by occasional scatological similes ("this young lady has hair as yellow as a small child's excrement"), is produced in Cologne. ( A performance of the work in concert form was presented in Cologne on 23 October 1948)

### 24 OCTOBER 1949

Joaquin NÍN Y CASTELLANOS, Spanish pianist and composer of sensitive Hispanic piano pieces and subtle arrangements of old Spanish songs, dies in his native Havana at the age of seventy.

### 25 OCTOBER 1949

*Concerto* for seven instruments, percussion and strings by the 59-year-old Swiss composer Frank MARTIN, in three movements, *Allegro, Adagietto, Allegro vivace,* each commencing with the same syncopated theme, which is successively introduced by oboe, clarinet, horn, trumpet, trombone, bassoon and flute, is performed for the first time in Bern.

### 28 OCTOBER 1949

Ginette NEVEU, 30-year-old French violinist whose technical perfection and masculine energy in performance earned her the renown of the greatest woman violin virtuoso of the first half of the 20th century, perishes in an airplane accident near the Azores on her way from France to the United States, carrying her Stradivarius violin with her to flaming destruction.

## 29 OCTOBER 1949

*Ollantay,* symphonic triptych by the 33-year-old Argentinian composer Alberto GINASTERA, dealing with an Inca soldier who violates the priest's daughter in the temple of the virgins and is slain by the celestial army of the Sun God, in a somberly tense setting in a resonant dissonant idiom overlaying the basic pentatonic melos of pre-Columbian America, is produced in Buenos Aires.

## 3 NOVEMBER 1949

*Seventh Symphony* by Gian Francesco MALIPIERO in four movements (*Allegro, Lento, Allegro impetuoso,* and *Lento*), subtitled *Delle canzoni* because it evokes the impressions of imagined old songs inaudibly streaming from distant hills, is performed for the first time in Milan.

## 6 NOVEMBER 1949

Alan BUSH, member of the left wing of the British Labor Party, conducts the Massed Choirs and Orchestra of the Workers' Music Association in London in the first performance of his *Song of Friendship* for bass, chorus and band, dedicated to the ideal of international cooperation with the socialist countries of Europe and Asia.

## 15 NOVEMBER 1949

*Song of the Forests,* oratorio for tenor, bass, boys' chorus, mixed chorus and symphony orchestra by Dmitri SHOSTAKOVICH, in seven sections, glorifying in heroic triadic stanzas the Soviet reforestation plan, composed according to the tenets of Socialist Realism, with the text voicing the optimistic expectations of the time when young trees will rise majestically on the banks of Russian rivers, and concluding with a perfervid expression of faith in the Leninist Party and in the limitless wisdom of sagacious Stalin, is performed for the first time in Leningrad.

## 16 NOVEMBER 1949

*Le Peintre et son Modèle,* ballet by Georges AURIC, in which a modern Pygmalion emulates in marble the carnal perfection of a living Parisian model, is produced in Paris.

## 19 NOVEMBER 1949

*The Enormous Room,* symphonic poem by the 34-year-old American composer David DIAMOND, after the novel of that name by E. E. Cummings, descriptive of an actual "enormous room" in a French military camp, with 40 mattresses, 40 urinal cans and 40 multiracial suspects, in which Cummings was detained himself for two months in 1917, set to music in the manner of an "unfolding song" expressive of the mood of "a new and beautiful darkness," in a starkly dissonant idiom, is performed for the first time by the Cincinnati Symphony Orchestra under the direction of Thor Johnson.

## 20 NOVEMBER 1949

*Third Concerto* for piano and orchestra by the Czech composer Bohuslav MARTINU, in three movements, *Allegro, Andante poco moderato* and *Moderato,* written in a neo-classical manner, is performed for the first time by Rudolf Firkusny with the Dallas Symphony Orchestra, Walter Hendl conducting.

## 22 NOVEMBER 1949

Guillermo URIBE-HOLGUÍN, dean of Colombian composers, conducts in Bogotá the first performance of his *Sinfonieta campesina.*

## 22 NOVEMBER 1949

*Hindustani Concerto* for piano and orchestra by the 45-year-old Scottish composer Erik CHISHOLM, presenting an artful fusion of Hindu ragas with modern harmonies, is played for the first time in a world première in Capetown, South Africa, where Chisholm was a resident composer and teacher.

## 25 NOVEMBER 1949

*Apocalypse,* oratorio by the 42-year-old Dutch composer Henk BADINGS, in two parts and seven chapters, scored for chorus, orchestra and a vocal quartet representing the four apocalyptic beasts, is performed for the first time in Rotterdam.

## 1 DECEMBER 1949

*David Symphony* by the 41-year-old Polish-born Israeli composer Menahem AVIDOM (who Hebraized his original Germanic cognomen Mahler-Kalkstein), is performed for the first time by the Israel Philharmonic Orchestra in Tel Aviv.

## 1 DECEMBER 1949

Hans Werner HENZE, 23-year-old German composer, conducts in Stuttgart the first performance of his *Second Symphony,* in three movements, cast in a proclamatory dramatic manner, with peals of distant drums and fanfares of declarative trumpets leading to a conglomerate of thundering polyharmonies and taciturn but eloquent silences, chromatic torsion of polythematic compaction and polyglot fugues in judiciously copulated invertible counterpoint, terminating in a magma of heteroousian sounds relentlessly increasing in saturation and finally erupting in an abrasive discord.

## 2 DECEMBER 1949

*Turangalîla* (Hindu word meaning love song), an expansive mystical symphony in ten movements by Olivier MESSIAEN (composed between 17 July 1946 and 29 November 1948), scored for piano, Ondes Martenot and large orchestra with an augmented percussion section, and abounding in sonorities redolent of the music of Bali and Java, with melorhythmic lines derived from Messiaen's theory of melodic and rhythmic modes as expounded in his mus-ico-philosophical treatise *Technique de mon langage musical,* is performed for the first time anywhere by the Boston Symphony Orchestra, Leonard Bern-stein conducting. (Three movements of *Turangalila* were first performed under the title *Trois Talas* in Paris on 15 February 1948)

## 2 DECEMBER 1949

*Viola Concerto* by Béla BARTÓK, in three movements, *Moderato, Adagio reli-gioso, Allegro vivace,* connected by interludes, left in incomplete sketches after his death on 25 September 1945, reconstructed and orchestrated by his friend Tibor Serly, is performed for the first time by William Primrose, at whose behest the work was originally planned, with the Minneapolis Sym-phony Orchestra, under the direction of Antal Dorati.

## 6 DECEMBER 1949

Huddie LEDBETTER, known as LEAD BELLY, Louisiana-born Negro balladeer who was a cotton picker on southern plantations, was jailed for felonious as-sault, but won a pardon from the Louisiana State Prison in 1934 after he sang for the Governor, and got into jail again in New York in 1939 for stabbing, al-beit unfatally, another man, dies in New York at the age of sixty.

## 7 DECEMBER 1949

*Fifth Symphony* by the 42-year-old Dutch modernist Henk BADINGS is per-formed for the first time by the Concertgebouw Orchestra in Amsterdam.

## 8 DECEMBER 1949

*Gentlemen Prefer Blondes,* musical comedy by Jule STYNE, after the exhilarat-ing book of that title by Anita Loos, dealing with an acquisitive American blonde who latches herself onto a substantial sugar daddy, embodying her credo in the declarative song *Diamonds Are A Girl's Best Friend,* is produced in New York.

## 10 DECEMBER 1949

*Krútňava* (*Whirlpool*), opera in six scenes by the 41-year-old Slovak composer Eugen SUCHOŇ, a folk drama in which the bride of a slain Slovak peasant re-luctantly marries his slayer who is tormented by the memories of the as yet undiscovered crime and is impelled to confess when he begins to suspect that his putative child is in reality the pre-marital offspring of his victim, set to music within the framework of traditional Slavonic melos with a patina of mellow Wagneromorphic harmonies, is produced in Bratislava.

## 16 DECEMBER 1949

Bernard WAGENAAR, 55-year-old Dutch-born American composer, conducts the Boston Symphony Orchestra in the world première of his *Fourth Sym-*

*phony* in five movements, couched in a prophylactic neo-classical idiom covered by lyrical emulsions and invigorated by mobile counterpoint.

17 DECEMBER 1949

Two centuries have passed since the birth in Aversa, near Naples, of Domenico CIMAROSA, the composer of harmonious melodramatic operas in the finest tradition of the Italian Baroque. (To commemorate Cimarosa's bicentennial the Italian Government issued a postage stamp of 20 lire with his portrait)

20 DECEMBER 1949

*Enchanted Citadel,* ballet by the Japanese composer Akira IFUKUBE, is performed for the first time in Tokyo.

22 DECEMBER 1949

*Ricercari* for orchestra by the 52-year-old Parisianized Polish composer Alexandre TANSMAN, consisting of four classical movements (*Notturno, Scherzo, Intermezzo, Toccata*) and one unclassical section (*Study in Boogie-Woogie*) is performed for the first time by the St. Louis Symphony Orchestra, Vladimir Golschmann conducting.

23 DECEMBER 1949

Juan José CASTRO, 54-year-old Argentinian composer, conducts in Montevideo the world première of his two-act opera *La Zapatera prodigiosa,* after the story by Federico García Lorca.

31 DECEMBER 1949

To commemorate the 50th anniversary of the death of the famous Viennese operetta composer Karl MILLÖCKER, the Austrian Government issues a postage stamp of one schilling bearing his portrait.

## ᘓ *1950* ᘒ

4 JANUARY 1950

*Judith,* choreographic poem for orchestra by the 39-year-old American composer William SCHUMAN, to the biblical story of the valorous Hebrew damsel who penetrated the camp of the Assyrian general Holofernes besieging her city and expertly decapitated him during his sleep, interpreted as "an ancient fertility ritual of rebirth, in which the woman casts off the garment of mourning and puts on her garments of gladness symbolic of her femininity thereby defeating the enemy, death," composed in a severely dissonant polyphonic idiom, rhythmically vivified by raucous outcries of triumph as Judith exhibits the bearded head of Holofernes for the delectation of the populace, is performed for the first time by Martha Graham and her dance group with the Louisville, Kentucky, Orchestra.

## 6 JANUARY 1950

Francis POULENC plays the solo part with the Boston Symphony Orchestra, Charles Munch conducting, in the world première of his *Piano Concerto*, set in a gallant Gallic style, in three mundane movements (1) *Allegretto*, a hedonistically lyric essay in rococo harmonies (2) *Andante con moto*, a pastoral interlude in salubrious march time (3) *Rondeau à la française*, on the theme of an old French song "À la claire fontaine."

## 7 JANUARY 1950

*Susanne*, opera buffa by the Danish composer Knudaage RIISAGER is produced in Copenhagen.

## 11 JANUARY 1950

*Piano Concerto* by the 43-year-old American composer Paul CRESTON, in three movements (1) *Allegro maestoso*, in a vigorously lyric and coherently rhapsodic tonal idiom (2) *Andante tranquillo*, a bucolic presentation of tranquil modalities, and (3) *Presto* in the rhythmic scheme of a tarantella, is performed for the first time in Washington.

## 12 JANUARY 1950

*Mondi celesti e infernali*, opera in three acts "con 7 donne" by Gian Francesco MALIPIERO, written in the style of a baroque Italian madrigal suite, is produced in concert form on the Turin Radio. (The first stage performance took place in Venice on 2 February 1961)

## 15 JANUARY 1950

*Auto da Barca do Inferno*, opera by the Portuguese composer Ruy COELHO, is produced in Lisbon.

## 17 JANUARY 1950

*4 Mouvements Symphoniques* by the 44-year-old Dutch composer Guillaume LANDRÉ are performed for the first time in The Hague.

## 21 JANUARY 1950

On the 60th anniversary of his first public appearance as a violinist at the age of eight, Georges ENESCO, prime Rumanian musician of the 20th century, gives his last American concert in New York in the multiple capacity of violinist, pianist, conductor and composer, in a program comprising Bach's concerto for two violins (as a dual soloist, with his pupil Yehudi Menuhin), his violin sonata (as pianist, with Menuhin), his *Second Suite* for orchestra in C major and his *First Rumanian Rhapsody* (as conductor).

### 22 JANUARY 1950

*Chiarina*, ballet-grotesque by Boris BLACHER, is produced in Berlin.

### 26 JANUARY 1950

Carlos SURINACH, 34-year-old Spanish composer, conducts in Paris the first performance of his *Second Symphony*.

### 27 JANUARY 1950

*Four Transylvanian Dances* for string orchestra by the 42-year-old Transylvanian composer Sándor VERESS is performed for the first time in Basel.

### 28 JANUARY 1950

*Französische Suite* for orchestra by Werner EGK, on themes by Rameau, is performed for the first time in Munich. (It was first performed as a ballet in Hamburg on 1 February 1952)

### 29 JANUARY 1950

*Das Spiel vom König Aphelius*, music drama for narrator and orchestra by Heinrich KAMINSKI, is performed posthumously for the first time in Göttingen.

### 30 JANUARY 1950

The widow of Camille SAINT-SAËNS (separated from him in 1881, but never legally divorced) dies in Bordeaux at the age of ninety-five.

### 1 FEBRUARY 1950

*Timon of Athens*, a symphonic portrait after Shakespeare, by the 34-year-old American composer David DIAMOND, is performed for the first time by the Louisville Orchestra.

### 1 FEBRUARY 1950

*Concerto* for piano and orchestra by the 52-year-old German-born Israeli composer Paul BEN-HAIM, in three movements, subtitled *Vision, Voices in the Night* and *Dance*, reflecting respectively a romantic image, a Mediterranean landscape and an Oriental festival, is performed for the first time in Tel Aviv.

### 5 FEBRUARY 1950

*Concerto* for violin and orchestra by the 53-year-old French composer Jean RIVIER, written in a virtuoso idiom of modern France, is performed for the first time by the Société des Concerts du Conservatoire in Paris.

## 7 FEBRUARY 1950

*The Enchanted Pear Tree,* one-act radio opera by Hall OVERTON, is produced in New York.

## 8 FEBRUARY 1950

*L'Orso Re,* musical fable in three acts by the 65-year-old Italian composer Luigi FERRARI-TRECATE, dealing with an ensorcelled King who assumes an ursine form and rules a nation of bears, but is restored to the human species after the sorcerer's invultuation loses its magic, set to music replete with atonal acerbities and polytonal acridities and ending on a chord of eight different notes, is produced at La Scala in Milan.

## 8 FEBRUARY 1950

The German Democratic Republic formally adopts the musical setting by Hanns EISLER of the socialist hymn of Johannes R. Becher, "Auferstanden aus Ruinen und der Zukunft zugewandt" (composed by Eisler during a visit to Warsaw in 1949 and played by him for the first time on Chopin's piano in the house where Chopin was born), as its national anthem.

## 10 FEBRUARY 1950

*Third Symphony* by the 44-year-old German master contrapuntist Karl Amadeus HARTMANN, in three movements, "rooted in the spiritual landscape of Alban Berg," with a magistral fugue flanked by two slow movements—a *Largo* for strings and an "ecstatically hymnal" *Adagio,* is performed for the first time in Munich.

## 10 FEBRUARY 1950

*Violin Concerto* by the 39-year-old American composer William SCHUMAN, in two movements (1) *Allegro risoluto,* set in bitonal major-minor triadic harmonies in which the mediant is ambivalent, ending on the E major-minor chord (2) *Introduzione Adagio, Poco più mosso, Presto subito, Allegretto,* in stark quintal-quartal counterpoint, resulting in organum-like sonorities and ending on a unison, is played for the first time by Isaac Stern with the Boston Symphony Orchestra, Charles Munch conducting.

## 12 FEBRUARY 1950

*Die Füsse im Feuer,* and *Fingerhütchen,* two ballad operas by the Swiss composer Heinrich SUTERMEISTER, are performed for the first time in Berlin.

## 20 FEBRUARY 1950

*Don Quixote,* ballet by the Spanish composer Roberto GERHARD, resident in England, is produced in London.

*Frol Skobeyev,* comic opera in four acts by the 36-year-old Soviet composer Tikhon KHRENNIKOV, dealing with a liberal Russian nobleman of the 17th century who buys off and frees the serfs of the father of his beloved, is produced in Moscow.

1 MARCH 1950

*The Consul,* musical drama in three acts by Gian Carlo MENOTTI, to his own libretto depicting the agonizing peril of an anti-Fascist couple in an anonymous European country trying desperately to obtain a salutary visa from the consul of an unnamed great nation, set to music with intense lyrico-dramatic expressiveness, rivalling Puccini in theatrical power, in a distinctly personal cosmopolitan idiom with a judicious application of vigesimosecular technical media, is produced in Philadelphia, staged by Menotti himself. (The first New York production took place on 15 March 1950)

1 MARCH 1950

Paul HINDEMITH conducts the Louisville Orchestra in the world première of his *Sinfonietta in E,* in four movements, conceived as a 20th-century replica of an 18th-century entertainment piece, and abounding in lively contrapuntal gambados.

3 MARCH 1950

*Fourth Piano Concerto* by Darius MILHAUD, in three movements conceived in contrasting meditative and joyous moods, and reaching polytonal polyphony at recurring climaxes, is performed for the first time by Zadel Skolovsky with the Boston Symphony Orchestra, Charles Munch conducting.

7 MARCH 1950

*Violin Concerto* by the 34-year-old Canadian composer Alexander BROTT is performed for the first time in Montreal.

10 MARCH 1950

Lukas Foss, 27-year-old Berlin-born American composer conducts the Boston Symphony Orchestra in the world première of his *Song of Anguish,* biblical solo cantata for baritone and orchestra to the text freely arranged from the Book of Isaiah: "Woe unto them that call evil good and good evil!"

16 MARCH 1950

*Fifth Symphony* by Ernst KRENEK, in five linked movements, written in a free dodecaphonic idiom, is performed for the first time by the Albuquerque Symphony Orchestra.

18 MARCH 1950

A concert of "Musique Concrète," glorifying the "dialectic of the fortuitous" fructified by "esthetic volition," and compiled of aleatory combinations of recorded noises and unrelated fragments of speech and melodies, played at different speeds and sometimes in reverse, is presented at the Ecole Normale de Musique in Paris, by Pierre SCHAEFFER and Pierre HENRY in a program of synthetic pieces entitled *Symphonie pour un homme seul, Bidule en ut,* and *Concerto des ambiguités.*

24 MARCH 1950

*Cello Concerto* by Virgil THOMSON in three movements, subtitled *Rider on the Plains, Variations on a Southern Hymn Tune,* and *Children's Games,* employing simple parallel major triads for straight harmonization, and mutually exclusive pairs of major and minor triads, with some bitonal, pentatonic, and hexatonic excrescences for more complex developments, is performed for the first time by the Philadelphia Orchestra.

31 MARCH 1950

*The First Waltz,* operetta by the 80-year-old Viennese composer Oskar STRAUS is performed for the first time in Munich, in the presence of the composer, with 28 curtain calls saluting him at the end.

31 MARCH 1950

*Metaphor,* ballet by Niels Viggo BENTZON, 30-year-old Danish composer, is performed for the first time in Copenhagen.

3 APRIL 1950

Kurt WEILL, German composer, creator of a new type of modern opera, in which simple melodies are set in the framework of complex and often raspingly dissonant harmonies, dies at the age of 50 in New York, at the height of his new American career as the composer of successful stage music in a witty, folk-wise American manner.

9 APRIL 1950

*Der spanische Rosenstock,* opera in three acts by the 29-year-old Swiss composer Armin SCHIBLER, is performed for the first time in Bern, Switzerland.

19 APRIL 1950

LORD BERNERS (originally Gerald Tyrwhitt), aristocratic English composer of humorous modernistic pieces, dies in London at the age of sixty-six.

19 APRIL 1950

*L'Inconnue,* ballet by the French modernist André JOLIVET, is produced in Paris.

4 MAY 1950

*Concerto de mai* for piano and orchestra by the 51-year-old French composer Marcel DELANNOY, so named because it was begun in May 1949 and its orchestration completed in May 1950, barely in time for performance, is performed in Paris by the Société des Jeunesses Musicales de France.

4 MAY 1950

*L'Allegra brigata,* "six novellas in one drama of three acts" with words and music by Gian Francesco MALIPIERO, six stories of zealous love and dark jealousy, narrated by six members of the "merry brigade," culminating in the murder of one of them, is produced at La Scala, Milan.

5 MAY 1950

*Le Chevalier Errant,* ballet with chorus by Jacques IBERT, musically miming the more salient sallies of the "Knight Errant" Don Quixote, is performed for the first time in Paris. (A symphonic suite in four movements from this ballet was first performed in Paris on 22 February 1952)

7 MAY 1950

*La Main de Gloire,* "macaronic history of an enchanted hand," opera in four acts by Jean FRANÇAIX, to the fantastic story by Gerard de Norval about a duelist who by artful magic makes his right hand unerringly effective in killing his rival in love, but who subsequently loses control over the "glorious hand" and is led by it, against his will, to crime and eventually to self-destruction, is produced in Bordeaux.

9 MAY 1950

*The Triumph of St. Joan,* chamber opera by the 37-year-old American composer Norman DELLO JOIO, is performed for the first time at Sarah Lawrence College, Bronxville, New York. (The musical material of the opera was subsequently used by Dello Joio in an orchestral work *The Triumph of St. Joan Symphony,* first performed in Louisville, Kentucky, as a ballet on 5 December 1951. With an entirely different score, *The Triumph of St. Joan* was produced as an opera in New York on 16 April 1959)

11 MAY 1950

*Rapsodia banateana* by the Rumanian composer Zeno VANCEA, based on the themes of the Banat region is performed for the first time in Bucharest.

12 MAY 1950

*Pohádka máje (Romance in May),* opera in three acts by the Czech composer Jaroslav KVAPIL, is produced in Prague.

12 MAY 1950

*Bolivar,* opera in three acts by Darius MILHAUD (completed at Mills College, California, on 3 June 1943), symbolically representing the struggles and the victory of the Spanish-American Liberator, with a musical score full of polytonal tension and vibrating with tropical rhythms, is performed for the first time at the Paris Opéra.

## 13 MAY 1950

*De Nachtwacht,* opera by the Dutch composer Henk BADINGS, inspired by the famous painting by Rembrandt representing a company of soldiers enveloped in nocturnal shadows dappled with light, is performed for the first time in Antwerp.

## 17 MAY 1950

Nine centuries have passed since the death in Pomposa of GUIDO D'AREZZO, the initiator of musical pedagogy by means of the syllabic vocalization on Ut, Re, Mi, Fa, Sol, La.

## 17 MAY 1950

Eduardo FABINI, Uruguayan composer of impressionistic music imbued with Latin American melorhythms, dies in Montevideo on the eve of his 67th birthday.

## 18 MAY 1950

*The Jumping Frog of Calaveras County,* opera in two scenes by the 27-year-old Berlin-born American composer, Lukas Foss, after Mark Twain's famous story of a frog race, is performed for the first time at the University of Indiana in Bloomington, during the week in May when actual jumping frog contests are held annually in Calaveras County, California.

## 18 MAY 1950

*Second Symphony* in C minor by the dean of Canadian composers Healey WILLAN, is performed for the first time in Toronto.

## 20 MAY 1950

*First Symphony* by the 29-year-old American composer William BERGSMA is performed for the first time on a radio broadcast from New York.

## 20 MAY 1950

*Il Prigioniero,* one-act opera with a prologue by the 46-year-old Italian modernist Luigi DALLAPICCOLA, to a libretto based on *La Torture par l'Espérance* from *Nouveaux Contes cruels* by Villiers de l'Isle-Adam and Charles de Coster's *La Légende d'Ulenspiegel* dealing with a prisoner of Philip II in Saragossa provoked and aided in his escape by a guard who turns out to be the Grand Inquisitor in person (the prisoner exclaims: "La speranza, l'ultima tortura!"), with musical materials based on three dodecaphonic themes, symbolizing prayer, hope and freedom (with a choral finale of four mutually exclusive triads, thus equating tonality with liberty), is produced at the May Festival in Florence. (The first concert performance of the work was given on the Turin Radio, 4 December 1949)

## 22 MAY 1950

*Vier Letzte Lieder* for soprano and orchestra by Richard STRAUSS, written in 1948, are posthumously performed for the first time in London by Kirsten Flagstad, with Wilhelm Furtwängler conducting.

## 26 MAY 1950

*Third Symphony* by the 46-year-old Japanese composer Saburo MOROI is presented for the first time in Tokyo.

## 27 MAY 1950

*Jan Hus*, opera by the Czech composer Karel HORKÝ, dealing with the life of the religious Czech martyr, is produced in Brno.

## 8 JUNE 1950

*Concerto* for French horn and orchestra by Paul HINDEMITH is performed for the first time in Baden-Baden.

## 11 JUNE 1950

*Ein Sommertag*, ballet by Werner EGK, is performed for the first time in Berlin.

## 11 JUNE 1950

*Don Juan und Faust*, opera by the 49-year-old German composer Hermann REUTTER, is performed for the first time in Stuttgart.

## 12 JUNE 1950

Manuel ROSENTHAL conducts the orchestra of Radiodiffusion Française in Paris in the world première of his *Sinfonia in Do*, in three classically shaped movements of French provincial life, including realistic animal cries, and carrying a carillon motto in percurration throughout the work.

## 15 JUNE 1950

*Il Nazzareno*, opera by the Italian religious composer Lorenzo PEROSI, is produced at La Scala, Milan.

## 23 JUNE 1950

*Philomela*, opera in seven scenes by the 57-year-old Dutch composer Hendrik ANDRIESSEN, to a libretto from the Greek myth of a tyrannical king who carnally violates the chastity of his sister-in-law Philomela and cuts out her tongue to prevent her from reporting the outrage to others, but suffers grim retribution when Philomela kills his child and serves its roasted body at the royal feast, for which deed she is metamorphosed into a nightingale, is performed for the first time at the Holland Festival in Amsterdam.

23 JUNE 1950

*La Pierre enchantée,* ballet by Georges AURIC, is performed for the first time in Paris.

23 JUNE 1950

The 24th Festival of the International Society for Contemporary Music opens in Brussels presenting the following program:

*Chamber Symphony* in five movements by Schoenberg's disciple Hanns EISLER; *Concerto* for piano and chamber orchestra by the 35-year-old Dutch composer Marius FLOTHUIS; *Concerto for String Orchestra* by the 45-year-old English composer Alan RAWSTHORNE; and *Second Cantata* op. 31, by Anton von WEBERN, for soprano, bass, chorus and orchestra, in six sections based on a single 12-tone series, two divisions of which are so fashioned that each division states each of the 48 avatars of the series once and once only.

24 JUNE 1950

The 24th International Society for Contemporary Music Festival in Brussels presents the following program of chamber music:

*String Quartet* in one movement by the 29-year-old English composer Peter Racine FRICKER; *Psalm CXXVII* for three voices, violin, viola and cello, by the 27-year-old Italian composer Camillo TOGNI; *String Quartet* in three movements by the 43-year-old Russian-born, ethnically Polish, Swiss resident composer Constantin REGAMEY; *Hommage à Schoenberg* by the 35-year-old Brazilian composeress Eunice CATUNDA, scored for clarinet, bass clarinet, viola, cello and piano, with Latin American rhythms punctuating the dodecaphonic thematic material; *Sonata for Cello and Piano* by the 42-year-old German composer Wolfgang FORTNER and *String Quartet* by the 34-year-old South African Arnold Van WIJCK (who sometimes spells his name simply WYK).

25 JUNE 1950

At the 24th International Society for Contemporary Music Festival in Brussels, the following program of Belgian music is presented:

*James Ensor,* orchestral suite in four movements, *L'entrée du Christ à Bruxelles, Aquelettes se disputant un pendu, Jardin d'amour, Cortège infernal,* by the 73-year-old composer Florent ALPAERTS, inspired by the lugubrious paintings of the Belgian artist Ensor (1860–1949); *Allegro Symphonique* by the 49-year-old neo-classicist Marcel POOT; *3 mouvements Symphoniques* by the 52-year-old neo-romanticist Fernand QUINET; *Chant d'angoisse* for cello and orchestra by Albert HUYBRECHTS (1899–1938); and *Second Symphony* in three movements by the 56-year-old modernist Jean ABSIL.

25 JUNE 1950

*Namus (Honor),* opera by the 39-year-old Soviet composer Nazib ZHIGANOV, to a patriotic libretto in the Tatar language, is produced in Kazan, which was the seat of the Tatar Golden Horde that subjugated Russia before Kazan was stormed by Ivan the Terrible in 1572.

27 JUNE 1950

The following program is presented at the International Society for Contemporary Music Festival in Brussels:

*Hai-kai de Basho* for chamber orchestra by the 54-year-old Japanese composer Shukichi MITSUKURI, in ten aphoristic sections inspired by the three-line Japanese verses; *Laudi,* a neo-medieval unaccompanied chorus by the 29-year-old Swedish composer Ingvar LIDHOLM; *5 Comptines* (children's counting nursery rhymes) for voice and 11 instruments by the 36-year-old Belgian composer Pierre FROIDEBISE; *3 Lieder* for six wind instruments by the 27-year-old Belgian composer Karel GOEYVAERTS; *L'Explication des Métaphores* for speaker, two pianos, harp and percussion by the apostle of dodecaphonic music, René LEIBOWITZ, conducted by the composer, and *Cantata of the Vistula River* by the 42-year-old Polish composer Roman PALESTER.


28 JUNE 1950

The following program of orchestral music is presented at the 24th International Society for Contemporary Music Festival in Brussels:

*Sinfonia giocosa* in three movements by the 43-year-old Norwegian composer Klaus EGGE; *Toccata and Fugue* for piano and orchestra by the 45-year-old Polish composer Artur MALAWSKY; *Psyché,* symphonic movement by the French modernist André JOLIVET) and *La Naissance du Verbe* for chorus and orchestra by the 45-year-old Italian composer Giacinto SCELSI, which contains a polytonal canon in 48 parts written in 12 different keys.


29 JUNE 1950

The following program is presented at the 24th International Society for Contemporary Music Festival in Brussels:

*String Quartet* by 47-year-old Swedish composer Hilding HALLNÄS; *Second Sonatina* for violin and piano by the 49-year-old Swiss composer Conrad BECK; *Quintet* for wind instruments by the 34-year-old Belgian composer Marcel QUINET; *Les Rêves de Jacob,* choreographic suite for oboe, violin, viola, cello and doublebass, by Darius MILHAUD; and *String Quartet* by the 28-year-old Czech neo-classicist Karel HUSA.


30 JUNE 1950

The 24th Festival of the International Society for Contemporary Music in Brussels concludes with a concert of orchestral music consisting of the following compositions:

*Fourth Symphony* for string orchestra, by the German master-contrapuntist Karl Amadeus HARTMANN, in three well-demarcated movements: *Lento con passione, Allegro di molto (Scherzo), Adagio appassionato,* written in an expressionistic manner of a quasiserial nature, and related to the usages of Alban Berg; *Concerto* for flute and orchestra by the 36-year-old Dutch composer Hans HENKEMANS; *Concerto* for 3 pianos and 8 instruments by the 30-year-old Danish neo-romanticist Niels Viggo BENTZON; and *Fifth Symphony* by Harold SAEVERUD of Norway.

### 1 JULY 1950

Émile JAQUES-DALCROZE, creator of Eurhythmics and composer of lyric pieces of an ethnomusicological nature, dies in Geneva five days before his 85th birthday.

### 3 JULY 1950

*Concertante* for piano left hand and orchestra by the British composer Arnold BAX, in three movements, written in a classical idiom, economically designed in its harmonic and contrapuntal techniques, is performed for the first time at the Cheltenham Festival, England, by Harriet Cohen, for whom it was written after she fell carrying a tray of glass dishes into the kitchen of her London home in 1948 and cut the wrist of her right hand damaging the nerve and causing it to wither. (Initially, the work was called a *Concerto*, but in view of the slenderness of the piano part limited to the left hand, its designation was changed to *Concertante*.)

### 5 JULY 1950

*First Symphony* by the 29-year-old English composer Peter Racine FRICKER, in four movements making use of a variety of modern devices, including dodecaphonic approximations, devoid of a key signature but tonocentric in its teleological design, is performed for the first time at the Cheltenham Festival in England, Sir John Barbirolli conducting.

### 9 JULY 1950

Hans CHEMIN-PETIT, 47-year-old Potsdam-born composer whose Germanic first name and French patronymic are reflected in the duality of his semi-Teutonic demi-Gallic style of composition, conducts in Potsdam (where he remained through the years of wartime devastation) the first performance of his *Second Symphony*, set in the bland key of C major.

### 12 JULY 1950

*Concerto for French Horn and Orchestra* by the 48-year-old Belgian composer Raymond CHEVREUILLE, is performed for the first time in Brussels.

### 18 JULY 1950

Josef KRIPS, Austrian conductor, is forced to fly back to Vienna from New York two days after landing, when the immigration officials refuse to honor his valid American visa, owing to undisclosed information regarding his alleged leftist associations.

### 20 JULY 1950

The first Estonian opera on a Soviet theme, *Vabaduse laulik* (*The Singer of Freedom*), by the 42-year-old Volga-born Estonian composer Eugen KAPP, dealing with turbulent years of the Nazi invasion of Soviet Estonia in 1941, the heroic death of the patriotic bride of the hero, and ending with the expulsion of the invaders by the victorious Red Army in the last act, is produced in Tallin.

### 28 JULY 1950

On the bicentennial of the death of BACH, the Government of the Federal German Republic issues two stamps, at 12 and 23 pfennigs, bearing his image.

### 29 JULY 1950

To commemorate the 900th anniversary since the death on 17 May 1050 of the initiator of modern musical notation GUIDO D'AREZZO, the Italian Government issues a stamp of 20 lire bearing his likeness.

### 9 AUGUST 1950

Nicolai MIASKOVSKY, Russian composer of 27 symphonies, the greatest number written by anyone since Haydn, and teacher of a generation of Soviet composers, dies in Moscow of an inoperable intestinal cancer, at the age of sixty-nine.

### 5 SEPTEMBER 1950

The Australian composer Arthur BENJAMIN plays the solo part in the first performance of his *Piano Concerto* with the Sydney Symphony Orchestra under the direction of Eugene Goossens.

### 8 SEPTEMBER 1950

An organ based on the division of the octave into 31 unequal degrees, originally proposed for acoustical reasons by the celebrated Dutch astronomer Christiaan HUYGENS (1629–1695) in his *Nouveau Cycle Harmonique,* in which the smallest interval is ⅕ of a tone, a system which permits sounds to be produced in pure Pythagorean intonation as well as in the traditional scales of tempered semitones, is demonstrated for the first time in Rotterdam.

### 10 SEPTEMBER 1950

*Second Symphony* by the 45-year-old German composer Karl Amadeus HARTMANN, in a single movement, *Adagio,* with a median contrasting section *Allegro,* cyclically evolved from a guiding germinal theme through multiple variations in a series of terraced dynamic arches, is performed for the first time at the annual festival of modern music in Donaueschingen. (Hartmann's *Third Symphony* and his *Fourth* were performed prior to the *Second*)

### 18 SEPTEMBER 1950

*Saga-Symphony* by the prime Icelandic composer Jón LEIFS, set in bleak pentatonic modalities arrayed in glacially immobile harmonies and arranged in arctically gelid instrumentation, is performed for the first time in Helsinki.

898

## 19 SEPTEMBER 1950

*Son of a Clown*, operetta by the Soviet composer Isaak DUNAYEVSKY, a satire exposing the unsocialistic conduct of a popular Soviet circus artist, with a happy ending as he yields to the power of dialectical persuasion by his proper colleagues and returns to the path of Communist virtue, is produced in Moscow.

## 20 SEPTEMBER 1950

*Rosaura*, romantic opera after Goldoni by the learned Danish music theorist Knud JEPPESEN, is produced in Copenhagen.

## 22 SEPTEMBER 1950

*Ballade* for orchestra by the 43-year-old Java-born Dutch composer Henk BADINGS is performed for the first time in Maastricht.

## 4 OCTOBER 1950

*Ekvinocij (Equinox)*, music drama in three acts by the 43-year-old Croatian composer Ivan BRKANOVIĆ, wherein a rich American immigrant returning to his native Dalmatia on June 21, 1867, is confronted by the abandoned mother of his illegitimate Dalmatian son who is in love with the ship captain's young daughter coveted by his natural father as well, with a tragic retribution meted out when the mother kills the American by a well-aimed stone so as to enable their son to marry the captain's daughter, set to music in a melodramatic idiom, modernistically titivated by polytriadic harmonies and non-corrosive dissonances, is produced in Zagreb.

## 12 OCTOBER 1950

*Call Me Madam*, musical comedy by Irving BERLIN, inspired by the appointment of Pearl Mesta, the Washington "hostess with the mostest" as the American envoy to Luxemburg, wherein the American ambassadress to a tiny European republic promises a billion-dollar American subsidy to its prime minister and gains his personal affection, the score containing the politically shrewd song by three vocal Congressmen, *They Like Ike*, destined to play a historic role in overcoming Eisenhower's reluctance to enter the presidential campaign and resulting in his election in 1952, is performed for the first time in New York.

## 15 OCTOBER 1950

On the 50th anniversary of the death of the Czech composer Zdenko FIBICH, the Czechoslovak post office issues two commemorative stamps in the denominations of 3 and 8 kronen bearing his image.

## 24 OCTOBER 1950

*La Morte dell'Aria*, opera by the 46-year-old Italian composer Goffredo PETRASSI, is produced in Rome.

**27 OCTOBER 1950**

*Third Symphony* by the 44-year-old American composer Paul CRESTON, subtitled *Three Mysteries*, with its three movements, *The Nativity, The Crucifixion,* and *The Resurrection,* thematically derived from Gregorian chants, developed in an austerely lyrical manner, is performed for the first time by the Philadelphia Orchestra, Eugene Ormandy conducting, at the Worcester, Massachusetts Music Festival.

**29 OCTOBER 1950**

*Quartet* for piano and strings by Aaron COPLAND, commissioned by the Elizabeth Sprague Coolidge Foundation, his first work in an overtly serial method of composition, with the opening theme constituting a hendecaphonic tonerow, and the second theme being its retrograde, containing also some jazzy inflections, in three movements, *Adagio serioso, Allegro giusto, Non troppo lento,* is performed for the first time at the Coolidge Festival at the Library of Congress in Washington.

**31 OCTOBER 1950**

Octavio PINTO, Brazilian composer of attractive piano pieces, husband of pianist Guiomar Novaēs, dies in his native town of São Paulo, three days before his 60th birthday.

**31 OCTOBER 1950**

*Job,* "sacra rappresentazione" by the 46-year-old Italian modernist Luigi DALLAPICCOLA, written in a consistent dodecaphonic idiom eschewed only in the solemn triadic harmonies to accompany the Lord's climactic peroration, is performed for the first time in Rome.

**2 NOVEMBER 1950**

George Bernard SHAW, great Irish dramatist who during his meteoric interlude as a London music critic in the 1880's initiated a new journalistic treatment of musical events, coloring his reviews with brilliant personal prejudices, dies at 4:59 in the morning at his home at Ayot-St.-Lawrence, at the age of ninety-four, leaving stern instructions that no cross "or any other instrument of torture" be erected on his grave and that his body be cremated and ashes strewn in the garden.

**3 NOVEMBER 1950**

*Third Symphony* by the 35-year-old American composer David DIAMOND, dedicated to his parents, in five sections, alternatingly fast and slow, unified by two basic motives which appear in augmentation, diminution, and retrograde movement, is performed for the first time by the Boston Symphony Orchestra, Charles Munch conducting. (Diamond's *Fourth Symphony* was performed before the *Third* at a Boston Symphony concert on 23 January 1948)

## 6 NOVEMBER 1950

*Concerto* for clarinet, string orchestra, harp and piano by Aaron COPLAND, in two sections marked *Slowly and Expressively* and *Rather Fast,* linked by a flamboyant jazz cadenza for the clarinet, is performed for the first time by Benny Goodman, "King of Swing" who commissioned the work, with the NBC Symphony Orchestra in New York, conducted by Fritz Reiner.

## 7 NOVEMBER 1950

*The Family of Taras,* opera in four acts by the 45-year-old Soviet composer Dmitri KABALEVSKY, to a libretto dealing with the heroic family of a metal worker whose two sons and daughter join the partisans to fight the Nazi occupation army in the Ukraine in 1942, with thematic materials derived from popular Soviet songs, is produced in Leningrad.

(The first version of the opera was given in Moscow on 2 November 1947; both versions included some material from a previous opera by Kabalevsky, *In the Fire,* produced in Moscow on 7 November 1947, which in turn was a revised version of the opera *At Moscow,* produced in Moscow on 28 November 1943)

I transferred some thematic materials from the opera *In the Fire* into *The Family of Taras,* namely the theme of the enemy, the motive of the mother, and some other melodic elements, but not a great quantity in all. The longest episode among these borrowed materials is the chorus of Russian women driven away into Fascist slavery. This episode remained without change in the subject and the text, but was modified only in some details of the orchestral scoring. (From a letter to the author from Kabalevsky, dated Moscow, 28 January 1960)

## 12 NOVEMBER 1950

*Concerto for Koto and Orchestra* (the koto is a Japanese zither) by the 40-year-old Japanese composer Kozaburo HIRAI is performed for the first time in Tokyo.

## 18 NOVEMBER 1950

*Concerto Grosso* by Ralph VAUGHAN WILLIAMS, in five movements, scored for string orchestra subdivided into three groups to be played by amateurs of various grades of skill, written in a melodious, harmonious, generally euphonious, sophisticatedly abecedarian musical language fortified by a plasma of nutritious triadic harmonies, and including a part in which only open strings are used, is performed for the first time by a massed ensemble of 400 semi-professional and manually unskilled members of the Rural Music Schools Association in London, under the direction of Sir Adrian Boult.

## 19 NOVEMBER 1950

*Hamlet,* ballet by Boris BLACHER, is produced in Munich.

## 20 NOVEMBER 1950

Francesco CILÈA, Italian composer of melodramatic operas in the tradition of Verismo, of which *Adriana Lecouvreur* became a repertory piece, dies in Varazza at the age of eighty-four.

21 NOVEMBER 1950

*Fifth Symphony* by the 53-year-old Danish composer Knudaage RIISAGER, subtitled *Sinfonia serena*, in four movements, *Allegro ardito, Vivace ilare, Lamentoso, Allegro spregiudicato*, set in a style of tempestuous tranquillity, traversing the moods of defiance, vivacious hilarity, lament and unprejudiced merriment, without overflowing the banks of tonality, is performed for the first time in Copenhagen.

23 NOVEMBER 1950

*Short Symphony* by the 41-year-old Negro composer Howard SWANSON, is performed for the first time by the New York Philharmonic Orchestra, Dimitri Mitropoulos conducting.

23 NOVEMBER 1950

A Japanese musical group HAKUTOKAI (WHITE WAVE SOCIETY), formed with the aim of "reworking traditional Japanese music into a thing to be proud of on the international level," presents in Tokyo its inaugural concert consisting of works by modern Japanese composers.

24 NOVEMBER 1950

*Guys and Dolls*, "a musical fable of Broadway," by Frank LOESSER, based on tales by Damon Runyon, with various picturesque characters milling around a Manhattan nightclub, into which blunders a starry-eyed Salvation Army lass, idiomatically set to music in the colorful lingo of Tin Pan Alley, including among its hit tunes the melosomatic ballad, *Adelaide's Lament* marked by onomatopoeic tonal sternutations caused by amorous frustrations, *If I Were a Bell, A Bushel and a Peck*, and a three-part *Fugue for Tinhorns*, is produced in New York.

29 NOVEMBER 1950

*Catharsis*, symphonic ballet by the 44-year-old Dutch composer Bertus van LIER, to a scenario in which mysterious intruders terrorize a married couple, their two children and a pregnant woman, is performed for the first time in Utrecht.

1 DECEMBER 1950

Ernest John MOERAN, 55-year-old Irish composer of pleasantly lilted instrumental music permeated by authentically inflected melodic patterns of Irish and East Anglian folk tunes, is found drowned in the Kenmare River, County Kerry, Ireland, possibly a victim of a sudden suicidal impulse.

2 DECEMBER 1950

*Facanapas*, opera written in 1935 by the Greek composer Denis LAVRANGAS, is produced in Athens, nine years after the composer's death.

## 2 DECEMBER 1950

Ernest BLOCH conducts the first performance with the Chicago Symphony Orchestra of his *Scherzo Fantasque* for piano and orchestra.

## 2 DECEMBER 1950

Dinu LIPATTI, Rumanian pianist whose frail physique and lapidary pianism made him a Chopinesque figure, dies in Geneva of lymphogranulomatosis, at the lamentable age of thirty-three.

## 3 DECEMBER 1950

*Symphonie de Numance* by the 50-year-old French composer Henry BARRAUD, inspired by a play of Cervantes about the capture of the Spanish town of Numantia by the Roman armies of General Scipio in 133 B.C. is produced in Baden-Baden. (An opera by Henry Barraud expanded from the materials of *Symphonie de Numance* was produced at the Opéra-Comique in Paris on 15 April 1955)

## 6 DECEMBER 1950

President TRUMAN, infuriated by the disparaging review by Paul HUME in the Washington *Post* of a song recital by Truman's daughter Margaret, dispatches a letter to him written in longhand on White House stationery, as follows: "Mr. Hume: I have just read your lousy review of Margaret's concert. I've come to the conclusion that you are an eight-ulcer man on four-ulcer pay . . . Some day I hope to meet you. When that happens, you'll need a new nose, a lot of beefsteak for black eyes, and perhaps a supporter below."

## 8 DECEMBER 1950

*Sinfonia concertante* for violin, oboe, bassoon, cello and orchestra by Bohuslav MARTINU is performed for the first time in Basel.

## 9 DECEMBER 1950

*Twenty-Seventh Symphony,* in C minor, the last of a long series by the most prolific symphonist of the 20th century, Nicolai MIASKOVSKY (completed by him on 2 November 1949), in three cyclically bound movements, (1) *Adagio-Allegro animato* (2) *Adagio—Molto elevato* (3) *Presto,* distinguished by a sense of symphonic dramaturgy following the Aristotelian dialectic of catharsis through tragedy and pity and couched in lyrical Russian modalities, is performed for the first time in Moscow, four months after Miaskovsky's death.

## 11 DECEMBER 1950

*Clarinet Concerto* by Paul HINDEMITH, in four neo-classically balanced movements, *Ziemlich schnell, Schnell, Ruhig, Heiter,* reflecting the moods of hedonism, optimism, lyricism, and gaiety, written in a translucent polyphonic idiom with a generous application of temperate dissonances, is performed for the first time by the Philadelphia Orchestra, Eugene Ormandy conducting, with the whilom killer-diller on the licorice stick, Benny Goodman, to whom the score is dedicated, as soloist.

## 12 DECEMBER 1950

*Ninth Symphony* by the foremost Swiss symphonist Fritz BRUN, in five movements subtitled *Einleitung, Serenade, Liebesruf, Lob der Freundschaft* and *Lob Gottes und der Natur,* is performed for the first time in Zürich.

## 14 DECEMBER 1950

*Moldavian Suite* for orchestra by the 34-year-old Moscow-born composer Nicolai PEYKO, based on folk themes of Moldavia, a region newly incorporated into the Union of Soviet Socialist Republics, is performed for the first time in Moscow.

## 18 DECEMBER 1950

*Max und Moritz,* dance-burlesque by the 46-year-old German composer Richard MOHAUPT, inspired by the fairy tales of Wilhelm Busch retailing in gaily rhymed verses the unspeakable outrages wrought by two sadistically inventive small boys, is performed for the first time in Karlsruhe.

## 19 DECEMBER 1950

*On Guard For Peace,* cantata by Sergei PROKOFIEV, in ten sections, to texts by the foremost Soviet writer of children's verse Samuel Marshak, inveighing against the American militarists importing "one hundred thousand tons worth of death" to Europe, is performed for the first time in Moscow.

## 20 DECEMBER 1950

*First Symphony* by the 63-year-old Austrian composer Ernst TOCH, bearing the epigraph from Martin Luther's anacoluthic oath "Und wenn die Welt voll Teufel wär' . . . ," containing the thematic use of tritones, the *diabolus in musica* of medieval theorists, in four movements (1) *Molto tranquillo,* (2) *Allegro molto,* (3) *Langsam, zart,* (4) *Allegro non troppo,* concluding on a hymnal D major chord, is performed for the first time in Vienna.

## 22 DECEMBER 1950

Walter DAMROSCH, German-born American musician, who conducted a great many American premières of famous works, dies in New York at the age of eighty-eight.

## 23 DECEMBER 1950

Vincenzo TOMMASINI, Italian composer of neo-romantic symphonic pieces touched with impressionistic color, dies in his native Rome at the age of seventy-two.

*904*

Charles Kœchlin, the bearded patriarch of French music, composer of numerous pieces of symphonic and vocal music in a highly personal idiom marked by brilliant eruptions of instrumental colors, dies in his villa, Le Canadel, in the province of Var, in Southern France, at the age of eighty-three.

## ❧ 1951 ❧

### 6 JANUARY 1951

*The Shadowy Waters,* opera by the 67-year-old dean of the traditional school of Greek composers Manolis Kalomiris, to a libretto drawn from an Irish tale of W. B. Yeats, is produced in Athens.

### 16 JANUARY 1951

*From the Bottom of My Heart,* opera in three acts by the 37-year-old Ukrainian composer Herman Zhukovsky, with action taking place on a Ukrainian collective farm, wherein an unsocialistically individualistic youth is won over to the collectivistic way of life by his proletarian bride and together they attend the unveiling of an electric power station, set to music modeled after Mussorgsky's realistic style, is produced at the Bolshoi Theater in Moscow.

Our nation expects Soviet composers to produce operas realistically reflecting the contemporary scene, in which the beauty and spiritual power of our people are revealed in full measure. Performances of new Soviet operas are eagerly awaited by the public. Great interest was aroused by the production at the Bolshoi Theater of the opera by Herman Zhukovsky, *From the Bottom of My Heart,* devoted to an important subject, the life on our collective farms, the Kolkhozs. But the authors of the opera and its producers failed to examine closely the Kolkhoz way of life. They failed to portray it adequately, in vivid artistic imagery, accompanied by colorful realistic music. The opera proved to be a feeble production marked by serious errors. Its melodic materials are largely deficient in characterization. The dramatic episodes are musically faceless. One has the impression of listening to essentially the same melodies over and over again. As a result, there is no realistic representation of our heroes of labor at the Kolkhoz . . . The composer's exclusive preoccupation with sentimental whimsicalities leads to incongruities. In the scene of the conference of the praesidium of the Kolkhoz, the contradiction between the action on the stage and the music becomes particularly obvious. Completely unnatural is also the ballad music in the scene in the tavern, which has nothing to do with the words of the aria about new man, about Communism. . . . Herman Zhukovsky's score, weak from a professional standpoint, compounds the ideological falsity of the libretto in its portrayal of the Soviet people as devoid of all individuality. In this respect the authors reveal their inability to achieve fidelity to life. (*Pravda,* Moscow, 19 April 1951)

The article in *Pravda* of 19 April 1951, regarding the opera *From the Bottom of My*

*Heart*, contains alongside some correct critical judgments of the music and the libretto of the opera, some instances of exaggerations and prejudice. . . . Its evaluation of the opera is incorrect and one-sided. (From the statement of the Central Committee of the Communist Party of the Soviet Union, published in *Pravda*, 8 June 1958)

### 19 JANUARY 1951

*Le Rire de Nils Halerius,* "lyric and choreographic legend" by the French composer Marcel LANDOWSKI is performed for the first time at Mulhouse, Alsace.

### 20 JANUARY 1951

*Dimnjiaci Uz Jadran (The Chimneys of the Adriatic Coast)*, opera in five acts by the 55-year-old Croatian composer Ivo TIJARDOVIĆ, to a story of mortal strife between Yugoslav partisans and Fascists on the Dalmatian coast in 1943, is produced in Zagreb.

### 22 JANUARY 1951

Ernst von DOHNÁNYI appears as soloist in the first performance anywhere with the Florida State Symphony Orchestra in Tallahassee (where he made his home in 1949 as professor of music at Florida State College) of his *Second Piano Concerto* in B minor, written in Austria in 1947.

### 24 JANUARY 1951

A century has passed since the death of Gasparo SPONTINI, Italian composer whose opera *La Vestale* was the rage of Napoleonic France, but whose fame declined to a historical footnote in the annals of grand opera.

### 25 JANUARY 1951

*Volpone* by the 52-year-old French composer Marcel DELANNOY, a symphonic suite of four scenes from the musical score to a film after the novel of Stefan Zweig, derived from the famous play of Ben Jonson, is performed for the first time on the Lyons Radio.

### 26 JANUARY 1951

*Fourth Piano Concerto* by Gian Francesco MALIPIERO, in three movements, a *Lento* flanked by two *Allegros*, written in a compact neo-baroque style, is performed for the first time in Turin.

### 27 JANUARY 1951

To mark the 50th anniversary of the death of Giuseppe VERDI, Toscanini conducts in New York a performance of Verdi's *Manzoni Requiem*.

### 29 JANUARY 1951

*Bogdan Khmelnitzky,* opera in four acts by the Ukrainian composer Konstantin DANKEVICH, centering on the 17th-century Cossack chieftain who fought against the Polish invaders, is produced in Kiev, evoking an outraged condemnation in *Pravda* on 20 July 1951, after its performance at the Ukrainian Music Festival in Moscow, for its erroneous treatment of historic realities in the relationship between the Russians and Ukrainians and its inadequate musical characterization. (The libretto of the opera was radically revised, the motive of Ukrainian separatism softened and the patriotic element of struggle against the Polish feudal imperialism strengthened, with the finale depicting the joy of the reunion of the Ukraine and Great Russia announced on 8 January 1654; this revised version was first performed, with the musical score essentially unchanged, in Kiev on 21 June 1953)

3 FEBRUARY 1951
The CANADIAN LEAGUE OF COMPOSERS is formed in Toronto, with John Weinzweig as chairman.

6 FEBRUARY 1951
*Concerto* for French horn and string orchestra by the Swiss composer Othmar SCHOECK, written in a neo-Schubertian lyrical manner, is performed for the first time in Winterthur.

11 FEBRUARY 1951
*Lady Hamilton,* opera by the 64-year-old German composer Robert HEGER, dealing with Lord Nelson's Mediterranean romance, is produced in Nuremberg.

22 FEBRUARY 1951
*Second Symphony* by Charles IVES, composed between 1897 and 1901, in five movements *Andante moderato, Allegro, Adagio cantabile, Lento maestoso, Allegro molto vivace,* expressing "the musical feelings of the Connecticut country in the 1890's" and embodying an extraordinary variety of thematic resources, including a mockingly distorted quotation of a chromatic passage from the *Third Symphony* of Brahms, all this immersed in an ocean of American tunes, jigs, gallops, reels and ragtime, culminating with the oriflamme of brass, vociferating *Columbia, The Gem of the Ocean,* is performed for the first time, half a century after its composition, by the New York Philharmonic, Leonard Bernstein conducting.

23 FEBRUARY 1951
*Symphonie concertante* for oboe and string orchestra by Jacques IBERT is performed for the first time in Basel.

28 FEBRUARY 1951
*Suite Archaïque* by Arthur HONEGGER, in four movements, *Ouverture, Pantomime, Ritournelle et Serenade, Processional,* written in architecturally proportioned measures of the French rococo, is performed for the first time by the Louisville Orchestra.

*Auto Accident,* by the American composer Harold G. DAVIDSON, inspired by the magazine article "And Sudden Death" (whose author himself died in an automobile accident), scored for percussion, a siren, and glass plates to be smashed at the climax, is performed for the first time at the University of Illinois School of Music, in Urbana.

## 2 MARCH 1951

*La Vita Nuova* for voices and orchestra by the 47-year-old Russian-American composer Nicolas NABOKOV, inspired by Dante, is performed for the first time by the Boston Symphony Orchestra, Charles Munch conducting.

## 9 MARCH 1951

*Il était un petit Navire,* satirical opera in three acts by Germaine TAILLEFERRE, the only woman member of the French Six, based on the popular French children's song of that name, is performed for the first time at the Opéra-Comique in Paris.

## 9 MARCH 1951

*Fifth Symphony* by Arthur HONEGGER, completed in Paris on 10 November 1950, subtitled *Di tre re* (because each of its three movements, *Grave, Allegretto, Allegro marcato,* terminates on an unadorned *Re* in the lower strings and timpani), devoid of a key signature and marked by atonal intervallic saltation, is performed for the first time as a commissioned work, by the Boston Symphony Orchestra, Charles Munch conducting.

## 13 MARCH 1951

*Amphitryon,* a neo-classical opera by the Swiss composer Robert OBOUSSIER, to a libretto based on the classical Greek myth of Zeus making a visitation of Amphitryon's wife in the guise of Amphitryon himself and inadvertently procreating Heracles, is performed for the first time in Berlin.

## 17 MARCH 1951

*Das Verhör des Lukullus,* opera by the German composer Paul DESSAU, to a radio play by Bertolt Brecht, originally broadcast by a Swiss station in 1939, representing the trial of the Roman General Lucullus (c.110–56 B.C.) in Hades, by the victims of his aggressive wars, is performed for the first and last time at the German Opera in East Berlin, and then banned by the authorities of the German Democratic Republic as ideologically false in its libretto and decadently discordant in its music.

The world peace camp with its 800 million people, led by the Soviet Union, is not a court presided over by ghosts, but one wielding realistic power to put war criminals on trial down on earth. What at the outbreak of Hitler's war may have been an expression of the uncertain political stand on the part of an exiled anti-Fascist dramatist, such as Brecht, registers in our minds in 1951 as a relapse into doubt and weakness . . . As for the music, it follows Igor Stravinsky, a composer resident in the U.S.A., who is a fanatical destroyer of all European musical traditions. Paul Dessau has missed the opportunity to arouse the spirit of the masses against a new war of conquest. A musical work that drowns the listener in a flood of dissonances and intellectualistic tricks lends support to reactionary groups in the audience and is repugnant to the progressive elements of our society. (*Neues Deutschland*, East Berlin, 22 March 1951)

Look at the orchestra of *Das Verhör des Lukullus*. There are no violins. This most noble of all instruments, capable of producing the most beautiful tonal designs is missing from the score. Instead, there is a piano doctored with drawing-pins set up on the strings and nine different kinds of percussion instruments, among them metal sheets struck by rocks. (ibid., as quoted in *Deutsche Zeitung,* Berlin, 1 January 1953)

(A revised version of the opera, under the more explicit title *Die Verurteilung des Lukullus*, i.e. condemnation, rather than a mere trial, was produced in East Berlin on 12 October 1951, with a notation in the program stating that the verdict of the dead is to be interpreted as the judgment of posterity, and that the more objectionable modernistic devices, were removed from the score, dissonances replaced whenever possible by consonances, and *Sprechgesang* changed to arias)

### 19 MARCH 1951

*Croquis Egyptiens,* orchestral suite by the Egyptian composer Alberto HEMSI, is performed for the first time by the Alexandria Symphony Orchestra.

### 21 MARCH 1951

*Eighth Symphony* by Gian Francesco MALIPIERO, subtitled *Di un tempo* to indicate that the work should be played without pause between clearly demarcated movements connected by transitional passages, is performed for the first time in Rome.

### 22 MARCH 1951

Willem MENGELBERG, German conductor, who excelled in performances of Beethoven, Mahler and Strauss (the score of *Ein Heldenleben* is dedicated to him), dies in Chur, Switzerland, an exile from his native Holland, where he was barred from conducting for his cultural collaboration with the Nazis during the Hitlerian occupation.

### 26 MARCH 1951

*Fourth Symphony* by the Japanese composer Saburo MOROI is performed for the first time by the Nippon Symphony Orchestra in Tokyo.

### 28 MARCH 1951

*Giants in the Earth,* opera in three acts by Douglas MOORE, to a story of Norwegian pioneers in the Dakota Territory in 1873, is produced by the Columbia University Opera Workshop in New York.

29 MARCH 1951

*The King and I,* a musical play by Richard RODGERS, with book and lyrics by Oscar Hammerstein II, based on the historically true account of a Victorian lady engaged by the King of Siam to teach Western amenities to his multiple children by his many wives and concubines, written in a cosmopolitan idiom flavored with Westernized orientalisms and stylized pentatonicisms, the most famous numbers being *Getting to Know You, I Whistle a Happy Tune, Hello, Young Lovers!* and *Shall We Dance?,* is produced in New York.

30 MARCH 1951

*Fourth Symphony* by the 57-year-old American composer Walter PISTON, commissioned by the University of Minnesota on the occasion of its centennial, in four movements: *Piacevole, Ballando, Contemplativo* and *Energico,* written in a compact neo-classical manner calculated to solve "the problem of balance between expression and formal design," is performed for the first time by the Minneapolis Symphony Orchestra, Antal Dorati conducting.

31 MARCH 1951

*München: ein Gedächtniswalzer* for orchestra by Richard STRAUSS, a nostalgic reminiscence of waltz time in old Munich, revised in 1945 from a film score of 1939, is performed for the first time in Vienna.

2 APRIL 1951

The Russian pianist Simon BARÈRE collapses and dies on the stage of Carnegie Hall in New York, while playing Grieg's *Piano Concerto.*

4 APRIL 1951

*Kállai Kettós (Kálló Double)* by Zoltán KODÁLY, scored for chorus, three clarinets, two cimbaloms and strings, with occasional humming effects in the voice parts, based on a Hungarian tune from the locality of Kálló, usually danced by a couple (*Kettós,* double, in the title), is performed for the first time by the Hungarian People's Ensemble in Budapest.

4 APRIL 1951

*Ballade* for cello and orchestra by the Swiss composer Frank MARTIN is performed for the first time in Geneva.

6 APRIL 1951

*Kerkeb,* opera by the 68-year-old French composer Marcel SAMUEL-ROUSSEAU, is produced at the Opéra-Comique in Paris.

6 APRIL 1951

*Sinfonia* in one movement by the 47-year-old American composer Vittorio GIANNINI, dedicated to the memory of his mother who taught him the violin (his father was a singer from Florence, Italy), built on an autogenetic theme ramified into four derivative subjects, culminating in a magistral quadruple fugue and vanishing in *pianississississimo* in immaculately white C major, is performed for the first time by the Cincinnati Symphony Orchestra, Thor Johnson conducting.

## 12 APRIL 1951

On the sesquicentennial of the birth of Joseph LANNER, Austrian pioneer in the art of the waltz, the Austrian Government issues a 60-groschen stamp bearing his likeness.

## 14 APRIL 1951

*Zeybek, Interlude* and *Horon*, three national orchestral dances by the Turkish composer Ahmed Adnan SAYGUN are performed for the first time in Ankara.

## 20 APRIL 1951

*Petite Suite* for orchestra by the Polish composer Witold LUTOSLAWSKI, his most successful piece, is performed for the first time by the Radio Orchestra in Warsaw.

## 21 APRIL 1951

Olive FREMSTAD, Swedish prima donna of ample pectoral powers, who sang the title role in the first American performance of *Salomé* by Richard Strauss, dies in Irvington-on-Hudson, New York, at the age of eighty.

## 21 APRIL 1951

*Fifth Symphony (Symphonie Concertante)* by the 45-year-old German polyphonist Karl Amadeus HARTMANN, scored for wind instruments, cellos and doublebasses, in three movements, a kinetically functional *Toccata*, a tonally parsimonious *Melodie*, subtitled *Hommage à Stravinsky*, and a *Rondo* is performed for the first time in Stuttgart.

## 21 APRIL 1951

Alexander KREIN, Russian-Jewish composer of operatic and symphonic music, much of it based on traditional Hebrew chants, dies in Moscow at the age of sixty-seven.

## 22 APRIL 1951

Commemorating the sesquicentennial of the birth of the German opera composer Albert LORTZING, the Government of the Federal German Republic issues a 20-pfennig stamp in his honor.

## 26 APRIL 1951

*The Pilgrim's Progress*, a "morality", in four acts, prologue and epilogue by Ralph VAUGHAN WILLIAMS, with his own libretto adapted from John Bunyan's famous Christian allegory, being an expansion and amplification of his one-act pastoral *The Shepherds of the Delectable Mountains*, first performed in London on 11 July 1922, with the additions of the episodes of the City of Destruction, the Valley of Humiliation, and the climactic Celestial City, set to music in illustrative neo-medieval modalities, associating valor with pentatonic trumpet calls, temptation with claudicant atonal steps, and sin with strident counterpoint, is produced at Covent Garden in London.

### 26 APRIL 1951

John Alden CARPENTER, American railroad shipping magnate and composer of ballets and instrumental music in a distinctive modernistic manner (the score of his jazzified ballet *Skyscrapers*, one of the earliest examples of American urbanistic music, was deposited in the cornerstone of Hampshire House, a forty-story New York skyscraper erected in 1931, as a symbol of the jazz age), dies in Chicago, the site of his gratifying financial successes, at the age of seventy-five.

### 28 APRIL 1951

*Die weisse Rose*, ballet by the 43-year-old German composer Wolfgang FORTNER, after Oscar Wilde's story *Birthday of the Infanta*, interpreted on two planes, realistic and surrealistic, in which the Infanta dances boogie-woogie in the sensual fantasy of the court dwarf enamored of her, is performed for the first time at the State Opera in Berlin.

### 1 MAY 1951

Camargo GUARNIERI, 44-year-old Brazilian composer, conducts in Rio de Janeiro the first performance of his orchestral suite *Brasiliana*, in three movements: *Entrada, Moda, Dansa*.

### 2 MAY 1951

*Dark Waters*, one-act opera by Ernst KRENEK, to his own libretto in English, dealing with a neurotic heiress who runs away from her wealthy parents in quest of adventure and meets accidental death of a gunshot wound in a river barge in the American South, is performed for the first time by the Opera Workshop at the University of Southern California School of Music in Los Angeles.

### 2 MAY 1951

*Symphony in E* by the 34-year-old American Negro composer Ulysses KAY, in three classically constructed movements, is performed for the first time in Rochester, Howard Hanson conducting.

### 4 MAY 1951

Ildebrando PIZZETTI conducts in Florence the first stage performance of his one-act opera *Ifigenia*, to the story of the immolation of Agamemnon's daughter to placate the goddess Artemis. (The opera was performed for the first time in concert form over the Italian Radio on 3 October 1950)

## 6 MAY 1951

*The Sons of Light*, cantata by Ralph VAUGHAN WILLIAMS, is performed in London for the first time by a chorus of 1000 school children and the London Philharmonic Orchestra.

## 8 MAY 1951

*Das Vokaltuch der Sängerin*, ballet-pantomime by the 24-year-old German composer Hans Werner HENZE, is performed for the first time, in concert form, in West Berlin.

## 12 MAY 1951

*First Symphony*, by the 35-year-old New Zealand composer Douglas LILBURN, is performed for the first time at Wellington, New Zealand.

## 15 MAY 1951

In observance of the centennial of the birth of Vincent d'INDY, the French Post Office issues a 25-franc stamp with his likeness.

## 15 MAY 1951

*John Socman*, opera by the 37-year-old English composer George LLOYD, to his father's libretto dealing with an unscrupulous 15th-century British magistrate, active amid a plethora of yeomen, bowmen, glee-men, friars and lollards, who tries to entice a farmer's daughter into marriage but yields her to her beloved archer, hero of the battle of Agincourt, when a wandering glee-maiden reveals herself as the magistrate's undivorced French wife, written in an abecedarian operatic idiom in which dramatic tension is created by an antiphony of brassy bombast and meretricious melodrama, is produced in Bristol.

## 15 MAY 1951

Felix Robert MENDELSSOHN, German cellist, great-grandnephew of Felix Mendelssohn, collapses and dies on the stage during his recital in Baltimore while playing a piece by Ernst von Dohnányi.

## 25 MAY 1951

*Symfonia Pokoju* (*Symphony of Peace*) for chorus and orchestra by the 36-year-old Polish composer Andrzej PANUFNIK in three sections, (1) *Lamentoso*, with a folk melody intoned amid the ruins of European cities (2) *Drammatico*, an agonizing appeal for world peace accentuated by purposefully concentrated syncopation (3) *Solenne*, an impassioned declaration that peace must be enforced by the will of the people, with an ending on a promissory chord of E major, is performed for the first time in Warsaw.

## 27 MAY 1951

Theodor ROGALSKI, 50-year-old Rumanian composer, conducts in Bucharest the first performance of his most successful work, *Three Dances for Orchestra*:

(1) *Dansure Rominesti*, based on a Transylvanian melody (2) *Gayda*, a Macedonian slow dance, with a trumpet making "wa-wa" sounds by muting it intermittently with the hand (3) *Hora*, a rapid Balkan dance.

### 29 MAY 1951

Josef Bohuslav FOERSTER, Nestor of Czech music, composer of numerous operas and symphonic works imbued with Bohemian melorhythms, within the matrix of Germanic operatic arts, dies in Nový Vestec at the venerable age of ninety-one.

### 30 MAY 1951

On the occasion of the inauguration of the First International Music Festival "Pražske Jaro" (Prague Spring), Czechoslovakia issues four commemorative postage stamps with the portraits of the founding fathers of Czech music, Bedřich SMETANA (1.50 and 3 kronen) and Antonín DVOŘÁK (1 and 2 kronen).

### 30 MAY 1951

Dimitri LEVIDIS, Greek composer of impressionistically flavored instrumental and vocal music, the first to use electronic instruments in symphonic works, dies in Athens at the age of sixty-five.

### 1 JUNE 1951

*Madame Bovary*, opera in three acts by the 52-year-old French composer Emmanuel BONDEVILLE, after Flaubert's famous novel of provincial adultery, is performed for the first time at the Opéra-Comique in Paris.

### 1 JUNE 1951

Two days after the death of the Moldavian composer Stepan NIAGA, his oratorio *The Song of Rebirth*, in eight sections traversing the history of Moldavia, from the period of Ottoman subjugation through Fascist domination and final liberation by the Soviet Army, is performed for the first time in Kishinev, capital of the Soviet Socialist Republic of Moldavia.

### 2 JUNE 1951

The Soviet Government issues two stamps, at 40 kopecks and one ruble, to honor the Viennese composer of ballets Leon MINKUS who spent most of his life in Russia.

### 2 JUNE 1951

*Festlicher Hymnus* for orchestra by the dean of Swiss composers Othmar SCHOECK, based on the tune of an Alpine shepherd's horn which develops into a Gregorian cantus firmus, ending on a resonant C, is performed for the first time in Grossmünster, on the occasion of the 600th anniversary of the entry of Zürich into the confederation of Swiss towns.

Serge KOUSSEVITZKY, Grand Seigneur of the baton, who ardently promoted the cause of modern music in Moscow, Paris and Boston, founder of the Edition Russe de Musique which published a series of works by Russian composers, including those of Scriabin, Stravinsky and Prokofiev, and who commissioned a whole generation of American composers to write symphonic works for him which he faithfully brought out during the quarter of a century of his conductorship of the Boston Symphony Orchestra (1924–1949), dies in Boston at the age of seventy-six.

7 JUNE 1951

*Symphonie* by the 35-year-old French composer Henri DUTILLEUX, in four movements, *Passacaglia, Scherzo, Intermezzo, Finale,* each developing autogenetically from thematic structures derived from the intervals of the major seventh and the tritone, making use of bitonal harmonies and frequently resorting to powerful ostinato figures, is performed for the first time by the Orchestre National in Paris, under the direction of Roger Desormière.

11 JUNE 1951

*Belgrade,* symphonic poem by the Serbian composer Dragutin GOSTUSKI, a historical musicorama of Belgrade, resolutely preserving its national Slavic aspects through centuries of invasion, subjugation and exploitation, is performed for the first time in Belgrade.

12 JUNE 1951

*Monopartita* by Arthur HONEGGER, in eight linked movements, indicating its antinomy of structure, the unifying aspect expressed by the prefix *mono,* and the divisive element implicit in the word *partita,* is performed for the first time in Zürich as a commissioned work on the occasion of the 600th anniversary of the entrance of the Canton of Zürich into the Helvetic Confederation.

13 JUNE 1951

*Stabat Mater,* a polyptych of intercessionary prayers by Francis POULENC, austerely scored for soprano solo, mixed choir and orchestra, is performed for the first time at the Music Festival in Strasbourg.

16 JUNE 1951

*Third Symphony* by the 46-year-old Dutch composer Guillaume LANDRÉ is performed for the first time by the Concertgebouw Orchestra in Amsterdam, Rafael Kubelik conducting.

17 JUNE 1951

*Second Piano Concerto* by the 46-year-old neo-classical English composer Alan RAWSTHORNE, in four movements (1) *Allegro piacevole* (2) *Allegro molto*

(3) *Adagio semplice—Poco Allegro* (4) *Allegro*, traversing in classical modalities a variety of moods creating an equilibrium of contrasting themes, firmly adhering to the triadic idiom, and concluding with a fugato building up into a jubilant oriflamme of exclamatory fanfares, is performed for the first time by Clifford Curzon and the London Symphony conducted by Sir Malcolm Sargent, as a commissioned work for the Festival of Great Britain of 1951.

### 19 JUNE 1951

André JOLIVET plays in Strasbourg the piano part in the first performance of his *Piano Concerto*, subtitled *Equatoriales*, evoking in its three movements the statically placid, humidly erotic and pacifically contemplative geographical regions lying on the equator, Central Africa, the East Indies and Polynesia, making colorful use of drums, bells, shakers, vibrators, and other indigenous percussion instruments.

### 22 JUNE 1951

The 25th Festival of the International Society for Contemporary Music opens in Frankfurt, presenting the following program of works by modern German composers:

*Third Symphony* in three movements by Karl Amadeus Hartmann (first performed in Munich on 10 February 1950); *Catulli Carmina* for two solo voices and mixed choir by Carl ORFF (first performed in Leipzig on 6 November 1943); *Concerto* for two pianos and orchestra in one movement by Hermann REUTTER, written in a free diatonic idiom, with an influx of polytonal harmonies; and *Sonata for Orchestra* by Werner EGK, the title emphasizing the neo-classical aspect of the work.

### 23 JUNE 1951

The 25th Festival of the International Society for Contemporary Music in Frankfurt presents two concerts:

Morning Program: *Chant funèbre à la mémoire des jeunes femmes défuntes* for mixed choir, orchestra and organ, by the veteran French modernist Charles KŒCHLIN, to the Latin words of the Requiem; and *D'un diable de briquet* by the 49-year-old Belgian composer Raymond CHEVREUILLE, a "radiophonic tale after Hans Christian Andersen," incorporating an imitation of a phonograph record played at 33 revolutions a minute, abruptly switching to 78 revolutions a minute, resulting in an effect of rhythmic diminution.

Evening program: *First Symphony* by Ernst TOCH (first performed in Vienna on 20 December 1950), in four movements unified by a thematic parabolic "ballistic curve"; *6 Chants* for chorus and orchestra by the 34-year-old French composer Jean-Louis MARTINET, written in the manner of medieval madrigals; *Coro di Morti*, dramatic madrigal for men's voices, three pianos, brass instruments, doublebasses and percussion, by Goffredo PETRASSI, written in 1941, to a text by the Italian romantic poet Leopardi, expressing the notion that to the dead the land of the living is as mysterious and horrifying as the dead are to those who are alive; *Symphonic Fragments* from the ballet *L'Auberge ensorcelée* by the 44-year-old Polish composer Antoni SZALOWSKI, written in a neo-classical manner.

## 24 JUNE 1951

*Fifth Symphony* by the 54-year-old French composer Jean RIVIER is performed for the first time in Strasbourg.

## 24 JUNE 1951

The 25th Festival of the International Society for Contemporary Music in Frankfurt presents the following program of symphonic music:

*Third Symphony* by the 34-year-old Swedish composer Karl Birger BLOMDAHL, subtitled *Facets* to indicate the pluralistic appearance of its five movements within a monistic entity; *Piccola Sinfonia giocosa* in four movements by the 51-year-old Swiss composer Willy BURKHARD; *Spiritual Chants* for mixed choir and organ by the 44-year-old Corsican composer Leo PREGER, written in emulation of medieval chants; and *Four Symphonic Movements* by the 46-year-old Dutch composer Guillaume LANDRÉ, in which thematic unity is maintained by periodic recurrence of the principal motive.

## 25 JUNE 1951

At the 25th Festival of the International Society for Contemporary Music in Frankfurt, the following program of chamber music is given:

*String Quartet* in six contrasting movements by the 26-year-old English composer Robert CRAWFORD; *Four Ancient Greek Poems* by the 26-year-old Brazilian composeress Nininha GREGORI, for soprano, woodwind quartet and celesta, conceived as an essay of ethnomusicological fidelity, but allowing some atonal discursions; *String Quartet* by the 25-year-old German composer Giselher KLEBE, in six short movements, based on the idea of "permanent variation," verging on dodecaphony without rigidity; *Sphenogramme* by the 22-year-old Japanese composer Toshiro MAYUZUMI, for contralto, flute, saxophone, marimba, violin, violoncello and piano, in five movements of widely contrasting materials, from Hindu liturgy to Bebop; and a neo-classical *Sextet* for woodwind instruments by the 30-year-old English composer John ADDISON.

## 26 JUNE 1951

At the 25th Festival of the International Society for Contemporary Music in Frankfurt the following program is presented:

*Concerto* for string orchestra in two movements by the 40-year-old German composer Helmut DEGEN; *5 Rechants* for 12 voices by the 42-year-old French composer Olivier MESSIAEN (*Rechant* being the 16th-century French word for *Refrain*), conceived in a neo-medieval style, with an admixture of Hindu rhythms; *Variations on a Haydn Theme* by the 50-year-old Austrian composer Hans Erich APOSTEL, in which the innocuous theme from the slow movement of Haydn's *Pauken-Symphonie* is subjected to intervallic translocations, procrustean melodic elongations and dodecaphonic torsions; and *Sonata* for Violin and Orchestra by the 36-year-old Polish composer Michal SPISAK.

## 27 JUNE 1951

As part of the 25th Festival of the Society for Contemporary Music in Frankfurt, the world première of the opera *The Duenna*, after Sheridan's play, by the Spanish composer Roberto GERHARD, resident in England, is given at the State Opera Theater in Wiesbaden.

## 28 JUNE 1951

The following works are presented at the 25th Festival of the International Society for Contemporary Music in Frankfurt:

*Das hohe Lied* for soprano and orchestra by the 27-year-old Polish composer and conductor Stanislaw SKROWACZEWSKI, in four sections, to the biblical text relating to King Solomon's young Shulamite concubine; *Piano Concerto* in four movements by the 46-year-old German composer Richard MOHAUPT; symphonic poem *La Isla de las Calmas* by the 63-year-old Norwegian composer Fartein VALEN, written in a tense atonal idiom within an impressionistic framework; *Nocturne for Orchestra* by the Polish-American composer Jerzy FITELBERG (1903–1951), in the form of a theme with four variations; and *Three Psalms of King David* for tenor, chorus and orchestra by the 42-year-old Danish composer Herman KOPPEL, dedicated to the memory of the sufferings endured by humanity during World War II.

## 29 JUNE 1951

The following program is presented at the 25th Festival of the International Society for Contemporary Music in Frankfurt:

*String Quartet* in three movements by the 41-year-old Danish composer Vagn HOLMBOE, illustrating the dialectical principle of antithetical motivic development in the first two movements and their synthesis in the third movement; *Gethsemane* for women's voices and a string trio by the 59-year-old Austrian composer Felix PETYREK, conceived as a 20th-century replica of a medieval religious play; *String Quartet* in four movements by the 35-year-old Argentinian composer Alberto GINASTERA, couched in the baroque idiom vivified by an injection of Argentinian melorhythms; and *Quintet* for wind instruments by the 39-year-old French composer Jean FRANÇAIX, written in a hedonistically Gallic manner.

## 29 JUNE 1951

On the 1900th anniversary of St. Paul's arrival in Athens, the 58-year-old Greek composer Petro PETRIDIS conducts in Athens the first performance of his oratorio *St. Paul.*

## 30 JUNE 1951

At the 25th Festival of the International Society for Contemporary Music in Frankfurt, the following works are performed:

*Ulysses*, cantata after James Joyce's novel of that name by the 46-year-old Hungarian composer, resident of England, Mátyás SEIBER (first performed in London on 27 May 1949), and *Il Prigioniero*, opera by Luigi DALLAPICCOLA (first performed in a concert version, on Radio Turin, 4 December 1949 and on the stage in Florence on 20 May 1950)

## 1 JULY 1951

*L'Apostrophe*, comic opera in one act by Jean FRANÇAIX, to a libretto from Balzac's *Contes drôlatiques*, dealing with a hunchback's fateful infatuation with a married belle, is performed on the stage for the first time, in Amsterdam, in the course of the Holland Music Festival.

918

1 JULY 1951

A program of contemporary German works is presented at the 25th Festival of the International Society for Contemporary Music in Frankfurt:

*Orchestral Variations on a Paganini Theme* by the 48-year-old Manchuria-born German-Estonian composer Boris BLACHER, in which the variations develop only the basic tonal elements of the theme, derived from Paganini's *Capriccio,* op. 26; *Violin Concerto* in four movements by the German composer Hans Werner HENZE (the performance took place on his 25th birthday), written in a discursively rhapsodic style, abandoning his youthful dodecaphony; *Fantasy on the Theme of B-A-C-H* for two pianos and orchestra by the 43-year-old neo-classicist Wolfgang FORTNER, where the Bach motive is construed as part of a 12-tone series; and the *Symphonic Dances* in four sections by Paul HINDEMITH, written in 1937. (The Festival concluded on the evening of 1 July 1951 with the stage performance of the five-act opera *The Life of Orestes* by Ernst KRENEK)


2 JULY 1951

The Soviet Government issues a series of stamps with pictures of the Bolshoi Theater and portraits of GLINKA, TCHAIKOVSKY, MUSSORGSKY, RIMSKY-KORSAKOV and BORODIN.


6 JULY 1951

Malcolm ARNOLD conducts at the Cheltenham Festival the first performance of his *First Symphony,* in three movements, *Allegro, Andantino* and *Vivace con fuoco,* written in an aggressively vitalistic and ostentatiously extrovert idiom, with a fugal finale marked by a proliferation of *stretti,* and punctuated by loud drum beats.


7 JULY 1951

*Terres du Rhône,* festive symphonic suite by the 50-year-old Swiss composer Hans HAUG, depicting in ethnomusicological modalities the glories of the river Rhône, flowing from the Alps through the Lake of Geneva into the Mediterranean, is performed for the first time under the composer's direction during the course of the Swiss Athletic Festival in Basel.


13 JULY 1951

Arnold SCHOENBERG, revolutionary genius, creator of the epoch-making method of composition with twelve tones related only to one another that has profoundly influenced a whole generation of composers in all parts of the world, dies at the age of seventy-six in Los Angeles, his American home from 1935. (Profoundly affected by triskaidekaphobia, Schoenberg regarded the date of his birth, 13th of September, as inauspicious; fearfully aware that the sum of the digits of 76, his age at his last birthday, was 13, he observed during his terminal illness in July 1951, that should he survive the fateful 13th of the month, all would be well, but he died on that day at 13 minutes before midnight)

## 14 JULY 1951

*Bunt Zakow* (*Rebellion of Clerks*), opera by the Polish composer Tadeusz SZELIGOWSKI, with the action evolving in Cracow in 1549, after the accession to the throne of King Sigismund II of Poland and his conflict with the powerful scribes of the state, employing some Gregorian canticles in the score to characterize the Catholic priesthood and the general harmonic scheme in the Mussorgsky style, is performed for the first time at Wroclaw.

## 21 JULY 1951

*Kappa*, ballet by the Japanese composer Yasushi AKUTAGAWA, symphonic poem depicting a Japanese mermaid, is performed for the first time by the Tokyo Philharmonic Orchestra.

## 26 JULY 1951

*Second Symphony* by the 30-year-old English composer Peter Racine FRICKER, in three movements, in an astutely synthetic idiom, frugal in sonorities and expressionistic in melodic atonality, is performed for the first time by the Liverpool Philharmonic Orchestra.

## 1 AUGUST 1951

*The Great Campaign*, opera by the Chinese woman composer Lee BO-CHAO, portraying in monodic tones the impressions of the 7,000-mile military trek of the Chinese Red Army in which she participated in 1935, is performed for the first time in Peking.

## 10 AUGUST 1951

*La Cuarterona*, opera by the Argentinian composer Juan García ESTRADA, to a libretto telling the story of a beautiful quadroon slave girl beset by amorous vicissitudes in colonial Argentina, is produced at the Teatro Colón, in Buenos Aires.

## 15 AUGUST 1951

Artur SCHNABEL, Austrian pianist and renowned pedagogue whose interpretations of German classics established a tradition among generations of his disciples and pupils of his disciples, who also wrote works in an extremely advanced atonal and polytonal idiom, dies in Axenstein, Switzerland, at the age of sixty-nine.

## 21 AUGUST 1951

Constant LAMBERT, English composer of sophisticated modern pieces, conductor, and writer of provocative essays, dies in London two days before his 46th birthday.

## 24 AUGUST 1951

MODERN JAZZ QUARTET is founded in New York by John LEWIS (pianist), Milt JACKSON (vibraphonist), Percy HEATH (bassist) and Kenny CLARKE (drummer), with the aim of establishing a fruitful coalition of classical music and jazz. (The official beginning of the Modern Jazz Quartet is reckoned from their first recording session of 22 December 1952)

## 26 AUGUST 1951

*Fifth Symphony* in four movements by the Chicago resident Czech composer Karel Boleslav JIRÁK, "an autobiographical work expressing the feelings of a human being who, after the tribulations of the great war has finally found a secure haven," is performed for the first time at the Edinburgh International Festival.

## 28 AUGUST 1951

The Soviet Government issues two commemorative musical postage stamps of 40 kopecks each, to mark the centennial of the death of the Russian song composer Alexander ALIABIEV bearing a musical quotation from his most famous song *The Nightingale*, and the 50th anniversary of the death of the symphonic composer Vassili KALINNIKOV.

## 5 SEPTEMBER 1951

*Heroic Oratorio*, by Vojislav VUCKOVIĆ, Serbian composer who fell victim of the Nazis in 1942, melorhythmically derived from native folksongs, is performed for the first time, posthumously, in Cetinje, in an orchestration completed by Alexander Obradović.

## 11 SEPTEMBER 1951

Igor STRAVINSKY conducts in Venice the world première of his opera in three acts, subdivided into nine scenes, *The Rake's Progress*, to the text of W. H. Auden and Chester Kallman, after Hogarth's eight engravings dealing with a profligate young man who concludes a pact with a gentleman-like Beelzebub, is tempted by him to marry a bearded lady, then gambles for the price of his soul, eventually landing in Bedlam, the whole summarized in a moral in the Epilogue, "For idle hearts and hands and minds the Devil finds a work to do," set to music in a mannered neo-baroque idiom, with rhythmic and melodic formulas reverting to the Italian settecento, artfully seasoned with pandiatonic spice.

## 23 SEPTEMBER 1951

*Third Symphony* by the 55-year-old Latvian-born German pianist and composer Eduard ERDMANN, is performed for the first time in Essen.

## 30 SEPTEMBER 1951

*Lysistrata*, ballet by Boris BLACHER (after the comedy by Aristophanes, in which the heroine stops the Peloponesian war by inducing the women of Athens to refuse marital favors to their soldier husbands unless peace is promptly made), is performed for the first time in Berlin.

## 1 OCTOBER 1951

Herbert EIMERT broadcasts a lecture, *Die Klangwelt der elektronischen Musik,* over the radio network Nordwestdeutscher Rundfunk, in which he makes use of the term "electronic music," coined by him, for the first time.

## 3 OCTOBER 1951

To commemorate the tenth anniversary of the death of the Austrian composer Wilhelm KIENZL, who wrote the first National Anthem of the Austrian Republic in 1920, the Austrian Government issues a stamp of one and a half schillings bearing his portrait.

## 4 OCTOBER 1951

*The Dybbuk,* opera by the American composer David TAMKIN, to the play by Ansky based on a medieval Jewish legend in which the spirit of a dead bridegroom invades the mind of his bride, is produced in New York.

## 6 OCTOBER 1951

Five world premières are presented at the opening day of the Donaueschingen Festival of Contemporary Music:

*Double Concerto* for violin, piano and small orchestra, in seven short movements, by Ernst KRENEK; *Piano Sonata* by the 40-year-old Swiss composer, Rolf LIEBERMANN; *Polyphonie X* for 17 solo instruments by the 26-year-old French composer Pierre BOULEZ, in three movements, set in a highly dissonant idiom (the audience reacted violently, and one outraged woman blew a police whistle, described by a reporter as "a nice, clean sound"); *Der himmlische Vagant,* a lyrical portrait of François Villon, for two voices and instruments, by the 51-year-old German composer Hermann REUTTER; and *Etude* in two parts for piano, wind instruments and percussion by the 52-year-old Rumanian-French composer Marcel MIHALOVICI.

## 7 OCTOBER 1951

Lukas Foss, 29-year-old Berlin-born American composer plays in Venice the solo piano part in the world première of his *Second Piano Concerto* in three movements, written in the manner of a 19th-century virtuoso piece, in extended tonality with the final C-major chord encrusted with a supplementary D, warranted here as the acoustically consonant ninth overtone.

## 7 OCTOBER 1951

The second and last concert of the Donaueschingen Music Festival presents the following works:

*Piccolo Concerto Notturno* in five movements by the Italian composer Guido TURCHI; *Konzertstück* for piano and orchestra in two movements by the Hungarian-Parisian composer Tibor HARSANYI; *Symphonia Brevis* in four movements by the Austrian composer Hanns JELINEK written in a neo-baroque idiom with superinduced atonalities; *Fifth Symphony* by Arthur HONEGGER; and the first performance of *Third Symphony* by the 25-year-old German composer Hans Werner HENZE, conducted by him, written in a turbulent idiom, saturated with atonal plaints, noxious dissonances and containing unconsummated fugatos, erupting at points of critical tensions into a multitude of incorporeal tintinnabulations out of which a jazzy orgy is spontaneously generated, ultimately coming to rest on a pacific concord.

### 7 OCTOBER 1951

For the first time in nineteen centuries the Colosseum in Rome is used for a public spectacle, with selections from VERDI's operas performed by the orchestra and the chorus of the Opera House of Rome.

### 10 OCTOBER 1951

JIYU SAKKYOKUKA (Free Composers Association) is formed in Japan.

The Association of Free Composers is trying to create a new music to suit the modern taste. It does not subscribe to the philosophy of destruction and rejection for their own sake. Instead, it tries to foster a firm belief in the free will of creation. (From the inaugural statement of the Association)

### 11 OCTOBER 1951

*Violin Concerto* in two movements by the 54-year-old Danish composer Knudaage RIISAGER is performed for the first time in Copenhagen.

### 11 OCTOBER 1951

*Il Principe felice,* opera after Oscar Wilde, by the Italian composer Renzo BOSSI, is performed for the first time in concert form on the Milan Radio.

### 12 OCTOBER 1951

*Ivan le Terrible,* opera in four acts by Georges BIZET, the score of which, believed to have been destroyed by Bizet in 1865, was discovered intact among the possessions of the family of the nephew of the second husband of Bizet's widow, is given a world première in Bordeaux.

### 14 OCTOBER 1951

Pablo CASALS conducts in Zürich an all-violoncello orchestra comprising of 123 French, German, Italian, English and Belgian violoncellists, male and female, in a program including the world première of his multicellistic score *La Sardana.*

### 18 OCTOBER 1951

*Seventh Symphony* by the 41-year-old Danish composer Vagn HOLMBOE, in four movements separated by three intermezzi, is performed for the first time in Copenhagen.

### 19 OCTOBER 1951

*Apocalypse,* symphonic poem by the 40-year-old Italian-born American composer Gian Carlo MENOTTI, is performed for the first time in Pittsburgh.

### 23 OCTOBER 1951

*Romantic Overture* by the 52-year-old Russian composer Alexander TCHEREPNIN, domiciled in America, inspired by "the sound of horses' hooves on the pavement" evoking "the romantic era to which it belongs," written in the virtually unobstructed key of C major and surcharged with equine kinetic energy, is performed for the first time in Kansas City.

### 25 OCTOBER 1951

Manuel ROSENTHAL, French composer and conductor, is summarily dismissed as music director of the Seattle Symphony Orchestra for moral turpitude in his unsanctified cohabitation with Claudine Pillard Verneuil, French singer whom he engaged as a soloist featured as Mme. Rosenthal, disregarding the existence of his undivorced wife in Paris.

### 2 NOVEMBER 1951

*Bonampak,* ballet by the 46-year-old Mexican composer Luis SANDI, inspired by the archaeological discovery in 1949 of Mayan frescoes in the jungle village of Bonampak, is performed for the first time in Tuxtla Gutiérrez, in the province of Chiapas, where Bonampak is situated.

### 5 NOVEMBER 1951

*Virginia Symphony* by the 69-year-old Virginian composer John POWELL is performed for the first time in Richmond, Virginia, and the day is declared by Governor John S. Battle of Virginia as John Powell Day, in appreciation of Powell's achievement as composer and as a valiant champion of white race supremacy. (Powell was a chief sponsor of Virginia's Racial Integrity Act of 1924 which barred the marriage of a white person and a person having a single platelet of Negro blood or more than one-sixth of Indian blood, all of which does not alter the fact that the only piece he is known for is *Rapsodie nègre*)

### 7 NOVEMBER 1951

*Erosion,* or *The Origin of the Amazon River,* symphonic poem by Heitor VILLA-LOBOS, is performed for the first time by the Louisville Orchestra.

### 9 NOVEMBER 1951

Sigmund ROMBERG, 64-year-old Hungarian-born American composer of 78 operettas to English libretti, among them such perennial favorites as *The Stu-*

*dent Prince* and *The Desert Song,* dies suddenly of cerebral hemorrhage at 11:15 P.M. in his hotel room in New York, a week after he arrived there from his residence in California.

### 10 NOVEMBER 1951

*Le Voyage de Magellan,* symphonic suite by the Parisianized Polish composer Alexandre TANSMAN, drawn from an unperformed opera of the same title, tracing the semicircumnavigation of Magellan in six colorful episodes, ending in the Philippine Islands which he inadvertently discovered and where he was butchered and devoured by the xenophagic aborigines, is performed for the first time by the St. Louis Symphony Orchestra, Vladimir Golschmann conducting, 430 years after Magellan's death.

### 13 NOVEMBER 1951

Nicolai MEDTNER, Russian composer of expressive piano pieces fashioned with exquisite lapidary care, convinced believer in the eternal verities of music as a profoundly humanistic art (he was of German extraction, and his brother was a philosopher of mystical orientation), dies at 4:50 A.M., at the age of seventy-one, in London where he settled after the debacle in the turmoil of the Russian Revolution of everything he held dear.

### 13 NOVEMBER 1951

Hugo LEICHTENTRITT, German-born scholar educated at Harvard University, author of a standard book on motets, biographer of Handel, and an unfortunate composer of Regeromantic instrumental pieces, dies in Cambridge, Massachusetts, at the age of seventy-seven.

### 14 NOVEMBER 1951

*Blanche Neige,* ballet by the French operetta composer Maurice YVAIN, is produced at the Paris Opera.

### 15 NOVEMBER 1951

The Government of Poland issues stamps at 45 and 90 groschen, honoring CHOPIN and MONIUSZKO.

### 16 NOVEMBER 1951

*Eastward in Eden,* opera in four acts by the Czech-born American composer Jan MEYEROWITZ, is produced in Detroit.

### 17 NOVEMBER 1951

*Marion, La Belle au tricorne,* comic opera in three acts by the 36-year-old Swiss composer Pierre WISSMER, is produced at the Opéra-Comique in Paris.

### 19 NOVEMBER 1951

To mark the semicentennial of the death of Giuseppe VERDI, the Italian Government issues three stamps, at 10, 25 and 60 lire, bearing his likeness.

## 22 NOVEMBER 1951

*Der rote Stiefel,* "picture book for music" in two parts by the Swiss composer Heinrich SUTERMEISTER (with an invisible vocal quartet substituted for the customary chorus), is performed for the first time, with a Swedish libretto, at the Stockholm Royal Opera.

## 27 NOVEMBER 1951

Henri COLLET, French music critic who coined the title "Les Six Français," dies in Paris at the age of sixty-six.

## 28 NOVEMBER 1951

Le Cercle Culturel du Conservatoire de Paris presents a concert of advanced music, featuring quarter-tone compositions by Ivan WYSCHNEGRADSKY, Russian emigre resident in Paris, for two and four pianos tuned a quarter-tone apart; three melodies "en langue imaginaire" by Marina SCRIABIN, daughter of Alexander Scriabin; *Suite monodique* for piano by Jéhan ALAIN, French composer and organist killed in France in June, 1940; and *Prelude and fugue* by Jean-Louis MARTINET.

## 29 NOVEMBER 1951

*Ein Landarzt,* radio cantata by the 25-year-old German composer Hans Werner HENZE, written in a free dodecaphonic idiom, after Kafka's story of a surrealistic country doctor's life, with symptomatic atonal vocalization to hemorrhagingly discordant harmonies and polyrhythmic chorea in syncopated singultation accentuating the neurasthenic malaise of the music, is performed for the first time on the Hamburg Radio.

## 30 NOVEMBER 1951

*Horizontes* by the Mexican pioneer of fractional tonalities Julian CARRILLO, scored for violin and cello in quarter-tones, a specially constructed zither-harp tuned in 16th-tones, and an accompanying normal orchestra playing mostly in semitones, is performed for the first time by the Pittsburgh Symphony Orchestra, Leopold Stokowski conducting.

## 30 NOVEMBER 1951

*Ugrum-Reka (River Ugrum),* opera in four acts by the 45-year-old Soviet composer Daniel FRENKEL, with its action set in Tsarist Siberia in 1910, wherein a mine owner strangles his bride when he finds out that she is a member of the Bolshevik party, and is driven to suicide by the outraged proletarian masses, set to music in a socialistically realistic style rooted in Russian melorhythms, is performed for the first time in Leningrad.

## 1 DECEMBER 1951

Felix PETYREK, Brno-born composer of progressively modernistic music who consistently employed a scale of alternating whole-tones and semitones in the conviction that this scale, cultivated by Rimsky-Korsakov, was his own invention, dies in Vienna, at the age of fifty-nine.

1 DECEMBER 1951

*Billy Budd,* opera in four acts by Benjamin BRITTEN, after the unfinished novel of Herman Melville depicting the hanging of a young sailor on an 18th-century British man-o'-war in 1797, scored for men's voices only, with orchestra, and set in emphatic triadic harmony (the pronouncement of the death sentence is illustrated in the orchestra by a succession of 34 triads, related only by the presence in each of them of at least one note of the F major triad), is produced in London.

5 DECEMBER 1951

*Incognita,* opera by Egon WELLESZ, 66-year-old Viennese composer and music scholar, to a libretto after Congreve, dealing with a masked lady (the *Incognita* of the title) in a man's attire who is saved from a male annoyant by her fiancé unaware of her identity, set to music in neo-archaic modalities acidulated by Viennese atonalities, is performed for the first time in Oxford, England, where he settled in 1938 after the Nazi Anschluss of Austria.

7 DECEMBER 1951

*Concerto for Two Pianos and Orchestra* by the 48-year-old Russian-American composer Nikolai LOPATNIKOFF, in three movements, set in a percussively neo-baroque style, is performed for the first time by Victor Babin and his wife Vitya Vronsky as soloists, with the Pittsburgh Symphony Orchestra.

13 DECEMBER 1951

Selim PALMGREN, Finnish composer of impressionistic miniatures permeated by Suomian melorhythms, dies in Helsinki at the age of seventy-three.

14 DECEMBER 1951

*Sinfonia Giocosa* in two movements by the Parisianized Rumanian composer Marcel MIHALOVICI, set in a hedonistically bland melodious and harmonious idiom, is performed for the first time by the Chamber Orchestra of Basel, Paul Sacher conducting.

14 DECEMBER 1951

Pedro SANJUÁN conducts the St. Louis Symphony Orchestra in the world première of his "ritual symphony" *La Macumba* derived from Afro-Cuban rhythms and chants.

22 DECEMBER 1951

*Huszti kaland (Adventure in Huszt),* comic opera in two acts by the 48-year-old Hungarian composer Pál KADOSA, dealing with a Magyar 17th-century student who captures a Hapsburg general in a castle in Huszt and as a reward gains the hand of his professor's daughter, is produced in Budapest.

**24 DECEMBER 1951**

*Amahl and the Night Visitors,* opera in one act by the 40-year-old Italian-American composer Gian Carlo MENOTTI, the first opera especially written for television, to his own libretto, inspired by the painting by Hieronymus Bosch, "The Adoration of the Magi," wherein a poor Arab boy whose dwelling is visited by the three Kings on their way to see the Infant Jesus, is cured of his lameness, set to music with a poignant sense of melodramatic tension and lyric expression, containing some implosive modernities under the tonal surface of Puccinian melos, is produced by the National Broadcasting Company as a special Christmas offering, becoming an annual event to be repeated every Christmas Eve during the second half of the twentieth century, as long as television exercises its lure.

**29 DECEMBER 1951**

*Drums of Japan,* ballet by the Japanese composer Akira IFUKUBE, is performed for the first time in Tokyo.

# ◈ *1952* ◈

**11 JANUARY 1952**

*Second Symphony* by Ernst TOCH in four movements, dedicated to Albert Schweitzer, as "the only victor in a world of victims," and presenting a musicorama of romantic moods passing through impassioned assertion of religious faith (*Allegro fanatico*), skeptical philosophy (*Sehr leicht, huschend, schatten-haft*), an introspective *Adagio,* and a proclamatory *Allegro,* in a tonal idiom with islands of dramatic dissonance in transit, is performed for the first time in Vienna.

**14 JANUARY 1952**

*Violin Concerto* by the 37-year-old Dutch composer Marius FLOTHUIS is performed for the first time in Utrecht.

**17 JANUARY 1952**

*The Cowherd and the Sky Maiden,* opera in one act by John VERRALL, is produced in Seattle.

**20 JANUARY 1952**

Arthur FARWELL, American composer of ethnomusicologically inspired instrumental pieces and songs, a fervent champion of musical Americanism, dies in New York at the age of seventy-nine.

## 23 JANUARY 1952

*Sinfonia dello Zodiaco* by Gian Francesco MALIPIERO, completed by him on 8 November 1951, subtitled "della Primavera all'Invierno," in four parts, beginning in a vernal pentatonic manner in the oxygenated key of C, and ending on a damp and gelid hibernal dissonance, is performed for the first time in Lausanne. (The work bears no numerical index; a symphony designated by Malipiero as "Ottava sinfonia" was written in 1964; there is therefore no justification to classify the present symphony as his ninth, as in some music reference books)

## 23 JANUARY 1952

Two centuries have elapsed since the birth in Rome, of an Italian father and a German mother (née Kaiser), of Muzio CLEMENTI, the sagacious reformer and innovator of pianistic techniques, whose *Gradus ad Parnassum* has become an emblem of excellence for young pianists aspiring to perform a gradual ascent to the summit of the mountain of the Muses.

(Clementi's baptismal certificate obtained by the author from the Archivio Segreto Vaticano bears the date 24 January 1752 and states "infantem *hieri* natum baptizavi" thus establishing 23 January 1752 as Clementi's true date of birth; the date 24 January 1752 encountered in some music dictionaries is tardy)

## 24 JANUARY 1952

On the occasion of the 25th anniversary of the Kammerorchester of Basel, its founder and conductor Paul Sacher presents a program of world premières:

*Die Harmonie der Welt* a symphony in three movements by Paul HINDEMITH, drawn from the orchestral portions of his opera on the life of the astronomer Johannes Kepler: (1) *Musica Instrumentalis* (not in the sense of instrumental music but as a category in the philosophy of Boethius indicating the instrumentality of art in the relationship between man and God) (2) *Musica humana,* expressing the harmony between the spiritual and the material aspects of man (3) *Musica mundana,* world harmony, depicting the concord of the planetary spheres; *Violin Concerto* by the 61-year-old Swiss composer Frank MARTIN, in three movements, *Allegro, Andante, Presto,* in a *sui generis* tonal idiom, in which octaves are excluded in melodic and harmonic structures, thus asymptotically approaching dodecaphony; and *Second Concerto for Orchestra* by Goffredo PETRASSI.

## 26 JANUARY 1952

*Second Violin Concerto* by the self-exiled Hungarian master of romantic music Ernst von DOHNÁNYI (completed on 7 January 1950, in Tallahassee, Florida) in C minor, in four movements, scored for orchestra without violins, is performed for the first time in San Antonio, Texas.

## 26 JANUARY 1952

Reinhold GLIÈRE conducts in Moscow the first performance of his *Concerto* for horn and orchestra.

## 30 JANUARY 1952

*Yuzuru,* romantic opera by the 27-year-old Japanese composer Ikuma DAN, to a libretto from the ancient Japanese legend about a crane flying home in the twilight, with singsong melodies in Nipponese modes accoutred in European harmonies, is produced in Tokyo.

## 30 JANUARY 1952

*Fourth Symphony* by the 45-year-old American composer Paul CRESTON in four well-contrasted movements (1) *Maestoso,* leading to a spirited *Allegro* (2) *Andante pastorale,* in a cyclic triune form, with a dancing episode as the middle section (3) *Allegretto giocoso,* a hedonistic scherzo (4) *Vivace saltellante,* a tarantella-like finale, is performed for the first time by the National Symphony Orchestra in Washington, Howard Mitchell conducting.

## 31 JANUARY 1952

*Sinfonia* by the 33-year-old American composer Leon KIRCHNER is performed for the first time by the New York Philharmonic.

## 1 FEBRUARY 1952

*Rondo vom goldenen Kalb,* ballet "in three night pieces" by the 34-year-old Austrian composer Gottfried von EINEM, to the biblical story of the worship of the golden calf, is performed for the first time in Hamburg.

## 5 FEBRUARY 1952

*Symphony in D* by the 49-year-old American composer John VINCENT is performed for the first time in its initial version by the Louisville Orchestra, Robert Whitney conducting. (In its revised version it was performed for the first time by the Philadelphia Orchestra, Eugene Ormandy conducting on 12 April 1957)

## 7 FEBRUARY 1952

*Přehedra Socialismu (Overture to Socialism)* by Emil František BURIAN, Czech composer of modernistically colored choral and instrumental music, composed in 1949 to salute the advent of the Communist government in Czechoslovakia, and containing quotations from the Soviet National Anthem, is performed for the first time in Prague.

## 8 FEBRUARY 1952

*String Quartet* in D major by Arnold SCHOENBERG, composed in 1897, the score of which was regarded as lost, is performed for the first time in the 20th century, after a hiatus of 55 years, at the Library of Congress in Washington.

This is the first publicly performed work of Schoenberg . . . played in Vienna during the season 1897–98. Grove and Leibowitz erroneously state that the score has been lost! In fact not only the score, but also the parts (written by Schoenberg himself) are preserved. (From a note by Schoenberg, in English, using third person singular, accompanying the manuscript of the score and parts of the *String Quartet* in D, which he offered for sale to the Library of Congress, and which was purchased shortly before his death)

## 8 FEBRUARY 1952

*L'Uragano,* opera in three acts by the 56-year-old Italian composer Lodovico ROCCA, after Ostrovsky's somber Russian play about a 19th-century merchant woman Katia Kabanova, whose drinking husband and oppressive mother-in-law drive her to suicide, is produced at La Scala in Milan.

## 11 FEBRUARY 1952

Hugo WEISGALL, 39-year-old Czech-born American composer, conducts in Baltimore the first performance of his short opera *The Tenor,* to a libretto drawn from the novella *Der Kammersänger* by Franz Wedekind, dealing with a self-centered tenor who steps over the dead body of one of his multitudinous mistresses in his haste to get to the opera theater in time to sing Tristan, set to music in a tense style between a narrative ballad and atonal expressionism, with several quotations from *Tristan und Isolde.*

## 13 FEBRUARY 1952

Alfred EINSTEIN, eminent German music scholar and lexicographer, first cousin of Albert Einstein, dies in his California retreat at El Cerrito, at the age of seventy-one.

## 17 FEBRUARY 1952

*Boulevard Solitude,* lyric drama in seven scenes by the 25-year-old German composer Hans Werner HENZE, to the story of Manon Lescaut interpreted in an existentialistically surrealistic manner, written in an expressionistically synthetic idiom, ranging from triadic constructions in plain C major to overt dodecaphony, a conception radically different from the melodramatic lyricism of the operas by Massenet and Puccini on the same subject, is performed for the first time in Hannover.

## 18 FEBRUARY 1952

Mstislav Rostropovich, prime Soviet cellist, plays the first performance in Moscow of *Symphonie Concertante in E minor* for cello and orchestra, by Sergei PROKOFIEV, written especially for him and dedicated to him, with much thematic material taken from Prokofiev's *First Cello Concerto* of 1938, and combining in its score the most felicitous qualities of Prokofiev's energetically lyrical and dramatically individual style, with flashes of irony illuminating the music, in three movements:

(1) *Andante,* in 2/4 time, in E minor, intoning, after a thunderous orchestral introduction, a spacious melody in the solo cello part, soon reaching a maximal saturation of so-

norous matter, with the cello scaling the heights of its range before subsiding to a lyrical ending. (2) *Allegro giusto*, in 4/4 time, in C major, in the manner of a toccata, with tennis-like tossing of chordal balls across the contrapuntal net, and basic tonality enhanced by particles of chromatic dust clinging to strategic points (3) *Andante con moto*, in 3/2 time, in E major, beginning with a chorale-like recitative, then embarking on a kinesthetic *Vivace* in 3/4 time, erupting in asymmetrical blasts of brass, and coming to rest on a unison E.

### 21 FEBRUARY 1952

The South African Musical Festival, celebrating the tricentennial of the Boer settlement, opens at Cape Town with a program of ballet music, including a world première of *Legend of Princess Vlei* by the 24-year-old South African composer John JOUBERT.

### 22 FEBRUARY 1952

*The Meeting of the Volga with the Don River,* festive overture by Sergei PROKOFIEV, written to celebrate the completion of the Volga-Don Canal, is performed for the first time on the Moscow radio.

### 22 FEBRUARY 1952

*Violin Concerto* by the 50-year-old Russian-born American composer Boris KOUTZEN, in three movements, written in a traditional 19th-century manner, with the employment of some hidden contrapuntal devices such as the superposition of a theme on its alter ego in reverse progression, is performed in a world première by Koutzen's daughter Nadia with the Philadelphia Orchestra, Eugene Ormandy conducting.

### 29 FEBRUARY 1952

Carlos CHÁVEZ conducts in Mexico City the world première of his *Violin Concerto,* with Viviane Bertolami as soloist, in eight linked movements of which the last four, separated from the first four by a florid violin cadenza, recapitulate in reverse the basic four movements, so that the entire work becomes an equilibrated specular octad possessing a perfect chirality.

### 3 MARCH 1952

The Austrian Government issues a stamp for $1\frac{1}{2}$ schillings in honor of the Viennese violinist and organizer of a popular quartet of two violins, guitar and accordion, Johann SCHRAMMEL (1850–1893).

### 3 MARCH 1952

*Seljaci (The Peasants),* comic opera in three acts by the Croatian composer Petar KONJOVIĆ, picturing rustic life, love and drama in a Serbian village at the end of the 19th century, written in a socialist realistic tradition with copious quotations of ethnic elements in Balkanized asymmetrical melorhythms, is produced in Belgrade.

## 4 MARCH 1952

*Tartiniana* for violin and orchestra by the 48-year-old Italian modernist Luigi DALLAPICCOLA, based on themes of Giuseppe Tartini, the initiator of the virtuoso school of Italian violin playing, is performed for the first time in Bern, Switzerland.

## 7 MARCH 1952

Albert COATES, Russian-born English composer-conductor resident in South Africa conducts at Cape Town the first performance of his opera *Tafelberg se Kleed* (*Van Hunks and the Devil*), to a libretto in the Afrikaans language, drawn from a native legend of a Dutchman holding a smoking contest with the devil on top of 3550-foot Table Mountain near Cape Town, causing violent winds and interfering with navigation in the harbor, set to music in an intelligently ethnomusicological idiom, with a generous application of rational dissonances.

## 7 MARCH 1952

*Twelfth Symphony*, with a choral ending, by the 56-year-old Swiss-American composer Ernst LÉVY, written in an austerely sonorous, frugally romantic style, is performed for the first time in Chicago under the composer's direction.

## 14 MARCH 1952

*Second Symphony* by the Hawaiian composer Dai-Keong LEE is performed for the first time in San Francisco.

## 14 MARCH 1952

Harry PARTCH, 50-year-old Californian composer, presents at Mills College, Oakland, his musical score to *King Oedipus* of Sophocles (in the version by William Butler Yeats), built on a 43-note scale in non-tempered pitch and employing specially constructed instruments: a modernized kithara with 72 strings, a Harmonic Canon with 44 strings, each of which is a freely tunable monochord; Marimba Eroica; Bass Marimba; two altered guitars; two flexible saxophones; microtonal string bass; microtonal violoncello and a set of Cloud Chamber Bowls, borrowed from the atomic laboratory of the University of California.

## 17 MARCH 1952

Juan José CASTRO, 56-year-old Argentinian composer, conducts at La Scala in Milan the world première of his opera *Proserpina e lo Straniero*, awarded the first prize of 4 million lire in a contest on the occasion of the semicentennial of Verdi's death, to an Italian libretto translated from the original Spanish, a modern rendition of the classical myth, wherein Proserpina appears as a Buenos Aires prostitute, and Pluto, the "stranger" of the, title, is transferred from the nether to the upper regions, as an aviator in World War II who is compelled to lead an air raid on a monastery in which his own wife had taken shelter, kills her, and expiates his crime by being himself killed by one of Proserpina's lovers, set to music in a tense melodramatic style, vitalized by South American melorhythms.

### 18 MARCH 1952

At the South African Festival in Cape Town, Szymon Goldberg plays the first performance of the *Violin Concerto* by the resident Scottish composer Erik CHISHOLM, in four substantial movements, inspired by Hindu modes, but clothed in a modern technique.

### 19 MARCH 1952

*Overture for the Dedication of a Nuclear Reactor* by the atomic physicist Arthur ROBERTS, in four movements representing the design, construction, and modus operandi of a nuclear reactor, derived from the motto A–E–C (for Atomic Energy Commission) with subsidiary parameters indicating specific weights in the periodical table of elements, C-12 (graphite or carbon), U-235 (uranium) and Pu-239 (plutonium), wherein the numbers represent intervals from the tonic, undergoing transmutation in a jazzified scherzo until the theme of the Atomic Energy Commission ominously cautions the operators to keep the reactor under control, is performed for the first time at Oak Ridge, Tennessee, the atomic research center. (The score itself was designated as not musically or atomically classified and conveying no secret diatonic, pandiatonic or dodecaphonic information)

### 20 MARCH 1952

*Second Symphony* by the 53-year-old Russian composer Alexander TCHEREPNIN, in four movements, written in 1945–1951 as a musical memorial of his father Nicolas Tcherepnin who died in Paris in 1945, is performed for the first time by the Chicago Symphony Orchestra, Rafael Kubelik conducting.

### 22 MARCH 1952

To mark the centennial of the birth of the notable Bohemian violinist and famous teacher, Ottakar ŠEVČÍK, the Czechoslovak government issues postage stamps for 2 and 3 kronen.

### 25 MARCH 1952

*Leonore 40/45*, opera in two acts and eight scenes by the Swiss composer Rolf LIEBERMANN, to a libretto drawn from the true story of a love affair between a German soldier and a French girl during the Nazi occupation of Paris and their separation after the liberation in August 1944 (the title alludes to the crucial years 1940–1945, and the name Leonore connotes fidelity, as in Beethoven's opera *Fidelio*), is performed for the first time in Basel.

## 26 MARCH 1952

To mark the 125th anniversary of BEETHOVEN's death, both West Germany and East Germany issue a series of stamps with his portrait.

## 27 MARCH 1952

The world première of the ballet *Chemin de Lumière* by Georges AURIC, to an existentialist human scenario in which love triumphs over death, in a symbolic setting designated as "somewhere in the world," is given in Munich.

## 28 MARCH 1952

*Walt Whitman,* symphonic essay by Paul CRESTON, is performed for the first time in Cincinnati.

## 30 MARCH 1952

*Don Perlimplin,* one-act opera by the 54-year-old Italian composer Vittorio RIETI, making his home in America, after the poem by Francisco García Lorca, is performed for the first time at the University of Illinois in Urbana.

## 1 APRIL 1952

*Atlanta,* symphonic suite by the American composer and arranger Don GILLIS, in six topographical movements descriptive of the historic landmarks of Atlanta, Georgia, is performed for the first time by the Atlanta Symphony Orchestra.

## 3 APRIL 1952

*Wat Tyler,* socio-historical opera by the left-wing member of the British Labour Party Alan BUSH, glorifying the leader of the peasant uprising in England in 1381, set to music steeped in English folk rhythms, is performed for the first time in a broadcast production in East Berlin.

## 3 APRIL 1952

Cemal REŞID REY, Turkish composer, conducts in Paris the first performance of his symphonic poem *L'Appel.*

## 5 APRIL 1952

*Inês Pereira,* opera by the Portuguese composer Ruy COELHO, is produced in Lisbon.

## 13 APRIL 1952

Morton GOULD conducts the United States Military Academy Band at West Point in the world première of his *Fourth Symphony,* written for the sesquicentennial of West Point, in two movements, *Epitaphs,* an elegiac fantasy about absent femininity, and *Marches,* a virile fanfaronade, hoisting a brassy oriflamme in the Army regulation time of 132 steps a minute, metronomed by a "marching machine."

The Brazilian Government issues a postage stamp of 60 milreis to mark the centennial of the birth of the Brizilian composer Henrique OSWALD.

*Fifth Symphony* in A minor by the dean of Swedish composers Hugo ALFVÉN is performed for the first time in Stockholm.

*Water Music* by the leader of the musical avant-garde John CAGE, scored for a pianist, who also uses a radio, whistles, water containers and a deck of cards, with thematic elements drawn from I-Ching, a Chinese book of oracles, is performed for the first time by David Tudor in New York.

Unlike Handel's, it actually splashes. (From a letter of invitation to the author to attend a performance of *Water Music*)

During a televised tour of the White House, President TRUMAN, acting as an amiable guide, obligingly plays a few bars from MOZART's *Ninth Sonata in A major* on the Steinway piano (installed in the White House on 11 December 1938), then goes over to the second piano (a Baldwin) to improvise a series of harmonious chords (boldly modulating from C major to D-flat major) adding for color, a series of chromatically ascending diminished seventh-chords.

*Romance* in D flat for harmonica, string orchestra and piano by Ralph VAUGHAN WILLIAMS, in three contrasting movements, is performed for the first time by the American mouth harmonica virtuoso Larry Adler with the Little Symphony Orchestra in New York. (The first English performance of the *Romance* took place in Liverpool on 16 June 1952)

*Ritmo Jondo* for clarinet, trumpet, xylophone, and percussion by the Catalan-American composer Carlos SURINACH, based on *Canto flamenco* rhythms, is performed for the first time in New York. (An extended version, in ballet form, was produced in New York under the title *Deep Rhythm* on 15 April 1953)

President Theodor Heuss of West Germany sanctions the restoration of the HAYDN melody of the Emperor's Hymn, used during the pan-Germanic period from Wilhelm II to Hitler as the vehicle of the geophagous anthem *Deutschland über alles* (it was originally written by Professor August Hoffmann von Fallersleben about 1840, with the intended meaning *Germany before all else*, rather than the imperialistic *Germany above all*, and expressing a patriotic feeling for the unification of individual German states), to a revised text eliminating the ambiguous words.

### 6 MAY 1952

The Boston Symphony Orchestra makes its first appearance abroad, with Charles Munch conducting it at the opening concert of the Paris Festival of 20th-century Music, sponsored by the Congress for Cultural Freedom, in a program listing DEBUSSY's *La Mer*, RAVEL's *Daphnis et Chloé* (second suite), HONEGGER's *Second Symphony*, Samuel BARBER's mellifluously neo-classical *Overture to the School for Scandal*, and the tersely contrapuntal *Toccata* by Walter PISTON.

### 7 MAY 1952

*Cordélia*, ballet by Henri SAUGUET, to the story of a little girl's daylight nightmare in which she is pursued by a man with a whip and a woman with a cudgel, is performed for the first time at the Paris Festival of 20th-century Music, on the same program with the première of a ballet by Georges AURIC, *Coup de feu*, in which two lovers literally set each others' hearts on fire which rages until a torrential rain extinguishes them, and the lovers return to a life of controlled amours.

### 7 MAY 1952

*Acres of Sky*, ballad opera by the 45-year-old American composer Arthur KREUTZ, dealing with subnormal rural family life in Arkansas, set to music in a sophisticatedly simplicistic ballad manner, is performed for the first time at Columbia University in New York.

### 11 MAY 1952

*The Revelation of the Fifth Seal*, apocalyptic symphonic poem by the Greek composer Yorgo SICILIANOS, is performed for the first time in Athens.

### 13 MAY 1952

*Cantata from Proverbs* by Darius MILHAUD, scored for women's chorus, oboe, cello and harp, in three movements (1) *Who crieth "Woe"?* an emotional exortation against the use of stimulants, dramatically underlined by the warning "Thine eyes shall behold strange things" (2) *The Woman Folly*, a pandiatonic portrait of females circa 1,000 B.C. (3) *A Woman of Valor*, extolling the virtues of a righteous and submissive housewife in orthodox society, is performed for the first time by the United Temple Chorus of Lawrence, Long Island, Isadore Freed conducting.

15 MAY 1952

Italo MONTEMEZZI, Italian composer of operas, among which *L'Amore dei tre re* became a perennial favorite, dies in Vigasio at the age of seventy-six.

18 MAY 1952

*Mila Gojsalića*, opera by the Croatian composer Jakov GOTOVAC, is performed for the first time in Zagreb.

18 MAY 1952

KING FREDERICK of Denmark, an amateur musician and pupil in conducting of Nikolai Malko, conducts the Danish State Radio Orchestra in an adequate performance of the *Second Symphony* by Sibelius, deferentially helped along by his faithful subjects in the orchestra, whenever he falters in beating time.

19 MAY 1952

Josef Matthias HAUER, the bearded Viennese prophet of 12-tone music, makes public in Vienna his *Zwölftonspiel-Manifest*, proclaiming, with a defiant display of unsophrosyne hubris, his priority and supremacy as the only begetter of 12-tone music, "der geistiger Urheber und trotz vielen schlechten Nachahmern immer noch der einziger Kenner und Könner der Zwölftonmusik."

The Builder of the Universe created Absolute Music in final fulfillment, once and for all. We, sons of men, have endeavored for eons of time to learn this divine primordial language. *Zwölftonspiel* regulates the physiological premises of pure intuition which alone enables us to perceive immutable Absolute Music as the revelation of the world order in all eternity. Tones with their overtones are suns with their planets. Solar systems temper one another. Their intervals are ordered with cogent necessity in the Harmony of the Spheres. *Zwölftonspiel* performs the functions of galaxies and constitutes the formative dynamic centers of organic processes. The language of the Builder of the Universe, with its 479,001,600 vocables, the Art of the Arts, the Science of Sciences, the Most Holy, the Most Spiritual, the Most Exalted in the world, is Music. But this Music must be distinguished from mere music-mongering, such as tone-paintings and symphonic poems, and suchlike "new" modern cultural dung heaps. Absolute Music is the link with Eternity, Religion, Spiritual Reality, different from various parochial denominations, philosophical systems and political ideologies. Music is of prime importance in directing the people along the right path. . . . You, 12-tone ignoramuses, learn the Tropes! (Text of Hauer's manifesto, translated from Hermann Progner's book *Die Zwölfordnung der Töne*, Vienna, 1953, pp. 231–232)

23 MAY 1952

On the 80th anniversary of his first public appearance as a child prodigy, Gustave L. BECKER, 91-year-old American pianist and composer presents at Steinway Hall in New York a concert in a program including Beethoven's *Appas-*

*sionata,* Chopin's *Polonaise* in A-flat, and five innocuous pieces by Becker himself: *Fugue* in G major, *Gavotte-Humoresque, Étude mélodique, Rondo-Scherzino* and *Flight of the Swallows.*

### 24 MAY 1952

*Defender of the Peace,* pacifist symphonic essay by the English composer Alan BUSH, is performed for the first time on the Vienna Radio.

### 26 MAY 1952

*Second Piano Concerto* by the 50-year-old Belgian composer Raymond CHEVREUILLE, is performed for the first time in Brussels.

### 30 MAY 1952

On the occasion of its sesquicentennial, the United States Military Academy Band, assisted by the Dialectic Society of the Corps of Cadets, presents at West Point, New York, a program of specially commissioned works for band, including *Fantasy* by Henry COWELL, derived in its thematic contents from separate segments of the Alma Mater melody; *West Point Suite* in three movements by Darius MILHAUD; and *Symphony in One Movement* for wind instruments by Roy HARRIS, expressive of the "idealism which has motivated the fighting men of our nation" and ending with a fugal dance.

### 2 JUNE 1952

*Aucassin et Nicolette,* marionette play by Mario CASTELNUOVO-TEDESCO, to the story of the medieval love of Aucassin, a nobleman, for the Saracen girl Nicolette captured during a Crusade, who is revealed as daughter of the King of Carthage, scored for soprano and 11 instruments, with a mimodrama enacted by marionettes on the stage, is performed for the first time, 14 years after its composition, at the Festival Maggio fiorentino, in Florence.

### 4 JUNE 1952

*Travesti,* comic ballet by the French composer Marcel DELANNOY is performed for the first time at Enghien-les-Bains.

### 7 JUNE 1952

*Merlijn,* symphonic drama in three scenes by Willem PIJPER, left unfinished after his death (only six episodes were completed, corresponding to six of the twelve signs of the Zodiac), inspired by the magician Merlin of King Arthur's legend, is performed posthumously for the first time in Rotterdam.

### 12 JUNE 1952

At the opening of the Festival of Creative Arts at Brandeis University in Waltham, Massachusetts, Leonard BERNSTEIN conducts the world première of his one-act opera *Trouble in Tahiti,* written in a modernistically titivated jazz idiom, to his own libretto descriptive of a marital collision in a suburban American home with mutual recriminations appeased when the married couple attends a motion picture depicting the delights of simple life on the pacific Pacific Island of Tahiti.

### 14 JUNE 1952

An Americanized version of Kurt WEILL's *Dreigroschenoper* set in a slangy dialogue by Marc Blitzstein, under the title *The Three-penny Opera*, is given in a world première, on the same program with a ballet, *Symphonie pour un homme seul*, acoustically compiled by the creator of "musique concrète" Pierre SCHAEFFER, at the Festival of Creative Arts at Brandeis University.

### 14 JUNE 1952

A nine-day festival of choral music opens at Aldeburgh, England, with Benjamin BRITTEN conducting a visiting Boys' Choir from Copenhagen in his *Ceremony of Carols,* and presenting modern arrangements of 18th-century music made by the 25-year-old Englishman Arthur Oldham, France's "jeune Français" Jean Françaix and others.

### 16 JUNE 1952

The German pianist Heinz ARNTZ sets a world record of continuous piano playing in a Düsseldorf restaurant by completing a keyboard marathon of 224 hours, allowing a minimal amount of time each day for dormition, micturition, defecation and ingestion of food.

### 17 JUNE 1952

Alberto WILLIAMS, cultured and prolific Argentinian composer (his grandfather was an Englishman), a student of César Franck in Paris, who upon return to Argentina made Buenos Aires a veritable Conservatoriopolis by opening several music schools there, writing nine romantic symphonies and hundreds of piano pieces inspired by Argentinian melorhythms, and publishing them all in his own publishing house, dies in his native city of Buenos Aires in his 90th year.

### 20 JUNE 1952

The 26th Festival of the International Society for Contemporary Music opens in Salzburg (where it was founded in 1923) in a program of orchestral works by German composers:

*Symphony* in three movements by Wolfgang FORTNER, in a neo-baroque style with tangential atonalities, conducted by the composer; *Fifth Symphony* by Karl Amadeus HARTMANN, in three movements of neo-classical inspiration; a *Choral Fantasy* by the 47-year-old Schoenberg disciple Winfried ZILLIG, written in a determined dodecaphonic technique; *Allegria,* by the 51-year-old German composer Werner EGK, in the form of a classical suite, conducted by the composer.

20 JUNE 1952

Paul HINDEMITH conducts in Zürich a revised version of his opera *Cardillac*, with a completely revised libretto drawn from E. T. A. Hoffman's story *Madame de Scuderi*, containing new episodes, including the insertion of a Lully opera segment, expertly Hindemithized in scoring and harmonization.

21 JUNE 1952

At the second concert of the 26th Festival of the International Society for Contemporary Music in Salzburg, the following works are presented:

*Sixth Symphony* by the Swiss neo-classicist Conrad BECK, in five movements, of which two pairs are linked reducing the whole to three larger movements; *Phantasie* for clarinet, piano and orchestra by the Vienna dodecaphonist Hanns JELINEK, paying homage to classicism by including the B-A-C-H motive in the introduction and at the conclusion; *Mythological Figurines* by the 49-year-old German composer Rudolf WAGNER-RÉGENY, in three sections, *Ceres, Amphitrite,* and *Diana*, designed in a free dodecaphonic idiom in variable meters, intended to unify archaic modes, asymmetric rhythms and euphonious dissonances; tripartite *Concertino* for oboe, bassoon and orchestra by the Vienna-born 47-year-old composer Paul CSONKA, introduced as a representative of Cuba, whither he emigrated in 1938, after the Austrian Anschluss; and *Three Pieces for Orchestra* by the 37-year-old Belgian composer Marcel QUINET, written in an eclectic neo-romantic vein daubed with impressionistic colors.

22 JUNE 1952

A concert of music by Arnold SCHOENBERG is given as part of the 26th Festival of the International Society for Contemporary Music in Salzburg, presenting his *Five Orchestra Pieces*, the monodrama *Erwartung* and *Variations for Orchestra*.

23 JUNE 1952

The following program of chamber music is presented at the 26th Festival of the International Society for Contemporary Music in Salzburg:

*Violin Sonata* by the Posen-born 41-year-old Israeli composer Josef TAL, based on Jewish melodies; *Three Invocations* for voice and piano by the Rumanian-born 32-year-old Italian composer Roman VLAD, couched in a neo-ecclesiastical modal idiom; *Sonata* for clarinet and violoncello by the 41-year-old British composeress Phyllis TATE, set in a pleasantly feminine neo-classic manner; *Variations* for piano by the 39-year-old Chilean composer Alfonso LETELIER; *Duo* for violin and violoncello by the 28-year-old Australian composer Don BANKS, written in a motoric modernistic style; *Sonata* for trumpet and piano by the 51-year-old Icelandic composer Karl Otto RUNOLFSSON, in a candidly classical idiom; and *String Quartet* by the 42-year-old French composer Jean MARTINON, set in the classical matrix with impressionistic discursions.

24 JUNE 1952

The following program is presented at the 26th Festival of the International Society for Contemporary Music in Salzburg:

*Canto de amor e paz* by the 32-year-old former dodecaphonist Claudio SANTORO of Brazil, couched in an Italianate neo-romantic manner; *Sextet* for wind instruments by the 45-year-old Finnish composer Nils Erik RINGBOM, in three movements disposed in an academic form, with fugal developments and concatenated variations; *Poem* for 22 string instruments by the 36-year-old British composer Humphrey SEARLE, written in a vertically-horizontal dodecaphonic manner, with the thematic 12-note chords melodically terraced in the development; *Piano Concerto* by the 45-year-old Norwegian composer Klaus EGGE, in a single compact movement with the accompaniment of string instruments only, couched in the form of seven variations on a folk-like Norwegian theme; *Variations* for wind instruments by the 44-year-old Swiss composer Edward STAEMPFLI, in a free dodecaphonic style in which the seventh and last variation is the mirror of the first; and *Sinfonia serena* for string instruments and kettledrums by the 55-year-old Danish composer Knudaage RIISAGER, in four movements of neo-classical inspiration.

## 24 JUNE 1952

Lodewijk MORTELMANS, Belgian composer, whose congenital Wagnerophilia did not deter him from viable utilization of folk music and lyric settings of Flemish poems, dies in his native city of Antwerp, at the age of eighty-four.

## 25 JUNE 1952

*Third Symphony* by the half-a-century-old Belgian composer Raymond CHEVREUILLE, is performed for the first time in Brussels.

## 25 JUNE 1952

The following program of chamber music is presented at the 26th Festival of the International Society for Contemporary Music in Salzburg:

*Piano Sonata* by the 34-year-old Sumatra-born naturalized American composer Claus ADAM; *Music* for clarinet, trumpet and viola by the 36-year-old Hungarian-born Viennese composer Karl SCHISKE, in a cosmopolitan neo-classical idiom; *Theme and Variations* for two violins, an essay in double counterpoint by the 29-year-old New Zealander Ronald TREMAIN; *Three Religious Chants* for soprano and string trio by the 22-year-old Belgian composer Henri POUSSEUR, to Latin texts in ecclesiastical modes encased in a dodecaphonic matrix; *Sonata* for unaccompanied violin by the 53-year-old Parisianized Rumanian composer Marcel MIHALOVICI, in four brief divisions in a neo-classical mold; *Three Piano Pieces* by the 29-year-old South African composer Stefans GROVÉ, in a neo-classical idiom; *Duo* for flute and harp by the 32-year-old Dutch composer Lex van DELDEN, in three classically-inspired sections; and *String Trio* by the 37-year-old Austrian-born Argentinian composer Guillermo GRAETZER.

## 26 JUNE 1952

At the 26th Festival of the International Society for Contemporary Music in Salzburg, the following program of orchestral music is presented:

*Symphony* in C major by the 53-year-old Hungarian-born Parisian composer Tibor HARSÁNYI, written in a cosmopolitan classical style; *Violin Concerto* by the 34-year-old German composer Bernd Alois ZIMMERMANN, in the spiritual manner of instrumental classicism with the thematic interpolation of *Dies Irae* in the middle movement; *Piano Concerto* by the Italian composer Mario PERAGALLO, classical in form and modernistically atonal in content; and *Le Soleil des Eaux* for voices and orchestra by the 27-year-old French radical composer Pierre BOULEZ, conceived in an agglutinatory motivic manner, in which each phrase is split into sections consecutively sung or played by different voices or instruments.

### 28 JUNE 1952

While conducting the third of the *Three Little Orchestra Pieces* by Wilhelm Heubner in a program of modern Austrian music at the 26th Festival of the International Society for Contemporary Music in Salzburg, Herbert HAEFNER, 46-year-old Austrian conductor collapses and dies on the podium.

(The scheduled program included a *Suite* for two flutes and string orchestra by Georg GRUBER, *Piano Concerto* by Cesar BRESGEN, *Three Little Orchestra Pieces* by Wilhelm HUEBNER, *Violin Concerto* by S. C. ECKHARDT-GRAMATTE, and *Hymn* for chorus, alto solo and orchestra by Gottfried von EINEM; the concert was interrupted after Haefner's dramatic death, and the last two works of the program remained unperformed)

### 29 JUNE 1952

The 26th International Society for Contemporary Music Festival in Salzburg concludes with a concert of orchestral music in the following program:

*Symphonic Antithesis* by the 55-year-old Yugoslav composer Matija BRAVNIČAR (first heard in Ljubljana on 9 February 1948) based on two antithetical concepts, sacred and profane, in native folk music, set in canonic and fugal forms with variations; *Theme and Variations* by the 45-year-old Japanese composer Yoritsune MATSUDAIRA, derived from old Japanese modes, and varying in melodic content from pentatonicism to dodecaphony, and in rhythm from asymmetrical Japanese meters to syncopated patterns of jazz and boogie-woogie; *Hymns to Beauty* for chorus and orchestra by the 32-year-old Swedish composer Göte CARLID, to Baudelaire's poems on the subject of debilitude of man, set to music of impressionistic colors; *Violin Concerto* by the 37-year-old Dutch composer Marius FLOTHUIS, in three parts, in a neo-classical vein; and *Canzoni* by the 60-year-old Italian composer Giorgio Federico GHEDINI, a neo-Renaissance essay in old Italian forms.

### 11 JULY 1952

A three-day Festival of national Swiss music opens at St. Gall, featuring concerts on long Alpine horns, and a yodeling contest with 2800 participants, 95 of them receiving silver buttons for excellence.

### 22 JULY 1952

*Tankred und Cantylene*, ballet by the 26-year-old German composer Hans Werner HENZE, is performed for the first time in Munich.

### 22 JULY 1952

*Pas de cœur*, ballet by the Austrian composer Gottfried von EINEM, is produced in Munich.

## 22 JULY 1952

*Don Fortunio,* one-act opera by the American composer Hamilton FORREST, is produced at Interlochen, Michigan.

## 27 JULY 1952

*Uvertura bohaterska (Heroic Overture)* by the 37-year-old Polish composer Andrzej PANUFNIK, written in an optimistic, socialist realistic style, with brass and drums accentuating the import of the theme, and ending on the heroic chord of E flat major, consanguine to the key of Beethoven's *Eroica,* is performed for the first time during the International Olympic Games in Helsinki, conducted by the composer.

## 9 AUGUST 1952

Hugo WEISGALL, Bohemian-born 39-year-old American composer, conducts in Westport, Connecticut, the first performance of his one-act opera *The Stronger,* after Strindberg's play in which a provincial matron taunts a former matrimonial rival about her inability to find a husband, while the other silently fixes her gaze on the audience with a meaningful smile suggesting that she is the stronger one, set to music in an expressionistically atonal idiom with jazzy interpolations illustrating the surrealistic mysteries of life.

## 13 AUGUST 1952

*The Farmer and the Fairy,* whimsical opera by Alexander TCHEREPNIN, dealing with a preternaturally promiscuous female whiling away twenty years of human cohabitation with a terrestrial farmer before returning to the phantom world, with the pentatonic scale used to express the simplicity of the tale, is performed for the first time at the Music Festival in Aspen, Colorado.

## 14 AUGUST 1952

*Die Liebe der Danae,* opera in three acts by Richard STRAUSS, portraying in a "psychological counterpoint" the Milesian tale of a concupiscent Zeus who descends upon the virginal Danaë in the form of a rain of gold, is produced posthumously in Salzburg.

(Strauss completed the score on 28 June 1940; the opera was initially scheduled for performance in Salzburg in August 1944, and the final rehearsal took place on 16 August 1944, when the Nazis closed all German and Austrian theaters.)

## 18 AUGUST 1952

Henry EXPERT, expert French music scholar, who spent much of his life editing and publishing French and Flemish music of the 15th and 16th centuries, dies in Tourettes-sur-Loup in the Alpes-Maritimes, in his 90th year.

## 19 AUGUST 1952

*Estancia,* ballet by the prime modern composer of Argentina, Alberto GINASTERA, illustrating a day spent on a farm in the pampas, set to music in

vivid subtropical colors, is performed for the first time in its entirety in Buenos Aires.

## 29 AUGUST 1952

*4' 33"* by John CAGE, for piano, two pianos, or any instrument, or any combination of instruments, in three movements *tacet*, with no sounds intentionally
produced, the length of time for each non-performed and unheard movement
determined by chance, is unplayed on the piano by his loyal famulus David
Tudor, at Maverick Concert Hall in Woodstock, New York.

The difficulty to judge John Cage's *4' 33"* is that it is impossible to tell what music has
*not* been played. (From an unidentified newspaper report of a New York non-perform-
ance of *4' 33"* of 14 April 1956)

## 1 SEPTEMBER 1952

*Der Idiot*, ballet-pantomime after Dostoyevsky, by the 26-year-old German
composer Hans Werner HENZE, is performed for the first time in Berlin.

## 14 SEPTEMBER 1952

*Concerto* for harpsichord and orchestra by the prime Swiss modernist Frank
MARTIN is performed for the first time at the International Festival of Contemporary Music in Venice.

## 15 SEPTEMBER 1952

*Second Piano Concerto* by the Manchurian-born half-Estonian half-German
composer Boris BLACHER, in three movements, based on the concept of form-
rhythm, so that metric formulas based on the arithmetic progressions (e.g.
1,2,3,4,5,4,3,2,1,), and summation series (1,2,3,5,8,13, etc.) determine the melodic and rhythmic pattern, is performed for the first time in Berlin.

## 17 SEPTEMBER 1952

*Die Witwe von Ephesus*, one-act chamber opera by the 44-year-old German
composer Wolfgang FORTNER, is performed for the first time in Berlin.

## 23 SEPTEMBER 1952

*Preussisches Märchen*, ballet-opera by Boris BLACHER, after a famous play
*Captain of Koepenick*, wherein a humble and frustrated government clerk
successfully impersonates a captain of the guard and arrests the mayor of his
home town for corruption, set to music in an appropriately comic, harmonically crude manner, with military rhythms subjected to asymmetrical dislocation, is performed for the first time at the Municipal Opera in West Berlin as
part of a month-long Music Festival.

## 4 OCTOBER 1952

*Noctambulation* for orchestra by the 26-year-old American composer Lee
HOIBY is performed for the first time in New York.

## 11 OCTOBER 1952

*Seventh Smphony* by Sergei PROKOFIEV, in C sharp minor, his last (completed on 5 July 1952), stylistically summarizing the entire course of his musical esthetics, declaratively lucid, ironically optimistic, tonally firm despite constant modulatory translocations, animated by irresistible rhythms, and humanized by pervasive lyric sentiment, in four classically designed movements: *Moderato, Allegretto, Andante expressivo* and *Vivace*, with an expansive, very Russian finale, is performed for the first time in Moscow.

Prokofiev's *Seventh Symphony* is full of joy of life, lyricism. It arouses admiration by its lucid and luminous material and its uncommonly fresh harmonic language. (Dmitri Shostakovich, in *Sovietskaye Iskusstvo,* Moscow, 12 November 1952)

## 11 OCTOBER 1952

The Danish State Symphony Orchestra arrives in New York for an American tour of 38 concerts.

## 15 OCTOBER 1952

*Symphonic Etude* by the 60-year-old Dutch composer Hendrik ANDRIESSEN, in four movements based on a 12-tone series consisting of converging groups of chromatic intervals, is performed for the first time by The Hague Philharmonic Orchestra, Willem van Otterloo conducting.

## 18 OCTOBER 1952

The French Government issues two stamps, for 4 francs and 15 francs, in honor of Camille SAINT-SAËNS.

## 20 OCTOBER 1952

*Concertato for Orchestra* by the 29-year-old American composer Peter MENNIN (né Mennini), subtitled *Moby Dick* (its musical materials were to form the skeleton of an inchoate cetacean opera inspired by Melville's famous novel), is performed for the first time in the town of Mennin's birth, Erie, Pennsylvania.

## 20 OCTOBER 1952

Erik CHISHOLM, 48-year-old Scottish composer, conducts at the University of Capetown, South Africa, the first performance of his monodrama *Dark Sonnet*, in 14 sections, corresponding to the 14 lines of a sonnet, to the scenario suggested by Eugene O'Neill's playlet *Before Breakfast*, in which a nagging housewife drives her adulterous poet-husband to suicide (he cuts his throat, while shaving, in the 14th movement), scored for two pianos and chamber orchestra and written in highly dissonant harmonies.

## 22 OCTOBER 1952

*Lord Inferno,* "harmonious comedy" in one act by the 60-year-old Italian composer Giorgio Federico GHEDINI, to a libretto after *The Happy Hypocrite* of Max Beerbohm, is performed for the first time in concert form over the Italian Radio. (A stage production of the opera was first given by La Scala in Milan on 10 March 1956, under a more precisely translated title *L'Ipocrita felice*)

## 26 OCTOBER 1952

Richard COBURN (whose real name was Frank De Long), American song writer who wrote the hit tune *Whispering*, dies in Los Angeles at the age of sixty-six.

## 27 OCTOBER 1952

*My Darlin' Aida*, musical play by Charles FRIEDMAN, in which Aida is transferred from Memphis, Egypt, to Memphis, Tennessee, A.D. 1861, and becomes a Negro slave, while Radames, whose name is transmogrified into Raymond Demarest, is reincarnated as a dashing confederate officer, with the famous aria *Celeste Aida* colloquially rendered "My Darlin' Aida," is produced in New York.

## 2 NOVEMBER 1952

*Ein Sommernachtstraum*, musical play after Shakespeare's *A Midsummer Night's Dream*, by Carl ORFF, is performed for the first time in Darmstadt.

## 4 NOVEMBER 1952

*Jadranski Kapričo* (*Adriatic Capriccio*) for violin and orchestra by the Croatian composer Petar KONJOVIĆ, in three movements making use of euphonious Dalmation folk melodies, is performed for the first time in Belgrade.

## 5 NOVEMBER 1952

*Cagliostro*, radiophonic drama in four acts by Ildebrando PIZZETTI, to his own libretto depicting in resonantly eloquent tonalities the adventures of the famous Sicilian charlatan who captivated the court of Marie Antoinette, is produced by the Italian Radio. (The first stage performance as an opera was given at La Scala, Milan, on 24 January 1953)

## 7 NOVEMBER 1952

*Dolores*, "roman musical" in three acts by Michel-Maurice LÉVY (who gained popularity as a comic artist "Betove," i.e. Beethoven), is produced at the Opéra-Comique in Paris.

## 9 NOVEMBER 1952

*Capitaine Bruno*, comic opera by the Swiss composer Pierre WISSMER, is performed for the first time in Geneva.

## 11 NOVEMBER 1952

Igor STRAVINSKY conducts in Los Angeles the world première of his *Cantata* for soprano, tenor, female chorus and five instruments, to the texts of four anonymous English poems of the 15th and 16th centuries, artfully set in a gentle archaizing manner, in a melodically modal and harmonically pandiatonic idiom, interspersed in its interstices with a multiplicity of canonic devices including the cancrizans heretofore shunned by Stravinsky.

### 16 NOVEMBER 1952

Morton GOULD conducts in Rochester, New York, the first performance of his *Concerto for Tap Dancer and Orchestra,* in four movements, *Toccata, Pantomime, Minuet* and *Rondo,* with pedal percussion of the solo tap dancer on a resonant floorboard, variegated by shoe shuffling and heel glissando.

### 16 NOVEMBER 1952

*20th Century Folk Mass* ("Jazz Mass") for cantor and congregation by the Rev. Geoffrey BEAUMONT, M.A., M.B.E., Vicar and Warden of Trinity College Mission, Cambridge, England, based on mundanely American jazz rhythms (the composer warns expressly against "ecclesiasticising" his unchurchly hymns), is performed for the first time at St. Luke's Church, Chesterton, Cambridge, as part of a Sunday service.

### 20 NOVEMBER 1952

*Gilgamesj,* opera by Ture RANGSTRÖM (1884–1947), Swedish composer of somberly turbulent romantic music (left incomplete at his death and orchestrated by John Fernström), based on the Babylonian epic of King Gilgamesh's quest in the world of the dead for his dearest enemy Enkidu, a lion-muscled man tamed by a lithesome temple maiden, is produced in Stockholm.

### 20 NOVEMBER 1952

The first version of the *Seventh Symphony* by Roy HARRIS, in a single movement, constituting a passacaglia with five variations couched in a clear tonal idiom with polyharmonic extensions, is performed for the first time by the Chicago Symphony Orchestra, Rafael Kubelik conducting. (A new and more compact version eliminating some of the complexities of the original, was first performed on 15 September 1955 by the Philadelphia Orchestra, Eugene Ormandy conducting, in Copenhagen, during its European tour)

### 20 NOVEMBER 1952

Francis POULENC plays the solo piano part in the first performance of his *Aubade,* "concerto choréographique," at the Opéra-Comique in Paris.

### 22 NOVEMBER 1952

The Government of the Federal German Republic issues a stamp for 4 marks in honor of Carl Friedrich ZELTER (1758–1832), the master of the Lied.

## 25 NOVEMBER 1952

*Seventh Symphony* for chamber orchestra by Henry Cowell, in four movements, is performed for the first time in Baltimore.

## 5 DECEMBER 1952

The Polish Government issues a series of stamps at 45 and 60 groschen commemorating the romantic Polish violinist and composer Henryk Wieniawski.

## 5 DECEMBER 1952

*Violin Concerto* by Gian Carlo Menotti is performed for the first time by Efrem Zimbalist and the Philadelphia Orchestra.

## 10 DECEMBER 1952

*Sea Piece with Birds* for orchestra by Virgil Thomson, a portrait of "the undertow of the sea, the surface tension of waves, and the flight of birds as they sail back and forth," with trumpet calls imitating the cries of seagulls, engulfed in a sea of whole-tone scales and mutually exclusive augmented triads, is performed for the first time in Dallas.

## 11 DECEMBER 1952

For the first time in history, a regularly scheduled opera performance is televised on the screens of 31 movie houses in 27 cities in the United States, when the Metropolitan Opera broadcasts the complete performance of *Carmen* over a closed television circuit not yet reachable in private homes.

## 12 DECEMBER 1952

*Second Symphony* by the Swedish modernist Karl-Birger Blomdahl is performed for the first time in Stockholm.

## 14 DECEMBER 1952

Fartein Valen, Norwegian composer of symphonies, symphonic poems and other works written in a highly individual manner, employing a dissonant idiom of atonal polyphony, and yet redolent of characteristically Scandinavian romanticism, dies at Haugesund at the age of sixty-five.

## 23 DECEMBER 1952

*Second Symphony*, subtitled *Victory,* by the American composer Harold Morris is performed for the first time in Chicago.

## 25 DECEMBER 1952

Bernardino Molinari, Italian conductor who brought out many works by modern Italian composers, including Respighi and Malipiero, dies in his native city Rome at the age of seventy-two.

## 28 DECEMBER 1952

Pope Pius XII attends, for the first time as Pontiff, a concert at the Vatican to hear the 80-year-old Master of the Pope's music Lorenzo PEROSI conduct his oratorio *Il Natale del Redentore* (The Birth of the Redeemer), first performed in Como on 12 September 1899.

# ᘿ *1953* ᘾ

## 1 JANUARY 1953

*Suite Hebraïque* for viola and orchestra by Ernest BLOCH is performed for the first time by the Chicago Symphony Orchestra, Rafael Kubelik conducting.

## 1 JANUARY 1953

THREE MEN'S CLUB to promote modern music is organized in Tokyo.

By intimate contact with each other, the three men of the Club, Ikuma DAN, Yasuki AKUTAGAWA and Toshiro MAYUZUMI, different in tendencies, try to stimulate each other into fuller fruition in their objectives. The three men are in honor bound to act in unison against the present-day commercialism. (From the statute of the Three Men's Club.)

## 7 JANUARY 1953

*Symphony for 42 String Instruments* by the 27-year-old German composer Gishelher KLEBE is performed for the first time in Hamburg.

## 9 JANUARY 1953

*Volpone,* opera in three acts by George ANTHEIL, freely adapted from the famous play of Ben Jonson dealing with a foxy old man who deludes his expectant heirs, is performed for the first time at the University of Southern California, Los Angeles.

## 14 JANUARY 1953

Sir John Barbirolli conducts the Hallé Orchestra in Manchester in the world première of *Seventh Symphony,* subtitled *Sinfonia Antartica,* by Ralph VAUGHAN WILLIAMS, derived from his music for the film *Scott of the Antarctic,* which opened in London on 30 December 1948, as an homage to Sir Robert Scott who perished with his group of Antarctic explorers on his return from the South Pole in 1912, in five movements:

(1) *Prelude (Andante Maestoso),* bearing a motto from Shelley's *Prometheus Unbound,* moving in stately progressions of alternating whole-tones and semitones harmonized

by unrelated major and minor triads and, after a chromatic constriction, rarefied into pentatonic patterns, projecting ominous wordless voices and pouring cascades of purlingly pearly tintinnabulations on the celesta and Glockenspiel; crashing into fortississimo, and concluding on a congealed oblique cadence (2) *Scherzo (Moderato)*, in pendulously barcarolling lolling rhythms in pentatonic and hexatonic scale patterns with shifting dominants and yet gravitationally tonal, ending in pianississississimo (3) *Landscape (Lento)*, with a motto from Coleridge's *Hymn Before Sunrise*, pictorializing the "motionless torrents" and "silent cataracts" in glacial triadic harmonies, static unisons and tritone-bound scales, ending on a tremulous cymbal receding into inaudibility (4) *Intermezzo (Andante sostenuto)* in an oscillating major and minor tonalities with hymnal tunes made austere by frigid Phrygian modalities (5) *Epilogue (Alla marcia moderato)*, with a motto from Captain Scott's last entry in his journal, in which he noted, before his frozen death, his serene acceptance of it, testified by brave trumpet calls in boldly ascending perfect fourths, and, as the gelid respiration of the Antarctic blizzard is registered in the accelerating turns of the wind machine, the wordless chorus intones its crying cryogenic semitones and the music freezes on a glacier-like minor sixth, in soundless *niente*.

### 17 JANUARY 1953

*La Capanna dello zio Tom*, opera in three acts by the Italian composer Luigi FERRARI-TRECATE, freely adapted from the famous abolitionist novel of Harriet Beecher Stowe, depicting the piteous state of Negro slaves in ante-bellum Kentucky, wherein the malevolent Signor Legree roars in impervious basso profundo and Zio Tom expatiates in tenor bel canto, is produced in Parma.

### 18 JANUARY 1953

The scheduled performance of Aaron COPLAND's *Lincoln Portrait* at the concert by the National Symphony in Washington for Eisenhower's inauguration as President, is cancelled at the instigation of Congressman Fred E. Busbey, Republican of Illinois, on the ground of Copland's alleged association with subversive political organizations.

There are many patriotic composers available without the long record of questionable affiliations of Copland. The Republican Party would have been ridiculed from one end of the United States to the other if Copland's music had been played at the inaugural of a President elected to fight Communism, among other things. (From Busbey's statement)

No American composer, living or dead has done more for American music and the growth of the reputation of American culture throughout the civilized world than Aaron Copland. To bar from the Inaugural Concert his music, and especially music about Abraham Lincoln, will be the worst kind of blunder and will hold us up as a nation to universal ridicule. (Statement by the League of Composers of New York City)

### 18 JANUARY 1953

Louise Nguyen VAN TY, Indo-Chinese composeress, plays the piano part in the first performance with the Lamoureux Orchestra of Paris, of her coloristic work *La Fête du Têt*, celebrating the lunar calendar holiday by an artful code of instrumental symbolism (trombone representing a tiger, bass drum a dragon, etc.) and nativistic pentatonicism.

### 25 JANUARY 1953

*Concerto for Kettledrums and Orchestra* by the 36-year-old French composer Gabriel Pierre BERLIOZ (no relation to Hector Berlioz) is performed for the first time by the Lamoureux Orchestra, Jean Martinon conducting.

### 29 JANUARY 1953

*La Luna dei Caraibi,* one-act opera by the 67-year-old Italian composer Adriano LUALDI to the libretto based on Eugene O'Neill's drama *The Moon of the Caribbees,* with an Italianate score Americanized by the presence of syncopating saxophones and tropical West Indian drums, is performed for the first time in Rome.

### 31 JANUARY 1953

*The Taming of the Shrew,* Shakespearean opera by the 49-year-old American composer Vittorio GIANNINI, an opulent Italianate score generously endowed with an attractive melodic curvature encompassed by sensuously carnal harmonies in a Wagneroverdian general idiom, is performed for the first time in concert form in Cincinnati.

(A color television production, the first of its kind, of this opera was broadcast by the National Broadcasting Company from New York on 13 March 1954)

### 1 FEBRUARY 1953

Dmitri KABALEVSKY conducts in Moscow the first performance of his *Third Piano Concerto* in D major, with Vladimir Ashkenazy as soloist, the last of a "trilogy of concertos" and, like the other two (for violin and for cello), set in three movements, fast, slow, very fast, full of accessible musical virtues, predictable melodic sequences, rhythmic vivacity and formal cohesiveness, sharpened by modulatory saltation from one tonal orbit into another in its chromatic proximity, creating a sense of pleasing disequilibrium.

### 7 FEBRUARY 1953

Ralph VAUGHAN WILLIAMS, recently widowed octogenarian dean of English composers marries his secretary, Mrs. Ursula Wood, a World War II widow.

### 7 FEBRUARY 1953

*The Marriage,* one-act television opera by Bohuslav MARTINU, to an English libretto after Gogol's play dealing with a hesitant bridegroom who jumps out of a ground-level window to escape matrimony, with a veristically Mussorgskian vocal dialogue in a vigorous rhythmic style, is performed for the first time by the National Broadcasting Company Television Network in New York.

### 11 FEBRUARY 1953

Carlos CHÁVEZ, prime Mexican composer, conducts the Louisville Orchestra in the first performance of his *Fourth Symphony,* subtitled *Sinfonia roman-*

*tica,* in three movements: *Allegro, Molto lento, Vivo,* with the melodic line dominated by the tritone, imparting to the music a stark Lydian color, and harmonized with pragmatic economy of means.

### 13 FEBRUARY 1953

*Trionfo di Afrodite,* "scenic concerto" by Carl ORFF, to poems by Catullus (in Latin), Sappho and Euripides (in Greek), scored for a large orchestra of strings, winds and percussion, and realized in a typical Orphean Orffian manner, with a motionless melody ornamented by a floridly antiquarian melisma (the "Hymn to Hymen" is represented by an unchangeable major third repeated 235 times in succession) and an immobile harmony barely shifting its gears (the Nuptial Cortège consists of a pattern of two chromatically expanding and contracting three-note chords, repeated 80 times before moving elsewhere), is produced in Milan.

(Orff designated this work ex post facto as the third part of a trilogy under the general title *Trionfi di Afrodite,* the first being *Carmina Burana,* a secularly profane medieval ode to the goddess of love, the second, *Catulli Carmina,* a classically Roman and sensuously personal dedication to Aphrodite's simulacra on earth)

### 17 FEBRUARY 1953

Three centuries have passed since the birth at Fusignano, Imola, of Arcangelo CORELLI, the initiator of the modern school of violin playing, himself a virtuoso of great powers, teacher of many other virtuosos, and a composer of numerous works for string instruments in the purest Italian style. (To commemorate the Corelli tercentenary, the Italian Government issued on 30 May 1953 a 25-lire stamp bearing Corelli's likeness)

### 18 FEBRUARY 1953

*The Book of Mormon,* oratorio by Leroy ROBERTSON, Utah-born composer, is performed for the first time at the Mormon Tabernacle in Salt Lake City.

### 19 FEBRUARY 1953

*Rhapsody-Concerto for Viola and Orchestra* by Bohuslav MARTINU in two principal movements, *Moderato* and *Molto Adagio,* with a cadenza introducing a subsidiary *Allegro* and ending in an *Andante molto tranquillo,* is performed for the first time in Cleveland.

### 21 FEBRUARY 1953

On the eve of the 50th anniversary of the death of Hugo WOLF, the Austrian Government issues a commemorative stamp for one and a half schillings bearing his portrait.

### 21 FEBRUARY 1953

*Babar the Elephant,* children's opera by the Russian-American composer, Nicolai BEREZOWSKY, is performed for the first time in New York.

## 25 FEBRUARY 1953

*Wonderful Town*, second musical comedy by Leonard BERNSTEIN based on the play *My Sister Eileen* and dealing with two ambitious sisters who come to New York from Ohio and get involved with a variety of dubious characters, including a whole contingent of the visiting Brazilian navy, set to music saturated with happy nostalgia and desperate merriment, is performed for the first time in New York.

## 1 MARCH 1953

*Gaudia Mundana*, a "secularly joyful oratorio" by the 32-year-old German composer Johannes DRIESSLER, is performed for the first time in Frankfurt.

## 1 MARCH 1953

*Eighth Symphony* by Henry COWELL, in four movements, with a mixed chorus singing nonsensical syllables, but blossoming forth in the finale into a typically Cowellian recreation of a fuguing tune to the text "Behold a voice angelic sounds," is performed for the first time at Wilmington, Ohio.

## 5 MARCH 1953

Sergei PROKOFIEV, Russian composer whose music, capable of a great variety of expression—mercurial, martial, jovial, saturnine—has brought new vigor to twentieth-century composition, whose musical language is marked by elastic tonality, plastic rhythmology, tensile polyphony and ductile harmony, within the ambience of euphonious dissonance, without losing its profound Russian quality, dies of a cerebral hemorrhage at 9 o'clock in the evening, in his home in Moscow, at the age of sixty-one, less than an hour before Stalin, whose reactionary views on music contributed to Prokofiev's harassment.

## 5 MARCH 1953

*Midas*, ballet in two acts by Jean FRANÇAIX, is performed for the first time in its orchestral version by the Paris Radio Orchestra.

## 11 MARCH 1953

*First Symphony* by the 25-year-old Serbian composer Aleksander OBRADOVIĆ, in two movements, the first depicting the sacrifice of Yugoslav men and women in their heroic struggle against the Nazis and the second expressing their joy at the ultimate victory, is performed for the first time in Belgrade.

## 11 MARCH 1953

*Johannes Faustus*, opera by the proletarian-minded 54-year-old German composer Hanns EISLER, in which the legendary island of Atlantis is raised from the ocean by the 16th-century alchemist Dr. Faustus, is produced in East Berlin, arousing sharp criticism in the Communist press for the characterization of the utopian life of Atlantis resembling the urban culture of capitalist America.

## 11 MARCH 1953

*A Parable of Death,* cantata for narrator, tenor and chorus by the 30-year-old Berlin-born American composer Lukas Foss, in six sections, to a text from thanatological poems and stories of Rainer Maria Rilke, set to music in neo-ecclesiastical modalities in starkly dissonant counterpoint, is performed for the first time in Louisville, Kentucky.

## 13 MARCH 1953

*Medea* for contralto and orchestra by Ernst KRENEK, an expressionistic cantata recounting in anguished dodecaphonic figurations the Greek tragedy of demented infanticide, is performed for the first time by the Philadelphia Orchestra.

## 17 MARCH 1953

*Le Loup,* ballet by the 37-year-old French composer Henri DUTILLEUX, a choreographic fantasy to a scenario in which a wolf abducts a young bride on her wedding night and inflames her with animalistic passion so that the hunters are forced to kill them both as they are locked in a bestial embrace, is produced in Paris.

## 22 MARCH 1953

Joseph ORECCHIO, Italian bootmaker who was the chief of the claque at the Metropolitan Opera House for twenty seasons (1915–1935) until a ban was put on such catalytic practices, dies in New York at the age of seventy-two.

## 27 MARCH 1953

Narciso GARAY, the first educated composer of the Republic of Panama, author of a treatise on native music, and formerly Minister of Foreign Affairs of the Republic, dies in Panama City at the age of seventy-three.

## 6 APRIL 1953

Gerard VICTORY, 31-year-old Irish composer, conducts the first performance in Dublin of his opera *An Fear a Phós Balbhín (The Silent Wife),* dealing with a deaf mute woman who spectacularly regains her power of speech and drives her husband to distraction by her continuous vociferation, whereupon he forces the physician who has cured her to restore her to her erstwhile blissful state of muteness.

## 9 APRIL 1953

*The Temptation of St. Anthony,* "dance symphony" by the 40-year-old American composer Gardner READ, containing a Prelude and four scenes, portraying a series of temptations, culminating in a sinuously seductive, sensually serpentine dance of the Queen of Sheba, set to music marked by concentric implosions of increasingly dissonant conglomerations of sound, with a bitonal chord of two minor triads distanced by a tritone serving as a harmonic motto, is performed for the first time by the Chicago Symphony Orchestra.

### 11 APRIL 1953

Two new works by Ernest BLOCH are performed for the first time by the BBC Symphony Orchestra, Sir Malcolm Sargeant conducting:

*Sinfonia breve* (completed in Oregon on 3 December 1952) in four movements: (1) *Moderato*, written in an anxious tritone-laden dramatic manner, with atonal melodic protrusions (2) *Andante*, an elegiac eclogue (3) *Allegro molto*, in a dissonantly chromatic idiom, with an emphasis on major ninths in contrapuntal texture (4) *Allegro deciso*, ending on a pallid C major in pianissimo.

*Second Concerto Grosso* for strings, in G minor, designed in a neo-baroque style, in three sections, *Maestoso, Andante, Allegro*, ending in rubicund B major.

### 11 APRIL 1953

*Ideas of Order* for orchestra by the 40-year-old American composer Arthur BERGER, inspired by poems of Wallace Stevens, is performed for the first time by the New York Philharmonic, Dimitri Mitropoulos conducting.

### 16 APRIL 1953

McNair ILGENFRITZ, wealthy amateur musician, holder for decades of Box 1 at the Metropolitan Opera House, dies in New York, bequeathing the bulk of his estate (about $150,000) to the Metropolitan Opera on condition that it should produce within two years of his death one of his two unorchestrated operas, *Phèdre*, in three acts or *Le Passant*, in one act, the piano scores of which he submitted to the management in 1943. (Upon examination of the music, the Board of Trustees of the Metropolitan Opera House declined the posthumous offer)

### 17 APRIL 1953

*Trághadh na Taoide* (*Ebbtide*), Irish opera by Tomás O'COILEAIN, is performed for the first time in Dublin.

### 17 APRIL 1953

*A Tale of Two Cities*, "romantic melodrama" in six scenes by Arthur BENJAMIN (completed by him in London on 17 February 1950), to a libretto after the famous biurban novel of Dickens with its violent action taking place between 1783 and 1790 in revolutionary Paris and apprehensive London, with the inclusion of topical quotations from contemporary songs, such as *Ça ira* and *La Carmagnole*, concluding with a dramatic cadenza on the drum as the heroic Englishman, sacrificing his own life for his beloved Frenchwoman, ascends the guillotine, is performed for the first time in concert form, in London, by the British Broadcasting Corporation Symphony Orchestra and soloists.

## 17 APRIL 1953

Jascha HEIFETZ is slugged on his right hand with an iron bar by an unidentified Jewish assailant in Jerusalem after his performance of the *Violin Sonata* by Richard STRAUSS, objectionable to Israelis on account of the composer's dubious associations with the Nazi regime.

## 21 APRIL 1953

*Seventh Symphony* by the Danish composer Niels Viggo BENTZON is performed for the first time in Copenhagen.

## 24 APRIL 1953

*Sixth Symphony* by the 47-year-old German master polyphonist Karl Amadeus HARTMANN, in two movements, an expressionistic *Adagio* presenting a shimmering interplay of somber sonorities rising to fiery *Allegro moderato con fuoco*, receding to pianississimo and reverting to *Adagio;* and *Presto*, comprising three fugues forming a terraced sequence of dynamic and rhythmic elements, each fugue opening in *pianississimo* and ending in *fortississimo,* is performed for the first time in Munich.

## 27 APRIL 1953

*Second Symphony* by the 29-year-old Vienna-born composer Robert STARER, now a citizen of Israel, is performed for the first time, in Tel Aviv, Erich Leinsdorf conducting.

## 28 APRIL 1953

The pianist Robert SERGIL completes a stretch of non-stop piano playing of 255 hours in Le Havre, France, beating by 31 hours the record of pianofortitude established by Heinz Arntz on 16 June 1952.

## 4 MAY 1953

Sixty years after its composition, *Irmelin,* posthumous opera in three acts by Frederick DELIUS, to his own libretto, dealing with a romantic princess who keeps vigil for an ideal lover and meets a swineherd who follows a silver stream in the hope of finding true love, is performed for the first time anywhere in Oxford, under the direction of Sir Thomas Beecham.

## 4 MAY 1953

*The Mighty Casey,* baseball opera by the 42-year-old American composer William SCHUMAN, dealing with the legendary pitcher for the Phillies who on 21 August 1887 struck out in the ninth inning in a game with the New York Giants, thus inspiring Ernest L. Thayer to write his poem *Casey at the Bat* ("Oh! Somewhere in this favored land the sun is shining bright . . . But there is no joy in Mudville—Mighty Casey has struck out!"), is performed for the first time at Hartford, Connecticut.

## 6 MAY 1953

*Die chinesische Nachtigall*, ballet by Werner EGK, after Hans Christian Andersen's tale, is performed for the first time in Munich.

## 7 MAY 1953

*Can-Can*, musical comedy by Cole PORTER, recalling the highlights of the 1890's in Paris, when the can-can was regarded as the nadir of depravity, featuring such nostalgic tunes as *C'est magnifique*, is produced in New York.

## 9 MAY 1953

*Israeli Country Dances* by the Latvian-born Israeli composer Marc LAVRY, a symphonic group of contrasting dance movements in an effective manner of Jewish musical folklore, is performed for the first time in Nazareth.

## 16 MAY 1953

*Piano Concerto* by the 43-year-old Rumanian composer Paul CONSTANTINESCU, in three movements: (1) *Allegro,* ingratiatingly utilizing authentic Rumanian melorhythms (2) *Andante,* marked by a characteristic Balkan rhythmic asymmetry (3) *Presto,* with thematic material derived from Transylvanian folk dances, is performed for the first time in Bucharest.

## 17 MAY 1953

*Guernica,* symphonic poem by the 27-year-old French-Canadian composer Clermont PEPIN, inspired by Picasso's *Guernica,* surrealistically conveying the sense of horror of the bombing of Guernica by the Nazi-Fascist planes during the Spanish Civil War with the angular atonal melodies expressing the animal cruelty of Picasso's distorted bull, and polytonal sequences reflecting the despair of massed humanity, is performed for the first time in Quebec, Wilfred Pelletier conducting. (The American première was given by the National Broadcasting Company Symphony Orchestra, on 23 August 1953)

## 17 MAY 1953

Leon XANROF, French Composer who wrote the sentimental chansonette *Le Fiacre* launched by Yvette Guilbert in the 1890's which became a nostalgic souvenir of the pre-automotive era (his real name was Fournier, which he translated into Latin, Fornax, which, read backwards, makes Xanrof), dies in Paris at the age of eighty-five.

## 22 MAY 1953

*Der Tod zu Basel,* oratorio by the 51-year-old Swiss composer Conrad BECK, tracing the history of disasters in Basel beginning with the polytonally dissonant unmelodious earthquake of 1356, is performed for the first time in Basel.

## 25 MAY 1953

A demonstration of electronic music is given for the first time in the world at the opening of the Music Festival of the Cologne Radio.

## 25 MAY 1953

*The Harpies,* one-act opera by Marc BLITZSTEIN, to his own libretto dealing with an oracular ancient Greek hounded by vengeful harpies, written in 1931, comes to a belated world première in New York.

## 25 MAY 1953

*Second Symphony* by the 31-year-old English composer Malcolm ARNOLD, in four movements: *Allegretto, Vivace, Lento* and *Allegro con brio,* written in the traditional symphonic idiom, is performed for the first time in Bournemouth, England.

## 26 MAY 1953

*Kontra-Punkte* for ten instruments by the 24-year-old German innovator Karlheinz STOCKHAUSEN, organized so that the interplay of the horizontal (melodic) and vertical (contrapuntal) lines results in a homogeneous dissonant florid counterpoint, with the instruments dropping out one by one until at the end the piano is left to fend for itself, is performed for the first time in the Electronic Studio of the West German Radio in Cologne.

## 26 MAY 1953

*The Barber of New York,* one-act opera by the Viennese composer Kurt MANSCHINGER, written under his pen name Ashley Vernon, dealing with a New York barber who refuses to shave the commander of a British ship, set to music in an ingratiatingly melodious and pleasingly harmonious manner, is performed for the first time in New York.

## 28 MAY 1953

*Zoya Kosmodemyanskaya,* symphony-legend by the 44-year-old Soviet composer Sergei RAZORYONOV, inspired by the heroic deed of a Soviet guerrilla girl hanged by the Nazis for arson in occupied Ukraine during World War II, with quotations from authentic guerrilla songs, is performed for the first time in Moscow.

## 28 MAY 1953

The 27th Festival of the International Society for Contemporary Music opens in Oslo, Norway, with the following program of orchestral music and instrumental concertos:

*Passacaglia 1952* by Gian Francesco MALIPIERO; *Violin Concerto* by Arnold SCHOENBERG (first performed in Philadelphia on 6 December 1940); *Piano Concerto* in three movements by the Norwegian romantic composer Harald SAEVERUD; *Second Symphony* by the 32-year-old English composer Peter Racine FRICKER, in three movements which increase progressively in length, each presenting a different aspect of rondo form.

### 28 MAY 1953

*Me and Juliet,* musical comedy by Richard RODGERS, with book and lyrics by Oscar Hammerstein II, wherein a chorus girl enamored of the assistant manager of a theater has to resist the dastardly machinations of a desperate electrician who covets her, featuring the successful tango tune *No Other Love,* borrowed by Rodgers from his own score for the documentary film, *Victory at Sea,* is produced in New York.

### 30 MAY 1953

At the second concert of the 27th Festival of the International Society for Contemporary Music in Oslo the following program of chamber music is given:

*Viola Sonata* by the 26-year-old South African composer John JOUBERT, in five movements, in a neo-baroque style; *Partita* for unaccompanied flute by the 23-year-old Japanese composer Makoto MOROI, in six sections thematically derived from six dodecaphonic series; *Sextet* for wind instruments by the 41-year-old Chilean composer René AMENGUAL; *Piano Sonatina* in four movements by the 41-year-old Finnish composer Erik BERGMAN; *Du,* cycle of seven songs for voice and piano by the 37-year-old American mathematician Milton BABBITT with the vertical, horizontal and motivic organization subordinated to a unifying dodecaphonic series; *Piano Sonata* by the 37-year-old Argentinian composer Alberto GINASTERA, in four movements (first performed by Johana Harris in Pittsburgh on 29 November 1952) in which the structural elements reflect dodecaphonic procedures while the melorhythmic substance relates to ethnic Argentinian sources; and *Third String Quartet* in three movements by the 43-year-old Danish composer Vagn HOLMBOE.

### 30 MAY 1953

*Dudaray (The Curly One),* opera in four acts by the 47-year-old Soviet composer Evgeny BRUSILOVSKY, on the subject of interracial social comity among pre-revolutionary fishermen in a Khazakstan village, with a profusion of Russian and Khazak folk tunes, is produced in Alma-Ata.

### 31 MAY 1953

At the third concert of the 27th Festival of the International Society for Contemporary Music in Oslo, the following program of music for chamber orchestra is presented:

*Le cimetière marin* by the impressionistic Norwegian composer Fartein VALEN (1887–1952), inspired by the symbolist poem of Paul Valéry, and presenting an antinomy of the serenity of the dead in a seaside cemetery and the constant movement of the life-giving sea; *Octet* by the 46-year-old Java-born Dutch composer Henk BADINGS, in three movements of neo-classical provenance; *Concerto da camera* for piano and string orchestra by the 35-year-old Swiss composer Julien-François ZBINDEN, in three neo-Bachian movements; *Opus 3 aux son frappés et frottés* by the 29-year-old Belgian empiricist Karel GOEYVAERTS, for piano, violin, viola, cello, vibraphone, and percussion, written in the pointillistic technique of thematic dismemberment; and *Salutatio Angelis* for mezzo-soprano and 12 instruments by the English composer Anthony MILNER, to the Latin text of the 130th Psalm, in the form of a passacaglia.

## 2 JUNE 1953

At the fourth concert of the 27th Festival of the International Society for Contemporary Music in Oslo, the following program of symphonic music is presented:

*Sixth Symphony* in three movements, by the 60-year-old Swedish composer Hilding ROSENBERG; *Piano Concerto* by the 26-year-old German composer of dodecaphonic tendencies, Hans Werner HENZE; *Concertino* for trumpet and orchestra by the French avant-garde composer André JOLIVET; and *Le Zodiaque*, cantata by the 59-year-old Belgian composer of moderately modern music Jean ABSIL.

## 2 JUNE 1953

At the Coronation Services for Elizabeth II of England, a new *Te Deum* by Sir William WALTON, is performed, and his March, *Orb and Sceptre*, is played during the procession.

## 2 JUNE 1953

*Variaciones Concertantes*, suite for chamber orchestra by the 37-year-old Argentinian composer Alberto GINASTERA, containing eleven whimsical variations (one of them for doublebass solo), on an original theme of Argentinian flavor, is performed for the first time in Buenos Aires, with Igor Markevitch conducting.

## 3 JUNE 1953

At the fifth concert of the 27th Festival of the International Society for Contemporary Music in Oslo, the following concert of chamber music is given:

*Sonatina* for clarinet and piano, in three movements by the 33-year-old Norwegian composer Hjort ALBERTSEN; *Piano Sonata 1952* by the 23-year-old Brazilian composer Roberto SCHNORRENBERG, in three movements, set in a free dodecaphonic idiom; *String Quartet* by the almost 31-year-old Scottish composer Iain HAMILTON, in three contrasting movements; *Second Piano Sonata* in three movements by Busoni's disciple Phillipp JARNACH; *Sonata in G* for violin solo by the Israeli composer Paul BEN-HAIM, in three classically outlined movements; and *Das Nasobém*, a divertimento for chorus a cappella by the 32-year-old Swiss composer Franz TISCHHAUSER, to the macabre texts by Christian Morgenstern.

## 5 JUNE 1953

At the sixth and last concert of the 27th Festival of the International Society for Contemporary Music in Oslo, the following program of symphonic music is given:

*Variazioni breve* by the 33-year-old Danish composer Niels Viggo BENTZON, a theme with five baroque variations and a coda forming a synthesis of the whole work; *I speglarnas sal (In the Hall of Mirrors)*, nine sonnets for solo singers, chorus and orchestra by the 36-year-old Swedish modernist Karl-Birger BLOMDAHL; *Flute Concerto* by the 72-year-old Dutch romanticist Sem DRESDEN, in three movements of a classical type; and *Concerto for Orchestra* by the grandmaster of Hungarian music Zoltan KODÁLY, written in the baroque manner, alternating motoric and lyric sections, with the principal theme of a pentatonic structure in an ancient Magyar mold.

### 8 JUNE 1953

*Gloriana,* opera in three acts by Benjamin BRITTEN on the subject of the unqueenly affair between Queen Elizabeth I and Essex to a libretto after Lytton Strachey's biographical study *Elizabeth and Essex,* written specially for the Coronation ceremony, glorying in Britannically shaped grandly confident triadic proclamations, is produced at a Gala Performance at Covent Garden in London, in the presence of Elizabeth II and the royal family, the first opera by a British composer so honored since King George II attended the performance of Handel's *Atalanta* in 1736.

### 9 JUNE 1953

*Second Symphony* by the 31-year-old Scottish composer Iain HAMILTON, in four movements of a classical formation and modernistic connotations, is performed for the first time at the Cheltenham Festival in England.

### 19 JUNE 1953

The Government of Czechoslovakia issues postage stamps honoring Leoš JANÁČEK (1.60 kronen) and Joseph SLAVÍK, renowned as the Paganini of Bohemia (75 hellers).

### 23 JUNE 1953

The Bolshoi Theater of Moscow presents the first complete performance of the grand opera *Decembrists* by the 63-year-old Soviet composer Yuri SHAPORIN, glorifying the five hanged conspirators in the abortive rebellion of 14 December 1825 (hence the historical nickname, Decembrists, Men of December) against the incumbent Tsar Nicholas I, set to music in a grand Russian style reaching a climax in the vocal quintet of the doomed Decembrists, to the rousing words of the poet Alexander Pushkin: "Have faith, comrade, our star will rise in happy rapture when Russia awakens from her slumber and will write our names on the ruins of autocracy."

### 26 JUNE 1953

*Concerto for Oboe and Strings* by the 31-year-old English composer Malcolm ARNOLD, in three neo-classical movements, is performed for the first time in London.

### 26 JUNE 1953

In the course of a series of concerts of modern music, *Die Woche für Neue Musik* at Frankfurt, two world premières are given:

*Spiegelungen* for orchestra by the 57-year-old Swiss-resident Moscow-born half-Russian half-German composer Vladimir VOGEL, in two movements, based on a dodecaphonic series consisting of two mutually inverted six-note groups (hence the title, mirrorings), with a tonifugal first movement *Lento espressivo*, and a firmly tonipetal second movement, *Allegro;* and *Cantata seculare* by the 48-year-old Hungarian composer resident in England Mátyás SEIBER, with its four movements titled after the four seasons, to a medieval Latin text, set to music in modernized ecclesiastical modes.

### 28 JUNE 1953

*Abstrakte Oper No. 1* by the 50-year-old China-born Estonian-German Boris BLACHER, scored for three vocalists, two speakers, chorus and orchestra, to a libretto by Werner EGK set in a surrealistically unintelligible language projected in a stream of syllabic glossolalia with the component scenes identified only by their emotional content, e.g. Fear, Love No. 1, Pain, Panic, Love No. 2, to denote the abstraction from the concrete, is performed for the first time in the course of *Die Woche für Neue Musik* in Frankfurt.

### 9 JULY 1953

The French Government marks the 250th anniversary of the birth of Jean-Philippe RAMEAU by issuing a postage stamp for 15 francs bearing his likeness.

### 17 JULY 1953

On the occasion of the quadricentennial of the birth of the Russian patriot Ivan SUSANIN, glorified in Glinka's opera *A Life for the Czar,* a group of Russian opera singers stage a celebration in Susanin's native village of Domnino by performing several arias from Glinka's opera.

### 19 JULY 1953

Marie ASHTON, an Irish housewife, completes a 133-hour marathon of piano playing, claiming the world record for female pianofortitude, exceeding by one hour the previous record established by Syncopating Sandy of Bolton, England.

### 26 JULY 1953

*Concerto d'Orphée* for violin and orchestra by the 52-year-old French composer Henri SAUGUET, in one protracted movement set in a curiously un-Orphean chromatic idiom, is performed for the first time at the Festival of Aix-en-Provence, in France.

### 26 JULY 1953

*Concerto Grosso for Band* by the 53-year-old American composer Joseph WAGNER, one of the earliest pieces in classical concerto grosso form written for band, is performed for the first time by the U.S. Marine Band in Washington.

## 31 JULY 1953

The Covent Garden Opera Company, on its South African tour, presents VERDI's *Aida* as the opening spectacle in Bulawayo, Southern Rhodesia, the first opera to be performed in the South African hinterland, a thousand miles from the coast, the singers and musicians having been transported by air.

## 15 AUGUST 1953

O. C. CASH, tax consultant for an oil company, founder of the Society for the Preservation and Encouragement of Barber Shop Quartet Singing in America (SPEBSQSA), dies in Tulsa, Oklahoma, at the age of sixty-one.

## 15 AUGUST 1953

Larry Adler plays the mouth harmonica with the London Symphony Orchestra, Basil Cameron conducting, in the first performance of the *Concerto for Harmonica and Orchestra* by the Australian-born composer Arthur BENJAMIN.

## 17 AUGUST 1953

*Der Prozess*, opera in nine scenes by the 35-year-old Austrian composer Gottfried VON EINEM, to a libretto from the surrealist tale of Franz Kafka, in which a deracinated Central European adrift in the disoriented world of 1919 is awaiting a trial on unspecified charges by anonymous judges, set to music in an economically dissonant idiom animated by rhythmic propulsion, is produced in Salzburg.

## 18 AUGUST 1953

*Captain Lovelock*, one-act opera by the American composer John DUKE, is produced at Hudson Falls, New York. (The first New York performance took place on 20 February 1956)

## 27 AUGUST 1953

Nicolai BEREZOWSKY, 53-year-old Russian-born American composer of ingratiatingly euphonious symphonies and chamber music breathing the simple joys of artistic self-expression, is found dead by his second wife in his New York apartment, a victim of intestinal congestion caused by a suicidal dose of powerful sedatives.

## 1 SEPTEMBER 1953

On his way to Indo-China to play for the embattled French Army there, the famous French violinist Jacques THIBAUD perishes in an airplane crash at Mount Cemet in the French Alps, carrying with him to fiery destruction two of his Stradivarius violins.

## 3 SEPTEMBER 1953

*Viola Concerto* by the 32-year-old English composer Peter Racine FRICKER is performed for the first time at the Edinburgh Festival by William Primrose, who commissioned the work, with the Philharmonia Orchestra conducted by Sir Adrian Boult.

## 8 SEPTEMBER 1953

*La Partita a Pugni (Prize Fight),* chamber opera by the 32-year-old Italian composer Vieri TOSATTI, dealing with a prize fight and a riot in the stadium ensuing in protest against the referee's decision, is performed for the first time at the Venice Festival.

## 15 SEPTEMBER 1953

*Ornaments,* for orchestra by Boris BLACHER, built on a series of metric progressions from 2 to 9 beats to a measure, then 2 to 8 beats, 2 to 7, 2 to 6, 2 to 5, etc., is performed for the first time at the Venice Festival.

## 17 SEPTEMBER 1953

Henry Holden HUSS, American composer and pianist, who once played his pieces at a reception for Tchaikovsky in New York in 1891, dies in New York at the age of ninety-one.

## 1 OCTOBER 1953

*Ein-Geb (Ein-Gev),* symphonic fantasy by the 46-year-old Budapest-born Israeli composer Ödön PARTOS, composed during the bitter fight between Jews and Arabs in the valley of Ein-Gev, and based on the musical letters of Ein-Gev (E, G, B-flat), melodically developed in oriental scales, is performed for the first time by the Israel Philharmonic Orchestra in Ein-Gev, Leonard Bernstein conducting.

## 3 OCTOBER 1953

Sir Arnold BAX, English composer of loftily designed impressionistically flavored symphonies and symphonic poems, dies in Cork, Ireland (where he was on an educational mission) at the age of sixty-nine.

## 11 OCTOBER 1953

*Le Réveil des Oiseaux,* ornithological symphony for piano and orchestra by Olivier MESSIAEN, with its melodic material drawn from an aviary of 37 song birds, exhibiting a remarkable similarity of atonal intervallic structures among such different species as a robin, a thrush, and a blackcap, with a universal preference for major sevenths and minor ninths, appearing also in such combinatory progressions as two perfect fourths separated by a tritone, is performed for the first time in the course of the Music Festival in Donaueschingen.

## 15 OCTOBER 1953

*La porta verde,* musical tragedy in four acts by the 70-year-old Italian composer Francesco SANTOLIQUIDO, is produced in Bergamo.

### 16 OCTOBER 1953

Darius MILHAUD conducts over the Italian Radio in Turin the world première of his *Fifth Symphony,* in four movements, *Vif et cinglant, Lent et tendre, Clair et leger, Alerte et rude.*

### 19 OCTOBER 1953

An aphoristic *Praeludium* by Igor STRAVINSKY, written in 1937 and scored for four saxophones, three trumpets, two trombones, strings, celesta, guitar and drums, is performed for the first time in the concert series of "Evenings on the Roof," in Los Angeles, conducted by Stravinsky's musical amanuensis Robert Craft, on the same program with Stravinsky's new orchestral setting of his piano piece *Tango,* written in 1940, his *Ragtime, Piano Rag Music, Ebony Concerto,* and three dances from *L'Histoire du Soldat.*

### 19 OCTOBER 1953

On the occasion of the centennial of the Steinway Piano Company, 35 pianists, in teams of four to ten for each number, give a polypianic rendition of CHOPIN's *Polonaise* in A major, SOUSA's march *Stars and Stripes Forever,* and the first performance of Morton GOULD's *Inventions* for four pianos and orchestra.

### 20 OCTOBER 1953

*Astutuli,* "A Bavarian comedy" by Carl ORFF, in the form of a "Sprechstück," to his own text in a rustic Bavarian dialect, arranged for rhythmically inflected voices and 24 assorted percussion instruments, including musical glasses and a beer stein, with the timpani and the xylophone providing the dominant-tonic cadences, dealing with a cunning charlatan who inveigles local farmers to supply liquor and women for him, astutely addressing them in kitchen Latin "O Vos astutuli" (Oh you, little clever people), is performed for the first time in Munich.

### 21 OCTOBER 1953

*The Inland Woman,* one-act opera by the 49-year-old Scottish composer Erik CHISHOLM, is performed for the first time in Cape Town, South Africa.

### 30 OCTOBER 1953

Emmerich KÁLMÁN, Hungarian composer of exhilarating operettas, among them the perennial favorite, *The Gypsy Princess,* dies in Paris at the age of seventy-one.

### 4 NOVEMBER 1953

Elizabeth Sprague COOLIDGE, munificent American music patroness, herself a composeress, who despite her deafness (she could hear music only with a powerful hearing-aid apparatus) diverted a generous portion of her fortune as a Chicago canned-pork heiress to the promotion of modern music and performance of specially commissioned chamber music works at the Coolidge Festivals, dies in Cambridge, Massachusetts, in her 90th year.

### 6 NOVEMBER 1953

*Atomic Bomb,* symphonic fantasy on an extremely realistic subject by the 52-year-old Japanese composer Masao OKI is performed for the first time in Tokyo.

### 6 NOVEMBER 1953

*Cello Concerto* by the 50-year-old Russian-American composer Nicolas NABOKOV, subtitled *Les Hommages,* in three movements named *Serenata di Pietro* (for Peter Tchaikovsky), *Ballata d'Allessandro* (for Alexander Dargomyzhsky), and *Corale di Michele* (for Michael Glinka), purporting to portray an impoverished Russian émigré driving a taxicab in Paris and humming tunes by Tchaikovsky, Dargomyzhsky and Glinka, is performed for the first time by the Philadelphia Orchestra, Eugene Ormandy conducting.

### 18 NOVEMBER 1953

The Government of Czechoslovakia issues a 30-heller stamp in honor of the famous Bohemian dramatic soprano Emmy DESTINN (1878–1930).

### 18 NOVEMBER 1953

*Sixth Symphony* by the 30-year-old American composer Peter MENNIN, animated by a neo-Baroque Italian spirit (Mennin's original name was Mennini), in three movements of functional music spiced with non-corrosive dissonances (1) *Maestoso,* as a prelude to an *Allegro* (2) *Grave,* marked by an economically applied emotive force (3) *Allegro vivace,* set in an energetic aggressive manner and terminating in an abrupt cadential configuration, is performed for the first time as a commissioned work, by the Louisville Orchestra.

### 1 DECEMBER 1953

Carlos CHÁVEZ conducts the Chamber Orchestra of Los Angeles in the world première of his *Fifth Symphony* for string orchestra, in three linked movements, *Allegro molto moderato, Lento, Allegro con brio,* marked by astutely drawn contrasts of thematic and dynamic factors, ranging in contents from loftily elegiac to powerfully elemental structures.

### 3 DECEMBER 1953

*Kismet,* musical extravaganza by Robert WRIGHT and George FORREST, derived from music by Alexander Borodin, disjoined, altered, dislocated and mutilated with the hit song *Stranger in Paradise* utilizing the lyrical portion of one of the *Polovetsian Dances* in *Prince Igor,* is produced in New York.

### 4 DECEMBER 1953

Daniel Gregory MASON, American composer of scrupulously academic symphonies and chamber music, one-time chairman of the Music Department of Columbia University, dies in Greenwich, Connecticut, at the age of eighty.

### 4 DECEMBER 1953

*Das Ende einer Welt,* radiophonic opera in two acts by the 27-year-old German composer Hans Werner HENZE, representing a jazzy Doomsday to the accompaniment of a disoriented and disharmonious heterogeneous assemblage of instruments, is performed for the first time in Hamburg.

### 6 DECEMBER 1953

*Rural Antiphonies* by the American experimental composer Henry BRANT, scored for five conductors and five orchestras, each operating at its own autonomous tempo and meter, is performed for the first time in New York City.

### 6 DECEMBER 1953

Ivo CRUZ conducts in Lisbon the first performance of his *Sinfonia de Amadis,* in four romantically programmatic movements descriptive of the love of Amadis for Oriana, his retirement to a monastery at a crisis of their romance, and his return as a defrocked impenitent monk for a sensualized reunion at the Portuguese royal court festival.

### 6 DECEMBER 1953

*First Symphony* by the Swedish composer Gunnar BUCHT is performed for the first time in Stockholm.

### 8 DECEMBER 1953

*The Dress,* one-act opera by Mark BUCCI, is produced in New York.

### 9 DECEMBER 1953

The Hungarian Government issues a series of postage stamps honoring LISZT, MOSONYI, ERKEL, BIHARI, GOLDMARK, BARTÓK and Zoltán KODÁLY, a rare distinction for the latter, still living and active.

### 11 DECEMBER 1953

Albert COATES, Russian-born English conductor, dies in Milnerton, near Cape Town, South Africa, at the age of seventy-one.

### 12 DECEMBER 1953

*Une Cantate de Noël* by Arthur HONEGGER, for baritone solo, children's voices, mixed chorus, organ and orchestra (sketched in 1941, but interrupted by the war, and not finished until 5 January 1953), with an instrumental intermezzo of popular Christmas songs containing special effects, e.g. singing *bouche fermée,* is performed for the first time by the Chamber Orchestra of Basel, Paul Sacher conducting.

## 16 DECEMBER 1953

The Rumanian Government issues a 55-lei postage stamp to commemorate the centennial of the birth of the Roumanian song composer Ciprian PORUMBESCU.

## 17 DECEMBER 1953

The first performance is given in Leningrad of the *Tenth Symphony* by Dmitri SHOSTAKOVICH (completed on 27 October 1953), thematically based on the musical letters of his name in German notation (D.SCH, in which S stands for Es, that is, E-flat, and H stands for B), in four movements:

(1) *Moderato* in E minor, wherein the monogram first appears in the form of initials (D, Es), is trilled over with the ascending semitone retaining its thematic connotations, reaching a climax in the recapitulation, supported by powerful drums (2) *Allegro,* in B-flat minor, in constant motoric agitation in an almost constant fortissimo (3) *Allegretto,* in C Minor, opening with a permutated monogram, then stating the four signature notes explicitly in the violins (4) *Andante,* wherein the oboe, the flute, the bassoon and the clarinet echo each other with a broadly Russian theme, which subsequently grows into a fugato in the strings, leading to a kinetic *Allegro,* and accumulating momentum driving relentlessly towards the *Finale* in which the personal monogram is revealed in full power of declarative utterance, ending with an ostinato on four kettledrums, reiterating and pounding the four notes in mighty augmentation.

## 25 DECEMBER 1953

*Sevil,* opera in three acts by the 31-year-old Azerbaijan composer Fikret AMIROV, to a libretto centered on an emancipated Soviet woman of Baku named Sevil who renounces the traditional ways of Moslem life, abandons her obsolete polygamous husband, goes to Moscow for a scientific education, publishes a book and returns home in feminine glory, set to music with a profusion of native melorhythms encased in mellifluous Russian harmonies, is performed for the first time in Baku. (A revised version was produced in Baku on 8 May 1955)

## 27 DECEMBER 1953

*The Capital of the World,* ballet by George ANTHEIL, is produced in New York.

## 29 DECEMBER 1953

*Wandering in Sorrow,* opera in three acts by Antonio SPADAVECCHIA, 46-year-old Odessa-born Soviet composer of Italian descent, after the revolutionary trilogy by Alexei Tolstoy, is performed for the first time in Perm. (A new version, titled *The Flaming Years,* was produced in Perm on 8 April 1966)

# ~ 1954 ~

*Notturno*, an elegiac piece of nostalgic inspiration by Ernst TOCH is performed for the first time as a commissioned work by the Louisville Orchestra.

9 JANUARY 1954

*Sinfonietta flamenca* by Carlos SURINACH, 38-year-old Spanish composer, now resident in America, based on the flamenco rhythms of his Catalan birthplace, is performed for the first time in Louisville.

11 JANUARY 1954

Oskar STRAUS, Austrian composer of merry Viennese operettas including *The Chocolate Soldier*, freely modeled after the fantasmagorical Shavian comedy *Arms and the Man*, dies at Bad Ischl, at the age of eighty-three.

15 JANUARY 1954

*Fourth Symphony* by the foremost Polish woman composer Grazyna BACEWICZ is performed for the first time in Cracow.

17 JANUARY 1954

*Sixth Symphony* by the industrious English symphonist Edmund RUBBRA, written in a rhapsodically neo-romantic idiom charged with dissonant counterpoint, but strongly anchored in tonal centers, is performed for the first time in London.

23 JANUARY 1954

*Alvorado na Floresta Tropical* (*Dawn in a Tropical Forest*), overture by the prime Brazilian composer Heitor VILLA-LOBOS, depicting in luscious instrumental colors the ornithological pandemonium in the Brazilian jungle at dawn, marked by a cornucopia of native melorhythms, is performed for the first time in Louisville, Kentucky.

23 JANUARY 1954

*Septet* by Igor STRAVINSKY for violin, viola, cello, clarinet, horn, bassoon and piano (or harpsichord), in three movements modeled after the baroque dance forms, *Allegro*, *Passacaglia* and *Gigue*, serving the functional purpose of a classical ensemble, couched in a frugal fugal polyphony and a parsimonious harmonic setting, is performed for the first time at the private estate of Dumbarton Oaks in Washington, with Stravinsky himself conducting.

## 28 JANUARY 1954

*Kaspers Fettisdag,* opera by the 61-year-old dean of Swedish composers, Hilding ROSENBERG, is performed for the first time in Stockholm.

## 1 FEBRUARY 1954

*Eighth Symphony* by the 78-year-old English composer Havergal BRIAN, in a single movement, in the key of B-flat minor, composed in 1949, and inspired by Goethe's ballad *Die Braut von Corinth,* set in constantly changing tempi, with the inclusion of two autocephalous passacaglias, is performed for the first time by the London Philharmonic Orchestra, Sir Adrian Boult conducting.

## 10 FEBRUARY 1954

Salvino de SILVA sets a world record for continuous guitar playing after 16 hours of supervised strumming in Lisbon.

## 12 FEBRUARY 1954

*The Legend of a Stone Flower,* ballet by Sergei PROKOFIEV, to a scenario from Ural fairy tales in which a piece of green malachite blossoms forth in melodious efflorescence, is produced posthumously at the Bolshoi Theater in Moscow.

## 13 FEBRUARY 1954

*Variations for Piano and Orchestra* by Wallingford RIEGGER, set in a vigorous vigesimosecular style, is performed for the first time as a commissioned work by the Louisville Orchestra.

## 21 FEBRUARY 1954

Ernst VON DOHNÁNYI, 76-year-old expatriate Hungarian composer, conducts in Athens, Ohio, the first performance of his first American orchestral piece, *American Rhapsody.*

## 23 FEBRUARY 1954

*Atlantide,* lyric and choreographic opera in four acts, by the 52-year-old French composer Henri TOMASI, after the novel of Pierre Benoit dealing with the polyandrogynous Queen of Atlantis (who has only a dancing, non-singing part), is produced in Mulhouse, Alsace.

## 27 FEBRUARY 1954

*Triskelion,* symphonic suite by the 45-year-old American composer Halsey STEVENS, symbolizing the relationship existing between the thematic ideas of the three movements of the suite, and their synthesis in a triskelion, a geometric figure of three branches radiating from the center, is performed for the first time in Louisville, Kentucky.

### 4 MARCH 1954
*Cello Concerto* by Ernst KRENEK is played for the first time in Los Angeles.

### 8 MARCH 1954
*Three Songs from William Shakespeare* for mezzo-soprano, flute, clarinet and viola by Igor STRAVINSKY are performed for the first time in Los Angeles.

### 12 MARCH 1954
The Radio Hamburg broadcasts the first performance of the two completed acts of the posthumous opera *Moses und Aron* by Arnold SCHOENBERG, written in 1930–1932, scored for voices, bass, tenor, chorus and orchestra, with a profusion of percussion instruments, to his own biblical text dissecting the dialectical antinomy between Moses (inflected *Sprechstimme* in the bass register) as prophet of monotheistic Judaic philosophy and Aaron (tenor) as the pragmatic materialist, opening with the voice of God chanting the single vowel O, evolving in an intricate hermetic dodecaphonic polyphony of allegorical motives in a Schoenbergian relativistic musical space, where there is no absolute up or down, right or left, forward or backward, and culminating in the Dance Around the Golden Calf (Act II, scene 3) in which four naked virgins (two sopranos and two contraltos) are throttled and slaughtered by priests, while other girls, some clad, pass butcher knives and hold receptacles for the jets of blood from the coronary aortas of the victims, followed by a universal quaquaversal erotic orgy, with multifutuent youths shouting dodecaphonically, "Human procreativity is sanctified!"

(The original title of the work was *Moses und Aaron*, but Schoenberg, oppressed by triskaidekaphobia, aware that the number of letters in the title aggregates to 13, deleted the second A in Aaron, reducing the total to 12, an ideal dodecaphonic module. The *Dance Around the Golden Calf* was performed separately on 2 July 1951 in the course of the International Summer Course of New Music in Darmstadt. The first stage performance of the entire opera took place on 6 June 1954 in Zürich)

### 13 MARCH 1954
*Piano Concerto* by the 23-year-old Spanish composer Cristóbal HALFFTER, nephew of Ernesto and Rodolfo Halffter, written in a neo-baroque manner with some atonal protuberances, is performed for the first time in Madrid.

### 13 MARCH 1954
*Toccata Giocosa* for orchestra by Gardner READ is performed for the first time as a commissioned work by the Louisville Orchestra.

## 14 MARCH 1954

Ludomir ROGOWSKI, Polish composer of colorful symphonic works scented with Slavonic suffusions further individualized by the use of a scale of alternating wholetones and semitones, which he believed to be of his invention, but which in chronological fact was used by Rimsky-Korsakov long before, dies at the age of 72, in Dubrovnik, Yugoslavia, where he spent most of his life.

## 17 MARCH 1954

*Concerto for Two Pianos and Orchestra* by Quincy PORTER, which won the Pulitzer Prize, is performed for the first time as a commissioned work by the Louisville Orchestra.

## 21 MARCH 1954

*Piano Concerto* by the 33-year-old English composer Peter Racine FRICKER is performed for the first time in London.

## 23 MARCH 1954

*Slovo od Mladosti* (*Message of Youth*), opera in three acts by the Yugoslav composer Danilo SVARA, is produced in Ljubljana.

## 24 MARCH 1954

Two one-act operas by Italian composers, *La Figlia del diavolo* by Virgilio MORTARI, and *La Gita in campagna* by Mario PERAGALLO, are performed for the first time at La Scala in Milan.

## 24 MARCH 1954

Willy FERRERO, American-born Italian conductor, who as a child prodigy before World War I astounded music lovers by actually conducting Mozart and Beethoven, dies in comparative obscurity in Rome at the age of 47, professionally reduced to the position of a provincial opera conductor.

## 26 MARCH 1954

*Les Voix de la mer*, opera by the 60-year-old Belgian composer Jean ABSIL, to a libretto mystically identifying the sea as an abstract female figure which lures a mariner from his fleshly wife to the submarine realm of fluvial sensuality and oblivion in death, is performed for the first time at the Théâtre de la Monnaie in Brussels.

## 1 APRIL 1954

*The Tender Land,* opera in three acts by Aaron COPLAND, to a libretto by Horace Everett, with a locale in the American Midwest, dealing with a harvester who breaks his promise to elope with a farmer's daughter, and she decides to leave her family to wander in the tender land of the cornfields alone, set to music imbued with American melorhythms, including some quotations from actual folk tunes, and accoutred in economic but tonally resonant pandiatonic harmonies, is produced at the New York City Opera.

### 4 APRIL 1954
In his last public appearance, ten days after his 87th birthday, Arturo TOSCANINI conducts in Carnegie Hall, New York, a program of Wagner's music with the Symphony Orchestra of the National Broadcasting Company, and becomes pathetically confused in the *Tannhäuser* Overture, necessitating an interruption of the broadcast and the incongruous substitution of a recording of the *First Symphony* by Brahms.

### 4 APRIL 1954
*The Transposed Heads*, opera in six scenes by the 41-year-old Australian-born American composeress Peggy GLANVILLE-HICKS, after a story by Thomas Mann, dealing with two Brahmins who are beheaded in a thanatolatrous ritual, leading to a capital confusion of decapitated torsos when the widow of one magically restores the head of her minifutuent husband to the more attractively muscular torso of the other and then decides to immolate herself with both Brahmins in a spectacular suttee, set to music in a synthetic semi-Oriental demi-Occidental idiom, ornamented with a cincture of Hindu drumlets, is performed for the first time in Louisville, Kentucky.

### 5 APRIL 1954
Claude DELVINCOURT, 66-year-old French composer of operas, ballet and instrumental music in a hedonistic Gallic manner, dies in an automobile accident, at Bivio di Albinia, Orbetello, Italy.

### 1 MAY 1954
The Government of the Netherlands issues a postage stamp to commemorate the Dutch composer Willem PIJPER (1894–1947), the foremost impressionist of Holland.

### 6 MAY 1954
*Ode an den Westwind* for cello and orchestra by the 27-year-old German composer Hans Werner HENZE inspired by Shelley's poem, is performed for the first time in Bielefeld.

### 7 MAY 1954
*Perfume Set to Music*, for voices and orchestra, an olfactory pastiche by Harry REVEL, in six movements glorifying in wafting aural emanations six famous scents conjured up by the French perfumer Corday: *Jet, Toujours Moi, Possession, L'Ardente Nuit, Zigane* and *Fame*, is performed for the first time at the opening night of a special series of modernistic Pop Concerts in Carnegie Hall, in New York.

## 13 MAY 1954

*Pajama Game,* musical comedy by Richard ADLER and Jerry Ross, based on Richard Bissell's novel 7½¢ (with reference to a demand by the union for a raise of 7½¢ per hour), retailing the high-jinks at the Sleep-Tite Pajama Factory, wherein the superintendent sings a duet with his own dictaphone-recorded voice (*Hey There*), the syncopated puffs of the steam heat pipes are transformed into a rhythmic dance, and both labor and management repair to Hernando's Hideaway to loll in tango rhythms in an intermittent illumination provided by lighted matches, is produced in New York.

## 14 MAY 1954

*Concerto for Orchestra,* by Tadeusz BAIRD, is first performed in Lodz.

## 15 MAY 1954

*The Voice,* and *The Pumpkin,* two one-act operas by the Hungarian-American composer Leslie KONDOROSSY are performed for the first time by the American New Opera Theater Society in Cleveland, Ohio.

## 15 MAY 1954

*Invocation and Dance* for orchestra by the 47-year-old American composer Paul CRESTON is performed for the first time in Louisville.

## 16 MAY 1954

Clemens KRAUSS, Austrian conductor, scholarly interpreter of classical and romantic operas and symphonic works and a close associate of Richard Strauss, dies suddenly at the age of 61, in Mexico City.

## 19 MAY 1954

Charles IVES, solitary genius on the American musical scene who, shunning the crowds wrote the prophetic works limning the greatness, the humility and the daily joys of American life in an idiom presaging by many years the developments of modern techniques of composition, dies in New York at the age of seventy-nine.

## 20 MAY 1954

*Il Contrabasso,* one-act opera-grotesque after Chekhov's short story, by the Italian composer Valentino BUCCHI, is given for the first time in Florence.

## 22 MAY 1954

*Le petit Faune,* symphonic extracts from a ballet score by the 81-year-old French composer ROGER-DUCASSE, wherein the surviving Grecian divinities in the forest of Marly are dispersed by the intrusion of modern civilization, and the little faun is mortally stabbed by a polytechnical student who finds him innocently cuddled at his fiancée's flank in the grass, set to a delicately contrived impressionistic score with neo-Grecian modalities pierced by poly-harmonies, is performed for the first time in the composer's home town of Bordeaux.

## 29 MAY 1954

*Eleventh Symphony* by Henry COWELL subtitled *Seven Rituals of Music,* in seven stylistically disparate sections reflecting in a broad spectrum of instrumental colors the seven melosomatic phenomena—grief, work, love, dance, magic, war and death, is performed for the first time in Louisville.

## 30 MAY 1954

The 28th Festival of the International Society for Contemporary Music opens in Haifa, Israel, in the following program of orchestral music performed by the Israel Philharmonic Orchestra:

World Première of *Odisseia de uma raça (The Odyssey of a Race),* symphonic poem by Heitor VILLA-LOBOS, expressive of his admiration for Israel: "When the Universe was formed, God created a heroic race which lived and suffered, and became victorious in Israel"; *Fourth Piano Concerto* by Darius MILHAUD, in three contrasting movements, written in a highly complex polytonal idiom demanding a maximum of pianofortitude, with Zadel Skolovsky as soloist; *Due Invenzioni* by the Italian neo-classicist Adone ZECCHI and the first performance of *Symphonie* in four movements by André JOLIVET.

## 31 MAY 1954

At the 28th Festival of the International Society for Contemporary Music in Israel, the following program of chamber music is given in Haifa:

*Violin Sonata* in three movements by the 54-year-old Italian composer Antonio VERETTI, dedicated "to an imaginary girl"; *5 Songs* by the 38-year-old South African composer Arnold VAN WYK; and *Second String Quartet* by Roger SESSIONS, in five movements based on three tetradecaphonic thematic groups consisting of 14 notes, of which 12 are different and two are duplicates, a dodecaphonic series of 12 non-repeated notes and a hendecaphonic series of eleven non-repeated notes, with numerous fugal developments in dissonant counterpoint.

## 1 JUNE 1954

Switzerland issues a commemorative postage stamp to mark the centenary of the death of the Swiss hymn composer Alberich ZWISSIG, with a musical quotation from his *Schweizer Psalm* which has attained the status of the Swiss National Anthem.

## 1 JUNE 1954

At the 28th Festival of the International Society for Contemporary Music in Israel, the world première of *David,* opera in five acts by Darius MILHAUD, is given in Jerusalem in oratorio form, to commemorate the three thousand years of the establishment of Jerusalem as the capital of Judea, with a chorus commenting on the event from the historical point of view.

## 2 JUNE 1954

At the 28th Festival of the International Society for Contemporary Music in Israel, the following program of orchestral and choral music is given in Haifa:

*Capriccio* for string orchestra by the 39-year-old Dutch composer Marius FLOTHUIS, in three movements written in rococo manner; *3 Psalms* for chorus a cappella by the 27-year-old Danish composer Bernhard LEWKOWITCH; *Third String Quartet (Quartetto lirico)* by Mátyás SEIBER, Hungarian composer resident in London, imbued with the spirit of lyrical desolation and based on a pessimistically atonal hypododecaphonic series; and *La Resa di Calais*, ballad for soloists, chorus, strings and piano by the Italian composer Mario PANATERO.

## 3 JUNE 1954

At the 28th Festival of the International Society for Contemporary Music, the following program of orchestral and choral music is given in Haifa:

*5 Variants of Dives and Lazarus* by Ralph VAUGHAN WILLIAMS; *Violin Concerto* by Riccardo MALIPIERO, dodecaphonic nephew of Gian Francesco Malipiero; the world première of *Metamorphoses on Saibara* for voice and instruments by the 47-year-old Japanese composer Yoritsune MATSUDAIRA, based on dodecaphonically dislocated modalities of ancient pentatonic Japanese dance tunes; the world première of the *Viola Concerto* by the Posen-born 43-year-old Israeli composer Josef TAL (who abridged his name from the German Grünthal); and *Symphonie Concertante* by the dean of Swedish composers Hilding ROSENBERG.

## 4 JUNE 1954

At the 28th Festival of the International Society for Contemporary Music in Israel, the following program of chamber music is given in Haifa:

*Variations on a Bach Chorale* by Michael GIELEN of Germany, resident in Buenos Aires; *First String Quartet* by the 63-year-old Israeli composer Erich-Walter STERNBERG; *Le Tombeau de Ravel* for harpsichord and five instruments by the 42-year-old Dutch composer Rudolf ESCHER; *Divertimento* for wind quintet by Saikkola LAURI of Finland; and *String Quartet* by the American composer Leon KIRCHNER.

## 6 JUNE 1954

At the 28th Festival of the International Society for Contemporary Music in Israel, the following program of orchestral music is given in Haifa:

*Sinfonia Piccola* by the Polish-Parisian composer Alexandre TANSMAN (performed for the first time in Paris on 27 November 1952); *Piano Concerto* by Arnold SCHOENBERG, played in a two-piano version; *Violin Concerto* by the 47-year-old Norwegian composer Klaus EGGE; and the world première of *4 Danzas* for orchestra by the Chilian composer Carlos RIESCO.

## 6 JUNE 1954

HAYDN's skull, which disappeared from his casket two days after his funeral in 1809, came into the possession of the Vienna Male Singing Society and eventually of the Society of Friends of Music in Vienna, where it was publicly exhibited in a glass case, is restored in solemn ceremony (after being sprinkled with holy water by Cardinal Innitzer of the Roman Catholic diocese of Vienna) to the rest of his skeleton in the marble sarcophagus at Eisenstadt, at the ancestral estate of Prince Esterhaz, where Haydn spent thirty years of his productive life. (The date 12 June 1938, assigned to the skeletal integration of Haydn in the Third Edition of *Music Since 1900,* is premature).

### 7 JUNE 1954
At the concluding concert of the 28th Festival of the International Society for Contemporary Music in Israel, the following program is presented in Haifa:

*Violin Sonata* by Ahmed Adnan SAYGUN (Turkey); *Threnody* for piano by Jean COULTHARD (Canada); *Fourth Suite* for piano by Nikolas SKALKOTTAS (Greece); *Suite* of songs by Avraham DAUS (Israel); *Violin Sonata* by Hector TOSAR (Uruguay); *Variations on a Yugoslav Folk-Tune* for piano by Mirko CIPRA (Yugoslavia); *Second Piano Sonata* by Paul HINDEMITH (U.S.A.); *Leyenda del Ariel Criollo* for cello and piano by Aurelio DE LA VEGA (Cuba) and *Violin Sonata* by Don BANKS (Australia).

### 12 JUNE 1954
The First International Council of Composers opens in Rejkjavik, Iceland, presenting a program of Scandinavian and other music.

### 13 JUNE 1954
Nicolas OBOUHOV, the Russian expatriate who wrote ecstatic religious music and marked his scores with blood symbolic of that shed during the Russian Revolution and who signed his name "Nicolas l'illuminé," dies in Paris at the age of sixty-two.

### 13 JUNE 1954
*Concerto* for tuba and orchestra by Ralph VAUGHAN WILLIAMS, in three classical movements, *Prelude, Romance, Rondo alla tedesca,* with two grand cadenzas of elephantine capers and borborygmic burps, is performed for the first time by the London Symphony Orchestra, with Philip Catelinet as tuba soloist, Sir John Barbirolli conducting.

### 17 JUNE 1954
*Die Heimkehr,* one-act opera by the Rumanian-Parisian composer Marcel MIHALOVICI, after Guy de Maupassant's novelette *Le Retour,* a tale of a soldier returning from the wars surrealistically greeted by a chorus of walls, doors, and windows of his own house, set to music with considerable dissonant angst and atonal disorientation, is performed for the first time in concert form on the Frankfurt Radio, to a German libretto. (The first stage performance took place in Düsseldorf on 9 November 1954; a revised version was produced in Hamburg on 23 January 1955.)

## 17 JUNE 1954

*A Dinner Engagement,* comic opera in one act by the 51-year-old English composer Lennox BERKELEY, to a libretto concerning an attempt of avaricious impoverished parents to marry their daughter to a certifiably authentic prince, unexpectedly succeeding through a fortuitous series of felicitous coincidences, written in an appropriately hedonistic modernistic manner, is performed for the first time at the Aldeburgh Festival.

## 19 JUNE 1954

The Italian Government issues a 25-lire postage stamp commemorating the centennial of the birth of the Italian opera composer Alfredo CATALANI.

## 6 JULY 1954

*Murder in Three Keys,* three compact one-act operas, *Black Roses, Dark Sonnet, Simoon,* each with a bizarre case of dubiously motivated homicide, by the 50-year-old Scottish composer Erik CHISHOLM, set in a modernistic idiom of high complexity, are performed for the first time in Greenwich Village, in New York.

## 8 JULY 1954

*Circus,* overture by Ernst TOCH, written in an artfully stylized mock-popular manner, with an ostentatiously vulgar march tune as a motto and an interlude of free improvisation in the brass, is performed for the first time at the summer season in Ravinia, Chicago, Isler Solomon conducting.

## 14 JULY 1954

*Third Symphony* by the 42-year-old English composer Stanley BATE, written in 1940, is performed for the first time at the Cheltenham Festival.

## 19 JULY 1954

Jean-Jules Aimable ROGER-DUCASSE, French composer of agreeable impressionistic music, dies in Le-Tallan-Médoc, near Bordeaux, at the age of eighty-one.

## 20 JULY 1954

*Les Caprices de Marianne,* opera by the 53-year-old French composer Henri SAUGUET, is performed for the first time in Aix-en-Provence.

## 21 JULY 1954

*Daelia,* one-act opera by the American composer Hamilton FORREST, is produced in Interlochen, Michigan.

## 26 JULY 1954

The Soviet Government issues two commemorative postage stamps at 40 and 60 kopecks, bearing the likeness of the "father of Russian opera" Michael GLINKA on the occasion of the sesquicentennial of his birth.

**27 JULY 1954**

*The Audition,* one-act opera by the 34-year-old German-born American composer Alfred Grant GOODMAN, dealing with an aging actor who refuses to accept fatherly roles on the stage, but is finally persuaded by a kindly widow to reconcile himself to his age, written in a moderately modern idiom, is performed for the first time at the Ohio University Summer Opera Workshop, in Athens, Ohio.

**28 JULY 1954**

*The Brothers,* short opera by George ANTHEIL, is produced for the first time in Denver.

**7 AUGUST 1954**

*Paris à nous deux,* or *Le nouveau Rastignac,* opera-farce by Jean FRANÇAIX caricaturing the pretentiousness of modern Paris society, typified by Balzac's pompous *arriviste* Rastignac *redivivus* with a quartet of uncouth saxophones representing self-propelled geniuses among artists and musicians, is performed for the first time at the American Conservatory in Fontainebleau, an elegant Paris suburb.

**14 AUGUST 1954**

*Concerto* for mouth harmonica and orchestra by the English composer Malcolm ARNOLD is performed for the first time at the Promenade Concerts in London, with Larry Adler as soloist.

**14 AUGUST 1954**

*The Lost Flute* by the 55-year-old Russian-born composer Alexander TCHEREPNIN for narrator and orchestra, is presented for the first time at the Peninsula Music Festival at Fish Creek, Door County, Wisconsin, conducted by Thor Johnson, with the composer's wife Hsien Ming reciting the six Chinese poems of the text.

**17 AUGUST 1954**

*Penelope,* "opera semiseria" in two parts by the 43-year-old Swiss-born composer Rolf LIEBERMANN, taking place the 3137th year after the end of the Trojan war, written in the style of modern antiquity, with baroque recitatives reflecting the Odyssean peripeties, contrasted with the dissonant counterpoint and stark bitonalities characterizing modern life, the score incorporating a recorded session of boogie-woogie, is performed for the first time in Salzburg.

**25 AUGUST 1954**

*La Victoire de Guernica,* oratorio for chorus and orchestra by the Italian modernist Luigi NONO, to the words by Paul Eluard descriptive of the inner meaning of the victory of man's spirit over evil, as illustrated by the spiritual victory of the victims of the Fascist air assault upon the Basque village of Guernica, written in an apocalyptically agonizing atonal idiom, is performed for the first time at the International Festival for New Music in Darmstadt.

## 26 AUGUST 1954

*Practical Cats,* "an entertainment for children" for speaker and orchestra by the 49-year-old British composer Alan RAWSTHORNE, to the text by T. S. Eliot, is performed for the first time at the Music Festival at Edinburgh.

## 28 AUGUST 1954

*Fifth Symphony (Symphony for Strings),* in one movement, by the 39-year-old American composer Vincent PERSICHETTI, is performed for the first time by the Louisville Orchestra.

## 4 SEPTEMBER 1954

*Study in Pianissimo,* a dynamic symphonic essay by Boris BLACHER, is performed for the first time in Louisville.

## 7 SEPTEMBER 1954

*Western Symphony* by the 34-year-old Philadelphia-born composer Hershy KAY, in four movements based on authentic American tunes, ending with a symphonic barn dance subtitled *Saturday Night,* is performed for the first time as a ballet by the New York City Ballet Company, choreographed by George Balanchine, who commissioned the work.

## 8 SEPTEMBER 1954

Ralph VAUGHAN WILLIAMS conducts at the Three Choirs Festival in the Worcester Cathedral the first performance of his Christmas Cantata *Hodie,* for soprano, tenor, baritone, mixed chorus, boys' voices and orchestra, to texts from the Bible, Milton and other English poets.

## 11 SEPTEMBER 1954

Licinio REFICE, 71-year-old Italian composer of sacred music, collapses and dies on the podium while conducting his mystery play *Santa Cecilia* in Rio de Janeiro.

## 11 SEPTEMBER 1954

Four grandchildren of Robert SCHUMANN living in the United States bring a suit for libel in New York for nine million dollars against Loew's Inc., producers of the motion picture *Song of Life,* charging that it slanders the memory of their grandfather represented as insane and their grandmother Clara Schumann portrayed as having a non-platonic relationship with a clean-shaven Brahms, causing them "to suffer a loss of social standing, humiliation, mortification, chagrin and other mental anguish." (The suit was dismissed in view of the historical truth of Schumann's insanity)

## 12 SEPTEMBER 1954

Leonard BERNSTEIN conducts at the International Festival of Contemporary Music in Venice the world première of his *Serenade* for violin solo, with Isaac Stern as soloist, string orchestra and percussion, inspired by Plato's *Symposium*, and set in five interrelated movements:

(1) *Phaedrus: Pausanias*, in which an initial fugato symbolizes the principle of erotic duality (2) *Aristophanes*, expatiating satirically on human love (3) *Erixymathus*, a rapid scherzo giving a physician's view on love as a scientific model of harmony of carnal components (4) *Agathon*, chanting a melodious paeon to Eros in all aspects of amorous passion (5) *Socrates: Alcibiades*, in which Socrates speaks of the daemon of love in measured didactic tones, while the mundane Alcibiades hurls at him a jazzified challenge.

## 14 SEPTEMBER 1954

*The Turn of the Screw*, chamber opera in two acts by Benjamin BRITTEN, after the somber novel of Henry James in which a Victorian governess battles manorial ghosts seemingly intent on subverting the souls of the children in her charge, scored for boy treble, girl treble, three sopranos, tenor and a 13-member orchestra in which the piano serves as harmonic backbone, the "screw" of the title being represented by a subject that "turns" through 15 variations, evolved during instrumental interludes between the 8 scenes of each act, the entire score encompassed within a vast modulatory scheme of alternating perfect fifths and thirds (or their inversions), forming a thematic dodecaphonic series, which is subjected to a whole lexicon of technical operations, transmutations and metamorphoses, creating a tense atmosphere of expressionistic Angst, is produced in Venice.

## 18 SEPTEMBER 1954

The Government of the Federal German Republic commemorates the fifth anniversary of the death of Richard STRAUSS by issuing a 40-pfennig stamp bearing his likeness.

## 18 SEPTEMBER 1954

*Concerto* for flute, strings, harp, celesta and percussion by Virgil THOMSON, "a portrait conceived as a concerto for nightingale and strings," in three movements, making use of mutually exclusive whole-tone scales as well as triadic harmonies according to an elaborate intervallic scheme, is performed for the first time at the Festival of Contemporary Music in Venice.

## 20 SEPTEMBER 1954

*In Memoriam Dylan Thomas, Dirge, Canons and Song*, for tenor, string quartet and four trombones by Igor STRAVINSKY, set in reverberant tones evocative in their sonorous prosody of the lamented poet's Welsh voice, to the text of his celebrated poem "Do not go gentle into that good night," in which the apostrophe "Rage, rage against the dying of the light" recurs as an anguished refrain, evolving bio-melodically from a molecule of five thematic notes subjected to serialistic transmutations, is performed for the first time at the Monday Evening Concerts, Los Angeles, Robert Craft conducting.

22 SEPTEMBER 1954

*Nelson,* opera in three acts by the 51-year-old English composer Lennox BERKELEY, dealing with the great admiral's celebrated romantic affair with Lady Hamilton, is performed for the first time at Sadler's Wells in London. (A partial performance, with piano accompaniment, was given in London on 14 February 1953)

2 OCTOBER 1954

Two operas by Gian Francesco MALIPIERO, *Il Festino* (originally broadcast over the Turin Radio on 6 November 1937) and *Donna Urraca,* are given their first stage performances in Bergamo.

3 OCTOBER 1954

*Variazioni per orchestra* by Luigi DALLAPICCOLA, with a subject built on a tone-row in which the first and last notes are related by a tritone, ranging in mood from a lyrical *Amoroso* to a raging *Con violenza,* is performed for the first time in Louisville.

17 OCTOBER 1954

*Concerto* for jazz band and symphony orchestra by the 44-year-old Swiss-born composer Rolf LIEBERMANN, written in the strict dodecaphonic idiom, in 8 movements (*Introduction, Jump, Scherzo I, Blues, Scherzo II, Boogie-Woogie, Interludium* and *Mambo*), in which the 12-note tone-row appears horizontally (melodically) in the piano, and vertically (harmonically) in the muted divisi strings, is performed for the first time at the Donaueschingen Music Festival.

17 OCTOBER 1954

In the course of the Donaueschingen Festival of Contemporary Music a program for prepared pianos is given including the world premières of two American works:

34′ 46.776″ for two pianists by John CAGE, the title indicating duration of the music in minutes and seconds, the method of composition being derived from two sources, the Chinese book of oracles, *I Ching,* enabling one to tell fortune by six throws of coins, and observation of imperfections on a sheet of paper, so that a work is created which is completely free from the impedimenta of personal taste, knowledge of musical literature, and tradition; and *Intersection for Magnetic Tape* by Morton FELDMAN, the title referring to a street intersection at the moment when the green light is flashed, the score (in the form of a topographical diagram) indicating the approximate pitch (high, middle or low), the number of notes to be used, and determining the total duration of the work.

### 19 OCTOBER 1954

The era of Electronic Composition dawns with a broadcast from the Funkhaus of Cologne of seven works synthetically put together from fragments recorded on magnetic tape, mutated by the alteration of pitch, acceleration and deceleration of tempo, diffraction of tone color, denaturalization of the overtone series, dislocation of rhythmic symmetry and reversal of direction (forward to retrograde):

*Glockenspiel,* and *Etüde über Tongemische* by Herbert EIMERT; *Studie I* and *Studie II* by Karlheinz STOCKHAUSEN; *Komposition No. 5* by Karel GOEYVAERTS; *Seismogramme* by Henri POUSSEUR; and *Formanten I and II* by Paul GREDINGER, all stemming from dodecaphonic esthetics, symbolized by the dodecahedron structure of the loudspeaker, suspended from the ceiling in the broadcasting studio.

### 19 OCTOBER 1954

*Analfabeta,* musical burlesque in one act by the 41-year-old Croatian composer Ivo LHOTKA-KALINSKI, to a libretto focused on an analphabetic municipal clerk who believes that analphabet is the name of a secret subversive political party and proceeds to take police action when he hears someone being called an analphabetic fellow, written in a satirically dissonant idiom in utilitarian modernistic harmonies marked by propulsive asymmetric rhythms, is produced in Belgrade.

### 20 OCTOBER 1954

*Sisyphus,* choreographic suite for orchestra by the 38-year-old Swedish composer Karl-Birger BLOMDAHL, depicting the atonal anguish of the frustrated Greek forced to roll a boulder uphill only to have it roll down again, is performed for the first time in Stockholm.

### 20 OCTOBER 1954

*Pampeana No. 3,* a symphonic pastorale by the 38-year-old Argentinian composer Alberto GINASTERA, making use of acrid polyharmonic complexities, a simulated *scordatura* on a guitar and a dodecaphonic series, while preserving the essential melorhythms of the pampas, is performed for the first time in Louisville.

### 23 OCTOBER 1954

*Fifth Symphony* by the 63-year-old Hungarian composer László LAJTHA, in two movements (*Très modéré* and *Vite et agité*), with their thematic consanguinity emphasized by the identical 16-bar endings of both movements, replete with lyrical and motoric Transylvanian melorhythms, is performed for the first time in Paris.

## 24 OCTOBER 1954

*Bakhtior and Nisso,* music drama in four acts by the Soviet composer Sergei BALASANIAN, dealing with the struggle of Tadzhik peasantry against the obsolescent feudal lords in Pamir supported by the decaying imperialist powers, with a didactic epilogue of the tragic Tadzhik situation, is performed for the first time in Stalinabad.

## 26 OCTOBER 1954

Franco ALFANO, Italian composer of effective melodramatic operas, dies in San Remo at the age of seventy-eight.

## 29 OCTOBER 1954

*La Magicienne de la Mer,* lyric legend in three scenes by the 73-year-old French composer Paul LE FLEM, wherein a modern siren, semi-undine demi-midinette lures fishermen of the city of Ys to her den of amphibious iniquity, eventually submerging the entire community, so that only the eternally resonant bells of the sunken cathedral give evidence of its former glories, is produced at the Opéra-Comique in Paris.

## 30 OCTOBER 1954

Claudio SANTORO, 34-year-old Brazilian composer, conducts in Rio de Janeiro the first performance of his Fourth Symphony, *Da Paz,* consecrated to the cause of international peace, set in optimistically consonant modalities, representing a distinct departure from his previous dodecaphonic proclivities and signalizing his adoption of the Soviet doctrine of Socialist Realism. (Santoro conducted *Da Paz* in Moscow on 21 March 1955)

## 4 NOVEMBER 1954

*A Tale of a Mask Maker,* one-act opera by the 43-year-old Japanese composer Osamu SHIMIZU, dealing with a disfranchised samurai's love for the beauteous daughter of a lowly mask-maker in 1204, and ending in the death of both, set to music derived from ancient Nipponese melorhythms, is performed for the first time in Osaka.

## 10 NOVEMBER 1954

*Juro Jánošík,* opera in six scenes by the 43-year-old Czech composer Jan CIKKER, with action taking place in Slovakia during the turbulent years 1711–1713 and focused on a rebellious idealistic youth Juro Jánošík betrayed into the hands of the Austrian gendarmerie and sentenced to hang, written in an expansive folkloristic idiom with spacious melorhythms of Slavic content and invigorated by asymmetrical rhythms and admissible dissonances, is produced in Bratislava.

## 10 NOVEMBER 1954

*Die stumme Serenade,* comic opera by Erich Wolfgang KORNGOLD, composed in 1946, is performed for the first time in Dortmund, Germany.

17 NOVEMBER 1954

*Sixth Symphony* by the English composer Edmund RUBBRA, in four move-ments, with thematic substance derived from a tetraphonic motive, E-F-A-B, in various transmutations developed in tangentially tonal modalities spiced with non-toxic resolvable dissonances, (1) *Lento-Allegretto*, displaying a conti-nuity of romantic development, in unobfuscated polyphony (2) *Canto*, set in spacious harmonies with unimpeded melorhythmic current (3) *Vivace impetu-oso*, an unpretentious lyric scherzo (4) *Poco Andante-Allegro moderato*, ending in a plagally approached unadulterated C major, is performed for the first time in London.

21 NOVEMBER 1954

Karol RATHAUS, Polish-born German-bred composer and scholar whose mod-ernistic music attracted brief attention in the period between the two wars, dies in New York, where he took refuge from European turmoil, at the age of fifty-nine.

23 NOVEMBER 1954

*Sandhog*, "ballad in three acts" based on the short story *St. Columbia and the River* by Theodore Dreiser, dealing with a true adventure of an Irishman, fa-ther of twins, employed as a "sandhog" in digging the tunnel under the North River in New York City in the 1880's, and who is blown up through the muck to the surface of the river, but escapes unscathed, featuring a *Work Song* and a *Sweat Song*, is produced in New York, with a folksy musical score by Earl ROBINSON.

26 NOVEMBER 1954

*Concerto for Orchestra* by the 41-year-old Polish composer Witold LUTOSLAWSKI, in three compactly functional movements, (1) *Intrada* (2) *Ca-priccio, Notturno ed Arioso* (3) *Passacaglia, Toccata e Chorale*, couched in classical forms, with melorhythmic contents derived from Polish folk sources, is performed for the first time in Warsaw.

29 NOVEMBER 1954

*Concerto for Orchestra* by the 32-year-old Greek composer Yorgo SICILIANOS, written in a compact and resonant idiom of neo-Grecian baroque, is per-formed for the first time in Athens.

30 NOVEMBER 1954

Wilhelm FURTWÄNGLER, German conductor, cultured interpreter of the mas-terpieces of German music and a liberal champion of moderate modern music, dies in Baden-Baden at the age of sixty-eight.

2 DECEMBER 1954

*Déserts*, symphonic poem by Edgar VARÈSE, scored for wind instruments, per-cussion and electronic sounds, the first work ever composed for orchestral instruments combined with a pre-recorded magnetic tape and conceived in an athematic idiom of agglutinated melorhythmic molecules, according to Varèse's doctrine of "organized sound," is performed for the first time in Paris.

(*Poem in Cycles and Bels* for tape recorder and orchestra by Otto Luening and Vladimir Ussachevsky was composed later than *Déserts*, but had its first performance two weeks earlier than Varèse's work)

## 2 DECEMBER 1954

Enrique SORO, Chilean composer of easily assimilable piano pieces tinted with local Andean color, dies in Santiago at the age of seventy.

## 3 DECEMBER 1954

*Troilus and Cressida*, opera in three acts by William WALTON, to a libretto derived from Chaucer, wherein Prince Troilus of Troy perishes in his attempt to rescue the daughter of a treasonous high priest from Greek captivity, and she stabs herself to death, set to music in a dramatically impassioned neo-Handelian manner, intensified by an uninhibited use of modern dissonance, is produced at Covent Garden in London.

## 3 DECEMBER 1954

*Prayers of Kierkegaard*, oratorio by Samuel BARBER for soprano solo, chorus and orchestra, to the texts from the writings of the melancholy Danish philosopher whose fatalistic theology paradoxically influenced the deterministic trends of his preeminently mechanistic century, set to music with an authentic sentiment of Protestant hymnody and frequent flights into atonal and bitonal formations, is performed for the first time by the Boston Symphony Orchestra, Charles Munch conducting.

## 4 DECEMBER 1954

*La Figlia di Iorio*, "pastoral tragedy" in three acts by Ildebrando PIZZETTI (composed between 11 July 1953 and 18 April 1954), to a mystical libretto of Gabriele d'Annunzio, wherein the beautiful daughter of a self-styled magus is forced to flee from a massed assault of harvesters "intoxicated by the sun and wine" and finds refuge in the family of a young bridegroom who, inflamed by her, carries her to an oceanside grotto and kills his own father with an axe when the latter intrudes to ravish her, but is saved from the vengeance of the villagers when she assumes the guilt as a psychological incendiary, and goes to her death in the "purifying flames" of a sacred fire, set to music in rhapsodically pyromantic modalities, is performed for the first time in Naples.

## 4 DECEMBER 1954

*Double Trouble*, one-act opera by the 50-year-old expatriate German composer Richard MOHAUPT, in which a pair of identical twins named Hocus and Pocus are involved in a series of amatory imbroglios, set to music in the manner of an Italian opera buffa, is performed for the first time as a commissioned work by the Louisville Orchestra, vocal soloists and chorus.

### 10 DECEMBER 1954

*Third Symphony* by the 51-year-old Russian-born American composer Nikolai LOPATNIKOFF is performed for the first time in Pittsburgh.

### 11 DECEMBER 1954

Carlos CHÁVEZ conducts at the Music Festival in Caracas the world première of his *Third Symphony*, commissioned for this occasion by the playwright Clare Boothe Luce, in four movements, *Introduzione, Allegro, Scherzo,* and *Finale,* based on classical models without overt ethnical Mexican references. (The Fourth and Fifth symphonies of Chávez, though written later than the Third, were performed on earlier dates, the Fourth on 11 February 1953, the Fifth on 1 December 1953)

### 14 DECEMBER 1954

*Second Symphony* by the 47-year-old French composer Tony AUBIN, is performed for the first time in Paris.

### 17 DECEMBER 1954

*Fourth Symphony* by Vincent PERSICHETTI, cast in the classical four movements (1) *Adagio–Allegro* (2) *Andante* (3) *Allegretto* (4) *Presto,* and conceived in a cyclically constructed form, judiciously equilibrated between lyric consonant episodes and dramatic dissonant interludes, is performed for the first time anywhere by the Philadelphia Orchestra, Eugene Ormandy conducting.

### 18 DECEMBER 1954

*Die Brücke von San Luis Rey,* radio opera by the 54-year-old German composer Hermann REUTTER, after Thornton Wilder's novel tracing back the lives of several people united in a catastrophe when a bridge collapses in Peru carrying them to their deaths, is given in its stage performance, in Essen. (First radio performance was given by the Frankfurt Radio on 20 June 1954)

### 23 DECEMBER 1954

*A Christmas Carol,* musical television play by Bernard HERRMANN, is produced by the Columbia Broadcasting System in New York.

### 25 DECEMBER 1954

A commemorative stamp of 15 dinars to mark the centennial of the death of the Serbian composer Vatroslav LISINSKY (1819–1854) is issued in Yugoslavia.

### 27 DECEMBER 1954

*The Saint of Bleecker Street,* music drama in three acts by Gian Carlo MENOTTI, to his own libretto dealing with a mystically illuminated young woman in the Italian section of Greenwich Village in New York, whose religious frenzy causes psychosomatic stigmata to appear on her hands and feet on Good Friday at the conclusion of her aria in the first act, emulating the wounds of Christ, and whose brother strangles his fiancée when she taunts him regarding his quasi-incestuous brotherly love, and the "Saint of Bleecker Street" falls lifeless to the ground as she receives the nun's veil, set to music combining elements of religious chants with mundane balladry, and including a scene in a subway station in the best tradition of Italian Verismo, is produced in New York, with Menotti himself acting in the multiple capacities of coordinator and stage director.

# ᘓᕟ 1955 ᕟᘖ

**7 JANUARY 1955**

*Fantaisies symphoniques* (*Sixth Symphony*) by Bohuslav MARTINU (completed on 23 April 1953), in three movements consisting of sections alternatively marked *Lento* and *Allegro,* with a germinal motive taken from Martinu's opera *Julietta,* and developed as a rhapsodic fantasy in a romantically impressionistic vein, is performed for the first time by the Boston Symphony Orchestra under the direction of Charles Munch, as a commissioned work for its 75th anniversary.

**7 JANUARY 1955**

Marian ANDERSON makes her debut at the Metropolitan Opera in New York, as Ulrica in Verdi's *Un Ballo in maschera,* the first Negro singer to be so distinguished.

**14 JANUARY 1955**

Heitor VILLA-LOBOS conducts the Philadelphia Orchestra in the world première of his *Eighth Symphony* in four movements, *Andante, Lento assai, Allegretto scherzando, Allegro giusto,* in which a spacious cantillation in the manner of Brazilian melorhythms is brought in contrast with stark dissonant harmonies, creating intermittent dramatic tension, and the world première of his *Concerto for Harp and Orchestra,* in four movements, *Allegro, Andante moderato, Scherzo, Allegro non troppo,* containing a long cadenza linking the third and fourth movements, with the eminent modernistic harpist Nicanor Zabaleta as soloist.

**14 JANUARY 1955**

Monaco issues a five-franc postage stamp to mark the 80th anniversary of the great humanist Albert SCHWEITZER.

## 15 JANUARY 1955

*Third Symphony*, in F sharp, by the 55-year-old Russian-born composer Alexander TCHEREPNIN, in four movements, *Lento, Allegro pesante, Adagio* and *Allegro*, written in a propellent rhythmic style, is performed for the first time by the Indianapolis Symphony Orchestra, Fabien Sevitzky conducting.

## 19 JANUARY 1955

Guillermo URIBE-HOLGUÍN, prime composer of Colombia, conducts in Bogotá the first performance of his *Third Symphony*.

## 23 JANUARY 1955

*Symphonie de chambre*, in E major, for 12 instruments, last work by Georges ENESCO (completed by him 28 May 1954), written in a rhapsodically elaborated rococo manner, is performed for the first time in Paris.

## 23 JANUARY 1955

*Tudor Vladimirescu*, opera-oratorio by the 40-year-old Rumanian composer Gheorghe DUMITRESCU dealing with the tragic hero of the Rumanian war for independence executed in 1821 by the Greek leader Ypsilanti on account of conflicting national aims, set in a sociologically realistic idiom, leaning strongly on folk music, is performed for the first time in Bucharest. (A partial performance of the work was given in Bucharest on 24 September 1951)

## 25 JANUARY 1955

*A Letter to Emily*, chamber opera by the American composer Lockrem JOHNSON, is produced in Seattle.

## 27 JANUARY 1955

*The Midsummer Marriage*, opera in three acts by the 50-year-old English composer Michael TIPPETT, to his own libretto, dealing with two pairs of lovers mating symbolically with their own antinomic selves representing the masculine element in a woman and a feminine element in a man, set to music in a capaciously diatonic idiom diversified by opulently terraced dissonances, is produced at Covent Garden in London.

## 16 FEBRUARY 1955

*La Conchiglia*, short opera by the Italian composer Lino LIVIABELLA, after Robert Louis Stevenson's *The Bottle Imp*, is produced in Florence.

## 18 FEBRUARY 1955

*Fifth Symphony*, subtitled *Sinfonia Sacra*, by Howard HANSON (completed by him on 8 August 1954), inspired by the story of the first Easter in the Gospel according to St. John, and conceived as an architectonic triptych, consisting of a triune introduction, a trithematic middle section, and variants and mutations of these materials forming a third division, founded on ecumenical ecclesiastical modalities and evolving with dramatic passion in powerfully resonant harmonies, is performed for the first time by the Philadelphia Orchestra under the direction of Eugene Ormandy.

## 21 FEBRUARY 1955

*Four Russian Songs* for soprano, flute, harp and guitar by Igor STRAVINSKY are performed for the first time at the Monday Evening Concerts in Los Angeles, Robert Craft conducting.

(Two of these songs are arrangements for voice and instruments of songs from *Four Russian Songs* for voice and piano completed on 23 October 1919; the other two are orchestrations of songs from *Three Tales for Children* for voice and piano completed on 21 June 1917)

## 24 FEBRUARY 1955

*Silk Stockings*, musical comedy by Cole PORTER, inspired by the motion picture *Ninotchka*, urbanely satirizing the Soviet ways of Stalinist life (when a Soviet bureaucrat is informed that Prokofiev is dead, he observes: "I didn't even know he was arrested" and a commissar carries with him a copy of "Who's Still Who"), is produced in New York.

## 24 FEBRUARY 1955

*Susannah*, musical drama in two acts by the 28-year-old American composer Carlisle FLOYD, to his own libretto, fashioned after the biblical story of Susannah and the elders transferred to rural Tennessee, wherein a fire-breathing Baptist preacher defiles a virginal cornfed farm girl after watching her swim innocently in the nude, whereupon her brother slays him during a baptism exhibit, set to music in a simplicistically hymnal triadic idiom, with a modicum of modernistic bitonalities, is performed for the first time at Florida State University in Tallahassee. (The first New York performance of the opera was given at the New York City Center on 27 September 1956)

## 27 FEBRUARY 1955

*Mitologia*, symphonic poem by the 62-year-old Portuguese composer Maurice SANDOZ, in two sections, *The Aeolian Harp* and *Sybil's Grotto*, is performed for the first time in Lisbon.

## 2 MARCH 1955

*Le Serment*, opera by the Parisianized Polish composer Alexander TANSMAN, is produced in Brussels.

## 13 MARCH 1955

*First Symphony* for strings by the 60-year-old Corsican-born French composer Henri MARTELLI, is performed for the first time in Paris.

## 14 MARCH 1955

*Hand in Hand,* opera by the Estonian composer Gustav ERNESAKS, dealing with the attempted sabotage of an Estonian electric power station by unliquidated Estonian counterrevolutionaries, with a jubilant finale as foes are foiled and the station begins to generate electricity, is produced in Tallin.

## 18 MARCH 1955

*A Trip to Nahant,* fantasy for orchestra by the America composer Randall THOMPSON, nostalgically depicting an excursion to the small town northeast of Boston, making use of euphoniously harmonized Americanistic tunes, is performed for the first time by the Philadelphia Orchestra, Eugene Ormandy conducting.

## 21 MARCH 1955

Olivier MESSIAEN, organist since 1932 at the Trinité in Paris, presents there the first integral performance of his *Livre d'Orgue,* in seven movements, *Reprise par interversion, Pièce en trio, Les Mains de l'Abîme, Chants d'oiseaux, Pièce en trio, Les Yeux dans les roues* and *64 durées,* written according to his theory of interrelated modalities, in which not only the notes, but durations and dynamic intensities are distributed according to a master plan of coordinated combinatorial parameters.

## 31 MARCH 1955

The first complete performance of Sergei PROKOFIEV's revised and abbreviated version of his opera *War and Peace,* after Tolstoy's epic novel, set to music with a natural fluency of modulating tonalities, rhythmically ebullient and rich equally in nostalgic lyrical quality and dramatic tension, is given posthumously in Leningrad.

## 2 APRIL 1955

*The Wish,* one-act opera by George ANTHEIL, to his own libretto about the death of a young couple in love in Greenwich Village in New York City, accentuating the fateful element in somber modalities, upon which the sounds of ubiquitous popular songs mundanely intrude, in a "synthesis of the mystic and the realistic," is performed for the first time in Louisville.

## 2 APRIL 1955

*Il Giudizio Universale,* opera in three acts by the 34-year-old Italian composer Vieri TOSATTI, in which members of the world bourgeoisie attend the Day of Judgment and confess their abominations perpetrated while maintaining a posture of social respectability, is produced at La Scala, Milan.

## 15 APRIL 1955

*Numance,* opera by the 54-year-old French composer Henry BARRAUD, based on a play by Cervantes dealing with the patriotic resistance of the Spanish town of Numantia to Roman invaders in 133 B.C., is performed for the first time at the Paris Opéra. (The symphonic predecessor of *Numance* was Barraud's *Symphonie de Numance,* performed at Baden-Baden on 3 December 1950)

24 APRIL 1955

*Dance Overture* by Paul CRESTON, a quadrinational musical tribute derived from the rhythms of the four powers that shaped the destiny of Florida, Spain (bolero), England (country dance), France (loure), and the United States (square dance), is performed for the first time at the convention of the National Federation of Music Clubs in Miami, Florida.

25 APRIL 1955

*Die Füsse im Feuer,* music drama by the 34-year-old Swiss composer Armin SCHIBLER, is produced in Zürich.

27 APRIL 1955

*The Magic Mirror,* opera in 3 acts by Wheeler BECKETT, is produced in Newark, New Jersey.

28 APRIL 1955

*Fifth Symphony* by the 45-year-old Rumanian composer Alfred MENDELSOHN is performed for the first time in Bucharest.

30 APRIL 1955

*Dawn,* operetta in three acts by the Albanian composer Kristo KONO, to a libretto depicting the successful discovery and condign lethal punishment of an unliquidated Albanian kulak scheming to murder a newly-wed socialistic couple, is produced in Tirana.

1 MAY 1955

Heinz ARNTZ sets a world record for playing the piano without stopping, except for necessary physiological functions of ingestion, imbibation, elimination and brief dormition, for 423 hours (17 days and 15 hours).

4 MAY 1955

Georges ENESCO, prime composer of modern Rumania, who began his career as an incredible child prodigy of fantastic natural gifts and became a virtuoso violinist and whose youthful *Rumanian Rhapsody* represents the most successful symphonic stylization of indigenous motives, dies in Paris at the age of seventy-three.

5 MAY 1955

*Damn Yankees,* musical comedy by Richard ADLER and Jerry ROSS, based on Douglass Wallop's novel *The Year the Yankess Lost the Pennant,* a modern Faust story in which an elderly baseball fan sells his soul to the devil in exchange for the career of a rejuvenated pitcher, enabling his favorite team, the Washington Senators, to win the pennant from the New York Yankees with psychosomatic assistance from a reincarnated witch Lola, and then cheats the

Devil by refusing to play in the World Series, regains his soul and returns to his proper age, is produced in New York.

### 5 MAY 1955

*Sixth Symphony* by the 45-year-old Danish composer Vagn HOLMBOE, commemorating the tenth anniversary of the liberation of Denmark from Nazi occupation, is performed for the first time in Copenhagen.

### 9 MAY 1955

*The Pot of Fat*, chamber opera in six scenes by the American composer Theodore CHANLER, a fable of a cat and a mouse living in congenial matrimonial concubinage, who store a pot of fat away in the church as communal property, with the cat poaching on it surreptitiously, set to music in a gently satirical Gallic vein, with asymmetrical melorhythms supporting a tonal vocal line, is performed for the first time at the Longy School of Music in Cambridge, Massachusetts. (The first New York performance was given 22 February 1956)

### 10 MAY 1955

*A Childhood Miracle*, one-act opera by the American composer Ned ROREM, based on Hawthorne's story *The Snow Image*, set to music in a simple tonal idiom adorned with tolerable non-toxic dissonances, and *The Nightingale*, one-act opera by Bernard ROGERS, after Hans Christian Andersen's tale of the Chinese Emperor saved from a mortal illness by the singing of a forest nightingale, sustained in an impressionistic style, are performed for the first time by Punch Opera in New York.

### 11 MAY 1955

*Violin Concerto* by the dean of modern British composers Sir Arthur BLISS is performed for the first time in London.

### 12 MAY 1955

Two centuries have passed since the birth at Fontanetto da Po of Giovanni Battista VIOTTI, Italian virtuoso violinist and composer who dazzled the royal court of Marie Antoinette and fled from the French Revolution to London to die in penury and distress.

(Viotti had a brother, also named Giovanni Battista, who was born on 23 May 1753, and died in infancy on 10 July 1754. The surviving Viotti, who was given the same first names, was born on 12 May 1755. Through confusion, Viotti's bicentennial was widely celebrated on 23 May 1953, on the anniversary of the birth of the dead child)

### 13 MAY 1955

*The Ruby*, a short opera by the American composer Norman DELLO JOIO, is performed for the first time in Bloomington, Indiana.

994

17 MAY 1955

Robert METZLER, 50-year-old Chicago church organist, obtains a court injunction against Miss Harriet Davis, 35, who, accompanied by her mother, systematically pursued him wherever he went after they met while walking their respective dogs, specifically charging her with blocking his car as he was leaving the church and creating a traffic jam. (Miss Davis claimed she was interested only in the inspiration received from his organ playing)

18 MAY 1955

Francesco Balilla PRATELLA, futurist Italian composer who wrote the first opera about an aviator and whose futuristic idiom was anchored mainly on the whole-tone scale, dies in Ravenna, at the age of seventy-five.

20 MAY 1955

*What Men Live By*, one-act opera-pastorale by Bohuslav MARTINU, adapted to an English libretto from Tolstoy's moralistic tale wherein a kindly cobbler tenders a helping hand to a pilgrim, a widow and a boy, and then learns in a veridical dream that he thereby received Christ, set to music with an equilibrated infusion of lofty modalities and mundane balladry, is performed for the first time on the stage at Hunter College in New York.

25 MAY 1955

*The Committee*, comic opera in four scenes by the 33-year-old American composer Matt DORAN, detailing an examination for a Music Doctor's degree in a Western American university, with a multiplicity of academically inane questions, including one asking which symphony ends with a timpani beat on the dominant (the correct answer is the first symphony by the chairman of the committee), is produced for the first time at the Del Mar College of Music in Corpus Christi, Texas.

25 MAY 1955

*The Fatal Oath*, opera by the 54-year-old Russian-born American composer Boris KOUTZEN, to a libretto derived from Balzac's horror story *La Grande Bretèche*, is performed for the first time anywhere in New York.

26 MAY 1955

Michel MAGNE conducts in Paris the first performance of his *Symphonie Humaine*, employing 150 players and making use of instruments producing inaudible sounds of slow low frequencies calculated to make a painful impact on the abdominal region of the listener.

30 MAY 1955

*Incontri* for 24 instruments by the Italian avant-garde composer Luigi NONO is performed for the first time in Darmstadt.

## 9 JUNE 1955

*First Symphony* by the Rumanian composer Sigismond TODUȚA is performed for the first time in Bucharest.

## 11 JUNE 1955

Marcel SAMUEL-ROUSSEAU, French composer of operas, ballets and other works, son of Samuel-Alexandre Rousseau, whose first Christian name he added to his own last name to avoid confusion, dies in his native Paris at the age of seventy-two.

## 15 JUNE 1955

*Feltámadt a tenger (The Sea Is Rising)*, oratorio by the Communist Hungarian composer Ferenc SZABÓ, descriptive of the revolutionary upheaval of 1848 and dedicated to the "unforgettable memory of the Hungarian Soviet Republic of 1919," is performed for the first time in Budapest.

## 17 JUNE 1955

The 29th Festival of the International Society for Contemporary Music opens at Baden-Baden with the following program:

*Seventh Symphony* by the 45-year-old Danish composer Vagn HOLMBOE, in a neo-classical setting, in seven sections, *Allegro con fuoco, Intermezzo I, Adagio, Intermezzo II, Presto, Intermezzo III, Coda,* in which the intermezzi serve as intervallic mutations and rhythmic variants of the principal movements; *Variazioni per Orchestra* by the 51-year-old Italian expressionist Luigi DALLAPICCOLA (first performed as a commissioned work in Louisville on 3 October 1954); *Lied der Kentauren,* cantata for soprano and orchestra by the German composer Markus LEHMANN; *Musique pour cordes* by the Swiss composer Constantin REGAMEY, in three movements, *Andante, Marcia giocosa, Vivace assai,* in a conciliatorily tonal idiom in which the modulatory factor is replaced by dodecaphonic relativity, with the retention of a definitely sensed tonal barycenter in each movement: and *Third Symphony* by Carlos CHÁVEZ (first performed at the Festival of Caracas, on 11 December 1954)

## 17 JUNE 1955

At a meeting of the International Standards Organization in Stockholm, delegates of 37 nations agree to raise the pitch of the basic tuning note "A" from 435 (adopted at an international congress in Vienna in 1885) to 440 cycles.

## 18 JUNE 1955

At the 29th Festival of the International Society for Contemporary Music at Baden-Baden, the following works are presented:

*Actus Tragicus* for ten violins by the German-American composer Erich Itor KAHN, derived from a dodecaphonic subject but provided with a triadic epilogue as a tonal atonement of the atonal peripeties of the "tragic act" and constituting an Aristotelian catharsis; *Kammerkonzert* for piano, woodwinds and percussion by the Swedish avantgarde composer Karl Birger BLOMDAHL, in four movements, *Lento, Allegro, Adagio,*

*Presto; Arpiade* by the Moscow-born German-Russian composer Vladimir VOGEL of Switzerland, scored for soprano and a small ensemble, to dadaistic texts of eight poems, four in German and four in French, by the surrealist poet Hans Arp, athematically set to music, with syllabic values determining a corresponding instrumental color; the world première of *Le Marteau sans Maître* by the emergent leader of the avant-garde, 30-year-old Pierre BOULEZ, scored for contralto, alto flute, vibraphone, xylorimba (a heterozygotic product of xylophone and marimba), viola, guitar, and a covey of unloud drumlets, shakers and metallic percussion instruments, to the surrealistic texts of René Char, in nine sections containing three instrumental "commentaries" on the masterless martellation of the title.

19 JUNE 1955

At the 29th Festival of the International Society for Contemporary Music in Baden-Baden, two concerts of chamber music are given, one in the afternoon, one in the evening:

Afternoon concert: *String Quartet* in three movements by Herbert BRÜN of Israel, based on a dodecaphonic series; *Alpha and Beta*, a dodecaphonic piano piece by the Japanese composer Makoto MOROI, the title alluding to the most conspicuous stars in the Gemini constellation; *Piano Sonatina* by the Australian composer Peter SCULTHORPE; *5 Lieder* for voice, flute, clarinet and bassoon by the 54-year-old Austrian composer Hans Erich APOSTEL; *Trio* for oboe, clarinet and bassoon by the 29-year-old Danish composer Jan MAEGAARD; and *Third String Quartet*, subtitled *Quartetto Lirico*, by the Hungarian-born naturalized British composer Mátyás SEIBER, in three contrasting movements, ending on a pessimistic note of cosmic desolation symbolized by an atonally disjunct melodic motto.

Evening concert: *Orchester-Ornament* by the 52-year-old China-born half-Estonian half-German composer Boris BLACHER, consisting of two fast and two slow movements, derived from an arithmetic series governing intervallic, metrical and rhythmic factors; *String Quartet* by the 28-year-old German composer Hans Werner HENZE, in three classically proportioned movements; *Chanson et Romance* for soprano and orchestra by the German composer Werner EGK, to the text of an old French love song; *The Creation* for baritone and orchestra by the German composer Wolfgang FORTNER, to the text by the American Negro poet Weldon Johnson, explaining the act of creation as the result of God's loneliness in a world without people; and *Variations for orchestra*, op. 31, by Arnold SCHOENBERG.

20 JUNE 1955

At the 29th Festival of the International Society for Contemporary Music at Baden-Baden, the following program of chamber music is presented:

*Sonata* for two pianos by the Italian modernist Riccardo NIELSEN, in three parts thematically built on a 12-tone series; *Quartet* for flute, clarinet, bassoon and piano by the Norwegian composer Knut WIGGEN, in a paradodecaphonic idiom; *Sonata* for cello and piano by the 46-year-old American composer Elliott Carter, in which he applies systematically the technique of "metric modulation" whereby an independent and usually incommensurate rhythm is superposed on the dominant meter and subsequently supersedes it as the main time signature; *Concertino* for flute, oboe, English horn and cello by the 34-year-old Swedish composer Ingvar LIDHOLM, in four movements, with the subject matter being derived from serialistic premises; and *Second String Quartet* in four movements by the English composer Francis BURT.

## 21 JUNE 1955

At the last concert of the 29th Festival of the International Society for Contemporary Music in Baden-Baden, the following program of symphonic music is presented:

*Rhapsody* for orchestra by the renowned pianist Arthur SCHNABEL, written in a neoclassical style with atonal excrescences in dissonant counterpoint; *Divertimento No. 1* for two violins and chamber orchestra by the Parisian Hungarian composer Tibor HARSÁNYI, in three movements of a classical countenance; *Suite* for string orchestra, piano and percussion by the Italian composer Gino CONTILLI, with a passacaglia based on a 12-tone series; and *Sinfonia* by the Spanish composer resident in England Roberto GERHARD, in three movements, derived from a basic 12-tone series with concomitant serial procedures in the intervallic and dynamic parameters.

## 26 JUNE 1955

*Musicwriter,* a machine that can efficiently and speedily type in musical notation, invented by the American composer Cecil EFFINGER, is demonstrated for the first time at the exhibit of the National Office Machine Dealers Association, in Denver, Colorado.

## 26 JUNE 1955

*The Hudson River Suite* by Ferde GROFÉ, inspired by Washington Irving's story, the score of which includes a part for a trained dog's barking, a rescue squad siren, a police whistle and a set of bowling pins to represent the rumble of the ghostly group encountered by Rip Van Winkle in the Catskill Mountains, is performed for the first time in Washington, with Sally Herman as soloist, barking in lieu of a dog.

## 5 JULY 1955

To commemorate the centennial of the birth of the Russian composer Anatoly LIADOV, the Soviet government issues a postage stamp at 40 kopecks bearing his portrait and a few notes from a Russian song arranged by him.

## 5 JULY 1955

*Zarya nad Dvinoi (Dawn over the Dvina)*, opera by the Ukrainian composer Yuli MEITUS, is performed for the first time in Kiev.

## 8 AUGUST 1955

*The Rope,* opera by the American composer Louis MENNINI, brother of Peter Mennin (who cut off the last letter of his Italian name), commissioned by the Koussevitzky Music Foundation, is presented for the first time at the Berkshire Music Festival at Tanglewood, Massachusetts.

## 11 AUGUST 1955

*A Lament for April 15,* fiscal madrigal by the retired banker Avery CLAFLIN, who had some lessons with Erik Satie in Paris, to the text, verbatim, of the tax instruction sheet for filing statements of income on April 15 each year, set to music with gravity befitting the subject, in the polyphonic style of a secular oratorio, is performed for the first time at the Berkshire Center in Tanglewood, Massachusetts.

## 17 AUGUST 1955

*Irische Legende,* opera by the German composer Werner EGK, is performed for the first time in Salzburg.

## 22 AUGUST 1955

Olin DOWNES, for many years chief music critic of the New York *Times,* earnest defender of the ideal of good music marked by melodious godliness and harmonious cleanliness, of which Sibelius was a paradigm and Schoenberg its principal defiler, dies of cancer in New York at the age of sixty-nine.

## 7 SEPTEMBER 1955

After five years of residence in America, 78-year-old Hungarian composer Ernst VON DOHNÁNYI, sobbing with joy (as reported by his third wife), becomes a citizen of the United States.

## 13 SEPTEMBER 1955

*Seventh Symphony,* by Darius MILHAUD, in three contrasting movements, *Animé, Grave, Vif,* completed by him in California on 15 May 1955, and written in a characteristically direct Gallic manner, without a key signature, but built around D, which is the first and the last note in the score, is performed for the first time in the course of the International Music Festival in Venice by the Orchestra of the Belgian Institute National de Radiodiffusion, as a commissioned work, conducted by Franz André.

## 15 SEPTEMBER 1955

*The Flaming Angel,* opera in five acts by Sergei PROKOFIEV, composed between 1919 and 1927, to a libretto from the medievalistic story by the Russian novelist Valery Bryusov, dealing with a young maiden tortured by the Inquisition for iniquitous communion with the Devil, comes to a belated posthumous stage production in the course of the Festival of Contemporary Music in Venice.

## 17 SEPTEMBER 1955

The German Federal Republic issues a 40-pfennig postage stamp commemorating the conductor Wilhelm FURTWÄNGLER.

## 18 SEPTEMBER 1955

*Variazioni concertanti* for piano and orchestra by the 35-year-old Rumanian-born Italian composer Roman VLAD, based on a succession of 12 different notes artfully extracted from a pseudo-dodecaphonic passage in Mozart's *Don Giovanni,* is performed for the first time in Venice.

## 24 SEPTEMBER 1955

*Suite transocéane* for orchestra by André JOLIVET is performed for the first time in Louisville, Kentucky, as a commissioned work, by the Louisville Orchestra.

## 7 OCTOBER 1955

Darius MILHAUD conducts the first performance, with the Boston Symphony Orchestra, of his *Sixth Symphony* in four movements, *Calme et tendre, Tumulteueux, Lent et doux,* and *Joyeux et robuste,* written in his characteristic cultured manner, vitalized by a constant influx of harmonious dissonances.

## 9 OCTOBER 1955

The Hungarian Government issues two stamps at 60 fellers and one forint honoring Béla BARTÓK, and bearing his portrait.

## 17 OCTOBER 1955

*Pallas Athene Weint,* opera in three acts with a prologue by Ernst KRENEK (completed in Los Angeles on 2 January 1955), to his own libretto, in which Pallas Athene sheds dodecaphonic tears over the subjugation of her city of Athens by the Spartans during the last phase of the Peloponnesian War in 404 B.C., with Socrates offering her diatonic consolation against a pentatonic accompaniment in gymnosophistical vigesimosecular counterpoint, is performed for the first time by the Hamburg State Opera.

## 23 OCTOBER 1955

*Only a Dream,* operetta by the Estonian composer Boris KYRVER, dealing with the love between an unemployed young architect and a salesgirl during the period between the two world wars, with local bourgeois color provided by interludes of obsolete jazz, is performed for the first time in Tallin.

## 28 OCTOBER 1955

*Saeta,* ballet by the 25-year-old Spanish composer Cristóbal HALFFTER, nephew of Ernesto and Rodolfo Halffter, is performed for the first time in Madrid.

## 29 OCTOBER 1955

*Violin Concerto* in A minor by Dmitri SHOSTAKOVICH, in four movements, a tranquil *Nocturne,* a limpid *Scherzo,* a stately *Passacaglia* leading by means of an extended cadenza into a whimsical *Burlesca,* is performed for the first time in Leningrad with David Oistrakh, to whom the Concerto is dedicated, as soloist.

## 4 NOVEMBER 1955

*Credendum* for orchestra by William SCHUMAN, in three movements, *Declaration, Chorale, Finale,* commissioned by the Department of State for UN-

ESCO, couched in a grandly declarative oratorical manner and ending with a festive affirmation of faith in a lofty oriflamme of sonorous masses, is performed for the first time by the Cincinnati Symphony Orchestra, conducted by Thor Johnson.

### 5 NOVEMBER 1955

The new hall of the Vienna State Opera, rebuilt according to the plan of the old building destroyed in the Allied air raid, and equipped with a headlight suspended from the ceiling in lieu of the ornate chandelier of the romantic past, opens with a performance of BEETHOVEN's *Fidelio*.

### 6 NOVEMBER 1955

*Griffelkin*, fantasy opera in three acts by the 33-year-old American composer Lukas Foss, to a German folk tale dealing with a mischievous adolescent devil who is given a day on earth as a reward for nasty behavior and decides to defect from Hell and embark on a life of humanistic endeavor, set to music in an inventively modernistic vein, including a skit of a discordant but basically diatonic Hell Conservatory, is produced as a commissioned work for television by the National Broadcasting Company in New York.

### 22 NOVEMBER 1955

Guy ROPARTZ, bearded patriarch of French music, composer of flamboyantly romantic operas and symphonic works, dies in his native mansion, Lanloup, not far from Guingamp, Côtes-du-Nord, Bretagne, at the age of ninety-one.

### 24 NOVEMBER 1955

*White Acacia*, operetta in three acts by the Soviet composer Isaak DUNAYEVSKY (who died in Moscow on 25 July 1955), to a story of romantic love between a harpoonist and a girl radio operator on a Soviet whaling ship bound for the Antarctic, embellished by pseudo-tropical dance tunes characterizing the ship's passage through the equatorial zone, is produced posthumously in Moscow.

### 25 NOVEMBER 1955

*Sixth Symphony* by Walter PISTON, written in a distinct tonal idiom but devoid of an overt key signature, in four movements (1) *Fluendo espressivo*, in sophisticated waltz time, opening with a permutated Bachian motto C-A-B-H and concluding with its conversion C-H-B-A (2) *Leggerissimo vivace*, scherzo in 2/4 time, with muted trumpets contributing moments of jazzy syncopation (3) *Adagio sereno*, with congested chromatic progressions alleviated by diatonic oxygenation, ending on an unadulterated B-A-C-H motto (4) *Allegro energico*, a symphonic hallelujah in march time concluding on a focal A, is performed for the first time by the Boston Symphony Orchestra, as a commissioned work for its 75th anniversary, under the direction of Charles Munch.

### 26 NOVEMBER 1955

*Grazina,* symphonic ballad by the 60-year-old Ukrainian composer Boris LIATOSHINSKY, inspired by the poem by the great Polish writer Adam Mieckiewicz, descriptive of a 13th-century Polish girl who dons the armor of a friendly knight at night and perishes in a victorious combat against the invading crusaders, is performed for the first time simultaneously in Kiev and in Moscow.

### 27 NOVEMBER 1955

Arthur HONEGGER, French composer of noble gifts, who launched the first symphonic locomotive in his *Pacific 231,* and created a new type of the modern biblical and historical cantata in *Jeanne d'Arc au bûcher* and *Le Roi David,* whose musical language naturally absorbed dissonance as part of new euphony, dies in Paris at the age of sixty-three.

### 30 NOVEMBER 1955

Josip SLAVENSKI, Yugoslav composer whose music presents native rhythms in modern dress, dies in Belgrade at the age of fifty-nine.

### 30 NOVEMBER 1955

*Pipe Dream,* musical play by Richard RODGERS, with book and lyrics by Oscar Hammerstein II, dealing with a vagrant girl who is saved from arrest by the madam of a fashionable bordello, and eventually finds happiness with a marine biologist, is produced in New York.

### 2 DECEMBER 1955

*Third Symphony* by Ernst TOCH, in three movements, *Molto Adagio, Andante tranquillo* and *Allegro impetuoso,* commissioned by the American Jewish Tercentenary Committee of Chicago, is performed for the first time by the Pittsburgh Symphony Orchestra. (It received the Pulitzer Prize in 1957)

### 26 DECEMBER 1955

*La Piccola Scala,* a miniaturized adjunct of La Scala, is inaugurated in Milan with CIMAROSA's opera *Il Matrimonio segreto.*

### 26 DECEMBER 1955

*Porgy and Bess,* folk opera by George GERSHWIN, is performed for the first time in Russia, at the Leningrad Palace of Culture, by an all-Negro cast, the first American theatrical company to visit the Soviet Union.

### 31 DECEMBER 1955

*Haru no Umi (Sea at Springtime),* concerto for *koto,* flute and orchestra by the blind Japanese composer Michio MIYAGI, is performed for the first time by Shinichi Yuize, a member of the Kabuki Dance Group, as soloist on the *koto,* and the New York Philharmonic, André Kostelanetz conducting.

# ℒ 1956 ℒ

3 JANUARY 1956

Alexandre GRETCHANINOFF, the last Mohican of the second generation of the Russian National School of composers, whose songs, imbued with the melodious melancholy of old Russia, have become perennial favorites, dies in New York, an expatriate for three decades, at the patriarchal age of ninety-one.

5 JANUARY 1956

*Violin Concerto* by the 48-year-old Hungarian-born American composer Miklós RÓZSA, written in a brilliant virtuoso style, replete with admissible modernities, and non-toxic polyharmonies, is performed for the first time by Jascha Heifetz with the Dallas Symphony Orchestra.

14 JANUARY 1956

*Idyll of Theocritus* for soprano and orchestra by the 59-year-old American composer Roger SESSIONS, to the text of an English translation of the second idyll by Theocritus, in which a Grecian damsel, deserted by her lover, manipulates, with the aid of Selene, a series of lunar invultuations to secure his return, set to music of impassioned austerity in a sui generis serial idiom, is performed for the first time in Louisville.

21 JANUARY 1956

On the occasion of the forthcoming bicentennial of MOZART's birth, Austria issues a commemorative stamp for two schillings 40 hellers with his image.

22 JANUARY 1956

*Palamas Symphony* for chorus and orchestra by the 72-year-old Greek composer Manolis KALOMIRIS, inspired by the poem of the modern Greek writer Kostis Palamas which pictures a decaying Balkan community revitalized by a masculine invasion of optimistic Gypsies, set to music with a profusion of exotic melorhythms accoutred in Italianate harmonies, is performed for the first time in Athens.

25 JANUARY 1956

*Etruscan Concerto* for orchestra, in three movements, by the Australian-born American composer Peggy GLANVILLE-HICKS, written in neo-archaic modalities purported to reflect the ethos of the ancient Etruscans, is performed for the first time in New York.

## 26 JANUARY 1956

*Mtzyri,* symphonic poem by the 31-year-old Georgian composer Otar TAKTAKISHVILI, inspired by a melodramatic tale of the Russian poet Mikhail Lermontov, descriptive of passionate mysteries in the forbidding chasms of the Caucasian mountains, is performed for the first time in Tbilisi.

## 27 JANUARY 1956

Erich KLEIBER, Austrian conductor, cultured interpreter of the classics and a valiant champion of modern music, who was the first to conduct Alban Berg's *Wozzeck,* dies in Zürich at the age of sixty-five.

## 27 JANUARY 1956

On the bicentennial of MOZART's birth, West Germany and East Germany issue commemorative stamps bearing his likeness.

## 1 FEBRUARY 1956

*Le Fou,* opera in three acts by the 40-year-old French composer Marcel LANDOWSKI, dealing with the inventor of a powerful war weapon capable of destroying the besiegers of his city who refuses to divulge the secret of its manufacture to his concitoyens for fear that it would kill innocents as well as the guilty in the enemy camp, is produced in Nancy, France.

## 13 FEBRUARY 1956

*Peter Pan,* symphonic fairy tale for orchestra by Ernst TOCH, inspired by J. M. Barrie's children's classic, in three sections reflecting in whimsical modalities and winged rhythms the adolescent antics of Peter Pan, is performed for the first time in Seattle.

## 14 FEBRUARY 1956

*Zaria,* opera in four acts by the 33-year-old Soviet composer Kirill MOLCHANOV, depicting in socialistically realistic modalities the revolutionary action on board the Russian cruiser Zaria (Dawn) in Petrograd harbor on the eve of the Soviet Revolution of October 1917, is produced in Perm.

## 15 FEBRUARY 1956

*Symphony in E flat* by Ernest BLOCH (completed on 8 March 1955), written in an energetically emotional style, in four movements, (1) *Tranquillo-Allegro deciso* (2) *Allegro* (3) *Andante* (4) *Allegro deciso,* in cyclic construction, returning to the tonic base after a number of caracoles into distant keys, is performed for the first time in London.

## 17 FEBRUARY 1956

*Second Symphony* by the 47-year-old Chilean composer Juan ORREGO-SALAS is performed for the first time in Minneapolis.

## 18 FEBRUARY 1956

Gustave CHARPENTIER, French composer whose "roman musical" *Louise* made history as the first French opera of the realistic school, dies in Paris at the patriarchal age of ninety-five.

## 18 FEBRUARY 1956

*Dr. Heidegger's Experiment,* one-act opera by the American composer Sam RAPHLING, is produced in New York.

## 23 FEBRUARY 1956

Leon KIRCHNER, 37-year-old American composer, plays with the New York Philharmonic Orchestra, Dmitri Mitropoulos conducting, the solo part in the first performance of his *Piano Concerto,* written in a functional neo-classical manner, in three movements, *Allegro, Adagio* and *Rondo.*

## 25 FEBRUARY 1956

*Mario e il Mago,* "choreographic action" in two acts by the 33-year-old Italian composer Franco MANNINO, to a scenario from a story of Thomas Mann taking place in an Italian spa in 1935, and dealing with the romantic competition between a balletmaster and a magician, is performed for the first time at La Scala in Milan.

## 25 FEBRUARY 1956

*La Guerra,* one-act opera by the 48-year-old Italian composer Renzo ROSSELLINI, to his own libretto portraying the horrible fate of a paralytic Italian mother with a Fascist-raped daughter and a Nazi-blinded son, is produced in Rome.

## 25 FEBRUARY 1956

*Piano Concerto* by the 30-year-old Vienna-born American composer Richard HOFFMANN, Schoenberg's last musical amanuensis in Los Angeles, thematically based on a dodecaphonic row and containing a rhythmic serialization, in international Morse code (.—..—.—), of Mozart's scatological letter to his father dated 17 October 1777, and other verbal serialisms, is performed for the first time at the annual Contemporary Music Festival in Oberlin, Ohio.

## 2 MARCH 1956

Heitor VILLA-LOBOS conducts the Boston Symphony Orchestra in the world première of his *Eleventh Symphony,* in four movements, *Allegro moderato, Largo, Scherzo, Molto Allegro.*

## 9 MARCH 1956

Eugene GOOSSENS, English conductor of the Sydney Symphony Orchestra and director of the New South Wales State Conservatorium of Music is detained at Sydney Airport on the charge of importing 1,100 sexual photographs and other articles of an uninhibited nature into puritanical Australia, and in consequence is forced to resign both posts.

### 10 MARCH 1956

*Séquence* by the 28-year-old French composer Jean BARRAQUÉ, scored for soprano, piano, harp, violin, cello, celesta, glockenspiel, vibraphone, xylophone and percussion, to a French text translated from Nietzsche's philosophical works, in an atonal idiom in which the intervals of a tritone and a major seventh are the formative factors, is performed for the first time in Paris.

### 11 MARCH 1956

Sergei VASSILENKO, Russian composer of flamboyant symphonic and vocal music exuding the aura of orientalized Russianisms, dies in his native Moscow at the age of eighty-three.

### 14 MARCH 1956

*Symphonie 1953* by the 69-year-old Dutch modernist Daniel RUYNEMAN, in three movements, *Robusto e vivo, Largo, Allegro energico,* bearing a motto from François Villon, "Rien ne m'est sûr que la chose incertaine," with the opening theme built on consecutive perfect fourths, is performed for the first time in Utrecht.

### 14 MARCH 1956

*Feria Magica* for orchestra, by the 41-year-old Spanish-American composer Carlos SURINACH, is performed for the first time in Louisville.

### 15 MARCH 1956

*My Fair Lady,* musical play by Frederick LOEWE with lyrics by Alan Jay Lerner, adapted from George Bernard Shaw's play *Pygmalion,* in which a Cockney flower girl is transfigured into a modern Galatea by a fanatical phonetician and learns to enunciate the sentence "the rain in Spain stays mainly on the plain," with correct vowels, containing such ingratiating tunes as *I Could Have Danced All Night* and *I've Grown Accustomed to Her Face,* is produced in New York. (A preliminary performance of the play was given in New Haven on 4 February 1956)

### 22 MARCH 1956

*Porträttet,* opera by the 63-year-old Swedish composer Hilding ROSENBERG, after Gogol's horror tale of a gold-laden portrait that comes to life to haunt its avaricious owner, is performed for the first time in concert form on the Stockholm Radio.

### 29 MARCH 1956

*Don Juan de Mañara,* radio opera by the 54-year-old French composer Henri TOMASI, is produced in Munich.

## 31 MARCH 1956

*Comoedia de Christi Resurrectione,* Easter passion play by Carl ORFF, scored for soloists, mixed chorus and children's voices, 3 pianos, 2 harps, 4 double-basses and percussion, a surrealistic interlingual tale of the Resurrection, with historical planes translocated and parasynchronized, in which the Roman soldiers guarding the tomb are Bavarians, and the devil objurgates Christ in ecclesiastical Latin, is performed for the first time on the Munich Radio. (The first stage performance took place in Stuttgart on 21 April 1957)

## 4 APRIL 1956

*Symphony for Trombone and Orchestra* by Ernest BLOCH, in three movements, (1) *Maestoso,* with the trombone solo making a series of eloquent declarations in quartal intervallic outcries (2) *Agitato,* in which the trombone assumes the role of a prophet in exclamatory Hebraic incantations (3) *Allegro deciso,* a rhetorical proclamation leading to a chromatic convergence to the cadential A major, is performed for the first time in Houston.

## 4 APRIL 1956

*Fifth Symphony* by the 49-year-old American composer Paul CRESTON, in three movements, *Con Moto,* flaunting the energy of monorhythmic challenge, *Largo,* expressive of passion, and *Maestoso-Allegro,* voicing poignant tenderness, the entire thematic material being derived from the initial subject by melorhythmic shifts, is performed for the first time in Washington.

## 7 APRIL 1956

*Second Symphony* by the 41-year-old American composer Gail KUBIK is performed for the first time in Louisville.

## 8 APRIL 1956

*The Trial at Rouen,* opera by the 43-year-old American composer Norman DELLO JOIO, a variant of his opera *Joan of Arc,* is performed for the first time on television by the National Broadcasting Company in New York.

## 13 APRIL 1956

Guillermo URIBE-HOLGUÍN, prime composer of Colombia, conducts in Bogotá the first performance of his *Fourth Symphony.*

## 16 APRIL 1956

*Sixth Symphony (Symphony for Winds)* by the 40-year-old American composer Vincent PERSICHETTI, in four classically arrayed movements, is performed for the first time by the Washington University Band in St. Louis.

## 21 APRIL 1956

*Variations for Orchestra,* a set by the 47-year-old American composer Elliott CARTER, based on the principle of topological congruity of thematic intervals, is performed for the first time in Louisville.

24 APRIL 1956

*I Sette peccati,* "musical mystery," with choreography and singing, by the 56-year-old Italian composer Antonio VERETTI, is produced at La Scala, in Milan.

26 APRIL 1956

*First Piano Concerto* by the 32-year-old Manchurian-born American composer of Russian parentage Benjamin LEES, couched in a civilized neo-classical manner vaccinated with immunologically prophylactic dissonances, is performed for the first time in Vienna.

2 MAY 1956

*Eighth Symphony* in D minor by Ralph VAUGHAN WILLIAMS, in four movements, of which the first, *Fantasia,* is a set of seven variations without a palpable theme, the second, *Scherzo alla marcia,* is an essay for wind instruments, the third, a *Cavatina,* a lyrical eclogue for strings, and the finale, *Toccata,* a festival of saccadic sonorities enhanced by a proliferation of percussion, vibraphone, xylophone, gongs and bells, is performed for the first time in Manchester, England, under the direction of John Barbirolli.

3 MAY 1956

*The Most Happy Fella,* musical play by Frank LOESSER, to a story in which a senescent Californian wine grower courting a restaurant waitress by mail, sends her a photograph of his handsome farmhand in lieu of that of his own unprepossessing self, and is distressed when she meets the proxy and becomes pregnant by him, set to music containing elements of grand opera and of Tin Pan Alley, and featuring the ingratiating love ballad *My Heart Is So Full of You,* is produced in New York.

6 MAY 1956

*Sampiero Corso,* lyric drama in three acts by the 54-year-old French composer Henri TOMASI, depicting in melodramatic colors the tempestuous career of the famous Corsican patriot who fought the encroachments of Genovese invaders in the 16th century, is produced in Bordeaux.

11 MAY 1956

*Images of Youth,* cantata in ten movements by the Polish-American composer Felix LABUNSKI, is performed for the first time in Cincinnati.

12 MAY 1956

On the occasion of the International Music Festival in Prague, Czechoslovakia issues postage stamps bearing portraits of MOZART (30 hellers), Joseph MYSLIVEČEK (45 hellers), and Jiři BENDA (60 hellers).

17 MAY 1956

*Pantaloon,* opera in three acts by the American composer Robert WARD, based on the play by Leonid Andreyev, *He Who Gets Slapped,* narrating the classically sad tale of a circus clown's infatuation for a bareback dancer, set to music in a sparse infra-modern triadically oriented idiom seasoned with euphonious dissonances, is performed for the first time by the Columbia University Opera Workshop in New York. (A revised version of the opera, under the title *He Who Gets Slapped*, was produced by the New York City Opera Company on 12 April 1959)

19 MAY 1956

*Seventh Symphony*, the last work of the Czech composer Jaroslav ŘÍDKÝ, in four classically designed movements, conceived in a slightly modernized Dvořákian manner, devoid of key signatures, but opening and closing with a unison F sharp, is performed for the first time in Prague, a few weeks before Řídký's death on 14 August 1956.

20 MAY 1956

*La Vérité de Jeanne*, oratorio by the 50-year-old French composer André JOLIVET, to the texts from the actual transcripts of the trial of Joan of Arc, is performed for the first time at the Festival of Domrémy, where she was born and where she first heard the acoustically implausible but subjectively convincing voices.

25 MAY 1956

*Rona*, opera in three acts by the 50-year-old German-born Croatian composer of Greek origin Boris PAPANDOPULO, dealing with the tragic love of a country girl for a non-peasant, is produced in Rijeka (Fiume).

27 MAY 1956

Igor STRAVINSKY's arrangement for chorus and orchestra of J. S. Bach's *Choral-Variationen über das Weihnachtslied* "Vom Himmel hoch da komm' ich her" is performed for the first time at the Ojai Festival, in Ojai, California.

30 MAY 1956

At a concert of electronic music presented at Cologne by the Westdeutscher Rundfunk the world premières of the following works are presented:

*5 Stücke* by the German theorist of modern musical trends Herbert EIMERT; *Doppelrohr* by the 28-year-old Swedish modernist Bengt HAMBRAEUS; *Klangfiguren II* by the geometrically inclined German composer Gottfried Michael KÖNIG; *Elektronische Komposition I* by the 58-year-old German composer of athematic, abstract and electronic music Hermann HEISS; *Interferenzen* by the 30-year-old German modernist Giselher KLEBE, portraying heterodynamic phenomena in wave mechanics; *Der Gesang der Jünglinge* by the German apostle of "total" music 27-year-old Karlheinz STOCKHAUSEN, to the text from the Book of Daniel relating the miraculous survival of three monotheistic Hebrew youths in the midst of the Babylonian fiery furnace, in a polymetric and polydynamic setting with a voice singing topologically contorted and intervallically translocated infantiloquent rhymes antiphonally echoed by an undistorted children's choir subsequently translated by electronic manipulation to the infrasonic inaudible range; and *Spiritus Intelligentiae Sanctus* by Ernst KRENEK, containing an electronic interlude in a scale of 13 equal degrees, with canonic imitation obtained by re-recording the original materials at different speeds, thus raising or lowering the pitch, with the macrorhythm governing the general architectonic scheme of the work and auxiliary microrhythms determining the duration of thematic tones.

## 3 JUNE 1956

The 30th Festival of the International Society for Contemporary Music opens in Stockholm with the following program:

*Concerto da camera* for flute, English horn and string orchestra by Arthur HONEGGER, in three movements, written in 1948; *Suite* for brass instruments, percussion and string orchestra by the 24-year-old Swiss composer Rudolf KELTERBORN, in four neo-baroque movements; *Spisak (Inventory)*, 13 sketches for 13 performers, including two female voices, by the Yugoslav composer Dušan RADIĆ, surrealistically depicting animals, plants and pieces of furniture; *Sinfonia da camera* by the Swedish composer Sven Erik BÄCK, thematically built on a liberated dodecaphonic formula and developed in a neo-classical style; *El amor pasa* for soprano, flute and chamber orchestra by the Finnish composer Ahti SONNINEN, to texts from Spanish poems; and *Triple Concerto* for oboe, clarinet and bassoon in three movements by the Danish neo-baroque composer Niels Viggo BENTZON.

## 4 JUNE 1956

A *Vision of Aeroplanes*, motet for chorus and organ by Ralph VAUGHAN WILLIAMS, to a text from the Book of Ezekiel, describing the prophet's vision of manned flying machines propelled by a wheel in the middle of a wheel, is performed for the first time in London.

## 4 JUNE 1956

At the second concert of the 30th Festival of the International Society for Contemporary Music in Stockholm the following program of chamber music is presented:

*Second String Quartet* by the Corsican-born French composer Henri MARTELLI; *Kontra-Punkte* by Karlheinz STOCKHAUSEN, scored for 10 instruments, written in a pragmatic serialistic idiom calculated to correlate the factors of pitch, duration, dynamic strength and instrumental color in both horizontal (melodic) and vertical (contrapuntal) aspects; *Chorale-Motet* for chorus a cappella by the Austrian composer Anton HEILLER, written in a neo-ecclesiastic modal idiom; *Quintet* for wind instruments by the Norweigan composer Finn MORTENSEN, in three movements cast in a neo-classical form; *Violin Sonata* in three movements by the 21-year-old Icelandic composer LEIFUR; and *Sixth String Quartet* in four movements by the dean of Swedish composers Hilding ROSENBERG.

## 5 JUNE 1956

At the third concert of the 30th Festival of the International Society for Contemporary Music in Stockholm the following program of orchestral music is presented:

*Variations for Orchestra* by the 26-year-old New Zealand composer Barry Moss; *Ectoplasm* for electronic instruments, percussion and strings by the 27-year-old Japanese composer Toshiro Mayuzumi, intended to effect a synthesis of preternatural psychic phenomena, Japanese Zen philosophy and Occidental ultra-modern techniques; *Idyll of Theocritus* for soprano and orchestra by Roger Sessions (first performed in Louisville on 14 January 1956); *Violin Concerto* in three movements by the 46-year-old Italian composer Mario Peragallo, written in 1953 and first performed at a contest in Rome in 1954, at which it carried the first prize; and *Fourth Symphony* by the 51-year-old Dutch composer Guillaume Landré, subtitled *Symphonie concertante*, in five movements, written in the dodecaphonic technique.

### 7 JUNE 1956

At the fourth concert of the 30th Festival of the International Society for Contemporary Music in Stockholm, the following program of Swedish music is given:

*Ritornell for Orchestra* by Ingvar Lidholm, in four movements, in which the term Ritornell indicates the return of the basic dodecaphonic theme in the form of an inversion or cancrizans; *Cantata* for soprano, flute, clarinet, cello and piano by Hilding Hallnäs; *Missa Brevis* for chorus *a capella* by Lars Erik Larsson; and *Sinfonia espressiva*, in four movements by Gösta Nystroem.

### 8 JUNE 1956

At the fifth concert of the 30th Festival of the International Society for Contemporary Music in Stockholm, the following program of chamber music is presented:

*Second String Quartet* by the 44-year-old Canadian composeress Barbara Pentland; *Trio* for flute, oboe and bass clarinet by Joaquín Homs Oller of Spain; *Psalm VIII* for soprano, flute, cello and piano by the 56-year-old Italian composer Luigi Cortese; *Elegia appassionata* for piano, violin, and cello by the 30-year-old German composer Giselher Klebe; and *Second String Quartet* by Alan Rawsthorne of England.

### 9 JUNE 1956

The French government issues a 15-franc postage stamp in honor of Maurice Ravel, bearing his portrait.

### 9 JUNE 1956

*Grozovan*, opera in four acts by the 44-year-old Moldavian composer David Gershfeld, to a libretto in the Moldavian language, dealing with the patriotic uprising of native guardsmen against the Turkish overlords of Moldavia in the middle of the 18th century, with a central dramatic episode touching on the fate of the heroic Grozovan and his young bride who is monstrously coveted by a lecherous janizary, set to music with a profusion of asymmetric Balkan melorhythms, is produced for the first time at the opening of the National Moldavian Theater in Kishinev, the capital city of the Soviet Socialist Republic of Moldavia.

## 10 JUNE 1956

At the sixth and last concert of the 30th Festival of the International Society for Contemporary Music in Stockholm, the following program of orchestral music is given:

*Sinfonia concertante* in five movements by the foremost Austrian theoretician and practitioner of dodecaphonic music Hanns JELINEK; *Violin Concerto* in four movements by the English composer Benjamin FRANKEL dedicated "to the memory of the six million" with the mournful motto of the falling minor second symbolizing the tragic fate of the Jews murdered by the Nazis; *Music for Orchestra* by the French composeress Marcelle DE MANZIARLY, in four movements set in order of a classical suite; *Piano Concerto* by the Russian-born American composer Alexei HAIEFF, in three movements, centering on the key of C major with pandiatonic ramifications; and the coloristic *Pampeana No. 3* by the Argentine composer Alberto GINASTERA (first performed in Louisville on 20 October 1954), painting the pampas in palpitating melo-rhythms and modernistic polyharmonies.

## 10 JUNE 1956

Four hundred years have passed since the death in Magdeburg of the erudite German music theorist Martin AGRICOLA.

## 15 JUNE 1956

*Passacaille* for orchestra by Maurice JARRE, written in memory of Arthur Honegger, using the musical letters (H - - e g g e -) in Honegger's name in the principal subject, is performed for the first time at the Music Festival in Strasbourg.

## 17 JUNE 1956

*Der Sturm*, magic fairy tale in three acts, by Frank MARTIN, to a German libretto translated from the French version of Shakespeare's play *The Tempest*, written in an economically tonal idiom, with the application of polytriadic progressions, and ending in clear F sharp major, is produced in Vienna.

## 21 JUNE 1956

*Cain and Abel*, electronic ballet by the Dutch composer Henk BADINGS, depicting the story of the first human murder with the aid of five acoustical layers and an optical siren which transforms an oscillating beam of light passed through a rotating disc to a photo-electric cell into melodies of varied timbres, with numerous other sonic effects produced by intermodulators of sinusoidal tones, is performed in The Hague for the first time.

## 23 JUNE 1956

Reinhold GLIÈRE, Russian composer of remote French extraction, who excelled in the melodious genre of harmoniously fashioned songs and whose grandiose symphony *Ilya Murometz* portrays the legendary giant of Russian folklore in grandisonant splendor, dies in Moscow at the age of eighty-one.

## 25 JUNE 1956

*Fifth Piano Concerto* by Darius MILHAUD is performed for the first time at the Lewisohn Stadium, New York, with Stell Andersen as soloist and Pierre Monteux conducting the Stadium Symphony Orchestra.

## 26 JUNE 1956

Michio MIYAGI, 62-year-old blind Japanese virtuoso player on the *koto*, who composed a thousand pieces for it, dies in a railroad accident near Tokyo.

## 27 JUNE 1956

*Pane Lesna Rusalim,* opera in three acts by the 47-year-old Rumanian composer Paul CONSTANTINESCU, dealing with an early 19th-century peasant girl participant in a Rumanian rebellion against the Turkish overlords, is performed for the first time in Bucharest.

## 7 JULY 1956

*The Ballad of Baby Doe,* folk opera in two parts by the 62-year-old American composer Douglas MOORE, to a libretto drawn from the real story of a historic personage named Elizabeth McCourt Doe, "the miner's sweetheart" of the American West, second wife of the "Silver Dollar King" Horace Tabor who built a fortune on silver but lost it when the U.S. went on the gold standard and died destitute in 1899, set to music in a melodious Americanistic idiom, imparting a flavor of authenticity by using actual tunes of the period, modernistically enlivened by shrewd rhythmic translocation and euphoniously dissonant counterpoint while maintaining a fine contrast of lyrical arias, dramatic duets, and individualized vocal ensembles, and further enhancing its realistic sense of history by introducing President Chester A. Arthur and silver-throated William Jennings Bryan singing of the economic glories of silver dollars, is performed for the first time at the Tabor Opera House in Central City, Colorado (elevation 8,500 feet) where the real Baby Doe luxuriated in the golden era of her silver prosperity, near Leadville (elevation 11,500 feet), where she spent 36 long years after her husband's death and was found frozen to death in a shack on 7 March 1935.

## 20 JULY 1956

The postal authorities of the German Democratic Republic (East Germany) issue two stamps, of the values of 10 and 20 pfennigs, commemorating the centennial of SCHUMANN's death, featuring a portrait of Schumann superimposed, through a fantastic dereliction of scholarship, on the reproduction of a few bars from Schubert's setting of Goethe's *Wanderers Nachtlied.* (The issue was withdrawn as soon as the misattribution was discovered, and a new set of stamps, with a musical example from a Schumann work, was issued on 8 October 1956)

## 29 JULY 1956

The first demonstration of music produced by stalactites is given in the 65-acre Luray Caverns in Virginia on the Great Stalacpipe Organ by Leland W.

SPRINKLE, its inventor, playing the Lutheran chorale *A Mighty Fortress Is Our God*, with five miles of wire electrically connecting the plungers that strike the stalactites tuned by careful grinding, and stereophonic effects achieved by staggered stalactites in natural cavernous air-conditioning maintaining the constant temperature of 54° Fahrenheit.

### 1 AUGUST 1956

Howard BRUBECK, 40-year-old Californian composer, conducts the San Diego Symphony in the first performance of his *Four Dialogues for Jazz Combo and Orchestra*, with the combo (combination of piano, alto saxophone, drums and doublebass) performing improvised patterns of notes and rhythms in jazzily logical coordination with the pre-composed orchestral parts, mostly adhering to metrical periods in powers of 2 ($2^2$, $2^3$, $2^4$, $2^5$ bars each), and the last section, *Blues* in a 12-bar pattern.

### 5 AUGUST 1956

*Second Symphony* by the 32-year-old American composer Ned ROREM is performed for the first time at La Jolla, California.

### 9 AUGUST 1956

*Bodas de Sangre*, opera in three acts by the 61-year-old Argentinian composer Juan José CASTRO, to a libretto after the mystical play *The Blood Wedding* of Federico García Lorca, is performed for the first time in Buenos Aires.

### 20 AUGUST 1956

*Edinburgh Overture* by the 65-year-old English composer Sir Arthur BLISS, is performed for the first time as a festive introduction to the Edinburgh Festival of Music and Drama.

### 3 SEPTEMBER 1956

To commemorate the tenth anniversary of the death of the German operetta composer Paul LINCKE (1866–1946), the government of West Germany issues a 20-pfennig stamp reproducing his portrait against the background of a musical quotation from his famous march song *Das macht die Berliner Luft* from his operetta *Berliner Luft*.

### 5 SEPTEMBER 1956

*Fourth Piano Concerto* by Sergei PROKOFIEV for left hand alone, originally commissioned by the amputated Austrian pianist Paul Wittgenstein, but never played by him, in four movements: (1) *Vivace*, a virtuoso type of toccata artfully confined to the left-hand range of the solo part (2) *Andante*, a tranquil essay making use of the entire keyboard (3) *Moderato*, a vivacious scherzo marked by saltatory melodic exuberance (4) *Finale*, cyclic metempsychosis of the initial *Vivace*, is performed for the first time in Berlin, 25 years after its composition, by the one-armed pianist Siegfried Rapp (who, like Paul Wittgenstein, lost his right arm from a shrapnel wound on the Russian front in World War I.)

6 SEPTEMBER 1956

An audience of 2,200 persons gathers in the concert hall of the Leningrad Conservatory to hear the Boston Symphony Orchestra, conducted by Charles Munch (the first American orchestra to play in the Soviet Union), in a program opening with the Soviet and American national anthems, and including BEETHOVEN's *Eroica*, Walter PISTON's *Sixth Symphony* and the Second Suite from RAVEL's *Daphnis and Chloe*, arousing spontaneous enthusiasm expressed in tumultuous applause, forcing the conductor to break his ingrained opposition to the playing of encores, and to oblige the audience with the rendition of *L'Apprenti Sorcier* by Paul DUKAS.

11 SEPTEMBER 1956

*Concerto* for harmonica and orchestra by the 57-year-old Russian-born composer Alexander TCHEREPNIN, is performed for the first time at the Venice Festival.

13 SEPTEMBER 1956

Igor STRAVINSKY conducts in the basilica of San Marco in Venice the first performance of his *Canticum Sacrum ad Honorem Sancti Marci Nominis*, composed in the spirit of a devout offering on the bimillennium of St. Mark, patron saint of Venice, scored for tenor, baritone, chorus and orchestra, consisting of an introductory *Dedicatio* and five sections: (1) *Euntes in Mundum* (2) *Surge aquilo* (3) *Ad tres Virtutes Hortationes* (4) *Brevis Motus Cantilenae* (5) *Illi autem profecti sunt*, set to Latin texts from the Vulgate, the three inner sections being the first works composed by Stravinsky entirely in a strict dodecaphonic technique, while the non-dodecaphonic sections 1 and 5 stand in palindromic relation to each other.

MURDER IN THE CATHEDRAL. (TIME magazine headline for review of the concert)

23 SEPTEMBER 1956

*König Hirsch*, opera in three acts by the 30-year-old German composer Hans Werner HENZE, after Carlo Gozzi's play *Il Re Cervo*, in which a king dethroned by an impostor lives in the deep forest as a stag, but reassumes his human form, overthrows the usurper and returns to his people as their rightful king, scored for singers, speakers, chorus, and orchestra, is produced in Berlin.

25 SEPTEMBER 1956

*Johannesburg Festival Overture* by William WALTON, a jubilee piece written for the 70th anniversary of Johannesburg as a hedonistic rondo, devoid of an explicit key signature but eloquently oriented towards a focal D, making use of genuine South African tunes, is performed for the first time in Johannesburg, South Africa.

### 2 OCTOBER 1956

*Ruth,* one-act opera by Lennox BERKELEY, to a libretto after the Book of Ruth, is produced in London.

### 4 OCTOBER 1956

*Fourth Piano Concerto,* subtitled *Incantation,* by Bohuslav MARTINU, is performed for the first time at the Metropolitan Museum of Art, New York City, with Rudolf Firkušny as soloist and Leopold Stokowski conducting.

### 6 OCTOBER 1956

*Piano Concerto* by the 38-year-old Austrian composer Gottfried VON EINEM, in three cyclic movements, *Molto moderato, Adagio* and *Con spirito,* written in a neo-baroque idiom spiced by non-toxic dissonances, is performed for the first time in Hamburg.

### 10 OCTOBER 1956

The first "Warsaw Autumn" International Festival of Contemporary Music opens in Warsaw, inaugurating a series of concerts concluding on 21 October 1956, presenting works by STRAVINSKY, SCHOENBERG, Alban BERG, Béla BARTÓK, SZYMANOWSKI, RAVEL, HONEGGER, ENESCO, Benjamin BRITTEN, SHOSTAKOVICH, KHACHATURIAN, MIASKOVSKY, PROKOFIEV, Jacques IBERT, Darius MILHAUD, Georges AURIC, Henri DUTILLEUX, André JOLIVET, Jean MARTINON, Jean-Louis MARTINOT, Olivier MESSIAEN, Henri BARRAUD, Leoš JANÁČEK, Bohuslav MARTINU, László LAJTHA, and a number of contemporary Polish composers: Grazyna BACEWICZ, Tadeusz BAIRD, Andrzej DOBROWOLSKI, Wojciech KILAR, Stefan KISIELEWSKI, Witold LUTOSLAWSKI, Artur MALAWSKI, Zygmunt MYCIELSKI, Piotr PERKOWSKI, Teodor ROGALSKI, Kazimierz SEROCKI, Stanislaw SKROWACZEWSKI, Michal SPISAK, Boleslaw SZABELSKI, Antoni SZALOWSKI, Zbigniew TURSKI, Stanislaw WIECHOWICZ, Stanislaw WISLOCKI, and Boleslaw WOYTOWICZ.

### 10 OCTOBER 1956

The Belgian Congo and Ruanda-Urundi issue sets of stamps commemorating the bicentennial of the birth of MOZART.

### 12 OCTOBER 1956

Lorenzo PEROSI, elective composer of several pontiffs, whose professed goal was to recreate the reverential and scholarly spirit of Palestrina in his own oratorios, which he often performed at the Vatican, but whose recurrent mental aberrations interrupted his ecclesiastical and musical activities, dies in Rome at the age of eighty-three.

## 17 OCTOBER 1956

*Fourth Symphony* by the 51-year-old Soviet composer Dmitri KABALEVSKY, in four traditional movements outlining a dramaturgic scenario of dialectic conflicts and an ultimate festive synthesis (1) *Lento,* an evocatively bucolic introduction to the mainstream of a bithematically developed *Allegro molto* (2) *Largo,* a solemn procession with the undertones of an undecided struggle (3) *Allegretto capriccioso,* a humanistic scherzo in cyclic rondo form (4) *Allegro,* a finale animated by the rhythms of a vigorous march reinforced by a masculine fugato, is performed for the first time in Moscow.

## 18 OCTOBER 1956

*Portrait* for violin and orchestra by the American composer Bernard ROGERS is performed for the first time in Cleveland.

## 18 OCTOBER 1956

*The Sweet Psalmist of Israel* by the 59-year-old Israeli composer Paul BEN-HAIM (who Hebraized his original German name Frankenburger), in three sections (1) *David Before Saul,* for harpsichord and wind instruments, representing David's playing upon a lyre to pacify King Saul (2) *Invocation,* for harp solo and strings, reflecting the spirit of the Lord speaking through David (3) *Song of Degrees,* a set of variations for harpsichord, harp and orchestra, is performed for the first time in Tel Aviv.

## 19 OCTOBER 1956

*Pokondirena tikva (Preening Pumpkin),* comic opera in three acts by the 54-year-old Yugoslav composer Mihovil LOGAR, to a libretto recounting the absurd behavior of a self-inflated matron in a provincial central European town, set to music in the manner of a Viennese operetta, is performed for the first time in Belgrade.

## 21 OCTOBER 1956

Two one-act operas, *Unexpected Visitor* and *The Two Impostors,* by the 41-year-old Czech-born American composer Leslie KONDOROSSY, are produced in Cleveland.

## 21 OCTOBER 1956

*The Unicorn, the Gorgon and the Manticore,* a madrigal fable for chorus, 10 dancers and nine instruments by Gian Carlo MENOTTI, subtitled *The Three Sundays of a Poet,* to his own libretto descriptive of a magically endowed poet, who thrice emerges from his seclusion on Sundays, leading successively a promenade with a pet unicorn, a gorgon and a manticore, and creating such a demand among local women to obtain similar pets, that the populace is driven to distraction, set to music in a translucidly euphonious manner, making use of dramatic dissonances to point the surrealistic quality of the tale, is performed for the first time at the Library of Congress, in Washington, as a commissioned work by the Elizabeth Sprague Coolidge Foundation.

21 OCTOBER 1956

*Second Symphony* in D minor by the Rumanian composer Sigismond TODUȚA is performed for the first time in Cluj.

22 OCTOBER 1956

*In the Drought,* opera by the 29-year-old South African composer John JOUBERT, is performed for the first time in Johannesburg.

22 OCTOBER 1956

*Déploration de Tonton, Chien Fidèle,* solo cantata for voice and orchestra by Jean FRANÇAIX, deploring the death of a faithful dog named Tonton in somber neo-medieval modalities, is performed for the first time in Paris.

24 OCTOBER 1956

At the opening of the concert series Musik der Zeit at Cologne, the world première is given of *Il Canto Sospeso (Broken Song)* for three voices, chorus and orchestra by Luigi NONO, to the texts selected from letters written by members of European resistance groups in Nazi-occupied countries condemned to death, among them a 14-year-old Greek schoolboy and two young Russian girls, set to music in the manner of a modern litany, making use of the hoquet technique, in which words, broken into syllables, are given separately to different voices creating an anguished effect of human discontinuity, employing as serial determinants the row derived from the horizontalization of the *Grossmutterakkord* consisting of all 12 different tones of the chromatic scale and all 11 different intervals and the Fibonacci series in which each number is the sum of the two preceding numbers.

26 OCTOBER 1956

Walter GIESEKING, eloquent master of the piano, born of German parents in Lyon, France, a superlative interpreter of German classics and French impressionists, dies in London at the age of sixty.

30 OCTOBER 1956

*Composition No. 6 aux objets sonores* by the 33-year-old Belgian composer Karel GOEYVAERTS, an electronic montage based on a mode of 180 units of duration, resulting in such time signatures as $11/4 + 1/8 + 1/64$, with this temporal-tonal continuum being subdivided into five sonorous agglomerations, is performed for the first time on the Brussels Radio.

10 NOVEMBER 1956

*Hécube,* opera in two acts by the 46-year-old French composer Jean MARTINON, is performed for the first time in Strasbourg.

12 NOVEMBER 1956

*Irma la Douce*, comedy with music by Marguerite MONNOT, in which a Montmartre *poule* supports an indigent art student in his Paris studio out of her illicit earnings, with surrealistic developments ensuing when he grows a beard and masquerades as her maquereau and after a pogonotomy accuses the artist, i.e. himself, of killing the pimp, his alter ego, receives a life sentence for this pseudonymous ipsocidal crime, but escapes, returns to Sweet Irma and discloses his true artistic identity, is produced in Paris.

15 NOVEMBER 1956

*Americana*, a symphonic pastiche of American tunes, from old balladry to jazz, by the 72-year-old American composer Louis GRUENBERG, is performed for the first time in Cleveland.

16 NOVEMBER 1956

Two symphonic poems by the 70-year-old Belgian neo-romanticist Robert HERBERIGS, *Les Quatres Saisons* (after Breughel) and *La petite Sirène* (after Hans Christian Andersen) are performed for the first time in Brussels.

18 NOVEMBER 1956

*The Men of Blackmoor*, sociological opera in three acts by the 55-year-old English composer Alan BUSH, to a libretto by his wife Nancy Bush, dealing with a strike of English mine workers in the early period of industrial expansion, with a tragic romance developing between a downtrodden miner and the owner's liberal daughter, set to music in the spirit of socialist realism and harmonized in broad triadic modalities, is produced for the first time in Weimar, in the German version, under the title *Die Männer von Blackmoor*.

23 NOVEMBER 1956

*Études pour orchestra à cordes*, a symphonic suite for strings by Frank MARTIN, is performed for the first time in Basel.

24 NOVEMBER 1956

Guido CANTELLI, 36-year-old Italian conductor whose great talent earned for him the appellation "piccolo Toscanini," dies in an airplane crash at Orly, near Paris, en route to America to conduct a series of concerts with the New York Philharmonic.

29 NOVEMBER 1956

*Bells Are Ringing*, musical comedy by Jule STYNE, dealing with a sympathetic telephone switchboard operator who invades the apartment of a neurotic playwright and provides the feminine ministrations he physiologically and psychologically needs to finish his play, is produced in New York.

### 1 DECEMBER 1956

*Candide,* musical comedy by Leonard BERNSTEIN based on Voltaire's novella retailing the extraordinary adventures of an unregenerate idealist who retains his optimism through all the tortuous peripeteia during his forced peregrinations, set to music with a sense of hedonistic persiflage, and incorporating parodies on classical dance music, as well as the first detected 12-tone row in any musical comedy (in the introduction to the second act), is produced in New York.

### 4 DECEMBER 1956

*The Intruder,* one-act opera by the 32-year-old Vienna-born composer Robert STARER, is performed for the first time in New York.

### 14 DECEMBER 1956

*Anabasis,* cantata by the 40-year-old Swedish composer Karl-Birger BLOMDAHL, after Xenophon's classic battle epic, is performed for the first time in Stockholm.

### 26 DECEMBER 1956

*1804,* cantata by the Serbian composer Božidar TRUDIĆ, written to commemorate the sesquicentennial of the Serbian uprising against the Turkish janizaries, set in Slavic diatonic modalities and nutritiously triadic harmonies and containing recitatives to the accompaniment of the Balkan instrument gusli, is performed for the first time in Sarajevo.

### 26 DECEMBER 1956

*Spartak,* ballet by Aram KHACHATURIAN, to a scenario glorifying the Roman gladiator Spartacus who led the slaves in a temporarily successful uprising in 73–71 B.C., but was eventually defeated and killed, set to music in a series of dramatic numbers, abounding in marching rhythms and colorful harmonies rooted in firm pedal points, with spacious melodies and chromatic rivulets forming gratifying contrasts, is performed for the first time in Leningrad.

### 29 DECEMBER 1956

The Rumanian government issues two stamps of 55 bani and of 1.75 lei in honor of Georges ENESCO, the prime modern Rumanian composer who died in Paris on 4 May 1955.

### 30 DECEMBER 1956

*Krakatuk,* fantastic opera in three acts by the 60-year-old Polish composer Tadeusz SZELIGOWSKI, after E.T.A. Hoffmann's fairy tale *The Nutcracker,* with the action transferred to old Warsaw and centered on the search, eventually successful after many an eerie peripeteia, of the magic nut Krakatuk, written in an ingratiatingly infantiloquent idiom, set in nutritious triadic harmonies, and spiced with non-toxic chromatic condiments, is produced in Gdańsk.

# ∾ *1957* ∽

1 JANUARY 1957

*The Prince of the Pagodas,* a ballet by Benjamin BRITTEN, is performed for the first time in London.

10 JANUARY 1957

*Caino,* one-act opera by the 74-year-old Italian composer Felice LATTUADA, after Byron's poem, is produced at La Scala, Milan.

11 JANUARY 1957

*Eighth Symphony* by the 49-year-old Java-born Dutch composer Henk BADINGS is performed for the first time in Hannover, Germany.

16 JANUARY 1957

Arturo TOSCANINI, "The Maestro," sublime Italian conductor whose fanatically meticulous interpretations of great musical masterworks and flaming devotion to his art set the loftiest standard of orchestral and operatic perfection, dies in his sleep at 8:40 A.M. in New York, a few weeks before his 90th birthday.

20 JANUARY 1957

*Declaration,* symphonic narrative by the 43-year-old American composer Morton GOULD, scored for two narrators, speaking chorus and orchestra, to the text of the Declaration of Independence, is performed for the first time by the National Symphony Orchestra, Howard Mitchell conducting, at the Inaugural Concert of the second Eisenhower administration held in Constitution Hall, Washington, D.C. (*A Declaration Suite* extracted from this work in five movements, *Liberty Bell, Midnight Ride, Concord Bridge, Summer '76,* and *Celebration,* was first performed by the Symphony of the Air, New York, on 14 February 1957)

25 JANUARY 1957

*Cello Concerto* by William WALTON, in three movements, *Moderato, Allegro appassionato* and *Epilogue,* in which the interval of a major seventh governs melodic and harmonic parameters, is performed for the first time by Gregor Piatigorsky, by whom it was commissioned, and the Boston Symphony Orchestra, Charles Munch conducting.

## 26 JANUARY 1957

*Dialogues des Carmélites*, opera in three acts by Francis POULENC, dealing with the martyrdom of Carmelite nuns during the French Revolution, set to music in a reverential sentiment, with devout accents of Latin hymns and the turmoil of the revolutionary populace standing in dramatic contrast, culminating in the horrifying stroke of the guillotine, is produced at La Scala, Milan, with an Italian libretto translated from a French play adapted from an unproduced motion picture based on a German novel.

## 30 JANUARY 1957

*Aculeo*, symphonic suite by Alfonso LETELIER of Chile, is performed for the first time in Louisville.

## 1 FEBRUARY 1957

*First Symphony* by the 36-year-old American pianist and conductor Leo SMIT, in four neo-classical movements, is performed for the first time by the Boston Symphony Orchestra, conducted by Charles Munch.

## 2 FEBRUARY 1957

*Jekyll and Hyde Variations* for orchestra by Morton GOULD, portraying in an artfully atonal vein the mutation of a humane physician into a bestial murderer by way of a fugally agitated stretto and schizophrenically waltzing memories, is performed by the New York Philharmonic, Dimitri Mitropoulos conducting.

## 7 FEBRUARY 1957

TCHAIKOVSKY's *Symphony in E-flat Major*, integrated and collated from uncoordinated sketches, is performed for the first time in Moscow. (The material from the symphony was used by Tchaikovsky in other works: the first movement in the *Third Piano Concerto*; two other movements in *Andante* and *Finale*, op. 79; another movement became *Scherzo-Fantasy*, op. 72)

## 9 FEBRUARY 1957

*Mother Margarita*, opera by the Yugoslav composer Krsto ODAK, is performed for the first time in Zagreb.

## 10 FEBRUARY 1957

*La Grande Bretèche*, television opera, after Balzac, by the 32-year-old American composer Stanley HOLLINGSWORTH, is performed for the first time by the National Broadcasting Company Television in New York.

## 11 FEBRUARY 1957

*Great River (The Rio Grande)*, symphonic poem for orchestra and narrator by the 58-year-old American composer Ernst BACON, in twelve movements, to a text by the American novelist Paul Horgan, tracing the flow of the Rio Grande from its sources in New Mexico to the Gulf of Mexico, is performed for the first time in Dallas.

### 16 FEBRUARY 1957

*Beg Bajazid,* opera by the 45-year-old Slovak composer Ján CIKKER, dealing with a Turkish-reared Slovak boy who at the age of thirty becomes commander of an Ottoman punitive battalion in his native village and cruelly carries its entire population into slavery, discovering that his own old mother was among his victims, the realization of which enormity makes him abandon his promising military career and return to Slovakia to fight his former masters, set to music with a proliferation of Slavic melorhythms set in polytriadic harmonies, is produced in Bratislava.

### 16 FEBRUARY 1957

Josef HOFMANN, great romantic Polish-born pianist, who began his career as a child prodigy (when he toured America in 1887, the Boston Society for Prevention of Cruelty to Children succeeded in preventing pianistic cruelty to him, forcing a temporary suspension of his career), and an affable composer of unpretentious romantic trifles under the nom de plume Dvorsky, a Russian equivalent of the German word Hofmann, i.e. yardman, dies in Los Angeles at the age of eighty-one.

### 19 FEBRUARY 1957

*Maskal,* symphonic suite by the Yugoslav composer Rudolf BRUČI (the title is derived from the Ethiopian folk festival of flowers), in three movements, is performed for the first time in Belgrade.

### 23 FEBRUARY 1957

*La Donna è mobile,* opera buffa by Riccardo MALIPIERO, dodecaphonic nephew of Gian Francesco Malipiero, the title alluding with ironic condescension to the famous aria from Verdi's *Rigoletto,* is performed for the first time in Milan.

### 23 FEBRUARY 1957

Ethel LEGINSKA, 70-year-old English-born pianist, composeress and conductoress (her real name was Liggins, but she adopted a Polish feminine surname, to improve her chances of success in a musical career), conducts in Los Angeles the world première of her opera *The Rose and the Ring* (after Thackeray's story).

### 24 FEBRUARY 1957

*Lydian Ode,* symphonic essay by Paul CRESTON, set in a mournful Lydian mode, is performed for the first time by the Wichita Symphony Orchestra as a commissioned work in memory of the donor's pianist sister.

## 26 FEBRUARY 1957

*Sinfonia visionaria* (*Ninth Symphony*), "in modo di rondo espansivo," by the Swedish composer Kurt ATTERBERG, scored for mezzo soprano, baritone, chorus and orchestra, is performed for the first time anywhere in Helsinki.

## 28 FEBRUARY 1957

*Third Symphony* by the 42-year-old American composer Gail KUBIK, with its thematic material extracted from his film music, in three movements, (1) *Slowly, broadly,* containing a long trumpet cadenza (2) *Slowly, sadly* (3) *Masquerade,* a vivacious polytonal charade, is performed for the first time by the New York Philharmonic, Dimitri Mitropoulos conducting.

## 28 FEBRUARY 1957

Sven-Erik BÄCK, 37-year-old Swedish composer, conducts at the Swedish Radio in Stockholm the first performance of his radio opera *Tranfjädrarna* (*Crane Feathers*), in one act and five tableaux, to a libretto after a Japanese Noh drama, in which a captive girl-crane sheltered by a farmer makes exquisite fabric for him from her own gossamer feathers, but flies away when he breaks his solemn promise never to look at her while she works when she assumes an aviohuman appearance, with her ornithoantropoheterogenation represented by an optimistic dodecaphonic series, containing some triadic elements within a stark ambience of monodic ostinati and tintinnabulating dynamics. (The first stage performance was conducted by Bäck at the Swedish Royal Opera in Stockholm on 9 February 1958)

## 28 FEBRUARY 1957

Ian PARROTT, 40-year-old British composer, conducts at the University College of Wales in Aberystwyth the concert version of his two-act opera *The Black Ram,* to a libretto in the Welsh language, dealing with an 18th-century baronet who drops his prize ram down the chimney of a stubborn Welshman when the latter refuses to sell his land, charges him with theft and gets him hanged in 1762, set to music with melorhythmic materials drawn from Welsh folk songs.

## 2 MARCH 1957

*Wild Bara,* opera in three acts by the 68-year-old Russian composer Anatoly ALEXANDROV, in which the proletarianized daughter of a disfranchised Carpathian peasant in the early 19th century starts a social upheaval, is performed for the first time in Moscow, in concert form.

## 2 MARCH 1957

A concert of Chinese music is given in Shanghai, presenting a *Mongolian Suite* for orchestra by U TSE-YUN, *New Year's Eve* for strings by YAN-TSE and *Nostalgia for Fatherland* for chorus and orchestra by MA-SA-TZUNG.

## 8 MARCH 1957

*Sixth Symphony* by the 41-year-old American composer David DIAMOND, in three movements, (1) *Introduzione—Adagio interrotto—Allegro* (2) *Adagio interrotto* (3) *Deciso: Poco Allegro—Fuga,* with their thematic materials related to the initial opening theme of 12 non-different notes and the conjugate theme of 11 non-different notes, dynamically sustained as a succession of diastolic and systolic phrases and periods, and culminating in a magistral fugue, is performed for the first time by the Boston Symphony Orchestra, conducted by Charles Munch.

## 8 MARCH 1957

*Boleslav I,* opera by the 69-year-old Bohemian composer Boleslav VOMÁČKA, dealing with the historical struggle between Duke Wenceslaus and his brother Boleslav, and ending with the murder of the former by the latter, is performed for the first time in Prague.

## 8 MARCH 1957

Othmar SCHOECK, Swiss composer of operas and symphonic works, a minor master of lyric Lieder in the purest romantic tradition, dies in Zürich at the age of seventy.

Schoeck is a type rather like Beckett who gets up at 2:30 P.M. his wife says . . . But he can write music all right. (James Joyce in a letter to his son George, 15 January 1935)

## 15 MARCH 1957

*Second Symphony* in E major by the 79-year-old Hungarian composer Ernst von DOHNÁNYI, is performed for the first time in its revised form by the Minneapolis Symphony Orchestra, Antal Dorati conducting. (The original version, written in 1944 was first performed in London on 23 November 1948)

## 17 MARCH 1957

*Fiesta,* ballet by Morton GOULD, is produced in Cannes, France.

## 17 MARCH 1957

At the University of Illinois, in Urbana, two short operas are performed for the first time: Ernst KRENEK's *The Bell-Tower,* after Melville, and Jan MEYEROWITZ's biblical music drama *Esther.*

## 19 MARCH 1957

The Second Festival of American Music opens in Caracas, Venezuela, and a prize of $10,000 for the best work submitted for performance is divided between Camargo GUARNIERI of Brazil for his orchestral *Chôro* and the Mexican composer Blas GALINDO for his *Sinfonía.*

## 21 MARCH 1957

*1907*, oratorio by the 47-year-old Rumanian composer Alfred MENDELSOHN, picturing in operatically dramatic tones the heroic rebellion of Rumanian peasantry against the oppressive landed gentry in 1907, is performed for the first time in Bucharest.

## 25 MARCH 1957

Camille ROBERT, French composer of the famous marching song of World War I, *Madelon*, which he wrote in 1911, dies at the age of 85 in Paris. (He was born inside the building of the Grand Opéra in Paris, where his father, the architect of the theater, made his residence)

## 4 APRIL 1957

*Tenth Symphony*, by Heitor VILLA-LOBOS, written to celebrate the 400th anniversary of the founding of the Brazilian metropolis of São Paulo, scored for soloists, chorus and orchestra, to a text by a 16th-century Brazilian priest, is performed for the first time in Paris.

## 5 APRIL 1957

Guillermo URIBE-HOLGUÍN, 77-year-old Colombian composer, conducts in Bogotá the first performance of his *Sixth Symphony*, written in a spaciously harmonious and chromatically melodious manner of his venerated teacher Vincent d'Indy.

## 9 APRIL 1957

Howard HANSON conducts in Washington his choral *Song of Democracy*, to words by Walt Whitman, composed for the centennial celebration of the National Education Association of America in the spirit of assertion of democratic tonality, with polytriadic harmonies expressing the ideal of unity in American diversity, and concluding in an envoi in the patriotic key of E flat major.

## 12 APRIL 1957

*Fourth Symphony* by the American composer Wallingford RIEGGER, in three movements, (1) *Allegro moderato* (2) *Allegretto con moto* (3) *Sostenuto—Presto*, written in an advanced polytriadic idiom marked by stimulating dissonant counterpoint, is performed for the first time as a commissioned work at the Festival of Contemporary Arts, organized at the University of Illinois, in Urbana.

## 13 APRIL 1957

*Second Symphony* for orchestra and chorus by the 40-year-old American composer Ellis KOHS, and the cantata *To the God Who Is in the Fire* by the 46-year-old American composer of Armenian-Scottish extraction Alan HOVHANESS are performed for the first time at the Festival of Contemporary Arts, at the University of Illinois, in Urbana.

## 16 APRIL 1957

*Narodne zagonetke (Folk Riddles)*, cantata by the 71-year-old Croatian composer Stevan HRISTIĆ, set to lively music in Balkanized asymmetrical meters, is performed for the first time in Belgrade, conducted by the composer.

## 19 APRIL 1957

Antal DORATI conducts the Minneapolis Symphony Orchestra (of which he is music director) in the first performance of his dramatic cantata *The Way of the Cross*, to the English text after Paul Claudel, in 14 sections, descriptive of the successive stages of the Via Dolorosa.

## 1 MAY 1957

*The Prodigal Son*, ballet by the veteran Swedish composer Hugo ALFVÉN, on the scenario from the New Testament, with the inclusion in the score of some Swedish dances, is produced in Stockholm on his 85th birthday.

## 2 MAY 1957

Tadeusz KASSERN, 53-year-old Polish composer of numerous competent choral and instrumental pieces, commits suicide in New York under the double pressure of inoperable cancer and his inability to obtain a permit to remain in the United States after his defection from the Polish Consulate.

## 6 MAY 1957

Michael GNESSIN, Russian-Jewish composer of expressive choral and instrumental music in a nostalgic Hebraic manner, dies in Moscow at the age of seventy-four.

## 9 MAY 1957

*Der Revisor*, comic opera in five acts by the German composer Werner EGK, to a libretto drawn from Gogol's comedy deriding the corruption and incompetence of Tsarist bureaucracy, with municipal officers lavishing honors and money on an inconspicuous and impecunious stranger in the belief that he is a government inspector traveling incognito, culminating in the dramatic appearance of the real Revisor, arranged in the form of an Italian opera buffa, sprinkled with innocuous dissonances and introducing stylizations of Russian folksongs for couleur locale, is performed for the first time in Schwetzingen.

## 9 MAY 1957

*Panfilo and Lauretta*, opera in three acts by Carlos CHÁVEZ, dealing with a group of 14th-century aristocrats hiding in a Tuscan villa hoping to escape the raging pestilence, diverting themselves by impersonating their true natures in uninhibited play, during which a soldier gives a demonstration of carnal intercourse with a Florentine noblewoman, the socio-sexual egalitarianism reaching the climax when a pestiferous monk invades their refuge with a theatrical troupe and infects guests and hosts alike with the bubonic plague, is produced at Columbia University in New York. (A revised Spanish version, under the title *El Amor propiciado,* was performed under the composer's direction in Mexico City on 28 October 1959)

### 10 MAY 1957

Maxim SHOSTAKOVICH, son of Dmitri SHOSTAKOVICH, plays the piano part in the first performance in Moscow of his father's *Second Piano Concerto,* dedicated to him, in three movements: (1) *Allegro,* in propulsive 4/4 time, with discursive lyric episodes (2) *Andante,* in a ruminating Chopinesque manner in 3/4 time, and (3) *Allegro,* an energetic essay in optimistic major keys, with its predominant 2/4 time occasionally disequilibrated by asymmetric measures in compound 7/8 time.

### 11 MAY 1957

Two short operas, *Il Figliuol prodigo* and *Venere Prigioniera,* by Gian Francesco MALIPIERO, are produced at the Florence May Festival to honor the composer on the attainment (on 18 March) of the age of seventy-five. (A concert performance of *Il Figliuol prodigo* took place on the Italian Radio on 25 January 1953)

### 12 MAY 1957

On the occasion of the annual Prague Spring Music Festival, the Government of Czechoslovakia issues a set of six postage stamps of the denominations of 60 hellers, bearing the portraits of eminent Bohemian composers and performers: Jan STAMIC (1717–1757) with a musical quotation from his *Frühlingssinfonie;* the virtuoso violinist Ferdinand LAUB (1832–1875); Joseph FOERSTER (1859–1951), with a musical quotation from the third act of his opera *Eva;* Vítězslav NOVÁK (1870–1949), with a musical quotation from his symphonic poem *In the Tatra Mountains,* and Otakar OSTRČIL (1879–1935) with a musical quotation from his opera *Poupe* in which the first note is erroneously printed as D-sharp instead of F-sharp.

### 15 MAY 1957

*Dzhalil,* opera in two acts by the 46-year-old Tatar Soviet composer Nazib ZHIGANOV, to a libretto by the Tatar composer Dzhaudat Faizy on the subject of the heroic life of the Tatar poet Musa Dzhalil, executed by the Nazis in 1944 after he was taken prisoner of war on charges of participation in underground activities, is performed for the first time in Kazan, with a Russian libretto. (A new revised version was produced in Kazan on 30 April 1964)

### 17 MAY 1957

The definitive version of HAYDN's *Concerto in D major* for violoncello and orchestra, is performed for the first time in Vienna by Enrico Mainardi from the newly found authentic manuscript, signed in Haydn's own hand, "di me

Giuseppe Haydn," thus settling beyond doubt Haydn's authorship of the work long attributed by doubting Haydnologists to Anton Kraft, Haydn's first cellist of Prince Esterházy's Orchestra.

### 20 MAY 1957

The Soviet Union issues a stamp of 40 kopecks in honor of Mili BALAKIREV, the enlightened mentor of the Russian National School.

### 22 MAY 1957

*Una domanda di matrimonio,* one-act opera buffa by the Italian composer Louis CHAILLY, after Anton Chekhov's playlet in which a youth about to propose to a girl becomes entangled in an abstract debate with her and only after making an angry departure recollects the object of his visit and mends matters by an immediate return and proposal in marriage, is produced at the Piccola Scala in Milan.

### 24 MAY 1957

*Venus in Africa,* fantasy-opera by George ANTHEIL, to a libretto about a virginal American youth traveling in Tunis who appeals to the statue of Venus for instruction in love, whereupon a native girl opportunely materializes to initiate him into advanced sexual techniques, with a musical score marked by saccadic rhythms and sophisticated balladry, fertilized by innocuous amorous dissonances, is performed for the first time by the opera group of the University of Denver.

### 24 MAY 1957

*The Moon and Sixpence,* opera in three acts by the 40-year-old English composer John GARDNER, based on Somerset Maugham's novel suggested by the life of Paul Gauguin, taking place in London, Paris and on a Pacific island, set to music in a colloquially simplicistic vein with some pseudo-exotic inflections, is performed as the first commissioned work of the Sadler's Wells Opera in London.

### 24 MAY 1957

*Simonida,* opera in three acts by the 46-year-old Yugoslav composer Stanojlo RAJIČIĆ, to a story of the 14th-century Byzantine damsel who is affianced to an aged Serbian king but falls in love with his son and, when the latter is blinded by the king's orders, dies from a psychosomatic inanition, is performed for the first time in Sarajevo. (A revised version was first performed in Belgrade on 17 April 1958)

### 25 MAY 1957

*A Feira,* opera by the Portuguese composer Ruy COELHO, is produced in Lisbon.

## 25 MAY 1957

*The Taming of the Shrew,* comic opera in four acts, after Shakespeare, by the 54-year-old Soviet composer Vissarion SHEBALIN, written in a realistic idiom modeled after Mussorgsky, but containing a considerable admixture of modernistically enhanced tonal harmonies and polyharmonies, is produced in Kuibishev. (The first Moscow performance of the opera, in concert form, took place on 1 October 1955)

## 31 MAY 1957

The 31st Festival of the International Society for Contemporary Music opens in Zürich, Switzerland, with a program of electronic music, comprising the following works:

*Scambi* by the 27-year-old Belgian composer Henri POUSSEUR; *Notturno* and *Syntaxis* by the 37-year-old Italian composer Bruno MADERNA; *8:37 Perspectives* and *Mutazioni* by the 31-year-old Italian composer Luciano BERIO.

## 1 JUNE 1957

The following orchestral works are presented at the 31st Festival of the International Society for Contemporary Music in Zürich, Switzerland:

*Corales criollos* by Juan José CASTRO of Argentina; *Scythian Suite* by PROKOFIEV; *Figures Sonores* by Yoritsune MATSUDAIRA of Japan; and *Sixth Symphony* by Karl Amadeus HARTMANN of Germany, in two large sections, a greatly protracted *Adagio,* Mahlerian in its proportions and philosophical concentration, and *Toccata,* generated by the motive of three notes, B-flat, B and A, with highly intricate variations and fugues.

## 2 JUNE 1957

The following works are presented at the third concert of the 31st Festival of the International Society for Contemporary Music in Zürich:

*3 Volkstexte,* op. 17, by Anton von WEBERN, for soprano, violin, clarinet and bass clarinet, written in 1924, in which the method of composition with 12 tones is employed by Webern for the first time after Schoenberg; *Concert Piece* for violin and piano by Mátyás SEIBER of Hungary and England; *Sonata* for trumpet, guitar and piano by the 32-year-old Italian composer Aldo CLEMENTI, employing the method of rhythmic serialism on repeated notes of natural harmonics, calculated to produce the effect of mechanized static immobility; *Contrasts* for clarinet, violin and piano by Béla BARTÓK; and *Frequencies* for piccolo, flute, guitar, doublebass, xylophone, vibraphone and percussion by the 20-year-old Swede Bo NILSSON, in which the dodecaphonic subject is presented in serial treatment in dynamics, tempi, coloration, duration, rhythms, and other aspects of musical composition, according to the formula:

$$\int (a + bx)^n dx = \frac{(a + bx)^{n+1}}{(n + 1)b} + C \qquad (n \neq -1)$$

## 3 JUNE 1957

During the course of the 31st Festival of the International Society for Contemporary Music in Zürich the following works are presented:

(1) *Concerto breve* for orchestra by Vittorio FELLEGARA of Italy, in a free non-classical, non-romantic, non-diatonic, non-chromatic, non-dodecaphonic but thematically coherent and sonorously integrated idiom; (2) *Eine Gotthard-Kantate* for baritone solo and string orchestra by the Russian-born Swiss resident composer Wladimir VOGEL, illustrating in expressively dodecaphonic melodies the vision of the poet Friedrich Hölderlin as he stood in contemplation at the St. Gotthard pass in the Alps; (3) *Recitativo ed Aria* for clavecin and orchestra by the 37-year-old Polish-born composer Roman HAUBENSTOCK-RAMATI, conceived as a neo-classical serial idea; (4) *5 Neapolitanische Lieder* for voice and chamber orchestra by the 30-year-old German expressionist composer Hans Werner HENZE, who took up residence on the island of Capri; (5) *Passacaglia* for small orchestra by the 32-year-old French composer Maurice JARRE, dedicated to the memory of Arthur Honegger; and (6) *Kammermusik No. 1* by Paul HINDEMITH, first performed in Donaueschingen on 31 July 1922.

## 3 JUNE 1957

*Die Räuber,* opera in four acts after Schiller by the 31-year-old German composer Giselher KLEBE, written in a heroic modern manner within a framework of unencumbered dissonances, is produced in Düsseldorf.

## 4 JUNE 1957

The 31st Festival of the International Society for Contemporary Music continues in Zürich with a concert presenting the following works:

*3 Psalmen* for soprano, tenor, chorus and orchestra by the Swiss composer Robert OBOUSSIER (who was fated to be assassinated five days later) composed in 1946–1947 under the impact of fresh memories of Nazi horrors and expressing in terms of simple tonal lyricism the successive sentiments of deep despair, nascent hope and liberating joy; *Concerto* for piano and orchestra by the 38-year-old American composer Leon KIRCHNER, of a sharply accentuated musical consistency within a classically clear formal design; *First Symphony* by the 31-year-old Chilean composer Gustavo BECERRA SCHMIDT, written in a volitionally synthetic idiom of tonal serialism; *Epitaph* for orchestra by the 33-year-old Austrian composer Karl-Heinz FÜSSL, dedicated to the memory of Anton von Webern, in 13 brief variations in the lapidary style of Webern himself with a maximum of dissipation in the distribution of orchestral registers and rhythmic units; and a *String Quartet* by the 32-year-old American composer Billy Jim LAYTON.

## 5 JUNE 1957

The 31st Festival of the International Society for Contemporary Music continues in Zürich with the following concert of Swiss music:

*4 Etudes* for string orchestra by Frank MARTIN; *Etudes* for voice and orchestra by Constantin RÉGAMEY; *Violin Concerto* by Willy BURKHARD; *Tre Mutazioni* for chamber orchestra by Jacques WILDBERGER; and *Amores* for tenor, trumpet, percussion and strings by Franz TISCHHAUSSER.

## 5 JUNE 1957

*The Curious Fern,* one-act opera by the American composer Meyer KUPFERMAN, is produced in New York.

## 6 JUNE 1957

The 31st Festival of the International Society for Contemporary Music in Zürich concludes with the first stage performance of Arnold SCHOENBERG's posthumous opera *Moses und Aron.*

## 8 JUNE 1957

*Bluthochzeit,* lyric tragedy in two acts by Wolfgang FORTNER, after *Bodas de Sangre* by Federico García Lorca, written in an eclectic dodecaphonic technique with symbolic overtones (the mother's impassionate apostrophe to the knife suggests atonal schizophrenia, a dodecaphonic canon of two violins alludes to the mystery of the forest, etc.) is performed for the first time in Cologne. (The world première was originally scheduled for 25 May 1957 but was deferred on account of the illness of one of the performers; *Der Wald,* a section of the complete opera was first performed in its original version in Frankfurt on 25 June 1953.)

## 9 JUNE 1957

Robert OBOUSSIER, 56-year-old Swiss composer, is stabbed to death 17 times by his room companion at dawn, in their apartment in Zürich.

## 10 JUNE 1957

*Putovanje (The Journey),* the first television opera to be given in Yugoslavia, a satirical musical burlesque by the 43-year-old Croatian composer Ivo LHOTKA-KALINSKI, dealing with a petty functionary vegetating about 1900 who nourishes an unfeasible desire to travel to distant places, set to music in the tonally dissonant manner of utilitarian opera, is produced in Zagreb.

## 17 JUNE 1957

On the 75th birthday of Igor STRAVINSKY, his ballet *Agon* (completed on 27 April, 1957, in Los Angeles, his dwelling place since World War II), an antiphonally designed realization of the ancient Greek *agon,* a prize contest, scored for 12 dancers, in 12 movements (the numbers symbolically signaling the incipient dodecaphony of Stravinsky's Third Style), is performed for the first time in Los Angeles in concert form, conducted by Stravinsky's loyal famulus, Robert Craft, and forming the following divisions:

(1) *Pas de Quatre* for 4 male dancers in diatonic ostentation (2) *Double Pas de Quatre,* for 8 female participants, marked by petulant minor seconds in argumentative heterophony (3) *Triple Pas de Quatre* for 8 female and 4 male dancers, with chromatic infol-

iation around the bisexual focal D (4) *Prelude* in triadic disposition (5) *First Pas de Trois*, containing a pandiatonic Saraband (6) *Gaillarde*, a pantriadic neo-archaic divertissement (7) *Coda* in faux-bourdon counterpoint (8) *Interlude*, an aimbivalent equilibrium of C major and B flat minor triads (9) *Second Pas de Trois*, in the form of a simple canonic bransle (10) *Bransle Gay*, with the orchestra in vacillating meter against the steady triple rhythms of a single castagnette (11) *Bransle de Poitou*, in the meter of a courante (12) *Interlude* (13) *Pas de Deux*, marked by wide intervallic saltation (14) Four choreographic *Duos*, monophonically serialistic, in propulsive quarter-note motion (15) Four choreographic *Trios* in paraserialistic melos, leading to a coda as a reprise of the initial *Pas de Quatre* and concluding on a gymnosophistically quartal-quintal chord C-F-D-G-C. (The first stage performance of *Agon* took place in New York on 1 December 1957)

### 26 JUNE 1957

*Dos movimientos* for a kettledrum and string orchestra by the 27-year-old Spanish composer Cristóbal HALFFTER, written in a constructivistically polyrhythmic manner, is performed for the first time in Madrid.

### 29 JUNE 1957

Ede POLDINI, Hungarian composer of pleasant piano pieces, of which *La Poupée valsante* became a semiclassical classic, dies in Vevey, Switzerland, at the age of eighty-eight.

### 3 JULY 1957

Richard MOHAUPT, German composer of various operatic and symphonic works in an enlightened modern manner, dies in Reichenau, Austria, at the age of fifty-two.

### 6 JULY 1957

Henry FÉVRIER, French composer of romantic operas touched with Wagneromorphic drama, dies in Paris at the age of eighty-one.

### 20 JULY 1957

Guillermo URIBE-HOLGUÍN, 77-year-old prime composer of Colombia, conducts in Bogotá the first performance of his *Seventh Symphony*.

### 23 JULY 1957

Two centuries have passed since Domenico SCARLATTI, originator of modern keyboard technique, died in Madrid, where he became a court composer, and where he successively married two Spanish ladies who bore him nine children, who in turn propagated in a geometric progression right into the 20th century, so that there are dozens of Scarlattis in the Madrid telephone book.

### 26 JULY 1957

*Jacob and the Indians*, opera in three acts by the 33-year-old American composer Ezra LADERMAN, is produced in Woodstock, New York.

## 31 JULY 1957

Sem DRESDEN, prime Dutch composer, author of romantic songs and instrumental pieces, dies at The Hague, at the age of seventy-six.

## 2 AUGUST 1957

*The Tower,* one-act opera by the American composer Marvin David LEVY, is performed for the first time by the Santa Fe Opera Company on his 25th birthday.

## 3 AUGUST 1957

Pablo CASALS, 80-year-old grand maestro of the violoncello, takes in marriage as his third wife, his 20-year-old pupil, Martita Montañez, in a ceremony held in San Juan, Puerto Rico, an island which was to become his permanent residence and the site of the Casals Music Festivals.

## 11 AUGUST 1957

At the opening of the Munich Festival, Paul HINDEMITH conducts the world première of his opera *Die Harmonie der Welt,* in five acts, to his own text, dealing with the life and theories of planetary motion of the astronomer Johannes Kepler, reverting also to the astrological ideas of the Harmony of the Spheres. (A symphonic suite from the opera was performed in Basel on 24 January 1952)

## 17 AUGUST 1957

*Schule der Frauen,* opera buffa in three acts by Rolf LIEBERMANN, after Molière's play *L'École des Femmes,* scored for six singers and chamber orchestra, in a German version, with Molière himself presiding over the action and expressing curiosity as to how his comedy would work out as an opera, is produced in Salzburg. (The original smaller concert version was first produced as a commissioned work in Louisville, Kentucky, on 3 December 1955; another version was presented in Zürich on 9 November 1957)

## 17 AUGUST 1957

Gunther SCHULLER, 31-year-old American composer and jazzologist, spontaneously invents, during a lecture at Music Inn at the Berkshire Music Center in Tanglewood, near Lenox, Massachusetts, the term *Third Stream,* to define a type of composition in which elements of jazz are organized within a classical matrix, so that popular music becomes ennobled and respectable without losing its innate vitality and classical music acquires an indigenous vivacity of rhythmic progress. (The exact date and circumstances of the portentous epiphany communicated to the author, with proper certification, by Gunther Schuller himself)

## 1 SEPTEMBER 1957

Dennis BRAIN, 36-year-old British virtuoso horn player, a scion of the family of horn players, is killed in an automobile accident after hitting a tree on a winding road in Hatfield, Hertfordshire, while driving at night at high speed from Birmingham to London.

## 11 SEPTEMBER 1957

*Concerto* for two pianos and orchestra by Gian Francesco MALIPIERO, written in a fine pandiatonic manner, is performed for the first time at the music festival of Besançon, France, by the matrimonial duo pianists Janine Reding and Henri Piette.

## 20 SEPTEMBER 1957

Jean SIBELIUS, great Finnish composer whose tall physical stature and granitically noble countenance seemed to mirror the spiritual character of his music and the spacious melorhythms of Suomi folksongs, dies in his home at Järvenpää at the age of 91 as his poignant *Swan of Tuonela* is mournfully broadcast over the Finnish radio.

## 23 SEPTEMBER 1957

Two postage stamps in the denominations of 40 kopecks and one ruble, are issued by the Soviet Union in honor of the great proponent of national Russian music Vladimir STASOV (1824–1906).

## 24 SEPTEMBER 1957

*Maratona di danza,* ballet by Hans Werner HENZE, is performed for the first time in Berlin.

## 26 SEPTEMBER 1957

*West Side Story,* musical play by the protean 39-year-old Leonard BERNSTEIN, presenting an American counterpart of Romeo and Juliet, wherein two youthful gangs collide murderously in the tenements and playgrounds of West Side, Manhattan, between 80th and 90th Streets, engulfing the tragic romance across the fighting lines between an American boy and a Puerto Rican girl, the score containing the modern sentimental ballads *Maria* and *I Feel Pretty,* is produced in New York, marking a musical event without precedent, a highly popular show with music written by the conductor of a major symphony orchestra, the Philharmonic of New York.

## 28 SEPTEMBER 1957

*Third Symphony* by the Rumanian composer Sigismond TODUŢA, subtitled *Ovid,* written in the commemoration of the second millennium of the birth of the Roman poet Ovid who was exiled by Emperor August to Rumania, is performed for the first time in Cluj, Rumania.

## 29 SEPTEMBER 1957

*La Dame aux camélias,* ballet by Henri SAUGUET, to a scenario after the famous melodrama of Alexandre Dumas, is produced at the Berlin Festival.

## 1 OCTOBER 1957

*Fourteen Minutes Before the Start,* a song by the Soviet composer Oscar FELTSMAN, depicting the expectant atmosphere before an aviator takes off on an important mission, destined to become the favorite air of the Soviet cosmonauts, is broadcast for the first time on Radio Moscow, three days before the launching of the first Sputnik. (Date and information obtained by the author from Oscar Feltsman)

1 OCTOBER 1957

*Thyl de Flandre,* opera by the 47-year-old French composer and musicologist Jacques CHAILLEY, is produced in Brussels.

1 OCTOBER 1957

*Seventh Symphony* by the English composer Edmund RUBBRA, couched in polycentric modalities invested with polytriadic harmonies containing a generous injection of non-toxic dissonances, in three cyclic movements (1) *Lento–Allegro moderato,* ending on "niente" in C major (2) *Vivace e leggiero,* a quasi-Vindobonic waltz-scherzo with a cadence on a thirdless C triad (3) *Passacaglia and Fugue,* in circular construction, the last two bars being identical with the first two, and concluding in unpigmented C major, is performed for the first time in Birmingham, England, by the Birmingham Symphony Orchestra under the direction of the Polish composer-conductor resident in England, Andrzej Panufnik.

10 OCTOBER 1957

Three unnamed short pieces for chamber orchestra by Arnold SCHOENBERG, written in 1910, untitled and unpublished, but historically important since they demonstrate the transitional period from athematic atonality to organized panthematic dodecaphony, are performed for the first time by members of the Berlin Philharmonic Orchestra in West Berlin.

10 OCTOBER 1957

*Seventh Symphony* by the 61-year-old Austrian composer Johann Nepomuk DAVID is performed for the first time at Stuttgart.

11 OCTOBER 1957

*Gauche, the Violoncellist,* one-act opera buffa by the 45-year-old Japanese composer Osamu SHIMIZU, is produced in Osaka.

16 OCTOBER 1957

The centennial season of the Hallé Orchestra in Manchester, founded by Charles HALLÉ in 1858, opens with a *Flourish for Glorious John* written for the conductor John Barbirolli by Ralph VAUGHAN WILLIAMS.

17 OCTOBER 1957

Ralph BENATZKY, Czech-born composer of tuneful German operettas, of which *Im weissen Rössl* became a universal favorite, dies in Zürich at the age of seventy-three.

*Toccata* for orchestra by Paul CRESTON is performed for the first time by the Cleveland Orchestra.

*Gorski Vijenac* (*Mountain Bouquet*), oratorio in three acts by the 46-year-old Herzegovinian composer Nikola HERCIGONIA, descriptive of the 1817 rebellion of Montenegro against its Ottoman overlords, in which the hero performs a personal sacrifice by subordinating his passion for a girl to his patriotism, containing 11-beat rhythms characteristic of the region, is produced in Belgrade.

Jean MARTINON conducts in Paris the first performance of his cantata *Le Lis de Saron* (*Rose of Sharon*), an impassionate Solomonian cantillation with a polytonal accompaniment.

*Fantasy* for piano by Aaron COPLAND, written for the 50th Anniversary of the Juilliard School of Music, receives its initial performances played twice (for better penetration and comprehension) in New York by William Masselos.

*Mother,* opera in four acts by the 44-year-old Soviet composer Tikhon KHRENNIKOV, after Maxim Gorky's novel, dealing with a protest strike by factory workers against a one-kopeck monthly tax, resulting in the strike leader's deportation to Siberia, where he is followed by his faithful beloved while his formerly apolitical mother takes over his work in distributing anti-Tsarist propaganda leaflets, set to music making ample use of the *Marseillaise,* the *Warsaw Funeral March,* the *Prison Ballad,* and other revolutionary songs popular during the period of the abortive Russian revolution of 1905, is produced at the Bolshoi Theater in Moscow.

*Milana,* opera in four acts by the Ukrainian composer Georgi MAIBORODA, dealing with a beautiful Soviet girl and her young Communist lover working in the resistance groups from 1939 to 1944 in the Fascist-governed part of Transcarpathia, until it was liberated by the Red Army and subsequently incorporated into the Ukrainian Soviet Socialist Republic, is performed for the first time in Kiev.

The world première is given in Moscow of the *Eleventh Symphony* by Dmitri SHOSTAKOVICH, subtitled *1905* (the year of the tragically abortive and yet romantically inspiring Russian revolution), set in four descriptive movements:

(1) *Palace Square*, postulating a static theme expressive of the inhumanity of the Tsarist regime interspersed with inchoate fragments of anguished church anthems, trumpet calls and ominous drum beats as background for the popular ballads *Listen!* and *The Prisoner* (2) *January the Ninth*, the "Bloody Sunday" in St. Petersburg when the Cossack troops dispersed the crowd advancing on the Winter Palace to petition the Tsar for redress of grievances, musically portrayed by an eerie *scherzo fugato*, interrupted by outcries of prayer and agony, with a militant workers' song *Boldly, Comrades, Step Forward!* marking the turn towards revolutionary decisions (3) *Perpetual Remembrance*, opening with the melody of the revolutionary funeral march *You Fell a Victim to Fateful Struggle*, changing to the strains of *Welcome the Free Word of Liberty* and leading to the finale (4) *The Alert*, using the melodies of *Warsaw March, Rage You Tyrants*, and *Let Us Uncover Our Heads*, with growing growls in the brass presaging the victorious revolution of 1917.

### 31 OCTOBER 1957

*Baptism of Fire*, opera in five scenes by the 48-year-old Estonian composer Gustav ERNESAKS, dealing with the abortive Russian Revolution of 1905, symbolized by the contrapuntal syncrasy of the old Tsarist anthem with the Marseillaise, popular among the revolutionary masses and sung to Russian words, is produced in Tallin.

### 2 NOVEMBER 1957

*The Voice of Lenin*, cantata for mixed chorus, children's chorus and orchestra by the Rumanian composer Alfred MENDELSOHN, is performed for the first time in Bucharest.

### 4 NOVEMBER 1957

Joseph CANTELOUBE, known as Canteloube de Malaret, after his family estate, French composer, whose tasteful quasi-impressionistic settings of songs from his native Auvergne have become favorites among singers, dies in Paris at the age of seventy-eight.

### 8 NOVEMBER 1957

*The Gadfly*, opera by Antonio SPADAVECCHIA, 50-year-old Odessa-born Soviet composer of Italian descent, to the novel of that name written in 1897 by the English novelist Ethel Voynich, dealing with an inspired British revolutionary who helped Garibaldi in the Italian struggle for independence, is produced in Perm.

### 16 NOVEMBER 1957

*Medusa*, ballet by the 39-year-old Austrian composer Gottfried von EINEM, is performed for the first time in Vienna.

### 18 NOVEMBER 1957

*The Throne of God*, cantata for mixed voices and orchestra by the 62-year-old American composer Leo SOWERBY, commissioned by the National Cathedral in Washington for its 50th anniversary, is performed for the first time in Washington.

22 NOVEMBER 1957

The government of the Democratic Republic of Germany issues two postage stamps in honor of two prominent Leipzig musicians, one for 10 pfennigs commemorating the organist Günther RAMIN who died on 27 February 1956, and for 25 pfennigs for the conductor Hermann ABENDROTH who died on 29 May 1956.

22 NOVEMBER 1957

*The Sweet Bye and Bye,* opera in three acts by the American composer Jack BEESON, to a discreetly fictionalized libretto suggested by the scandalous disappearance on 18 May 1926 of the famous female revivalist Aimée MacPherson, the builder of a personal temple in Southern California, is produced in New York.

22 NOVEMBER 1957

*Fourth Symphony* by Ernst TOCH in three movements, *Molto dolce, Molto tranquillo* and *Molto igualmente,* commissioned by the Women's Association of the Minneapolis Symphony Orchestra, and dedicated to the memory of Marion MacDowell (1857–1956) with a motto by the composer, addressing her as "indomitable, incandescent soul," and describing his symphony as a letter "written wholly upon your dictation," is performed for the first time by the Minneapolis Symphony Orchestra, Antal Dorati conducting.

25 NOVEMBER 1957

The Republic of Liberia issues a postage stamp bearing the musical notation of its National Anthem.

25 NOVEMBER 1957

*Logaritmos No. 3* by the Italian composer Giorgio GASLINI, for string quartet concertante with string orchestra, xylophone and chimes, in two parts, in which the quartet is treated as a dodecaphonic logarithm to the duodecimal base of the ripieni, is performed for the first time in Rome.

28 NOVEMBER 1957

*Othello,* Shakespearean ballet by the foremost romantic composer of Soviet Georgia Alexei MACHAVARIANI, written in romantically melodramatic tones, is produced in Tbilisi.

29 NOVEMBER 1957

Erich Wolfgang KORNGOLD, once a *Wunderkind* who aroused enthusiasm by his precocious talent and was hailed by reputable musicians as a modern Mozart, dies in Hollywood, his refuge after the Nazi darkness descended on his native Vienna, as the result of debilitating apoplexy, at the age of sixty.

**2 DECEMBER 1957**

*Smrt Stefana Dečanskogo* cantata by the Yugoslav composer Enriko JOSIF, in the form of a lamentation upon the death of the Serbian 14th-century king Stefan dethroned by his son, set to music in a neo-medieval style, is performed for the first time in Belgrade.

**3 DECEMBER 1957**

Yugoslavia issues a postage stamp of 70 dinars in honor of the Serbian composer Stevan MOKRANJAĆ (1856–1914).

**6 DECEMBER 1957**

*Third Symphony* by Roger SESSIONS, completed by him on 23 September 1957, in which a guiding dodecaphonic series is formed by a gradual accretion of thematic units, in four movements, *Allegro grazioso e con fuoco, Allegro un poco ruvido, Andante sostenuto e con affetto* and *Allegro con fuoco,* concluding on a seminal statement of the cumulative tone-row in decisive unisons, ending on a proleptic tonic B, is performed for the first time by the Boston Symphony Orchestra, under the direction of Charles Munch.

**9 DECEMBER 1957**

*Konjanik (The Horseman),* "cavalcade" for mixed chorus and chamber orchestra by the 39-year-old Trieste-born Yugoslav composer Emil COSSETTO, depicting a knight's night ride to a mysteriously receding battlefront, written in melodramatic march time, is performed for the first time in Zagreb.

**21 DECEMBER 1957**

Eric COATES, English composer of descriptive symphonic pieces, of which the *Knightsbridge* march from his *London Suite* became widely popular, dies at the age of seventy-one in Chichester.

**25 DECEMBER 1957**

*Labinska Vještica (The Witch of Labin),* opera in two acts by the 43-year-old Croatian composer Natko DEVČIĆ, with the action centered on the religious strife between Protestants and Catholics in 16th-century Istria, is produced in Zagreb.

# ᘀ *1958* ᘁ

**10 JANUARY 1958**

Alec ROWLEY, 65-year-old English composer of gracefully unpretentious music in smaller forms, collapses and dies during a tennis game in London.

## 15 JANUARY 1958

The Metropolitan Opera presents in New York the world première of *Vanessa*, opera in four acts by Samual BARBER, to the libretto by Gian Carlo Menotti, recounting the melodramatic tale of "a lady of great beauty" (Vanessa is a genus of butterflies to which an American variety, the "painted beauty," belongs) languishing "in a northern country about 1905," and the handsome young son of her dead lover who seduces her niece Erika, nearly causing her death as she tries to abort the fruit of their liaison, and who in the end marries Vanessa herself as a symbolic redemption of his father's defection long ago, set to music of colorful opulence freely applying chromatic, atonal, polytonal, and pandiatonic devices, with aerostatic melodies reposing on long-stemmed chords rooted in deep overtone-fertile basses, and with the vocal line varying from impassionate cantilena to ostentatiously prosaic spoken lines.

## 23 JANUARY 1958

*Mosaics* for orchestra by Howard HANSON, suggesting the interplay of colors, lights and shadows in a mosaic design by an astute polarization of instrumental timbres, is performed for the first time as a commissioned work by the Cleveland Orchestra in celebration of its 40th anniversary.

## 24 JANUARY 1958

Paul SACHER conducts the Chamber Orchestra of Basel in two world premières:

*The Epic of Gilgamesh*, cantata by Bohuslav MARTINU, in three parts, to the texts of newly deciphered Babylonian poems relating the story of a simple man of nature seduced by a dancer of the temple of Istar who dies to expiate his delinquency and posthumously warns King Gilgamesh of the lamentability of carnality and inexorability of perdition, with a musical score based on a brief archaically sounding theme artfully mutated into a series of variations; and *Kette, Kreis und Spiegel*, a "symphonic drawing" by Ernst KRENEK, wherein the "chain" in the title refers to the interlocking arrangement of 48 forms of the basic dodecaphonic series, "circle" to the principle of rotation underlying it, and "mirror" to the ultimate inverted form of the original configuration resulting from the preceding concatenations and rotations.

Whatever morphological kinship may be detected between adjacent sections is a result of similarities of intervallic shapes that may occur in neighboring forms of the tone-row, the vicinity of which, however, is a consequence of the premeditated serial arrangement and not dictated by requirements of a so-called musical nature. (Ernst Krenek, in *Extents and Limits of Serial Techniques* in *The Musical Quarterly*, April, 1960)

## 30 JANUARY 1958

*Partita for Orchestra* by William WALTON, in three movements: (1) *Toccata*, with thematic contents determined by the contraction of the octave to a major seventh and its subsequent fission into a tritone and a perfect fourth (2)

*Pastorale Siciliana,* in a luminescently Italian vein with a proliferation of trilled protuberances and (3) *Giga burlesca,* a hedonistic rondo, is performed for the first time by the Cleveland Orchestra.

### 5 FEBRUARY 1958

*Second Symphony* by the 53-year-old English composer of Cornish stock Michael TIPPETT (completed after five years of work on 13 November 1957), in four movements: (1) *Allegro vigoroso,* opening with a round of impressive beats on low C's, immediately challenged by the gymnosophistical fifths in the horns a tritone away and proceeding thence along polytriadic lines (2) a lyrically contemplative *Adagio molto e tranquillo* (3) a scherzo, *Presto veloce,* built on additive rhythms in asymmetrical meters, and (4) *Allegro moderato,* a fantasia in four unrelated sections, ending on the pandiatonic conglomerate C-G-D-A-E, is performed for the first time by the British Broadcasting Corporation Symphony Orchestra, under the direction of Sir Adrian Boult (who had to restart the work after something went amiss in the exposition in the first movement, and apologized to the public for an incidence of unintentional polyrhythmic polyharmony resulting from a contrapuntal contretemps)

### 6 FEBRUARY 1958

*The Dragon,* one-act chamber opera by Deems TAYLOR, to a story of an Irish princess saved from a green Irish dragon by a prince masquerading as a cook, set to music in a flowingly melodious and ingratiatingly harmonious idiom, with occasional euphonious modernities injected for melodramatic effect, is performed for the first time by the New York University Opera Workshop, in a version accompanied by piano and organ in lieu of the original orchestral instrumentation.

### 8 FEBRUARY 1958

*Il Vortice,* opera in three acts by the 50-year-old Italian composer Renzo ROSSELLINI, is produced in Naples.

### 12 FEBRUARY 1958

The inaugural concert of *Structures Sonores,* an ensemble of sound-producing objects fashioned of glass and steel in modernistically asymmetrical shapes by François BASCHET, is given at the Schola Cantorum in Paris in a program of works specially written by Jacques Lasry, the co-builder of *Structures Sonores,* and including *Two Dances for the Crystal, Coil-spring Dance, Metalic Preludium, Cosmotony, Bolide* and *Mister Blues.*

### 14 FEBRUARY 1958

*Hungaria 1956,* symphonic poem by the Polish composer Artur MALAWSKI, descriptive in somber tones of the sanguinary pacification by the Soviet Army of the Hungarian insurrection of 1956, is performed for the first time in Warsaw.

## 15 FEBRUARY 1958

*The World of Paul Klee*, symphonic suite by David DIAMOND, evoking by congenial melorhythmic configurations the impressions of four paintings by Klee: (1) *Grieving Child*, waltzing sadly in muted strings and muted brass (2) *Black Prince*, strutting in dislocated march time (3) *Pastorale*, in multiple triple meters, like a bark a-rolling in a barcarolle (4) *Twittering Machine*, with disconnected gears set a-flutter by means of a large sheet of heavy paper shaken longitudinally to produce the sonic simulacrum of a miniaturized thunderclap, is performed for the first time by the Portland, Oregon, Junior Symphony Orchestra, Jacob Avshalomov conducting.

## 20 FEBRUARY 1958

Isidor PHILIPP, 94-year-old French pianist and famous pedagogue, dies in Paris of injuries sustained in a fall at the entrance of the Metro, which he continued to use despite his nonagenarian fragility.

## 25 FEBRUARY 1958

*Aeneas-Silvius Symphonie* by the 56-year-old Swiss composer Conrad BECK (his *Seventh Symphony*), written as an homage to the 15th-century humanist Aeneas-Silvius Piccolomini of Siena who became Pope Pius II and founded the University of Basel, set in a series of four variations, alternately rhetorical, hieratic, nostalgic and impetuous, is performed for the first time in Zürich.

## 27 FEBRUARY 1958

*Miorița*, oratorio by the 31-year-old Rumanian composer Anatol VIERU, to the words of a folk ballad about a stray sheep, based on two mutually exclusive tropes of six notes (C,D,F-sharp, G,B,C-sharp and E-flat, E,F,A-flat, A,B-flat), aggregating to a 12-tone series, set in effectively acerbic harmonies, is performed for the first time in Bucharest.

## 1 MARCH 1958

*Assassinio nella Cattedrale*, opera-oratorio by the Italian grandmaster Ildebrando PIZZETTI, based on T.S. Eliot's play *Murder in the Cathedral*, and dealing with the assassination of Thomas à Beckett on the orders of Henry II of England in 1170, drawn in heroic modalities and resonant unencumbered harmonies, performed for the first time at La Scala, Milan.

## 1 MARCH 1958

*First Symphony* by the 35-year-old Greek composer Yorgo SICILIANOS, written in a neo-classical idiom revitalized by ambitonal, atonal and polytonal exfoliations, is performed for the first time by the New York Philharmonic Symphony Orchestra, Dimitri Mitropoulos conducting.

## 4 MARCH 1958

*Pre-Classic Suite* for orchestra by Paul CRESTON, in three movements (*Courante, Pavane* and *Galliard*) is performed for the first time in New Orleans.

## 5 MARCH 1958

*Orchestral Variations* by Aaron COPLAND, a symphonic transcription of his *Piano Variations* of 1930, derived, as was the original work, from an eleven-bar theme of a dramatically atonal nature, with an involute four-note figure, E, C, E-flat, C-sharp, constituting the thematic nucleus, is performed for the first time in Louisville.

## 7 MARCH 1958

*Third Symphony* by the 57-year-old French composer Henry BARRAUD, in four contracting movements freely conceived in a median modernistic manner, utilizing enriched tonality, polytonality, atonality, and occasionally non-thematic dodecaphony, is performed for the first time by the Boston Symphony Orchestra, Charles Munch conducting, on the same program with the première of Walter PISTON's *Viola Concerto.*

## 9 MARCH 1958

*Second Symphony* for strings and celesta by the 59-year-old French composer Marcel DELANNOY, in three well-balanced movements, is performed for the first time in Paris.

## 19 MARCH 1958

*Gallantry,* one-act "soap opera" by Douglas MOORE, in which a hospital nurse is libidinously coveted by a lascivious surgeon about to perform an appendectomy on her fiancé, set to music in mock-melodramatic tones, is performed for the first time in New York.

## 16 MARCH 1958

*Doubles,* a set of symphonic variations by the apostle of ultramodern music Pierre BOULEZ, scored for a normal classical orchestra, in which the spatial positions of musical chairs are periodically shifted, with the application of novel dynamic effects such as simultaneous crescendo and diminuendo in the same chord, is performed for the first time in Paris.

## 22 MARCH 1958

*Ninth Symphony* by the 82-year-old English composer Havergal BRIAN, written in 1951, in three movements, *Allegro vivo* (prefaced by a slow introduction), *Adagio* and *Allegro moderato,* set in a modernistically individual experimental manner without overflowing the tonal boundaries of classical forms, scored for full orchestra and a substantial pod of drums, is performed for the first time by the London Symphony Orchestra, under the direction of Norman Del Mar.

## 25 MARCH 1958

Emerson WHITHORNE, American composer, who in 1920 wrote the first piece of airplane music, dies in Lyme, Connecticut, at the age of seventy-three.

## 26 MARCH 1958

*Ongaku,* a symphonic suite on Japanese themes by Henry COWELL, is performed for the first time in Louisville.

## 26 MARCH 1958

*Musique Funèbre* by the 45-year-old Polish composer Witold LUTOSLAWSKI, dedicated to the heroes and victims of Polish resistance groups against the Nazis, based on a symbolic tonal emblem of ascending tritones and descending semitones, is performed for the first time in Katowice, Poland.

## 27 MARCH 1958

*The Heart of the Taiga,* opera in four acts by the 59-year-old Soviet composer Lev KNIPPER, to a libretto dealing with the conflicts and achievements in the collective farms of Eastern Siberia, set to music in accordance with the doctrine of Socialist Realism, national in thematic materials and socialist in treatment, is performed for the first time, in concert form, in Moscow. (The first version of the opera, originally entitled *The Root of Life,* written in 1949, was not produced)

## 28 MARCH 1958

W. C. HANDY, "Father of the Blues," who learned to play the cornet by practicing on a cow's horn as a child, and whose *Memphis Blues,* which he published at his own expense ($32.50) in 1912, created a new genre of American music, dies in New York at the age of eighty-four. (A commemorative stamp of 6 cents, showing W. C. Handy playing the trumpet, was issued in Memphis on 17 May 1969 on the occasion of the sesquicentennial of the city and to honor the birth place of *Memphis Blues*)

## 28 MARCH 1958

*First Symphony* by the 39-year-old American composer George ROCHBERG, in three movements, (1) *Allegro risoluto,* written in an exclamatory triadic idiom with atonal implosions and onomatopeic ornithological episodes (2) *Tema e variazioni,* a sepulchrally Calvinistic chorale drenched in lachrymal magma (3) *Adagio–Allegro giocoso,* a marching procession in maximal dissonances ending in reiterative caudal chords, is performed for the first time in Philadelphia.

## 1 APRIL 1958

Alexander TCHEREPNIN, 59-year-old Russian composer, becomes an American citizen in Chicago.

## 2 APRIL 1958

*Ninth Symphony* in E minor by Ralph VAUGHAN WILLIAMS, his last, written at the age of 85, in four movements: (1) *Allegro moderato,* in a whimsically variegated sonata form with a rhapsodically wrought recapitulation (2) *Andante sostenuto*, introduced by a romantic flügelhorn solo, with a meaningful stroke of the gong ushering in a clonic march tune (3) *Allegro pesante*, a sophisticated scherzo in which three saxophones disport themselves with saltatory felinity, ending with a funereal side-drum tap (4) *Andante tranquillo*, in two sections, exuding a species of tragic optimism, concluding with periodically inturgescent and detumescent E-major chords, vanishing into nothingness, marked *niente* in the score, is performed for the first time, a few months before the composer's death, by the London Philharmonic Orchestra, Sir Adrian Boult conducting.

2 APRIL 1958

*Nirvana-Symphony* by the 29-year-old Japanese composer Toshiro MAYU-ZUMI, in six movements, comprising three Buddhist hymns and three "campanologies" (temple bell tones), symbolizing the ideal Buddhist state Nirvana, with a male chorus in 12 parts singing Zen chants, is performed for the first time in Tokyo.

3 APRIL 1958

A century has elapsed since the death in Paris at 79, of Sigismund Ritter von NEUKOMM, "fruitful composer, world famous conductor and organist, all-round musician and scholar" (as he is described on a plaque on the wall on the house in which he was born around the corner from Mozart's birthplace in Salzburg).

4 APRIL 1958

*Ett Spel om Maria* (*A Play on Mary*), scenic oratorio by the 38-year-old old Swedish composer Sven-Erik BÄCK, with dodecaphonically serialized Holy Family supported by the diatonic choral commentary, is performed for the first time in Stockholm.

5 APRIL 1958

*Minotauros*, choreographic suite for orchestra by the 41-year-old Swedish composer Karl-Birger BLOMDAHL, descriptive of the Cretan half-bull half-man devouring virgins in a dodecaphonic fury, is performed for the first time in Stockholm.

11 APRIL 1958

*Second Symphony* by the 43-year-old Siberian-born American composer Alexei HAIEFF, in three movements, transcribed from his piano sonata written in 1955, in a modernistically mannered neo-baroque style, is performed for the first time by the Boston Symphony Orchestra, Charles Munch conducting.

13 APRIL 1958

Van CLIBURN, 23-year-old Louisiana-born Texan pianist, spectacularly wins the first prize in the Tchaikovsky Contest in Moscow for his performance of

Tchaikovsky's *First Piano Concerto* and Rachmaninoff's *Third Piano Concerto,* victoriously overtaking a number of young Russians, and arousing tremendous enthusiasm among music-loving Muscovites. (On 20 May 1958, a Van Cliburn Day was declared in New York, and he was given a ticker-tape parade, the first musician so honored)

## 14 APRIL 1958

*Titus Feuerfuchs, oder Liebe, Tücke und Perücke,* burlesque opera by the Swiss composer Heinrich SUTERMEISTER, is produced in Basel.

## 14 APRIL 1958

Two one-act operas are performed for the first time by the opera workshop and orchestra of the Mannes College of Music in New York:

*The Robbers* by the 34-year-old American composer Ned ROREM, to his own libretto, involving multiple internecine slaughter among three murderers in a fight over their initial victim's money, set to music in a grimly dissonant idiom, with recurrent detonations of homicidal harmonies, and *The Pet Shop* by the 60-year-old Egyptian-born Italian composer Vittorio RIETI, wherein the daughter of a New York society woman marries a member of the canine jury influential in awarding first prize to her mother's dog, set to music in an appropriately hedonistic manner with a cornucopia of vivacious melorhythms.

## 15 APRIL 1958

The *Second Quintet* for piano and strings by Ernest BLOCH is performed for the first time at the opening concert of a music festival arranged by the Department of Music of the University of California, Berkeley.

## 17 APRIL 1958

*The Rock,* a symphonic prelude by Bohuslav MARTINU, is performed for the first time in Cleveland.

## 18 APRIL 1958

*First Symphony* by the 24-year-old American composer Easley BLACKWOOD (completed by him on 9 December 1952, at the age of 19) conceived "along completely abstract lines," in four movements, *Andante maestoso, Andante comodo, Scherzo, Andante sostenuto,* written in a rhapsodically romantic vein, with a tropism towards triadic points of repose, sensitized by atonal divagations in a euphonious polyharmonic setting, is performed for the first time by the Boston Symphony Orchestra, Charles Munch conducting.

## 18 APRIL 1958

The First Inter-American Music Festival opens in Washington under the auspices of the Pan American Union, with a program including the first performance of *New England Episodes,* a symphonic suite by Quincy PORTER.

## 20 APRIL 1958

Two Brazilian works, *Twelfth Symphony* by Heitor VILLA-LOBOS, and *Chôro* for clarinet and orchestra by Camargo GUARNIERI, are performed for the first time at the First Inter-American Music Festival in Washington.

## 21 APRIL 1958

*Dugme (The Button)*, musical grotesque in one act by the 44-year-old Croatian composer Ivo LHOTKA-KALINSKI, dealing with the desperate predicament of a petty functionary invited to an influential dinner, who cannot find the crucial collar button for his formal dress, set to music in an utilitarian modernistic idiom replete with non-corrosive polytriadic dissonances, is performed for the first time in Zagreb.

## 22 APRIL 1958

*Eighth Symphony* by Darius MILHAUD, subtitled *Rhodanienne*, depicting in its four movements the progress of the river Rhône, from its source in the Swiss glacier through Lake Geneva to its emergence as a French river, and its division into several streams forming a conspicuous delta, is performed for the first time by the San Francisco Symphony, Enrique Jordá conducting, on the same program with the first performance of the *First Violin Concerto* by the 37-year-old American composer Andrew IMBRIE.

## 23 APRIL 1958

*The Good Soldier Schweik*, opera by the American composer of Czech origin Robert KURKA (who died of leukemia at the age of 35, on 12 December 1957), to a colloquial American libretto drawn from the Czech novel of Jaroslav Hasek, depicting the misadventures of a Czech soldier of the Austro-Hungarian Army in World War I, whose irrepressible habit of good-natured equivocation embroils him in fantastic troubles with the military, written in an unaffected folkloristic manner and scored for wind instruments and percussion only, is posthumously performed for the first time at the City Center in New York.

## 26 APRIL 1958

*Seventh Symphony* by the 66-year-old Hungarian composer László LAJTHA, in three movements devoid of key signatures but essentially tonal, scored for an orchestra with multiple percussion to be used in a genteel manner without "brutal noise," and couched in a modern style with a modicum of civilized dissonances, using a heraldic motto trumpeted in naked fifths, is performed for the first time anywhere in Paris, prior to the initial production on Lajtha's earlier *Sixth Symphony*.

## 29 APRIL 1958

*Fifth Symphony, Jerusalem* (with chorus), by the Russian-born American composer Lazare SAMINSKY, in two sections, (1) *The City of Solomon*, "of strife, tumult and pristine splendor" (2) *The City of Christ,* "of a creed born in disillusion, transfigured into light," composed in 1929–1930, comes to a belated first performance in New York.

2 MAY 1958

*The Lady of Shalott,* ballet by Sir Arthur BLISS, dealing with the love-death of a maiden from the Arthurian legends, who dies of unrequited love for Sir Lancelot of the Lake, is produced at the University of California, Berkeley.

4 MAY 1958

*Escurial,* one-act opera by the 25-year-old American composer Marvin David LEVY, is produced in New York.

15 MAY 1958

*Concert for Piano and Orchestra* by the prime mover of the American avant-garde John CAGE, in which miniaturized precision is antinomially achieved through the application of the principle of indeterminacy of melorhythmic parameters, is performed for the first and (by definition) last time in its non-precognitive unreproducible form by the pianist David Tudor with Merce Cunningham as choreographic conductor, in New York.

*The Concert for Piano and Orchestra* is without a master score, but each part is written in detail in a notation where space is relative to time determined by the performer and later altered by a conductor. Notes are of three sizes referring ambiguously to duration or amplitude. As many various uses of the instruments as could be discovered were subjected to the composing means which involved chance operations and the observation of imperfections in the paper upon which the music was written. The pianist's part is a "book" containing 84 different kinds of composition. The pianist is free to play any elements of his choice, wholly or in part, and in any sequence. (From John Cage's annotation in the catalogue of his works)

22 MAY 1958

The Music Festival at the University of California, Berkeley concludes with the first performance of *Requiem* by Randall THOMPSON, for double chorus *a cappella.*

28 MAY 1958

The Central Committee of the Communist Party of the Soviet Union issues a declaration amending its Resolution of 10 February 1948 which assailed the state of Soviet music and singled out PROKOFIEV, SHOSTAKOVICH, KHACHATURIAN and MIASKOVSKY for specific derogation as submissive followers of the decadent Western trends. (Complete text in the section LETTERS AND DOCUMENTS)

30 MAY 1958

*First Violin Concerto* by Béla BARTÓK (composed between 1 July 1907 and 5 February 1908) in two contrasting movements, *Andante Sostenuto* (later incorporated into the first section of *Two Portraits* for orchestra), representing an Ideal and based on a "personal" leitmotiv, D—F-sharp—A—C-sharp, of the Hungarian violinist Geyer Steffy for whom the Concerto was written, and who was in possession of the unpublished and unperformed manuscript until her death in 1957, and *Allegro giocoso,* a hedonistic rondo, is performed for the first time in Basel.

5 JUNE 1958

*Sixth Symphony* by the Rumanian composer Alfred MENDELSOHN is performed for the first time in Bucharest.

6 JUNE 1958

*Geigy Festival Concerto* for a "Basel Drum" and orchestra, by Rolf LIEBERMANN, commissioned by the chemical firm J. R. Geigy & Co., of Basel, Switzerland, on the occasion of its bicentennial, set in a hedonistically dodecaphonic idiom, is performed for the first time in Basel.

7 JUNE 1958

*Zoologica,* a symphonic suite by the 55-year-old German composer Günther RAPHAEL, is performed for the first time in Duisburg.

9 JUNE 1958

*The Sun Over the Steppe,* opera in three acts by the 55-year-old Soviet composer Vissarion SHEBALIN, dealing with the civil war in the Don River basin in 1919, depicting in strong contrasts the militant heroism of the Bolsheviks and the black treachery of the counterrevolutionary forces in a socialistically realistic melodic style making use of authentic Cossack folk tunes, is performed for the first time in Moscow, in concert form. (The first stage production took place in Moscow on 22 December 1959)

9 JUNE 1958

The 32nd Festival of the International Society for Contemporary Music opens in Strasbourg with the following program:

*Septuor* by Peter SCHAT of Holland; *Oratio Mechtildis* for chamber orchestra by Klaus HUBER (Switzerland); *Développements raréfiants,* suite for voice and small ensemble by Makoto MOROI (Japan); *Les Jeux* for baritone and string orchestra by Milko KELEMEN (Yugoslavia); and *Concerto* for clarinet, horn, violin, cello, piano and percussion, by Ralph SHAPEY (U.S.A.).

11 JUNE 1958

The following works are presented at the 32nd Festival of the International Society for Contemporary Music in Strasbourg:

*Concertino* for three trumpets and string orchestra by Egil HOVLAND (Norway); *Ritornell* for orchestra by Ingvar LIDHOLM (Sweden); *Sept Poèmes de René Char* for vocal quartet and orchestra by Jean-Louis MARTINET (France); and *Concerto* for jazz band and orchestra by Rolf LIEBERMANN (Switzerland).

## 12 JUNE 1958

The following program is presented at the 32nd Festival of the International Society for Contemporary Music in Strasbourg:

*Fantasia seria* for string quartet by Fleming WEIS (Denmark); *No. 5 Zeitmasse* for wind quintet, by Karlheinz STOCKHAUSEN (Germany); *Variations* for violin, cello, and piano by Yori-Aki MATSUDAIRA (Japan); *Alma Redemptoris Mater* for six wind instruments by Peter Maxwell DAVIES (England); and *String Quartet* by Valentino BUCCHI (Italy).

## 13 JUNE 1958

The following works are presented at the 32nd Festival of the International Society for Contemporary Music in Strasbourg:

*Ouverture in tre tempi*, by Niccolò CASTIGLIONI (Italy); *Prevariata* for orchestra, by Einojuhani RAUTAVAARA (Finland); *Concerto* for piano, sixteen wind instruments, and percussion, by Miches CIRY (France); *Fourth Symphony* in one movement, by Bernd Alois ZIMMERMANN (Germany); and *Variations symphoniques* by Miloš SOKOLA (Czechoslovakia).

## 14 JUNE 1958

The following works are presented at the 32nd Festival of the International Society for Contemporary Music in Strasbourg:

*Third Symphony* by Henry BARRAUD (France); *Jeux* by DEBUSSY; and *Sixth Symphony* by Darius MILHAUD (France).

## 14 JUNE 1958

The 32nd Festival of the International Society for Contemporary Music in Strasbourg continues with the following program:

*Second String Quartet* by Herbert BRÜN (Israel); *Piano Fantasy* by Aaron COPLAND (U.S.); *Second String Quartet* by Hans Erich APOSTEL (Austria); *Dialogues* for two violins by John EXTON (England); and *Trio* for piano, violin and cello, by Artur MALAWSKI (Poland).

## 15 JUNE 1958

At the 32nd Festival of the International Society for Contemporary Music in Strasbourg, Charles Munch conducts the world première of the *Second Symphony* by the 87-year-old French modernist Florent SCHMITT, op. 137 (the First Symphony being the *Symphonie Concertante* for orchestra and piano written in 1932), his last work (excepting a Mass for mixed chorus and organ performed after his death), in three movements (*Assez animé, Lent sans excès, Animé*), set in a vigorously youthful style, full of rhythmic propulsion in the animated sections and harmoniously lyrical in the slow movement, without transcending, however, the admirably respectable modernity of his early works, generously coloristic in the scoring and ostentatiously somber in the savagely rhythmed primitivistic episodes. (Other works on the program were BACH's *Violin Concerto* in A minor, Sergei PROKOFIEV's *Second Violin Concerto* and *Suite en fa* for orchestra by Albert ROUSSEL)

### 15 JUNE 1958

The posthumous opera *François Villon* by the Dutch composer Sem DRESDEN opens the Holland Festival at Amsterdam.

### 18 JUNE 1958

*Noye's Fludde*, one-act opera by Benjamin BRITTEN after a 14th-century English miracle play dealing with Noah's Ark and the Flood, and scored for a pleasingly bruitous ensemble of recorders, bugles, handbells, drums, cups hit by wooden spoons, string instruments and piano, with singing parts for the principal characters, a spoken part for the Voice of God (accompanied by a wind machine), and children's voices for seven groups of seven pairs of animals—lions, oxen, swine, camels, asses, dogs, cats, polecats, etc. and birds—is performed for the first time in the church of the village of Orford, England, during the course of the annual Aldeburgh Music Festival.

### 20 JUNE 1958

*The Scarf*, one-act opera by the 32-year-old American composer Lee HOIBY, with a libretto drawn from Chekhov's short story *The Witch*, dealing with a frustrated wife cheered by a young mailman seeking shelter in their house during a blizzard, with a murderous ending (not in the original story) when she strangles her uninteresting husband with her long scarf, set in a moderately modern vein, is performed for the first time at the First Festival of Two Worlds, in Spoleto, Italy.

### 23 JUNE 1958

Armas JÄRNEFELT, Finnish composer of melodious and harmonious instrumental pieces tenderly interwoven with Suomian folksong patterns within a Germanic framework, dies in Stockholm, where he made his home for many years, at the age of eighty-eight.

### 27 JUNE 1958

Cuba issues a postage stamp of 4 centavos honoring the 19th-century musician and pedagogue Ignacio CERVANTES.

### 10 JULY 1958

Italy issues postage stamps commemorating the approximate centennial of the birth of PUCCINI and that of LEONCAVALLO, the two Italian composers who, with Mascagni, created *Verismo*, the modern type of operatic realism, with denominations of 25 lire each.

### 16 JULY 1958

*Wuthering Heights,* opera in three acts with a prologue by the 32-year-old American composer Carlisle FLOYD, after Charlotte Brontë's emotional story of dark passions in the inhibited atmosphere of the bleak heath in the moorlands of Northern England, with a musical score of balladic design uncluttered by polyphonic complexity and limited to functional melodic elements, is performed for the first time as a commissioned work by the Santa Fe Opera Company, in Santa Fe, New Mexico. (A revised version with the third act entirely rewritten, was produced by the New York City Opera on 9 April 1959)

### 17 JULY 1958

*Second Symphony* for string orchestra by the 63-year-old Corsican-born French composer Henri MARTELLI, is performed for the first time in Paris.

### 18 JULY 1958

*Homenaje a Bolívar,* for voices, chorus and orchestra by the prime composer of Colombia Guillermo URIBE-HOLGUÍN, is performed for the first time in Bogotá.

### 31 JULY 1958

Percy A. SCHOLES, enlightened English writer on music, whose *Oxford Companion to Music* is a unique example of imaginative lexicography and a treasure trove of wide-ranging information, dies a week after his 81st birthday in Vevey, Switzerland, his home for many long years.

### 5 AUGUST 1958

Josef HOLBROOKE, English composer of ambitious stage works, in which he tried to block the modernistic tide and adopted a simplified tonal idiom to please the great masses (who failed to respond), dies in London a month after his 80th birthday.

### 17 AUGUST 1958

Florent SCHMITT, "le sanglier des Ardennes," as he was once called to describe his emotional impetuosity and boar-like animal power associated with the inhabitants of his native Ardennes, composer of numerous symphonic and choral works in a bold modern style which enjoyed a certain succès d'estime and who continued to write until the end (his last work, a symphony, was performed in his presence at the Strasbourg Festival on 15 June 1958), dies in Neuilly near Paris at the patriarchal age of eighty-seven.

### 20 AUGUST 1958

*Maria Golovin,* opera in three acts by Gian Carlo MENOTTI, to his libretto, dealing with a blinded Italian veteran of World War II who falls in love with the beautiful wife of a Russian prisoner of war presumed dead, attempts to shoot her when her husband materializes, and departs in quest of a new life, set to music in a gorgeously Italianate idiom, burnished with modernistic atonalities and vitalized by incidental spurts of euphonious jazz, is performed for the first time at the International Exposition in Brussels, Belgium.

### 24 AUGUST 1958
Leo BLECH, German composer and conductor, dies in Berlin at the age of eighty-seven.

### 26 AUGUST 1958
Ralph VAUGHAN WILLIAMS, grand seigneur of English modern music, whose many symphonic and choral works combined enlightened nationalism with superlative mastery of technical resources, dies in London at the age of 85, shortly after the first performance of his *Ninth Symphony*.

### 1 SEPTEMBER 1958
Belgium issues a postage stamp of 30 centimes honoring the Belgian violinist Eugène Ysaÿe on the occasion of the centennial of his birth.

### 3 SEPTEMBER 1958
The Congregation of Rites of the Vatican issues an Instruction on Sacred Music, prohibiting the use in liturgical services of mechanical devices such as radio, phonograph, tape recorder or automatic organ players even in transmitting sermons or performances of sacred music.

### 12 SEPTEMBER 1958
*Léonidas ou la cruauté mentale*, opéra-bouffe by the Swiss composer Pierre WISSMER, is performed for the first time in Paris.

### 15 SEPTEMBER 1958
Egypt issues a postage stamp to honor the Arab musician Sayed DARWISH (1892–1923).

### 23 SEPTEMBER 1958
At the final concert of the International Festival of Contemporary Music in Venice, Igor STRAVINSKY conducts the first performance of his sacred work to the Latin text from the Lamentations of the Prophet Jeremiah, entitled *Threni*, scored for six soloists, chorus and orchestra, his first integrally serial composition, evolved from a unifying 12-tone subject.

### 3 OCTOBER 1958
*The Diary of a Madman*, opera in one act by Humphrey SEARLE, after Gogol's story descriptive of the inner state of a demented Russian government clerk, with the madman intoning his fantasties and delusions in insanely atonal in-

tervallic leaps while the dissonant orchestra observes a schizophrenically logical dodecaphonic structure, and an eerie electronic tape accompanies the madder moments of the psychological bedlam, leading to a final outcry in an integral twelve-note blob, is performed for the first time at the Berlin Music Festival, Hermann Scherchen conducting.

### 3 OCTOBER 1958

Guillermo URIBE-HOLGUÍN, 78-year-old Colombian composer, conducts in Bogotá the first performance of his *Eighth Symphony.*

### 7 OCTOBER 1958

*Fiesta,* minuscule one-act opera by Darius MILHAUD, dealing with a shipwrecked sailor rescued by villagers who seduces the wife of one of them and is ignominiously thrown back into the sea, is performed for the first time in Berlin.

### 7 OCTOBER 1958

*Genèse,* electronic music for five oscillators by the prime composer of the Dutch avant-garde Henk BADINGS, tape-recorded in Eindhoven on four tracks of spatial sound, is performed in public for the first time in Brussels. (It was produced as a ballet under the title *Der Sechste Tag* in Innsbruck on 7 November 1959, and under the title *Mikrobiologisches* in Linz on 22 February 1960)

### 13 OCTOBER 1958

*A Vision of Judgment,* oratorio by Peter Racine FRICKER, is performed for the first time at the Leeds Festival.

### 14 OCTOBER 1958

The RCA ELECTRONIC MUSIC SYNTHESIZER, capable of producing any musical tone in any instrumental color, and of manipulating them by repetition, reverberation, dynamic intensification, rhythmic variegation, acceleration and deceleration, is patented by its inventors, H. F. OLSON and H. BELAR, of the Acoustical and Electromechanical Research Laboratory of the Radio Corporation of America. (The first public presentation of the RCA Electronic Music Synthesizer and music produced by the machine was made at the American Institute of Electrical Engineers Meeting in New York on 31 January 1956 by General David Sarnoff)

### 16 OCTOBER 1958

*Nocturne,* a linked series of songs for voice and small orchestra, by Benjamin BRITTEN, to texts from poems by Shakespeare, Shelley, Keats, Tennyson, Coleridge, Middleton, Wilfred Owen and Wordsworth, with night being represented by the perennially incandescent key of C major and dawn by intrusive inflections of D-flat major, is performed for the first time at the Centennial Music Festival at Leeds.

## 18 OCTOBER 1958

*Minnesota Symphony* by the Norwegian composer Harald SAEVERUD, commissioned for the celebration of the centennial of the statehood of Minnesota, in four movements with subtitles suggesting the ethnic aspects of Scandinavian Minnesotans (*Once Upon a Time, Hope and Longing, Gay Day, Man and the Machine*) is performed for the first time by the Minneapolis Symphony Orchestra, Antal Dorati conducting.

## 19 OCTOBER 1958

*Poésie pour pouvoir* by Pierre BOULEZ, scored for two orchestras conducted by two synchronized conductors (Hans Rosbaud and Boulez himself), with four large and four small loudspeakers placed on each wall and a rotating loudspeaker suspended from the ceiling (the rate of rotation is specified as a serial parameter), with a recorded narration of French poetry, electronically distorted so as to render it unintelligible, rising from a dehumanized sinusoidal sound to a limit of sonic variety, is presented for the first time at the Donaueschingen Festival.

## 21 OCTOBER 1958

*Un Ballo in Maschera* by VERDI, is brought out in Swedish at the Stockholm Opera, with the original libretto dealing with the assassination of Gustave II of Sweden in March 1792, instead of that of the absurd "governor" of Boston of the traditional version made under the pressure of the authorities in turbulent Italy fearing the dangers of the representation of regicide on the stage.

## 24 OCTOBER 1958

Lukas Foss conducts the Pittsburgh Orchestra in the first complete presentation of his *Symphony of Chorales for Orchestra*, in four movements based respectively on Bach's chorales No. 90, No. 77, No. 139, No. 133 and containing in the second movement a fugue on the motive B-A-C-H, with consecutive entries at the interval of a tritone.

## 25 OCTOBER 1958

*Osud*, opera in three "romantic tableaux" by Leoš JANÁČEK, written in 1903–1904, and depicting symbolically and autobiographically the tragic frustrations of a composer Zivny (i.e. living) amid the inappreciative hordes of uncomprehending society, is performed on the stage for the first time in Brno, thirty years after the composer's death. (A concert performance of the work given by the Brno Radio on 18 September 1934)

## 27 OCTOBER 1958

*Undine*, a ballet by Hans Werner HENZE, is performed for the first time anywhere in London.

## 3 NOVEMBER 1958

*Tenth Symphony* by the 82-year-old English composer Havergal BRIAN, in a single compound movement entailing constant changes of tempi and set in a modernistic romantic idiom, scored for a large orchestra including a phalanx of drums requiring the services of ten players, is performed for the first time in London.

Completion of each of my symphonies is realized by Symmetry and Balance of Design. The Symphonies compose themselves. (From Havergal Brian's declaration of purpose made at the age of 94, on 7 May 1970, at the author's request)

## 7 NOVEMBER 1958

*Variazioni Concertanti* for orchestra by the 55-year-old Russian-born American composer Nikolai LOPATNIKOFF, consisting of the theme enunciated by strings pizzicato, four variations, and an energetic finale, is performed for the first time in Pittsburgh.

## 10 NOVEMBER 1958

*Adventures of King Arthur,* one-act opera buffa by the foremost woman composer of Poland Grazyna BACEWICZ, is performed for the first time on the Warsaw Radio.

## 27 NOVEMBER 1958

Artur RODZINSKI, fiery conductor of Dalmatian birth and Jewish-Polish origin, who acquired fame as a symphonic perfectionist and disciplinarian, and notoriety as a recalcitrant and intransigent artist, constantly at odds with the managerial world (he was discharged successively by the New York Philharmonic and the Chicago Symphony Orchestra in the middle of the season for violations of contractual agreements), dies of heart failure in Boston, while on a brief American engagement, at the age of sixty-six.

## 3 DECEMBER 1958

*Mrika,* first national Albanian opera, written by the Albanian composer Prenk JAKOVA, wherein a young Albanian girl named Mrika is sabotaged in her work involving the construction of a collective hydro-electric power plant by her treacherous temporary bridegroom acting at the behest of foreign imperialists, with the socialistically realistic ending vouchsafed when she overcomes all interventionist wiles and, as the plan is completed, marries a progressive co-worker, set to music in a congenially optimistic idiom, based on proletarian Albanian tunes, is produced in Shkodra.

## 3 DECEMBER 1958

*Second Symphony* by the 34-year-old Harbin-born Russian-American composer Benjamin LEES, in three movements, *Andante mesto, Scherzo* and *Adagio,* in a contrastingly lyrical, hedonistic and meditative style, vitalized by propulsive rhythms, is performed for the first time in Louisville.

## 5 DECEMBER 1958

*Fourth Symphony* by the 59-year-old Russian-American composer Alexander TCHEREPNIN, in three movements, *Moderato, Allegro, Andante con moto*, melodically based on his favorite 9-note scale constructed by dividing the octave into three equal parts and interpolating two passing notes in each division with the polyphonic structure governed by the method described by him as *Interpoint (punctus inter punctum)*, is performed for the first time by the Boston Symphony Orchestra, Charles Munch conducting.

## 11 DECEMBER 1958

Ikuma DAN, Japanese composer, conducts in Tokyo the world première of his grand opera *Yang Kwei-fei*, on an ancient Chinese tale dealing with a concubine of the Chinese Emperor who falls in love with the Emperor's eunuch, featuring a Mongolian wrestling dance as a choreographic interlude.

## 11 DECEMBER 1958

*Sixth Symphony* by Jean RIVIER is performed for the first time in Paris.

## 22 DECEMBER 1958

A century has passed since the birth in Lucca of Giacomo PUCCINI, who introduced into the world of Italian operatic melodrama a number of novel modernistic procedures, such as whole-tone scales, consecutive triads and ninth-chords, unresolved suspensions, sustained dissonances and even polytonality, without impairing the popular appeal and great commercial success of his productions.

# ∽ *1959* ∾

## 3 JANUARY 1959

*Thirteenth Symphony* by the 73-year-old prolific Rumanian composer Dimitrie CUCLIN is performed for the first time in Arad.

## 4 JANUARY 1959

*O Vestido de Noiva*, opera by the 67-year-old Portuguese composer Ruy COELHO, is produced in Lisbon.

## 24 JANUARY 1959

*Moskva Tcheryomushki*, the first operetta by Dmitri SHOSTAKOVICH, depicting the urban predicament of the newly wed Sasha and Masha, trying to obtain an apartment in the new housing development in the Moscow suburb of

Tcheryomushki, with a score full of dulcet waltzes and hedonistic tunes, is produced in Moscow.

### 27 JANUARY 1959

*The Volcano*, opera in three acts by the Soviet composer Evgeny UTZEVICH, wherein a wily American capitalist named Octopus and his daughter who is employed by the Central Intelligence Agency are exposed by a native woman school teacher with the aid of the downtrodden Polynesian masses groaning under the yoke of the American military forces occupying, since 1945, a volcanic island in the South Pacific, is produced in Donetz.

### 30 JANUARY 1959

Paul HINDEMITH conducts the Pittsburgh Symphony Orchestra in the first performance of his *Pittsburgh Symphony*, composed for the bicentennial celebration of the city, in three movements, of which the first exploits quartal melodic patterns and their inversions, the second is a slow angular march ending with six instrumental variants of the Pennsylvania Dutch tune *"Hab lumbedruwwel mit me lumbeschatz"* and the last movement is based on an ostinato figure of six different notes, with a final somewhat jazzy subject to the words: "Pittsburgh is a great old town."

The Pennsylvania Dutch are very familiar to me; their German dialect is almost the same as that of my old home. I have always been acquainted with their way of life. And their Lieder are those which to this very day are sung in the countryside where they once originated. (Hindemith's statement in the program book)

### 31 JANUARY 1959

*Fantasia Concertante* for piano and orchestra by Bohuslav MARTINU in three movements, in a translucent neo-baroque style, is performed for the first time in Berlin, with Margrit Weber, to whom the work is dedicated, as soloist.

### 5 FEBRUARY 1959

Curt SACHS, learned German musicologist, expert in Oriental musical cultures, dies in New York at the age of seventy-seven.

### 6 FEBRUARY 1959

*La Voix humaine*, one-act opera by Francis POULENC, a monologue for soprano, to a text by Jean Cocteau, in which a dejected girl vainly tries to regain the affection of her lover in a long responseless telephone monologue reaching its climax when she learns of his impending marriage, and still cries, "Je t'aime!" written in a monodically sensual simplified Debussyan idiom, with aerostatic harmonies supporting a fleshless and denuded vocal line (a Paris critic described the action as "Mélisande au téléphone") is produced at the Opéra-Comique in Paris. (Date from the announcement of the work as "création" in *Le Figaro* of 6 February 1959; the date given in the *Enciclopedia dello Spettacolo*, 17 February 1959, is tardy.)

## 7 FEBRUARY 1959

*A Guide to the Life Expectancy of a Rose,* one-act opera-fantasy by the 37-year-old American composeress Vivian FINE, to her own libretto, written in a sophisticated vigesimosecular idiom vitalized by prudential dissonances, is produced in concert form in New York.

## 12 FEBRUARY 1959

George ANTHEIL, the whilom enfant terrible of American music whose *Ballet mécanique* depicts in expressive noises the ambience of the modern world amidst American-made machines, but whose later compositions reflect his disillusion in conventional modernity and a militant espousal of the eternal verities of tonal music, and whose lovelorn column "Boy Meets Girl" helped to patch up many a broken romance, dies in New York at the age of fifty-eight.

## 13 FEBRUARY 1959

*Ivailo,* opera in seven scenes by the 50-year-old Bulgarian composer Marin GOLEMINOV, to a libretto dealing with the Bulgarian uprising against their Mongolian overlords in 1280, led by the shepherd Ivailo, written in an expansive Italianate manner, with the inclusion of authentically Slavic popular chants of the period, is produced in Sofia.

## 13 FEBRUARY 1959

*Parables* by Bohuslav MARTINU, a symphonic suite in three sections, *Parable of a Sculpture* (after Saint-Exupéry, alluding to a mystical change in one who looks at a statue), *Parable of a Garden* (with reference to a psychic meaning of floral scent), and *Parable of a Labyrinth* (inspired by *Le Voyage de Thésée* by Georges Neveux, which postulates the mythological truth that without the aid of Ariadne and her guiding thread, Theseus would have never found his way out of the Cretan labyrinth), is performed for the first time by the Boston Symphony Orchestra, Charles Munch conducting.

## 24 FEBRUARY 1959

*Second Symphony* by the English composer Lennox BERKELEY, in four movements of neo-classical content vitalized by an infusion of non-toxic dissonances, is performed for the first time in Birmingham.

## 25 FEBRUARY 1959

Gustave BECKER, American pianist and composer, who continued to give annual concerts even after he became a nonagenarian, dies at the age of 97 while visiting his daughter in Epsom, Surrey, England.

## 26 FEBRUARY 1959

*Second Symphony* by the 40-year-old American composer George ROCHBERG, in four sections, derived from a symmetrical 12-tone row of two groups of hexachords but free of dodecaphonic asceticism and admitting even explicit triadic formations, is performed for the first time by the Cleveland Orchestra, George Szell conducting.

## 28 FEBRUARY 1959

*The Sons of Aaron,* opera in two acts by the 37-year-old German-born American composer Siegfried LANDAU, to his own libretto from the Bible, is performed for the first time in Scarsdale, New York.

## 1 MARCH 1959

*Capriccio* for soprano, violin and orchestra by Rolf LIEBERMAN, in the form of a compact *Rondo* in which the main subject is taken from his opera *Leonore 40/45,* another theme is a dodecaphonic *Adagio* from a love song in his opera *Penelope,* and still another theme borrowed from his piano sonata, is performed for the first time in Paris.

## 1 MARCH 1959

*Das Stundenlied,* choral suite with orchestra by Gottfried von EINEM, to nine poems by Bertolt Brecht on the nine hours of the Passion, in which Jesus appears as the Socialist victim of reactionary priests, is performed for the first time in Hamburg.

## 3 MARCH 1959

*Thirteenth Symphony* in five movements, subtitled *Madras Symphony,* by Henry COWELL, written during his sojourn in Madras, India, in the course of a world tour, in 1956, and completed in New York in 1958, inspired by the Indian *talas* (rhythmic patterns) and the *ragas* (scales or modes), is performed for the first time in Madras by the Little Orchestra of New York City under the direction of Thomas Scherman, during its Asian tour.

## 4 MARCH 1959

*Third Symphony* by the Norwegian composer Klaus EGGE, inspired by the spectacular display of aurora borealis during a transatlantic flight, in one movement opening and ending with an evocative *Adagio misterioso,* with an intermediate rapid section in asymmetrical rhythms, illustrative of the changing colors of the phenomenon, is performed for the first time in Louisville.

## 10 MARCH 1959

*Summer Seascape,* symphonic sketch by Howard HANSON, is performed for the first time by the New Orleans Symphony Orchestra.

## 15 MARCH 1959

*Seventh Symphony* by the 53-year-old German master of polyphonic dodecaphony, Karl Amadeus HARTMANN, in three movements, *Ricercare, Adagio Mesto* and *Virtuoses Scherzo,* is performed for the first time in Hamburg.

## 17 MARCH 1959

Rafaele d'ALESSANDRO, Swiss composer of pleasantly modern pieces, dies in Lausanne on his 48th birthday.

## 17 MARCH 1959

*Quotations in Percussion* by Arthur COHN, a quinquepartite suite for 103 percussion instruments, the largest phalanx of its type ever assembled for performance, among them a gigantic bass drum, a microsonic triangle, hydrophonic gong, the Brazilian concussion instrument reco-reco, cracked glass in a glass container, a double-bass placed on sawhorses and struck with drumsticks, a cat's meow and friction utensils such as a washboard, with a text from anonymous and non-anonymous authors, inter alia Walt Whitman and James Joyce, is performed for the first time in New York.

## 20 MARCH 1959

*Symphonic Poem After Descartes* by the 56-year-old American composer John VINCENT, in two parts of four sections each wherein the Cartesian principle of actuality is reflected by the thematic notes of the natural harmonic series, with the opening phrase by the solo timpani prosodically rhythmed in the basic words of Descartes, *Cogito ergo sum*, continuing through the musical representation of the Cartesian theory of planetary motions in *Vortex*, and of the geometric *Folium*, a Cartesian knot, and allusions to the philosopher's Catholic faith in quotations from medieval hymnody, concluding on a chord containing a series of overtones, is performed for the first time by the Philadelphia Orchestra, Eugene Ormandy conducting.

## 21 MARCH 1959

*Monsieur Jabot*, opera by the Swiss composer Roger VUATAZ, is performed for the first time in Geneva.

## 24 MARCH 1959

*Gruppen*, spatial work by the 30-year-old German apostle of the avant-garde Karlheinz STOCKHAUSEN, for three chamber orchestras, each governed by individual serial parameters determining meter, rhythm, intervallic structure, dynamics, instrumentation and differentiated noises, with three synchronized conductors beating time in three different tempi ($M_1 = 70$, $M_2 = 113.5$, $M_3 = 94$), is performed for the first time at Cologne.

## 3 APRIL 1959

*Fourth Symphony* by the Swedish composer Gunnar BUCHT is performed for the first time in Stockholm.

## 5 APRIL 1959

Marie ASHTON, 238-pound housewife in Slough, England, completes 133 hours of uninterrupted (except for necessary physiological functions) piano pounding, establishing a world record of pianofortitude for the female of the species, although still falling far behind the accomplishment of Heinz Arntz of Germany who completed a piano marathon of 255 hours on 28 April 1953.

## 11 APRIL 1959

Eric BLOM, urbane, witty and caustic English writer on music, whose life of musical journalism culminated in the formidable accomplishment of editing the Fifth Edition of Grove's *Dictionary of Music and Musicians* in nine volumes, the largest music dictionary in the English language, dies in London at the age of seventy.

## 13 APRIL 1959

Eduard van BEINUM, energetic and imaginative Dutch conductor, who commuted by plane via the North Pole between Los Angeles, where he was permanent conductor, and Amsterdam, where he was similarly engaged, dies suddenly at the age of fifty-seven while conducting a rehearsal of the Concertgebouw Orchestra in Amsterdam.

## 19 APRIL 1959

*Third Symphony* by the 35-year-old American composer Ned ROREM, in five classically designed movements, opening with a Passacaglia, and couched in a euphonious idiom with an invigorating injection of non-toxic dissonances, is performed for the first time in New York.

## 23 APRIL 1959

*On the Far Shores,* opera in four acts by the Estonian composer Willem REJMAN, the action taking place in a country on the Indian Ocean "controlled by the military forces of a certain imperialist power" represented by a Mr. Lockhart and a Mr. Brown, whose sinister schemes of military and economic subjugation are foiled by a socialistic local teacher and an employee of the Soviet Embassy, is produced at Tallin.

## 25 APRIL 1959

*Second Symphony* by the 52-year-old Soviet Georgian composer Andrei BALANCHIVADZE is performed for the first time in Tbilisi.

## 26 APRIL 1959

*Aurelia,* opera in three acts by the 47-year-old Moldavian composer David GERSHFELD, to a Moldavian text, dealing with a local girl who dies a heroic death fighting the Nazis in Bessarabia, is produced in Kishinev.

## 26 APRIL 1959

*Six Characters in Search of an Author,* musical play by the 46-year-old Czech-born American-educated composer Hugo WEISGALL, after Pirandello's symbolic drama, with the dramatis personae being members of an opera company, so that the product represents a controlled and strictly circumscribed opera rehearsal, set to music in a quasi-dodecaphonic idiom, is produced by the New York City Opera.

*1063*

## 26 APRIL 1959

*Kádár Kata,* opera in two acts by the Hungarian composer Mihály HAJDU, after a grim Transylvanian tale in which the possessive mother of a youth in love with Kata drowns her in a pond, and as her body is incarnated in a flower, he follows her into the dark waters, is produced in Budapest.

## 12 MAY 1959

*Fantaisie concertante* for violin and piano by the 65-year-old Belgian composer Jean ABSIL is performed for the first time in Brussels.

## 15 MAY 1959

*Mérope,* opera in three acts by the Portuguese composer Joly Braga SANTOS, with the vocal line set in conformity with the natural prosody of the Portuguese language, is produced in Lisbon.

## 17 MAY 1959

*Mirandolina,* opera by Bohuslav MARTINU, after Carlo Goldoni's comedy *La locandiera (The Mistress of the Inn),* is produced in Prague.

## 21 MAY 1959

*Symphonic Epitaph,* for narrator, chorus and orchestra by the 31-year-old Serbian composer Aleksander OBRADOVIĆ, extolling the heroism of mobilized workers who held off the Nazi assault during the invasion of Yugoslavia in 1941, is performed for the first time in Belgrade.

## 23 MAY 1959

*Joshua,* biblical oratorio by the 52-year-old German-born American composer and conductor Franz WAXMAN, is performed for the first time in Dallas, Texas.

## 31 MAY 1959

*Aniara,* "revue of mankind in space-time," by the 42-year-old Swedish composer Karl-Birger BLOMDAHL, wherein an animated female electronic brain Mima guides the space ship Aniara to Mars after the atomic disintegration of the earth, with the passengers delivering themselves nostalgically to the last terrestrial pleasures (a sex orgy in a hall of mirrors, a jazz session, etc.), the music running the entire gamut of expression from a Lesbian waltz to a jazz solo in 7/16, with some weird sounds on magnetic tape creating a suitable interplanetary mood, and recordings of the voices of Hitler, Khrushchev and Eisenhower remindful of the past forces of evil, half-evil and good, the nuclear musical motif being an involuted *Grossmutterakkord,* consisting of 12 different notes and 11 different intervals spiralling out of the central C, and ever returning to it, is performed for the first time at the Royal Opera in Stockholm.

## 3 JUNE 1959

*Doña Beatriz, la Sinventura*, opera by the Guatemalan composer Felipe SILIÉZAR, depicting the great inundation of 1541 in Guatemala during which a volcanic lake engulfed the palace of the Spanish colonial regents carrying Doña Beatriz, "the Luckless One," to her death, is produced in Guatemala City.

## 8 JUNE 1959

The PURCELL-HANDEL Festival opens in London (both composers were buried in Westminster Abbey) under the combined auspices of The Arts Council, the British Council, the British Broadcasting Corporation and the British Museum, continuing through 27 June, and featuring performances of operatic works, oratorios and solo compositions.

## 10 JUNE 1959

The 33rd Festival of the International Society for Contemporary Music opens in Rome with the following program of symphonic music:

*Cheltenham Concerto* for chamber orchestra by George ROCHBERG of the U.S.A.; *Skaldens Natt* for soprano, chorus and orchestra by the Swedish composer Ingvar LIDHOLM *Omnia tempus habent*, cantata for soprano and 17 instruments by the German composer Bernd Alois ZIMMERMANN; and *Prolation* for orchestra by the 24-year-old English composer Peter Maxwell DAVIES.

## 10 JUNE 1959

*Seraphine oder die stumme Apothekerin*, opera by the Swiss composer Heinrich SUTERMEISTER, after Rabelais, is performed for the first time over the Zürich Radio.

## 11 JUNE 1959

At the 33rd Festival of the International Society for Contemporary Music in Rome, the following program of chamber music is given:

*Eighth String Quartet* by the dean of Swedish composers, Hilding ROSENBERG; *Serenata* for flute, viola, doublebass, harpsichord and percussion by Goffredo PETRASSI of Italy; *Nocturnos* for soprano and instruments by Hans Ulrich ENGELMANN of Germany; and *Three Blue Sketches* for nine instruments by Hanns JELINEK of Austria, written in a dodecaphonic jazz style with a serial sequence of meters and rhythms.

## 12 JUNE 1959

At the 33rd Festival of the International Society for Contemporary Music in Rome, the following chamber works are presented:

*Mati (Mother)* for voice and string quartet by the 28-year-old Yugoslav composer Alojz SREBOTNJAK; *Second String Quartet* by the Argentinian composer Alberto GINASTERA; *Three Studies* for cello and piano by the 35-year-old Australian composer Don BANKS;

*Two Sonnets* for baritone, clarinet, viola and cello by the American composer Milton BABBITT; and *Ein irrender Sohn* for contralto and instruments by the 22-year-old Swedish composer Bo NILSSON.

### 13 JUNE 1959

At the 33rd Festival of the International Society for Contemporary Music in Rome, the following works by the winners of the International Competition of 1958 are presented, in an afternoon concert:

*String Quartet* by the 25-year-old American composer Ramiro CORTES; *Des Engels Anredung an die Seele* for tenor, accompanied by flute, horn, clarinet and harp, by the 34-year-old Swiss composer Klaus HUBER; *Six Poems of Dylan Thomas* for voice and instruments, by Riccardo MALIPIERO; and the cantata *Canticum Psalmi Resurrectionis* by the 28-year-old German composer Dieter SCHÖNBACH.

### 13 JUNE 1959

The 33rd Festival of the International Society for Contemporary Music in Rome presents an evening concert of the following symphonic works:

*Sinfonia in Do,* written by Manuel ROSENTHAL of France during his sojourn in America in 1949, and first performed in Paris on 12 June 1950; *Tartiniana Seconda* for violin and orchestra by Luigi DALLAPICCOLA (his first *Tartiniana* was written in 1951), on material from Tartini's unpublished works; *Quatre Essais* for orchestra by the 30-year-old Polish composer Tadeusz BAIRD (first performed in Katowice on 12 August 1958), wherein each of the four parts uses different instrumentation, in a profusion of emancipated dodecaphony; *Impromptus* for orchestra by Wolfgang FORTNER of Germany, built on a sequence of serial parameters, and Stravinsky's *Agon,* in which *sui generis* serial procedures and polyrhythmy form a synthesis of Stravinsky's earliest and latest methods.

### 14 JUNE 1959

*Die tödlichen Wünsche,* opera by the 33-year-old German composer Giselher KLEBE, after Balzac's novel *La Peau de Chagrin,* in which the owner of a magical piece of shagreen that fulfills his wishes is consumed by the inanition of success, is performed for the first time in Düsseldorf.

### 14 JUNE 1959

The 33rd Festival of the International Society for Contemporary Music in Rome continues with the following program of chamber works:

*Suite de Kurpie* for contralto and 9 instruments by the 32-year-old Polish composer Witold SZALONEK; *Trio* for clarinet, cello and piano by the 42-year-old Swedish composer Karl-Birger BLOMDAHL; and *Improvisations sur Mallarmé* for soprano and instruments by the French apostle of intransigent antideterminism in a calculated aleatory system of composition, Pierre BOULEZ.

### 15 JUNE 1959

At the 33rd Festival of the International Society for Contemporary Music in Rome the following works for chamber orchestra are presented:

*Konstellationen,* suite for strings by the 35-year-old Danish composer Per Nörgaard (first performed on the Danish Radio on 3 November 1958), spiritually and technically derived from the early period of Schoenberg, middle period of Alban Berg, and late period of Béla Bartók; *Concertino* for piano and chamber orchestra, by the 39-year-old French composer André Casanova; *Incontri* for 24 instruments by the 35-year-old Italian experimentalist Luigi Nono (first performed at the Darmstadt Festival on 30 May 1955); *Tre Studi* for chamber orchestra by the 34-year-old Italian composer Aldo Clementi (first performed at the Festival for New Music in Darmstadt in 1957); *Oiseaux exotiques* for piano and orchestra by Olivier Messiaen, composed in 1955, conjuring up in sophisticated idealization the tweets, chirps, warbles, twitters and trills of polychromatic birds of Asia and America; and *Samai* for chamber orchestra by the Japanese composer Yoritsune Matsudaira, a palimpsest of old Japanese court dance themes and serial parameters.

## 16 JUNE 1959

The 33rd Festival of the International Society for Contemporary Music in Rome concludes with a program of the following symphonic and choral works:

*Permutazioni sinfoniche* by the Dutch composer Guillaume Landré based on the medieval idea of hexachordal mutations, with centripetal tonal inflections; *Vier Gedichte von Stefan George* for mixed chorus with instrumental accompaniment, by the German composer Michael Gielen, derived from a dodecaphonic radix, tonally solidified by recognizable repetitions of focal elements; *Trittico sinfonico* by the Finnish composer Nils-Eric Fougstedt; and *Nachtstücke und Arien* for soprano and orchestra by the 32-year-old German modernist Hans Werner Henze, depicting, with a modicum of modified dodecaphony, the passage from crepuscular to auroral hours.

## 17 JUNE 1959

*A Hand of Bridge,* for four solo voices and chamber orchestra by Samuel Barber, to a libretto by Gian Carlo Menotti, revealing in audible asides the wishes, anxieties and fantasies of a bridge foursome: a florid businessman conjuring up an alabaster palace at Palm Beach with "twenty naked girls and twenty naked boys tending to my pleasures," a lawyer wondering where his unstabilized blond-tressed mistress was, and their vacuous wives engaged in inconsequential chatter, set to music in a tense polyrhythmic idiom, is performed for the first time at the Festival of Two Worlds in Spoleto, Italy.

## 17 JUNE 1959

The American popular pianist Liberace is awarded by a London tribunal the sum of 10,000 pounds in damages in his suit for defamation of character against the *Daily Mirror* of London and its columnist W. Connor (Cassandra) for suggesting in print that Liberace was a homosexual.

## 19 JUNE 1959

*Salto Mortale,* electronic opera by Henk Badings for five voices with electronic accompaniment, to the composer's libretto, in which a professor of biochemistry (lyric tenor) restores to life a recent suicide poet by using an elixir perfected by him and enabling him to vitalize dead bodies, if not too decayed, and who kills him again when the poet, whose voice suddenly changes from tenor to bass, forms a mutual attraction with the professor's favorite young laboratory assistant (a high soprano), is produced by the Dutch Television Network, as the first opera totally accompanied by an electronically recorded score.

### 21 JUNE 1959

On the occasion of the bicentennial of the foundation of the City of Pittsburgh, the Pittsburgh Symphony Orchestra presents the world premières of *Adagio and Scherzo* by Quincy PORTER, and *Paeans and Dances of Heathen Iberia* by Carlos SURINACH.

### 25 JUNE 1959

*Clarinet Concerto* by Guillaume LANDRÉ is performed for the first time in Amsterdam as part of the Holland Festival.

### 3 JULY 1959

*Concerto* for viola, strings and percussion in four movements by the 35-year-old Vienna-born Americanized Israeli composer Robert STARER, written in techniques suggested by similarly instrumented works by Béla Bartók and Frank Martin, is performed for the first time in Geneva.

### 5 JULY 1959

*Concerto Grosso* for orchestra by Heitor VILLA-LOBOS is performed for the first time in Pittsburgh.

### 7 JULY 1959

Ernest Newman, nonagenarian English music critic who started out as a Liverpool bank clerk named William Roberts, adopted the symbolic pseudonym "earnest new man" and sailed forth on a brilliant career of musical journalism (he was columnist of *The Sunday Times* of London for 38 years until his retirement on his 90th birthday in 1958), author of a monumental Wagner biography and several books on opera, dies at Tadworth, Surrey.

### 14 JULY 1959

GROCK, Swiss-born musical clown whose real name was Adrian Wettach, who provided entertainment for half a century by playing on a tiny violin kept in a huge fiddle case, or trying to move the piano towards the bench before starting to play, dies at Imperia, Italy, at the age of seventy-nine.

### 15 JULY 1959

Ernest BLOCH, Swiss-born composer of impassioned Jewish-inspired music clad in sonorous modern harmonies, dies of cancer in Portland, Oregon, nine days before his 79th birthday.

In my works termed "Jewish" I have not approached the problem from without, by employing melodies more or less authentic or "Oriental" formulae, rhythms or intervals . . . No! I have but listened to an inner voice, deep, secret, insistent, ardent, an instinct much more than cold and dry reason, a voice which seemed to come from afar beyond myself, far beyond my parents. This entire Jewish heritage moved me deeply; it was reborn in my music. To what extent it is Jewish, to what extent it is just Ernest Bloch, of that I know nothing. The future alone will decide. (From Bloch's article in *Musica Hebraica,* 1938)

## 17 JULY 1959

*Janus* by Paul CRESTON, a diptych consisting of a lyric prelude and a fast dance with a single theme for both sections, in unvarying triple time but greatly variegated as to rhythms and polyrhythms, is performed for the first time in Denver.

## 22 JULY 1959

*Missa Brevis* for 3-part boys' voices and organ by Benjamin BRITTEN, according to the Catholic rite, to Latin words (*Credo* is omitted) is performed for the first time at Westminster Cathedral in London.

## 23 JULY 1959

The Bayreuth Festival opens with a performance of *Der Fliegende Holländer,* staged in an expressionistic and inherently unWagnerian manner by Wagner's grandson Wieland Wagner.

## 29 JULY 1959

The Union of Soviet Socialist Republics issues a postage stamp representing the statue of TCHAIKOVSKY.

## 9 AUGUST 1959

Emil František BURIAN, modern Czech composer who initiated voice bands performing in a prescribed rhythmic pattern but without definite pitch, dies in Prague at the age of fifty-five.

## 9 AUGUST 1959

A *Fawn in the Forest,* one-act opera by the English composer Gerald COCKSHOTT, is produced at the rustic White Barn Theater, in Westport, Connecticut.

## 16 AUGUST 1959

Wanda LANDOWSKA, grande dame of the clavecin, a noble instrument which she lovingly resuscitated from its Baroque quietus, and brought forth a bevy of pupils, dies at the age of 82 in her American retreat (where she lived since she was forced to abandon France as the German armies converged on Paris) at Lakeville, Connecticut.

## 16 AUGUST 1959

Pedro Humberto ALLENDE, Chilean composer who combined in his works the peculiar melorhythms of the Chilean countryside with impressionistic harmonies, dies in Santiago at the age of seventy-four.

## 17 AUGUST 1959

*Julietta,* "opera semiseria" by the 35-year-old German composer Heimo ERBSE, based on the short story of Heinrich von Kleist, *The Marquise of O.,* relating the plight of a young Italian widow cast adrift during the Napoleonic wars and rescued from the rapacious soldiery by a noble German aristocrat, who however, takes advantage of her fainting spell to incontinently ravish and impregnate her, redeeming himself by a proposal of honorable marriage, set to music in an appropriately hedonistic vein, is produced in Salzburg.

## 19 AUGUST 1959

*Symphonic Prayer* by Alexander TCHEREPNIN, thematically based on the 9-tone "Tcherepnin scale," a symmetrical progression of three groups, each containing a whole tone and two semitones, contrapuntally treated in his sui generis technique of *Interpunctus,* in which two-part complexes enter the interstices between wider two-part complexes, all immersed in euphonious dissonances, is performed for the first time as a commissioned work at the opening concert of the Pan American Festival in Chicago.

## 24 AUGUST 1959

The Eleventh International Edinburgh Festival opens with a presentation by the Royal Opera of Stockholm of Verdi's *Un Ballo in Maschera,* with the libretto restored to its original, in which King Gustav II of Sweden, and not the preposterous Riccardo, Governor of Boston, is assassinated by his secretary, in a Swedish translation and adaptation from the primary source, *Gustave III ou Le Bal masqué* by Eugène Scribe.

## 25 AUGUST 1959

On his 41st birthday, Leonard BERNSTEIN conducts in Moscow a concert of the New York Philharmonic Symphony Orchestra, on its grand tour of Europe, presenting the first Moscow performance of STRAVINSKY's *Le Sacre du Printemps* since the Soviet Revolution, and the first Soviet performance of *The Unanswered Question* by Charles IVES, encored in response to an ovation.

## 28 AUGUST 1959

*Sinfonia* for two orchestras by the British composer Iain HAMILTON is performed for the first time at the Edinburgh Festival.

## 28 AUGUST 1959

Bohuslav MARTINU, Czech composer of classically wrought symphonies animated by a deep emotional current and of many instrumental concertos and chamber music pieces, cast in a judiciously modernistic manner without ever relinquishing the basic sense of tonality, dies at the age of 68 in Liestal, Switzerland.

8 SEPTEMBER 1959

A souvenir sheet containing postage stamps for HANDEL (10 pfennigs), HAYDN (25 pfennigs), SPOHR (15 pfennigs), BEETHOVEN (20 pfennigs), and MENDELSSOHN (40 pfennigs) is issued in West Germany in conjunction with the opening of the Beethoven Hall in Bonn.

11 SEPTEMBER 1959

The 22nd International Festival of Contemporary Music opens in Venice, continuing through 26 September, and featuring opera, ballet, chamber music and electronic demonstrations, including three ultra-modern stage works by Italian composers: *Allez-hop,* mimed tale by Luciano BERIO; *Diagramma Circolare,* abstract melodrama by Alberto BRUNI, AND *Il Circo Max,* a contemporary satire on café society by Gino NEGRI.

12 SEPTEMBER 1959

*Prometheus,* opera by Rudolf WAGNER-RÉGENY, is performed for the first time in Kassel.

12 SEPTEMBER 1959

The Third Festival of Contemporary Music opens in Warsaw with the world première of Tadeusz BAIRD's *Expression* for violin and orchestra, and works by SHOSTAKOVICH (*First Piano Concerto*), Anton VON WEBERN (*Six Pieces* for orchestra), SZYMANOWSKI (*Third Symphony*), and Boleslaw SZABELSKI (*Toccata* for orchestra).

14 SEPTEMBER 1959

At the Third Festival of Contemporary Music in Warsaw, the world premières of *Music for Strings, Horn and Percussion* by Grazyna BACEWICZ and *First Symphony* by Henryk GÓRECKI are given, as well as SZYMANOWSKI's Fourth Symphony and Luigi NONO's *Composizione per Orchestra.*

17 SEPTEMBER 1959

*Strophes* by the 25-year-old Polish avant-garde composer Krzysztof PENDERECKI, scored for soprano, speaker and ten instruments, to words from the Bible, Sophocles and other great sources, written in a highly complex athematic idiom, making use of serial and aleatory procedures, is performed for the first time at the "Warsaw Autumn" Festival.

20 SEPTEMBER 1959

*Die Ermörderung Cäsars,* one-act opera by the 34-year-old German composer Giselher KLEBE, is performed for the first time in Essen.

## 22 SEPTEMBER 1959

Josef Matthias HAUER, Viennese pioneer of 12-tone music based on symmetric six-note tropes (he had a rubber stamp made, which he used on his stationery, signed "the spiritual protagonist of 12-tone music and, despite many poor imitators, still the only one who knows and understands it"), dies in solitude and obscurity in a furnished room in Vienna, at the age of seventy-six.

## 25 SEPTEMBER 1959

Gunther SCHULLER conducts in New York the first performance of his *Conversations* for string quintet and jazz quartet (piano, percussion, vibraphone and double-bass), containing aleatory interludes.

## 3 OCTOBER 1959

*Plautus in Nonnenkloster,* opera by the 70-year-old German composer Max BUTTING, is produced in Leipzig.

## 3 OCTOBER 1959

*Second Symphony* by André JOLIVET in three movements (1) *Heurté,* marked by colliding sonorities (hence the subtitle) (2) *Fluide,* in a slow tempo with serially developed lyric motives (3) *Vigoureux,* a hedonistic finale, is performed for the first time in Berlin.

## 4 OCTOBER 1959

A series of 18 autogenetic meetings is launched by the American writer, painter and musician Allan KAPROW at the Reuben Gallery in New York, with a cast of participants including visitors "who sit in various chairs," described as HAPPENINGS, thereby adding a winged word to the modern vocabulary.

The name "Happening" is unfortunate. It was not intended to stand for an art form, originally. It was merely a neutral word that was part of a title of one of my projected ideas. It was the word which I thought would get me out of the trouble of calling it a "theater piece," a "performance," a "game," a "total art," or whatever, that would evoke associations with known sports, theater, and so on. But then it was taken up by other artists and the press to the point where now all over the world it is used in conversation by people unaware of me, and who do not know what a "Happening" is. (From a recorded interview with Allan Kaprow, reproduced in *Happenings,* an anthology, published in New York, 1966)

## 4 OCTOBER 1959

*Concerto* for cello and orchestra, op. 107, by Dmitri SHOSTAKOVICH, in four sections, *Allegretto, Moderato, Cadenza,* and *Allegro con moto,* beginning and ending in E-flat major, characteristically Shostakovichian in its contrasts of relentless animation and ruminating lyricism, is performed for the first time in Leningrad by Mstislav Rostropovich, to whom the piece is dedicated.

## 4 OCTOBER 1959

*Der arme Konrad,* opera in five acts by the 50-year-old German composer Jean Kurt FOSTER, dealing with the peasant rebellion in Southern Germany in 1514, is produced in East Berlin.

## 17 OCTOBER 1959

*Epitaphium für das Grabmal des Prinzen Max Egon zu Fürstenberg,* a dodecaphonic offering by Igor STRAVINSKY on the tomb of the prince patron of the Donaueschingen Festival, scored for flute, clarinet and harp and consisting of eight statements of its unifying dodecaphonic theme, including inversion, retrograde and inverted retrograde, is performed for the first time at the opening of the annual Musiktage in Donaueschingen.

## 18 OCTOBER 1959

*Vlast (Authority),* third musical burlesque by the 46-year-old Croatian composer Ivo LHOTKA-KALINSKI, dealing with a pompous prime minister whose authority is deflated by ridicule, set to music in a utilitarian polytriadic manner making melodic use of a specially devised heterotonal scale in the range of a minor ninth, is performed for the first time on the television network in Zagreb.

## 19 OCTOBER 1959

Stanley BATE, English composer of rhapsodic symphonies and neo-romantic chamber music, dies in London at the age of forty-seven.

## 21 OCTOBER 1959

*Concertino* for doublebass and strings by the 35-year-old Croatian composer Milko KELEMEN is performed for the first time in Zagreb.

## 21 OCTOBER 1959

*Violin Concerto* by the 46-year-old Soviet composer Tikhon KHRENNIKOV, written in an optimistically vigorous manner, consonant with the ideals of Socialist Realism, is performed for the first time in Moscow.

## 22 OCTOBER 1959

A century has passed since the death in Kassel of Ludwig SPOHR, grand master of German music whose fame rivaled that of Beethoven and Mendelssohn, but whose obsolescent operas, oratorios, symphonies, concertos, chamber music, and songs rapidly decayed into archeological desuetude.

## 23 OCTOBER 1959

*Beatrice,* music drama in three acts by the 33-year-old American composer Lee HOIBY, based on Maeterlinck's play *Sœur Béatrice,* and dealing with a ravished nun driven to bordellos, who returns to the convent in her old age and meets a saintly prioress in whom she recognizes her other self as she might have been, and dies absolved of shame, is performed for the first time in Louisville.

### 23 OCTOBER 1959

*Three New England Sketches,* suite for orchestra by Walter PISTON, with romantic subtitles, *Seaside, Summer Evening* and *Mountains,* reflecting the "impressions, reminiscences, even dreams, that pervaded the otherwise musical thoughts of one New England composer," with coloristic sonorities permeating the essentially symphonic design, is performed for the first time at the 100th Worcester, Massachusetts Festival by the Detroit Symphony Orchestra, Paul Paray conducting.

### 23 OCTOBER 1959

*Eagles,* symphonic poem by Ned ROREM, is performed for the first time by the Philadelphia Orchestra, on his 36th birthday.

### 24 OCTOBER 1959

*Seventh Symphony (Liturgical)* by the 44-year-old American composer Vincent PERSICHETTI is performed for the first time by the St. Louis Symphony Orchestra.

### 28 OCTOBER 1959

*Second Symphony* by Roberto GERHARD, Catalan composer radicated in England since the Spanish Civil War, written in a serial polyphonic idiom, is performed for the first time in London.

### 28 OCTOBER 1959 ·

*La Vida de la Misión,* posthumous Spanish-American opera by the German-born Texan composer Carl VENTH, is performed by the Symphony Society of San Antonio for the first and last time, a few months before his centennial, using the funds left by Venth's widow to satisfy the dead composer's lifelong desire to let the world hear it.

### 30 OCTOBER 1959

*Kassiani,* opera in four acts by the Greek composer George SKLAVOS, dealing with a Byzantine noblewoman who resolved to become a nun, is performed for the first time in Athens.

### 5 NOVEMBER 1959

The first performances of two symphonies by the 83-year-old English composer Havergal BRIAN are given in London: *Eleventh Symphony,* written in 1954, consisting of three contrasting movements and ending with a festive march; and *Twelfth Symphony*, written in 1957, in a single movement subdivided into three sections and concluding serenely after a fierce climax.

### 9 NOVEMBER 1959

Heeding the protest made by the Moslem population of Djakarta, the Indonesian Army Commander of the Fourth Military District of West Java issues a decree banning rock 'n' roll, cha-cha, and other American "social dances" as violating the Indonesian norm of decency. (Date and details communicated by the Embassy of Indonesia, Washington, D.C., in a communication to the author dated 21 June 1961)

### 15 NOVEMBER 1959

*Third Symphony* by Ned ROREM is performed for the first time by the Denver Symphony.

### 16 NOVEMBER 1959

*The Sound of Music*, musical comedy by Richard RODGERS to the lyrics of Oscar Hammerstein II, suggested by the true story of Baroness Maria von Trapp, governess to the seven singing children of the widowed Austrian Baron Georg von Trapp (whom she subsequently married), who fled Austria en masse after the Nazi Anschluss in 1938 to find fame as the Trapp Family Singers, with a variety of eminently singable songs in the score, including the modernized solfa ditty, *Do-Re-Mi*, is produced in New York.

### 17 NOVEMBER 1959

Heitor VILLA-LOBOS, great innovator of Brazilian music, inventive creator of the pan-Brazilian *Chôros* and of *Bachianas Brasileiras*, in which Bach-like polyphony forms the background for Brazilian melorhythms, and who believed that science, love of country and music form the triune entities expressing the idea of *Brasilidade*, dies in his native Rio de Janeiro at the age of seventy-two.

### 19 NOVEMBER 1959

*La Notte di un Nevrastenico*, opera buffa by the 47-year-old Italian composer Nino ROTA, dealing with sexual frustrations of a neurasthenic youth bedeviled by the amorous groans made by a heterosexual couple occupying an adjacent room in his hotel, is performed for the first time in concert form in Turin.

### 26 NOVEMBER 1959

Albert KETÈLBEY, English composer of remote Danish origin, whose exotic pieces, such as *In a Persian Market*, *In a Monastery Garden*, *In a Chinese Temple Garden*, became fantastically popular among the musical bourgeoisie all over the world, and even penetrated via radio into the proletarian masses of the young Russian Soviet Socialist Republic, causing Soviet spokesmen for the arts to declare Ketèlbey's alluring exoticism a piece of cleverly masked imperialist propaganda, dies in Cowes, Isle of Wight, at the age of eighty-four.

## 27 NOVEMBER 1959

*Der Tod des Grigori Rasputin,* opera in three acts by Nicolas NABOKOV (grown out of the one-act opera *The Holy Devil* first performed in Louisville on 18 April 1958), describing in naturalistic detail the astounding story of the painstaking murder in 1916 of the Russian "mad monk," by poison, bullets and drowning under ice, with quotations and stylizations of contemporary salon music (an old-fashioned phonograph is played on the stage), is produced at Cologne.

## 27 NOVEMBER 1959

*Seven Studies on Themes of Paul Klee* by the 34-year-old American composer Gunther SCHULLER, in seven movements depicting in various heterotonal colors seven paintings by Paul Klee, one of them, *The Twittering Machine,* lubricated with some quarter-tones, is performed for the first time by the Minneapolis Symphony Orchestra, Antal Dorati conducting.

## 6 DECEMBER 1959

*Stanac,* opera by the 64-year-old Croatian composer Jakov GOTOVAC, to a libretto from a 16th-century Croatian fable in which an aged shepherd named Stanac is induced by cunning swindlers to shave his beard and give his sheep away to nubile town girls in the expectation that these actions would rejuvenate him, but who remains as phallically fallible as prior to his pogonotomy, is performed for the first time in Zagreb.

## 9 DECEMBER 1959

*Legend,* symphonic poem by the 38-year-old American composer Andrew IMBRIE, is performed for the first time by the San Francisco Symphony Orchestra.

## 11 DECEMBER 1959

*Second Symphony* by the 43-year-old French composer Henri DUTILLEUX, in three movements, *Animato, ma misterioso, Andantino sostenuto, Allegro fuocoso,* scored for 12 solo instruments and orchestra, with the two groups collectively independent of each other, resulting in a stereophonic antiphony and instrumental echolalia, is performed for the first time as a commissioned work by the Boston Symphony Orchestra, Charles Munch conducting.

## 11 DECEMBER 1959

*Oedipus der Tyrann,* "funeral play," after Sophocles, by Carl ORFF, is produced at Stuttgart.

## 11 DECEMBER 1959

*Mela and Fair,* orchestral essay by Henry COWELL, designed to effect a compatible blend of Hindu melorhythms (Mela is the Hindu word for country fair) with Americanistic fiddling tunes, is performed for the first time at the opening of the United States exhibit at the World Agricultural Fair in New Delhi, as a musical manifestation of the Fair's motto, "Food, Friendship, Freedom and Family."

### 13 DECEMBER 1959

*The Sofa,* a modern opera by the 52-year-old English composeress Elizabeth MACONCHY, is produced in London.

### 15 DECEMBER 1959

*Blue Flame,* opera in four scenes by the 48-year-old American composer Alan HOVHANESS, is performed for the first time in San Antonio, Texas.

### 18 DECEMBER 1959

Two days after his 77th birthday, Zoltán KODÁLY, veteran of Hungarian music, marries his 19-year-old pupil Sarolta Péczely. (His first wife, pianist and composer of salon music which she published in 1900–1905 under her first married name Emma Gruber, and whom Kodály married in 1910, died on 12 November 1958 at the age of ninety-nine)

(Date of Kodály's second marriage and the age of the bride at the time was communicated to the author by Sarolta Kodály during a visit at the Kodály home in Budapest on 25 March 1963)

### 18 DECEMBER 1959

*Oratorio of Our Time* for narrator, solo voices, chorus and orchestra by the Bulgarian composer Lubomir PIPKOV, to the words of six imaginary letters from a girl to a soldier, set to music in the effective manner of Socialist Realism and collective individualism, vitalized by a profusion of asymmetrical Balkan rhythms, is performed for the first time in Plovdiv.

### 24 DECEMBER 1959

*Le Mystère de la Nativité,* oratorio by the prime composer of Switzerland Frank MARTIN, to a text from a 15th-century nativity play, picturing heaven (modally) and hell (atonally and dissonantly), and concluding with the presentation of Jesus in the temple, is performed for the first time in Geneva.

### 28 DECEMBER 1959

Three tenors, Ramon Vinay of Chile, Karl Liebl of Germany, and Albert Da Costa of the United States sing at the Metropolitan Opera House in New York the role of Tristan in the first, second and third acts of *Tristan und Isolde* respectively, all three being successively disabled by debiliating colds but making this valiant effort in order to prevent the cancellation of a sold-out performance, with the unaffected Swedish soprano Birgit Nilsson imperturbably singing the part of Isolde.

# ⚡ *1960* ⚡

## 2 JANUARY 1960

*Fourth Symphony* by Roger SESSIONS, written in celebration of the centennial of the State of Minnesota, in three movements: (1) *Burlesque*, a satirically atonal piece, punctuated by asymmetrical stresses (2) *Elegy*, a somberly passionate invocation, receding into elegiac reverie (3) *Pastorale*, a bucolic musical landscape in barcarolle-like rhythms, in a euphonious dissonant setting, is performed for the first time by the Minneapolis Symphony Orchestra, Antal Dorati conducting.

## 5 JANUARY 1960

*Poem for Tables, Chairs and Benches* by the 24-year-old Idaho-born experimentalist La Monte YOUNG, a visual and aural action in which furniture is moved, audibly by dragging or pushing on the floor, or inaudibly by lifting, with pre-programmed parameters indicating the timing of entrances and exits of the furniture movers and duration of each manipulation of a specific piece of furniture, is performed for the first time as part of the series of experimental music, at the University of California, Berkeley.

## 10 JANUARY 1960

*Jabadao*, choreographic tone-poem by the Corsican composer Henri TOMASI evoking the ancient Celtic action in Brittany, in which the devil (represented by five oboes in unison to emulate the obsolete instrument *bombarde*) captures the souls of incautious maidens who venture out on a midnight dance, is performed for the first time in Paris.

## 10 JANUARY 1960

Igor STRAVINSKY conducts in New York the world première of his *Movements for Piano and Orchestra*, in five divisions, written according to a personally furbished and punctiliously fashioned dodecaphonic method of composition, with the serial rows spaced horizontally while polyrhythmic patterns are designed for vertical perception.

Perhaps the most significant aspect of my new work is its "anti-tonality." I am amazed at this myself, in view of the fact that in *Threni*, triadic references occur in every bar. This new work is the most advanced, from the point of view of construction, of anything I have ever composed. Every aspect of the composition of the *Movements* was guided by the forms of the series—the sixes, the quadrilaterals, the triangles, etc. To me, the fact of the 12 tones is not as important as the fact of the serial function. The *Movements* have made me see that I am becoming not less but more of a serial composer. The rhythmic language of the *Movements* is also the most advanced I have so far used. I compose my polyrhythmic combinations to be heard vertically. . . . The five movements are related more by tempo than by "mood" or "character" . . . Construction replaces contrast. (From Stravinsky's program note)

### 15 JANUARY 1960

*Spectra* by the American composer Gunther SCHULLER, scored for a septuple orchestra, in seven parts, to convey the impression of the seven principal colors reflecting the heptatonic nature of the rainbow, is performed for the first time anywhere by the New York Philharmonic, Leonard Bernstein conducting.

### 22 JANUARY 1960

*Tahmeela*, symphonic poem by the Egyptian composer Halim EL-DABH, is performed for the first time by the Cairo Symphony Orchestra.

### 25 JANUARY 1960

*La Coupole*, symphonic poem by the 32-year-old French composer Jacques BONDON, subtitled *Tableaux fantastiques d'un monde étrange* and presenting scenes of an extra-terrestrial world with scintillating metallic percussion, undulating tropes of woodwinds, oscillating divided strings, and vociferating brass, is performed for the first time in Paris.

### 1 FEBRUARY 1960

*Arjuna*, symphonic poem by Alan HOVHANESS, scored for small European-type orchestra with the Indian instrument *mridangam*, and couched in the Carnatic classical style, is performed for the first time at an all-Hovhaness concert in Madras, India, with the composer participating as pianist.

### 2 FEBRUARY 1960

*Second Symphony* by the Czech-born Canadian composer Oscar MORAWETZ is performed for the first time by the Toronto Symphony Orchestra.

### 5 FEBRUARY 1960

*A Igreja do mar*, opera by the Portuguese composer Frederico DE FREITAS, is performed for the first time in Lisbon.

### 9 FEBRUARY 1960

Ernst von DOHNÁNYI, grand old man of Hungarian music, the last of the Mohicans of the Central European romantic school of music, whose first steps in composition received the blessings of Brahms, dies of a heart attack in New York City at 10:40 in the morning, at the age of eighty-two.

### 12 FEBRUARY 1960

*Attis*, cantata by 38-year-old Wisconsin-born American composer Robert W. MOEVS, to the erotic Latin verses from Catullus bemoaning the fate of a

Phrygian youth who is compelled to sacrifice his virility to the Earth Goddess, is performed for the first time by the Boston Symphony Orchestra, Richard Burgin conducting.

### 13 FEBRUARY 1960

*Sixth Symphony* by Jean RIVIER, in four contrasting movements, embanked within the bounds of traditional symphonic forms, is performed for the first time in Warsaw.

### 22 FEBRUARY 1960

*Concerto for Piano* with wind instruments and percussion by the 30-year-old Welsh composer Alun HODDINOTT, in four movements set in a traditionally dissonant modern idiom, is performed for the first time in London.

### 25 FEBRUARY 1960

*Music for Amplified Toy Pianos* by John CAGE, the keyboard of each being limited to nine white keys with microphones attached to the instruments and wired loudspeakers distributed among the audience so that deafening decibels enter each human auricle, is performed for the first time by David Tudor, Cage's authorized pianist and faithful famulus, at Wesleyan University in Middletown, Connecticut.

### 26 FEBRUARY 1960

*Il Dottore di vetro,* radiophonic opera by the 40-year-old Rumanian-born Italian composer Roman VLAD, dealing with a senescent Spanish doctor, dissuaded by a scheming barbering surgeon from marrying a nubile damsel who diagnoses the gout from which he suffers as a case of incipient vitrification resulting from unbridled sexual fantasies, is produced in Rome.

### 29 FEBRUARY 1960

*Bursać Nikoletina,* symphonic poem by the Yugoslav composer Dragutin ČOLIĆ, named after a roguish character of northwestern Bosnian folklore, set to music permeated with asymmetrical Balkan dance rhythms, is performed for the first time in Belgrade.

### 1 MARCH 1960

*Second Symphony* by the 60-year-old American composer Joseph WAGNER, in four movements bearing self-explanatory titles: (1) *With dramatic intensity* (2) *With continuous restless energy* (3) *With dignified noble simplicity* (4) *With strong drive,* is performed for the first time in Wilmington, Delaware. (A revised version was first performed in Providence in 12 February 1963)

### 1 MARCH 1960

*Sinfonietta in E,* in four movements, by Paul HINDEMITH, is performed for the first time, as a commissioned work, by the Louisville Orchestra, Robert Whitney conducting.

#### 4 MARCH 1960

*Hunchback-Horse,* ballet by the 27-year-old Soviet composer Rodion SHCHEDRIN, after the famous Russian fairy tale dealing with an omnipotent pony, is produced in Moscow. (A revised version was produced in Leningrad on 21 December 1963)

#### 4 MARCH 1960

The American baritone Leonard Warren is fatally stricken on the stage of the Metropolitan Opera in New York at 9:55 P.M., after completing Don Carlo's aria *Urna fatale del mio destino* in the third act of Verdi's *La Forza del Destino,* and dies a few minutes later, at 10:03 P.M., of a massive cerebrovascular hemorrhage.

#### 10 MARCH 1960

*Svätopluk,* historical opera by the 51-year-old Slovak composer Eugen SUCHOŇ, dealing with a Moravian prince who ordered the expulsion of followers of the Thessalonian brothers Cyril and Methodius, founders of the Slavic branch of the Greek Orthodox Church, and restored the Catholic liturgical service in Moravia, is performed for the first time in Bratislava.

#### 18 MARCH 1960

*Concertino* for cello and orchestra, op. 132, by Sergei PROKOFIEV, left incomplete at his death, is performed for the first time in Moscow, in an idiomatically supplemented version by Mstislav Rostropovich.

#### 18 MARCH 1960

Antal DORATI, 53-year-old Hungarian conductor, conducts the Minneapolis Symphony Orchestra, of which he is musical director, in the first performance of his *Fifth Symphony,* in five movemements, designated by formal content: Sonata (*Vivace con brio*), Variazioni (*Andante*), Scherzo (*Presto*), Adagio (*Notturno*), and Rondo Finale (*Allegro robusto*), without key signatures but converging centripetally on a focal A, with thematic elements derived from chromatic permutation and containing spacious pentatonic melodies of millennial antiquity redolent of the primeval modes of the Szekels and Magyars in immemorial Pannonia, culminating in a terse and curt finale.

#### 23 MARCH 1960

*Magische Quadrate,* symphonic fantasy by the 64-year-old Austrian composer Johann Nepomuk DAVID, intervallically derived from magic squares in which the sums of the horizontal, vertical and diagonal rows of numbers are constant, and depicting in its three movements the *Saturn Square* (constant sum 15), *Melancholia Square* (constant sum 34), and the *Witch Square* (constant sum 15), with the augends and the addends computed in semitones from an arbitrarily selected ground note designated by unity, is performed for the first time in Recklinghausen, Germany.

### 23 MARCH 1960

The Radio Station WEOK at Poughkeepsie, New York, issues a directive, replacing the term "Disk Jockey" for radio announcers who "ride" recordings of popular songs by "Musicaster" to avoid "unpleasant associations" resulting from revelations that disk jockeys accepted "payola" (payment by interested parties to promote particular songs on the air by broadcasting them at prime time with eloquent "plugs").

### 26 MARCH 1960

*Concerto for Kazoo and Orchestra* by the 36-year-old New York composer Mark BUCCI, originally titled *Concerto for a Singing Instrument* (so that any instrument with the range of a twelfth, including the human voice can perform it), accompanied by strings, harp and celesta, and written in an uninhibitedly hedonistic manner, replete with unapologetically tonal melody dipped in a nontoxic dissonant sauce, is performed for the first time by the New York Philharmonic at a concert for young people, Leonard Bernstein conducting, with Anita Darian as Kazoo soloist.

### 28 MARCH 1960

*Twelfth Symphony* by Henry COWELL is performed for the first time by the Houston Symphony Orchestra, Leopold Stokowski conducting.

### 28 MARCH 1960

Fife and Drum Corps is organized in the U.S. Army to play on festive occasions on the fife and on the drums, colorfully attired in the costumes of Spirit of 1776.

### 28 MARCH 1960

Austrian Airlines inaugurate the flights of three Vickers Viscount planes carrying the name of Beethoven, Bruckner and Johann Strauss.

### 29 MARCH 1960

*Ninth Symphony* by Darius MILHAUD, commissioned by the Fort Lauderdale, Florida, Symphony Orchestra, in three movements, *Modérément animé, Lent et sombre* and *Alerte et vigoureux,* without key signatures but gravitating towards a barycentric F, is performed for the first time in Fort Lauderdale, under the direction of Mario di Bonaventura.

### 31 MARCH 1960

Joseph HAAS, whose liturgic works written in a grand Germanic manner (*Deutsche Singmesse, Deutsche Kindermesse, Deutsche Gloria*) with their emphasis on the hypostatic Germanism of God, seem to justify the appellation "Der Spielmann Gottes" bestowed on him by his admirers, dies in Munich 12 days after his 81st birthday.

## 5 APRIL 1960

*Night Blooming Cereus,* chamber opera in two scenes by the 33-year-old Ca nadian composer John BECKWITH, in which a gardening lady receives a visi by her daughter's daughter as an act of contrition to expiate her mother' elopement a generation before, with an emotional finale as the nocturnal cer eus suddenly blossoms forth in the afternoon, set to music in a moderatel: modern idiom decussated with asymmetrical meters, and copulated in innoc uous dissonant counterpoint, is produced in Toronto. (A concert performanc took place on the Ontario Radio on 4 March 1959)

## 14 APRIL 1960

*The Woman of Andros,* electronic ballet by Henk BADINGS, realized in the Philips Laboratory at Eindhoven on four tracks of spatial sound, is performe for the first time in Hannover, Germany.

## 23 APRIL 1960

Ferde GROFÉ leads the San Francisco Symphony Orchestra as guest conduc tor in the world première of his musicoramic *San Francisco Suite,* in four pic torial movements, *Gold Rush, Bohemian Nights, Mauve Decade* an *1906–1960,* the latter opening with a concentrated blast of ultra-seismologica percussion to illustrate the famous San Francisco earthquake.

## 26 APRIL 1960

*Boréal,* an impressionistically Arctic symphonic poem by the 34-year-old Ca-nadian composer François MOREL, is performed for the first time in Montreal.

## 2 MAY 1960

Three centuries have passed since the birth in Palermo of Alessandro SCARLATTI, founder of the Neapolitan School of composition, composer of nu-merous effective oratorios and operas, and father of Domenico Scarlatti.

## 2 MAY 1960

*Jugando al toro,* ballet inspired by a bull fight, by the 30-year-old Spanish composer Cristóbal HALFFTER, is performed for the first time in Barcelona.

## 4 MAY 1960

*Chvala Světla (Praise of Light),* cantata in eleven sections by the 35-year-old Czech composer Svatopluk HAVELKA, marked by optimistically diatonic melo-dies and polytriadic harmonies, with a profusion of tritones in a section enti-tled "In Praise of Modern Fashion," is performed for the first time in Prague.

## 8 MAY 1960

*Second Symphony* by the 53-year-old American composer Ross Lee FINNEY is performed for the first time by the Philadelphia Orchestra at the 67th Annual May Festival at Ann Arbor, Michigan.

8 MAY 1960

Hugo ALFVÉN, Swedish composer of five symphonies and of a well-known Swedish orchestral rhapsody, *Midsommarvaka,* which he wrote in 1904, dies a week after his 88th birthday, at Faluns, Sweden.

9 MAY 1960

Botho von Steegan, 60-year-old refugee from East Prussia, sets fire to Beethoven's birthplace in Bonn, destroying the furniture and two early Beethoven autographs, a song *An Laura,* and the piano score of an early ballet, as a gesture of protest against the order by the West German authorities for his forcible deportation to East Germany.

10 MAY 1960

*Goran,* cantata by the Croatian composer Krešimir BARANOVIĆ, in five movements to the words by a Croatian poet who fell in the battle against the Nazis, is performed for the first time in Belgrade under the composer's direction.

14 MAY 1960

Lucrezia BORI, famous Spanish-born soprano, whose real name, Borja, she changed to avoid any association with the murderous Lucrezia Borgia, dies in New York at the age of seventy-two.

14 MAY 1960

Virgil THOMSON conducts at the State University College of Education in Potsdam, New York, the first performance of his *Missa pro Defunctis,* for chorus and orchestra, embodying elements ranging from earliest Christian chants to the jazzy inflections of modern America, harmonically dominated by the spirit of the major triad, moving in parallel formations and creating "evanescence and iridescence" in shifts of unstable tonality.

16 MAY 1960

*Ludas Matyi,* ballet by the 57-year-old Hungarian composer Ferenc SZABÓ, after a Hungarian fairy tale dealing with a proletarian youth who forces a dishonest merchant to pay him the price of his wild geese, set to suitably picaresque music, infused with melorhythms of Hungarian folksongs, is performed for the first time in Budapest.

19 MAY 1960

*Tobias and the Angel,* opera in two acts by Sir Arthur BLISS, on the biblical subject wherein the Archangel Raphael exorcises the demon who has been annoying the bride of Tobias, is produced in London.

20 MAY 1960

*Les Amants captifs,* opera by the 54-year-old French composer Pierre CAPDEVIELLE, in which Vulcan imprisons Venus and Mars in an invisible net on their adulterous bed, is performed for the first time in Bordeaux.

21 MAY 1960

*Eighth Symphony* by the 68-year-old Hungarian composer László LAJTHA, classically constructed in four movements, devoid of key signatures, with the basic tonal materials exfoliating in ostentatiously dissonant secundal concatenations, fertilized by an insemination of Transylvanian modalities, is performed for the first time in Budapest, anticipatorily to the first performance of his earlier *Sixth Symphony* which took place in Brussels on 12 December 1960.

22 MAY 1960

*Der Prinz von Homburg*, opera in three acts by the German composer Hans Werner HENZE, after an old melodrama by Heinrich von Kleist discoursing upon the peripeties of a German prince sentenced to die for neglecting his military duties in favor of love, reprieved at the last moment and given a victor's laurel, with a musical score of dynamic incandescence increasing in complexity from Italianate beginnings to a dodecaphonic climax, is produced in Hamburg.

24 MAY 1960

*Primavera*, symphonic suite in four vernal movements by the 44-year-old South African composer Arnold van WYK, thematically derived from songs by the 13th-century German minnesanger Neithart von Reuenthal, is performed for the first time in Bloemfontein, South Africa.

25 MAY 1960

Malcolm Frager, 25-year-old American pianist, plays at the Queen Elisabeth International Music Competition in Brussels the first performance of the *Piano Concerto* by the Belgian composer Marcel POOT specially written for the competition, and wins first prize, outdazzling a number of formidably equipped Russian pianists.

26 MAY 1960

*Noc a Naděje (Night and Home)*, symphonic poem by the 38-year-old Czech composer Otmar MÁCHA, dedicated to the memory of the victims of the ghetto of Theresienstadt, the Nazi camp near Prague, with the anguished mood sustained by a monothematic progression of alternating semitones and sesquitones, is performed for the first time in the course of the International Music Festival in Prague, bearing the allusively vernal name Prague Spring (Prague was liberated from the Nazis in the spring).

27 MAY 1960

*Fourth Symphony* by the 56-year-old American composer Vittorio GIANNINI is performed for the first time at the Juilliard School of Music in New York.

## 27 MAY 1960

*Violin Concerto* by the 35-year-old ex-dodecaphonic French composer Serge NIGG, written in an eclectic idiom conforming to the doctrine of Socialist Realism adopted by him under the influence of the French Communist Party, is performed for the first time in Paris.

## 28 MAY 1960

*Fifth Symphony* by the Dutch composer Léon ORTHEL is performed for the first time in Rotterdam.

## 28 MAY 1960

*Nazar Stodolya,* opera in three acts by the Ukrainian composer Constantin DANKEVICH, to a libretto reciting the dramatic story of a valiant young Cossack in love with a glorious girl whose infamous father is bent on leading her to the connubial bed of an unspeakable colonel of the Tsarist Army, with true young love triumphant in the E-flat major finale, set to music in soaring modalities with melodramatic Slavic verve, is produced in Kharkov.

## 3 JUNE 1960

*Der Zauberfisch,* operatic ballad in two acts by the 68-year-old Bohemian-born Austro-German composer Fidelio FINKE, to a libretto drawn from a fairy tale by the Grimm brothers dealing with a shrewish fisherwoman who is endowed with worldly goods by a magic fish, but keeps demanding more until the fish deprives her of all her gains, set to music in a burlesque manner laden with sharp but tonal polyphonic dissonances, is performed for the first time in Dresden.

## 10 JUNE 1960

The 34th Festival of the International Society for Contemporary Music opens in Cologne with a program comprising two basic works by the founders of dodecaphonic and serial music, *Fünf Orchesterstücke* by Arnold SCHOENBERG and *Fünf Sätze* for string orchestra by Anton von WEBERN.

## 11 JUNE 1960

A postage stamp of 30 centimes (with the overprint plus 10 francs) honoring BIZET, bearing his bewhiskered and bespectacled image and facsimiles of the title pages of *L'Arlésienne* and *Carmen,* with a Spanish fan and a tambourine shown in the foreground, is issued by the Administration des Postes et Télécommunications of France. (The date of issue of the stamp was to mark the 3000th performance of *Carmen* in Paris, but the jubilee performance was postponed)

## 11 JUNE 1960

Benjamin BRITTEN conducts at the opening of the 13th Aldeburgh Festival the world première of his operatic setting in three acts of Shakespeare's *A Midsummer Night's Dream,* to a libretto by Britten himself and his favorite tenor Peter Pears, with a heterogeneous musical score, containing atonal melodic devices to illustrate the surrealistic scene and animistic fantasy, while leaving the triadic foundations intact.

## 11 JUNE 1960

The 34th Festival of the International Society for Contemporary Music in Cologne presents the following program of chamber music:

*Cori di Didone,* for chorus and percussion, by the 36-year-old Venetian Luigi NONO, to the story of Dido's self-immolation, written in an expressive paradodecaphonic style; *Anagram* for four voices, speaking chorus and instruments, by the 28-year-old Argentinian-born avant-garde composer Mauricio KAGEL, conducted by him in world première, the anagram being represented in four surrealistic poems in German, in French, in Italian and in Spanish, in which only the consonants and vowels of the Latin palindrome from Dante's *Divina Commedia* "In girum imus nocte et consumimur igni" are used (thus the sounds *a, b, d, f, h, l, p, v* and *z* are excluded); and *Kontakte* for electronic sounds, piano and percussion, by the 31-year-old German innovator Karlheinz STOCKHAUSEN.

## 12 JUNE 1960

*Spring,* opera in two acts by the Albanian composer Tish DAIJA, taking place in Albania in the spring of 1944, and centered on a heroic partisan dying "with the name of the Communist Party on his lips" before the firing squad of the Nazi occupying forces, betrayed by an Albanian Fascist who failed in love rivalry for the hand of a beautiful mountain maiden, set to music in melodramatic colors of the traditional opera, with a stimulating injection of asymmetrical Albanian rhythms, is produced in Tirana.

## 12 JUNE 1960

The 34th Festival of the International Society for Contemporary Music in Cologne presents an orchestral concert in the following program:

*Skolion* by the Yugoslav Milko KELEMEN (Skolion being the Greek word for a table song or a round), with a considerable element of isorhythmic improvisation; *Mosaiken* by the 25-year-old Dutch-dodecaphonist Peter SCHAT; *Eighth Symphony (Rhôdanienne)* by Darius MILHAUD, (first performed at the Berkeley, California, Festival on 22 April 1958); *Poem* for viola and chamber orchestra by the 38-year-old American Czech Karel HUSA, based on a self-consistent tone-row; and *Spectra* by the American 34-year-old composer Gunther SCHULLER, in which the orchestra is subdivided into seven groups (as the spectrum is analyzed into seven principal colors), originally performed by the New York Philharmonic on 15 January 1960.

## 13 JUNE 1960

The 34th Festival of the International Society for Contemporary Music in Cologne presents a concert of orchestral music with three world premières:

*Quaderni per Orchestra* by the 34-year-old Italian modernist Luciano BERIO, which reflects five pictorial images built according to the principle of a freely gyrating mobile; *Motus Colores* by the 39-year-old Swedish composer Ingvar LIDHOLM, based on a twofold serial and aleatory structure, rhythmic and timbric; and *Pli selon pli,* "portrait de Mallarmé" by Pierre BOULEZ, containing three improvisations derived from specific tonal data, but statistically indeterminate and multivalent.

## 14 JUNE 1960

The 34th Festival of the International Society for Contemporary Music in Cologne presents a concert of orchestral music in the following program:

*Chorikon* by the 36-year-old Greek composer Argyris KOUNADIS, based on three mutually invertible symmetric tone-rows; *Fourth Symphony* by the American composer Roger SESSIONS, originally written for the Minnesota Centennial in 1957, in three movements, *Burlesque, Elegy* and *Pastorale; Aprèsludes,* "after-play" by the 27-year-old Italian composer Niccolò Castiglioni, in which four interrelated fragments, built on a dichotomy of two different tempi (one metronomic, one motoric), are integrated into a functionally dialectic succession of discrete sonorous units, with dynamic elements maintaining a euphoniously aerostatic equilibrium; *Piano Concerto* by the 35-year-old Rumanian Parisian Marius CONSTANT, cast in a cyclic monothematic tripartite form; and *Musique en Relief* by the 34-year-old Pole Wlodzimierz KOTOŃSKI, in five short movements, written in a serial technique.

## 15 JUNE 1960

*Martin Korda, D.P.,* opera in three acts by Henk BADINGS, to a symbolically realistic story of a displaced person (D.P.) impaled on the diagonal of a parallelogram of opposing political, social and economic forces after World War II, illustrated by irrational polyharmony, and culminating in a schizophrenic vision, scored for voices with electronic accompaniment, is produced at the opening of the Holland Festival in Amsterdam.

## 15 JUNE 1960

The 34th Festival of the International Society for Contemporary Music in Cologne continues with a chamber music concert comprising the following works:

*Maqamat* for flute and string quartet by the 52-year-old Hungarian-born Israeli composer Ödön PARTOS, Maqamat being an Arabic type of thematic melody serving as cantus firmus for improvisation; *Fantasy and Fugue* for piano by the 38-year-old Norwegian composer Finn MORTENSEN, written in a free dodecaphonic idiom; *String Quartet* by the American composer Arthur BERGER, conceived in a modified dodecaphonic idiom, with the serial row assembled cumulatively by discrete units; *Auf die ruhige Nachtzeit,* for soprano, flute, viola and cello by the 35-year-old Swiss composer Klaus HUBER, built in a mirror-like symmetric framework to a text of seven stanzas, each line of which contains seven syllables, while the nucleus of the thematic series is fissioned into mutually imitative halves; *Third String Quartet* by the 43-year-old Korean composer Isang YUN; and *Mobiles* for two pianos by the 30-year-old Belgian composer of serial music Henri POUSSEUR.

## 16 JUNE 1960

An orchestral concert is presented at the 34th Festival of the International Society for Contemporary Music in Cologne with the following program:

*Omaggio* by the 34-year-old German composer Giselher KLEBE, a neo-baroque homage to Italy; *Der Wein* for soprano and orchestra by Alban BERG, to the text of the German translation of Baudelaire's vinous poems, *L'âme du vin, Le vin des amants* and *Le vin du solitaire,* set in an impassionately expressionistic vein, composed in 1929, and first performed in Königsberg on 4 June 1930; *Aulodie* for oboe and orchestra by the 52-year-old German composer Wolfgang FORTNER, emulating the character and the sound of the ancient Greek wind instrument Aulos, written in an appropriately bland monodic idiom; and *Canti di Liberazione* for mixed chorus and orchestra by Luigi DALLAPICCOLA, written in an individualized dodecaphonic style.

### 17 JUNE 1960

The 34th Festival of the International Society for Contemporary Music in Cologne continues with a program of orchestral music, presenting the world première of *Fioritura* by the 43-year-old Swedish ultra-modernist Karl-Birger BLOMDAHL; *Movements for Piano and Orchestra* by STRAVINSKY (first performed in New York on 10 January 1960); and *Requiem* for soprano and baritone solo, chorus and orchestra by the China-born Russian-Estonian composer acclimatized in Berlin, Boris BLACHER.

### 18 JUNE 1960

The 34th Festival of the International Society for Contemporary Music in Cologne presents the following program of miscellaneous music:

*Ricercar and Doubles* for 8 instruments by the 25-year-old English composer Peter Maxwell DAVIES, based on the old song *To Many a Well,* treated with the techniques of *Hoquetus, Isorhythmics, Mensuration* and *Prolation* applied to a paradodecaphonic radix derived from the notes of the song, and scored for flute, oboe, clarinet, bassoon, horn, viola, cello and cembalo; *Introduzione-Sequenze-Coda* for 3 flutes, chimes and percussion by the 32-year-old Swedish composer Bengt HAMBRAEUS, based upon the acoustic concept of "Music in Space"; *Selektion I* for four groups of loudspeakers utilizing five basic sonorous units, by the pioneer atonalist and dodecaphonist Herbert EIMERT; *Cantata sacra* for tenor and six instruments by the 33-year-old Danish composer Bernhard LEWKOWITCH, a Latin hymn with a serial cyclic setting, with the number 12 playing the fundamental role in temporal division; *De la muerte a la mañana,* cantata by the 35-year-old German-born Chilean composeress Leni ALEXANDER, to words of Dylan Thomas, Thomas Wolfe and the Psalms, written in a paradodecaphonic idiom; and *Cantata* by the 29-year-old Catalan composer Xavier BENGUEREL, conceived in a neo-medieval manner.

### 19 JUNE 1960

The 34th Festival of the International Society for Contemporary Music concludes in Cologne with an orchestral concert comprising the following works:

*Sixth Symphony* by the veteran Dutch composer Matthijs VERMEULEN, subtitled *Les Minutes heureuses* (after a hemistichon from *Le Balcon* of Baudelaire, *Je sais l'art d'évoquer les minutes heureuses*), in three continuous movements, with the thematic base derived from the syllables *La, do, ré,* phonetically spelling *L'Adoré,* for the Supreme Being, culminating in a canon for three trumpets on this theme; *Nobody knows de Trouble I seen* for trumpet and orchestra by the German composer Bernd Alois

ZIMMERMANN, molded after a Negro Spiritual, with elements of pentatonicism inherent in the blues section; *Apparitions* by the 37-year-old Hungarian composer György LIGETI, wherein the title is taken in the French sense as a transitory manifestation or an ephemeral phenomenon, and connotes a reduction of the role of the height of pitch and the concomitant intervallic structure, melodic line and harmonic investiture, replaced by the sonic dimension of *Klangfarbe* in the taxonomic athematic distribution of discrete quanta within a given aural spectrum, in several acoustical layers of different densities ceaselessly colliding in their labyrinthine courses; and *Seventh Symphony* in three movements by the German master polyphonist Karl Amadeus HARTMANN.

### 21 JUNE 1960

In the course of the Music Festival in Strasbourg, the first complete performance is given of *Hieronymous Bosch* for orchestra by the 36-year-old French composer Serge NIGG, inspired by Bosch's famous triptych *The Garden of Terrestrial Delights* in the Prado Museum at Madrid, in three contrasting movements tonally limning the landscape of Hell, a man contemplating a rat through a glass tube, and the rosary of sin, written in Nigg's eclectic "third" manner (the first was dodecaphonic, the second, folklorically realistic, dictated by Nigg's Communist allegiance), reaching the point of dissonant paroxysm in the surrealistic portrayal of abomination of desolation and perversion of body and soul.

### 22 JUNE 1960

*Tapshyrylmagan Hatlar* (*Unposted Letters*), opera in four acts by the 50-year-old Tatar composer Dzhaudat FAIZY (real name Faizullin), to his own libretto in the Tatar language, is performed for the first time in Kazan.

### 23 JUNE 1960

The Ninth Annual Festival of Music and Dance in Granada, Spain, opens with the first performance of a posthumous work by Bohuslav MARTINU, *Suite on the Frescoes of Piero della Francesca*, in three movements, representing the varying moods portrayed by the painter, musically translated into the form of a free fantasia.

### 1 JULY 1960

On the occasion of the quincentenary of the University of Basel, *Cantata Academica* by Benjamin BRITTEN, to a Latin text taken from the university charter, and subdivided into 12 sections, each dominated by a different tonal center according to a premeditated 12-tone series (which appears discretely in direct and retrograde forms), written in an emphatically diatonic style dominated by major chords, and ending with a coda recapitulating the first section, is performed for the first time in Basel.

### 3 JULY 1960

The Newport Jazz Festival is ordered by the City Council of Newport, Rhode Island, to close down after a night of terror when thousands of young jazz lovers, failing to gain admission because Newport's Freebody Park was full to capacity, rioted, threw beer cans and bottles at the police, National Guardsmen, and Navy militia summoned to quell the disturbance with tear gas and strong firemen's hoses, leaving some fifty injured on both sides and necessitating the declaration of emergency and sealing off Newport County to all incoming vehicles, banning liquor sales, and cancelling the remaining concerts of the Festival at which several jazz luminaries were scheduled to appear.

## 7 JULY 1960

On the centennial of birth of Gustav MAHLER, Austria issues a postage stamp for one and a half schillings with his portrait.

## 9 JULY 1960

At a seminar on electronics in Darmstadt, the first public performance is given of the definitive version of *Etude concrète pour un seul coup de cymbale* lasting 2 minutes 35 seconds, by the 34-year-old Polish composer Wlodzimierz KOTOŃSKI, constructed in an integral serial technique by transposing the original sounds of the cymbal electronically to 11 different pitches of the chromatic scale and assigning to them different durations and dynamic intensities.

## 9 JULY 1960

Edward Burlingame HILL, American composer of impressionistic orchestral scores of subtle cerulean charm, an early follower of French modernism, teacher of many an American composer at Harvard University, whose father was a professor of chemistry there and whose grandfather was once its president, dies in his summer home in Francestown, New Hampshire, at the age of eighty-seven.

## 14 JULY 1960

*The Lodger,* opera in two acts by the English composeress Phyllis TATE, relating in nostalgically somber tones the predicament of an elderly couple who discover that their lodger is Jack the Ripper and who charitably let him leave and vanish into the London fog as a young detective on his trail takes time off to pay court to their daughter (thus protecting her from Jack's disembowelling propensities), is performed for the first time at the Royal Academy of Music, of which the composer was an alumna.

## 14 JULY 1960

On the last day of the 16th Festival of British Contemporary Music at Cheltenham, the world première is given of *Cosmos,* symphony in four movements by Reginald SMITH-BRINDLE, depicting the "everlasting infinities," "numberless firmaments," "confraternity of souls" and other cosmic and spiritual things, with the application of a variety of eclectic infra-modern technical devices.

## 15 JULY 1960

*Hercules furens,* music for the tragedy by Euripides by the Greek composer Yorgo SICILIANOS, is performed for the first time under the composer's direction in the ancient open arena in Epidaurus, in Greece.

## 23 JULY 1960

*Ballet of Lights,* with music by the Egyptian composer Halim EL-DABH, is presented in world première in front of the great Sphinx in Cairo.

## 27 JULY 1960

In commemoration of the 83rd anniversary of the birth of Ernst von DOHNÁNYI, the Governor of Florida proclaims it Dohnányi Day "in recognition of the pride felt by our citizens that he chose to live among them for the last twelve years of his life and chose Florida for his final resting place." (A similar proclamation was issued by the Governor of Florida on Dohnányi's 84th birthday in 1961)

## 30 JULY 1960

The Fifth Annual Jazz Festival in Great Britain held on the green lawns of Lord Montagu of Beaulieu's estate, 68 miles south of London, is broken up at 11:15 P.M. when some ten thousand youths erupt in mass savagery under the influence of Americanized British jazz, and haul down the bandstand and the floodlights for the British Broadcasting Corporation filming the festival.

## 1 AUGUST 1960

Bolivia issues a series of 12 stamps (6 regular and 6 airmail) to honor the 19-year-old Bolivian violinist Jaime LAREDO (with the insignia of his name spelled in the musical notes, La, Re, Do), winner of the 1959 International Music Competition in Brussels, when he was selected as best among 37 contestants, playing a Stradivarius violin lent to him for the occasion on 31 May 1959, a week before his 18th birthday.

## 4 AUGUST 1960

*Port Town,* one-act opera by the 47-year-old German-born American composer Jan MEYEROWITZ, to a libretto by Langston Hughes, telling a symbolic tale of platonic love of a sailor in port for a dreamy schoolgirl quickly squelched by horrified townsfolk, with a musical score full of romantic vocalizing in lush harmonies, is performed for the first time at the Berkshire Music Center at Tanglewood, Massachusetts.

## 7 AUGUST 1960

André BLOCH, French composer of numerous operas and instrumental pieces, of which the *Suite palestinienne* for cello and orchestra, written by him at the age of seventy-five, gained considerable popularity, dies at Viry-Châtillon, near Paris, at the age of eighty-seven.

## 14 AUGUST 1960

The first musical broadcast via an artificial earth satellite is accomplished during the twenty-first pass of the American orbiting balloon Echo I between 2:44 and 2:55 A.M., when a taped recording of the patriotic hymn *America the Beautiful* is transmitted from the Bell Telephone laboratory at Holmdel, New Jersey, to the Jet Propulsion Laboratory at Goldstone, California.

## 20 AUGUST 1960

Rudolf MOSER, 68-year-old Swiss composer of classically organized and romantically inspired instrumental and vocal music, perishes in a 275-foot plunge during an Alpinist excursion near St. Moritz.

## 23 AUGUST 1960

Czechoslovakia issues a 40-heller postage stamp in honor of the Czech composer and conductor Oskar NEDBAL (1874–1930) and a 60-heller stamp in honor of the Czech opera composer Otakar Ostrčil (1879–1935).

## 2 SEPTEMBER 1960

At the 14th Edinburgh International Festival, the Royal Liverpool Orchestra conducted by John Pritchard gives the world première of the *Second Symphony* by Sir William WALTON (completed on 22 July 1960), set in three well-balanced movements:

(1) *Allegro molto,* with propulsively masculine rhythms and resiliently leaping melody (2) *Lento assai,* an elegiacally dulcet evocation (3) *Passacaglia,* thematically proclaiming the three notes of the G minor triad plus nine more notes without duplication thus forming a 12-note series, and after ten variations, leading through an accelerated fugato to a Coda-Scherzando, and a grandiloquently unmitigated G major ending, with brass sonorities in triumphant fanfares.

## 3 SEPTEMBER 1960

*Third Symphony* by Humphrey SEARLE, psychologically tense in its darksomely upsurging calls (inspired by a visit to Mycenae and the sight of the ruins of the palace in which Agamemnon was supposed to be killed), is performed for the first time at the Edinburgh Festival.

## 8 SEPTEMBER 1960

*Derby Day,* a race-track overture by William ALWYN, is performed for the first time in London.

## 8 SEPTEMBER 1960

The Stockholm festival of modern Scandinavian music opens with a concert of orchestral works by the Swiss-born Gunnar BERG, 66-year-old Stockholm-born Maurice KARKOFF, 28-year-old Dane Per NÖRGAARD and the 40-year-old Finn, Nils-Eric FOUGSTEDT.

## 10 SEPTEMBER 1960

*Purloined Happiness,* opera in three acts by the Ukrainian composer Yuli MEITUS, wherein a rural damsel, believing her bridegroom to be dead, marries another and finds herself in a painful dilemma when he returns to reclaim his purloined happiness, is produced in Lvov.

## 14 SEPTEMBER 1960

Two centuries have passed since the birth in Florence of Luigi CHERUBINI, prolific composer of impeccable craftsmanship, who became a formidable disciplinarian as director of the Paris Conservatory.

## 18 SEPTEMBER 1960

First performances of two new works by two modern Polish composers are presented for the first time in the course of the Fourth International Festival of Contemporary Music, "The Warsaw Autumn," in Warsaw:

*Wymiary czasu i ciszy (Dimensions of Time and Silence)* for chorus and instruments by the 26-year-old leader of the Polish avant-garde Krzysztof PENDERECKI, intended as a musical counterpart of paintings by Paul Klee and other expressionist artists and creating a "space of sonic matter," with entrances of various instrumental bodies indicated in the score by red lines, the text vocalized on the decasyllabic Latin pentameter of the palindromic magic square

SATOR
AREPO
TENET
OPERA
ROTAS

and in addition introducing permutations and rotations of consonants in the vocal line, converting the chorus into a percussion ensemble supplemented by sibilation and purified bruitism; *Tertium datur* by the 31-year-old ultra-modernist Boguslaw SCHAEFFER, subtitled "Treatise of composition for clavichord and instruments," following a method of facture neither classical nor modern (hence the title contradicting the rule of Aristotelian logic, *Tertium non datur,* in syllogisms of mutually exclusive terms), making use of novel techniques with a free displacement of tonal centers and metrical stresses and written out in a pictorial notation in diagrams and geometric figures.

## 20 SEPTEMBER 1960

Ida Rubinstein, urbane and enterprising Russian-Jewish dancer and choreographer, who dazzled Paris for many years by her well-financed ballet presentations, for whom Debussy wrote *Le Martyre de Saint-Sébastien,* Ravel wrote *Boléro* and Stravinsky *Le Baiser de la fée,* dies at an uncertain age (but old) in seclusive obscurity in the village of Vence on the French Riviera.

## 21 SEPTEMBER 1960

*Rosamunde Floris,* opera in three acts by Boris BLACHER, to a libretto wherein a promiscuous damsel premaritally impregnated by an unscrupulous galant and abandoned by him, marries an aspiring librarian, after the latter defenestrates his previous fiancée, with a polymonotonous tension created by solitonal system of repetitious effects in variable meters, is produced at the Berlin Music Festival.

24 SEPTEMBER 1960

Mátyás SEIBER, 55-year-old Hungarian composer, resident in England from 1935, whose music astutely combines Magyar melos, baroque formality and dodecaphonic techniques, is killed in an automobile crash in Krueger National Park in Johannesburg, South Africa, during his stay there as visiting lecturer and composer.

25 SEPTEMBER 1960

*Capriccio* for piano and orchestra by the Israeli composer Paul BEN-HAIM, is performed for the first time in Tel Aviv.

27 SEPTEMBER 1960

At the 23rd Festival of Contemporary Music in Venice, Igor STRAVINSKY conducts the world première of his *Monumentum Pro Gesualdo di Venosa ad CD Annum*, an instrumental surrealization of three madrigals by Gesualdo, Prince of Venosa, composer, lutenist, and murderer by proxy (he is reputed to have hired assassins to overtake and kill his fleeing wife and her lover), on the occasion of the quadricentennial of his birth, the Stravinsky touch clearly pointed (*ex ungue leonem*) by the colloidal suspension of ornamental dissonances and forceful translocation of metric incipits, creating a distinctly vigesimosecular form of triune chirality.

27 SEPTEMBER 1960

At the opening concert of the Paris Festival (*Semaines Musicales de Paris*), the Philharmonic Orchestra of Leningrad presents a program of Russian music, under the auspices of the Comité National de la Musique and the patronage of the City of Paris, the Department of Seine, the Radiodiffusion française, and administered by the Chambre Syndicale des Organisateurs de Concerts. (Other foreign orchestras participating in Les Semaines Musicales de Paris were the Israel Philharmonic, the Orquesta Nacional of Madrid, and the Tokyo Radio Orchestra)

30 SEPTEMBER 1960

*Toccata Festiva*, a dedicatory piece by Samuel BARBER, commissioned by Mrs. Mary Curtis Zimbalist on the occasion of the unveiling of a large cathedral organ, costing $175,000, at the inaugural concert of the 61st season of the Philadelphia Orchestra, is performed for the first time, with Eugene Ormandy, starting on his 25th season as music director, conducting.

### 30 SEPTEMBER 1960

Ernst KRENEK conducts in Hamburg the world première of his orchestral work *Quaestio Temporis* for chamber orchestra, based on a 12-tone series containing all eleven different intervals in symmetrically invertible positions so that two intervals equidistant from the center are complementary to an octave, and the central interval, a tritone, is complementary to itself, with the sum of these eleven intervals (66 semitones) taken as the basic temporal parameter determining six different speeds of the eleven principal sections of the work according to six terms of the Fibonacci series (in which each term equals the sum of the two preceding terms) from 2 to 21, decupled and metronomically applied to the duration of a quarter-note (20, 30, 50, 80, 130, and 210 to a minute) with further parameters of vertical density and horizontal spissitude reaching the ne plus ultra compression in the finale with 12 vertical layers and a sensory maximum of 14 successive notes per second, in the individual parts.

### 30 SEPTEMBER 1960

*Le Taillis ensorcelé*, symphonic poem by the 32-year-old French composer Jacques BONDON, depicting a vegetable universe on another planet, possessing complex polyrhythmies of non-logarithmic growth rate, in a hyperserial melodic idiom, is performed for the first time in Paris.

### 1 OCTOBER 1960

*Nigerian Folk Symphony* by the prime Nigerian composer Fela SOWANDE, is performed for the first time in a broadcast by the British Broadcasting Corporation in London on the day of the proclamation of Nigeria's independence.

### 2 OCTOBER 1960

*Free China,* symphonic poem by the 55-year-old Soviet composer Boris ARAPOV, depicting in four connected movements the happy life, felicitous labor, festive jubilation, and earnest struggle for a still brighter Chinese future, making use of pentatonic Sinological materials, is performed for the first time in Leningrad.

### 7 OCTOBER 1960

*Les Adieux,* one-act opera by the 45-year-old French composer Marcel LANDOWSKI, in which a young woman refuses to open the door for her lover when he comes for his daily session, realizing that her infatuation with him is not sufficiently compelling, is produced in Paris.

### 8 OCTOBER 1960

The United States Post Office issues two stamps in the series Men of Liberty in honor of Ignace Paderewski, great Polish composer and statesman, who went into exile after Hitler's attack on Poland, and died in America.

8 OCTOBER 1960

*A Story of a Real Man,* posthumous opera in four acts by Sergei PROKOFIEV, to a documentary libretto from the heroic life of a Soviet fighter pilot who returned to active service in combat in World War II, after having lost both legs, receives its first performance for the general public at the Bolshoi Theater in Moscow, with the actual hero of the opera, the flyer Maresyev, present in the audience. (A semi-private performance was given for selected public in Leningrad on 3 December 1948, but the score was summarily rejected by Soviet officials and music critics as inadequate to its theme and too dissonant in musical substance.)

In the modernistic antimelodic music of Prokofiev's opera *A Story of a Real Man,* the composer retains his old positions, condemned by the Party and by Soviet society. The spiritual world of the Soviet man who performs miracles of valor and heroism for the love of his fatherland holds no attraction for Prokofiev. He is still interested solely in the external effects of dramatic action and in naturalistic details. (Tikhon Khrennikov in *Pravda,* 4 January 1949)

Melodic generosity of this music, the bright songful arias, the especially powerful chracterization of the image of the hero made the production of *A Story of a Real Man* a great event in the cultural life of the capital. (*Pravda,* 9 October 1960)

"I am deeply moved" said the Hero of the Soviet Union Alexey Petrovich Maresyev. "Prokofiev's opera brought back to me the unforgettable events of the Great Patriotic War." He said this after attending the final rehearsal of Prokofiev's opera *A Story of a Real Man* on the stage of the Bolshoi Theater. After the end of the rehearsal, A. P. Maresyev warmly congratulated the artists, embraced and kissed the interpreter of the part of Alexey. (Report of the impression received by the real pilot Maresyev whose story served as the foundation of the libretto, in *Izvestia,* 6 October 1960)

10 OCTOBER 1960

The Philharmonic Orchestra of Israel opens its international tour in Paris under the direction of Carlo-Maria GIULINI in a program containing a *Psalm* by the 25-year-old Israeli composer Noam SHERI.

14 OCTOBER 1960

*Second Violin Concerto* by Walter PISTON, distinguished by characteristically Pistonian directness of musical speech, translucency of contrapuntal fabric, and contrastfulness of the three ideally equilibrated movements, *Moderato, Adagio,* and *Allegro,* is performed for the first time by the Pittsburgh Symphony Orchestra, Joseph Fuchs soloist, William Steinberg conducting.

15 OCTOBER 1960

At the opening of the Musiktage für die zeitgenössische Tonkunst at Donaueschingen, a chamber music concert is presented with the following program of world premières:

5 *Bagatellen* for wind quintet (flute, oboe, clarinet, bassoon, horn) by Wolfgang FORTNER, written in an unaffected vein of *Gebrauchsmusik;* first performance of the

posthumous *Fourth String Quartet* by Bohuslav MARTINU, written in 1937 for a Paris friend, but never performed in public; *Szene I* for a chamber ensemble (2 flutes, 2 trumpets, harp, piano, percussion, and two empty wine bottles) by the precociously ultra-modernistic 23-year-old Bo NILSSON of Sweden whose serialistically conceived and surrealistically constructed music postulates the orderliness of systematic disorder; *Twelfth String Quartet* in quarter-tones by Alois HÁBA of Prague, in three movements designated by the traditional Italian terms, *Allegro energico, Andante cantabile, Allegro risoluto* but constructed athematically in melody, asymmetrically in periodicity and agglutinatively in successiveness, with the intervallic structure using the entire gamut of quarter-tones and their multiples, including "neutral" seconds (a quarter-tone larger than a minor second and a quarter-tone smaller than a major second), neutral thirds, sixths and sevenths, and pairs of neutral perfect intervals (fourths, fifths, octaves); *Tropi per complesso da camera* by the Milanese modernist Niccolò CASTIGLIONI, for flute, clarinet, violin, cello, piano and percussion, serially conceived as tropes of sonority, tempo, and even of bel canto; and *Kammermusik 1960* for 14 instruments by the 29-year-old Pomeranian composer Dieter SCHÖNBACH, in five movements with sonorously meaningless titles *Akuo, Siri I, Melog, Siri II, Khor,* selected to inspire constructivistically coloristic associations to help form an auditively subjective organization of the music.

### 16 OCTOBER 1960

On the second and last day of the Musiktage für die zeitgenössische Tonkunst at Donaueschingen, the world premières are given of the following works:

*Suite of Dances* by the 53-year-old Japanese modernist Yoritsune MATSUDAIRA, for three orchestras conducted by three conductors in non-coincidental tempi and meters, written in a serialistically procrusteanized style of ancient Japanese court music Bugaku (a genre of Gagaku); *Anaklasis* for strings and percussion by the 26-year-old Pole Krzysztof PENDERECKI, a serial interpretation of the anaclastic transposition of short and long syllables in the Ionic rhythms of Greek prosody, with associative tonal and metrical ideas (arithmetical progressions, rotation of tone-rows, etc.), introducing quarter-tones as part of an intervallic series, making use of instrumental innovations such as the prepared piano, and resorting to diagrammatic notation for metric and rhythmic factors (the piece was hissed by the audience, but punitively encored by the conductor Hans Rosbaud); and *Chronochromie* for orchestra by Olivier MESSIAEN in 7 sections evolved from the considerations of time (*chronos*) and color (*chroma*), comprising 32 different note-values (durations) subjected to symmetrical permutation and melodic colors supplied by songbirds of France, Sweden, Japan, Mexico, and noise elements of waterfalls of the French Alps, the chronos and the chroma being mutually interactive, individual chroma being determined by corresponding chronos so that *Chronochromie* becomes the color of time.

### 19 OCTOBER 1960

Haiti issues a series of stamps (10 centimes, 20 centimes and 1 franc 50 centimes) in honor of the Haitian composer Occide JEANTY (1860–1936) with a musical quotation from his *1804 Marche Militaire,* commemorating the proclamation of independence of Haiti from France.

### 20 OCTOBER 1960

*Time Cycle,* by Lukas Foss, a suite of four songs for soprano and orchestra to the texts by Auden, Housman, Kafka and Nietzsche, all of them concerned with clocks, bells and timepieces, and written in a highly rarefied pointillistically sharpened idiom beyond the borders of tonality, with interludes for a heterogeneous quartet (clarinet, cello, percussion and piano) improvising simultaneously but without collective precognition following individually subjective semi-aleatory ideas within the deterministic parameters of thematic matrices and serial instrumental rotation, is performed uniquely (for any other performance would inevitably be different in the improvised interludes) by the New York Philharmonic, Leonard Bernstein conducting, Adele Addison soprano, with Lukas Foss himself as piano aleatorist (the composed part of the piece without optional interludes was repeated at the end of the concert.)

21 OCTOBER 1960

*Le Roi David,* biblical music drama by Arthur HONEGGER, first performed in Mézières, near Lausanne, on 11 June 1921, and later revised as a symphonic psalm and oratorio, is presented for the first time as an opera at the Grand Opéra in Paris, arranged in 31 scenes interspersed by choral numbers and supplied with an additional dialogue, but without in any way altering the original musical score.

21 OCTOBER 1960

*Seventh Symphony* by William SCHUMAN, in four movements, *Largo assai, Vigoroso, Cantabile intensamente* and *Scherzando brioso,* conceived in a vigorous and intense 20th-century idiom replete with austere intervallic structures with a predilection for major sevenths and minor ninths, but ending unapologetically in sonorous E flat major, is performed for the first time by the Boston Symphony Orchestra, Charles Munch conducting.

22 OCTOBER 1960

*Time-Span,* symphonic movement by George ROCHBERG, conceived in an abstractly constructivistic style in a serial technique of durations, with tonal elements in dodecaphonic distribution ascetically sampled in widely contrasting instrumental monosyllables in dynamic chiaroscuro, commissioned by the Junior Division of the Women's Association of the St. Louis Symphony Society on funds obtained through the sale of art by local modernist painters auctioned off on a Mississippi steamboat, is performed for the first time by the St. Louis Symphony Orchestra. (A revised version of the work was performed, under the title *Time-Span II,* on 19 January 1964 in Buffalo, the composer conducting)

23 OCTOBER 1960

*Preamble to Peace* by Earl ROBINSON, oratorio based on the Preamble to the United Nations Charter, is performed for the first time by the Trenton Symphony Orchestra.

## 25 OCTOBER 1960

The Symphony Orchestra of Radio Tokyo presents, during its international tour, a program in Paris, featuring two Japanese works:

*Euburi*, 2 tableaux by the 31-year-old Michio MAMIYA, composed in 1957, and representing a stylized impression of the dances and prayers at the Enburi festival during harvest time, with a profuse percussion section, including an enormously huge gong and an extraordinarily minuscule drum; and *Mandala*, symphonic poem by the 31-year-old Toshiro MAYUZUMI, attempting to translate Buddhist philosophy into musical terms, and based on a series of 10 notes derived from two sets of overtones of sacred bells of Japanese temples, each forming a pentatonic scale, with the tonics of the two sets distanced by a minor ninth, designed to achieve a schematic tonal representation of the sacred symbol of Oriental art, the mandala, with its concentrically arrayed geometric figures, and at the same time to suggest the concept of collective subconscious as promulgated by Carl Jung.

## 25 OCTOBER 1960

*Thai*, symphonic rhapsody by the 34-year-old Dutch composer Jurriaan ANDRIESSEN, based on four jazz tunes by King Phumiphol Aduldet of Thailand, is presented by the Royal Military Band of the Netherlands as a surprise for the musical monarch during a concert given by the municipality of The Hague at which he and Queen Juliana of Holland were guests of honor.

## 25 OCTOBER 1960

José PADILLA, Spanish composer of the popular tunes *Valencia* and *El Relicario*, ubiquitously played and sung in the 1920's, dies in Madrid at the age of seventy-one.

## 28 OCTOBER 1960

The North German Radio Network presents the world première of *Carré* by Karlheinz STOCKHAUSEN, for four orchestras and four choruses placed on four podia and conducted by four conductors along the four walls of a square mess hall in Hamburg with the audience seated in a carré of rows of chairs at 90° to each other, the music based on a one-to-one correspondence of duration (macro-time) and height of pitch (micro-time).

## 30 OCTOBER 1960

Alfred HILL, Nestor of Australian composers, who wrote ballets, symphonic poems and chamber music utilizing melodic and rhythmic materials of the aboriginal Maoris, dies in Darlinghurst, near Sydney, a few weeks before his 90th birthday.

## 2 NOVEMBER 1960

Malcolm ARNOLD conducts the British Broadcasting Corporation Symphony Orchestra in London in the world première of his *Fourth Symphony*, in four movements, cast in his customary infra-modern but hedonistically vigorous style, with the inclusion of some Caribbean percussion used "non-exotically," and introducing in the *Scherzo* a 12-note palindrome "to express unpleasant emotion."

2 NOVEMBER 1960

Dimitri MITROPOULOS, 64-year-old Greek conductor of ecstatic genius, prodigious musician with a photographic memory and champion of ultra-modern music, dies suddenly of a heart attack, collapsing and falling on the podium of La Scala, Milan, after conducting 45 beats of the first movement of Mahler's *Third Symphony*. (According to his will, his body was cremated in Switzerland, since Italian law prohibits cremation, and flown by a Greek government plane to Athens for a non-religious ceremony, cremated bodies being unacceptable to the ritual of the Greek Orthodox Church, and placed in an urn in the Athens Conservatory of Music)

6 NOVEMBER 1960

On the occasion of the sesquicentennial of the birth of the Hungarian pioneer of national opera, Ferenc ERKEL, the Hungarian government issues a 60-feller postage stamp.

6 NOVEMBER 1960

*The Arsenal*, opera by the Ukrainian composer Georgy MAIBORODA, is produced in Kiev.

7 NOVEMBER 1960

To commemorate the centennial of the birth of the Spanish national composer Isaac ALBÉNIZ, the Spanish government issues two postage stamps with his likeness, at 25 centavos and one peseta.

8 NOVEMBER 1960

*Third Symphony* by the 40-year-old English composer Peter Racine FRICKER is performed for the first time in London.

11 NOVEMBER 1960

The Brazilian Coffee Institute stages at the Music School of the University of Brazil in Rio de Janeiro the first Brazilian performance of Bach's *Coffee Cantata*, recounting the tribulations of a young German maiden whose father will not let her indulge in drinking such an aphrodisiac beverage which she herself finds "better tasting than a thousand kisses."

17 NOVEMBER 1960

*Second Violin Concerto* by Paul CRESTON is performed in a world première by Michael Rabin and the Los Angeles Philharmonic.

18 NOVEMBER 1960

A century has passed since the birth in the village of Kurylówka in Podolia (which was part of Poland until the Second Partition of 1793, when it was ceded to Russia) of Ignace Jan PADEREWSKI, the great piano virtuoso who thrilled multitudes in Europe and America during the Golden Age of romantic artistry at the turn of the century, composer of the perennially popular *Minuet* and also bigger things in various genres, Polish patriot and statesman who was briefly Prime Minister of Poland after World War I.

(Paderewski's date of birth is 6 November 1860 according to old style Russian calendar, or 18 November new style. The Government of Poland issued a commemorative stamp of 2 zloty 50 groszy on the correct date 18 November 1960. Paderewski stamps for 4 and 8 cents were issued by the U.S. Post Office, in the Liberty Champions Series on 8 October 1960, not stated to be centennial, but several governors proclaimed the date of 6 November 1960 as Paderewski Day with specific reference to the centennial, among them Governor Nelson Rockefeller of New York. Governor Michael V. DiSalle of Ohio, issued a proclamation stating: "Whereas November 6, 1960 marks the one hundredth anniversary of the birth of Ignace Paderewski, noted Polish statesman and artist and Whereas, as a great piano virtuoso and composer Paderewski contributed countless hours of musical entertainment to the peoples of the world, Whereas, this great orator and patriotic leader fought continuous never-faltering battle for Polish independence, and Whereas, in this centennial year of the birth of Paderewski, the Government of the United States is honoring him by issuing a stamp bearing his likeness in the Champion of Liberty series, Now, therefore, I, Michael V. DiSalle, Governor of the State of Ohio, do hereby proclaim November 6, 1960 as Paderewski Day." Similar statements, giving the centennial date as 6 November 1960 were issued by the governors of Illinois and Nebraska. Governor Price Daniel of Texas stated in his declaration that "October 1960 will mark the one hundredth anniversary of the birth of Ignace Paderewski." Maryland, Colorado, and Michigan held celebrations of Paderewski Day; the State of Minnesota proclaimed an American-Polish Friendship Day. The proclamation of the governor of Michigan included the reminder that Podolia was "occupied" by Russia at the time of Paderewski's birth)

### 25 NOVEMBER 1960

The era of soap operas, daily radio broadcasts telling stories of heartbreak, mental and physical illnesses, frustrated female amours, and teetering business enterprises (usually sponsored by manufacturers of soaps and detergents, hence also known as sudsy programs), formally comes to an end as the Columbia Broadcasting System removes from the ether the long enduring serials, *Ma Perkins,* veteran of 27 years of struggle to maintain her lumber mill (inaugurated 13 August 1933), *The Right to Happiness,* 20-year-old story of a nubile widow and perpetually adolescent son (inaugurated 22 January 1940), *Young Dr. Malone,* wise and lovable, medically and socially (inaugurated 29 April 1940) and *The Second Mrs. Burton,* a widow infatuated with a young and unscrupulous artist (inaugurated 7 January 1946), the final episodes all provided with happy or at least morally gratifying endings, to the accompaniment of saturated diminished seventh-chords on the organ, the instrument indissolubly linked to radio serials from time immemorial.

### 25 NOVEMBER 1960

*Hachatur Abovian,* opera in three acts by the Armenian composer Gebork ARMENIAN (changed from his real name Khachaturian in order to avoid confu-

sion with his famous namesake), recounting in romantic tones the life and social activities of the bringer of enlightenment to Armenia in the first half of
the 19th-century, is produced in Erevan, capital of the Armenian Soviet Socialist Republic.

## 3 DECEMBER 1960

*Marko Polo*, opera by the Yugoslav composer Ivo TIJARDOVIĆ, encompassing
in three acts the epic travels of Marco Polo to China and back to Venice in
the years 1271–1292, set to songful Italianate melodies with some pentatonic
discursions in the scenes set in fabulous Cathay, is performed for the first time
in Zagreb.

## 3 DECEMBER 1960

*Camelot*, musical revue by Frederick LOEWE, with book and lyrics by Alan
Jay Lerner, drawn from the novel *The Once and Future King* by T. H. White,
in which the fabled court of King Arthur at the legendary town of Camelot in
West England is modernized and melodramatized in an ingratiatingly sentimental manner, with Guinevere familiarly called Jenny and Lancelot dubbed
Lance, concluding with the nostalgic envoi, "Don't let it be forgot/ That once
there was a spot/ For one brief shining moment/ That was known as Camelot," is produced in New York.

## 5 DECEMBER 1960

*Violin Concerto* by the 38-year-old Czech composer Zdeněk LIŠKA, written in
a modern virtuoso manner, is performed for the first time in Leningrad at a
demonstration of the Czechoslovak theatrical spectacle *Laterna magica*, in
which the violinist appears in a dual function as a performer in the flesh on
the stage and as an actor in the film in close succession without losing the continuity of the action or of the music.

## 11 DECEMBER 1960

Carl ORFF conducts in Stuttgart the world première of his nativity play *Ludus
de nato infante mirificus*, to his own libretto in the Upper Bavarian dialect intermingled with ecclesiastical Latin, employing toneless rhythmoloquy with
a gymnosophistically monochromatic and an ascetically homophonic instrumental accompaniment.

## 12 DECEMBER 1960

*Sixth Symphony* by the Hungarian composer László LAJTHA, in four romantically lyric movements, assertively tonal in spite of constant melismatic chro-
matization and conspicuous absence of key signatures, scored for a modern
orchestra with an imposing battery of percussion instruments, which, the
composer warns "messieurs les chefs d'orchestre" in a printed note are not to
be allowed to produce "brutal noise," is performed for the first time in Brussels.

## 15 DECEMBER 1960

*Lysistrata,* comic opera with serious pacifist intent by the Rumanian composer Gherase DENDRINO, ending with a realistic release of actual white doves and cast in a Viennese manner with a lot of waltzing tunes, is performed for the first time in Bucharest under the composer's direction.

## 16 DECEMBER 1960

*The Golden Child,* television opera in three sections by Philip BEZANSON to a Christmas libretto by Paul Engle wherein a child's rag doll magically leads a California gold rusher of 1848, his pregnant wife, and a small daughter out of a snowy wilderness to a mining camp, with a subsequent birth of a male child in a manger, making use of some special effects such as an authentic moo of a cow, is produced in a 90-minute television broadcast from New York.

## 17 DECEMBER 1960

*Ninth Symphony* for string orchestra by Henk BADINGS is performed for the first time in Amsterdam.

## 17 DECEMBER 1960

Paul HINDEMITH conducts in Mannheim the world première of his opera *Das lange Weihnachtsmahl,* in one act, after Thornton Wilder's plotless play *The Long Christmas Dinner,* translated into German by Hindemith, recounting the tale of 90 Christmas dinners in a single American family through several generations between 1840 and 1930, the dead departing and the newly born arriving, with a musical score of formal self-sufficiency and tonal directness wherein resolvable dissonances are subordinated to the basically triadic harmony.

## 17 DECEMBER 1960

Eleven days before his 84th birthday, Pablo CASALS conducts in Acapulco, Mexico, the world première of his oratorio *El Pesebre* (*The Manger*), composed in the 1940's for a performance in celebration of the unconsummated downfall of General Franco, and conceived as a nativity play interwoven with Catalan folksong material.

## 19 DECEMBER 1960

A "realization" of MAHLER's unfinished *Tenth Symphony* in F-sharp major and minor, by the British musicologist Deryck Cooke (of the five movements of the work, the first, *Adagio,* the second, a *Scherzo,* and 28 measures of the third, *Purgatorio,* exist in full score; the rest in "short score"), is performed for the first time by the Philharmonia Orchestra of London under the direction of Berthold Goldschmidt. (On 28 April 1963, Alma Mahler, his widow, wrote to Deryck Cooke, expressing her admiration for his intuitive but authentic completion, and rescinding her earlier prohibition of further performances of the work in this version)

30 DECEMBER 1960

*The Invitation*, ballet by Mátyás SEIBER, Hungarian composer, long resident in London, to a libretto focused on two adolescents in love befriended by a perverse married couple, with the boy being seduced by the wife, and the girl raped by the husband, set to music in an expressionistically concentrated, schematically sensual quasi-dodecaphonic idiom, is produced at Covent Garden in London, three months and six days after Seiber's tragic death.

30 DECEMBER 1960

*Symphonic Engravings*, a suite for orchestra by the Soviet composer of Azerbaijan, Kara KARAEV, drawn from his music to the film *Don Quixote*, and picturing the knight of the sorrowful countenance in funereal tones, grotesquely changing to an asymmetrically rhythmed galop, with Sancho Panza represented by a rude, crude march, is performed for the first time in Baku.

30 DECEMBER 1960

*Mariuta*, opera in three acts by the Soviet composer Dmitri TOLSTOY, after the story *Forty-First* by Boris Lavrenev, dealing with a Soviet girl guerrilla fighter who is left to guard a White Russian officer taken prisoner during the civil war in Central Asia, falls in love with him, but despite their intimacy, kills him unhesitantly when he tries to join the crew of an anti-Bolshevik motor boat on the Aral Sea, as she did forty previous enemies, is performed for the first time in Perm.

# ✍ *1961* ✍

1 JANUARY 1961

*Deseret*, television opera by the 31-year-old American composer Leonard KASTLE, based on a romanticized episode in the life of Brigham Young, founder of the Mormon colony in the Utah desert called Deseret, dealing with his magnanimous surrender of his 25th bride-to-be to a young Union Army officer whom she loves, set to music in a liltingly melodious and meltingly harmonious manner with pleasing arias, vocal duets, trios, quartets, quintets and sextets, is produced by the National Broadcasting Company Television Opera in New York.

5 JANUARY 1961

*Second Symphony*, written by the 27-year-old American composer Easley BLACKWOOD, on a commission from the G. Schirmer music publishing firm to commemorate its centennial, set in a rhapsodically romantic vein with a cornucopia of exclamatory and proclamatory fanfares, mitigated by atonally chromaticized melodic lines and nervously agitated rhythms, in three movements, *Largo, Scherzo* and *Toccata*, well within the classical mold, each ending on a unisonal E, is performed for the first time by the Cleveland Orchestra, George Szell conducting.

## 8 JANUARY 1961

CLARINEN, accurate modern replicas of Bach trumpets, capable of performing baroque music with great agility, celerity and perfect articulation along the natural scale of the harmonic series, are sounded over the Cologne Radio.

## 9 JANUARY 1961

In a Vienna court, Heinrich SCHMID, vocal coach of the Vienna State Opera, is awarded 1000 schillings damages in his lawsuit against the critic Franz Endler for unfairness in his review of a song recital by Elisabeth Schwarzkopf given in Vienna on 19 May 1960 accompanied by Schmid, in which Endler said that Schmid "struggled sullenly with the notes and limped unsteadily" in Hugo Wolf's song *Das Köhlerweib ist trunken (The Collier's Wife Is Drunk)*, maliciously or ignorantly disregarding the fact that these supposed lapses were intentional for a vivid illustration of drunkenness in the syncopated piano part.

## 13 JANUARY 1961

An evening of electronic opera and other musical essays in time, space, and sound, is produced by David Johnson at the Cooper Union for the Advancement of Science and Art in New York in a program opening with *Cough Music* (a recorded montage of actual coughs nervously emitted by the audience during a New York ballet recital, electronically altered and rhythmically rearranged and magnified); *Two Sounds* (violin scrapings amplified to screeches); *Amazing Grace* (electronically scrambled Negro spirituals) and an opera, *The Peaceable Kingdom* by Dick HIGGINS, dedicated to the composer's brother Mark "murdered by Lumumba's racists" in the Congo, scored for speaking voices representing tropical animals, accompanied by electronically amplified sounds of three toy pianos.

## 15 JANUARY 1961

George BARATI, Hungarian-born American composer conducts the Honolulu Symphony Orchestra in the first performance of his symphonic poem *The Dragon and the Phoenix*, suggested by a Polynesian legend, with the Phoenix redivivus illustrated by ornithological echolalia in the woodwinds and the dragon evoked by pyrophoric eruptions in the brass accompanied by sonorific clangors of pythonic gongs.

## 20 JANUARY 1961

*Gloria* by Francis POULENC for soprano solo, chorus and orchestra, comprising six parts of the Catholic Mass, conceived in a perfervid religious spirit and set in exalted triadic modalities, is performed for the first time by the Boston Symphony Orchestra, Charles Munch conducting.

2 FEBRUARY 1961

*Dance and Invocation* for orchestra by the Israeli composer Paul BEN-HAIM is performed for the first time in Tel Aviv.

8 FEBRUARY 1961

*Collages* by the Catalan composer Roberto GERHARD, resident in England, a serial work for orchestra and tape-recorded noises, composed in emulation of the principles of abstract expressionism in modern art, with the organic music represented by humans while electronic sound generators take an independent course, except at nine specified points at which the two sonic streams cross each other, is performed for the first time in London by the Orchestra of the British Broadcasting Corporation.

The tape recording consisted entirely of noises; gusty escaping winds, the steam exhaust of a train, rattles, bangs, and moans, tappety-tapping, all without form, shape, rhythm or sequence, cropping up here and there. . . . To this hideous counterpoint the orchestra added its quota of unmelodic, unharmonious, unrhythmical music, notes snatched out of the blue, dissonances mercifully overwhelmed by the greater cacophony of noise issuing from the loudspeaker. Mr. Gerhard's composition was an attempt to imitate that form of painting known as collage, in which extraneous bits of material are stuck on to the painted canvas in the name of abstract art. The musical result was as meaningless as the graphic one. If ever the BBC has wasted public money on the rehearsal and performance of absolute rubbish, it was on this occasion. One might as well have taken the orchestra to the Hungerford Bridge and allowed them to improvise to the chance noises of the railway and the river. Perhaps this is just what happened and Mr. Gerhard was just deceiving us. (*Musical Opinion*, London, March 1961, in a leading article entitled *Rubbish!*)

9 FEBRUARY 1961

*Symphonic Dialogues* for orchestra by the Polish-born American composer Felix LABUNSKI, inspired by Arthur Schnitzler's *Reigen*, an erotic farce of overlapping fornication, in which a member of one couple becomes heterosexually involved with a member of another, and the last of the series with the initial adulterer with whom the round originated, forming a pericyclically proleptic dichotomy, represented in the score by nine bithematic sections (a + b, b + c, c + d . . . h + a) flanked by mutually reversible prelude and postlude, is performed for the first time by the Cincinnati Symphony Orchestra, Max Rudolf conducting.

10 FEBRUARY 1961

As part of the ceremony marking the opening of the first part of the Niagara Power Project, Ferde GROFE conducts the Buffalo Philharmonic in Niagara Falls in the first performance of his symphonic *Niagara Falls Suite*, in four movements reflecting historical, social and political aspects of the mighty cataract: *The Thunderer of the Waters, Devil's Hole Massacre, The Honeymooners,* and *Power of Niagara 1961.*

## 10 FEBRUARY 1961

The Philadelphia Orchestra, conducted by Eugene Ormandy, gives the world première of the *Seventh Symphony* by Walter PISTON, written in a kinesthetic neo-baroque manner, with clear tonal epicenters but without explicit key signatures, in three movements:

(1) *Con moto,* in non-waltz 3/4 time, melodically perambulating the circumference of mutant tonalities, gravitating towards A (2) *Adagio Pastorale,* in 6/8, an elegiac eclogue with exterior decorations in the woodwinds, agitated towards the middle but subsiding into a floatingly fluent fluvial flute solo in the envoi (3) *Allegro festevole,* in 2/4, a vivacious essay in the manner of a symphonic toccata.

## 10 FEBRUARY 1961

*1941,* opera in three acts by the 58-year-old Croatian composer Mihovil LOGAR, to a libretto glorifying the patriotic resistance groups fighting the Nazis in occupied Belgrade, containing in the action a choreographic hallucination, is produced in Serajevo.

## 17 FEBRUARY 1961

*Purgatory,* opera in one-act by the Bohemian-born American composer Hugo WEISGALL, to a libretto from a mystagogical play by William Butler Yeats, wherein a man slays his father to avenge his mother's death in childbirth, and many years later kills his own son to prevent him from victimizing the women of the future, set to music in parsimoniously dissonant counterpoint, and frugally arranged harmonies is performed for the first time in concert form at the Library of Congress in Washington.

## 20 FEBRUARY 1961

Percy GRAINGER, romantic Australian-born pianist and composer whose first steps in music were tenderly fostered by Grieg, and who wrote folksy pieces with homely English titles making ostentatious use of colloquial musical terms (such as "dished up for piano" instead of arranged, "louden lots" instead of crescendo, "middle fiddle" instead of viola, "room-music" for chamber music, "foursome" for quartet, and even "twenty-two-some" for an ensemble of twenty-two instruments), and whose own life as a wandering artist was full of heartache (his adored mother jumped to her death from the 18th floor of the Aeolian Hall Building on 42nd Street in New York in 1922), romance (he married the Swedish painter and poet Allea Viola Stroem in the Hollywood Bowl before an audience of 22,000 people and wrote a bridal song for her entitled *To a Nordic Princess*), virtue (he was utterly unmercenary, a vegetarian, teetotaler, and non-smoker, and never owned a hat), and eccentricity (he was once arrested as a suspicious character when he arrived for a concert in Wausau,

Wisconsin, in 7° below zero weather wearing white ducks, a knapsack, but no hat or coat), dies in White Plains, New York, at the age of seventy-eight.

## 22 FEBRUARY 1961

Nick La Rocca, jazz cornetist, founder in New Orleans of the Original Dixieland Band, the first white ensemble of this genre, who blazed his syncopated trail to Chicago, New York and the world, dies in his native New Orleans at the age of seventy-one.

## 2 MARCH 1961

*Ariadne,* lyric opera in one act by Bohuslav Martinu, in which Theseus appears as the Freudian *superego* that kills its own *id* personified by Minotaur with the aid of Ariadne's psychoanalytic umbilical cord, set to music in an orderly succession of recitatives, ensembles, and instrumental interludes in a neo-Monteverdian monody, is produced posthumously in Gelsenkirchen, Germany.

## 2 MARCH 1961

*Nonet for Strings* by Aaron Copland, scored for three violins, three violas and three cellos, with a discrete distribution of contrapuntal entities in polytriadic harmonies gradually accelerating in canonic imitation, then subsiding into serene polyharmony, is performed for the first time at the Dumbarton Oaks Research Library as a commissioned work in honor of the 50th wedding anniversary of Mr. and Mrs. Robert W. Bliss, owners of the Dumbarton Oaks estate in Georgetown, D.C.

## 2 MARCH 1961

An American music program of works by members of the Southeastern Composers' League is presented by the George Peabody College for Teachers in Nashville, Tennessee, comprising twelve innocuous pieces for various instrumental groups and a set of six *Fallopian-Tube Waltzes* by Peter Ford, a microsonic anatomical percussion piece, in which the process of ovulation is illustrated by a dozen raw eggs solo dropped from a stepladder into a metal basket on the floor.

## 3 MARCH 1961

Paul Wittgenstein, amputated Austrian pianist who, after losing his right arm in Russia during World War I, began a unique career as a left-hand virtuoso and who commissioned Ravel, Richard Strauss, Prokofiev and others to write left-hand piano concertos for him, dies at the age of 73 in Manhasset, Long Island.

## 4 MARCH 1961

A partial concert performance is given at Yankton College in South Dakota of *The American Volunteer,* an opera in four acts composed in 1889 by the Italian bandmaster Felice VINATIERI who served with the Union Army in the Civil War and joined General Custer, to leave him just before his last stand in the battle with Sitting Bull at Little Big Horn. (Vinatieri commemorated the famous battle in his band piece *General Custer's Last Indian Campaign*)

8 MARCH 1961

Sir Thomas BEECHAM, autocratic British grandee of the conductorial baton whose revenue from hereditary wealth accumulated through the opulent sales of Beecham's liver pills enabled him to organize and maintain a symphony orchestra and a Beecham Opera Company early in the century, and whose insouciant disdain for good manners (he remarked, after a horse defecated on the stage in *Aida* during a tenor aria, "the beast is rude, but a good music critic") was condoned in deference to his sovereign musicianship revealed in his impeccable interpretations of classical music and his championship of early modernists, dies in London of a cerebral hemorrhage at the age of eighty-one.

10 MARCH 1961

*Per un Don Chissiotta,* opera by the 31-year-old French composer Jean-Pierre RIVIÈRE, is produced by the Piccola Scala in Milan as the winning work in the international opera competiton held by the Ricordi publishing firm to mark the 150th anniversary of its existence.

11 MARCH 1961

*Uno Sguardo dal Ponte,* opera by Renzo ROSSELLINI, to a libretto after Arthur Miller's play *A View from the Bridge,* dealing with a tragedy of concupiscence among illicit Italian immigrants in New York, is produced in Rome.

19 MARCH 1961

*The Unattainable Woman,* opera in three acts by the 52-year-old Estonian composer Eugen KAPP, is produced in Tartu.

23 MARCH 1961

*Il Calzare d'argento,* sacred play in two acts by Ildebrando PIZZETTI, dealing with a medieval pauper who is accused of the theft of a sacred relic when a silver shoe falls into his hands from a crucifix in the Lucca Cathedral but is exonerated by Jesus descending from the cross to testify in his defense, is produced at La Scala in Milan.

31 MARCH 1961

*L'Horloge de Flore,* suite for solo oboe and small orchestra by Jean FRANÇAIX, in seven movements each named after a specimen in the Flower Clock of Linnaeus, classified according to the hour of expected bloom, from poisonberry (flowering at 3 A.M.) to Silene Noctiflore (flowering at 9 P.M.), and set in an appropriately floriated neo-classical manner, is performed in a world première by the Philadelphia Orchestra, Eugene Ormandy conductor, with John de Lancie, first oboist of the orchestra, who commissioned the work, as soloist.

2 APRIL 1961

Wallingford RIEGGER, American composer of extraordinary independence of spirit and broadness of outlook, whose creative catalogue ranged from pragmatic studies in the simplest possible forms and idioms (most of them published under a variety of common-sounding pseudonyms) to sharply dissonant atonal pieces of experimental but immediately effective works, dies in New York at the age of 75, after an emergency operation for a clot on the brain as the result of head injuries sustained after he tripped on a leash of one of two quarreling dogs which he tried to separate and fell on the pavement near his home as he went out for a luncheon appointment with Otto Luening.

4 APRIL 1961

Tenth Symphony by Darius MILHAUD, in four movements, Décidé, Expressif, Fantasque, Emporté, conceived in Milhaud's characteristic style of sharp contrasts, formal cohesion, and harmonic bitonality, with resilient rhythms animating the fast episodes, is performed for the first time by the Portland, Oregon, Symphony Orchestra, as a commissioned work for the centennial of the State of Oregon.

5 APRIL 1961

Len LYE demonstrates at the Museum of Modern Art in New York his tangible motion sculptures creating their own musical compositions through incidental collisions of rods and rings and music-box flanges attached to them.

11 APRIL 1961

Revelation in the Courthouse Park, scenic extravaganza by Harry PARTCH, after The Bacchae of Euripides (in which a horde of nymphomaniacal Bacchantes kill and dismember the King of Thebes for trying to suppress their orgiastic cult), in a theatrical setting featuring folk singers, dancers, tumblers, drum girls, and an assortment of exotic instruments producing non-tempered scales and Greek modes and musique concrète on a tape recorder, is staged at the University of Illinois, Urbana, during its Festival of Contemporary Arts.

12 APRIL 1961

For the first time a song is sung in outer space, as Yuri GAGARIN, 27-year-old Soviet cosmonaut, sings the patriotic air by Shostakovich, "My homeland hears, my homeland knows where in the skies her son soars on," to voice his elation as gravity gradually returns to his weightless body and his spaceship Vostok, decelerated by retro-rockets, begins its parabolic descent over Central Africa a few minutes before landing in a fallow plowed field of the collective farm, Lenin's Way, near the city of Engels, some 400 miles southeast of Moscow, after the completion of the first circumterrestrial manned flight.

## 13 APRIL 1961

*Intolleranza 1960,* "scenic action" in two parts, political opera-oratorio by the 37-year-old Italian modernist Luigi NONO, to texts by Eluard, Mayakovsky, Brecht, and other revolutionary poets integrated into a realistically allegorical continuity of nightmarishly unconnected tableaux, in which a refugee is dodecaphonically tortured by four choruses electronically transmitted from the four points of the compass, and a magnificently irrelevant ballet in a mythical "Dummyland" culminates in the atomic explosion of a polydodecaphonic chord, is produced during the course of the XXIV International Festival of Contemporary Music in Venice, amid protests in the audience and shouted mutual insults, as a Neo-Fascist group "Ordine Nuovo" stages a demonstration, showering from a gallery typewritten copies of an anti-dodecaphonic manifesto, proclaiming that "the only thing that is missing in this season of festivals, is Music," refusing to believe that "this confusion of sound and dissonances called dodecaphony represents even a minimal musical manifestation," declaring that "in it there is no concept of hierarchy, the fulcrum around which the principles are formed that have made traditional music an imperishable art" and concluding with the assertion that dodecaphony is "only a distribution of notes contrasting with one another and demonstrating what happens when democracy is carried into the field of music."

## 20 APRIL 1961

*Symphonic Prelude* by Walter PISTON, designed in four musical "facets" contrasted by tempo, density of motion and mood, but united by a basic tonal center F, is performed for the first time by the Cleveland Orchestra, George Szell conducting.

## 22 APRIL 1961

Belgium issues a 6-franc postage stamp honoring the famous Belgian violinist Henri Vieuxtemps (1820–1881) and 2-franc postage stamp honoring the Belgian organist and song composer Willem de Mol (1846–1874).

## 24 APRIL 1961

*Jeux Vénitiens,* symphonic suite by the 48-year-old Polish composer Witold LUTOSLAWSKI, written in a complex polyphonic idiom subordinated to an interrelated system of thematic subjects according to a *sui generis* serial procedure, including aleatory episodes within a predetermined duration, is performed for the first time in Venice by the Cracow Symphony Orchestra.

## 27 APRIL 1961

In the course of the Second Inter-American Music Festival in Washington, Howard Hanson conducts the Eastman School Philharmonic in the first performances of two American works: *Fourteenth Symphony* in four movements by Henry COWELL and *Give Me the Splendid Silent Sun* for baritone and orchestra by Roy HARRIS, to the words of Walt Whitman.

30 APRIL 1961

Two world premières are given in the course of the Second Inter-American Music Festival in Washington, D.C.:

*Symphony in Four Parts (Overture, Hymn, Ostinato, Toccata)* by the Cuban-born Californian composer Aurelio de la VEGA and the grandiose *Cantata para América Mágica* for dramatic soprano and percussion orchestra of 53 instruments to ancient pre-Columbian texts by the Argentinian composer Alberto GINASTERA, in six divisions, invoking the magical powers of the dawn, love, warfare, phantasmagoria, agony and prophecy.

30 APRIL 1961

In the course of the Second Inter-American Music Festival in Washington, the Orquesta Sinfónica Nacional de Mexico gives the first performances of two symphonic works: *Lyric* by the Canadian vanguardist Harry SOMERS and *Third Symphony*, in four movements, by the Mexican composer Blas GALINDO.

1 MAY 1961

At a concert of works by Edgar VARÈSE in New York, his electronic scores *Déserts* and *Poème électronique* are performed, as well as a new version of *Ecuatorial* for men's chorus and orchestra, originally conceived in 1934.

1 MAY 1961

*Forest Song*, ballet by the Ukrainian composer Herman ZHUKOVSKY, on the subject of Soviet youth working on the virgin soil of intellect and emotion, abounding in mellifluous melodies and rich gingerbread harmonies and quickened by stimulating dance rhythms, is produced in Moscow during a festival of Ukrainian music.

5 MAY 1961

Jean-Michel DAMASE, 33-year-old French composer conducts in Bordeaux the world première of his lyric comedy *Colombe*, to a libretto by Anouilh, dealing with an undeflowered flower girl named Colombe who marries into a middle-class family, then becomes an actress and is successively seduced by the director, by an actor, by a poet, and finally by her husband's half-brother, but is forgiven when she agrees to renounce the theater and return to her florist's stand.

7 MAY 1961

*Tkalci*, opera in two acts by the Czech composer Vít NEJEDLÝ, after Gerhard Hauptmann's drama *Die Weber*, dealing with the desperate sabotage action of German weavers, who destroy not only the factory of their oppressive employer but also his private house, set to music in an expressive melodramatic vein, is posthumously performed for the first time in Plzeň.

## 15 MAY 1961

*Krakatit,* opera in two parts by the Czech composer Václav KASLÍK, after a novelette of Karel Čapek wherein the inventor of a powerful explosive Krakatit has a vivid hallucination that a group of anarchists forces him to use his invention to destroy society, and upon awakening becomes a militant pacifist, set to music in an explosively dynamic score including electronic sound, is produced in Ostrava.

## 18 MAY 1961

The Chopin Express, operating between Vienna and Warsaw, is inaugurated by the Austrian Federal Railways, leaving Vienna at 10 P.M. and arriving in Warsaw the next day at 11:09 A.M.

## 19 MAY 1961

*Lancelot,* two-act opera by the 25-year-old Czech composer Luboš FIŠER, to a libretto from the Arthurian legend dealing with a knight in love with a queen, is produced in Prague.

## 20 MAY 1961

*Silas Marner,* opera in three acts by the 34-year-old South African composer John JOUBERT after the novel of that name by George Eliot, dealing with an unjustly maligned village weaver who is vindicated through industry, prosperity, and love for a foundling, set to music in a triadic tonal idiom spiced with prudential non-corrosive dissonances, is produced at the South African College of Music in Cape Town.

## 20 MAY 1961

*Elegie für junge Liebende,* opera in three acts by the 34-year-old German composer Hans Werner HENZE, to a libretto (originally in English) by W. H. Auden and Chester Kallman, dealing with an egocentric old poet who sends the younger of his two mistresses and her lover to their deaths in an expected snowstorm, in the Alps in 1910, calculated to provide the needed catalytic impulse for the completion of his literary masterpiece, an "elegy for young lovers," the score making use of a variety of expressive vocal resources, from whispers to screams, is performed for the first time in Schwetzingen. (The opera was first performed in English in Glyndebourne on 13 July 1961 under the original title *Elegy for Young Lovers*)

## 25 MAY 1961

*Rapsodie Cartésienne,* orchestral rhapsody by the 61-year-old French composer Henry BARRAUD, written according to putative principles of Descartes, is performed for the first time in Paris.

## 25 MAY 1961

*Il Mercante di Venezia,* grand opera in three acts by Mario CASTELNUOVO-TEDESCO, the winning work in an international competition sponsored by the

Italian manufacturer of the bitter-sweet apéritif Campari, greatly condensed from Shakespeare's play and equisyllabically translated by the composer into Italian (so that the opera can be performed in English or Italian without rhythmic readjustments) and supplemented by Shakespeare's sonnet "O! Never say that I was false of heart" but with Shylock's forced conversion to Christianity omitted (being Jewish, Castelnuovo-Tedesco himself was compelled to leave Italy in 1939 when Mussolini espoused Hitler's antisemitic policy), the music soaring rhapsodically in the grandest Puccinian manner and the melodious vocal line immersed in luxuriant but never unduly dissonant harmonies, with but a single instance of explicit modernity when a dodecaphonic chord is erected to illustrate the wrong guesses of two pretenders to Portia's hand (the chord is resolved into the purest C major when the lucky Bassanio guesses right), is performed for the first time at the Maggio Musicale in Florence, where the composer's ancestors were bankers at the time when Shylock was a usurer in Venice.

### 31 MAY 1961

Radio Warsaw broadcasts the first performance of *Tren pamięci ofiar Hiroszimy* (*Lament in Memory of the Victims of Hiroshima*) by the 27-year-old Polish composer Krzysztof PENDERECKI, scored for 24 violins, 10 violas, 10 cellos and 8 double-basses, in graphic notation indicating special effects, such as the highest possible note, arpeggios on strings below the bridge, tapping, rapping, rasping, rattling, scraping and snapping at the body of the instruments, with the duration of individual measures marked by the actual time, from 4 to 30 seconds each, comprising sections of stochastic playing in a directed aleatory procedure, and calculated to give a distant impression of the atomic annihilation of the Japanese town of Hiroshima on 6 August 1945, with a simulacrum of human outcries of disembodied anguish and unsynchronized heartbeats of disarticulated infantiloquy in a tremor of microsonic formication in quarter-tones, concluding with a massive tonal cloud of gray matter, encompassing two octavefuls of icositetraphonic harmony.

### 3 JUNE 1961

*The Right Hand of a Great Master*, opera by the 57-year-old Georgian composer Shalva MSHVELIDZE, to a libretto from the time of the internecine strife in the 11th century for the possession of Georgia, wherein the young Georgian king engages a captive architect to build a temple on the confluence of the Aragva and the Kura rivers, and upon finding out that he has seduced his favorite concubine, orders his right hand to be cut off, driving both him and her to suicide, is produced in Tbilisi.

### 5 JUNE 1961

*Concerto* for mouth harmonica and orchestra by Heitor VILLA-LOBOS, written in 1955, in three contrasting movements replete with humid Brazilian melo-rhythms and containing a tropically luxuriant cadenza, is performed posthumously for the first time during a Music Festival in Cartágena, Colombia, conducted by Guillermo Espinosa, with John Sebastian, the virtuoso harmonica player to whom the work is dedicated, a soloist.

### 5 JUNE 1961

In a deliberate hoax aimed at gullible listeners and uncritical music critics, the British Broadcasting Corporation presents a *Mobile for Tape and Percussion* by a non-existent 22-year-old Polish composer Piotr ZAK, consisting of a montage of random noises and other débris of *Musique concrète* gathered around the studio.

The British Broadcasting Corporation policy of giving the musical avant-garde a hearing needs no justification, but there are bound to be occasional lapses: Piotr Zak's *Mobile* for electronic tape and two partially improvising percussion players, broadcast twice last night, sounded like one of them. The composer's refusal to publish a score suggests that he considers a consciously analytic approach a waste of the listener's time. It was certainly difficult to grasp more than the music's broad outlines, partly because of the high proportion of unpitched sounds and partly because of their extreme diversity. Without some idea of what could be relevant, it is not easy to say what is not. (*The Times*, London, 6 June 1961)

### 7 JUNE 1961

On his 50th birthday, Franz REIZENSTEIN, German-born English subject, plays in London the solo part in the first performance of his *Second Piano Concerto*, in three movements, written in a neo-romantic vein marked with diversified lyrico-dramatic episodes setting the tone of melancholy exhilaration.

### 9 JUNE 1961

*The Greek Passion* for voices and orchestra, last work by Bohuslav MARTINU, after the novel by the Greek writer Nikos Kazantzakis, *Christ Recrucified*, in which a bearded shepherd, acting Christ in a passion play in a Greek village about 1900 A.D., identifies himself so completely with his role that he begins to preach unpopular sermons attacking capitalism and imperialism and is slain by a villager impersonating Judas, set to music embodying elements of Greek folksongs and Byzantine liturgical chants, is brought out posthumously at the Zürich Opera, under the direction of Paul Sacher on whose estate in Switzerland Martinu completed the work on 15 January 1959, shortly before his death.

### 11 JUNE 1961

The 35th annual Festival of the International Society for Contemporary Music opens in Vienna with a program dedicated to the works of Anton von WEBERN:

*Cantata, Das Augenlicht*, op. 26, written in 1935, scored for mixed chorus and chamber orchestra, including a saxophone, xylophone, celesta, harp and mandolin, based on a 12-tone radix with predominantly small intervals, spelling the name B-A-C-H in its exposition, undodecaphonically harmonized in quartal formations superimposed on thematic major sevenths and their concomitant minor ninths; *First Cantata*, op. 29, for soprano solo, mixed chorus and orchestra, in three parts, written in 1939, based on a symmetrical 12-tone row composed of two 6-note tropes, of which the second constitutes a melodically inverted cancrizans, with the text of the third part referring to the transfiguration of the Three Graces represented by a fugue in the form of a Scherzo with variations; Webern's orchestral arrangement of Bach's *Ricercata* (the second fugue of the *Musikalisher Opfer* written for Frederick the Great); Bach's motet *Singet dem Herrn*, in four sections with a parallel instrumental accompaniment; and Webern's *Second Cantata*, op. 31, his last completed work, containing a complex four-part canon derived from a dodecaphonic radix.

### 12 JUNE 1961

The 35th Festival of the International Society for Contemporary Music in Vienna presents a special concert in a program comprising a *Rondino giocoso* for string orchestra by the Viennese composer Theodor BERGER, Mozart's *Violin Concerto* in G major, PROKOFIEV's *Second Violin Concerto* and MAHLER's *First Symphony*.

### 13 JUNE 1961

At the third concert of the 35th Festival of the International Society for Contemporary Music in Vienna, the following program is given:

*Musik* for 22 solo string instruments by the Swiss composer Jacques WILDBERGER (a world première); *Sonata* for piano, five wind instruments, timpani and strings by the Czech composer Václav DOBIÁŠ, written in a harmonious neo-baroque style; *Variationen* for 40 instruments by Michael GIELEN of Austria, with its theme represented by a tone row *in nuce*, followed by twelve variations governed by an arithmetical progression in a serial arrangement of instrumental groupings; and the eloquently sonorous *Arcana* by the grand maître of new music Edgar VARÈSE, consistently dissonant in its polyphonic fabric, with the exception of two bars of C major before the end inserted to create the sense of shattering discordance.

### 14 JUNE 1961

*Forma Ferritonans*, symphonic poem by the Swedish modernist Karl-Birger BLOMDAHL, written on commission from the Oxeloesund Steel Corporation in Sweden to celebrate the opening of its new manufacturing plant, illustrated by a progression beginning softly in the bass to symbolize the presence of unprobed iron ore in the bowels of the earth, and rising to a thundering "ferritonans" climax, picturing the rolling sheets of manufactured metal, is performed for the first time in Oxeloesund.

### 15 JUNE 1961

At the fourth concert of the 35th annual Festival of the International Society for Contemporary Music in Vienna, the following program of vocal and instrumental music is given:

Four *a cappella* choruses by the serialistic West German composer Winfried ZILLIG, derived from a dodecaphonic series, subjected to a rigorous canonic treatment; *Serenata* for chamber orchestra by Vittorio FELLEGARA of Italy, in one neo-baroque movement, set in unaltered 3/8 time; *Wymiary Czasu i Ciszy* by the 27-year-old Polish experimenter Krzysztof PENDERECKI, scored for a wordless and toneless 40-part chorus, singing, whispering, whistling (glissando), and fluttertonguing on the voiceless gutturals, sibilants and labials (e.g. G B P K T) arranged in artfully contrived canonic configurations, wherein the "dimensions of time and silence" of the title are measured in precisely indicated durations, the entire piece lasting exactly 8 minutes and 40 seconds; *3 Lieder* by the 31-year-old Icelander Fjölnir STEFANSSON, with each song built on a symmetrically constructed dodecaphonic radix, and transpositions limited to the tritone; *Monody for Corpus Christi* by the 26-year-old British composer Harrison BIRTWISTLE, to the text from 16th-century English church songs, for soprano, flute, violin, and horn; *O, O, O, O, That Shakespeherian Rag* (the title being a line from T. S. Eliot's poem *The Waste Land*), scored for mixed chorus and a jazz combo, by the American composer Salvatore MARTIRANO, to four excerpts from Shakespeare, with words unnaturally syllabilized and abnormally articulated to cause the disjected members of the poetic line to form adventitious verbalities.

## 16 JUNE 1961

In the course of the 35th Festival of the International Society for Contemporary Music in Vienna, the world première is given of *Die Jakobsleiter*, unfinished oratorio by Arnold SCHOENBERG to his own theologically mystical text, derived from the biblical story of Jacob's dream of a celestial ladder, placing unclean souls of rationalists, skeptics and cynics at the bottom of the ladder, and geniuses at the top, with ascending and descending traffic maintained by the Archangel Gabriel busily reincarnating skeptics into believers and vice versa, the composition of which, begun in 1915, continued fragmentarily throughout 35 years almost until Schoenberg's death, the germinal musical idea already adumbrating the 12-tone method (the basic row being the sum of two hexachords: D, C-sharp, E, F, G, A-flat, plus C, E-flat, B, B-flat, F-sharp and A, the first group being used in different rhythms and registers), set in score according to Schoenberg's sketches and subsequent elucidations by Winfried Zillig, with the application of stereophonic "music in space," in accordance with the suggestion made by Schoenberg in a note written in English in 1944: "Today, October 1944, the problem of the *Fern-Orchester* and *Fern-Chöre* would best be resolved by being played behind the scene, by soundproof materials inaudible at the stage, but by microphones distributed so as to appear at different places of the hall," and a previous note written in German in 1921: "Chorus and soloists, at first chiefly on the platform, then gradually joined by the choruses stationed with the offstage orchestras, so that in the end the music streams from all sides of the hall."

## 17 JUNE 1961

At the sixth concert of the 35th Festival of the International Society for Contemporary Music in Vienna, the following works are performed:

*Felder* for flute, vibraphone, tubular chimes, piano and a large assortment of percussion instruments by the Norwegian composer Björn Wilho HALLBERG, the "fields" of the title referring to units of the dimension of time during which each player is aleatorically independent, with the application of numerous special effects, such as the toneless clapping of the flute keys; *Calligraphy* for piano by the Japanese composer Keyiro Sato, calculated to express in a complex serialistic design the "pure vitality" of the music, comparable to the perfection of Zen-Buddhist calligraphy, attaining in the final stretto the intensity and internal concentration of the exalted state "kihaku"; *Haiku Settings* for voice and piano by the American composer Mel Powell, to English tristychs from Japanese originals consisting of 5—7—5 syllables each, to be sung with head-tones changing to falsetto; *Canzone da sonare* for piano and percussion by the Japanese composer Shin-ichi Matsushita, written with the application of aleatory concepts, in which each player is free to select any thematic fragments within a strict time limit, in a manner corresponding to the technique of Japanese brush painting; *Relazioni fragili* for cembalo and chamber orchestra by the Austrian composer Friedrich Cerha, in four parts, devised according to a complex serial concept, in which all elements of music are ordered and organized in their interdependent actions, with two women's voices treated as instruments and producing reverberations in the orchestra that change their secondary sexual characteristics to male sonorities; and *Composizione 3* for 12 instruments by the Italian composer Egisto Macchi, an essay in tone color, opening with an "extended zone of inconceivable pianissimo" and making use of quarter-tones.

## 18 JUNE 1961

The 35th Festival of the International Society for Contemporary Music in Vienna continues with the following program:

Three works by Anton von Webern: *Passacaglia*, op. 1, *Variationen* for orchestra, op. 30, and *6 Stücke* for orchestra, op. 6; *Metamorphosen* for 23 solo string players by Richard Strauss, written by him during the last days of the fall of Germany, as a mournful testament of an 80-year-old German master of romantic music; *Second Piano Concerto* by the German-born Israeli composer Josef Tal, in one tripartite movement, based on a traditional modal cantillation of Jeremiah's lament, developed according to serial principles; and the world première of *Von der Liebe*, lyric fantasy for voice and orchestra by Gottfried von Einem, consisting of four chromatically inflected songs about love with correspondingly romantic instrumental interludes.

## 19 JUNE 1961

At the 35th Festival of the International Society for Contemporary Music in Vienna, the following works are performed:

*Tre Pezzi* for cello and orchestra, *Fantasia, Capriccio* and *Epilogue* by the Hungarian-born British-naturalized composer of atonally inflected music, Mátyás Seiber, who perished in an automobile accident in South Africa on 24 September 1960; *Monosonata* by the autodidact experimenter in the ultimate complexities of the musical language within humanly performable limits, 32-year-old Boguslaw Schäffer of Poland, written for six string quartets subdivided into three uneven groups of one, two and three each, the whole work based on a single melodico-harmonic matrix, consisting of 8 different notes and 7 different intervals, with the contrapuntal and harmonic materials built from units from a single note to twice twelve notes, while other dimensions and parameters parallel these radices; *Strophes* by the 34-year-old Italian composer Franco Donatoni, empirically developed from an organic serial concept, with instrumental complexes built on the principle of the labyrinth the intersections of which constitute a matrix of unpredictable topographic events compounded of tone-clusters of various degrees of spissitude; *Sequences* for violin and four orchestral groups by the 42-year-old Polish composer living in Vienna, Roman HAUBENSTOCK-RAMATI, constructed according to the concept of a two-dimensional continuum of contrasting qualities—perpendicularity and linearity, staticism and mobility—in completely emancipated dissonant counterpoint; and *Chronochromie* for orchestra by Olivier MESSIAEN, making thematic use of song patterns of French, Swedish, Japanese and Mexican birds and of the rustling noises of waterfalls in the French Alps, with 32 different divisions of time (*chronos* of the title) and corresponding diversities of color (*chromos* of the title) forming a chronochromic hypostasy.

### 20 JUNE 1961

The 35th annual Festival of the International Society for Contemporary Music in Vienna concludes with the performance of three works by Béla BARTÓK: *Dance Suite, Violin Concerto* and *Concerto for Orchestra.*

### 22 JUNE 1961

At the Holland Festival in Amsterdam, Otto KLEMPERER, 76-year-old German conductor, leads the Concertgebouw Orchestra in the world première of his newly composed symphony in two movements, with an ending in which the *Marseillaise* is irrelevantly projected against a variation of an original theme, creating an element of surprise in polytonal counterpoint.

### 24 JUNE 1961

*Gothic Symphony* by the 85-year-old English composer Havergal BRIAN, in four movements, the last of which is an enormously protracted Te Deum, and the second movement a funeral march, written for a huge orchestra requiring a choir of 8 flutes (including a bass flute), 11 clarinets of various sizes (including a contrabass clarinet), 8 instruments of the oboe family (including the oboe d'amore and heckelphone), 16 kettledrums, a thunder machine and other noisemakers, 2 separate brass orchestras, 4 large choruses, a children's chorus and vocal soloists, is performed for the first time in Westminster, 42 years after the composition of the work.

### 30 JUNE 1961

Lee de FOREST, Iowa-born "Father of Radio" (as the title of his autobiography proclaimed), the Aladdin of the Audion, the magical lamp which he invented in 1906, which made radio possible by the addition of an essential third element, the grid, to the anode and the cathode of a vacuum tube; who courted a lady by closed-circuit radio (he married her, but the marriage was annulled shortly afterwards; his subsequent wives were a suffragist, a concert singer, and a motion picture actress), and who on 3 April 1909 engineered the first broadcast of a human voice when he installed two microphones along the footlights of the stage at the Metropolitan Opera House in New York and transmitted the singing of Enrico Caruso in *Cavalleria Rusticana* to a receiver in his home, dies in Hollywood whose flowering owed so much to his inventions in the field of the sound motion pictures and television, at the age of eighty-seven.

You have debased my child . . . You have made him a laughingstock of intelligence . . . a stench in the nostrils of the gods of the ionosphere . . . (From Lee de Forest's letter to the National Association of Broadcasters on the 40th anniversary of the Audion tube, 1946)

### 12 JULY 1961

Irving CONN (real name Cohn), piano player who in 1922 set to music the fascinatingly self-contradictory verse, *Yes, We Have No Bananas,* which Frank Silver wrote down after talking to a Greek fruit-vendor at Lynnbrook, Long Island, and which became the great hit of the 1920's (the first four notes of the song are identical with Handel's *Halleluja* from *Messiah,* but the similarity was in all probability coincidental), dies at Hudson, New York, at the age of sixty-three.

### 20 JULY 1961

*Lavinia,* opéra-bouffe by Henry BARRAUD, to a modern story about a Neapolitan fruit-vendor who names his newly-born daughter Lavinia, and when a local journalist points out that Lavinia was the wife of Aeneas, ignorant neighbors decide that the child was the fruit of an illegitimate affair of the vendor's wife with Aeneas, leading to all kinds of amusing contretemps, with an appropriately light but sophisticated musical score, is performed for the first time in the course of the summer festival at Aix-en-Provence.

### 23 JULY 1961

Grace Bumbry, "die schwarze Venus," 24-year-old American Negro mezzo-soprano, sings the role of Venus in *Tannhäuser* at the opening of the sacrosanct Wagner Festival in Bayreuth, the first black woman to appear in a Wagner opera, directed by Wagner's grandson Wieland Wagner and appearing not as an ample-bodied symbol of medievalistic sensuality, but as a magical presence clad in gold-black attire and standing immobile with outspread arms in the foreground of the stage.

### 3 AUGUST 1961

John CAGE conducts at the International Week of Today's Music in Montreal, Canada, the first performance of his *Atlas Eclipticalis* notated so that each part occupies space equal to a time at least twice as slow as clock time, with loudness being proportional to the size of notes on paper, the score being the product of chance operations by the placing of transparent templates on the pages of an astronomical atlas and inscribing the positions of stars.

### 16 AUGUST 1961

*Szimfónia* by Zoltán KODÁLY, his first symphony, completed in May 1961 at the age of 78, with a dedication to the memory of Arturo Toscanini in a line from a psalm " . . . is etenim saepenumero me adhortatus est . . ." (for indeed Toscanini often encouraged Kodály and voluntarily played his music), in three movements, *Allegro, Andante moderato* and *Vivo,* the outer movements in unobstructed C major in a virile binary march time, the inner movement a set of variations on an ancient quintuple-metered pentatonic Magyar chant melismatically situated in the proximity of G-sharp minor, is performed for the first time at the Lucerne Festival for which it was written, in the presence of the composer and his 20-year-old bride.

### 16 AUGUST 1961

*Das Bergwerk zu Falun,* opera by the 57-year-old German composer Rudolf WAGNER-RÉGENY, after a story by Hugo von Hofmannsthal painting in dark undertones the doom-laden progress of a death-obsessed collier, saturated with atonal forebodings, with occasional tonal relief brought about by rustic rhythms, is performed for the first time at the Salzburg Festival.

### 17 AUGUST 1961

*C'est la guerre,* opera in one act by the Hungarian composer Emil PETROVICS, to the verisimilitudinous story of a Hungarian deserter given refuge by a friend in Budapest in 1944, who is betrayed to the Nazis by her landlady avenging the loss of her two sons in battle, and is executed with his host whose wife, who has in the meantime fallen in love with him, defenestrates herself as the Nazi officer observes in French, "C'est la guerre," set to music in expressionistically dissonant harmonies replete with dramatic bitonalities, is performed for the first time in concert form on the Budapest Radio. (The first stage performance took place in Budapest on 11 March 1962)

### 19 AUGUST 1961

*Nausicaa,* opera by the Australamerican composeress Peggy GLANVILLE-HICKS, to a libretto by Robert Graves from his book *Homer's Daughter,* advancing the frivolous notion that the epic *Odyssey* was created not by Homer but by his daughter, set to music in homophonic pseudo-Grecian modalities, ending in a sudden explosion of declarative C major, with soloists singing in English and the commentating chorus in Greek, receives its world première in Athens, in the Herodes Atticus amphitheater built in 161 A.D., situated on the southern slope of the Acropolis.

### 23 AUGUST 1961

*Lembitu,* opera in two acts by the 47-year-old Estonian composer Villem KAPP, relating the defeat administered to the crusading German Knights by the Estonians in the 12th century, is produced in Tallin.

### 5 SEPTEMBER 1961

The government of Rumania issues a 3-lei postage stamp to honor Georges ENESCO on the occasion of the Enesco Festival in Bucharest, and showing Enesco playing the violin and the initial bars of his *Third Violin Sonata.*

## 6 SEPTEMBER 1961

*Double Concerto* for harpsichord, piano and two chamber orchestras by Elliott CARTER, antiphonally constructed so that the two ensembles are mutually exclusive (except that each has a French horn), and are further musically separated by coopting different sets of preferred intervals, metronomic speeds and polyrhythmic schemes (the harpsichord group cultivates harsh dissonances and polyrhythmic combinations of 4 against 7 temporal units while the piano ensemble favors lighter dissonances and clearer consonances as well as less complex polyrhythms, viz. 5 against 3), the mutual exclusivity leading to complementality, synchronization, syncretism, synthesis and ultimately esthetic fusion, the whole continuous work subdivided into seven linked movements and forming in the process one of the most complex and yet most self-consistent works of modern music in a non-dodecaphonic though mainly atonal matrix, is performed for the first time in the course of the 8th Congress at the International Society for Musicology in New York.

Craft: What composition by an American-born composer has most attracted you to date?

Stravinsky: Elliott Carter's *Double Concerto*. But analysis as little explains a masterpiece or calls it into being as an ontological proof explains or causes the existence of God. There, the word is out. A masterpiece, and by an American composer. (From a colloquy between Robert Craft and Igor Stravinsky in *Musical America*, New York, June 1962)

## 17 SEPTEMBER 1961

In the course of the First Music Festival of Israel (inaugurated on 26 August 1961), an open-air concert is presented in the amphitheater of Caesarea, built by Herod in 12 B.C., and dug up from the sands in 1959, in a program of instrumental music, with Pablo CASALS playing a Bach sonata for viola da gamba.

## 18 SEPTEMBER 1961

*Blood Moon,* opera by the 48-year-old American composer Norman DELLO JOIO, to a libretto dealing with the famed octoroon actress Adah Menken who prospered in New Orleans and New York at the time of the Civil War until her favorite lover discovered the $12\frac{1}{2}$% of denigrating Negro blood in her veins, set to music within the framework of Civil War tonality, varnished with a pandiatonic patina, is performed for the first time in San Francisco.

## 20 SEPTEMBER 1961

To mark the sesquicentennial year of the birth of Franz LISZT, the Hungarian Post Office issues a series of six perforate and six imperforate postage stamps in his honor.

(The German Democratic Republic issues a set of four Liszt stamps on 19 October 1961; Austria issued one Liszt stamp at 3 schillings on 20 October 1961, and Russia issued a 4-kopeck Liszt stamp on 31 October 1961)

## 20 SEPTEMBER 1961

On the occasion of the centennial of the birth of the Australian-born prima donna Nellie MELBA, the Australian government issues a postage stamp in her honor.

## 24 SEPTEMBER 1961

An architectonically utilitarian and ostentatiously non-baroque building of the Deutsche Oper, constructed according to the modern findings of the science of acoustics, is officially opened on Bismarckstrasse in West Berlin to take the place of the renowned Städtische Oper, destroyed by aerial bombardment but restored in its original site on Unter den Linden in East Berlin.

## 25 SEPTEMBER 1961

*Alkmene,* opera by the 36-year-old German composer Giselher KLEBE, dodecaphonically dealing with Zeus who assumes the likeness of Amphitryon and materializes in his wife's bedroom to claim his marital right by Olympian proxy, is performed for the first time at the newly built Deutsche Oper in West Berlin.

## 28 SEPTEMBER 1961

*Scherzo* for piano and orchestra, an early work by Béla BARTÓK, written by him at the age of 23, and consisting of an introductory *Adagio* and a typically Hungarian *Allegro vivace,* with the influx of a considerable amount of rational dissonance, is performed for the first time in Budapest as part of the gradual process of Bartók's canonization in his native country.

## 30 SEPTEMBER 1961

*A Man's Destiny,* music drama by the 52-year-old Soviet composer Ivan DZERZHINSKY, dealing with a Soviet prisoner of war who escapes from Nazi captivity in 1943 and returns to his native village only to find that his wife and daughters were killed in an air raid but saves himself from suicidal despair by adopting an orphan boy, set to music in an illustratively realistic idiom (the Nazis are characterized by quotations from Kurt Weill's *Dreigroschenoper*), employing the Soviet accordion Bayan for realistic effect, is produced at the Bolshoi Theater in Moscow.

## 1 OCTOBER 1961

The world première is given in Leningrad of the *Twelfth Symphony* by Dmitri SHOSTAKOVICH, dedicated to the memory of Lenin, and subtitled *1917,* a triumphant sequel to his *Eleventh Symphony* (which commemorates the idealistically romantic and therefore unsuccessful revolution of 1905), encompassing in four movements the historic milestones of Lenin's life:

(1) *Revolutionary Petrograd (Allegro),* reflecting in opulent triadic harmonies the period from the abortive Russian revolution of 1905 to Lenin's arrival in Petrograd in

April 1917 (2) *Razliv* (*Adagio*), descriptive of Lenin's hiding place in a Finnish retreat under an assumed name in the summer of 1917 when his arrest was ordered by the Russian Provisional Government (3) *The Aurora* (*Allegro*), glorifying the cruiser *Aurora* which fired the first shots of the Soviet Revolution (4) *Dawn of Humanity* (*Allegretto*), portraying in eloquent sonorities and impassioned colors the Soviet victory of 7 November 1917.

### 7 OCTOBER 1961

*Fifteenth Symphony* by Henry COWELL, subtitled *Thesis*, is performed for the first time at Bowling Green, Kentucky.

### 12 OCTOBER 1961

*The Wings of the Dove*, opera in two acts by Douglas MOORE, after a psychological novel by Henry James wherein a British girl persuades her fiancé to ingratiate himself with a dying American heiress and induce her to bequeath her fortune to him, ending with an empty victory as the plan succeeds but their love is dead, set to a deliberately infra-modern, melodious and harmonious score, is performed for the first time in New York.

### 16 OCTOBER 1961

*Do Russians Want War?* a song by Eduard KOLMANOVSKY, to the bitterly ironical words of the prime Soviet poet Eugeny Evtushenko, destined to become the most popular anti-war song, widely used at Soviet festivals and official celebrations, is broadcast for the first time on Radio Moscow. (Date obtained by the author from Kolmanovsky)

### 17 OCTOBER 1961

*Third Symphony* by the 53-year-old Yugoslav composer Milan RISTIĆ, in four movements tracing chronologically the four stages of his life—youth, political struggle, Nazi occupation and liberation in a new socialist world—written in a neo-classical manner unified by a twelve-tone serial row without forsaking the essential tonality, is performed for the first time in Belgrade.

### 21 OCTOBER 1961

Peter RONNEFELD, 26-year-old German composer, conducts at the Festival of the Music Theater of the 20th Century in Düsseldorf the world première of his four-act opera *Die Ameise*, wherein a voice teacher formicatingly enamored of his pupil Formica, strangles her in the middle of a coloratura aria, in his remorse cultivates a queen ant in his prison cell (hence the title *The Ant*, or in Latin, *Formica*) whom he teaches to sing, is released for good behavior and tries to get her into a ballet show dealing with the life in an anthill, collapses and dies when his incautious impresario steps on her, set to music in an eclectically dissonant style with such realistic episodes as a colloquy of convicts reminiscing about their sexual experiences and a male chorus lecturing in vulgar Latin on the mating modus operandi of ants.

21 OCTOBER 1961

The annual Donaueschingen Festival of Contemporary Music opens with the following program:

*Monades III* for chamber orchestra (world première) by Jacques GUYONNET (Switzerland); *Permutazioni* for wind quintet by Mátyás SEIBER (1905–1960) of Hungary and England; *Entelechie I* for 5 instrumental groups (world première) by Peter SCHAT (Holland); *Credentials or think, think lucky,* for voice and instruments (world première) by Roman HAUBENSTOCK-RAMATI (Poland); *Structures* for 2 pianos (vol. 2; world première) by Pierre BOULEZ (France)

22 OCTOBER 1961

The second concert of the two-day Donaueschingen Festival of Contemporary Music presents the following program:

*Atmospheres* for orchestra (world première) by György LIGETI (Hungary); *Epifanie* for orchestra (world première) by Luciano BERIO (Italy); *Contrasts* for orchestra (world première) by Gunther SCHULLER; *Variations* for orchestra by SCHOENBERG.

23 OCTOBER 1961

*Torquilla,* oratorio by the Danish composer Niels Viggo BENTZON, to texts from Nevil Shute's tale of the atomic war between China and Russia ultimately engulfing the world in lethal cobalt radiation, is performed for the first time in Aarhus, Denmark.

26 OCTOBER 1961

*Eighth Symphony* by David DIAMOND (completed on 15 November 1960, on the day after the 60th birthday of Aaron Copland, to whom the work is dedicated), in two movements: (1) *Moderato-Adagio-Allegro vivo,* neurotically agitated and languidly anguished (2) *Theme, Variations* and *Double Fugue,* derived from a 12-tone radix, is performed for the first time by the New York Philharmonic, Leonard Bernstein conducting.

26 OCTOBER 1961

*The Crucible,* opera by Robert WARD after Arthur Miller's play, dealing with the hysterical witch-hunt in Salem, Massachusetts, in 1692, set to music in a traditional operatic style, is produced in New York.

5 NOVEMBER 1961

*The Flower of Remembrance,* opera in three acts by the Albanian composer Kristo KONO, dealing with an Albanian youth fighting the oppressive Turkish rule in 1907, erroneously reported to have been torn apart by wild wolves, the news causing his faithful beloved to lose her reason thus saving her from a repugnant forced marriage, with a happy dénouement vouchsafed when she receives from him a symbolic flower of remembrance, instantly curing her amnesia, while her obtrusive suitor is frozen to death in the mountains, is produced in Tirana.

## 11 NOVEMBER 1961

Two short Flemish operas, *Jonker Lichthart* by Jef van HOOF, written in 1928 for a radio performance, and *St. Anthony's Great Temptation* by Louis de MEESTER, a modernistic interpretation of the horror-laden painting of Hieronymous Bosch, with electronic jazz symbolizing the agony of seduction, are performed in the Flemish language in Antwerp.

## 13 NOVEMBER 1961

At the invitation of President John F. Kennedy, Pablo CASALS takes part in a concert of chamber music in the White House, given in honor of Governor Luis Muñoz of Puerto Rico, the adoptive residence of Casals, his first appearance in the White House since he played for President Theodore Roosevelt in 1904.

## 14 NOVEMBER 1961

*Concerto accelerato* for violin and orchestra by the Serbian composer Dragutin GOSTUSKI in which the tempo is accelerated from *Largo* to *Allegretto* to *Presto* through its three atonally oriented movements, is performed for the first time in Belgrade.

## 20 NOVEMBER 1961

*Gráficos* for guitar and chamber orchestra by the 47-year-old Gibraltar-born Spanish composer Maurice OHANA, in three movements, based on melorhythms of the Andalusian *Cante hondo,* is performed for the first time in London.

## 25 NOVEMBER 1961

Vittorio GIANNINI conducts the Chicago Lyric Opera Company in the world première of his opera *The Harvest,* dealing with a somber tale of multilateral lust on an American farm circa 1900, wherein two brothers covet the third brother's young bride, who is ultimately strangled by their blind father when she rejects his groping advances.

## 20 DECEMBER 1961

*The Golden Bird,* operatic fairy tale by the Bulgarian composer Marin GOLEMINOV, is produced in Sofia.

## 21 DECEMBER 1961

*Covek je vidik bez kraja* (A Man Is a Horizon Without End), cantata by the Yugoslav composer Rudolf BRUČI, to texts from letters written by doomed inmates of Nazi concentration camps, set to music in anguished chromatic convolutions, culminating in a heroic finale in optimistic major keys, proclaiming the ultimate faith in freedom, is performed for the first time in Belgrade.

25 DECEMBER 1961

*Not Love Alone,* opera in three acts by the 29-year-old Soviet composer Rodion SHCHEDRIN, is performed for the first time at the Bolshoi Theater in Moscow.

## ᘀ *1962* ᘁ

9 JANUARY 1962

*Seventh Symphony,* subtitled *Les Contrastes,* by the French composer Jean RIVIER, written in a cultivated style of Gallic romanticism, is performed for the first time in Paris.

10 JANUARY 1962

*Orchestral Abstractions,* symphonic suite by the 33-year-old American composer William SYDEMAN, in three movements written in a dramatically atonal idiom, is performed for the first time in New York.

11 JANUARY 1962

*Princesse Pauline,* opera-masque by the French composer Henri TOMASI, dealing with the amours of Napoleon's sister, is performed for the first time in concert form in Paris. (The first stage performance took place at the Opéra-Comique in Paris, on 21 June 1962.)

14 JANUARY 1962

*Fifth Symphony* by the Swedish composer Gunnar BUCHT is performed for the first time in Stockholm.

17 JANUARY 1962

*Eighth Symphony* by Roy HARRIS, commissioned by the San Francisco Symphony Orchestra on the occasion of its 50th anniversary, purporting to represent in stately modalities the five principal stages of the life of St. Francis, patron saint of San Francisco—Childhood and Youth, Renunciation of Mundane Joys, The Building of the Chapel with His Own Hands, Pantheistic Joy, Ecstasy after Premonition of Death—and concluding on a pandiatonically amplified C-major chord, is performed for the first time by the San Francisco Symphony Orchestra, Enrique Jordá conducting.

## 19 JANUARY 1962

*Violin Concerto* by the 76-year-old Austrian composer and music scholar Egon WELLESZ set in four classically designed movements, written in a post-romantic atonal idiom, is performed for the first time in Vienna.

## 20 JANUARY 1962

*Fourth Symphony* by Dmitri SHOSTAKOVICH, in three movements, *Allegretto poco moderato, Moderato con moto* and *Largo,* his most uncompromisingly dissonant work containing some remarkable canonic writing, which he composed in 1936 but withdrew after an unfavorable impression it produced on Soviet musicians during tentative rehearsals in Leningrad, is performed in public for the first time after an interval of 25 years in Moscow.

## 25 JANUARY 1962

*Bold Island,* symphonic suite by Howard HANSON, inspired by Bold Island off the coast of Maine, where Hanson spends his summers, is performed for the first time by the Cleveland Symphony Orchestra.

## 26 JANUARY 1962

*Seventh Symphony* by the 36-year-old American composer David DIAMOND, in three movements (1) *Andante,* serving as a prelude to *Allegro ma non troppo* (2) *Andante* (3) *Allegro moderato,* accelerating through a succession of prodding indications of *Più mosso,* and reaching double quick time at the end, written in a tense dynamic idiom marked by anxious chromatic torques within a broadly diatonic framework, but invariably observing a classically designed cyclic thematic structure, is performed for the first time by the Philadelphia Orchestra, Eugene Ormandy conducting. (Diamond's *Eighth Symphony* was performed earlier, on 26 October 1961, by the New York Philharmonic)

## 29 JANUARY 1962

Fritz KREISLER, one of the greatest violinists of the 20th century and composer of perennial favorites (*Liebesleid, Liebesfreud, Caprice Viennois*), as well as a number of original pieces which he ascribed to Vivaldi, Couperin, and several lesser classics, dies in New York City of a heart ailment four days before his 87th birthday.

## 5 FEBRUARY 1962

Jacques IBERT, French composer, consummate master of impressionistic tone painting, whose *Escales,* depicting in lavish instrumental colors the sun-drenched ports of call in the Mediterranean basin, became a minor master-piece of modern music, dies in his native Paris at the age of seventy-one.

## 5 FEBRUARY 1962

*Kragujevac,* symphonic poem with chorus by the Serbian composer Dušan KOSTIĆ to the text of the poem *Bloody Fairy Tale* by a contemporary poetess dealing with the shooting by the Nazis of Serbian schoolboys in Kragujevac in occupied Yugoslavia in September 1941, with the application of modified dodecaphonic motives to express horror and anxiety, is performed for the first time in Belgrade.

### 14 FEBRUARY 1962

*Chôro* for violoncello and orchestra by Camargo GUARNIERI, written in the typical manner of Brazilian folksong rhapsody, with some astringent but always tonal harmonies, is performed for the first time in New York.

### 15 FEBRUARY 1962

*Rehearsal Call,* opera buffa in three acts by Vittorio GIANNINI, retailing the vicissitudes of three boys and three girls trying to find menial operatic jobs, such as ushers, in New York, with bits from Wagner and atonal arias illustrating their aspirations, is performed for the first time at the Juilliard School of Music in New York.

### 16 FEBRUARY 1962

*Twelfth Symphony* by Darius MILHAUD, subtitled *Rural,* is performed for the first time by the San Francisco Orchestra, Enrique Jordá conducting, on the Davis campus of the University of California, by which it was commissioned.

### 17 FEBRUARY 1962

Bruno WALTER, German conductor who excelled in exemplary interpretations of the classics, devoted champion of the music of Mahler, dies at the age of eighty-five in Beverly Hills, California, where he settled after being forced to leave the darkness of Nazified Europe.

### 19 FEBRUARY 1962

*Un amour électronique,* opéra-bouffe by the 56-year-old Hungarian-born French composer Joseph KOSMA, in which a lady is enamored of a homuncular electronic robot who collapses when her husband asks him to square the circle, is produced in Paris.

### 22 FEBRUARY 1962

A month and six days after his 90th birthday, Henri BÜSSER, prolific French composer who remained faithful to the melodious and harmonious legacy of his teacher Gounod through all the vicissitudes of the ultra-modern era in music, conducts the first performance of his *Concerto* for trumpet and string orchestra specially written for a nonagenarian concert in his honor at the Paris Conservatory.

### 23 FEBRUARY 1962

*A Sermon, A Narrative* and *A Prayer,* triptych by Igor STRAVINSKY to texts from St. Paul, The Acts of the Apostles, and a poem by Thomas Dekker, completed on 31 January 1962, scored for contralto, tenor, speaker, chorus and a medium-size orchestra including three gongs, piano and harp, written in a hermetic serial idiom, with a dodecaphonic radix germinating melodic, contrapuntal and harmonic integumenta, is performed for the first time by the Basel Chamber Orchestra, Paul Sacher (who commissioned the work) conducting.

## 26 FEBRUARY 1962

*Eighteenth Symphony* by the 86-year-old English composer Havergal BRIAN, in three movements, with two outer movements in marching time flanking a lyric middle movement, organically connected but thematically diversified, composed in 1961, receives its first performance at the opening concert of the St. Pancras Arts Festival in London, by the Polyphonia Symphony Orchestra, Bryan Fairfax conducting.

## 26 FEBRUARY 1962

Czechoslovakia issues two 10-heller postage stamps to mark the centennial of the birth of Czech composer and conductor Karel KOVAŘOVIC and the centennial of the death of Czech composer František ŠKROUP.

## 1 MARCH 1962

*The Alcestiad*, opera by the American composeress Louise TALMA to a libretto by Thornton Wilder, dealing with the ancient myth of a Greek woman whose devotion to Apollo won her release from Hades, is performed for the first time anywhere in Frankfurt, Germany.

## 6 MARCH 1962

*Pervy Kosmichesky (The First Cosmic Ship)*, symphonic poem by the 57-year-old Ukrainian composer Gleb TARANOV, commemorating in optimistically triadic harmonies the first orbital flight of the Soviet Sputnik launched in 1957, and using the exact rhythmic formula of the Sputnik beep as a motto, is performed for the first time in Kiev.

## 9 MARCH 1962

*Fantasy and Variations* for piano and orchestra by Norman DELLO JOIO, with six variations on a thematic four-note cell, is performed for the first time by the Cincinnati Symphony Orchestra.

## 11 MARCH 1962

*Symphony* by 29-year-old Sergei SLONIMSKY, Soviet nephew of Nicolas Slonimsky, in three movements: *Lento, Vivace bruscamente, Largo-Allegro,* written in a melodically tense, rhythmically intense, and contrapuntally tensile idiom, ending with a magisterial triple fugue, is performed for the first time by the Leningrad Philharmonic, Arvid Jansons conducting.

*The Singing Skeleton,* one-act opera by the 50-year-old Japanese composer Osamu SHIMIZU, based on a harrowing horror tale of old Japan, is performed for the first time in Osaka.

20 MARCH 1962

*Violin Concerto* by the Israeli composer Paul BEN-HAIM (who changed his real name Frankenburger to the Hebrew patronymic Ben-Haim which means Son of Life, when he fled to Palestine in 1933 from his native Munich darkened by the Hitlerian cloud) in three movements, *Allegro, Andante affettuoso, Cadenza e Finale,* set in the focal tonality of B major, but without an explicit key signature, neo-classical in form, but embodying occasional scintillae of Judaic cantillation in the solo violin part, is performed for the first time in Tel Aviv by Zvi Zeitlin, for whom the work was written, accompanied by the Israel Philharmonic.

22 MARCH 1962

*The Golem,* opera in four acts by Abraham ELLSTEIN, to a libretto derived from the famous Jewish legend of a rabbi who by the magic of alchemy creates a destructive human creature, set to music in a Wagneromantic idiom seasoned with Judaic melismas, is produced by the New York City Opera, as a commission of the Ford Foundation.

23 MARCH 1962

*Symphony (1962)* by the 47-year-old American composer Irving FINE, in three movements, *Intrada,* suggestive of an ordered choreographic action, *Capriccio,* a hedonistic scherzo, and *Ode,* a dithyrambic fantasia with an epilogue, is performed for the first time by the Boston Symphony Orchestra, Charles Munch conducting.

26 MARCH 1962

A set of four airmail stamps is issued by Fidel Castro's government in Cuba to celebrate the opening of the Cuban international broadcasting service, containing the initial notes of the *Hymn of the 26th of July,* the Cuban national anthem commemorating the first act of Castro's victorious insurgence on 26 July 1953.

31 MARCH 1962

*Meditationen über die Totenmaske von Amedeo Modigliani,* cantata by the Moscow-born Swiss composer Wladimir VOGEL, aurally limning the visual art and the dramatic career of the Italian modernist painter Modigliani, from his humble beginnings to his death in Paris at the threshold of success and the suicide of his beloved model Jeanne, the musical scheme based on a 12-tone row and developed by a serial distribution of characteristic intervals (large atonal spans symbolizing the Greco-like elongation of Modigliani's portraits), is performed for the first time by the Radio Svizzera Italiana in Lugano.

## 31 MARCH 1962

*Den gefundne Ofelia*, electronic opera by the Danish composer Jorgen PLAETNER treating Orphelia and Hamlet in modern psychoanalytic terms, is performed for the first time in Copenhagen.

## 3 APRIL 1962

Manolis KALOMIRIS, Greek composer of Wagneromantic operas on ancient and modern Greek subjects, teacher of a generation of young Greek composers, dies in Athens at the age of seventy-eight.

## 5 APRIL 1962

*The Communist Manifesto*, oratorio by the Prague-born composer Erwin SCHULHOFF, written in 1932, to the classical text of Karl Marx, beginning with the celebrated sentence: "A ghost is walking across Europe, the ghost of Communism," set in declarative triadic harmonies, and ending with the appeal "Proletarians of all nations, unite!" in a virile Dorian mode, is performed posthumously in Prague, from a manuscript copy discovered in Russia.

## 5 APRIL 1962

*Il buon soldato Svejk*, opera in three acts by the 45-year-old Italian composer Guido TURCHI, to a libretto from the famous novel of Jaroslav Hašek, dealing with a marvelously passive Czech soldier Schweik whose demoralizing indifference exercises a salutary influence on the heterogeneous Austro-Hungarian Army in World War I of which he was a reluctant member, set to music in an aggressively atonal idiom and corrosively discordant harmonies and vitalized by pseudo-popular rhythmic patterns, is produced at the Teatro alla Scala in Milan.

## 6 APRIL 1962

*Cyrnos*, opera in three acts by the 50-year-old French composer André AMELLER, dealing with the political struggle in 16th-century Corsica (Cyrnos is its Greek name) during which a Corsican soldier of fortune slays his wife who threatens to expose his scheme to deliver Corsica to the French, set to music in a melodramatically explosive style dulcified by a cerulean Mediterranean couleur locale, is produced in Nancy.

## 6 APRIL 1962

*Transfigurations* for piano and orchestra, a serial composition based on the principle of permutations, by the Yugoslav composer Milko KELEMEN, is performed for the first time by the Hamburg Radio.

### 9 APRIL 1962

*Consort* by John VINCENT, in three movements, scored for piano and strings in a neo-Elizabethan style in copulative antiphony with superimposed harmonic acridities and rhythmic asymmetries, is performed for the first time by the Seattle Symphony Orchestra, Milton Katims conducting.

### 12 APRIL 1962

*Il Tamburo di panno*, one-act opera by the Italian composer Orazio FIUME, modeled after the classical Japanese genre of *No*, is produced in Rome.

### 16 APRIL 1962

In the course of the Fifth International Festival of Music and Drama at Osaka, Japan, three Japanese composers conduct their own works:

Symphonic suite *The Silk Road* by the 38-year-old Ikuma DAN, in four movements, *Prelude, Pastorale, Dance* and *March*, a baroque treatment of old Japanese modes; *Nirvana Symphony* by the 33-year-old Toshiro MAYUZUMI, in six movements for orchestra, chorus with orchestrally imitated campanology, ending with a Zen hymn; and *Dark Mirror*, subtitled *Young Orpheus on a Theme of the Atomic Bomb*, by Yori-Aki MATSUDAIRA, wherein a Japanese youth disfigured by radiation burns in Hiroshima meets a spiritual prostitute who gives him a magic mirror showing his face as it was before the atomic holocaust and who decides to have plastic surgery performed by a phantom surgeon from the land of the dead which may either cure or kill him.

### 16 APRIL 1962

*Polymorphie* by the 28-year-old Polish modernist Krzysztof PENDERECKI, scored for 48 string instruments in pluralistic counterpoint, in copulative synchronization and maximal harmonic combinatoriality, making use of diatonic, pandiatonic, pentatonic, chromatic and icositetraphonic progressions, is performed for the first time in Hamburg.

### 22 APRIL 1962

*Majstori su prvi ljudi* (*Masters Are First Among Men*), a musical comedy by the Serbian composer Dušan KOSTIĆ, dealing with a modern Figaro manipulating the love affairs of his employers, is produced in Belgrade.

### 10 MAY 1962

*In seinem Garten liebt Don Perlimplin Belison*, comic opera by the 54-year-old German composer Wolfgang FORTNER, his third on the subject drawn from García Lorca's *Bodas de Sangre* (the first two were *Der Wald* and *Die Bluthochzeit*) wherein the minifutuent husband of an unusually mobile donna performs a self-induced schizophrenia, so that half the time he is a magnificently potent youth, his real self ultimately killing his fantasy ego in a semi-homicidal demisuicide, set to music in an appropriately divisive serial idiom, is performed for the first time at the opening of the Music Festival at Schwetzingen, Germany.

## 10 MAY 1962

*Legend of Comrade Tito,* cantata by the Yugoslav composer Boris PAPANDOPULO, tracing in heroic verse and music the patriotic struggle against the Nazis of Yugoslav partisans under the command of President Tito of Yugoslavia, is performed for the first time in Zagreb.

## 15 MAY 1962

*Sonority Canon for Four Solo Flutes Accompanied by 33 Flutes on Tape* by Otto LUENING, the flutiest piece since Pan blew his syrinx, is performed for the first time at a concert of contemporary flute music at Columbia University in New York.

## 15 MAY 1962

*Chorikon,* symphonic tetraptych by the 38-year-old Greek composer Arghyris KOUNADIS, in four serially organized movements, artfully incorporating the modalities of popular Greek songs, is performed for the first time by the Berlin Philharmonic, with the composer's teacher, Wolfgang Fortner, conducting.

## 15 MAY 1962

*Vision of Poets,* a cantata for soloists, chorus and orchestra by the 38-year-old Manchurian-born American composer Benjamin LEES, in ten sections to words by Walt Whitman, is performed for the first time as a commissioned work at the dedication concert of the World's Fair Festival in Seattle, by the Seattle Symphony Orchestra, under the direction of Milton Katims.

## 18 MAY 1962

*Vzkriesenie (Resurrection),* opera in three acts by the 50-year-old Slovak composer Jan CIKKER, after Tolstoy's moralistic novel centered on the sufferings of a debauched orphan girl in 1886, set to music in an expressionistically atonal idiom to reflect the psychic contradictions of her reformed seducer, is produced in Prague.

## 19 MAY 1962

*Concerto for Violoncello and Orchestra* in C major by Joseph HAYDN, in three cyclic movements, *Moderato, Adagio, Allegro di Molto,* long regarded as lost, is performed for the first time during the Spring Festival in Prague, from an 18th-century copy of the original, discovered in the archives of the National Museum of Prague.

## 24 MAY 1962

*Srbija,* cantata by the 45-year-old Serbian composer Rudolf BRUČI, patriotically extolling the valor of Serbia, set to music in a proclamatory triadic idiom, with occasional dodecaphonic arabesques in wordless solos and choral vocalises, is performed for the first time in Belgrade.

### 25 MAY 1962

The Coventry Cathedral Festival opens in the newly constructed church replacing the old historic shrine destroyed in the Nazi air attack of 1941, with the first performance of *The Beatitudes*, religious cantata by Sir Arthur BLISS to texts drawn from the Bible and from the writings of John Donne and other English poets.

### 25 MAY 1962

The first International Anton von Webern Festival opens at the University of Washington in Seattle with the first performance from the manuscript, recently discovered by Hans Moldenhauer, of the symphonic poem by Anton von WEBERN *Im Sommerwind*, written by him in 1904 at the age of nineteen.

### 29 MAY 1962

*King Priam*, opera in three acts by the 57-year-old English composer Michael TIPPETT, to his own libretto relating in colloquial prose the vicissitudes of the Trojan ruler whose son Paris abducted Helen, precipitating the Homeric wars, set to music in a frugal monodic idiom accompanied by a skeletonized instrumental group and percussion supporting the tonal spinal vertebrae while the guts of string instruments are often conspicuously absent, is performed for the first time in Coventry, England.

### 30 MAY 1962

At the consecration of the functionally modernized Cathedral of Coventry replacing the old Gothic edifice destroyed by the Germans from the air during World War II, Benjamin BRITTEN conducts the first performance of his *War Requiem* to the texts of the Latin *Missa pro defunctis* and nine poems by the young British poet Wilfred Owen killed a week before the Armistice of 1918, the musical setting anchored in the medieval diabolus in musica, the tritone, symbolizing the horror and the pity of war (Benjamin Britten himself was a conscientious objector during World War II), but remaining firmly within the framework of modulatory tonality.

### 31 MAY 1962

The 36th Festival of the International Society for Contemporary Music opens in London with the following program:

World première of *Espejismos* (from *espejo*, mirror) by the nearly 38-year-old Argentine composer Carlos VEERHOFF, based on a dodecaphonic motto of two mutually exclusive whole-tone scales, one ascending, the other descending; STRAVINSKY's cantata *A Sermon, a Narrative and a Prayer* (first performed in Basel on 23 February 1962), to the texts from St. Paul's Letter to the Romans (VIII, 24-25), his Letter to the Hebrews (XI, 1; XII, 29), Acts of the Apostles, VI-VII, and a prayer written by the playwright

*1136*

Thomas Dekker, culminating in a choral Alleluia, the thematic material being serially constructed with a dodecaphonic motto related to rhythmic values; *Antifone* for orchestra by Hans Werner HENZE, the antiphonal elements including not only thematic responses but the contrasts of tempi, dynamic tensions, articulation, and timbre, and even the seating arrangement, while the dodecaphonic series results from cumulation rather than exposition of melodic and harmonic elements; *Cujus Legibus Rotantur Poli* by the 37-year-old Swiss composer Klaus HUBER, to the Latin text from Aurelius Augustinus, wherein the central idea of the divine laws governing the terrestrial rotation around the polar axis is represented by spiral intervallic structures; and Arnold SCHOENBERG's *Variations for Orchestra*, op. 31.

2 JUNE 1962

To mark the centennial year of the birth of Gustave CHARPENTIER, whose *Louise* was a landmark of French operatic realism, the French Post Office issues a commemorative stamp of 30 centimes with an overprint of additional 10 centimes.

2 JUNE 1962

In the course of the 36th Festival of the International Society for Contemporary Music in London, a concert of British music is given comprising the following works:

*Partita* for string quartet by John EXTON, 29-year-old disciple of Luigi Dallapiccola, written in 1957 in a free dodecaphonic idiom and consisting of seven movements in variation form; *The Queen's Epicedium* by PURCELL, written for the funeral of Queen Anne in 1694, multilaterally "realized" by Benjamin Britten; *The Deluge*, cantata for soprano, contralto and chamber ensemble by the Berlin-born 29-year-old naturalized English composer Alexander GOEHR to texts from the notes of Leonardo da Vinci dealing with the Flood; *Boyhood's End*, cantata with alternating sections of recitative and arioso, by Michael TIPPETT, composed in 1943 to texts from W. H. Hudson's autobiography reminiscing about adolescing in Argentina; *String Quartet* by Peter Maxwell DAVIES, 27-year-old member of the avant-garde, composed in 1961 according to a *sui generis* serial method, in one movement comprising four demarcatable sections; *Canticle No. 3* by Benjamin BRITTEN for voice and piano with interludes for French horn with piano, composed in 1954 to Edith Sitwell's *Canticle of the Rose* subtitled *The Raids, 1940, Night and Dawn*, wherein the inexorability of war, the ineluctability of night, and the indeterminacy of dawn are conjured up by spasmodic contractions of thematic intervals in variation forms.

3 JUNE 1962

*Blackwood & Co.*, burlesque opera by the Swiss composer Armin SCHIBLER, in which a bed manufacturing company of New York City awards a free bed de luxe to a young honeymoon couple as part of a publicity campaign ("We stand behind every bed we sell"), with other companies advertising Sweetsex and Pepsi-Cola in neon signs next to Merry's Hotel, is produced in Zürich.

3 JUNE 1962

The following program for chamber orchestra is presented in London in the course of the 36th Festival of the International Society for Contemporary Music:

*Lyric Variations* by Reuben Radica, 31-year-old Yugoslav composer, for string orchestra, in which the thematic notes and rhythmic values are subjected to integral organization; *Two Epigrams* for chorus a cappella by the 32-year-old Sicilian-born composer Girolamo Arrigo, composed in 1957, to texts relating to Michelangelo's statue *La Notte*; *Suoni estremi* for speaker and string quartet by the 47-year-old Swiss composer Philipp Eichenwald, to a text from the report of a landslide by an illiterate Sicilian woman illustrating the human reaction to catastrophic extremities (hence the title, Extreme Sounds); *Propos d'Alain*, for baritone and 12 instruments by Goffredo Petrassi to words from the writings of the 12th-century French theologian Alain, the musical setting derived from postulated micro-structures as non-integral serial parts; and Darius Milhaud's pioneer jazz ballet *La Création du Monde* of 1922 for 18 instruments. (*Constellation III* for organ and magnetic tape by the Swedish composer Bengt Hambraeus listed in the printed program book of the Festival was not performed due to technical difficulties)

### 4 JUNE 1962

In the course of the 36th Festival of the International Society for Contemporary Music in London the following program of orchestral music is presented:

*Helian di Trakl*, by the 39-year-old Italian composer Camillo Togni, a cycle of five songs for voice and chamber orchestra to poems of the German poet Georg Trakl, first performed in a version with piano in Darmstadt on 1 June 1955, and derived from a fundamental dodecaphonic series; *Mobiles* for violin and orchestra by the 37-year-old French composer Maurice Jarre, first performed at the Strasbourg Music Festival in 1961, consisting of six elements which the soloist is free to play in any order of ten prescribed permutations while the accompaniment remains an invariant, analogously with structural mobile arrangements of Alexander Calder; *Erotics*, a set of six songs for soprano and orchestra by the 33-year-old Polish composer Tadeusz Baird, first performed at the Warsaw Autumn Music Festival on 16 September 1961; *Double Concerto* for harpsichord, piano and two chamber orchestras by Elliott Carter, written in 1961, according to an enormously complex and relentlessly logical scheme in which each of the two antiphonal instrumental groups is multilaterally organized in respect to intervals, rhythms, and tempi, without reference to a basic tone row or a common theme, in seven interconnected movements (first performed in New York on 6 September 1961); and Benjamin Britten's *Violin Concerto*, composed in America in 1939.

### 6 JUNE 1962

The 36th Festival of the International Society for Contemporary Music in London concludes with a chamber music concert comprising the following works:

*Moving Pulses* for three voices and percussion by the 35-year-old Formosan composer Kejiro Esaki, with three vocalists moving freely, on stage, under the stage and among the audience, written in the intonations of *No* in no known or unknown language; *Constructions* for two pianos by the 27-year-old Dutch composer Jan van Vlijmen, totally serialized in pitch, meter and rhythm; *Haggadah* (*Legend*) for viola, percussion and piano by the Budapest-born Israeli composer Ödön Partos, in five short movements of oriental thematic provenance systematized in a dodecaphonic series; *Trio* for violin, cello and piano in three movements by Leopold Spinner, 56-year-old Galician Pole resident in England since 1938; *Formantes* for two pianos by the Spanish composer Cristóbal HALFFTER, nephew of Rodolfo and Ernesto HALFFTER, in eight sections, of which the inner six are played in any order, in any form, and in any tempo, while the pitch, durations of notes and dynamics are fixed; and *Trio* for flute, guitar and percussion by the 36-year-old Polish composer Wlodzimierz KOTOŃSKI.

## 8 JUNE 1962

*Alea* for 8 loudspeakers, 8 tape recordings and 8 composers, compiled at random by the Danish composer Jorgen PLAETNER, is performed for the first time in Copenhagen.

## 10 JUNE 1962

*Cabeza de Vaca*, cantata by George ANTHEIL, his last major work, completed in 1957, to the text by Allan Dowling, drawn largely from the reports of the Spanish explorer Alvar Nuñez Cabeza de Vaca to King Charles V beginning with 17 June 1527 after his shipwreck in the Gulf of Mexico, his spiritual and medicinal help to Indians, adjudged by a papal encyclical to possess redeemable souls, set to music in a triadic harmony amplified at tense moments into tertian pyramids and dramatized by dissonant pandiatonicism, with topical and historical references made in singsong see-sawing from the tonic to the dominant, pentatonic Indian chants, and ecclesiastical hymns (*Dies irae* is plainly alluded to), is presented in a posthumous world première in observance of Whitsuntide on the television network of the Columbia Broadcasting Company.

## 12 JUNE 1962

John IRELAND, English composer of instrumental and vocal pieces rooted in austere Celtic modalities accoutred in impressionistically colored harmonies, dies in Washington, England, at the age of eighty-two.

## 13 JUNE 1962

Eugene GOOSSENS, English composer and conductor, whose expertly fashioned operas and symphonies set a mark of impressionistic modernism in England in the first third of the 20th century, for many years conductor of the Cincinnati Symphony Orchestra and later of the Sidney, Australia, Symphony Orchestra, dies in London at the age of sixty-nine.

## 14 JUNE 1962

*Samsara*, symphonic poem by Toshiro MAYUZUMI, is performed for the first time in Tokyo.

## 14 JUNE 1962

*Noah and the Flood*, biblical spectacle by Igor STRAVINSKY, narrated, mimed, sung, and danced, with literary material taken from the Book of Genesis and a collection of medieval miracle plays of Chester, England, is performed for the first time three days before Stravinsky's 80th birthday at a special television production by the Columbia Broadcasting Company, with Stravinsky himself presented visually as the conductor of the previously recorded and video taped performance and a highly stylized choreography by George Balanchine, Stravinsky's associate in numerous ballets for many years, wherein Noah and his human companions in the Ark are introduced wearing neo-troglodytic two-dimensional expressionless masks and the paired animals are portrayed by artfully artless toys, the basically dodecaphonic musical score exhibiting utmost economy of design and maximalized individuality of instrumental parts, while hymnal choral numbers to Latin texts are set in heterophonically harmonious and diatonically melodious modalities.

Of hundreds of reviews of my New York work *Noah and the Flood*, most of them, like my every opus since 1905, were gratifyingly unfavorable, I found only yours entirely stupid and suppurating with gratuitous malice. The only blight on my 80th birthday is the realization that my age will probably keep me from celebrating the funeral of your senile music columnist. (A cable dispatched by Igor Stravinsky from Hamburg, Germany, and published in the New York *Herald Tribune*, of 24 June 1962)

Stravinsky is a man trapped in his own narrowness and intolerance, so blinded by the praise of sycophants who want to vindicate his joining the twelve-tone camp that he leaps to an instantaneous attack upon everyone who dares to express an independent opinion about his work. . . . As to Noah . . . it was nothing but a slight pièce d'occasion of 20-minute duration embedded in a television medley both silly and artificial, and interrupted by repellent commercials. (Response to Stravinsky's cable by the music critic of the New York *Herald Tribune*, Paul Henry Lang, in the same issue)

### 17 JUNE 1962

On the occasion of Stravinsky's 80th birthday, Ernst KRENEK presents to him a musical offering, inscribed *Carissimo amico sapientissimo magistro*, a two-part vocal canon in Latin, containing 80 words, both words and music ending on C.

### 18 JUNE 1962

*Atlántida*, unfinished "scenic cantata" by Manuel DE FALLA (begun on 29 December 1928 and interrupted on 8 July 1946, four months and a week before his death), to the text from the Catalan poem by Mosé Jacinto Verdaguer describing the salvation of Spain by Hercules who tore it asunder from the continent of Africa to let the flood that submerged the island of Atlantis pass through the Pillars of Hercules into the Mediterranean, and culminating with the voyage of Columbus across the Ocean Sea, combining in the score the elements of a medieval miracle play, a mimodrama for the parts of Hercules and Columbus, and Spanish folklore (Queen Isabella dreams her prophetic dream of the New World to the strains of two folksongs, one Catalan, one from Granada), is performed for the first time, in a version completed by Falla's pupil Ernesto Halffter, at La Scala, Milan, Thomas Schippers conducting.

### 24 JUNE 1962

A fountain in honor of Richard STRAUSS is erected in Munich on the site of the house in which he was born and which was destroyed during air raids of 1943, with scenes from his opera *Salomé* sculptured on the central column.

## 25 JUNE 1962

*Cuba's Daughter,* opera by the 61-year-old Soviet composer Konstantin LISTOV, depicting in realistically romantic terms the heroic life of Angela Alonso, Cuban girl guerrilla, who fought in the ranks of Fidel Castro's insurrectionary forces in 1958, and who gave poison to her beloved to save him from torture after he was captured by the police, is performed for the first time in Voronezh.

A statuesque figure, black locks of hair falling on her shoulders; a handsome, courageous, and at the same time coquettish face; her hands naturally and decisively grasping an automatic rifle . . . (From a description of Angela Alonso's appearance on a Soviet poster, 1961)

It is a great honor for me, a simple soldier of my country, that my life should be the subject of an opera. With the death of my beloved, all dreams of personal happiness were ended for me, but this news from Moscow made me happy once more. I am convinced that the opera will be a tremendous success because I am aware of the enormous talents of the Soviet people and of their sincere love for Cuba. (From Angela Alonso's letter addressed to the Moscow correspondent of the Havana daily newspaper *Revolución*)

## 26 JUNE 1962

*Psalmy Dawida (Psalmus),* cantata by the 28-year-old Polish composer Krzysztof PENDERECKI, to texts from the Psalms of David, based on a neo-Gregorian cantus firmus diversified by atonal protuberances and employing the dramatic effects of shouting and whispering in highly dissonant counterpoint, is performed for the first time in Cracow.

## 27 JUNE 1962

*Ausgerechnet und verspielt,* "Spiel-Oper" for television by Ernst KRENEK, to his own libretto in which a mathematician loses a lot of hard-earned-money using his highly scientific theory of probability at the roulette table, but breaks the bank by playing a series of consecutive numbers taken from the intervals in semitone units in a tone-row selected at random by a humanoid computer, is performed for the first time on television in Vienna.

## 5 JULY 1962

*Five Movements,* suite for orchestra by the 39-year-old American composer Leslie BASSETT, derived from the concept of "pyramid sounds" in which the symmetrical portions in relation to the apex in each movement are thematically and dynamically related, is performed for the first time in Rome.

## 9 JULY 1962

*Heterophonie,* a compound of five successive and/or simultaneous heterophonic symphonic variations on a theme by the Argentinian-born German composer Mauricio KAGEL, is performed for the first time in its third version at the International Summer Festival in Darmstadt. (The world première of the combined Versions I/II was given over the Cologne Radio on 22 May 1962)

## 12 JULY 1962

A 20-pfennig postage stamp honoring Michael PRAETORIUS, German music theorist who died on his 50th birthday on 15 February 1621, with the reproduction of a tuning fork superimposed over three bars of a three-voice motet from his *Musae Sionae* (1614), is issued by West Germany.

## 21 JULY 1962

Robert STOLZ, 81-year-old Austrian composer, conducts at the open-air amphitheater in Bregenz, on Lake Constance, the world première of his 43rd operetta, *Trauminsel*, dealing with a Canadian archeologist infatuated with an Aztec belle, with the score incorporating the explosive sounds of actual fireworks.

## 23 JULY 1962

During the first intercontinental transatlantic telecast relayed by the American artificial satellite Telstar, the 312-voice Mormon Tabernacle Choir transmits its performance of *The Battle Hymn of the Republic* from the foot of Mount Rushmore on which the heads of Washington, Jefferson, Lincoln and Theodore Roosevelt are imposingly hewn from the rock, at noon of local sidereal time (7:00 P.M. Greenwich time) during Telstar's 123rd orbit, and Ferruccio Tagliavini presents an aria from *Tosca* in the open theater of the Baths of Caracalla in Rome at 11:00, local sidereal time (6:00 P.M. Eastern daylight saving time) during Telstar's 124th orbit.

## 24 JULY 1962

The Wagner Festival in Bayreuth opens with a novel production, by Wagner's grandson Wieland WAGNER, of *Tristan und Isolde* wherein King Mark becomes Tristan's father thus intensifying the incestuous element and introducing an Œdipus complex (justified by the archeological discovery of an inscription on the gravestone of a putative counterpart of Tristan as the son of a putative counterpart of King Mark) and Isolde languishes in her *Liebestod* but does not die, with an abstract stage set dominated by an enormous shaft as a phallic symbol.

## 6 AUGUST 1962

On the 17th anniversary of the atomization of Hiroshima, a grand cantata by the Japanese composer Masao OKI to a poem by Sankichi Toge in six movements: *August 6th* (with the atom bomb exploding on a dominant seventh-chord in triple forte), *At the First-Aid Stations, See My Eyes, For an Infant Soul, We Call to You, Take Back the Human* (ending on a C-major chord in triple forte), is performed for the first time in Tokyo.

Everybodies in the world should keep the verses from the bottom of Toge's heart in memory. This is, I believe, the straight-forward approach to make a restate for the continued existence and the well-being of the mankind, to take back the humanity being lost in our days. And this passage can be cut open only by the well-intentioned combination of the people, the honest and frank, innocent of flattering to power and wealth. This grand cantata is a today's art to be made out only by the Japanese. Through the creation and propagation of this work we, the today's Japanese, I believe, can fulfill one of our grave responsibilities for the peace of the mankind. And it is the desire of the Japanese heart in our time of the terror of atomic weapons. (From the introductory note in English in the printed score)

### 9 AUGUST 1962

*Phonologie Symphonique* by the Japanese composer Toshiro MAYUZUMI is performed for the first time in West Berlin.

### 12 AUGUST 1962

*Constantin Palaeologus,* last opera by the Greek composer Manolis KALOMIRIS, dealing with the Emperor of Byzantium whose defeat by the Turks in 1453 marked the end of the Eastern Empire, is produced in Athens, three months after the composer's death.

### 14 AUGUST 1962

The first vocal duet in outer space is heard around the world when Major Andrian Nikolayev and Lieutenant Colonel Pavel Popovich, the "heavenly twins" of the Soviet Cosmos orbiting the earth in tandem in their spaceships Vostok 3 and Vostok 4, establish radio contact and sing the *Astronaut Song* by the Soviet composer Oscar FELTSMAN: "I know, my friends that caravans of rockets/Will hurl us forward from star to star/And that on the dusty pathways of distant planets/Our footprints will leave their mark!"

Comrades Nikolayev and Popovich had more fun than their predecessors Gagarin and Titov. Not only did they maintain communication with Earth, but they could talk to each other and watch each other at work. And as you know, they even gave a sort of improvised concert for the Cosmos and sang a duet with a refrain which suits the occasion perfectly and corresponds to our future plans in the Cosmos. (From a speech by the Soviet Premier Minister Nikita Khrushchev in Moscow, delivered on 18 August 1962)

### 15 AUGUST 1962

The Second Israel Music Festival opens in Jerusalem with a grand spectacle called Folklore of a Nation, presenting the folkloric patterns of various communities of Israel in song and dance, with the participation of immigrants from Yemen, Kurdistan, North Africa, Arabia and India, culminating in an exhibition by the native-born Israelis, the Sabras.

### 19 AUGUST 1962

The Edinburgh Festival of Music and Drama opens with programs of varied fare and performers from all over Europe, featuring a grand presentation of works by Dmitri SHOSTAKOVICH, with the composer in attendance, including his ten symphonies, eight string quartets, cello concerto, violin concerto, cello sonata, piano quintet, songs and his orchestration of MUSSORGSKY's opera *Khovanshchina*, performed by the Belgrade Opera Company.

### 22 AUGUST 1962

The Edinburgh Festival of Music and Drama presents the world première of *Three Songs of Life and Love* by the Italian avant-garde composer Luigi NONO:

(1) *Sul Ponte di Hiroshima* for orchestra, picturing in angry dissonances the atomic annihilation of a man with a guitar standing on a bridge in Hiroshima on 6 August 1945 when the bomb fell (2) an anguished solo for unaccompanied soprano vaulting atonal intervals in the narrative of an Algerian girl tortured by the French colons to secure information (3) a protest against war, set in discordantly pacifistic heterophony.

### 23 AUGUST 1962

Irving FINE, American composer of fine instrumental music exquisitely equilibrated in a modernistic manner with occasional dodecaphonic explorations, dies in Boston of a massive heart attack at the age of forty-seven.

### 31 AUGUST 1962

On the day of the Independence of Trinidad and Tobago, the government of the new nation within the British Commonwealth adopts as their national anthem a song by the Trinidad musician Patrick CASTAGNE, the winner in a competition among 1,150 entries, to his own words declaring the love of their "Islands of the blue Caribbean Sea" where "every race finds an equal place."

### 2 SEPTEMBER 1962

Igor STRAVINSKY conducts, sharing the podium with his constant assistant Robert Craft, in the course of the Second Israel Music Festival in Haifa, a concert of his orchestral music including the *Symphony in Three Movements* of 1945, the *Violin Concerto* of 1931, the *Ode* of 1943, and a symphonic suite from *The Firebird*, in the third revision made in 1945. (He conducted the same program in Jerusalem on 4 September 1962 and in Tel Aviv on 6 September 1962)

### 6 SEPTEMBER 1962

Hanns EISLER, German composer of introspective atonal and dodecaphonic music according to the doctrine of his master Arnold Schoenberg and of optimistically triadic socialistic marches for the Soviet Army and proletarian choruses for East Germany, dies in East Berlin at the age of sixty-four.

### 11 SEPTEMBER 1962

John LENNON, Paul McCARTNEY, George HARRISON and Richard STARKEY ("Ringo Starr"), four young, brash and pert Liverpudlians destined to ascend the empyrean heights of fame, fortune and ubiquitous adulation under the inspired sobriquet THE BEATLES phonemically related to the rhythmic beat and the order of coleoptera, make their first recording together in a hallucinogenic rendering of two vocal quartets, *Love me, do!* and *P.S. I Love You.*

## 20 SEPTEMBER 1962

In the course of the Sixth Music Festival in Warsaw ("Warsaw Autumn") comprising a series of concerts of empiric, experimental, atonal, athematic, gymnosophistical, but invariably autocephalous and aggressively vigesimosecular music, three works by modernistic Polish composers are given for the first time:

*Musica Ipsa* by the 33-year-old composer Boguslaw SCHÄFFER, an instrumental concerto in three parts posing and resolving the problems of progressive variability of thematic material and a novel type of symphonic emotionalism, as opposed to formalized serialism; *Capriccio* for 24 instruments by the 36-year-old Jan KRENZ, subdivided into six groups of players and written in a polythematic succession of phrases and ideas governed by discrete dodecaphonic motives; and *Canon* by the 28-year-old Krzysztof PENDERECKI for orchestra and magnetic tape, scored for 52 string instruments and developed in three layers in canonic imitation among themselves, culminating in a stretto of 208 voices involving the recorded parts, making use of diatonic, pandiatonic, chromatic and icositetraphonic resources. (At other concerts of the Sixth Warsaw Festival the following works by Polish composers were presented: *Riff 62* by Wojciech KILAR, based on a constantly repeated jazzified refrain to characterize the spirit of the modern year 1962; *Variations Without a Theme* by Tadeusz BAIRD, presenting inconstant variants of an asomatous subject; *Concerto for Orchestra* by Grazyna BACEWICZ; and *Aphorisms* by Boleslaw SZABELSKI)

## 23 SEPTEMBER 1962

At the inauguration of Lincoln Center for the Performing Arts in New York City, Leonard BERNSTEIN, conductor and music director of the New York Philharmonic, presents in the new Philharmonic Hall a concert televised by the Columbia Broadcasting System in the following program:

*Gloria* from BEETHOVEN's *Missa Solemnis*; the first performance of the specially commissioned work by Aaron COPLAND, *Connotations for Orchestra*, intended to express "the tension, aspirations, and drama inherent in the world today" set in a *sui generis* dodecaphonic technique, with the basic statement made by four spacious but highly dissonant chords of mutually exclusive groups of three notes, and an agitated rhythmic section in which the notes of the tone row are allowed free repetition, and the first movement of Mahler's *Eighth Symphony*, nicknamed *Symphony of a Thousand*, here performed by about 500 instrumentalists, soloists and choristers, including a children's choir.

## 24 SEPTEMBER 1962

At the second concert given in the Philharmonic Hall in Lincoln Center for the Performing Arts in New York City, the Boston Symphony Orchestra, under the direction of its newly appointed conductor Erich Leinsdorf of

Vienna, presents the world première of *Piano Concerto* by Samuel BARBER, with John Browning as piano soloist, an exuberantly romantic, comprehensively pianistic work set in a centripetally tonal idiom in a peripheral tonal diaspora, with thematic phrases uncoiling in a diachromatic modality cadentially dissolving in triadic formations, in three movements:

(1) *Allegro appassionato*, opening with a somber germinal phrase for piano solo, evolving antiphonally with the orchestra in palpitatingly dramatic exchanges (2) *Canzona*, a meditative adumbration of the old Italian contrapuntal form, with a prominent flute solo, accompanied by the piano playing guitar-like figurations (3) *Allegro molto*, in unremitting 5/8 time, in the manner of a virtuoso toccata.

### 25 SEPTEMBER 1962

At the third concert given in the Philharmonic Hall at Lincoln Center for the Performing Arts in New York City, the first performance of Walter PISTON's *Lincoln Center Festival Overture* is presented by the Philadelphia Orchestra, Eugene Ormandy, conductor, on the same program with Aaron COPLAND's *Lincoln Portrait* with the United States Ambassador to the United Nations, Adlai Stevenson, acting as the narrator reciting Abraham Lincoln's words to the music, the program rounded off by both suites from *Daphnis et Chloé* by RAVEL, and Van Cliburn's playing of RACHMANINOFF's *Third Piano Concerto*.

### 26 SEPTEMBER 1962

After forty-eight years of absence from his native Russia, Igor STRAVINSKY appears in Moscow in a program of his music, conducting the Moscow State Symphony Orchestra in performances of his symphonic *Ode* of 1944, and his ballet suite *Orpheus* of 1947, with his assistant Robert Craft leading *Le Sacre du Printemps*, and Stravinsky concluding the concert with an encore, his arrangement of 1917 of the *Volga Boatmen's Song*.

### 28 SEPTEMBER 1962

At the Philharmonic Hall in Lincoln Center for the Performing Arts in New York the Juilliard School Orchestra presents the first performances of two commissioned works: *Toccata for the Sixth Day* by William BERGSMA, dean of the Juilliard School of Music, and *Song of Orpheus* for cello and orchestra by William SCHUMAN, President of Lincoln Center.

### 30 SEPTEMBER 1962

Leonard Bernstein conducts at Philharmonic Hall in Lincoln Center for the Performing Arts in New York the first Young People's Concert of the season, including the first public performance of *Catacoustical Measures* by Daniel PINKHAM of Boston, originally composed as an acoustical test of the new Philharmonic Hall.

### 3 OCTOBER 1962

*The Master of Boyana*, opera in four acts by the 38-year-old Bulgarian composer Konstantin ILIEV, depicting the legendary story of an anonymous painter of 13th-century frescoes in the church at the village of Boyana near Sofia and his artistic victory over iconographic reactionaries who objected to the realistic interpretation of religious subjects and a concomitant consummation of his love for a chosen mate, set to music in an advanced idiom containing traits of Stravinsky's neo-Grecianism, Prokofiev's stylized Slavism and atonally oriented expressionism of Alban Berg, with unabashed Italian cantilena persisting in the vocal parts, is produced in Sofia.

## 4 OCTOBER 1962

*Eighth Symphony* by William SCHUMAN, President of Lincoln Center in New York, in three movements, the first and second in a slow tempo, and the finale a rapid rhapsodic rondo, written in a tensile polyharmonic idiom, is performed for the first time as a commissioned work by the New York Philharmonic Orchestra, Leonard Bernstein conducting on the same program with a memorial performance of the *Adagio* from *Notturno for Strings and Harp* by Irving FINE.

## 9 OCTOBER 1962

*Fifth Symphony* in C major by the Soviet composer Vissarion SHEBALIN, in the classical four movements, is performed for the first time in Moscow.

## 11 OCTOBER 1962

*The Passion of Jonathan Wade,* opera in three acts by Carlisle FLOYD, to his own libretto dealing with a noble-souled Yankee commander who marries a Southern belle in the post-bellum turmoil of 1866 undismayed by a rude raid of the Ku Klux Klan during their wedding, to a musical score bathed in lyrical melodiousness and set in the traditional sequences of arias, duets, and dramatic interludes in the orchestra, with some nice plantation ballads sung by a mamma named Nicey, is produced by the New York City Opera Company.

## 15 OCTOBER 1962

Leopold STOKOWSKI, eighty years old, but vigorous in his assertive musicianship, presents at Carnegie Hall in New York City the opening concert of his newly organized American Symphony Orchestra.

## 18 OCTOBER 1962

*Concerto* for Wind Quintet and Orchestra by the 49-year-old American composer Alvin ETLER, in three movements, in the style of a modern concerto grosso, is performed for the first time anywhere by the Tokyo Philharmonic with the New York Woodwind Quintet as quintuple soloists.

## 22 OCTOBER 1962

*Bonjour Max Ernst,* surrealistic cantata by the Danish composer Niels Viggo BENTZON is performed for the first time in Aarhus, Denmark, as a tribute to the modern master of abstract art.

## 24 OCTOBER 1962

*0'00''* (zero silence) "to be performed in any way by anyone," composed by John CAGE in Tokyo, as No. 2 after his longer silent work *4'33''*, receives its instantaneous first performance simultaneously with the writing of the first margination of the blank-page manuscript with the following instructions on the title page: "With any interruptions. Fulfilling in whole or part an obligation to others. No two performances to be of the same action, nor may that action be the performance of a 'musical' composition. No attention to be given the situation (electronic, musical, theatrical). In a situation provided with maximum amplification (no feedback), perform a disciplined action." (The title page is followed by three blank pages in the printed copy, retailing at 50 cents)

## 25 OCTOBER 1962

Jacques PERROT, Parisian music hall artist known as "Tête de bois," gives an opening performance at the Olympia in Paris of his *Concerto pour une grande tête et orchestre,* for skull solo accompanied by doublebass, piano, xylophone and 20 violins, the cranial melodic range extending to three and a half octaves in dry weather and only one octave in case of rain, the dynamics gauged by tapping fingers for piano effect and a mallet for *mezzo forte,* a maximum of loudness, the finer nuances depending on the locality, the resonance areas including the parietal and occipital bones, maxilla, mandible, zygomatic arch, eye socket and mental process (bony promontory, forming the chin).

## 25 OCTOBER 1962

*Opéra d'Aran* by Gilbert BÉCAUD, a Parisian crooner nicknamed "Monsieur 100,000 volts" for his high electric potential with young audiences, to a libretto inspired by Robert Flaherty's film of the same name wherein two lovers on a bleak island outpost in the North Sea are forced to sail away in an unseaworthy boat into the ocean after they are charged with a local murder, with a musical score coagulating operatic ideas from Gounod to Puccini, is produced at the composer's own expense, accompanied by a gushing flood of crimson publicity, at the Théâtre des Champs-Elysées in Paris.

## 26 OCTOBER 1962

*Piano Concerto* by Gunther SCHULLER is performed for the first time by the Cincinnati Symphony Orchestra.

## 27 OCTOBER 1962

*L'Opéra de Poussière,* opera in two acts by the French composer Marcel LANDOWSKI, dealing with an ironic fate of an opera composer who kills himself when his fiancée leaves after a series of fruitless attempts to have his opera produced, with the attendant publicity arousing sudden interest in his opera which is produced posthumously with sensational success, is performed for the first time in Avignon, under the composer's direction.

## 2 NOVEMBER 1962

*Albena,* opera in five tableaux by the Bulgarian composer Parashkev KHADZHIEV, to a libretto from the village life in Dobrudja of early 20th-century, based on a true story of an aberrant wife who becomes a passive accomplice in the murder of her husband by her lover, is performed for the first time in Varna. (In real life she was stoned by the villagers, but in the opera she is allowed to depart.)

## 3 NOVEMBER 1962

*Concerto-Rhapsody* for violin and orchestra by Aram KHACHATURIAN (originally named simply *Rhapsody*) is performed for the first time in Moscow, with Leonid Kogan as soloist.

A concerto is music with chandeliers burning bright; a rhapsody is music with chandeliers dimmed (a description Khachaturian used during his meeting with the author in Moscow on 7 December 1962)

## 4 NOVEMBER 1962

*Second Symphony* by the Soviet composer Andrei ESHPAY, conceived in a broadly Russian style with melodic inflections of his own ancestral pentatonicism of the Mongol Mari strain, and developed in an energetically lyrical vein, is performed for the first time in Moscow.

## 8 NOVEMBER 1962

Humphrey SEARLE conducts in Birmingham, England, the first performance of his *Fourth Symphony* in four movements on a monothematic idea of a dodecaphonic nature.

## 9 NOVEMBER 1962

*Hamlet,* Shakespearean opera in three acts by the 53-year-old Russian-born American composer Sergius KAGEN, is performed for the first time in Baltimore.

## 11 NOVEMBER 1962

*The Legend of a Lake,* ballet in three acts by the Bulgarian composer Pantcho VLADIGEROV, to a story of a patriotic Bulgarian damsel who opens the dikes to drown the foe attacking the village perishing herself in the flood, is produced at the Sofia National Opera, under the direction of the composer's son.

## 13 NOVEMBER 1962

*Barcarolla fantastica,* symphonic picture by the 48-year-old Dutch composer Hans HENKEMANS, written in a coloristically impressionistic manner influenced by the style of his teacher Willem Pijper, divisible into five episodes, all in the steady rhythms of 6/8 and 9/8, suggesting the Venetian gondola song, is performed for the first time by the Northern Philharmonic Orchestra in Groningen, Holland, on the occasion of its centennial.

### 26 NOVEMBER 1962

*Synthesis* for strings and percussion by the 40-year-old Greek composer Yorgo SICILIANOS, constructed according to a serial concept in which both melodic components and rhythmic units are coordinated in contrapuntal and harmonic complexes, is performed for the first time in Athens.

### 29 NOVEMBER 1962

*Seventh Symphony* by Jean RIVIER, in three movements, the inner a *Lento malinconico* the outer two, *Allegros,* economically constructed and centered on a single principal motive, is performed for the first time in Paris.

### 30 NOVEMBER 1962

*Ouverture Philharmonique* by Darius MILHAUD is performed for the first time by the New York Philharmonic at its new home in Lincoln Center for the Performing Arts in New York, as a specially commissioned work.

### 4 DECEMBER 1962

*Concerto* for two guitars and orchestra by Mario CASTELNUOVO-TEDESCO is performed for the first time in Toronto.

### 6 DECEMBER 1962

Gunther SCHULLER conducts in New York a concert of music entitled "American Iconoclasts" which includes works by Henry Cowell (*Polyphonica*) Stefan Wolpe, Edgar Varèse, John Cage and Charles Ives, the latter represented by short pieces arranged by Gunther Schuller from undecipherable manuscripts in the Ives collection of the Yale University Library: *Chamber Orchestra Set No. 3* (*At Sea, Luck and Work, Premonitions*) and *Chromatimelodtune* written between 1913 and 1919 and prophetically containing motives of 12 different notes each.

### 8 DECEMBER 1962

Four centuries have passed since the death in Venice of Adrian WILLAERT, master of the secular madrigal, the instrumental ricercar, and the sacred motet, initiator of antiphonal writing for the two symmetrical choirs at San Marco, Venice, where he was *maestro di cappella* from 12 December 1527, teacher of Andrea Gabrielli Zarlino, and many foreign musicians of renown.

### 18 DECEMBER 1962

*Thirteenth Symphony* by Dmitri SHOSTAKOVICH, scored for bass soloist, male voices and orchestra, op. 113, to words by the 29-year-old Soviet poet

Evgenyi Evtushenko, in five movements (1) *Adagio, "Babi Yar"* (2) *Allegretto, "Humor"* (3) *Adagio, "Women"* (4) *Largo, "Fears"* (5) *Allegretto, "Career"* of which the first includes an eloquent remembrance of the fate of thousands of Jews put to death by the Nazis at Babi Yar in Kiev in 1941 and a passionate appeal against anti-Semitism, is performed for the first time in Moscow. (Reacting to criticisms from high Communist quarters pointing out that not Jews alone were killed at Babi Yar, Evtushenko added a few words of the martyrdom of Russian and Ukrainian young men and women, along with the Jews)

20 DECEMBER 1962

*Katerina Ismailova,* a new version of SHOSTAKOVICH's opera *Lady Macbeth of the District of Mzensk,* minus the naturalistic sexual intermezzo in the orchestra, is produced in Moscow.

30 DECEMBER 1962

Emil SIMON, Bessarabia-born 26-year-old Rumanian composer, conducts in Bucharest the world première of his cantata *Partidului (To the Party)* based on a musical anagram HBCA of Bach, and written in a realistically socialistic manner rich in optimistically opulent harmonies as an offering of thanks to the Communist Party "which has given a purpose to our lives and glory to our land."

# ❧ 1963 ❧

4 JANUARY 1963

*Percussion Concerto* by Henry COWELL is performed for the first time by the Pittsburgh Symphony Orchestra.

18 JANUARY 1963

*Ninth Symphony* by Roy HARRIS, "dedicated to the City of Philadelphia as the Cradle of American Democracy," in three movements bearing subtitles from the Constitution of the United States; (1) *Prelude,* "We the People" (2) *Chorale,* "To form a more perfect Union" (3) *Contrapuntal Structures,* "To promote the general welfare," in three sections, concluding on an optimistic bitonal chord of B major over G major, is performed for the first time by the Philadelphia Orchestra, Eugene Ormandy conducting.

18 JANUARY 1963

*Riolama, Ten Places for Piano and Orchestra,* by Ernst BACON is performed for the first time in Syracuse.

23 JANUARY 1963

*Les Jumeaux*, opera in three acts by the Rumanian-born Parisian composer Marcel MIHALOVICI, is performed for the first time in Brunswick, Germany.

25 JANUARY 1963

*Mouvement Symphonique*, subtitled *Bostoniana*, by Jacques IBERT, which constitutes the first movement of a larger work commissioned by the Boston Symphony Orchestra but left unfinished at Ibert's death, is performed for the first time by the Boston Symphony Orchestra, Charles Munch conducting.

25 JANUARY 1963

*Eighth Symphony* by the German master of symphonic modernism Karl Amadeus HARTMANN, in two principal parts, *Cantilena*, with a passionate, penetrating theme, derived from a structure of dispersed tritones, and *Dithyrambe*, motoric and frugally fugal, is performed for the first time in Cologne.

30 JANUARY 1963

Francis POULENC, second youngest of the French Six, "Musicien de la doulce France," as he was once poetically described, whose gift evolved from nihilistic beginnings to pure melodic poetry, and who knew how to combine mundane hedonism with religious contemplation, dies suddenly of a heart attack in Paris at the age of sixty-four.

Like his name, he was both dapper and ungainly. His clothes came from Lanvin but were unpressed; his hands were scrubbed but the fingernails were bitten to the bone . . . His social predilections were for duchesses and policemen . . . He was deeply devout and uncontrollably sensual. (Ned Rorem in *Poulenc—A Memoir*, in *Tempo*, London, Spring 1963)

5 FEBRUARY 1963

*Emancipation Symphony* by the 46-year-old American composer Robert KELLY, written to celebrate the centennial of the Proclamation of Emancipation by Abraham Lincoln, written in an abstract 12-tone dodecaphonic idiom to demonstrate the democratic principles of tonal equality, is performed for the first time, in Washington.

6 FEBRUARY 1963

*Piano Concerto* in three movements by the 35-year-old French composer Jean-Michel DAMASE, written in the manner of Gallic baroque, is performed for the first time in Paris.

8 FEBRUARY 1963

*Violin Concerto* by the 39-year-old American composer Benjamin LEES, born in Manchuria of Russian parents, in three movements of a classical nature, with the contrapuntal and harmonic elements forming a reticle of euphonious dissonance, is performed for the first time by the Boston Symphony Orchestra, Erich Leinsdorf conducting, Henryk Szeryng soloist.

## 9 FEBRUARY 1963

*Requiem* by Dmitri KABALEVSKY, commemorating the supreme sacrifice of the Soviet soldiers and citizens fallen victims to the Fascist aggression in eleven sections similar to the subdivisions of the Russian service for the dead, among them *Eternal Glory, I Shall Not Die, Remember,* and concluding with a prayerfully powerful appeal to the world to renounce war intoned by a children's chorus, is performed for the first time in Moscow.

## 15 FEBRUARY 1963

*Spirit of the Avalanche,* opera by the American composer Alan HOVHANESS, is performed for the first time anywhere in Tokyo.

## 16 FEBRUARY 1963

László LAJTHA, Hungarian composer of nine well-regulated symphonies, some of them revealing a deep melorhythmic sense of authentic Magyar music, dies suddenly of a heart attack in Budapest, at the age of seventy.

## 17 FEBRUARY 1963

*Violin Concerto* by the Czech pioneer of microtonal music Alois HÁBA, composed in 1954 and based on athematic but homeorhythmic motives, exuberantly hendecaphonic and dodecaphonic in its melodic materials and paradoxically classical in form, is performed for the first time in Prague.

## 18 FEBRUARY 1963

*Sinfonia montana,* dodecaphonic symphony with programmatic content by the German composer Jürg BAUR, who was born on Armistice Day in 1918, is performed for the first time in Hagen.

## 22 FEBRUARY 1963

The Delta Chi Fraternity of Wayne State University in Detroit, Michigan, sets the world record for demolishing an upright piano and passing all its *disjecta membra* through a 9-inch hole in 4 minutes 51 seconds. (A group of British firemen in Christchurch, England, smashed 17 pianos on 12 July 1966 in a vain attempt to beat the world record of Wayne University, but their best time was 5 minutes 48 seconds)

## 23 FEBRUARY 1963

*The Darkened City,* opera in three acts by the 52-year-old Americanized German-born composer Bernhard HEIDEN, dealing with the year of the plague, 1319, in East Anglia, during which a lethargic victim Lazarus rises from the mass of presumed cadavers frightening the populace and precipitating ecclesiastical hysteria, set to music in a measurably tonal, rhythmically propulsive manner, verisimilitudinarily illustrated by authentic passages of Gregorian chant, is produced by the Indiana University Opera Theater in Bloomington, Indiana.

### 28 FEBRUARY 1963

*Il Diavolo in giardino,* "historical pastoral comedy" in three acts by the 38-year-old Italian composer Franco MANNINO, centered on the famous swindle of a diamond necklace at the court of Marie Antoinette in Versailles, with the inclusion in the score of some popular airs of the time, written in a modernistically polyharmonic idiom, and ending on a dissonantly salinated chord of D major, is produced in Palermo.

### 3 MARCH 1963

*Labyrinth,* surrealist opera by Gian Carlo MENOTTI, to his own libretto in which a distraught bridegroom misplaces the key to his hotel room on his wedding night, gets lost in a maze of nightmarish corridors, meanders into a non-adjacent spatial continuum, is suspended weightless in an orbiting spaceship, and is measured for interment by an ultra-dimensional mortician while holding in his hand the crucial hotel room key, set to music with a somewhat atonal lilt, reverting to terrestrial tonality in non-cosmic scenes, is performed for the first time as a commissioned work by the National Broadcasting Company Television Opera Theater.

### 8 MARCH 1963

On the 150th anniversary of the first concert of the Royal Philharmonic Society, William WALTON conducts the London Philharmonic in the first performance of his *Variations on a Theme by Hindemith,* derived from 36 bars of the opening section of the second movement of Hindemith's *Cello Concerto,* comprising nine variations and a fugal finale and concluding with the trumpet call from Hindemith's opera *Mathis der Maler,* astutely constructed as an amiable colloquy between the two composers, preserving under Walton's British patina Hindemith's characteristic tonal inflections.

### 8 MARCH 1963

Nikita KHRUSHCHEV, Premier of the Union of Soviet Socialist Republics, airs his views on music at a meeting of Communist Party leaders and representatives of Soviet literature and arts, in which he states his unalterable opposition to abstractionism, formalism and other petty bourgeois tendencies, and says that dodecaphony to him is plain cacophony, the pun being possible in Russian as well as in any other language. (Full text in LETTERS AND DOCUMENTS)

### 13 MARCH 1963

*Alceste,* opera by the Dutch composer-engineer Ton de LEEUW, commissioned by the Netherlands Television Foundation, is performed for the first time on the Holland National Television network.

## 14 MARCH 1963

Frances McCANN, 41-year-old American operatic soprano, is slain in a hotel room in Rome by her impresario Ernest Boxman who shoots himself too, dying a few days later.

## 16 MARCH 1963

*Il Capitan Spavento,* one-act opera by Gian Francesco MALIPIERO, is produced in Naples.

## 18 MARCH 1963

*Concerto for Violin, Piano and Orchestra* by the American composer Robert Russell BENNETT, is performed for the first time in Portland, Oregon.

## 19 MARCH 1963

*Stereophony for Orchestra* by the Canadian composer Harry SOMERS, based on a 12-tone series subdivided into three groups of four notes each, with orchestral instruments distributed in different places in the concert hall for stereophonic effect, is performed for the first time in Toronto.

## 21 MARCH 1963

*Sixteenth Symphony* in five movements by Henry COWELL, subtitled *Icelandic,* making thematic use of the open fifths characteristic of ancient runic chants projected on the tritone bases of the indigenous Lydian mode and integrated in a dodecaphonic series, is performed for the first time in Reykjavik.

## 27 MARCH 1963

*Cello Concerto* by the 36-year-old Rumanian composer Anatol VIERU, in one compact movement, written in an individually advanced idiom with the application of thematic tropes adumbrating dodecaphony, is performed for the first time in Geneva, as the prize-winning work for an international competition.

## 28 MARCH 1963

*Fifteenth Symphony* subtitled *Silver Pilgrimage,* by Alan HOVHANESS, is performed for the first time in New York.

## 1 APRIL 1963

To supplement the previously enforced prohibition of singing sad songs that undermine the nation's morale, the government of South Vietnam issues an order forbidding performances of American twist music.

## 2 APRIL 1963

*Prophecy of Isaiah,* last work by Bohuslav MARTINU, for chorus and orchestra is performed posthumously in Jerusalem, with the original Biblical text in English changed to corresponding verses in Hebrew.

## 4 APRIL 1963

*Andromache's Farewell*, scena for soprano and orchestra by Samuel BARBER, after an episode in *The Trojan Woman* by Euripides, relating to Andromache's tragic fate after she is carried to Greece by the victors as a war prize, set to music in a highly tense, euphoniously discordant idiom, is performed for the first time by the New York Philharmonic, Thomas Schippers conducting.

## 11 APRIL 1963

*Sept Répons des Ténèbres*, last work by Francis POULENC, commissioned by the New York Philharmonic in celebration of its opening season in Lincoln Center for the Performing Arts, scored for a boy soprano, boys' choir and orchestra, to Latin texts descriptive of the tenebrous days of Christ's Passion, with an atonally refracted medieval chant figure as a motto, is performed for the first time by the New York Philharmonic, under the direction of Thomas Schippers.

## 13 APRIL 1963

In the course of the 26th International Festival of Contemporary Music in Venice, the world premières are given of *Quintet* for piano and strings by Alberto GINASTERA (Argentina), *Diagramma IV* for flute solo by Henryk GÓRECKI (Poland), *Polyphonie I* for alto flute and piano by Jacques GUYONNET (Switzerland), and *Recíproco* for flute, piano and percussion by Luis de PABLO (Spain).

## 14 APRIL 1963

In the course of the 26th International Festival of Contemporary Music in Venice, the Groupe de Recherches Musicales, led by the Paris electrical engineer Pierre SCHAEFFER, originator (in 1948) of musique concrète, presents a program of orchestral music with electronic montages in absolute world premières:

*Collages* by Philippe CARSON (France), *Alternances* by Bernard PARMEGIANI (France), *L'expérience ambigue* by Jean-Etienne MARIE (France), *Tutti* by Ivo MALEC (Yugoslavia), *Synergies* by François-Bernard MACHE (France), *D'un bout à l'autre* by Edgardo CANTON (Argentina), *Éventail* by N'Guyen Van TUONG (Vietnam), *Pluriel* by François BAYLE (France), *Compose-Composite* by Luc FERRARI (France).

## 16 APRIL 1963

In the course of the 26th International Festival of Contemporary Music in Venice, a chamber music concert presents the world premières of the following works:

*Musica da camera* for 9 instruments by Angelo PACCAGNINI; *Informel 2* for 15 instruments by Aldo CLEMENTI; *A Solemn Music* for voice and small ensemble to the words of Milton's poem by Niccolò CASTIGLIONI; *Elegie* for voice, violin, clarinet and guitar by Antonio VERETTI; and *Serenade No. 2* by the 30-year-old Californian avant-garde composer Morton SUBOTNICK.

23 APRIL 1963

In the course of the 26th International Festival of Contemporary Music in Venice, a concert of symphonic music is given comprising the following works:

World première of *Abracadabra* by the 81-year-old Italian grandmaster of music Gian Francesco MALIPIERO, for baritone and orchestra, in 8 episodes of neo-pastoral inspiration with the thematic material derived from the letters of the medieval magic word Abracadabra; Bruno MADERNA's *Concerto* for oboe and orchestra, and the world première of *Stratégie* by the Greek composer Iannis XENAKIS, a "musical competition" for two orchestras playing two different pieces comprising 19 musical divisions, the durations of which are determined by an IBM 7090 computer in Paris, each constituting a matrix of the game, with the conductor who carries out the stochastic data more efficiently being declared the winner (Maderna won on this occasion by *viva voce* acclamation against the Yugoslav conductor Konstantin Simonovic)

23 APRIL 1963

*Monsieur de Pourceaugnac*, opera by Frank MARTIN, after Molière's farce, in which a pompous landlord to whom an ambitious bourgeois wants to give his daughter in marriage is beset by machinations organized by the unwilling bride, is declared debile by false doctors and bigamous by false lawyers until he is driven back to his country estate and the bride is free to marry her true lover, with a musical score written in a classical comic style and the orchestra supplemented by a xylophone, celesta, piano, harp, harpsichord and vibraphone, is produced at the newly rebuilt Grand-Théâtre in Geneva, Ansermet conducting. (The previously announced date for the première, 13 December 1962, was postponed)

24 APRIL 1963

*Novae de infinito laudes*, cantata by the German composer resident in Italy, Hans Werner HENZE, to the texts of six essays of the martyr of science Giordano Bruno, discoursing learnedly upon celestial bodies, the basic four elements, the continuous mutation, the pleasure of motion, the sunrise and the Summum Bonum, set to music in a correspondingly catholic idiom, tonal, atonal, polytonal, serial, is performed for the first time in the course of the 26th International Festival of Contemporary Music in Venice.

25 APRIL 1963

Paul HINDEMITH conducts the New York Philharmonic in the world première of his *Concerto for Organ and Orchestra*, commissioned by the New York Philharmonic in celebration of its opening season in Lincoln Center and consisting of four movements: (1) *Crescendo—Moderato maestoso* (2) *Allegro assai* (3) *Canzonetta in Triads and Two Ritornelli*, with interludes for solo organ traversing 22 different major and minor triads in unrelated succession (4) *Phantasy on Veni Creator Spiritus*, set to music in a resplendent neo-gothic Regeromorphic idiom (the score was completed on 1 February 1963 in the Upper Palatinate, once the home ground of Max Reger).

## 26 APRIL 1963

*Media in vita,* symphonic oratorio by the Swiss composer Armin SCHIBLER, to the text of a patrological Latin poem reminding that middle life is half death and written in a neo-ecclesiastical style with two antiphonal choruses representing the dead and the living, is performed for the first time in Zürich.

## 30 APRIL 1963

*Noah and the Flood,* ballet with singing, by Igor STRAVINSKY, receives its first stage performance in Hamburg.

## 2 MAY 1963

*Ninth Symphony,* the last work by the Hungarian composer László LAJTHA, written in a structurally lucid, classically designed form, with melismatic melos suggesting the Magyar origins of its inspiration, is given a posthumous world première in Paris.

## 5 MAY 1963

On the 18th anniversary of the liberation of Holland from the Nazi occupation, Radio Hilversum presents the first performance of the oratorio entitled *5 mei: Zij (Fifth of May: They)* by Bertus VAN LIER.

## 12 MAY 1963

The Bonn Council opens a Robert SCHUMANN Museum, housing his manuscripts and letters, in the private clinic in Endenich, now a suburb of Bonn, where Schumann was confined during the last three years of his life and where, during his intervals of lucidity, he wrote his last compositions.

## 13 MAY 1963

*Highway No. 1, U.S.A.,* one-act opera by the American Negro composer William Grant STILL, glorifying in epic tones the main North-South automobile artery leading along the coast from Maine to Florida, is performed for the first time in Miami, Florida.

## 16 MAY 1963

*Fifth Symphony* by the 36-year-old German composer Hans Werner HENZE, in three movements: *Movimentado, Adagio, Moto perpetuo,* scored for orchestra sans clarinets and sans bassoons and couched in a searchingly atonal but tonipetal idiom keeping clear of totally organized dodecaphony which was Henze's preferred style before he settled on the island of Ischia in the Bay of Naples, is performed for the first time as a commissioned work by the New York Philharmonic, Leonard Bernstein conducting.

## 16 MAY 1963

*One Hundred Devils and One Girl,* operetta by Tikhon KHRENNIKOV, is produced in Moscow.

## 18 MAY 1963

*Death of the Bishop of Brindisi,* dramatic cantata by Gian Carlo MENOTTI, scored for orchestra, two soloists and a chorus of 525, including 325 children, dealing with the historic episode of the Children's Crusade of A.D. 1212, which was blessed by the Bishop of Brindisi who subsequently was tortured by conscience and responsibility for the tragic death of the adolescent crusaders when their ships foundered and sank, is performed for the first time in Cincinnati.

## 20 MAY 1963

*Die Soldaten,* opera in four acts by the German composer Bernd Alois ZIMMERMANN, is performed for the first time in Cologne.

## 22 MAY 1963

To commemorate the sesquicentennial of the birth of Richard WAGNER, the Soviet Union issues a 4-kopeck postage stamp with his portrait.

## 27 MAY 1963

To mark the bicentennial of the birth of the French opera composer Etienne-Nicolas MÉHUL, France issues a 60-centime postage stamp in his honor.

## 28 MAY 1963

*La Celestina,* opera by Flavio TESTI, is produced in Florence during the Maggio Fiorentino Festival.

## 29 MAY 1963

Exactly fifty years after the world première of STRAVINSKY's *Le Sacre du Printemps* at the Théâtre des Champs-Elysées in Paris, Pierre Monteux, the original conductor, now 88, leads the London Symphony Orchestra in the Royal Albert Hall, London, in the presence of the composer.

It was a moving experience to watch these octogenarian partners in a 50-year-old crime receiving their ovation together. (*The Times,* London, 30 May 1963)

The short, bald composer sat forward eagerly, although in the shadows, as the orchestra presented a performance that the reviewers agreed came up to the occasion. Then it was all over and the audience exploded in applause . . . Monteux turned to face the delirious audience and then immediately looked around the hall for his fellow octogenarian. Stravinsky, in a box, noticed the conductor's confusion, and whipped out a handkerchief to catch his attention . . . As Monteux began the slow climb to the box through an admiring throng, Stravinsky continued to wave his handkerchief at the delighted audience . . . After the two old friends embraced each other in the box, Monteux returned to the podium. (New York *Times,* 31 May 1963)

## 31 MAY 1963

*Dualities,* ballet by Humphrey SEARLE, is performed for the first time in Wiesbaden.

4 JUNE 1963

*Byzantine Concerto* for piano and orchestra by the 54-year-old Serbian composeress Ljubica MARIĆ, in three movements, thematically derived from elements of ancient Byzantine chants, set in baroque form and embellished by atonal and polytonal techniques, is performed for the first time in Belgrade.

7 JUNE 1963

*Concerto* for guitar and orchestra by Alfonso LETELIER is performed for the first time in Santiago, Chile.

8 JUNE 1963

The 37th Festival of the International Society for Contemporary Music opens in Amsterdam with the following program:

*Ombres* for orchestra by Ton DE LEEUW, 36-year-old Dutch composer of highly advanced music with philosophical undertones, in four movements utilizing some Indian ragas; *Les symphonies de timbres* by the 43-year-old Polish-born composer Roman HAUBENSTOCK-RAMATI, an essay in forms and sonorities and thematic metamorphoses in a peritonal idiom; *4 Songs*, op. 22 by Arnold SCHOENBERG; and *Eighth Symphony* by Karl Amadeus HARTMANN.

9 JUNE 1963

The second concert of the 37th Festival of the International Society for Contemporary Music in Amsterdam presents the following program:

*Flökt (Fluctuations)* for chamber orchestra by the 25-year-old Icelandic composer Thorkell SIGURBJÖRNSSON built on the scheme of expanding intervals and freely fluctuating instrumental sonorities; *Studio per 24*, an experimental sketch for 24 instruments by the 30-year-old Italian composer Giacomo MANZONI; *Um Mitternacht*, for chorus by the Viennese composer Hans Erich APOSTEL, written in dynamically dimmed sonorities between pianissimo and mezzo forte, in a free chromatic idiom; *Aphorismes 9* by the 66-year-old Polish composer Boleslaw SZABELSKI, a succinct suite for 9 instruments in a somewhat impressionistic manner; *Improperia per voci*, by the 36-year-old Danish composer Bernhard LEWKOWITCH, to the Latin text of the Good Friday ritual containing the Lord's reproaches to his people, with an element of free improvisation in the inflected speech and requiring the audience to heave a deep sigh during the cadential fermata; *Constellations III*, by the 35-year-old Swedish composer Bengt HAMBRAEUS written for an electronically enriched organ with the application of the aleatory technique of calculated improvisation; and *Bugaku* by the 56-year-old Japanese composer Yoritsune MATSUDAIRA, in four movements for small orchestra based on melorhythms of ancient Japanese court dances with the application of the principle of indeterminacy as to the order of components and instrumentation.

10 JUNE 1963

The third concert of the 37th Festival of the International Society for Contemporary Music at Amsterdam presents the following program:

*Elegia II* by the 23-year-old Argentinian composer Armando KRIEGER for contralto, 2 flutes, piano and percussion, wherein the verticality of harmony is contrasted with the horizonatality of the melorhythmic line and both are balanced by their common perpendicularity to instrumental timbre; *Sonata for flute and piano* by the 30-year-old Australian composer Richard MEALE opposing the static and dynamic aspects of symmetry and asymmetry and injecting elements of indeterminacy in contrapuntal combinations; *Erde und Himmel,* cantata by the 24-year-old Swiss composer Heinz HOLLIGER, in three movements, to words by a young Swiss suicide hovering between death and existence, the morbid oscillation portrayed by the devices of inversion and retrograde canon in an atonalized serialistic idiom; *Favola per clarinetto e batteria grande* by the 43-year-old Swedish composer Sven Erik BÄCK, in the narrative style of responsorial fabulation, with the clarinet speaking and assorted chimes and drums offering colorful comment; *Second String Quartet* by the Dutch composer Kees VAN BAAREN, written in a pre-classical form of a suite rich with improvised but premeditated cadenzas; *Second Sonata* for piano by the prophet of French ultramodernism Pierre BOULEZ, written in 1948 when he was 22 and based on a cellular type of composition through cohesive agglutination and melorhythmic coagulation of component thematic ingredients.

### 12 JUNE 1963

The fourth concert of the 37th Festival of the International Society for Contemporary Music in Amsterdam presents the following program:

*Variations on an Old Song* by the great Dutch organist Sweelinck (1562–1621) orchestrated by Jan MUL; *Concerto* for two pianos and orchestra by the 49-year-old Belgian-born composer Luctor PONSE, in three movements, based each on a group of thematic intervals according to a serial technique; *Concerto for Orchestra No. 3* by the Indonesian-born 34-year-old Dutch composer Will EISMA, in three movements, with the thematic foundation of mutually exclusive symmetrically posited six-note tropes; *De Vogels,* overture by the Dutch composer Alphons DIEPENBROCK (1862–1921), after *The Birds* of Aristophanes; *Anagrams* for chamber orchestra by the 58-year-old Dutch composer Guillaume LANDRÉ, in four sections, in which the thematic materials are anagrammatically permutated; *6 Symphonic Epigrams,* extremely brief, by the Dutch impressionist Willem PIJPER (1894–1947).

### 12 JUNE 1963

In the course of the 25th International Music Festival in Strasbourg, the world première is given of *Cantates pour une démente* by Maurice JARRE, scored for soprano, contralto, chorus and orchestra to texts from authentic letters by inmates of insane asylums, with the score notated both acoustically and pictorially, as a "partition-tableau," which can be read from left to right or from right to left, wherein the notes are represented by colors, dynamic intensity by the size of a color disc, 2 centimeters being the unit of time according to a chosen tempo so that 4,920 different versions could be produced in performance (hence the plural form of the title, *Cantates*)

### 13 JUNE 1963

The Fifth Concert of the 37th Festival International Society for Contemporary Music at Amsterdam presents the following program:

*Serenade* for flute, clarinet and bassoon by the 32-year-old Yugoslav composer Alojz SREBOTNJAK, written in the 12-tone technique, in six brief movements; *Quintet No. 2*

*1161*

for piano, clarinet, violin, viola and cello by the 30-year-old Czech composer Ilja ZELJENKA, written in a modified 12-tone idiom, with tonipetal tendencies; *Trio* for violin, clarinet and piano by the 32-year-old American composer Donald MARTINO, in 7 symmetric sections and derived from a series of consequential permutations of a predetermined set of 12 different notes; *Sonata* for cello solo by the 45-year-old German composer Bernd Alois ZIMMERMANN, in 5 sections, purporting to illustrate the passage from Ecclesiastes commenting upon planetary movements: " . . . et suis spatiis transeunt universa sub caelo"; *4 Studies* for wind quintet by the 44-year-old Swiss composer Robert SUTER, in 4 sections: *Couleurs, Mouvements, Improvisations* and *Polyphonie*, the content corresponding to the explicit intentions of the titles; *String Quartet No. 6* by the 53-year-old Danish composer Vagn HOLMBOE, in four movements monothematic in ultimate derivation, but morphologically diversified in treatment.

## 14 JUNE 1963

The sixth and last concert of the 37th International Society for Contemporary Music Festival at Amsterdam presents the following program:

*Canzone per orchestra* by the 32-year-old Norwegian composer Arne NORDHEIM, in three movements in a terse contrapuntal idiom with the basic melorhythmic motto stated explicitly in the first six bars; *Three Movements for Orchestra* by the 48-year-old American composer George PERLE, set in a serial technique in which the rhythmic impulses are symmetrically distributed; *Arabescata* for orchestra by the 35-year-old Finnish composer Einojuhani RAUTAVAARA, in 3 graphic variations in which tones, durations, intervals, instrumental colors and dynamics are serially distributed; *Symphonie concertante* by Jacques IBERT for oboe and string orchestra couched in a neo-classical vein with coloristic effects and *Threnody for the Victims of Hiroshima* by Krzysztof PENDERECKI for 52 string instruments.

## 15 JUNE 1963

*Le Silence de la Mer,* lyric drama in one act by the French composer Henri TOMASI, to a dramatic libretto from the time of Nazi occupation of France, in which a German officer of uncommon sensibilities who lodges in a French home tells the story of his life to an old man of the house and his niece, and then kills himself, is performed for the first time in Strasbourg.

## 18 JUNE 1963

The government of the People's Democratic Republic of Germany issues two postage stamps, at 20 and 25 pfennigs, marking the 75 years of the composition of the *Internationale.*

## 23 JUNE 1963

*Die Errettung Thebens,* opera in three acts by the Swiss composer Rudolf KELTENBORN, to his own libretto drawn freely from Aeschylus, in which seven princes from Argos assail the seven gates of Thebes, is produced in Zürich.

## 25 JUNE 1963

*A Frenchman in New York*, symphonic suite by the Gallic Novoeboracophile Darius MILHAUD, in six sightseeing sections: (1) *New York with Fog on the Hudson* (impenetrably static in windless wind instruments) (2) *The Cloisters* (devotionally hymnal in neo-medieval polymodalities) (3) *Horse and Carriage in Central Park* (quadripedally nostalgic in equine saunter) (4) *Times Square* (cacophonously polychordal in quaquaversal commotion) (5) *Gardens on the Roof* (an urbanely aerated aerie) (6) *Baseball in Yankee Stadium* (fugally competitive, with pitcher and batter in vernacular antiphony), is performed for the first time by the Boston Pops Orchestra, Arthur Fiedler conducting.

## 28 JUNE 1963

*Figaro lässt sich scheiden*, opera in two acts by the German composer Giselher KLEBE, a non-Mozartian projection, wherein characters of the famous Beaumarchais play are placed in the tourbillon of the French Revolution, with Figaro singing atonal arias in a dodecaphonic idiom, is produced by the Hamburg State Opera.

## 2 JULY 1963

*Our Man in Havana*, opera in three acts by the 31-year-old composer Malcolm WILLIAMSON of New Zealand, after the melodramatic novel by Graham Greene, with spies and counterspies matching wits in wry atonalities over ostentatious pseudo-Cuban rhythms, is produced in London.

## 4 JULY 1963

On the occasion of the Fourth Centennial of the founding of El Escorial, the Spanish Ministry of Information and Tourism inaugurates an international festival of music with the participation of groups of artists from Europe and America.

## 4 JULY 1963

The new Presidential Medal of Freedom, established by President John F. Kennedy's executive order to reward annually those "who contribute significantly to the quality of American life," is awarded among 31 recipinents to the great Spanish violoncellist Pablo CASALS, outstanding Negro singer Marian ANDERSON and the Austrian pianist Rudolf SERKIN.

## 6 JULY 1963

*Little Symphony* by the 30-year-old German-born English composer Alexander GOEHR, written in memory of his father Walter Goehr and couched in a euphonious atonal idiom, is performed for the first time in York, England.

## 6 JULY 1963

*Variations for Orchestra* by the 40-year-old Californian composer Leslie BASSETT, each based on a quadripartite phrase, the segments of which possess an individual dynamic and color scheme, but are not related to a hypothetical theme conceivably implied in the variants, are performed for the first time in Rome. (Its first American performance was given by the Philadelphia Orchestra, Eugene Ormandy conducting, on 22 October 1965; in 1966 the work received the Pulitzer Prize in Music)

### 25 JULY 1963

Wagner's grandson Wieland WAGNER is roundly booed by the Wagnerolatrous audience in Bayreuth after his modern production of *Die Meistersinger*, in which the fight scene in the second act becomes a donnybrook, and the polka and the samba are danced in the third act.

### 1 AUGUST 1963

*Elemental* by the American jazz pianist Dave BRUBECK, subtitled "Concerto for Anyone Who Can Afford an Orchestra," is performed for the first time by Brubeck's jazz quartet with the Arrangers Workshop Orchestra in Rochester.

### 20 AUGUST 1963

A six-concert series of avant-garde music opens in New York with the following program:

*Dreams* for piano by the American composer Frederic RZEWSKI; *Pour Clavier* by the Italian composer Silvano BUSSOTTI; *Klavierstück* by Karlheinz STOCKHAUSEN, inviting the pianist to dust the keyboard with talcum powder and perform glissandos with a pair of women's white gloves; and *Teatrino* by Giuseppe CHIARI, a multi-media presentation for five squeaking dolls, ping-pong balls, drums, electronic tape, an alarm clock and a lumber jack's saw with the piano *obligato* playing snatches from BEETHOVEN's *Fifth Symphony*.

### 21 AUGUST 1963

The avant-garde concert series continues in New York presenting John CAGE's *Variations II and III*, with electronically amplified sounds of various actions, such as drinking water, with a microphone pressed against his throat aggregating to the decibel count of the Niagara Falls, and a piece by Cage's Japanese disciple Toshi ICHIYANAGI activating the denuded piano wires and the wooden parts of two pianos manned by John Cage and his accommodating clairaudient famulus David Tudor.

### 26 AUGUST 1963

The third of the six concerts of avant-garde music is presented in New York, including *Water Music* and *Densities* by the 22-year-old American musician Joseph BYRD, for various instrumental ensembles; *High Contrasts* by Philip CORNER for an amplified harpsichord, with a profusion of silences between massive agglomerations of sonic materials; *Ludlow Blues* by Malcolm GOLDSTEIN, for a heterophonic group of wind instruments; and *Ergodos /2/3* by James TENNEY for electronic tape recording of animal noises.

The fourth concert of the avant-garde series in New York presents the following program:

*Two pieces for piano* by the Swedish composer Bo NILSSON; *Schlagfiguren und Quantitäten* and *Zyklus* for percussion by Karlheinz STOCKHAUSEN; *Music for 3 pianos* by Toshi ISHIYANAGI, the Japanese composer; *Action Music* for piano by the American composer Alvin LUCIER, in which digital aleatorics are combined with bodily gestures; *Sonata* for 3 pianos by Christian WOLFF; *Two Piano Pieces* by Morton FELDMAN; *From Place to Place* for two pianos by David BEHRMAN; *Nursery Fable with Exegesis* for piano by Bertram BALDWIN; *Corona for Pianists* by the Japanese composer Toru TAKEMITZU.

28 AUGUST 1963

In the course of the Edinburgh Festival of Music and Drama, the first performance is given of the *Concerto for Orchestra* by the British composer Michael TIPPETT, commissioned by the Edinburgh Festival Society, in three movements of neo-baroque consistency: (1) *Allegro*, without string instruments (2) *Largo*, without wind instruments (3) *Allegro*, for full orchestra.

1 SEPTEMBER 1963

*Cantata Misericordium* by Benjamin BRITTEN (completed on 25 May 1963), scored for piano, harp, timpani, solo string quartet, tenor, baritone, and chorus and string orchestra, written for the centenary of the International Red Cross, to a Latin dramatization of the parable of the Good Samaritan, in a tonal style with bitonal excrescences, is performed for the first time in its spiritual birthplace, Geneva, at a Red Cross celebration, by the Orchestre de la Suisse Romande, Ernest Ansermet conducting.

2 SEPTEMBER 1963

*Mary of Magdala*, cantata for chorus and orchestra by Sir Arthur BLISS, is performed for the first time at the Three Choirs Festival, at the Worcester Cathedral.

3 SEPTEMBER 1963

Hungary issues a 40-forint postage stamp in honor of the Hungarian composer Leo WEINER, who died on 13 September 1962.

3 SEPTEMBER 1963

The avant-garde musical festival continues in New York City with the following program of young adventurous music:

*Composition 1960, No. 13* by the 27-year-old Idaho-born composer La Monte YOUNG for cello solo letting the performer play anything at all to his taste (a Sammartini *Adagio* was actually played); *Projection 1* by Morton FELDMAN; *City Minds and Country Hearts* by Ornette COLEMAN; *Music for Cello and Piano* by Earle BROWN (partly aleatory), and *34′46.776″* for violin and piano by John CAGE, during which both players blow whistles, hurl cymbals, and perform other seemingly random actions, circumscribed by temporal parameters indicated in a sheet of instructions.

### 7 SEPTEMBER 1963

*Second Symphony* by Louis MENNINI, subtitled "da Festa," is performed for the first time by the Erie Philharmonic, as part of the sesquicentennial celebration of the founding of Erie, Pennsylvania.

### 9 SEPTEMBER 1963

The New York Festival of avant-garde Music concludes with a non-stop performance of Erik SATIE's piano piece *Vexations*, which according to Satie's instructions is to be played unremittingly 840 times, with the total duration of 18 hours 40 minutes at the estimated length of a single hearing of 80 seconds. (The event began at 6:00 P.M. on Monday 9 September and ended at 12:40 P.M. on Tuesday, 10 September with ten crepuscular, nocturnal, matutinal and diurnal pianists playing in relay).

### 10 SEPTEMBER 1963

The Soviet Post Office issues commemorative postage stamps to honor Giuseppe VERDI and Alexander DARGOMYZHSKY on the sesquicentennial of their births, and the Ukrainian singer-composer Semyon GULAK-ARTEMOVSKY on the 100th anniversary of his birth.

### 21 SEPTEMBER 1963

The newly erected Place des Arts opens in Montreal, Canada, with a concert by the Montreal Symphony Orchestra, featuring the world première of *Miroir* by the Canadian composer Jean-Papineau COUTURE; RAVEL's *La Valse* and MAHLER's *First Symphony*, led by the newly appointed music director of the Montreal Symphony, the youngest ever to head a major orchestra, 27-year-old Indian conductor Zubin MEHTA, to the extrinsic accompaniment of protesting French-Canadian nationalists clamoring for entrance outside the hall and carrying placards saying "Étatisation de la Place des Arts," "Vive la nation Québecoise" and "Le Québec se réveille."

### 22 SEPTEMBER 1963

*Don Giovanni*, one-act opera by Gian Francesco MALIPIERO, after Pushkin's drama *The Stone Guest*, is produced in Naples.

### 3 OCTOBER 1963

*Violin Concerto* by the prime Argentinian composer Alberto GINASTERA, is performed for the first time as a commissioned work by the New York Philharmonic, Leonard Bernstein conducting, Ruggiero Ricci soloist, set in three formalistically modernistic movements:

(1) *Cadenza e Studi,* opening with a prolonged cadenza, leading to six technical studies, unified by a common dodecaphonic series, the first exploiting multiple stops in

the violin solo, the second in tertian formations, the third in changing intervals, the fourth in free figurations, the fifth employing high harmonics, and the sixth making use of tropes in quarter-tones, followed by a magistral coda summarizing the devices of all six studies (2) *Adagio* for 22 soloists, a lyric interlude intended as an homage to the virtuosi of the New York Philharmonic (3) *Scherzo pianissimo e Perpetuum mobile*, opening with a prologue for exotic drums and assorted chimes, played on the threshold of audibility at a very rapid tempo, with thematic fragments from Paganini's *Capriccios* passing fleetingly through the orchestra before the final precipitous flight of perpetual motion.

### 4 OCTOBER 1963

*Sogno d'un tramonto d'autonno (Dream of an Autumn Sunset)*, one-act opera by Gian Francesco MALIPIERO originally written in 1913 as incidental music to a play by Gabriele d'Annunzio, dealing with a Venetian Dogaressa who schemes to destroy her love rival through ceraceous invultuation and acuminulate perforation of her waxen image, and induces an internecine carnage of carnally aroused men on the barges in the canals of Venice, is performed half a century after its composition on the Milan radio, in concert form.

### 6 OCTOBER 1963

*Symphonie marine* by Jacques IBERT, written in 1931 in a Gallically elegant, coloristic aquamarine manner but withheld by him from performance, is performed for the first time posthumously in Paris.

### 9 OCTOBER 1963

Hans Werner HENZE conducts in Berlin the first performance of his *Fourth Symphony*, with its material taken wholly from the discarded finale of the second act of his opera *König Hirsch*, in one movement which disperses its tonal energy in tangential atonalities, coming to rest on a soft multiple unison.

### 10 OCTOBER 1963

On the occasion of the sesquicentennial of Verdi's birth, a 30-lire stamp with his portrait is issued by Italy.

### 10 OCTOBER 1963

*Gentlemen, Be Seated!* opera in two acts from the time of the American Civil War by the 50-year-old American composer Jerome MOROSS, which combines elements of a minstrel show, dance, and drama, with a "Mister Interlocutor" supplying commentary on the historic, social, and fictional characters and events, is produced in New York.

### 11 OCTOBER 1963

A concert of ultra-avant-garde American music is presented in New York City in a program comprising the world premières of the unpremeditated *Vertical Thoughts* in five perpendicular movements by Morton FELDMAN, abounding in non-aforethought canons, with players entering whenever they have a chance and of his *Straits of Magellan,* a circumnavigatory "graph piece" with the compass pointing towards a tonal pole exercising great latitude of altitude of sound, as well as his threnody to the dead abstractional painter Franz Kline, *The Swallows of Salangan;* and four partially prepense pieces by Earle BROWN: *December 1952, Pentathis* (a demonstrative nonaseity derived from the pentathionate, a sulphur solution, with allusions to the five-event athletic contest Pentathlon), *Available Forms I,* in 27 accidental events, and *From Here,* the title referring to the common schizophrenic phrase, "You can't get there from here."

#### 11 OCTOBER 1963

President John F. KENNEDY announces the formation of a new permanent national company of the Metropolitan Opera in association with the National Cultural Center in Washington.

#### 11 OCTOBER 1963

Jean COCTEAU, Gallic inspirer of the arts, poet, dramatist, painter, stage designer, and newly elected member of the august French Academy (*Vu,* a Paris periodical, listed among the future impossibilities man's landing on the moon and Cocteau's election to the Academy), dies of a heart attack in his suburbanly Parisian country seat at Milly-la-Forêt at 1:30 P.M., at the age of 74, a few hours after the death caused by the hemorrhage of the spleen of Edith Piaf, 47-year-old, 90-lb., 4-ft., 10-in., French street singer, who was brought up in a brothel run by her grandmother and nicknamed Piaf (argot for a sparrow) by her souteneur, a cabaret owner shot to death in 1937.

#### 13 OCTOBER 1963

Alexander TCHEREPNIN plays in Berlin the piano part in the world première of his *Fifth Piano Concerto.*

#### 15 OCTOBER 1963

The new Philharmonic Hall, designed by the German architect Hans SCHAROUN, shaped as an asymmetrical polygon, with a seating capacity of 2,200, and acoustically accoutred with 136 pyramidal ceiling reflectors for sound (Helmholz resonators), festooned with neon light tubes, opens in West Berlin with a gala performance of Beethoven's *Ninth Symphony* by the Berlin Philharmonic Orchestra, under the direction of Herbert von Karajan.

#### 16 OCTOBER 1963

*Carmen Vitale,* cantata by Alan RAWSTHORNE, to a medieval English text exhorting the hearers to practice carnal abstinence, with the hymn to St. John *Ut queant laxis,* used by Guido d'Arezzo as the foundation of the syllabic singing method, serving here as the cantus firmus, so that musical phrases enter a degree higher in each succeeding stanza, is performed for the first time in London.

## 20 OCTOBER 1963

The opening of the new Nisei Theater with a capacity of 1,350 seats and equipped with the most advanced electronic systems takes place in Tokyo, with the presentation of BEETHOVEN's *Fidelio* by the Deutsche Oper of West Berlin, comprising its entire personnel of 280 members.

## 20 OCTOBER 1963

*Ut Unum Sint,* symphonic piece by the Italian composer Renzo ROSSELLINI, inspired by the last words of Pope John XXIII uttered before his death, "That they may be one," from the Latin text of the Gospel according to St. John, Chapter 17, Verse 11, is performed for the first time by the Miami Symphony Orchestra, Fabien Sevitzky conducting.

## 21 OCTOBER 1963

*The Last Savage,* opera buffa by Gian-Carlo MENOTTI, to his own libretto dealing with a whimsical American heiress who undertakes a search for the abominable snowman in the high Himalayas, locates a putative specimen, imports him to her native Chicago and when he recoils in horror from abstract impressionist art, dodecaphonic music and beatnik poetry, takes him back to his mountain habitat and eventually marries him, set to music in urbane satirical tones, with illustrative persiflage of American avant-garde pursuits, is produced at the Opéra-Comique in Paris.

## 22 OCTOBER 1963

*Synthesis for Orchestra and Electronic Sound* by Otto LUENING is performed for the first time by the Erie, Pennsylvania, Philharmonic.

## 23 OCTOBER 1963

*Symphony for Metal Orchestra (Seventeenth Symphony)* by the American composer Alan HOVHANESS, is performed for the first time in Cleveland.

## 28 OCTOBER 1963

*Second Piano Concerto* by Leon KIRCHNER, in two connected movements, written in a rhapsodically exhortatory style, gravid in its dissonant condensation, with a decoratively baroque piano part and minatory percussion, is performed for the first time by the Seattle Symphony Orchestra with the composer conducting, Leon Fleischer soloist.

## 1 NOVEMBER 1963

Two Negro music students are arrested in Jackson, Mississippi, by the city police and are held overnight on a charge of disturbing the peace in trying to attend, with two valid tickets, a concert given by the Royal Philharmonic Orchestra of London, under Sir Malcolm Sargent, at a segregated hall.

I understand that Sir Malcolm received a telephone call during the interval of his concert telling him of the arrest of the two students and asking him not to carry on with the concert. Unfortunately, the terms of our contract still applied, and no doubt he felt it his duty to play the advertised concert in full. (From a letter by the concertmaster of the Royal Philharmonic Orchestra, in the *Manchester Guardian Weekly*, 5 December 1963)

11 NOVEMBER 1963

*Echoi*, suite of four movements by Lukas Foss, scored for piano, clarinet, cello, assorted percussion and a garbage can, written according to a stochastic formula in which temporal freedom is given to the percussion player controlling the actions of his colleagues, is performed for the first time in New York, with Lukas Foss presiding at the piano.

12 NOVEMBER 1963

*Anniversary Concerto: 75* by the 40-year-old American composer Robert EVETT, commissioned for the 75th anniversary of the Basic-Witz Furniture Industries of Wayneseboro, Virginia, in seven movements with instrumental solos expressive of individual pieces of mass-produced furniture, set in a fittingly automated rhythmic idiom, is performed for the first time in Washington.

12 NOVEMBER 1963

Paul HINDEMITH makes his last public appearance, conducting the Vienna Chamber Chorus in the first performance of his last work, a *Mass* for mixed choir *a cappella*, written in an austere neo-medieval polyphonic idiom, with transitional discords occasionally perturbing the reticent ambience of the music.

15 NOVEMBER 1963

Fritz REINER, Hungarian-born conductor, master technician of the baton, distinguished both in symphonic and operatic repertory, sympathetic interpreter of modern music, dies in New York at the age of seventy-four.

17 NOVEMBER 1963

*This Sacred Ground* by David DIAMOND, a symphonic setting of Lincoln's Gettysburg Address, scored for orchestra, chorus and male voice is performed for the first time by the Buffalo Philharmonic Orchestra.

20 NOVEMBER 1963

*Sixth Symphony* by the Swedish composer Gunnar BUCHT is performed for the first time in Stockholm.

## 20 NOVEMBER 1963

The National Theater of Munich, housing the Staatsoper, opens its doors in a building reconstructed stone by stone, stucco by stucco, to produce an architectural facsimile of the original structure with its Corinthian columns and a 180-light chandelier destroyed in an Allied air attack on 18 October 1943, with a performance of *Die Frau ohne Schatten* by Richard STRAUSS, born in Munich 99½ years before. (This was a preliminary opening for invited guests; the official opening for the general public took place on 23 November 1963 with a performance of Wagner's *Die Meistersinger* which had its première at the Munich National Theater in 1868)

## 22 NOVEMBER 1963

At the Friday afternoon concert of the Boston Symphony Orchestra, having completed the first performance of the torturously atonal and minatory *Study for Orchestra No. 2* by the American composer William SYDEMAN, Erich Leinsdorf is apprised of the assassination of President Kennedy and announces the tragic news to the audience (there are cries: "No, no!"), then conducts the *Marcia funèbre* from Beethoven's *Eroica*.

## 23 NOVEMBER 1963

Twenty-five days before his unexpected death, Winfried ZILLIG conducts in Linz the world première of his seventh opera, in one act, *Das Verlöbnis*, depicting in an ironically solemn dodecaphonic idiom the joys and heartaches of rural love.

## 27 NOVEMBER 1963

Werner EGK conducts in the newly rebuilt National Opera Theater in Munich the world première of his opera in two acts, *Die Verlobung in San Domingo*, to his own libretto fashioned after a novella by Heinrich Kleist dealing with a miscegenational love affair in San Domingo during the native uprising against the French in the early 19th century, ending in tragedy with the innocent death at the hands of the white lover of the lovely mulatto girl unjustly suspected of spying, containing a half-hour interlude of tape recorded indigenous music.

## 2 DECEMBER 1963

*The Knife*, opera in two acts by the Welsh composer Daniel JONES, commissioned by the Welsh Committee of the Arts Council, to his own libretto, wherein a Negro accused of raping and murdering a white girl in a Southern mining town in 1866 is saved from lynching when a conscience-stricken white miner confesses the crime, is produced at Sadler's Wells in London.

## 2 DECEMBER 1963

*The Sojourner and Mollie Sinclair*, one-act opera by Carlisle FLOYD, to his own libretto delineating the conflict between an old-fashioned clan chieftain and a progressive-minded lass among the early Scottish settlers in the Carolinas, commissioned by the Carolina Charter Tercentenary Commission is produced in Raleigh, North Carolina.

### 2 DECEMBER 1963

*Murder of a Great Chief of State, In Memory of John F. Kennedy,* a brief symphonic piece by Darius MILHAUD composed in Paris on the day after the assassination, is performed for the first time in Oakland, California.

### 3 DECEMBER 1963

Aaron COPLAND conducts at the Munich National Opera Theater the world première of his ballet *Dance Panels in Seven Movements,* built in a translucidly intricate polyphonic reticle, with some jazzy interpolations.

### 5 DECEMBER 1963

Karl Amadeus HARTMANN, German master of modern polyphony, who adopted a viable individual style incorporating elements of pure classicism and prudential modernism, dies in his native town of Munich at the age of fifty-eight.

### 7 DECEMBER 1963

A commemorative stamp honoring the centennial of Pietro MASCAGNI's birth, is issued in Italy.

### 9 DECEMBER 1963

Leonard BERNSTEIN conducts in Tel Aviv the world première of his choral *Third Symphony* subtitled *Kaddish,* inspired by the traditional Jewish prayer for the dead, originally commissioned by the Boston Symphony Orchestra, and re-dedicated to the memory of President John F. Kennedy.

### 10 DECEMBER 1963

*Song of Human Rights,* cantata by Howard HANSON commissioned by the United Nations Human Rights Organization, to texts from various sources including excerpts from the Inaugural Address of President John F. Kennedy, is performed for the first time as part of the observance honoring the United Nations Human Rights day in Washington.

### 10 DECEMBER 1963

Ronald STEVENSON, 35-year-old English pianist and composer, plays at Cape Town, South Africa, the first performance of his brobdingnagian *Passacaglia* for piano solo, lasting one hour and 20 minutes, and written as a tribute to Dmitri Shostakovich, based on the theme of Shostakovich's musical monogram, D.S.C.H. (D, Es, C, H in German notation), used by Shostakovich himself in his *Tenth Symphony.*

## 20 DECEMBER 1963

The Lithuanian Soviet Socialist Republic issues a 4-kopeck stamp in honor of the prime modern composer of Lithuania, Mikas PETRAUSKAS (1873–1937).

## 20 DECEMBER 1963

*Pacem in terris,* choral symphony, op. 404, by Darius MILHAUD, to the Latin text from the 1963 encyclical of Pope John XXIII, in seven sections, proclaiming the imperative necessity of peace in a scientific age, rights of free movement, obedience to divine authority, spirit of justice, protection of political dissenters, disarmament and brotherhood of man, is performed for the first time at the inauguration of a new hall of the Paris Radio under the direction of Charles Munch. (It had its first church performance in the cathedral of Notre Dame in Paris on 1 June 1964, on the occasion of the 800th anniversary of the inception of its construction.)

## 21 DECEMBER 1963

*Shaúra,* opera in three acts in the Bashkir language by the 46-year-old Bashkir Soviet composer Zagir ISMAILOV, is produced in Ufa.

## 28 DECEMBER 1963

Paul HINDEMITH, supreme musical craftsman of 20th-century Germany, whose ideals of immanent esthetics rooted in the mastery of tonal techniques has bridged the Bachian past with the logic of modern music, dies in Frankfurt, Germany, at the age of 68, following a series of four consecutive cerebro-vascular strokes.

## 28 DECEMBER 1963

*Triple Concerto* for violin, piano, cello and orchestra, the last work by the Rumanian composer Paul CONSTANTINESCU, is performed for the first time in Bucharest eight days after his death.

## 31 DECEMBER 1963

The Government of South Africa bans the musical play *South Pacific* by Richard RODGERS on the ground that it encourages miscegenation.

# ❧ 1964 ❧

## 10 JANUARY 1964

Pierre BOULEZ conducts in Basel the first performance of a fragment from his *Figures, Doubles, Prismes* for orchestra, conceived in blocks of double sonic prisms in *fortissimo* separated by cylindrical pillars of zero sonority in the "temps strié" (striated time), and representing the creative desire to "seize and organize the delirium."

### 13 JANUARY 1964

*The House of Atreus,* ballet by the Canadian composer Harry SOMERS, depicting the murder of Agamemnon and Electra's avenging wrath, written in an ironically philosophical manner with jazzy vignettes on a neo-Grecian canvas, is performed for the first time in Ottawa.

### 14 JANUARY 1964

*Second Symphony* by Quincy PORTER, in four classical movements, set in a dignified neo-baroque style with some atonal excrescences and polytonal protuberances, is performed for the first time in Louisville.

### 14 JANUARY 1964

*Voyage Four,* "spatial concert piece" by the American composer Henry BRANT, scored for 83 instrumentalists and a singer, is performed for the first time in New Haven, led by three conductors, with the players seated in different parts of the hall, on the balcony and on the stage, so as to create the impression of a stereophonic environment.

### 20 JANUARY 1964

*Fourteenth Symphony* by the prolific Swiss-American composer Ernst LÉVY is performed for the first time in Basel.

### 22 JANUARY 1964

Marc BLITZSTEIN, 58-year-old American composer of operas of social significance, dies in a hospital at Fort-de-France, Martinique, as a result of a savage beating arising out of a political altercation at the hands of three sailors the night before.

### 23 JANUARY 1964

*Seventh Symphony* subtitled *Variation Symphony,* by the American composer Peter MENNIN, in five concise movements, charged with kinetic energy, is performed for the first time by the Cleveland Orchestra, George Szell conducting.

### 7 FEBRUARY 1964

*Fifth Symphony* by Roger SESSIONS, a compact single-unit work written in a neo-classically formal serialistic idiom, and scored for a colorful orchestra, including xylophone, marimba, vibraphone, piano, harp and celesta, is performed for the first time by the Philadelphia Orchestra, Eugene Ormandy conducting.

## 14 FEBRUARY 1964

*Concerto in C minor* for cello and orchestra by the French composer Henri SAUGUET, is performed for the first time in Moscow by Mstislav Rostropovich, to whom the work is dedicated, under the direction of the composer.

## 17 FEBRUARY 1964

*Athaliah,* opera in two parts by the 51-year-old Czech-born American composer Hugo WEISGALL, based on Racine's play about Jezebel's murderous daughter, set in a lyrico-dramatic expressionistic idom with dodecaphonic parameters, is performed for the first time by the Concert Opera Association in New York, conducted by its founder and director Thomas Scherman.

## 18 FEBRUARY 1964

*Alexander bis,* opera buffa in one act by Bohuslav MARTINU, is posthumously produced for the first time in Mannheim.

## 25 FEBRUARY 1964

*Concerto-Monologue* for cello and orchestra by the Soviet composer Lev KNIPPER, is performed for the first time in Moscow by Mstislav Rostropovich to whom the concerto is dedicated.

## 6 MARCH 1964

*Third Symphony* by Ross Lee FINNEY, in three movements, each subdivided into three sections, each of the latter containing three themes of dodecaphonic connotations, is performed for the first time by the Philadelphia Orchestra, Eugene Ormandy conducting.

## 12 MARCH 1964

Benjamin BRITTEN conducts in Moscow the world première of his *Cello Symphony,* with Mstislav Rostropovich, to whom it is dedicated, as soloist.

## 13 MARCH 1964

*Concerto* in E major for cello and orchestra by the Soviet composer Boris TCHAIKOVSKY, unrelated to his great namesake, is performed for the first time in Moscow by Mstislav Rostropovich, to whom the work is dedicated.

## 13 MARCH 1964

*Fifth Symphony* subtitled *Jephtha's Daughter,* by Ernst TOCH, in one movement (completed on 18 May 1963), coloristically scored for large orchestra that includes gong, chimes, xylophone, vibraphone, Chinese temple blocks and an anvil, depicting in melodramatic tones the tragic Biblical story of Jephtha's sacrifice of his daughter in obedience to the cruel command of the barbarous Jehovah, is performed for the first time by the Boston Symphony Orchestra, Erich Leinsdorf conducting.

### 15 MARCH 1964

*Yolimba, oder Die Grenzen der Magie,* opera "in one act and four love songs" by the 36-year-old German composer Wilhelm KILLMAYER, dealing with a televisonary robotesse scientifically furnished with supernumerary aphrodisiac organs, who shoots every man uttering or muttering the word love, but reaches the limits of her magic (hence the title) in her encounter with a sexless technician, and retreats to her native electronic world, is produced in Wiesbaden.

### 25 MARCH 1964

The octogenarian composer Robert STOLZ conducts at the Volksoper in Vienna the première of his 51st operetta, *Frühjahrs-Parade,* depicting the power of Viennese love in three different age groups, with 400 soldiers of the Austrian Army participating as non-singing marching uniformed auxiliary forces.

### 31 MARCH 1964

*Umbrian Scene,* tone poem by the 47-year-old American Negro composer Ulysses KAY, a tranquil symphonic work evoking the landscape of the Italian province of Umbria, is performed for the first time in New Orleans.

### 1 APRIL 1964

*The Plague,* oratorio by the Catalan composer Roberto GERHARD, resident in England since the Spanish Civil War, to a text from the novel of the same name by Albert Camus describing an imaginary outbreak of virulent pestilence in Oran, Algiers, in the 1940's, scored for singing, whispering, shouting, moaning and wailing voices, orchestra and air-raid sirens, is performed for the first time by the British Broadcasting Corporation in London, Antal Dorati conducting.

### 1 APRIL 1964

Božidar KUNC, 60-year-old Zagreb-born pianist and composer, who made his home in America from 1951, dies of a heart attack at 10:45 P.M., in a Detroit hospital, half an hour after completing a performance with the Detroit Symphony Orchestra of his *Piano Concerto* in B minor (of which he played the world première in Zagreb on 27 April 1934) at a special concert sponsored by the Croatian Board of Trade, in a program which also featured his sister, the singer Zinka Milanov.

### 6 APRIL 1964

*Elegy for J.F.K.* by Igor STRAVINSKY, scored for baritone, two clarinets and corno di bassetto, to a poem by W. H. Auden, lamenting in the reverential tones of a liturgical threnody the death of an admired President fallen on 22 November 1963, based on a 12-tone series containing a proliferation of wholetone progressions, symbolic of evil, and ending with a 3/8 bar of absolute silence, is performed for the first time at one of the Monday Evening Concerts in Santa Monica, California.

## 15 APRIL 1964

*La Venus d'Ille,* lyric drama in two acts by the nonagenarian French composer Henri Büsser, to his own libretto relating the story of a statue of Venus found in the French provincial town of Ille who stuns a youth to death with a bracelet he playfully placed on her hand, is produced in Paris.

## 17 APRIL 1964

*Notturno ungherese* for orchestra by Miklós Rózsa, Hungarian composer prospering in Hollywood, drawn from the remembered melorhythms of his Magyar adolescence, is performed for the first time by the Philadelphia Orchestra, Eugene Ormandy conducting.

## 19 APRIL 1964

*Montezuma,* opera in three acts by Roger Sessions, dealing in atonally anguished colors with the fall of the last Aztec emperor, is performed for the first time anywhere in West Berlin.

## 20 APRIL 1964

*Concerto-Symphony* for cello and orchestra by the Bulgarian composer Lubomir Pipkov, is performed for the first time in Moscow by Mstislav Rostropovich to whom the work is dedicated.

## 22 APRIL 1964

*October,* opera by Vano Muradeli, depicting in heroic Russian modalities the glorious Bolshevik Revolution of 25 October 1917, according to the Julian calendar of old Russia, corresponding to 7 November, Gregorian style, containing in the cast, for the first time on the stage, a singing part for Lenin, is performed for the first time in its complete stage version at the Palace of Congresses in the Kremlin in Moscow. (The concert version was first heard on the Moscow Radio on 5 December 1962)

## 22 APRIL 1964

*World's Fair Suite* for orchestra by Ferde Grofé, in five movements epitomizing the main points of attraction of the New York World's Fair—*Unisphere, International, Fun at the Fair, Pavilions of Industry* and *National*—is performed as a specially commissioned work for the first time at the opening of the Fair, in rainy weather, for an audience of 63 people, and in the presence of the semi-paralyzed 72-year-old composer (he suffered a stroke in 1962).

## 24 APRIL 1964

The Swiss Exposition of Industry opens in Lausanne, architecturally reflecting the modern world in its wall-less Pavillon Échange, with the world première of *Les Échanges* by Rolf Liebermann, scored for 52 machines, including teletypes, cash registers, staplers and copying devices, timed by an electronic computer to last exactly 195 seconds.

## 2 MAY 1964

A memorial exhibition to mark the centennial of the death of Giacomo MEYERBEER, the sublime melodramatist of ultra-romantic operatic art, opens in his native Berlin.

## 7 MAY 1964

*Sixth Symphony* by the prime Mexican composer Carlos CHÁVEZ, in three movements, *Allegro risoluto, Adagio* and a *Passacaglia* with 43 variations, is performed for the first time as a commissioned work by the New York Philarmonic, Leonard Bernstein conducting.

## 8 MAY 1964

Under the auspices of the Elizabeth Sprague Coolidge Foundation, the Library of Congress presents the world premières of the piano quintets by Roberto CAAMAÑO of Argentina, Gustavo BECERRA SCHMIDT of Chile and *Structures* for piano and string quartet by the Cuban-born American composer Aurelio de la VEGA, in five movements, containing three structures with two intervening "mobiles."

## 10 MAY 1964

*Epilogue to Profiles in Courage: J.F.K.*, a "symphonic dedication" by Roy HARRIS, lamenting in dark bitonalities punctuated by slow drum beats the loss to the world of a young American president, ending softly on the half-fulfilled promise of a G-major triad over a C-major chord, is performed for the first time in Los Angeles.

## 13 MAY 1964

*Concerto for Cello and Orchestra* by the Soviet composer Tikhon KHRENNIKOV is performed for the first time in Moscow by Mstislav Rostropovich, to whom the work is dedicated.

## 20 MAY 1964

At the opening concert of the Basel Festival of New Music from Germany and Switzerland, the first performance is given of *Épitaphe pour Évariste Galois*, "documented action" for soprano, baritone, narrators, speaking chorus, magnetic tape and orchestra by the 42-year-old Swiss composer Jacques WILDBERGER, depicting in six sections the tragically brief life of the French mathematician Évariste Galois, killed at the age of 20 in a duel in Paris, on 30 May 1832:

(1) *The Autopsy*, to the words of the official registry of death, detailing the exact nature of the mortal head wound (2) *The Night before the Duel*, to the text of the last letter which Galois wrote, and concluding with the statement "Je meurs victime d'une infâme coquette," the word "coquette" being scanned to the rhythm of a mocking in-

fernal dance (3) *Mathematics,* depicting in a scientifically serial idiom the mathematical speculations of Galois as a schoolboy, punctuated by marginal remarks of his teachers (4) *Politics,* presenting the facts of his republican agitation after the mild Paris revolution of 1830, resulting in his arrest and imprisonment (5) *The Death,* in which Galois voices his hatred of all authoritarianism and sketches the ideas of his revolutionary mathematical theory of groups (6) *Évariste Galois Illustre Mathématicien Français,* to the text of the inscription on the wall of the house in which Galois was born.

The mathematical achievement of Galois lies in the field of the theory of equations. He proved, with the aid of his newly developed theory of groups, that algebraic equations containing exponential powers higher than 4, cannot be solved in their general form. His discoveries formed the foundation of modern algebra. The group theory touches upon the problems of ornamentation, symmetries and permutations. Since these concepts, and particularly that of permutation, are integral parts of contemporary musical grammar, I became preoccupied with Galois. My work is an *hommage* to the unfortunate youth whose ideas are so important to us. These ideas are not "illustrated" in the music, but are present in its principle of organization. Thus, in the third section of my work, *Mathematics,* there are numerous interrelated permutation groups serving as a hidden steering system. (Elucidatory statement by Jacques Wildberger prepared at the author's request)

## 26 MAY 1964

*A Vision of Therese,* two-act opera by the 38-year-old Swedish composer Lars Johan WERLE, after Emile Zola's short story *Pour une nuit d'amour,* dealing with a provincial femme fatale who brings passion into the life of a flute-playing postal clerk, written in an idiom of anguished atonal tension, with realistic effects contributed by phonograph recordings, is performed for the first time during the Stockholm Festival of Music, Drama and Dance.

## 26 MAY 1964

Aaron COPLAND conducts the London Symphony Orchestra in the first performance of his *Music for a Great City* (commissioned by that orchestra on the occasion of its 50th anniversary), a symphonic cyclorama of sights and sounds of New York City, intensely realistic in its illustrative effects, in four tableaux, *Skyline, Night Thoughts, Subway Jam* and *Towards the Bridge.*

## 27 MAY 1964

The first International Seminar of Marxist Musicology opens in Prague, with delegates from the countries of the Socialist bloc, including the Soviet Union, East Germany, Hungary, Yugoslavia, Rumania and Bulgaria, assembled to discuss the dialectically correct interpretation of musical phenomena, in accordance with the Marxist doctrine of the identity of the real and epistemological worlds, and in the light of Lenin's theory of the sociological determinism of art.

## 28 MAY 1964

*Taras Shevchenko,* opera in four acts by the 50-year-old Ukrainian Soviet composer Georgi MAIBORODA, to his own Ukrainian libretto on the subject of the revolutionary life of the Ukrainian poet Shevchenko (1814–1861), is produced in Kiev.

## 28 MAY 1964

*4 x 5,* concerto for four quintets by the 57-year-old Russian-born Swiss composer Constantin REGAMEY, in five movements, *Perotinamente* (i.e. in the manner of Perotin), *Quasi una monodia, Condensazioni in moto, Mosaica e Corale, Concertando,* is performed for the first time at the Basel Festival of New Music.

## 28 MAY 1964

The 38th Festival of the International Society for Contemporary Music opens in Copenhagen with the following program:

*Konzertmusik für Blasorchester* by Paul HINDEMITH, written in 1927, a defiant fanfaronade in blatant sonic outbursts of wind instruments, containing quotations from popular German music; *Muzyka epifaniczna* by Tadeusz BAIRD of Poland, first performed under the French title *Musique épiphanique* in Montreux, Switzerland, on 12 September 1963, a musical stream of consciousness, emulating the inspired glossolalia of the Apostles and the grammatic epiphany of James Joyce; *Ricercari* for orchestra by the 33-year-old Argentinian composer Antonio TAURIELLO; *Mutazioni,* four choreographic fragments for orchestra by the 37-year-old Italian composer Vittorio FELLEGARA, based on serial structures of tones and intervals; and *Fragment VI* for six orchestral groups by the 31-year-old Danish composer Per NÖRGAARD, realized in optical notation for microchronous divisions and metrical notation for macrochronous progressions.

## 29 MAY 1964

At the second concert of the 38th Festival of the International Society for Contemporary Music in Copenhagen, the following program of chamber music is presented:

*Second Quintet* for piano, clarinet, violin, viola and cello by the 31-year-old Czech composer Ilja ZELJENKA, set in a *sui generis* punctualistic idiom in which serialism is liberalized and dodecaphony mitigated by tonal centralism while rhythmic organization is governed by the contrast of symmetrical and asymmetrical figurations; *4 Pieces for String Trio* by the 34-year-old Polish modernist Boguslaw SCHÄFFER, a suite of four short essays in virtuosity, demonstrating the execution of twisted sonorities, percussive effects on instrumental bodies, maximum velocity in glissandi, and diversification of pizzicati; *Being Beauteous* by the German expressionist Hans Werner HENZE, resident in Italy, for coloratura soprano, 4 cellos and harp to a poem of Rimbaud; *Pour violon et piano* by the 55-year-old Swiss-born Danish composer Gunnar BERG; *Sonant* for guitar, harp, doublebass and percussion by the Argentine-born German experimentalist Mauricio KAGEL, conceived *in statu nascenti* so that the complete execution of the work is immanently impossible, and the players are instructed to act, gesticulate and read aloud irrelevant texts borrowed from roulette (Faites votre jeu!) and from chess (Pièce touchée, Pièce jouée), with instantaneous and simultaneous translation into their respective mother tongues; and *Bolos* for 4 trombones, written in collaboration by two Swedish composers, Jan BARK and Folke RABE.

## 30 MAY 1964

At the third concert of the 38th Festival of the International Society for Contemporary Music in Copenhagen, the following program of chamber music by Danish composers is given:

*Passacaglie* for flute, violin, cello and piano by the 41-year-old Poul Rovsing LOSEN, in five movements, each based on a different rhythmic mode; *Direction: inconnue* by 33-year-old Ib NORHOLM, inspired by a one-way street sign in which the direction of the arrow is ambiguous; *Cantata* for contralto and seven instruments by 40-year-old Axel BORUP-JORGENSEN, and *In Terra Pax* for clarinet, piano and percussion by 32-year-old Pelle GUDMUNDSEN-HOLMGREEN.

## 30 MAY 1964

In the course of the 18th Festival at Ojai, California, a program of international avant-garde and electronic music is given:

*Samstirni* by the Icelandic composer Magus Blondal JOHANNSSON; *Ensembles for Synthesizer* by Milton BABBITT, of the Columbia-Princeton Electronic Music Center; *Duo for Clarinet and Recorded Clarinet* by William O. SMITH, originally produced at the Studio di Fonologia Musicale in Milan; *Mikrostruktury* by the Polish composer Wlodzimierz KOTOŃSKI, recorded at the Experimental Studio of the Polish State Radio in Warsaw; *Rhythm Studies* on perforated piano tape by the American-born composer Conlon NANCARROW, living in Mexico and recorded in his home studio; *Events* by Mel POWELL, prepared at the Electronic Music Studio at Yale University; *Tautalogos II* by Luc FERRARI, produced at the Centre de Recherche of the Radiodiffusion-Télévision Française in Paris; *La Sonate et les trois messieurs ou comment parler musique*, a surrealistic glossolalia by the French actor Jean TARDIEU, in which three people talk colloquially about the phenomenon of sonata form and its effect on the impressionable mind; *Selektion I* by Herbert EIMERT, produced at the Studio für Elektronische Musik in Cologne; and *Coordinates for Magnetic Tape* by the Cuban-Californian composer Aurelio DE LA VEGA, produced at the San Fernando Valley State College Electronic Laboratory in Northridge, California, in three movements: *Polynomial, Acoustical Measurements* and *Vectors*.

## 31 MAY 1964

The Mozart Express is launched by the Austrian Federal Railways, running between Vienna and Paris, leaving Vienna at 8:10 A.M., and after a stop at Salzburg, Mozart's birthplace, arriving in Paris at 11 P.M. (A train named Mozart Express was also run by the U.S. Occupation Forces between Munich and Vienna, during the period of 1946–1955).

## 1 JUNE 1964

At the fourth concert of the 38th Festival of the International Society for Contemporary Music in Copenhagen, the following program is presented:

*Diaglyphen* for chamber orchestra by the 40-year-old German composer Günther BECKER, in which the sonorous materials are arranged in three categories, alpha, beta and gamma, corresponding to the horizontality, verticality and diagonality of spatial and temporal parameters; *Concerto rapsodico* for voice and orchestra by the 40-year-old Austrian composer Karl Heinz Füssl, esthetically conceived on the geodesic line connecting Mahler with Berg; *Hi-Kyo* for flute, piano, strings and percussion by the 34-year-old Japanese composer Kazuo Fukushima, the title meaning literally a flying mirror, the music combining traditional oriental elements with western serialism; *Tre occasioni* for soprano and orchestra by the 34-year-old Italian composer Girolamo Arrigo, written to demonstrate that creative action may result from occasional opportunities; *Offrandes* for soprano and chamber orchestra by Edgar Varèse; and *Genesis II* for 15 performers by the 30-year-old Polish avant-garde composer Henryk Górecki.

## 2 JUNE 1964

At the fifth concert of the 38th Festival of the International Society for Contemporary Music in Copenhagen, the following program is presented:

*Movimento* for harpsichord, piano and 9 wind instruments by the 36-year-old Italian composer Franco Donatoni, conceived as a serialized set of variations, in which the antagonism between the harpsichord and piano is neutralized by the intervention of the brass; *Lyric Songs* for mezzo soprano and 2 pianos by the 33-year-old German composer Dieter Schönbach in which the German verses are treated as sonic verbalities to be integrated into the musical fabric; *Alpha-Beth* for six wind instruments by the 27-year-old French composer Gilbert Amy, written as an exercise in modern sonorities; *String Quartet* by the 38-year-old Hungarian composer György Kurtag, in six movements with free thematic associations in non-dodecaphonic atonalities; *Impressions d'un Choral* for harpsichord by the 29-year-old Bulgarian-born Israeli composer Yitshak Sadai, in which the melodic materials of Bach's chorale *O Haupt voll Blut und Wunden* is organized hendecaphonically in two unequal tone-rows of six and five notes; and *The World Is Discovered*, instrumental motet in 6 movements by the 29-year-old English composer Harrison Birtwistle.

## 3 JUNE 1964

The 38th Festival of the International Society for Contemporary Music in Copenhagen concludes with the following program of orchestral music:

*Metamorphose II* by the 32-year-old Catalan composer Enrique Raxach, in 15 sections forming three main divisions, organized according to contrasts of rhythms and timbres; *Equivalences* by the 25-year-old French composer Jean Claude Éloy, striving to achieve a serene equilibration of contrasting dynamic, rhythmic and instrumental elements with Zen-like pauses of total immobility; *7 Haikai*, Japanese sketches by Olivier Messiaen, with the participation of the electronic keyboard instrument, Ondes Martenot; *Wisnania (Confessions)*, three symphonic poems by the 37-year-old Polish composer Witold Szalonek, for narrator, chorus and orchestra, in expressionist colors; *Faglarna (The Birds)* by the 52-year-old Finnish composer Erik Bergman, for baritone and a chamber ensemble in which coloristic instruments predominate, designed to picture the human desire to fly away into the light of outer space; and *Nausikaa ensam* for soprano, chorus and orchestra by the 43-year-old Swedish composer Ingvar Lidholm, written in a neo-romantic quasi-expressionistic style.

## 3 JUNE 1964

*Martin's Lie*, chamber opera by Gian Carlo Menotti, to his own libretto, in which a 12-year-old medieval orphan boy shelters a heretic and refuses unto death to reveal his hiding place to the inquisitors, is performed for the first time anywhere at the opening of the 17th consecutive Music Festival in Bath, England.

### 3 JUNE 1964

*The Photo of the Colonel,* opera in three acts by the English composer Humphrey SEARLE, to a play by the Rumanian-Parisian dramatist of the theater of the absurd Eugene Ionesco, dealing with a maniacal killer who terrorizes the townspeople by inquiries about "the photo of the colonel" and then murdering them, with the music based on three groups of four chromatically adjacent tones aggregating to a dodecaphonic series, is performed for the first time on the stage in Frankfurt. (The first concert performance was broadcast by the British Broadcasting Corporation on 8 March 1964, the composer conducting)

### 4 JUNE 1964

*Demeter,* ballet by Boris BLACHER, is performed for the first time in Hannover.

### 6 JUNE 1964

*Karl Marx,* oratorio by the 31-year-old Estonian composer Jään RÄÄTS, to texts from Marx, employing spoken words as well as singing voices with an orchestral accompaniment, is performed for the first time in Tallin.

### 7 JUNE 1964

In the course of the centennial celebration of the birth of Richard STRAUSS, his unfinished mythological opera, *Des Esels Schatten,* focused on an ass's currier at the time of the "laughing philosopher" and father of the atomistic theory of matter Democritus, featuring a fauna of frogs, storks, tooth extractors and didactic scholars, arranged in six scenes from an incomplete manuscript by Karl Haussner, is presented for the first time in Ettal.

### 9 JUNE 1964

Louis GRUENBERG, Russian-born American-bred composer, whose opera *The Emperor Jones* momentarily gave the illusion of an American epic of the musical theater, and whose experiments in symphonic jazz earned him a footnote in modern music history, dies in Los Angeles in his 80th year.

### 11 JUNE 1964

A century has elapsed since the birth of the great German master of modern romantic music Richard STRAUSS.

### 11 JUNE 1964

*English Eccentrics,* "an entertainment in two acts" by the 32-year-old Australian composer Malcolm WILLIAMSON, a review in music of the history of British social non-conformists, is performed for the first time at the Aldeburgh Festival.

## 13 JUNE 1964

*Curlew River,* "parable for church performance" by Benjamin BRITTEN, inspired by a medieval Japanese *No* play, with the action transferred to an ungeographic Curlew River in East Anglia, wherein a woman searching for her lost son learns that he has drowned in it, with an all-male cast, an orchestra of seven players, and singers voicing their parts in half-spoken sounds, while the contrapuntal fabric is decussated into sparse Spartan patterns, is performed for the first time in Orford Church as part of the Aldeburgh, England, Music Festival.

## 16 JUNE 1964

Ernst KRENEK conducts in Hamburg the first performance of his opera *Der goldene Bock (The Golden Ram),* to his own libretto in which the Argonaut Jason inadvertently breaks the time barrier, finds himself on Route 66 in the United States, marries the termagant Medea, divorces her after she serves him a dish of human soup made of the flesh of a Greek shipping magnate and flies back in time and space to ancient Greece in a jet plane called Chrysomallos (i.e. golden fleece), which is attacked by Medea transformed into a dinosaur-sized dragon (she is thrown off the liner and perishes), with an ironic finale when Greek customs officers seize the golden fleece as contraband, the music written in a complex but logically impeccable serial idiom embellished by pre-recorded electronic sounds.

## 21 JUNE 1964

*Faust III,* operatic trilogy by the Danish composer Nils Viggo BENTZON, to his own libretto, in which Goethe's *Faust,* James Joyce's Bloom in *Ulysses* and Kafka's Josef K. in *The Trial* are psychologically related through their fantasies of feminine projections and magical Mephistos, is produced for the first time in Kiel at the opening of a Scandinavian-German Music Festival.

## 27 JUNE 1964

*Tongues of Fire,* oratorio by the 38-year-old Greek composer Jani CHRISTOU, to a text from the liturgical ritual of Epiphany, composed in a *sui generis* serial technique of isotones and isochrones and culminating in a magisterial canonic glossolalia uttered by intrapuntally involved speaking chorus, is performed for the first time at the Bach Festival in Oxford, England.

## 1 JULY 1964

Pierre MONTEUX, grand old man of French music, whose unobtrusive command of the orchestra inspired respect of his musicians and admiration of his composers, dies in his American summer home at Hancock, Maine in his 90th year, a few months after the conclusion of his last tour as guest conductor of European orchestras.

## 3 JULY 1964

*The Lady from Colorado,* one-act opera by the American composer Robert WARD, dealing with a real-life Irish immigrant girl whose spectacular marriage to a titled Englishman in a booming Colorado mining town in 1875 created a sensation in American society, is performed for the first time at the restored old opera house in Central City, Colorado.

## 4 JULY 1964

*Concerto for Two Pianos and Orchestra* by Walter PISTON is performed for the first time at the Second Congregation of the Arts at Dartmouth College, Hanover, New Hampshire.

## 15 JULY 1964

*Morvoren,* opera by the 34-year-old English composer Philip CANNON, to a libretto concerning an attractive Cornish mermaid who lures a susceptible altar boy to her aquatic realm, set to music in an expressionistically serialistic idiom, is performed for the first time in London.

## 24 JULY 1964

*Don Rodrigo,* opera by the prime composer of Argentina, Alberto GINASTERA, in nine scenes, each designated by a classical form (Rondo, Suite, Melodrama, Caccia and Scherzo, Nocturne and Duo, Aria Ternary Form, Canon and Aria, Arch Form), dealing with the semi-legendary 15th-century Spanish warrior Don Rodrigo who wages a patriotic war against the Moors, written in a dodecaphonic idiom enhanced by spatial serialism (12 dodecaphonic hunting horns are sounded from different points of compass in the hall to illustrate Don Rodrigo's desperate search for his beloved running in nude terror in the crepuscular forest; prophetic bells of liberty fill the hall ubiquitously in the scene of his death), is performed for the first time at the Teatro Colón in Buenos Aires as a specially commissioned work by the Argentine government.

## 2 AUGUST 1964

*Piano Concerto* by Vincent PERSICHETTI is performed for the first time at the Congregation of the Arts, Dartmouth College, Hanover, New Hampshire.

## 12 AUGUST 1964

*Sinfonia Sacra,* by Andrzej PANUFNIK, Polish composer resident in England, is performed for the first time at the Palace of Monaco as the prize-winning work in an international competition.

## 23 AUGUST 1964

*Abraham and Isaac,* sacred ballad for baritone and chamber orchestra by Igor STRAVINSKY, written in an expressive dodecaphonic idiom, to the original Hebrew text from Genesis, is performed for the first time in Jerusalem, in a concert hall situated in the immediate vicinity of Mt. Moriah where an angel of the Lord stayed Abraham's hand as he was about to carry out the abominable act of filicide as originally ordered by the inhuman and treacherous Jehovah, with Stravinsky's Boswellian famulus Robert Craft conducting in the presence of the composer.

### 30 AUGUST 1964

*Concertino* for piano, strings and percussion by the 29-year-old Greek composer Theodore ANTONIOU, written in a serial idiom in which the fundamental tone row grows cumulatively from an embryonic diatonic cellule, is performed for the first time in Athens.

### 3 SEPTEMBER 1964

*Cello Concerto* by the 61-year-old South African composeress Priaulx RAINIER is performed for the first time in London.

### 5 SEPTEMBER 1964

The entire company of La Scala of Milan opens its month-long guest season with a performance of PUCCINI's opera *Turandot*, at the Bolshoi Theater in Moscow, the first major European opera company to visit Soviet Russia.

### 5 SEPTEMBER 1964

A set of four stamps with portraits of the prime Rumanian composer of modern times, Georges ENESCO, is issued by Rumania on the occasion of the Third International Enesco Festival of Music and Drama in Bucharest.

### 6 SEPTEMBER 1964

*The Water and the Fire,* dramatic oratorio in four scenes by the English composer Anthony MILNER, on the theme of man's alienation from God, is performed for the first time in Herford, England, in the course of the Three Choirs Festival.

### 10 SEPTEMBER 1964

*Vox Maris,* symphonic poem by Georges ENESCO, his last work, completed by him a year before his death, symbolizing in romantic modalities the fate of a sailor lured by the "voice of the sea" to a watery grave, is performed for the first time in Bucharest.

### 17 SEPTEMBER 1964

*Der Zerrissene,* opera in two acts by Gottfried von EINEM, to a libretto arranged by Boris Blacher from a novel by Johann Nestroy, dealing with a disillusioned capitalist who finds that capital cannot buy happiness, set to music in an ostentatiously tonal manner immersed in a plasma of non-toxic dissonances and polytriadic parallelisms, is produced in Hamburg.

18 SEPTEMBER 1964

Carlos Chávez conducts in Mexico City the first performance of his orchestral *Resonancias*, commissioned by the Secretariat of Public Education in Mexico to celebrate the inauguration of the National Archeological Museum in Chapultepec, a polyphonic essay in ordered thematic resonances and rationally copulated dissonances, in a sui generis serial technique in which melorhythmic patterns are never duplicated, concluding with a serenely placed hendecaphonic chord.

1 OCTOBER 1964

*The East Is Red*, militant song of the Chinese Communist Party, is sung for the first time in Peking by a myriad of young Socialist voices. (Date obtained from Guozi Shudian, China Publications Center in Peking. A recording of the song was broadcast from space by the first Chinese satellite launched on 23 April 1970)

1 OCTOBER 1964

Ernst Toch, enlightened composer of symphonies, concertos, chamber operas, string quartets and other music, written in a cultured manner of modern romanticism, dies at the age of 76 in Los Angeles where he found his third home after his native Vienna and adoptive Berlin.

5 OCTOBER 1964

*Meditation on Zeami*, symphonic poem by the American composer Alan Hovhaness, glorifying in pentatonic sonorities of massed trumpets accompanied by clangorous bells the legendary founder of the Japanese No drama, is performed for the first time by the American Symphony Orchestra in New York, Leopold Stokowski conducting.

7 OCTOBER 1964

*Fifth Symphony* by the English composer Humphrey Searle, written in a serial technique in the spirit of Anton von Webern to whose memory the score is dedicated, is performed for the first time by the Halle Orchestra in Manchester, England.

8 OCTOBER 1964

*Natalia Petrovna*, opera in two acts by the 38-year-old American composer Lee Hoiby, to a libretto from Turgenev's play *A Month in the Country*, characterizing in romantic modalities distilled in modernistic ambitonalities the emotional turmoils of 19th-century Russian women, is performed for the first time at the City Center in New York.

14 OCTOBER 1964

The First Festival of American and Spanish Music opens in Madrid in the following program of orchestral music:

*Symphony No. 12* by Heitor VILLA-LOBOS (written in 1957 and first performed at the First Inter-American Music Festival in Washington on 20 April 1958); *Violin Concerto* by the Spanish-born Mexican composer Rodolfo HALFFTER, on his first visit of his native land; *Sinfonia* by the Cuban-American composer Aurelio de la VEGA (first performed at the Second Inter-American Music Festival in Washington on 30 April 1961), in four movements, *Obertura, Himno, Ostinato, Toccata,* based on four distinct dodecaphonic series fertilized by luxuriant rhythms; and *Lyric* for orchestra by the Canadian composer Harry SOMERS.

### 15 OCTOBER 1964

On the occasion of the 50th anniversary of the American Society of Composers, Authors and Publishers the United States Post Office issues a commemorative 5-cent stamp, depicting a lute, a clarion and an oblong music box.

### 15 OCTOBER 1964

Cole PORTER, American lyricist-composer, author of the nostalgic chromatic song *Night and Day*, the tropically pulsating, punningly sophisticated dance *Begin the Beguine*, and a number of other great melodies, dies of a kidney ailment in Santa Monica, California, at the age of seventy-one.

### 15 OCTOBER 1964

At the second concert of the First Festival of Music of America and Spain in Madrid, the following program of chamber music is given:

*Música para Muñecos de Trapo* for clarinet and string quartet by the 64-year-old Spanish composer Victorino ECHEVARRIA, in five picturesque episodes depicting life among puppets; *String Quartet,* subtitled *Carlos III* by the estimable Spanish composer of folkloristic Iberian music Conrado DEL CAMPO (1879–1953); *Quintet* for wind instruments by the prime composer of Chile Domingo SANTA CRUZ; and *Quintet* for piano and string quartet by the Mexican composer Blas GALINDO.

### 17 OCTOBER 1964

At the third concert of the First Festival of Music of America and Spain in Madrid, the following program of orchestral music is given:

*Preludio Sinfónico* by the Colombian composer Roberto PINEDA-DUQUE; *Canticum in P. P. Johannem XXIII* by Ernesto HALFFTER of Spain; *Sinfonía* by Celso GARRIDO LECCA of Peru (first performed at the Second Interamerican Music Festival in Washington on 22 April 1960), in three contrasting movements based on a 12-tone series; and *10 Melodías Vascas* for orchestra by the Basque composer Jesús GURIDI (1886–1959) originally performed on 12 December 1941 by the Madrid Symphony Orchestra, based on authentic Basque tunes.

### 19 OCTOBER 1964

At the First Festival of American and Spanish Music in Madrid the following program is given:

*Nonet for Solo Strings* by Aaron COPLAND (first performed in Dumbarton Oaks on 2 March 1961), dedicated to Nadia Boulanger and performable by groups of 24, 36, or

48 instrumentalists; *Suite* for harp, strings and percussion by Virgil Thomson, in three movements, in a world première, with Nicanor Zabaleta as soloist; *Capriccio* for harp and string orchestra by Walter Piston, a world première, performed by Zabaleta; *Partita* for strings by Enrique Solares of Guatemala, in four movements of atonal connotation; and *Concerto Breve* of considerable duration by the Catalan composer Xavier Montsalvatge.

### 21 OCTOBER 1964

At the First Festival of American and Spanish Music in Madrid the following program of orchestral music is given:

*Obertura Grotesca* by the Spanish-born Argentinian composer Julian Bautista (1901–1961), composed in 1932; *Concerto* for piano and orchestra by the Argentinian composer Roberto Caamaño in three neo-classical movements; *Rutas* by the Dominican composer Manuel Simo, in four movements in the neo-classical vein; *New England Episodes* by Quincy Porter (first performed at the First Interamerican Music Festival at Washington on 18 April 1958); and *Concerto for Orchestra* by the Venezuelan composer Antonio Estevez.

### 22 OCTOBER 1964

At the First Festival of American and Spanish Music in Madrid the following program is given:

*Cesuras* by the Spanish composer Luis de Pablo, for double trio of woodwind and string instruments consisting of freely serialized episodes separated by important pauses (hence the title); *Sincronismos No. 2* by the Argentinian composer Mario Davidovsky in which the basic instrumental quartet (flute, clarinet, violin and cello) is synchronized with a pre-recorded magnetic tape; *Lamentos* by the Peruvian composer Pozzi Escot, for voice and instruments, to the disembodied, dismembered and disfigured verbal elements taken from James Joyce and other authors, in five sections, each containing seventeen sound events; *Preludio* for magnetic tape by José Vicente Asuar of Chile; *Composition for IBM Computer 7090* by Gerald Strang of the U.S.; *Mixturas* by Carmelo A. Bernaola of Spain, representing a painter's color mixtures; and *Constantes Rítmicas en el Modo Primero* by José Soler of Spain.

### 24 OCTOBER 1964

*The Virgin and the Faun,* one-act opera by the Hungarian-born Californian composer Eugene Zador, wherein an impoverished family is compelled to sell their prized possession, a Renaissance painting of a shepherdess and a faun, with a happy ending secured when its young purchaser proposes to the daughter of the family, retaining the painting in their common home, written in a candidly harmonious and ostentatiously melodious manner, is performed for the first time anywhere by the Opera Workshop at the University of California, Los Angeles, with a piano accompaniment in the absence of an orchestra.

### 24 OCTOBER 1964

At the First Festival of American and Spanish Music in Madrid the following program is given:

*Third Symphony* in four movements, by the Chilean composer Juan ORREGO SALAS; *Variaciones sobre un Tema Nordestino* for piano and orchestra by the Brazilian composer Camargo GUARNIERI; *Te Deum* by the Uruguayan composer Hector TOSAR; and *Sinfonia Sevillana* by the Spanish composer of the old nationalist school Joaquín TURINA.

### 26 OCTOBER 1964

At the First Festival of American and Spanish Music in Madrid the following program of chamber music is presented:

*Second String Quartet* by Roberto GERHARD, Catalan composer residing in England; *String Quartet* by Francisco ESCUDERO of Spain; *Soli II* for wind quintet by Carlos CHÁVEZ of Mexico; and *Quintet* for piano and string quartet by the Chilean composer Gustavo BECERRA SCHMIDT.

### 27 OCTOBER 1964

To reciprocate the visit of the La Scala troupe in Russia in September 1964, the Bolshoi Theater Opera Company of Moscow goes to Milan for a season of 23 performances, opening with a spectacularly colorful presentation of the unabridged version of Mussorgsky's *Boris Godunov*, the only alteration being the elimination from the cast of characters of the name Khrushchev (odious since Nikita Khrushchev's fall from Soviet power on 14 October 1964), which appears in Pushkin's drama and in Mussorgsky's opera, replacing it with an anonymous designation "nobleman."

### 28 OCTOBER 1964

At the First Festival of American and Spanish Music in Madrid the following program is given:

*El Retablo de Maese Pedro*, puppet play by Manuel DE FALLA; *Concierto de Estio* for violin and orchestra by the blind Spanish composer Joaquín RODRIGO; and *Improperios*, a sacred chorus by the Spanish composer Federico MOMPOU.

### 30 OCTOBER 1964

*Vérnász*, opera in three acts by the 33-year-old Hungarian composer Sándor SZOKOLAY, after the mystical play *Bodas de Sangre* by Federico García Lorca, dealing with a bloody feud between two village families, culminating in an elopement of a married man with his rival's lethal bride (she is a symbol of Death incarnate) on her wedding day, leading to the death of both contenders and the retribution in blood dealt to her as well, is produced in Budapest.

### 30 OCTOBER 1964

The 13th Festival of Chamber Music opens in the Coolidge Auditorium of the Library of Congress in Washington to commemorate the centennial of the birth of Elizabeth Sprague Coolidge, the founder of the festival, with a program including PURCELL's ode, *Celebrate This Festival*, and three world premieres:

*Parole di San Paolo* by Luigi Dallapiccola, for voice and instruments, set in a dramatic dodecaphonic style of Italian provenance, with the composer conducting; *In Time of Daffodils* by Riccardo Malipiero, dodecaphonic nephew of Gian Francesco Malipiero, a set of five songs to the texts by E.E. Cummings, scored for soprano, baritone and a chamber ensemble; and *Miserere Nobis*, a Mass for 18 wind instruments by the German modernist Giselher Klebe, set in uncompromisingly dissonant Gothic counterpoint. (Aaron Copland's *Appalachian Spring*, originally commissioned by the Coolidge Foundation and performed for the first time at the 10th Coolidge Festival on 30 October 1944, was also included in the program)

### 31 october 1964

The First Festival of American and Spanish Music in Madrid concludes with the following program of orchestral music:

*Second Symphony* by the Panamanian composer Roque Cordero; *Sinfonía de Don Rodrigo*, comprising three excerpts from the opera *Don Rodrigo* by Argentina's prime modernist Alberto Ginastera; *Secuencias* by Cristóbal Halffter, ultra-modernistic nephew of Rodolfo and Ernesto Halffter, opening with an explosion of undifferentiated homogeneous noise as a manifestation of the primordial sonic universe, and progressing toward total organization and serialization of sonorous elements (first performed in Madrid on 16 June 1964); and the world première of *Sinfonia Aitana* (surnamed after a lofty mountain chain in the Levant), by the 78-year-old Spanish composer Oscar Esplá, subtitled *A la música tonal, in memoriam*, as a gesture of resignation in the face of the decline of time-honored tonal concepts.

### 31 october 1964

The second concert of the 13th Coolidge Festival in Washington continues with an afternoon program containing vocal pieces by Mozart and Beethoven and the following pieces by modern composers:

*Quartetto per Elisabetta*, dedicatory piece by Gian Francesco Malipiero, in one movement, for string quartet; first performance of *Amaryllis*, variations for string trio by William Schuman, based on an old English round and dedicated to the memory of Elizabeth Sprague Coolidge; *First String Quartet* by Prokofiev, originally composed for an early Coolidge festival in 1930; and the world première of *String Septet* by Darius Milhaud, in four movements of which the second, subtitled *Étude de hasard dirigé*, represents a modernistic interplay of directed chance.

(The evening program of 31 October 1964 contained a cantata by Schubert; the first performance of *Sonata a quattro* by the Chilean composer Juan Orrego-Salas, scored for flute, oboe, doublebass and harpsichord, in four movements; first performance of *Four Psalms* by Howard Hanson for baritone, two violins, two violas and two cellos; *Fifth String Quartet* by Béla Bartók, originally composed for a Coolidge Festival in 1934; and the first performance of *String Sextet* by Walter Piston, in three movements of varied content in a neo-baroque manner.

### 1 november 1964

At the afternoon concert of the 13th Coolidge Festival in Washington, the following program is given:

*Come, Ye Sons of Art*, cantata by Henry PURCELL; the world première of *Cantata* by the Cuban-Californian composer Aurelio de la VEGA, scored for two sopranos, contralto and chamber orchestra, in three movements, based on a dodecaphonic series: *Introduction, Contrapunctus primus, Contrapunctus secundus;* the world première of *The Feast of Love* by Virgil THOMSON for baritone and chamber orchestra, to the text from *Pervigilium Veneris*, written in an evocatively archaizing manner; *Herodiade*, orchestral recitation by Paul HINDEMITH; and the world première of *Bomarzo*, cantata for narrator, baritone and chamber orchestra by the prime composer of Argentina Alberto GINASTERA, in six sections, *The Horoscope, The Metaphysical Anxiety, The Portrait, In Search of Love, The Monsters of the Sacred Forest* and *Eternity of Bomarzo*, a dramatic hexalogy recounting the fateful career of the 16th-century hunchbacked Prince Pier Francesco Orsini, Duke of Bomarzo, whose quest for immortality leads him to murder in the company of mystical alchemists and caballistic astrologers, eventuating in the transformation of the rocks in his garden into giant monsters in the gaping mouth of one of which he perishes, set to music employing a number of ultra-modern serial techniques, including the application of the involutes, evolutes and spirals of the *Grossmutterakkord* (invertible dodecaphonic all-interval chord invented by Nicolas Slonimsky on 13 February 1938).

## 6 NOVEMBER 1964

Carnegie Hall is proclaimed a "Registered National Historic Landmark," and an appropriate plaque is unveiled in a special ceremony by Mayor Wagner of New York and representatives of the National Parks Service.

## 12 NOVEMBER 1964

*One-Man Show*, chamber opera by the 29-year-old British composer Nicholas MAW, dealing with an impecunious young art student whose back is discovered to be tattooed in a theoretically abstract pattern (actually it spells JOE upside down), and who therefore becomes the target of covetous art dealers, is performed for the first time in London.

## 13 NOVEMBER 1964

*Gesangszene* for baritone and orchestra, last work by the German master of symphonic counterpoint Karl Amadeus HARTMANN, to texts from the German translation of *Sodome et Gomorrhe* by Jean Giraudoux, is performed for the first time at Frankfurt, with an ending in speaking voice, following indications given by Hartmann himself at his deathbed on 5 December 1963.

## 15 NOVEMBER 1964

At the annual World Series of Roller Canaries in New York City, a quartet of canaries from Stony Creek, Ontario, is declared the winner for their excellence in schockels (a chuckling ha-ha-ha-ho-ho-ho), glucks (vocalized hen-like clucks), water rolls (gurgling trills) and flageolets (do-de-do-de), and for their scarcity of point-losing schwirrs (tearing sounds), locken (whistling), schnarrs (unvocal sibilation), aufzug (wheezing), schnatters and schnetters (a variety of schnarrs).

## 18 NOVEMBER 1964

*Shunkan (The Banishment)*, one-act opera by the 53-year-old Japanese composer Osamu SHIMIZU, based on the folk tale of a rebellious priest exiled in 1177 to a desert island by the Japanese feudal lords, is produced in Tokyo.

## 21 NOVEMBER 1964

*Willem van Saeftinge*, opera by the 35-year-old Dutch composer Freddy DEVREESE, to a historical libretto, portraying the pragmatism of ecclesiastical authorities in medieval Flanders, is performed for the first time in Antwerp.

## 21 NOVEMBER 1964

*Concerto* for clarinet and orchestra by the American composer Easley BLACKWOOD is performed for the first time in Cincinnati.

## 26 NOVEMBER 1964

*La nuit foudroyée*, opera in four acts by the 36-year-old French composer Jacques BONDON, in which a diurnal man is held in thrall by a nocturnal woman who disintegrates in his arms with the dawn, is performed for the first time in concert form on the Paris Radio. (A stage production took place in Metz on 10 February 1968)

## 30 NOVEMBER 1964

*The Sun of the Incas*, suite in six sections for soprano and 11 instruments by the 35-year-old Soviet modernist Edison DENISOV (he was named Edison because of his father's admiration for the inventive genius of Thomas Alva Edison), to the words of the Chilean Nobel-prize laureate Gabriela Mistral, and derived autonomously from a single series of 12 different notes, is performed for the first time in Leningrad.

## 30 NOVEMBER 1964

*Tartuffe*, fourth and last opera by the British composer Arthur BENJAMIN, completed shortly before his death in 1960 in vocal score, written in a relaxed opera-bouffe manner to suit Molière's comedy of hypocrisy, is performed for the first time in London under the direction of Alan Boustead who completed the orchestration of the opera.

## 3 DECEMBER 1964

*Three Against Christmas*, one-act opera by the American composer Andrew IMBRIE, dealing with the abolition of Christmas in a mythical town of Peebles, is performed for the first time at the workshop of the University of California in Berkeley.

## 6 DECEMBER 1964

The Pavilion of the Music Center for the Performing Arts in Los Angeles, one of the three structures erected at the cost of $33.5 million, opens its Dedication Week with a concert by the Los Angeles Philharmonic Orchestra, under the direction of its 28-year-old Indian conductor Zubin Mehta, officiating in his third season as musical director, in a program including *Fanfare* for massed brass and drums by Richard Strauss written by him for the Vienna Philharmonic in 1924, William Schuman's *American Festival Overture*, Ottorino RESPIGHI's *Feste Romane* and Beethoven's *Violin Concerto*, with Jascha Heifetz as soloist.

## 8 DECEMBER 1964

During the Dedication Week of the Pavilion of the Music Center for the Performing Arts in Los Angeles, the Los Angeles Philharmonic Orchestra, under the direction of Zubin Mehta, presents a program containing the First and the Ninth Symphonies of Beethoven and the world première of *Elytres* (French for *elytra*, anterior pair of wings in the Coleoptera serving to protect the posterior pair) by Lukas Foss, for twelve instruments playing only in the G clef and employing only the high half of the audible range to suggest the aleatorily aleate motion of the insect wings, and based on the principle of controlled stochastic musical data, resulting in 12 times 24 probabilistic events during actual performance.

## 11 DECEMBER 1964

Alma Mahler Gropius Werfel, widow of Gustav Mahler, the divorced wife of the architect Walter Gropius (with whom she became amorously involved while still married to Mahler who was aware of this relationship and was moved to write "beautiful poems" about it), widow of the writer Franz Werfel, self-confessed inamorata of many another genius (in her memoirs, *And the Bridge is Love*, she names as her lovers Oskar Kokoschka, the painter, Paul Krammerer, the biologist, and Ossip Gabrilowitsch, the pianist), dies in New York in the fullness of her days, at the age of eighty-five.

## 18 DECEMBER 1964

*Concerto* for koto and chamber orchestra by Henry COWELL, in three movements, the first using the characteristic descending Japanese mode (major third, minor second, major second, major third, minor second), the second set in a Western idiom, and the third combining the elements of both East and West, is performed for the first time in Philadelphia by the blind virtuoso koto player Kimio Eto, with Leopold Stokowski and the Philadelphia Orchestra.

## 28 DECEMBER 1964

*The Execution of Stepan Razin*, cantata for solo bass, chorus and orchestra by Dmitri SHOSTAKOVICH, to the text by the Soviet poet Evgeny Evtushenko, glorifying the career of the 17th-century rebel from Volga who rose against the power of the Tsar, is performed for the first time in Moscow.

# ∽ 1965 ∽

8 JANUARY 1965

*Five Contrasts for Orchestra,* a suite by the Hungarian-American composer Eugene ZADOR, presenting a quinquefoil of varied moods and culminating in a precipitous fugal avalanche, is performed for the first time by the Philadelphia Orchestra, Eugene Ormandy conducting.

14 JANUARY 1965

*5 Métaboles,* suite for orchestra by the 48-year-old French composer Henri DUTILLEUX, in five movements expressive of rhetorical metabolism in which the principal theme of each *métabole* undergoes topological translocations suggested by the individual titles, *Incantatoire, Linéaire, Obsessionnel, Torpide, Flamboyant,* written in the dissonant counterpoint of modern euphony, is performed for the first time by the Cleveland Orchestra, under the direction of George Szell.

19 JANUARY 1965

*Third Symphony* for string quartet and orchestra by Benjamin LEES, 41-year-old Manchurian-born American composer of Russian parentage, is performed for the first time in Kansas City.

20 JANUARY 1965

Alan FREED, American disc jockey who popularized the term Rock 'n' Roll to describe the stultifyingly monotonous type of syncopated music, originally known as rhythm-and-blues, whose ministrations at the turntable moved post-adolescent mobs to frenzy, and who was arrested, indicted and pleaded guilty to taking bribes, colloquially known as "payola" from publishers and recording companies to promote their inane ballads (he received a suspended sentence), dies at Palm Springs, California, at the age of forty-three.

20 JANUARY 1965

*Requiem für Lumumba* by Paul DESSAU, in 28 convulsive movements glorifying the martyred leader of Congo masses Patrice Lumumba, scored for two speakers, a speaking chorus and a wordless soprano voice, with a profusion of Central African percussion instruments, set in a dialectical dodecaphonic idiom but ending in triumphantly socialistic C-major, is performed for the first time in East Berlin.

## 24 JANUARY 1965

*Cello Concerto* by Jean MARTINON, French composer and conductor of the Chicago Symphony Orchestra, in three modernistic movements opening with a luxuriant cadenza and progressing through a passable labyrinth of asymmetrically rhythmed, polyharmonically integrated serial themes with conjugate tonal foci, is performed for the first time in Hamburg.

## 30 JANUARY 1965

*Ukiyo (Floating World)*, ballad for orchestra by Alan HOVHANESS inspired by an old Japanese Buddhist concept of the unpredictability of fate, the music exfoliating from a single dramatic theme, and ending in a state of "controlled chaos", is performed for the first time in Salt Lake City.

## 2 FEBRUARY 1965

*Antiphonies* by the 28-year-old French composer Gilbert AMY, written for two orchestras in antiphonal competition, with a third orchestra entering the musical tournament to arbitrate polyphonic differences, is performed for the first time in Paris, with the composer and Bruno Maderna as synchronized conductors.

## 8 FEBRUARY 1965

*Appassionato* for orchestra by the German-born American composer Lothar KLEIN is performed for the first time in Dallas, Texas.

## 8 FEBRUARY 1965

*First Symphony* by the American composer Gunther SCHULLER, combining elements of formal classicism with the ingredients of the Third Stream (the term of his own invention denoting civilized jazz), is performed for the first time in Dallas.

## 24 FEBRUARY 1965

*The Mines of Sulphur*, opera by the 28-year-old English composer Richard Rodney BENNETT (the title is from one of Iago's speeches in Shakespeare's Othello), wherein a band of 18th-century English gypsies murder a rich old man but are driven to terrified confessions when a phantom theatrical troupe performs a play reenacting the murder, in addition contaminating them with plague, set to music in a suitably melodramatic modern idiom, permeated with non-infectious dissonances, is produced in London.

## 1 MARCH 1965

*Clitennestra*, music drama by Ildebrando PIZZETTI, depicting the classic tragedy of Clytemnestra, from her murder of Agamemnon to her death at the hands of her own children, Electra and Orestes, is produced at the Teatro alla Scala in Milan.

4 MARCH 1965

*Narrative for Orchestra* by the 41-year-old American composer William FLANAGAN is performed for the first time by the Detroit Symphony Orchestra.

4 MARCH 1965

In the course of the Buffalo Festival of the Arts Today a *Poème Symphonique* for 100 metronomes by the Hungarian composer György LIGETI is given its first American performance, at the Buffalo Festival of the Arts Today, with ten performers assigned the task of winding up the metronomes set at different speeds, the ending signalized by the expiration of the beats of the terminal metronome.

I composed my piece for 100 metronomes in 1962, partly as a sort of persiflage of chance music (believing that the little automatons can do this job better than human performers), partly as an experiment in "continuous form" resulting in a gradual "rhythmic diminuendo," the metronomes stopping one by one. Different polymetric patterns arise automatically; the slowest oscillating metronome remains alone at the end. The world première took place in September 1963 at the official party given by the burgomaster of Hilversum. All performers, with myself as conductor, wore full dress. The production was taped for television, but the film was never shown because the Senate of the City of Hilversum protested against the public showing and the burgomaster himself felt deeply offended. (From Ligeti's letter to the author, dated 21 May 1965)

5 MARCH 1965

*Eighth Symphony* by Walter PISTON, his first major work containing explicit dodecaphonic processes, scored for a full symphonic contingent and two non-arpeggiating harps, in three movements: (1) *Moderato mosso*, evolving from a somberly involuted 12-tone motive, with harmonic configurations anchored in tritones and perfect fourths (2) *Lento assai*, a suite of variations marked by thematic imbrication in fugal progressions (3) *Allegro marcato*, a propulsive rhythmic rondo, thematically purified by recurrent diatonic statements, and concluding on an ascetic thirdless C triad, is performed for the first time by the Boston Symphony Orchestra conducted by Charles Munch.

7 MARCH 1965

*Third Symphony* by the 31-year-old American composer Easley BLACKWOOD is performed for the first time in Chicago.

9 MARCH 1965

Gunther SCHULLER conducts the New Orleans Philharmonic Symphony Orchestra in the first performance of his orchestral *American Triptych: Three Studies in Texture*, in the following divisions:

(1) *Calder's Four Directions*, a musical realization of Alexander Calder's rotating mobiles representing a three-dimensional spatial counterpoint, with an intussusception of instrumental groups on the stage written in serial melodic formations (2) *Pollock's Out*

*of the Web,* illustrating Jackson Pollock's drip method of painting, applying an analogous aleatory dripping of notes and tone-colors (3) *Davis's Swing Landscape,* written in an enriched jazz technique to convey the visual impression of paintings of Stuart Davis, with the musical course following three different tempo levels.

15 MARCH 1965

*Inferno 1944,* oratorio by Hellmuth Christian WOLFF, commemorating the massive Allied air assault on Dresden in 1944, is performed for the first time in Gera, East Germany.

19 MARCH 1965

*The Emperor of Ice Cream,* music drama by the 31-year-old American composer Roger REYNOLDS, derived from stochastically calculated probabilities of sonic incidence, is performed for the first time at the third 20th-Century Innovations Concerts in New York City, under the direction of Gunther Schuller.

25 MARCH 1965

*Atomtod,* opera by the 32-year-old Italian composer Giacomo MANZONI depicting in a surrealistically apocalyptic spirit the atom death of Planet Earth, with a handful of men surviving in ultra-scientific shelters but perishing in the end of mental inanition, is produced at the Piccolo Scala in Milan.

25 MARCH 1965

*Lizzie Borden,* opera by the 43-year-old American composer Jack BEESON, drawn from the famous parenticidal case of the 1890's in New England ("she gave her father forty whacks, and when she saw what she had done, she gave her mother forty-one"), written in a flippantly melodramatic vein, with topical allusions to hymnal chants, seasoned with expressionistic atonalities, is produced in New York.

26 MARCH 1965

On his 40th birthday Pierre BOULEZ conducts, at the Monday Evening Concerts in Los Angeles, the world première of his *Éclat* for divers instruments.

28 MARCH 1965

*The Passion According to Saint Luke,* oratorio by Randall THOMPSON, is performed for the first time in Boston.

2 APRIL 1965

The first stage performance of the opera *Deirdre* by the dean of Canadian composers, Healey WILLAN, to a libretto from the Irish legend of the Red Branch Knights of Ulster, set to music in a flamboyant Wagneromantic style, is presented in Toronto.

7 APRIL 1965

*Der junge Lord,* opera buffa in two acts by Hans Werner HENZE, dealing with a 19th-century Byronic English gentleman dallying in a provincial German town who manhandles a girl by mammary palpation, tears off his clothes and reveals himself as a circus ape, set to music in a mock-Verdian style, is performed for the first time in Berlin.

8 APRIL 1965

*Calder Piece,* by Earle BROWN for four percussion instruments silently accompanied by a mobile by Alexander Calder, is performed for the first time in Paris.

10 APRIL 1965

*Philidor's Defense,* symphonic poem by the 55-year-old Prague-born American composer Paul REIF, describing a famous chess game in 1858, is performed for the first time in New York.

11 APRIL 1965

*The Final Ingredient,* opera by the 34-year-old American composer David AMRAM, to the story of a Passover celebration by Jewish prisoners in a Nazi concentration camp, is performed for the first time as a commissioned work by the American Broadcasting Company, with the composer conducting.

14 APRIL 1965

On the centennial day of Lincoln's assassination, *Abraham Lincoln Symphony* by Roy HARRIS, chronologically his tenth, for chorus, brass ensemble, two amplified pianos and percussion, in five movements, relating to five aspects of Lincoln's career, is performed for the first time at Long Beach, California.

17 APRIL 1965

A concert of Igor STRAVINSKY's music is given by the Chicago Symphony Orchestra, including two new pieces: *Variations,* based on a linear succession of twelve different thematic notes representing "musical mobiles" and *Introitus: T. S. Eliot in Memoriam,* scored for six male voices, harp, piano, viola, double bass, four kettledrums and two gongs.

25 APRIL 1965

*Concerto for Orchestra* by the Catalan-born composer Roberto GERHARD, resident in England since 1936, is performed for the first time anywhere by the British Broadcasting Corporation Symphony Orchestra, in Boston during its American tour.

26 APRIL 1965

The American Symphony Orchestra, under the direction of Leopold Stokowski, gives the first integral performance of the grandiose *Fourth Symphony* by Charles IVES, composed between 1910 and 1916, in four movements:

(1) *Prelude: Maestoso adagio,* a solemnly intimate evocation of the American scene, with the hymn *Watchman, Tell Us of the Night,* as a central melodic idea (2) *Allegretto,* derived from the music of the second movement of the *Concord Sonata,* depicting Hawthorne's transcendental ride in the "Celestial Railroad," and set in a fantastically complicated, polymetric, polyrhythmic, polyharmonic, and polycontrapuntal palimpsest, with particles of American songs, ballads and hymns strewn over the orchestral musicorama (3) *Fugue, Andante con moto,* transcribed from Ives's First String Quartet written in 1896, subtitled A Revival Meeting, and fugally treated in a euphoniously dissonant vein (4) *Largo maestoso,* derived from Ives's *Memorial Slow March* for organ composed in 1901 and based on the melody of the hymn *Nearer, My God, to Thee,* concluding on a philosophical concord, with drums marking time in the distance.

The esthetic program of the work is that of the searching questions of What? and Why? which the spirit of man asks of life. This is particularly the sense of the prelude. The three succeeding movements are the diverse answers in which existence replies. (From a program note written by Charles Ives for the performance of the second movement given in New York under the direction of Eugene Goossens on 29 January 1927)

### 30 APRIL 1965

*The Torch of Prometheus,* opera by the Czech composer Jan HANUŠ, wherein a modernized Prometheus steals atomic fire from heaven thus challenging the power of the monopoly of the dictatorial and imperialistic Olympus, is produced in Prague.

### 30 APRIL 1965

The Symphony Orchestra of the British Broadcasting Corporation presents the first of a series of six concerts of 20th-Century music at Carnegie Hall in New York with Antal Dorati, musical director, conducting. (The last concert of the series took place on 15 May 1965)

### 2 MAY 1965

The Early Bird Satellite, launched by the American Telegraph and Telephone Company, transmits selections of hedonistically cosmopolitan band music from radio stations in Washington, Québec and Portsmouth, England, and a chorus from Stockholm, in a synchronized rendition with Washington, of *Auld Lang Syne,* with 1/6 second's lag required for the radio signal to reach the satellite and bounce back to earth.

### 2 MAY 1965

The Seattle Symphony Orchestra, Milton Katims conductor, presents a Contemporary Festival Concert under a grant from the Rockefeller Foundation and under the auspices of the University of Washington School of Music, in the following program of first performances by American composers: *Oracles* by William BOLCOM; *Elegiac Symphony* by Donald KEATS; *Graffiti* by Roger REYNOLDS and *Symphony of Overtures* by Donald ERB.

## 4 MAY 1965

*Intimation to the Living,* cantata for narrator, chorus and orchestra by the Dutch composer Hans HENKEMANS, commissioned by the Artists Resistance Movement 1942–1945 of Holland, is performed for the first time in Amsterdam on the National Remembrance Day, marking the 20th anniversary of the liberation of Holland from the Nazis.

## 7 MAY 1965

The Third Inter-American Music Festival opens in Washington with a program comprising the world premières of the following works:

*Little Symphony* by Luis Antonio ESCOBAR of Colombia; *Second Symphony,* subtitled *Billy Ascends,* by Robert EVETT of the United States, symbolizing the spiritual ascent of Billy Budd after his hanging in Herman Melville's classic story; *Concerto* for five timpani and orchestra by Jorge SARMIENTOS of Guatemala; *Concerto a tre* for violin, cello, piano and orchestra by Juan ORREGO-SALAS of Chile; and the first American performance of the *Sinfonia de Don Rodrigo* for dramatic soprano and orchestra by Alberto GINASTERA of Argentina.

## 8 MAY 1965

In the course of the Third Inter-American Music Festival in Washington, five world premières of the following pieces of chamber music for strings are presented:

*String Trio* by Joaquín ORELLANA of Guatemala; *String Quartet* by Eduardo MATURANA of Chile; *Invention* for string trio by Carlos CHÁVEZ of Mexico; *Three Poems* for narrator and string quartet by Pozzi ESCOT of Peru and *Second String Quartet* by Ezra LADERMAN of the United States.

## 9 MAY 1965

In the course of the Third Inter-American Music Festival in Washington the following works are performed for the first time:

*Rondo Rhapsody* for orchestra by John VINCENT of the United States; *Dúo Trágico* for piano and orchestra in memory of John F. Kennedy by Hector CAMPOS-PARSI of Puerto Rico; *Nueva York* by Leon SCHIDLOWSKY of Chile; *Third Symphony* by Domingo SANTA CRUZ of Chile; *Violin Concerto* by Roque CORDERO of Panama; *Symphonic Suite* by Pedro SANJUÁN of the United States.

## 11 MAY 1965

In the course of the Third Inter-American Music Festival in Washington, the following program of orchestral world premières is presented by the Buffalo Philharmonic Orchestra conducted by Lukas Foss:

*Laudes* by Celso GARRIDO-LECCA of Peru; *Concertino de cámara* by Alfonso MONTECINO of Chile; *Stray Birds,* triptych for baritone and eleven instruments by Hector TOSAR of Uruguay; *Vivencias I-IV* by Enrique ITURRIAGA of Peru; and *Violin Concerto* by Juan José CASTRO of Argentina.

## 12 MAY 1965

At the last concert of the Third Inter-American Music Festival in Washington the following program of first performances is given:

*Sejatpar* by Marina SAIZ of Panama; *Cello Concerto* by Claudio SANTORO of Brazil; *Transparencias* for six instrumental groups by Antonio TAURIELLO of Argentina; *Orchestra Variations* by Gerardo GANDINI of Argentina; and *Music for Piano and Orchestra* by Juan Carlos PAZ of Argentina.

## 12 MAY 1965

The Spring Festival of Czechoslovakia opens in Prague, inaugurating a series of 71 concerts with the participation of Sadler's Wells Opera Company of London; Cleveland Orchestra, George Szell conducting; London Symphony Orchestra, George Solti conducting, Moscow Radio Symphony Orchestra, and the Czech Philharmonic (the Festival closed on 11 June 1965)

## 20 MAY 1965

The 39th Festival of the International Society for Contemporary Music opens in Madrid with the following program of symphonic music:

*Stasimon B !* by the Greek composer Yorgo SICILIANOS, for chorus and orchestra, to words from Euripides, constituting an attempt to revive ancient Greek modes with the aid of modern serial techniques; *Piano Concerto* by the 58-year-old Japanese composer Yoritsune MATSUDAIRA, in three movements, inspired by ancient Japanese court music, but constructed according to dodecaphonic procedures, lubricated by quartertones and diversified by aleatory devices; *Spiegel II* by the 39-year-old Austrian composer Friedrich CERHA, a cycle of six pieces for 55 string instruments, forming multiple reflecting surfaces of sonic chirality; and *Second Symphony*, in three movements, *Heurté, Fluide, Vigoureux*, by the 59-year-old French composer André JOLIVET, employing a free, eclectically atonal and adumbratively serial method of composition with an infusion of subtropical rhythms.

## 21 MAY 1965

At the 39th Festival of the International Society for Contemporary Music in Madrid, the following program of chamber music is performed:

*3 Fantasias* for clarinet and piano by the 32-year-old Berlin-born British composer Alexander GOEHR, combining the "fantastic" element in the Miltonian sense in a proliferation of fugal fancies with a modernistic profusion of unmitigated dissonances; *In Time of Daffodils* for soprano, baritone and a chamber group of instruments by the 50-year-old Italian composer Riccardo MALIPIERO, nephew of Gian Francesco Malipiero, to the texts, in English, of five surrealist poems by the American poet, E. E. Cummings; *Alpha-Beth* for six instruments by the 28-year-old French composer Gilbert AMY, in five movements illustrating various combinations of instruments and rhythms; *Polar* by the 35-year-old Spanish composer Luis de PABLO, in which heterogeneous groups of instruments are mutually polarized (hence the title); *Concerto for String Instruments* by the 25-year-old Japanese composer Motohiko ADACHI, derived from a single agogic pattern; *Glühende Rätsel (Glowing Riddles)* by the 26-year-old Swiss composer Heinz HOLLIGER, for contralto and a small group of instruments, in five sections unified by a common melorhythmic pattern; and *Contrasts* for piano, violin and clarinet by Béla BARTÓK, in three dance movements.

## 22 MAY 1965

*The Happy Prince,* opera by the 33-year-old New Zealand composer Malcolm WILLIAMSON, after Oscar Wilde, scored for 8 soloists, chorus, semi-chorus, piano duet and percussion, is performed for the first time at the Farnham Festival in England.

## 22 MAY 1965

At the 39th Festival of the International Society for Contemporary Music in Madrid, the following program of symphonic music is performed:

*Eufonia 64* by the 48-year-old Hungarian composer Rudolf MAROS for 24 wind instruments, two harps and percussion, in four symmetrical movements subordinated to the idea of an equilibrium of sound, form and notation; *In Nuce* by the 42-year-old Swedish composer Ake HERMANSON, consisting of a series of parallel variations in indeterminate notation, evoking an embryo's evolution into a foetus (hence the title, "in a nutshell"); *Hölderlin-Fragmente* by the 29-year-old German composer Aribert REIMANN, for soprano and instruments, to the mystical texts of Friedrich Hölderlin's poems, built on a free serial basis and developed in pointillistic images; *Music for Orchestra* by the 43-year-old Polish composer Andrzej DOBROWOLSKI constructed in spatial matrices of instrumental groups; *Violin Concerto* by Alban BERG; and *Secuencias* by the 35-year-old Spanish composer Cristóbal HALFFTER, representing a succession of acoustical phenomena, beginning with white noise without rhythmic organization, and progressing towards increasingly complex integration of thematic sonorities.

## 24 MAY 1965

At the 39th Festival of the International Society for Contemporary Music in Madrid, the following program of chamber music is performed:

*Music for Brass Quintet* by the 39-year-old American composer Gunther SCHULLER, in three movements representing the integral calculus of differential melorhythmic fragments with a series of brief cadenzas improvised by the players in the jazz idiom; *Rondeaux per Dieci* by the 42-year-old Italian composer Camillo TOGNI, for soprano and nine instruments (aggregating to ten performers thus justifying the title), written in the manner of serialistic neo-classicism; *Sonata Canonica,* by the 28-year-old Czech composer Peter KOLMAN, an aphoristic composition for clarinet and bass clarinet thematically built on a permutating dodecaphonic series; *Divisions* by the 29-year-old Swiss composer Jürg WYTTENBACH for piano and strings in four movements, following the Baroque forms with improvised permutations of principal themes in free cadenzas; *Fresque sonore* for 7 instruments by the 43-year-old Japanese composer Shin-Ichi MATSUSHITA, evocative of oriental frescos with varied instrumental colors in an acoustical space; *Einst dem Grau* by the 28-year-old Dutch composer Ton DE KRUYF, inspired by a mystical poem of Paul Klee, and involving the application of dodecaphonic techniques; *Destination 5* by the 30-year-old Israeli composer Noam SHERIFF, for two trumpets, two trombones, tuba and percussion, the duration of performance stipulated to be precisely five minutes, and the metric arrangements being derived from the geometric properties of the golden mean section.

## 25 MAY 1965

At the 39th Festival of the International Society for Contemporary Music in Madrid, the following program of Spanish music is performed:

*Homenaje a Miguel Hernández* for bass voice and orchestra to the words of Miguel Hernández, by the 32-year-old Spanish composer Antón García ABRIL; *Sonata del Sur* by the dean of Spanish composers Oscar ESPLÁ, for piano and orchestra, in three movements, permeated with melorhythms of Spanish secular and sacred music; *Ausencias de Dulcinea* by the blind Spanish composer Joaquín RODRIGO, a symphonic poem inspired by Cervantes and his vision of Dulcinea; *Canticum in P. P. Johannem XXIII* for soprano, bass and chorus, by the Spanish composer Ernesto HALFFTER; and *Desintegración morfológica de la Chacona de Bach* by the 53-year-old Spanish composer Xavier MONTSALVATGE, in which Bach's famous Chaconne for violin solo is morphologically fissioned, then reassembled in a new form.

## 26 MAY 1965

At the 39th Festival of the International Society for Contemporary Music in Madrid, the following program of symphonic music is presented:

*Szene II* by the 28-year-old Swedish composer Bo NILSSON, one of his three *Scenes for Orchestra* written in an abstractly theatrical manner; *Epitaffio* for orchestra and magnetic tape by the 34-year-old Norwegian composer Arne NORDHEIM, with only three words used in the text culled from the verses of the Italian poet Salvatore Quasimodo (Solo, Terra, Sera) interpreted as emotional signals for the music; *Freski symfoniczne* by the 43-year-old Polish composer Kazimierz SEROCKI, in four sections, each representing an imaginary fresco; *Symphony* by Anton VON WEBERN, in two movements, op. 21, his masterpiece of dodecaphonic chirality; *Abraham and Isaac* by Igor STRAVINSKY for baritone and orchestra; and *A Survivor from Warsaw,* for narrator, chorus and orchestra, by Arnold SCHOENBERG.

## 27 MAY 1965

*The Judas Tree,* "musical drama of Judas Iscariot," by the 30-year-old British composer Peter DICKINSON, for speakers, singers, chorus and chamber orchestra, wherein the tree on which Judas hanged himself is mystically identified with the tree of the true cross, utilizing in the score various forms of serial devices and electronic effects and simplicistically tonal harmonies, with the tritone (the medieval "diabolus in musica") representing Judas, progressing through a series of excruciating (*ex cruce*) discords to a theologically immaculate unison symbolizing the sacrificial identity of Jesus and Judas, is performed for the first time in the College of St. Mark and St. John in London.

## 28 MAY 1965

The 39th Festival of the International Society for Contemporary Music concludes in Madrid with the following program of music for chamber orchestra:

*Iter inverso* by the 40-year-old Italian composer Domenico GUACCERO, in two sections, *Da monodia a linee* and *Da linea a sfera,* illustrating a geometric expansion from linear melody to spherical harmony in a spatial distribution of instrumental sonorities; *Bo-*

*marzo*, cantata for narrator, baritone and instruments by the prime Argentinian composer, 49-year-old Alberto GINASTERA, revolving around a mad Florentine Duke and written in a serial idiom; *Combat T 3 N* by the 25-year-old French composer René KOERING, depicting in serially designed melodies and rhythms the composer's impression of the French Army maneuvers in which he participated; *Stabat Mater* for 3 unaccompanied choruses by the 31-year-old prime modernist of Poland, Krzysztof PENDERECKI, using liturgical chant patterns of the Catholic ritual surrounded by a raging stream of anguished dissonance; and *El Retablo de Maese Pedro* by Manuel DE FALLA, a "musical and scenic adaptation of the story of the ingenious Knight Don Quixote of La Mancha."

## 5 JUNE 1965

*24 Hours*, a festival of environmental anti-music is proffered in Wuppertal, Germany, featuring the following non-events:

*String Quartet* by George BRECHT (the four players shake hands mutually and depart); *Danger Music Number Six* by Dick HIGGINS (a silent piece); *Collective Composition* by György LIGETI, entitled *The Future of Music* (the composer appears with a stopwatch and scrutinizes the audience whose reaction constitutes the content of the composition); *Creep into the Vagina of a Living Whale* by the Korean composer Nam June PAIK (free improvisation with any animate object); *Count the Waves of the Rhine* by Nam June PAIK (a notated piece of music containing only rests and repeat signs); *Two Sounds* by La Monte YOUNG, a verbal piece containing the words "Two Sounds" but no actual sounds; *Music for the Ear* by Dick HIGGINS; *Composition 1960, No. 15* by La Monte YOUNG, a piece to be imagined only.

## 8 JUNE 1965

Erik CHISHOLM, Scottish composer of a number of sophisticated works in various genres, including expert stylizations of Oriental modes, dies in Rondebosch, South Africa, at the age of sixty-one.

## 15 JUNE 1965

The 18th Holland Festival of Music and Drama opens in Amsterdam with a concert by the Concertgebouw Orchestra featuring the posthumous performance of *Salutation Joyeuse* by Anton van der HORST, Dutch composer who died in Amsterdam on 7 March 1965.

## 16 JUNE 1965

In the course of the Holland Music Festival two operas by Dutch composers are presented for the first time in Amsterdam:

*De Droom (The Dream)* by Ton de LEEUW, in which dreams are induced by a somnificent pillow, featuring a ballet based on 13 *Haikai* in English, set to music in an orientalistically modernistic vein, in a scientific notation so that the linear dimensions are proportional to the duration of each note; and *Jean Léveck* by Guillaume LANDRÉ, to Guy de Maupassant's story *Le Retour*, wherein a vagabond returning to his abandoned and long remarried wife, agrees to disappear again so as not to disturb her new happiness, set in a euphoniously dissonant idiom.

## 20 JUNE 1965

*L'Hymne aux Morts* by Olivier MESSIAEN, commemorating the dead of the two world wars, is presented for the first time at the Cathedral of Chartres, on the occasion of the visit there of President Charles de Gaulle.

## 20 JUNE 1965

*Traumspiel*, first opera by the 28-year-old German composer Aribert REIMANN, after August Strindberg's symbolically realistic psychological drama *Ett Drömspel* (*The Dream Play*), couched in a lyrically expressionistic modern idiom asymptotically tending towards shifting tonal foci, is produced in Kiel.

## 24 JUNE 1965

*Second Symphony* by the French composer Marcel LANDOWSKI is performed for the first time in Strasbourg.

## 28 JUNE 1965

*Moses und Aron*, Arnold SCHOENBERG's unfinished expressionistic opera, is given its first London performance at the Royal Opera House in Covent Garden, eliciting shocked and prurient comments regarding the realistic mise-en-scène of the climactic orgy depicting the sacrifice to the golden calf of three bare-bosomed virgins, who were, however, asked to turn their backs to the audience. (The fiery immolation of live animals was left out of the production owing to safety regulations forbidding the setting of fires on the stage)

## 14 JULY 1965

Leonard BERNSTEIN conducts the New York Philharmonic in the world première of his *Chichester Psalms*, for chorus and orchestra, commissioned by the Chichester Cathedral, to the Hebrew texts of Psalms 100, 23 and 131, set in a neo-ecclesiastical idiom of ascetic severity, marked by a proliferation of ominous harmonic collisions and asymmetrical rhythmic phrases. (The first performance in Chichester, England, took place at the Tri-Choir Festival, on 31 July 1965)

## 21 JULY 1965

*Le Rossignol de Boboli*, one-act operatic "fable" by Alexandre TANSMAN, in which a nightingale, accidentally mutated into a human, is restored to his original avian identity thanks to the efforts of a devoted love bird, is produced in Nice.

## 4 AUGUST 1965

*Cantos for orchestra* by the 43-year-old Scottish composer Iain HAMILTON, designed according to the principles of instrumental serialism, in 5 sections: *Parade, Nocturne I, Sonata, Nocturne II, Declarations*, is performed for the first time in London.

## 10 AUGUST 1965

An estimated horde of 70,000 people gathers at the Sheep Meadow in Central Park, New York, to hear the first performance of a newly established series of outdoor concerts by the New York Philharmonic, in a program comprising the first performance of William SCHUMAN's *Philharmonic Fanfare*, WAGNER's *Meistersinger Overture* and BEETHOVEN's Ninth Symphony, William Steinberg conducting. (Eleven more concerts were given by the New York Philharmonic in New York, Brooklyn and Queens attracting great crowds)

## 25 AUGUST 1965

The third annual Avant-Garde Festival opens in New York in a program of *Action Music* by the Korean composer Nam June PAIK, including an *Ommaggio a Cage* scored for a destructible upright piano, a dozen eggs, scissors for an instant haircut and tape-recorded noises, with the participation of the cellist Charlotte Moorman wearing a cellophane sheath and playing *Le Cygne* by SAINT-SAËNS in an oil drum filled with water. (The series concluded on 11 September 1965)

## 2 SEPTEMBER 1965

*Herr von Hancken*, second opera in three acts by the Swedish composer Karl-Birger BLOMDAHL, dealing with a Swedish paterfamilias pursued by God for his blasphemous outrecuidance and saved from perdition by the devil whom he encounters in a European spa in 1806, set to music in a serialistic technique, in which the leading motives of God, man and devil are formed by permutated ingredients of the governing tonal series, is produced in Stockholm.

## 4 SEPTEMBER 1965

Albert SCHWEITZER, great Alsace-born humanitarian, who began his career as an organist and a Bach scholar, winner of the Nobel Peace Prize, who went to West Africa to serve the ailing natives as a physician, dies in the jungle hospital of Lambaréné in Cabon, founded by him, at the age of ninety.

## 5 SEPTEMBER 1965

*La Passion selon Sade,* theatrical action for mixed media by the prime Italian avant-garde composer Sylvano BUSSOTTI evolving from a dodecaphonic motto and ramifying into varied atonal, polytonal, rhythmically dispersed, serialistically surrealistic musical motion purported to portray the sadistic bedroom philosophy of Marquis de Sade (1740–1814), is produced in the course of the Modern Music Festival in Palermo, Sicily.

The work is not all here; when the performers absorb the text they may recapitulate from memory all fragments that they remember, in order or in disorder, including errors of memory, without mutual communication, or any point of reference, gradually yielding and groping more and more during lapses of remembrance; only when memory is completely extinct can the performance come to a FINE. (From Bussotti's postscript in the score of his *Tableaux vivants avant la Passion selon Sade*)

## 9 SEPTEMBER 1965

Julian CARRILLO, Mexican composer, pioneer in composition in quarter-tones, eighth-tones, sixteenth-tones and other fractional intervals, who promulgated the earliest theory of micro-intervals in his publication *Sonido 13* (i.e. sound beyond 12), dies in Mexico City at the age of ninety.

## 14 SEPTEMBER 1965

*Violin Concerto*, composed in 1963, by the 83-year-old dean of Italian composers, Gian Francesco MALIPIERO, in three classically equilibrated movements, with a profusion of delicate violinistic filigree, is performed for the first time in Venice.

## 16 SEPTEMBER 1965

The Commonwealth Arts Festival opens in London with a concert by the Sydney, Australia, Symphony Orchestra featuring the first performance of *Violin Concerto* by the New Zealand composer Malcolm WILLIAMSON.

## 21 SEPTEMBER 1965

*Piano Concerto* by the Russian-born, quarter-French, quarter-Scottish, quarter-Russian, quarter-German, naturalized American composer Avenir de MONFRED, subtitled *Trois Aspects de la France*, in three movements, *France classique, France romantique* and *France populaire*, cast in an intensely melodious and harmonious idiom, redolent of the spirit of Liszt, Rachmaninoff and Debussy, diffused in a Gallic ambiance, is performed for the first time, 21 years after its composition, by the Bulgarian pianist Yury Boukoff and the Norddeutscher Rundfunk Orchestra in Hamburg.

## 23 SEPTEMBER 1965

*Oba ko so* (*The King Did Not Hang*), Nigerian folk opera for mixed media, including singing, dancing and acting, telling the story of the Nigerian god Shango, is performed at the Cardiff Commonwealth Arts Festival.

## 23 SEPTEMBER 1965

The Toronto Symphony presents at the Commonwealth Arts Festival in Glasgow, Scotland, a program of orchestral music, including the first performance of *Suite* for harp and chamber orchestra by Harry SOMERS of Canada.

## 25 SEPTEMBER 1965

On the 20th anniversary of the death of Béla BARTÓK, the Budapest Radio presents a program of his music relayed by the American Communications Satellite Telstar to both hemispheres.

## 25 SEPTEMBER 1965

*Der Traum des Liu-Tung*, opera in four dream sequences by the 48-year-old Korean composer Isang YUN, after a medieval Taoist fable centered on a Zenstarred youth who lapses into catalepsy and awakens 16 years later, scored for a modern orchestra with a large array of oriental instruments, with singers oscillating between tempered intonation and oriental sing-song, is produced for the first time in West Berlin.

### 29 SEPTEMBER 1965

*Balkan Rhapsody* for orchestra by the Bulgarian-born American composer Boris KREMENLIEV, written in a neo-romantic manner diversified by Balkan melorhythmic asymmetries, is performed for the first time in Munich.

### 29 SEPTEMBER 1965

*Petite Symphonie*, subtitled *Scultura*, by the 36-year-old Polish composer Boguslaw SCHÄFFER, in five minuscule movements notated diagrammatically, in curvilinear, rectilinear and spiral geometric designs, conceived as a study in plastic forms (hence the association with sculpture in the subtitle) and exploring the entire sonic and dynamic spectrum, from fortississimo to pianissimo, ending in an ascending icositetraphonic glissando in the massed strings, is performed for the first time in the course of the 9th International Festival of Contemporary Music in Warsaw ("Warsaw Autumn").

### 30 SEPTEMBER 1965

In the course of the Commonwealth Arts Festival in London, the Sydney Symphony Orchestra presents the first performance of *Sun Music* by the 36-year-old Tasmanian composer Peter SCULTHORPE, climaxed by an integrated icositetraphonic sonic aggregate of 59 adjacent quarter-tones for string instruments.

### 2 OCTOBER 1965

*A Bridge*, Bulgarian opera by Alexander RAICHOV, depicting the Communist revolutionary and military action on the eve of the liberation of Sofia by the Soviet Army from the Nazis, is produced in Rusa, Bulgaria.

### 14 OCTOBER 1965

*Sud*, opera by the expatriate 34-year-old American composer Kenton COE to a libretto concerning homosexual practices in South Carolina on the eve of the Civil War, written in an incongruously eupeptic manner, is produced in Marseilles.

### 18 OCTOBER 1965

*Die Ermittelung (The Inquest)*, oratorio by the Italian avant-garde composer Luigi NONO, to a text by Peter Weiss based entirely on the court transcript of trials of minor Nazi criminals, dramatized by electronic effects, consisting of eleven songs, each illustrating a bestial episode of murderous inhumanity, culminating with an account of the crematorium, is performed for the first time in Berlin.

### 18 OCTOBER 1965

*Nineteenth Symphony* by Henry COWELL, his last completed major work, in five movements cast in a rhythmically propulsive, melodically expansive and harmonically pellucid manner with occasional agglomerations of tone-clusters diversified by multifarious percussion including porcelain bowls, is performed for the first time by the Nashville, Tennesse, Symphony Orchestra, conducted by Willis Page.

### 24 OCTOBER 1965

On the 20th anniversary of the founding of the United Nations, *Voices for Today* for two choirs by Benjamin BRITTEN, specially written for the occasion, to a collage of anti-war texts ranging in period from Jesus and Socrates to Camus and Evtushenko, and concluding with a setting of Virgil's fourth eclogue which was believed by medieval theologians to be a prediction of the coming of Christ, used by Britten as a symbol of the coming of Peace, is performed for the first time in the General Assembly Hall in the United Nations Building in New York.

### 25 OCTOBER 1965

The Norwegian government issues a commemorative stamp in honor of the bicentennial of the Philharmonic Society of Bergen.

### 28 OCTOBER 1965

The Third International Festival of Visiting Orchestras opens in Carnegie Hall, New York, with a concert by the Detroit Symphony, conducted by Sixten Ehrling and featuring the first performance of *Lions,* symphonic poem by the 42-year-old American composer Ned ROREM, with a motto from Shakespeare, "The hind that would be mated by the lion must die for love," characterized by maundering blues played by a meandering jazz combo.

### 28 OCTOBER 1965

*Requiem* by Wilfred JOSEPH, a memorial choral symphony to the Jews slain by the Nazis, with the motto "Requiescant pro defunctis iudaeis," set to a Hebrew text of the Kaddish, is produced at La Scala, as the winner of the First International Composition Competition of the City of Milan.

### 2 NOVEMBER 1965

*Jacobowsky und der Oberst,* opera in four acts by Giselher KLEBE, after Franz Werfel's ironic play detailing the tragicomic adventures of a Jewish Pole who saves a snobbish Polish aristocrat after the military débacle in France in 1940, is produced at the Hamburg State Opera.

### 4 NOVEMBER 1965

*Miss Julie,* opera in two acts by Ned ROREM, after Strindberg's play dealing with a liaison between an aristocratic Scandinavian lady and her father's servant, set to music in a euphonious modernistic vein, with the application of rational dissonances, is produced in New York.

## 6 NOVEMBER 1965

Edgar VARÈSE, magisterial genius of new music, whose scientifically inspired works—*Intégrales, Hyperprism, Ionisation*—weave a magic carpet of "organized sound" and whose flamingly cryogenic symphonic pageants—*Amériques, Arcana, Déserts*—have established the principle of sonic illation and additive athematic development, the first modern composer to combine electronic elements with conventional instrumental timbres, dies in New York at the age of eighty-one. (Varèse was born on 22 December 1883, not 1885, as he himself believed and as all biographical dictionaries indicate; from 1950 on he spelled his first name with a final *d*, Edgard, which was the original spelling in his birth certificate)

## 16 NOVEMBER 1965

*Pine Tree Fantasy* for orchestra by the dean of American music, 71-year-old Walter PISTON, written as a tribute to his native state of Maine, in three cyclic sections, with an *Allegro deciso* flanked by two elegiac expositions, and modally converging on a focal C, is performed for the first time by the Portland, Maine, Symphony Orchestra.

## 19 NOVEMBER 1965

The National Polish Opera House, rebuilt and restored after its fiery destruction by the Nazi air force during the devastating onslaught on Poland in September 1939, is reopened in Warsaw.

## 21 NOVEMBER 1965

*Eighth Symphony* by the 69-year-old Austrian composer Johann Nepomuk DAVID, is performed for the first time in Stuttgart.

## 2 DECEMBER 1965

The New Music Workshop at the University of California, Los Angeles, presents a program of avant-garde music comprising the following manifestations:

*Piano Piece No. 1* by George MACIUNAS, consisting of bringing an upright piano onto the stage; *Piano Piece No. 1* by La Monte YOUNG, composed at 2:10 A.M. on 8 November 1960 and containing the following instructions: "Push the piano up to a wall and put the flat side flush against it. Then continue pushing into the wall. If the piano goes through the wall, keep pushing in the same direction regardless of new obstacles," and *Playable Music No. 4* by the Korean composer Nam June PAIK, performed by Joseph Byrd for the first time anywhere, fulfilling to the letter the directions "Cut your left arm very slowly with a razor (more than 10 centimeters)," shedding 7 cubic centimeters of blood in the process. (Someone in the audience shouted the exhortation "Encore! Use your throat!")

### 3 DECEMBER 1965

A second manifestation of the New Music Workshop of the University of California, Los Angeles, presents the world première of a patriotic octet for 8 or more instruments, *The Defense of the American Continent from the Viet-Cong Invasion* (subtitled *Communist Aggression Music No. 1*) by the 27-year-old American composer Joseph BYRD, culminating with a polyphonic synchronization of *America the Beautiful* with *Deutschland, Deutschland über alles.*

### 5 DECEMBER 1965

*The Cancelling Dark*, radio opera by the British composer Christopher WHELEN, based on the true story of an aircraft crash-landing in the desert in which the doomed pilot and his sole passenger engage in a philosophical dialogue and self-induced hallucinations of women in their lives, is performed for the first time in London.

### 10 DECEMBER 1965

Henry COWELL, American composer, builder of novel sonic edifices, theorist of new musical resources, inventor of the tone-clusters played on the piano keyboard with elbows and forearms, animator and devoted champion of artistic innovations and modern techniques, dies in Shady, New York, at the age of sixty-eight.

### 11 DECEMBER 1965

*La Princesse de Clèves*, opera in five acts by Jean FRANÇAIX, reviving in a hedonistically modernistic neo-classical idiom the age of royal France, is performed for the first time in Rouen.

### 14 DECEMBER 1965

*Mara*, opera by the British composer John HASTIE, dealing with a sea nymph who induces a non-aqueous prince to marry her, set to music in an appropriately fanciful simplistic manner, modernized by atonal melismas in asymmetrical rhythms, is produced in Croydon, England.

### 24 DECEMBER 1965

*Ayikuli*, Chinese opera composed collectively by a group of Communist musicians, adapted from a film entitled *Red Blossom on Tien Shan Mountains*, and dealing with a heroic Kazakh woman, a former slave, who becomes a revolutionary leader, is produced in Peking.

### 30 DECEMBER 1965

Jean MARTINON conducts the Chicago Symphony Orchestra in the first performance of his *Altitudes*, symphony in three movements, *La Porte des Étoiles, Le Jardin Vertical* and *La Traversée des Dieux*, written for its Diamond Jubilee Season of the Orchestra, of which he is musical director.

# ☙ 1966 ❧

## 4 JANUARY 1966

*Julius Caesar Jones,* opera in two acts by the 34-year-old New Zealand-born English composer Malcolm WILLIAMSON, dealing with imaginative children who conjure up a surrealistic Polynesian fantasy, set to music in a deceptively unsophisticated manner, is produced at a children's theater in London.

## 19 JANUARY 1966

The 61-year-old British composer Michael TIPPETT conducts in London the first performance of his cantata in three parts, *The Vision of St. Augustine,* to Latin texts from St. Augustine's confessions, in which he comments on his instant realizations of the persistence of volition, evanescence of reified material objects and the relativity of time, making use of a variety of techniques, including vocal glossolalia, medieval hocket syncopation and thematic serialism, set in the classical forms of rondo and toccata, and concluding with a pious Alleluia.

## 4 FEBRUARY 1966

*Zwischenfälle bei einer Notlandung,* "reportage" for electronic devices, instruments and singers, in two phases and 14 situations, by Boris BLACHER, with an acoustically realistic aural report of incidents at a forced landing of an aircraft, introducing the contrasting characters of survivors, among them a cybernetics scientist, a journalist, a prima donna, a financier and a girl secretary, is produced in Hamburg.

## 5 FEBRUARY 1966

*Sixth Concerto* for piano and orchestra by the 83-year-old grand master of Italian music Gian Francesco MALIPIERO, in three cyclic movements, *Allegro, Lento, Allegro,* bearing the subtitle *delle macchine,* and ending with a stroke on the bass drum, is performed for the first time in Rome.

## 5 FEBRUARY 1966

*Concerto* for cello, seventeen woodwind instruments, percussion and harmonium by the 26-year-old Soviet composer Boris TISHCHENKO, in one monothematically conceived movement, written in an advanced modernistic dialectical style, is performed for the first time in Leningrad, Igor Blazhkov conducting, with Mstislav Rostropovich, to whom the Concerto is dedicated, as soloist.

## 9 FEBRUARY 1966

*Kardiogram I* by the 23-year-old Swedish avant-garde composer Gunnar VALKARE, in the form of a coroner's report, to the French text, "Il meurt a Paris en 1867. . . ." scored for four vocalists of different sexes, chorus and chamber orchestra, is performed for the first time in Stockholm.

## 10 FEBRUARY 1966

*First Symphony* by the 29-year-old English composer Richard Rodney BENNETT, in three movements, *Allegro, Andante* and *Molto vivace*, scored for a large orchestra and employing a rich assortment of exotic percussion instruments, written in an expressionistic continental manner and a free serial idiom peculiar to the modern Albion while not renouncing tonality and hedonistically colorful means of musical expression within a distinctly vigesimo-secular Weltanschauung, is performed for the first time in London.

## 11 FEBRUARY 1966

*Psalm 140* for soprano and orchestra by Roger SESSIONS, in which David's prayer for deliverance from evil is expressed with eloquently dissonant and atonally explosive fervor, is performed for the first time by the Boston Symphony Orchestra, Erich Leinsdorf conducting.

## 12 FEBRUARY 1966

*The Eternal Theme,* symphonic poem by the 68-year-old Israeli composer Paul BEN-HAIM, in six movements, *Intrada, Fanfare, Prayer for the Innocent, Meditation, Rondo, Conclusion,* written in a neo-baroque formal manner, with six trumpets proclaiming the rabbinical belief in the eternal "song of all songs at the end of all time," is performed for the first time by the Israel Philharmonic Orchestra in Tel Aviv.

## 21 FEBRUARY 1966

*The Phoenix, Fabulous Bird,* tone poem by John VINCENT dedicated to the city of Phoenix, Arizona, and based on a soaring theme symbolizing the eternal rebirth of the fiery bird, is performed for the first time in Phoenix.

## 25 FEBRUARY 1966

*Piece for Allison Knowles* by the Korean composer Nam June PAIK, instructing the performer, a female, to take off 25 pairs of multicolored silk pieces of underwear and lift her remaining skirt to mark the coda, is demonstrated for the first time at an avant-garde happening in Los Angeles.

## 3 MARCH 1966

*Relata I* for symphony orchestra by the 49-year-old American composer-mathematician Milton BABBITT is performed for the first time, in Cleveland.

5 MARCH 1966

*Excursion* for orchestra by the 43-year-old American composer Irwin
BAZELON is performed for the first time in Kansas City.

21 MARCH 1966

*Mr. and Mrs. Discobbolos,* minuscule opera by the 34-year-old American composer Peter WESTERGAARD, for two singers and six instrumentalists, to the
whimsical poem by Edward Lear, with the aleatorically serial idiom of the
music illustrating the rhymed glossolalia of the text, is performed for the first
time at a concert of the Group for Contemporary Music at Columbia University in New York.

24 MARCH 1966

The First Inter-American Festival of the Arts opens in San Juan, Puerto Rico,
with a program of choral music by Puerto Rican composers.

30 MARCH 1966

*St. Luke Passion,* oratorio by the 32-year-old Polish avant-garde composer
Krzysztof PENDERECKI, to the Latin text of the Passion and Death of Jesus
Christ according to St. Luke, composed in a fervidly devotional style, making
use of the millennial devices of the Gregorian chant as well as of serial procedures of the mid-20th century, written in a special graphic notation, indicating the highest possible note by an isosceles triangle, and the lowest by an inverted one, with special symbols for various percussion effects, is performed
for the first time at the Cathedral of Münster, Germany.

31 MARCH 1966

*Markheim,* opera in three acts by the 39-year-old American composer Carlisle
FLOYD, after Robert Louis Stevenson's tale of a pawnbroker who is given a
specious promise of a life of pleasure by a diabolical stranger, is produced in
New Orleans.

2 APRIL 1966

The First Inter-American Festival of Arts in San Juan, Puerto Rico, concludes
with a program of Latin American music, including the first performance of
*Musica Festival* for chamber orchestra by the Puerto Rican composer Amaury
VERAY.

3 APRIL 1966

*Terrêtektorh* for orchestra by Iannis XENAKIS, 43-year-old Rumanian-born
Greek electronic engineer, active in Paris, foremost exponent of stochastic
music, with the etymology of the title indicating earth (*terre*), tectonic (*tekt*)
and action suffix *orh,* conceived as a sonotron, i.e. accelerator of sonic particles, disintegrator of acoustic masses and a synthesizer, covering the entire

spectrum of sound, with an emphasis on noise elements, is performed for the first time at the Festival of Contemporary Music at Royan, France, conducted by Hermann Scherchen, with 88 musicians strewn among the audience, each equipped with a consortium of drumlets and policemen's whistles, "producing sounds similar to flames."

If desired, a rain of hail can surround each of the listeners, or perhaps a murmuration of a pine forest, or any other atmosphere or linear concept, static or in motion. The individual listeners will then find themselves as though sailing in a frail boat on a turbulent sea, or in a pointillistic universe of sonorous sparks moving in cumulous or isolated clouds. (Xenakis in a descriptive note, reproduced in the program book of the 1967 Warsaw Festival)

### 4 APRIL 1966

*Luna 10*, circumlunar unmanned orbiting "cosmic ship" launched by the Soviets, is activated to broadcast the *Internationale* to the earth for the opening of the sixth session of the 23rd Congress of the Communist Party of the USSR.

### 5 APRIL 1966

*Cantata* by Sergei PROKOFIEV, written in 1937 to glorify the 20th anniversary of the Soviet Revolution, scored for two choruses, military band, ensemble of accordions and percussion, to texts from Marx, Engels, Lenin and Stalin, judged ideologically and musically inadequate and therefore withheld from performance, is finally given a hearing at a public concert in Moscow, nearly thirty years after its composition, with the significant omission of the section of Stalin's texts in conformity with the process of de-Stalinization in Soviet politics and art.

### 6 APRIL 1966

*Cello Concerto* by the 60-year-old English composer Alan RAWSTHORNE, in three movements, *Allegro lirico, Mesto*, and *Allegro*, set a luminously bitonal harmonic idiom, gravitating towards a focal C, is performed for the first time in London.

### 14 APRIL 1966

The First Hellenic Week of Contemporary Music opens in Athens, Greece, in programs including the string quartets of SCHOENBERG, several works by Anton VON WEBERN and Olivier MESSIAEN and eleven world premières by modern Greek composers, among them *Trittys* for guitar, percussion and 2 doublebasses by the 37-year-old empiricist Nikos MAMANGAKIS (15 April) and *Praxis for 12* for strings, piano and percussion by the 40-year-old avant-gardist Jani CHRISTOU (18 April).

### 16 APRIL 1966

After 83 years of operatic splendor of the gilded age of America, the old baroque building of the Metropolitan Opera House of New York, inaugurated on 22 October 1883, where the golden voices of the past had resounded gloriously for the delectation of tax-free millionaires and aristocratic opera lovers, closes its antiquated doors with a final nostalgic performance of Puccini's opera *La Bohème,* before moving to a new home in the modernistically functional Lincoln Center for the Performing Arts.

## 28 APRIL 1966

In the series of "Symphonic Forms in the Twentieth Century," the New York Philharmonic under the direction of Leonard Bernstein presents the world premières of two works by the 50-year-old American composer David Diamond:

*Fifth Symphony,* composed intermittently between 1947 and 1964, and completed on the Island of Ponza, Italy, on 30 September 1964 (after the completion and performances of his 6th, 7th and 8th Symphonies) in two large sections: (1) *Adagio-Allegro energico,* opening with an unaccompanied English horn solo, achieving a dynamic climax in the second subject (2) *Andante; Fuga; Allegretto; Adagio,* with an intervallically angular but tonally centered fugue ending in a rhetorical solo cello summarizing thematic ideas from both movements; and *Concerto for Piano and Orchestra,* composed in 1949–1950, in three movements: (1) *Andante-Allegretto-Allegro,* set in an amalgamated form of sonata and rondo (2) *Adagio, molto espressivo,* couched in a quasi-devotional mood (3) *Allegramente,* a spirited rondo launched by a gay piccolo solo, in an unequivocal A major (conducted by David Diamond himself with Thomas Schumacher as soloist).

## 28 APRIL 1966

*Concerto buffo* for chamber orchestra by Sergei SLONIMSKY, written in an advanced technical style making use of serial and aleatory procedures in two movements, *Canonic Fugue* for 14 string instruments and trumpet and *Improvisation,* opening with a protracted flute solo and concluding with a tumultuous dance, is performed for the first time in Leningrad.

## 28 APRIL 1966

*Carry Nation,* opera in two acts by Douglas MOORE, nostalgically recreating the stormy career of Carry Nation, the redoubtable American lady who led a crusade against demon rum by smashing saloons and bars with her little hatchet, written in a fittingly grandiloquent idiom with a profusion of florid arias, is produced at the University of Kansas in Lawrence, Kansas.

## 28 APRIL 1966

*Analigus,* orchestral triptych by the Cuban-born American composer Aurelio de la VEGA, in four movements, *Phases, Serenade, Pauses* and *Partitus,* athematic in structure and designed as an exposition of contrasting sonorities (including the novel effect of the entire string section shuffling their feet to produce a rhythmic noise), but possessing nevertheless a logic of analogy (the title *Analigus* is a deliberate distortion of the word), is performed for the first time in Fullerton, California.

## 1 MAY 1966

*Sinfonia* by the 30-year-old English composer Nicholas MAW, in three movements, with an embryonic fourth movement fertilized in utero in the finale, conceived as a compressed cellular organism, expressionistically developed along atonal thematic lines, is performed for the first time at the Rutheford College of Technology in Newcastle-upon-Tyne, England.

## 6 MAY 1966

The Third Festival of Music opens in Caracas, Venezuela with a program of orchestral works by Latin American composers:

*Partita 3* by Julian ORBÓN of Cuba; *New York* by Leon SCHIDLOWSKY of Chile; *Fantasia de Bolsillo* by José Luis MUÑOZ of Venezuela; *Sands* by Pozzi ESCOT of Peru and *Abyssus* by Carlos TUXEN-BANG of Argentina.

## 8 MAY 1966

At the second concert of the Third Festival of Music in Caracas, the following works by Latin American composers are performed:

*Homogramas I* by Gustavo BECERRA SCHMIDT of Chile; *Música III* by Antonio TAURIELLO of Argentina; *12 Mobiles* by Jacqueline NOVA of Colombia; and *Sinfonía en Cuatro Partes* by Aurelio DE LA VEGA of Cuba and the United States.

## 11 MAY 1966

*First Symphony* by the 45-year-old American composer Andrew IMBRIE is performed for the first time in San Francisco.

## 11 MAY 1966

During the course of the Third Festival of Music in Caracas, the following works for various ensembles are performed for the first time anywhere:

*Continuidades* by Juan Carlos PAZ of Argentina; *Laudate Servum Domine,* cantata by Leopoldo BILLINGS of Venezuela; *Resonancias Tres* by Hilda DIANDA of Argentina and *Discrepancia* by Lukas Foss of the United States.

## 13 MAY 1966

During the course of the Third Festival of Music in Caracas, the Philadelphia Orchestra under the direction of Eugene Ormandy presents the world premières of *Concerto per corde* by Alberto GINASTERA of Argentina and *4 Piezas para orquesta* by Hector TOSAR of Uruguay.

## 14 MAY 1966

At the Third Festival of Music in Caracas, the Philadelphia Orchestra, under the direction of its guest conductor Stanislaw Skrowaczewski, presents the following program:

*Variaciones concertantes* by Alberto GINASTERA of Argentina; *Sensemayá* by Silvestre REVUELTAS of Mexico; the world première of *Ludus Symphonicus* by Edino KRIEGER of Brazil; *Medea's Dance of Vengeance* by Samuel BARBER of the United States and *Canto for Orchestra* by Peter MENNIN of the United States.

### 14 MAY 1966

*The Magic Chair,* one-act opera by the Hungarian-born American composer Eugene ZADOR, in which a malingering bureaucrat is seated in a magic chair that forces him to tell scandalous truths about his management of municipal affairs, is performed for the first time (with piano instead of the orchestra) at Louisiana State University in Baton Rouge.

### 15 MAY 1966

At the Third Festival of Music in Caracas, two works by Venezuelan composers are given for the first time: *Sinfonietta Satirica* by Inocente CARREÑO and *Ballet Miniatura* by Blanca ESTRELLA.

### 15 MAY 1966

*15 Prints After Dürer's Apocalypse,* suite for orchestra by the 30-year-old Czech composer Luboš FIŠER, abstractly related to the apocalyptic visions embodied in the engravings of Albrecht Dürer, with melodic and harmonic materials serially derived from the basic mode of six notes, while the musical current is carried forward within precisely determined time units, is performed for the first time at the Prague Spring Music Festival.

### 16 MAY 1966

The Philadelphia Orchestra under the direction of Eugene Ormandy presents in the course of the Third Festival of Music in Caracas the world première of the posthumous *Ninth Symphony* by Heitor VILLA-LOBOS and the world première of *Sinfonia* by Roque CORDERO of Panama.

### 18 MAY 1966

*Violin Concerto* by William BERGSMA is performed for the first time under the composer's direction at Tacoma, Washington.

### 18 MAY 1966

The Third Festival of Music in Caracas closes with an orchestral program of music by Venezuelan composers, including *First Symphony* by Carlos FIGUEREDO; *Fantasia* for piano and orchestra by Nelly Mele LARA; *Giros Negroides* by Antonio LAURO; and *El Rio de las Siete Estrellas* by Evencio CASTELLANOS.

### 21 MAY 1966

*Professor Mamlock,* opera by the 52-year-old Slovak composer Ladislav HOLOUBEK to a libretto inspired by the European resistance movement against the Nazi occupation written in an angst-filled dodecaphonic idiom is performed for the first time in Bratislava, under the direction of the composer.

### 23 MAY 1966

*Die schwarze Spinne,* opera in three acts by Josef Matthias HAUER, after a mystical tale by the Swiss cleric Albert Bitzius (1797–1854), dealing with a peasant woman who attempts to outwit the devil incarnate by pretending to submit to his hideous proposal to surrender to him her unbaptized child for his iniquitous purposes, but who is transformed into a black spider and brings forth a proliferation of horrible arachnids instead, with thematic materials derived from a single tone-row, E, G sharp, D, F, A, C, D sharp, F sharp, B, C sharp, B flat and G, is performed posthumously for the first time in Vienna.

### 27 MAY 1966

*Lake Ukereve,* opera in five scenes by the 44-year-old Czech composer Otmar MÁCHA, to his own libretto dealing with the medical missionaries combating the effects of sleeping sickness in Central Africa in 1900, with eloquent arias and choruses supported onomatopoeically by stylized drums suggesting primitivistic rites, is produced in Prague.

### 29 MAY 1966

*Der Tod des Empedokles,* "scenic concerto" in one act by the German composer Hermann REUTTER, to the romantic poem by Friedrich Hölderlin, in which the ancient wise philosopher finds his private truth in a voluntary death in the crater of the volcano Aetna, is performed for the first time in Schwetzingen, on the same program with the revised version of Reutter's one-act opera buffa *Die Witwe von Ephesus* (first performed in Cologne on 23 June 1954).

### 31 MAY 1966

The Metropolitan Opera Company of New York opens its European season in Paris, its first visit since 1910.

### 2 JUNE 1966

*17 Tage und 4 Minuten,* opera buffa in three acts by Werner EGK, a fanciful version of Calderón's comedy *El mayor encanto amor,* with wandering Ulysses and nymphomaniacal Circe making love for exactly 17 days and 4 minutes surrounded by half-mythological, quarter-realistic and quarter-surrealistic creatures, is produced in Stuttgart.

### 4 JUNE 1966

*Symphonie de marches* by Henri SAUGUET is performed for the first time as a commissioned work at the International Congress of Railroads, in Paris, to stimulate the popular appreciation of train travel.

## 8 JUNE 1966

*Der mysteriöse Herr X,* opera in three acts by the Austrian composer Alfred UHL, is performed for the first time at the Vienna Festival of Music.

## 9 JUNE 1966

*The Burning Fiery Furnace,* a church parable by Benjamin BRITTEN, set for male voices, organ and instruments, to the biblical story of Shadrach, Meshach and Abednego and their miraculous survival in the Babylonian oven, written in an esthetically devotional, tensely modern musical idiom, is performed for the first time by the English Opera Group, without a conductor, in the course of the annual Aldeburgh Festival, founded by Britten.

## 10 JUNE 1966

*Jeppe,* opera by the Norwegian composer Geirr TVEITT, is performed for the first time in Bergen, Norway.

## 13 JUNE 1966

*La Mère coupable,* opera in three acts by Darius MILHAUD, to a libretto from a comedy by Beaumarchais, in which Figaro settles the amorous troubles of the daughter of the "culpable mother" Rosina, is performed for the first time in Geneva.

## 14 JUNE 1966

*Doppio Concerto Grosso* by the Japanese composer Michio MAMIYA, in three movements, scored for a violin and a percussion group as soloists with a large orchestra, opening in a neo-Nipponese manner with an explosive polycacophonous sound, but concluding with a pacifically Baroque perpetuum mobile, is performed for the first time by the Japan Philharmonic Symphony Orchestra in Tokyo.

## 18 JUNE 1966

Half a millennium has passed since the birth of Ottaviano PETRUCCI, the Venetian printer who was the first to publish a complete collection of part-songs from movable type.

## 23 JUNE 1966

In the course of the 18th International Music Festival in Strasbourg, three world premières are presented:

*Expressions contrastées* for orchestra, piano and percussion, by Charles CHAYNES, depicting the kaleidoscopic sensations induced by a psychic visit to an astral territory; *Le Marcheur Solitaire,* a monologue for orchestra by the 42-year-old American composer Eugene KURTZ, written in a "spatial idiom" derived from harmonic aggregates of 3, 6 and 8 serially arranged sounds; and *Chant après Chant,* a fragment from a projected but uncomposed epic *La Mort de Virgile* by the problematic French composer Jean

BARRAQUÉ scored for 6 groups of percussion, piano and soprano and based on a series of varied rhythmic cells arranged in permutations and translocations.

### 23 JUNE 1966

In the course of the Holland Festival in Amsterdam the 31-year-old Dutch modernist Peter SCHAT conducts the first performance of his operatic triptych *Labyrinth* dealing with the three aspects of a woman (sexual, ideological, naturalistic) and intended as "a total theater" calculated to impose "disorientation by simultaneity of incongruities" through the use of mixed media, containing films, ballet, electronic sound, and chants in Latin, accompanied by an orchestra without violins, but with several double-bassoons, doublebasses and bass clarinets.

### 23 JUNE 1966

*Sixth Symphony* by the 80-year-old Austrian composer Egon WELLESZ, "an idea presented in three aspects," in three movements of cyclic facture, an introspective *Lento*, a light-hearted Viennese *Scherzo* and a philosophic *Adagio*, written in a Mahlerian style with dodecaphonic excrescences, is performed for the first time in Nuremberg.

### 28 JUNE 1966

*Akrata* by Iannis XENAKIS, 44-year-old Rumanian-born Greek engineer, architect and composer, scored for 15 wind instruments and a vibraphone, written according to his individual method of stochastic composition, in which the creative impulse delegates the process of composition to probabilistic events, and in which the melodic, rhythmic and dynamic parameters are of axiomatic subsumption and strict organization (the Greek title denotes total consistency), is performed for the first time during the English Bach Festival in Oxford.

### 3 JULY 1966

Deems TAYLOR, versatile American composer and writer whose operas *The King's Henchman* and *Peter Ibbetson* flashed with momentary brilliance at the Metropolitan Opera, articulate master of ceremonies on radio programs and in whimsical movies (such as Walt Disney's *Fantasia*), literate music critic of an astute conservative persuasion, dies in New York at the age of eighty.

### 10 JULY 1966

The 17th Annual Music Festival opens in Dubrovnik, Yugoslavia, with the participation of the Zagreb Philharmonic, the Belgrade Philharmonic, the Cincinnati Symphony Orchestra and ensembles of Serbo-Croatian folk singers.

### 13 JULY 1966

*Kinesis* by the 31-year-old Greek composer Theodor ANTONIOU, for two groups of strings, is performed for the first time at the Athens Festival.

### 27 JULY 1966

The annual Israel Festival opens in Jerusalem with a specially commissioned work *A Festival Sinfonietta* by the Israeli composer Menahem AVIDOM, and the first performance in Israel of *Requiem* by BERLIOZ. (The Festival concluded on 23 August with a concert of chamber music.)

### 28 JULY 1966

*Esculapio al Neon,* musical fantasy by Ennio PORRINO, is performed posthumously in concert form, in Naples.

### 30 JULY 1966

Walter KAUFMANN conducts the Indiana University Opera Group in the world première of his opera *A Hoosier Tale,* to his own libretto, dealing with the marital miscegenation between a white trader and an Indian girl in old Indiana (Hoosier is a folksy epithet for inhabitants of Indiana), set in ostentatiously simplicistic harmonies, with quotations from American songs.

### 5 AUGUST 1966

The Israel Philharmonic Orchestra embarks on a tour in the Far East, terminating on 19 September, presenting 16 concerts in Australia, 8 in New Zealand and 3 in Hong Kong, under the direction of Eliyahu Inbal, Zubin Mehta and Antal Dorati, and with the participation of the Israeli violinist Zvi Zeitlin.

### 6 AUGUST 1966

*Die Bassariden,* neo-Grecian opera by Hans Werner HENZE, to an English libretto by W. A. Auden and Chester Kallman, based on *The Bacchae* of Euripides, set to music in the form of a symphony in four movements within a single act, depicting the conflict between the Germanically tense dodecaphonic asceticism of a sexually repressed King of Thebes and the Italianate incandescent sensualism of the multifutuent, yet diatonically conditioned god of wine Dionysus, all this refracted through a prism of rococo mannerisms, is produced in Salzburg in the German version.

### 16 AUGUST 1966

*Melorhythmic Dances* by Carlos SURINACH, an orchestral suite of seven movements (Fervid, Festive, Poignant, Tragic, Voluptuous, Vehement, Mournful) is performed for the first time at the Meadow Brook Music Festival at Oakland University in Rochester, Michigan.

### 18 AUGUST 1966

*Markings,* symphonic essay by Ulysses KAY, dedicated to the memory of Dag Hammarskjöld, Secretary General of the United Nations until his death in a plane accident in the Congo in 1961, with the title taken from his own posthumous writings, in a single movement subdivided into four contrasting but interrelated sections, opening with an *Allegretto agitato* and progressing through a number of quietly turbulent moods, and ending on a pandiatonic question mark, is performed for the first time at the Meadow Brook Music Festival of Oakland University, in Rochester, Michigan for which it was written.

### 21 AUGUST 1966

*Pavane Variations* for orchestra by Paul CRESTON, written in a dissonantly rhapsodic, sonorously explosive manner, ingratiatingly mitigated by lyrical moments of harmonic candor, is performed for the first time at the La Jolla Music Festival in California.

### 4 SEPTEMBER 1966

*Le metamorfosi di Bonaventura,* fantastic opera by the dean of Italian composers Gian Francesco MALIPIERO, in three acts tracing the madness of a Seville jester, written in a characteristic modern baroque style, is performed for the first time at the opening of the Festival of Modern Music in Venice.

### 6 SEPTEMBER 1966

*Metamorphoses Ebrietatis,* symphonic poem by the Swiss composer Armin SCHIBLER, is performed for the first time in Montreux, Switzerland.

### 9 SEPTEMBER 1966

The 40th Festival of the International Society for Contemporary Music opens in Stockholm with the following program of orchestral music played by the Stockholm Philharmonic Orchestra:

*Improvisations symphoniques* for piano and orchestra by the 55-year-old Hungarian composer Gabor DARVAS, in two movements, *Cadenza* and *Notturno,* in which the intervallic scheme is governed by the Fibonacci series, with improvised permutations; *Gesangsszene* by Karl Amadeus HARTMANN (1905–1963) of Germany, for baritone and orchestra, written in the manner of free recitative with euphonious dissonant accompaniment; *Transparencias* for 6 instrumental groups by the 35-year-old Argentinian composer Antonio TAURIELLO, based on a general serial principle; and *Syntagma* for orchestra by the 34-year-old Spanish modernist Enrique RAXACH, derived from a complex of parameters. (*Choros I* by Henryk GÓRECKI of Poland was listed in the program, but the performance was cancelled when it was discovered that the orchestral parts were contaminated by a plague of errors.)

### 10 SEPTEMBER 1966

The Royal Opera of Stockholm presents, in the framework of the annual Stockholm Festival, the world première of the two-act opera *Tronkrävarna* (*The Pretenders*) by the Swedish composer Gunnar BUCHT, after Ibsen's play *Kongsemnerne.*

### 11 SEPTEMBER 1966

The second concert of the 40th Festival of the International Society for Contemporary Music in Stockholm presents the following program:

*Octandre* (the title means an 8-stamen plant) by Edgar VARÈSE (1883–1965), a florid instrumental octet in dissonant harmonies, composed in 1924; *Preludes* by the 69-year-old Polish composer Boleslaw SZABELSKI, in three movements unified by a 12-tone row; *Alveare vernat* for flute and instruments by the 41-year-old Swiss composer Klaus HUBER, written in a metamorphic serial idiom (the title means "spring appears in a beehive"); *Diaphonie I* for chorus and orchestra by the Argentine-born 34-year-old German-domiciled composer Mauricio KAGEL, set for chorus, orchestra and two film projectors casting the musical score derived from random photographic impressions on the screen; *Antistixis* by the 30-year-old Greek composer Yorgos APERGIS, written for three string quartets, in six consecutive events; *Improvvisazione* by the 34-year-old Italian composer Fausto RAZZI, for viola, 18 wind instruments and kettledrums, written as a free interplay of neo-baroque elements; and *Prologues* by the 27-year-old Polish composer Tomas SIKORSKI for a wordless female choir and a small ensemble.

## 12 SEPTEMBER 1966

The third concert of the 40th Festival of the International Society for Contemporary Music in Stockholm presents the following program of chamber music:

*Second Wind Quintet* by the 22-year-old Australian composer Ross EDWARDS, written in a freely atonal idiom, economically treated for an optimum effect; *De Profundis* by the 50-year-old Norwegian composer Knut NYSTEDT, for chorus *a cappella; Songs* by Charles IVES (U.S.A.); *Epitaphe* for two sopranos and flute, kettledrums, vibraphone, drums, piano and celesta, written in an expressionistically anguished atonal idiom by the 39-year-old Italian composer Vittorio FELLEGARA; *Music for Albion Moonlight* for soprano and instruments by the 28-year-old English composer David BEDFORD, based on thematic clusters of notes; and *Prisme* by the 33-year-old Danish composer Per NÖRGAARD, for mezzo-soprano, tenor, baritone, guitar and orchestra, in 8 movements.

## 13 SEPTEMBER 1966

At the fourth concert of the 40th Festival of the International Society for Contemporary Music in Stockholm the following program of chamber music is given:

*Quattrodramma* by the 71-year-old German composer Paul DESSAU, for four cellos, two pianos and a battery of percussion, written in a free serialistic idiom with aleatoric interludes; *The Tomb at Akr Caar* by the 52-year-old Finnish composer Bengt JOHANSSON, for voice and chamber chorus, to texts by Ezra Pound, set in a moderate polytonal idiom; *This Is Thy Glorification* by the 22-year-old Jerusalem-born Israeli composer Ron LEWY, for narrator, chorus and instruments; *Third String Quartet* by the 34-year-old Czech composer Marek KOPELENT, written as a study in altering tensions; *Elegie in friulano* by the 66-year-old Italian composer Antonio VERETTI, to words in the Frioulian dialect of North Italy, scored for voice, violin, clarinet and guitar, in 9 short movements; *Oro No. 2* by the 32-year-old Icelandic composer Leifur THORARINSSON, based on a free serial technique in aleatoric turbulence (hence the name, Oro, disturbance); *Torso* by the 42-year-old Danish composer Axel BORUP-JÖRGENSEN, written for two string quartets, one of which is tape recorded in advance; and *Kanon* by the 29-year-old Norwegian composer Alfred JANSON, written for a chamber orchestra and prerecorded tape.

14 SEPTEMBER 1966

At the fifth concert of the 40th Festival of the International Society for Contemporary Music in Stockholm, a program of Swedish music is given:

The first performance of *Il Cantico del sole* by the 47-year-old composer Siegfried NAUMANN, for soloists, chorus and orchestra, to the words of Francesco d'Assisi; *Coloratura IV* by the 26-year-old composer Jan W. MORTHENSON, representing a coloristic study of harmonic textures; and *Poesis* by the 45-year-old composer Ingvar LIDHOLM, a lyrico-dramatic study in contrasting sonorities of orchestral timbres.

15 SEPTEMBER 1966

The 40th Festival of the International Society for Contemporary Music in Stockholm presents its sixth and last concert in the following program:

*Un día sobresale,* by the 39-year-old German-born Argentinian composer Michael GIELEN, serialistically conceived as a pentaphony for five solo instruments, and five groups of five musicians each (of which one group is comprised of vocalists); *Les Sons* by the 39-year-old Polish composer Witold SZALONEK, scored for orchestra without violins and cellos, and conceived as a series of tonal tensions from pianississississimo to fortississississimo; *Etude III* by the 28-year-old French composer Jean-Claude ÉLOY, conceived as a concertino for 5 percussion players, piano, harp, celesta and a classical orchestra; *22 Pages* by the 32-year-old Dutch composer Joep STRAESSER, for wind instruments, 8 doublebasses, percussion and male voices, to a text by John Cage, for tenor, baritone, bass and an assorted ensemble of instruments; and *Transfiguration* by the 38-year-old Swedish composer Bengt HAMBRAEUS, a cycle of movements of instrumental and electronic music, in which any movement can be played individually or synchronously with any other.

16 SEPTEMBER 1966

The new Metropolitan Opera House, erected in Lincoln Center, New York, at the cost of $45,700,000, opens with a spectacular production of the specially commissioned opera *Antony and Cleopatra* by the American composer Samuel BARBER, in three acts and 16 scenes, conducted by Thomas Schippers and staged with flamboyant extravagance by Franco Zeffirelli (special prices were set at $250 for a single seat in rows A through M) requiring the participation, besides the soprano Leontyne Price (first Negro singer to take the part of Cleopatra in any opera), the bass Justino Diaz as Antony and tenor Jess Thomas as Octavian, of three horses, three goats and a camel, the scenery, including a sphinx, arrayed on multiple rotating platforms, making it possible to change the scene of action from Alexandria to Rome with cinematic celerity, and a musical score combining Italianate fervor of bel canto with a flair for intellectually modern melodic configurations, quartal intervallic progressions and acridly euphonious polyharmonies.

17 SEPTEMBER 1966

*TIS-MW-2,* a metamusical audio-visual spectacle by the 37-year-old Polish modernist Boguslaw SCHÄFFER, to a non-ontological alogical oneirological scenario for an illusory narrator reciting a series of discrete surrealistic fragments of irrationally oriented non-temporal events to the accompaniment of an indeterminate instrumental ensemble, with demoniac illuminations scintillating in sudden silences, anguished outcries, implosive borborigmuses and choreic singultations, is performed for the first time in the course of the 10th International Festival of Contemporary Music in Warsaw ("Warsaw Autumn").

## 18 SEPTEMBER 1966

*Tomorrow*, lyric drama in one act by the 38-year-old Polish composer Tadeusz BAIRD, to a libretto after Joseph Conrad's story of dark passions in a fishermen's village, ending with the murder of a seaman by his own father for an attempt to violate a girl who was the object of the father's senescent adoration, is produced in Warsaw in the course of the 10th International Festival of Contemporary Music ("Warsaw Autumn").

## 20 SEPTEMBER 1966

*Muses of Sicily*, cantata by the 40-year-old German composer Hans Werner HENZE is performed for the first time in Berlin as a commissioned work to mark the 175th anniversary of the Berlin Singakademie.

## 21 SEPTEMBER 1966

*Ninth Symphony* in three movements by the prime Italian symphonist Gian Francesco MALIPIERO, subtitled *Hélas* because a presentiment of the death of his wife interrupted the composition of the finale and inspired an elegiac interlude, is performed for the first time in the course of the 10th Festival of Contemporary Music in Warsaw ("Warsaw Autumn").

## 21 SEPTEMBER 1966

*Sixth Symphony*, surnamed *Sinfonia Tragica*, by the 90-year-old English composer Havergal BRIAN, composed in 1948, consisting of three movements played without pause, receives its first performance, in London. (*Sinfonia Tragica* was originally an unnumbered work, but at the age of 92 the composer renumbered his earlier symphonies and discarded the *First Symphony* written in 1908; this ellipsis made *Sinfonia Tragica* his *Sixth Symphony*)

## 23 SEPTEMBER 1966

George BARATI conducts the Honolulu Symphony Orchestra in the world première of his festival ode, *The Waters of Kane*, for chorus and orchestra, a symphonic invocation of the millennial legend of the magic waters struck from the rainbow of the Polynesian demiurge Kane, written in a primitivistic modernistic idiom, with thematic materials drawn from authentic Hawaiian chants, fertilized by hula rhythms tapped out on the native drum *puili* made of the split bamboo plant.

## 24 SEPTEMBER 1966

*Altisonans,* avian tone poem by Karl-Birger BLOMDAHL, produced by an electronic transmutation of elements of bird songs superimposed on the reduction to the audible spectrum of satellite signals and the impact of cosmic rays, is recorded in the Swedish Television Center in Stockholm.

## 25 SEPTEMBER 1966

On his 60th birthday Dmitri SHOSTAKOVICH is nominated Hero of Socialist Labor by the Soviet Government, and a concert of his music is given at the Moscow Conservatory, presenting the first performance of his *Second Violoncello Concerto* under the direction of his son Maxim Shostakovich, with Mstislav Rostropovich as soloist.

## 1 OCTOBER 1966

The 67-year-old German pianist Heinz ARNTZ plays, at the Long Island fair in Westbury, New York, his favorite march *Alte Kameraden,* establishing at 1 P.M. the world record of pianofortitude with 1054 hours of continuous piano playing (with two hours off each day for the physiological necessities of sleeping, eating and elimination), a pianistic marathon begun at 8:00 P.M. on 18 August 1966, in a Düsseldorf cafe, continued in a truck from Düsseldorf to Bremerhaven, in the salon of the liner United States and in another truck from the pier to the fair at Roosevelt Raceway in Westbury.

## 3 OCTOBER 1966

The new Jesse H. Jones Hall for the Performing Arts opens in Houston, Texas, with the Houston Symphony Orchestra, conducted by Sir John Barbirolli in a program including the first performance of a commissioned American work, *Ode to the Temple of Sound* by Alan HOVHANESS.

## 8 OCTOBER 1966

*Amerika,* opera by Roman HAUBENSTOCK-RAMATI, after Kafka, written in an advanced serial idiom, with the application of electronic techniques, is produced at the Berlin Festival.

## 8 OCTOBER 1966

*Requiem Canticles* by Igor STRAVINSKY, for mixed chorus, vocal soloists and orchestra, in 9 sections (6 vocal and 3 instrumental), set to abbreviated extracts from the Requiem in the Latin ritual, and written in a reverential neo-ecclesiastical spirit but set in a specific serial idiom, is performed for the first time at a semi-private gathering at Princeton University.

## 12 OCTOBER 1966

*Esther,* opera in two acts by the German composer Robert HANELL, in which the non-Aryan animal warmth of a young Jewish girl violinist is used by the

Nazi doctors to restore the life of an experimentally frozen Aryan youth, with anti-fascist love blossoming forth between the two enabling the girl to go to her death in a gas chamber with a renewed hope in the inherent decency of at least one German in a flood of Hitlerian diabolism, is produced at the German State Opera in East Berlin.

12 OCTOBER 1966

Gunther SCHULLER conducts the Hamburg State Opera in the world première of his three-act opera *The Visitation,* inspired by the faceless terrors of Kafka's novel *Der Prozess* and dedicated "to all men who, through hate, injustice and oppression are denied freedom in their pursuit of happiness," with the action transferred to the American South and focused on the tragic fate of a black student suspected of harboring a miscegenating sentiment towards a white girl, set to music in a plenitude of modern techniques, ranging from triadic serenity to integral serialism, and incorporating a jazz combo in the orchestral score, the action subdivided into the following sections:

ACT I. Scene 1. *A Warning* (jazzy portents and discordant omens against the background of Negro chants). Scene 2. *Miss Hampton* (atonal coloratura voicing anxiety and sympathy). Scene 3. *A Summoning* (brassy tumult in a drug store where the intended victim is employed as a soda jerk). Scene 4. *An Interrogation* (massive incursion of authoritarian brass reinforced by traumatic drumbeats). ACT II. Scene 1. *The Court House* (ostentatiously egalitarian jurisprudential disharmonies). Scene 2. *An Encounter* (police cars cruising permissively past groups of racist men mobilizing in darkening streets). Scene 3. *The Lawyer* (tranquilizing legalities in pseudo-humanitarian concordant counterpoint). ACT III. Scene 1. *The Nightclub Operator* (polytonal tides of inexorable inhumanity). Scene 2. *The Preacher* (a specious paraclete radiating phony euphony). Scene 3. *The Sacrifice* (polychordal onslaught by brutalized killers, with the recorded voice of Bessie Smith, the Queen of the Blues, heard on a distant phonograph providing sorrowful commentary). *Epilogue* (a funereal procession intoned by a toneless chorus receding into timeless space).

16 OCTOBER 1966

Wieland WAGNER, grandson of Wagner and great-grandson of Liszt, who with his brother Wolfgang assumed the directorship of the Bayreuth Festivals in 1951, and revolutionized the production of Wagner's music dramas, doing away with the stuffy Teutonic costumery which was once *de rigueur* and introducing stark scenic symbolism (e.g., the erection of a phallic totem pole in *Tristan und Isolde*), dies in Frankfurt at the age of forty-nine.

29 OCTOBER 1966

*Music for Indiana,* a symphonic sketch by Darius MILHAUD, written for the sesquicentennial of the State of Indiana, is performed for the first time in Indianapolis.

### 30 OCTOBER 1966

*Sinfonia Tramontana,* the last symphony by the Swedish romantic composer Gösta NYSTROEM (1890–1966) is performed posthumously in Stockholm.

### 4 NOVEMBER 1966

*In Memoriam John F. Kennedy* by the 38-year-old American composer William SYDEMAN, for narrator and orchestra, to a text including extracts from Kennedy's speeches and comments by Kennedy's associates, containing allusions to the funeral march from Beethoven's *Eroica* and to the U.S. National Anthem, is performed for the first time by the Boston Symphony Orchestra, Erich Leinsdorf conducting.

### 5 NOVEMBER 1966

*Együtt és egyedül (Together and Alone),* allegorical opera by the 48-year-old Hungarian composer András MIHÁLY, in which a perpetual wanderer seeking the location of Dante's Inferno finds it in Hungary under the Nazi-dominated Fascistic regime, set to music in somberly discordant harmonies and ominously asymmetrical rhythms, is produced in Budapest.

### 8 NOVEMBER 1966

*Die Flucht,* dramatic oratorio by the Russian-born, German-educated Swiss composer Wladimir VOGEL is performed for the first time in Zürich.

### 12 NOVEMBER 1966

Quincy PORTER, American composer of highly cultured symphonic music set in a neo-classical style, dies in Bethany, Connecticut, at the age of sixty-nine.

### 15 NOVEMBER 1966

*Puntila,* opera by Paul DESSAU, after a play by Bertolt Brecht, in 12 scenes with a prologue and an epilogue, dealing with four resolute women who expose the wickedness of an alcoholic landlord, written in a burlesque manner, including a series of ariosos and half-spoken dialogues, is produced in East Berlin.

### 17 NOVEMBER 1966

*Fourth Symphony* by the 64-year-old Swedish composer Sten BROMAN, in two sections *Fantasia* and *Finale,* unified by a permanent rhythmic pulse of 63 beats per minute, with all changes of tempo being multiples of this number and the melodic material drawn from a mono-serial dodecaphonic matrix, the score containing a large complement of percussion instruments, including exotic drums, is performed for the first time by the Detroit Symphony Orchestra under the direction of its Swedish conductor Sixten Ehrling.

### 19 NOVEMBER 1966

*Sixth Symphony* by Roger SESSIONS, in three movements, written in a highly complex contrapuntal idiom, fertilized by the spermatic infusion of asymmetrically ejaculated rhythms, commissioned by the State of New Jersey for the celebration of its tercentenary, is performed for the first time in its entirety in Newark. (The first two movements were performed for the first time, before the third movement was completed, in Newark, on 19 January 1966)

## 29 NOVEMBER 1966

*The Violins of Saint-Jacques,* opera in three acts by the 35-year-old Australian composer Malcolm WILLIAMSON, his fifth opera, in which phantom violins emerge from the sea on each anniversary of the cataclysmic eruption in 1902 of Mont Pelée on the Island of Martinique, with assorted zombies, among them a convertible Lesbian and an effeminate captain, arising from the foam in voodoo rituals, set to music in a sophisticatedly simplicistic triadic idiom vivified by Caribbean rhythms, is produced by the Sadler's Wells Opera Company in London.

## 2 DECEMBER 1966

*Double Concerto* for oboe, harp and 18 string instruments by Hans Werner HENZE, written in a dissonant neo-baroque idiom, is performed for the first time in Zürich.

## 11 DECEMBER 1966

*Guayana Johnny (The Sugar Reapers),* opera in two acts by the English socialist composer Alan BUSH, dealing with the downtrodden sugar plantation workers in British Guiana who successfully overwhelm the British colonial power in 1953, containing an episode of interracial passion of a handsome Negro for a diminutive Hindu maiden, set to music steeped in indigenous melorhythms, is performed for the first time in Leipzig.

## 11 DECEMBER 1966

*Laura,* comic opera by Béla TARDOS, Hungarian composer of meloromantic music, is produced posthumously in Debrecen, 23 days after the composer's death.

## 15 DECEMBER 1966

*Triplum* by Wolfgang FORTNER, a triptych in which the thematic condominium of component trinities is scored for a triune consortium of wind instruments, strings, percussion and three pianos, set in serially calculated triplicities of tripartite forms, is performed for the first time by the Basel Chamber Orchestra, Paul Sacher conducting.

## 17 DECEMBER 1966

*Apocalypse* for narrator, chorus and instruments by the 26-year-old Polish composer Edward BOGUSLAWSKI, written in an expansive grandiloquent manner, with allusions to ecclesiastical chants providing an eschatological ambience, is performed for the first time in Warsaw.

### 18 DECEMBER 1966

*Fourth Symphony* by the English composer Benjamin FRANKEL is performed for the first time in London.

### 21 DECEMBER 1966

*It Is Snowing,* cantata by the Soviet composer Georgy SVIRIDOV, to words by Boris Pasternak, is performed for the first time in Moscow.

### 29 DECEMBER 1966

*Concerto for Percussion and Orchestra* in three movements by the 42-year-old American composer Donald ERB, is performed for the first time by the Detroit Symphony Orchestra.

# ◅ 1967 ▻

### 4 JANUARY 1967

Mary GARDEN, Scottish soprano singer who captured the imagination of the Paris public as Mélisande in Debussy's opera at its first performance in 1902 despite her burring accent, dies in her native town of Aberdeen in Scotland, a few weeks before her 93rd birthday. (She was born on 20 February 1874, not 1877, as she self-rejuvenatingly claimed)

### 6 JANUARY 1967

*Piano Concerto* by the 58-year-old American composer Elliott CARTER, in two movements, *Fantastico* and *Molto giusto,* conceived in the form of a double concerto grosso, in which a group of seven instruments acts as a polyphonic mediator between the piano and orchestra, with thematic materials organized in a serial totality of metrical, rhythmical, melodic, harmonic and contrapuntal parameters, is performed for the first time by Jacob Lateiner with the Boston Symphony Orchestra, Erich Leinsdorf conducting.

### 12 JANUARY 1967

*Fourth Symphony* by the 63-year-old Hungarian neo-classicist Paul KÁDOSA is performed for the first time in Budapest.

### 24 JANUARY 1967

A symphony concert in a program of four specially commissioned works by American composers is presented at the University of Chicago to mark its 75th anniversary:

*Music for the Magic Theater,* by George ROCHBERG, a musical collage of quotations from compositions by masters from Mozart to Varèse, interlinearly perlustrated by connective tissue of original motives; *Inflexions* for 14 players by the Argentine composer, resident in America, Mario DAVIDOVSKY, written in a modernistic idiom within the normal tempered scale; and *Un Voyage à Cythère* for soprano and ten instruments by Easley BLACKWOOD, depicting in impressionistic tones a journey to the island of Aphrodite.

### 27 JANUARY 1967

*Concerto for Cello and Orchestra* by Frank MARTIN in three movements: *Allegro moderato, Adagietto* and *Vivace,* written in a pantonal style ranging from immaculate diatonicism to quasi-dodecaphonic chromaticism, is performed for the first time in Basel.

### 29 JANUARY 1967

*Die Doppelgängerin,* opera in three acts by the Czech-American composer Jan MEYEROWITZ, based on Gerhardt Hauptmann's play *Winterballad,* to a libretto of murderous violence and preternatural revenge by an alter ego of the victim (hence the title) in 16th-century Sweden, set to music in neo-medieval modalities, is performed for the first time in Hannover, Germany.

### 7 FEBRUARY 1967

*Les Quasars (Third Symphony)* for chorus and orchestra by the Canadian composer Clermont PEPIN, to his own poem extolling man's boldness in probing the mysterious quasi-stellar objects in remote space, in four movements, *Symphonie de lumières, Poésie de couleurs, Trajectories invisibles de présences* and *Lancinantes décorations de silence,* set in hyperimpressionistic harmonies, is performed for the first time in Montreal.

### 14 FEBRUARY 1967

*Fourth Symphony* by the 46-year-old English composer Peter Racine FRICKER, in one continuous movement, subdivided into ten sections, written in a freely atonal idiom containing mutually independent dodecaphonic episodes, but gravitating towards a focal A as a key center, dedicated to the memory of his Hungarian teacher Mátyás Seiber (who died in an automobile catastrophe in South Africa on 24 September 1960) and embodying translucently veiled thematic allusions to several of Seiber's works, is performed for the first time in Wolverhampton, England.

### 15 FEBRUARY 1967

*Nausikaa* and *Die Bauerhochzeit,* scenic cantatas by Hermann REUTTER, newly arranged for the stage from his vocal cycle *Hochzeitslieder,* are performed for the first time on the stage in Mainz.

### 16 FEBRUARY 1967

Anis FULEIHAN, 66-year-old American composer, conducts the New York Philharmonic in the world première of his *Second Symphony* in five movements: *Moderato, Vivace, Andante con moto, Tempo di marcia* and *Allegro,* the latter based on a Greek song retained in Fuleihan's childhood memories in his native island of Cyprus.

### 24 FEBRUARY 1967

*Kardiogram IV* by the 23-year-old Swedish avant-garde composer Gunnar VALKARE, scored for four vocalists of different sexes, chorus and a chamber orchestra, is performed for the first time in Helsinki, Finland.

### 1 MARCH 1967

The inaugural concert is given in the newly built Queen Elizabeth Hall, London, in the presence of Queen Elizabeth II, presenting a program of music by English composers, from Henry PURCELL to Benjamin BRITTEN, including the first performance of Britten's *Hankin Booby* for chamber orchestra, based on English folksongs.

### 2 MARCH 1967

*Variations for Cello and Orchestra,* in one continuous movement, by Walter PISTON, written in his newly adopted dodecaphonic technique of composition, opening with a widely-spaced 12-tone chord, with the perfect fourth, tritones and their summational major sevenths being the principal "tendency intervals," the entire panchromatic panoply opened to include episodes in diatonic modalities and nutritious triadic harmonies, concluding on a starkly thirdless triad on D, is performed for the first time by the prime Soviet violoncellist Mstislav Rostropovich, with the London Symphony Orchestra on its American visit, conducted by Gennady Rozhdestvensky, in Carnegie Hall, New York.

### 4 MARCH 1967

*Kaiser Jovian,* opera in four acts by the 35-year-old Swiss composer Rudolf KELTERBORN, wherein Jupiter assumes the identity of the ephemeral Roman emperor Jovian (reigned 363–364 A.D.), marries his bride, and ultimately reveals himself and returns to Mt. Olympus, opening and ending with a vociferous dodecaphonic chord, is produced in Karlsruhe.

### 4 MARCH 1967

*Arden muss sterben,* a "political opera about ourselves" in two acts by the 34-year-old German-born English composer Alexander GOEHR, to a German libretto after an anonymous 16th-century English play *Arden of Feversham,* dealing with the murder of a faceless man by his wife and her lover, set to music as a series of interconnected variations immersed in an atonal magma, is performed for the first time by the Hamburg State Opera.

### 5 MARCH 1967

*Eli,* opera in 12 scenes by the German composer Walter STEFFENS, after a story by the Nobel laureate Nelly Sachs, dealing with a Jewish boy named Eli

*1234*

slain by an Ebreocidal Nazi as he plays a tune on his shepherd's pipe in the childish hope of summoning angels from heaven to his aid, set to music in "intervallically coherent atonal counterpoint" is produced in Dortmund.

## 5 MARCH 1967

Lukas Foss conducts in New York, with the Soviet cellist Mstislav Rostropovich as soloist, the first performance of his *Concerto* for violoncello and orchestra, written in a highly advanced modern idiom and containing aleatory passages.

## 6 MARCH 1967

Zoltán KODÁLY, great master of modern Hungarian music who together with Béla Bartók early in the century traveled through the hills and dales of Southeastern Europe to collect thousands of authentic multinational folk melodies, composer of operas, symphonic, choral and instrumental music, dies in Budapest of a heart ailment at the age of eighty-four.

## 9 MARCH 1967

*The Servant of Two Masters*, posthumous opera by Vittorio GIANNINI (who died in New York on 28 November 1966 at the age of 63), after the play by Carlo Goldoni, written in an effusively euphonious, harmonious and melodious idiom as a legacy of the composer's Italian ancestry, is brought out for the first time by the New York City Opera Company.

## 11 MARCH 1967

Geraldine FARRAR, American soprano, who rose to fame as a heart-rending Madama Butterfly, a role which she sang at the Metropolitan Opera with Caruso a hundred times, and colored her career by sensationally publicized affairs of the heart, dies at the age of 85 at her farmland retreat in Ridgefield, Connecticut, surviving by decades the purple era of her stardom.

## 17 MARCH 1967

*Mourning Becomes Electra*, opera in three acts by the 34-year-old American composer Marvin David LEVY, to the libretto condensed from Eugene O'Neill's trilogy, in which the scene of action is shifted from ancient Greece to a New England village in 1865, Agamemnon is phonetically anglicized into Ezra Mannon returning home from the Civil War, Clytemnestra becomes Christine, her lover Aegisthus is Adam Brant, Electra is Lavinia and her brother Orestes is Orin, set to music in an anguished atonal idiom embanked in compact dissonant counterpoint, is produced by the Metropolitan Opera Company as a commissioned work, at Lincoln Center, New York.

## 23 MARCH 1967

*Stronger Than Death*, opera in three acts by the Soviet composer Kyrill MOLCHANOV, focused on a Soviet hero of the defense of Brest-Litovsk against the Nazi assault in June 1941, is produced in Voronezh in the presence of the actual prototype of the story, Pyotr Gavrilov, Hero of the Soviet Union.

## 24 MARCH 1967

*Quintet for Groups* by the 40-year-old American composer Benjamin Burwell JOHNSTON, in which the orchestra is divided into five contrasting sections of instruments, is performed for the first time by the St. Louis Symphony Orchestra.

## 25 MARCH 1967

To mark the centennial of the birth of Arturo TOSCANINI, the Italian government issues a 40-lire yellow and lavender commemorative stamp depicting the Maestro with a baton in his right hand.

## 31 MARCH 1967

*The Bridge*, "anti-opera" by the Czech composer Jaromil BURGHAUSER, to a symbolic libretto placed simultaneously at two points in time, in the revolutionary year of 1848 and in the socialist year of 1963, and located in space on a bridge which divides a town into two parts, set to music in modern serial techniques, is produced in Prague.

## 1 APRIL 1967

*Polymorphie* for 106 musicians by the French composer Michel DECOUST is performed for the first time in the course of the musical festival in Royan, France.

## 5 APRIL 1967

Mischa (a diminutive Slavic form for Michael) ELMAN, 76-year-old Russian-Jewish violinist whose playing was distinguished by an emotional richness of tone and romantic absorption in the music, dies suddenly of a heart attack in New York.

## 6 APRIL 1967

*Los Caprichos*, symphonic fantasy by the 40-year-old German composer Hans Werner HENZE, inspired by Goya's drawing of a witch riding a broom at the altitude of about 2,000 feet, is performed for the first time in Duisburg.

## 6 APRIL 1967

*Concerto for Piano and Orchestra* by Miklós RÓZSA, Hungarian-born composer domesticated in Hollywood, in three well-contrasted movements, vibrant with colorful Lisztian pianism, saturated with euphonious dissonances and vitalized by explosively asymmetrical rhythms, is performed for the first time by the Los Angeles Philharmonic Orchestra, with Zubin Mehta conducting and Leonard Pennario playing the solo part.

**6 APRIL 1967**

*Chthonic Ode* for orchestra by the American composer Paul CRESTON, a homage to the modern British sculptor Henry Moore, extolling in tersely dissonant harmonies the immanent chthonicism of his primitivistically transcendental sculptures, is performed for the first time in Detroit.

**13 APRIL 1967**

*La Chanson de Roland,* lyric opera in three acts by the 72-year-old French composer Henri MARTELLI, to the composer's own libretto after the medieval French epic, is performed for the first time in Paris.

**14 APRIL 1967**

*Dies Irae,* "Oratorium ob memoriam in perniciei castris in Oswiecim necatorum inexstinguibilem reddendam," for solo voices, chorus and orchestra, by the 33-year-old Polish modernist Krzysztof PENDERECKI, dedicated to the memory of men, women and children exterminated in Auschwitz (Oświęcim) by the Nazis, to Latin texts from Psalms and Apocalypse and Latin translations of poems by Louis Aragon, Paul Valéry and others, as well as Greek texts of Aeschylus, is performed for the first time in Cracow. (Three days later it was performed at the inaugural of the Monument of Struggle and Martyrdom in Oświęcim)

**15 APRIL 1967**

In honor of the 20th anniversary of UNESCO, the Republic of Togo issues a set of commemorative postage stamps of seven values (5, 10, 15, 20, 30, 45 and 90 francs) featuring portraits of Bach, Beethoven, Debussy and Duke Ellington.

**16 APRIL 1967**

*Les Hauts de Hurlevent,* opera in seven scenes after Emily Brontë's novel *Wuthering Heights,* by the French composer Thomas STUBBS, set to an appropriately romantic score in an ingratiatingly old-fashioned operatic idiom, is produced for the first time in Rouen, France.

**17 APRIL 1967**

*The Crook,* comic opera in two acts by the Israeli composer Menahem AVIDOM, the first musical satire on the government of Israel, wherein its fiscal troubles lead to the promulgation of a decree forbidding the population to breathe after the expiration of the deadline for payment of taxes, is produced in Tel Aviv.

**18 APRIL 1967**

*Cosmic Mist,* symphonic poem by the Texas-born composeress Radie BRITAIN, in three movements, (1) *In the Beginning* (2) *Nebula* (3) *Nuclear Fission,* illustrative of cosmogonic mysteries by means of chromatic implosions amidst tritone-laden harmonies, culminating in a subatomic fortissississimo, is performed for the first time at an unrehearsed orchestral symposium in Houston.

### 19 APRIL 1967

*Cello Concerto* by the Hungarian ultra-modernist György LIGETI, is performed for the first time in Berlin.

### 27 APRIL 1967

*La Duchesse de Langeais,* opera in three acts by the French-Italian conductor Eugène BOZZA, written in a Puccinian lyrico-dramatic style, is performed for the first time in Lille, France.

### 27 APRIL 1967

*Phorion* for orchestra, electronic organ, harpsichord and guitar by the 44-year-old ultra-modern American composer Lukas Foss, a metamorphosis of Bach's violin *Partita in E (Phorion* means stolen goods in Greek, and the idea came to Foss in a dream when he heard, and observed on paper, "torrents of Baroque 16th-notes washed ashore by ocean waves and sucked in again"), with the thematic materials transmogrified by aleatory permutations, acrobatic inversions, congenial perversions and melorhythmic singultations, is performed for the first time by the New York Philharmonic, under the direction of Leonard Bernstein.

### 29 APRIL 1967

*Geschäftsbericht,* minimal opera (duration 600 seconds) by the prime German Communist composer Paul DESSAU, a "business report" to the text of the indictment of the American aggression in Vietnam by the International Tribunal for War Crimes in Stockholm, with an epilogue in which dead American soldiers curse President Johnson for depriving them of their lives, is produced in Leipzig.

### 29 APRIL 1967

The Universal and International Exhibition Expo 67, opens in Montreal to mark Canada's Centennial year with the presentation of specially composed oratorio *Terre des hommes,* to a French text, for orchestra, chorus and two narrators, by the Canadian composer André PREVOST, written in an infra-modern idiom enlivened by rational dissonances, with the message exhorting mankind to regain the "perfumes of dawn."

### 30 APRIL 1967

At the World Festival of Music given in conjunction with Expo 67 in Montreal, the Stockholm Royal Opera makes its North American debut with Verdi's opera *Un Ballo in Maschera,* to the original libretto describing the assassination on 16 March 1792 of King Gustavus of Sweden, rather than that of the mythical "Governor of Boston" of the revised version.

### 2 MAY 1967

*Venice*, "an audiograph" for double orchestra and brass choirs by the American composer Morton GOULD, portraying, in seven "sonic postcards" the topography of Venice, its cafés, its canals and its pigeons, is performed for the first time by the Seattle Symphony Orchestra.

### 9 MAY 1967

A Criminal Court Judge in New York City gives a suspended jail sentence to Charlotte MOORMAN, 28-year-old American cellist for playing a recital in New York on 9 February 1967 in "topless" attire, with her rounded bosoms fully exposed to potentially innocent eyes.

### 13 MAY 1967

*Concerto* for flute and orchestra by Jean FRANÇAIX is performed for the first time in Schwetzingen, Germany.

### 14 MAY 1967

*Galileo*, oratorio by the American composer Ezra LADERMAN, depicting the prosecution by the Church of the great astronomer Galileo, is performed for the first time as a television drama with music by the Columbia Broadcasting Company in New York.

### 15 MAY 1967

*Antiparallele*, for piano and orchestra by the 46-year-old Slovenian composer Primoz RAMOVS, is performed for the first time at the Zagreb Festival.

### 17 MAY 1967

*Jonah*, dramatic cantata by the American composer Daniel PINKHAM, is performed for the first time at the New England Conservatory of Music in Boston, as part of the celebration of its centennial.

### 19 MAY 1967

*Bomarzo*, opera in two acts by the 51-year-old Argentinian modernist Alberto GINASTERA, subdivided into 15 scenes saturated with effulgent sex, ecstatic violence and psychedelic hallucinations, dealing with the 16th-century Italian Duke of Bomarzo, to a libretto fashioned after a novel by the Argentine writer Manuel Mujica Lainez, featuring a seduction in a bordello, mass voyeurism, latent sodomy and ineffable perversions leading to Bomarzo's poisoning, set to music with the application of various serial techniques, a chord of 12 different notes and 11 different intervals being of germinal importance, is performed for the first time on the stage in Washington. (A cantata *Bomarzo* by

Alberto Ginastera, with the same plot but a different score, was performed for the first time on 1 November 1964, also in Washington)

### 22 MAY 1967

At the opening concert of the 11th Gulbenkian Music Festival in Lisbon, *Concerto for Violin, Piano and Orchestra* by the 69-year-old Brazilian composer Francisco MIGNONE is performed for the first time.

### 26 MAY 1967

*Madame Bovary*, opera in two acts by the Swiss composer Heinrich SUTERMEISTER, after Flaubert's famous novel analyzing the adulterous life and pitiful death of a provincial Frenchwoman, is performed for the first time in Zürich.

### 2 JUNE 1967

*To Vishnu*, tone poem by the 56-year-old American composer Alan HOVHANESS, depicting the solar god of the Hindus as the controlling deity of the galactic spheres, opening with a musical landscape of mildly dissonant chaos and culminating in a sonic pandemonium of bells and trumpets in a fiery orbit, is performed for the first time by the New York Philharmonic.

### 2 JUNE 1967

*Sequencia, Coral e Ricercare*, a neo-baroque symphonic suite by the 60-year-old Brazilian composer Camargo GUARNIERI is performed for the first time at the 11th annual Gulbenkian Music Festival in Lisbon.

### 2 JUNE 1967

Queen Elizabeth of England opens the 20th Music Festival of the Suffolk fishing village of Aldeburgh, with the Royal Artillery Band sounding fanfares from the opera *Gloriana* by Benjamin BRITTEN, founder of the Aldeburgh Festival, followed by a brief concert featuring Britten's choral overture *The Building of the House* written for the occasion.

### 3 JUNE 1967

Two chamber operas by British composers receive their first performances at the Aldeburgh Festival in England:

*Castaway* by Lennox BERKELEY, dealing with the dalliance of Odysseus with Nausicaa; and *The Bear* by William WALTON, after a comic play by Anton Chekhov in which an ill-mannered intellectual, about to propose to the lady of his heart, nearly ruins their future marital bliss by starting a polemical discussion with her.

### 12 JUNE 1967

*Magic Prison* for two narrators and orchestra by the 43-year-old American composer Ezra LADERMAN, based on the writings of Emily Dickinson, is performed for the first time by the New York Philharmonic, André Kostelanetz conducting.

17 JUNE 1967

*Heroine,* opera in two acts by the Albanian composer Vangjo Novo, in which an Albanian girl guerrilla heroically refuses, despite inhuman torture, to disclose the names of the Communist-led partisans to the Nazi invaders in 1943, culminating in a total liberation of the land and the execution of local traitors, set to music according to the romantic formula of socialist opera, with tragedy and sacrifice in minor modes leading to a triumphant finale in marching major keys, is produced in Tirana.

18 JUNE 1967

*Blumine,* excised movement from Gustav MAHLER's *First Symphony,* redolent of the flowery scent of the neologism of the title (taken by Mahler from a literary essay *Herbst-Blumine* of the romantic German writer Jean Paul), is performed for the first time in the 20th century, from a recently discovered manuscript, at the Aldeburgh Music Festival, in England, conducted by Benjamin Britten. (The first complete 20th-century performance of Mahler's *First Symphony,* in five movements, including *Blumine,* was given on 9 April 1968, in New Haven, Connecticut, by the New Haven Symphony Orchestra, Frank Brieff conducting)

24 JUNE 1967

*Die Blumen von Hiroshima,* musical chamber play by the German composer Jean Kurt FOREST, dealing with a militant American pacifist who in 1955 marries a Japanese girl, survivor of the atom bombing of Hiroshima, despite the ominous possibility that the genes of their children might be affected by latent radiation, is produced in Weimar, conducted by the composer.

28 JUNE 1967

*Triplum* by Gunther SCHULLER, scored for orchestra in which the strings, the woodwinds and the brass constitute three self-sufficient entities (hence the title) functioning in the manner of a concertino, with a polyphonally effulgent climax, in conformity with the titular concept *e tribus unum,* is performed for the first time in Philharmonic Hall, Lincoln Center, New York.

2 JULY 1967

The Fifth Congregation of the Arts opens at Dartmouth College in Hanover, New Hampshire, under the direction of Mario di Bonaventura, with Aaron COPLAND, Hans Werner HENZE and Frank MARTIN participating as visiting composers, inaugurating a series of concerts comprising the following world premières:

*Endecatode* (eleven melodies) for chamber orchestra, in 11 visions, by the 85-year-old dean of Italian composers Gian Francesco MALIPIERO (5 July); *Estri* (improvisational fancies), a chamber symphony by Goffredo PETRASSI of Italy (2 August); *Clarinet Concerto* by Walter PISTON (6 August); *Soli No. 4* for trumpet, horn and trombone by Carlos CHÁVEZ (9 August) and *Virtuose Musik (Second Violin Concerto)* by Boris BLACHER of West Germany (19 August).

## 7 JULY 1967

*Toyon of Alaska (The Lord of Alaska)* historical pageant-opera in three acts by Williard STRAIGHT, dealing with the Russian overlord of the Arctic Alexander Baranov who established the first settlement in Alaska in 1792, is produced in Anchorage during the centennial celebration of the purchase of Alaska by the United States from the Russian government in 1867 for the sum $7,500,000.

## 9 JULY 1967

A month after the glorious conclusion of Israel's six-day war against the overwhelmingly more populous adversaries of the surrounding Arab nations, the Israel Philharmonic Orchestra, under the direction of Leonard Bernstein and with Isaac Stern as the soloist, gives a concert on Mount Scopus on the Northeastern side of Jerusalem in a program including two works by converted Jewish composers, *Violin Concerto* by Felix MENDELSSOHN and *Second Symphony* by Gustav MAHLER, the latter with the final chorus sung in Hebrew.

## 18 JULY 1967

*Aequora Lunae*, symphonic suite in seven movements by the 64-year-old South African composeress Priaulx RAINIER, symbolically portraying the astrological characteristics of the principal seven "seas" of the moon, is performed for the first time in Cheltenham, England.

## 20 JULY 1967

*Concerto* for trombone and orchestra by the Hungarian-American composer Eugene ZADOR, is performed for the first time in Meadow Brook, Michigan.

## 21 JULY 1967

The Bayreuth Festival opens its annual Wagner series, including three cycles of *The Ring of the Nibelung* in Wieland WAGNER's production as designed by him before his death in 1966.

## 23 JULY 1967

*Doña Barbara*, opera by the 43-year-old American woman composer Caroline LLOYD, resident in Venezuela for 15 years, is performed for the first time in Caracas.

## 29 JULY 1967

The Israel Philharmonic Orchestra commences a three-week tour of the United States and Canada, with an opening concert at Philharmonic Hall, Lincoln Center, in New York under the direction of William Steinberg, in a program of classical German music prefaced by an exultant *Fanfare to Israel* by the German-born Israeli composer Paul BEN-HAIM.

## 3 AUGUST 1967

*The Rise and Fall of the Third Reich,* cantata by the 35-year-old Argentinian-born American composer of Russian-Jewish parentage, Lalo (Boris) SCHIFRIN, adapted from his musical score to the moving picture of that name after the historical book by William Shirer, in which Satan sends his special envoy Adolf Hitler to Germany, and containing an actual recording of Hitler's rasping voice, couched in a musical style pervaded by atonal anxiety, is performed for the first time at the Hollywood Bowl by the Los Angeles Philharmonic Orchestra, chorus and soloists under the direction of Lawrence Foster.

## 6 AUGUST 1967

On the 22nd anniversary of the atomic obliteration of Hiroshima, a cantata entitled simply *Hiroshima* by the Italian composer Gaetano ZUFFRE, is performed for the first time as a dedicatory work by the Japanese Broadcasting Corporation in Tokyo.

## 8 AUGUST 1967

The production of the opera *Bomarzo* by the prime Argentinian composer Alberto GINASTERA, scheduled for performance at the Teatro Colón in Buenos Aires, is cancelled on orders of the military government of Argentina as "obsessed by sex and violence."

*Bomarzo* contains an excessive dose of scenes of violence and sex, which makes it unacceptable for the Argentine public. Perhaps the opera can be successful in Europe and in the United States, but it is our duty to protect our own people. I repeat that this measure was taken for strictly moral reasons, for we believe that the action of *Bomarzo* is not suitable for production in the Teatro Colón. (Statement of the Secretary of Culture of the Municipality of Buenos Aires)

## 8 AUGUST 1967

Jaromir WEINBERGER, 71-year-old Czech composer of one of the most durable comic operas of the twentieth century, *Schwanda,* driven to despondency because of his inability to produce further successful works, commits suicide by swallowing an overdose of barbiturates at his home in St. Petersburg, Florida, where he settled in 1939.

## 10 AUGUST 1967

At the Expo 67 World Festival in Montreal, the Bolshoi Theater Opera Company of Moscow, in its first appearance in North America, presents MUSSORGSKY's great national opera *Boris Godunov.*

## 10 AUGUST 1967

*Gita,* electronic piece for chorus, brass ensemble and prerecorded tape by the Canadian engineer-composer R. Murray SCHAEFER is performed for the first time at the Berkshire Festival, in Lenox, Massachusetts.

12 AUGUST 1967

*War and Peace*, monumental opera by Sergei PROKOFIEV is presented by the Bolshoi Opera as its second offering on its first tour in the Western Hemisphere, at Montreal, during the music festival of the Canadian Expo 67.

14 AUGUST 1967

At the Canadian Expo 67 World Festival in Montreal, the Bolshoi Theater Opera Company of Moscow presents the first Canadian performance of RIMSKY-KORSAKOV's mystical opera *The Legend of the Invisible City of Kitezh*, popularly known as the Russian *Parsifal* (indeed, Wagnerian undertones are peculiarly discernible underneath the multicolored Russian harmonies).

25 AUGUST 1967

*Die Sonnenfinsternis*, cantata by the Swiss composer Conrad BECK, for contralto and chamber orchestra, philosophically reflecting upon the wonder of a solar eclipse, is performed for the first time at the International Musical Festival of Lucerne, Switzerland.

25 AUGUST 1967

*Historien om en Moder (Story of a Mother)*, opera by the Danish composer Thomas KOPPEL, written by him when he was 17, to a sentimental story by Hans Christian Andersen, is produced in Copenhagen.

31 AUGUST 1967

*Oxus*, dramatic scene for voice and orchestra by Humphrey SEARLE, to the text from the final stanza of Matthew Arnold's poem *Sohrab and Rustum* relating the ancient Persian tale of Rustum fighting a tournament to the death against the young Tatar Sohrab on the river Oxus (Amu-Darya) in Central Asia, only to discover, after killing him, that he is his natural son by a Tatar concubine, set to music in a strict dodecaphonic idiom in disregard of the ethnomusicologically proper pentatonicism of Asian modalities, is performed for the first time in London.

2 SEPTEMBER 1967

*Labyrinth*, phantasmagoric opera in two acts by the 35-year-old Danish composer Per NÖRGAARD, in which the guide of a labyrinth in a sideshow at a country fair imagines himself in Dante's Inferno with a tape recorder blaring popular songs, is produced in Copenhagen.

3 SEPTEMBER 1967

*The Death of Moses*, cantata by the 56-year-old Israeli composer Josef TAL, written in the manner of a modern miracle play and combining mystic elements with allusions to historical reality, scored for voices, orchestra and electronic sound generators, is performed for the first time in Jerusalem.

## 4 SEPTEMBER 1967

*Visage d'Axel*, symphonic poem by the 43-year-old French composer Serge NIGG, in two sections, *Le monde visionnaire*, and *Le monde passionel*, after a poem by Villiers de l'Isle Adam, is performed for the first time in Paris.

## 13 SEPTEMBER 1967

*Inscape*, for orchestra by Aaron COPLAND (the title comes from a poem by Gerard Manley Hopkins), a "quasi-mystical illumination," with thematic materials derived from two basic 12-tone rows, is performed for the first time by the Orchestra of the University of Michigan in Ann Arbor. (The work, commissioned by the New York Philharmonic in observance of its 125th anniversary, came to its first New York performance by that orchestra on 20 October 1967)

## 14 SEPTEMBER 1967

The Los Angeles Philharmonic Orchestra, under the direction of its 31-year-old Indian conductor Zubin Mehta, undertakes its first world tour with concerts in Belgium, Luxembourg, Rumania, Greece, France, Austria, Germany, Italy, Yugoslavia, Turkey, Cyprus, Iran and India. (The tour was completed on 6 November 1967, with a concert in Mehta's native city of Bombay)

## 15 SEPTEMBER 1967

*The Luck of Ginger Coffey*, opera in three acts by the Canadian composer Raymond PANNELL, to a libretto retailing the vicissitudes of an Irishman in search of a newspaper job in Canada, set to music in an ingratiatingly eclectic idiom, containing rock 'n' roll, hymnology and French-Canadian folksongs, is produced in Toronto.

## 23 SEPTEMBER 1967

*Louis Riel*, music drama in three acts by the Canadian composer Harry SOMERS, centered on the dramatic career of the French-Canadian rebel who espoused the cause of the Metizo Indians in 1869 (he was 1/8 redskin and married a squaw), tried to overthrow the government and was hanged in 1886, to a bilingual libretto, set to music in a highly diversified idiom, containing serial devices, electronic effects and contemporary folksongs, is produced in Toronto.

## 30 SEPTEMBER 1967

*Virineia*, music drama by the 35-year-old Soviet composer Sergei SLONIMSKY, depicting the social and personal upheavals in the Russian countryside during the first year of the Russian Revolution, in seven ideologically and politically significant scenes—*The End of the Autocracy, The End of the Family, The End of Religious Faith, The Night, The Dawn, Political Meetings, Farewell*, centering on the fate of a simple Russian woman Virineia who breaks away from the chains of dull matrimony and obsolete religious faith, set to music deeply rooted in Russian melos, with the interpolation of purely illustrative orchestral tableaux—a blizzard, a night's silence, a people's rumblings—is produced in Leningrad.

### 1 OCTOBER 1967

*Seventh Symphony* by Roger SESSIONS, written to observe the sesquicentennial of the University of Michigan, in three classically conceived movements, *Allegro con fuoco, Lento e dolce* and *Allegro misurato*, followed by a brief epilogue, set to music in dissonant polyphony with thematic strands formed by a serial pattern, is performed for the first time in Ann Arbor, the site of the University of Michigan, by the Chicago Symphony Orchestra, conducted by Jean Martinon.

### 4 OCTOBER 1967

The 41st Festival of the International Society for Contemporary Music opens in Prague with the following program of symphonic music:

*Configurations* by the Japanese composer Yori-Aki MATSUDAIRA; *Perspectives* by the Greek neo-classicist Yorgo SICILIANOS; *Iniciativas* by the Spanish neo-classical abstractionist Luis de PABLO; and *Triplum* by the German modernist Wolfgang FORTNER.

### 5 OCTOBER 1967

At the second concert of the 41st Festival of the International Society for Contemporary Music in Prague the following orchestral works are given:

*Shadows* by the Italian modernist Girolamo ARRIGO; *Sigma* by the Yugoslav abstractionist Ivo MALEC; *Contra fidem* by the Polish neo-classicist Zbigniew RUDZINSKI, intended to exemplify "a struggle for a concise form in the non-traditional field of musical expression;" and *Symphony* for three instrumental groups by the Spanish modernist Cristóbal HALFFTER.

### 7 OCTOBER 1967

On Jazz Day in New York City, so designated by Mayor Lindsay, the orchestral *Jazzhattan Suite* by Oliver NELSON, specially composed for the occasion, has its first performance in Central Park, a natural location for Manhattanese jazzification, embanked between the protective towers of East Side and West Side and flanked by jazz-fecund maternal Harlem and an aggressively erectile paternalistic downtown genus.

### 7 OCTOBER 1967

At the 41st Festival of the International Society for Contemporary Music in Prague two fairy-tale operas by the Czech composer Jiří PAUER, *The Talkative Snail* and *The Red Riding Hood,* are presented, on the same day with the following program of chamber music:

*Dialogues* for flute and harp by Jan KAPR of Czechoslovakia; *Fragment IV from Shakespeare Sonnets* by Ton de KRUYF of Holland; *String Quartet* by Atilla BOZAY of

Hungary; *String Quartet No. 15* by the 74-year-old Czech modernist Alois HÁBA, written in fifths of a tone; *Réseaux* by Francis MIROGLIO of France, and *Aria da capo* by Yitzhak SADAI of Israel.

## 8 OCTOBER 1967

At the 41st Festival of the International Society for Contemporary Music in Prague the following program of chamber music is presented:

*For Two Violins* by Robert du BOIS of Holland; *Trio* for oboe, viola and harp by Heinz HOLLIGER of Switzerland; *Presence* by Bernd Alois ZIMMERMANN of Germany; *Springtime* by Erik BERGMAN of Finland and *Eufemias Mysterion* by Miloslav KABELÁČ of Czechoslovakia.

## 9 OCTOBER 1967

*Concerto à ballo* for orchestra by the 58-year-old Austrian composer Alfred UHL, in four movements set in a neo-baroque idiom diversified by modern harmonies, is performed for the first time by the Vienna Symphony Orchestra in New York, during its American tour.

## 9 OCTOBER 1967

At the 41st Festival of the Society for Contemporary Music in Prague, the following program of music by Czech composers is presented:

*15 Prints After Dürer's Apocalypse* by the 32-year-old composer Luboš FIŠER (first performed in Prague on 15 May 1966); *6 Etudes* for chamber orchestra by Miloslav ISTVAN; *Foam* for orchestra by Svatopluk HAVELKA; and *Transformations* by Roman BERGER.

## 10 OCTOBER 1967

At the last concert of the 41st Festival of the International Society for Contemporary Music in Prague the following program of symphonic music is presented:

*Tsukishiro* by the Japanese composer Kazuo FUKUSHIMA; *Métamorphose d'Écho* for voice and orchestra by the French composer Claude PREY, incorporating the natural inflections of conversation in French in the vocal part, echoed by the instruments; *Aura* by the Swedish composer Arne MELLNÄS, scored for a heterogeneous ensemble, including a clavier of beer bottles and exploding toy balloons, and set in a free aleatory idiom; *Studio No. 2* by the Italian composer Giacomo MANZONI; and *Sub rosa* by the Yugoslav composer Milko KELEMEN.

## 14 OCTOBER 1967

*Meer der Stürme*, symphonic poem by the foremost Communist composer of East Germany Paul DESSAU, an expansively optimistic fanfaronade, presaging in a proleptically realistic idiom the landing of Soviet cosmonauts in the Sea of Storms on the surface of the moon, is performed for the first time in East Berlin, on the occasion of the 50th anniversary of the Soviet Revolution. (In actual history, American astronauts made the first lunar landing, on 20 July 1969, in the Sea of Tranquility rather than in the Sea of Storms)

15 OCTOBER 1967

*Vertige d'Éros,* symphonic poem by Gunther SCHULLER, written by him in 1945, at the age of twenty, in an erotically impressionistic idiom, achieves its belated first performance in Madison, Wisconsin.

17 OCTOBER 1967

Shulamith RAN, 20-year-old Israeli composeress, plays in Jerusalem the solo part in the first performance of her *Piano Concerto.*

17 OCTOBER 1967

*Hair,* a rollicking rock 'n' roll musical, with lyrics by several hands including William Shakespeare (in Hamlet's complaint about air pollution, smog and "a foul and pestilent congregation of vapors"), and music mostly by Galt Mac-Dermot, a spontaneously designed far-out mass spectacle in which the audience is invited to get it on with the cast and vocally participate, featuring for the first time in the musical theater a scene of total nudity mitigated only by stroboscopically freaked-out lights, including such mind-blowing songs as *Let the Sunshine In,* the title song *Hair* and the psychedelically astrological chorus *Aquarius,* couched in the bemused plagal modalities of old English balladry with incredibly heavy raps laid on the audience by uninhibited proliferation of Anglo-Saxon profanity, opens in New York under the aegis of the Shakespeare Festival Public Theater. (It subsequently moved to the discotheque The Cheetah, and on 29 April 1968 inaugurated its highly auspicious Broadway run, proceeding thenceforward on a triumphant cephalotripsical tour of world capitals)

19 OCTOBER 1967

On its first visit to the United States, the La Scala Company of Milan gives, in Cargenie Hall, New York, a performance of VERDI's *Requiem.*

21 OCTOBER 1967

*Seven Counterpoints,* orchestral suite by the English composer Peter Racine FRICKER, temporarily in residence at the University of California, Santa Barbara, is performed for the first time in Pasadena, California.

21 OCTOBER 1967

The first performance of the stage version of the scenic cantata *Nochebuena del Diablo* by the dean of Spanish composers Oscar ESPLÁ is given in Madrid.

22 OCTOBER 1967

*Capriccio* for violin and orchestra by the 33-year-old Polish modernist Krzysztof PENDERECKI is performed for the first time at the Donaueschingen Festival, with Wanda Wilkomirska as soloist.

### 22 OCTOBER 1967

*Lontano* for orchestra by the Hungarian ultra-modern composer György LIGETI, is performed for the first time at the Donaueschingen Music Festival.

### 29 OCTOBER 1967

*Eighth Symphony* by the 52-year-old American composer Vincent PERSICHETTI, in four classically ordered movements vitalized by picaresque instrumental colors (including a lyric aria on the tuba) and an active percussion section, is performed for the first time at Baldwin-Wallace College in Berea, Ohio.

### 31 OCTOBER 1967

*A Penny for a Song*, comic opera by the 31-year-old English composer Richard Rodney BENNETT, to a story about a British eccentric who dresses up like Napoleon to issue the counter order cancelling the imagined invasion of Southern England by the French Army in 1804, precipitating a number of military alarms and absurdities, is produced in London.

### 2 NOVEMBER 1967

*Concerto* for doublebass and orchestra by Hans Werner HENZE, is performed for the first time as a commissioned work by the Chicago Symphony Orchestra, with Gary Karr soloist and Jean Martinon conducting.

### 3 NOVEMBER 1967

*White Nights* (the title refers to the subhorizontal sunlight during the summer nights in the sub-Arctic St. Petersburg), "musical chronicle" by Tikhon KHRENNIKOV, a pasquinade satirizing the last years of the Tsarist rule in Russia, with a cast of historical characters including the last Tsar Nicholas II, his Tsarina, and her coterie maneuvered by the sinister monk Gregory Rasputin (his last name derives from the Russian word for debauchery), set to music in the manner of Russian burlesque profusely interlarded with pseudo-Gypsy balladry, is performed for the first time in Moscow.

### 4 NOVEMBER 1967

*The Gallant King*, opera by the 61-year-old Slovak composer Alexander MOYZES, is produced in Bratislava.

### 6 NOVEMBER 1967

*Tovarishch Andrei*, opera-oratorio in ten scenes, with a prologue and an epilogue, by the 56-year-old Soviet composer Boris GIBALIN, a series of musical tableaux illustrating the revolutionary life of Jacob Sverdlov, known in the Tsarist underground as "Tovarishch Andrei," is performed for the first time in Sverdlovsk, the Ural city, formerly Ekaterinburg, renamed Sverdlovsk after Sverdlov was assassinated by an anti-Bolshevistically inspired Russian Charlotte Corday in 1918.

## 7 NOVEMBER 1967

*Der letzte Schuss,* opera by the 33-year-old German composer Siegfried MATTHUS, to a libretto dealing with the romance between a Red Army girl guerrilla and a captured White Army officer during the civil war in Central Asia in 1919, whom she is assigned to guard and whom she shoots down (the "last shot" of the title) when he attempts to join the crew of an enemy motor boat in the Aral Sea, written in a modernistically decorative manner including electronic sounds, is produced in East Berlin as part of the celebration of the semicentennial of the Soviet Revolution.

## 9 NOVEMBER 1967

*La Fille de l'homme,* lyric tragedy in three acts by the 61-year-old French composer Pierre CAPDEVIELLE, to a libretto dealing with an Italian railroad magnate who incites a woman employee to kill her lover, is performed for the first time in concert form on the Paris Radio. (A complete stage performance was given in Paris on 1 December 1967)

## 9 NOVEMBER 1967

*November Steps,* symphonic sketch by the 37-year-old Japanese composer Toru TAKEMITSU, for solo biwa (lute) and shakuhachi (bamboo flute) and orchestra, creating in its static homophony the impression of autumnal immobility, with special effects in the percussion section, is performed for the first time by the New York Philharmonic under the direction of the Japanese conductor Seiji Ozawa.

## 14 NOVEMBER 1967

The newly organized Orchestre de Paris makes its initial appearance in Paris under the direction of Charles Munch, in a program of works by Berlioz, Debussy and Stravinsky.

## 21 NOVEMBER 1967

*Hodaya Min Hamidbar (Thanksgiving from the Desert),* oratorio by the 70-year-old Israeli composer Paul BEN-HAIM, is performed for the first time at the Kibbutz Yagour in Israel.

## 25 NOVEMBER 1967

*The Brothers Ulyanov,* opera in three acts by the 64-year-old Ukrainian Soviet composer Yuli MEITUS, based on the life story of Vladimir Ulyanov (Lenin) and his brother who was hanged for the participation in the attempt to assassinate the Tsar Alexander III, is produced in Ufa.

## 30 NOVEMBER 1967

The first performance is given in the German Radio Studio in Cologne of *Hymnen,* electronic piece by the foremost proponent of new music Karlheinz

STOCKHAUSEN, for a heterophonic ensemble, including an electronic accordion, recorded shrieks, wheezes and audible exhalations, a tacit viola played by moving the bow across the strings without touching them, a tamtam rubbed by paper rolls, subdivided into four parts with thematic materials derived from a number of national anthems, opening with dislocated versions of *Internationale* and the *Marseillaise* and concluding with a "hymunion in the harmondy of a Utopian Pluramon State," under the direction of Stockhausen himself, manipulating a circular rectangle of a rigorously indeterminate digital computer.

### 30 NOVEMBER 1967

*The Decision*, opera by the 39-year-old Scottish composeress Thea MUSGRAVE, to a libretto based on an actual case of a miner entombed for 23 days following a cave-in of rock in Scotland in 1835 (he died three days later), which so shocked the stolid British establishment that a government decision (hence the title) was made to ameliorate the conditions of mine workers and to prohibit the employment of women and children in the Scottish mines, is performed for the first time in London.

### 1 DECEMBER 1967

*Neutron Star*, by the 27-year-old Swedish composer Jan W. MORTHENSON, a sonic construction of the hypothetical neutron star created by an implosion of a decayed supernova, with its entire mass contracted to an electrically neutral body of about ten kilometers in diameter and a fantastic density of $10^{11}$ g/cm$^3$ constituting the specific weight of the atomic nucleus denuded of electrons, in which the condensation of matter is symbolically represented by constantly increasing frequencies, beginning with the subsonic and ending in a heterodynamic echo, is constructed by means of multiple superpositions of electronic tapes at the Electronic Music Studio of the Swedish Broadcasting Station in Stockholm, with the aid of Computer SAAB D-21.

### 9 DECEMBER 1967

*Die Witwe des Schmetterlings*, opera in three scenes by the modernistically minded 50-year-old Korean composer Isang YUN, to an oneiric libretto in German based on an old lepidopteromorphic Chinese tale about a defunct functionary whose metempsychotic memory of having been a giant butterfly is reified when he emerges from his coffin as from a chrysalis and scares away his perfidious "butterfly widow" and her lover, set to music in an orientalized serial idiom, marked by angst-laden vocal atonalities and pierced by acute instrumental discords and horrendous asymmetric rhythms in an ample battery of percussion, is performed for the first time in Bonn in the absence of Isang Yun himself who was abducted with his wife from his West Berlin apartment on 17 June 1967 by South Korean agents, flown to Seoul to stand trial as a North Korean spy and sentenced to life imprisonment, but reprieved in March 1969 after the West German government threatened to cut its economic aid to South Korea in retaliation for illegal acts on German soil, with a contributory pressure exerted by the aroused intellectual community supported by a letter of protest signed by Igor Stravinsky and 23 other important composers.

### 12 DECEMBER 1967

On the 80th birthday of the Swedish composer Kurt ATTERBERG, his *Sinfonia visionaria* is performed for the first time in Malmö.

### 14 DECEMBER 1967

*Cello Concerto* by the 70-year-old Israeli composer Paul BEN-HAIM is performed for the first time in Limburg, Holland.

### 14 DECEMBER 1967

*Fourth Symphony,* subtitled *New York,* by the 71-year-old Spanish-born naturalized English composer Roberto GERHARD, in one movement, written in an idiosyncratic serial idiom, cohesive in form, but free in the agglutination of its additive thematic elements, dedicated to the New York Philharmonic on the occasion of its 125th anniversary, is performed for the first time by that orchestra, William Steinberg conducting.

### 26 DECEMBER 1967

Two new operas by Yugoslav composers are presented for the first time in Zagreb:

*Svjetleći Grad (The Town of Light),* seventh opera by the 54-year-old Croatian composer Ivo LHOTKA-KALINSKI, probing the minds of mental patients in an asylum in a wide-ranging atonal idiom departing decisively from the Italianate musical language of his previous works; *Adam i Eva* by the 51-year-old Slovenian composer Silvije BOMBARDELLI, dealing with man and wife meeting in the astral world after their respective terrestrial suicides, and settling their differences in an intentionally vulgarized monorhythmic manner with polytonal protuberances calculated to produce a surrealistic effect.

### 27 DECEMBER 1967

*Landschaft aus Schreien,* cantata by the 40-year-old Swedish composer Maurice KARKOFF, to the text of the Nobel-prize winning German Jewish poetess Nelly SACHS, recalling the horrors of the Nazi extermination camps, where "the landscape of screams tears the black bandage of the night," written for singing and spoken voice in an anguished atonal idiom, is performed for the first time by the Swedish Radio Station in Stockholm.

# ∽ 1968 ∾

**4 JANUARY 1968**

*Third Symphony* by the 64-year-old Russian-born American composer Nicolas Nabokov, subtitled *A Prayer* and composed in memory of Pope John XXIII and J. Robert Oppenheimer, written in a solemn neo-medieval idiom distilled in impressionistic harmonies, is performed for the first time as a commissioned work by the New York Philharmonic, on its 125th anniversary, with Leonard Bernstein conducting.

**5 JANUARY 1968**

*Piano Concerto* by the Canadian composer Jean Papineau-Couture, is performed for the first time in Quebec.

**8 JANUARY 1968**

*Babels Torn (The Tower of Babel)*, ballet by the Swedish composer Hilding Rosenberg, is performed for the first time as a commissioned work at the Swedish Television Station.

**8 JANUARY 1968**

Rezsö Seress, 68-year-old Hungarian composer of the song *Gloomy Sunday*, which precipitated a wave of Sunday suicides in the 1930's and was temporarily banned in Hungary and in the United States, jumps out of the window from the second floor of his apartment in Budapest (on a Monday), in a fit of despondency caused by a painful case of aortic stenosis in his head. (He died in a hospital on 12 January 1968. Information received from his widow)

**11 JANUARY 1968**

*The Equation* ($x = 0$), opera in one act by the 47-year-old English composer Geoffrey Bush, scored for voices, cello solo, wind ensemble, organ and percussion, dealing polytonally with the incompatibility of war with morality or common sense, is performed for the first time in a London church.

**11 JANUARY 1968**

*Chimes* for orchestra by the 35-year-old Soviet composer Rodion Shchedrin, in the form of a concerto for orchestra, written in a highly dissonant chromatic style with the orchestra in a state of constant furfuraceous commotion, punctuated by sounds of bells and culminating with a pistol shot, is performed for the first time as a commissioned work by the New York Philharmonic, Leonard Bernstein conducting.

### 18 JANUARY 1968

*Second Symphony* by the 31-year-old English composer Richard Rodney BENNETT, in a single economically compact movement with a pluralistic network of thematic groups derived from a guiding dodecaphonic series and forming multifarious dissonant harmonies, is performed for the first time as a commissioned work by the New York Philharmonic, Leonard Bernstein conducting.

### 25 JANUARY 1968

*Alpine Ballad,* lyric opera in one act by the 84-year-old Soviet composer Andrei PASHCHENKO, to a libretto recounting the story of an affectionate international romance spontaneously exfoliating between a Russian soldier and an Italian girl during their flight from a Nazi concentration camp, is performed for the first time in Leningrad.

### 2 FEBRUARY 1968

On his 60th birthday, the Italian composer Renzo ROSSELLINI conducts in Monte Carlo the first performance of his seventh opera, *L'Avventuriere,* to a libretto dealing with a penitent retiring businessman who pays farewell visits to his estranged wife, his mistress and others whom he has wronged in his life, set to music in a peculiarly unadventurous Italianate idiom.

### 4 FEBRUARY 1968

*Stephen Crane,* cantata for chorus and orchestra by the 51-year-old Negro American composer Ulysses KAY, to the texts of four poems by the short-lived American poet Stephen Crane (1871–1900), *Black Riders, Mystic Shadow, A Spirit* and *War Is Kind,* is performed for the first time in Chicago as a commissioned work in honor of the centennial of the Chicago Musical College.

### 5 FEBRUARY 1968

*A Study in the Story of Human Stupidity,* symphonic poem by the 24-year-old Swedish composer Gunnar VALKARE, is performed for the first time in Aarhus.

### 5 FEBRUARY 1968

*Le Voyage,* "musique électro-acoustique" by the pioneer of musique concrète Pierre HENRY, is produced in Grenoble as a ballet.

### 8 FEBRUARY 1968

*Eleventh Symphony* by Roy HARRIS, in a single cyclically constructed movement, commissioned by the New York Philharmonic on its 125th anniversary, and written as the expression of "emotional rather than intellectual ethos," is performed for the first time by the New York Philharmonic under the composer's own direction.

### 13 FEBRUARY 1968

Ildebrando PIZZETTI, Italian composer whose music combined the expansive melodiousness of his national heritage with modern chromatic harmonies, and whose operas revived the style of medieval mystery plays, dies in Rome at the age of eighty-seven.

### 29 FEBRUARY 1968

Howard HANSON conducts the New York Philharmonic in the world première of his *Sixth Symphony*, in six compact movements, conceived in a broad neo-romantic style seasoned with euphonious dissonances and invigorated by stimulating asymmetrical rhythms.

### 29 FEBRUARY 1968

*The Light in the Wilderness*, oratorio by the American jazz pianist and composer Dave BRUBECK, in 12 sections, to segments of the New Testament, written in an ostentatiously elevated Handelian manner, vivified by jazzy inflections and incorporating neo-baroque cadenzas and free improvisations, is performed for the first time in Cincinnati.

### 5 MARCH 1968

*Hamlet*, opera by Humphrey SEARLE, to a libretto compressed from Shakespeare's play, with the thematic texture derived melodically and methodically from a 12-tone series, except for the scene of the tragedians, which is set in an ostentatiously tonal idiom in euphonious harmonies, is produced in Hamburg with a German libretto.

### 7 MARCH 1968

*Ricercare*, symphonic essay in a time-honored Baroque form by Walter PISTON, is performed for the first time as a commissioned work by the New York Philharmonic.

### 11 MARCH 1968

*Schooltime Compositions* by the English modernist Cornelius CARDEW, with "matrices arranged around vocal sounds, triangles, newspapers, balloons, noises, desire, keyboard, with many people working," in optative adaptation of a set of melodic, rhythmic and instrumental parameters, aiming by guessing, grasping, gasping, gaping, aping and ping, at creating dissipating pullulating "beautiful bodies in rags" in multidimensional media, are performed uniquely (first time is last time, each random a meander), by the Focus Opera Group at the International Students House in London, on the same bill with

*Aventures* by the Hungarian ultra-avantgardist György LIGETI for three non-sensically syllabificating singers and seven instruments, and *Sur scène* by the Argentinian-born aleatorist Mauricio KAGEL for an omnivocal singer, three instruments and a mime.

## 13 MARCH 1968

*Seventh Symphony* by the 92-year-old English composer Havergal BRIAN, written in 1948, in four elongated movements, (1) *Allegro moderato,* opening with an ebullient brass fanfare and proceeding with ponderous concentration (2) *Allegro,* with discursive episodes (3) *Allegro* alternating with *Adagio* (4) *Moderato,* marked *Epilogue Once Upon a Time,* in an appropriately narrative romantic manner, is performed for the first time in London. (It was on this occasion announced as Brian's *Sixth Symphony,* owing to the variable numbering; in the final list of works made by Brian in 1968, the work was described as *Seventh Symphony*)

## 14 MARCH 1968

*Ordure dans l'air après la passion,* instrumental nonet by the 24-year-old Swedish modernist Gunnar VALKARE, an atonally postcoital malefaction in malfecation, is performed for the first time in Stockholm.

## 15 MARCH 1968

*Second Piano Concerto* by the 44-year-old Manchurian-born American composer of Russian parentage Benjamin LEES, in three movements, *Allegro enfatico, Adagio vago* and *Allegro tempestoso,* set in an individually synthetic idiom incorporating heterogeneous elements redolent of the rhapsodic elegance of Rachmaninoff, the percussive volatility of Prokofiev and the primitivistic modernity of Béla Bartók, is performed for the first time by Gary Graffman and the Boston Symphony Orchestra, Erich Leinsdorf conducting.

## 16 MARCH 1968

Mario CASTELNUOVO-TEDESCO, Italian-born composer of harmonious operas, overtures, concertos, piano works and songs, whose spirit of cultured modernism transcended the bounds of tenacious traditions and inconstant fashions alike, dies at the age of 72, in Los Angeles, where he settled at the outbreak of the Second World War.

## 17 MARCH 1968

*Votre Faust,* opera by Henri POUSSEUR, treating the Faust legend in contemporary terms, with audience participation in the form of a vote in favor of one of the four proffered dénouements, is performed for the first time in concert form in Buffalo.

## 21 MARCH 1968

*Fra Angelico,* symphonic poem by the 57-year-old half-Armenian half-Scottish American composer Alan HOVHANESS, his opus 220, written as a tribute to the mystical medieval Italian master of the fresco and couched in a harmoniously translucent, orientalistically modal idiom, is performed for the first time by the Detroit Symphony Orchestra, Sixten Ehrling conducting.

## 24 MARCH 1968

*Prometheus,* opera by Carl ORFF, the third part of his trilogy of Greek tragedies, after *Prometheus Bound* of Aeschylus, set to the original ancient Greek text, in one continuous act, constituting a series of homophonic monologues, dialogues, trialogues, tetralogues and choruses in neo-Grecian diatonic modalities accoutred in rudimentary triadic harmonies and orchestrated for 4 pianos, 6 flutes, 6 oboes, 6 trumpets, 6 trombones, 4 banjos, 4 harps, 2 organs, 9 doublebasses, 5 kettledrums and an ensemble of 70 percussion instruments, is performed for the first time in Stuttgart.

## 28 MARCH 1968

*Symphony* by the 51-year-old American Negro composer Ulysses KAY, commissioned by the Illinois Sesquicentennial Committee, written in a classical manner, in the traditional four movements, with hypersensitive applications of dissonant counterpoint underlying the melodic flow, vivified by frequent detonations of jazzy syncopation, but shunning topical melodic references to the musical past of Illinois, is performed for the first time by the Chicago Symphony Orchestra, Jean Martinon conducting, in Macomb, Illinois.

## 31 MARCH 1968

*La Symphonie pastorale,* opera by the Dutch composer Guillaume LANDRÉ, after the autumnal novel by André Gide, dealing with the crepuscular passion of an aging Swiss minister for a blind orphan girl adopted by him, who recovers her sight and selects his son as her spiritual bridegroom, dying of mystical inanition just as the world of sight and love is uncovered for her, is performed for the first time in Rouen, France.

## 31 MARCH 1968

The Vancouver Symphony Orchestra, in British Columbia, with Meredith Davies conducting, gives the first performance of *Estudios Sinfónicos* by the prime Argentinian composer Alberto GINASTERA, titled in homage to Robert Schumann, and in emulation of his *Etudes symphoniques,* presented as a commissioned work on the occasion of the centennial of Canada, containing nine studies based on three chords, two of which are formed by six different notes, and one is pandodecaphonic, each serving as a biomusical nucleus.

## 7 APRIL 1968

Oliver KNUSSEN, 15-year-old English schoolboy, conducts the London Symphony Orchestra in the first performance of his ambitious *First Symphony,* in four movements, *Allegro brillante, Lento, Scherzo-Satira* and *Theme and Variations,* written in a thematically pluralistic hemidemisemiserial idiom redolent of Mahler, Shostakovich and Alban Berg, and culminating in a respectable fugato.

## 7 APRIL 1968

*Piano Concerto* by the American composer John CORIGLIANO is performed for the first time by the San Antonio Symphony, conducted by Victor Alessandro.

## 8 APRIL 1968

*Concerto for Violoncello and Orchestra* by Bernd Alois ZIMMERMANN, "en forme de pas de trois," in five movements, the "trois" being the three dramatic personae—the soloist, the orchestra and the ballet, employing, in addition to a regular orchestra, a cimbalom, a glass harp, a mandolin, a guitar and an electronic doublebass, is performed for the first time in Strasbourg, in concert form. (The first performance as ballet took place in Wuppertal on 12 May 1968)

## 10 APRIL 1968

*Full Circle,* one-act opera by the 58-year-old Scottish composer Robin ORR, dealing with an inadvertent killer of a Scottish policeman in 1930 who is tracked down to his middle-class habitat, written in the form of a dramatic ballad, emphasizing the elegiac element in the killer's family life and his devotion to his loyal wife, is performed for the first time in Perth, Scotland.

## 21 APRIL 1968

*Concerto for Synket and Orchestra* in three movements by Jerome ROSEN, the first of its genre, with a portable electronic instrument, invented by the Russian acoustician in Rome named Paul Ketoff, is performed for the first time on the campus of the University of Washington in Seattle.

## 2 MAY 1968

*Eighth Symphony* by Roger SESSIONS, set in an austerely euphonious dissonant idiom, in one movement subdivided into contrasting sections, statically propulsive in its emotional tonus, thematically governed by a cybernetically functional dodecaphonic series, occasionally apocopated in hendecaphonic or decaphonic forms, is performed for the first time by the New York Philharmonic Orchestra as a commissioned work on the occasion of its 125th anniversary, William Steinberg conducting.

## 18 MAY 1968

*The Choir Invisible,* choral symphony in three movements by the 41-year-old South African composer John JOUBERT, after a poem by George Eliot, wherein true immortals form an ethereal chorus in the ionosphere radiating spiritual goodness residual from the terrestrial virtues of its members before death, is performed for the first time in Halifax, England, with the composer conducting.

## 24 MAY 1968

*Invocation-Concerto* for violin and orchestra by the 47-year-old American composer Ralph SHAPEY, written in a pluralistic serial technique, with individual melodic ingredients limited to a few intervallic distances between two consecutive thematic notes, is performed for the first time in New York.

## 30 MAY 1968

*The Marriage of Nyakato,* one-act opera by the prime composer of Uganda Solomon MBABI-KATANA, to the story of a beautiful country girl Nyakato whose family witch doctor correctly interprets, in a psychedelic solo on an indigenous central African long horn, a Freudian dream of her father as a precognitive revelation of her becoming the bride of the tribal King, containing a number of African dances, with the music derived from original pentatonic and tetratonic African melodies, is performed for the first time in the City of Kampala in Uganda, with the composer himself presiding at the piano.

## 8 JUNE 1968

*Punch and Judy,* puppet show for sadistic children, in which Punch throws a baby into the fire, kills Judy, his doctor and his lawyer and escapes the hangman by a stratagem, with a deliberately oxymoronic score by the British composer Harrison BIRTWISTLE, in which murderous action is illustrated by elegiac music and human kindness by shattering discords, is produced at the Aldeburgh Festival in England.

## 10 JUNE 1968

*The Prodigal Son,* "parable for church performance," by Benjamin BRITTEN, to a Latin text, and based on a plainchant in the Phrygian mode, accompanied by a small orchestra including some exotic percussion instruments, is performed for the first time at the Aldeburgh Festival.

## 14 JUNE 1968

Karl-Birger BLOMDAHL, Swedish composer of original ideas and mastery of modern techniques, who made intelligent and effective use of electronic resources, and whose pessimistic views of the terrestrial destinies are reflected in his dodecaphonic interplanetary opera *Aniara,* dies of a heart ailment in Kungsängen, at 51 (His ashes were strewn over nearby Lake Mälaren).

## 19 JUNE 1968

The Fourth Inter-American Music Festival opens in Washington under the general direction of Guillermo Espinosa, Chief of the Music Division of the Pan American Union, with the following program of Latin American music:

*Cantus Creationis* for four instrumental groups by José Almeida PRADO of Brazil (a world première); *Xilofonías* for flute, oboe, bass clarinet, bassoon and percussion by Mario KURI-ALDANA of Mexico, in three movements, with the "wooden sound" of the xylophonic concept of the title provided by the drum section; *Contrasts* for two pianos and chamber orchestra by Gerardo Gandini of Argentina (a world première); *Concertante* for timpani and chamber ensemble by Blas E. Atehortua of Colombia (a world première); *Divertimento III (Density I)* by Cesar Bolanos of Peru; and *Quodlibet III* for chamber ensemble, an aleatory composition within a given set of cybernetical temporal parameters, by Gabriel Brncic of Chile (a world première).

20 JUNE 1968

In the course of the Fourth Inter-American Music Festival in Washington, the following program of electronic music is given:

*Animus I* for trombone and tape by Jacob Druckman of the United States; *Dialogues I* by Francisco Kroepfl of Argentina, with a sonic material based on sinusoidal waves and filtered white sound; *Cross-Fire* for piano and taped piano by Carman Moore of the United States, a "pièce de résistance for the entire family, rhythmically simple, based on Italian folksongs, complete with a home-cooked Chinese dinner" constituting a game of statement by the recorded tape and stochastic response by the human pianist; *Of Wood and Brass* by Vladimir Ussachevsky of the United States, in four distinct sections, electronically metamorphosed by topological translocations and soniferous dispersion of original sounds of trombones, xylophones and a Korean gong; musical score from the Polish documentary film, *The World in Which We Live* by Mesías Maiguashca of Ecuador, beginning with sound of a giant rocket; *Juegos (Games)* for piano and magnetic tape by Gustavo Becerra Schmidt of Chile, with the pianist superposing an unpremeditated solo on the recorded sound, including the applause and voices of an audience taped in 1966; and *Synchronisms No. 2* for four instruments and electronic sounds by Mario Davidovsky of Argentina, aiming at a consistent integration of volitional and mechanistic media.

21 JUNE 1968

On the 100th anniversary of the first production of Wagner's *Die Meistersinger*, West Germany issues a 30-pfennig stamp with a facsimile reproduction of the initial 12 bars of the Overture to the opera.

21 JUNE 1968

In the course of the Fourth Inter-American Music Festival in Washington, the following program of avant-garde music of Latin America is presented:

*Elegy for Strings* by Rafael Aponte-Ledée of Puerto Rico; *Canticum Instrumentalis* by Marlos Nobre of Brazil, with the sonic materials subjected to multiserial treatment (a world première); *Eidesis II (1967–III)*, for 13 instruments by Alcides Lanza of Argentina, the title being derived from the Greek word "eidos" (idea) and from the oneiric phenomenon known in medicine as "eidetic dreams," wherein the kinetic energy of enormous charges of sensuality leads to a series of sonic orgasms, with some instruments tuned in quarter-tones resulting in orgiastic icositetraphonic implosions; *Fissions* by Edgar Valcárcel of Peru, in four sections and three cadenzas, in which the sonic nuclei are fissioned with liberation of soniferous energy; and *Métamorphose d'après une Lecture de Kafka*, for piano and 15 instruments, by Armando Krieger of Argentina (a world première), in which the superimposition of various instrumental groups symbolize the anthropozoic metamorphoses in Kafka's tales.

*Die Geschichte von einem Feuer,* opera by the German composer Dieter SCHÖNBACH, a multi-media spectacle for chorus, orchestra and functional kinetic sculpture cybernetically directed by an electronic computer, to a libretto portraying three anonymous men engaged in quest of instances of nobility through eight periods of time, from ancient Greece to the present, is performed for the first time in Kiel.

23 JUNE 1968

In the course of the Fourth Inter-American Music Festival a program of orchestral and choral music is presented, in Columbia, Maryland, including the first performances of the *Piano Concerto* by Robert WARD of the United States, *Recitative and Variations for Orchestra* by Hector TOSAR of Uruguay, and *Hymn to the Americas* for soprano, chorus and orchestra by Rudolph SCHIRMER of Schirmer Inc., to a Spanish text, set in abecedarian triadic harmonies in the manner of rudimentary hymnody.

24 JUNE 1968

In the course of the Fourth Inter-American Music Festival in Washington, a program of string quartet music is presented, including the world premières of *Zinctum* by Sergio CERVETTI of Uruguay and *Quartet 1967* by Leon SCHIDLOWSKY of Chile.

25 JUNE 1968

In the course of the Fourth Inter-American Music Festival in Washington, the following world premières are given:

*Myth of Dreams and Cosmogonies* for wood-wind quintet by Alexis RAGO of Venezuela, in four movements, *Amavalica, Totemic Animals, The Venus of Seas and Constellations,* and *Petroglyphs,* suggested by ancient Indian legends; and *Divertimento on Themes by Paul Klee* by Roberto GARCÍA-MORILLO of Argentina for woodwind quintet, inspired by 21 sketches of the expressionistic Swiss painter Paul Klee, set to music in a synthetically codified style of sophisticated infantiphony.

27 JUNE 1968

In the course of the Fourth Inter-American Music Festival in Washington, a concert of avant-garde music of Spain is given, presenting the following program:

*Objetos Sonoros* by Ramón BARCE, in four divisions, derived from the concepts of plane geometry and spherical trigonometry, with centripetal filaments rotating around a central tonic G; *Geometrías* by Leonardo BALADA, derived from pointillistic tonal topology and linear homophony, introduced by a symbiotic exposition of both; *Three Pieces for Double Quintet and Percussion* by Antón GARCÍA-ABRIL, evolving from parameters of spontaneous cellular generation; *Antiphonismói* by Cristóbal HALFFTER, exploring the limits of compressibility of recurring improvisatory passages; *Caesuras* by Luis DE PABLO, for flute, oboe, clarinet, violin, viola and cello, the structure of which is determined by the aleatoric phenomena before and after thematic caesuras, or pauses; *Vertices* by Miguel Angel Coria, derived from the serial principle of interchangeable vertical and horizontal parameters; *Car en effet* by Tomás Marco, inspired by an inductive syllogism propounded by Pierre Boulez as a stochastic non sequitur after a lecture in Darmstadt in 1965, set to music emphasizing freedom of creative emission; *Surface No. 1* for woodwind quartet, string quartet, piano and percussion by Carmelo A. Bernaola, illustrating a non-rigid codification of the formal elements of two-dimensional surfaces of three-dimensional solids.

## 27 JUNE 1968

*Concerto* for double-bass and orchestra by Gunther Schuller is performed for the first time in New York, conducted by the composer.

## 30 JUNE 1968

The Fourth Inter-American Music Festival concludes with a concert by the Washington National Symphony Orchestra, conducted by Walter Hendl, in the following program:

*Sonic Landscape* by Lester Trimble of the United States, conceived as an abstract composition, which became concrete in the composer's mind when a jet airplane flew over his New York apartment with a deafening sonic boom (a world première); *Piano Concerto* by Antonio Tauriello of Argentina, subdivided into 11 structures with an optional synchronization between the soloist and the orchestra (a world première); *Poem of Itabira* for contralto and orchestra by Heitor Villa-Lobos (first performed in Rio de Janeiro on 30 December 1946); *Mount Gilboa* for tenor and orchestra, subtitled *Lamentations of David for the Death of Saul and Jonathan* by Julián Orbón of Cuba, dedicated to a Catholic nun of Jewish ancestry who perished in a Nazi concentration camp in Poland; and *Symphony with Theme and Five Variations (Third Symphony)* by Roque Cordero of Panama, based on the concept of concentric specular reflections of the pluralistic structure inherent in the concept of variations (first performed in Caracas on 16 May 1966)

## 6 JULY 1968

On the occasion of the 70th anniversary of the birth of Hanns Eisler, a disciple of Schoenberg who also wrote proletarian choruses and other socialist music, the government of the German Democratic Republic issues 8,000,000 postage stamps of 20 marks with his portrait, wearing glasses.

## 9 JULY 1968

*The Great Digest* for chorus and organ, and *Missa Brevis*, to the Latin text, by Anthony Gilbert, with special effects, such as permanent tone-clusters produced by placing weights on the organ keyboard, and with the chorus clicking pebbles and whistling, are performed for the first time at the Cheltenham Festival.

## 16 JULY 1968

*Naboth's Vineyard*, a brief theatrical play with music by the 35-year-old Berlin-born English composer Alexander Goehr, to a Latin text, with singers placed behind a partition while action is mimed on the stage, is performed for the first time in London.

### 28 JULY 1968

*Concerto for Flute and String Orchestra* by the 35-year-old American composer Easley BLACKWOOD is performed for the first time in the course of the 1968 Congregation of the Arts at Dartmouth College, Hanover, New Hampshire, with Robert Willoughby as soloist and Mario de Bonaventura conducting.

### 30 JULY 1968

The Festival of Israel is inaugurated in Jerusalem with the world première of the oratorio *Testimonium,* traversing the history of Jerusalem through the ages, with music by Zvi AVNI, Sergiu NATRA, Roman HAUBENSTOCK-RAMATI, Yitzhak SADAI and Jehoshua LAKNER. (The Festival concluded on 31 August 1968 with a concert by the New York Philharmonic, Leonard Bernstein conducting)

### 1 AUGUST 1968

Ernst KRENEK conducts at the 1968 Congregation of the Arts at Dartmouth College, Hanover, New Hampshire, the first performance of his *Augenblick erinnert (Instant Remembered)* for soprano and orchestra. (At the same concert, the first public performance is given of the posthumous *Rondo* for string quartet by Anton VON WEBERN, written in 1906)

### 4 AUGUST 1968

*Concerto for Violino Grande and Orchestra* by the prime Polish modernist Krzysztof PENDERECKI, written for a 5-stringed violin, tuned c-g-d-a-e, composed in 1967 on a commission from the Swedish government for the Swedish lutier Hans Olof Hanson, the inventor of the Violino Grande, in a formally monistic but thematically pluralistic movement, is performed for the first time in its final version at the Congregation of the Arts at Dartmouth College, Hanover, New Hampshire, with Bronislaw Eichenholz as soloist.

### 10 AUGUST 1968

*Virginia City, Requiem for a Ghost Town,* symphonic poem by Ferde GROFÉ, a tribute to the centennial celebration of St. Mary's of the Mountain Catholic Church, is performed for the first time in Virginia City, Nevada, where the famed Comstock City once throve on the Comstock lode of silver ore.

### 11 AUGUST 1968

*Chamber Symphony* by the American composer Andrew IMBRIE is performed for the first time at the Congregation of the Arts, at Dartmouth College, Hanover, New Hampshire.

### 13 AUGUST 1968

*The Growing Castle*, opera by the 36-year-old Australian composer Malcolm WILLIAMSON, his sixth, to his own libretto after Strindberg's mystical drama *A Dream Play*, dealing with a neurotic Scandinavian young woman who lives in an animated world of fantasy, set to music in a neo-Verdian manner of simplicistic sophistication, is performed for the first time in Dynevor Castle, Wales, as a commissioned work by Lord Dynevor, in concert form, with solo singers accompanied alternatively at the piano and at the harpsichord by the composer.

### 23 AUGUST 1968

*Nomos* for orchestra by the 34-year-old English composer Harrison BIRTWISTLE is performed for the first time in London.

### 24 AUGUST 1968

Rafael KUBELIK, Czech conductor and composer, launches an appeal to world musicians to boycott the nations which invaded Czechoslovakia with military force on the night of 20–21 August 1968—Russia, Poland, Hungary, Bulgaria and East Germany, and to refuse to maintain cultural relations with them until they evacuate the country. (The appeal was joined by Igor Stravinsky, Artur Rubinstein, Yehudi Menuhin, Otto Klemperer, Bernard Haitink and Claudio Arrau.)

### 3 SEPTEMBER 1968

Juan José CASTRO, 73-year-old Argentinian composer of cultured symphonic and operatic works reflecting the melorhythmic resources of his country, dies in his native Buenos Aires after years of inanition caused by multiple apoplectic attacks.

### 5 SEPTEMBER 1968

*La Femme et son Ombre*, ballet by the 35-year-old French composer Jacques CHARPENTIER, after the mimodrama of Paul Claudel, is performed for the first time in Paris.

### 21 SEPTEMBER 1968

The 42nd Festival of the International Society for Contemporary Music opens in Warsaw in conjunction with the 12th Festival of the "Warsaw Autumn," in the following program:

*Symphonies* for wind instruments by the 41-year-old Dutch composer Ton DE LEEUW; *Capriccio* for violin and orchestra by the 34-year-old Polish composer Krzysztof PENDERECKI (first performed at the Donaueschingen Festival on 22 October 1967); *Spiegel I* for orchestra by the 42-year-old Viennese composer Friedrich CERHA, the first of the seven works of that title suggesting a mirrorable musical structure; and *Requiem* for soloists, chorus and orchestra by the Translyvanian-born Hungarian composer György LIGETI (first performed in Stockholm on 14 March 1965).

## 22 SEPTEMBER 1968

At the 42nd Festival of the International Society for Contemporary Music in Warsaw, two concerts of instrumental and vocal music are given, one at noon and one in the evening in the following programs:

Noon: *Concerto for Six Musicians* by the 49-year-old Danish composer Niels Viggo BENTZON; *Rondo* by the 36-year-old Danish composer Per NÖRGAARD; *Quattro Monologhi* for oboe solo by the 41-year-old Polish composer Witold SZALONEK; *Song II* for mezzosoprano and percussion by the 25-year-old English composer Tim SOUSTER; *Amores* for "prepared piano" by the chief prophet of the American avant-garde John CAGE; *Espace et Rythme* for a percussion ensemble by the 40-year-old Rumanian composer Tiberiu OLAH; *Solo* for sliding trombone by John CAGE; *Sequenza V* for trombone solo by the 42-year-old Italian composer of the Italian avant-garde Luciano BERIO; and *Ricercare a 5* for trombone solo by the 51-year-old American composer Robert ERICKSON.

Evening: *Pantalan* for orchestra by the 38-year-old Spanish composer Agustin BERTOMEU; *Canti* for violin and orchestra by the 37-year-old Argentinian composer Antonio TAURIELLO; *Stabil-Instabil* for orchestra by the 44-year-old German composer Günther BECKER; and *Aielet, fille de Iephte*, opera-mysterium by the Polish composer Augustin BLOCH.

## 23 SEPTEMBER 1968

At the 42nd Festival of the International Society for Contemporary Music in Warsaw, a concert of electronic music is given in the afternoon and two ballets by Polish composers in the evening with the following programs:

Afternoon: *Symphonie* by the 39-year-old Polish composer Boguslaw SCHÄFFER, an electronically constructed work represented in score by diagrammatic homologues suggesting alternative stochastic procedures, and employing generators of sinusoidal waves, saw-tooth oscillators, impulsions, filters, cyclic modulators, amplitude discriminators and white noise integrators comprising the entire spectrum of audible sounds; *Philomel* for mezzosoprano and a synthesized double-track magnetic tape by Milton BABBITT, 52-year-old American pioneer of integral musical serialization and advanced electronic techniques, in three sections, to the words of John Hollander after the classical myth of the metamorphosis of Philomel into a nightingale, in which the songs of other birds are represented by the vocal palimpsest on magnetic tape; *Telemusik* by the 40-year-old apostle of the German avant-garde Karlheinz STOCKHAUSEN, an electronic work conceived during insomnia in Tokyo and realized as a dream of omniterrestrial music reflecting the human melorhythms of Asia, America, Africa and Europe; *Treni d'onda a modulazione di intensità* by the 42-year-old Italian ultramodernist Vittorio GELMETTI, consisting of 21 sonorous lines, each employing five different frequencies of sinusoidal, rectangular and irregular waves as well as filtered and white sounds, governed by statistical data; *Hétérozygote* by the 39-year-old French composer Luc FERRARI, illustrating the growth of organisms of mixed chromasomal provenance, and comprising heterogeneous sound sources, such as speech, the barking of dogs, the bleating of sheep, the howling of winds, the splashing of water and other polyphonic ingredients of natural origin.

Evening: *Tytania i osiol (Titania and the Ass)*, ballet by the 60-year-old Polish composer Zbigniew TURSKI; and *Pancernik Potiomkin (Dreadnaught Potemkin)*, ballet for orchestra and magnetic tape by the 41-year-old Polish composer Juliusz Luciuk, based on the historical episode of the mutiny on the Tsarist warship of that name.

## 24 SEPTEMBER 1968

At the 42nd Festival of the International Society for Contemporary Music in Warsaw two concerts of orchestral music are given in the following programs:

Afternoon: *Crescendo e diminuendo* for harpsichord and 12 string instruments by the 39-year-old Siberian-born Soviet composer Edison Denisov (he was named in honor of Thomas Alva Edison) designed as a bivalve palindrome, opening with a single B-flat of the first violin (*non vibrato*), growing in sonorous amplitude, and after reaching the peak, reverting in precise palindromic ending on the initial B-flat of the first violin (*non vibrato*), the total duration being six minutes, and all temporal parameters being divisible by six (the central orchestral tutti lasts 48 seconds, the number of instruments is 12, the harpsichord being a supernumerary free agent), first performance having been given in Zagreb on 14 May 1967, and first American performance on 18 May 1967 by the New York Philharmonic under the direction of Leonard Bernstein; *Mouvements* by the 34-year-old Bulgarian composer Ivan Spasov, for 12 string instruments; *Divertimento d'Improvisation* for chamber orchestra by the 46-year-old Bulgarian composer Lazar Nikolov, giving aleatoric freedom to players within the determined parameters of the music; *Symphonie des timbres* by the 34-year-old Bulgarian composer Vasil Kazandzhiev, an essay in diversified instrumental timbres; *Requiem pour un jeune homme inconnu* for chamber orchestra by the 41-year-old Bulgarian composer Simeon Pironkov, a tribute to unknown men who died young; *Musica concertante* for chamber orchestra by the 44-year-old Bulgarian composer Georgi Tutev, based on a dodecaphonic series, with applications of aleatoric tone colors; *Divertimento for String Orchestra* by Béla Bartók.

Evening: *Iris* for orchestra by the 36-year-old Danish composer Per Nörgaard, an essay in instrumental iridescence (hence the title), in which the themes are the headlines of an "electric newspaper," employing collages of musical clichés; *Banka* for soprano and orchestra by the 34-year-old Korean-born Japanese composer Hiroaki Minami, to words by an ancient Japanese poet, meditating on the death of his wife, infant children and his own; *Tenebrae* for orchestra by the 43-year-old Swiss composer Klaus Huber, in three parts without pause, suggesting three aspects of tenebrousness: solar eclipse, constant obscuration of life, and the Golgotha, making use of quartertones; *Et exspecto resurrectionem mortuorum* for orchestra, by Olivier Messiaen of France, in five movements with biblical exergues for each, making use of Indian ragas, and including an imitation of a Brazilian jungle bird Uirapurú (*Leucolepis modulator*).

## 25 SEPTEMBER 1968

At the 42nd Festival of the International Society for Contemporary Music in Warsaw, two concerts of chamber music are given in the following programs:

Afternoon: *Training 68* for clarinet, trombone, cello and piano by the 36-year-old Polish composer Wojciech Kilar; *Pour quatre*, for clarinet, trombone, cello and piano by the 43-year-old Polish composer Wlodzimierz Kotoński; *Spirale I per uno* by the 38-year-old Polish composer Leoncjusz Ciuciura, for voice and percussion, to the words of an existentialist monologue, written in the graphic notation of musical ideograms, with aleatoric latitude; *Polychromie* for clarinet, trombone, cello and piano by the 30-year-old Polish composer Zygmunt Krauze exploiting the polychromatic potentialities of different instrumental combinations; *Keyboard Studies* by the 33-year-old Californian composer Terry RILEY, a part of a vast work guided by intervallic and melodic parameters of indefinite duration (a record length achieved being eight hours in 1967); *Plus-minus*, for clarinet, trombone, cello and three pianos by Karlheinz STOCKHAUSEN, subtitled *2 x 7 Pages for Workout*, in which the diagrammatic instructions are deliberately latitudinous as though "transmitting the voice of deeply hidden anonymity undiscoverable even by the composer himself."

Evening: *Quick Are the Mouths of Earth* by the 34-year-old American composer Roger REYNOLDS, for chamber orchestra, in six parts, each subdivided into six sections, the instrumental ensemble comprising three mutually independent groups operating distinct types of spatial interludes, making allowance for aleatoric interpretation; *Cadencias II* by the 32-year-old Argentinian composer Gerardo GANDINI, written for 15 instruments as an essay of thematic mobility in indetermined expositions; *The Approach to the Hidden Man* by the 35-year-old Swiss composer Jacques GUYONNET, for mezzo-soprano and chamber orchestra, written in graphically stochastic notation; *Canticum Zachariae* by the 31-year-old Czech composer Tadeáš SALVA, for soprano and chamber orchestra, to a biblical text, using various modern techniques but preserving a fixed tonal center; *Músicas de cámara* by the Spanish composer Carmelo Alonso BERNAOLA with a graphic notation indicating the stable parameters of the music; *Tragoedia* by the 34-year-old English composer Harrison BIRTWISTLE, planned as a symbiotic form of absolute and theatrical music based on concentric layers.

Evening: *La passion selon Sade*, mimed oratorio by the 36-year-old Italian avant-garde composer Sylvano BUSSOTTI, in four suggestive tableaux vivants, *Mistico, Libertina, Demoniaco* and *Mortale*, with Marquis de Sade represented by a panerotic serial arrangement of the musical letters of Sade and Bach.

## 26 SEPTEMBER 1968

At the 42nd Festival of the International Society for Contemporary Music in Warsaw, two concerts of chamber music are given, one in the afternoon and one in the evening, with the following program:

Afternoon: *Rondo* for string quartet by the 38-year-old Yugoslav composer Stanko HORVAT, in which the rondo form is treated serialistically with an ordered succession of instrumental rather than thematic entries; *Due Lamenti* for soprano and piano by the 35-year-old Hungarian composer Miklós KOCSÁR, in two movements, *Clamor* and *Malagueña*, to the texts of Federico García LORCA, using serialistic and aleatoric procedures; *Manzit* for clarinet, trombone, cello and piano by the 34-year-old Swedish composer Karl-Erik WELIN, a study in sonority in free serial techniques; *Crystals* for chamber orchestra by the 45-year-old Austrian composer, Jacob GILBOA, who emigrated to Palestine in 1938, arranged in dodecagenic serial divisons, comprising 12 sections, each lasting 12 seconds, and each integrally mirrorable; *Cantata* by the 48-year-old Czech composer Zbyněk VOSTŘÁK, to the text by Kafka dealing with the frustration of an average man incapable of penetrating the mystery of reality (first performed under the composer's direction in Prague on 24 September 1966); *Improvvisazione III* for two sopranos, bass, percussion, flute, double-bass and harpsichord by the 36-year-old Italian composer Fausto RAZZI, the improvisatory element referring to the latitude given to the players to extend or reduce the duration of each note and raise or lower the pitch, but leaving other parameters stabilized; *Continuum* by the 46-year-old Polish composer Kazimierz SEROCKI, scored for 123 percussion instruments, including xylorimbas, bottles, gourds, bells, gongs and drums, subdivided into 36 sections, the shortest lasting 4 seconds, and the longest 45 seconds (first performed at the Stockholm festival on 17 September 1967).

Evening: *Parades* for orchestra and two pianos by the 31-year-old Polish composer Zbigniew BARGIELSKI, in four movements, burlesquing the stolid stultification of salon music; *Piano Concerto* by the 61-year-old Dutch composer Kees van BAAREN, in one movement, written in a moderately modern idiom; *Paroles tissées* for tenor and orchestra by the 55-year-old Polish composer Witold LUTOSLAWSKI, in four contrasting divisions, to the text by the surrealist French poet Jean-François Chabrun, set in a lyrically expressionistic idiom (first performed at the Aldeburgh, England, Festival on 25 June 1965); *Second Symphony* by Sergei PROKOFIEV.

### 27 SEPTEMBER 1968

At the 42nd Festival of the International Society for Contemporary Music in Warsaw three concerts are given with the following programs:

Afternoon: *Spheroon* by the 36-year-old Yugoslav composer Vladan RADOVANOVIĆ, for chorus and tape, in palimpsest, glorifying the primordial dust of a chaotic tourbillion; *Labiryntus II* by the prime Italian avant-gardist Luciano BERIO, for soprano, chamber orchestra, percussion and a vocal ensemble, superimposed on a tape recording.

Evening: *4 x 5*, concerto for four quintets by the 61-year-old Russian-born Swiss composer Constantin REGAMEY, scored for four contrasting groups of five instruments each, and based on a single series containing all different intervals, in five movements suggesting a millennial link with the Ars antiqua: *Perotinamente* (i.e., in the manner of Perotin), *Quasi una monodia, Condensazioni in moto, Musica e Corale,* and *Concertando; Epifanie* for mezzosoprano and orchestra by Luciano BERIO, a cycle of heterogeneous songs set to texts in French, English, Spanish and German, in an artful montage; *Serenata II* for flute and four instrumental groups by the 32-year-old Dutch composer Jan VAN VLIJMEN, in a single movement subdivided into five fragments of varied connotations; *Figures, Doubles, Prismes* for orchestra by the French magus of modern music, Pierre BOULEZ, composed in 1958 and representing a deep probe into sonorous structures.

Late evening: Film music: *Altisonance* by the Swedish avant-garde composer Karl-Birger BLOMDAHL (1916–1968), in which the visual images from outer space are translated into altisonant frequencies, with the terrestrial ornithological sounds of the songs of the nightingale and the blackbird combined in an audio-visual montage with the static noise from the sun and the aurora borealis (first performed at the Festival of Art and Technology in Stockholm on 20 September 1966); *Match,* and *Solo* by the 36-year-old Argentinian-born German experimentalist Mauricio KAGEL obtained as a result of electronic synchronization, desynchronization and postsynchronization.

### 28 SEPTEMBER 1968

At the 42nd Festival of the International Society for Contemporary Music in Warsaw two concerts are given, one in the afternoon and one in the evening, in the following programs:

Afternoon: *14 Arten den Regen zu beschreiben* for flute, clarinet, violin, viola, cello and piano by the politically and musically radical composer Hanns EISLER (1898–1962), a cycle of 14 brief variations on a theme, written by Eisler in 1941; *Morsima-*

*Amorsima* for piano, violin, cello and double-bass by the 46-year-old Rumanian-born Greek composer and engineer Iannis XENAKIS, prime theorist of the scientifically organized stochastic method of composition (*Morsima* means an event ordained by fate; *Amorsima*, by virtue of the privative *a*, means not ordained by fate) with parameters derived from the statistical findings of probabilities of tonal events calculated by a computer; *Triad III* for oboe, viola and cello by the 35-year-old English composer Justin CONNOLLY, the word triad here meaning simply a triunity of timbres; *Quartet* Op. 22, for violin, clarinet, tenor saxophone and piano by Anton VON WEBERN, in two movements of color melody, canonic polyphony and serialistic pointillism; *Moments* for flute, clarinet, viola, cello and piano by the 27-year-old Polish composer Piotr WARZECHA, in a single movement written in a variety of modern techniques; and *Kammersymphonie*, op. 9, by Arnold SCHOENBERG.

Evening: *Tenth Symphony* by Dmitri SHOSTAKOVICH; *Second Piano Concerto* by the 35-year-old Soviet composer Rodion SHCHEDRIN (first performed by him with the Moscow Radio Orchestra on 5 January 1967), in three movements: (1) *Dialogues*, opening with an exergue in piano, echoed by the orchestra (2) *Improvisation*, a toccata-scherzo, in which two dominant themes are freely copulated in versatile improvisatory manner (3) *Contrasts*, wherein the piano plays single notes and chords as if tuning up the instrument, eliciting an antiphonal reaction from the orchestra; *To the Memory of the Dead During the Years of the Siege of Leningrad*, symphonic poem by the 38-year-old Soviet composer Andrei PETROV, scored for strings, trumpets, two pianos and percussion, a musical dedication to the heroic human spirit to be recalled when "men will explore new planets and abolish war forever."

### 29 SEPTEMBER 1968

On the last day of the 42nd Festival of the International Society for Contemporary Music in Warsaw, two concerts are given, one at noon and one in the evening, with the following programs;

Noon: *Sonata per archi* by the 42-year-old German expressionist Hans Werner HENZE (first performed in Zürich on 21 March 1958), in two linked movements, *Allegro* and a theme with 32 variations, each having 8 bars; *Jubilus* by the 37-year-old French composer André LAPORTE, scored for brass and percussion, with the thematic material based entirely on the serial principle of 12 different notes and different dynamic and instrumental elements, incorporating organized aleatoric episodes; *5 Chants* for mezzo-soprano and chamber orchestra by the 40-year-old Polish composer Tadeusz BAIRD, to the words of a Polish poetess who died young; *The Dorian Horizon* by the 37-year-old Japanese composer Toru TAKEMITSU, scored for two string ensembles; *Lineas y puntos* for 20 wind instruments and a double-track magnetic tape by the 38-year-old Spanish composer Cristóbal HALFFTER (first performed at the Donaueschingen Festival on 22 October 1967); *Eufonia III*, for orchestra, by the 51-year-old Hungarian composer Rudolf MAROS, intended to create a euphonious modernistic impression, with a mirrorable section in the center of the piece.

Evening: *La Peau du Silence* for orchestra by the 33-year-old French composer François-Bernard MÂCHE, in five movements, *Plages, Manipulations, Poème, Migrations* and *Montage*, employing the imitation of the animal noises of marine life and nocturnal birds, in a montage of human sounds; *Canti* for soprano and orchestra by the 28-year-old Polish composer Edward BOGUSLAWSKI, for soprano and orchestra, based on a dodecaphonic series; *Second Concerto* for oboe and orchestra by the 48-year-old Italian composer Bruno MADERNA (first performed in Cologne on 10 November 1967) and

*Fifth Symphony* by the 71-year-old Polish composer Boleslaw SZABELSKI, in a single movement, with a choral ending set to the text of abstract syllables.

## 29 SEPTEMBER 1968

*Second Piano Concerto* by Hans Werner HENZE, in one movement, subdivided into three sections, the first representing the auditory impressions of the Orient and evoking the clangs of the Japanese Gagaku orchestra in a pluralistic setting with specular intervallic reflections, the second, a scherzo with thematic elements intervallically refracted and prismatically dispersed, and the finale, a polyphonic fantasy inspired by the line from Shakespeare's sonnet, "the expense of spirit in a waste of shame," the whole intended to convey the existentialist philosophy derived from the optimistic realization of the inevitability of human decay, is performed for the first time in Bielefeld, Germany.

## 29 SEPTEMBER 1968

*Ulisse,* opera in two acts with a prologue by the 64-year-old Italian modernist Luigi DALLAPICCOLA, to his own Italian libretto after Homer's *Odyssey,* centered on Princess Nausicaa's insular interlude with Ulysses, and set in a sui generis dodecaphonic technique, with a fissile 12-tone-series forming two thematic hexachords, each subject to interior permutations, is performed for the first time at the Berlin Music Festival in a German version under the title *Odysseus,* conducted by Lorin Maazel.

## 2 OCTOBER 1968

*Three Mysteries,* opera-triptych by Niccolò CASTIGLIONI, based on three separate texts, *Silence,* inspired by a Japanese Noh play, *Chordination* in a setting of a medieval English morality play, *The Fall of Lucifer and Aria,* developed from a scene in Shakespeare's *Romeo and Juliet,* written in an austere atonal manner with the utmost economy of sonic materials, is performed for the first time in Rome.

## 3 OCTOBER 1968

*To Thee Old Cause,* symphonic evocation by William SCHUMAN for oboe, brass, timpani, piano and strings, inspired by Walt Whitman's poem, and dedicated to the memory of the slain leaders of American society Martin Luther King and Robert F. Kennedy, is performed for the first time by the New York Philharmonic, Leonard Bernstein conducting.

## 7 OCTOBER 1968

*I Have a Dream,* solo cantata for voice and orchestra by Elie SIEGMEISTER, to the text based on the famous speech by Martin Luther King, is performed for the first time in Omaha.

## 9 OCTOBER 1968

*Nine Rivers from Jordan,* opera in three acts by the Czech-born American composer Hugo WEISGALL, to a libretto saturated with religious symbolism, in which a Christ-like British soldier in World War II lets a Judas-like German war prisoner escape, the first opera in history to employ four-letter words for sexual intercourse in dialogue, set to music in intransigently dissonant counterpoint, with some topical insertions, such as the singing of *Lili Marlene,* a song popular with both sides in the conflict, is produced by the New York City Opera.

### 10 OCTOBER 1968

Luciano BERIO, 42-year-old Italian avant-garde composer, conducts the New York Philharmonic and Swingle Singers in the first performance of his *Sinfonia,* surrealist musicorama in four parts: the first, making use of a text from an anthropological treatise on Brazilian mythology with dodecaphonic boulders crashing into the tidal waves of a totality of discordance; the second, in which the name of Martin Luther King is fissioned into its syllabic atoms; the third, a montage of thematic molecules in a disoriented version of Mahler's Resurrection Symphony, with disembodied motives from disemboweled Bach and Berlioz, Debussy and Stravinsky juxtaposed and superimposed in multidimensional counterpoint, while voices recite excerpts from the writings of Samuel Beckett and James Joyce subjoined to French graffiti from the walls of the Sorbonne during the student insurrection of May 1968; and the last, a sonic collage beginning with a whispering of atomized vocables and concluding with a panacoustical coagulation of aleatory matrices.

### 19 OCTOBER 1968

*Hamlet,* opera in three acts by the 37-year-old Hungarian composer Sándor SZOKOLAY, after Shakespeare, in a Hungarian translation adapted by the composer, is performed for the first time in Budapest.

### 26 OCTOBER 1968

*The Scarlet Mill,* opera in two acts by the 73-year-old Hungarian-born American composer Eugene ZADOR, after Ferenc Molnar's play *The Red Mill* having to do with an infernal red mill capable of corrupting the most virtuous man in Hell's epicenter, but failing when the only certifiably virtuous man found in the whole world proves to be absolutely incorruptible, set to music in a functionally modernistic manner saturated with tolerable discords, is performed for the first time by the Brooklyn College Opera Theater.

### 27 OCTOBER 1968

*Fifth Symphony* by the Austrian composer Karl WEIGL (1881–1945), surnamed *Apocalyptic,* in four movements, (1) *Evocation* (2) *The Dance around the Golden Calf* (3) *Paradise Lost* (4) *The Four Horsemen,* conceived in a megasymphonious Bruckneromantic manner, polyphonically elaborated and harmonically inspissated, is performed for the first time, 23 years after its composition, by the American Symphony in New York under the direction of its sesquioctogenarian founder Leopold Stokowski.

## 30 OCTOBER 1968

*L'Apocalypse de Jean,* electronic oratorio by the Parisian pioneer of concrete music Pierre HENRY, is performed for the first time in Paris.

## 6 NOVEMBER 1968

Charles MUNCH, 77-year-old Alsatian-born conductor, known as "le beau Charles" for his patrician demeanor and sartorial elegance, who rose to the highest position in the music world after a late start (he made his conducting début at 42) and held the prestigious post of music director of the Boston Symphony Orchestra from 1949 to 1962, whose aristocratic insouciance in interpretations of the classics and idiosyncrasies of treatment (his irrepressible penchant for fast tempi gave rise in the orchestral milieu to the quip that the three degrees of musical celerity are *Presto, Prestissimo, Munchissimo*) aroused occasional perplexity, dies of a sudden heart attack in the early morning, in Richmond, Virginia, on the day he was to lead a concert there with the touring Orchestre de Paris, founded by him in 1967. (Date and hour of death from the official verdict by the Virginia State Medical Examiner. The obituary in The New York *Times* of 7 November 1968 erroneously datelined the Richmond dispatch about Munch's death as 5 November 1968)

## 6 NOVEMBER 1968

Guillaume LANDRÉ, Dutch composer of nobly intentioned music in various genres, greatly esteemed within the confines of his native land, dies in Amsterdam at the age of sixty-three.

## 8 NOVEMBER 1968

*The Passion of Oedipus,* opera in two acts by the American composer Roy TRAVIS, written in an advanced dissonant idiom, is performed for the first time by the Opera Workshop of the University of California, Los Angeles.

## 17 NOVEMBER 1968

*Epitaph for the Victims of Katyn,* symphonic elegy by the 54-year-old Polish composer resident in England Andrzej PANUFNIK, dedicated to the memory of hundreds of Polish officers and soldiers slain in Katyn, Lithuania, in 1941, during the rapid advance of the Nazi armies into Russia, is performed for the first time in New York by the American Symphony, Leopold Stokowski conducting.

## 18 NOVEMBER 1968

*Concerto for Two Pianos and Orchestra* by Paul CRESTON is performed for the first time in Montavallo, Alabama, by the New Orleans Philharmonic Symphony, Werner Torkanowsky conducting.

## 24 NOVEMBER 1968

*Kesa and Morito,* opera in three acts by the Japanese composer Kan ISHII, to a horrendous tale of medieval Japanese passions, in which the reckless suitor of a friend's beauteous wife, scheming to murder the husband in the darkness of the night, severs with his sword the head of his beloved, and holding it aloft in faint moonlight realizes the enormity of his miscalculation, set to music in a cosmopolitan vigesimosecular idiom without ostentatious Nipponisms, is produced in Tokyo by an all-Japanese company of singers and instrumentalists.

### 3 DECEMBER 1968

*Ars amatoria,* cantata by the 45-year-old Austrian composer Gerhard WIMBERGER, in five parts to selected texts from Ovid's classical manual of sexual gymnastics written ca. 8 A.D., scored for soprano, baritone, chorus, jazz combo and chamber orchestra with the focal word *amor* intoned by the soprano in a long solo embracing a two-octave range, is performed for the first time in Berlin.

### 9 DECEMBER 1968

*Musique pour l'homme* by the Dutch composer Joep STRAESSER, for singing, speaking, shouting and whispering voices and a large orchestra, to the text in French of the Universal Declaration of the Rights of Man adopted by the United Nations in 1948, with quodlibets rendered deliberately unintelligible by heterosyllabification, is performed for the first time by the Concertgebouw Orchestra in Amsterdam.

### 9 DECEMBER 1968

A scheduled first performance in Hamburg of *Das Floss der Meduse (The Raft of the Medusa)*, "oratorio volgare e militare" by the German composer Hans Werner HENZE, dedicated to Ché Guevara, the fiery Cuban guerrilla fighter executed by the Bolivian soldiery during an abortive revolutionary operation, a setting of the story of the dramatic shipwreck of the French frigate Medusa in 1816 revealing a shocking lack of humanity among its superior officers who left 154 seamen and passengers to die on the raft made from the hulk of the wrecked ship, to a libretto in which the living sing in German while their dead comrades call to them in untranslated lines from Dante's *Divina Commedia,* is canceled when the chorus refuses to sing under a red banner installed on the stage. (Henze had said that world revolution was more important than world premières of new music.)

### 15 DECEMBER 1968

*Epicycle,* a continuum for mixed media by the 42-year-old Greek composer Jani CHRISTOU, designed to last any duration of time (millennia, decennia, lustra, years, months, weeks, days, hours, minutes, seconds, milliseconds, nanoseconds, picoseconds) "in a climate of total impassivity," with optional audience participation, is given its first finite presentation at a session of the Hellenic section of the International Society for Contemporary Music in Athens.

19 DECEMBER 1968

*Help! Help! The Globolinks!* a space opera by Gian Carlo MENOTTI, to his own libretto in English depicting the invasion of the earth by extraterrestrial globolinks (i.e. global links) who speak an electronic language of dodecaphonic provenance but who are vulnerable to the sounds of human music and are eventually routed by a school band playing a diatonic march, is produced at the Hamburg State Opera.

24 DECEMBER 1968

*The Story of Ivan the Fool,* cantata by Alexander TCHEREPNIN, for narrator, vocalists, chorus, orchestra and electronic devices, after Tolstoy's moralistic tale of a simpleton who outwits wiseacres, written in a folkloristic Russian style, is performed for the first time in a broadcast by the BBC in London, from a previously recorded tape conducted by the composer.

29 DECEMBER 1968

Sixty years after the devastating earthquake in Sicily on 28 December 1908, when some 75,000 people perished, a newly decorated Vittorio Emanuele Theater reopens in Messina, the epicenter of the tremor, with the production of Verdi's *Aida,* the opera which was last performed on the eve of the disaster, in the presence of several survivors, with the conductor using the same baton as the one wielded by the last maestro to conduct at the theater.

31 DECEMBER 1968

*False Relationships and the Extended Ending* for cello, violin, trombone, three pianos and chimes, by the 42-year-old American avant-garde composer Morton FELDMAN, is performed for the first time in the course of the Festival of New Music in Palermo, Sicily.

## ℘ *1969* ℘

10 JANUARY 1969

*Ninth Symphony* by William SCHUMAN, subtitled *Le Fosse Ardeatine,* written under a deep impression of a visit at the Ardeatine Caves in Rome where the Germans shot, bombed and suffocated 335 Italians in 1944 in reprisal for the killing of 32 German soldiers by the Italian resistance groups, is performed for the first time by the Philadelphia Orchestra, Eugene Ormandy conducting.

14 JANUARY 1969

*Asterism* for piano and orchestra by the Japanese modernist Toru TAKEMITSU, written for a normal orchestra with a plethora of percussion, containing episodes of aleatoric sound and improvisation, is performed for the first time by the Toronto, Canada, Symphony orchestra, with Yuji Takahashi at the piano and Seiji Ozawa on the podium.

### 16 JANUARY 1969

Vladimir DUKELSKY, Russian composer who was born in a railroad station during his mother's journey to Pskov and became famous in America under an abbreviated cognomen Vernon Duke (which was suggested to him by George Gershwin), whose ballets and rarely played symphonies exhibit a cultured brand of listenable vigesimosecular modernism and whose popular songs, such as *April in Paris,* are poetic perennials of urban American music, dies in Santa Monica of a cardiac arrest during the second operation for a fulminant cancer of the lung, at an unfulfilled age of sixty-five.

### 16 JANUARY 1969

*Relata II* for orchestra by the articulate enunciator of advanced musicomathematical techniques Milton BABBITT, a sequel to his *Relata I,* based on the idea of an intimate relationship between contrapuntal voices and concomitant rhythmic values in their mutual combinatoriality, is performed for the first time by the New York Philharmonic, Leonard Bernstein conducting.

### 17 JANUARY 1969

*Third Symphony* by the Manchuria-born 45-year-old American composer Benjamin LEES, is performed for the first time by the Detroit Symphony Orchestra, Sixten Ehrling conducting.

### 24 JANUARY 1969

*Andrea del Sarto,* opera in two acts by the 60-year-old French composer DANIEL-LESUR, inspired by the life of the famous Florentine painter, known as "Andrea senza errore," because of the impeccability of his fresco technique, is performed for the first time in Marseille.

### 14 FEBRUARY 1969

Hans Werner HENZE conducts in London the world première of his spoken cantata *Versuch über Schweine,* scored for speaker, chamber orchestra and jazz combo, the swine of the title being the contemptuous sobriquet for the rebellious West Berlin students in the restless days of 1968, accepted by them as an honorific title, to texts by the Chilean theorist of the doctrine of the Students for Democratic Society Gaston Salvatore, as a testimony of "the necessity of rebellion against the acceptance of the supposedly unalterable conditions of life."

### 19 FEBRUARY 1969

*Photoptosis,* prelude for orchestra by Bernd Alois ZIMMERMANN, limning the fluctuating light absorption by various color surfaces, with the inclusion in the orchestra of quarter-tone passages, is performed for the first time in Gelsen-kirchen, Germany.

## 20 FEBRUARY 1969

Ernest ANSERMET, Swiss conductor of high cultural attainments whose inter-pretations of old and new masterpieces were marked by elegance and preci-sion and who served as an apostle of early modern music but turned against the ultimate vigesimosecular trends and denounced dodecaphony in a dog-matic musicosophical tract, dies in Geneva at the age of eighty-five.

## 28 FEBRUARY 1969

*Luisella,* opera in four acts by the 44-year-old Italian composer Franco MANNINO, expanded from his original one-act opera, to the libretto from a short story by Thomas Mann, in which a cuckolded husband dressed up as a woman at a beer party in a German provincial town in 1897 suffers a fatal cardiac arrest while singing the song Luisella composed by his wife's lover, with a lethally dissonant polychord serving as his epitaph, is performed for the first time in Palermo, conducted by the composer.

## 2 MARCH 1969

*Die Reise,* opera by the Swedish composer Lars Johan WERLE representing a dichotomy of reality and fantasy, written in an eclectic idom embracing tonal-ity, serialism, electronic sound and sonic montage, and embellished by judi-ciously selected non-corrosive dissonances, is performed for the first time in Hamburg.

## 14 MARCH 1969

*Muko Erabi (The Marriage Contest),* comic opera in one act by Osamu SHIMIZU, to a libretto based on a folk-tale involving a contest of three suitors for the hand of the beauteous daughter of a prosperous landowner, won by a pauper who guesses rightly by choreographic palpation that his dance partner wearing a hideous demon's mask is his nuptial objective, is produced for the first time in Tokyo.

## 16 MARCH 1969

*Hommage à Gauss* for violin and orchestra by the 24-year-old French com-poser Alain LOUVIER, serially derived from the probability curve of the fa-mous German mathematician Karl Friedrich Gauss, with a polyrhythmic per-cussion section portraying the differential calculus involved in the Gaussian equations, is performed for the first time in Paris.

## 16 MARCH 1969

*The Plough and the Stars,* opera in three acts by the American composer Elie SIEGMEISTER, based on the play of Sean O'Casey, depicting the agonies, the joys and human humor of the dramatic days during the Irish rebellion of 1915 and 1916 against the British domination, is performed for the first time at the 26th Festival of Contemporary Music of Louisiana State University in Baton Rouge, conducted by Peter Paul Fuchs.

### 23 MARCH 1969

*Sixth Symphony* by the 63-year-old English composer Benjamin FRANKEL, of Polish-Jewish parentage, in five movements unified by a common dodecaphonic series, in five movements, a spacious *Andante,* a waltzing *Allegro,* a ruminating *Adagio,* an elegiac *Intermezzo* and a rapid *Allegro* in quintuple time, immersed in resonant impressionistic carillons reflecting his philosophical "attitudes to things and people" and realistically directed towards progressive society, is performed for the first time by the Philharmonia Orchestra in London, Denis Vaughan conducting.

### 3 APRIL 1969

*Nomos gamma,* for orchestra and percussion by Iannis XENAKIS, with performers strewn quaquaversally among unsuspecting members of the audience, sonically ranging from the gentlest coo to massive teratological borborygmuses, is performed twice in succession for maximum traumatic effect at the Music Festival in Royan, France.

### 22 APRIL 1969

Peter Maxwell DAVIES, 35-year-old English avant-garde composer, conducts in London the first performance of his *Eight Songs for a Mad King* for voice and instruments, including a large biscuit tin filled with glass fragments, illustrating the schizophrenic state of King George III and notated in the form of a cage with criss-crossed music staves.

### 29 APRIL 1969

*The Lion, the Witch and the Wardrobe,* opera in four acts, prologue and epilogue, by the English composer John MCCABE, to a libretto from a Christian parable of C. S. Lewis, with a cast of characters on three hypostatic levels, human (4 schoolboys), preternatural (a leonine Christ figure) and a bestiary (of superanimals), is performed for the first time at the Manchester, England, Cathedral Festival.

### 17 MAY 1969

The United States Post Office issues a six-cent stamp honoring W. C. HANDY, "Father of the Blues", and concomitantly celebrating the sesquicentennial of the City of Memphis, the scene of Handy's early triumphs, in which he is portrayed playing trumpet in deep blue against a purple background.

### 29 MAY 1969

*Under Western Eyes,* opera in three acts by the 42-year-old South African composer John JOUBERT, to a libretto fashioned from Joseph Conrad's tale of

Russian revolutionary exiles in Geneva early in the 20th century, set to music in a sophisticated melodramatic manner salinated by the ingestion of Slavoromantic songs, is performed for the first time in the course of the Camden, England, Music Festival.

## 1 JUNE 1969

Rosemary BROWN, middle-aged British housewife and amateur pianist, gives the first performance, televised by the British Broadcasting Corporation Television Studio, of a *Moment Musical* for piano by Franz SCHUBERT, composed by him in 1969 and transmitted to her by posthumous telepathy. (A number of piano pieces by BACH, MOZART, BEETHOVEN, CHOPIN, LISZT, BRAHMS, DEBUSSY and RACHMANINOFF were similarly dictated to her at various times, proving that a prolonged state of death fatally affects the sense of elementary harmony even among musicians once known for their unerring skill in composition)

## 2 JUNE 1969

The newly constructed auditorium of the Canadian National Arts Center, with a seating capacity of 2,373 persons, is inaugurated in Ottawa with a presentation of a specially commissioned ballet *Kraanerg* ("perfected energy") by the world's foremost cybernetic composer Iannis XENAKIS, to his own scenario depicting the domination of the earth by the youth in 2069 A.D. who decree the extermination of all humans over thirty years of age, with an apocalyptic accompaniment of a fantastically varied electronic score.

## 20 JUNE 1969

The Hamburg State Opera presents, as part of the program of the 43rd Festival of the International Society for Contemporary Music, the world première of the demonological music drama in three acts *Die Teufel von Loudun* by the 35-year-old Polish magus of ultra-modern music Krzysztof PENDERECKI, to a libretto drawn from Aldous Huxley's novella dealing with the implosion of the *furor uterinus* among 17th-century Ursuline nuns in the southern French town of Loudun, whose latent sexuality was aroused to a feverish pitch by the virile presence of a macrophallic and multifutuent neighbor cleric whom they accused of invading their bodily orifices in the immund shape of a homuncular incubus, leading to a searching inquest by the Holy Inquisition and ultimately to his execution for communion with the devil on 18 August 1634, set to music with a maximal number of stylistic resources, from copulative heterophony of dissonant counterpoint in a plasma of pantechnical parameters to eschatological scatology in naturalistic onomatopoeia illustrated, e.g., by the sonic simulation of the expulsion of flatulent demons from the gastro-intestinal tract of the prioress in an icositetraphonic series of brobdingnagian borborygmuses.

## 21 JUNE 1969

In the course of the 43rd Festival of the International Society for Contemporary Music in Hamburg, the following program of chamber music is given:

*Redundanz II* for string quartet by the 38-year-old Austrian composer Josef Maria HORVATH, based on the principle of stastical changes of melodic, rhythmic and esthetic parameters and involving thematic redundancies applicable in cybernetic calculus; *Trio* for flute, marimbaphone and guitar by the 37-year-old Hungarian composer László KALMÁR, written in linear counterpoint, in three linked movements; *Distributions* for strings by the 38-year-old Japanese composer Yori-Aki MATSUDAIRA, based on a gradual accumulation of discrete distributions of sonic materials, beginning with a simulacrum of tuning; *Paraphrase* for flute and piano by the 33-year-old Swiss composer Jürg WYTTENBACH, in six cyclical movements, with a motto of an invertible and reversible theme; *Serenata* for a chamber ensemble by the 31-year-old Dutch composer Ton de KRUYF, in two movements representing a polythematic collage.

## 22 JUNE 1969

At the 43rd Festival of the International Society for Contemporary Music in Hamburg, two programs are given, one in the afternoon and one in the evening:

Afternoon program: *Mutatis Mutandis* for six players by the 32-year-old Rumanian-born Israeli composer Yehuda YANNAY, a study in intermutation of thematic parameters in horizontal and vertical dimensions, with an intussusception of independent elements at climactic points, eventually returning to the purified essences; *Übungen für Gydli*, for soprano, flute and harp, by the 55-year-old Czech composer Jan KAPR, to the words by his infant daughter nicknamed Gydli, with a congenially infantiloquacious onomatopoeic instrumental accompaniment; *Still Life* for chamber ensemble by the 37-year-old Czech composer Marek KOPELENT, with a thematically serial, aerostatically ethereal suspension of single notes analogous with paintings of fruits, flowers and inanimate objects; *Crystals* for chamber ensemble by the 49-year-old Czech-born and Vienna-educated Israeli composer Jacob GILBOA, illustrating the symmetrical principles of crystallography in serial parameters; *Cantata* for mixed choir, wind instruments and percussion by the 49-year-old Czech composer Zbynek VOSTRAK, to the words by Franz Kafka in Czech translation of the original German text, expressing the surrealistic anguish of quotidian reality in acute dissonant counterpoint.

Evening program: *Heterophonika idiomela* by the 45-year-old Constantinople-born Greek composer Arghyris KOUNADIS, exploring the combinatorial techniques of individual (*idio*) melos (*mela*) in heterophonic structures, in three individualized movements: (1) *The other Sebastian*, i.e. a non-Bach (2) *La polonaise interrompue*, an essay, in an established form (3) *The holy man of Arcueil*, a tribute to the musical grand seigneur of Arcueil, Erik Satie; *Siebengesang* by the 30-year-old Swiss composer Heinz HOLLIGER, a suite in seven sections for oboe, orchestra, voices and a loudspeaker, to amplify and alter the character of the oboe sound, with the composer himself playing the oboe; *Paraboles* for dramatic soprano and chamber orchestra by the 32-year-old French composer Paul MÉFANO; and *Septem Tubae* by the polished Polish composeress Bernadetta MATUSZCZAK, for chorus, orchestra, percussion and organ, to texts from the Apocalypse.

## 23 JUNE 1969

The 43rd Festival of the International Society for Contemporary Music in Hamburg presents a concert of choral and instrumental music with the following program:

*Sonata* for 5 woodwind instruments by the 33-year-old Danish composer Mogens Winkel HOLM, conceived as an instrumental drama in one act, with a considerable latitude in interpretation without actual improvisation; *Cantate pour elle* for soprano, harp and four magnetic tapes by the 44-year-old Zagreb-born French composer Ivo MALEC, in which the instruments are contrapuntally counterposed to their recorded images without identity of thematic substance; *Portrait* for two pianos and two percussion players by the 62-year-old Japanese composer Yoritsune MATSUDAIRA, an abstract portrait projected in five albums, with their order to be decided aleatorically by the players, but all must play the same number, involving free intussusception of themes and rhythms; *Halleluja* for voices by the 37-year-old Argentine-born German composer Mauricio KAGEL, set to words in pseudo-Latin of liturgical type and verbalization until a freely chosen fermata, serving as a turning point to another section.

## 24 JUNE 1969

At the 43rd Festival of the International Society for Contemporary Music in Hamburg the following concert of choral and orchestral music is presented:

*4 Novelettes for Chamber Orchestra* by the 40-year-old Polish composer Tadeusz BAIRD, written in a cyclic form, in four movements, with the finale outlined in strictly controlled aleatoric distribution of sonic components; *Consolation II* for 16 voices by the 34-year-old German composer Helmut LACHENMANN, with the syllabification of the text obtaining thematic significance as tonal material; *Break* for piano by the 30-year-old German composer Hans-Joachim HESPOS, an essay in syncopated rhythms and polyharmony; *AMB* by the 39-year-old German composer Dieter SCHÖNBACH, for 7 groups of speaking vocalists, to the text of a liturgy (AMB is the vowelless Hebrew spelling of Amen); *Continuum* by the 47-year-old Polish composer Kazimierz SEROCKI, for 123 percussion instruments manned by six players, placed stereophonically as autonomous sonic transmitters, in 36 sections, the shortest of which lasts four seconds (first performed at the Stockholm Festival on 17 September 1967)

## 25 JUNE 1969

The 43rd Festival of the International Society for Contemporary Music in Hamburg presents the following program of symphonic music:

*Symphony K* by the 49-year-old Polish composer Roman HAUBENSTOCK-RAMATI, in which the letter *K* stands for Kafka's "everyman" oppressed by the incomprehension and incomprehensibility of the outside world and by the unanalizability of the subjective Angst, in three sections based on the instrumental portions of HAUBENSTOCK-RAMATI's opera *Amerika; Concerto* for violoncello and orchestra by the 51-year-old German composer Bernd Alois ZIMMERMANN, in five movements, *Introduzione, Allegro, Adagio, Tempo di marcia, Blues and Coda*, designed as a choreographic "pas de trois", with an optional ballet representation being the third performing entity; *Mutazioni* by the 42-year-old Polish composer Witold SZALONEK, for chamber orchestra, in three sections marked *Gajo, Espressivo, Molto agitato*, with "combined sonic effects" in the woodwind instruments, produced by an abnormal manipulation of keys: *Imaginario II* by the 39-year-old Spanish composer Luis de Pablo, an essay in timelessness, without a determinate beginning or ending, with the thematic material treated as an infinity of combinatoriality, so that the piece may last a mystical chiliad, a hebdomad of lustra, a quindecillion of picoseconds, a bissextile year, a sidereal day, or an imaginary number of non-zero moments.

27 JUNE 1969

The 43rd Festival of the International Society for Contemporary Music in Hamburg presents the following concerts of instrumental and vocal music:

*La Musiquette II* by the 35-year-old Polish composer Henryk Mikolaj GÓRECKI, a "musical crooked mirror of everyday life" scored for trumpets, trombones, two pianos and multiple percussion; *Reflection* by the 39-year-old Japanese composer Hifuni SHIMOYAMA, for 66 string instruments divided into three equal groups, reflecting one another in a sonic mirror; *Echo* for soprano, boys' chorus, mixed chorus and orchestra by the 38-year-old Norwegian composer Arne NORDHEIM, to the texts in Italian by Salvatore Quasimodo, reflecting the oppression of Nazi occupation of Europe; *Le Roman de Kapitagolei* for orchestra by the 42-year-old Italian-born Swiss composer Giuseppe Giorgio ENGLERT, conceived in the form of a musical discourse, to a text of meaningless vowel-rich phonemes suggesting a multiplicity of possible meanings; *In alium* by the 25-year-old English composer John TAVENER, for soprano, string orchestra, organ, percussion and four tape recordings, to French, German, English and Latin texts sung by quadrilingual children simultaneously on four tapes (the title comes from the sentence, "Spem in alium nunquam habui," the first line of a choral motet by Thomas Tallis), first performed by the British Broadcasting Corporation Promenade Concert in London on 12 August 1968.

20 JULY 1969

The HARMONY OF THE SPHERES of the Pythagorean doctrine that interprets the position and movement of celestial bodies in terms of musical concordance is mystically manifested as first men step on the silent surface of the moon.

# Letters
# and
# Documents

# *Motu Proprio* of Pope Pius X on Sacred Music

INSTRUCTION ON SACRED MUSIC

### I. GENERAL PRINCIPLES

§ 1. Sacred music, being a complementary part of the solemn liturgy, participates in the general scope of the liturgy, which is the glory of God and the sanctification and edification of the faithful. It contributes to the decorum and the splendor of the ecclesiastical ceremonies, and since its principal office is to clothe with suitable melody the liturgical text proposed for the understanding of the faithful, its proper aim is to add greater efficacy to the text, in order that through it the faithful may be the more easily moved to devotion and better disposed for the reception of the fruits of grace belonging to the celebration of the most holy mysteries.

§ 2. Sacred music should consequently possess, in the highest degree, the qualities proper to the liturgy, and in particular *sanctity* and *goodness of form*, which will spontaneously produce the final quality of *universality*.

It must be *holy*, and must, therefore, exclude all profanity not only in itself, but in the manner in which it is presented by those who execute it.

It must be *true art*, for otherwise it will be impossible for it to exercise on the minds of those who listen to it that efficacy which the Church aims at obtaining in admitting into her liturgy the art of musical sounds.

But it must, at the same time, be *universal* in the sense that while every nation is permitted to admit into its ecclesiastical compositions those special forms which may be said to constitute its native music, still these forms must be subordinated in such a manner to the general characteristics of sacred music that nobody of any nation may receive an impression other than good on hearing them.

### II. THE DIFFERENT KINDS OF SACRED MUSIC

§ 3. These qualities are to be found, in the highest degree, in Gregorian Chant, which is, consequently, the Chant proper to the Roman Church, the only chant she has inherited from the ancient fathers, which she has jealously guarded for centuries in her liturgical codices, which she directly proposes to the faithful as her own, which she prescribes exclusively for some parts of the liturgy, and which the most recent studies have so happily restored to their integrity and purity.

On these grounds Gregorian Chant has always been regarded as the supreme model for sacred music, so that it is fully legitimate to lay down the following rule: *the more closely a composition for Church approaches in its movement, inspiration and savor the Gregorian form, the more sacred and liturgical it becomes; and the more out of harmony it is with that supreme model, the less worthy it is of the temple.*

The ancient traditional Gregorian Chant must, therefore, in a large measure be restored to the functions of public worship, and the fact must be accepted by all that an ecclesiastical function loses none of its solemnity when accompanied by this music alone.

Special efforts are to be made to restore the use of the Gregorian Chant by the people, so that the faithful may again take a more active part in the ecclesiastical offices, as was the case in ancient times.

§ 4. The above-mentioned qualities are also possessed in an excellent degree by Classic Polyphony, especially of the Roman School, which reached its greatest perfection in the sixteenth century, owing to the works of Pierluigi da Palestrina, and continued subsequently to produce compositions of excellent quality from a liturgical and musical standpoint. Classic Polyphony agrees admirably with Gregorian Chant, the supreme model of all sacred music, and hence it has been found worthy of a place side by side with Gregorian Chant, in the more solemn functions of the Church, such as those of the Pontifical Chapel. This, too, must therefore be restored largely in ecclesiastical functions, especially in the more important basilicas, in cathedrals, and in the churches and chapels of seminaries and other ecclesiastical institutions in which the necessary means are usually not lacking.

§ 5. The Church has always recognized and favored the progress of the arts, admitting to the service of religion everything good and beautiful discovered by genius in the course of ages—always, however, with due regard to the liturgical laws. Consequently modern music is also admitted to the Church, since it, too, furnishes compositions of such excellence, sobriety and gravity, that they are in no way unworthy of the liturgical functions.

Still, since modern music has risen mainly to serve profane uses, greater care must be taken with regard to it, in order that the musical compositions of modern style which are admitted in the Church may contain nothing profane, be free from reminiscences of motifs adopted in the theatres, and be not fashioned even in their external forms after the manner of profane pieces.

§ 6. Among the different kinds of modern music, that which appears less suitable for accompanying the functions of public worship is the theatrical style, which was in the greatest vogue, especially in Italy, during the last century. This of its very nature is diametrically opposed to Gregorian Chant and classic polyphony, and therefore to the most important law of all good sacred music. Besides the intrinsic structure, the rhythm and what is known as the *conventionalism* of this style adapt themselves but badly to the requirements of true liturgical music.

### III. THE LITURGICAL TEXT

§ 7. The language proper to the Roman Church is Latin. Hence it is forbidden to sing anything whatever in the vernacular in solemn liturgical functions—much more to sing in the vernacular the variable or common parts of the Mass and Office.

§ 8. As the texts that may be rendered in music, and the order in which they are to be rendered, are determined for every liturgical function, it is not lawful to confuse this order or to change the prescribed texts for others selected at will, or to omit them either entirely or even in part, unless when the rubrics allow that some versicles of the text be supplied with the organ, while these versicles are simply recited in the choir. However, it is permissible, according to the custom of the Roman Church, to sing a motet to the Blessed Sacrament after the *Benedictus* in a Solemn Mass. It is also permitted, after the Offertory prescribed for the Mass has been sung, to execute during the time that remains a brief motet to words approved by the Church.

§ 9. The liturgical text must be sung as it is in the books, without alteration or inversion of the words, without undue repetition, without breaking syllables, and always in a manner intelligible to the faithful who listen.

### IV. EXTERNAL FORM OF THE SACRED COMPOSITIONS

§ 10. The different parts of the Mass and the Office must retain, even musically, that particular concept and form which ecclesiastical tradition has assigned to them, and which is admirably brought out by Gregorian Chant. The method of composing an *introit*, a *gradual*, an *antiphon*, a *psalm*, a *hymn*, a *Gloria in excelsis*, etc., must therefore be distinct from one another.

§ 11. In particular the following rules are to be observed:

(a) The *Kyrie, Gloria, Credo,* etc., of the Mass must preserve the unity of composition proper to their text. It is not lawful, therefore, to compose them in separate movements, in such a way that each of these movements form a complete composition in itself, and be capable of being detached from the rest and substituted by another.

(b) In the office of Vespers it should be the rule to follow the *Cæremoniale Episcoporum*, which prescribes Gregorian Chant for the psalmody and permits figured music for the versicles of the *Gloria Patri* and the hymn.

It will nevertheless be lawful on greater solemnities to alternate the Gregorian Chant of the choir with the so-called *falsi-bordoni* or with verses similarly composed in a proper manner.

It is also permissible occasionally to render single psalms in their entirety in music, provided the form proper to psalmody be preserved in such compositions; that is to say, provided the singers seem to be psalmodising among themselves, either with new motifs or with those taken from Gregorian Chant or based upon it.

The psalms known as *di concerto* are therefore forever excluded and prohibited.

(c) In the hymns of the Church the traditional form of the hymn is preserved. It is not lawful, therefore, to compose, for instance, a *Tantum ergo* in such wise that the first strophe presents a romanza, a cavatina, an adagio and the *Genitori* an allegro.

(d) The antiphons of the Vespers must be as a rule rendered with the Gregorian melody proper to each. Should they, however, in some special case be sung in figured music, they must never have either the form of a concert melody or the fullness of a motet or a cantata.

V. THE SINGERS

§ 12. With the exception of the melodies proper to the celebrant at the altar and to the ministers, which must be always sung in Gregorian Chant, and without accompaniment of the organ, all the rest of the liturgical chant belongs to the choir of levites, and, therefore, singers in church, even when they are laymen, are really taking the place of the ecclesiastical choir. Hence the music rendered by them must, at least for the greater part, retain the character of choral music.

By this it is not to be understood that solos are entirely excluded. But solo singing should never predominate to such an extent as to have the greater part of the liturgical chant executed in that manner; the solo phrase should have the character or hint of a melodic projection (*spunto*), and be strictly bound up with the rest of the choral composition.

§ 13. On the same principle it follows that singers in church have a real liturgical office, and that therefore women, being incapable of exercising such office, cannot be admitted to form part of the choir. Whenever, then, it is desired to employ the acute voices of sopranos and contraltos, these parts must be taken by boys, according to the most ancient usage of the Church.

§ 14. Finally, only men of known piety and probity of life are to be admitted to form part of the choir of a church, and these men should by their modest and devout bearing during the liturgical functions show that they are worthy of the holy office they exercise. It will also be fitting that singers while singing in church wear the ecclesiastical habit and surplice, and that they be hidden behind gratings when the choir is excessively open to the public gaze.

VI. ORGAN AND INSTRUMENTS

§ 15. Although the music proper to the Church is purely vocal music, music with the accompaniment of the organ is also permitted. In some special cases, within due limits and with proper safeguards, other instruments may be allowed, but never without the special permission of the Ordinary, according to prescriptions of the *Cæremoniale Episcoporum*.

§ 16. As the singing should always have the principal place, the organ or other instrument should merely sustain and never oppress it.

§ 17. It is not permitted to have the chant preceded by long preludes or to interrupt it with intermezzo pieces.

§ 18. The sound of the organ as an accompaniment to the chant in preludes, interludes, and the like must be not only governed by the special nature of the instrument, but must participate in all the qualities proper to sacred music as above enumerated.

§ 19. The employment of the piano is forbidden in church, as is also that of noisy or frivolous instruments such as drums, cymbals, bells and the like.

§ 20. It is strictly forbidden to have bands play in church, and only in special cases with the consent of the Ordinary will it be permissible to admit wind instruments, limited in number, judiciously used, and proportioned to the size of the place—provided the composition and accompaniment be written in grave and suitable style, and conform in all respects to that proper to the organ.

§ 21. In processions outside the church the Ordinary may give permission for a band, provided no profane pieces be executed. It would be desirable in such cases that the band confine itself to accompanying some spiritual canticle sung in Latin or in the vernacular by the singers and the pious associations which take part in the procession.

VII. THE LENGTH OF THE LITURGICAL CHANT

§ 22. It is not lawful to keep the priest at the altar waiting on account of the chant or the music for a length of time not allowed by the liturgy. According to the ecclesiastical prescriptions the *Sanctus* of the Mass should be over before the elevation, and therefore the priest must here have regard for the singers. The *Gloria* and the *Credo* ought, according to the Gregorian tradition, to be relatively short.

§ 23. In general it must be considered a very grave abuse when the liturgy in ecclesiastical functions is made to appear secondary to and in a manner at the service of the music, for the music is merely a part of the liturgy and its humble handmaid.

VIII. PRINCIPAL MEANS

§ 24. For the exact execution of what has been herein laid down, the Bishops, if they have not already done so, are to institute in their dioceses a special Commission composed of persons really competent in sacred music, and to this Commission let them entrust in the manner they find most suitable the task of watching over the music executed in their churches. Nor are they to see merely that the music is good in itself, but also that it is adapted to the powers of the singers and be always well executed.

§ 25. In seminaries of clerics and in ecclesiastical institutions let the above-mentioned traditional Gregorian Chant be cultivated by all with diligence and love, according to the Tridentine prescriptions, and let the superiors be liberal of encouragement and praise toward their young subjects. In like manner let a Schola Cantorum be established, whenever possible, among the clerics for the execution of sacred polyphony and of good liturgical music.

§ 26. In the ordinary lessons of Liturgy, Morals, Canon Law given to the students of theology, let care be taken to touch on those points which regard more directly the principles and laws of sacred music, and let an attempt be made to complete the doctrine with some particular instruction in the aesthetic side of sacred art, so that the clerics may not leave the seminary ignorant of all those subjects so necessary to a full ecclesiastical education.

§ 27. Let care be taken to restore, at least in the principal churches, the ancient *Scholæ Cantorum,* as has been done with excellent fruit in a great many places. It is not difficult for a zelous clergy to institute such *Scholæ* even in smaller churches and country parishes—nay, in these last the pastors will find a very easy means of gathering around them both children and adults, to their own profit and the edification of the people.

§ 28. Let efforts be made to support and promote, in the best way possible, the higher schools of sacred music where these already exist, and to help in founding them where they do not. It is of the utmost importance that the Church herself provide for the instruction of her choirmasters, organists, and singers, according to the true principles of sacred art.

§ 29. Finally, it is recommended to choirmasters, singers, members of the clergy, superiors of seminaries, ecclesiastical institutions, and religious communities, parish priests and rectors of churches, canons of collegiate churches and cathedrals, and, above all, to the diocesan ordinaries to favor with all zeal these prudent reforms, long desired and demanded with united voice by all; so that the authority of the Church, which herself has repeatedly proposed them, and now inculcates them, may not fall into contempt.

Given from Our Apostolic Palace at the Vatican, on day of the Virgin and Martyr, St. Cecilia, November 22, 1903, in the first year of Our Pontificate.

PIUS X, POPE

# *Mediator Dei* of Pope Pius XII on the Sacred Liturgy

### THE ADORNMENT OF CHURCHES AND ALTARS

§ 191. As regards music, let the clear and guiding norms of the Apostolic See be scrupulously observed. Gregorian chant, which the Roman Church considers her own as handed down from antiquity and kept under her close tutelage, is proposed to the faithful as belonging to them also. In certain parts of the liturgy the Church definitely prescribes it; it makes the celebration of the sacred mysteries not only more dignified and solemn but helps very much to increase the faith and devotion of the congregation. For this reason, Our predecessors of immortal memory, Pius X and Pius XI, decreed—and We are happy to confirm with Our authority the norms laid down by them—that in seminaries and religious institutes, Gregorian chant be diligently and zealously promoted, and moreover that the old *Scholæ Cantorum* be restored, at least in the principal churches. This has already been done with happy results in not a few places.

### GREGORIAN CHANT AND CONGREGATIONAL SINGING

§ 192. Besides, "so that the faithful take a more active part in divine worship, let Gregorian chant be restored to popular use in the parts proper to the people. Indeed it is very necessary that the faithful attend the sacred ceremonies not as if they were outsiders or mute onlookers, but let them fully appreciate the beauty of the liturgy and take part in the sacred ceremonies, alternating their voices with the priest and the choir, according to the prescribed norms. If, please God, this is done, it will not happen that the congregation hardly ever or only in a low murmur answer the prayers in Latin or in the vernacular." A congregation that is devoutly present at the sacrifice, in which our Saviour together with His children redeemed with His sacred blood sings the nuptial hymn of His immense love, cannot keep silent, for "song befits the lover" and, as the ancient saying has it, "he who sings well prays twice." Thus, the Church militant, faithful as well as clergy, joins in the hymns of the Church triumphant and with the choirs of angels, and, all together, sing a wondrous and eternal hymn of praise to the most Holy Trinity in keeping with words of the preface, "with whom our voices, too, thou wouldst bid to be admitted."

§ 193. It cannot be said that modern music and singing should be entirely excluded from Catholic worship. For, if they are not profane nor unbecoming to the sacredness of the place and function, and do not spring from a desire of achieving extraordinary and unusual effects, then our churches must admit them since they can contribute in no small way to the splendor of the sacred ceremonies, can lift the mind to higher things and foster true devotion of soul.

§ 194. We also exhort you, Venerable Brethren, to promote with care congregational singing, and to see to its accurate execution with all due dignity, since it easily stirs up and arouses the faith and piety of large gatherings of the faithful. Let the full harmonious singing of our people rise to heaven like the bursting of a thunderous sea and let them testify by the melody of their song to the unity of their hearts and minds, as become brothers and the children of the same Father.

§ 211. Given at Castel Gandolfo, near Rome, on the 20th day of November in the year 1947, the 9th of Our Pontificate.

Pius XII

## The Black List of Disapproved Music

At the Convention of the Society of St. Gregory of America, held in Rochester, New York, May 4–6, 1922, the publication of a list of music not in accordance with the MOTU PROPRIO was authorized. The works of the following composers and the particular compositions listed below are clearly antagonistic to the principles enunciated in the document issued by Pope Pius X.

In preparing this section it was considered sufficient to mention the titles of only a few of the "most popular" of the objectionable Hymnals, Choir-Books, etc., still to be found in so many choir lofts.

It would be manifestly impossible to print a complete list of all the works which fall under this head. The purpose of the Society is to draw attention to the type of composition which is clearly opposed to the principles of the MOTU PROPRIO.

All the Masses by the following composers:

| | | |
|---|---|---|
| ASHMALL | GENERALI | MARZO |
| BATTMANN | GIORZA | MERCADANTE |
| BORDESE | KALLIWODA | MERLIER |
| BROWN (WILL. M. S.) | LA HACHE | MILLARD |
| CONCONE | LAMBILLOTTE | PONIATOWSKI |
| CORINI | LEJEAL | SILAS |
| DURAND | LEONARD | STEARNS |
| FARMER | LEPREVOST | TURNER |
| GANSS | LOESCH | WIEGAND |

Of CHARLES GOUNOD's, the following Masses:

| | | |
|---|---|---|
| St. Cecilia | Sacred Heart | De Paques (No. 3) |

The musical value of the religious compositions of MOZART, JOSEPH HAYDN, SCHUBERT, G. ROSSINI,* C. M. VON WEBER does not enter into the question. The exception taken is their purely liturgical unfitness according to the principles declared in the MOTU PROPRIO.

All the Vespers and Psalms, by

| | | |
|---|---|---|
| ALDEGA | GIORZA | MODERATI |
| BRIZZI | LEJEAL | STEARNS |
| CAPOCCI | MARZO | WIEGAND |
| CERRUTI | McCABE | ZINGARELLI |
| CORINI | MERCADANTE | |
| GENERALI | MILLARD | |

* Not to be confused with Rev. Carlo Rossini, whose compositions stand approved.

The Requiem Masses by

CHERUBINI      MADONNA      GIORZA      OHNEWALD

Hymn- and Choir-Books

ST. BASIL'S HYMNAL
BERGE HYMNALS
CANTICA PUERORUM, Eduardo Marzo
LAUS ET PRECES, Eduardo Marzo
COLLECTION FOR SODALISTS, A. H. Ro-
    sewig
CONCENTUS SACRI, A. H. Rosewig
CATHOLIC CHOIR BOOK, P. Giorza
CATHOLIC CHOIR MANUAL, G. M. Wynne
SALVE, VOLUME I, P. Giorza
GLORIA, VOLUME II, P. Giorza
LAUS DEO, VOLUME III, P. Giorza

THE CHAPEL HYMN BOOK
CATHOLIC YOUTH'S HYMN BOOK, Chris-
    tian Brothers
MAY CHIMES, Srs. Notre Dame
PETER'S CLASS BOOK
PETER'S CATHOLIC HARMONIST
PETER'S CATHOLIC HARP
PETER'S SODALITY HYMN BOOK
SUNDAY SCHOOL HYMN BOOK
VADE MECUM, Kelly
WERNER'S COLLECTION OF SEVEN PIECES
WREATH OF MARY

## MISCELLANEOUS DISAPPROVED MUSIC

STABAT MATER—G. ROSSINI

All of Rossini's compositions should be excluded from the Catholic choir. These works are unchurchly, to say the least. The "Stabat Mater" is most objectionable from a liturgical standpoint.

REGINA COELI—P. GIORZA

All compositions by P. Giorza should be eliminated from the repertoire of the Catholic choirs. The composer wrote any number of "Ballets." He did not change his style one iota when he put sacred words to these utterly secular melodies. The worst example of this "Ballet" style in church is the setting of the "Regina Coeli," which, sad to relate, is still sung in many of our churches.

JESU DEI VIVA—G. VERDI

Taken from the opera "Attila." This number is another favorite among Catholic choirs. Verdi did not write this for use in the Church, but for one of his operas. He would have been the first to object to its use in its present form, since it is neither fitting nor appropriate.

THE AVE MARIAS by

LUZZI, MILLARD, VERDI, BACH-GOUNOD, MASCAGNI, LAMBILLOTTE, KAHN, ETC.

All arrangements and adaptations of Operatic Melodies, such as Sextet from "Lucia di Lammermoor," Quartet from "Rigoletto," arias from "Tannhäuser," "Lohengrin," "Othello," etc.

SALVE REGINA, C. Henshaw-Dana
BORDESE'S COMPOSITIONS . . . ALL

Songs in English, such as
    The End of a Perfect Day
    Face to Face
    Beautiful Isle of Somewhere
    O Promise Me
    I Love You Truly
    There's a Beautiful Land on High

Good Night, Sweet Jesus
Wedding Marches
From "Lohengrin"—R. Wagner
From "Midsummer Night's Dream"—F. Mendelssohn

NOTE: The Society of St. Gregory, at its convention held in Rochester, New York, May 4–6, 1922, registered an emphatic protest against the efforts made by certain publishers of Catholic Church Music to create an impression that "revised editions" of Masses by Mozart, Haydn, Schubert, Weber, Gounod, Millard, Giorza, Farmer, Kalliwoda and other composers of the operatic school were edited to conform to the requirements of the MOTU PROPRIO.

Because a certain number of repetitions have been eliminated from these unacceptable works it does not follow that they are metamorphosed, through this process, into liturgical compositions. No amount of revision, editing or truncating can create a devotional composition out of a work that is intrinsically secular in character. Pope Pius X, in his MOTU PROPRIO, made clear the distinction between the secular and the sacred style.

The attempt of certain publishers to "hoodwink" a gullible public by using in an indiscriminate manner the caption "In accordance with the MOTU PROPRIO" deserves the condemnation of every friend of liturgical art. A flagrant example of this attempt to pull wool over the eyes of the innocent is found in the publication of the popular song "Silver Threads Among the Gold" as an "Ave Maria Stella" under the caption "In accordance with the MOTU PROPRIO."

What the Society of St. Gregory has condemned in the way of unliturgical music applies to those so-called Revised Hymnals which have merited the disapproval of the authorities simply because the compilers and editors have chosen to disregard the very plain recommendations contained in the MOTU PROPRIO.

# Three Anti-Modernist Poems: 1884, 1909, 1924

1

DIRECTIONS FOR COMPOSING A WAGNER OVERTURE

(From an American newspaper, *ca.* 1884)

A sharp, where you'd expect a natural.
A natural, where you'd expect a sharp.
No rule observe but the exceptional
And then (first happy thought) bring in a Harp!

No bar a sequence to the bar behind,
No bar a prelude to the next that comes.
Which follows which, you really needn't mind:—
But (second happy thought!) bring in your Drums!

For harmonies, let wild discords pass;
Let key be blent with key in hideous hash;
Then (for last happy thought!) bring in your Brass!
And clang, clash, clatter—clatter, clang and clash.

A Sufferer

2.

(From the New York *World*, inspired by some music of Richard Strauss,
*ca.* January 1909)

> Hark! from the pit a fearsome sound
>   That makes your blood run cold.
> Symphonic cyclones rush around—
>   And the worst is yet untold.
>
> No—they unchain those dogs of war,
>   The wild sarrusophones,
> A double-bass E-flat to roar
>   Whilst crunching dead men's bones.
>
> The muted tuba's dismal groan
>   Uprising from the gloom
> And answered by the heckelphone,
>   Suggest the crack of doom.
>
> Oh, mama! is this the earthquake zone?
>   What ho, there! stand from under!
> Or is that the tonitruone
>   Just imitating thunder?
>
> Nay, fear not, little one, because
>   Of this sublime rough-house;
> 'Tis modern opera by the laws
>   Of Master Richard Strauss.
>
> Singers? they're scarcely heard nor seen—
>   In yon back seat they sit,
> The day of Song is past, I ween;
>   The orchestra is it.

3.

(From the Boston *Herald*, February 1924, inspired by Stravinsky's
*Sacre du Printemps*)

> Who wrote this fiendish "Rite of Spring,"
> What right had he to write the thing,
> Against our helpless ears to fling
> Its crash, clash, cling, clang, bing, bang, bing?
>
> And then to call it "Rite of Spring."
> The season when on joyous wing
> The birds melodious carols sing
> And harmony's in everything!
>
> He who could write the "Rite of Spring"
> If I be right, by right should swing!

# Manifesto of Futurist Musicians

I address myself to the young, for only the young will listen to me and understand me. But there are those who are born old, coming into the world like a somber spectre of the past, a tumid cryptogram of venom. Neither words nor ideas have any meaning for them. Their destiny is imposed on them. It is death.

I address myself to the young, because they become naturally excited about new things, present and living. They must follow me, faithfully, ardent, through the pathways of the future, where our intrepid brothers, Futurist poets and painters, precede us in glory, beautiful in their rage, violent in their rebellion and luminous in their animating genius.

A year ago a committee composed of Pietro Mascagni, Giacomo Orefice, Guglielmo Mattioli, Rodolfo Ferrari and the critic Gian Battista Nappi, selected my Futurist opera *La Sina d'Vargoun*, written to my own libretto in free verse, as the winner of the prize of 10,000 lire in a contest, the money to be used to defray the expenses of the production of my work recognized as superior to other entries. The first performance, given in December, 1909, at the Teatro Communale in Bologna, was received with great enthusiasm, some insipid and stupid criticisms, generous support of friends, and the high honor of vituperation by numerous enemies.

Having triumphantly entered the Italian musical scene, and established contact with audiences, publishers and critics, I could judge with a maximum of self-possession the intellectual mediocrity and mercantile ignorance which have reduced Italian music to a uniform genre of vulgar melodrama, placing it in absolute inferiority in comparison with the Futurist developments in other countries.

In Germany, after the glorious revolutionary era dominated by the sublime genius of Wagner, Richard Strauss elevated the most bizarre type of instrumentation to the level of a vital artistic achievement. Yet even Strauss is unable to disguise the aridity, the mercantilism and the banality of his soul under harmonic mannerisms and clever acoustical effects. He attempts, however, to redeem his past by ingenious innovations.

In France, Claude Debussy, a profound artist, is a man of literature rather than a musician, swimming in a serene lake of tenuous, delicate, azure harmonies, immersed in an instrumental symbolism of monotonous polyphony by means of a whole-tone scale. It is a novel system, but still a device implying a voluntary limitation, and Debussy does not always succeed in covering up the indifferent quality of his thematic and rhythmic invention and his almost total lack of ideological development. In his music, this development becomes a primitive and infantile periodic repetition of a short and poverty-stricken theme, or of a monotonous and vague rhythmic pattern. He resorts in his operatic formulas to the obsolete concepts of the Florentine Camerata, which in 1600 gave birth to melodrama, but has not achieved a complete reform of the art of music drama even in its own country. Nonetheless, more than any one else, Debussy valiantly fights against the past and often emerges victorious. Charpentier may be ideologically stronger than Debussy, but musically he is inferior.

In England, Edward Elgar, who presides over the destruction of the past with considerable élan by amplifying the classical symphonic forms, attempting a thematic development in multiform variations on the same subject, and seeking equilibrated effects to satisfy our complex sensibilities in a variety of instrumental combinations, if not in their exuberance.

In Russia, Modest Mussorgsky, innovating the spirit of Rimsky-Korsakov, repudiates the tradition by instilling the national primitive element in formulas inherited from others and by seeking dramatic truth and harmonic freedom. In Finland, a new art is being nurtured against the background of national poetry. The music of Sibelius testifies to its strength.

And in Italy? Music schools, conservatories and academies of music are vegetating miserably. In these sanctuaries of impotence, teachers and professors, illustrious defectives, are perpetuating the old traditions and are fighting every attempt to extend the musical ambience. The result is a cautious repression, elimination of all liberal and bold tendencies, unceasing mortification of impetuous intelligence; unconditional support of mediocrity which knows how to copy and criticise; prostitution of great musical glories of the past. It is an arsenal of deadly weapons against the growing genius; the reduction of study to futile acrobatics, practiced in the perpetual agony of a retarded and already dead culture.

Young musical talents, stagnating in the Italian conservatories, set their sights on the alluring mirage of opera under the auspices of important publishing firms. The majority reduces this art to a very low level through lack of basic ideas and poor technique; very few new operas reach the stage and of these many have to be financed by the composers for the sake of an ephemeral success and polite tolerance.

Pure instrumental composition is the final refuge of these frustrated opera composers, and, to exonerate themselves, they predict the end of music drama as an obsolete and anti-musical form. At the same time they confirm the universal belief that Italians are not born to write orchestral music, and demonstrate their ineptness in this noble and vital genre of composition.

The fortunate few who overcome all obstacles and obtain the favors of large publishing houses to whom they become bound by illusory and humiliating contracts, are slaves who sell their art. The merchant publishers issue orders, assign commercial limits to forms of music drama and set up as models the low, sickly and vulgar operas of Giacomo Puccini and Umberto Giordano. They are willing to pay the librettists, particularly those who manufacture their scripts according to the manner of a pasticcio baked by such writers as Luigi Illica, fetid cakes called operatic librettos. These publishers reject all works that transcend mediocrity; with their vested monopoly they make profit from their merchandise and forestall even a timid attempt at rebellion. They assume the tutelage and the privilege over popular tastes, and in complicity with the critics maintain the monopoly of bel canto in Italian opera, strangling and suffocating the throat of the nation.

Only Pietro Mascagni, himself the creation of a publisher, has enough courage to rebel against traditional art, against publishers and the deceived and spoiled public. By his personal example, first and the only one in Italy, Mascagni has torn the veil off the shame of publishing monopolies and the venality of the press and has hastened the day of our liberation from the mercantile Tsarism of the dilettantes. With a force of genius Pietro Mascagni has made real attempts at innovation in the music and librettos of his theatrical works, even though he has not as yet succeeded in freeing himself from traditional forms.

Futurism is a rebellion of life, of intuition and of sentiment, a thundering and impetuous spring. It wages implacable war on musicians who repeat, prolong and exalt the past to the detriment of the future. It proclaims the conquest of artistic action, amoral, free and imaginative.

I raise the red banner of Futurism to the sun in open air, sounding a clarion call under this flaming symbol to those among young composers who have a heart with which to love and to fight, a mind to conceive ideas, and boldness immune to cowardice. I rejoice in setting myself free from the chains of tradition, of doubt, of opportunism and of vanity.

I repudiate the title of Maestro, which is a stigma of mediocrity and ignorance, and hereby confirm my enthusiastic adherence to Futurism. For the young, for the ardent, for the courageous, I issue these irrevocable instructions:

1. We must convince young composers to desert music schools, conservatories and academies, and to adopt free study as the only means of regeneration.

2. We must combat with assiduous energy the fatally venal and ignorant critics, to free the public from the maleficent influence of their writings and to found for this purpose an independent musical journal, resolutely opposing the criteria of conservatory professors and of those who have been degraded by them.

3. We must abstain from the participation in any contest with the usual sealed envelopes and compulsory fees of admission, denouncing publicly the mystifications involved in them and exposing the incompetence of juries, generally composed of cretins and imbeciles.

4. We must keep aloof from commercial or academic circles, treating them with contempt, and preferring a modest life to the affluence of those through whom art is being sold.

5. We must liberate the individual musical consciousness from all imitation of the past, we must feel and sing with one's soul directed towards the future, receiving inspiration from nature in all its manifestations, human and extrahuman, and exalt man as a symbol of perennial regeneration in intimate relationship with nature.

6. We must destroy the pretense of well-made music, that rhetoric of impotence, and proclaim the unique ideal of Futurist Music, absolutely different from any written before. We must create in Italy a Futurist musical taste. We must destroy pedantic, academic and soporific values, and to regard the phrase, "Let us turn to the past" as odious, stupid and vile.

7. We must proclaim the reign of the singer as finished and demand that the vocal part in a work of art should correspond to that of an orchestral instrument.

8. We must change the term "opera libretto" to "dramatic and tragic poem set to music," substituting free verse for metrical prosody. Every opera composer must be the author of his own literary text.

9. We must combat categorically the historical reconstructions and the traditional mise en scène, and condemn the opposition to the use of contemporary dress in opera as stupid.

10. We must deprecate ballads in the manner of Tosti and the loathsome Neapolitan songs, as well as sacred music which has no reason to exist now that the decline of religious faith is complete, and which has become a monopoly of impotent conservatory directors and incompetent priests.

11. We must generate in the audiences a constantly increasing hostility against the exhumations of old operas, which hamper the chances of modern composers; we must exalt in music all that is revolutionary and original, treat the insults and the ridicule of the moribund opportunists as an honor.

And now let the defenders of the past turn against me with all the fury they are capable of, while I stand serenely smiling, not caring a whit. I climb over the past and in a loud voice I issue a summons to young musicians to gather under the banner of Futurism, launched by the poet Marinetti in Paris last year, which has since conquered the greatest intellectual centers of the world.

BALILLA PRATELLA, MUSICIAN
MILAN, 11 OCTOBER 1910

(Translated from the Italian by Nicolas Slonimsky)

## Technical Manifesto of Futurist Music

All innovators are futurists in relation to their own times. Palestrina would have thought that Bach was mad. Bach would have rendered a similar judgment about Beethoven, and Beethoven would have described Wagner as crazy. Rossini claimed that he finally understood Wagner's music by playing it upside down. Verdi, after he heard the overture to *Tannhäuser*, said in a letter to a friend that only an insane person could have written it.

Today we find ourselves at the threshold of a glorious madhouse, for we declare without hesitation that counterpoint and fugue, still considered the most important branch of the musical curriculum, represent nothing more than the ruins of the history of polyphony of the period between the Flemish School and Bach.

We hear laments that young musicians are no longer capable of inventing melodies, doubtless alluding to the type of melodies cultivated by Rossini, Bellini, Verdi or Ponchielli. But melody is now conceived harmonically; harmony is felt through complex combinations and successions of sounds, thus creating new melodic resources. This development marks the end, once and for all, of paltry imitators of the past, who have no longer any reason to exist, and of various venal purveyors to the low tastes of the public.

We, the Futurists, proclaim that the traditional modes derived from major, minor, augmented, and diminished intervals, and even the novel scales of whole tones, are merely special cases of the harmonic and atonal chromatic scale. We also declare as invalid the concepts of consonance and dissonance. From the innumerable combinations and varied relations derived from the chromatic scale there will blossom forth a Futurist Melody. Such a melody will be a synthesis of harmony, similar to an ideal line formed by the incessant flowering of thousands of ocean waves with unequal crests.

We, the Futurists, predict progress and eventual victory over the chromatic atonal mode, after a search and the realization of an enharmonic mode. While chromaticism makes use of all sounds contained in a scale made up of semitones, the enharmonic mode, by incorporating small subdivisions of tones, offers to our renewed sensibilities a maximum of determinable combinatorial sounds and novel relations of chords and timbres. Above all, the enharmonic mode makes it possible to use natural instinctive intonations and modulations of enharmonic intervals, unavailable to us because of the artificial structure of our tempered scale, a condition we intend to change. We, Futurists, have for a long time cherished these enharmonic intervals found only in the natural dissonances of orchestral instruments which are differently tuned and in the spontaneous songs of the people sung without preoccupation with art.

The rhythms of modern dances, monotonous, limited and decrepit, must yield to a free polyrhythmic art. The alternation and succession of all possible meters and rhythms will achieve an equilibrium only in the genius and esthetic sense of the creative artist. Technical mastery of instrumentation must be acquired experimentally.

All this will be possible when conservatories, music schools and academies of music are deserted and are forced to close down, so that musical studies can be pursued in absolute freedom. Teachers of today will become experts of tomorrow, objective guides and collaborators of students; they will cease the unconscionable corruption of nascent geniuses by forcing them to drag themselves behind their personality and by imposing on them their own errors and their own criteria. We conclude:

1. Melody is a synthesis of harmony, in which major, minor, augmented and diminished triads are special cases of a generic chromatic atonal mode.

2. Enharmonic relationships are magnificent victories of Futurism.

3. The monopoly of the modern dance must be broken, since its rhythms are special cases of free rhythm, in the sense that the rhythm of a hendecasyllable is a special case of a strophe in free verse.

4. By effecting a fusion of harmony and counterpoint, we must create polyphony in the absolute sense, such as has never been attempted before.

5. We must master all expressive technical and dynamic elements of instrumentation and regard the orchestra as a sonorous universe in a state of constant mobility, integrated by an effective fusion of all its constituent parts.

6. All musical forms are created by generative emotional motives.

7. A revival of traditional forms, dead and buried, of a classical symphony must be prevented.

8. All stage works must be regarded as symphonic forms.

9. It is imperative that opera composers should write their own librettos, their own dramatic theatrical poems. The symbolic action of such a poem must spring from the composer's own creative imagination, reinforced by the determination to develop emotional motives. Librettos written by others would force the composer to accept from others the rhythms of his own music as well.

10. Free verse is the only means of obtaining polyrhythmic freedom.

11. All forces of nature, tamed by man through his continued scientific discoveries, must find their reflection in composition—the musical soul of the crowds, of great industrial plants, of trains, of transatlantic liners, of armored warships, of automobiles, of airplanes. This will unite the great central motives of a musical poem with the power of the machine and the victorious reign of electricity.

BALILLA PRATELLA, MUSICIAN
MILAN, 11 MARCH 1911

(Translated from the Italian by Nicolas Slonimsky)


## The Art of Noises

### FUTURIST MANIFESTO

MY DEAR BALILLA PRATELLA, GREAT FUTURISTIC COMPOSER:
In the crowded Costanzi Theater, in Rome, while I was listening with my futurist friends Marinetti, Boccioni, and Balla to the orchestral performance of your overwhelming MUSICA FUTURISTA, there came to my mind the idea of a new art: the ART OF NOISES, a logical consequence of your marvelous innovations.

Life in ancient times was silent. In the nineteenth century, with the invention of machines, Noise was born. Today Noise is triumphant, and reigns supreme over the senses of men. For many centuries life evolved in silence, or, at the most, with but a muted sound. The loudest noises that interrupted this silence were neither violent nor prolonged nor varied, since—if we overlook such exceptional phenomena as hurricanes, tempests, avalanches, waterfalls—nature is silent.

*Noises* being so scarce, the first *musical sounds* which man succeeded in drawing from a hollow reed or from a stretched string were a new, astonishing, miraculous discovery. By primitive peoples musical sound was ascribed to the gods, regarded as holy, and entrusted to the sole care of the priests, who made use of it to enrich their rites with mystery. Thus was born the conception of musical sound as a thing having an independent existence, a thing different from life and unconnected with it. From this conception resulted an idea of music as a world of fantasy superimposed upon reality, a world inviolate and sacred. It will be readily understood how this idea of music must inevitably have impeded its progress, as compared with that of the other arts. The Greeks themselves—with their theory of music (systematized mathematically by Pythagoras) which permitted the use of a few consonant intervals only —greatly limited music's scope and excluded all possibility of harmony, of which they knew nothing.

The Middle Ages, with their modifications of the Greek tetrachord system, with their Gregorian chants and their folk songs, enriched the art of music. Yet they continued to regard music from the point of view of *linear development in time*—a narrow view of the art which lasted several centuries and which persists in the more complicated polyphony of the Flemish contrapuntists. The *chord* did not exist: the flow of the individual parts was never subordinated to the agreeable effect produced at any given moment by the ensemble of those parts. In a word, the medieval conception of music was horizontal, not vertical. An interest in the simultaneous union of different sounds, that is, in the chord as a complex sound, developed gradually, passing from the perfect consonance, with a few incidental dissonances, to the complex and persistent dissonances which characterize the music of today.

The art of music at first sought and achieved purity and sweetness of sound; later, it blended diverse sounds, but always with intent to caress the ear with suave harmonies. Today, growing ever more complicated, it seeks those combinations of sounds that fall most dissonantly, strangely, and harshly upon the ear. We thus approach nearer and nearer to the MUSIC OF NOISE.

This musical evolution parallels the growing multiplicity of machines, which everywhere are assisting mankind. Not only amid the clamor of great cities but even in the countryside, which until yesterday was ordinarily quiet, the machine today has created so many varieties and combinations of noise that pure musical sound—with its poverty and its monotony—no longer awakens any emotion in the hearer.

To excite and exalt our senses, music continued to develop toward the most complex polyphony and the greatest variety of orchestral timbres, or colors, devising the most complicated successions of dissonant chords and preparing in a general way for the creation of MUSICAL NOISE. This evolution toward noise was hitherto impossible. An eighteenth-century ear could not have endured the dissonant intensity of certain chords produced by our modern orchestras—triple the size of the orchestras of that day. But our own ears—trained as they are by the modern world, so rich in variegated noises—not only enjoy these dissonances but demand more and more violent acoustic emotions.

Moreover, musical sound is too limited in qualitative variety of timbre. The most complicated of orchestras reduce themselves to four or five classes of instruments differing in timbre: instruments played with the bow, plucked instruments, brass winds, wood winds, and percussion instruments. So that modern music, in its attempts to produce new kinds of timbre, struggles vainly within this little circle.

We must break out of this narrow circle of pure musical sounds, and conquer the infinite variety of noise-sounds.

Everyone will recognize that every musical sound carries with it an incrustation of familiar and stale sense associations, which predispose the hearer to boredom, despite all the efforts of innovating musicians. We futurists have all deeply loved the music of the great composers. Beethoven and Wagner for many years wrung our hearts. But now we are satiated with them and derive much greater pleasure from ideally combining the noises of street-cars, internal-combustion engines, automobiles, and busy crowds than from re-hearing, for example, the "Eroica" or the "Pastorale."

We cannot see the immense apparatus of the modern orchestra without being profoundly disappointed by its feeble acoustic achievements. Is there anything more absurd than to see twenty men breaking their necks to multiply the meowling of a violin? All this will naturally infuriate the musicomaniacs and perhaps disturb the somnolent atmosphere of our concert halls. Let us enter, as futurists, into one of these institutions for musical anemia. The first measure assails your ear with the boredom of the already-heard and causes you to anticipate the boredom of the measure to come. Thus we sip, from measure to measure, two or three different sorts of boredom, while we await an unusual emotion that never arrives. Meanwhile we are revolted by the monotony of the sensations experienced, combined with the idiotic religious excitement of the listeners, Buddhistically intoxicated by the thousandth repetition of their hypocritical and artificial ecstasy. Away! Let us be gone, since we shall not much longer succeed in restraining a desire to create a new musical realism by a generous distribution of sonorous blows and slaps, leaping nimbly over violins, pianofortes, contrabasses, and groaning organs. Away!

The objection cannot be raised that all noise is loud and disagreeable. I need scarcely enumerate all the small and delicate noises which are pleasing to the ear. To be convinced of their surprising variety one need only think of the rumbling of thunder, the howling of the wind, the roar of a waterfall, the gurgling of a brook, the rustling of leaves, the receding clatter of a horse's hoofs, the bumping of a wagon over cobblestones, and the deep, solemn breathing of a city at night, all the noises made by wild and domesticated animals, and all those that the human mouth can produce, apart from speaking or singing.

Let us wander through a great modern city with our ears more attentive than our eyes, and distinguish the sounds of water, air, or gas in metal pipes, the purring of motors (which breathe and pulsate with an indubitable animalism), the throbbing of valves, the pounding of pistons, the screeching of gears, the clatter of streetcars on their rails, the cracking of whips, the flapping of awnings and flags. We shall amuse ourselves by orchestrating in our minds the noise of the metal shutters of store windows, the slamming of doors, the bustle and shuffle of crowds, the multitudinous uproar of railroad stations, forges, mills, printing presses, power stations, and underground railways.

Nor should the new noises of modern warfare be forgotten. Recently the poet Marinetti, in a letter from the trenches of Adrianopolis, described to me in admirably unfettered language the orchestra of a great battle:

*"every 5 seconds siege guns splitting the belly of space with a TZANG-TUMB-TUUUMB chord revolt of 500 echos to tear it to shreds and scatter it to infinity In the center of these TZANG-TUMB-TUUUMB spied out breadth 50 square kilometers leap reports knife-thrusts rapid-fire batteries Violence ferocity regularity this deep bass ascending the strange agitated insane high-pitched notes of battle Fury panting breath eyes ears nostrils open! watching! straining! what joy to see hear smell everything everything taratatata of the machine guns frantically screaming amid bites blows traak-traak whipcracks pic-pac pum-tumb strange goings-on leaps height 200 meters of the infantry Down down at the bottom of the orchestra stirring up pools oxen buffaloes goats wagons pluff plaff rearing of horses flic flac tzing tzing shaak hilarious neighing iiiiii stamping clanking 3 Bulgarian battalions on the march croooc-craaac (lento) Shumi Maritza or Karvavena TZANG-TUMB-TUUUMB toctoctoctoc (rapidissimo) crooc-craac (lento) officers' yells resounding like sheets of brass bang here crack there BOOM ching chak (presto) chachacha-cha-chak up down back forth all around above look out for your head chak good shot! Flames flames flames flames flames collapse of the forts over behind the smoke Shukri Pasha talks to 27 forts over the telephone in Turkish in German Hallo! Ibrahim!! Rudolf! Hallo! Hallo, actors playlists echos prompters scenarios of smoke forests applause smell of hay mud dung my feet are frozen numb smell of saltpeter smell of putrefaction Timpani flutes clarinets everywhere low high birds chirping beatitudes shade cheep-cheep-cheep breezes verdure herds dong-dang-dong-ding-baaaa the lunatics are assaulting the musicians of the orchestra the latter soundly thrashed play on Great uproar don't cancel the concert more precision dividing into smaller more minute sounds fragments of echos in the theater area 300 square kilometers Rivers Maritza Tundja stretch out Rudopi Mountains standing up erect boxes balconies 2000 shrapnel spraying exploding snow-white handkerchiefs full of gold srrrrrrrr-TUMB-TUMB 2000 hand-grenades hurled shearing off black-haired heads with their splinters TZANG-srrrrrr-TUMB-TZANG-TUMB-TUUUMB the orchestra of the noises of war swells beneath a long-held note of silence in high heaven gilded spherical balloon which surveys the shooting , , ."*

We must fix the pitch and regulate the harmonies and rhythms of these extraordinarily varied sounds. To fix the pitch of noises does not mean to take away from them all the irregularity of tempo and intensity that characterizes their vibrations, but rather to give definite gradation or pitch to the stronger and more predominant of these vibrations. Indeed, noise is differentiated from musical sound merely in that the vibrations that produce it are confused and irregular, both in tempo and in intensity. Every noise has a note—sometimes even a chord—that predominates in the ensemble of its irregular vibrations. Because of this characteristic note it becomes possible to fix the pitch of a given noise, that is, to give it not a single pitch but a variety of pitches, without losing its characteristic quality—its distinguishing timbre. Thus certain noises produced by rotary motion may offer a complete ascending or descending chromatic scale by merely increasing or decreasing the speed of the motion.

Every manifestation of life is accompanied by noise. Noise is therefore familiar to our ears and has the power to remind us immediately of life itself. Musical sound, a thing extraneous to life and independent of it, an occasional and unnecessary adjunct, has become for our ears what a too familiar face is to our eyes. Noise, on the other hand, which comes to us confused and irregular as life itself, never reveals itself wholly but reserves for us innumerable surprises. We are convinced, therefore, that by selecting, co-ordinating, and controlling noises we shall enrich mankind with a new and unsuspected source of pleasure. Despite the fact that it is characteristic of sound to remind us brutally of life, the ART OF NOISES must not limit itself to reproductive imitation. It will reach its greatest emotional power through the purely acoustic enjoyment which the inspiration of the artist will contrive to evoke from combinations of noises.

These are the futurist orchestra's six families of noises, which we shall soon produce mechanically:

| 1 | 2 | 3 | 4 | 5 | 6 |
|---|---|---|---|---|---|
| Booms Thunder-claps Explosions Crashes Splashes Roars | Whistles Hisses Snorts | Whispers Murmurs Mutterings Bustling noises Gurgles | Screams Screeches Rustlings Buzzes Cracklings Sounds obtained by friction | Noises obtained by percussion on metals, wood, stone, terracotta | Voices of animals and men: Shouts Shrieks Groans Howls Laughs Wheezes Sobs |

In this list we have included the most characteristic fundamental noises; the others are but combinations of these.

The rhythmic movements within a single noise are of infinite variety. There is always, as in a musical note, a predominant rhythm, but around this may be perceived numerous secondary rhythms.

CONCLUSIONS

1.—Futurist musicians must constantly broaden and enrich the field of sound. This is a need of our senses. Indeed, we note in present-day composers of genius a tendency toward the most complex dissonances. Moving further and further away from pure musical sound, they have almost reached the *noise-sound*. This need and this tendency can only be satisfied *by the supplementary use of noise and its substitution for musical sounds.*

2.—Futurist musicians must substitute for the limited variety of timbres of the orchestral instruments of the day the infinite variety of the timbres of noises, reproduced by suitable mechanisms.

3.—The musician's sensibility, liberating itself from facile, traditional rhythm, must find in noises the way to amplify and renew itself, since each noise offers a union of the most diverse rhythms, in addition to the predominant rhythm.

4.—Since every noise has in its irregular vibrations a general, predominating tone, it will be easy to obtain, in constructing the instruments which imitate it, a sufficiently wide variety of tones, semitones, and quarter-tones. This variety of tones will not deprive any single noise of its characteristic timbre but will merely increase its tessitura, or extension.

5.—The practical difficulties in the construction of these instruments are not serious. Once the mechanical principle producing a given noise is found, one may vary its pitch by applying the general laws of acoustics. For example, in instruments employing rotary motion the speed of rotation will be increased or diminished; in others, the size or tension of the sounding parts will be varied.

6.—Not by means of a succession of noises imitating those of real life, but through a fanciful blending of these varied timbres and rhythms, will the new orchestra obtain the most complex and novel sound effects. Hence every instrument must be capable of varying its pitch and must have a fairly extensive range.

7.—There is an infinite variety of noises. If, today, with perhaps a thousand different kinds of machines, we can distinguish a thousand different noises, tomorrow, as the number of new machines is multiplied, we shall be able to distinguish ten, twenty, or thirty thousand different noises, not merely to be imitated but to be combined as our fancy dictates.

8.—Let us therefore invite young musicians of genius and audacity to listen attentively to all noises, so that they may understand the varied rhythms of which they are composed, their principal tone, and their secondary tones. Then, comparing the varied timbres of noises with those of musical tones, they will be convinced how much more numerous are the former than the latter. Out of this will come not merely an understanding of noises, but even a taste and an enthusiasm for them. Our increased perceptivity, which has already acquired futurist eyes, will then have futurist ears. Thus the motors and machines of our industrial cities may some day be intelligently pitched, so as to make of every factory an intoxicating orchestra of noises.

I submit these statements, my dear Pratella, to your futuristic genius, and invite you to discuss them with me. I am not a professional musician; I have therefore no acoustic prejudices and no works to defend. I am a futurist painter projecting into an art he loves and has studied his desire to renovate all things. Being therefore more audacious than a professional musician could be, caring nought for my seeming incompetence, and convinced that audacity makes all things lawful and all things possible, I have imagined a great renovation of music through the Art of Noises.

LUIGI RUSSOLO
MILAN, 11 MARCH 1913

(Translated from the Italian by Stephen Somervell)

# Down with the Tango and Parsifal!

*Futurist Circular Letter to Certain Cosmopolitan Friends who Arrange Tango Tea Parties and Parsifalize.*

A year ago, responding to a questionnaire, I denounced the debilitating poison of the tango. This epidemic swinging gradually invades the whole world. It threatens to corrupt all races by gelatinizing them. We must therefore inveigh with full force against the imbecility of this fad and turn back the sheepish current of snobbism.

The ponderous English and German tangos are mechanized lusts and spasms of people wearing formal attire who are unable to exteriorize their sensibilities, and plagiarize Parisian and Italian tangos. They are copulated mollusks, who stupidly alter, morphinize and pulverize the felinity and savagery of Argentina.

To possess a woman one does not rub against her but penetrates her! A knee between the buttocks? It should be mutual! You will say, this is barbarism! All right then, let us be barbarians! Down with the tango and its languid thrills! Do you believe that it is exciting to look into each other's mouth and ecstatically relish each other's teeth like a couple of hallucinating dentists? Do you find it amusing to uncork one another to get a spasm out of your partner without ever achieving it yourself, or maneuver the pointed toes of your shoes like a hypnotized cobbler? It is like Tristan and Isolde who delay their *frissons* to excite King Mark. It is a medicinal dropper of passion, a miniature of sexual anguish, a sugared pastry of desire, lust in open air, delirium tremens, hands and feet of alcoholics, coitus mimed for the cinema, a masturbation waltz! Fie on this skin diplomacy! Hail the savagery of brusque possession and the fury of muscular, exalting and fortifying dance! Tangos are slow and patient funeral processions of sex that is dead! In the name of health, force, will power and virility we split on the tango and its superannuated enervations!

If the tango is bad, *Parsifal* is worse, because it inoculates an incurable neurasthenia with its floods and inundations of mystical lachrimosity. *Parsifal* is a systematic depreciation of life, a cooperative factory of gloom and desperation, an unmelodious discharge of squeamish stomachs, indigestion and heavy breath of virgins at forty, complaints of queasy and constipated old priests, sales in bulk and retail of remorse and elegant ennui for snobs. It is an insufficiency of blood, kidney weakness, hysteria, anemia and chlorosis! It is a brutalization of man in ludicrous progressions of vanquished and wounded notes, snorting of drunken organs, wallowing in the vomit of bitter leitmotives, tears and false pearls of Mary Magdalene sitting in décolletage at Maxim's, polyphonic purulence of the wound of Amfortas, lachrymose somnolence of the Knights of the Holy Grail and preposterous satanism of Kundry. Away with all that obsolete offal!

Mesdames et Messieurs, Queens and Kings of Snobbism, you owe absolute obedience to us, the Futurists, the living innovators. Surrender to the enthusiastic putrefaction of the crowds the corpse of Wagner, this innovator of fifty years ago, whose music, surpassed today by Debussy, by Strauss, and by our own great Futurist Pratella, no longer means anything. We will teach you to love the living, oh dear slaves and sheep of snobbism! And here is the most persuasive argument: It is no longer fashionable to love Wagner and *Parsifal*, played everywhere, even in the provinces, or to give tango tea parties like all the good petits bourgeois. So quit the mollifying dances and rumbling organ sounds. We have something more elegant to offer you! Tango and *Parsifal* are no longer chic!

F. T. MARINETTI
MILAN, 11 JANUARY 1914

(Translated from the French by Nicolas Slonimsky)


# Futurist Manifesto of Aeromusic

## SYNTHETIC, GEOMETRIC, CURATIVE

Our futurist temperament, accelerated by the dynamic quality of mechanical civilization, has attained a hypersensitivity thirsting after essence, speed, and trenchant decision.

Long declamations, hesitating analyses and endless trains of words-lamentations-and-bells die in boredom for the ears of those who are swiftly rising in the air.

The futurist movement, created by a synthesis of Italian innovators inspired with originality and speed, has taught and continues to teach the religion of speed, that is, the attempt to synthesize the world from above.

For, beyond all prosody, beyond free verse and outside the bonds of syntax, we have been able to obtain the synthesis and the synoptic simultaneity of unconstrained tables of words of a new poetry. Furthermore, we shall create a new futurist aeromusic whose law is synthesis—brevity beyond all music.

Music, by its very nature sensuous, enveloping, penetrating and persisting in the nerves after the fashion of a vapor or a perfume, tends towards analysis, while showing itself apt at summing up all the infinity of sensations in a stirring moment—thanks to its harmonic densities.

As futurist poets and musicians

a) We condemn music for music's sake which borders fatally on the fetishism of a set form, on virtuosity or technicism. Virtuosity and technicism have alienated Bach, Beethoven and Chopin from synthesis, and they have confined their genius in a maniacal pursuit of musical architecture and of music for music's sake, scattering and chilling the stirring ardor, the themes and the "finds" in the midst of tiresome development and depressing repetitions.

b) We condemn the custom of setting to music obsolete poems and subjects, the kind that composers, with their usual incompetence, are fatally bound to choose.

Only synthesis of free words can enable music to fuse with poetry.

c) We condemn imitation of classical music. In art, every return is a defeat, or disguised impotence. We must invent, that is to say, extract a personal musical emotion from life.

d) We condemn the use of popular songs, which has led spirits as perspicacious and cultivated as Stravinsky and most inspired talents, as Pratella and Malipiero, away from synthesis in an artificial and monotonous primitivism.

e) We condemn imitations of jazz and negro music, killed by rhythmic uniformity and the absence of inspired composers, long Pucciniesque lamentation asthmatically interrupted by slaps and by the syncopated tom-tom of railway trains.

Futurist music, a synthetic expression of great economic, erotic, heroic, aviational, mechanical dynamism, will be a curative music.

We shall have the following types of syntheses, which will enable us to live sanely in speed, to fly, and to win in the greatest war of tomorrow.

Sonorous block of feelings. Decisive crash. Spatial harmony. Howling interrogation. Decision framed by notes. The regularity of the air motor. The caprice of the air motor. Interpenetration of joyful notes. Triangle of songs suspended at a thousand metres. Musical ascension. Fresh fan of notes over the sea. Aerial simultaneity of harmonies. Anti-human and anti-impressionist expression of the forces of nature. Coupling of echoes.

Italian musicians, be futurists, rejuvenate the souls of your listeners by swift musical syntheses (not exceeding a minute), thunderously arousing the optimistic and active pride of living in the great Italy of Mussolini, which will henceforth be at the head of the Machine Age!

F. T. MARINETTI
MAESTRO GIUNTINI

(From the Italian monthly magazine, *Stile futurista*, August 1934)

# History of the Dalcroze Method of Eurhythmics

1ST PERIOD—GENEVA, 1903–1910
It was as a professor of solfège at the Conservatory of Geneva that Jaques-Dalcroze became interested in the difficulty his students had in singing accurately. In an attempt to correct this fault, he began to make them walk in rhythm. This formed the basis of the exercise known as "stepping the time-values" ("faire des pas") which has slowly developed into eurythmics.

It was in 1903 that the first "steps" were taken. In 1904 Dalcroze continued to improve and elaborate his exercises, although the refusal of the Conservatory to accept his ideas had forced him to give private lessons. In 1905 the Conservatory allowed him to give his first demonstration (15 April), and on the first of July he expounded the principles of his method before a Conference held at Soleure (VI Tagung der Schweizerischen Tonkünstler). In spite of this, official institutions still denied him their support, and he continued to give private courses, constantly attracting more and more pupils.

After frequent conferences and demonstrations, the study of eurythmics was introduced into the conservatories at Zurich and Basel (autumn of 1905 and spring of 1906).

The first summer class took place between 23 August and 8 September 1906, at Geneva, with 77 enrollments. It was followed by three more, also in Geneva: from 1 to 15 August 1907 (115 students); 1–15 August 1908 (130 students); and 2–16 August 1909 (140 students).

Meanwhile Dalcroze and several of his pupils were giving demonstrations outside Switzerland, and in 1907 a course of eurythmics was opened at Paris and at Brussels. The year 1907 also witnessed the first meeting of the Society of Eurythmics (Société de Gymnastique Rythmique) at Geneva.

In 1908 conferences and demonstrations took place in Berlin, Dresden, Munich, and Husum. In 1909 other courses were started and the demonstrations increased, including Paris, Heidelberg, and Vienna.

The method was launched. In 1910, at the beginning of the year, Dalcroze gave other demonstrations at Paris and Brussels, then in Berlin, Leipzig, and Dresden. As a result of this last visit he was offered the Institut de Dresde-Hellerau, so that he might have a place in which to put his theory into practice, and on 3 October Dalcroze and fifteen of his pupils left Geneva for Hellerau.

2ND PERIOD—HELLERAU, 1910–1914
Jaques-Dalcroze arrived in Dresden in October 1910, and it was in this city, at Ständehaus, that the first lessons were given. The cornerstone of the buildings of Hellerau was laid on 26 April 1911, and in November of the same year began a course in eurythmics. But it was in 1912 that Hellerau, garden city of Europe built by Germany's greatest architects, was fittingly dedicated. In June and July of that year the great Festival of Jaques-Dalcroze took place, with a musical program composed of Gluck's *Orpheus* and *Echo et Narcisse* by Dalcroze himself. It was a landmark in the history of the art: 4141 people came from Germany and other countries to take part in the celebration. The second Festival was held a year later. *Orpheus* was performed in its entirety, and more than 5000 people attended.

It is difficult to convey an impression of the brilliance of this period in the history of Hellerau. All the artists of Europe were there at one time or another, including such outstanding figures as Paul Claudel, Karl Storck, Bernard Shaw, Prince Wolkonsky (Director of the Imperial Theatres of Russia), Adolphe Appia, Nijinsky, as well as all the stars of Diaghilev's Ballet Russe, Max Reinhardt, and many others.

The history of eurythmics was not concentrated, however, at Hellerau. In 1913 alone, Dalcroze gave demonstrations in six cities of Germany and seventeen cities outside, while other professors were introducing his method in 36 other cities. Foreign governments sent commissions to Hellerau to study this new educational system. Dalcroze was invited to present his innovation at the International Congress of Physical Education at Paris; before the royal family of Belgium; and at the International Congress of Music Professors at Berlin.

In Europe and elsewhere the study of eurythmics was growing; 23 cities (9 countries) introduced it into their public schools, and 19 cities (7 countries) into their Conservatories of Music. There are Dalcroze schools in Berlin, Breslau, Budapest, Dresden, Frankfort, Kiev, London, Moscow, Nürnberg, St. Petersburg, Prague, Warsaw, and Vienna; and eurythmics is taught in 127 cities of the following countries: Germany, America, England, Austria, Belgium, Spain, Finland, France, Holland, Hungary, Italy, Poland, Russia, Sweden, and Switzerland.

The year 1914 marks the end of the splendid activity of Hellerau. On 4 February, Wolf Dohrn, the great organizer of the Institute, died as the result of a mountain-climbing accident. At the beginning of the year Jaques-Dalcroze had come to Geneva to direct the preparations for the great "Fête de Juin." The war came, and he never returned to Hellerau.

3RD PERIOD—GENEVA, 1915–1935

After several months of confusion, when all hope had been lost of reorganizing a center for eurythmics, the Institute of Geneva was finally opened (12 October 1915). In spite of the war, its enrollment for the first year included 397 pupils, representing 16 nationalities.

Everywhere there was a similar effort to keep the new movement alive. In Switzerland eurythmics was taught in fourteen cities, and included in the curricula of the conservatories at Berne, Basel, and Zurich.

In England there were 1392 pupils in March, 1916; and all during the war Dalcroze continued, in spite of the danger of crossing the Channel, to visit the English schools.

Although there was no large school in France at this time, there was a Club de Gymnastique Rythmique at 52 rue de Vaugirard, Paris.

In the United States instruction was now given in seven cities, beginning in 1915 with the first Jaques-Dalcroze Institute.

Sweden, Holland, and Russia continued the work and sent reports to Geneva. Each year one or the other of these countries distinguished itself by an increase in the number of students or by expansion into more and more cities.

In 1919 Geneva held its first postwar summer course, which has been followed by many others, and relations were renewed with Germany.

In 1926 the first Congrès du Rythme was held in Geneva, a huge demonstration which held out great hope for the future of eurythmics. In August of the same year was founded the International Union of Professors of the Jaques-Dalcroze Method. On this occasion the approximate number of pupils throughout the world was estimated at 22,700.

In 1927, Dalcroze was invited to Frankfort to give conferences and demonstrations at the International Exposition of Music. It marked his triumphal return to Germany, and the press welcomed him with great enthusiasm.

The United States announced in 1927 that 22 cities had courses in eurythmics; and in 1929 England counted 5574 pupils divided among 144 schools.

From 1915 to 1935 more than 125 demonstrations were given in Switzerland; from 1920 to 1935 Dalcroze gave more than sixty demonstrations in nine other countries.

Eurythmics can be said to exist in more than thirty countries, among which are South Africa, Germany, England, Australia, Austria, Belgium, Canada, Chile, Denmark, Egypt, Spain, United States, Finland, France, Greece, Holland, Italy, Ireland,

Japan, Lithuania, Morocco, the Natale, Norway, New Zealand, Palestine, Poland, Portugal, Russia, Sweden, Switzerland, Czechoslovakia, and Yugoslavia.

From 1915 to 1934 the Institute at Geneva had 7253 pupils, representing forty-six nationalities.

(From the *Association Jaques-Dalcroze* at Geneva)

# Society for Private Musical Performances in Vienna

(A STATEMENT OF AIMS, WRITTEN BY ALAN BERG)

The Society was founded in November, 1918, for the purpose of enabling Arnold Schoenberg to carry out his plan to give artists and music-lovers a real and exact knowledge of modern music.

The attitude of the public toward modern music is affected to an immense degree by the circumstance that the impression it receives from that music is inevitably one of obscurity. Aim, tendency, intention, scope and manner of expression, value, essence, and goal, all are obscure; most performances of it lack clarity; and specially lacking in lucidity is the public's consciousness of its own needs and wishes. All works are therefore valued, considered, judged, and lauded, or else misjudged, attacked, and rejected, exclusively upon the basis of one effect which all convey equally—that of obscurity.

This situation can in the long run satisfy no one whose opinion is worthy of consideration, neither the serious composer nor the thoughtful member of an audience. To bring light into this darkness and thus fulfill a justifiable need and desire was one of the motives that led Arnold Schoenberg to found this society.

To attain this goal three things are necessary:

1. Clear, well-rehearsed performances.
2. Frequent repetitions.
3. The performances must be removed from the corrupting influence of publicity; that is, they must not be directed toward the winning of competitions and must be unaccompanied by applause, or demonstrations of disapproval.

Herein lies the essential difference revealed by a comparison of the Society's aims with those of the everyday concert world, from which it is quite distinct in principle. Although it may be possible, in preparing a work for performance, to get along with the strictly limited and always insufficient number of rehearsals hitherto available, for better or worse (usually the latter), yet for the Society the number of rehearsals allotted to works to be performed will be limited only by the attainment of the greatest possible clarity and by the fulfillment of all the composer's intentions as revealed in his work. And if the attainment of these minimum requirements for good performance should necessitate a number of rehearsals that cannot be afforded (as was the case, for example, with a symphony of Mahler, which received its first performance after twelve four-hour rehearsals and was repeated after two more), then the work concerned should not, and will not, be performed by the Society.

In the rehearsal of new works, the performers will be chosen preferably from among the younger and less well-known artists, who place themselves at the Society's disposal out of interest in the cause; artists of high-priced reputation will be used only so far as the music demands and permits; and moreover that kind of virtuosity will be shunned which makes of the work to be performed not the end in itself but merely a means to an end which is not the Society's, namely, the display of irrelevant virtuosity and individuality, and the attainment of a purely personal success. Such things will be rendered automatically impossible by the exclusion (already mentioned) of all demonstrations of applause, disapproval, and thanks. The only success that an artist can have here is that (which should be most important to him) of having made the work, and therewith its composer, intelligible.

While such thoroughly rehearsed performances are a guarantee that each work will be enabled to make itself rightly understood, an even more effective means to this end is given to the Society through the innovation of weekly meetings* and by frequent repetitions of every work. Moreover, to ensure equal attendance at each meeting, the program will not be made known beforehand.

Only through the fulfillment of these two requirements—thorough preparation and frequent repetition—can clarity take the place of the obscurity which used to be the only impression remaining after a solitary performance; only thus can an audience establish an attitude towards a modern work that bears any relation to its composer's intention, completely absorb its style and idiom, and achieve that intimacy that is to be gained only through direct study—an intimacy with which the concert-going public can be credited only with respect to the most frequently performed classics.

The third condition for the attainment of the aims of the Society is that the performances shall be in all respects private; that guests (foreign visitors excepted) shall not be admitted, and that members shall be obligated to abstain from giving any public report of the performances and other activities of the Society, and especially to write or inspire no criticisms, notices, or discussions of them in periodicals.

This rule, that the sessions shall not be publicized, is made necessary by the semipedagogic activities of the Society and is in harmony with its tendency to benefit musical works solely through good performance and thus simply through the good effect made by the music itself. Propaganda for works and their composers is not the aim of the Society.

For this reason no school shall receive preference and only the worthless shall be excluded; for the rest, all modern music—from that of Mahler and Strauss to the newest, which practically never, or, at most, rarely, is to be heard—will be performed.

In general the Society strives to choose for performance such works as show their composers' most characteristic and, if possible, most pleasing sides. In addition to songs, pianoforte pieces, chamber music, and short choral pieces, even orchestral works will be considered, although the latter—since the Society has not yet the means to perform them in their original form—can be given only in good and well-rehearsed 4-hand and 8-hand arrangements. But the necessity becomes a virtue. In this manner it is possible to hear and judge a modern orchestral work divested of all the sound-effects and other sensuous aids that only an orchestra can furnish. Thus the old reproach is robbed of its force—that this music owes its power to its more or less opulent and effective instrumentation and lacks the qualities that were hitherto considered characteristic of good music—melody, richness of harmony, polyphony, perfection of form, architecture, etc.

A second advantage of this manner of music-making lies in the concert style of the performance of these arrangements. Since there is no question of a substitute for the orchestra but of so rearranging the orchestral work for the piano that it may be regarded, and should in fact be listened to, as an independent work and as a pianoforte composition, all the characteristic qualities and individualities of the piano are used, all the pianistic possibilities exploited. And it happens that in this reproduction—with different tone quality—of orchestral music, almost nothing is lost. Indeed, these very works, through the sureness of their instrumentation, the aptness of their instinctively chosen tone-colors, are best able to elicit from the piano tonal effects that far exceed its usual expressive possibilities.

At the first nine meetings, the following works were performed:

* At that time, every Sunday morning from 10 to 12, in the Society's small concert hall.

Béla Bartók, 14 Bagatelles, Op. 6 (twice)
Alban Berg, Piano Sonata, Op. 1
Claude Debussy, Two Song Cycles: Proses Lyriques (twice) and Fêtes galantes
(twice); Trois Nocturnes pour orchestre, arr. for 2 pianos 4 hands by Maurice
Ravel (twice)
Josef Hauer, Nomos in seven parts, Op. 1, and Nomos in five parts, Op. 2
Gustav Mahler, 7th Symphony, arr. for piano 4 hands (twice); Five songs from "Des
Knaben Wunderhorn" (twice)
Hans Pfitzner, Five Songs, Op. 26
Max Reger, Introduction, Passacaglia, and Fugue for 2 pianos 4 hands, Op. 96
(twice); Sonata for piano and 'cello in A minor, Op. 118 (twice)
Franz Schreker, Vorspiel zu einem Drama, arr. for piano 4 hands (twice)
Alexander Scriabin, Sonata for piano No. 4 (twice); Sonata for piano No. 7 (twice)
Richard Strauss, Don Quixote, Op. 35, arr. for 2 pianos 4 hands (twice)
Igor Stravinsky, Trois pièces faciles and Cinq pièces faciles pour piano à 4 mains
(twice)
Anton von Webern, Passacaglia for orchestra, Op. 1, arr. for 2 pianos 6 hands
Alexander von Zemlinsky, Four Songs, Op. 8

The following works are in rehearsal and are (among others) planned for performance:

Alban Berg, Vier Lieder, Op. 2
Julius Bittner, Sonata for piano and 'cello
Ferruccio Busoni, Six Elegies for piano
Gustave Charpentier, Poèmes Chantés, for solo voice and chorus
Claude Debussy, La Mer, 3 esquisses symphoniques, arr. for 2 pianos 4 hands
Fidelio Finke, Piano pieces
Egon Kornauth, Violin sonata
E. W. Korngold, Violin sonata, Op. 6
Gustave Mahler, 6th Symphony, arr. for piano 4 hands by A. von Zemlinsky
Viteslav Novak, Erotikon, piano pieces
Hans Pfitzner, Piano quintet in F minor, Op. 23
Maurice Ravel, Two Hebrew Songs
Max Reger, Suite for 'cello, Op. 131c; Sonata for violin and piano, Op. 139, Sonata
for clarinet and piano, in B minor, Op. 107
Franz Schreker, Kammersymphonie, arr. for 2 pianos 4 hands
Cyril Scott, Sonata for violin and piano, Op. 57
Richard Strauss, Symphonia domestica, Op. 53, arr. for 2 pianos 4 hands
Igor Stravinsky, Berceuses du chat, Chansons avec ensemble, Pribaoutki, Chansons
plaisantes
Josef Suk, "Erlebtes und Erträumtes," piano pieces; "Ein Sommermärchen," sym-
phonic poem arr. for piano 4 hands
Anton von Webern, "Entflieht auf leichten Kähnen," mixed chorus a capella, Op. 2
Karl Weigl, String quartet in E major
Alexander von Zemlinsky, Six Songs (Maeterlinck), Op. 13; 2nd String Quartet, Op. 15

Finally it should be mentioned that, in addition to the performances listed, there
were lectures and other meetings serving the purposes of the Society.
The financial means for accomplishing these ends were obtained in the following
ways:
1. Through the regular membership dues.
2. Through voluntary contributions over and above these dues.
3. Through occasional voluntary gifts from non-members.
Following are the official membership rates:

The weekly evening meetings of the Society count as concerts to which members subscribe for a season. The subscription rates for the selected category of seats may be paid in advance for the whole season, or in quarterly, monthly, or even weekly installments, although the member obligates himself to pay all the installments for a complete season. In addition, upon joining the Society and at the beginning of each season, introductory fees must be paid, their amount varying with the location of the seats.

There are four categories of seats. The least expensive (IV) cost 1 Krone a week; the next (III) 2 Kronen; the next (II) 3 Kronen; the first category is reserved for those who voluntarily pay more.

In accordance with these rates, membership dues are as follows:

| annually | | Payment in | | | | | |
|---|---|---|---|---|---|---|---|
| | | a) 52 Weekly Rates | | b) 12 Monthly Rates | | c) Quarterly Rates | |
| | | Introductory | Weekly | Introductory | Monthly | Introductory | Quarterly |
| | | Kr. | Kr. | Kr. | Kr. | Kr. | Kr. |
| 4th category | 60. | 8. | 1. | 6. | 4.50 | 6. | 13.50 |
| 3d    " | 120. | 16. | 2. | 12. | 9. | 12. | 27. |
| 2nd   " | 180. | 24. | 3. | 18. | 13.50 | 18. | 40.50 |
| 1st   " | 300. | 34. | 5. | 30. | 22.50 | 30. | 67.50 |
| or | 400. | 36. | 7. | 40. | 30. | 40. | 90. |
| or | 500. | 40. | 9. | 80. | 35. | 80. | 105. |
| etc. | | | | | | | |

This grading of dues was devised in order to share the considerable expenses of the Society equitably and in proportion to the ability of members to pay. It is naturally expected that those who are in a position to make greater sacrifices will avail themselves of the first two categories.

Upon joining this Society, members must fill in and mail the appended form, declaring knowledge of and willingness to abide by the statutes.

PRESIDENT: ARNOLD SCHOENBERG
16 FEBRUARY 1919

EXTRACT FROM THE STATUTES
4. Any person of honorable and unblemished character and willing to accept the regulations may become a member.
6. The members of the Society are obligated
   a) to further the aims of the Society and to avoid acts prejudicial to them.
   b) to pay membership dues for the current year, even in case of premature cessation of membership.
   c) not to injure the cause served by the Society.
8. The direction of the Society consists of
   a) the President, Arnold Schoenberg, the duration of whose tenure is not limited;
   b) a committee of from ten to twenty (chairman, secretary, etc.) chosen by the General Assembly in agreement with the President.
9. The President has a completely free hand in the direction of the Society. He decides upon the kind and amount of the expenditures necessary to the work

of the Society: fees paid to participants and the committee members specified in section 10, rental of halls, payment for lectures, administrative expenses, etc. He has also the right to remit wholly or in part the dues of worthy and needy members.

12. All decisions of the General Assembly, including elections, changes in statutes, dissolution of the Society, etc., require for their validity the consent of the President.

(Translated from the German by Stephen Somervell)


# What Is Atonality?

(A radio talk given by Alban Berg on the Vienna *Rundfunk*, 23 April 1930, and printed under the title *"Was ist atonal?"* in 23, the music magazine edited by Willi Reich, No. 26/27, Vienna, 8 June 1936)

*Interlocutor:* Well, my dear Herr Berg, let's begin!

*Alban Berg:* You begin, then. I'd rather have the last word.

*Int.:* Are you so sure of your ground?

*Berg:* As sure as anyone can be who for a quarter-century has taken part in the development of a new art—sure, that is, not only through understanding and experience, but—what is more—through faith.

*Int.:* Fine! It will be simplest, then, to start at once with the title of our dialogue: What is atonality?

*Berg:* It is not so easy to answer that question with a formula that would also serve as a definition. When this expression was used for the first time—probably in some newspaper criticism—it could naturally only have been, as the word plainly says, to describe a kind of music the harmonic course of which did not correspond to the laws of tonality previously recognized.

*Int.:* Which means: In the beginning was the Word, or rather, a word, which should compensate for the helplessness with which people faced a new phenomenon.

*Berg:* Yes, that, but more too: This designation of "atonal" was doubtless intended to disparage, as were words like arhythmic, amelodic, asymmetric, which came up at the same time. But while these words were merely convenient designations for specific cases, the word "atonal"—I must add, unfortunately—came to stand collectively for music of which it was assumed not only that it had no harmonic center (to use tonality in Rameau's sense), but was also devoid of all other musical attributes such as melos, rhythm, form in part and whole; so that today the designation as good as signifies a music that is no music, and is used to imply the exact opposite of what has heretofore been considered music.

*Int.:* Aha, a reproach! And a fair one, I confess. But now tell me yourself, Herr Berg, does not such a distinction indeed exist, and does not the negation of relationship to a given tonic lead in fact to the collapse of the whole edifice of music?

*Berg:* Before I answer that, I would like to say this: Even if this so-called atonal music cannot, harmonically speaking, be brought into relation with a major-minor harmonic system—still, surely, there was music even before that system in its turn came into existence. . . .

*Int.:* . . . and what a beautiful and imaginative music!

*Berg:* . . . so it doesn't follow that there may not, at least considering the chromatic scale and the new chord-forms arising out of it, be discovered in the "atonal" compositions of the last quarter-century a harmonic center which would naturally not be identical with the old tonic. . . . We already have today in the "composition in twelve tones related only to each other" which Schoenberg has been the first to practice, a system that yields nothing in organization and control of material to the old harmonic order.

*Int.:* You mean the so-called twelve-tone rows? Won't you tell us something more about them in this connection?

*Berg:* Not now; it would lead too far afield. Let us confine ourselves to this notion of "atonality."

*Int.:* Agreed. But you have not yet answered my question whether there does not indeed exist a distinction such as that implied in the word between earlier music and that of today, and so whether the giving up of relationship to a keynote, a tonic, has not indeed unsettled the whole structure of music?

*Berg:* Now that we have agreed that the negation of major and minor tonality does not necessarily bring about harmonic anarchy, I can answer that question much more easily. Even if certain harmonic possibilities are lost through abandonment of major and minor, all the other qualities we demand of a true and genuine music still remain.

*Int.:* Which, for instance?

*Berg:* They are not to be so quickly listed, and I would like to go into that more closely—indeed, I must do so, because the point in question is to show that this idea of atonality, which originally related quite exclusively to the harmonic aspect, has now become, as aforesaid, a collective expression for music that is no music.

*Int.:* No music? I find that expression too strong; nor have I heard it before. I believe that what the opponents of atonal music are most concerned with is to emphasize the implied antithesis to so-called "beautiful" music.

*Berg:* That view you take from me. Anyhow, this collective term "atonality" is intended to repudiate everything that has heretofore made up the content of music. I have already mentioned such words as arhythmic, amelodic, asymmetric, and could name a dozen more expressions derogatory of modern music: like cacophony and manufactured music, which are already half forgotten, or the more recent ones like linear music, constructivism, the new factuality, polytonality, machine music, etc. These terms, which may perhaps properly apply in individual special instances, have all been brought under one hat to give today the illusory concept of an "atonal" music, to which those who admit no justification for this music cling with great persistence, purposing in this single word to deny to the new music everything that, as we said, has heretofore constituted music, and hence its right to exist at all.

*Int.:* You take too black a view, Herr Berg! You might have been entirely justified in that statement of the case of a while ago. But today people know that atonal music for its own sake can be fascinating, inevitably in some cases— where there is true art! Our problem is only to show whether atonal music may really be called musical in the same sense as all earlier music. That is, to show, as you have said, whether if only the harmonic foundation has changed, all the other elements of former music are still present in the new.

*Berg:* That I declare they are, and I could prove it to you in every measure of a modern score. Prove above all—to begin with the most important—that in this music, as in any other, the melody, the principal voice, the theme, is fundamental, that the course of the music is in a sense determined by it.

*Int.:* But is melody in the traditional sense at all possible in atonal music?

*Berg:* Yes, of course, even vocal melody.

*Int.:* Well, so far as song is concerned, Herr Berg, atonal music surely does follow a new path. There is certainly something in it that has never been heard before, I would almost like to say, something temporarily shocking.

*Berg:* Only as concerns harmony: on that we agree. But it is quite wrong to regard this new melodic line as taking a path entirely new, as you declare, in comparison with the usual characteristics of melodic procedure, or even as never before heard and shocking. Nor is this true of a vocal line, even if it is marked with what someone recently described as intervals of an instrumental chromaticism, distorted, jagged, wide-spaced; nor that it thereby totally disregards the requirements of the human voice.

*Int.:* I never said that, but I cannot help feeling that vocal melody and melody in general does seem never to have been treated like that before.

*Berg:* That is just what I am objecting to. I maintain on the contrary that vocal melody, even as described, yes, caricatured, in these terms, *has always existed,* especially in German music; and I further maintain that this so-called atonal music, at least in so far as it has emanated from Vienna, has also in this respect naturally adhered to the masterworks of German music and not— with all due respect—to Italian bel-canto opera. Melody that is linked with harmony rich in progressions, which is almost the same thing as being bold, may naturally, so long as one doesn't understand the harmonic implications, seem "distorted"—which is no less the case with a thoroughly chromatic style of writing, and for which there are hundreds of examples in Wagner. But take rather a melody of Schubert, from the famous song "Letzte Hoffnung." Is that distorted enough for you? [Berg here gives further examples—from Schubert: "Wasserfluth," bars 11–12, "Der stürmische Morgen," bars 4–8, 15–18; and from Mozart, *Don Juan* in particular to show that even in the classics vocal melody may be constantly on the move, expressive in all registers, animated and yet capable of declamation—indeed, an ideal instrument.] But you will also see by these examples from the classics that it has nothing to do with atonality if a melody, even in opera-music, departs from the voluptuous tenderness of Italian cantilena—an element you will furthermore seek in vain in Bach, whose melodic potency nobody will deny.

*Int.:* Granted. But there seems to be another point in which the melody of this so-called atonal music differs from that of earlier music. I mean the asymmetrical structure of melodic periods.

*Berg:* You probably miss in our music the two- and four-bar periodicity as we know it in the Viennese classicists and all the romantics, including Wagner. Your observation is correct, but you perhaps overlook the fact that such metrical symmetry is peculiar to this epoch, whereas in Bach, for example, it is only to be found in his more homophonic works and the suites that derive from dance-music. But even in the Viennese classics, and especially in Mozart and Schubert, we observe again and again—and quite particularly in their most masterly works—efforts to break away from the restraints of this square symmetry. [Here Berg cites examples from *Figaro*.]

This art of asymmetric melodic construction developed still further in the course of the nineteenth century (just think of Brahms . . . "Vergebliches Ständchen," "Am Sonntagmorgen," or "Immer leiser wird mein Schlummer"), and while the four-bar period preponderates in Wagner and his followers (they clung to this earlier style-factor in favor of other innovations, notably in the harmonic field), even at this time there is a very clear tendency to give up the two- and four-bar form. A direct line runs here from Mozart through Schubert and Brahms to Reger and Schoenberg. And it is perhaps not without interest to point out that both Reger and Schoenberg, when they discussed the asymmetry of their melodic periods, pointed out that these follow the prose of the spoken word, while strictly square-rhythmed melody follows, rather, metrical speech, verse-form. Yet, as with prose itself, unsymmetrical melodies may be no less logically constructed than symmetrical melodies. They too have their half and full cadences, rest and high points, caesuras and bridges, introductory and concluding moments which, because of their directional character, may be compared with modulations and cadences. To recognize all this is to feel in them melody in the truest sense of the word.

*Int.:* . . . and perhaps even find them beautiful.

*Berg:* Quite right! But let us go on: This freedom of melodic construction is naturally accompanied by freedom of rhythmic organization. Because the rhythm of this music has undergone a loosening process—let us say through contraction, extension, overlapping of note-values, shifting of strong beats, as we see it quite particularly in Brahms—does not mean that the laws of rhythm are dispensed with; and the term "arhythmic" for this treatment, which after all represents just another refinement of the artist's means, is just as silly as "amelodic." This rhythmic treatment is particularly conditioned too by the multilinearity of the new music; we seem, indeed, to be finding ourselves in a time which very much resembles Bach's. For as that period, through Bach himself, wrought a change from pure polyphony and the imitative style (and the concept of the church modes), to a style of writing built on major-minor harmony, so now we are passing out of the harmonic era, which really dominated the whole Viennese classic period and the nineteenth century, slowly but incessantly into an era of preponderantly polyphonic character. This tendency to polyphony in so-called atonal music is a further mark of all true music and is not to be dismissed just because it has been nicknamed "linear structure."

*Int.:* Now I think we have arrived at a most important point.

*Berg:* Yes, at counterpoint!

*Int.:* Right! The essence of polyphony of course consists in the interordination and subordination of voices, voices, that is, which have a life of their own. Here again we are dealing with the harmonic aspect; I mean, the individual lives of all the voices give rise to a second, a new life, that of the collective sound. . . .

*Berg:* . . . which is of course not accidental, but consciously built and heard.

*Int.:* Now that is just what surprises me. Then is that elemental interplay of atonal voices, which seem to me to lack any such essential contrast as would give rise to a strong internal life, also achieved by conscious construction, or is it the play of some admittedly highly inspired chance?

*Berg:* That question—to be brief and not too theoretical—I can answer with a truth won from experience, an experience that springs not only from my own creative work but from that of other artists to whom their art is as sacred as it is to me (so anachronistic are we of the "atonal" Viennese school!). Not a measure in this music of ours—no matter how complicated its harmonic, rhythmic, and contrapuntal texture—but has been subjected to the sharpest control of the outer and the inner ear, and for the meaning of which, in itself and in its place in the whole, we do not take the artistic responsibility quite as much as in the case of some very simple form—as a simple motive or a simple harmonic progression—the logic of which is at once clear to the layman.

*Int.:* That explanation seems to me to make sense. But if so, it almost seems as though the word "atonal" must be a misnomer for this whole tendency in music.

*Berg:* Why, that's what I've been saying the whole time, trying to make it clear to you.

*Int.:* But then you, that is, your music, must somehow have some relation to the *formal* elements of earlier music too? If my guess is correct, this very music— the word "atonal" doesn't sound right after what we've said—strives to keep in close touch with older forms?

*Berg:* With form itself; and is it any wonder then that we should turn back to the older forms as well? Is this not a further proof of how conscious contemporary practice is of the entire wealth of music's resources? We have just seen that this is the case in all serious music. And since this wealth of resources is apparent in every branch of our music simultaneously—I mean, in its harmonic development, in its free melodic construction, in its rhythmic variety, in its preference for polyphony and the contrapuntal style, and finally in its use of all the formal possibilities established through centuries of musical development— . . . no one can reproach us with our art and tag it as "atonal," a name that has become almost a byword of abuse.

*Int.:* Now you have made an important declaration, Herr Berg. I am somewhat relieved, for even I thought that the word "atonal," whencesoever it came, had given rise to a passing theory foreign to the natural course of musical development.

*Berg:* That would suit the opponents of this new music of ours, for then they would be right about the implications which really lie in the word "atonal," which is equivalent to anti-musical, ugly, uninspired, ill-sounding and destructive; and they would furthermore be justified in bemoaning such anarchy in tones, such ruination of music's heritage, our helpless state of deracination. I tell you, this whole hue and cry for tonality comes not so much from a yearning for a keynote relationship as from a yearning for familiar concords—let us say it frankly, for the common triads. And I believe it is fair to state that no music, provided only it contains enough of these triads, will ever arouse opposition even if it breaks all the holy commandments of tonality.

*Int.:* So it is still sacred to you, after all, good old tonality?

*Berg:* Were it not, how could such as we—despite the skepticism of our generation —maintain faith in a new art for which Antichrist himself could not have thought up a more diabolical appellation than that word "atonal"!

(Translated from the German by M. D. Herter Norton)


# Letter from Arnold Schoenberg on the Origin
# of the Twelve-Tone Method of Composition

DEAR MR. SLONIMSKY:
The "Method of composing with twelve tones" had many "first steps" (*Vorversuche*). The first step happened about December 1914 or at the beginning of 1915 when I sketched a symphony, the last part of which became later the "Jakobsleiter," but which never has been continued. The Scherzo of this symphony was based on a theme consisting of the twelve tones. But this was only one of the themes. I was still far away from the idea to use such a basic theme as a unifying means for a whole work.

After that I was always occupied with the aim to base the structure of my music *consciously* on a unifying idea, which produced not only all the other ideas but regulated also their accompaniment and the chords, the "harmonies." There were many attempts to achieve that. But very little of it was finished or published.

As an example of such attempts I may mention the piano pieces op. 23. Here I arrived at a technique which I called (for myself) "composing with tones," a very vague term, but it meant something to me. Namely: In contrast to the ordinary way of using a motive, I used it already almost in the manner of a "basic set of twelve tones." I built other motives and themes from it, and also accompaniments and other chords—but the theme did not consist of twelve tones. Another example of this kind of aim for unity is my "Serenade." In this work you can find many examples of this kind. But the best one is the "Variationen," the third movement. The theme consists of a succession of fourteen tones, but only eleven different ones, and these fourteen tones are permanently used in the whole movement. With lesser strictness still I use the tones of the first two measures in "Tanzszene."

The fourth movement, "Sonett," is a real "composition with twelve tones." The technique is here relatively primitive, because it was one of the first works written strictly in harmony with this method, though it was not the very first—there were some movements of the "Suite for Piano" which I composed in the fall of 1921. Here I became suddenly conscious of the real meaning of my aim: unity and regularity, which unconsciously had led me this way.

As you see, it was neither a straight way nor was it caused by mannerism, as it often happens with revolutions in art. I personally hate to be called a revolutionist, which I am not. What I did was neither revolution nor anarchy. I possessed from my very first start a thoroughly developed sense of form and a strong aversion for exaggeration. There is no falling into order, because there was never disorder. There is no falling at all, but on the contrary, there is an ascending to higher and better order.

ARNOLD SCHOENBERG

Hollywood, California
3 June 1937

# Letter from Anton Von Webern

ANTON VON WEBERN
MARIA ENZERSDORF
BEI WIEN, IM AUHOLZ 8
AUSTRIA

14 January 1937

MUCH ESTEEMED MR. SLONIMSKY:

Your friendly letter with enclosures brought me very special joy. To realize that you have taken the trouble of making my music accessible to children and that you have actually *succeeded* in doing so gives me uncommon satisfaction and real consolation. That you used my own score to arrange it for children is a friendly thought on your part, and it makes me happy that the notes that I have written appear on the Children's Page, dedicated specially to children.* Yes, it is true that if the so-called adults, the grown-ups, had as few prejudices as children, then everything would be quite different.

I am glad to give you the dates of composition of my 5 *Orchesterstüke* Op. 10, which you want. I wrote, in the years between 1911 and 1913, with long interruptions, about twenty pieces, as expressions of musical lyricism, and selected five of them to include in opus 10. The dates of composition of these five pieces are 28 June 1911, 13 September 1913, 8 September 1913, 19 July 1911 and 6 October 1913. The first performance of these pieces took place at the Festival of the International Society for Contemporary Music in Zürich on 22 June 1926, under my direction. I am very much interested in the book on modern music that you are writing.** Do you need more dates about my works? I hope to hear from you again soon, and I salute you most cordially.

Yours,<br>ANTON VON WEBERN

* In 1936, Slonimsky reproduced in its entirety No. 4 of Op. 10 containing only six bars, with an upbeat, in 3/4 time, on the Children's Page of the *Christian Science Monitor*, and arranged it graphically, with the pictures of the instruments used in the score—clarinet, trumpet, trombone, mandoline, celesta, harp, snare drum, violin and viola—drawn next to the clef.

** This book was the first edition of *Music Since 1900*, published in 1938.

# Gebrauchsmusik and Gemeinschaftsmusik

(From a letter to the author from B. Schott's Sons, dated Mainz, 16 June 1936)

The word *Gebrauchsmusik* seems to have come into use in the postwar period. It is hard to define its meaning exactly. With the mechanization of music through radio and gramophone, with the increasingly organized musical life in Germany, and also owing to political circumstances, many composers, some on their own initiative, some because they were commissioned, began writing music for special purposes. The most obvious examples were compositions for the radio and musical illustrations for films; in brief, all compositions which called for no independent value in themselves but served only a special use (*Gebrauch*). When the expression *Gebrauchsmusik* was first used it is not possible to establish. It is not an official description, such as might head a section of a catalogue; its opposite would be art music, concert music, absolute music.

With *Gemeinschaftsmusik* the case is somewhat different. The postwar trend towards a polyphonic style gave rise to a new type of musicmaking, cultivated especially by the youth, and distinguished from the customary orchestral style in that every voice has an importance of its own, i.e., all voices are equal, forming a new *Gemeinschaft* (community) in which new joy is found. This was true not only of instrumental music but also of all sorts of vocal music or the combination of both. In this connection we speak of "activating" the listener; as distinguished from the old "middle-class concert life," the main emphasis in the new youth is put less on listening to compositions written for the concert hall than on making music themselves. Correspondingly, it is no longer the virtuoso who plays the leading role, but the group, the community. This group arose, as we said above, out of the spirit of the new music itself and would not have been possible had not the composers of the day been turning always further from the romantic style, back to the *Spielmusik* of the middle ages and of the eighteenth century.

As a leader of modern music Hindemith was probably the first important composer to write for these purposes. He published such compositions under the title of *Das Neue Werk* in 1927 [Schott], so that it is justifiable to regard this time as approximately the birth-hour of the concept of *Gemeinschaftsmusik*. The expression must have been first used in Schott's catalogue about this time.

We understand that in the United States *Gemeinschaftsmusik* is translated by "sociable music." We no longer use this expression in our catalogues but speak instead of *Sing- und Spielmusik* (music to be sung and played), which seems to correspond better to the spirit of the music than the former term. We believe that the word *Gemeinschaftsmusik* went out of fashion with the political turn in Germany in 1933, perhaps because it came into being in the era just preceding.

# Letter from George Bernard Shaw

4, WHITEHALL COURT (130) LONDON, S.W.1.                    2nd September 1936
PHONE: WHITEHALL 3160.
TELEGRAMS: SOCIALIST, PARL-LONDON.

DEAR SIR,
Within my lifetime there has been a complete liberation of modulation from its old rules. All the composers, great and small, have now availed themselves fully of this.

New modes have been tried, like the whole-tone (or organ tuner's) scale of Debussy; and the obsolete modes have been played with a little. But all this music was in terms of some tonality or other, however sudden and frequent its modulations and transitions might be. And the harmonic practice was so free that the scale became a 12 note scale with nothing of the old tonality left but a keynote. Still, as long as there was a keynote there was no fundamental difference between Bach and Richard Strauss.

Schönberg tried to get loose from the keynote by writing pieces in listening to which you could not guess which was to be the final chord, because there was no tonal cadence. The revolutionary young composers rushed in at this new game and dropped key signatures; so that their scores were a mass of accidentals; but Schönberg exhausted the fun of this and relapsed more and more into tonality. This drift is apparent in all the big composers now. It is hard to say that the symphonies of Sibelius are in this key or that; but when we come to know his symphonies by heart as we know those of Mozart and Beethoven they will appear as tonal to us as Elgar's.

In short the post-Wagnerian anarchy is falling into order as all anarchies do pretty soon; and I expect soon to hear the Wagnerian flood of endless melody getting embanked in the melodic *design* of Bach and Handel.

Faithfully,<br>G. BERNARD SHAW

Nicolas Slonimsky Esq.
238 Hemenway Street
Boston
Massachusetts
U.S. America.

# Letters from Charles E. Ives

WEST REDDING
CONNECTICUT
14 JULY 1929

DEAR MR. SLONIMSKY:

Last Spring Henry Cowell told me that you had been kind enough to ask for a score of mine which your orchestra* might play. I should have written before but have been laid up for some months back and haven't been able to attend to things— even correspondence; and also was not sure I could get anything ready by next fall, as all of my scores are for larger orchestras. But I have one** which I got out the other day and played for Henry Cowell who liked it and thought it should be played, and could be, with some revisions reducing it to the chamber group. The 1st and last movement lend themselves quite readily, but the 2nd which has some old "brass-band and town-tune" things in it, has a considerable brass part. But, I remember, this (in part) was first played by a theater orchestra as a kind of topical march. They made it go quite well with only a cornet and trombone,—a piano taking off the rest of the brass. So, I think, it can be brought down with the help of a piano part. At any rate I'm going ahead with it on this basis and should have it ready to send you in September. I am glad to do this anyway and you must not feel at all obligated to play it. You may not like it, and even if you do, you may not think it advisable or practicable to present—that will be quite alright. This score was written quite some years ago and won't loosen up much of a modern "sword-swallower"—but the subject matter I feel justifies its existence. It has some colloquial spots which the older generations of New Englanders (including mine) will get. But please feel perfectly free to do whatever you think best with it.

I have heard with pleasure that you and your organization are making a valuable contribution to music and to Boston. I wish I could hear it and also am very anxious to hear some of your music. I'm glad *New Music* will publish some of it soon.***

Henry Cowell left last week for California, after spending a few days with us. You will like to hear his experiences abroad, especially in Russia. He is a courageous "advance guard" all in himself. I tell him he is a better ambassador than some of our more famous ones.

Hoping to have the pleasure of meeting you before long, I am with best wishes,

Sincerely yours,
CHAS. E. IVES

* The Chamber Orchestra of Boston.
** *Three Places in New England.*
*** *Studies in Black and White* for piano published by New Music Quarterly in its October 1929 issue.

164 EAST 74 STREET
NEW YORK
29 DECEMBER 1929

DEAR MR. SLONIMSKY:

The copy of the score* is being photographed and will be sent you this week. I hope you may like it. It adapted itself more readily than I supposed to the smaller orchestra. There are some places where the woodwind may be too heavy for the number of strings—for instance, at the end of the 3rd movement there is a rather mean, off-rhythm, inner part for the oboe, which may be omitted, letting the oboe play along with the trumpet on the main tune—there were originally 3 trumpets here. However, do anything you think best.

There will be a pianist and in the middle movement an extra drum player to be engaged, if you decide to play it; and I shall want to take care of this and any other extra expense that you may be put to in playing it. I would also appreciate it if you will have the parts copied in Boston and get some careful person to correct them and send me the bill.

I hope you have been well and that your work is going along successfully.

I am, with best wishes for the New Year,

Sincerely yours,
CHAS. E. IVES

* *Three Places in New England.*

164 EAST 74TH STREET
NEW YORK
16 JANUARY 1930

DEAR MR. SLONIMSKY:

Thank you much for your letter. I greatly appreciate what you say and that you feel the music* is worth playing. It doesn't seem right that you should be placed in so much uncertainty about carrying on the concerts**—it is work that should not be circumscribed. The Boston Symphony Directors ought to lend more of a hand, if only from their sense of duty to music in Boston (we won't say from their sense of music). However, anything that's any good, works out slowly—usually, I suppose.

I was very sorry not to go to your concert Sunday, but I have not been able to get out at all recently. Was glad to see that the critics were favorably impressed—and I hope you felt the same way.

Your comment in the Boston *Evening Transcript* is very interesting and so well put. It seems to me that Paul Rosenfeld's interest in words is keener than his judgment of music. Probably I ought not to say that as I know very little of the music he talks about. Something I read of his some years ago rather gave me that impression. When you come to New York again I hope to have the pleasure of seeing you.

I am, with kind regards,

Sincerely,

CHAS. E. IVES

* *Three Places in New England.*
** With the Chamber Orchestra of Boston, founded by Slonimsky in 1927.

164 EAST 74TH STREET
NEW YORK
8 FEBRUARY 1930

DEAR MR. SLONIMSKY:

Henry Cowell telephoned us this morning, that you will come down for the rehearsals on the 16th. It is good of you to do so. Mrs. Ives and I would like very much to have you stay with us while you are here and we hope you can and will come as soon as you can before Sunday and stay over the weekend at least.

Looking forward to your visit I am, with best wishes.

Sincerely,

CHARLES E. IVES

164 EAST 74 STREET
NEW YORK
FEBRUARY 1930

BIOGRAPHY OF CHARLES E. IVES:

Born in Danbury, Conn. U.S.A., Oct. 20, 1874. Studied with his father, who was a music teacher and bandmaster. Played, as a boy, in the town bands and churches. Graduated from Yale College in the Class of 1898; while in college took the courses in music under Prof. Horatio W. Parker; Organ master, Centre Church, New Haven, Conn., 1892–98; Organ master and Director of Music, Central Presbyterian Church, New York to 1902. Entered business in 1898. Member of the firm of Ives & Myrick, 46 Cedar St., New York.

(See over for "nice" music)

For smaller orchestra or chamber music:
1. Theater or Chamber Orchestra Set
2. 2nd movement for *Holiday* set (strings, 1 horn, 1 flute, bells)
3. 1st Violin Sonata
4. 3 Pieces for Trumpet and Piano
5. Movements from 1st and 2nd Piano Sonatas
6. Book of 114 Songs

For larger orchestra:
7. 4th Symphony; 2nd movement published by New Music Edition, San Francisco
8. 1st Orchestra Set, *Three Places in New England*
9. 2nd Orchestra Set (no name)
10. *Decoration Day* (from *Holiday* set)
11. *Fourth of July* (from *Holiday* set)
12. Orchestra & Chorus: *Lincoln, the Great Commoner*

DEAR MR. SLONIMSKY:

I must write just a line to tell you what a fine time I had yesterday—it was quite a memorable occasion, for us, at least. It was good of you to come. Mrs. Ives and I will expect you in 2 weeks; we would like to have you stay with us while you are here—but you must do whatever is most convenient for you. You must be here part of the time, at least—and all the time if you can. We want you to feel free to come and go as you would in your own home.

I can't write as I would like to, the lame hands make it hard.—So good-bye for a short while.

Sincerely,
CHAS. E. IVES

You left your baton here. It feels rather ethereal so I won't mail it for it may be broken—unless you want me to.

DEAR MR. SLONIMSKY:

We are very glad you will be with us. Don't trouble to telephone, but come right up—we are not going out.

I think Henry Cowell told you that both his and my things were accepted by the committee*—you did it as far as my music was concerned.

Sincerely,
CHAS. E. IVES

* The Pan American Association of Composers, which sponsored Slonimsky's concerts in New York and in Europe.

DEAR MR. SLONIMSKY:

I was sorry to miss you last week—I found your letter here upon getting back Saturday. We got out to hear Henry's concerto with the Conductorless Orchestra. It was strongly stimulating and carried us high in many places—will tell you more about it when I see you which I hope will be soon. Was glad to hear that the date for the concert next year has been arranged.* Please let me know whenever I can do anything in the matter. Will send along the suggested songs as soon as I can get to it.

Yours sincerely,
CHARLES E. IVES

* 10 January 1931, in New York.

DEAR MR. SLONIMSKY:

We are up here now for the summer—and so I'm afraid we missed you again in New York—but Mrs. Ives and I hope you may find it convenient to come down here and will be, but we expect to be here right along. It's too bad you won't be in France this see us some time this summer. I suppose it's too early to know just what your plans summer—you see how the virtuous sins of committees and men (assuming committees are men) throw their "long shadows o'er innocent humanity." * But we won't be cast down by this particular Inter-Rational Committee—and they may see Casey driving his own hearse some day! Personally I put it up to the Republican Party of ours—it's just one of the many hard-boiled, old-lady, soft-stuff things they are responsible for. They kept us out of Geneva—and you can't blame Europe much for wanting to keep us out of everything—except their hotels.

I wrote to Dr. Goldberg** saying I was mailing the book of songs to him—but as I looked for one to wrap up, I found there were no complete copies here—only those that I'd cut single copies from—so some of the pages are missing—but not many. I will send him one of these now and a complete copy later—as soon as I can get hold of one. I think next fall I'll get some more printed, perhaps adding some others.

Sincerely yours,
CHAS. E. IVES

* Slonimsky had some difficulties in traveling with his Russian passport before he became a citizen of the United States in 1931.

** Isaac Goldberg (1887–1938), American writer who planned to do an article on Ives.

WEST REDDING
CONNECTICUT
30 MAY 1930

DEAR MR. SLONIMSKY:

Our letters crossed—I guess. I'm glad the ring is cleared for the first bout. I don't know that I'm much qualified to give suggestions, but will do the best I can. The original plan that you and Henry Cowell had of giving 3 things and repeating them is by far the best. From what I hear from all sides—especially from the ears that have been most of their lives fed on the consonant heritage—is that a long program of modern pieces leaves them confused and tired—which is a bad thing for them (and the music) and all concerned. A short program they get better—sometimes!

When you come to New York in June perhaps you can run up here, but if you haven't the time I can come to New York for a day and meet you—I have to go down every so often. Do whatever you find most convenient. With best wishes, I am

Sincerely,
CHAS. E. IVES

WEST REDDING
CONNECTICUT
8 JUNE 1930

DEAR MR. SLONIMSKY:

We're very glad you will make us a visit—it will be fine to have you here. It won't do you any harm to get away from the routine, Boylston Street and city noise. This is a good place to rest if you feel like it or to work if you feel like it or to meditate or all three at once. Bring some old clothes and your bathing suit—on a hot day you may like to dive into "My Little Pool" (but it has nothing on yours).*

We're a little uncertain about the last part of June—we may have to be away for a few days—but how about the first week in July—or if more convenient for you the second week. Suit yourself—only be sure to come.

There used to be a way of getting down via Boston, Albany and Pittsfield and down the Housatonic River—but probably the best way to come down is the main line to South Norwalk, and we will meet you there. If you are to go to New

York first, there are several good trains up here—we're about 60 miles from New York.

I didn't have in mind so much scaring away the "gentler part" of the audience, by the quality of the program (they will have to stand for that) as by the "quantity." If they get too much they go home groggy.

Have just gone through the book of songs and will mail it today. Some of the pages are gone. I can't seem to find any more whole copies.

Sincerely,
CHAS. E. IVES

\* Reference to Slonimsky song *My Little Pool*.

WEST REDDING
CONNECTICUT
6 SEPTEMBER 1930

DEAR MR. SLONIMSKY:

Thank you for sending the magazines. Your "conductorless conductor" philippic is fine\*—and a swinging comment on the history and evolution of this species—his rise and fall—rather his ups and downs. Though I doubt if he is any more to blame than most of the lady patrons! When you say "some conductors have mastered the art of beginning and stopping with the orchestra"—you made "some hit off"—Mark Twain could do no better.

It was fine to have you here with us—we enjoyed your visit exceedingly—both the old and young generation—you project yourself generously into each. We hope to see you here again before long—come anytime, only let us know 2 or 3 days before, so we can be sure to be here. We are thinking of making a few days family visit up the state. Don't let the arranging of the songs take up any time you need for other work—do it entirely at your convenience—there's no hurry.\*\*

Sincerely yours,
CHAS. E. IVES

\* Slonimsky's article on conductors and conducting in the magazine *Plain Talk*, published in the fall issue of 1930.
\*\* Ives asked Slonimsky to orchestrate the accompaniment of some of his songs.

QUEBEC, CANADA
OCTOBER 1930

DEAR MR. SLONIMSKY:

Your letter came when we were leaving. We didn't intend as much of a trip as this but Mrs. Ives seemed pretty much tired out with the long job of housekeeper, chaffeur, nurse and general caretaker—and needed a rest. We will probably stay around here until the latter part of the month, depending on how we feel and will probably stop over for a little family visit at Williamstown, Mass. on the way back. I'm sorry not to be more certain as we want to see you in Redding again. But if that isn't possible will hope to see you in New York the first part of November. Will write when our plans are more certain.

This city is the cliff, the country about and the waters in the river all seem beautiful to us. Looking at the inscriptions on the monuments and all the children only 2 years old and speaking French—make us feel in a foreign land—and we are. We went to the old English church this morning. The "Plain Chant" and canticles, sung by everybody in unison, each one making a little music of his own to Mr. Tallis—may stand as a point of departure into collective composing—and the universal "Lyre." I'll now stop this and say good night.

Sincerely yours,
CHAS. E. IVES

DEAR MR. SLONIMSKY:

We're back from the North Pole.* I was about to write that we were to stay on here longer when a water shortage came along and it looked as if we would have left to New York before this—and may have to any day now. If you are down there next week or so, please call up the house (Butterfield 5449)—if we're not there, perhaps you can run up here—if you don't mind drinking skimmed milk and washing in the dew. Telephone here is 43-5 Redding. At any rate I'll let you know as soon as we get to New York.

I want to thank Dr. Goldberg for his article in the Mercury.** Mrs. Ives and I appreciated it greatly. He has a way of putting things that is not common to most writers of music criticism, or to writers in general for that matter. We hope that we may have the pleasure of meeting him before long.

How are you and how are things going? If I can do anything about the concert,*** please let me know.

Sincerely,
CHAS. E. IVES

* Ives had just returned from a trip to Quebec.

** *The American Mercury,* edited by H. L. Mencken, of which Isaac Goldberg was a regular contributor.

*** The concert of the Chamber Orchestra of Boston in New York, scheduled for 10 January 1931.

WEST REDDING
CONNECTICUT
23 NOVEMBER 1930

DEAR MR. SLONIMSKY:

Our letters crossed, I think—and probably you didn't get mine before leaving for Washington. We fully expected to have had to leave for New York last week, but just after writing, a three days' rain came, and the spring is up and we're going to stay here until after Thanksgiving. Will be at 164 West 74 on December 1st, and shall hope to see you there soon after. Mrs. Ives and I want you to stay with us when in the city and we hope you can.

As I remember you thought to start rehearsals about December and so think it just as well to send the enclosed now.*

Thank you much for sending the Phonograph Monthly article—you hit things off —and make that which may be somewhat uninteresting to the general reader, interesting to him. We will have to work out some plan this winter to have your orchestra make some records—through a company, if they'll undertake it—if not, we'll go it alone.

We've had an exciting day—a new grandniece, a fight with a polite skunk, and in between—Sir Jim Jeans which Mrs. Ives has been reading to me.

Sincerely yours,
CHAS. E. IVES

* A substantial check toward expenses connected with the New York concert of the Chamber Orchestra of Boston, scheduled for 10 January 1931.

DEAR MR. SLONIMSKY:
If it isn't too late, this might be put in the first paragraph* after "in 1914": "it was arranged, by the writer's request a while ago, for chamber orchestra." It won't do any harm to have people know, if only by a slight inference, that you aren't afraid to ferret out a nonentity and do the unpopular thing etc. You're the only conductor that ever asked me to do anything. This score would never have gotten off the shelf, if it hadn't been for you.—Come down soon.

Sincerely,
CHAS. E. IVES

* In Nicolas Slonimsky's program notes on *Three Places in New England,* performed for the first time by Slonimsky and his Chamber Orchestra of Boston in New York on 10 January 1931.

164 EAST 74 STREET
NEW YORK
26 DECEMBER 1930

DEAR MR. SLONIMSKY:
Thank you for your card and letter and enclosures. It seems to me there is no particular hurry in having the notice of the "repetitions" printed. Henry will be here Sunday and I'll find out how he feels about it. Personally, I should just say that these will be separated and let it go at that—with possibly a paragraph to the effect that as these 3 things happen to be made to a great part of new materials etc., in general structure, rhythm, harmony etc., which may not be easy to get on the first hearing, they are repeated. Also, I don't know that we ought to assume if a listener stays to hear something repeated it is a sign of his approval—it may be just the opposite—or at least a willingness to give it another chance. Radio: Art and business all hitched up together. 91%% (I like to be precise) of all radio and phonograph records—are "sebaceous cysts," and soft ones at that—and they sell—though if a 3-year-old is always fed candy for breakfast he will always be a 3-year-old—and the oatmeal market will die. The letter from the Victor Co.—"all commitments are made by themselves" —unnecessary statement!—just look at them, g— d— soft-headed lists!—94%% "ta ta" stuff. However, in a day or so, I'm going to see how we can get in touch and at least take a crack at both the ether and Victor. Please don't worry about the concert— either the business part or wrong-note part. Hope to see you soon.

Hastily,
CHAS. E. IVES

164 EAST 74 STREET
NEW YORK
30 DECEMBER 1930

DEAR MR. SLONIMSKY:
Yours just at hand. Take out the oboe, by all means, in 1st–2 measures, p. 27 before letter H; these notes were originally for a 2nd flute (ad lib.)*
At letter O, p. 39, do as you think best. Perhaps if the violins and piano could pound the waltz out somewhat it might do—I used to find if 2 countertunes in about same register were played by 2 brass instruments the contrast was sometimes lost. However, the quality of the trumpets seems different today than when I played one. But do anything in this or other places you think advisable. Will see you tomorrow—

come right up—if convenient—but come up anyway. Will let you know about the repetition notice** as soon as I see Henry. He has not come yet.

Sincerely,<br>
Chas. E. Ives

* Slonimsky conducted the first performance of *Three Places in New England* in New York on 10 January 1931, with his Chamber Orchestra of Boston, composed of Boston Symphony Orchestra players with one of each of the wind instruments.

** Slonimsky proposed a program of three pieces by American composers to be played twice, at the beginning and at the end of the concert, so as to give the audience a second chance to become acquainted with the unfamiliar American idiom, but eventually it was decided not to do so.

164 EAST 74 STREET<br>
NEW YORK<br>
5 JANUARY 1931

DEAR MR. SLONIMSKY:

Henry is back, looking strong for action, after a very successful turn in Havana.

We are looking forward to seeing you here. The radio plan looks more possible. Will tell you all about it on Wednesday.

Am sending the enclosed * right on so you can deposit in your account before you leave. The records will be made alright—Victor** or Vanquished notwithstanding.

Hastily,<br>
Chas. E. Ives

* A personal check towards expenses for Slonimsky's European trip.
** The Victor Recording Company.

164 EAST 74 STREET<br>
NEW YORK<br>
26 FEBRUARY 1931

DEAR MR. SLONIMSKY:

I'm glad you have a pain in the throat and not in the heart—but if you had it would be quite alright. I'll learn you how to give a cuss word a good "vita propria."

We are glad you'll be down next week and will expect you. Remember you have the right key, not a strange key in your pocket.

Now here is an important job for you. Mrs. Ives wrote today to Mrs. Prof. Kingsley Porter about the Paris concerts, asking her and his help, saying that you would call her up and try to see her—we hear they are going abroad shortly. They live at Elmwood, Cambridge, in the old James Russell Lowell house. Prof. Porter is connected now with Harvard.

Sincerely,<br>
Chas. E. Ives

WEST REDDING<br>
CONNECTICUT<br>
8 MAY 1931

Mons! Mon Dieu!—Mon' Lisa—Bon Ami (not the mild sapolio)—Bon Soir—Cher—Chez—French is a too violent language for me—no *good* cuss words—I understand it perfectly (when it's translated).

I hope attending to so many difficulties etc. at one time won't tire you all out, and that the managers will do their part. A friend of mine who is gradually getting interested in American music (seeing that article of Henry's started it*) and may be of substantial help later—suggests that programs, notices etc. be put in "steamers" sailing from New York to France between now and June.** Your manager, he says, can get in touch with the "pursers" etc. sailing for Cherbourg—and also that notices be distributed to the hotels etc. However this is not advice—do anything you think best. Don't worry too much about the situation (that's good advice which I hate to have anyone give me—g— d——)

If not too much trouble please have a dozen or so programs and notices sent to me as soon as possible—as we have heard of a few friends who are going abroad this month.

Now that you are a regular Yankee,*** you will spit through your teeth, talk through your nose, cuss between syllables and let 'em "learn you" in Paris how to compose real American stuff. Our best wishes to you.

Sincerely,
CHAS. E. IVES

* A reference to an article by Henry Cowell, entitled (amazingly enough), *Four Little Known Modern Composers: Chávez, Ives, Slonimsky, Weiss,* published in the ephemeral magazine *Aesthete,* New York, August 1928.
** Slonimsky's Paris concerts took place on 6 and 11 June 1931.
*** Slonimsky received his American citizenship papers in April 1931.

WEST REDDING
CONNECTICUT
28 MAY 1931

DEAR MONSIEUR—BEAUCOUP!

We were glad to get your letters. Both came this A.M. It's 'most mail time—and just a line, so it will catch tomorrow's boat.

That's quite alright about Varèse. I don't blame him for wanting something new played. Have arranged with the Chase National Bank to cable their Branch Office in Paris a credit of $250 to you, which you can draw on by your personal check whenever you need any. Do whatever is necessary to be done, please, and don't worry. Nobody can read by Roman Candles. I agree with Henry that now you are over there, there's no need of hurrying back if there are things that can be done—for instance, the English concert. And if there isn't enough left to carry out the work, let me know. The concert will go alright. Just kick into the music as you did in the Town Hall—never mind the exact notes or the right notes, they're always a nuisance. Just let the spirit of the stuff sail up to the Eiffel Tower and on to Heaven. Never mind the ladybirds, male and female, in the audience—they're dear and nice—or the cuffs—they never should be worn.* But you are a good boy.

I hope you can get in enough rehearsals, and if you can't, do it anyway and we will fix it up somehow. Don't bother with mine too much because it is harder—the others won't get any too much rehearsing.

I think probably it is advisable to put at least one notice in the leading papers; they do a lot for music and a lot against it.

Hastily,
CHAS. E. IVES

* Slonimsky complained that the cuffs of his shirt in full dress kept sticking out during the concert.

WEST REDDING
CONNECTICUT
12 JUNE 1931

DEAR "VERY GOOD EDDIE":*

We much appreciated your thought in sending the cables.** I sent the long one on to Henry. All I can say is that you are a good boy—with or without cuffs.*** Mrs.

*1327*

Ives is rejoicing to know and so am I that your courage, genius and character are receiving recognition and appreciation. You had a hard job—music-wise, other-wise and business-wise—and rather heavy responsibility. I hope all the composers will realize what you have done for them. To the public, a composer can say, no matter how it goes "my music *is* what it is"—regardless of what Geo. says—but a conductor has to break it into the existence of others—some of whom are "nice-pussy-boys"—ta-ta—some job! We wouldn't have been much surprised if the "Françoises" had hung a "blot" on the "Amerricaine." I wouldn't have blamed them much if they had—to my way of thinking "these U.S." during the last 10 years or so politically, and otherwise have been backward in coming forward. If Wilson had been running things—"bigger" things would have gone on. Your cables indicate that the French have been quite open and fair-minded—thanks to you to a great extent. The "old gals" over here ( I mean music critics—I often get them mixed up) are pretty soft under the "ears"—some, at least, are.

I hope now you can "let down" a little and get in some vacation days. It will be fine to see you again, but I hope you feel justified in staying as long as you want. How about the English and other concerts?

Please give my thanks to Varèse for all he has done. I hope his music went well and was appreciated. The enclosed **** is but a mark of respect between one citizen and another. When I see that so many get too much for doing so little (Josie Hoff-"frau",***** for instance) and you nothing for doing so much, then I like to have a hand in the opposition. I hope you had enough to get by on. If convenient, will you save me a dozen or so program notes.

What do you think of trying to make a few records?

Kindest greetings to your mother and you from all of us.

Sincerely,
CHAS. E. IVES

* A colloquialism current in the 1920's meaning "a good guy," popularized by Jerome Kern's 1915 musical of that name.

** Reporting his Paris concerts of American music.

*** Slonimsky had trouble with the cuffs of his full-dress suit which kept sticking out in the sleeves when he conducted an agitated passage.

**** A substantial personal check.

***** Josef Hofmann.

WEST REDDING
CONNECTICUT
10 JULY 1931

DEAR COLUMBUS ET VESPUCCIUS:*

We understand you continue your Voyage of Discovery and take sail again soon. But Uncle Deac, your "rustic" friend, says there are some things that should not be discovered in America—so don't bother—discover only a new move in chess—and, we hope, Redding. Will you stop here on your way to Boston or come down later? We expect to be away late in August till perhaps around the second week in September. Do whatever is convenient—but we all want to see you.

The papers, notes, etc., just at hand.** Your accomplishment has been remarkable. It is fine to have those estimates of your work and the rest. The French writers seem to listen and think more carefully than many do over here—we have too much snap judgment—without the "snap."

Philip Hale has it in for the American moderns—says they are just trying to pull same stuff as European moderns are, etc., etc. The thing seems to me not only unfair but it is not by any means all the truth—and half-truths are more insidious than an "honest lie." He says your program should have been much finer: E. B. Hill, Loeffler, Deems Taylor, and Arthur Foote. He forgets all about Vick Herbert and Carrie

Bond, also Richard Wagner and Puccini. Well—your trunk will contain evidence enough to smother that "nice old lady." * * *

Henry is much pleased with your success and says he hopes to have you conduct some concerts in California this fall. If there is anything I can do, let me know. The enclosed is just to be on the safe side (not towards the sofa).* * * *

There is much to talk with you about, but I will have to stop here—my hands and arms have been bothering again* * * * *—it's hard to handle a pen—but the meanest part is not to be able to play the piano when I want. However—am better now than I was last week.

With cordial greetings and congratulations,
Yours sincerely,
CHAS. E. IVES

* Reference to the opening paragraph of an article in the Paris publication *Le Canard enchaîné* by André Cœuroy, entitled *Découverte de l'Amérique*: "Nous venons, sans blague, de découvrir l'Amérique, grâce à un Christophe Colomb qui, parti de Russie, est allé à Boston recueillir pour nous des témoignages authentiques de la création musicale américaine. Ce Christophe Colomb s'apelle Nicolas Slonimsky."

* * Reports and reviews of Slonimsky's Paris concerts of American music given on 6 and 11 June 1931.

* * * Philip Hale, music and drama editor of *The Boston Herald*, published on 7 July 1931 an editorial article entitled *Mr. Slonimsky in Paris,* in which he wrote: "Nicolas Slonimsky of Boston, indefatigable in furthering the cause of the extreme radical composers, has brought out in Paris orchestral compositions by Americans who are looked on by our conservatives as wild-eyed anarchists. Are these Parisians to be blamed if they say that the American composers thus made known to them are restless experimenters or followers of Europeans whose position in the musical world is not yet determined?"

* * * * A substantial check.

* * * * * Ives suffered from a severe diabetic condition and a muscular tremor.

WEST REDDING
CONNECTICUT
18 AUGUST 1931

DEAR MR. SLONIMSKY:

Thank you very much for the program note. Mrs. Ives and I think it is excellent—and one of the best things you've done. You "get in 'em good." The enclosed is just about as you had it, with a few corrections in details—one about Prof. Parker—whom I don't want to be unfair to. Parker seldom got horrified or mad, usually he'd just "smile" and not say much, sometimes he'd get a little bothered or puzzled.*

Well, we think of you and Miss Adlow** (who "was" and "is") with a very great and deep satisfaction. It's really a source of happiness to us, to think of you both—and of your new life.

In the "Barn dance" let 'em git it going—no pretty tones and long bowing. I think one violin (off stage) *pppp* plays in "off part" with the song, will be best. Hope you can make out my unclear writing. I'm quite ashamed of it.

Greetings, to you both,
CHAS. E. IVES

* Slonimsky wrote in his program note that Horatio Parker, with whom Ives studied at Yale University, was "horrified" by unresolved dissonances in the music Ives submitted to him.

* * Slonimsky married Dorothy Adlow, art critic of *The Christian Science Monitor*, in Paris, on 30 July 1931, with Varèse as best man.

DEAR COLUMERICA:

You're back, I guess, about now from shooting the buffalo—with robes and scalps.° And if not—it's quite alright, too. I hope you had a satisfactory time and found Henry well and sitting on the end of his summer symphony, loafing.

We came up here for a boat ride. It seems great to us to get back to this wilderness, a log cabin and living with the moose again. And we're staying longer than we expected.

Am sending the enclosed according to your instructions. Some Tombstone inscriptions°° and pieces, to be or not to be played, and a "face." And when I look at it, I apologize. When is a man, not a man? Answer: When he has his picture taken. However, this is the last picture I'll ever have taken. So I'll stop talking.

We all send best wishes to you both, and shall hope to see you both soon. Will probably go back sometime next week.

As ever, Sincerely,
CHAS. E. IVES

° Slonimsky was conducting in the West in the fall of 1931.
°° Biographical data requested by Slonimsky.

DEAR MR. AMBASSADOR,°

As I learn that this is my birthday, I will celebrate by sitting down in a moderately comfortable chair and writing you. As you know, birthdays should be either forgotten or celebrated—I always do both—it's far better—for what.

We are wondering how you both are. We greatly appreciated the letter from your wife—and her art articles. They are extremely interesting, so clearly thought and beautifully written. It is a comment on the ways of the layman—and human nature (in her "Art and Publicity")—the congenital habit of man, "thinking for himself," after the "nice" teacher has told him *what* to think for himself—and his art of enjoying something he never can enjoy. I hope your plans for the work abroad are coming on as you want, and as soon as there is anything I can do, you will let me know. Last week Ich hatte, morgen früh ein froelich blatt (one of the best words in the English language) vom liebe Heinrich er sagt°°—that (and you probably have already heard) the Berlin Philharmonic Orchestra to give two concerts of American music, and you are to conduct one of them and the regular German conductor the other— why don't you do both! Henry was here on the day before he sailed. He seemed quite in sympathy with your foreign plans—and also said that, thanks to you the San Francisco concert was more of a success than usual and I hope you felt the same. We will be in New York before long—depending on how far the thermometer and water goes down—probably around the first part of November and we hope to see you there and to have the pleasure of a visit from you both—all of my family want to be most kindly remembered to all of your family.

Sincerely,
CHARLES E. IVES

° A Paris reviewer referred to Slonimsky as the American ambassador of music.
°° Ives' own brand of German. "Heinrich" is Henry Cowell.

WEST REDDING
CONNECTICUT
17 NOVEMBER 1931

DEAR AMERICAIN:

As you see we're still here, the weather holding up and some warm days staying around, kept us longer than we expected. But we expect to go to New York next week—probably not later than the 20th and we hope you and Mrs. Slonimsky can come down to see us soon.

We have lots of things to talk over—and cuss about. No, I remember I've turned over a new leaf (page 7), and have locked all the best cuss words in the cellar closet and thrown the key down the well.

The new circulars are good ones. I'd like a few more, to send to some philistines, though it will probably make some bellow. My arms have been bothering again, and I can't write or play much and I'm sour. So good-bye.

Hoping to see you both soon,

Sincerely,
CHAS. E. IVES

I had a letter from Robert Schmitz, who is going to be in Paris after the first of the year, and who says he will be glad to play the piano at the Paris concerts. He knows that set of mine which I gave to you (a semi-piano concerto). Schmitz is well known in Paris—he's a friend of Monteux and has played with him. He's also the discoverer of Milhaud. How's that soft-seat Koussevitzky, the lily? Is he still bothering you and hornswoggling the puritans?

164 EAST 74 STREET
NEW YORK
JANUARY 1932

DEAR N.S.A.*—this doesn't mean "no swearing allowed" nor "no silence aloud,"

I had a long talk with Henry the day after you left. I told him what I told you about the "Rhythmicon" situation as I had got to thinking about it after our meeting—and we went into it from all angles. It relieved my mind to know especially that the new one would really be nearer to an instrument, than a machine. There will be a "lever" that can readily change the "tempo" with pedals and also the "tones" etc. It wasn't so much the question of having another made—as I think it ought to—it will be improved, transported, and studied on—but the main question is whether it is yet time to present it at Paris—and if so how is the best way to do it. Henry feels as I do about that—and after the demonstration at the New School for Social Research next Tuesday we can know better how to do it. I sent the remitted check to Mr. Theremin yesterday—and he's started the building. It will be yours and Henry's—I just want to help—and sit under its "shadow" on a nice day.**

I was glad to hear that you feel better about the 3 other pieces of mine at the Paris concert. Good, clear parts are made. It can be put like this: Three Pieces for (Large) Orchestra: I. *The Cage,* II. *The 4th of July,* III. *An Elegy.* Hoping to see you soon.

Sincerely,
CHAS. E. IVES

* The initials stand for Nicolas Slonimsky Adlow (Dorothy Adlow-Slonimsky).
** The "Rhythmicon" was constructed by Leon Theremin in New York, at Henry Cowell's specifications. Cowell wrote a special piece *Rhythmicana* for it, but it was too late to be used at Slonimsky's second series of concerts in Paris, given on 21 and 25 February 1932.

DEAR N.S. AM. AMBAS!

I felt very, *very* badly in not seeing you again that time in New York. I was just about in the end of one of those g— d— low sloughs, when a man can't be anything and doesn't know it—couldn't eat, sleep, think, or even cuss moderately!

We have been in Westmoreland living "slow with the sheep." The lakes and mountains and country are beautiful. We admire the English ways. When they get run over, they smile and say sorry ( C# → B♭ ) to the taxi driver!

Our plans are indefinite—but are going to Germany (and will see Henry) and probably to France. I will write a long and a nice letter to you soon—when I can lose the vibrato.*

I appreciate deeply all you have done, your interest, help and above all your friendship—which will last through Eternity even to the day after the "4th of July." **

I am glad to report that I am much better than I've been for sometime. You see, I have a remarkable doctor in New York (he's no good when you're sick)—but when I told him on leaving that I was going to take a pint of ale every night he said—"Don't do that—remember, three pints a day keep the doctor away—and drink good ale when you can." He was quite right. Eat, drink and be merry, for tomorrow we live on Main Street.

Sincerely,<br>
CHAS. E. IVES

* Ives had increasing difficulties handling the pen, but insisted on writing in longhand to friends.
** Title of Ives' symphonic piece, from the *Holidays* set.

DEAR MR. SLONIMSKY:

To play the "Washington B.D." * in New York as you propose seems to me much Have you ever been in "Zwitzerland?" Well—I have!—for a month! And we think the best! I hope the players don't give too much trouble—or flat tires. seriously of staying on till 1974.** We are in a little place just out of the village— nobody around but 2 goats and this "young frau." *** Traveling doesn't seem to agree with us, and we may stay here for some while—perhaps go to Italy later.

Sincerely,<br>
CHAS. E. IVES

* *Washington's Birthday*, from Ives' *Holidays* set, which Slonimsky conducted and recorded for the New Music Records.
** Ives was born in 1874.
*** Mt. Jungfrau.

Remembrance to you both from this family. Best wishes for the New Year and many of them—but of course, not too many! We are in this country of great beauty —living in a little stone hut, on a side hill overlooking the Ionian toward the boot of Italia. We hope to stay here till Spring. We hear you did heroic work at the last concert against the opposition of the Union and "Premature Comment" girls.*

It is much appreciated. You see I'm getting so I can write (almost nice) and will send you a nice long letter soon, writin' regular.

CHAS. E. IVES

* Slonimsky was to conduct a concert in New York sponsored by the Pan American Association of Composers on 1 November 1932, but there were difficulties with the Musicians' Union, and the concert had to be postponed until 4 November. However, the New York Evening *Sun* published a disparaging account of the event in its issue of 2 November 1932, two days before it took place.

TAORMINA, SICILY
5 FEBRUARY 1933

IO TE SALUTO SIGNORE!

"Buona Bonaparte di Batone"—and you are a good boy, even if you shoot old ladies in the elbow. You have been doing great work—and the Los Angeles battle was an extraordinary feat—a literal triumph for you. I'm glad they speak of your courage as well as your genius—Questo mi piace—and all the family who read with enthusiasm the tributes to your Napoleonic Forelock,* your rostrumic authority, your imagination, to say nothing of your "Riding master" ability. That article "An Old Lady Gets 3 Shots" etc. is one of the best of its kind we have ever seen.** José Rodriguez writes as though he were writing to get something off his chest and not to fill up a newspaper column. In spite of its ploy of comedy, it is convincing and dignified: of a man who thinks, and thinks for himself, and a literary "something" besides. Everybody in Boston aged over 38 years 6 months ought to read it***— but "Parlo troppo presto!"

It can't be long now before you get a permanent job with some big orchestra, I hope in the East—you've done so much for practically nothing—it makes me mad —and Mrs. Ives too. "Mi dia una hatto!" **** Though many a true word lodges in the teeth and though it's a long road that has no saloon, thou'll be there, with Aurora!—Non posso aspetto tanto!! ****

It was good to know that the Pan American concert has been arranged for the 1934 Italian Festival—"Guggenheim" or not, you will have to be there—even if we have to train a nice eagle to fly you over. "Vogliamo anche un salotto"—when you're there—"Swatta di woppo, non troppo!"

We are here on a side hill of lemons and oranges—have you been in Sicily?— that is, early in the morning?—The sun comes out of Greece over the Ionian sea— which is quite alright and then a nice breeze over Calabria, brings it to your eye —but with it lemons, and madamigelle on the other eye! "Mi mandi un barbiere alle otto!" But this is a place of great beauty—and we can lead a quiet, "peasant" kind of life, which agrees with us. When the sun shines it is as our June—when not, it is like "Election Day" and Republicans! It is the color "buono mollo"—in everything and everywhere that makes up scenery here. There are many artists here—no musicians. "Lo voglio molto forte!" Will probably stay here until the first part of March or so, and then go to some of the Italian cities for a while and may sail back from Naples—or possibly, a boat to England and back that way—"desidero un sigaro forte." When you write again it would be best to mail to our London address, the Guaranty Trust Co., 50 Pall Mall.

EX LIBRIS—SCRIPTOR ROMANUS
401 B.C.

"Signore, io te saluto—ancora e ancora!"

* A woman reporter in California said that Slonimsky had a "Napoleonic forelock."
** José Rodriguez published in a local magazine a review of Slonimsky's Los Angeles concerts of December, 1932 under the title "Old Lady Gets Three Shots in the Arm," the old lady being the Los Angeles Philharmonic and the three shots being Ives, Cowell and Slonimsky.
*** Slonimsky was 38½ years old when he conducted his Los Angeles concerts.
**** Samples of Ives' own brand of Italian.

DEAR "NAP"—CON FORELOCK: *

Thank you very much for your letters—which we all enjoyed. We wanted to see more of Italy—but traveling around, hotels, etc. don't seem to agree with me somehow. So we came more directly on to England. Will stay here, "quiet and slow" until we sail—probably in July.

I hope things are going forte with you. When do you get back from Russia and are you going there? Is Russia a musical nation—like Italy—I mean is Russia a musical nation?—or do they like nice voices? I hear from Henry occasionally—he is now in California and says that America *is* a musical nation (out there). I didn't intend to get this old subject in this letter—but an article in an English paper this morning—"Are we a musical nation?" brought it—I am sorry. There is nothing in a musical nation—not even music! for a nation is only a nation—but a good cigar is et al!

It seems a long time since we've seen you—and it is. I hope next year things will work out better for all of us. Just now it seems a bad time for "carrying on" the work—all armies are apparently out of breath and supplies—but another year we must resume.

Yours as ever,
CHAS. E. IVES

P.S. Am not sure, but think before leaving I told you that in cleaning house preparatory to being away so long, I found several of the old scores, etc.—from which some of the songs were taken—I had forgotten some of them or thought they were not kept—so before arranging any songs it would be better to wait until we can get together again and look over these manuscripts. I also found some other things—or parts of them—that might do for short, chamber pieces, some of only 4 or 5 instruments—among them was a set of half-dozen pieces called "Cartoons," "A 3 minute Yale-Princeton Football Game," "Gyp the Blood & Hearst!" (which is worst?) "The Gen. Slocum Disaster," "Mike Donlin at the Bat," "Central Park in the Dark," etc. Some of them are topics of "those days," but why not!—"D.K.E. & ΦU," "Yale Campus," "Calcium Light Night." When we get back will have Hanke** copy what he can—they were mostly in lead pencil, some rather indistinct—I think you will like some of them. One thing, they won't take much rehearsal and only a very few players. I'm looking these over. I was impressed with this—that I now have good advice for young composers—"If you write anything you think is good, copy it out in ink" and "If you write anything you think is no good, copy it out in ink!"

Auf wiedersehn—but not yet "good-bye"—and if you go to Russia come back before sunset—for it's long since we've seen you around the table.

* A reference in a Los Angeles newspaper review which said that Slonimsky's forelock was Napoleonic.
** Ives' regular copyist.

DEAR PATER-FAMILIAS!

The new message this morning was received by all the Ives family with enthusiasm—we send warmest congratulations to her father and mother—and also to Electra! *—may good health (even in the 1st tooth) be hers—may she live in happiness and not behold tragedy—except over the footlights! We were just about to write—in fact, Mrs. Ives had pen in hand—to see if Mrs. Dorothy Adlow and Mr. Nicolas

Slonimsky could not come and see us over the Labor Day Holidays—but Electra steps in—as "Generations and Destiny" have done before—but won't it be possible for you to run down sometime before long? It has been far too long since we've seen you. Just let us know 2 or 3 days ahead—and we can meet you either in Bridgeport (Bridgeport is better for most trains) or South Norwalk if you come from Boston. We have been settled in America for a few weeks, gradually getting our bearings on household Penates back into place. Have seen no one yet but the family etc., though have heard from Henry Cowell and Carl Ruggles—they're both well—one seething, and one cussing.

Well—as soon as the family situation warrants your departure, please come down and see us in Redding—there's a new Eddington book—a new hammock and some mice—(not nice) moth-eaten scores, old and sore, for you to look at. Give our love to the baby and the mother—and keep some for the "Ole man—Papa!"

Ever yours,<br>
Chas. E. Ives

* Electra Slonimsky was born in Boston on 16 August 1933.

WEST REDDING<br>
CONNECTICUT<br>
1 NOVEMBER 1933

PADRE BON APPETITO DI ELECTRA! *

We were glad to get your letter and know that the family keeps well—that Electra thrives under you as "Dispenser of Rations" speaks well for her "toleration!"

To be in Mr. Birchard's catalogue is more of an honor to *me* than to him—that is, I consider myself the honored one—as he is the only American publisher, as far as I know, who has published music he believed should be published, yet knowing it would bring him certain loss and the ridicule, or at best a "nice smile" from the trade. Please, tell him how much I appreciate his interest. You told him, I presume, that we wanted parts engraved and he should include this in the amount.**

We expect Henry up for a day soon—next to N.S. he is the busiest man in New York.

A letter from Mr. Aaron Copland says he is writing an article about my songs for "Modern Music" and I am sending him some of those old manuscripts (photos) to help him get the facts straight, etc.

Chas. E. Ives

* Infant daughter of Slonimsky, who occasionally took care of her feeding.
** Slonimsky arranged with the C. C. Birchard Co. of Boston to publish *Three Places in New England,* with Ives paying for the engraving and other expenses in full.

WEST REDDING<br>
CONNECTICUT<br>
4 NOVEMBER 1933

DEAR PADRE:

I am answering your 3 letters "to once"—2 came yesterday and one this morning. I don't know exactly what to say about the score. The estimate is somewhat more than I had thought of "laying out" just at the present time.* The score, of course, will have to be engraved—but would this other process in making the parts, come out just as clearly as the engraved parts? ** Also, another point that I've heard about through Henry's troubles and others, is the question of "performance fees." It apparently often means a law suit and prevents performance. Henry says Stokowski returned a score recently saying that the Philadelphia Orchestra would not pay fees, etc. I would be willing to make any business arrangement that Mr. Birchard would suggest, so that "performance fee" could be cut out. If this can be done, I think I might as well go ahead and have the score made, on the estimate in letter. Also please ask them to let me know a few days in advance when payments are to be made.

I greatly appreciate your willingness to help me correct the proofs. I can't see that green-white proof paper. Can't find a score here but have one in New York. Our best to family,

Ever yours,<br>
CHAS. E. IVES

Have extra pencil—I revert to it—can steer it with less vibrato than pen.

° The arrangement with the Birchard Co. was that Ives would pay for the engraving and printing of the score and parts of *Three Places in New England.*

°° Slonimsky had suggested photographing parts individually from the score.

WEST REDDING<br>
CONNECTICUT<br>
5 DECEMBER 1933

DEAR PADRE:

I would have written before but have been somewhat out of shape for the last few weeks, and am still kept on "my back" most of the time—to much "ritin', talkin', playin' and cussin'," they say.

Thank you much for what you have done, and also Mr. Birchard. Am sending the enclosed check for $200 on account.

Am not sure I'd make any changes in the score—the drum part at beginning of the second movement, I wrote that way, so the "down beat" bass drum, would go along as they play it on main beats, not after beats. On Page 27 think it might be easier for drum and piano to play as it is written, or both ways might be printed—would also keep 2nd viola here. There are 2 or 3 places (short phrases only), when it might be better for horn than trumpet. But I will look it through again in a few days and write more. Generally speaking, I don't like to change anything after once finished. But you may be right.° We can tell better when we see the proofs.

It was fine to hear that Mrs. Slonimsky had such a success in Pittsburgh. We do hope to see you both—wrong—you 3, soon after we get to New York. But we may stay here till after Christmas. Our love to Electra and you all. As ever,

Sincerely,<br>
CHAS. E. IVES

Please excuse paper, pencil and ritin'. As you see there is no "tremolo" with nice pencil. The enclosed was sent me by an unmusical friend and you may like to see it. Needn't send back.

° Slonimsky had made several suggestions for uniform notation in various parts of the score of *Three Places in New England.*

WEST REDDING<br>
CONNECTICUT<br>
12 DECEMBER 1933

DEAR PADRE:

You are a good boy to take so much trouble over the score.° Most of the ways you suggest are advisable I think. The work looks well done—I will start today to go over the proofs, etc. and will get them back in a week or so.

I meant to have written you before, but forgot to say that Mrs. Ives says she will get you a copy of the Kodak picture for the "Transcript" ° °—if you can't get it from "Modern Music"—and that is none of my business to remark upon!

Ever yours,
CHAS. E. IVES

° *Three Places in New England.*
° ° Slonimsky was writing an article on Ives for the Boston *Evening Transcript.*

WEST REDDING
CONNECTICUT
16 DECEMBER 1933

DEAR N.S.P.

I've started in on going over the proofs—and I ran right into a "mess" that I thought was straightened out when Hanke made the parts. In all the strings mostly I, II and Viola, there should be some consistent way of showing when they play together and in parts. I asked Hanke to both "down and up" stems on all strings (except Bass) unless there were long passages of a page or more where there is only one part, then just one stem would do, if "unis." or "a due" or "non div." or some indication to that effect, was put. I will do the best I can to straighten these out, but it will take a little time. You will probably know the best way to make it clearest to the players. There are also mistakes I didn't correct, for instance on p. 2—note tied to another, but a dot over 1st note which of course is impossible. I am sorry to give you and the engraver so much trouble—but it's better to get it right now—even if it takes longer—and there is no hurry anyway.

Another point: As there is no staff for tuba at beginning of movements, there should be some note to indicate to conductor that tuba plays only when separate staff occurs. I haven't a tuba part here. The old score that had this was cut up and pasted when the photo-copy was made. I think you have the tuba copy I made from that. Haven't had time to cover all the points in your "questionnaire" but will in a few days and will then send.

Your conductor's note is "well put"—for some conductors it will be a help and others it will (according to what I hear of some conductors)—it will mix them up so they will "sidestep" the whole job—it will make others "sour."—If used, I think it better than sent out when parts are asked for—or sent only to conductors that I'd send it to just as it stands, but there are others who I wouldn't like to have think (as it came ostensibly from me) that I underrate their intelligence—for instance Goossens. The last paragraph, as it stands, would seem to doubt one's ability to learn something new ("unable" could be the word). However, we can decide about that later. There are very few, if any, conductors with your "gifts"—I think most of them could not learn to beat 2 ups, and if they try to, would make things worse. I sent your copy of conductor's note to my brother's office to have a copy made, and will send it back with one or 2 suggestive changes.

Ought to get the proofs here corrected and back to you in a week or so. I hope my corrections etc., can be made out, I have used lead pencil, as my pen wobbles so. With our best to all the family,

Yours as ever,
CHAS. E. IVES

WEST REDDING
CONNECTICUT
19 DECEMBER 1933

DEAR PADRE:

Mrs. Ives has been expecting to go down and do some Christmas shopping, but hasn't for one reason or another. She wanted to get something for Electra's first

Christmas—something that she (Electra) would be willing to have in her wardrobe—or has she already started her library? So we are sending the enclosed—and it may be just as well—as Mater (not Padre) will know better what will be the things for her.

Haven't been able to do much on the proofs yet*—have had a few off days—but will get the first movement back to you soon—also questionnaire etc.

But we send our kindest remembrances, with care and affection to you "three."

Ever yours,
CHAS. E. IVES

* Of *Three Places in New England,* in the process of publication by the C. C. Birchard Co. in Boston.

WEST REDDING
CONNECTICUT
24 DECEMBER 1933

DEAR N.S.P.:

Electra's Christmas letter is a poem—and so is her signature. May her first New Year's be a happy one and may she have many nice ones, but not too nice!

The newspaper clipping with a list of composers, etc.—didn't mention Henry Cowell and made us sore, and we were about to burn it up when a fine and illuminating article came to our eye—by a Boston lady—Dorothy Adlow* (you will remember seeing her in Paris, I think)—so it went into our archive and not the fire.

Am about to send you the proofs of the first movement—all corrected—sometime. There are many minor things as stems, bows, etc. which I should have fixed before sending to engraver. They may kick about the extra work, I'm making them and I wouldn't blame them. Am sending a check for Birchard Co.—please ask them to let me know what the balance is, after January 1st and I'll settle the 2nd week in January and will hope to see you. Will let you know definitely later. We then can go over everything, notes etc. before final printing.

Sincerely,
CHAS. E. IVES

* Mrs. Nicolas Slonimsky, art critic of *The Christian Science Monitor.*

WEST REDDING
CONNECTICUT
26 DECEMBER 1933

More—Proofs, etc.

1) Stems, bow marks, etc. for div. strings—(my fault—thought this had been done when parts were made)—as there are already so many double stems (up and down)—might be better to do this all through instead of "unis."

2) Last measure p. 19—have put 2nd Cello part in 1st Bass (this is better I think—sometimes a Cello sounds too loud and scratchy down there).

3) Would have title and name only on cover and title page and not in very large print.

4) On page 15—would put metronome at 80 as 72 seems too big a jump from preceding.

5) p. 17—metronome marks changed a little.

6) p. 19—bottom corner—date in very small print (1911). Henry thinks all dates should go in.

7) p. 14—memo over RH piano in small print suggesting—2 players ad lib.

8) Opposite p. 19—(last music page of I)—would put verse (program) in small print—would have these programs at end and not at beginning of movements. Rather not feature the programs etc. before the music.

9) Think that whatever conductor's instructions should go in a note printed on separate sheet and be sent out when parts are sent and not in score. I think your "note"

1338

about beating the 2 rhythms is excellent and well put, even as it stands, if it got before men of your genius, brains and courage—but where are they? Most conductors, if they should be told to beat 2 together would fall over in a nice-looking swoon and give up the whole job—and it gives them another excuse for not playing anything. The 2 slight revisions I've made, would make it more optional and not sound quite so much as if I were laying the law down. And from some experience, asking most men to do a new way, only makes them do it worse.

There are 2 or 3 other points that might go into conductor's note—for instance, about playing the piano at places—optional 2 players and when also, way of playing end of the third movement, holding ff chord till *sordini* are put on, etc. Also organ part. But we can decide about these things when we get together again.

Will send answers to your questionnaire soon—after going over the second movement about which it refers to most.

My corrections, etc.—are not any too clear—and if you or the engraver can't make some out, let me know—there's no great hurry about the job exactly—is there? We might take our time and do it as well as possible.

C. E. I.

WEST REDDING
CONNECTICUT
3 JANUARY 1934

DEAR "NAP" *

I take my pen in hand to write you a long tiresome letter about why A is quite natural & ¾ nice but wrong—but Happy New Year, first, to you all!

The engraver, when he sees my marks on the proofs of the II movement, which I'm mailing you today, may get quite sore—I wouldn't blame him. I should have gone through them, specially the strings before it was sent to him. I've done the best I could to straighten it out—& I hope you & he can make out the corrections, etc., for instance:

1) If div. bow marks up & down are in one measure & then only the "up" in the next, the "down" players might not know what to do always—keep on—or stop— All these things I've tried to fix with the least trouble to the engraver. But he may have a better way.

2) If parts are to be made from the score, as you suggested, all the marks will have to go in each staff—a great many are in—but not all—for instance the "roller" . . . just before letter A.

3) In II movement, a piccolo often plays with a flute, sometimes in unison, sometimes, octave higher. I tried to show this by a "note" over flute part. But a separation in II in percussion part should be made for the player.

4) In some places, an extra player for the piano is better—so have put at beginning (Piano for 2 players ad lib)—the passages etc. can be suggested in the conductor's note, to go with parts—I do not like too many observations in score.

5) Horn parts were all left out on pages 53-54 (didn't try to copy them in)—engraver can take it from photo score.

6) 2 measures before Q—would put in the regular parts—not the *ossia*—or both.

7) At H. p. 35—when the 2 bands play. Your plan of the separate time for each is good and a great improvement. But I think it's important to show in the score, where each fits into the other—so have kept Piano as it was with dotted lines up to show how it stands with the II and have put back II Viola part as it was to show how II Viola stands with I.

8) Have kept the first 5 measures of II as it was. So the drum parts keep the bass drum on main beat—the rest of the orchestra miss the beats.

There are other things but can't think of them now. When they send the corrected proofs back, I wish they could be with the black notes on white paper—these white notes blur my eyes—and I can't work as steadily as on black on white, which is not very steadily at that. Am not starting over the III proofs for a little while—to give the eye a let-up.

What concert is to be in March, which Varèse spoke to you about? It's very good of him to have you play something of mine. I might suggest 2 short but active songs— and the quiet "In the Night" for orchestra: 1) "The New River" (p. 42, New Music edition, about 40 seconds), 2) "December," p. 40 (about 30 seconds), 3) "In the Night" (3rd movement, Theater Orchestra Set, New Music edition, about 2 minutes). This gives a contrasting group—short (about 4 minutes), not many players, not many rehearsals, & not very expensive!

The "December" ought to be sung by 3 to 10 fat basses (raucous voiced) and the "New River" by 1 or 2 men or 1 man and a lady (to A-sharp). "In the Night" without a voice.

But the "New River" and "December" will have to have the old scores copied and parts made (you have I think photos of these which you might look over.) When you get back will have this done. As I remember there are some measures in the old scores that are rather indistinct, but not many—and it won't take long to have copies made. Also I think the "New River" takes 2 Saxophones, but one and a trombone would do it. Good night.

C. E. I.

° Again a reference to the "Napoleonic forelock" that a California reporter found in Slonimsky's physical appearance.

164 EAST 74 STREET
NEW YORK
11 JANUARY 1934

DEAR INTERPRETER (of tongues and Sounding Brass—not the Psalmist's kind—but all nice music)—

Do you beat 2 rhythms when interpreting a lecture? We would have liked to have seen its setting. We're back in this gas-grained city. If we didn't have this house on our hands, we wouldn't come at all. When are you coming down? We hope soon— only we're sorry that just now, as our nephew is living with us, and in the only spare room—but we're having a room fixed for him in the attic (my floor), which Mrs. Ives thinks will be ready about the first of next month—as they have to run heating pipes, etc. up—but the next time you must stay with us.

Am returning the 2 pages— This (ossia place) way is good, I think & would go ahead with it. Haven't started going over the III yet. Haven't been quite in shape for a week or so and getting back to this "onus" doesn't help. Will you please ask them to send me another proof of the III in black & white (& charge it to me). After I look at those white notes on green, for about 10 minutes they all start to move around —like rice in green soup to my eyes—but you are a good boy to take so much trouble and we hope to see you soon.

Our love to all the family and Electra and Matre and Padre.

C. E. I.

I haven't seen anybody yet—and won't until I can get up to an 84 = ♩—except you.

164 EAST 74 STREET
NEW YORK
5 FEBRUARY 1934

DEAR PADRE!

Since writing you we have had some low days—Uncle Deac died—quite suddenly after a stroke. You remember him living with us in Redding—the oldest of our generation—and one of the last of the old type, now quite vanishing—and the world loses something undefinable.

Weiss & Riegger came in—and also Varèse—they are all full of plans—which I hope will work out. They told me first that Reiner was to conduct the Town Hall concert—that made me *sore*—but Varèse telephoned the other day that *you* were to conduct it—which is *quite* right—very much quite alright!!

Have been rather slow correcting the last movement,* but have now got it cleared up and am mailing it to you today. On last page, the quotation from the poem should be printed in small print, in the way the other movements were done —have put in last page of photo to show. Please tell the engraver that I want to see the last proofs of the whole thing, including verses, programs, etc. before it goes to press. And also please ask them to send the balance of the bill as soon as they know what it is. I put in a few things about playing the piano, etc. that ought to go with "conductor's note." Will show these to you later. When are you coming down, and how much does Electra weigh today?

Chas. E. Ives

N.S.P.! Atoms are indivisible—so are 32nd-notes. From p. 74 each 2 measures are put down as such, through p. 80. In other words these "backwater waves" are put in a prescriptive formula which exists only on paper—so when played exactly right— it's wrong—like Arthur Evans' cow. Don't read the above again but just tell the engraver I've tried to make as little trouble as I could—and the attached sheet makes the lower staff piano, from p. 74 to 80, clear, uniform and nice. The real music is all put in the footnote to p. 74.

C. E. I.

* Of *Three Places in New England.*

164 EAST 74 STREET<br>NEW YORK<br>6 FEBRUARY 1934

DEAR N.S.P.

We thank you—Mr. Parker* and the Transcript—for your effort, interest and space. Do you handle the pen, the baton or the nursing bottle the best? Electra may have her special vote—but we vote for all three! Will you please ask them to save a dozen (or 25 better, because old copies are hard to get) copies and have them sent here whenever convenient—and we will send you a London Spectator** some-day. I turned in the corrected proofs of the third movement*** yesterday to the proper department (= N.S.P.) We can talk about pagination and other matters when you come down—as you say that will be soon. Don't bother about the score, am having clean copies made from the manuscript of the 2 chorus songs "New River" and "December," which Varèse says are on the program together with the "In the Night" set.**** Good night to you all.

Chas. E. Ives

Please ask Birchard Co. to let me see final proofs before sending to press.

* H. T. Parker, drama and music editor of the Boston Evening *Transcript.*

** The only periodical that Ives and Mrs. Ives ever read; they did not subscribe to any American newspaper or magazine.

*** Of *Three Places in New England.*

**** New York concert under the auspices of the Pan American Association of Composers scheduled for 15 April 1934 in Town Hall, New York.

DEAR PADRE:

It was fine to have you with us around the family—and we hope it won't be in the distant future before Madre and the Papina, may join around it too—Electra will be quite old enough to travel soon—having a birthday every 6 months.

The final proofs to the second movement* came today. Have only as yet looked at the first page—and the *ossia* drum part there probably will be of help, and would let it stay. It shouldn't take me long to check it all over and will send it back next week. I suppose they haven't forgotten that I haven't seen the final proofs of the first movement yet and will send it—also proofs of the written pages, i.e. verses, programs etc.

The notes you ask about on page 60 last measure are right now, the oboe and viola are OK. As I see it, here it is more a matter of where the voices lead to than their relation vertically to others. In the R.H. piano the upper A's are all flat and the lower A's natural. If the upper staff piano is taken by one player 2 hands it's quite easy to play. In fact 2 players (except in a very few places) are better than one. This week there have been several more instances of need of some "résumé"—but comprehensive and under one cover, & covenient to mail—a teacher and lecturer in Philadelphia writes for something like that, a pianist and lecturer etc. in a college in Louisville, in a letter which came this A.M. asks for data, etc. for his lectures and yesterday a letter from Homeyer & Co., 458 Boylston St., Boston saying they have requests for my music and ask where it is published and for description pamphlets, etc. etc. I have had many requests etc. like this, and nothing to send—except odds and ends, scraps, and now the Musical Quarterly are all out, 1 copy left**—no more copies—so to have what is wanted under one cover and convenient to mail is quite necessary. Also the booklet should help sell both the new score*** and the songs etc.

The enclosed photo MSS of the original organ piece, later the "In the Night" will show in the upper manual the general idea of the 2 upper string parts which were left out—and which should get in. I will copy out these 2 measures later and send. I'm sorry to bother you with this long badly written letter. If you can't read it—it will be quite alright! It reminds me of a "Raphaelic Sky"—it's so different.

Our love to the family,
Sincerely,
CHAS. E. IVES

* Of *Three Places in New England.*
** *The Musical Quarterly* of January 1933 with an article on Ives by Henry Bellamann.
*** *Three Places in New England,* published by C. C. Birchard Co. of Boston.

DEAR N.S.P.*

The final corrected proofs were mailed to you this A.M.—so the job is done—most—only the prose and conductor's note, which is short and only to be copied. Will send it soon. I want to thank you for your help, interest and eyes—you were a good boy—and how is Electra!

We rather looked for you last week, but hope to see you soon. The parts are being made for the 2 choruses and a photo of "New River" score in your own handwriting is to be sent you. There was one measure (when they sing "Tara-boomdeay") that I thought the strings better play with piano. You have, I think the score to the other song—"December." If not, will have one sent or give you one when you come down, which I hope will be soon.**

Another letter came in this A.M. from a music school asking for data, biography, then half lost—so that a booklet will save me a lot of trouble and cussing—it is digest of criticism, notes, etc. It takes me a whole day to get things together, and really needed.

How does Electra like it here in America? Our love to her and her mother and Padre.

Sincerely,
CHAS. E. IVES

\* Nicolas Slonimsky Padre.
\*\* Slonimsky arranged some songs of Ives for voice and orchestra to be performed at his concert in April 1934 in New York.

164 EAST 74 STREET
NEW YORK
22 FEBRUARY 1934

DEAR N.S.P.\*

In writing you yesterday I meant to have sent the enclosed which Henry sent me. It might help in the booklet. It's from the "Music Lovers Guide" of February 3rd. And I also meant to have asked you to look at the last 15 pages to the end of the 2nd movement of my 4th Symphony which Henry published some years ago. Playing only the percussion group and a piano, or both pianos, would do for a piece or study in rhythms and percussion:

10 players, besides piano player (1, 2 or 3):

| | |
|---|---|
| 1 Gong | 1 Indian drum |
| 1 Light Gong or Cymbal hung up | 1 Timpani |
| 1 Cymbal | 1 Low Bell |
| 1 Bass Drum | 1 High Bell |
| 1 Snare Drum | 1 Triangle |

And to get the wood percussion, a xylophone would go well playing the piccolo part.

If you have a copy you might look it over and see what you think about it. It seems to me it makes a coherent musical sense, this way, even without the orchestra. In fact, this and other parts of this symphony I remember playing when I was working on it, with a few drums, kitchen tables, bells, etc. and the rhythmic lines seemed to hold up by its own. However, it may not do, but look it over. Will send a copy I have here to you marked as suggested when I mail back the proofs of the second movement\*\* within a few days. The final proof to the first movement will be ready for any time. When you have the song scores copied, let me know what it will be and I'll send the check.

CHAS. E. IVES
Good night to all,

\* Nicolas Slonimsky Padre.
\*\* Of the score of *Three Places in New England*.

164 EAST 74 STREET
NEW YORK
24 FEBRUARY 1934

DEAR N.S.P.S.—2ND S = "SCRIBA"—

You were a good boy to make copies—but am sorry for the misunderstanding about "Duty"—that isn't to be sung, and besides it's for a large orchestra. I'd no idea of having it copied, as I remember it was on the desk and just gave it to you for future reference. I hope it didn't take much time. The "December" looks well done and plain but I can't correct the last part until you send me the ink copy I made for the last photo page. I can't see that old copy now—happen to be going through one of those "bad eye" periods when everything blurs, unless very clear.

Am sending tomorrow the second movement* finished. There were a few mistakes but unimportant—have put a snare drum in that 11/8 measure that always bothered so—a drum was there once to make it clear to players.

Does Electra like New England winter? Love to all the family,

Ever yours,
CHAS. E. IVES

* Of *Three Places in New England.*

164 EAST 74 STREET
NEW YORK
5 MARCH 1934

DEAR N.S.P.

Am sending back the 6 pages you sent of the III * proofs. You are right—let them take p. 77 from correct copy (correct on paper, though you can't make me play it that nice way except Sat. P.M.)—am quite sure, in sending the copy back with these 2 measures, I explained to the engraver to go by these—if he had he would have saved himself and us trouble. When they send the I and III final proofs, if the former proofs, with corrections in, could be sent also it would save time in checking up. The other engravers (New Music) always did that.

I don't care about the cover page—as long as the letters aren't = (are not) big, especially my name. Would just have *Three Places in New England* (an orchestral set) and the separate titles of each movement inside.

You are a good copyist—but I had no intention of having you take so much trouble and time to copy those scores. All I thought was that you would go over them with the copyist and perhaps go over a measure or passages that seemed indistinct, etc.

I've gone over the "December" as best I could. There are a few places, I can't quite make out in the old copy but its near enough and have had a photostat made, which will save time making parts etc. This and your copy will be sent back to you in a day or so.

A letter from Henry says some 70 people subscribed last month to the New Music Quarterly Records at $5 a person—it is surprising! In these Pan American concerts some good recordings ought to result. I hope so. Apparently the time, according to Henry's expression, is a problem—4½ minutes or less to each side.

Good night to all,

Yours,
CHAS. E. IVES

* Third movement of *Three Places in New England.*

164 EAST 74 STREET
NEW YORK
7 MARCH 1934

DEAR N.S.P.

The scores and the voice parts of the songs came today.* Didn't mean to have you do all that work—I thought you'd just look or lean over the "scribe's" shoulder and point to a bad note. They are all plain and I'll have the parts copied here and your voice pages photostated. Now don't do anymore copying, you have more to do than that. They will probably send the proofs to the first movement of *Three Places* soon and then the worst of the job will be done. Please excuse this very bad letter. Will hope to see you soon.

CHAS. E. IVES

° Orchestral arrangements made by Nicolas Slonimsky for his New York concert on 15 April 1934.

164 EAST 74 STREET
NEW YORK
24 APRIL 1934

DEAR N.S.P.

Are you there—with both arms! et al. Please be sure to come in and see us if you're down Sunday, the 29th. Thanks for the notices from the Boston paper. The printed proof copy for Birchard Co. came yesterday, mostly O.K. Am mailing back today.

Ever yours,
CHAS. E. IVES

Is it nice to like music?

164 EAST 74 STREET
NEW YORK
1 MAY 1934

DEAR N.S.P.

Mrs. Ives was disturbed that you have to come way down here to do those recordings, perhaps several times and instead of getting paid for it you even have to pay your own traveling expenses. She doesn't think it fair—nor do I, and I'm enclosing something to make us feel better.°

Your plan for the recording seems the best. One side *Lilacs*°° 4 minutes, other side *Barn Dance*,°°° *In the Night*°°°° about the right time—and better to have time and space than otherwise.

Ever yours,
CHAS. E. IVES

° A characteristic Ivesian way of blaming Harmony Ives for his own noble impulses.
°° By Carl Ruggles.
°°° From *Washington's Birthday* of Ives.
°°°° By Ives.

WEST REDDING
CONNECTICUT
5 JUNE 1934

DEAR N.S.P.

Riegger writes that the records went well, and that you did "nice work, old boy!" and the players were *serious and enthusiastic*—also that a few days ago Salzedo told him that *In the Night* was one of the best records he had ever heard—Riegger adds: "Salzedo is *very* critical." I hope Henry will like them and that they will help in this work.°

We are all glad to be back on the hill again and for me more sleep—less cuss. We hope you can get down before the summer is over.

We all send our best to you both,

Sincerely,
CHAS. E. IVES

° The recordings of *Washington's Birthday* and *In the Night* were made by Slonimsky for the New Music Edition, founded and edited by Henry Cowell.

DEAR PADRE!

I've been on the point of writing you for many days back—but I'll have to admit for sometime I didn't seem to be able to keep in decent shape—and had to give up doing about everything. It's humiliating and makes me mad. Mrs. Ives has decided, backed up by all the family plus the M.D., that the best thing to do now is to sail over to England and stay there for 2 or 3 months—anyhow for good or otherwise, we're going to sail on August 10. Our address (as before) is c/o Guaranty Trust Co., 50 Pall Mall, London.

Everybody seems to like the records*—you did a good job—a hard one. I appreciate all you have done deeply and "I take off my hat."

I've been wondering if I owe Birchard and Co. anything. The data, etc. for the little brochure (is that spelled OK? My Irish is bad!) will be sent in a few days to you from the office typewriter. It has (1) a short biography (including name and date of birth) (2) a list of compositions, etc. (3) Digest of Comment. Besides these, the verses and program for the "3 Places in New England" which are printed in the score might go in, and I suppose whatever (but short) forenote the publisher thinks ought to be made—but *Please NO Picture* of me or any nice man anywhere!

The digest of comment has been arranged in preferential order by one who thinks he knows—but I suppose—(Here Ives had to stop. His handwriting was so shaky that the words were hardly intelligible, and his adopted daughter Edith took over: "Dear Mr. Slonimsky: I am now writing for daddy. Here is a hug, etc.")

* Slonimsky recorded *Washington's Birthday* for New Music Records.

DEAR N.S.P.

Was just about to write you when your letter came. We were glad to know you all are well and that Electra is learning how to talk, or not how to talk, I can't quite make out—but both are best. We've been back for a while—as yet haven't been able to do anything I wanted to, but am getting better now and expect to be a human being soon—whatever that is! I appreciate the trouble you have taken about the printing etc. I don't know how many copies of the score should be printed. I remember that you said both you and Mr. Birchard thought a certain number should be sent to conductors, libraries, schools etc. Perhaps 300 would be enough to start with. But do whatever seems advisable and please let me know about a week ahead and I'll send the check for it. I will be glad to look over the proofs for the brochure any time. A few later things have been sent me that might go in or perhaps you may have something too. I feel the need of this, as I'm getting an increasing number of inquiries, etc. from papers, teachers, students, et al.—asking for data this book will give and which I'm never able to put my hands on when wanted—and some of the letters, I'm ashamed to say, I haven't even answered.

Mrs. Ives and Edie join me in kindest remembrances to you and yours.

Ever yours,
CHAS. E. IVES

DEAR N.S.P.

Here is the printed matter corrected as well as I can, and with some suggestions. Would vote for the outside page not to be in gaudy, loud-mouthed colors that all nice* magazines and books have, but rather in plain letters and color. Mrs. Ives says a light grey—and if I were you I would take her advice. Ask Electra's mother to tell her husband that wives know more about color than men. And how do you like it in America and when are you coming to New York?

C. E. I.

* It should be remembered that Ives used the word "nice" with a strong feeling of revulsion.

164 EAST 74 STREET<br>NEW YORK<br>APRIL 1935

DEAR N.S.P.!

Thanks for your letter and for sending the proofs of the conductor's note. There are some references to pages, etc. I can't quite make out—so think I'll wait for a copy of the printed score to check up with. And there's no hurry I think, about this proof, as it is only to be sent out with the parts.

I'm very glad you are to conduct the concert in Denver. Robert Schmitz was here about a month ago but was not certain about the concert. Schmitz is a fine man—brains and courage. Milhaud told me that Debussy said that Schmitz had more music sagacity than most young men he knew. Please ask Birchard Co. to send me the bill for the printing, etc. as soon as it is done.

Hoping to see you again before long—and with kindest wishes from us all to Electra, her mother and you.

I am yours ever,<br>CHAS. E. IVES

WEST REDDING<br>CONNECTICUT<br>11 MAY 1935

DEAR N.S.P.!! *

You are a good boy to send me the article and translation**—they were well written. I can see how you can write good English—but how did you learn Russian?

Am glad our parts*** came out so well. There is just one place I noticed that might help. It's the drum part in the 2nd movement, when playing the "off rhythm" —it might help the drummer if his part was cued in as the piano part in the score is. However, this can be easily done later.

Everybody at church—except the one who ought to be—"arreta prodita"—bad Latin for Electra to correct! **** I expected to send back a score from New York. Will do so soon. There's one item in it, that makes no sense. "Don't play first measure unless there are 3 trombones"—now if it had said—"don't play first measure unless there is a good conductor" that would be the most sensible note ever written—the only conductor's note ever needed!

Please ask Birchard and Co. to send a copy of score to the 2 names enclosed. And if they also will send a half dozen (or more) copies to me, I'll appreciate it. Will also pay for the postage if I should. We all send best wishes to you and yours,

Ever yours,<br>CHAS. E. IVES

* N.S. Padre.
** An article on American music published in the Moscow monthly "Sovietskaya Musica."
*** Makeshift photocopies of individual parts from the published score of *Three Places in New England*.
**** Electra's first language was Latin.

Dear W. S. R—

You are a Good Boy
A gigantic and difficult job — the
Book came. Many Thanks.
Anybody can write a Good
Symphony — yet it takes a better
man to conduct it — But
only you & Sam Johnson
can write a Good Encyclopaedia.
Now give your mind & body a
good rest — take it easy — just
conduct the Boston Symphony for
the Ladies for a season — then
you will be able to do your
big work again — a memorable
Day — Ahoy!

Ever yours
Chas E. Ives

DEAR N.S.P.

This is just a line of welcome home. Will write in more detail as soon as I get in better pen-handling (not pan-handling) shape. We all send our best remembrances to Electra, her mother and dad.

Ever yours,
C.E.I.

164 EAST 74 STREET
NEW YORK
NOVEMBER, 1935

DEAR N.S.P.

I'm sorry to report that I haven't been able to attend to those various things you wrote me about last summer— For some time past haven't been in shape to do anything I want to— As for music, sometimes for days at a time—can't see it, hear it or play it—not even a nice wrong note! But am getting somewhat out of this spell and hope soon to be more like a human being. May things go well with all of you. Best wishes again.

Ever yours,
CHAS. E. IVES

WEST REDDING
CONNECTICUT
23 NOVEMBER 1937

DEAR N.S.P.

You are a good boy! A gigantic and difficult job! The book* came. Many thanks. Anybody can write a good symphony—yet it takes a better man to conduct it. But only you and Sam Johnson can write a good Encyclopedia. Now give your mind and body a good rest—take it easy—just conduct the Boston Symphony for the old ladies for 10 seasons—then you will be able to do your big work again. A memorable day! Ahoy!

Ever yours,
CHAS. E. IVES

* First edition of *Music Since 1900.*

# Letters from Edgar Varèse

PARIS
26 APRIL 1931

DEAR MR. SLONIMSKY,

I have just received the program of your New York concert with the Pan-American Association of Composers, and it is very gratifying for me to know from your program notes how you feel about my music. I hope that when you have your own orchestra you will conduct my big works.

Cowell writes me of a prospective concert in Paris. May I suggest—may I even insist—that you play *Intégrales* instead of *Octandre*. I have already written Cowell and Salzedo my reasons for it. *Intégrales* was played here only once two years ago —not under favorable conditions—and yet provided a sensation. There is a demand for a repeat performance, and I think that the announcement of *Intégrales* on your program would help fill your hall.

I am looking forward to seeing you soon here in Paris—and having at last the pleasure of hearing you conduct.

With kindest regards.

Yours sincerely,
EDGAR VARÈSE

PARIS
12 OCTOBER 1931

CHER AMI,
Merci pour votre lettre. Cowell wrote me from Hamburg immediately after his landing. If I can, I will go to Berlin to see him, but it is rather problematical on account of the depletion of my "gold mines." He told me about your success in California, which does not surprise me but does not prevent me from congratulating you most sincerely.

*Orchestre Symphonique de Paris.* The February concerts* must be made an immense success, and they must be given with all possible assurance of artistic results —with all the necessary rehearsals, etc. I will occupy myself with the task of molding the orchestra—a labor of slow penetration which is of absolutely prime importance. Good will on earth is secure, but as for the stars, it is up to us to reach them. Such a success will be the trampoline which will enable us to jump. Without it we cannot start. It is therefore imperative that you should take steps to obtain the necessary resources to realize this project.

*Arcana.* There is a great deal of talk about it, and an atmosphere of great and sympathetic expectation is created around this score. It will be published within a fortnight and I will send you a copy at once.

Everything moves along, and it is only the question of time—and perseverance in the imposed discipline, but—and I have the bad taste of Cato in insisting on it— Paris in February and the repercussions of this event is the condition *sine qua non* of the future successes. The road is open—but we must not start in the spirit of adventure—everything must be calculated in the preparation of this effort.

Cowell writes me—and it makes me happy—about the interest that certain important women in Southern California show for your appearances there.

To recapitulate, and to make use of your own words: it is imperative to organize a series of concerts of great musical importance in Europe. True—but the launching start must be in Paris. We have two immediate goals: intense concentration on the two February concerts—and their triumph. Am content with the projected concerts culminating in the performance of my *Amériques.* Do not forget to bring your own set of Chinese blocks for *Arcana.* If you find a good tamtam—deep—sonorous— warm—gargantuan—bring it along too. I work a great deal. Full of ideas fight and energy.

VARÈSE

* Slonimsky was engaged to conduct two concerts with the Orchestre Symphonique de Paris on February 21 and 25, 1932, featuring Varèse's *Arcana*.

PARIS
21 NOVEMBER 1931

CHER AMI,
Thank you for your kind letter, article, translation and photograph.

*Havana.* If you will have, as Caturla* told Alejo Carpentier,** an orchestra large enough for *Le Sacre du Printemps,* I would like very much that my *Amériques* should be included in the program. See what you can do about it, and allow me to remind you of what I insist upon in regard to *Intégrales* for Paris. This is a psychological strategy. I know where I am going and what will follow. But, after all, we have a common cause, and I am happy that it is so. Have faith in my "hard-boiled" experience and don't mind this renewed insistence. My plan is clearly drawn—its development is logical—its results assured. You, Cowell, Salzedo, Ruggles, Riegger, Ives, Weiss—we must group together in a bloc. So you can see that there is no question of personal vanity. You know me well enough to realize that prima donna posturing is the least of my preoccupations. So try to do everything possible, and also the *impossible.*

*Berlin.* Let us decide on *Arcana.* You will have full knowledge of the score after the concert of the Orchestre Symphonique de Paris. The score has been sent to you. Despite all my care I am sure that your lynx eye will still find some errors. Let me know. People already talk about this concert—there are great expectations, and we must make it a resounding success—not only for our own satisfaction but also as a point of departure for further activities.

*Russia.* I saw the Soviet attaché who is doing all he can. He said that great interest in my works is developing there. I told him that I was very happy to hear about that, but that they should be played in such a way as to render them justice. I told him that you were the "mechanic" of my choice<sup></sup>*** and that I wanted to have my works revealed in Russia by you. Some friends who just came from Russia brought some very flattering reports concerning me. But they also anticipate a great deal of red tape which is rampant in the U.S.S.R. This proves that the countries of old Europe and the U.S. have no reason to envy the Russians. But I am doing my best. Naturally, there is no question about defraying the expenses for the Russian concerts.

I am glad that you are seeing Salzedo—he is a dear and an old friend of mine. I am happy that my modest opinion about your person and your talents has moved you. I had a long conversation about you with Florent Schmitt, and you have his complete sympathy. He also is a wonderful comrade. Needless to say, you are free to quote all that is of interest to you in my letter to Salzedo. My opinions are not divided according to categories, and my admiration for you is expressed in public as well as in private.

Votre
VARÈSE

---

° Cuban composer.
°° Cuban novelist and writer on music.
°°° Varèse used to call Slonimsky "mon mécanicien," voicing his belief that performers should be regarded as mechanics carrying out the composer's engineering plans.

PARIS
24 DECEMBER 1931

CHER AMI,

O.K. for *Intégrales* in Berlin and Budapest. The only thing on which I insist in that only the players should be on the stage, as you did in Paris, and that the rest of the orchestra should remain back stage and return to their seats after the performance of this work. Please get a string drum from Carl Fischer in New York—it costs only a dollar or two—and take it with you, because it is impossible to find one in Europe. They call it Lion's Roar, a stupid name, more suitable to describe the rumblings of a Methodist minister. O.K. also for Cuba to do *Amériques* after the fusion of the two orchestras in Havana. Merci. You and the score look like Siamese Twins on the photograph.

*Arcana.* We will correct the mistakes in the score together in Paris. I am glad that you are beginning to study it and I will be happy to hear this première of the new version under your intelligent and precise direction. Your progress does not surprise me. I have opened an unlimited credit for your future.

Do you think that there might be persons in New York interested in our group who could lend us support? Speak about it to Salzedo—he could give you good advice concerning the matter. Here, in Paris, unfortunately nothing. Crisis . . . Crisis < $ff$ Crisis. But you will have a full house for your concerts in February. Not only myself but my friends will make sure of it. Amical souvenir.

Varèse

# Letter from the Japanese League of Composers

TOKYO<br>
22 March 1936

DEAR SIR!

I am a master of Hacsoh-ha composer's Society. I have read your letter with great rejoice. Hacsoh-ha is a group of my students, so all members are yet young about 20 years old, because I am yet 30 years. They have no interesting national compositions in their past. I have also no works in pure Japanese style. We Japanese composers, now and past, are studying European Harmony and Theory.

Of course, we have a earnest desire to complete our pure national music in future. We have many mystic melodies and wonderful scales in past, but we have no theories now and past. So we must at first, anyhow, study the perfect theories by West. We young Japanese composer is trying every test to using our old scales on our work. But non of them succes about it.

It is necessary to Japan, or it is a duty of Japanese composers, to complete a work and theories about it. We must compose or find new Japanese pure music in Western high style, in its instrumentation, systems and theorical elements.

Every group of Japanese composers or privatly earnestly trying this new work, but non of them complete it.

For instance, I send my score "Thema and Variations" for string trio to you. You will find easily from it only a European music, not a Japanese colour you needed. I know you will disappointed after reading my score. There will exist only a imitation of Western music.

I am very sorry, that you must wait a complete Japanese works in future; four or five years after. I believe that we will complete it recently.

Mr. Yokota, Nakano, Hirai are all my student and they are yet poor as young, so this time I will not send their works to you. But, I have many students about 150 members, and I will heartily send you when they will complete it.

Many thanks to your kind letter to our Japanese composer in far East. We feel so many happies that we are musician, such a international artist. Please remember me and teach us as long as possible. I have a riliance on my hard will to complete our new National music.

My honourable conductor! please encourage me hereafter. Good by!

from your<br>
Taijiro Goh

# The Ideological Platform of the Russian
# Association of Proletarian Musicians

## MUSIC AND THE CLASSES

(This is the third and last formulation of the platform of the RAPM, adopted in 1929. The first formulation was published in the magazine *Musikalnaya Nov*, No. 12, 1924; the second in No. 1 of the magazine *Music and October* for 1926. The RAPM was dissolved by government decree 23 April 1932.)

Reflecting the general evolution of class society, the music of the past evolved along two main paths: on the one hand the music of the toilers, the exploited, and the oppressed classes (the so-called folk music), on the other hand the feudal bourgeois music, which comprises virtually the entire bulk of written "cultured" music.

The position of this or that class at a given historical moment determines the development of these two musical cultures.

The brilliant spread of the musical culture of the ruling classes was determined by its possession of the tools of material, technical culture in the domain of everyday life as in that of the special musical field (complicated musical instruments, special technique of their manufacture, special educational institutes, music printing, etc.).

On the contrary, the music of the oppressed and exploited classes, despite its deep musical significance, remains at a primitive stage as far as cultural, technical and material means are concerned.

The above conditions give the ruling classes the possibility of utilizing the creative forces of the exploited masses. At certain moments of history musicians of the ruling classes address themselves to the art of the oppressed classes and, taking their most valuable possession, nourish their own music entirely with the vitalizing juice of folk music.

The bourgeoisie of the period of well-developed capitalism exerts, as a ruling class, profound moral influence on all strata and classes of the population, systematically poisoning the worker's mind. This influence is shown in the ideology of a certain fraction of the working masses and in their everyday life, as a result of which we find tendencies of degeneration and disintegration in the artistic tastes of some of its members. In the field of music this degeneration follows on the one hand the line of urban romance, on the other that of religious petty bourgeois estheticism, and very recently, the erotic dance of the contemporary capitalist city (fox-trot, Charleston, jazz music, etc.).

Since the emergence of social differentiation and stratification in the country, similar tendencies may be noted in folk music; having undergone the influence mentioned above, it becomes contaminated with songs alien to its nature (all sorts of "patriotic," "religious" songs and also those mentioned above), and, inasmuch as it reflects the psychology of different social strata in the country (on the one hand that of toilers, workers, on the other hand that of the exploiting parasitical elements), it ceases to be uniform.

While defining the class nature of one or another musical composition, it is imperative to consider its ideological emotional content expressed by corresponding sonorous material.

## MUSICAL CULTURE OF THE PAST

During the bourgeois revolution and its struggle with remnants of feudal society, the bourgeoisie appeared as the bearer of economic and cultural progress, and its ideologists, among them composers, expressed the aspirations of a great majority of the population. At that time the bounds of cultural intercourse among men were comparatively wide and the bourgeois artists reflected the views of this wide community. This could not but affect in a beneficial way the artistic output of the bourgeois artists, inasmuch as inspiration, enthusiasm, and creative power increase in the direct ratio to the number of recipients among the popular masses.

The creative production of composers reflecting active and heroic sentiments of the revolutionary bourgeoisie, compared to the rest of the musical legacy, appears nearest to the psychology and world outlook of the contemporary proletariat, inasmuch as it possesses a more realistic, a more objective attitude.

This musical legacy, representing the best in musical culture of the past, has also evolved the highest type of musical form. The creative production of Beethoven and Mussorgsky may be cited as specimens of this highly-developed culture.

Bourgeois music in its latest period (that of the entrance of capitalism into its highest stage, financial capitalism) has reflected the process of general decay and disintegration of bourgeois culture. During this period music begins to cultivate decadent moods, and engages in the following pursuits:

a. Cultivation of sensual and pathologically erotic moods emerging as a result of narrowing interests of a bourgeoisie degenerating morally and physically; cultivation of musical materials reflecting primitive psychology of the nations "colonial" exotic music, etc.).

b. Mysticism, feeling of oppressiveness as a premonition on the part of the bourgeoisie of the impending social catastrophe and the end of bourgeois rule.

c. Reproduction in a musical work of the movement of the contemporary capitalist city with its milling humanity and industry. This naturalistic streak in contemporary music is a symptom of its decay and of the inner devastation of the bourgeoisie, the inadequacy of its ideological-emotional world to serve as whose cultural evolution has stopped at early stages ("barbarism," specific a "means of communication among men" and inspiration for composers. Hence, the so-called "emotionalist" trends in music and, specifically, urbanist music that reduces itself to a more or less successful reproduction of noises.

d. Cultivation of primitive coarse subjects as a means, on the part of the bourgeoisie, to slow up the process of degeneration and to fight the proletariat that threatens "anarchy" for the bourgeoisie after the Revolution.

The decadent subject-matter of bourgeois music determines its form. Under the influence of decadent moods the inner meaning of music becomes diluted; technical elements gain ascendancy and music splits into factions according to its formal elements. In contemporary decadent bourgeois music the most characteristic elements are:

a. Hypertrophy of harmonic, vertical concepts, resulting in utter monotony and poverty of metrical, rhythmical design, which leads towards distortion of the musical phrase and loss of dynamic power, and disappearance of melos that causes the vocal crisis of bourgeois opera.

b. Hypertrophy of the polyphonic principle, accompanied by complete negation of the modal groundwork of music (so-called linear music).

c. The pursuance of alogical spasmodic rhythms.

d. The striving towards so-called absolute self-dependent "constructivistic" music, mechanistically built, and claiming to produce an emotional response of a predetermined nature. The school of composition inculcating this attitude (the so-called theory of "manufacture" of musical compositions) contributes to the complete disappearance of creative urge, replaced by dead mechanical schematicism.

During this last period the bourgeoisie, disguising its class interests under convenient slogans, makes claim to "objective," formal, technical "attainments," rejects the legacy of the classical past, and promotes "novelty," "contemporaneity" and "progress" in a narrow, formal, technical sense. These trends in contemporary bourgeois music, symptomatic of the psychological distress of the bourgeoisie, are a direct result of its decay and degeneration.

## THE PROLETARIAN REVOLUTION AND THE CONTEMPORARY SITUATION ON THE MUSICO-IDEOLOGICAL FRONT

A long chain of circumstances prevents the proletariat from mastering the fine arts, music and literature, and from producing their own protagonists in the arts, and specifically in music. These circumstances are:

First, the proletariat has begun the social revolution not waiting for the complete development of its culture within the framework of capitalistic society (despite the fact that the process of cultural development has started long before the acquisition of power by the proletariat, and that in certain fields proletarian culture has attained great heights).

Second, the social revolution of the proletariat has started in a land whose working class was at a very low cultural level.

Third, a great deal of creative power has been spent during a long civil war, and an industrial upbuilding accompanied by the greatest difficulties.

In view of this and many other circumstances the proletariat which exercises hegemony in social policy and general economy, does not exercise this hegemony in cultural pursuits, and, in particular, in the arts.

The absence, at this moment of the hegemony of the proletariat in the arts gives the opportunity to ideologists of intermediate and even openly inimical social strata to pursue their artistic aims along bourgeois lines and even influence the policies of proletarian institutions by foisting their ideology on them. The NEP [New Economical Policy] and the numerous bureaucratic distortions of the Soviet State apparatus contribute to the process of this insidious penetration. Besides, a great majority of proletarian artistic groups, in contrast with the proletariat which openly proclaims the class character of its artistic organizations, strives to conceal this affiliation under the guise of societies "scientific," "interpretative," "creative" and such, while actually serving enemy ideology. In music, for instance, the reactionary character of the right wing of musical society and its connection with the bureaucratic circles of the old regime force this group to maintain secret solidarity without forming any open organizations.

Social organizations and trends existing in music reflect on the one hand the general class differentiation and the existence of social stratification among these classes, on the other hand the various peripeteia of class struggle, uniting and disuniting, as they do, the heterogeneous social formations.

At the present time there exist among musicians the following trends reflecting the ideology of fundamental social groups:

a. A group of musicians that has been formed under the influence of the bureaucratic circles of the old regime, sponsors of art and music.

At the present time this group, in view of absence of all connection with living art in all fields, has completely degenerated into a dead and retrograde epigonism incapable of contributing anything vital to music. Members of this group have managed, however, to entrench themselves in several important educational institutions.

b. A comparatively significant force, represented by a so-called group of "contemporaries" that reflects the ideology of the one-time "vanguard" young Russian bourgeoisie and bourgeois intelligentsia and that defends the tenets of modern decadent bourgeois art.

The vitality and significance of this group stand in undeniable connection with the presence in the economy of our land, along with a socialistic section, of a comparatively strong capitalist current productive of bourgeois ideology. In some measure the ideology of this group is sustained by the penetration into the U.S.S.R. of bourgeois influences from the capitalist countries.

c. In the course of the next few years there must be expected a rise of the intermediate strata and classes, the village and city intelligentsia. Being a motley conglomeration of heterogeneous phenomena, this grouping requires that we discriminate in passing judgment on them. Along with sincere and honest companion-of-the-road citizenry striving to understand the proletariat and reflect its world outlook in its creative production and musical activity, there exist here certain grossly adaptationist trends that do not go beyond outward exhibitionistic "revolutionariness," and are essentially alien or even inimical to the proletariat.

d. In the course of the last five years there has been considerable progress of proletarian art contributing to penetration of proletarian influence among the artistic intelligentsia.

This proletarian group of musicians is potentially strong, thanks to its connection with a class now in the vanguard of history.

## RAPM

The non-enforcement of hegemony of the proletariat in the divers ideological fields and specifically in the domain of art cannot, of course, continue for any considerable time. After the very first successes in the task of economic recuperation, the proletariat will assemble and solidify its cultural powers to repel the petty-bourgeois influences and heighten the cultural level of the masses, in which there is observable a huge growth of independent activity, not solely in the political and economical fields but also in general culture. Voluntary proletarian organizations have contributed to this growth in no small measure and art at the same time a determining factor in this growth. Such are, in the domain of the arts, the Associations of Proletarian Artists, organizations historically given to the proletariat as conscious expressions of the historical process.

The fundamental task of the Proletarian Artistic Associations is to establish the hegemony of the proletariat in various fields of the arts.

In the domain of music, such an organization is embodied in the Russian Association of Proletarian Musicians (RAPM) which unites musicians active in the proletarian advance-guards on the various sections of the front of class war, among them on the musico-ideological section.

The ultimate aim of the RAPM is extension of the hegemony of the proletariat to the music field. At present it sets the following concrete tasks:

a. Extension of the proletarian Communist influence to the musical masses, reeducation and reorganization of these masses in order to direct their work and creative talents towards Socialist upbuilding.

b. Creation of Marxist musicology and Marxist musical criticism, critical absorption of the musical culture of the past and of contemporary musical literature from the viewpoint of the proletariat.

c. Demonstration of proletarian musical creative productions and creation of necessary conditions for complete development and growth of proletarian music.

Toward the accomplishment of these tasks the RAPM

    a. poses at its open meetings the most urgent problems in the domain of creative work, Marxist musicology, mass action and pedagogical musical work;

    b. expounds, through the medium of the Soviet professional and party press, and also the organs of the RAPM, its fundamental ideas, heightens the social, scientific-musical and artistic level of the musical masses, analyzes and gives a musico-sociological evaluation of musical literature, pointing out the path of new musical work in city and country;

    c. while helping the working and peasant masses to create their own music, organizes musical education of these masses for which purpose it encourages proletarianization of music schools and formation of music-teaching cadres in the conservatories, and also discusses in special conferences, problems of method in musical work among the masses and the individual circles in workers' clubs;

    d. poses and discusses the problems of formation of new interpretative ways and begins the work of sanitation of our concert masses, organizing its own exemplary choral and orchestral collectives, and also groups of individual performers.

In its interrelations with various groupings of musicians, the RAPM is guided by the general policy of the proletariat and the party in relation toward various social categories. Neither the circumstance that the working class has already acquired power, nor the special character of musical problems deters the proletariat from fighting against ideological influences opposed to the proletariat on the musical front. As to the intermediate, the so-called companion-of-the-road groupings, the RAPM deems it necessary and useful to attract these groups unquestioningly into creative, scientific and educational work in the domain of music and to utilize them in practical work.

"While weeding out the antiproletarian and the counter-revolutionary elements and fighting the ideology of the new bourgeoisie among some of the companions-of-the-road, it is imperative to exercise tolerance towards the intermediate ideological forms, patiently helping them to form comradely relationship with the cultural powers of Communism." (From the resolution of the Central Committee of the All-Russian Communist party on the party policy in literature)

In their creative work, composers, members of the Association of Proletarian Musicians, strive above all to reflect the rich, full-blooded psychology of the proletariat, as historically the most advanced, and dialectically the most sensitive and understanding class.

Following the dialectical and not the mechanistic laws of evolution, composers, members of the RAPM, strive to create gradually new musical forms and a new style born of its artistic subject matter.

The interrelation of content and form is regarded by the RAPM as a dialectical unity.

Thus, while not accepting any form of contemporary bourgeois music that in its content is opposed to the proletariat, the RAPM proclaims the slogan of learning the craft first of all from those among composers of the past who reflected in their creative output the subject matter close to the revolutionary ideas of the proletariat.

New musical forms are created and will be created by the proletariat. Proletarian music must "penetrate into the innermost masses of workmen and peasants, unite the thought and the will of these masses and raise them" for further struggle and construction, organizing their class consciousness in the direction of the ultimate victory of the proletariat as builder of Communist society.

    (Translated from the Russian by Nicolas Slonimsky)

# Resolution of the Union of Soviet Composers
# Condemning Anti-Soviet Activities

The composers of Moscow, musical activists and members of the Union of Soviet Composers, assembled at a session on the occasion of the trial of the anti-Soviet Trotskyist Center, express their profound indignation at the criminal activity of the Trotskyists, the vilest column of the world Fascist counter-revolution. Inveterate sworn enemies of socialism, dastardly enemies of the working class and its great Party of Lenin and Stalin, attempted to take away from us the achievements of the proletarian revolution, restore capitalism, and impose upon the country the Fascist yoke.

The enemies miscalculated again. In the land of victorious socialism, they failed to find support for their heinous designs, and, having sunk to the lowest level of degradation, became a direct agency of German and Japanese Fascism.

The murder of the best sons of the working class, espionage and diversion, sabotage of the defensive power of the Soviet Union, auctioning off piecemeal the great Soviet fatherland—there is no infamy of which these monstrous Trotskyist outcasts are not capable of perpetrating. There is no room on earth for this vile band!

Soviet composers join their voices to the unanimous demand of the Soviet people —to shoot down every one of these traitors who attempted to destroy our happy life. We are convinced that Soviet justice will expose all the criminal nests of the Trotskyists and their accomplices from the Bukharinovite camp, and will cleanse our Fatherland of this scum of Fascism.

RESOLUTION

United by the great idea of socialism, its ranks closed around the Communist Party and our beloved leader and friend, Comrade Stalin, the Soviet people, having crushed the Fascist beast, strengthening and fortifying revolutionary vigilance, will continue its heroic struggle for the happy future of human kind.

(Published in *Sovietskaya Musica*, Moscow, January 1937)


# Soviet Musical Policy, 1948

RESOLUTION OF THE CENTRAL COMMITTEE
OF THE ALL-UNION COMMUNIST PARTY
(BOLSHEVIKS) OF 10 FEBRUARY 1948

The Central Committee of the All-Union Communist Party (Bolsheviks) considers that the opera *Great Friendship* (music by Muradeli, libretto by Mdivani), produced by the Bolshoi Theater of the Union of Soviet Socialist Republics on the

1358

Thirtieth Anniversary of the October Revolution, is a defective anti-artistic work, in its music and its libretto.

The basic defects of the opera are rooted, first of all, in the music. The music of the opera is inexpressive and weak. It has not a single memorable melody or aria. It is confused and discordant; it is built on continuous dissonances, and ear-splitting combinations of sounds. Occasional lines and scenes, making a pretense of melodiousness, are suddenly interrupted by discordant noises, alien to a normal human ear, which produce a depressing effect on the listener. There is no organic connection between the music and the stage action. The vocal part of the opera, choruses, solos, and ensembles, make a distressing impression. As a result, the resources of the orchestra and the singers remain unused.

The composer did not take advantage of the richness of folk melodies, songs, refrains and dance airs, so abundant in the art of the nations of the USSR, and especially in the art of the nations of North Caucasus, where the action represented in the opera takes place.

In the pursuit of false "originality" in his music, the composer Muradeli ignored the best traditions of classical opera in general, and particularly of Russian classical opera distinguished by inner substantiality, melodic richness, breadth of range, national spirit, and elegant, attractive and clear musical form, the qualities which made Russian operas the best in the world, an art beloved by and accessible to broad strata of the people.

The libretto of the opera is historically false and artificial; it pretends to represent the struggle for the establishment of Soviet power and amity of nations in North Caucasus in 1918–1920. In this opera the wrong impression is created that such Caucasian nations as the Georgians and Osetins were at that time inimical to the Russian people, which is historically false inasmuch as the obstacle blocking the establishment of the friendship of nations during that period in North Caucasus were the Ingushs and Chechens.

The Central Committee of the All-Union Communist Party (Bolsheviks) considers that the fiasco of Muradeli's opera is the result of the fallacious, and, for the art of a Soviet composer, fatal formalistic path taken by Comrade Muradeli.

As was demonstrated at the conference of Soviet musicians, held in the Central Committee of the All-Union Communist Party (Bolsheviks), the fiasco of Muradeli's opera is not an isolated case, but is closely connected with a precarious condition of contemporary Soviet music and with the spread among Soviet musicians of formalistic tendencies.

As far back as 1936, in connection with the appearance of the opera by D. Shostakovich, *Lady Macbeth of the District of Mzensk, Pravda,* the organ of the Central Committee of the All-Union Communist Party (Bolsheviks), subjected to sharp criticism the anti-national formalistic distortions in the music of Shostakovich, and exposed the harm and danger of this trend for the destinies of the development of Soviet music. *Pravda,* acting upon the instructions of the Central Committee of the All-Union Communist Party (Bolsheviks), clearly formulated the demands presented by the Soviet people to their composers.

Despite these warnings, and despite the directives given by the Central Committee of the All-Union Communist Party (Bolsheviks) in its resolutions regarding the magazines *Zvezda* and *Leningrad,* the cinema film *Great Life,* and measures for improvement of the repertoire of dramatic theaters, no reorientation of any kind was made in Soviet music. Occasional successes of some Soviet composers in the field of song writing that received recognition and attained wide popularity in our country, in film music, etc., do not alter the general picture of the situation. Particularly bad are the conditions in symphonic and operatic production, with reference to composers who adhere to the formalistic anti-national movement. This movement has found its fullest expression in the works of composers such as Comrades Shostakovich, Prokofiev, Khachaturian, Shebalin, Popov, Miaskovsky, and others, in whose music formalistic distortions, and anti-democratic tendencies which are alien to the Soviet people and its artistic tastes, are represented with particular obviousness. The characteristic features of this music are the negation of basic principles of classical music; the preachment of atonality, dissonances and disharmony, supposedly representative of "progress" and "modernism" in the development of musical forms; the rejection of such all-important concepts of musical composition as melody, and the infatuation with the confused, neuropathological combinations which transform music into cacophony, into a chaotic agglomeration of sounds. This music is strongly reminiscent of the spirit of contemporary modernistic bourgeois music of Europe and America, reflecting the dissolution of bourgeois culture, a complete negation of musical art, its impasse.

An essential trait of the formalistic movement is also the rejection of polyphonic music and polyphonic singing, based on simultaneous combination and development of a series of independent melodic lines, and the cultivation of a monotonous type of unison music and song, often without words, in violation of the system of many-voiced singing harmony peculiar to our people, all of which leads to impoverishment and decline of music.

Trampling upon the best traditions of Russian and western classical music, rejecting these traditions as supposedly "obsolete," "old-fashioned," and "conservative"; haughtily snubbing those composers who are conscientiously trying to absorb and develop the concepts of classical music as adherents of "primitive traditionalism" and "epigonism," many Soviet composers, in their pursuit after a false conception of novelty, have in their music torn themselves away from the ideals and artistic tastes of the Soviet people, have cloistered themselves in a narrow circle of specialists and musical epicures, have debased the lofty social role of music and narrowed its significance, limiting it to the gratification of the perverted tastes of esthetizing egocentrics.

The formalistic movement in Soviet music has engendered among some Soviet composers a one-sided cultivation of complex forms of instrumental wordless symphonic music, and a supercilious attitude towards such musical genres as opera, choral music, popular music for small orchestras, national instruments, vocal ensembles, etc.

All this inevitably leads to a loss of fundamentals of vocal culture and dramatic mastery, so that the composers forget how to write for the people, as evidenced by the fact that no Soviet operas comparable to Russian classical operas have been produced in recent years.

The break between some Soviet musicians and the people has led to the formulation of the corrupt "theory" that the people fail to understand the music of many contemporary Soviet composers because they have not "grown up" enough to appreciate their intricate compositions; that they will understand it a few centuries hence, and that one should not be embarrassed if some musical works do not find an audience. This thoroughly individualistic and radically anti-national theory has contributed even more to the segregation of some composers and musicologists from the people, from the criticism of Soviet society, and has driven them into their shells.

The cultivation of all these and similar views causes the greatest harm to Soviet musical art. A tolerant attitude towards these views means the spread among those active in Soviet musical culture of tendencies alien to it, leading to an impasse in musical development, to the liquidation of musical art.

The fallacious, anti-national, formalistic tendency in Soviet music exerts a pernicious influence on the preparatory study and education of young composers in our conservatories, especially in the Moscow Conservatory (Director Comrade Shebalin) where the formalistic tendency is predominant. Students are not inculcated in the respect for best traditions of Russian and western classical music; they are not brought up to love national art and democratic musical forms. The creative output of many students of our conservatories consists in blind imitation of the music of Shostakovich, Prokofiev, and others.

The Central Committee of the All-Union Communist Party (Bolsheviks) finds an altogether intolerable situation in Soviet music criticism. The leading posts among critics are occupied by opponents of Russian realistic music and adherents of decadent formalistic music. Every new work by Prokofiev, Shostakovich, Miaskovsky, Shebalin, is acclaimed by these critics as "a new victory of Soviet music" and they glorify in this music its subjectivism, constructivism, extreme individualism, and technical complications of the idiom, i.e., exactly that which should be subjected to criticism. Instead of combating the harmful views and theories alien to the principles of socialist realism, music critics promote them, hailing the composers who share these false artistic concepts as the advance guard in art.

Musical criticism has ceased to express the opinion of Soviet society, the opinion of the nation, and has become a mouthpiece of individual composers. Some music critics, instead of writing objective criticisms, have begun, because of personal friendship, to fawn upon this or that musical leader, glorifying their works in every conceivable way.

All this means that a section of Soviet composers has not yet outlived the vestiges of bourgeois ideology, nourished by the influence of contemporary decadent western European and American music.

The Central Committee of the All-Union Communist Party (Bolsheviks) considers that this unfavorable situation on the front of Soviet music has resulted from the incorrect line in Soviet music, pursued by the Committee of the Fine Arts attached to the Council of Ministers of the USSR, and the Organizational Committee of the Union of Soviet Composers.

The Committee of the Fine Arts of the Council of Ministers of the USSR (Comrade Khrapchenko) and the Organizational Committee of the Union of Soviet Composers (Comrade Khachaturian), have failed to propagandize realistic concepts in Soviet music, the basis of which is the recognition of the tremendous progressive role of classical heritage, and especially of traditions of the Russian musical school, the utilization of this heritage and promotion of its further development, combining high ideational values with the artistic perfection of musical form, the genuineness and realism of music, its profound organic connection with the people, and with the people's musical and vocal art; a high professional mastery, and at the same time simplicity and accessibility of musical works—instead of all this, they have actually encouraged the formalistic movement alien to the Soviet people.

The Organizational Committee of the Union of Soviet Composers has become the tool of a group of composer-formalists, the hotbed of formalistic distortions. The Organizational Committee has created a suffocating atmosphere in which creative discussions are absent. The leaders of the Organizational Committee, and the musicologists grouped around them, heap praise upon anti-realistic, modernistic products undeserving of support, whereas works distinguished by their realistic character and by an effort to continue and to develop the classical heritage, are declared of secondary importance, remain unnoticed and are ignored. Composers who flaunt their "advanced" and "arch-revolutionary" ideas in music act in the Organizational Committee as proponents of the most backward and provincial conservatism, revealing a supercilious intolerance towards the slightest manifestations of criticism.

The Central Committee of the All-Union Communist Party (Bolsheviks) considers that the atmosphere, and the attitude towards the problems of Soviet music, created in the Committee of the Fine Arts at the Council of Ministers of the USSR and in the Organizational Committee of the Union of Soviet Composers, cannot be tolerated any longer, for they inflict the greatest harm upon the development of Soviet music. In recent years the cultural demands and the standard of artistic taste of the Soviet people have grown to an extraordinary degree. The Soviet people expect from their composers products of high quality in all forms, in opera, in symphonic music, in vocal art, in choral and dance music. In our country, composers are given unlimited opportunities, and all necessary conditions have been created for a genuine flowering of musical culture. Soviet composers have a listening audience such as no composer ever knew in the past. It would be unforgivable not to take advantage of all these richest potentialities, and not to direct one's creative efforts along the correct realistic path.

The Central Committee of the All-Union Communist Party (Bolsheviks) resolves:

(1) To condemn the formalistic movement in Soviet music as anti-national and leading to liquidation of music.

(2) To urge the Department of Propaganda and Agitation of the Central Committee and the Committee of the Fine Arts to correct the situation in Soviet music, to liquidate the defects pointed out in the present Resolution of the Central Committee, and to secure the development of Soviet music in the realistic direction.

(3) To call upon Soviet composers to realize fully the lofty requirements of the Soviet people upon musical art, to sweep from their path all that weakens our music and hinders its development, and assure an upsurge of creative work that will advance Soviet musical culture so as to lead to the creation in all fields of music of high-quality works worthy of the Soviet people.

(4) To approve organizational measures of the corresponding Party and Soviet organs, designed to improve the state of musical affairs.


# Discussion at a General Assembly of Soviet Composers Moscow, 17–26 February 1948

SPEECH OF A. A. ZHDANOV

Comrades, the Central Committee of the All-Union Communist Party (Bolsheviks) has decided to assemble a conference of Soviet musicians for the following reasons.

Recently the Central Committee took part in the social preview of the new opera by Comrade Muradeli, *Great Friendship.* You can well imagine with what attention and interest the Central Committee anticipated the very fact of the appearance of a new Soviet opera. Unfortunately, the hopes of the Central Committee were not justified. The opera *Great Friendship* turned out to be a failure.

What were, in the opinion of the Central Committee, the reasons, and what were the circumstances which led to the bankruptcy of this opera? What are the basic defects of this opera?

Speaking of the basic defects of the opera, one must first of all mention its music. In the music of this opera there is not a single memorable melody. The music does not reach the listener. It is not by accident that a rather considerable and sufficiently qualified audience, consisting of no fewer than five hundred people, did not respond during the performance to any part of the opera.

The music of the opera turned out to be very poor. The substitution of inharmonious and at the same time noisy improvisations for melody transformed the opera into a chaotic assortment of screeching sounds. The resources of the orchestra in the opera are utilized to a very limited extent. Throughout a major portion of the opera, the musical accompaniment consists of but a few instruments, and only once in a while, sometimes in the most unexpected places, the whole orchestral ensemble enters in stormy, discordant, and often cacophonic interventions, getting on the nerves of the listener and violently perturbing his mood. This disharmony, this lack of correspondence between the music and the actions, moods, and events, represented on the stage in the course of the opera, produces a depressing effect. A drum intrudes on the most lyrical moments of intimate sentiments; on the other hand, in the scenes of fighting and excitement, when the action on the stage portrays heroic events, the music for some reason becomes soft and lyrical. This creates a break between the musical accompaniment and the moods which the artists are supposed to reflect on the stage.

Despite the fact that the opera treats a very interesting period, the epoch of the establishment of Soviet power in North Caucasus, with all the complexity of its multinational society, and the diversity of forms of class struggle, demanding an adequate picture of the eventful life of the nations of North Caucasus, the music of the opera is alien to the national art of the peoples of North Caucasus.

When Cossacks are on the stage (and they play an important role in the opera), their appearance is not signalized in the music or in the singing by anything characteristic of the Cossacks, of their songs and their music. The same is true in regard to the people of the mountains. If the action includes the dancing of a Lezghinka, its melody does not remind us of any popular rhythms of the Lezghinka. In his pursuit of originality, the composer introduces his own music for the Lezghinka, an unimpressive, tedious music, which is much poorer, much less attractive than the traditional popular music of the Lezghinka.

The pretense of originality permeates the entire score of the opera. The music produces, I should say, a stultifying impression on the listener. Some stanzas and scenes of a lyrical or semi-melodious nature, or those that pretend to be melodious, are suddenly interrupted by noise and shrieking in fortissimo, reminding us of the noise on a building lot, at the moment when excavators, stone crushers and cement mixers go into action. These noises, alien to the normal human ear, demoralize the listener.

A few words regarding the vocal part of the opera: choral, solo, and ensemble singing. Here, too, one must mention the poverty of the entire vocal line of the opera. They say that this opera has complex singing melodies. We do not find it so. The vocal part of the opera is poor, and cannot stand a critical comparison with that wealth of melody and breadth of range to which we are accustomed in the classical operas. In this opera the largest orchestral capacities of the Bolshoi Theater and the magnificent vocal abilities of its singers are left unused. This is a great error. It isn't right to bury the talents of the singers of the Bolshoi Theater, giving them the range of half an octave, or two thirds of an octave, when they can sing two octaves. One should not impoverish art, and this opera represents the impoverishment, the drying-up of art, musical as well as vocal art.

The Committee of the Fine Arts, and particularly its chairman Comrade Khrapchenko, holds the chief responsibility for this affair. He widely publicized the opera *Great Friendship*. More than that, even before the opera was reviewed and approved by listeners, it was announced for production in a number of cities, in Sverdlovsk, Riga, and Leningrad. In the Moscow Bolshoi Theater alone, according to the Committee's statement, six hundred thousand rubles were spent on its production.

This means that the Committee of the Fine Arts, having passed a bad opera for a good one, not only proved itself incompetent in the task of leadership in art, but demonstrated its irresponsibility in having induced the State to expend large sums of money without justification.

If the Central Committee of the All-Union Communist Party (Bolsheviks) is not correct in defending the realistic direction and classical heritage in music, let it be said openly. It may be that the old musical norms have outlived their time; perhaps they should be rejected and be replaced by a new, more progressive direction. One must declare it openly, without hiding in the corner, and without smuggling anti-democratic formalism in music as contraband under the slogan of supposed devotion to the classics, and loyalty to the ideals of socialist realism. It is bad, it is not quite honest. One must be frank and declare outright whatever Soviet musicians have to say on this question. It would be dangerous, and downright fatal for the interest of the development of Soviet art, if the repudiation of the cultural heritage of the past, and the adoption of degraded music, were cloaked in a toga of supposedly genuine Soviet music. Here we must call things by their true names.

## DECLARATION OF TIKHON KHRENNIKOV

The Central Committee of our Party in its Resolution of 10 February 1948 severely branded the anti-democratic formalistic tendencies in Soviet music. The immediate reason for the intervention of the supreme Party organs into musical affairs was the new opera *Great Friendship* by Muradeli, staged by the Bolshoi Theater of the USSR in the days of the thirtieth anniversary of the October Revolution.

It was established that repeated directives of the Party on the problems of art were not carried out by the majority of Soviet composers. All the conversations about "reconstruction," about switching of composers to folkways, to realism, remained empty declarations. Almost all composers who worked in the field of large forms kept aloof from the people, and did not enjoy popularity with the broad audiences. The people knew only songs, marches and film music, but remained indifferent towards most symphonic and chamber music. Concerts in which Soviet symphonic novelties were performed were attended very poorly, whereas classical programs almost invariably filled the hall. Soviet people, in their letters to concert organizations and to the Radio Committee, often voiced their perplexity and at times their protests against the incomprehensible and complicated music of a number of Soviet composers.

The leading figures of our Party and the Central Committee of the All-Union Communist Party (Bolsheviks) have frequently expressed themselves on the subject of Soviet art, directing its development along the path of Socialist realism, and cleansing it of harmful influences and alien ideology. Let us recall the words of V. I. Lenin on the tasks of Soviet art, his appeals in favor of a folk direction in art, his defense of Russian classical heritage against the assaults of the Association of Proletarian Culture; let us further recall the conferences of the Committee for Agitation and Propaganda at the Central Committee of the All-Union Communist Party (Bolsheviks) on the problem of music, held in 1925 and 1929 at the peak of the activity of the Association for Contemporary Music; the Resolution of the Central Committee of the All-Union Communist Party (Bolsheviks) of 23 April 1932 regarding the reorientation of literary and artistic organizations; the articles in the newspaper *Pravda,* "Confusion Instead of Music," and "Ballet Falsification" in 1936; the resolutions of the Central Committee of the All-Union Communist Party in 1946 concerning the periodicals *Zvezda* and *Leningrad,* the film *Great Life,* and the repertory of the drama theaters. We cannot fail to mention the utterances of Comrade Zhdanov at the philosophical discussions of June 1947, and particularly the principal thesis of his declaration: the thesis of the intransigent struggle for the purity of Soviet ideology as the most advanced and the most progressive in the world.

Among the directives of the Central Committee of the All-Union Communist Party (Bolsheviks) dealing with art, the Resolution on Muradeli's opera *Great Friendship* is particularly important for the destinies of Soviet music. This Resolution deals a decisive blow to the anti-democratic formalist movement which has spread in Soviet music. It administers a crushing blow to modernist art as a whole. At the same time this Resolution directs Soviet music onto the path of realism leading to the development and integration of the best traditions of musical classicism and musical art of the nations of the USSR, the path of truly democratic art, the creation of which the Soviet people expects from its composers.

The Central Committee of the All-Union Communist Party (Bolsheviks) points out in its Resolution that formalistic distortions and anti-democratic tendencies have found their fullest expression in the works of such composers as Shostakovich, Prokofiev, Khachaturian, Popov, Miaskovsky, Shebalin, and others. In the music of these composers we witness a revival of anti-realistic decadent influences calculated to destroy the principles of classical music. These tendencies are peculiar to the bourgeois movement of the era of imperialism: the rejection of melodiousness in music, neglect of vocal forms, infatuation with rhythmic and orchestral effects, the piling-up of noisy ear-splitting harmonies, intentional illogicality and unemotionality of music. All these tendencies lead in actual fact to the liquidation of music as one of the strongest expressions of human feelings and thoughts.

In Soviet music, particularly during the last three or four years, there has been increasingly noticeable a break between the listener and musical art. Indicative in this respect is the fiasco with the public of the majority of works written by Soviet composers in recent years: Muradeli's opera *Great Friendship*; Prokofiev's *Festive Poem*, his cantata *Blossom Forth the Mighty Land* and the *Sixth Symphony*; Miaskovsky's *Pathetic Overture* and the cantata *Kremlin at Night*; Shostakovich's *Poem of Fatherland*; Khachaturian's *Symphonie-Poème*, and others.

In the music of the majority of Soviet composers there is noted an over-emphasis on purely abstract instrumental forms, not characteristic of the classical Russian movement in music, and a lack of interest in program music on concrete subjects of Soviet life. Exaggerated attention is given to chamber music written for a handful of connoisseurs, while ignoring such mass consumption forms as the opera.

The composers became engrossed in formalistic experimentation with artificially inflated and impracticable orchestral combinations (such as the inclusion of twenty-four trumpets in Khachaturian's *Symphonie-Poème*, or the incredible scoring for sixteen double-basses, eight harps, four pianos, to the exclusion of the rest of the string instruments, in Prokofiev's *Ode on the End of War*). Such music could not be performed by any of the provincial orchestras; and the gala performances in the Moscow Philharmonic evoked nothing but bewilderment among the listeners by the irrational use of orchestral sonorities, at times actually causing physical suffering. Musical instruments were not used in their natural medium. Thus, the piano was converted into a percussion instrument (as in the fist blows on the keyboard in Prokofiev's *Sixth Sonata*); the violin was transformed from a songful, tender instrument into a grunting, percussive one. The clarity and logic of harmonic progressions were sacrified in favor of intentional complexity of acoustical combinations; natural chords were turned into "timbre-sounds," into blots and inkspots of sound.

A peculiar writing in code, abstractness of the musical language, often reflected images and emotions alien to Soviet realistic art—expressionistic tenseness, neuroticism, escape into a region of abnormal, repulsive, and pathological phenomena. This defect is noticeable in many pages of Shostakovich's *Eighth* and *Ninth Symphonies*, and the *Piano Sonatas* of Prokofiev. One of the means of escape from reality was also the "neo-classical" tendency in the music of Shostakovich and his imitators, the resurrection of melodic turns and mannerisms of Bach, Handel, Haydn, and other composers, which were reproduced in a decadently distorted manner.

The musical art of the people and, above all, Russian folk songs were not favored by the aforementioned composers. When occasionally they turned toward folk melodies they arranged them in an overcomplex decadent manner alien to folk art (as in Popov's *Third Symphony on Spanish Themes*, and in some arrangements of Russian folk songs by Prokofiev).

All these creative faults are typical expressions of formalism.

Formalism is a revelation of emptiness and lack of ideas in art. The rejection of ideas in art leads to the preachment of "art for art's sake," to a cult of "pure" form, a cult of technical devices as a goal in itself, a hypertrophy of certain elements of the musical speech at the price of a loss of integrity and harmoniousness of art.

The Resolution of the Central Committee of the All-Union Communist Party (Bolsheviks) indicates that one of the traits of formalist music is the rejection of singing polyphony and a retreat towards a cerebral, dry, artificial counterpoint in the so-called linear style, or else the adoption of primitive unison writing.

The cultivation of form as a goal in art leads in the end to the disintegration of form itself and to the loss of high-quality professional mastery.

As Comrade Zhdanov has profoundly pointed out, the philosophical background of these views is subjective idealism. The artist imagines himself to be the appraiser and final judge of his art. He cares little about the listening human society. Personal caprice, a random whim, an extreme inconsiderateness, and the subjectivism of the isolated author are sharply contrasted with the requirements and expectations of his environment: "This is the way I feel, and I don't care what my listeners think about it."

Comrade Zhdanov has said in this connection that if an artist does not expect to be understood by his contemporaries, it leads to desolation, to an impasse. If a true artist, says Comrade Zhdanov, finds that his work is not understood by the listeners, he must figure out first of all why he failed to please the people, why the people cannot understand him.

The theory and practice of formalism is a complete negation of democratic aspirations of the Russian classical composers and of the progressive representatives of music criticism. Great musicians of the past addressed their art to a contemporary audience, to their people, and not to their remote descendants.

Soviet composers of the formalistic persuasion ignored these progressive traditions of Russian classicism. It is not by accident that Comrade Zhdanov said to the composers-formalists present at the conference in the Central Committee: "One must admit that the landlord Glinka, the government clerk Serov and the member of nobility Stasov were more democratic than you are."

The anti-democratic formalistic direction of Soviet music is closely connected with the bourgeois decadent music of the contemporary West and the modernistic music of pre-revolutionary Russia.

The present musical art of western Europe and America reflects the universal dissolution and spiritual impoverishment of bourgeois culture. One cannot name a single composer of the West who is not infected with formalistic diseases, subjectivism and mysticism, and lack of ideological principles. The apostle of reactionary forces in bourgeois music, Igor Stravinsky, with equal impartiality writes a Catholic Mass in a stylized decadent style, or jazz pieces for the circus. The latest musical "genius" of contemporary France, Olivier Messiaen, writes mystical music on subjects from the Bible and medieval Catholic works. Contemporary operas of the German composers Hindemith, Krenek, Alban Berg, the Englishman Britten, the American Menotti, are a conglomeration of wild harmonies, far removed from natural human song. In this music there is frankly proclaimed a reversion to the primitive savage cultures of prehistoric society; eroticism is glorified along with psychopathology, sexual perversion, amorality and the shamelessness of the contemporary bourgeois heroes of the twentieth century.

In the well-known opera by Krenek, *Sprung über den Schatten,* nearly all the characters are absolutely amoral individuals. In that opera there is even a special chorus of sexual psychopaths-masochists. In the opera by the German composer Max Brand, *Machinist Hopkins,* the principal characters are murderers and erotomaniacs. Machinist Hopkins himself is a vile fascist caricature of a leader in a workers' movement, and is represented as a lustful beast, a base exploiter of women.

In Hindemith's *Sancta Susanna* religious erotomania is portrayed with repulsive naturalism. Similar pathology characterizes the neurotic operas of Alban Berg, and, among recent operas, *The Medium* by Gian-Carlo Menotti which enjoys tremendous success with the bourgeois public in America. The central character of this opera is a professional swindler, a woman spiritualist who suffers from alcoholism, and in addition is a murderess.

In Russian music formalistic ideas flourished particularly during the reaction after the Revolution of 1905. Among characteristic examples of decadent art in music are Stravinsky's *Le Sacre du Printemps,* Prokofiev's *Buffoon,* and a number of other works by these composers. The man who inspired and commissioned the majority of these works was Serge Diaghilev, one of the most prominent ideologists of Russian modernism.

Diaghilev was the organizer of a modernistic group of artists, known as "The World of Art." He urged artists and musicians to sever connections with the great realistic traditions of Russian art: "Down with the traditions of the Mighty Five, of Tchaikovsky. They are obsolete and limited national phenomena; it is time to merge Russian art in a common European culture"—such was the frank and cynical slogan of Diaghilev and other representatives of the modernistic camp.

The modernist element in Russian music is the revelation of frank sycophancy before the Western music market, a desire to gain favor with the foreign audience, to titillate the nerves of the surfeited bourgeois listener-snob with exotic Russian "Asianism."

For Diaghilev's ballet in Paris, Stravinsky wrote *Petrouchka, Le Sacre du Printemps, Les Noces,* the opera *Le Rossignol,* and Prokofiev wrote his ballet *The Buffoon,* and other works.

The principal goal of the composers of these works is to escape from the contemporary world of humanity into the world of abstraction. Stravinsky himself, in his article, "What I Wished to Express in *Le Sacre du Printemps*" (*Music,* monthly magazine, 1913), writes: "I evoke neither human joy nor human sadness; I move towards a greater abstraction." His reversion to the images of "primordial earth" he explains by a desire to reflect "that fear which lives in every sensitive soul in contact with mysterious forces." This reversion to antediluvian barbaric images, the depiction of savagery and bestial instincts of a prehistoric man, of a Scythian, is found in some poems of the Russian writers of the bourgeois-modernistic type. In these poems, there is sounded an alarm before the "coming Ham," the plebeian who must come and destroy the beauty and the well-being of the bourgeois regime. In *Le Sacre du Printemps* Stravinsky expressed these moods in boisterous, chaotic, intentionally coarse, screaming sonorities. "Rhythm and motion, not the element of feeling, are the foundations of musical art," asserted Stravinsky. With Diaghilev's blessings Stravinsky uses, in *Petrouchka* and *Les Noces,* some elements of Russian life to mock at Russian customs and to please the European spectator by the express emphasis on Russian "Asianism," crudity, animal instincts, sexual motives. Ancient folk strains are here grotesquely distorted, twisted, and are served as if reflected in a crooked mirror. These so-called "irony and grotesque" are in evidence also in Prokofiev's ballet *The Buffoon,* in which the "exoticism" of old Russian folkways is relished in a decadent manner. The musical language of this work is related to the above-named ballets of Stravinsky. The continuation of the same line of "Russian grotesque" is seen in Stravinsky's comic opera "after Pushkin," *Mavra,* written in 1922. From this opera there is a direct line to the two defective operas by Shostakovich, *The Nose* and *Lady Macbeth.*

Paralleling this line Stravinsky and other new composers of the West, such as Hindemith in Germany, launched in the 1920's a "new" slogan (actually it is closely connected with the first line): "Back to Bach!" This meant that in a number of works there were revived polyphonic devices mechanically transplanted from Bach. They were ornamented by "new" harmonies, transforming the whole thing into cacophony. This reversion to Bach led to the composition by Stravinsky of the so-called *Symphony of Psalms,* in which there are stridently combined the old Bachian devices of polyphonic writing with the ear-splitting "contemporary" harmonies. The meaning of this mixture is well expressed in the composer's dedication of this Symphony: "Dedicated to the Almighty Lord and to the American Philharmonic Society." *

The music of Soviet composers of the 1920's and 1930's offers numerous instances of formalistic tendencies in Soviet music: Shostakovich: opera *The Nose, Second Symphony, Third Symphony;* Prokofiev: the ballets *The Prodigal Son, On the Boristhenes, Pas d'acier,* the opera *The Flaming Angel, Third Symphony, Fourth Symphony, Fifth Piano Concerto, Fifth Piano Sonata;* Mossolov: *Iron Foundry, Newspaper Advertisements;* Knipper: the opera *North Wind, Tales of a Porcelain Buddha;* Deshevov: the opera *Ice and Steel;* Miaskovsky: *Tenth Symphony, Thirteenth Symphony, Third Piano Sonata, Fourth Piano Sonata;* Feinberg: *Piano Sonatas, First Piano*

* The inscription in the score of Stravinsky's *Symphony of Psalms* reads: "Composed for the glory of God and dedicated to the Boston Symphony on the occasion of the fiftieth anniversary of its existence."

*Concerto*; Shebalin: *Lenin Symphony, Second Symphony*; Popov: *First Symphony*; Liatoshinsky: *Second Symphony*, songs; Boelza: *First Symphony, Second Symphony*, songs; Polovinkin: *Telescopes* for orchestra, *Accidents* for piano; Litinsky: Quartets and Sonatas; Shcherbachev: *Third Symphony*, etc.

The formalistic element in music is particularly strong in the *Eighth Symphony*, the *Ninth Symphony*, and the *Second Piano Sonata* by Shostakovich; in the *Sixth Symphony*, the opera *War and Peace*, and a number of piano works by Prokofiev; in *Symphonie-Poème* by Khachaturian; in the Quartet and String Trio by Shebalin, and in the *Third Symphony* by Popov. In Miaskovsky's music we find a one-sided preoccupation with instrumental music and a lack of interest for vocal and operatic music, which had a detrimental effect on the melodic idiom of his instrumental compositions, particularly the *Third Piano Sonata* and the *Fourth Piano Sonata*, written in the 1920's, but newly revised by the composer in recent years.

The influence of formalism is strongly felt in the creative work of young composers. The imitation of negative traits of the music by Shostakovich and Prokofiev, the infatuation with decadent thematics, exoticism and mysticism became almost a routine phenomenon in the creative output of the young generation of Soviet composers.

Formalistic distortions are also strongly reflected in the education of young composers in conservatories, particularly in the Moscow Conservatory. This is obviously connected with the fact that some composers mentioned in the Resolution of the Central Committee of the All-Union Communist Party (Bolsheviks) as representative of the formalistic movement (Shostakovich, Shebalin and Miaskovsky) are professors of the Moscow Conservatory, and Shebalin is its director.

The almost total contamination of young composers with the harmful influence of western music, the imitation of negative qualities of Soviet composers belonging to the formalist school, neglect of the traditions of musical classicism, particularly Russian classicism, and of the art of the nations of the USSR, testifies to the fact that the formalist movement plays a decisive role in the education of the young cadres of composers.

The Central Committee of the All-Union Communist Party (Bolsheviks) notes an altogether intolerable condition of Soviet music criticism. Our critics have lost the most important quality of Russian progressive criticism. They have ceased to fight for the high aspirations of art, for the ideals of realistic and democratic art.

The orientation towards Stravinsky as the most progressive phenomenon in contemporary music is found in the treatise of A. Ogolevetz, *Introduction to Contemporary Musical Thought*. In essence the entire "theory" of A. Ogolevetz is, objectively speaking, a theoretical support of formalism, and is an anti-Leninist and anti-Marxist work.

The musical departments of the periodical, *Soviet Art*, and other newspapers, and the monthly *Sovietskaya Musica* did not fight for the ideals of democratic art but lent their pages to apologists for the formalist movement. The Committee of Fine Arts has often shown the inclination to stifle even the most timid attempts to criticize the formalist movement. Thus, at the personal directive of Comrade Khrapchenko, chairman of the Committee of Fine Arts, critical articles about the *Ninth Symphony* of Shostakovich (among them an article by Keldysh strongly condemning this Symphony) were not allowed for publication in *Sovietskaya Musica*.

The policy of the Committee of Fine Arts, the Organizational Committee, and the Musical Fund, in the Section for Promotion and Propaganda of Soviet music, reflected above all the interests of the formalist school. Thus, the Musical Fund published the obviously fallacious formalistic compositions of the type of the *Second Symphony* of Boelza and the *Fourth Symphony* of Shostakovich, not to mention numerous editions of different versions of works by a narrow group of composers of the formalist school.

The Committee on Fine Arts did not take suitable measures toward the development of Soviet music in the realistic direction; it failed to promote the composition of operas, choral music, popular music for small orchestras, music for national instruments, vocal ensembles, etc. Commissions given to composers by the Committee of Fine Arts did not direct Soviet music along the correct path. The system of commissions was basically a form of material security for the leading group of composers of the formalist school. The major part of State commissions for the year 1947 was taken up by abstract, textless, instrumental forms. Prokofiev alone received eight commissions, among them one for the preparation of a "new" version of his *Fourth Symphony* derived from his ballet *The Prodigal Son*, which was condemned by Soviet society.

The decisive role in the Music Section of the Committee for Stalin Prizes was played by the same composers, representatives of the formalist movement. Some products of decadent art, which failed to find recognition with the general public, were nominated for a prize on the basis of a hearing by the narrow circle of specialists. Almost every new work by "leading" composers was automatically promoted as a prize work, year after year.

Soviet composers must reject as useless and harmful garbage all the relics of bourgeois formalism in musical art. They must understand that the creation of high-quality works in the domain of the opera, symphonic music, song-writing, choral and dance music, is possible only by following the principles of socialist realism.

Our duty is to mobilize all our creative strength and to give a worthy response, in the shortest possible time, to this appeal of our Party, to the appeal of our great leader Comrade STALIN.


STATEMENT BY VANO MURADELI

The Central Committee of our Party in its historic Revolution has subjected my opera *Great Friendship* to a just and severe criticism.

The Resolution establishes the fact that my opera is an anti-artistic composition, corrupt both from the musical and political standpoint. I fully agree with this absolutely correct evaluation of my opera.

A. A. Zhdanov, in his historic report to the General Assembly of Soviet Composers, exposed in clear terms the false formalistic tendencies in my opera *Great Friendship*.

The speech of Zhdanov will remain forever in my memory as an impassioned appeal to Soviet composers to serve our people with honesty and devotion, and to fight determinedly and unswervingly for the great ideals of building up Communist society in our country.

Addressing the Union of Soviet Composers, I wish to state the causes of my major creative errors. There are several reasons for my failure. I shall attempt to analyze them in full.

(1) Although I have been a convinced exponent of composition inspired by folk songs, I was unable to pursue this realistic path. Instead, attracted by false innovations, I have accepted the formalistic techniques of musical modernism.

(2) My isolation from other composers, which was a result of my "aristocratic" position in the Organizational Committee, deprived me of the opportunity of heeding their Bolshevik criticism, and receiving their professional advice.

(3) I have not made adequate study, and have not acquired sufficient professional knowledge of the operatic heritage of the great Russian and Western classics.

(4) Having been completely engrossed in the composition of my opera, I neglected to work on the improvement of my ideological political education.

(5) My over-confidence and self-complacency, my exaggerated preoccupation with professional activities, carelessness and haste, resulted in retarding the progress of my work.

(6) I failed to pay attention to the voice of the people and to their ideological and spiritual requirements. I lost the sense of true actuality and its vital imperatives. My opera *Great Friendship* failed to portray the life of the people, or its art, in any of its native phases. This shows that I have lost contact with the life of our people.

I grew up in the atmosphere of folk music. My first compositions hardly differed from simple songs of the people. In my later works—*Four Georgian Songs, Symphonic*

*Dance,* and *Ten Heroic Songs*—I again turned for inspiration to these sources of people's music.

How could it have happened that I failed to introduce a single folk song in the score of my opera? It seems strange and almost incredible to me, and can be explained only as a manifestation of my inherent snobbishness. Apart from that, I did not possess sufficient mastery and craftsmanship for writing a large operatic work and building a music drama. In a number of places in my opera I indulged in technical tricks to obtain novel effects. Thus my opera was deprived of natural feeling and logical development.

There is no justification for these techniques in my opera, for the absence of folk songs, for the over-elaborateness, and at times crudity of my musical language. All this deprives my opera of the sense of reality, leading me towards a false formalistic path.

I have before me a definite task, to realize fully and unequivocally the seriousness of my creative errors, and to correct these errors with ideological honesty in my future works. The Resolution of the Central Committee of the All-Union Communist Party (Bolsheviks) is a new and vivid manifestation of interest and solicitude shown by our Party for the destinies of Soviet socialist culture. This historic Resolution constitutes for Soviet composers a clear creative program presaging a mighty uplift of Soviet musical culture. I will try with all my heart to earn the right to continue my devoted service to our Soviet music.

## STATEMENT OF DMITRI SHOSTAKOVICH

As we look back on the road traversed by our art, it becomes quite clear to us that every time that the Party corrects errors of a creative artist and points out the deviations in his work, or else severely condemns a certain tendency in Soviet art, it invariably brings beneficial results for Soviet art and for individual artists.

The directives of the Central Committee of the All-Union Communist Party (Bolsheviks) are inspired by the desire to raise the standard and the significance of art in the development of our Soviet society.

When in 1936 the central organ of our Party, *Pravda,* severely condemned my opera *Lady Macbeth of the District of Mzensk* and pointed out my serious aberrations, my formalism, this creative failure affected me profoundly. I gave it a great deal of thought, trying hard to derive from it all the necessary lessons. It seemed to me that in the years following, my art began to develop in a new direction. I strove to provide an answer in my work to the great and stirring problems that faced the whole Soviet land, the whole Soviet people. It seemed to me that to a certain extent I managed to eradicate the pernicious elements pointed out in *Pravda*: the over-complication of the musical language, the elaboration of musical thought, etc.

This severe but just criticism by the Party made me study more intensely the works of the Russian classics and Russian national art. In that light I regarded my work on Mussorgsky's opera *Boris Godunov* when I worked on its orchestration and on its editing.

As I look back mentally at all I have written after *Lady Macbeth,* it seems to me that in my symphonic works and chamber music there appeared elements new to my art, which when developed should have given me the opportunity of finding a path to the heart of the Soviet people. However, this did not materialize. I now can clearly see that I overestimated the thoroughness of my artistic reconstruction; certain negative characteristics peculiar to my musical thought prevented me from making the turn that seemed to be indicated in a number of my works of recent years. I again deviated in the direction of formalism, and began to speak a language incomprehensible to the people.

Now, when the Party and our entire nation, speaking through the Resolution of the Central Committee of the All-Union Communist Party (Bolsheviks), condemn this tendency in my music, I know that the Party is right; I know that the Party shows solicitude for Soviet art and for me as a Soviet composer.

All the resolutions of the Central Committee of the All-Union Communist Party (Bolsheviks) regarding the art of recent years, and particularly the Resolution of 10 February 1948 in regard to the opera *Great Friendship*, point out to Soviet artists that a tremendous national uplift is now taking place in our country, our great Soviet nation.

Some Soviet artists, and among them myself, attempted to give expression in their works to this great national uplift. But between my subjective intentions and objective results there was an appalling gap.

The absence, in my works, of the interpretation of folk art, that great spirit by which our people lives, has been with utmost clarity and definiteness pointed out by the Central Committee of the All-Union Communist Party (Bolsheviks).

I am deeply grateful for it and for all the criticism contained in the Resolution.

All the directives of the Central Committee of the All-Union Communist Party (Bolsheviks), and in particular those that concern me personally, I accept as a stern but paternal solicitude for us, Soviet artists.

Work—arduous, creative, joyous work on new compositions which will find their path to the heart of the Soviet people, which will be understandable to the people, loved by them, and which will be organically connected with the people's art, developed and enriched by the great traditions of Russian classicism—this will be a fitting response to the Resolution of the Central Committee of the All-Union Communist Party (Bolsheviks).

In my *Poem of Fatherland* I attempted to create a symphonic work infused with songfulness and melodiousness. It proved to be unsuccessful.

On the basis of the principles clearly given in the Resolution of the Central Committee of the All-Union Communist Party (Bolsheviks), I shall try again and again to create symphonic works close to the spirit of the people from the standpoint of ideological subject matter, musical language and form.

I shall still more determinedly work on the musical depiction of the images of the heroic Soviet people.

I am now at work on the music for a cinema film, *Young Guard,* and I have begun an opera of the same title. I hope that in these compositions I shall partially achieve the aims of which I spoke here.

Some of my songs have attained a certain popularity among the people. Now, equipped with the directives of the Central Committee of the All-Union Communist Party (Bolsheviks), I shall again and again try to create Soviet mass songs.

I have no doubt whatsoever that Soviet music is on the eve of a tremendous creative uplift. This uplift will develop on the basis of the realization in the art of Soviet composers of the wise and just directives of the Central Committee of the All-Union Communist Party (Bolsheviks).

I appeal to all composers to bend their efforts to the task of the realization of this remarkable Resolution.


## STATEMENT OF ARAM KHACHATURIAN

The Resolution of the Central Committee of the All-Union Communist Party (Bolsheviks) is the expression of the will of our people and fully reflects the opinion of the Soviet people regarding our music.

The Resolution of the Central Committee of the All-Union Communist Party (Bolsheviks) brings liberation to us, Soviet musicians. Indeed one feels as if we have thrown off the chains that have held us for many years. Despite my depressed moral state (for understandable reasons), I have a feeling of joy and satisfaction.

We feel easier, more free; there is before us a clear path, a road for Soviet music to pursue its swift progress. I see this path clearly, and I have only one desire, to correct by creative work all my previous errors.

How could it happen that I have come to formalism in my art? I made use of many folk songs, particularly my native Armenian songs. I have also used other national songs, Russian, Ukrainian, Georgian, Uzbekian, Turkmenian, and Tartar songs. I wrote a number of compositions based on these songs.

I have always declared that I do not recognize non-melodic music; I have always maintained that melody is the foundation of musical composition. But despite the fact that I stood on these seemingly correct creative positions, I have committed formalistic errors.

I see two reasons for these errors. The first is my preoccupation with technique. I have often been reproached for my insufficient technical equipment. This was reflected in my consciousness. My desire to achieve a complete technical mastery imperceptibly resulted in an over-emphasis on technique, which is particularly evident in my *Symphonie-Poème*.

I have reached formalism because of my cultivation of abstract technique.

When music critics and musicologists were telling me that it was about time for me to go beyond the national confines, to renounce the supposedly narrow stylistic direction of my music, I listened attentively to these ideas. I failed to repudiate these harmful creative positions in time. In recent years I have moved farther and farther away from my native Armenian element; I wanted to be cosmopolitan.

Andrey Adreyevitch Zhdanov in his statement at the meeting in the Central Committee of the Party said that internationalism in music can develop only on the basis of enrichment and flowering of national music, and not by erasing the national elements.

Creative errors and formalistic leanings in our music could not but influence my work in the Organizational Committee, which became a hotbed of formalism. It could not fight formalism with members who either fully or partly stood on formalistic positions, or else were sympathizers. As the principal leader of the Organizational Committee, I had every opportunity to inaugurate and lead the struggle with this phenomenon in music. But I failed to do so.

I turned out to be a poor leader, and my methods of work in the Organizational Committee were undemocratic. In recent years I stood aloof from our composers' life. Members of the Organizational Committee became "grands seigneurs" proud of their "creative achievements," and as a result found themselves generals without an army. Criticism and self-criticism in the Organizational Committee were stifled.

The Resolution of the Central Committee declares that the Organizational Committee maintained a suffocating atmosphere, devoid of all creative discussion. One of the chief reasons interfering with the work of the Organizational Committee was a lack of unity among its members. We were preoccupied with petty quarrels and our personal interrelations. We forgot that we were appointed to guide the Union of Soviet Composers, that we were expected to lead all other composers. Hypocritically paying compliments to one another, we, the members of the Organizational Committee, actually were highly antagonistic to each other.

I accept full responsibility for the unfavorable situation on the front of Soviet music, which was created as a result of the incorrect line in the domain of Soviet music, established by the Organizational Committee.

I wish to point out another very serious danger. I want to warn those comrades who, like myself, hoped that their music, which is not understood by the people today, will be understood by the future generations tomorrow. It is a fatal theory. In our country, millions of people, the entire Soviet nation, are now arbiters of music. What can be higher and nobler than writing music understandable to our people and to give joy by our creative art to millions?

I urge all Soviet composers, and above all, Shostakovich, Prokofiev, Shebalin, Popov, Miaskovsky, and Muradeli, to answer the stern but just Resolution of the Central Committee of the All-Union Communist Party (Bolsheviks) by a decisive reorientation of their musical views, and to prove by their artistic production the thoroughness and the sincerity of their reorientation.

Our principal task is now to unite on the basis of the Resolution of the Central Committee, to work as much as possible, and as well as possible, and to prove by deeds that Soviet composers are marching in the vanguard of victorious Soviet culture.

## LETTER FROM PROKOFIEV

The state of my health prevents me from attending the General Assembly of Soviet Composers. I therefore wish to express my ideas in regard to the Resolution of the Central Committee of the All-Union Communist Party (Bolsheviks) of 10 February 1948, in the present letter. I request that you read it at the Assembly if you find it expedient.

The Resolution of the Central Committee of the All-Union Communist Party of 10 February 1948, has separated decayed tissue in the composers' creative production from the healthy part. No matter how painful it may be for many composers, myself included, I welcome the Resolution of the Central Committee of the All-Union Communist Party (Bolsheviks) which establishes the necessary conditions for the return to health of the whole organism of Soviet music. The Resolution is particularly important because it demonstrates that the formalist movement is alien to the Soviet people, that it leads to impoverishment and decline of music. It points out with ultimate clarity the aims that Soviet composers must attain to be of the greatest service to the Soviet people.

As far as I am concerned, elements of formalism were peculiar to my music as long as fifteen or twenty years ago. Apparently the infection caught from contact with some western ideas. When formalistic errors in Shostakovich's opera *Lady Macbeth of the District of Mzensk* were exposed by *Pravda,* I gave a great deal of thought to creative devices in my own music, and came to the conclusion that such a method of composition is faulty.

As a result, I began a search for a clearer and more meaningful language. In several of my subsequent works—*Alexander Nevsky, A Toast to Stalin, Romeo and Juliet, Fifth Symphony*—I strove to free myself from elements of formalism and, it seems to me, succeeded to a certain degree. The existence of formalism in some of my works is probably explained by a certain self-complacency, an insufficient realization of the fact that it is completely unwanted by our people. The Resolution has shaken to the core the social consciousness of our composers, and it has become clear what type of music is needed by our people, and the ways of the eradication of the formalist disease have also become clear.

I have never questioned the importance of melody. I love melody, and I regard it as the most important element in music. I have worked on the improvement of its quality in my compositions for many years. To find a melody instantly understandable even to the uninitiated listener, and at the same time an original one, is the most difficult task for a composer. Here he is beset by a great multitude of dangers: he may fall into the trivial or the banal, or into the rehashing of something already written by him. In this respect, composition of complex melodies is much easier. It may also happen that a composer, fussing over his melody for a long time, and revising it, unwittingly makes it over-refined and complicated, and departs from simplicity. Undoubtedly, I fell into this trap, too, in the process of my work. One must be particularly vigilant to make sure that the melody retains its simplicity without becoming cheap, saccharine, or imitative. It is easy to say, but not so easy to accomplish. All my efforts will be henceforth concentrated to make these words not only a recipe, but to carry them out in my subsequent works.

I must admit that I, too, have indulged in atonality, but I also must say that I have felt an attraction towards tonal music for a considerable time, after I clearly realized that the construction of a musical work tonally is like erecting a building on a solid foundation, while a construction without tonality is like building on sand. Besides, tonal and diatonic music lends many more possibilities than atonal and chromatic music, which is evident from the impasse reached by Schoenberg and his disciples. In some of my works in recent years there are sporadic atonal moments. Without much sympathy, I nevertheless made use of this device, mainly for the sake of contrast, in order to bring tonal passages to the fore. In the future I hope to get rid of this mannerism.

In my operatic production I have been often criticized for the predominance of recitative over cantilena. I like the theater as such, and I believe that a person who attends the opera has a right to expect not only auditory, but also visual impressions; or else he would go to a concert and not to the opera. But every action on the stage is closely associated with recitative; on the other hand, cantilena induces a certain immobility on the stage. I recall the painful experience of watching the action in some of Wagner's operas, when during a whole act, lasting nearly an hour, not a single person moved on the stage. This fear of immobility prevented me from dwelling on cantilena too long. In connection with the Resolution, I thought over this problem with great care, and came to the conclusion that every operatic libretto has elements demanding the use of the recitative, while other elements imperatively require a treatment in the arioso style. But there are also sections (and these sections take up considerable space, adding up perhaps to one-half of the entire opera) which the composer may treat as he wishes, either as a recitative or as an arioso. Let us consider, for example, the scene of Tatiana's letter from *Eugene Onegin*. It would have been quite simple to write most of it in the form of a recitative, but Tchaikovsky preferred cantilena, and so made the letter scene into a sort of aria, which has this additional advantage that it is accompanied by stage action, giving satisfaction not only to the ear but also to the eye. This is the direction which I intend to take in my new opera on a contemporary Soviet subject, *A Tale of a Real Man* by Polevoy.

I am highly gratified that the Resolution has pointed out the desirability of polyphony, particularly in choral and ensemble singing. This is indeed an interesting task for a composer, promising a great pleasure to the listener. In my above-mentioned opera, I intend to introduce trios, duets, and contrapuntally developed choruses, for which I will make use of some interesting northern Russian folk songs. Lucid melody, and as far as possible, a simple harmonic language, are elements which I intend to use in my opera.

In conclusion, I should like to express my gratitude to our Party for the precise directives of the Resolution, which will help me in my search of a musical language, accessible and natural to our people, worthy of our people and of our great country.


## LETTER TO STALIN

DEAR IOSIF VISSARIONOVICH:

The composers and musicologists of the Soviet capital, assembled for the discussion of the historic Resolution of the Central Committee of the All-Union Communist Party (Bolsheviks) of 10 February 1948 regarding the opera by Muradeli, *Great Friendship,* send to you, our beloved leader and teacher, a warm salute and wishes for good health.

We are tremendously grateful to the Central Committee of the All-Union Communist Party (Bolsheviks) and personally to you, dear Comrade Stalin, for the severe but profoundly just criticism of the present state of Soviet music, and for the interest which you and the Central Committee of our Party have shown for the progress of Soviet music, and for us, Soviet musicians.

The conference of Soviet musicians with the Central Committee of the All-Union Communist Party (Bolsheviks), and particularly the speech of Comrade Zhdanov, and the Resolution of the Central Committee of the All-Union Communist Party (Bolsheviks) of 10 February 1948, are events of historical significance; the extraordinarily powerful, profound and precise analysis of the contemporary state of Soviet music, the clear directives for the elimination of defects in Soviet music give us inestimable help, a testimony of the great power and prophetic vision of the Communist Party.

We, composers and musicologists of the city of Moscow, recognize the complete justice of the Party's criticism of Soviet music, which is now freeing itself from the deadening impact of bourgeois-formalist routine, from the influence of decadence.

It is obvious to us that, having entered the path of formalistic pseudo-modernism, the representatives of the movement condemned in the Resolution of the Central Committee of the All-Union Communist Party (Bolsheviks) have disassociated themselves from folk music and song, have forgotten the musical language of their native land, have debased themselves to the point of subjecting their talents to models and dogmas of western European and American modernism. Confronted with the Soviet people, whose voice sounds in every line of the Resolution of the Central Committee of the All-Union Communist Party (Bolsheviks), we admit that many of us have forgotten the great traditions of Russian musical realism. The words of the great genius, Glinka, who declared "Music is created by the people, and we, artists, only arrange it," have not found their adequate expression in the art of Soviet composers. As a result, the national element has been ignored in our operatic and symphonic production, and the fallacious "theory," subjectively idealistic in its essence, has been circulated to prove that broad masses of listeners are supposedly not "grown up" enough to understand contemporary music.

For us, Soviet musicians, it is all the more painful to realize that we have failed to draw correct and logical conclusions from the warnings that have been repeatedly sounded by our Party whenever Soviet music has deviated from its true realistic path. The articles, Confusion Instead of Music and Ballet Falsification, published in Pravda twelve years ago, the Resolutions of the Central Committee of the All-Union Communist Party (Bolsheviks) concerning the magazines Zvezda and Leningrad, and the motion picture Great Love, and the article, Regarding the Repertory of Dramatic Theatres and Measures for Its Improvement, were not followed, as it was with profound justice pointed out in the Resolution of the Central Committee of the All-Union Communist Party (Bolsheviks), by any reorientation in Soviet music. Soviet composers and critics have failed to appreciate duly the timely and precise directives of the Central Committee of the All-Union Communist Party (Bolsheviks), and so have caused the heaviest detriment to Soviet musical culture. Only their lack of contact with the life of the nation can account for the fact that our composers were unable to evaluate in full the colossal and unprecedented growth of artistic tastes and requirements of the broad popular masses, and for that reason were unable to satisfy these tastes and requirements of the great Soviet people.

Your personal suggestions, dear Iosif Vissarionovich, regarding the task of building the Soviet classical opera, given by you in your talk with the composer Dzerzhinsky in connection with his opera, Quiet Flows the Don, remain a fighting program of our creative effort. We shall bend every effort to apply our knowledge and our artistic mastery and to produce vivid realistic music reflecting the life and struggles of the Soviet people.

The creative isolationism of composers must be ended once and for all. There is no place for bourgeois individualism in the musical art of a country where the artist is given every opportunity for a full development of his creative individuality, where he is surrounded with solicitude and care, of which the artists of bourgeois countries dare not even dream. In no country has a composer such an audience as in our land.

The Soviet artist is the servant of the people. This is the first conclusion that all Soviet composers and musicologists ought to make, and the creative art of every Soviet musician must be subordinated entirely to this lofty democratic principle.

Not for the snobs should sound our music, but for our whole great people.

We assure you, our beloved leader and teacher, that the appeals of the Central Committee of the All-Union Communist Party (Bolsheviks) addressed to us, Soviet musicians, will become a fighting program of our creative art. We shall give all our strength to the new and unparalleledly great flowering of Soviet musical art.

We give to you and to the whole Soviet people a sworn pledge that we shall direct our work along the path of socialist realism, tirelessly laboring to create, in all musical forms, models worthy of our great epoch, striving to make our music beloved by the whole great Soviet people, so that the great ideas that inspire our nation in its universally historic deeds of valor shall find living and vivid expression in our art.

Long live the Lenin-Stalin people, the nation-worker, nation-victor that has earned the right for the most progressive socialist art in the world!

Long live the Lenin-Stalin Central Committee of the All-Union Communist Party (Bolsheviks)!

Long live our leader and teacher, father of the nation, great STALIN!

## Letter of Protest from Four Soviet Composers

TO THE EDITOR OF IZVESTIA:

American newspapers have reported the release of the film *The Iron Curtain*. We know that this film pursues the aim of slandering our homeland, of fanning enmity and hatred for the Soviet people, in order to please the enemies of world peace and security.

With deep indignation we have learned from a report of the *New York Times* that excerpts from our musical works are being used in this film.

Needless to say, none of us ever gave, or could have given, his consent for the use of our music in any form whatsoever in the picture *The Iron Curtain*.

Knowing beforehand that Soviet composers would indignantly reject any such offer, the agents of the American Twentieth Century-Fox Corporation resorted to a swindling trick in order to steal our music for their outrageous picture. American reactionaries decided to supplement, by the theft of our works, the anti-Soviet forgeries on which their film is based.

The fact that these gentlemen enjoy full opportunity for political blackmail, that they ignore elementary rights of composers in making unwarranted use of their creative work, proves once more that manners and morals exist in the United States under which the rights of the individual, freedom of art, and democratic principles, to which allegiance is solemnly vowed, are in reality most unceremoniously trampled underfoot.

While expressing categorical protest against such methods, against this cynical infringement on the freedom of art, we resolutely insist that our music be removed from the film *The Iron Curtain*.

D. SHOSTAKOVICH, S. PROKOFIEV
A. KHACHATURIAN, N. MIASKOVSKY

April 1948

## Declaration of the Central Committee of the Communist Party of the Soviet Union Amending and Cancelling the Resolution of 10 February 1948 and Restoring the Dignity and Integrity of Soviet Composers Attacked in That Resolution

The Central Committee of the Communist Party of the Soviet Union notes that the Resolution of the Central Committee dated 10 February 1948, and dealing with the opera by V. Muradeli, *Great Friendship*, has on the whole played a positive role in the development of Soviet music. In this Resolution the aims in the development of Soviet musical art were defined on the basis of the principles of Socialist Realism, with emphasis placed on the significance of the relationship between art and the life of the Soviet people, as on the importance of the best democratic traditions of musical classicism and folk art. The Resolution justly condemned the formalistic tendencies in music and ostensible innovations which took it away from the people into a circle of estheticizing gourmands. The development of Soviet music during the subsequent years confirmed the correctness and the timeliness of the Party's judgment.

However, the evaluation of the creative work of individual composers contained in this Resolution was in a number of instances unfair and unjustified. The opera by Vano Muradeli, *Great Friendship*, had faults that merited specific criticism, but these faults did not justify the description of this opera as formalistic. Talented composers, comrades Prokofiev, Shostakovich, Khachaturian, Shebalin, Popov, Miaskovsky and others who showed faulty tendencies in some of their works, were peremptorily described as representatives of the formalist trends inimical to the people.

In this Resolution, specifically in the criticism of Muradeli's opera, there was made, contrary to historical facts, an artificial discrimination against some of the peoples of the northern Caucasus. Some incorrect evaluations in the Resolution reflected the subjective approach towards certain works of art on the part of J. V. Stalin. It was further demonstrated in the one-sided judgment of individual works of art and in the biased criticism of the operas *Bogdan Khmelnitsky* by Konstantin Dankevich and *From the Bottom of My Heart* by Herman Zhukovsky in the editorial articles of the newspaper *Pravda* published at J. V. Stalin's behest in 1951. As is well known, in his judgments regarding these problems, Stalin was under the negative influence of Molotov, Malenkov and Beria. Despite the fact that the libretto and the music of the opera *Bogdan Khmelnitsky* had faults, there was no justification in describing them as "gross ideological errors." The unwarranted reproaches contained in this article in *Pravda* were repeated later on in a number of other articles and statements. The editorial article of *Pravda* regarding the opera *From the Bottom of My Heart*, which included some correct critical judgments of its music and of its libretto, also included obvious exaggerations and bias.

The Central Committee of the Communist Party of the Soviet Union resolves: (1) to note that the Resolution of the Central Committee of 10 February 1948 with regard to the opera by Vano Muradeli *Great Friendship*, while correctly tracing the direction of the development of Soviet art along the lines of folk forms and realism, and containing just criticism of erroneous formalistic tendencies in Soviet music, passed unjust and unjustifiably harsh judgment on works by many talented Soviet composers, disclosing the negative traits that marked the period of the cult of personality (2) to rule that the evaluation of the operas *Bogdan Khmelnitsky* and *From the Bottom of My Heart*, given in the editorial articles of the newspaper *Pravda*, is incorrect and one-sided and to recommend to the editorial board of the newspaper *Pravda*, on the basis of the present decision, to prepare an editorial article containing a many-sided and profound analysis of the fundamental problems of the development of Soviet musical art (3) to suggest to the regional and local committees and to the Central Committees of the Communist Parties of the Republics of the Union, and to the Ministry of Culture of the Union of Soviet Socialist Republics, to initiate in the professional unions of creative art workers and in the institutes of the arts the requisite explanatory work in connection with the present Resolution, with the view of raising the ideological and artistic level of Soviet musical art, and the further solidarization of the creative intelligentsia on the basis of Communist ideology and the strengthening of the links connecting Soviet arts with the life of the people. (Dated 28 May 1958)

# Declaration of the Second International Congress
## of Composers and Musicologists
## in Prague, 29 May 1948

We, composers and musicologists of different countries, gathered at the Second International Congress of Composers and Musicologists in Prague from 20 May to 29 May 1948, organized by the Union of Czech Composers, have, after discussions and conferences lasting for ten days, unanimously agreed on the following declaration.

Music and musical life of our epoch are undergoing a profound crisis. This crisis is characterized by the sharp conflict between so-called serious music and so-called light music.

So-called serious music is becoming increasingly individualistic and subjective in its content, and increasingly complex and constructivistic in its form.

So-called light music is becoming increasingly banal, impersonal, and standardized; in many countries it is made the object of a monopolized commercial industry, and becomes a piece of merchandise.

So-called serious music has lost the proper balance of its individual musical elements. In some cases, rhythmic and harmonic elements are over-emphasized, and the melodic elements rejected; in others, formally constructivistic elements are the determinants; or else, the logical development of the musical thought is replaced by a formless melodization and esthetizing imitation of old contrapuntal writing. But no formal ingenuities can conceal the ideational vacuity of the majority of these works.

On the other hand, so-called light music confines itself exclusively to primitive melodies, entirely ignoring all other elements. It is usually based on the most vulgar, most commonplace melodic formulas, exemplified particularly by American popular music.

These tendencies, supposedly opposite, are in reality two sides of the same nefarious phenomenon, and are conditioned by the same social process.

The more evident these defects are in contemporary serious music, the more complex its form and subjective contents, the smaller is its audience, while vulgar popular music penetrates deeper and deeper the musical life of different countries and peoples, contributing to the debasement and banality of perception of its many millions of listeners and perverting their musical tastes.

We, the delegates gathered at the Second International Congress of Composers and Musicologists in Prague, note that this situation is particularly inadmissible in our time when new social forms are being created, and when human culture enters a new era, posing before the creative artist new and urgent tasks.

The International Congress does not intend to give any concrete recipes or instructions for writing music; it is understood that each nation must find its own ways and methods. However, the reasons and the essence of the contemporary crisis in music ought to be understood by all, and we must apply a united effort to solve it.

A successful solution of the crisis in contemporary music seems to be possible under the following conditions:

(1) If composers renounce in their art the tendencies of extreme subjectivism; then their music would express great, new, and progressive ideas and aspirations of the popular masses and progressive ideals of contemporary life.

(2) If creative artists turn decisively towards national culture of their lands and become its true defenders against the cosmopolitan tendencies of contemporary life, for true internationalism in music is attained only on the basis of the strengthening of national culture.

(3) If the attention of composers is directed first of all towards musical forms that are most concrete in their contents, particularly operas, oratorios, cantatas, songs, mass choruses, etc.

(4) If composers and music critics become active and practical workers in the musical education of their peoples.

The Congress urges composers of the whole world to write music in which high artistic qualities combine with creative individuality and deep and genuine folk art.

The Congress considers that exchange of experience and ideas among progressive composers and musicologists of all nations is now an acute and urgent necessity. To achieve this, progressive musicians must unite their forces, first of all in their own countries, which ought to lead in the nearest future to the formation of a union of progressive composers and musicologists of all countries.

The Congress states its conviction that such an association of progressive composers and musicologists of all countries, by arduous and determined work will solve the protracted contemporary musical crisis, and will restore to music its lofty and noble role in society. Only under such conditions will music become a mighty factor in the solution of the great historic tasks facing all progressive mankind.

For the Praesidium of the Second International Congress of Composers and Musicologists in Prague:

A. Estrella (Brazil); V. Stojanov (Bulgaria); St. Lucky, A. Kypta, A. Sychra, Jar. Tomásek (Czechoslovakia); Roland de Candé (France); M. Flothuis, M. Rebling (Holland); O. Danon, N. Devcic (Yugoslavia); Denés Bartha (Hungary); Zofia Lissa (Poland); Hanns Eisler (Austria); A. Mendelsohn (Rumania); Tikhon Khrennikov, Boris Yarustovsky, Yuri Shaporin (USSR); Georges Bernard (Switzerland); Alan Bush, Bernard Stevens (Great Britain).

# Declaration Made by Nikita Khrushchev
# on 8 March 1963 Stating His Views on
# Music in Soviet Society

In music, as in other arts, there are many genres, styles and forms. No one proposes to declare a ban on any of these styles and genres. But we want to stipulate our own attitude towards music, its tasks and its creative direction. To put it briefly, we are for melodic music, rich in content, which stirs the souls of men, generating strong feelings. We are against cacophonic music. . . . When I hear the music of Glinka, tears of joy appear in my eyes. Perhaps it is no longer fashionable, and I am not a young man, but I like to listen to David Oistrakh when he plays the violin, and I like to hear the massed collective of violins in the orchestra of the Bolshoi Theater. I do not know what this violin collective is called in professional terms. I have heard it many times, and always had great pleasure. Of course, I have no pretensions to claim that my feeling for music should become a general norm for everyone. But we refuse to encourage people who pass off cacophony for real melody and who regard music universally loved by the people as obsolete. Every nation has its musical traditions and loves its popular songs. I was born in a Russian village and was brought up in an atmosphere of Russian and Ukrainian music, of its folk songs. I derive great pleasure from listening to songs by Solovyov-Sedoy, or to Kolmanovsky's song to the words of the poet Evtushenko, "Do Russians Want War?" I like many Ukrainian songs, for instance *Rushnitchok* by Maiboroda. I listen and want to listen more and more. We have many good composers who have written many fine songs, but as you understand I cannot enumerate them all. In musical composition there are serious defects. One cannot consider the current infatuation with jazz music as a normal phenomenon. We are not against all jazz music; there are all kinds of jazz music. Dunayevsky knew how to write good music for jazz orchestra. I like some songs performed by the jazz orchestra conducted by Leonid Utyosov. But there is also music which makes one feel like vomiting, and causes colic in one's stomach.—After the recent plenum of the Union of Composers of the Russian Socialist Federal Soviet Republic, comrade Shostakovich invited us to a concert at the Kremlin Convention Hall. Although we are all very busy we went to hear it, because we were told that it was going to be an interesting concert. And indeed there were some interesting numbers on the program. But then they put on a jazz band, then another, then another, and then all three together. Even good jazz is hard to take in quantity, but this kind of jazz bombardment was beyond endurance. And there was no place to hide. Music in which there is no melody produces nothing but irritation. They tell us that such opinions as mine reveal a lack of understanding. It is true that it is impossible to understand some jazz music which is repugnant to the ear. We must object also to so-called modern dance seeping through from the west into our land. I traveled through the country a great deal. I watched Russian, Ukrainian, Kazakh, Uzbek, Armenian and Georgian dances. They are beautiful dances and pleasant to watch. But what they call modern fashionable dance is simply indecent, an orgy and the devil knows what. They say that such obscenities one can witness only among the shakers. I cannot vouch for it because I never attended shakers' meetings. But it seems that among our creative workers there are young people who are eager to prove that melody in music has lost its right to exist and that it ought to be replaced by some new kind of music, dodecaphonic music, music of noises. A normal person finds it difficult to understand what is hidden behind the word dodecaphonic, but in all probability it is the same as cacophonic. Well, this cacophonic music we totally reject. Our people cannot include such trash in our ideological armament. (Shouts in the audience: "Right!") We need music that inspires, that calls for heroic deeds and for constructive labor. When a soldier goes to war, he takes all that he needs with him, and the regiment band never leaves him. It inspires him during the army march. Music for such bands can be written only by composers who adhere to positions of socialist realism, who remain close to everyday life and to the problems of national struggle, those who are supported by the people. Our political stand in art is that of intransigent opposition to abstractionism, formalism and other bourgeois perversions of this type. It is Lenin's line, which we have unswervingly followed, and which we will continue to follow. (APPLAUSE)


# Charter of the Union of Soviet Composers

CONFIRMED BY THE SECOND ALL-UNION CONGRESS OF SOVIET COMPOSERS, 1957

I. GENERAL STATEMENT

The Union of Soviet Composers is a voluntary social organization which unites composers and musicologists actively participating in the development of Soviet musical art. Having creatively mastered the Marxist-Leninist theory which equips an artist with the capacity of observing the authentic truth of life in all its complexity and totality, Soviet composers are guided by the method of Socialist Realism. This method demands from composers a faithful reflection of reality in its revolutionary development and high mastery in the artistic representation of life's images. In opening many-sided opportunities for the revelation of individual peculiarities of one's talent, Socialist Realism predicates a wealth and variety of artistic styles and a broad creative initiative in the struggle for ideals of Communism and for the national essence of the multi-national Soviet art of music.

II. TASKS OF THE UNION OF COMPOSERS OF THE USSR

The Union of Composers of the USSR sets the following tasks for itself:

1. Cooperation and unionization of Soviet composers and musicologists with the purpose of creating ideologically valid musical works of high artistic content which would contribute to the building of Communism in our country.

2. Creative development of the best traditions of Russian and other national musical cultures of the Soviet Union as well as those of foreign classical music and intensive promotion of Soviet musical culture, socialist in content and national in form.
3. Development of Soviet musicology, analysis of foremost problems of musical aesthetics on the basis of Marxism-Leninism, as well as of important questions of musical history and theory.
4. Establishing Soviet music as a progressive force of world music culture and irreconcilable struggle against the influences of bourgeois ideology.
5. Ideological and political education of Soviet composers and musicologists, aiding them in their creative growth and the evolution of their professional mastery, and an intensive spread of creative discussion as a fundamental method of the Union's activities.
6. Establishment of creative and organizational contacts with Soviet performers.
7. Establishment of creative contacts with the representatives of literature, cinema, the theater and fine arts.
8. Establishment of creative contacts with composers and musicologists of the nations of people's democracies and with progressive musical organizations and representatives of other foreign countries; promotion of the best works of Soviet music abroad and the best works of foreign music in the USSR.
9. Socio-creative advice to musical institutions and organizations which are connected with music, such as orchestras, radio, television, music publishing firms, musical educational institutions, clubs, palaces of culture, professional musical press and musical sections of the general press.
10. Aid to the members of the Union of Soviet Composers in a deep and many-sided study of the life and culture of the peoples of the USSR and of foreign countries.
11. Aid to the members of the Union of Soviet Composers in the improvement of the cultural and material conditions of their life and work and in the safeguarding of their authors' rights.

To carry out these aims the Union of Soviet Composers takes the following course of action:

1. Organizes discussions about important creative and scientific problems, musical compositions and musicological works.
2. Promotes the progress of young composers and musicologists, aiding their ideo-political growth and perfecting their artistic mastery.
3. Organizes expeditions for study and recording of the creative music of the nations of the USSR.
4. Promotes intensively the development of musical creativity of non-professional groups.
5. Organizes creative visits of the Union's members at plants and factories, at construction sites, at collective farms and state farms, at service branches of the Soviet Army and Soviet Navy; and arranges creative meetings with listeners.
6. Organizes exchanges of creative experiences among composers and musicologists of the fraternal republics of the USSR.
7. Organizes exchanges of creative experiences among composers and musicologists of the Soviet Union and musical representatives of foreign countries.
8. Organizes competitions for the best works in different types of musi-

cal composition and musicology and for the best performance of works by Soviet composers.

9. Propagandizes the achievements of Soviet music by means of publishing musical works and musicological books, organizing concerts, discussions, lectures, etc.

III. CONTINGENT OF THE UNION OF COMPOSERS OF THE USSR

1. The following are qualified for membership of the Union of Soviet Composers:

    (a) Composers of works of a high professional caliber possessing individual socio-artistic significance.
    (b) Music critics and musicologists whose scientific works, critical essays and activity as lecturers and propagandists have actively contributed to the development of creative practical work and to the theory of Soviet musical art.

2. Members of the Union of Soviet Composers enjoy the right of a decisive vote at general assemblies; of electing and of being elected as delegates to congresses, plenary meetings and conferences; of electing and being elected to the guiding and controlling organs of the Union.

3. Members of the Union of Soviet Composers must take active part in the work of the Union, must contribute to the attainment of its goals, must observe discipline established by the Union and must fulfill all requirements of the present Charter.

4. Application for membership must be submitted to local branches of the Union of Composers of the USSR, enclosing works and other materials relating to the creative musical, musicological and social activity of the applicant.

    The Directorate of a regional or local union numbering fewer than twenty members has a right to accept for membership composers and musicologists having special musical and educational qualifications. An applicant is accepted by a majority of no less than two-thirds of the total membership.

    Composers' unions of fraternal republics of the USSR numbering fewer than twenty members each, much submit the candidacy of applicants accepted for membership in the Union of Soviet Composers to the Secretariat of the Union of Composers of the USSR for confirmation.

    Admission to the membership of composers and musicologists not having special musical and educational qualifications must be confirmed by the Secretariat of the Union of Composers of the USSR. Rejection of candidacy is subject to appeal to the Directorate of the Union of Composers of the USSR.

5. Persons admitted to membership in the Composers' Union are assessed annual dues of 36 rubles and receive a membership card of the Union of Composers of the USSR.

6. Expulsion from membership of the Composers' Union is effected by a majority of no less than two-thirds of the membership of the Directorate of the corresponding local branch of the regional Union of Composers in the following cases:

    (a) Deprivation of rights to vote by court action.
    (b) Incompatability of a member's activities with the aims and policies of the Union of Composers of the USSR.
    (c) Perpetration of anti-social actions.
    (d) Creative inactivity over a period of three years when not induced by illness or other justifiable cause, and also unconscientious attitude towards professional work.

(e) Systematic avoidance of participation in the socio-creative work of the Union.

(f) Failure to pay membership dues for a year.

(g) A member's own desire to leave the Union.

7. The decisions of the Directorate of the Union of Composers regarding expulsion from membership can be appealed to a superior organization, including the Congress of Soviet Composers.

IV. GUIDING ORGANS OF THE UNION OF COMPOSERS OF THE USSR

1. The highest guiding organ of the Union of Composers of the USSR is the Congress of Composers which convenes every four years.

2. Election of delegates to the All-Union Congress of Composers is conducted according to the rules established by the Directorate of the Union of Composers of the USSR. These delegates are elected by secret ballot in national assemblies. When a Soviet republic includes regional branches, delegates are elected at regional meetings or general assemblies.

3. The Congress of Soviet Composers performs the following functions:

(a) Passes on the questions of ideologically creative policy of Soviet music and Soviet musicology.

(b) Discusses and rules on the reports of the Directorate and the Control Committee of the Union of Composers of the USSR.

(c) Discusses and rules on the acceptance of the Charters of the Union of Composers and of the Musical Fund of the USSR.

(d) Elects central guiding and control organs of the Union of Soviet Composers.

4. Besides the periodical congresses of the Union of Soviet Composers, extraordinary congresses may be called to consider questions of an urgent nature. Such extraordinary congresses are summoned by the Directorate of the Union of Soviet Composers of the USSR for the following considerations:

(a) For its own reasons.

(b) At the request of not less than one-half of the membership of the Union of Soviet Composers.

(c) At the request of the Control Committee.

(d) At the request of Directorates of no fewer than five branches in Soviet republics or regional bodies, each of which numbers no fewer than fifty members of the Union of Soviet Composers.

When such requests are made, the Directorate of the Union of Composers of the USSR is obliged to summon an extraordinary congress within sixty days.

5. In the interval between congresses, the Directorate of the Union of Soviet Composers elected by secret ballot at the Congress, performs the functions of the executive organ.

6. In the interval between congresses, the Directorate of the Union of Soviet Composers performs the following functions:

(a) Provides guidance for the entire creative activity of the Union of Soviet Composers.

(b) Rules on fundamental problems touching on the creative, organizational and financial activities of institutions and enterprises of the Union of Composers.

(c) Guides the activity of all composers' unions in the fraternal republics of the USSR.

(d) Considers and confirms the accounts of the activities of the Directorate of the Musical Fund of the USSR.

Congresses of composers' unions of the republics of the

USSR are summoned by the Directorate of the corresponding local branches of the Union of Soviet Composers.

7. Plenary sessions of the Union of Composers of the USSR are assembled at least twice a year.

8. The Directorate of the Union of Composers of the USSR elects a Secretariat from among its members, composed of a First Secretary and subordinate secretaries the number of which is determined by the Directorate.

9. The Directorate of the Union of Soviet Composers performs the following functions during the period between plenary sessions:

    (a) Organizes and provides constant guidance for the ideologically creative activities of the Union of Soviet Composers on the entire territory of the USSR.

    (b) Provides guidance for the current activities of the Union of Composers of the USSR.

    (c) Provides representation in behalf of the Directorate of the Union of Composers of the USSR at all state and social institutions.

    (d) Considers creative accounts of organizations of composers of fraternal Soviet republics.

    (e) Provides guidance for the activity of the Directorate of the Musical Fund of the USSR.

10. The Secretariat of the Union of Soviet Composers must present an accounting of its activities to the Directorate of the Union of Soviet Composers at least twice a year.

11. In the autonomous Soviet republics, as well as in regional districts, local unions of composers may be organized when a minimum of five members of the Union of Soviet Composers are available there.

    In the autonomous Soviet republics and regional districts in which there are available fewer than five members of the Union of Soviet Composers, a general assembly of the latter elects a plenipotentiary of the Union of Composers in that particular Soviet republic or regional district. The candidacy of such a plenipotentiary is confirmed by the Directorate of the corresponding local union of composers.

12. The Charter of the Union of Composers of the USSR is binding for all republican and regional branches. The quantitative contingent and the constitution of guiding organs of local unions of composers as well as the schedules of congresses and regional meetings are determined by the resolutions of such congresses and of regional meetings, taking into account the peculiarities of each particular organization.

13. The Directorate of each of the regional branches of the Union of Soviet Composers provides guidance for the activities of the Union of Composers on the territories of the corresponding Soviet republics or regions.

    The resolutions of the All-Union congresses and of the Directorate of the Union of Composers of the USSR are binding for all branches of the Composers' Union.

14. For the purpose of checking on the management of the property and finances of the Union of Soviet Composers and its subsidiary institutions, a Control Committee is elected at each congress by secret ballot. Members of the Control Committee cannot concurrently be members of the Directorate of the Union of Soviet Composers.

    The Control Committee must submit reports of its activities to the Congress of Soviet Composers.

15. Republican and regional controlling organs are elected at correspond-

ing congresses and general assemblies. In organizations of composers numbering fewer than twenty members, control organs are not elected.

V. PROPERTY RIGHTS AND OTHER PRIVILEGES OF THE UNION
OF COMPOSERS OF THE USSR

1. The Union of Composers of the USSR and those of individual republics and regions assume the rights of juridical persons, with all corollaries thereof, in pursuance of established laws, including possession, acquisition of property, signing of contracts, legal claims and liabilities, arbitration, etc.

2. The Directorate of the Union of Soviet Composers assumes the duty of safeguarding of authors' rights of the members of the Composers' Union in the territory of the USSR and, through corresponding Soviet organs abroad, takes necessary measures to protect other rights of members of the Union of Soviet Composers.

3. The Union of Soviet Composers maintains, with joint responsibility before the Directorate and the Secretariat of the Union of Soviet Composers, a financially autonomous organization possessing the rights of a juridical person, the Musical Fund of the USSR, whose principal task is to render aid for the creative activities of composers and musicologists, and which concentrates the entire administrative and financial services for the improvement of the material and cultural needs of members of the Union of Soviet Composers.

4. The Directorate of the Musical Fund of the USSR is appointed by the Directorate of the Union of Soviet Composers.

5. The Union of Soviet Composers maintains the following organizations:
   (a) A publishing press, *The Soviet Composer*, whose task is the publication and wide distribution of Soviet musical literature of all types, as well as of scientific and popularizing works by Soviet musicologists.
   (b) All-Union Bureau for Propaganda.
       Both organizations are financially independent and have the rights of juridical persons.

6. The Secretariat of the Union of Composers of the USSR takes charge of the activity of the Central House of Composers which constitutes an independent organization possessing the rights of juristic persons.

7. The financial funds of the Union of Soviet Composers are provided from the following sources:
   (a) Budgetary appropriations from State organs.
   (b) Membership dues.
   (c) Income from the property of the Union of Soviet Composers.

8. The Union of Soviet Composers and its subsidiary organizations are exempt from State or local taxes, dues or custom fees.

9. The Union of Soviet Composers extends its activity throughout the territory of the USSR.

10. The Directorate of the Union of Soviet Composers is domiciled in Moscow.

11. The Union of Soviet Composers has its seal inscribed THE UNION OF COMPOSERS OF THE USSR.

12. Unions of composers in other Soviet republics and regions have corresponding seals.

# Appeal for Peace Addressed to Musicians
## of the World at the International Manifestation
## Held in East Berlin on 2 November 1961

*On the 2nd November, 1961, leading composers and musicologists from the Soviet Union the People's Republic of Poland, the Czechoslovak Socialist Republic, the People's Republic of Bulgaria, the People's Republic of Rumania, and the People's Republic of Hungary, met in the Apollo Hall of the German State Opera in Berlin to give their names, together with their colleagues from the German Democratic Republic to a Manifestation for the Conclusion of a German Peace Treaty, for the securing of peace in the world. In an Appeal, the musicians from seven Socialist countries call on composers, musicians and musicologists of the whole world to help them realise this aim, which is for the wellbeing of mankind.*

*Nathan Notowicz, Secretary of the Union of German Composers and Musicologists, welcomed the foreign guests, as well as leading representatives of public and cultural life in the German Democratic Republic. The delegates of the various countries then made the following statements.*

DMITRI SHOSTAKOVICH, SOVIET UNION

DEAR FRIENDS,

The question of the conclusion of a Peace Treaty with Germany and the final removal of the remnants of the Second World War is a question which today deeply moves all simple people in the world—moves the whole of mankind.

We Soviet people follow with great attention events in the heart of Europe, where the forces of progress, freedom, and peaceful creation fight against the forces of reaction, revanchism and militarism. It is well known that the West German revanchists do not want peace for Germany. They want to plunge the German people again into the terrible hellfire of a war. Can we, who are dedicated to peaceful and humanistic creative work, accept that the gigantic riches which are created by the working people, be transformed into a death-dealing weapon of horror and destructiveness never before known? No! No! and once again No! Every one of us to whom the joys of peaceful work are so dear has the duty today to raise his voices in defense of peace and justice. There must not be a single painter, actor or musician in the world who does not passionately protest against the preparations for an atomic battle.

Of great importance for the maintenance and consolidation of peace is the problem of the removal of the remnants of the Second World War, the peaceful solution of the German question, and on this basis, the normalisation of the situation in West Berlin.

The fact that there is no German Peace Treaty creates an uncertain situation and is a help to the aggressive forces.

We are of the opinion that a Peace Treaty is the only correct solution of the German question and we stand firm for the conclusion of this Peace Treaty based on mutually acceptable terms. We are convinced that the Peace Treaty will contribute towards normalising the mutual relations of States, will prevent a new world war and will relax international tension.

Our country is an enormous industrial power but we do not threaten anyone and we are of the opinion that all differences can be solved peacefully.

We musicians have the fate of the German people particularly at heart—the people of outstanding workers, great scholars, thinkers and eminent composers. We have only to remember that Germany presented the world with the genius Beethoven, who passionately called on the peoples of the earth to unite.

We long for the time when the whole of Germany will be united under the banner of peace and progress and will be forever a peace-loving happy country.

I shall never forget the tragedy of my birthplace, Leningrad, which suffered barbarous bombing and a cruel hunger blockade. Hundreds of thousands of the people of Leningrad, including women, children and old people, died of hunger or through the bombs. Can we allow mankind to suffer an even more terrible fate?

My dear friends—musicians from various countries, we stand passionately for the defence of peace and the happiness of the peoples, for the peaceful solution of the German question. Let us defend the right of the peoples for a peaceful happy life. Let beautiful and inspiring music sound all over the world rather than the hateful wailing of the sirens.

I call upon my colleagues in all countries of the earth to follow our appeal and raise your voices to defend peaceful creative work for the happiness and freedom of the people.

STEFAN SLEDZINSKI, PEOPLE'S REPUBLIC OF POLAND

DEAR COLLEAGUES,

Sixteen years have already passed since the ending of the Second World War, but the whole world still feels the terrible results of this war.

The frightful irreplaceable losses in people and in goods which Polish culture and the whole of mankind suffered during the last war, during the fascist occupation, are for us—the representatives of Polish culture and Polish musical life—not only a past burdening us like a nightmare, but also a painful lesson showing us what fascism and imperialism lead to.

We shall never forget this lesson, just as many other peoples, including the German people, have not forgotten. For that reason we shall always be found in the forefront with those who stand for the right of mankind to peace and who work for that peace, no matter which country and in what form the hydra of fascism and imperialism raises its head.

Sixteen years ago when the whole world made the firm decision "Never again War," it looked as though the shadow of war had been banished for ever. It looked as though not only all the peoples, but also those who had been responsible for their fate, had drawn the correct lessons of history.

Time has shown however that for certain states and imperialist circles the terrible destruction was not enough. They place the world in danger of a new war, incalculable in its consequences and which threatens the existence of life on the earth altogether. We composers and musicians of all countries cannot wait indifferently for such a destructive war which would mean the destruction of all life and the highest achievements of the creative human spirit. We believe that works of art and not destructive tools are the expression of the endeavours of a true man.

Therefore we have the duty to defend peace which is so necessary for the development of art. And therefore we have the right to raise our voices for its defense.

Despite the frightful destruction of the last war—and may it be the last—we have developed art and science to a high degree in our country, thanks to our work and thanks to the care of the party and government. We Polish artists and musicians understand that we are also defending all achievements in the sphere of music when we call for a fight for peace. We do not want the destruction of our Philharmonic and Symphonic Orchestras, opera houses and music schools, reconstructed with such effort and more beautiful than before. We do not want that our rich musical creations be destroyed so that in Poland music is silenced as it was during the dark years of the war and the occupation.

We want every citizen of our country to be able to hear music in peace, to be receptive to its beauty and obtain joy from it. And we believe that musicians of all countries have the same aim.

We think that the more people in the world correctly understand music and its message the less will brutal actions be able to provoke conflicts and wars.

Allow me, on behalf of the Union of Polish Composers and all representatives of musical life in Poland to express our complete agreement with the initiative of the Composers Union of the GDR for the signing of an Appeal for the Conclusion of a Peace Treaty with Germany and the peaceful settlement of the German problem. We believe that in this way the source, from which the unleashing of a new war threatening the existence of mankind stems, will be removed.

At the same time I take this opportunity of conveying warmest greetings to our colleagues in the German Democratic Republic on behalf of the Polish cultural workers, and wish you victory in your noble fight for a just cause, which is also ours.

ANTONIN SYCHRA, SOCIALIST REPUBLIC OF CZECHOSLOVAKIA

LADIES AND GENTLEMEN,
This is my 18th visit to Berlin and today I want to speak about my experiences and memories.

I first visited the German Democratic Republic in 1950. At that time the situation was very complicated and, in many respects unfavourable. The food shops, and others were pretty empty. Everywhere there were ruins. And when you spoke to someone about the political situation, and particularly with the young people, you had the impression that you heard the correct opinion but that actually you were hearing meaningless phrases which had no clear and live content. Of course it only looked like this from the outside. For instance at the musicological congresses on the life and work of Johann Sebastian Bach it was quite different. There you felt the clear, ideological, purposeful position. Together we created a new picture of J. S. Bach and in so doing, unexpectedly found that we were seeing a reflection of the new forceful life in the GDR, a reflection of the new political path which the German Democratic Republic was taking.

During the World Festival I saw the GDR, and particularly Berlin, in another light. Berlin was international, full of life, joy and movement. Some other festivals, especially in Moscow, were perhaps more colourful and also bigger, but none of them could be compared with the Berlin Festival in the matter of fighting spirit. When you spoke there with someone on topical questions, you felt—and this was bound up with the whole atmosphere—that you were no longer hearing phrases but real experiences which formed the basis of a firm world outlook.

Then there were other meetings, the Beethoven Congress, the Schubert celebrations, lectures at the Humboldt University, discussions and meeting of the Composers Union. We made many valuable new friendships and gathered many deep impressions and fought many fights together.

One thing I find particularly important. In the German Democratic Republic you see how every question of science and art is bound up with life and the political struggle. Sometimes it happens that we cultural workers are too liberal. We are not always vigilant enough when we judge new western trends in art, new experiments or opinions. In the GDR the situation is different. Here all conflicts and contradictions seem to be sharper and more immediate. When you get to know the present situation here well, you have to agree with our German colleagues that it is necessary to have all these things out—thoroughly and from the party point of view.

When we speak today of the help of the socialist states for the German Democratic Republic we must bear in mind that this is a mutual help. It is help for those who are holding the outpost of our whole socialist camp. Through this help we shall all be stronger and firmer. With this in mind I welcome this meeting, which is bound up with an important turning point in world history, on behalf of the Union of Czechoslovak Composers and of the whole Czechoslovak people.

PETKO STAINOFF, PEOPLE'S REPUBLIC OF BULGARIA

LADIES AND GENTLEMEN,

The whole of mankind is experiencing exciting and fateful days. At this critical moment all peace-loving and honest people are looking to the leading statesmen of the big powers. We know that war destroys all the prerequisites for the development of science and culture, together with the well-being and progress of mankind. We, the Bulgarian musicians, follow with deep sympathy all events in connection with the maintenance of the dearest possession of mankind—peace. If we undertake all efforts and do all in our power—however little that is—to contribute towards the maintenance of peace, we fulfill the most urgent duty of all responsible musicians. The Bulgarian composers and musicologists are united in assuring their German colleagues, and the whole world, that they fight side by side with them for the solution of this serious problem—the security and well-being of the German people.

Our peace-loving and industrious Bulgarian folk works for our beloved homeland and leads it along the road to Socialism with an enthusiasm and energy it never before possessed. The Bulgarian people, who took this road to the bright future of Communism out of conviction and at the price of its own blood, will guard this precious thing. This does not merely concern the Bulgarian people. It is a question of the maintenance of peace in the whole world, for the road of one people to Socialism and Communism is reached only through firm and fraternal friendship with other nations who work for peace.

In the present critical period the Berlin question appears to be one of the most dangerous problems out of which a world of conflict can arise. We are of the opinion that this problem must be solved as quickly as possible and that the danger of conflagration for a new world war be removed. Every possibility that Berlin would be used as the starting point of any conflict must, from the start, be prevented. The German people long for peace and quiet in order that they can still better use their strength and capabilities, which they have proved over the centuries, for the building up of their material and spiritual life. More than ever before the German people need peace in order to be able to work.

We, the Bulgarian musicians, stand firmly behind the decision of the German and Soviet peoples to sign the Peace Treaty with Germany, because we are convinced that this will be beneficial not only to the German people but to the whole of mankind.

My dear German colleagues, the Bulgarian composers, who respect and esteem your creative work, greet, through you, the whole German people, and promise to you and to the whole world not to desert you at this time, no matter what the difficulties which may arise in the solution of such an important question for you and the whole of mankind. We are prepared to declare our solidarity with the delegates of all countries at this congress and to sign the Appeal in which artists all over the world are called upon to stand for a speedy successful solution of the German question, and for the settlement of all problems in connection with the maintenance of world peace. With all our hearts we wish our esteemed German colleagues strength and confidence in their creative social-political work and determination in the defense of our mutual cause.

FERENC SZABÓ, PEOPLE'S REPUBLIC OF HUNGARY

DEAR COLLEAGUES, DEAR FRIENDS,

In the course of its thousand years of history our people had to fight for hundreds of years against the German aggressors, who under the slogan "Drang nach Osten" continuously attacked our fatherland in order to destroy its national state and to plunder and subject our people so that our country could become part of the German Reich.

At the turn of the 17th century the superior force was victorious and our national state was destroyed. Our vanquished and plundered fatherland became an Austrian colony for almost three centuries.

All this reached a pinnacle in the frightful flood of death and destruction of the Second World War. The reactionary rulers of Hungary of that time drove the suppressed Hungarian workers and peasants by the hundreds of thousands into the battlefield, forcing them to die for the interests of German imperialism. German imperialism and fascism devastated our country, sent hundreds of thousands of our sons to their deaths and supported, with its whole power, the reactionary rulers of our country.

We do not nourish resentment against the German working people. Humanist German thought, which is rooted in the people, German literature and music, decisively influence the development of Hungarian culture. The great classics of German music —Bach, Handel, Beethoven, Mendelssohn, Schumann, Wagner—are continuously performed in our concerts and opera houses. We Hungarian composers learned the laws of beauty of the classical music from Bach's chorale. Through intensive study of the Bach Fugues and of his two and three-part inventions we completed our knowledge of counterpoint. The wealth of forms and the perfection of Beethoven's works was, and is, the highest ideal for every Hungarian composer.

We esteem and love all that is valuable which the German people in the fields of science, thought, art and literature have created. We are bound by ties of friendship to the working people of the German Democratic Republic. We gladly visit them because we know and see that militarism and fascism have been torn out by the roots in the German Democratic Republic. With trust and sympathy we observe the impressive development of their country and are prepared to fully support all efforts and the fight of the working people in the interest of their sovereignty and their socialist achievements.

We must not forget however that on the other side of the borders of the German Democratic Republic there exists another Germany, where aggressive German militarism and fascism lives on and prepares a new world war. We have no right to forget that the rulers of the present West Germany again dream of the conquest and plundering of other countries. An official organ of the government of the German Federal Republic issued a map—and it is still being distributed—on which one half of the Hungarian People's Republic, which was never German soil and which has belonged to Hungary for a thousand years, appears as "stolen" German territory.

It becomes ever more clear that the imperialist powers have given West Germany the role of ignition button to press, which is to unleash a new world war. It can explode tomorrow setting the world in flames and bringing the danger of death to mankind. The aggressive revanchists, who were once Hitler's generals, can take over the ignition button tomorrow and there is only one possibility of saving mankind from a third devastating and bloody world war—the settlement of the German question through the conclusion of a Peace Treaty.

We, Hungarian composers, musicologists and artists want to live and work with all artists in the world in peace and security. We have many plans and we wish to finish the works we have begun. We want to further develop the art and musical culture of our people who are building Socialism. We want to give our people and the whole world still more beauty, confidence, faith and strength. That is what we are living and working for. And for that we need peace and security. That is why we demand that the German Peace Treaty be concluded.

On behalf of the Hungarian composers, musicologists and musicians I declare that we are in agreement with the aims, and with the content and text of the Appeal. We are prepared to sign this Appeal and to support it with all our strength in Hungary and in the whole world.

HANNS EISLER, GERMAN DEMOCRATIC REPUBLIC

With grief and care I turn, above all, to my colleagues in West Germany. Their situation is difficult. First because of the peculiarities of the profession. Music—in contradistinction to the other arts—has still retained archaic traits of the unconscious, bluntness. To a certain extent the ear is more backward than the quick eye. This has contributed to form the musician type, who seeks to remain outside the quarrels of the world, who does not recognise his social situation and does not want to be involved in the great discussions of our time. He does not want to have anything to do with politics but he forgets that politics have to do with him—that the general interests are also his interests and that you can't live outside society but only vegetate. Such an attitude also harms his art. But to take part in the fight for the noblest task of our century—the defence and maintenance of peace—means also to look after his own private interest.

The pressure which is put on him, the pressure of the state apparatus of the Federal Republic, the newspapers, radio and television stations, which make anyone who shows only sympathy for Socialism, or who in the most modest way stands for recognition of the German Democratic Republic and for the Peace Treaty, into a suspected, dangerous person, who, if nothing worse happens to him, will be forced down to earth through economic boycott. Add to this that young composers are driven into a style of music, through the music critics, through the radio and by the juries of musical festivals, which separates them from their listeners and leads to sectarianism. So it happens that often young talented people, appear like old men in their works and experienced composers behave like experimental beginners, in order to appear on the music markets. Such an attitude changes into a social attitude and the isolated composer isolates himself from social life.

So as not to be misunderstood—I was and I am for what is new in music. But experiments must have a meaning and not be pseudo experiments such as were discarded long ago—artistically and therefore also socially meaningless. The danger is that those who do not play the game do not get performed and are thrown overboard as useless, or they remain silent. If they play the game they deform or squander their talent in sectarian circles.

I do not say this in order to begin a debate on esthetics, but only to describe the difficulties of the West German composers. Because however they compose and whatever differences we have, everything gives way today to the decisive question of peace. Music is made by people for people and if the people are destroyed then music is destroyed also.

In the western world they speak of the great crisis and the danger of a new terrible war which threatens to wipe out the world. We do not believe that there is real ground for a world crisis. What are the grounds?

I find it difficult to repeat what is said daily. The words are bitter in my mouth and I repeat them, only they should be said here and by me: the Government of the Soviet Union proposes that both German States should be recognised, that a Peace Treaty be signed with both German States and that the situation in West Berlin be normalised. It is prepared to give the Treaties into the custody of the United Nations and to guarantee adherence to them in every possible way.

The answer of a number of western governments—above all the Federal Republic— was a threat of war, hate propaganda against the people of the socialist camp and particularly against the German Democratic Republic—threats of which Goebbels need not have been ashamed. That gangsters spit out their hate against the Soviet Union is not new but the heat and the vulgarity of this propaganda is no accident. A former SS general said "The post-war period is at an end and we are now in the pre-war period." In West Germany you can write, print and distribute such criminal sayings. West German politicians speak of the highest risks which must now be taken. Fascists and revanchists sit in high and the highest government posts. Judges once again stretch out their blood-stained shoes under High Court benches and the fascist scum once again greedily looks toward the East. The big bankers, the monopolists and the big landowners again speak of freedom. What do they mean? The basic folly of our epoch—anti-Communism—as Thomas Mann said, has been made the leading idea of the State. Why? Because the Soviet Union wants tò conclude a Peace Treaty with both German States. This propaganda of hate has increased since the 13th August when our government took measures which were absolutely necessary.*

In their own interests the West German colleagues must tear down the veil which hangs over the truth. They must resist. They must immunise themselves against the hatred of big business—hatred against the most noble idea of mankind—Socialism and Communism. Just imagine what possibilities will exist for us all when there is such a Peace Treaty and normalisation of the situation in West Berlin—no worry about the future, an atmosphere freed of poison, peaceful competition between the nations.

So, we musicians are also called upon to take our part in the fight for peace with our works, and—wherever we are—through our personal stand.

May we not be lacking in strength and courage.

* Reference to the Berlin Wall, built on 13 August 1961.


APPEAL ADOPTED BY ALL WHO ATTENDED THE MANIFESTATION:

TO COMPOSERS, MUSICOLOGISTS AND MUSICIANS ALL OVER THE WORLD

Mankind is threatened by the danger of a new war—the most terrible and perhaps the last in history. Yet the possibility exists of turning aside the danger and of banning war and weapons for ever.

In this situation we address ourselves to our colleagues all over the world. When, 25 years ago, the anti-fascists stated that Hitler meant war, many did not believe it. Today, we who have experienced the horrors of war and the fiends in the shape of man who unleashed it, we affirm that the West German revanchists and generals, made more cunning but no wiser as a result of the last war, are preparing a new one. They do not even attempt to hide the fact. The identical mad plans of 25 years ago, and for the most part the same men, are used. In barely disguised terms they speak of a new order in Europe and of a military attack on the German Democratic Republic and other socialist countries, which they call "liberation," just as Hitler did in similar cases. Openly and shamelessly they demand an army of 400,000 armed with atomic weapons. They have, already, leading positions in NATO.

However, not only has the relation of forces in the world changed in favour of peace—in Germany also the situation has changed. There were always millions who wanted peace and they are also there today in West Germany. Up to now they have not had the strength to thwart the German militarists' war policy. The measures taken by the government of the German Democratic Republic on 13th August saved world peace and were a mighty blow by the German people, on German soil, against German militarism. With this action, against which German militarism curses and groans, the fight against war has entered a new phase in the whole world. The next thing will be the conclusion of a German Peace Treaty. Through the existence of the German Democratic Republic the forces of peace inside Germany are, for the first time in history, so strong, so confident, and so organised that they are in a position to prevent a war—together with the peaceloving people of the whole world.

In the western countries various factors combine to show the people what happens in the socialist countries in a completely false light. We, the citizens of the socialist countries, assure you that war will never be started by a socialist country. No-one here can profit from the making of atom bombs or other war material. The production of weapons is a necessity for our countries, and one which we would gladly renounce. Our countries, especially the Soviet Union, have made gigantic plans during the course of which the face of the earth and the fate of the people will be thoroughly changed in the next few years. In order to realise those plans we need peace and nothing but peace.

In the countries of western Europe and the United States the argument that a new war would be so terrible that no-one can want it or begin it, is often heard. It is true that this argument has validity if it depended on reason and clear consideration. But the militarists have plans which, it is true, envisage millions of dead in their own country (the "specialists" call it "Megadead"), but which principally reckon with the complete destruction of the socialist countries. It is of course a false speculation as sensible people in all leading countries understand. But those who expect that the West German militarists and the militarists of other capitalist countries think clearly and soberly, are themselves guilty of false speculation. War cannot be avoided by relying on the good sense of those whose object in life it is to make war.

The idea still prevails that nothing can be done against a threatening war or, that at the best, only professional politicians know what ought to be done. Protected by such arguments war is prepared. However, recently, and particularly since the 13th August the recognition that peace can be saved when millions of people make it their business, has grown in many countries. The comprehension that there are two German States and that this reality must be recognised, is coming to be accepted in the neutral countries of Asia and Africa, but also in England, the United States and other countries.

The neutralisation of the West Berlin conflagration centre, the confirmation by Treaty of the existing Oder-Neisse-frontier, an atomic-weapon-free zone in Central Europe and the acceptance of both German States in UNO, can be achieved by peaceful negotiations. They are reasonable demands which serve peace and are therefore in the best interests of us all.

Dear colleagues your voices carry weight. Appeal to your people, to the public and to the government of your countries. It is high time that the remains of the Second World War be removed and the preparations for a third war be smashed.

We none of us can imagine a life without music! Do not let us forget that without life there is no music!

(Official English text)


# Musical Ideology of the Nationalist Socialist (Nazi) Party

I propose to show to German musicians what used to be and then to call for their help to establish what ought to be.

A great heritage ran the peril of being undone. A whole generation grew up which had to a large degree lost the zeal for the strength and purity of German art as it was created by the masters, a generation which all too often as in everyday life confused freedom with license, which placed the brain above the heart, which preferred to cultivate all that is alien and international rather than native. No longer did their hearts beat faster—the German true beat—they called this concept "reactionary."

Then, as National Socialism captured more and more hearts, the firmament of art began to be streaked with lightning flashes. Those among us who had always identified themselves with German art, felt that the power which emanated from this movement had to do not only with the realities of life but also possessed a deeper spiritual world concept, a nucleus from which a new hope was blossoming also for German art. Thus we, too, became comrades-in-arms, and so there arose the *Kampfbund für deutsche Kultur*, indissolubly connected with the names of Alfred Rosenberg and Hans Hinkel, their founders and first leaders, and WE BEGAN TO MARCH. From one place to another, everywhere there were things to be cleaned up—there was enough dirt! Meanwhile, there the great work of the Reichskulturkammer was slowly unfolding, which embraced all artistic professions, and which reached its peak in the unforgettable speech of its founder, Minister Goebbels, at its inauguration in November 1933. Thus was painstakingly created an instrument which in its great idea of steady progress could put art and artists to service as well. This betokens not alone an organizational reform but also the watch over the spiritual and artistic life of the nation under the guidance of the Reichskulturkammer, and especially, the Reichsmusikkammer, a watch not to impose restrictions to art but to protect it from influences that degrade and alienate it from the German soul.

And this must be the wish and the hope of all of us, invoking the unforgettable words of Adolf Hitler: "Had the artists known what I will some day do for them, they would all be on my side."

(From a chapter in *Rückblick und Ausblick,* by Paul Graener, German composer, published in *Deutsche Kultur im Neuen Reich,* Berlin, 1934)

# Hearings Regarding Hanns Eisler
## Committee on Un-American Activities
## House of Representatives
## Washington, D.C.
## 24, 25 and 26 September 1947

J. Parnell Thomas, New Jersey, Chairman*

Karl E. Mundt, South Dakota
John McDowell, Pennsylvania
Richard M. Nixon, California**
Richard B. Vail, Illinois

John W. Wood, Georgia
John E. Rankin, Mississippi
J. Hardin Peterson, Florida
Herbert C. Bonner, North Carolina

Robert E. Stripling, Chief Investigator
Donald T. Appell, Special Investigator

STRIPLING: When and where were you born?
EISLER: 6 July 1898, in Leipzig, Germany.
STRIPLING: What is your occupation?
EISLER: I am a composer.
STRIPLING: Musical composer?
EISLER: Musical composer—may I add, of international reputation.
STRIPLING: Of international reputation?
EISLER: Yes.
STRIPLING: In what institutions did you receive your musical education?
EISLER: In Vienna, at the Academy. I am the pupil of the famous composer Arnold Schoenberg, one of the greatest living masters of modern music.

* On 3 December 1949, J. Parnell Thomas was sentenced to 6–18 months imprisonment, after pleading no contest and throwing himself on the mercy of the court on charges of misappropriation of government funds, putting on the Congressional payroll a number of his relatives who never did any work, including a bed-ridden 71-year-old aunt of his wife, and extorting kickbacks from employees. He was released on 9 September 1950 on parole, and subsequently obtained full pardon from President Truman.

** In 1968 Richard M. Nixon was elected President of the United States.

STRIPLING: Mr. Chairman, the loudspeaker equipment doesn't seem to be working, and I am sure everyone is having a good bit of difficulty in hearing. Could I ask for a slight recess to see if it is possible to get the equipment working?

THE CHAIRMAN: All right.

STRIPLING: Mr. Eisler, on August 5, 1938, the Acting Secretary of Labor issued an order permitting you and your wife to remain until January 21, 1939, before departing from the United States. On January 9, 1939 you filed an application to extend the time of your temporary stay for six months. In March 2, 1939, the Assistant Secretary of Labor ordered your deportation from the United States.

EISLER: Yes, I remember this quite well.

STRIPLING: And you were given an extension until April 7, 1939.

EISLER: Yes, Hitler was already in Austria, and being deported to Germany would have meant my execution.

STRIPLING: During 1940 you were employed in various capacities. Will you outline these for the committee?

EISLER: I was employed as professor of music at the New School for Social Research. And I got a grant from the Rockefeller Foundation.

STRIPLING: Now, Mr. Eisler, are you now, or have you ever been a Communist?

EISLER: I am not now a Communist. I remember I made, when I was a young man, in 1926, an application for the German Communist party, but I found out very quickly that I couldn't combine my artistic activities with the demands of any political party, so I dropped out.

STRIPLING: Mr. Eisler, you have been the foremost figure in the revolutionary movement of the Soviet Union in the musical field, have you not?

EISLER: No, sir. The Soviet Union has wonderful composers and I never was in the foreground of the movement of the Soviet Union at all.

STRIPLING: Mr. Chairman, I have here a copy of *The Daily Worker* of January 15, 1935. I should like to introduce this into the record. It states: "Hanns Eisler will arrive here January 27. The famous revolutionary composer, who has been living in exile in Paris and London since the advent of Hitler, is well known in Europe and America for his brilliant compositions, which include K-u-h-l-e W-a-m-p-e." Would you pronounce it for us?

EISLER: *Kuhle Wampe.* This is a motion picture which I did in 1932 in Berlin.

STRIPLING: *Hell on Earth, Comintern, M-a-s-s-n-a-h-m-e.*

EISLER: What is that last one, please?

STRIPLING: M-a-s . . .

EISLER: M-a-s . . . Would you be so kind, please?

STRIPLING: M-a-s . . . (exhibits printed paper).

EISLER: *Massnahme,* which is a German word meaning Expedient.

STRIPLING: And the next one?

EISLER: *Tempo der Zeit,* which means The Tempo of our Times.

STRIPLING: And the next one?

EISLER: *Rot Front,* which means Red Front.

STRIPLING: Red Front?

EISLER: Yes.

STRIPLING: Did you compose all of them?

EISLER: Yes.

STRIPLING: Mr. Chairman, I have here *The Daily Worker* of February 18, 1935, which contains an article entitled "Noted Composer of Comintern Arrives for U.S. Concert Tour—Hanns Eisler Exiled from Germany and His Music Banned."—The Communist Party in Germany had to fight the old beer garden atmosphere and nationalistic ditties of the middle class which had gone their way to the masses. In this cultural and musical development, the German workers were led by Hanns Eisler. The class struggle in Germany, strikes, barricades, May First celebrations, and other demonstrations are bound up with his name. Eisler, however, was not happy in the surroundings of the musical bourgeoisie. To be one of a great number of decadent musicians meant a futility stagnating to his talents. Only when Eisler came into the struggle of the working class did he find his medium and with it grew his power of composing music which expressed not only the life and battles of the German workers but of the working class of the entire world.

THE CHAIRMAN: What is it you are reading from now?

STRIPLING: From The *Daily Worker,* Mr. Chairman, concerning Mr. Eisler's arrival in the United States in 1935.

THE CHAIRMAN: Is that the Communist *Daily Worker,* the organ of the Communist Party in the United States?

STRIPLING: It is the official organ of the Communist Party.

THE CHAIRMAN: That is what I wanted the record to show.

STRIPLING: Mr. Eisler, have you on a number of occasions said, in effect, that music is one of the most powerful weapons for the bringing about of the revolution?

EISLER: Napoleon said . . .

THE CHAIRMAN: Never mind Napoleon. You tell what you said.

EISLER: I consider myself, in this matter, a pupil of Napoleon. I think in music I can enlighten and help people in distress, in their fight for their rights . . .

STRIPLING: You have written a lot of songs, Mr. Eisler, have you not?

EISLER: I have written not only songs. Here is a book printed by a subversive organization, the Oxford University Press, but I cannot say that I am a member of the Oxford University Press.

STRIPLING: Mr. Chairman, I should like to introduce a translation of an article which appeared in *Sovietskaya Musica,* in March and April of 1933 issue, "For a Solid Front of all Proletarian and Revolutionary Musicians." (Reads)

EISLER: May I object to the reading of articles of this kind, old articles from a different time, because it can only create a kind of hysteria against me.

THE CHAIRMAN: Mr. Stripling, what is the purpose of your reading these excerpts?

STRIPLING: The purpose is to show that Mr. Eisler is the Karl Marx of Communism in the musical field and he is well aware of it.

EISLER: I would be flattered.

STRIPLING: Mr. Chairman, I intend to show that the International Music Bureau, as a section of the Communist International, was a major program of the Soviet Union in their effort to bring about a world revolution and establish a proletarian dictatorship. This International Music Bureau, which Mr. Eisler conceived and re-organized in 1935, after he had been in the United States, carried on extensive activities, which I shall be glad to introduce into the record. Now, I would like to question Mr. Eisler about the origin of it.

EISLER: It was my idea and the idea of my friends.

STRIPLING: Mr. Eisler, who composed the Internationale?

EISLER: A man called Pierre Degeyter. It was written around 1888.

STRIPLING: Did you ever belong to an organization known as the Pierre Degeyter Music Club?

EISLER: I gave a lecture there once.

STRIPLING: In the United States?

EISLER: In the Pierre Degeyter Club.

STRIPLING: Do you consider it to be a Communist organization?

EISLER: Mr. Stripling, I don't ask anybody if he is a Communist or not when I go to a club and speak.

STRIPLING: I have here a song book, entitled *Red Song Book.* This was published, prepared by the Workers Music League, with the hammer and sickle on the front, and they feature on the back the song Comintern by Hanns Eisler. Would you like to read the words?

EISLER: You have a better pronunciation than I.

STRIPLING (reading):

Oh, you who are missing,
   Oh, comrades in dungeons,
You're with us, you're with us,
   This day of our vengeance.
No Fascists can daunt us,
   No terror can halt;
All lands will take flame
   With the fire of revolt,
All lands.

The Comintern calls you,
   Raise high Soviet banner,
In steeled ranks to battle.
   Raise sickle and hammer,
Our answer: Red Legions
   We raise in our might;
Our answer: Red Storm Troops
   We lunge to the fight.
Our answer Red Storm Troops.

From Russia victorious
   The workers' October
Comes storming reactions
   Regime the world over
We're coming with Lenin
   For Bolshevik work
From London, Havana,
   Berlin and New York,
From London.

Rise up, fields and workshops!
   Come out workers, farmers!
To battle march onward,
   March on world stormers!
Eyes sharp on your guns,
   Red banners unfurled,
Advance Proletarians
   To conquer the world.
Advance Proletarians.

Is this one of your little ditties that someone adopted?

EISLER: This song was written in 1926. This is a translation. When was the song printed here?

STRIPLING: Beg pardon?

EISLER: When was it printed here?

STRIPLING: This was published in 1932 in New York.

EISLER: In 1932 I was in Berlin. I am not responsible for literary translations. My song was written in Germany for a theater performance on the anniversary of the German revolution in 1918.

MCDOWELL: Who wrote the words, Mr. Stripling?

STRIPLING: By Victor Jerome.

EISLER: In 1932.

STRIPLING: Other songs which appear in this issue are the Internationale, The Barricades, The Builders, Comrades, The Bugles Are Sounding, Solidarity, The Workers Funeral March, and others.

EISLER: Very beautiful melody there.

STRIPLING: I have another one here, Mr. Eisler, entitled "America Sings."

EISLER: Yes.

STRIPLING: That was published by the Workers Book Shop, in New York, which is the official publishing house of the Communist Party. Among the songs which are contained in *America Sings* are *Comintern, Comrades, The Bugles Are Sounding, Internationale, Red Air Fleet, Red Flag, Rounds, Salute to Life, Scottsboro Boys, Solidarity Forever,* and for some unknown reason, *The Star Spangled Banner.* I have here, Mr. Chairman, an article entitled *The Revolutionary Musical Front,* by Gregory Schneerson, which appeared in the magazine *Sovietskaya Musica* of May 1933. It says: "The Workers League has published songs by Hanns Eisler and by Soviet composers which have been translated into the English language. The American comrades have succeeded in getting into the movement a number of outstanding musicians and theorists. Great assistance in theoretical courses has been given by the Pierre Degeyter Music Club in New York, organized by the League. The work in the club is being conducted by such great musicians as Henry Cowell, Charles Seeger, and others. The League has over 6,000 active members. A number of large choruses and orchestras make the league one of the strongest and outstanding factors in the International Musical Revolutionary front." Mr. Eisler, when you were in Moscow in 1935, did you give out some interviews or write some articles?

EISLER: I think I gave interviews, as usual. Mostly ideas about Germany.

STRIPLING: I have an article here written by you, which appeared in *Sovietskoe Iskusstvo,* July 29, 1935, and it has your picture, and is printed in Russian. The title is *The Destruction of Art.* You state: "Still, I am an optimist with regard to the future because I believe in the inexhaustible strength of the organized masses. The dark epoch of Fascism makes it clear to every honest artist that close cooperation with the working masses is the only way of dealing with creative art. Only in a revolutionary struggle will an artist find his own individuality. Similar developments can be observed in America where the well-known composer Aaron Copland has written a mass song *The First of May.* An active role is also played in the workers' musical movement by Henry Cowell, of San Francisco. These events, which only three years ago could hardly have been imagined, proved that for a real artist there is only one way, the road toward revolution. It would not be long before there would not be left a single great artist on the other side of the barricades. Revolutionary music is now more powerful than ever. Its political and artistic importance is growing daily." Mr. Eisler, what do you mean by "on the other side of the barricades"?

EISLER: Will you repeat the title of this article?

STRIPLING: The title of it was *The Destruction of Art.*

EISLER: By whom?

STRIPLING: By Hanns Eisler.

EISLER: No, I didn't destroy art. I spoke on how Fascism has destroyed art.

THE CHAIRMAN: I don't think that is responsive to the question. What was your question, Mr. Stripling?

STRIPLING: I asked him what he meant when he referred to "the other side of the barricades."

EISLER: I meant, in Germany, to fight against Hitler. That was my real belief.

STRIPLING: The next matter, Mr. Chairman, I would like to introduce, is a translation of an interview with Hanns Eisler, which appeared in the *Evening Moscow* of June 27, 1935. This is quoting you, Mr. Eisler: "I left Germany after the Reichstag fire. Therefore, I have only second-hand information about the latest events in the musical life of Germany. It is natural and logical that all efforts to promote the workers' musical movement are radically suppressed by the Fascist regime. Not only are the workers' unions persecuted by the Fascists but also the leftist elements among the bourgeois composers. Even Paul Hindemith who, in view of the tragic shortage of people on the musical front, was hurriedly reinstated by the Hitlerites, has now lost their confidence. Considerable time must pass before a young generation of second-class musicians will grow up who will satisfy the political and artistic expectations of Adolf Hitler. For the time being the leadership in the musical world of Germany is divided between Hans Pfitzner and the very old Richard Strauss. Actually, Pfitzner's popularity was never significant. But Strauss was once great. The scores which he is composing now do not add any glorious pages to the history of his creative art. Recently the first performance of his new opera based on a libretto by Stefan Zweig took place at Dresden. The permission to produce a play by Zweig, who is a Jew, in present-day Germany reveals the pressing desire to compensate Strauss for his obedience. Alas, this seems to have been the only compensation for all his efforts. His opera had a dubious success. In London, where I went directly from Germany, I wrote a symphony in which I tried to solve a number of purely technical musical problems. There, an outstanding conductor, Ernest Ansermet, conducted the first performance of my symphony. I intend to follow up this musical work by a new symphony dedicated to the victims of the Fascist terror. From England I proceeded to America. I have the most pleasant recollections about this trip. First of all, I succeeded in giving there a great number of concerts for the benefit of political prisoners. Secondly, I gave a whole series of popular lectures on German Fascism. These lectures were always attended by very large audiences. For instance, in New York about 5,000 people listened to the lectures. In Hollywood and Los Angeles the audience consisted not only of workers but of numerous representatives of the progressive intelligentsia. I am extremely pleased to report a considerable shift to the left among American artists. I do not believe it would be an exaggeration to say that the best people in the musical world of America (with very few exceptions) share at present extremely progressive ideas. Their names? They are Aaron Copland, Henry Cowell, Wallingford Riegger, the outstanding musical theoretician Charles Seeger, the greatest specialist on modern music Nicolas Slonimsky, and finally the brightest star on the American musical horizon, the great conductor, Leopold Stokowski. Recently he even dared to play the Internationale at a concert. This nearly caused a riot." Mr. Eisler, did you write a song entitled *In Praise of Learning*?

EISLER: Yes.

STRIPLING: I will read the words to this one verse. It says:

> Learn now the simple truth,
> You, for whom the time has come at last.
> It is not too late.
> Learn now the A, B, C,
> It is not enough, but learn it still.
> Fear not, be not downhearted,
> Begin, you must learn the lesson,
> You must be ready to take over,
> You must be ready to take over.

What do you mean, "You must be ready to take over"?

EISLER: This song appeared in a play which I wrote the music for. It was written in 1929 in Berlin. The play was based on the famous novel by Maxim Gorki. This theater piece was sung by workers on the stage.

THE CHAIRMAN: You didn't mean that you must be ready to take over now, did you?

EISLER: I can't understand your question.

THE CHAIRMAN: You said that it applied to Germany.

EISLER: Not only to Germany. It was a song in a show. It applied to the situation on the stage.

STRIPLING: It was shown in the United States. He wrote the music for it in the United States.

EISLER: No, I wrote the music in 1929 or 1930 in Berlin. It was produced in Copenhagen, in New York and in Paris. It was a theater play.

THE CHAIRMAN: It doesn't apply only to Germany but applies to France and Italy and the United States?

EISLER: This song applies to the historical structure of the Russian people from 1905 until 1917.

THE CHAIRMAN: Would you write the same song here in the United States now, about "You must take over" here in the United States?

EISLER: No.

THE CHAIRMAN: You have changed your opinion, then?

EISLER: No, but I am a guest, a stranger here, and the labor movement can handle their affairs themselves. That is what I mean.

STRIPLING: Mr. Eisler, did you ever send greetings to the Soviet Union?

EISLER: Sure.

STRIPLING: You don't hate Stalin, Mr. Eisler?

EISLER: Pardon?

STRIPLING: Do you hate Stalin?

EISLER: No.

STRIPLING: Why did you tell the immigration authorities that you hated Stalin?

EISLER: I cannot remember the fact. If I really made such a stupid remark I was an idiot.

STRIPLING: You said, "I hate Stalin just as I hate Hitler" when you were before the immigration authorities.

EISLER: I am surprised. There must be a misunderstanding, or it is a completely idiotic, hysteric remark.

THE CHAIRMAN: Do you remember?

EISLER: I don't remember the remark. I think that Stalin is one of the greatest historical personalities of our time.

STRIPLING: This message, Mr. Chairman, refers to Stalin's Constitution, by Hanns Eisler, and reads: "Hearty greetings to the Constitution of the great socialist state, based on the great principle, From Each According to his Abilities, to Each According to his Work. It is almost impossible to encompass the tremendous consequences which your Constitution will have for future instruction of the new socialist culture. Each success for the Soviet Union is success for the international proletariat. It gives us courage in struggle and binds us to give all our strength in the defense of the Soviet Union."

EISLER: Did I write this?

STRIPLING: It says "By Hanns Eisler, hearty greetings."

EISLER: I cannot remember. It is quite possible that I did.

STRIPLING: The Great Soviet Encyclopedia, Mr. Eisler, published in Moscow, in 1933, prints your picture and says: "Hanns Eisler, born 1898, composer, Communist, is at the head of the proletarian movement in German music." Is that an error on the part of this Great Soviet Encyclopedia to refer to you as a Communist?

EISLER: It is an error. They call everybody a Communist who is active like me. I would be a swindler if I called myself a Communist. The Communist underground workers in every country have proved that they are heroes. I am not an hero. I am a composer.

STRIPLING: Did you write the music for a play *Die Massnahme*?

EISLER: Sure.

STRIPLING: Would you describe it to the committee.

EISLER: It goes back to an old Japanese play. I wrote the music for it.

STRIPLING: It dealt with party strategy?

EISLER: Yes.

STRIPLING: It had to do with four young Communists, did it not?

EISLER: Yes, sir.

STRIPLING: And three of the Communists murdered the fourth one because they felt he would be a menace to the cause, is that correct?

EISLER: Yes.

1400

STRIPLING: That is the theme of it?

EISLER: Yes.

STRIPLING: The real title of the play is *Disciplinary Measure,* isn't that right?

EISLER: Yes, it is a poetical philosophical play.

STRIPLING: Mr. Chairman, I don't think we can finish with Mr. Eisler before lunch. We will have to call him back to the stand.

THE CHAIRMAN: All right, we will recess.

STRIPLING: Mr. Eisler, you stated that you have a sister in the United States.

EISLER: Yes.

STRIPLING: By the name of Ruth Fischer.

EISLER: Yes.

STRIPLING: Do you recall receiving a letter from her on April 27, 1944, addressed to you and your wife?

EISLER: I don't recall it. What kind of letter was it, please?

STRIPLING: In this letter she accused you and her brother Gerhard of being agents of the GPU. She stated as follows (reading): "If the local branches of the GPU can succeed in making clever arrangements for a natural death it will not succeed this time. Not for you nor for Gerhard Eisler, Chief of the German GPU division in the United States. . . . This time it will not be made so easy for you. You always play with terror and are always afraid to take your responsibility for your acts. I have made the following preparations: Three physicians have given me a thorough examination. I am now in good health. There is no cause for natural death. I am constantly under a physician's care and am taking care of myself in a sensible manner. The doctors are informed and in case of any trouble they will testify accordingly. A number of reputable journalists and politicians have been informed and possess a copy of this letter. A number of German emigrants have also been apprised." Do you recall receiving this letter?

EISLER: Really not. I don't recall getting such a letter. I think the letter is absolutely idiotic.

THE CHAIRMAN: If I had received a letter like that, or anyone in this room, particularly if it was from our sister, they would remember.

EISLER: Maybe my wife put it away. But let us say, for the sake of the record, that I received this letter.

MCDOWELL: Mr. Eisler, did you write the *Ballad to Paragraph 218?*

EISLER: I write only music.

MCDOWELL: You remember the words?

EISLER: Sure.

MCDOWELL: Did you write the *Ballad of the Maimed?*

EISLER: Of what, please?

MCDOWELL: *Ballad of the Maimed,* the hurt, the injured.

EISLER: I wrote music to it.

MCDOWELL: Have you read the words?

EISLER: Yes.

MCDOWELL: Did you write *Ballad of Nigger Jim?*

EISLER: I wrote the music.

MCDOWELL: You didn't write the words.

EISLER: No.

MCDOWELL: Did you read the words?

EISLER: I read the words.

MCDOWELL: Did you write *Song of the Dry Bread?*

EISLER: Yes, it was in a play.

MCDOWELL: Did you write the words?

EISLER: No. I never write the words.

MCDOWELL: Did you read the words?

EISLER: Sure.

MCDOWELL: Did you write *Song of Demand and Supply*?

EISLER: It is one of the songs of the . . .

MCDOWELL: Did you write the words?

EISLER: No.

MCDOWELL: Did you read the words?

EISLER: Yes.

MCDOWELL: I would like to say, Mr. Chairman, that I think all members of the committee should examine these exhibits that I have here, and that I have just named to Mr. Eisler, who maintains he is a composer of the music. This is matter that couldn't be sent through the mails in the United States. It deals with affairs that are entirely out of political matters, entirely out of anything except perhaps that of medicine. Obscenity is a poor word for it. I don't know what the custom is in Germany or in Austria, but such words as are in those sheets have no place in any sort of a civilisation.

EISLER: They are considered as great poetry.

MCDOWELL: They are considered as what?

EISLER: Great poetry.

MCDOWELL: Great poetry?

EISLER: Yes.

MCDOWELL: Well, great poetry as we are taught in America has nothing to do with that kind of truck. Among other things there is a song in there apparently dedicated or written because of the laws prohibiting abortion.

EISLER: Yes.

MCDOWELL: In Germany.

EISLER: Yes.

MCDOWELL: This song ridicules the law . . .

EISLER: Yes.

MCDOWELL: Opposing the prohibition of abortions.

EISLER: Yes.

MCDOWELL: In other words, this song would, I presume, in your Communist fashion of thinking, urge that the law opposing abortion be disregarded.

THE CHAIRMAN: I would suggest that we don't get very deep into the question of abortion.

RANKIN: I understand that you have complained that this committee has smeared you.

EISLER: Yes, Mr. Rankin.

RANKIN: When you make that charge you are making that charge against a Committee of the Congress of the United States. You realize that, do you?

EISLER: Yes.

MCDOWELL: This Committee is governed by the rules of the House of Representatives. Nothing that this Committee has done is in violation of the rules of the House, or in conflict with the laws of common decency. Now, where do you get any authority for saying that this committee has smeared you?

EISLER: I haven't any authority at all, but if you had made such a hearing without giving, every week the last 12 months, things about me which are not even sometimes the truth, it would be different. But when you have distortions or inventions of somebody which told it to one of the members of the committee, when you go into this fantastic press campaign against an artist, I am sure every red-blooded artist will be, after one year, after you nearly ruined him, very angry about this.

RANKIN: I am conscious, when I look at this filth here, to which Mr. McDowell has referred . . .

EISLER: Pardon me, Mr. Rankin. It is not filth.

RANKIN: I am conscious that anybody that would write that stuff would certainly not have much respect for the Congress of the United States. But this Committee has given you more than a fair deal, more than a fair trial, more than you would have gotten in any other country in the world. In any other country in the world you would have fared worse than you have in the United States, if you had carried on the same class of conduct that has been brought out by the testimony here.

EISLER: I don't know, Mr. Rankin, how you are familiar with American poetry.

RANKIN: American what?

EISLER: Poetry.

RANKIN: Poetry.

EISLER: An American writing. This is not American poetry or American writing. This was written in German. It is not translated. It was written in Berlin in 1927 or 1928 or 1929. I say, again, it is great poetry. We can have different tastes in art, but I cannot permit, Mr. Rankin, that you call my work by such names. I protest against that.

RANKIN: I suppose that I am as familiar with American poetry and with English poetry generally as any Member of either House. And anybody that tries to tell me that this filth is poetry certainly reads himself out of the class of any American poet that has ever been recognised by the American people.

EISLER: I am sorry . . .

RANKIN: I don't believe I have anything further, Mr. Chairman.

MCDOWELL: Mr. Eisler, you wrote the poem *About Killing?*

EISLER: No. I put it together from poetry. I cannot write words, you know.

MCDOWELL: Mr. Chairman, I would like permission to read these nine lines, which is the entire poem, that Mr. Eisler put together.

RANKIN: I reserve the right to object. But we will hear him read it.

MCDOWELL (reading):

> Terrible it is to shed blood,
> Hard it is to learn to kill
> Bad it is to see people die before their time,
> But we must learn to kill,
> We must see people die before their time,
> We must shed blood,
> So that no more blood may be shed.

EISLER: This is a correct anti-Fascist statement. When Heydrich was killed by the Czech people, I agreed with this. He was a gangster, and he killed innumerable good people. This is poetry and not reality. The difference between art and real life has to be reconsidered. Take Hollywood—at every street corner you can see the most cruel pieces of art, and you can read stories in mystery magazines that you can buy in every drug store, which are horrible. I don't like such stuff. This is a little philosophical poem directed against gangsters.

RANKIN: Mr. Chairman, the American people, of course, have just whipped Hitler, but the thing that shocks me is that while our boys were dying by the thousands over there to get Hitler's heel off their necks, some of these people come here and attempt to foment revolution in the United States. It is about time the American people woke up and put a stop to it.

THE CHAIRMAN: Mr. Eisler, the Chair wishes to direct you to remain in the United States.

STRIPLING: Mr. Appell, were you directed by the Committee to make an investigation as to Mr. Eisler's status as a visiting lecturer and professor with the New School for Social Research in New York?

APPELL: I was, sir.

STRIPLING: I may say, Mr. Chairman, the purpose of Mr. Appell's testimony is to show that Mr. Eisler's position with the New School for Social Research was used merely as a subterfuge in order for him to remain here.

APPELL: On May 2, 1935, Dr. Alvin Johnson, the director of the school, wrote Eisler that he was appointed visiting professor of music for the academic year 1935–36. On March 29, 1938, Dr. Johnson, with the apparent purpose of qualifying Eisler as a non-quota visa applicant, changed Eisler's status from lecturer in music to professor in music. In this letter, Dr. Johnson stated that the New School and its students were so enthusiastic over his work as a visiting lecturer that they wanted him to remain permanently. Mr. Chairman, with respect to this appointment which was prompted by the overwhelming enthusiasm of the New School and its students, I should like to refer to the pay record and attendance cards of the New School for Social Research in substantiation of the overwhelming enthusiasm. In the two courses conducted by Eisler from October 5, 1935 to January 18, 1936, no more than eight students attended the course of Musical Composition, and only three attended the course on the Crisis of Modern Music. . . . When Dr. Johnson wrote the letter prompted by the overwhelming enthusiasm, Eisler had seven students attending the lecture on Musical Composition, one student attending the lecture on Counterpoint, with the third course having been cancelled after the first lecture.

STRIPLING: Mr. Chairman, a number of the songs which Mr. Eisler composed the music for, the words were provided by Bertolt Brecht, who will be one of the witnesses in the Hollywood investigation, who is a Communist. Did your investigation disclose that Bertolt Brecht has also been brought to this country in a similar manner by the New School?

APPELL: Apparently, he was.

RANKIN: Mr. Appell, would you say this was a Communist school of instruction?

APPELL: No sir, I do not say that it is a Communist school.

RANKIN: It was spreading Communist propaganda?

APPELL: I have no evidence that the school itself has put out any Communist propaganda, but I know that the members of the faculty of the New School for Social Research are very prominently displayed in our files.

RANKIN: Do you know whether or not Mrs. Eleanor Roosevelt was familiar with this situation when she urged the admission of Hanns Eisler into the United States?

APPELL: I do not, sir.

RANKIN: Did you read her recent article in the *Ladies Home Journal?*

APPELL: No sir, I haven't.

RANKIN: It is the most insulting communistic piece of propaganda that was ever thrown in the faces of the women of America. I am just wondering if she was familiar with all of this Communist infiltration when she was trying to get Hanns Eisler into the United States.

APPELL: I do not know that, sir.

RANKIN: I want to point out that her action was not official. She did not represent the party in power in trying to get these Communists returned or readmitted to the United States. And she certainly doesn't represent the better element of the American people in this Communist propaganda that she has written in the *Ladies Home Journal.*

## The Birth of Jazz

Come on there, Professor, string up the big harp and give us all a tune! The Seals are down from Boyes Springs for tomorrow's first engagement with the Sox and now we'll get a round of real baseball. The squad numbers fifteen men and reached the city shortly after 10 o'clock, having departed from the Spa before the camp was awake. Everybody has come back to the old town full of the old "jazz" and they promise to knock the fans off their feet with their playing.

What is the "jazz"? Why, it's a little of that "old life," the "gin-i-ker," the "pep," otherwise known as the enthusiasalum. A grain of "jazz" and you feel like going out and eating your way through Twin Peaks. It's that spirit which makes ordinary ball players step around like Lajoies and Cobbs. The Seals have it and we venture to say that everybody in the big town who has ever stopped to "pan" the San Francisco club in the past several months will be inoculated with it by the time the coming string of games is over.

"Hap" Hogan gave his men a couple of shots of "near-jazz" last season and look at what resulted—the Tigers became the most ferocious set of tossers in the league. Now the Seals have happened upon great quantities of it in the quiet valley of Sonoma and they're setting the countryside on fire. The team which speeded into town this morning comes pretty close to representing the pick of the army. Its members have trained on ragtime and "jazz" and Manager Del Howard says there's no stopping them. Class will not be denied, and whether they are ball players or not the members of the first squad will not be wanting in spirit and determination.

For the fans' information it is sufficient to state that Del Howard while he is manager of that San Francisco club will give them a first-class run for their money. He's a real ball player, excelling in several branches of the sport—the most important of all of which is—baseball sense.

Meanwhile, keep your eye on the Seal outfit. The players are just brimming over with that old "Texas Tommy" stuff and there is a bit of the "jazz" in everything they do.

("Scoop" Gleeson, *The Bulletin,* San Francisco, 6 March 1913)

Spring in a baseball training camp is all too often a season of sore arms, "charley horses" and crushed hopes. But that of 1913, when the San Francisco Seals took up a temporary abode at Boyes Springs, in Sonoma County, was different. For one thing Del Howard was installed as manager and the change ushered in a new spirit of enthusiasm and anticipation. For another, Art Hickman had arrived on the scene in the guise of a camp follower. He came up ostensibly to take a rest, but really to do a little fraternizing with his friends the newspaper correspondents.

It was this happy set of circumstances that launched Hickman on his career as a popular orchestra leader and marked the birth of a new syncopation in dance tunes, which soon won its way under the name of "jazz."

Hickman, whose home originally was in Oakland, had spent some time in his youth, dancing with his sister, Pearl, in professional engagements. He had played trap drums and picked at a piano in one of the city's places of amusement. Then had been named entertainment manager at the Chutes Theater. During his stay at the springs he went on several outings with the newspaper crowd. Up to Jack London's ranch at Glenn Ellen, where Jack was working away on "John Barleycorn." Over to the winery and the early California landmarks at Sonoma. But mostly he turned up to sit in the sun in the bleachers when the Regulars and Yannigans, selected from the baseball squads, put in their afternoons playing practice games. It was a pleasant and indolent way to enjoy a vacation. Perhaps Hickman had the idea all the time and was only awaiting such an opportunity to try it out. But it was his suggestion that it might be a good plan to put on a couple of dances and relieve the tedium of the evenings. He said it wouldn't cost much and that if the management at the springs would cooperate, with room and board, he thought he could induce several musicians out of work, to come up for a vacation. That was how his first group of players was assembled. As a feature Hickman included a banjo player in his orchestra—some one said he got the notion from watching one of the Negro orchestras at Purcell's on the Barbary Coast.

Similarly the very word "jazz" itself came into general usage at the same time. We were all seated around the dinner table at Boyes one evening and William ("Spike")

Slattery, then sports editor of *The Call*, spoke about something being the "jazz," or the old "gin-iker fizz."

"Spike" had picked up the expression in a crap game. Whenever one of the players rolled the dice he would shout, "Come on, the old jazz."

For the next week we gave "jazz" a great play in all our stories. And when Hickman's orchestra swung into action for the evening's dances, it was natural to find it included as "the jazziest tune tooters in all the Valley of the Moon." On one of the evenings James Woods, then manager of the Hotel St. Francis, and former Police Judge Jack Sullivan, visitors to the camp, attended the dance. Woods was at once struck by the melody of the band. "How long has this been going on?" he asked. He was introduced to Hickman and forthwith the latter was engaged to assemble an orchestra for the St. Francis. Soon all San Francisco was dancing to the "Rose Room Fox Trot" by Art Hickman.

("Scoop" Gleeson, *The Call Bulletin*, San Francisco, 3 September 1938)

# Resolution of the Fire and Police Research Association of Los Angeles on the Subversive Perils of American Folk Music

October 4, 1963

MR. NICOLAS SLONIMSKY
295 BEACON STREET
BOSTON, MASSACHUSETTS

DEAR MR. SLONIMSKY;

Thank you for your letter of September 28, 1963 requesting a copy of our resolution which we sent to the House Committee on Un-American Activities regarding communist infiltration into the field of folk singing. We are enclosing a copy of this resolution and we have no objection to your reproducing it, provided it is reproduced in toto and without any alterations.

Very truly yours,
PAUL R. JACKSON, MEMBER
BOARD OF DIRECTORS

RESOLUTION

WHEREAS, there is increasing and cumulative evidence indicating a deep interest in, and much activity by the Communist Party, USA, in the field of Folk Music, and

WHEREAS, Folk Music has been successfully used in the past by great political movements in history, particularly in the USSR, and

WHEREAS, the dialectics of the Communist movement have successfully used, and are now using all modes and media of communication with young people, including the subtleties and the verbal subterfuges of applied dialectics in both poems and songs, and

WHEREAS, it is becoming more and more evident that certain of the "Hootenannies" and other similar youth gatherings and festivals, both in this country and in Europe have been used to brainwash and subvert, in a seemingly innocuous but actually covert and deceptive manner, vast segments of young people's groups, and

WHEREAS, the youth of our nation is acknowledged to be a major target of the Communist Conspiracy, and

WHEREAS, there is much evidence indicating an accelerated drive in the Folk Music field is being made on or near the campuses of a number of high schools and colleges by certain individuals of questionable motivation, including members of the Communist Conspiracy,

THEREFORE, be it resolved that the Fire and Police Research Association of Los Angeles in its regular monthly meeting of August, 1963, hereby formally requests the Congress of the United States, through its House Committee on Un-American Activities, to investigate Communist subversive involvement in the Folk Music field, that the continued, effective misuse of this media may not be made, and that it may not be further used as an unidentified tool of Communist Psychological or Cybernetic Warfare to ensnare and capture youthful minds in the United States as it has so successfully and effectively captivated them abroad.

Adopted by the Board of Directors, August 7, 1963.


# United States Senate

REMARKS OF SENATOR KENNETH B. KEATING AND OTHERS ON FOLKMUSIK (FROM CONGRESSIONAL RECORD, THURSDAY SEPTEMBER 26, 1963, VOLUME 109, NO. 154).

October 7, 1963

MR. NICOLAS SLONIMSKY
295 BEACON STREET
BOSTON, MASSACHUSETTS

DEAR MR. SLONIMSKY:

Thank you for requesting a copy of my recent speech on hootenannies.
I am very pleased to enclose a copy of the complete text for your information.

Very sincerely yours,
KENNETH B. KEATING

## MINE ENEMY—THE FOLK SINGER

Mr. KEATING. Mr. President, it will come as a shock to many Senators, but according to a resolution of a certain Los Angeles civic organization the Communists have developed a new secret weapon to ensnare and capture youthful minds in America—folk music.

No one who serves in Congress could reasonably entertain any illusions, no matter what might be the thrust of Soviet policy at any given time, about any possible letup in the intensity and earnestness of the Soviet pursuit toward its ultimate goal of world domination. Nor, based on our experiences with and knowledge of Soviet tactics, can one ever safely underestimate the capacity of communism for devising and employing whatever techniques are necessary to accomplish its long-range ends, from outright military takeover and occupation and the violent coup d'etat, to espionage, sabotage, subversion, propaganda, economic warfare, and perversion of the political and social processes of free societies to its own evil purposes. Nevertheless, I am stunned by the revelation that folk music is part of the Communist arsenal of weapons.

The resolution adopted by this organization, called the Fire and Police Research Association of Los Angeles, Inc., describes folk music as—and I quote from the resolution—"an unidentified tool of Communist psychological or cybernetic warfare."

For the benefit of any Senators who may not be fully familiar with the term "Cybernetics," I looked it up in the dictionary, and it means "a comparative study of the control system formed by the nervous system and brain and mechano-electrical communication systems, such as computing machines."

I ask unanimous consent that the text of the resolution be printed in the RECORD following my remarks.

The PRESIDING OFFICER (Mr. KENNEDY in the chair). Without objection, it is so ordered.

Mr. KEATING. Mr. President, this amazing document maintains that "the dialectics of the Communist movement have successfully used, and are now using all modes and media of communication with young people, including the subtleties and the verbal subterfuges of applied dialectics in both poems and songs" and that "it is becoming more and more evident that certain of the 'Hootenannies' in this country and in Europe have been used to brainwash and subvert"—and now, listen to this—"in a seemingly innocuous but actually covert and deceptive manner, vast segments of young people's groups." It closes with a fervent plea for a congressional investigation of this "unidentified tool of Communist psychological and cybernetic warfare" which is being used "to ensnare and capture youthful minds in the United States as it has so successfully and effectively captivated them abroad."

I had always had the impression that if anything was thoroughly American in spirit, it was American folk music. To be sure, I was perfectly aware of certain un-American influences in it, like Elizabethan balladry, English Protestant hymns and spirituals, and, with respect to jazz and in some cases the Negro spiritual, native African rhythms. But in my naivete I had never considered these un-American influences to be of a sinister nature and simply passed them off as part and parcel of the melting-pot tradition which has contributed so much in the way of variety and interest to the American cultural heritage.

In the light of this resolution, however, I have given this subject renewed attention. Have we ever considered, for example, that the music of our national anthem, the Star-Spangled Banner, is based upon an English folk melody—a drinking song, no less—"To Anacreon in Heaven"?

Of course, I realize that folk music tradition is grounded in movements of political, economic, and social unrest and I did not expect to find in music which originated among sharecroppers, miners, union organizers, factory workers, cowboys, hill folk, wanderers, and oppressed Negroes—a pattern of tribute and praise to such symbols of orthodoxy as the gold standard, the oil depletion allowance, and the standing rules of the U.S. Senate.

I knew that in reviewing the evidence I would be in for a share of lyrical protest against war, depression, economic exploitation, the plight of the Negro, the farmer, the worker, the railroaded convict, and, generally, the poor and down-trodden. I knew I would also come across music, as I actually did, dedicated to Robin Hood folk heroes like Jesse James, Pretty Boy Floyd, and Billy the Kid. And so I made allowances for the basic cultural factors operative in the folk music field. No one could possibly imagine the members of the board of directors of General Motors sitting around a conference table composing ditties in honor of defense contracts, while it is not surprising that coal miners should have come up with a protest song, "Sixteen Tons," crying "Saint Peter, don't call me, 'cause I can't go; I owe my soul to the company store."

I might interject at this point that the reason I recite rather than sing these words is that I know I would be breaking the Senate's rules if I did anything to provoke a Senate "hootenanny."

Mr. HUMPHREY. Mr. President, will the Senator yield?

Mr. KEATING. I yield.

Mr. HUMPHREY. I have examined the rules of the Senate, knowing of the Senator's speech. I do not recall seeing anything in the rules which would prohibit the Senator from singing, except his own good judgment.

Mr. AIKEN. Are there any other reasons?

Mr. KEATING. My voice is not of the best. Some of the citations bearing out this thesis are better sung than said. There is in the gallery an old friend and associate of my office who could sing them. But I think it best that I do not sing them.

Mr. HUMPHREY. Particularly without musical accompaniment.

Mr. KEATING. I would not be able to do that, anyway. If I used a guitar, I would have to use a left-handed guitar.

Mr. HUMPHREY. Let us not do anything "left" here.

Mr. KEATING. No; let us do everything right.

But when I began to look into the folk music business, I began to find that where there is smoke, there is fire—which perhaps explains how the Fire and Police Research Association gets into the act, too.

The first significant discovery I made was that from this Nation's very beginnings folk music had indeed been used, "in a seemingly innocuous but actually covert and deceptive manner, to incite violations of the laws of the United States." Why, even "Yankee Doodle" has fallen victim to misuse in this fashion, as it did during President Jefferson's embargo of 1808 imposed to prevent our embroilment in the Napoleonic wars. Just listen to this plea to run the embargo:

> Attention pay ye bonny lads
> And listen to my Fargo
> About a nation deuced thing
> Which people call Embargo
>
> Yankee doodle, keep it up
> Yankee doodle, dandy
> We'll soak our hide in home-made rum
> If we can't get French brandy
>
> I've got a vessel at the wharf
> Well loaded with a cargo
> And want a few more hands to help
> And clear the cursed Embargo

Yankee doodle, keep it up
Yankee doodle, dandy
We'll soak our hide in home-made rum
If we can't get French brandy

Now it seems perfectly obvious to me that if people went around singing this to-day, we would be in a pretty fix with our shipping ban against Castro. Before we knew it, we would have rum-running out of Cuba in American bottoms.

While we are on the subject of the whisky trade, this is another area for grave concern. Apparently, some of our folk music takes a pretty cavalier attitude toward the enforcement of our Internal Revenue laws and could easily brainwash our young people into total disrespect for all law and order. The song, "Darlin' Cory," is a prime example of this:

Wake up, wake up, darlin' Cory
What makes you sleep so sound?
The revenue officers a-comin'
Gonna tear your still house down

Or, for another example, the now very popular, "Copper Kettle," which contains the lines:

My daddy he made whisky
My granddaddy did, too
We ain't paid no whisky tax
Since 1792

If enough people went around singing this at hootenannies, Americans might soon get the idea that they don't have to pay their taxes. After all, the family in the song got away without paying them for 171 years. And if the Government loses its ability to collect taxes to pay for our defense effort, we would be wide open for a Communist takeover, would we not?

This sinister folk music plot for disarmament takes more direct form than merely inciting Americans not to pay their taxes. Consider, for example, this pacifist Negro spiritual:

Gonna lay down my sword and shield
Down by the river-side
Down by the river-side
Down by the river-side
Gonna lay down my sword and shield
Down by the river-side
And study war no more.

It should be especially noted that this song tells us not only to lay down our arms, but also—in the words of the Fire and Police Research Association—it uses "the subtleties and the verbal subterfuges of applied dialectics" by implying, by the words "And study war no more," that we should close down West Point, Annapolis, the Air Force Academy, and the War College, get rid of our ROTC program in our Nation's colleges and universities, and thus cut off our supply of trained military officers to lead us in our defense against communism. If we do not realize that this "seemingly innocuous" Negro spiritual is "actually covert and deceptive," we have obviously been duped.

Now the Communists have also been known to sow the seeds of dissension in capitalist countries by turning people against their own political leaders. There's an Ozark folk song—and perhaps one of the Senators from Arkansas can enlighten me as to its origin—that goes like this:

> Yes, the candidate's a dodger, yes, a well-known dodger
> Yes, the candidate's a dodger, and I'm a dodger, too
> He'll meet you and greet you and ask you for your vote
> But look out, boys, he's dodging for a note.

To be quite honest, I am not sure I understand all the "subtleties and verbal subterfuges" of these "applied dialectics." For example, what does the fellow mean when he sings, "And I'm a dodger, too"? Is he saying he is a draft-dodger and advocating resistance to the enforcement of the selective service laws? And then, what is meant by the words that the candidate is "dodging for a note"? Is he trying to undermine American faith and confidence in America's political leaders by implying that all they are interested in are "notes," that is to say, campaign contributions? I hope Senators will read the RECORD carefully tomorrow and fill me in on what may be an example of subtle regional dialectics.

These examples must give pause to every patriotic American who may have taken folk music for granted in the past. But there is one concern I still have about a congressional investigation of folk music proposed by the Fire and Police Research Association of Los Angeles. What I fear is that such an investigation would stimulate the writing of new folk music making fun of congressional investigations. This shows how devious the Communists really are. First they subtly use the verbal subterfuges of applied dialectics in folk music, knowing full well that organizations like the Fire and Police Research Association of Los Angeles are always on guard against them and sooner or later will demand a congressional investigation. Then, once a congressional investigation of folk music is held, the Communists set about composing new folk music impugning the integrity of congressional investigations, like this folk song of a few years ago:

Who's gonna investigate the man who investigates me?
I don't doubt my loyalty
But how about what his may be?
Who'll check the record of the man who checks the record of me?
Seems to me there's gonna be an awfully long line.

One more problem puzzles me
Pardon my strange whim
But who's gonna investigate the man who investigates the man who investigates him?

This shows that there may be no logical stopping place once an investigation of folk music goes forward. Any such investigation would ultimately have to be extended ad infinitum, to take in a study of the folk songs composed in response to the investigation itself, which can go on indefinitely. But perhaps all this simply shows how devious the Communists are, perpetually tying up the valuable time of our elected officials and diverting their attention from other subversive activities which they engage in.

It all boils down to a gigantic plot, one that has been brought to our attention before, most notably, by the assistant minority leader, the senior Senator from California [Mr. KUCHEL], based on letters he has received from constituents whose keen alertness to matters involving our national security is fully equal to that of the Fire and Police Association of Los Angeles, Inc. And so, now, to the list of subversive individuals, institutions, and ideas, which presently includes the United Nations, the income tax, the Chief Justice of the United States, the Girl Scouts of America, fluoridation of the water supply, the last four Presidents of the United States, beatniks, Harvard University, civil rights demonstrations, expenditures for mental health, the Arms Control and Disarmament Agency, coffee houses, every Secretary of State since William Jennings Bryan, professors of anthropology, back-door spending, metro government, Jews, Time magazine, the Council on Foreign Relations, firearms registration, the Protestant clergy, the two United States Senators from New York plus between 77 and 83 of their colleagues and proposals for Federal aid to mass transportation—to this list of Communist-inspired persons and ideas we must now add, merciful heavens, American folk music. And who knows what lies ahead?

Already there are signs that the Communists are going beyond folk music in their plot to subvert America, but I shall not dwell on that. Consider for a moment the inroads which have been made into the popular music field by such songs as "The Moon Belongs to Everyone. The Best Things in Life Are Free."

Mr. President, we ought to be grateful that we have a Constitution—that it protects the right of everyone to sing out as well as speak out whenever the spirit moves him. There is a fire of freedom in this document called the Constitution which no amount of researching by organizations such as the Fire and Police Research Association of Los Angeles will ever succeed in putting out.

This resolution is but another demonstration of the absurd lengths to which the amateur ferrets of the radical right will go in their quixotic sallies against the Communist menace. As the great FBI Director J. Edgar Hoover has often warned, vigilante charges such as these can breed the atmosphere of suspicion and confusion which tends not only to undermine free institutions but, of equal concern, to divert our energies from tackling the real threats posed by international communism to our liberty and security. With devotion to our freedoms, with trust in the American ideal of cultural diversity, with, above all, a sense of proportion and discernment in meeting the challenges of our times, I for one have every faith that—in the words of that inspiring song—we shall overcome.

Mr. Russell. Mr. President, will the Senator from New York yield?

Mr. Keating. I yield to the Senator from Georgia.

Mr. Russell. The remarks just made by the Senator from New York are a valuable contribution to the permanent record of the Senate. They bring to the attention of the American people the deep tolerance of these days and also show that the sense of humor has not been entirely extinguished by the complexities of the age in which we live.

But having paid tribute to the Senator's tolerance, I must express regret that he did not include in his magnificent defense of some of the things we have known in years gone by the song "Dixie." I did not hear him include that song in the list of things he defended. I am sure he would not desire to conclude his remarks without extending the mantle of Keating tolerance to overlap "Dixie" because it was written by a constituent of one of his predecessors in the Senate.

Mr. Keating. That is my understanding. "Dixie" was written by a New Yorker and is, of course, one of the great songs of the folk tradition. I am happy to include it in the engulfing embrace of these remarks. I am sure the Fire and Police Research Association of Los Angeles would find something subversive in it, but I fail to see how "Dixie" could undermine our security in any way.

Mr. Pell. Mr. President, I wish to congratulate the Senator from New York [Mr. Keating] on his spoof of the charges that folk music is a subversive wing of the Communist conspiracy.

The past summer we had the most successful music festival in the form of a folk festival that we have ever had in Newport. More people came to it, they were better shaved, and more enjoyment was received by our local citizens than had ever before been the case in any form of public entertainment.

When it is suggested, because of political reasons, that we should clamp down on forms of art expression, I think we are treading dangerously close to totalitarianism.

This approach is very akin to that of the Kremlin with regard to impressionist artists and jazz musicians. Certainly it is not an approach that we should emulate.

Accordingly, I am very glad indeed that the Senator from New York has spoken as he has.

# Letter from Ralph Nader
# Sounding Alarm at the Noise Pollution
# of the Aural Environment
# by the Rock-'n'-Roll Bands

May 31, 1969

HON. WARREN G. MAGNUSON
CHAIRMAN, SENATE LABOR-HEW APPROPRIATIONS SUBCOMMITTEE
U.S. SENATE

HON. PHILIP HART
CHAIRMAN, SUBCOMMITTEE ON THE ENVIRONMENT
SENATE COMMERCE COMMITTEE
U.S. SENATE

DEAR SENATORS MAGNUSON AND HART:

Noise trauma is being viewed as an increasingly serious environmental hazard by scientists as the noise level of our working and public surroundings continues rising. Acoustic trauma from rock and roll music is emerging as a very real threat to the hearing quality of young people who expose themselves to substantial durations of this music by live rock groups with high amplification. The nature of this hazard and its avoidance merit your attention if only to foresee and forestall even more aggravated risks and to focus public concern on noise traumas of all kinds in our occupational and public environments. This country may be producing a new generation of young Americans with impaired hearing before they reach the age of 21. It is in this context that the following information may be helpful:

The American Medical Association, the Workmen's Compensation Board of New York State and other similar groups consider exposure to noise levels over time between 85–90 db (decibels) to be hazardous to an individual's hearing. Some individuals are more susceptible to ear damage than others. The degree of hearing loss depends on a variety of important noise characteristics—most prominently the noise intensity, the frequency composition of the noise and the distribution and length of exposure to the noise. These are crucially important relationships. For example, given equivalent intensities, high frequencies are more harmful than lower frequencies. If high frequencies are prominent, as they are in rock and roll music, the risk of damage to the hearing is 100 times greater at 120 decibels than at 90 decibels. Other factors which have greater or different effects upon the hearing mechanism include rhythm, resonance and reflection. For rock-and-roll music bands, reflection is high because of the customary bare, hard walls, floors and ceilings that permit such reflection back to the microphones of the individual instruments and of the hall amplification systems. There are few absorptive surfaces. The worst sound pressure levels come from the playing of "hard rock" as distinguished from "folk rock" and "soul music."

The typical rock band's instruments are provided with high gain amplifiers and large speaker systems whose output is usually reamplified by two or more powerful hall sound reinforcement systems. Decibel level measurements in several Washington, D.C. establishments ranged between 100 to 116 decibels. With headphones, 125 decibels were attained. Readings in other areas of the country have shown similar levels but also higher levels, reaching on occasion in some discotheques levels of 125 to 138 decibels. The pain threshhold level is 140 decibels for most people.

A number of recent studies by specialists have comprised a basis for urging further studies. Highly amplified rock music in relatively small, high reflection rooms has been around for several years. Studies are just beginning to catch up with this electronically facilitated acoustic assault, however.

In 1967, a study by Charles P. Lebo, M.D., Kenward S. Oliphant, E.E., and John Garrett, M.D., based on measurements obtained in two rock-and-roll music establishments in San Francisco, concluded that noise levels and frequency distributions therein "can produce temporary auditory threshold shifts and is of an order that has been recognized as entailing risk of permanent ear damage." These sound measurements exceeded the State of California ear damage risk criteria for industrial establishments. Dr. Lebo et al. noted that "noise greater than 92 decibels in sound pressure composed of frequencies primarily between 500 and 8,000 Hz (cycles per second) and sustained for a period of one hour will produce as much as 40 decibels threshold shift in the area of 4,000 Hz in approximately 10 per cent of the ears exposed, no measurable shift in another 10 per cent, and between 5 and 30 db shift in the remaining 80 per cent of ears. Their data showed sound pressures with these frequencies to prevail in the musical establishments they studied. Their final conclusion is noteworthy:

> "We believe that we have demonstrated that the noise levels produced by some live rock-and-roll bands with the aid of high amplification unmistakably exceed those considered safe for prolonged exposure. Attenuation of the amplification to safe levels would substantially reduce the risk of ear injury in the audience and performers and, in the opinion of the authors, would still permit enjoyment of the musical material."

A later study (1968) by Dr. Lebo and K. P. Oliphant declared that "the sound pressure levels produced by a typical symphony orchestra in a typical concert hall during fortissimo passages for full orchestra are well below the acoustic trauma hazard strata." "The noise output of the rock groups is likely to be particularly ototraumatic because of factors other than sound pressure peaks alone. These factors include compressed dynamic range, narrow band amplification, and continuity from the addition of amplified and reamplified reverberation to the early arrival sound." Indicating a path of further inquiry, the authors suggest that the "use of certain drugs by some rock and roll listeners may further reduce the effectiveness of the protection afforded by the stapedius and the tonsor tympani."

Another study by Dr. David M. Lipscomb, director of audiology clinical services at the University of Tennessee, showed damage and destruction to the cells in an unprotected ear of a guinea pig exposed to 90 hours of go-go music spread over a three month period at intervals similar to the habits of the average teen-ager. The cells in the unprotected right ear were either displaced, collapsed or totally missing, while the left ear, protected by a plug, showed no signs of damage. (The guinea pig was chosen because its ear's biochemical process was very similar to that of man.) In the tests, go-go music was recorded and played back to the guinea pig at the identical sound level measured at a Knoxville discotheque. Dr. Lipscomb said that he "used 120 decibels as the sound level for these tests," but sound in various discotheques were measured at a peak of 138 decibels, "only two decibels below the pain threshold."

Quite significantly, what prompted Dr. Lipscomb's experiment was the routine screening of entering freshmen at the University of Tennessee which discovered a large number with measurable hearing loss. "We were shocked to find that the hearing of many of these students had already deteriorated to a level of the average 65-year-old person," said Dr. Lipscomb. Tests were then conducted involving 3,000 Knoxville public school students and showing a marked increase in the prevalency of high frequency hearing loss as the student moves from the sixth grade to high school senior—a period during which his exposure to recreational noises increases, according to Professor Lipscomb. Five per cent of the 1,000 students tested at the sixth grade level suffered measurable hearing loss. This prevalence rose to 14 per cent of the 1,000 students at the ninth grade level and approximately 20 per cent of the 1,000 high school seniors. Professor Lipscomb believes that we have reached the point that "the young people are losing sufficient hearing to jeopardize their occupational potential." He urged entering into "a program or the consequences are going to be pretty dire."

A University of Florida audiologist, Dr. George T. Singleton, tested the hearing of ten 14-year-olds before a rock-and-roll dance. During the dance he measured the sound intensity of the room and found the sound level to be 106–108 db in the middle of the floor and 120 decibels next to the bandstand. It did not fall below the established safety limit of 90 db until he was forty feet outside the building. All ten teenagers showed some temporary loss of hearing with the greatest hearing loss occurring in the high-frequency range involving consonantal sounds.

An exceptional hazard for rock fans comes through the headphone. Damage, both temporary and permanent, can be extraordinary with headphones. Serious symptoms during usage of high volume headphones are: buzzing or tickling of the ear, tinnitus or ringing in the ear or temporary loss of hearing.

The hazard to the musicians is of course the greatest because of their longer exposure time. A recently published study (February 1969) observed five members of a rock-and-roll musical combo in Michigan before, during and after a rehearsal. Peak sound levels generated in the practice room ranged from 120 to 130 decibels (compared to the 120 decibels from a Saturn moon rocket measured at the press site). All the players reported ringing in the ears after the rehearsal with the head noises persisting for two of the players from one to two days. The authors warned that such exposure may produce progressive, accumulative and permanent inner ear damage. They recommend that such musicians wear customized ear defenders to reduce by 20 to 30 db the intensity of noise reaching the ears. (Rupp, R. R., & Koch, L. J., Univ. of Michigan) Similar findings come from Dr. James Jenger of the Houston Speech and Hearing Center who tested a five man combo, all under 23 years of age and three of whom suffered slight permanent damage. Although discussion with discotheque performers and workers produce regular admissions of hearing loss, surprisingly little attention has been given this problem by occupational safety specialists and labor unions.

Why is rock music played so loudly? This question also has received little study. Some light was shed in a Michigan State study by Dr. William F. Rintelmann, who showed less alarm than other researchers. He asked 66 college students last year why such music was played so loudly. Here is his report:

"The most commonly given response was that the high intensity makes up for the mediocre quality, that mistakes are not as readily noticed when the volume is so high and that musicians 'drown out their own mistakes.' The second most often given response was that the very loud music commands the attention of the listeners, 'takes control of their minds' by blocking out any environmental sounds such as talking, glasses rattling, etc. and almost forces them to dance in a manner that they feel releases tension. Following are some quotes from the responses gathered which may express this concept more clearly: 'It surrounds the people totally in the rock and roll atmosphere; it turns them on,' 'It makes you get worked up into a frenzy that serves to release a lot of tension and energy,' 'The type of dancing that is popular today would look a little strange with soft music.' A third frequently given response concerned the physical effect of the music on the body, the actual vibration of the body to the beat of the music. As one student said, 'It is supposed to captivate the body physically.' A fourth frequently given response was that the musicians feel that the louder they play, the better they are. Since the more powerful amplifiers are more expensive, louder music also implies a successful group. The authors also received this impression from the musicians themselves. . . . As a final point, perhaps the classic comment of all, given by one of the students who felt that the music was played at about the right intensity level, was 'It provides people of this age with the opportunity to congregate without having to communicate.' "

Rock band music impairing hearing involves both occupational and consumer issues. It typifies the growing pervasiveness of a trauma too charitably called noise pollution. The federal government should be concerned about it, but is doing little. Congress has done almost nothing. I believe it would be most salutary for you, in your respective official positions noted above, to conduct brief hearings that will bring together the relevant knowledge, etch the major problems, educate the public and the states and municipalities which have the immediate legal responsibility. Whether these jurisdictions wish to classify such musical performances, above a certain sound pressure and frequency level, as public nuisances, or whether they wish to require ear protectors for musicians and band hall workers, or whether they may require certain absorptive surfaces in the halls or rooms, will depend on sound, public information and awareness. Your Subcommittees can provide this important service as well as prod the Executive Branch into greater activity in this area of acoustic abuse and other areas as well.

Thank you for your consideration and your continuing interest in the well-being of the consumer.

Sincerely yours,<br>RALPH NADER

# Statement on the Mobilization of the Masses to Use Mao Tsetung's Thought to Transform the Literary, Musical, Art and Theater Front in China

Following Chairman Mao's great teaching that "there is no construction without destruction," the workers' Mao Tsetung Thought propaganda team stationed at the China Opera and Dance-Drama Theatre has mobilized the masses there to carry out protracted and deep-going revolutionary mass criticism. This was to help the literary and art workers to raise their consciousness of class struggle and the struggle between the two lines and change their old ideology, so that they would gradually shift their stand over to the side of the workers, peasants and soldiers.

In the past year, the mental outlook of the literary and art workers in this theatre has undergone a profound change.

The China Opera and Dance-Drama Theatre was one of the literary and artistic organizations under the direct control of the arch renegade Liu Shao-chi and the counter-revolutionary revisionist Chou Yang and their gang. In the decade and more before the cultural revolution, the handful of capitalist roaders there made use of this theatre in their frantic opposition to Chairman Mao's revolutionary line in literature and art. They actively pushed Liu Shao-chi's counter-revolutionary revisionist line and energetically peddle feudal, bourgeois and revisionist trash in literature and art. As a result, emperors, kings, generals and ministers, scholars and beauties and foreign mummies overran the stage. The theatre thus became one of the places used for restoring capitalism and creating counter-revolutionary public opinion.

After the propaganda team entered this theatre, it followed Chairman Mao's instruction to "thoroughly criticize and repudiate reactionary bourgeois ideas in the sphere of academic work, education, journalism, literature and art and publishing, and seize the leadership in these cultural spheres" and his other great teachings and analysed the specific conditions there. Members of the team were of the opinion that, to ensure that the proletariat firmly occupies and transforms this position, it is essential to take a firm grasp of the class struggle in the ideological and political spheres, use the powerful weapon of revolutionary mass criticism to eliminate the pernicious influence of Liu Shao-chi's counter-revolutionary revisionist line in literature and art, get rid of the bourgeois individualist ideology, and use Mao Tsetung Thought to thoroughly remould the world outlook of the literary and art workers.

The propaganda team successively ran several Mao Tsetung Thought study classes which made the proletarian revolutionaries and other revolutionary masses in the theatre even more determined to carry out deep-going revolutionary mass criticism. In these classes, they studied Chairman Mao's great theory of continuing the revolution under the dictatorship of the proletariat and came to a clearer understanding of the fact that, since the great cultural revolution, although organizationally the proletariat has already seized back that portion of power usurped by the bourgeoisie, its struggle against the bourgeoisie in the ideological and political spheres has not ended. Only by waging protracted and deep-going revolutionary mass criticism to thoroughly criticize the counter-revolutionary revisionist line in literature and art and eliminate its pernicious influence, and by letting Mao Tsetung Thought occupy all positions can the dictatorship of the proletariat be effectively consolidated and strengthened and the restoration of capitalism prevented. Only thus can we ensure that our literature and art will always advance triumphantly along Chairman Mao's revolutionary line.

On the basis of such an understanding, the revolutionary masses of the whole theatre were filled with enthusiasm and the tide of their revolutionary mass criticism surged higher and higher.

Having repeatedly studied Chairman Mao's great teaching "This question of 'for whom?' is fundamental; it is a question of principle," the propaganda team deeply realized that the focus of the struggle between the two lines in literature and art is the question of whom literature and art should serve. In order to transform the literary and art ranks with Mao Tsetung Thought, the fundamental thing to do is to unfold criticism of the sinister counter-revolutionary revisionist line in literature and art so that the literary and art workers can gradually shift their stand over to the side of the workers, peasants and soldiers, to the side of the proletariat.

Through revolutionary mass criticism, the revolutionary masses of the theatre ascertained more fully the perfidious ambition of the arch renegade Liu Shao-chi in frenziedly pushing a sinister counter-revolutionary revisionist line in literature and art in a vain attempt to subvert the dictatorship of the proletariat and restore capitalism. They further heightened their consciousness of class struggle and the struggle between the two lines.

Accusation of the sinister revisionist line in literature and art which had poisoned them was a profound education for the revolutionary literary and art workers on the question of whom to serve.

One opera singer had worked as a cowherd for a landlord in the old society when he was only 13. In 1946, he jumped out of this pit of misery and joined the revolution. He became an actor in an army cultural troupe. In the difficult years of the War of Liberation, his heart was wholly dedicated to the revolution and the cause of saving China, and he portrayed only the workers, peasants and soldiers. After the liberation of the whole country, he came to the cities. Poisoned by the sinister counter-revolutionary revisionist line in literature and art, his thoughts and feelings changed. For many years before the cultural revolution, he was preoccupied with making a reputation for himself and took the revisionist road of desiring only to improve his art while remaining aloof from politics. His roles were confined to those of young nobles and bourgeois and feudal talents. Once, the theatre put on the big poisonous weed *The Peddler and the Lady*. He played the title role and was acclaimed by the capitalist roaders. He later became a member of the national stage artists' association. In this way, his thoughts and feelings became further divorced from the working people, and he sank even deeper in the mire of revisionism.

The revolutionary mass criticism woke him up with a start. Recalling how his thoughts and feelings had changed from the time he was a poor cowherd to his rise as the actor in the role of the peddler in the play, he said indignantly: "It was Liu Shao-chi's counter-revolutionary revisionist line which influenced me to divorce myself from the working people, forget the revolution and, through 'peaceful evolution,' embark on the revisionist road. It is the Great Proletarian Cultural Revolution personally initiated and led by Chairman Mao that saved me. I am determined to study Mao Tsetung Thought well, thoroughly rid myself of the poison of Liu Shao-chi's sinister literary and art line, and serve the workers, peasants and soldiers with all my heart."

Deliberately "honoring" some of the literary and art workers with the titles of "well-known actor," "well-known director" or "well-known script writer," the handful of capitalist roaders in the theatre gave them high pay and provided them with lucrative means of livelihood. This lured those literary art workers whose bourgeois world outlook had not been remoulded well into chasing after personal fame and gain and taking the revisionist road of concentrating on raising their level of artistic skill and of keeping aloof from proletarian politics. As the days went by, they became more and more divorced from the labouring people, from productive labour and revolutionary practice and slid farther and farther down the revisionist road.

One young dance-drama actress was a typical representative of the "three well-knowns and three highs." After enjoying her performance in the sinister dance-drama *Mermaid,* Liu Shao-chi lavished praises on her and personally instructed the theatre's capitalist roaders to increase her salary by three grades and gave her membership in the national dance association. Indeed, they spared no effort to corrupt her.

During the revolutionary mass criticism, the masses deeply realized from this young woman's vivid example that "the 'three well-knowns and three high's' were truly arsenic used by Liu Shao-chi to poison the literary and art workers. It was a soft sword which drew no blood but killed people." From her own painful experience, the dancer who was deeply poisoned by the revisionist line came to understand that the criminal aim of Liu Shao-chi and his agents in promoting this vile policy was to use fame and gain as bait to drag the literary and art workers into the mire of revisionism and turn them into tools for restoring capitalism. She said: "To be revolutionary literary and art workers, it is imperative first of all to solve the question of whom to serve. If this fundamental question is not solved, we will lose our bearings, go astray and run counter to Chairman Mao's revolutionary line in literature and art. And the result will be that the harder we work, the greater the harm we do to the revolution."

Revolutionary mass criticism has enabled the theatre's revolutionary masses to bring about a tremendous change in their mental outlook. Led by the workers' propaganda team, they often go to factories, mines and rural people's communes to take part in manual labour and receive re-education by the proletariat. They have gradually raised their level of class consciousness and consciousness of the struggle between the two lines, and their thinking and feelings are merging more and more with those of the workers, peasants and soldiers. Recently, while helping the rural communes with the summer harvest, sowing and field management, they joined the poor and lower-middle peasants in farm work and lived, studied and carried on the cultural revolution together with them. During work breaks, they gave performances for the poor and lower-middle peasants, enthusiastically propagating Mao Tsetung Thought, extolling the poor and lower-middle peasants' profound proletarian feelings of cherishing ardent love for the great leader Chairman Mao and their advanced deeds displaying love of the socialist collective economy. In addition to carrying water and sweeping courtyards for the poor and lower-middle peasants, they helped them mend and sew clothes and wash quilts and beddings. Full of praise, the commune members said: "We poor and lower-middle peasants welcome such literary and art workers."

(*Peking Review*, 1 August 1969)

# Dictionary
# of
# Terms

**Abecedarianism.** As the etymology of the word indicates, ABECEDARIANISM (A-B-C-D-ari-anism), is alphabetarian in its nature. But ABECEDARIANISM is not necessarily a pejorative term. It takes a highly trained intellect and technical skill to create a truly Abecedarian masterpiece, as demonstrated, for instance in the self-inverted redundant prose of Gertrude Stein. Musical ABECEDARIANISM is far from tonal INFANTILOQUY. Stravinsky's *Piano Pieces for 5 Fingers*, Bartók's *Mikrokosmos* and Casella's *Valse diatonique* from his *Pezzi infantili* are illustrations of sophisticated ABECEDARIANISM. Abecedarian effects are naturally pro-duced by small children banging at random on the white keys of the piano keyboard at the level of their heads, often resulting in the unintentional formation of interesting pandiatonic patterns vivified by asymmetrical rhythms. The walk across the keys by Domenico Scarlat-ti's cat provided the inspiration for a fugue; the critics who described the music they did not like as puerile or cat music had an imperfect understanding of the constructivist poten-tialities of random tonal juxtaposition.

**Ablation.** Extreme luxuriance of decorative and ornamental elaborations in the post-Ro-mantic period of modern music resulted, through surfeit, in a profound repugnance to such practices. An inevitable consequence was a drastic ABLATION of all non-essential thematic excrescences and protuberances from a finished composition. A process of subjective ABLATION impelled some modern composers to revise their early works and reduce their in-strumental luxuriance to an economic functional organization. The most striking instance of such ABLATION is Stravinsky's reorchestration of the score of his ballet *The Firebird*, remov-ing some supernumerary instruments, excising florid cadenzas and in effect plucking the fiery bird of its iridescent plumage. Most audiences prefer the original luxuriant version to this later parsimonious arrangement.

**Absolute Music.** The term ABSOLUTE MUSIC is applied to music that is free from pro-grammatic designs, psychological affiliations or illustrative associations; its Latin etymology connotes independence. In its function ABSOLUTE MUSIC is parasynonymous with ABSTRACT MUSIC, but the two terms are differentiated in their temporal points of reference. ABSOLUTE MUSIC is of ancient heritage, while ABSTRACT MUSIC is a relatively recent phe-nomenon, marked by structural athematism in an atonal context.

**Abstract Music.** Abstraction in music implies a separation of sonic structures from representational images, whether pictorial or psychological. ABSTRACT MUSIC is the anto-nym of all musical styles that are concrete or naturalistic; abstract works are usually short, athematic and rhythmically asymmetric. Intellectual fantasy, rather than sensual excitation, is the generating impulse of ABSTRACT MUSIC; its titles are derived from constructivistic and scientific concepts: Structures, Projections, Extensions, Frequencies, Sound. The Ger-man composer Boris Blacher has developed a successful form of ABSTRACT OPERA, in which concrete action takes place in a swarm of discrete sonic particles, disjected words in several languages and isolated melodic fragments. ABSTRACT EXPRESSIONISM, a term applied to non-objective painting, is sometimes used to describe musical works of abstract quality with expressionistic connotations. A subsidiary genre of ABSTRACT MUSIC is ALEATORY MUSIC, in which the process of musical cerebration is replaced by a random interplay of sounds and rhythms.

**Absurd Music.** The vocable *surd*, cognate with *sourdine*, implies a muted sound; *Absurd* suggests a becalmed truth, but not necessarily nonsense. There are mathematical equations that seem to contradict common sense; in fact, square roots that cannot be resolved pre-cisely, are called irrational numbers, or by the now obsolete term surd, a cousin of ABSURD. The inner validity of absurd logic was enunciated by Tertullian when he said: "Credo quia absurdum est." Oxymoronic pairs, such as "passionate indifference," or "glacial fire," are intrinsically absurd, and yet eloquent in their self-contradiction. ABSURD MUSIC cultivates analogous incompatibilities. It is particularly effective in modern opera, where a scene of horror may be illustrated by a frivolous waltz, or a festive celebration by the somber strains of a funereal march. The modern techniques of POLYTONALITY and ATONALITY represent MUSIC OF THE ABSURD to the withered sensitivity of an old-fashioned ear.

**Accompaniment.** In modern music, ACCOMPANIMENT transcends its traditional ancillary function and becomes an integral part of the entire composition. The simplest form of modern ACCOMPANIMENT is that of POLYTONALITY, in which the melody is set in one key and the harmony in another. Rhythmically, the modern ACCOMPANIMENT rarely follows the inflections of the melody; deliberate oxymoronic usages are enhanced by translocated accents.

**Acousma.** An auricular disturbance induced in hostile audiences by ULTRA-MODERN MUSIC, is known as ACOUSMA. Music critics, even those not suffering from professional indigestion, are chronically prone to ACOUSMA, and their discomfort is often reflected in their reviews.

**Acoustics.** By definition, acoustical phenomena are fundamental to all music. The overtone series, which is the generator of the basic major triad, is also the source of nominal dissonances. The tritone, deprecated as "diabolus in musica" by medieval scholiasts, is the foundation stone of ATONALITY, POLYTONALITY and other modern techniques. Acoustically, it is the 45th overtone at the distance of $6\frac{1}{2}$ octaves from the fundamental note, with which it forms a concord. Scriabin, theorizing ex post facto, regarded his MYSTIC CHORD as a consonance, because its constituents approximate the high overtones. An interesting practical application of the acoustical properties of the overtone series is found in Ravel's *Boléro*, where at one point the melody is accompanied by a group of flutes and piccolos constituting the 6th, 8th, 10th and 12th overtones progressing in parallel formations. In the score Ravel marks the gradually decreasing dynamics of these high notes, corresponding to a natural tapering of the strength of overtones in higher elevations. This calculated enhancement of natural overtones affects the timbre of the solo instrument. If performed correctly with the dynamics scrupulously observed, the solo player will find to his dismay that his instrument has undergone a curious change in its tone color. With the aid of electronic means of tone production, this effect can be produced artificially, generating hybrid sonorities such as a half-bassoon and a half-trombone, or a timbre which is a third-oboe, a third-clarinet and a third-violin.

Rhythms can be combined in special proportions with the overtone series. In 1932 Henry Cowell, in collaboration with Leon Theremin, constructed the *Rhythmicon,* an instrument which generates a series of rhythmic beats in an overtone series, the number of beats being proportional to the position of each overtone, so that the octave has two beats per time unit, the interval of the 12th, three beats, the major third over two octaves, five beats, etc. This arrangement makes it possible to devise polyrhythmic counterpoint of great variety and unique sonority. Acoustical innovations and improvements in the purity of intonation are not without musical perils, however. Perfect tuning in orchestral performance would generate differential tones and make a sonic jungle out of a classical symphony. The desire of modern architects to attain acoustical perfection often leads to orchestral pollution in the concert hall. Old-fashioned rococo architecture, with its ornate brocades and heavy curtains, contributed the necessary dampening of sounds and echoes that secured harmonious euphony. Modern acousticians eliminated the decorations, removed the tasselled seat covers and cushioned surfaces, replacing them by plywood and plastic, and added an array of mobiles suspended from the ceiling to eliminate microsonic impurities. But these elaborations resulted in some unwelcome side-effects. Parasitical noises were neutralized, but a variety of unsuspected musical micro-organisms, overtones and differential tones, rose from the instruments themselves, flooding the hall in a harmonious plasma that all but destroyed the natural equilibrium of tonal imperfections and mutual reverberations that were responsible for the rich resonance intuitively achieved by the musical architects of the past. The consequences of such modernization were painfully evident in the scientifically designed Philharmonic Hall at Lincoln Center in New York. The resulting acoustical anarchy was fortunately corrected by an ingenious rearrangement of the physical properties of the auditorium and the stage, so that the natural heterogeneity of sonic euphony was restored.

**Action Music.** The term ACTION MUSIC is applied to compositions resulting from an impulsive melosomatic urge. Like IMPRESSIONISM, the term itself arose by analogy with painting. ACTION ART implies a free wielding of the brush in which the unpremeditated splash of color becomes a creative enzyme for the next projection. In ACTION MUSIC there is no calculated design; the initial reflex generates a successive series of secondary reflexes in a network of musico-neural synapses, resulting in the formation of dynamically propelled sounds.

ACTION MUSIC is primarily a manifestation in MIXED MEDIA, or HAPPENINGS, with audience participation, in which the spontaneous psychological and physiological excitations determine the course of events. Composers of ACTION MUSIC usually provide a set of instructions, leaving specific decisions to the performers. ACTION MUSIC is a mass phenomenon, which transcends national boundaries and energies in similar forms in many lands, like self-flagellation of medieval penitents and tergiversations of the whirling dervishes. This ubiquity of incidence is paralleled by the SYNCRETISM of cultures in ACTION MUSIC. Western practitioners of the genre tend to annex the contemplative philosophies of the East, while Oriental composers of ACTION MUSIC adopt serialistic methods and mathematical parameters. In mass manifestations, ACTION MUSIC often finds its audible expression in the ululations of pullulating populations.

**Additive Composition.** As the term implies, ADDITIVE COMPOSITION is effectuated by a series of successive additions to an initial thematic statement. The connection is mechanistic by definition, but if by chance, or subliminal design, a dominant melorhythmic figure emerges, a paradoxical rondo is the result.

**Adjunction.** Melodic, rhythmic or harmonic ADJUNCTION is produced by a juxtaposition of compatible thematic particles. Such a method suggests a less mechanistic connection than in ADDITIVE COMPOSITION, and a possibility of a thematic unity is not excluded. The Belgian composer Désiré Pâque used the term *Adjonction constante* to describe an episodic use of recurrent or non-recurrent motives.

**Aerostatic Suspension.** In Impressionistic scores, the shimmering interference of euphonious dissonances generates a sonic inversion which forces the lighter elements to ascend into the upper harmonic regions. At some point an equilibrium of overtones and differential tones is established. This euphony, with ethereal sonorities wafted by the winds of flutes, oboes, clarinets and flageolet-like upper strings, suggests a physical convection which may be described as AEROSTATIC SUSPENSION.

**Agglutination.** When successive melorhythmic particles are not unified by common tonality or melorhythmic similarity, the resulting type of composition may be described as AGGLUTINATION, a gluing together. The method differs from ADDITIVE COMPOSITION in possessing a greater malleability in the process of coalescence. On the other hand, it lacks the inherent compatibility that is present in the method of ADJUNCTION.

**Aleatory Music.** The word ALEATORY is derived from the Latin "alea," that is, a die. (Julius Caesar exclaimed after crossing the Rubicon, "Alea jacta est.") ALEATORY MUSIC in the literal sense is not a new invention. "Dice music" was a popular parlor game in the 18th century. A celebrated example is *Musikalisches Würfelspiel*, attributed to Mozart. In the second half of the 20th century, composers of the AVANT-GARDE introduced true ALEATORY methods. A pioneer work was *Music of Changes* by John Cage, derived from chance operations found in the ancient Chinese book of oracles *I-Ching*, in which random numbers are obtained by throwing sticks. By drawing an arbitrary table of correspondences between numbers and musical parameters (pitch, note-value, rests) it is possible to derive a number of desirable melorhythmic curves. Human or animal phenomena may also serve as primary data. Configurations of fly specks on paper, pigeon droppings on a park bench, the design of crushed mosquitoes on wallpaper, the parabolic curve of an expectoration directed towards a spittoon, dissection of birds as practiced in ancient Rome, etc. are all excellent materials for ALEATORY MUSIC. At a HAPPENING in an American mid-western university, the anal discharge of a pig, which was administered a clyster, was used as an Aleatory datum. Mauricio Kagel has made use of partially exposed photographic film for ALEATORY composition. The composer-engineer Iannis Xenakis organizes ALEATORY MUSIC in STOCHASTIC terms, which possess the teleological quality absent in pure ALEATORY pursuits. Among affiliated subjects of ALEATORY MUSIC are PROBABILITY, INFORMATION THEORY, STOCHASTIC COMPOSITION, CYBERNETICS, EXPERIMENTAL MUSIC, COMPUTER MUSIC, EMPIRICAL MUSIC and INDETERMINACY.

**Algorithm.** In mathematical usage, an ALGORITHM is an operator devised for the solution of problems arising in the theory of numbers. Directions given in puzzle canons to indicate the time and the interval of entry are ALGORITHMS. The most ubiquitous ALGORITHM in modern music is the TRITONE. It compasses a chord containing 11 different intervals, for the sum of the first 11 numbers equals 66, which corresponds in semitone units to 5½ octaves, the tritone being half an octave. The TRITONE is also the operating ALGORITHM in the problem of distributing 12 different notes of the chromatic scale into four mutually exclusive triads. Here the modus operandi is to build two major triads separated by a tritone, and two minor triads a whole tone higher whose tonics are also at a distance of a tritone (e.g., C major, F-sharp major, D minor, G-sharp minor). Magical properties emerge from such operations. It is remarkable, for instance, that four mutually exclusive triads can be arranged only by using a pair of major triads and a pair of minor triads, and that no other distribution is possible. But it is also possible to split the chromatic scale into a group of diminished, minor, major and augmented triads, one of each, a symmetric and elegant solution, suggesting similarly elegant formulas in mathematics. Algorithmic composition is a virgin field for experimentation in modern techniques.

**Allusive Quotation.** Folk songs, contrapuntal elaborations on a given cantus firmus, quotations from the doom-laden chant *Dies irae*, have been for centuries a favorite resource of ALLUSIVE QUOTATIONS. Richard Strauss inserted the theme of the funeral march from Beethoven's *Eroica* in the score of his *Metamorphosen*, a dirge on the death of Germany, written during the last weeks of World War II. Alban Berg quoted Bach's chorale *Es ist genug* at the conclusion of his *Violin Concerto* as a memorial for Manon Gropius, daughter of Mahler's widow by a second marriage, who died young. Quotations from a composer's own scores are not rare; a notorious modern example is the egocentric series of quotations used by Strauss in the score of his tone poem *Ein Heldenleben*. But perhaps the most extraordinary assembly of assorted thematic memos, memories and mementos is found in *Sinfonia* by Luciano Berio, in which he quotes metamorphosed fragments from works of Mahler, Debussy, Ravel and others.

**Alphabetical Monograms.** The origin of musical notation is alphabetical or syllabic. The names of the notes of the initial hexachord of the major scale were taken by Guido d'Arezzo from the first syllables of a Latin hymn, and this syllabic nomenclature is still in use in the Latin countries and in Russia. In German, the musical notes are designated by letters from A to H; thanks to this alphabetic denomination, it is possible to contrive musical themes out of words and names comprising these letters, the most illustrious example being the theme B-A-C-H. That such an artificial method of thematic invention does not hamper a composer of genius, is proved by Schumann's *Carnaval*, which is based on the spelling of the name of the town of ASCH (in German nomenclature either A-flat, C, B or A, E-flat, C, B). Dmitri Shostakovich based the main themes of his *Tenth Symphony* and the *Eighth String Quartet* on his ALPHABETICAL MONOGRAM, in German nomenclature, D.SCH. Mario Castelnuovo-Tedesco extended his system of ALPHABETICAL MONOGRAMS to 25 letters of the Italian alphabet, arranging the notes chromatically and filling two full octaves from A to Z.

**Ambulation.** AMBULATORY activities by performers during a concert in the process of playing is a particular case of SPATIAL DISTRIBUTION, in which the position of the players in physical space is treated as an independent parameter. AMBULATION is also related to VECTORIALISM; in both the direction of the source of sound depends on the placement, stationary or kinetic, of the performers. In an AMBULATORY composition, the players are usually instructed to make their entrances on the stage while playing the initial bars upon their instruments which they carry with them. Some avant-garde composers even demanded the pushing of a grand piano on the stage while performing a one-arm composition on the keyboard. Rational AMBULATION is practiced in *Antiphones* for string quartet by the Soviet composer Sergei Slonimsky. In the opening of the work the cello player, originally seated in the middle of the last row of the concert hall, is instructed to walk with his instrument to the stage, while playing passages in a non-tempered scale; the other players are engaged in walking movements one after another, in a manner of an ambulatory fugato.

**Anagrams.** By analogy with literal ANAGRAMS, in which words and sentences are derived

*1426*

from a given matrix (e.g., "Flit on, cheering angel" from Florence Nightingale), notes of a musical subject can be rearranged in order to generate plausible thematic variations. The 12 notes of the chromatic scale yield 479,001,600 possible permutations suitable for dodecaphonic usages. Polyanagrams, formed by linear (melodic), vertical (harmonic) and oblique (fugal) parameters, are comprised in the generic term COMBINATORIALITY, introduced by Milton Babbitt. Perhaps the most intricate Polyanagram is *Anagrama* by the Argentineborn avant-garde composer Mauricio Kagel, scored for speaking chorus, 4 vocalists and instruments, to the text derived from Dante's *Divina Commedia*, subject to a number of permutations forming plausible sentences in different languages.

**Analphabetism.** There is a marked difference between musical ANALPHABETISM and ABECEDARIANISM. While ABECEDARIANISM is the art of using artless formulas, ANALPHABETISM is the inability to use even a limited tonal vocabulary owing to a faulty technique of composition. The most obnoxious type of ANALPHABETISM is FRAUDULENT MODERNISM, mimicking advanced idioms and putting wrong notes in elementary harmonies. In its most innocent and disarming form, ANALPHABETISM approaches INFANTILOQUY. It is only when it raises its turgid tentacles above the level of harmless romantic indulgence that ANALPHABETISM becomes its literal self, i.e. illiteracy.

**Anamnesis.** A vivid memory of a psychologically important event that passes the mind simultaneously with another seemingly identical experience is popularly attributed to METEMPSYCHOSIS, a remembrance of a previous incarnation. ANAMNESIS is a similar explosion of memory, but it is devoid of any mystical notions. In music, an unexpected appearance of a thematic motive amid irrelevant melorhythmic events is ANAMNESTIC.

**Anarchy and Autarchy.** Innovating composers since the time of Wagner have been accused of promoting musical ANARCHY. An educated French music critic wrote after attending the first performance of Debussy's *Pelléas et Mélisande*, "No, I will never have anything to do with these anarchists of music!" But when Schoenberg enunciated his method of composition with 12 tones related only to one another, the outcries against atonal ANARCHY changed to charges of esthetic AUTARCHY. To refute such accusations, Schoenberg wrote, in a letter from Hollywood dated 3 June 1937, and addressed to Nicolas Slonimsky: "What I did was neither revolution nor anarchy. I possessed from my very first start a thoroughly developed sense of form and a strong aversion for exaggeration. There is no falling into order, because there was never disorder. There is no falling at all, but on the contrary, there is an ascending to a higher and better order."

**Animal and Human Noises.** The introduction of parts for animals into musical composition is an old and cherished fantasy. Imitations of bird songs have been part of music since the Middle Ages; but an actual sound of a bird occurs for the first time in Ottorino Respighi's *Pines of Rome* which includes a phonograph recording of a Roman nightingale. When a dog incidentally barked during a recording of Walter Piston's ballet suite *The Incredible Flutist*, the conductor decided to keep it in the final recording. A part for cat's meow appears in the score of Nicolas Slonimsky's piece *Anatomy of Melancholy*, to be enacted by a real cat whose tail is pulled during the performance. Electronic transcriptions provide an opportunity to supply recorded or synthetic animal noises. The tape recording of the cetacean song of a humpback whale has been incorporated into the symphonic poem *And God Created Great Whales* by the American composer Alan Hovhaness. Human noises—whistling, shrieking, grunting—were cultivated by the Italian Futurists and further propagated by the cosmopolitan AVANT-GARDE.

**Anti-Music.** ANTI-MUSIC is a concept formulated by analogy with the hypothetical phenomenon of Anti-Matter, in which the electrical charges of subatomic particles are reversed, so that the physical encounter between matter and Anti-Matter would result in mutual annihilation. ANTI-MUSIC reverses the acoustical charges of consonances and dissonances. The valences in the series of overtones are similarly reversed, so that the diminishing intervals in the upper part of the harmonic series are regarded as increasingly euphonious concords, and those close to the fundamental tone as discords, requiring a resolution. A manual of ANTI-MUSIC is yet to be written. Triadic formations, tonal sequences,

*1427*

symmetric periods and harmonious cadences would be ruled out in such a textbook. ANTI-MUSIC of this nature would then be taught in elementary schools along with the physical principles of anti-matter. But old music would not be entirely excluded. In special seminars, courses will be given in ANTI-ANTI-MUSIC, in which consonances will regain their respected status, while dissonances will once more be relegated to a dependency. It is even possible that in the fantastic world of ANTI-MUSIC, tolerance will be granted to such teratological practices as those of Bach, Beethoven, Brahms, Debussy and Schoenberg.

**Anti-Opera.** While ANTI-MUSIC is still in its embryonic stage, ANTI-OPERA flourishes on the contemporary scene. Its modest beginnings consisted in the reversal of the Aristotelian unity of place and action. In the world of ANTI-OPERA, it is not enough to use librettos that make no sense; this has long been achieved in classical Italian opera. What is required is deliberate violence wrought on logic, drama and comedy. Withal, ANTI-OPERA must be utterly solemn. The vocal parts must be written in an anti-larynx idiom. After the completion of an ANTI-OPERA, the score must be fractured, splintered, fragmented and then reassembled in a random montage, making sure that no inadvertent euphony or any non-Anti-Musical matter would result. ANTI-OPERA may include elements of the opera of the absurd, but there are differences. In the opera of the absurd, there is drama in the very absurdity of the libretto, while in ANTI-OPERA the dialogue is an *actus interruptus,* without any continuity. ANTI-OPERA belongs to the category of MIXED MEDIA, approaching in its total absence of cohesion the improvisatory qualities of a HAPPENING.

**Aposiopesis.** In oratorical practice, APOSIOPESIS is a sudden interruption of a speech as if in a state of overwhelming emotion. A locus classicus is Neptune's exhortation to his disobedient winds, "Quos ego. . . ." in Virgil's *Aeneid.* In music, APOSIOPESIS is used to best effect in opera. In Neo-Classical works, a dramatic break in a cadence or a rhythmic elision of a beat is a counterpart of APOSIOPESIS.

**Asomatous Variations.** Etymologically, the adjective ASOMATOUS signifies incorporeality, the lack of a soma, a material body. In composition, ASOMATOUS VARIATIONS are metamorphoses of an absent theme. Often a theme is cumulative, building up part by part, a practice as frequent among classical composers as in ultra-modern music. In DODECAPHONIC MUSIC, the principal series is sometimes evolved by such a cumulative thematic accretion. ASOMATOUS VARIATIONS serve a descriptive purpose in Vincent d'Indy's *Istar Variations.* In this work, portraying the passage of the Babylonian goddess Istar through seven gates, at each of which she deposits a part of her garments, the theme does not appear in its totality until the final gate is reached. Elgar's *Enigma Variations* are based on a clearly outlined subject, but Elgar repeatedly hinted that this visible theme is but a counterpoint to a prime motive, which remains ASOMATOUS. Composers of the AVANT-GARDE cultivate the art of ASOMATOUS VARIATIONS with such determination that, in some ultra-modern works, an accidental repetition of a motive automatically marks the end of performance.

**Asymmetry.** Classical music is based on an orderly succession of symmetric periods and phrases; modern composers relish asymmetrical patterns. Often a simple, quasi-abecedarian tune is deliberately thrown out of symmetry by the addition or elision of a rhythmic unit, while the accompanying figure continues its preordained course. Compound meters are intrinsically asymmetric, as are the subdivisions of binary and ternary meters into unequal groups. Such subdivisions are typical of Serbian, Croatian, Bulgarian, Macedonian and Rumanian folk music. Béla Bartók makes artistic use of such meters derived from the multiethnic folkways of his native Transylvania.

**Athematic Composition.** ATHEMATIC COMPOSITION is the product of a deliberate effort to separate the melodic line into segregated groups of phrases and motives bearing no relation to one another. ATHEMATIC MUSIC does not adhere to any formal organization; a work without connected themes can therefore start and end at any point. Karlheinz Stockhausen arranges some of his works in segments which can be played in any order whatsoever, with this stipulation that when a performer, accidentally or intentionally, arrives at the same segment, it marks the ending. ATHEMATIC COMPOSITION tends towards atonal designs, in which the principle of non-repetition of melodic material is paramount. An athematic work need not be incoherent or inchoate; successive melodic statements may be related by a preferential use of a certain interval or a certain rhythmic configuration. In this sense, it may be said that an ATHEMATIC COMPOSITION has either zero or an indefinitely large number of themes.

**Atonality.** Etymologically, ATONALITY is a negative concept which connotes the absence of tonality. The term was first applied by hostile critics as a derisive description of a type of modern composition in which tonality was almost entirely disfranchised and integral chromaticism served as the guiding principle of melodic writing. Atonal composers avoid the repetition of a particular tone in order to preclude the appearance of an adventitious tonic. By natural predisposition such melodies invited a dissonant harmonization. Under such circumstances the key signature becomes superfluous. The desire to obviate the tonic-dominant relationship in atonal writing has led to the replacement of the perfect fifth by the tritone and of the octave by a major seventh. One of the most frequently occurring chordal formations in ATONAL MUSIC is a contraction of the four-part major triad, with the octave reduced to a major seventh, the fifth to a tritone and the major third to a sesquitone: C-E-G-C→C-D-sharp-F-sharp-B. The same chord can be obtained by raising the lowest note a semitone and leaving the upper three notes unaltered: C-E-G-C→C-sharp-E-G-C. This chord may also be analyzed as a diminished-seventh chord with an unresolved appoggiatura. Consecutive blocks of such chords at a distance of a minor third are favorite devices of IMPRESSIONIST composers.

The gradual atrophy of tonality has resulted in the non-repetition of essential melodic notes, culminating in the organization of melodic writing making use of all 12 different tones. Tertian melodies and harmonies, affiliated with triadic structures, gave way to quartal and quintal progressions. Ascending or descending melodic fourths became the hallmark of atonal writing, gradually approaching the asymptote of integral dodecaphony in a cumulative PANDIATESSARON, an edifice of perfect fourths comprising all 12 tonics of the cycle of scales in the counterclockwise direction. Atonal structures guided by the principle of non-repetition are found in many works by 20th-century composers. An interesting example is an ornamental passage in Stravinsky's opera Le Rossignol, introducing the song of the Chinese nightingale. It traverses two ascending perfect fifths, a descending minor sixth, an ascending major seventh, an ascending minor third, a descending major third and an ascending major seventh. Not a single note is repeated, and the characteristic atonal interval of a major seventh occurs twice.

Tonal scales and modes derive their individuality from asymmetry of the pattern of tones and semitones. Atonal progressions are formed by the division of the octave into equal parts: two tritones, or three major thirds, four minor thirds, six major seconds, or 12 semitones. An augmented triad consisting of two major thirds is regarded as a dissonance in traditional harmony. When in 1903 the Russian composer Vladimir Rebikov used an augmented triad as the concluding chord of his opera The Christmas Tree, his daring was decried by academic critics. The diminished-seventh chord, consisting of minor thirds, is also an atonal dissonance, requiring a resolution into a triad. An atonal scale of 8 notes, obtained by the interpolation of symmetrically placed major or minor seconds in the sesquitone scale, is a frequently used coloristic device. It is described in Russian music dictionaries as Rimsky-Korsakov's scale. The WHOLE-TONE SCALE, representing the division of the octave into six equal parts, is a progression of a distinctly atonal nature, for it lacks the tonic-dominant complex and the leading tone.

The musical notation of ATONAL MUSIC, which in the larval phase of chromatic harmony bristled with double-sharps and double-flats, has been functionally simplified. When the fiction of a phantom tonality could no longer be maintained, double-sharps, double-flats and such vestigial tonal symbols as E-sharp and B-sharp, F-flat and C-flat were replaced by their enharmonic equivalents.

The cradle of ATONALITY is Central Europe, the birthplace of Freud's psychoanalysis, Kafka's existential Angst, the asymmetrical imagery of Kandinsky and the relativistic universe of Einstein. It seems fitting that these artistic and scientific developments occurred at about the same time. The controlled hesitancy, directed anxiety and Hesychastic omphaloskepsis of the period could be musically expressed with congenial intimacy only by atonal constructions. The circumstance that the TRITONE, the "diabolus in musica" of the medieval theorists, became the cornerstone of ATONALITY is a most significant reversal of musicosophical concepts of good and evil. It is also interesting to note that the tritone, being half an octave, is a neutral interval. On the psychological level this neuter quality suggests sexlessness. In his *Harmonielehre* Schoenberg remarks that "angels, our higher nature, are also sexless." In this assertion Schoenberg contradicts St. Thomas Aquinas who argued that angels must be of the masculine gender because Jacob wrestled with one and he would not have wrestled either with a woman or with a neuter hermaphrodite.

ATONAL melodies cultivate wide intervallic leaps, in order to avoid the monotony of consecutive small intervals. Although individual phrases in ATONAL MUSIC are usually short, the cumulative melodic curve appears long and sustained. Moreover, there is a singular sense of equilibrium inherent in a good atonal melody, in which the incidence of high notes is balanced by a countervailing group of low notes, with the solid central range representing a majority of essential notes. The computation of the relative frequency of individual notes in an ATONAL MELODY reveals the characteristics of the bell-shaped probability curve of Gauss. Since the duration of an individual note affects the general equilibrium of a melody, the sum of the products of duration in arbitrary units multiplied by the distance in semitones from the center of the melodic range must be zero, if the intervals below the central line are to be counted with a minus sign.

Several systems of atonal notation have been proposed in which accidentals are replaced by special symbols. Joseph Matthias Hauer suggested a multilineal staff. Jefim Golyscheff, a Russian who was active in Germany after World War I as composer and painter, and who eventually settled in Brazil, notated sharps with a cross inside a white circle and designated note values by stems. A similar notation was adopted by the Russian composer Nicolas Obouhov. He gave a demonstration of it at a concert of his works in Petrograd on 3 February 1916; he called his system "Absolute Harmony."

Herbert Eimert gives the following description of the essence of ATONALITY in his *Atonale Musiklehre* (1924): "Atonality, as the word itself implies, lacks modes, major and minor keys, and eliminates the entire harmonic apparatus of tonal music—cadences, leading tones, anticipations, resolutions, enharmonism, altered tones, etc.—as well as the concept of consonance and dissonance in their technical harmonic, but not psychological, aspects. The 12 mutually unrelated and independent tones of the tempered scale form the material of ATONAL MUSIC. The foundation of atonal material is therefore not a scale, or a progression of tones, but a group of tones, a complex, and specifically the only possible number of different tones, namely 12 tones." Hauer has this to say about ATONALITY: "In atonal music there are no tonic, dominant, subdominant, degrees, resolutions, consonances, dissonances, but only the 12 intervals of equal temperament; its scales consist therefore of 12 tempered semitones. In an ATONAL MELODY all purely physical, sensual, as well as trivial and sentimental elements, are eliminated, and its law, its *nomos*, is only that the 12 tones of the tempered scale must be played again and again."

Schoenberg and Alban Berg deprecated the use of the term ATONALITY. Berg concluded his talk on the subject, broadcast over the Vienna Radio on 8 June 1936, with these words: "Antichrist himself could not have thought up a more diabolical appellation than ATONAL!"

**Aud Music.** Optical art has given rise to a concentrated type of visual craft known as Op Art. By analogy, auditory art in its intense modern organization may be termed Aud Music. Op Art makes its impact felt by a direct assault on the visual nerve. Aud Music directs its onslaught against the auditory nerve. If *trompe l'oeil* in Op Art deceives the eye by rotating spirals, three-dimensional palimpsests, etc., the technique of *trompe l'oreille* in Aud Music confuses the ear by an unnerving succession of explosive musical fragments and sudden silences. Op Art and Aud Music freely combine in Audio-Visual syndromes. Fascinated by the optically concentric grooves of a phonograph disc, the painter Picabia called it Optophone.

To paraphrase Apollinaire, AUD MUSIC explores "a rational use of non-similitudinarianism." It makes music out of elements that are non-musical. Op Art tends to become music; modern artists often depict musical objects, such as a realistic metronome with an eye on the pendulum by Man Ray, which he entitled *Object of Destruction*, or a burning tuba by

René Magritte. AUD MUSIC makes use of sound producing objects that are not musical instruments, as exemplified by the symphonic poem for 100 metronomes of György Ligeti. Other examples of Aud and Op Art acting in concert are Sculptures Sonores, sound-producing sculptures. Engineering applications of Aud Music are illustrated by the *Rhythmicon*, constructed by Theremin and Henry Cowell and the *Sonotron*, an acoustical accelerator built by Iannis Xenakis on the model of the Cyclotron and designed to synthesize sonic particles into a sound mass.

Jean Cocteau spoke of "oreilles myopes," referring to those suffering from auditory astigmatism. White light, analyzed by the spectroscope into primary colors, has inspired Op Art; by analogy, a linear evolution of a sonic complex generates AUD MUSIC.

**Augenmusik.** Music for the Eye is a term of opprobrium often applied to works that look orderly and plausible on paper but are unimpressive to the ear. Yet visual symmetry usually corresponds to a fine musical organization. Composers of the AVANT-GARDE have adopted the patterns of AUGENMUSIK as points of departure for their musical inspiration. Anestis Logothetis, a Bulgarian-born Greek composer, exhibited his scores of AUGENMUSIK in Vienna, bearing characteristic geometric titles, such as Cycloid, Culmination, Interpolation, Parallax, Concatenation. Villa-Lobos experimented with MILLIMETRIZATION by transferring a chart, a curve, or a silhouette onto a piece of graph paper, with the ordinate corresponding to intervals in semitones and the abscissa to the duration of a note.

**Auricular Stimuli.** Some musical ears are so sensitive that they perceive sonic stimuli at the threshold of audibility; they are also capable of generating such impulses from within, while reading a musical score, providing a realistic illusion of audible sounds. The secret of the process of composition, particularly of IMPRESSIONISTIC music, may lie in this type of inner stimulation. Such AURICULAR STIMULI perhaps explain the enigmatic title of a piece by Ravel, *Sites auriculaires*. The phenomenon of inner AURICULAR STIMULI may well be measurable and ought to be investigated by otologists.

**Autogenetic Composition.** AUTOGENETIC COMPOSITION, especially in modern music, is the function of melodic invention that makes the development of the basic idea seem inevitable. Bach anticipated the process in his riddle canons; modern composers, proceeding from premises entirely different from those of Bach, apply the method in advanced techniques. AUTOGENETIC COMPOSITION is an intelligent evaluation of the potentialities of an original invention.

**Automatic Composition.** True AUTOMATIC COMPOSITION can become a reality only with a considerable advance of electronic music. A photoelectric cell may be used to trigger selected groups of notes and to imprint them on a rotating roll of paper. A coordinating device can be constructed to dictate rhythms. An automatic musical typewriter can recapitulate whole sections of a composition. AUTOMATIC MUSIC should not be confused with automatic writing as employed by spiritualists. A British housewife appeared on television in the summer of 1969 and claimed that her diluted imitations of works by Schubert and Liszt were dictated to her by them, and that she wrote them down automatically. Her claims were never subjected to controlled examination, but if substantiated they would prove that a prolonged state of death fatally affects the ability to compose even among celebrated musicians.

**Avant-Garde.** The term AVANT-GARDE is the heir to a long series of terms descriptive of progressive art—Modern, Ultra-Modern, New, Modernistic, Experimental, Empiric. The unfortunate derivation from the military vocabulary does not seem to dismay progressive composers who accept the term as an honorable profession of artistic faith. The paradox is complicated by the fact that many AVANT-GARDE composers move in the direction of nullification of music as a complex art, with absolute zero as prospective Doomsday, as music diminishes in bulk and mass. There is an advantage to this minimusification, since the diminution in sonic mass, motion and duration, leads to a corresponding increase in the sensitivity of perception. When a composer writes a work consisting of a sustained note continuing indefinitely, the listener learns to appreciate the slightest variations in dynamics and pitch. After this, even a simple succession of two different tones would appear diversified and attractive.

**Bebop.** BEBOP, Rebop, or simply BOP, is one of the many onomatopoeic vocables descriptive of jazz techniques. The most striking characteristic of BEBOP is its maximal velocity, sometimes reaching 20 notes a second in clear articulation, with a strong off-beat stress. The invention of the term and the technique is generally attributed to the American Negro jazz player Dizzy Gillespie. BEBOP is marked by irregular syncopation, a widely ranging melody of quasi-atonal configurations and, most importantly, by an accompaniment in rapidly changing modernistic harmonies, making use of unresolved dissonances and polytonal combinations. The verbalization of BEBOP can be traced to a counting jingle *Four or Five Times,* a disc issued by the Victor Company in 1928, in which the following line occurs, "BEBOP one, BEBOP two, BEBOP three." BOP as a verb was used in the comic strips in the 1920's, meaning to hit or to clobber. An erudite discussion of BOP is found in an article by Peter Tamony in the Spring, 1959, issue of the San Francisco periodical *Jazz.*

**Bitonality.** As the term indicates, BITONALITY is the simultaneous use of two different keys. The most effective type of BITONALITY is the combination of two polarized major triads whose tonics lie on the diametrically opposite points in the cycle of scales, and form the interval of a tritone. The sum of the absolute values of sharps or flats in the key signatures of such triads is always six (e.g. C major and F-sharp major, with zero sharps and six sharps respectively, or A-flat major and D major with key signatures of 4 flats and 2 sharps). The most frequently employed type of BITONALITY is the complex of C major and F-sharp major triads, which forms the harmonic foundation of Stravinsky's *Pétrouchka,* and is often called "Pétrouchka Chord." It is also known as "Parisian Chord," on account of the vogue that it subsequently acquired among Paris composers. The chord is of a clearly pianistic origin, with the white keys of C major contrasted with the black keys of F-sharp major; indeed, Stravinsky had originally planned to use these bitonal materials in a *Konzertstück* for piano and orchestra, and this accounts for the important piano part in the score of *Pétrouchka.* Acoustically, the most advantageous position of these two chords is the spacing of one in open harmony, in root position in the low register, and of the other in close harmony in the first inversion of the triad (e.g. C, G, E, A-sharp, C-sharp, F-sharp). In this disposition, the outer voices, the middle voices and the inner voices are all in the relationship of a tritone. It is of importance to note that the major hexachords based on such polarized scales aggregate to 12 different notes. BITONALITY of minor triads is encountered more seldom owing to poor acoustical balance of such combinations. In NEO-CLASSICAL music, a modal type of BITONALITY has come into existence, as exemplified by such complexes as C major and D major, in the Lydian mode. Such cases of BITONALITY are also part of PANDIATONICISM. Another type of BITONALITY is a combination of two major or minor triads with a tone in common, for instance C major combined with E major or E-flat major, favored particularly by composers of ethnic associations, among them Vaughan Williams and Roy Harris. It is interesting that a decreasing progression of intervals, beginning with 9 semitones and ending with 3 semitones, will form a bitonal major chord consisting of triads in second inversions (e.g. G, E, C, G, C-sharp, F-sharp, A-sharp, C-sharp) and that an increasing progression from 3 semitones to 9 semitones will form a bitonal combination of two minor triads in root positions (e.g., D, F, A, D, G-sharp, D-sharp, B, G-sharp). All these types of BITONALITY pursue the aims of euphony, either by polarization or by Pandiatonic approximation. A very important non-euphonious type of BITONALITY is homonymous BITONALITY of major and minor triads in close harmony (e.g., C, E, G, C, E-flat, G), with a friction point at a semitone between the major and the minor third of the same triad. It was cultivated assiduously by Stravinsky from his earliest period. In its linear devolution, it offers a stimulating quasi-atonal melodic design.

In his variations on the tune of *America,* written in 1891, Charles Ives combines F major with A-flat major. In order to bring out the bitonal resonance, he marks one of the tonalities *pianissimo* and the other *fortissimo.*

**Blues.** The word Blue is an old American colloquialism expressing melancholy. The BLUES, in plural, is an American ballad form, marked by leisurely syncopation, in 4/4 time, in slow tempo. In its melancholy lilt, the BLUES forms the counterpart of the Elegy, the Bohemian Dumka or the Brazilian Modinha. Its distinctive characteristic is the "blue note" of the flatted seventh in major keys; the third is often flatted too. The sentiment of the BLUES reflects the long history of the suffering of the Negro people in the South; some elements in the Negro Spirituals and in Stephen Foster's songs are direct progenitors of the BLUES. The first composer of the BLUES in the modern sense was W. C. Handy; his songs, *The Memphis Blues* (1911) and *The St. Louis Blues* (1914), established the genre. On 17 May 1969 the United States Post Office issued a commemorative 6-cent stamp showing W. C. Handy playing the trumpet, with the legend "Father of the Blues." Ravel has a BLUES movement in his *Violin Sonata*. The most famous concert piece in the BLUES idiom is Gershwin's *Rhapsody in Blue*.

In its classic form, BLUES consists of a series of 12-bar strophes, with the following harmonic progression: 4 bars of tonic, 2 bars of subdominant, 2 bars of tonic, 1 bar of dominant, 1 bar of subdominant and 2 bars of tonic; the plagal cadence is *de rigueur*. As in all jazz, there are infinite variations on this harmonic succession, with atonal protuberances in the melody and pandiatonic excrescences in the accompaniment.

**Boogie-Woogie.** Like most terms of JAZZ music, BOOGIE-WOOGIE is an onomatopoeic alliterative word suggesting a certain type of rhythmic beat. BOOGIE-WOOGIE invaded the public arena at a concert of popular American music given in Carnegie Hall in New York on 23 December 1938. It is the only JAZZ form that has adopted an explicit classical model, of the type of passacaglia and chaconne, with the principal theme given in the bass and thus determining the harmonic scheme. The pattern of BOOGIE-WOOGIE is remarkably regular. It consists of a 12-bar period: 4 bars of tonic harmony, 2 bars of subdominant harmony, 2 bars of tonic harmony, 2 bars of dominant harmony and again 2 bars of tonic harmony. As in all JAZZ forms, the meter is in 4/4 time, but the rhythmic pattern is set in rapid motion, most often with dotted-eighth notes followed by sixteenth-notes. The bass is usually written in even eight-notes, in broken octaves, and is sometimes described as "walking bass." The persistent eighth-notes, rhythm is suggested by the title of an early BOOGIE-WOOGIE song, Beat Me Daddy, Eight to the Bar.

**Bop.** BOP is an apocope of BEBOP; possibly it preceded BEBOP, for the exclamatory flagellant expletive BOP appears in American comic strips in the 1920's, invariably followed by an exclamation point.

**Boustrophedon** is an ancient system of writing and reading in alternate directions, one line from left to right, and the next from right to left. The Greek etymology of the word derives from oxen turning around as in plowing a field. Ophthalmologists find the BOUSTROPHEDONIC alignment beneficial in relieving the strain of shifting of the eye from right to left at the end of a line. In modern times, books have been published in a BOUSTROPHEDONIC arrangement, but no attempt has been made to publish music according to similar principles. The retrograde form of a thematic series is, to all effects and purposes, BOUSTROPHEDONIC.

**Bruitism.** BRUITISM is a genre of musical composition consisting of noises. The pioneer work of BRUITISM was *Arte dei Rumori* by the Italian Futurist Luigi Russolo, in which he codified the noises of friction, attrition, sibilation, percussion and concussion. Edgar Varèse elevated the inchoate BRUITISTIC scheme to a purely musical form in his epoch-making work *Ionization*.

**Chirality.** The etymology of CHIRALITY (from the Greek *cheir*, hand) connotes the symmetry of human hands. Lord Kelvin, who coined the term, proposed the following definition: "I call any geometrical figure, or a group of points, CHIRAL, and say it has CHIRALITY if its image in a plane mirror, ideally realized, cannot be brought to coincide with itself." Since music evolves in time and not in space, a composition that possesses CHIRALITY must consist of two symmetrical halves, the first note or chord being identical with the last, the second with the penultimate, the third with the antepenultimate, etc. In other words, musical CHIRALITY is achieved by the technique of specular reflection, or retrograde imitation. In spatial terms of musical performance, CHIRALITY exists between the first violin and second violin sections in an orchestra, if they are placed traditionally to the left and to the right of the conductor.

**Chromatic Torsion.** Chromatic melodies are most effective when they are involuted towards a central tone in a spiral. The effect of constant vectorial changes during which such a central tone is approached alternately from above and from below, may be described as CHROMATIC TORSION. An interesting example is the theme of the Queen of Shemaha in Rimsky-Korsakov's opera *Le Coq d'or*, in which CHROMATIC TORSION (and contortion) is effectively applied along the stems of diminished-seventh chord harmonies.

**Circatonalitarianism.** The employment, whether successive or quaquaversal, of all 12 minor and major modalities in a single composition may be called CIRCATONALITARIAN, by analogy with the biological term Circadian. CIRCATONALITARIAN structures are present literally in POLYTETRACHORDS, which traverse 12 major or minor tetrachords.

**Circuitry.** Modern scores for MIXED MEDIA performances often have the appearance of blueprints for the electric circuits in scientific instruments and digital computers. An early example of musical CIRCUITRY is the part marked *Luce* in Scriabin's *Prometheus*, intended to fill the concert hall with changing colors corresponding to fluctuations in instrumental timbre. The detailed directions as to lighting given by Schoenberg in his monodrama *Erwartung* are in the same category. The Russian composer Nicolas Obouhov, who called himself "Nicolas l'Illuminé," designed an electronic instrument in the form of a cross, called *Croix Sonore*. In the CIRCUITRY of some ultra-modern scores the SPATIAL DISTRIBUTION of instruments becomes a musical parameter. Elliott Carter, Lukas Foss, Krzysztof Penderecki, Jani Christou, Sylvano Bussoti, Iannis Xenakis, John Cage and others, wrote works stipulating the position of each instrument in relation to the rest of the ensemble.

**Collective Nouns.** The following are suggestions for COLLECTIVE NOUNS to designate groups of musical instruments: a fluviality of flutes, an exhalation of piccolos, a conviviality of clarinets, a scabrosity of bassoons, a promiscuity of saxophones, an oriflamme of French horns, a plangency of oboes, an ambrosia of harps, a flourish of trumpets, a pomposity of trombones, a phlogiston of tubas, a circumspection of pianos, an enfilade of violins, a reticence of violas, an elegance of cellos, a teratology of double-basses, a titillation of triangles, and the Brobdingnagian borborygmuses of bass drums.

**Combinatoriality.** In general topology the concept of COMBINATORIALITY applies to the functional congruence of geometrical figures of the same order of continuity. Thus a square can be brought into topological congruence with a circle because all the points of the former are in an enumerable correspondence of the other. On the other hand, the geometry of figure 8 cannot be made congruent with a square or a circle without cutting. The American composer and theorist Milton Babbitt extended the term COMBINATORIALITY to serial techniques. The parameter of continuity in dodecaphonic writing is the order of succession of the 12 thematic notes in their four forms, basic, retrograde, inversion and inverted retrograde, all of which are combinatorially congruent. Furthermore, the tone-row can be functionally divided into two potentially congruent groups of six notes each, or three groups of four notes each, or four groups of three notes each, with each such group becoming a generating serial nucleus possessing a degree of subsidiary COMBINATORIALITY. Extending the concept of COMBINATORIALITY to other parameters of serial music, a state of total SERIALISM is attained, in which not only the actual notes of a series, but also meter, rhythm, intervalic configurations, dynamics and instrumental timbres are organized in sets and subsets. The subsets in turn are organized as combinatorial derivations, possessing their own order of continuity and congruence. Of these, the most fruitful is the principle of rotation, in which each successive set is obtained by the transposition of the first note of the series to the end of a derived set. Thus the first set, 1, 2, 3, . . . 12, appears after rotation as subset 2, 3, 4, 5, . . . 12, 1, or as 3, 4, 5, 6, . . . 12, 1, 2, etc. Inversion, retrograde and inverted retrograde can be subjected to a similar type of rotation. The additive Fibonacci series, in which each number equals the sum of the two preceding numbers, as in 1, 1, 2, 3, 5, 8, 13, 21, is another fertile resource for the formation of sets, subsets and other derivations. The Fibonacci numbers can be used for building non-dodecaphonic tone-rows, in which case the numbers will indicate the distance from the central tone in semitones, modulo 12, so that 13 becomes functionally identical with 1, 21 with 9, etc. The numerical field of COMBINATORIALITY is circumscribed by 12 different notes. But experiments have been conducted, notably by Ernst Krenek, with artificial scales of 13 equal degrees, obtained with the aid of electronic instruments. Potential uses of COMBINATORIALITY operating with sets of more than 12 notes in an octave are limitless.

**Commodious Nomenclature.** The musical avant-garde does not oppose euphony on general principle. Harmonious progressions are tolerated in modern music. The compromise between the prospective music of the future and the modality of the past is often achieved by resorting to COMMODIOUS NOMENCLATURE, as exemplified by the neologisms NEO-CLASSICAL, NEO-BAROQUE, NEO-ROMANTIC, and beyond that by the exotic terms VECTORIALISM, LIPOGRAMMATICISM or SPATIAL SERIALISM. New Music, Modern Music, Contemporary Music, etc., once progressive slogans, have long been overgrown with a fungus of obsolescence. Futurism itself, a rebellious cry of the dawn of the century, is now an academic object of historical study.

**Computer Music.** Digital computers are ideal purveyors of random numbers, which in turn can be converted into musical parameters. Such data furnish the natural sources for ALEATORY MUSIC. Care should be taken, however, not to program COMPUTER MUSIC excessively, for such input would amount to the dictation of the programmer's own musical ideas, which are often lamentable.

**Conjugated Counterpoint.** By definition, counterpoint is a conjugation of two or several melodic parts, but too often in common practice contrapuntal techniques follow harmonic formulas, to the detriment of the interdependence of component voices. It is therefore useful to introduce the term CONJUGATED COUNTERPOINT in its etymological sense of "opposite notes yoked together." The locus classicus of CONJUGATED COUNTERPOINT is the second movement of Béla Bartók's *Concerto for Orchestra*, in which conjugated pairs of wind instruments are arrayed in succession and intussusception.

**Contrapuntal Intussusception.** In many modern scores contrapuntal groups are arranged in pairs, and each pair becomes an individual entity which is subsequently combined with another prefabricated pair, and yet another. When two such pairs are widely separated in their ranges, an opportunity is presented for an intussusception of a new pair, forming a structure of six contrapuntal voices in three subdivisions. Alexander Tcherepnin made systematic use of this technique in his method of INTERPOINT (Contrapunctus inter punctum).

**Controlled Improvisation.** An arrangement of available thematic elements, following a definite formal design and confined within a specified period of time, has been described as CONTROLLED IMPROVISATION. Accordingly, the performer selects attractive or significant motives and phrases of an otherwise non-integrated work, as though drawing pre-set lines from a printer's tray, resetting them at will, duplicated, fragmented, or upside-down. Karlheinz Stockhausen, Lukas Foss, Earle Brown, and others have availed themselves of this manner of composition.

**Country Music.** As it is practiced in the American South, COUNTRY MUSIC is deeply imbued with sentimental balladry, with curiously oblique cadences that impart an archaic flavor to the melody. The syncopated beat, characteristic of RAGTIME and JAZZ, is practically absent in these bland songs. Through the medium of radio and television, COUNTRY MUSIC spread far and wide in the United States, eventually coalescing with ROCK 'N' ROLL.

**Cubism.** The musical counterpart of CUBISM in art is the erection of massive sonorous complexes moving *en bloc* at different speeds and angular motion. Such harmonic boulders produce the best effect in POLYTRIADIC STRUCTURES. CUBISTIC music must be static, with a low potential. There should be no intermediate melodic or harmonic shifts between CUBISTIC complexes, but tremolo effects within each unit may contribute to resonant power congruent with massive sonic structures.

**Cybernetics.** The word CYBERNETICS is derived from the Greek root for governing. As defined by its originator Norbert Wiener, CYBERNETICS is the exercise of human control over mechanical and electrical apparatus, especially in the field of communication. In music, CYBERNETICAL data are collected by various ALEATORY, intuitive or other means; the resulting materials are translated into a system of musical parameters, and a viable outline is drawn. It is in the selection and the programming of CYBERNETICAL elements that a composer can assert his personality. In music, CYBERNETICAL SERENDIPITY plays a beneficial part. Novel ideas often suggest themselves during the process of mutation and permutation of thematic elements, contributing to the all-important problem of musical communication.

**Cyrenaic Hedonism.** Hedonistic traits in modern music developed as a natural psychological reaction to the cataclysm of World War I. Composers and the public sought relaxation in hedonistic dalliance, Cyrenaic in its complete orgiastic abandon and Sybaritic in its quest for mindless comforts. The center of this cult of music for pleasure was France; it enjoyed a particular vogue between 1920 and 1935, when the slogan of NEW SIMPLICITY was launched as an antidote to post-Romantic solipsism. In form and content this new music cultivated the elegant conceits of the French rococo period, with an emphasis on Epicurean qualities designed to please the palate. Historically, it was the long-delayed fruition of the musical cuisine of Rossini, with occasional polyharmonies and asymmetric rhythms used for modern seasoning.

**Dadaism.** The word DADAISM was invented by Tristan Tzara of 8 February 1916 at a congenial gathering of friends in a Zürich café. According to one of the many versions, the word Dada owes its origin to French infantiloquy as a sort of dental lallation. Esthetically, DADAISM was the product of the frustrations endured during the First World War. Its philosophy was entirely negative. Derived from the vociferously proclaimed detestation of all art, music and poetry, DADAISM stood close to FUTURISM in its furious onslaught on all established values, but failed to offer a new art to replace the old. Despite its violently negative code, DADAISM prepared a well-manured ground for the flowering of such fertile stylistic vegetation as SURREALISM. DADAISM also cast its proleptic shadow on the AVANT-GARDE of the 1960's and the improvisatory art of the HAPPENINGS.

**Decomposition and Reassembly.** The technique of DECOMPOSITION AND REASSEMBLY is suggested by the title of a painting by the Futurist artist Umberto Boccioni, "Scomposizione," in which the normal head of a woman is fragmented and reassembled in a topologically non-congruent shape. The idea is applicable to modern music. A melody can be fractured and its elements redistributed in a different configuration. Variations, tonal and atonal, can be experimentally rearranged, melodically, harmonically and rhythmically. DECOMPOSITION AND REASSEMBLY may provide interesting and novel combinations of thematic materials and stimulate a disadvantaged composer to explore the laws of musical congruence far beyond his ordinary capabilities.

**Demolition.** Public DEMOLITION of musical instruments as part of new techniques of the American and British AVANT-GARDE came into vogue shortly after the conclusion of World War II, possibly as a sado-masochistic exercise of aggressive tendencies, frustrated by the unconditional surrender of the ex-enemies. Contests in the swiftness of destroying upright pianos have been held in clubs and colleges. According to the established rules of the game, a piano had to be reduced to comminuted fragments that could be passed through an aperture of specified dimensions (usually a circle 6 inches in diameter.) In Stockholm, Sweden, a young pianist concluded his recital by igniting a dynamite charge previously secreted inside the piano, blowing it up. An exploding splinter wounded him in the leg. The American AVANT-GARDE composer La Monte Young set a violin on fire at one of his exhibits.

Bakunin, the scientific anarchist, said, "Die Lust der Zerstörung ist eine schaffende Lust." This "creative impulse of destruction" has received its full vindication in the anti-piano activities of the modern times.

**Demotic Music.** DEMOTIC MUSIC is a generic category that comprises all genres of popular music—rural, urban, pop, country, folk, western, jazz, tin-pan alley, commercial jingles. Modern applications of the resources of DEMOTIC MUSIC are obtained by diatonic translocation, atonal dismemberment and rhythmic compression. Hexachordal diatonic melodies may be metamorphosed into complex melorhythmic progressions without losing their DEMOTIC morphology. ABECEDARIAN MUSIC for children is a fruitful source of such topological transformation. Not all simple music is necessarily DEMOTIC, unless the folk quality is expressed in a composed work with utmost fidelity. Some obscure composers have succeeded in producing tunes that seem to be authentically DEMOTIC. The universally popular tune, *Dark Eyes*, regarded by many as an autochthonous Russian Gypsy song, is actually a violin piece, entitled *Valse-hommage* composed by a German band leader active in Russia in the 1880's. The Neapolitan ballad *Funiculi-Funicula*, mistaken by many for a genuine folk tune, was written by an Italian vocal teacher resident in London.

**Dialectics.** Etymologically, DIALECTICS is a discourse. Musical DIALECTICS may be a useful term to describe a kind of meaningful antiphony, an orderly exchange of melodic statements, sufficiently divergent to imply the sense of a debate and yet unified by a general melodic, rhythmic or harmonic idea. Music in a dialectical form ought to be by definition a succession of free associations, not too strict in grammar and syntax, replete with asymmetrical rhythms and unresolved dissonances. The term is large enough to cover many idioms and techniques, from NEO-CLASSICAL structures to SERIAL COMPOSITION.

**Dilapidation of Tonality.** The disappearance of explicit key signatures from the notation of modern composition was the first symptom of the DILAPIDATION OF TONALITY and deterioration of traditional harmony. The key signature has a reason for existence in NEO-CLASSICAL works in which the tonic-dominant relationship is still extant and triadic modulations strong. But the dormant chromaticism erupts all the more viciously against tonal restraints, and the key signature, if it is set down at all, exists only to be denied. The chromaticization of the modern idiom during the last decades of the 19th-century resulted in an enormous proliferation of double-sharps and double-flats. As enharmonic modulation reared its multicolored head, the antinomy between the tonality symbolized by the key signature and the florid panchromatic display reached the point of arithmetical incompatibility. Seven notes of the diatonic scale represented by seven positions on the music staff and seven letters of the alphabet were to provide notation for the 12 different notes of the chromatic scale. Academic musicians, eager to preserve the fiction of eminent tonality, and being unable to find a common denominator between 7 and 12, erected a fantastic network of accidentals; triple sharps and triple flats pollulate in the *Canons and Fugues* of Wilhelm Middelschulte. A whole section, acoustically equivalent to C major, masquerades in intervalic enharmonies as B-sharp and D-double-flat major in the piano part of Ravel's *Trio*. Debussy was similarly involved in exotic structures of double-flats and double-sharps in a triadic passage of his *Feuilles mortes*.

Even in the 19th century, tonality was often nominal and the key signature an armature without a function. *Intermezzo No. 4*, op. 76, by Brahms is ostensibly in B-flat major, but the tonic triad is not reached until the final two bars. This type of tonal convention may be described as teleological tonality in which the tonic is the goal rather than the point of departure. The language of ATONALITY arose from the products of the decay of tonal relationships. Genuinely atonal melodies lack the homing instinct; they meander and maunder without the beacon of a tonic in sight. The attraction of the tonic does not exist in atonal writing; the members of an atonal melody are weightless. This atonal assembly deprived of tonal gravity, came to be organized by Arnold Schoenberg in a mutually gravitating dodecaphonic complex. Key signatures are obviously superfluous in atonal and dodecaphonic music, but not in POLYTONALITY where different key signatures are used simultaneously.

The supremacy of tonality demanded that each composition should end in the same key, or in a related key, in which it began. How strong the prerequisite of this tonal uniformity was felt by composers of the 19th century is illustrated by a whimsical annotation of Richard Strauss in his song entitled *Wenn*, published in 1897. In the original version, the principal key is D-flat major, but the final seven bars and the concluding chord are in D major. Strauss supplied an alternative coda in which the transition was made to the original key, with the following footnote: "Vocalists who may perform this song before the end of the 19th century are advised by the composer to transpose the last seven bars a semitone lower so as to arrive at the end of the song in the same key in which it began."

**Dislocation of Melodic Lines.** A special case of modern variation is a linear DISLOCATION OF A MELODIC LINE. A high note may be pulled upwards and a low note may be pulled downwards without disrupting the intervalic balance of the melody itself. Virtually any tonal melodic line can be topologically transformed into a dodecaphonic series, with ascending intervals retaining their upward direction and descending intervals conserving their downward motion. Stationary notes in the melody may be pulled upwards or downwards at will. Examples of intervalic and modulatory translocation can be found in NEO-CLASSICAL compositions. Translocation is also an excellent resource of modern burlesque.

**Displaced Tonality.** A modernistic resource in tonal techniques which has been successfully applied by composers who are reluctant to abandon tonality altogether, is a DISPLACEMENT of the tonic by an instant modulation a semitone higher or a semitone lower. Translocation by larger intervals is not effective. Major scales are more suitable for such translocation because of the greater intervalic strength within a major tetrachord, while minor tetrachords are often ambiguous. Transposition of the initial three notes of a major scale a semitone higher or lower forms a group of six different notes; a similar translocation in a minor key will entail a duplication of one member of the series. Examples of melodic translocations are found in many works of Prokofiev and Shostakovich.

**Dissonant Counterpoint.** The term DISSONANT COUNTERPOINT came into usage in the 1920's as a sort of apologetic declaration by proponents of ATONAL MUSIC. It emphasized the functional equality of dissonance and consonance in all types of contrapuntal techniques. In fugal writing, in particular, a strong tendency was evinced to use the tritone as the interval of entry, instead of the traditional perfect fifth of the tonic-dominant complex. DISSONANT COUNTERPOINT does not exclude consonances but puts them on probation. However, the perfect octave, as a cadential interval, is generally shunned by the theoreticians of DISSONANT COUNTERPOINT, and is usually replaced by a major seventh.

**Dodecaphonic Music.** In historical perspective, DODECAPHONIC MUSIC is the product of a luxuriant development of chromatic melody and harmony. A conscious avoidance of all tonal centers led to the abolition of key signature and a decline of triadic harmony. The type of composition in which all tonal points of reference have been eliminated became known as ATONALITY. It was from this paludous atmosphere of inchoate ATONALITY that the positive and important technical idiom of dodecaphonic composition was gradually evolved and eventually formulated by Arnold Schoenberg as the "method of composing with 12 tones related only to one another." Schoenberg's first explicit use of his method occurs in his *Serenade*, op. 24, written in 1924. Five fundamental ideas underlie Schoenberg's method: (1) Dodecaphonic monothematism in which the entire work is derived from a 12-tone row (*Tonreihe*) which comprises 12 different notes of the chromatic scale. (2) The tone-row is utilized in four conjugate forms: the original, retrograde, inversion, and retrograde inversion. (3) Although the order of the notes in the tone-row is rigidly observed, the individual members of the series can be placed in any octave position, a peculiar feature of dodecaphonic music which results in the wide distribution of the thematic ingredients over the entire vocal or instrumental range of a single part or over sections of different parts. (4) Since each of the 4 forms of the basic 12-tone series can be transposed to any starting point of the chromatic scale, the total of all available forms is 48. (5) Melody, harmony and counterpoint are functions of the tone-row, which may appear in all its avatars, horizontally as melody, vertically as harmony and diagonally as canonic counterpoint. It may also be distributed partly in melodic progressions, partly in harmonic or contrapuntal structures, creating DODECAPHONIC MELOHARMONY or MELOCOUNTERPOINT. Because of the providential divisibility of number 12, the 12-tone row can be arranged in 6 groups in 2-part counterpoint, 4 groups in 3-part counterpoint (or harmony), 3 groups in 4-part harmony or 2 groups in 6-part harmony.

In a communication sent to Nicolas Slonimsky in 1939, Ernst Krenek describes the relationship between ATONALITY and the method of composing with 12 tones as follows: "ATONALITY is a state of the musical material brought about through a general historical development. The 12-tone technique is a method of writing music within the realm of ATONALITY. The sense of key has been destroyed by ATONALITY. The method of composing with 12 tones was worked out in order to replace the old organization of the material by certain new devices."

Schoenberg was not alone in his dodecaphonic illumination. Several musicians, mostly in Austria and Germany, evolved similar systems of organizing the resources of the chromatic scale in a logical and self-contained system of composition. Jef Golyscheff, Russian composer and painter who lived in Germany and eventually settled in Brazil, worked on the problem as early as 1914, and in 1924 published a collection which he called *12 Tondauer Musik*, making use of 12 different tones in thematic structures. At about the same time Nicolas Obouhov invented a system which he called "Absolute Harmony" and which involved the use of all 12 chromatic tones without doubling; he played his piano pieces written in this system at a concert in Petrograd on 3 February 1916.

Passages containing 12 different notes in succession, apart from the simple chromatic scale, are found even in classical works. There is a highly chromaticized passage in Mozart's *G Minor Symphony* derived from three mutually exclusive diminished-seventh chords, aggregating to 12 different notes. The main subject in the section "Of Science" in the score of *Also sprach Zarathustra* by Richard Strauss contains all 12 different notes of the chromatic scale, but they remain uninverted, untergiversated and otherwise unmetamorphosed, and thus cannot be regarded as a sampler of dodecaphonic writing.

Liszt's *Faust Symphony* opens with a theme consisting of four successive augmented triads descending by semitones comprising all 12 different tones, but it cannot be meaningfully described as an anticipation of the dodecaphonic method. Charles Ives has a 12-tone series of different chromatic notes in his instrumental piece *Tone Road No. 3*, which he wrote in 1915. This intuitive invention is important not only as an illustration of his prophetic genius, but also as another indication that dodecaphonic ideas appeared in the minds of musicians working in different parts of the world, completely independent of each other.

Among scattered examples of 12-tone composition of the pre-dodecaphonic years is *L'adieu à la vie* for piano by Alfredo Casella, which ends on a chord of 12 different notes. An amusing example of dodecaphonic prevision is the *Hymn to Futurism* by César Cui, written in 1917, when the last surviving member of the Russian Mighty Five was 82 years old. Intended as a spoof, the piece contains a passage of three mutually exclusive diminished-seventh chords in arpeggio adding up to 12 different notes, and another passage comprising two mutually exclusive augmented triads with a complementary scale of whole tones passing through the unoccupied six spaces, forming another series of 12 different notes. The fact that Cui had two dodecaphonic series in his short composition demonstrates that even in a musical satire the thematic use of 12 different notes was a logical outcome of the process of tonal decay, serving as a fertilizer for the germination of dodecaphonic organisms.

Schoenberg was intensely conscious of the imperative need of asserting his priority in the invention of the method of composition with 12 tones. Among contenders for the honor was Fritz Klein, the author of an extremely ingenious composition for orchestra, *Die Maschine*, subtitled "eine extonale Selbstsatire," published in 1921 under the characteristic pseudonym "Heautontimorumenos" (i.e., Self-Tormentor). This pseudonym Klein took from the title of a play by Terence, which contains the famous aphorism: "Homo sum; humani nil a me alienum puto." Klein's score contains a remarkable array of inventions: a "Mutterakkord" containing 12 different notes and 11 different intervals, a "Pyramidakkord," patterns of rhythmically repeated 12 notes, etc., all presaging the future developments of integral serialism. When queried by Nicolas Slonimsky regarding Klein's role in the history of Dodecaphonic composition, Schoenberg replied (in English): "Although I saw Klein's 12-tone compositions about 1919, 1920 or 1921, I am not an imitator of him. I wrote the melody for *Scherzo* composed of 12 tones in 1915. In the first edition of my *Harmonielehre* (1911), there is a description of the new harmonies and their application which has probably influenced all these who now want to become my models."

A much more formidable challenge to Schoenberg's dodecaphonic priority was made by Joseph Matthias Hauer of Vienna, who had experimented with 12-tone composition independently from Schoenberg. But his method differed from Schoenberg's in essential aspects. He built 12-tone subjects from 6-tone "tropes," and allowed free permutation of each trope, a concept that was entirely alien to Schoenberg's fundamental doctrine of thematic ordering of the tone-row. Still, Schoenberg regarded Hauer's theories as sufficiently close to his own method to take notice of them. Schoenberg described the dodecaphonic situation in Vienna in a retrospective note published in the program book of a concert of his chamber music given in New York in 1950: "In 1921 I showed my former pupil Erwin Stein the means I had invented to provide profoundly for a musical organization granting logic, coherence and unity. I then asked him to keep this a secret and to consider it as my private method with which to do the best for my artistic purposes." (The arcane character of this report calls to mind a Latin cryptogram in which the astronomer Huygens encoded his discovery of the rings of Saturn to insure the priority of his observations.) "If I were to escape the danger of being his imitator," Schoenberg continued, "I had to unveil my secret. I called a meeting of friends and pupils, to which I also invited Hauer, and gave a lecture on my new method, illustrating it by examples of some finished compositions of mine. Everybody recognized that my method was quite different from that of others." Hauer refused to surrender his own claims as the spiritual protagonist of 12-tone music. A man of an irrepressible polemical temper, he even had a rubber stamp made, which he used in his private correspondence, and which carried the following legend: "Josef Matthias Hauer, der geistiger Urhaber und trotz vielen schlechten Nachahmern immer noch der einziger Kenner und Könner der Zwöftonmusik."

Although Schoenberg's title to the formulation and practical application of the method of composing with 12 tones was finally recognized, in 1948 he came into an unexpected collision with a fictional claimant, Adrian Leverkühn, the hero of Thomas Mann's novel *Doktor Faustus*, described as the inventor of the 12-tone method of composition. In an indignant letter to the editors of the *Saturday Review of Literature* Schoenberg protested against this misappropriation of his invention. The idea that Leverkühn might be considered as a fictional portrait of Schoenberg himself infuriated him. "Leverkühn is depicted," Schoenberg wrote, "from beginning to end, as a lunatic. I am seventy-four and I am not yet insane, and I have never acquired the disease from which this insanity stems. I consider this an insult."

John Stuart Mill once expressed fears that musical invention might soon exhaust its resources, considering the limited number of melodies that could be derived from the eight degrees of the major or the minor scale. He reckoned without the eventual proliferation of chromatic melodies. There are 479,001,600 permutations of 12 units, and as many possible melodies consisting of 12 different notes each. In the dodecaphonic firmament, the melodic horizon is practically unlimited.

The properties of 12-tone composition are truly magical. A priori, it would seem impossible that the 12 notes of the chromatic scale could be arranged in four mutually exclusive triads, considering that its organization was the product of negation of tonality. Yet it has been found empirically that there are two basic solutions of this problem, each capable of three transpositions. But there is a limiting condition: two of these triads must be major and two minor. On the basis of C, these solutions are: (1) C major, D minor, F-sharp major, G-sharp minor; (2) C major, B-flat major, G-sharp minor and F-sharp minor. The ever-present tritone is the interval between the tonics of each pair in the first solution, and between the tonics of the first and last triad in the second solution. It is also possible to distribute the 12 chromatic tones in a group containing a diminished triad, a minor triad, a major triad and an augmented triad. Furthermore it is possible to arrange four mutually exclusive triads in a continuous chain of major and minor thirds, forming a chord of the minor 23rd, e.g. F-sharp major, E major, D minor, C minor in an ascending series. This is the unique solution of this particular problem. The symmetry of these arrangements is extraordinary. These findings were first published in 1947 in Nicolas Slonimsky's *Thesaurus of Scales and Melodic Patterns*, and have been since verified by a digital computer without adding any new solutions.

Far from being sterile excogitations, the theory of mutually exclusive triads has had its practical application long before it was explicitly formulated. A passage including four mutually exclusive triads occurs in the concluding section of Debussy's *Prélude à l'Après-midi d'un Faune* (E major, C minor, D major, B-flat minor, with the melody descending chromatically from G-sharp down to F.)

The method of composing with 12 tones related only to one another did not remain a rigid dogma. Its greatest protagonists, besides Schoenberg himself, were his disciples Alban Berg and Anton von Webern. Somewhat frivolously, they have been described as the Vienna Trinity, with Schoenberg the Father, Berg the Son, and Webern the Holy Ghost. Both Berg and Webern introduced considerable innovations into the Schoenbergian practice. While Schoenberg studiously avoided triadic constructions, Alban Berg used the conjunct series of alternating minor and major triads capped by three whole tones as the principal subject of his last work, the *Violin Concerto* (1935). Schoenberg practically excluded symmetric intervallic constructions and sequences, but Alban Berg inserted, in his opera *Lulu*, a dodecaphonic episode built on two mutually exclusive whole-tone scales. Anton von Webern dissected the 12-tone series into autonomous sections of 6, 4 or 3 units in a group, and related them individually to one another by inversion, retrograde and inverted retrograde. This fragmentation enabled him to make use of canonic imitation much more freely than would have been possible according to the strict Schoenbergian doctrine.

The commonly used term for DODECAPHONIC MUSIC in German is *Zwölftonmusik*. In American usage it was translated literally as 12-tone music, but English music theorists strenuously object to this terminology, pointing out that a tone is an acoustical phenomenon and that DODECAPHONY deals with the arrangement of written notes, and that it should be consequently called 12-note music. In Italy the method became known as *Dodecafonia* or *Musica dodecafonica*. Incidentally, the term *Dodecafonia* was first used by the Italian music scholar Domenico Alaleona in his article *L'armonia modernissima* published in *Rivista Musicale* in 1911 but it was applied there in the sense of total chromaticism as an extension of Wagnerian harmony.

The proliferation of dodecaphony in Italy was as potent as it was unexpected, considering the differences between Germanic and Latin cultures, the one introspective and speculative, the other humanistic and practical. Luigi Dallapiccola was one of the earliest adepts, but he liberalized Schoenberg's method and admitted tonal elements. In his opera *Il Prigioniero*, written in 1944, he made use of four mutually exclusive triads.

The greatest conquest of Schoenberg's method was the totally unexpected conversion of Igor Stravinsky whose entire esthetic code had seemed to stand in opposition to any predetermined scheme of composition; yet he adopted it when he was already in his seventies. Many other composers of world renown turned to dodecaphonic devices as a thematic expedient without full utilization of the four basic forms of the tone-row. Béla Bartók made use of a 12-tone melody in his *Second Violin Concerto*, but he modified its structure by inner permutations within the second statement of the tone-row. Ernest Bloch, a composer for whom the constrictions of modern techniques had little attraction, made use of 12-tone subjects in his *Sinfonia Breve* and in his last string quartets. English composers who have adopted the technique of 12-tone composition with various degrees of consistency are Michael Tippett, Lennox Berkeley, Benjamin Frankel, Humphrey Searle and Richard Rodney Bennett. William Walton makes use of a 12-tone subject in the fugal finale of his *Second Symphony*. Benjamin Britten joined the dodecaphonic community by way of tonality. In his expressionist opera *The Turn of the Screw*, he adopts a motto of alternating perfect fifths and minor thirds (or their respective inversions), aggregating to a series of 12 different notes. The Spanish composer Roberto Gerhard, who settled in England, wrote in a fairly strict dodecaphonic idiom. In France the leader of the dodecaphonic school is René Leibowitz, who also wrote several books on the theory of 12-tone composition. Wladimir Vogel, a Russian-born composer of German parentage, making his home in Switzerland, has adopted Schoenberg's method in almost all of his works. The Swiss composer Frank Martin has extended the principles of dodecaphonic writing to include a number of tonal and modal ramifications.

In America Schoenberg's method has found a fertile ground, not only among his students but also among composers who had pursued different roads. Roger Sessions, Virgil Thomson and David Diamond have followed Schoenberg's method with varying degrees of fidelity. Aaron Copland used the dodecaphonic technique in some of his chamber music works; in the orchestral compositions entitled *Connotations* commissioned for the opening concert of Lincoln Center, New York, in 1962, he applied the totality of DODECAPHONY to characterize the modern era of music. Walter Piston interpolated a transitional 12-tone passage in his ballet suite *The Incredible Flutist*. He resisted integral dodecaphony until his septuagenarian calendae, when in his *Eighth Symphony* he adopted Schoenberg's method in all its orthodoxy. Leonard Bernstein inserted a 12-tone series in the score of his *Age of Anxiety* to express inner agitation and anguished expectancy of the music. Samuel Barber made an excursion into the dodecaphonic field in a movement of his *Piano Sonata*. Gian Carlo Menotti turned dodecaphony into parody in his opera *The Last Savage* to illustrate the decadence of modern civilization into which the hero was unexpectedly catapulted from his primitivistic habitat.

In Soviet Russia dodecaphony still remains officially unacceptable as a "formalistic" device. (In a speech delivered in Moscow on 8 March 1963, Nikita Khrushchev, then Prime Minister of the Soviet Union, observed: "They call it dodecaphony, but we call it cacophony.") Nevertheless, some blithe spirits of the young Soviet generation, among them Andrei Volkonsky, Valentin Silvestrov and Sergei Slonimsky, have written and published works in the 12-tone idiom.

The following is a summation of theoretical postulates, subsidiary lemmata and practical usages of dodecaphonic techniques.

(1) The generating dodecaphonic series must be constructed in such a way as to establish a strong mutual valence of the component members, relating them only to one another in accordance with Schoenberg's prescription, and avoiding any suggestion of chordal derivation, particularly that of a triadic nature.

(2) Intervals most suitable for the construction of a viable series are those that carry no tonal affiliation, with particular preference for the major seventh, the minor ninth, and the tritone. Since the intervallic difference between the major seventh and the tritone is a perfect fourth and the difference between the minor ninth and the tritone is a perfect fifth, these differential intervals have acquired a peculiar structural importance in DODECAPHONIC MUSIC, provided they do not appear poised strategically in the potential relationship of the tonic and dominant, or tonic and subdominant. Melodic successions of perfect fourths or perfect fifths are favored since they tend towards atonal asymptotes. Historically, such quartal and quintal progressions led to the distinctive evolution of atonal patterns preceding the formation of strictly dodecaphonic conformations.

(3) Identical intervals between successive pairs of thematic tones are to be used with circumspection so as not to impair the individuality of members of the tone-row and prevent their degeneration and entropic coalescence into chromatic or diatonic scales or into easily decipherable chordal combinations.

(4) Although the original tone-row must be stated in full in the exposition, immediate repetition of a single tone in the series is not to be regarded as a disruptive factor, for such repetition may be simply a synonym for a rhythmic prolongation.

(5) Since the concept of tonality is irrelevant to DODECAPHONIC MUSIC, the key signature is automatically eliminated. For the same reason chromatic alterations pertinent to tonal usages and modulation are reduced to their simplest enharmonic equivalents; double sharps and double flats are completely eliminated. Some dodecaphonic composers insist on prefixing every note with a sharp, flat or natural, but this type of notation is visually distracting and wasteful.

(6) Functional and operative equivalence of melody, harmony and counterpoint is of fundamental importance to the Dodecaphonic techniques and constitutes its most innovative feature; thus the 12 tones of the series may be distributed either horizontally in melodic lines, vertically in harmonic columns, or diagonally in contrapuntal formations becoming different dimensions of a unified dodecaphonic space.

(7) Triadic chordal formations are unacceptable in vertical constructions as well as in horizontal melodies. Major triads, particularly in root positions, are inadmissible; their inversions are to be avoided in conspicuous positions. Only slightly less objectionable are minor triads in root positions, but inversions of minor triads in an atonal context are often tolerated. Explicit dominant-seventh chords, implying as they do the presence of the leading tone, are incompatible with the atonal essence of dodecaphony. Similarly obnoxious are diminished-seventh chords because of their connotations as leading-tone harmonies and also because of their uniform intervallic structure.

(8) PANDIATONICISM and POLYTONALITY have no place in the dodecaphonic vocabulary on account of their tonal derivation. Generally speaking, acoustical euphony, inflated sonorities and facile fluidity of harmonic progressions are contrary to dodecaphonic esthetics; any external effects of a melodious or harmonious nature are in conflict with the austere spirit and philosophical severity of the serial designs.

(9) Although the fundamental series and its derivations are available in 12 transpositions, such exhaustive utilization of serial materials is rarely found in actual works. Paradoxically,

the most favored transpositions, particularly in sections corresponding to recapitulation in classical forms, stand in a quartal-quintal relationship, demonstrating once more the strength of the classical legacy in dodecaphonic composition. One would expect frequent transpositions at a tritone, but such is not the case, because the tritone is apt to be of strategic use in the original series, and would duplicate itself in such a transposition.

(10) The formal structure of works written in the 12-tone idiom is remarkably conservative, following the classical models of variations, passacaglia, prelude, suite, or serenade. The most striking instance of this classical consciousness is the organization of Alban Berg's expressionistic opera *Lulu,* a definitely serial work, which nevertheless contains individual sections bearing titles of Baroque forms. Variations are especially congenial to dodecaphonic organization, with the 12-tone row representing the theme and the retrograde, inversion and inverted retrograde being the three basic variations.

(11) Large forms, such as sonatas and symphonies, are not suited to dodecaphonic treatment owing to the essentially tonal thematic relationship between the exposition, the development and the recapitulation. For similar reasons, dodecaphonic treatment cannot be applied to fugal forms. Canonic imitation is possible when the 12-tone row is fragmented into subdivisions of 3, 4, or 6 notes each, as in some works by Anton von Webern, where such infradodecaphonic segments stand in a structural symmetric relationship of inverted and retrograde correspondence to one another.

(12) Polymetric and polyrhythmic developments are but rarely encountered in DODECAPHONIC compositions. Binary and ternary time signatures of the classical type are prevalent, while compound meters are rare. Triplets, quintuplets and other groups of prime divisions of note values are virtually absent because of the difficulty of fitting such groups into the serial melodic-harmonic scheme. Certain rhythmic predilections may be noted, especially the "Schoenberg Sigh," consisting of a short note on the strong beat immediately followed by an unstressed long note.

(13) In orchestration, traditional scoring prevails. There is no inclination to introduce exotic or unusual instruments; the flexaton in the score of Schoenberg's *Variations for Orchestra* is an exception. Special percussion effects are alien to the spirit of DODECAPHONIC MUSIC. On the other hand, there is a great variety of sound-color (*Klangfarbe*), with a fine gradation of dynamic elements.

(14) Historically, esthetically and structurally, 12-tone music is an evolutionary product of the ultra-chromatic modalities of the post-Wagnerian school of composition. The algorithms of chromatic convergence and divergence in DODECAPHONIC harmony are common. An experimental proof of this evolutionary origin of DODECAPHONIC melody and harmony may be provided by a calculated cancellation of a minimal number of sharps or flats, never exceeding a shift of a semitone, with the resulting product being an essentially diatonic composition with functional chromatic passing notes. Conversely, a simple diatonic melody may be metamorphosed into a DODECAPHONIC series provided that invariance of the vectorial factor is observed, so that the directional intervalic design remains unaltered. Repeated notes in the original diatonic melody can be replaced by their immediate neighbors. Operating according to these procedures, the Viennese melody *Ach du lieber Augustin,* the initial refrain of which happens to contain 12 notes if the last repeated note is omitted, can be transmuted dodecaphonically according to the following formula, in which the capital letters represent the notes of the original tune, ascending intervals are designated by the plus sign, descending intervals by the minus sign, and the numbers are semitone units: G, A, G + 1, F + 1, E + 1, C + 2, C + 1, D + 2, G + 4, G + 3, E − 1, C. It is to be observed that in this case a conscious effort has been made to retain the first and last notes of the original melody, thus preserving an explicit dominant-tonic relationship.

(15) The hereditary characteristics of the DODECAPHONIC techniques strongly point to their ultimate classical origins. The very foundation of the thematic arrangements in inversions and retrograde forms is an old classical and even pre-classical method of varying a thematic subject. Furthermore, there seems to be a tendency in the works of Schoenberg, Berg and Anton von Webern to extend the field of classical devices, particularly in the use of ostinati composed of a segment of the 12-tone row. Thus the tolerance of an immediate repetition of a thematic tone is extended to the repetition of a thematic fragment.

In view of the possibility of such DODECAPHONIC self-pollination, there is no reason to fear that DODECAPHONIC COMPOSITION would degenerate into an endless permutation of the available 479,001,600 combinations resulting from the factorial algorithm (12!) The second and the third generations of composers of 12-tone music have devised other methods of serial construction, the most interesting of them being a sort of DODECAPHONIC amputation, which reduces the 12-tone row to a hendecaphonic or decaphonic group of thematic notes. An attractive resource is to leave the amputated member of the series completely out of the account until the very end of a composition, when it would suddenly appear like a *tonus ex machina* and, suspended in a protracted fermata, would assert itself as a triumphantly recessive prodigal tonic.

**Duodrama.** DUODRAMA is a modern type of dramatic presentation, in which only two actors conduct a dialogue, usually reciting their reciprocal experiences retrospectively without coming to a dramatic clash. It lends itself naturally to chamber opera.

**Electronic Music.** ELECTRONIC MUSIC was revealed to the world on 5 August 1920 when the Russian engineer and cello player Leon Theremin gave a demonstration of his *Thereminovox* at the Moscow Technological Institute. The apparatus consisted of a set of cathode tubes, a vertical antenna and a metal arc; the sound was produced heterodynamically by the movement of the right hand which changed the electric potential in the area, creating a differential tone which determined the height of pitch. The left hand manipulated the field in the vicinity of the metal arc, regulating the power and the timbre of the sound. In constructing this instrument Theremin seemed to carry out Lenin's dictum that "socialism is proletarian dictatorship plus electrification." Theremin's invention was followed by a number of electronic instruments, among which the most successful was *Les Ondes Martenot*, a keyboard instrument for which a number of modern French composers wrote special works. In Germany, Joerg Mager constructed an electronic instrument which he called *Sphärophon*, and later developed other models, *Partiturophon* and *Kaleidophon*. A more practical and a more successful electronic instrument was *Trautonium* manufactured by Friedrich Trautwein; Hindemith wrote some music for it. Oscar Sala introduced some innovations into the *Trautonium* in an electronic organ which he called *Mixtur-Trautonium*.

Unlimited musical horizons opened to ELECTRONIC MUSIC with the introduction of the so-called *Synthesizers*, capable of producing any frequency with the utmost precision and distribute the relative strength of the overtones so as to create any desired instrumental timbre. With the aid of *Synthesizers* it becomes possible to construct scales of any number of equal degrees. Ernst Krenek wrote a piece of music containing 13 equal parts of the octave. Among the capacities of the modern *Synthesizer* is the reproduction of a recorded composition at any speed without altering the pitch. No problem of articulation arises, for the generation of the sound is electronic, completely independent of all mechanical elements. In 1969 the American engineer, providentially named Moog, perfected a portable synthesizer which advanced the techniques of ELECTRONIC MUSIC still further. The *Moog*, as it came to be called, may well become the house instrument of the second half of the 20th century.

ELECTRONIC MUSIC requires special notation. One of the earliest attempts at a practical system was made in 1937 by Percy Grainger in his *Free Music* for 4 electronic instruments constructed by Theremin, indicating pitch and dynamic intensities in a four-part score on graph paper.

**Elegant Variation.** In his *Modern English Usage*, Fowler describes frivolous verbal substitutions as ELEGANT VARIATIONS. The phrase is suitable, with the application of similar gentle scorn, to some musical procedures. Variations that vary for the sake of variance, with an objective of sophisticated elegance of expression, are as offensive in their tautological and often teratological variety as their counterparts in literary diction. Reger's *Variations on a Theme by Mozart* are typical examples of ELEGANT VARIATION, turgid in reference, redundant in treatment. On the other hand, Rachmaninoff's 18th variation in his *Rhapsody on a Theme of Paganini* is both elegant and varied, for it represents an exact inversion of the minor triadic theme, resulting in a completely transformed, yet morphologically congruent melody, in which the ascending minor triadic figure of the theme becomes a descending major triadic figure.

**Empirical Music.** In application to modern techniques of composition, EMPIRICAL MUSIC suggests a pragmatic rather than an inspirational approach. It is, however, less cerebral, less laboratorian than EXPERIMENTAL MUSIC.

**Enharmonic Ambivalence.** The Janus-like nature of an enharmonic tone, performing two different functions at a modulatory junction, opens the portals of chromatic modulation and establishes a democratic omnivalence of the 12 different tones in dodecaphonic melody and harmony. In this view, chromatic harmony is a functional derivative of ENHARMONIC AMBIVALENCE.

**Entropy.** The luxuriant development of chromatic harmony and the concomitant equalization of enharmonic pairs may be described as musical ENTROPY, in which the component thematic particles become evenly distributed in melody and harmony. In physics, ENTROPY signalizes the dissipation of KINETIC ENERGY, the neutralization of electric potentials and an ultimate thermodynamic stability of inertial matter. The pessimistic cosmology that postulates the eventual end in a total passivity of the universe does not, however, constitute a categorical imperative for composers. Nothing prevents them from reversing the process of ENTROPY and reinstating the primacy of selected modalities. Verdi said: "Torniamo all 'antico: sarà un progresso."

**Environment.** The concept of musical ENVIRONMENT embraces the totality of technical resources. Ideally, the function of a composer is to establish a favorable ENVIRONMENT for these techniques, and apply powerful detergents to remove the accumulated tonal impurities. Particularly toxic is chromatic supererogation; conversely, a fine atonal work may suffer from excessive triadic infusion. The ENVIRONMENT also includes the parameters of VECTORIALISM; spatial arrangement of instruments on the stage is clearly environmental in its function. In this larger sense, the function of ENVIRONMENT comprises not only every technical aspect of musical composition but also the conditions of the performance itself.

**Ethnic Resources.** National musical cultures have developed from two distinct resources: the ethnic legacy and universally adopted techniques of composition. When Villa-Lobos was asked "What is folklore?" he replied, "I am folklore!" By this declaration he meant to say that in his original melodic inventions he gave expression to the artistic consciousness of the Brazilian people. In his *Bachianas brasileiras*, Bachian counterpoint gives ancillary service to ethnic Brazilianism. Charles Ives created single-handedly a modern American idiom that employs ETHNIC RESOURCES in a perfect SYNCRETISM of substance and technique. In Russia, the primacy of ETHNIC RESOURCES is maintained partly by the national spirit of the people and partly by the ideological principles of SOCIALIST REALISM which prescribes the realistic style of music within the framework of national modalities.

Ethnic musical materials are not necessarily incompatible with modern techniques. It is possible to arrange a popular tune dodecaphonically by applying various intervalic extensions and compressions, while retaining the vectorial parameters of the original melody. Perhaps the most congenial modern technique in making use of ETHNIC RESOURCES is PANDIATONICISM, in which the tonal functions are preserved and enhanced.

**Etiology.** The study of causation, or ETIOLOGY, is of importance not only in medicine and physics, but also in the fine arts. Particularly informing is the ETIOLOGY of ultra-modern music which is often likened by hostile observers to a symptom of mass dyscrasia. But to its adepts new music is the revelation of a superior psyche. Dostoyevsky, who suffered from epilepsy, advances the daring notion that during an epileptic *grand mal* the mind penetrates the ultimate mysteries of life and death. Similarly, the manifestations of the musical AVANT-GARDE, whether in the popular or technically complex field, are to their participants the proleptic vistas of the new universal art. Schoenberg, more than any other composer, endured endless abuse on the part of uncomprehending critics, but he never doubted the correctness of his chosen path. Edgar Varèse, who was similarly abused, wrote in a personal letter in 1931: "I know where I am going, and what will follow. My plan is clearly drawn, its development logical, its result assured." In the perspective of history, both Schoenberg and Varèse proved right. The ETIOLOGY of their genius is a lesson for the future.

**Euphony.** Etymologically, EUPHONY implies a happy sound, but it is not necessarily synonymous with consonant harmony. A succession of dissonances, if they follow a natural tonal sequence, may sound entirely euphonious to the ear, while a progression of disembodied open fifths or disemboweled multiple octaves could register as uneuphonious and unsettling. Psychological apperception is the determining factor in this aural impression. Generally speaking, soft dissonances are tolerated better than loud consonances. Even more decisive is the factor of linear EUPHONY. A single line of an atonal melody impresses an untutored ear as an unacceptable dissonance, even though no simultaneous complex of sounds is involved. If an atonal melody were to be performed at a very slow tempo with long silences between the individual notes, no linear disharmony could then result. But the faster the tempo, the more disruptive to the peace of mind does an atonal melody become. It should be remembered that the word *harmonia* meant a melody in ancient Greek music. A rapid succession of tones unconnected by a uniform tonality will appear as a meaningless jumble of notes to an inexperienced listener. On the other hand, a musician trained in the art of listening to serial music will accept atonal melodies as legitimate expressions of a musical sentiment. The linearity of melody depends exclusively on the instant dampening of a sound in the cochlea without a tinnitus, but the memory of the previous sound persists, much in the manner that the retina of the eye retains the static images of a cinematographic film. It would be interesting to speculate on the possible course of music as an art if the cochlea, too, possessed the ability to retain sounds for a fraction of a second. Suffice it to say that all music, vocal, instrumental or percussive, would then become polyphonic.

**Evolution and Devolution.** In a famous definition, Herbert Spencer describes the process of EVOLUTION as an integration of matter and concomitant dissipation of motion, during which matter passes from an indefinite, incoherent homogeneity to a definite, coherent heterogeneity. He specifically included music in this process, with reference to the increasing complexity resulting from rhythmic changes and modulatory progressions, its specialization and its gradual differentiation from poetry, drama and dance. In recent times, however, the evolutionary process has been reversed. Once more, as in antiquity, music has entered into an intimate association with the theater and dance in the modern genre of MIXED MEDIA. ALEATORY procedures have accentuated the DEVOLUTION of music by increasing the element of homogeneity and the degree of randomness of distribution of constructive elements. It may be argued that DEVOLUTION was unavoidable since the integration of music in the Spencerian sense has achieved its maximum of coherence in such techniques as the dodecaphonic method, and that a recoil from the stone wall of determinism reversed the evolutionary process, resulting in an esthetic passivity, in which kinetic energy is reduced to zero. In the practice of the AVANT-GARDE, the demobilization of technical resources has reached the point of melorhythmic asceticism, with only a few different notes being used in an entire work, as though emulating the legendary philosopher Cratylus who spent his declining years by moving the index finger of his right hand to and fro in front of his nose in the firm belief that this motion was the only demonstrable truth.

**Experimental Music.** All music is EXPERIMENTAL; tradition is merely a congealed experiment. Chromatic harmony was EXPERIMENTAL in Wagner's time, and its ultimate dodecaphonic development became the most important type of EXPERIMENTAL MUSIC of the 20th century. Perhaps the most literally correct application of EXPERIMENTAL MUSIC is represented by aleatory operations, in which the manipulator merely sets the scene of action and nature supplies an EXPERIMENTAL answer. With every turn of the esthetic wheel, EXPERIMENTAL MUSIC was decried and deprecated by the adepts of the preceding prevalent style as repugnant to normal senses. In the second half of the 20th century, EXPERIMENTAL MUSIC finally moved into its proper enclave, that of the laboratory, where composers and experimenters conducted their research with electronic instruments and computers. There is a danger, however, that an imaginative computer may be hampered in its inventive productions by the limitations of the musical engineer who would program the data so as to adapt them to a preordained order, and in so doing would convert the machine into a mere servant. In one of such man-made pseudo-computerized compositions, the ending consists of a protracted C major coda which no computer in its right mental circuit could possibly turn out. The only valid programming of musical composition is that generated by a collection of random numbers ejaculated like so many embryonic sea-horses out

1446

of their male parent's pouch, to be translated into notes and rhythms according to a predetermined code. In all such experiments caution should be taken to prevent a disgorgement of data from becoming a personal regurgitation of the programmer.

**Expressionism.** EXPRESSIONISM stands in a reciprocal relationship to IMPRESSIONISM, as its functional and psychological counterpart. IMPRESSIONISM derives its source of inspiration from external sources, whereas EXPRESSIONISM conjures up its images in the inner world of the human psyche and exteriorizes its states as an intimate subjective report. IMPRESSIONISM tends to be pictorial and exotic; EXPRESSIONISM is introspective and metaphysical. Impressionistic literature, art and music are easily projected outside; EXPRESSIONISM is an arcane medium, born in the deepest recesses of the psychic complex and cannot easily be translated into the common language of the arts. The receiver of colorful images of Impressionist art or music has the means of comparing the precise reality with the artist's impressions of it. No such scale of comparison is available to an outside recipient of Expressionist art, for it is a product of the artist's dream in which the dreamer experiences shock and surprise despite the fact that he is both the author and the victim of his own dreams. Because of this duality of the Expressionistic process, the art of EXPRESSIONISM itself suffers from the trauma of illogic; it is characterized by the breakdown of illation and by the disruption of the consequential processes of psychic transmission. The unreality of EXPRESSIONIST drama, poetry, painting and music, is the greatest obstacle for general comprehension. But once the curtain is removed and the secret images of a dreamer reach the observer in the form of poetry, art or music, EXPRESSIONISM becomes a universal medium of mass communication and the greatest multiplier of artistic emotion.

It is natural that because of the basic antinomy between the sources of IMPRESSIONISM and EXPRESSIONISM, each should generate a distinctive musical language. IMPRESSIONISM thrives on equilibrated euphony of harmonious dissonances, while EXPRESSIONISM prefers the harsh syntax of ATONALITY. The coloristic opulence of Impressionist music is obtained through the expansion of tonal materials into the spacious structures of resonant harmonies and exotic scales. EXPRESSIONISM, on the other hand, communicates its deep-seated anxieties through chromatic congestion and atonal dispersion. IMPRESSIONISM builds its thematic contents on fluctuating modality, block harmonies and parallel progressions of triadic formations. EXPRESSIONISM rejects modality, tonality and all diatonic textures. Its melodies are constructed parabolically, away from a putative tonic. In its evocation of the classical past, IMPRESSIONISM integrates the diatonic materials into the enhanced edifices of PANDIATONICISM. The harmonic idiom of EXPRESSIONISM is formed by the superposition of fourths and fifths. Progressions of consecutive perfect fourths or fifths result in the formation of 12 different notes in a panchromatic complex, preparing the foundation of the method of composing with 12 tones related only to one another, as formulated by Schoenberg.

There are profound differences in the historic, cultural and geographic factors in the development of IMPRESSIONISM and EXPRESSIONISM. IMPRESSIONISM is Gallic, EXPRESSIONISM Germanic. The French syllabification of IMPRESSIONISTIC poetry is a paradigm of euphonious instrumentation, with the vowels acquiring specific weights and distinctive colors. The German texts of EXPRESSIONIST songs offer no sonorous gratification of resonant vocables, but in their guttural strength they seem to deepen the penetration of the philosophical and often mystical notions underlying the words.

Though IMPRESSIONISM in music is a close counterpart of pictorial art, no Impressionist composer of any stature has ever tried his hand at painting pictures. EXPRESSIONISM is basically a psychic development with no esthetic contact with painting, and yet composers of the Expressionist school, notably Schoenberg and Berg, possessed a striking talent for painting in the EXPRESSIONIST style. Jef Golyscheff, the composer of early atonal music, emigrated to Brazil and became an Expressionist painter. Carl Ruggles, an American composer who developed a sui generis EXPRESSIONIST style in an atonal idiom, abandoned composition entirely and devoted himself to abstract painting.

**Fasciculation.** In view of the vagueness of such terms as section, part, division, subdivision, period, phrase, etc., it might be useful to introduce into musical nomenclature the term FASCICLE to designate a self-sufficient fragment of a musical work. Particularly, it is useful in application to serial music. In dodecaphonic exposition, FASCICLE I, FASCICLE II, FASCICLE III and FASCICLE IV would indicate the four forms of the basic tone-row. In NEO-CLASSICAL compositions FASCICULATION may easily replace the conventional Baroque designations of sequences, modulatory digressions and the like. This type of nomenclature may also contribute to the analytical clarity of theoretical discussion.

**Fetishes and Taboos.** In the inexorable course of history and of the arts, FETISHES of yesterday become TABOOS of tomorrow. The following modernistic FETISHES of the recent musical past have become TABOOS: (1) The diminished-seventh chord, once favored by Italian opera composers, the *Accorde di Stupefazione*, used to melodramatize the high points in operatic action. Verdi, who was responsible for some of the most effective applications of this "Chord of Stupefaction," often in parallel chromatic progressions, in his own operas, issued a stern warning to young composers not to abuse it. No self-respecting composer of today would resort to such unsophisticated practices, except for musical persiflage. (2) Tonal sequences, particularly those rising or descending by degrees, known as *Rosalias*, after an old popular Italian ballad, "Rosalia, mia cara." Indeed, sequences of any kind have virtually disappeared from 20th-century music. (3) The WHOLE-TONE SCALE, once a FETISH of IMPRESSIONISM, has now sunk into noxious desuetude as a cinematic effect used to portray strutting Nazis, mad scientists or schizoid females on the sound track. (4) Parallel progressions of major-ninth chords and consecutive formations of second inversions of major triads at intervals of minor thirds, one of the most prized formulas of IMPRESSIONISM. (5) The *Pétrouchka Chord*, known also as *Parisian Chord*, consisting of two major triads at the distance of a tritone. This early instance of BITONALITY, which became a FETISH of modern French music in the second quarter of the 20th century has been disfranchised and relegated to the category of FRAUDULENT MODERNISM. There are even signs and tokens on the firmament that the sacrosanct FETISH of the 20th century, the DODECAPHONIC method of composition, is on the point of deciduous decay, losing its dodecuple integrity and degenerating into the lipogrammatic hendecaphonic or decaphonic series.

**Formalism.** The term FORMALISM has acquired a specific pejorative meaning in Soviet esthetics, as a method inimical to the essence of desirable art. The *Encyclopedic Music Dictionary*, published in Moscow in 1966, defines FORMALISM as follows: "FORMALISM represents an artificial separation of form from content, and the attribution to formal elements of self-sufficient primary values to the detriment of musical content. . . . In contemporary esthetics, FORMALISM becomes a method of art hostile to realism and cultivated especially by the adepts of MODERNISM. FORMALISM is based on the theory of art for art's sake, counterposing the artist to society and art itself to life, seeking to create an artistic form detached from objective reality. The governing precepts of FORMALISM are the negation of ideological and realistic content of a work of art, a construction of arbitrary new forms, combined with the denial of national cultural heritage. In the final analysis, FORMALISM results in the abolition of artistic imagery and disintegration of formal coherence. In musical practice, FORMALISM rejects the ideational and emotional musical values and denies the capacity of a musical work to reflect reality. Proponents of FORMALISM attempt to justify their fallacious doctrine by pointing out the specific nature of music as an art lacking the external connection with the world of real objects, such as is present in painting or sculpture, and intrinsically incapable of conveying a concrete narrative characteristic of literature. The esthetic teaching of Marxism refutes FORMALISM by a scientific approach to music as a special form of social ideology. The reactionary theories of FORMALISM are assiduously cultivated in books and articles by the apologists of musical MODERNISM. The struggle for the correct formulation of SOCIALIST REALISM leads to the removal of FORMALISM from its pedestal. One should not confuse FORMALISM, however, with genuine individual originality or with true innovation in the field of musical forms and in the inner substance of a composition, which constitute an unalienable part of authentic realistic art."

**Formant.** FORMANT is an acoustical term, indicating the relative strength of partial overtones that determines the timbre of a musical instrument. In ultra-modern nomenclature, a FORMANT is the catalytic element that forms, deforms and transforms a given timbre into another by means of electronic manipulation.

**Fraudulent Modernism.** Commercially successful composers of marketable semi-classical music, eager to gain esthetic equality with sophisticated musicians, like to inject dissonant notes into their ABECEDARIAN and often ANALPHABETIC productions; proudly, they exhibit pieces using 12 different notes in a more or less chromatic order to earn membership in socially distinguished DODECAPHONIC circles. A combination of emaciated melodies in a spurious atonal manner and dietetic harmonies heavily spiced with discordant irrelevancies, is the essence of FRAUDULENT MODERNISM. Its adepts often parade in panel discussions, glibly bandying about mispronounced names of the latest celebrities of the AVANT-GARDE. FRAUDULENT MODERNISM fails because of the technical inadequacy of its practitioners and of their naive belief that wrong notes are the credentials of advanced sophistication.

**Frugal Ankyloglossia.** Art thrives on economy of means, but modernistic frugality must not be allowed to reach the point of tonal ANKYLOGLOSSIA. The criterion is a freedom of expression without cacuminal retroflection.

**Furniture Music.** In his sustained effort to degrade music and to reduce it to a menial level, Erik Satie was prompted to inaugurate a demonstration of *Musique d'ameublement,* which he defined as "new music played during intermission at theatrical events or at a concert, designed to create a certain ambience." At an actual performance at the Paris Art Gallery, Satie placed his musicians in separate groups, and urged the public to treat them as functional objects, to speak loudly and not to listen with professional attention. The performers were free to play anything they wished regardless of the repertoire selected by their confrères.

**Futurism.** FUTURISM is a modern movement in the arts that emerged in Italy early in the 20th century, under the aegis of the Italian poet Marinetti. Its musical credo was formulated by Balilla Pratella in his *Manifesto of Futurist Musicians* issued in Milan on 11 October 1910 and supplemented by a *Technical Manifesto of Futurist Music* of 11 March 1911. On 11 March 1913 Luigi Russolo published his own *Futurist Manifesto.* In these declarations the Italian FUTURISTS proclaimed their complete disassociation from classical, romantic and IMPRESSIONIST music and announced their aim to build an entirely new music inspired by the reality of life in the new century, with the machine as the source of inspiration. And since modern machines were most conspicuous by the noise they made, Pratella and Russolo created a new art of noises, *Arte dei Rumori.* Russolo designed special noise instruments and subdivided them into six categories. His instruments were rudimentary and crude, with amplification obtained by megaphones, but there is no denying that the Futurists provided a prophetic vision of the electronic future of fifty years later. It is interesting to note that most Futurist musicians and poets were also painters. Their pictures, notably those of Luigi Russolo, emphasized color rather than machine-like abstractions, and generally approximated the manner of Abstract EXPRESSIONISM. In the music by Pratella and others we find a profusion of modern devices of their Futurist day, with a foremost place given to the WHOLE-TONE SCALE. The Futurists gave monody preference over polyphony, and steady rhythm to asymmetry. The future of the Futurists appears passé, but they opened the gates to the experimenters of the actual chronological future, which none of them lived to witness.

**Game Music.** Games of musical compositions, in which cards, each containing a musical phrase, are put together according to special rules, are of considerable antiquity. One such game, *Musikalisches Würfelspiel,* was put on the market in London in 1806 and was announced as "Mozart's musical game, enclosed in an elegant box instructing in a system of easy composition by mechanical means of an unlimited number of waltzes, rondos, hornpipes, reels and minuets." The attribution to Mozart is spurious, but the game itself has a certain ingenuity. The players were to throw a pair of dice, and the number indicated the particular card containing a musical phrase. Since the sequence was arranged so that each card was interchangeable with other cards containing melodies in approximately the same range set in similar harmonies, there was obviously no danger of running into difficulties. A much more modern conceit was suggested by an English musician William Hayes in his book entitled *The Art of Composing Music by a Method Entirely New, Suited to the Meanest Capacity,* published in 1751, in which the author, with a rather crude satirical intent, explained the principle of the game: "Take a brush with stiff bristles (like a toothbrush), dip it into an inkwell, and, by scraping the bristles with the finger, spatter with one sweep a whole composition onto the staff paper. You have only to add stems, bar lines, slurs, etc., to make the opus ready for immediate performance. Whole and half-notes are entirely absent, but who cares for sustained tones anyway!" This is indeed a proleptic anticipation of methods of composition used by the AVANT-GARDE 200 years after the publication of this lively manual.

An interesting modern game can be devised using several sets of dodecaphonic cards, each set containing all 12 notes of the chromatic scale. The deck is shuffled and distributed among players. One after another, the players put down duplicates in their hands and collect a missing note of the next dodecaphonic series from the cards put down by other players. The winner is the player who first assembles all 12 different notes.

The most ambitious musical game of the modern era is *Stratégie* by Iannis Xenakis, first performed at the Venice Festival on 23 April 1963. In it, two conductors lead two different orchestras in two uncoordinated works. The audience declares the winner, taking into consideration the excellence of each orchestral group, marking points on the scoreboard for most striking rhythms, best color effects and finest instrumental solos.

Modern scores descriptive of games are numerous. Arthur Honegger wrote a symphonic movement *Rugby*, Arthur Bliss composed a ballet entitled *Checkmate*, Paul Reif selected *Philidor's Defense* as the title of a work for a chamber orchestra, inspired by a chess game played in 1858. Stravinsky portrayed a poker game in his *Jeu de Cartes*, a ballet in three deals in which the joker is defeated by a royal flush in hearts. A more abstract score by Stravinsky, entitled *Agon*, also portrays a game. Debussy's ballet score *Jeux* depicts an allegorical game of tennis.

**Gauche Dexterity.** Satire and burlesque depend for their effect on a deliberate violation of traditional rules of melodic structure, rhythmic symmetry and harmonic euphony. A sophisticated imitation of such semi-literate gaucherie often becomes an art in itself. Examples are many: Stravinsky reproduces the heterogeneous harmony of the barrel organ in *Pétrouchka*; Darius Milhaud tonalizes the natural cacophony of a barroom in the score of *Le Bœuf sur le toit*. Erik Satie elevated the dexterity of his gaucherie into a high art of musical persiflage; he was helped in it by his lack of an academic technique of composition; it was easier for him than for real masters to imitate ineptitude.

**Gebrauchsmusik.** The term GEBRAUCHSMUSIK, or Utilitarian Music, came into vogue shortly after the end of World War I; its earliest mention is found in the German magazine *Signale für die Musikalische Welt* of December 1918. GEBRAUCHSMUSIK promoted the utilization of new mechanical instruments, the radio, the phonograph and music for the films. A variety of GEBRAUCHSMUSIK was GEMEINSCHAFTSMUSIK, Community music, which cultivated choral singing. The term GEMEINSCHAFTSMUSIK was later changed to Sing- und Spielmusik, in the generic category of HAUSMUSIK. Probably the first work written specially for such groups by a modern composer was *Das neue Werk* by Paul Hindemith. Stylistically, GEBRAUCHSMUSIK has developed a type of modern melody, rhythm, harmony and orchestration making free use of utilitarian dissonance, polytonal combinations and polymetric arrangements. An innovation in GEBRAUCHSMUSIK is spoken rhythmic song, a variant of SPRECHSTIMME. In opera, the librettos were usually satirical and political, with a radical bent, especially PROLETARIAN MUSIC. From Germany, operatic GEBRAUCHSMUSIK was transplanted to America, where economic impoverishment contributed to its popularity. GEBRAUCHSMUSIK had little success in Russia, France or Italy, countries with a rich operatic culture, in which there was no necessity of reducing operatic productions to miniature dimensions. HAUSMUSIK, and GEBRAUCHSMUSIK in general, relied on the participation of the audience. Children's music is a natural product of GEBRAUCHSMUSIK. Hindemith wrote the first piece of GEBRAUCHSMUSIK designed specially for singing and acting by children, *Wir bauen eine Stadt*.

**Gemeinschaftsmusik.** GEMEINSCHAFTSMUSIK is a term used by German composers to designate communal singing or playing; although of ancient origin, the practice was popularized as part of the program of HAUSMUSIK, in the generic category of GEBRAUCHSMUSIK.

**Gestalt.** GESTALT is a fashionable psychological term which, in an attractively misapprehended scientific German nomenclature, connotes an ensemble of apperceptions produced by a series of sensory stimuli. The word, which can be literally translated as form, figure or appearance, indicates a psychological interaction between the physical nature of a given phenomenon and the inner interpretation of it by a receptive mind. The shape of a white vase against a uniformly black background, may be perceived as two human figures facing each other if the symmetric sides of the vase are drawn to resemble silhouettes. In music, GESTALT is capable of many interpretations, of which the most literal is enharmonic ambivalence, as for instance the perception of a triad as a dissonance in the context of alien harmonies. Thus, if a C major triad is sounded immediately after an unrelated dominant-seventh chord based on E-flat, the ear would demand its resolution into the dissonant syndrome of the preceding dominant-seventh chord. Generally speaking, GESTALT is apprehended as an entire ensemble of musical parameters, comprising form, proportional distribution of consonances and dissonances, diatonic or chromatic tropism, symmetry or asymmetry of melorhythmic figurations, etc.

**Graphic Notation.** Ever since 1000 A.D. when Guido d'Arezzo drew a line to mark the arbitrary height of pitch, musical notation has been geometric in its symbolism. The horizontal coordinate of the music staff still represents the temporal succession of melodic notes, and the vertical axis indicates the simultaneous use of two or more notes in a chord. Duration values have, through the centuries of evolution, been indicated by the color and shape of notes and stems to which they were attached. The composers of the AVANT-GARDE, eager to reestablish the mathematical correlation between the coordinates of the musical axes have written scores in which the duration was indicated by proportional distance between the notes. Undoubtedly such geometrical precision contributes to the audio-visual clarity of notation, but it is impractical in actual usage. A passage in whole-notes or half-notes followed by a section in rapid rhythms would be more difficult to read than the imprecise notation inherited from the past. In orchestral scores, there is an increasing tendency to cut off the inactive instrumental parts in the middle of the page rather than to strew such vacuums with a rash of rests. A graphic system of tablature notation was launched in Holland under the name *Klavarskribo*, an Esperanto word meaning keyboard writing. It has been adopted in many schools in Holland.

New sounds demanded new notational symbols. Henry Cowell, who invented tone-clusters, notated them by drawing thick vertical lines attached to a stem. Similar notation was used for similar effects by the Russian composer Vladimir Rebikov. In his book, *New Musical Resources*, Cowell tackled the problem of non-binary rhythmic division and outlined a plausible system that would satisfy this need by using square, triangular and rhomboid shapes of notes. Alois Hába of Czechoslovakia, a pioneer in microtonal music, devised special notation for quarter-tones, third-tones and sixth-tones.

As long as the elements of pitch, duration, intervalic extension and polyphonic simultaneity remain in force, the musical staff can accommodate these elements more or less adequately. Then noises were introduced by the Italian Futurists into their works. In his compositions, the Futurist Luigi Russolo drew a network of curves, thick lines and zigzags to represent each particular noise. But still the measure and the proportional lengths of duration retained their validity. The situation changed dramatically with the introduction of ALEATORY processes and the notion of indeterminacy of musical elements. The visual appearance of aleatory scores assumes the aspect of ideograms. John Cage, in particular, remodeled the old musical notation so as to give improvisatory latitude to the performer. The score of his *Variations I* suggests the track of cosmic rays in a cloud chamber. His *Cartridge Music* looks like an exploding supernova, and his *Fontana Mix* is a projection of irregular curves upon a strip of graph paper. The Polish Avant-Garde composer Krzysztof Penderecki uses various graphic symbols to designate such effects as the highest possible sound on a given instrument, free improvisation within a certain limited range of chromatic notes, or icositetraphonic tone-clusters.

In music for MIXED MEDIA, notation ceases to function per se, giving way to pictorial representation of the actions or psychological factors involved. Indeed, the modern Greek composer Jani Christou introduces the Greek letter *psi* to indicate the psychology of the musical action, with geometric ideograms and masks symbolizing changing mental states ranging from complete passivity to panic. The score of *Passion According to Marquis de Sade* by Sylvano Bussotti looks like a surrealistic painting with musical notes strewn across its path. The British Avant-Garde composer Cornelius Cardew draws black and white circles, triangles and rectangles to indicate musical action. Iannis Xenakis prefers to use numbers and letters indicating the specific tape recordings to be used in his musical structures. Some composers abandon the problem of notation entirely, recording their inspirations on tape.

The attractiveness of a visual pattern is a decisive factor. The American avant-garde composer Earle Brown draws linear abstractions of singular geometric excellence. Karlheinz Stockhausen often supplements his analytical charts by elucidatory (or tantalizingly obscurative) annotations.

The chess grandmaster Tarrasch said of a problematical chess move: "If it is ugly, it is bad." *Mutatis mutandis*, the same criterion applies to a composer's musical graph.

**Gymnosophistical Homophony.** The description Gymnosophist is applied to an Indian sect that flourished about 1,000 A.D. who preached abstinence from carnal delights, refused to wear clothes and limited themselves to the simplest modes of communication. Etymologically, the word is derived from the Greek roots for "naked" and "wisdom." Archaizing usages and affectation of utmost simplicity in musical composition may well be called GYMNOSOPHISTICAL; naked fifths, in particular, when applied ostentatiously in modern works, creating the impression of luxurious abstemiousness, are GYMNOSOPHISTICAL. Erik Satie, in his sophisticated practice of GYMNOSOPHISTICAL harmonies in such works as *Gymnopédies*, provides a perfect example of the style, deliberately bleak in its renunciation of harmonious carnality and yet thoroughly modern in its invocation of secret rites and suggested aberrations. For different reasons, Stravinsky adopted GYMNOSOPHISTICAL modalities in his neo-Grecian works, as a reaction against the proliferation of colorful sonorities in instrumental music, including his own. GYMNOSOPHISTICAL HOMOPHONY is a natural medium also for neo-ecclesiastical composition in quintal or quartal gemination.

**Happenings.** A HAPPENING is a colloquial gerund that has assumed a substantive value as a result of collective activities among American theater workers, painters, poets and musicians in the 1950's. The word itself was first used in this sense in the 1959 issue of the *Anthologist*, a review published by Rutgers University. It featured an article by Allan Kaprow, teacher of Art History at Rutgers, entitled *The Demiurge*, in which he announced his aim of creating an entirely new art. As an illustration he appended the outline of a script, with a caption, "Something to Take Place: a HAPPENING." Kaprow and others staged in October 1956 in a New York art gallery, a production under the name 18 HAPPENINGS in 6 parts. The audience was distributed in 14 groups seated in chairs at random, and its participation in the action was earnestly solicited. The spectacle was synesthetic, with sound, multicolored lights, and peripheral tactile and olfactory impressions. There were also "visual poems," of the graffiti type, randomly lettered in crayon on walls and placards, with such communications as "My Toilet is Shared by the Man Next Door who is Italian." The musical part consisted of aleatory superfetations of loudspeaking musical and anti-musical sounds. Activities included various commonplace HAPPENINGS performed with the meaningful air of an artistic act. Allan Kaprow made an ex post facto statement bemoaning his choice of the word HAPPENING as unfortunate, but conceded that it helped him to achieve an all-embracing inclusivity in describing the uninhibited exhibits of the AVANT-GARDE. In the meantime, HAPPENING entered the language, penetrating the common speech so deeply that everyday events are often described as HAPPENINGS simply because they have taken place at all. The term became popular in Europe as Le Happening, El Happening, Il Happening or Das Happening.

**Hausmusik.** After a long period of alienation from the masses, modern composers in Germany came to the conviction that music should cease to be a hermetic art for select audiences and should be returned to its source, the home. HAUSMUSIK, as such "home music" became known, was a development parallel to GEBRAUCHSMUSIK. Dissonant harmony and asymmetric rhythms were not excluded, as long as the performance did not present technical difficulties. Usually HAUSMUSIK was written for voices or SPRECHSTIMME, with piano accompaniment and obbligato parts for instruments easy to play, such as recorders, clarinets and violins.

**Hebetude and Lubricity.** A recipe for a musical work providing sensory and intellectual gratification is a judicious mixture of dissonant HEBETUDE and euphonious LUBRICITY. As a product of intellectual elucubration, hebetudinous abstruseness results from indiscriminate use of Dodecaphonic, Hendecaphonic, Pandiatonic or Polymodal Combinatorialities. Modernistic LUBRICITY, on the other hand, flows from an incontinent evacuation of artificially flavored euphonious fluids sublimated in a feculent plasma. Hebetudinous excogitations by Hesychastically minded introverts occasionally reveal serendipitous technicalities of interest, as demonstrated by tonal inventions in *Die Maschine* by Fritz Klein, while lubriciously scabrous effluvia of an ABECEDARIAN composer are usually productive of homogeneous sonic matter of glutinous consistency, fetid, infertile and degenerate.

**Hendecaphonic Serialism.** With the gradual relaxation of dodecaphonic strictures in the orthodox Schoenbergian doctrine, serial composers have begun to resort to a lipogrammatic device of omitting a member of a 12-tone subject, reducing the series to a HENDECAPHONIC form, containing only 11 tones. The missing tone, conspicuous by its absence, may be introduced in the coda with a panache suggesting the apparition of an actual tonic.

**Hirsute Chromaticism.** A judicious mixture of chromatic and diatonic modes in a serial work is entirely valid as a mode, idiom or a style. What cannot be tolerated in a modern composition of any pretensions to self-consistency is the hairy growth of chromatics upon a diatonic or pandiatonic melodic and harmonic surface, with membranous pellicles obscuring the melorhythmic lines without protecting them. When instances of such HIRSUTE CHROMATICISM occur inadvertently, a depilatory agent should be applied in order to restore the basic musical design. At the same time, care should be taken not to fall into the extremes of unesthetic alopecia.

**Homeological Variations.** Modern variations are often derived from a subject by topological extensions and compressions of the constituent intervals and rhythms, a process known as HOMEOLOGICAL. This term denotes the compatibility of geometric figures which can be topologically altered without disrupting the continuity of their perimeters. Thus, a triangle can be stretched or crumpled like rubber and brought into congruity with a square or a circle, but not with a torus which is morphologically non-congruent with triangles, squares or circles. In modern music, a diatonic melody may be analogously compressed and extended by intervalic changes, but it cannot be converted into a pointillistic configuration or a hocketus, without violating topological laws.

**Homonymity.** In music, as in verbal communication, identical sounds often acquire different connotations according to the context. For example, *mental process* in anatomy refers not to the state of mind but to the bony promontory that forms the chin, the key word being derived from *mentum*, chin, not from *mens*, mind, while the word *process* comes from proceed in the sense of outgrowth. A C-major chord, if written with an F-flat instead of E, loses its white immaculacy and becomes a dissonant suspension over the A-flat major triad. HOMONYMITY plays a particularly significant role in DODECAPHONIC MUSIC. A segment of a 12-tone series may prove to be homonymous with another segment of another form of the same series. This fragmentary replication is of great structural importance in the theory and practice of COMBINATORIALITY.

**Hörspiel.** In search of a term that would apply to a great variety of musical works, the practitioners of GEBRAUCHSMUSIK in Germany selected the generic appellation HÖRSPIEL. Literally, HÖRSPIEL means a play for hearing: usually it is a short composition for a solo instrument, a small instrumental ensemble, or a choral group. In its idiom, a HÖRSPIEL should not appear strange to untutored ears, but non-toxic dissonances should not be shunned. A HÖRSPIEL is related to the practice of HAUSMUSIK.

**Icositetraphony.** As the etymology of the term indicates, ICOSITETRAPHONY deals with music using 24 equal intervals in an octave (icosi = 20; tetra = 4; phone = sound), i.e., in quarter-tones. A tone-row composed of 24 different notes in quarter-tones is an icositetraphonic series. In modern works ICOSITETRAPHONY usually occurs in conglomerates, as in the coda of Krzysztof Penderecki's *Threnody for the Victims of Hiroshima* and in Sergei Slonimsky's *Concerto Buffo*.

**Illation.** In logic and rhetoric, ILLATION is a conclusion drawn from given premises. In music, ILLATION represents a consistent development of thematic ideas, a logical progression from one idea to the next. ILLATION is particularly important in DODECAPHONIC structures, in which the basic series serves as a postulate from which all subsequent patterns are derived.

**Imbricated Counterpoint.** Canonic imitation in stretto formation may be described as IMBRICATED COUNTERPOINT, because it follows the pattern of roof shingles or tiles, all of the same size and all partly covered by adjacent shingles.

**Immaculacy.** The irresistible attraction that C major exercises on many modern composers is a curious phenomenon. Scriabin ends his *Poème de l'Extase* with a protracted coda of IMMACULATE C major in a veritable sunburst of white-hot flame on the waves of the luminiferous ether. C major was also the favorite key of Prokofiev, a composer whose esthetic precepts were diametrically opposed to Scriabin's; to him C major was simply a pianistic convenience lying naturally under the fingers. Pianistically, C major is associated with whiteness, but on many old keyboard instruments the keys of diatonic C major were black. Also pianistic in origin is PANDIATONICISM; a great many pandiatonic constructions in piano works are examples of C-major IMMACULACY. Even Schoenberg, for all of his anti-triadic teachings, succumbed to the temptation: his *Piano Concerto* ends on an enhanced C-major chord.

**Impressionism.** The term IMPRESSIONISM was first used in an article by Louis Leroy published in the Paris journal *Charivari* in its issue of 25 April 1874, to characterize the type of painting cultivated by French artists who exhibited at the Paris Salon des Refusés, with specific reference to *Sunrise* by Claude Monet, subtitled "an impression." This painting was Impressionistic in the sense that it brought out the subjective impact of the landscape on the artist, as it registered in his inner eye. Far from being offended by the irony implied in the word IMPRESSIONISM, the French modernists of the time accepted it as an honorable title. It was not the first time in cultural and political history that a sobriquet intended as a pejorative appellation was elevated to the dignity of a dictionary definition. When the French aristocrats dismissed the Paris revolutionaries as sans-culottes, because they did not wear the culottes, the knee breeches, the expression was adopted triumphantly by the populace. When the German Kaiser described the British expeditionary force in World War I as "a contemptible little army," the English gleefully accepted this depreciative nomination, turning its sharp point against the Germans themselves as their vaunted superiority began to crumble. A group of American realistic painters, active in the first decade of the 20th century was described as Ashcan School by reactionary critics, and it was under that name that the group had proudly entered the annals of American art. The term Baroque originally meant uncouth, ungainly or bizarre, but it has risen in its semantical evolution to represent the noblest period in the history of fine arts.

Only slightly less derisive than IMPRESSIONISM was the term Symbolism, applied to modern French poets whose imagery dealt with symbols rather than with realities. The word Symbolism appeared for the first time in print in the Paris daily *Le Figaro* of 18 September 1886. As IMPRESSIONISM in art, Symbolism was the product of a reaction against the hegemony of academic realism. The painter Courbet said, "Le réalisme c'est la négation de l'idéal." To poets and to painters alike, music was the supreme medium of artistic expression. Paul Verlaine formulated this belief in the famous line, "De la musique avant toute chose." He insisted that words themselves should be selected for the quality of their sound: "Les mots seront choisis en tant que sonores." Gauguin declared that he sought to achieve a musical expression in his exotic paintings: "Je cherche plus la suggestion que la description, comme le fait la musique." Conversely, the spectrum of light appears as a determining factor of musical expression to composers of the Impressionist school. Debussy spoke of "lumière sonore," such as is produced by an analytical diffraction of tones. The constant interchange of auditory and visual aspects in music and in art is illustrated by the titles both of Impressionist paintings and musical compositions. Whistler gave musical captions to his paintings—Symphonies, Nocturnes—while titles of Debussy's works are often taken from painting—Esquisses, Images. Poets were apt to speak of music that can be seen and of paintings that can be heard. After hearing Debussy's *Prélude à l'Après-midi d'un Faune*, Stéphane Mallarmé, whose poem inspired the work, inscribed the book to Debussy, with a quatrain, which equates word, light and sound in one sensation: "Sylvain d'haleine première/ Si ta flûte a réussi/ Ouïs toute la lumière/ Qu'y soufflera Debussy!" In a modern tale of fantasy a scientist transplants the optical nerve to the ear and the auditory nerve to the eye, so that the human subjects on whom he performed this experiment heard colors and saw tones.

In *Les Fleurs du Mal*, Baudelaire said: "J'aime avec fureur les choses où le son se mêle à la lumière."

The interpenetrability of all senses, including the olfactory and the gustatory, was the dream of poets, artists and musicians. Baudelaire wrote: "Les parfums, les couleurs et les sons se répondent." In his essays *À rebours*, Huysmans conjures up an organ of liqueurs. As the organist pulls out the stops, each discharges a drop of wine accompanied by the sound of corresponding instrumental color. The clarinet gives the taste of curaçao sec; the oboe serves kummel; for the flute there is anisette; for the trombone gin and whiskey, while the tuba filters strong vodka.

The flight from nominalism among poets, painters and musicians of France a hundred years ago had a touch of mystical taboo which forbade the naming of the deity in primitive religions. Mallarmé wrote: "To name an object is to suppress three quarters of the enjoyment of a poem; to divine gradually, to suggest, that is the dream." In order to be effective, art had to be a matrix of uncertainties. The French poet Charles Brugnot wrote the lines which Ravel selected as an epigraph for his piano suite *Gaspard de la nuit*: "Je croyais entendre/ une vague harmonie enchanter mon sommeil/ et près de moi s'épandre un murmure pareil/ aux chants entrecoupés d'une voix triste et tendre."

Above all, Impressionism should not serve a utilitarian purpose or perform a function. Henri de Regnier spoke of "le plaisir délicieux et toujours nouveau d'une occupation inutile." Ravel put these words in the score of his *Valses nobles et sentimentales*.

If the aim of Impressionism is to suggest uncertain images, then such images must be clothed in uncertain sounds; in music such sounds are dissonances. The yearning desire for dissonant harmonies can be traced back to Horace's pithy oxymoron, "Concordia discors," and to Keats, who said that "discords make the sweetest airs." Verlaine was explicit when he spoke poetically of "accords harmonieusement dissonants." Dissonances are indeed harmonious in Impressionist music as discordant tones are suspended in airy equilibrium above the sustained basses that support columns of natural overtones.

Walter Pater said: "Impressionism is a vivid personal reflection of a fugitive effect." Spectral evanescence lies in the nature of Impressionist art and music. Sounds that suggest perfumes are ephemeral; they shimmer, they waver, and they vanish. Impressionist melodies are transparencies of a magic lantern; the images succeed each other without organic cohesion. There is no thematic development; the progress of the music depends on contrasts of contiguous thematic statements and colorful juxtapositions of sound. Impressionism shuns the grandiosity of epic arts and the emotionalism of romance. No human passions invest the scores of Impressionist music, and the sonorities are never overwhelming. It is characteristic of Impressionist composers that in the selection of their subjects they favor the moon over the sun. Verlaine's poem *Clair de Lune* inspired Debussy's famous piano piece. Schoenberg, in his *Pierrot lunaire*, a work that possesses distinct Impressionistic qualities, selected a group of poems focused on a moonstruck lover with the pale disk of the moon projected on the back of his garment.

A suggestion of sensuality is often more forceful than a realistic description of carnality. Whispered words are more enervating than raucous outcries. Distant rhythms of throbbing drums, brief effervescences of quickly extinguished melodic phrases, muted instrumental colors, all this suggests faint mementos of passionate events. Debussy's most dyspeptic critic Camille Bellaigue (who was Debussy's classmate at the Paris Conservatoire) grudgingly admitted that Debussy's music "fait peu de bruit," but, he added malevolently, it makes "un vilain petit bruit." John Ruskin exploded in righteous indignation against modern French music: "Musicians, like painters, are almost virulently determined in their efforts to abolish the laws of sincerity and purity, and to invent, each for his own glory, new modes of dissolute and lascivious sound." When Debussy's Prélude à l'après-midi d'un Faune was first performed in Paris in 1894, a cautionary notice was inserted in the program: "The poem of Mallarmé, which inspired Debussy, is so sadistic that the management decided not to print it in the program book, because young girls attend these concerts." The great romanticist of French music Gounod, addressing students at the Paris Académie des Beaux Arts on 20 October 1883, warned them: "Do not be seduced by those hollow words, Realism, Idealism, Impressionism. They belong to the nihilist vocabulary, which now constitutes modern art."

Paul Verlaine described IMPRESSIONISM in a line of singular intimacy as "la chanson grise où l'Indécis au Précis se joint." And he summarized the esthetic code of Symbolist poetry and Impressionist art in a challenging invitation, "Pas la Couleur, rien que la Nuance!" The formula fits the music of French IMPRESSIONISM to perfection: in it the indecisiveness of the design is mitigated by the precision of execution. Bright colors are relinquished in favor of infinitesimally subtle nuances. Just as the eye is trained to differentiate between light and shadow in Impressionist art, so the ear is disciplined to discriminate between the measured quanta of sonic impulses in Impressionist music.

IMPRESSIONISM is the differential calculus of music, in which the infinitesimal particles of coloristic sound are integrated into a potent musical factor. Debussy himself insisted that he was a realistic composer and he deprecated the term IMPRESSIONISM. He wrote to his publisher Durand, in March 1908: "I am trying to create musical reality, the kind that some imbeciles call IMPRESSIONISM, a term which I consider most unfitting."

IMPRESSIONISM has created its own tonal vocabulary and harmonic syntax. Its inspiration came from remote antiquity in time and far distances in space. When the Paris Exposition of 1889 presented Oriental dancers from Indochina with their strange bell-like musical instruments, Debussy and his friends found new resources in the polychromatic monody of the exotic modes from the East, free from contrapuntal and harmonic artificiality of western music. At the same time manufactured products from Japan began to arrive at the Paris markets, wrapped in Japanese rice paper with the symbolic prints by unknown masters. It was this wrapping paper, rather than the goods it enveloped, that provided pictorial resources to many French painters. Debussy selected a Japanese drawing of a typhoon wave for the cover of his score of La Mer. James Gibbons Huneker was not far wrong in his horrified contemplation of Debussy as a revenant from the East. "If the western world ever adopted eastern tonalities," he wrote, "Claude Debussy would be the one composer who would manage its system. I see his curious asymmetrical face, the pointed fawn ears, the projecting cheekbones. The man is a wraith from the East. His music was heard long ago in the hill temples of Borneo; was made as a symphony to welcome the head-hunters with their ghastly spoils of war!"

The innovations introduced by Impressionist techniques are as significant in the negation of old formulas as in the affirmation of the novelties. They may be summarized in the following categories:

MELODY: (1) Extreme brevity of substantive thematic statements. (2) Cultivation of monothematism and the elimination of all auxiliary notes, ornaments, melodic excrescences and rhythmic protuberances. (3) Introduction of simulacra of old Grecian and ecclesiastical modes calculated to evoke the spirit of serene antiquity in stately motion of rhythmic units. (4) Thematic employment of pentatonic scales to conjure up imitative sonorities and tintinnisonant Orientalistic effects. (5) Coloristic use of the scale of whole tones for exotic ambience. (6) Rapid iteration of single notes to simulate the rhythms of primitive drums.

HARMONY: (1) Extension of tertian chord formations into chords of the eleventh, or raised eleventh, and chords of the thirteenth. (2) Modulatory schemes in root progressions of intervals derived from the equal division of the octave into 2,3,4,6 and 12 parts in preference to the traditional modulations following the order of the cycle of fourths and fifths. (3) Motion by block harmonies without transitions. (4) Preferential use of plagal cadences either in triadic harmonies or extended chordal formations. (5) Quartal harmonies used as harmonic entities which move in parallel formations. (6) Modal harmonization in root positions of perfect triads within a given mode, with the intervalic relationships between the melody notes and the bass following the formula 8, 3, 5, 8, etc. when harmonizing an ascending scale or mode, and the reverse numerical progression 8, 5, 3, 8, etc. in harmonizing a descending scale or mode, excluding the incidence of the diminished fifth between the melody and the bass; the reverse numerical progression, 8, 5, 3, 8, 5, etc. for an ascending scale results in a common harmonization in tonic, dominant and subdominant triads in root position; the same common harmonization results when the formula 8, 3, 5, 8, 3, etc. is applied to the harmonization of a descending scale; this reciprocal relationship between a modal and a tonal harmonization is indeed magical in its precise numerical formula. (7) Intertonal harmonization in major triads, in which no more than two successive chords belong to any given tonality, with the melody moving in contrary motion to the bass; since only root positions of major triads are used, the intervals between the melody and the bass can be only a major third, a perfect fifth and an octave. In harmonizing an ascending scale, whether diatonic, chromatic or partly chromatic, the formula is limited to the numerical intervalic progression 3, 5, 8, 3, 5, etc., and the reverse in harmonizing a descending scale, i.e., 8, 5, 3, 8, 5, 3, etc. Cadential formulas of pre-Baroque music are often intertonal in their exclusive application of major triads in root positions. A remarkable instance of the literal application of the formula of intertonal harmonization is found in the scene of Gregory's prophetic vision in Mussorgsky's opera *Boris Godunov*, in which the ascending melodic progression, itself intertonal in its peculiar modality, B, C-sharp, E, F-sharp, G, is harmonized successively in the major triads in root positions, E major, C-sharp major, A major, F-sharp major, E-flat major. Another instance of intertonal harmonization occurs in the second act of Puccini's opera *Tosca*, in which the motto of the chief of police, a descending whole-tone scale in the bass, is harmonized in ascending major triads in root positions, in contrary motion; the intervalic relationship between the melody and the bass follows the formula 8,3,5,8,3,5,8,. (8) Parallel progressions of inversions of triads, particularly second inversions of major triads, with the root progression ascending or descending in minor thirds, so that the basses outline a diminished-seventh chord. (9) Parallel progressions of major ninth-chords, also with a bass moving by minor thirds. (10) Parallel progressions of inverted dominant-seventh chords, particularly 6/5/3 chords. (11) Free use of unattached and unresolved dissonant chords, particularly suspensions of major sevenths over diminished-seventh chords. (12) Cadential formulas with the added major sixth over major triads in close harmony.

COUNTERPOINT: (1) A virtual abandonment of Baroque procedures; abolition of tonal sequences and of strict canonic imitation. (2) Reduction of fugal processes to adumbrative thematic echoes, memos and mementos. (3) Cultivation of parallel motion of voices, particularly consecutive fourths and organum-like perfect fifths.

FORM: (1) Desuetude of sectional symphonies of the classical or romantic type, and their replacement by coloristic tone poems of a rhapsodic genre. (2) Virtual disappearance of thematic development with its function being taken over by dynamic elements. (3) Cessation in the practice of traditional variations, discontinuance of auxiliary embellishments, melodic and harmonic figurations whether above, below or around the thematic notes and the concomitant cultivation of instrumental variations in which the alteration of tone color becomes the means of variegation. A theme may be subjected to augmentation or diminution and in some cases to topological dislocations of the intervalic parameters. Thus the tonal theme of Debussy's *La Mer* is extended in the climax into a series of whole tones. (4) Homeological imitation of melorhythmic formulas of old dance forms, often with pandiatonic amplification of the harmony. (5) A general tendency towards miniaturization of nominally classical forms, such as sonata or prelude.

INSTRUMENTATION: (1) Coloristic employment of unusual instrumental combinations. (2) Predilection for attenuated sonorities, with muted strings and muted brass, and considerable expansion of the role of woodwind instruments and of the decorative sonorities of the harp and the celesta. (3) Projection of evocative but brief solos, often in unusual registers. (4) The planting of deep pedal points over which the strings and the woodwinds are suspended in aerostatic equilibrium, often with a muted horn, trumpet or trombone, penetrating the euphonious mist. (5) Careful cultivation of multiple divided strings. (6) Periodic sonic expansions and compressions, massive heavings and sudden recessions. (7) Fluctuation of dynamic rhythms and constant oscillation of thematic particles. (8) Fragmentation of melodic patterns and pulverization of ingredients in tremolos. (9) Heterogeneous instrumental combinations tending to alter the natural tone color of an individual instrument. (10) Frequent application of dynamic antiphony of homogeneous or heterogeneous instrumental groupings.

**Inaudible Music.** Since electronic instruments are capable of generating any frequency, it is possible to reproduce sounds below and above the audible range. The first work for such infrasonic and ultrasonic wavelengths was the INAUDIBLE symphony entitled *Symphonie Humaine* by the French composer Michel Magne, conducted by him in Paris on 26 May 1955. Its movements were entitled *Epileptic Dance, Thanatological Berceuse* and *Interior View of an Assassin*. The INAUDIBLE version was unheard first, followed by a hearing of an audible transcription. The mystical Russian composer Nicolas Obouhov devised in 1918 an INAUDIBLE instrument which he named Ether, theoretically capable of producing infrasonic and ultrasonic sounds ranging from five octaves below the lowest audible tone to five octaves above the highest audible tone. But Obouhov's instrument was never constructed. Avant-garde composers working in mixed media often compose visual music, which can be seen but not heard. A poetic example is the act of releasing a jar full of butterflies "composed" by La Monte Young. Imagination plays a crucial part in the appreciation of INAUDIBLE MUSIC. An interviewer on a broadcast of the British Broadcasting Corporation was sent a defective copy of John and Yoko's Wedding Album (John Lennon was a member of a Liverpudlian vocal quartet, since fallen into innocuous desuetude, known as The Beatles) in which two sides were blank except for an engineer's line-up tone. The broadcaster gave it a warmly favorable review, noting that the pitches differed only by microtones, and that "this oscillation produces an almost subliminal uneven beat which maintains interest on a more basic level," and further observing that the listener could improvise an Indian raga, plainsong or Gaelic mouth music against the drone. John and his Japanese bride Yoko sent him a congratulatory telegram, announcing their intention to release the blank sides for their next album. "Heard melodies are sweet, but those unheard are sweeter."

**Indeterminacy.** In nuclear physics, the principle of INDETERMINACY states that it is inherently impossible to determine both the position and velocity of any subatomic particle beyond the liminal degree of accuracy. This notion has impressed some modern composers and moved them to apply the INDETERMINACY principle to composition with aleatory or stochastic elements. If the position of a note is indicated precisely, then the rhythm must be optional, and vice-versa. The performing musicians are free to improvise either the actual notes in the nucleus considered indeterminate, or its rhythm, but not both.

**Induction and Deduction.** In new music, which flaunts its affinity with exact sciences and mathematical logic, the terms INDUCTION AND DEDUCTION may be applied with some profit. In serial composition, in particular, the method allows to complete a series by the process of INDUCTION. The Bach theme, B-flat, A, C, B, for instance, can be an inductive clue to a 12-tone series, to be completed by using the intervalic content of the subject in transposition by inversion and retrograde. The process of DEDUCTION also possesses a certain validity in composition. With the aid of thematic INDUCTION AND DEDUCTION, it is easy to construct logical sequences of tones. Suppose we have a dodecaphonic series designated by the first 12 integers, 1, 2, 3 . . . 12; in its second appearance it assumes the succession 2, 3, 4 . . . 12, 1. By inductive reasoning the third series should be 3, 4, 5, 6 . . . 12, 1, 2, etc. This type of DODECAPHONIC COMPOSITION is known as ROTATION. Conversely, it is possible to derive identical serial rows by DEDUCTION from the principle of rotation, while other morphological variants can be obtained by omitting parts of the series.

**Inertial Guidance.** Borrowed from navigation, the term INERTIAL GUIDANCE denotes an automatic sequence which depends entirely on previously accumulated data. At its most elementary level, INERTIAL GUIDANCE is a signal of repeat, as in the recapitulation section of sonata form. In the original manuscript of Schubert's *Unfinished Symphony*, the initial 64 bars of the first movement are repeated in the recapitulation, but rather than writing them out, Schubert simply marked them numerically, 1–64. A conversion formula could be devised to take care of INERTIAL GUIDANCE for transpositions to another key, augmentations of a theme, diminutions and even fugal stretti, with symbolical directions according to a set code. For instance, S₂(I), where S stands for Subject and I denotes Tonic Harmony, would indicate that the second subject is to be transposed to the tonic from its original appearance in the dominant. In dodecaphonic techniques, a symbolic system for INERTIAL GUIDANCE would save the drudgery of writing out the basic forms of the tone-row. It would be possible, for instance, to program the composition of a tone-row consisting of three groups of identical intervallic conformations, the first of which spells BACH. In order to complete the 12-tone series, BACH would have to be transposed 4 semitones higher and 4 semitones lower. The formula would then appear as follows: BACH, (BACH + 4), (BACH − 4). If the second or the third group is to be inverted or reversed, it can be indicated by the subscripts *i* and *r*. In addition to INERTIAL GUIDANCE, a set of formulas can also be devised for a Command Guidance, which would interrupt the automatic processes of INERTIAL GUIDANCE, and dictate a new set of directives. It must be kept in mind, however, that the formula must not be allowed to be more complex than ordinary notation.

**Infantiloquy.** Onomatopoeia, whether tonal or electronically produced, is the most effective means of instrumental INFANTILOQUY. Borborygmic rumbles and oral ejaculations of sonic particles in an asymmetric pattern are infantiloquacious by nature, and they can be easily imitated by an instrumental ensemble. An infantiloquent modern piece may include fragments from nursery rhymes. An example of successful INFANTILOQUY is Karlheinz Stockhausen's *Gesang der Jünglinge,* in which a child's voice is combined with electronic sounds.

**Information Theory.** In relevant application to modern music, INFORMATION THEORY touches on the problems of GRAPHIC NOTATION, semantics of certain melorhythmic figures, dynamic levels of various parts of a musical work and instrumental color, etc. A composer must be able to convey a maximum amount of information with optimum efficiency. Composers of complicated music have without exception insisted that the knowledge of their modus operandi is unnecessary for the complete comprehension of the musical message. The quality of performance cannot elevate a poorly constructed musical composition to a higher degree of excellence; nor can an indifferent execution of a great masterpiece impair its inherent validity. Musical information can be conveyed with considerable impact by playing a four-hand arrangement of a Beethoven symphony, but would fail to register even in a virtuoso performance of a work lacking in power of communication.

**Infra-Modern Music.** If Ultra-Modern Music transcends the outer limits of modernism, INFRA-MODERN MUSIC fails to reach even its lowest boundaries, and dwells in the penumbra of pretentious self-inflation. Composers of INFRA-MODERN MUSIC make frequent incursions into the alluring land of dissonant harmonies, but they seldom succeed in manufacturing even a similitudinarian counterfeit. Their attempts to inject atonal or polytonal elements in the effete body of their productions remain as sterile as their imaginations are impotent.

**Integration.** Harmonic INTEGRATION of a linear progression in dodecaphonic works is an essential factor in Schoenberg's method of composition with 12 tones related only to one another. Melody and harmony become two dimensions of dodecaphonic space, thus contributing to a higher unity of the compositional design. True, melody and harmony are intimately associated in classical music theory in conformity with the laws of chordal relationship, but the great difference between the two concepts lies in the fact that in classical harmony the chordal accompaniment performs the function of melodic tonality, while in serial music it is an integral part of the entire meloharmonic scheme.

**Interpoint.** INTERPOINT, or PUNCTUS INTER PUNCTUM, is a term devised by the Russian composer Alexander Tcherepnin to describe a special kind of contrapuntal technique, in which pairs of conjugated contrapuntal voices enter a vacancy between another pair of contrapuntal parts without overlapping. The resulting four-part counterpoint becomes in turn the intussusception between a still more dehiscent coupling. In order to achieve interpuntal polyphony, it is obviously necessary to plan in advance the upper and lower limits of the range of each pair, recalling to mind Swift's verses: "So, naturalists observe, a flea/ Hath smaller fleas that on him prey/ And these have smaller still to bite 'em/ And so proceed *ad infinitum.*"

**Intervallic Symbolism.** Symbolical associations between intervals and ideas are rooted in scholastic theories. An anonymous medieval tract explains the acoustical perfection of the octave by the circumstance that "octavo die Abraha circumcisus erat." The tritone was "diabolus in musica." Bach had correlated certain intervals to specific subjects with considerable precision. Since words could not always be heard, an intervallic equation contributed to the clarity of the meaning. The ascent to heaven was depicted by a rising diatonic scale. Torment was expressed by involuted chromatic passages. The descent into hell was intervallically related to the falling diminished-seventh. Essentially, Wagner's system of leading motives is a species of INTERVALLIC SYMBOLISM. Some modern composers have revived a medieval symbolism of intervals. In Luigi Nono's spectacle for MIXED MEDIA, *Intolleranza*, the characters are associated with specific intervals: the woman with minor seconds and their inversions, major sevenths; the refugee with the tritone and perfect fourths; and his friend with perfect fourths and major seconds. As in Bach's day such associations help to follow the leading motives of the score.

**Invariants.** With the growing fascination shown by modern composers for the theory of sets, the term INVARIANTS has acquired a certain practical validity. Its relevance is obvious. The 12 tones of the dodecaphonic series are INVARIANTS within a certain set; the derivatives of the tone-row are variables. Number 4 is the INVARIANT in a set of instruments of a string quartet. A flute part interchangeable with that of the piccolo is a variable. Besides the advantage of scientific jargon, the system of musical INVARIANTS clarifies some processes of serial composition. Particularly frequent is the use of the term for segments of different forms of a tone-row, for instance, the basic series and its retrograde, transposed, which happen to have several notes in common, by accident or structural serendipity.

**Jazz.** The word JAZZ appeared for the first time in print in the sports column in *The Bulletin* of San Francisco in its issue of 6 March 1913. Describing the arrival of a baseball team, the writer "Scoop" Gleeson reported: "Everybody has come back to the old town, full of the old 'jazz' and they promise to knock the fans off their feet with their playing." Gleeson then asks himself a rhetorical question: "What is this jazz? Why, it's a little of that 'old life,' the 'gin-i-ker,' the 'pep,' otherwise known as the enthusiasalum." Reminiscing about the occasion in an article published in the same San Francisco newspaper in its issue of 3 September 1938, "Scoop" Gleeson volunteered the information that the expression "jazz" had been picked up by the Sports editor during a crap game. According to Gleeson, it was first applied to music when a bandleader named Art Hickman launched his dance band, but there is no evidence of such use in any published source. The next verified appearance of the word JAZZ was in *Variety* of 27 October 1916 in a brief communication from Chicago, reporting a concert of JAZZ music, with the word spelled *jass*. Another item in *Variety* followed on 5 January 1917 when it was spelled *Jaz*. An engagement of the Dixie Jass Band of New Orleans in a Chicago cabaret was noted in *Variety* of 16 January 1917. A week later JAZZ reached New York, and it was spelled with two z's in a report in *Variety*. An item in the Victor Record Review of 7 March 1917 reads: "Spell it *Jass, Jas, Jaz,* or JAZZ—nothing can spoil a *Jass* band . . . It has sufficient power and penetration to inject new life into a mummy, and will keep ordinary human dancers on their feet till breakfast time . . ." It was about the same time that the Victor Co. issued the first recording bearing the word *Jass—Dixieland Jass One-Step*.

A number of writers have attempted to connect the word JAZZ with old slang. The word *Jasm* is found in an American novel published in 1860, and a claim has been made without support that its colloquial meaning was male sperm. Other equally unfounded guesses were that the word came from the French slang expression current in New Orleans in the 19th century, and that its verbal form meant to copulate. The determination to track the word down to some kind of sexual meaning has been the motivation of many imaginative but unsupported etymologies. Some have tried to trace it to native African languages. However, considering the specific, clear and plausible description of the word JAZZ as it appeared in print for the first time in 1913, there is no reason to doubt that it was a spontaneous colloquialism generated around San Francisco. The entire history of the word JAZZ is thoroughly covered in the pioneer article by Peter Tamony in an ephemeral periodical *Jazz*, a quarterly of American music, in its issue of October 1958. Analytically, JAZZ may be described as a modern development of the counterpoint of the fourth species. Its rhythmic formula is related to the medieval *Hocketus,* in which the singing line is freely transferred from one voice to another in syncopated singultation. (The word *hocketus* itself is an etymological cognate of hiccups.) Another historical antecedent of JAZZ is the *Quodlibet,* a freely improvised interlude within a definite metrical framework. As practiced by untutored performers, JAZZ produces the collective impact of glossolalia, tonolalia or rhythmolalia.

The paradoxical nature of JAZZ is its combination of unlimited variety of rhythmic patterns with a metric and modal uniformity. JAZZ melodies, almost without exception, are set in major keys, in 4/4 time. But the major tonality is modified by the use of "blue" notes, the lowered seventh and the lowered third in the melody. Some theorists speculate that the systematic incidence of the "blue" seventh is an approximation of the seventh overtone, and is therefore a natural consonance. The lowered third, however, cannot be explained on acoustical grounds. It may well represent a true case of harmonic equivocation, in which the melodic minor third is projected on the major complex in some sort of polytriadic superfetation. It is significant that this major-minor SUPERFETATION is the constant resource of Stravinsky's tonal harmonies.

The basic characteristics of JAZZ are the symmetrical divisions of binary meters and the strong tonality in major keys. Within this framework, the melody, of a syncopated nature, often departs widely from its harmonic connotations.

Historically JAZZ evolved from RAGTIME, a syncopated type of American music that flourished in the last decade of the 19th century and during the first years of the new century. A parallel development is BLUES, a distinctively American ballad form, suffused with nostalgia and redolent of the remembered sufferings of the Negro race, as expressed in the Negro spirituals. Semantically, the term is connected with the colloquialism "to have the blues." The "blue note," that is the flatted seventh in a major key, remains a paramount feature in the BLUES. The acknowledged creator of the genre was W.C. Handy whose song *The Memphis Blues,* published in 1911, was the first of its type.

In the meantime, the temperature of JAZZ music kept rising, and soon acquired the sobriquet HOT JAZZ, as contrasted with the more leisurely type of SWEET JAZZ. HOT JAZZ gave way to COOL JAZZ, which actually a hotter product, as though the hot water and cold water faucets became switched around in the process of transition.

A new era of JAZZ music dawned in 1935 with a riotous explosion of SWING, which signalized a certain rhythmic manner of performance rather than a definable structural form.

JAZZ, SWING and other types of popular American music of the 1930's coalesced into a general category of JIVE, a generic form that describes the playing style in the 1940's. SWING and JIVE were largely improvisatory in nature; a novel way of organizing popular forms emerged in 1938 with BOOGIE-WOOGIE, based on an orderly harmonic progression in the bass, relating it to the classical formulas of the passacaglia and the chaconne.

A lateral form, BEBOP, Rebop or simply Bop, appeared in the 1940's; in it the main emphasis was on the strong off-beat. With its raucous sound and crude assault on the musical sensorium, SWING music had no room for such poetic refinements as the "blue notes" which vanished from the Swing horizon.

For more than half a century, JAZZ in its various forms was separated from folk music. JAZZ was an urban product; folk music, or country music, remained stagnant in its rural recesses. The instrumentation of JAZZ was based on the trumpet, the saxophone, the banjo, the piano and the drums, with the clarinet emerging as its flamboyant chanticleer in SWING. Country music replaced the piano by the guitar and the trumpet by the rustic fiddle. When country music invaded the radio airwaves, the television channels and the sound movies, it gradually developed into a horrendously successful creation that became known as ROCK 'N' ROLL. Marked by an unrelenting, unremitting beat, ROCK 'N' ROLL reduced the rhythmic wealth of early syncopated music to a two-dimensional construction of bland uniformity. Its cumulative impact is apt to be as powerful as the rhythmic tramp of a regiment of soldiers which can bring down a suspension bridge by generating pendulum-like vibrations of increasing amplitude.

Throughout the history of American popular music, systematic incursions were made into the stylistically distant territory of classical and romantic music, carrying away loot and booty from the uncopyrighted remains of Chopin, Tchaikovsky and Rachmaninoff. Some products of these predatory forays, such as *Russian Rag*, fashioned from Rachmaninoff's defenseless C-sharp minor *Prelude*, are not devoid of inventive cleverness. Indignant outcries arose from the classical-minded musicians against such barbarous practices, but eventually this musical cannibalism subsided of its own accord.

A reconciliation between popular and serious music was effected with taste and vitality in a movement known as the THIRD STREAM, making it possible to introduce JAZZ into serious music.

**Jive.** JIVE is a collective noun that describes the action of JAZZ. A JIVE session is a display of coordinated glossolalia or tonolalia, spontaneous and self-conscious in their manifestation. A jam session is conducted in the language of JIVE. The semantic distinctions and confluences of these terms are illustrated by the jazzy glossolalia in a song recorded by Columbia in 1940: "Romp it, stomp it, ride it too. Jam it, Jump it, Jive it through."

**Kaleidophonia.** By analogy with kaleidoscopic images, the term KALEIDOPHONIA may be used to describe a musical composition derived from multiple mirror-like reflections of a central subject. By selecting a code of parameters determining intervals and durations, a Kaleidophonic structure can be designed as a harmonic complex composed of contrapuntal lines in quaquaversal rhythmic dispersion. Joseph Schillinger published in 1940 a volume of musical patterns which he entitled *Kaleidophone*.

**Kinetic Energy.** When applied to music, KINETIC ENERGY during a given interval of time connects the velocity (number of notes per time unit), amplitude (degree of loudness in decibels) and the height of pitch expressed in semitones counting from the lowest note in the audible range. KINETIC ENERGY is the product of all these parameters. From this it follows that the auditory impact is directly proportional to velocity, loudness and frequency of vibrations per second. There is also a psychological factor that affects the subjective measurement of KINETIC ENERGY. The off-beat chord in Haydn's *Surprise Symphony*, though in itself possessing a modest impact, carries a relatively greater charge of psycho-kinetic energy because it is unexpected. Generally speaking, a greater impression is produced by detonations of sonic quanta in asymmetrical rhythms than much stronger discharges occurring at regular intervals of time.

**Kitsch.** The German patois word KITSCH denotes a pretentiously manufactured object, an unimaginative arrangement of artifacts or a heterogeneous collection which is more tasteless than artless. Christmas cards with rhymed doggerel and tinctured flowers, religious gypsum figurines with a clock in the center of the torso, a motion picture representing muscular men lifting rubber weights, chrome gargoyles, dinner plates with reproductions of members of the presidential family and all sorts of tinsel and fustian, are examples of middle-class KITSCH. In music, KITSCH is represented by so-called semi-classical compositions made up of harmonic detritus and melodic debris from the mutilated remains of Rachmaninoff's *Second Piano Concerto*, or Beethoven's *Moonlight Sonata*, or from a mixture of both. KITSCH products are usually given colorful titles such as "Purple Piano" or "Sentimental Violin," and favor for some unfathomable reason the keys of D-flat major or C minor. KITSCH is the degenerate descendant of the German Biedermeier movement. At the distance of a century, the Biedermeier products possess a certain charm of old-fashioned sentiment and the musical compositions of the period were invariably correct from the technical standpoint. Modern KITSCH is usually devoid of the most elementary type of technical proficiency and appeals to the lowest classes of commercially conditioned eyes, noses and ears.

**Klangfarbe.** In its present semantical usage, KLANGFARBE is a special dimension of the musical sound. "It must be possible," Schoenberg states in his *Harmonielehre*, "to form a succession of KLANGFARBEN possessing a mutual relationship of a logical type equivalent to that of the melody formed by a succession of different tones." This melody of tone colors is exemplified in Schoenberg's movement originally entitled *The Changing Chord* in his *Five Orchestral Pieces*. Anton von Webern developed the idea in the direction of serialism of KLANGFARBEN, almost reaching the ultimate dodecaphonic order, in which the fundamental KLANGFARBE series is formed by the successive sounding of 12 different notes by 12 different instruments.

**Lehrstück.** The problems of writing music in a modern idiom adaptable for educational purposes among workers and young people preoccupied a number of German composers in the 1920's. The idea of a LEHRSTÜCK for accompanied chorus with the liberal application of inflected voice, SPRECHSTIMME, arose in Germany about that time. Paul Hindemith, Ernst Toch and Kurt Weill wrote several such works. Often the "teaching" element in a LEHRSTÜCK was political, as exemplified in the "instruction pieces" of Hanns Eisler.

**Lipograms.** An omission of an essential member of a melodic series, be it a simple diatonic tune or a dodecaphonic tone-row, a musical apocopation or an APOSIOPESIS, or any other similar rhetoric device that interrupts the normal progress of a musical sentence, may be described as a LIPOGRAM, a vocable derived from Greek nomenclature, that denotes a deficiency of a letter. A LIPOGRAM in a dodecaphonic series results in the formation of a Hendecaphonic row. When the last note of a series is omitted, a melodic apocope results; when an interruption occurs dramatically in the middle of a melorhythmic paragraph, the effect is similar to that of an APOSIOPESIS. Lipogrammatic techniques provide ample resources for novel melodic, rhythmic, contrapuntal, harmonic and instrumental patterns.

**Machine Music.** The modern machine became an object of artistic inspiration early in the 20th century. The Italian Futurists made a cult of automobiles and airplanes. George Antheil's *Ballet mécanique* shocked concert audiences by its bruitism. Max Brand produced the first machine opera in *Machinist Hopkins.* Honegger made a declaration of love for powerful American locomotives in his symphonic movement *Pacific 231.* Frederick S. Converse glorified the Ford car in his automobilistic musicorama *Flivver 10,000,000.* But locomotives, automobiles and airplanes soon lost their glamor and became public nuisances. By mid-century the machine as an artistic object became obsolete. It is ironic that no composer was moved to extol in lofty tones the greatest machine adventure of all ages, the landing on the moon.

**Major-Minor Syndrome.** It was a traditional convention in Baroque music to end a work in a minor key on a major triad; a major third that replaced a minor third in the final triad acquired the name *Tierce de Picardie.* The preference for the major third in final chords is explained by its privileged position as the fifth partial note of the harmonic series, whereas a minor third of the fundamental tone does not occur acoustically. In the practice of modern composers, a major third is often superimposed on a minor third. Scriabin employed such a MAJOR-MINOR SYNDROME in his last opus numbers, but he spread the harmony widely, so that the frictional dissonance of a semitone was avoided. It was Stravinsky who cultivated a true MAJOR-MINOR SYNDROME in placing both the minor and the major third within a triad. He made use of it as a motto in his early choral work *Zvezdoliky.* It occurs also in *Le Sacre du Printemps.* Most importantly, Stravinsky uses it as a melodic palimpsest, breaking up the combined chord, with both the major and the minor third assuming a thematic significance.

**Meloharmony.** In a triadically constructed melody, the harmonic arrangement is clearly outlined. In such instances, it is proper to speak of MELOHARMONY as a two-dimensional entity. In DODECAPHONIC MUSIC, MELOHARMONY acquires a particular significance, because the fundamental series can be distributed horizontally, i.e. melodically, and vertically, i.e. harmonically, and still preserve its continuity. It is also possible to speak of melocontrapuntal structures, arranged vertically, horizontally, or diagonally. A cognate term is MELORHYTHM, in which melody and rhythm are combined into a dual entity.

**Melorhythm.** The term *Meloritmo,* frequently used by Spanish and Latin American writers on music, and signifying a synthetic two-dimensional entity possessing both melodic and rhythmic attributes, is sufficiently useful to be adopted in other languages. It is also a convenient substitute for the definition of a musical phrase, which must necessarily have the dual MELORHYTHMIC consistency. In serial music, MELORHYTHMS may be regarded as the integrals of the melodic and rhythmic differential series.

**Melosomatic Effect.** The neologism MELOSOMATIC suggests an interaction between Melos and the physical Soma. It may be traumatic when loud music is played without relief.

But a more insidious psychological lesion is produced by personal associations. In his short story, *The Black Monk*, Anton Chekhov, who was a professional physician, describes the deadly effect produced on a young intellectual by the playing of *Angel's Serenade* by Gaetano Braga, resulting in a fatal cerebral hemorrhage when the piece is played again after a long interval of time. Autosuggestion may have been responsible for the death of the Hungarian composer Rezsö Seress, author of the pessimistic popular song *Gloomy Sunday* (it was banned in various localities after numerous suicides were purportedly engendered by it.) By a delayed reaction, forty years after writing this song, the composer himself jumped out of a window. The Russian pianist Alexander Kelberine took a lethal dose of barbiturates after his last concert on January 27, 1940 in Town Hall in New York, for which he arranged a funereal program, consisting entirely of works in minor keys, the last number being Liszt's *Totentanz.* Sexual stimulation is highly melosomatic, as amply demonstrated by the reactions of the young to concerts of popular music, particularly ROCK 'N' ROLL. Tolstoy, who turned against sex after a lifetime of indulgence and sixteen illegitimate children, presented a philosophical study of musical sexuality in his novel *The Kreutzer Sonata*, wherein he tells how the last movement of Beethoven's work, with its propulsive syncopation, overwhelms the natural restraints of the performers, a middle-class married Russian woman pianist and a male violinist, hurling them into a frenzy of illicit passion. It may be questioned that amateurs could ever master the technical difficulties of that diabolically intricate last movement, let alone create enough excitement to carry them away. (There is a famous painting illustrating the climactic scene of the novel, showing the mustachioed violinist implanting a passionate kiss on the lips of a lady pianist while holding both the violin and the bow in his left hand, suggesting that he had the presence of mind to switch the bow from the right hand to the left, but leaving it unexplained as to why he did not deposit the instrument on the lid of the piano in that crucial moment. The painting is widely used as an advertisement for a brand of perfume with a sexy name.)

Melosomatic associations were responsible for the extraordinary vogue of the piano piece *A Maiden's Prayer* by a Polish composeress named Thekla Badarzewska, a wishfulfilling favorite of several generations of unmarried females. In 1937 Stravinsky instituted in Paris a suit against Warner Brothers for the production of a film entitled *The Firebird*, in which a submissive young girl is so unnerved by the phonograph playing of the *Pagan Dance* from Stravinsky's *Firebird* that she wanders into the flat of a professional seducer, who had the piece played continually with malice aforethought, and yields to his infamous desires. The judge failed to appreciate Stravinsky's attitude, since the seductive power of music is supposed to be the composer's greatest pride, and adjudicated the case by granting Stravinsky a token sum of one French franc in compensation for the offense.

**Metamusic.** Metaphysical visions have obsessed composers through the ages. They dreamed of a METAMUSICAL symphony in which all mankind would participate as a responsive reverberating assembly of congenial souls. Shortly before he died, Scriabin wrote an outline of a METAMUSICAL Mysterium that would embrace all senses in a pantheistic mystical action. Much more earthbound, but musically fascinating, was the project of a *Universe Symphony* by Charles Ives, a work that he hoped to see performed by several orchestras stationed on hilltops overlooking a valley. The Russian mystical composer Nicolas Obouhov envisioned a METAMUSICAL union of all religions. He completed a major part of this work which bore the title *Le Livre de Vie.* He kept the manuscript on a self-made altar under an ikon, in a corner of his small room in Paris. Since this was to be the book of his own life, body and soul, he made all annotations in the original scores in his own blood. He tried to interest American music lovers to have this work produced in a specially built temple in Hollywood, but died with his dream unfulfilled.

Composers of the AVANT-GARDE have at their disposal the means of producing METAMUSICAL scores with the aid of electronic synthesizers. They may even plan to hitch their METAMUSICAL chariot if not to the stars then at least to the planets. There is nothing mystical in the term METAMUSIC. It simply means an art transcending traditional music, by analogy with Aristotle's Metaphysics, which indicates the position of a chapter dealing with philosophy, directly after a discussion of physics in his *Organon.*

**Metempsychosis.** A recurrence of a theme in an altered melorhythmic shape, suggesting the effect of *déjà entendu* without literal resemblance, may be called musical METEMPSYCHOSIS. The *idée fixe* in the *Symphonie Fantastique* of Berlioz does not fall into this category, because here it was deliberately implanted and reproduced in a clearly recognizable form. The discovery of melorhythmic revenants may give a clue to the composer's inner impulses, and it is particularly fruitful in serial compositions, where METEMPSYCHOSIS may appear subliminally, despite the composer's efforts to guard himself against unintentional thematic references.

**Metric Modulation.** In a general sense of the word, METRIC MODULATION is a change of time signature. In special modern usage, proleptically applied by Charles Ives and systematically cultivated by Elliott Carter, METRIC MODULATION is a technique in which a rhythmic pattern is superposed on another, heterometrically, and then supersedes it and becomes the basic meter. Usually, such time signatures are mutually prime, e.g., 4/4 and 3/8, and so have no common divisors. Thus the change of the basic meter decisively alters the numerical content of the beat, but the minimal denominator (1/8 when 4/4 changes to 3/8; 1/16 when, e.g., 5/8 changes to 7/16, etc.) remains constant in duration.

**Microtonality.** Intervals smaller than semitones were used in ancient Greece, but were abandoned in western music with the establishment of the ecclesiastical modes. When greater sensitivity towards tonal elements developed in modern times, composers and theorists began investigating the acoustical, coloristic and affective aspects of intervals smaller than a semitone, particularly quarter-tones. The Mexican composer Julián Carrillo experimented with microtonal intervals as early as 1895, when he published his *Sonido 13 (13th Sound)*; the title referred to the tonal resources beyond the 12 notes of the chromatic scale. Later he organized an international society for the exploration of MICROTONALITY under the grandiose name "Cruzada Intercontinental Sonido 13." He devised special instruments for performance of microtonal intervals and proposed a numerical notation of 96 divisions of the octave, which enabled him to designate precise intervalic values for 1/3-tones, 1/4-tones, 1/6-tones, 1/8-tones and 1/16-tones. As an exercise in MICROTONALITY he arranged Beethoven's *Fifth Symphony* in quarter-tones by dividing each interval into two, so that the octave became a tritone, and the entire range of the work shrank to about three octaves, like some monstrous simulacrum of a physical universe in which the sensorium of auditory frequencies undergoes an extraction of the square root.

The English musician John Foulds experimented with quarter-tones in 1898. He writes in his book *From Music Today* (1934): "In the year 1898 I had tentatively experimented in a string quartet with smaller divisions than usual of the intervals of our scale, quarter-tones. Having proved in performance their practicability and their capability of expressing certain psychological states in a manner incommunicable by any other means known to musicians, I definitely adopted them as an item in my composing technique. . . . Facetious friends may assert roundly that they have heard quarter-tones all their lives, from the fiddle strings and larynxes of their mutual friends, who produced them without any difficulty."

The most systematic investigation of the theory and practice of quarter-tones was undertaken by Alois Hába in Czechoslovakia. "As a boy of 12," he writes, "I played with my three older brothers in my father's village band. We were poor; there were ten children in the family, and I had to contribute to household expenses. When we played for village festivals it often happened that folk singers used intervals different from the tempered scale, and they were annoyed that we could not accompany them properly. This gave me the idea to practice at home playing non-tempered scales on my violin in intervals smaller than a semitone. This was my first 'conservatory' for music in quarter-tones and in sixth-notes."

Probably the first entirely self-consistent work in quarter-tones was the string quartet written by Hába in 1919. He also compiled the first manual containing detailed instructions on composing in quarter-tones, third-tones and sixth-tones, which he published under the fitting title *Neue Harmonielehre* in 1928. Under Hába's supervision the August Foerster piano manufacturing company of Czechoslovakia constructed the first model of a quarter-tone piano which was patented on 18 March 1924. At the same time Hába established the first seminars of MICROTONAL MUSIC at the Prague Conservatory. He and his students published a number of works in quarter-tones, in Hába's special notation containing symbols for half a sharp, a sharp and a half, half a flat, and a flat and a half. A quarter-tone upright piano was constructed by Willi Möllendorf even before Foerster's, but it was only an ordinary piano tuned in quarter-tones and not a specially built instrument. It is now placed in the Deutsches Museum in Munich as a historical relic. The same museum also possesses a quarter-tone Harmonium built by Foerster and a harmonium of 19 divisions of the octave designed by Melchior Sachs.

In 1917 the Russian composer Ivan Wyschnegradsky devised a system of quarter-tones with a motto, inspired by Heraclitus, "Everything flows." In 1924, then living in Paris, he formulated the concept of "pansonority," which in his nomenclature meant a discrete continuum of quarter-tones. To produce fairly accurate quarter-tones he used two pianos or two pairs of pianos tuned a quarter-tone apart. On 10 November 1945 he conducted in Paris an entire program of his works, including a symphonic poem for four pianos entitled *Cosmos*.

In Russia itself quarter-tone music had a brief period of success in the early 1920's, cultivated by the Quarter-Tone Society of Leningrad, founded by Rimsky-Korsakov's grandson Georg.

Charles Ives, whose universal genius touched on many aspects of modern composition, contributed some pieces written in quarter-tones. He tells us that he became aware of the new resources of MICROTONAL MUSIC when his father, a band leader in the Union Army during the Civil War, experimented in tuning band instruments a quarter-tone apart.

Probably the earliest published composition containing quarter-tones was a group of two pieces for cello and piano by Richard H. Stein, composed in 1906, but quarter-tone passages in them were used only as occasional ultra-chromatic interludes. Ernest Bloch inserted quarter-tones in his first piano quintet mainly for their affective value in coloristic appoggiaturas.

American composers David Zeikel and William Harold Halberstadt investigated the potentialities of quarter-tones in the 1940's and wrote special works, mostly for the violin, in quarter-tones. For the sake of completeness it may be mentioned that Nicolas Slonimsky composed an overture for strings, trumpet and percussion in the Phrygian Greek mode using as his theme an extant version of an ancient Greek tune from the accompaniment to the tragedy *Orestes* produced in Athens in 400 B.C.; he conducted this arrangement at the Hollywood Bowl on 13 July 1933. In order to produce the needed two quarter-tones, the open upper strings of the violins, violas and cellos were tuned a quarter-tone up, with the rest of the string instruments preserving the ordinary pitch.

The first quarter-tone piano manufactured in the United States was patented by Hans Barth on 21 July 1931. His instrument had two keyboards of 88 notes each. The upper keyboard was tuned at the regular international pitch and had the usual five black keys and seven white keys. The lower keyboard was tuned a quarter-tone down, and its keys were blue and red.

James Paul White, a Boston musician, constructed in 1883 a microtonal keyboard which he called *Harmon*, and used a notation in which deviations from regular pitch were indicated by plus and minus signs. He theorized that 612 equal divisions of an octave would provide the most practical approximation to pure intonation. His instrument is preserved at the New England Conservatory of Music.

Perhaps the most ambitious project in MICROTONAL MUSIC has been undertaken by the American composer Harry Partch who devised a scale of 43 intervals in an octave, and constructed a number of special instruments, among them a microtonal cello, a reed organ with 43 registrations, and a modern version of the Greek kithara.

Musicologists have made numerous attempts to reconcile the tempered scale with Pythagorean intonation. Perhaps the most complete research in this direction was done by Joseph Yasser in his book *A Theory of Evolving Tonality*, published in New York in 1932, in which he proposed a system of "supra-tonality," with accidentals designated by special symbols for supra-sharp, supra-flat and supra-natural of the synthetic scale.

Quarter-tones were used by composers to suggest the Greek enharmonic mode through the centuries. Halévy incorporated a few quarter-tones in his symphonic poem *Prométhée enchaîné*, and Berlioz wrote an interesting account of its first performance in *Revue et Gazette Musicale de Paris* of 25 March 1849: "The employment of quarter-tones in Halévy's work is episodic and very short, and produces a species of groaning sound in the strings, but its strangeness seems perfectly justified here and enhances considerably the wistful prosody of the music."

The Rumanian composer Georges Enesco inserted a transitional passage in quarter-tones in his opera *Oedipe* produced in Paris in 1936. In this case, too, the composer's intention was to evoke the effect of the ancient Greek enharmonic scale.

It must be said that in actual performance on instruments manipulated by humans, quarter-tones and other microtonal divisions are only rough approximations of their true acoustical value. With the advent of electronic instruments, it became possible to reproduce microtonal intervals with absolute precision. Ernst Krenek experimented with a scale of 13 equal intervals in an octave. But despite the extraordinary resources offered by electronic instruments, composers of the Avant-Garde remained singularly indifferent to microtones. The Polish modernist Krzysztof Penderecki has used quarter-tones in massive multi-octave tone-clusters, creating sonorous complexes in icositetraphonic harmony.

A curious disquisition on quarter-tones and other fractional intervals as a logical extension of Chopin's sensitive use of chromatic harmony is contained in a pamphlet by Johanna Kinkel, *Acht Briefe an eine Freundin über Clavier-Unterricht,* published in Stuttgart in 1852: "As we wonder what it is that grips us and fills us with foreboding and delight in Chopin's music, we are apt to find a solution that might appear to many as pure fantasy, namely that Chopin's intention was to release upon us a cloud of quarter-tones, which now appear only as phantom doppelgänger in the shadowy realm within the intervals produced by enharmonic change. Once the quarter-tones are emancipated, an entirely new world of tones will open to us. But since we have been accustomed to the long established divisions into semitones, these new sounds will seem weird, suggesting a splash of discordant waves. Yet the children of the next generation, or the one after next, will suck in these strange sounds with mother's milk, and may find in them a more stimulating and doubly rich art. Chopin seems to push at these mysterious portals; his melodies stream in colliding currents through the semitones as if groping for finer and more spiritual nuances than those that were available for his purposes. And when this door is finally sprung open, we will stand a step nearer to the eternal domain of natural sounds. As it is, we can only give a weak imitation of the Aeolian harp, of the rustle of the forest, of the magical ripple of the waters, unable to render them in their true impressions, because our so-called scales made up of whole tones and semitones are too coarse and have too many gaps, while Nature possesses not only quarter-tones and eighth-tones but an infinite scale of split atoms of sound!"

**Migratory Tonics.** When tonalities are in a state of constant flux, the laws of probability will still lead to the accidental formation of tonal centers, notes that occur more frequently than others, much in the line of the well-known paradox that if only three dozen individuals are assembled at a party, the odds are even that two of them will have the same day and month for a birthday. Such statistically established keynotes in an otherwise free modulatory environment may be called MIGRATORY TONICS, a term particularly suitable for works in which tonality is not renounced unequivocally.

**Millimetrization.** This is a term introduced by Villa-Lobos to describe the transfer of mathematical curves or outlines of photographs onto graph paper, precise to a millimeter. His best known piece arranged according to MILLIMETRIZATION is *New York Skyline.*

**Mixed Media.** Musicians of the AVANT-GARDE are increasingly laboring towards the coordination and unification of modern musical productions with those of other arts—painting, sculpture, phonograph recording, theater, radio, television, electronics—activities that are often generalized under the category of MIXED MEDIA. The practice represents in fact a return to the ancient ideal of unity of liberal arts, with music occupying the honorable position as *ancilla artis.* This tendency has generated a number of novel developments of catalytic artistic powers.

**Mobile.** In modern sculpture, a MOBILE is a delicately balanced construction of metal or wood, which can easily be swayed by gentle flow of air. Modern composers have adopted this term to describe a similarly flexible melorhythmic structure, usually scored for a small number of instruments, and characterized by a fine intervallic equilibrium, most often maintained by serial arrangements.

**Modern Music.** In the card catalogue of the British Museum, works written after 1800 are included in a section marked MODERN MUSIC. In American usage, MODERN MUSIC is a colloquialism for dance tunes, and popular songs. Medieval manuscripts dealing with musical theory often open with the phrase, "Brevitate gaudent moderni." The moderns that relished brevity were, in the opinion of the anonymous authors of these treatises, the adherents to Ars Nova. In present usage, MODERN MUSIC refers to that written since 1900. The variants are 20th-century music, New Music, Music of Our Time, Music of Today and Contemporary Music.

**Modernistic Music.** The flexion "istic" denotes a depreciation in the purity of the original product. Hellenistic art is inferior to that of the Golden Age of Greece; PRIMITIVISTIC paintings or compositions suggest a less virile version of the artistic qualities of primitive man; IMPRESSIONISTIC idioms are dissipated derivatives of IMPRESSIONISM. To describe a piece of music as MODERNISTIC has an aura of indulgent condescension, suggesting an adoption of models of modern music and a facile pastiche "à la manière de. . . ."

**Monism.** MONISM is a philosophical doctrine postulating the existence of a basic element that is the prime constituent of all material objects. In music MONISM denotes an analogous primacy of a concept or a function. The dodecaphonic series is a MONISTIC factor which determines the development of an entire work. A set of variations is intrinsically MONISTIC since it is derived from a primary source, but it is pluralistic if the variations are regarded as mutually independent entities.

**Monodrama.** MONODRAMA is a stage work in which only one actor, speaker, or singer acts, recites or sings. Schoenberg introduced a type of singing recitation, SPRECHSTIMME, in which the actor enunciates his lines in an inflected manner following the melorhythmic design of the music, a technique that came to its full fruition in his *Pierrot Lunaire*. The classical example of a staged MONODRAMA is Schoenberg's *Erwartung*. The Russian composer Vladimir Rebikov evolved a novel type of MONODRAMA which he described as Psychodrama; in it an actor recites his state of mind with a musical accompaniment. In Schoenberg's *Die glückliche Hand*, the central character sings and mimes the story, and a chorus comments on the action in SPRECHSTIMME.

**Monothematism and Polythematism.** "Brevitate gaudent moderni," medieval theorists said of the moderns of their own time. In the 20th century, this "joy of brevity" assumed the form of MONOTHEMATISM, in which a single subject governs the entire composition. MONOTHEMATISM is basic to the structure of a theme with variations; but if variations depart too widely from the theme, the result may be POLYTHEMATIC. Rigid MONOTHEMATISM carries an intrinsic danger of monotony; on the other hand, extreme POLYTHEMATISM courts the opposite danger of discontinuity. In MONOTHEMATISM the single theme must recur a sufficient number of times to produce an impression of uniformity; in POLYTHEMATIC constructions, similarities among successive themes must be avoided.

**Monte Carlo Method.** Statistical laws govern games of chance as well as the parameters of ALEATORY MUSIC. The MONTE CARLO METHOD is the most convenient of all gambling devices for easy musical application. The numbers from 1 to 36 of roulette, of the type used in the casino of Monte Carlo, can be equalized to the 36 chromatic tones of three octaves and notated accordingly as the roulette ball finds its niche, with zero corresponding to the lowest note of an arbitrarily selected progression. Rhythmic figures can be derived from a similar process by equalizing the 36 numbers to 36 different note values; if a smaller number of different rhythms is needed, then a dozen or a half-dozen sets on the roulette table can be selected as primary units. In the MONTE CARLO METHOD the probability of occurrence of a certain number depends on the frequency of previous incidences; thus certain notes may accumulate greater statistical probability of incidence and determine the tonal tropism. Harmonization and contrapuntal lines can be obtained by combining the single melorhythmic lines determined by individual Monte Carlo runs. Normally, atonal melodies and dissonant harmonies would result, but a spontaneous appearance of a dodecaphonic series is as unlikely as picking 12 different cards from a pack at random.

**Morphology.** The emergence of a great variety of new forms of composition makes it difficult to classify them according to traditional categories. It may be desirable therefore to substitute the term MORPHOLOGY for the formal analysis, with the nomenclature of botany replacing that of traditional historic terminology. The geometrical rubrics of botanical classification would add imaginative metaphors suitable to modern musical usages. It would be possible, for instance, to speak of radial symmetry in neo-classical music, of a chromatic inflorescence in an atonal melody, or even of agamogenetic axes in dodecaphonic cross-pollination. The advantage of such botanical similes lies in precision and specificity of the terms and in their easy applicability to intervalic structures.

**Musicorama.** This is a telescoped word descriptive of a continuously variegated panorama of connected musical episodes.

**Musique Concrète.** MUSIQUE CONCRÈTE was discovered and named on 15 April 1948 in Paris by Pierre Schaeffer, a French radio engineer. Experimenting with the newly invented magnetic tape, he found that a heterogeneous collection of songs, noises, conversations, radio commercials, etc. recorded on tape, presented a realistic phonomontage which may serve for actual composition by superimposing fragments of tape recordings in a polyphony of random sounds, splicing the tape in various ways, running it at different speeds, or backwards, etc. The raw materials of "concrete music" are susceptible to all kinds of treatment and are therefore capable of unlimited transformations. The technique of double and triple recording on the same length of tape makes it possible to create a polyphony of concrete music of great complexity. In fact it is possible to recompose a classical symphony from a recording of a single note, which can subsequently be changed in pitch and arranged in the requisite rhythmic order, superimposed on other tones derived from the original note, altered in tone color by additional electronic manipulation, until a whole work is reconstructed from these constituent tonal dynamic and instrumental elements. The Polish composer Wlodzimierz Kotoński composed an *Etude concrète* for orchestra using as his material a single stroke of the cymbal electronically altered and transposed. The American experimenter Richard Maxfield collected 30 seconds of coughs at a modern ballet recital and expanded these bronchial sonorities into a five-minute orchestral work entitled *Cough Music*.

**Mutations.** In search for synonyms or paronyms to replace the ambiguous nomenclature of academic musicology, some modern composers have begun using the scientific sounding words VARIANTS or MUTATIONS for Variations. MUTATIONS may be beneficial, musically speaking, when the mutant genes add to the brilliance of thematic adornment, as in some variations in the diaphanous music of Ravel; or they may be detrimental to the bio-musical organism, as in the cluttered polyphony of Max Reger. Recessive MUTATIONS, such as Stravinsky's neo-Baroque ornamentation, may become dominant characteristics, with uncertain benefits. In human terms, MUTATIONS are found in large musical families, in which the embryo develops fully conditioned by the genetic complex of his parents. A striking example is that of Siegfried Wagner, a musical mutant who fully absorbed the musical genes of his father but acquired MUTATIONS that made him sterile. Some MUTATIONS are products of defective genes of the theme itself, a condition that may lead to melodic dyscrasia, harmonic dyslogia and contrapuntal dyskinesia. There is no relief in such cases but to destroy the theme *in statu nascendi* in order to eliminate mutagenic elements and build afresh an untainted homunculus.

**Mystic Chord.** In conformity with his mystical beliefs, Scriabin described the basic chord of *Prometheus,* C, F-sharp, B-flat, E, A, D, as the MYSTIC CHORD. Ex post facto, he regarded these components, seriatim, as 8th, 9th, 10th, 11th, 13th, and 14th overtones. Analytically, the MYSTIC CHORD belongs to the category of the dominant-ninth in a major key with two suspensions, as is made clear by resolving F-sharp to G and A to B-flat.

**Narcolepsy.** Symphony concerts are notoriously conducive to NARCOLEPSY, and their attendance is sometimes recommended by psychologists as an effective cure of insomnia. Statistical surveys indicate that the narcogenic factors are mainly the pendulum-like rhythmic beats in classical music, particularly when there is no change in dynamics. An unexpected sforzando will wake up even the most inveterate narcoleptic, as illustrated by the story of Haydn's *Surprise Symphony* with its famous chord in the slow movement that was supposed to arouse the somnolent London concert goers from their middle-aged slumber. On the other hand, modern works rarely put people to sleep because of the constant changes in rhythm and dynamics. NARCOLEPSY is also an inevitable outcome of lectures on musicology; according to observations conducted by a trained psychologist at a session of the International Musicological Congress in New York, a deep coma overtook practically the entire audience during the first twenty seconds of a reading from manuscript of a paper by an eminent Dutch musicologist. At the same occasion, attention was suddenly increased by the appearance on the podium of the inventor of a double-bass flute and an ultra-sonic piccolo. He could never succeed in blowing through the long tube of the big flute, which met with sympathy in the audience. The hyper-piccolo could not be heard by humans, but a terrier dog who strayed into the hall showed agitation at the ultra-sonics that canines can hear easily. Both the dog and the inventor were rewarded by hearty applause.

**Naturalism.** In musical usage, NATURALISM appears as an extreme case of VERISMO. Naturalistic opera emphasizes the negative phenomena of life without the redeeming quality of romance. In Soviet parlance NATURALISM has acquired a pejorative meaning; the word was used as a verbal missile in the attacks on Shostakovich's opera *Lady Macbeth of the District of Mzensk*, particularly with reference to the scene of adultery illustrated in an orchestral interlude by sliding trombones.

**Negative Music.** NEGATIVE MUSIC is synonymous with ANTI-MUSIC, but there is a scintilla of a difference between the two terms. ANTI-MUSIC stresses its opposition to any musical actions, whereas NEGATIVE MUSIC operates on the supposition that there may exist negative frequencies as mathematical abstractions, related to audible music as a negative to the positive in photography. NEGATIVE MUSIC would reverse dynamic values; a vocal text containing tender sentiments would be harmonized by loud dissonant noises; conversely, a symphonic poem on the subject of the nuclear war would be depicted by the minutest distillation of monodically concentrated tones. The field for experimentation in NEGATIVE MUSIC is limitless, precisely because it is impossible to speculate about its nature.

**Neo-Classicism.** When the luxuriance of IMPRESSIONISM reached its point of saturation, it became clear to many composers that further amplification of coloristic devices was no longer stimulating or novel. The Weber-Fechner law postulates that the force of physical impact must be increased exponentially in order to produce an arithmetical increase in the sensory impression, so that a hundredfold magnification of sound is needed to provide a tenfold increase in the physiological effect. It was to be expected that composers and audiences alike would rebound from such sonic inundation. This reaction coincided with the economic collapse following World War I so that it became financially impossible to engage large orchestras or grandiose operatic companies. The cry went all over Europe, "Back to Bach!" To this was added the slogan of NEW SIMPLICITY. Since it was no longer feasible to move forward, musical tastes with the aid of intellectual rationalization made a 180° turn towards the past. But the past could not be recaptured in its literal form, and the new retrograde movement was launched under the name of NEO-CLASSICISM. It was characterized by the following traits: (1) Rehabilitation of diatonicism as the dominant idiom, enhanced by pandiatonic constructions, in which all seven degrees of the diatonic scale are functionally equal (2) Elimination of all programmatic and romantic associations either in the titles or the tonal content of individual works (3) A demonstrative revival of the Baroque forms of Sonata, Serenade, Scherzo, Passacaglia, Toccata and the florid type of variations (4) Demotion of chromatic elements of the scale to their traditional role as passing notes (5) Restrained use of massive sonorities and renunciation of all external and purely decorative effects, such as non-thematic melismas and non-essential harmonic figurations (6) Cultivation of compact forms, such as symphonies and sonatas having a single movement and operas without a chorus and with a reduced orchestral contingent (usually containing 13 instruments), with an important piano part performing the function of the cembalo in Baroque music (7) Reconstruction of old Baroque instruments, particularly the harpsichord and their employment in modernized classical techniques (8) Exploration of canonic and fugal writing without adherence to strict rules of classical polyphony (9) Radical curtailment of the development section in Baroque forms with a purely nominal recapitulation, and a concise coda free from redundant repetition of final tonic chords.

**Neo-Medievalism.** NEO-CLASSICISM resuscitated Baroque music in a new guise of pandiatonic harmonies and asymmetrical rhythms. Retreating still further into the past, some modern composers discovered a world of surprisingly modernistic devices such as hocketus, heterophony and quodlibet, and the techniques of inversion and retrograde composition which are basic to SERIAL MUSIC. Modernization of these resources resulted in the stylized idiom of NEO-MEDIEVALISM, which adopted not only the old musical modalities, but the verbal usages of ecclesiastical Latin for texts. The most remarkable example of this trend is Stravinsky's oratorio *Oedipus Rex*, with a specially written text in medieval Latin. Carl Orff produced a number of successful works in a NEO-MEDIEVAL style, notably *Carmina Burana*, to texts in Latin and German dialects. A significant trait of these works is their imaginative repetitive technique. The liberating power of literal repetition has a particular attraction for composers of the AVANT-GARDE who follow oriental religious practices, exemplified by the interminable turning of the Tibetan prayer wheel.

**Neo-Modality.** The system of modes, so potent for centuries, nearly lost all its binding power under the impact of ATONALITY and DODECAPHONY. Dormant strains have achieved a new Renaissance in the ethnically deep-rooted works of Béla Bartók. A surprising revival of modality was its adoption by the purveyors of ROCK 'N' ROLL. Roy Harris has built a sui generis *ethos* of modes by assigning specific emotions to each, according to the intervalic magnitude of the opening tetrachord, ranging from the most spacious, Lydian mode, expressing optimism, to the least spacious, Locrian mode, expressing pessimism. Avenir H. Monfred has developed a practical method of modern modal composition, diatonic NEO-MODALITY, in which a modal change is effected by altering the key signature. Thus the Dorian mode on D can be transformed, either during the process of composition or by spontaneous improvisation, into any other mode by adding sharps or flats to the key signature; it would be transmuted into D major by placing two sharps in the key signature, into the Phrygian mode by two flats, etc.

**Neo-Mysticism.** The words "Laus Deo" which Haydn used to append to every manuscript upon its completion were simply the expression of his piety and did not imply a claim of direct communication with the Deity. Mystical composers of the 20th century, on the other hand, believed that they were oracles of higher powers. Mahler thought he was possessed by Beelzebub. He scrawled appeals to Satan in the manuscript of his unfinished *Tenth Symphony*; he believed in the mystical magic of all of his music. But it was left to Scriabin to formalize his mystical consciousness in musical terms. His symphony *Prometheus* is based on a six-note chord which he called MYSTIC CHORD. Shortly before his death he sketched out the text for a Mysterium, which he envisioned as a synaesthetic action which would comprise all human senses as receiving organs. A large ensemble of bells was an instrumental feature of this eschatological creation, to be performed high over the Himalayan Mountains.

**Neophobia.** Musical NEOPHOBIA is a neurotic fear of radical innovations. Professional music critics are particularly prone to suffer from it, a condition that they attempt to disguise as profound devotion to the immutable laws of music. Like mental patients, they regard themselves as the only rational human beings in a mad world. The more enlightened among them often correct their former misapprehensions. At the first American performance of *Don Juan* by Richard Strauss, Philip Hale described it as "a good deal of a bore." Eleven years later he called it a work of "fascinating, irresistible insolence and glowing passion." Heinrich Strobel, who became the great panjandrum of the AVANT-GARDE, had contributed some choice invectives against the American moderns in his report of a concert in Berlin in 1932: "For two hours Nicolas Slonimsky bore down on the musicians of the Berlin Philharmonic, until finally they could no longer refrain from openly showing their disgust. For an hour and three quarters the public tolerated the noise, but by the cacophonous melee of *Arcana* by Varèse the audience lost their patience. A scandal broke loose. It was understandable. No ear can endure this sort of noise for any length of time. It has nothing to do with music. It does not shock and it does not amuse. It is simply senseless."

**Neo-Primitivism.** An art saturated with culture is invariably tempted to return to its simple origins, chronologically to the cave paintings of primitive man and to the haunting drum rhythms of Homo Protomusicus, and biologically to Infantiloquy. Supreme mastery of design is used by abstract expressionist painters to emulate pre-historic color drawings, and a sophisticated instrumental technique is utilized by modern composers for children's pieces in asymmetrical rhythms.

From these dual resources, intuitively developed by primitive man and by a human child, grew the language of NEO-PRIMITIVISM. Discarding the civilized garments of romantic images and impressionistic colors, it seeks to attain the crude power of massively arrayed sonorities, asymmetrical rhythms and percussive instrumentation. In NEO-PRIMITIVISM, melodies are brief refrains, often limited to the range of a major tetrachord. Reiteration of single notes in unchanged speed is cultivated to the point of stupefaction. Vacuous progressions of naked fifths and fourths are used to form an impression of inarticulate eloquence. Heterophony, in which a mobile voice elaborates on the principal subject ignoring the niceties of counterpoint, is encountered in numerous scores of NEO-PRIMITIVISTIC music, as a curious recessive characteristic.

NEO-PRIMITIVISM is almost invariably nationalistic in character. The greatest masterpiece of NEO-PRIMITIVISM, Stravinsky's *Le Sacre du Printemps,* bears the subtitle *Scenes of Pagan Russia.* Béla Bartók's music evokes the Neo-Primitivistic landscape of immemorial Pannonia. Villa-Lobos recreates the inchoate sound of the Brazilian jungle in his symphonies. NEO-PRIMITIVISM is nurtured on the essential character of the race, but the composer himself need not be an archeologist; he derives his inspiration from the art of his own time. The French painter Henri Rousseau copied the subjects and color patterns of his exotic paintings from illustrations in a French children's book. Paul Gauguin painted his Tahitian women from photographs, preferring them to living models. Nonetheless, both created a genuinely novel type of pictorial NEO-PRIMITIVISM. In music, however, NEO-PRIMITIVISTIC representation cannot be effected without a complete mastery of modern techniques of composition. The theory that an analphabetic musician can write primitivistically authentic works by simply disregarding the civilized rules of harmony and counterpoint is false.

**Neo-Romanticism.** NEO-ROMANTICISM represents a secondary phase of the modern stylistic upheaval, following the repudiation of programmatic music as a valid medium. The frustrations of World War I sharpened a general disenchantment among poets, artists and musicians, but the purely negative intellectual movements, such as DADAISM, soon exhausted their shock power and gave way to a mitigated type of romantic music in the form of NEO-ROMANTICISM. Coloristic elements, so ingratiatingly used in the symphonies of Sibelius, in the tone poems of Richard Strauss and in the early ballet scores of Stravinsky were applied with apprehensive circumspection by Neo-Romantic composers. Representational onomatopoeia and literal reproduction of natural sounds replaced the subjective effusions of modern pictorialism. Benjamin Britten's sea gulls in the interludes of his opera *Peter Grimes,* Olivier Messiaen's bird-songs in his score *Chronochromie* and the phonograph record of the song of a real nightingale in Ottorino Respighi's *Pines of Rome* are modern instances of NEO-ROMANTICISM.

**New Music.** Newness is a recurring motive in musical nomenclature. The emergence of rhythmic modalities in the 14th century became historically known as Ars Nova. The monodic type of composition used by the Florentine initiators of opera was published under the name *Nuove musiche.* In painting, *Art Nouveau* was the description given the French art that flourished in the 1890's. The term NEW MUSIC became current about 1920; it denoted a type of modern music marked by a dissonant counterpoint, ATONALITY and brevity of expression. Later, NEW MUSIC became synonymous with ULTRA-MODERN MUSIC.

**New Simplicity.** During the NEO-CLASSICAL flowering of the 1920's, the slogan NEW SIMPLICITY was raised among composers eager to divest themselves of an enforced sophistication of the period. In practice, NEW SIMPLICITY meant a return to elementary and sometimes ABECEDARIAN melodic and harmonic practices, barely covered with a patina of NON-TOXIC DISSONANCES.

**Non-Toxic Dissonances.** DISSONANCES can be said to be NON-TOXIC or non-corrosive if they are embanked within a tonal sequence, or if their candential illation corresponds to traditional modalities. It is the harmonic context that determines the toxicity of a dissonance for an untutored ear. Among the most corrosive dissonances are atonal combinations in which intervals of a high degree of discordance, such as major sevenths, minor seconds and the tritone, are combined with acoustically euphonious intervals of a perfect fifth and a perfect fourth. The absence of thirds, whether major or minor, is the distinctive feature of corrosive harmony, but toxic sonic effects result also from the simultaneous use of two homonymous major and minor triads on account of the interference between the major and minor thirds. Changes in bio-chemical balance and nervous reactions to the impact of toxic dissonances can be measured on a neurograph, providing a scientific clue to the apperception of modern music.

**Numbers.** The Latin word *Numeri* had a second meaning, music, for it was governed by the law of proportions between two different sounds. In Shakespearean English, NUMBERS refer to musical composition. St. Augustine drew a distinction between *Numeri sonantes*, the actual musical tone that is perceived by the senses, and *Numeri recordabiles*, music that is remembered. In St. Augustine's concept, a melody was formed by a single sound instantaneously perceived and memorably associated with several preceding sounds. Long before St. Augustine, Aristoxenus likened the musical tones of a melody to letters in a language. So intimate was the connection felt between NUMBERS and music that in medieval universities music was taught as part of the Quadrivium of exact sciences, along with arithmetic, geometry and astronomy. This association with NUMBERS was lost in classical and romantic music. Not until the 20th century did the numerical element in music regain its status. Mathematical parameters lie at the foundation of serial music. The calculus of sets is an important tool in rhythmic serialization. Some composers have applied the Fibonacci NUMBERS, in which each term is the sum of its two predecessors, to metrical, rhythmic and intervalic parameters. Simple arithmetical progressions also yield material for rhythmic arrangements. The application of NUMBERS to composition is limitless; the difficulty is to select numerical sets that would provide material for purely musical structures.

**Objets Trouvés.** Ready-made objects are often incorporated by modern artists as part of a sculpture or a montage. Ultra-modern composers sometimes insert passages from works by other composers as a token of homage and partly as an experiment in construction. Such OBJETS TROUVÉS need not harmonize with their environment which may be completely alien to the nature of the implant. An early example is the sudden appearance of the tune *Ach du lieber Augustin* in Schoenberg's *Second String Quartet*.

**Omnitonality.** In search of terms signifying various degrees of modulatory freedom, modern musicologists have chanced upon OMNITONALITY, to indicate a totality of tonalities entailing frequent collisions of different keys. OMNITONALITY enjoyed a certain vogue as a compromise definition for modern techniques that retained the basic sense of tonality but expanded it to the entire cycle of major and minor scales. It is almost synonymous with PANTONALITY.

**Open Form Composition.** Works based on CONTROLLED IMPROVISATION, in which materials are selected from available resources, have a venerable ancestry; classical composers supplied alternative versions for transitions and endings as a matter of course. In its modern avatar, OPEN FORM COMPOSITION often delegates the ordering of component parts to the performer. Chronological priority in developing such techniques belongs to the American composer Earle Brown whose *Folio*, written in 1952, affords great latitude in the arranging of given materials. Karlheinz Stockhausen further developed this technique in his *Klavierstücke*, consisting of separate sections which can be performed in any order.

**Organized Sound.** Sound is an acoustical phenomenon, which all by itself does not make music. Composition begins at the point when two sounds are connected in linear succession or vertical superposition. But the nature of these links is not circumscribed by any rules of melody and harmony. With the emancipation of dissonances in the 20th century, the vertical combinations became free from restraints imposed on them by tradition. Linear progressions, once bound within the framework of modes and scales, are developed in atonal designs. Schoenberg replaced diatonic melody and consonant harmony by the new dodecaphonic discipline. Edgar Varèse advanced the concept of ORGANIZED SOUND, as a complex of successive acoustical phenomena unrelated to one another except by considerations of sonic equilibrium. Dissonant combinations are preferred because they constitute a probabilistic majority and therefore are entitled to greater representation in ORGANIZED SOUND. For the same statistical reasons, successions of melodic notes are apt to generate atonal configurations. The form of works written according to the doctrine of ORGANIZED SOUND is athematic, and the rhythms are usually asymmetric. The valence between successive units, in melody, harmony and rhythm, under such conditions, is an idempotent.

**Palimpsest.** In musical semantics, the term PALIMPSEST may be used as a substitution for an intentionally erased composition. This erasure may be complete or partial, with some elements of the original idea left under the sonic surface. The hidden design may be discovered by intervalic analysis, comparable to the use of ultra-violet rays in detecting the old text in a parchment covered by a newer piece of writing.

**Palindrome.** Palindromic words and sentences do not change when they are read backwards. Max Reger, whose last name is a PALINDROME, replied wittily to an admirer who complained that he could see only his back while he conducted a concert: "I am no different front or back." Musical PALINDROMES are synonymous with retrograde movements. In a PALINDROMIC section in Alban Berg's opera *Lulu*, the music revolves backwards to depict the story of Lulu's incarceration and escape. Samplers of PALINDROMIC canons are found in Nicolas Slonimsky's *Thesaurus of Scales and Melodic Patterns*.

**Palingenesis.** The meaning of the word PALINGENESIS is rebirth, and it is parasynonymous with METEMPSYCHOSIS. In modern musical usage PALINGENESIS corresponds to a reprise, with the important difference that the original material is not recapitulated literally but appears metempsychotically in a form as dissimilar from its progenitor as a reincarnated cat is from its former human avatar. PALINGENESIS is a particularly convenient term to designate an electronically altered sonic substance, or a topologically metamorphosed thematic idea.

**Pandiatessaron.** This is a vertical column consisting of perfect fourths (from *Diatessaron*, the interval of a fourth in ancient Greek music). The PANDIATESSARON contains all 12 notes of the tempered scale and represents a dodecaphonic integration of quartal melodies.

**Pandiatonicism.** The term PANDIATONICISM was coined by Nicolas Slonimsky and was first used in the first edition of his book *Music Since 1900* published in 1937. It is a technique in which all seven degrees of the diatonic scale are used freely in democratic equality. The functional importance of the primary triads, however, remains undiminished in PANDIATONIC harmony. PANDIATONICISM possesses both tonal and modal aspects, with the distinct preference for major keys. The earliest PANDIATONIC extension was the added major sixth over the tonic major triad. A cadential chord of the tonic major seventh is also of frequent occurrence. Independently from the development of PANDIATONICISM in serious music, American JAZZ players adopted it as a practical device. Concluding chords in piano improvisations in Jazz are usually PANDIATONIC, containing the tonic, dominant, mediant, submediant and supertonic, with the triad in open harmony in the bass topped by a series of perfect fourths. In C major, such chords would be, from the bass up, C, G, E, A, D, G. It is significant that all the components of this Pandiatonic complex are members of the natural harmonic series. With C as the fundamental generator, G is the third partial, E the fifth partial, D the 9th, B the 15th and A the 27th. The perfect fourth is excluded both theoretically and practically, for it is not a member of the harmonic series, an interesting concordance of actual practice and acoustical considerations. With the dominant in the bass, a complete succession of fourths, one of them an augmented fourth, can be built: G, C, F, B, E, A, D, G, producing a satisfying Pandiatonic complex. When the subdominant is in the bass, the most euphonious result is obtained by a major triad in open harmony, F, C, A, in the low register, and E, B, D, G in the upper register. Polytriadic combinations are natural resources of Pandiatonicism, with the dominant combined with the tonic, e.g. C, G, E, D, G, B, making allowance for a common tone; dominant over the subdominant, as in the complex, F, C, A, D, G, B, etc. True Polytonality cannot be used in Pandiatonicism, since all the notes are in the same mode. Pedal points are particularly congenial to the spirit of Pandiatonicism, always following the natural spacing of the component notes, using large intervals in the bass register and smaller intervals in the treble. The esthetic function of Pandiatonicism is to enhance the resources of triadic harmony; that is the reason why the superposition of triads, including those in minor, are always productive of a resonant diatonic bitonality. Although Pandiatonicism has evolved from tertian foundations, it lends itself to quartal and quintal constructions with satisfactory results. Pandiatonicism is a logical medium for the techniques of NEO-CLASSICISM. Many sonorous usages of PANDIATONICISM can be found in the works of Debussy, Ravel, Stravinsky, Casella, Malipiero, Vaughan Williams, Aaron Copland and Roy Harris. The key of C major is particularly favored in piano music, thanks to the "white" quality of the keyboard. Indeed, Pandiatonic piano music developed empirically from free improvisation on the white keys. Small children promenading their little fingers over the piano keyboard at the head level produce Pandiatonic melodies and Pandiatonic harmonies of excellent quality and quite at random.

**Panpentatonicism.** By analogy with PANDIATONICISM, which denotes a free use of the seven diatonic degrees, PANPENTATONICISM grants a similar dispensation to the five notes of the pentatonic scale. Consecutive fourths and fifths are frequent contrapuntal resources. Since the leading tone is missing in the pentatonic scale, plagal cadences are the only available endings. PANPENTATONIC tone-clusters are more euphonious than the pandiatonic ones; when projected against a perfect fifth in the bass, they create an attractive sonority of a modernistic PANPENTATONIC chinoiserie.

**Pantonality.** The term PANTONALITY denotes the use of all major and minor keys with complete freedom and without preference for any particular tonality. PANTONALITY is almost synonymous with OMNITONALITY, the only difference being that PANTONALITY includes atonal melodic progressions and uninhibited dissonant textures, while OMNITONALITY tends to enhance the basic sense of tonality.

**Parerga & Paralipomena.** Like Schopenhauer, who published fragments of his philosophical writings under the high-sounding name PARERGA & PARALIPOMENA, Richard Strauss gathered some residual materials from his *Symphonia domestica,* and incorporated them in a work commissioned by the amputated pianist Paul Wittgenstein, denominated *Parergon zur Symphonia domestica,* and scored for piano left-hand and orchestra. While such creative thrift is justified when Schopenhauer or Strauss practice it, collections and arrangements of *disjecta membra* put together by composers of lesser endowment, and particularly those whose technical progress was arrested at the Abecedarian or Analphabetic niveau, are clearly objectionable.

**Permeability.** PERMEABILITY is a factor that determines the degree of interpenetrability of thematic, non-thematic and bruitistic elements, reinforcing the structure of a given tonal complex, and occasionally coming to a mutually annihilating collision, in which the resulting GESTALT becomes a terraced and tesselated ziggurat. The term PERMEABILITY is also used to describe the process of mutual osmosis among parameters of ORGANIZED SOUND.

**Pernicious Interference.** The law of contrasts is basic to every piece of modern music, but supererogatory acervation and ornamental promiscuity of melodic and harmonic elements constitute PERNICIOUS INTERFERENCE. Taste and technical skill are the sole means to avoid this danger.

**Planarianism.** A musical composition which can be dissected into two or more parts, with each growing out into a separate independent body may be called PLANARIAN, by analogy with the flatworm of that name that possesses a trifid intestine and is capable of regenerating each of its severed parts into new flatworms. The structure of a work in the style of PLANARIANISM may reach great complexity. Karlheinz Stockhausen has written autogenetic works that can be cut up, with each musical PLANARIAN becoming a self-sufficient sonic organism. This process of vermiculation and its concomitant divisibility has been further advanced by John Cage; at his hands each musical platyhelminth becomes a unique and irreproducible species.

**Plastic, Elastic and Spastic Variations.** Plasticity of texture is essential in modern Variations, securing a malleability of tonal materials. Tonal Elasticity adds intervallic flexibility

1475

to a plastic theme. A rhythmic effect can be achieved by Spastic convulsions of the melodic line, producing implosions which impart a stimulating sense of disquiet to the music.

**Pluralistic Structures.** Pluralism is an epistemological concept connoting a multiplicity of causes and events. Developments of modern music support the pluralistic view in such styles as NEO-CLASSICAL, IMPRESSIONISTIC or EXPRESSIONISTIC, in which the factors of melody, rhythm, and intervalic values are of different formulation. But the same type of structure becomes monistic if it is derived from a uniform set, as for instance in Variations. Pluralism and Monism are mutually specular, but they are reconciled in serial music. Analogies with the visible spectrum invite themselves. White light is monistic in its sensory perception, but pluralistic when it is analyzed into the prismatic constituents of the rainbow. WHITE SOUND is a monistic aggregation of sonic particles, which can be separated into a pluralistic collection of its tonal components.

**Pointillism.** In the nomenclature of modern art, POINTILLISM is a method of applying colored dots to the canvas, forming a cumulative design. In modern music, the term is descriptive of atonal and athematic idioms, in which separate notes are distributed individually rather than as parts of an integral melorhythmic curve. The maximal dispersion of members of a dodecaphonic series in different octave positions is an example of serial POINTILLISM.

**Political Symbolism.** In the affective usages of the Renaissance, major keys symbolized joy and minor keys sadness. Such correspondence of emotional states and sounds has an acoustical foundation, for the major third is the fifth overtone of the fundamental tone, while the minor third is not a member of the harmonic series and produces interference. This natural preference for major keys as acoustically superior to minor tonalities was the subject of an interesting philosophical exposition of POLITICAL SYMBOLISM given by Anatoly Lunacharsky, Soviet Commissar of Education in an introductory speech at a Moscow concert on 10 December 1919: "Major keys lift the sound; they raise it a semitone up, and its power grows. By analogy with laughter, with its exultant feeling of joy, major keys elevate the mood and cheer us up. Minor keys, on the other hand, droop, leading to a compromise, to a surrender of positions; the sound is lowered, and its power diminishes. Allow me, as an old Bolshevik, to put it this way: major tonality is Bolshevik music; but a minor key is a deeply rooted inner Menshevik. Cultural history chose to call major and minor two different species of modes in the world of sound. Bolsheviks and Mensheviks are the two parties which have not only determined the fate of Russia in the greatest years of her life, but became a world phenomenon, and brought out, along with reactionary and bourgeois slogans, the two most important banners around which all humanity gathers."

**Pollution.** Harmonic POLLUTION is characterized by indiscriminate disposal of chromatic refuse in a diatonic landscape. The process is vividly illustrated by a fetid organ arrangement of Chopin's *Nocturne* in E-flat major, in which the initial ascending interval of a major sixth, from B-flat to G, is infested by noxious chromatic runs. A polluted version of Prokofiev's *Peter and the Wolf* has been published in America in the absence of a copyright agreement with the Soviet Union; it is characterized by vulgar insertion of auxiliary material in every available melodic or harmonic vacancy. Orchestral POLLUTION manifests itself in a general sonic flatulence and an infarction of supernumerary thirds and sixths. The rhythmic line, too, is an easy victim of POLLUTION. In the remarkable compound rhythmic design in Gershwin's song *I Got Rhythm*, the original asymmetric line is often grossly mutilated, reducing it to Abecedarian syncopation. Erudite arrangements of works of Bach and other classics, made by musicians of intelligence and taste, cannot be cited as examples of musical POLLUTION. Even hyperchromatic pullulation found in some transcriptions by Max Reger, possesses validity, although they should be labelled "artificially flavored with chromatic additives." Some morphological transformations and homeological modifications are legitimate means of modernization. Examples of such artistic enhancement are *Symphonic Metamorphoses on Themes of Carl Maria von Weber* by Hindemith and the ballet *Le Baiser de la Fée* by Stravinsky, imaginatively deformed from themes of Tchaikovsky.

**Polymetry.** In a linear application, POLYMETRY is a succession of changing meters; polyphonically, POLYMETRY is the simultaneous use of several different meters. POLYMETRY dates back to the Renaissance, exemplified in the double time signature of Spanish dance music, 3/4 against 6/8. In operatic usage, POLYMETRY is encountered in scenes descriptive of simultaneous uncoordinated action, known under the name Imbroglio (literally, entanglement). The concluding section of Stravinsky's *Le Sacre du Printemps*, with its constantly changing time signatures, represents linear POLYMETRY at its greatest complexity. (It is characteristic of changing fashions that in 1940 Stravinsky rearranged this section in more uniform time signatures.) The unequal division of binary and ternary meters, which is a species of linear POLYMETRY, is found in Rimsky-Korsakov's opera *The Legend of the City of Kitezh*, in which the invading Mongols are characterized by the irregularly divided measures of $2/8 + 2/8 + 2/8 + 3/8 = 9/8$ and $3/8 + 2/8 + 3/8 = 8/8$. Linear POLYMETRY of this type is also characteristic of Balkan popular dances. Modern composers, fascinated by purely numerical properties of fractions representing traditional time signatures, often follow a pre-determined arithmetical formula to establish a desired metrical progression. Boris Blacher makes use of the series of numerators 1, 2, 3, 4, 5, 4, 3, 2, 1, in his orchestral *Ornaments*. Elliott Carter employs "metric modulation" by changing meter and tempo in polyphonic writing. The Welsh composer Daniel Jones has developed a system of complex time signatures based on repeated numerical patterns, some of them of extraordinary length, e.g. $32322322232232332332332/4$ and $9864323468/8$, both used in his *Sonata for Three Kettledrums*. He also has elaborated the techniques of augmentation, diminution and retrograde in changing time signatures, designated by such arithmetical ALGORITHMS as $6432/8$ and $3464/8$. The numerators in all these examples represent the succession of repeated or changing numbers of beats in a bar.

Perhaps the most remarkable instance of contrapuntal POLYMETRY is found in the second movement of *Three Places in New England* by Charles Ives, illustrating the meeting of two marching bands, with similar marching tunes played simultaneously at different tempi, in the ratio 4/3, so that four bars of the faster march equal three bars of the slower tempo. In his original manuscript Ives coordinated these different tempi within the uniform measures in 4/4 time, marking cross-accents wherever they occurred. At the suggestion made by Nicolas Slonimsky, Ives agreed to incorporate in the published score an alternative arrangement with non-coincidental barlines, in clear polymetric notation. In his performances of the work, Nicolas Slonimsky conducted three bars in 4/4 time with his right hand and four bars in *alla breve* time with his left hand. In this polymetric coordination, the downbeat of the left hand coincides successively with the downbeat of the right hand, then with the fourth beat of the right hand, with the third beat, with the second beat and again with the downbeat of the right hand. In the first bar the upbeat of the left hand falls between the second and the third beats of the right hand; in the next bar the upbeat of the left hand occurs between the downbeat and the second beat of the right hand, and so on. Those in the orchestra who had parts with the faster march were to follow the conductor's left hand and the rest his right hand. (A critic remarked that Slonimsky's performance was evangelical, for his right hand knew not what his left hand was doing.)

**Polymodality.** POLYMODALITY is a special case of POLYTONALITY in which the principal melodic lines are modal rather than explicitly major or minor. Polymodal harmonies are disposed with the best effect by the use of a triple pedal point in open harmony in a minor key, suggesting Dorian, Phrygian or Aeolian constructions.

**Polyrhythmy.** As the etymology of the word indicates, POLYRHYTHMY is the simultaneous occurrence of several different rhythms. POLYRHYTHMY differs from POLYMETRY in that the former indicates a combination of two rhythmic groups, usually consisting of mutually prime numbers of notes or irregular groups of non-coincident patterns, while the latter merely indicates the superposition, or a palimpsest, of two different meters usually having the same note values as their common denominator. If two measures of different time signatures are isochronous, then the effect is both polymetric and polyrhythmic. The problems of the polyrhythmic notation have been solved by composers of the AVANT-GARDE who prefer to indicate the duration of individual notes or rhythmic groups in seconds rather than note values. Another possible solution of polyrhythmic notation would be to introduce time signatures with denominators not limited to the powers of two. A time signature of 2/3 or 4/7 would replace triplets or septuplets in binary meters, but attempts to introduce such numerical innovations have been unsuccessful.

**Polytetrachord.** A term introduced by Nicolas Slonimsky in his *Thesaurus of Scales and Melodic Patterns*, POLYTETRACHORD is omnitonal. A major POLYTETRACHORD consists of 12 conjunct major tetrachords, traversing all 12 keys of the cycle of major scales. A minor POLYTETRACHORD consists of 12 keys of the cycle of minor scales. A partial use of the POLYTETRACHORD affords a rapid linear modulation into any major or minor key.

**Polytonality.** POLYTONALITY is the simultaneous use of several keys. In actual practice, it is difficult to sustain the acoustical separation of more than two different keys, thus reducing POLYTONALITY to BITONALITY. Four mutually exclusive triads are workable in linear arpeggios (e.g., C major, F-sharp major, D minor, G-sharp minor, distributed in ascending quadritonal passages), but the same four keys in columnar superposition could be made effective only by careful differentiation of instrumental groups (e.g., C major in the strings, F-sharp major in muted horns, D minor in clarinets and oboes and G-sharp minor in flutes and piccolos, with optional support of the strings by the bassoons and double-bassoons.)

Simultaneous linear progressions of two or more different tonalities are in the category of POLYTONALITY. Bitonal scales with their tonics at a distance of major or minor thirds or sixths are entirely consonant, even though they run along different tonalities. But even scales in parallel major sevenths, if played at sufficiently large distances, become technically consonant. Theoretically, C major scale played in the lowest available register of the piano and B major scale at a distance of four, five or six octaves, minus a semitone, will form consonant harmony, because B in relation to the low C at such distances constitutes the 15th, 30th and 60th partial of the harmonic series. The coda of *Also sprach Zarathustra* of Richard Strauss contains a B major triad in the high treble with a double-bass playing a low C, an instance often referred to as the first explicit use of POLYTONALITY. Actually, the members of the B major triad in the treble represent the 60th, 75th and 90th partials of the harmonic series, generated by the low C, and are therefore consonant combinations. Genuine, acoustically pure polytonal combinations can be provided by playing the triads of D major, E major, G major and others against C major in the deep bass without falling into dissonance. Beyond the audible range, even F-sharp major, the farthest key in the cycle of scales from C major, can be brought into the harmonic series. Most polytonal combinations, however, are not even theoretically consonant. An amusing example of POLYTONALITY is Mozart's *Ein musikalischer Spass*, where he makes the horns play in different keys from the rest of the orchestra. But Mozart's professed intention in this "musical joke" was to ridicule the ignorance of village musicians. He could not have anticipated the time when such musical jokes would become a new technique.

**Polytriads.** POLYTRIADIC harmony may be regarded as a special case of POLYTONALITY, with mobile parts containing complete triads. If the triads move along a single scale or a mode, the resulting technique is POLYMODALITY. Homonymous triads, major and minor, encased within the compass of a perfect fifth (e.g. C, E-flat, E-natural, G), are often found in modern works. Such POLYTRIADS are *e duobus unum*, giving rise to modes possessing the characteristics of both major and minor keys.

**Pop Music.** The colloquial abbreviation of the term Popular Music into POP MUSIC corresponds to the depreciation and devaluation of materials and resources of the original product. POP MUSIC is a counterpart of Pop Art, with its appeal directed mainly towards the heterogeneous musical, unmusical and antimusical masses. Its effects are achieved by the application of raucous and blatant sound amplified by electronics. POP MUSIC annexes numerous forms from the vast arsenal of sentimental ballads and country music and it manages to instill a tremendous amount of kinetic energy into its public manifestations. While POP MUSIC belongs in the category of DEMOTIC MUSIC, it tends to be more cosmopolitan in its appeal and capable of attracting miscellaneous groups of people without requiring special adaptation to the changing tastes of the audiences.

**Pornographic Music.** It was Eduard Hanslick who said that the last movement of Tchaikovsky's *Violin Concerto* suggested to him the hideous notion that music can actually stink to the ear. The literal depiction of an episode in *Symphonia Domestica* by Richard Strauss, which illustrates his retirement to the bed chamber with Frau Strauss, to the suggestive accompaniment of two conjugated trumpets, impressed some listeners at its first performance as indecent. In a symphonic interlude in Shostakovich's opera *Lady Macbeth of the District of Mzensk*, with the marital bed occupying the center of the stage, the trombone glissandi seem to give an onomatopoeic representation of sexual intercourse. Graphic notation offers excellent opportunities for suggestive pictorial pornography. The tetraphallic score *Mooga Pook* by the American composer Charles Amirkhanian is a fine example.

**Potential Techniques.** The number of POTENTIAL TECHNIQUES of musical composition is unlimited, as is the number of mathematical sets or matrices. The best-known numerical set in music is the method of composition with 12 tones, or DODECAPHONIC MUSIC. But it is possible to devise a hendecaphonic method, or decaphonic method, generated respectively by eleven or ten tones in a series. Any technique of composition is valid provided it is self-consistent. It is entirely justified to postulate a system in which only dissonant intervals are used. It is also conceivable to devise a method of composing only with nominal consonances (such a system was applied by Nicolas Slonimsky in his piano suite *Studies in Black and White*, in which only consonant intervals are used in a scheme of mutually exclusive counterpoint of pandiatonic sets in the right hand played on the white keys and panpentatonic figurations in the left hand played on the black keys). Any number of deficient or lipogrammatic systems of composition can be constructed by stipulating the omission of a note or a group of notes. Some modern poets experimented with omitting certain vowels or consonants in order to achieve a special effect. An American writer tied down the E key on his typewriter and wrote a whole novel without ever using that most frequent letter of the English alphabet, thus dispensing with the definite article, most personal pronouns, etc. The following techniques may be tabulated as possessing a workable rationale and some attractive coloristic features which might give them statistical chances of survival:

(1) Exclusive use of a limited number of notes in a scale, exemplified by the five-note scale, or Pentatonic scale and the Whole-Tone scale of six notes, the so-called Rimsky-Korsakov scale of alternating whole tones and semitones, a scale of nine notes consisting of three disjunct minor thirds with passing notes within the interval of each minor third, etc. (2) Various lipogrammatic or lipographic scales, including the hendecaphonic scale and decaphonic scale, often used by serial composers who do not wish to be restricted to the orthodox dodecaphonic method (3) Residual scales, in which the notes left over in a lipogrammatic composition are used as a matrix in a coda or a cadential codicil. In a hendecaphonic composition, such a codicil would contain a single note repeated in unison, in octave duplications, or in triplicate, quadruplicate, quintuplicate, sextuplicate and septuplicate, using all available octave points. Residual scales are legitimate devices in the building of dodecaphonic series. Thus the seven notes of the C major scale joined by the five notes of the pentatonic scale of the black keys would form a 12-tone matrix. Such a complex may also be called a conjugated diatonic-pentatonic complex (4) Intervallic lipographs, in which certain intervals are deliberately avoided in a serial set. Thirds and sixths, being most intimately associated with classical harmony, may be peremptorily excluded in favor of the seconds and sevenths in order to secure a prevalence of dissonant intervals. Emphatic use of naked fourths and fifths, to the exclusion of all other intervals, is a lipographic device to conjure up an archaic effect. A growing fashion in modern music is the selective assignment of a certain interval to a specific instrument. Béla Bartók made such a selective distribution of intervals in the second movement, *Game of the Couples*, of his *Concerto for Orchestra*, in which five pairs of wind instruments are each given a distinct interval to cultivate. Several modern composers apply such intervallic lipographs to instruments in chamber music (5) Derivative sets, made available as functions of a certain melodic figure differentiated by a given intervallic modulus. Let us differentiate a descending whole-tone scale in the bass by an ascending set of the following intervals: octave, major tenth, perfect 12th, two octaves, etc. Its derivative function will be the ascending melodic line of the following intervals: whole tone, semitone, sesquitone, whole tone, etc. This is a very important progression governing the harmonization in major triads in root position in contrary motion, which is found in Liszt's symphonic poem *Divine Comedy* and in the second act of Puccini's opera *Tosca*, announcing the entrance of the Chief of Police. Let us now harmonize the ascending whole-tone scale in the melody using the same function, that is harmonization by major triads in root position in contrary motion following the intervallic distances between the

melody and the bass at a perfect octave, a major tenth, a perfect 12th, a double octave, etc. The function in the bass will be a descending pattern of the following intervals: whole tone, semitone, sesquitone, whole tone, whole tone. This is the inversion of the melodic function obtained by differentiating by the same modulus the descending whole-tone scale in the bass. We find then that the whole-tone scale differentiated either in a descending bass or in an ascending melodic line will result in an identical function, inverted, and will thus constitute a reciprocal function, or an idempotent. Most interesting of all such reciprocal sets are those in which the principal equation is tonal and the derivative is atonal. A good example is an ascending diatonic scale in the melody arranged in two-part counterpoint with the stipulation that the derivative function should be a descending set seeking the nearest available nominal consonance. Under such conditions the differentiated ascending C major scale in the melody will result in a quasi-chromatic descending derivative set in the bass: C, B, A, A-flat, G, F-sharp, E and E-flat. But an ascending C major scale in the bass, under similar conditions will produce a different descending derivative in the melody, C, B, G-sharp, F, E, C-sharp, B, A. The different results are explained by the fact that while a perfect fifth is a consonance, its inversion, a perfect fourth, is not. Using consonant intervals as the functional operator is of interest because of the possibility of arranging atonally shaped melodies in triadic harmonies. There is a fertile field for experimentation along these lines, for instance harmonizing the ascending chromatic scale in the melody using only members of a single major triad in the bass. (Beginning with C in the melody, it is possible to harmonize the ascending chromatic scale up to A by using only members of the F major triad in the bass, descending and ascending without producing any dissonant intervals, e.g., C, A, F, C, A, F, A, C, F, A.) Such exercises in consonant counterpoint provide unexpected illumination on the nature of diatonic and chromatic scales in their relationship to triadic tonality (6) Intervallic progressions using only consonant intervals with certain specifications can provide a fresh resource for new contrapuntal techniques. A very fertile set of conditions is this: select two consonant intervals and use them in an unbroken series of alternations, with this proviso, that one of the voices must move by degrees, that is a major or a minor second up or down, the other voice adjusting itself accordingly to form the next interval. Let us take the octave E-E and the fifth as the next interval. We now move the upper E to F; since the next interval must be a perfect fifth, the lower voice must move to B-flat. Now let us move the upper note back to E, and since the next interval is again an octave, then the lower voice must go down to E as well. It is now the turn of the lower voice to move up and down gradually. It moves up to F; since the next interval must be a perfect fifth, the upper voice must come down from E to C. The F in the lower voice now returns to E, and since the next interval must be an octave, then the upper voice ascends from C to E. Now the lower voice goes down to D; the next interval is a perfect fifth, so the upper voice comes down from E to A. Trying again, while observing the same conditions of gradual progression vs. free intervallic leaps, the upper voice may go a major second up to F-sharp; in this case the lower voice must respond by moving up to B, forming a perfect fifth with F-sharp; after a return to the octave on E, the upper voice may descend to D-sharp, which will be seconded by the lower voice going up to G-sharp. Then both voices return to their respective E's, and the lower voice will take over the role of the *cantus firmus*. It will move, as the upper voice did before, to F-sharp, forcing the upper voice to move to C-sharp, and after passing through the octave, will descend to D-sharp, necessitating the lowering of the upper voice to A-sharp. The final interval will again be the octave. What is remarkable in this little exercise is that every note of the chromatic scale will be covered, and nine minor triads will be outlined by their tonics and dominants. By adding the missing mediants for each one of these chords in different octaves, one would obtain a third voice of surprising melodiousness. The next experiment may be conducted with a dissonant interval alternating with a consonant interval and finally with two dissonant intervals. The addition of supplemental contrapuntal voices will supply a further resource. (7) Homeological variations, obtained by extensions or compressions of thematic intervals provide a novel method of structural variations. The simplest case is exemplified by a uniform duplication of all intervals. Such an operation would convert Bach's *Chromatic Fugue* into an impressionistic piece of music, because all its semitones would be replaced by progressions of exotic sounding whole-tone scales. If the intervals of the same fugue are halved, the outcome will be a complex of icositetraphonic harmony.

**Prepared Piano.** PREPARED PIANO is an instrumental technique, which alters the sound by placing various small objects, such as bolts, nuts, metal clips, coins, on the piano strings. The idea may be traced to the old schoolboy trick of putting a piece of paper on the piano strings to produce a tinkling, harpsichord-like sound. The first modern composer to experiment scientifically with such devices was Henry Cowell, who initiated the technique of playing directly on the piano strings, mostly glissando, and developed an extraordinary skill in stopping the strings so as to change their pitch, enabling him to play an ascending scale on the keyboard which, because of the alteration of the length of strings, resulted in a descending scale in actual sound. His disciple John Cage explored further possibilities along these lines, and gave the name to the altered instrument of PREPARED PIANO.

**Prepense Music.** This is music aforethought; it is the antonym of UNPREMEDITATED MUSIC.

**Probability.** The PROBABILITY of incidence of certain intervals, notes and rhythms in a given piece of music depends on its predetermined melorhythmic idiom. The PROBABILITY of occurrence of an unresolved major seventh in a composition written before 1900 is virtually nil, while the PROBABILITY of such incidence in DODECAPHONIC MUSIC is very high. Similarly, the PROBABILITY of a concluding chord being a dissonance is zero for the 19th century, but it increases exponentially after 1900. The commanding importance of the tritone in ATONAL and DODECAPHONIC MUSIC makes its appearance a probable event in compositions in which the key signature is absent. The PROBABILITY of incidence of all 12 different notes and 12 different intervals in relation to the starting tone in a full chromatic scale is obviously 100%. Some problems of PROBABILITY lead to paradoxical solutions. Here is an example. How many tone-rows of 12 different notes and 11 different intervals is it possible to build within the range of the octave that would form an increasing or a decreasing arithmetical progression if only the absolute value of each interval is taken into consideration irrespective of its direction, whether ascending or descending? The surprising answer is 2. Taking C as the point of departure, the rows will be: C, B, D-flat, B-flat, D, A, E-flat, A-flat, E, G, F, F-sharp, and its retrograde, each one changing intervalic direction in alternation, pendulum-like.

**Progressive Jazz.** In the first half of the century JAZZ was principally a spontaneous product of mass improvisation with untutored instrumentalists achieving fantastic virtuosity simply because they were not told by any teacher that the technical tricks they performed were unplayable. In 1950 a natural desire arose among the second generation of JAZZ players to acquire gloss, polish and even theoretical knowledge. They studied with eminent European composers resident in the United States and they listened to records of modern music. They became conversant with such terms as ATONALITY and POLYTONALITY and even DODECAPHONY. They discarded the lowly banjo of the early jazz period as though ashamed to confess their plebeian social origin; they annexed a full complement of the Baroque ensemble in their orchestras. With full credentials, a movement was launched, grandly described as PROGRESSIVE JAZZ. Technical resources kept pace with the dignity of the orchestral presentation. The WHOLE-TONE SCALE was rediscovered as an ultra-modern device and played in unison by the violins. Two different keys were used simultaneously in a daring display of POLYTONALITY. The square time was diversified occasionally by asymmetric rhythms; sometimes compound meters were inserted. But despite these adornments and borrowings from respectable sources, PROGRESSIVE JAZZ could never attain distinction and soon gave way to a more homely but less pretentious style of jazzification.

**Prolepsis.** Schlegel said: "Der Historiker ist ein rückwärts gekehrter Prophet." The notion that a historian might be a prophet of the past is most provocative. The modern cultivation of some of the recessive traits of the musical past represents such a prophecy turned backwards. Consecutive fifths were the rule before the advent of tertian counterpoint; they were strictly forbidden in classical music, but returned early in the 20th century in the guise of neo-archaic usages, and were further reinforced in the practice of consecutive triadic harmonies. The dissonant heterophony of ancient modalities was incorporated as a novelty in NEO-PRIMITIVISM. The "Wicked Bible" became a collector's item because of a negative particle inadvertently omitted from the commandment forbidding adultery. Erik

Satie drew a table of anti-commandments in his *Catéchisme du Conservatoire* in which he ridiculed the elevation of once forbidden practices to the status of harmonic laws: "Avec grand soin tu violeras/ Des règles du vieux rudiment./ Quintes de suite tu feras/ Et octaves pareillement./ Au grand jamais ne résoudras/ De dissonance aucunement./ Aucun morceau ne finiras/ Jamais par accord consonnant." The exclusion of major triads in the Schoenbergian table of commandments is the most striking instance of PROLEPSIS. Indeed, every determined violation of the academic rules becomes a case for PROLEPSIS if such a violation becomes itself a rule.

**Proletarian Music.** The ideological upheaval that accompanied the Soviet revolution of 1917 posed an immediate problem of creating arts that would be consonant with the aims and ideals of socialist society. Since the political structure of the Soviet government was that of the dictatorship of the proletariat, it was imperative to postulate a special type of literature, drama, art and music, that would be proletarian in substance and therefore accessible to the popular masses. Some Soviet theoreticians proposed to wipe off the slate of the arts the entire cultural structure that preceded the revolution and to create a *tabula rasa* on which to build a new proletarian edifice. Among suggestions seriously offered by some musicians in the early days of the Soviet revolution was the confiscation of all musical instruments in order to abolish the tempered scale and to construct new instruments based on the acoustically pure intervals. A more appropriate suggestion was made to compose music which included sounds familiar to a proletarian worker. A symphony of the factory was actually staged in an experimental demonstration, with singers and players placed on rooftops. Shostakovich included a factory whistle in the score of his *May First Symphony*. Alexander Mossolov wrote a ballet called *Iron Foundry*, in which a large sheet of steel was shaken to imitate the sound of the forge. Unsuccessful attempts were made to proletarianize the librettos of old operas. In one production, Puccini's opera *Tosca* was advanced from the Napoleonic times to those of the Paris Commune. Tosca kills not the chief of the Roman police but the anti-Communard general Gallifet, disregarding the fact that the actual general Gallifet died in bed long after the fall of the Commune. Meyerbeer's opera *The Huguenots* was renamed *The Decembrists* and the action transferred to December 1825 to celebrate the rebellion of a group of progressive-minded aristocrats against the accession to the throne of the Czar Nicholas I. The notorious Russian Association of Proletarian Musicians (RAPM) was founded in 1924 to pass judgment on the fitness and unfitness of all music for proletarian consumption. It stipulated an arbitrary code of desirable musical attributes, among them unrelenting optimism, militant socialism, proletarian class consciousness, representational programmaticism and the preferential use of major keys. Beethoven was commended by the RAPM for his rebellious spirit; among Russian composers Mussorgsky was singled out as a creator of realistic art. A difficult problem was posed by Tchaikovsky. His profound pessimism and fatalism, his reactionary political views and particularly his homosexuality seemed an insurmountable barrier for the RAPM theoreticians to overcome. But Tchaikovsky was a favorite composer not only of the popular masses but also of the entire Presidium of the Soviet of People's Commissars. Even from the purely musical standpoint Tchaikovsky was theoretically unacceptable. His preference for minor keys and for melancholy moods in his operas and symphonies were the very antinomy of all that the new society of Soviet Russia stood for. In their attempt to rationalize the popularity of the *Pathétique Symphony*, the RAPM reached the acme of casuistry. In this work, so the argument went, Tchaikovsky delivered a magnificent funeral oration on the tomb of the bourgeoisie, and the superb artistic quality of this lamentation could not fail to please proletarian listeners. But soon the dialectical self-contradictions became evident even to the most obdurate members of the RAPM and factional strife pulled their ideology apart. There were also signs of repugnance against the vicious attacks led by the RAPM against the surviving composers of the pre-revolutionary times, greatly esteemed Conservatory professors and any others who dared to oppose its untenable ideology. The entire controversy was suddenly resolved when the Soviet government summarily disbanded the RAPM. As one composer expressed the nearly unanimous satisfaction at this action, "We could once again dare to write music in 3/4 time," alluding to the RAPM's ridiculous insistence that proletarian music ought to be written in march time.

The valid residue of PROLETARIAN MUSIC found its way to Germany and to America assuming special national idioms. Simplicity of form, utilization of popular dance rhythms and, in theatrical music, a selection of subjects from Revolutionary history or class warfare, were the main characteristics of music for the Proletariat. In America, Proletarian opera flourished briefly in the 1930's with Marc Blitzstein as its chief proponent. In Germany, Kurt Weill, working in close collaboration with the dramatist Bertolt Brecht, created a type of music drama that in its social consciousness had a strong affinity with PROLETARIAN MUSIC. In Russia itself, after the disbandment of the RAPM, viable ideas of PROLETARIAN MUSIC were absorbed in the doctrine of SOCIALIST REALISM.

**Prolixity.** Brevity is not necessarily an ideal; PROLIXITY is not always a fault. In classical music, PROLIXITY was ingrained in the forms of sonata and court dances, with the required repetitions of complete sections. Only the impatience of modern performers impels them to disregard such redundancies. "Brevitate gaudent moderni," to quote a recurring *incipit* of medieval musical treatises. Beethoven's *Eroica* concludes with the tonic chord repeated 28 times. By contrast, Prokofiev's *March* from *Love for Three Oranges*, ends abruptly on a single C major triad. The natural aversion of modern musicians to restatement and overstatement extends also to tonal sequences with their predictable turns. This homologophobia led finally to the collapse of the tonal system itself, and inspired Schoenberg to promulgate the principle of non-repetition of thematic notes and the formulation of his method of composition with twelve tones related only to one another.

**Proportional Representation.** Among thousands of conflicting musical theories, each claiming superiority over the others, no attempt has yet been made to conduct a statistical survey of the frequency of occurrence of every note of the scale in a given composition. Yet such a computation might well provide an illuminating insight into PROPORTIONAL REPRESENTATION of diatonic and chromatic notes, and the role of tonal centers. In serial composition, in particular, a statistical analysis can measure the strength of the gravitational force that attracts atonal and serial groups to a putative keynote. The duration of each note will have to be considered as a multiplying factor. Thus, if the least common denominator is an eighth-note, then a half-note would carry the same specific weight as four eighth-notes. It would also be possible to evaluate the relative hierarchy of the members of a tone-row. A serial composer may plan in advance a PROPORTIONAL REPRESENTATION of specific notes, intervals and durations. If desired, an artificial tonic can be posited by assigning to it the greatest frequency of incidence. This technique is applicable to all serial sets, even those containing only three or four notes. Rhythmic sets can be similarly arranged according to a predetermined formula of PROPORTIONAL REPRESENTATION. The method is particularly fruitful in building melodies and rhythms of a primitivistic type, in which the repetition is of the essence.

**Pseudo-Exoticism.** To an imaginative composer, the attraction of exotic lands is in inverse ratio to available information about such lands and in direct ratio to the square of the distance from the non-beholder. "Turkish" music, which had nothing in common with real Turkish modalities, enjoyed a great vogue in the 18th century and was used as a PSEUDO-EXOTIC resource by Mozart. When dancers from Indochina came to perform at the Paris Exposition of 1889, French musicians were fascinated by the unfamiliar sounds of resonant bells and muffled drums in the percussion group that accompanied the dancers. The emergence of IMPRESSIONISM in France owes much to this dance music from the Orient as refracted through the "auricular sites" of a European. The legends of the East provided poetic materials for song texts and operatic librettos. These tenuous impressions were transmuted into a *musique nouvelle*, vibrant with voluptuous *frissons*. Oriental scales were represented in the works of Debussy, Ravel and their imitators by the pentatonic scale which could be conveniently played on the black keys of the piano keyboard. Great composers were able to create a new art derived, however inaccurately, from Oriental sonorities; in fact, several composers, natives of Asia, who studied music in Paris, began to mold their own authentic modes in the Impressionistic manner. When the novelty began to fade, the pentatonic scale, the tinkling bells and other paraphernalia of Oriental music, found their way into the commercial factories of vulgar musicians plying their trade with much profit in the semi-classical division of "modern" music, in Broadway shows and on the soundtrack of exotic movie spectaculars. The proliferation of this PSEUDO-EXOTICISM resulted in the contamination of the genuine product, so that Orientalistic music eventually disappeared from decent practice.

**Pseudo-Music.** PSEUDO-MUSIC differs from ANTI-MUSIC in that the latter is a rebellious inversion of all musical values, while PSEUDO-MUSIC is an imitative product of specious validity. PSEUDO-MUSIC of the modern type is manufactured by semi-professionals who possess a modicum of Abecedarian talent for sentimental melody and hymn-book harmony. Feminine PSEUDO-MUSIC, usually produced by women pianists and singing teachers, has some documentary value as an illustration of neo-Biedermeier culture. Some such pieces of salon music have achieved tremendous popularity, among them, the romances of Carrie Jacobs Bond, the pianistic trivialities of Cécile Chaminade, and, the greatest of them all, *Prière d'une vierge* by Thekla Badarzewska.

**Punitive Music.** Relentless playing of a trivial tune arranged in repellent harmonies may well be used, and possibly has been used by dictatorial regimes, to extract confessions from suspected music lovers. A similar practice is pursued in the form of a musical massage in democratic countries, by means of juke boxes or other instruments of torture, in public restaurants, in jet planes waiting for a chance to make a scheduled departure, at bus terminals and railroad stations, with the ultimate intention of weakening the sales resistance to a commercial product among captive listeners. For an entirely different purpose, Erik Satie, who detested audiences, directed to have his piano piece, pointedly titled *Vexations*, to be performed 840 times in succession. His punitive design, however, was circumvented by a group of sado-masochists who carried Satie's instructions to the letter and had, on 9–10 September 1963, arranged in New York 840 performances of Satie's piece, played without interruption by a relay of willing pianists who obtained thereby not only a measure of secret gratification but also a great deal of publicity.

**Quaquaversal Dispersion.** Macropolysyllables are not necessarily frivolous when they define a phenomenon in a memorable or picturesque phrase. QUAQUAVERSAL DISPERSION is a convenient macropolysyllable to describe a radial expansion of the central cumulus of sonic matter, similar to the process of gradual sliding of geological layers, to which the term QUAQUAVERSAL (literally, turning in different directions) is applied in science.

**Quarter-Tones.** QUARTER-TONES are not modern inventions; they are found in the ancient Greek enharmonic scale. Many romantic composers of the 19th century thought of reviving QUARTER-TONES as a unit of an icositetraphonic scale. George Ives, father of Charles Ives, who was Army band leader during the Civil War, experimented with tuning his instruments a quarter-tone apart. A systematic investigation of QUARTER-TONES began about 1900; among its pioneers were the Mexican composer Julián Carrillo and Alois Hába of Czechoslovakia. Further details are found in the entry on MICROTONALITY.

**Radial Distribution.** RADIAL DISTRIBUTION of a linear series is a maximum dispersion of the constituent tones, such as occurs in a technique commonly described by a term borrowed from art, POINTILLISM. The visual impression from an actual score is a picture of tonal particles appearing and disappearing in the outer registers of orchestral instruments, or extreme octaves on the piano keyboard. The geometry of this image is particularly striking in the appearance of the instrumental works by Anton von Webern.

**Ragtime.** RAGTIME is the earliest manifestation of American syncopated music, which was soon to rise to glory in JAZZ. It was RAGTIME that gave prominence to the piano in popular music. Its rhythmic formula approximates that of the Toccata, with rapid motion and cross-accents. Henry F. Gilbert and Charles Ives cultivated RAGTIME rhythms early in the century. Debussy made use of RAGTIME rhythms in his *Golliwog's Cake Walk* in the piano suite *Children's Corner*. The proliferation of RAGTIME must have been pervasive, considering the outcries of shock and indignation in the music periodicals in the dying days of the old century. An editorial writer fulminated in an article entitled "Degenerate Music," published in *The Musical Courier* of 13 September 1899: "A wave of vulgar, filthy, and suggestive music has inundated the land. The pabulum of theater and summer hotel orchestras is 'coon music.' Nothing but RAGTIME prevails, and the cake-walk with its obscene posturings, its lewd gestures. . . . One reads with amazement and disgust of the historical and aristo-cratic names joining in this sex dance. Our children, our young men and women, are contin-ually exposed to the contiguity, to the monotonous attrition of this vulgarizing music. It is artistically and morally depressing, and should be suppressed by press and pulpit." In 1901 the American Federation of Musicians adopted a resolution that its members "shall hence-forth make every effort to suppress and discourage the playing and publishing of such musi-cal trash by substituting the works of recognized and competent composers, thereby teach-ing the general public to appreciate a wholesome, decent, and intellectual class of music." When the famous prima donna Nordica included a song by the American composer Ethel-bert Nevin in her Chicago recital in 1901, the Chicago *Tribune* deplored her "sense of the fitness of things" in singing a "coon song" alongside a group of German lieder. The monthly *Journal of the International Music Society*, in its issue of June 1905, described RAGTIME in the following words: "It suggests the gait of a hurried mule among anthills; there is a cross-rhythm, with a kind of halting contrapuntal ornamentation in the accompaniment which sometimes brings a stress onto the fourth beat of the bar. The phrases being no longer pre-sented with regular and recurrent pulsations, give rise to a sense of disorder, which, com-bined with the emotional expression of the music, suggests an irresponsibility and a sense of careless jollity agreeable to the tired or vacuous brain."

As late as 1916, RAGTIME was still a phenomenon to be abhorred, to judge by a letter to the editor from the writer Ivan Narodny published in the New York *Evening Sun:* "The rhythm of RAGTIME suggests the odor of the saloon, the smell of backyards and subways. Its style is decadent. It is music meant for the tired and materially bored minds. It is essentially obvious, vulgar, and yet shockingly strong for the reason that it ends fortissimo." But there were also some philosophically analytic voices in the press. Rupert Hughes wrote soberly in the *Musical Record* of Boston of 1 April 1899: "If RAGTIME were called *tempo di raga* or *rague-temps*, it might win honors more speedily. If the word could be allied to the harmonic *ragas* of the East Indians, it would be more acceptable. The Negroes call their clog-dancing 'ragging' and the dance a 'rag.' There is a Spanish verb *raer* (to scrape), and a French naval term, *ragué* (scraped), both doubtless from the Latin *rado*. RAGTIME will find its way gradu-ally into the works of some great genius and will thereafter be canonized, and the day will come when the decadents of the next, the 20th century, will revolt against it and will call it 'a hidebound, sapless, scholastic form, dead as its contemporaries, canon and fugue.' Mean-while, it is young and unhackneyed, and throbbing with life. And it is racial."

**Realism.** Generally speaking, the term REALISM as applied to music describes a type of programmatic romanticism, which is intended to picture a landscape or represent a psycho-logical state. REALISM has acquired a special meaning in the nomenclature of Soviet music, usually appearing in the dual formula of SOCIALIST REALISM whose function is to give a re-alistic reflection of contemporary life from the standpoint of Socialist society. Soviet com-posers are constantly urged to cultivate musical REALISM, to write music of concrete images rather than abstract formalism, to preserve the national tradition of each of the constituent members of the Soviet Union, using the melodic and harmonic language accessible to the masses and contributing to the realistic understanding of life itself.

**Redundancy.** In electronics guidance systems, REDUNDANCY is a safety factor in the proper functioning of the machine. If a part fails, its redundant replacement immediately goes into action; and if that one fails, still another part is activated to perform the same function. In music, REDUNDANCY is represented by an ostentatious repetition of a thematic motive. It has its application in serial complexes of intervalic, rhythmic and coloristic pa-rameters. By assigning a certain interval for a redundant use by an instrument, an associa-tive equation is established, so that the interval becomes the identifying motto of the instru-ment itself. Some serial composers assign a single note to an instrument, so that the instrument and the note become inalienably bound. This evokes the memories and prac-tices of serf orchestras in Tsarist Russia, consisting of wind instruments, of which each could produce but a single note, so that each serf playing that instrument often became known under the nickname of E-flat, F-sharp, etc. (When several serfs escaped from the es-tate of a music-loving Russian landlord, he put out an official notice asking the police to be on the lookout for the fugitives, giving their musical names as identification.)

**Replication.** In their search for effective and direct musical formulas, modern composers have increasingly turned back to the primitivistic pattern of simple repetition, a sort of bio-musical REPLICATION of a subject keeping its identity as unalterable as the design on an ancient Peruvian poncho. The most celebrated instance of such REPLICATION is Ravel's *Boléro* in which the variations are limited to changes from one instrumental color to another. A less literal type of REPLICATION is MONOTHEMATISM, of which Debussy's *String Quartet* is a perfect example. Still another variant is the thematic REPLICATION of a musical monogram, which spells out a name or a common word in letter-notes, usually in German notation. A modern example is the *Eighth String Quartet* by Shostakovich, which is built on his initials in German spelling, D, S, C, H, the letter S representing E-flat (Es). Shostakovich uses the same personal monogram in his *Tenth Symphony*. Some members of the AVANT-GARDE have carried the principle of REPLICATION to the ultimate limit of a single note recorded on tape without any change in dynamics and without a rhythmic interruption.

**Rescue and Escape Terms.** Many new musicological terms ambiguously descriptive of a modern style, idiom or technique are RESCUE AND ESCAPE TERMS, words and phrases used as nebulous definitions of uncertain musical events. The term OMNITONALITY belongs to this category; others may be found by industrious perusal of music magazines beginning in 1910.

**Retardation.** The device of RETARDATION, melodic, harmonic or contrapuntal, consists of holding over a certain note or a harmonic complex while other parts of the musical fabric are shifted. In modern music RETARDATION is not developed in accord with the moving elements but continues indefinitely in order to create a sustained discord. In pandiatonic techniques, this procedure results in a chain of superpositions of the principal triadic harmonies.

**Rock 'n' Roll.** American popular music has evolved from the dual resources of urban and rural folksongs. Urban popular music found its primary inspiration in the unique modalities of the Negro Spirituals, with their lowered third and seventh, which constitute the foundation of the BLUES. RAGTIME, JAZZ, SWING and such lateral developments as BEBOP and BOOGIE-WOOGIE, all preserve the character of city music. Quite different was the type of popular music cultivated in the rural regions of the country, which represented mostly the tradition of European, and particularly English, folksongs. This country music was marked by a leisurely pace devoid of the nervous excitement and syncopated beat peculiar to the popular productions of city life. With the advent of the electronic age, the barriers between urban and rural music were brought down. In the ensuing implosion and fusion of both genres, a new art was born, which found its fullest expression in the phenomenon of ROCK 'N' ROLL.

The combination of the words ROCK and ROLL appears for the first time on a Columbia phonograph record issued in the early 1930's; the rhythm of this specimen was that of a barcarolle, and the words Rock and Roll obviously referred to the gentle swaying of a boat on the river. This rural serenade was gradually transformed into a much more aggressive type of popular music, ROCK 'N' ROLL, or simply ROCK. Its cradle was in the radio broadcasting studios of Tennessee about 1950. In it, the weaker rhythms of country music overflowed the syncopation of classical JAZZ and reduced the aggressive asymmetry of the urban product to the monotony of an even beat in square time. In ROCK 'N' ROLL the pendulum-like rhythmic motion produces a tremendous accumulation of KINETIC ENERGY, leading to a state of catatonic stupefaction among the listeners and the players themselves. The effect of this constant rhythmic drive is similar to that of the sinusoid wave with a steadily increasing amplitude created by the march of a regiment of soldiers across a suspension bridge, which can break the strongest steel. Thanks to the electronic amplification, ROCK 'N' ROLL became the loudest music ever heard. Otologists have warned that its addicts may lose the sensitivity to the higher harmonics of the human voice and become partially deaf. Ralph Nader, the American Cassandra of urban civilization, has cautioned the public against the danger of sonic pollution by ROCK 'N' ROLL in a letter addressed to a member of the Congress of the United States.

The protagonist of ROCK 'N' ROLL was Elvis Presley, who developed the pelvic technique of rhythmic swing. (He became known as Elvis the Pelvis.) Four Liverpudlians, who became celebrated under the cognomen The Beatles (a palimpsest of Beat and Beetles), joined the ROCK 'N' ROLL movement but evolved a distinctive style of their own, with some characteristics of the English ballad.

The remarkable feature of ROCK 'N' ROLL is the revival of archaic modality with its characteristic plagal cadences, the Dorian mode being a favorite. In harmony, the submediant is lowered in major keys and becomes the minor third of the minor subdominant triad. Parallel triadic progressions, adopted by ROCK 'N' ROLL, also impart an archaic modal quality to the music. It may well be that the fusion of old modes and modern rhythms will create a new type of SYNCRETISM of musical folkways.

*Time* magazine commented on ROCK 'N' ROLL in its issue of 18 June 1956: "An unrelenting, socking syncopation that sounds like a bull whip; a choleric saxophone honking mating-call sounds; an electric guitar turned up so loud that its sound shatters and splits; a vocal group that shudders and exercises violently to the beat while roughly chanting either a near-nonsense phrase or a moronic lyric in hillbilly idiom."

The Canadian underground newspaper, grandly named *Logos*, gave in 1969 this description of ROCK 'N' ROLL as a social force: "Rock is mysticism, revolution, communion, salvation, poetry, catharsis, eroticism, satori, total communication, the most vibrant art form in the world today. Rock is a global link, as young people everywhere plug into it and add to the form. What this new music suggested was raising your level of consciousness away from the fragmented, intellectual, goal-oriented time and material world to a unified sensual direction in a timeless spiritual environment."

The greatest mass demonstration of ROCK 'N' ROLL, and perhaps the greatest manifestation of the attractive power of music in all history, was the Woodstock, N.Y., Festival in August 1969, when an enormous crowd of young people, estimated at quarter of a million heads, congregated in a farmland to hear their favorite Rock groups. The happening had a profound sociological significance as well, for the audience consisting of youthful non-conformists, popularly known as hippies, seemed to be infused with the spirit of mutual accommodation, altruism and love of peace. ROCK 'N' ROLL music, at least on that occasion, proved that it has indeed the power to soothe a savage breast.

**Rotation.** In post-Schoenbergian developments of DODECAPHONIC MUSIC the 12-tone series is often modified by ROTATION. As the term implies, the series is shifted a space, so that at its next occurrence, it begins with the second note, and ends with the first; in the subsequent incidence, it starts on the third note, and ends on the second, etc. ROTATION in its various further developments is a fertile device of dodecaphonic techniques.

**Scales.** The American pedagogue Percy Goetschius used to play the C major scale for his students and ask them a rhetorical question, "Who invented this scale?" and answer it himself, "God!" Then he would play the WHOLE-TONE SCALE and ask again, "Who invented this scale?" And he would announce disdainfully, "Monsieur Debussy!"

Debussy did not invent the WHOLE-TONE SCALE, but he made ample use of it. Other scales, built on quaquaversal intervalic progressions, engaged the attention of composers: the so-called Hungarian Gypsy scale, the pentatonic scale suitable for orientalistic melismas, and the scale of alternating whole tones and semitones, which is classified in Russian encyclopedias as Rimsky-Korsakov's scale. The modern Dutch composer Willem Pijper made prolix use of it, and his disciples, believing that it was his own invention called it Pijper's Scale. In fact, this scale, formed by the insertion of passing notes in the melodically spaced diminished seventh chord, was used by Liszt, Tchaikovsky and many other composers. Scriabin derived a scale of six notes from his MYSTIC CHORD, composed of three whole tones, a minor third, a semitone and a whole tone. Alexander Tcherepnin has devised a scale of nine notes consisting of a whole tone, a semitone, a semitone, a whole tone, a semitone, a semitone, a whole tone, a semitone, a semitone. The Spanish composer Oscar Esplá wrote music based on the scale of the following intervals: semitone, whole tone, semitone, semitone, semitone, whole tone, whole tone, whole tone.

Verdi was impressed by an exotic scale which he found in an Italian music journal, where it was described as "Scala enigmatica." It consists of a semitone, a minor third, three consecutive whole tones, and two consecutive semitones. At the age of 85 Verdi wrote a choral piece based on this "enigmatic" scale.

Ferruccio Busoni experimented with possible scales of seven notes and stated that he had invented 113 different scales of various intervalic structures. The first theorist to examine and classify scales based on the symmetrical division of the octave was Alois Hába, in his book *Neue Harmonielehre*. Joseph Schillinger undertook a thorough codification of all possible scales having any number of notes from two to twelve, working on the problem mathematically. In his *Thesaurus of Scales and Melodic Patterns*, Nicolas Slonimsky has tabulated some two thousand scales within the multiple octave range, including such progressions as the Polytetrachord, bitonal scales of eight notes, scales of three disjunct major or minor pentachords aggregating to two octaves, etc.

Progressions of large intervals, thirds, fourths or fifths, cannot be properly described as scales, without contradicting the etymology of the word derived from scala, a ladder. But helix-like constructions, involving spiraling chromatics may well be called scales. Quartertone scales and other microtonal progressions also belong in this category.

**Scotophilia.** In biology, SCOTOPHILIA denotes the receptive phase of circadian rhythm in which the chief activity is performed in the dark; vampire bats, usually nocturnal, are outstanding examples of Scotophiliac animals. As applied to musical composition, SCOTOPHILIA is the love of dark and somber sonorities marked by a statistically certifiable prevalence of low registers and slow tempi, as in the symphonies of Sibelius. Interestingly enough, avantgarde composers, whose chosen self-appellation connotes a rapid movement forward, betray a curious addiction to static, somber and darksome moods and compositorial habits. Such composers may well be called Scotophiliacs.

**Secundal and Septimal Harmonies.** A distinct shift in harmonic structures occurred early in the 20th century as the tertian harmonies of triadic derivation began to give way to the more acute progressions in SECUNDAL HARMONIES and their SEPTIMAL inversions. Debussy wrote special studies in consecutive major seconds, treating them as concords requiring no resolution. SECUNDAL HARMONIES are also represented in Impressionistic works in the form of consecutive last inversions of seventh chords. SEPTIMAL HARMONIES are the familiar devices in early JAZZ cadences, in which the seventh was the "blue note." Composers of the later generation used tonic major sevenths as cadential chords. SECUNDAL AND SEPTIMAL HARMONIES are commonly used in PANDIATONIC structures.

**Sensory Impact.** The quantitative expansion of technical devices in modern music led to a corresponding SENSORY IMPACT on the listeners, often reaching the threshold of physical pain. Incessant playing of modern dance music, electronically amplified beyond the endurance of an average person, may well produce a positive conditioned reflex among the young. Professional music critics have for a century complained about the loudness of modern music, beginning with that of Wagner, but in their case the SENSORY IMPACT is measured not so much by the overwhelming volume of sound as by the unfamiliarity of the idiom. The epithets such as "barbaric" were applied with a fine impartiality to Wagner, Tchaikovsky, Berlioz and Prokofiev, while Debussy, Strauss and Mahler were often described as "cacophonous." It is the relative modernity that makes the SENSORY IMPACT intolerable to a music critic. "This elaborate work is as difficult for popular comprehension as the name of the composer," wrote the Boston *Evening Transcript* in its review of Tchaikovsky's *First Piano Concerto*. An index of vituperative, pejorative and deprecatory words and phrases, the Invecticon appended to Nicolas Slonimsky's *Lexicon of Musical Invective*, demonstrates the extraordinary consistency of the critical reaction to unfamiliar music. Even the gentle Chopin did not escape contumely; he was described in a daily London newspaper as a purveyor of "ranting hyperbole and excruciating cacophony."

**Serendipity.** SERENDIPITY is a nonce word, coined by Horace Walpole in 1754, and derived from the Arabian tale of the princes of Serendip who made important discoveries and found fortune by opportune accident and sagacious surmise. In music, SERENDIPITY is almost equivalent to intuition or inspiration, but it is applicable particularly to the realization of melodic, harmonic and intervalic relationships seemingly unconnected with the primary aim of a composer or theorist. Examples of SERENDIPITY are tabulated in the article on POTENTIAL TECHNIQUES.

**Serialism.** SERIALISM is a method of composition in which thematic units are arranged in an ordered set. Tonal SERIALISM was promulgated by Schoenberg in 1924, as the culmination of a long period of experiments with atonal chromatic patterns; in retrospect, Schoenberg's method may be regarded as a special case of integral SERIALISM, much as the special theory of relativity is a subset of general relativity. Schoenberg's method deals with the 12 different notes of the chromatic scale; integral SERIALISM organizes different intervals, different rhythmic values, dynamics, etc. in autonomous sets. Fritz Klein expanded the serial concept of dodecaphonic sets to different rhythmic and intervalic values. In his score, *Die Maschine*, published in 1921, he employs sets of 12 identical notes in irregular rhythms, "Pyramid Chords" consisting of intervals arranged in a decreasing arithmetical progression of semitones, and a harmonic complex consisting of 12 different notes and 11 different intervals, the *Mutterakkord.* The mathematical term "set," for a tone-row, was introduced by the American composer Milton Babbitt in 1946. He experimented with techniques of tonal, rhythmic and intervalic sets. George Perle proposed the term "set-complex" to designate 48 different forms generated by a fundamental dodecaphonic series. In all these sets the magic number 12 plays a preponderant role. In the general concept of SERIALISM, sets may contain any number of pitches, in any scale, including non-tempered intervals.

A summary of serial parameters comprises the following: (1) Twelve different pitches as developed by using the method of composition with 12 tones, including apocopated sets, hendecaphonic, decaphonic, enneaphonic, octophonic, heptaphonic, hexaphonic, pentaphonic, tetraphonic, triphonic, diphonic, monophonic and zerophonic. (2) Organization of melody containing 12 different intervals, from a semitone to the octave and the concomitant chords containing 12 different notes and 11 different intervals. (3) Twelve different rhythmic values, which may contain a simple additive set of consecutive integers, a geometrical progression, a set of Fibonacci numbers, etc. (4) Twelve different KLANGFARBEN, in which a melody consists of a succession of disparate notes played by 12 different instruments either in succession, in contrapuntal conjugation, or harmonic coagulation. (5) Spatial SERIALISM, in which 12 different instruments are placed in quaquaversal positions, with no instruments in close proximity. (6) Vectorial SERIALISM, in which the sound generators are distributed at 12 different points of the compass, according to 12 hour marks on the face of a clock, or else arranged spatially on the ceiling, on the floor, in the corners of the auditorium. (7) Dynamic SERIALISM, with 12 different dynamic values ranging from pianississississimo to fortississississimo, including the intermediate shadings of mezzo-piano and mezzo-forte. (8) Ambulatory SERIALISM, in which 12 musicians make their entrances and exits one by one, in contrapuntal groups, in stretto, or in the fugue, the latter being understood in the literal sense of running. (9) Expressionistic SERIALISM, in which actors and singers assume definite facial expressions marking their psychological identity. (10) SERIALISM of 12 different sound generators, including steamrollers, motor lawn mowers, steam pipes, radiators, ambulance sirens, etc. (11) SERIALISM of 12 visually different mobiles, each producing a distinctive noise. (12) SERIALISM of 12 teratological borborygmuses and sonic simulacra of various physiological functions.

**Sesquipedalian Macropolysyllabification.** Quaquaversal lucubration about pervicacious torosity and diverticular prosiliency in diatonic formication and chromatic papulation, engendering carotic carmination and decubital nyctalopia, causing borborygmic susurration, teratological urticulation, macroptic dysmimia, bregmatic obstipation, crassamental quisquiliousness, hircinous olophonia and unflexanimous luxation, often produce volmerine cacumination and mitotic ramuliferousness leading to operculate onagerosity and testaceous favillousness, as well as faucal obsonation, parallelepipedal psellismus, pigritudinous mysophia, cimicidal conspurcation, mollitious deglutition and cephalotripsical stultitiousness, resulting despite Hesychastic omphaloskepsis, in epenetic opistography, boustrophedonic malacology, lampadodromic evagination, chartulary cadastration, merognostic heautotimerousness, favaginous moliminosity, fatiscent operosity, temulencious libration and otological oscininity, aggravated by tardigrade inturgescence, nucamentacious oliguria, emunctory sternutation, veneficial pediculation, fremescent dyskinesia, hispidinous cynanthropy, torminal opitulation, crapulous vellication, hippuric rhinodynia, dyspneic nimiety and favillous erethism, and culminating in opisthographic inconcinnity, scotophiliac lipothimia, banaustic rhinorrhea, dehiscent fasciculation, oncological vomiturition, nevoid paludality, exomphalic invultuation, mysophiliac excrementatiousness, flagitious dysphoria, lipogrammatic bradygraphy, orectic aprosexia, parataxic parorexia, lucubicidal nutation, permutational paranomasia, rhoncial fremitus, specular subsaltation, crapulous crepitation, ithyphallic acervation, procephalic dyscrasia, volitional volitation, piscine dermatology,· proleptic pistology, verrucous alopecia, hendecaphonic combinatoriality, microaerophilic pandiculation and quasihemidemisemibreviate illation.

**Sesquitone Scales.** Sesquitone is an interval of three semitones. The Sesquitone Scale is a progression of minor thirds, or augmented seconds, depending on notation, and is identical with the arpeggiated diminished-seventh chord. Attractive ornamental effects can be obtained by infrapolation, interpolation and ultrapolation, or a combination of these processes. An infra-inter-ultrapolation of the Sesquitone Scale produces a chromatically inflected melodic pattern of an orientalistic type. The interpolation of a single note between the successive degrees of the Sesquitone Scale forms a scale of alternating whole tones and semitones, widely used by many composers, beginning with Liszt and Tchaikovsky. In Russian reference books it is described as Rimsky-Korsakov's Scale.

**Silence.** Poets often spoke of the eloquent and the harmonious quality of Silence. The lines in Félicien David's *Symphonic Ode* are appropriate: "Ineffables accords de l'éternel silence!/ Chaque grain de sable/ a sa voix/ Dans l'ether onduleux le/ concert se balance:/ Je le sens, je le vois!" The longest Silence explicitly written out is the five-bar rest in the score of *L'apprenti Sorcier* by Paul Dukas. György Ligeti composed a work consisting of a quarternote rest. The most ambitious composition utilizing the effect of total silence is 4′ 33″ by John Cage, scored for any combination of instruments, *tacet*, and subdivided into three movements during which no intentional sounds are produced. It was unheard for the first time at Woodstock, New York, on 29 August 1952, with David Tudor at the silent piano.

**Singultation.** The modern practice of onomatopoeic Singultation is derived from the medieval hocketus in which the singing line is interrupted by a syncopated translocation of thematic components, producing hocketus or a singultus (both words mean hiccups). Brief detonations of kinetic energy in modern works are forms of Singultation.

**Socialist Realism.** The Soviet Union is the first modern state that has attempted to regulate its art, literature, drama and music according to explicitly defined ideological principles. Since the structure of the Soviet government was derived from the doctrine of the dictatorship of the proletariat, a Russian Association of Proletarian Musicians (RAPM) arrogated to itself the right to dictate the proper musical forms suitable for the consumption of proletarian masses. It was disbanded by the Soviet government in 1932 after its failure to help in the creative formulation of mass music became evident. With the rise of the national consciousness in the component republics of the Soviet Union, it was realized by Soviet authorities that proletarian internationalism was no longer sufficient to serve as an enduring ideology. Surviving masters of old Russian music had to be accepted as representatives of the Russian masses; their classical precursors were glorified as exponents of progressive ideals consonant with the new Socialist reality of the Soviet era. Soviet composers were urged to create an art national in form and Socialist in content, a method which eventually became known as Socialist Realism. Stylistically, Socialist Realism requires the retention of the tonal system of composition, broadly based on the folk modalities of Russian songs and the native chants of other Republics of the Soviet Union. The doctrine of Socialist Realism concentrates on the national development of operas and secular oratorios, in which revolutionary ideals can be expressed verbally as well as musically. The Aristotelian formula of catharsis through pity and terror underlies the librettos of most Soviet operas and the scenarios of most Soviet ballets. Patriotic subjects are particularly recommended; they lend themselves readily to the triune formula which opens with a scene of happiness, goes through a period of sudden horror and concludes in a victory over adverse circumstances. The so-called "Leningrad Symphony" of Shostakovich is a remarkable example of this Aristotelian construction, particularly so because it was written during continued retreats of the Soviet armies before the Nazis, and yet its finale predicts Victory. The classical tradition of the *Tierce de Picardie*, with its major cadence, suits perfectly the Soviet preference for major keys. Anatoly Lunacharsky, first Commissar of Education of Soviet Russia explained the political advantage of major keys by comparing them with the convictions of the Bolshevik party, while minor keys were reflecting the introvert pessimism of the Mensheviks.

The doctrine of SOCIALIST REALISM does not preclude lyrical expression or individual allusions. Shostakovich uses the monogram D.S.C.H., corresponding, in German notation, to the notes D, E-flat, C and B as the main subject of his *Tenth Symphony*. However, many among Soviet composers, even as eminent as Miaskovsky, were often criticized by the exponents of SOCIALIST REALISM for their musical morbidity, anxiety and solipsistic introspection. In the domain of rhythm, marching time is a natural medium for the optimistic attributes of SOCIALIST REALISM, but it is reserved for its proper position in the finale of a symphony or the final chorus of an opera. In this respect, SOCIALIST REALISM merely continues the old tradition of Russian music. Even such melancholy composers as Tchaikovsky and Rachmaninoff excelled in triumphant march-time movements.

In authoritative Soviet declarations, SOCIALIST REALISM is opposed to FORMALISM, which is described as an artificial separation of form from content and the excessive cultivation of purely external technical devices, particularly ATONALITY, POLYTONALITY, and DODECAPHONY. The statutes of the Union of Soviet Composers provide a specific guidance to Soviet composers for their ideological concepts: "The greatest attention of Soviet composers must be given to the victorious progressive foundations of reality, to the heroic and luminous beauty that distinguishes the spiritual world of Soviet man, which must be incarnated in musical images full of life-asserting force. SOCIALIST REALISM demands an implacable opposition against anti-social modernistic movements, expressive of the decadence and corruption of contemporary bourgeois art, against genuflection and slavish obsequiousness before the culture of the bourgeoisie."

**Sonic Exuviation.** The effectiveness of a modernistic climax depends on an astute interplay of contrasts. One of the most effective dynamic devices is SONIC EXUVIATION, the shedding of old skin of instrumental sonority, a return to a state of primordial nakedness and a new dressing-up of musical materials and a gradual building of another climax, a cut-off of sonic matter, leaving a soft exposed bodily shape. Such a dramatic EXUVIATION occurs at the end of the last movement of *Three Places in New England* by Charles Ives, where a tremendously powerful heterogeneous complex of sound suddenly crumbles, and a residual gentle chorale is heard in the quiet air.

**Sonic Organization.** Varèse defines music as ORGANIZED SOUND. It is logical to describe any musical composition, especially of the modern constructivist type, as a Sonic Organism which follows bio-musical laws. It is autogenetic, capable of natural replication induced by contrapuntal interpenetration of contrasting melorhythmic entities. SONIC ORGANIZATION presupposes an engineering plan, which takes into consideration an appropriate cross-pollination of musical themes.

**Spatial Distribution.** The placement of musicians on the stage, long a matter of tradition, has assumed an unexpected significance in modern times in the guise of musical vectorialism. Elliott Carter specifies the exact position of the players in his string quartets. Lukas Foss, in his *Elytres* for 12 instruments, places the musicians at maximum distances available on the stage. The use of directional loudspeakers in performances of ultra-modern works is an electronic counterpart of SPATIAL DISTRIBUTION. In German broadcasting studios experiments have been made in distributing a 12-tone row in serial works among 12 electronic amplifiers placed in a clock-like circle, with each amplifier being assigned an individual note of the series. Empirical applications of the principle of SPATIAL DISTRIBUTION have been made by various composers early in the century, notably by Erik Satie in his *Musique d'ameublement*.

**Spectrum.** By analogy with the prismatic SPECTRUM of primary colors, a totality of KLANGFARBEN can be described as a tonal SPECTRUM. Before the era of ELECTRONIC MUSIC, the colors of the auditory SPECTRUM were limited to the available instruments of actual manufacture. With the aid of electronic generators it is possible to build a SPECTRUM possessing an infinite capacity of instrumental colors, and the style and idiom of an entire work can be programmed by the proportional strength of such instrumental colors. The metaphor of a musical SPECTRUM is therefore justified by the actuality of its realization.

**Specular Reflection.** The mirror image in Baroque counterpoint is applied to mutually conjugated melodic inversions, in which the ascending intervals are reflected by descending intervals, and vice versa. It is theoretically possible to construct an infinite SPECULAR REFLECTION, in which the intervallic distance between the two mirrors recedes, so that intervals are inverted in the outer regions of the instrumental range, extending even into the inaudible spectrum of ultra-sonic and infra-sonic sounds. In some modern works written specially for dog audiences, ultra-sonics can achieve considerable effectiveness. Beyond the canine auditory range, a gap occurs until the frequency of light waves is reached. Mystically inclined composers may find pantheistic inspiration in these notions of passing from men through dogs to infinity.

**Sprechstimme.** SPRECHSTIMME—literally a speech-voice—is a term popularized in its expressive use by Schoenberg in *Pierrot Lunaire* and later works. It is an inflected speech, notated on the regular music staff by special symbols indicating the approximate height of the note. The method was used systematically for the first time in 1897 in the operatic melodrama *Königskinder* by Engelbert Humperdinck.

**Static Music.** Although the general trend of music since 1900 has been towards greater complexity of texture and greater variety of dynamics, an opposite movement has manifested itself in some circles of the Avant-Garde, aimed at total tonal immobility and static means of expression. STATIC MUSIC finds its logical culmination in works that are limited to a single note in unchanging dynamics, usually in pianissimo. The melosomatic impact of such a production may be considerable if the listener is forced to hear a single note played by an instrumentalist for a long time. The expectation of some change, constantly deceived, may cause an emotional perturbation of great psychological interest.

**Stochastic Composition.** The term STOCHASTIC was introduced into music by the Greek engineer and composer Iannis Xenakis, to designate an aleatory projection in which the sonic trajectory is circumscribed by the structural parameters of the initial thematic statement. (The word itself comes from the Greek root meaning "the aim of an arrow.") STOCHASTIC procedures are in actual practice equivalent to controlled improvisation.

**Strategy and Tactics.** Modern composers are forever seeking metaphors from other fields to enrich the rapidly obsolescent musical nomenclature derived from vague Italian words indicating form, speed, dynamic force or expression. Among such new metaphors are STRATEGY AND TACTICS. The general scheme of a modern symphony or a sonata is Strategical, while variations, cadenzas and contrapuntal elaborations are Tactical devices. Iannis Xenakis, the originator of the STOCHASTIC method of composition, extended the concept of STRATEGY AND TACTICS into an actual tournament between two orchestras and two conductors, exemplified in his antiphonal symphony entitled *Stratégie*. According to the composer's specifications, two orchestras perform simultaneously two different compositions, following the uncoordinated pair of conductors, and stopping at climactic points to survey the mutual gains and losses. At the end of the maneuver the audience votes to nominate the winner of this instrumental encounter.

**Superfetation.** When several viable musical ideas occur simultaneously and are contrapuntally conjugated without a preliminary statement, a melorhythmic SUPERFETATION is the result. The thematic embryos may then be separated to pursue their different courses; or else, the non-identical geminal subjects may remain unified like Siamese twins, treated collectively as bipartite entities which subsequently may enter into a secondary SUPERFETATION. Given a complete freedom of dissonant counterpoint, SUPERFETATION can be extended to thematic triplets, quadruplets, quintuplets, sextuplets, septuplets, octuplets, etc., interpenetrating and disengaging themselves in a multiplicity of instrumental or vocal lines.

**Surrealism.** The word SURREALISM was coined in 1903 by the French poet Guillaume Apollinaire in his fantastic play *Les Mamelles de Tirésias*, in which he treated the problem of a transsexual transplantation of mammary glands, and which he subtitled "drame surréaliste." SURREALISM became a fashionable movement when André Breton published a surrealist manifesto in 1924. In it, he described SURREALISM as "psychic automatism," anti-rationalistic in essence and completely spontaneous in its creative process. Fantasy and free association were the normative factors of Surrealistic literature and art. Apollinaire described SURREALISM as the rational technique of the improbable. Jean Cocteau equated it with the essence of poetry; in his film *Le Sang du Poéte* he proposed to give a "realistic account of unreal phenomena." The famous French handbook, *Nouveau Petit Larousse*, defines SURREALISM tersely as "tendance d'une école à négliger toute préoccupation logique." Surrealism is oxymoronic in essence, thriving on the incompatibility of the opposites, exemplified by such images as cold flame, thunderous silence, painstaking idleness, quiet desperation. Names of persons often have a surrealistic ring. A Boston dentist, Dr. Toothacher, a Chicago gangster Alturo Indelicato, a Canadian insurance salesman John Death, were living examples of SURREALISM. The furlined cup and saucer, created by the 23-year-old artist Megret Oppenheim in 1936, is a typical surrealistic artifact. Surrealistic incongruity was exemplified also in a piece called Bagel Jewelry, a composition by a New York artist, in which a real bagel was encased in a jewelry box, with a pricetag of $100.

In a modern production of *Hamlet*, the King's line, "We shall call up our friends," acquired a surrealistic twist because of a telephone receiver placed on the table. The Renaissance paintings representing Biblical scenes in which musicians perform on the lute and the theorbo, are both anachronistic and surrealistic in their effect. SURREALISM possesses an oneiristic quality, in which dreams become more real than life. The etymology of the word implies a higher degree of realism, penetrating into the subliminal human psyche.

Surrealist artists are fascinated by musical subjects. Salvador Dali humanized musical instruments. In one of his paintings, a faceless cellist plays on the spinal column of a human cello mounted on a pin. On its buttocks there are the familiar resonators in the forms of symmetric gothic F's. (Life imitates art. At an avant-garde concert in New York a lady cellist performed a solo on the spine of a fellow musician, using a regular bow and applying occasional pizzicatti to his epidermis.) Another musical painting by Dali, bearing the surrealistic title *Six Apparitions of Lenin on a Piano*, represents several heads of Lenin crowned with aureoles strewn across the keyboard. The Belgian surrealist René Magritte painted a burning bass tuba. In the art work *Object for Destruction* by the American surrealist Man Ray, a print of a human eye was attached to the pendulum of a metronome. Real metronomes are the instruments in the score by the Hungarian modernist György Ligeti, containing 100 metronomes all ticking at different speeds. In his vision of socialist music of the future, the Soviet poet Vladimir Mayakovsky conjured up a symphony with rain conduits for flutes. The American band leader Spike Jones introduced a latrinophone, a surrealistic lyre made of a toilet seat strung with violin strings.

Apollinaire urged artists, poets and musicians to cultivate "the insane verities of art." No one has followed his advice more ardently than Erik Satie. He incarnated the spirit of inversion. He entitled his utterly surrealistic score *Parade* "ballet réaliste." Jean Cocteau wrote: "Satie's *Parade* removes the sauce. The result is a completely naked object which scandalizes by its very nakedness. In the theater everything must be false in order to appear true." Satie was very much in earnest when he wrote, "J'emmerde l'art—c'est un métier de con." The titles of his piano pieces are typical of surrealistic self-contradiction: *Crépuscule matinal de midi, Heures séculaires et instantanées, Tyrolienne turque, Sonatine bureaucratique, Fantaisie musculaire, Trois morceaux en forme de poire* (the latter, printed under a cover representing a pear, was a defiant response to criticism that his music was formless.)

**Swing.** Among the many ephemeral terms descriptive of varieties of JAZZ, SWING has gained a permanent historical position. It is not a new slang expression. The word SWING appears in the titles of old American dance tunes: Society Swing of 1908, Foxtrot Swing of 1923, Charleston Swing of 1925. In 1932 Duke Ellington wrote a song with the incipit, "It Don't Mean a Thing if It Ain't Got That Swing." SWING music achieved its first great boom in 1935, largely through the agency of the jazz clarinet player Benny Goodman, introduced to the public as the King of Swing. The American magazine *Downbeat* described SWING in its issue of January 1935 as "a musician's term for perfect rhythm." The November 1935 issue of the magazine carried a glossary of "Swing terms that cats use," in which SWING was defined as "laying it in the groove." This metaphor, borrowed from the phonograph industry, gave rise to the once popular adjective "groovy," in the sense of neat, perk and pert.

SWING music must have exercised a hypnotic effect on the youth of the 1930's. The New York *Times* of 30 May 1938 ran the banner headline, "Swing Band Puts 23,400 in Frenzy. . . . Jitterbugs Cavort as 25 Orchestras Blare in Carnival." Self-appointed guardians of public morals lamented the new craze: "Pastor Scores Swing as Debasing Youth, Declares it Shows an Obvious Degeneracy in our Culture and Frothiness of Age," the New York *Times* headlined. Stravinsky, then a recent American citizen, endorsed Swing. *Time* Magazine quoted him as saying in January, 1941: "I love swings. It is to the Harlem I go. It is so sympathetic to watch the Negro boys and girls dancing and to watch them eating the long, what is it you call them, frankfurters, no—hot dogs—in the long rolls. It is so sympathetic. I love all kinds of swings."

**Symbolic Analysis.** An overwhelming compulsion on the part of many modern composers to return the art of music to its source, mathematics, is behind many manifestations of the Avant-Garde. Yet no attempt has been made to apply symbolic logic to the stylistic and technical analysis of modern music. A simple statistical survey can determine the ratio between unresolved dissonances and consonant structures in modern works as compared to those of the past. Such an analysis would indicate in mathematical terms the process of the emancipation of dissonances. The next step would be to tabulate certain characteristics of a given modern school of composition and note their presence in another category, which would help to measure the extent of its influence. The Whole-Tone Scale, for instance, was cultivated particularly by the French Impressionists, but it can be found in works of composers who do not subscribe to impressionist esthetics. Progressions of second inversions of major triads in parallel formation, moving by sesquitones, are typical of IMPRESSIONISM. But the same formations can be encountered in the music of non-impressionists. Ravel concludes his string quartet with such triadic progressions, and so does Gustav Holst in his suite *The Planets*, but they are never found in the works of Hindemith, a paragon of Neo-Classicism, or in those of Prokofiev. The index of tonality is very strong, amidst dissonances, in Stravinsky, but is totally absent in Schoenberg. All these styles, idioms and techniques can be designated by a system of symbols; intervals would be numbered in semitones; upward motion would be symbolized by the plus sign, and downward motion by the minus sign. In this scheme the whole-tone scale would be shown by the formula 6 (2), denoting six degrees of two semitones each, with a plus or minus sign indicating the direction of the movement. A bitonal chord such as formed by C major and F sharp major, can be indicated by the symbol, MT for major triad and the number 6 for the tritone. The synchronization of these triads can be indicated by brackets: (MT) (MT + 6). More importantly, symbolic formulas can describe a style. The music of Hindemith, which lacks the Impressionistic element entirely, can be formulated as 50% NC (for Neo-Classical) + 50% NR (Neo-Romantic), with dissonant content and strength of tonal centers indicated by additional symbols or subscripts. Stravinsky's early music could be circumscribed by symbols ED for Ethnic Dissonance. Dodecaphonic method could be indicated by the coefficient 12. Other symbols would denominate metric and rhythmic symmetry or asymmetry. In the SYMBOLIC ANALYSIS of an eclectic composer such as Delius, with basic romanticism modified by a considerable influx of impressionistic harmonies and colors, the following formula would be satisfactory, with R for Romanticism, C for Classicism, E for Ethnic quality and I for Impressionism: 40% R + 20% C + 30% E + 10% I. A table of styles, idioms and techniques, may be drawn in the manner of the periodical table of elements. Just as vacant spaces in Mendeleyev's schematic representation indicated unknown elements which were actually discovered at a later time, so new techniques of modern composition may well come into being by searching application of SYMBOLIC ANALYSIS.

**Synaesthesia.** Color associations with certain sounds or tonalities are common subjective phenomena. It is said that Newton chose to divide the visible spectrum into seven distinct colors by analogy with the seven degrees of the diatonic scale. Individual musicians differed greatly in associating a sound with a certain color. The most ambitious attempt to incorporate light into a musical composition was the inclusion of a projected color organ in Scriabin's score *Prometheus,* in which the changes of instrumental coloration were to be accompanied by changing lighting in the concert hall. The most common association between tonality and color is that of C major and whiteness. It is particularly strong for pianists for the obvious reason that the C major scale is played on white keys. However, Scriabin who had a very strong feeling for color associations correlated C major with red. By all conjecture F-sharp major should be associated with black, for it comprises all five different black keys of the piano keyboard, but Scriabin associated it with bright blue and Rimsky-Korsakov with dull green. Any attempt to objectivize color associations is doomed to failure if for no other reason than the arbitrary assignment of a certain frequency to a given note. The height of pitch rose nearly a semitone in the last century, so that the color of C would now be associated with C-sharp in relation to the old standards. Some composers dreamed of a total SYNAESTHESIA in which not only audio-visual but tactile, gustatory and olfactory associations would be brought into a sensual synthesis. Baudelaire said: "Les parfums, les couleurs et les sons se répondent." J. K. Huysmans conjured up an organ of liqueurs. He describes it in Chapter IV of his book *A Rebours:* "Interior symphonies were played as one drank a drop of this or that liqueur creating the sensations in the throat analogous to those that music pours into the ear. In this organ of liqueurs, Curaçao sec corresponded to the clarinet with its somewhat astringent but velvety sound; Kummel suggested the oboe with its nasal quality; Menthe and Anisette were like the flute, with its combination of sugar and pepper, petulance and sweetness; Kirsch recalled the fury of the trumpet; Gin and Whiskey struck the palate with the strident explosions of cornets and trombones; Vodka fulminated with deafening noise of tubas, while raki and mastic hurled thunderclaps of the cymbal and of the bass drum with full force." Huysmans continued by suggesting a string ensemble functioning in the mouth cavity, with the violin representing vodka, the viola tasting like rum, the cello caressing the gustatory rods with exotic liqueurs, and the double-bass contributing its share of bitters.

Composers in mixed media, anxious to embrace an entire universe of senses, are seeking ultimate SYNAESTHESIA by intuitive approximation, subjective objectivization and mystical adumbrations. Schoenberg was extremely sensitive to the correspondences between light and sound. In the score of his monodrama *Die glückliche Hand* he indicates a "crescendo of illumination" with the dark violet light in one of the two grottos quickly turning to brownish red, blue green and then to orange yellow.

**Synchrony.** Metric or rhythmic SYNCHRONY is an inclusive term of which POLYMETRY AND POLYRHYTHMY are specific instances. Synchronization demands absolutely precise simultaneity of sets of mutually primary numbers of notes within a given unit of time, e.g. 3:2, 5:3, 11:4, etc. Triplets and quintuplets are of course common in free cadenzas since Chopin's time. (There is a consistent use of 4 beats against 3 in Chopin's *Fantaisie-Impromptu.*) But arithmetical precision in synchronizing larger mutually primary numbers of notes cannot be obtained by a human performer no matter how skillful, or by several performers playing different rhythms at once. Such SYNCHRONY becomes feasible with the aid of electronic machines. In 1931, Henry Cowell, working in collaboration with the Russian electric engineer, Leon Theremin, constructed a device, in the form of concentric wheels, which he called Rhythmicon. By manipulating a rheostat with a rudimentary crank, the performer automatically produced precise synchronization of the harmonic series, the number of beats per time unit being equal to the position in the series, so that the fundamental tone had one beat per second, or any other time unit, the second partial note had 2 beats, the third, 3 beats, etc. up to 32 beats produced by the rim of the Rhythmicon. The result was an arithmetically accurate SYNCHRONY score of 32 different time pulses. Since only the mutually non-primary numbers of beats coincided in the process, the collateral effect of rotating the machine was the production of an eerie scale of upper overtones, slower in its initial notes, faster as the position of the overtone was higher. The speed of rotation of the Rhythmicon wheel could be regulated at will, so as to create any desired alteration in tempo or pitch. The initial chord of each main division contains, necessarily so, the entire spectrum of overtones, and their simultaneous impact is of tremendous power, a perfect concord of multitonal consistency in non-tempered intonation.

An entirely novel idea of producing SYNCHRONY with mathematical precision was initiated by Conlon Nancarrow, an American composer living in Mexico City. He worked with a player-piano roll, punching holes at distances proportional to the desired rhythms. He wrote a series of etudes and canons, which could be performed only on the player piano, and which achieved the synchronization of different tempi that could not be attained by living instrumentalists. In his works he was free to select numbers with a fairly low common denominator, in which case there were occasional coincidences between the constituent parts. But the majority of his chosen proportions of the pulse tempi are such that the common denominator was not attained until the end of the piece, if at all. He also wrote a composition in which the relationship of the tempi was 2 to $\sqrt{2}$, and since the latter is an irrational number (which Nancarrow approximated to 3 decimal points) the contrapuntal parts could, at least theoretically, never meet.

**Syncretism.** In history and theology, SYNCRETISM denotes the coalescence of incompatible elements or concepts. Etymologically, the word is derived from the union of ancient Greece with Crete. SYNCRETISM is a useful term in music as well, applied to describe the affinity between autogenetic ethnic melodies and cultivated triadic harmonies. A typical example of SYNCRETISM is the arrangement of pentatonic tunes in tonal harmonies, often resulting in the alteration of the intervalic content, as for instance in *Londonderry Air*, a pentatonic melody which has been altered by its arranger by changing the opening interval of a minor third to a semitone in order to provide the leading tone and to convert the modality of the song into a familiar major key. In modern music, SYNCRETISM assumes a polytechnical character through the application of widely incompatible techniques in a single work. An example is Alban Berg's opera *Lulu*, a serial work, which contains also triadic progressions, as well as harmonic figurations and tonal sequences.

**Synergy.** SYNERGY is defined by the American architect Buckminster Fuller, the discoverer of new principles of spherical stability in designing structures, as the "behavior of a whole system unpredicted by the behavior of any of its separate parts, or the subassemblies of its parts." SYNERGY in music is a technique whereby the last note of a segment of several thematic notes is the first note of the second segment. These segments can be separated, in which case the conjunctive note is repeated. The method is of considerable value in building serial chains, in which the concatenations of adjacent links may be freely dissolved. With this separation of links, the function of the connecting tone becomes ambiguous, serving as the imaginary tonic of the first segment or an imaginary dominant of the second segment. The specification "imaginary" is important because of the esthetic differences created by such a split of the chain.

**Temporal Parameters.** The conjectural duration of a musical composition is a factor of importance per se, a TEMPORAL PARAMETER which has a decisive bearing on the cohesion and relative stability of the constituent parts of the entire work. The 20th century cultivated a type of Brobdingnagian grandiosity which seemed to equate quantity with quality. Among relatively well known symphonic works, the *Alpine Symphony* by Richard Strauss held the record for absolute length, but it was eclipsed by the *Gothic Symphony* of the English composer Havergal Brian, containing 529 pages of full score. The longest piano work of the century is *Opus Clavicembalisticum* by the English-born Parsi composer Kaikhosru Sorabji, which he played for the first and last time in Glasgow on 1 December 1930. The work consists of 12 movements in the form of a theme with 44 variations and a passacaglia with 81 variations. Characteristically, it is dedicated "to the everlasting glory of those few men blessed and sanctified in the curses and execrations of those many whose praise is eternal damnation."

While some composers kept expanding the duration of their individual works, their contemporaries followed the opposite trend towards extreme brevity of musical utterance. The pioneer of this modern concision was Anton von Webern; one of his pieces written in 1911 for several instruments lasts only 19 seconds. The Hungarian composer György Ligeti wrote a movement consisting of a single quarter-tone rest. The ultimate in the infinitesimally small musical forms was achieved by John Cage in his 0 ' 00 ", "to be performed in any way by anyone," and first presented in this ambiguous form in Tokyo on 24 October 1962.

**Teratological Borborygmus.** Modern works of the first quarter of the 20th century systematically increased the amount of massive sonorities as though their intention was to produce an otological ACOUSMA, or some other tonitruant Brobdingnagian TERATOLOGICAL BORBORYGMUS, a huge and monstrous intestinal rumbling issuing from the mouthpieces of brass instruments, shrill flageolets of the piccolos and high harmonics in the strings. It was inevitable that a reaction against this loss of all moderation should have set in among composers of the avant-garde. This reaction was made necessary because of the catastrophe of World War I, when it was no longer feasible to place huge orchestral apparatus at the service of composers of macrosonic works. The era of TERATOLOGICAL BORBORYGMUS seemed to end without a hope of recurrence, but the emergence of electrically amplified popular music of the ROCK 'N' ROLL type generated an electronic circus that promised to eclipse the deafening potentialities of the past.

**Third Stream.** THIRD STREAM denominates a combined art of popular music and modern techniques of composition. The term itself was used for the first by Gunther Schuller at his lecture at the Berkshire Music Center in Tanglewood, given on 17 August 1957. If the first stream is classical, and the second stream is Jazz, THIRD STREAM is their Hegelian synthesis, which unites and reconciles the classical thesis with the popular antithesis. Instances of such synthetic usages are found in a number of modern works. The Third Stream flows in *Golliwog's Cake Walk* from Debussy's *Children's Corner,* where bits of syncopated ragtime animate the music. Gershwin's *Rhapsody in Blue* is the most important precursor of THIRD STREAM. In constructive application of THIRD STREAM, ultra-modern techniques, including serialistic procedures, can be amalgamated with popular rhythmic resources.

**Tinnitus.** A sustained pressure on the auditory nerve causes a condition known as TINNITUS, a persistent tintinnabulation in the cochlea in the inner ear. Schumann experienced it during the final stages of his mental illness; he heard a relentless drone on high A-flat. Smetana suffered a similar aural disturbance, but the note he heard was a high E, and he too eventually went insane. He introduced this high E in the violin part at the end of his string quartet, significantly entitled *From My Life.*

Some clinically sane composers active in the last third of the 20th century, who never suffered from a pathological TINNITUS, experimentally created an artificial one. Morton Feldman wrote a violin part with an interminable F-sharp calculated to generate a psychic TINNITUS in the outer and inner ears of performers and listeners alike. La Monte Young devised a TINNITUS of a perfect fifth with a notation, "to be held for a long time." Other ways of affecting the listener is a tape recording of a dripping faucet, or a simulacrum of "white noise" prolonged without a prospect of ever ending. Physical action may be added to a TINNITUS, such as measured drops of lukewarm water on the occipital bone of the head held down by clamps, a device helpful to keep in subjection a particularly recalcitrant listener to a piece of avant-garde music. This method was widely practiced to subdue difficult patients in the 18th-century insane asylums.

**Tonal Aura.** Aura is a medical term used to describe a premonitive sensation before an epileptic seizure. TONAL AURA is a useful metaphor for a coloristic hypertension created in modern technical innovations, such as playing below the bridge of stringed instruments, fluttertongue on the flute, glissando in the French horn, or a particularly unsettling borborygmus in the bass trombone. Schoenberg's score *Begleitungsmusik zu einer Lichtspielscene,* written for an unrealized abstract motion picture, contains striking instances of Musical Aura, beginning with the sections marked *Threatening Danger* and *Fear* and culminating in the finale, *Catastrophe.*

**Tonal Tropism.** By computing the frequency of recurrence of each particular note in an atonal work and finding which of the 12 notes of the chromatic scale has a marked preponderance over the others, it may be asserted that such a frequently recurrent note represents a tonal focus, and that other members of an atonal melody have a TONAL TROPISM towards such a putative tonic. Other aspects of TONAL TROPISM are: the approach to the most frequently occurring tone by a semitone from below, suggesting a leading tone; a preferential placement of a note in the bass; an extended duration of a certain tone; its appearance at the end of a musical fascicle; a simulated cadence or some other kind of privileged position at strategic points, at a strong beat of the measure, etc. In verbal descriptions of a composition containing such features, the term TONAL TROPISM may be used with justification.

**Tone Clusters.** The technique of Tone Clusters was demonstrated for the first time in public by Henry Cowell at the San Francisco Music Club on 12 March 1912, on the day after his fifteenth birthday. It consists of striking a pandiatonic complex of two octaves on white keys using one's forearm or a panpentatonic set of black keys, as well as groups of 3 or 4 notes struck with the fists or the elbow. Cowell notated the Tone Clusters by a thick black line on a stem for rapid notes or a white-note rod attached to a stem for half-notes. By a remarkable coincidence, the Russian composer Vladimir Rebikov made use of the same device, with an identical notation, at about the same time, in a piano piece entitled *Hymn to Inca*. Still earlier, Charles Ives made use of tone clusters in his *Concord Sonata*, to be played with a wood plank to depress the keys. Béla Bartók used Tone Clusters to be played by the palm of the hand in his *Second Piano Concerto*, a device that he borrowed expressly from Cowell, by permission.

**Tonolalia.** Glossolalia is a preternaturally inspired manifestation of spontaneous and simultaneous multilingual intercourse. Tonolalia is an analogous verbal neologism, in black different instruments and voices disport themselves in a modernistic quodlibet. Particularly effective are antiphonal uses of Tonolalia in which an improvised interlude is echoed by another instrument or a group of instruments.

**Tonotripsical Impact.** A cephalotripsical blow crushes the skull. A Tonotripsical Impact is produced by an implosion of sonic matter calculated to stun into submission and psychically incapacitate the listeners to an ultra-modern concert. At a "happening" in New York, the complete Sunday edition of the New York *Times* was thrown on the floor of a chamber music hall, and a power lawn mower was wheeled in and proceeded to chew up the newspaper with cephalotripsical effect. A literal example of Tonocephalotripsical music is the *Concerto for the Hammer and the Skull*, by a French composer who performed it himself by striking different parts of the bones of his head producing different tones, and opening his mouth as a resonator.

**Total Music.** In ancient Greece music was an inalienable part of drama and literature. In medieval universities, it formed a division of the quadrivium, which included also arithmetic, geometry and astronomy. In modern times, music lost this intimate connection with sciences and liberal arts. It maintained its proud independence until the middle of the 20th century when the Avant-Garde brought music out of its isolation into the condominium of Mixed Media. The slogan of Total Music was launched, and the once exclusive art became at various Happenings an action to be performed on equal terms with conversation, consumption of food, sexual intercourse and sleep. Performing musicians willingly surrendered even their physical separation from the audience, and invited the collaboration of the public on the stage. Formal attire that placed musicians on a higher plane was abandoned. Since nudity became admissible in the theater, musicians followed suit. A topless female violoncellist gained notoriety by exposing her upper half to sophisticated music lovers. Total Music, which embraces all aspects of human behavior, is a counterpart of the French "roman total," a fictional form which combines factual reportage with unbridled fantasy.

**Translocations.** By altering the intervallic structure of a given musical subject and by translocating its tonal constituents, it is possible to bring any melorhythmic figure into topological congruity with any other. The number of such changes, in which the intervalic unit is a semitone and the rhythmic unit is the smallest note value occurring in the subjects, will indicate the degree of affinity existing between such two subjects. In isometric melodies, the index of rhythmic exchangeability will obviously be zero, so that only the index of the necessary intervalic changes measured by the number of semitones need be considered. In isotonal pairs only the rhythmic changes remain to be computed. The smaller the number of alterations required to transform the melorhythmic outline of one subject into that of another, the greater is the intrinsic similarity between the two. A cursive statistical survey indicates that virtually all principal leading motives in Wagner's music dramas are closely related. Thus we find that it requires but a few changes of intervals and rhythms to transmute the motive of erotic love in *Tristan und Isolde* to that of faith in *Parsifal*. The main motives of most tone poems of Richard Strauss are also topologically similar, no matter what the programmatic design is. On the other hand, the index of interchangeability of dodecaphonic tone rows is extremely high, characteristic of the numerical diversity of dodecaphonic themes. This result should not be surprising, for the works of Wagner and Richard Strauss (to take only these two composers as examples) are based on triadic formations with auxiliary chromatic notes, whereas serial music does not depend on tonality and the intervalic structure in the serial idiom is free of all restrictions. A composer, writing in any modern style, whether serial or non-serial, is in a position of selecting any desired table of approximations of main subjects, in relation to inervalic, melodic, metric and rhythmic parameters, planning in advance such incidental factors as repetition of thematic notes, lipogrammatic omissions, and thus achieving any degree of variety. ALEATORY methods can be limited in advance by numerical parameters, thus imparting to the music an individual physiognomy. Intuition, being an aleatory mental state, may also enter this preliminary outline of substantive parameters. Ernst Krenek has pointed out that the German word *Einfall,* inspiration, connotes in its etymology a falling in as though by chance. The word inspiration itself has aleatory connotations, which is drawing in of breath. Once such a tabulation is set up, the composer can proceed to operate the field of desirable TRANSLOCATIONS, the topology of form, the degree of thematic cohesion or dispersion, etc. Thus the techniques of TRANSLOCATION and its cognate, that of computation of similarities, possess practical validity from both the analytical and synthetical viewpoints. A study of translocations may eventually become an integral branch of musical didactics in perfecting the skill of manipulating and coordinating a multiplicity of technical factors.

**Tritone.** The medieval theorists described the TRITONE as "diabolus in musica" and ejected melodic progressions involving the TRITONE from the body of church music as the work of the devil, encompassing as it did the discordant interval of the augmented fourth unfit for a proper tetrachord. In German schools in Bach's time a music student who inadvertently made use of the augmented fourth was punished in class by a rattan blow on the knuckles of the hand.

The earliest suggestion that the use of the TRITONE may not be a *peccatum mortale* was made by Ramos de Pareja in *Musica Practica* published in 1482, but his leniency received little approbation. It was in the natural course of events that the stone rejected by the medieval builders should become the cornerstone of modern music, in all its principal aspects, POLYTONALITY, ATONALITY, DODECAPHONY. The importance of the TRITONE is derived from the very quality that disenfranchised it before, namely its incompatibility with the tonic-dominant complex. Two major triads at the distance of a tritone formed the bitonal "Parisian chord" so popular in the first quarter of the century; complementary hexachords in major keys with tonics distanced by a tritone redound to the formation of a symmetrical 12-tone row; a series of intervals diminishing by a semitone beginning with a major sixth and ending with its inversion, the minor third, forms a bitonal major chord with tonics at a tritone's distance; a chord containing all eleven different intervals is encompassed by five octaves and a tritone from the lowest to the highest note.

**Ultra-Modern Music.** In the early 1920's it became evident to composers using advanced techniques that the term MODERN MUSIC was no longer sufficiently strong to describe the new trends. In search of further emphasis, they chose the term ULTRA-MODERN MUSIC, that is music beyond the limits of traditional modernism. In announcing the publication of *New Music* magazine, Henry Cowell, its founder and editor, declared that only works in the Ultra-Modern idiom would be acceptable for publication. Some decades later, it was realized that ULTRA-MODERN Music, too, began to show unmistakable signs of obsolescence. Still, certain attributes of ULTRA-MODERN MUSIC have retained their validity: dissonant counterpoint, atonal melodic designs, polymetric and polyrhythmic combinations and novel instrumental sonorities.

**Unpremeditated Music.** Strictly speaking, no piece of music can be composed with an absolute lack of premeditation. Great improvisers of the past always had a proleptic image, in definite sounds, of what they were going to play. However, the composers of ALEATORY MUSIC in the second half of the 20th century have made serious attempts to create music without a shadow of melody aforethought, or harmony prepense. The absence of premeditation in such cases becomes as essential as in capital crime.

**Unwasity.** UNWASITY is an etymological transliteration of the Russian word *nebylitsa*, a fairy tale. This English neoterism may be used as an imaginative figure to describe a modernistic fairy tale, or a palingenetic form so dissimilar from its original that it becomes a literal UNWASITY, something that never was.

**Urbanism.** URBANISM is the music of the modern city. It derives its inspiration from urban phenomena, governed by the cult of the machine, and comprising the art of the motion pictures, automobile traffic, newspapers and magazines. Inter-urban machines (locomotives, airplanes) also enter the general concept of URBANISM. Among the most durable works of Urbanist music was Honegger's symphonic movement, *Pacific 231*, glorifying the locomotive. Luigi Russolo wrote a suite for noise instruments, subtitled "a demonstration of automobiles and airplanes," in 1913; it was the first work which contains a reference to airplanes in the title. The American composer Emerson Whithorne composed the earliest piece of airplane music for orchestra, entitled *The Aeroplane*, in 1926. Sports (prize fights, football, rugby) also attracted composers by their new urbanistic romanticism. "Machine" music received its greatest expansion in the 1920's; its typical products were the opera *Jonny Spielt Auf* by Ernst Krenek, *Machinist Hopkins* by Max Brand, and *Lindbergh's Flight* by Kurt Weill. In Russia musical URBANISM coalesced with the development of PROLETARIAN MUSIC, in which the machine was the hero of the production; an example is *The Iron Foundry* by Alexander Mossolov. *Technical Symphony* by the Hungarian composer Eugen Zador and *Poderes de Caballo*, ballet by Carlos Chávez are examples of urbanist symphonic and ballet music. Prokofiev's ballet *Le Pas d'acier*, representing the life in a Soviet factory, is also urbanist in its subject matter. The ostentatious realism of urbanist music fell out of fashion after World War II, but as late as 1964 Aaron Copland wrote a symphonic suite, entitled *Music for a Great City*, descriptive of the sounds of New York City.

**Vectorialism.** The modern preoccupation with mathematical factors in music has resulted in the formation of novel concepts and techniques, among them VECTORIALISM, which specifies the angular value of the vector-radius from the center of the concert hall to musical instruments or electronic transmitters, so that each ingredient of a melodic or harmonic pattern receives its identifying index. VECTORIALISM of sonic sources is an aspect of SPATIAL DISTRIBUTION.

**Verbalization.** Karlheinz Stockhausen was the first to introduce the concept of VERBALIZATION in lieu of musical notation. One of his pieces represents a parabolic curve with the following inscription: "Sound a note. Continue sounding it as long as you please. It is your prerogative." John Cage has elevated VERBALIZATION to the degree of eloquent diction. Earle Brown and Morton Feldman are inventive verbalizationists. La Monte Young tells the player: "Push the piano to the wall. Push it through the wall. Keep pushing." Nam June Paik dictates: "Cut your left arm very slowly with a razor (more than 10 centimeters)." Philip Corner limits himself to a simple command: "One anti-personnel type CBU (Cluster Bomb Unit) will be thrown into the audience."

**Verismo.** The term VERISMO became popular in the 1890's when it was used to describe the type of operatic naturalism exemplified by Mascagni's opera *Cavalleria Rusticana* and Leoncavallo's *Pagliacci*. The obvious etymological derivation of VERISMO is from vero, true, with reference to the realistic quality of the libretto. Soon the vogue spread into France with the production of *Louise*, a "musical romance" by Gustave Charpentier. In Germany VERISMO assumed satirical and sociological rather than naturalistic forms; in England, Benjamin Britten's *Peter Grimes* may be described as veristic in its subject and execution. VERISMO had no followers in Russia, where nationalistic themes preoccupied the interests of opera composers.

**Vigesimosecular Music.** A Latinized form of a common word often imparts precision lacking in its vernacular counterpart. The neologism VIGESIMOSECULAR compounds the Latin ordinal numeral 20 with the word for century. By the very ponderosity of its

Sesquipedalian Macropolysyllabification, the term evokes deep erudition and concentrated anfractuosity of elucubration. It is therefore reserved for advanced theories and practices of 20th-century music.

**Wagneromorphism.** An obsessive idolatry of Wagner, common among composers around the turn of the century, a mass genuflection and humicubation before the unquestionable genius of Wagner, produced the phenomenon of Wagneromorphism. It is characterized by a total absorption of all familiar traits of Wagner's melody and harmony, particularly chromatic suspensions, triadic fanfares, modulatory sequences and dynamic explosions followed by protracted recessions.

**Wagneromanticism.** This is a telescoped word to describe a style of composition much in vogue late in the 19th century, in which romantic program music is invested in Wagnerian harmonies.

**White Sound.** By analogy with the complementary colors of the visual spectrum, White Sound can be described as a sonic continuum containing all available tones within a certain auditory range, or a complex consisting of prescribed intervals, a pandiatonic or panpentatonic Tone Cluster, a dodecaphonic or icositetraphonic cumulus, etc. White Sound can be prismatically analyzed into a linear progression forming a scale of discrete tones.

**Whole-Tone Scales.** The Whole-Tone Scale gained ephemeral popularity early in the 20th century as an exotic resource cultivated by the Impressionist school of composers. If major tonality is masculine, and minor is feminine, then the Whole-Tone Scale is of the neuter gender. It lacks modality; the intervalic progression in the Whole-Tone Scale remains the same in melodic rotation. The perfect fifth and the perfect fourth, the cornerstones of tonality, are absent in the Whole-Tone Scale; there is no dominant or subdominant, and no leading tone. Analytically, the Whole-Tone Scale is atonal. It can also be regarded as the linear function of two mutually exclusive augmented triads. The Tritone, the "diabolus in musica" of the medieval scholiasts is fundamental to the Whole-Tone Scale, which can be built as the intussusception of three mutually exclusive tritones at the distance of a whole-tone from one another. Because of this association, the Whole-Tone Scale itself became a favorite device of early modernism to portray diabolical forces, menacing apparitions and ineffable mysteries.

The earliest mention of an intentional employment of the Whole-Tone Scale occurs in Mozart's comical divertimento *Die Dorfmusikanten*, subtitled "a musical joke." But Mozart used the Whole-Tone Scale here not to illustrate a malevolent agency, but to ridicule the incompetence of village musicians and their inability to play in tune. The Whole-Tone Scale came into its own as an ominous symbol in Glinka's opera *Ruslan and Ludmila*, in which it is used as a motto of the magician Chernomor. Rossini made use of the Whole-Tone Scale in a song written in 1864 entitled *L'Amour à Pékin*, in which it was described as "gamme chinoise." The possible reason for this reference is that an ancient Chinese panpipe contains two mutually exclusive Whole-Tone Scales in symmetrically disposed tubes. Liszt was fascinated with the Whole-Tone Scale, and was greatly impressed by the *Fantastic Overture* which the Russian amateur composer Baron Vietinghoff-Scheel sent him, and in which Whole-Tone Scales were profusely employed. In his comment on the work, Liszt described the effect as "terrifying to all long and protruding ears." Liszt himself made use of the Whole-Tone Scale in his symphonic poem *Divina Commedia*, illustrating the Inferno; and he used it systematically in his posthumously published organ pieces.

The problem of harmonizing the Whole-Tone Scale tonally was solved by Glinka in a sequence of modulations. Liszt harmonized a descending Whole-Tone Scale which occurs in the bass, by a series of divergent major triads in root positions. It is doubtful whether Puccini was aware of Liszt's application of this harmony, but he used a precisely identical triadic harmonization of the descending Whole-Tone Scale in his opera *Tosca*, as an introduction to the appearance of the sinister Roman chief of Police.

The Russian composer Vladimir Rebikov was probably the first to have written an entire composition derived exclusively from the Whole-Tone Scale and its concomitant series of augmented triads, in his *Les Démons s'amusent* for piano; its title suggests that Rebikov was fully aware of the demoniac association of the WHOLE-TONE SCALE. But it was Debussy who elevated the WHOLE-TONE SCALE from a mere exotic device to a poetic and expressive medium. Its Protean capacity for change and adaptability greatly attracted Debussy and his followers, as an alternative variation of a diatonic scale. A very interesting application of the WHOLE-TONE SCALE occurs in *La Mer*; the principal theme of the first movement is in the Aeolian mode; in the third movement it appears isorhythmically as a progression of whole-tones. The first and the last sections of Debussy's *Voiles* for piano consist of whole tones with the middle section providing a contrast in the pentatonic scale.

A whole catalogue can be compiled of incidental usages of the WHOLE-TONE SCALE. Even Tchaikovsky, not usually given to modern inventions, made use of the WHOLE-TONE SCALE in a modulatory sequence illustrating the appearance of the ghost of the old Countess in his opera *The Queen of Spades*. Rimsky-Korsakov filled the second act of his opera *Le Coq d'or* with WHOLE-TONE SCALES and augmented triads to convey the impression of death and devastation of the battlefield. The entrance of Herod in *Salomé* of Richard Strauss is announced by a leading motive composed of whole-tones. Gustav Holst characterized Saturn in his symphonic suite *The Planets* by a series of whole-tone passages to evoke the mystery of Saturn's rings. Apart from astronomy, the whole-tone scale serves pure fantasy. In his symphonic fairy tale *Kikimora* Liadov paints the mischievous sprite in whole-tones. Paul Dukas introduces the hapless amateur magician in his *L'Apprenti Sorcier* in a series of whole-tones. The English composer Edward Maryon assigns the WHOLE-TONE SCALE to the changelings in his opera *Werewolf*, reserving the diatonic scale for normal children. Another English composer, Havergal Brian, has a chorus singing in WHOLE-TONE SCALES in his opera *The Tigers*, to illustrate the aerial bombardment of London by the Zeppelins during World War I. There are bits of whole-tone figures in Gian Carlo Menotti's children's opera *Help, Help, the Globolinks!* to describe the creatures from outer space. The earthlings in the opera overcome the invading globolinks in victorious C major.

The symbolism of the WHOLE-TONE SCALE is strong in Soviet music. In the opera *Battleship Potemkin* by Oles Tchisko, the Tsarist officers proclaim their authority in whole-tones. In the *Anti-Fascist Symphony* by Boris Mokrousov, the Fascists march in whole-tone steps.

A remarkable demonstration of the perdurability of the whole-tone scale as a symbol of evil is provided by Stravinsky's *Elegy for J. F. K.*, which contains within a 12-tone row two intervallically congruous groups of whole tones, each embanked in a tritone, itself a symbol of deviltry.

With the gradual decline of pictorial and sensorial programmaticism in contemporary music, the WHOLE-TONE SCALE sank into innocuous desuetude. It found its temporary outlet and a stylistic rehabilitation in dodecaphonic usages in the form of two mutually exclusive hexachords. Eventually it joined the subculture of film music. The Nazis advance on the screen to the sound of WHOLE-TONE SCALES in the trombones. Mad scientists hatch their murderous schemes to blow up the world in mighty progressions of whole-tones. Mentally disturbed maidens pluck WHOLE-TONE SCALES on the harp. When Jean Harlow, in her screen biography, climbs up the ladder in the studio before her final collapse, she is accompanied by delicate whole-tone pizzicati. The WHOLE-TONE SCALE is also used, wittily so, in satirical comment on pompous personages in animated cartoons.

**Zen.** The philosophy of ZEN is at once an infinitely complex and fantastically simple doctrine that accepts irrelevance of response as a legitimate and even elevating part of human discourse. This paradoxical liberating trait exercises a compelling attraction for composers of the Avant-Garde, eager to achieve a total freedom of self-expression combined with the precision of indeterminacy. The verbal and psychological techniques of ZEN can be translated into music through a variety of means which may range from white noise of (theoretically) infinite duration to (theoretically) instantaneous silences. In the field of MIXED MEDIA, in particular, ZEN provides a rich vocabulary of gestures, facial expressions, inarticulate verbalization, ambulatory exercises, performance of physiological functions, etc. In the composition of instrumental music, ZEN expands perception of the minutest quantities of sonic material and imparts eloquence to moments of total impassivity, in which the audible tones become interlopers between areas of inaudibility. Imagination and fantasy in the mind of a practitioner of ZEN may subjectively become more expressive than the realization of the creative impulse in written musical symbols.

# Index

# INDEX

A (pitch), 630, 996
Aarons, Alfred M., 680
Abato, Vincent, 779
Abecedarianism (term), 1423
Abendroth, Hermann, 1039
Ablation (term), 1423
Abraham, Paul. *Die Blume von Hawaii,*
535; *Victoria und ihr Hussar,* 522
Abrányi, Emil, 106
Abril, Antón García, 1204
Absil, Jean. Concerto, piano, 670; *Fan-
taisie concertante,* 1064; symphony
#2, 895; *Variations symphoniques,*
835; *Les Voix de la mer,* 973; *Le
Zodiaque,* 961
Absolute music (term), 1423
Abstract Expressionism (term), 1423
Abstract music (term), 1423
Absurd music (term), 1423
Académie des Beaux-Arts. *See* Prix de
Rome
Accademia di Santa Cecilia (Rome), 315
Accompaniment. Discussed, 1423–1424
Achron, Joseph. Concerto, violin, #2,
636; *Golem,* 553
Acousma (term), 1424
Acoustics. Discussed, 1424
Action music (term), 1424–1425
Adachi, Motohiko, 1202
Adam, Charles-Adolphe, 48
Adam, Claus, 942
Addison, Adele, 1099
Addison, John, 917
Additive composition (term), 1425
Adjunction (term), 1425
Adler, Guido, 460; death, 729
Adler, Larry. Plays Arnold, 980; Benja-
min, 964; Berger, 750; Milhaud, 834;
Vaughan Williams, 936
Adler, Richard. *Damn Yankees,* 993;
*Pajama Game,* 975
Aeromusic (Futurist), 1303–1304
Aerophor, 193, 229

Aerostatic suspension (term), 1425
Aetherophone. *See* Theremin
Agglutination (term), 1425
Agricola, Martin, 1012
Air conditioning, 671
Akutagawa, Yasuki, 920, 950
Alain, Jéhan, 715, 926
Alaleona, Domenico, 179, 326; death,
486; 1303
Albéniz, Isaac. Death, 145; teacher, 363;
stamp, 1101. Works: *Iberia,* 118;
*Triana,* 627
Albert, Eugene d'. Sues *Allgemeine
musikalische Zeitung,* 399; death, 544.
Works: *Flauto solo,* 81; *Der Golem,*
440; *Der Improvisator,* 27; *Izeïjl,* 150;
*Kain,* 4; *Liebesketten,* 213; *Mareike
von Nymwegen,* 380; *Mister Wu,* 553;
*Revolutionshochzeit,* 316–317; *Die
schwarze Orchidee,* 482; *Sirocco,* 340;
*Der Stier von Olivera,* 295; *Tiefland,*
50; *Die toten Augen,* 266; *Tragal-
dabas,* 117; *Die verschenkte Frau,* 197
Albertsen, Hjort, 961
Aleatory music (term), 1425
Alesandrescu, Alfred, 401
Alessandro, Rafaele d', 1061
Alessandro, Victor, 1258
Alexander, Leni, 1089
Alexandrov, Alexander, 487, 783
Alexandrov, Anatoly, 1024
Alexei, Patriarch, Russian Orthodox
Church, 859
Alfano, Franco. Completes Puccini, *Tu-
randot,* 431; judges Schubert centen-
nial contest, 479; 985. Works: *Cyrano
de Bergerac,* 618; *Hymn to Bolivar,*
522; *La Leggenda di Sakuntala,* 349;
*Madonna Imperia,* 454; *L'Ombra di
Don Giovanni,* 237; *Il Principe Zilah,*
138; *Risurrezione,* 68; sonata, cello,
477; symphony #2, 584; *L'Ultimo
Lord,* 508

1505

Alfvén, Hugo. 1937 Dresden festival, 646; death, 1084. Works: *Midsommervaka*, 420; *The Prodigal Son*, 1027; symphony #5, 936
Algorithm (term), 1426
Aliabiev, Alexander, 921
All-American Youth Orchestra, 733
Allegra, Salvatore, 416
Allen, Paul, 266
Allende, Humberto. Death, 1070. Works: concerto, cello, 256–257; *Concierto sinfónico*, violin, 763; *La Voz de las Calles*, 341
Allusive quotation. Discussed, 1426
Alonso, Angela, 1141
Alpaerts, Flor, 230, 895
Alphabetical monograms, 1426
Alsace-Lorraine festival of, 1905, 76
Altschuler, Modest. Conducts first concert, Russian Symphony Orchestra, 55; conducts Scriabin, *Poème de l'Extase*, 131; *Prometheus*, 252
Altshuler, Ira M., 860
Alwin, Karl, 362
Alwyn, William, 734, 1093
Ambulation (term), 1426
Ameller, André, 1133
Amengual, René, 960
American Academy, Rome, 346, 373
American Composers' Alliance, 660
American Composers' Contest, 685
American Federation of Musicians, 756, 763, 1347
American Guild of Musical Artists, 624
American Legion, 317
American Musicological Society, 590
American Society of Composers, Authors and Publishers, 234, 277–278, 660, 700–701, 725, 803, 1188
Amirkhanian, Charles, 1479
Amirov, Fikret, 859, 969
Amram, David, 1199
Amy, Gilbert, 1182, 1196, 1202
Anagrams, 1426–1427
Analphabetism (term), 1427
Anamnesis (term), 1427
Ananda, Sondet Phra Chao Yu Hua Buhimbol Adulyadej, 462, 1100
Anarchy, 1427
Andersen, Stell, 1013
Anderson, Marian, 688, 989, 1163
Anderson, Maxwell, 707
André, Franz, 999
Andreae, Volkmar, 395, 513
Andreyev, Vasily, 90
Andriessen, Hendrik. *Christus Rex*, 856;

*Philomela*, 894; sinfonia, organ, 856; *Symphonic etude*, 946
Andriessen, Jurriaan, 1100
Animal and human noises, 1427
Anna (horse). Death, 710
Annunzio, Gabriele d', 181–182, 185, 232, 235, 252, 304
Ansermet, Ernest. First concert, Orchestre de la Suisse Romande, 306; death, 1276. Works conducted: Beck, *Innominata*, 542; Britten, *Cantata Misericordium*, 1165; Honegger, *Christophe Colomb*, 711; idem, *Horace Victorieux*, 348; Martin, *Monsieur de Pourceaugnac*, 1157; Stravinsky, *Capriccio*, 499; idem, *Le Chant du Rossignol*, 241; idem, *L'Histoire du Soldat*, 302; idem, mass, 862; idem, *Volga Boatmen's Song*, 283
Antheil, George. Birth, 7; letters, 452, 510; death, 1060. Works: *Ballet Mécanique*, 434, 452; *The Brothers*, 980; *Cabeza de Vaca*, 1193; *The Capital of the World*, 969; concerto, violin, 829; *Decatur at Algiers*, 793; *Helen Retires*, 582; *Jazz Symphony*, 452; *Nocturne*, 793; sonata, violin, piano and drums, 452; string quartet, 452; symphony #4, 781; symphony #5 (*Joyous*), 867; symphony #6, 869; *Transatlantic*, 509–510; *Venus in Africa*, 1029; *Volpone*, 950; *The Wish*, 992
Antill, John, 820
Anti-music (term), 1427–1428
Anti-opera (term), 1428
Antoniou, Theodore, 1186, 1222
Apergis, Yorgos, 1225
Apollinaire, Guillaume, 836, 1354
Aponte-Ledée, Rafael, 1260
Aposiopesis (term), 1428
Apostel, Hans Erich. Works: 5 *Lyric Pieces*, 586; *Four Melodies*, 650; 5 *Lieder*, 997; string quartet #1, 873; #2, 1051; *Um Mitternacht*, 1160; *Variations on a Haydn Theme*, 917; wind quartet, 876
Ara, Ugo, 83
Arakishvili, Dmitri, 308, 464
Arányi, Jelly d'. And Schumann violin concerto, 659. Works played: Holst, double concerto, 507; Ravel, *Tzigane*, 388–389; Smyth, concerto, 449; Vaughan Williams, *Concerto accademico*, 421
Arapov, Boris, 1096

chestra, 1145; *Music for Strings, Horn and Percussion,* 1071; symphony #1, 855; #4, 970

Bach, Johann Sebastian, 3, 111, 121, 232, 260, 263, 366, 378, 437, 625, 679, 712, 721, 750, 878, 888, 898, 941, 1009, 1052, 1056, 1101, 1106, 1117, 1123, 1182, 1204, 1237, 1238, 1271, 1278, 1279, 1288, 1322, 1332, 1338, 1342; as B-A-C-H, 693, 1001, 1056, 1117, 1151, 1267; Bach monogram, 1426; "Back to Bach," 1470

Bach Society of New Jersey, 679

Bachelet, Alfred. *Hymne Védique,* 751; *Un Jardin sur l'Oronte,* 555; *Quand le cloche sonnera,* 365; *Scemo,* 239

Bäck, Sven-Erik. *Crane Feathers,* 1024; *Favola,* 1161; sinfonia da camera, 1010; *Ett Spel om Maria,* 1046

Bacon, Ernst. *A Drumlin Legend,* 875; *Great River,* 1022–1023; *Riolama,* 1151; *A Tree on the Plains,* 752

Badarzewska, Thekla, 1326, 1346

Badings, Henk. And MANETO, 648; at 1937 Dresden festival, 646. Works: *Apocalypse,* 884; *Ballade,* orch., 899; *Cain and Abel,* 1012; *Genèse,* 1055; *Martin Korda, D.P.,* 1088; *De Nachtwacht,* 893; octet, 960; *Prelude to a Tragedy,* 734; *Salto Mortale,* 1067–1068; sonata, violin & piano, 609; string quartet, 693; *Symphonic Variations,* 856; symphony #1, 512; #2, 572; #3, 605; #4, 839; #5, 885; #8, 1021; #9, 1104; trio, piano and strings, 650; *The Woman of Andros,* 1083

Bagier, Guido, 362

Baird, Tadeusz. At 1956 Warsaw Autumn, 1016. Works: *5 Chants,* 1269; concerto for orchestra, 975; *Expression,* 1071; *Erotics,* 1138; *Muzyka epifaniczna,* 1180; *Quatre Essais,* 1066; *Quatre Novelettes,* 1280; *Tomorrow,* 1227; *Variations Without a Theme,* 1145

Bajić, Isidor, 175

Baker, Ray Stannard, 94

Baker, Theodore, 593

Bakunin, Mikhail, 1436

Balada, Leonardo, 1261

Balakirev, Mily. Death, 164; centennial, 637; stamp, 1029. Works: symphony #2, 144

Balalaika, 90, 487

Balanchine, George, 981, 1140

Balanchivadze, Andrei, 1063

Balanchivadze, Meliton, 430

Balasanian, Sergei, 985

Balazs, Frederic, 757

Baldwin, Bertram, 1165

Baliev, Nikita, 123

Baloković, Zlatko, 657

Baltimore Symphony Orchestra. First concert, 265

Bandur, Jovan, 854

Banks, Don. Duo, violin and cello, 941; sonata, violin, 978; 3 studies, cello and piano, 1065

Bantock, Granville. Conducts Delius, *Brigg Fair,* 119; death, 821. Works: *Dante and Beatrice,* 186; *Hebridean Symphony,* 263; *Pagan Symphony,* 622; *Pilgrim's Progress,* 482; *The Seal Woman,* 399

Baranović, Krešimir, 550, 1084

Barati, George, 1106, 1227

Barber, Samuel. Birth, 159. Works: *Adagio for Strings,* 679; *Andromache's Farewell,* 1156; *Antony and Cleopatra,* 1226; *Capricorn Concerto,* 788; *Cave of the Heart,* 816; *Commando March,* 774; concerto, cello, 814; concerto, piano, 1146; concerto, violin, 728; *Essay for Orchestra,* #1, 679, 801; #2, 751; *A Hand of Bridge,* 1067; *Knoxville, Summer of 1915,* 851; *Medea's Meditation and Dance of Vengeance,* 816, 1219; *Music for a Scene from Shelley,* 603; *Prayers of Kierkegaard,* 987; *School for Scandal Overture,* 571, 937; *The Serpent Heart,* 816; sonata, piano, 1303; *A Stopwatch and an Ordnance Map,* 790; string quartet, 679; symphony #1, 636; #2, 783; *Toccata Festiva,* 1095; *Vanessa,* 1040–1041

Barbershop, 53, 667, 707

Barbirolli, John. Honored by Vaughan Williams, 1036. Conducts: Benjamin, symphony #1, 858; Britten, *Sinfonia da Requiem,* 731; Castelnuovo-Tedesco, *King John,* 750; idem, piano concerto, 701; Fricker, symphony #1, 897; Herrmann, *Moby Dick,* 711; Hovhaness, *Ode to the Temple of Sound,* 1228; Mason, *Lincoln Symphony,* 657; Read, symphony #1, 656; Vaughan Williams, *Fantasia on Sussex,* 505; idem, symphony #8, 1008; idem, tuba concerto, 978; Weinberger, *Variations and Fugue,* 700

Barce, Ramón, 1261
Barcelona. Orquesta Sinfónica, 171
Bardi, Giovanni de', 580
Barère, Simon, 910
Bargielski, Zbigniew, 1268
Bark, Jan, 1180
"Barn Dance" (radio program), 422
Barraine, Elsa, 689, 818
Barraqué, Jean, 1006, 1221
Barraud, Henri. At 1956 Warsaw Autumn, 1016. Works: *La Farce du Maître Pathelin*, 858; *Lavinia*, 1121; *Numance*, 992–993; *Rapsodie Cartésienne*, 1114; *Symphonie de Numance*, 903; symphony #3, 1044, 1051
Barrère, Georges, 318
Barth, Hans, 534, 1466
Bartlett, Ethel, 743
Bartók, Béla. Ravel on, 269; and Cowell, 457, 1498; and 1937 Dresden festival, 646; on Ravel, 661; death, 803; Turchi, in memoriam, 860; stamp, 968, 1000; and 1956 Warsaw Autumn, 1016; and 1961 ISCM festival, Vienna, 1120; via Telstar, 1208; and neo-modality, 1471; and neo-primitivism, 1472. Works: *Bluebeard's Castle*, 299; *Cantata Profana*, 589; concerto for orchestra, 792, 819, 1120, 1435, 1479; concerto, piano, #1, 457; #2, 1498; #3, 811; concerto, viola, 885; concerto, violin, #1 (early work posthumously published), 1049–1050; #2, 694–695, 1120, 1441; *Contrasts*, 684, 1030, 1203; *Dance Suite*, 413, 1120; *Deux Images*, 217, 1050; *Divertimento*, 714–715, 756, 1266; *A Fábol faragott királyfi*, 285; *Five Dances*, 381; *Four Orchestral Pieces*, 350–351; *A Kékzakállú Herceg Vára*, 299; *Kossuth*, 54; *Mikrokosmos*, 1423; *The Miraculous Mandarin*, 440–441; *Music for Strings, Percussion and Celesta*, 638; rhapsody, violin and orch., 585; *Scherzo*, orch., 58; *Scherzo*, piano and orch., 1124; sonata, 2 pianos and percussion, 663, 674; sonata, violin and piano, #1, 361; #2, 376, 401; string quartet #5, 626, 1191; suite, orch., #2, 151; *Two Portraits*, 217, 1050; *The Wooden Prince*, 285
Bartók, Ditta, 663
Bartóš, František, 568, 674
Barzin, Leon, 701

Baschet, François, 1042
Basic-Witz Furniture Industries, 1170
Bassett, Leslie, 1141, 1163
Bate, Stanley, 756, 979; death, 1073
Bath, Hubert, 230, 381
Battle, John S., 924
Baudelaire, Charles, 1455, 1495
Baudrier, Yves, 628
Bauer, Harold, 125, 133, 564, 565
Baur, Jürg, 1153
Bautista, Julian. *Obertura Grotesca*, 1189; *4 Poemas Callegos*, 857; *Tres Ciudades*, 673
Bax, Arnold. 1922 Salzburg festival, 362; on Henry Wood, 787–788; quoted by V. Williams, 560; death, 965. Works: *Concertante*, piano left hand and orch., 897; *The Garden of Fand*, 332; *Ode to the Red Army*, 782; sonata, viola, 397; symphony #1, 366, 393; #2, 500; #3, 505, 560; #4, 545; #5, 578; #6, 614; #7, 697
Bayle, François, 1156
Bayreuth, 396, 1069, 1121, 1142, 1242
Bazelon, Irwin, 1215
Beatles, 1144–1145, 1458, 1487
Beaumont, Geoffrey, 948
Bebop (term), 1432
Becaud, Gilbert, 1148
Becerra Schmidt, Gustavo. *Homogramas I*, 1218; *Juegos*, 1260; piano quintet, 1178, 1190; symphony #1, 1031
Becher, Johannes R., 889
Bechstein, Carl, 5
Beck, Conrad. *Chamber Cantata*, 692; *Innominata*, 542, 551; *Oratorio über die Sprüche des Angelus Silesius*, 590; sonatina, violin and piano, #2, 896; *Die Sonnenfinsternis*, 1244; string quartet #3, 458; symphony #5, 514; #6, 941; #7 (*Aeneas-Silvius*), 1043; *Der Tod zu Basel*, 958
Becker, Günther, 1181, 1265
Becker, Gustave, 938–939, 1060
Becker, Hugo, 89
Beckett, Wheeler, 993
Beckwith, John, 1083
Bedford, David, 1225
Beecham, Sir Thomas. Death, 1110. Works conducted: Bax, symphony #5, 578; Brian, *Hero and Leander*, 130; Delius, *Irmelin*, 957; idem, *A Mass of Life*, 146; Delius festival, 497–498; Dohnányi, piano concerto #2, 844; Scott, piano concerto, 255;

idem, *Two Passacaglias*, 247; Thomson, symphony #2, 743; Vaughan Williams, *In the Fen Country*, 141

Beeson, Jack, 1039, 1198

Beethoven, Ludwig van, 11, 76, 155, 260, 263, 308, 356, 384, 437, 451, 629, 676, 685, 688, 691, 736-737, 744, 810, 824, 828, 935, 938, 1001, 1015, 1071, 1082, 1084, 1145, 1164, 1168, 1169, 1171, 1191, 1194, 1207, 1230, 1237, 1278, 1288, 1324, 1326, 1327, 1345

"Beethoven," Michel-Maurice Lévy, 947

Behrend, Jeanne, 706

Behrman, David, 1165

Beidler, Isolde, 242

Beinum, Eduard van, 807, 1063

Belaieff, Mitrofan Petrovich, 54, 68

Belar, H., 1055

Bellaigue, Camille, 182, 1317-1318

Bellini, Vincenzo, 21, 611, 639

Benatzky, Ralph, 506, 518, 1036

Benda, Jiří, 1008

Benguerel, Xavier, 1089

Ben-Haim, Paul. *Capriccio*, piano and orch., 1095; concerto, cello, 1252; concerto, piano, 888; concerto, violin, 1132; *Dance and Invocation*, 1107; *The Eternal Theme*, 1214; *Fanfare to Israel*, 1242; *Hodaya Min Hamidbar*, 1250; sonata, violin solo, 961; *The Sweet Psalmist of Israel*, 1017; symphony #1, 736; #2, 847

Benjamin, Arthur. Plays Howells, piano concerto, 244. Works: concerto, harmonica, 964; concerto, piano, 898; *Cotillon*, 686; *The Devil Take Her*, 540; *Jamaican Rumba*, 747; *Prelude to a Holiday*, 758; *Prima Donna*, 870; symphony #1, 858; *A Tale of Two Cities*, 956; *Tartuffe*, 1193

Bennett, Richard Rodney. And dodecaphony, 1441. Works: *The Mines of Sulphur*, 1196; *A Penny for a Song*, 1249; symphony #1, 1214; #2, 1254

Bennett, Robert Russell. At Yaddo, 549; rescores *Carmen*, 776; and Stravinsky, 793. Works: concerto, violin, piano and orch., 1155; *Eight Etudes for Orchestra*, 745-746; *The Enchanted Kiss*, 809; *The Four Freedoms*, 772; *Maria Malibran*, 604; *Symphony in D for the Dodgers*, 733

Bennett, William Sterndale, 700

Benoît, Peter. Death, 16; 589

Bentzon, Jörgen. *Racconto*, 674; *Sat-*

*urnalia*, 793; sonatina, flute, clarinet and bassoon, 458

Bentzon, Niels Viggo. *Bonjour Max Ernst*, 1147-1148; *Concerto for Six Musicians*, 1265; concerto, oboe, clarinet and bassoon, 1010; concerto, 3 pianos and 8 instr., 896; *Faust III*, 1184; *Metaphor*, 891; *Partita*, piano, 835; symphony #4 (*Metamorphosen*), 877; #7, 957; *Torquilla*, 1126; *Variazioni breve*, 961

Berezowsky, Nicolai. Wins NBC prize, 549; plays Diamond violin concerto, 641; death, 964. Works: *Babar the Elephant*, 953; concerto, viola, 741, 756; *Gilgamesh*, 834; string quartet, 549; symphony #2, 581-582; #3, 638; #4, 774

Berg, Alban. Prague ban, 441; 1932 ISCM festival, 552; death, 616-617; in "Entartete Musik," 670; and the 1956 Warsaw Autumn, 1016; on atonality, 1311-1315, 1430; and dodecaphony, 1440; and expressionism, 1447. Works: concerto, violin, 625, 1203, 1426, 1440-1441; *Drei Orchesterstücke*, 508; *Kammerkonzert*, 450-451, 458; *Lulu*, 596-597, 610, 646, 1443, 1474, 1496; *Lyric Suite*, 443, 585; *Orchesterlieder* (Altenberg), 219; sonata, piano, 345; string quartet, 376; *Der Wein*, 1089; *Wozzeck*, 423-425, 431, 441, 625

Berg, Gunnar, 1093, 1180

Berg, Natanael. *Engelbrekt*, 496; *Genoveva*, 840; *Judith*, 621; *Lelia*, 199

Berger, Arthur. *Ideas of Order*, 956; string quartet, 1088

Berger, Jean, 749-750

Berger, Roman, 1247

Berger, Theodor, 1117

Bergman, Erik. *The Birds*, 1182; sonatina, piano, 960; *Springtime*, 1247

Bergsma, William. Concerto, violin, 1219; *Paul Bunyan*, 695; symphony #1, 893; *Toccata for the Sixth Day*, 1146

Berio, Luciano. *Allez-hop*, 1071; *Epifanie*, 1126, 1268; *Labiryntus II*, 1268; *Mutazioni*, 1030; *8:37 Perspectives*, 1030; *Quaderni per Orchestra*, 1087; *Sequenza V*, 1265; *Sinfonia*, 1271, 1426

Berkeley, Lennox. And dodecaphony, 1441. Works: *Castaway*, 1240; concerto, piano, 873; *A Dinner Engage-*

#1, 963; *Chiarina*, 888; *Concertante Musik*, 659; concerto, piano, #1, 849; #2, 945; concerto, strings, 760; concerto, violin, #2, 1241; *Demeter*, 1183; *Die Flut*, 825; *Fürstin Tarakanowa*, 728; *Hamlet* (ballet), 901; *Hamlet* (symphonic poem), 720; *Lysistrata*, 921; *Die Nachtschwalbe*, 848–849; *Ornaments*, 965, 997, 1477; *Preussisches Märchen*, 945; *Requiem*, 1089; *Rosamunde Floris*, 1094–1095; *Study in Pianissimo*, 981; *Variations for Orchestra on a Paganini Theme*, 843, 919; *Virtuose Musik*, 1241; *Zwischenfälle bei einer Notlandung*, 1213

Black-list, 357, 1290–1292

Blackwood, Easley. Concerto, clarinet, 1193; concerto, flute and strings, 1263; symphony #1, 1047; #2, 1105–1106; #3, 1197; *Un Voyage à Cythère*, 1233

Blanc, Giuseppe, 145, 215

Blancafort, Manuel, 626

Bland, James, 181

Blauvelt, Lillian, 313

Blazhkov, Igor, 1213

Blech, Leo. Conducts d'Albert, *Mister Wu*, 553; death, 1054. Works: *Alpenkönig und Menschenfeind*, 49; *Das war ich*, 38; *Rappelkopf*, 49; *Versiegelt*, 130

Bleyle, Karl, 126

Blind Tom, 126

Bliss, Arthur. Conducts Stravinsky, *Ragtime*, 304. Works: *Adam Zero*, 814; *The Beatitudes*, 1136; *Checkmate*, 648, 1312; *Colour Symphony*, 364; concerto, piano, 697; concerto, violin, 994; *Conquest of the Air*, 676; *Edinburgh Overture*, 1014; *The Lady of Shalott*, 1049; *Mary of Magdala*, 1165; *Miracle in the Gorbals*, 790; *Morning Heroes*, 516; *The Olympians*, 881; quintet, oboe and strings, 551; *Rhapsody*, 377; *Rout*, 360–361; *Tobias and the Angel*, 1084

Bliss, Robert Woods, 669, 1109

Blitzstein, Marc. Translates Weill, *Dreigroschenoper*, 940; assailed and killed, 1174; and proletarian music, 1483. Works: *Airborne*, 812; *The Cradle Will Rock*, 648; *Freedom Morning*, 772; *The Harpies*, 959; *No For an Answer*, 726; *Regina*, 881; string quartet, 549

Bloch, André, 1092. Works: *Au Béguinage*, 537; *Guignol*, 622; *Kaa*, 565; *Maïda*, 148; *Suite palestinienne*, 864

Bloch, Augustin, 1265

Bloch, Ernest. New York Society of the Friends of Music concert, 284: in "Entartete Musik," 670; death, 1068. Works: *America*, 485; *Baal Shem*, 741; concerto, violin, 682–683; concerto grosso #1, 414; #2, 956; *Concerto symphonique*, piano, 879; *Evocations*, 664; *Helvetia*, 543; *Hiver-Printemps*, 87; *Israel* symphony, 284; *Macbeth*, 172; *Poems of the Sea*, 757; quintet, piano and strings, #1, 380, 477, 1466; #2, 1047; *Sacred Service*, 578; *Schelomo*, 284, 362; *Scherzo Fantasque*, 903; *Sinfonia breve*, 956, 1441; sonata, piano, 757; sonata, violin, 362; string quartet #2, 836; suite, viola and orch., 333; *Suite Hebraïque*, 950; *Suite Symphonique*, 804; symphony in E flat, 1004; symphony, trombone and orch., 1007; *Three Psalms*, 284; *Trois Poèmes Juifs*, 281, 284; *22nd Psalm*, 393; *Vivre Aimer*, 18; *Voice in the Wilderness*, 637

Blockx, Jean. Death, 202. Works: *Baldie*, 120; *De Bruid der Zee*, 24; *Thyl Uylenspiegel*, 2

Blom, Eric, 1063

Blomdahl, Karl-Birger. Death, 1259. Works: *Altisonans*, 1228, 1268; *Anabasis*, 1020; *Aniara*, 664, 1064; chamber concerto, piano, winds and percussion, 996–997; concerto, violin, 857; *Fioriture*, 1089; *Forma Ferritonans*, 1117; *Herr von Hancken*, 1207; *Minotauros*, 1046, *Sisyphus*, 984; *I speglarnas sal*, 961; symphony #1, 795; #3, 917; trio, clarinet, cello and piano, 1066; trio, strings, 835

Bloom, Leopold, 63, 1184, 1465

Blow, John, 674

Blues (term), 192, 1432

Blum, Robert, 477, 625

Blume, Friedrich, 878

Blüthner, Julius Ferdinand, 161

Boccioni, Umberto, 1436

Bo-Chao, Lee, 920

Bodanzky, Artur, 284, 564, 565

Boero, Felipe. *Ariana y Dionisios*, 331; *El Matrero*, 495; *Tucumàn*, 300

Bogatyrev, Anatoly, 699

Boguslawski, Edward, 1231, 1269

Bohemian Club, 98
Bois, Robert du, 1247
Boito, Arrigo. Death, 299; libretto, *Basi e Bote*, 449; and La Scala reopening, 816. Works: *Nerone*, 389
Bolanos, Cesar, 1260
Bolcom, William, 1200
Bolshoi Theater. Milan visit, 1190; American debut, 1243
Bombardelli, Silvije, 1252
Bonaventura, Mario di, 1082, 1241, 1263
Bond, Carrie Jacobs, 826, 1484
Bondeville, Emmanuel, 914
Bondon, Jacques. *La Coupole*, 1079; *La nuit foudroyée*, 1193; *Le Taillis ensorcelé*, 1096
Bongos, 467
Bonn. Beethoven-Hall, 1071
Bononcini, Giovanni, 838
Boogie-woogie (term), 683, 1433
Bop (term), 1433
Borchard, Leo, 802
Borck, Edmund. Killed in war, 781. Works: *Fünf Orchesterstücke*, 569; *Napoleon*, 759; *Prelude and Fugue*, 624
Bori, Lucrezia, 1084
Bořkovec, Pavel. Concerto, piano, 610; *Start*, 514; string quartet #4, 873
Borland, W. J., 591
Borne, Fernand le. *See* Le Borne
Borodin, Alexander, 574, 632–633, 634, 919, 967
Borovsky, Alexander, 473
Borowski, Felix. *Boudour*, 318–319; *Fernando del Nonsentsico*, 639–640; *Peintures*, 293
Börrensen, Hakon. *Kaddara*, 338; *Den kongelige Gast*, 318; *Thor korer til Jotunheim*, 193; *Tycho Brahes Dröm*, 386
Borup-Jørgensen, Axel, 1181, 1225
Boscovich, Uriah, 666
Bosmans, Henriette, 491
Bossi, Enrico. Death at sea, 409
Bossi, Renzo. *Passa la Ronda!*, 309; *Il Principe felice*, 923; *La Rosa rossa*, 705; *Volpino il Calderaio*, 421
Boston Opera House. Opening, 150
Boston Society for Prevention of Cruelty to Children, 1023
Boston. Symphony Hall, 9
Boston Symphony Orchestra. Plays for Panama-Pacific Exposition, 255;

Muck's resignation demanded, 293; unionized, 763; Soviet tour, 1015
Boughton, Rutland. *Alkestis*, 363; *Bethlehem*, 261; *The Immortal Hour*, 245; *The Lily Maid*, 591; *The Queen of Cornwall*, 398
Boukoff, Yury, 1208
Boulanger, Lili, 227; death, 295
Boulanger, Nadia. Prix de Rome, 227; conducts A. Tcherepnin, 383; plays Copland, 407; conducts Stravinsky, 669; plays Stravinsky, 818; dedicatee, Copland nonet, 1188
Boulez, Pierre. Birth, 410; lecturer, 1262. Works: *Doubles*, 1044; *Éclat*, 1198; *Figures, Doubles, Prismes*, 1173–1174, 1268; *Improvisations sur Mallarmé*, 1066; *Le Marteau sans Maître*, 997; *Pli selon pli*, 1088; *Poésie pour Pouvoir*, 1056; *Polyphonie X*, 922; *Le Soleil des Eaux*, 943; sonata, piano, #2, 1161; *Structures*, vol. II, 1126
Boulnois, Joseph, 303
Boult, Adrian. Works conducted: Bantock, *Pagan Symphony*, 622; Bartók, concerto, 2 pianos, percussion and orch., 663; Bax, symphony #7, 697; Bliss, piano concerto, 697; Brian, symphony #8, 971; Fricker, viola concerto, 965; Goossens, oboe concerto, 697; Medtner, piano concerto #3, 781; Scott, violin concerto, 465; Tippett, symphony #2, 1042; Vaughan Williams, concerto grosso, 901; idem, *Five Variants on Dives and Lazarus*, 697; idem, piano concerto, 560; idem, symphony #3 (*Pastoral*), 352; #4, 604; #6, 852; #7 (*Antarctica*), 950; #9, 1046
Bourgault-Ducoudray, Louis, 166
Bourguignon, Francis de, 415–416
Bousquet, Francis, 472
Boustead, Alan, 1193
Boustrophedon (term), 1433
Boutnikoff, Ivan, 550
Bowles, Paul, 549
Boxman, Ernest, 1155
Bozay, Attila, 1246
Bozza, Eugène, 1238
Braga, Gaetano, 116, 1464
Brahms, Johannes, 566–567, 594, 739, 907, 974, 1079, 1278, 1437
Brailey, W. T., 201
Brain, Aubrey, 449
Brain, Dennis, 1034

Brand, Max, 492, 1500
Branly, Edouard, 710
Brant, Henry. At Yaddo, 549. Works: concerto, saxophone, 800; concerto, violin, 730; *Rural Antiphonies*, 968; symphony #1, 847; *Voyage Four*, 1174
Braunfels, Walter. *Don Gil von den grünen Hosen*, 403; *Galatea*, 503; *Prinzessin Brambilla*, 143; *Die Vögel*, 334
Bravničar, Matija, 943
Brazil. Parliament requires programing of Brazilian works, 639
Brazilian Coffee Institute, 1101
Brecht, Bertolt, 475, 495, 505, 512, 1404
Brecht, George, 1205
Brediceanu, Ion, 401
Brehme, Hans, 730
Breil, Joseph Carl. *The Asra*, 422; *The Birth of a Nation*, 250; *The Legend*, 309
Breitkopf und Härtel, 1, 3, 6, 246, 777
Brenta, Gaston, 415–416, 694
Bresgen, Cesar, 943
Breton, André, 1493
Bretón, Tomás, 2
Bréville, Pierre de, 159
Brian, Havergal. Declaration of purpose, 1057. Works: *Doctor Merryheart*, 214–215; *English Suite #3*, 354; *For Valor*, 114; *Gothic Symphony*, 1120, 1496; *Hero and Leander*, 130; symphony #1, 1227; #6 (*Tragica*), 1227; #7, 1256; #8, 971; #9, 1044; #10, 1057; #11, 1074; #12, 1075; #18, 1131; *The Tigers*, 1502
Bricoux, R., 201
Bridge, Frank. Varied by Britten, 674; 726. Works: *Rebus*, 730; *The Sea*, 209; string quartet #3, 477; *Summer*, 267
Brieff, Frank, 1241
Britain, Radie, 1237
British Music Society, 344
Britten, Benjamin. Birth, 230; modernizes *Beggar's Opera*, 855; and 1956 Warsaw Autumn, 1016; "realizes" Purcell, *The Queen's Epicedium*, 1137; conducts Mahler, *Blumine*, 1241. Works: *Albert Herring*, 837; *Ballad of Heroes*, 691; *Billy Budd*, 927; *A Boy Was Born*, 660; *The Building of the House*, 1240; *The Burning Fiery Furnace*,

1221; *Cantata Academica*, 1090; *Cantata Misericordium*, 1165; *Canticle #3*, 1137; *Cello Symphony*, 1175; *A Ceremony of Carols*, 754, 940; concerto, piano, 676; concerto, violin, 1138; *Curlew River*, 1184; *Diversions on a Theme*, 746; *Gloriana*, 962, 1240; *Hankin Booby*, 1234; *Les Illuminations*, 706, 734; *Let's Make an Opera*, 877; *The Little Sweep*, 877; *A Midsummer Night's Dream*, 1086–1087; *Missa Brevis*, 1069; *Nocturne*, 1055–1056; *Noye's Fludde*, 1052; *Paul Bunyan*, 732; *Peter Grimes*, 800, 1472, 1500; *Phantasy Quartet*, 585; *The Prince of the Pagodas*, 1021; *The Prodigal Son*, 1259; *The Rape of Lucretia*, 819; *Saint Nicolas*, 855; *Scottish Ballad*, 743; *Serenade*, 773; *Sinfonia de Requiem*, 731, 758; *Spring Symphony*, 878; suite, violin and piano, 625; *The Turn of the Screw*, 982, 1441; *Variations on a Theme of Frank Bridge*, 674; *Voices for Today*, 1210; *War Requiem*, 1136; *The Young Person's Guide to the Orchestra*, 823
Brkanović, Ivan, 899
Brncic, Gabriel, 1260
Broadcast Music, Inc., 700–701
Brod, Max, 833
Brogi, Renato, 327
Broman, Sten, 674, 1230
Brown, Earle. And controlled improvisation, 1435; notation, 1452; and verbalization, 1500. Works: *Available Forms I*, 1168; *Calder Piece*, 1199; *December, 1952*, 1168; *Folio*, 1473; *From Here*, 1168; *Music for Cello and Piano*, 1165; *Pentathis*, 1168
Brown, Rosemary, 1278
Browning, John, 1146
Brubeck, Dave, 1164, 1255
Brubeck, Howard, 1014
Bruch, Max, 331–332
Bruči, Rudolf. *Covek je vidik bez kraja*, 1127–1128; *Maskal*, 1023; *Srbija*, 1135–1136
Bruck, Henrik, 487
Bruckner, Anton. Stamps, 356, 880; centennial, 398; Bruckner Society of America, 523; airplane, 1082. Works: symphony in F minor, 370; symphony #0, 400; #4, 665; #9, 44, 547; *Te Deum*, 44
Bruckner Society of America, 523

Cage, John. Birth, 208; "American Iconoclasts" concert, 1150; homage by Paik, 1207; text for Straesser, 22 *Pages*, 1226; and spatial distribution, 1434; as planarian, 1475; and the prepared piano, 1481; and verbalization, 1500. Works played: Ichiyanagi, 1164. Works: *Amores*, 1265; *Atlas Eclipticalis*, 1121; *Cartridge Music*, 1313; concert, piano and orchestra, 1049; *Fontana Mix*, 1451; *Imaginary Landscape #1*, 704; *#3*, 749; *Music for Amplified Toy Pianos*, 1080; *Music of Changes*, 1425; *The Seasons*, 834; *Solo for Trombone*, 1265; *Variations I*, 1451; *II*, 1164; *III*, 1164; *Water Music*, 936; *0'0"*, 1148, 1496; *4'33"*, 945, 1148, 1490; *34'46.776"*, 983, 1166

Cagney, James, 761
Cahill, Thaddeus, 94; death, 586
"California Nature Singer," 879
Cambert, Robert, 338
Cameron, Basil. Works conducted: Bax, symphony #4, 545; Benjamin, harmonica concerto, 964; Malipiero, symphony #2, 639
Campari, 1115
Campos-Parsi, Hector, 1201
Camusse, Ezio, 212
Canadian League of Composers, 907
Canaries, 1192–1193
Cannon, Philip, 1185
Cantelli, Guido, 1019
Canteloube, Joseph. Death, 1038. Works: *Le Mas*, 490–491; *Vercingétorix*, 570
Canton, Edgardo, 1156
Cantor, Eddie, 382
Capdevielle, Pierre, 1084, 1250
Caplet, André. Prix de Rome, 19; orchestrates Debussy, *Children's Corner*, 179; conducts Debussy, *Boîte à joujoux*, 320; death, 411. Works: *Miroir de Jésus*, 389, 435
Cardew, Cornelius, 1255–1256, 1452
Carlid, Göte, 943
Carlton, Effie Canning, 705
Carmi, Avner, 843–844
Carnegie Hall. Becomes Registered National Historic Landmark, 1192
Carpenter, John Alden. Death, 912. Works: *Adventures in a Perambulator*, 251–252; *The Anxious Bugler*, 776; *The Birthday of the Infanta*, 320; concertino, piano, 267; concerto, vio-

lin, 657; *Krazy Kat*, 350; *Patterns*, 554; *Pilgrim Vision*, 334; *Sea-Drift*, 575; *The Seven Ages*, 807; *Skyscrapers*, 428, 912; symphony #1, 719; #2, 760
Carr, Michael, 699
Carreño, Innocente, 1219
Carreño, Teresa. Death, 287; 665, 672
Carrillo, Julián, 1208; and microtonality, 1465, 1484. Works: Concertino, 449; *Horizontes*, 926; *Preludio a Cristóbal Colón*, 409; *Sonido 13*, 523
Carson, Philippe, 1156
Cartan, Jean, 535, 568
Carter, Elliott, 133; and spatial distribution, 1434; and metric modulation, 1465, 1477. Works: concerto, piano, 1232; *Double Concerto*, 1123, 1138; *The Minotaur*, 831; *Pocahontas*, 696; sonata, cello and piano, 997; string quartet #2, 1491; symphony, 785; variations, orchestra, 1007
Carter, Ernest, 386, 540
Caruso, Enrico. First American record, 55; San Francisco earthquake, 91; molestation charge, 97; first broadcast of human voice, 143; first opera broadcast, 155; sings Puccini, *Fanciulla del West*, 173; death, 346; horse, 710; invoked, 829
Carvalho, Eleazar de, 739, 870
Caryll, Ivan, 49, 177
Casadesus, François, 293
Casals, Pablo. Marries, 1034; at first Israel Music Festival, 1123; White House concert, 1127; Presidential Medal of Freedom, 1163. Works played: Tovey, cello concerto, 595; Vaughan Williams, *Fantasia on Sussex*, 505. Works: *El Pesebre*, 1104; *La Sardana*, 923
Casanova, André, 1067
Casavola, Franco, 493, 619
Casella, Alfredo. American debut, 347; on Ravel, 661; death, 830; and pandiatonicism, 1475. Works conducted: Malipiero, *Impressioni dal Vero*, 379; Stravinsky, *Les Noces*, 477; Walton, *Façade*, 477. Works: *L'Adieu à la vie*, 1301; *Chorale and March*, 650; *Concerto Romano*, 449; concerto, piano, violin, cello and orch., 575; concerto, strings, 798; concerto, violin, 478; *Il Convento veneziano*, 408; *Il Deserto tentato*, 644; *La Donna Serpente*, 545–546; *Elegia Eroica*, 277;

La Favola di Orfeo, 552, 872; La Giara, 403; Introduction, Aria and Toccata, 585; Italia, 162; Notte di Maggio, 237; Paganiniana, 874; partita, piano and orch., 435; Pezzi infantili, 1423; Scarlattiana, 444; Serenata for Five Instruments, 477, 513; suite in C, 162; symphony #2, 162; #3, 731
Casella, Enrique M., 437, 699
Cash, O. C., 667, 964
Cassadó, Gaspar, 418
Cassadó, Joaquín, 323
Cassone, Leopoldo, 364
Castagne, Patrick, 1144
Castaldi, Alfons, 401
Castellanos, Evencio, 1219
Castelnuovo-Tedesco, Mario. At 1922 Salzburg festival, 361; at 1924 ISCM festival, Salzburg, 398; at 1934 ISCM festival, 586; death, 1256; musical alphabet, 1426. Works: Aucassin et Nicolette, 939; Bacco in Toscana, 530; The Birthday of Infanta, 828; Cipressi, 719; concerto, cello, 601; concerto, guitar, 701; concerto, 2 guitars, 1150; concerto, piano, #1, 484; #2, 701; concerto, violin, #1 (Concerto Italiano), 427; concerto, violin, #2 (The Prophets), 565–566; Le Danze del Re David, 457; King John, 750; La Mandragola, 431–432; Il Mercante di Venezia, 1114–1115; Noah's Ark, 806; Il Raggio verde, 378; Variazioni sinfoniche, 507
Castiglioni, Niccolò. Aprèsludes, 1088; Ouverture in tre tempi, 1051; A Solemn Music, 1156; Three Mysteries, 1270; Tropi, 1098
Castillo, Jesús, 396
Castillo, Ricardo, 747
Castrato, 356
Castro, José María, 757
Castro, Juan José. Death, 1264. Works: Bodas de Sangre, 1014; concerto, violin, 1201; Corales criollos, 1030; Mekhano, 651; Proserpina e lo Straniero, 933; 3 Symphonic Pieces, 536; La Zapatera prodigiosa, 886
Castro, Ricardo, 10, 96
Catalani, Alfredo, 979
Catelinet, Philip, 978
Cattelani, Ferruccio, 5
Cattozzo, Nino, 580
Catunda, Eunice, 895

Caturla, Alejandro García, 533; murdered, 721
Caudella, Eduard, 9
Cavalieri, Lina. Killed in air raid, 780
Cerha, Friedrich. Relazioni fragili, 1119; Spiegel I, 1264; Spiegel II, 1202
Cerón, José, 747
Cervantes, Ignacio, 1052
Cervetti, Sergio, 1261
Chabrier, Emmanuel, 227, 753
Chadwick, George Whitefield. Death, 528. Works: Adonais, 3; Aphrodite, 202–203; Cleopatra, 79; Judith, 20; Pilgrim pageant music, 344; Symphonic Sketches, 121
Chailley, Jacques, 1036
Chailly, Louis, 1029
Chaliapin, Feodor. Signs protest, 72; Paris debut, 110; in Gunsbourg, Le vieil Aigle, 140; in Massenet, Don Quichotte, 157; sings God Save the Tsar, 175; deprived of title People's Artist, 459; death, 668
Chamberlain, Houston Stewart, 135; death, 443–444
Chaminade, Cécile. Death, 785; 1484
Champagne, Claude, 480
Chanler, Theodore, 994
Chapí, Casal, 747
Chapí, Ruperto, 36, 141, 143
Chaplin, Charles, 717
Charpentier, Gustave. Alsace-Lorraine festival, 76, 1005; stamp, 1137. Works: Impressions d'Italie, 76; Julien, 225; Louise, 3, 1500
Charpentier, Jacques, 1264
Chasins, Abram, 529
Chauve-Souris, 123
Chávez, Carlos. At 1942 ISCM festival, Berkeley, 757. Works conducted: Copland, El Salón Mexico, 653; Halffter, violin concerto, 755; Huízar, symphony #2, 630; Ponce, Chapultepec, 496; idem, Ferial, 717; idem, violin concerto, 771. Works: El Amor propiciado, 1028; Caballos de Vapor (H.P.), 547, 1500; concerto, piano, 745; concerto, violin, 932; Los Cuatros Soles, 512; Dark Meadow, 809; Energía, 533; El fuego nuevo, 480; H.P., 547, 1500; Hija de Cólquide, 809; invention, string trio, 1201; Llamadas, 592; Obertura Republicana, 611; Panfilo and Lauretta, 1027; Resonancias, 1187; Soli II, 1190; IV, 1241; Sinfónia India, 618; Sinfónia de Antígona

test, 479; protests anti-Semitism, 564; reply, 565; death, 904. Works conducted: Copland, symphony for organ and orch., 407; Gershwin, concerto, 422; idem, *An American in Paris*, 484; Holst, *Egdon Heath*, 466; Rachmaninoff, piano concerto #3, 151; Sibelius, *Tapiola*, 422; Taylor, *Through the Looking Glass*, 309. Works: *Cyrano de Bergerac*, 217; *Dove of Peace*, 210; *Dunkirk*, 769; *Man Without a Country*, 645; *The Opera Cloak*, 761

Dan, Ikuma. Founds Three Men's Club, 950. Works: *The Silk Road*, 1134; *Yang Kwei-Fei*, 1058; *Yuzuru*, 930

Dance Educators of America, 739

Daniel, Price, 1102

Daniel-Lesur. *See* Lesur, Daniel

Daniels, Mabel, 531–532

Danish State Symphony Orchestra. U.S. tour, 946

Dankevich, Konstantin, 906, 1086

Darewski, Herman, 836

Dargomyzhsky, Alexander, 967, 1166

Darian, Anita, 1082

Darnton, Christian, 691, 692

Darrell, Jack, 715–716

Darrieux, Marcel, 379

Darvas, Gabor, 1224

Darwish, Sayed, 1054

Da Silva, Oscar. *See* Silva, Oscar da

Daughters of the American Revolution, 688

Daus, Avraham, 978

David, Félicien, 1490

David, Johann Nepomuk. *Magische Quadrate*, 1081; partita, 632; symphony #4, 881; #7, 1036; #8, 1211

David, Karl Heinrich, 466

Davidenko, Alexander, 411, 487

Davidovsky, Mario. *Inflexions*, 1233; *Synchronisms #2*, 1189, 1260

Davidson, Harold G., 908

Davies, Meredith, 1257

Davies, Peter Maxwell. *Alma Redemptoris Mater*, 1051; *Eight Songs for a Mad King*, 1277; *Prolation*, 1065; *Ricercar and Doubles*, 1089; string quartet, 1137

Davies, Walford, 192, 247, 731

Davis, Ellabelle, 831

Davis, Harriet, 995

Day, Charles Russell, 4

Debussy, "Chouchou," 314

Debussy, Claude. As "Monsieur Croche,"

16; Légion d'Honneur, 41; and Satie, 48; pro-Rameau outburst, 63; and Lili Texier, 64; and Ravel, 88; marriage, 119; conducts, London, 120; conducts, Budapest, 172; conducts, Moscow, 231–232; work misattributed to, 279; last appearance, 284; death, 296; Stravinsky homage, 343; stamps, 697, 721, 1237; Falla homage, 702; substituted for Wagner, 709; Orchestre de Paris opening, 1250; in Berio, *Sinfonia*, 1271; spirit messages, 1278; as Impressionist, 1454–1456; and pandiatonicism, 1475; and pseudo-exoticism, 1483; Goetschius on, 1487; and secundal harmony, 1488; sensory impact, 1488. Works: *Berceuse Héroïque*, 258; *La Boîte à joujoux*, 320; *Chansons de Bilitis* (melodrama), 14; *Children's Corner*, 133, 179, 1484, 1497; *Clair de Lune* (*Suite Bergomasque*), 1455; *Estampes*, 54; *Études*, 259; *Feuilles Mortes*, 1437; *General Lavine-Eccentric*, 812; *Ibéria*, 157; *Images* (orchestra), 157, 158–159, 232; *Jeux*, 222–223, 1051, 1450; *Khamma*, 403, 831; *Marche écossaise*, 232; *Le Martyre de Saint-Sébastien*, 181–182, 185–186; *La Mer*, 80–81, 105–106, 120, 232, 937, 1318, 1319, 1502; *Nocturnes*, 12, 20, 232; *Pelléas et Mélisande*, 30–36, 109, 122, 323, 1427; *Prélude à l'Après-midi d'un Faune*, 120, 202, 232, 1455; preludes, piano, book 1, 163–164; preludes, piano, book 2, 226, 812, 1437, 1502; rhapsody, clarinet and orch., 232; rhapsody, saxophone and orch., 312; *Rondes de Printemps*, 158–159; *Six Épigraphes antiques*, 14; sonata, violin and piano, 284; string quartet, 1348; *Syrinx*, 361; *Trois Chansons de Charles d'Orléans*, 144

Decomposition and reassembly (terms), 1436

de Coppet, Edward. *See* Coppet, Edward de

Decoust, Michel, 1236

de Falla. *See* Falla

Defauw, Désiré, 822

"Defense Swing," 738

de Forest, Lee, 107, 143, 260–261; death, 1120–1121

Degen, Helmut, 917

Degeyter, Pierre, 366

de Hartmann, Thomas. *See* Hartmann, Thomas de
de Keyser. *See* Kaiser
Dekhterev, Vasily, 766
De Koven, Reginald. Death, 322. Works: *The Beauty Spot,* 144; *The Canterbury Pilgrims,* 280; *Maid Marian,* 21; *Rip van Winkle,* 321
de Kruyf, Ton. *See* Kruyf, Ton de
Delage, Maurice, 491
De Lamarter, Eric, 277, 414–415
de Lancie, John, 1111
Delannoy, Marcel. *Arlequin Radiophile,* 813; *Cinderella,* 536; *Concerto de mai,* 891–892; *L'Éventail de Jeanne,* 489; *Le Fou de la Dame,* 491, 510; *Ginevra,* 756; *Pantoufle de vair,* 536, 605; *Le Poirier de Misère,* 447–448; *Puck,* 868; string quartet, 535; symphony #1, 583; #2, 1044; *Travesti,* 939; *Volpone,* 906
de Lara. *See* Lara
Delbos, Claire, 616
del Campo, Conrado, 1188
Delden, Lex van, 942
Delgadillo, Luis A. *Escenas Pastoriles,* 695; *Sinfonia Incaica,* 455; *Los Tincos,* 695
Delibes, Léo, 621, 644
Delius, Frederick. Companion of Honour, 489; Delius festival, 497–498; death, 590; symbolic analysis of, 1494. Works: *Air and Dance,* 497; *Appalachia,* 497; *Arabesque,* 497; *Brigg Fair,* 118–119, 497; concerto, piano, 497; concerto, violin, 497; *Cynara,* 497; *Dance Rhapsody #1,* 148, 497; #2, 497; *Eventyr,* 307, 497; *Fennimore and Gerda,* 316, 497; *Idyll,* 572; *In a Summer Garden,* 133, 497; *Irmelin,* 957; *Koanga,* 61; *A Late Lark,* 497; *Lebenstanz,* 213; *A Mass of Life,* 146–147, 498; *North Country Sketches,* 497; *On Hearing the First Cuckoo in Spring,* 229; *Requiem,* 355; *Sea Drift,* 92, 497; *A Song of Summer* 536; *Songs of Sunset,* 497; string quartet, 497; *Summer Night on the River,* 229; *A Village Romeo and Juliet,* 105, 497
Dello Joio, Norman. *Blood Moon,* 1123; concerto, harp, 840; fantasy and variations, piano and orch., 1131; *Joan of Arc,* 1007; *Ricercari,* piano and orch., 825; *The Ruby,* 994; *The Trial at Rouen,* 1007; *The Triumph of St. Joan,* 892; *Wilderness Stair,* 859
Del Mar, Norman, 864, 1044
Delmas, Marc, 227
Delvincourt, Claude. Prix de Rome, 227; death, 974. Works: *Bal Vénitien,* 551, 735; *La Croisière jaune,* 615; *La Femme à Barbe,* 672; *Films d'Asie,* 615; *Lucifer,* 865; *Offrande à Silva,* 458; *Pamir,* 615
de Manziarly, Marcelle, 569
de Mol, Willem, 1112
Demolition (term), 1436
Demotic music (term), 1436–1437
Demuth, Norman, 691
Dendrino, Gherase, 1104
Denisov, Edison, 1193, 1266
*Denkmäler der Tonkunst in Bayern,* 6
*Denkmäler deutscher Tonkunst,* 6
Dent, Edward J., 363
Denza, Luigi. Judges *Feis Ceoil,* 62, 352. Works: *Funiculi-Funicula,* 115, 162
de Rogatis, Pascual. *Anfion y Zeto,* 257; *Huémac,* 270; *La Novia del Hereje,* 607
de Roos, Robert. *See* Roos, Robert de
de Sabata, Victor. *See* Sabata, Victor de
de Séverac, Déodat, 339. Works: *Cœur du Moulin,* 153, 185; *Danse des Treilles et du Chevalet,* 185; *Fête des Vendanges,* 185; *Héliogabale,* 166
Deshevov, Vladimir, 401, 509
Désormière, Roger. "École d'Arcueil," 375. Conducts: Dutilleux, symphony #1, 915; Koechlin concert, 557
Des Prez, Josquin, 346
Dessau, Paul. *Geschäftsbericht,* 1238; *Meer der Stürme,* 1247; *Puntila,* 1230; *Quattrodramma,* 1225; *Requiem für Lumumba,* 1195; *Das Verhör des Lukullus,* 908–909; *Les Voix de Paul Verlaine à Anatole France,* 735
Destinn, Emmy, 967
Dett, Robert Nathaniel, 644–645
Deutsch, Karl Alfred, 626
Devčić, Natko, 865, 1040
Devreese, Freddy, 1193
Diaghilev, Serge. "Historic concerts" of Russian music, 110; ancestry, 473; death, 496; and Markevitch, *Rebus,* 541. Works produced: Auric, *Les Matelots,* 416; idem, *La Pastorale,* 433; Chopin, *Les Sylphides,* 91; Debussy, *L'Après-midi d'un Faune,* 202; idem, *Jeux,* 223; Dukelsky, *Zéphyr*

Composers, 401; conducts Rumanian concert, Paris, 647; stamps, 814, 1020, 1122, 1186; and Little Orchestra Society, 840; 60th anniversary concert, 887–888; death, 993; and 1956 Warsaw Autumn, 1016. Works played or conducted: Bartók, violin sonata #2, 401; Golestan, *Rumanian Symphony*, 155; Lipatti, *Divertissement*, 647–648; Mihalovici, *Caprice roumain*, 647; Ravel, sonata, violin and piano, 455. Works: *Oedipe*, 622–623, 1467; *Rumanian rhapsody* #1, 45, 888; #2, 45; sonata, violin and piano, 888; #3, 1122; suite, orchestra, #1, 45; #2, 888; *Symphonie de chambre*, 990; symphony, D major (juvenilia), 582; symphony #1, 86; #2, 252; #3, 312; *Vox Maris*, 1186

Enescu. *See* Enesco

Engel, Carl, 785

Engel, Lehman, 643

Englemann, Hans Ulrich, 1065

Englert, Giuseppe Giorgio, 1281

English Folk-Dance and Song Society, 557

Enharmonic ambivalence (term), 1445

Enna, August. *Gloria Arsena*, 283; *Komedianter*, 326; *Nattergallen*, 212; *Princessen paa Aerten*, 8

"Entartete Musik" (Düsseldorf exhibition), 670–671

Entropy (term), 1445

Environment (term), 1445

Eppert, Carl, 549

Epstein, Sol, 504

Er, Nie, 629

Erb, Donald, 1200, 1232

Erbse, Heimo, 1070

Erdmann, Eduard. Serenade, 551; sonata, violin solo, 377; symphony #2, 393; #3, 921

Erickson, Robert, 1265

Erkel, Franz, 968, 1101

Erkin, Ulvi Cemal. *Bairam*, 588; concerto, violin, 850

Erlanger, Camille, 311. Works: *Aphrodite*, 90; *L'Aube rouge*, 196; *Bacchus triomphant*, 149; *Icare*, 195; *Le Juif polonais*, 5; *La Sorcière*, 214; *Tess*, 91

Ernesaks, Gustav. *Baptism of Fire*, 1038; *Hand in Hand*, 992; *Puhajarv*, 819; *Tormida Rand*, 881

Erskine, John, 539, 582

Esaki, Kejiro, 1138

Escher, Rudolf. *Arcana Musae Dona*, 836; *Musique pour l'Esprit en Deuil*, 857; *Tombeau de Ravel*, 977

Escobar, Luis Antonio, 1201

Escorial, 1163

Escot, Pozzi. *Lamentos*, 1189; *Sands*, 1218; *Three Poems*, 1201

Escudero, Francisco, 1190

Eshpay, Andrei, 1149

Espinosa, Guillermo, 628, 1116, 1259

Esplá, Oscar. Scale, 1349. Works: *Nochebuena del Diablo*, 626, 1248; *Sinfonia Aitana*, 1191; *Sonata del Sur*, 1204

Espoile, Raúl, 474, 629

Esposito, Arnaldo d', 739

Estevez, Antonio, 1189

Estrada, Juan García, 920

Estrella, Blanca, 1219

Ether (instrument), 1458

Ethnic resources. Discussed, 1445

Etiology (term), 1445

Etler, Alvin, 1147

Ettinger, Max, 470

Euphony (term), 1445–1446

Eurhythmics, 75, 169, 181, 258, 1305–1307

Europe, James Reese, 236; murdered, 312

*Even Hitler Had a Mother*, 690

Everett, Horace, 973

Evett, Robert, 1170, 1201

Evolution and devolution. Discussed, 1446

Evtushenko, Eugeny, 1125, 1151

Experimental music (term), 1446–1447

Expert, Henry, 944

Expo 67, 1238, 1243, 1244

Exposition Internationale de l'Eau, 698

Exposition Universelle, Paris, 5

Expressionism (term), 1447

Exton, John, 1051, 1137

Eysler, Edmund, 44, 256; death, 881

Fabini, Eduardo, 893

Fachiri, Adila, 507

Fairbanks, Douglas, 419

Fairfax, Bryan, 1131

Faizullin. *See* Faizy

Faizy, Dzhaudat, 1090

Fall, Leo. Death, 419. Works: *Die Dollarprinzessin*, 115; *Der fidele Bauer*, 112; *Irrlicht*, 70; *Der liebe Augustin*, 197; *Madame Pompadour*, 369; *Die Rose von Stamboul*, 274

certino, 2 pianos, 609; *Marionettes,* 361; *Eine Reiterburlesque,* 377; sonata, flute, 551; string quartet, 360; *Der Zauberfisch,* 1086

Finney, Ross Lee. *Barbershop Ballad,* 707; symphony #2, 1083; #3, 1175

Fino, Giocondo, 97

Fire and Police Association, 1406–1407

Firkušný, Rudolf. Works played: Hanson, concerto, 867; Martinu, concerto #3, 884; #4, 1016; Menotti, concerto, 805

Fišer, Luboš, 1114, 1219, 1247

Fisher, Fred, 746

Fitelberg, Gregor. Conducts: Fitelberg, violin concerto #2, 649; Lutoslawski, symphony, 692; Szymanowski, symphonie concertante, 554; idem, violin concerto #2, 573

Fitelberg, Jerzy. Concerto, violin, #1, 551; #2, 649; *Nocturne,* 918; string quartet #2, 491; #4, 734; #5, 818; string quartet (unspecified), 694

Fitzgerald, John F., 102

Fiume, Orazio, 1134

Flagstad, Kirsten, 894

Flamenco, 359

Flanagan, William, 1197

*Flat Foot Floogie,* 677

Fleischer, Leon, 1169

Flier, Jacob, 670

Flint, Seth, 730

Flonzaley Quartet, 83

Floridia, Pietro, 166

Flothuis, Marius. Capriccio, strings, 977; concerto, flute, 809; concerto, piano and chamber orch., 895; concerto, violin, 928, 943

Floyd, Carlisle. *Markheim,* 1215; *The Passion of Jonathan Wade,* 1147; *The Sojourner and Mollie Sinclair,* 1171–1172; *Susannah,* 991; *Wuthering Heights,* 1053

Flügel, Gertrude, 747

Flute as rat-catcher, 857

Flying piano recital, 627

Foerster, August, 387, 1465

Foerster, Josef Bohuslav. Death, 914; stamp, 1028. Works: *Bloud,* 621; *Eva,* 1028; *From Shakespeare,* 176; *Jessica,* 75; *Nepřemoženi,* 307; *Srdce (The Heart),* 381; symphony #4 (*Easter Eve*), 82; #5, 498

Fontainebleau. American Conservatory, 344

Foote, Arthur, 345. Death, 642

Ford, Peter, 1109

Forest, Jean Kurt, 1241

Forest, Lee de. See de Forest

Formalism (term), 1448

Formant (term), 1448

Forrest, George, 787, 967

Forrest, Hamilton. *Camille,* 520; *Daelia,* 979; *Don Fortunio,* 944

Fortner, Wolfgang. Conducts Kounadis, 1135. Works: *Aulodie,* 1089; *Bluthochzeit,* 1032; *The Creation,* 997; *Fantasy on the Theme of B-A-C-H,* 919; *5 Bagatellen,* wind quintet, 1097; *Impromptus,* 1066; *In seinem Garten liebt Don Perlimpin Belison,* 1134–1135; *Nuptiae Catulli,* 687; sonata, cello and piano, 895; symphony, 940; *Triplum,* 1231, 1246; *Die weisse Rose,* 912; *Die Witwe von Ephesus,* 945

Foss, Lukas. Birth, 363; at Inter-American Music Festival (1965), 1201; spatial distribution, 1434; and controlled improvisation, 1435. Works: concerto, cello, 1235; concerto, piano, #2, 922; *Discrepancia,* 1218; *Echoi,* 1170; *Elytres,* 1194, 1491; *Griffelkin,* 1001; *The Jumping Frog of Calaveras County,* 893; *A Parable of Death,* 955; *Phorion,* 1238; *The Prairie,* 773; *Recordare,* 867; *Song of Anguish,* 890; *The Song of Songs,* 830–831; symphony, 796; *Symphony of Chorales,* 1056; *Time Cycle,* 1098–1099

Foster, Jane, 42

Foster, Jean Kurt, 1073

Foster, Lawrence, 1243

Foster, Stephen Collins, 42, 436, 712, 871

Fougstedt, Nils-Eric, 1067, 1093

Foulds, John, 208, 380, 1465

Fourdrain, Félix, 108, 215, 237

Fournier, Léon. See Xanrof

Fox-Strangways, Arthur Henry, 321

Frager, Malcolm, 1085

Françaix, Jean. At Aldeburgh, 940. Works: *L'Apocalypse,* 753; *L'Apostrophe,* 918; concertino, piano, 598; concerto, flute, 1239; concerto, piano, 633, 650; *Les Demoiselles de la Nuit,* 855; *Déploration de Tonton, chien fidèle,* 1018; *Le Diable boiteux,* 872–873; *Divertissement,* 616; *L'Horloge de Flore,* 1110–1111; *Huit Bagatelles,* 552; *Le Jeu sentimental,* 632;

*La Main de gloire,* 892; *Les Malheurs de Sophie,* 848; *Midas,* 954; *Paris à nous deux,* 980; *La Princesse de Clèves,* 1212; quadruple concerto, 618; quintet, winds, 918; *Le Roi nu,* 629; sonata, 2 violins and cello, 585; symphony, 555

Francescatti, Zino, 806

Franchetti, Alberto. *La Figlia di Jorio,* 90; *Germania,* 28; *Notte di Leggenda,* 249

Franchetti, Aldo, 423

Franck, César, 76, 366–367, 940

Franckenstein, Clemens von, 332

Frankel, Benjamin. And dodecaphony, 1441. Works: concerto, violin, 1012; string quartet #2, 835; symphony #4, 1232; #6, 1277

Frankenburger, Paul. *See* Ben-Haim, Paul

*Frankie and Johnny,* 690

Fraudulent modernism (term), 1449

Frederick, King of Denmark, 938

Frederick, Kurt, 862

Free Composers Association, Japan, 923

Freed, Alan, 1195

Freed, Isadore, 937

Freeman, Harry Lawrence. *African Kraal,* 47; *Vendetta,* 381; *Voodoo,* 476

Freitas, Frederico de, 1079

Fremstad, Olive, 911

Frenkel, Daniel, 926

Frescobaldi, Girolamo, 766

Fricker, Peter Racine. Birth, 331. Works: concerto, piano, 973; concerto, viola, 964–965; string quartet, 895; symphony #1, 897; #2, 920, 959; #3, 1101; #4, 1233; *Seven Counterpoints,* 1248; *A Vision of Judgment,* 1055

Friedman, Charles, 947

Friml, Rudolf. *The Firefly,* 210; *Katinka,* 261; *Rose Marie,* 398; *The Vagabond King,* 419

Froidebise, Pierre, 896

Frolov, Markian, 719

Frugal ankyloglossia (term), 1449

Frumerie, Gunnar de, 709

Fuchs, Joseph, 1097

Fuchs, Lukas. *See* Foss, Lukas

Fuchs, Peter Paul, 1277

Fuentes. *See* Sánchez de Fuentes

Fukai, Shiro, 663, 879

Fukushima, Kazuo, 1182, 1247

Fuleihan, Anis. Concerto, 2 pianos, 726; concerto, Thereminovox, 797; symphony #1, 637; #2, 1233–1234; *Three Cyprus Serenades,* 824

Fuller, Buckminster, 1496

Fuller, Donald, 757

Fumet, Dynam-Victor, 867

Furniture music (term), 1449

Fürstenberg, Max Egon zu, 1073

Furtwängler, Wilhelm. Plea for Jewish artists, 565; plea to Hubermann, 571; general music director, Reichsmusikkammer, 575; resigns conductorship of Berlin Philharmonic, 579; resumes conductorship, 604; withdraws from New York Philharmonic engagement, 623; denazified, 824; death, 986; stamp, 999. Works conducted: Hindemith, *Mathis der Maler,* 583; Prokofiev, piano concerto #5, 554; Schoenberg, variations for orchestra op. 31, 483; Strauss, *Vier letzte Lieder,* 894; Toch, *Kleine Theater-Suite,* 525; idem, *Komödie für Orchester,* 461; Trapp, symphony #3, 401. Works: symphony #2, 848

Füssl, Karl-Heinz, 1031, 1182

Futurism (term), 1449

Futurist manifestoes, 1294–1304

Gabrieli, Andrea, 641

Gabrilowitsch, Ossip, 11, 564–565; death, 631, 1194

Gade, Jacob, 419

Gadzhibekov, Uzeir. *Kyor-Oglu,* 644; *Leili and Medzhnun,* 120; *Sheikh Senan,* 152

Gadzhiev, Dzhevdet, 800

Gafurius, Franchinus, 306

Gagarin, Yuri, 1111

Gaito, Constantino. *Caio Petronio,* 206; *Flor de Nieve,* 360; *Ollantay,* 436; *La Sangre de las Guitarras,* 552

Gál, Hans, 372, 431

Galajikian, Florence, 549

Galeotti, Cesare, 4, 161

Galindo, Blas. Quintet, piano and strings, 1188; sinfonia, 1025; symphony #3, 1113; *Two Preludes,* orch., 736

Gallois, Victor-Léon, 77

Game music (term), 1449–1450

Gandhi, 867

Gandini, Gerardo. *Cadencias II,* 1267; *Constrasts,* 1260; *Orchestra Variations,* 1202

Ganne, Louis, 91

Ganz, Rudolf, 559, 729
Garay, Narciso, 955
Garbousova, Raya, 814
García, Manuel, 93
García-Abril, Antón, 1261
García-Morillo, Roberto, 1261
Garden, Mary. Sells kisses, 192; death, 1232. Works performed: Debussy, *Pelléas et Mélisande*, 31, 36, 323; Février, *Gismonda*, 308; Forrest, *Camille*, 520
Gardner, Isabella Stewart, 116
Gardner, John, 1029
Gardner, Samuel, 314
Garretta, Juli, 627
Garrido-Lecca, Celso, 1188, 1201
Gasco, Alberto, 217, 558
Gaslini, Giorgio, 1039
Gatty, Nicholas Comyn. *Duke or Devil*, 154; *Greysteel*, 89; *Prince Ferelon*, 341
Gaubert, Philippe, 77, 452
Gauche dexterity (term), 1450
Gauguin, Paul, 1472
Gauk, Alexander, 503
Gavrilov, Pyotr, 1236
Gay, Noel, 659
Gebrauchsmusik (term), 1317, 1450
Gebrauchsoper (term), 303
Gedalge, André, 427
Geigy, J.R. & Co., 1050
Geiser, Walther, 434
Gelmetti, Vittorio, 1265
Gemeinschaftsmusik (term), 1317, 1450
*Genesis* suite, 806
*George White's Scandals of 1924*, 395
George II, King of England, 962
George V, King of England, 618
George VI, King of England, 645
Georges, Alexandre. *Charlotte Corday*, 15; *Miarka*, 81; *Sangre y Sol*, 199
Gerhard, Roberto. And dodecaphony, 1441. Works conducted: Cartan, *Pater Noster*, 568; Walton, *Belshazzar's Feast*, 568. Works: *Ariel*, 624-625; *Aubade, Interlude and Dance*, 675; *Collages*, 1107; concerto for orchestra, 1199; *Don Quixote*, 836, 889; *The Duenna*, 917; *Melodies of Catalonia*, 551; *Passacaglia and Chorale*, 568; *The Plague*, 1176; string quartet #2, 1190; *Sinfonia*, 998; symphony #2, 1074; #4 (*New York*), 1252
Gericke, Wilhelm, 1, 12, 46
Gerlach, Horst, 574

Gerlach, Theodor, 50
German, Edward. Death, 655. Works: *Merrie England*, 30; *Tom Jones*, 108; *Welsh Rhapsody*, 65
German State Philharmonic Orchestra (Soviet), 577
German Tonkünstlerverein dissolves, 648
Germany. Third Reich (fl. 1933-1945). (N.B.: actions against individual musicians are indexed under those musicians rather than here.) Bans jazz, 563, 611; *Reichsmusikkammer* formed, 574; consolidates singing societies, 587; bans foreign pseudonyms, 592; commissions replacement for Mendelssohn, 594; bans non-Aryans from orchestras, 608; article, *Der Jude als Musik-Fabrikant*, 622; establishes International Music Festival, 624; curbs critics, 635; and *Nibelungen-Marsch* 636; and *Gleichschaltung*, 648; forces withdrawal of piece from ISCM festival, 650; board of examiners on recordings, 660; bans teaching of Jews by Aryans, 669; "Entartete Musik" exhibit, 670; bans *Frankie and Johnny*, 690; songs of Nazi party prohibited, 801
Germany (BRD), national anthem, 936-937
Germany (DDR), national anthem, 889
Gernsback, Hugo 261, 380
Gershfeld, David, 1011, 1063
Gershwin, George. Death, 651; paintings exhibited, 660; and Schillinger, 767. Works: *An American in Paris*, 110, 484-485, 535; concerto in F, 422-423, 699; *Cuban Overture*, 552; *Delishious*, 543; *Funny Face*, 462; *Girl Crazy*, 515, 578; *I Got Rhythm*, 1476; *Lady Be Good*, 404; *Let 'em Eat Cake*, 573; *Mischa, Jascha, Toscha, Sascha*, 512; *Of Thee I Sing*, 541, 549-550, 558; *Oh Kay*, 439; *Porgy and Bess*, 610, 1002; *Rhapsody in Blue*, 384-385, 801, 1433, 1497; rhapsody #2, 543; *Rhumba*, 552; *Somebody Loves Me*, 395; *Strike up the Band*, 487; *Swanee*, 294; *Sweet Little Devil*, 385; *Variations on "I Got Rhythm,"* 578
Gershwin, Ira, 541, 610
Gerster, Ottmar. *Enoch Arden*, 633; *Festliche Toccata*, 759; *Die Hexe von*

Graener, Paul. In *Reichsmusikkammer*, 575; and 1937 Dresden festival, 646; death, 791; *Byzanz*, 299; *Don Juans letztes Abenteuer*, 240; *Friedemann Bach*, 539; *Hanneles Himmelfahrt*, 447; *Der Prinz von Homburg*, 602; *Schirin und Gertrude*, 327; *Schwanhild*, 745; *Theophano*, 299; *Wiener Symphonie*, 743

Graeser, Wolfgang, 474

Graetzer, Guillermo, 942

Graffman, Gary, 1256

Graham, Marian, 204

Graham, Martha. American Dance Festival, 1948, 859. Works: *Appalachian Spring*, 790–791, 1191; *Cave of the Heart*, 816; *Dark Meadow*, 809; *Judith*, 887; *Night Journey*, 833; *The Serpent Heart*, 816; *Wilderness Stair* (*Diversion of Angels*), 859

Grainger, Percy. Collects *Brigg Fair*, 119; on Delius, 149; wedding, 475; death, 1108. Works played: Carpenter, concertino, 267. Works: *British Folk-Music Settings*, 691; *Free Music*, 1444; *In a Nutshell*, 269–270; *Mock Morris*, 164; *Molly on the Shore*, 362; *To a Nordic Princess*, 475

Granados, Enrique. Performed by Sociedad Nacional de Música, 250; death in a torpedoed ship, 267. Works: *Gaziel*, 96; *Goyescas* (piano), 177; *Goyescas* (opera), 264, 627; *Picarol*, 15

*Grand Ole Opry*, 422

Graphic notation (term), 1451–1452

Grasse, Eugène, 325

Graves, Robert, 1122

Grechaninoff, Alexander. *See* Gretchaninoff

Gredinger, Paul, 984

*Greensleeves*, 490, 592

Gregori, Nininha, 917

Gregorian chant, 17, 51, 54, 59, 78, 200, 485, 511, 842

Gregory I, Pope, 59

Gretchaninoff, Alexandre. Signs protest, 72; death, 1003. Works: *Dobrinya Nikitch*, 49; *Missa Oecumenica*, 782; *19 February 1861*, 177; *Sœur Béatrice*, 211–212; symphony, E major, 392

Grieg, Edvard. And Dreyfus case, 46; Oxford doctorate, 93; death, 113; fatal to Barère, 910; stamp, 770. Works:

concerto, piano, 203; *Olav Trygvason*, 129; *Song of Norway*, 787

Griffes, Charles Tomlinson. Death, 326. Works: *The Kairn of Koridwen*, 279; *The Pleasure Dome of Kubla Khan*, 319; *Poem*, flute and orch., 318; *Roman Sketches*, 313; *The White Peacock*, 313

Griffith, David Wark, 250

Grignon, Lamote de. *See* Lamote de Grignon

Grimaud, Yvette, 873

Grock, 1068

Grofé, Ferde. Scores Gershwin, *Rhapsody in Blue*, 384. Works: *Grand Canyon Suite*, 539; *Hudson River Suite*, 998; *Niagara Falls Suite*, 1107–1108; *San Francisco Suite*, 1083; *Virginia City*, 1263; *World's Fair Suite*, 1177

Gropius, Manon, 625, 1426

*Grossmutterakkord*, 664, 1018, 1064, 1192

Grosz, Wilhelm, 345, 362, 417

*Groupe du Zodiaque*, 874

Grove, George, 6

Grové, Stefans, 942

Gruber, Emma, 1077

Gruber, Franz Xaver, 866

Gruber, Georg, 943

Gruenberg, Louis. Death, 1183. Works: *Americana*, 1019; concerto, violin, 793; *The Creation*, 441; *Daniel Jazz*, 419; *The Emperor Jones*, 559; *Four Diversions*, 549; *Green Mansions*, 655; *Jack and the Beanstalk*, 539; *Jazz Suite*, 490; symphony #1, 581

Grünewald, Mathias, 583

Grünthal, Josef. *See* Tal, Josef

Guaccero, Domenico, 1204

Guarino, Carmine, 449

Guarnieri, Camargo. *Abertura Concertante*, 769; *Brasiliana*, 912; *Chôro*, orch., 1025; *Chôro*, cello and orch., 1130; *Chôro*, clarinet and orch., 1047–1048; concerto, violin, 759; *Dansa Brasileira*, 730; *Sequencia, Coral e Ricercare*, 1240; symphony, 824; *Variaciones sobre un Tema Nordestino*, 1190

Gudmundsen-Holmgreen, Pelle, 1181

Guerrini, Guido, 336, 558

Gui, Vittorio, 454

Guido d'Arezzo, 485, 893, 898, 1451

Guilbert, Yvette, 780

Guilmant, Alexandre, 179

Hubermann, Bronislaw, 571
Hucbald, 511
Hüe, Georges. *Dans l'ombre de la Cathédrale*, 349; *Le Miracle*, 174; *Riquet à la Houppe*, 485; *Le Roi de Paris*, 17; *Siang-Sin*, 387
Hughes, Langston, 1092
Hughes, Rupert, 1485
Hugo, John Adam, 310
Huízar, Candelario, 630
Hull, Arthur Eaglefield. Suicide, 480
Hülsenbeck, 266, 270
Hume, J., 201
Hume, Paul, 903
Humperdinck, Engelbert. Death, 346. Works: *Dornröschen*, 39; *Gaudeamus*, 310; *Hänsel und Gretel*, 647; *Die Heirat wider Willen*, 75; *Königskinder* (melodrama), 1354; *Königskinder* (opera), 174; *Die Marketenderin*, 240; *The Miracle*, 195
Humpert, Hans, 772
Huneker, James Gibbons. Death, 337; 1318
Huré, Jean, 534
Husa, Karel. *Poem*, viola and chamber orch., 1087; string quartet, 896
Huss, Henry Holden, 965
Hutchison, Miller R., 110
Huybrechts, Albert. *Chant d'angoisse*, 895; string quartet #2, 513
Huygens, Christian, 898
Huysmans, Joris Karl, 1495
Hypnosis, 204

Ibert, Jacques. At 1956 Warsaw Autumn, 1016; death, 1129. Works: *L'Aiglon*, 640; *Amours de Jupiter*, 812; *Angélique*, 445; *Ballade de la Geôle de Reading*, 364; *Barbe-Bleue*, 773; *Chapeau de paille d'Italie*, 519; *Chevalier errant*, 892; concerto, cello and winds, 429; concerto, flute, 582; concerto da camera, saxophone, 625; *Danton*, 629; 2 mouvements, 2 flutes, clarinet and bassoon, 418; *Diane de Poitiers*, 587; *Divertissement*, 519; *Donogoo*, 553; *Escales*, 383; *L'Éventail de Jeanne*, 489; *Féerique*, 423; *Mouvement symphonique* (*Bostoniana*), 1152; *Paris*, 553; *Persée et Andromède*, 493; *Les Petites Cardinal*, 665; *14 Juillet*, 629; *Les Rencontres*, 408; *Roi d'Yvetot*, 502; *Symphonie concertante*, oboe and strings, 907, 1162; *Symphonie Marine*, 1167

Ichiyanagi, Toshi, 1164, 1165
Icositetraphony (term), 1453–1454
Ifukube, Ikira. *Arctic Forest*, 785; *Drums of Japan*, 928; *Enchanted Citadel*, 886
Ihlert, Heinz, 575
Ilgenfritz, McNair, 956
Iliev, Konstantin, 1146–1147
Illation (term), 1454
Imbricated counterpoint (term), 1454
Imbrie, Andrew. Chamber symphony, 1263; concerto, violin, #1, 1048; *Legend*, 1076; symphony #1, 1218; *Three against Christmas*, 1193
Impressionism (term), 1454–1458
Inaudible music. Discussed, 1458
Inbal, Eliyahu, 1223
Indeterminacy. Discussed, 1458
Indonesia. Bans American dance music, 1075
Induction and deduction (terms), 1458
Indy, Vincent d'. President of Schola Cantorum, 9; and Academy of Santa Cecilia, 248; teacher, 282; death, 540; stamp, 913. Works: *Chant de la Cloche*, 214; *Choral varié*, 62; concerto, flute, cello and strings, 451; *Diptyque méditerranéen*, 442; *Étranger*, 42; *Istar*, 201, 1428; *Jour d'Été à la Montagne*, 88; *Légende de Saint Christophe*, 329; *Poème des rivages*, 348; *Rêve de Cyniras*, 456; *Souvenirs*, 108; symphony #2, 58; #3 (*Sinfonia brevis de Bello Gallico*), 319–320
Inertial guidance (term), 1458–1459
Infantiloquy (term), 1459
Information theory (term), 1459
Infra-modern music (term), 1459
Ingelbrecht, Désiré Émile, 334
*The Instruments of the Orchestra* (film), 823–824
Insull, Samuel, 498
Integration (term), 1459
Inter-American Festival of the Arts, San Juan, 1215
Inter-American Music Festival. First, in 1958, 1047–1048; second, in 1961, 1112–1113; third, in 1965, 1201–1202; fourth, in 1968, 1259–1262
International Composers' Guild, 342, 371
International Congress of Composers and Musicologists, Prague, 855, 1378–1379

975; ISCM 1966 festival, Stockholm, 1225; ethnic aspect, 1445; and metric modulation, 1465; and microtones, 1466; and ragtime, 1484. Works: *Chamber Orchestra Set #3*, 1150; *Charlie Rutlage*, 549; *Chromatimelodtune*, 1150; *March 1776*, 64; *Orchestral Set #1*, see *Three Places in New England; Orchestral Set #2*, 254; *Serenity*, 549; sonata, piano, #2 (*Concord, Mass., 1840–1860*), 685, 1498; symphony #2, 907; #3, 813; #4, 446, 1199–1200; *Three Places in New England*, 64, 523–524, 532, 1477, 1491; *Tone Roads #3*, 1439; *The Unanswered Question*, 1070; *Universe Symphony*, 1464; variations on *America*, 1432. LETTERS to Nicolas Slonimsky, 1318–1348
Ives, George, 1484

Jackson, Milt, 920
Jacob, Maxim, 375
Jacobi, Frederick. String quartet, 434; symphony #1, 402; *Two Assyrian Prayers*, 420
Jacquet, Maurice, 262
Jadassohn, Salomon, 27
Jakova, Prenk, 1057
James, Philip. *Bret Harte*, 637; *Station WGZBX*, 549
Janáček, Leoš. Death, 475; 1929 ISCM festival, 491; stamp, 962; and 1956 Warsaw Autumn, 1016. Works: *Balada blanická*, 326; capriccio, piano (left hand) and winds, 466; concertino, piano and chamber orch., 428, 457; *Glagolithic Mass*, 463; *Její Pastorkyna (Jenufa)*, 55; *Katá Kabanová*, 348; *Osud*, 1056; *Příhody Lišky Bystroušky (Cunning Little Vixen)*, 403; *Šárka*, 421; sinfonietta, 436; sonata, violin and piano, 377; string quartet, 418; *Šumařovo dítě*, 290; *Taras Bulba*, 347; *Věc Makropulos*, 442; *Výlety páně Broučkovy (Flights of Mr. Brouček)*, 327; *Z mrtvého domu (From a House of the Dead)*, 507
Janson, Alfred, 1225
Jansons, Arvid, 1131
Janssen, Werner. Conducts: *Genesis* suite, 806; Harris, prelude and fugue, 622
Japanese Composers' League. Letter, 1352

Jaques-Dalcroze, Émile. Eurhythmics, 75, 1305–1307; Hellerau school, 169; cornerstone laid, 181; Geneva institute, 258; death, 897. Works: *Onkel Dazumal*, 76
Jarnach, Philipp. Completes Busoni, *Doktor Faust*, 414. Works: sonata, piano, #2, 961; sonatina, flute and piano, 377; string quartet, 345, 398
Järnefelt, Armas, 1052
Jarre, Maurice. *Cantates pour une Démente*, 1161; *Mobiles*, 1138; *Passacaille*, 1012, 1031
Jass (term). *See* jazz
Jaubert, Maurice. Death in war, 715. Works: *Jeanne d'Arc*, 647; *Sonata a due*, 826
Jazz (not including individual performers and works with jazz influences). First use of term, 218; 236, 272–273, 276, 278, 279, 281, 305, 336, 365, 427, 454, 475, 563, 577, 611, 670, 679, 681, 1090–1091, 1092, 1404–1406, 1460–1462
*The Jazz Singer*, 460
Jeanty, Occide, 1098
Jefferson, Thomas, 682
Jehin, Léon, 140
Jelinek, Hanns. *Phantasie*, clarinet, piano and orch., 941; sinfonia concertante, 1012; *Symphonia brevis*, 922–923; *Symphony for Brass*, 551; *Three Blue Sketches*, 1065
Jemnitz, Alexander. Serenade, string trio, 491; sonata, harp, 609; sonata, violin and piano, 458
Jemnitz, Sándor, 857
"Jena symphony," 155
Jensen, Ludvig Irgens, 838
Jeppesen, Knud, 899
Jeremiáš, Jaroslav, 311
Jeremiáš, Otakar. *Bratři Karamazovi*, 478–479; *Till Eulenspiegel*, 875
Jessel, Leon, 288
*La Jeune France*, 628
Jezek, Jaroslav, 586
Jiménez, Bernal, 729
Jirák, Karel Boleslav. At 1924 Salzburg ISCM festival, 398. Works: quintet, winds, 513; symphony #3, 689; #4, 832; #5, 921
Jive (term), 1462
*Jiyu Sakkyokuka*, 923
Joachim, Joseph, 113, 658
Johansson, Bengt, 1225

Johannson, Magus Blondal, 1181
John XXIII, Pope, 1253
Johnson, David, 1106
Johnson, Howard, 283
Johnson, Lockrem, 990
Johnson, Lyndon Baines, 1238
Johnson, Pete, 683
Johnson, Thor. Conducts: Brant, symphony #1, 847; Diamond, *The Enormous Room*, 883; Giannini, sinfonia, 911; Schuman, *Credendum*, 1001; Tcherepnin, *The Lost Flute*, 980
Johnston, Ben, 1236
Johnston, Mary, 670
Jokl, Otto, 535
Jolivet, André. And *La Spirale*, 616; and *La Jeune France*, 628; 1956 Warsaw Autumn, 1016. Works: *Cinq Danses rituelles*, 754; *Complaintes du Soldat*, 766; concertino, trumpet, 961; concerto, ondes Martenot, 852; *Cosmogonie*, 842; *Dolores*, 826; *Guignol et Pandore*, 785; *L'Inconnue*, 891; *Le Livre de Christophe Colomb*, 830; *Psyché*, 896; *La Queste de Lancelot*, 779; sonata, piano, 836; *Suite delphique*, 861; *Suite transocéane*, 1000; symphony #1, 976; #2, 1072, 1202; *La Tentation dernière*, 760; *La Vérité de Jeanne*, 1009
Jolson, Al, 460, 477
Jommelli, Niccolò, 246
Joncières, Victorin de, 3
Joncker, Théo de, 415–416
Jones, Charles, 757
Jones, Daniel. *The Knife*, 1171; sonata, 3 kettledrums, 1477
Jones, Edward German. *See* German, Edward
Jones, Sidney, 810
Jones, Spike, 1493
Jongen, Joseph, 513
Jongen, Léon. *Malaisie*, 614; *Thomas l'Agnelet*, 385
Jora, Mihail, 401, 546
Jordá, Enrique. Conducts: Harris, symphony #11, 1128; Milhaud, symphony #8, 1048; #12, 1130
Joseph, Wilfred, 1210
Josif, Enriko, 1040
Josten, Werner. *Jungle*, 497; sonata, violin, 674
Joteyko, Tadeusz. *Grajek*, 318; *Królowa Jadwiga*, 476
Joubert, John. *The Choir Invisible*,

1258; *In the Drought*, 1018; *Legend of Princess Vlei*, 932; *Silas Marner*, 1114; sonata, viola, 960; *Under Western Eyes*, 1277–1278
Joyce, James, 61, 63, 1025
*Der Jude als Musik-Fabrikant* (article), 622
Judge, Jack, 675
Judson, Arthur, 828
Jürgens, Fritz, 257
Juilliard, Augustus D., 101, 311
Jurgenson, Peter, 54

Kabalevsky, Dmitri. *At the Approaches to Moscow*, 761, 901; *Colas Breugnon*, 665; concerto, cello, 862, 871; concerto, piano, #1, 540; #2, 627; #3, 862, 952; concerto, violin, 862; *The Family of Taras*, 901; *In the Fire*, 901; *Requiem*, 1153; symphony #1, 555–556; #2, 559; #3 (*Lenin*), 579; #4, 1017
Kabasta, Oswald, 577; suicide, 811
Kabeláč, Miloslav. *Eufemias Mysterion*, 1247; *Neustupujte*, 804; symphony #2, 856, 873
Kabos, Llona, 663
Kacinkas, Jeronimas, 674
Kadosa, Paul. Concerto, piano, 568; *Huszti kaland*, 927; string quartet #2, 734; symphony #4, 1232
Kagel, Mauricio. *Anagram*, 1087, 1427; *Diaphonie I*, 1225; *Halleluja*, 1280; *Heterophonie*, 1141; *Match*, 1268; *Solo*, 1268; *Sonant*, 1180; *Sur Scène*, 1256
Kahn, Erich Itor, 996
Kaiser, Alfred, 172
Kajanus, Robert, 7
Kaleidophonia (term), 1462
Kalinnikov, Vassili, 12, 921
Kallman, Chester, 921, 1114, 1223
Kálmán, Emmerich. Death, 966. Works: *Czardasfürstin*, 259; *Gräfin Maritza*, 386; *Herbstmanöver*, 136; *Herzogin von Chicago*, 470; *Zirkusprinzessin*, 430
Kalmár, László, 1279
Kalninš, Alfreds. *Banjuta*, 329; *Dzimtenes Atmoda*, 428; *Salinieki*, 428
Kalninš, Janis, 621
Kalomiris, Manolis. On Ravel, 661; death, 1133. Works: *Constantin Palaeologus*, 1143; *Palamas Symphony*, 1003; *Protomastoras*, 267; *Rapsodie*

*grecque,* 430; *Shadowy Waters,* 905; *Symphony of the Brave Young Men,* 798; *Virgin of Sparta,* 726
Kamieński, Lucjan, 283
Kaminski, Heinrich. Concerto grosso, 413; *Drei geistliche Lieder,* 397; *Jürg Jenatsch,* 492; *Magnificat,* 458; *Spiel vom König Aphelius,* 888
Kaminski, Joseph, 810
Kanitz, Ernst, 362, 397
Kapp, Eugen. *Kalevipoeg,* 842; *Tuleelegid,* 801; *Unattainable Woman,* 1110; *Vabaduse laulik,* 897
Kapp, Villem, 1122
Kapr, Gydli, 1279
Kapr, Jan. *Dialogues,* 1246; sonata, piano, 835; *Übungen für Gydli,* 1279
Kaprál, Václav, 625
Kaprálová, Vitězslava, 673
Kaprow, Allan, 1072, 1452
Karaev, Kara. *Don Quixote,* 1105; *Symphonic Engravings,* 1105; *Veten,* 800
Karajan, Herbert von, 1168
Karel, Rudolf. Death, 797. Works: *Demon,* 413; *Ilseino Srdce,* 402; *Smrt Kmotřička,* 560; *Tři Vlasy Děda Všlvěda,* 862
Karg-Elert, Sigfrid, 565
Karkoff, Maurice, 1093, 1252
Karlowicz, Mieczyslaw, 138
Karnevicius, Jurgio, 561
Karr, Gary, 1249
Kashnitsky, Vladimir, 402
Kaslík, Václav, 1114
Kassern, Tadeusz, 821, 1027
Kastle, Leonard, 1105
Katims, Milton. Conducts Bolcom, Erb, Keats, Reynolds, 1200; conducts Lees, *Vision of Poets,* 1135; conducts Vincent, *Consort,* 1134
Kauder, Hugo, 362
Kauffmann, Leo Justinus. Killed in air raid, 788. Works: *Berlenhemd,* 787; *Geschichte vom schönen Annerl,* 754; *Symphonic Suite,* 568
Kaufmann, Walter, 677
Kaufmann, Werner, 1223
Kaun, Hugo. Death, 547. Works: *Der Fremde,* 325; *Hiawatha,* 44; *Menandra,* 420; *Minnehaha,* 44
Kay, Hershy, 981
Kay, Ulysses. *Markings,* 1223; *Of New Horizons,* 787; *Stephen Crane,* 1254; symphony in E, 912; symphony (1968), 1257; *Umbrian Scene,* 1176
Kazandzhiev, Vasil, 1266

Kâzim Akses, Necil. *Ankara Castle,* 760; ballade, 850; *Bayönder,* 599
Kazoo, 1082
Keats, Donald, 1200
Kelberine, Alexander. Suicide, 706; 1464
Kelemen, Milko. Concertino, doublebass and strings, 1073; *Les Jeux,* 1050; *Skolion,* 1087; *Sub rosa,* 1247; *Transfigurations,* 1133
Kelley, Edgar Stillman. *Gulliver,* 642; Pilgrim pageant music, 345; symphony #2, 225
Kellogg, Charles, 879
Kelly, Frederick Septimus, 273
Kelly, Robert, 1152
Kelterborn, Rudolf. *Die errettung Thebens,* 1162; *Kaiser Jovian,* 1234; suite, brass, percussion and strings, 1010
Kemal Pasha, Mustafa, 475
Kennedy, Jimmy, 699
Kennedy, John Fitzgerald, 102, 1127, 1163, 1168, 1171, 1172, 1176, 1178, 1201, 1230
Kennedy, Robert, 1270
Kentner, Louis, 663
Kerensky, Alexander, 284
Kern, Jerome. Death, 806. Works: *The Cat and the Fiddle,* 537; *Leave It to Jane,* 288-289; *Mark Twain,* 752; *Music in the Air,* 555; *Roberta,* 575; *Sally,* 335; *Show Boat,* 464; *Sunny,* 419; *Sweet Adeline,* 496
Ketèlby, Albert, 1075
Ketoff, Paul, 1258
Ketting, Piet. Fugue, piano, 694; *Three Sonnets from Shakespeare,* 734
Khachaturian, Aram. Birth, 47; wife, 837; accused of "decadent formalism," 847; at 1956 Warsaw Autumn, 1016; cleared of Westernism, 1049; declaration on personal ideology, 1371-1373. Works: concerto, cello, 822; concerto, piano, 651; concerto, violin, 722; concerto-rhapsody, violin, 1149; *Gayane,* 763; film on Lenin, 866; *Poem about Stalin,* 682; *Saber Dance,* 763; *Spartak,* 1020; symphony #2, 778
Khachaturian, Gebork. *See* Armenian, Gebork
Khadzhiev, Parashkev, 1149
Khodzha-Einatov, Lev, 670
Khrennikov, Tikhon. Birth, 226; judges Soviet music, 866; on Prokofiev, *Story of a Real Man,* 1097; statement on musical policy, 1364-1369. Works:

concerto, cello, 1178; concerto, violin, 1073; *During the Storm,* 700; *Frol Skobeyev,* 890; *Mother,* 1037; *One Hundred Devils and One Girl,* 1158; symphony #1, 610–611; #2, 764; *White Nights,* 1249

Khristov, Dobry, 99

Khrushchev, Nikita, 1064, 1154, 1190, 1379–1380, 1452

Kiddie music notation, 836

Kienzl, Wilhelm. Death, 740; stamp, 922. Works: Austrian national anthem, 329; *Kuhreigen,* 194; *Das Testament,* 275

Kilar, Wojceich. And 1956 Warsaw Autumn, 1016. Works: *Riff 62,* 1145; *Training 68,* 1266

Killmayer, Wilhelm, 1176

Kilpinen, Yrjö, 377

Kindler, Hans. Conducts: Piston, symphony #2, 783; Ward, symphony #2, 846

Kinetic energy (term), 1324

King, Martin Luther, 1270, 1271

Kinkel, Johanna, 1329

Kirchhoff, P. Kilian, 785

Kirchner, Leon. Concerto, piano, #1, 1005, 1031; #2, 1169; sinfonia, 930; string quartet #1, 977

Kiriac, Dmitri, 401

Kiriwina Island, 770

Kirkpatrick, John, 685

Kisielewski, Stefan, 1016

Kitsch (term), 1324

Klangfarbe (term), 1324–1325

Klavarskribo, 538, 1313

Klaxon, 110

Klebe, Giselher. *Alkmene,* 1124; *Elegia appassionata,* 1011; *Ermörderung Cäsars,* 1071; *Figaro lässt sich scheiden,* 1163; *Interferenzen,* 1009; *Jacobowsky und der Oberst,* 1210; *Miserere Nobis* mass, 1191; *Omaggio,* 1089; *Die Räuber,* 1031; string quartet, 917; symphony, strings, 950; *Die tödlichen Wünsche,* 1066

Klee, Paul, 1043, 1076, 1261

Kleiber, Erich, 596; death, 1004

Klein, Fritz, 335–336, 406–407, 1439, 1489

Klein, Lothar, 1196

Klein, Walter, 362

Klemperer, Otto. Furtwängler pleads for, 565; attacked as Jew, 622; Czech boycott, 1264. Works conducted: Achron, violin concerto #2, 636;

Bloch, *Voice in the Wilderness,* 637; Casella, *Scarlattiana,* 444; Schoenberg, *Begleitungsmusik,* 517; idem, suite for strings, 606; Toch, *Pinocchio,* 636. Works: symphony, 1120

Klenau, Paul von. *Elisabeth von England,* 690; *Kjartan und Gudrun,* 297; *Michael Kohlhass,* 574; *Rembrandt von Rijn,* 638

Klindworth, Karl, 270

Klingsor, Tristan, 62

Klose, Friedrich, 47

Kneisel, Franz, 430

Knipper, Lev. Concerto, violin, 781; *Concerto-Monologue,* 1175; *The Heart of the Taiga,* 1045; *Lyric Suite,* 534; *Meadowland,* 582; *North Wind,* 507; *Overture,* 701; *Revolutionary Episode,* 440; *Root of Life,* 1045; symphony #3, 561; #4 (*Four Études for Orchestra:* now withdrawn), 562; #5 (#4) (*Ballad about a Komsomol Fighter,* 1934), 582; #6, 621; #7, 702

Knorr, Iwan, 129, 263

Knowles, Allison, 1214

Knussen, Oliver, 1257

Kobbé, Gustav, 300

Kobune, Kojiro, 693

Kochanski, Paul. Works performed: Harty, *Variations on an Irish Folk Tune,* 215; Szymanowski, violin concerto #2, 573

Kocsár, Miklós, 1267

Koczalski, Raul, 38

Kodály, Zoltán. Ravel on, 269; on Bartók, 299; visits U.S., 823; Kossuth prize, 849; stamp, 968; marriage, 1077; death, 1235. Works: Concerto for orchestra, 728, 961; *Czinka Panna,* 849; *Dances of Galánta,* 823; *Dances of Marosszék,* 519; duo, violin and cello, 397; *Háry János,* 438; *Kállai Kettós,* 910; *Matra Pictures,* 691; *Peacock Variations,* 703; *Psalmus Hungaricus,* 381, 434; serenade, 2 violins and viola, 362; sonata, cello solo, 378; string quartet #2, 735; *Summer Evening,* 507; *Székely Fonó,* 548–549; symphony, 1121–1122; *Te Deum of Budavár,* 630

Koeberg, Frits Adriaan, 333

Koechlin, Charles. On Societé Nationale de Musique, 100; on Satie, *Socrate,* 325; orchestrates Debussy, *Khamma,* 403, 831; death, 905. Works: *L'Âme* heureuse, 847; *Chant funèbre à la Mémoire des jeunes Femmes défuntes,* 916; *Cinq Chorals dans les Modes du Moyen-Age,* 557; *Danton,* 629; *La Forêt païenne,* 416; *Fugue symphonique,* 557; *Jacob chez Laban,* 413; *Primavera,* 857, 873; *14 Juillet,* 629; sonata, 2 flutes, 361; sonata, piano, 378; *Trois Poèmes du Livre de la Jungle,* 557

Koehler, Emil, 735

Koëlla, Gustave-Adolphe, 78

Koellreutter, Hans Joachim, 873

Koering, René, 1205

Koffler, Josef. 15 Variations, 568; string trio, 534; symphony #3, 673

Kogan, Leonid, 1149

Kohs, Ellis. Concerto for orchestra, 758; symphony #2, 1026

Kokoshka, Oskar, 1194

Koliada, Mikola, 608

Kolisch String Quartet, 443, 460

Kolman, Peter, 1203

Kolmanovsky, Eduard, 1125

Kondorossy, Leslie. *The Pumpkin,* 975; *The Two Impostors,* 1017; *Unexpected Visitor,* 1017; *The Voice,* 975

Kondracki, Michal, 693

König, Gottfried Michael, 1009

Konjović, Petar. *Jadranski Kapričo,* 947; *Knez od Zete,* 494; *Koštana,* 529; *Makar Čudra,* 811; *Seljaci,* 932; *Ženidba Miloša Obilića,* 283

Kono, Kristo. *Dawn,* 993; *The Flower of Remembrance,* 1126

Kopelent, Marek. *Still Life,* 1279; string quartet #3, 1225

Koppel, Herman. Sextet, winds, 835; *Three Psalms of King David,* 918

Koppel, Thomas, 1244

Korchmarev, Klimenty, 618

Koreshchenko, Arseny, 11

Kornauth, Egon, 362

Korngold, Erich Wolfgang. Death, 1039. Works: concerto, violin, 829; *Die Kathrin,* 700; *Much Ado about Nothing,* 343; piano trio, 171; *Der Ring des Polykrates,* 267; *Schauspiel Ouvertüre,* 194–195; *Der Schneemann,* 169; *Sinfonietta,* 230–231; string quartet, 418; *Die stumme Serenade,* 985; *Die tote Stadt,* 334; *Violanta,* 267; *Das Wunder der Heliane,* 460

Kósa, Georg. *6 Pieces for Orchestra,* 413; trio, 2 violins and viola, 835

Kosma, Joseph, 1130

Kostelanetz, André. Conducts: Copland, *Lincoln Portrait,* 752; Creston, *Frontiers,* 773; Kern, *Mark Twain,* 752; Laderman, *Magic Prison,* 1240; Miyagi, *Haru no Umi,* 1002; Thomson, *Mayor LaGuardia Waltzes,* 752

Kostić, Dušan. *Kragujevac,* 1129–1130; *Majstori su prvi ljudi,* 1134

Kotoński, Wlodzimierz. *Etude concrète pour un seul coup de cymbale,* 1091, 1469; *Mikrostruktury,* 1181; *Musique en Relief,* 1088; *Pour quatre,* 1266; trio, flute, guitar and percussion, 1139

Kounadis, Argyris. *Chorikon,* 1088; *Heterophonika idiomela,* 1279

Koussevitzky, Serge. Russian Music Publishing House, 142–143; Volga tour, 163; Debussy conducts K's orchestra, 231–232; conductor of former Imperial Court Orchestra, 284; inaugurates Paris Concerts Koussevitzky, 339; conductor, Boston Symphony Orchestra, 399; protests anti-Semitism, 564; reply, 565; Berkshire Music Center, 716; Bernstein as disciple, 775; death, 915. Works conducted: Barber, cello concerto, 814; idem, *Commando March,* 774; idem, *Knoxville, Summer of 1915,* 851; idem, symphony #2, 783; Bartók, concerto for orchestra, 792; Bax, symphony #2, 500; Bernstein, *Age of Anxiety,* 872; Carpenter, *Patterns,* 554; Castelnuovo-Tedesco, *Cipressi,* 719; Converse, *Flivver 10,000,000,* 453; Copland, *Music for the Theatre,* 422; idem, piano concerto, 444; idem, *Symphonic Ode,* 544; idem, symphony #3, 822; idem, *Two Pieces for String Orchestra,* 485; Diamond, symphony #2, 788; Dukelsky, *Dédicaces,* 683; Foss, *The Prairie,* 773; idem, *Song of Songs,* 830–831; Gershwin, concerto in F, 699; idem, rhapsody #2, 543; Glière, symphony #2, 119; Gretchaninoff, *Missa Oecumenica,* 782; Gruenberg, symphony #1, 581; Hanson, symphony #2, 519; Harris, symphony #1, 580; #3, 688, 699; #5, 766; #6, 784; Hill, concertino, 712; idem, *Lilacs,* 451; idem, symphony #1, 469; #2, 526; #3, 659; idem, violin concerto, 680; Hindemith, cello concerto, 728; idem, *Konzertmusik,*

Lincke, Paul, 29, 1014
Lindberg, Oskar, 776
Lindbergh, Charles, 459, 462, 495–496
Lindsay, John (mayor), 1246
Lindsay, John (string bass), 437
Lipatti, Dinu, 647, 903
Lipkovska, Lydia, 158
Lipograms (term), 1463
Lisinsky, Vatroslav, 988
Liška, Zdeněk, 1103
Lissenko, Nikolai, 52; death, 212
List, Eugene, 745
Listov, Konstantin, 1141
Liszt, Franz, 192, 648, 706, 739, 808, 820, 853, 968, 1123, 1278, 1439, 1464, 1479, 1487, 1490, 1501
Lithuanian National Opera. Organized, 335
Liuzzi, Fernando, 641
Liviabella, Lino. La Conchiglia, 990; Il Vincitore, 630
Lloyd, Caroline, 1242
Lloyd, George. Iernin, 594; John Socman, 913; The Serf, 678
Lockwood, Normand. Informal Music, 757; The Scarecrow, 800
Loeffler, Charles Martin. Protests anti-Semitism, 464; reply, 565; death, 606. Works: Canticle of the Sun, 420; Divertissement espagnol, 13; Evocation, 524–525; Memories of My Childhood 392; A Pagan Poem, 116
Loesser, Frank. Guys and Dolls, 902; The Most Happy Fella, 1008; Where's Charley?, 861
Loewe, Ferdinand, 44
Loewe, Frederick. Brigadoon, 831; Camelot, 1103; My Fair Lady, 1006
Logar, Mihovil. Pokondirena tikva, 1017; 1941, 1108
Logothetis, Anestis, 1431
London. Queen Elizabeth Hall. Inaugural program, 1234
London Promenade Concerts. In World War I, 244
London Symphony Orchestra formed, 63
Long, Marguerite. Works played: Debussy, Études, 259; Milhaud, piano concerto #1, 596; Ravel, piano concerto, 542
Longy, Georges, 14
Lopatnikoff, Nicolai. Concerto, piano, #1, 551; #2, 515; concerto, 2 pianos, 927; concerto, violin, 751; sinfonietta, 756; symphony #1, 486;

#2, 704; #3, 988; Variazioni Concertanti, 1057
Lopez-Buchardo, Carlos, 363
Lorca, Federico García, 359
Lorenzi-Fabris, Ausonio de, 69
Lortzing, Albert, 911
Los Angeles. Pavilion for the Performing Arts. Opening, 1194
Los Angeles Philharmonic Orchestra. First concert, 316; world tour, 1245
Losen, Poul Rovsing, 1181
Lothar, Mark, 576
Loucheur, Raymond, 819
Louis, Rudolph, 80
Lourens, J. P., 19
Lourié, Arthur, 529
Louvier, Alain, 1276
Lovreglio, Ernesto, 650
Lualdi, Adriano. At 1929 ISCM festival, Geneva, 491; and Dresden festival, 1937, 646. Works: Il Diavolo nel Campanile, 411; La Figlia del Rè, 354; La Luna dei Caraibi, 952; Le Nozze di Haura, 768; La Rosa di Saaron, 254–255
Lübeck bombed, 750
Luboshutz, Pierre, 775
Lubricity (term), 1453
Luce, Clare Boothe, 988
Lucier, Alvin, 1165
Luciuk, Juliusz, 1265–1266
Lucký, Stepan, 857
Luders, Gustav, 65
Ludwig, August, 814
Luening, Otto. And Riegger, 1111. Works: Evangeline, 853; Poem in Cycles and Bels, 987; Sonority Canon, 1135; Synthesis for Orchestra and Electronic Sound, 1169
Luigini, Alexandre, 94
Lully, Jean-Baptiste, 556
Lumumba, Patrice, 1106, 1195
Lunacharsky, Anatoly, 332, 1476
Luray, Virginia, 1013
Lusitania, 254
Lustgarten, Egon, 362
Lutheal, 389
Luther, Martin, 811
Lutoslawski, Witold. And 1956 Warsaw Autumn, 1016. Works: concerto for orchestra, 986; Jeux Vénitiens, 1112; Musique Funèbre, 1045; Paroles tissées, 1268; Petite Suite, 911; symphony, 850; Variations Symphoniques, 697
Lutyens, Elizabeth. Festival of Music

*tions,* 1279; variations, violin, cello and piano, 1051

Matsudaira, Yoritsune. *Bugaku,* 1160; concerto, piano, 1202; *Figures sonores,* 1030; *Metamorphoses on Saibara,* 977; *Portrait,* 1280; *Samai,* 1067; *Suite of Dances,* 1098; theme and variations, 943

Matsushita, Shin-ichi. *Canzone da sonare,* 1119; *Fresque sonore,* 1203

Matthus, Siegfried, 1250

Mattoli, Guglielmo, 152

Maturana, Eduardo, 1201

Matuszczak, Bernadetta, 1279

Mauri, José, 342–343

Maw, Nicholas. *One-Man Show,* 1192; *Sinfonia,* 1218

Maxfield, Richard, 1469

Mayakovsky, Vladimir, 579

Mayuzumi, Toshiro. Founds Three Men's Club, 950. Works: *Ectoplasm,* 1011; *Mandala,* 1100; *Nirvana-Symphonie,* 1046, 1134; *Phonologie Symphonique,* 1143; *Samsara,* 1139; *Sphenogramme,* 917

Mbabi-Katana, Solomon, 1259

Mc. *See* Mac

Meale, Richard, 1161

*Mediator Dei,* 842

Medinš, Jānis. *Deevi un Cilveki,* 358; *Uguns un Nakts,* 342

Medtner, Nikolai. Dedicatee, Rachmaninoff, piano concerto #4, 450; death, 925. Works: concerto, piano, #2, 449; #3, 781

Meester, Louis de, 1127

Méfano, Paul, 1279

Mehta, Zubin. Opens Montreal Place des Arts, 1166; opens Los Angeles Pavilion, 1194; and 1966 Israel Philharmonic tour, 1223; and Los Angeles Philharmonic world tour, 1245. Works conducted: Couture, *Miroir,* 1166; Foss, *Elytres,* 1194; Rózsa, piano concerto, 1236; Schuman, *American Festival Overture,* 1194; Vega, *Analigus,* 1218

Méhul, Etienne-Nicolas, 1159

Meitus, Yuli. *The Brothers Ulyanov,* 1250; *Purloined Happiness,* 1094; *The Young Guard,* 841; *Zarya nad Dvinoi,* 998

Melartin, Erkki, 153

Melba, Nellie, 526; stamp, 1124

Melcer, Henryk, 56

Mellnäs, Arne, 1247

Meloharmony (term), 1463

Melorhythm (term), 1463

*Melos,* 324

Melosomatic effect (term), 1463–1464

Menasce, Jacques de, 757

Menchaca, Angel, 390

Mendelsohn, Alfred. Symphony #5, 993; #6, 1050; *The Voice of Lenin,* 1038; *1907,* 1026

Mendelssohn, Arnold, 3

Mendelssohn, Felix Robert, 913

Mendelssohn-Bartholdy, Felix, 3, 138, 594, 622, 628, 738, 1071, 1242

Mendès, Catulle, 41

Mengelberg, Willem. Musical portrait, 262; conducts first recording by New York Philharmonic, 356; death, 909. Works conducted: Bartók, violin concerto, 694; Delius program, 229; Hindemith, *Der Schwanendreher,* 613; idem, violin concerto, 709; Kodály, *Peacock Variations,* 703; Milhaud, *Carnaval d'Aix,* 442; Pijper, symphony #1, 298; #2, 365; Reger, *Konzert im alten Stil,* 209; Saminsky, symphony #2, 366

Mennin, Peter. Birth, 373. Works: *Canto,* 1219; *Concertato for Orchestra (Moby Dick),* 946; symphony #3, 830; #6, 967; #7 (*Variation Symphony*), 1174

Mennini, Louis. *The Rope,* 998; symphony #2, 1166

Menotti, Gian Carlo. Birth, 191; libretto, Barber, *Vanessa,* 1041; libretto, Barber, *A Hand of Bridge,* 1067. Works: *Amahl and the Night Visitors,* 928; *Amelia Goes to the Ball,* 641; *Apocalypse,* 924; concerto, piano, 805; concerto, violin, 949; *The Consul,* 890; *Death of the Bishop of Brindisi,* 1159; *Help! Help! the Globolinks!,* 1274, 1502; *The Island God,* 748; *Labyrinth,* 1154; *The Last Savage,* 1169, 1441; *Maria Golovin,* 1053–1054; *Martin's Lie,* 1182–1183; *The Medium,* 815, 829; *The Old Maid and the Thief,* 694; *The Saint of Bleecker Street,* 988–989; *The Telephone,* 829; *The Unicorn, the Gorgon, and the Manticore,* 1017–1018

Menuhin, Yehudi, 888, 1264

Merikanto, Oskar. *Elinan Surma,* 171; *Regina von Emmeritz,* 323

Messager, André. Conducts Debussy, *Pelléas,* 36; 489. Works: *L'Amour*

1554

masqué, 368; *Coups de roulis,* 478; *Les Dragons de l'Impératrice,* 71; *Fortunio,* 111–112; *Monsieur Beaucaire,* 310; *Passionément,* 427

Messiaen, Olivier. Birth, 131; and *La Spirale,* 616; and *Jeune France,* 628; and 1956 Warsaw Autumn, 1016; and Hellenic Contemporary Music Week, 1216; as Neo-Romantic, 1472. Works: *Cinq Rechants,* 917; *Chronochromie,* 1098, 1120; *Et exspecto resurrectionem mortuorum,* 1266; *L'Hymne aux morts,* 1206; *Livre d'orgue,* 992; *La Nativité du Seigneur,* 674; *Les Offrandes oubliées,* 526; *Oiseaux exotiques,* 1067; *Quatuor pour le fin du temps,* 726–727, 818–819; *Le Réveil des Oiseaux,* 965; *Sept Haikai,* 1182; *Le Tombeau resplendissant,* 561; *Trois petites liturgies de la Présence Divine,* 799; *Trois Talas,* 885; *Turangalila,* 884

Messina. Vittorio Emanuele Theater. Reopens, 1274

Metamusic (term), 1464

Metempsychosis (term), 1464–1465

Metric modulation (term), 1465

Metronomes, 1197

Metropolitan Opera. Bans claque, 616; National Company founded, 1168; old building closes, 1216–1217; new house opens, 1226; European tour, 1220

Metz, Theodore, 617

Metzler, Robert, 995

Meulemans, Arthur, 706

Mexico City. Orquesta Sinfónica, 503

Meyerbeer, Giacomo, 622, 632, 1178, 1344

Meyerowitz, Jan. *Die Doppelgängerin,* 1233; *Eastward in Eden,* 925; *Esther,* 1025; *Port Town,* 1092

Miaskovsky, Nicolai. Teaching condemned, 847; death, 898; and 1956 Warsaw Autumn, 1016; cleared of Westernism, 1049; criticized as formalist, 1491. Works: *Birthday Overture,* 704; concerto, cello, 797–798; concerto, violin, 680; *Silence,* 187; sonata, piano, #4, 435; *Symphonie-Fantaisie,* 721; symphony #1, 242; #2, 204; #3, 251; #4, 408; #5, 330; #6, 389–390; #7, 408; #8, 433; #9, 471; #10, 470; #11, 559; #12 (*Collective Farm Symphony*), 550; #13, 593; #14, 602; #15,

612; #16, 631; #17, 660; #18, 655; #19, 687; #20, 722; #21, 721; #22, 746; #23, 755; #24, 777; #25, 830; #26, 866; #27, 903

Michel, Erhard, 513

Mickey Mouse, 477, 721

Microtonality (term), 1465–1467

Microtonality (uses), 25, 146, 208, 345, 372, 378, 380, 387, 409, 447, 449, 520, 523, 534, 551, 638, 642, 662, 692, 758, 805, 842, 873, 898, 926, 933, 1098, 1115, 1134, 1247, 1260, 1266

Mignan, Edouard, 227

Mignone, Francisco. *Alegrias de Nossa Senhora,* 878; *Caramurú,* 301; concerto, violin, piano and orch., 1240; *Contractador dos Diamantes,* 399; *O Espantalho,* 746; *Festa das Igrejas,* 751; *L'Innocente,* 476; *Mizú,* 653; *Momus,* 566; *Quadros Amazonicos,* 878; *Sonho de um Menino Travesso,* 737

Migot, Georges. And *La Spirale,* 616. Works: *La Fête chez la Bergère,* 421; *Hagoromo,* 357; *La Jungle,* 542; *Le Rossignol en amour,* 640; symphony #1 (*Agrestides*), 357; *Trois Epigrammes,* 421

Migratory tonics (term), 1467

Miguez, Leopoldo, 19

Mihalovich, Ödön, 121

Mihalovici, Marcel. *Caprice roumain,* 647; *Concerto quasi una Fantasia,* violin, 626; *Etude,* piano, winds and percussion, 922; *Fantaisie,* orch., 514; *Die Heimkehr,* 978; *L'Intransigeant Pluton,* 691; *Les Jumeaux,* 1152; *Prelude et Invention,* 694; *Sinfonia Giocosa,* 927; sonata, violin alone, 942; variations, brass and strings, 874

Mihály, András, 1230

Mikorey, Franz, 160

Milan. Teatro alla Scala. Reopens, 350; bombed, 771; reopens, 816; Piccola Scala, 1002; Soviet tour, 1186; North American debut, 1248

Milhaud, Darius. As one of *Les Six,* 322; flees France, 716; talk on *Les Six,* 757; as Hamid-al-Usurid, 769; and 1956 Warsaw Autumn, 1016. Works: *L'Abandon d'Ariane,* 470; *Actualités,* 474–475; *Agamemnon,* 453; *Le Bal Martiniquais,* 808; *The Bells,* 815; *Le Bœuf sur le Toit,* 325,

757, 1450; *Bolivar,* 892; *La Brebis égarée,* 381–382; *Cain and Abel,* 806; *Cantata from Proverbs,* 937; *Le Carnaval d'Aix,* 442; *Catalogue de Fleurs,* 398; *Les Choéphores,* 313; *Christophe Colomb,* 508; concerto, cello, #2, 823; concerto, clarinet, 810; concerto, marimba, vibraphone and orch., 869; concerto, percussion and chamber orch., 520; concerto, piano, #1, 596; #2, 745; #3, 817; #4, 890, 976; #5, 1013; concerto, 2 pianos, 762; concerto, viola, 500; concerto, violin, #2, 862; *Le Cortège funèbre,* 716; *La Création du Monde,* 379, 1138; *Danton,* 629; *David,* 976; *La Délivrance de Thésée,* 470; *L'Enlèvement d'Europe,* 459; *Les Euménides,* 462; *L'Éventail de Jeanne,* 489; *Fanfare de la Liberté,* 763; *Fiesta,* 1055; *A Frenchman in New York,* 1163; *L'Homme et son désir,* 343; *Kentuckiana,* 868; *La Libération des Antilles,* 808; *Les Malheurs d'Orphée,* 432; *La Mère coupable,* 1221; *Les Mariés de la Tour Eiffel,* 344; *Maximilien,* 541–542; *Médée,* 699; *Murder of a Great Chief of State,* 1172; *Music for Indiana,* 1229; octet, strings, 879; *L'Oiseau,* 663; *Opus Americanum,* 777; *Ouverture philharmonique,* 1150; *Pacem in Terris,* 1173; *Le Pauvre matelot,* 463–464; *Protée,* 332, 413; *14 Juillet,* 629; *Les Rêves de Jacob,* 896; *Sabbath Morning Service,* 876; *Salade,* 391, 442; *Scaramouche,* 651, 769; septet, strings, 1191; sonata, flute, oboe, clarinet, piano, 360; string quartet #4, 378; #9, 650; #14, 879; #15, 879; suite, harmonica and orch., 834; suite, orch., #2, 332, 413; suite, violin and orch., 806, 834; *Suite Française,* 800; *Suite Provençale,* 654; symphony #1, 718; #2, 825; #3 (*Hymnus Ambrosianus*), 841; #4 (*1848*), 854; #5, 966; #6, 1000, 1051; #7, 999; #8 (*Rhodanienne*), 1048, 1087; #9, 1082; #10, 1111; #12 (*Rural*), 1130; *Le Train bleu,* 395; *West Point Suite,* 939
Millimetrization (term), 1467
Millöcker, Karl, 886
Milner, Anthony. *Salutatio Angelis,* 960; *The Water and the Fire,* 1186

Milojević, Miloje. Death, 817. Works: *Grimaces rythmiques,* 651; *Smrt majke Jugovića.* 359
Minami, Hiroaki, 1266
Minhejmer, Adam, 6
Minkus, Leon, 914
Minneapolis Symphony Orchestra formed, 50
Minsky's, 573
Miroglio, Francis, 1247
Missa, Edmond. *Maguelone,* 47; *Muguette,* 45
Mitchell, George, 437
Mitchell, Howard. Conducts: Creston, symphony #4, 930; Gould, *Declaration,* 1021
Mitropoulos, Dimitri. Death, 1101. Works conducted: Barber, *Medea's Meditation and Dance of Vengeance,* 816; Berger, *Ideas of Order,* 956; Bloch, violin concerto, 683; Chávez, piano concerto, 745; Copland, *Statements,* 746; Diamond, *Rounds,* 792; idem, symphony, #1, 745; Gould, *Jekyll and Hyde Variations,* 1022; idem, symphony #3, 829; Hindemith, symphony in E flat, 743; Kirchner, piano concerto, 1005; Krenek, piano concerto #3, 823; idem, symphony #4, 843; Kubik, symphony #3, 1024; Milhaud, piano concerto #1, 682; Nabokov, *Sinfonia Biblica,* 725; Piket, *Curtain Raiser,* 867; Rey, *Concerto Chromatique,* 563; Schnabel, symphony #1, 824; Sicilianos, symphony #1, 1043; Siegmeister, *Ozark Set,* 791; Swanson, *Short Symphony,* 902. Works: *Sœur Béarice,* 312
Mitsukuri, Shukichi, 896
Mixed media (term), 1467
Miyagi, Michio, 1002; death, 1013
Mlynarski, Emil, 388, 479
Mobile (term), 1467
Modern Jazz Quartet, 920
Modern music (term), 1468
*Modern Music* (magazine), 386
Modernistic music (term), 1468
Moeran, Ernest John. Death, 902. Works: rhapsody, piano and orch., 771; symphony, 662
Moeschinger, Albert, 818
Moevs, Robert W., 1070–1080
Mohaupt, Richard. Banned by Nazis, 664; death; 1033. Works: *Die Bremer Stadtmusikanten,* 877; con-

certo, piano, 918; *Double Trouble,* 987–988; *Max und Moritz,* 904; *Stadtpfeiffermusik,* 818; *Die Wirtin von Pinsk,* 664

Mokranjać, Stevan, 246, 1040

Mokrousov, Boris, 652, 1502

Molchanov, Kyrill. *Stronger Than Death,* 1235; *Zaria,* 1004

Moldenhauer, Hans, 1136

Molina, Antonio J., 295

Molinari, Bernardino. At 1928 ISCM festival, Siena, 476; 949. Works conducted: Barber, symphony #1, 636; Respighi, *Ballata delle Gnomidi,* 327; idem, *Pini di Roma,* 406

Möllendorf, Willi, 1466

Mompou, Federico, 1190

Moncada. *See* Hernández Moncada

Moncayo, Pablo, 861

Monet, Claude, 1454

Monfred, Avenir de, 1208, 1471

Monism (term), 1468

Moniuszko, Stanislaw, 925

Monleone, Domenico. *Cavalleria Rusticana,* 103; *La Giostra dei Falchi,* 103; *Il Mistero,* 340

Monnot, Marguerite, 1019

Monodrama (term), 1468

Monothematism and polythematism. Discussed, 1468

Montañez, Martita, 1034

Monte Carlo method (term), 1468

Montecino, Alfonso, 1201

Montemezzi, Italo. Death, 938. Works: *L'Amore dei tre re,* 221; *Giovanni Gallurese,* 71; *Hellera,* 143; *L'Incantesimo,* 773; *La Nave,* 304; *La Notte di Zoraima,* 524

Monteux, Pierre. Death, 1184. Works conducted: Antheil, symphony #6, 869; Bloch, *Evocations,* 664; idem, *Suite Symphonique,* 804; Ferroud, symphony, 527; Françaix, symphony, 555; Gilbert, *Indian Sketches,* 337; Gould, *Fall River Legend,* 852; Griffes, *Pleasure Dome of Kubla Khan,* 319; Markevitch, piano concerto, 527; Milhaud, concerto, piano, #5, 1013; idem, concerto, viola, 500; idem, *Opus Americanum,* 777; Nabokov, *Symphonie lyrique,* 504; Pijper, concerto, piano, 464; idem, symphony #3, 439; Poulenc, *Concert champêtre,* 492; Prokofiev, symphony #3, 493; Rivier, symphony #1, 559; Rudhyar, *Poèmes ironiques* and *Vis-*

*ion végétale,* 282; Scelzi, *Rotative,* 541; Schelling, *Suite variée,* 695; Sessions, symphony #2, 827; refuses to conduct Strauss, *Till Eulenspiegel,* 271; conducts Stravinsky, *Pétrouchka,* 188; idem, *Le Rossignol,* 241; idem, *Le Sacre du Printemps,* 237, 1159

Monteverdi, Claudio, 491, 603, 776

Montsalvatge, Xavier, 1204

Moog, Robert, 1444

Moon landing, American (actual), 1281

Moon landing, Soviet (putative), 1247

Moór, Emanuel, 537. Works: *Andreas Hofer,* 39; concerto, piano, 125; *Hochzeitsglocken,* 127; *La Pompadour,* 27

Moor, Karel. *Hjoerdis,* 81; *Viy,* 47

Moore, Carman, 1260

Moore, Douglas. *The Ballad of Baby Doe,* 1013; *Carry Nation,* 1217; *The Devil and Daniel Webster,* 696; *The Emperor's New Clothes,* 869; *Farm Journal,* 840; *Gallantry,* 1044; *Giants in the Earth,* 909; *The Headless Horseman,* 640; *Pageant of P. T. Barnum,* 430; symphony #2, 815; *White Wings,* 869; *The Wings of the Dove,* 1125

Moore, Grace, 827

Moore, Mary Carr. *David Rizzio,* 550; *The Flaming Arrow,* 355; *Narcissa,* 201

Moorman, Charlotte, 1207, 1239

Morawetz, Oscar, 1079

Morax, André, 428

Morel, François, 1083

Morera, Enrique, 86

Moreschi, Alessandro, 356

Moret, Ernest, 328

Morgan, J. P., 102

Morgan, Jimmie, 260

Mormon Tabernacle Choir, 1142

Moroi, Makoto. *Alpha and Beta,* 997; *Développements raréfiants,* 1050; partita, flute solo, 960

Moroi, Saburo. Symphony #3, 893; #4, 909

Moross, Jerome. *Ballet Ballads,* 853–854; *Gentlemen, Be Seated!,* 1167

Morphology (term), 1468–1469

Morris, Harold. Concerto, piano, 537; symphony #2 (*Victory*), 949; #3 (*Amaranth*), 849

Morrison, H., 352

Mortari, Virgilio. *La Figlia del diavolo,* 973; *Rapsodia,* 535

Mortelmans, Lodewijk, 942
Mortensen, Finn. Fantasy and fugue, piano, 1088; quintet, winds, 1010
Morthenson, Jan W. *Coloratura IV*, 1226; *Neutron Star*, 1251
Morton, Jelly Roll, 437
Moser, Rudolf, 1093
Moses-Tobani, Theodore, 576
Mosonyi, Mihály, 968
Moss, Barry, 1011
Mossolov, Alexander. Expelled from Union of Soviet Composers, 620. Works: concerto, harp, 702; *The Hero*, 475; *The Iron Foundry*, 461, 514, 1482, 1500; string quartet, 457
Moszkowski, Moritz, 409
Mottl, Felix, 56, 79; death, 191
*Motu Proprio*, 51, 485, 842
Moulaert, Raymond, 513
Moussorgsky. *See* Mussorgsky
Moyzes, Alexander, 610
Mozart, Wolfgang Amadeus, 71, 356, 368, 422, 578, 692, 727, 766, 822, 837, 936, 999, 1003, 1004, 1005, 1008, 1016, 1117, 1181, 1191, 1232, 1278, 1425, 1439, 1449, 1478, 1483, 1501
Mraczeck, Joseph Gustav, 446
Mravinsky, Evgeny, 775
Mshvelidze, Shalva. *Legend of Tariel*, 812; *The Right Hand of a Great Master*, 1115
Muck, Karl. Conducts Panama-Pacific Exposition, 255; World War I troubles, 293, 295, 296, 297; death, 708. Works conducted: Busoni, piano concerto, 67; Chadwick, *Symphonic Sketches*, 121; Debussy, *La Mer*, 105; Hadley, *Salome*, 108; Loeffler, *Pagan Poem*, 116; Schelling, *Impressions from an Artist's Life*, 262; Smyth, *Der Wald*, 30
Mul, J. N., 568, 1161
Mulè, Giuseppe. Anti-modernist manifesto, 558. Works: *La Baronessa di Carini*, 201; *The Cyclops*, 874; *Dafni*, 467; *Liola*, 601; *La Monacella della Fontana*, 369; *Two Sicilian Songs*, 585
Müller, Gottfried, 784
Müller, Johannes, 492
Munch, Charles. Debut as conductor, 555; American debut, 825–826; first foreign tour, Boston Symphony, 937; at 1958 ISCM festival, Strasbourg, 1051–1052; first Orchestre de Paris concert, 1250; death, 1272. Works conducted: Barber, *Prayers of Kierkegaard*, 987; Barraud, symphony #3, 1044; Blackwood, symphony #1, 1047; Brod, *Two Rustic Dances*, 833; Diamond, symphony #3, 900; #6, 1025; Dutilleux, symphony #2, 1076; Fine, symphony, 1132; Haieff, symphony #2, 1046; Honegger, *Symphonie Liturgique*, 820; idem, symphony #5, 908; Ibert, *Mouvement symphonique*, 1152; Jaubert, *Sonata a Due*, 826; Martinu, *Fantaisies symphoniques*, 989; idem, Parables, 1060; Milhaud, concerto, piano, #4, 890; idem, *Pacem in Terris*, 1173; Nabokov, *La Vita Nuova*, 908; Poulenc, concerto, organ, strings and timpani, 736; idem, concerto, piano, 887; idem, *Gloria*, 1107; Piston, symphony #6, 1001, 1015; #8, 1197; idem, *Toccata*, 861; Ropartz, symphony #5, 823; Schmitt, symphony #2, 1051; Schuman, concerto, violin, 889; idem, symphony #7, 1099; Sessions, symphony #3, 1040; Smit, symphony #1, 1022; Tcherepnin, *Suite Georgienne*, 711; idem, symphony #4, 1058; Walton, concerto, cello, 1021
Munich. Staatsoper. Destroyed, 773; reopens, 1171
Muñoz, José Luis (composer), 1218
Muñoz, Luis (governor), 1127
Munter, Charles, 204
Muradeli, Vano. Exonerated from taint of formalism, 866; statement on personal policy, 1369–1370. Works: *Friendship of Peoples*, 839; *Great Friendship*, 839; *October*, 1177; symphony #1, 681–682
Musgrave, Thea, 1251
*Music and Letters*, 321
*Music Review*, 706
Music Therapy Project, 591
Music typewriter, 630, 998
*The Musical Quarterly*, 248
Musical saw, 412
Musicorama (term), 1469
*Musicwriter*, 998
*Die Musik*, 19, 622
*Die Musik in Geschichte und Gegenwart*, 878
"Musique Concrète," 851, 890–891, 1469
Mussolini, Benito, 584, 644, 669, 744
Mussorgsky, Modeste. Centennial, 690;

O'Hara, Geoffrey, 271
Oistrakh, David, 1000
Oki, Masao. *Atomic Bomb,* 967; *Hagoromo,* 710; Hiroshima cantata, 1142
Olah, Tiberiu, 1265
Oldberg, Arne, 450
Oldham, Arthur, 940
Olenin, Alexander, 260
Oller, Joaquín Homs, 1011
Ollone, Max d'. *L'Arlequin,* 406; *Georges Dandin,* 505; *La Samaritaine,* 650
Olson, H. F., 1055
Olympiad, Berlin, 1936, 630
Omnitonality (term), 1473
Ondes Martenot, 471, 485–486, 588, 662, 791, 799, 852, 861, 873, 884, 1182
Ono, Yoko, 1458
Oosterzee, Cornelie van, 163
Open form composition (term), 1473
Opieński, Henryk. *Jakub lutnista,* 464; *Maria,* 372
Oppenheimer, J. Robert, 1253
Oransky, Victor, 506–507
Orbón, Julián. *Mount Gilboa,* 1262; *Partita 3,* 1218
Orchestre de la Suisse Romande. First concert, 306
Orchestre Symphonique de Paris. First concert, 479
Orecchio, Joseph, 955
Orefice, Giacomo. Prize committee member, 152. Works: *Chopin,* 24; *Radda,* 212
Orff, Carl. *Antigonae,* 879; *Astutuli,* 966; *Die Bernauerin,* 837; *Carmina Burana,* 647, 1471; *Catulli Carmina,* 775, 916; *Comoedia de Christi Resurrectione,* 1007; *Die Kluge,* 766; *Ludus de nato infante mirificus,* 1103; *Der Mond,* 686; *Oedipus der Tyrann,* 1076; *Prometheus,* 1257; *Ein Sommernachtstraum,* 947; *Trionfi,* 647, 775, 953; *Trionfo di Afrodite,* 953
Orgad, Ben-Zion, 870
Organized sound (term), 1473–1474
Original Dixieland Jazz Band, 272, 277
Orlansky, Yakob, 764
Ormandy, Eugene. Televised concert, 849. Works conducted: Antheil, symphony #5, 867; Barber, *Cave of the Heart,* 816; idem, *Toccata Festiva,* 1095; idem, violin concerto, 728; Bartók, piano concerto #3, 811; Bassett, variations for orch., 1164; Cordero,

sinfonia, 1219; Creston, symphony #3, 900; Diamond, symphony #7, 1129; Finney, symphony #3, 1175; Françaix, *L'Horloge de Flore,* 1111; Fuleihan, *Three Cyprus Serenades,* 824; Ginastera, concerto for strings, 1218; Hanson, symphony #5, 991; Harris, symphony #7, 948; #9, 1151; idem, *When Johnny Comes Marching Home,* 599; Hindemith, clarinet concerto, 904; idem, *Cupid and Psyche,* 774; Koutzen, violin concerto, 932; Martinu, concerto for 2 pianos, 775; idem, symphony #4, 807; Milhaud, suite, violin and orch., 806; Nabokov, cello concerto, 967; Persichetti, symphony #3, 842; #4, 988; Piston, *Lincoln Center Festival Overture,* 1146; idem, symphony #7, 1108; Rachmaninoff, piano concerto #4, 450; idem, *Symphonic Dances,* 726; Schuman, symphony #9 (*Le Fosse Ardeatine*), 1274; Sessions, symphony #5, 1174; Thompson, *A Trip to Nahant,* 992; Thomson, *Louisiana Story,* 865; Tosar, *4 Piezas para Orquesta,* 1218; Villa-Lobos, symphony #9, 1219; Vincent, *Symphonic Poem after Descartes,* 1062; idem, symphony, 930; Zador, *Five Contrasts,* 1195
Ornstein, Leo, 408
Orr, Robin, 1258
Orrego-Salas, Juán. *Canciones castellanas,* 874; *Concerto a tre,* 1201; *Sonata a quattro,* 1191; symphony #2, 1004; #3, 1190
Orrelana, Joaquín, 1201
Orthel, Léon. *Sinfonia piccola,* 856; symphony #5, 1086
Ory, Kid, 437
Osterc, Slavko. Concerto, piano, 609; *Four Songs,* 585; *Mouvement symphonique,* 675; *Passacaglia-Chorale,* 692
Ostrčil, Otakar. Stamps, 1028, 1093. Works: *Honzovo Královstvi,* 589; *Kunálovy ocj,* 130; *Legenda z Erinu,* 344; *Poupě,* 175, 1028; sinfonietta, 393; *Vlasty Skon,* 69
Oswald, Henrique, 936
Otlet, Robert, 415–416
Otterloo, Willem van, 946
Overton, Hall, 889
Ovsianniko-Kulikovsky, Dimitri, 867
Ozawa, Seiji, 1250, 1275

Pablo, Luis de. *Cesuras,* 1189, 1261; *Imaginario II,* 1280; *Iniciativas,* 1246; *Polar,* 1202; *Recíproco,* 1156
Paccagnini, Angelo, 1156
Pacchierotti, Ubaldo. *L'Albatro,* 82; *Eidelberga Mia!,* 122
Pachmann, Vladimir de, 559
Paderewski, Ignace. Paderewski Fund established, 6; at White House, 46; teacher, 260; musical portrait by Schelling, 262; Premier of Poland, 308; stamps, 313, 1096; resigns premiership, 319; in film, 629; first radio concert, 688; banned in Germany, 690; leaves Europe, 720; death, 737; centenary, 1101–1102. Works performed: Saint-Saëns, concerto #4, 139. Works: *Manru,* 17; symphony, 139
Padilla, José, 1100
Paganini, Nicolò, 421, 594, 714, 919
Paganini String Quartet, 879
Page, Willis, 1210
Pahissa, Jaime. *Gala plácida,* 215; *Marianela,* 370; *Monodía,* 419–420; *Suite intertonal,* 438
Paik, Nam June. *Action Music,* 1207; *Count the Waves of the Rhine,* 1205; *Creep into the Vagina of a Living Whale,* 1205; *Omaggio a Cage,* 1207; *Piece for Allison Knowles,* 1214; *Playable Music #4,* 1211, 1500
Paine, John Knowles, 92
Paisiello, Giovanni, 713
Paladilhe, Émile, 19, 427
Palau, Manuel, 698
Palester, Roman. *Cantata of the Vistula,* 896; *Danse Polonaise,* 626; *Little Overture,* 735; *Symphonic Music,* 535
Palestine Symphony Orchestra, 637; conductorless concerts, 702
Palestrina, Giovanni Pierluigi, 412
Paliashvili, Zakhar. *Abesalom e Etheri,* 309; *Daisi,* 382; *Latavra,* 467
Palimpsest (term), 1474
Palindrome (term), 1474
Palingenesis (term), 1474
Palma, Athos. *Los Hijos del Sol,* 481; *Nazdah,* 395
Palmer, Geoffrey, 376
Palmer, Robert, 756
Palmgren, Selim, 927. Works: concerto, piano, #3, 355; *Daniel Hjört,* 161; *Metamorphoses,* 355
Pan American Union, 392
Panatero, Mario, 977

Pandiatessaron (term), 1474
Pandiatonicism (term), 1474–1475
Panizza, Ettore. *Aurora,* 128; *Medio Evo Latino,* 11
Pannell, Raymond, 1245
Panotrope, 457
Panpentatonicism (term), 1475
Pantonality (term), 1475
Panufnik, Andrzej. Conducts Rubbra, symphony #7, 1036. Works: *Berceuse,* 842, 858; *Epitaph for the Victims of Katyn,* 1272; *5 Folk Tunes,* 819; *Sinfonia Rustica,* 875–876; *Sinfonia Sacra,* 1185; *Symfonia Pokoju,* 913; *Tragic Overture,* 871; *Uvertura bohaterska,* 944
Paolantonio, Franco, 598
Papandopulo, Boris. *Legend of Comrade Tito,* 1135; *Rona,* 1009; *Sunčanica,* 736; symphony #2, 815
Papineau-Couture, Jean, 1253
Pâque, Désiré, 702–703, 1425
Paray, Paul, 709, 1074
Parelli, Attilio, 199
Parerga & paralipomena (terms), 1475
Paris Exposition, 1937, 649
Paris Opéra. Performance cancelled due to shelling, 295; reopens, 296
Paris. Orchestre Symphonique de Paris. Initial concert, 479
Parker, Horatio. Doctorate, Cambridge, 37; death, 320. Works: *Fairyland,* 256; *Mona,* 199–200
Parmegiani, Bernard, 1156
Parris, Herman M., 854
Parrott, Ian, 1024
Parry, Hubert Hastings. Death, 303. Works: *The Love That Casteth Out Fear,* 65; *Symphony-Fantasy,* 213
Parry, Joseph, 311
Partch, Harry. As microtonalist, 1466. Works: *King Oedipus,* 933; *Revelation in the Courthouse Park,* 1111
Partos, Edmund, 735
Partos, Ödön. *Ein-Gev,* 965; *Haggadah,* 1138; *Maqamat,* 1088
Pashchenko, Andrei. *Alpine Ballad,* 1254; *The Black Cliff,* 533; *Eagles in Revolt,* 421; *Symphonic Mystery,* 389
Pater, Walter, 1455
Patti, Adelina, 315
Pauer, Jiří. *Red Riding Hood,* 1246; *The Talkative Snail,* 1246
Paul, Dean, 542–543
Paumgartner, Bernhard, 623

Paunović, Milenko, 387
Pavlova, Anna, 262, 378
"Payola," 1082, 1195
Paz, Juan Carlos. *Continuidades*, 1218; *Music for Piano and Orchestra*, 1202; *Music for Trio*, 735; passacaglia, 650; sonatina, flute and clarinet, 570
Pears, Peter, 1087
Pedrell, Carlos, 286
Pedrell, Felipe. Death, 363; homage by Falla, 702. Works: *El Conte Arnau*, 627; *I Pirenei*, 25
Pedrollo, Arrigo. *L'Amante in Trappola*, 631; *Delitto e castigo*, 440; *L'Uomo che ride*, 326; *La Veglia*, 321
Penderecki, Krzysztof. And spatial distribution, 1434; and notation, 1451; microtonalist, 1467. Works: *Anaklasis*, 1098; *Canon*, 1145; capriccio, violin and orch., 1248, 1264; concerto, violino grande, 1263; *Dies Irae*, 1237; *Polymorphie*, 1134; *Psalmy Davids*, 1141; *St. Luke Passion*, 1215; *Stabat Mater*, 1205; *Strophes*, 1071; *Die Teufel von Loudun*, 1278; *Tren pamieci ofiar Hiroszimy*, 1115, 1162, 1454; *Wymiary Czasu i Ciszy* (*Dimensions of Time and Silence*), 1094, 1118
Pennario, Leonard, 1236
Pentland, Barbara, 1011
Pepin, Clermont. *Guernica*, 958; symphony #3 (*Les Quasars*), 1233
Pepping, Ernst, 514
Pepusch, Johann Christoph, 855
Peragallo, Mario. Concerto, piano, 943; concerto, violin, 1011; *La Gita in campagna*, 973
Pergolesi, Giovanni Battista, 328, 647, 656
Peri, Jacopo, 9, 454
Perkin, Helen, 514
Perkowski, Piotr, 1016
Perle, George, 1162, 1489
Permeability (term), 1475
Pernicious interference. Decried, 1475
Perosi, Lorenzo. Death, 1016. Works: *Il Natale del Redentore*, 950; *Il Nazzareno*, 894; *Pompeii*, 200
Perpignan, F., 252
Perrin, Pierre, 338
Perrot, Jacques, 1148, 1498
Persichetti, Vincent. Concerto, piano, #1, 804; #2, 1185; symphony #1, 840; #3, 842; #4, 988; #5, strings, 981; #6, winds, 1007; #7 (*Liturgical*), 1074; #8, 1249
Persico, Mario, 525
Persymfans, 353
Peru. Orquesta Sinfónica Nacional, 682
Pessard, Émile-Louis-Fortuné, 279
Peters, Rudolf, 345
Peterson-Berger, Wilhelm. *Adils och Elisiv*, 448; *Arnljot*, 160
Petit, Raymond, 458
Petrassi, Goffredo. Concerto, orchestra, #2, 929; *Il Cordovano*, 875; *Coro di Morti*, 740, 916; *Estri*, 1241; *La follia di Orlando*, 832; introduction and allegro, violin and chamber orch., 609; *La Morte dell'Aria*, 899; partita, 569; *Propos d'Alain*, 1138; *Il Ritratto di Don Chisciotte*, 873; *Serenata*, 1065
Petrauskas, Mikas, 96, 1173
Petridis, Petro. *Berceuse*, 433; *Danse de Kleftes*, 432; *Le Petit vaisseau*, 433; *Prélude de Zemfira*, 432; *St. Paul*, 918
Petrillo, James C., 756
Petrov, Andrei, 1269
Petrovics, Emil, 1122
Petrucci, Ottaviano, 1221
Petrželka, Vilém. *Námořník Mikuláš*, 520; *Věčný Návrat*, 384
Petyrek, Felix. Death, 927. Works: *Gethsemane*, 918; *Litanies*, 435; passacaglia, piano, 360; sextet, 360
Peyko, Nicolai, 904
Pfitzner, Hans. Musical portrait by Schelling, 262; death, 876. Works: *Das Christ-Elflein*, 291; *Das Herz*, 538; *Kleine Sinfonie*, 702; *Palestrina*, 287; *Die Rose vom Liebesgarten*, 21
Philadelphia Orchestra. Inaugural concert, 11; Association incorporates, 39; renounces German music, 290; renounces "debatable" music, 552
Philately. *See* Stamps
Philipp, Franz, 345
Philipp, Isidor, 1043
Phillips, Burrill, 875
Phillips, Montague, 337–338
Phonograph, 55, 406, 459, 677, 916, 1054, 1076, 1179. *See also* Recordings
Phumiphol Aduldet. *See* Ananda, Sondet Phra Chao Yu Hua Buhimbol Adulyadej
Piaf, Edith, 1168
Piano demolition, 1153, 1436

Powell, John. Sponsors Racial Integrity Act, 924. Works: Pilgrim pageant music, 345; *Rapsodie nègre*, 295, 924; symphony, 833; *Virginia Symphony*, 924
Powell, Mel. *Events*, 1181; *Haiku Settings*, 1119
Prado, José Almeida, 1259
Praetorius, Michael, 243, 1142
Prague Spring festival, 1951, 914; 1965, 1202
Pratella, Francesco Balilla. Manifestoes, 170, 177, 204, 1294–1298, 1449; death, 995. Works: *L'Aviatore Dro*, 333; *Lilia*, 79; *Ninna nanna della bambola*, 373; *La Sina d'Vargöun*, 152–153; *Sinfonia della Vita*, 216
Pratt, Silas Gamaliel, 273
Preger, Leo, 917
Prepared piano (term), 1481
Prepense music (term), 1481
Presley, Elvis, 1486
Prevost, André, 1238
Prey, Claude, 1247
Price, Leontyne, 1226
Primrose, William. Works played: Bartók, concerto, 885; Fricker, concerto, 964
Pringsheim, Klaus. Conducts Lapham, *Mount Mihara*, 599. Works: concerto, piano, 611; overture to Sullivan's *The Mikado*, 820
Printemps, Yvonne, 478
Pritchard, John, 1093
*Pritomnost*, 642
Prix de Rome, 10, 19, 47, 76, 77–78, 98, 227, 235, 480
Pro Arte Quartet, 554
Probability (term), 1481
Production Collective (Procoll), 411, 487
Progressive jazz (term), 1481
Prohibition, 306
Prokofiev, Serge. Graduates, 149; unperformed piece reviewed, 275–276; Tokyo recital, 300; in New York, 301; American debut, 305; sues Lifar, 558; on *Grossmutterakkord*, 664; accused of "decadent formalism," 847, 866; and Koussevitzky, 915; death, 954; and Cole Porter, 991; and 1956 Warsaw Autumn, 1016; cleared of Westernism charge, 1049; letter on personal policy, 1373–1374; and displaced tonality, 1438; and symbolic analysis, 1492. Works: *Ala and Lolli*, 264, 275, 1030; *Alexander Nevsky*, 695–696, 702; *Autumn*, 191; *Ballad of a Boy Who Remained Unknown*, 782; *Betrothal in a Convent*, 822; *Cantata*, 1216; *Chout*, 341; *Cinderella*, 806; concertino, cello, 1081; concerto, cello, #1, 681, 931; concerto, piano, #1, 205; #2, 227–228; #3, 349; #4, 1014; #5, 554–555; concerto, violin, #1, 379, 393; #2, 615, 1052, 1117; *Divertissement*, orch., 501; *Dreams*, 172; *L'Enfant prodigue*, 494, 518; *The Flaming Angel*, 493, 999; *The Gambler*, 492–493; *Humorous Scherzo*, 275; *Legend of a Stone Flower*, 971; *Lieutenant Kijé*, 639; *The Love for Three Oranges*, 350, 1483; *The Meeting of the Volga with the Don*, 932; *Ode to the End of the War*, 805, 818; *On Guard for Peace*, 904; *Overture on Hebrew Themes*, 323, 377; *Le Pas d'Acier*, 456, 1500; *Peter and the Wolf*, 627, 1476; *The Prodigal Son*, 494, 518; quintet, winds and double bass, 477; *Romeo and Juliet*, 705; *Russian Overture*, 631; *Scythian Suite*, 264, 275, 1030; *Semyon Kotko*, 715; *Seven Are They*, 393; sonata, flute, 835; sonata, piano, #1, 172; sonata, violin, #2, 835; sonata, 2 violins, 558; *Songs of Our Day*, 662; *Story of a Real Man*, 866, 1097; string quartet #1, 1191; *Suggestions diaboliques*, 135; *Sur le Borysthène*, 558, 583; *Symphonic Song*, 586; symphonie concertante, cello and orchestra, 681, 931; symphony #1 (*Classical*), 143, 298; #2, 415, 1268; #3, 493; #4, 518; #5, 794–795; #6, 839; #7, 946; *The Ugly Duckling*, 275; *War and Peace*, 789, 992, 1244; *Zdravitza*, 704; *1941*, 765
Prolepsis (term), 1481–1482
Proletarian music (term), 1482–1483
*The Proletarian Musician*, 486
Prolixity (term), 1483
Proportional representation (term), 1483
Proust, Marcel, 828
Prout, Ebenezer, 153
Prunières, Henry, 332
Prussak, Eugene, 411
Pseudo-exoticism (term), 1483–1484
Pseudo-music (term), 1484

1566

Puccini, Giacomo. And *Avalon*, 336–337; bolshevized, 399; death, 404; and La Scala reopening, 816; stamp, 1052; centenary, 1058; and Telstar, 1142. Works: *La Bohème*, 1217; *La Fanciulla del West*, 173; *Gianni Schicchi*, 306–307; *Madama Butterfly*, 56–58; *La Rondine*, 281–282; *Suor Angelica*, 306; *Il Tabarro*, 306; *Tosca*, 1, 336–337, 339, 1142, 1457, 1479, 1482, 1501; *Turandot*, 431, 1186

Pulitzer prize, 814, 1002

Punitive music (term), 1484

Purcell, Henry, 806, 1065, 1137, 1190, 1192, 1234

Quaquaversal dispersion (term), 1484

Quarter-tones (term), 1484. For mentions in body of book *see* Microtones

Queen's Hall, London. Destroyed, 732–733

Quinet, Fernand. *Moralités non légendaires*, 513; 3 mouvements symphoniques, 536, 895

Quinet, Marcel. Quintet, winds, 896; *Three Pieces for Orchestra*, 941

Quiroga, Manuel, 677

RAPM. *See* Russian Association of Proletarian Musicians

R.C.A. synthesizer, 1055

Raabe, Peter, 608, 798

Rääts, Jään, 1183

Rabaud, Henri. Director, Paris Conservatory, 331; death, 880. Works: *L'Appel de la Mer*, 388, *La Fille de Roland*, 59; *Marouf*, 240; *Le Miracle des loups*, 402; *Rolande et le mauvais garçon*, 589

Rabe, Folke, 1180

Rachmaninoff, Serge. Glinka prize, 69; signs protest, 72; American debut, 150; leaves Russia, 292; arranged by Respighi, 538; on Chaliapin, 668; jazzed, 681, 1462; increases production, 717; American citizenship, 765; death, 768; spirit messages, 1278; and Socialist Realism, 1491. Works: concerto, piano, #2, 21, 69, 110, 1462; #3, 151–152, 1047, 1146; #4, 450; *Etudes-Tableaux*, 538–539; *Francesca da Rimini*, 87; *Kolokola* (*The Bells*), 232; *The Island of the Dead*, 144–145; *Liturgy of St. John Chrysostom*, 172; *The Miserly Knight*, 87; *Rhapsody on a Theme of Paga-*

*nini*, 594–595, 1444; *Russian Rag*, 298; *The Scythians*, 725–726; *Symphonic Dances*, 725–726; symphony #2, 121; #3, 633; *Vesper Mass*, 251

Radeglia, Vittorio, 294

Radial distribution (term), 1484

Radić, Dušan, 1010

Radica, Reuben, 1138

Radio (NB: after 1929 indexing is selective), 24–25, 63, 107, 143, 155, 330, 331, 336, 360, 366, 367, 368, 380, 392, 422, 440, 495, 508, 549, 554, 566, 570, 592, 611, 646, 652, 655, 677, 688, 694, 700, 703, 705, 710, 725, 830, 878, 926, 947, 1054, 1093, 1102

Radio photography, 661

Radoux, Charles, 200

Radovanović, Vladan, 1268

Raff, Joseph Joachim, 358

Rago, Alexis, 1261

Ragtime (term), 1484–1485

Raichov, Alexander, 1209

Railroad trains. Chopin, 1114; Mozart, 1181

Rainier, Priaulx. *Aequora Lunae*, 1242; concerto, cello, 1186

Rajičić, Stanojlo, 1029

Rameau, Jean Philippe, 63, 963

Ramin, Günther, 1039

Ramos de Pareja, 1499

Ramovs, Primos, 1239

Ran, Shulamith, 1248

Rangström, Ture. And 1922 Salzburg festival, 361. Works: *Gilgamesj*, 948; *Kronburden*, 316; *Middelalderig*, 340

Raphael, Günther, 1050

Raphling, Sam, 1004

Rapp, Siegfried, 1015

Rascher, Sigurd, 596

Rasse, François, 91

Rathaus, Karol. Death, 986. Works: concerto, piano, 756; *Fremde Erde*, 520; string quartet, 674; suite, orch., 514; *Vision dramatique*, 850

Rautavaara, Einojuhani. *Arabescata*, 1162; *Prevariata*, 1051

Ravel, Maurice. And Prix de Rome, 19, 47, 76, 77–78; on piano innovations, 88; on Schoenberg, 220–221, 269; and Russolo, 239; protests ban on German music, 269; on Bartók, 269; on Kodály, 269; refuses Légion d'Honneur, 322; on Obouhov, 395; death, 661; substituted for Wagner, 709; Haussermann elegy, 729; Escher

Rejman, Willem, 1063
Replication (term), 1486
Rescue and escape terms. Discussed, 1486
Respighi, Elsa Olivieri, 640
Respighi, Ottorino. Arranges Rachmaninoff, 538; anti-modernist manifesto, 558; arranges Monteverdi, *Orfeo,* 603; at Mussolini prizegiving, 605; death, 624. Works: *Ballata delle Gnomidi,* 327; *Belfagor,* 371–372; *Belkis, regina di Saba,* 542; *La bella addormentata nel bosco,* 356; *La Boutique fantasque,* 313; *La Campana sommersa,* 462; *Concerto gregoriano,* 352; *Concerto in modo misolidio,* 426; *Feste Romane,* 488, 1194; *La Fiamma,* 580; *Fontane di Roma,* 280; *Impressioni Brasiliane,* 474; *Lucrezia,* 640; *Maria Egiziaca,* 545; *Metamorphoseon,* 517; *Pini di Roma,* 405–406, 1289, 1472; *La Primavera,* 369; *Re Enzo,* 73; *Scherzo veneziano,* 334; *Semirama,* 171; *Sinfonia drammatica,* 249; *Vetrate di chiesa,* 448
Retardation (term), 1486
Reti, Rudolf, 362, 413
Reutter, Hermann. *Die Bauerhochzeit,* 1233; *Die Brücke von San Luis Rey,* 988; concerto, 2 pianos, 916; *Doktor Johannes Faust,* 628; *Don Juan und Faust,* 894; *Der himmlische Vagant,* 922; *Hochzeitslieder,* 1233; *Nausikaa,* 1233; *Odysseus,* 759; *Saul,* 845; *Der Tod des Empedokles,* 1220; *Der verlorene Sohn,* 489–490; *Die Witwe von Ephesus,* 1220
Revel, Harry, 974
*La Revue Musicale,* 332
Revueltas, Silvestre. Death, 718. Works: *La Coronela,* 718; *Homenaje a Federico García Lorca,* 654–655; *Música de Feria,* 735; *El Renacuajo Paseador,* 718; *Sensemayá,* 1219; string quartet, 549
Rey, Cemal, Reşid. *L'Appel,* 935; concerto chromatique, 563; *Karagueuz,* 543; symphony, 850
Reyer, Ernest, 19, 136
Reynolds, Roger. *The Emperor of Ice Cream,* 1198; *Graffiti,* 1200; *Quick Are the Mouths of Earth,* 1267
Rezniček, Emil Nikolaus. Death, 802. Works: *Donna Diana,* 574; *Der Gondoliere des Dogen,* 538; *Holofernes,*

380; *Ritter Blaubart,* 323; *Satuala,* 462; *Spiel oder Ernst?,* 518; *symphonietta (Ironische Symphonie),* 74; *Till Eulenspiegel,* 26
Rheinberger, Josef, 24, 690
Rhené-Baton, 526
Riadis, Emile, 608, 661
Riausov, Sergei, 487
Ricci, Ruggiero, 1166
Riccitelli, Primo, 371
Richter, Hans. Leads first London Symphony Orch. concert, 63; death, 275. Works conducted: Elgar, *Dream of Gerontius,* 9; idem, symphony #1, 131
Řídký, Jaroslav, 1009
Riegger, Wallingford. Death, 1111. Works: *Canon and Fugue,* 756; *March in Memoriam,* 801; suite, flute alone, 549; symphony #3, 854, 876; #4, 1026; *Three Canons,* 533; variations, piano and orch., 971
Riemann, Hugo, 127, 268, 314
Riesco, Carlos, 977
Rieti, Vittorio. *Barabau,* 423; concerto, wind quintet and orch., 393; *Concerto du Loup,* 758; *Don Perlimpin,* 935; *Noah's Ark,* 413; *The Pet Shop,* 1047; serenata, 552; sonata, flute, oboe, bassoon and piano, 418; symphony #4 (*Sinfonia Tripartita*), 793–794
*The Right to Happiness,* 1102
Riisager, Knudaage. *Benzin,* 522; concertino, saxophone, 692; concerto, trumpet and strings, 674; concerto, violin, 923; *Étude,* 846; *Phoenix,* 816; *Primavera,* 601; *Qarrtsiluni,* 689, 873; *Slaraffenland,* 635; *Sinfonia serena,* 942; sonata, piano, 585; *Summer Rhapsody,* 780; *Susanne,* 887; symphony #1, 436; #2, 449; #3, 615; #4, 719; #5, 902; *T-DOXC,* 459; *Tivoli-Tivoli,* 771
Riley, Terry, 1267
Rimsky-Korsakov, Andrei, 164
Rimsky-Korsakov, Georgy, 25, 372, 1466
Rimsky-Korsakov, Nikolai. On Scriabin, 27; judges Glinka prizes, 69; signs protest, 72; fired from conservatory, 74; appeal for unionization, 82; asked to rejoin conservatory, 85; *Chronicle of My Musical Life,* 95; conducts at Diaghilev concert, 110; and Richard Strauss, 111; and Stra-

Rolón, José, 502
Romani, Romano, 252
Romberg, Sigmund. Death, 924. Works:
*Blossom Time*, 346; *Blue Paradise*,
256; *Desert Song*, 441; *May Wine*,
615; *Maytime*, 288; *The Midnight
Girl*, 235; *My Maryland*, 459–460;
*The New Moon*, 478; *The Rose of
Stamboul*, 354; *The Student Prince*,
404; *Up in Central Park*, 795
Rome. Accademia di Santa Cecilia, 315
Rome. Colosseum, 923
Ronnefeld, Peter, 1125
Roos, Robert de. Concerto, piano, 818;
*Five Etudes*, 693
Roosevelt, Eleanor, 688, 850; de-
nounced as Communist, 1403
Roosevelt, Franklin Delano, 679, 682,
737, 816, 827
Roosevelt, Theodore, 46, 88, 95, 682,
1127
Rootham, Cyril, 666. Works: symphony
#2, 666; *The Two Sisters*, 353
Ropartz, Guy. Restores Magnard, *Guer-
cœur*, 530; death, 1001. Works: *Le
Pays*, 197; symphony #3, 97; #5,
823
Rorem, Ned. On Poulenc, 1152. Works:
*A Childhood Miracle*, 994; *Eagles*,
1074; *Lions*, 1210; *Miss Julie*, 1210;
*The Robbers*, 1047; symphony #2,
1014; #3, 1063
Rosbaud, Hans. Co-conducts Boulez,
1056; conducts Penderecki, 1098
Rose, Billy, 793
Roselius, Ludwig. *Godiva*, 571; *Gudrun*,
695
Rosen, Jerome, 1258
Rosenberg, Hilding. *Babels Torn*, 1253;
concerto, strings, 835; *Kaspers Fettisdag*, 971; *Joseph and his Brethren*,
849; *Lycksalighetens*, 795; *Porträttet*,
1006; *Resan till Amerika*, 556; string
quartet #6, 1010; #8, 1065; symphonie concertante, 649, 977; symphony #6, 961; *De två Kungadöttrarna*, 717–718
Rosenthal, Manuel. Dismissed, 924.
Works: *Bootleggers*, 566; *Hop! Signor*, 546; *Jeanne d'Arc*, 673; *Musique de Table*, 821; *Rayon de
soieries*, 510; *Saint Francis d'Assisi*,
791; sonatina, 2 violins and piano,
491; symphony, 894, 1066
Rosenthal, Moriz, 820

Roslavetz, Nicolas, 461; death, 788
Ross, Jerry. *Damn Yankees*, 993; *Pajama Game*, 975
Rossellini, Renzo. *L'Avventuriere*, 1254;
*La Guerra*, 1005; *Uno Sguardo dal
ponte*, 1110; *Ut Unum Sint*, 1169;
*Il Vortice*, 1042
Rossini, Gioacchino, 107, 313, 518, 632,
644, 713, 762, 775, 816, 1364
Rostropovich, Mstislav. Works played:
Britten, *Cello Symphony*, 1175; Foss,
concerto, 1235; Khrennikov, concerto,
1178; Knipper, concerto-monologue,
1175; Pipkov, concerto-symphony,
1177; Piston, variations, 1234; Pro-
kofiev, concertino, 1081; idem, con-
certo, 681; idem, symphonie concer-
tante, 931; Sauguet, concerto, 1175;
Shostakovich, concerto #1, 1073;
#2, 1228; Tchaikovsky (B.), con-
certo, 1175; Tishchenko, concerto,
1213
Rota, Nino, 1075
Rotation (term), 1487
Rothwell, Walter, 316
Rottenberg, Ludwig, 260
Rouget de l'Isle, Claude Joseph, 7
Rousseau, Henri, 1472
Rousseau, Marcel Samuel. *See* Samuel-
Rousseau
Rousseau, Robert, 698
Rousseau, Samuel-Alexandre, 159, 995
Roussel, Albert. Grades Satie, 126;
death, 653; preferred to Ravel, 661.
Works: *Aeneas*, 608; *Bacchus et
Ariane*, 531; concertino, cello, 639;
concerto, piano, 473; *Danton*, 629;
*Divertissement*, 377; *L'Éventail de
Jeanne*, 489; *Évocations*, 202; *Le
Festin de l'Araignée*, 221; *Joueurs de
Flûte*, 418; *La Naissance de la Lyre*,
416; *Padmâvatî*, 373–374; *Petite
Suite*, 504; *Pour une Fête de
Printemps*, 347–348; *Psalm, 80*, 536;
*14 Juillet*, 629; *Résurrection*, 62;
string quartet, 558; *Suite en Fa*,
444, 650, 1052; symphony #1
(*Poème de la Forêt*), 124; #2, 347,
354, 394; #3, 516; #4, 611, 626; *Le
Testament de la Tante Caroline*, 633–
634; trio, flute, viola and cello, 513
Rowley, Alec, 1040
Rozhdestvensky, Gennady, 1234
Rozkošný, Josef Richard, 86
Rózsa, Miklós. Concerto, piano, 1236;
concerto, violin, 1003; *Notturno un-*

*gherese*, 1177; *Variations on a Hungarian Peasant Song*, 775

Rózycki, Ludomir. *Beatrix Cenci*, 446; *Boleslaw Smialy*, 139; *Casanova*, 372; *Eros und Psyche*, 280; *Lili Spiewać*, 563; *Meduza*, 212; *Mlyn diabelski*, 526; *Pan Twardowski*, 340

Rubbra, Edmund. Festival of Music for the People, 691. Works: symphony #1, 644; #2, 683; #3, 724; #4, 758–759; #5, 868; #6, 986; #7, 1036

Rubinstein, Anton, 499

Rubinstein, Artur, 1264

Rubinstein, Ida. Death, 1094. Works danced or produced: Auric, *Les Enchantements d'Alcine*, 494; Debussy, *Le Martyre de Saint-Sébastien*, 181, 185–186; Honegger, *Amphion*, 534; idem, *Jeanne d'Arc au Bûcher*, 670; idem, *Sémiramis*, 588; Ibert, *Diane de Poitiers*, 587; Ravel, *Boléro*, 481; Stravinsky, *Le Baisier de la Fée*, 482; idem, *Perséphone*, 587

Rudhyar, Dane. Casts Scriabin's horoscope, 254; *The Astrology of Personality*, 635. Works: *Poèmes ironiques*, 282; *Vision végétale*, 282

Rudolf, Max, 1107

Rudzinski, Zbigniew, 1246

Ruera, Josep M., 624

Ruggles, Carl. And expressionism, 1447. Works: *Angels*, 418–419; *Men and Mountains*, 405, 460, 532; *Sun-Treader*, 544, 626

Runolfsson, Karl Otto, 941

Rupnik, Ivan, 844

Russian Association of Proletarian Musicians, 486, 548, 562, 1353–1357, 1482, 1490

Russian Music Publishing House, 142–143

Russian Orthodox Church. Condemns worldliness in church music, 859

Russian Symphony Orchestra, 55

Russolo, Luigi. Manifesto, 218; introduces *intonarumore*, 225; Paris concert, 344; death, 828; as "bruiteur," 1433; and Futurism, 1449; notation, 1450; as Urbanist, 1500; Futurist manifesto, 1298–1302. Work: *Networks of Noises*, 238

Ruyneman, Daniel. *Amphitryon Overture*, 856; concerto, violin, 766; *Hieroglyphs*, 307; *De Roep*, 307; sonata, chorus, 539; *Symphonie 1953*, 1006

Rytel, Piotr, 500

Rzewski, Frederick, 1164

Sabaneyev, Leonid, 275–276

Sabata, Victor de, 282

Sabbatini, Niccolo, 158

Sabine, Wallace, 9

Sacher, Paul. Works conducted: Bartók, *Divertimento*, 715; idem, *Music for Strings, Percussion and Celesta*, 638; Beck, *Oratorio über . . . Angelus Silesius*, 590; idem, symphony #5, 514; Burkhard, *Das Jahr*, 748; idem, *Genug ist nicht Genug*, 714; idem, *Das Gesicht Jesajas*, 621; Honegger, *Cantate de Noël*, 969; idem, *Danse des Morts*, 708; idem, *Jeanne d'Arc au Bûcher*, 670; idem, symphony #2, 753; #4 (*Deliciae Basilienses*), 827; Krenek, *Kette, Kreis und Spiegel*, 1041; Malipiero, symphony #6, 869; Martin, *Ballade*, 743; idem, *Petite Symphonie Concertante*, 817; Martinu, concerto da camera, 747; idem, double concerto, 707; idem, *Epic of Gilgamesh*, 1041; idem, *Greek Passion*, 1116; idem, *Toccata e due Canzoni*, 827; Mihalovici, *Sinfonia giocosa*, 927; Stravinsky, concerto, 827; idem, *A Sermon, a Narrative, and a Prayer*, 1131

Sachs, Curt, 1059

Sachs, Melchior, 1328

Sachs, Nelly, 1252

Sadai, Yitzhak. *Aria da capo*, 1247; *Impressions d'un choral*, 1182; *Testimonium*, 1263

Saeverud, Harald. Conducts, 214. Works: concerto, piano, 959; *Galdreslätten*, 835; *Peer Gynt*, 849; symphony #5, 896; #6 (*Dolorosa*), 769; symphony, *Minnesota*, 1056

St. Cyr, Johnny, 437

St. Petersburg. Conservatory, 72, 74, 85, 300

St. Petersburg. Opera, 319

Saint-Saëns, Camille. Prix de Rome, 19; on *Motu Proprio*, 51; Oxford degree, 112; Légion d'Honneur, 215; denounces German art, 246; Athens festival, 328; death, 349; widow dies, 888; stamp, 946. Works: *Les Barbares*, 20; *Caprice andalou*, 68; *Carnaval des animaux*, 353, 1207; concerto, cello, #2, 71; concerto, piano, #4, 139; *Déjanire*, 178; *Hail, Cali-*

444; *Habeyssée,* 831; mass, 1051; *Oriane et le Prince d'Amour,* 662; *Le Palais hanté,* 70; *Le Petit elfe Ferme-l'Œil,* 384; *Psalm XLVII,* 98; *Rondo burlesque,* 514; *Sémiramis,* 10; *Sonate libre en deux parties enchaînées,* 377; *Suite en rocaille,* 649; *Suite sans esprit de suite,* 663; symphonie concertante, 556; symphony #2, 1051; *Tragédie de Salomé,* 115–116, 201
Schnabel, Arthur. Death, 920. Works: *Piano Pieces in Seven Parts,* 735; *Rhapsody,* 998; sonata, piano, 418; symphony #1, 824
Schnorrenberg, Roberto, 961
Schoeck, Othmar. Death, 1025. Works: concerto, horn and strings, 907; *Don Ranudo de Colibrados,* 311; *Festlicher Hymnus,* 914; *Gaselen,* 398; *Hafislieder,* 377; *Penthesilea,* 443; *Das Schloss Dürande,* 768; *Venus,* 357; *Vom Fischer un seiner Fru,* 515; *Das Wandbild,* 336; *William Ratcliffe Overture,* 125–126
Schoemaker, Maurice, 415–416, 513
Schoenberg, Arnold. Paintings exhibited, 169; and Mahler, 184; *Harmonielehre,* 190, 1430; Russian tour, 214; conducts Academic Society for Literature and Music concert, 219–220; and Ravel, 220–221, 269; London visit, 233; and *Verein für musikalische Privataufführungen,* 304, 1307–1311; on *Mutterakkord,* 407; and *Wozzeck,* 424; in Berg motto, 450; theme varied by Ullman, 450; dedicatee, Berg, *Drei Orchesterstücke,* 508; at 1932 ISCM festival, Vienna, 552; dismissed as non-Aryan, 567; returns to Judaism, 570; arrives in U.S., 574; U.S. debut, 583; attacked in *Die Musik,* 622; on Gershwin, 651; in "Entartete Musik," 670; U.S. citizen, 732; on Zemlinsky, 750; and Mann, 863–864; greets Congress of Dodecaphonic Music, 876; quoted by Seiber, 876; Catunda homage, 895; death, 919; ISCM concert, 941; and Downes, 999; amanuensis, 1005; and 1956 Warsaw Autumn, 1016; and Hellenic Week of Contemporary Music, 1216; on anarchy, 1427; and dilapidation of tonality, 1437; and Klein, 1439; etiology, 1445; and expressionism, 1447; and harmonic integration, 1459; and organized sound, 1473; Satie as prolepsor, 1482; homologophobe, 1483; and serialism, 1489; symbolic analysis 1494. Works: Bach arrangements, 366; *Begleitungsmusik zu einer Lichtspielszene,* 517, 1497; *Das Buch der hängenden Gärten,* 376; chamber symphony #1, 104, 219, 790, 1269; #2, 724; concerto, piano, 780, 977; concerto, violin, 723–724, 959; *Drei Satiren,* 426; *Erwartung,* 394, 941, 1468; *Four Songs,* op. 22, 1160; *Friede auf Erden,* 107, 691; *Fünf Orchesterstücke,* 206–208, 233, 941, 1086, 1462; *Die glückliche Hand,* 400, 1468, 1495; *Gurrelieder,* 216, 790; *Die Jakobsleiter,* 1118; *Kammersymphonie, see* chamber symphony; *Klavierstücke* op. 11, 140, 141, 148; *Moses und Aron,* 972, 1032, 1206; *Ode to Napoleon Buonaparte,* 792, 819; *Pelleas und Melisande,* 70, 214, 790; *Pierrot Lunaire,* 210–211, 872; Prelude, *Genesis* suite, 806; quintet, winds, 434; *Sechs kleine Klavierstücke,* 757, 876; *Serenade,* 396, 418, 1438; string quartet (1897), 930; string quartet #1, 104; #2, 134–135, 362, 606, 1473; #3, 460; string trio, 833; suite, piano, 876; suite, strings, 606, 790; *A Survivor from Warsaw,* 862, 1204; *Theme and Variations,* orch., op. 43b, 789–790; three pieces, chamber orch., 1036; variations, orch., op. 31, 482–483, 609, 941, 1126, 1137, 1443; *Verklärte Nacht,* 29, 343, 790; *Vielseitigkeit,* 426; *Von Heute auf Morgen,* 503. LETTER to Nicolas Slonimsky on the 12-tone method, 1315–1316
"Schoenberg sigh," 1443
Schola Cantorum, Paris, 9
Scholes, Percy A., 480, 1053
Schönbach, Dieter. *AMB,* 1280; *Canticum Psalmi Resurrectionis,* 1066; *Die Geschichte von einem Feuer,* 1261; *Kammermusik 1960,* 1098; *Lyric Songs,* 1182
Schrammel, Johann, 932
Schrecker, Franz. *See* Schreker, Franz
Schreker, Franz. Conducts Schoenberg, *Guerrelieder,* 216; dismissed by the Nazis, 567; death, 583–584; in "Entartete Musik," 670. Works: *Der ferne Klang,* 205–206; *Die Gezeichneten,* 298; *Irrelohe,* 388; *Der Schatzgräber,*

1491; and displaced tonality, 1438.
Works: *Age of Gold*, 516; *Bolt*, 529;
concerto, cello, #1, 1072–1073; #2,
1228; concerto, piano, #1, 573,
1071; #2, 1028; concerto, violin,
1000; *The Execution of Stepan
Razin*, 1194; *Katerina Ismailova*, 1151
(*see also* Lady Macbeth. . . .);
*Lady Macbeth of the District of
Mzensk*, 579–580, 600, 618–619,
1469, 1479 (*see also* Katerina Ismailova); *Leningrad*, 759; *The Limpid Stream*, 604; *Moskva Tcheryomushki*, 1058–1059; *The Nose*, 502;
quintet, piano and strings, 722; *Song
of the Forests*, 883; suite, jazz orch.,
681; symphony #1, 432; #2 (*To
October*), 461, 1482; #3 (*May
First*), 503; #4, 1129; #5, 657–
658; #6, 701–702; #7, 749, 1490;
#8, 774–775; #9, 805; #10, 969,
1407; #11 (*1905*), 1037–1038; #12,
1124–1125; #13, 1150–1151; *Young
Guard*, 866
Shostakovich, Maxim, 1028, 1228
Sibelius, Jean. Teacher, 90; visits U.S.,
242; doctorate, Yale, 242; dedicatee,
Bax symphony #5, 578; in time cap-
sule, 677; appeals to U.S. against
Soviet invasion, 737; stamp, 808; and
Downes, 999; death, 1035; and the
Neo-Romantics, 1472. Works: *Chris-
tian II*, 242; concerto, violin, 56; *Fin-
landia*, 7, 677; *Oceanides*, 242, 261;
*Origin of Fire*, 661; overture, A minor,
28; *Pohjola's Daughter*, 99, 242;
*Scaramouche*, 357; *Suomi*, 7, 677;
*The Swan of Tuonela*, 242, 1035;
symphony #2, 28, 938; #3, 113–
114; #4, 180; #5, 261; #6, 369;
#7, 387–388; *Tapiola*, 442–443;
*Valse Triste*, 61
Siccardi, Honorio, 693
Sicilianos, Yorgo. Concerto, orchestra,
986; *Hercules furens*, 1092; *Perspec-
tives*, 1246; *The Revelation of the
Fifth Seal*, 937; *Stasimon B*, 1202;
symphony #1, 1043; *Synthesis*, 1150
Siegmeister, Elie. *I Have a Dream*,
1270; *Ozark Set*, 791, 801; *The
Plough and the Stars*, 1276–1277;
*Prairie Legend*, 827; symphony #1,
841; *Western Suite*, 807
Siena pianoforte, 843–844
Sigtenhorst-Meyer, Bernhard van den,
568

Sigurbjörnsson, Thorkell, 1160
Sigward, Botho, 255
Sikorski, Tomas, 1225
Silence. Discussed, 1490
Siliézar, Felipe, 1065
Siloti, Alexander. Signs protest, 72; ap-
peal to unionize Russian musicians,
82; cancels Bach performance, 260;
death, 808. Works conducted: Liadov,
*From the Apocalypse*, 214; idem,
*Kikimora*, 153; Rachmaninoff, piano
concerto #2, 21; Roger-Ducasse,
*Orphée*, 234; Stravinsky, *Scherzo
fantasque*, 138; Szymanowski, sym-
phony #3, 277
Silva, Luigi, 752
Silva, Oscar da, 19
Silva, Silvano da, 971
Silver, Charles, 352
Silvestri, Luigi, 409
Silvestrov, Vladimir, 1442
Simeon, Omer, 437
Simo, Manuel, 1189
Simon, Emil, 1151
Simonovic, Konstantin, 1157
Simpson, Robert, 44
Sinding, Christian. Award, 262; death,
744. Works: *Der heilige Berg*, 238;
symphony #2, 107; #3, 336; #4
(*Winter and War*), 617
Singer, André, 757
Singultation (term), 1490
Sinigaglia, Leone. *Danze piemontese*,
76; *Piemonte*, 156
Širola, Božidar, 458
Sitson, Ma. *See* Ma-Sa-Tsung
Sitwell, Edith, 374
Sitwell, Osbert, 536–537
Sitwell, Sacheverell, 500
Sitzplatz, Siegfried, 832
*Les Six*, 322, 375, 757
Skalkottas, Nikos, 880, 978
Skilton, Charles Stanford. *The Sun
Bride*, 508; *Two Indian Dances*, 273
Sklavos, George. *Kassiani*, 1074; *Kyra
Frossini*, 339; *Lestenitza*, 831
Skolovsky, Zadel, 890, 976
Škroup, František, 1131
Skrowaczewski, Stanislaw. And 1956
Warsaw Autumn, 1016; and Caracas
festival, 1218, 1219. Work: *Das
hohe Lied*, 918
Skull solo, 1148, 1498
Slavenski, Josip, 1002. Works: *Bal-
kanofonia*, 487–488; *Oriental Sym-
phony*, 589–590

Slavický, Klement, 386
Slavik, Josef, 962
Sledzinski, Stefan. Appeal for peace, 1387–1388
Slezak, Leo, 817
Slonimsky, Nicolas. And Obouhov, 395, 433; Paris concerts of American music, (1931) 532–533; discovers *Grossmutterakkord*, 664; and microtones, 1466. Works conducted: Castillo, *La Doncella Ixquic*, 747; Caturla, *Bembé*, 533; Chávez, *Energía*, 533; Cowell, *Synchrony*, 532; Gershwin, *Cuban Overture*, 552; Harris, *Overture from the Gayety and Sadness of the American Scene*, 599; Ives, *Three Places in New England*, 523, 532, 1477; Riegger, *Three Canons*, 533; Ruggles, *Men and Mountains*, 532; idem, *Sun-Treader*, 544; Salzedo, *Préambule et Jeux*, 533; Sanjuán, *Sones de Castilla*, 533; Varèse, *Arcana*, 1333; idem, *Ecuatorial*, 587; idem, *Intégrales*, 533; idem, *Ionisation*, 563; Weiss, *American Life*, 532. Writings: *Lexicon of Musical Invective*, 1488; *Music Since 1900*, 656, 1474; *Thesaurus of Scales and Melodic Patterns*, 1440, 1474, 1478, 1488. Works: *The Anatomy of Melancholy*, 1427; *My Toy Balloon*, 755; *Studies in Black and White*, 1479; suite, 742. Mentioned at Eisler hearings, 1399
Slonimsky, Sergei. And dodecaphony, 1442. Works: *Antiphones*, 1426; *Concerto buffo*, 1217, 1454; symphony, 1131; *Virineia*, 1245
Smareglia, Antonio. *Abisso*, 234; *Oceana*, 43
Smetana, Bedřich, 386, 393, 584, 786, 1497
Smit, Leo, 1022
Smith, Bessie. *Downhearted Blues*, 369; 655; and Schuller, 1229
Smith, Carleton Sprague, 590
Smith, David Stanley, 575
Smith, Julia, 687
Smith, Kate, 680
Smith, Pine Top, 683
Smith, William O., 1181
Smith-Brindle, Reginald, 1091
Smyth, Ethel. Arrest, 204; death, 785. Works: *The Boatswain's Mate*, 264; concerto, violin, horn and orch., 449; *Entente Cordiale*, 438; *Fête galante*,

374; *March of the Women*, 179; *Odelette*, 362; *Der Wald*, 30; *The Wreckers*, 96
Socialist realism (term), 1490–1491
Sociedad Nacional de Música (Buenos Aires), 259
Sociedad Nacional de Música (Madrid), 250
Société des Compositeurs, 365
Société Française de Musicologie, 281
Société Indépendante de Musique, 100, 161, 182
Société Nationale de Musique, 100
Society for the Preservation and Encouragement of Barbershop Quartet Singing in America. *See* SPEBSQSA
Society for Private Performances, Vienna, 1307–1311
Society for the Promotion of Proletarian Music, Production Collective, 411, 487
Society of Quarter-Tone Music, 372
Society of Recorder Players, 655
Society of Rumanian Composers, 401
Society of St. Gregory, 357
Sodero, Cesare, 511
Sokola, Miloš, 1051
Solares, Enrique, 1189
Soler, José, 1189
Solesmes, France. Saint-Pierre (Benedictine Abbey), 17, 51, 54, 356
Solomon, Isler, 979
Soltys, Mieczyslaw, 389
Somers, Harry. *The House of Atreus*, 1174; *Louis Riel*, 1245; *Lyric*, 1113, 1188; *Stereophony for Orchestra*, 1155; suite, harp and chamber orch., 1208
Sommer, Hans, 61
Sonic exuviation (term), 1491
Sonic organization (term), 1491
Sonneck, Oscar, 37, 248
Sonninen, Ahti, 1010
Sonntag, Gottfried, 636
Sonzogno, Giulio Cesare, 871
Sorabji, Kaikhosru, 519–520, 1496
Soro, Enrique, 987
Soto, Felipe, 838
Soulima-Stravinsky, Sviatoslav, 614
Sound film (early history), 460, 477, 479
Souris, André. *Hommage à Babeuf*, 649; *Quelques Airs de Clarisse Juranville*, 626; *Rengaines*, 692–693
Sousa, John Philip. Death, 544; in time capsule, 677; stamp, 712. Works: *The*

1579

1071; Herbert, 713; Indy, 913; Janáček, 962; Jeanty, 1098; Kalinnikov, 921; Kienzl, 922; Kodály, 968; Kovařovic, 1131; Kreutzer, 879; Lanner, 911; Laredo, 1092; Laub, 1028; Leoncavallo, 1052; Liadov, 998; Lincke, 1014; Lisinsky, 988; Liszt, 968, 1123; Lortzing, 911; MacDowell, 713; Mahler, 1091; Mascagni, 1172; Massenet, 755; Méhul, 1159; Melba, 1124; Mendelssohn, 1071; Millöcker, 886; Minkus, 914; Mokranjać, 1040; Moniuszko, 925; Mosonyi, 968; Mozart, 356, 1003, 1004, 1008, 1016; Mussorgsky, 919; Mysliveček, 1008; Nägeli, 636; Nedbal, 1093; Nevin, 714; Nordraak, 754; Novák, 1028; Ostrčil, 1028, 1093; Oswald, 936; Paderewski, 1096; Pergolesi, 656; Petrauskas, 1173; Pijper, 974; Porumbescu, 969; Praetorius, 1142; Puccini, 1052; Rameau, 963; Ramin, 1039; Ravel, 1011; Rheinberger, 690–691; Rimsky-Korsakov, 786, 919; Rossini, 763, 775; Saint-Saëns, 946, Schrammel, 932; Schubert, 356, 1013; Schumann, 1013; Schweitzer, 989; Ševčík, 934; Sibelius, 808; Škroup, 1131; Slavík, 962; Smetana, 584, 786, 914; Soto, 839; Sousa, 712; Spohr, 1071; Spontini, 656; Stamic, 1028; Stasov, 1035; Strauss, J., 356, 880; Strauss, R., 982; Tchaikovsky, 919, 1069; Toscanini, 1236; Verdi, 925, 1166, 1167; Vieuxtemps, 1112; Wagner, 769, 1159, 1260; Weiner, 1165; Wieniawski, 949; Wolf, 356, 953; Ysaÿe, 1054; Zelter, 948; Ziehrer, 846; Zwissig, 976

Stanford, Charles Villiers. Death, 388. Works: *The Critic*, 262; *Much Ado about Nothing*, 18; *Ode to Discord*, 147; *The Traveling Companion*, 411–412

Starer, Robert. Concerto, viola, strings and percussion, 1068; *The Intruder*, 1020; symphony #2, 957

Starkey, Richard. *See* Starr, Ringo

Starokadomsky, Mikhail. Concerto, orch., 649; concerto grosso, 603

Star Opera Company, N.Y., 317

Starr, Ringo, 1144–1145, 1487

*Star-Spangled Banner*, 462, 506, 527, 779, 1230

Stasov, Vladimir, 96, 1035

Statham, Heathcote, 631

Static music (term), 1492

Statkowski, Roman, 65

Steber, Eleanor, 851

Steegan, Botho von, 1084

Stefansson, Fjölnir, 1118

Steffens, Walter, 1234

Stein, Erwin, 1439

Stein, Fritz, 155, 575

Stein, Gertrude, 581, 834

Stein, Richard H., 146, 758, 1466

Steinberg, Maximilian, 126, 576

Steinberg, William. Works conducted: Ben-Haim, *Fanfare to Israel*, 1242; Copland, *Billy the Kid*, 678; Creston, saxophone concerto, 779; Gerhard, symphony #4, 1252; Piston, violin concerto #2, 1097; Schuman, *Philharmonic Fanfare*, 1207; Sessions, symphony #8, 1258; Toch, piano concerto #2, 600

Steinert, Alexander, 522

Steinway Piano Company, 966

Stepanian, Aro, 671

Stepanov, Lev, 684

Stephan, Rudi, 257, 329

Stephen Foster Society, 499

Stereophony, 710, 721

Stern, Isaac. Works played: Bernstein, *Serenade*, 982; Mendelssohn, concerto, 1242; Schuman, concerto, 889

Sternberg, Erich Walter. String quartet #1, 977; *Twelve Tribes of Israel*, 752

Steuermann, Eduard, 780

Stevens, Halsey. Symphony #1, 812; *Triskelion*, 971–972

Stevenson, Adlai, 1146

Stevenson, Ronald, 1172

Stewart, Reginald, 811

Stiedry, Fritz, 563, 724

Still, William Grant. *Afro-American Symphony*, 538; *And They Lynched Him on a Tree*, 715; *Darker America*, 441; *From the Black Belt*, 451; *La Guiablesse*, 566; *Highway No. 1, U.S.A.*, 1158; *In Memoriam: The Colored Soldiers Who Died for Democracy*, 778; *Lenox Avenue*, 645; *Poem for Orchestra*, 793; *Sahdji*, 531; *The Troubled Island*, 871

Stimmer, Karl, 513

Stochastic composition (term), 1492

Stock, Frederick. Works conducted: Bloch, *Helvetia*, 543; Carpenter, *Krazy Kat*, 350; idem, *Sea-Drift*, 575;

Casella, symphony #3, 731; Ganz, piano concerto, 729; Kodály, concerto for orchestra, 728; Oldberg, symphony #3, 450; Sowerby, symphony #1, 356; #3, 730; Walton, *Scapino*, 732. Works: cello concerto, 488; *Festival Fanfare*, 718; *Rhapsodic Fantasy*, 420

Stockhausen, Karlheinz. And controlled improvisation, 1435; notation, 1452; and open form composition, 1473; as planarian, 1475; and verbalization, 1500. Works: *Carré*, 1100; *Der Gesang der Jünglinge*, 1009, 1459; *Gruppen*, 1062; *Hymnen*, 1250–1251; *Klavierstück*, 1164; *Kontakte*, 1087; *Kontra-Punkte*, 959, 1010; *Plus-Minus*, 1267; *Schlagfiguren und Quantitäten*, 1165; *Studie I-II*, magnetic tape, 984; *Telemusik*, 1265; *Zeitmässe*, 1051; *Zyklus*, 1165

Stockhoff, Walter, 405

Stockholm. Konsertfoerening, 38

Stockholm. Royal Opera, 1238–1239

Stoessel, Albert, 440, 640, 769

Stojanović, Petar, 82, 604

Stokowski, Leopold. Philadelphia Orchestra debut, 209; in *Fantasia*, 721; and All-American Youth Orch., 733; and American Symphony Orch., 1147. Works conducted: Antheil, symphony #4, 781; Carrillo, concertino, 449; idem, *Horizontes*, 926; idem, *Sonido* 13, 523; Chávez, *Caballos de Vapor*, 547; Cowell, symphony #12, 1082; idem, *Tales of the Countryside*, 733; Fuleihan, Thereminovox concerto, 797; Griffes, *The White Peacock*, 313; Hovhaness, *Meditation on Zeami*, 1187; Ives, symphony #4, 1199; McDonald, symphony #2, 610; Malipiero, *Pause del Silenzio*, 451; Martinu, piano concerto #4, 1016; Ornstein, piano concerto #2, 408; Panufnik, *Epitaph for the Victims of Katyn*, 1272; Rachmaninoff, piano concerto #4, 450; idem, *Rhapsody on a Theme by Paganini*, 594; idem, symphony #3, 633; Schoenberg, piano concerto, 780; idem, violin concerto, 723; Scott, piano concerto, 333; Siegmeister, *Prairie Legend*, 827; idem, symphony #1, 841; Stravinsky, *Le Sacre du Printemps*, 721; does not conduct Stravinsky, *Zvezdoliki*, 693–694; con-

ducts Varèse, *Amériques*, 430; idem, *Arcana*, 452; Weigl, symphony #5, 1271

Stoll, Peter, 504

Stolz, Robert. *Frühjahrs-Parade*, 1176; *Trauminsel*, 1142; *Zwei Herzen in 3/4 Takt*, 572

Stradivari, Antonio, 660

Stradivarius violin. Buried, 860; crashes, 882, 964

Straesser, Joep. *Musique pour l'homme*, 1273; *22 Pages*, 1226

Straight, Williard, 1242

Strang, Gerald, 1189

Strang, Walter, 594

Stransky, Joseph. Conductor, N.Y. Philharmonic, 182. Works conducted: Schoenberg, Bach arrangements, 366; Varèse, *Bourgogne*, 173

Strategy and tactics (terms), 1492

Straus, Oskar, 970. Works: *The Chocolate Soldier*, 130; *The First Waltz*, 891; *Hugdietrichs Brautfahrt*, 89; *Die lustigen Nibelungen*, 67; *Mariette*, 478; *Das Tal der Liebe*, 154; *Der tapfere Soldat*, 130; *Ein Walzertraum*, 106

Strauss, Franz, 77

Strauss, Johann, Jr., 356, 420, 644, 698, 880, 1082

Strauss, Richard. Visits U.S., 59; Alsace-Lorraine festival, 76; accused of plagiarism, 83, 142; and Rimsky-Korsakov, 111; Noren quotes, 112; and Mahler, 168; and Schoenberg, 207; *Légion d'Honneur*, 242; removed from London program, 244; Monteux refuses to conduct, 271; Salzburg festival, 1922, 360; president, Reichsmusikkammer, 575; receives Hitler's and Goebbels' pictures, 590; resigns Reichsmusikkammer post, 608; and International Society for Promoting Cooperation among Composers, 645–646; on Ravel, 661; as precursor of Stravinsky, 684; 80th birthday, 786; denazified, 857; death, 880; and Mengelberg, 909; stamp, 982; memorial, 1140; centenary, 1183; and neo-romanticism, 1472; sensory impact, 1488; and translocation, 1499. Works: *Die ägyptische Helena*, 473; *Alpensinfonie*, 258, 1496; *Also Sprach Zarathustra*, 1439, 1478; *Arabella*, 570; *Ariadne auf Naxos*, 211, 760, 786; *Aus Italien*, 115; *Le bourgeois*

certo, 830; Mennin, symphony #7, 1174; Piston, *Symphonic Prelude*, 1112; Rochberg, symphony #2, 1060
Szendrei, Aladar, 324
Szeryng, Henryk, 1153
Szigeti, Josef. Works played: Bartók, *Contrasts*, 684; Bloch, *Baal Shem*, 741; idem, violin concerto, 683; Casella, violin concerto, 478
Szokolay, Sándor. *Hamlet*, 1271; *Vérnász*, 1190
Szulc, Jósef Zygmunt, 232
Szymanowski, Karol. Death, 641; and 1956 Warsaw Autumn, 1016. Works: *Concert Overture*, 88; concerto, violin, #1, 393–394; #2, 573, 626; *Hafis Songs*, 377; *Hagith*, 357; *Harnasie*, 605; *Król Roger*, 434, 872; *Polish Songs*, chorus, 536; *Stabat Mater*, 693; string quartet, 418; symphonie concertante, 554, 649; symphony #1, 143; #2, 180; #3, 277, 1071; #4, 554, 1071; *Tantris le bouffon*, 361; 12 etudes, 398

Taboos. Discussed, 1448
Tagliaferro, Magda, 524
Tailleferre, Germaine. *Nouveaux jeunes* program, 292; as one of *Les Six*, 322; and *La Jeune France*, 628. Works: *Chansons Françaises*, 513; concerto, piano, 414; *Il était un petit Navire*, 908; *Les Mariés de la Tour Eiffel*, 344; *Paris-Magie*, 875
Takagi, Toroko, 864
Takahashi, Yuji, 1275
Takata, Shin-Ichi, 864
Takemitsu, Toru. *Asterism*, 1274–1275; *Corona for Pianists*, 1165; *The Dorian Horizon*, 1269; *November Steps*, 1250
Taktakishvili, Otar, 1004
Tal, Josef. Concerto, piano #2, 1119; concerto, viola, 977; *The Death of Moses*, 1244; *Exodus*, 844; sonata, violin, 941
Tallis, Thomas, 1281
Talma, Louise, 1131
Tamkin, David, 922
Tamony, Peter, 1323
Taneyev, Sergei. Glinka prize, 69; signs protest, 72; death, 255. Works: symphony, 69; *Upon Reading the Psalms*, 253
Tanglewood, 716
Tango forbidden, 291
Tansman, Alexandre. *Adam and Eve*,

806; concerto, piano, #1, 433; #2, 464–465; *Danse de la Sorcière*, 435; *Impressions of a Big City*, 526; *Rapsodie Polonaise*, 742; *Ricercari*, 886; *Le Rossignol de Boboli*, 1206; *Le Serment*, 991; *Sinfonia Piccola*, 977; *Sonatine transatlantique*, 526; string quartet #5, 757; symphony #1, 450; #5, 765; #7, 840; *Le Voyage de Magellan*, 925
Taranov, Gleb, 1131
Tardieu, Jean, 1181
Tardos Béla, 1231
Tarnopolsky, Vladimir, 487
Tárrega, Francisco, 154
Tartini, Giuseppe, 751, 933, 1066
Tashkent. National Opera House, 480
Tate, Phyllis. *The Lodger*, 1091; sonata, clarinet and cello, 941
Tauriello, Antonio. *Canti*, 1265; concerto, piano, 1262; *Música III*, 1218; *Ricercari*, 1180; *Transparencias*, 1202, 1224
Tavener, John, 1281
Taylor, Deems. Narrates *Fantasia*, 721; death, 1222. Works: *The Dragon*, 1042; *The King's Henchman*, 447; *Marco Takes a Walk*, 762; *Peter Ibbetson*, 525; *Ramuntcho*, 748; *Through the Looking Glass*, 309
Taylor, P. C., 201
Taylor, Samuel Coleridge. See Coleridge-Taylor, Samuel
Tchaikovskaya, Antonina Ivanovna, 280
Tchaikovsky, Boris, 1175
Tchaikovsky, Modest, 263
Tchaikovsky, Peter Ilich, 11, 244, 664, 681, 712, 721, 744, 853, 919, 965, 967, 1047, 1069, 1462, 1476, 1478, 1482, 1487, 1488, 1490, 1491, 1502. Work first performed after 1900: symphony #7, 1022
Tchaikovsky Museum, Klin, 744
Tchemberdzhi, Nicolai, 487
Tcherepnin, Alexander. Completes Mussorgsky, *The Marriage*, 654; U.S. citizen, 1045; "interpoint," 1435, 1459; Tcherepnin scale, 1487. Works: *The Ajanta Frescoes*, 378; concerto, harmonica, 1015; concerto, piano, #2, 383–384; #3, 560; #5, 1168; *Les Douze*, 842; *The Farmer and the Fairy*, 944; *La Femme et son Ombre*, 858; *Die Hochzeit der Sobeide*, 564; *L'Homme à la Peau de Léopard*, 815; *The Lost Flute*, 980; *Ol-Ol*, 466;

Romantic Overture, 924; The Story of Ivan the Fool, 1274; Suite Georgienne, 711; Symphonic Prayer, 1070; symphony #1, 461; #2, 934; #3, 990; #4, 1058; Training, 607; Trepak, 678

Tcherepnin, Nicolas. On Prokofiev, 298; son's symphony in memoriam, 934. Works conducted: Liadov, Enchanted Lake, 141. Works: The Masque of the Red Death, 264; Narcisse, 181; Le Pavillon d'Armide, 117

Tchishko, Oles. Dreadnaught Potemkin, 649, 1502; In the Captivity of Apple Trees, 529

Teatro Augusteo, 628

Teatro Colón, Buenos Aires, 473

Tebaldini, Giovanni, 142

Tel Aviv. First Hebrew opera house, 382

Television, 646, 708–709, 849, 928, 936, 949, 952, 988, 1001, 1007, 1022, 1073, 1104, 1105, 1139, 1140, 1142, 1154, 1197, 1199, 1239, 1253

Telmányi, Emil, 199

Telstar, 1142, 1208

Temporal parameters (term), 1496

Tenney, James, 1164

Tenor, female, 680

Teodorini, Elena, 289–290

Teratological borborygmus (term), 1496–1497

Terrasse, Claude. La Botte secrète, 43; Chonchette, 30; Le Cochon qui sommeile, 307; Faust en ménage, 382; Le Mariage de Télémaque, 163; Monsieur de la Palisse, 67; La Sire de Vergy, 46

Tertis, Lionel, 595

Terzi, Louisa, 860

Testi, Flavio, 1159

Tetrazzini, Luisa, 712

Texier, Rosalie, 64

Thalberg, Sigismond, 196

Theater of People's Art, 623

There'll Be a Hot Time in the Old Town Tonight, 617

Theremin, Leon. Exhibits Aetherophone (theremin), 330–331; patent, 466; performs Schillinger, First Airphonic Suite, 499; and rhythmicon, 1424, 1431, 1495; and theremin, 1444

Theremin (instrument), 330, 389, 466, 468, 499, 586, 797

Thibaud, Jacques, 463, 964

Third stream (term), 1034, 1497

Thomas, Ambroise, 191

Thomas, Dylan, 982

Thomas, Jess, 1226

Thomas, Kurt, 630

Thomas, Theodore, 70

Thompson, Randall. Jazz Poem, 482, 730; Requiem, 1049; Solomon and Balkis, 751; symphony #1, 504; #2, 546, 699; #3, 876; The Testament of Freedom, 768; A Trip to Nahant, 992

Thomson, Virgil. At Yaddo, 549; on Harris symphony #3, 688; and dodecaphony, 1441. Works: concerto, cello, 891; concerto, flute, 982; Fanfare for France, 765; The Feast of Love, 1192; Filling Station, 662; Four Saints in Three Acts, 581; Louisiana Story, 864–865; The Mayor LaGuardia Waltzes, 752; Missa pro Defunctis, 1084; The Mother of Us All, 834; Portraits, symphonic suite, 791; Sea Piece with Birds, 949; The Seine at Night, 848; suite, harp, strings and percussion, 1189; Symphony on a Hymn Tune, 797; symphony #2, 743; Wheat Field at Noon, 865

Thorarinsson, Leifur, 1225

Three Men's Club, 950

Thuille, Ludwig, 15, 104

Tierney, Harry. Irene, 318; Kid Boots, 382; Rio Rita, 446

Tiessen, Heinz, 477

Tigranian, Armen, 205

Tijardović, Ivo. Dimnjiaci uz Jadran, 906; Marko Polo, 1103

Tikotsky, Evgeny, 794

Tilzer, Harry von. See von Tilzer, Harry

Time capsule, 677

Tinel, Edgar, 141–142

Tinnitus (term), 1497

Tipperary, 675

Tippett, Michael, 69; imprisoned as conscientious objector, 770; and dodecaphony, 1441. Works: Boyhood's End, 1137; A Child of Our Time, 784; concerto for orchestra, 1165; King Priam, 1136; The Midsummer Marriage, 990; symphony #2, 1042; The Vision of St. Augustine, 1213

Tischhauser, Franz. Amores, 1031; Das Nasobém, 961

Tishchenko, Boris, 1213

S.S. Titanic, 201

Toch, Ernst. Attacked as Jew in Die Musik, 622; in "Entartete Musik," 670; U.S. citizenship, 716; death,

1187; and the *Lehrstück*, 1468. Works: *Big Ben*, 598; *Bunte Suite*, 488–489; *Die chinesische Flöte*, 375; *Circus Overture*, 979; concerto, cello and chamber orch., 416; concerto, piano, #1, 438, 458; #2, 600; *The Covenant*, 806; *Der Fächer*, 510; *Five Pieces for Chamber Orch.*, 413; *Fuge aus der Geographie*, 511; *Gesprochene Musik*, 511; *Die Heilige aus U.S.A.*, 539; *Kleine Theater-Suite*, 525; *Komödie für Orchester*, 461; *Notturno*, 970; *Peter Pan*, 1004; *Pinocchio*, 636; *Die Prinzessin auf der Erbse*, 459, 510; *Spiel*, 513; symphony #1, 904, 916; #2, 928; #3, 1002; #4, 1039; #5, 1175; symphony, unnumbered, piano and orch., 591; *Das Wasser*, 511

Toduța, Sigismond. Symphony #1, 996; #2, 1018; #3, 1035

Tofft, Alfred, 472

Toge, Sankichi, 1142

Togni, Camillo. *Helian di Trakl*, 1138; *Psalm CXXVII*, 895; *Rondeaux per Dieci*, 1203

Tokyo. Nisei Theater, 1169

Toldrá, Edouardo, 480

Tollins, Jan, 568

Tolstoy, Dmitri, 1105

Tom, Blind. *See* Bethune, Thomas

Tomasi, Henri. *Atlantide*, 971; *Don Juan de Mañara*, 1006; *Jabadao*, 1078; *Princesse Pauline*, 1128; *Sampiero Corso*, 1008; *Le Silence de la Mer*, 1162; *Tam-tam*, 569; *Vocero*, 560

Tommasini, Vincenzo. Completes Boito, *Nerone*, 389; 904. Works: *Il Carnevale di Venezia*, 497; concerto, strings, 873; *Les Femmes de Bonne Humeur*, 283; *Medea*, 91; string quartet, 476; *Uguale Fortuna*, 215–216

Tonal aura (term), 1497

Tonal tropism (term), 1497

Tone clusters (term), 1498

Toni, Aleco, 558

Tonolalia (term), 1498

Tonotripsical impact (term), 1498

Torkanowsky, Werner. Works conducted: Creston, 2 piano concerto, 1272

Tosar, Hector. *4 Piezas para Orquesta*, 1218; *Recitative and Variations for Orchestra*, 1261; sonata, violin, 978; *Stray Birds*, 1201; *Te Deum*, 1190

Tosatti, Vieri. *Il Giudizio universale*, 992; *La Partita a Pugni*, 965

Toscanini, Arturo. U.S. debut, 130; medal for courage under fire, 271; performance of Wagner protested, 274; U.S. tour with La Scala, 335; conducts La Scala reopening, 350; conductor, New York Philharmonic-Symphony, 469; refuses to conduct *Giovinezza*, 530; protests anti-Semitism, 564; reply, 565; cancels Bayreuth engagement, 568; conducts first concert of Palestine Symphony Orchestra, 637; conducts first concert of NBC Symphony, 660; South American tour, 714; conducts La Scala reopening, 771, 816; televised concert, 849; Verdi memorial, 906; last appearance, 974; death, 1021; dedicatee of Kodály, *Szimfónia*, 1122; stamp, 1236. Works conducted: Barber, *Adagio for Strings*, 679; idem, *First Essay for Orchestra*, 679; Boito, *Nerone*, 389; Castelnuovo-Tedesco, cello concerto, 601; idem, *Variazioni sinfoniche*, 507; idem, violin concerto #2, 566; Chasins, *Three Chinese Pieces*, 529; Giordano, *Madame Sans-Gêne*, 250; Gnecchi, *Cassandra*, 83; Leoncavallo, *Zazà*, 11; Kodály, *Summer Evening*, 507; Pizzetti, *Concerto dell'Estate*, 489; idem, *Fra Gherardo*, 473; idem, *Rondo veneziano*, 505; Puccini, *La Fanciulla del West*, 173; idem, *Turandot*, 431; Respighi, *Feste Romane*, 488; idem, *Fontane di Roma*, 280; Siegmeister, *Western Suite*, 807; Sinigaglia, *Danze piemontesi*, 76; Strong, *Die Nacht*, 701; Tommasini, *Il Carnevale di Venezia*, 497; Zandonai, *I Cavalieri di Ekebù*, 410

Toselli, Enrico, 427

Tosti, Paolo, 162

Total music (term), 1498

Tournemire, Charles. *Les Dieux sont morts*, 387; symphony #3 (*Moscou*), 229; #5 (*Dans les Alpes*), 326

Tovey, Donald Francis. Judges Schubert centennial contest, 479; death, 716. Works: *The Bride of Dionysius*, 549; concerto, cello, 595–596

Toyama, Michigo, 649

Toye, Geoffrey, 236

Translocations (term), 1498–1499

Trapp, Maria Augusta, 1075

Trapp, Max, 401

Trautwein, Friedrich, 1444
Travis, Roy, 1272
Tremain, Ronald, 942
Trimble, Lester, 1262
Trinidad and Tobago. National anthem, 1144
*Triton,* 557–558
Tritone (term), 1499
Trouhanova, Natacha, 201
Trudić, Božidar, 1020
Truman, Harry S, 682, 903, 936
Truman, Margaret, 903
Trunk, Richard, 575–576
Tuba, centennial of, 610
Tubi, Angelo. *Benvenuto Cellini,* 88; *Thermidor,* 410
Tudor, David. Works played or unplayed: Cage, concert, 1049; idem, *Music for Amplified Toy Pianos,* 1080; idem, *Water Music,* 936; idem, *4'33",* 945, 1490; Ichiyanagi, 1164
Tuong, N'Guyen Van, 1156
Turchi, Guido. *Il Buon soldato Svejk,* 1133; concerto, strings, 860; *Piccolo Concerto Notturno,* 922
Turina, Joaquín. Performed by Sociedad Nacional de Música, 250; 868. Works: *Canto a Sevilla,* 451; *El Castillo de Almodovar,* 581; *Evangelio,* 252; *Jardín de Oriente,* 370; *Margot,* 246; *Por el Río Guadalquivir,* 627; *La Procesión del Rocío,* 219; *Rapsodia sinfónica,* 563; *Rítmos,* 480; *Sinfonia sevillana,* 331, 1190; trio, piano and strings, 458
Turkish State Opera inaugurated, 850
Turner, Godfrey, 758, 865
Turski, Zbigniew, 1016, 1265
Tutev, Georgi, 1266
Tuthill, Burnet, 782
Tuttle, Stephen, 768
Tutunkhamen, 693
Tuxen-Bang, Carlos, 1218
Tveitt, Geirr, 1221
Twelve-tone music. *See* dodecaphonic music
Twist forbidden, 1155
Tzara, Tristan, 265, 310, 1298

U Tse-Yun, 1024
Ugarte, Floro, 330
Uhl, Alfred. *Concerto à ballo,* 1247; *Der mysteriöse Herr X,* 1221
Ukulele, 289
Ullman, Viktor. *Five Variations and a Double Fugue on a Theme by Schoen-*berg, 491; sonata, piano, 734; string quartet, 674
Ultra-modern music (term), 1499
Union, musicians, first, 346
Union of Polish Composers, 802
Union of Soviet Composers, 482, 866. Charter, 1380
U.S. House of Representatives. Committee on Un-American Activities, 850, 1394–1404
U.S. Senate. Debate on folk music, 1407–1413
Universal edition, 18
Unpremeditated music (term), 1499–1500
Unwasity (term), 1500
Urbanism (term), 1500
Uribe-Holguín, Guillermo. *Homenaje a Bolívar,* 1053; *Sinfonietta campesina,* 884; symphony #1, 314; #2, 400; #3, 990; #4, 1007; #6, 1026; #7, 1033; #8, 1055
Usandizaga, José María. Death, 257. Works: *Las Golondrinas,* 234; *Mendi Mendiyan,* 163
Uspensky, Victor, 620
Ussachevsky, Vladimir. *Of Wood and Brass,* 1260; *Poem in Cycles and Bels,* 987
Usurid, Hamid-al, 769
Utzevitch, Evgeny, 1059

Valcárcel, Edgar, 1260
Valen, Fartein. Death, 949. Works: *Le Cimetière marin,* 960; concerto, violin, 858; *La Isla de las Calmas,* 918; *Sonetto di Michelangelo,* 835–836
Valkare, Gunnar. *Kardiogram I,* 1214; *Kardiogram IV,* 1234; *Ordure dans l'air après la passion,* 1256; *A Study in the Story of Human Stupidity,* 1254
Valle-Riestra, José María, 12
Vallée, Rudy, 19
Valls, Josep. Concerto, string quartet and orch., 650; symphony, 692
van Beinum. *See* Beinum
Vancea, Zeno, 892
Van Cliburn. *See* Cliburn
Vanderbilt, William K., 102
van Dieren. *See* Dieren
van Lier, Bertus. And Maneto, 648. Works: *Catharsis,* 902; little suite, violin and piano, 674; *5 Mei: Zij,* 1158; symphony #2, 569
Van Ty, Louise Nguyen, 951

Van Vactor, David. *Gothic Impressions*, 749; symphony, 685
van Wijck. *See* Wyk
van Wyk. *See* Wyk
Varèse, Edgar. Organizes International Composers' Guild, 342; "American Iconoclasts" concert, 1150; death, 1211; quoted by Rochberg, 1232; etiology, 1445; and organized sound, 1473, 1491. Works: *Amériques*, 430; *Arcana*, 452, 1117, 1471; *Bourgogne*, 173; *Déserts*, 986–987, 1113; *Ecuatorial*, 586–587, 1113; *Hyperprism*, 370; *Intégrales*, 533; *Ionisation*, 562–563, 1433; *Octandre*, 1225; *Offrandes*, 1182; *Poème électronique*, 1113. LETTERS to Nicolas Slonimsky, 1350–1352
Vassilenko, Sergei, 1006. Works: *The Garden of Death*, 125; *Hircus Nocturnus*, 138; *The Legend of the Great City of Kitezh and the Calm Lake Svetoyar*, 28; *Mirandolina*, 868; *Son of the Sun*, 494; *Suvorov*, 749; symphony #4 (*Arctic*), 595
Vatican, 545, 1054. *See also* popes by name
Vaughan, Denis, 1277
Vaughan Williams, Ralph. Festival of Music for People, 691; marriage, 952; death, 1054; pandiatonicism, 1475. Works: *Benedicite*, 536; *Bucolic Suite*, 28; concerto, oboe and strings, 788; concerto, piano, 560; concerto, tuba, 978; *Concerto accademico*, 421; concerto grosso, strings, 901; *English Folk Song Suite*, 375–376; *Fantasia on a Theme by Thomas Tallis*, 167; *Fantasia on Greensleeves*, 592; *Fantasia on Sussex*, 505; *Festival Te Deum*, 645; *Five Tudor Portraits*, 631; *Five Variants on Dives and Lazarus*, 697, 977; *Flos Campi*, 420, 492; *Flourish for Glorious John*, 1036; *Hodie*, 981; *Hugh the Drover*, 396; *In the Fen Country*, 141; *Job*, 534; *The Lark Ascending*, 344; *Merciless Beauty*, 418; *Norfolk Rhapsody #1*, 94; *#2 & #3*, 95, 114; *Old King Cole*, 374; *On Wenlock Edge*, 151, 397; *Pilgrim's Progress*, 359, 770, 911–912; *The Poisoned Kiss*, 627–628; *Riders to the Sea*, 659; *Romance*, harmonica and orch., 936; *The Running Set*, 577; *Sancta Civitas*, 432; *Scott of the Antarctic*, 865, 950; *Serenade to Music*, 678; *The Shepherds of the Delectable Mountains*, 359, 912; *Sir John in Love*, 490; *The Sons of Light*, 913; *Story of a Flemish Farm*, 801; suite, viola and small orch., 595; symphony #1 (*A Sea Symphony*), 170; #2 (*A London Symphony*), 236; #3 (*Pastoral*), 352, 413; #4, 604; #5, 770; #6, 851–852; #7 (*Antarctic*), 950–951; #8, 1008; #9, 1045–1046; *Thanksgiving for Victory*, 800; *Two English Folk Songs*, 691; *A Vision of Aeroplanes*, 1010; *The Wasps*, 151
Vaurabourg, Andrée, 414
Vectorialism (term), 1500
Veerhoff, Carlos, 1136
Vega, Aurelio de la. *Analigus*, 1217; cantata, 1192; *Coordinates* (magnetic tape), 1181; *Leyenda del Ariel Criollo*, 978; *Structures*, 1178; symphony, 1113, 1188, 1218
Velasco Maidana, José María, 713
Venth, Carl, 1074
Veray, Amaury, 1215
Verbalization (term), 1500
Verdi, Giuseppe. Death, 13; 130, 248, 350, 633, 640, 816, 906, 923, 925, 947, 964, 989, 1023, 1056, 1070, 1081, 1166, 1167, 1238, 1248, 1274, 1445, 1448, 1487
*Verein für musikalische Privataufführungen*, 304
Veress, Sándor. *Four Transylvanian Dances*, 888; string quartet #1, 609; #2, 650
Veretti, Antonio. *Burlesca*, 546; *Elegie in Friulano*, 1156, 1225; *Il Favorito del rè*, 546; *Il Galante tiratore*, 560; *I Sette peccati*, 1008; *Sinfonia Italiana*, 514; sonata, violin, 976
Verger, Christine, 161
Verismo (term), 1500
Verlaine, Paul, 1455
Vermeulen, Matthijs; symphony #4, 881; #6, 1089
Verneuil, Claudine Pillard, 924
Vernon, Ashley, 959
Verrall, John, 928
Vianna, Fructuoso, 757
Viardot García, Pauline, 163
Victoria, Tomás Luis de, 191
Victory, Gerard, 955
Vidal, Paul, 94
Vidu, Ion, 401
Vienna. Opera House. Bombed, 797; reopens, 1001

Wagner, Joseph. Concerto grosso, band, 963; *Hudson River Legend*, 782–783; symphony #1, 789; #2, 1080

Wagner, Richard, 22, 52, 52–53, 67, 134, 176, 223, 242, 244, 246, 250, 265, 273, 274, 317, 336, 342, 373, 396, 443, 515, 571, 636, 647, 682, 704–705, 709, 709–710, 722, 769, 787, 837, 849, 931, 974, 1069, 1077, 1121, 1130, 1142, 1159, 1171, 1207, 1242, 1260, 1488, 1498, 1501

Wagner, Robert, 1192

Wagner, Siegfried. Protests American Parsifal, 53; death, 512; and mutation, 1469. Works: *An allem ist Hütchen Schuld*, 291; *Banadietrich*, 156; *Bruder Lustig*, 80; *Der Heidenkönig*, 576–577; *Herzog Wildfang*, 16; *Der Kobold*, 55; *Schwarzschwanenreich*, 304; *Sternengebot*, 119; symphony, 739

Wagner, Wieland, 1069, 1121, 1142, 1164, 1229; death, 1242

Wagner, Winifred, 837

Wagner-Régeny, Rudolf. *Das Bergwerk zu Falun*, 1122; *Die Bürger von Calais*, 686; *Der Günstling*, 602; *Johanna Balk*, 732; *Midsummer Night's Dream*, 594; *Mythological Figurines*, 941; *Prometheus*, 1071

Wagneromanticism (term), 1501

Wagneromorphism (term), 1501

Wajditsch Verbovac von Dönhoff, Gabriel, 684

Wald, Max, 549

Waldteufel, Emil, 251

Walker, Johnny, 602

Wallenstein, Alfred. Plays Stock, cello concerto, 488. Works conducted: Benjamin, *Jamaican Rumba*, 747; Krenek, cello concerto, 972; Levant, piano concerto, 748

Walpole, Horace, 1350

Walter, Bruno. Concert cancelled due to W's Judaism, 564; Furtwängler pleads for, 565; last concert before *Anschluss*, 665; death, 1130. Works conducted: Barber, *Second Essay for Orchestra*, 751; Bruckner, symphony #4, 665; Carpenter, symphony #2, 760; Mahler, *Das Lied von der Erde*, 193; idem, symphony #9, 204; Pfitzner, *Palestrina*, 287; Weill, symphony #2, 593; Wellesz, *Prosperos Beschwörung*, 665

Waltershausen, Hermann von, 196

Walton, William Turner. Birth, 29. Works: *The Bear*, 1240; *Belshazzar's Feast*, 536–537, 568; concerto, cello, 1021; concerto, viola, 497, 514; concerto, violin, 703; *Crown Imperial*, 645; *Façade*, 374, 477; *In Honour of the City of London*, 655; *Johannesburg Festival Overture*, 1015; *Orb and Sceptre*, 961; partita, orch., 1041–1042; *Portsmouth Point*, 435; *Scapino*, 731; string quartet #1, 377; symphony #1, 613; #2, 1093, 1441; *Te Deum*, 961; *Troilus and Cressida*, 987; *Variations on a Theme by Hindemith*, 1154; *The Wise Virgins*, 712

Ward, Robert. Concerto, piano, 1261; *The Crucible*, 1126; *He Who Gets Slapped*, 1009; *The Lady from Colorado*, 1185; *Pantaloon*, 1008–1009; symphony #1, 733; #2, 846

Warlock, Peter. See Heseltine, Philip

Warren, Leonard, 1081

Warsaw Autumn. First, (1956), 1016; sixth, (1962), 1145; tenth, (1966), 1226–1227; twelfth, (1968), 1264–1270

Warsaw. National Opera House. Reopens, 1211

Warzecha, Piotr, 1269

Watanabe, Hisaharu, 841

Watch and Ward Society, 102

Waxman, Franz, 1064

Weber, Carl Maria von, 180, 433, 515, 1476

Weber, Margrit, 1059

Webern, Anton. On Schoenberg's paintings, 169; Berg *Kammerkonzert* motto, 450; conducts Vienna Arbeiter-Sinfonie, 552; and Berg concerto, 625; killed, 802; Füssl piece in memoriam, 1031; and 1961 ISCM festival, 1116, 1119; arranges Bach, 6-part ricercar, 1117; International Webern Festival, 1136; dedicatee, Searle, symphony #5, 1187; and First Hellenic Week of Contemporary Music, 1216; and dodecaphony, 1440; fragmentation of rows, 1443; *Klangfarbenmelodiker*, 1462–1463; radial distribution in, 1484; miniaturist, 1496. Works: *Das Augenlicht*, 673, 1116; cantata #1, 819, 1117; #2, 895, 1117; concerto, 609; *Drei Volkstexte* (op. 17), 1030; *Fünf Sätze für Streichquartett*, 361, 1086;

*Fünf Stücke für Orchester,* 191, 435; *Im Sommerwind,* 1136; passacaglia, 343, 1119; quartet, piano, clarinet, saxophone and violin, 1269; rondo, string quartet, 1263; *Sechs Stücke für Orchester,* 219, 1071; string quartet (op. 28), 693, 734; string trio, 477; symphony, 500–501, 535, 1204; variations, orch., 767, 1119. LETTER to Nicolas Slonimsky, 1316

Wedekind, Frank, 646

Wegelius, Martin, 90

Wehrli, Werner, 306

Weigl, Karl, 362, 1271

Weill, Kurt. Birth, 4; stink-bombed, 493, 516; lawsuit, 515–516; attacked as Jew in *Die Musik,* 622; in "Entartete Musik," 670; death, 891; music used to characterize Nazis, 1124; and the *Lehrstück,* 1463; and proletarian music, 1483. Works: *Aufstieg und Fall der Stadt Mahagonny,* 505, 516, *see also* Mahagonny (Songspiel); *The Ballad of Magna Carta,* 706–707; *Die Bürgschaft,* 544; concerto, violin, 435; *Down in the Valley,* 858–859; *Die Dreigroschenoper,* 475–476, 493, 515–516, 940, 1124; *Frauentanz,* 397; *Der Jasager,* 512; *Johnny Johnson,* 634; *Knickerbocker Holiday,* 677; *Lady in the Dark,* 727; *Lindberghflug,* 495–496, 1500; *Mahagonny* (Songspiel), 459, *see also* Aufstieg und Fall der Stadt Mahagonny; *Der Neinsager,* 512; *One Touch of Venus,* 772; *Der Protagonist,* 430; *Quodlibet,* 428; *Royal Palace,* 448; *Die Sieben Todsünden der Kleinbürger,* 569; *Street Scene,* 826; symphony #2, 593; *Der Zar lässt sich photographieren,* 466

Weinberger, Jaromir. Suicide, 1243. Works: *A Bird's Opera,* 742; *Czech Rhapsody,* 742; *Die geliebte Stimme,* 526–527; *Lidé z Pokerflatu,* 556; *Lincoln Symphony,* 741; *Švanda Dudák,* 454; *Variations and Fugue,* 700; *Wallenstein,* 657

Weiner, Leo, 1165

Weingartner, Felix. Works conducted: Bizet, symphony, 602; Korngold, sinfonietta, 230; Marx, *Romantisches Klavierkonzert,* 352. Works: *Dame Kobold,* 266; *Die Dorfschule,* 327; *Kain und Abel,* 240–241; *Meister Andrea,* 327; *Orestes,* 27

Weinzweig, John. And Canadian League of Composers, 907. Works: *Edge of the World,* 811; *Red Ear of Corn,* 870

Weis, Fleming, 1051

Weis, Karel. *Die Dorfmusikanten,* 69; *Lešetínský Kovář,* 329; *Der polnische Jude,* 15; *Útok na Mlýn,* 200

Weisgall, Hugo. *Athaliah,* 1175; *Nine Rivers from Jordan,* 1270; *Purgatory,* 1108; *Six Characters in Search of an Author,* 1063; *The Stronger,* 944; *The Tenor,* 931

Weismann, Julius. *Midsummer Night's Dream,* 594; *Die pfiffige Magd,* 687; *Schwanenweiss,* 379

Weiss, Adolph, 532

Weissberg, Julia, 432

Welin, Karl-Erik, 1267

Wellesz, Egon. *Alkestis,* 387; *Die Bakchantinnen,* 533; concerto, violin, 1129; *Five Sonnets of Elizabeth Browning,* 625; *Incognita,* 927; *Die Prinzessin Girnara,* 340; *Prosperos Beschwörung,* 665; *Short Suite,* 398; string quartet, 361; symphony #6, 1222; *Three Choruses,* 534

Wendland, Waldemar, 816

Wenrich, Percy, 283

Werfel, Alma. *See* Mahler, Alma

Werfel, Franz, 400

Werle, Lars Johan. *Die Reise,* 1276; *A Vision of Therese,* 1179

Werrenrath, Reinald, 305

Wessel, Horst, 504

West Virginia Folklore Society, 256

Western Union, 727

Westhreen, P. A. van, 330

Wettach, Adrian, 1068

Wetz, Richard, 107

Whelen, Christopher, 1212

White, Clarence Cameron, 877

White, James Paul, 1328

White sound (term), 1501

White Wave Society, 902

Whiteman, Paul. Works conducted: Copland, *Letter from Home,* 789; Gershwin, *Rhapsody in Blue,* 384–385; Grofé, *Grand Canyon Suite,* 539; Stravinsky, *Scherzo à la Russe,* 812

Whithorne, Emerson. Death, 1044. Works: *Aeroplane,* 427, 1500; *Moon Trail,* 576; *New York Days and Nights,* 378, 436; *Saturday's Child,* 429; symphony #1, 577; #2, 641

Whitney, Robert. Works conducted: Hindemith, sinfonietta in E, 1080; Vincent, symphony, 930

Whittaker, William, 458

Whole-tone scale. Discussed 1501–1502

Widor, Charles Marie. Prix de Rome, 19; death, 641. Works: *Nerto*, 401; *Les Pêcheurs de Saint-Jean*, 85; *Symphonie antique*, 178

Wiechowicz, Stanislaw, 693, 1016

Wieniawski, Adam Tadeusz, 214

Wieniawski, Henryk, 949

Wieprecht, Wilhelm, 610

Wiggen, Kurt, 997

Wihtol, Joseph, 852

Wijck. See Wyk

Wildberger, Jacques. *Épitaphe pour Évariste Galois*, 1178; *Musik*, strings, 1117; *Tre Mutazioni*, 1031

Wilder, Thornton, 1104, 1131

Wilfred, Thomas, 351

Wilkomirska, Wanda, 1248

Willaert, Adrian, 1150

Willan, Healey. *Brébeuf and His Brethren*, 772; *Deirdre of the Sorrows*, 815, 1198; symphony #1, 631; #2, 893

Williams, Alberto. Death, 940. Works: symphony #6 (*Death of the Comet*), 658; #7 (*Eternal Repose*), 658

Williams, Gerrard, 362

Williamson, Malcolm. Concerto, violin, 1208; *English Eccentrics*, 1183–1184; *The Growing Castle*, 1264; *The Happy Prince*, 1203; *Julius Caesar Jones*, 1213; *Our Man in Havana*, 1163; *The Violins of Saint-Jacques*, 1231

Willner, Arthur, 345

Willoughby, Robert, 1263

Willson, Meredith, 717

Wimberger, Gerhard, 1273

Wind Massive (Soviet wind orchestra), 627

Winter, Paul, 667

Wislocki, Stanislaw, 1016

Wissmer, Pierre. *Capitaine Bruno*, 947; *Léonidas ou la cruauté mentale*, 1054; *Marion, ou la Belle au Tricorne*, 832, 925

Witkowski, Georges Martin. *Mon Lac*, 348; *Poème de la Maison*, 308; *La Princesse lointaine*, 584

Witmark, Isidore, 301

Witt, Friedrich, 155

Wittgenstein, Paul. Does not play Prokofiev concerto #4, 1014; death, 1109; commissions Strauss, *Parergon*, 1475. Works performed: Britten, *Diversions on a Theme*, 746; Ravel, concerto, piano left hand, 539–540, 585; Schmidt, *Concertante variationen*, 384; idem, concerto #2, 601; Strauss, *Parergon*, 420

Woestyne, David van de, 835

Wolf, Hugo, 45, 356, 953, 1106

Wolf-Ferrari, Ermano, 846. Works: *Gli Amanti sposi*, 409; *L'Amore medico*, 231; *Il Campiello*, 620; *Cenerentola*, 4; *La Dama boba*, 686; *Gli Dei a Tebe*, 770; *Le Donne curiose*, 51; *I Gioielli della Madonna*, 195–196; *I Quattro rusteghi*, 90; *Il Segreto di Susanna*, 153; *Sly*, 464; *La Vedova scaltra*, 527; *Veste di cielo*, 453; *La Vita nuova*, 45

Wolff, Albert, 320

Wolff, Christian, 1165

Wolff, Hellmuth Christian, 1198

Wolfurt, Kurt von, 709

Wolpe, Stefan, 734, 1150

Wolzogen, Ernst von, 22

Wolzogen, Hans von, 81; death, 672

Wood, Henry. Death, 787. Works conducted: Bax, symphony #3, 505; Brian, *For Valor*, 114; Bridge, *Rebus*, 730; idem, *The Sea*, 209; Britten, piano concerto, 676; Delius, *Eventyr*, 307; idem, *Idyll*, 572; Ireland, *London Overture*, 652; Schoenberg, *Fünf Orchesterstücke*, 206; Scott, symphony #2, 48; Smyth, concerto, violin, horn and orch., 449; Vaughan Williams, *Serenade to Music*, 678

Wood, Ursula, 952

Woodstock, N. Y., 945, 1487

Woodward, J. W., 201

Works Progress Administration. *See* Federal Music Project

World War I. Deaths: Boulnois, 303; Butler, 254; Butterworth, 271; Écorcheville, 251; Farrar, 301; Granados, 267; Jürgens, 257; Kelly, 273; Magnard, 245; Novotný, 299; Sigward, 255; Stephan, 257. Draft-exempt orchestra, 247. Popular songs, 249, 259–260, 270, 271, 278, 282, 283, 286, 287, 297, 298, 299, 304, 305

World War II. Deaths: Alain, 715; Borchard, 802; Borck, 781; Cavalieri, 780; Humpert, 772; Jaubert, 715; Kauffmann, 788; Krasa, 782; Laparra, 768; Leigh, 754; Marinuzzi, 802; Orlansky, 764; Schulhoff, 759; Vučković, 763; Vuillermoz, 715; Webern, 802. Draft-exempt orchestra, 709. Popular songs, 699

World's Fair, New York (1939–1940), 668, 677, 695, 697, 710

World's Fair, New York (1964–1965), 1177

World's Fair, Seattle (1962), 1134, 1135

Woronow, Wladimir, 873

Woytowicz, Boleslaw. And 1956 Warsaw Autumn, 1016. Works: *Berceuse*, 609; *Children's Cantata*, 551; symphony #2, 821; *Twenty Variations in Symphonic Form*, 694

Wright, Robert. *Kismet*, 967; *Song of Norway*, 787

Wyk, Arnold van. At 1954 ISCM festival, Haifa, 976. Works: *Primavera*, 1085; string quartet, 895

Wyschnegradsky, Ivan. Cercle Culturel concert, 926. Works: *Cosmos*, 805, 1466; *Etude en forme de Scherzo*, 638; *5 Variations*, 805; *Linnite*, 805; *Symphonic Fragments*, 638; *Thus Spake Zarathustra*, 638; *24 Preludes*, 638

Wyttenbach, Jürg. *Divisions*, 1203; *Paraphrase*, 1279

Xanrof, Leon, 958

Xenakis, Iannis. And aleatory music, 1425; "Sonotron," 1431; and spatial distribution, 1434; notation, 1452; and stochastic composition, 1492. Works: *Akrata*, 1222; *Kraanerg*, 1278; *Morsima-Amorsima*, 1268–1269; *Nomos gamma*, 1277; *Stratégie*, 1157, 1450, 1492; *Terrêtektorh*, 1215–1216

Yaddo, 549, 687

Yamada, Kosçak, 154

Yan-Tse, 1024

Yannay, Yehuda, 1279

Yasser, Joseph, 1466

Yates, Victor, 691

Yodeling, 943

Youmans, Vincent. Death, 814. Works: *Hit the Deck*, 454; *No No Nanette*, 410; *Wildflower*, 368

Young, La Monte. Ignites violin, 1436; artificial tinnitus, 1497; and verbalization, 1500. Works: *Composition 1960, #5*, 1320; *#13*, 1165; *#15*, 1205; *Piano Piece #1*, 1211; *Poem for Tables, Chairs and Benches*, 1078; *Two Sounds*, 1205

*Young Dr. Malone*, 1102

Ysaÿe, Eugène, 527; death, 530; 1054

Yuize, Shinichi, 1002

Yun, Isang. Abduction, 1251–1252. Works: string quartet #3, 1088; *Der Traum des Liu-Tung*, 1208–1209; *Die Witwe des Schmetterlings*, 1251–1252

Yvain, Maurice. *Blanche neige*, 925; *La Dame en décolleté*, 382; *Pas sur la bouche*, 409; *Ta bouche*, 356

Zabaleta, Nicanor. Works performed: Piston, capriccio, 1189; Thomson, suite, 1189; Villa-Lobos, concerto, 989

Zach, Max, 197

Zádor, Eugen: *Asra*, 621; *Biblical Scenes*, 777; *Columbus*, 700; concerto, trombone, 1242; *Diana*, 382; *Dornröschens Erwachen*, 529; *Five Contrasts for Orchestra*, 1195; *A Holtak Szigete*, 468; *The Magic Chair*, 1219; *Maschinenmensch*, 590; *The Scarlet Mill*, 1271; *Sinfonia Tecnica*, 550, 1500; *Tanzsymphonie*, 639; *Ungarisches Capriccio*, 601; *Variations on a Hungarian Folksong*, 446; *The Virgin and the Faun*, 1189; *X-mal Rembrandt*, 509

Zajc. *See* Zaytz

Zak, Piotr, 1116

Zandonai, Riccardo. Accused of high treason, 255; anti-modernist manifesto, 558; Mussolini prize, 605; death, 786. Works: *I Cavalieri di Ekebù*, 410; *Conchita*, 192; *La Farsa amorosa*, 561; *Francesca da Rimini*, 235; *Giulietta e Romeo*, 353; *Il Grillo del focolare*, 130; *Melenis*, 213; *La Via della finestra*, 314

Zanella, Amilcare. *Aura*, 166; *Il Revisore*, 707

Zarlino, Gioseffo, 281

Zavadil, Jozef, 694, 818–819

Zaytz, Giovanni von, 248

Zbinden, Julien-François, 960

Zebre, Demetrij. *Toccata*, 650; *Trois poèmes lyriques*, 694

Zecchi, Adone. *Duae fugae*, 835; *Due invenzioni*, 976

Zeffirelli, Franco, 1226

Zehme, Albertine, 210
Zeikel, David, 1466
Zeiler, Richard, 538
Zeitlin, Zvi, 1132, 1223
Zeleński, Wladislaw. *Janek,* 9; *Stara Baśń,* 107
Zeljenka, Ilja, 1161–1162, 1180
Zelter, Carl Friedrich, 948
Zemlinsky, Alexander. Orchestrates Korngold, *Der Schneemann,* 169; quoted by Berg, 443; death, 750. Works: *Es war einmal,* 2; *Eine florentinische Tragödie,* 278; *Four Songs* (Maeterlinck), 219; *Kleider machen Leute,* 172; *Der Kreidekreis,* 573; string quartet, 476; *Der Zwerg,* 358
Zen (term), 1502
Zenk, Ludwig, 625
Zhelobinsky, Valery. *Her Name Day,* 603; *Kamarinsky Muzhik,* 571
Zhiganov, Nazib. *Altyntchetch,* 738; *Dzhalil,* 1028; *Ildar,* 761; *Irek,* 708; *Katchkyn,* 698; *Namus,* 895; *Tulyak,* 801
Zhukovsky, Herman. *Forest Song,* 1113; *From the Bottom of My Heart,* 905
Zich, Otakar. *Guilt,* 354; *Malířský Nápad,* 159
Zichy, Géza, 74; death, 383

*Ziegfeld Follies of 1919,* 313
Ziegler, Hans, 504
Ziehn, Bernhard, 209
Ziehrer, Karl Michael, 846
Zilcher, Hermann. *Doktor Eisenbart,* 358; symphony #5, 847
Zillig, Winfried. At 1961 ISCM festival, Vienna, 1118; realizes Schoenberg, *Die Jakobsleiter,* 1118. Works: *Choral Fantasy,* 940; *Das Opfer,* 633; *Rossknecht,* 560; *Das Verlöbnis,* 1171; *Die Windsbraut,* 733
Zimbalist, Efrem, 949
Zimbalist, Mary Curtis Bok, 1095
Zimmermann, Bernd Alois. Concerto, cello, 1258, 1280; concerto, violin, 942; *Nobody Knows de Trouble I Seen,* 1089–1090; *Omnia tempus habent,* 1065; *Photoptosis,* 1275–1276; *Presence,* 1247; *Die Soldaten,* 1159; sonata, cello alone, 1162; symphony #4, 1051
Zirra, Alexandru, 726
Zöllner, Richard, 360
Zolotarev, Vasily, 425
Zuckermann, Augusta. *See* Mana-Zucca
Zuffenato, Guido, 558
Zuffre, Gaetano, 1243
Zweig, Stefan, 608
Zwissig, Alberich, 976